THE OFFICIAL ENCYCLOPEDIA OF BRIDGE

Newly revised, Sixth Edition

Published by the American Contract Bridge League, Inc., 2990 Airways Boulevard, Memphis, Tennessee, 38116-3847. Manufactured in the United States of America.

Library of Congress Cataloguing in Publications Data.

Main entry under title:

The Official Encyclopedia of Bridge

ISBN   0-943855-44-6

CONTRIBUTING EDITORS

To this edition

Phillip Alder
Carlos Cabanne
Gabriel Chagas
Hugh Darwen
Herman De Wael
Elly Ducheyne-Swaan
Albert Field
Santanu Ghose
Anna Gudge
Mazhar Jafri
Per Jannersten
Danny Kleinman
Eric Kokish
Sandra Landy
Jean-Paul Meyer
Svend Novrup
Julian Pottage
Barry Rigal
Giannarigo Rona

To earlier editions

*Jean Besse
Larry N. Cohen
Eric Crowhurst
Albert Dormer
Sue Emery
Robert Ewen
Richard Grenside
Olof Hanner
*M. Harrison-Gray
Diane Hayward
*Monroe Inberman
*Jane Johnson
Jared Johnson
Patrick Jourdain
*Edgar Kaplan
*Fred Karpin
Sami Kehela
*Rhoda Barrow Lederer
Phillip Martin
Marshall Miles
*Victor Mollo
David Parry
*Anthony Priday
Jeff Rubens
Bill Sachen
Ton Schipperheyn
Frank Stewart
Jess Stuart
Alec Traub
Dorothy Truscott
*Ray Telfer
Sol Weinstein

* Deceased

THE OFFICIAL ENCYCLOPEDIA OF BRIDGE

Newly revised Sixth Edition

*Authorized by the American Contract Bridge League
and prepared under its supervision*

HENRY G. FRANCIS
Editor-in-Chief

ALAN F. TRUSCOTT
Executive Editor

DORTHY A. FRANCIS
Editor, Sixth Edition

FOREWORD

This Encyclopedia was the brainchild of the late Richard Frey, who suggested the project to the American Contract Bridge League in 1962. His aim was to "Provide an official and authoritative answer to any question a reader might ask about the game of contract bridge and its leading players." He brought Alan Truscott from England to do the research and compilation. The first edition was published in 1964. Frey was the editor-in-chief of the first three editions, and Truscott has been the executive editor of all six editions.

The first edition included much new technical, biographical and bibliographical material, and one *tour de force* – the suit combinations section by Eric Crowhurst — was remarkable in its depth and accuracy. It has continued virtually unchanged in subsequent editions.

The second edition (1971) was supervised by Thomas Smith, the third (1976) by Amalya Kearse, the fourth (1984) by Diane Hayward, and the fifth (1994) by Dorthy Francis. Henry Francis, editor-in-chief of this edition, also served in that capacity for the third, fourth and fifth editions.

This edition, has been prepared primarily by Henry Francis, with major contributions and help from Alan Truscott and Barry Rigal. Once again Dorthy Francis has updated American biographies and world-wide tournament results. Tim Bourke, who owns one of the world's most complete bridge libraries and who assembled the Morehead Library at ACBL Headquarters, prepared the bibliography. Many others made contributions, and some of these are listed as contributing editors. A complete list is impossible, but our thanks go to all who have helped in any way.

This book was published by the American Contract Bridge League under the authority of its Board of Directors and its Chief Executive Officer, David Silber.

— HENRY FRANCIS
Editor-in-Chief

How to use this Encyclopedia

For easy reference, this book has been divided into five main parts: I. General information: technical (bidding and play); historical, procedural, laws, and terminological; II. Bridge organizations; III. Biographies; IV. International and national results; V. Bibliography.

I. General Information.

Technical. When more than one name is in use for a specific system, convention, etc., the major entry is usually under the name most commonly used in North America. Other names are provided via cross-references.

The reader who wishes to study a particular field is advised to consult one of the following group headings: BIDDING; BIDDING SYSTEMS; COLLOQUIALISMS; DEFENSE; DEFENSE TO ONE NOTRUMP; DOUBLES; DUMMY PLAY; DUPLICATE BRIDGE; LEADS; MATHEMATICS OF BRIDGE; OPENING BID; REBIDS; RESPONSE; SIGNALS; SLAM CONVENTIONS; SQUEEZE; SUIT COMBINATIONS; TROPHIES; TRUMP PLAY; VALUATION.

Historical. Every effort has been made to record the history of bridge and games that led to the invention of bridge.

Procedural. The Laws of Contract Bridge (1993) and the Laws of Duplicate Contract Bridge (1997) are presented in full. Various aspects of tournament organization also are dealt with in detail.

Terminological. Terms and colloquialisms in common use in the English-speaking world are explained.

II. Bridge Organizations.
National and international bridge organizations throughout the world are listed, often with some description and history. Contact information also is included.

III. Biographies.
Approximately 3000 bridge personalities from around the world are listed. Far stricter criteria have been enforced for inclusion.

IV. Championship Results.
Winners through the years of world championships, zonal championships, ACBL and ABA championships, European Championships and many others are listed.

V. Bibliography.
Significant books on all aspects of bridge are listed by subject.

A

ABA. See AMERICAN BRIDGE ASSOCIATION.

ABL. See AMERICAN BRIDGE LEAGUE.

ABOVE THE LINE. A phrase denoting all scores in rubber bridge entered above a horizontal line on the scoresheet, including penalties and the premiums for honors, slams, rubbers, overtricks and fulfilling a doubled or redoubled contract. See BELOW THE LINE, PREMIUM SCORE.

ABSOLUTE FORCE. A bid which makes it incumbent on partner to guarantee that another bid can be made by the player making the absolute force. Unless the bid is overcalled or doubled immediately, the partner is under conventional obligation to make some call other than a pass. See DEMAND BID, FORCING BID.

ABTA. See AMERICAN BRIDGE TEACHERS ASSOCIATION.

ACBL. See AMERICAN CONTRACT BRIDGE LEAGUE.

ACBL ACE OF CLUBS CONTEST. For a variety of reasons, the vast majority of ACBL members play mostly in club games, seldom venturing out to tournaments. Many are fine players who simply do not like to, or cannot afford to, travel — or who simply prefer the intimate atmosphere of the club.

To recognize achievement at the club level, the ACBL created the Ace of Clubs competition in 1984. As with the winners in the MINI-McKENNEY races, the Ace of Clubs champions are recognized at the Unit level as well as ACBL-wide.

All points won at the club level are counted except for North American Open Pairs and Grand National Teams. For winners, see Appendix II.

ACBL BOARD OF DIRECTORS. The body that manages and controls the business and activities of the ACBL. The Board is composed of one director elected by each DISTRICT for a three-year term. The terms of the directors are staggered, with approximately one-third of the directors being elected each year. Each year the Board of Directors elects from among incumbent members a president of the ACBL to serve for one year. Usually the Board meets three times a year, usually just before the Spring, Summer and Fall NABCs.

ACBL BOARD OF GOVERNORS. A body that has the power to make recommendaticns to the BOARD OF DIREGTORS OF THE ACBL, to propose amendments to the BYLAWS OF THE ACNL and tg receive reports from and to ratify certain actions taken by that Board. The Board of Governors is composed of five members from each DISTRICT and members-at-large. Two of the five representatives from each District are designated First Alternate Director and Second Alternate Director from such District during their terms of office. The members-at-large, who have full voting rights, consist of past presidents of the ACBL and past chairmen of the Board of Governors. They are permanent members of the Board of Governors. Three regular meetings a year are held, usually during the North American Bridge Championships.

ACBL BRIDGE BULLETIN. A monthly magazine that is the official organ of the American Contract Bridge League. It has by far the largest circulation of any bridge periodical, since it goes to all ACBL members, totaling approximately 160,000. It was published originally as *The Bulletin of the American Bridge League* in 1934. The word "Contract" was added when the name of the organization was changed in 1937. It became *The Contract Bridge Bulletin* in 1962. This was simplified to *The Bulletin* in the Seventies. To include the concept of bridge in the title, the name was changed to *The Bridge Bulletin* in 1993.

Earliest issues, edited by Geoffrey Mott-Smith and William Huske, consisted of a four-page tabloid newspaper listing tournament results and facts concerning upcoming tournaments. In subsequent years it was edited by George Beynon and then by Alfred Sheinwold.

In May 1958, editorship was assumed by Richard L. Frey, who instituted radical changes in format and content. In June of 1958 the directory of bridge clubs was included for the first time. In June 1959, increasing circulation made possible a switch to offset printing. In 1960, the publication went from 10 issues a year to a full 12-issue monthly. Pages jumped from 408 in 1958 to 968 in 1969.

A Master Pointers section was begun in February 1964. Frey also instituted the insert plan by which various ACBL districts and units could have their own publication inserted into the parent magazine and mailed with it.

In 1970, Frey retired and his duties were assumed by three of his assistants. Steven Becker was appointed executive editor; Tannah Hirsch became the editor; and Thomas Smith was named business manager. Major changes in the top editorial positions took place again in 1972, when the ACBL moved its headquarters from Greenwich CT to Memphis TN. Late in 1972 Henry Francis became executive editor; Sue Emery was appointed editor; and Richard Oshlag became business and advertising manager. Oshlag became head of the ACBL computer department in 1983 and Frank Stewart became managing editor. Stewart resigned in 1989, at which time Brent Manley took over as managing editor.

Under Francis the *Bridge Bulletin* again made major strides. Extensive coverage of major events throughout the world became the rule. The Master Pointers section was expanded, and two new special areas were added – one for new players and one for intermediates. In-depth interviews of bridge stars, corporate giants who play bridge and tournament directors were introduced. The Mail Box became the springboard for all sorts of high-spirited discussions, with controversial letters setting off interesting and informative debates. Book reviews were enhanced to include reviews of computer programs. A new feature, "It's Your Call," quickly became the magazine's most popular feature. Front covers highlighted important bridge happenings. The insert plan inaugurated by Frey was expanded. Each December issue featured a complete index of the year's articles.

When Francis retired as executive editor in 1997 after 25 years in that post, Manley was promoted to executive editor and Paul Linxwiler was hired as managing

editor. Manley's first act was to give the magazine a new look. In line with the greatly increased interest in computer bridge, Manley also began an annual review of the products available along with pertinent comments concerning the performance of the products. He also added many features, including crossword puzzles, cartoons and humorous stories and anecdotes.

The *Bridge Bulletin* has continued its growth. In 1981 the page total climbed to 1304, and the record was set in 1994 when there was a total of 1712 pages. In 2000 the magazine consisted of 132 pages per issue, for an annual total of 1584 pages. The magazine also is available on the ACBL web page.

ACBL BRIDGE SERIES. A set of five books used by the ACBL for teaching and authored by Audrey Grant. The books: *Bidding (The Club Series), Play (The Diamond Series), Defense (The Heart Series), Commonly Used Conventions (The new Spade Series), More Commonly Used Conventions (The Notrump Series)*. The original *Spade Series (Duplicate)* was reworked into two Play courses. They are called *Play Course for the Advancing Student - 1* and *Play Course for the Advancing Student - II*.

ACBL has developed E-Z Deal decks of cards for each basic course. These cards are coded so that a student can deal the lesson hands found at the end of each chapter. The E-Z Deal cards eliminate the need for a teacher to pre-duplicate hands used in the classroom. There are in addition E-Z Deal booklets for the series which offer the chapter summaries for each text in a format that students can use for easy reference.

ACBL has developed a television series, *The Bridge Class*, based on *The Club Series* text. This program contains 13 half-hour shows and is distributed by the Public Broadcasting System (PBS). ACBL has developed a second series for television known as *Play Bridge with Audrey Grant*. This program contains 13 half-hour shows based on *The Diamond Series* and 13 half-hour shows based on *The Heart Series*. See also TELEVISION.

Interest in the ACBL Teaching Series is widespread. Foreign translations of these books into Spanish, French Canadian and Japanese have been authorized by ACBL.

ACBL BULLETIN. Now called ACBL BRIDGE BULLETIN. See ACBL BRIDGE BULLETIN.

ACBL CHAMPIONSHIPS. Championships in the American Contract Bridge League take place on many levels. At the top are the three North American Bridge Championships, all of which feature many events of national ranking. The districts of the ACBL stage more than 100 regional championships each year. Such events regularly draw competitors from a wide area. The third level is sectional championships, which usually draw from a fairly concentrated area. Next is the local championship, which usually involves an area encompassing only a few clubs. The most common championships are those run by clubs. These games are primarily for the players who regularly play at the sponsoring club.

The ACBL sponsors several special championships – ACBL-wide charity games, International Fund games, ACBL-wide Senior games, International Team Trials, Women's International Team Trials, special Junior games, etc.

ACBL CHARITY FOUNDATION. See ACBL CHARITY PROGRAM.

ACBL CHARITY PROGRAM. The program whereby the ACBL makes major contributions to charity. Funds collected for charity are turned over to the ACBL Charity Foundation for distribution. A board of trustees makes grants to local and national charities. Many of the donations are made to charities who primary purpose is research.

The charity program has three main purposes: (1) to make important contributions to worthy charities; (2) to foster good public relations, and (3) to provide a promotional tool to clubs and units so that they can stimulate interest and extend their activities. The program includes all kinds of games at the club, unit, district and national levels.

Bridge-related charity efforts began in 1934 on the initiative of William McKenney. The chief beneficiaries were children's charities such as the Children Cancer Fund and the War Orphans Scholarship Fund. From 1951 to 1964, the ACBL designated one or two national charities per year as charity recipients. The desire to aid less well-known but thoroughly worthy causes with smaller contributions led the ACBL Board of Directors to establish the ACBL Charity Foundation on July 1, 1964. This foundation donates more than $125,000 per year to various charities that include the ACBL's Charity of the Year. Charities that have been the Charity of the Year:

1982-83	National Kidney Foundation, $240,000.	
1984-85	National Committee for the Prevention of Child Abuse, $312,834.	
1986-87	Arthritis Foundation, $300,000.	
1988-89	American Foundation for AIDS Research, $200,000.	
1990-91	Hospice, $200,000.	
1992-93	Multiple Sclerosis, $200,000.	
1994-95	Alzheimer's, $200,000.	
1996-97	National Council on Alcohol and Drug Dependency, $200,000.	
1998	Crohn's and Colitis, $100,000.	
1999	Autism Foundation, $100,000.	
2000	American Parkinson's Disease Foundation, $100,000.	

The original trustees were Gen. Alfred Gruenther, president; Benjamin Johnson, John Simon, Jeffy Lewis and Sidney Fink. The following have been honored as trustees emeriti: Percy Bean, Richard Hewitt, Ruth McConnell, John Norwood, Abner Parker, Carl Rubin, Leo Seewald, Nate Silverstein, Sam Stayman, Edgar Theus, Kathie Wei-Sender and Joseph Weintraub. Presidents:

1964-65	Alfred Gruenther
1965-67	Sidney Fink
1968-73	Benjamin Johnson
1973-74	Joseph Stedem
1975-80	Percy Bean
1981-82	Jerome Silverman
1983	Ruth McConnell
1984	Jerome Silverman
1985-86	Kathie Wei-Sender
1987	Richard Hewitt
1988-89	Joan DeWitt McKean
1990	Percy Bean
1991	Richard Hewitt

ACBL EDUCATIONAL FOUNDATION. A charitable trust fund established as a nonprofit organization in 1987. The foundation provides grants to promote the education of bridge that support the current needs of the bridge community. Its goal is to make bridge a game played by people of all ages and walks of life. Contribution are in the form of gifts from individuals, families and corporations. The foundation once relied on donations only for its funds, but in 2000 the ACBL Board of Directors approved changes in the use of funds raised at ACBL special games. Until then, money raised in certain special games at North American championships was given to the ACBL Charity Foundation. In 2000 the game on the opening night of the championships was renamed the Educational Foundation Pairs and Teams, and money raised in this event goes to the Educational Foundation. The game held during NABCs formerly called the Charity Pairs was renamed the Educational Pairs, with the money raised now going to the Educational Foundation. 2001 officers:

ACBL GENERAL CONVENTION CHART. The conventions listed below must be allowed in all ACBL sanctioned tournament play (other than in events with an upper restriction of 20 or fewer masterpoints and events for which the ACBL conditions of contest state otherwise) and at club-level events with multiple-site overall masterpoint awards. Clubs have full authority to regulate conventions in games conducted solely at their clubs.

DEFINITIONS

1. An opening suit bid or response is considered natural if in a minor it shows three or more cards in that suit and in a major it shows four or more cards in that suit. A notrump opening or overcall is natural if not unbalanced (generally, no singleton or void and only one or two doubletons).
2. An overcall in a suit is considered natural if, by agreement, it shows four or more cards in the denomination named.
3. A sequence of relay bids is defined as a system if,

after an opening of one of a suit, it is started prior to opener's rebid.

ALLOWED

★ ★ **Unless specifically allowed, methods are disallowed ★ ★**

OPENING BIDS

1. ONE CLUB OR ONE DIAMOND may be used as an all-purpose opening bid (artificial or natural) promising a minimum of 10 high-card points.
2. FORCING 1NT OPENING BID indicating a balanced or unbalanced hand and a minimum of 16 HCP.
3. TWO CLUBS ARTIFICIAL OPENING BID indicating one of:
   a) a strong hand.
   b) a three-suiter with a minimum of 10 HCP.
4. STRENGTH SHOWING OPENING AT THE TWO LEVEL OR HIGHER that asks for aces, kings, queens, singletons, voids or trump quality and responses thereto.
5. TWO DIAMOND ARTIFICIAL OPENING BID indicating one of:
   a) both majors with a minimum of 10 HCP.
   b) a strong hand.
   c) a three-suiter with a minimum of 10 HCP.
6. OPENING SUIT BID AT THE TWO LEVEL OR HIGHER indicating two known suits, a minimum of 10 HCP and at least 5-4 distribution in the suits.
7. OPENING NOTRUMP BID AT THE TWO LEVEL OR HIGHER indicating at least 5-4 distribution in the minors.
8. OPENING THREE NOTRUMP BID indicating one of
   a) a solid suit or
   b) a minor one-suiter.
9. OPENING FOUR-LEVEL BID transferring to a known suit.

RESPONSES AND REBIDS

1. ONE DIAMOND as a forcing, artificial response to 1♣.
2. ONE NOTRUMP response to a major suit opening bid forcing one round; cannot guarantee game invitational or better values.
3. CONVENTIONAL RESPONSES WHICH GUARANTEE GAME FORCING OR BETTER VALUES. May NOT be part of a relay system.
4. TWO CLUBS OR TWO DIAMONDS response to third or fourth-seat major-suit openings asking the quality of the opening bid.
5. SINGLE OR HIGHER JUMP SHIFTS AND/OR NOTRUMP BIDS AT THE TWO LEVEL OR HIGHER to indicate a raise or to force to game.
6. ARTIFICIAL AND CONVENTIONAL CALLS after strong (15+ HCP), forcing opening bids and after opening bids of 2♣ or higher. (For this classification, by partnership agreement, weak two-bids must be within a range of 7 HCP and the suit must contain at least five cards – *See #7 under DISALLOWED*.)
7. ALL CONSTRUCTIVE CALLS starting with the opening bidder's second call.
8. CALLS THAT ASK for aces, kings queens, singletons, voids or trump quality and responses thereto.
9. ALL CALLS AFTER A NATURAL NOTRUMP opening bid or direct overcall, EXCEPT for natural notrump opening bids or overcalls with a lower limit

of fewer than 10 HCP or with a range of greater than 5 HCP (including those that have two non-consecutive ranges). *See #7 under DISALLOWED.*

COMPETITIVE

1. CONVENTIONAL BALANCING CALLS.
2. CONVENTIONAL DOUBLES AND REDOUBLES and responses (including free bids) thereto.
3. NOTRUMP OVERCALL for either
   a) two-suit takeout showing at least 5-4 distribution and at least one known suit (At the four level or higher there is no requirement to have a known suit.) or
   b) three-suit takeout (at least three cards in each of the three suits.)
4. JUMP OVERCALLS INTO A SUIT to indicate at least 5-4 distribution in two known suits and responses thereto.
5. CUEBID of an opponent's suit and responses thereto, except that a cuebid that could be weak (fewer than 10 HCP) directly over an opening bid, must show at least one known suit.
6. DEFENSE TO:
   a) conventional calls (except see #9 RESPONSES and REBIDS above and #7 under DISALLOWED below),
   b) natural notrump opening bids and overcalls, except that direct calls, other than double and 2♣ must have at least one known suit.
   c) opening bids of 2♣ or higher.
7. Numbers 4 through 8 under RESPONSES AND REBIDS above APPLY TO BOTH PAIRS.

DISALLOWED

1. Conventions and/or agreements whose primary purpose is to destroy the opponents' methods.
2. Psyching of artificial or conventional opening bids and/or conventional responses thereto. Psyching conventional suit responses, **which are less than** 2NT, to natural openings.
3. Psychic controls (Includes ANY partnership agreement which, if used in conjunction with a psychic call, makes allowance for that psych.)
4. Forcing pass systems.
5. Relay (tell me more) systems.
6. Opening one bids which by partnership agreement could show fewer than 8 HCP. (Not applicable to a psych.)
7. CONVENTIONAL RESPONSES, REBIDS AND A CONVENTIONAL DEFENSE TO AN OPPONENT'S CONVENTIONAL DEFENSE after natural notrump opening bids or overcalls with a lower limit of fewer than 10 HCP or with a range of greater than 5 HCP (including those that have two non-consecutive ranges) and weak two-bids which by partnership agreement are not within a range of 7 HCP and do not show at least five cards in the suit.

CARDING

Dual-message carding strategies are not approved except on each defender's first discard. Except for the first discard only right-side-up or upside-down card ordering strategies are approved. Encrypted signals are not approved. In addition, a pair may be prohibited from playing any method (such as suit preference systems at trick one), when they are deemed to be playing it in a manner which is not compatible with the maintenance of proper tempo (much like dual message signals). This decision may be appealed to the tournament committee.

ACBL GOODWILL COMMITTEE. A group of ACBL members dedicated to promoting goodwill and good manners everywhere that bridge is played. The committee was organized in 1955 with John E. Simon as chairman and Louise Durham as co-chairman. In 1957 the committee was made permanent, with two members, one man and one woman, being appointed from each district by the district director to hold permanent membership on the Committee. In 1963 three assistant chairmen were designated: Ethel Keohane (East), Louise Durham (Central) and Evelyn Piro (West). In 1972 John T. Murphy was added as another assistant chairman. In 1975 Jerome Silverman was named chairman, succeeding Simon who became Honorary Chairman Emeritus. In 1977 Kay Moody became chairman. She was succeeded in 1979 by Dr. John Pratt. In 1985, Aileen Osofsky, the present chairman, took the post. Under her tenure the committee has significantly expanded its endeavors, taking on promotion of Active Ethics, awareness of the hearing impaired, support of Junior, Youth and Charity programs, naming of a GOODWILL MEMBER OF THE YEAR and other projects.

Each member of the ACBL Board of Directors is entitled to appoint two members from his or her district annually to the committee. Meetings are held on Monday during each North American championship tournament. Assisting Osofsky as assistant chairpersons are Sharon David, Valley Village CA; Korene Geffen, Aurora CO; Judy Kay, Narberth PA; George Rosenkranz, Mexico City; Carol Sanders, Nashville TN; Aidan Ballantyne, Vancouver BC; and Penny Augustine, Toronto. See GOODWILL MEMBER OF YEAR.

ACBL GOODWILL MEMBER OF THE YEAR. An award begun in 1990 by Goodwill Committee Chairman Aileen Osofsky to honor the ACBL member whose actions and philosophy embody the principles of goodwill: a promoter of bridge, a courteous and friendly opponent and a gentle and considerate partner. Recipients:

1990 Doris O'Grady
1991 Julian Slager
1992 Dorothy and Norman Edwardson
1993 Jack Boehne
1994 Gladys Hodge
1995 Kara Jarman
1996 Tom Gardner, Mayme Lawrence
1997 Dick Shaver
1998 Jay Brown
1999 Miriam Martin
2000 Joan Weinrott
2001 Louise Wiegman, John Keech
See ACBL GOODWILL COMMITTEE.

ACBL HALL OF FAME. The original Hall of Fame was started by *The Bridge World* in 1964. The original members were Ely Culbertson, Charles Goren, Harold Vanderbilt, Oswald Jacoby, Milton Work, Sidney Lenz, Waldemar von Zedtwitz, Howard Schenken and Sidney Silodor. When *The Bridge World* discontinued its work on the Hall, no members were added until the ACBL inducted the original nine into its own Hall in 1995, then added eight more. The new members were Edgar Kaplan, Al Roth, Bobby Wolff, B. Jay Becker, Easley Blackwood, Barry Crane, John Crawford and Helen Sobel Smith. Additional members were added each year thereafter as follows:

1996 – Eddie Kantar, Norman Kay, Alfred Sheinwold, Josephine Culbertson, Victor Mitchell, Sam Stayman, David Bruce (von Zedtwitz Award) and Lee Hazen (Blackwood Award).

1997 – Edith Freilich, George Rapee, Bill Root, Dick Frey, Jim Jacoby, Lew Mathe, P. Hal Sims (von Zedtwitz Award) and Albert Morehead (Blackwood Award).

1998 – Bill Eisenberg, Mary Jane Farell, Dorothy Truscott, John Gerber, Sonny Moyse, Peter Pender, Alvin Landy (von Zedtwitz Award) and Dave Treadwell (Blackwood Award).

1999 – Bobby Goldman, Bob Hamman, Theodore Lightner, Al Sobel, Margaret Wagar, Michael Gottlieb (von Zedtwitz Award) and Kathie Wei-Sender (Blackwood Award).

2000 – Sidney Lazard, Ira Rubin, Lou Bluhm, Harry Fishbein, Charles Solomon, Meyer Schliefer (von Zedtwitz Award) and George Rosenkranz (Blackwood Award).

2001 – Richard Freeman, Lew Stansby; Peter Leventritt, Bobby Nail, Sally Young, Sami Kehela and Eric Murray (each received von Zedtwitz Award), Alan Truscott (Blackwood Award).

The von Zedtwitz Award is given to a deceased player who made outstanding contributions to bridge either as a player or in some area outside of playing expertise. The Blackwood Award is given to a player, living or deceased, who has made major contributions to bridge outside the area of bridge expertise. Portraits of all members are housed in a gallery at ACBL Headquarters in Memphis, Tennessee.

ACBL HANDBOOK. A handbook that includes the regulations and practices followed by the American Contract Bridge League in several important phases of its activities. Covered in detail are the regulations and practices involving membership, clubs, units, districts, tournaments and discipline. Interested persons or groups may secure copies from ACBL HEADQUARTERS.

ACBL HEADQUARTERS. The headquarters building, located at 2990 Airways Boulevard, Memphis, Tennessee, has been the home of the ACBL since 1989. Hundreds of members visit the building each year to meet the staff and to see the ACBL HALL OF FAME display, the ALBERT MOREHEAD MEMORIAL LIBRARY and the magnificent collection of trophies. The walls on all four floors are adorned with photos of bridge greats and bridge administrators through the years. The grounds outside are landscaped in such a way that the four suit symbols are sculptured in flowers and plants. More than 90 persons in the Headquarters building take care of day-to-day ACBL activities.

Over the years the ACBL has had many homes. After being housed in New York City since its inception, it moved to Greenwich, Connecticut, in 1967. This became the sole home of the ACBL when the Western office was closed in 1968. When the Board of Directors decided that the organization should be located somewhere near the center of the United States because so much of its business was shipping, the ACBL was moved to Memphis, Tennessee late in 1972. A building constructed specifically for the ACBL was built at 2200 Democrat Road. However, because of additional member services and programs, the ACBL outgrew this location and moved to the Airways address in 1989.

Principal Headquarters personnel:
Chief Executive Officer – Wayne Hascall
Controller – Jack Zdancewicz
Bridge Administration – Gary Blaiss
Bridge Bulletin editor – Brent Manley
Sales – Jim Miller
Education – Julie Greenberg
Membership – Carol Robertson
Important ACBL e-mail addresses:
Chief Executive Officer – ceo@acbl.org
Bridge Bulletin – editor@acbl.org
Masterpoints – masterpoints@acbl.org
Tournaments – tournaments@acbl.org
Education – education@acbl.org
Club Department – club@acbl.org
Membership – membership@acbl.org
ACBLscore – acblscore@acbl.org
North American Bridge Championships – nabc@acbl.org
International events – internationalevents@acbl.org

ACBL INSTANT MATCHPOINT GAME. A special game staged once a year, usually in September, which is scored by preassigned matchpoints. The hands are taken from a long-ago tournament. An expert checks each hand for possible results and then assigns specific matchpoints for all possible scores.The game is set up so that all contestants play exactly 24 boards, no matter what the size of the event. Games are sanctioned at clubs as requested throughout the ACBL. Since the North-South and East-West pairs are not in direct competition with each other, winners are proclaimed for each direction. See EPSON PAIRS, WORLD-WIDE PAIRS.

ACBL INTERNATIONAL OPEN TEAM SELECTION. Many methods have been tried for selection of the North American team for Bermuda Bowl contests or of the United States team for World Olympiads.

1950-60 - Team Performance

From 1950 to 1960, the ACBL selected the winners of the SPINGOLD, or the victors in a playoff between the Spingold and VANDERBILT winners.

In 1960 the United States was entitled, by virtue of the size of the ACBL membership, to send four teams to the first World Team Olympiad. Two of the teams selected were the winners of the Vanderbilt and the Spingold. Each of the other teams consisted of three pairs selected by a committee (the five most recent ACBL presidents attend- ing the 1959 Fall Nationals) from among the contestants remaining in the seventh or eighth round of the Vanderbilt and Spingold respectively.

1961 - Direct Selection

The 1961 team consisted of three pairs selected by the ACBL Board of Directors from among the winners and runners-up in major national events.

1962-69 - Trials by Pairs

In an effort to select pairs in effective current form, pairs trials were instituted in 1961. From 1961 to 1966, the first three pairs in each trial were nominated as the inter- national team for the following year, and the fourth-place pair became the alternate pair. Beginning with the 1967 trials, this automatic selection method was dropped and the non-playing captain was permitted to select any two of the top four pairs, and the third and alternate pair from among the remaining finalists. Julius

Rosenblum exercised this option in 1967 when he named Edgar Kaplan and Norman Kay, who had finished fourth in the trials, to the team. Philip Feldesman and Ira Rubin, the third-place pair, became alternates, the only time the top three pairs were not selected as the international team.

1970 – Vanderbilt – Spingold Playoff

The Pair-Team trials were discontinued in order to allow selection of an entire team rather than individual pairs to comprise a team. The 1970 International Team was selected by a direct 180-board playoff between the winners of the 1969 Vanderbilt and Spingold. This reduced the prestige of the Fall North American Championships, which previously had two events that qualified pairs for the trials.

1971-72 - Placing-Points Playoffs

Beginning with the 1969 Fall NABC, the ACBL adopted a playoff among the teams with the best records over the course of a year. Teams placing high in the three major team championships (Reisinger, Vanderbilt, and Spingold) were awarded points according to the following scale: Vanderbilt and Spingold: 1st -10 points; 2nd - 4; 3rd - 2. Reisinger: 1st - 6 points; 2nd - 4; 3rd - 2. If a team accumulated 20 points it was to be automatically designated the International Team; otherwise teams with lesser numbers of points were to playoff.

1973-1979 – Vanderbilt, Spingold, Reisinger, Grand Nationals Winners Playoff

With the introduction of the GRAND NATIONAL CHAMPIONSHIPS in 1972, the selection of the North American international team became a simple matter of a four-team playoff among the winners of the ACBL's four major team events: the Vanderbilt, Spingold, Reisinger, and Grand Nationals.

1980-1983 – Vanderbilt, Spingold, Reisinger, Grand National, Canadian National Winners Playoff

At the request of the CANADIAN BRIDGE FEDERATION, that section of the Grand National Teams involving Canadian players was separated from the main event and changed into a Canadian National Teams Championship. The Canadian champions became a fifth entry in the trials in those years when a Bermuda Bowl team was being chosen. The trials started with a round-robin, with one team being eliminated. The usual knockout format was used from that point on, with a carryover formula applied.

1985-1990 – Tri-Country Trials

In 1985 it was decided that one team from Zone 2 to the Bermuda Bowl would be a United States team. This team would be the winner of the United States Bridge Championship (USBC), a contest among the victors of the Vanderbilt, Spingold, Reisinger and Grand National. The other team would be the winner of a tri-cornered contest among the other three nations in Zone 2 – Canada, Mexico and Bermuda.

1991 – Three Zone 2 representatives

As a result of WBF action increasing the total entry in the Bermuda Bowl, Zone 2 was authorized to send three teams. These teams were the winners of the USBC and the tri-country trials plus the top three pairs from the Pan North American Bridge Championships.

Starting in 1995 the United States representatives were determined in the International Team Trials. Many teams are entered each year, and a carefully constructed screening process is used to decide what teams play which, and when. In Olympiad years (years divisible by four), one team is chosen; in Bermuda Bowl years (odd-numbered years) two teams are selected.

ACBL INTERNATIONAL WOMEN'S TEAM SELECTION. The United States has used several different methods to determine the team to send to the World Women's Team Olympiad. In 1960, a committee consisting of the five most recent ACBL presidents attending the 1959 Fall Nationals selected the team by choosing three pairs of women who finished first or second in any national championship event during 1959. For 1964, a trial by pairs was held, similar to the trials held during that period for the ACBL INTERNATIONAL OPEN TEAM SELECTION. In 1968 four pairs qualified for a round-robin. Each pair played a 32-board match in partnership with each of the other pairs, and Margaret Wagar, the non-playing captain, was empowered to select any three of the four pairs. For 1972, teams earned points in the major national team championships to determine the team. However, one team amassed so many points that it was designated without a playoff. For 1976, women earned "selection points," either as teams or as pairs, on all-women teams in the Vanderbilt, Spingold, Reisinger and Spring National Women's Teams. Available points ranged from 1 point for being runner-up in the Spring Women's teams to 28 for winning the Vanderbilt or Spingold. To be selected intact, a team must have won more qualification points than any individual pair, except that if there were only one higher pair, a four-person team plus the high-ranking pair would form the six-member team. This method was continued through 1988. When the WBF began staging Venice Cup contests for odd-numbered years opposite the Bermuda Bowl in 1985, the same selection process was in effect.

The selection point method was discontinued in 1989, and the North American Women's Bridge Team Championships (NAWBTC) were inaugurated. The 1989 winning team gained a bye to the Venice Cup semifinals, while the second-place team (Canada) had to compete in round-robin qualifications. In 1991, three ACBL teams were selected — first and second in the U.S. Women's Trials plus Canada, which won a playoff with Mexico. In 1992 the United States Women's Bridge Championships (USWBC) were held to select a team for the Olympiad. Zone II once again had three representatives for the Venice Cup in 1993.

Automatic qualifiers for the women's trials include the reigning NEC Venice Cup champion, if the team is intact at the time of the trials; first and second in the Women's Knockout Teams; first in the Women's Swiss Teams; first in the Women's Board-a-Match Teams; any all-woman team reaching the semifinals of the Vanderbilt or Spingold; any all-woman team finishing first through fourth in the Reisinger Board-a-Match Teams. See also TRI-COUNTRY TRIALS, VENICE CUP, WOMEN'S TEAM OLYMPIAD. For results see Appendix III.

ACBL JUNIOR CORPS. The ACBL established the Junior Corps as a part of its Junior program in 1990. Members of the Junior Corp are ACBL's elite Junior players who are the future of the organization. This group is charged with working together with Unit officials and tournament organizers to promote bridge among young people. New members are inducted at the Junior Day receptions held at each of the three annual NABCs.

ACBL LAWS COMMISSION. See LAWS COMMIS-SION OF THE ACBL.

ACBL LIBRARY. See ALBERT MOREHEAD ME-MORIAL LIBRARY.

ACBL LIFE MASTER. Once the highest ACBL player rank. (For qualification for this rank, see RANKING.) The category was created by the AMERICAN BRIDGE LEAGUE in 1936 and selection of the first Life Masters was based on national tournament successes, although a masterpoint program had been in effect since 1934. Initially, the rank was conferred on a group of 10 players, ranked in order according to the number and importance of their national victories, and an eleventh player was made Life Master shortly thereafter. There are now six separate categories of Life Master (see RANKING). The first 100 players to achieve the rank were:

1.	David Bruce	1936
2.	Oswald Jacoby	1936
3.	Howard Schenken	1936
4.	Waldemar K. von Zedtwitz	1936
5.	P. Hal Sims	1936
6.	B. Jay Becker	1936
7.	Theodore A. Lightner	1936
8.	Richard L. Frey	1936
9.	Michael T. Gottlieb	1936
10.	Sam Fry Jr.	1936
11.	Merwin D. Maier	1936
12.	Charles S. Lochridge	1937
13.	Charles H. Goren	1938
14.	A. Mitchell Barnes	1938
15.	Harry J. Fishbein	1939
16.	Charles J. Solomon	1939
17.	Sally Young	1939
18.	Fred D. Kaplan	1939
19.	John R. Crawford	1939
20.	Walter Jacobs	1939
21.	Morrie Elis	1939
22.	Phil Abramsohn	1940
23.	Edward Hymes Jr.	1940
24.	Alvin Landy	1940
25.	Helen Sobel Smith	1941
26.	Sherman Stearns	1941
27.	Robert A. McPherran	1941
28.	Jeff Glick	1942
29.	Arthur Glatt	1942
30.	Dr. Richard Ecker Jr.	1942
31.	Albert Weiss	1942
32.	Lee Hazen	1942
33.	Peggy Solomon	1942
34.	Alvin Roth	1942
35.	Sidney Silodor	1943
36.	Olive Peterson	1943
37.	Margaret Wagar	1943
38.	Peter A. Leventritt	1943
39.	Edson T. Wood	1944
40.	Ralph Kempner	1944
41.	Arthur S.Goldsmith	1944
42.	Simon Becker	1944
43.	Stanley O. Fenkel	1944
44.	George Rapee	1944
45.	Ruth Sherman	1944
46.	Robert Appleyard	1945
47.	M. A. Lightman	1945
48.	Samuel Stayman	1945
49.	Edward N. Marcus	1945
50.	Charles A. Hall	1945
51.	Emily Folline	1946
52.	Joseph E. Cain	1946
53.	Harry Feinberg	1946
54.	Ambrose Casner	1946
55.	Samuel Katz	1946
56.	Jack Ehrlenbach	1946
57.	J. Van Brooks	1946
58.	Simon Rossant	1946
59.	Edward G. Ellenbogen	1946
60.	Sidney B. Fink	1946
61.	Bertram Lebhar Jr.	1946
62.	Meyer Schleifer	1947
63.	Louis Newman	1947
64.	Elinor Murdoch	1947
65.	Paula Bacher	1947
66.	Florence Stratford	1947
67.	Jules Bank	1947
68.	William McGhee	1947
69.	Maynard Adams	1947
70.	Edith Kemp	1947
71.	David Carter	1947
72.	Jack Cushing	1947
73.	Dr. A. Steinberg	1947
74.	Jane Jaeger	1947
75.	Cecil Head	1947
76.	S. Garton Churchill	1947
77.	Edward S. Cohn	1947
78.	John Carlin	1947
79.	Lawrence Welch	1947
80.	Frank Weisbach	1947
81.	Charlton Wallace	1944
82.	Dr. Louis Mark	1947
83.	Edward Taylor	1947
84.	Dan Westerfield	1947
85.	Tobias Stone	1947
86.	Mark Hodges	1947
87.	Leo Roet	1947
88.	Sol Mogal	1947
89.	Herbert Gerst	1947
90.	Lewis Mathe	1947
91.	Ludwig Kabakjian	1947
92.	Gratian Goldstein	1947
93.	Allen P. Harvey	1947
94.	Lewis Jaeger	1947
95.	Mildred Cunningham	1947
96.	Elmer J. Schwartz	1947
97.	Linda Terry	1947
98.	Maurice Levin	1948
99.	Dave Warner	1948
100.	Ernest Rovere	1948

ACBL LIMITED CONVENTIONS. (May be used in games with an upper limit of 20 or fewer MPs)
CLUBS
Club management shall determine the conventions permitted in club games with an upper limit of 20 or fewer masterpoints.
LOCAL & HIGHER EVENTS
The sponsoring organization of local and higher rated tournaments may determine the conventions permitted in games with an upper limit of 20 or fewer masterpoints.
OPENING BIDS
A 1♣ opening bid may be both artificial (says noth-

ing about clubs) and forcing (partner must respond at least once), but opener must have at least 10 HCP. A negative 1 ♦ response may be used.

A 2 ♣ opening bid may be artificial and strong. It may be balanced (a hand stronger than a traditional 2NT opening) or unbalanced (a hand with which you would open a strong two-bid if playing that way). Further bidding will describe the hand.

A 3NT opening bid may show a hand with a long, solid suit (gambling).

RESPONSES AND REBIDS

A jump shift of one or more levels (into a suit or into notrump) may be used either to force to game or to show a raise of partner's suit.

Any meaning may be given to the responses and rebids after an opening bid of 1NT. Exception: if the 1NT opening has a point range which exceeds 5 HCP, or if the 1NT opening has an agreed lower limit of fewer than 10 HCP, responses and rebids may not be conventional — they must be natural.

Any meaning may be given to the responses to and rebids after an opening bid of 2 ♣ or higher. Exception: if the opening bid is a weak two-bid with (a) an agreed point range of more than 7 HCP, (b) an agreement that the bid suit can contain fewer than five cards, or (c) an agreement that the hand can contain fewer than 5 HCP, responses and rebids may not be conventional — they must be natural.

Any call may be used to ask partner or to respond to partner about aces, kings, queens, singletons, voids or trump quality with the exceptions noted above.

COMPETITIVE AUCTIONS

Any meaning may be given to a double or a redouble.

A notrump overcall or jump overcall may be use to show a two-suited hand (at least 5–4 distribution in the two suits). At least one of the suits must be known. The second suit may be known or unknown.

Any meaning may be given to the cuebid of an opponent's suit.

Any meaning may be given to calls used to defend against opponents' conventional calls, notrump bids and opening bids of 2 ♣ or higher.

DISALLOWED

Conventions and /or agreements with a primary purpose of destroying the opponents' methods are not allowed (e.g., a bid telling nothing about the bidder's hand, made simply to use up bidding space).

Agreements allowing the partnership to open the bidding at the one level with fewer than 8 HCP are not allowed. This does not preclude a psychic opening bid.

Psyching of artificial opening bids or conventional responses to artificial opening bids is not allowed.

Psychic controls (bids designed to determine whether partner has psyched or to clarify the nature of the psych) are not allowed.

Relay systems (one player tells nothing about his own hand while interrogating partner about his hand through a series of conventional calls) are not allowed.

CARDING

A discard (a card played while not following suit) can convey a message to partner. The message can pertain to the length of the suit of the card discarded, to the attitude toward that suit (desire to have partner lead that suit) or to another suit (no information about the suit of the card discarded). A pair may decide to attribute the attitude message (good-bad) to the cards on either a

higher-to-lower basis (a higher card is more positive than a lower card) or a lower-to-higher basis (a low card is more positive than a higher card).

A discard may carry more than one message, but only at each defender's first discard of the deal. Dual-message discards are not permitted as second or subsequent discards. Encrypted signals (the order and /or message is based on information known to the other defender but not yet to declarer) are not allowed at any time.

ACBL MASTERPOINTS. At ACBL events, masterpoints can take many forms.

Club points - 100 club masterpoints are the equivalent of one masterpoint.

Black points - Awarded for overall positions, section positions, and match awards in ACBL sanctioned club games; in all unit events; and in all other levels of tournament competition except those in which gold, red or silver points or net points are awarded.

Net points - Awarded for online masterpoint events and are colorless. (No more than 1/3 of points required to achieve established ACBL status may be won from online play.)

Silver points - Awarded exclusively in all events at sectional tournaments and also at ACBL sanctioned sectional tournaments held at clubs.

Red points - Awarded for all regionally rated events at NABCs and for all events at a regional tournament when the masterpoints are not gold. In addition, red points are awarded for certain special events.

Gold points - Awarded at North American Bridge Championships (NABCs) in national-rated events that have an upper limit of at least 750 masterpoints. Gold points are awarded for overall positions and for section firsts in all two-session regional-rated events with an upper limit of at least 750 masterpoints at NABCs and regional tournaments. No more than two strats or flights of the same event may issue gold points with the exception of bracketed knockout teams. Partial gold points awards are given for certain special events.

Platinum points - Awarded for NABC+ events and include the national-rated senior and women's events with no upper masterpoint limit but not the junior, Flight B or other restricted events.

ACBL MID-CHART. This chart applies to:
1. All NABC+ events with no upper masterpoint restrictions played at an NABC.
2. All unrestricted Flight A regionally rated events at an NABC.
3. Any bracket of a bracketed KO at an NABC which contains no team with a bracket designator (average masterpoints of the entire team or top two players) of less than 1000 points.

This chart (or any part) may apply to any sectionally or regionally rated event or tournament at sponsor's option provided that this has been included in tournament advertising. (The requirement for advertising does not extend to use in Flt. A or high brackets of KOs.)

Pre-Alerts are required for all conventional methods not permitted on the ACBL General Convention Chart. **Except for those methods designated by an asterisk (*) which do not require a written suggested defense.** A written description of, and suggested defenses to such methods must be made available to opponents. A defense to a method which requires the above pre-Alert

may be referred to during the auction by opponents of the convention user.

AFTER JULY 1, 2001, pairs using a method permitted by the Mid-Chart and not noted by an asterisk must have available for the opponents the defense approved and listed in the ACBL Defense Database which is available at www.acbl.org. A hard copy may be purchased from the ACBL sales department (in the U.S. 1-800-264-2743; in Canada 1-800-264-8786.

A method may be approved experimentally for Mid-Chart events. In order to have a method approved experimentally, a complete description and suggested defense must be submitted to ACBL, attention Chief Tournament Director by regular mail or e-mail to chief.tournament.director@acbl.org

ALLOWED

★ ★ Unless specifically allowed, methods are disallowed ★ ★

1. All of the ACBL General Convention Chart.
2.* Relay (tell me more) systems that promise game-forcing values.
3.* All other constructive rebids and responses are permitted - except for:
   a. relay systems that show less than game-forcing values,
   b. conventional calls after natural notrump opening bids or overcalls with a lower limit of fewer than 10 HCP or with a range of greater than 5 HCP conventional calls *(see #9 under RESPONSES AND REBIDS and #7 under DISALLOWED on the General Convention Chart)* – however, this prohibition does not extend to notrumps that have two non-consecutive ranges neither of which exceeds 3 HCP - and
   c. conventional calls after a weak two-bid with an agreed range of more than 7 HCP or an agreement where the suit length may be four cards *(see #6 under RESPONSES AND REBIDS and #7 under DISALLOWED on the General Convention Chart).* THIS APPLIES TO BOTH PAIRS.
4. Any call that promises four or more cards in a known suit. (See items #6 and #8 in DISALLOWED below.)
5. Opening 2♦ showing a weak two-bid in an unspecified major and may include additional strong (15+ HCP) meaning(s).
6. A 2♠ or 2NT opening bid showing an unspecified minor or both minors.
7. Any strong (15+ HCP) opening bid.
8. Notrump overcall as a two-suit takeout showing at least 5-4 distribution.
9.* Defense to natural notrump opening bids and overcalls.
10. Any opening bid at the three level or higher showing an undisclosed solid suit.

DISALLOWED

1. Conventions and/or agreements whose primary purpose is to destroy the opponents' methods.
2. Psyching of artificial opening bids and/or conventional responses thereto.
3. Psychic controls. (Includes ANY partnership agreement which, if used in conjunction with a psychic call, makes allowance for that psych.)
4. Forcing pass systems.
5. Relay (tell me more) systems except those that are game-forcing.

6. Opening one-bids which by partnership agreement could show fewer than 8 HCP. (Not applicable to a psych.)
7. Psyching a conventional agreement which may show fewer than 10 HCP and which is not permitted by the General Convention Chart. This includes psyching responses to or rebids of these methods.
8. Any weak opening bid which promises an unknown suit may not include as the unknown suit the suit named (the suit opened).

CARDING

Same as listed on the General Convention Chart.

ACBL MINI-McKENNEY RACES. Annual competitions to determine the leading masterpoint winners in each ACBL rank classification. The group to which a player belongs is determined by his masterpoint holding at the start of the year. The McKENNEY TROPHY was established in 1938 to recognize the ACBL member who won the most masterpoints in a calendar year. In 1974 the ACBL Board voted to recognize masterpoint achievements among players of less than Life Master rank.Units may order Mini McKenney medallions from ACBL to be given to each winner of each category in their Unit. See ACBL RANK CLASSIFICATIONS. For winners see Appendix II.

ACBL NATIONAL APPEALS COMMITTEE. Committee appointed at each ACBL North American Championship to hear appeals of rulings of directors or complaints concerning conduct or ethics. See APPEALS COMMITTEE, COMMITTEE.

ACBL NORTH AMERICAN BRIDGE CHAMPIONSHIPS. The American Contract Bridge League stages three North American Bridge Championships (NABC) annually. These championships, held in the spring, summer and fall, last 10 + days. Special events such as the North American Pairs final (spring) and the late rounds of the Grand National Teams (summer) usually precede the NABC.

Each NABC features events for all players from the top experts to the absolute beginner. Many North American Championships with national rating, consisting of four, six or more sessions, are contested throughout. Every day there is at least one two-session championship with regional rating. Four-session regionally-rated knockout events take place during morning sessions as well as in an afternoon-evening format. One-session side games now are incorporated into CONTINUOUS PAIRS events. A full program of games for new and intermediate players takes place under tournament directors especially trained for this kind of game. Usually included are BRIDGE PLUS games for players who are totally new to duplicate bridge.

Nationally-rated championships: Spring NABC – Vanderbilt Knockout Teams, North American Pairs Flights A and B, North American Non-Life Master Pairs, Open Pairs I, Open Pairs II, Women's Pairs, Mixed Pairs, Silver Ribbon Pairs, Swiss Teams, Women's Swiss Teams, 49er Pairs; Summer NABC – Spingold Knockout Teams, Grand National Teams (Flights A, B and C), Wagar Women's Knockout Teams, Life Master Pairs, Mixed Teams, IMP Pairs, Fast Open Pairs, Senior Swiss Teams, Red Ribbon Pairs; Fall NABC – Reisinger Board-a-Match Teams, Blue Ribbon Pairs, North American

Swiss Teams, Life Master Open Pairs, Life Master Women's Pairs, Open Board-a-Match Teams, Women's Board-a-Match Teams, Non-Life Master Pairs, Senior Knockout Teams, 99er Pairs. Winners of these events are listed in Appendix I.

Each day all competitors receive a Daily Bulletin. Prior to each afternoon and evening session an expert delivers a 45-minute talk offered primarily for intermediates and new players. Many other special events and entertainments enhance each NABC program.

ACBL ONLINE. A computer service for playing bridge on the internet that started in 2001 and offers ACBL masterpoints. Features include complete records, vugraphs from major tournaments, bidding contests, bridge columns, chat room.

ACBL PLAYER NUMBER. See PLAYER NUMBER.

ACBL PLAYER OF THE YEAR. Awarded to the ACBL member who earns the most masterpoints during a calendar year in nationally-rated events. For winners see Appendix II.

ACBL PRESIDENTS. American Bridge League; American Contract Bridge League; and United States Bridge Association.

ABL

1927	Ralph R. Richards
1928	Henry P. Jaeger
1929	Robert W. Halpin
1930	Clayton W. Aldrich
1931	Capt. Fred G. French
1932	Waldemar K. von Zedtwitz
1933	Sir Derrick J. Wernher
1934	Ray H. Eisenlord
1935	Louis J. Haddad
1936	H. Huber Boscowitz

ACBL

1937	Gordon M. Gibbs
1938	Nate B. Spingold
1939	James H. Lemon
1940	Elmer J. Babin
1941	Robert J. Gill
1942	Morgan Howard
1943	Albert H. Morehead
1944	Richmond H. Skinner
1945	George A. Alderton, II
1946	Benjamin M. Golder
1947	J. McGrover
1948	Waldemar K. von Zedtwitz
1949	Dr. Louis Mark
1950	Rufus L. Miles, Jr.
1951	Julius L. Rosenblum
1952	Joseph Cohan
1953	Benjamin O. Johnson
1954	Peter A. Leventritt
1955	Jefferson Glick
1956	Rufus L. Miles, Jr.
1957	Joseph G. Ripstra
1958	Charles J. Solomon
1959	Winslow Randall
1960	Frank T. Westcott
1961	James P. Ferguson
1962	Max Manchester
1963	Jerry M. Lewis

1964	Leo Seewald
1965	Robin B. Mac Nab
1966	Eilif Andersen
1967	John W. Norwood
1968	Joseph J. Stedem
1969	Edgar G. Theus
1970	William A. Baldwin
1971	Carl Rubin
1972	Percy X. Bean
1973	Jerome R. Silverman
1974	Ruth McConnell
1975	Lewis L. Mathe
1976	Donald Oakie
1977	Louis S. Gurvich
1978	Walter K. O'Loughlin
1979	Leo J. Spivack
1980	Ira G. Corn, Jr.
1981	James E. Zimmerman
1982	Sydney A. Levey, Jr.
1983	William Gross
1984	Douglas Drew
1985	Chris Wilson
1986	Thomas K. Sanders
1987	Robert Wolff
1988	Herb Smith
1989	Phyllis Burke
1990	Edward Gould Jr.
1991	David McGee
1992	Joan Levy Gerard
1993	Barbara Nudelman
1994	Virgil Anderson Jr.
1995	Cecil Q. Cook
1996	Dudley B. Brown
1997	Howard J. Piltch
1998	Richard Anderson
1999	Val Covalciuc
2000	Glenn Smith
2001	James Kirkham

USBA

1932-4	Milton C. Work
1935-7	Ely Culbertson

ACBL RANK CLASSIFICATIONS. ACBL members are ranked according to the number of masterpoints won along with some other qualifications for most ranks. The classifications: Rookie, 0-4.99 points; Junior Master, 5-19.99; Club Master, 20-49.99; Sectional Master, 50-99.99, at least 5 silver; Regional Master, 100-299.99, at least 5 red or gold, 15 silver; NABC Master, 200-299.99, at least 5 gold, 15 red or gold, 25 silver; Life Master, 300, at least 25 gold, 25 red or gold, 50 silver. Ranking above this point require the player to have qualified as a Life Master: Bronze Life Master, 500 points; Silver Life Master, 1,000 points; Gold Life Master, 2,500 points; Diamond Life Master, 5,000 points; Grand Life Master, 10,000 points and one unlimited NABC championship.

ACBL SUPERCHART. This chart applies to all NABC+ events with no upper masterpoint limit played at an NABC in which contestants play segments (no change of opponents) of 12 or more boards. This chart (or any part) may be used at a sectionally or regionally rated event or tournament at sponsor's option in any event with 12-board or longer segments provided this has been included in tournament advertising.

Pre-Alerts are required for all conventional methods not permitted on the ACBL General Convention Chart. Description of, and suggested defenses to, such methods must be made in writing. A defense to a method which requires the above pre-Alert may be referred to during the auction by opponents of the convention user.

For NABC+ events in which this chart is permitted, pairs playing SuperChart methods must furnish the above descriptions of their methods to the Director-in-Charge of the event the day prior to the session in which they choose to play them.

ALLOWED

★ ★ Unless specifically allowed, methods are disallowed ★ ★

All of the ACBL MidChart plus any other non-destructive convention, treatment or method except that:
1. Artificial weak bids at the two or three level (including those with strong adjuncts) must possess,
   a) a known suit or
   b) one of no more than two possible suits not to include the suit bid.
2. Defenses over opponents' natural suit bids must promise,
   a) for non-cuebids showing a single suited hand, one of no more than two possible suits
   b) a cuebid which could show a weak hand with four or more cards in the suit bid must promise four or more cards in another known suit.
3. The prohibitions contained in item #9 under RESPONSES AND REBIDS on the General Convention Chart are effective for this Chart. (However, this prohibition does not extend to notrumps that have two non-consecutive ranges neither of which exceeds 3 HCP.)

DISALLOWED

1. Conventions and/or agreements whose primary purpose is to destroy the opponents' methods.
2. Psyching of artificial opening bids and/or conventional responses thereto.
3. Psychic controls (includes ANY partnership agreement which, if used in conjunction with a psychic call, makes allowance for that psych).
4. Forcing pass systems.
5. Opening one bids which by partnership agreement could show fewer than 8 HCP. (Not applicable to a psych.)
6. Psyching a conventional agreement which may show fewer than 10 HCP and which is not permitted by the General Convention Chart. This includes psyching responses to or rebids of those methods.

CARDING

Same as listed on the General Convention Chart.

ACBL YELLOW CARD. A CONVENTION CARD that lists specific CONVENTIONS that can be played in limited ACBL events.

ACBLSCORE. The computer program devised by the American Contract Bridge League to score bridge tournaments and club games, compute masterpoint awards, compile personnel records, prepare monthly club reports and provide reports on tournament events for publications. ACBLscore now is commonly used in many non-ACBL countries. The program is generally considered to be the most user-friendly and accurate scoring program.

ACBL-WIDE CHARITY PAIRS. Special one-session games staged twice a year to raise money for the ACBL Charity Foundation and the Canadian Bridge Federation Charitable Fund. All ACBL clubs are offered the opportunity to run a section of these games. Results are funneled to ACBL where overall and district winners are determined. For results see Appendix IV, ACBL-WIDE GAMES.

ACBL-WIDE GAMES. Many special games are played across the entire American Contract Bridge League. Included are charity games, International Fund games, Senior games and Instant Matchpoint games. Special hand records are distributed to all clubs, units and districts running such games so that all the competitors play exactly the same set of hands. Analysis sheets prepared by experts are distributed to all players at the conclusion of each game. Proceeds from the charity games go to the ACBL Charity Foundation or the Canadian Bridge Federation Charitable Fund. Proceeds from International Fund games are used to help cover the expenses of those selected to participate in world championship events. See ACBL CHARITY PROGRAM, ACBL-WIDE CHARITY PAIRS, ACBL-WIDE INSTANT MATCHPOINT GAMES, ACBL-WIDE INTERNATIONAL FUND PAIRS, ACBL-WIDE SENIOR GAMES, EPSON PAIRS, WORLD-WIDE PAIRS.

ACBL-WIDE INSTANT MATCHPOINT GAMES. This event was inaugurated in 1987 as part of the ACBL Golden Anniversary celebration. Royal Viking Cruise Lines sponsored the event in that year and in four of the six years that followed. This is the only event on the ACBL calendar where gold points are available at clubs. In the open contest the first point of the award for a section top is gold. ACBL-wide winners earn special prizes. Winners of a special Youth contest earn a $500 scholarship provided by the ACBL Educational Foundation. For winners, see Appendix IV.

ACBL-WIDE INTERNATIONAL FUND PAIRS. Special one-session games staged three times a year on an ACBL-wide basis by the American Contract Bridge League. All ACBL clubs are offered the opportunity to run a section of these games. Results are funneled to ACBL where overall and district winners are determined. These games raise funds that are used to help those qualifying for international play to cover their expenses while representing the ACBL in international competition.

ACBL-WIDE SENIOR GAMES. Once a year the American Contract Bridge League stages a one-session game for Seniors (55 years or older) on an ACBL-wide basis. All ACBL clubs are offered the opportunity to run a section of this game. Results are funneled to ACBL where overall and district winners are determined.

AWL. See AMERICAN WHIST LEAGUE.

ACCIDENTS. From time to time a player may suffer from some misfortune at the bridge table. He may miscount his points, missort his hand, mishear the bidding or pull out a wrong card. In such circumstances he should be particularly careful not to react in any way when he discovers his error.

ACCORDING TO HOYLE. A phrase indicating that a procedure is sanctioned both legally and ethically; in addition, that it has the backing of custom. The prestige of EDMOND HOYLE was so great that the phrase "according to Hoyle" came to mean correct procedure in general.

ACCREDITED TEACHERS. Accredited Teachers earn the title by successfully completing the ACBL's Teacher Accreditation Program (TAP). The TAP was created in 1986 as part of the ACBL's new BRIDGE EDUCATION PROGRAM. It is a ten-hour seminar designed by Audrey Grant, a Canadian educator, to develop new bridge teachers and to introduce them to the ACBL's TEACHING SERIES. Many established bridge teachers have participated in the TAP as a form of continuing education and are also Accredited Teachers. Interested ACBL members and volunteer workers have taken the TAP course and have earned the title of ACBL Accredited Teacher.

Special programs for Accredited Teachers are offered at each ACBL NABC. These include dinner meetings and special workshops/seminars. A quarterly newsletter, *The Bridge Teacher*, is published by ACBL and contains news of the organization's activities, teaching tips, special funded teaching programs and general information of interest to this group.

ACE. The suit card with only a single pip. In most games, including all those of the bridge family, it is the highest ranking card; hence, a top performer in any field.

In England, the ace of spades was the card which indicated that the duty had been paid and its printing was controlled by the government. Ever since the wrapper carried the duty or tax notation, the card has remained ornate in England and the United States, where each manufacturer developed an individual design to serve as a trademark.

In other countries, other aces have served to carry the trademarks: clubs in France, hearts in Germany. See ACE-SHOWING RESPONSES; HONOR TRICK; OPENING LEADS; POINT-COUNT.

ACE AND KING SHOWING RESPONSES. A method of showing aces and kings in response to an opening two bid. Some combinations can be shown in one bid; others require more rounds of bidding. With no aces and no kings, the responder bids 2NT. With one king and no aces, the first response is 2NT, and then if partner makes a bid below the game level, responder bids the suit with the king.

If responder has one ace and no kings, he bids the suit in which he has the ace. If he has two kings and no aces, he jumps to 3NT. If he has two aces and no kings, he jumps to 4NT. If he has one ace and one king, he first bids the suit in which he has the ace and later bids the suit in which he has the king.

ACE-ASKING BIDS. See BLACKWOOD, GERBER CONVENTION.

ACE FROM ACE-KING. The traditional lead of the king from an ace-king holding has been abandoned by many players in favor of the ace lead. Some players lead the ace against notrump contracts only, because an ace lead against notrump is unlikely to be attractive if the king is not held.

The argument in favor of leading the ace is that it avoids certain ambiguities which arise if the king is led:

(1) After the lead of the king against a suit contract, the opening leader's partner is unsure whether to indicate a small doubleton combination. He would wish to do so if the lead is from ace-king, but not if it is from king-queen. The same would apply if the leader's partner holds a doubleton jack.

(2) After the lead of the king against any contract, the opening leader's partner is uncertain whether to signal with his second card holding the jack and two small cards. In this situation he would wish to signal if the lead was from king-queen but not if it was from ace-king. (It is assumed in all cases that dummy holds three worthless cards.)

Against this, the proponents of the king lead point out that the lead of an unsupported ace is not uncommon against a suit contract, and the leader's partner may wish to know whether the king is held.

Holding a doubleton ace-king, this special procedure is reversed: the king is led followed by the ace. Other cases where the king is usually led: (1) when leading partner's suit or in bid and supported suits; (2) against six-level contracts (unless trying to deceive declarer) and five-level contracts; (3) when planning to shift to a singleton.

Whatever convention is being used, the ace lead may sometimes be tactically advisable against a slam contract: the king is too revealing when the opposing hands have a singleton opposite a combination headed by queen-jack.

For an alternative method of avoiding the ambiguity arising from the king lead, see RUSINOW LEADS. Also see OPENING LEADS.

ACE-GRABBER. A player who leads or takes his aces at his first opportunity, often making the play easier for the opponents.

ACE-HIGH. This describes a suit held by one player in which the ace is the top card without other top honors.

ACE IDENTIFICATION. An extension of the GERBER CONVENTION, devised by Norman Squire of England, to discover which ace a partnership is missing.

When responder has shown one or two aces in response to 4♣, 4NT asks for further information. If responder has one ace, he bids the suit of the ace. If he has two aces, he bids:

5♣ with aces of the same color
5♦ with aces of the same rank
5♥ with mixed aces

This may assist in deciding whether to bid a small slam, and possibly a grand slam if the 4NT bidder has a void. See also ROMAN GERBER.

ACE LEAD. Against notrump, by a convention of long standing, this lead requires partner to play his highest card of the suit led. This may be helpful if the opening leader has A-K-J-10-x-x, and his partner holds the queen, but these situations are not common. This is not applicable if a partnership uses ACE FROM ACE-KING as a standard lead.

ACE SHOWING. See CUEBIDS TO SHOW CONTROLS.

ACE-SHOWING RESPONSES. Answers to forcing opening bids that are based on the theory that the opener with a powerful unbalanced hand is more interested in his partner's first-round controls than in his long suit or general strength.

This is sometimes employed over FORCING TWO-BIDS, but is also common in conjunction with conventional TWO CLUBS STRONG ARTIFICIAL OPENINGS, especially in Europe. A minimum response, other than a negative one, shows the ace of the suit bid. The responses to a conventional 2♣ bid would be:

2♦	negative
2♥ or 2♠	ace-showing
2NT	8 points at least, but aceless
3♣ or 3♦	ace-showing
3NT	two aces

Some French experts vary this scheme in two ways. A 2NT response is permitted with two kings; and a hand holding two aces can make a more precise response:

3♥	two mixed aces (♠ and ♦, or ♥ and ♣)
3♠	two aces of the same color
3NT	two aces, both major or both minor

The opening bidder can subsequently ask for kings by using the bid normally employed to ask for aces — 4NT or 4♣ as appropriate.

An alternative scheme is to respond according to the step principle, showing aces and kings simultaneously. See STEP RESPONSES TO STRONG, ARTIFICIAL TWO-BIDS. See also BLUE TEAM CLUB; CAB; DYNAMIC NOTRUMP; SCHENKEN SYSTEM.

ACE VALUES. A method of distributional valuation developed as part of the BARON SYSTEM.

When valuing a hand for a raise, the HONOR TRICK value of the hand is added to the following distributional values:

	with 3 trumps	with 4 trumps
void	2	3
singleton	1	2
doubleton	$1/2$	1

(But a second shortage counts at half value unless five trumps are held.)

The total is the level to which responder should raise playing LIMIT RAISES. For example:

♠ Q J 3 2 ♥ K Q 6 ♦ K 6 5 2 ♣ 9 6

In response to a 1♠ opening bid, this hand counts three ace values (two for honor tricks plus one for the club doubleton) and therefore justifies a raise to 3♠.

If the opening bidder is planning to raise his partner's response, he subtracts two from his ace values and raises to the level of the answer: i.e., with four ace values he raises to the two level, with five to the three level, and so on. See DISTRIBUTIONAL COUNTS.

ACES OVER TWO-BIDS. See ACE-SHOWING RESPONSES.

ACES SCIENTIFIC SYSTEM. A detailed system formulated by the ACES TEAM with the aid of a computer for research and experimentation. Precise standards are set for all phases of bidding, including detailed methods for dealing with opponents' interference in constructive auctions. The main features of the system, as described by Bobby Goldman, are:

(1) $15^1/2$ to 18 point notrump openings. Responses of 2♦ and 2♥ are JACOBY TRANSFERS; 2♠ promises both minor suits and is a mild slam try; 3♣ and 3♦ are weak; 3♥ and 3♠, both artificial, are mild slam tries in clubs and diamonds respectively.

2♣ is non-forcing STAYMAN, following which responder may: rebid 3♣ to seek a 4-4 minor suit fit; or rebid 3♦ (artificial) to show a long minor suit and slam interest; or rebid three of the other major suit to show four-card support for opener's major, an unidentified singleton and slam interest.

(2) Major suit openings promise at least five cards; a 1NT response is forcing for one round; two-level responses are virtually forcing to game. Jump raises are limit, and forcing raises may be made in one of six ways to show specific point ranges and hands with and without singletons. See UNBALANCED SWISS RAISE, VALUE SWISS RAISE.

Jump shifts into minor suits show solid suits with at least $6^1/2$ playing tricks; opener's rebids below 3NT show stoppers rather than suits.

(3) Minor suit openings promise at least three-card suits. Immediate jump raises are limit; jumps to three of the *other* minor suit are forcing raises. These jump shifts and delayed jump raises are forcing to 3NT or four of a minor. Jump shift responses into major suits promise either a solid suit, an excellent suit in a notrump type hand or a strong suit with strong support for opener.

(4) 2♣ openings (strong and artificial) are usually forcing to game. A response of 2♦ is neutral; other suits are natural with good values in the suit; 2NT and 3NT deny any aces and show balanced hands with no suit worse than J-x-x. Two-level openings other than clubs are WEAK TWO-BIDS.

(5) Slam conventions include modern ROMAN BLACKWOOD responses to BLACKWOOD, plus a fifth step to show two aces and a useful void, and additional steps to show one ace and a useful void. Further slam tries may be made after the ace-asking response. 5NT, even after Blackwood, asks about trump quality whenever a fit has been agreed. See also GERBER and SUPER GERBER.

ACES TEAM. A full-time professional bridge team, organized in 1968 by Dallas financier Ira Corn for the express purpose of returning the world team championship to the United States.

Corn selected six players from among America's leading young experts, paying each a salary, plus tournament expenses, to undertake a full-time career of studying and playing bridge. He started with James Jacoby and Bobby Wolff, and shortly thereafter added Billy Eisenberg, Bobby Goldman and Michael Lawrence. Robert Hamman joined the team in 1969. Monroe Ingberman, mathematician and bridge writer, worked with the Aces as their first coach. In mid-1968 retired Air Force Colonel Joseph Musumeci was added as trainer and coach. The team was incorporated as the U.S. Aces, but was popularly known as the Dallas Aces and later simply as the Aces.

Using a computer to analyze results and to generate specific sets of hands to provide practice in given areas of the game — slam hands, preemptive openings, etc. — the Aces spent 50 to 60 hours a week perfecting the bidding systems and discussing problems encountered at the table. Complete records of all hands played were compiled for critical analysis. From the intensive study and analysis emerged various bidding styles including

the ORANGE CLUB, used by Wolff and Jacoby; the similar BLACK CLUB, used by Hamman and Eisenberg; and the ACES SCIENTIFIC SYSTEM, used by Goldman and Lawrence. Besides competing in North American Championships and Regional knockout team-of-four contests, the Aces also engaged many of America's top experts in practice matches in Dallas and staged a series of exhibition matches. See SHARIF BRIDGE CIRCUS.

In 1969, the team achieved the first major goal set by Corn by winning the Spingold Knockout Teams and later a playoff match that earned the Aces the right to represent North America in the 1970 BERMUDA BOWL in Stockholm, Sweden. With Italy's BLUE TEAM in temporary retirement, the Aces returned the BERMUDA BOWL to North America for the first time since 1954. The Aces successfully defended their world title in 1971.

In 1971 Eisenberg left the team and was replaced by Paul Soloway. By June of 1972 the team had become a part-time effort, with the players being paid only their expenses rather than salaries. Thereafter the makeup of the Aces began to change. In 1972 the Aces were runner-up to Italy in the Team Olympiad. Jacoby-Wolff played the Orange Club; Hamman-Soloway, the Green Club and Goldman-Lawrence, Standard American with special treatments. In early 1973 Soloway was replaced by Mark Blumenthal. The Aces were second to Italy in the Bermuda Bowl, playing as two threesomes: Wolff-Hamman-Jacoby playing Aces Club and Goldman-Lawrence-Blumenthal playing Standard American with special treatments. Soon thereafter Lawrence and Jacoby left the team and were replaced by Eric Murray and Sami Kehela. In 1974 the Aces were second to Italy with Hamman-Wolff playing the Aces Club, Blumenthal-Goldman, Aces Scientific, and Kehela-Murray, Colonial Acol.

In 1975 Eddie Kantar and John Swanson made their first appearances in international play with the Aces and Soloway-Eisenberg were back on the team. The Aces were second to Italy in the Bermuda Bowl and the team was Hamman-Wolff (Aces Club); Eisenberg-Kantar, Soloway-Swanson (Standard American with special treatments).

In 1976 North America did not fare well in the Team Olympiad, but won the Bermuda Bowl. On the team were two former Aces — Soloway and Eisenberg.

The Aces won the 1977 Bermuda Bowl as Zone 2 representatives, and another team from North America finished second. Playing for the Aces once again were Hamman-Wolff, Soloway-Swanson and Eisenberg-Kantar. In 1979 four ex-Aces won the Bermuda Bowl in Rio on a team captained by Malcolm Brachman (Eisenberg, Goldman, Kantar, Soloway). The next year, in the 1980 World Team Olympiad, Corn captained the Aces to second place behind France. His team was Hamman-Wolff, still playing the Aces Club; Soloway-Ira Rubin (Standard American with special treatments) and Fred Hamilton-Mike Passell (five-card majors, two-over-one game force). In 1981 for the first time in many years no Ace or former Ace was present on the U.S. International Team.

In the fall of 1981 Corn put together one more Aces team. He had great hopes for Hamman-Wolff (the only players to remain constantly with the Aces throughout a 13-year period), Alan Sontag-Peter Weichsel and Mike Becker-Ronnie Rubin. Just three months after Corn's sudden death of a heart attack in April, 1982, the Aces

won the Spingold in Albuquerque and qualified for the International Team Trials in Minneapolis that November.

Hamman, in summing up the history and the victory of this Aces team, reported, "Just say that we won one for big Ira." The Aces name stuck with them. In the Minneapolis trials, which they won, they were known as the Aces and their non-playing captain was Musumeci. The team went on to win the Bermuda Bowl in 1983 in Stockholm, Sweden.

From that point on the Aces Team as such disappeared into history. But members of the team continued to have many successes. Hamman and Wolff headed the WBF rankings in 1992. Lawrence and Kantar are prolific bridge authors. Soloway became the first player to break the 50,000-point barrier in 1998. Jacoby was a syndicated bridge columnist.

ACOL DIRECT KING CONVENTION. A bid of 4NT to ask for kings by a player whose partner has already made a bid specifically showing the number of aces he holds (which might be zero). This convention may be used after an ACOL TWO-BID has been raised directly to the game level, or after the GAMBLING THREE NO TRUMP if this opening denies a side-suit ace but may include side-suit kings, or after STEP RESPONSES TO STRONG, ARTIFICIAL TWO-BIDS.

ACOL 4NT OPENING. A specialized bid asking for aces. The responses are:

5♣ = no ace	5♠ = ♠A
5♦ = ♦A	5NT = two aces
5♥ = ♥A	6♣ = ♣A

ACOL SYSTEM. This system is standard in British tournament play and widely used in other parts of the world. The originators were a group of players that included Maurice Harrison-Gray, Iain Macleod, J. C. H. Marx, Terence Reese and S.J. Simon. It was called Acol because it was first played in 1934 in the small North London bridge club on the street of the same name. Many of the ideas were derived from the early writings of Ely Culbertson. The chief features of the system are:

(1) The weak notrump not vulnerable and the strong notrump vulnerable. The original ranges were 13-15 and 16-18, but 12-14 has become standard for the weak range, and 15-17 is often preferred to 16-18. The system is frequently used with a weak or strong notrump at all vulnerabilities (see also THREE-QUARTER NOTRUMP).

(2) LIMIT RAISES and notrump responses. Raises and notrump responses are never forcing in their own right. After an opening bid of 1♣, a response of 2NT or 3♣ is encouraging but not forcing, showing about 11 points or the distributional equivalent.

(3) Jump rebids are not forcing unless in a new suit.

(4) Opening suit bids tend to be slightly weaker than in American methods, especially if a six-card major suit is held. Opening a major holding a four-card suit is relatively common.

(5) Two-over-one responses were made very freely, perhaps with 8 points, in the early days of the system but now correspond more closely to traditional Standard American. Some play this response as forcing to 2NT.

(6) Fourth-suit bids are used conventionally by most Acol experts. See FOURTH SUIT FORCING.

(7) 2♣, artificial strong opening, forcing to 2NT.

(8) ACOL TWO-BID, forcing for one round.

(9) GAMBLING 3NT. A long strong minor suit with at least two other suits protected.

(10) 4NT opening asks for specific aces. See ACOL 4NT OPENING.

Other regular features of the system are listed separately: CULBERTSON 4-5NT or BLACKWOOD; STAYMAN CONVENTION; GRAND SLAM FORCE; TRIAL BID. Optional features of Acol listed separately include: ACOL DIRECT KING CONVENTION; BARON SLAM TRY; BENJAMIN; CROWHURST; FLINT; GERBER CONVENTION; INTEREST-SHOWING BIDS; KOCK-WERNER REDOUBLE; RESPONSIVE DOUBLE; ROMAN BLACKWOOD; ROMAN 2♦; SHARPLES; SHORT-SUIT GAME TRY; STRONG NOTRUMP AFTER PASSING; SWISS CONVENTION; TEXAS CONVENTION; UNUSUAL NO-TRUMP; VOID-SHOWING BIDS; WEISSBERGER.

ACOL TWO-BID. A type of INTERMEDIATE TWO-BID, strong and forcing for one round. A strong distributional hand is required with at least eight playing tricks:

(a)	(b)
♠ A K Q 8 7 5 4	♠ 8
♥ A J 4	♥ A Q J 10 5 4
♦ 9 6	♦ A K 9 8 5
♣ 2	♣ 9
Bid: 2♠	Bid: 2♥

A suit of six or more cards is normal, but the bid can be used with two strong five-card suits.

The negative response is traditionally 2NT but the modern style is to use the next highest suit, a HERBERT NEGATIVE. After the negative, a simple rebid or a bid of a lower-ranking suit at the three level is non-forcing.

A suit takeout response approximates to a standard two-over-one takeout, but can be weaker at the level of two. A single raise is highly constructive, suggesting a slam. A double raise shows about 10 points but no ace. If responder has moderate strength but no marked distributional feature and no slam ambitions, he can make a negative response and then bid game. See BENJAMIN.

ACORNS. One of the suits in old-time PLAYING CARDS. See also PACK.

ACRONYM. Initials to make a word used to identify anything connected with bridge. See CAB, COI, DONT, EFOS, EHAA, KISS, LOL, MUD, RONF, SID, TAP, TTASL.

ACTIVE DEFENSE. A risky defensive policy aiming to develop or cash tricks quickly, usually because dummy has a suit that will provide discards for declarer's losers.

ACTIVE ETHICS. Actions to enable all players to have equal access to methods and understandings used by their opponents. The concept was first broached by Bobby Wolff during his tenure as president of the American Contract Bridge League. According to Wolff, Active Ethics has nothing to do with such items as score corrections — players are supposed to make sure they have the right scores whether or not the adjustment favors them. Instead Wolff characterizes Active Ethics

as the desire not to take advantage — the desire to make sure that the opponents are privy to all of a partnership's conventions, treatments, habits and idiosyncrasies. "The game itself is more important than winning" said Wolff, subsequently president of the World Bridge Federation.

ADEQUATE TRUMP SUPPORT. See TRUMP SUPPORT.

ADJUSTED SCORE. There are two types of Adjusted Score: (1) Artificial, when no result can be estimated. The score will normally be 40%, 50% or 60% according to circumstances. The total adjusted score for both sides will not always add up to 100%. (2) Assigned Adjusted Score. The non-offending side gets the most favorable result that was likely; the offending side gets the most unfavorable at all probable. See LAWS OF CONTRACT BRIDGE, Law 12.

The application of an adjusted score often will affect other scores. See FOULED BOARD.

ADVANCE. The first action by the partner of the player who makes the first move for the defensive side, and the player who makes it. An example is a response to an overcall. See RUBENS ADVANCES.

ADVANCE CUEBID. A cuebid of a first-round control (in rare cases, a second-round control) made before the cuebidder's partner knows the agreed trump suit. The purpose of this cuebid is to distinguish between a normal raise and a raise based on controls plus a good distributional fit that offers some hope for slam if partner has the right distribution or high-card structure.

For example the bidding goes:

South	North
1♠	2♥
3♠	4♣

North holds:

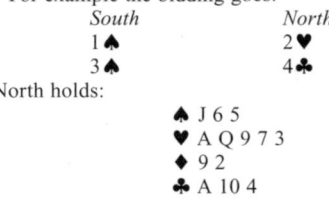

If South holds a solid spade suit, the ♥K and a diamond control, slam at spades will be a reasonable undertaking, but might not be reached unless North shows his slam interest by cuebidding the ♣A before supporting spades. From South's seat, however, the 4♣ bid is ambiguous. North could have a heart-club two-suiter or be making an advance cuebid.

The cuebid might also be used after a jump shift:

South	North
1♠	1NT
3♦	4♣

North holds:

♠ 7
♥ Q 10 6 4
♦ K 8 7 3 2
♣ A 5 2

North's hand has grown to slam proportions after South's jump shift, so he makes a slam try by cuebidding the ♣A before raising diamonds. Here also South is not yet certain whether North has a legitimate club suit or is cuebid-ding in support of diamonds or possibly spades.

Variations of this cuebid occur in many notrump sequences, but cannot be considered true advance cuebids

because the trump suit is set by implication.
For example:

South	North	South	North	South	North
1NT	3♠	2NT	3♥	1♣	1♠
4♦		4♣		2NT	3♥
				4♦	

The logical interpretation of South's last bid in each of these auctions is that he has strong support for partner's last named suit, a maximum for his previous bid(s), a reasonable collection of first- and second-round controls, possibly a ruffing value, and the ace of the cuebid suit. Without these features, South would support North's suit or rebid 3NT, as North's bidding requested.

Certain "impossible" bids can logically be interpreted as advance cuebids.

North	South
3♣	3♥
4♦	

South's 3♥ response is forcing; North will usually rebid 4♣ or raise to 4♥. Since North is unlikely to have a diamond suit worth suggesting as trumps, he can bid 4♦ on:

```
        ♠ 9 5
        ♥ Q 7 4
        ♦ 3
        ♣ A Q 9 8 5 3 2
```

After North has opened 3♣, he can hardly hold a better hand in support of hearts. See also ADVANCE SAVE, SACRIFICE. CUEBID TO SHOW CONTROL.

ADVANCED LEBENSOHL. Variant of LEBENSOHL over 1NT interference, invented by Glenn McIntyre of Boston. Bids from 2NT through 3♥ are transfers showing invitational or better values. Opener may accept the transfer to deny game interest or make another bid to force to game. 2NT, the club transfer, may also be the start of slow Stayman or a prelude to a signoff in 3♦ or 3♥ if those suits were not available at the two level. See LEBENSOHL.

ADVANCED PRECISION. A form of the Precision Club system in which ROMAN ASKING BIDS (alpha through omega) are used.

ADVANCER. See ADVANCE.

ADVANCE SAVE. A SACRIFICE bid made before the opponents have reached their probable optimum contract. The ploy is also known as a premature or anticipatory save. The opponents will usually know that the sacrificer does not expect to make his bid; hence, his objective is to make them guess at a high level without giving them full opportunity to exchange information.

For example, East-West are vulnerable, and the bidding goes:

West	North	East	South
1♣	2♥	3♥	6♥

South holds:

```
        ♠ J 10 7 4
        ♥ K 10 7 5 3
        ♦ 7 4 2
        ♣ 6
```

North's 2♥ bid is preemptive. East-West are probably headed for slam in clubs, so South wants to set them a problem. South is prepared to concede a penalty of 1100 or thereabouts, which may be an accurate sacrifice and

may also goad East-West into attempting an impossible contract.

Dlr: North　　Vul: N-S

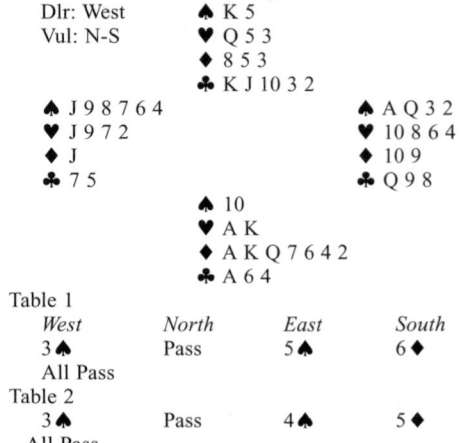

West	North	East	South
	1♠	Pass	2♥
Pass	4♦(1)	Dbl	4NT
7♦	7♥	All Pass	

(1) Heart fit, diamond shortness.

In the 1980 U.S. International Team Trials, East's double of 4♦ was turned into an advance save by West. North, with massive extra strength, guessed wrong by bidding 7♥.

The scoring changes in the 1987 edition of *Laws of Duplicate Bridge* make violent advance saves less desirable. Indeed, the possibility of quixotic results at IMP scoring was a catalyst for those changes. With pre-1987 scoring, if North-South could make 7♣ for +2140, East-West stood to gain 6 IMPs by going down ten doubled at 7♦ for –1900.

Tactics

An advance sacrificer must avoid pushing the opponents into a cold contract. On the deal which follows, East had to preempt just enough: high enough to keep North-South from learning they had a slam, low enough to give them room to stop at game.

Dlr: West
Vul: N-S

```
              ♠ K 5
              ♥ Q 5 3
              ♦ 8 5 3
              ♣ K J 10 3 2
♠ J 9 8 7 6 4              ♠ A Q 3 2
♥ J 9 7 2                 ♥ 10 8 6 4
♦ J                       ♦ 10 9
♣ 7 5                     ♣ Q 9 8
              ♠ 10
              ♥ A K
              ♦ A K Q 7 6 4 2
              ♣ A 6 4
```

Table 1

West	North	East	South
3♠	Pass	5♠	6♦
All Pass			

Table 2

West	North	East	South
3♠	Pass	4♠	5♦
All Pass			

At Table 1, East's strenuous efforts goaded South into the cold slam, and then East failed to save at 6♠ for –900 (old scoring). At Table 2, East beat par with a restrained raise to 4♠.

ADVANCED SENIOR MASTER. A rank once used by ACBL to denote a player just below Life Master rank. This rank is now known as NABC Master.

ADVERSARY. Either opponent of declarer, or, during the auction, a player on the opposing side.

AFRICA. The World Bridge Federation incorporated Africa as Zone 8 at its meeting in Maastricht in 2000. Africa now is eligible to be represented as a zone in such events as the Bermuda Bowl and the Venice Cup. Prior to 2000, African nations had to compete with nations in Zone 4, the Bridge Federation of Asia and the Middle East zone. The following nations became part of the African zone in 2000: Botswana, Egypt, Kenya, Mauritius, Morocco, Reunion, South Africa, Tanzania, and Zimbabwe.

AGGREGATE SCORE. See TOTAL POINT SCORING.

ALBERT MOREHEAD MEMORIAL LIBRARY. The largest bridge library in the world, containing more than 2,000 different volumes in addition to many artifacts and historical items. The library was dedicated by the ACBL in memory of Albert Morehead, a bridge bibliophile. His excellent collection of bridge books provided the ACBL with an excellent basis for the library. In later years the ACBL acquired the personal libraries of Edgar Kaplan and Alfred Sheinwold.

In addition to rare books, the library houses a fine collection of games, teaching aids, cassettes, records and magazines. The memorabilia include five-suit decks of cards, score tallies of all kinds, top-score pins, all kinds of duplicate boards, Culbertson bridge chips, dealing machines – even a copy of the 1958 *Time Magazine* that featured Charles Goren on the cover as the King of the Bridge Aces.

The library is located in the ACBL Headquarters building in Memphis, Tennessee, near the ACBL HALL OF FAME display. Also nearby is the ACBL's magnificent collection of trophies. Five of the most prestigious are in glass cases in the library. The reminder are in two large glass display cases adjacent to the library. The trophies are valued at more than half a million dollars.

ALCATRAZ COUP. This is a form of bridge robbery that almost warrants a trip to Alcatraz for the perpetrator. The following is an example:

Dummy
A J 10

Declarer
K x

Declarer, to make three tricks in the suit, calls the jack from dummy and, receiving a small card from right-hand opponent, fails to follow suit. Fourth hand either produces the queen or a small card. If a small card, declarer corrects his revoke by substituting the small card, leads to his king, and has the ace in dummy for the third trick. If fourth hand produces the queen, declarer corrects his revoke by producing the king, sweetly permitting his left-hand opponent to change his play, and finesses the located queen on the next play.

Whenever the coup occurs, the defenders are entitled to redress and should receive an adjusted score in accordance with LAWS OF DUPLICATE (Laws 12A, 47F). Declarer must not gain an advantage, and any such swindle attempted deliberately should meet with a serious penalty on ethical charges.

Coincidentally, bridge was played at Alcatraz. See BRIDGE IN PRISONS.

ALERT. The word used by a player to call attention to the opponents that partner has made a bid that has a conventional or unusual meaning. See ALERTING, ANNOUNCEMENT.

ALERTING. A method of drawing opponents' attention to the fact that a particular bid has a conventional or unusual meaning. In 1971 the ACBL adopted a CONVENTION CARD that provided boxes for a partnership to check off its basic bidding agreements, thereby eliminating the need to list all partnership understandings. The revised 1994 card had a similar configuration. The World Bridge Federation now has its own convention card, and most national bridge organizations also have prepared convention cards along the same lines as the ACBL card. The recommended Alert procedure is for a player to announce to his right-hand opponent, "Alert" whenever a bid occurs that is either conventional or a private understanding. The opponent can request an explanation at that time by saying, "Please explain," or can reserve the right to inquire at any later time when it is his turn to call or play. See EXPLANATION OF ANY CALL OR PLAY. A player must use the Alert procedure unless his opponents specifically request him not to do so before the auction begins. Some organizations insist on the use of the Alert procedure at all times. See CONVENTION.

A player who gains information from his partner's Alert is not permitted to use this information to his advantage. If it is determined that this has happened, the director is empowered to award an adjusted score and to impose a penalty if he thinks the situation calls for it.

If a player Alerts in error, fails to Alert or gives a wrong explanation of the Alert, his partner cannot correct the error immediately, nor can he indicate in any way that a mistake has occurred. At the conclusion of the auction, the declarer or the dummy should clarify any necessary points concerning that side's Alerts. However, the defending side must wait until the conclusion of play before making any statements of correction — an earlier explanation could easily give partner information to which he is not entitled. If declarer believes he has been damaged by the Alert mistake, and the director agrees, the director is empowered to adjust the score. If declarer or dummy makes a clear bidding error, breaking the agreement shown on the convention card or in the partnership notes, there is no obligation to explain it.

The following represents the ACBL's rules and views concerning the Alert procedure. For a full explanation of WBF rules concerning Alerting, see WORLD BRIDGE FEDERATION ALERTING POLICY.

Most natural bids are not Alertable. Natural bids that represent an unusual treatment are Alertable. For example, if you play that a two-over-one response is non-forcing, you must Alert it. Natural bids in a suit are defined as follows:

Any offer to play in a suit for the first time with 3+ cards in a minor, 4+ in a major, 4+ for an overcall, 5+ for a weak two-bid, 6+ for a weak three-bid; a notrump opening or overcall if not unbalanced (in general, no singleton or void and a maximum of two doubletons).

Conventional calls above 3NT beginning with opener's rebid are not Alertable during the auction. At the end of the auction these calls must be Alerted, and explained on request, before the opening lead is made. This ap-

plies to both the declaring side and the defenders. When explaining bids, tell what they mean rather than giving its name. For instance, say "5♣ showed zero or three key-cards" not "Roman Keycard." Before the opening lead, the opponents are entitled to know the complete meaning of all conventional calls. "Yes" is not the right answer to the question "Is 2♠ Michaels?" You must say something like: "Two spades showed at least 5-5 in hearts and a minor, any strength." If the declaring side is aware that there is a natural but unusual component in the auction, they should volunteer the information before the opening lead is made. For example, "His negative double of 1♥ denied four spades."

Bids or calls usually become Alertable when made, but some especially unusual methods require pre-Alerts. These include two-system methods, systems based on very light openings or other highly aggressive methods or preempts, systems that may be unfamiliar to the opponents (such as a system based on canapés), and SuperChart and MidChart conventions.

Natural bids are Alertable when they show unusual strength, shape or limitations. All conventional bids are Alertable except Stayman, Blackwood, and Gerber, plus certain bids that call for an Announcement instead of an Alert. A 1NT response to a major that is a one-round force calls for an Announcement — "Forcing for one round." If 1NT is semi-forcing, this also must be Announced. The same is true of a transfer bid in response to an opening 1NT bid – "2♥ is a transfer to 2♠."

Strong, natural openings and overcalls of 1NT that are completely within the 15-18 range do not require an Alert. If 1NT is not within the 15-18 range but is natural, the partner of the notrump bidding must Announce the range. Conventional 1NT openings and overcalls of course are Alertable. As for responses to 1NT, Stayman asking for a four-card major, forcing suit bids at the three level and signoff bids at the two-level are not Alertable. Transfers to hearts and spades call for an Announcement. All other responses are Alertable.

If the partnership is playing very light opening bids (fewer than 10 HCP), this must be Alerted. So must an opening bid of 2♣ if it is not forcing (such as the Precision 2♣). All canapé systems are subject to pre-Alerts.

The following responses to suit bids are Alertable: (1) 1NT over 1♥ that shows four spades; (2) non-forcing suit bids by an unpassed hand; (3) natural jump shifts that are not game forcing; (4) conventional jump shifts; (5) preemptive jump raises; (6) non-forcing 2NT; (7) 1NT response to minor opening that does not deny holding a four-card major. If opener rebids 1NT showing a strong hand or which might have bypassed a four-card major by agreement, these also are Alertable. A limit or forcing jump raise over a double is Alertable.

Some defensive bids are Alertable – (1) non-jump Unusual Notrump; (2) very light overcalls (fewer than 6 HCP); (3) weak jump advances; (4) jump overcalls that are intermediate or better.

The ACBL defines two types of doubles. Type 1 occurs when partner has made no call other than Pass, it's early in the auction, and the level is below 4♠ or when it's the usual negative double below 4♠ after partner has opening one of a suit. If such doubles are penalty or unusual non-penalty, they must be Alerted. Takeout doubles and doubles for the lead of a suit are not Alertable. Type 2 doubles occur when partner has made any call other than Pass or the double is of

notrump or the call is above the 4♥-level. This usually occurs late in the auction. Doubles that are penalty (or penaltyish) are not Alertable. Non-penalty doubles are Alertable.

Use of bidding screens makes it necessary for a player to Alert his own bid to the player on his side of the screen. The recommended procedure is to place the Alert card on the bidding tray. Some players merely point to the Alert card, a practice that often leads to disputes.

ALLIGATOR COUP. See CROCODILE COUP.

ALL-STAR GAMES. In the late Eighties and early Nineties, considerable attention was given to promotion of bridge with the aim of reawakening the kind of widespread interest the game enjoyed in the Forties and Fifties. One strategy for accomplishing this goal was to attract the attention of the news media by conducting competitions patterned after the professional tennis tour. Thus was born the all-star circuit. Matthew Granovetter, editor of *Bridge Today Magazine*, developed the concept and executed several successful all-star tournaments — with cash prizes for the winners — in the early Nineties. The schedule was sporadic, however, and Granovetter's ultimate goal was to secure a major sponsor so that the tournaments could be conducted on a regular basis. This sponsor never materialized. The all-star games — usually individual movements with about 20 participants — were held in such varied locations as Albany NY, Novato CA and Boca Raton FL. Sponsors included a health club, a shopping mall and Perrier, the French bottler of mineral water. For winners see *BRIDGE TODAY*, ALL-STAR GAMES, Appendix IV.

ALPHA ASKING BIDS. (1) Asking bids in the ROMAN SYSTEM concerned with controls in a side suit. See ROMAN ASKING BIDS. (2) Asking bids in the SUPER PRECISION system concerned with responder's support for the suit opened at the one level. See SUPER PRECISION ASKING BIDS.

ALTERNATE THREAT SQUEEZE. See COMPOUND SQUEEZE.

ALTERNATIVE SQUEEZE. (Either-Or Squeeze). A simple squeeze played as a double squeeze.

```
        ♠ A K Q x
        ♥ K
        ♦ —
        ♣ —

        ♠ x x
        ♥ x
        ♦ K
        ♣ A
```

Suppose West has the ♥A, and East has the ♦A. Spades cannot be guarded by both opponents, so North's small spade technically cannot be a DOUBLE MENACE because it is not possible for opponents to hold four spades each. However, when South leads the ♣A, whichever opponent is actually guarding spades must unguard that suit in order to keep his ace. If West keeps his ♥A, North discards the ♥K. If West started with four or more spades the squeeze has worked on him. Alternatively, if West started with fewer than four spades, East is now squeezed.

AMBER. British colloquialism indicating that both sides are vulnerable. See GREEN, RED, WHITE.

AMBIGUOUS BIDS. See GENERAL UNDER-STANDINGS; PARTNERSHIP MISUNDERSTAND-INGS.

AMBULANCE SERVICE. Rescuing partner from an impending large penalty.

AMERICAN AUCTION BRIDGE LEAGUE. See AMERICAN BRIDGE LEAGUE.

AMERICAN BRIDGE ASSOCIATION. Founded in 1932 when a group of black tennis enthusiasts decided to relax after a tournament and play bridge. After constructing some ugly black wooden boxes (duplicate boards) and debating endlessly over which direction was North, the director decreed North was wherever he said it was – and thus was the ABA founded in Hampton VA with a membership of 20. The first National took place in Buckroe Beach VA in 1933. At the time black players were not welcome at ACBL tournaments. When the ACBL opened its doors wide some three decades later, members of the ABA opted to continue their organization, a source of great fun and fine fellowship. Many blacks also joined the ACBL and played in major tournaments sponsored by each organization.

The ABA conducts two National tournaments annually, a Spring National inaugurated in 1968 and a Summer National, first held in 1934. These championships feature open, mixed, men's and women's pairs, an individual and team championships for open, mixed, men's and women's teams. The premier event is the knockout teams which often draws in excess of 200 teams. The earliest Nationals were held in New York City, but now they are held in many major cities in the United States, Canada and the Islands. For past results of the ABA Open Teams and Open Pairs, see Appendix I. In addition, the ABA also conducts more than 100 lower-rated tournaments each year.

Dr. M.E. DuBissette (president, 1932-35), Horace R. Miller (president, 1936), L.C. Collins and John W. Cromwell were the men responsible for the formation and early success of the ABA. In 1936 the ABA merged with the Eastern Bridge League, a group of New York City clubs headed by Morgan S. Jensen. Steady expansion continued under the presidency of Dr. E. L Belsaw (1936-49). The original four geographical sections were subsequently expanded to eight, and each conducted Sectional tournaments equivalent to ACBL regionals. A masterpoint system was established and the quarterly *ABA Bulletin,* edited by William Tatum from 1944-53, became an outstanding publication. Its high standards were maintained under succeeding editors: C.G. Fredd (1954-59), Clarence and William Farmer (1960-69), Bobbye Caldwell (1970-75 and 1978-82), Maxine Daly (1975-77), William Furr (1982-94), Barbara Vinzant (1995-98) and Estelle Lavender (1999 on). The *Bulletin* contains winners, races, tournament trails, bridge instruction, ABA business items, special newcomer features, and photos. Voting for national officers is conducted through the *Bulletin.* The magazine is supplemented by periodic newsletters from the ABA's eight sections.

Official recognition of the growing acceptance of participation by blacks in ACBL tournaments came in 1952 when the ACBL passed an amendment proposed by Gen. Robert Gill by which each unit became the sole judge of membership qualifications in its territory. Enactment of federal legislation which forbade the exclusion of blacks from hotels, etc., was speedily followed in 1964 by an ACBL regulation ensuring the right of any ACBL member to play in any North American championship tournament no matter where held. The last barrier to ACBL membership was removed in 1967 when the ACBL included in its bylaws the proviso that "no person shall be denied membership because of race, color, or creed."

An outstanding achievement of the ABA administration under Victor Daly of Washington DC (president 1949-64) was the conduct of negotiations leading to the building of mutual rapport and respect between the ACBL and the ABA. Hundreds of ABA members joined the ACBL, with a high percentage achieving the rank of Life Master. The first black ACBL Life Master was Marion Wildy (1956). The first ABA Life Master to achieve Life Master ranking in the ACBL was Leo Benson (1962). The close association of the ACBL and the ABA continued under the ABA presidency of Maurice Robinson, New York City (president 1964-69). At the suggestion of the ABA, representatives of the ABA and the Greater New York BA, a unit of the ACBL, met in two exhibition matches in New York in 1969. This resulted in one win for each organization. Starting in the Nineties, leading representatives of both organizations met regularly to promote interaction and solve problems. At the ACBL Summer Championships in Anaheim CA in 2000, a special ABA-ACBL two-session event was held. Players who earned points were free to choose which organization would award them the points.

Since 1977 Robert J. Price, Chicago, has been the ABA's No. 1 player. His partner, Joyce Williams, also of Chicago, has been the leading woman player. Sara Pearson is the leading player on the West Coast. Successful partnerships include Reginald Chapman, Washington DC, and Roscoe Rigmaiden, Philadelphia; Lionel Barton, Missouri City TX, and Dwight Galley, Houston; Chester Johnson and Herbert Taylor, Chicago; Sara Pearson of Culver City CA and Mae Clark of Arlington TX; Naomi and Heyward Ballard, Detroit; George Johnson, Charlotte NC, and Edna Cravanas, Oakland CA; Bill and Berry Thompson, Detroit; Willis Troy; Henderson NV, and Robert Friend, Irvine CA; Worth and Gloria Christler, Atlanta; Beverly and Samuel Lucas, Yellow Springs OH; Clarice Reid, Bethesda MD, and Dorothy Sides, Cincinnati OH; Milton and Bessie Haley, Dayton OH; John Washington and Julius Fields, New York; Lawrence Berkley, New York; and George Hudson, St. Louis; Melvin Rhone, Chicago, and Harold Bickham, Indianapolis, Allie Raines and J.T. McGhee, Detroit; and Lee Pennington, Nashville, and Mary Moragne, New York.

The William Friend Award is awarded to the top-point winner in a calendar year. In 1987 the Powder Puff award for the top woman point winner was renamed the Joyce Williams Deroy in honor of the woman who was the ABA's top woman player for more than 15 years.

The ABA's five Grand Masters have dominated the association for many years, and all five have done well in ACBL competition as well. Robert Price of Chicago

was the highest point holder as of 2000 when he had 28,000. Next was Lionel Barton of Houston, followed by Charles Johnson of Chicago, Reginald Chapman of Washington DC, and Arnold Jones of Chicago.

The ABA instituted a Hall of Fame in 2000 – two living and two posthumous members were to be chosen based on their bridge performance. Two others whose dedication to the ABA superseded the masterpoint will be honored with the Kenneth Cox Award.

The ABA also has an active charity program, issuing eight scholarships annually and making major contributions to such charities as the Sickle Cell Foundation, NAACP, Urban League, Red Cross and Operation Push.
ABA Headquarters
2828 Lakewood Avenue SW, Atlanta GA 30315
Elise Gilman, Headquarters Keeper
Phone 404-768-5517
Fax 404-767-1871
Gloria Christler, National Secretary
The following have served as ABA presidents:

M.E. DuBissette	1932-35
E.T. Belsaw	1936-49
Victor Daly, Washington DC	1949-63
Maurice Robinson, New York	1964-69
Pauline Taylor, Detroit	1970-73
Arnold Jones, Chicago	1974-75
Jacqueline Sheppard, Philadelphia	1976-78
Arnold Jones, Chicago	1979-82
Arthur Reid, Bethesda MD	1982-84
George Johnson, Charlotte NC	1984-86
Geraldine Wilson, Cromwell CT	1986-88
Thelma Woodson, Detroit	1988-90
Robert Price, Chicago	1990-92
Anita Troy, Henderson NV	1992-96
George Love, Harrisburg PA	1996-98
Cleo Terrell, Chicago	1999-

2000 officers:
President: Cleo Terrell
8030 S. Indiana Ave., Chicago IL 60619
773-483-1348
Vice President: Richard Bowling
1806 Sharpe Rd., Greensboro NC 27406
336-272-1246
Executive Secretary: Gloria Christler
2828 Lakewood Ave. SW, Atlanta GA 30315
404-768-5517
Treasurer: Edward High
1709 Patton Ave., Charlotte NC 28216
704-375-3176
Executive Committee: Eastern – Crawley Arrington; Mid-Atlantic – Leola Rucker; Southern – Vernice Whitfield; Northwest – Edward West; Great Lakes – Mary Sirmons; Midwest – Dorris West; Southwest: Henry Irwin; Western: Harley Wyatt.
National Tournament Authority: Executive Secretary – Gloria Christler; NTA Chairman – Robert Friend; Tournament and Conventions Manager – Phyllis Heard; Tournament Chairman – Harold Bickham; Chief Scorer – Worth Christler; Supervising Director – Carole Patton; Supplies and Logistics – William Beasley.
Website: www.americanbridge.com

AMERICAN BRIDGE LEAGUE. An organization founded in 1927 as the American Auction Bridge League. The word "auction" was dropped in 1929. The League joined with the UNITED STATES BRIDGE ASSOCIATION in 1937 to form the AMERICAN CONTRACT BRIDGE LEAGUE. See PRESIDENTS. See results in Appendix I.

AMERICAN BRIDGE OLYMPICS. American winners of the WORLD PAR CONTESTS are listed in Appendix IV.

The Culbertson organization staged a national Olympic in 1932, distinct from the world event. The winners were: North-South, Dr. and Mrs. Monte F. Meyer; East-West, James M. Magner, Jr., and William C. Campbell.

AMERICAN BRIDGE TEACHERS ASSOCIATION. A nonprofit professional organization composed primarily of bridge teachers, but including tournament directors and bridge writers, dedicated to promoting higher standards of bridge teaching and playing.

The ABTA was founded in 1957 by a charter membership of 150. At the initial meeting, held in New York City, the 14 members attending, including Deborah N. Glover, the organizing secretary, and George S. Coffin, the organizing treasurer, proposed that the goal of the organization be "to provide and protect the standards of bridge teaching and its practitioners, to establish a code of ethics and minimal fees insofar as is practical, and to make known in the public and professional interest any information in the bridge profession."

The association is divided into 10 regions, each headed by a regional director. The regional directors, in collaboration with state chairmen, set up frequent meetings at which teachers discover new techniques that are made available and also examine the latest teaching equipment.

A general meeting is held once a year just prior to the ACBL Summer North American Championships at the site of the tournament. Outstanding speakers and teachers offer ideas and thoughts throughout the three-day meeting. Most of the game's leading personalities have addressed the organization at least once, and many have appeared several times.

Applicants for membership have to submit information to an ABTA committee regarding their professional bridge teaching experience, bridge affiliations, experience and knowledge for acceptance in the organization. After five years a member can apply for designation as a Master Bridge Teacher.

Honorary members: Charles Goren (1960), Oswald Jacoby (1977), Harold Schenken, Richard Frey, Easley Blackwood (1978), Sam Stayman Alfred Sheinwold (1980), Fred Karpin (1982), Max Hardy (2001).

The ABTA *Quarterly Magazine* now is edited by Leslie Shafer, who took over in 1998 when Frank Thomas retired after being on the job for 30 years. Earlier editors were George Coffin and Harold Shaw.
Presidents of the ABTA have been:

1958-59	Jo Woods
1960-61	Margaret M. Wales
1962	Deborah N. Glover
1963	George S. Gooden
1964	Dorothy Jane Cook
1965	Kenneth B. Turner
1966	Nellie Harrington
1967	Helen D. Albano
1968-69	Thelma Smith
1970-71	Helen Cale
1972-73	Effie Lindsay Long White
1974-75	Edward L. Gordy

1976-77	Eloene Griggs
1978-79	Antha Mallander
1980-81	Dr. T. B. Lyons
1982-83	Frank Thomas Jr.
1984-85	Antha Mallander
1986-87	Bert Gilliken
1988-89	Ruth De More
1990-91	Roberta Salob
1992-93	Harry Lampert
1993-95	Ginny Schuett
1995-97	Edward Gentino
1997-99	Dr. George Speigel
1999-2001	Dr. F.R. (Ted) Applegate

Other officers as of June 2001
First Vice President - Mary Jane Von Moss
Second Vice President - Lynn Berg
Secretary - Libby Brawn
Business Secretary/Treasurer - Pat Harrington
14840 Crystal Cove Court #503
Fort Myers, FL 33919

AMERICAN CONTRACT BRIDGE LEAGUE. The governing body for organized bridge activities and promotion on the North American continent. Duplicate bridge in the United States, Canada, Mexico and Bermuda is managed by ACBL, by far the largest bridge organization in the world. ACBL traces its history from the organization of the American Auction Bridge League in Hanover NH at the 1927 congress (tournament) of the American Whist League, by a group sparked by Ralph R. Richards, including E. J. Tobin, Robert W. Halpin, Henry P. Jaeger and Clayton W. Aldrich. Tobin was named executive secretary. Contract bridge was introduced at the second congress held in Cleveland in 1928, during which year the infant organization acquired the services of William E. McKenney, whose originality, drive and organizational ability did much to establish ACBL.

The increased popularity of contract bridge led to the name change to American Bridge League in 1929. A merger of this group with the United States Bridge Association was effected in 1937, with McKenney, first named executive secretary in 1929, remaining at the helm of the organization until 1947.

In 1948-49 a major reorganization of the ACBL was carried out by Waldemar von Zedtwitz, as president and chairman, aided by the steering committee of Robert J. Gill, Ralph Gresham, Lee Hazen, Bertram Lebhar Jr., Raymond J. McGrover, and Albert H. Morehead and the Bylaws Committee headed by Lawrence Weiss of Boston.

McKenney was succeeded by Russell J. Baldwin, who was business manager until his recall to active duty with the U. S. Army in 1951, at which time Alvin Landy was named acting business manager. In 1952, Landy was advanced to the position of executive secretary, remaining in that post until his death in 1967. Tom Stoddard, then executive administrator, served briefly as executive secretary pro tem until Easley Blackwood was appointed to that post in 1968. Blackwood retired after three years, as he had planned, on March 1, 1971. Richard Goldberg, assistant executive secretary under both Landy and Blackwood, was named as Blackwood's successor. Goldberg served as executive secretary until he retired in 1984. His successor was Ralph Cohen, who served for two and a half years. Cohen had served as

Goldberg's assistant from 1971 to 1984. He was succeeded by William Gross, a former member of the Board of Directors who also had served a term as ACBL president. Gross held this position until he retired in 1991. He was replaced by Stephen Signaigo, a Memphis businessman. Signaigo's successor was Denis Howard of Australia, former president of the World Bridge Federation. Howard served as pro tem chief executive officer for six months in 1992, at which time Roy G. Green became the chief executive officer. Green's background was in banking and real estate. When Green retired in 1998, he was replaced by David Silber.

ACBL membership grew spectacularly from the 270 who joined the American Auction Bridge League to more than 15,000 at its 20th birthday in 1947. Following the 1956 merger with the Pacific Bridge League, which became the ACBL's Western Division, growth accelerated to 170,000 in 1970 and approached 200,000 in 1993.

ACBL's scope and influence has increased substantially. Beyond the authorization and supervision of bridge tournament activities from the level of North American and Regional Championship tournaments to the games run in some 4,200 duplicate clubs, ACBL activities include: formulation and publication of the Laws, both of Contract (Rubber) Bridge and of Duplicate Contract Bridge; conduct of charity games and other activities which have raised millions of dollars for hundreds of charitable purposes; publication of a monthly magazine on bridge activities around the world; cooperation with other national bridge organizations through membership in the World Bridge Federation; hosting three World Team Olympiads (1964, 1972 and 1984), three World Pair Olympiads (1978, 1986 and 1994), two Venice Cups (1978 and 1981) and nine world championships for the Bermuda Bowl.

Two major forces in ACBL's growth are the MASTERPOINT PLAN and the RANKINGS, both of which were important considerations in ACBL's consolidation with USBA and the Pacific Bridge League. In 1961, the huge task of issuing and recording members' masterpoints was computerized. In 1975, when this service had grown to require mailing some 38,000 notification postcards per semi-monthly cycle, it was streamlined to a once-a-month operation. Masterpoint mailings are now made every other month. In 1992 the ACBL inaugurated a system whereby the masterpoint notifications were included in a polybag with the monthly ACBL publication, the *Bridge Bulletin*. Many other jobs formerly done manually now are done by the computer — mailing labels, new member welcome cards, membership cards, membership renewal notices, Unit report forms, special lists such as new Life Masters and Top 500 leaders, club sanction renewal forms, transaction journals, newsletters, masterpoint updating, scoring at tournaments, inventory control, sales, cash receipts, accounts payable, etc. The *Bridge Bulletin* is the most widely distributed and one of the most highly respected publications in its field. ACBL also compiled and published records and selected hands of all world championships and team Olympiads from 1953 to 1989 and also in 1995.

An additional service was added to ACBL in 1993 — the MAD (Member Assistance Department) line. This is two 800 telephone lines, one for the United States and one for Canada, that members can call to learn their

masterpoint holdings, get answers to their questions, offer suggestions and make complaints. ACBL also is very much into the business of bridge education. The Education Department staff actively supports Junior bridge programs in colleges, high schools and grade schools; trains bridge teachers; provides special publications for teachers and students; prepares special videotapes for public television, and runs special competitions such as college championships. The teacher and student texts used in classes sponsored by ACBL were written by Audrey Grant.

In 2000 Memphis headquarters for ACBL employed approximately 90 persons. In addition there were more than 200 tournament directors of various ranks on staff. Members of the ACBL Board of Directors and Board of Governors are chosen by the membership. The Board of Directors elects the presidents and Honorary Members of the ACBL.

AMERICAN CONTRACT BRIDGE LEAGUE GOLDEN ANNIVERSARY.

In 1987 the ACBL held a year-long celebration of its golden anniversary, commemorating the 1937 merger of Ely Culbertson's UNITED STATES BRIDGE ASSOCIATION and Bill McKenney's AMERICAN BRIDGE LEAGUE. Features of the Golden Anniversary Year: (1) a series of articles on the first 50 years of the ACBL was printed in the *Bridge Bulletin* (which had progressed from a four-page leaflet to a full-sized monthly magazine of 132 pages); (2) a slick Golden Anniversary edition of the *Bridge Bulletin* was published in 1988, sketching features of the anniversary and highlighting events and personalities of the half century; (3) the first ACBLwide Instant Matchpoint Pairs was inaugurated as part of the Golden Anniversary observance – for the first time, gold points were awarded to section winners at club games; (4) ACBL celebrated its own Jubilee by winning both the Bermuda Bowl and the Venice Cup at the World Championships in Jamaica; (5) the Golden Anniversary Year culminated with a Golden Jubilee Gala held at the Anaheim NABC in November. It was a fitting finale. The total of 13,948 tables broke all previous Fall records for attendance. From the opening earthquakes to an unprecedented four-nation win in the Reisinger, it was a scintillating tournament. The Jubilee Gala was a full dress affair with thousands of players taking part in the festivities.

AMERICAN LEADS.

Leads devised at whist to give partner a count when a solid suit was being led. The lead of the jack followed by the queen, for example, showed a solid seven-card suit. The inventor was Nicholas Browse Trist of New Orleans. Although they have long been obsolete, American leads were a milestone in the development of defensive signals.

AMERICAN WHIST LEAGUE.

The AWL was founded in Milwaukee in 1891 as a central organization to control and promulgate the laws of WHIST. Its sponsorship of tournaments between representatives of member clubs did much to stimulate the competitive aspects of games of the bridge family. Within the first few years of the life of this league its members worked out official laws, rules, a code of ethics, boards, methods of scoring, and movements of boards and players for all sorts of games up to teams of sixteen.

By the end of the Thirties, the League existed in name only, although whist congresses, attended by a few lifelong devotees, continued into the Fifties. The careers of many of the players prominent in whist continued into auction bridge and contract, including Robert F. Foster, Robert W. Halpin, Nathan Kelly, Sidney S. Lenz, Winfield S. Liggett Jr., Andrew J. Mouat, Charles L. Patton, Ralph R. Richards, P. Hal Sims, Charlton Wallace, Wilbur C. Whitehead and Milton C. Work.

The AWL prolonged its life by adding an Auction Team event in 1924 and an Auction Pair event in 1930. A Contract Whist event in 1934 did not prove popular and was dropped, but the Contract Pair event began in 1930 and the Team event in 1932 continued through 1937.

AMERICAN WHIST MOVEMENT.

A schedule for conducting duplicate contests between teams-of-four originated for tournaments at whist, later adapted to auction and contract bridge.

The movement is primarily designed for an odd number of teams. The contest starts with one team and one set of boards at each table. The N-S pairs are stationary and the E-W pairs move. Before the first round the E-W pairs skip one table in the lower direction and the boards are dealt (at this moment only). The progression between the rounds is regular: the moving pairs skip one table in the lower direction and the boards are moved down one table. For a shorter movement, even number of rounds, either in the beginning and the end, or in the middle, can be omitted.

The movement may be adapted to an even number of teams with two irregularities in the progression. At the first irregularity the moving pairs skip an extra table (the E-W pairs move down three tables), at the second irregularity both the pairs and the boards skip an extra table (the boards are then moved down two tables). The times for the irregularities are given under SIX TABLES, EIGHT TABLES, etc.

In this adaptation for an even number of teams each team will miss one team. To avoid this, a round may be added, in which each match has it own boards, shared between the two tables in the match. See TEAM-OF-FOUR MOVEMENTS.

AMSTERDAM CLUB SYSTEM.

Bidding system once used mainly in the Netherlands; now obsolete.

ANALYSIS.

The appraisal of a bidding or playing situation. It is generally used in reference to the play of the cards. A good analyst will recognize the possibilities inherent in a particular deal and act accordingly, so as to give his side the best mathematical or psychological chance in either dummy play or defense.

ANALYSIS SHEETS.

Printed matter giving analyses of deals played in a specific contest, such as an ACBL-wide game. Since the hands are computer dealt, and since they are the same at all sites, it is possible to arrange for an expert to be given a set of the deals months in advance. The expert then makes a thorough study of each deal before writing a short synopsis of what is likely to happen and what should happen. This material is typeset and printed in advance and sent to the persons in charge at each site where the deals will be played. The package of analysis sheets is opened immediately after the game and each player receives a copy, enabling him

to check his results against what the expert considers to be par.

ANCHOR SUIT. When a two-suited bid specifies one suit but leaves the other unspecified, (See ASTRO and MICHAELS) the specified suit is called the anchor suit.

ANGLO-AMERICAN MATCHES. Teams representing Great Britain (or England) and the United States (or North America) have met on many occasions. The official meetings in World Championship competition are given in Appendix V under WORLD CHAMPIONSHIP with these headings: BERMUDA BOWL, WOMEN'S TEAM OLYMPIAD, WORLD WOMEN'S PAIRS, WORLD MIXED PAIRS, VENICE CUP, ROSENBLUM TEAMS. For results of semi-official and unofficial matches, see Appendix IV. See also JOSHUA CRANE.

ANNOUNCEMENT. A method used (predominantly in ACBL sanctioned play) to indicate the meaning of a call. Presently, an Announcement is used instead of an Alert in these situations: 1♠-Pass-1NT. If the 1NT is forcing for one round by partnership agreement, the opening bidder should Announce, "Forcing." 1NT-Pass-2♥. If the partnership is playing transfer bids, then the opening bidder should Announce, "Transfer." When 1NT is opened, the partner of the opener should Announce the range. For example, 1NT (11-14 HCP); partner announces, "11-14." The Announcement is not required if 1NT shows a range in the 15-18 point area.

ANTICIPATION. See PREPAREDNESS, PRINCIPLE OF.

ANTI-FRAGMENT BID. See SPLINTER BID.

ANTI-LEMMING BIDS. A method of avoiding 3NT with a major-suit weakness following a 1NT opening. Devised by Alan Truscott. A 3♥ response to 1NT shows a three-card heart holding, a weak doubleton spade, and the values for a normal raise to 3NT. Similarly, 3♠ shows a three-card spade suit and a weak doubleton heart. Opener can select a final contract, perhaps 3NT, a 4-3 major game, or four of a minor, non-forcing. This assumes that transfers are being used. Similarly, after 1NT-2♣-2♦, 3♥ or 3♠ shows a four-card suit and a weak doubleton in the other major. See *The Bridge World* July 1996.

ANTI-SPLINTER BIDS. Various bids used in responding to an opening of a major to show opening values but no short suit. See SPLINTER BID.

APPEAL. An appeal is of a director's ruling. (See Laws 92 and 93, and Law 79C for expiration period). Any ruling by a director may be appealed, but an Appeals Committee does not have the authority to overrule the Director on a point of law. In team events, the captain must concur in the appeal. See APPEALS COMMITTEE.

APPEALS COMMITTEE. A committee appointed to hear and rule on appeals by contestants and other disputed matters that may arise during the course of a tournament. The committee usually is appointed in advance at major tournaments such as world championships and zonal championships. Such committees are usually named as necessary at lesser tournaments.

When a pair or team appeals a tournament director's ruling, the committee first listens to and asks questions of the tournament director who gave the ruling being appealed. The director is then dismissed and the committee listens to and asks questions of the players involved in the situation causing the appeal. After gaining as much relevant information as possible, the players are dismissed. The committee then deliberates and makes its decision which is then transmitted to the tournament director, the appellants and the side appealed against. An appeals committee also may hear cases involving conduct and ethics.

APPENDIX MOVEMENTS. Frequently it is necessary to alter various game movements for various reasons — late arriving pairs, a desire to have all pairs play exactly the same boards, etc. See APPENDIX PAIR, APPENDIX TABLE , BUMP MOVEMENT, ROVER.

APPENDIX PAIR. A method of adding an extra pair in a movement. The appendix pair will be stationary at some point, replacing the pair scheduled for that position who sit out for a round. A pair cannot be appended at a table which already has a stationary pair. See also ROVER.

APPENDIX TABLE. A method of expanding sections to accommodate extra tables without increasing the number of boards in play; particularly useful for adding late pairs or tables to HOWELL MOVEMENTS. The result of adding appendix tables to the seven-table Howell game has led to the THREE-QUARTER MOVEMENT for eight, nine, and up to 12 tables.

Appendix tables in Mitchell movements are used when it is necessary for all the pairs to play all the boards. The method is ideally suited for 7, 11 and 13 tables. A further use is to append a Newcomer table to a regular game where inexperienced players may be accommodated without delaying the regular game. The application of the appendix table principle by former National Tournament Director Paul Marks has made the RAINBOW INDIVIDUAL MOVEMENT adaptable for numbers of tables one or even two greater than prime numbers such as 7, 11, 13, 17, etc.

The technique of handling an appendix table is simple. In a Howell movement, a table (or tables) may be appended to any table where there are two moving pairs. The North-South pair at the base table is instructed to remain stationary as is the East-West pair at the appended table. Boards are constantly relayed from the base table to the appended table, and as moving pairs arrive at the base table to sit North-South, they are instructed to play at the appended table, then to resume their regular progression. In a Mitchell game, a table (or tables) may be appended to any section that consists of a prime number of tables. Boards are placed on the base table (or tables) and are relayed with the appended table (or tables). Throughout the game the boards move regularly to the next lower table within the prime section. The East-West pair at the base table remains stationary, as does the North-South pair at the appended table. All other pairs move each round; East-West moves to the next higher table and North-South skips one table to the next higher table.

APPROACH-FORCING SYSTEM. A term applicable to most standard methods of bidding, including GOREN SYSTEM or STANDARD AMERICAN. The CULBERTSON SYSTEM was the earliest of these, and was the basis on which many other systems were built. The original objective of Ely Culbertson was to emphasize the need for slow suit exploration, in preference to an early excursion into notrump. See APPROACH PRINCIPLE.

APPROACH PRINCIPLE. The precept of Ely Culbertson favoring opening suit-bids and a slow exchange of information in preference to notrump opening bids and responses. He described it this way:

"In view of the fact that in making an opening bid, the player is venturing into unknown territory, it is wise for him to proceed cautiously, to feel his way, and thus, protected by a network of approach suit-bids of one, act with care until he learns something about the distribution of honor strength held by his partner and his adversaries.

"The Approach Principle, as applied to contract, may be stated as follows: *Whenever a hand contains a biddable suit, even a shaded four-card minor, that suit and not notrump should usually first be bid.* The *notrump complex,* which suggests that the opening bid on a hand should be notrump even when the hand contains a biddable suit, is a disease especially prevalent among advanced players. The logical place for notrump bidding is after information has been exchanged as to suit lengths and distribution. Notrump bids in the early stages crowd the bidding too much and eliminate many valuable suitbids, while the bid of a suit always leaves the alternative of notrump without increasing the contract. The use of the Approach Principle does not decrease, but, as a matter of fact, increases the number of safe notrump contracts undertaken."

Culbertson's dislike of indiscriminate notrump bids stemmed from experience. Too many of his contemporaries carried over from auction the phobia created by the scoring table (where if the opponents held three honors in a suit they might outscore the declarer who made only two-odd or three-odd). Thus they tended to bid 1NT with almost any hand lacking a suit headed by three honors. Hampered by lack of a Stayman convention to discover a 4-4 fit after the notrump opening, far too often the wrong contract was reached. In support of the approach idea, Culbertson quoted the following hands:

West (dealer)	East
♠ A Q x x	♠ J x x x
♥ A x	♥ x
♦ A J x	♦ K x x x
♣ A 10 x x	♣ K x x x

Culbertson's suggested bidding was:

West	East
1♠	2♠
3NT	4♠
Pass	

A few years later, most good players — including Culbertsonites — would open with 1♣, and arrive at the same final contract. But in citing this example, he was shooting at the flaw of opening a notrump with more than the desirable strength, as well as the danger of missing the spade fit.

In the beginning, Culbertson recommended notrump openings on a range of three honor tricks not vulnerable to four-plus honor tricks vulnerable. His zeal for approach principles caused him to limit the bid to 4-3-3-3 distribution with an occasional exception for 4-4-3-2, including a strong doubleton not less than Q-x.

Thus, analysis of the 1937 prototype World Championship reveals that the Culbertson team did not use a single opening bid of 1NT. As methods of responding to 1NT were improved so as to discover suit fits after the notrump opening, Culbertson gradually relaxed his strictures against opening notrumps on hands of the wrong distribution in order to use the bid on more hands of the right high-card strength. Thus, by 1949, 4-4-3-2 and 5-3-3-2 distributions (but not five-card majors) were officially included in the notrump family — no longer as exceptions. But while the distributional range was spread, the high-card range was narrowed, standardized at three and one-half to four-plus honor tricks which were later interpreted — by Culbertson as well as by others — as 16-18 high-card points, with even 6-3-2-2 distributions admitted to the notrump family on hands of proper high-card strength and strong doubletons.

Over a span of more than 30 years the Culbertson Approach Principle remained, with but little alteration, a basic principle of bidding. A few more hands containing biddable suits were opened with 1NT; the standards for biddable suits in the responder's hand were shaded down. But it remained standard practice to avoid indiscriminate notrump openings, and especially to avoid responses of 1NT to partner's suit bid if a response could be given at the one level in another suit. The notrump response sometimes results in a suit fit being missed, and may lead to the weak hand becoming the declarer at notrump. Many experts play that a response of 1NT to 1♦, for example, absolutely denies holding a four-card major suit. Others, however, would not choose to respond in a worthless four-card suit. See BIDDABLE SUIT.

ARNO. See LITTLE ROMAN CLUB (ARNO SYSTEM).

ARRANGEMENT OF CARDS. The act of sorting the cards in one's own hand or (by the declarer) in the dummy's hand, which includes the conventional placing of trumps to the declarer's left in the dummy's hand. Most players sort their cards into suits, red and black alternately, and place the cards in each suit according to rank. It is regarded as an offense against the proprieties of bridge for any player to draw inferences about another player's hand by noting the position of the cards. But some players split suits and avoid singletons at the end of the hand to protect themselves against players with better eyesight than ethics.

ARRANGEMENT OF TABLES. At a duplicate tournament, the arrangement of tables depends on the size and shape of the playing space and the expected number of tables which must be accommodated (see TABLE SPACING). A hairpin type arrangement is more desirable than a straight line arrangement for sections in order to bring the last table into proximity with the first in each section.

ARRANGEMENT OF TRICKS. In duplicate bridge, the act of turning a card face down on the edge of the

table immediately in front of a player after four cards have been played to a trick, with the long axis of the card pointing to the players who won the trick. In rubber bridge, the act of collecting the cards played to a trick by a member of the side that won the trick and then turning them face down on the table so that the tricks are identifiable in proper sequence. See LAWS (Law 65); LAWS OF DUPLICATE (Law 65).

ARRANGING. (1) A term having reference to the aligning of the cards of the dummy as that hand is being spread on the table just after the opening lead has been made. The declarer may arrange the cards to his own satisfaction when he states that he is doing so.

(2) A statement by a player before he has bid in the first round of bidding meaning that he has been lax in picking up his hand or looking at it, and is not in a position to act when it becomes his turn. A call of some sort should follow this remark with reasonable dispatch.

(3) The act of sorting one's own cards. See ARRANGEMENT OF CARDS.

ARROW. The symbol on the duplicate board which indicates the alignment required so that the North player receives the hand designated for him. Table cards have the compass points printed on the edges; the boards have the arrow symbol pointing to the North hand; the arrow point and the printed direction coinciding, each player's hand is directly in front of him in the board. See: ARROW SWITCH; SCRAMBLED MITCHELL MOVEMENT.

ARROW SWITCH. The right-angle switch of the boards in some rounds of a tournament to get increased balance. In a Mitchell movement, the arrow switch is used to obtain a single winner. See SCRAMBLED MITCHELL MOVEMENT.

ARTIFICIAL INTELLIGENCE. Non-trivial decision-making by a computer. Many programs for bidding and play have been prepared for bridge. Some programs for bidding are highly sophisticated, but as of this writing the play programs are at best at the intermediate level.
Incomplete information. Chess and checkers are games of complete information, as each player can see everything about the current situation. Bridge is a game of incomplete information because some cards are hidden from each player. Of course this complicates the decision making.
Decision tree (or game tree). A program makes a series of decisions which can be diagrammed in the form of a tree, with the current situation being the root. Each possible immediate decision is a separate branch. Subsequent decisions are sub-branches. *Look-ahead, tree-search* and *mini-max* are names for the process of *traversing* this tree in order to make the root decision. *Alpha-Beta* is the name for an improved version of this process. The size of the tree is huge (especially with incomplete information), too large for any computer to deal with in a reasonable length of time until part way into the play of the hand. So *pruning* (ignoring seemingly irrelevant possible plays) and possibly stopping the search at a certain *depth* (number of plays into the future) is normally done.
Expert systems. Programs look up the first few bids from a table, much as a person memorizes the responses

to STAYMAN or the meanings of JACOBY TRANSFERS. But most tables use huge tables of bids to help them bid, before they actually have to make a decision later in the auction. The use of such tables makes this portion of a bridge program an *expert system*.
Machine learning. This is the process by which a program automatically changes its decision-making rules, based on the results of actual situations it has encountered in the past. Few bridge programs use learning.
Pattern matching. A human bridge player readily recognizes that a hand or suit fits a certain pattern, and has a repertoire of possible techniques for dealing with such a hand or suit. A program must do this, too. But pattern matching is difficult to teach to a program.
Monte Carlo sampling. Some programs use Monte Carlo sampling. In the case of bridge, the computer considers a number (maybe even thousands) of random hypothetical estimates of the unseen hands in choosing its next play. The name *Monte Carlo* was apparently the code name of the project that John von Neumann and Stanislaw Ulam were working on when he invented this sampling method (for *simulation* of nuclear processes) for the Manhattan (atomic bomb) Project.

ARTIFICIAL BIDS and CALLS. An artifical bid or call can be correctly interpreted by partner only if agreement has been reached about its meaning in advance.

Certain artificial bids and calls are now so standard that their apparent normal meaning would be considered as an artificial convention. For example: a takeout double; a 2NT negative response to an opening two-bid, etc.

At the extreme of artificiality are cipher bids which bear no relation to the suit named or to any other suit. The most common examples are the Stayman responses of 2♣ and 3♣ over 1NT and 2NT respectively, and the responses to Blackwood.

Cipher bids are developed to the maximum by a RELAY SYSTEM, in which one player can make a series of artificial bids to discover the details of his partner's hand. In extreme cases, an original pass can be used artificially. See WEAK OPENING SYSTEMS.

The proliferation of artificial bids of all kinds in the postwar years led to some objections. The AMERICAN CONTRACT BRIDGE LEAGUE, the FRENCH BRIDGE FEDERATION and the ENGLISH BRIDGE UNION, among others, restrict the use of artificial systems and conventions, such as the Italian systems and others of similar complexity, in normal tournament play. It is considered that the users of such systems gain an unfair advantage against opponents unfamiliar with the methods employed. This is particularly true in pair tournaments and other events in which only a few boards are played in each round.

Defensive bids take on a different meaning against artificial systems, and the meanings of doubles, notrump bids and bids in the opponent's suit have to be carefully considered. A further point is that a defender can afford to pass over an artificial forcing bid holding a strong hand, knowing that he will get a further opportunity to bid.

At the international level the use of artificial bids and systems is restricted by the WBF.

In the early Thirties there was some doubt about the legality of certain artificial bids. In 1933 the Portland Club in London, one of the law-making bodies, ruled

that the Culbertson 4-5NT convention and others that could indicate the possession of specific cards were illegal. The decision was based on the idea that a bid that showed possession of a particular card amounted to the exposure of that card.

This ruling was quickly challenged in America, and the Whist Club gave an opposite verdict.

ARTIFICIAL CLUB BID. See ONE CLUB SYSTEMS.

ARTIFICIAL RESPONSES AND REBIDS AFTER NATURAL NOTRUMP. See NOTRUMP BIDDING.

ASBURY PARK. The scene of many of the most important national championships in the early years of contract bridge. The nine-day Summer championships of the ABL and later of the ACBL were held there from 1930 to 1941 inclusive, making it the focal point of the bridge tournament year. In the early Forties the Asbury Park Convention Hall became too small to accommodate a national championship.

ASCHERMAN. Method of calculation for pair tournaments. One extra scoring unit is awarded to every pair. This makes the formula for fouled boards (see NEUBERG formula) far easier to apply, and the final percentages of every tournament are significant and unbiased by the number of tables. As an example, a sole top in a tournament of 10 tables will score 100% in the classical method, but only 95% in Ascherman. A sole top in a tournament of 100 tables is also 100% in the classical method, but 99.5% in the Ascherman method. Thus, the Ascherman method reflects more truly the accomplishment of the players. Developed in 1987 by Herman De Wael, but named after Ir. Wim Ascherman of the Netherlands, who had developed something similar in the Fifties.

ASEAN BRIDGE CLUB CHAMPIONSHIP. Contested annually since 1979 in October-November among Brunei, Indonesia, Malaysia, Philippines, Singapore and Thailand. Indonesia won the Open Team title each year 1979-1994. For results, see Appendix IV.

ASKING BID. A method by which one player can discover specific information about distribution, controls or trump quality held by his partner. These bids usually are used when exploring for a slam contract, but sometimes are used when checking the feasibility of a game contract. The original Asking Bids were devised by Albert Morehead and developed by Ely Culbertson.

For many years Asking Bids fell into disuse. They were not a part of Standard American or any of the major systems used. However, in recent years various forms of Asking Bids have very much returned to favor. Many of the leading Italian players who consistently won world championships in the Fifties, Sixties and Seventies employed Asking Bids. All of the RELAY SYSTEMS now in vogue all over the world rely heavily on Asking Bids. Most of these relay systems have one member of a partnership asking a long series of questions by making relay bids and the other partner responding in a predetermined pattern. Using these sophisticated methods, it often is possible for the asking partner to announce his partner's exact distribution plus the location of all honor cards.

Several Asking Bids are commonly used by most partnerships. The GRAND SLAM FORCE is an Asking Bid as ace-asking bids like BLACKWOOD and GERBER. The WESTERN CUEBID is an Asking Bid, attempting to ferret out the possibility of a notrump game. A raise to five of a suit after an opponent has overcalled usually asks partner to bid the slam if he has first-round or second-round control of the opponents' suit. Even the Stayman 2♣ response to 1NT is an Asking Bid.

However, the Asking Bids used by those employing relay methods go far beyond these simple applications. Usually letters of the Greek alphabet, such as alpha, beta, gamma and delta, are used to describe various levels.

Various Asking Bids can be used in responding to a major-suit preemptive openings. Possible are:

(1) In response to 3♥ or 3♠, 4♣ can be used as Blackwood or to ask for suit quality. Rebids are: 4♦ denies ace or king; 4♥ promises ace or king; 4♠ promises ace and king; 4NT shows solid suit.

(2) Combined with (1), 4♦ can ask for a short suit. Then opener signs off in his suit to deny a short suit; bids a singleton; bids 4NT with an unidentified void, and 5♣ asks for its location (after 3♠ - 4♦; 4NT - 5♣, 5♠ is a club void.)

(3) New-suit response to a three or four of a major suit can ask about the suit bid. First step by opener shows at least two losers in the suit; second step shows second-round control; third step shows first-round control. This treatment became standard in BWS 1994.

See also AUSTRALIAN ASKING BID, AUSTRALIAN TRUMP ASKING BID, BETA ASKING BID, FULWILER, GAMMA SLAM BID, LEBOVIC, MATHE ASKING BID, SUPER-PRECISION ASKING BID, WANG TRUMP ASKING BID.

ASPRO. A method of defending against 1NT openings based on ASTRO, devised by Terence Reese. (The name is borrowed from a popular British brand of aspirin.)

The term *astronaut* is used to designate the overcaller, and the term *relay* to describe the responses in the neutral suit. Aspro is varied in three respects:

(1) *Major two-suiters* are bid differently. With five spades and four or five hearts, the astronaut bids 2♣ and follows with 2♠ over the 2♦ relay.

With four spades and five hearts the treatment varies with the strength of the overcaller's hand. Normally he bids 2♣ followed by 2♥ giving responder the opportunity to show spades. With a stronger hand he bids 2♦ followed by 2NT.

(2) *Pronounced two-suiters* (6-5 or 6-6 distribution). Specific bids are laid down for each two-suited hand:

2NT	black suits
3♣	minor suits
3♦	red suits
3♥	major suits

With the odd two-suiters (spades-diamonds or hearts-clubs), bid two of the minor suit and follow with a jump in a six-card suit.

(3) *A redouble* by the astronaut or the responder is an SOS. For alternative methods of defending against 1NT, see DEFENSE TO ONE NOTRUMP.

ASPTRO. A defense to 1NT which takes an element from ASPRO and ASTRO. 2♣ shows hearts and another suit and 2♦ shows spades and another suit.

ASSETS. A method of distributional valuation originated by Alan Truscott and described by him in several books. It provides for automatic re-evaluation by opener and responder as the bidding develops.

For a long suit (5 or more cards), count one asset

For a singleton, count one asset

For a void, count two assets

Each asset, or distributional point, is counted at the start, and may bring the high-card points up to the 13 points required for an opening. This gives a sound result, for it distinguishes between 4-3-3-3 and 4-4-4-1, which the long-suit method does not, and between 5-4-2-2 and 5-4-3-1, which neither the long-suit method nor the short-suit method does.

Both opener and responder adjust their assets in the light of the auction:

If there appears to be no fit, assets disappear

If there is an 8-card fit, assets count normally

If there is a 9-card fit, assets double

If there is a 10-card fit, assets triple

Suppose that after a 1♠ opening showing a five-card suit responder holds:

♠ J x x x x
♥ x x x x x
♦ —
♣ x x x

Four assets triple, and the jack gives a total of 13 for a bid of 4♠.

ASSIGNMENT OF SEATS. Methods of assigning seats vary from country to country. In ACBL events the assignments are on the entry blanks that contestants purchase. In many other areas of the world, entries must be purchased early. The tournament personnel gather all the entries and assign seats. A sheet is posted indicating the seating assignment of each pair or team. See SEED, SEEDING.

ASSIST. To raise a suit first bid by partner. See RAISE.

ASSOCIATION. National organizations with names beginning in this way are listed under the names of the countries.

ASSUMPTION IN PLAY. Assumption is a basic element of dummy play and defense. Any finesse, for example, may be taken on the assumption that it will win. In planning the play or defense of an entire deal, declarers and defenders must often assume that the cards lie so the contract can be made or defeated; they proceed on the assumption that such a lie of the cards exists.

♠ 10 6 4 2
♥ A 3
♦ A Q 5 4
♣ K 9 3

♠ Q
♥ K J 9 6 4 2
♦ K 3 2
♣ 6 4 2

South plays at 4♥ after opening a weak 2♥ bid. West leads the ♠3. East wins the ace and shifts to a club, and West takes the ace and returns the ♣Q. East ruffs dummy's king and leads a low spade. South ruffs and leads a heart to the ace, West following with the ten.

Should South finesse the jack on the next heart or put up the king?

South knows that West held six clubs and at least three spades, and South must assume a 3-3 diamond break, since he needs a discard for his losing club. South should therefore play West for 3-1-3-6 distribution and finesse the ♥J.

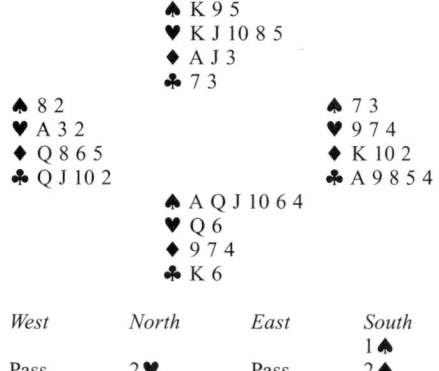

West	North	East	South
			1♠
Pass	2♥	Pass	2♠
Pass	4♠	All Pass	

West leads the ♣Q, and East wins the ace. East knows the defense cannot prevail if South has solid trumps and the ♥A. East must assume that West has one major-suit trick, but it is too much to expect him to have two. Hence, East must assume that West has the ♦Q. It is essential to shift to a diamond at the second trick, giving declarer no time to draw trumps and set up the hearts for discards.

When a contract depends on the position of two or three key cards, it often helps to make a definite assumption about one of them. If you can afford to have it wrong, assume that it is wrong; if you must have it right, assume that it is right and build up your picture of the opposing hands on that basis.

Here is a difficult example of a second-degree assumption, quoted from *The Expert Game* by Terence Reese.

♠ A K 10 6 3
♥ Q 5
♦ Q 4
♣ K Q 6 2

♠ Q J 9 4 2
♥ 7
♦ A J 6 3
♣ 8 7 4

West deals at game all and the bidding goes:

West	North	East	South
1♥	Dbl	2♥	3♠
Pass	4♠	All Pass	

West leads the ♥K and continues with the ♥A. South ruffs and draws trumps in two rounds. What should he play next? The contract will fail only if South loses two tricks in clubs and one in diamonds. Suppose that he leads a club, which looks obvious. If East holds the ♣A, then surely West will hold the ♦K and South will be defeated. Playing a diamond first, on the other hand, South is completely safe. If West holds the ♦K, and puts it up, there will be two club discards on declarer's ♦A-J. But if East holds the ♦K, then assuredly West will hold the ♣A. It is a puzzling but instructive hand. This is the distribution against which South has to guard:

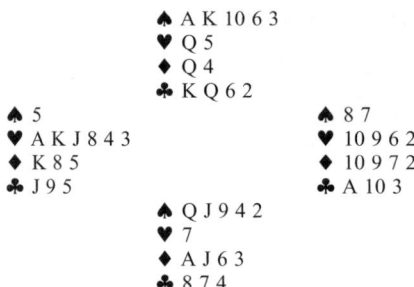

```
            ♠ A K 10 6 3
            ♥ Q 5
            ♦ Q 4
            ♣ K Q 6 2
♠ 5                         ♠ 8 7
♥ A K J 8 4 3               ♥ 10 9 6 2
♦ K 8 5                     ♦ 10 9 7 2
♣ J 9 5                     ♣ A 10 3
            ♠ Q J 9 4 2
            ♥ 7
            ♦ A J 6 3
            ♣ 8 7 4
```

ASSUMPTIONS, MATHEMATICAL. See MATH-EMATICAL ASSUMPTIONS.

ASTRO. Over 1NT, a specialized use of minor-suit over-calls to show two-suited hands. The name of the convention is derived from the initial letters of the inventors' names: **A**llinger-**ST**ern-**RO**sler. After a strong or a weak notrump, in the direct or the reopening position:

2♣ shows *hearts* and a minor suit

2♦ shows *spades* and another suit

The Astro bidder promises at least nine cards in two suits, and his suits must have some solidity if he is vulnerable.

The Astro bidder's partner has a choice of these actions:

(1) Two of the anchor major (i.e., the particular major suit guaranteed by the overcaller): shows at least three cards in the suit and no further ambitions.

(2) Three of the anchor major: a game invitation with at least four-card support. The strength depends mainly on the vulnerability situation, and to a lesser extent on the strength of the notrump opening.

(3) Four of the anchor major: natural.

(4) Pass: a weak hand and a long suit (probably of six cards) in the minor bid by partner.

(5) Two of the neutral suit (i.e., the next suit above the Astro bid): a negative action, denying the ability to make any other response. Indicates at least a doubleton in the neutral suit and usually fewer than three cards in the anchor suit.

(6) 2NT: artificial and forcing. Shows some support for the anchor major, and suggests game prospects without guaranteeing a further bid.

(7) New suit takeout or jump (including a jump in the neutral suit and a raise of the takeout bid): shows a six-card or longer suit.

The Astro bidder has a choice of rebids after a neutral response. He may pass with five cards in the neutral suit, or show five cards in the anchor suit by bidding it. He may show his second suit at the level of three, indicating a probable six-card suit and more than minimum playing strength.

In most sequences, 2NT by either player is artificial and forcing. As responder's second bid, it is likely to be weak:

West	East
♠ A 5 2	♠ Q 4 3
♥ A J 10 5 4	♥ 6
♦ 6	♦ Q 8 5 3 2
♣ K 10 8 5	♣ Q 9 6 4

West	North	East	South
			1NT
2♣	Pass	2♦	Pass
2♥	Pass	2NT	Pass
3♣	All pass		

Astro Variations

Some partnerships use a variation of Astro similar to the BROZEL convention, called Pinpoint Astro, which is more explicit as to the two suits held.

2♣ shows hearts and clubs

2♦ shows hearts and diamonds

2♥ shows hearts and spades

2♠ shows spades and a minor suit

A modification adopted by many Roth-Stone players uses both two-level and three-level overcalls in order to show precisely which suits are held:

2♣ shows clubs and spades

2♦ shows diamonds and spades

3♥ shows clubs and hearts

3♠ shows diamonds and hearts

Double shows hearts and spades

Yet another variation, devised by Matthew Granovetter, uses a double to show spades and another suit. 2♣ shows clubs and hearts; 2♦ shows diamonds and hearts.

Defense

The opening bidder's partner has several choices if his side appears to have the balance of strength. He can double with a defensive hand, usually with a good holding in the anchor major and the suit he doubles; cuebid the anchor major when his hand is unsuited to defense; or pass to await developments (remembering that there might not be any). A non-jump new-suit bid (including a raise in the Astro bidder's minor) would be unconstructive. 2NT would be natural. For an alternative defense to Astro, see LEBENSOHL CONVENTION.

For alternative defensive conventions against notrump openings, see DEFENSE TO ONE NOTRUMP.

ASTRO CUEBID. Devised by the authors of the ASTRO convention, these are used to show certain two-suited hands.

An immediate cuebid in the suit bid by the opener shows a long minor together with a shorter major suit. The bid shows clubs and hearts unless one of these suits has been bid, in which case the next-higher suit is assumed.

(a)	(b)
♠ 5 3	♠ 5
♥ A K J 6	♥ K 10 6 5 2
♦ 7	♦ Q 10 9 7 4 3
♣ A Q 10 8 5 2	♣ 6

With hand (a), the cuebid would be used over 1♦ or 1♠. This is an inconvenient hand to bid with standard methods. Note that the problem is less acute if the minor suits are reversed. Over 1♠, for example, a double would then be appropriate, followed by a diamond bid over a club response.

With hand (b), 2♣ can be bid over 1♣ at favorable vulnerability. As clubs have been bid, the cuebid must show the red suits.

ASTROLITE. A defense to 1NT with the following features: (1) double: penalties; (2) 2♣: heart one-suiter or hearts and a minor; (3) 2♦: spades and a minor; (4) 2♥: majors; (5) 2NT: minors or strong with both ma-

jors. Other bids natural. After 2♣, partner may: (a) pass with club length and no heart fit; (b) bid 2♦ with limited strength and no heart fit; (c) bid 2♥ with limited strength and heart fit; (d) bid 2♠, natural with no heart fit; (e) bid 2NT forcing. See ASPRO, ASTRO.

ATTACK. To take the initiative in bidding or play at some risk. Used particularly with reference to the opening lead.

ATTACKING LEAD. A risky lead from a high-card combination such as A-Q, K-J or an unsupported high honor in an active attempt to win or establish fast tricks. This is common against a notrump contract, but less common against a suit contract when a passive lead is often called for. See OPENING LEADS.

The term *attacking lead* used to be applied to a lead from an honor sequence, but this meaning is obsolete. Several situations deserve special mention:

(1) An attacking lead is desirable when the leader holds four or more trumps or can deduce that his partner holds four or more trumps.

(2) An attacking lead is desirable when the opponents have reached a suit game tentatively after bidding three suits. For example:

West	East
	1♣
1♥	1♠
3♣	4♣
5♣	

The opening leader can expect his partner to have any missing high diamond honor because both West and East have avoided notrump. It is probably desirable to take diamond tricks before declarer can get discards.

(3) An attacking lead has to be considered against a contract at a high level, either in a suit or notrump, if the bidding suggests that declarer will have a long side suit in his hand or the dummy.

(4) An attacking lead should not be made against a grand slam but is far more attractive against a small slam. See LEADS, TEMPO (1).

ATTITUDE SIGNAL. The interest or lack of interest of a defender in having a suit led or continued by his partner. The usual method of encouraging the lead or continuation of a suit is a HIGH-LOW SIGNAL. Low-high is discouraging. See also ODD-EVEN DISCARDS and UPSIDE-DOWN SIGNALS.

AUCTION. The bidding by the four players for the contract. The dealer is the first bidder after the cards are dealt. He may pass or bid. The bidding proceeds clockwise around the table. Each player may pass, make a bid or raise a preceding bid, double an opponent's bid or redouble an opponent's double. The bidding ends when three players have passed in succession (or four players on the first round of bidding).

AUCTION BRIDGE. The third step in the evolution of the general game of bridge. Its predecessors were WHIST and BRIDGE WHIST. The great innovation in auction bridge was the introduction of competitive bidding. It was first played in 1903 or 1904, but the precise circumstances are disputed. The first code of laws governing the play of auction was set forth in 1908, the product of a joint committee of the Bath Club and the Portland Club. The popularity of auction bridge increased enormously, and the activity in whist and bridge whist decreased proportionately. After the introduction of contract bridge in 1926, auction bridge lost favor rapidly.

In auction bridge the aim was to keep the contract as low as possible because the declarer's side was credited with the number of tricks won, whether contracted for or not. For example, the declarer might have bid 2♠ and actually won six tricks over his book. He was credited with making a small slam. Penalties and premiums in auction are the same without regard to vulnerability. Honor scoring in auction bridge is different from contract bridge — so important, in fact, that it may distort the bidding, especially in duplicate auction.

Auction bridge scoring is as follows:

Scoring. Provided declarer has won at least the number of odd tricks named in his contract, declarer's side scores for each odd trick won:

	Undoubled	Doubled	Redoubled
With notrump	10	20	40
With spades trump	9	18	36
With hearts trump	8	16	32
With diamonds trump	7	14	28
With clubs trump	6	12	24

Game and Rubber. When a side scores, in one or more deals, 30 points or more for odd tricks, it has won a game and both sides start fresh on the next game. When a side has won two games, it wins the rubber and adds to its score 250 points.

Doubles and Redoubles. If a doubled contract is fulfilled, declarer's side scores 50 points bonus plus 50 points for each odd trick in excess of his contract. If a redoubled contract is fulfilled, declarer's side scores 100 points bonus plus 100 points for each odd trick in excess of his contract. These bonuses are additional to the score for odd tricks, but do not count toward game.

Undertricks. For every trick by which declarer falls short of his contract, his opponents score 50 points; if the contract is doubled, 100 points; if it is redoubled, 200 points.

Honors. The side which holds the majority of the trump honors (A, K, Q, J, 10), or of the aces at notrump, scores:

For 3 trump honors (or aces) 30
For 4 aces in one hand at notrump 100
For 5 trump honors in one hand 100
For 4 trump honors in one hand 80
For 4 trump honors in one hand, 5th in partner's hand 90

Slams. A side which wins 12 of the 13 tricks, regardless of the contract, scores 50 points for a small slam. A side which wins all 13 tricks, regardless of the contract, scores 100 points for a grand slam.

Points for overtricks, undertricks, honors and slams do not count toward game. Only odd tricks count toward game, and only when declarer fulfills his contract.

Contract Bridge for Auction Players by Ely Culbertson gives the complete details of auction bidding contrasted, in parallel columns, with contract bidding. See also *Auction Bridge Complete* by Milton C. Work.

AUGUST CONVENTION. See TWO-WAY STAYMAN.

AUSTRALIAN ASKING BID. A slight modification of the original CULBERTSON ASKING BIDS. Holding a singleton in the asked suit and two aces, a jump is made in the suit of the lower-ranking ace. In some cases the asking bid can be made below the four level: 2♠ in response to 1♥, for example, is used as an asking bid.

AUSTRALIAN BRIDGE. An independent magazine with six issues a year founded by Denis Howard in 1970. It was managed and edited by Ron Klinger 1972-84, and since then by Paul Marston and Stephen Lester. Address: P.O. Box 1426, Double Bay NSW 1360, Australia.

AUSTRALIAN TRUMP-ASKING BID. A trump-asking bid initiated by either partner's use of the cheapest bid in notrump immediately after a major suit has been agreed. The inquiry, which could be made as low as the two level, focuses on the king and queen of trumps. Lacking both king and queen, the partner of the asking bidder signs off in the trump suit. The other responses are in steps, not counting the trump suit as a step:

1st step	queen
2nd step	king
3rd step	king and extra length
4th step	king and queen
5th step	king and queen and extra length

For alternative methods see TRUMP ASKING BID.

AUSTRIAN SYSTEM. See VIENNA SYSTEM.

AUTHORIZED INFORMATION. Information legally available. This includes information such as meanings of calls, explanations of the Laws and methods used to show count and attitude.

AUTOBRIDGE. A commercial device, invented in the Thirties and still popular. Lesson hands can be used for self-teaching bidding and play. A deal sheet is inserted in a special board so that only the player's own cards are shown. As the deal progresses, the player finds that his own bids and plays are automatically corrected, and that the bids and plays of the other players are automatically revealed. The board and deal sheets are accompanied by a booklet, in which the hands are set out and the bidding and play explained by experts.

Experts who have composed *Autobridge* hands include Ely and Josephine Culbertson, Albert Morehead, Richard Frey, Charles Goren, Alfred Sheinwold, Alan Truscott and Barry Rigal.

AUTOMATIC HAND REGISTERS. In original duplicate whist before 1883 each hand was written on a *register* (hand-record slip), then tricks were scooped in as usual. So the players had to reconstruct their hands from registers for replay at the next table. The four loose hands were carefully piled atop each other crosswise into a small box, a device too unstable to move without mixing up or scrambling the cards. So after every round *all* players had to move to new tables.

In 1883 James Allison invented the automatic hand register simply by having players keep all their played cards face down in front of themselves as today we still do. Each perpendicular card marked a trick won, a *live* soldier; else it was placed horizontally. But players still put their played hands in the little box *in stasis* on the table.

In order to correct this second problem special card trays were introduced, each equipped with rubber bands to hold each hand more securely for passing the boards to the next table. Soon a company in Kalamazoo MI manufactured the world's first duplicate board with card pockets sold as Paine's Whist Trays. These were cumbersome, but at least they aided the growing popularity

of duplicate whist, especially in the great whist tournaments held 1894 through 1936 by the AMERICAN WHIST LEAGUE.

AUTOMATIC SQUEEZE. A simple squeeze which will operate against either opponent.

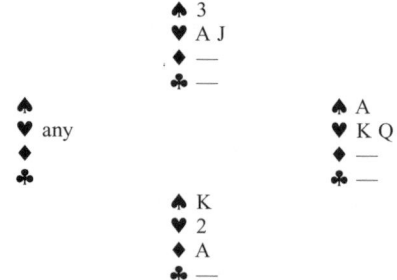

The lead of South's ♦ A squeezes East, and would also squeeze West if the defenders' hands were exchanged. Whatever West discards, the ♠ 3 is thrown from dummy.

This situation contrasts with a POSITIONAL SQUEEZE, when only the player who plays immediately after the squeeze card is under pressure, and the declarer's discard from the third hand varies with the defender's discard. See also SQUEEZE.

AUTOMATIC TWO DIAMONDS RESPONSE. See TWO DIAMONDS ARTIFICIAL RESPONSE TO FORCING TWO CLUBS OPENING.

AUTOMATON CONTRACT BRIDGE PLAYER. An obsolete electric machine designed by William Patzer to play a specific bridge hand against anyone who would put a coin into the machine to start the proceedings. The machine would make winning plays against various stratagems used by the declarer — i.e., the paying customer. See also ROBOT BRIDGE PLAYER.

In the days of whist there were several very popular machines which, it was claimed, were able to play whist. The first, invented by an American named Balcom and adapted for exhibition by Maelzel, was exhibited circa 1829-31. An automaton called "Psycho" was exhibited by John Maskelyne at the Egyptian Hall, Piccadilly, London for several decades starting in 1875. The *New York Journal* exhibited an automaton whist player, named the "Yellow Kid," in New York in 1896.

AVERAGE EXPECTANCY. The term applied to the expected holding of the partner of the opening bidder; it may refer to one-third of the missing cards of a suit or one-third of the missing honor strength. The fraction will vary as the bidding progresses. It was much used in the CULBERTSON SYSTEM in his arguments for preemptive bids.

AVERAGE HAND. A hand that contains ten high-card points. An ace, king, queen, and a jack, or one-fourth of all the high honors, is the average expectation of each player before the hands are seen. This basic assumption furnishes the player with a simple yardstick for measuring the relative high-card strength of a given hand, and may assist materially in estimating the game potential or penalty expectancy of any bid. Hence, two or three points added to an average hand is the valuation of a hand with a minimum opening bid.

AVERAGE SCORE. One-half the matchpoints possible on a given deal or in a particular session of a matchpoint pairs tournament.

In IMP pair games average on a given board is the arithmetical mean of all scores on that board, usually excluding the highest and the lowest. This constructed average is called a *datum*. See INTERNATIONAL MATCHPOINTS.

The average score is usually the basis on which adjusted scores are awarded when a particular deal cannot be properly played. When the deal cannot be played through no fault of one pair, the adjustment is usually 60% of the available matchpoints. Deduction from the average score is made by the tournament director when one of the pairs is at fault. These adjustments are referred to as Average-plus and Average-minus.

AVOIDANCE. A plan of play designed to prevent a particular opponent from gaining the lead.

There are two main reasons for pursuing such a plan. First, it may be necessary to prevent a defender with established winners from gaining the lead, especially at notrump. Second, declarer may have a suit combination which is vulnerable to a lead from a particular side. Both aspects of avoidance arise if either of these suit combinations is held:

(a)	(b)
Dummy	*Dummy*
3 2	2
Declarer	*Declarer*
A J 4	K J 4 3

In each case South is playing 3NT and West leads the 5 to East's queen. If South wins the trick, East becomes the dangerous hand, but if South holds up twice, West becomes the opponent to be feared. South's play at the first trick must therefore be determined by an examination of the whole hand to discover which opponent is more likely to secure the lead. If a vital king or queen is missing in a side suit, it is usually obvious which opponent may gain the lead. If the missing card is an ace, there will often be an inference available from the bidding. In the examples above, West would be likely to have a side ace if he has volunteered a bid, and unlikely to have one if he has passed throughout.

The suit combination which most commonly indicates the need for an avoidance play is a guarded king or the equivalent: a guarded queen when one top honor has been played, or, as in the examples above, a guarded jack when two top honors have been played; a guarded 10 would operate in the same way if three honors have been played.

But if declarer may have to lose the lead twice, the danger suit may be one in which he has one sure guard and a partial guard:

(a)	(b)	(c)
Dummy	*Dummy*	*Dummy*
J 4 3 2	A 3 2	K 3 2
Declarer	*Declarer*	*Declarer*
A 10	Q 4	Q 4

In each case the right-hand opponent is the danger hand. In (a) and (b) there is a certainty of two stoppers if the suit is led from the left. In (c), suppose that the left-hand opponent holds the ace. Declarer then has two tricks if the suit is led from his left, but only one trick if it is led from the right.

The danger hand may suddenly change. Suppose that in (a) the danger hand secures the lead and plays a low card. The 10 loses to an honor, and the ace is knocked out. The left-hand opponent has suddenly become the danger hand: he may have one small card remaining, which he can lead to allow his partner to score two tricks. Similarly, in (c), the right-hand opponent may gain the lead and play a low card. Declarer puts up the queen, which holds the trick. It is now the case that the left-hand opponent must not be permitted to gain the lead.

Avoidance play may require unusual handling of a suit which needs development.

(d)	(e)	(f)
Dummy	*Dummy*	*Dummy*
K J 8	K 9 2	K 9
Declarer	*Declarer*	*Declarer*
A 10 9 5 2	A J 4 3	A Q 4 3 2

The left-hand opponent is the danger hand. In (d) declarer runs the 10 or 9: it would be quite wrong to play the ace first, because the queen may have three guards. In (e) a deep finesse of the 9 is taken if South is trying for three tricks. The danger hand can secure the lead only if it has both the missing honors. In (f) the 9 is finessed with the virtual certainty that it will lose. (If the danger hand held both honors, he would play one.) This ensures four tricks against any normal break, and keeps the danger hand from the lead unless it has J-10-x-x.

Another type of avoidance play is possible in this situation:

$$A K 3 2$$
$$Q 8 7 \qquad\qquad J 10 9$$
$$6 5 4$$

South needs three tricks in this suit, but must not permit East to gain the lead. Declarer leads twice from his hand, permitting West to win a trick with the queen if he plays it at any stage. If West is able to make a discard on the suit led from dummy back to declarer's hand, he can thwart South's plan by the spectacular discard of his queen.

Avoidance play can also be effected by LOSER-ON-LOSER technique or by DUCKING. Also see DANGER HAND.

B

BA. Bridge Association.

BABY BLACKWOOD. The use of a 3NT bid conventionally to discover the number of aces held by partner. The convention was originally used after a forcing double raise in a major suit but can be used after a limit raise. For example:

South	North
1♥	3♥ (forcing)
3NT	

South's 3NT bid is a request for aces. North bids 4♣ with no aces (or four aces), 4♦ with one ace, and so on. Similarly, an immediate jump to 3NT in response to a 1♥ or 1♠ opening may be used as Baby Blackwood. Those using BERGEN RAISES and similar methods which locate a fit below 3NT can use Baby Blackwood.

An alternative proposal is to use 2NT to uncover the number of aces partner holds. Whenever either player

bids 2NT, partner bids 3♣ with no aces, 3♦ with one ace, etc. Subsequent bids of 3NT, 4NT and 5NT can then be used to locate the number of kings, queens and jacks, respectively held by partner. See BLACKWOOD.

BACK IN. To make the first bid for one's side, after passing on a previous round, in the face of opposing bidding. See BALANCING.

BACK SCORE. The summary sheet on which the results of each rubber are credited to the winners and debited against the losers, in rubber bridge or Chicago. Results are entered in hundreds of points, with 50 points ignored in England but counted as 100 in the United States. The back score is referred to by more colorful names in England, as "flogger" or "washing list," while many American clubs refer to it as a "ledger."

BACKWARD FINESSE. An unnatural finessing maneuver which may sometimes be made for special reasons.

(a)

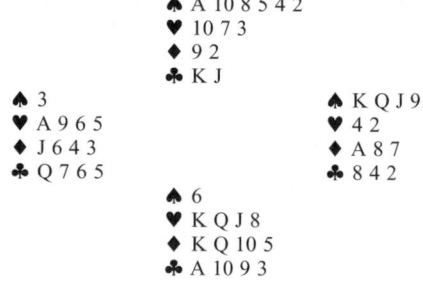

(b)

In (a), the normal play is to finesse the jack, which is an even chance. As the cards lie, it is easy to see that the winning play is to lead the jack. If this is covered, South finesses the 9 on the way back.

Similarly in (b), the normal play is to finesse the 10 after leading to the king, but the lead of the 10 is essential in the position given, with a finesse of the 8 to follow. (The position of the ace is irrelevant.)

There are three possible reasons for selecting the backward finesse. First, there may be a good reason to believe that the natural finesse will fail, based on an inference from an opening bid, for example, or a failure to open the bidding.

Second, the backward finesse may be an AVOIDANCE play. Suppose that in both of the above cases the declarer has an extra small card in his own hand and in the dummy, and needs three tricks without allowing West to gain the lead. His best play is the jack in (a) and the 10 in (b). It is doubtful whether this should be classified as a backward finesse, because South may well reject the finesse on the way back.

Third, the play may be selected when SHOOTING for a top in a pair event or playing for a SWING in a team-of-four match.

In defense the backward finesse can be a natural play dictated by cards visible in dummy. See SANDWICH DEFENSE.

BACKWASH SQUEEZE. A unique type of TRUMP SQUEEZE in which both menaces are in the same hand and the player sitting behind the hand with the menaces holds both guards plus a losing trump, and is caught in the backwash of a squeeze by means of a ruff taken in the hand holding the menaces. Analyzed and described by Geza Ottlik in the February 1974 issue of *The Bridge World*, the backwash squeeze can have any of a number

of other end-game characteristics. Three of his hands are used here by permission of *The Bridge World*.

Occasionally the backwash squeeze can be used as a DISCOVERY play. The following example requires a VIENNA COUP for the execution of the squeeze.

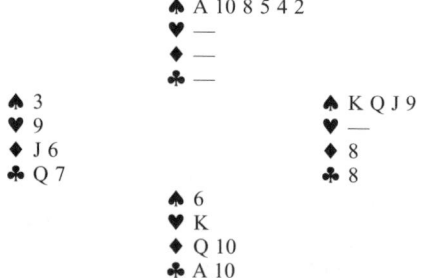

South plays in 4♥ after East doubled 3NT for a spade lead. West leads a heart and East plays low. South wins with the 8 and leads a club to the jack, which holds. So far, so good. Declarer leads a diamond to the king, which wins, a club to the king and another diamond. East plays the ♦A and leads a trump. West plays the ace and another trump while East throws a spade. The lead is in the South hand, and declarer needs five of the last six tricks, in this position:

```
                ♠ A 10 8 5 4 2
                ♥ —
                ♦ —
                ♣ —
   ♠ 3                          ♠ K Q J 9
   ♥ 9                          ♥ —
   ♦ J 6                        ♦ 8
   ♣ Q 7                        ♣ 8
                ♠ 6
                ♥ K
                ♦ Q 10
                ♣ A 10
```

If either minor-suit honor were unguarded the contract could be made by guessing which, dropping it and drawing the last trump. But the bidding suggests that West has the hand shown. The solution is to lead a spade to the ace, and ruff a losing spade with the master trump, setting up an unnecessary trump trick for West (Vienna Coup), but squeezing him in the process. When the spade is ruffed, West is backwash-squeezed. South may, of course, misguess the position — he still has to read West's holding correctly. But he is no worse off than before; he will have seen another card played before making the decision and will have confirmed the exact spade count. No other play will work in the above ending.

The backwash squeeze can be used to strip a defender of his exit cards preparatory to a throw-in play.

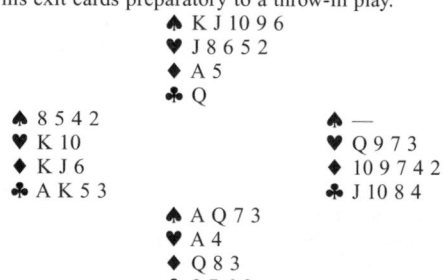

South has arrived in 4♠ after a 13-15 notrump opening by West and an Astro 2♦ bid by North, showing spades and another suit. West led the ♣K and forced dummy with a second club. Planning to set up dummy, declarer led ace and another heart. West won and forced dummy again in clubs. Declarer ruffed a heart high, then led a low spade to dummy and discovered the unfortunate spade division. Suddenly a simple hand had become complicated. North was on lead, with declarer needing five of the last six tricks:

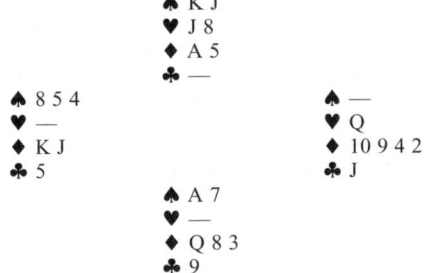

```
                    ♠ K J
                    ♥ J 8
                    ♦ A 5
                    ♣ —
   ♠ 8 5 4                        ♠ —
   ♥ —                            ♥ Q
   ♦ K J                          ♦ 10 9 4 2
   ♣ 5                            ♣ J
                    ♠ A 7
                    ♥ —
                    ♦ Q 8 3
                    ♣ 9
```

Declarer ruffed a heart with the ♠A — and the backwash caught West in its undertow. An underruff would let declarer draw trumps; and a diamond pitch would allow South to cash the ♦A and then lead the ♥J, throwing a club. Thus, West had to part with his club — his only exit card. South cashed the ♠K-J and led the last heart. West ruffed, but was endplayed.

```
                    ♠ Q J 9
                    ♥ 3
                    ♦ 10 8 4 3
                    ♣ Q 7 5 4 2
   ♠ A 10                        ♠ K 6 4
   ♥ A 6                         ♥ 8 7 5 2
   ♦ 9 7 6 5 2                   ♦ A Q J
   ♣ 10 9 8 3                    ♣ A K J
                    ♠ 8 7 5 3 2
                    ♥ K Q J 10 9 4
                    ♦ K
                    ♣ 6
```

South has arrived in 2♠ doubled after a strong 1♣ opening by East showing 17 or more points, and a CARD-SHOWING DOUBLE by West promising 6-8 points. Clubs were led and continued, with South ruffing the second round. South tried to slip the ♥9 through, but West took his ace and shifted to the ace and another spade. When East won his trump king he cashed the ♦A and continued with the queen. Declarer had lost five tricks and apparently had one more to lose — if he drew the last trump he could not return to the closed hand to run the hearts. Because of the blockage in the North-South spades, East's ♠6 prevented ordinary suit-establishment. However, South ruffed the ♦Q and cashed three top hearts, East being forced to follow suit, leaving this position:

```
                    ♠ Q
                    ♥ —
                    ♦ 10
                    ♣ Q
   ♠ —                            ♠ 6
   ♥ —                            ♥ —
   ♦ 9 7                          ♦ J
   ♣ 9                            ♣ A
                    ♠ 8
                    ♥ K 4
                    ♦ —
                    ♣ —
```

South led a heart, ruffed it with dummy's ♠Q and East was squeezed. If he underruffed, the South hand would be high. If he discarded a plain suit he would promote one of dummy's cards which would be led, forcing East to ruff and allowing South to overruff.

BAD CARD HOLDER. A player who seems consistently to hold less than his fair share of honor cards at rubber bridge. Although many losing players explain their losses by claiming to be bad card holders, lack of skill is a more likely explanation. Both mathematics and practical tests suggest that any given player and any given partnership will hold close to an average holding over a long period in terms of percentage.

BAD CARDS. (1) Consistently inferior cards in a session of rubber bridge. (2) Cards that are expected, on the basis of the bidding, to be of little or no value to partner. If partner shows an unbalanced distribution with one very long suit or two long suits, minor honors in the other suits are unlikely to be of value to him. Similarly, tenace holdings or single honors other than the ace deteriorate if the suit is bid by the left-hand opponent. See WORKING CARDS.

BAD HANDS. Hands containing little or no honor strength.

S. J. Simon pointed out that underbidding with a bad hand is a common error of the average player. He gave this spectacular example of the need to bid with a weak hand:

```
                    East
                    ♠ 4 3 2
                    ♥ K 2
                    ♦ 5 4 3 2
                    ♣ 5 4 3 2
```

West	North	East	South
	1♦	Pass	2♣
2♦	3♣	Pass	3♦
4♣	4♦	Pass	5♣
5♦	Pass	5♠	Pass
6♠	Pass	?	

East has been forced to express a choice between the major suits, and has shown no strength whatever. He has the vital ♥K, and West must be confident of making 12 tricks without that card. Therefore the ♥K must be the 13th trick, and East should bid the grand slam.

If partner shows great strength, a player should always ask himself whether his hand is better than it might be in the light of his earlier bidding.

BAD POINTS. See BAD CARDS (2).

BALANCE OF POWER. A concept first put forth by S. Garton Churchill involving the calculation of the safety of entering the auction based on actions taken by the opponents. See BALANCING.

BALANCE OF STRENGTH. The concept of calculating which side holds the majority of the high-card points. If a player adds his own point-count to the minimum shown by his partner, and the total is more than 20, he knows his side has the balance of strength. Sometimes he can infer that his side is likely to have the balance of strength by relying on the normal expectation of strength values in his partner's hand.

BALANCED COMPARISONS. A principle embodied in most types of duplicate movement. A movement is perfectly balanced if any two competing pairs are compared (i.e. play in the same direction) on the same number of boards, independent of which two competing pairs are being compared.

Any full MITCHELL MOVEMENT is automatically balanced because the players do not change direction, and the stationary players, like the moving players, compare with each other throughout.

A Scrambled Mitchell, giving one winner among all pairs, cannot be completely balanced. This is a general phenomenon when the number of rounds is far fewer than the number of competing pairs.

The original HOWELL MOVEMENTS were not balanced, nor were the later schedules prepared by Col. Russell J. Baldwin and William C. McKenney. The first balanced Howell schedules were prepared by Jacques Ach and Charles Kennedy in 1935.

BALANCED DISTRIBUTION (or pattern). A hand that appears suitable for notrump rather than trump contracts. Standard types are 4-4-3-2, 4-3-3-3 and 5-3-3-2; 5-4-2-2 and 6-3-2-2 are borderline cases. See EXPECTED NUMBER OF CONTROLS IN BALANCED HANDS. The completely balanced 4-3-3-3 distribution can be described colloquially as flat, square or round, an example of the strangeness of bridge geometry.

Balanced distribution can also refer to an even division of one suit around the table.

BALANCING. (or protection, which is the normal term in England). Reopening with a bid or double when the opposing bidding has stopped at a low level.

After a suit opening

West	North	East	South
1 ♦	Pass	Pass	?

East's hand is known to be extremely weak, so South can balance with a hand of medium strength on the assumption that his partner has unrevealed strength.

The normal range for a simple suit bid by South in this situation would be 8-13 points in high cards. The spade suit is particularly significant: possession of spades favors balancing action, and lack of spades counts against it.

In more general terms, a shortage in an unbid suit, especially a major, militates against balancing, and a shortage in the opponent's suit favors it.

> ♠ 3
> ♥ A Q 6 4
> ♦ K J 5 3
> ♣ Q 6 4 2

South has sufficient strength to bid 1 ♥, but that would be dangerous. The opponents almost certainly have a spade fit, which they are likely to discover if given the opportunity. It is perhaps better policy to allow them to play 1 ♦, which may be a poor contract for them.

But if the opening bid had been 1 ♠, balancing action (in this case a double) would be automatic. It is now probable that East-West are in their best denomination, that North-South have a fit somewhere, and that North has some strength. North will frequently pass a strong hand with length and strength in the opponent's suit, but South can discount that possibility if he himself has the opponent's suit.

If South jumps in a new suit, he shows a hand too good for a simple balancing bid, probably a six-card or strong five-card suit and about 12-16 points.

A balancing double closely resembles a takeout double by the second player: there is virtually no upper limit, but with only moderate strength it should usually indicate a shortage in the opponent's suit and at least three-card support for each unbid suit. A balancing double may be slightly weaker (a minimum of about 9 points with ideal distribution) than an immediate takeout double. A balancing double is unattractive with a void in the opponent's suit and 5-4-4-0 distribution because the doubler's partner will often pass for penalties. Marshall Miles suggests that the cuebid in the opponent's suit should be used freely in this position: it does not guarantee a game or even a second bid, and cuebidder's partner bids as he would in response to a takeout double.

A balancing bid of 1NT is a weakish action, but exactly how weak is a matter of opinion. Standard treatment suggests the equivalent of a weak notrump opening, (BWS 1994) with about 10-14 points. KAPLAN-SHEINWOLD indicates an 8-10 point range because a stronger hand would double. Others advise a 12-16 point range because hands of this strength may otherwise present problems. A double may not be convenient with three or four cards in the opponent's suit and a doubleton in an unbid suit. A balancing jump to 2 NT shows 18-19 in traditional methods.

After a suit opening and response

The most important consideration is whether the opening side seems to have a fit. If the opening bid is raised to the two-level and the opener passes, balancing action is strongly indicated, especially if the opening bid was in a minor suit.

West	North	East	South
1 ♣	Pass	2 ♣	Pass
Pass	?		

In this situation North should almost invariably balance. Holding:

> ♠ A J 5 3
> ♥ K J 4 2
> ♦ J 3
> ♣ 6 4 2

he doubles. If South bids 2 ♦, North passes or perhaps corrects to 2 ♥, leaving South the option of continuing with 2 ♠.

When one side has a fit, their opponents are almost sure to have a fit also. If the opening bid was 1 ♦ raised to 2 ♦, balancing is usually called for. For this reason many players, as opener, continue to three of the minor suit as a preemptive maneuver to forestall balancing action.

West	North	East	South
1 ♣	Pass	2 ♣	Pass
3 ♣			

or

West	North	East	South
1 ♦	Pass	2 ♦	Pass
3 ♦			

See PREEMPTIVE RE-RAISE.

Balancing action is desirable in theory but more difficult in practice if a major suit has been opened and raised. The player who balances must be prepared for his side to land at the three-level, although a balancing bid of 2 ♠ over 2 ♥ can occasionally be risked with a four-card suit. Partner will suspect a four-card suit because

of the failure to make an immediate overcall.

There is a case for "balancing" in the live position with minimal values:

West	North	East	South
1♥	Pass	2♥	2♠

If the opponents have a fit, you are likely to have a fit.

> ♠ K Q J 10 3
> ♥ 5
> ♦ 8 7 6 2
> ♣ 9 4 3

Such a bid has lead-directing value. It also helps pertner who may be unable to balance because he has heart length.

When an opening bid is raised directly, the opening side usually has a combined eight-card or better fit (though pairs that employ FOUR-CARD MAJORS may sometimes land in a 4-3 fit). The same applies if the responder's suit is raised. Balancing action is indicated after:

West	North	East	South
1♣	Pass	1♥	Pass
2♥	Pass	Pass	?

South may benefit, however, from a knowledge of his opponents' style: If East-West often raise a response with three-card support, South cannot be sure that East-West have an eight-card fit.

There are other situations in which the opening side probably has an eight-card fit:

(a)		(b)	
West	East	West	East
1♥	1NT	1♦	1♥
2♥		2♥	

In both cases, North-South are likely to have a spade fit and should usually try to contest the auction, either with a spade bid or a balancing double.

Balancing actions need not be restricted to the pass-out position:

(c)	
West	East
1NT	2♥

If East's 2♥ bid is natural and non-forcing, both West and East have limited their strength, and West will normally pass. Therefore, either North or South may be obliged to take balancing action. If South holds:

> ♠ K J 10 7 5 3
> ♥ 7 4
> ♦ Q 7 4
> ♣ 6 3

he should bid 2♠. If South passes, North may decline to balance because he lacks length in spades and is reluctant to compete at the three level.

Similarly, on auctions (a) and (b), above, both North and South are in a position to balance. East-West are probably about to drop the auction at the two-level.

If the opening side fails to locate a trump suit (perhaps after bidding three suits) or stops at 1NT, balancing is less attractive.

West	North	East	South
1♣	Pass	1♥	Pass
2♣	Pass	2♥	Pass
Pass	?		

North cannot act safely. East-West may have substantial high-card strength; they may have retired only because the hands fit poorly. If the deal is a misfit, North probably does better to defend.

West	North	East	South
1♥	Pass	1NT	Pass
Pass	Dbl		

or

West	North	East	South
1♥	Pass	1♠	Pass
1NT	Dbl		

In these sequences, North is implying that he passed originally on a strong hand because he holds strength and length in the opener's heart suit. He is hoping for a penalty, although South may choose to bid if his hand is very weak and he has a long suit.

Balancing actions need not be confined to low levels.

Dlr: East
Vul: E-W

> ♠ K Q 7 2
> ♥ K J 8 5 4 3 2
> ♦ 7
> ♣ 2

> ♠ 8 6 4 3   ♠ —
> ♥ 10   ♥ Q 6
> ♦ A K 6 3   ♦ J 10 9 5 4 2
> ♣ A Q 9 8   ♣ K 10 7 6 5

> ♠ A J 10 9 5
> ♥ A 9 7
> ♦ Q 8
> ♣ J 4 3

West	North	East	South
		Pass	1♠
Pass	4NT	Pass	5♥
Pass	5♠	Pass	Pass
Pass			

In the 1968 Olympiad Open Teams final, West's final pass came only after long study. The winning decision — easier with all four hands in view — was to balance with 5NT, unusual for the minor suits.

After a 1NT opening

A 1NT bid passed by the opener's partner produces a situation in which balancing is often not expedient. The probabilities are that the opening side has no good fit, and therefore that the defending side also has no good fit. The best policy, therefore, generally is to remain silent. To bid a five-card suit in the passout position may produce a double from opener's partner and a singleton trump in the dummy. However, some risks may have to be taken at board-a-match or pair scoring; conventional machinery such as ASTRO, HAMILTON (Cappelletti) or LANDY can prove helpful. See also DEFENSE TO ONE NOTRUMP, UNUSUAL NOTRUMP.

BALDWIN TROPHY. Awarded to the winners of the NORTH AMERICAN OPEN PAIRS. The trophy honors Russell Baldwin, former director and treasurer of the ACBL and co-inventor, with Bill McKenney, of the McKenney-Baldwin movements used in tournament bridge.

BAMBERGER POINT-COUNT. See ROBERTSON POINT-COUNT and VIENNA SYSTEM.

BANGKOK CLUB. A system devised by Somboon Nandhabiwat and used by Thailand in world championships in 1966, 1967 and 1969. It is a relative of the VIENNA SYSTEM.

1♣ opening is a one-round force, showing 12-20 points and denying a 5-card suit outside clubs. 1♦ is a negative response, 1NT is an artificial game-forcing response, and other responses are semi-positive.

1 ♦, 1 ♥ and 1 ♠ show 11-17 points with a 5-card suit. 1NT is artificial and strong with 18+ points. Two-bids are natural and game-forcing.

BAR, BARRED. (1) The penalty for certain types of infractions sometimes calls for the partner of the offender to make a forced pass on his next turn. At other times the partner of the offender must pass whenever it is his turn to bid for the rest of the auction. Such situations arise when a player bids out of turn, corrects an insufficient bid in various permissible ways and exposes a card during the auction.

(2) An ethical player, when his partner has hesitated and then passed at some point during the auction, is expected to bar himself from taking any action on his cards that is in any way questionable; that is, he will lean over backwards to avoid taking advantage of his partner's hesitation.

(3) A player may be technically *barred* from further bidding, especially if he has limited his hand previously. See, e.g., PREEMPTIVE RE-RAISE, SIGN-OFF BID.

(4) A player may be prohibited by the methods he is using from making a certain bid. For example, pairs using psychic responses to WEAK TWO-BIDS may agree that opener is barred from rebidding past three of his own suit. The opponents are entitled to know if this is the case, so such a sequence calls for an Alert.

BARCO SQUEEZE. A triple-double squeeze, exerting pressure on both opponents in three suits. The most famous example was played by Edward T. Barco, and described by him in *The Bridge World* (Dec. 1935).

```
                  ♠ A 5 4
                  ♥ K J 3
                  ♦ A J 8
                  ♣ A 10 7 2
  ♠ Q 10 3 2                  ♠ J 9 8
  ♥ 8 4                       ♥ 2
  ♦ 10 9 5 3 2                ♦ Q 6 4
  ♣ K 8                       ♣ J 9 6 5 4 3
                  ♠ K 7 6
                  ♥ A Q 10 9 7 6 5
                  ♦ K 7
                  ♣ Q
```

West led a trump against South's contract of 7 ♥, and declarer ran five trump tricks to reach this ending:

```
                  ♠ A 5 4
                  ♥ —
                  ♦ A J 8
                  ♣ A 10
  ♠ Q 10 3 2                  ♠ J 9 8
  ♥ —                         ♥ —
  ♦ 10 9 5                    ♦ Q 6 4
  ♣ K                         ♣ J 9
                  ♠ K 7 6
                  ♥ 7 6
                  ♦ K 7
                  ♣ Q
```

South led a further heart, on which West and North discarded a spade. East was squeezed, and had to discard a spade also. The last trump squeezed West in three suits. However, if he had discarded a diamond, declarer would have had to make the double-dummy play of entering dummy and leading the ♦ J. See HEXAGON SQUEEZE and OCTAGONAL TWO-TRICK SQUEEZE.

BAROMETER. A method originated in Sweden in which all groups of boards are played simultaneously. Running scores are posted on the Barometer shortly after the conclusion of each round, thus heightening the interest for both players and spectators. Toward the end of an event, the known positions of the pairs in contention often will influence the tactics they choose in attempting to win. A Barometer contest can be arbitrarily split into a number of sessions.

The best movement for a Barometer for pairs is Barometer Howell (or Endless Howell) where the pairs each time move to the next table, up or down, in the way described for a FLOWER MOVEMENT.

For individual contests there are barometer movements (for up to 13 tables) in which each player has every other player as a partner once and as an opponent twice. Individual barometer movements also exist for 14 and 15 tables.

BAROMETER PAIRS. Differentiated from other pair games by the method of distributing the boards and by the scoring. In the usual type of pair event, all or most of the boards are in play every round. The boards are moved from table to table on a predetermined schedule so that eventually all pairs play most of the boards at some time during the session. In a barometer game the boards do not move from table to table after each round. All pairs play the same boards at the same time throughout the event. The director and his staff will have preduplicated many sets of boards prior to the game. Quite often each table will have its own set of boards; equally often two or three tables will share one set of boards. Each set of boards goes out of play after one round.

As a result, all scores for a given set of boards are available as soon as the round is over. The director retrieves the score tickets and enters them immediately. Quite often the scores will be posted for inspection by the players after each round, so each pair knows where it stands at all times. Any given pair's fortunes will rise and fall as the game goes on — hence the name Barometer.

BARON BARCLAY BRIDGE SUPPLIES. The world's largest bridge supply company, Baron was founded in 1975 by Randy and Mary Baron of Shelbyville KY. In 1990, Baron merged with Barclay Bridge Supplies of Port Chester NY which was founded in 1944. Baron Barclay sends its catalog to almost 100,000 customers twice annually. They carry virtually every bridge book in print as well as software, playing cards and gift items. Address: 3600 Chamberlain Lane, Louisville KY 40241. Phone 1-800-274-2221. E-mail: baronbarclay@baronbarclay.com

BARON COROLLARY. An adjunct to TWO-WAY STAYMAN, of increasing popularity in Canada, that is designed to discover 4-4 minor suit fits. After responder has bid 2 ♦ (forcing to game), and opener has bid 2NT, denying a four-card major or a five-card minor, a 3 ♣ rebid by responder asks opener's precise distribution. Opener rebids 3 ♦ with 3-3-4-3, 3NT with 3-3-3-4 or three of his longer major if he has two four-card minors.

BARON NOTRUMP OVERCALL. An equivalent to a weak takeout double. It is usually made with a single-

ton or void in the opponent's suit, and the most likely distribution is 4-4-4-1. The maximum strength is 13 points, and the minimum depends on vulnerability. It has achieved little popularity because 1NT is valuable as a natural overcall. For an alternative method of making a weak takeout double, see MICHAELS CUEBID.

BARON SLAM TRY. An invitation to a slam contract if partner holds good trumps. A bid of the suit next below the agreed suit at the five or six level specifically asks partner whether he holds good trumps. So if spades are agreed, 5♥ invites 6♠, and 6♥ invites 7♠. What constitutes good trumps depends on the previous auction. Partner must ask himself how much worse his trump holding might be in the light of his previous calls.

BARON SYSTEM. An English system developed in the Forties by Leo Baron, Adam Meredith and others. Its exponents have had considerable success in British tournament play, and many of the system ideas have taken root in the general theory of the game. Examples are: (1) the weak notrump opening bid combined with a 1NT constructive rebid; (2) bidding UP THE LINE with four-card suits; (3) relaxed requirements for BIDDABLE SUITS; (4) the five-card suit requirement for a response of 2♥ to an opening of 1♠; (5) the lead of ACE FROM ACE-KING.

Other distinctive features of the system are: (6) a bid of the third suit by the opener is forcing (e.g., 1♣-1♥-1♠). Some experts using standard methods follow this theory when the response is at the level of two. (7) an immediate raise requires at least four-card trump support. (8) suit opening bids are highly prepared, with a four-card spade suit being opened ahead of a five-card heart suit regardless of quality. (9) simple overcalls are strong and jump overcalls weak. See also: ACE VALUES; BARON NOTRUMP OVERCALL; BARON SLAM TRY; 2NT OPENING; 2NT RESPONSE.

BARON TWO NOTRUMP RESPONSE. See TWO NOTRUMP RESPONSE.

BARRAGE. The French term for PREEMPTIVE BID. Sometimes used by English writers to describe a series of obstructive bids.

BARRED. See BAR, BARRED.

BARRICADE. An obsolete term for PREEMPTIVE BID or BARRAGE, coined by P. Hal Sims.

BARRY CRANE TOP 500. The race to determine the ACBL member who accumulates the most masterpoints during a calendar year. Originally the McKenney Trophy, it was put into play by William E. McKenney, ACBL executive secretary. It was known as the McKenney Trophy contest from 1937-1981. When the list was expanded to include the leading 500 players it was called the Top 500 from 1982-1985. It became the Barry Crane Top 500 in 1986. Crane, who was murdered in July 1985, was ACBL's top masterpoint holder and was acknowledged by his peers to be unequalled as a masterpoint winner and a matchpoint player. His influence on the race was dominant for more than three decades. Grant Baze broke the record for the most

masterpoints in a year in 1974 when he earned 3270. This mark stood the test for 15 years, but it finally was shattered in 1999 when Jim Barrow earned 3584.26 points. No records are available for the first 15 years of the Top 500, but point records are available from 1957 on. Record holders over the years with their point totals: 1957, Edgar Kaplan, 808; 1960, Robert Jordan, 873; 1963, Oswald Jacoby, 1034; 1964, Hermine Baron, 1370; 1969, Paul Soloway, 1434; 1971, Barry Crane, 1443; 1973, Barry Crane, 1562; 1974, Kerri Shuman, 1619; 1976, Mike Passell, 1815; 1977, Ron Andersen, 2009; 1979, Clarence Goppert, 2118; 1980, Ron Andersen, 2725; 1983, Ron Andersen, 2994; 1984, Grant Baze, 3270; 1999, Jim Barrow, 3584. For winners see Appendix II.

BART. An artificial forcing two-diamond bid used in this sequence:

Opener	Responder
1♠	1NT
2♣	2♦

This shows various hands, many of them including a five-card heart suit. The opener makes that assumption, and will often bid 2♥ with a doubleton, perhaps ending the bidding.

The responder may continue with: (a) 2♠ with a doubleton spade and 8-10 points; (b) 2NT with four-card club support and 10-11 points; (c) 3♣ with five-card club support and 10-11 points; (d) 3♦, to play.

Immediate bids of 2♠ or 3♣ by responder are similar to the direct actions, but weaker.

BASE III. A powerful computer program, created by Fred Gitelman of Toronto, for creating, storing and analyzing bridge problems, which may be complete deals or end-positions. A unique feature is the program's ability to take a 52-card diagram and decide whether a given contract can or cannot be made, and show how. This procedure may, however, take a long time. End-positions are solved very quickly. Another feature helps in the analysis of suit combinations and the calculation of percentages. The user can input his own hands, or he can create hands for bidding practice or simulations in a similar fashion to BOREL.

The creator of the program hopes eventually to produce a high-level program that will bid, play and defend, but formidable obstacles must be faced. It is not easy to teach a computer to draw inferences from opposing bids that may be artificial, stylistic or psychic.

BASTILLE. Method of calculation for pair tournament, similar to BUTLER. The average is not rounded, and the difference of every table's score with this average is converted into IMPs by means of a linear extrapolation of the IMP scale (15 points = 0.5 IMPs, 45 points = 1.5 IMPS, etc.) Utilization of this method would have prevented the strange occurrences in The Hague in 1994 (see DEN HAAG BUTLER INCIDENT). The very nature of duplicate means that every good thing one pair does also helps those playing at other tables in the opposite direction. In the Butler system it is possible that these helps can be greater than your benefit. In the Bastille method that is impossible. The system was developed in 1989 by Herman De Wael and was first used in Antwerp on July 14 of that year, hence the name. Subsequently, some improvements have been added, mainly

to the formula that is used for the calculation of the average.

BATH COUP. A simple hold-up of the ace when the jack is also held:

(a)

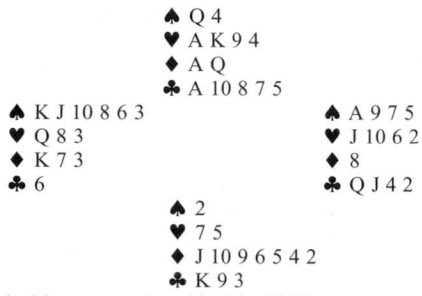

```
              4 3 2
  K Q 10 9 6              7 5
              A J 8
```

(b)

```
              A 3 2
  K Q 10 9 6              7 5
              J 8 4
```

In each case the king is led and is allowed to win. If declarer holds two small cards, as in (b), he should generally play the higher one. This play may cause West to think that East has begun a high-low, and induce him to continue the suit to South's advantage.

The play dates from the days of whist, and is presumably named after the English watering place of Bath.

BATTLE, SARAH. A character invented by Charles Lamb to embody his idea of what a perfect whist player should be. In his *Essays of Elia* he wrote: "She loved a thorough-paced partner, a determined enemy. She took and gave no concessions. She never made a revoke nor even passed it over in her adversary without exacting the utmost forfeiture. She fought a good fight — cut and thrust.

"She sat bolt upright, and neither showed you her cards, nor desired to see yours. I never in my life — and I knew Sarah Battle many of the best years of it — saw her take out her snuffbox when it was her turn to play, or snuff a candle in the midst of a game or ring for a servant until it was fairly over. She never introduced or connived at miscellaneous conversation during its progress. As she emphatically observed, 'cards are cards,' and if I ever saw mingled distaste in her fine last-century countenance, it was at the airs of a young gentleman of a literary turn, who had been with difficulty persuaded to take a hand, and who, in his excess of candor, declared that he thought there was no harm in unbending the mind now and then, after serious studies, in recreations of that kind! She could not bear to have her noble occupation, to which she wound up her faculties, considered in that light. It was her business, her duty, the thing she came into the world to do — and she did it. She unbent her mind afterwards over a book."

BATTLE OF THE CENTURY. See CULBERTSON-LENZ MATCH.

BATTLE OF THE SEXES. A marathon trans-Atlantic match played April 1 to April 15, 1989. More than 1000 players took part, playing 24 hours a day with a pair of men against a pair of women. The companion table, in Paris, had the opposite seating. A record number of boards, 2352, was played, and after seesaw exchanges the men won by 196 IMPs, a small margin in view of the length of the match. The match was conceived and organized by Alan Truscott, with Claire Tornay in charge in New York and José Damiani in charge in Paris.

On the following deal Damiani as East was the victim of fine play by Danielle Gaviard.

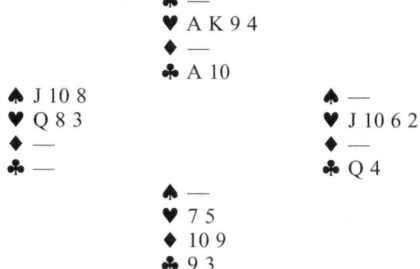

Both sides were vulnerable. The bidding:

West	North	East	South
2♠	Dbl	4♠	5♦
Pass	Pass	Pass	

Gaviard landed in 5♦ as shown, after a weak opening two-bid on her left. It might seem that she was due to lose a trump trick, a spade trick and a club trick, but she took advantage of a subtle defensive error.

West led his singleton club, South played low from dummy and captured East's jack with the king. She finessed the ♦ Q successfully, cashed the ace and led a spade. East put up the ace, and continued with a spade ruffed by the declarer.

A diamond was surrendered to West, who routinely played another spade and gave Gaviard her chance. She ruffed and reached this ending:

```
              ♠ —
              ♥ A K 9 4
              ♦ —
              ♣ A 10
  ♠ J 10 8                    ♠ —
  ♥ Q 8 3                     ♥ J 10 6 2
  ♦ —                         ♦ —
  ♣ —                         ♣ Q 4
              ♠ —
              ♥ 7 5
              ♦ 10 9
              ♣ 9 3
```

On the next trump lead the ♣10 was thrown from the dummy and Damiani, in the East seat, was subjected to a trump squeeze. He had to choose between throwing a heart and allowing South to establish a heart winner in the dummy, and throwing a club and permitting the ♣9 to score.

West was left to discover that he should have shifted to a heart after winning the ♦ K. And the women gained 10 IMPs: in the replay the men with the North-South cards in New York played 3♣ and scored 110.

BEAN TROPHY. Awarded to the winners of the RED RIBBON PAIRS. The trophy honors Percy Bean, former president of the ACBL and the ACBL Charity Foundation.

BECKER. Over an opponent's 1NT opening, a simple conventional method of showing certain two-suited hands. A 2♣ overcall promises length in both minor suits, and a 2♦ overcall promises length in both major suits. The overcaller suggests limited high-card strength, since a penalty double is available with a strong hand. Overcaller also suggests at least five cards in each suit, but players often employ Becker, as well as other two-suited overcalls, with 4-5 distribution, especially at matchpoint duplicate.

For alternative defenses to an opposing 1NT opening, see DEFENSE TO ONE NOTRUMP.

BED. See GO TO BED.

BEER CARD. The ♦7 under certain special circumstances. If declarer wins the trick 13 with the ♦7 in a successful contract, he claims "Beer Card!" and his partner must buy him a beer. You cannot claim "Beer Card!" if you go down. If a defender wins the last trick with the ♦7 and declarer has been set, the defender may also claim "Beer Card!" and his partner must buy him a beer. A defender cannot claim "Beer Card!" if declarer makes his contract. Greg Morse, with help from Jeff Goldsmith and Sheri Winestock, has unearthed the Beer Card history. The ♦7 has a special role in a Danish game called "Boma-Loma". Partly because of this, bridge players in Copenhagen were the first bridge players to use the Beer Card term. It became quite common in Europe and reached London by the Eighties. The term was imported into North America by the American Junior team after they made a visit to Poland for a Junior Bridge Camp. It has since spread around the world, mostly via World Junior Championships.

BELATED SUPPORT. Support for the opening's original suit during the second round of bidding. Sometimes it is very similar to PREFERENCE and JUMP PREFERENCE. Some examples:

West	East
1♥	1♠
1NT	2♥

West	East
1♠	1NT
2♣	2♠

West	East
1♠	1NT
2♣	3♠

Sometimes the opener offers belated support to the responder's suit.

West	East
1♦	1♥
1NT	2♣
2♥	

BELONG. An expression to indicate which side can legitimately expect to buy the contract. A player who says he knew that "the hand belonged to the opponents" indicates that he judged the opposition could make the highest positive score on the deal. In such circumstances, it may pay to take an ADVANCE SAVE or other preemptive action. Alternatively, a player who judges that he will be outgunned in high cards may prefer to remain silent on the theory that he will end up as a defender and does not wish to give information that may help the declarer.

An alternative meaning of the word in modern bridge jargon, especially in a POST-MORTEM, is to indicate the most desirable contract for a side: "We belong in 5♦".

BELOW THE LINE. Points at RUBBER BRIDGE entered below the horizontal line on the score sheet. These points are solely those made by bidding and making partscores, games or slams. All other points are scored above the line only. Points scored below the line count toward winning a game or rubber. At DUPLICATE BRIDGE or CHICAGO, the term may be used loosely to refer to trick score. See ABOVE THE LINE, SCORING.

BENJAMIN. Convention permitting an Acol player to use weak WEAK TWO-BIDS in the major suits; invented by Albert Benjamin (Scotland). Opening bids of 2♠ and 2♥ are weak. An opening bid of 2♦ is equivalent to an Acol bid of 2♣ and almost guarantees game. The negative response is 2♥ and the sequence 2♦-2♥-2NT, showing 23-24 points, can be passed.

An opening bid of 2♣ shows a normal Acol one-round forcing two-bid in an unspecified suit and promises at least eight playing tricks. The negative response is 2♦ and any positive response is forcing to game. With this method it is possible to use an ACOL TWO-BID when clubs is the primary suit. See ACOL SYSTEM.

BENNETT MURDER. A historic tragedy which took place in Kansas City KS in 1929. The victim was John S. Bennett, a prosperous perfume salesman, who met his death as a result of a game of contract in which he played with his wife against another married couple. His wife became so infuriated at her husband's play that she shot him following a bitter quarrel. She was tried for murder later the same year, and acquitted.

The following account of the episode appeared in the *New York Evening Journal*:

"As the game went on," Mrs. Hoffman said, "the Bennetts' criticism of each other grew more and more caustic. Finally a spade hand was bought by them in the following manner: Bennett bid a spade. My husband overcalled with 2♦. Mrs. Bennett promptly boosted the original spade bid to four. I passed. Mrs. Bennett, as dummy, laid down a rather good hand. But her husband was set. This seemed to infuriate his wife and she began goading him with remarks about 'bum bridge players.' He came right back at her. I don't remember the exact words. This kept up for several minutes. We tried to stop the argument by demanding cards, but by this time the row had become so pronounced that Bennett, reaching across the table, grabbed Myrtle's arm and slapped her several times. We tried to intervene, but it was futile. While Mrs. Bennett repeated over and over in a strained singsong tone, 'Nobody but a bum would hit a woman,' Her husband jumped up and shouted, 'I'm going to spend the night at a hotel. And tomorrow I'm leaving town.' His wife said to us: 'I think you folks had better go.' Of course, we started to do so."

While the Hoffmans were putting on their things Mrs. Bennett dashed into the bedroom of her mother, Mrs. Alice B. Adkins, and snatched the family automatic from a dresser drawer. "John's going to St. Joseph," she explained to the older woman, "and wants to be armed." Bennett had gone to his "den," near the bathroom, to pack for the intended trip. Hoffman, adjusting his muffler, turned back and saw his friend alone for the moment. While Mrs. Hoffman waited in the doorway, her husband advanced toward Bennett, hoping to say a word or two that would dispel this angry depression. The two men were in conversation as Mrs. Bennett darted in, pistol in hand. Bennett saw her, ran to the bathroom, slammed the door just as two bullets pierced the wooden

paneling. Hoffman, rigid with astonishment, remained in the den. His wife, hearing the shots, ran down the hall and began pounding on the door of the next apartment. It is thought Bennett died from two bullets fired as he neared the door leading to the street. He staggered to a chair — the Hoffmans agree — moaning, "She got me." Then he slumped, unconscious, to the floor. Mrs. Bennett was standing at the other side of the living room, the gun dangling loosely from her fingers. As Bennett fell, her daze broke. She ran toward him. Police found her bent over him, giving vent to wild sobs.

The alleged hand was as follows:

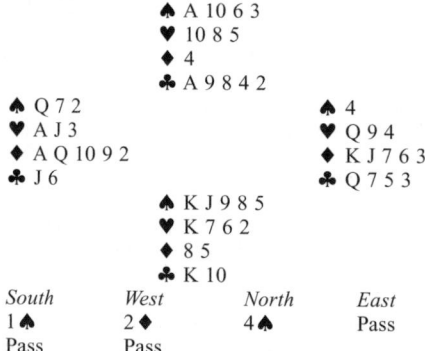

South	West	North	East
1 ♠	2 ♦	4 ♠	Pass
Pass	Pass		

Mr. Bennett opened the bidding without sufficient values for an opening bid, and suffered an unusually heavy penalty. However, 4 ♠ was not an impossible contract, and Ely Culbertson analyzed the deal as follows:

We have heard of lives depending on the play of a card. It is not often that we find that figure of speech literally true. Here is a case in point. Mr. Bennett had overbid his hand. Of that there can be no doubt, but even with this, so kind were the gods of distribution that he might have saved his life had he played his cards a little better. Mr. Hoffman opened the ♦ A, then shifted to the club suit when he saw the dummy void of diamonds, and led the ♣ J. This Mr. Bennett won with his king and started to pull the adverse trumps. Here again he flirted with death, as people so frequently do when they fail to have a plan either in the game of bridge or the game of life. He still could make his contract and save his life. The proper play before drawing the trumps would have been to establish the club suit after ruffing the last diamond. Suppose Mr. Bennett, when he took the club trick with his king, had led his last diamond and trumped it with one of dummy's small trumps. He could then lead a trump and go up with the king. Now he would lead the ♣ 10, and, when Mr. Hoffman followed suit, his troubles would be over. He would play the ♣ A and lead the nine or eight. If Mrs. Hoffman put up the queen, Mr. Bennett should trump and let Mr. Hoffman overtrump if he pleased. If Mr. Hoffman, after winning this trick, led a heart, the contract and a life would be saved. If he led a diamond the same would be true. A lead of the trump might still have permitted the fatal dénouement but at least Mr. Bennett would have had the satisfaction of knowing that he had played the cards dealt him by fate to the very best of his ability.

The episode was entertainingly described at length by Alexander Woollcott in *While Rome Burns*.

BERGEN OVER NOTRUMP. See DONT.

BERGEN RAISE. A method devised by Marty Bergen to give responder more ways to raise opening bidder's major suit. This method enables responder to distinguish among raises of various strengths with either three- or four-card support.

West	East
1 ♠	2 ♠ = three trumps, 7 to 10 points
	3 ♣ = four trumps, 7 to 10 points
	3 ♦ = four trumps, a limit raise
	3 ♠ = four or more trumps, 0 to 7 points, preemptive

The responses are similar if the opening bid is 1 ♥.

Many partnerships reverse the meanings of 3 ♣ and 3 ♦. The theory is that using 3 ♣ for the stronger bid allows more room for exploration.

This method is based on the idea that it is "safe" to go to the three-level with a 9-card fit. See LAW OF TOTAL TRICKS.

In defense, following a response of 3 ♣ or 3 ♦, double is usually lead-directing, but may be the first move with a major-minor two-suiter, with the major suit to be bid later; a cuebid of opener's major shows the other major and the unbid minor; pass and double is takeout.

BERMUDA. Host to the first BERMUDA BOWL (1950) and later to the Silver (1975) and Golden Anniversary (2000) Bermuda Bowls. The BERMUDA INCIDENT occurred during the 1975 event. The Bermuda unit stages a regional every year in late January.

BERMUDA BOWL. A World Team Championship; the trophy at stake therein.

The first postwar world contract bridge team championship was played in Bermuda in 1950 on the initiative of Norman M. Bach. The contest was a three-cornered match among teams representing the United States, Great Britain (the European champion) and Europe (a combined Sweden-Iceland team).

The next six Bermuda Bowl contests were two-team events between the United States and the winners of the European Championships.

In 1958, the contest became a three-cornered event with the inclusion of the South American champions.

In 1960, 1964, 1968 and 1972, which were Team Olympiad years, there was no Bermuda Bowl competition. In 1974 the WORLD BRIDGE FEDERATION voted to conduct the Bermuda Bowl in odd-number years only. To provide a transition, the Bermuda Bowl and the World Team Olympiad were played consecutively in Monte Carlo in 1976.

Starting in 1961, the defending champion was invited to compete. This practice was discontinued after the 1977 Bermuda Bowl, when two teams from the United States met in the final. One was the team that qualified through the Trials method, the other was the defending champion. The Executive Council of the WBF decided it was not good for two teams from the same zone to compete in the final.

From 1950 to 1963 inclusive, the Bermuda Bowl was organized under the auspices of the ACBL and the EBL, with the collaboration of the South American Bridge Confederation starting in 1958. Since 1963, the Bermuda Bowl has been conducted by the WBF. In 1965 the WBF voted to expand the event to a five-team contest by including the Far East champions, who became eligible for the first time in 1966. The Bermuda Bowl became a

six-sided affair for the first time in 1971 when Australia exercised its right to represent the South Pacific Zone. The Central American-Caribbean Zone was represented for the first time in the 1979 championship. And the Bridge Federation of Asia and the Middle East fielded a representative in the Bermuda Bowl for the first time in 1981. The European Zone was allotted a second spot in the competition in 1981.

The pattern for Bermuda Bowl competition was changed radically, starting with the 1983 competition. The winners of the North American Team Trials and the European champions advanced automatically to the semifinals. The North American runner-up and the second-place European team also qualified for Bermuda Bowl play, but they had to take part in a round-robin with the winners of the other zones to determine the other two semifinalists. Also eligible to play in the round-robin were the victors from South America, Far East, Central America-Caribbean, Australia-New Zealand and Asia-Middle East. In addition, the host country had the right to enter a team if that country had not already qualified as a Zonal representative.

In order to insure that two teams from the same Zone did not meet in the final, the WBF stipulated that if two teams from the same Zone reached the semifinals, they had to oppose each other in a semifinal.

The WBF also decided in 1981 that future Bermuda Bowls, starting in 1985, would not be held in either Europe or North America. World Team Olympiads and World Pair Championships would be held in even years in either North America or Europe, while Bermuda Bowls would be held elsewhere in odd years.

The pattern changed again in Yokohama, Japan, in 1991. The number of teams was enlarged to permit the inclusion of four teams from Europe, three from North America, one from the South Pacific, two from all other zones plus one from the host country. The policy of exempting one European team and one North American team from the qualifying stage was abandoned, as was the restriction which required the final to be between two teams from different zones. (However, a final between two teams from the same country was not permitted, a restriction affecting only ACBL.) Teams were in two qualifying groups, with four from each advancing to quarterfinal playoffs.

The same format was followed in Santiago, Chile, in 1993, but the method of setting up the quarterfinals was changed. In earlier Bermuda Bowls with double round-robins, the winner of one would play the fourth-place finisher in the other, and the second-place finishers would oppose the third-placers. Starting in 1993, the winner in each of the round-robins could select their opponent from the teams that finished second, third and fourth in the other round-robin. Since carryover was involved, this gave a considerable edge to the teams finishing first in the round-robin.

China proved to be an outstanding host in 1995, with many outstanding electronic advances. A major first was the live broadcasting of some match segments over nationwide television on a major TV network. Chinese officials estimated that more than a million viewers watched the bridge show.

Once again the size of the field was increased for the 33rd Bermuda Bowl in Hammamet, Tunisia, in 1997. Eighteen teams were in play, and they competed in a complete round-robin instead of two small round-rob-

ins as in earlier contests. The WBF zones were represented as follows: Europe 5, North America 3, South America 2, Far East 2, Oceana 2, Middle East-Africa 2, Central America-Caribbean 1, host country 1. Pairings for the quarterfinals were set up as follows: The round-robin winner could choose its opponent from among those teams that finished fifth through eighth. The second-place team could take its choice from those remaining from the 5-8 pool. The same was true for the third-place teams, and the fourth-place teams got whoever was left.

1999 was an unusual year for the Bermuda Bowl – it didn't take place. Bermuda, which hosted both the opening and the silver anniversary Bowls, also wanted to be the host for the golden anniversary. However, the anniversary year – 2000 – was not a Bowl year because Bowls are played in odd-numbered years. The Bermuda committee petitioned the WBF to allow the Bowl to be played in January, 2000, so that it would be a true golden jubilee. The WBF approved this plan.

The field was increased to 20, with an extra qualifier from both Europe (now with six entries) and the Far East (now with three entries). Players throughout the world were able to follow the championships on their computers. Some matches were described as they were happening, and there were frequent updates on the remaining matches.

For a full listing of Bermuda Bowl results, see Appendix V.

BERMUDA INCIDENT. In 1975, the Bermuda Bowl was played in Bermuda in celebration of the 25th anniversary of the Bermuda Bowl. During the early qualifying stages, Gianfranco Facchini, a member of the Italian team, was observed apparently giving foot signals to his partner, Sergio Zucchelli.

The first person to notice unusual foot movements was Bruce Keidan, an American news correspondent monitoring the match between Italy and France. Keidan reported his observation to the North American npc, Alfred Sheinwold, and to Edgar Kaplan, a member of the WBF Appeals Committee. Kaplan informed WBF President Julius Rosenblum. Rosenblum observed for a time, then assigned special observers from the Appeals Committee, Johannes Hammerich of Venezuela and James O'Sullivan of Australia, to monitor the Italian pair.

According to Keidan, Hammerich and O'Sullivan, Facchini reached out with his feet on several occasions during auctions and before opening leads, and apparently touched Zucchelli on the toes once or more; Zucchelli's feet remained completely immobile, and Facchini did not move his feet at other times. Rosenblum, Hammerich and WBF Vice President Jaime Ortiz-Patiño of Switzerland therefore decided to monitor Italy's next qualifying match, using European observers. Before this plan could be implemented, however, the WBF was informed that the North American team would refuse to play against Zucchelli and Facchini in the next scheduled match. This, plus the fact that rumors of the foot movement accusation were already rampant, caused the WBF to inform all team captains of what had transpired, to postpone the Italy-North America match and to convene a hearing immediately.

The WBF Appeals Committee heard testimony from observers Keidan, Hammerich, O'Sullivan, Rosenblum and Tracy Denninger of Bermuda. Facchini did not deny

moving his feet, but attributed his movements to nervous tension. Zucchelli testified that he was unaware of any foot actions by his partner. Oswald Jacoby, who had analyzed some of the hands, was called as a witness, but the Committee was unable to find specific correlation between the foot movements observed and the bidding or play of the hands — a factor usually considered essential to conclusive proof of cheating. The WBF therefore resolved that Facchini and Zucchelli "…be severely reprimanded for improper conduct with respect to the actions of Mr. Facchini moving his feet unnaturally and touching his partner's feet during the auction and before the opening lead." Coffee tables were thereafter placed beneath the card tables to block any possibility of further such movements.

Sheinwold promptly issued a statement: "The North American team endorses the verdict of *guilty* but deplores the failure of the World Bridge Federation to bar this pair from further international competitions." The word guilty had not appeared in the original verdict, but a later statement from Rosenblum corrected this omission by declaring that the accused pair "had been found guilty only of improper foot movements." The first meeting between the Italian and North American teams, postponed from Sunday afternoon, was played that evening. Italian npc Sandro Salvetti kept the suspect pair out of the lineup, saying that their nerves were frayed by the accusations. Two days later, the pair also sat out the second qualifying match against North America, although they had played in other matches in the interim.

On the morning of the first session of the final between Italy and North America, when Sheinwold learned that Facchini and Zucchelli were listed in Italy's starting lineup, he announced that the North American team would not play against this pair unless instructed to do so by the ACBL. ACBL representatives in Bermuda unanimously ordered the team to play. Italy fared poorly with the accused pair in the lineup, and it was only after they had been benched at the request of Benito Garozzo and Giorgio Belladonna that Italy staged an "impossible" rally to retain the world title.

The partnership of the accused players was broken up and the WBF advised Italian bridge officials that it would not welcome the nomination of either player to any event it conducted in the immediately foreseeable future. See BUENOS AIRES AFFAIR; CAPTAIN; CHEATING; CHEATING ACCUSATIONS.

BESSE PAR CONTEST. An extremely difficult contest staged during the 1998 World Championships in Lille, France. The event was named the Jean Besse Foundation Par Contest in honor and memory of the late Jean Besse of Switzerland, one of the outstanding personalities in world bridge for many years. The problems were formulated by Pietro Bernasconi of Switzerland. One computer program (GIB) plus 34 international stars competed. The winner was Michael Rosenberg of the United States, although he made one more error than runner-up Bart Bramley of the United States. However, his speed at solving the 12 problems overcome the cost of the error. Eric Rodwell of the United States was third. The computer program performed well, leading the field at the halfway point. However, the computer was unable to make the necessary inferences from the bidding during the second half and dropped in the standings as a result. Rosenberg received 50,000 Swiss francs (approxi-

mately $35,000 U.S.) for his victory. See PAMP PAR CONTEST, PAR CONTEST.

BETA ASKING BID. (1) Asking bids in the ROMAN and SUPER PRECISION SYSTEMS concerned with responder's support for the suit bid by the 1♣ opener. After the negative response of 1♦, opener initiates the inquiry by jumping in a major suit (or, in Roman, by simply rebidding a minor suit). The responses are as set out in ROMAN ASKING BIDS.

(2) Asking bids in the SUPER PRECISION system concerned with the quality of a side suit after responder has made a positive response in notrump are also sometimes called Beta Asking Bids, although the difference in schedule of responses has led them to be designated Delta Asking bids in the version of Super Precision used by Giorgio Belladonna and Benito Garozzo. See SUPER PRECISION ASKING BIDS.

BETTER BRIDGE. A publication produced by Audrey Grant and David Lindop and distributed by the American Contract Bridge League. The material in general is aimed at newcomer and intermediate players.

BETTING. Betting is illegal in tournament play sanctioned by the American Contract Bridge League or any of its affiliated groups.

Occasionally rather sizable bets have been made on the results of challenge bridge matches, notably the CULBERTSON-LENZ MATCH of 1931-32 and the CULBERTSON-SIMS MATCH of 1935.

Bets on the outcome of a rubber or match are based on the side winning the larger number of points rather than the rubber bonus or bonuses, and are thus distinguished from STAKES, which are based on the difference in points earned at so much per point.

BF. Bridge Federation.

BFAME. See BRIDGE FEDERATION OF ASIA AND THE MIDDLE EAST.

BIBLIOGRAPHY. See section V of this *Encyclopedia*.

BID. A call by which a player proposes a contract that his side will win at least as many odd tricks (one to seven) as his bid specifies, provided the hand is played at the denomination named. See LAWS (Laws 17 through 40). See BID BOX.

BID OF MORE THAN SEVEN. A call by a player contracting for more than seven-odd tricks, and one which is, therefore, inadmissible. See LAWS (Law #38).

BID OUT OF ROTATION. A call by a player, not in turn. See LAWS (Law #31).

BID WHIST. A form of whist in which the players bid for the right to name the trump suit. The player to the left of the dealer bids first and the dealer bids last. The second and third players must pass or make a higher bid, but the dealer can take the contract by matching the bid of the third player. Bids are in numbers, from one through seven, indicating the number of tricks to be taken above book (six tricks). The player who wins the bidding then names the trump suit and makes the opening

lead. If he chooses notrump instead of a suit, scoring for the hand is doubled. There are many minor variations from place to place in bidding and scoring rules.

BIDDABLE SUIT. The minimum requirements for a bid in terms of the length and strength of the suit.

In the Thirties, the CULBERTSON SYSTEM laid down Q-J-3-2 as a minimum biddable suit, but permitted this to be shaded slightly in certain circumstances. Modern writers tend to reject a generalized rule for biddable suits, recognizing that the requirements must depend on the circumstances in which the bid is made. Four main situations can be listed.

Opening bid

The higher the rank of the suit, the higher the suit requirements tend to be. 1♣ is often used as a prepared bid with 4-3-3-3, 3-4-3-3 or 4-4-2-3 distribution. (The advent of FIVE-CARD MAJORS has seen this tendency grow.) Some authorities require that a three-card suit be headed by an honor, but this is not always possible:

> ♠ A J 8 5
> ♥ A K J
> ♦ 5 4 2
> ♣ 8 5 3

Many players using standard methods would bid 1♣ and hope for the best.

If the red suits were reversed in this example, some experts would open 1♦, regarding the quality of the suit as of greater importance than the convenience of rebid provided by an opening of 1♣. But this is an exceptional case. A bid of 1♦ usually shows at least a four-card suit, but no guarantee is made about the quality of the suit. Four small cards may be sufficient in certain circumstances. Opening on a three-card diamond suit occurs occasionally when opener, playing five-card majors, has 4-4-3-2 distribution.

Standards are generally higher for major-suit openings (not taking into account players who favor FIVE-CARD MAJORS). A few players distinguish between hearts and spades, opening four-card heart suits more readily than four-card spade suits.

Responses to suit bids

A similar principle applies: the most economical bid may sometimes be made with a three-card suit, especially a minor suit, while the most space-consuming bid usually indicates a five-card or longer suit.

	(a)	(b)	(c)
♠	K 7 5	9 7 5	9 7 5
♥	A 5 2	A 5 4 2	A K 4
♦	A 6 3	K 6 3	6 4 3
♣	9 6 4 3	A 6 3	8 7 4 3

With hand (a), most experts would select a response of 1♦ to an opening bid of 1♣. This is a waiting bid which can come to little harm, and there is no good alternative unless a 2NT response is being used as a limit bid.

Hand (b) presents a problem when responding to an opening bid of 1♠ if a 1NT response is not forcing. 2♥ is clearly ruled out because nearly all experts reserve this space-consuming response for hands containing a five-card or longer heart suit. The hand is not strong enough for 2NT (unless this is played as limit). So the general expert choice would be 2♣.

It is usually dangerous to bid a three-card major suit, but Pierre Jais of France used to recommend 1♥ in response to 1♦ with hand (c), or 1♠ in response to 1♥

if the major suits are reversed. This is an extreme treatment, but illustrates the general principle of striving to make the most economical bid.

Conversely, a response at the two-level in the suit ranking immediately below the opener's almost always shows a minimum of five cards, as with the response of 2♥ to 1♠.

The most controversial problem concerning biddable suits is whether a weak four-card major suit should be bid at the one-level in preference to 1NT.

The authorities who favor five-card majors require a four-card suit of any strength to be shown at the level of one, but other leading writers are divided or noncommittal on this point. See WALSH SYSTEM.

Rebids

This is similarly controversial when the choice lies between showing a weak four-card major suit and rebidding 1NT. In 1959, a panel of American experts were asked whether they subscribed to the idea of "giving highest priority to finding a major-suit fit." There were 29 panelists who answered yes, without reservations; 38 panelists answered yes, with reservations; 17 replied that they would bid the four-card major suit only if it was worth showing. On this specific hand:

> ♠ 7 4 3 2
> ♥ 5 3
> ♦ A Q 7
> ♣ A Q J 7

the panelists were asked to choose between a rebid of 1♠ and a rebid of 1NT after opening 1♣ and receiving a response of 1♥. There were 49 votes for 1♠ and 43 for 1NT.

In a survey conducted by *The Bridge World* magazine in 1967, 90 leading experts were asked whether a 1NT rebid after an opening bid of 1♣ and a response of 1♥ denied a four-card spade suit. Sixty percent replied yes, indicating that the tendency at that time favored rebidding major suits regardless of quality.

In 1984, *The Bridge World* asked experts whether they approved of the 1♠ rebid on these hands:

	(a)	(b)	(c)
♠	A J 6 4	A K J 6	J 5 3 2
♥	J 4 3	K 4 3	K 6 4
♦	K 6 4	10 4 2	A Q 10
♣	A J 4	Q 4 3	K 10 3

Fifty-nine percent approved on (a), 66 percent on (b), but only 47 percent on (c). On such hands, therefore, it seems that experts are increasingly willing to use judgment and rebid 1NT to give a general picture of their strength and pattern. This is affected by the increasing number of players who use the Walsh idea of responding in a major suit and concealing a diamond suit of any length unless the hand is strong.

The problem is different at the level of two, when the choice lies between rebidding a five-card suit and introducing a weak four-card suit. Almost all experts would prefer to show the four-card suit, if lower ranking.

Overcalls

In most situations, the overcaller can apply the standards of a rebiddable suit (see OPENER'S REBID), but standards must vary widely in accordance with such factors as vulnerability, level of the auction, and preemptive effect. See OVERCALL, REBIDDABLE SUIT.

BIDDER. A player who states or indicates a bid. Occasionally the term is used to indicate a player who is prone

to overbid, or one who will prefer trying a doubtful contact rather than defending in a competitive bidding situation. Also, any player during the auction period.

BIDDING. The period following the deal and ending after the third successive pass of any bid, double or redouble. Aspects of this phase of the game are listed under the following group headings: COMPETITIVE BIDDING; COMPETITIVE DOUBLE; CUEBID; DEFENSE TO ONE NOTRUMP; DEFENSIVE BIDDING; DOUBLES; FOUR CLUB CONVENTIONS; FOUR NOTRUMP CONVENTIONS; NOTRUMP BIDDING; OPENING BID; OVERCALLS; REBIDS; RESPONSE; SLAM BIDDING; TWO-SUITER CONVENTIONS; VALUATION.

Other articles include: APPROACH PRINCIPLE; BIDDABLE SUIT; BIDDING SPACE; CANAPÉ; CAPTAINCY; COMMAND BID; CONVENTIONS; DISCOURAGING BID; ENCOURAGING; FORCING; GENERAL UNDERSTANDINGS; HERBERT NEGATIVE; IDLE BIDS; IMP TACTICS; IMPOSSIBLE BIDS; INFERENCE; LAW OF TOTAL TRICKS; LEAD-INHIBITING BID; LIMIT BID; MATCHPOINT BIDDING; PARTNERSHIP BIDDING; PARTSCORE BIDDING; PSYCHIC BIDDING; PSYCHIC CONTROLS; RUBBER BRIDGE TACTICS; RULE OF TWO AND THREE; SAFETY LEVEL; SIGN-OFF BID; THREE-SUITER; WEAK SUIT.

BIDDING BOX. A device that enables players to bid without speaking. It consists of a box that has one card for each possible bid plus additional cards for pass, double, redouble, Stop and Alert. The box either sits on the table or is attached to the table. To make a call, the player removes the appropriate card from the box and places it on the table in front of him. For subsequent calls, the player removes the appropriate cards and places them over earlier calls in such a manner that all calls are visible. All BIDDING CARDS remain on the table until the end of the auction, thus avoiding most requests for reviews of the bidding. The possibility of mishearing a bid also is eliminated.

Bidding boxes were used for the first time in world championships during the World Pair Championships in Sweden in 1970. Beginning with the world championships in Las Palmas, the Canary Islands, in 1974, bidding boxes have been used exclusively in world championship competition. In recent years bidding boxes have been used in virtually all major championships throughout the world. They also are used almost exclusively at thousands of bridge clubs throughout the world. At North American Championships, bidding boxes are used in all events. With few exceptions, everyone agrees that bidding boxes are a great improvement over verbal bidding.

BIDDING CARD. The card with a bid or a call printed on it that is part of the collection of such cards in a BIDDING BOX.

BIDDING CHALLENGE. Feature of some bridge magazines, providing readers with pairs of hands to bid and a comparison with the efforts of a panel of experts. Called "Challenge the Champs" in *The Bridge World*.

BIDDING CONTESTS. See INTERNATIONAL BRIDGE ACADEMY.

BIDDING SCREEN. See SCREEN.

BIDDING SPACE. The amount of room used in terms of bids which have been skipped. A response of 1 ♥ to 1 ♦, for example, uses no bidding space, but a response of 2 ♣ would use up a good deal of bidding space. The general theory is that the length of a suit tends to increase as the bidding space consumed in bidding increases.

(1) In opening the bidding, 1 ♣ is infrequently a three-card suit, and the length expectancy increases up the line. 1 ♠ is usually a five-card suit, even for players who do not require five-card majors.

(2) Similarly in responding, a response using no bidding space, e.g., 1 ♣-1 ♦, may occasionally be a three-card suit. A response using maximum bidding space (e.g. 1 ♠-2 ♥) is nearly always a five-card suit.

(3) In rebidding by the opener, a rebid in the original suit can be played as a five-card suit if it consumes no space (1 ♥-2 ♦-2 ♥), but is almost sure to be a six-card suit if maximum bidding space has been used (1 ♥-1 ♠-2 ♥).

(4) Overcalls represent exceptions, for tactical reasons. 1 ♠ over an opposing bid of 1 ♣ is slightly more likely to be a four-card suit than it would be over 1 ♥. In the former case the overcaller may be taking a calculated risk in the hope of shutting the opponents out of a heart fit. See USEFUL SPACE PRINCIPLE.

(5) The entire available range of bids into which many bidding sequences must be squeezed.

BIDDING SYSTEM. Specific methods of bidding are discussed under the following headings:

ACES SCIENTIFIC; ACOL; AMSTERDAM CLUB; APPROACH-FORCING; BANGKOK CLUB; BARON; BIG DIAMOND; BISSELL; BLUE TEAM CLUB; BRIDGE WORLD STANDARD; CAB; CANAPÉ; CANARY CLUB; CARROT CLUB; CHURCHILL STYLE; COLONIAL ACOL; CRANE; CULBERT-SON; DUTCH SPADE; EASTERN SCIENTIFIC; EFOS; EHAA; FOUR ACES; FRENCH CLUB; GOREN; HUM SYSTEMS; KAMIKAZE NOTRUMP; KAPLAN-SHEINWOLD; LEGHORN DIAMOND; LITTLE MAJOR; LITTLE ROMAN CLUB; MARMIC; MONACO; MOSCITO; NEW SOUTH WALES; NOTTINGHAM CLUB; OFFICIAL; ORANGE CLUB; PRECISION CLUB; PRO SYSTEM; REITH ONE-OVER-ONE; RELAY SYSTEMS; ROMAN; ROMEX; ROTH-STONE; SCHENKEN; SIMPLIFIED CLUB; SIMPLIFIED PRECISION; SIMS; STANDARD AMERICAN; STONEAGE ACOL WITH PAKISTANI PREEMPTS; SUPER PRECISION; SYMMETRIC RELAY; TWO OVER ONE; ULTIMATE CLUB; VANDERBILT CLUB; VIENNA; WALSH; WEAK OPENING SYSTEMS; WESTERN SCIENTIFIC; WINSLOW.

BIDDING TO THE SCORE. See PARTSCORE BIDDING.

BIDDING TRAY. See TRAY.

BIFF. Colloquial for trumping the led suit, particularly a winning card on an early lead.

BIG CLUB. See BLACK CLUB; BLUE TEAM CLUB; ORANGE CLUB; NEAPOLITAN; PRECISION CLUB;

SCHENKEN SYSTEM; SUPER PRECISION; VANDERBILT CLUB SYSTEM.

BIG DIAMOND SYSTEM. A method introduced by G. Robert Nail and Robert Stucker, the cornerstone of which is a forcing 1♦ opening, promising an unbalanced hand with at least 17 points. 1♥ is the negative response (0-9), and 1NT is an artificial positive response in hearts.

Other openings: 1♣, forcing, showing a balanced hand not suitable for a 1NT opening (14-16) or 2NT opening (20-21). A 1♦ response is negative (0-10); 2♣, nonforcing, showing 12-15 points with 4-4 or longer in the minor suits; 2♦, showing 14-16 points and 4-4 or 5-4 in the major suits.

BIOGRAPHIES. See Section III.

BIONIC BRIDGE. A plan to use computers to play bridge without cards. It was conceived by C.C. Wei and developed in Taiwan by Patrick Huang and others. It was a forerunner of more sophisticated methods now available. See COMPUTER PLAY

BIRITCH, or Russian Whist. The historic four-page pamphlet, thought to be the earliest publication of the rules of bridge. Authorship has now been traced to John Collinson of London, in whose name copyright was entered July 14, 1886. A reproduction, made available through the courtesy of Cambridge University Library, is in the ACBL library. The principal innovations from short whist are described as follows:

No card is turned up for trumps.

The dealer, after the cards have been looked at, has the option of declaring the suit he elects for trumps, or of saying "Pass," in which latter case his partner must declare trumps.

In either case, the one declaring may, instead of declaring trumps, say "BIRITCH," which means that the hands shall be played without trumps.

Either of the adversaries may say "Contre," in which case the value of all tricks taken is doubled. The dealer or his partner may however thereupon say "Surcontre," in which latter case the value of all tricks taken is quadrupled, and so on ad infinitum.

The person to the left of the dealer leads a card. Then the partner of the dealer exposes all his cards, on the table, which are played by the dealer as at Dummy Whist.

GAMES AND RUBBERS

A game is won by the first side which scores 30 points in play. The honors do not score toward game. The Rubber consists of two games out of three.

SCORING

The odd tricks count as follows:

If "Biritch" is declared .... each 10 points
If "Hearts" are made trumps .... each 8 points
If "Diamonds" are made trumps .... each 6 points
If "Clubs" are made trumps .... each 4 points
If "Spades" are made trumps .... each 2 points

If all the tricks are taken by one side they add 40 extra points. This is called "GRAND SLAMM."

If all the tricks but one are taken by one side they add 20 extra points. This is called "PETIT SLAMM."

The winners of each rubber add 40 points to their score. This is called "CONSOLATION."

There are four honors if "BIRITCH" is declared, which are the four aces.

Equality in aces counts nothing.
3 aces .... 3 tricks
4 aces .... 4 tricks
4 aces in one hand .... 8 tricks

There are five honors, viz: Ace, King, Queen, Knave, and Ten, if trumps are declared.
Simple honors (3) .... 2 tricks
4 simple honors .... 4 tricks
4 simple honors in one hand .... 8 tricks
5 simple honors in one hand .... 1 trick additional to the score for four honors

If one hand has no trumps (trumps having been declared), his side, in case of it scoring honors, adds the value of simple honors to its honor score, or, in case of the other side scoring honors, the value of simple honors is deducted from the latter's honor score. This is called "CHICANE."

Despite existence of the historic pamphlet, derivation of the name *bridge* from *Biritch* was long disputed on the ground that no such word existed in Russian. Research by Robert True in the early Seventies found that earlier Russian dictionaries did include the term, defined as *herald*, town crier, announcer, making it a logical name for a game which introduced the new idea of announcing the declaration at which the hand was to be played. It is interesting to observe the designation of Biritch for the declaration of notrump, a feature never part of whist. Use in the pamphlet of the French terms for double and redouble would tend to confirm that bridge was played earlier in France, or in those diplomatic circles where French was the prevailing language. See also HISTORY OF BRIDGE.

BISSELL. An original method for showing distribution with the first bid, devised by Harold Bissell of New York and published in 1936. It attracted favorable attention from B. Jay Becker, Louis Watson and Edward Hymes, and anticipated some modern European systems, such as ROMAN and RELAY.

Valuation. This was by a distributional point-count which ingeniously took into account the strength of combined honors as well as suit lengths. Honor cards were valued at 3, 2 and 1 point respectively if there were 0, 1 or 2 higher honors missing in the same suit.

To these were added distributional points: 1 for the fourth card in any suit; and 4 for the fifth and succeeding cards in any suit.

The grand total bore a direct relation to the playing-trick strength of a hand (three times the number of playing tricks) and was therefore an accurate measure of the power of the hand.

BIT. British colloquialism for a small card. "Ace-bit" means a doubleton ace.

BL. Bridge League.

BLACK CLUB. Bidding system used by Bob Hamman and Billy Eisenberg when they were members of the ACES TEAM.

BLACK POINTS. Points won at club games and Unit championships. See "GOLD POINTS; PLATINUM POINTS; RANKING OF PLAYERS; RATING POINTS; RED POINTS; REGIONAL AND NATIONAL POINTS; SILVER POINTS.

BLACK AND RED GERBER. A variation of the GERBER convention devised by Irving Cowan which

uses 4♣ as the ace-asking bid only when a red suit has been agreed on as trumps. When clubs or spades are to be trumps, the ace-asking bid is 4♦. This modification retains a lower-level ace-asking bid than BLACKWOOD, while avoiding the ambiguity of using 4♣ as Gerber, with clubs as the agreed suit.

BLACKPOOL MOVEMENT. A movement popular in England in which 10 tables play 24 boards. Two boards are played in each round, and bye stands are placed between tables 1 and 10, and between 5 and 6. Players and boards move as in a normal MITCHELL MOVEMENT for 11 rounds, so that in the eleventh round original opponents are again in opposition. For the twelfth round East-West pairs deduct their pair number from 11 and move to the indicated table.

BLACKWOOD. A convention in which a 4NT bid is used to discover the number of aces held by partner. It was invented by Easley Blackwood in 1933 and has attained worldwide popularity.

The conventional responses to the 4NT bid are:

5♣	no ace or four aces
5♦	one ace
5♥	two aces
5♠	three aces

If the 4NT bidder continues by bidding 5NT, he asks for kings in a similar fashion. As this must be an attempt to reach a grand slam, the 5NT bid guarantees that the partnership holds all four aces. (At matchpoint duplicate scoring, this idea might be disregarded in the interest of seeking a contract of 6NT.)

Some players use the next meaningless bid, instead of 5NT, to ask for kings. This is called ROLLING BLACKWOOD.

However, the traditional use of the follow-up 5NT bid to ask for kings has been abandoned by most experts. In BWS94, 73% of experts preferred 5NT to be a general grand slam try and a request for a cuebid. Among American experts, this traditional version of the convention has been largely replaced by ROMAN KEYCARD BLACKWOOD (RKCB). When there is no agreed trump suit, RKCB cannot be used. Experts strongly favor (73% in BWS 2001) use of a modified responding scheme: 5♣ — no ace or three aces, 5♦ — one ace or four aces, 5♥ — two aces. However, the traditional use of the follow-up 5NT bid to ask for kings has been abandoned by most experts. In BWS 1994 73% of experts preferred 5NT to be a general grand slam try and a request for a cuebid.

Requirements

There are no specific requirements, but the 4NT bidder should feel safe at the level of five and have an expectation of 12 playing tricks in the combined hands. He should expect to be able to make a successful decision on the basis of his partner's response and should therefore usually be well provided with second- and third-round playing tricks in the combined hands.

It is seldom wise to use the convention when holding a void suit or worthless doubleton in an unbid suit, or when matters such as trump quality remain unresolved.

If the intent is to play in a minor-suit slam, a Blackwood bidder must use discretion if he has fewer than two aces. He may use Blackwood if the intended trump suit is diamonds, but not if it is clubs. (One variation of responses when clubs is the agreed trump suit caters to this difficulty: the 4NT bidder assumes that his partner

has at least one ace; hence, there is no response to show no aces. A 5♣ response shows one, 5♦ shows two, etc.)

In some circumstances it may be possible to play in 5NT. If the Blackwood bidder next bids an unbid suit at the five-level, he is requesting responder to bid 5NT. However, this is rarely necessary since a Blackwood bidder is normally intending to play in a suit.

Void suits

Void suits may not be counted as aces, but there are several methods by which voids can be indicated.

(1) Make the normal response, but at the level of six, to show the indicated number of aces and an unspecified void. Thus 6♣ shows no ace and a void; 6♦ shows one ace and a void, etc.

(2) Bid 6♣ to show one ace and a void; 6♦ to show two aces and a void.

(3) Bid 5NT to show two aces and a void; six of a suit ranking below the agreed trump suit to show a void in that suit and one ace; six of the agreed trump suit to show one ace and a higher-ranking void.

(4) Holding two aces, make the response that normally shows no aces; holding three aces, make the response that normally shows one ace. When the 4NT bidder signs off, the responder does not pass, but now bids the suit of his void. Responses at the six level show one ace and a void, as in (3) above.

(5) Using a three-step set of normal responses to Blackwood in which 5♣ shows 0 or 3 aces, 5♦ shows 1 or 4, and 5♥ shows two aces, make a bid higher than 5♥ to show a void. 5♠ shows a spade void and one ace; other responses are as in (3) above.

Interference bidding

See BLACKWOOD AFTER INTERFERENCE.

Non-conventional

There are a number of situations in which 4NT should be treated as a natural bid. Experts sometimes disagree on specific situations, but there is general agreement on the following rule:

A 4NT bid is a natural bid whenever the partnership has not bid a suit genuinely. For example:

South	North	South	North	South	North
1NT	4NT	2♣	2♦	1NT	2♣
		2NT	4NT	2♦	4NT
		(using an			
		artificial			
		2♣ bid)			

But there are other circumstances in which the 4NT bid should be treated as natural. Careful partnership agreement is needed. The following rule is generally valid: If, during the auction, one player bids 3NT and his partner bids four of a minor suit as a slam suggestion, a subsequent 4NT bid by either player should be a natural sign-off bid. For example:

South	North	South	North
1♠	2♥	1♠	2♣
3NT	4♦	3NT	4♣
4NT		4NT	

In these sequences the final bid rejects the slam invitations and expresses a desire to play in 4NT.

A more general rule is recommended by Terence Reese; 4NT is natural when no suit has been agreed, either directly or by inference. This covers a wide range. For example:

South	North
1♠	2♥
3NT	4NT

Many players would regard this as conventional, but on Reese's rule it would be natural.

South	North
1♥	2NT
4NT	

This type of 4NT bid is listed as conventional by Blackwood himself, but would be natural on Reese's rule. If South wishes to bid 4NT conventionally, he can make a forcing bid at the level of three and follow with 4NT on the next round.

By agreement, a raise from 2NT to 4NT at any stage can be regarded as natural: a conventional 4NT can always be postponed. But judgment may be required when 3NT is followed by 4NT.

South	North
1♠	3♥
3NT	4NT

This is clearly conventional. North may be planning to play in either major suit, but has had no opportunity to fix a suit below game level.

A survey of experts in BWS2001 sought a consensus on the meaning of non-competitive 4NT bids that were clearly forcing. The panel voted overwhelmingly in favor of such a bid being Blackwood or Roman Keycard Blackwood rather than a control showing bid or general slam encouragement. However, if a competitive 4NT can logically be interpreted as either takeout, a general slam try or natural, takeout prevails.

However:

West	North	East	South
			1♥
4♠	4NT		

When there is no jump, the consensus in BWS 1994 was that 4NT is for takeout.

A survey of experts in BWS 2001 sought a consensus on the meaning of non-competitive 4NT bids that were clearly forcing. The panel voted overwhelmingly in favor of such a bid being Blackwood or Roman Keycard Blackwood, rather than a control-showing bid or general slam encouragement. However, if a competitive 4NT can logically be interpreted as a takeout, a general slam try or natural, takeout prevails.

Also, any sudden jump from a suit bid to 4NT is of necessity conventional. See also: ACE IDENTIFICATION; BABY BLACKWOOD; BLACKWOOD AFTER INTERFERENCE; BYZANTINE BLACKWOOD; CULBERTSON 4-5NT; DECLARATIVE-INTERROGATIVE 4NT; FOURTEEN THIRTY; GERBER CONVENTION; KEY CARD BLACKWOOD; KICKBACK; NORMAN 4NT; ROLLING BLACKWOOD; ROMAN BLACKWOOD; ROMAN GERBER; ROMAN KEYCARD BLACKWOOD; SUPER BLACKWOOD; SUPER GERBER; SUPPRESSING THE BID ACE.

BLACKWOOD AFTER INTERFERENCE. The traditional method for dealing with opponents who overcall a Blackwood bid has been to double whenever the size of the prospective penalty is attractive, and otherwise to pass with no aces and bid the cheapest suit with one ace, and so forth up the line. Modern conventions recognize that the penalty will rarely be sufficiently lucrative to warrant a double, and therefore give that call an artificial meaning related to the number of aces held by the Blackwood responder. The most common such conventions are:

(1) DEPO, which stands for Double Even, Pass Odd. A double shows zero, two, or four aces; a pass shows one or three.

(2) DOPI, which stands for Double Zero, Pass 1. A double shows no aces, pass shows 1 and two or more aces are shown by bidding up the line.

(3) PODI, which stands for Pass Zero, Double 1. The double and the pass have the reverse of the meanings they have using DOPI; other bids are the same. Similarly, DOPE is the reverse of DEPO.

DOPI is more widely used than PODI. A number of experts agree to use DOPI when the overcall is below the trump suit at the five-level, allowing room for bidding two or more aces up the line, and to use DEPO when the overcall is at five of the trump suit or higher and space is scarce.

The BWS 2001 expert consensus was for DOPI at the five-level and DEPO at the six-level.

It is also possible to use Roman responses with DOPI or PODI. The first step shows 0 or 3 aces, the second step shows 1 or 4 while the first bid other than pass or double shows 2. Pairs that play KEYCARD BLACKWOOD would be well advised to discuss whether or not the trump king counts in responding after interference.

Some experts play a variation of DOPI when 4NT is doubled. ROPI (redouble zero, pass one) or its reverse, RIPO can be used. This can lead to occasional misunderstandings, and the more popular choice is to act as if the double had not taken place.

BLACKWOOD THEORY OF DISTRIBUTION. A formula applied when missing four cards including the queen.

♠ K J 10 7 4
♠ A 8 6 2

South lays down the ace and both defenders play low. On the second round West plays low, and South has to decide whether to finesse or play for the drop.

Mathematically it is extremely close. Easley Blackwood suggested a rule based on the LAW OF SYMMETRY: If the combined North-South holding in their shortest suit is:

(a) five cards, or four cards divided 2-2: play for the drop;

(b) four cards divided 3-1 or 4-0, or fewer than four cards: finesse. This formula was tested on a large number of published hands and produced excellent results. However, it can apply only when there are no indications from the bidding and play, which is rarely the case.

See BLACKWOOD AFTER INTERFERENCE.

BLANCHARD CASE. Just after the 1984 Fall NABC in San Diego, Robert and Jill Blanchard of New York City filed suit against the ACBL in Los Angeles. The Blanchards' claim was that gender-based events such as the Men's Pairs violated California's Unruh Act, an antidiscrimination statute. Five years later, the Los Angeles Superior Court, in which the suit was filed, dismissed the suit for lack of prosecution. As part of a settlement with the Blanchards, in which they agreed not to appeal, the ACBL's insurance carrier paid $15,000 toward the couple's legal expenses. The insurance carrier paid all of ACBL's legal expenses.

Beginning in 1990, three nationally-rated events formerly restricted to men were changed to open events.

The Life Master Men's Pairs at the Spring NABC is now one of two Open Pairs; the Men's Swiss Teams, also contested in the Spring, is now the Open Swiss Teams; and the Men's Board-a-Match Teams, contested in the Fall, is now the Open Board-a-Match Teams.

Around the time of the Blanchards' suit — and in response to complaints by the couple — the ACBL also eliminated gender-based events from those used to qualify ACBL pairs for WBF competition. The Blanchards claimed that they could not qualify together in events restricted to men or women. The ACBL Board of Directors agreed and changed the qualifying policy.

BLANK. A void. Used as an adjective, it indicates lack of a protecting small card for an honor, as a blank king. As a verb, it means to discard a protecting small card, as to blank a king.

Blank honors, whether singleton or doubleton, are slightly devalued in most POINT-COUNT methods.

BLANK HAND. A hand with seemingly no trick-taking potential (see YARBOROUGH).

BLANK SUIT. See VOID.

BLIND LEAD. The first lead on any hand, so called because the opening leader has not seen the dummy. This term is particularly applied when the leader's partner has not bid, and the declarer's side has bid only one denomination. Terence Reese is quoted as saying, "Blind leads are for deaf players." See OPENING LEAD.

BLIND PLAYERS. Blindness is not an insurmountable obstacle to bridge playing. The cards are marked with Braille symbols, and sighted players in turn call the card played to each trick. A blind player may at any time ask that the remaining cards in the dummy be called out. Early Braille markings were not standardized and often players could not read one another's Braille.

J. Patrick Dunne and Dr. Arthur Dye were the first blind players to participate in major American Contract Bridge League tournaments. Dr. Lois Zwart (later Wiley) commenced playing a few years later, accompanied by her seeing eye dog. Dr. Dye and Dr. Wiley both earned Life Master rating as have other blind players — John Larsen of Minneapolis, Anne Cunningham of Charlotte NC, Sarah Howard of Newport News VA and Michael Andrew Levinson of Daly City CA who, though legally blind, won the Life Master Men's Pairs at the Fall 1981 North American Championships.

John Schuler of San Diego suffered severe macular degeneration in 1991, but he kept on playing bridge regularly, thanks to the computer internet. In fact he was a member of the winning team in the first OKbridge Internet World Bridge Championship in 1999.

BLITZ. To crush your opponents, usually in a session of team play in which their score is zero or to beat an oppenent 20-0/25-0/30-0 in Victory Points.

BLIZZARD. British colloquialism for a worthless hand.

BLOCK. A situation in which entry problems within a particular suit make it difficult or impossible to cash winners or possible winners in that suit. This occurs when both members of a partnership (the declaring side or the defense) hold significant honor cards, and one of them has no accompanying small cards. For example:

North	North
K Q J 10	Q J 3 2
South	South
A	A K

In these cases the block is complete, and the honor cards in dummy cannot be utilized unless a side entry is available. Sometimes the block may be less embarrassing:

North	North
A J 4 3 2	A 4 3 2
South	South
K Q	K Q J

If there is no side entry to dummy, South must overtake his last honor with dummy's ace. He needs a 3-3 division of the defenders' cards to make more than three tricks.

The general rule for resolving blocked situations, or for avoiding unnecessary blocks, is that high cards must be played from the shorter hand as quickly as possible. See also BLOCKING, UNBLOCKING and INTERNAL BLOCK.

BLOCKBUSTER. A bridge hand of seemingly tremendous trick-taking potential. From time to time, however, these hands have a weakness and give rise to very large sets when the partner's hand contains no protective features and the trump suit divides unfavorably. See also MONSTER and ROCK-CRUSHER.

BLOCKED SQUEEZE. See CRISS-CROSS SQUEEZE, under SIMPLE SQUEEZE. For other types of blocked squeeze, see ENTRY SQUEEZE and STEPPINGSTONE SQUEEZE.

BLOCKING. Playing so as to create a block in the opponent's suit. For example:

```
              ♠ A 5 2
♠ K 10 8 6 3              ♠ Q 9
              ♠ J 7 4
```

West leads the ♠6 against 3NT. The normal play is to hold up the ace twice, but this is useless if West rather than East is likely to gain the lead. In that case South should put up dummy's ace, abandoning the chance that the lead is from king-queen. Whenever East holds a doubleton honor the spade suit is blocked for the defense.

Notice that if the defensive entry was held by East, he would need to unblock with the queen on the first trick. Other positions:

```
              ♠ A 6 4
♠ Q 9 8 5 3              ♠ K J
              ♠ 10 7 2
```

In this position West leads the five and South puts up dummy's ace, hoping for East to hold two honors doubleton. When the defenders gain the lead, they can cash only one spade trick.

```
              ♠ 8 6
♠ A 9 4 3 2              ♠ K J 10
              ♠ Q 7 5
```

When East wins the lead of the three with the king, and returns the jack, South should cover and thus block the suit. He assumes that West's three is an honest fourth-

best lead, in which case West cannot have six spades, and East cannot have a doubleton.

If there were two small spot cards missing, suggesting a six-card suit with West, South should play low on the jack.

♠ A 3

♠ K J 7 5 4   ♠ Q 8

♠ 10 9 6 2

On the lead of the five, South blocks the suit by putting up dummy's ace. This permits a triumph for the rare player who underleads K-Q-J-x-x (see OPENING LEADS).

♠ 7 5

♠ Q 6 2   ♠ A 10 9 8 4

♠ K J 3

West leads the two to East's ace, and the 10 is returned. If South judges that West had led from an honor, he puts up the king and achieves a block. See also UNBLOCKING.

BLUE PETER. A humorous term for a high-low signal invented in 1834 by Lord Henry Bentinck. This was probably the first defensive signal in any game of the whist family. The name is nautical in origin, referring to a signal hoisted in harbor to denote that a ship is ready to sail. Bentinck's signal was used in a side suit to indicate to partner a desire to have trumps led. For uses of the high-low or echo in contract, see SIGNALS, SIGNALING and PETER.

BLUE RIBBON PAIRS, NORTH AMERICAN CHAMPIONSHIP. A championship event contested annually at the Fall NABC, under which heading past results are listed. Entry is limited to (1) players who, within a specified period of time, have finished high in North American Championship events, or have finished first or second in regionally rated events, (2) the top 100 masterpoint holders, (3) members of current official teams representing the ACBL or any of its member countries in international competition and (4) winners of Grand National District championships. For winners, see Appendix I. See CAVENDISH TROPHY.

BLUE TEAM. The popular name of the Italian international bridge team which gained a remarkable series of successes beginning in 1956. The name is apparently derived from the 1956 Italian Trials, when the Blue Team defeated the Red Team.

Federico Rosa, the late Secretary of the Italian Bridge Federation, explained that the successes of the Blue Team were closely connected with the name of Carl' Alberto Perroux, the Technical Commissioner of the Italian Bridge Federation. He undertook this duty in 1950, and scored his first success in the following year when the team which he had selected won the European Championship in Venice. But the subsequent World Championship encounter with the United States at Naples showed that the young Italian champions were lacking in experience and team discipline.

But this did not cause Perroux to lose heart. He wrote then that the Italians had wished to reach the moon too quickly. This was a promise and a threat. From that day, two groups of enthusiasts, under the paternal leadership of the Technical Commissioner, dedicated themselves to a profound and detailed study of the game. As a result the two schools — the Neapolitan and the Roman

— gave birth not only to two of the most accurate bidding systems ever devised, NEAPOLITAN and ROMAN, plus LITTLE ROMAN, but also to the great story of the Blue Team, made up of men such as Walter Avarelli, Giorgio Belladonna, Eugenio Chiaradia, Massimo D'Alelio, Pietro Forquet, Benito Garozzo, Camillo Pabis-Ticci and Guglielmo Siniscalco.

The Italians did not have to wait too long before avenging the 1951 defeat. From 1956 the Blue Team, captained by Perroux through 1966, then by others, went from victory to victory, and finally reached the moon. They set an international record which will probably never be equalled: four consecutive European Championship wins, ten consecutive World Championship victories in the Bermuda Bowl and three consecutive World Team Olympiad victories.

With the universe theirs, the Blue Team announced its retirement after winning the 1969 World Championship. After the Aces' victories in the 1970 and 1971 Bermuda Bowls, the Blue Team briefly returned to world competition for the 1972 World Team Olympiad. Using modifications of the Precision Club system, the Blue Team won the round-robin and went on to defeat the Aces in the finals 203-138. Italy continued its domination of the Bermuda Bowl in 1973, 1974 and 1975 but with only two or three members of the traditional Blue Team in the lineup.

BLUE TEAM CLUB. An increasingly popular offspring of the NEAPOLITAN system, developed principally by Benito Garozzo. See BIBLIOGRAPHY C. The chief features of the Blue Team Club are:

1♣ opening is forcing and normally shows 17 or more points (4-3-2-1 count). Occasionally distributional factors may dictate a 1♣ bid with slightly less than 17, or a weaker opening with exactly 17.

Responses show controls by steps, counting an ace as 2 controls and a king as 1. 1♦ shows 0-2 controls, less than 6 points; 1♥ shows 0-2 controls, 6 points or more; 1♠ shows 3 controls, and so on up to 2♦, which shows 6 controls and 2NT showing 7. Jump responses of two of a major show a six-card suit headed by two honors but less than 6 points.

If 1♣ is overcalled at the one-level, a pass is equivalent to the first step response and a double to the second. Other responses are control-showing, except that 2♥ and 2♠ retain the same meaning as if there were no intervention. After a jump overcall the responses follow a similar pattern: pass is the weakest bid, double shows 6 or more points, suit responses are forcing for a round, a response in notrump shows 3 or 4 controls, and a cuebid shows 5 or more controls.

1♣ is generally forcing to 1NT if the response is 1♦, or to 2NT if the response is 1♥. The partnership is committed to game after any other control-showing response.

The opener can force to game by a jump rebid in a suit. If he rebids 1NT or 2NT, the responder can use Stayman. Responder usually makes his first rebid in his best suit, and subsequently shows significant features.

1♦, 1♥, and 1♠ openings are natural limited bids, showing 12-16 points and at least a four-card suit. Occasionally 1♦ may be opened on a three-card suit. With two suits of equal length, opener bids the higher-ranking. With two suits of unequal length, the shorter suit is bid first unless the hand is a minimum and the long suit is higher-ranking.

Most responses are normal. Jump raises are limited. A 2NT jump response is invitational, showing 11-12 points and 4-3-3-3 distribution. Jump shifts show solid or near-solid suits and 13 points or more. Strong hands are bid according to the Canapé principle. Responder's first suit may not be a real suit if his second is higher-ranking.

A response at the two-level is forcing for one round, or to 2NT. Opener must rebid a five-card suit if he has one. After a 1 ♥ or 1 ♠ opening, a second-round jump by responder to 4♣ or 4 ♦ agrees opener's suit is trump and shows a control in the bid suit. See BLUE TEAM FOUR CLUBS-FOUR DIAMONDS CONVENTION.

If opener has a maximum opening, usually 14-16 points, he may make a jump rebid or reverse. Concentration of points in the bid suits favors the selection of a strong rebid.

1NT opening shows a balanced hand, either 13-15 points with a club suit and exactly three cards in each major, or 16-17 points. Minor-suit responses are artificial. 2♣ normally shows 8-11 points and requests opener conventionally to rebid 2♠ with the strong notrump, or make some other two-level bid to describe the strength and club length of the 13-15 notrump. After a 2♠ rebid, 2NT by responder asks for majors; minor-suit rebids are non-forcing. After any other rebid by opener, responder's rebids are mostly non-forcing, though encouraging in some cases.

A 2 ♦ response shows a minimum of 12 points and is forcing to game. With a strong notrump, opener bids a four-card major or bids 3♣ with no major, after which 3 ♦ by responder inquires about the minors. With a weak notrump, opener rebids 2NT, after which 3 ♦ by responder requests opener to describe his strength and number of clubs in four steps.

Jump responses to the three-level show six-card suits headed by two of the top three honors with 6-7 points. Jump responses of 4♣ and 4 ♦ are transfers to 4 ♥ and 4 ♠ respectively.

2♣ opening shows a good club suit of at least five cards and 12-16 points. If a second suit is held, opener will usually have a minimum of 15. A response of 2 ♦ is artificial and asks opener to bid a secondary suit. If he does not have one, he rebids either 2NT with stoppers in two of the outside suits, or 3♣ with a stopper in only one outside suit. 3 ♦ by responder then requests opener to pinpoint his stoppers. Other two-level responses are natural and non-forcing. Jump responses are forcing to game. 2 ♦ opening shows a powerful three-suited hand (4-4-4-1) with 17-24 points. See BLUE TEAM TWO DIAMONDS. 2♥ and 2♠ openings are WEAK TWO-BIDS with a normal range of 8-11. 2NT is the only forcing response.

3♣ opening is a natural preempt and shows a minimum of seven playing tricks, including one outside the club suit.

Gambling 3NT.

Other opening bids are standard.

Blackwood is used on the first and second rounds of bidding, or in later rounds if a jump bid. Responses are ROMAN BLACKWOOD style, with 5♣ showing one ace or four, and 5 ♦ showing none or three. In other situations 4NT is a natural slam invitation. Partner can cooperate by showing an additional feature. He may pass, but more often signs off in the agreed suit. See DECLARATIVE INTERROGATIVE FOUR NOTRUMP.

Defensive bidding is normal, but overcalls are made freely, especially at the one-level. Jump overcalls are intermediate. In response to takeout double, the cheapest bid may be a HERBERT NEGATIVE. See also TRANSFER OVERCALLS OF ONE NOTRUMP. Also See NEAPOLITAN.

BLUE TEAM FOUR CLUB-FOUR DIAMOND CONVENTION. A delayed game raise used in the BLUE TEAM CLUB system to describe responder's minor suit controls. When opener bids and rebids a major suit or opens a major suit and rebids in notrump and responder has excellent support for opener's suit, he responds as follows:

(1) 2♣ followed by 4♣ shows first- or second-round control of clubs and denies first- or second-round control of diamonds;

(2) 2 ♦ followed by 4 ♦ shows first- or second-round control of diamonds and denies first- or second-round control of clubs;

(3) 2♣ followed by 4 ♦ shows either first-round control of both clubs and diamonds or second-round control of both suits;

(4) 2 ♦ followed by 4♣ shows first-round control of one minor and second-round control of the other.

See also NEAPOLITAN FOUR DIAMONDS CONVENTION.

BLUE TEAM TWO DIAMONDS. An opening bid showing a hand worth 17-24 high-card points, with 4-4-4-1 distribution.

An integral part of the BLUE TEAM CLUB system, this convention can also be used with standard methods.

Responses fall into one of four categories:

(1) *Immediate sign-off:* with a very weak hand (about 0-5 points) and three or more spades, responder bids 2♠. Opener will normally pass unless he has either a singleton spade or a maximum hand with four spades. With a singleton spade, opener rebids 2NT, allowing responder to select one of the other three suits.

(2) *Discouraging response with long broken suit:* with a hand worth 5-6 points containing a broken six-card suit, responder bids three of his suit. If that suit is opener's singleton he will pass unless he has a maximum. If opener has four cards in responder's suit he may either bid game or try for slam by cuebidding his singleton. After the cuebid, responder bids in steps to show whether he has the ace or king of his suit, and whether or not he has any singleton.

(3) *Encouraging response with long good suit:* with a hand worth about 6-7 points containing a six-card suit headed by any three honors or two of the top three honors, responder bids 2NT. This bid asks opener to bid the suit below his singleton. At his next turn responder bids his suit (or bids 3NT if his suit is clubs and opener has shown a singleton club by rebidding 3♠). If opener's singleton is in responder's long suit, opener may pass with a minimum, or may bid game in notrump or in responder's suit with a maximum. If opener has four cards in responder's suit the partnership is committed to game, and opener may try for slam by cuebidding. Responder then cuebids a singleton if he has one.

(4) *Relay response:* with a hand unsuitable for any of the above responses, responder bids 2♥, an artificial bid that asks opener for information. With a minor suit

singleton and/or a maximum (21-24), opener bids the denomination below his singleton; rebids of 2NT and 3♣ show minimum hands and rebids of 3♦ through 3NT show maximums. If opener has instead a minimum (17-20) and a major suit singleton, he rebids 2♠; responder then rebids 2NT asking opener to bid 3♣ with a singleton heart, 3♦ with a singleton spade and 17-18 HCP, or 3♥ with a singleton spade and 19-20. Responder may then cuebid opener's known singleton to ask about various features of opener's hand such as point count, controls and queens.

BLUFF. A bid or play made with deceptive intent. See PSYCHIC BID and DECEPTIVE PLAY.

BLUFF FINESSE. See CHINESE FINESSE.

BOARD. (1) A duplicate board. (2) The table on which the cards are played. (3) The dummy's hand, so called because it lies on the table. See LAWS OF DUPLICATE (Law #2).

BOARD, DUPLICATE. An oblong or square board or packet used in various forms of duplicate bridge, slotted with four sections, each deep enough to hold one quarter of a standard deck of playing cards.

The face, or top, of each board has listings appropriate to the board's use, as follows: numbered so that it can be quickly distinguished from companion boards of the same set, one slot marked to indicate the dealer, vulnerability conditions marked both in the slot itself (usually in red) and on the face of the board.

Sometimes the cards to be placed in the slots are shuffled by the players and dealt at the beginning of each contest, but for larger tournaments organizers usually obtain preshuffled or machine-prepared hands to be put into play instead of player-dealt hands.

As adapted for use in contract bridge, the boards are usually packed in sets of 32 or 36 in a carrying case designed for them. Dealer and vulnerability follow a standardized pattern, with North dealing the first board, East the second, South the third and West the fourth with the same rotation repeated for every subsequent set of four. Vulnerability is arranged in a 16-board pattern as follows:

Board	1	2	3	4	5	6	7	8
Dealer	N	E	S	W	N	E	S	W
Vulnerability	No	N-S	E-W	Both	N-S	E-W	Both	No

Board	9	10	11	12	13	14	15	16
Dealer	N	E	S	W	N	E	S	W
Vulnerability	E-W	Both	No	N-S	Both	No	N-S	E-W

Thus every player deals in each of the four possible vulnerability situations. George Beynon noted that this pattern can be put into a magic square, in which N means N-S vulnerable; E, E-W; B means Both; and O for no vulnerability thus:

> O N E B
> N E B O
> E B O N
> B O N E

The first duplicate boards (then called trays) were devised by Cassius M. Paine and J. L. Sebring in 1891. They were square boards, called Kalamazoo after the company that manufactured them. The first oblong boards were produced by William McKenney in 1928 using paper, and the first metal boards were manufac-

tured in 1931 by F. Dudley Courtenay. The first plastic boards were used by the ACBL at the North American Championships in Salt Lake City in 1976. The ACBL now uses plastic boards exclusively.

Square and circular boards are also used, and paper, cardboard, wood and plastic are alternative materials. Wallets made of plastic and foldable when not in use are popular in Europe and South America.

BOARD-A-MATCH. A method of playing multiple team matches in which each team plays against a variety of opponents and each board has exactly the value of 1 point. Although this method used to be prevalent in North America, it has been replaced in large part by INTERNATIONAL MATCHPOINTS with SWISS MOVEMENT pairing.

The movement is so arranged that if the North-South pair of a given team plays a board against the East-West pair of an opposing team, the East-West pair of the given team plays the same board against the North-South pair of the same opposing team. If the total of a team's North-South and East-West scores on the same board is positive, that team receives 1 point. If it is negative, the team receives 0 points. If the total is exactly zero (that is, if both teams achieve the same score), both teams receive ¹/₂ point.

Some National events are still played in this fashion: the REISINGER TEAMS; the OPEN BOARD-A-MATCH TEAMS, the WOMEN'S BOARD-A-MATCH TEAMS and the MASTER MIXED TEAMS. It is occasionally scheduled at the regional and sectional levels.

Top-flight players claim board-a-match is the toughest type of bridge event, requiring intense concentration for every card played. The event's popularity diminished over the years when it became apparent that the skill involved is so high that the same teams were winning almost all the time.

Board-a-match is virtually unknown in Europe, where it is sometimes termed "point-a-board." For movements employed see AMERICAN WHIST MOVEMENT, STAGGER MOVEMENT, NEW ENGLAND RELAY.

BOARD-A-MATCH SWISS TEAMS. The difference between this type of SWISS TEAMS event and others is the method of scoring (see TEAM GAMES). After play is finished and the teams compare scores, one matchpoint is awarded for each board won and half a matchpoint for each board tied. The margin of difference on any board is of no consequence — winning a board by 10 is the same as winning a board by 4000 — it's one. This type of game is rare. Occasionally it is run at a North American Championship, but seldom elsewhere. See FLIGHTED TEAMS, MIXED TEAMS, OPEN TEAMS, ROUND-ROBIN TEAMS, SPEEDBALL SWISS TEAMS, STRATIFIED TEAMS, STRATIFLIGHTED TEAMS, TEAM GAMES, VICTORY POINT SWISS TEAMS, WIN-LOSS SWISS TEAMS, ZIP SWISS TEAMS.

BOARD-A-MATCH TEAMS. This is the toughest type of event in tournament bridge, which may account for its lack of popularity. A team plays a small number of boards against one opponent — usually two, three or four — then moves on to take on another opponent. The movement is set up in such a way that any team always plays any given board against two opposition pairs of

the same team. Often the movement is similar to the MITCHELL MOVEMENT used in pair games, but with some major differences that are always explained by the tournament director. At the end of a session, the members of a team gather to compare scores. Each board is scored separately as a win, tie or loss.

The reason why the game is so tough is that every board is equally important. Some boards in Swiss and knock-out events are not all that important — very little may be at stake. But every board in a board-a-match game is worth one full matchpoint, and a high degree of concentration is necessary throughout every board of a session. See BOARD-A-MATCH.

BODY. A term used to describe a hand with useful intermediate cards such as 10s, 9s and 8s. Some authorities advocate counting a 10 as half a point, sometimes only for notrump purposes. The 10 is of greatest value in combination with one or two higher honors, such as K-10-x, Q-10-x or K-Q-10. It has least value when isolated (10-x-x) or in a solid suit (A-K-Q-J-10). Similarly a 9 may be valuable in combination (Q-10-9) but almost worthless in isolation.

Body may be a decisive factor in making a bidding decision:

♠ K 10 5 4
♥ A Q 9
♦ Q 10 9
♣ K J 8

This hand counts 15 points in high cards, but the intermediate cards make it a "good" 15, and most experts would treat it as a 16-point hand and open with a 16-18 notrump if playing that range.

Body is a factor to consider when making BORDER-LINE OPENING BIDS. As the bidding proceeds, a player can often revalue his intermediate cards. A holding of 10-9-x is certainly worthless if the bidding marks partner with a singleton or a void, and very probably worthless opposite a doubleton. But there is a good chance that the 10-9 will be valuable opposite a probable three card suit: partner may have something like A-J-x, K-J-x, or Q-8-x.

BOLS BRIDGE TIPS. A series of annual contests invented by the late Herman Filarski and subsidized by the Bols Company of The Netherlands. Players of international stature submitted bridge tips for publication in periodicals all over the world. A panel of judges voted each year to decide the winner. The tips were distributed to members of the INTERNATIONAL BRIDGE PRESS ASSOCIATION and became a popular feature in most bridge magazines and many newspaper columns worldwide. The articles appeared in 19 languages. Later the tips were gathered together, expanded and made into a book, *Bridge Tips by World Masters*, with Terence Reese as editor. Sally Brock and Barry Rigal also produced *Fit for a King*, a book made up of Bols Brilliancies. The contest was suspended from 1978 to 1986. Winners:

1974-5	Terence Reese
1975-6	Jean Besse
1976-7	Jeff Rubens
1987	Steen Moller
1988	Michael Lawrence
1989	Zia Mahmood
1990	Gabriel Chagas

1991	Chip Martel
1992	Eric Crowhurst
1993	Larry Cohen

BOLS BRILLIANCY AWARD. See INTERNATIONAL BRIDGE PRESS ASSOCIATION AWARDS.

BONNEY'S SQUEEZE. A triple squeeze against one opponent combined with a simple squeeze against the other. Analyzed by Norman Bonney of Boston.

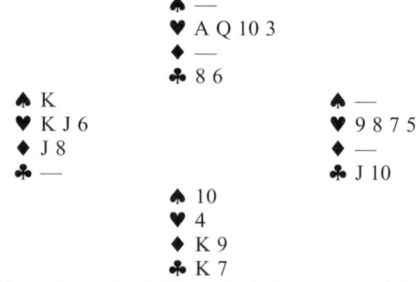

♠ —
♥ A Q 10 3
♦ —
♣ 8 6

♠ K   ♠ —
♥ K J 6   ♥ 9 8 7 5
♦ J 8   ♦ —
♣ —   ♣ J 10

♠ 10
♥ 4
♦ K 9
♣ K 7

South leads the ♦ K on which he throws a club from dummy. East is squeezed and must discard a heart. Now the lead of the ♣K squeezes West in three suits. At the start South has all but two of the remaining tricks, but he manages to win all six by means of the squeeze.

BONUS. A term used in all types of bridge to describe various premiums given under the scoring rules to sides or partnerships who accomplish specified aims.

In rubber bridge, bonuses are awarded for the winning of the rubber by scoring two games before the opponents have scored two games. A bonus of 700 points is credited to the side winning a two-game rubber before the opponents have won even one game. If the opponents have won a game, the bonus becomes 500 points. A bonus of 50 points is paid any side scoring a successful doubled contract, and similarly 100 for making a redoubled contract. A bonus is scored above the scoring line for a side which, in the given hand, has held honors in trump, or all the aces in one hand at notrump. This bonus is either 100 or 150 points. (See HONORS.) Bonus scores are given to sides who successfully bid and make any slam contract. (See SLAM.) If a rubber of bridge has to be terminated before its regular conclusion, a bonus of 300 points is given to a side that is a game ahead, and a partscore earns a 100-point bonus.

In CHICAGO bridge, bonuses can occur on each of the four hands, inasmuch as in this type of contest each deal is really almost a separate game of itself. A nonvulnerable side scoring a game in Chicago is credited with 300 points immediately, and a vulnerable side, 500. Slam bonuses are the same as in rubber bridge, and honors are likewise scored. A partial score achieved on the fourth or final deal, however, acquires an extra bonus of 100 points. This bonus is awarded only for partials actually acquired on the last deal — there is no premium for a partial remaining open at the conclusion of a four-deal chukker.

In duplicate bridge, a bonus is awarded for the making of any partia score (a below-game score) on a given deal. The bonus is 50 points. The regular slam premiums apply in duplicate scoring as explained above, but there are no bonuses for honors, except in total-point scoring. In duplicate, the regular Chicago bonuses for

games bid and made apply, e.g., 300 for making a non-vulnerable game and 500 for making a vulnerable game.

BOOK. The tricks won by a side which have no value in the score. For the declarer, the first six tricks taken constitute his book; for the adversaries, the amount of the declarer's bid subtracted from seven, or the maximum number of tricks the adversaries may take without defeating declarer's contract. The origin of the term apparently lies in the old practice of forming the first six tricks into a "book" by placing them all in one stack.

BOOK GAME. Style of a player who is acquainted with the situations described in the books about bridge, and rigorously follows this pattern of bidding and play. It features theoretical knowledge, but implies lack of skill from practice and lack of versatility.

BOOK PLAYER. A player who plays a BOOK GAME. "The book player is a safe partner, but is not very dangerous as an adversary." (A. W. Drayton: *Art of Practical Whist*).

BOOKS. See BIBLIOGRAPHY.

BORDERLINE OPENING BIDS. When the decision seems to be close between opening the bidding with one of a suit and passing, a number of considerations may influence a good player. A poll of experts in BWS 2001 favored a moderate style, with a conservative style favored by nearly as many.

Position at the table
The third player can open relatively freely, with a point or two fewer than normally required. This may inconvenience the fourth player, who is likely to have the best hand at the table. The third player can open light because there is no necessity to rebid. Indeed, to do so would suggest a sound opening; hence, a desirable feature of a light opening is the ability to pass any response in comfort. A light opening should still contain acceptable defensive values. It should be based on a good suit, since lead direction is a principal reason to risk such an opening.

Vulnerability
This may sway a borderline decision, especially at matchpoints. With a 5-3-3-2 hand, for example, when the five-card suit is weak, there is a distinct possibility of playing a part-score down two to save an opposing part-score. The vulnerability would then make the difference between a good score and a bad one.

Quality and location of honors
In general, a hand with honors in its long suits is well placed in attack, while a hand with honors in its short suits is more effective in defense. This factor is allowed for to some extent in most point-count systems, which devalue singleton kings, queens, and jacks, and doubleton queens and jacks.
Consider the following two hands:

(a)	(b)
♠ 9 4 3	♠ A J 4
♥ A J 7 5 3	♥ J 7 5 3 2
♦ A Q 5 4	♦ J 5 4 3
♣ 3	♣ A

The distribution and point-count are the same, but hand (a) has a sound opening bid, and hand (b) does not — although it could represent an acceptable opening bid in

some situations. The difference lies in the location of the honor cards. Hands with supporting honors are generally stronger than hands with scattered honors.

(a)	(b)
♠ A 8 6 4	♠ A K 5 3
♥ K 5 3	♥ 6 4 2
♦ K 4	♦ 8 5
♣ Q 7 4 2	♣ K Q 4 2

More players would rather open hand (b) than hand (a).

Hands that contain PRIMARY HONORS (aces and kings) are more attractive to open than hands filled with queens and jacks. Aces and kings will win tricks on defense if the opponents compete and obtain the contract. See PRIMARY HONORS and SECONDARY HONORS.

Rebid prospects
The ease or difficulty of the rebid will often be a determining factor.

      ♠ 6
      ♥ A Q J
      ♦ K 9 4 2
      ♣ Q 8 6 4 2

If this hand is opened 1♣, the likely 1♠ response leaves opener with no attractive rebid; nor it is desirable to open 1♦ and rebid 2♣ with minimum values and weak suits. An original pass avoids these difficulties.

Majors or minors
The possession of a major suit, and particularly spades, favors an opening bid. An opening bid in a major has some obstructive value, and the prospects of outbidding the opponents and of scoring a game are slightly improved.

Playing tricks and body
The prospect of winning tricks, regardless of how many high-card points are held, is a logical argument for opening the bidding. In 1984, *The Bridge World* magazine polled experts on their standards for opening bids. Ninety percent said they would open:

      ♠ 8 6
      ♥ 7
      ♦ A Q 4 2
      ♣ A J 10 8 4 2

as dealer, neither vulnerable. Fifty-one percent would open:

      ♠ 8 6
      ♥ 7
      ♦ A J 10 3
      ♣ A J 10 8 4 2

However, experts also pay attention to body, or the presence of intermediate cards. Only 16 percent would open:

      ♠ 8 6
      ♥ 7
      ♦ A J 8 3
      ♣ A J 8 7 4 2

Presumably, for the reasons given earlier, more experts would open if the long suits were spades and hearts.

Pearson point count
This is a method used by many players to determine whether or not to open a borderline hand in fourth position. The count works this way: the number of high-card points is added to the number of spades. If the total is 14 or more, the recommendation is to open the bidding. The spade suit often is the key when bidding for pluses on partials.

BOREL. A powerful computer program designed by John Lowenthal. It was the first program to generate deals which could be specified in any desired way. This permitted hands to be printed out for partnership practice in a given area. As an example, the program could give South a 15-17 point notrump opening facing a hand with at least five spades and at least 6 points. It is also used by theorists for simulations to test the desirability of a particular bidding action, or to compare opening lead choices in a given situation. See BASE III.

BOSTON CHESS CLUB. This club, founded in 1857 in Boston MA, was the oldest club devoted to games in the United States. In 1926, bridge-playing replaced chess as the chief activity at the club. In modern times contract was played almost exclusively. When the club encountered severe difficulties in 1981 due to a split over acceptance of a player who had been expelled from ACBL for cheating, the interests in the club were sold to the Cavendish Club in Brookline MA.

BOTH VULNERABLE. A term applied to the situation when both sides are subject to larger awards and penalties. In rubber bridge, a side becomes vulnerable by winning a game during the rubber. The side that wins the second game out of three wins a 500-point bonus. In Chicago, the vulnerability situation is predetermined – both sides are vulnerable only on the fourth deal. In duplicate, once again the vulnerability is predetermined. The vulnerability is set up in 16-board segments. Both sides are vulnerable on boards 4, 7, 10 and 13. Only North-South is vulnerable on board 2, 5, 12 and 15. East-West is vulnerable on boards 3, 6, 9 and 16. Neither side is vulnerable on boards 1, 8, 11 and 14. A side that is vulnerable has to be more careful about taking chances and saves because the penalties are substantially higher. At the same time, in team play it pays to go for the game because the bonus points are substantially higher.

BOTTOM. In tournament play, the lowest score on a particular hand in the group in direct competition. It is extended, in conversation, to indicate an excruciatingly bad result.

BOUGHT. See BUY.

BOURKE RELAY. A device invented by Tim Bourke of Australia, used to clarify the auction after opener rebids his suit:

North	South
1 ♦	1 ♠
2 ♦	?

2 ♥ asks for clarification, and subsequent 3 ♦ or 3 ♠ by South is forcing. Direct bids of 3 ♦ and 3 ♠ are invitational. See *Bridge World*, July 1996.

BOX A CARD. To place a hand in a duplicate board with a card, usually not the top card, turned face up.

BRACKETED KNOCKOUT TEAMS. A method of seeding based on ability and experience is used to divide the total field into two or more groups. Sometimes the breakdown is according to the average masterpoints of all players on each team. In other cases the total of the masterpoints of the two players on the team with the most masterpoints is used as the criterion. Each bracket comprises a separate event with its own masterpoint awards. There is no interplay between brackets. The size of each bracket and the number of brackets depend on the number of teams entered. The purpose of bracketing is to establish groups within which each team is competitive. See COMPACT KNOCKOUT TEAMS, DOUBLE ELIMINATION KNOCKOUT TEAMS, HANDICAP KNOCKOUT TEAMS, MINI KNOCKOUT TEAMS, MIXED TEAMS, OPEN TEAMS, RANDOM DRAW KNOCKOUT TEAMS, TEAM GAMES, ZIP KNOCKOUT TEAMS.

BREAK. The distribution of the outstanding cards in a suit in a manner favorable to the declarer. This may imply that a suit was divided evenly or nearly so, or that an adversely held honor was positioned so that it did not develop into a winning trick. The term "break" is also used to indicate the actual distribution of the cards outstanding in the suit; or with the adjective "bad" to indicate unfavorable distribution from the declarer's standpoint.

In most contexts, "split" may be used as a synonym for "break," both as a noun and a verb: "the suit split (or broke) badly (or well)." "There was a bad split (or break) in spades." For expectations as to how a suit will break, see MATHEMATICAL TABLES 4, 4A.

BREAK ROUND. Breaks, usually five minutes, for smoking, bathroom, etc This has the added benefit of enabling the slow pairs to catch up.

BREAKAGE. A rubber bridge term for rounding off the score to the nearest 100 points.

BREAKING TIES. The breaking of ties in duplicate contests, when it is a question of the winner, is done for the purpose of awarding of trophies when it is not feasible to award duplicate prizes to the tying pairs or teams. Masterpoint awards in ACBL tournaments are awarded equally to each tying group, the amount being one-half the sum of the awards for first and second places. The main occasion for breaking of ties during the course of the competition is to determine which of two or more pairs, tied for the last qualifying position or positions, is entered into the final session. In either case, for pair events, the method is similar. All boards played by all tying groups are considered, and 1 point is awarded for an above average score and ½ point for an average score if the board or boards were not played in direct comparison. If the tying pairs are in direct comparison on any board, 1 point is awarded to the pair with the better matchpoint result on that board, ½ point if their matchpoint result is a tie. In team events, the result of the match between the two tying teams is used with Board-a-Match scoring.

In head-to-head team competition, such as knockout events, additional boards are played. In Swiss Teams, ties usually are broken by means of Swiss Points. The total of scores of all opponents are tallied for the tied teams, and the winner is the team with the highest total. Sometimes only matches played in the second half of the event are used to compute Swiss Points. The use of victory points has substantially reduced the number of ties in Swiss Team events. The method of breaking ties should be approved by the Sponsoring Organization or announced in the Conditions of Contest before being used.

Ties are now much rarer in ACBL events. Until 1992, two pairs were considered tied if the difference in score was less than half a matchpoint; two teams in board-a-match events were considered tied if the difference in score was less than a quarter of a matchpoint. The Board of Directors passed a regulation changing this so that only an exact tie is considered a tie in board-a-match team events. In pair events pairs are not considered to be tied unless the difference between their scores is less than .01 matchpoints. The same is true in individual events.

BRIDGE. A partnership game of cards derived from WHIST and played by four persons. The term can refer to three distinct games, which are listed under BRIDGE WHIST, AUCTION BRIDGE and CONTRACT.

All these games have been referred to simply as *bridge* during their periods of dominance, and the term "bridge whist" was not used when the game was in vogue (1894-1904). It was coined subsequently to distinguish the game from its successors.

The earliest printed mention of *bridge* appears to be in a pamphlet published in 1886 entitled "Biritch, or Russian Whist." Although there is no certainty that the game is Russian, the fact that it was christened "Russian Whist" gave weight to the idea that it originated in Russia. It does, as a matter of fact, bear a close resemblance to Vint, Preference and similar games; and Vint certainly is of Russian origin. See BIRITCH; HISTORY OF BRIDGE.

BRIDGE BATTLE OF THE CENTURY. See CULBERTSON-LENZ MATCH.

BRIDGE BUCKS. Special scrip produced by the ACBL for use as money at bridge tournaments and to buy bridge supplies.

It has been produced in three denominations — $1 (Charles Goren), $5 (Oswald Jacoby) and $10 (Helen Sobel Smith).

BRIDGE BUFFS' BULLETIN. A bulletin published quarterly since 1973 by Bill Sachen in the interests of bridge book collectors. New and old books and periodicals are reviewed, master lists of all known bridge and whist books have been published, and subscribers can publicize lists of books they wish to purchase or sell. See BIBLIOGRAPHY.

BRIDGE BULLETIN. See ACBL BRIDGE BULLETIN.

BRIDGE COLUMNS. Ever since the game of auction bridge became popular, newspapers and periodicals have had columns in which bridge is featured. These columns are quite varied, frequently containing local bridge news including results of local duplicate contests, anecdotes, interesting results; other columns are of a didactic nature such as quizzes and problems. Others feature outstanding and unusual bridge hands with explanations of bidding and play and sidelights on the personalities involved. Some are distributed to newspapers through national syndicates, appearing in hundreds of papers; others are produced locally for one, two or three papers.

The popularity of bridge columns is attested to by the fact that very few papers have ever dropped one permanently because every such attempt met with violent protest from the readers.

In the United States, syndicated columnists write most of the bridge columns in mainstream newspapers. The work of some syndicated columnists appears in thousands of newspapers daily. These include Omar Sharif, assisted by Tannah Hirsch and Tom Smith; Bobby Wolff, assisted by Joe Musumeci; Frank Stewart; Phillip Alder; Steve Becker, and Alan Truscott. In earlier years such outstanding bridge personalities as Charles Goren, Alfred Sheinwold, B.Jay Becker, Oswald Jacoby and James Jacoby authored syndicated columns. Other American bridge columnists include Eddie Kantar, Jared Johnson, Billy Miller, Marty Bergen, Mike Lawrence, Richard Kaplan, Barry Rigal, Henry Francis and Bernard Trippett.

Great Britain has many bridge columnists. The following write daily columns: Tony Forrester, Andrew Robson, Peter Donovan, David Bird, Elena Jeronimidis and Patrick Jourdain. Weekly columnists include Zia Mahmood, Boris Schapiro and Paul Mendelson.

Other major columnists around the world: Australia – Jim Borin, Ron Klinger, Tony Jackman, Dennis Priest, Denis Howard, Roger Penny, Philip Gue, David Lusk, David Shockman and Nigel Rosendorff. Belgium – Hans Gelder. Bermuda – David Ezekiel. Canada – Eric Kokish, Beverly Kraft, Jude Goodwin-Hanson, Audrey Grant, A. Trudelle, Jeff Blond, Dave Willis and Paul Thurston. Denmark – Peter Lund, Ib Lundby, Svend Novrup and Hans Werge. France – Guy Dupont, Michel Lebel, Jean-Paul Meyer and Herve Pacault. Italy – Dino Mazza and Fulvio Manno. Netherlands — Jan van Cleeff, Cees Sint, Kees Tammens, Toine van Hoof, Max Rebattu, Henk Willemsens, Jan Worm and Ad Oskam. Norway – Geir Helgemo, Tommy Sandsmark, Jon Sveindal, Geir Olav (Geo) Tislevoll, Knut Palmstrom, Knut Kjarnsrod, Tore Mortensen and Alf Helge Jensen. South Africa –Douglas Ettlinger. Sweden — Tommy Gullberg, Sven-Olov Flodqvist, Anders Brunzell and Anders Wirgren.

BRIDGE D'ITALIA. A beautifully produced magazine published by the Italian Bridge Federation. Edited by Riccardo Vandoni, earlier by Guido Barbone and Dino Mazza. Address: Via Ciro Menotti ^{11}/c-20129, Milan, Italy. Phone 39-2-70000483 Fax 39-2-70001398.

BRIDGE EDUCATION PROGRAM. ACBL established a Bridge Education Program in 1986. The goal of this new program was ultimately to ensure the future of the organization. Faced with an aging membership and a general decline in the popularity of bridge, the ACBL designed the Bridge Education Program (1) to teach new people to play the game, and (2) to lead these new players to ACBL membership.

ACBL's Bridge Education Program has grown into a strong arm of the organization. It supports many successful programs including: (1) The development of four textbooks and teacher manuals which compose the ACBL TEACHING SERIES and produce considerable income for the ACBL through sales and foreign translations; (2) a bridge teaching program for schools (SBLS - School Bridge Lesson Series), administered by ACBL and funded by the ACBL EDUCATIONAL FOUNDATION, which led to the development of the ACBL Junior Program and many new young ACBL members; (3) new player membership programs such as the Reduced

Price Membership program which make ACBL membership meaningful for the new player.

BRIDGE FEDERATION. NCBOs with names starting in this way are listed under the country name in section V.

BRIDGE FOR BEGINNERS. A special form of duplicate for players with little playing experience and no experience with duplicate. The play is informal, with instructors ready to offer advice at all times.

BRIDGE GOLF. See GOLF.

BRIDGE HISTORY. See HISTORY OF BRIDGE.

BRIDGE I NORGE (BIN). Independent Norwegian bridge magazine known for its bridge political editorials, founded 1975 by Sverre Frich, William B. Herseth, Leif-Erik Stabell and Tommy Sandsmark. Published by Sverre Frich 1975-85. Published and edited by Tommy Sandsmark 1985-1999. Published and edited from 1999 by Boye Brogeland. Web site: http://www.bin.no. E-Mail address: boye@bin.no

BRIDGE IN PRISON CAMPS. The absorbing character of bridge to such an extent that one is unaware of the passage of time has made it an ideal activity for prisoners of war confined in military prison camps. WORLD WAR II. Allied prisoners in German camps in Europe often played bridge, including a future Dutch star, Herman Filarski. The most remarkable games, in terms of quantity and quality, took place in Java where Dutch prisoners of the Japanese struggled with a limited supply of cards. The following astonishing deal, recalled by C. Th. de Booy, was from an eight-table duplicate.

```
Dlr: East        ♠ 10 8 7 3
Vul: Both        ♥ 9 6 4 2
                 ♦ A 8 3
                 ♣ 7 4
   ♠ 5 2                    ♠ Q
   ♥ 5                      ♥ K Q J 10 8
   ♦ 7                      ♦ K Q J 10 6 4
   ♣ K Q J 10 8 6 5 3 2     ♣ 9
                 ♠ A K J 9 6 4
                 ♥ A 7 3
                 ♦ 9 5 2
                 ♣ A
```

At some tables South played 4♠ (1♦ -Dbl; 4♣-P-4♥-4♠; all pass). In one case South won the club lead, played the trump ace and unblocked the 7 from dummy. He cashed the ♥A, led to the ♦A and ruffed a club high. West was thrown in with his ♠5 and was allowed to win two club tricks as South discarded diamonds from the dummy and hearts from the his hand, making his contract. He lost no red-suit tricks.

At another table it occurred to West to play his ♠5 under the ace, but this did not help him. South drew the remaining trump and cashed the red aces. He then threw West in with a club, again achieving a double ruff-sluff position.

The Hanoi Duplicate Club. When Lt. Col. William Means was returned to the U.S. from Vietnam, he gave an extraordinary account of how he and the prisoners on his cellblock were able to conquer boredom and other afflictions — at least part of the time — with a duplicate bridge game.

It was six years and seven months from the time his plane was shot down in July 1966 until his release with the first contingent of freed POWs in February 1973. During the last three years of that time, Means was in charge of entertainment for his cell block. He had been part of a group that played party bridge at Shaw Air Force Base in Sumter SC in 1963 and had a brief exposure to duplicate. In prison in Hanoi, one of his fellow prisoners had experienced duplicate and was able to help in setting up and scoring the games.

There were only five decks of cards. There were no duplicate boards, no traveling score sheets, no table cards, no tables. So the same five decks of cards were played at each table, then shuffled and played over again. Duplicate boards were porcelain covered metal plates that often served as the duplicate board and the traveling score. When there were no pencils for scoring on the plates, toilet paper was used for score sheets with scores entered by use of cotton-tipped bamboo sticks dipped in homemade ink. For tables they used their POW blankets, folded into the shape of a table. The hands, each wrapped with a scrap of paper showing its compass position, were stacked atop an upside down plate for passing from one "table" to another.

These duplicate contests were held regularly on Wednesday and Sunday nights and pairs stayed intact for one month. Session scores for each pair were accumulated and at the end of a month, North-South and East-West winners were declared. In lieu of masterpoints, the players put up candy and cigarettes from their personal ration and these were awarded to the winners. At the beginning of a new month partners were redrawn and a fresh series of games began.

Duplicate games of from three to six tables were a regular semi-weekly feature for the last three years before the POWs were released. Ground rules were established and administered according to bridge laws as they were remembered from the old days at Shaw, with Col. Means either directing the games himself or appointing a substitute.

Hostages played bridge too. While American hostages were being held in Iran (Nov. 4, 1979-Jan. 20, 1981) many of them learned to play bridge to help pass the time. One hostage in solitary confinement dealt out thousands of hands and got quite upset because East-West were getting most of the high cards — he identified with North-South.

BRIDGE IN PRISONS. In 1972, recognizing that bridge is such an absorbing and constructive activity that it might assist in the rehabilitation of prisoners, the ACBL Board of Directors and the ACBL Charity Foundation instituted a policy of encouraging the playing of duplicate bridge in penal institutions.

The ACBL and various member units have donated cards, boards, bridge books and other instructional materials to prison duplicate clubs. In 1973 the ACBL Charity Foundation made a $5,000 contribution to the Foundation for the Advancement of Inmate Rehabilitation and Recreation. The American Bridge Teachers' Association has assisted the program by waiving its initiation fees and dues for prison inmates who qualify as bridge teachers and pass the ABTA examination. Local clubs have encouraged their players to participate in

prison duplicate games. By early 1982 there were some two dozen duplicate clubs in penal institutions.

It is perhaps fitting that bridge be encouraged in prisons since the idea of playing with one hand exposed as the dummy may have originated in Newgate Prison, where whist was played in this manner as a three-handed game prior to 1820.

A remarkable account of bridge playing in Alcatraz was provided in 1992 by Morton Sobell of San Francisco, who was an inmate there from 1952 to 1958 as a result of his involvement in the Rosenberg espionage case.

"It was the only card game. We used a special deck of dominoes, rather than cards. They came in four colors to denote suits and the values were denoted by the number of dots: jack was 11 etc. And we had a wooden board with a ledge for holding the dominoes so that they could not be seen by others.

"Play was out in the small yard, behind the first and third base lines, so that on frequent occasions a softball would land in the middle of the table, which was a blanket-covered folding-leg bridge table cut down to about 20 inches in height. We sat on hassocks.

"With a population of 250 men it was not unusual to have 20 games going on weekends. It was a sight to behold: The men all bent over in their thin pea coats in the foggy drizzly cold, playing all weekend long, about five or six hours each day.

"Usually the men arranged the game Friday night for a 25,000 or 50,000 point series. Whoever reached the figure first won. The bets were usually the moth-eaten stale Wings cigarettes which were distributed, three packs a week to each of the men.

"I am not a card player, but for want of anything else to do I played some. What amazed me was that each night, on returning to the cellhouse, many of the men would replay each of the hands from memory, discussing the bidding and the play. These were men who had never played bridge until they came to the Rock, but obviously they had card-sense which I didn't.

"The bridge was not very sophisticated, and as I recall nobody engaged in any artificial bids. Nor was there any real intensity in the play. It was just something to pass the time." See TURGENEV.

BRIDGE JOURNAL, THE. A bimonthly magazine intended for the edification of and exchange of ideas by serious players, founded and first published in 1963 by Paul Heitner and Jeff Rubens and aimed at improving technical and mechanical aspects of the game, especially at tournament level. Some of the regular features of this publication were a *Spotlight on Bidding* match between experts, a problem forum on bidding and play, and a *Systems Corner*. When Rubens became associate editor of *The Bridge World* in 1967, the *Journal* ceased independent publication and merged with *The Bridge World*. See BIBLIOGRAPHY.

BRIDGE LAWS MAILING LIST (BLML). Mailing list on the Internet on which tournament directors around the world can discuss the Laws of Bridge. Originally started in 1997 by David Stevenson of Liverpool and six other directors who had been having e-mail conversations on the Laws, the list had grown in 1999 to more than 200 members, including some of the leading directors in the WBF and several members of the WBF Laws Committee.

BRIDGE MATHEMATICS. See MATHEMATICS OF BRIDGE.

BRIDGE MUSEUMS. The Nils Jensen Bridge Museum in Stockholm contains an outstanding collection of technical devices. E.g. dealing machines of all times, a "Bridge Rama" (the first vugraph system) from 1960, the first Bidding Box from 1963, etc. What is unique with Jensen's collection is that most objects are in working order. Bruno Sacerdotti of Milan, Italy, has a collection of approximately 1,000 trump indicators and markers. These can be seen after making an appointment to visit the shop "La Chouette" in Milan.

BRIDGE OLYMPICS. See WORLD PAR CONTESTS and Appendix IV.

BRIDGE PERSONALITY OF THE YEAR. See INTERNATIONAL BRIDGE PRESS ASSOCIATION AWARDS.

BRIDGEON. An internet bridge magazine edited by David Lusk of Adelaide, Australia. Features include bridge columns, a bidding panel, bridge news from around the world, editorials.

BRIDGE PLUS. A special form of duplicate play devised for students. It is patterned after the students' classroom experience. The games usually last two hours, allowing the students to play 10-14 hands. The games are supervised by accredited teachers.

BRIDGE PLUS MAGAZINE. Monthly bridge magazine published in Great Britain.

BRIDGE TODAY DIGEST ONLINE. A magazine sent by e-mail twice a week. Includes the bridge controversy of the day, letters and hands.

BRIDGE TODAY MAGAZINE. A bi-monthly publication, edited by Matthew and Pamela Granovetter, featuring articles about the game, tournaments, new ideas, humor and insights into the people behind the cards. Feature writers include Alvin Roth, Eddie Kantar, Martin Hoffman, Marshall Miles, Roselyn Teukolsky, Pete Kichline and Scott Cardell.

Bridge Today, Att: Griffin Enterprises,
3329 Spindletop Dr NW, Kennesaw, GA 30144-7336.
Phone: 770-529-8088. Fax: 770-529-5289.
E-mail: pam@bridgetoday.com
Website: Bridgetoday.com

BRIDGE TODAY UNIVERSITY. Offers advanced bridge classes for the tournament player and some beginner courses as well. Classes taught by Pamela and Matthew Granovetter, Larry Cohen, Marshall Miles and Larry King. These 11-week courses are by e-mail and are available through the Bridgetoday.com website.

BRIDGE TOURNAMENT FOR CLUBS IN COPENHAGEN. The world's oldest yearly bridge event, played every year since 1927. Invitations are issued to all clubs in Copenhagen, of any sort, including clubs promoting relations between countries, clubs of doctors, engineers, women's liberation, etc. Each year the tournament is

played on the second Monday of each month from November through April.

BRIDGE WHIST. The game which succeeded WHIST in popularity until AUCTION BRIDGE became the vogue early in the twentieth century. Chief differences between bridge whist and whist are the manner of selection of the trump suit, the introduction of play at notrump, the exposure of the dummy hand, and the innovation of the double and redouble calls, which could continue indefinitely. This endless redoubling feature introduced the element of gambling for very high stakes into the staid game of whist, which caused a storm of disapproval. The *Whist Reference Book*, published in 1898, called doubling "the most objectionable feature of the game." Instead of the trump suit being selected by the turn of the last card dealt, the dealer or his partner has the privilege of naming the trump suit or notrump. It was a requirement of the game that the leader ask, "Partner, may I lead?" to which his partner, if he did not plan to double, was required to respond, "Pray do." The play then proceeded as in auction or contract bridge.

The scoring is different from whist, in which each trick counted only one point. In bridge whist, the four suits and notrump have varying values. Spades are the lowest of the suits in value, followed in ascending order by clubs, diamonds, hearts, and notrump. Honors, games, rubbers, and slams are also scored. The greatest exponent of the strategy and tactics of bridge whist was Joseph B. Elwell, who wrote many books on the subject, chief among them, *Advanced Bridge*, published in 1904.

Contemporary players and writers referred to the game simply as "bridge." As the shorter term was also used later to refer to auction bridge and contract bridge, card historians invented the term "bridge whist" to identify the original form of bridge.

BRIDGE WORLD STANDARD. A consensus system developed in 1967 and periodically updated, most recently in 1994 and 2001. It is based on the majority preferences of leading experts and thousands of readers of *The Bridge World*. If the experts expressed a clear preference, their choice became the treatment or convention. If the vote was close, the poll of the readers determined what became part of the system. Because it is a consensus system, BWS is rarely used in its entirely by any partnership. However, it is invaluable when new partners are developing their bidding system. BWS interpretations, either 2001 or 1994, are included in the definitions of bids and calls throughout this book. Check the bid or call in question to determine the BWS method concerning it.

BRIDGE WORLD, THE. The oldest *continuously* published magazine dealing with contract bridge, founded and first published by Ely Culbertson in October, 1929. Published monthly, it was a comparative success from the start, and such events as the Culbertson-Lenz Match of 1931-1932 and the Culbertson-Sims match later did much to further interest.

Culbertson, who held the post of editor-in-chief until September, 1943, founded the magazine with the idea of making it a widely popular publication, and for a short time it was placed on newsstand sale. However, this proved uneconomical. It soon became what it has remained — a magazine for better than average players and a sounding board for new and improved theories.

The magazine was the first to present such ideas as the Stayman Convention, the Roth-Stone and Kaplan-Sheinwold systems, Lavinthal suit-preference signals, Unusual Notrump bids, Key Card Blackwood, many modern uses of transfers and doubles, etc. The Master Solvers Club features a panel of experts who vote for and explain why they chose what they consider to be the correct bid in a monthly series of problems. This idea has been copied by bridge publications all over the world.

Publication was taken over from Culbertson in 1943 by Albert H. Morehead, who edited it in association with Richard L. Frey, Josephine Culbertson, Alphonse Moyse Jr. and others until 1946 when it was taken over by Moyse. Moyse ran it under the Culbertson aegis until the death of the Culbertsons — December 1955 and March 1956, when he became sole owner and editor.

In November 1963 the magazine was bought by the McCall Corporation, with Moyse retained as editor. When Moyse retired in 1966, McCall's divested itself of the magazine. Edgar Kaplan and Jeff Rubens became sole owners, with Kaplan assuming the role of editor and Rubens co-editor. Much of the material that Rubens had been publishing in *Bridge Journal* appeared in *The Bridge World*, including a highly popular series of bidding matches between expert partnerships. Since Kaplan's death, Rubens has been editor.

The list of sometime editors and contributing editors includes many famous bridge writers — B. Jay Becker, Sam Fry Jr., Charles Goren, William Huske, Oswald Jacoby, Theodore Lightner, Walter Malowan, Geoffrey Mott-Smith, Alfred Sheinwold, Alexander Sobel, Alan Truscott, Bobby Wolff, Waldemar von Zedtwitz, Edwin Kantar, Eric Kokish, Kit Woolsey, Phillip Alder and others.

BRIDGE WORLD TEAM. A name applied to several teams in the early Thirties whose members were particularly associated with *The Bridge World*. The most famous of these teams comprised Ely and Josephine Culbertson, Waldemar von Zedtwitz, and Theodore Lightner. Their successes included the VANDERBILT CUP of 1930 and the first of the ANGLO-AMERICAN MATCHES.

BRIDGERAMA. The European term for BRIDGE-O-RAMA.

BRIDGETTE. A bridge game for two players invented by Prince Joli Kansil (the former Joel D. Gaines), with the assistance of Waldemar von Zedtwitz. It is played with a 55-card deck — the standard pack plus three extra cards called *colons*. The colons are used in the play to force the opponent to discontinue the suit he is leading. In an advanced version of Bridgette, *cuebids* are used to elicit specific information about the opponent's distribution.

BRIDGE-O-RAMA. A method of displaying bridge competition to a large audience. The technique was devised in Italy and first used in the 1958 Bermuda Bowl. The forerunner of this development was used in the Thirties when an electric display board was used in ex-

hibitions in department stores. The features of Bridge-O-Rama include a large display board on which the hands can be placed in frames, so that the representations of the actual cards are lighted, along with devices for indicating the winning card, tricks won by declarer or defender, the contract and other information. In addition to the display board there is a console, or bank of light switches, by which the lights of the display board are controlled. Explanations and comments on the bidding and play are provided by an expert panel.

The largest audience for a Bridge-O-Rama showing was the crowd of 1,500 that attended the finals of the 1964 Olympiad in the Hotel Americana in New York City. The size of the crowd made necessary the simultaneous vugraph screening of the hands for spectators too far away to see the Bridge-O-Rama board.

Because setting up the deals for Bridge-O-Rama slowed up the play and required a large staff, exhibitions since the 1971 Bermuda Bowl in Taiwan have been almost exclusively by means of vugraph. Usually the Vugraph show also features closed circuit television of the play in the open room, often with a camera focused on each of the players. See VUGRAPH.

BRILLIANCY. Exceptional play or defense that qualifies the player for honor awards. See BOLS BRILLIANCY AWARDS.

BRING IN. To establish a suit and make effective use of the established winners. The ability to bring in a suit may be affected by considerations of ENTRIES, TEMPO, CONTROLS, or DUCKING, or by the SUIT COMBINATION in the suit being established.

BRITISH BRIDGE. Direct methods of bidding advocated in the Thirties by a group of English players headed by Walter Buller and Ewart Kempson, as opposed to the approach-forcing methods popularized by Ely Culbertson.

BRITISH BRIDGE WORLD. An English monthly publication (1932-1939) founded by Hubert Phillips. It was revived in 1956 as a successor to the *Contract Bridge Journal*, and continued until 1964 when it merged with *Bridge Magazine*. See BIBLIOGRAPHY.

BRITISH PARLIAMENT MATCHES. Matches between the House of Commons and the House of Lords held annually since 1975. This unique event was founded by Rixi Markus with the assistance of the Right Honourable Harold Lever, MP, and is staged by *The Guardian*, national daily newspaper for which Markus was bridge editor. The matches are played under the conditions of rubber duplicate: that is, the same hands are played at each of the two tables in the match but the scoring is rubber-bridge scoring.

BROKEN SEQUENCE. Combination of at least three high cards which has at least two of the cards in sequence. Some authorities say that the non-touching honor must be the highest honor of the sequence (A-Q-J, K-J-10, Q-10-9). They say that combinations where the non-touching honor is below the other honors (A-K-J, K-Q-10, etc.) is an INTERIOR SEQUENCE. However, many other authorities claim that Broken Sequence applies to both kinds of sequences.

BROKEN SUIT. A suit containing no honor cards in sequence.

BROMAD. (Bergen Raises Over a Major-suit After a Double). Bromad is designed to identify the precise degree of major suit fit in competitive auctions. When one of a major is doubled, redouble denies three trumps in principle, while 2♣ shows a constructive raise, 2♦ shows a limit raise with three trumps, a simple raise is preemptive, and jumps are normal Bergen raises with four trumps. 2NT can be used to show a preempt in one minor.

An alternative approach is to use 2♣ and 3♦ as both slightly less strong than limit raises with three and four trumps respectively, and to retain 2NT as the limit raise. Now 2♦ and 3♣ are natural and non-forcing.

BROZEL. Developed by Bernard Zeller as a defense against an opposing 1NT opening, and may be used either in the direct or balancing position.

A double shows a one-suited hand. If partner does not wish to defend, he bids 2♣ and passes the doubler's next bid. All overcalls on the two-level show two suits as follows:

2 ♣	shows hearts and clubs
2 ♦	shows hearts and diamonds
2 ♥	shows hearts and spades
2 ♠	shows spades and a minor
2NT	shows clubs and diamonds

An overcall at the three-level shows a singleton or void in the bid suit and support for the other three suits.

After a weak response to a 1NT opening, a double again describes a one-suited hand. Without suitable defense, partner bids the next higher-ranking suit, then passes the doubler's next bid. All simple overcalls shows the bid suit and the next higher-ranking unbid suit. 2NT is a takeout for the three unbid suits, and a cuebid is a stronger takeout, implying game possibilities.

For alternative defensive conventions against notrump openings, see DEFENSE TO ONE NOTRUMP.

BUENOS AIRES AFFAIR. In 1965, the international bridge world was rocked by a widely publicized charge that Terence Reese and Boris Schapiro, representing Great Britain in the Bermuda Bowl at Buenos Aires, Argentina, had transmitted information about the heart suit by finger signals.

The original observations were made by B. Jay Becker and Dorothy Hayden, members of the North American team, and Alan Truscott, bridge editor for *The New York Times*. They testified that the British pair were observed to be holding their cards in a varying manner, with a different number of fingers, either closed or spread, showing at the back of their hands from deal to deal.

After comparing findings, it was suggested that Reese and Schapiro were signaling the number of hearts they held (two fingers for two or five hearts, depending on whether the fingers were closed or spread, three fingers for three or six hearts, and so forth). The evidence was presented to John Gerber (npc, North American team), who in turn brought it to the attention of Ralph Swimer (npc, British team) and Geoffrey Butler, chairman of the British Bridge League and member of the World Bridge Federation Executive Committee and chairman of its Appeals Committee. After an independent investigation, Butler called a meeting of the Appeals Committee to present his observations, to study the evidence further and to inform Reese

and Schapiro of the charges against them. Both denied the allegations. The matter was then brought to the attention of the WBF Executive Committee. On the last day of the World Championship, by a vote of 10-0 (Carl'Alberto Perroux abstaining, one absentee), the Executive Committee found Reese and Schapiro guilty of using illegal signals, and the evidence was turned over to the British Bridge League for final disposition. Swimer conceded the Great Britain-Argentine match, which Great Britain had won 380-184, and the Great Britain-North American match, in which Great Britain was leading 288-242 with twenty boards to play.

After receiving the WBF report, the British Bridge League set up an independent inquiry to study the charges, headed by Sir John Foster, Queens Counsel, and General Lord Bourne, assisted on the technical aspects of the case by Alan Hiron and Tony Priday. The Foster report, released after more than ten months' consideration, found Reese and Schapiro "not guilty" of the cheating allegation. In the opinion of Sir John Foster, who required the highest standard of proof, the technical evidence appeared to indicate that Reese and Schapiro had not profited in the bidding or play from a foreknowledge of the heart suit, and thus failed to substantiate the testimony of the prosecution's witnesses.

After learning of this verdict, which was released after the 1966 WBF meeting, WBF President Charles Solomon stated, "It is doubtful that the WBF can accept the decision of the London hearing . . ." His position was that the WBF had rendered the verdict in Buenos Aires and had submitted its report to the British Bridge League to determine what punitive action would be taken.

At its annual meeting in 1967, the WBF Executive Committee reaffirmed its earlier guilty verdict and passed a resolution that the chairman of the Credentials Committee refer applications of any player found guilty of irregular practices in WBF-sponsored tournaments to the Executive Council. The implication was that applications by Reese and Schapiro would not be accepted, and the implication became fact in 1968 when the Executive Council so answered a query from the British Bridge League concerning possible entry of Reese and Schapiro in the 1968 World Team Olympiad. As a result, the British Bridge League elected not to participate in the Olympiad.

In 1968, the Executive Council restored Reese and Schapiro to good standing on the ground that the three-year ban that had been in effect since 1965 constituted adequate punishment.

The repercussions of the episode during the years of controversy spanned the American and European continents. An article by Rixi Markus defending Reese that appeared in *The Bridge World* resulted in a libel suit by Swimer, and the reluctance of Reese and Swimer to play against each other created problems in the 1968 British Team Trials. The evidence for both sides was presented in books by two of the controversy's leading figures: Reese's *Story of an Accusation* and Truscott's *The Great Bridge Scandal*. See BERMUDA INCIDENT, CHEATING, CHEATING ACCUSATIONS, HOUSTON AFFAIR, SION-COKIN AFFAIR.

BULLETIN. See DAILY BULLETIN, BRIDGE BULLETIN.

BUMBLEDOG AND BUMBLEPUPPY. Humorous terms applied to bad players or bad play in whist.

BUMP MITCHELL. An adaptation of the MITCHELL MOVEMENT invented by Forrest Sharpe for the accommodation of a half table. The game is set up as if there were no half table (extra pair) and boards are distributed to all the full tables only. If the number of full tables is even, a skip at the normal time will be necessary.

The extra pair plays North-South, sitting out the first round and taking the highest North-South number. At round two this pair replaces the North-South pair at Table 1 and stays at Table 1 for the rest of the session. The North-South pair originally at Table 1 sits out the second round and bumps the North-South pair originally at Table 2 on the third round, remaining at Table 2 for the rest of the session. In like fashion pair 2 bumps pair 3, pair 3 bumps pair 4, etc., until the end of the session. It is convenient and logical, but not necessary, to actually change the number of a table to match the number of the North-South pair that is sitting there. It also is not necessary for the pair that was sitting out to physically supplant another pair. The pair with the highest North-South number keeps their own table.

At round 2 the North-South pair at Table 1 sit with no opponents and no boards (as if they did not exist). On round 3 the North-South pair at Table 2 sit with no opponents and no boards, etc.

The pairs that sit out must be factored up the proper amount so that their scores may be compared with those of the ones who did not sit out.

All boards are in play every round, so all have the same matchpoint top, no matter how many rounds are played. A complete movement is not required.

The total number of rounds possible is one fewer than the number of full tables. For example: nine rounds are possible with $10^1/_2$ tables.

This movement is not acceptable if $7^1/_2$, $9^1/_2$ or $13^1/_2$ tables are in play and one desires to play seven rounds of four boards, nine rounds of three boards and 13 rounds of two boards, respectively. Now rarely used.

BURNER. A colloquialism used in bridge tournaments to refer to a photocopy of raw scores (i.e., not matchpointed) made available to players a few minutes after the end of a session or the machine used to produce it. Now made obsolete by computer scoring.

BUSINESS DOUBLE. See PENALTY DOUBLE.

BUSINESS PASS. See PENALTY PASS.

BUST. Bridge slang term for a seemingly valueless hand. See YARBOROUGH.

BUSY CARD AND IDLE CARD. These terms were originated by Ely Culbertson, and used in his *Red Book on Play* (see BIBLIOGRAPHY). His definitions are:

A busy card is one which will have a definite duty in the play of the hand, either as a trick winner or as a guard to a card which will or may eventually win a trick. The idle cards have no such function; they serve the holder only in that he may discard them and save his busy cards for a better purpose.

If a suit is distributed as shown in the diagram, then West's small card is idle, but both the king and queen are busy.

```
              A J 10
    K Q x              x x x x
              x x x
```

The terms arise in connection with squeeze play, whose object is to force the discard of a busy card by an opponent.

BUTCHER. Colloquialism to indicate a bad misplay: "He butchered the hand." An alternative term is 'MISERE'.

BUTLER SCORING. See IMP PAIR SCORING.

BUY. In a competitive auction, to make a bid that the opponents do not contest. "He bought it for three hearts."

BWS. See BRIDGE WORLD STANDARD.

BYE. (1) In team-of-four competition, an advance to a later round without the necessity of winning or playing a match. This occurs at some point in the play in order to reduce the field to a power of two.

(2) In pair contests, a BYESTAND is used as a temporary resting place for boards not in play during a particular round.

(3) In pair matches, when an uneven number of pairs compete, there is one table, a bye table, at which traveling pairs find no opponents, or where a stationary pair has no opponents come to them.

(4) A slang term, unsanctioned by law, for "I pass". Sometimes also "Bye me," or "I go bye". Such terms are to be avoided since, unless they are always used, they infringe the warning against different designations for the same call.

BYESTAND. A stand (it may be a chair or small side table) where one or more sets of boards rest during rounds in which they are not in play. The byestand is usually placed in such position that the boards will be conveniently available to the table where they will be in play next.

The most common use of a byestand is described under MITCHELL MOVEMENT. A pamphlet (available on request from the ACBL office) instructs the tournament director what procedure to follow to correct the omission or misplacement of the byestand in a Mitchell movement. The use of a byestand in a Mitchell game is necessary only when it is desired to play all the boards. (See EIGHT TABLES; TWELVE TABLES.) If one or more sets of boards are not to be played, the SKIP MOVEMENT eliminates the need for the byestand.

Byestands also are common in all HOWELL and THREE-QUARTER movements as well as some team movements.

BYLAWS. Regulations by which national organizations, clubs and other bridge entities govern their membership and activities.

BYLAWS OF THE ACBL. The ACBL Bylaws govern principally such matters as elections; meetings; powers of the Board of Directors, Board of Governors and officers; structure; membership; standing and special committees, and the Laws Commission. With respect to membership in the ACBL, the Bylaws provide as follows:

Any person is eligible for membership in the ACBL. There shall be the following categories of membership:

1. *Member.*

Upon application and payment of annual dues as established by the Board of Directors, an applicant shall become and remain a member unless:

a. The member has failed to pay dues in accordance with regulations established by the Board of Directors; or

b. The member has been censured or expelled in accordance with regulations established by the Board of Directors; or

c. The member has been reclassified as an honorary or life member.

2. *Life Member.*

A member who meets the qualifications and requirements as established by the Board of Directors shall be reclassified as a life member upon ratification by a majority vote of the Board of Governors. Life members shall not be required to pay dues but may be required, in order to maintain an active status and receive services from the ACBL, to pay such annual service charges as may be established by the Board of Directors.

3. *Honorary Member.*

The Board of Directors may elect honorary members according to guidelines adopted by the Board of Directors. Honorary members shall be exempt from the payment of dues or annual service charges, shall retain an active status and shall receive services from the ACBL.

Any member, including a life member, shall be a member of the Unit within whose jurisdiction he or she resides unless there are District regulations creating exceptions. Any member or life member of the ACBL may be censured, suspended, expelled or otherwise disciplined in accordance with regulations established by the Board of Directors. Every member in each category of membership shall be subject to regulations established by the Board of Directors establishing binding and compulsory arbitration to settle disputes involving the ACBL and its members.

BYZANTINE BLACKWOOD. A complex variation of the 4NT ace-asking convention, devised by J.C.H.Marx of Great Britain, in which the responses are given in the style of ROMAN BLACKWOOD and may be based on a key-suit king instead of one of the aces normally shown. Key suits include the trump suit, any genuine side suit that has been bid and supported, and any suit bid by a player whose partner's first bid was in notrump. Byzantine is not used when there are more than two key suits. If there is only one key suit, a king of a half-key suit, i.e., a genuine suit that has been bid but not supported, may be shown.

For example, when there is only one key suit, a Byzantine 5♣ response shows no aces, or three aces, or two aces plus the key-suit king.

C

CAB. A British system of bidding that incorporates some features of STANDARD AMERICAN: a strong 1NT opening with GLADIATOR responses (but responses of 2♦, 2♥ and 2♠ are constructive though non-forcing); forcing jump raises and 2NT response (except in compe-

tition); a conventional 2♣ opening with ace-showing responses; ACOL TWO-BIDS; opening bids of 3♣ and 3♦ that suggest a solid or nearly solid suit and invite 3NT. The initials CAB stand for Two Clubs, Ace-asking and Blackwood. Leslie Dodds was the principal contributor to the development of CAB, now virtually obsolete.

CAC or CACBF. See CENTRAL AMERICAN AND CARIBBEAN BRIDGE FEDERATION.

CADDY. An assistant at a bridge tournament. Duties of the caddy are to dress the tables (putting pickup slips, pencils and private scores on the tables); picking up the completed entry blanks and score tickets; assembling the boards at the conclusion of play, and otherwise being useful. In pair events or team events scored by BOARD-A-MATCH, the caddy picks up the scoreslips at the completion of each round and assists the scorer in checking doubtful slips. In a KNOCKOUT TOURNAMENT or a team game with a SWISS MOVEMENT there are no scoreslips to be picked up, and the caddy's chief duty during the session is to transport the boards played at one table of each match to the other table of the same match.

Assignment of caddies to work various sessions of a duplicate tournament is the responsibility of the local tournament committee. Generally selection is made from interested high-school boys and girls. Some caddies become expert players.

CALCUTTA. A duplicate tournament with a feature making possible a fair-sized financial gain to any player or other participant. After the entries have been made, an auction is held at which players, spectators and others bid for and buy the contesting pairs. The total of the moneys bid for the players is put into a pool which is distributed to the purchasers of the winning entries. In addition, cash prizes or other worthwhile stimuli are provided so that the contestants themselves have a stake in the results. It is usually a proviso that a contestant may purchase from the buyer up to a 50% interest in his own partnership at the original price.

The most famous calcutta, attracting many of the world's best players, is that staged each May in Las Vegas by New York's Cavendish Club, and continued after that famous body closed its doors in 1991. See CAVENDISH.

Because of the gambling feature involved in the auctioning of the participants, the AMERICAN CONTRACT BRIDGE LEAGUE does not sanction calcuttas and masterpoints are not awarded. However, ACBL directors are permitted to run these tournaments. See GAMBLING AT BRIDGE.

CALIFORNIA CUEBID. See WESTERN CUEBIDS; CUEBIDS IN OPPONENT'S SUIT.

CALIFORNIA SCORING. A method of computing the East-West pairs' matchpoint score by assigning them the same score as their North-South opponents, rather than the reciprocal. Using this method the East-West pair with the lowest score is the winner. Alternatively, each East-West score may be subtracted from the maximum possible matchpoint total to produce the same score that would have been achieved using regular matchpoint scoring methods. California Scoring derived its name from its popularity primarily in California and other Western clubs. Computer scoring has made it obsolete. See TRAVELING SCORESLIP.

CALL. Any bid, double, redouble or pass. See LAWS.

CALL AFTER THE FINAL PASS. See LAWS (Law 35).

CALL IN ROTATION AFTER AN ILLEGAL CALL. See LAWS (Law 34).

CALL OUT OF TURN. See LAWS (Laws 28-35).

CALLING A CARD OR A SUIT. The privilege of compelling an opponent to lead or play a certain card or a certain suit, to play his highest or lowest, or to win or lose a trick. See LAWS (Laws 26, 27c, 30b, 31b, 32, 36a, 37, 38, 39b, 50, 52, 52, 55b, 56, 57, 73). See LAWS OF DUPLICATE (Laws 46, 51).

CAMROSE TROPHY. The Home International series competed for annually among England, Scotland, Wales and Southern Ireland and Northern Ireland under the auspices of the BRITISH BRIDGE LEAGUE. Southern Ireland withdrew from the series in 1951 and rejoined in 1999. The trophy was presented by Lord Camrose in 1936 and play began in 1937, with a wartime break 1939-45. The 50th series was in 1993. As of 1999, England had won 41 times and Scotland 12 times. These two countries tied twice. Ireland won in 2000. The Junior Camrose (under 25) has been regularly won by England. The Peggy Bayer (under 20) has usually been won by England, but Scotland won in 1995 and 1997. For results, see Appendix IV.

CANADIAN BRIDGE FEDERATION. Although Canada is part of the American Contract Bridge League, the nation also has its own national contract bridge organization, the Canadian Bridge Federation (CBF). The CBF deals with its own national championships, its own charity organization and representation in world championships. The CBF was founded in 1967 in order to promote a national identity and union of Canadian players. It stages annual open and women's championships. The CBF determines which teams will represent Canada in the World Olympiads. It also determines the teams that compete with Mexico and Bermuda in odd-numbered years to decide which of the three countries will compete in Bermuda Bowl and Venice Cup world competition. The CBF publishes a magazine, the *Canadian Bridge Digest*, and has its own charity organization, the Canadian Charitable Fund.

CANADIAN NATIONAL TEAMS. Until 1980 teams representing Canada competed in the Grand National Teams. In 1980 Canada separated from the Grand National Teams and staged its own national championship, a practice that has continued since that time. The format calls for grass-roots contests at clubs in the fall, with succeeding qualifications leading to the national finals. The winning team qualifies to represent Canada in the World Team Olympiad in Olympic years and in the tri-country playoffs for a berth in the Bermuda Bowl with Bermuda and Mexico in odd-numbered years. In the fourth year the winners represent Canada in the Rosenblum Teams.

As a result of a controversial regulation passed by the World Bridge Federation Executive Council, there was no tri-country playoff for a berth in the 2001 Bermuda Bowl. To be eligible a country had to finish in the top half of the standings in the 2000 World Team Olympiad. Canada, Mexico and Bermuda all failed to finish in the top half.

See Appendix I for results.

CANAPÉ. A bidding method in which the long suit is usually bid on the second round. This was developed by Pierre Albarran (1894-1960) in France, where it has had a considerable following. By contrast, standard methods are described in France as la longue d'abord (long suit first).

Canapé has influenced Italian bidding theory; it is incorporated in both the ROMAN and BLUE TEAM CLUB systems, and in offspring systems such as the ORANGE CLUB and the SIMPLIFIED CLUB, which is a total canapé system.

Albarran's definition of canapé was: "With a two-suited hand of more than minimum strength, the higher-ranking suit must be bid on the first round if it has four cards, and on the second round if it has more than four cards."

Four-card major suits are usually bid ahead of any minor suit; five-card major suits are bid on the first round if the hand is a minimum. Normal reverse sequences are inverted (inversé):

    ♠ A Q 10 x x
    ♥ K Q x x
    ♦ K x
    ♣ x x

Using canapé, the opening bid is 1♥, and 2♠ is bid on the next round. A heart preference is highly improbable, so the canapé player can stay safely at the level of two.

Admittedly canapé is in difficulty with certain minimum hands, such as those with four spades and five clubs. 1♠ followed by 3♣ would exaggerate the strength, and 1♣ followed by 1♠ would imply a five-card spade suit.

A modified version called "canapé tendency" (tendance canapé) was used successfully in international competition by Pierre Jaïs and Roger Trézel. They bid minimum hands in normal fashion, but adopt the canapé principle for hands of maximum strength and some hands of intermediate strength.

CANARY CLUB. An artificial bidding system, now obsolete, developed in 1964 by John Lowenthal and Paul Heitner. The name of the system is derived from its chief features: Canapé, Relay and 1♣ forcing.

CANNIBAL SQUEEZE. See SUICIDE SQUEEZE.

CANSINO. A defense to 1NT in which an overcall of 2♣ shows clubs and two other suits, and 2♦ shows both majors. See DEFENSE TO ONE NOTRUMP.

CAP GEMINI WORLD TOP TOURNAMENT. Played annually in The Hague, Netherlands, the invitational event routinely has one of the strongest fields in international competition.

The tournament debuted in 1987 as the Staten Bank Invitational. It underwent two name changes before Cap Gemini, a computer company, took on sponsorship in

1991 after co-sponsoring the tournament with Staten Bank the year before.

In the tournament, 16 pairs play 15 head-to-head matches in round-robin style. Scoring originally was by IMPs converted to Victory Points. In later tournaments, scoring was by IMPs compared to a datum derived from scores across the field. See Appendix IV.

CAP VOLMAC WORLD TOP TOURNAMENT. See CAP GEMINI WORLD TOP TOURNAMENT. See Appendix IV for results.

CAPPELLETTI. (Also called HAMILTON, and in Britain, POTTAGE). A defense against a 1NT opening devised by Michael Cappelletti. Over an opponent's 1NT opening, in either the direct or balancing seat, 2NT shows the minors; 2♥/2♠ shows that suit plus a minor; 2♦ shows both majors; 2♣ shows any one-suited hand. Double is penalty-oriented. This was the BWS 1994 expert consensus.

All these overcalls suggest fewer than 15 good points; better hands usually double, although a 2NT overcall is available to show a strong distributional hand. Overcalls at the three level or higher are natural.

The structure may be played soundly or aggressively.

A conservative pair would probably require a good six-card suit or better to bid 2♣, 5-5 in the majors to bid 2♦, and a five-card major to overcall in a major, all with substantial high-card values. Active pairs may frequently bid 2♦ with 4-4 in the majors, 2♥/2♠ with any four-card major and a five-card minor, and 2♣ on hands that would have opened a weak two-bid (including good five-card suits).

Responses (in an active style) are:

(i) After 2♣: Pass, possible, with at least six clubs; 2♦, the normal response, allowing the 2♣ bidder to pass or bid his suit; 2♥/2♠, possible, with at least a strong five-card suit; 2NT: 11 or more points, plus support for all four suits. The 2♣ bidder is invited to bid game with a maximum.

(ii) After 2♦: Pass, requires at least six strong diamonds; 2♥/2♠ choice of suit, unconstructive; 2NT, asks for the 2♦ bidder's better minor; 3♣, requires at least six strong clubs; 3♥/3♠: invitational, promising four or more trumps. It is possible, however, to play this bid as preemptive.

(iii) After 2♥/2♠: New suit, natural, non-forcing; Raise, 7 to 10 points; 2NT, asks for the minor, but if followed by three of the major, promises 10 to 12 points and invites game.

After 1NT-2♣-Dbl, a redouble shows 7 or more high-card points with some support for all suits; it invites the 2♣ bidder to compete to the three-level.

It is also possible to play Cappelletti after 1NT overcalls of partner's minor-suit opening. See DEFENSE TO ONE NOTRUMP; DONT, HAMILTON, POTTAGE TRANSFER OVERCALLS OF ONE NOTRUMP.

CAPPELLETTI AFTER THE OPPONENTS' DOUBLE OF ONE OF A MAJOR. The concept of using transfers in response to an opening of one of a major, after a double by responder's RHO. It was invented approximately simultaneously by Eric Rodwell and Mike Cappelletti Sr. The methods set out by the former extend to interference over a Precision 1♦ opening bid.

The general philosophy is that all actions by responder of 1NT or higher are transfers. Transfers into a new suit at the two-level show either a single-suited hand, or act as a lead-director with at least secondary support of partner's major. Responder has both a constructive and a destructive raise to two of partner's major. The direct raise is destructive (generally less than 6 HCP) as is the jump raise, while the transfer into partner's suit is generally 7-9 HCP with typically exactly three-card support. Jumps by responder are most usefully played as fit-showing (four or more cards in support of partner with a good second suit) but an alternative treatment of preemptive jumps is also playable. So after the sequence:

1♥   Dbl

1♠ is natural, 1NT transfers to clubs, 2♣ transfers to diamonds, 2♦ and 2♥ are both heart raises, 2♠ 3♣ and 3♦ are fit-showing jumps, 3♥ is a preemptive heart raise, and 2NT shows a limit raise or better, generally in a balanced hand.

Opener tends to complete the transfer unless very unsuitable for play in that suit; responder will then pass with the single-suited hand and make a natural descriptive continuation with any other hand-type.

CAPPELLETTI CUEBIDS. When the opponents have bid two suits, the lower-level cuebid shows both unbid suits with greater length in the lower-ranking suit. The higher-level cuebid shows both unbid suits with greater length in the higher-ranking suit.

CAPTAIN. Teams representing major bridge countries in international play normally have a nonplaying captain (although Great Britain won three successive European Championships 1948-50 with Maurice Harrison-Gray as playing captain). The captain's chief function is to decide who shall play at each stage in the contest, taking into account such factors as the ability and stamina of the players at his command, the caliber of the opposition, the closed and open room, and VUGRAPH. In addition, the captain represents the team in discussions relating to the conditions of play, and in protests and appeals. He also acts as the team's spokesman on all social occasions.

The importance of the captain's role has been recognized in recent years, and it is usual for a World Championship contestant to appoint an experienced player whose decisions will be respected and accepted by the players in his charge. At one time the president of the ACBL was automatically designated nonplaying captain of its international team, but this practice was discontinued after 1961.

With the inception of the playoff method of ACBL selection from the winners of the four major team championships, each team was required to select a nonplaying captain from a panel of eligible captains selected by the ACBL Board of Directors, and the captain of the winning team was virtually an automatic selection for the World Championship, although subject to Board confirmation.

Carl'Alberto Perroux, of Italy, who made a considerable contribution to the remarkable series of victories compiled by the BLUE TEAM, earned a reputation as one of the most powerful and successful nonplaying captains in the history of bridge.

Dan Morse has been a highly successful captain of American teams. He was the American captain when North America finally ended Italy's Blue Team reign in the Bermuda Bowl in 1976. He also was captain of the United States team in 1988 when the U.S. won the World Team Olympiad for the first time.

Alfred Sheinwold also was an active captain for North America. He was catain of the American team in the 1975 Bermuda Bowl when the foot-tapping incident took place. Rather than have his team play against the foot-tappers, who were allowed to continue playing, Sheinwold withdrew his team from the competition. However, the ACBL tournament committee on hand at the tournament overruled him and sent the American team back into action. See BERMUDA INCIDENT.

CAPTAINCY. The control of the auction assumed by one partner in certain situations. The classical approach to constructive bidding is that each partner fully describes his hand; then the two partners act together to choose a contract.

West	East
1♠	2♥
3♣	3♠
4♦	4♥
4♠	5♣
6♠	

The above auction is a dialogue between equals: both players participate in the search for the best contract; both can use their judgment.

In many auctions, however, one player's bidding narrowly defines his strength and suggests a trump suit (or notrump); he is said to limit his hand. The basis of the limit approach is that the auction is easier if one player limits his hand quickly. His partner then becomes captain of the partnership and must place the contract at the proper level.

West	North	East	South
3♠	4♥	Dbl	Pass
4♠			

West has violated captaincy; his descriptive 3♠ opening put East in charge.

In Blackwood auctions the 4NT bidder is captain, and his partner merely follows instructions in making the agreed responses. But captaincy may shift from one partner to another in a single auction. For example, if the Blackwood bidder continues with 5NT, indicating his side's possession of all the aces, in some circumstances responder may bid a grand slam.

The idea of captaincy is best seen in relay systems: one player makes meaningless bids (relays) to obtain information about his partner's strength and distribution; he then places the contract all by himself.

The term also applies to the player in charge of the affairs of a team. The captain can be either a player or a non-player. The captain makes the key decisions for his team — who will sit out, who will play with whom, what table which players will sit at, whether to appeal a director's decision, etc.

CARD COMBINATIONS. See SUIT COMBINATIONS.

CARD COMMITTEE. In private clubs it is customary that a committee of two or more members is charged with the responsibility of order and decorum in the club's card room. Referred to this committee are disputes which arise in the play that cannot be settled by reference to the rules of the game in question. Also under the juris-

diction of this committee come such questions as what games will be permitted, rules of procedure for forming tables, maximum stakes and unpaid wagers. With respect to contract bridge tournaments, see COMMITTEE.

CARD, DAMAGED OR MARKED. See DAMAGED CARD.

CARD FEE. See ENTRIES.

CARD PLAYED. See PLAYED CARD.

CARD READING. Drawing correct inferences about the nature of the opponent's holdings and distribution from information disclosed by the auction and the fall of the cards.

♠ A 8
♥ K Q J 7 6
♦ J 8 7
♣ 6 5 3

♠ Q J 10 4 3 2
♥ A 5 3
♦ A K
♣ 10 7

South plays in 4♠ after East has opened the bidding with 1♣. West leads the ♣2 and East wins with the ace, and shifts to the ♥9. A seemingly secure contract is now in some jeopardy. East clearly has a singleton heart, and very likely three trumps including the king. Obviously his play is to win the second trump lead and put partner in with a club honor for a heart ruff. Declarer can foil this defense by playing East for the ♦Q (not unlikely on the bidding). Winning the heart in dummy, he plays off the ♦A-K before crossing to the ♠A. The ♦J is led from dummy, East covering and South discarding his last club, thus effectively severing communication between the defenders. The complete deal:

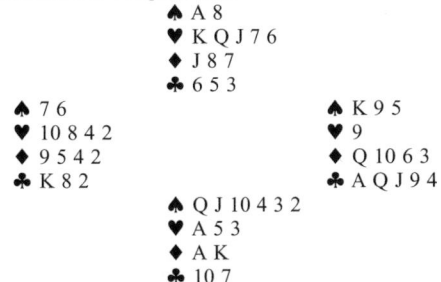

```
                ♠ A 8
                ♥ K Q J 7 6
                ♦ J 8 7
                ♣ 6 5 3
  ♠ 7 6                        ♠ K 9 5
  ♥ 10 8 4 2                   ♥ 9
  ♦ 9 5 4 2                    ♦ Q 10 6 3
  ♣ K 8 2                      ♣ A Q J 9 4
                ♠ Q J 10 4 3 2
                ♥ A 5 3
                ♦ A K
                ♣ 10 7
```

Combining accurate card-reading with counting often provides valuable clues for the defense. Careful examination of the evidence provided East with the opportunity to defeat the contract on this hand:

```
                ♠ 10 8 6 2
                ♥ K 6 5
                ♦ Q 5
                ♣ A J 7 6
  ♠ J 7 4 3                    ♠ A Q 9 5
  ♥ Q 7 4 2                    ♥ J 10
  ♦ 9 6 3 2                    ♦ A 8 7
  ♣ 8                          ♣ Q 5 4 3
                ♠ K
                ♥ A 9 8 3
                ♦ K J 10 4
                ♣ K 10 9 2
```

The bidding has been:

South	North
1♣	1♠
1NT	2NT
3NT	

West leads the ♥2, and East's 10 loses to declarer's ace. A club is led to dummy's ace, and the jack run, West discarding the ♦2. The ♦Q is taken by East, and he reviews the situation.

He knows that South has four club tricks, and at least two in hearts. What about the diamonds? West's diamond discard on the second club is revealing: he is unlikely to have parted with one from 10-x-x-x or J-x-x-x. Could West have started with five diamonds? Not very likely, for in that case he might have led one. South can therefore be assumed to have three diamond tricks, enough for his contract, should he regain the lead. The only hope for the defense seems to lie in spades. If East's estimate of the situation is correct, then West had started with a 4-4-4-1 distribution, marking declarer with a singleton spade — very likely the king, considering his bidding. Declarer's play of the club suit seems to bear this out; having a two-way finesse, he chose to take it into the hand that was less likely to shift to spades, if it lost. On this reasoning East lays down the ♠A, dropping declarer's king, and continues with a small card to his partner's jack. A third round of spades permits East to score the Q-9 to defeat the contract. Declarer would have been better placed by leading a diamond to the queen at trick 2. Now East would not have enough information to find the ♠A shift. See also COUNTING THE HAND and INFERENCE.

For full discussions of card reading, see: *Card Reading* by Eric Jannersten; *The Art of Card Reading at Bridge* by Fred Karpin; *Bridge Logic* by Hugh Kelsey; *All 52 Cards* by Marshall Miles; *How To Read Your Opponent's Cards* by Mike Lawrence.

CARD SENSE. A special aptitude for playing card games, specifically (in this context) bridge.

Until psychological research and Army selection procedures satisfactorily demonstrated the existence of special aptitudes, there was considerable controversy about whether card sense existed.

Although he changed his mind later, Ely Culbertson was originally among the skeptics, commenting as follows: "One hears a good deal about that elusive something called 'card sense.' It is spoken of as though it were some mysterious, deeply inborn faculty which cannot be taught. Lack of 'card sense' is always said to be the great bugaboo blocking the prospective bridge player's path to improvement. As a matter of fact, 'card sense' - whatever those who use the term mean - is a certain facility at cards shown by some players and entirely lacking in others."

Among good bridge players, it is virtually impossible to distinguish between what is the result of card sense and what is the result of experience. Card sense is more easily distinguishable among beginners, where it appears to be a compound of various elements: intelligence, interest and youth.

There is probably a high correlation between ability to learn the elements of bridge and mathematical aptitude, and a somewhat lower correlation with intelligence quotient. See also INTUITION, ASSUMPTIONS, RECTIFYING THE COURT.

CARDING AGREEMENTS. See COUNT, DISCARD-ING, FOSTER ECHO, HIGH-LOW, LENGTH SIG-NAL, ODD-EVEN DISCARDS, REVOLVING DIS-CARDS, SCANIAN SIGNAL, SMITH, SUIT PREF-ERENCE SIGNAL, TRUMP SIGNAL, UPSIDE-DOWN SIGNAL, VIJNE SIGNAL.

CARDS. Used in a colloquial sense, usually in describing the meaning of certain doubles, to mean high-card strength. See CARD-SHOWING DOUBLE.

CARDS, NEUTRAL AND POSITIVE. The only information disclosed by the play of a neutral card is the obvious point that the player has that particular card. The essence of this is that the player is not void of the suit, and even this knowledge will generally have little or no effect on problems of probability.

A card may be said to have positive value when:

(1) the holder was deemed certain to have played it, or;

(2) it indicates the position of one or more other specified cards, or suggests their probable location, or;

(3) it indicates the distribution of all the outstanding cards of a suit.

> *North*
> ♠ 5 4 3
> ♥ A K 2
> ♦ A J 8 6 5
> ♣ K 3
>
> *South*
> ♠ A J 2
> ♥ Q 8 4 3
> ♦ K 10 7
> ♣ A J 5

South plays in notrump, and West leads the ♠K. South assumes that West holds the ♠ K-Q-10. If he also assumes that West was certain to make this lead, there will be odds of 13 to 10 that East has the ♦ Q:

(a) If East follows with a low spade, these odds are only very slightly altered. East's card is neutral, and indicates only that West does not have seven spades. The elimination of all distributions where West holds seven spades removes more cases favorable to East's holding the ♦ Q than unfavorable cases. The odds are a very little less than 13 to 10, and the difference may be disregarded.

(b) If East plays a heart at trick one, there will be positive significance in the fact that he has played a nonspade, though the card itself is neutral. The odds are 13 to 6 that East holds the ♦ Q. We know now that East is not void of hearts, but we cannot say that he was certain to play a heart whatever cards he holds.

(c) If East discards a club at trick one, the odds are again 13 to 6 that he has the ♦ Q.

CARDS OF A SUIT IN OPPONENT'S HAND. See SUIT, NUMBER OF CARDS IN.

CARD-SHOWING DOUBLE. A double that does not promise any particular distribution but instead shows general high-card strength. The amount of strength promised by a double that shows cards obviously varies according to the circumstances in which the double is made. For example, the DOUBLE OF TWO CLUBS RESPONSE to a WEAK NOTRUMP can be played to show strength equivalent to that of a double of a 1NT opening. The double of interference of a PRECISION CLUB opening bid, however, promises about 5-8 points.

CAREY LIMOUSINE AWARD. A prize given by the INTERNATIONAL BRIDGE PRESS ASSOCIATION for the best defense of the year. George Jacobs set up this award in 2000.

CARIBBEAN CHAMPIONSHIPS. Organized in 1964 as an informal international championship for countries in the Caribbean area. See CENTRAL AMERICAN AND CARIBBEAN CHAMPIONSHIPS. See Appendix III.

CARROT CLUB. A forcing club system invented by Hans Göthe and Anders Morath of Sweden.

CARRYOVER SCORES. Methods for determining carryover scores are the responsibility of the sponsoring organization.

Under the regulations of the AMERICAN CONTRACT BRIDGE LEAGUE, certain events in tournaments of sectional or higher rating are conducted in more than one session. These events may or may not involve elimination of some of the contestants from the main event (see CONSOLATION EVENT).

If no players are eliminated from the event, their matchpoint score is carried over from one session to the succeeding session, and the event decided upon the total score in all sessions. Regulations require that if a later session of a playthrough multi-session event has a different top score on a board, provision is made for adjusting to the top score in the first session. See FACTORING.

When the original starting field is reduced for later sessions, regulations provide that scores in the early (qualifying) round or rounds be carried over into the final session on the basis of this formula:

$$\text{carryover} = \frac{M \cdot QFD \cdot A \cdot B}{E \times S}$$

where M represents the number of matchpoints in the qualifying round or rounds which a contestant scores, QFD is the square of the number of pairs in the final session, A is the average on a board in the finals, B is the number of boards in the qualifying round or rounds, E is the number of pairs entered in the event, and S is the sum of all qualifying scores of pairs eligible for the finals.

If there is one qualifying round and one final, the total spread from top to bottom score is reduced to twice the top score on a board in the finals; if there are two qualifying rounds and one final, the total is reduced to three boards; and for two qualifying rounds and two final rounds, four boards. The formula may give a smaller spread.

The carryover method also is used in some ACBL team events. In board-a-match events at North American Championships, such as the Reisinger Teams, a carryover formula along lines similar to the ones outlined above is applied. In the North American Swiss Teams event, different carryover formulas are applied from qualifying to semifinal and from semifinal to final. Half of any score greater than 5 is carried over from qualifying to semifinal. However, Victory Points are used in the fi-

nal. Each finalist is given a carryover equivalent to 1 Victory Point for each full quarter over 5 a team scores in the semifinal.

At the world level, a special carryover formula has been applied in some Bermuda Bowl contests. Half the IMP difference from the round-robin is carried over to the final or semifinal if the team that finished higher in the round-robin has the plus; only one-third of the IMP difference is carried over if the team that finished lower in the round-robin has the plus.

Carryover also is applied from the qualifying to the semifinal and from the semifinal to the final of the World Open Pairs and from the qualifying to the final of the World Women's Pairs. A special carryover formula also is used in the Swiss Teams portion of the Rosenblum Teams. Another special carryover plan was used in the semifinals of the 1980 World Team Olympiad.

CARVE. To badly misplay, or butcher, a hand (British).

CASH. To play a winning card while on lead.

CASH IN (also CASH OUT). To take a series of tricks by playing winning cards one after another. The term is usually applied to a situation where a player realizes that he is on lead for what is probably going to be the last time during that particular hand, and while in control, he will now take his tricks. The term can be applied to a declarer as well as defenders.

CAVALIER. A fourth COAT CARD, which is still maintained in some playing cards as an alternative to the JACK. See PACK.

CAVENDISH CLUB (New York City). Founded in 1925 by Wilbur C. Whitehead, in association with Gratz M. Scott, and Edwin A. Wetzlar, the Club was housed for the first eight years at the Mayfair House, and then moved to the Ambassador Hotel. It was at the Ritz Tower Hotel 1950-65 and occupied premises on Central Park South 1965-74. In 1974 it moved to the Carlton House, stayed until 1983, and after a brief stop on 48th Street, ended in a townhouse on 73rd. St. Rent escalations and falling membership forced the Club to cease operations on May 31, 1991.

From 1941 the Cavendish Club was a not-for-profit membership corporation, managed by B. Jay Becker 1941 to 1947 and Rudolf Muhsam 1947 to 1973, who were also club secretary, Thomas M. Smith from 1973 to 1987, Thomas L. Snow, 1987 to 1990 and Richard Reisig, 1990 to 1991.

In 1975, the Club inaugurated the CAVENDISH IN-VITATIONAL PAIRS, which has become one of the strongest and most prestigious invitational events in the world.

Presidents were: Gratz M. Scott 1925-35; Frank Crowninshield 1935-47; Nate Spingold 1948-58; Samuel Stayman 1958-61 and 1981-82; Howard Schenken 1961-64; Harold Ogust 1964-67; Leonard Hess 1967-70; Edward Loewenthal 1970-73; Roy V. Titus 1973-76 and 1980-81; Archie A. Brauer, 1976-79; Yehuda Koppel 1979-80 and 1985-86; William Roberts 1982-85; Sidney Rosen 1986-87; Claire Tornay 1987-90; and Thomas M. Smith 1990-91.

Members included many players of international reputation.

CAVENDISH INVITATIONAL PAIRS. The biggest money bridge tournament in the world, with the total pool exceeding $1 million. Now an annual event played in Las Vegas in May, the tournament was born in 1975 when it was organized by Thomas M. Smith and Michael Moss and sponsored by the Cavendish Club. A scoring method called Cross-IMPs now used in many cash-prize tournaments was used from the beginning for this event. Every result on every deal is IMPed against all other results for that deal. Although the IMP scale goes as high as 24, an upper limit of 17 IMPs has been set for this event. The top pairs in the world are invited, and the schedule is set up in such a way that each pair plays a short match against every other pair. (The size of the field in 2000 was 50 pairs, too large for a complete round-robin. As a result, each pair played only 45 of the other 49 pairs during the two-day, four-session event.)

On the evening preceding the event, a calcutta auction takes place. Each pair is put up for auction, and the money bid is placed in the calcutta pool. This money is awarded to the owners (usually a consortium rather than an individual makes the bids) of the top-ranking pairs. Each pair has the right to buy a portion of the pool bid on their pair. There is also a prize pool which is divided among the top finishers.

Until the mid-Nineties, the tournament was staged in New York City, home of the Cavendish Club. However, the club was dissolved and no longer exists. Prior to the club's demise, the Cavendish Invitational Pairs was established as a separate corporation so as to insure the continuation of the event. Shortly after the founding of the corporation, the tournament was moved to Las Vegas.

For results, see Appendix IV.

CAVENDISH INVITATIONAL TEAMS. A major cash-prize event for the Jack Dreyfus Trophy staged just prior to the annual CAVENDISH INVITATIONAL PAIRS in Las Vegas in May. Outstanding teams from around the world are invited to compete – the field today usually consists of 24 teams. The prize fund in 2000 amounted to more than $300,000.

CAVENDISH TROPHY. Awarded to the winners of the NORTH AMERICAN BLUE RIBBON PAIRS. Donated by the CAVENDISH CLUB.

CBA. CONTRACT BRIDGE ASSOCIATION.

CBL. CONTRACT BRIDGE LEAGUE.

CELEBRITIES. Many persons who are outstanding in their own spheres of activity also find much enjoyment playing bridge. Heads of state who put bridge high on their activities schedule include U.S. President Dwight D. Eisenhower and Chinese Premier Deng Xiaoping. The International Bridge Press Association once recognized Deng as Bridge Personality of the Year. Wan Li, at one time the #2 man in China, once won a World-Wide Simultaneous Pairs game. Many other high-ranking officials in China also play bridge regularly. Mahatma Ghandi of India enjoyed a good game of bridge, as did Winston Churchill, Great Britain's prime minister.

Bill Gates, founder of Microsoft Corporation, liked the game well enough to compete in the North American Mixed Teams championship in 2000 – and he even qualified for the final. Warren Buffett, perhaps the most

successful investor over the years as head man of Berkshire-Hathaway, capped several appearance in Congress vs. Corporate matches by playing the Mixed Pairs world championship in 1994. He too qualified for the final. Jaime Ortiz-Patino, now of Spain and formerly of Switzerland, a top world business leader and regular international competitor, served for 10 years as president of the World Bridge Federation. Marc Hodler, president of the Switzerland Bridge Federation for many years, is a vice president of the International Olympic Committee. George Rosenkranz of Mexico, a top scientist in the medical world who often is called the inventor of the birth control pill, not only has won many North American championships – he even invented a system of bidding – the Romex System.

Several other business leaders have embraced bridge as a hobby. Laurence Tisch, for many years CEO of the CBS television network, was a regular on the Corporate team in each of their successful matches against Congress. Malcolm Forbes, founder of *Forbes* magazine, also was a serious bridge player. Jimmy Cayne, president of Bear Stearns, plays the game at its highest levels, including the Bermuda Bowl in 1995, and has several North American championships to his credit. Ace Greenberg, chairman of the board of Bear Stearns, is an ACBL Life Master who has won the Reisinger Teams.

The U.S. Congress team usually fielded at least nine players, since it was common for them to be called away from their matches against Corporate because of important votes in Congress. Congress has been represented by Arlan Stangeland, Bob Packwood, Rudy Boschwitz, Hank Brown, Robert Kastenmeier, Bob Kerry, Jim Leach, Lynn Martin, Howard Neilson, Robert Zion, James Jeffords, Robert Smith and Judge Melvin Welles. Carl Albert, former speaker of the House, frequently found time for a rubber or two. Supreme Court Justice John Paul Stevens has been a frequent player at clubs and tournaments and is an ACBL Life Master. Federal Judge Carl Rubin not only became a Life Master – he served several terms on the ACBL Board of Directors and was president of the ACBL when the Board made the decision to move the league from Greenwich CT to Memphis in 1971. Another federal bridge, Amalya Kearse, has the best record of all the celebrities in bridge – she won a world championship, a Women's Pairs. She also was editor of the Third Edition of the *Bridge Encyclopedia* and has authored other bridge books.

Bridge also is popular among top politicians in Great Britain. Every year there is a match between the House of Lords and the House of Commons. There even has been a match between British Parliament and the U.S. Congress.

Many top-flight performers of stage, screen and television have found bridge to be special. The most outstanding of these is Omar Sharif, a movie idol who was quoted as saying, "Acting is my living, bridge is my passion." He is an outstanding player who has played successfully at the top levels.

George Burns loved the game so much that he tried to play daily, right up to the day he died. He donated a trophy that is given annually to the ACBL senior who has the best year. George Kaufman, the playwright, even wrote short stories and articles about bridge. The Marx Brothers often got together for a rubber or two between takes on the set. Movie and TV cameraman George Clemmens met his wife while they were playing a couple of rubbers on the set. Les Brown, leader of his Band of Renown, also played bridge frequently.

Telly Savalas, TV's Kojak, enjoyed a strong rubber or two, as do Elizabeth Taylor, Ronnie Cox, Dick Yarmy, Casa Williams, Don Adams, Robert Quarry and Ray Walker.

In the world of literature, Somerset Maugham not only played the game – he injected bridge situations into some of his books. Ian Fleming, author of the James Bond books, and Agatha Christie, the noted mystery writer, also worked bridge into their books. C.S. Forester and Charles Dickens could not write about bridge – the game had not been invented yet – but whist situations appeared in their works. One of the books written by author Terry Quinn, *The Great Bridge Conspiracy*, is entirely about bridge. Novelist Don Von Elsner made the name of Jake Winkman well-known in his books that featured bridge.

Bridge is major in the sports world – it is one of the favorite games when teams are making long trips. The list includes baseball stars like Tom Seaver, Jim Bunning, Tim McCarver, Richie Ashburn, Pinky Higgins, Norm Cash and Dizzy Dean. Life Master Pauline Betz Addie was a tennis great, and many-time champion Martina Navritalova always enjoys a good game of bridge. Althea Gibson, another tennis all-time star, belonged to the American Bridge Association while attending Lincoln University in Jefferson City MO.

Many top chess stars play bridge – and many bridge champions play chess. Only one person, Irina Levitina, formerly of Russia but now of New York City, has won world championships in both sports. Other chess experts who enjoy bridge include Viktor Korchnoi, Bent Larsen and Anatoly Karpov.

This article in no way should be considered to be a complete list of celebrities interested in bridge – it is only the tip of the iceberg. It is intended as an indication of the widespread interest in bridge. See also LITERATURE AND BRIDGE, POLITICIANS.

CENTRAL AMERICAN-CARIBBEAN CHAMPIONSHIPS. Formerly CARIBBEAN CHAMPIONSHIPS. Held annually for the member nations of the CENTRAL AMERICAN AND CARIBBEAN BRIDGE FEDERATION. For results, see APPENDIX III.

CHAIRMAN. The chief elected official of the AMERICAN CONTRACT BRIDGE LEAGUE prior to the reorganization in 1949. Subsequently the title was revived, in the form of Chairman of the BOARD OF DIRECTORS. Since 1963 the title has regularly been accorded to the immediate past-president of the ACBL. Chairmen before that date were:

1938-42	Nate Spingold	1955	Charles Solomon
1943-45	Albert H. Morehead	1956	J.G. Ripstra
1946-47	Brig. Gen. Robert J. Gill	1957	Charles Solomon
1948-49	Waldemar von Zedtwitz	1958	Winslow H. Randall
1950-52	Curt Reisinger	1959	Frank T. Westcott
1953	Peter Leventritt	1960-61	Max Manchester
1954	Julius Rosenblum	1962	Jerry Lewis

See PRESIDENTS.

Chairmen also can be the head of a committee, such as a tournament appeals committee. The leading planner for a tournament frequently is referred to as the tournament chairman.

CHALLENGE. A declaration proposed by Sidney Lenz in 1929 to replace the Takeout Double. It was used ex-

perimentally in one New York club, but received little support.

In the Fifties the term was revived in a different sense, as an attempt to check artificial bidding. When any one player has made two bids, a positive bid can be *challenged*. The bidding then ends, and the contract reached is played redoubled. This plan, originated by Col. Cyril Rocke, also received little support.

CHAMPIONSHIP TOURNAMENT. The principal function of bridge governing bodies is to provide interesting bridge competitions for its members, and to record accurately the achievements made by each member in competitive play. Championship tournaments are staged at various levels in nations throughout the world. Some are cash-prize tournaments such as the Cavendish Invitational and the Cap Gemini. Others such as the Bermuda Bowl, Venice Cup, World Team Olympiad, etc., determine world champions. The eight World Bridge Federation zones use zonal competitions to determine which teams will compete in major world championships. Most nations hold tournaments to determine national champions. Championship tournaments also are held at several lower levels in most nations.

The ACBL sponsors and conducts more than 1000 tournaments a year at which masterpoints are awarded. These tournaments are divided into several classes depending on the importance of the event, the territory represented, the movement employed, the conditions of sponsorship and the number of entries. Classification of each event is published in advance, and masterpoints are awarded according to formulas that take into consideration various factors.

(1) *North American Bridge Championships (NABC)*. These championships are conducted by the ACBL. Each major event is held only once a year, split among the three North American tournaments. For results, see Appendix I.

(2) *Regional Championships.* ACBL membership is divided into 25 geographical districts, each strictly limited as to territory. Regional championships are conducted by ACBL districts under the supervision of a rated director appointed by the ACBL. These tournaments offer the players of the area an opportunity to earn a substantial number of gold and red points, awards that are necessary to achieve the rank of Life Master. In addition, at each NABC a large number of secondary events, most of which are flighted or stratified, are conducted, all with regional championship status.

(3) *Sectional Championships.* These events are conducted by ACBL units under the supervision of a rated director appointed by the ACBL. Each unit is expected to conduct at least one Sectional tournament a year. Additional tournaments are allocated on the basis of membership and history of previous sectional tournament scheduling. The points awarded at Sectionals are silver, a very important fact for those interested in becoming Life Masters. A would-be Life Master must win at least 50 silver points, and silver points are available only at Sectionals.

(4) *Unit Championships.* Each unit may conduct 16 sessions of Unit Championship-rated events annually.

Further information is contained in the *ACBL Handbook*, latest copies of which are available from ACBL Headquarters.

Championship tournaments are staged in countries throughout the world. Many determine national championships, and many decide area or continental championships, such as the South American Championships, the European Championships, etc. Tournaments also are held at the world level: Bermuda Bowl, Venice Cup, Team Olympiad, etc. For results, see Appendices III, IV and V.

CHANCE. The element of luck or hazard present in almost all card games but materially reduced in potency as a feature in bridge. Chance in bridge is usually concerned with the quality of the cards dealt one in rubber contests, but even this should become relatively equal to both sides over a long period of time. The number of points held by a player or partnership tends to approach the theoretical expectation over a long period, although the absolute difference may increase. In play situations chance can be a factor, but the expert player will tend to be able to reduce its influence by applying skill and mathematical deliberation to situations where a lesser player would merely play on and attribute any failure to bad luck.

In duplicate, chance can be a considerable factor in the short run. Good contracts fail and bad contracts succeed; hands which represent borderline games and slams are likely to favor one side at the expense of the other. Less obvious, but equally important, is the chance of playing the right opponents at the right moment. With luck you will play against good opponents when they have no control of the bidding and play, and against weaker players when the bidding and play are slightly too difficult for them. See also FORTUNE.

CHANGE OF SUIT. The first mention of a suit not previously bid by any player; used on a wide variety of hands in which exploration is called for. In standard methods, the general rule is that a change of suit by the responder is forcing for one round; a change of suit by the opener is nonforcing. This is subject to many exceptions.

Changes of suit by the responder are nonforcing in the following cases:

(1) If responder passed originally. But a jump shift by a passed hand is a doubtful case. Most authorities treat this bid as forcing for one round, implying a fit with the opener's suit. But some players reserve the right to pass, especially if the jump is from a minor suit to a major.

(2) If the second player doubled at the one level (However, most players consider a change of suit over a double as forcing. Some vary their treatment according to the level at which responder acts).

(3) If the second player overcalls 1NT. Similarly, when the second player overcalls with a conventional bid, such as a Michaels Cuebid, responder can double to show strength; a bid in a new suit is non-forcing.

(4) If the opener rebids 1NT and responder's new suit is not a reverse; for example:

West	East
1♣	1♠
1NT	2♦

However, most tournament competitors play this sequence as forcing. The new minor is conventional, asking partner to clarify his holdings in the major suits. See NEW MINOR FORCING.

(5) In response to a 1NT opening at the level of two if transfers are not in use.

(6) After a 1NT response and a two-level rebid by opener:

West	East
1♠	1NT
2♣	2♥

Changes of suit by the opener are forcing in the following cases:

(1) A jump shift below the game level.
(2) A reverse below the game level.
(3) After a single raise by responder:

West	East
1♥	2♥
3♦	

(4) After responder has shown strength:

West	East
1♥	2NT
3♦	

West	East
1♥	2♠
3♣	

West	East
1♠	2♣
2♥	

CHANGING A CALL. The act of substituting a call for a call made previously at the same turn. See LAWS (Law 25).

CHANGING PROBABILITIES DURING PLAY. See PROBABILITIES A POSTERIORI and PROBABILITIES A PRIORI.

CHARITY EVENT. A regular game, usually either pairs or teams, from which a portion of the proceeds, sometimes all, from the selling of entries and other sources, is earmarked for a specified charity.

CHARITY FOUNDATION. See ACBL CHARITY PROGRAM.

CHARLES GOREN FOUNDATION. See INTERCOLLEGIATE BRIDGE TOURNAMENT.

CHEAPER MINOR. See DEFENSE TO OPENING THREE-BID; SECOND NEGATIVE RESPONSE AFTER ARTIFICIAL FORCING OPENING.

CHEAPEST BID. The most economical bid available at any particular point in the auction, such as 1♦ in response to 1♣. Many conventional bids and systems make use of this principle of economy by attaching special meanings to club bids at various levels, and occasionally to diamond bids. The same principle of economy is followed in making natural opening bids and responses. See CHOICE OF SUIT, RELAY, UP THE LINE.

CHEATING. Throughout history, card cheats have always been held in contempt. It is so with bridge.

The Laws of Contract Bridge are not designed to prevent cheating or to provide redress. The lawgivers have taken the view that it would be wrong to accord cheats a status by providing legal remedies against their activities. This also is the policy of the ACBL: exclusion from membership is the penalty for premeditated cheating, but cases of momentary weakness often are dealt with by temporary suspension. ("The penalty of cheating is exclusion from society," wrote the great whist authority, Cavendish.)

Cheating at Rubber Bridge. At rubber bridge, cheating is not a problem. Short of actually manipulating or marking the cards, it is impracticable for a lone player to cheat effectively. The fact that good bridge is so exact an art militates against cheating, for a player who makes bids or plays which are against the odds but which prove consistently successful soon excites suspicion. Cheating in clubs is therefore rare.

Traditional forms of cardsharping are unrewarding in bridge because each deal is almost equally important. A sharper can hardly make a killing by awaiting a suitable opening as in such games as poker, and if he just happened to pick up good cards every time he dealt, his career would be shortlived.

The dealing of seconds, therefore, the classic technique of the cardsharping aristocracy, is not an effective means of winning. (An accomplished sharp, dealing from a marked pack, sees when a high card is about to go to an opponent, and deals that opponent the next card instead, keeping the high card for himself or his partner.) For the same reason, another time-honored device of sharps, ringing in a cold deck, will not yield a reward commensurate with the risk.

Cheating at Duplicate. The fact that duplicate is a game for fixed partnerships as opposed to the cut-in style of rubber bridge makes dishonesty more practicable.

Cheating at duplicate is by no means easy to define. Although the Laws do not recognize cheats, the section called *The Proprieties* defines two main types of improper conduct: breaches of ethics and breaches of etiquette. Breaches of ethics are commonly thought of as unfair practices which fall short of deliberate cheating, but it is possible for the difference to be one of degree only. For example, a pair who take note of inflections in bidding would be considered unethical, while a pair who set out to impart similar information by secret signals would be considered cheats. (See also ETHICS, ETIQUETTE and PROPRIETIES.)

The following are some examples of infringements peculiar to the tournament world. By their aggravated nature they can be classified as cheating. Methods used by cheats have involved cigarettes, cigars, pens, pencils, scorecards, finger positions, grip on cards, use of left or right hand. All these were eliminated by the use of bidding screens, which restrict the cheater to noises and electronic devices.

Players have been caught using stacked decks, sometime by inserting decks that have been previously prepared. In other cases, players in Swiss Teams have refrained from redealing boards with which they were familiar from a previous round. In still other cases, players have been observed shuffling the cards in such a way that the dealer or the dealer's partner is dealt a specified card.

Many tournament procedures have been devised that are unobtrusive but effective safeguards against cheating. Thus, in the Laws of Duplicate, some of the examples cited as irregularities are anticheating safeguards. These are:

90 B.3. Any discussion of the bidding, play or result of a board, which may be overheard at another table.

90 B.4. Any comparison of scores with another contestant during a session.

90 B.5. Any touching or handling of cards belonging to another player.

See BERMUDA INCIDENT, BUENOS AIRES AFFAIR, CHEATING ACCUSATIONS, HOUSTON AFFAIR, SION-COKIN AFFAIR.

CHEATING ACCUSATIONS. Accusations of cheating are rare in serious tournament bridge, and substantiated accusations are even rarer. It is generally recognized that an allegation that is not supported by solid evidence should not be made, and that accusation by rumor is highly improper.

At the international level there have been very few cases of charges being brought. Most of these were disposed of, without widespread publicity, by the national or international committees concerned. The notable exceptions occurred in the 1965 and 1975 BERMUDA BOWLS. See BERMUDA INCIDENT, BUENOS AIRES AFFAIR.

Several suggestions have been made aimed at preventing cheating and forestalling accusations of cheating. Screens called FRANCO BOARDS were introduced in Italian events years ago, but did not find general acceptance. In 1974, the proposal of WBF President Julius Rosenblum to use BIDDING SCREENS in the 1975 Bermuda Bowl in order to eliminate accusations of cheating met with a sharp division of opinion, with many taking the position that such screens would be demeaning to the players and to bridge itself. Nevertheless, in 1975 bidding screens were used for the first time in World Championship play, and their use in combination with bidding boxes virtually eliminated any problems relating to the inadvertent exchange of unauthorized information and the ethical problems resulting from hesitations. The response of the players to the screens and boxes was overwhelmingly positive. The irony of the 1975 Bermuda Bowl was, however, that while the screens designed to eliminate cheating accusations were being enthusiastically received, an Italian pair were accused of cheating by using foot signals under the tables. See BERMUDA INCIDENT.   Another accusation of cheating was leveled at two members of Italy's 1973 and 1974 Bermuda Bowl champions. Leandro Burgay, who was passed over by the Italian Bridge Federation as a choice for the 1976 Bermuda Bowl and World Team Olympiad team, presented a tape to the FIB. Burgay claimed the tape contained a telephone conversation between him and Benito Bianchi in which Bianchi had openly discussed illegal signaling methods. According to the tape, Bianchi explained how he and Pietro Forquet had used cigarettes to convey signals during the 1973 and 1974 Bermuda Bowl contests. The case came to the attention of the WBF, but nothing ever came of it because it was never proved that the tapes were authentic. See also HOUSTON AFFAIR and SION-COKIN AFFAIR.

CHECKBACK STAYMAN. A common conventional agreement following a 1NT rebid, searching for an unbid major suit or a preference to responder's major.

Opener	Responder
1♣	1♥
1NT	2♣

This asks opener to give preference to hearts, or show

an unbid four-card spade suit. With neither he bids 2♦. 2♣ followed by 2♥ or 2♠ is invitational, whereas those bids made directly would be weak.

Some use 2♦ as a game-forcing Stayman and 2♣ as a weak Stayman. If the latter, responder has invitational values if he bids again.

See CROWHURST, NEW MINOR FORCING, STAYMAN ON SECOND ROUND.

CHESS PLAYERS. Nobody has ever reached the highest levels at both chess and bridge, but many have been expert at one game and near-expert at the other. High-ranking bridge players who are also classed as strong chess players include Alan Truscott and Louis Levy. Sol Rubinow and Oswald Jacoby also were fine chess players. Among chess players, two former world champions, Emanuel Lasker and José Raoul Capablanca, once were contributing editors to *The Bridge World*.

Guillaume le Breton Deschapelles of France was acknowledged as the finest player of his day at both chess and whist. A modern Frenchman has done even better. Pierre Ghestem won two world bridge team titles, was world champion at dames (i.e. checkers or draughts), and was French chess champion, an astonishing triple. Viktor Korchnoi also enjoys a good game of bridge.

Irina Levitina, now of New York but formerly of the Soviet Union (St. Petersburg and Leningrad), has earned superior honors in both games. In 1984 she reached the final of the World Women's Chess Championships, and she was ranked as the Soviet Union's No. 1 female player. As a representative of the United States, of which she is now a citizen, she won the World Women's Team Olympiad in 1996. She has won several North American championships, the first coming in 1993 (Women's Knock-out Teams). Jonathan Mastel of Great Britain was No. 1 board for Britain and a well-regarded bridge player.

CHEST YOUR CARDS. Hold your cards close to your chest so that they are not visible to an opponent, usually a request by another player. The culprit may have a vision problem, or simply be careless. An alternative solution is to "lap the cards" — hold them in the lap where they are hidden by the table.

CHICAGO (Four-Deal Bridge). A form of the game much played in clubs and well suited to home play. Its effect is to avoid long rubbers of uncertain duration; a member never need wait longer than the time (about twenty minutes) required to complete four deals. The game is called "Chicago" for the city in which it originated, and sometimes "club bridge."

Basic rules. The LAWS OF CONTRACT BRIDGE and rules for CLUB PROCEDURE are followed, except as modified by the following rules.

The rubber. A rubber, sometimes called a chukker, consists of a series of four deals that have been bid and played. If a deal is passed out, the same player deals again and the deal passed out does not count as one of the four deals.

A fifth deal is void if attention is drawn to it at any time before there has been a new cut for partners or the game has terminated; if the error is not discovered in time for correction, the score stands as recorded. A sixth or subsequent deal is unconditionally void and no score for such a deal is ever permissible.

In the event that fewer than four deals are played, the

score shall stand for the incomplete series and the fourth deal need not be played unless attention is drawn to the error before there has been a new cut for partners or the game has terminated.

When the players are pivoting, the fact that the players have taken their proper seats for the next rubber shall be considered a cut for partners. (In a pivot game, partnerships for each rubber follow a fixed rotation.)

Vulnerability. Vulnerability is not determined by previous scores but by the following schedule:

First deal: neither side vulnerable.

Second and third deals: dealer's side vulnerable, the other side non-vulnerable.

Fourth deal: both sides vulnerable.

Premiums. For making or completing a game (100 or more trick points), a side receives a premium of 300 points if on that deal it is not vulnerable or 500 points if on that deal it is vulnerable. There is no additional premium for winning two or more games, each game premium being scored separately.

The score. As a reminder of vulnerability in Four Deal Bridge, two intersecting diagonal lines should be drawn near the top of the score pad, as follows:

The numeral "1" should be inserted in that one of the four angles thus formed that faces the first dealer. After play of the first deal is completed, "2" is inserted in the next angle in clockwise rotation, facing the dealer of the second deal. The numerals "3" and "4" are subsequently inserted at the start of the third and fourth deals, respectively, each in the angle facing the current dealer.

A correctly numbered diagram is conclusive as to vulnerability. There is no redress for a bid influenced by the scorer's failure to draw the diagram or for an error or omission in inserting a numeral or numerals in the diagram. Such error or omission should, upon discovery, be immediately corrected, and the deal or deals should be scored or rescored as though the diagram and the number or numbers thereon had been properly inserted.

Partscores. Partscores made previously may be combined with a partscore made in the current deal to complete a game of 100 or more trick points. The game premium is determined by the vulnerability of the side that completes the game. When a side makes or completes a game, no previous partscore of either side may thereafter be counted toward game.

A side that makes a partscore in the fourth deal, if the partscore is not sufficient to complete a game, receives a premium of 100 points. This premium is scored whether or not the same side or the other side has an uncompleted partscore. There is no separate premium for making a partscore in any other circumstances.

Deal out of turn. When a player deals out of turn, and there is no right to a redeal, the player who should have dealt retains his right to call first, but such right is lost if it is not claimed before the actual dealer calls. If the actual dealer calls before attention is drawn to the deal out of turn, each player thereafter calls in rotation. Vulnerability and scoring values are determined by the position of the player who should have dealt, regardless of which player actually dealt or called first. Neither the rotation of the deal nor the scoring is affected by a deal out of turn. The next dealer is the player who would have dealt next if the deal had been in turn.

Optional rules and customs. The following practices,

not required, have proved acceptable in some clubs and games.

(i) Since the essence of the game is speed, if a deal is passed out, the pack that has been shuffled for the next deal should be used by the same dealer.

(ii) The net score of a rubber should be translated into even hundreds (according to American custom) by crediting as 100 points any fraction thereof amounting to 50 or more points: e.g., 750 points count as 800; 740 points count as 700 points.

(iii) No two players may play a second consecutive rubber as partners at the same table. If two players draw each other again, the player who has drawn the highest card should play with the player who has drawn the third-highest, against the other two players.

(iv) To avoid confusion as to how many deals have been played: Each deal should be scored, even if there is no net advantage to either side (for example, when one side is entitled to 100 points for undertrick penalties and the other side is entitled to 100 points for honors). In a result that completes a game, premiums for overtricks, game, slam, or making a doubled contract should be combined with the trick score to produce one total, which is entered below the line; for example, if a side makes 2♠ doubled and vulnerable with an overtrick, 870 should be scored below the line, not 120 below the line and 50, 500, and 200 above the line.

In some clubs, particularly in New York City, the vulnerability on the second and third deals is reversed. The objective is to give the non-vulnerable side an opportunity to preempt as dealer. Two variations popular in England are: (1) Undoubled overtricks do not count, called Illinois; (2) Undoubled undertricks beyond one do not count, called California.

Tactics. Suppose that on the fourth deal, South is declarer at 4♠ with:

> ♠ Q J 8 3
> ♥ 8 5 4 3
> ♦ A J 6
> ♣ 8 5

> ♠ A K 10 7 5 2
> ♥ A 2
> ♦ K 3
> ♣ K 6 4

West leads the ♣Q. East wins the ace and shifts to a heart. South checks the score; his side is ahead by 190 points. South can take the ♥A, draw trumps and claim 11 tricks for +650 and victory by 840 points; N-S will win an 8-point chukker. If South makes an extra overtrick, however, N-S will win a 9-point rubber, and if South takes only ten tricks for +620, N-S will still win an 8-point rubber. South should therefore win the ♥A, draw trumps and finesse the ♦J in pursuit of a second overtrick.

In the auction, overbidding the score has the same significance as at rubber bridge: if N-S have a 60 partial, an auction such as 1♠-2♠-3♠ suggests slam. At Chicago, however, the changing vulnerability affects tactics. Suppose that on the third deal, there are three passes to South, who holds:

> ♠ J 7 5
> ♥ A Q 10 7 2
> ♦ K 7 5
> ♣ J 5

If South passes, E-W get a redeal and retain their vul-

nerability. South should open 1 ♥ to deprive the opponents of their chance to make a vulnerable game or slam.

Suppose that on the third deal South holds:

♠ 8 4
♥ K 7 4
♦ A J 9 5 2
♣ K J 4

N-S are vulnerable. After two passes, South should pass. Since North has passed, game is unlikely. South hopes the deal will be passed out, giving N-S another chance to take advantage of their vulnerable status.

If it is agreed that partnerships will rotate, which is normal, there is a psychological element with marginal third and fourth-seat hands: bid with a relatively weak partner, willing to end the wheel, but pass with a relatively strong partner. Rubber is a misnomer, because it should refer to the traditional best-of-three games format. Alternative words that have some currency are "chukker", originally a period of polo, and "wheel" from the X diagram used to track the dealer on the scorepad. Curiously and coincidentally, chukker is derived from a word meaning "wheel". See COMPENSATION.

For determination of partners, see last section of PIVOT BRIDGE, LAWS OF.

CHICAGO TROPHY. Awarded for the MIXED BOARD-A-MATCH TEAMS. Formerly awarded for the North American Open Team Championship (board-a-match scoring) until 1965 when it was replaced by the REISINGER MEMORIAL TROPHY; contested at the Fall NABC (under which heading past results are listed). The Chicago Trophy was donated by the Auction Bridge Club of Chicago in 1929. (In 1928, the open team competition was for the Harold S. Vanderbilt Cup.) See Appendix I for results.

CHICANE. A term from BRIDGE WHIST referring to a hand that is void of trumps. It was scored the same as three honors. In contract bridge, the term is obsolete in its original sense, though it is occasionally used to describe a void suit, as "chicane in hearts."

CHICO TWO DIAMONDS. A slightly simplified or modified version of the MULTI. An opening bid of 2 ♦ shows either a weak two-bid in a major or a strong (20+) 4-4-4-1.

CHINA CUP. An invitational championship offered by the China Bridge Association from 1996 to 1999. The event came about as a result of the tremendously successful Bermuda Bowl championship in Beijing in 1995. Four teams were invited each year – one from China, one from the European Bridge League, one from the ACBL and one to represent the World Bridge Federation. The team event consisted of two round-robins in both the Open and the Women's event. The players also participated in a three-session pairs championship. The event was discontinued after 2000 for lack of sponsorship. For results see Appendix IV.

CHINESE FINESSE. An attempt to win a trick by leading an unsupported honor.

```
              ♠ A 5
♠ K 8 6 2              ♠ J 10 7
              ♠ Q 9 4 3
```

If South needs to avoid a loser in this suit, he may

dismiss the remote chance of dropping the singleton king and try the effect of leading the queen from his hand. In the diagrammed situation West may well decide to duck, fearing that South has Q-J-10, with or without the 9.

CHINESE TAIPEI. See TAIWAN.

CHOICE, RESTRICTED. See RESTRICTED CHOICE.

CHOICE OF PACKS AND SEATS. The winner (or highest card) of the cut for first deal has the choice of which seat he will take and which of the two packs he wishes to deal.

CHOICE OF SUIT. In opening the bidding and responding, a long suit is normally bid ahead of a short one, but a few exceptions should be noted:

(1) A three-card minor suit, particularly clubs, is often bid ahead of a four-card major suit. Using FIVE-CARD MAJORS, the prepared minor-suit bid is made in all situations. In traditional methods the major suit will usually be preferred if the suit is biddable and there will not be any rebid difficulty. In practice a four-card major is rarely bid with a 4-3-3-3 distribution: a minimum hand needs to keep the bidding at a low level; a hand of medium strength normally opens 1NT; and a maximum hand bids 1 ♣ in order to make it easy for partner to respond.

(2) A strong four-card suit is often bid ahead of a five-card suit that ranks immediately beneath it. (However, with strong hands, a REVERSE from the long suit into the short suit becomes possible.) An acute problem can arise if both suits are of poor quality:

♠ A 6 4 2
♥ A 8 5 4 3
♦ A J 6
♣ 8

To bid 1 ♠ followed by 2 ♥ would be risky. One solution is to open 1 ♥ and improvise a 2 ♦ rebid if responder bids 2 ♣.

♠ Q
♥ A J 4
♦ K 7 5 2
♣ A 10 8 5 2

Since the diamond suit is weak, the best plan may be to open 1 ♣ and rebid 1NT over the likely 1 ♠ response. This sequence does not accurately describe opener's pattern, but neither does a 1 ♦ opening followed by 2 ♣; furthermore, a 1NT rebid better limits opener's strength.

♠ 4
♥ A K 4
♦ K Q 9 5
♣ K J 7 5 3

A 1 ♦ opening is desirable. If the response is 1 ♠, opener rebids 2 ♣. If responder then returns to 2 ♦, opener has enough extra strength to act again by bidding 2NT.

♠ 7 5
♥ A K 5 4
♦ A K 6 5 4
♣ Q 6

Players whose style allows a reverse on hands of this strength can open 1 ♦. If a reverse promises more strength, opener must start with 1 ♥ or, more likely, 1NT. With 3-3 in the minors, 70% of the BWS 2001 experts

voted to bid 1♣ uniformly. 30% voted to exercise judgment. The BWS 2001 consensus was to use judgment when opening minimum hands with 4-5 in the minors. A small minority (19%) favored 1♣ in all cases.

Cases are on record in world-championship play where players opened in a strong four-card minor suit ahead of a weak five-card major, as a U.S. player did when he bid 1♦ on:

> ♠ 10 7 5 3 2
> ♥ 8
> ♦ A K J 10
> ♣ K 4 3

(3) A five-card suit may be bid ahead of a six-card suit ranking immediately below it if the hand is a minimum:

> ♠ x
> ♥ A J x x x
> ♦ A Q x x x x
> ♣ x

1♦ followed by a heart bid would not be justified by the strength of the hand, and opposing bidding might shut out the heart suit. Most players will bid 1♥, treating the hand as a 5-5 distribution.

(4) In response to 1♠, a three-card club or diamond suit is sometimes bid in preference to a four-card heart suit.

(5) In response to an opening bid in a red suit, a major suit is sometimes bid at the one-level in preference to a five- or six-card minor suit at the two-level. This may be because the hand is not strong enough to bid at the level of two, or to avoid concealing the major suit when the hand is not worth two constructive bids.

See also BIDDABLE SUITS; CANAPÉ; THREE-CARD SUITS, BIDS IN; WALSH.

With two or three suits of equal length, the choice is more complicated:

(6) With two five-card black suits, expert opinion favors bidding 1♠ in all cases (39% in BWS 2001). A substantial minority (27%) favored bidding 1♠ unless the hand is very strong. With a five-card suit and a lower-ranking six-card suit, the expert consensus was to bid the higher-ranking if the suits are touching, but not otherwise.

(7) With two or three four-card suits, opener at one time would usually begin with the suit below the shortage, or most nearly below it, to prepare an economical rebid after the expected response in his short suit.

> ♠ 6 5 2   ♠ 5 4
> ♥ A K 6 4   ♥ A K 6 4
> ♦ 5 4   ♦ 6 5 2
> ♣ A Q 7 5   ♣ A Q 7 5

Opener would start with 1♣ on the first hand and 1♥ on the second. But with hands containing two strong four-card major suits, such as:

> ♠ A Q 10 6
> ♥ A K 10 5
> ♦ 5 4 3
> ♣ J 3

experts disagree on the better opening bid. And if the "rule" dictated opening in a weak four-card major suit, most players would search for another bid.

> (a)   (b)   (c)
> ♠ 7 5   ♠ 7 4   ♠ 6 4 3
> ♥ Q 8 6 4 ♥ J 5 4 3 ♥ K 10 5 3
> ♦ A 4 2   ♦ A Q 6 4 ♦ A Q 7 5
> ♣ A K 6 4 ♣ A K 4   ♣ A 4

> 1♣   1♦   1♦

In all three cases, opener could comfortably rebid 1NT over a response of 1♠.

The advent of FIVE-CARD MAJORS further eroded the "rule"; pairs using this style found the choice of a suit limited by system. However, the five-card-major style is not trouble-free. On hand (c), above, and on the two hands below,

> ♠ J 5 4 3   ♠ J 7 5 3
> ♥ J 7 4 2   ♥ A K 5
> ♦ A K 3   ♦ J 8 5 3
> ♣ A 10   ♣ A 10

opener has a doubleton club; he therefore used to have a problem after a response of 2♣ to a 1♦ opening. In the modern style there is no difficulty, since opener's 2NT rebid after a two-over-one response suggests no extra strength.

If the opener's hand is extremely strong, he rarely has a rebid problem. In that case, a minor suit is often bid in preference to a major, with the idea of keeping the bidding low and giving partner maximum opportunity to respond if his hand is weak.

If the opener holds both minor suits, he often has a free choice and may be guided by tactical or lead-inhibiting (or lead- directing) considerations. Since opener will seldom wish to bid both suits, he need not open 1♦ to prepare a 2♣ rebid. However, 1♦ may be preferable holding a worthless tripleton heart:

> ♠ A J
> ♥ 10 6 4
> ♦ K J 10 3
> ♣ K J 5 3

A 1♣ opening would leave opener with an awkward rebid after an overcall of 1♥ and a response of 1♠.

> ♠ 6 5
> ♥ J 6 4
> ♦ A Q 7 5
> ♣ A K 6 5

Here, opener must plan his rebid after a 1♥ response. If he is willing to raise to 2♥ or rebid 1NT, he can start with 1♣; otherwise, he must open 1♦, planning to rebid 2♣.

Hands with three four-card suits are often difficult to describe. To open in the "middle" suit may sometimes fare better than the traditional "suit below the shortage":

> ♠ K Q 9 4
> ♥ K Q 10 4
> ♦ A 9 5 3
> ♣ 3

A 1♥ opening avoids the awkward rebid that opener faces if he opens 1♠ and receives a response of 1NT or 2♣. (Again, a 1♦ opening is required in a FIVE-CARD MAJOR style.)

> ♠ Q
> ♥ K J 9 3
> ♦ K 7 6 4
> ♣ A J 7 3

If opener expects a 1♠ response and is willing to rebid 1NT, he can open 1♣. To open 1♦, keeping a 2♣ rebid in reserve, would work well if the response were 1NT. A 1♥ opening might lose if the response were 1NT; opener would have to guess which minor suit to bid next.

(8) With five-card suits, responder invariably prefers the higher-ranking for his response. For

responder's choice with four-card suits, see UP THE LINE.

CHUKKER. A term for four deals of CHICAGO. It is also used in a long team match for a group of boards followed by comparison of scores. The term is borrowed from polo.

CHURCHILL STYLE. The methods of bidding advocated by S. Garton Churchill of New York. The main features are:

(1) A weak notrump opening. Churchill was among the first leading American theorists to advocate this bid and his followers were the exclusive advocates of it for many years.

(2) A "utility" 1NT response with a wide variety of weak hands. This was the forerunner of the forcing ROTH-STONE 1NT response.

(3) Light opening bids with distributional patterns such as 5-4-3-1, 5-4-4-0, 4-4-4-1, 6-4-3-0, 5-5-3-0, 6-5-1-1, etc.

(4) Frequent bids in short suits; Churchill was well before his time in using such bids as all-purpose bids for exploring for games and slams, or steering the contract into a particular hand, etc.

(5) Constructive overcalls; forcing jump overcalls.

(6) Four-card openings in suits of any strength.

(7) "Picture Bidding"; jump rebids and responses used essentially to describe solid or near-solid suits as well as slam aspirations.

(8) No strength-showing forcing opening bid.

(9) Sparing use of preemptive bids.

(10) Balance of Power bidding (see BALANCING).

CIPHER BID. See ARTIFICIAL BID.

CIRCUS. See SHARIF BRIDGE CIRCUS.

CLAIM OR CONCESSION. A suggestion that play be curtailed; a statement to the effect that a player will win (claim) or lose (concession) a specific number of tricks. The definition is the same for both duplicate and social bridge, but the procedure following a claim or concession is quite different.

In social bridge, the player who claims, or concedes, must put his cards face up on the table, and then make a comprehensive statement of his intentions. If the claim is disputed, play continues with claimer's cards exposed. Claimer is restricted by the statement he made: He may not take an unannounced finesse, except one proven or virtually proven; If he may have been unaware that a trump remained out, his opponents may require him to draw, or not to draw, trump. He may adopt only a routine line of play, not an unannounced unusual line.

If claimer is declarer, either defender (or both) may face his cards for partner's inspection without penalty. If claimer is a defender, declarer may prohibit the other defender from making a play that could be suggested by seeing partner's cards.

In duplicate bridge a claim or concession ends play. When there is any dispute the Director is called to hear the claimer repeat his statement and to adjudicate the result. In adjudicating, the Director restricts claimer's proposed line of play as in rubber bridge.

A concession may be withdrawn if the player has conceded a trick he has already won, or must win on any possible play of the remaining cards. In rubber bridge this right lapses when all players have called on a subsequent deal. In duplicate it lapses with the expiration of the normal protest period. If a conceded trick cannot be lost by any probable play, the concession may be withdrawn: in rubber bridge until the cards are mixed together; in duplicate until the conceding side calls on a subsequent deal or the round ends. In duplicate, agreeing to an opponent's claim, "acquiescing", is not conceding: an acquiescence may be withdrawn within the normal protest period. In either game, a concession by one defender is withdrawn if the other objects immediately.

In both codes of law this general principle is established: After any disputed claim, the objective is to settle the issue as equitably as possible to both sides, but any doubtful point should be resolved in favor of the claimer's opponents.

CLASH SQUEEZE. A squeeze in three suits, distinguished by the presence of a special type of long menace called a clash menace, analyzed and named by Chien-Hwa Wang (in *Bridge Magazine* articles 1956-57).

```
              A 2
K                      J 10
              Q
```

South's queen is a clash menace against West's king.

```
              A x x
Q J                    9 x x
              K 10
```

South's 10 is a clash menace against West's queen and jack.

The following are the basic positions for a clash squeeze.

(1) Simple Squeeze-Positional

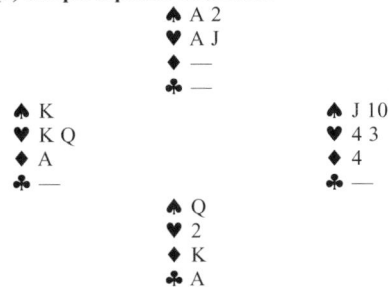

South leads the ♣A, which squeezes West in three suits (if West discards a spade, South cashes the queen and then crosses to the ♥A in order to take the ♠A).

Delayed (secondary)

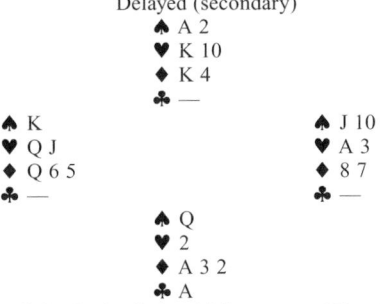

South leads the ♣A, which squeezes West in three suits. West must discard a heart, and North throws a

spade. Now South can lead a heart and establish a trick in that suit. See also VICE SQUEEZE.

(2) Double Squeeze (nonsimultaneous and positional). A double clash squeeze consists of two parts: a clash squeeze against one opponent, then a simple squeeze against the other.

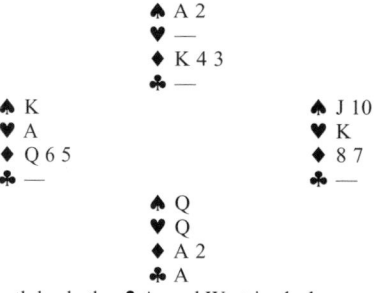

South leads the ♣A, and West is clash squeezed. He must discard a heart, after which South plays the ♦K then ♦A to squeeze East in the majors.

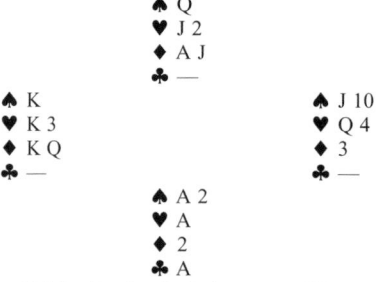

The ♣A lead by South clash squeezes West, and forces him to discard a heart. South cashes the ♥A (VIENNA COUP), then crosses to the ♦A, squeezing East in the majors.

(3) Double Squeeze (simultaneous)

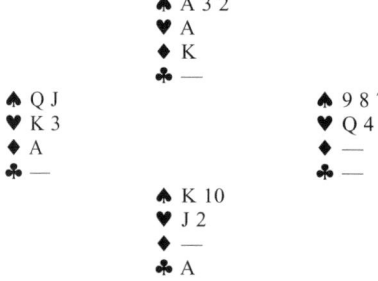

On the lead of the ♣A West must discard a heart, North throws a diamond, and East is squeezed in the majors. This is a positional squeeze.

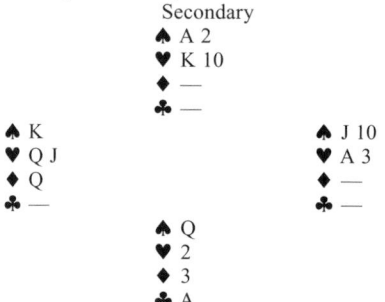

South leads the ♣A. If West discards a heart, North throws a spade, and East throws a spade. South leads a heart to establish a trick in that suit, with the ♠A for an entry. If West throws a spade, North throws a heart as does East. South cashes the ♠Q and leads a heart to throw in East who must give the last trick to North's ♠A.

(4) Trump Squeeze

Single

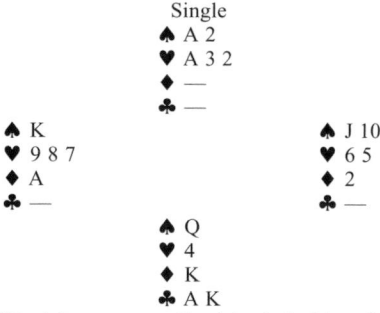

With clubs as trumps, South leads the king of that suit. West can do no better than discard a heart, but now South can ruff out that suit, using the ♠A as a re-entry. This squeeze is positional.

Double

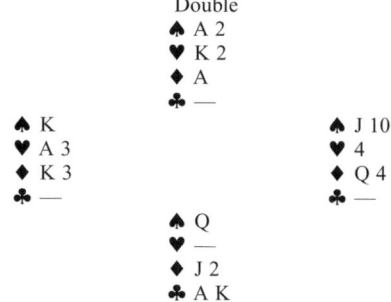

Clubs are trumps. South leads the trump king, and West must throw a diamond. North and East discard hearts. South cashes the ♦A and ruffs a heart, squeezing East in spades and diamonds. See HEDGEHOG SQUEEZE.

CLEAR A SUIT. At notrump play, to clear a suit is to force out, by continued leads of the suit, adversely held high cards so that the remainder of the cards in that suit are winners. At suit play, the term is used also to indicate a line of play which cashes winners in one side suit and trumps out the balance of the cards in that suit so as to eliminate all cards of the suit from both the declarer's and dummy's hand. Then if a trick is lost to the defense later, a further lead of this suit gives declarer the option of trumping in one hand while discarding a potential loser in the other. See also ELIMINATION.

CLOCK. Devices used at tournaments to indicate to the players how much time is left in the round and when the round is ended. The clocks usually are large display boxes with the time indicated by lights. A sound usually is emitted when two minutes remain in the round, and a second sound occurs when the round is over.

Clocks also are used to time pairs in a team event. Since there may be penalties for slow play, it becomes necessary to determine who was responsible for the slow play. The only realistic way to do this is to time the individual pairs with clocks such as chess clocks.

CLOSED HAND. The hand of the declarer, as distinct from the OPEN HAND, which is now legally referred to as the DUMMY. The term dates from BRIDGE WHIST, which introduced the idea of an exposed hand visible to the other players.

CLOSED ROOM. In team-of-four matches, particularly in knockout matches, the two pairs of a team play in different rooms or different areas of the same room. One of these rooms is designated the open room, one the closed room. Normally, spectators are permitted in the open room, and these spectators are free to come and go, without hindrance. However, if spectators are permitted in the closed room, they are restricted to one table and are not permitted to leave until the match they are watching is terminated. As soon as one of the matches in the closed room has been terminated, the original open room becomes a closed room to which no other spectators are permitted entrance, and to which no contestant or spectator may be readmitted after leaving until the last open room contest has terminated.

In important matches where arrangements are made for play-by-play relaying of information to a large group of spectators, the boards are originally played in a closed room with a starting time appreciably earlier than that for the replay. Thus information may be kept from the players in the replay but made available to spectators, who can contrast the results of the first play with what is going on in the replay. Spectators thus are more fully informed of what has gone on than are any of the actual contestants.

In some major events such as the European Championship, the open room is always open, but players are not permitted to leave the closed room until the open half of their match is completed. See BRIDGE-O-RAMA.

CLUB. (1) The symbol ♣, which appears on the 13 cards of the lowest ranking of the four suits in a bridge deck, stems from the French (trefle), but the name seems to be of Spanish or Italian origin as a translation of basto or bastone. The outline of the club symbol suggests a cloverleaf, and therefore the peasantry. (2) The club suit consists of the 13 cards bearing this symbol. Since the club suit as trump is the least likely final declaration when a choice of trump suits is available, many systems make use of the naming of this suit to show conventional holdings. (3) See CLUBS. See CLUB CONVENTIONS.

CLUB BRIDGE. See CHICAGO.

CLUB CHARITY GAMES. See CHARITY PROGRAM OF THE ACBL.

CLUB CONVENTIONS. The low-ranking club suit is particularly well suited for conventional uses of various kinds. The VANDERBILT CLUB was the original "club convention" and has had many successors (see ONE CLUB SYSTEMS and TWO CLUB SYSTEMS). Conventional club bids at higher levels include TWO CLUBS STRONG ARTIFICIAL OPENING, NAMYATS, BERGEN RAISES, STAYMAN and GERBER.

CLUB PROCEDURES. See HOUSE RULES. Each bridge club will find that there are situations in its op-

eration that are not covered by the Laws or where the Laws do not agree with the desire of the members of the club on such points as precedence in entering a table, complement of a table, personal dislikes of certain players, methods of settling games for stakes and like problems. Procedures used in such cases should always be consistent and definitely formulated for future reference.

CLUB SYSTEMS. See ONE CLUB SYSTEMS, TWO CLUB SYSTEMS.

CLUBS. Organizations or groups of bridge players who form units acting as centers of interest for players in a particular community.

Clubs are so diversified today as to type of premises and rules of membership that a comprehensive description is impossible. Large cities all over the world have at least one and often many more such clubs. Those who prefer to play for stakes can usually be accommodated, providing they pass whatever standards are set up. Those who prefer duplicate can usually find an open-game club devoted to such purposes. In smaller towns throughout America, the emphasis has shifted to duplicate bridge, and a club for that purpose is almost always available to the players of the community. The ACBL issues directories of the 4000-plus clubs that operate games approved by ACBL. Games usually occur at regular periods, with specially scheduled club championship events every calendar quarter. Fees are charged for each participation, and in some cases annual dues as well. See OLDEST CLUBS.

CLUBS FOR TAKEOUT. A variation of CHEAPER MINOR TAKEOUT. The bid for takeout is always made in clubs. Even when the preempt is in clubs, the next higher club bid shows a hand worth a takeout double.

COAT CARDS. The original term in English for the three cards of each suit which represent costumed human figures: the king, queen and jack. In some countries a fourth coat card, variously the valet or courtier, is included in the deck. The term has been superseded by a corruption, "court cards." See COURT CARD, FACE CARDS.

CODED RAISES. When a major-suit opening is doubled, some artificial raises are often used.

West	North	East	South
1♠	Dbl	2♣	

This is often used to show a strong single raise with 7-9 points. A popular extension is to play this to show 3-card support and a jump to 3D to show similar values with four-card support. This leaves one natural non-forcing bid available in each minor.

COFFEEHOUSE BRIDGE. Card playing in European coffee houses frequently featured conversational or other gambits designed to mislead opponents, and the term "coffeehouse bridge" became a synonym for legal but unethical gambits. Such questions as "Did you bid a *spade*?" with a rising inflection to inform partner of a sound spade holding in one's own cards, or "What did you bid first over 1♦?" to right-hand opponent when one wants his partner to lead that suit against a notrump contract, are gambits that are easily caught. Such a player is ostracized at rubber bridge, and the offense is adjudi-

cated in duplicate bridge when a director is present. Action on a doubtful hand after a slow pass by partner is somewhat harder to classify, but the ethical player will pass all such doubtful hands after such a slow pass by partner.

Conversational gambits, even when made without any devious intent, have no place at the bridge table among serious, ethical players.

COFFEEHOUSING. Indulging in unethical actions with full intent to mislead opponents.

K J

Q 2   A 5

4 3

The 4 is led from the closed hand, and West hesitates before playing the obvious 2. This is coffeehousing — an attempt to make the declarer believe that West was thinking of playing the ace. If this happens in tournament play, South should call the director and is likely to get redress under Law 73D2, LAWS OF DUPLICATE CONTRACT BRIDGE. See COFFEEHOUSE BRIDGE.

COFFIN TROPHY. Awarded to the NORTH AMERICAN WOMEN'S BOARD-A-MATCH TEAMS. The trophy honors George Coffin, prolific bridge author.

C.O.I. See COMMITTEE FOR AN OPEN AND IMPROVED ACBL.

COLD. Bridge slang term describing an easily makable contract. In post-mortem heat, players tend to exaggerate the degrees of coldness. Frigid and icy are similar terms. A colorful variation is "colder than a creek rock" or "crick rock."

COLLECTION AND ARRANGEMENT OF TRICKS. See LAWS OF CONTRACT BRIDGE (Law 65); LAWS OF DUPLICATE (Law 65).

COLLECTIONS OF PLAYING CARDS. Collections, public and private, are fairly numerous; quite a few museums have cards as part of their material on graphic arts.

The largest collection in the United States, a gift of the United States Playing Card Company to the Museum of Art, is in Cincinnati OH. In New York City, the Morgan Library has a few of the oldest and most valuable cards. Yale University has a collection of more than 3000 packs, uncut sheets, and card printers' woodblocks acquired by the late Melbert and Mary Cary and willed to Yale University in 1967.

The French collection is in the Bibliotheque Nationale in Paris; London has a collection in the Guildhall; others are in Vienna, Nuremberg, Dresden, Munich, and Budapest. The Deutschspielkarten Museum in Leinfelden, Germany, south of Stuttgart, is a research center and an exhibition. The Museo "Fournier" de Naipes in Vitoria, Spain, has a collection of 6,000 packs and more than 12,000 books. The largest private collection, belonging to Albert Field, Astoria N.Y., has been willed to Columbia University.

COLLEGE BRIDGE. See INTERCOLLEGIATE BRIDGE TOURNAMENT. Also see Appendix IV for results.

COLLOQUIALISMS. Bridge has evolved or adopted its share of colloquialisms. For example, see the following: BIFF; BLOCKBUSTER; DEATH HOLDING; DUB; FIXED; FRAME; GAME HOG; GOULASH; HOOK; HORSE AND HORSE; JUNK; KIBITZ; KICK IT; KILLED; LAY-DOWN; LOCK; MAMA-PAPA BRIDGE; MAYONNAISE; PALOOKA; PHANTOM SACRIFICE; PIANOLA; PUMP; PUNCH; QUACK; RAGS; RIDE; SHAKE; SOCK; STIFF; SUCKER'S DOUBLE; TANK; UNDER THE GUN; and UPPERCUT.

COLONIAL ACOL. A version of ACOL popular in Canada; its basic elements were used by all three Canadian pairs in the 1972 World Team Olympiad.

Major features include four-card major suit openings (1♣ opening may be prepared). Jump raises are usually limit, with either SWISS, JACOBY 2NT or SPLINTERS used to show a strong raise. 1NT opening is 16-18, although some shade it to 15-17, with TWO-WAY STAYMAN. Opening bids of 2♦, 2♥, or 2♠ are ACOL TWO-BIDS; some partnerships use FLANNERY 2♦.

COLOR. A rarely used term that distinguishes suit-play from notrump play. In the bidding, to "change the color" means to bid a new suit. The term is virtually synonymous with "suit."In non-English languages, the common term is color, not suits.

Originally there were four colors – white, red, blue and black. The associated symbols – the spear, the heart, the rhombus and the clover – became dominant in France and spread to other countries.

COLORFUL CUEBID. An immediate overcall in the opponent's major suit to show two unbid suits of the same color. Devised by Dorothy Hayden Truscott. See also CUEBIDS IN OPPONENT'S SUIT; MICHAELS CUEBID.

COLUMNS. See BRIDGE COLUMNS.

COLUMNISTS. See BRIDGE COLUMNS.

COMBINATION FINESSE. See DOUBLE FINESSE and INTRA-FINESSE.

COMBINATION TEAM SCORING. A method of scoring team-of-four events that permits comparison of pair scores as well as team scores. After award of team scores on a win-half-loss basis, the North-South scores are matchpointed on the basis of the number of times the board was played, and the East-West scores are matchpointed on the same basis.

In theory this combination team scoring permits a team to analyze its game as to which of the pairs contributed to the winning or losing of boards by securing a less-than-average result.

This is also the method by which team scores are computed on a board that has been fouled between the times that the two halves of the team play it. The fields resulting from the fouling are matchpointed separately, and the combination of the percentages of the possible matchpoints totaled for the two team halves. Such a total of less than 70 loses the board, exceeding 130 wins the board, and between these percentages a half on the board is awarded.

COMBINATION. The idea of a combination is fundamental to bridge calculations. Examples where this conception is used are in calculating the probability of a specified hand pattern or the division of a suit among the four players. It is also frequently used in calculating the respective probabilities of (or the ratio between) the division of the combined holding of the defenders in a specified suit or with specified honor holdings.

Our general expression for a combination is $_nC_r$, which we read as "the number of combinations of n things taken r at a time". For example, $_4C_2$ means the number of ways in which we can select two articles out of a total of four articles.

We note that if r=n we can write $_nC_n$ in place of $_nC_r$. Whatever the number n represents $_nC_n$ is equal to 1. After all, there is only one way in which we can select n articles out of a total of n articles. There is also only one way in which we can select no (0) articles.

The values of a selected number of combinations are given in Mathematical Tables, Table 5.

If we wish to calculate the value of a combination we need to understand the concept of the 'factorial'. For bridge purposes the factorial of a number is the product of all numbers from 1 up to and including the specified number, e. g., five factorial (written 5!) is $1 \cdot 2 \cdot 3 \cdot 4 \cdot 5$. When using factorials in our calculations we often find it simpler to reverse the above order, setting out 5! as $5 \cdot 4 \cdot 3 \cdot 2 \cdot 1$.

Conventionally the value of 0! is taken as 1.

Consider the number of ways in which 13 cards can be selected from a pack of 52 cards. Our first can be any one of the 52 cards, our second any one of 51 cards, etc. We have the following calculation:

$$52 \cdot 51 \cdot 50 \ldots . 41 \cdot 40$$

which is the same as multiplying all the numbers from 52 down to 1 and dividing the answer by the product of all the numbers from 39 down to 1. We can express this calculation in mathematical shorthand as:

$$\frac{52!}{39!}$$

However, this is not the whole story. The answer we obtain would be correct if we were interested in the order in which we select the cards. This is not the case. The order in which the cards are selected is irrelevant for our purpose. Let us take one of the 13 cards at random. It could have been selected on any one of our 13 draws. A second of these cards could have been selected on any one of the remaining twelve draws, and so on. In other words, we have $13 \cdot 12 \cdot 11 \ldots . \cdot 1$ (or 13!) ways in which those 13 cards could be selected. This means that the total number of ways in which 13 cards can be selected from a pack of 52 cards is

$$\frac{52!}{39! \ 13!}$$

(See NUMBER OF POSSIBLE HANDS, DEALS).

Our general formula for this type of calculation is

$$\frac{n!}{r! \ (n-r)!}$$

Let us now look at a simple example where the defenders have a combined holding of four cards in a specified suit. This means that they hold 22 cards in the other three suits. A named player can have a holding in the specified suit of

0 cards in $_4C_0 \cdot {_{22}C_{13}}$ ways.
1 card in $_4C_1 \cdot {_{22}C_{12}}$ ways.
2 cards in $_4C_2 \cdot {_{22}C_{11}}$ ways.
3 cards in $_4C_3 \cdot {_{22}C_{10}}$ ways.
4 cards in $_4C_4 \cdot {_{22}C_9}$ ways.

Bearing in mind that 26 cards can be divided between the two defenders in $_{26}C_{13}$ (or 10,400,600) ways, we obtain the following table

			%.
$_4C_0 \cdot {_{22}C_{13}}$	$= 1 \cdot 497{,}420$		
	$= 497{,}420$	$=$	4.7826
$_4C_1 \cdot {_{22}C_{12}}$	$= 4 \cdot 646{,}646$		
	$= 2{,}586{,}584$	$=$	24.8696
$_4C_2 \cdot {_{22}C_{11}}$	$= 6 \cdot 705{,}432$		
	$= 4{,}232{,}592$	$=$	40.6957
$_4C_3 \cdot {_{22}C_{10}}$	$= 4 \cdot 646{,}646$		
	$= 2{,}586{,}584$	$=$	24.8696
$_4C_4 \cdot {_{22}C_9}$	$= 1 \cdot 497{,}420$		
	$= 497{,}420$		4.7826
TOTAL	10,400,600		100.0001

The extra 0.0001% is, of course, due to approximating.

We note that $_nC_r = {_nC(n-r)}$. In other words, $_4C_1$ is equal to $_4C_3$. This is obvious, for if one player can hold r cards in a specified number of ways his partner must be able to hold the remainder of the partnership cards in exactly the same number of ways.

Now let us examine the problem of a holding of specified cards. Let us assume that the four cards held by the defense in a named suit consist of K-Q-x-x. What is the probability that a named defender, e.g., West, holds both the king and the queen? He can hold

K-Q-x-x $= {_4C_4} \cdot {_{22}C_9}$
$= 1 \cdot 497{,}420$
$= 497{,}420$
K-Q-x $= {_2C_2} \cdot {_2C_1} \cdot {_{22}C_{10}}$
$= 1 \cdot 2 \cdot 646{,}646$
$= 1{,}293{,}292$
K-Q $= {_2C_2} \cdot {_{22}C_{11}}$
$= 1 \cdot 705{,}432$
$= 705{,}432$
$\underline{}$
2,496,144 Total

The respective percentages are: 4.7826; 12.4348; 6.7826. The total is exactly 24%.

When we compare the probability of his holding the doubleton K-Q with the probability of his holding the singleton K half our work is already done. We have

K-Q $= {_2C_2} \cdot {_{22}C_{11}}$ $= 1 \cdot 705{,}432$
$= 705{,}432$ $= 6.7826\%$
K $= {_1C_1} \cdot {_{22}C_{12}}$ $= 1 \cdot 646{,}646$
$= 646{,}646$ $= 6.2174\%$

We find that 705,432 and 646,646 have a highest common factor (HCF) of 58,786 giving us a ratio of 12:11.

As $_2C_2$ and $_1C_1$ are both equal to 1 we are really comparing $_{22}C_{11}$ and $_{22}C_{12}$. This comparison can be made without the above calculations if we note that

$$_nC \ (r+1) = \frac{_nC_r \ (n-r)}{r+1}$$

In our above example we have n = 22 and r = 11, so

$$_{22}C_{11} = \frac{_{22}C_{11} \ (22-11)}{11+1} \quad \text{or} \quad \frac{_{22}C_{11} \cdot 11}{12}$$

giving us a ratio of $_{22}C_{12}$ to $_{22}C_{11}$ or 11:12. Alternatively we can use the formula

$$_nC(r-1) = \frac{_nC_r \cdot r}{n-(r-1)} \quad \text{or} \quad _{22}C_{11} = \frac{_{22}C_{12} \cdot 12}{22-(12-1)}$$

giving us the ratio of $_{22}C_{11}$ to $_{22}C_{12}$ as 12:11. This method

may be used to draw other comparisons, e.g., which has the greater probability, and by how much, that a named player will hold two out of four missing cards or that he will hold three of such cards? We have a comparison between

$$_4C_2 \cdot {}_{22}C_{11} \text{ and } {}_4C_3 \cdot {}_{22}C_{10}.$$

We know that

$$_{22}C_{11} = {}_{22}C_{10} \cdot {}^{12}/_{11}$$

and that

$$_4C_2 = {}_4C_3 \times {}^3/_2$$

so $_4C_2 \cdot {}_{22}C_{11} = \left({}_4C_3 \cdot \dfrac{3}{2} \right) \left({}_{22}C_{10} \cdot \dfrac{12}{11} \right)$

The ratio is thus

$$_4C_2 \cdot {}_{22}C_{11} : {}_4C_3 \cdot {}_{22}C_{10} :: 18 : 11$$

This means that the chance of a named player holding two of four missing cards is higher than his chance of holding three of such cards. However, the overall chance of a 3-1 or 1-3 break is 22 : 18 (or 11 : 9) as there are two different (and equal) ways in which the defenders' cards can be divided so that one of them holds three cards, but only one way in which each of them holds two cards.

There are many other problems in which we can use this method of calculating the ratios between two (or more) different probabilities.

COME-ON, COME-ON SIGNAL. A defensive maneuver by which one player indicates to his partner that he wishes a suit, led by his partner, to be continued. The usual come-on is a HIGH-LOW SIGNAL, called also an ECHO and in England, a PETER. An alternative is the UPSIDE-DOWN SIGNAL. See ATTITUDE SIGNAL.

COMIC NOTRUMP OVERCALL. An overcall of 1NT to show a weak hand with a long suit. Partner bids 2♣ to locate the long suit. See also GARDENER NOTRUMP OVERCALL.

COMMAND BID. A term suggested by George Rosenkranz to describe a bid that commands partner to make a specific response, but (a) does not promise a holding in the commanded suit (compare TRANSFER BID); (b) promises no particular strength (compare DEMAND BID); (c) does not ask about the holding in any suit (compare ASKING BID). For example:

West	North	East	South
2♠	Dbl	Pass	2NT

By partnership agreement, South's bid of 2NT is LEBENSOHL. North is forced to bid 3♣, after which South has several options.

With the advent of conventions such as PUPPET STAYMAN, the alternative term "puppet bid" has come into use.

COMMITTEE. In tournaments of the American Contract Bridge League of sectional or higher rating, a committee from the sponsoring organization is charged with the responsibility of making necessary arrangements. This is known as the tournament committee. The work of this committee is divided into two parts, before and during the tournament. Among the pretournament duties are arrangements for location, dates, securing of sanctions, arrangements for services to the players, prizes, obtaining the services of a director, publicity and financing.

During the course of a tournament, the director may be called on to make a ruling where he is unable to se-cure agreement on the facts under question. In such cases, and in cases where the director uses his discretionary powers, a player may, through the director, appeal to the tournament committee. Such an appeal is based on questions of fact, not of law. See Chapter XI, LAWS OF DUPLICATE CONTRACT BRIDGE.

Appeals to the national authority on matters of conduct, deportment or ethics can be taken to the ACBL Conduct and Ethics Committee, and on questions of law to the ACBL Laws Commission.

Occasionally, the tournament committee delegates to a subcommittee (known as an appeals committee) its duties at a particular tournament. See NATIONAL APPEALS COMMITTEE.

At world championships, a specially appointed appeals committee is on duty during and after every session of play.

COMMITTEE FOR AN OPEN AND IMPROVED ACBL (COI). Organized in 1990 by a group of ACBL members interested in promoting openness in Board and Management functions and offering constructive criticisms. Besides the concentration on communications, the group focused specifically on cost containment, efficiency at headquarters, reducing the size of the Board of Directors and the costs of Board meetings, honorariums and expenses. They advocated Bylaw revision and redistricting. At the Boston NABC in the summer of 1990, the annual membership meeting was reconvened five times (probably the longest in history) as amendments to Bylaws were initiated. Four months later at the Fall NABC in San Francisco the membership and the Board of Governors voted in favor of four of five recommended Bylaws. Also at San Francisco COI participated in formation of the President's Advisory Committee on Policies and Procedures (PACPP) composed of three members each from the Board of Directors, the Board of Governors and the general membership with Jack Feagin, head of COI, as spokesman for membership. Four years later the *COI Newsletter* agreed that PACPP —presented as an alternative to the "war being waged by some of the members hoping to achieve changes in the ACBL government and management" — proved to be a flop.

At the Spring NABC in Atlantic City in 1991 the Bylaws changes were transformed into "Special Standing Rules" (a supplement to ACBL Bylaws) subject to cancellation by a simple majority vote of the Board of Directors. In Las Vegas in the Summer of 1991 COI endorsed Board of Governors recommendations and passed pertinent resolutions to save money and improve existing Bylaws. However, the annual membership meeting was declared a non-meeting because of lack of a quorum, so none of the resolutions could be brought up or voted upon. At the COI meeting in Washington DC in July 1993 the topics of discussion were the new club plan and alternate methods of reducing the size of the Board of Directors.

For many years the COI produced a newsletter just prior to each North American championship. However, the COI now has its own website where news and opinions are aired on an ongoing basis. The organization still produces one newsletter per year. Feagin is president, Jim Wood is the newsletter editor, and Tom Goodwin is the website administrator.

COMMON MARKET CHAMPIONSHIPS. See EUROPEAN COMMUNITY CHAMPIONSHIPS. For results, see Appendix IV.

COMMONSENSE SYSTEM. See CRANE SYSTEM.

COMMUNICATION BETWEEN PARTNERS. The act of conveying information within a partnership. It is a breach of ethics when information is conveyed intentionally by a remark, gesture or mannerism. See LAWS (Proprieties, 1). Information can of course be conveyed legitimately by bids and defensive plays.

COMMUNICATION PLAY. A play intended to preserve or establish communication (transfer of the lead) between partnership hands to make it possible at a strategic time to lead from a certain hand; or a play to destroy such means of communication between the opponents. Various plays of this nature are discussed in the following articles: DESCHAPELLES COUP; DUCKING; ENTRY; ENTRY-KILLING PLAY; HOLDUP; MERRIMAC COUP; SCISSORS COUP.

COMMUNICATIONS. The ability to transfer the lead from one hand to the opposite hand.

COMMUTER BRIDGE. A set-to at bridge on trains, popular in Boston, Chicago, New York, Philadelphia and other cities. Players who regularly use the same train for commuting arrange to have the first player to enter the train reserve a double seat, and the other players use the same car, joining the game as soon as they board the train. In New York, the cards are dealt as the last player boards, and play is continued until the train reaches the Newark or 125th Street station, after which no further hands are dealt.

Originally, running scores in the form of rubbers prevailed, continuing from day to day with settlement of the wagers made monthly, but in the Sixties four-deal bridge (CHICAGO) gained ground. In some groups it is common to make a Tunnel Bid: A wild action aimed at recovering lost ground as the train runs into the terminal.

COMPACT KNOCKOUT TEAMS. The usual match in a knockout event runs for at least one full session. However, in a compact event, the matches are shortened so that two matches can be played in one session. This makes it possible to determine a winner in a 16-team game in just two sessions. This means the entire event can be finished in one day. See BRACKETED KNOCKOUT TEAMS, DOUBLE ELIMINATION KNOCKOUT TEAMS, HANDICAP KNOCKOUT TEAMS, MINIKNOCKOUT TEAMS, MIXED TEAMS, OPEN TEAMS, RANDOM DRAW KNOCKOUT TEAMS, TEAM GAMES, ZIP KNOCKOUT TEAMS.

COMPARING SCORES. Discussion of results already achieved by contestants in a duplicate competition. Making such comparisons with other contestants playing the same board in tournament play before the session's play has been completed has long been held to be unethical. Since 1963 these comparisons have been declared illegal, and the director is authorized to assess penalties for such actions.

The private scores kept by many tournament players furnish material for long and involved discussions of what might have been, and are very useful for later study and as a reminder of holdings.

In club games where traveling scoreslips are used to facilitate the scoring of the game, knowledge of previous results on an individual board is legitimately available to the players after the board has been played. Courtesy requires that the player responsible for scoring the result make the slip available to the other players who are entitled to see it; discussion of previous results should be held in abeyance until both (or all) the boards of the current round have been completed. Score comparison is not regarded with disfavor in Europe. Players may compare scores on boards already played by both partnerships unless specifically instructed to the contrary. See ESTIMATION.

COMPARISONS. At duplicate, comparisons are made between pairs (or players) who played a board in the same direction, and consequently under similar conditions of dealer, vulnerability, and holding. See BALANCED COMPARISONS.

COMPASS POINTS. In discussing bridge hands, columnists describe the four players by using the points of the compass to distinguish the players. Thus North and South compete against East and West. In tournament play, too, the table markers designate the seating of the players for the original deals by compass directions at designated tables. In the usual Mitchell type of tournament competition, the North and South players remain in the same seats throughout, doing the scoring and passing the boards, while the East and West players move from table to table in a direction opposite that in which the boards are passed. In other types of competition, a pair of players may occupy either the North-South or the East-West seats for a portion of the session.

COMPENSATION. A method of playing a one-table game with the luck of the deal virtually eliminated. It was devised by players in Kharkov in the Ukraine and was developed by players in Moscow.

By analyzing thousands of deals with the aid of a computer, they calculated the scoring expectation with a given number of high-card points in the partnership hands. This established a table so that players can measure at the end of a deal whether they have met, fallen short or surpassed expectations.

Their table is: 20 points, 0; 21, 50; 22, 70; 23, 110. For higher point counts the expectation varies with vulnerability: 24 points, 200 not vulnerable, 290 vulnerable; 25, 300, 440; 26, 350, 520; 27, 400, 630; 28, 430, 630; 29, 460, 660; 30, 490, 690; 31, 600, 900; 32, 700, 1050; 33, 900, 1350; 34, 1000, 1500; 35, 1100, 1650; 36, 1200, 1800; 37+, 1300, 1950.

An example of how the scoring works: a vulnerable partnership that bids and makes 3NT for 600 with 24 points collects 600 - 290 = 310.

COMPETITION. (1) Any duplicate bridge contest. See TOURNAMENT. (2) A bidding situation in which both sides are active.

COMPETITIVE BIDDING. Bidding sequences in which both partnerships enter the auction. Grouped articles include DEFENSE TO ONE NOTRUMP, DEFENSIVE BIDDING, DOUBLES, OVERCALLS, TWO-

SUITER CONVENTIONS. Other entries include AD-VANCE SAVE, APSTRO, ASTRO, ASTPRO, BAL-ANCING, BECKER, BERGEN OVER NOTRUMP, BROMAD, BROZEL, CANSINO, CAPPELLETTI, CAPPELLETTI OVER OPPONENT'S DOUBLE OF ONE OF A MAJOR, CLUBS FOR TAKEOUT, COM-PETITIVE DOUBLE, CRASH, DEFENSE TO OPEN-ING FOUR-BIDS, DEFENSE TO OPENING THREE-BIDS, DEFENSE TO STRONG ARTIFICIAL OPEN-INGS, DEFENSE TO TWO-SUITED INTERFER-ENCE, DONT, DOUBLE FOR SACRIFICE, ESCAPE, ESCAPE SUIT, EXTENDED HERBERT NEGATIVES, FORCING PASS, GOOD-BAD TWO NOTRUMP, GRANO-ASTRO, HAMILTON, KOCK-WERNER REDOUBLE, LANDY, LEAD-DIRECTING BID, LEBENSOHL APPLICATIONS, LITTLE CUEBID (PETIT CUEBID), MITCHELL STAYMAN, MODI-FIED CRASH, OBAR BIDS, REDOUBLE, RESCUE, RIGAL OVER PROTECTIVE NOTRUMPS, RIPSTRA, RUBENS ADVANCES, SACRIFICE, SCRAMBLING, SCRAMBLING TWO NOTRUMP, SOS REDOUBLE, SUCTION, SUPER UNUSUAL NOTRUMP, SUPPORT DOUBLE, TAKEOUT DOUBLE, TRANSFERS OVER DOUBLES OF OPENING PREEMPTIVE BIDS, TRAP PASS, WOOLSEY, WRIGGLE.

COMPETITIVE DOUBLE. A double in a competi-tive auction which invites partner to bid game but gives him the option of signing off in a partscore or passing for penalties. One increasingly popular example is the MAXIMAL DOUBLE. Competitive doubles can be useful in contested auctions where the enemy suit has been bid and raised at a low level:

West	North	East	South
			1♥
2♣	2♥	3♣	Pass
Pass	?		

North may hold

  ♠ A 7 4 3   ♥ J 6 2   ♦ A 10 9 4   ♣ 8 3

He is too strong to pass and his holding in clubs is too weak to make either a penalty double or a cooperative double, but his aces are useful for either offense or de-fense. Since South will usually not have sufficient val-ues in the opponents' suit to double for penalties in such an auction, and since any unilateral action could easily be wrong, some experts prefer to use this double as competitive. It says: "Partner, I have a good hand with two-way values and don't know what to do; *you* decide."

Another typical competitive double occurs when the doubler's previous bidding shows that he cannot possi-bly be strong in the suit he is doubling.

West	North	East	South
			1♦
Pass	1NT	2♠	Pass
Pass	?		

North cannot have as many as four good spades in view of his original 1NT response, and his location in front of the spade bidder is hardly ideal for defensive purposes. Thus a double is competitive, showing a hand such as:

  ♠ A 6 3   ♥ J 6 4   ♦ A 6   ♣ 10 9 7 4 3

Partner is asked to decide whether to play for the pen-alty, or bid on in notrump.

COMPLEMENTARY SCORES. When two contes-tants play against each other in a matchpoint contest,

their combined matchpoint scores add up to the matchpoint top available on that board, and the two scores are complements of each other. For example, if top score is 12 points and the North-South pair earns 8 points, the opposing East-West pair earns 4 points. Simi-larly if one pair earns 2½ points, the opposing pair earns 9½ points.

COMPLETE THE CUT. See CUT (2).

COMPLETE TABLE. In rubber bridge, four or more players. In club bridge, club rules sometimes specify six players as constituting a complete table. When a table is complete, no other player may cut in until or unless one of the players withdraws.

The alternative procedure, common in England, is for players to cut into any table which has completed a rub-ber, provided only that three players may not cut in un-less there is only one table in play. This arrangement produces a greater circulation of players.

COMPOUND GUARD SQUEEZE. A squeeze in three suits, in which two suits are stopped by both opponents and the third suit holding requires a defender to retain certain cards to prevent declarer from taking a winning finesse.

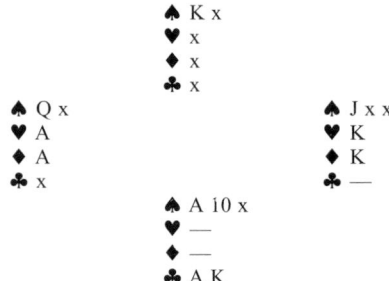

South leads the ♣A to squeeze East, who must dis-card a red card. On the continuation of the ♣K, West must discard the red suit which East has retained. North discards the suit which West has kept, and East is squeezed in spades and the red suit he has saved.

See COMPOUND SQUEEZE, COMPOUND TRUMP GUARD SQUEEZE, GUARD SQUEEZE.

COMPOUND SQUEEZE. A preparatory triple squeeze, followed by a double squeeze, analyzed exhaus-tively by Clyde E. Love. This ending requires two double menaces (guarded by both opponents) and a one-card menace. The one-card menace must be placed to the left of the opponent threatened. Declarer has all remaining tricks but one.

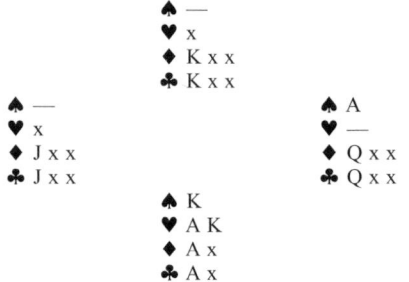

South leads the ♥A, and East is squeezed in three suits.

In order to avoid giving declarer a trick directly, East must unguard a minor suit. South cashes the king and ace of that suit, leaving West with the sole guard in that suit. Now the lead of South's remaining heart effects a double squeeze. Each of the double menaces must be accompanied by a winner in its suit to provide an entry.

The alternate threat squeeze is a hybrid form of compound squeeze with very special requirements.

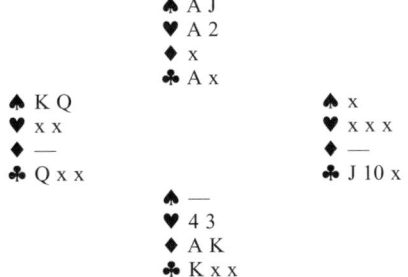

South leads the ♦ A, and West must discard one of his guards. Since a spade would give up a trick directly, West must throw a heart or a club. If he chooses a heart, the low heart is discarded by North on the ♦ K continuation. Meanwhile, East has thrown a heart and a spade. Now a heart lead squeezes West (in spades and clubs), and the ♠ A which follows squeezes East (in hearts and clubs). If West chooses to discard a club on the ♦ A, declarer leads a club to the ace, cashes the ♠ A and returns to his hand with the ♣ K. Now the lead of the ♦ K brings about a simultaneous double squeeze.

From this, the special requirements for this squeeze are: (1) a one-card menace accompanied by a winner and placed to the left of the threatened opponent; (2) a double menace (the alternate threat suit) accompanied by a winner and any two cards of that suit in the hand opposite.

In addition, the usual requirements for a compound squeeze must be present.

COMPOUND TRUMP GUARD SQUEEZE. A compound guard squeeze with a trump element.

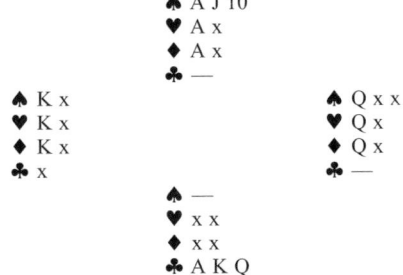

Clubs are trumps. On the lead of the ♣ A North throws a red-suit loser. East is squeezed in three suits and must discard a red card. On the next club lead West abandons the suit East has retained and the other red-suit loser is thrown from the dummy. East discards from the red suit he has already unguarded, and is trump squeezed by a lead to that ace. See COMPOUND SQUEEZE; COMPOUND GUARD SQUEEZE; GUARD SQUEEZE; TRUMP SQUEEZE.

COMPOUND TRUMP SQUEEZE. A compound squeeze in which at least one opponent is subject to a

trump squeeze. The following ending was posed is a double-dummy problem by William Whitfeld before 1900.

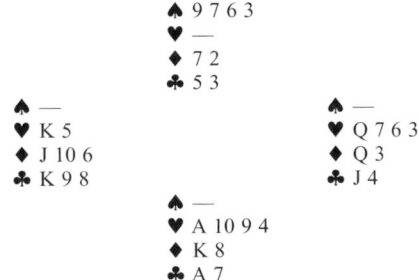

South has the lead with spades as trumps and needs all the tricks.

South leads a low heart and trumps in dummy. A trump is led from dummy and East must discard a club or a diamond to avoid letting declarer establish an extra heart trick by ruffing. South discards whichever suit East discards, and leads that suit from dummy, winning in his hand. Declarer now cashes the ♥ A, discarding a diamond from dummy, and leads a small heart, ruffing. When dummy's last trump is led, East obviously must keep his last heart and discard whichever minor suit he has retained. South discards his heart and West is squeezed in the minor suits.

COMPUTER CHALLENGE MATCH. Zia Mahmood won a challenge match against seven computers in London in 2000. The computer participants were GIB, Meadowlark Bridge, Q-Plus Bridge, Micro Bridge, Blue Chip Bridge, Oxford Bridge and a Saitek machine. GIB won the prize for the best played hand.

COMPUTER CHAMPIONSHIPS. World computer championships have been staged annually since 1997. The chief organizer has been Al Levy of New York City, with support from ACBL, WBF and various sponsors. Computer programs play head-to-head matches, each playing North-South at one table and East-West at the companion table. Each program inputs the opposing convention card. Human operators announce the bids and plays made by their program to the opposing operators. For the 2001 championships it is intended that four computers will be hooked into a central server, virtually eliminating human interaction. Appeals may relate to slow play or to convention misinformation, but there are no plays out of turn or revokes. For results, see Appendix IV.

COMPUTER HANDS. Deals prepared for play by a computer. First used in 1963 at the Eastern States Regional in New York City on the initiative of Martin Scheinberg. As a result of modern computer technology, computers now can make the necessary random selection, sort the cards and place them in the correct board. The machine that performs these actions is called the DUPLIMATE, and it is produced by Per Jannersten of Sweden. The machine makes it possible to preduplicate many sets of boards in preparation for a major event.

On a less sophisticated level, there are many computer programs that generate random hands and reproduce them on paper. This makes it possible for the tourna-

ment directors to pass out the hand records at the start of a session and have the players duplicate two or three boards from the hand records. Once again this makes it possible to have an entire field play exactly the same boards, of course with the exception for each pair of the boards they duplicated. And additional benefit is the ability to print hand records for distribution to the players immediately upon conclusion of the session.

Computer hands are the rule rather than the exception at tournaments throughout the world. Some players still complain that computer hands are "different," but every test made of a certified program has shown the resulting hands to be well within mathematical expectations.

COMPUTER PLAY. Bridge play on computers has become very sophisticated. It is possible to play a real game of bridge via the computer. Each player sits at his own computer and makes his individual bids and plays. His partner might be at a computer in the next room or he could be halfway around the world. The programs are set up so that the players can make their bids in turn just as they would at a table. During the play, the card that is played is displayed when it is played in turn. The programs are set up to keep track of the score whether the game is matchpoints or IMPs. Games can be set up for foursomes, for teams, for pair events and for individuals. Before play starts, pairs can exchange convention cards. When an unusual bid occurs, a player can ask for and get an explanation from his opponents. During play bids can be Alerted and explained.

Tournament play is not only possible – it takes place on a regular basis. In fact OKbridge staged the first Internet World Bridge Championship in 1999 in which teams from all corners of the world competed. The final, staged in Boston at the start of the ACBL Fall North American Championships, pitted the United States against Russia, and the Americans came from behind to win.

Playing programs often offer much more. It is possible for individuals to set up their own tables, for the players to converse, for kibitzers to watch, for directors to rule on judgment situations and Law violations. After the hand is completed, players can review the bidding and trick-by-trick play. If the deal is being played many times, players can see what results were achieved at other tables.

Many new friendships have been formed as a result of meeting in a computer setting. In fact, several marriages have resulted, some involving partners from different countries. If players get their first experience on the computer, quite often they will be interested in trying their luck against live opponents, a boon to club owners.

COMPUTER PROGRAMS. Many software programs have been produced that relate to the technical aspects of bridge. Some produce certain types of hands for practice purposes, some are playing programs, some are analytical programs. A program that has been extremely beneficial to bridge journalists is *Deep Finesse*. Once you load the hand and the bidding into this program, you can learn for sure whether the contract can be made. If it can be made, the program shows how in detail. If the hand can be beaten by perfect defense, the program shows how.

Many programs have been produced that play bridge

– in fact there have been several tournaments in which the only contestants were bridge programs. Usually at least eight software packages from many parts of the world compete. Such programs are capable of a reasonably high level of bidding, play and defense. Products using these programs have been generated, enabling individuals to play bridge against the computer.

The better programs are sophisticated enough to challenge even top-flight players. Zia played a challenge match against a computer program and was hard-pressed to win.

The first appearance of a computer program at a world championship occurred in Valkenburg, the Netherlands, at the 1980 Olympiad. The Volmac program for constructive bidding was demonstrated, and it did just about as well as the human experts. It used artificial bidding methods designed by Benito Garozzo.

COMPUTER SCORING. Almost all tournaments today are scored with the help of a computer. Many excellent programs have been devised that enable a game to be scored almost instantly once the last board has been played. The program used by the American Contract Bridge League is called ACBLScore. This and other programs are in use all over the world. Even most club games are scored by computer.

Computer scoring has made scoring across the field an easy process. When scoring was done manually, scoring across an entire field was an arduous process, requiring many hours and with the results prone to error. With computer scoring, the results are available almost instantaneously. And if an error is found, a couple of simple keystrokes usually is enough to make the correction.

Until the advent of computers, all scoring was done manually. The scorer would enter all results on a large recap sheet, do the necessary matchpointing (figuring the point score for each recorded result), add the scores for each pair and rank the fields.

The first serious attempt to score a tournament with computer assistance occurred in Ostend, Belgium, in the early Fifties. The players used sensitized pencils to enter the scores on punched cards that were fed directly into a machine. Besides calculating the overall standings, the machine furnished each pair with a virtual reproduction of their personal scorecard complete with the matchpoints on each board.

CONCEDE. To yield one or more of the remaining tricks to the opponents. See Laws (Laws 68, 69, 70, 71); LAWS OF DUPLICATE (Laws 68, 69, 70, 71).

CONCESSION. See CLAIM OR CONCESSION.

CONDITIONS OF CONTEST. A statement governing the competition in an event. In general there should be a preliminary statement as to the masterpoint requirements or other prerequisites for entry into the event, the number of sessions the event will run, the entry fee, how many qualifying sessions and how many final (or semifinal) sessions. In knockout team games there should also be a statement as to such matters as the number of boards to be played in each match; the seeding rights, i.e., the rights exercisable by the higher-ranked team with respect to the choice of seats and opponents; any restrictions on the right to have two pairs who played each

other in the first half of the match play against each other in the second half; the method of resolution of the match in the event of a tie, and so forth. In Swiss team games the conditions of contest must include statements as to the form of scoring used, including the scale of victory points, if any. In a pair event a final statement, made up after the event is under way, includes the setup of the game, number to be qualified and method of qualification, whether at-large pairs will be qualified, and computation of the carryover, and the setup of the final (or semifinal) session(s).

Under Law 78D and Law 80, all such conditions become Law, and therefore have the full backing of Law.

CONDONING. An action immediately following an irregularity by the opposition which would have been a proper one if the preceding action had been proper.

At rubber bridge, an irregular bid can be condoned in this way unless the non-offending side has drawn attention to the irregularity. In duplicate such a bid can be condoned as a matter of law. In both forms of the game an irregular lead can be condoned in all circumstances. If a declarer leads from the wrong hand, a defender may follow in proper sequence, either on his own initiative or if his partner so requires. See LAWS 34, 53, 60; LAWS OF DUPLICATE (Laws 27, 53, 60).

CONDUCT. See ETHICS AND CONDUCT.

CONFERENCE. A voluntary association of neighboring ACBL units or districts organized to further the purposes of the ACBL and of its member units. The powers of a Conference are limited to those delegated to it by the member units. Reasons for organizing an ACBL Conference include the promotion of matters of mutual interest, such as tournament attendance and the reduction of inter-unit and inter-district frictions.

CONGLOMERATE MAJOR RAISE. An extension of the SWISS CONVENTION designed to allow responder to make a forcing raise of a major suit opening while specifying whether it is based on a singleton somewhere in the hand, on great high card strength, on very good trumps or merely on general strength. Using the bids just beyond a jump raise (starting with 3♠ over 1♥, or 3NT over 1♠), responder bids as follows:

First step	shows a singleton (unidentified)
Second step	shows 17-18 HCP
Third step	shows four trumps headed by at least two of the top three honors, or more than four trumps headed by at least the ace or king
Fourth step	shows any hand worth a strong raise that does not meet the above criteria.

After responder has shown a singleton, opener can ask where it is by making the cheapest bid. Responder bids the suit of his singleton if he can do so without going past four of the trump suit; otherwise he bids four of the trump suit.

For alternative methods see SUPER SWISS, UNBALANCED SWISS RAISE, VALUE SWISS RAISES.

CONGRESS. Term for TOURNAMENT, dating back to the days of whist. The term no longer is used in North America but still is common as a synonym for tournament in other parts of the world.

CONGRESS, UNITED STATES. A team of players from the United States Congress played matches against CORPORATE AMERICA 1989, 90, 93, 96. Corporate America, made up of major business executives, defeated Congress in all four matches. Playing in 1989 were Rep. Arlan Stangeland (R-Minnesota), captain; Sen. Bob Packwood (R-Oregon); Sen.Rudy Boschwitz (R-Minnesota), Rep. Hank Brown (R-Colorado); Rep. Robert Kastenmeier (D-Wisconsin); Sen. Bob Kerrey (D-Nebraska); Rep. Jim Leach (R-Iowa); Rep. Lynn Martin (R-Illinois); Rep. Howard Nielson (R-Utah); Rep. Robert Zion (R-Wisconsin). On the 1990 team were Stangeland; Boschwitz; Brown; Rep. Jim Bunning (R-Kentucky); Sen. James Jeffords (Ind-Vermont); Kastenmeier; Leach; Nielson; Packwood; Rep. Robert Smith (R-Oregon); Zion. The 1993 team was made up of Leach; Stangeland; Brown; Bunning; Jeffords; Kastenmeier; Packwood; Judge Melvin Welles, and Zion. The 1996 team was made up of Leach, Brown, Bunning, Rep. Conrad Burns (R.-Montana), Sen. Kay Bailey Hutchinson (R-Texas), Rep. James Tallant (R-Missouri), Rep. Thomas Petri (R-Wisconsin), Judge Mel Welles, Packwood.

CONSOLATION PAIRS. Some multi-session pair games have qualifying sessions instead of being play-through. A certain number of pairs in each group qualify to play in the final session or sessions. Usually a special game for non-qualifiers is run alongside the final. This game, a regular pair game as far as movement and scoring are concerned, is called a consolation.

CONSTRUCTIVE. A description applied to a bid that suggests game prospects but is not forcing. The partner will take further action more often than not. See ENCOURAGING (1); INVITATIONAL.

CONSTRUCTIVE BIDDING. Auctions in which one side attempts to locate its best contract without interference from the opponents. See INTERFERENCE BID.

CONSTRUCTIVE RAISE. The use of an immediate raise from 1♠ to 2♠ or 1♥ to 2♥ to show 8-10 points. Weaker raises are shown by bidding 1NT forcing and then reverting to opener's major. This is a slightly weakened version of the Roth-Stone treatment, in which the raise was virtually forcing.

CONSULTATION. This practice between partners regarding a penalty is forbidden under Law 10C2, LAWS OF DUPLICATE, and any such discussion cancels the right to penalize.

CONTESTANT. One or more players competing for a combined score. In an individual contest, each player enters as an individual, changing partners as the movement requires and receiving credit for his own score on each board he plays. In a pair contest, players enter as pairs, playing with the same partner throughout for a common score on all boards played. In a team contest, players enter as a team of four or more, changing partners among their own teammates as permitted by the CONDITIONS OF CONTEST, but competing for a common score. In WBF events it is usual to classify the non-playing captain as a contestant.

CONTESTED AUCTION. See COMPETITIVE BIDDING.

CONTINENTAL CLUB of Amsterdam. Founded in 1889 as a meeting point for Amsterdam businessmen and their American colleagues to play whist and other card games. The Continental is the world's second-oldest bridge club after London's Portland Club. It was prominent in Dutch (and European) bridge in the thirties but the Holocaust in World War II deprived it of many Jewish members. Afterward the membership included the top echelon of Dutch bridge: the brothers Ernst and Frits Goudsmit, Martijn Cats, Herman Filarski, Bob Slavenburg, Jut Kramer, Kees Kaiser and, later, Jaap Kokkes, Arie van Heusden and Max Rebattu. Another member, Maurits Caransa, founded the tournament named after him. He was kidnapped in 1978 after a visit to the club and released after payment of 8,000,000 guilders. During the 100th anniversary celebrations in 1989, the club burned down. It was subsequently relocated.

CONTINUOUS PAIRS. A multi-session event in which each session is a regular pair game, and point awards usually are given for each individual session. The usual method to determine an overall winner is to give player credit for his best two scores, and the overall ranking is done from these figures. However, occasionally different conditions of contest are set up. Each player may play with as many different partners as there are sessions since the overall standings are determined on an individual basis. Continuous Pairs must consist of three or more sessions.Often called Bridge Series in ACBL.

CONTRACT. (1) The undertaking by declarer's side to win, at the denomination named, the number of odd tricks specified in the final bid, whether undoubled, doubled or redoubled. (2) The game of contract bridge, loosely. See TRUMP SUIT.

CONTRACT BRIDGE. Fourth in the succession of partnership card games that began with WHIST and continued with BRIDGE WHIST and AUCTION BRIDGE. The essential point of difference from its predecessor is that no tricks won in the play are counted toward game except those which are contracted for in the bidding. A declarer contracting for and making 100 points in trick score has made a game and becomes vulnerable. Game contracts are: 3NT (first trick worth 40, and subsequent tricks 30 each); four of a major suit, hearts or spades, worth 30 each; five of a minor suit, diamonds or clubs, worth 20 each. See SCORING; MAJORITY CALLING.

Sides may be predetermined if two partnerships are preestablished. Otherwise the cards are cut to establish partnerships and, in any case, to determine the first dealer. Partners face each other in seats arbitrarily named for compass points, North and South opposing East and West. The player at the dealer's left shuffles the cards and presents them to the dealer, who offers them to the player at his right for a cut. Normally, two decks of 52 cards are used, the dealer's partner shuffling the second deck and placing them after shuffling at his right, from where the next dealer offers the cards to the previous dealer for a cut. The dealer distributes the cards one at a time to each player in a clockwise manner beginning with the player on his left, and taking the last card himself, ending with each player having before him a hand of 13 cards. The players study their hands, and the bidding period begins.

The dealer has the opportunity to open the bidding, or he may pass. During the bidding, correct procedure requires that bids be made in a uniform manner, as, "pass," "1 ♠," "double," etc. Any variation from the standard formula is improper, as also are any gestures, remarks, mannerisms or grimaces. See PROPRIETIES. The auction proceeds until three players have passed in succession following the last bid, double or redouble. If all four players pass, the deal is abandoned and the next player deals. (In CHICAGO, the same dealer redeals.) At the end of the bidding, the declarer is determined as that player of the partnership who first named the denomination, suit or notrump, of the final bid. This completes the bidding phase of the hand.

The player to the left of the declarer makes the opening lead. After he has led a card, declarer's partner places his hand face up on the table, and the play of his cards is at the management of the declarer. See ARRANGING.

The play consists of 13 tricks, to each of which each player contributes one card in proper clockwise sequence. To each trick each player must play a card of the suit led, if able. If unable, he may play any card. Any trick containing a trump is won by the highest trump; any trick not containing a trump is won by the highest card of the suit led. The winner of each trick leads to the next trick.

The declarer then attempts to make his contract, by taking as many tricks in excess of six as his final contract specified he would take. If he succeeds, he enters his trick points BELOW THE LINE and any extra tricks or bonuses he may have earned ABOVE THE LINE. When a partnership's total of trick points exceeds 100, that partnership is vulnerable, and a new game is started from a zero trick score on each side. The side first winning two games gets the bonus for winning the rubber. See SCORING.

If the declarer fails to make his contract, his opponents score points above the line for each undertrick. These points are increased if the contract has been doubled or redoubled during the period of the auction. See HISTORY OF BRIDGE.

CONTRACT BRIDGE FORUM. The monthly bridge publication published for four districts of the Western Conference of the American Contract Bridge League. The publication, which appears in a newspaper format, was originated by Tom Stoddard as a private enterprise and later was the official publication of the Pacific Bridge League. The editor is Ken Monzingo, P.O. Box 33567, San Diego CA 92163.

CONTRACT BRIDGE GOLDEN ANNIVERSARY. The invention of contract bridge by Harold Vanderbilt in 1925 was celebrated at a Golden Anniversary party during International Team Trials in Palo Alto CA on Halloween weekend in 1975. Lew Mathe, ACBL president at the time, and Alan Truscott, *New York Times* bridge editor, paid tribute to Harold Vanderbilt whose ideas and talent brought us the game as we know it today. Appropriately, the party was held in the Bay Area where Vanderbilt's cruise ship *Finland* set sail in Octo-

ber 1925. On that cruise Vanderbilt put the finishing touches to his new scoring table with its concept of vulnerability, and contract was born.

The 60th anniversary was observed in Winnipeg, Manitoba, at the NABC in November 1985. The 60th birthday of contract bridge was celebrated with a 235-pound birthday cake designed to serve 1200 people. The *Bridge Bulletin* cover took note of the 60th anniversary with pictures naming "Stars of the Decades" – Harold Vanderbilt in the Twenties, Ely Culbertson in the Thirties, Charles Goren in the Forties, Howard Schenken in the Fifties, Oswald Jacoby in the Sixties, Bob Hamman in the Seventies and Barry Crane in the Eighties. See HISTORY OF BRIDGE

CONTRACT BRIDGE LAWS. For rubber bridge, see LAWS OF CONTRACT BRIDGE; for duplicate bridge, see LAWS OF DUPLICATE CONTRACT BRIDGE; for Chicago, see CHICAGO.

CONTRACT WHIST. A cross between WHIST and CONTRACT BRIDGE. The four players bid in turn for the contract, but the play is that of whist, with all four hands concealed. The principles of the game were set forth in *Contract Whist*, by HUBERT PHILLIPS, published in 1932. Although played only occasionally, it is considered by some to be a game requiring high skill.

CONTRACTING. A word which signifies the act of agreeing to take a certain number of tricks in a deal of bridge.

CONTRACTING SIDE. Declarer and his partner. The opponents are the defending side.

CONTROL ASKING BID. See ASKING BID.

CONTROL BID (see also CUEBID IN OPPONENT'S SUIT). The modern name, advocated by *The Bridge World*, for CUEBIDS TO SHOW CONTROLS. This is to avoid the ambiguous use of the word CUEBID, which more commonly refers to a bid in the opponent's suit. A bid in a suit in which the partnership cannot wish to play is usually a control bid if the partnership is already committed to a game contract. A slam invitation is implied:

	(a)		(b)
North	*South*	*North*	*South*
1♠	3♠	1♣	1♥
4♦		3♥	4♦

In each case the side is committed to game, and a suit has been firmly agreed. The final bid is a slam suggestion, and the cuebidder's partner acts accordingly. If his hand is completely unsuitable for slam purposes, he signs off in the agreed trump suit at the lowest level. If he is willing to cooperate in a slam venture, he can bid a slam directly or take some other strong action which would take the bidding past the game level. When in doubt, he can sometimes make a further control bid below the game level; in case (a), South can make a control bid of 4♥ in his turn without taking the bidding past 4♠.

The first control bid is assumed to show first-round control (usually the ace, but occasionally a void), although a hand which is known to be very weak might make a control bid with a king. Later control bids by either player may show second-round controls.

It is usual (and in some systems compulsory) to make the cheapest possible control bid. Therefore in case (a) above, North denies first-round club control, and in case (b), South denies first-round spade control.

An alternative recommended by Jeremy Flint is to control bid first the higher ranking of two touching aces and the lower of two nontouching aces. (The trump suit is excluded in determining which suits are touching.) The intent is to create extra room for the partnership to show all its controls. A hand given in illustration by Hugh Kelsey in his book on Slam Bidding is:

West	*East*
♠ A 7	♠ 3
♥ A 5 4	♥ K 8 6
♦ J 10 9 6 5 2	♦ A K Q 7
♣ K 4	♣ A Q 8 5 3

Using standard methods of bidding all controls as cheaply as possible, the auction would start:

West	*East*
1♦	3♣
3♦	4♦
4♥	5♣
5♠	?

East cannot be sure his partner has the ♣ K and cannot find out without committing himself. Using the Flint style, however, the auction would be:

West	*East*
1♦	3♣
3♦	4♦
4♠	5♣
5♥	5♠
6♣	7♦

CONTROL BIDS. Alternative name, advocated by *The Bridge World*, for CUEBIDS TO SHOW CONTROLS. This is to avoid the ambiguous use of the word CUEBID, which more commonly refers to a bid in the opponent's suit.

CONTROL MAINTENANCE. A strategy aimed at preventing a defender from gaining the mastery of a particular suit. In notrump hands, HOLD-UP PLAY is the key to control. In trump play, control usually refers to the struggle against a defender holding trump length. The following example is from *Reese On Play* by Terence Reese.

A fairly well-known stratagem to avoid losing control of trumps is to refuse to ruff until dummy can cope with the suit which the opponents have led:

```
              ♠ Q 10 8
              ♥ 9 8
              ♦ Q J 8 7
              ♣ K 9 8 7
♠ 7 6                      ♠ 5 4 3 2
♥ Q J 10 7 6               ♥ K 5 4 3 2
♦ A 9 4                    ♦ 10 5
♣ J 6 3                    ♣ 10 2
              ♠ A K J 9
              ♥ A
              ♦ K 6 3 2
              ♣ A Q 5 4
```

The ♥ Q is led against 4♠. If declarer draws three or four rounds of trumps, the 4-2 split is fatal for him. The right play is to draw two rounds of trumps and then clear diamonds. West wins with the ace and plays a second heart; South discards a club from his hand and any fur-

ther heart leads can be dealt with in dummy.

In the play of this hand declarer used two stratagems to protect himself from losing control; he cleared the side suit before drawing trumps, and he refused to ruff the second heart.

CONTROLLED PSYCHIC. See PSYCHIC CONTROLS.

CONTROLS. (1) Generally, holdings that prevent the opponents' winning one, two or conceivably three immediate tricks in a specified suit.

First-round control: ace, or a void in a trump contract.

Second-round control: king, or a singleton in a trump contract.

Third-round control: queen, or a doubleton in a trump contract.

Controls may be discovered or revealed by means of ASKING BIDS or CUEBIDS. Also see CUEBIDS TO SHOW CONTROLS.

(2) Specifically, aces and kings. An ace is normally counted as two "controls," and a king as one. See BLUE TEAM CLUB, SYMMETRIC RELAY SYSTEM and EXPECTED NUMBER OF CONTROLS IN BALANCED HAND.

CONVENIENT CLUB. See SHORT CLUB.

CONVENIENT MINOR. See SHORT CLUB.

CONVENTION. A call or play with a defined meaning, which may be artificial. The oldest convention is the fourth-best lead, which dates back to Hoyle about 1740. The oldest bidding convention is the takeout double, which was not as obvious when it originated about 1912 as it is today.

CONVENTION CARD. A printed card listing commonly used conventions. It is used by players in duplicate bridge to indicate to opponents the conventions and special understandings a pair has. A pair must fill out a set of convention cards before beginning play that lists offensive style and conventions, defensive conventions and understandings and lead agreements.

The card used by the American Contract Bridge League lists offensive bids on the front, defensive bids and lead understandings on the back. The common conventions are printed on the card so that players merely have to make checkmarks. Open areas also are provided so that players can write in any conventions or understandings that are not in the printed matter.

The card used by the World Bridge Federation is more complicated than the ACBL card. Pairs planning to play in major world events must submit their cards in advance for WBF approval. Failure to do so can result in penalties. Pairs competing in world events often have to submit additional pages reflecting any unusual methods.

Sponsoring organizations have a right to regulate conventions under Law 40E.

CONVENTIONAL. Describing a bid that is based on the use of a convention.

CONVENTIONS, ACBL. Following are the types of conventions permitted in ACBL tournaments. There are three lists — a general list that must be allowed in almost all ACBL tournaments, a limited list for use in games that have an upper masterpoint limit of 20, and a superchart that lists conventions that require a pre-Alert and can be used in specific North American Championship events.

CONVERSATION. Conversation is carried on at the bridge table in the language of the bidding and the play of cards. Any other conversation during the bidding or play of the hand is either distracting (and therefore discourteous), revealing (and therefore improper and even illegal), or misleading. (See COFFEEHOUSING) Although bridge is a social game, any socializing or gossiping should be confined to the short period of the deal, or prior to the start of the game or during a refreshment intermission. See BATTLE, SARAH.

COOPERATIVE DOUBLE. A double that leaves partner the option of passing for penalties or bidding further, a special type is the OPTIONAL DOUBLE. Originally used by Ely Culbertson to describe a double of an opening three-bid, the term is now better reserved for some more complicated situations:

West	North	East	South
Pass	Pass	1♥	Dbl
1♠	2♦	Pass	Pass
2♥	Pass	Pass	Dbl

Since South's first double suggested support for the unbid suits, he cannot be well-stocked in hearts. South's second double suggests a hand such as:

> ♠ A 10 6 3
> ♥ Q 5
> ♦ K 7 5
> ♣ A Q 10 6

South has good defensive values, a doubleton heart honor and moderate support for diamonds. The double is a suggestion that leaves the final decision to North.

West	North	East	South
			1♣
Pass	Pass	Dbl	1♠
2♦	Pass	Pass	Dbl

In the light of his previous bidding, South can hardly have any positive assurance of defeating 2♦. He obviously has a good hand and maybe 4-3-1-5 distribution.

This type of double can occur in many disguises, but the doubler has always limited his hand in such a way that he cannot be in a position to guarantee a penalty. See also COMPETITIVE DOUBLE; DOUBLE; MAXIMAL OVERCALL DOUBLE; OPTIONAL DOUBLE.

COPENHAGEN CLUBS, Bridge Tournament of the. The world's oldest regularly played event, founded in November 1927. It has been played every year since then, even during World War II, on the second Monday of each winter month.

COPENHAGEN CONVENTION. A defensive scheme devised by John Trelde and Gert Lenk of Denmark and popular there. After an opening bid of one of a suit, 2NT shows the low unbid suits, 3♣ shows the high and low unbid suits, and 3♦ shows the high unbid suits.

CORPORATE AMERICA. A Corporate America team, made up of major corporate executives, was formed in 1989 to play a challenge match against a team made up of members of the United States Congress. Matches were held in Washington DC in May of 1989,

90, 93, 96, and Corporate America was the victor in all four matches.

Playing for Corporate America in 1989 were Laurence Tisch, president and chief executive officer of the Columbia Broadcasting System, captain; Alan "Ace" Greenberg, chairman and chief executive officer of The Bear Steams Companies; James Cayne, president of Bear Steams; Warren Buffett, chief executive officer of Berkshire Hathaway; George Gillespie III, partner in Cravath, Swaine and Moore; the late Malcolm Forbes, chairman and editor-in-chief of *Forbes Magazine.* The 1990 team: Tisch; Buffett; Greenberg; Cayne; Gillespie; Jack Dreyfus, founder of the Dreyfus Fund and president of the Dreyfus Medical Foundation; Milton Petrie, chief executive officer of Petrie Stores Corporation. The 1993 team: Buffett; Gillespie; Cayne; Rita Shugart, president of the Monterey Airplane Co.; Nick Nickell, president of Kelso and Co., and Warren Spector, former KING OF BRIDGE. Playing in 1996 were Buffett, Cayne, Gillespie, Greenberg, Nickell and Tisch

Corporate America played a challenge match against the British Parliament team in February, 1990, at the London home of Forbes. Corporate America lost to the Lords but defeated the House of Commons. Playing for Corporate America were Tisch, Forbes, Gillespie, Cayne, Greenberg, Petrie and Buffett.

CORRECT THE COUNT. See RECTIFYING THE COUNT.

CORRECTION PERIOD. The time specified by the sponsoring organization during which corrections to the score may be sought.

Scoring errors may be made by a director (as when he wrongly transcribes a score) or by players at the table. The former must be corrected immediately if attention is drawn to them before the conclusion of the correction period. The latter require evidence that an error was in fact made; the director will often check the private scorecards of the players involved before changing a score.

The correction period's expiration is specified in the Conditions of Contest. (Before the advent of scoring by computer, it often appeared on the RECAPITULATION SHEET or, in a knockout event, on the bracket sheet.) Law 79C of the Laws of Duplicate Bridge states that, unless the sponsoring organization specifies a different time, the correction period expires a minimum of 30 minutes after the official score has been completed and made available for inspection.

Great latitude is allowed in handling scoring correction, in part because of the varying nature of tournament events. For instance, in the case of a club that meets once a week, the correction period may extend until the next weekly session. At a tournament, the correction period for a one-session event usually does not expire until 24 hours after the event (except on the last day of the tournament).

In a multi-session playthrough event, however, the correction period expires about an hour before the end of the next session. In an event with a qualifying stage, the correction period may be shorter; although the scores in a qualifying session — and the masterpoint awards — may be changed until the end of the tournament, the qualifying field must be determined at least 15 minutes prior to the beginning of the next stage of the event.

In a Swiss Teams, the result of each match must be reported quickly so assignments for the next match can be made. (In case of an appeal of a director's ruling in a Swiss Teams, pairings for the next match are made on the assumption that both sides win the appeal.) In an event such as the Vanderbilt Knockout Teams, the correction period may expire at the announced starting time of the next session of an ongoing match, or one hour before the announced starting time for the next match for the last two sessions of a completed match, or 30 minutes after the end of the match for the last two sessions of a final match.

A noted instance of a belated scoring appeal came in the 1990 World Knockout Teams in Geneva. In the third quarter of one semifinal match, a board was scored as down five doubled, -1100, when the actual result was down six. The error affected the result of the match, but was not brought before the tournament committee until the next day. Still, the losing team had a chance, since the Conditions of Contest permitted the committee to correct a manifestly incorrect score. The committee judged, however, that the error lay in what had been agreed to at the table. Had the deal been scored as down six, -1100, that would have been obviously — manifestly — incorrect. But the agreed result, though mistaken, had been scored correctly, so the outcome of the match stood. See PROTEST PERIOD and SCORE CORRECTIONS.

COUNT. A term used in three distinct senses, referring to: (1) the number of cards held in a suit, see COUNTING THE HAND, COUNT SIGNALS, FOSTER ECHO, TRUMP SIGNAL; (2) the strength of a hand, see DISTRIBUTIONAL COUNTS, POINT-COUNT, WORK POINT COUNT; (3) the number of tricks that must be lost for the operation of a squeeze; See RECTIFYING THE COUNT, SQUEEZE WITHOUT THE COUNT.

COUNT SIGNAL. (also called LENGTH SIGNALS.) A method by which one defender indicates to his partner the length held in a particular suit. The standard procedure is to play high-low with an even number of cards and to play the lowest with an odd number of cards.

The converse procedure, upside-down count signals, originated long ago in Sweden and became popular in North America in the Eighties. The advantage of this is that the defender is not in difficulty with some doubletons. One may not be able to spare the higher card, for signalling purposes, when it is a jack, a ten or a nine. With three cards one can normally spare the middle card if the top card would be extravagant.

The normal application occurs when declarer attacks a suit in which he is strong, but a signal can be made in a suit which is both led and dominated by the defenders. (See FOSTER ECHO.) In a high-level contract, the opening leader may need to know his partner's length in order to judge which tricks can be cashed quickly.

Accurate suit-length signals are the key to a golden treasury of defensive plays. After a few tricks have been played, good defensive signalers may know nearly everything about the unseen hands and should be able to play just as accurately as declarer.

A defender may decide not to echo for fear of giving information to declarer. Conversely he may echo with an odd number in an attempt to fool declarer.

When following a suit played by the declarer, always echo when using standard signals to show an even number of cards unless it appears that this may help declarer,

in which case do not echo at all. Occasional false signals should be made in situations where it will not matter that partner is misled. See TRUMP SIGNAL.

In this connection, there are two valid psychological points. First, it is not wise to try to outsmart declarer continually by making false signals. Declarer usually comes out of a guessing game better than the defenders. Therefore, false signals should be avoided unless the play has been thought out well in advance. However, some false signals must be made. It is essential not to become typed as a player whose echoes are always dependable. The second psychological point arises when a defender is afraid to signal for fear of tipping his hand. If it seems a borderline case, it is better to signal.

Usually the defenders must cooperate to lead declarer astray. In a situation such as the following, declarer is more likely to go wrong if both players falsecard.

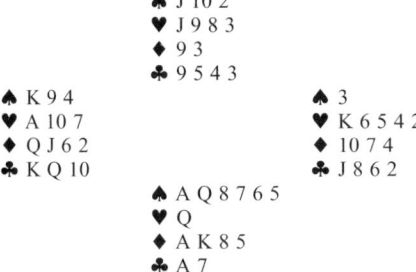

West's 1♦ opening is passed to South, who lands in 4♠. West leads the ♣K and South holds off in order to create a ruffing communication between dummy and the closed hand. South wins the second club and plays diamonds, intending to ruff the third round low and the fourth high. If East is awake, he will try to persuade declarer to ruff both diamonds high and rely on a 2-2 trump break. When South plays the ♦A and ♦K, East plays high-low with the 10 and 4. But West must keep up with the ball too and withhold his normal suit-length signal; he should play the 2 followed by the 6, supporting the theory that the diamonds are 5-2.

For a method by which declarer can play to take advantage of length signals, see DISCOVERY.

COUNTERING ONE TRUMP INTERFERENCE. See LEBENSOHL, NEGATIVE DOUBLE, RUBINSOHL.

COUNT SQUEEZE. A squeeze that operates on a player who does not guard a crucial suit in such a way as to give declarer a count of the suit, allowing him to drop an honor offside instead of taking a losing finesse.

```
              ♠ A Q
              ♥ K
              ♦ —
              ♣ —
  ♠ x x                    ♠ K
  ♥ A                      ♥ —
  ♦ —                      ♦ —
  ♣ —                      ♣ x x
              ♠ x
              ♥ x
              ♦ —
              ♣ A
```

Suppose that West is known to have the ♥A, South leads the ♣A and West discards a spade. North can safely

discard the ♥K. South leads a spade, and West follows low. North's ace must be played for it is known that West's remaining card is the ♥A. If West had guarded spades, he would have been caught in a SHOW-UP SQUEEZE.

COUNTING CARDS. It is each player's responsibility to determine that the hand he is about to play contains exactly 13 cards. This determination should be made before he looks at the face of any card. The Laws of Duplicate Bridge also require that 13 cards be replaced in the pocket of the board. (There is no longer a requirement to actually count the cards.)

COUNTING THE HAND. Deducing the distribution of the hidden hands from information gained during the bidding and early stages of play.

On many hands, the crucial play depends on the distribution of one particular suit. By observing or projecting the distributions of the other three suits, a player may be able to deduce how the key suit splits, *even if that suit has not yet been led*.

The procedure used is simple arithmetic, based on two facts: each suit has 13 cards; each player started with 13 cards in his hand.

The following is an elementary illustration of the basic technique of counting the hand: A decision which at first glance is a pure guess reduces to a certainty as a result of the play of the other suits.

West	East
♠ A Q 7	♠ K 5 3
♥ K Q 6	♥ A 4 2
♦ A K J 3	♦ Q 8 4 2
♣ A J 5	♣ K 10 3

West plays 7NT, with the ♠J led. He should delay his decision in clubs to the very end, by first cashing all his winners. South follows twice to each major, but discards clubs on the third round of each. He then follows to three rounds of diamonds, while North discards a heart on the third round. Now, by subtraction, North is known to have started with five cards in each major and two diamonds, hence only one club. So West cashes dummy's ♣K, and (unless North drops the queen) finesses through South with certainty.

In the above example, counting the hand made declarer's final play a sure thing. More often, counting will indicate which play has the highest probability of success.

Suppose South had followed to four diamonds. Now it would be known that he started with five clubs, and North with two clubs. Then West should finesse through South as before, this time with odds of five to two that South has the missing queen. (When declarer finally takes the finesse, each defender has only one unknown card, but the odds determined from the count of the *initial* distribution are unchanged.) See PROBABILITIES, A POSTERIORI and A PRIORI.

In the illustration above, declarer's problem was simply which way to take a finesse. Sometimes counting the hand will help declarer decide between a squeeze and a finesse. Sometimes it will point up the necessity to handle a problem suit in a way radically different from what he would otherwise have attempted.

West	East
♠ A K Q	♠ 7 5 3
♥ A K Q	♥ 6 4 2
♦ A Q 8	♦ K 7 3
♣ K Q 7 3	♣ A 10 4 2

Again West plays 7NT, with the ♠J led. Apparently West must cash king and queen of clubs, hoping that North has two or more clubs or that the jack is single-ton. But before playing clubs, West should cash his major-suit winners. On the third round of each, South discards diamonds. West then cashes the ♦A-Q, and both opponents follow. Counting North's hand — five spades, five hearts, and two diamonds — shows that he has at most one club, which must be the 8, 9, or jack if West is to make the contract. So West abandons the normal play in clubs, and instead leads the 3 to dummy's ace. If North follows with the 8 or 9, declarer leads a club from dummy and covers South's card, using the carefully preserved ♦K as a re-entry for a second fi-nesse if South splits his holding.

The preceding examples were played at notrump, so declarer could count the hand by cashing his winners and noting when the opponents showed out. In a suit contract, this type of play runs the risk of the opponents gaining a ruff. However, in a suit contract, declarer may be able to count the hand by using his own trumps for ruffing. For example, if dummy has A-K-x-x in a side suit, and declarer has two small, declarer may be able to ruff the suit twice in his hand. He does not gain any tricks by doing this, as his long trumps were winners anyhow. In fact, in the process of ruffing he destroys any squeeze or throw-in threat in the suit. But he is sure to obtain the count of the suit, if that is the crucial factor in the play of the rest of the hand.

So far, we have considered only cases where declarer's information on the count was gained during the play. Inferences about suit lengths may also be drawn from the opponents' bidding (or failure to bid), from the open-ing lead, or from defenders' plays or signals (see DIS-COVERY). These inferences are, of course, not as firm as when a player fails to follow suit.

Defensive Play. Counting the hand is as important for the defenders as for the declarer.

North (Dummy)
♠ K J
♥ 10 5 3
♦ A 8 6 3
♣ A 8 7 2

East
♠ A Q 6
♥ J 9 7 6
♦ Q J 10
♣ J 9 5

South plays in 5♦, no other suits having been bid. West leads the ♠5. East wins and leads a second high spade, which South ruffs. South cashes ♦K-A; West follows once, then discards a spade. South now cashes the ♥A-K-Q (West following three times), then leads a diamond. East wins and counts declarer's hand — one spade, three hearts, five diamonds, therefore four clubs. So East does not fall for declarer's trap – he does not return a club, jeopardizing West's doubleton king or queen. Instead he leads a major, yielding a useless ruff and sluff, and eventually sets the hand with a club trick.

In addition to absolute counts, as in the above example, and inferential counts from the bidding, the defenders have a counting aid not available to the declarer — the COUNT SIGNAL. Most experts use such signals spar-ingly, to help partner in the play of one specific suit. The policy of some experts is to signal length in all suits when they think partner will profit more than declarer

from a complete count of the hand.

In general, when partner is unlikely to be misled, a de-fender should make it as difficult as possible for declarer to count the hand. For instance, if a suit has gone around three times, the defender should retain the thirteenth card as long as possible, to keep declarer in doubt as to its location. It is usually wrong for a defender's first discard to be a worthless card in a suit where he has five cards and dummy has four cards — an astute declarer may be able to use this inference in counting the hand.

For a full discussion of counting, see *All Fifty-Two Cards* by Marshall Miles (BIBLIOGRAPHY, D). See also CARD READING; COUNTING TRUMPS; REC-TIFYING THE COUNT.

COUNTING TRUMPS. This does not present prob-lems for the expert, but the inexperienced player some-times has trouble. There are three methods, which in increasing order of efficiency are:

(1) Wait until you need to know and then add the cards played to the cards remaining in view and subtract from 13 — a lot of effort that often produces the wrong result.

(2) a. As declarer, note at the start how many trumps the defenders have, and mentally reduce that total as the cards appear.

b. As defender, make a guess from the bidding about the length of declarer's trumps. See how many this gives your partner. Then adjust your thinking if re-quired.

(3) Think in terms of distributional patterns, which are of course the same as the patterns of a particular hand. If you have a 4-4 trump fit you are thinking of the patterns 4-4-3-2 or 4-4-4-1. If one defender shows out on the second round you know automatically that the other defender began with four and has two more. Play-ers who are used to thinking in terms of patterns are able without difficulty to count all the suits. Two ele-ments of the pattern are known at the start. When the bidding or play reveals a third, the fourth element is known automatically.

This is the expert method, and intermediate players should take the trouble to acquire the knack. A conscious effort to note the pattern of any 13-card hand improves familiarity with the patterns. See COUNTING THE HAND.

COUP. A special play maneuver by declarer. More spe-cifically, without further designation, it refers to an endplay situation in which a defender's finessable trumps are trapped without a finesse. This may arise when there is no entry to take a finesse, or when there is no trump to lead for a finesse. Often the coup has to be prepared by shortening the trump length, reducing it to not more than the same length as the defender's. For example:

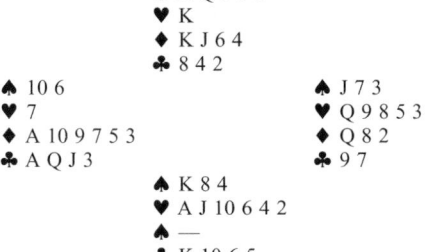

South plays in 4♥ after West has shown the minor suits by an unusual notrump overcall. The ♦A is led and ruffed, and a heart is led to the king. South cashes the ♦K, ruffs a diamond, and plays three rounds of spades ending in dummy. A spade is ruffed, and a club is played. South must eventually make his two remaining trumps.

When the preparation of the coup makes it necessary to ruff a winner, the term GRAND COUP is used. Single, double and triple grand coups refer to situations in which one, two, and three winners are ruffed respectively.

For the term coup applied in other special contexts, including some unusual defense maneuvers, see ALCATRAZ COUP; BATH COUP; COUP EN PASSANT; CROCODILE COUP; DESCHAPELLES COUP; DEVIL'S COUP; GRAND COUP; IDIOT'S COUP; MERRIMAC COUP; MORTON'S FORK COUP; PITT COUP; ROBERT COUP; SCISSORS COUP; SERPENT'S COUP; VIENNA COUP.

COUP EN BLANC. A term formerly used by some writers instead of DUCK.

COUP EN PASSANT. The lead of a plain suit card to promote a low trump behind a higher trump to a winning position. The term is taken from chess. See also ELOPEMENT.

In the following position, spades are trump. The lead is in the North hand.

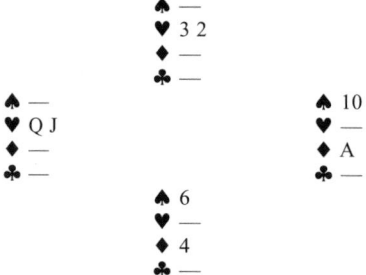

```
              ♠ —
              ♥ 3 2
              ♦ —
              ♣ —
♠ —                          ♠ 10
♥ Q J                        ♥ —
♦ —                          ♦ A
♣ —                          ♣ —
              ♠ 6
              ♥ —
              ♦ 4
              ♣ —
```

Declarer (South) holds no more winning cards. However, when a heart is led from the North hand, South makes a trick with the ♠6. If East discards, South ruffs the heart. If East ruffs with his master trump, the ♠6 wins the final trick. In the above example, if East held ♠10-5, South would score the ♠6 en passant in a similar manner, overruffing if East ruffed low and discarding if East ruffed high.

COUP WITHOUT A NAME. See SCISSORS COUP.

COURT CARD. The king, queen and jack of each suit are represented by coated figures rather than pips, giving rise to the expression coat card. This term was corrupted to court card, probably due to the association with the figures in a royal court, and sometimes wrongly extended to include the ace. See COAT CARDS, FACE CARDS.

COURTESY. See PROPRIETIES, Law 74.

COURTESY BID. A response made on a very weak hand to allow for the possibility that the opener has great strength. The courtesy response is never made in response to a major suit, partly because partner's next

action may be a game bid and partly because the contract of 1♥ or 1♠ will be playable. The courtesy response with a very weak hand is often indicated if the opening bid is 1♣ and responder is short in clubs. If he is 4-4-4-1, for example, a 1♦ response avoids the risk of playing in a 3-1 fit and may improve the contract. But there is some risk. This situation illustrates a weakness of standard bidding vis-à-vis strong-club methods.

COURTESY OF THE TABLE. A feature of the laws of auction bridge and the first laws of contract bridge. If dummy left the table, the defenders were required to take over dummy's duty of guarding declarer against the possibility of revoking. No penalty could be exacted against a declarer who revoked if the defenders had failed to ask the routine question, "Having no more?"

It was customary, although not legally necessary, for the dummy to ask for the Courtesy of the Table on leaving the table. This served to remind the defenders of their obligation in the matter.

This requirement was omitted from the first International edition of Laws, published in 1932.

COVER CARD. A method of valuation devised by George Rosenkranz as part of the ROMEX SYSTEM, but applicable in any method.

Aces and kings are cover cards — also queens if they are likely to be effective. If the opener's hand is measured in terms of losers, responder can judge how many of the losers he covers:

```
                  Responder
                  ♠ Q x
                  ♥ K Q x x
                  ♦ K x x x
                  ♣ x x x
Opener            Responder
1♠                1NT
2♥                4♥
```

The opening bidder should have at most seven losers, and responder has four cover cards: ♠Q, ♥K-Q and ♦K. Four of opener's losers are covered, leaving three, and game can be bid. If the ♠Q were the ♣Q it could not be counted as a cover card, and a raise to 3♥ would be sufficient. See LOSING TRICK COUNT.

COVERING HONORS. When an honor is led and the next player follows with a higher honor, he is said to have covered an honor with an honor. Second hand should usually cover an honor if he might establish a trick in that suit for himself or partner in the process.

If an honor is led from a sequence of touching honors, it is seldom proper to cover until the last of the sequentials is led. The following examples are typical:

```
(a)                      A x x
        K x x                            10 x x
                  Q J 9 x
```

The queen is led. If West covers, then South can take a finesse against the 10. West must duck the first honor lead but cover at the second opportunity.

If West does cover, he can be expected to hold K, K-x, or K-10.

```
(b)                      K x x
        Q x x                            A 9 x x
                  J 10 8
```

South leads the jack and makes two tricks if West covers. If West ducks, East can win or duck, and South

is held to one trick provided the defenders avoid leading the suit subsequently.

(c)

```
                    A x x
    Q 9 x                        K 8 x x
                    J 10 x
```

If West covers the jack he gives South two tricks.

The decision about whether to cover is usually more difficult when the honor is led by declarer. Generally, if dummy does not have the honor directly below declarer's card, it should be assumed that declarer has it, and the defender should wait and cover the next honor. If dummy has the honor below the card led by declarer, it is often proper to cover unless declarer is believed to have a TWO-WAY FINESSE. When in doubt, the best policy is usually to duck quickly. An exception to the rule about not covering a sequence occurs when the opposing suit can be blocked:

(d)

```
                    A K x x x
    Q 9 x                        x x x
                    J 10
```

If dummy has no entry, West must cover the jack or 10 immediately to prevent declarer from making five tricks.

(e)

```
                    Q J 10 9 x
    x x x                        K x x x
                    A
```

If the queen is led second hand must not cover. If he covers, the remainder of the suit is established in the North hand.

(f)

```
                    A x
    K x x                        x x x
                    Q J 10 x x
```

If the queen is led West must not cover. He can ensure a trick in the suit because the ace must be played on the second round.

There are numerous exceptions to this rule, and a clever declarer can pose the defenders many problems, as in the following examples:

(g)

```
                    A x
    K x x                        J 10 x x
                    Q x x x
```

If South needs to steal a trick in the suit, he can lead the queen — West may duck.

(h)

```
                    A x x
    K x                          10 9 x
                    Q J x x x
```

If South leads the queen, West must cover with a doubleton king; otherwise South can continue with a small card and drop the king.

(i)

```
                    Q J 10 8 x
    A x x x                      K 9 x
                    x
```

At a trump contract, North leads the queen in a side suit. East must play the king. If he ducks, the king may be ruffed out eventually.

CRACK. As an adjective, an expert player, partnership or team. As a verb, there are three meanings: (1) to obtain bad results after a period of success; (2) to double; (3) to open a new suit during the play of the hand. The latter two meanings are bridge colloquialisms.

CRANE SYSTEM. An obsolete bidding system devised by Joshua Crane in which the full value of the hand was bid immediately in accordance with its point-count. A hand counting to 12-15 was bid at the one level; a hand worth 16-19 was bid at the two level,

etc. This may have been the earliest published system to include a distributional point-count: both opener and responder counted three points for a singleton and six points for a void once the trump suit had been agreed.

CRASH. A method of bidding defensively against an artificial forcing 1♣ opening bid developed by Kit Woolsey and Steve Robinson. The word CRASH is an acronym for Color-RAnk-SHape. After an opening 1♣ forcing bid, a double or an overcall of 1♦ or 1NT show various types of two-suited hands. Double shows color — both suits are red or both are black. 1♦ shows rank — both suits are majors or both are minors. 1NT shows shape — both suits are pointed (spades and diamonds) or both are rounded. These bids are usually made on weak distributional hands — usually at least nine cards in the suits pinpointed. Bids of 1♥, 1♠, 2♣ and 2♦ show single-suited hands. Partner of the CRASH bidder usually responds as high as possible in the lowest suit possible. Overcaller passes if this is one of his suits, but bids the next higher suit in his own two-suiter if the overcaller has chosen the wrong pair of suits. For example:

West	North	East	South
1♣	Dbl	Pass	3♣
Pass	3♦	Pass	?

If South is 4-4 in clubs and hearts, he will correct to hearts because he knows partner has a heart-diamond hand. If North had a black hand, he would have passed 3♣.

The original version of this convention had 1♦ for color, 1♥ for rank and 1NT for shape, with a double reserved to show a hand of some strength and with all two-level overcalls showing one-suited hands.

CRASH can also apply to several conventions in which some pair of features (two aces, for example) are identified as being of the same color, rank or shape.

British CRASH uses 1♥, 1♠ and 1NT for the three two-suiters, with Double and 1♦ for hearts and spades respectively.

CRASHING HONORS. The deceptive play of a suit by declarer resulting in the defense wasting two high honors on one trick.

The most common situation in which the declarer can crash honors occurs when the declarer holds concealed length in his own hand. The lead of an honor from dummy may cause second hand to cover with an honor, crashing still a third honor in the other defender's hand. For example:

```
                    ♠ J 8 5 3
    ♠ A                          ♠ K 4
                    ♠ Q 10 9 7 6 2
```

If the ♠ J is led from dummy (North), East may play the king in the hope that West holds ♠ 10-x, 10-9, or 10-x-x.

Declarer may also crash honors with a lead from his own hand toward the dummy. This play is most likely to work if dummy is apparently (or actually) short of entries, as the defenders may believe declarer did not have the option of taking a finesse.

More subtle examples of crashing honors can be found in holdings in which the declarer is missing several top cards. The choice of card to lead might not seem too important in this suit:

♦ J 8 5 3

♦ 10 9 7 6 4

If possible, declarer (South) should start the diamond suit by leading the jack from dummy. East may play the ace from A-Q-2, or may split honors from K-Q-2.

Sometimes, it helps declarer's plan if the defenders know about his length in a suit. In the example below, South has indicated a six-card club suit.

♣ J 8

♣ Q 5 3   ♣ A K

♣ 10 9 7 6 4 2

South leads the ♣2 toward dummy's jack. As he would make the same play with A-K-7-6-4-2 of clubs in his hand, West is faced with a guess. If West takes the wrong view, the defense will crash honors in clubs.

In a slightly different sense, declarer may sometimes crash a single honor by making it fall on a trick with low cards, so it will not interfere with the trick-taking potential of declarer's honor cards.

♠ —

♠ A 5   ♠ J 10 9

♠ K Q 8 7 6 4 3 2

South, who has opened with 4♠, can afford to lose only one spade trick. His only chance is to lead the ♠Q from the closed hand. West may suspect that South has an even longer suit than he actually holds (or may make a mistake), and so play low. South can now crash the ace with one of East's minor honors by leading a low spade, preserving his king for the third round of the suit. See DECEPTIVE PLAY.

CRISS-CROSS RAISE. Players using limit raises in response to minor-suit openings have a problem with opening values and balanced distribution. One solution is the criss-cross jump shift: 1♣ – 2♦ shows a forcing raise in clubs, and 1♦ – 3♣ shows a forcing raise in diamonds. With an unbalanced hand a SPLINTER is usually available. Many players avoid the problem by using INVERTED MINOR SUIT RAISES. Many play the crisscross raises as limit bids when using Inverted Minor Raises.

CRISS-CROSS SQUEEZE. A blocked squeeze described under SIMPLE SQUEEZE.

CROCKFORD'S CLUB. In London, England, a famous proprietary club descending from a gambling club founded by William Crockford in 1827. In modern times it has been primarily a bridge club. In December 1961, Crockford's reverted to its gambling traditions by becoming the headquarters of chemin-de-fer in England.

CROCKFORD'S CLUB. Founded by Ely Culbertson in New York in 1932 and named after the English club of the same name. The club was famous for its high-quality cuisine and for its luxurious appointments, as was its sister club in Chicago. Many famous American players of the Thirties were members of Crockford's. Many members were drawn from high society rather than from the tournament bridge world. The club was in operation from 1932 to 1938.

CROCODILE COUP. A defensive maneuver to foil an impending endplay. Like a crocodile opening his jaws, a defender in second seat wins a trick with an unneces-

sarily high card, preventing his partner from being thrown in.

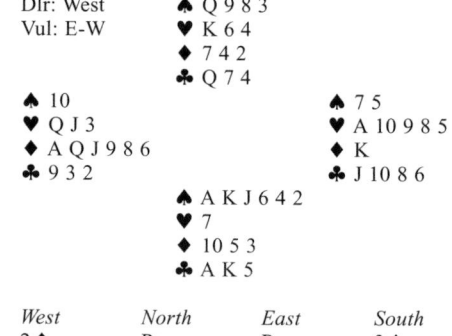

Dlr: West
Vul: E-W

♠ Q 9 8 3
♥ K 6 4
♦ 7 4 2
♣ Q 7 4

♠ 10   ♠ 7 5
♥ Q J 3   ♥ A 10 9 8 5 2
♦ A Q J 9 8 6 ♦ K
♣ 9 3 2   ♣ J 10 8 6

♠ A K J 6 4 2
♥ 7
♦ 10 5 3
♣ A K 5

West	North	East	South
2♦	Pass	Pass	3♠
Pass	4♠	All Pass	

West leads the ♥Q and ♥J. South ruffs, draws trumps, ruffs dummy's last heart and cashes his club tricks. He then leads a low diamond from his hand. If West plays the 9, East must win and concede a ruff-and-discard. West must count declarer's distribution, realize that the defense needs three diamond tricks to defeat the contract, and rise with the ♦A — a Crocodile Coup.

CROSS-IMP. See IMP PAIR GAMES.

CROSSRUFF. A method of play whereby ruffing tricks are made in each of a partnership's hands, thus using the trumps separately.

When a crossruff is played, ruffing tricks are being taken in two side suits. It is usually a good idea to cash winners in the remaining suit at an early stage.

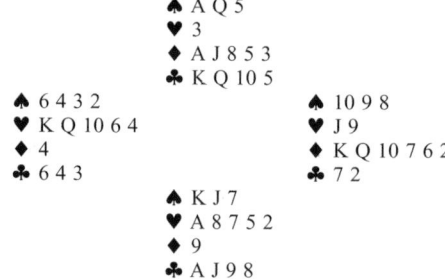

♠ A Q 5
♥ 3
♦ A J 8 5 3
♣ K Q 10 5

♠ 6 4 3 2   ♠ 10 9 8
♥ K Q 10 6 4 ♥ J 9
♦ 4   ♦ K Q 10 7 6 2
♣ 6 4 3   ♣ 7 2

♠ K J 7
♥ A 8 7 5 2
♦ 9
♣ A J 9 8

After East opens 3♦, West leads a trump against South's 6♣ contract. South can count only five top tricks outside of clubs and must therefore make all his remaining trumps separately. He must be careful to cash his three spade tricks immediately, else the defenders will discard spades when failing to follow to red-suit tricks. If this happens, declarer will lose his good spades to opposing ruffs. If the spades cannot be cashed at once, there is no hope for the contract.

CROWHURST. A secondary Stayman inquiry after a 1NT rebid by opener, devised by Eric Crowhurst and widely used by British tournament players. Opener is assumed to have 12-16 HCP; the 2♣ rebid by responder asks for further clarification. If opener has 15-16 he rebids 2NT or higher (game forcing); with 12-14 opener either (1) rebids a five-card major suit, (2) shows three-card support for responder's major suit, (3) shows an unbid four-card major suit, or (4) bids 2♦. See also STAYMAN ON SECOND ROUND.

CROWNINSHIELD TROPHY. Presented by Frank Crowninshield for British-American competition. It was contested only once, in 1949, when an unofficial U.S. team (John Crawford, Peter Leventritt, George Rapee, Samuel Stayman) played matches against two British teams. The result was a win for Britain by 330 aggregate points. See ANGLO-AMERICAN MATCHES. For results see Appendix IV.

CUDGELS. The club suit.

CUEBID. A forcing bid in a suit in which the bidder cannot wish to play. It is applied to (1) bids in the opponents' suit at any level; (2) bids to show controls at a high level after a suit has been agreed directly or by inference. It is possible to use the term "cuebid" for a bid that is neither in opponent's suit nor a show of control. See OUT-OF-THE-BLUE CUEBID.

Cuebids are also discussed under the following headings: ADVANCE CUEBID; ASTRO CUEBID; CAPPELLETTI CUEBID; COLORFUL CUEBID; CONTROL BID; CUEBID AS LIGHT TAKEOUT; CUEBID IN OPPONENTS SUITS; CUEBID TO SHOW CONTROLS; DIRECTIONAL ASKING BID; JUMP CUEBID; KANTAR CUEBID; MICHAELS CUEBID; UNASSUMING CUEBID; WESTERN CUEBID.

CUEBID AS LIGHT TAKEOUT. An immediate cuebid of an opponent's opening bid is a weak takeout bid for the other three suits. This method reserves the takeout double for stronger hands having greater defensive values. See CUEBID IN OPPONENT'S SUIT.

CUEBID IN OPPONENT'S SUIT. When a player bids a suit which has originally been called by his opponents, he is said to make a CUEBID. A cuebid is not made in the expectation of actually playing in the relevant suit; it is made for exploratory or control-showing purposes.

In the early days of contract bridge, a cuebid could be made in only two situations: the immediate overcall in the opponent's suit guaranteed a void (or at any rate, no losers) in the suit. This was later extended to strong hands with a singleton in the suit. At later stages in the auction, opposite a partner who had already bid, the cuebid in the opponent's suit was used to show control of the suit and suggest slam.

In the above form, the opportunity to make a cuebid rarely occurred. Theorists, particularly in England and California, developed the idea that any cuebid below game is simply forcing, and this idea eventually prevailed. It made use of many idle bids.

Cuebids are used much more extensively by experts than by others. In studying the meaning of various cuebids, the subject is considered (1) from opener's viewpoint, (2) from responder's viewpoint, and (3) from defenders' viewpoint.

Cuebid by Opener

The level at which the cuebid is made is a vital consideration. The meaning changes according to whether game has been reached.

Above the game level, there can be no doubt that the cuebid is a slam try. The same is true in this sort of situation:

West	North	East	South
			1♠
2♥	3♠	Pass	4♥

South has already committed the partnership to playing in at least a game in spades, so 4♥ must be a slam try, showing control of the heart suit. First-round control of hearts (ace or void) is virtually guaranteed. This sort of cuebid is also called a CONTROL BID.

But when a partnership is still searching for the safest game contract, the cuebid by opener is much less precise. He may or may not have slam ambitions. He may or may not have a control in the cuebid suit. Time will tell:

West	North	East	South
			1♣
1♥	1♠	Pass	2♥

All North can tell at this stage is that South has an enormous hand and wants to be in at least a game. North must make the most helpful bid he can think of, which is likely to be notrump if he has a heart stopper. If he has a double heart stopper and a weak hand he should jump to 3NT. This should serve as a warning to South that duplication is present. South may have any of the following hands:

(a)
♠ A Q 7 4
♥ 6
♦ A 6 3
♣ A K J 5 4

South's hand offers good slam prospects, and it would be wrong to raise immediately to 4♠. He plans to bid 4♠ on the next round, whatever rebid he gets from North. A delayed raise to game always promises more than an immediate game bid. See FAST ARRIVAL.

(b)
♠ A 4
♥ 7 5
♦ A J 5
♣ A K Q J 5 4

Here the cuebid is made, not as a slam try, but as a means of reaching the best game contract.

Although he has no spade fit and no heart control, South must insist on reaching game. He is too strong to bid 3♣, which could be passed. If North bids 2NT, South raises to 3NT. If North rebids 2♠, South simply bids 3♣, and awaits developments.

(c)	(d)
♠ A J 6	♠ A 6 5
♥ 5	♥ 5
♦ A J 7	♦ K Q J 6 4
♣ A K Q 9 5 4	♣ A K Q J

On both these hands South will bid 3♠ if North bids 2NT in response to South's 2♥ cuebid. In each case, the best contract may turn out to be 4♠, which North will bid if he has a five-card suit or a strong four-card suit.

In some circumstances, a cuebid is not even completely forcing to game. Consider the following:

West	North	East	South
			1♣
Pass	Pass	1♥	2♥

or

West	North	East	South
			1♣
1♥	Pass	2♥	3♥

South cannot be insisting on game here because he did not open with a forcing bid, and his partner's hand may be completely worthless. He may have either of these hands:

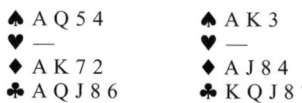

```
♠ A Q 5 4        ♠ A K 3
♥ —              ♥ —
♦ A K 7 2        ♦ A J 8 4
♣ A Q J 8 6      ♣ K Q J 8 7 3
```

This particular cuebid, even without a jump, suggests a void in hearts. (With a singleton heart, a takeout double would be the normal action: South would then be less reluctant to hear his partner pass the double for penalties.)

The following example shows the advantage of playing the low-level cuebid as a vague forcing bid, without any guarantee of control in the suit.

West	North	East	South
			1♣
2♠*	3♥	Pass	3♠
*weak			

South holds:

```
              ♠ 7 5
              ♥ J 3
              ♦ Q 8 3
              ♣ A K Q 7 4 3
```

This use of the cuebid to ask about stoppers first became popular on the West Coast of the United States. Hence it is called a WESTERN CUEBID and it has since become standard. It is the only way for South to steer the contract into 3NT if North has a spade guard. (If South had a spade stopper he could simply bid 3NT himself.) Unless the partnership has this understanding, South is forced to bid 4♣, or even 4♥, when the notrump game may easily be best (see DIRECTIONAL ASKING BID).

A cuebid must always be considered within the framework of the bidding. If the cuebidder and his partner have limited their hands by the earlier auction, the cuebid may be made even in a partscore situation, when there is no intention of reaching game. This is illustrated by the following example:

West	North	East	South
			1♣
1♦	Pass	1NT	Pass
Pass	Dbl	Pass	2♦

South's hand was:

```
              ♠ Q J 10 6
              ♥ A 7 5 4
              ♦ 6
              ♣ K J 8 4
```

As he had passed over 1NT and then refused to stand the double, it was clear that South was weak. With North also limited by his original pass, the cuebid was simply a useful maneuver to find a major-suit fit.

Cuebid by Responder

West	North	East	South
			1♣
1♠	2♠		

Classically this would have shown a club fit with no losers in spades, and a desire to reach at least game. In the modern style, this cuebid shows a strong hand with a four-card or better fit for opener's suit. There is no indication of control in the opponent's suit:

```
(a)              (b)
♠ 7 4 2          ♠ 7 4 2
♥ A 3            ♥ A 3
♦ K Q 7          ♦ Q 10 8
♣ A 8 7 3 2      ♣ K J 6 5 2
```

There are two schools of thought about the strength of the cuebid. A. Game-forcing, as in (a), with a jump to 3♣, as in (b) invitational.

B. Invitational or better. This treatment would use the cuebid for (a) and (b). If opener then bids 3♣ it suggests a final contract and responder will pass with an invitational hand. A direct jump to 3♣ is preemptive.

There is no upper limit to the strength of the cuebid, which will often be the start of a slam exploration. In principle, the cuebid denies length in the unbid major. The jump cuebid, 3♠ instead of 2♠ in this sequence, asks opener to bid 3NT with a stopper in the opponent's suit. However, some treat it as a splinter, probably a void. An alternative is to play that the jump cuebid requires a 3NT bid with or without a stopper. This allows 3NT to be played from the right side if responder has A x x or K x x and opener has Q x or J x x.

Having the contract played from the right side of the table is a consideration on this deal:

```
Dlr: S              ♠ Q 5
Vul: N-S            ♥ 6 2
                    ♦ K Q 3
                    ♣ A Q 8 7 6 4
♠ J 10 9 8 6 2              ♠ K 7 4
♥ A K 10 3                 ♥ 9 8
♦ 7 4                      ♦ J 9 8 5
♣ 5                        ♣ J 10 9 2
                    ♠ A 3
                    ♥ Q J 7 5 4
                    ♦ A 10 6 2
                    ♣ K 3
```

West	North	East	South
			1♥
Pass	2♣	Pass	2♦
2♠	3♠	Dbl	Redbl
Pass	3NT	All Pass	

If the cuebid were not available, North would be in trouble over 2♠. 3♣ or 3♦ would be substantial underbids, likely to lead to a missed game.

East's double of 3♠ strongly suggests that he has a top spade honor, so North-South are able to play 3NT from the North position. When a cuebid (in the opponent's suit or otherwise) is doubled, a redouble shows control of the suit; whether it is first or second-round control is a matter for partnership agreement.

There are often opportunities for using the cuebid after an original pass by the cuebidder:

West	North	East	South
	Pass	Pass	1♦
1♠	2♠		

This shows a near opening bid, a balanced distribution, and insufficient spade strength to bid 2NT. For example:

```
(a)              (b)
♠ 7 4 3 2        ♠ A 6 4
♥ A Q 6          ♥ A K 9
♦ Q 8 5          ♦ 10 9 8
♣ K 10 7         ♣ 10 9 7 3
```

Holding a fit with the opener's suit, the responder will rarely wish to look further than a raise of partner's suit. With the hands given, North would have an impossible bid to make. In each case he is hoping for 3NT, but he wants his partner to play it.

If North wishes to make a cuebid because he has a powerful diamond fit, he can still do so. But until North

clarifies the situation on the next round, South must bid on the assumption that North's hand is balanced. Any simple bid by South on the second round, such as 3♣ or 3♦, may be passed. So if South wants to be in game he must make a counter-cuebid of 3♠ or take some other strong action.

A cuebid in notrump. A cuebid in notrump is both rare and rarely understood. Suppose the bidding goes:

West	North	East	South
			1♦
1NT	2NT		

What does North's bid mean? It cannot be a balanced hand trying for a notrump game, because any such hand would simply double 1NT and take a penalty. 2NT in this situation should be regarded\ as a cuebid, simply forcing to game or perhaps forcing to four of a minor. It shows an unbalanced hand which does not wish to defend against notrump. A two-suiter is likely, such as:

    ♠ A Q 6 5 4 2
    ♥ A J 6 5 3
    ♦ 9
    ♣ 4

There should be game in one of the major suits, but a double will not work out well if, as is likely, West has a strong club suit.

Once the game level has been reached, the cuebid becomes a control bid, Almost invariably it will show the ace or a void, but might occasionally be made with a second-round control. This can be ventured if the controlbidder's trump holding is strong, as there is then no danger that partner will race for a grand slam missing a trick in the enemy suit.

Negative inferences. The failure to cuebid can be very significant:

West		East	
♠ A Q 7 5 4 3		♠ K J 8 5	
♥ A K J 6 3		♥ 7 2	
♦ —		♦ A Q 10 8 3	
♣ 9 4		♣ 10 6	

West	North	East	South
1♠	4♣	4♠	Pass
5♠	Pass	Pass	

This asks only for control of clubs. If West had any other worries he would make a suitable control bid.

Similarly, a player who holds

    ♠ 5 2
    ♥ A Q 7 6 4 2
    ♦ —
    ♣ A K 8 7 3

can bid 5♥ when his partner's 1♥ has been overcalled with 1♠.

There are numerous possibilities for cuebidding after partner's opening bid of 1NT. Frequently the cuebid has to take the place of a STAYMAN inquiry which has been frustrated by the intervening bid.

    ♠ A K 7 3
    ♥ Q 6
    ♦ A 10 6 2
    ♣ K J 6

South holds this hand and the bidding goes:

West	North	East	South
			1NT
2♥	3♥	Pass	3♠
Pass	3NT	Pass	?

North's bid of 3♥ could have any of three meanings.

He could be paving the way for a slam; he could be trying to find a 4-4 spade fit to play in 4♠; or he could be worrying about the presence of a heart guard for 3NT.

The 3NT bid makes it clear that he does not have spades, nor is he seeking a slam. His only reason for not bidding 3NT directly was because he has no heart guard.

In these circumstances, West would enjoy 3NT, so South must bid 4♦. He expects to play a game in spades, diamonds, or clubs. (But see LEBENSOHL).

Another curious cuebid can arise after a 1NT opening bid:

West	North	East	South
			1NT
Dbl	2NT		

This cannot be a natural bid because a hand which is ready to suggest 3NT would prefer to redouble. The redouble is almost sure to produce a good score, probably from a penalty when the opponents play in some doubled contract at the two-level. So 2NT must be a forcing bid with a very unbalanced distribution — probably a two-suiter on which game seems feasible. Over West's double, a jump to 3♠ for example, should be preemptive, not forcing, so 2NT is the only forcing bid at North's disposal.

Cuebid by the Defender

Cuebids by the side which did not open the bidding are considered under two headings; cuebids by second hand and cuebids by fourth hand.

Cuebids by second hand. The immediate overcall in the opponent's suit has been the subject of experiment in recent years. There are at least five varieties:

(1) *Classical* (Culbertson-Goren). The equivalent of an opening forcing bid, guaranteeing a game. Goren insisted the cuebid shows first-round control in the cuebid suit without explaining what to do if that feature is not present. Culbertson was less rigid, permitting the cuebid with a singleton and allowing for the possibility that the bidding may die short of game if the responding hand is very weak. Modern bidders contend that these interpretations weaken the value of the bid since there is so rarely an opportunity to use it.

(2) *Modern* (Reese and Dormer). Here the cuebid is used for most powerful hands with game prospects when a takeout double is unsuitable because a penalty pass would be unwelcome. *Blueprint for Bidding* gives these three examples of 2♦ after an opening 1♦:

(a)	(b)
♠ A K 10 8 4 3 2	♠ A Q 10 7 4
♥ K 4	♥ K J 8 7 5
♦ 7	♦ —
♣ A J 6	♣ A Q 5

        (c)
        ♠ K Q 9 5 4
        ♥ A
        ♦ 9
        ♣ A K J 8 3 2

In (a), the spades are bid and rebid, and the bidding can die at 3♠. If (b) gets a 3♣ response, a repeat cuebid of 3♦ is used to ask for a major suit. The bidding can stop at 3♥ or 3♠. If (c) gets a 2♥ response, which is likely, the rebid is 3♣, which can be passed.

(3) *Hypermodern* (the MICHAELS CUEBID). Here there is a two-suited hand, usually less than opening bid strength. Over a minor suit it shows major suits; over a major suit it shows the unbid major and an unspecified minor. In the latter case the hand may be stronger.

It is generally true that two-suited hands are difficult to bid in defense, and this has given rise to various attempts, such as the unusual notrump, to show two suits with one bid.

(4) *Artificial* (the ASTRO CUEBID). This method is described by its inventors, Larry Rosler, Roger Stern and Paul Allinger. It shows a minor-major two-suiter — the lower unbid minor and the lower unbid major. The minor suit is always long, and the distribution is likely to be 6-5, 6-4, or 5-4. The strength will vary wildly. At favorable vulnerability, it might be a 5-point hand hoping for a sacrifice, while at unfavorable vulnerability the cuebidder must have a sound hand able to play safely at the three-level. See also COLORFUL CUEBID.

(5) *Natural*. There is a strong argument for playing an immediate overcall in an opponent's minor suit as a natural bid to show a suit, especially if the opponents do not open four-card major suits. In that case they will frequently bid a three-card minor suit, and the second player may want to bid the suit naturally.

Against opponents who open freely with weak four-card major suits, or even three-card major suits, the cuebid may be used naturally at all times.

Of the five different methods listed above, the most popular, in expert circles, is the Michaels Cuebid.

The second player may make a delayed cuebid in a variety of circumstances. A common situation, when the second hand is strong, follows a takeout double:

West	North	East	South
			1♥
Dbl	Pass	2♣	Pass
2♥			

Many years ago this bid was used as a natural bid to show a strong heart suit, and it was not forcing. This treatment has been abandoned, partly because such hands usually pass the opening heart bid, and partly because it is needed as a cuebid with a variety of strong hands.

The precise meaning of the cuebid is influenced by the type of immediate cuebid being used. If this has the traditional strong meaning, then the delayed cuebid is certain to be less than a game-forcing hand. Using a specialized cuebid — (3), (4), or (5) above — the delayed cuebid has no upper limit. In either case the minimum should be a hand with about 20 points.

A pass followed by a bid in the opponent's suit may need a little study. Usually it is a natural bid, based on a strong suit which the opponent has stolen. For example:

West	North	East	South
			1♠
Pass	1NT	Pass	Pass
2♠			

This indicates a good six-card spade suit. South and North may well have only four spades and one spade respectively, so West cannot allow himself to be talked out of playing in spades. He would be less inclined to bid 2♠, perhaps, if the opening bid promised a five-card suit. See OVERCALL IN OPPONENT'S MAJOR SUIT.

The same would apply if the opening bid is in hearts, but the situation is different when the opening bid is in a minor suit:

West	North	East	South
			1♦
Pass	1NT	Pass	Pass
2♦			

Now it is much less likely that West will want to bid 2♦ naturally. North-South will almost always have six diamonds between them - usually more. It is more useful, therefore, to use the bid in the opponent's minor suit as a cuebid for a major-suit takeout on this type of hand:

- ♠ K 8 5 3
- ♥ A 10 6 3
- ♦ 7 5 4
- ♣ K 2

West could not afford to make an original double with this hand, partly because his strength is insufficient, and partly because he is not prepared for a club response. It is highly probable after this auction that East-West have a 4-4 fit or better in one of the major suits, and the 2♦ cuebid is an effective way for East-West to balance themselves into a major suit.

To complete the picture as far as cuebids by the second player are concerned, there is the rare notrump cuebid. A bid of 2NT over an opening bid of 1NT can, by agreement, be either: (a) an unusual notrump showing minor-suit length; or (b) a freak two-suited hand of any kind.

Cuebids by Fourth Hand. Six common cases need consideration.

(1) *After two passes.* If South bids 1♦ and East bids 2♦ in the pass-out position, the cuebid should mean the same as if made by second hand. East must bear in mind that West and North are limited by their original passes.

(2) *After a pass and a suit response.*

West	North	East	South
			1♦
Pass	1♠	2♦ or 2♠	

This requires partnership agreement. Many, would consider one or both of these as natural, indicating a good 6-card suit or better. Others consider them strong and forcing. The same problem arises when second-hand has overcalled.

(3) *After an overcall and a pass.*

West	North	East	South
			1♦
1♠	Pass	2♦	

This is back to the earlier pattern: a strong hand which expects to go to game but does not know where to go. East might hold:

- ♠ K 3
- ♥ Q J 6 2
- ♦ 10 3
- ♣ A K 7 5 4

East expects to reach game, but this could be in any denomination except diamonds. West may show any additional feature: a second suit if he has one; a diamond guard by bidding notrump; or a good overcall including a six-card spade suit by jumping to 3♠. If he can do no more than rebid 2♠, East raises to 3♠, which can be passed. If East-West are vulnerable, East might go to 4♠ over 2♠. This depends on the partnership's overcalling standards.

Alternatively, East may hold a hand which is worth a raise to 4♠, but offers some slam chances. If he bids 2♦, and follows with 4♠ West may be able to continue.

Another treatment that has become increasingly popular among modern players is to use this cuebid as responder's only strong bid, usually equivalent to a limit raise of the overcaller's suit.

For example, the bidding goes:

West	North	East	South
1♥	1♠	Pass	2♥

South holds:

♠ K 9 5
♥ A 7 2
♦ K J 9 8 3
♣ 10 6

In standard methods, South would express the value of his hand by jump raising to 3♠, but this may get his side too high. Employing the cuebid as an invitational measure permits South to explore accurately for game without endangering the partial contract. If North rebids 2♠, South passes, while if North shows additional values above a minimum overcall by jumping to 3♠ or introducing a new suit, South supports spades as cheaply as possible to describe the limited nature of his cuebid. With a stronger hand, South would again cuebid, but would take some further action over a minimum rebid by North. As a corollary, a double raise of an overcall is freed for use as a preemptive tactic.

Consider also the jump cuebid:

West	North	East	South
1♥	1♠	Pass	3♥

This is commonly used as a limit raise in spades, leaving 3♠ available as a preemptive move. Some prefer to use this as a good preemptive raise, with 7-9 points, spade length and a singleton. Stronger hands must start with a cuebid at the two-level, a method known as Mixed Raises. See also RESPONDING TO OVERCALLS and UNASSUMING CUEBID.

(4) *After a double and a pass*

This is very common:

West	North	East	South
			1♦
Dbl	Pass	2♦	

East can hold any hand on which he expects to get to game, but does not know where. A typical hand would be:

♠ K 7 6 3
♥ K 7 6 3
♦ 9 3 2
♣ A K

Over 2♦, West is almost sure to bid a major, which East raises to game. A raise to 3♠ (or 3♥) would not be forcing. It would be appropriate if the ♣K were turned into the jack or a small card.

This last point involves an important principle. In general, a cuebid is not completely forcing to game. It loses its forcing quality when a limited position is reached. A raise is always limited, so the bidding can die below game. A minimum double and a minimum cuebid may not have enough combined values for game. This allows East to make the cuebid freely on hands which would otherwise present a problem.

(5) *After a double and a bid*

West	North	East	South
1♦	Dbl	1♥	2♥

This is similar to (2), in that the opponents have bid two suits. 2♥ is a normal cuebid, with no interest in a heart contract. Holding four hearts or more, South would certainly double. But the only way to show diamonds at this point is to bid them, so 2♦ should simply mean a desire to play in that contract.

However, in Great Britain 2♥ would usually be natural, showing at least 5 hearts in response to partner's takeout double.

(6) *After a notrump overcall*

West	North	East	South
1♦	1NT	Pass	2♦

There are three schools of thought about this position. The normal interpretation is that it is a cuebid, which can be used as a Stayman substitute.

Alternatively, 2♣ can be retained as a Stayman bid, in which case 2♦ is a weak hand that wants to play in diamonds. This is not too unlikely because the notrump bidder has promised a good diamond holding.

The modern tendency is to play Systems On, in which case the responder acts as he would have over an opening 1NT bid. 2♦ is then a transfer.

The situation changes to some degree when the opening bid is 1♣.

West	North	East	South
1♣	1NT	Pass	2♣

Obviously this presents a dilemma. If 2♣ indicates a weak hand that should play in clubs, how does the partnership look for a major suit fit? Many players use CHEAPER MINOR, which means that 2♣ would show the weak club hand while 2♦ would probe for the major suit fit.

Natural cuebids

There are several situations in which a bid that appears to be a cuebid can be natural, non-forcing. These often occur after the opponent's have bid two suits.

1♣	Pass	1♠	?

Most experts would use 2♣ and 2♠ as natural, showing a six-card suit. Many use 1NT as a distributional takeout with at least 5-5 in the unbid suits.) The position is more complex if there has been an overcall:

1♣	1♥	1♠	?

Some players consider 2♣ and 2♠ to be cuebids, but many use 2♠ as the only cuebid since responder usually will have a five-card suit. 2♣ would be natural and non-forcing since West may have a three or four—card suit. A minority would use both bids as natural, with no cuebid.

A player who passes and then bids the opponent's suit usually shows a natural desire to play:

1♣	Pass	1♥	Pass
1♠	2♣		

North is likely to have a good six-card club suit.

Conclusion

Cuebidding is an extremely broad subject. There are hundreds of situations in which low-level cuebids can be used effectively. Most of them are impossible to classify because they occur on the second or third round of bidding. In these situations, cuebids may provide an answer to bidding problems which would otherwise be insoluble.

Other cuebid situations are listed under CONTROL BID and CUEBID. Also see ADVANCE CUEBID, ASKING BID, DOUBLE OF A CUEBID, GENERAL PURPOSE CUEBID, INTEREST-SHOWING BID, LAST TRAIN CUEBID, OUT-OF-THE-BLUE CUEBID, ROMAN ASKING BID, SPLINTER BID, TRIALBID, VOID-SHOWING BID.

CULBERTSON ASKING BID. See ASKING BID.

CULBERTSON FOUR-FIVE NOTRUMP. A slam convention showing aces and kings as well as asking for them. The 4NT bid promises either: three aces or two aces and a king of a suit genuinely bid by the partnership.

The responses: Holding two aces, or one ace and all the kings of genuinely bid suits, bid: 5NT. Holding no ace, bid: five of lowest genuinely bid suit. Holding one ace, usually bid the ace suit (but if this is the lowest bid suit, a jump to six is necessary).

Notice that the signoff is not in the agreed trump suit, but in the lowest suit which the partnership has genuinely bid. Responder can exercise some discretion when he holds one ace and no additional values. If his normal response would take the bidding above the five level in the agreed trump suit, he may invent some lower bid.

Holding two aces *and* a king, the responder is often interested in a grand slam. Provided his king is not in the agreed trump suit, he may bid the suit in which he holds a king. This may be temporarily misleading, but he can clarify the situation by making a constructive bid on the next round.

This convention was generally superseded by Blackwood and other conventions, but retained popularity among some leading British players. See BYZANTINE BLACKWOOD, TURBO.

CULBERTSON-LENZ MATCH. The *Bridge Battle of the Century*, as it was called when it took place between December 1931 and January 1932, was a genuine milestone in the history of the development and promotion of bridge as it is known today. Combining as it did every feature designed to capture and hold the interest of the then bridge-mad multitudes, and starring the greatest celebrities then prominent in bridge, it was predestined to be an exciting and long-remembered event. These were the years when bridge was making its impact felt keenly in the United States for the first time.

During the previous decade, many new styles of bidding and play had come to the forefront, and most prominent among these was the CULBERTSON SYSTEM. Conceived and popularized by a man who was a born molder of opinions and customs, and who was a superbly able practical psychologist as well, the Culbertson System took the nation by storm, and was indeed original in concept and, as practiced by its leading exponents, a successful and highly practical method of bidding in bridge. Naturally its success caused many rivalries and feuds among those players who were at the very top rungs of the bridge ability ladder. This resulted in a strange war — a Systemic War in which 12 leading authorities (including Sidney Lenz, Milton Work, Wilbur C. Whitehead and Edward V. Shepard) got together and organized a corporation, Bridge Headquarters — all forces joined to combat Culbertson's domination of contract bridge.

The principal leader of the various groups in opposition to the Culbertson methods was Lenz, a veteran of auction bridge. In his camp were other great luminaries of the game who also felt that their methods were superior to the Culbertson System. The name by which the Lenz forces' system was called was the Official System. A book on this system, which acknowledged its debt to Culbertson in that much of it was derived from his concepts, was later to be written by Work.

The actual match was the result of a challenge made earlier in 1931 by Culbertson to the Lenz faction. There were many complications to be ironed out before agreement as to conditions could actually be achieved, but essentially the match was finally played on a pair-against-pair basis, with Culbertson wagering $5,000 against Lenz's $1,000 on the outcome, with the money going to charity no matter who won. Culbertson promoted the match as the struggle of a young, loving married couple against the forces of adversity — 12 jealous authorities, the establishment, combined against them. Of course it was also billed as a grudge fight and a battle of systems. As a result the match was a topic of conversation at every bridge table and at many dinner tables long before it began.

In all, 150 rubbers were played, and during 88 of them Culbertson played with his wife, Josephine. His partners for the balance of the encounter were Theodore A. Lightner, Waldemar Von Zedtwitz, Howard Schenken, and Michael Gottlieb. Lenz played the first 103 rubbers with Oswald Jacoby, who then resigned because of a difference of opinion on the play of a defensive situation. Lenz's partner for the remainder of the session was Cmdr. Winfield Liggett Jr. Alfred Gruenther, then a lieutenant instructor at West Point, was chief referee of the match.

The Culbertson team won by 8,980 points. Careful and accurate records of cards held for each deal were kept, and at the conclusion it was determined that each side had held fairly much the same number of high cards as the other. The first half of the match was held at New York's Chatham Hotel, and the second part at the newly opened Waldorf-Astoria. The conditions of play and of protocol in general were governed by an agreement to which both Culbertson and Lenz were signatory, and the bridge laws under which the match was conducted were those published by the Whist Club of New York.

Coverage by the press of the nation was stupendous. Stories about the match were on the front pages of newspapers all over America. Regular correspondents were dispatched to the scenes of play, and some of the great newspaper personalities of the time wrote articles for their papers and for syndicates. The Associated Press laid heavy cables right into the Culbertson apartment at the Chatham Hotel, assigned reporters to the match and gave play-by-play coverage while Western Union and Postal Telegraph established branches in a spare room. The press missed the significance of the very first deal when Lenz failed in 5 ♦ because he thought the contract was notrump.

A continuous line of the rich and famous moved into the drawing room and out of it, viewing the action through cracks in a large leather screen, and trying to catch a glimpse of the players' faces or the flash of a card being played. Culbertson called it the greatest peepshow in history. A 438-page book *(Famous Hands of the Culbertson-Lenz Match)* was published in three sections with bidding and play analyzed by Culbertson and his partners, Jacoby, and Lt. Gruenther. Complete statistics were collated, and records of every phase of the match carefully kept. However, the single most significant feature of the entire proceedings was the enormous impetus it gave bridge when the game's popularity was already great.

	Culbertson	Lenz
Points won	122,925	113,945
Rubbers won	77	73
Number of two-game rubbers	37	32
Size of average rubber won	934	866
Largest rubber won	2,590	2,825
Games	195	186
Small slams bid and made	9	8
Small slams defeated		
(not including sacrifices)	9	5
Grand slams defeated	0	1

Opening suit bids of one	366	289
Opening 1NT bids	43	45
Opening forcing bids	5	5
Small slams made but not bid (many owing to lucky breaks)	20	19
Games made but not bid (many owing to lucky breaks)	15	13
Successful contracts	273	273
Defeated contracts	142	162
Number of (exact) game contracts voluntarily bid and defeated	48	49
Number of penalties of 600 plus	7	14
Points lost in penalties of 600 plus	5,900	11,500
Aces	1,745	1,771
Kings	1,775	1,741
Honor tricks	3,649 ¹/₂	3,648
Points (4-3-2-1)	18,091	17,898
Value of average rubber	899	
Hands dealt	879	
Hands passed out	25	

CULBERTSON NATIONAL STUDIOS. An organization of bridge teachers which flourished in the Thirties. Some 4,000 bridge teachers passed examinations in the CULBERTSON SYSTEM and were granted certificates attesting their fitness to teach the Culbertson methods. A similar organization was developed later by Charles Goren. See also AMERICAN BRIDGE TEACHERS ASSOCIATION.

CULBERTSON-SIMS MATCH. A 150-rubber pair match held in March and April of 1935 with Ely and Josephine Culbertson on one side against P. Hal and Dorothy Sims. On the next-to-last day of the match, Culbertson played with Albert H. Morehead and Sims with B. Jay Becker, while the ladies took a holiday. The match was won by the Culbertsons by a margin of 16,130 points. In this match, which took place as a result of a challenge issued by Sims, accurate records were kept of the proceedings and of the cards and deals held by the participants. Publicity for the contest was not as widespread as in the CULBERTSON-LENZ MATCH three years earlier, but the nation's interest was aroused. Both sides took to the airwaves on weekly radio broadcasts to describe various features of the games, and hands of particular merit were discussed. The match served to whet the public's already keen appetite for bridge and anything about it, as well as to reinforce the position of authority held by the Culbertson group.

CULBERTSON SYSTEM. The system of bidding developed by Ely Culbertson, revised periodically to incorporate new developments. For example, in 1930 Culbertson regarded a response in a new suit as nonforcing, which was a departure from his 1925 auction principles. He adhered to this in the 1933 *Blue Book*, which listed a one-over-one response as "99 ⁴⁴/₁₀₀% forcing", but abandoned the idea in 1935 when it became clear that the mass of bridge players would not be converted.

Other nonforcing bids were featured in the early Blue Books, abandoned shortly afterward, and revived by others as "modern" innovations. Examples are: LIMIT RAISES; limit 2NT response; and WEAK NOTRUMP openings, nonvulnerable. All these became features of the ACOL style; and limit raises and weak notrumps regained some popularity among American tournament players in the Sixties. The 1933 *Blue Book* also included the WEAK JUMP OVERCALL.

The Culbertson System, influenced both by the methods of the successful FOUR ACES and by pressure of public opinion, was crystallized in the 1936 *Gold Book*. The bidding set out in the *Gold Book*, with one notable exception, became standard practice in America for the next 15 years, and was only slightly modified by the GOREN SYSTEM, which won the allegiance of the bridge-playing masses in the Fifties. The chief features were:

(1) Valuation by HONOR TRICKS.

(2) Uniform standards for BIDDABLE SUITS, with Q-J-x-x a minimum four-card suit. This applied to the opening bidder, irrespective of whether the suit was a major or a minor. The responder could bid a shaded or conditional biddable suit.

(3) The APPROACH PRINCIPLE, emphasizing suit opening bids and responses in preference to notrump bids.

(4) The FORCING-TWO-BID; any opening suit bid of two requiring the partnership to reach game. (Later modified, 1952-53, so that responder could pass after a sequence such as 2♠-2NT-3♠.)

(5) The forcing takeout (or jump shift) showed 3¹/₂ honor tricks (or about 16 points). This requirement was raised by Goren and later authorities.

(6) STRONG NOTRUMP (4-4¹/₂ honor tricks) preferably limited to 4-3-3-3 distribution in accordance with the approach principle.

(7) Jump rebids by opener or responder (see OPENER'S REBIDS) not forcing unless in a new suit. (This principle was modified by later writers: see GOREN SYSTEM and STANDARD AMERICAN.)

(8) ASKING BIDS were introduced in 1936, and reintroduced in 1953 with amplifications, but never gained substantial support.

In 1952-53 Culbertson also introduced his own DISTRIBUTIONAL COUNT.

CULBERTSON TROPHY. Any of a number of trophies donated by Ely and Josephine Culbertson, all of them for minor events. In 1962 the name was given to the World Pair Championship trophy, first contested at Cannes, France.

CUMBERLAND HAND. See DUKE OF CUMBERLAND HAND.

CUMULATIVE SCORE. In tournament bridge, when an event is scheduled for more than one session of play and there is no elimination of players from the event, the winner of the event is decided by cumulative score, that is, the total of the scores made in each of the sessions. However, should there be a different average score for the two or more sessions (owing to playing a different number of boards, a no-show for the second session, or other reason), the later sessions' scores are factored by a multiplier that makes the sessions comparable to the first session, so that a particularly high score in any session would carry the same weight as in any other session.

In rubber bridge, where the partnerships change from rubber to rubber, a cumulative score of points won or lost in each rubber is kept so that each player's status of winnings or losses is shown at the termination of each rubber.

In progressive or party bridge, the cumulative score is the totality of points won at all tables at which the player played. Generally, only plus scores are considered, and

losses are not deducted before being entered onto the cumulative scoresheet.

In knockout team-of-four matches, all points are scored both plus and minus for both pairs of both teams, and the team with a greater plus total than minus total is the winner. This is referred to as AGGREGATE SCORE or TOTAL-POINT SCORING and has been almost completely supplanted in head-to-head matches by International Match Points.

CUPS, SWORDS, MONEY, WANDS. Names of suits in Tarot. Tarot was a special deck of cards used in ancient Italy and elsewhere for various games and for fortunetelling. Tarot cards are still in use today, mostly for parlor games.

CURIOSITIES. See FREAK HANDS.

CURSE OF SCOTLAND. A term applied to the ♦9, for which various explanations are given, none completely authoritative. The *Bridge Magazine* once listed six possible origins for the term as follows:

1. That in the once popular round game *Pope Joan*, the ♦9 was called the Pope, the antichrist of Scottish Reformers.

2. That the ♦9 was the chief card in the game *cornette*, introduced into Scotland by the unhappy Queen Mary.

3. That "Butcher" Cumberland wrote the orders for the Battle of Culloden, 1746, on the back of the card. This is very doubtful.

4. That the order for the Massacre of Glencoe (1692) was signed on the back of this card.

5. That the dispositions for the fatal field of Flodden (1513) were drawn up on it by James IV of Scotland. Both these last have only the slightest authority.

6. That it is derived from the nine lozenges that formed the coat of arms of the Earl of Stair, who was especially loathed for his connection with the Massacre of Glencoe and the union with England (1707).

CURTAILING MOVEMENT DURING PLAY. A method of terminating a game at a given time, without playing all the boards scheduled according to the movement in use. It is accomplished by omitting one or more of the rounds normally scheduled by the movement.

In general, any movement in which all boards in play at each round may be terminated at the end of any round, with no other defect than disturbance of balanced comparisons.

In a pair or individual movement involving either bye boards or relays, early termination also disrupts the scoring, for some boards will be played more often than others. This will result in a different top on certain boards, and a different possible score for some or all contestants. True results still can be obtained through factoring. See REDUCED HOWELL.

CURTAIN CARD. A record of a hand in a duplicate board. The curtain card is placed in the board with the hand; the player is thus able to determine that the hand he has taken from the board is the one that was to have been there. An advantage of curtain cards is that fouled boards are discovered immediately. See FOULED BOARD; HAND RECORD: MISSING CARD; TRUSCOTT CARD.

CUT. (1) At the commencement of rubber bridge play, a pack of cards is spread out, face downward, and each player draws one, turning it face up. Rank and suit of these cards determine the makeup of the first partnerships, and the original dealer. (2) At the conclusion of each hand, the cards are gathered together and reshuffled for the next deal. The new dealer presents the shuffled deck to the right-hand opponent, who cuts the pack by removing more than four but fewer than 48 cards from the top of the deck, and places the cards removed alongside the balance of the deck, nearer to the dealer. The dealer then completes the cut by placing the part of the pack which was originally on the bottom above the part originally on the top. (3) A colloquial term for the verbs "trump" or "ruff," used commonly in Scotland. (4) To terminate a movement before the scheduled completion.

CUT IN. To assert the right to become a member of an incomplete table, or to become a member of a complete table at such time as it may become incomplete.

CUTTHROAT BRIDGE. 1. A name applied to a traditional three-handed game (described under THREE-HANDED BRIDGE) and to a four-handed game with flexible partnerships.

In the four-handed version originated by S.B. Fishburne, Tulsa OK, and sometimes called "Reject" or "Let's Pick Partners," the opening bid must be natural and honest (at least 13 points in high cards, and at least four cards in the suit bid). The auction closes when a bid is followed by three passes; doubling and redoubling takes place later. No partscore contracts are played: the cards are thrown in, and the deal passes.

The player who makes the final bid is always declarer, and after the final pass he nominates one of the other three players as his partner. That player becomes the dummy, and moves into the seat opposite the declarer. Declarer's partner has the option of rejecting the partnership, in which case he scores with the defenders instead of with the declarer. Either defender may double and declarer (or dummy if he has not rejected) may redouble. A variation permits the dummy to reject and double.

A separate score is kept for each player, using normal contract scoring as far as possible. The rubber bonus is only 500 if either defender has a game. Only plus scores are recorded, so no entry is made on the score of the one, two, or three players who are on the losing end of a deal. In the final scoring, each player has a reckoning with each other player.

Honors are scored only by the player holding them. A player becomes vulnerable in the usual way. A non-vulnerable player scores 300 if his vulnerable partner scores rubber points.

A weak point in this version of the game was the rejection of partscores. 3NT was seldom played because a player with a weak hand could bid 4♣ or 4♦ without risk; unless someone made a higher bid, the hands were thrown in.

This gave rise to another version which gained considerable popularity in New York clubs: After the (natural) opening bid, the next player must make a bid of 4NT or higher. Some games include a GOULASH feature. For a variation including a nullo feature, see RAZZLE-DAZZLE.

2. A term used to describe the manner in which some bridge players play: To go after every possible trick, whether as declarer or defender.

CUTTING FOR DEAL, PARTNERS. At the beginning of each rubber, in order to establish partnerships and determine the original dealer, the four participating players each draw a card from an unfaced deck. The two players drawing the highest ranking cards play as partners, and the player with the higher of these two is the dealer on the first hand. An alternative method of determining deal and partners for second and subsequent rubbers is pivoting (see PIVOT BRIDGE).

At CHICAGO, a method combining both the cut and the pivot is frequently used, the cut establishing partnerships and deal for the first round, the highest cut card determining the pivot player. After the first round, the pivot player remains stationary and plays with his original right-hand opponent for the second round, and then with his original left-hand opponent for the third round. The pivot player, who deals the first hand of each of the three rounds, is often termed the wheel. See LAWS (Law 3).

CUTTING OUT. It is frequently impractical to have exactly four players. When five players form a table, an order of omission from the table is established by drawing. The player with the lowest card sits out the first rubber, and other players sit out in their turn in the order thus established.

Alternatively, a fresh draw can be made after each rubber, with the lowest to sit out; only players who have not sat out participate in the draw. This is a matter of club procedure.

The draw for participation in the rubber is usually quite distinct from the draw, or cut, for partners. But see PIVOT BRIDGE.

CYCLIC MOVEMENT. A movement in which contestants follow each other in a regular sequence or series. When a move is called, each contestant moves to a position previously occupied by a given other contestant, whose name or number is known in advance. The HOWELL MOVEMENT for pairs is a typical cyclic movement. Many other movements for pairs, teams or individuals use the cyclic feature in some form.

D

D.I. See DECLARATIVE-INTERROGATIVE FOUR NOTRUMP.

DAB. See DIRECTIONAL ASKING BID.

DAILY BULLETIN. Up-to-date reports on tournament activities produced and published on a daily basis and distributed to the contestants and onlookers. Daily Bulletins were introduced at the European Championships in Amsterdam, the Netherlands, in 1955. Today such bulletins are produced at all major international tournaments, at all North American championships, and at many lesser tournaments. Until the middle Nineties, these bulletins were printed and distributed at the tournament site. After some experimentation, the bulletins began to appear in electronic form. As of this printing, bridge fans all over the world can follow the tournament action – the bulletins at all major championships go on the web. Quite often it is possible for fans in far-away places to see the daily bulletins before the contestants receive their printed version.

Bulletins at major events offer a wide variety of material – winners, other results, standings, breaking news, analyzed hands, interviews, personality stories, etc. Outstanding journalists frequently contribute articles. Most bulletins today also feature excellent photos, something that was thought impossible back in the days before computers when every word in each bulletin had to be typed manually.

DAMAGED CARD. According to the LAWS OF CONTRACT BRIDGE, Law 7: A pack containing a card so damaged or marked that it may be identified from its back. It must be replaced if attention is drawn to the imperfection before the first card of the current deal is dealt.

DANGER HAND. The declarer often strives to prevent one opponent, the danger hand, from obtaining the lead. This may be because that player has established winners, or because he will be able to make a damaging lead through a vulnerable honor holding. See AVOIDANCE.

DATUM. A reference score from which the number of IMPs won or lost in an IMP pair game can be computed. See AVERAGE SCORE.

DE ROS CASE. Henry William Lord de Ros, the senior baron of England and a close friend of the Duke of Wellington, was a successful whist player. In 1836 he proposed to sue *The Satirist* for reporting that he had cheated at Graham's Club. Four members of the club wrote a letter supporting the charges, and one of them, John Cumming, was sued by de Ros for libel. The defense was that the statement about cheating was true. The Baron was accused of a trick known as *sauter la coupe*. This required the use of marked cards, some of which were produced in evidence. The aces and kings were marked by thumbnail. The dealer used sleight-of-hand to insure that the last card, which he dealt to himself, was a valuable one.

Two doctors swore that he suffered from stiffness and weakness in all his upper joints. The condition of his hands made it impossible for him to perform such a trick. The attorney-general contended that this was a conspiracy. The defense brought substantial witnesses to testify that when de Ros was about to deal, and only then, he had a fit of coughing which obliged him to put his hands under the table. An honor was always the turn-up card, going to the dealer.

The jury found for the defense, and de Ros was ruined socially. When he died three years later it was said that his tombstone would read *Here lies de Ros waiting for the Last Trump*. The episode was described in full by John Welcome in *Great Scandals of Cheating at Cards*.

DEAD. Bridge jargon to describe a player in a hopeless situation. It usually refers to the play of the hand, as in, "North made a killing shift, and I was dead." Also said of a hand, especially dummy, which has been robbed of (or never had) an entry.

DEAL. (1) To distribute the 52 cards at contract; (2) the privilege of thus distributing the cards; (3) the act of dealing; (4) the cards themselves when distributed.

The dealer distributes the cards face down, one at a time in rotation into four separate hands of 13 cards each,

the first card to the player on his left and the last card to himself. If he deals two cards simultaneously or consecutively to the same player, or fails to deal a card to a player, he may rectify the error, provided he does so immediately and to the satisfaction of the other players. The dealer must not allow the face of any card to be seen while he is dealing. Until the deal is completed, no player but the dealer may touch any card except to correct or prevent an irregularity.

In duplicate, the cards may be placed into any pocket. If the sponsoring organization wishes, the dealing may be from computer printouts or by dealing machine.

See LAWS (Laws 8, 9, 10), LAWS OF DUPLICATE BRIDGE (Law 6).

DEALER. The player who distributes the cards at a hand of bridge. At the start of a rubber of regular bridge or of CHICAGO, a cut is made for partners and for the deal privilege. The player who receives the highest card becomes dealer. The entire deck is given out one by one in turn to each player starting at the left of the dealer, each fourth card going to the dealer himself. The dealer speaks first in the auction by either bidding or passing. Subsequent calls proceed normally in a clockwise direction.

The term *dealer* is also a specialized slang word applying to a person who knows how to cheat at cards by arranging or stacking the pack in such fashion as to give himself and/or his partner by far the best of the cards continuously.

DEALING DEVICE. (1) A crank-operated machine which distributes the cards. (2) An electrically operated card table which accepts the used pack, shuffles it, and distributes the cards for the next deal. Neither has gained wide acceptance. (3) Various electronic devices, in Sweden, United States and France, intended to solve the problem of pre-dealing large numbers of identical hands. All use special bar coding on the cards. See DUPLIMATE.

DEALING MACHINES. As old as the game, if not older. An early example is the Hammond Electric Bridge Table, based on US Patent 1889-729. Curt Engvall of Stockholm constructed the first high-speed duplicating machine in 1969. In principle it was a punched-card sorter. In 1982 at the world championships in Biarritz, France, machine-dealt boards (with punched cards) were used in a WBF event for the first time. In 1988 (world championships in Venice, Italy), optical recognition made its first appearance in a world event. Since the 1990 world championships in Geneva, Switzerland, Per Jannersten's DUPLIMATE system (with bar-coded cards) has been standard at all major championships. Functional dealing machines of all times can be studied at the Nils Jensen Bridge Musuem in Stockholm.

DEATH HOLDING. A holding in a suit which seems an a priori certainty to kill the partnership's chances of playing or defending successfully. Among the most common examples are (1) a holding of x-x in the opponents' suit in a hand with slam possibilities; with a small doubleton in one hand it is likely that neither partner can adequately control the opponents' suit for slam play; (2) a defensive holding of Q-x in front of a long suit headed by A-K in the dummy's or declarer's hand; such a holding gives little hope of a trick on power, and no hope that declarer will misplay or misguess.

DECEPTION, MATHEMATICS OF. The rule of multiplication of probabilities (see PROBABILITY OF SUCCESSIVE EVENTS) is applicable when declarer has to decide whether a card is a DECEPTIVE PLAY. The probability that a suspected card is true is the probability that the player holds a distribution that leaves him no choice but to play it. The probability that it is false is the probability that he has a distribution from which the deceptive play would be attractive, multiplied by the probability that he would in fact decide to play the falsecard.

A 8 3 2

K Q 10 4

After winning the opening lead, South plays the king. West follows low, and East plays the 9. The probability that this is a singleton is approximately 2.8%. However, East may hold J-9-x-x, and the probability of this holding is about 8.4%. Consequently, if the probability that East would play the 9 from J-9-x-x is greater than 1/2, that distribution would be more likely than the singleton 9. Albert Dormer and Terence Reese have postulated that the play of the 9 from J-9-x-x is obligatory, in order to present South with a choice of plays on the second round. If South accepts this view, he must play the ace next time. (For simplicity, the assumption has been made that, if West held J-7-6-5, he would play the low cards indiscriminately.)

The problem should be pursued a little further. Suppose that the only deception envisaged is the play of the 9 from J-9-x-x, that is to say that East holds either J-9-x-x or the singleton 9 when he plays the 9. With a side entry to dummy, South can now give himself a better chance. He enters dummy and leads low toward the Q-10. If East shows out, South plays the queen, and has a marked finesse against West.

To counteract this, East must not merely play the 9 from J-9-x-x, but also from 9-x-x and 9-x. If he is deemed capable of this, there is little attraction for declarer in the play just described, since if East follows to a low card from dummy, declarer will have to guess whether to finesse the 10 or play the queen. As 9-x-x and 9-x each have a probability of about 10.2%, South would do better to play dummy's ace on the second round, unless he estimates only a very small probability of the 9 being played from a doubleton or tripleton.

A detailed explanation of this case is as follows: It is assumed that East will always play the 9 from J-9-x-x. The possible plans for South are:

A. Low to the ace, so as to be able to finesse against East if West shows out.

B. Enter dummy with a side-suit, lead toward Q-10, and finesse the 10 if East follows.

C. Enter dummy with a side-suit, lead toward Q-10, and play the queen if East follows:

The probabilities that the relevant distributions were dealt to East are: 9-x or 9-x-x, 64%; J-9-x-x, 27%; singleton 9, 9%. Let p = the probability that East will play the 9 if he has 9-x or 9-x-x. Then the chance of plan A succeeding is .64 times p + .27, and of plan B succeeding, .09 + .27. Therefore if p is less than 14%, plan A is preferable. That is, plan A should be preferred unless it is thought that West would not play the 9 from 9-x or 9-x-x at least seven times in fifty. The chance of plan C succeeding is .64 times p + .09, and plan C is thus clearly inferior to plan A. If entries permit, the two should be led from North's hand on the first round of that suit. It is

now more difficult for East to play the 9 from J-9-x-x. West may hold the 10 and the play of the 9 could concede a trick unnecessarily.

DECEPTIVE BID. See LEAD-INHIBITING BID and PSYCHIC BIDDING.

DECEPTIVE LEAD. See OPENING LEAD.

DECEPTIVE OPENING LEAD. See FALSE-CARDING and OPENING LEAD.

DECEPTIVE PLAY. The term deceptive play could well be used to describe any play that aims to mislead an opponent. Discriminating writers, however, tend to restrict the use of the term to plays by the declarer. Deceptive play by the defenders is more suitably described as FALSECARDING, and is dealt with under that title.

Deceptive plays by the declarer are analyzed under these headings:

(1) Weakness-concealing plays. Bluff is the basis of most of these plays; the declarer deliberately does something which is not correct technique, in the hope that the deceptive effect of his play will outweigh its mathematical shortcoming.

```
              ♠ 8 6 3
              ♥ 9 2
              ♦ Q J 10 6 4
              ♣ K Q 7

              ♠ A K 9 4
              ♥ A J
              ♦ K 9 8 3
              ♣ A 8 2
```

West leads a small heart against South's 3NT contract, and East puts up the queen. If perfect defense were to be assumed, South's best play would be to duck. After winning the next trick he would play diamonds, hoping that the defender with the ♦ A had no more hearts to play.

This plan has a slight but legitimate chance of success. In practice it is very much better to win the first trick, and drive out the ♦ A. If West has it, and the ♥ K as well, he may not find the right continuation. East's play of the ♥ Q on the opening lead has made it plain to West that declarer has the jack, but he does not know that it is bare. West may conclude that his best chance of defeating the contract is to find East with a black ace, so that he can lead hearts through declarer's jack.

On other occasions the declarer tries to bluff his way through by opening up a weak suit himself.

```
              ♠ J 6 2
              ♥ A K 10
              ♦ 8 6 3
              ♣ A 10 9 7

              ♠ Q 7 3
              ♥ Q 8 3
              ♦ A 10 2
              ♣ K Q 4 3
```

West leads the ♥ 4 against South's 3NT contract.

Declarer's ninth trick can come only from spades, and then only if both ace and king are in one hand. Further, if declarer attacks spades himself, and is lucky enough to find the cards suitably placed, the defender will probably shift to diamonds.

Declarer's best plan is to take the opening lead in dummy and lead diamonds himself, inserting the 10 if East plays low and ducking if East puts up an honor. There is a reasonable chance that the defenders will attack spades.

Many weakness-concealing plays involve releasing a high card earlier than need be. Against a notrump contract, West leads the two of a suit in which dummy holds J-x-x and declarer Q-x. If East plays the ace, it can do no harm for declarer to drop the queen. East will probably recognize that this is not a singleton, and he may assume that declarer's other card is the king. There are many variations of this theme.

Sometimes bluff is needed to extract tricks from an unpromising holding. A declarer who is reduced to the necessity of attempting to make two tricks with K-x-x in dummy and J-x-x in the closed hand does best to lead the king from the table. If the cards are distributed as follows:

```
                    K x x
      A 10 x                     Q x x x
                    J x x
```

West may conclude that South is trying to establish a suit headed by the queen and jack in the closed hand. If West seeks to molest declarer's communications by holding up the ace, South has every chance of two tricks, for East is unlikely to put up the queen on the second round and West may hold up the ace a second time.

(2) Strength-concealing plays. These are resorted to most frequently in notrump contracts. The usual occasion is when declarer wants the defenders to continue a suit which they have opened, rather than shift to a suit which he fears more.

```
              ♠ K J 7 3
              ♥ 10 7 2
              ♦ Q J 10 5
              ♣ 8 7

              ♠ A Q 2
              ♥ J 8
              ♦ A 9 7 4 3
              ♣ A Q 6
```

West leads a small club against 3NT and East plays the jack. Declarer can afford to win with the ace rather than the queen. He crosses to dummy with a spade and takes the diamond finesse, hoping that if it loses West will continue clubs rather than shift to hearts. The stratagem is a familiar one but can be effective.

Following is a play to conceal strength which can occur equally at a suit contract or at notrump:

```
                    Q 5 2


                    A 10 9 8
```

South needs to develop a second trick in the suit, but entry difficulties make it necessary to lead from the closed hand. He has no indication of where the king is located.

Some players will lead the 10 in the hope of putting pressure on West, but actually the 8 is better, especially if West can be expected to realize that South has the ace. By leading the 8, declarer conceals the fact that he has a possible finesse against the jack. Hence, if West has the king, he is more likely to put it up, for from his viewpoint the declarer may have no option but to play dummy's queen. It is, therefore, sound psychology to lead the 8, and run it if West plays low.

(3) Honor-crashing plays. Plays aimed at persuading the defenders to spend two honors — usually trumps — on one trick range from the simple to the subtle. Some examples are given under the title CRASHING HONORS, but others are more deceptive in flavor.

$$Q\ 7\ x\ x$$

$$10\ 8\ x\ x\ x$$

The usual way of playing this suit is by leading small toward the queen. Declarer loses only two tricks provided that the suit divides evenly, that West has the lone jack, or that West has A-K-x or A-K-J.

The fact that the defenders would expect declarer to play thus can make the lead of the queen from dummy effective. If the bidding rules out the possibility that East has a singleton, the queen lead cannot cost and may tempt a cover from East if he has K-J-x or A-J-x.

Sometimes the best way to crash the defenders' honors is to induce them to ruff with a small trump before the trump suit has been touched.

```
            ♠ Q 9 8 6
            ♥ A K 8
            ♦ K Q 7 6 4
            ♣ A
♠ K                       ♠ A 2
♥ J 10 9 7 5 4 3          ♥ 6 2
♦ 10                      ♦ 9 8 3 2
♣ Q J 9 6                 ♣ 7 5 4 3 2
            ♠ J 10 7 5 4 3
            ♥ Q
            ♦ A J 5
            ♣ K 10 8
```

In a pairs contest South plays 4♠ after West has made a preemptive bid in hearts. When West opens the ♥J, South's best deceptive play is to win in hand, cross to the ♣A, and continue hearts, throwing a diamond from hand. If East ruffs in small on the third round, South overruffs and drops the enemy trumps together for a high matchpoint score.

(4) Scrambling plays. When the declarer has pronounced views as to whether he wants the defenders to continue a suit or shift, he may be able to cut in on their signals. The general rule for declarer is to put out the same signals as he would if he were defending — a high card to encourage a continuation, a low card to discourage. The following is a basic position:

```
            9 7 4
A K J 3                 10 8 5
            Q 6 2
```

When West leads the king against a suit contract, South drops the 6 to make East's 5 look like the beginning of an echo.

If the declarer has more than two cards to signal with, it does not necessarily follow that he should play the highest.

```
            9 3 2
A K J                  10 8 5
            Q 7 6 4
```

When West leads the king and East plays the 5, South should drop the 6, not the 7. If he played the 7, West would realize that some deception was afoot, for it is a basic rule of defensive signaling that encouraging signals should be as high as is safely possible. East, therefore, would not start an echo with the 5 if he also held the 6. So, if South dropped the 7 in the above diagram, West would suspect that he held the 6 as well. Similarly:

```
            8 3
Q J 10 5               9 7
            A K 6 4 2
```

South is playing a notrump contract, having concealed this suit in the bidding. West leads the queen, and South, needing to develop the suit, encourages in the hope that West will continue. In this diagram, both the 4 and the 6 are apt to be effective, but against players who themselves always falsecard as high as possible the 4 is best; if West reasons that South would play the 6 to encourage, West will be all the more convinced that East's 7 is the beginning of a signal.

It can be good policy for declarer to scramble the signals even when he has no immediate objective in mind.

```
            K Q 4
J 9 5 2               10 8 6
            A 7 3
```

Suppose South wants to enter dummy to lead another suit. By leading the 7, rather than the 3, he may confuse West's count of the hand. East's 6 may appear to West as the beginning of an echo; it may even suggest to him that East is holding up the ace.

There are some more advanced situations where the declarer has not only to play the right card — he has to know also which hand to lead from.

```
            K Q J 8 2
9 6 5                 A 10 4
            7 3
```

South is playing a notrump contract, and has no entries to dummy. He needs two tricks from the suit.

If South starts by playing the 3 toward dummy's king, West will play the 5, and East will know that his partner has either three cards in the suit or a singleton. In neither case can it cost East to play his ace on the second round, so South will be thwarted in his endeavor.

Suppose instead that South leads the 7 from hand; now, from East's angle his partner's 5 could be the beginning of an echo, showing a doubleton. In any case, East allows dummy to win the first trick, but the critical point comes on the second round: provided that the second lead comes from dummy, East will have to make his decision without any sure guidance from partner.

On other occasions it can be better to make both leads from the closed hand:

```
            K Q J 2
A 8 6                 10 9 4
            7 5 3
```

This time South is playing a suit contract, and will be inconvenienced if the ace is held up until the third round. He leads the 5 from hand and dummy wins. Now he must re-enter the closed hand in another suit and lead the 7; West may place his partner with two or four cards, and in either event may release the ace. The principle followed is to make the defender with the stop card play second to the vital trick.

Also coming broadly under the heading of scrambling plays are those where the declarer has to follow suit with a particular card in order to make it more difficult for the defenders to gauge his holding.

```
            K J 6
8 5                  A Q 10 7 4 2
            9 3
```

South is playing a suit contract, and West leads the 8 of this side suit, which East has bid. Dummy plays the jack, East the queen, and South drops the 9. If he plays the 3 instead, East knows that it is safe to continue with

ace and another (unless the partnership is playing MUD leads). After the play of the 9, however, East has to take account of the possibility that declarer has a singleton.

In general, in such situations as above, the declarer follows suit with a card higher than the one led, but sometimes only a certain card will do.

```
              K 7 4 3
2                         A Q 8 6 5
              J 10 9
```

Again West leads a suit bid by his partner, and this time declarer wants to lose only one trick. (Discards are available elsewhere.) His best chance is to play low from dummy and drop the 10 from hand. East may still read the situation correctly, but his task would be easier if declarer played either the jack or the 9; he would then be able to infer that partner would not have opened the 2 from either J-10-2 or 10-9-2.

The same general good philosophy extends to falsecarding against reverse signals. Declarer attempts to scramble the defense's signals by imitating the defensive signal he wants.

(5) Miscellaneous deceptive plays. One group of situations which does not fall readily under any other heading, and which has been little explored is the following:

	West	East
(a)	10 7 3 2	A K Q 6 4
(b)	J 6 5 4	A K 10 7 3
(c)	10 5 4 3	A K 8 6 2

In each case East is declarer, and these are his trump holdings. It costs nothing to lead the high card from West each time, intending, if North plays low, to overtake and play normally for the drop. Occasionally the deceptive precaution will pay dividends, as where North covers the 10 with the jack from J-9-8-5 in example (a), enabling his cards to be picked up by subsequent finesses. Example (b) is similar, while in (c) East improves his chances not only when North has all four outstanding cards but also when he covers from J-9-7 or Q-9-7.

There are many similar positions, and the field is widened when account is taken of bidding inferences.

```
      West        East
      10 4 3 2    A K 8 6
```

The 10 lead costs only when North has the lone queen or jack. If the bidding precludes this possibility, the 10 is liable to prove doubly effective, since North will be expecting declarer to play him for trump length. Further, North may not care to outbluff the declarer by playing low from a holding headed by queen and jack, since declarer may well run the 10 in this situation.

The basis of another group of miscellaneous plays is that the lead should be made from dummy toward the closed hand:

```
              A Q x x

              x x x
```

South has to develop this suit at notrump but does not need immediate tricks. Best play is to lead small from dummy on the first round. East may put up the king from a variety of holdings which would have ruined the declarer had he played any other way.

Similarly:

```
              K x x x

              Q x
```

At a suit contract, South leads from dummy on the first round, and the queen holds. Ordinary technique is

to play low from both hands on the next round, and hope to ruff out the ace on the third. Entries permitting, however, it is better to re-enter dummy after the queen, and to lead again toward the closed hand. East may put up the ace, fearing that declarer started with both queen and jack.

DECK. (1) All 52 cards. In some sections of the world all 52 cards are called the PACK instead of the deck. (2) A wealth of high cards held either in one hand or over the period of many hands.

DECLARATION. (1) Contract, e.g., a heart declaration. (2) A statement of intent as to further line of play made by the declarer at some point previous to the play of the last trick of any given hand. See also CALL.

DECLARATIVE-INTERROGATIVE (D.I.) FOUR NOTRUMP. The use of 4NT as a general slam investigation, rarely as BLACKWOOD; developed originally as part of the NEAPOLITAN system. 4NT is Blackwood if it is a jump bid, or bid at the first opportunity after a sudden leap to game. Otherwise, it promises two aces if bid by an unlimited hand, or one ace by a limited hand, and requests partner to show an undisclosed feature (a first- or second-round control, or even a key queen) by bidding the suit containing the feature. The reply does not promise extra values unless it goes past five of the agreed trump suit. Responder may also answer by jumping to six of the agreed suit to deny interest in a grand slam, or by bidding 5NT to announce a complete maximum and strong interest in a grand slam. Over any normal five-level reply, a rebid of 5NT again asks for additional features in an effort to reach a grand slam and promises one more ace than originally guaranteed.

In several systems such as KAPLAN-SHEINWOLD and BLUE TEAM CLUB, D.I. 4NT asks for features without promising a specific number of aces. In Blue Team when 4NT is bid in the course of a series of cuebids it is a generalized slam try indicating that all suits are controlled, unless the player who bids 4NT bypasses a suit in which control has not been shown. Some expert partnerships have agreed that after a Blackwood 4NT and the ace-showing response, 5NT is always declarative-interrogative, asking for features rather than for the number of kings.

DECLARER. The player who first bid the denomination of the final bid. If the final bid is hearts, the player that first named hearts is the declarer. He becomes the declarer when the opening lead is faced, and controls the play of the dummy and his own hand as a unit.

DECLARER'S CLAIM OR CONCESSION OF TRICKS. See CLAIM OR CONCESSION and LAWS (Law 68); LAWS OF DUPLICATE (Laws 68-71).

DEEP FINESSE. A finesse when three or more cards are missing higher in rank than the card finessed. This is often made in order to execute a DUCK or AVOIDANCE play, but can be a genuine play necessary to achieve the best result. Well-known situations are:

	(a)	(b)	(c)
	Q 10 x	A J 9	A Q 9
	x x x	x x x	x x x

With (a) the 10 is finessed, although it might be right to put up the queen if West leads a low card: it would be unusual to lead from A-J or K-J with Q-10-x visible in dummy.

With (b) and (c) the 9 is finessed to give the maximum chance.

A rarer deep finesse can occur when a singleton is held opposite a five-card suit including J-10-8:

(d)	(e)	(f)
A J 10 8 x	K J 10 8 x	Q J 10 8 x
x	x	x

In each case the best chance of developing three tricks is to finesse the 8 on the first round. See also FINESSE and SUIT COMBINATIONS.

DEEP FINESSE PROGRAM. A computer program that thoroughly analyzes hands, indicating at any given point whether or not declarer can make his contract and whether or not the defense can defeat the contract with best defense. The program is used by many bridge journalists to make sure published hands are analyzed accurately.

DEFEAT THE CONTRACT. To prevent the declaring side from making as many tricks as required by the final contract.

DEFECTIVE TRICK. A trick that contains fewer or more than four legally played cards. See LAWS (Law 67); LAWS OF DUPLICATE (Law 67).

DEFENDER. An opponent of the declarer; one whose main aim is to attempt to prevent the declarer from making his contract or to hold declarer to the fewest tricks possible.

DEFENDER'S CLAIM OR CONCESSION OF TRICKS. See CLAIM OR CONCESSION and LAWS (Law 70); LAWS OF DUPLICATE (Laws 68, 69, 70, 71).

DEFENDING HAND. Either opponent of the declarer; occasionally used in the bidding to refer to an opponent of the player who opened the bidding.

DEFENSE, DEFENSIVE PLAY. The play by the opponents of the declarer. The primary object of defensive play is normally to defeat the contract, even at the expense of presenting declarer with overtricks if the chosen line of defense is unsuccessful.

At duplicate, however, particularly at matchpoint play, holding declarer to a minimum number of tricks can be important, indeed. Articles dealing with defensive play that should be consulted are: COVERING HONORS; DEFENSE TO A SQUEEZE; DESCHAPELLES COUP; DISCARDING; DISCOVERY; DUCK; ENTRY-KILLING PLAY; FALSECARDING; FORCING DECLARER TO RUFF; JETTISON; MATCHPOINT DEFENSE; MERRIMAC COUP; OPTIMUM STRATEGY; OVERRUFF; PLAY FROM EQUALS; RUFF AND DISCARD; RULE OF ELEVEN; SECOND HAND PLAY; SPOT CARDS; THIRD HAND PLAY; THROUGH STRENGTH; TRUMP PROMOTION; UNDERRUFF; UP TO WEAKNESS; UPPERCUT. For all topics relating to LEADS, OPENING LEADS, SIGNALS, see those headings.

DEFENSE TO DOUBLE OF ONE NOTRUMP. In standard practice the double of a 1NT opening bid is for penalties. The usual means of escape is for opener's partner to bid a suit, and the traditional meaning of a redouble is to penalize the doubler. See DOUBLES OF NOTRUMP BIDS (Third hand problems). However, several alternatives are designed either to locate the partnership's best escape suit, or to place the notrump opener as declarer, or both.

One suggested method is to use TRANSFER BIDS. Responder bids the suit next below his long suit. If responder's suit is clubs he redoubles to ask opener to bid clubs. If responder has no long suit but has seven or eight cards in the major suits, he can redouble, ostensibly transferring to clubs; but, after opener bids 2♣, responder bids 2♦, asking opener to choose between hearts and spades.

In a simpler method, suggested by Martin J. Cohn of Atlanta, suit bids by responder remain natural, and the redouble itself is used as a Stayman-type inquiry for the majors.

A third possibility is to use a response of 2♦ to ask opener to bid his better major suit, and to redouble to ask him to bid his better minor suit. In this method, responder's immediate run-out to 2♥ or 2♠ would be natural, and his bid of 2♣ would promise a long minor suit. If responder's suit is diamonds he runs to that suit over the double of 2♣ that will presumably be forthcoming.

Finally, a method proposed by Alan Truscott. A redouble forces 2♣ and may show club length. If the redoubler follows with two of a red suit he shows a four-card suit with at least one other four-card suit higher in rank. A direct 2♣ bid shows a four-card club suit with at least one other four-card suit in reserve. Direct bids of 2♦ and higher are natural. Unlike other methods, this enables the partnerships to find 4-4 fits in the minor suits with assurance. The method works equally well when a 1NT overcall is doubled. See EXODUS, SCRAMBLING, SWINE.

DEFENSE TO INTERFERENCE WITH BLACKWOOD. See BLACKWOOD AFTER INTERFERENCE.

DEFENSE TO MULTI. See MULTI.

DEFENSE TO ONE NOTRUMP. The general rule used to be to pass when in doubt. Since the notrump bidder has delineated his hand within limited bounds, it is easier for opener's partner to assess the situation and decide whether a double for penalties is in order.

In the passout position, it was argued that it paid to be especially conservative because the possibility is strong that the defenders do not have a worthwhile fit. The partner of the opening bidder is content to play in notrump, so chances are that all suits are reasonably balanced around the table. If the player in fourth seat has a long suit, chances are his partner is short in this suit because both opener and responder have indicated balanced hands. Nevertheless in the last decade many defenses such as DONT and Woolsey encourage bidding any time the player in the balancing seat has 13 cards.

If the opening bid is a strong notrump, chances are the opponents do not have game. The situation changes radically when the opening bid is a weak notrump – even

more so if the opening notrump shows 10-12 or 8-10 HCP. The opponents should make every effort to find their fit or punish the opening bidder if they can determine they have the fit or the power.

There are many specialized actions the opponents can take after an opening notrump bid, most of which are methods of showing a two-suited hand. These include ASPRO, APSTRO, ASTRO, ASTROLITE, BECKER, BROZEL, CANSINO, CAPPELLETTI, DONT, DOUBLES OF NOTRUMP BIDS, EXCLUSION BID, HAMILTON, GRANO-ASTRO, LANDY, RIPSTRA, SUCTION.

Actions by the opener's partner are affected by the meaning of the second player's action. The consensus in BWS94 is: Lebensohl applies; redouble is strength-showing; double is for penalties, forcing to 2NT, with later raises and 2NT not forcing; cuebid of shown suit forcing to 2NT or raise, at least invitational.

DEFENSE TO OPENING FOUR-BID. When an opponent opens the bidding with a four-level bid, the calls of double and 4NT are used in a variety of ways, depending on the suit opened. Against 4♣ or 4♦, a double is for takeout. A 4NT overcall is subject to partnership agreement – it's either BLACKWOOD or it's natural.

When the opening bid is 4♥, a double is for takeout and guarantees a reasonable spade holding. 4NT usually is considered to be a minor suit takeout. Against 4♠, the traditional meanings were double for penalties and 4NT as a general takeout. However, the modern expert consensus (68% in BWS 2001) is that this double should be for takeout, and 4NT should indicate a non-spade two-suiter. See PREEMPTIVE BID.

DEFENSE TO OPENING THREE-BID. The following methods can be used as a defense against Weak Two-bids also:

(1) Standard. A double is primarily for takeout, but is sometimes described as "cooperative" or "optional" because the doubler's partner may sometimes decide to pass in the expectation of a penalty. 90% of the world plays this way.

A normal minimum for the double would be 16 points in high cards, perhaps a little less in the pass-out seat. The double implies support for the unbid major or majors unless the doubler has considerable reserve strength. Other bids would be natural, including 3NT, which would be a minimum of 15½. Desirable features for this bid would be a double stopper in the opener's suit and a good minor suit. See TONTO for a modern method of responding.

(2) Fishbein. Devised by Harry Fishbein. A double of a three-bid is for penalties, and the doubler's partner should rarely take any action. A bid in the cheapest available suit is a conventional bid to replace a takeout double. 3♥ over 3♦, for example, would show a minimum of 16 points in high cards and a three-suited hand, or possibly a two-suited hand. The Fishbein takeout bid over 3♠ would be 4♣. The takeout bid is unconditionally forcing because it might be based on a two-suited hand. The convention does not apply in the pass-out position.

(3) Cheaper (or lower) minor. The use of the cheaper available minor suit as a takeout bid: 3♦ over 3♣, and 4♣ over other three-bids. As in the Fishbein convention, a double is for penalties, and the convention does not apply sitting under the three-bidder (although it can apply by partnership agreement).

This convention used to be common among English tournament players. A variation is known in America as the SMITH CONVENTION, devised by Curtis Smith. He recommends the use of 4♣ as the takeout bid in all circumstances, even over 3♣.

(4) Optional double. A double that promises a balanced hand with both support for the unbid suits and some strength in the opener's suit. It invites the doubler's partner to pass for penalties.

(5) Weiss. The use of the cheaper minor for takeout as in (3) above, with the double used as an optional double as in (4).

(6) 3NT for takeout. Rare in America, but combined with a double for penalties, this used to be but is no longer standard procedure in England at rubber bridge. A disadvantage is that 3NT is often needed as a natural bid.

(7) Reese. 3NT for a takeout over major-suit three-bids only, with a double for penalties. Double for takeout over minor suits and in fourth seat.

(8) Two-suiter takeouts. Overcalls of four in a minor suit after a major-suit three-bid can be used to show that suit and the unbid major. In combination with standard takeout doubles, this solves some difficult two-suiter problems. The single-suited minor-suit hand is often suitable for a 3NT overcall or a jump to the five-level. The two-suiter bids can be applied in both second and fourth seats. (A minor two-suiter can be shown by a jump to an "unusual" 4NT.)

(9) Cheaper minor over the blacks. 3♦ over 3♣ and 4♣ over 3♠ are for takeout. Double over these bids is therefore for penalties. Double over 3♦ and 3♥ is cooperative.

(10) FILO (British). A combination of *Fi*shbein over red suits and *lo*wer minor, or cheaper minor, over black suits. All doubles suggest a penalty. The BWS 1994 expert consensus is that the cuebid over any three-bid is MICHAELS. It therefore shows majors over a minor, the other major and and a jump to 4♦ over 3♣ is diamonds plus major.

DEFENSE TO PREEMPTIVE BIDS. See DEFENSE TO OPENING FOUR-BID; DEFENSE TO OPENING THREE-BID and WEAK TWO-BIDS.

DEFENSE TO A SQUEEZE. The prerequisites for a true squeeze are: menace cards, properly located and oriented; sufficient entries to these menaces; and correct timing. Unless all these elements are present, the squeeze will not be effective unless the opponents misdefend. There are several principles which can assist the defenders to discard correctly.

(1) Two-card menace. If one defender guards a two-card menace and two isolated menaces, then he should unguard the long menace when a choice must be made among the three suits.

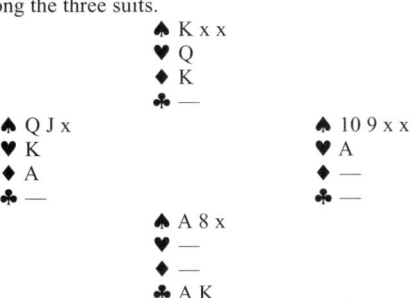

The lead of the ♣A squeezes West in three suits. If he discards a heart, the ending leads to a twin-entry DOUBLE SQUEEZE. West must discard a spade, his guard to the long menace.

(2) Unguarding a menace. When a defender guards two long menaces and one isolated menace, then he should unguard the long menace placed to his left.

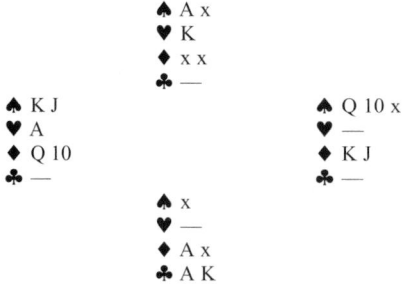

South leads the ♣A, which squeezes West in three suits. If he discards a diamond, then South cashes the ace of that suit, which leads to a positional double squeeze. West must discard a spade, the guard to the long menace situated to his left.

(3) Progressive squeeze defense. In this example, South leads the ♣A, which squeezes East in three suits.

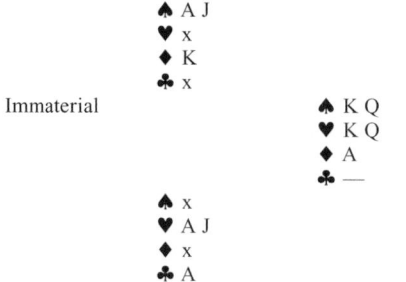

Any discard costs a trick, so East's primary objective is to protect himself from a progressive squeeze, which would cost him two tricks. A heart is the only discard that will achieve this end.

This resembles an automatic REPEATED SQUEEZE position, but it is faulty in that a one-card menace (the ♦K) is misplaced in the North hand. When South leads the ♣A, West must discard the ♦A. Otherwise South can win all the remaining tricks.

(4) Underruff. On rare occasions an UNDERRUFF proves to be a defender's only safe play. The following hand from a par contest illustrates the point. (Romanet).

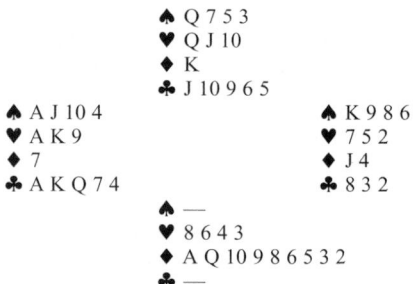

East is declarer in 6♠. South leads the ♦A, followed by the queen. West ruffs the second diamond with the ace and North must underruff. Any other discard would enable declarer to establish a trick. When the trumps are run off, North cannot be squeezed since he discards after West, the hand which contains all the menace cards.

Sometimes correct discarding will not save the defenders; an early attack against one of the basic elements of the squeeze may be the only means to break it up.

(5) Destruction of the menace. This can be effected in two ways: (1) by leading the suit at every opportunity, thus forcing declarer to play the menace card prematurely; and (2) by making it impossible to ISOLATE THE MENACE. This latter occurs usually at a trump contract. Terence Reese provides this example to illustrate the attack on menace cards.

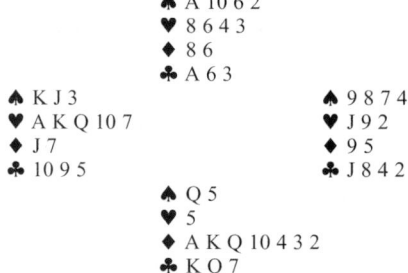

South is declarer at 6♦. West leads the ♥K. If West continues with another heart, South ruffs, and after drawing trumps, enters dummy with the ♣A to ruff a third heart, thus leaving West alone with the burden of guarding that suit as well as the spade suit. However, if West refrains from leading the second heart, then the heart menace cannot be isolated; East's jack cannot be ruffed out, and West can discard all his hearts, relying on East to guard that suit.

(6) Attack on entries. This defense consists of playing the suit where declarer has a long menace. In this way a two-card menace may become an isolated menace, a twin-entry menace may be transformed into an ordinary two-card menace, etc.

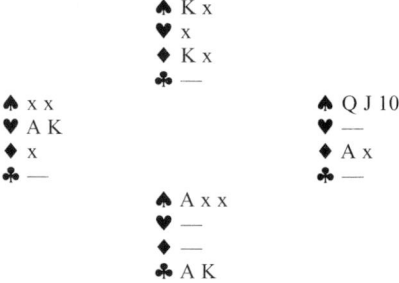

Clubs are trumps, and West has the lead. If West leads a heart or a diamond, South can ruff and play his last trump, and East will be squeezed in diamonds and spades. The ending is a twin-entry simple squeeze. However, if West leads a spade, the twin-entry menace is reduced to a two-card menace of the usual sort and the squeeze must fail.

(7) Failure to rectify the count. Many times declarer must lose one or two tricks to the opponents in RECTI-FYING THE COUNT for a squeeze. Defenders can withhold their cooperation in this maneuver, either by failure to cash established winners or by refusing to win a trick offered by the declarer. The example below, if permitted to succeed, is known as a SUICIDE SQUEEZE.

```
                  ♠ 6 3 2
                  ♥ 8 5 3 2
                  ♦ A Q 6
                  ♣ K 6 2
  ♠ K Q J 10 7                    ♠ 9 5
  ♥ J 9                           ♥ Q 10 7 4
  ♦ 7 3                           ♦ J 10 9 5
  ♣ Q J 8 4                       ♣ 10 7 3
                  ♠ A 8 4
                  ♥ A K 6
                  ♦ K 8 4 2
                  ♣ A 9 5
```

South is declarer at 3NT, and West leads a spade.

South wins the second round and returns the suit. If West cooperates with declarer and cashes all his spades, then East can discard his clubs, but the second club lead won in dummy later squeezes him in the red suits. West cannot even cash the fourth spade without putting pressure on his partner. East can let go of two clubs on the third and fourth spades, but when declarer cashes his ♣A-K, East must either unguard the diamonds or discard a heart, whereupon declarer will be able to set up dummy's fourth heart for his ninth trick. West can cash only two spades, but then he must switch and declarer cannot make his contract.

```
                  ♠ K Q J 4
                  ♥ A 4
                  ♦ 7 4 3 2
                  ♣ J 4 3
  ♠ 8 6                           ♠ A 10 9 7
  ♥ Q J 10 7 6 3 2                ♥ 9 8
  ♦ 8                             ♦ J 10 9 6
  ♣ 8 7 5                         ♣ 9 6 2
                  ♠ 5 3 2
                  ♥ K 5
                  ♦ A K Q 5
                  ♣ A K Q 10
```

South is declarer at 6NT after West opens 3♥. West leads the ♥Q. South takes the king and leads a spade to the king. If East wins the first or second spade lead, South can execute a spade-diamond squeeze against East. If East ducks two rounds of spades, however, the contract is unmakable. See also *Killing Defense at Bridge* by Hugh Kelsey.

DEFENSE TO STRONG ARTIFICIAL BIDS. Since systems based on a strong, artificial opening bid (usually 1♣) have become increasingly popular, the defending side needs new ways to enter the auction, both to prepare for a sacrifice and to obstruct the opponents. Several methods are in current use; they are based on the premise that the defending side can most profitably act with one long suit or a two-suiter.

A majority of tournament players employ a simple de-

fense: a double to show length in both major suits, 1NT to show length in both minors (MATHE). Other overcalls are natural; jump overcalls are preemptive. This method applies directly over a forcing 1♣ opening and following an artificial 1♦ response (favored by 65% of experts in BWS 2001). A double of a semi-positive or positive artificial response should show the suit doubled. (87%).

The same defense can in theory be used over an artificial, forcing 2♣ opening. Pairs seldom have this agreement, however, since (1) they must enter the auction a level higher; (2) a 2♣ opening suggests massive defensive values; hence, the chance of finding a paying sacrifice decreases, while the chance of giving the opening side information to use in the play increases.

Few pairs, in fact, have any special agreements over an opposing 2♣ opening. In the absence of any agreements, a double of 2♣ is logically lead-directing, promising club strength; 2NT shows length in the minor suits; suit overcalls are natural.

More methods are discussed under their own headings: See EXCLUSION BIDS, CRASH, IDAK, ROBINSON and WONDER BIDS.

Alan Truscott devised a method by which the defending side can show all possible one- and two-suited hands. A jump overcall is natural; a simple overcall shows length in the bid suit and the suit that ranks just above it. Hence, over 1♣, 1♦ = diamonds and hearts; 1♥ = hearts and spades; 1♠ = spades and clubs; 2♣ = clubs and diamonds. The two non-touching suit combinations are shown by double (clubs and hearts) and 1NT (spades and diamonds). Over a negative 1♦ response, the only change is that double shows diamonds and spades, 1NT shows clubs and hearts.

A modified version, preferred later by the author of the method, uses minimum actions to show one-suiters and jump bids, starting with 2♦, to show two-suiters. When defender has a balanced strong hand he should pass on the first round. See PANAMA, TRAP, TRUSCOTT DEFENSE.

DEFENSE TO TWO-SUITED INTERFERENCE. When an opponent conventionally shows a two-suited hand, as with a MICHAELS CUEBID or an UNUSUAL 2NT OVERCALL, the opening bidder's partner has several countermeasures: a double, a raise, at least one cuebid and a bid of a new suit not shown by the opponent's interference.

A double and a cuebid are strength-showing actions. A double suggests a hand that would have been worth a redouble of a takeout double. Responder should avoid this action, however, unless he seeks to penalize the opponents. A double may goad the opponents into further preemption, and if responder has a strong hand with several offensive features, he should begin to describe his hand.

A cuebid in a suit shown by the interference is a general force that begins investigation for the best contract; by partnership agreement, it may promise support for opener's suit or length in the fourth suit (see below).

A single raise in opener's suit is equivalent to a normal single raise. Responder needs no extra high-card values, but he should be careful of raising with poor trumps; the opponent's overcall increases the chance of a bad trump split.

West	*North*	*East*	*South*
1♥	2♥(1)	?	

(1) Spades and a minor

Neither side vulnerable. East should bid 3♥ with:

♠ 5 4   ♥ Q 10 6 2   ♦ A 9 6 4 2   ♣ J 4.

East could not raise to 3♥ (as a LIMIT RAISE) if North had passed, but he must stretch to compete over North's interference. A raise may show even less at favorable vulnerability.

A bid in a new suit is natural and non-forcing. If the opponent's action shows two suits, but one is unspecified, responder can cuebid only in the known suit.

West	North	East	South
1♠	2♠ (1)	?	

(1) Hearts and a minor

A 3♥ bid by East is a cuebid; both 3♣ and 3♦ are natural and non-forcing, since North's minor suit is unknown.

Practice varies among experts. This problem was presented to an expert panel in *The Bridge World* magazine:

IMP scoring, neither side vulnerable:

West	North	East	South
	1♣	2♣ (1)	?

(1) Michaels; both majors

What should South call with:

♠ 3   ♥ K 8 3   ♦ A K 10 6 3   ♣ K J 10 3

Sixteen of 30 panelists doubled despite the prospect of a leap in spades by West. Eight bid 2♦; some considered the bid forcing. One cuebid 2♠, and one jumped to 3♦.

Edgar Kaplan suggested a cuebid of 2♥. In Kaplan's style, 2♥ suggests a club fit, a stopper or control in hearts and unbalanced distribution; hence, it implies spade shortness. Ira Rubin preferred 3♠, a splinter bid suggesting spade shortness and club support. Marty Bergen uses a method over Michaels similar to Unusual over Unusual. His 2♥ cuebid shows a good club raise; a 2♠ cuebid would show a strong hand with diamonds.

When the opponents interfere with an Unusual 2NT overcall, many pairs employ the method known as Unusual over Unusual. They retain the strength-showing message of a double and the competitive nature of a single raise, but assign a specific meaning to each cuebid. Each cuebid shows the strength of a limit raise or better, plus length in a suit not promised by the overcall.

In Bergen's method, for example, the lower cuebid shows support for partner's suit; the higher cuebid shows a good hand with the fourth suit.

West	North	East	
1♠	2NT	3♣ = limit raise or better in spades	
		3♦ = good hand with hearts	
		3♥ = natural, non-forcing	
		3♠ = weak, competitive	

West	North	East	
1♣	2NT (1)	3♣ = weak, competitive	
		3♦ = limit raise or better in clubs	
		3♥ = good hand with spades	
		3♠ = natural, non-forcing	

(1) Hearts and diamonds

The alternative is to play that the lower cuebid shows the lower of the possible suits, and the higher the higher. Thus after a major opening 3♣ shows hearts and 3♦ shows spades, irrespective of the opening bid.

The modern expert consensus, determined by BWS94 is: Double is for penalties but does not create a force; double of artificial action suggests a later penalty double; new suit and 2NT are non-forcing; the cheapest cuebid is limit raise or better; the next cuebid shows forcing

bid in the remaining suit.

Where spades is the unbid fourth suit, it makes sense for a bid of 3♠ to be forcing (since you have gone past the security-blanket of three of partner's suit) and thus the cuebid to show spades is not forcing beyond three of partner's suit.

For a convention dealing in part with two-suited interference over 1NT openings, see LEBENSOHL.

DEFENSIVE BIDDING. Bidding by a partnership after the opponents have opened the bidding, although at times the bidding by the opening side could be termed defensive. The following main headings should be consulted: COMPETITIVE BIDDING, CONTROL BIDS, CUEBIDS, DOUBLES and OVERCALLS. Some specialized defensive systems are listed under various systems, such as ROTH-STONE and KAPLAN-SHEINWOLD.

Accurate defensive bidding requires considerable experience and judgment. It is in this area that the expert has the greatest advantage over less experienced players. Many factors have to be taken into consideration.

1. The risk involved. Possible gain has to be weighed against possible loss.

2. The prospects of gaining. Often the opening side can be outbid if you can find a fit. Often both sides can make a partial. Taking a small loss when the opponents can make a partial pays big dividends in duplicate. Sometimes the defensive side can make a game; sometimes they can take a good sacrifice; sometimes the opponents can be pushed too high; sometimes they can be pushed into the wrong contract.

3. Vulnerability. The defensive side is in a much better position for action when not vulnerable against vulnerable. Even at equal vulnerability it often pays to take reasonable risks. However, when vulnerable against non-vulnerable, you should use great care because of the risk of a heavy penalty.

4. Level of the auction. Heavy risk is often involved when the opponents have forced you to decide at a high level. Coming in at the one-level is relatively simple and safe, but the danger of being doubled rises as the level increases. So if you come in at a higher level, you should have a strong hand either in high cards or distribution.

5. Estimate of partner's hand. If the opponents rest at a low level, there is a greater chance that partner has something. If the opponents have found a low-level fit, the chances are greater that your side also has a worthwhile fit.

6. Positional prospects. A king in the suit of the bidder on your right is more valuable than the reverse because the bidder is more likely to hold the ace.

7. Length of suit. Clearly the longer the suit you hold, the better are your chances for a plus if you step in.

8. Holding in opponents' suit. A small doubleton or tripleton in the opponents' suit is a red flag – the chances of quick losers are greatly increased. However, if the opponents have strongly supported each other, your tripleton may be a plus – it may mean partner has a singleton or a void in the opponents' suit.

Many other factors are involved at times – the type of game, the status of your game or the match, wasted small honors in the opponents' suit, etc. Experts consider defensive bidding one of the most difficult areas of the game. See LAW OF TOTAL TRICKS.

Also see the following for specific information about

various types of defensive bidding:
COMPETITIVE BIDDING, DEFENSE TO ONE
NOTRUMP, DOUBLES, OVERCALLS, TWO-SUITER
CONVENTIONS. Other entries include ADVANCE
SAVE, APSTRO, ASTRO, ASTPRO, BALANCING,
BECKER, BERGEN OVER NOTRUMP, BROMAD,
BROZEL, CANSINO, CAPPELLETTI, CLUBS FOR
TAKEOUT, COMPETITIVE DOUBLE, CRASH, DE-
FENSE TO OPENING FOUR-BIDS, DEFENSE TO
OPENING THREE-BIDS, DEFENSE TO STRONG
ARTIFICIAL OPENINGS, DEFENSE TO TWO-
SUITED INTERFERENCE, DONT, DOUBLE FOR
SACRIFICE, FORCING PASS, GOOD-BAD TWO
NOTRUMP, GRANO-ASTRO, HAMILTON, KOCK-
WERNER REDOUBLE, LANDY, LEAD-DIRECTING
BID, LEBENSOHL APPLICATIONS, LITTLE
CUEBID (PETIT CUEBID), MITCHELL STAYMAN,
MODIFIED CRASH, OBAR BIDS, REDOUBLE, RES-
CUE, RIGAL OVER PROTECTIVE NOTRUMPS,
RIPSTRA, RUBENS ADVANCES, SACRIFICE,
SCRAMBLING, SCRAMBLING TWO NOTRUMP,
SOS REDOUBLE, SUCTION, SUPER UNUSUAL
NOTRUMP, TAKEOUT DOUBLE, TRANSFERS
OVER DOUBLES OF OPENING PREEMPTIVE
BIDS, TRAP PASS, WOOLSEY, WRIGGLE.

DEFENSIVE TRICK. A card or card combination that
may be expected to win a trick if an opponent becomes
the declarer.

In some situations a player with a solitary defensive
trick may need to take positive action. If 6 ♥ is reached
voluntarily and the bidding has indicated that 6 ♠ is a
possible SACRIFICE, a hand that is known to be very
weak may have the conventional agreement to double if
it has one defensive trick. This should help partner to
make the right decision (which may still be to bid 6 ♠),
and avoid a PHANTOM SACRIFICE. For artificial uses
of doubles and passes to reveal whether or not the partnership has enough defensive tricks to defeat the slam,
see DOUBLE FOR SACRIFICE. also see QUICK
TRICK.

DELAYED DUCK SQUEEZE. A particular form of
SECONDARY SQUEEZE.

DELAYED GAME RAISE. A bidding sequence
equivalent to a standard jump raise.

♠ K J 5 4
♥ A 5 3
♦ 8 2
♣ A Q 9 7

This hand is too strong to raise an opening 1 ♠ to 4 ♠
in any normal bidding style. Using LIMIT RAISES without a Jacoby 2NT, a substitute for the forcing double raise
is necessary, and 2 ♣ followed by 4 ♠ is the usual device.
This is not completely satisfactory if the opener's rebid is
2 ♠ because the nature of responder's hand is not clarified; but in that case the slam prospects are remote.

For alternative solutions to this problem, see SWISS,
THREE NOTRUMP RESPONSE, and TWO NOTRUMP
RESPONSE. These devices would be used on relatively
balanced hands, in which case the delayed game raise can
be reserved for markedly two-suited hands.

In modern bidding styles, a bid of 1NT, forcing, following by a jump to game in opener's suit, shows a balanced hand with 13-15 points and three-card support.

DELAYED RAISE. See BELATED SUPPORT; PREF-
ERENCE.

DELAYED STAYMAN. See STAYMAN ON SECOND
ROUND.

DELTA ASKING BID. See SUPER PRECISION ASK-
ING BIDS.

DEMAND BID. A FORCING BID. A term used occasionally to refer to a FORCING TWO-BID but otherwise obsolete.

DEMICOMA. A bidding system developed by Dr.
Prakash K. Paranjape of India and played primarily in
India. It is based on DEstructive MInors and
COnstructive MAjors designed to handle all opening
hands that hold four or more cards in a major suit in a
purely constructive way. As a corollary, hands with minor suit density are opened at higher level and serve a
mildly destructive purpose. The system uses a forcing
club (usually no long suit and no 5-5 distribution), five-
card majors (can have longer minor), opening 1 ♦ usually showing a four-card major, responses in a four-card
major even if holding a much longer minor, opening 2 ♣
and 2 ♦ 11-15 usually with no four-card major, 2NT
strong two-suiter or single-suiter, 3 ♣ at least 5-5 in
minors, weak two-bids in majors, slam bidding based
on integrated ace-asking with exclusion element built
in, 2NT response over 1 ♥ or 1 ♠ ace-asking, 1NT rebid after 1 ♣-1 ♦ strong and forcing.

DEN HAAG BUTLER INCIDENT. The strange ending to the Cap-Volmac tournament in 1994. In the last
round, a board had been scored 2NT+1: +180. The opponents on the board, HAMMAN-WOLFF, sought and got
a rectification. They expected to gain 1 IMP and consequently won one place, but instead lost one place and 2000
Dutch guilders. The rectification also caused a change of
the average with which all scores were compared, which
fell from +240 to +230. This made no change in Hamman-
Wolff's score, but it did give another pair, Leufkens-
Westra, 1 IMP and a lone sixth place (originally they had
been classed tied for sixth). This would not have happened if the BASTILLE system had been used. Under
that system, Hamman-Wolff would have gained 0.625
IMPs, while Leufkens-Westra would have gained 0.11
IMPs, so no reversal of positions would have occurred.

DENIAL BID. A bid that indicates lack of support for
partner's bid (an obsolete term).

DENIAL CUEBID. A method of showing honor-loca-
tion in the later stages of the auction. It was first used in
several relay systems, in differing formats. The procedure developed by Roy Kerr and others in New Zealand
as part of SYMMETRIC RELAYS has been adopted by
some standard bidders.

The method assumes that one player has already described his distribution, approximate strength, and controls (or possibly key-cards). He shows his high cards
by: bidding one step to deny a high honor in his primary
suit; two steps to deny in his second suit, etc. If two
suits are (or could be) equal in length, the higher-ranking is inspected first.

Here is an example based on a Flannery opening:

West	East
♠ K 6 5 3	♠ A Q 4
♥ K Q 8 7 5	♥ A
♦ A	♦ 6 5 3
♣ 6 5 4	♣ Q J 9 8 7 2

West	East
2 ♦ (1)	2NT (2)
3 ♣ (3)	3 ♦ (4)
3NT (5)	4 ♣ (6)
4 ♠ (7)	5 ♣ (8)
Pass	

(1) Flannery, four spades, five hearts, 11-16 points.

(2) The normal inquiry. In effect a relay.

(3) Tripleton club, so 4-5-1-3.

(4) Relay asking for controls.

(5) Four controls. (Two are assumed for the opening bid.)

(6) Relay, asking for denial cuebids.

(7) The third step, promising a high heart, a high spade but no high clubs. (The next relay would ask again about hearts. Suits known to be singleton or void are ignored.)

(8) Knowing ♣ AK are missing.

If the opener has a similar hand with ♣ AK and neither the king nor queen of hearts, he will show six working controls (a singleton king does not count) and no top honor in hearts. Responder will bid 7 ♣, knowing that the six controls are the ♠ K, ♦ A and ♣ AK.

The denial cuebid concept can be applied in many situations, including sequences that follow Roman Key-card Blackwood.

DENOMINATION. The suit or notrump specified in a bid. The modern term is STRAIN. See LAWS (Law 18).

DEPO. See BLACKWOOD AFTER INTERFERENCE, DOPI, REPO.

DESCENDING ORDER. The order of the rank of the denominations: notrump, spades, hearts, diamonds and clubs. The opposite order is UP THE LINE.

DESCHAPELLES COUP. The lead of an unsupported high honor in order to establish an entry to partner's hand. This sacrificial play was invented by Alexandre Louis Honore Lebreton Deschapelles.

```
              ♠ A Q 10 4
              ♥ A J
              ♦ 8 7 5 4
              ♣ 8 6 3
♠ 3 2                      ♠ 9 8 7 6 5
♥ Q 8 6                    ♥ K 10 7 5
♦ K Q J 9 6 3              ♦ A
♣ 7 5                      ♣ A 4 2
              ♠ K J
              ♥ 9 4 3 2
              ♦ 10 2
              ♣ K Q J 10 9
```

The blocked diamond position makes it very difficult to defeat South's highly optimistic 3NT contract. East overtakes the ♦ K lead with his ace, and must hope that his partner has a queen outside diamonds. If West has the ♣ Q, the contract will be defeated automatically, so East assumes that his partner holds the ♥ Q. The return of the ♥ K is the key play. Whether or not South ducks, West's

♥ Q is established as an entry, and South can be held to five tricks. Any other play by East at the second trick permits South to make his contract. Note that the play of the ♥ K cannot give South his contract if West has the ♣ Q: South's maximum would then be eight tricks.

For a similar defensive play aimed at destroying an entry instead of creating one, see MERRIMAC COUP.

DESPERATION LEAD OR PLAY. A lead or play made in defiance of the dictates of safety when defensive prospects seem poor. A tactic usually reserved for rubber bridge, not duplicate. For example, after this bidding:

West	North	East	South
	Pass	1 ♠	Pass
3 ♠	Pass	4 ♠	All Pass

South has to lead from:

```
              ♠ 8 7
              ♥ K 4
              ♦ J 8 5 4 2
              ♣ 9 7 4 3
```

The lead of the ♥ K is a desperation lead trying to promote a heart ruff in South's hand. North may hold ♥ A, or ♥ Q and ♠ A.

DEUCE. Another name for the 2, the card of lowest rank in a suit.

DEVIL'S BEDPOSTS. The ♣ 4.

DEVIL'S COUP. Often called the disappearing trump trick. The defenders' seemingly sure trump trick vanishes due to a certain lie of the cards. This is very low percentage play. It is difficult to formulate a general rule as to whether it is better or worse than the straightforward method of drawing trumps. The best play depends upon several factors. If you start by trying for the coup, there's often a chance of recovery when you see the coup cannot succeed. Two examples:

```
1.            ♠ A K Q 2
              ♥ K 7 3
              ♦ A
              ♣ 10 9 7 5 4

              ♠ 5
              ♥ A 10 9 4 2
              ♦ K Q J 9
              ♣ A 3 2
```

Contract 7 ♥. Opening lead ♠ J.

a. In the Devil's Coup line, declarer cashes three spades, discarding clubs; ruffs a spade; cashes the club and diamond aces; ruffs a club, cashes two diamonds; ruffs the last diamond, and leads a club from dummy hoping for this position;

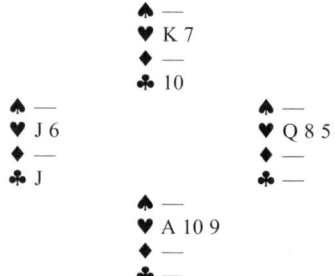

```
              ♠ —
              ♥ K 7
              ♦ —
              ♣ 10
♠ —                        ♠ —
♥ J 6                      ♥ Q 8 5
♦ —                        ♦ —
♣ J                        ♣ —
              ♠ —
              ♥ A 10 9
              ♦ —
              ♣ —
```

This succeeds when West is 4-2-4-3 with honor-small

in hearts, about 2.8%. It also succeeds when W is 4-3-4-2 with xxx of hearts, another .5%, for a total of about 3.3%.

b. Straightforward line. The only problem is trumps. Playing for QJ doubleton in East or honor singleton in West succeeds about 9%.

c. Combined line. If you try for the coup and East shows out on the fourth round of spades, you can still try for QJ tight in East or honor singleton in West. If either hand ruffs earlier, or West ruffs on the fourth round, you are down. The straightforward line is better.

2.
```
                    ♠ J 5 4 2
                    ♥ K 10 7
                    ♦ A 6
                    ♣ K 8 6 4
    ♠ A K 7 3                   ♠ Q 9 8 6
    ♥ Q 6 5                     ♥ J 8
    ♦ J 9 8                     ♦ Q 7 3 2
    ♣ J 10 7                    ♣ 5 3 2
                    ♠ 10
                    ♥ A 9 4 3 2
                    ♦ K 10 5 4
                    ♣ A Q 9
```
Here, there is work to be done besides picking up trumps. You need two diamonds ruffs in dummy or one ruff and a club split or a squeeze. That extra work reduces the percentages of the straightforward line to a bit over 4%. Here, it may well be worth starting with the devil's coup line and switching if it cannot work. The pure coup line is again 3.3%. The combined line may well be better. These factors are involved:

a. The trump spots. In the first hand, if West ruffs with the 8 from 8xx on the fourth round of diamonds, you can no longer pick up QJ tight in East. In the second hand, where both dummy and declarer have a high spot, that is not possible:

K 10 7

A 9 x x x

If West ruffs from either 8xx or QJ, you can overruff in North and still pick up trumps. Similarly, can you pick up stiff honor opposite honor-fourth? In the first hand, you can. In the second hand, you can't. In a *Bridge World* hand, the trumps were:

K 10

A 8 x x x x

Now there is no straightforward play. The only possible line is to play for West to hold honor-9 doubleton.

b. What else is to be done? If trumps are the only problem, as in the first hand, the straightforward line may well be better.

c. Card-reading. The lead may make it more or less likely that the distribution needed for the Devil's Coup exists. In the first hand, West's spade lead might suggest that West isn't short in spades, so there's less chance he will ruff. In grand slam contracts, West's failure to lead a trump might make the xxx-QJ distribution in trumps less likely.

DEVIL'S PICTURE BOOK, DEVIL'S TICKETS.

Names given to playing cards by New England Puritans. From the time of their introduction in Europe, gambling at cards had been opposed: in 1397, John I, King of Castille, forbade dice and cards; in 1397, the Provost of Paris forbade playing at dice or cards on workdays; in 1404, the Synod of Langres forbade clergymen to play at dice or cards; in 1423, St. Bernardino preached against cards and persuaded the people of Bologna to throw their cards into a fire; and in 1541, the Parliament of Paris forbade play at dice or cards in the homes of the town and suburbs.

The objections were usually against gambling or against working-men wasting their time; but the Puritans, for example, held that the Second Commandment (graven images) was violated by face cards. Hence, some churches permitted games using decks without court cards.

The opposition to cards has dwindled steadily, and the term is used humorously today except in a few isolated communities.

DEVYN PRESS. The publishing division of Baron Barclay Bridge Supplies was founded in 1979 by Randy Baron and Andrew Bernstein. Devyn Press has published more than 200 books on bridge and now has more than 100 books in print.

DIAMOND. (1) The suit second lowest in rank, next above the club suit, represented by the symbol ♦. This represents the third estate, although the symbolism is not obvious. (2) The symbol. The suit originated in France in the sixteenth century; its name obviously comes from the diamond-shaped lozenge used for the pips.

DIAMOND LIFE MASTER. An ACBL Life Master who has more than 5000 masterpoints. Also an ABA Life Master with more than 1000 masterpoints.

DINK. To shorten the trumps of either dummy or declarer by forcing him to ruff; an obselete colloquialism.

DIRECT COMPETITION. Such competition exists between two contestants when they play hands which are identical with respect to cards, relative location, dealer, and vulnerability. See BALANCED COMPARISONS.

DIRECT CUEBID. See CUEBID IN OPPONENT'S SUIT.

DIRECTION. The designation of North, South, East, West, or the hand held by these players.

DIRECTIONAL ASKING BID. A specialized use of a low-level CUEBID IN OPPONENT'S SUIT to invite partner to bid notrump. Partner must bid notrump if he holds Q-x, J-x-x, or better in the opponent's suit. The directional asking bidder may have two objectives. First, he may wish to discover whether his side has a combined stopper in the opponent's suit when he himself holds Q-x, J-x-x, or a singleton king. Second, he may wish to steer the contract into his partner's hand. A player with A-x-x or K-x-x should wish to be dummy if the right-hand opponent has bid the suit. The lead should come up to partner's possible Q-x or J-x-x.

However, the low-level cuebid is regularly used on the West Coast and in England as a general-purpose forcing bid (or WESTERN CUEBID). The cuebidder will often have no stopper of any kind in the opponent's suit, and his partner bids notrump if, and only if, he has a full stopper in his own right. (In general, the Western cuebid "asks" if opponents have bid only one suit, but shows a stopper if they have bid more than one.)

Each partnership must decide whether the low-level cuebid shows a guard (East Coast style), no guard (West Coast style), or half a guard (directional asking bid).

Players using the West Coast style, who are the great majority of American players, can sometimes use a repeat cuebid below the game level as a directional asking bid:

West	North	East	South
			1♣
Pass	1♦	1♥	2♥
Pass	3♣	Pass	3♥

South holds:

> ♠ A 4
> ♥ J 7 3
> ♦ 9
> ♣ A K Q 9 7 6 2

2♥ is a Western Cuebid asking for a stopper. 3♥ is a directional asking bid, asking for half a stopper. 3NT can still be reached if North has as little as a singleton heart king or queen.

DIRECTOR. (1) Tournament director, the person designated to supervise a bridge tournament and to apply and interpret the LAWS OF DUPLICATE BRIDGE. These duties are outlined in Laws 81-91, and his responsibilities set forth. (2) Director of ACBL governing body at national or lower level. Throughout this *Encyclopedia*, Director (capitalized) is used in sense (2). Tournament director is not capitalized.

DIRECTOR CLASSIFICATION. See TOURNAMENT DIRECTORS.

DIRECTOR'S INSTRUCTIONS. See INSTRUCTIONS, DIRECTOR'S.

DISAPPEARING TRUMP TRICK. See DEVIL'S COUP; SMOTHER PLAY.

DISCARD. (1) To play a card which is neither of the suit led, nor of the trump suit, or (2) the card so played. Colloquialisms for discard include DITCH, PITCH and SHAKE. Defenders can and do convey information to each other by the specific nature of certain discards. See DEFENSE; DISCARDING; SIGNALING.

DISCARDING. Deciding which cards to throw away and which to keep in the later stages of the play is one of the basic arts of the game. Although each case must be considered on its own merits, several general considerations are worth remembering.

(1) It is desirable to keep parity with a useful side suit in dummy.

> *North*
> ♠ A K Q 7 4
> *West*
> ♠ 10 8 5 3 2

West should avoid a spade discard. If South held the singleton jack or J-x, he would then win five tricks; if South held a low singleton, he could establish dummy's fifth spade.

> *North*
> ♠ A K 8 2
> *West*
> ♠ 9 7 6 4

If South has a doubleton queen, West's holding constitutes a stopper. To retain his spades, West should not hesitate, for example, to unguard a queen in another suit in which dummy is weak. Even if declarer has A-K-J, he may finesse.

West's spade holding could be significant with the 5 instead of the 9♠ if South held J-9-3 or 10-9-3, he would need a side entry to dummy to take four tricks.

The same consideration applies when declarer is known to have or may have a long suit.

(2) A defender who pays attention to the bidding can often reconstruct declarer's hand and decide whether his bidding would be consistent with or without a particular honor.

Suppose this is the position:

> *North*
> ♣ K J 5
>
> *East*
> ♣ Q 8 6 3

When discarding, East must make up his mind who holds the ♣A. If South holds it, East must retain three clubs; if West has the ace, East needs only to keep a doubleton.

If in the same situation East holds only low clubs, he should be careful to retain three clubs if he believes declarer holds the ace.

(3) Many discards are informative and contribute to accurate defense. The defenders should seldom worry about giving away information to declarer; declarers dislike being deceived, and many place no reliance on the defenders' plays.

A valuable rule is to signal with the highest card you can spare. Hence, a high encouraging discard denies the next higher card and promises the next lower.

> *North*
> ♣ 4 3 2
>
> *West*
> ♣ A 8 5

If East discards the ♣K, West can lead the suit happily. If East throws the jack, West can lead the 5♠ East must have started with K-J-10-9 or J-10-9-x. But if East throws the queen, West must leave clubs alone; South's king may be trapped later.

A player discarding from a worthless hand should try to help his partner, who may need information. If a defender has worthless holdings in two suits, he should normally discard from both suits as soon as possible. To discard low cards from only one suit would suggest that he has something to look after in the other.

If partner may be interested in length rather than strength, a possible maneuver is to discard one suit completely. Alternatively, it is possible to give COUNT SIGNALS at each stage. With 9-7-5-3-2, the sequence might be 2, 7, 3, 9, 5. The first discard is discouraging; subsequently, a low card indicates a odd number of cards remaining, a high card indicates an even number. See PRESENT COUNT.

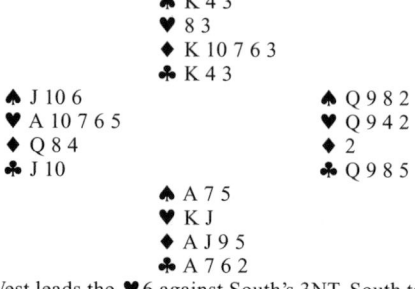

West leads the ♥6 against South's 3NT. South takes

East's queen with the king, leads a diamond to the king and returns a diamond. East should discard the ♥2, suggesting an original holding of four hearts, and West will know to lay down the ♥A when he gets in with the ♦Q.

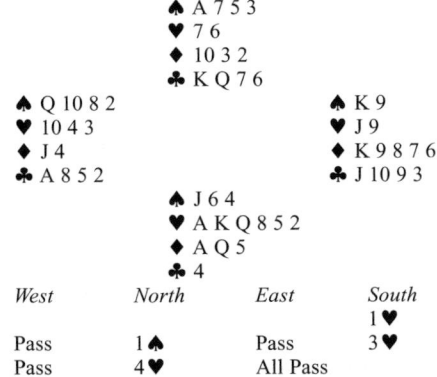

```
              ♠ A 7 5 3
              ♥ 7 6
              ♦ 10 3 2
              ♣ K Q 7 6
♠ Q 10 8 2                    ♠ K 9
♥ 10 4 3                      ♥ J 9
♦ J 4                         ♦ K 9 8 7 6
♣ A 8 5 2                     ♣ J 10 9 3
              ♠ J 6 4
              ♥ A K Q 8 5 2
              ♦ A Q 5
              ♣ 4
```

West	North	East	South
			1♥
Pass	1♠	Pass	3♥
Pass	4♥	All Pass	

West leads the ♠2. East wins the king and returns the ♠9: jack, queen, ace. South finesses the ♦Q and draws trumps. On the third trump, East should discard the ♣J to signal an even number. If South holds the ♣A, he has the rest of the tricks; if West has the ♣A, East wants him to take it at the right time. If West wins the first club and continues spades, South goes down.

Here is another example of an informative discard:

```
              ♠ K Q 3 2
              ♥ 9 8
              ♦ Q J 4
              ♣ K 7 5 2
♠ 8 7                         ♠ J 10 9 6 5
♥ A 10 7 6 4                  ♥ Q J 3
♦ K 8 6 3                     ♦ 7
♣ J 8                         ♣ Q 10 9 6
              ♠ A 4
              ♥ K 5 2
              ♦ A 10 9 5 2
              ♣ A 4 3
```

West	North	East	South
			1NT
Pass	2♣	Pass	2♦
Pass	3NT	All Pass	

West leads the ♥6: 8, jack, king. South goes to the ♣K and passes the ♦Q, winning. When he leads the ♦J next, East should discard the ♥Q. The RULE OF ELEVEN tells East that South has no more hearts higher than the 6, so West's suit is ready to cash. But West may not know; from his point of view, South's hand could be,

♠ J x   ♥ K Q x   ♦ A 10 9 x x   ♣ A Q x

making a spade switch necessary.

```
              ♠ 10 8 7 3
              ♥ 6 3
              ♦ K 6
              ♣ K J 10 7 3
♠ A J 4                       ♠ Q 9 6 2
♥ Q 10 8 5 4                  ♥ 9 7
♦ 10 8 4                      ♦ J 9 7 5
♣ 8 5                         ♣ A 6 4
              ♠ K 5
              ♥ A K J 2
              ♦ A Q 3 2
              ♣ Q 9 2
```

West	North	East	South

West leads the ♥5: 3, 9, J. South attacks clubs, and East holds off. On the third club, West can discard the ♥Q, disavowing interest in hearts, and East should shift to spades.

(4) A taxing situation arises when declarer forces discards by cashing a long suit, and a defender has more than one suit to guard.

Even if no squeeze threatens, cooperative discarding may be needed to prevent the loss of a trick. In this situation, a defender cannot and should not try to guard every suit; he must guard one and leave the other to his partner. The deal below is given by Marshall Miles.

```
              ♠ Q 5
              ♥ 10 9 6 3 2
              ♦ Q
              ♣ A Q 9 8 2
♠ J 9 7 6 3                   ♠ K 10 8
♥ K 5                         ♥ J 8 7 4
♦ K 8 5                       ♦ 10 9 7 2
♣ 7 6 3                       ♣ 5 4
              ♠ A 4 2
              ♥ A Q
              ♦ A J 6 4 3
              ♣ K J 10
```

West	North	East	South
			1♦
Pass	1♥	Pass	2NT
Pass	3♣	Pass	3NT
All Pass			

West leads the ♠6. South wins the third spade and runs the clubs. On the third club, East must decide which red suit to guard; suppose he judges to keep diamonds and therefore throws three hearts. West must discard twice; if he pitches a winning spade to guard both red kings, South is safe by passing the ♦Q. Hence, West must cooperate with East by keeping ♥K5 and blanking the ♦K. South must then guess well to make his game.

(5) A defender can safely discard winners for which he has no entry. An exception arises in this common position:

```
                North
                ♣ A Q
                       East
                       ♣ K 2
```

At the 12th trick South can try for an overtrick by taking a club finesse. If East has kept two clubs, South can take the finesse safely. But if East has kept one club and a winner, South may choose not to jeopardize his contract.

Another type of tactical discard may be necessary when a defender is threatened with a strip-squeeze:

```
              ♠ J 4
              ♥ 5 2
              ♦ A Q 8 6 3
              ♣ K J 6 4
♠ K 8 5 2                     ♠ 10 9 7 3
♥ K Q 10 7 3                  ♥ 9 8 6
♦ 7 2                         ♦ 10 9 4
♣ 9 3                         ♣ 8 7 5
              ♠ A Q 6
              ♥ A J 4
              ♦ K J 5
              ♣ A Q 10 2
```

West	North	East	South
			2NT
Pass	6NT	All Pass	

West leads the ♥K. South takes the ace and cashes nine tricks in the minor suits. If West's last three cards are the ♥Q and the guarded ♠K, South can lead a heart for an endplay. To mislead declarer, West does best to discard three low spades early, then the ♥3 and ♥10.

It will often be clear that unless partner has certain cards, nothing can be done. A defender can then discard on the assumption that partner has those cards.

```
              ♠ K J 6 3
              ♥ 8 7 3
              ♦ 9 6 5 2
              ♣ 6 5
♠ 5                          ♠ 9 8 4
♥ Q 10 6 2                   ♥ J 9 5 4
♦ Q 10 8 4                   ♦ J 7
♣ Q J 10 4                   ♣ A 9 3 2
              ♠ A Q 10 7 2
              ♥ A K
              ♦ A K 3
              ♣ K 8 7
```

West	North	East	South
			2♣
Pass	2♦	Pass	2♠
Pass	4♠	All Pass	

West leads the ♣Q. East takes the ace and returns a club. South wins, ruffs a club in dummy and runs his trumps, forcing West to unguard a red queen.

West knows that South held five spades and three clubs. If South had four diamonds, East would have switched to his singleton at the second trick. If South had four hearts, he would have led hearts earlier to ruff his fourth heart in dummy if necessary. Assuming South has three cards in one red suit and two in the other, West should keep diamonds. The reason is simple: If South has a diamond loser, only West can guard diamonds.

(6) A tactical discard may be used to create an entry.

```
              ♠ A K 4 3
              ♥ 10 4
              ♦ 7 5 2
              ♣ A Q 3 2
♠ Q 7 5 2                    ♠ J 10 9 8
♥ K J 9 7 3 2                ♥ Q 6
♦ Q 9                        ♦ K 3
♣ 10                         ♣ J 9 8 7 5
              ♠ 6
              ♥ A 8 5
              ♦ A J 10 8 6 4
              ♣ K 6 4
```

West	North	East	South
			1♦
Pass	1♠	Pass	2♦
Pass	3♣	Pass	3NT
All Pass			

West leads the ♥7 against South's 3NT, and South holds up the ace twice. On the third heart, East should discard the ♦K. If South's diamonds are headed by A-Q-J, the king is worthless; if West has the ♦Q, East must unblock.

(7) The so-called IDLE FIFTH CARD in a suit is always an attractive discard — so much so that declarer can often infer that a defender's first discard comes from a five-card suit.

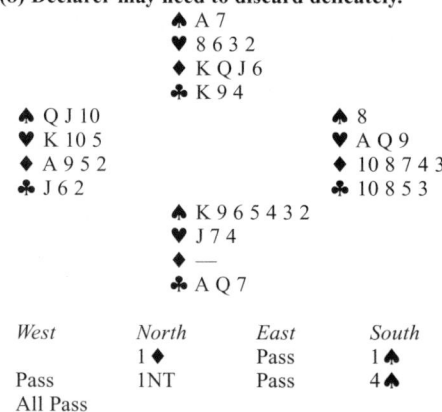

```
              ♠ Q 6 3
              ♥ K Q 9 4
              ♦ K 9 3 2
              ♣ 9 7
♠ A K 9 7 4 2                ♠ 8
♥ 6                          ♥ J 8 7 5 2
♦ 6 4                        ♦ J 10 8 5
♣ K 10 8 6                   ♣ Q 5 4
              ♠ J 10 5
              ♥ A 10 3
              ♦ A Q 7
              ♣ A J 3 2
```

West	North	East	South
			1NT
2♠	3NT	All Pass	

West led the ♠K and continued with the ace, on which East discarded the ♥2. South drew the inference, and after winning the third spade, he cashed the ♥K and led a heart to the ten to make the contract. East could lose nothing by throwing clubs on the spade leads.

(8) Declarer may need to discard delicately.

```
              ♠ A 7
              ♥ 8 6 3 2
              ♦ K Q J 6
              ♣ K 9 4
♠ Q J 10                     ♠ 8
♥ K 10 5                     ♥ A Q 9
♦ A 9 5 2                    ♦ 10 8 7 4 3
♣ J 6 2                      ♣ 10 8 5 3
              ♠ K 9 6 5 4 3 2
              ♥ J 7 4
              ♦ —
              ♣ A Q 7
```

West	North	East	South
	1♦	Pass	1♠
Pass	1NT	Pass	4♠
All Pass			

West led the ♠Q. South won with dummy's ace and led the ♦K, throwing a club. When West took the ♦A he naturally shifted to the ♣J, and South made his game. See DEFENSE TO A SQUEEZE. See also *More Killing Defense* by Hugh Kelsey.

DISCIPLINARY CODE. A set of rules and regulations drawn up by a bridge organization to cover acts by members that require discipline. Such codes are in effect at all levels, from the club to the national organizations to the World Bridge Federation.

DISCIPLINE. The ability of both members of a partnership to follow an agreed system when partnership action is called for.

The ROTH-STONE SYSTEM was the first to stress partnership discipline as a requirement for use of the system, although all systems had implied its necessity without actually stressing it. Selection committees for teams in international competition have stressed more and more the importance of discipline under the heading of established partnerships. Discipline also describes actions taken against players who break the rules of the

game. Disciplines run the gamut from reprimand to outright expulsion. See DISCIPLINARY CODE.

DISCOURAGING BID. A bid indicating that game or slam is unlikely but not impossible. Examples are: responder's raise of opener's suit from one to two, as a first response or as a rebid; responder's bid of 1NT as a first response or as a rebid; opener's minimum rebid of his suit after a one-round forcing response at the two level; and in some styles a suit takeout in response to an overcall.

The bidder expects a combined point-count in the range of 18-22, or the distributional equivalent, and partner continues only if he has considerable additional strength in terms of high cards, distribution or fit.

DISCOURAGING SIGNAL. A card played that by partnership agreement shows no interest in the suit led. See DISCARD, SIGNALS.

DISCOVERY. The process of maneuvering the play in order to learn vital information about the hidden hands.

Terence Reese gives this example in *The Expert Game*.

♠ 10 8 4 2
♥ K 9 8 3
♦ A Q 4 3
♣ Q

♣9 led

♠ A Q J 9 7 5
♥ —
♦ 6 5 2
♣ A K 7 4

With neither side vulnerable, South opens 1♠ in fourth seat. North raises to 4♠, and South bids 6♠.

South will look first to see if there is any reason for cashing the ♠A and play for some elimination position. The chances of this are obscure, so he may judge that the hand depends on one of two finesses and lead a spade for a finesse of the queen.

It is possible to improve on that play. At the second trick declarer should lead the ♥K from dummy. If East covers with the ace, South ruffs and finesses the ♦Q. East wins with the king and leads the ♠6. Now South has discovered for sure that East holds the ♥A and ♦K. Since West opened the ♣9 it is probable also that East holds ♣J-10; if South wants to look further, he can place East with intermediate cards in both hearts and diamonds, for had West held a solid sequence in either suit he would presumably have led it.

In short, South has built up for East a hand on which, if it contained the ♠K as well, he might well have opened the bidding third hand. Having reached this point, South may decline the spade finesse and play for the drop of the singleton king.

A different type of discovery play can be aimed at determining a suit division.

♠ Q 8 3
♥ 8 4
♦ 8 7 2
♣ K Q 8 4 3

♥3 led   ♥10 played

♠ A K 5
♥ K 9 6
♦ K Q J 10 5
♣ A 6

South opens 2NT and is raised to 3NT. He wins the first trick with the ♥K, and has to choose between playing diamonds and clubs. The diamond play wins if the heart suit is split 4-4; the club play wins if the clubs split 3-3.

The even club split is slightly more likely mathematically, and the heart lead increases the chance that West has a five-card suit. But instead of plunging on clubs, South can give himself both chances if the defenders are good players. At the second trick he leads the ♣6 to dummy's king, followed by a low club to the ace. West is likely to signal his club length (see COUNT SIGNALS) by playing low from a three-card holding or high from two or four. if West's club plays indicate that the suit will not break, South abandons clubs and tries diamonds. This preserves the chance of making the contract if the hearts are split evenly and avoids a possible two-trick defeat.

Discovery plays by the defenders are very rare. The following example is from the 1961 British International Trials.

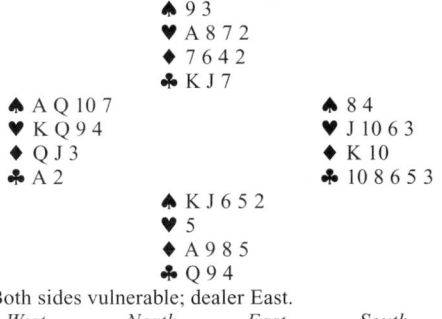

Both sides vulnerable; dealer East.

West	North	East	South
		Pass	Pass
1♥	Pass	2♥	2♠
Dbl	2NT	Pass	3♦
Dbl	All Pass		

West led the ♥K, captured by dummy's ace. South led a spade to his jack, and West won with the queen. It was clearly necessary for the defenders to lead trumps, but the lead of the queen would have blocked the suit, and prevented the defenders from playing three rounds advantageously. West judged that his partner must have a high diamond honor or the ♣Q. To learn which, he led the ♣A to get an attitude signal. When East dropped the ♣3 it was clear that he did not hold the ♣Q, so West shifted to the ♦3. South was held to six tricks, losing 800.

If in a suit contract dummy is weak and third-hand has K-J-x (x), he will usually play the jack. This may force the ace and indicate the location of the queen.

DISCRETIONARY POWERS. See ADJUSTED SCORE and Duplicate Law 12.

DISQUALIFICATION. Law 91, LAWS OF DUPLICATE BRIDGE, provides that a director is specifically empowered to suspend a player for the balance of a session, or subject to the approval of the tournament committee or the sponsoring organization, to disqualify a player, pair or team for cause in order to maintain discipline or order.

DISTRIBUTION. The manner in which the cards of a suit are dispersed among the four hands of a deal, or the manner in which the number of cards in the four suits are distributed in one hand. Variations in distribution are the basis of various bidding systems in use. See BIDDING.

DISTRIBUTIONAL COUNT. Distributional points added to high-card points are used to arrive at an overall hand valuation. There are various ways in which the standard 4-3-2-1 point-count can be supplemented:

Goren Count, devised by William Anderson of Toronto, and adopted and developed by Charles Goren.

void	counts 3 points
singleton	counts 2 points
doubleton	counts 1 point

This applies to the opener's hand, and these points are added to the high-card point-count (subject to the usual corrections).

If the responding hand plans to raise the opener's suit, he applies a different count:

void	counts 5 points
singleton	counts 3 points
doubleton	counts 1 point

In addition, the responder makes certain corrections, deducting a point for each of the following; (a) a raise with 3 trumps; (b) a 4-3-3-3 distribution; (c) an insufficiently guarded high card. Also, a point is added for a king, queen, or jack in the trump suit provided this does not bring the total number of high-card points in the trump suit to more than 4.

Karpin Count, popularized by Fred Karpin, who was the first to achieve a large following with a distributional point-count method.

Distributional points are assigned for length, one point for each card over four in any suit. Thus any five-card suit counts 1 point, any six-card suit 2 points, and so on.

Short suits are counted in raising partner according to the following schedule:

	with 4 or more trumps	with 3 trumps
void counts:	3	2
singleton counts:	2	1
doubleton counts:	1	0

These are in addition to points for length.

A simple version of the Karpin idea was published in 1947 by Richard Miller. An even earlier pioneer of distributional point-count was Victor Porter of Boston. His method, published in 1938, allowed 4 points for each singleton and void, and 2 points for a doubleton in both hands.

Culbertson Count, published by Ely Culbertson in 1952. For an opening suit bid, count each card over three in any suit as one point except that the fourth card does not count in the trump suit. When declarer's opening bid has been raised, he counts the fourth trump as a point, and adds 2 points when he holds six or more trumps. Responder also counts 2 points for holding six or more trumps when giving a raise and makes some minor correction: (a) 1 point is deducted for three-card trump support or 4-3-3-3 distribution; (b) 1 point is added for holding a void or two singletons.

Prior to Culbertson's adoption of point-count, he advocated a distributional count. Honor winners and long-suit winners were added, and the total of the combined hands represented the level to which the side could bid. A supporting hand counted ruffing values, but did not count length in side suits.

Roth Count, devised by Alvin Roth to quantify the point-count adjustments in hand evaluation which experts make in light of the bidding. The Roth system retains the 4-3-2-1 Work point-count for honor cards and

the basic 3-2-1 Goren count for shortness. It adds points for long suits: 1 point for any six-card major or for a good six-card minor; 2 points for any seven-card major or for a good seven-card minor.

Adjustments to shortness and length points are made in light of the degree of fit shown by partner's bidding. With 0-2 cards in partner's suit, no points are counted for shortness in a side suit; with 3 cards in partner's suit, the normal 3-2-1 scale of shortness count should be used; with 4 cards in partner's suit one extra point should be added for each singleton, plus one extra point if there are any doubletons. If one's own suit is raised by partner or if partner makes a notrump bid showing a balanced hand, one point is added for each card in the suit in excess of four.

Combination Count, devised in England, uses lengths and shortages immediately. Karpin length points are supplemented by 2 for a void and 1 for a singleton. This is applied to both opener and responder in all situations with two provisos: (a) the opening bidder may not count more than 3 distributional points; (b) in responses and rebids no player may count more distributional points than he has cards in his partner's suit.

All distributional counts are an attempt to reach by formula the bid which an expert will make on the basis of experience. Their chief value is in giving guidance to inexperienced players; experts seldom make any conscious calculation of distributional points. See VALUATION and ASSETS.

DISTRIBUTIONAL POINT-COUNT. For the distributional value of certain short suit holdings translated into point-count, see DISTRIBUTIONAL COUNTS, DISTRIBUTIONAL VALUES.

DISTRIBUTIONAL VALUES. The trick-taking possibilities of a hand that depend on the distribution of the cards in the other three hands rather than on the rank of the cards in their respective suits; low-card tricks in general, including long-suit tricks and ruffing tricks (short-suit tricks).

The classic example of the power of distribution versus points is the DUKE OF CUMBERLAND'S HAND. A slight variation, given below, has been immortalized by Ian Fleming in his *Moonraker*.

The famous James Bond, sitting North and partnering M, sets out to teach a lesson to the cheat Drax.

Having prearranged the pack, Bond sees to it that the evil Drax gets the West hand and it will be clear that, no matter which of his three suits East chooses to lead, the final contract of 7♣ doubled and redoubled by Bond cannot be defeated. Playing for enormous stakes, this costs Drax something like 15,000 pounds — a salutary lesson indeed!

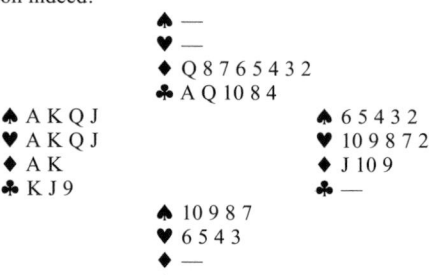

	North	
	♠ —	
	♥ —	
	♦ Q 8 7 6 5 4 3 2	
	♣ A Q 10 8 4	
West		East
♠ A K Q J		♠ 6 5 4 3 2
♥ A K Q J		♥ 10 9 8 7 2
♦ A K		♦ J 10 9
♣ K J 9		♣ —
	South	
	♠ 10 9 8 7	
	♥ 6 5 4 3	
	♦ —	
	♣ 7 6 5 3 2	

DISTINGUISHED MEMBER. A special award set up by the ACBL Board of Directors. No time schedule for awarding the honor was established, nor were there specific criteria set out for selecting the recipient except that the person should be a truly distinguished member of ACBL. The first was Lou Bluhm of Atlanta, who was singled out for his personal attributes and contributions to bridge, particularly in the area of ethics and courtesy. The only other choice by 2001 was James Zimmerman for his contributions to the game in many areas.

DISTRICT, DISTRICT ORGANIZATION. One of 25 sectors of the American Contract Bridge League. Each district is represented on the ACBL Board of Directors by a director, elected by the unit boards of the district. Each district also is allotted five representatives on the ACBL Board of Governors. Each district is governed by a district organization whose functions include the organization of regional tournaments, staging a district-wide contest to determine the district's representative in the Grand National Teams (United States districts only), staging a district-wide contest to determine the district's representatives in the three flights of the North American Pairs, staging a district-wide contest to determine the pair that will represent the district in the North American 49er Pairs, coordinating sectional tournaments with neighboring districts and handling special cases by means of an appointed district judiciary committee.

DISTRICT CHAMPIONSHIP. See GRAND NATIONALS CHAMPIONSHIPS (A, B and C) NORTH AMERICAN OPEN PAIRS (A, B and C).

DISTRICT JUDICIARY COMMITTEE. A committee of the DISTRICT ORGANIZATION whose rights and responsibilities include hearing appeals from disciplinary action imposed on a member by a unit board of directors, and conducting disciplinary hearings *ab initio*, which may result in censure, suspension or expulsion of a player.

DITCH. A colloquialism for DISCARD.

DOG. A very poor hand. (Colloq.)

DONT. (Disturb the Opponents' Notrump.) Invented by Marty Bergen, this is a method of maximizing the number of hands on which to come in over 1NT, while preserving a moderate amount of safety by describing two-suiters at a cheap level.

The basic framework involves using double as an unspecified one-suiter, with 2♣, 2♦ and 2♥ each promising a two-suiter with the bid suit and an unspecified higher suit. 2♠ is a normal spade overcall. Getting to 2♠ via the double suggests a strong hand with spades (or in some partnerships, spades and a four-card minor)

In response to the double, fourth hand can pass the double with better than opening values, or bid 2♣ to ask partner to name his suit. Other actions by fourth hand show a long suit and suggest a final contract.

In response to the two-suited bids, fourth hand can pass, (which he should generally do with three or more cards in the anchor-suit, or with two cards in the anchor-suit and a two-suiter of his own, suggesting a big misfit). Alternatively, he can bid the next suit up as a relay for overcaller's second suit, or bid his own suit.

2NT is a game invitation, asking overcaller to describe his suit lengths and range. A raise of overcaller's suit is no more than mildly invitational.

So in an auction such as (1NT) 2♦ (P) responder can pass, or bid 2♥ as a request for overcaller to pass or correct. 2♠ by responder would be to play, 2NT would be a relay with game interest.

A simple scheme of responses after the 2NT relay would be to play:

(After a 2♣ overcall) 3♣ is any minimum – responder passes or bids 3♦ as pass or correct. All other actions are natural and extra values.

(After a 2♦ overcall) 3♣/3♦ show minimums with hearts and spades respectively, 3♥/3♠ are natural and extras.

(After a 2♥ overcall) 3♣/3♦ are minimums, anchoring to the better major, 3♥/3♠ the same principle with a maximum.

If the opposition continue bidding after an overcall of double, 2♣ or 2♦, fourth hand's bids are natural rather than pass/correct while his doubles are always takeout, as indeed are further doubles by the overcaller.

DONT can also be played over a 2NT opening bid.

DOOP. A device developed by Ronald Andersen which permits "one table duplicate games," so that hands previously played in tournaments can be played in the home.

DOPE. See BLACKWOOD AFTER INTERFERENCE.

DOPI. See BLACKWOOD AFTER INTERFERENCE.

DOUBLE. A call that increases the scoring value of odd tricks or undertricks of an opponent's bid. See LAWS (Law 19). See DOUBLES.

DOUBLE AGAINST SLAM. See DOUBLE FOR SACRIFICE; LIGHTNER DOUBLE.

DOUBLE-BARRELED STAYMAN. A method of combining forcing and non-forcing STAYMAN. See TWO-WAY STAYMAN.

DOUBLE COUP. A trump coup in which two ruffs are necessary to achieve the required end position.

DOUBLE DUMMY. (1) Play of a hand that could not be improved upon, as though declarer were looking at all four hands as in DOUBLE DUMMY PROBLEMS. It can also be used to refer to perfect play by the defenders.

Originally, Double Dummy was a two-handed form of whist in which each player had a dummy. Some players exposed all four hands, thus giving rise to the modern usage.

Some bridge-playing computer programs can look at the cards of the other three players, during play, in order to play as well as possible.

(2) Trademark of a two-hand contract game, introduced in 1975, in which each player has a dummy. Since each player already sees two hands, no dummy hand is put down on the table.

DOUBLE DUMMY PROBLEM. Problems in the play of the hand in which the solver knows the holdings in all four hands. The contract and the opening lead are specified. Like chess problems, they are for the solitary

analyst. They require great skill in construction. Double dummy problems have a long history. They were constructed in the 19th century before bridge challenged the popularity of whist. They were often appended to bridge columns, usually in a miniature setting in which each player has played most of his cards. See WHITFELD SIX. The most common double dummy problem has a full 52-card layout. There is usually an unusual twist, perhaps involving a squeeze or endplay, and the solver needs to explore several variations. The opponents are assumed to play perfectly.

The genre thrived in the United States in the first half of this century. Since then it had been largely confined to British magazines, particularly *Bridge Magazine* (and its successors) which had a continuous double dummy solving contest with high quality problems. It was directed until 1965 by Ernest Pawle and subsequently by Hugh Darwen. It has now been abandoned because of the advent of the computer. The following is a classic Darwen construction: MAMMOTH ON A SEESAW

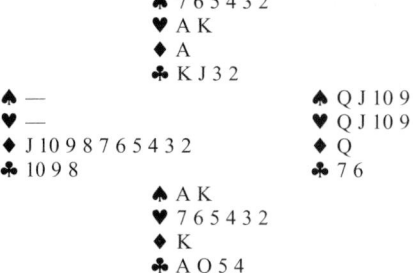

```
                 ♠ 7 6 5 4 3 2
                 ♥ A K
                 ♦ A
                 ♣ K J 3 2
  ♠ —                         ♠ Q J 10 9 8
  ♥ —                         ♥ Q J 10 9 8
  ♦ J 10 9 8 7 6 5 4 3 2      ♦ Q
  ♣ 10 9 8                    ♣ 7 6
                 ♠ A K
                 ♥ 7 6 5 4 3 2
                 ♦ K
                 ♣ A Q 5 4
```

South is required to make 10 tricks in notrump. The lead is the club 10. The solution is astonishing: South must allow West to win the first trick with the club ten. South wins the next two tricks in the dummy with the club jack and the diamond ace, with the order depending on West's play to the second trick. The lead of the club 2 then squeezes East out of two tricks. If he throws a heart, South wins with the club queen and works on hearts. If he throws a spade, South wins with the club ace and works on spades.

There are three major original collections of problems: *Sure Tricks* by George Coffin, based on work by Ivar Andersson; *Double Dummy Bridge* by George Coffin; and *Bridge Magic* by Hugh Darwen.

Recent times have seen the emergence of computer programs that can solve double dummy problems on an average computer in a matter of seconds. See DEEP FINESSE, INFERENTIAL PROBLEM, SINGLE DUMMY PROBLEM.

DOUBLE ELIMINATION. A method used in knockout team events by which a team is not eliminated until it has lost two matches.

Ordinarily in a knockout tournament, the team that loses a head-on match is eliminated from further competition.

The first competition between teams results in a group of losers and a group of winners (usually termed winners' bracket and losers' bracket). Matches continue in the winners' bracket, with half the competing teams continuing in the winners' bracket in the next round, the balance joining the losers' bracket. Eventually there is one surviving team from the winners' bracket.

In the losers' bracket, head-on play continues between

one-time losers. Winners of these matches continue play in the next round, with losers in this bracket being eliminated as they have then lost their second match. In each round of the losers' bracket, the winners of the previous round are joined for the next round by the losers in the preceding round from the winners' bracket. This can often lead to a possible rematch between two teams that have previously competed against each other. The CONDITIONS OF CONTEST are usually designed to provide as few as possible of such rematches.

Special provisions must usually be made in the conditions for the last few matches, depending on whether the losers' bracket ends up in a round of two, three, four, or five. See REPECHAGE.

DOUBLE ELIMINATION KNOCKOUT TEAMS. A KNOCKOUT TEAMS event in which a team must be defeated twice before being eliminated. See BRACKETED KNOCKOUT TEAMS, COMPACT KNOCKOUT TEAMS, HANDICAP KNOCKOUT TEAMS, MINI-KNOCKOUT TEAMS, MIXED TEAMS, OPEN TEAMS, RANDOM DRAW KNOCKOUT TEAMS, TEAM GAMES, ZIP KNOCKOUT TEAMS.

DOUBLE FINESSE. A finesse against two outstanding honors. The classic situation is:

A Q 10

x x x

The only serious chance of making three tricks is to finesse the 10. A more difficult situation is:

A J 4 3 2

10 9 6 5

With this holding some players would play the ace, hoping for an honor to fall or for a 2-2 division. But the better percentage play is to take two finesses. See also DEEP FINESSE, FINESSE, and SUIT COMBINATIONS.

DOUBLE FOR SACRIFICE. A double of an opponent's voluntary slam bid after the doubler's side has bid and raised a suit preemptively, designed to help the defenders decide whether they have enough tricks to defeat the slam or should sacrifice. The double indicates how many tricks the doubler expects to take. There are two variations of the convention.

One method, called the Negative Slam Double, or Unpenalty Double, requires the left-hand opponent of the slam bidder to double only if he has no defensive tricks. If his partner has fewer than two such tricks, he sacrifices. If the slam bidder's LHO has one or two tricks he passes and his partner doubles only if he has no tricks, allowing the slam to be played doubled if the pass was made with two tricks, or the sacrifice to be taken if the pass was made with one trick.

An alternative method, called the Positive Slam Double, requires the slam bidder's LHO to double only if he has two defensive tricks. If instead he passes, his partner will sacrifice with no tricks, pass with two tricks, or double with one trick, allowing the slam to be played doubled if the pass was made with one trick, or the sacrifice to be taken if the pass was made with no tricks.

These sacrificial maneuvers became less frequent with the introduction of increased penalties for non-vulnerable partnerships. See DEFENSIVE TRICK.

DOUBLE GRAND COUP. A play by which declarer twice ruffs winning cards in order to reduce the hand which is long in trumps to the same length as that of an opponent, in preparation for a coup.

DOUBLE IN SLAM-GOING AUCTION. See DEFENSE TO INTERFERENCE WITH BLACKWOOD; DOUBLE FOR SACRIFICE; DOUBLE OF A CUEBID; LEAD DIRECTING DOUBLE; LIGHTNER DOUBLE.

DOUBLE JUMP. A bid that skips over two levels. This may refer to a RAISE (1♥-4♥), a RESPONSE (1♥-3♠) or an OVERCALL (1♥-3♠ or 4♣). The term is obsolescent, partly because it is frequently misunderstood or misused by inexperienced players who confuse a DOUBLE RAISE (1♥-3♥) with a DOUBLE JUMP RAISE (1♥-4♥). See SPLINTERS.

DOUBLE JUMP OVERCALL. A preemptive jump after an opposing opening bid. As with all preemptive actions, the bidder must allow for the vulnerability and the level at which he has to bid. The bid normally requires a suit of at least seven cards, but some liberties may be taken at favorable vulnerability. Over 1♣, a jump to 3♠ may be tried with a hand as weak as:

♠ K Q J 10 3 2
♥ 3
♦ 10 9 7 5
♣ 8 4

This offers a definite possibility of shutting out the heart suit. In other situations the RULE OF TWO AND THREE should be applied. See PREEMPTIVE BID; PREEMPTIVE OVERCALL; and WEAK JUMP OVERCALL.

DOUBLE JUMP RAISE. See TRIPLE RAISE.

DOUBLE JUMP SHIFT REBID. See OPENER'S REBID.

DOUBLE JUMP TAKEOUT. A preemptive response one level higher than a JUMP SHIFT, such as 1♥-3♠, or 1♠-4♥. See PREEMPTIVE RESPONSES.

DOUBLE KNOCKOUT. See DOUBLE ELIMINATION.

DOUBLE MENACE. In a double squeeze situation, the threat card in the suit guarded by both opponents.

DOUBLE NEGATIVE. A bid or sequence of bids indicating a very weak hand. Once it was common to respond 2♦ to an opening strong 2♣ to show a poor hand, then to rebid in the cheaper minor to show a very weak hand. Another method was the HERBERT NEGATIVE, in which the responder bid the next higher suit over opener's rebid after responding 2♦ to the opening 2♣ bid. Many modern experts use 2♦ to show a hand with sufficient values for game. The initial response of 2♥ shows the super weak (0-3 points) hand. A response of 2NT is positive showing hearts. When 1♣ is strong and artificial, some players respond 1♦ and over 1♥ bid 1♠ to show the super-weak hand.

DOUBLE OF CONTROLBID OR CUEBID. At a high level, a double of a suit bid in which there is no intention of playing can be used for lead-directing purposes, or perhaps to suggest a save. This gives the left-hand opponent the possibility of a pass or a redouble, for which prior agreements can be made.

A double of a cuebid at a low level would be lead-directing by a side which is on the defensive. But a double of a normally preemptive cuebid such as a MICHAELS CUEBID would, in standard practice, show a strong defensive hand. See DEFENSE TO TWO-SUITED INTERFERENCE.

DOUBLE OF ONE NOTRUMP. This call can be natural or artificial. When used as a natural bid, the double usually shows a hand equal approximately to the level of the notrump bid. If the opponents are using 15-17 notrumps, the double shows at least 15 HCP and a willingness to defend if partner can stand the double. If the opponents are using weak notrump openings, the double usually shows at least the equivalent of the upper level of the opponents' notrump range. Some pairs play the double to be penalty at all times – the doubler feels he can defeat notrump on his own. If the partner of the opening notrump bidder is very weak but has a suit at least five cards long, he will usually run from the double to his suit, probably the only area where his hand can take any tricks. The most common use of the double as a conventional bid occurs in DONT, which is an Acronym for Disturb the Opponents' NoTrump. The double announces a one-suited hand, and partner is required to respond 2♣ so that the DONT bidder can show his suit. The double when BROZEL is being used also shows a one-suiter, and once again the responder bids 2♣ to let partner name his suit — unless he wants to take his chances and defend.

DOUBLE OF THREE NOTRUMP. See LEAD-DIRECTING DOUBLE. FISHER DOUBLE.

DOUBLE OF TWO CLUBS RESPONSE TO NO-TRUMP. The 2♣ response to an opening bid of 1NT is almost invariably the STAYMAN convention. When 2♣ is bid in response to a strong notrump, a double by the LHO of the 2♣ bidder is normally a lead-directing bid showing length and strength in clubs, but not promising overall strength. See DOUBLES OF ARTIFICIAL BIDS FOR PENALTIES.

When the opening notrump bid is of the weak variety, however, the responder sometimes has a very weak hand with which he wishes to escape into a suit. See WEAK NOTRUMP. The escape is frequently initiated by a 2♣ response. Consequently for many expert partnerships the double of the 2♣ response to a weak opening notrump simply shows general strength. The double does not promise any particular distribution, but suggests that the doubler has a hand with which it would have been appropriate for him to double the notrump opening had he been sitting over the opener.

DOUBLE OUT OF ROTATION. See LAWS OF DUPLICATE, Law 32.

DOUBLE RAISE. A bid in the suit bid by partner, raising the level of the bidding by skipping a level. The most common double raise occurs when re-

sponder jumps a level in support of partner's opening bid, e.g., 1♠-3♠. The Goren system used this raise to show good support for partner's suit – usually at least four-card support – and 13-15 HCP. Many rubber bridge players still use this method, but most tournament players have switched to either the limit raise or the weak raise. Using limit raises, the 3♠ bidder is showing good support with 10-12 support points. Using weak raises, he is showing very good trump support and some helpful distribution with very little in the way of high card points. Over an intervening takeout double, most players – even those who play limit jump raises, use the jump to show the weak hand. The limit raise is shown with a jump to 2NT. Other players use 2NT as the weak raise with the jump in partner's suit being a limit raise.

Over 1♠, bid 3♠ as a strong jump raise with
   ♠ A 10 5 4
   ♥ K Q J
   ♦ A 8 7 5
   ♣ 9 2
Over 1♠, bid 3♠ as a limit double raise with
   ♠ Q 8 4 2
   ♥ A Q 3
   ♦ 7 5 4 2
   ♣ K 10
Over 1♠, bid 3♠ as a weak double raise with
   ♠ J 10 5 4 2
   ♥ 6
   ♦ Q 8 5 3
   ♣ 9 8 6

Many tournament players now use BERGEN RAISES to show the limit and construction raises and use the weak jump raise to show the weak distributional hand.

When the suit involved is a minor, the traditional meaning of a jump raise is a limit bid – 10-12 points and at least four-card support – usually five-card support. However, a large number of tournament players have opted for INVERTED RAISES. A simple raise, as 1♣-2♣, is forcing, showing at least the values for a limit raise. A jump raise, as 1♣-3♣ is weak. Some players use the single raise as a force to game, using CRISSCROSS to show the limit raise.

If the opening bidder makes a jump raise in the suit bid by partner, he is showing a hand with enough reserve values to invite game.

See also DELAYED GAME RAISE, JACOBY TWO NOTRUMP, SPLINTER BIDS, SWISS CONVENTION, TWO NOTRUMP RESPONSE, THREE NOTRUMP RESPONSE.

DOUBLE RAISE IN MINOR, PREEMPTIVE. See INVERTED MINOR SUIT RAISES.

DOUBLE SHOWING ACES. See DEFENSE TO INTERFERENCE WITH BLACKWOOD.

DOUBLE SQUEEZE. A squeeze affecting both opponents. It involves three suits, which may be labeled A, B and C. One opponent is squeezed in suits A and B while the other is squeezed in suits B and C. Thus a double squeeze is a combination of two simple squeezes, one against each opponent. Every double squeeze requires a squeeze card, a double menace, and two isolated menaces, guarded by only one opponent. Declarer must have all but one of the remaining tricks. The following clas-

sifications are based on analysis by Bertrand Romanet.
(1) *Simultaneous*. In a simultaneous double squeeze both opponents are squeezed on the same trick. There are three basic positions:

(a) Balanced

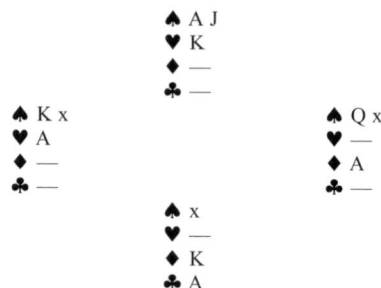

South leads the squeeze card, the ♣A. West is squeezed in the majors, and he must discard a spade. North throws a heart, and East is squeezed in spades and diamonds.

This is a positional squeeze.

(b) Automatic

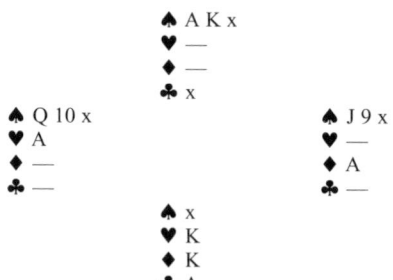

South leads the ♣A, squeezing West in the majors. West must discard a spade, and now East is squeezed in spades and diamonds.

(c) Twin Entry

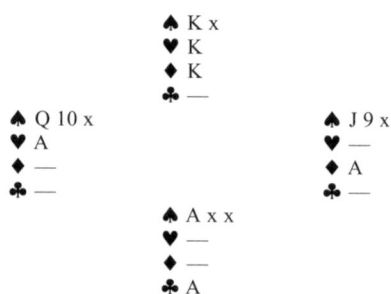

South leads the ♣A, West must throw a spade, North discards a heart, and East is squeezed in spades and diamonds. This is a positional squeeze.

(2) *Non-simultaneous*. In a non-simultaneous double squeeze there are two separate squeeze cards. Declarer's last established trick in the fourth suit squeezes one opponent; a trick or more thereafter, the second squeeze card disposes of the other opponent. The second squeeze card lies opposite the first squeeze card, and it accompanies the isolated menace guarded by the opponent who was squeezed initially. There are four basic positions (Romanet):

(a) Inverted Left

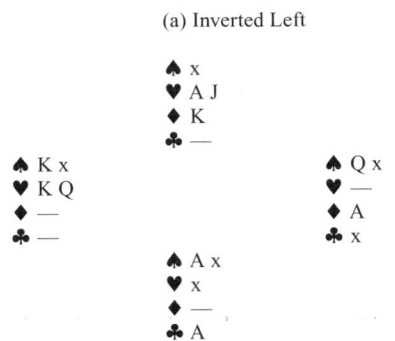

South leads the ♣A, forcing West to discard a spade, and North throws a low heart. Now South leads a heart to the ace which squeezes East in spades and diamonds. This is a positional squeeze.

The term *inverted* refers to the fact that the double menace accompanies the squeeze card, which is unusual since the double menace ordinarily lies opposite the squeeze card. Left indicates that the isolated menace guarded on the left is accompanied by a winner.

(b) Inverted Right

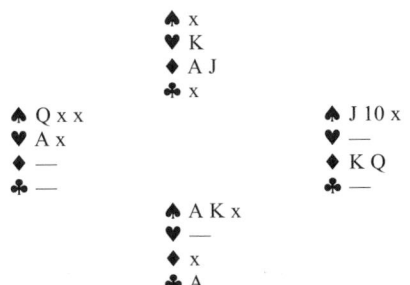

South leads the ♣A, forcing East to discard a spade. Now North wins the ♦A, squeezing West in spades and hearts. This is an automatic squeeze. For this squeeze an ordinary two-card menace against both opponents does not suffice; a recessed menace is required.

(c) Twin Entry Left

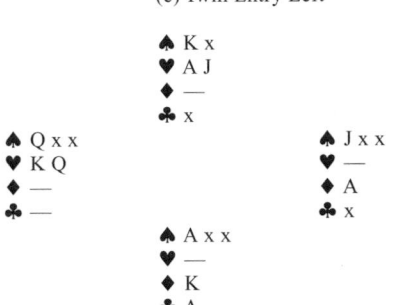

South leads the ♣A, which forces West to discard a spade. Now a lead to the ♠K, followed by the ♥A squeezes East in spades and diamonds. This is a positional squeeze.

It combines elements of the balanced and twin-entry positions discussed above.

(d) Inverted Left Recessed

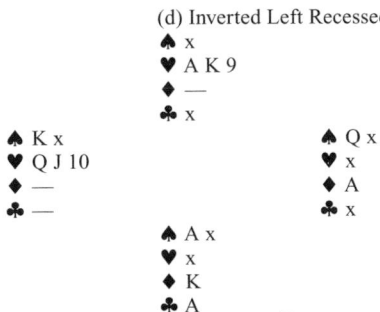

South leads the ♣A, which forces West to discard a spade. Now North wins two top hearts, the last of which squeezes East in spades and diamonds. This is a positional squeeze.

The isolated menaces are arranged as in a balanced double squeeze, but the double menace is inverted. As compensation, North must have two winners, one of which is an entry. The last two positions illustrate the available endings. See also BARCO SQUEEZE; BONNEY'S SQUEEZE; CLASH SQUEEZE; HEXAGON SQUEEZE; OCTAGON SQUEEZE; RECIPROCAL SQUEEZE.

DOUBLE TENACE. A tenace in which the sequence is broken in two places, such as A-Q-10, K-J-9.

DOUBLED INTO GAME. Making a doubled contract and collecting a game bonus that would not have been scored without the double. So it is any doubled contract, except 3NT, between 2♥ and 4♦.

DOUBLER. A player who has doubled.

DOUBLES. The two main categories are PENALTY DOUBLE and TAKEOUT DOUBLE, which are listed separately. Distinguishing between the two types is not always easy. The following is a sound general rule: A double of a suit bid below the game level is for takeout if partner has not bid. Conversely, a double is for penalties if:
(1) The bidding is at the game level or above; or
(2) The bid doubled is in notrump; or
(3) The doubler's partner has already bid. But these generalities require some qualification in particular cases.

(1) Even at the game level, a double may have a takeout flavor. If the bidding goes 1♥-pass-4♦-double, the doubler is unlikely to be loaded with hearts. He indicates a hand with considerable high-card strength and expects a takeout, although partner will often exercise his option of passing for penalties. If the suit were spades, the penalty aspect would be more dominant.

(2) A double of a response of 1NT is a special case (1♥-pass-1NT-double). This is primarily for takeout, although responder may exercise his option to pass.

(3) Doubles on the second round have to be considered on their merits, and are sometimes ambiguous. The old theory was that a double of a suit rebid is for penalties when the same suit could have been doubled on the first round. This is true in cases like:

West	North	East	South
			1♠
Pass	2♣/1NT	Pass	2♠
Dbl			

West must have spade length and strength, and was lying in wait. The situation would not be so clear in a minor suit:

West	North	East	South
			1♦
Pass	1NT	Pass	2♦
Dbl			

West may have diamond strength, but equally, since both opponents are limited, he may be looking for a major suit. East's diamond length will usually enable him to interpret the double correctly.

If another takeout action is available, a double is clearly for penalties. The following sequences only look similar:

(a)

West	North	East	South
			1♣
Pass	1♦	Pass	2♣
Dbl			

(b)

West	North	East	South
			1♦
Pass	2♣	Pass	2♦
Dbl			

Sequence (a) is clearly for penalties: West would make a cuebid of 2♦ holding the majors. (The same would apply to the sequence 1♦-pass-1NT-pass-2♣-double.)

In sequence (b) the cuebid is not available, so the double is ambiguous: it is likely to be for a takeout, but East must inspect his hand.

Experts disagree about the meaning of this rare sequence:

West	North	East	South
			1♥
Pass	1NT	Pass	2♣
Dbl			

The doubler can be expected to have some heart strength, but whether he has clubs is not clear.

Other delayed doubles are also rare, and tend to have length and strength in the opener's suit. For example

West	North	East	South
			1♣
Pass	1♥	Pass	1♠
Dbl			

West presumably has a hand worth a take-out double of one spade, with 1-4-4-4 a possible distribution.

West	North	East	South
			1♣
Pass	1♥	Pass	1NT
Dbl			

This has a penalty flavor. West has a strong hand with club length and strength. He is likely to be short in hearts.

A double is in principle for penalties if three suits have been bid around the table: there are no longer two or more suits between which the responder can choose. However, if made at a low level, some expert partnerships nevertheless use such doubles as takeout, and some treat the double as a COOPERATIVE DOUBLE. See NEGATIVE DOUBLES, SNAPDRAGON.

Doubles other than penalty doubles and takeout doubles may be used in a variety of situations to give information. In slam auctions, for example, doubles may be used offensively as a DEFENSE TO INTERFERENCE WITH BLACKWOOD. Defensively, doubles may be used to exchange information as to when to sacrifice against a slam. See DOUBLE FOR SACRIFICE.

Other doubling situations are discussed under: BALANCING; CARDSHOWING DOUBLE; COMPETITIVE DOUBLE; COOPERATIVE DOUBLE; DEFENSE TO DOUBLE OF ONE NOTRUMP; DOUBLE OF ARTIFICIAL BID FOR PENALTIES; DOUBLE OF CUEBID; DOUBLE OF TWO CLUB RESPONSE TO ONE NOTRUMP; DOUBLES OF NOTRUMP BIDS; FISHER DOUBLE; FREE DOUBLE; INHIBITORY DOUBLE; LEAD-DIRECTING DOUBLE; LIGHTNER DOUBLE; MAXIMAL OVERCALL DOUBLE; NEGATIVE DOUBLE; OPTIONAL DOUBLE; PENALTY PASS; RESCUE; RESPONSES OVER OPPONENT'S TAKEOUT DOUBLE; RESPONSIVE DOUBLE; SNAPDRAGON; STRIPED-TAILED APE DOUBLE; SUCKER DOUBLE; SUPPORT DOUBLE; TRANSFERS OVER DOUBLES OF ONE NOTRUMP; TWO NOTRUMP OVER TAKEOUT DOUBLE; WRIGGLE; as well as PENALTY DOUBLE and TAKEOUT DOUBLE.

DOUBLE OF ARTIFICIAL BID. At a high level the situation is clear-cut. A player who doubles a response to BLACKWOOD, or a GERBER 4♣ bid, for example, is showing strength in the suit he has doubled in the hope of directing his partner to the right opening lead. There is a negative inference which is sometimes overlooked: the player who does not double a conventional bid on his right usually does not want that suit led.

At a low level, other considerations come into play. The double for business is the standard treatment when the hand seems sure to belong to the side that is doubled. This would apply if the bid doubled is: a conventional 2♣; a conventional response (negative or ace-showing) to a conventional 2♣; or a Stayman response to 2NT or a standard (strong) notrump. See also FISHER DOUBLE.

When the doubling side may well have the majority of the high-card strength, the double may be put to better use by partnership agreement — either to show general strength or in some more specialized way. Each situation needs examination in relation to the convention used by the opponent. See DOUBLE OF TWO CLUB RESPONSE TO NOTRUMP; JACOBY TRANSFER BIDS; ONE CLUB SYSTEMS; ROMAN SYSTEM; TEXAS, and WEAK NOTRUMP. For an alternative treatment of all such situations, see TWO-SUITER conventions.

BWS 2001 summarized this by saying that the double shows the suit doubled. The meaning varies by common sense among penalty, value-showing and lead-directing.

DOUBLE OF NOTRUMP. A number of situations deserve separate comment:

(1) Doubles of strong notrump openings. A very rare action, seldom justified unless a long strong suit is held together with side entries. Partner should hardly ever take out the double. A player with a balanced 17-point hand should usually pass a notrump opening, because the likely losses from doubling exceed the likely profits. The meaning of the double does not vary in fourth seat, and the opening leader tends to lead a short suit. For alternative treatments, see DEFENSE TO ONE NOTRUMP.

(2) Doubles of weak notrump openings. A double by second hand should be at least as strong as the opening bid, and a good suit to lead is desirable but not essential. To pass a weak notrump with a balanced 15-

point hand runs a serious risk of missing a game; to double with less leads to trouble when the opener's side has the balance of strength.

The double by fourth hand is a theoretical problem. Apparently the fact that opener's partner has passed should encourage the fourth player, but this is deceptive. Experienced players do not pass very weak hands when their partners have opened with 1NT, instead they scramble out into a suit at the level of two in an attempt to avert disaster. So when 1NT has been passed, the opener's side is more likely than not to hold the balance of strength, and the fourth player should be cautious about doubling. (But this sort of thinking might permit the third player to try a doublecross by passing with a near-yarborough.) Conversely, the fourth player should double a two-level suit takeout by third hand with any hand he would have doubled an opening weak notrump on his right. Many players extend this treatment to a double of a Stayman response to allow for the possibility that third hand is taking evasive action. This gives up the lead-directing double of a Stayman bid based on clubs. The expert consensus in BWS 2001 was that a double of Stayman after a strong notrump should show clubs, strength unspecified, but that it should show general strength after a weak notrump.

The doubler's partner should take out only with a long suit and a very weak hand.

(3) Double of a 1NT overcall. By third player this is a simple indication that he has at least 8-9 points and therefore expects his side to have the balance of strength. This principle applies to most notrump doubles: the double is made when the doubler thinks it more likely than not that his side has more than 20 high-card points. If the opener doubles 1NT, either by second or fourth hand, he shows a maximum one-bid, probably 19-21 in high cards.

(4) Doubles of 3NT are often lead-directing. See LEAD-DIRECTING DOUBLE.

(5) Double of a notrump rebid.

West	North	East	South
			1♣
Pass	1♥	Pass	1NT
Dbl			

or

West	North	East	South
			1♣
Pass	1♥	Pass	1NT
Pass	Pass	Dbl	

In both sequences the double is intended for penalties. In the first case West has club strength, and in the second case East has heart strength.

(6) Third hand problems. When an opening 1NT bid is doubled, the opening bidder's partner has four standard options.

(a) Redouble. A call indicating that the opener's side has the majority of the high-card strength, and that a penalty should be available if the doubling side escapes into a suit. A frequent action holding 9 points or more opposite a weak (12-14) notrump. Opposite a standard (16-18) notrump, 5 points is theoretically sufficient, but slightly more is desirable in view of the likelihood that the doubler has a good suit to lead.

(b) Two notrump. A bid with no natural meaning, because a strong balanced hand would always redouble. It is therefore treated as a type of cuebid, and is likely to be based on a strong two-suited hand.

(c) Two clubs. Not necessarily Stayman after a double. It is normally a natural bid with a long club suit, and should be assumed to be so by the opener. However, the bid is often made on a weak unbalanced hand with the intention of making an SOS redouble when doubled. This would be an appropriate action with a 4-4-4-1 distribution, for example.

(d) Three of a suit. An unlikely action opposite a standard notrump. Opposite a weak notrump it would be preemptive, with a six-card suit and no game ambitions.

For other options available to the partner of the opening notrump bidder, see DEFENSE TO DOUBLE OF ONE NOTRUMP.

DOUBLETON. An original holding of two cards in a suit. If an opening lead is made from a doubleton, the top card is customarily led first. (A low lead from a doubleton is normal in Poland and also occasionally in Italy.) For evaluation of a doubleton, see DISTRIBUTIONAL POINT-COUNT.

DOUBLY IMPROPER CALL. A call which is irregular in two respects, such as an insufficient bid out of rotation. See LAWS (Law 31).

DOWN. Defeated; said of a declarer who has failed to make a contract. The term is used in various ways, such as "We are down two" or "down 800," meaning the side has failed to make a contract by two tricks or has incurred a penalty of 800 points.

DRAW FOR PARTNERS. Cut for partners. See LAWS (Law 3).

DRAWING TRUMPS. The action of removing the trumps from the opponents' hands. When he first gains the lead, declarer tends to draw trumps, but must be careful not to remove cards from his own hand or dummy that are necessary for some other purposes. There are various considerations which may persuade declarer to postpone drawing trumps.

Ruffs. Declarer may need to ruff some of his losers in the dummy. It may be necessary to give the lead to the opponents in the process of establishing and taking the ruffs, and they may lead trumps at every opportunity. Declarer must leave at least enough trumps in dummy to take care of his losers while allowing for such trump leads by the defense (see CROSSRUFF).

Entries. Often declarer can use trumps as entries. These entries may be required for finesses or development of a side suit. If no other entries are available, these plays must be made while drawing trumps.

Sometimes declarer plans to establish a suit. Once it has been established, the trump suit may provide the only entry to the suit. If this delayed entry would not be available after drawing trumps and taking ruffs, then either suit must be established first. Eventually the hand with the established suit may be entered by drawing the last trump, or by means of a ruff.

Stoppers. Dummy's trumps may serve as stoppers in a certain suit. However, it may not be expedient for declarer to ruff all his losers in that suit; instead he plans to establish discards, which may entail losing the lead to the opponents. Declarer seeks to leave one trump in dummy (to stop the opponents' suit) for each time he must lose the lead in this fashion.

Declarer may be able to use his trumps or dummy's trumps as stoppers. He may be unable to ruff in his hand lest he lose trump control. Therefore he must leave enough trumps in the dummy to cope with the opponents' suit while he proceeds with the development of the hand.

Timing. Declarer may put off drawing trumps because his play for the hand as a whole requires him to deal first with other matters:

(1) Declarer may seek to establish a quick discard for a potential loser before the defenders can establish and cash their trick in that suit.

(2) Declarer has a side-suit which is not solid. Unless he has abundant trumps it is best to test the side-suit before all the trumps are drawn. This is important if the trump suit is broken.

(3) Declarer has a choice between the ruffing game and the long suit plan (particularly if the long suit is in dummy). By leading the long suit at once, declarer can vary his plan according to circumstances.

Weakness. If the trump length and strength is shared about equally between the two sides, declarer should usually avoid trump leads:

North
J 5 4

South
K 9 7 2

In such situations South can hope to collect two or three trump tricks by leaving his holding intact for the end game.

But with extreme weakness in trumps, declarer is on the defensive. He may need to lead trumps to avoid opposing ruffs.

Master Trump. Declarer usually ceases to draw trumps when one defender has one or two master trumps. But a trump continuation may still be desirable to achieve a throw-in, or simply to get rid of the lead; and it may be necessary to drive out a master trump which would otherwise interrupt the run of dummy's established suit at a time when dummy has no remaining entry.

DRIVE OUT. To force the play of a high card, i.e., to lead or play a card sufficiently high in rank to force the play of an adverse commanding card to win the trick, or to continue until this result is achieved.

DROP. To capture an adverse potential winning card by the direct lead of a higher card or series of higher cards, as to drop an unguarded king by the play of an ace; also, the play which endeavors to capture an adverse card, as to "play for the drop," instead of finessing.

Whether to finesse or play for the drop is generally a case of determining the correct mathematical probabilities. However, this preference is considerably modified by information derived from the bidding and play, and it is the policy of good players to obtain as much information as possible, inferential as well as exact, before committing themselves. For example:

West	North	East	South
1♣	Pass	Pass	1NT
Pass	3NT	All Pass	

If during the play, East shows up with an ace or king, it is highly unlikely that he will hold another high honor, since he passed his partner in 1♣. It would therefore be indicated for South to disregard the mathematical prob-

abilities and confidently place all missing honors in the West hand.

DRURY. A conventional 2♣ response by a PASSED HAND after partner's major-suit opening.

West	East
Pass	1♠
2♣	

The 2♣ bid asks opener to clarify his strength. West might hold:

♠ Q 9 2		♠ J 10 5
♥ 10 6 4	or	♥ A 5 4 2
♦ A K 7 4		♦ A J 8 5
♣ Q 4 3		♣ 9 3

Without Drury, West has no attractive action: a single raise is an underbid; a double raise with only three trumps and poor distribution is inappropriate; a natural response of 2♦ might be passed, and even if opener bid again, responder might have to go to the three level to show the spade support.

The convention works similarly after a 1♥ opening, though its frequency of use may be very slightly lower because responder often bids 1♠.

Douglas Drury devised Drury, so the story goes, as protection from the feather-light third-hand openings of his partner Eric Murray. The convention as employed by most modern pairs differs in some respects from Drury's original version.

In the original, a 2♦ rebid by opener suggested a sub-minimum opening. Responder could then sign off at two of opener's major. However, a 1984 poll of experts showed a preference — by a margin of more than two to one — for a rebid of the major suit as opener's weak action. Any other rebid suggests a sound opening. Hence, the variation once known as REVERSE DRURY is now standard.

A few partnerships play Drury in competition (particularly after a double):

West	North	East	South
			Pass
Pass	1♥	1♠	2♣

Some players use 2♦ additionally, showing 4-card support, with 2♣ showing exactly 3-card support. This is useful to the opener if he has a distributional hand. (Suggested by Marty Bergen.) See PASSED HAND, STRONG NOTRUMP AFTER PASSING.

DROP-DEAD BID. A bid that tells partner to do no more bidding. The most common bid of this type is a two-level non-conventional response (2♦, 2♥ or 2♠) to 1NT showing a very weak hand. Another common variety is a 3NT response to 1NT.

DUB. (1) A player whose game is below the standards of the players with whom he competes. (2) A doubleton (colloquial).

DUCK. To play a small card, and surrender a trick which could be won, with the object of preserving an ENTRY. When the suit has been led by an opponent, the duck is mechanically identical to a HOLD-UP, in that a master card (or cards) is retained, but the objective is different. A player ducks in order to pursue his own aims, but holds up in order to thwart the opponents.

A COUP EN BLANC is a ducking play for the purpose of winning a later trick.

Apart from a considerable number of situations listed

under SAFETY PLAY, ducking plays may be listed under five main headings:

(1) *Suit combinations.* To make the maximum number of tricks in notrump with no side entry to dummy:

(a)	(b)
A K x x x	A Q x x x
x x or x x x	x x or x x x

In (a) the first trick is ducked and the declarer hopes for an even split to make four tricks; with three small, he may duck once to score four tricks, twice to insure making three tricks against a 4-1 split.

The situation in (b) is similar, but declarer finesses on the second round; if declarer has three small cards, the first-round duck is slightly better than a finesse followed by a duck because right-hand opponent might hold a singleton king.

(c)	(d)
K Q 10 7 x x	K J 8 x x x x
x x	x x

These are harder, and declarer needs more optimism. In each case he must duck the first trick completely in the hope of finding the right-hand opponent with a singleton ace. If the required situation does exist, it would be brilliant play for the left-hand opponent to play his highest card in an attempt to deflect declarer from his purpose.

(2) *Trap combination.* In notrump with no side entry in dummy:

(e)	(f)	(g)
A Q J x x x	A Q J x x	A Q 10 x x x
x x	x x x	x x x

In each case a small card is led, and left-hand opponent plays the king. A duck ensures the loss of only one trick and is essential in (e), (f), and (g) if LHO brilliantly played the king from king-fourth. If LHO has sneakily played the king from a doubleton or tripleton, he has gained a trick for his side.

(h)	(i)
A K x x x	A Q x x x
J 10	J 10

If declarer's lead is covered, he must duck and hope for a 3-3 division. The only hope of five tricks is for left-hand opponent to fail to cover holding Q-x-x (or K-x-x). It is therefore better to lead the 10, following the principle of leading low from a sequence when you wish to avoid a cover.

(j)	(k)
A x x x x	A x x x x
Q J x	J 10 9

In both cases declarer leads a high card and must duck if left-hand opponent covers. In (k) the jack is the best lead: declarer plans to follow with the 9. If left-hand opponent is left with a doubleton honor, he may make the mistake of playing low, and declarer makes four tricks.

(3) *Double and triple.* Again in notrump with no side entry to dummy:

(l)	(m)
A x x x x	A 9 x x x
x x x	x x x x

With (l) two ducks and a 3-2 split are needed to make three tricks. (m) requires one duck if the suit splits 2-2,

giving four tricks; a 3-1 split requires two ducks, and gives three tricks; a 4-0 split requires three ducks and gives two tricks. This is the only possible situation for a triple duck.

(4) *Control.* In a trump contract:

(n)	(o)	(p)
x x	A x	A x x
A x x	x x x	x x x

Declarer usually ducks with (n) unless there is a possibility of a 7-1 division. This prepares for a ruff in dummy without the need for a side entry, and retains control of the suit if the opponents shift: this may be most important if they are able to draw dummy's trumps.

Declarer would not duck with (o) if a ruff is the only consideration, but it may be right to duck for control reasons. If the defenders can prevent a ruff, declarer is better placed with the ace still in dummy.

The duck with (p) could also be described as a hold-up. It interferes with the defensive communications, and may prevent the defense taking a second trick if the suit is divided 5-2.

(5) *Defensive.* A defender in a trump contract often ducks to prepare for a ruff by his side or in order to prevent a ruff by declarer:

	(q)			(r)	
West	*East*		*West*	*East*	
x x	A x x x		x x	A x x	

In (q) West leads a doubleton in a side suit in the hope of getting a ruff. East ducks if he can judge that the lead is more likely to be a doubleton than a singleton, and if he thinks that West is more likely to secure the lead.

The objective is reversed in (r), although the mechanics are the same. West leads a doubleton trump aiming to prevent a ruff in the dummy. Again East ducks if he judges that West had a doubleton and the likely entry.

The suit combination plays described above for the declarer are also available for the defenders, almost always in notrump contracts. Some ducks that are simple for the declarer are very much harder for the defense:

	(s)			(t)	
	x x			J x x	
K x x		A x x x x	K x x x x		A x x
	Q J 10			Q x	

In (s) West leads low and an entryless East must duck. In (t) the duck can be on the first or second round. The first-round duck may have the advantage of depriving dummy of an entry, because declarer can drop the queen under the ace. This would only lose if the lead was from Q-x-x-x specifically. See also THIRD-HAND PLAY.

DUEL. A two-handed form of bridge invented by Norman B. Hasselriis, and described by him in *The Bridge World* magazine for February 1950. See HONEYMOON BRIDGE.

DUFFER. A bridge player of inferior ability.

DUKE OF CUMBERLAND HAND. A phenomenal hand at whist. The Duke of Cumberland, son of George III, King of England, was an inveterate gambler for high stakes. One day, at the notorious gaming rooms in Bath, it is said that he was dealt the following hand:

    ♠ A K Q   ♥ A K Q J   ♦ A K   ♣ K J 9 7

The game being whist, the last card, a club, was turned to set the trump suit. The Duke, sitting at dealer's left, had the opening lead. In accordance with sound whist pre-

cepts, he opened the ♣7. Obviously it was to his interest to knock out all the opponents' trumps as quickly as possible to avoid the ruffing of any of his solid top cards.

The Duke's opponents proceeded to assert that he would not win a single trick. This infuriated him and he made a bet. The complete deal was:

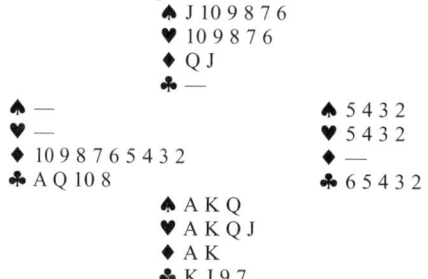

West won the ♣7 with the 8, and led a diamond which was trumped by his partner. East returned a club, the Duke's 9 being taken by the 10, and a second diamond was trumped by East. East led his last trump into his partner's tenace over the Duke, and West won and led the final trump from his hand, felling the Duke's king. West's seven established diamonds won the last seven tricks.

This display of virtuosity by East-West allegedly cost the Duke the sum of 20,000 pounds or nearly $100,000.

Such is the story of the Duke of Cumberland's Hand as related by Professor Richard A. Proctor in *How to Play Whist* (1885). One wonders why the Duke, an experienced whist player, did not speculate on how his opponents could foretell the outcome. (Remember that no hand is exposed in whist.) A more plausible version of this legendary episode suggests that the South hand was given to the Duke, who knew that it was manufactured and ventured to bet in the face of that knowledge.

The victim may have been an earlier duke, "Butcher" Cumberland, son of George II, but the scant evidence favors the later duke. See DISTRIBUTIONAL VALUES.

DUMB BIDDER or SILENT BIDDER. A British device to permit silent bidding. It consists of a small board placed in the center of the table on which the four suits, notrump, numbers from 1 to 7, double, redouble, and pass are inscribed. Each player makes his bid by tapping the appropriate sections with a pencil. This avoids any possible revealing inflections. The BIDDING BOX, has supplanted this device today. Also see SLIDING BOX, WRITTEN BIDDING.

DUMMY. (1) The declarer's partner after he has placed his cards face up on the table, which is done immediately after the opening lead is faced by the opponent on the declarer's left; (2) the cards held by the declarer's partner, also called the dummy's hand. The name originated in dummy whist, in which there were only three players, the fourth hand being exposed as the "dummy," an imaginary and silent player (see HISTORY OF BRIDGE). The dummy in bridge takes no part in the play; he may not suggest by word or gesture any lead or play, but at the conclusion of play he may call attention to violations of law. In North America, dummy may ask partner if he has any or none of the suit led, to prevent a revoke. If the dummy looks at his partner's hand or the hand of either adversary, he forfeits his right to protect his partner from revoking. See LAWS (Laws 42, 43).

DUMMY BRIDGE. A form of bridge for three. The player cutting low plays as dummy's partner for the entire game or rubber. Usually only single games are played before a new cut, the winner scoring a bonus of 50 points. Dealer or his partner names the trump suit. Dummy deals first and partner declares, having looked only at the dummy hand. When an opponent deals, however, he may pass to his partner the right to name trumps. Dealer's left-hand opponent is the only player who may double. The dummy is not exposed until after the opening lead. Otherwise, play is as in BRIDGE WHIST.

One theory of the origin of AUCTION BRIDGE attributes it to a game in which three British officers in a post in India remote from any fourth player evolved the idea of bidding for the dummy.

DUMMY PLAY. The management of the assets of the declarer and the dummy; synonymous with "declarer's play." The subject is dealt with under the following general headings: COUP; ENDPLAY; FINESSE; MATHEMATICS OF BRIDGE; SQUEEZE; TRUMP PLAY. Also under the following particular titles: ASSUMPTIONS IN PLAY; AVOIDANCE; BACKWARD FINESSE; BLACKWOOD THEORY OF DISTRIBUTION; BLOCK; BLOCKING; CARD READING; CARDS, NEUTRAL AND POSITIVE; CONTROL; COUNTING THE HAND; CRASHING HONORS; CROSSRUFF; DECEPTION, MATHEMATICS OF; DECEPTIVE PLAY; DEEP FINESSE; DESPERATION LEAD OR PLAY; DISCOVERY; DRAWING TRUMPS; DROP; DUCK; DUMMY REVERSAL; DUMMY'S FIRST TRICK PLAY; ECONOMY OF HONORS; ENTRY; EXIT PLAY; EXPECTATION; FALSECARDING; GAMBIT; GROSVENOR GAMBIT; HOLD UP; IMP TACTICS; INFERENCE; JETTISON; LOSER ON LOSER; MATCHPOINT PLAY; NEGATIVE INFERENCE; OBLIGATORY FINESSE; OPTIONS; OVERTAKE; PERCENTAGE PLAY; PLAY FROM EQUALS; PROBABILITIES; RESTRICTED CHOICE; RUFF AND DISCARD; RUFF AND RUFF; RUFFING FINESSE; RULE OF ELEVEN; SAFETY PLAY; SHOOTING; SINGLE-DUMMY PROBLEMS; SINGLETON KING; SMOTHER PLAY; SPOT CARDS; SUIT COMBINATIONS; THROW-IN; TRUMP PICK-UP; TRUMP SUIT MANAGEMENT; TWO-WAY FINESSE; UNBLOCKING; UNDERRUFF.

DUMMY REVERSAL. A procedure by which the dummy is made the master hand. Generally speaking, it is advantageous to ruff only in the hand that contains shorter trumps, but in a dummy reversal extra tricks may sometimes be developed by ruffing in the long hand and later using dummy's trumps to extract those of the opponents.

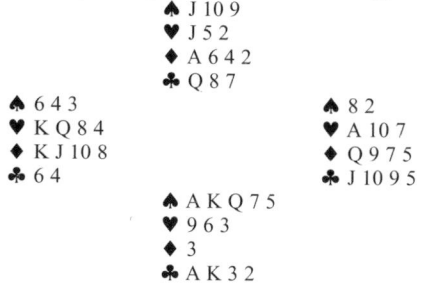

South plays in 4♠, and the defense cash their three heart tricks before shifting to a diamond. Superficially

it seems that declarer must bank on an even division in clubs or alternatively draw two rounds of trumps and then attempt to ruff the fourth club in dummy in case they divide unevenly. Both these lines are inferior to the dummy reversal which requires only a 3-2 break in trumps. Dummy wins the diamond, and a low diamond is ruffed with the ♠A. Dummy is re-entered twice in spades — declarer conserving his small trumps for that purpose — to ruff the remaining diamonds with the king and queen, leaving this position:

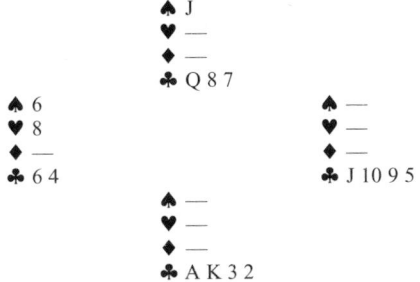

Declarer now crosses to dummy's ♣Q, and leads the ♠J, extracting the last trump upon which he discards his losing club, and takes the last two tricks with the ♣A-K. Note that declarer can switch plans after drawing two spades if they are 4-1.

Sometimes the decision to "reverse," or establish the dummy in preference to his hand, is forced upon declarer by the character of his trump suit.

```
              ♠ A K J
              ♥ 10 2
              ♦ A J 8 7 3
              ♣ A 9 8
♠ 3 2                      ♠ 10 9 4
♥ 7 5 4                    ♥ Q J 9 3
♦ Q 9 5 4                  ♦ K 10 6
♣ Q J 10 2                 ♣ 6 5 4
              ♠ Q 8 7 6 5
              ♥ A K 8 6
              ♦ 2
              ♣ K 7 3
```

The contract is 6♠, and West leads the ♣Q. If declarer attempts to ruff his losing hearts in dummy he will promote a trump trick for East which together with the club loser will spell defeat. However, by ruffing three of dummy's diamonds in his hand — establishing the fifth diamond in the process — he can utilize dummy's trumps for drawing purposes. That way he makes his slam, losing only a club trick.

DUMMY WHIST. A variety of WHIST for three. The player who draws the lowest card plays with the dummy as his partner. The last card dealt is turned as trumps. Dummy is not exposed until after the opening lead is made. Each trick over book (6) counts as one point. Seven points are game.

DUMMY'S FIRST TRICK PLAY. Most of the problems concerning the choice of plays from dummy at the first trick relate to doubleton honors. An interesting rule, suggested by M. D. Macdonald of Greensboro NC, covers the play with Q-x and J-x when declarer has at least one honor:

Play low from dummy if the opponents have *exactly* two significant honors. In table form:

	doubleton queen	
declarer has	significant honors	play
A-10-x	K-J	low
K-10-x	A-J	low
J-x-x	A-K	low
A-x-(x)	K	high
A-9-x	K-J-10	high
10-x-x	A-K-J	high
A-J-x	K	high
K-x-(x)	A	high

(doubtful case K-9-x, in which the right play varies with circumstances.)

	doubleton jack	
declarer has	significant honors	play
A-10-x	K-Q	low
Q-x-x	A-K	low
K-10-x	A-Q	low
A-K-x	Q	high
A-Q-x	K	high
A-9-x	K-Q-10	high
K-9-x	A-Q-10	high

(Two obvious exceptions: A-x-x and K-x-x.)

When dummy has more than two cards, it is usually right to play low at the first trick, but there are some obvious exceptions. Play high, for example, with Q-x-x facing nothing, or J-x-x facing A-K-x.

Special circumstances may call for special plays:

(a)	(b)	(c)
A-x-x	K-10-x	10-5-4 or J-5-4
J-x-x	Q-x-x	A-K-9

In (a) the play of the ace may block the suit. East would have to have a doubleton king or queen for this to matter. But if he has a quick entry he can unblock effectively.

In (b) it is sometimes right to play the king from dummy. If East has A-J-9-x-x he will have to win and cannot continue. If dummy plays low East can play the 9, ready to run the suit if West gains the lead.

In (c) the 10 should be played. If the 10 is covered with the jack and declarer wins, opening leader will not know the position of the 9 and may continue the suit when he gains the lead.

DUMMY'S FORFEITURE OF RIGHTS. This is invoked if the player whose hand is the dummy intentionally looks at his partner's or an opponent's hand. He then forfeits his privileges as far as protecting his partner against revokes or leading from the wrong hand. See LAWS (Laws 42, 43).

DUMMY'S HAND. It is the responsibility of all the players equally that dummy's hand shall be a proper one. No revoke can be claimed as a result of an improper play from the dummy. See DUMMY.

DUMMY'S RIGHTS AND LIMITATIONS. Dummy has certain absolute and limited rights as described in LAWS OF DUPLICATE (Laws 42, 43). In a rubber bridge game, particularly under social conditions in the home, the old rule of courtesy of the table required that the opponents inquire of the declarer whether a play to a trick constituted a revoke, and failure to so inquire waived the right to a penalty for such a revoke.

DUOBRIDGE. A four-handed bridge game for two players invented by Art Kaplan of Merrick NY in 1977.

The game is played with a regular 52-card deck. It is unique as a two-player bridge game in that the players play as partners against imaginary opponents. The key to the game is the DuoBridge Deal, a semi-random deal of the cards based on mathematical principles that enable the players to feel they are actually participating in a four-handed game. See HONEYMOON BRIDGE.

DUPLICATE. A term applied to the playing of the same deal of cards by more than one table of players; successively applied to whist, auction bridge and contract bridge. See DUPLICATE BRIDGE and HISTORY OF BRIDGE.

DUPLICATE BOARD. See BOARD, DUPLICATE.

DUPLICATE BRIDGE. The form of bridge in which the same hand is played more than once. Each competing unit (which may be an individual, pair or team) seeks to perform better than one or more other units playing the identical deals in similar circumstances. The luck of the deal, so important in rubber bridge, is therefore eliminated to a large extent, and bridge becomes a satisfactory test of skill. (But see CHANCE.)

Cavendish, the great whist authority, organized what amounted to a duplicate whist match by getting four experts, sitting North-South at one table and East-West at the other, against four ordinary players. As he predicted, the experts won far more than half the tricks available.

The first application of the duplicate idea dates from whist. The pioneer in this field was JOHN T. MITCHELL, who invented the first pair movement and whose book on duplicate whist appeared in 1891. The long series of American Whist League Championships began in the same year. (See HISTORY OF BRIDGE.)

The duplicate principle was never applied to the original game of bridge (see BRIDGE WHIST) which flourished in the decade 1894-1904. It was generally believed that bridge, unlike whist, was not a suitable game for serious competition. This was perhaps partly because at this stage of its development bridge permitted unlimited redoubles, which emphasized the gambling element in the game and gave it a poker-like character.

The first games of duplicate auction bridge were apparently held in 1914 under the auspices of the American Whist League, but another 10 years elapsed before a national auction tournament was staged.

The application of duplicate to contract bridge was a rapid development, and the first national championship was held in 1928, when the game was less than three years old, under the auspices of the AMERICAN (auction) BRIDGE LEAGUE.

The most popular form of duplicate is the weekly club game. This usually consists of a pair event of 21 to 28 boards, lasting some 3-3½ hours. The number of tables varies widely. Usually the players pay a card fee. Many clubs run several games a week, and a few clubs in large metropolitan areas run games each afternoon and evening throughout the year.

North American players wishing to join a club can obtain copies of a Directory of Clubs for a small fee by applying to ACBL HEADQUARTERS. In other nations interested persons should apply to the national contract bridge organization. Most such organizations are listed in this book under the name of the country.

Duplicate bridge can be a satisfying home game for eight players. (See TWO TABLES.) It is also very popular as part of the recreation program of commercial and industrial organizations.

For the more complex organization of tournaments above the club level, see AMERICAN CONTRACT BRIDGE LEAGUE and CHAMPIONSHIP TOURNAMENTS.

The mechanics of play at duplicate are covered in LAWS OF DUPLICATE BRIDGE, Laws 2-8. In order to make replay of the hand possible, some modification of the mechanics of the deal, shuffle and gathering of tricks from those of RUBBER BRIDGE or CHICAGO is necessary.

Essentially, the mechanics of duplicate require the following steps:

(1) Getting the right boards and correct opponents to the table. See MOVEMENTS.

(2) Withdrawal of the hand to be played from the board, counting the cards to ascertain the correctness of the hand.

(3) Determination of vulnerability and dealer on the board (see BOARD, DUPLICATE). The bidding then proceeds as in rubber bridge.

(4) The play to the trick. Instead of playing to the center of the table, each player faces his contribution or lead face up, in front of him, in turn. When the four cards have been played to the trick, each player turns his card face down, in a line, in front of him. The card is pointed toward his partner if they have won the trick, but placed with the length from right to left if the trick was won by the opposition.

(5) Determination of and agreement about the result. All four players should, as a result of the preceding paragraph, agree as to the number of tricks won by the declarer. If disagreement exists, the cards should not be disturbed, but the result should be determined by the director, who should be summoned.

(6) Recounting the cards and replacing them in the pockets of the duplicate board.

At duplicate every deal is scored separately. Neither partscores nor games bid and made carry over to the next deal. Whenever one side scores a game or a partscore they collect, in addition to the trick score, an immediate bonus:

For making a vulnerable game	500
For making a nonvulnerable game	300
For making a part score	50

Honors do not count at duplicate. In all other respects the scoring is the same as at rubber bridge. Articles dealing with various aspects of handling duplicate tournaments are: ACROSS-THE-FIELD SCORING; ADJUSTED SCORE; AMERICAN WHIST; APPENDIX TABLE; ARROW SWITCH; ARROW; ASSIGNMENT OF SEATS; BALANCED COMPARISONS; BLACKPOOL; BREAKING TIES; BUMP MITCHELL; BYESTAND; CALIFORNIA SCORING; CARRYOVER SCORES; COMPUTER HANDS; COMPUTER SCORING; CONVENTION CARD; CURTAILING MOVEMENT DURING PLAY; CYCLIC; DUPLICATE SCORING; ENTRIES; FACTORING; FOULED BOARD; HALF TABLE; HAND RECORDS; HOWELL; HYBRID SCORING; INDIVIDUAL; INTERNATIONAL MATCHPOINTS; MATCHPOINT; McKENNEY-BALDWIN; MOVEMENT; POSTING THE SCORE; PROVIDE SCORING; RAINBOW IN-

DIVIDUAL; RECTIFICATION; ROUND-ROBIN; ROVER; SCORING CORRECTION; SCRAMBLED MITCHELL; SEEDSEEDING; SHORT HOWELL; SLOW PLAY; STARTING TIME; SUBSTITUTE; SUSPENSION; SWISS; TEAM-OF-FOUR MOVEMENTS FOR BOARD-A-MATCH TEAMS; THREE-QUARTER HOWELL; TOURNAMENT DIRECTOR; TRAVELING SCORESLIP; TWO, THREE-FOUR, ETC., to FIFTEEN TABLES

DUPLICATE BRIDGE LAWS. See LAWS OF DUPLICATE.

DUPLICATE, MATHEMATICS OF MATCHPOINT. See MATHEMATICS OF MATCHPOINT PLAY.

DUPLICATE SCORING. The scoring of each deal is covered by the provisions of Laws 77 and 78 of the LAWS OF DUPLICATE. The following scoring table lists all possible duplicate results:

Bid Made	Made	Not Vulnerable Undbl	Dbl	Rdbl	Vulnerable Undbl	Dbl	Rdbl
1♣ - 1♦	1	70	140	230	70	140	230
	2	90	240	430	90	340	630
	3	110	340	630	110	540	1030
	4	130	440	830	130	740	1430
	5	150	540	1030	150	940	1830
	6	170	640	1230	170	1140	2230
	7	190	740	1430	190	1340	2630
1♥ - 1♠	1	80	160	520	80	160	720
	2	110	260	720	110	360	1120
	3	140	360	920	140	560	1520
	4	170	460	1120	170	760	1920
	5	200	560	1320	200	960	2320
	6	230	660	1520	230	1160	2720
	7	260	760	1720	260	1360	3120
1NT	1	90	180	560	90	180	760
	2	120	280	760	120	380	1160
	3	150	380	960	150	580	1560
	4	180	480	1160	180	780	1960
	5	210	580	1360	210	980	2360
	6	240	680	1560	240	1180	2760
	7	270	780	1760	270	1380	3160
2♣ - 2♦	2	90	180	560	90	180	760
	3	110	280	760	110	380	1160
	4	130	380	960	130	580	1560
	5	150	480	1160	150	780	1960
	6	170	580	1360	170	980	2360
	7	190	680	1560	190	1180	2760
2♥ - 2♠	2	110	470	640	110	670	840
	3	140	570	840	140	870	1240
	4	170	670	1040	170	1070	1640
	5	200	770	1240	200	1270	2040
	6	230	870	1440	230	1470	2440
	7	260	970	1640	260	1670	2840
2NT	2	120	490	680	120	690	880
	3	150	590	880	150	890	1280
	4	180	690	1080	180	1090	1680
	5	210	790	1280	210	1290	2080
	6	240	890	1480	240	1490	2480
	7	270	990	1680	270	1690	2880
3♣ - 3♦	3	110	470	640	110	670	840
	4	130	570	840	130	870	1240
	5	150	670	1040	150	1070	1640
	6	170	770	1240	170	1270	2040
	7	190	870	1440	190	1470	2440
3♥ - 3♠	3	140	530	760	140	730	960
	4	170	630	960	170	930	1360
	5	200	730	1160	200	1130	1760
	6	230	830	1360	230	1330	2160
	7	260	930	1560	260	1530	2560
3NT	3	400	550	800	600	750	1000
	4	430	650	1000	630	950	1400
	5	460	750	1200	660	1150	1800
	6	490	850	1400	690	1350	2200
	7	520	950	1600	720	1550	2600
4♣ - 4♦	4	130	510	720	130	710	920
	5	150	610	920	150	910	1320
	6	170	710	1120	170	1110	1720
	7	190	810	1320	190	1310	2120
4♥ - 4♠	4	420	590	880	620	790	1080
	5	450	690	1080	650	990	1480
	6	480	790	1280	680	1190	1880
	7	510	890	1480	710	1390	2280
4NT	4	430	610	920	630	810	1120
	5	460	710	1120	660	1010	1520
	6	490	810	1320	690	1210	1920
	7	520	910	1520	720	1410	2320
5♣ - 5♦	5	400	550	800	600	750	1000
	6	420	650	1000	620	950	1400
	7	440	750	1200	640	1150	1800
5♥ - 5♠	5	450	650	1000	650	850	1200
	6	480	750	1200	680	1050	1600
	7	510	850	1400	710	1250	2000
5NT	5	460	670	1040	660	870	1240
	6	490	770	1240	690	1070	1640
	7	520	870	1440	720	1270	2040
6♣ - 6♦	6	920	1090	1380	1370	1540	1830
	7	940	1190	1580	1390	1740	2230
6♥ - 6♠	6	980	1210	1620	1430	1660	2070
	7	1010	1310	1820	1460	1860	2470
6NT	6	990	1230	1660	1440	1680	2110
	7	1020	1330	1860	1470	1880	2510
7♣ - 7♦	7	1440	1630	1960	2140	2330	2660
7♥ - 7♠	7	1510	1770	2240	2210	2470	2940
7NT	7	1520	1790	2280	2220	2490	2980

DEFEATED CONTRACTS

Down	Not Vulnerable Undbl	Dbl	Rdbl	Vulnerable Undbl	Dbl	Rdbl
1	50	100	200	100	200	400
2	100	300	600	200	500	1000
3	150	500	1000	300	800	1600
4	200	800	1600	400	1100	2200
5	250	1100	2200	500	1400	2800
6	300	1400	2800	600	1700	3400
7	350	1700	3400	700	2000	4000
8	400	2000	4000	800	2300	4600
9	450	2300	4600	900	2600	5200
10	500	2600	5200	1000	2900	5800
11	550	2900	5800	1100	3200	6400
12	600	3200	6400	1200	3500	7000
13	650	3500	7000	1300	3800	7600

After the score on any hand has been determined according to this table, a comparison of results becomes possible.

Most pair individual events are scored on a matchpoint basis. After all the scores have been determined on a board, in American scoring 1 matchpoint is awarded to a team, pair or individual for every score that they have bettered, and $^1/_2$ matchpoint for every score that they have duplicated. In the rest of the world 2 matchpoints are awarded to a team, pair or individual for every score they have beaten and 1 point for every score they tie. Totaling of the matchpoint scores determines the winner for the session. When an event is held in two or more sessions without elimination, the total score is carried forward. The event winner is determined by the largest total score.

Scores for a multi-session event where elimination is involved, however, do not carry over totals from the qualifying round. Carryover depends on the number of qualifying rounds and the number of final rounds and is provided for by conditions of contest. For details of the formula used in ACBL tournaments, see CARRYOVER SCORES.

For team-of-four play, there are three methods of scoring in use: BOARD-A-MATCH, TOTAL POINTS, and INTERNATIONAL MATCHPOINTS. (Other methods in use in Europe include COMBINATION TEAM SCORING and QUOTIENT SCORING.)

In board-a-match, the most common type of team competition in the United States until the introduction of the enormously popular SWISS MOVEMENT in 1967, each board is scored as 1, $^1/_2$ or 0 matchpoints, depending on whether the total score on the two plays is greater than zero, zero, or less than zero. This system of scoring over-emphasizes the extra trick, the notrump versus suit play, the hair-trigger partscore double. An alternative, particularly in longer matches, is total-point scoring, which, however, has the defect of being able to determine the outcome of a match on two or so major SWING hands. The International Matchpoint method, which has gained almost universal currency, is designed to eliminate the defects of both board-a-match and total-point scoring methods. In the present IMP scale (see Law 78), the small swings are rewarded with fewer points than larger swings, but the award to a large swing hand is still great in comparison.

IMP scoring may be used for pair events, where a pair's score on a board is determined by its reference to a mean score on the board (by averaging all except the upper and lower scores made) with an IMP award based on the difference. (See INTERNATIONAL MATCHPOINTS; INTERNATIONAL OPEN TEAM SELECTION.)

In Swiss Teams, scoring is based on International Matchpoints. Sometimes the win-tie-loss method is used; sometimes the IMP total is converted to Victory Points. See BUTLER SCORING.

DUPLICATE TECHNIQUE. See IMP TACTICS; MATCHPOINT BIDDING; MATCHPOINT PLAY.

DUPLICATE TOURNAMENT. See DUPLICATE BRIDGE and CHAMPIONSHIP TOURNAMENTS.

DUPLICATE TRAY. See BOARD, DUPLICATE.

DUPLICATE WHIST. The oldest form of duplicate competition, in which movements such as the MITCHELL and HOWELL were developed.

DUPLICATING BOARDS. See TWINNING.

DUPLICATION OF DISTRIBUTION. This occurs where the suit lengths in a partnership's hands are evenly matched. A distributional flaw that limits the trick-taking potential of a pair of hands, it manifests itself in the absence of a long suit that can be developed.

♠ A Q 10	♠ K J 9
♥ K Q J 9	♥ A 10 6 2
♦ A 10 3	♦ 9 7 6
♣ 6 4 2	♣ Q 7 3

The presence of a long card in either hand would permit the development of an additional trick, but with the above distribution, no game contract is likely to be fulfilled, though sufficient values are held. Also called MIRROR DISTRIBUTION.

DUPLICATION OF VALUES. A concentration of strength and control in the same suit between two partners. When too much of the combined strength of the partnership is concentrated at one point there are likely to be serious weaknesses elsewhere and an unsound contract is often reached.

West	East
♠ A K	♠ Q J
♥ K Q J 10 4	♥ A 9 7 5
♦ A 7 5	♦ K 6 4 3
♣ 4 3 2	♣ 8 6 5

The above hands contain sufficient values to warrant a game contract in hearts, which has to fail owing to the poor division of strength in the black suits.
Another form of duplication:

West	East
♠ 6 4	♠ A K Q 8 7
♥ A J 10 4 3	♥ K Q 7 6
♦ K Q 8 5	♦ 9
♣ 9 7 5	♣ 6 4 2

A contract of 4 ♥ would be almost impossible to avoid, though declarer has four quick losers. Both hands contain, in effect, second-round control in spades and diamonds, leaving a glaring weakness in clubs. If West's ♦ K-Q (5 points) were changed to the ace (4 points), the game would be a laydown, for now East's singleton diamond would be pulling its weight.

Certain sequences have been devised to identify duplication of values at the slam level — for example, keeping out of six where there is a prospect of two immediate losers in a suit:

West	East
1 ♠	3 ♠
4 ♦	4 ♥
5 ♠	

Here the opener's last bid asks partner to bid a slam if he has as good as a second-round control in the unbid suit, clubs.

In a general way, duplication can be detected when a player has a void or singleton in a suit in which his partner has indicated some strength. For example:

West	North	East
1 ♥	1 ♠	1NT

West holds:

♠ —
♥ K Q 8 6 2
♦ A Q 9 3
♣ K J 7 4

and must tread warily, for his partner's values (in spades) seem to be misplaced for purposes of a suit contract.

DUPLIMATE. Modern dealing machine consisting of computer software that governs a card-sorting machine. Each card, usually after selection by means of a random dealing program, is placed in the North, South, East or West slot of a duplicate board at a speed of approximately 7 seconds for 52 cards. It is also possible to load selected deals (not computer-generated) that the machine will duplicate into boards.

DUTCH COUP. A maneuver setting up a PSEUDO SQUEEZE, suggesting an unblocking play like the VIENNA COUP without the presence of the necessary one-card menace in the closed hand. This coup was described for the first time by Gerrit-Jan Forch of the Netherlands in 1972.

Declarer, who held a singleton club originally, cashed dummy's ♣A early in the play. After he cashed his long spades he reached this ending:

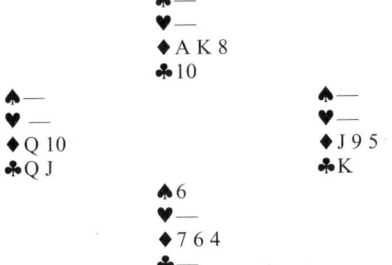

When he cashed the last spade, he pitched dummy's ♣10. East, under the impression that declarer held the ♣Q and that West consequently had three diamonds, discarded a diamond, setting up a third diamond trick for declarer. See DUTCH SQUEEZE.

DUTCH ENTRY. An entry card in dummy that is not real because declarer has a void in that suit. When declarer fails to cash this card the last time he is in dummy, declarer reinforces the impression that the card in a genuine entry.

```
                ♠ 9 5
                ♥ 7 6
                ♦ A 9 8
                ♣ A 10 8 7 4 2
♠ —                            ♠ K J 4
♥ K J 9 8 5                    ♥ A Q 10 3
♦ Q 10 5 4                     ♦ J 6 2
♣ K J 9 3                      ♣ Q 8 5
                ♠ A Q 10 8 7 6 3 2
                ♥ 4 2
                ♦ K 7 3
                ♣ —
```

West	North	East	South
		1♥	4♠
5♥	5♠	Dbl	All Pass

West led a heart to East's ace. East cashed the ♥Q and shifted to the ♦2. South expected all three missing trumps to be with East because East had doubled, attempting to keep West from bidding 6♥. However, he needed two entries to dummy if East covered the ♠9. But South took advantage of the fact that East did not know that the ♣A was not an entry. He won the ♦A in dummy and led the ♠9. East could not see the point of giving away the situation, so he played low. And of course so did South, who cashed the ♣A for a

diamond discard and then took a second trump finesse through East.

DUTCH SPADE. A transfer system, developed by Max Rebattu of the Netherlands. The opening shows the next higher suit: Pass = 1♣, 1♣ = 1♦, 1♦ = 1♥, 1♥ = 1♠. The 1♠ opening is used as random, 0-10 points, any distribution. The inventor and his partner, Anton Maas, used it in finishing second in the 1982 World Pairs.

DUTCH SQUEEZE. A form of the PSEUDO SQUEEZE. The card combination in dummy that includes the entry card and the card(s) to be promoted creates the impression of a threat even no such threat exists. The card that looks like an entry card in fact is not because declarer has a void in that suit. Former Netherlands world champion Bob Slavenburg reached the following ending in the 1965 Sunday Times Tournament:

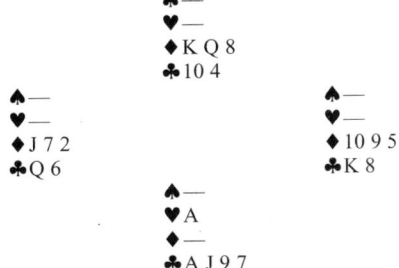

Earlier Slavenburg had deliberately not cashed his diamond tricks. At this point in the play he cashed the ♥A. Both West and East, looking at the visible diamond threat, thought they had to hold onto to their diamonds, so both pitched a club.

DYNAMIC NOTRUMP. A 1NT opening bid to show an unbalanced hand with 18-21 points. Developed by George Rosenkranz as a cornerstone of the ROMEX SYSTEM.

Responses are control-showing as in the BLUE TEAM style, counting an ace as two controls and a king as one. 2♣ shows no more than one control with 0-6 points; 2♦ shows less than two controls with 7 or more points; 2♥ shows two controls; 2♠ shows three controls, etc.

Opener's rebids are natural except that after a 2♣ response, 2♦ asks responder to bid a major. A notrump rebid describes a minor two-suiter.

With a balanced hand of less than 19 points, opener opens in a suit, then rebids either 1NT with 12-16 points or 2NT with 17-18 points.

E

EAST. One of the four hands at the bridge table. East is the partner of West and the left-hand opponent of North.

EASTERN CUEBID. A low-level cuebid in an opponent's suit, showing a stopper in the suit. The converse, a WESTERN CUEBID, asks partner for a stopper.

EASTERN SCIENTIFIC. A style of bidding in which

the principal features are strong notrump openings with non-forcing Stayman and Jacoby Transfer bids, five-card major-suit openings with a forcing 1NT response and limit raises. Two-over-one responses are strong but not necessarily forcing to game. Other elements are weak two-bids, with a strong artificial 2♣ opening forcing to 2NT or three of a major suit; also negative and responsive doubles. See STANDARD AMERICAN and BRIDGE WORLD STANDARD.

EASY ACES. The four aces are divided 2-2 between the opposing pairs.

E-BRIDGE. A subscriber-supported international web site that provides live online tournament and social bridge for players anywhere; full coverage (including vugraph with expert commentary) of major tournaments and events around the world; bridge news from all World Bridge Federation zones; and complete resources for bridge information, education and entertainment. It is the host for ACBLonline. Conceptually, e-bridge is a bold attempt at creating a comprehensive and universal site where bridge is the only nationality.

ECATS BRIDGE. A website developed by Anna Gudge and Mark Newton (a non-bridge player!) to provide world-wide bridge information. Launched in April 1999, it uses database-to-web technology to enable players to find information about their own bridge organization, to learn details about bridge personalities and to discover what events are being played where. It is also a comprehensive source of documents relating to major championships, the Laws, conditions of contest for world and zonal events and other such data. Gudge and Newton also developed the ECats Scoring System, which is used to score the World Wide Bridge Contest. This system enables players to follow the results as they are uploaded by individual clubs and re-scored across the whole field. Some 31,000 players from all WBF Zones participated in the inaugural event in 2000. and it is hoped that this will be exceeded in the 2001 Tournament. The system makes it possible for players to watch the scores change as new clubs submit results. They can also see their own scorecard giving details of their matchpoints, percentage board-by-board.and overall ranking. This scoring system is now used for other Zonal and national events.More information is available in the 'Sim Pairs' section of the site. www.ecatsbridge.com is the website address. The e-mail address is anna@ecatsbridge.com

ECHO. See HIGH-LOW SIGNAL.

ECONOMY OF HONORS. A playing technique intended to preserve honor cards from capture by opposing honors or trumps. The opponents can sometimes be encouraged to give up their high cards in exchange for low ones.

K Q x x

J x x

South leads twice from his own hand in order to make three tricks when West holds A-x. See ACE GRABBER, which illustrates the opposite principle.

Michael Sullivan gave these examples of economy of honors.

(1)
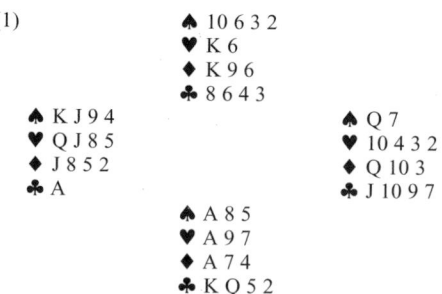

South plays 1NT and receives the lead of the ♦ 2 from West. Needing two club tricks and holding actual or potential stoppers in all other suits, South wins the ♦ A and, as insurance against the bare ♣A in the West hand, leads a low club. The ace drops and all is well, but even if it had not, the entries and tempos are available for two subsequent leads toward the ♣K-Q-x.

(2)
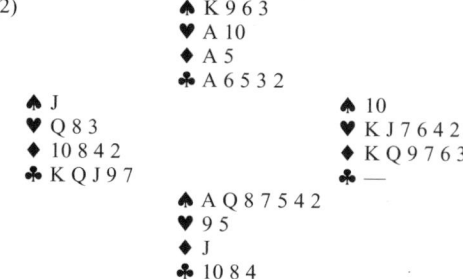

West leads the ♣K against South's contract of 4♠. Unless the ♣A is ruffed, South has 10 certain tricks. To guard against that lone possibility, declarer ducks the first round of clubs and subsequent club leads until West either shifts to another suit or permits South to ruff the fourth round of clubs. Eventually declarer gets to discard his losing heart on the carefully preserved ♣A.

EDUCATIONAL FOUNDATION. Foundations established by the American Contract Bridge League and the World Bridge Federation to foster the spread of bridge awareness through education. See ACBL EDUCATIONAL FOUNDATION and WORLD BRIDGE FEDERATION.

EFOS. The "economical forcing system" used in international championships by leading Swedish players. A minimum suit response, such as 1♠ in reply to 1♥, is treated as artificial. The object is to give the opener every opportunity to make a natural descriptive rebid. A single raise of responder's artificial suit response is a strong bid indicating reversing values. For a similar idea, see RELAY SYSTEM.

EHAA (Every Hand An Adventure). A highly natural system developed in the early Sixties, which became quite popular during the Seventies and is still in widespread use today. Its salient features are four-card majors, sound opening bids, weak two-bids in all four suits and an opening bid of 1NT that shows less than an opening bid of one of a suit (most players use a 10-12 HCP range). In general, EHAA players tend to use a minimal number of conventions, relying heavily on bidding judgment rather than a scientific approach. Most forego the use of any artificial forcing opening bid, although some use a 3♣ opening as an artificial game force.

The heart of the system is an undisciplined weak two-bid, showing almost any kind of hand pattern, promising 6-12 HCP and a minimum of five cards, possibly as little as x-x-x-x-x, in the suit bid. All responses and rebids are natural, with a single raise or 2NT response played as constructive but not forcing.

EIGHT or EIGHT-SPOT. The seventh highest ranking card in each suit, having eight pips of the suit to which it belongs on the face. See: DISCARD; HIGH-LOW SIGNALS; OPENING LEADS; RULE OF ELEVEN.

EIGHT TABLES. At duplicate, eight tables provide for competition among 32 players as individuals, 16 pairs or eight teams-of-four. See IRREGULAR RAINBOW.

An eight-table individual movement can be constructed, based on a seven-table RAINBOW MOVEMENT, with the addition of stationary players numbered 29, 30, 31 and 32.

As a team-of-four contest the choice is between a THURNER movement and a SWISS TEAM movement. Alternatively, you may start the game with four boards on each table and let the moving (E-W) pairs skip down one table. Following the first round the boards move to the next lower table but the East-West pairs skip two tables instead of one. East-West 1 skips from table 7 to table 4; East-West 2 skips from 8 to 5; etc.

Following the second, third and fourth rounds the East-West pairs skip a table in the lower direction and the boards move to the next lower table. After the fifth round the East-West pairs skip two tables and the boards skip one table. East-West pair 1 skips from 6 to 3; East-West 2 skips from 7 to 4; etc. To save confusion the director can pick up the boards, put them in order, and redistribute them, four to a table, starting with 25 to 28 on table 1.

If a seventh round is advisable, have East-West pairs 1 to 4 add 4 to their number and go to that table. East-West 5 to 8 will subtract 4 from their number and go to that table. Boards in play will be reshuffled. This is the only time during the game the boards are reshuffled. Tables 1 and 5 will relay boards 1 to 4, tables 2 and 6 will relay boards 5 to 8, tables 3 and 7 will relay 9 to 12 and 4 and 8 will relay 13 to 16.

As a pair game, eight tables can be either a MITCHELL or a REDUCED HOWELL movement. If the movement chosen is a Mitchell, the preferred method is to play four-board rounds with a skip after the fourth round. The game consists of either 24 or 28 boards. A better movement, but one which is more difficult to run, uses a byestand and relay. When the boards are distributed for three-board rounds, two adjoining tables are assigned to share boards. Exactly halfway around the field, a set of boards is placed on a bye table, and these boards sit out the first round. Boards and players move as in a normal Mitchell with no skip round. All eight rounds should be played, so every pair plays all 24 boards.

Two types of Reduced Howells are available, one for a 26-board game and one for 22 boards (SHORT HOWELL). There are three stationary pairs in the longer game, five in the shorter game.

For 7½ or 8½ tables, see HALF TABLE MOVEMENTS.

EITHER-OR SQUEEZE. See ALTERNATIVE SQUEEZE.

ELEVEN, RULE OF. See RULE OF ELEVEN.

ELEVEN TABLES. At duplicate, 11 tables afford excellent competition for either 44 individuals, 22 pairs or 11 teams-of-four.

As an individual tournament, 11-table games usually are conducted under the RAINBOW MOVEMENT. Twenty-two boards are in play for 11 rounds, and top is 10, average 110. It is also possible to extend the number of partnerships and boards to 24 or 27 by playing eight or nine rounds of three boards each. An interchange of partnerships by an exchange of seats between East and South, for two-board rounds, or by a counterclockwise movement by West in a three-board round, increases the number of partnerships, but usually slows down the speed with which the game can be conducted.

As a pair contest, a MITCHELL is usually the choice. Three boards are given out at each table, and each pair plays either 27 or 24 boards, depending on the number of rounds. It is also possible to give out two boards to a table, in which case each pair meets every pair playing in the opposite direction for a total of 22 boards. It is possible to play a THREE-QUARTER MOVEMENT — nine stationary pairs and 26 boards — but this is rarely chosen. An alternative to playing a truncated Howell is to play two boards per round in an EXPANDED MITCHELL with 12 or 13 rounds.

The standard team-of-four movement requires 10 rounds. At 30 boards, it is too long, at 20 boards, too short for most sessions. Usually 24 boards are played, with the two middle rounds eliminated. After four rounds, traveling pairs return the boards just played to their home table and subtract three (or add eight) to their number to get their fifth-round assignment. If it is advisable to play 10 rounds of three boards each, distribute three boards to a table with 1-3 on table 1, 4-6 on table 2, going around to 31-33 on table 11. The boards are shuffled before the first round and not shuffled again during the game. To start the game have the East-West pairs skip a table in the lower direction. East-West 1 skips to 10, East-West 2 skips to 11, etc. After each round the East-West players skip a table in the lower direction and the boards move one table in the lower direction.

A method that permits each team to play 26 boards works as follows. The movement is the same as for the 30-board game listed above. The teams play three boards a round for the first three rounds. At this point the director removes the highest numbered board from each table, and the teams play two boards per round for the next four rounds. The director then returns the third board to each set and the final four rounds are three-board rounds. This method allows each team to play every other team, albeit not the same number of boards against each.

For 10½ tables or 11½ tables, see HALF TABLE MOVEMENTS.

ELIMINATION. A type of endplay in which (1) neutral suits are all played from both declarer's and dummy's hand, the last of such plays (2) saddling a defender with the lead in order to force the defender to make a lead desired by the declarer. The play of the neutral cards is referred to as a STRIP PLAY, the saddling of a defender with the lead as a THROW-IN PLAY. See the latter for a discussion of various types and illustrations. See also PARTIAL ELIMINATION.

ELOPEMENT. A term coined by Geza Ottlik of Budapest, Hungary, in a series of *Bridge World* articles

to describe coups by which a player scores a trick or tricks with trumps that would not ordinarily have sufficient rank to take a trick. The simplest type of elopement is a COUP EN PASSANT. In the following elopement, spades are trump:

```
                    ♠ K 2
                    ♥ K
                    ♦ x
                    ♣ —
    ♠ A                             ♠ Q
    ♥ A                             ♥ Q
    ♦ A K                           ♦ Q
    ♣ —                             ♣ A
                    ♠ 3
                    ♥ —
                    ♦ x
                    ♣ x x
```

South leads a club and, remarkably, takes three tricks. If West ruffs, a diamond is discarded from dummy. If West throws a diamond, the club is ruffed in dummy and a heart is ruffed in the South hand, and the lead of South's last club is a coup en passant. If West instead throws the ♥ A, the club is ruffed and the ♥ K provides a discard for South's losing diamond while West ruffs with his master trump.

EMPTY. A colloquial term indicating that the spot cards in a suit are of no value. "King empty fourth" means a four-card suit headed by the king with the spot cards unimportant.

ENCOURAGING. (1) A term applied to a bid which strongly urges partner to continue to game. See INVITATIONAL.

(2) A term applied to a defensive signal by which a player urges his partner to continue playing the suit led. See COME-ON, HIGH-LOW SIGNAL, ODD-EVEN SIGNALS, UPSIDE-DOWN SIGNALS.

ENCRYPTED SIGNAL. Devised by Peter Winkler. Using such signals, information can be passed both covertly and legally between partners, adding a new dimension to the theory of the game. They are banned by the ACBL and many other official bodies.

Suppose that in the course of bidding toward a slam South wishes to tell his partner that he holds the ♣A. He can usually do this by making an appropriate bid (e.g., a cuebid of 4♣), but the opponents also may benefit from this information.

Nonetheless, the information that South has the ♣A is sometimes passed to North in unwittingly covert fashion; if North, holding the other three aces, employs an ace-asking convention (such as Blackwood) and South gives the one-ace reply, North can then see that his partner's ace is in clubs, but no law requires North to reveal to the opponents what he can deduce from looking at his own hand.

Once one piece of information has been passed covertly, it can be used as key for another; e.g., conceivably South's next bid might carry the message "I hold the king of the suit ranking one below the suit in which I hold the ace."

To clarify the situation consider the following gross simplification. Suppose that there are only three players, A, B and C, and each is randomly dealt a card from a deck which consists only of the three cards x, y and z. A wishes to communicate a single bit of information (e.g., whether or not he dyes his hair) to B but not to C. Suppose that A holds x and he "guesses" that B holds y; A then makes the following public announcement: "I hold either x or y." If B responds "So do I," then key is established. If A dyes his hair he is now in a position to say "I dye my hair if my card is x, otherwise I do not." C remains in the dark.

On the other hand if A misguesses and B holds z, B will respond "Sorry; I have neither x nor y"; the key is now blown and A cannot attain his objective. It thus appears that the situation is worth, on the average, $1/2$ bit of key to A and B. It should be noted, however, that if C had for some reason revealed his holding, then no guessing by A would have been necessary.

Using a similar strategy at the bridge table, with four players and 52 cards, suggests an average of $4^1/3$ bits of key available for covert partnership communication. That may not sound like much to a cryptographer, but to a bridge player the ability to transfer even a single bit of information covertly to his partner could be crucial.

Of course, the guessing needed to establish key at the bridge table has to be coded by legal bids. Since there are barely enough of these for sufficient communication to arrive at a good contract, bids cannot be wasted solely for the purpose of establishing key. Hence we attempt to establish key only when the attempt simultaneously passes information valuable in the selection of a contract. Key established in this manner will be termed active key.

When the opponents are doing the bidding we must be content to listen; frequently they will reveal a piece of information which establishes our key "for free." This passive key can then be used to encrypt defensive signals.

Here is a simple example of an active crypto-convention. A jump raise of partner's opening suit traditionally shows a strong hand with trump support; suppose we require in addition either the ace or king of trumps. (With both or neither some other response, e.g., 3NT, can be employed.) This is useful by itself, since trump quality is important in slam bidding, but it is also an attempt to establish key. If opener is missing both top trumps he rebids 3NT and key is lost, but otherwise, if interested in slam, he rebids as follows: with the ace of trumps, he cuebids normally (i.e., bids a suit in which he has control); but with the king of trumps, he cuebids a suit in which he lacks control. Responder can tell which by looking at his own top trump, but the opponents have not been tipped off as to the killing opening lead.

Certain modern conventions which guarantee specific holdings make key establishment an easy second step. An example is disciplined weak two-bids, in which an opening two-bid in first or second position guarantees two of the top three honors in the trump suit. Why not have some response (say, 2NT) guarantee the missing honor? This provides key for a three-way encryption of opener's "feature" rebid; e. g. the sequence 2♠ - 2NT - 3♥ might be used to show "either A-K of trumps and a high heart or A-Q of trumps and a high club or K-Q of trumps and a high diamond." Only partner knows for sure.

To take advantage of passive key one needs at least two different opening lead agreements (e.g., fourth-best, and third/fifth best) and at least two signaling systems (e.g., low card encourages, high card encourages.) One of the systems is selected for use whenever no key is obtained.

Key is obtainable whenever the opponent who eventually becomes declarer gives an exact count of some quantity. Examples: declarer answers the Stayman convention, showing four cards of a certain suit, or uses the splinter

convention, showing one card; declarer shows his aces or kings in a Blackwood reply; declarer shows his exact pointcount in a notrump sequence; declarer shows out of a suit early in the play. In each case the exposure of the dummy will enable each defender to count the number of the objects in question that his partner holds. The opening leader can, for example, use one lead agreement when holding an odd number of "objects" and the other when holding an even number. His partner can "read" the lead as soon as dummy is spread, but hopefully the declarer cannot until too late in the play.

When key is obtained because declarer has shown out of a suit, it is too late to encrypt the opening lead but perhaps not too late to encrypt the defensive signals. Here a fancy encryption scheme can be used because the defenders may have a lot of key; they, and only they, know the exact spot-card distribution of the suit in question.

It should be noted that although passive key is more easily obtained than active key, it must be used with discretion. Some forms are not completely reliable (e.g. Stayman, point-count). Worse, it may occasionally happen that the key can be "turned" - declarer determines during the play what system is in use and deduces the location of cards involved in the key. On balance, though, most forms of passive key are safe and effective.

EN PASSANT. See COUP EN PASSANT.

ENDLESS HOWELL. See FLOWER MOVEMENT.

ENDPLAY. A play taking place usually toward the end of the hand, though sometimes earlier. The preparation for an endplay may begin as early as the first or second trick; its object is to win at least one additional trick. They are essentially of three types; the forced lead or throw-in play, the coup or trump-reducing play, and the squeeze play. Many variations of each type occur. Endplay is often given a restricted meaning as a synonym for throw-in: "East was now endplayed." Articles dealing with various endplays are listed under the general headings COUP and SQUEEZE, and under the particular headings RUFF AND DISCARD, SMOTHER PLAY, THROW-IN, TRUMP PICK-UP, UNDERRUFF.

ENTRIES. Sold for events at a bridge tournament to provide a control of seating assignments. Each entry blank designates an individual's, pair's or team's original seating assignment as to table number (and direction if appropriate) and section.

In the U.S.A. particular seating assignments are usually separated from others at multi-sectioned events for assignment to known expert players to distribute such players equitably throughout the field. See ENTRY, SEED, SEEDING and ASSIGNMENT OF SEATS.

ENTRY. A means of securing the lead in a particular hand. Careful and effective use of entries is one of the basic arts of card play. In most situations it is sound strategy to maintain entries in both hands, which means preserving entries in the weaker hand where possible.

When both hands hold high cards, and there are more high cards than tricks, declarer should try to preserve a flexible entry situation:

♠ A Q 10

♠ K J 9

Suppose the first spade trick is won with the ace. If South will need entries to dummy, he should drop his king; if he needs entries to his hand, he should drop the 9. The jack is definitely intrinsically inferior. Declarer should aim to have the sequence of cards alternate from hand to hand: dropping the jack would leave dummy's Q 10 in effective sequence.

Similarly when drawing trumps, declarer may leave himself with two low trumps in one hand and one in the other. He should try to arrange that the single trump ranks between the trumps in the opposite hand.

A 4-4 fit will often provide an entry with a spot card if the suits divides 3-2.

A Q 10 3

K J 9 2

If dummy needs every possible entry, South should start by overtaking any high card as economically as possible. Later he repeats the process, and if the suit splits 3-2, he does so a third time, giving dummy a fourth-round entry with the 3.

The same is true if the defenders have one, two, or three winners in the suit. If declarer has four small cards in each hand, he can arrange to win the fourth round in either hand, except in the rare case when the spot cards do not overlap at all.

Some special situations involving entries are dealt with under the following headings: BLOCK; BLOCKING; DESCHAPELLES COUP; ENTRY-KILLING PLAY; ENTRY-SHIFTING SQUEEZE; ENTRY SQUEEZE; GAMBIT; HOLD UP; MERRIMAC COUP; SCISSORS COUP; STEPPINGSTONE SQUEEZE; UNBLOCKING; UNBLOCKING SQUEEZE.

ENTRY-KILLING PLAY. A play made with the object of cutting the opponents' entry to a particular hand. Special varieties of this are discussed under MERRIMAC COUP (by the defense) and SCISSORS COUP (by the declarer).

The following are typical maneuvers by second hand when dummy is entryless:

♠ A J 10 x x

♠ Q x x   ♠ K x x

♠ x x

When South leads the suit, West must play the queen to hold South to one trick in the suit. If he plays low, East must allow the 10 or jack to hold to prevent South making four tricks.

♠ A J 9 x

♠ K 10 x   ♠ Q 8 x x

♠ x x

When South leads, West must again play high. If he plays low, South can make a second trick in the suit by finessing the nine.

Similarly, plays can be made by the declarer. If East were declarer in these two cases, he would play high from dummy on a lead from South if he could judge the situation accurately.

ENTRY-SHIFTING SQUEEZE. An entry-shifting squeeze is a positional squeeze in which the squeeze card is a winner accompanied by additional winners in the same suit that provide communication between declarer's hand and dummy. Declarer manages his entries in the suit of the squeeze card so that he can take advantage of the discards chosen by the defender under pressure.

I. Trumps
  A. One opponent guards two suits

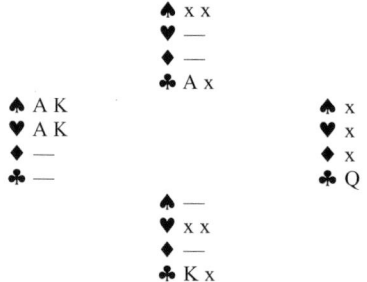

Clubs are trumps, and South leads. If East's trump were the deuce, declarer could claim the remaining tricks on a crossruff. In the actual end position, South leads the ♣K and West is squeezed in the majors: If West discards a heart, South retains the lead, and a heart ruff establishes a long card in that suit; if West discards a spade, declarer overtakes with dummy's ♣A, and he ruffs a spade to establish a winner in dummy.
  B. One opponent guards three suits

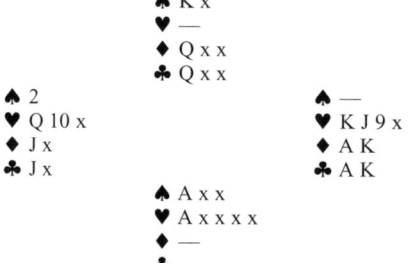

With spades as trumps, North leads the ♠K, and East is squeezed in three suits for two additional tricks: If he discards a club or a diamond, North retains the lead to ruff out the remaining honor in that suit; if he discards a heart, then South overtakes with the ♠A in order to establish hearts.

The two-suit squeezes require a balanced trump holding (equal length in both hands) when declarer has all but one of the remaining tricks, but they require an unbalanced trump holding if a trick must be lost after the squeeze.

The three-suit squeezes require an unbalanced trump holding, unless a throw-in menace is involved, in which case a balanced trump holding is needed.

II. Notrump
  A. One opponent guards two suits

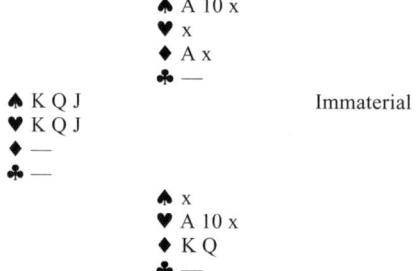

South is declarer in a notrump contract. When the ♦K is led, West is squeezed in the majors. If West discards a heart, declarer overtakes with the ♦A and then plays ace and another heart, establishing the long heart in his hand, with the ♦Q as entry to cash it. If West discards a spade,

dummy's low diamond is played, retaining the ♦A as entry to the long spade, established by playing ace and another.
  B. One opponent guards three suits

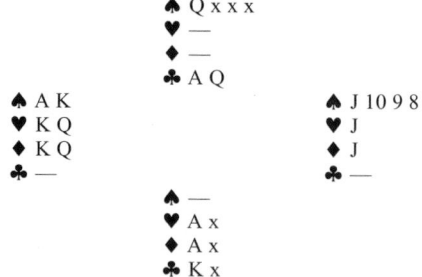

In a notrump contract, South leads a low club, squeezing West in three suits: If West unguards a red suit, North wins the ♣A, and returns a club to the king, allowing South to cash the red aces, and the long card in the suit unguarded by West; after a spade discard by West, North wins the ♣Q, concedes a spade to West, wins the forced return of a red suit, cashes the other red ace, and returns a club to the ♣A in order to cash the ♠Q.
  Stepping-Stone:

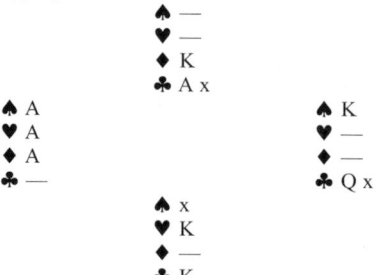

Needing two tricks at notrump, South leads the ♣K, and West is squeezed in three suits: discarding a red ace establishes the corresponding king for declarer, so West discards the ♠A. (If South held the ♠K, this discard would concede a trick directly.) South retains the lead and exits with a spade to East's king, forcing him to lead a club to North's ♣A.

ENTRY SQUEEZE. A squeeze that is aimed at forcing a defender, or both defenders, to discard from a seemingly worthless holding so that declarer can create an extra entry to one hand or the other by overtaking a card of winning rank. Analyzed and described by Geza Ottlik in the December 1967 issue of Bridge World. His article, entitled "The Quest," won the first International Bridge Academy "Article of the Year" award in 1968. Two of the hands from this article follow.

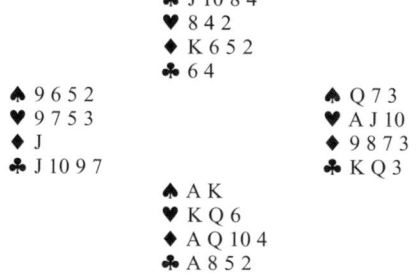

South declares 3NT after East has opened the bidding,

and West leads the ♣J. East overtakes with the queen and continues with the king and a third club as declarer holds up the ace until the third round. The ♦ A-Q reveal the 4-1 division, but South can still get home if he concedes a club to West, which crushes East in three suits. Clearly East cannot let go of a spade, and if he discards a heart, one heart lead from dummy suffices to establish two tricks in that suit for declarer. So East is forced to discard one of his "useless" diamonds. Now declarer has two diamond entries to dummy by overtaking the 10 with the king and can lead twice toward his heart honors. As Ottlik noted in his article: "Those silly little diamonds in East's hand have a function after all. Nondescript, irrelevant, or immaterial as they may be called, by their sheer existence they also serve. They stand and wait in the way, blocking traffic, hindering enemy lines of communication. And having this value, however silent, taciturn and hidden, they are subject to the pressure of a squeeze."

The entry squeeze can also operate against both opponents in the form of a double squeeze.

```
                ♠ A 6 4
                ♥ 10 6 5
                ♦ J 8 7 4
                ♣ 9 4 2
  ♠ J 10 8                    ♠ 9 7 5 2
  ♥ Q 7 4 2                   ♥ K 8 3
  ♦ 10 6 5 2                  ♦ Q 9 3
  ♣ 7 6                       ♣ 10 8 5
                ♠ K Q 3
                ♥ A J 9
                ♦ A K
                ♣ A K Q J 3
```

West leads the ♠J against South's contract of 6NT. Rather than bank everything on finding East with both heart honors, or guessing which opponent might hold a doubleton honor, declarer wins the spade in hand and cashes five rounds of clubs, discarding a diamond and a heart from dummy. On the last club West is in some difficulty. If he holds fewer than three hearts, South can lead a heart from his hand to establish two tricks in that suit. Alternatively, if West comes down to fewer than three diamonds, declarer can cash the ♦ A-K, the ♠K-A, then take the heart finesse; West, marooned with nothing but hearts, must then return a heart into declarer's tenace. So West is "squeezed" down to a singleton spade. East, in turn, is squeezed on the last club, for he must also hold three cards in each red suit and can hold no more than one spade. South has thus squeezed both opponents in a suit in which he started with three top winners and now makes his slam by overtaking the ♠K with the ace for a heart finesse. The ♠6 provides entry to dummy for the second heart finesse. See also ENTRY-SHIFTING SQUEEZE, OVERTAKING SQUEEZE, STEPPING-STONE SQUEEZE, and UNBLOCKING SQUEEZE.

EPSON WORLDWIDE BRIDGE CONTEST. See WORLDWIDE BRIDGE CONTEST.

EQUALS. Cards that are in sequence, or cards that are in effect in sequence because all cards of intervening rank have been played. See PLAY FROM EQUALS.

EQUAL VULNERABILTY. Either both sides are vulnerable or both side are not vulnerable. Preempts and sacrifices require some care because the vulnerability is not favorable. This is especially true for partscores when both sides are vulnerable. See FAVORABLE VULNERABILITY, UNFAVORABLE VULNERABILITY.

EQUITY. The equity rule for adjusting scores. See LAWS OF DUPLICATE (Law 12).

ERRORS IN SCORING. See LAWS OF DUPLICATE (Law 79) and SCORING CORRECTIONS.

ESCAPE MECHANISM. See SOS REDOUBLE and WRIGGLE.

ESCAPE SUIT. A long suit held in reserve by a player making a gambling or psychic bid. An overcall of 1NT by a player with a weak hand and a long broken suit is a well-worn tactic. It is not difficult to expose the maneuver by doubling and forcing the overcaller to escape into his suit, but the tactic has some positive value: a weak hand with a long suit might otherwise be shut out of the auction unless WEAK JUMP OVERCALLS are being used.

Psychic bids in a short suit with an escape suit in reserve are seldom tried because they tend to be more dangerous to partner than to the opponents.

For a regular systemic use of a bid with an escape suit, see GAMBLING THREE NOTRUMP.

ESTABLISH. To make a suit or an individual card good by forcing out the opponent's guards or winners. Thus one may establish K-Q-J-10-9 of a suit for four tricks after conceding one to the ace.

ESTABLISHED CARD. A card that has been promoted to winning rank after all higher-ranking cards in the other hands have been played.

ESTABLISHED ENTRY. An entry developed by driving out a higher card.

ESTABLISHED PARTNERSHIP. Two players who compete as partners often enough to have a thorough understanding of the methods they use. Some of the more famous partnerships include Eric Rodwell-Jeff Meckstroth, Benito Garozzo-Giorgio Belladonna, Gabriel Chagas-Roberto Branco, Edgar Kaplan-Norman Kay, Lorenzo Lauria-Alfredo Versace, Adam Zmudzinski-Cezary Balicki, Chip Martel-Lew Stansby.

ESTABLISHED REVOKE. A revoke which may not be corrected. A revoke becomes established as soon as the revoking player or his partner leads or plays to the next trick, or, if the revoke is made in leading, as soon as the revoking player's partner plays to the trick on which the revoke is made; or by the act of making a claim. A revoke made on the 12th trick must be corrected. See LAWS (Law 62D).

ESTABLISHED SUIT. A long suit in which a player holds all the remaining high cards, which at notrump or after trumps have been drawn at a suit contract will all be winners when the suit is led and run. The object of notrump play is essentially to establish one or more long suits by drawing or forcing out whatever high cards the opponents may hold in that suit.

ESTIMATION. The attempt to judge the score that one is likely to have earned in a duplicate game. Generally a

player estimates by comparing his result on a hand with those likely to be obtained elsewhere. As a result of this procedure, one can often alter one's tactics toward the end of a session, playing a somewhat chancier game if behind and needing "tops" to win, or playing "down the middle" if well ahead. See SHOOTING.

ETHICS AND CONDUCT. The term "ethics" is commonly used in relation to the observance of fair play. Breaches of ethics are generally thought of as unfair practices which fall short of deliberate cheating.

The Laws deal with the whole question of proper behavior at bridge under the general heading, "Proprieties." See Laws of Duplicate #72-4. This includes ETIQUETTE. In the Laws of Contract Bridge the Proprieties are in a separate section following Law #81.

ETIQUETTE. Much of the popularity of contract bridge is attributable to the high standards of etiquette which are observed by the players. No other modern game leans so heavily on the expectation that participants will conduct themselves in a highly civilized manner.

In tournament bridge, violations of proper etiquette are to be expected from inexperienced players, either through ignorance or inadvertence. A well-mannered opponent who is the victim of such a violation will, if he considers that comment is called for, be at pains to make it clear that his comment is intended to be helpful rather than admonitory.

At the other end of the scale is the noxious violation by the experienced player who complains loudly - but unofficially — of a violation of ethics or etiquette committed against him. "I wuz robbed!" is never heard from a player of high standards of etiquette; he either makes an official protest or says nothing.

The LAWS OF CONTRACT BRIDGE deal with the whole question of proper behavior under the heading, "Proprieties." Matters of etiquette, as distinct from questions of ethics, are dealt with in Part III of the Proprieties.

Among the breaches of good manners frequently observed are the following: discussion between two partners of a board just played when there is another board to play; looking at an opponent's hand after it has been placed in the board without asking permission; criticism of an opponent's bidding or any implication of bad faith on the part of the opponents without having previously called the director to the table.

EUROPEAN COMMUNITY CHAMPIONSHIPS. These championships, also known as the European Common Market Championships, were held every two years from 1967 to 1998. Italy had the best record, winning the overall championship in 1967, 1971, 1973, 1977, 1979, 1981, 1985 and 1993. France was the overall champion four times. Championships were played for Open Teams, Womens Teams, Mixed Teams, Junior Teams, Open Pairs, Womens Pairs, Mixed Pairs and Junior Pairs. For results see Appendix IV.

EUROPEAN YOUTH CHAMPIONSHIPS. Held every even-numbered year, and played in two series for National Teams (one per country) comprising: (a) Junior players (who have at most their 25th birthday in the year of the tournament), and (b) Schools players (who have at most their 21st birthday in the year of the tourna-

ment). The format in each series is a simple round-robin (no semifinals and final). The Junior series also serves as Europe's qualifier to the following year's World Junior Teams Championship.

EVEN. A term applying to the equal distribution of the outstanding cards in a suit, as a 3-3 division of six outstanding cards.

EVENT. A contest of one or more sessions in duplicate bridge played to determine a winner.

EXCESS POINTS. When cumulative scoring was used in pair competition, the limit placed on the number of points that could be scored was, for the defenders, 600 if not vulnerable, 900 if vulnerable; for the declarer, 800 if not vulnerable, 1,000 if vulnerable. No limitation was placed if the contract was for a slam. Losers lost total points, winners were credited only with the maximum and the balance carried to a special "excess points" column used only for breaking ties. In England, the 600 maximum for defenders was 700. Since matchpoint scoring has almost totally replaced total-point scoring, this provision was omitted from the Laws of 1943 and subsequently.

EXCLUSION. A Unit board of directors may vote to exclude a member of another Unit from its tournaments for cause. See also SUSPENSION.

EXCLUSION BID. A bid which shows a holding in every suit except the one named. This is a feature of the ROMAN SYSTEM. After an opening bid of 2♣ or 2♦, showing a three-suited hand, the opener rebids in his short suit if he receives the conventional positive response of 2NT (see ROMAN TWO DIAMONDS). Similarly, the Roman System prescribes a bid in the shortest unbid suit in response to a takeout double; this has a transfer effect, permitting the stronger hand to become declarer. A takeout double is itself an exclusion call in a wide sense: it implies support for all suits except the one already bid.

Exclusion bids have been adopted by some partnerships as a defense against strong artificial opening bids. This device is useful for competing on three-suited hands in which no suit has been bid naturally. An extension of this convention devised by Andrew Bernstein, which he calls the "Super Convention," is to use an overcall of an opponent's notrump opening as a two-way exclusion bid. The overcall thus shows either length in the suit bid, or shortness in the suit bid and support for all other suits. The partner of the overcaller is expected to treat the overcall as natural if he has fewer than three cards in the suit. Otherwise he is expected to take his choice of the other suits. See EXCLUSION BLACKWOOD.

EXCLUSION BLACKWOOD. This is an extension of Blackwood to permit one hand to exclude an ace from the responses to Blackwood because that player has a void in a named suit. The normal responses played are those used with Roman Keycard Blackwood. Most typically, those pairs who use Texas responses to 1NT or 2NT play that Texas followed by a new suit is Exclusion Blackwood, with the transfer suit as trumps and the second suit as the excluded suit. Thus:

1NT	4♥
4♠	5♥

is Roman Keycard Blackwood for spades, with hearts excluded, rather than a confession of forgetting Texas! Responses here would be 5♠ with 0 or 3 keycards, 5NT with 1 or 4 keycards, 6♣ with 2 but no queen of trumps and 6♦ with 2 and the queen of trumps.

Similarly, unusual jumps where a lower bid would be a splinter are also Exclusion Blackwood. A sequence such as:

1♠	2♥
5♣	

would be Exclusion for hearts, since 4♣ would have shown a splinter in clubs.

EXHAUST. To draw all cards of a suit from the hand of any player. A player becoming void of a suit during the play is said to be exhausted of that suit, as distinguished from holding no cards of that suit originally.

EXHIBITION MATCH. Special events set up as attractions for spectators. Sometimes these take place at major tournaments; sometimes they are an event that stands alone, such as the matches between leading American businessmen and the U.S. Congress, also those between the Houses of Parliament. Also see BRIDGE-O-RAMA and VUGRAPH.

EXIT. To "get out of one's hand," particularly when it is undesirable to lead from one's hand, usually by making a lead which is not likely to jeopardize the value of any partnership holding.

EXIT CARD. A card by which one can exit from one's hand, offering an escape from an opponent's attempted THROW-IN or ELIMINATION play.

EXIT PLAY. A defensive UNBLOCKING maneuver executed in order to avoid a THROW-IN.

```
              ♠ K Q 10 9
              ♥ Q 10 3
              ♦ K 4 2
              ♣ 9 4 3
♠ 7 2                        ♠ 6 5
♥ A K 8 5                    ♥ 7 6 2
♦ Q J 9                      ♦ 10 8 7 5
♣ K J 8 6                    ♣ 10 7 5 2
              ♠ A J 8 4 3
              ♥ J 9 4
              ♦ A 6 3
              ♣ A Q
```

South is in 4♠ after an opening bid on his left, and West leads three rounds of hearts. Declarer wins, draws trumps, and plays ace, king, and another diamond, hoping to throw West in for a favorable club lead. West, however, makes an exit play, unblocking the queen and jack on the first two diamond leads, and retaining the 9, which his partner overtakes on the third round to play a club, defeating the contract.

EXODUS. A method of responding after partner's opening 1NT bid has been doubled. A redouble forces opener to rebid 2♣. The redouble indicates that responder has a suit he wishes to play at the two-level. If it is clubs he passes partner's forced 2♣. If he bids another suit, opener passes.

If responder bids a suit at the two level over the double,

he is asking opener to choose between the suit bid and the suit immediately higher, i.e., opener's choice over 2♥ would be either hearts or spades. If responder's suits are not touching, he bids two of his lower-ranking suit. If opener bids the next higher suit, responder bids his higher-ranking suit, allowing opener to make a choice.

If responder, after redoubling, bids 2NT over opener's forced 2♣, he is using a form of FORCING STAYMAN. If responder bids 2♠ over the double, opener must rebid 2NT, and responder now bids his minor, guaranteeing a hand good enough for 3NT or at least four of the minor. See DEFENSE TO DOUBLE OF ONE NOTRUMP and DOUBLES OF NOTRUMP BIDS.

EXPANDED MITCHELL (or HESITATION MITCHELL). A way to play one round, or more than one extra round, in a MITCHELL MOVEMENT introduced by E. E. Blandon. The expansion is obtained by decreasing the number of stationary pairs and letting the moving pairs visit not only E/W places but also some N/S places. See also REDUCED HOWELL.

EXPECTANCY. What a player is entitled to expect in various circumstances governed by mathematical probabilities. (1) In the deal, a player's expectancy is one ace, one king, one queen and one jack. (2) After looking at his hand and before any bidding has taken place, a player may expect his partner to hold one-third of the outstanding honor cards. (3) In some bidding situations, a player's expectation of partner's strength may be clear-cut. If a player with 17 points hears a bid of 1NT (16-18) bid on his right, the expectation of his partner's hand is three points. (4) In the play, expectancy depends on more complex mathematical calculations. (See MATHEMATICAL TABLES.) The trick expectancy from the most promising line of play in many situations is given under SUIT COMBINATIONS. See also EXPECTATION.

EXPECTATION. The average result which would be achieved over a long trial period. In order to compute the expectation of a particular play, it is necessary to consider not only the frequency of gain or loss but the amount that is being risked. For example, let us compute the expectation of a pair that reaches a contract of 4♠, not vulnerable, at rubber bridge. This contract, we will say, depends on winning one of two finesses (a 75% chance). Assuming the contract will either make or fail by one trick and that the pair will receive 300 points for making the game. The pair's expectation is:

(75%)	•	(+ 420)	+	(25%)	•	(-50)
chance		result		chance		result
of		of		of		of
success		success		failure		failure

This sum is 315 - 12.5 = 302.5. In making this computation we take into account that 75% of the time the pair will score + 420 and 25 % of the time the pair will score -50.

Let us contrast this expectation with that of a pair with the same cards that stops in 3♠. The expectation of the latter is (assuming 50 points for a part score):

(75%)	•	(+ 170)	+	(25%)	•	(+ 140)
chance		result		chance		result
of an		of		of		when just
overtrick		overtrick		making		making

This sum is 127.5 + 35.0 = 162.5. Thus, the expectation of the pair bidding game is higher. This indicates that it is favorable to attempt the game under these conditions.

By bidding the game, a pair will win an average of 302.5 points whereas by stopping short it will win an average of only 162.5. A similar calculation will indicate that it is not profitable (in the long run) to bid such a game which depends on two successful finesses (only a 25% chance).

In the play of the hand, the declarer may sometimes be unable to determine the correct play without resorting to at least a rough calculation of the expectation of different lines.

West	East
♠ A K 6 2	♠ 5 4
♥ A K 6 2	♥ 5 4
♦ A K 2	♦ 5 4
♣ 3 2	♣ A K Q 7 6 5 4

West plays 6NT against the opening lead of the ♦ Q. East-West are vulnerable. How should West play?

A safety play for the contract is available. West needs only six club tricks for his contract. By ducking the first round of clubs he ensures his contract without an overtrick (+ 1440). By trying to run the clubs, he will make an overtrick (+ 1470) unless North holds all four clubs. If declarer fails to make the safety play and North has four clubs, he will be down three tricks (minus 300).

The expectation of the safety play is:

$$(100\%) \cdot (+\,1440) = 1440$$

The expectation of trying to split the clubs is:

$$(5\%) \cdot (-300) + (90\%) \cdot (+1470)$$

chance	chance
North has	clubs are
four clubs	not 4-0

$$+\,(5\%) \cdot (1440)$$

chance
South has
four clubs

This expectation is only 1380. Therefore, the safety play is the superior play.

West	East
♠ Q 5 4 3	♠ J 2
♥ Q 5 4 3	♥ J 2
♦ A K 2	♦ 5 4
♣ 3 2	♣ A K Q 7 6 5 4

West plays in 1NT against an opening lead of the ♦ Q. East-West are not vulnerable. Once again the safety play guarantees the contract (with an overtrick) for + 120. If West fails to employ the safety play and North has all four clubs, he will be set two tricks for –100.

The expectation of the safety play is

$$(100\%) \cdot (+\,120) = 120$$

while the expectation of trying to run the clubs without loss is

$$(5\%) \cdot (-100) + (90\%) \cdot (+\,150)$$
$$+\,(5\%) \cdot (+\,120) = 136$$

(assuming the defenders will discard correctly on the run of clubs).

In this case, the safety play is not the superior play. (This does not take into account the fact that if the clubs were 4-0 there might have been some North-South bidding. Such a consideration makes the safety play even less desirable.)

EXPECTED NUMBER OF CONTROLS IN BALANCED HANDS. A table of the number of controls statistically predictable in balanced hands of varying strength was analyzed and described by GEORGE ROSENKRANZ in the December 1974 issue of *The Bridge World* (see tabulation nearby). Knowledge of the average expectations of numbers of aces and kings for the strength in pointcount already shown is useful in determining whether or not to bid aggressively.

The table shows the approximate frequencies of specific numbers of controls (Ace = 2, King = 1) in all hands with 4-3-3-3, 4-4-3-2 or 5-3-3-2 distribution. Blanks indicate zero frequency; asterisks indicate less than one-half of 1 percent frequency.

EXPECTED NUMBER OF CONTROLS IN BALANCED HANDS

hcp	Relative Freq.	0	1	2	3	4	5	6	7	8	9	10	11	12
3	1216	67	33											
4	1891	40	39	21										
5	2505	23	48	29										
6	3129	12	41	47										
7	3795	5	30	46	19									
8	4192	2	19	44	28	7								
9	4377	*	10	35	44	1 1								
10	4379	*	5	24	44	27								
11	4179	*	2	14	40	33	11							
12	3755	*	1	8	30	42	17	2						
13	3242		*	3	20	39	34	4						
14	2687		*	1	11	33	38	17						
15	2115		*	*	5	24	42	23	6					
16	1596			*	2	14	36	37	10	1				
17	1155			*	1	8	27	39	24	1				
18	799			*	*	3	18	39	30	10				
19	526				*	1	10	32	40	15	2			
20	333				*	*	5	22	38	31	4			
21	201				*	*	2	13	35	35	15			
22	115					*	1	6	26	43	20	4		
23	62.9					*	*	3	17	38	35	7		
24	32.6					*	*	1	9	31	38	21		
25	16.0						*	*	4	21	43	26	6	
26	7.32							*	1	12	37	41	9	
27	3.21							*	*	6	28	41	25	
28	1.28							*	*	2	18	44	32	4
29	0.48								*	1	9	35	49	6

EXPERT. A player of conceded skill. The caliber of the player accorded this title will vary with the circles in which he regularly plays.

EXPLANATION OF CALL OR PLAY. Also see ALERTING, PRIVATE CONVENTION. During the auction and before the final pass any player may, at his own turn to call, ask for a full explanation of any call made by an opponent. After the auction, a question such as "Is there anything we should know about this?" is appropriate. After the auction and throughout the play, any player except dummy may, at his own turn to play, ask for an explanation of opposing calls or card play conventions. See FACE DOWN LEADS; LAWS OF DUPLICATE (Laws 20, 41).

A player who asks for an explanation of a bid should beware of giving information to his partner by his question. For example, a player who asks the meaning of a normal 1♣ opening bid when he holds great club strength may be subject to penalty under Law 16. It is better to ask a question in general terms, rather than draw attention to one particular suit-bid and so expose oneself to the suggestion that the question may be lead-directing.

When the auction is over, it is recommended that dummy volunteer any explanation about his side's bidding which he may think necessary. Voluntary explanations during the auction are not advisable because they may enlighten partner (or appear to enlighten him). If a player gains information as a result of his partner's explanation, he must carefully avoid taking advantage of it. However, it would be improper to offer an immediate correction of partner's incorrect explanation of the partnership understanding. More often than not, this would give unauthorized information to partner. If the offending side is also the declaring side, the mistaken information should be corrected before the opening lead is made. If the offending side is the defending side, no correction can be offered until the completion of the hand — again to correct earlier could result in unauthorized information for partner. If the non-offending side feels they have been injured by the incorrect information given, they have the right to seek adjudication of the board by the director, and failing that, by the Appeals Committee. See LAWS OF DUPLICATE (Laws 73,75).

A tournament director may direct a player to leave the table while his partner gives an explanation; and it may be proper for him to depart voluntarily (at his partner's request or of his own volition) if a possibility of a misunderstanding exists.

EXPOSED CARD. For cards exposed during the bidding, see Law 24. Cards exposed during the play are covered by Laws 48, 49, and 68; LAWS OF DUPLICATE (Laws 48, 49, 68).

EXPOSED HAND. A hand placed in full view of all the players. This usually refers to dummy's hand, but it may also apply to the hand of declarer or a defender, which may become exposed by accident or in the process of making a claim. See Laws 48, 49, 62, 64, 68; LAWS OF DUPLICATE (Laws 48, 49, 62, 64, 68).

EXTENDED GERBER. A method of pinpointing certain key cards in slam bidding, devised by Jerold A. Fink of Cincinnati. See GERBER.

After a trump suit is established, a bid of 4♣ requests partner to show controls (ace-2 controls, king-1 control). 4♦ shows 0 or 1♠ 4♥ shows 2♠ 4♠ shows 3♠ 4NT shows 4. With 5 or more controls, responder subtracts 5 and bids accordingly. After the conventional 4♦ response, a 4♥ bid asks responder to clarify whether he holds 0 or 1 controls by bidding 4♠ with 0 controls (or 5 or 10), or 4NT with 1 control (or 6 or 11).

Other four-level bids by the asking bidder are sign-offs. The asking bidder may also sign off by bidding 5♣ and passing partner's forced 5♦ response, or by bidding 5♦ and passing partner's forced 5♥ response or correcting it to 5♠. Other combinations of rebids on the five level are conventional, asking partner to show points (king-2 points, queen-1 point) in two specific suits by seven steps, ranging from 0 points for the first step to 6 points for the seventh step.

EXTENDED HERBERT NEGATIVE. A further use of HERBERT NEGATIVES was noted roughly simultaneously by Richard Granville and Barry Rigal in the Seventies, although its origin is certainly older than that. The use occurs in the sequence where second hand makes a takeout double at his first turn and then cuebids in his opponent's suit. In these auctions the first step by responder at his second turn is unrelated to suit lengths and simply shows 0-4 HCP. Thus in the auction:

1♦	Dbl	Pass	1♠
Pass	2♦	Pass	2♠

2♠ shows moderate values. With nothing, responder would bid 2♥ at his second turn. With spades and hearts and a moderate hand responder cand jump to 3♥. This method can also be used when opener rebids his suit and the takeout doubler makes a second double to show significant extra values.

EXTENDED LANDY. The LANDY convention is a 2♣ takeout for the major suits over an opponent's notrump opening. An extension was proposed by Ira Rubin in 1947, using a two-club bid as a takeout request after a response or rebid of one notrump after a suit opening. It implies more distribution and less strength than a double. It also applies in the passout seat:

West	North	East	South
1♦	Pass	1♠	Pass
1NT	2♣		

This shows five or more clubs and exactly four hearts, based on North's failure to overcall immediately.

Other similar uses were developed later by Martin Cohn.

EXTRA TRICK. A trick scored in excess of the number of tricks required to fulfill a contract. Such tricks are scored above the line and do not count toward game at their trick value. Extra tricks carry premium values if the contract has been doubled or redoubled. See OVERTRICK and SCORING.

F

FACE (of a card). The front of a playing card, containing the suit and rank of the card.

FACE CARD. The cards which have a representation of a human figure, called originally coat cards, later court cards. Their design is virtually the same for all manu-

facturers in America and Britain, deriving from eighteenth century French patterns.

Earlier designs depended on the skill of the artists who carved the wood blocks, and gradually degenerated from representation of recognizable people and objects into meaningless figures. It has been said that Henry VIII was the model for all four kings; the oldest extant English cards have the same curling moustache and divided beard on the four kings, and legend has it that the queens were likenesses of Elizabeth of York, Henry VII's queen. The remainder of the design is clearly derived from cards made in Rouen, France; the faces differ, but the costumes, position of the hands, and weapons all show similarities.

The French packs developed along their own lines until 1813, when an official design was promulgated; the cards were named, and even today the names appear on many packs:

	SPADES	HEARTS	DIAMONDS	CLUBS
KING	David	Charles	César	Alexandre
QUEEN	Pallas	Judith	Rachel	Argine
JACK	Hogier	Lahire	Hector	Lancelot

All represent real or mythical figures except Argine, an anagram of Regina.

In the Hungarian pack, eight of the face cards represent characters in Schiller's drama, *Wilhelm Tell*, set in Switzerland:

SUITS	OBER	UNTER
Acorns	Wilhelm Tell	Reszö Harras
Leaves	Ulrich Ruden	Walter Fürst
Bells	Vadász Stüssi	Itel Reding
Hearts	Herman Gezler	Pásztor Kuoni

But an oddity exists; the cards were never used in Switzerland.

The usual German packs do not have a queen, but have two jacks (or knaves), the Ober and the Unter. Some German packs, however, have four face cards, king-queen-jack-jack. The Italo-Spanish pack uses a cavalier in place of a queen.

FACE-DOWN LEAD. A procedure first introduced experimentally by the WBF in 1972 and adopted by the ACBL in 1975, recommending that the opening leader place his opening lead face down on the table, after which his partner may ask questions about the auction. This ensures that the partner of the leader will have the opportunity to ask questions about the auction before dummy is tabled, and that his questions will not influence the opening leader in his choice.

However, a face-up lead does not deprive the leader's partner of the right to ask questions. The face-down lead has a secondary purpose: If the lead is out of turn, the card can be retrieved without penalty.

This is now a requirement under Law 41 but there is no penalty for failure to lead face down. Sponsoring organizations may opt for face-up leads.

FACED CARD. A card exposed to all the players, which may be a card in the dummy, a penalty card, or a card exposed by a player making a claim or his opponent. No revoke penalty can be exacted for failure to play a faced card. See also PLAYED CARD.

FACT. A happening at a bridge table. When the facts are in dispute, or their interpretation is a matter of judgment, the matter may be referred to the tournament committee. This includes the significance or otherwise of

hesitations. The committee may not overrule the director on a point of law, although an appeal may be forwarded to the NATIONAL LAWS COMMISSION.

FACTORING. The process of adjusting matchpoint scores to the same base to make them comparable for ranking purposes. This used to be a monumental mathematical chore. However, factoring is automatic with computer scoring.

When scores are to be compared for ranking within a group of contestants, it is necessary that the comparison be on the same base. For instance, in a $12\frac{1}{2}$ table Mitchell game, the usual procedure is to have a phantom pair 13 in one of the two fields. Consequently all the pairs in one direction have a bye round, playing only 24 boards, while the pairs in the other direction play all 26 boards. Top on a board in such a case is 11. The pairs that did not sit out have a possible of 286, but those who sat out have a possible of only 264. To make the scores comparable, the scores of the pairs that sat out must be multiplied by the fraction $^{286}/_{264}$ ($^{13}/_{12}$). To facilitate the computation, add $^{1}/_{12}$ of the score obtained to the scores of the pairs that sat out.

Some half-table movements are more complicated. For instance, with $15\frac{1}{2}$ tables, there would be 16 pairs in one direction and 15 in the other, but usually only 12 or 13 rounds would be played. The best method of handling this situation is to set up a ROVER movement — one pair successively replaces pairs sitting in their direction after sitting out the first round according to a formula set up to guarantee that no pair plays another pair twice and that no pair plays the same set of boards twice. All pairs in the direction in which the rover pair is not playing would not sit out. In the other direction, the rover pair plus all the pairs the rover replaced for a round would sit out one round. To determine a winner it is necessary to factor the scores of those who played the lower number of rounds up to the number of rounds played by the rest of the field.

In all half-table games it is possible to set up a movement where top on a board is the same for all boards. Whenever possible, the director should attempt to set up such a movement. However, from time to time a situation arises where certain boards are played more or less frequently than other boards, resulting in a higher top score on certain boards. When this happens, it is necessary to factor all boards with a lower top by a fraction that will make those boards have a top equivalent to the top of the boards with the higher top. If some boards have a top of six and others have a top of five, then it is necessary to multiply the matchpoint scores on the boards with the five top by $^{6}/_{5}$.

For one-session events in more than one section where there is a different top score in each section (an example would be one 14-table Mitchell section, top 12, average 156, and one 7-table three-quarters movement, top 6, average 78), the scores in the section with the lower top score must be factored up to those of the larger section (in this case, by simply doubling, $^{312}/_{156}$ or 2 being the factor applied).

If the smaller section were an 11-table game with a three-quarters movement, 10 top, 130 average, the factor would be $^{312}/_{260}$ or $^{6}/_{5}$.

In two-session events (without elimination) in which there are more or fewer contestants in the second session, and consequently top on a board is different, the second

session is always adjusted to the score of the first session.

If a half-table movement winds up with different tops on some boards, then it is necessary to do a double factoring. First the tops on the boards should be factored so that there is the same top on all boards. Then a second factoring should equalize the scores based on the number of boards each pair played.

FAILURE TO COMPLY WITH A LEAD OR PLAY PENALTY. The act of playing an INCORRECT CARD when a player is able to lead or play from an unfaced hand a card or suit required by law or specified by an opponent in accordance with an agreed penalty. See LAWS OF DUPLICATE, Law 52.

FALL, FALL OF THE CARDS. The play of a card or cards on a trick; the order in which they are played.

FALL NATIONALS. See FALL NORTH AMERICAN BRIDGE CHAMPIONSHIPS.

FALL NORTH AMERICAN BRIDGE CHAMPION-SHIPS. Formerly called the Winter Nationals or the Fall Nationals. This annual tournament held since 1927 takes place in November or early December. These championships were originally under the auspices of the American Bridge League, and since 1937 have been controlled by the American Contract Bridge League. The Fall NABC began as a four-day tournament and was enlarged to eight days four years later. Nine-day tournaments became standard in postwar years. In 1963, the addition of the International Fund Pairs lengthened the tournament to nine and one-half days. It became a full ten-day tournament when ACBL rescheduled major events in 1969. In 1981 a pre-tournament Charity Gala was added. The Thursday evening Charity game now consists of the Charity Pairs games and the first rounds of Charity Knockout Teams.

In 1928 the major event of the ABL's "Winter Congress" was the Open Pairs played for the Cavendish Trophy. The Chicago Trophy (now the Reisinger) for the Board-a-Match Teams-of-Four was put in play in 1929. The Reisinger Teams and the Blue Ribbon Pairs (inaugurated in 1963) are the premier (six-session) events at the Fall NABC along with the North American Swiss Teams event which was added to the schedule in 1977. The four-session Life Master Women's Pairs, formerly held simultaneously with the Life Master Men's Pairs, has, since 1990, played opposite a new Life Master Open Pairs. The four-session Women's Board-a-Match Teams, formerly held simultaneously with the Men's Board-a-Match Teams, has, since 1990, played opposite an Open Board-a-Match Teams. For past results of Fall Championships, see Appendix I.

Fall North American Championships Attendance (an asterisk indicates the record was broken that year; table counts not available until 1952)

Year	Site	Tables
1927	Chicago	
1928	Cleveland	
1929	Chicago	
1930	Cleveland	
1931	Philadelphia	
1932	New York	
1933	Cincinnati	
1934	New York	
1935	Chicago	
1936	Chicago	
1937	Washington	
1938	Cleveland	
1939	Pittsburgh	
1940	Philadelphia	
1941	Richmond	
1942	Syracuse	
1943	New York	
1944	Atlantic City	
1945	Atlantic City	
1946	Hollywood FL	
1947	Atlantic City	
1948	Philadelphia	
1949	Philadelphia	
1950	New Orleans	
1951	Detroit	
1952	Miami	2,017
1953	Dallas	1,798
1954	Atlanta	1,775
1955	Miami	2,359*
1956	New Orleans	2,777*
1957	Los Angeles	6,154*
1958	Detroit	4,046
1959	Coronado CA	5,838
1960	New York City	6,391*
1961	Houston	4,967
1962	Phoenix	6,468*
1963	Bal Harbour FL	7,129*
1964	Dallas	8,686*
1965	San Francisco	11,198*
1966	Pittsburgh	8,896
1967	New Orleans	8,904
1968	Coronado CA	7,858
1969	Bal Harbour FL	9,069
1970	Houston	7,994
1971	Phoenix	7,080
1972	Lancaster PA	11,545*
1973	Las Vegas	13,464*
1974	San Antonio	8,419
1975	New Orleans	11,705
1976	Pittsburgh	8,787
1977	Atlanta	10,701
1978	Denver	9,467
1979	Cincinnati	9,262
1980	Lancaster PA	13,521*
1981	San Francisco	11,377
1982	Minneapolis	7,465
1983	Bal Harbour FL	10,555
1984	San Diego	12,072
1985	Winnipeg MB	5,534
1986	Atlanta	11,285
1987	Anaheim CA	13,948*
1988	Nashville	13,214
1989	Lancaster PA	12,580
1990	San Francisco	13,239
1991	Indianapolis	9,298
1992	Orlando FL	14,980*
1993	Seattle	11,456
1994	Minneapolis	7,181
1995	Atlanta	10,269
1996	San Francisco	12,894
1997	St. Louis	8,632
1998	Orlando	12,053
1999	Boston	12,531
2000	Birmingham	8,215

FALSECARD. A card played with the intention of deceiving the opposition.

Defenders normally play true cards in order to provide each other with information. The declarer, with no partner to worry about, is not obliged to play true cards, so for him there is no such thing as a falsecard.

Deceptive play by the declarer may extend to the conduct of the whole hand, whereas in practical play the defenders are usually limited to the play of a single falsecard to one trick. It is, therefore, convenient to treat the subject of deceptive play by the defenders under the title "Falsecarding," dealing with declarer play under the title DECEPTIVE PLAY.

The defenders' advantage

Although the defenders are usually restricted to the choice of a single card, rather than a complete tactical play, they have many more opportunities for skillful deception than the declarer. Consider this situation:

```
            K 7 3
  J 9 6 2          A Q 4
            10 8 5
```

East is the declarer, and clearly there is no way for him to bring in the suit without loss. If dummy's jack is led, North covers and South's 10 is promoted.

Now suppose instead that the declarer is South and that West is on lead. If West leads the jack, the declarer cannot be sure whether or not it is right to cover; he cannot see the defenders' cards. In the diagram, the king must be put on to make the 10 a guard; but it may turn out that West has made a clever play from the Q-J, the true position being:

```
            K 7 3
  Q J 9 2          A 6 4
            10 8 5
```

Now if the king is played on the first lead from West, East wins with the ace and returns the suit through South's 10♠ the defenders take all the tricks.

Suppose that in the second diagram the declarer is East once more, and that he again leads an honor from dummy. If North covers, he allows declarer all the tricks, but North has no difficulty in playing low; seeing the Q-J in dummy, he ducks the first lead, following the maxim that a defender should cover the last of touching honors - a complete answer to problems of this sort.

Clever falsecarding aims at exploiting the defenders' advantage in situations of that kind. Falsecarding is analyzed under these headings: DECEPTIVE OPENNG LEADS; FALSE SIGNALS; FALSECARDING IN THE MIDDLE OR END GAME; PLAYING A KNOWN CARD; RANDOM FALSECARDS WHICH CANNOT DECEIVE PARTNER; TRUMP SUIT FALSECARDING.

Playing a known card

A well-established principle of defensive play is that a defender in a critical position should play a card he is known to hold or will soon be known to hold, if he can do so without sacrificing a trick. Example:

```
            A J 5
  Q 10 3           8 6 2
            K 9 7 4
```

South leads low, finesses dummy's jack, and continues with ace and another. When the ace is played, West can follow suit with two cards of equal value, the queen and 10. He should play the card he is known to hold, the queen, offering declarer the possibility of finessing the 9 on the third round.

Such maneuvers are common in a keen game, even when the defender has no specific objective in mind.

```
            A K J 6
  Q 5 4            10 8 3 2
            9 7
```

South finesses dummy's jack. West should play the queen on the next round, for until he releases the queen, declarer knows that the suit cannot possibly be ruffed on his left. Similarly:

```
            A Q 7 5
  K J 10 3          8 6 4 2
            9
```

Playing a crossruff, South finesses dummy's queen and continues with ace and another, ruffing. Until West parts with the card he is known to hold, the king, declarer can safely ruff low.

More difficult to gauge is the early release of a high card whose position is not marked but soon will be.

```
            A K J 3 2
  Q 8 4            10 9 6 5
            7
```

At a trump contract, this is a side suit. South cashes the ace and ruffs a low card. West, who can see that his queen will fall under the king next, plays it on the second round, and South will think only three tricks are available.

It may be necessary to have a grasp of the strategy of the entire hand before this sort of play is safe.

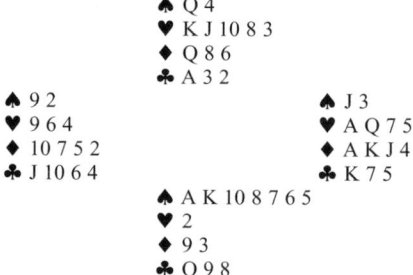

```
                ♠ Q 4
                ♥ K J 10 8 3
                ♦ Q 8 6
                ♣ A 3 2
  ♠ 9 2                      ♠ J 3
  ♥ 9 6 4                    ♥ A Q 7 5
  ♦ 10 7 5 2                 ♦ A K J 4
  ♣ J 10 6 4                 ♣ K 7 5
                ♠ A K 10 8 7 6 5
                ♥ 2
                ♦ 9 3
                ♣ Q 9 8
```

South plays in 4♠ after East has opened the bidding. Diamonds are led and South ruffs the third round. Needing to establish two heart tricks, he finesses dummy's 10.

East wins with the ace, not the queen, and returns a trump. East judges that declarer will expect him to have the ace for his opening bid, so if he wins the first trick with the queen, declarer will take a ruffing finesse against the ace on the next round and make his contract. After East's deceptive play of the ace, however, declarer may try to bring down the queen in West by ruffing the second round. If he tries that, shortage of entries prevents him from establishing a second heart trick.

The following hand illustrates a different reason for releasing a high card whose location will soon be known to the declarer.

```
                ♠ 7 5 3
                ♥ 7 2
                ♦ A Q J 8 6 3
                ♣ 6 5
  ♠ 10 8 6                   ♠ Q J 9
  ♥ A 10 8 6 3               ♥ Q 9 5
  ♦ K 10                     ♦ 9 7 2
  ♣ 8 7 2                    ♣ J 10 9 4
                ♠ A K 4 2
                ♥ K J 4
                ♦ 5 4
                ♣ A K Q 3
```

In a pairs contest, West leads a small heart against 3NT, and the queen is topped by the king. South returns a diamond, and West, knowing that his king is lost, plays it immediately. Now South has a problem, even if he knows West as a guileful player. If he takes the trick and it turns out that the king is singleton, he may take only nine tricks; by ducking, he could have won 11 tricks by establishing the long cards without letting East gain the lead.

Trump suit falsecarding

The suit combinations illustrated in the following can exist in any suit, whether trumps or not, but it is best to consider them as being trump. The fact that in every case the declarer has the majority of cards means that the suit usually will be trumps; also, the deceptive maneuvers require an exact appreciation of the layout of the suit, and in practical play this condition is seldom met unless the suit is trumps.

The essence of most of the following plays is that a falsecard is obligatory; failure to falsecard leaves declarer no option but to adopt the winning line of play. The falsecard presents him with the possibility of following an alternative line, which will lose. This type of falsecard is still purposeful even if the declarer is unlikely to fall into the trap set for him. Had the falsecard not been played, there would have been no possibility of declarer's going wrong; after the falsecard there is such a possibility, however slight.

```
        A J 8 3
K 2              10 9 6
        Q 7 5 4
```

South leads small and finesses dummy's jack. If East plays the 6, declarer has no choice but to play the ace on the next round, making all the tricks. If East plays the 9 or 10, declarer may enter the closed hand to lead the queen, which would be the winning play if East had 10-9 doubleton or a singleton.

There are some plays which appear dangerous at first sight but which in fact are obligatory if a high standard of play is assumed.

```
        A Q 6 2
4                K 10 8 3
        J 9 7 5
```

When declarer leads small and finesses dummy's queen, only the 8 from East offers hope of a second trick. If East wins with the king, the ace will be played on the next round, and a third-round finesse will pick up the suit. After the play of the 8, declarer may come to hand and lead the jack, which would be a good play if East held 10-8 alone, but costs a trick in the actual diagram. Following is one of many variations of the theme.

```
        K Q 9 4
10 8 6 3         A
        J 7 5 2
```

Unless West plays the 8 when a low trump is led toward dummy's king, he has no chance of a second trick.

Many falsecarding positions are associated with the holding of J-9 doubleton and related holdings:

```
        Q 8 3
A 7 6            J 9
        K 10 5 4 2
```

South attacks this suit by leading low from dummy. East follows with the jack, and South's king loses to West's ace. South is likely to finesse the 8 next, playing West for A-9-7-6.

```
        K 8 3
7 6 5            A J 9
        Q 10 4 2
```

If South leads low from dummy, East may gain by playing the jack.

This next position also has variations:

```
        J 9 3
8 5 4            Q 10
        A K 7 6 2
```

Whether South lays down the ace from hand or leads the 3 from dummy, East can probably read the position well enough to gauge that it is safe to drop the queen.

The following play is liable to score:

```
        Q 2
J 10             A 7 3
        K 9 8 6 5 4
```

When South leads small to the queen, East ducks smoothly and the declarer probably continues by finessing the 9 in his own hand. Had East taken the queen with the ace, South would have played to drop the jack on the next round, recognizing that there would be no purpose in finessing against A-J-7-3 in East's hand. A similar position:

```
         7
J 10 6           A 5
        K Q 9 8 4 3 2
```

Dummy's 7 is led and the king wins. Unless West plays the 10 or jack, declarer has no choice but to lead a low card to the next trick.

Many falsecards have a better chance of succeeding in a pairs contest, where declarers are willing to take measured risks for an extra trick.

```
        J 8 6 2
Q 10 9 5          3
        A K 7 4
```

When South plays the ace, West drops the 9 or 10. If declarer can afford to lose one trick, he does best to play small toward the jack, which preserves the position against any lie of the defenders' cards, but in a pairs contest he may decide instead to cross to dummy and lead the jack. This is equally safe against four cards in East's hand, and nets a big matchpoint score if West holds 10-9 alone.

Occasionally it is possible to forestall these defensive wiles.

```
        Q 8 4 2
 3               J 9 6 5
        A K 10 7
```

When declarer plays the ace from hand, the standard falsecard for East is the 9. If he fails to play the 9, declarer is bound to continue by leading toward the queen, discovering the finesse against the jack. After the play of the 9, declarer may continue with the king from hand, with the idea of finessing against West if he has J-6-5-3.

Entries permitting, declarer in the above situation should make the first lead from dummy. Now it is dangerous for East to drop the 9, for partner could have the singleton 10.

There is another type of falsecard which, though not occurring in the trump suit, is associated with suit contracts. This is the play of a high card perhaps setting up winners for declarer - to dissuade declarer from following a line of play which the defender knows must win. A bold player may sacrifice a high card in this way even though he may be unable to en-

visage the likely effect; it is sufficient for him that the declarer must be deflected from the course which he has apparently set. A classic hand of this kind was defended by the British player, Terence Reese, in his Oxford days.

```
            ♠ Q 9 6 3
            ♥ K J 5
            ♦ 9 7 4 2
            ♣ J 3
♠ J 10 4                      ♠ 5
♥ Q 8 7 2                     ♥ 10 4 3
♦ A K J                       ♦ 10 8 6 5 3
♣ 8 5 4                       ♣ Q 9 6 2
            ♠ A K 8 7 2
            ♥ A 9 6
            ♦ Q
            ♣ A K 10 7
```

West led diamonds against South's 6♠ contract.

South ruffed the second round and played three rounds of clubs, ruffing in dummy. Since it was evident that the fourth club could be ruffed with impunity, Reese dropped the queen on the third round.

The declarer continued with the ♠Q-A. When East showed out on the second trump, it appeared safe to lead the ♣10, intending to discard a heart in dummy and subsequently ruff a heart. However, West made his trump jack to defeat a contract that would have been made routinely had East not falsecarded.

Random falsecards which cannot deceive partner

The previous situations have been mainly those where an immediate purpose could be discerned. There are, however, situations where it is permissible for a defender to falsecard with the more general aim of harrying the declarer and spoiling his count of the hand. The most common is where declarer has shown out of a suit. Since both defenders know the exact distribution of the suit, they may falsecard with no specific aim in mind.

Falsecards of that type are more effective if made before declarer actually shows out of the suit, since he is then more inclined to take them at face value.

```
            ♠ K 10 7
            ♥ A 5
            ♦ K 4 3 2
            ♣ 10 8 6 5
♠ Q 9 8                       ♠ 6 5 3 2
♥ Q 10 4 3                    ♥ J 6 2
♦ 9 5                         ♦ J 6
♣ J 9 7 3                     ♣ A K Q 2
            ♠ A J 4
            ♥ K 9 8 7
            ♦ A Q 10 8 7
            ♣ 4
```

South plays 6♦ after East has dealt and passed. When West leads the ♣3, East falsecards, winning with the king rather than the queen. Declarer ruffs the ace, and has to guess the spade position to make his contract. Had East won the opening lead with the queen, South would have reflected (after finding the red jacks in East) that East might have opened the bidding had he held the ♠Q and 13 points in all.

False Signals

The defenders labor under the disadvantage that most of their signals are sent "in clear" and so are liable to enemy interception. On a hand like the following, the declarer's task is easier if his opponents are known as conscientious signalers.

```
            ♠ 8 7
            ♥ K 8 7 5 4
            ♦ 8 6 2
            ♣ A 9 5

            ♠ A K Q 10 6 5
            ♥ A 2
            ♦ A Q J
            ♣ K 7
```

South plays 6♠ in a pairs contest. Having won the club lead with the king and drawn trumps, South's problem is whether to try to ruff out the hearts for two discards or to finesse diamonds; shortage of entries means that he cannot try both. But, if the defenders echo to show two or four cards, declarer knows what to do after playing ace and another heart.

Best results are obtained by defenders who keep up with the game and at a given time are conscious whether a false signal could mislead partner. Very often it can be recognized that partner will not be misled. In such cases, defenders should vary their signals between true and falsecards rather than try to outsmart the declarer.

False signals can be used to persuade the declarer to ruff unnecessarily, or to ruff high, in a critical trump situation.

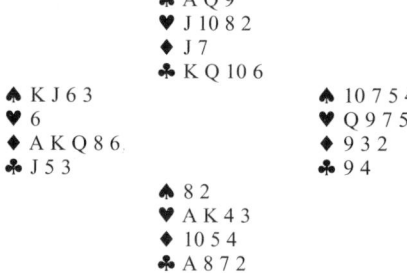

```
            ♠ A Q 9
            ♥ J 10 8 2
            ♦ J 7
            ♣ K Q 10 6
♠ K J 6 3                     ♠ 10 7 5 4
♥ 6                           ♥ Q 9 7 5
♦ A K Q 8 6                   ♦ 9 3 2
♣ J 5 3                       ♣ 9 4
            ♠ 8 2
            ♥ A K 4 3
            ♦ 10 5 4
            ♣ A 8 7 2
```

South plays 4♥ after West has opened 1♦. On the ♦A-K, East echoes with the 9 and 2. Since it is quite possible that East has a doubleton diamond, declarer may judge to ruff with the 10 when West plays the third round. If he does so, he loses two trump tricks instead of one.

A defender must occasionally falsecard his partner to direct the defense.

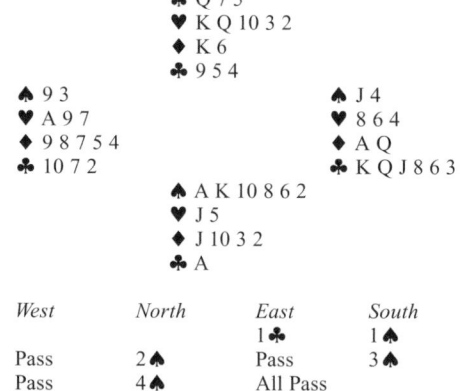

```
            ♠ Q 7 5
            ♥ K Q 10 3 2
            ♦ K 6
            ♣ 9 5 4
♠ 9 3                         ♠ J 4
♥ A 9 7                       ♥ 8 6 4
♦ 9 8 7 5 4                   ♦ A Q
♣ 10 7 2                      ♣ K Q J 8 6 3
            ♠ A K 10 8 6 2
            ♥ J 5
            ♦ J 10 3 2
            ♣ A
```

West	North	East	South
		1♣	1♠
Pass	2♠	Pass	3♠
Pass	4♠	All Pass	

West leads the ♣2. East can see that his defense is moot unless West has a trump trick or the ♥A. Even

then, West must shift to diamonds. East therefore plays the ♣K at the first trick, denying the queen. When West takes the ♥A, he should find the diamond switch.

Deceptive Opening Leads

Defenders should seldom depart from the accepted conventional leads. To underlead an ace against a suit contract, or to lead an honor from the middle of a sequence, may score on a particular hand, but if it is done frequently, the loss in partnership accuracy and confidence will outweigh the gain thus made.

Because that is generally recognized as true, the occasional deceptive lead can be all the more effective. Some leads, such as the jack from Q-J doubleton, are so well known as to lack any element of surprise. The following is also far from fresh:

```
                 J 6 4
      10 9 2                  Q 3
               A K 8 7 5
```

Left to himself, the declarer loses no tricks in this trump suit when he plays to drop the doubleton queen. Some authorities have commended the opening lead of the 9, the theory being that declarer may put on the jack and play East for Q-10-3-2 or Q-10-x.

Declarer's protection against being duped too often is the knowledge that a good defender seldom leads a trump other than his lowest. To lead the 9 from 9-2, for example, can never gain as compared with leading the 2, and can cost in more than one way. Since most defenders are averse to leading a singleton trump, the declarer should look suspiciously at the lead of a 9 or card of similar rank; particularly when, as in the preceding diagram, he himself holds the card of next lower rank, and knows that the card led cannot be the top of a sequence.

The deceptive lead of fifth-best instead of fourth-best against notrump is a more persuasive maneuver. It is likely to gain in many situations like the following:

```
                    ♠ K 9 8
                    ♥ Q 6
                    ♦ J 10 3 2
                    ♣ K Q 8 5
   ♠ A 5                          ♠ J 10 7 6 3
   ♥ A 10 8 4 2                   ♥ 9 7 5
   ♦ K 9 6                        ♦ 5 4
   ♣ J 9 3                        ♣ 10 6 2
                    ♠ Q 4 2
                    ♥ K J 3
                    ♦ A Q 8 7
                    ♣ A 7 4
```

West's own wealth of high cards makes it unlikely that his partner can contribute to the defense, so he leads the ♥2 against 3NT. Dummy wins, the ♦J runs to West's king, and a small heart comes back. Declarer cashes his diamonds, and both defenders discard spades. Now South has to decide whether to set up a spade or to seek his ninth trick in clubs. After cashing two rounds of clubs he is none the wiser and, taking the opening lead at its face value, he may think that hearts are 4-4 and that it is safe to play a spade.

No less effective is the lead of third-best in an attempt to create the impression that a five-card suit is held. This is the other side of the picture from the previous deal:

```
                    ♠ Q 10 9
                    ♥ Q 6 2
                    ♦ A K 6
                    ♣ Q 9 7 5
   ♠ A 7 3 2                      ♠ 8 5 4
   ♥ A 9                          ♥ 7 5 4 3
   ♦ J 10 5 3                     ♦ 7 4
   ♣ A 8 4                        ♣ J 6 3 2
                    ♠ K J 6
                    ♥ K J 10 8
                    ♦ Q 9 8 2
                    ♣ K 10
```

Again West knows that partner has little to fight with, so he leads the ♠3 against South's 3NT contract. After driving out the ♥A and receiving the return of the ♠2, South has only eight tricks, and has to decide whether to play a club or test diamonds. If he knew West had only four spades, he could safely play a club. After the deceptive lead, however, he may decide to try for the diamond break, in which case he establishes the setting trick for the defenders.

Other opportunities for a deceptive lead are sometimes missed. Suppose the declarer in a notrump contract opened the bidding with 1NT, and subsequently showed a spade suit in response to Stayman. Since both defenders know declarer has precisely four spades, there is no reason why the defender, if he decides to open up the suit, should give declarer free information by leading a conventional fourth-best; he can simply lead his lowest card.

Falsecarding in the Middle or End Game

In the middle game, it is possible for both defenders to know the exact lie of the cards while declarer is still in doubt. When this is the case, defenders can deceive declarer without deceiving each other.

The position illustrated under the heading *The Defenders' Advantage* is a basic one to which there are many variations. Example:

```
                 K 7 3
      A Q 8                  J 9 6 2
               10 5 4
```

Judging in the middle game that three tricks are needed from this suit, West leads the queen followed by the 8. Declarer may duck twice, playing him for Q-J.

```
                 A J 9 4
      Q 10 5                  K 8 6
               7 3 2
```

South leads low, intending to follow the percentages by finessing the 9 the first time and the jack the second. By putting up the queen, West may persuade declarer that he has the king as well, and deflect him from his course. Similar positions arise when West is on lead:

```
                 J 9 6
      K 10 5 2                  Q 8 3
               A 7 4
```

If circumstances compel West to open this suit, the king is the card. Conversely, in a position such as the following, it may be best to lead small:

```
                 J 9 7
      K Q 3                  10 6 5 2
               A 8 4
```

In the end game there are occasions when a desperate lead offers the only hope of escaping from an elimination.

```
                 A 9 7
      Q 8 2                  J 6 4 3
               K 10 5
```

If South has staged an elimination which compels West to open this suit, the queen is best, offering declarer the possibility of winning in hand and finessing against the jack. If West leads small instead, declarer can play only for split honors. Similarly:

```
                    Q 9 7
        J 8 4                   K 10 6 2
                    A 5 3
```

If West leads small, declarer may play low in dummy and capture the 10 with the ace; on the next round he probably finesses the 9. If West leads the jack on the first round, declarer may cover on the assumption that the 9 sits behind the 10.

Suppose that in the above example the declarer is on lead, and plays small toward the table. Suppose also that East is marked with the king, and the declarer intends to insert dummy's 9, forcing East to lead away from the king or concede a ruff-sluff. On South's lead, West puts in the jack to make it appear that he has the 10 as well, in which case declarer's play would be to duck in dummy.

For declarer's counter-weapon, see DECEPTION, MATHEMATICS OF. See also *Deceptive Play at Bridge* by Hugh Kelsey; *Falsecards* by Mike Lawrence; *Step by Step Guide to Deception* by Barry Rigal.

FALSE PREFERENCE. A return to partner's original suit at the lowest level when holding greater length in the second suit. See PREFERENCE BIDS.

FAMILY. Perhaps the biggest, greatest and most successful family in bridge is the family anchored by Gail Greenberg of New York City. A World Grand Master, Greenberg is a four-time world champion. Her daughter, Jill Blanchard, also is a world champion – she won the Women's Team Olympiad in 1996. Her son, Brad Moss, is a winner at the ACBL national level and was named King of Bridge in 1989. Another son, Andrew Moss, was King of Bridge in 1991. Her second husband, Mike Moss, finished second in the 1990 Rosenblum Teams. Jack Greenberg, her present husband, and Steve Shane, her first husband, also have performed well at the North American level.

Another family with two world champions is the Becker family. B.Jay Becker was on the winning Bermuda Bowl team in 1951 and 1953, and he was second in 1958 and 1965. His son Michael was a Bermuda Bowl victor in 1983. Father and son were both on the American team in the 1973 Bermuda Bowl, but this team did not qualify for the final. Anoather son, Steve, has been successful in North American events, and he also was executive editor of the *Bridge Bulletin* from 1969-1972. Michael's wife Judy has an NABC victory to her credit. His brother Simon also was an outstanding player.

The Hamman family also has two world champions. Bob Hamman, rated by the WBF as the top bridge player in the world, has nine world championships under his belt. His wife Petra won the Women's Team Olympiad in 2000. Hamman's first wife, Barbara, won Women's KO Teams in 1985. His son Chris has won several regionals.

The Seamon family also has a proud history. The late William Seamon and his sister, the late Anne Burnstein, both had outstanding records in NABC events. Edith Freilich, their sister, has won North American championships in each of six different decades. Seamon's daughter, Janice Seamon-Molson, is one of the leading American women players, and her husband, Mark Molson, finished second in the 1995 Bermuda Bowl. His son, Michael Seamon, has been among the leading American players for many years. His wife Rita also has won her share of major events.

The Schaltzes of Denmark are a successful three-generation family. Lizzie Schaltz won the European Women's Teams in 1955. Her son Peter and Peter's wife Dorthe regularly represent Denmark in international competition – Dorthe won the Women's Team Olympiad in 1988. In 2000 his son, Martin, aged 14, received an IBPA award for the best play by a Junior. Peter had many early successes playing with his cousin Knud-Aage Boesgaard.

The Jacoby family boasted two of the finest players ever to play in North America. Oswald, the father, was an original member of the Four Aces and was a prolific winner on the North American circuit. His son Jim won three world championships – two Bermuda Bowls and a Team Olympiad. Oswald's wife Mary Zita and Jim's wife Judy both earned Life Master status.

The three Hsieh brothers – David, Bill and Doug — all became Life Masters while in their teens and while playing primarily with their father George. Bill, the 1983 King of Bridge, became a Life Master at age 13, and Doug got his gold card when he was only 11.

Ralph Cohen, former CEO of the ACBL, has won several NABC championships, as has his son Bill. Ralph has represented both his native Canada and the United States in world competition. His wife Joan, his son Jordan and Jordan's wife Fran are all Life Masters.

The Cappellettis and the Pavliceks also have powerful father-son combinations. Both Mike Sr. and Mike Jr. have put the Cappellettis at the top of NABC standings, as have Richard Sr. and Richard Jr. for the Pavliceks. Mike Sr.'s first wife, now Kathie Walvick, and his present wife, Susan Green, both have won North American titles. Richard Sr.'s wife Mabel is a Gold Life Master.

Joel Wooldridge, one of the youngest players ever to become a Life Master, and his mother Jill were a strong combination during Joel's teen and pre-teen years. Joel became a Life Master at age 11. Sam Hirschman, the 1994 King of Bridge, was the youngest Life Master prior to Wooldridge. Marty Hirschman, his father, a fine player, spent years working with Sam and his brother Dan, who won his first regional at the age of 9 and later became the ACBL's youngest Life Master at the age of 10. His mother, Marcy Abramson, also is a Life Master.

Steve Weinstein, one of America's top players, had many early successes playing with his stepfather, Fred Stewart. They won the Life Master Pairs in 1981 when Weinstein was only 17 – he was the youngest player ever to win an NABC.

The Kasle family includes Gaylor, one of the leading masterpoint winners of all time; his wife Barbara, a Gold Life Master; his mother Lee, a North American champion in 1959, and his father Sidney, Life Master #525.

The Hackett trio – Paul Hackett and his twin sons, Jason and Justin, play regularly on the world circuit with major success. Jason and Justin were members of the Great Britain team that won the World Junior Championship in 1995.

Other significant families are: the Gardeners of Great Britain, Nico and daughter Nicola Smith; the Bianchis and Valentis of Italy; Peter Gill and sister Barbara Travis of Australia and the Passells of the United States.

FAMOUS HANDS. This was the most dramatic hand of the 1975 Bermuda Bowl final between Italy and North America, perhaps the most dramatic of the century – Board 92 of the 96-board match. It was already known that no big swing was likely on the final four deals, and Italy was ahead by 13. As soon as the deal was flashed on the vugraph screen, everyone realized the huge potential for a swing.

Board 92. Dealer West. E/W vul.

```
                ♠ A K 10 9
                ♥ —
                ♦ A 9 7
                ♣ J 9 8 6 3 2
   ♠ 4 3                        ♠ 7 6 5 2
   ♥ Q 10 8 7                   ♥ K 4 3 2
   ♦ Q 10 6 4                   ♦ J 5 3
   ♣ 7 5 4                      ♣ K 10
                ♠ Q J 8
                ♥ A J 9 6 5
                ♦ K 8 2
                ♣ A Q
```

Closed Room bidding:

West	North	East	South
Franco	Hamman	Pittala	Wolff
Pass	1♠	Pass	2♥
Pass	3♣	Pass	4NT
Pass	5♥	Pass	6NT
All Pass			

Bidding on vugraph:

Eisenberg	Belladonna	Kantar	Garozzo
Pass	2♣	Pass	2♦
Pass	2♠	Pass	3♥
Pass	3NT	Pass	4♣
Pass	4♦	Pass	4NT
Pass	5♦	Pass	5♥
Dbl	Redbl	Pass	5♠
Pass	5NT	Pass	7♣
All Pass			

Writeups of this hand have appeared in just about every major bridge periodical in the world. The vugraph room was a cauldron of tension as the 31 calls were written on the screen. When the involved sequence was closed by the grand slam bid, there was an audible gasp from the 700 in attendance, then a wild cheer from the predominantly pro-Italian audience.

When the king-10 of clubs appeared onside, and when Kantar failed to falsecard the king, Belladonna had no trouble bringing home the slam — and with it the world championship. The Italians gained 12 IMPs to win, 214-189. However, if the club position had been different — or if Kantar had falsecarded and Belladonna had gone for it — North America would have been the world champion instead. In subsequent interviews, Belladonna stated that he would have played for a 4-1 split if Kantar had falsecarded with the king at his first turn.

North America led by 68 IMPs against Pakistan in the 1981 Bermuda Bowl final when along came this deal, which featured an incredible swing that depended on the opening lead.

Board 72. Dealer West. None vul.

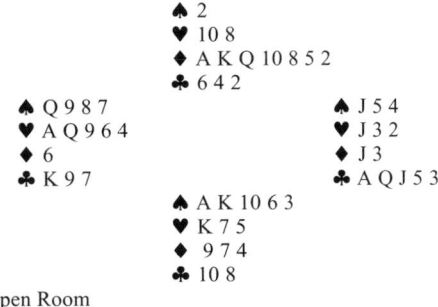

```
                ♠ 2
                ♥ 10 8
                ♦ A K Q 10 8 5 2
                ♣ 6 4 2
   ♠ Q 9 8 7                    ♠ J 5 4
   ♥ A Q 9 6 4                  ♥ J 3 2
   ♦ 6                          ♦ J 3
   ♣ K 9 7                      ♣ A Q J 5 3
                ♠ A K 10 6 3
                ♥ K 7 5
                ♦ 9 7 4
                ♣ 10 8
```

Open Room

West	North	East	South
Solodar	Masood	Levin	Zia
2♦ (1)	Pass	2♠	Pass
Pass	3♦	3♥	Pass
Pass	4♦	All Pass	

(1) Four spades, five hearts, 12-17 HCP.

Levin had a virtually automatic trump lead on the auction. This gave Masood a chance to pitch a heart on the second high spade, and after drawing trumps he was able to ruff his third club. Just making.

Closed Room

West	North	East	South
Munir	Meckstroth	Fazli	Rodwell
1♥	3♥ (1)	Dbl	3NT
Pass	Pass	Dbl	Pass
Pass	Redbl (2)	Pass	Pass (3)
Pass			

(1) Asks partner to bid 3NT if he has hearts stopped.
(2) SOS showing strong doubts about 3NT.
(3) "I think my chances of making 3NT are good."

A heart lead would mean 950 (13 IMPs) for Pakistan, but no one expected Munir to lead a heart. His real choices were the black suits. A spade would mean minus 750 (12 IMPs), but a club would lead to *ten* tricks for the defense for plus 2200 and 20 precious IMPs. But there was much more riding on the opening lead. Meckstroth and Rodwell had been getting away with murder throughout the match, but a 2200-point penalty would surely take some wind out of their sails.

But Munir led a spade. Rodwell took Fazli's jack with the king and cashed the spade ace. Then he ran the diamonds, but the defenders kept the right cards and Rodwell settled for nine tricks!

Munir describes his thoughts about this deal in India's *Bridge Digest*:

"…Conscious that an enormous number of points hung on the lead I took time to think matters over. What would partner's first-round pass followed by a later double show? How does that differ from the situation where partner has doubled both 3♥ and 3NT? What conclusions could I draw from South's *pass* of the SOS redouble?

"If partner had passed 3♥ and then doubled 3NT, I would have treated that as a Lightner type asking for a surprise lead. The double of 3♥ clearly showed some heart support and the subsequent double must guarantee at least a black ace, with or without a good suit. It was too much to hope the opponents had gone mad and partner had a diamond stopper. In the circumstances I decided one lead through South would enable us to run the hearts and I concentrated on trying to work out which black ace partner held. If South held stoppers in both black suits then partner held the spade ace and declarer the club ace and the spade king.

So I led a spade and Rodwell was +750. If I had led a club we would have been +2200. I now know how Bob Hamman must have felt in the last Olympiad when he had to choose which ace to lead against a grand slam and chose the wrong one!"

This is the deal Masood was talking about. It was the key deal against France in 1980 World Team Olympiad in Valkenburg, the Netherlands. The French were the victors, in good part due to the 19-IMP swing on this deal.

Board 52
Dlr: West
Vul: Both

```
                    ♠ 10
                    ♥ K Q 9
                    ♦ A 10 9 8 3 2
                    ♣ K 9 8
  ♠ Q 9 5 3 2                      ♠ A K J 8 7 6
  ♥ J 8 5 4                        ♥ A 10 7 6 3 2
  ♦ Q 6 4                          ♦ —
  ♣ 7                              ♣ 2
                    ♠ 4
                    ♥ —
                    ♦ K J 7 5
                    ♣ A Q J 10 6 5 4 3
```

Open Room

West	North	East	South
Perron	Rubin	Lebel	Soloway
Pass	1 ♦	1 ♠	2 ♣
4 ♠	Pass	5 ♣	6 ♣
Pass	Pass	6 ♠	Dbl
All Pass			

The auction started quietly enough, but Perron's leap to 4 ♦ added some impetus. Rubin's pass was forcing and Lebel chose to make his slam try in clubs, a cunning psychological ploy. Soloway bid what he thought he could make, and Lebel bid the 6 ♠ he was always going to bid. Soloway knew he was playing with fire when he doubled – 6 ♠ might easily be frigid if he guessed the wrong opening lead or if he didn't get his heart ruff. However, he was unwilling to take out unilateral insurance and he couldn't very well *invite* the grand by passing with a spade loser. As it happened, this was the par spot.

Soloway could have arranged a third defensive trick by underleading his ♣ A for a heart ruff, but this was a real shot, particularly given Lebel's club cuebid. Soloway tried a diamond and raised his eyebrows (behind the screen) when Lebel ruffed. Lebel drew trumps and led a low heart out of his hand, holding his losers to one in that suit. Rubin ducked the ♥ J but when forced to take his heart trick, he cashed the king for one down.

Closed Room

West	North	East	South
Wolff	Mari	Hamman	Chemla
Pass	1 ♦	2 ♦	2 ♥
4 ♠	4NT	5 ♠	6 ♣
Pass	6 ♦	6 ♠	7 ♦
Pass	Pass	Dbl	All Pass

Hamman tried Michaels, and Chemla cuebid to show his diamond fit. After Wolff leaped to 4 ♠, Mari tried 4NT to show his strong hand. Hamman sandbagged with 5 ♠, hoping to buy the contract at the six-level. Chemla brought out his secret weapon and Mari converted 6 ♣ to 6 ♦, the agreed trump suit. Hamman followed through with 6 ♠ as planned and this put Chemla on the spot. Since he had a shrewd idea about Hamman's devious approach, he was unwilling to double and collect what promised to be a small penalty at best and an unbearable tragedy at worst. Besides, if he bid the grand, Hamman might

be *forced* to save, or he might guess the wrong lead.

Hamman, like Soloway, knew his position was precarious, but he too was unwilling to take out unilateral insurance when his opponents were guessing at the seven-level. He doubled!

But what to lead? If Chemla's cuebid and Mari's 4NT were truthful, the ♠ A would live; but look at the Open Room -singletons are sometimes cuebid! In *Le Bridgeur* Chemla was quoted as being sure Hamman would double and might well misguess the lead. The French rated to hold more spades than hearts, so the ♥ A seemed safer. It wasn't. Mari ruffed in dummy, found the trump queen and claimed for 19 IMPs.

FAST ARRIVAL. The idea that the faster a contract is reached, the weaker the hand that places the contract; and, conversely, the slower the approach, the stronger the suggestion that a higher contract may be appropriate.

(a)		(b)	
West	East	West	East
1 ♠	2 ♣	1 ♠	2 ♣
2 ♠	4 ♠	2 ♠	3 ♦
		3NT	4 ♠

East's bidding is more encouraging in (b) than in (a).

For decades, constructive bidding was based on the idea that the better your hand, the higher you bid. In the Fifties and Sixties, a minimum-bidding style arose that espoused slow, scientific investigation for the best contract. The principle of Fast Arrival was a logical product of this style. Since jumps to game left less room for slam investigation, they implied an absence of slammish values and discouraged more bidding.

The significance of the two auctions above is indisputable, but the implications of other auctions are less clear and a matter for partnership discussion.

West	East
1 ♥	2 ♦
2 ♠	4 ♠

After East's response at the two-level and West's reverse, East-West are assured of game. In the classical approach, East's raise to 4 ♠ promises excellent spade support and willingness to hear West bid again. In Fast Arrival, East's 4 ♠ promises minimum values, trumps that may be only fair and no slam aspirations. If East wanted to leave room for slam investigation, he would raise to 3 ♠.

West	East
1 ♥	2 ♦
2 ♠	3 ♠

In the classical approach, East promises spade support, but the rest of his hand is not clearly defined. Using Fast Arrival, East implies interest in slam.

Though Fast Arrival often shows to advantage, a jump bid may be needed to emphasize a crucial feature. For example, trump quality is a major factor in slam bidding, and a jump in trumps should promise strong support.

West	East
♠ A 9 4	♠ J 10 8 7
♥ A	♥ K 9 5 4
♦ A Q J 9 4	♦ K 10 8 2
♣ A 9 7 3	♣ K
1 ♦	1 ♥
3 ♣	3 ♦
3 ♠	4 ♣
4 ♦	5 ♦
Pass	

This auction occurred in a U.S. Team Trials. At the other three tables, East followed his first response with a jump preference in diamonds, promising strong support, and reached the excellent slam.

Fast Arrival auctions also sustain a loss when they end in the wrong contract.

	West	East
	♠ A 8 5	♠ J 6 3
	♥ J 9 6 4 2	♥ A 7 3
	♦ A Q 5	♦ K 10 9 6 2
	♣ K 2	♣ A 7

Table 1

West	East
1♥	2♦
2NT	4♥

Table 2

West	East
1♥	2♦
2NT	3♥
3NT	

The auction at Table 1 was Fast Arrival. A spade opening lead sank 4♥, while 3NT made at Table 2. However, the BWS2001 consensus was for SLOW ARRIVAL. Fast arrival is an integral part of some conventions. However, it should not be assumed without partnership agreement.

See an article in the *The Bridge World*, Dec. 1978. See also TWO OVER ONE GAME FORCE.

FAST PAIRS. The speed of play is increased by a major factor. Instead of the usual seven to eight minutes allowed to play each board, the game is set up so that boards must be completed in five minutes. Sometimes this permits more boards to be played; more often this type of game results in a game finishing at an earlier time. Such a game often is called SPEEDBALL PAIRS.

FAST PASS. A lightning action which may improperly and unethically convey weakness. The prevention of a fast pass is one of the reasons for the SKIP-BID WARNING. See also RHYTHM.

FAVORABLE VULNERABILITY. Not vulnerable against vulnerable. Since penalties are smaller, there are more opportunities for competitive bidding and sacrifices. Preempts are much more likely to prove effective. See EQUAL VULNERABILITY, UNFAVORABLE VULNERABILITY.

FEATURE, FEATURE SHOWING. A feature is a particular holding of an ace or king (occasionally a queen) which may be of particular importance in a given hand. Showing of features in a hand through the bidding commences only when a suit is agreed on and a game is assured. Among the conventions that are in common use to determine features are ACE-SHOWING RESPONSES, ASKING BIDS, GERBER, BLACKWOOD, and other 4NT bids, the GRAND SLAM FORCE, CUEBIDS, and various combinations or modifications thereof. See also WEAK TWO-BIDS.

FEDERATION, FEDERACION, FEDERAÇÃO. See country name in Section II.

FERT. The weak opening in STRONG PASS systems, called a "bid of misery" by Edgar Kaplan. Fert is short for "fertilizer," which describes this type of bid quite

graphically. The usual range is 0-7, and a variety of one-level suit-bids are used. A major-suit fert is more risky than a minor-suit fert, but more difficult to handle.

A fert at unfavorable vulnerability is decidedly risky, but only if the opponents are prepared to take advantage of it. They must decide whether action over a strong pass is equivalent to an overcall or an opening bid. If the former, it is possible to make an "overcall" of one club. One aggressive counter-measure is fert over fert: A minimum suit bid announces that the next player has a fert range. This allows him to pass with moderate balanced hands and double with strong hands, maximizing the chance of emerging with a big penalty. Some fert users therefore abandon them at unfavorable vulnerability.

The fert causes great confusion for the opponents, who seldom get an opportunity for a normal constructive auction. But the purpose is not simply destructive: The strong pass gains a step when compared with a strong club method. See WEAK OPENING SYSTEMS.

FIBONACCI NUMBERS. The number of items of information (different distributions, for example) that can be shown with efficient (usually highly artificial) relays and responses, in any given bidding space, is always a Fibonacci number. Fibonacci numbers are members of this sequence:

$$1, 1, 2, 3, 5, 8, 13, 21, 34, 55, 89, 144...$$

Each number is the sum of the previous two numbers.

If you have a bidding space of ten bids (1♣ through 2NT, for example), then the total number of items of information that can be shown by relays is 55, the tenth Fibonacci number.

This kind of information can help you modify your relay structure. It can help you decide if you should improve the efficiency of the relay structure.

If you would gain only one bid, you may not want to increase the number of artificial bids to improve efficiency. But if the bid you would gain keeps you under game, you may want to improve the efficiency. This information can also help you decide if you should try to pack more information into the same bidding space. It may even indicate that it is impossible to show the information that you want to show in the available bidding space.

FICTION. See LITERATURE AND BRIDGE.

FIELD. All the players entered in an event.

FIELD REPRESENTATIVE. An ACBL tournament director assigned to supervise bridge activity at the tournament and club level in one of the ACBL's seven areas.

FIELDING A PSYCHIC. An abnormal or unexpected action by the partner of a psychic bidder which protects the partnership and makes it appear that the player is aware of the psychic before it can legitimately be shown to have been exposed by the course of events. For example:

South	West	North	East
1♠	Pass	2♥	3♦
Pass	Pass	Pass	

If South has opened with a psychic bid and North has 12 points, the psychic has been fielded and the partner

will face action by a director and perhaps a committee. But if East does not act and South passes, the psychic has been exposed and North can take any action he pleases. See PSYCHIC BIDDING.

FIFTEEN TABLES. At duplicate, 15 tables provide for competition among 60 players, 30 pairs, or 15 teams-of-four. It is a very good movement for 15 teams-of-four for board-a-match. It is inconvenient for 15 tables of Swiss Teams, requiring one three-way match each round to solve the odd number problem.

As an Individual tournament, a group of 60 players used to be extremely awkward. The movement usually used was a 52-player RAINBOW with a double appendix. However, Tournament Director Maury Braunstein devised a movement that allows for 26 boards to be played in 13 rounds, with a top of 12. The movement through most rounds is similar to that used in other Individuals: South up one table, East up two tables, West down two tables, boards down one table, North stationary. After Rounds 5 and 7, East and West skip an extra table. After Round 12, South, West, East and the boards all move an extra table. If hand record duplication is used, the duplication round is counted as the first round and only 24 boards are played, with a top of 11. This duplication round counts as a playing round as far as the irregular moves are concerned.

As a pair game, a MITCHELL, either straight or scrambled is used. There are guide cards available for treating 14 to 20 tables as appendix movements using only 26 boards. This is standard in many countries where direct comparison on all the boards in play is desired. It is also sometimes used as the last session of multi-session events, although twinned seven-, eight-, or nine-table sections give comparable results with proper seeding of the sections.

In a team game, 28 boards are required to complete the movement. When 24 boards are desired, either the middle two, or the first and last rounds, can be omitted.

For 14½ or15½ tables see HALF TABLE MOVEMENTS.

FIFTH ACE. See KEY CARD BLACKWOOD and ROMAN KEY CARD BLACKWOOD.

FIFTH CHAIR TROPHY. Awarded to the winners of the NORTH AMERICAN FORTY-NINER PAIRS. See FIFTH CHAIR.

FIFTH HONOR. The ten-spot of the trump suit.

FILO. See DEFENSE TO OPENING THREE BIDS.

FINAL BID. The last bid in the auction, followed by three consecutive passes. There can be no further bidding. The final bid becomes the contract.

FINESSE. The attempt to gain power for lower-ranking cards by taking advantage of the favorable position of higher-ranking cards held by the opposition.
The most common uses of the finesse are:
(1) *To avoid losing a trick.*

♣ A Q

♣ 3 2

South cannot afford to lose a club trick. He therefore leads a club to North's queen, finessing against the king. If West has the king, the queen will win, and South will avoid a club loser.

♠ Q 10 6 2
♠ J 9 3   ♠ K 8 7 5
♠ A 4

West leads the ♠ 3, and South must avoid a spade loser. If South reads the position correctly, he will play the ♠ 10 from dummy, finessing against the ♠ J. This enables South to avoid a spade loser.
(2) *To gain a trick with low-ranking cards*

♥ A 3 2

♥ Q 6 5

Needing two heart tricks, South cashes North's ace and leads toward his queen. If East holds the king, the queen will score a trick for South.

♦ Q 3 2

♦ 7 6 5

South needs one diamond trick. His best chance is to find West with both the A-K. He therefore leads toward the queen in the North hand.
(3)*To prepare for a second finesse in the same suit.* A finesse can often be used to create a second finesse. When this is done successfully, the second finesse usually results in the direct gain of a trick.

♣ A J 10

♣ 4 3 2

Needing two club tricks, South leads low to dummy's 10. If this finesse loses to an honor in the East hand, declarer is in position to take two tricks via a second finesse if West has the remaining high honor.

♠ A J 9

♠ 4 3 2

Needing two spade tricks, South leads low toward the North hand. When West follows low, he finesses the 9. If West started with K-10 or Q-10, this will drive a high honor from the East hand and a second finesse of the jack will result in two tricks for South.
(4) *To prepare for a pinning play in the same suit.* A finesse can also be preparatory to a different form of trick-gaining play in a suit. By taking an early finesse, it may be possible to reduce the length of the suit in one enemy hand.

♥ Q 9 8 7
♥ J 5   ♥ K 10 6
♥ A 4 3 2

Needing three heart tricks, South leads low, and finesses dummy's 7. East wins with the 10, but declarer later enters the North hand, and pushes the queen through East, blotting out the entire defensive holding. This combination of plays is now called an INTRA-FINESSE.

♦ Q 10 8 3 2
♦ J 9 4   ♦ A K 7 6
♦ 5

With some other suit as trump, South must develop two diamond tricks. He leads low from his hand, finessing North's 8. Later, the queen is led from the North hand to ruff away East's remaining honor. The suit will now fall after the second ruff (see FALSECARDING).
(5) *As an avoidance play.* A finesse may prove useful for keeping a particular opponent off lead.

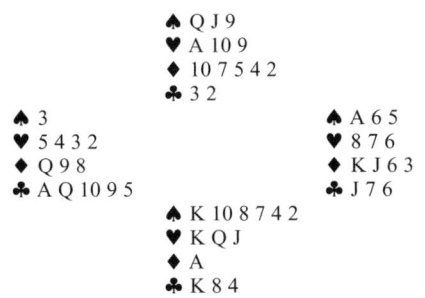

```
              ♠ Q J 9
              ♥ A 10 9
              ♦ 10 7 5 4 2
              ♣ 3 2
♠ 3                              ♠ A 6 5
♥ 5 4 3 2                        ♥ 8 7 6
♦ Q 9 8                          ♦ K J 6 3
♣ A Q 10 9 5                     ♣ J 7 6
              ♠ K 10 8 7 4 2
              ♥ K Q J
              ♦ A
              ♣ K 8 4
```

Against South's 4♠ contract, West leads the ♠3. East plays two round of spades.

South now leads a club from dummy. If East follows low, South should finesse the 8! This is an avoidance play, designed to keep East off lead and avoid the killing play of the third trump.

If East has the ♣A, the next club lead will score the ♣K, and produce the game-going trick. However, if West has the ace, East can be prevented from leading the third round of trump. South later enters dummy with a heart, and leads a club to his king. This loses to West's ace, but declarer cannot be prevented from ruffing his third club in dummy.

(6) *As a safety play.* A finesse is often part of a safety play.

```
              ♠ K 9 2

              ♠ A J 5 4 3
```

South wishes to avoid losing two spade tricks. He cashes the ace and then leads toward dummy. If West follows with a small card, he finesses dummy's 9 to guard against West having started with Q-10-x-x (See SAFETY PLAY).

```
              ♠ A 10 9 8

              ♠ K 7 6 5 4
```

South wishes to avoid losing two spade tricks. He leads from either hand, and finesses by playing low from the opposite hand. In this way, Q-J-x-x in either hand can be picked up with only one loser.

(7) *To gain one or more entries*

```
              ♠ K 7 4
              ♥ J 8 7
              ♦ A 9 7 6 5
              ♣ J 10
♠ 8 5 2                          ♠ —
♥ A K 10 9                       ♥ Q 6 5 4 2
♦ Q 2                            ♦ J 10 3
♣ A Q 9 8                        ♣ 7 6 5 3 2
              ♠ A Q J 10 9 6 3
              ♥ 3
              ♦ K 8 4
              ♣ K 4
```

This hand demonstrates many techniques in the play of the cards. With best play on both sides, it hinges on repeated finesses to gain entries. South opens 4♠ in third position, and all pass. West leads the ♥K which holds. West cannot continue with the ♥A, for declarer will discard a diamond from his hand, later establishing the diamond suit by ruffing (see LOSER-ON-LOSER), preventing a lead through the ♣K. If West leads a lower heart, declarer will play the ♥J to force East's queen. He will later pass the ♥8 to West while discarding a diamond and will thereby make his contract (see AVOIDANCE).

Nor can West profitably shift to diamonds. If West leads the ♦Q, declarer lets him hold the trick; if West leads the ♦2, declarer wins the king, draws trumps, leads a diamond and ducks West's queen. (Declarer cannot succeed in this deal if he leads diamonds himself. He can lead to the ♦A and play a low diamond from both hands next, forcing West to win, but declarer cannot then unblock the ♦K before he draws trumps.)

Since West cannot profitably lead clubs, his only chance is to shift to a trump. Because of the recurring finesse for entry position in the trump suit, it makes no difference which trump West plays.

Suppose West leads the ♠2. Declarer finesses dummy's 4, which holds. The ♥J is played from dummy, East covers with the queen, and declarer ruffs with an honor. Now the ♦K and ♦A are cashed, West unblocking the ♦Q under the ♦K to avoid being thrown in with that card. The ♥8 is played. When East cannot cover, declarer's last diamond is discarded.

West wins and cannot lead a club or a heart, so he plays another trump. Declarer finesses the 7 (or wins the king while unblocking from his hand if West plays the 8), underplaying with his 6, ruffs a diamond to establish the suit, re-enters dummy with the remaining spade, and runs the diamonds.

On this deal, two finesses were taken against West's trump cards to obtain a third entry to dummy. Notice that if South must lead spades himself, he can enter dummy only twice against best defense by West.

See also BACKWARD FINESSE; CHINESE FINESSE; DEEP FINESSE; DOUBLE FINESSE; INTRA-FINESSE; OBLIGATORY FINESSE; RESTRICTED CHOICE; RUFFING FINESSE; SAFETY PLAY; SUIT COMBINATIONS; TWO-WAY FINESSE.

FINESSE, OBLIGATORY. See OBLIGATORY FINESSE.

FINESSE AGAINST PARTNER. See THIRD-HAND PLAY.

FINESSE PROBABILITIES. These and all finessing situations are listed under SUIT COMBINATIONS.

FIRST HAND. The dealer.

FIRST UP. A bidding system devised by Berl Stallard of the United States. The system called for the opening bidder to bid his lowest four-card suit, and the responder then bid his lowest four-card suit. Fit was all-important, suit quality was less so. Although several experiments with the system proved moderately successful, First Up never achieved wide usage.

FISHBEIN CONVENTION. See DEFENSE TO OPENING THREE-BID.

FISHBEIN TROPHY. This trophy is awarded every year to the player with the best overall individual performance record in the American Contract Bridge League Summer North American Bridge Championships. The trophy, in memory of Sally Fishbein, was donated by ACBL in recognition of the untiring efforts of Harry Fishbein who served as treasurer of ACBL and refused to accept the customary compensation. For winners see Appendix II.

FISHBOWL. A sealed, soundproofed room with space for one table and four players. It had a one-way glass front, permitting a Bridgerama audience to see in but preventing the players from seeing out. It was used in some world and European Championships in the Sixties, and was later replaced by closed-circuit television monitors to permit the spectators to see the players more clearly.

FISHER DOUBLE. A LEAD-DIRECTING DOUBLE of a notrump contract asking for a minor-suit lead, developed by Dr. John Fisher. After an opening bid of 1 or 2NT, if there have been no legitimate suit bids, a double of the final notrump contract asks for a club lead if Stayman has not been used and a diamond lead if it has.

A slightly simpler version is to play that a double always asks for a diamond lead, making the opponents' use of Stayman irrelevant.

FIT. A term referring to the effectiveness or ineffectiveness of two partnership hands in combination commonly used to refer specifically to the TRUMP SUIT, under which heading various trump fits are discussed.

When the hand as a whole is considered, the fit may be distributional. With a sound trump fit, a shortage in each hand in different suits is likely to lead to an effective CROSSRUFF. (For an unsatisfactory fit, see DUPLICATION OF DISTRIBUTION.)

Fit can also be considered in terms of honor cards, which may or may not be effective in play (see GOOD CARDS).

FIT-SHOWING JUMP. With the opponents silent throughout, you pass, your partner opens in third or fourth position and you make a jump-shift response; perhaps:

West	North	East	South
	Pass	Pass	1 ♦
Pass	2 ♥		

What does this jump shift signify?

The normal expert agreement is that it is a fit-showing jump. It describes a hand with the following characteristics:

a. a maximum pass: 9-11 points

b. at least nine cards (5-4 or 4-5) in the two suits bid

c. virtually all the points concentrated in the two suits.

An ideal hand for the auction given above would look something like this:

♠ 5 3　♥ A Q J 8 7　♦ K 10 7 6　♣ 6 2

Whether the bid is totally forcing is a debatable point. If the jump is from a minor to a major, a pass may be best if the opener is weak and has three cards in the major. That, in essence, is the fit-showing jump in action. But there are some other situations worth considering.

Suppose your partner's third-seat opening bid was 1 ♥. What do you respond with each of these hands?

1. ♠ K 3　♥ Q 7 6 4　♦ K Q 6 5　♣ 7 6 2
2. ♠ 5 3　♥ 6 2　♦ A 7 3　♣ K Q J 8 7 2
3. ♠ A K 8 5 4　♥ Q J 7 4 3　♦ 5 4　♣ 2
4. ♠ 2　♥ Q J 7 4 3　♦ 5 4　♣ A K 8 5 4

Assuming that you are using the REVERSE DRURY convention, 2 ♣ would be your choice with the first hand. If you do not employ Drury, you would make a limit raise of 3 ♥.

Because 2 ♣ is an artificial bid when using Drury, you must make a jump response of 3 ♣ with the second hand.

This shows a maximum pass with six respectable clubs. (Bid a simple 2 ♣ if not using Drury.)

The third hand is an ideal fit-showing jump: you bid 2 ♠. (You could make a splinter bid, but the second suit is a more important feature of your hand. You can cuebid the shortage later if partner is interested in a slam.)

The problem comes with the fourth hand. If 2 ♣ is Drury and 3 ♣ natural, how do you make a fit-showing jump in clubs? Most experts keep the 2NT response for this hand.

However, there are alternative agreements. Some pairs ignore the possibility altogether! They normally use the 2NT response for a maximum minor two-suiter. And others, a small minority, use the jump raise to three of the agreed major for the fit-showing jump in clubs.

Finally, suppose you pick up this hand:

♠ 4　♥ K J 10 4　♦ 8 3　♣ K Q J 7 6 3

The vulnerability is unfavorable for your side. The auction begins like this:

West	North	East	South
			1 ♥
2 ♠(a)	?		

(a) Weak

What would you do?

You could bid a simple 4 ♥, but will you or your partner be able to judge the auction correctly when East bids 4 ♠?

You could bid 3 ♣, but that commits you to bidding 5 ♥ over 4 ♠. You can hardly ignore your heart support for the whole auction.

The ideal answer is a bid of 4 ♣ as a fit-showing jump. You tell partner that you have a hand worth 4 ♥ with a good side suit as well. Now he should be able to make an intelligent decision over 4 ♠. (True, for most pairs this jump would be treated as a SPLINTER BID, but perhaps that is not such a wise agreement in this sort of situation unless the jump is in the opponent's suit.)

It is even possible to use this type of fit-showing jump at a lower level.

West	North	East	South
			1 ♥
1 ♠	3 ♣/4 ♣		

The 3 ♣ response shows a hand worth a limit raise in hearts with a reasonable club suit. The 4 ♣ jump shows the same hand except that it is worth game in hearts. (Here, some pairs who treat 3 ♣ as fit-showing play that 4 ♣ is a splinter bid. For these pairs, 3 ♣ shows a hand worth *at least* a limit raise in hearts.) See PASSED HAND.

FIVE or FIVE-SPOT. The tenth ranking card in a suit, having five pips of the suit to which it belongs.

FIVE NOTRUMP. In the modern style, this bid is often an instruction to partner to "pick a suit". Usually this occurs when at least three strains are in play. Suppose that responder to 1NT has this:

♠ x
♥ A J x x
♦ K Q J x
♣ K Q J x

West	East
1NT	2 ♣
2 ♠	5NT

In general, 5NT is not needed as a Grand Slam Force since such hands can be handled with a 4NT Roman

Keycard bid. 5NT bid is often useful in a competitive auction.

♠ —
♥ K x
♦ K Q x x x
♣ A Q x x x x

West	North	East	South
2♠	3♥	4♠	5NT

North is invited to bid 6♣, 6♦ or 6♥.

This use of the 5NT bid has diminished the use of the GRAND SLAM FORCE.

FIVE NOTRUMP BID. If an undiscussed but clearly forcing non-competitive 5NT bid might logically have more than one interpretation, the BWS 2001 expert consensus was a request to partner to "pick a slam." A substantial minority chose the GRAND SLAM FORCE.

FIVE NOTRUMP OPENING. A very rare opening bid, showing a balanced hand which can guarantee 11 tricks. Responder is asked to raise the bidding one level for each ace, king or queen he holds.

FIVE OF A MAJOR OPENING. Shows a hand missing both top honors in the trump suit, but with no outside losers. Partner is invited to raise to small slam with one of the missing key cards, to grand slam with both. Probably the rarest bid in bridge.

FIVE OR SEVEN. A phrase indicating the type of partnership holdings on which a successful play makes a grand slam, but if the play is not successful, the opponents can cash a second trick immediately, holding the result to five-odd. For a hand of this type, see MATCHPOINT BIDDING. In rubber bridge, probably the grand slam contract should be preferred, but there may be situations at duplicate where a six-odd contract is tactically better, even though this is neither the maximum nor the safest contract.

FIVE TABLES. At duplicate five tables provide competition for 20 players, 10 pairs, or five teams-of-four.

As an Individual, the 20-player RAINBOW Movement is recommended. Begin the game by putting five boards on each table. 1-5 go on table 1, 6-10 go on table 2, right around to 21-25 on table 5. The boards are shuffled before the first round only.

In a pair event, a Mitchell of five rounds of five boards can be used. However, the HOWELL MOVEMENT with nine rounds of three boards is preferable.

For team-of-four contests, see TEAM-OF-FOUR MOVEMENTS; the standard team-of-four progression (pairs skip a table down while boards move one table down) completes the game in four rounds, usually of six boards each. TOTAL POINT, BOARD-A-MATCH, or IMP scoring can be used.

For 4½ tables or 5½ tables, see HALF TABLE MOVEMENTS.

FIVE-ACE BLACKWOOD. See KEYCARD BLACKWOOD.

FIVE-BID. Any bid at the five level, to take 11 tricks if it becomes the final contract. As an opening bid, it indicates a hand of unusual power. As a bid made during the

auction, it may be a slam invitation or part of a specialized slam convention. To play 5♠ or 5♥ voluntarily and fail is one of the most ignominious results possible at the bridge table. Experts prefer to estimate slam possibilities below the game level. See: ADVANCE SAVE; BLACKWOOD; FIVE OF A MAJOR OPENING; 5NT OPENING; PREEMPTIVE BID; SUPER GERBER.

FIVE-CARD MAJORS. The concept according to which an opening bid of one of a major guarantees at least a five-card suit. This method has become standard in American tournament play, but European methods vary. The five-card major guideline applies only in first and second position. The overwhelming expert consensus (95% in BWS 2001) was that a bid in a four-card major suit is acceptable in third and fourth positions if the auction rates to be manageable thereafter.

The knowledge that partner has five cards in the suit when he opens with a major simplifies responder's problems, especially if there is competitive bidding. Now a jump raise to three (either forcing or limit) can be made with only three-card support, and sometimes a single raise can be made with only a doubleton honor.

Problems can arise when using the five-card major system. First, it can force opener to make frequent prepared, and slightly unnatural, minor suit opening bids. Opening bids on three-card club and diamond suits become common. When opener has 4-4-4-1 or 4-4-3-2 and must open 1♦, the bidding can get sticky if partner responds 2♣ and the partnership is not playing a two-over-one-forcing-to-game system. More important, the more frequent use of minor suit openings makes it much easier for the opponents to get into the bidding. An opening bid of 1♠ is especially preemptive in nature.

The expert consensus in BWS 2001 was to use judgment in deciding which suit to bid with 4-4 in the minor suits. A small minority (14%) favored bidding one diamond in all cases. In BWS 94, experts favored a bid of 1♦ with 4-5 if, and only if, the diamonds were strong and the clubs were weak. They were neutral on the question of whether a 1NT rebid with a singleton in partner's major suit was acceptable.

Because of the rebid problems that often arise using five-card majors, most users also employ the 1NT response as forcing for one round. They also tend to use negative doubles, which makes it easier to uncover fits that might stay hidden otherwise.

Five-card majors were introduced into American tournament bidding in the Fifties by the ROTH-STONE and KAPLAN-SHEINWOLD systems. See BRIDGE WORLD STANDARD, EASTERN SCIENTIFIC, WALSH SYSTEM.

FIVE-CARD SPADES. Some systems, mainly in Britain, Netherlands and Norway, require that a 1♠ opening must have at least five cards, while four-card heart openings are acceptable.

FIVE-CARD STAYMAN. See PUPPET STAYMAN.

FIVE-ODD. A term indicating five tricks over the book, or 11 tricks in all.

FIVE-SUIT BRIDGE. This game, devised in 1937 by Dr. Walter H. W. Marseille, a Viennese psychologist and mathematician, used a special 65-card deck. There were

five suits of 13 cards and each of the four players was dealt 16 cards. The remaining card was called the "widow" and placed face upwards on the table. After the dummy was exposed the declarer was entitled to exchange any card in his own hand or the dummy for the widow.

The fifth suit was green in color (except in England where it was blue) and was called "leaves" in Austria, "crowns" or "royals" in England and "eagles" in America. Public interest was aroused when George VI bought some decks at an exhibition and several books were written about the game, but it did not achieve lasting popularity.

One authority gives the inventor's name as Dr. Marculis.

FIXED. A colloquial term to designate a pair (or a team) that has received a bad score through no fault of its own. Initially applied to a situation in which an opposing player has made a technical error or suffered a legal misadventure, and gained a good result thereby. His innocent opponents, who suffered, but probably not in silence, can say that they have been fixed. Now it can be any successful good play by a bad player.

FLAG-FLYING. An obsolete colloquialism for a bid made with full consciousness of its failure if allowed to stand, in the hope of avoiding a greater loss if the opponents are permitted to play the contract. The term was used to describe a bid made after the opponents had apparently reached their final contract, rather than one interjected during the auction. In this way it is distinguished from preemptive action (see PREEMPTIVE BID). SACRIFICE and SAVE are the modern terms.

FLANNERY TWO DIAMONDS. Developed by William Flannery to show an 11-15 point hand with five hearts and four spades. In BWS2001 one-fourth of the experts favored this convention.

Major-suit responses on the two-level are signoffs, though opener may raise with a maximum and a minor-suit void. Jump responses in the majors are invitational, and jumps to 4♣ and 4♦ are transfers to 4♥ and 4♠ respectively. If responder bids a minor on the three-level, opener bids 3NT with a fit (ace or king doubleton, or queen third). A 2NT response asks opener to clarify his strength and distribution. Opener rebids 3♥ with 11-13 points or 3♠ with 14-15 points and two cards in each minor (or 3NT with 14-15 if his strength is concentrated in his minor suit doubletons), 3♣ or 3♦ with three cards in the bid suit, or 4♣ or 4♦ with four cards in the bid suit.

The standard defense to Flannery 2♦ is to play that a 2♥ overcall is a three-suited takeout (with shortness in hearts). Double of 2♦ shows the equivalent of a strong notrump opener and is penalty oriented. A 2NT overcall is unusual for the minors, while suit overcalls other than 2♥ are natural.

An alternative is to play that a double shows a balanced hand in the 13-16 range, and 2NT shows a stronger balanced hand. See also FLANNERY TWO HEARTS.

FLANNERY TWO HEARTS. An opening bid of 2♥ to show a hand worth 11-15 points with five hearts and four spades. Responses and rebids are the same as for the FLANNERY 2♦ convention, except that to sign off in hearts responder simply passes.

The Flannery 2♥ bid is not as easy to defend as its 2♦ counterpart. The usual practice is to play that the double of 2♥ shows the strong notrump and that 2♠ shows a three-suited takeout. The assumption (not always valid) is that the long spade suit is the least likely hand one might hold.

Here also it is possible to use a double and a 2NT overcall to show moderate and strong balanced hands.

FLAT. (1) Hand: A hand without distributional values, particularly one with 4-3-3-3 distribution. "Square" and "round" are also used to describe this type of hand.

(2) Board: A deal on which no variations in result are expected in the replays. In team play, a board in which the two scores are identical and therefore do not affect the score. Also called a PUSH.

FLIGHT. A division of a game in which competitors are separated according to the number of masterpoints held. Usually the top flight is open to all comers, while lower flights have an upper masterpoint limit.

FLIGHTED PAIRS. See PAIR GAMES.

FLIGHTED TEAMS. An event that is broken down into two or three fields based on masterpoints. Each field competes as a separate event. The flight for which a team is eligible is determined by the masterpoint holding of the player with the most points. Teams may opt to play in a higher classification but not in a lower one. Often the breakdown in ACBL events is as follows: Flight A — 0 to infinity; B — 0-750; C — 0-300. All teams are eligible to compete in Flight A; only teams with fewer than 750 points for each player (Flight B limit) are eligible to play in Flight B; only teams with fewer than 300 points for each player (Flight C limit) are eligible to play in Flight C. Teams eligible for Flight A only may compete in Flight A only. See HANDICAP TEAMS, STRATIFIED TEAMS, STRATIFLIGHTED TEAMS, TEAM GAMES.

FLINT. An artificial 3♦ response to a 2NT opening, devised by Jeremy Flint of England to permit a partnership to stop below game. (Though this author is credited with other conventions — see below — the 3♦ convention is the one known simply as Flint.)

Opener is forced to rebid 3♥. Responder passes if his long suit is hearts; otherwise, he bids 3♠, 4♣ or 4♦. Opener is then expected to pass, but may continue to game if his hand is particularly suitable.

Responder can still bid 3♦ in a natural sense if he follows with any action other than a minimum suit bid. If responder next bids 3NT, for instance, he shows a diamond suit and mild slam interest.

A modification, the Flint 3♣, allows a partnership to rest in 3♦ or three of a major suit after a 2NT opening. A 3♣ response forces opener to bid 3♦, and responder then passes or signs off in a major suit. A 3♦ response is used as a Stayman inquiry for a major suit.

Another convention, the Flint 2♦, is used to investigate game in notrump or a minor suit after a WEAK NOTRUMP opening. A 2♦ response shows either a hand with a solid minor suit or an unbalanced hand with at least four cards in each minor. Opener rebids a four-card major suit if he has one or bids 2NT otherwise.

Responder's next bid clarifies his hand.

The popularity of transfer bidding has made these Flint conventions obsolescent.

FLIP-FLOP. A reversal of the usual meaning of a 2NT response when a minor-suit opening is doubled. The idea is to use it preemptively, reserving the jump raise to show invitational values. See TWO NOTRUMP RESPONSE (Over opponent's takeout double).

FLOAT. A colloquialism meaning that three passes follow. "1NT float" means 1NT - pass - pass - pass. A similar term is SWISH. In the play, declarer may be said to float a card when he leads it and passes it for a finesse.

FLOGGER. See BACK SCORE.

FLOWER MOVEMENT. An adaptation of the HOWELL MOVEMENT so that the apparently haphazard movement of the players is replaced by an orderly progression. One pair (North-South at table 1) remains stationary throughout. All other pairs progress, East-West moving toward the higher-numbered table, until they reach the highest-numbered table. After that round they merely switch directions at that table and thereafter move to the next lower-numbered table. As the players reach table 2, North-South, their next progression is to table 1, where they will sit East-West, then to table 2, East-West.

The movement has simple player moves. There are two disadvantages, however. One is that the movement cannot be made as balanced as an ordinary Howell. The other is that board progression is irregular, which is why the movement is best played with a central table for all idle boards. Board movement should be by the director. With board duplication so much easier today, it is common for the same boards to be played at all tables each round. This method is used in many major events such as the CAVENDISH PAIRS.

FLUKE. A fortuitous profit. An extreme case would be represented by a player dropping a card that appears disastrous but produces a brilliant result.

FOLLOWING SUIT. The legal obligation of each player to play a card of the suit led if possible.

FORCE. (1) Noun: Any bid making it incumbent upon the bidder's partner to bid at least once more. (2) Verb: To cause to ruff; to cause a player to use a high card.

FORCED BID. A bid a player must make according to the system being played. When playing CAPPELLETTI, for instance, partner of the player who overcalled 1NT with 2♣ must normally bid 2♦ if there is no intervening bid. See DONT, CAPPELLETTI, FORCING PASS, GLADIATOR, HAMILTON, LEBENSOHL.

FORCING. A bid or call requiring further action by partner.

FORCING BID. A bid which, because of system or convention, requires the partner to keep the bidding open, by making some call other than a pass if there is no intervening call. Examples can be found under FORCING SEQUENCES and FORCING PASS.

Perhaps the most widely used forcing bids are the JUMP SHIFT by an unpassed hand and the ONE-OVER-ONE or TWO-OVER-ONE responses by an unpassed hand.

FORCING CLUB. See ONE CLUB, ARTIFICIAL AND FORCING.

FORCING DECLARER TO RUFF. A method of defensive play, usually sound strategy when other forms of defense seem inadvisable or doubtful. When a defender, by the play of an established side suit, forces declarer to use his valuable trumps, it sometimes causes the declarer to lose control of the play. This is sometimes called "pumping" declarer. In the following deal the insistent forcing of the declarer's strong trump hand enabled the defending partnership to defeat an otherwise sure game.

```
              ♠ 6 4 3 2
              ♥ K 10 8
              ♦ A Q J
              ♣ A J 10
♠ K Q 10 9 5              ♠ A 7
♥ A 5 4 3                 ♥ 7
♦ 10 3                    ♦ 7 6 5 4 2
♣ 7 2                     ♣ 9 6 5 4 3
              ♠ J 8
              ♥ Q J 9 6 2
              ♦ K 9 8
              ♣ K Q 8
```

West	North	East	South
1♠	Dbl	Pass	3♥
Pass	4♥	All Pass	

West's opening lead was the ♠K, which East won with the ace to unblock his partner's suit. East returned the ♠7, which West won with the queen. West continued the suit, forcing South to ruff. South now led a heart, and when West won with the ace he led another spade, forcing South to ruff a second time. South led a second round of hearts. At this point, it is obvious that South could not make his contract, for West's greater length in trumps gave him a trump winner. This was brought about by West's continued forcing play, which destroyed declarer's trump fortress.

FORCING LEADS. Plays by the opening leader aimed at weakening the declarer's trump suit. The lead is most effective when the leader has four trumps and can visualize the declarer being forced to ruff prematurely and perhaps lose trump control.

Generally a forcing lead is made from a long suit. Declarer may have to exhaust his attenuated trump suit to extract the defender's trumps. Subsequently, if the defense regains the lead, they will be in a position to cash the established cards in their suit, for the hand will have been reduced to notrump.

```
              ♠ 7 6 5
              ♥ A 9 8 4
              ♦ K 8 6 3
              ♣ A 10
♠ A 9 3 2                 ♠ 8
♥ K Q 10 7                ♥ J 6 5 2
♦ 7                       ♦ A 5 4 2
♣ 8 7 6 5                 ♣ J 9 4 3
              ♠ K Q J 10 4
              ♥ 3
              ♦ Q J 10 9
              ♣ K Q 2
```

The contract is 4♠ by South. If the singleton diamond is led, the declarer has an easy ride, but holding four trumps, West should resist this temptation and attack in hearts. Declarer wins and forces out the ♠ A. West continues hearts, reducing South's trump length to his own. Declarer is now fixed — if he draws West's trumps and plays diamonds, East wins, and the defense secures two heart tricks. Alternatively, if he abandons trumps after discovering the bad break, West will score two of his small trumps.

Often the opening leader can diagnose the proper occasion for a forcing lead from the auction:

South	North
1♠	2♣
2♦	2NT
3♣	3♠
4♠	Pass

West holds: ♠ 9 8
       ♥ K J 6
       ♦ 10 5 3 2
       ♣ Q 7 6 3 2

South's bidding has pinpointed a singleton or void in hearts; East almost certainly has at least four trumps. West should start a forcing game by leading the ♥ K (pinning a possible singleton queen in the South hand). See also ATTACKING LEADS, OPENING LEADS.

FORCING ONE NOTRUMP RESPONSE. See ONE NOTRUMP RESPONSE TO MAJOR, FORCING

FORCING PASS. A pass which forces partner to take action. Such a pass may be made in the following situations:

(1) The opponents have taken an obvious sacrifice. A forcing pass denotes the desire to bid toward a higher contract if partner is willing.

(2) The opportunity for a sacrifice has arisen. A forcing pass denotes the desire to sacrifice, and asks partner to do so if he cannot double the opponents and defeat their contract.

(3) A safety level has been established below which the contract cannot be sold. A forcing pass denotes inability to find a suitable call, or the desire to see if partner can double the enemy bid.

(4) After a slam-level sacrifice, a forcing pass sometimes denotes control of the enemy suit and requests partner to bid a slam if he has the necessary outside values.

An important situation arises at a high level:

West	North	East	South
1♥	2♦	3♦	5♦
Pass	Pass	Dbl	Pass
5♥			

The expert consensus in BWS94 is that this sequence is strong, inviting 6♥. A direct 5♥ bid is weaker, confirming to the principle of FAST ARRIVAL. But the converse agreement is possible.

(5) Some bidding systems employ a forcing pass in first or second position as a form of opening bid. If the bidder opens the bidding by bidding a suit or notrump, he is indicating that his hand is lower than opening-bid range. Usually each bid has a special conventional meaning. If the opener has a full opening bid, he must pass, and it is up to partner to open the bidding, knowing his partner has good values. The system causes serious disruption to opposition bidding. Most players do not know how to cope with this method that is the reverse of the usual. Such systems are not permitted in ACBL play or in world pair tournaments. These systems are allowed, however, in major world team championships such as the Bermuda Bowl. In the past, pairs from the Netherlands, New Zealand, Brazil and Poland, among others, have used forcing pass systems. The ACBL does not allow them because it has a policy against destructive systems — systems aimed at disrupting the opponents rather than at arriving at the correct contract. See FERT, PASS-DOUBLE INVERSION.

FORCING RAISE. Perhaps nothing in bidding has changed as much in recent years as the way in which responder makes a forcing raise of opener's suit. A DOUBLE RAISE used to be the only way to indicate a forcing raise. Today, however, in a non-competitive auction the double raise usually is a LIMIT BID. Diverse methods of showing the forcing raise have been developed, including JACOBY TWO NOTRUMP, MINI-SPLINTERS, SPLINTERS, STRONG PASS, THREE CLUBS RESPONSE AS A MAJOR RAISE, THREE NOTRUMP RESPONSE, and various forms of SWISS. See also INVERTED MINOR SUIT RAISE, CRISS-CROSS RAISE and WEAK OPENING SYSTEM.

FORCING REBID. See OPENER'S REBID and RESPONDER'S REBID.

FORCING SEQUENCE. A series of bids that requires the bidding to continue. Some sequences cannot be passed because the last bid showed strength; in such cases, the bidding may be forcing for one round only. Other sequences are forcing because the partnership has established that they have the values for game or slam; they are committed to continue until they reach game (or extract a worthwhile penalty).

Examples of forcing sequences follow. No unanimity of opinion exists as to the nature of many sequences. With the plethora of bidding systems and styles, sequences admit to varying interpretations, not only from system to system, but from pair to pair.

Sequences that are forcing for one round:

1. A new suit by responder:

(a) 1♥ 1♠

(b) 1♣ 1♠
   2♣ 2♥

(c) 1♣ 1♥
   1♠ 2♦

(See FOURTH SUIT ARTIFICIAL.)

(d) 1♣ 1♦
   1NT 2♥ (but not 1♣-1♥-1NT-2♦

unless playing NEW MINOR FORCING)

(e) 1♠ 2♦
   2♠ 3♣

(f) 3♣ 3♠

2. A reverse by opener:

(a) 1♣ 1♠
   2♥ (but not absolutely forcing for traditionalists)

(b) 1♠   2♦
    3♣ (sometimes called a high reverse)

3. A new suit by opener after a two-over-one response:
    1♠   2♣
    2♥

4. A new suit bid after the trump suit is agreed:
(a) 1♥   2♥
    3♣

(b) 1♠   3♠
    4♣

(c) 1♦   1♠
    2♠   3♣

5. A strength-showing sequence by opener:
    1♦   1♠
    2♣   2NT
    3♦ (but not 1♦-1♠-2♦-2NT-3♣)

6. A new suit bid by responder after responder redoubles at his first turn:

West	North	East	South
	1♦	Dbl	Redbl
Pass	Pass	1♥	1♠

7. A passed-hand jump shift after a major suit opening:
    Pass   1♥
    3♦

The 3♦ bid by the passed hand implies a heart fit, so most pairs treat it as forcing. See DRURY and FIT-SHOWING JUMPS.

Game-forcing sequences

1. A first-round jump by responder:
(a) 1♠   2NT (natural)

However, an 11-12 point 2NT response is standard in ACOL after any opening bid. In North America it is common after an opening bid in a minor suit.

(b) 1♥   2NT (an artificial forcing raise)

(c) 1♥   2♠ (But See WEAK JUMP-
               SHIFT RESPONSE.)

2. A jump rebid by opener after a two-level response:
    1♥   2♣
    3♥ or 4♣

3. A jump shift by opener:
    1♥   1♠
    3♣

4. Miscellaneous sequences:
(a) 1♥   1♠
    3♥   3♠

(b) 1♥   2♦
    2NT   3♥

However, if opener's 2NT rebid suggests no extra strength, this sequence also could be played as invitational, according to partnership agreement.

(c) 1♦   1♥
    3♦   4♦

The modern style is to play this as forcing, perhaps inviting the start of a cuebid sequence. However, there are still many pairs who play this sequence as merely invitational to game. (If opener's 2NT rebid suggests no extra strength, this sequence may be played as invitational.)

(d) 1♠   2♥
    3♦   3NT
    4♣

Many modern pairs use a style in which a response in

a new suit at the two-level usually commits the partnership to game. An advantage of this style is to create more forcing sequences and permit leisurely investigation for the best contract. In this style, the sequence:
    1♠   2♣
    2♠   3♠
is forcing to game. (See TWO OVER ONE GAME FORCE; and FAST ARRIVAL.)

The above discussion centers on forcing sequences after opening bids of one of a suit. For other forcing sequences, see FORCING TWO-BID and 1NT OPENING. Furthermore, JUMP REBIDS BY RESPONDER, a controversial topic, is treated separately.

FORCING STAYMAN. See STAYMAN.

FORCING TAKEOUT. See JUMP SHIFT.

FORCING TWO-BID. The traditional use of an opening two-bid in a suit to show a hand which can virtually guarantee game, or even slam. (Also referred to as Culbertson two-bid, DEMAND BID or STRONG TWO-BID). It was a cornerstone of the CULBERTSON system and remained standard practice in the U.S. and many other parts of the world. In postwar years virtually all experts abandoned the Forcing Two in favor of the WEAK TWO-BID, the ACOL TWO-BID, and other treatments.

A variety of formulas have been put forward to determine whether a hand is worth a forcing two. Goren gives this schedule:

With a good five-card suit	25 high-card points.
With a good six-card suit	23 high-card points
With a good seven-card suit	21 high-card points.

With a second good five-card suit, one point less is needed. If the game is to be in a minor suit, two points more are needed. Two more formulas were devised by Hy Lavinthal: (a) More honor tricks than possible losers. (This rule was incorporated into the Culbertson System.) (b) Rule of 24: add to the high-card point count two points for every card over four in any suit; then subtract a point for any king or queen not in sequence with a next-ranking honor; bid two if the answer is 24 or more. However, the expert does not normally use such rules; he employs the forcing two-bid if he has reasonable game prospects opposite a worthless or nearly worthless hand.

Another consideration is that a hand may be slightly too weak for a forcing two, but at the same time distinctly too strong for an opening bid of one in a suit. In such circumstances, a slightly shaded two-bid may be a lesser evil than an over-strength one-bid.

However, the likelihood that a one-bid may be passed out is a further consideration. Highly distributional hands may safely be opened with a bid of only one, because if opener's partner passes it is most unlikely that both opponents will do so. Lacking controls of three suits therefore, the expert will tend to open with a one-bid and jump later to show distribution.

Culbertson later modified the unconditionally game-forcing character of the bid to permit partner to pass a bust hand if opener's call after a 2NT response was a simple rebid of his first suit, i.e.:
    2♥-2NT-3♥

Responses. The conventional negative response is 2NT. Other responses are positive and natural, showing at least 7-8 points and seldom less than one quick trick (i.e., an

ace, a king-queen, or two kings)

However, other responding treatments are used, including ACE-SHOWING RESPONSES and HERBERT NEGATIVE.

FORESIGHT. Looking ahead in the bidding or play. Examples of this are the prepared minor-suit opening bid to provide a convenient rebid over partner's or opponents' action, the early loss of a trick in order to set up a squeeze position, and a switch by defenders to a new suit in order to break up a possible throw-in play. See BIDDING; ENDPLAY; PREPAREDNESS, PRINCIPLE OF.

FORFEIT. To cancel a right or turn to call. See LAWS OF CONTRACT BRIDGE (Law 15), LAWS OF DUPLICATE (Law 11).

FORK. See FOURCHETTE, MORTON'S FORK COUP.

FORTUNE TELLING. Predicting the future of an individual by giving significance to a pattern of playing cards spread before him. Standard packs can, of course, be used, but the TAROTS, with their individuality, provide a greater opportunity for imaginative divination.

FORWARD GOING. See CONSTRUCTIVE.

FOSTER ECHO. A third-hand unblocking play against notrump, intended at the same time to show count. With a four-card holding, the first play is the second highest, followed by the third highest, with the lowest saved for last. With a three-card holding, the first play is second highest and the second is the highest, again saving the lowest for last. However, this method has disadvantages and is not widely used by experts. See COUNT SIGNALS.

FOULED BOARD. A board in which a card or cards or hands have been interchanged into incorrect pockets. Usually a fouled board occurs when the board is being discussed after the play and various hands are interchanged across the table.

Fouling a board is a major misdemeanor in bridge competition because the scores prior to and after the fouling cannot be compared. When a board has been reported as fouled, the director must determine at what point in the competition the fouling occurred. He then must matchpoint the results in some fair manner in the two fields thus created.

The WBF formula for scoring fouled boards and those needing adjusted scores was adopted by the ACBL in 1990. It is:

$$M = \frac{(N \cdot S)}{n} + \frac{(N - n)}{2n}$$

M = Final matchpoints on the board
N = Number of scores on the board
S = Matchpoint score in the group
n = number of scores in the group
Specifications:

The formula applies to groups of 3 or more scores on a fouled board.

The formula applies to a group of 3 scores when it is the larger group, otherwise the scores in a group of 3 are awarded matchpoint scores of 70%, 60% and 50%.

The scores in a group of 2 are awarded matchpoint scores of 65% and 55%.

Equal scores in groups of 3 and 2 share the arbitrary matchpoint awards.

A single score is awarded a matchpoint score of 60% in each direction.

Matchpoint scores are rounded to the nearest 100th with .005 rounded up.

To guard against the possibility of fouling a board, no more than one hand should be removed from the board at a time during discussions. This is particularly true when the opponents are not at the table.

In board-a-match team play, the correct manner of handling a fouled board is a matter of regulation, which has been changed from time to time. Under 1976 regulations of the ACBL, the scores, both North-South and East-West, are divided into two fields, before and after the fouling, each field is matchpointed independently, and the percentage of possible match points for each pair then is determined. For each team that played the board in different positions, the percentages are added and the board is won if the total is 120 or more, halved from 80 to 120, and lost with 80 or less. Results for teams that played the board in identical form are computed in the usual way, since the fouling occurred either before both halves of the teams had played it, or after both halves of the teams had played it.

A board with two hands having an incorrect number of cards, for example 12-14, is not fouled since no result can be achieved on this deal. The Law: "Incorrect Number of Cards" applies and the pair(s) who looked at their incorrect hands should receive average minus.

ACBL policy provides that the players who created the fouled board and made it necessary to apply the formula should be penalized one full board. (A foul in duplication that applies to one section only, and does not invoke the formula, is not so penalized.)

FOUR or FOUR-SPOT. The eleventh ranking card of each suit, designated by four pips of the suit symbol on the face.

FOUR ACES SYSTEM. Methods used by the FOUR ACES TEAM in winning many championships during the Thirties. The main features of the system were:

(1) Point count of ace=3; king=2; queen=1; jack=$^1/_2$. This makes a total of 26 points in the pack, and $6^1/_2$ represent an average hand; $9^1/_2$ points represent a mandatory opening bid.

(2) Limited 1NT opening with a range of $11^1/_2$-13 points. (Hands with less than seven honor cards are devalued by $^1/_2$ point for each honor, and hands with more than seven honors similarly increased in value.) Establishment of this notrump range solved major rebidding headaches. In combination with point-count and rigidly prescribed responses, it precluded many of the notrump bidding faults that plagued inexpert players.

(3) Minor-suit bids, if need be in a three-card suit, as exploring maneuvers, either by the opener or the responder.

(4) WEAK JUMP OVERCALLS.

(5) PSYCHIC BIDS by third hand and occasionally first hand showing some high-card strength in the suit bid and little else.

(6) JUMP SHIFT to the level of two or three as a psychic control. The opener rebids 2NT with a psychic, and

with any other rebid a slam is reached.

The Four Aces' book included a number of other original ideas, many of which have become standard practice.

FOUR ACES TEAM. The team that dominated tournament competition in the mid-Thirties. The first appearance of this team was at the Summer NAC in Asbury Park in 1933, when David Burnstine (Bruce), Richard Frey, Oswald Jacoby, and Howard Schenken won the forerunner of the Spingold Teams. Michael Gottlieb joined the team immediately afterward, and during 1934 the Four Aces' major wins included the Vanderbilt, the Spingold, the Grand National and the forerunner of the Reisinger. They successfully defended the Grand National 1935, and also repeated in the Vanderbilt, with Sherman Stearns replacing Frey, who had resigned. Burnstine, Jacoby, Schenken and Gottlieb defeated France in the first world championship match, played in Madison Square Garden. Gottlieb retired in 1936 and was replaced by Merwin D. Maier. B. Jay Becker and other experts played occasionally as members of the team, which did not play after December 1941 but continued as an entity for purposes of book and newspaper publication until 1945.

The Four Aces played their own system, and wrote a book, *The Four Aces System of Contract Bridge* (see BIBLIOGRAPHY, C) which presented their original expert methods. Though the system was widely followed by tournament players, the book was not a commercial success.

FOUR CLUB CONVENTIONS. See GERBER, NAMYATS, RUBIN TRANSFERS, SOUTH AFRICAN TEXAS, SWISS CONVENTION. See also SPLINTER BID, VOID-SHOWING BIDS.

FOUR CLUBS AND FOUR DIAMONDS OPENING PREEMPTS. Such bids usually are based on an eight-card minor in a poor hand. If the partnership is using a GAMBLING THREE NOTRUMP to show a solid minor, then an opening of 4♣ or 4♦ would show a broken suit. See NAMYATS.

FOUR CLUBS AND FOUR DIAMONDS OPENING TRANSFERS. See NAMYATS.

FOUR DIAMOND CONVENTIONS. See BLUE TEAM 4♣-4♦ CONVENTION; NAMYATS; NEAPOLITAN FOUR DIAMONDS CONVENTION; RUBIN TRANSFERS; SOUTH AFRICAN TEXAS; TEXAS.

FOUR HORSEMEN. A champion team of the early Thirties. It was formed by P. Hal Sims in 1931 to challenge the earlier success of the Culbertson team. The other "horsemen" were Willard S. Karn, David Burnstine (Bruce) and Oswald Jacoby. They won the two major team championships, the Vanderbilt and the Asbury Park, by large margins in 1932, and won the Reisinger convincingly in 1933. Sims' efforts to develop and promote his own system in opposition to Culbertson did not suit Jacoby and Bruce, who successively left the team (See FOUR ACES TEAM).

FOUR NOTRUMP CONVENTIONS. Since a 4NT bid is the lowest bid possible above the major-suit game level, it is a bid that is frequently used to initiate slam inquiries. Among the specialized uses of this bid are the following, dealt with in the following articles: ACOL DIRECT KING; ACOL FOUR NOTRUMP OPENING, BLACKWOOD, BYZANTINE BLACKWOOD, CULBERTSON FOUR-FIVE NOTRUMP, DECLARATIVE-INTERROGATIVE FOUR NOTRUMP, DEFENSE TO OPENING FOUR-BID, GENERAL PURPOSE CUEBID; KEY-CARD BLACKWOOD, KING CONVENTION, NORMAN, R/H 4NT CONVENTION, ROMAN BLACKWOOD, SAN FRANCISCO, SMITH CONVENTION; SUPPRESSING THE BID ACE.

For a discussion of the distinction between the quantitative and conventional uses of 4NT, see BLACKWOOD.

FOUR NOTRUMP OPENING. In standard methods, shows a balanced hand too strong to open 3NT. It should be a ten-trick hand with perhaps 28-30 points. This rare bid is in disuse in standard practice, because an opening 2♣ bid followed by 4NT serves equally well. For alternative treatments, see ACOL FOUR NOTRUMP OPENING; BLACKWOOD; FOUR NOTRUMP OPENING PREEMPT; RUBIN TRANSFERS.

FOUR NOTRUMP OPENING PREEMPT. Devised by Terence Reese and Jeremy Flint as part of the Little Major System and subsequently adopted by several American experts to distinguish between a strong and weak minor-suit game preempt.

An opening bid of 4NT shows a weak preempt of 5♣ or 5♦ with fewer than five controls, counting an ace or void as two controls and a king or singleton as one control. Consequently, an opening bid of 5♣ or 5♦ would show a stronger preempt, five or more controls. For an alternative treatment see RUBIN TRANSFERS.

FOUR NOTRUMP OVERCALL. A bid of 4NT after an opposing opening bid is usually a form of the UNUSUAL NOTRUMP, calling for a minor suit. This could not apply after an opening bid of 3♣, 3♦, or a weak 2♦, in which case the bid would be Blackwood. For treatment of 4NT overcall after an opening bid at the four level see DEFENSE TO OPENING FOUR-BID.

FOUR OF A SUIT OPENING. A natural opening bid of four to show a long, strong suit with little side strength. A typical hand would contain a seven- or eight-card suit, but a six-card suit is possible.

An opening four in a minor would seldom be based on a solid suit, because of the possibility of 3NT. For alternative treatments, see NAMYATS, LITTLE MAJOR, RUBIN TRANSFERS.

FOUR TABLES. At duplicate, four tables provide for competition among 16 (or 17) players as individuals, eight pairs of players, or four teams of four.

A full individual tournament, with all possible partnerships, has the difficulty of being very short (15 or 17 boards) or very long (30 or 34 boards). A reduced tournament in 12 or 13 rounds, 24 or 26 boards, is usually preferable. See INDIVIDUAL MOVEMENTS.

As a pair game, the HOWELL MOVEMENT, with seven rounds, is preferable to the MITCHELL MOVEMENT, with only four rounds. Either three or four boards may be played per round.

If the Mitchell movement is used, Tables 1 and 4 should relay boards throughout, with a byestand between tables

2 and 3. Boards move from 4 to 3 to byestand to 2 to 1 where they are shared with 4. East-West pairs move up.

The board-sharing can be avoided by using this schedule:

	Table 1			Table 2			Table 3			Table 4		
Round	NS	EW	B	NS	EW	B	NS	EW	B	NS	EW	B
1	1	5	1	2	6	2	3	7	3	4	8	4
2	1	6	4	2	5	3	3	8	2	4	7	1
3	1	7	2	2	8	1	3	5	4	4	6	3
4	1	8	3	2	7	4	3	6	1	4	5	2

As a team-of-four event, three stanzas are required; in the first stanza, traveling pairs of teams 1 and 2 exchange places, as do the traveling pairs of 3 and 4; boards are relayed between tables 1 and 2 and between tables 3 and 4; in the second stanza, traveling pairs of team 1 play at 3 and of team 3 at 1; similarly with teams 2 and 4; in the third stanza, teams 1 and 4 and teams 2 and 3 interchange traveling pairs, and relay the boards. Boards are reshuffled at the end of each stanza, and the six matches are scored individually. BOARD-A-MATCH, TOTAL POINT, or INTERNATIONAL MATCHPOINT SCORING can be used, and ties broken with summation from the three matches at board-a-match or total point or by quotient of points won divided by points lost at International Match Points. You may instead use the following way of playing, where 1-4 are the teams and a and b denote the two pairs in each team:

	Table 1			Table 2			Table 3			Table 4		
Round	NS	EW	B	NS	EW	B	NS	EW	B	NS	EW	B
1	1a	2b	1	2a	3b	2	3a	4a	4	4b	1b	5
2	2a	1b	1	3a	2b	2	4b	3b	4	1a	4a	5
3	4a	3b	1	3a	1b	3	1a	2a	4	2b	4b	6
4	3a	4b	1	1a	3b	3	2b	1b	4	4a	2a	6
5	1a	4b	2	4a	2b	3	2a	3a	5	3b	1b	6
6	4a	1b	2	2a	4b	3	3b	2b	5	1a	3a	6

For 3½ and 4½ tables, see HALF TABLE MOVEMENTS.

FOUR-BID. A bid at the four-level, to take 10 tricks if it becomes the final contract.

FOUR-CARD MAJORS. Systems which include opening the bidding in a major that consists of only four cards. In North America most players use FIVE-CARD MAJORS systems, but four-card majors are much more common in the rest of the world. Even in North America, many systems incorporate the four-card majors idea – ROTH-STONE, KAPLAN-SHEINWOLD, and many canapé relay systems. In the days of auction bridge, players were expected to have five cards in the suit if they opened a major. In the early days of contract bridge, opening four-card majors was very common. In the Seventies experts and other tournament players reverted to five-card majors. Most modern bridge teachers teach five-card majors, but many old-time rubber bridge players still play four-card majors. The BIDDABLE SUIT requirements govern whether or not such players will open a four-card major suit.

FOUR-CARD SUIT BID. See BIDDABLE SUITS.

FOURCHETTE. An obsolete term for a tenace such as A-Q, K-J or Q-10.

FOUR-DEAL BRIDGE. See CHICAGO.

FOUR-FIVE NOTRUMP CONVENTION. See CULBERTSON FOUR-FIVE NOTRUMP.

FOUR-ODD. Four tricks over book, or ten tricks in all.

FOUR-SUIT TRANSFER BIDS. Transfer bids into all four suits achieved some popularity in tournament play in the 80s. The usual plan, in response to 1NT, is:

2 ♦ shows heart length
2 ♥ shows spade length
2 ♠ shows club length
2NT shows diamond length

This method was favored by one-third of the respondents in BWS1994. Far less popular (13%) was the alternative in which 2NT shows clubs and 3 ♣ shows diamonds.

After 2 ♠ and 2NT, the opener should accept the transfer if he has a fit with responder's suit and make the intermediate bid if he does not. (Some partnerships reverse this procedure.) If responder has a good minor suit, perhaps A Q x x x x, he can play 3NT with a fit and three of his suit without one. If responder has a weak minor two-suiter he can bid 2NT and pass the rebid.

The responder will often have a strong hand and will continue bidding. The meaning of a subsequent major-suit bid needs agreement, the simple option being to use bids of the major as natural or as shortage.

Using this method, a direct 2NT bid by responder is not available as a natural invitation. To give such a message, the responder must use STAYMAN and follow with 2NT, which does not, therefore, imply possession of a four-card major suit. See MINOR SUIT STAYMAN.

Other schemes are possible. (1) 2 ♠ shows clubs, 2NT natural, 3 ♣ shows diamonds; (2) 2 ♠ shows minors, 2NT shows clubs, 3 ♣ shows diamonds.

FOURTEEN TABLES. At duplicate, 14 tables provide competition among 56 players as 56 individuals, 28 pairs, or 14 teams. The team-of-four can be board-a-match or Swiss team competition — either is a good contest.

As an individual tournament, twinned RAINBOW sections of seven tables can be used with a 13 top. This provides 21 boards with the same number of partnerships. Also possible is an Appendix Rainbow as described in TWELVE TABLES, where the bumped players will play boards 27 and 28 at table 14, with all other players moving and all players playing 13 rounds, 26 boards, top 12, average 156. The Appendix Rainbow movement could be cut at 11 or 12 rounds if desired.

As a pair game, 14 tables has become the basic unit for a section where there are many sections. When it is desired to preduplicate the hands from prepared hand records, the players who do the duplicating do not play the hands they duplicate; therefore it is necessary to have at least 14 tables in each section in order to play the standard 26 boards.

A possibility is to duplicate, let the board set be moved down one table, have the EW pairs remain and play a Skip Mitchell. After seven rounds of play (the duplication round is not counted), the moving pairs will skip the boards they duplicated.

As a team contest the THURNER MOVEMENT with two boards a round is available. Alternatively, you may start by having East-West skip a table in the lower direction and the boards are shuffled. After the first and second round the boards move to the next lower table and the East-West pairs skip a table in the lower direction. After the third round the boards move normally but the moving pairs skip an extra table. The East-West pairs move normally for the next six rounds. After the ninth round the moving pairs skip an extra table and the boards

skip a table. For the remaining rounds the moving pairs make the regular team-of-four move.

If a 13th round is advisable, the moving pairs 1 to 7 add 7 to their table number and go to that table. Moving pairs 8 to 14 subtract 7 from their table number and go to that table. Tables 1 and 8, 2 and 9, 3 and 10, 4 and 11, 5 and 12, 6 and 13, and 7 and 14 relay boards for that round. For the 13th round the boards are reshuffled.

A STAGGER MOVEMENT also is possible.

For 13½ or 14½ tables see HALF TABLE MOVEMENTS.

FOURTEEN-THIRTY. A variation of Roman Key Card Blackwood in which the normal responses in a minor suit are inverted: 5♣ shows one key card or four, and 5♦ three or zero. The name is 1430, rather than 1403, because that is a familiar score. The advantage arises when hearts are trumps and responder has one ace: A five-diamond relay bid is then available to ask for the trump queen.

FOURTH BEST. See FOURTH HIGHEST LEAD.

FOURTH HAND. The fourth player to have the opportunity to make a call or play to a trick; the player to the dealer's right.

FOURTH HIGHEST LEAD. Traditionally the fourth-highest card of a long suit is led to develop long card tricks in a suit or to give partner the count in the suit led. The application of the RULE OF ELEVEN when the card led is the fourth highest is a determining factor in play by third-hand and declarer. This is probably the oldest convention in the game. See OPENING LEADS, THIRD HIGHEST LEADS, THIRD AND FIFTH.

FOURTH SUIT ARTIFICIAL. See FOURTH SUIT FORCING.

FOURTH SUIT FORCING. The popular term for the idea that a bid by responder of the only unbid suit at his second turn is an artificial force. The term, introduced by Norman Squire, England, in magazine articles in the Fifties, is a misnomer. Fourth Suit Artificial would be more accurate since there is little disagreement about whether or not such bids are forcing. The disagreement is in the details of the treatment, which is used by the vast majority of experts. When used artificially, the responder tends to have two or three losers in the fourth suit or to have doubts about strain or level. The opener should not bid notrump unless he has a stopper in the fourth suit, which is in effect an unbid suit.

The one area concerning fourth-suit forcing where there is a major difference of opinion occurs when spades is the fourth suit after an auction that has gone 1♣-1♦-1♥. Is 1♠ fourth suit forcing or is it a natural spade bid? Each method has many adherents. If it is natural, it is only a one-round force and shows at least a four-card spade suit. If it is fourth-suit forcing, then it is forcing to game. It may or may not show spades. If the 1♠ is played as natural, then most players using fourth suit forcing bid 2♠ as the fourth-suit force. In BWS 1994 just under half the respondents wanted 2♠ to be the fourth-suit forcing bid.

♠ 7 5 4
♥ A 6 2
♦ A K Q 4
♣ 8 4 3

After 1♣-1♦-1♥, responder will bid 2♠ if the agreement is that this is fourth-suit forcing – otherwise responder will bid 1♠.

At the two-level, most experts in BWS 1994 favored the idea that the fourth-suit bid promises another bid but were neutral on the possibility of stopping in 2NT. Many now play that the fourth-suit bid is game-forcing, so it is necessary to have an agreement with partner.

North	South	North
♠ 4 3 2	1♣	1♦
♥ 4 3 2	1♠	?
♦ A K 4 3 2		
♣ A 2		

A fourth-suit bid of 2♥, the only convenient action, is unattractive if North promises another bid or, worse, if it is game-forcing. If the agreement is that 2NT by South after 2♥ is non-forcing, he must jump to 3NT with extra values and a heart stopper.

If the response is at the two-level, those who play two-over-one forcing methods are already committed to game, or virtually so. Other bidders must decide how far the fourth-suit is forcing. At the three-level, the usual agreement is that a fourth-suit bid is game-forcing.

North	South	North
♠ A K Q 3 2	1♥	1♠
♥ 3 2	2♦	3♣
♦ A 3 2		
♣ 4 3 2		

If the fourth-suit bid is by a passed hand, the partnership needs to have an agreement. There was no consensus in BWS 1994, with opinions divided among forcing, non-forcing, and forcing only if a reverse.

FOURTH-HAND BID. For a discussion of minimum openings in fourth seat, see BORDERLINE OPENING BIDS.

The idea that the fourth player must have additional strength to open the bidding is now quite obsolete, and at duplicate a player may open slightly light in the hope of snatching a partscore.

Opening three-bids and weak two-bids in fourth position show maximum values, close to an opening bid, but rarely occur. Other opening bids are not affected by the positional factor. See also PASSED HAND.

FOUR-THREE-TWO-ONE COUNT. See POINT-COUNT.

FRACTIONAL MASTERPOINT CERTIFICATE. See RATING POINTS.

FRAGMENT. A term describing a suit of two or more cards that is not long enough to bid naturally; usually a three-card holding. The bid of a fragment is designed to imply shortness in an unbid suit. See FRAGMENT BID.

FRAGMENT BID. An unusual bid — usually a double jump — in a new suit on the second round of bidding, showing a fit with partner's suit and a shortage in the fourth suit (devised by Monroe Ingberman). The last bid in each of the following sequences is a fragment bid:

(a)		(b)		(c)	
North	South	North	South	North	South
1♣	1♥	1♣	1♥	1♣	1♥
3♠		1♠	4♦	1♠	4♣

The fragment bidder usually has two or three cards in the fragment suit, and must have a singleton or void in the fourth suit — clubs in (b).

The fragment idea can be extended to this situation:

North	South
1♥	2♣
2♦	3♠

Here the bid shows a fit with hearts and a diamond shortage. (The more orthodox treatment is to use this sequence to show a fit with diamonds, because South's hand has been improved by North's rebid.)

For alternative treatments of such sequences, see ASKING BIDS, SPLINTER BIDS, SWISS CONVENTION, and VOID-SHOWING BIDS.

Although fragment bids were originally devised as a use for the double jump shift, which was otherwise usually an idle bid, when a player has made a bid that denies a two-suited hand, a fragment bid may be made in a suit without jumping. The implication of the fragment bid is that the bidder has support for his partner's suit and a singleton in the remaining suit. See Soloway theory of JUMP SHIFTS.

FRAME. A colloquialism for a game. The term probably came from the appearance of the scoring pad used in rubber bridge: the vertical and horizontal lines, the edge of the single column pad, and the line drawn underneath the score when the game is completed "frame" the trick-score constituting the game.

FRANCO-AMERICAN MATCHES. Teams representing France and the United States (or North America) have met on many occasions. For results, see Appendix IV.

FREAK HAND. A single hand or a complete deal of abnormally unbalanced distribution. Usually a hand in which one player has more than seven cards in one suit, or more than eleven cards in two suits.

The expert has a tremendous advantage in bidding for he has learned how to handle virtually every possible bidding situation. There is one type of bidding situation, however, that even the veriest of tyros handles as well (or as badly) as the expert. This is in the field of freak hands– hands that contain extremely long suits plus a void or two. (See DUKE OF CUMBERLAND HAND, HEARTBREAKER, MISSISSIPPI HEART HAND, and SWING HAND.) These hands defy scientific evaluation, and past experiences are of no help in appraising these anomalies. So the expert, like the average player, has to guess what he should bid; and when it comes to guessing, anybody is as good as anybody else.

Consider a few freak hands. The two deals which follow were all taken from North American Championships events. The first one arose in the Master Mixed Teams Championship of 1961.

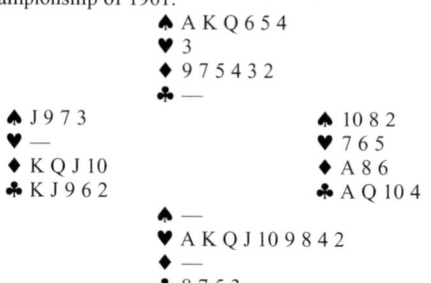

Note that 7♥ by South is unbeatable because West has no trump to lead. South can ruff the probable diamond opening lead and ruff a club in dummy. The top spades enable declarer to pitch his other three clubs In the unlikely event that North was declarer, a trump lead would defeat 7♥ four tricks.

We have all run into situations comparable to the one contained in this final deal, and there is not a thing we can do about it in preparing ourselves to handle it in the future.

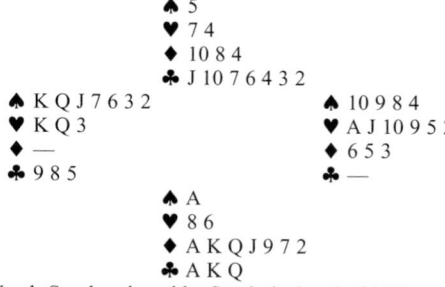

North-South vulnerable, South dealer, the bidding:

West	North	East	South
			2♦
2♠	Pass	4♠	5♦
5♠	6♦	6♠	Dbl
All Pass			

West's only loser was the ace of trumps.

FRED FRIENDLY AWARD. The annual award given by the PROFESSIONAL TOURNAMENT DIRECTORS ASSOCIATION to the ACBL tournament director who best evidences the qualities of courtesy and friendliness to players. The award was named for Paul Stehly, whose nickname was Fred Friendly. For winners see PROFESSIONAL TOURNAMENT DIRECTORS ASSOCIATION.

FREE BID. A bid made by a player whose partner's bid has been overcalled by right-hand opponent. In such circumstances partner will have another chance to bid, so it would seem unnecessary to bid with minimum values. Traditional theory therefore prescribed elevated standards for all "free" actions, equivalent to perhaps an additional king.

However, experts have long since abandoned this requirement except when the bid is 1NT.

There are three separate categories.

(1) 1NT (e.g. 1♣-1♥-1NT). The traditional range is 10-12 or 9-12, but many players reduce this by partnership agreement, sometimes to as little as 7-10. In that case the minimum would apply only when holding a double stopper in the opponent's suit.

(2) Suit Response (e.g.1♣-1♥-1♠). A minimum of 9 points according to old textbooks, but the modern expert style is to bid as if there has been no interference. There is a strong tendency for the free response, and this one in particular, to show a five-card suit (especially playing NEGATIVE DOUBLES), or at least a strong four-card suit. But in the ROTH-STONE SYSTEM, added values are necessary for a free bid; a negative double is used with weaker hands.

A free two-over-one response (e.g. 1♣ 1♥ 2♦) usually shows 11 points, or even 12; the standard should be slightly higher when the opener cannot rebid his suit at

the level of two. How far this bid is forcing is debatable. The BWS 94 consensus was that it was forcing as far as three of responder's suit, i.e., 3 ♦ in the above sequence.

(3) Raises. In this category (e. g. 1 ♦ -1 ♠ -2 ♦) almost all experts have abandoned the idea that the raise shows greater strength than it would without the overcall. There is no disadvantage in raising exactly as if there had been no overcall, and there is a considerable tactical loss in adopting a waiting policy. See FREE RAISE, NEGATIVE FREE BID.

FREE DOUBLE. A double of a contract which represents a game if undoubled. Usually confined to rubber bridge, when a partscore will convert an earlier partscore into game. If both sides have a partscore, judgment of a high level is required; all players may be straining their resources.

Doubles of game and slam contracts cannot properly be described as free. See PENALTY DOUBLE and SUCKER'S DOUBLE.

FREE FINESSE. A defensive lead which allows declarer to take a finesse without the risk of losing the trick, or which allows him to take a finesse that could not normally be taken at all.

FREE RAISE. A single raise of opener's suit after an overcall. The classical theory that a free raise implies extra strength (8-10 points) has been generally abandoned; most experts maintain the normal range (6-9 points) irrespective of the overcall. However, the overcall may make it necessary to relax the requirements for trump support, especially if the overcall is in the suit ranking immediately below opener's:

(a)	(b)
♠ A x	♠ x x
♥ x x	♥ A x x x
♦ x x x x	♦ Q x x x
♣ A J x x x	♣ K x x

In (a), a raise to 2 ♠ would be appropriate when 1 ♠ has been overcalled by 2 ♥. In (b), 1 ♣ should be raised to 2 ♣ after an overcall of 1 ♠. In each case the trump length is one card below standard. These examples assume that NEGATIVE DOUBLES are not being used. See FREE BID.

FRENCH CLUB. A simple 1 ♣ forcing system once in common use in France and other parts of the world.

FRENCH SCORING. A method formerly used in tournaments sanctioned by the French Bridge Federation, now obsolete. The value of the fourth trick in notrump was reduced to 20, so that making 10 or more tricks gave the same score in notrump or a major suit.

FREQUENCY CHART. Informational sheets produced for the players when computer scoring is used on across-the-field tops. The charts tell the number of times each score is achieved on each deal and also list the matchpoints each score is worth. Players use these charts to check their scores, but one drawback is that a player cannot tell whether or not he was credited with the correct result on any given board.

FRIEND AWARD. The annual award given by the AMERICAN BRIDGE ASSOCIATION to the player who earns the most ABA masterpoints in a calendar year.

FRIGID. See COLD.

FRUIT MACHINE SWISS. If responder has opening values and a fit in response to a major opening he can bid:

(1) Four clubs showing either: two aces and a singleton; three aces; or two aces and the trump king. After a 4 ♦ relay, the responder bids, respectively, the singleton, 4NT, or the trump king.

(2) Four diamonds with two aces and none of the above. See SWISS CONVENTIONS.

FULFILLING A CONTRACT. Taking as many tricks, in the play of the hand, as contracted for in addition to the book of six, i.e., eight tricks in a contract of two. A bonus of 50 points is awarded for a less-than-game contract in duplicate, 300 for a nonvulnerable game, and 500 for a vulnerable game.

G

GABARRET CUP. This Argentine award donated in memory of Adolfo Gabarret is the equivalent of the ACBL BARRY CRANE TOP 500 TROPHY. For winners, see Appendix IV.

GADGET. An artificial bidding device which can be grafted on to standard bidding methods but is not an integral part of any system. The term applies to nearly all the articles listed under ARTIFICIAL BIDS and SLAM CONVENTIONS.

GAMBIT. A deliberate sacrifice of a trick in order to gain additional tricks. The term is borrowed from chess.

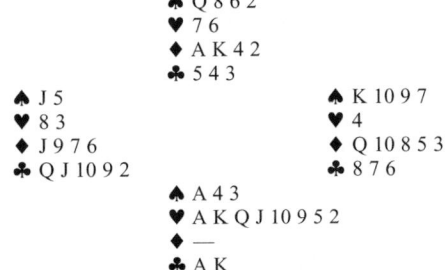

West leads the ♣ Q against South's contract of 6 ♥.

Declarer, at trick two, must play one of his two small trumps and concede an otherwise unnecessary trick to the 8. This forces a trump entry to the dummy, and permits South to discard his two spade losers on dummy's diamond winners. A spade lead would have defeated the contract. See GREEK GIFT.

GAMBLING AT BRIDGE. Playing for stakes is quite common in social bridge games around the world, either in clubs or privately. The game is normally Chicago, or four deals, in North America, and traditional rubber bridge in Europe and other parts of the world. GOULASH games are common in France. In some countries, particularly Scandinavia, duplicate play is normal and bridge for a stake is very rare.

In a home game in North America the stake may be as

little as 1/20th of a cent and is rarely more than three cents. In club games the lowest stake is usually one cent, and a game in New York City in which many of the players are millionaires is regularly played for a dollar or more.

Gambling is prohibited in contests sanctioned by the American Contract Bridge League and other NCBOs. However a hybrid between social bridge and duplicate is popular in some clubs, particularly in New York City. A group of eight or more players cut to form teams and then play a short duplicate match for a predetermined stake. Losers pay winners according to the IMP score. Then a fresh cut produces new teams.

GAMBLING THREE NOTRUMP. An opening bid based on a long, solid minor suit, a feature of the ACOL SYSTEM that has been adopted by many players using an artificial 2♣ forcing opening bid.

(a)	(b)
♠ A 5	♠ 7
♥ K 2	♥ Q 8 3
♦ J 3	♦ A K Q 8 4 3 2
♣ A K Q J 7 4 3	♣ J 3

The amount of outside strength required to make this bid varies with the individual partnership. In its original form stoppers were needed in at least two side suits, as in (a). The modern tendency is to make the bid (except in fourth position) with little or no outside strength, as in (b). This was the choice of the BWS2001 expert panel. Responses:

(1) 4♣ shows extreme weakness and a desire to play at the four-level in opener's suit.

(2) 4♦ is usually used artificially. A common arrangement is to use it as a singleton inquiry. Opener bids a major-suit singleton, bids 4NT without a singleton, and bids his minor with a singleton in the other minor.

(3) 4♥ and 4♠ are natural, with a self-sufficient six-card suit or better.

(4) 4NT is conventional, with responses downgraded because the opener has already shown an ace. A 5♦ rebid would therefore show two aces.

(5) 5♣ shows a desire to play in five of opener's suit - possibly for preemptive reasons.

(6) 5♦ is natural, implying that responder has a club honor and has therefore deduced that opener's suit is diamonds.

(7) 6♣ shows a desire to play a minor-suit slam.

The most effective method of bidding against a gambling 3NT opening bid is to use the RIPSTRA convention. Assuming adequate high-card strength, the bid of four of the better minor suit as a takeout for the majors gives the partnership the best chance of finding its best suit.

If 3NT becomes the final contract, the best chance to defeat the contract is usually for the opening leader to cash a winner in order to take a look at dummy and to obtain information from his partner as to which hand controls which side suits.

If the opening bid denies an outside ace, a 4NT response can be used to ask opener to bid a slam holding an eighth trump.

GAME. The winning of 100 points below the line in bridge. Game can be attained by bidding and winning a succession of two or more partscores, or can be bid in one contract after it is determined that the partnership has sufficient values in the combined hands. The first team to win two such games wins the rubber and the premium. In CHICAGO, a game may be bid and scored on each of four deals and it is theoretically possible for a side to win four games in one CHUKKER.

GAME ALL. The situation when both sides are vulnerable. The term is rare in the United States but standard in England.

GAME BID. A bid for just enough odd tricks to complete the requirement for game in a particular suit or notrump. In duplicate bridge this is a bid for 3NT, four of a major suit or five of a minor suit. In rubber bridge if a pair has a partscore, a game bid usually requires fewer tricks; a partscore of 40 points, for example, would make 2NT, two of a major or three of a minor into game bids.

GAME BONUS. Points awarded for bidding and making a game. In duplicate and Chicago, the award is 500 if vulnerable, 300 if not vulnerable. In rubber bridge, the award is 700 for winning a rubber two games to none and 500 for winning a rubber two games to one.

GAME CONTRACT. An undertaking of a contract which, if successful, will earn enough points in trickscore to make or complete the 100 required for a game. In notrump, three-odd, in hearts or spades, four-odd, in clubs or diamonds, five-odd tricks produce at least the 100 points necessary from a love score. With a partscore, lower contracts become game contracts. Some rubber bridge players will double a game contract more freely than below-game contracts, although such tactics are misconceived. See SUCKER'S DOUBLE.

GAME DEMAND BID. A bid which, once made, imposes an obligation upon the partnership to keep the bidding alive until game is reached or a satisfactory penalty inflicted upon the opponents. An obsolescent term. See FORCING TWO-BID.

GAME-FORCING BID. A bid which announces that the partnership should reach a game contract or higher, and thereby establishes a GAME-FORCING SITUATION.

GAME-FORCING SITUATION. A sequence of bidding which has committed both members of a partnership to reach a game contract. Many such types of sequences are listed under FORCING SEQUENCES.

GAME-GOING. A term applied to any hand or bidding situation which promises to develop a game for the partnership.

GAME IN. A colloquial expression meaning vulnerable.

GAME INVITATION. See BERGEN RAISES; COMPETITIVE DOUBLE; DRURY; INVITATIONAL BID; JUMP RAISE BY RESPONDER; LIMIT JUMP RAISE; LIMIT JUMP RAISE TO SHOW SINGLETON; MAXIMAL DOUBLES; MAXIMAL OVERCALL DOUBLE; SHORT-SUIT GAME TRIES; TWO-WAY GAME TRIES; WEAK-SUIT GAME TRY.

GAME-TRY DOUBLE. See MAXIMAL OVERCALL DOUBLE.

GAMMA TRUMP ASKING BID. An ASKING BID in the ROMAN and SUPER PRECISION systems concerned with the quality of responder's suit, which is inferentially agreed as trumps. The Roman responses are as follows:

1st step - Queen or worse
2nd step - King
3rd step - Ace
4th step - Two top honors
5th step - Three top honors

For responses in the SUPER PRECISION system, which are identical to the trump-asking responses in standard PRECISION CLUB, see PRECISION ASKING BIDS.

GARBAGE. A colloquial term for a minimum type of holding whose majority values are in unsupported queens and jacks.

GARDENER NOTRUMP OVERCALL. A two-way bid which may be either a natural notrump overcall with 16-18 points or a weak hand with a long suit. Partner usually bids 2♣ to find out which type of overcall was made, and the overcaller rebids 2NT if he has the natural strong type. There is a technical reason for this procedure if strong jump overcalls are being used: a weak hand with a long suit has no convenient way to enter the auction. Devised by Nico Gardener, London. See COMIC NOTRUMP.

GATHERING TRICKS. The taking in of tricks won by a side. The tricks taken by a side should be arranged in such a way that their number and sequence are apparent. See LAWS (Law 65).

GENERAL PURPOSE CUEBID. A bid of 4NT used as a general purpose slam try when a cuebid is not available or convenient. Since it is difficult to distinguish this from Blackwood and similar bids, it is rarely employed.

GENERAL UNDERSTANDINGS. There are a number of areas in which it pays a partnership to have a general agreement to cover situations that have not been specifically discussed. BWS 2001 determined that the following are the consensus choice of the experts, which should apply as a default without discussion. In some cases the vote was for an ad hoc decision about which choice is more sensible. Alternatives that partners can agree are shown in order of preference.

(1) If a call could logically be considered forcing or non-forcing, whichever seems more sensible prevails. Forcing was a popular second choice.

(2) If the choice is between natural and artificial, natural prevails. 2nd choice, whichever seems more sensible.

(3) If the choice is between a double being penalty or non-penalty, whichever seems more sensible prevails. Non-penalty was a popular second choice.

(4) If the choice is between a double being lead-directing (Lightner) or not, whichever seems more sensible prevails. 2nd choice, lead-directing.

(5) If the choice is between a redouble being for business or escape, whichever seems more sensible prevails. 2nd choice, escape.

(6) If there is a pass over an opposing redouble, whichever meaning, penalty or escape, seems more sensible prevails. 2nd choice, almost as popular, was penalty or non-forcing.

(7) If the choice in a competitive auction is between a situation being forcing for the partnership or non-forcing, non-forcing prevails. 2nd choice, whichever seems more sensible.

(8) When a pass would be forcing in a competitive situation, a double should discourage further offensive bidding in all cases. A popular second choice was penalty double when partner is limited, and discouraging further offensive bidding when unlimited. Third choice, penalty when a suitable hand is a live possibility, discouraging otherwise. Fourth choice, penalty otherwise.

For the following four items concerning doubles in a competitive situation: (a) means penalty; (b) means undescribed high-card values with no further definition; (c) means undescribed high-card values but with sufficient length in the suit doubled, based on the level of the auction, to sustain a penalty pass on ordinary distribution; (d) means a relatively strong offensive hand with sufficient defense to expect a set when partner passes with a normal hand.

(9) When a pass would be non-forcing in a competitive situation and both partners are unlimited: (c) prevails; (d), (a) and (b) are acceptable alternatives in that order of preference.

(10) When a pass would be non-forcing in a competitive situation and the doubler is unlimited and his partner limited: (a) prevails; (c) and (d) are acceptable alternatives in that order of preference.

(11) When a pass would be non-forcing in a competitive situation and the doubler is limited and his partner unlimited: (a) prevails; (c) is an acceptable alternative.

(12) When a pass would be non-forcing in a competitive situation and both partners are limited: (a) prevails. Alternatives unacceptable.

(Summary: penalty is the consensus choice except when both partners are unlimited.)

(13) When a forcing bid is doubled, pass and redouble are both non-forcing, suggesting a contract.

GENERALI WORLD MASTERS INDIVIDUAL. A biennial invitational competition to determine open (52 players), women's (28 players) and Junior (20 players) Individual champions. It was first held in 1992. For results see Appendix IV.

GENEVA. A method of showing any pair of unbid suits with an overcall of 2NT (or higher) by a player whose side has not yet bid. The bidder moves to his cheaper suit if his partner does not locate a fit. Many low-level doubles become penalty doubles. A danger is that the fit, if any, will be found at an excessively high level. Devised by Dr. William Konigsberger and Derrick Deane of Geneva, Switzerland.

GEORGE BURNS TROPHY. This trophy, inaugurated in 1993, is given annually to the ACBL Senior Player of the Year. It is named for George Burns, famous comedian who was still playing bridge daily at his country club well into his late nineties. For winners see Appendix I.

GERBER CONVENTION. A 4♣ bid to ask partner how many aces he holds. The traditional responses are:
4♦ no ace 4♥ one ace 4♠ two aces 4NT three aces 5♣ four aces.
4♦ can be used instead of 5♣ to show the rare holding

of four aces. Experts strongly favor (62% in BWS 2001) use of a modified responding scheme:

4♦ no ace or three aces
4♥ one ace or four aces
4♠ two aces

This is analogous to the responses to ROMAN KEY-CARD BLACKWOOD.

As originally written (ROLLING GERBER), the 4♣ bidder uses the next available bid to ask for kings on the same principle, but cannot use the agreed trump suit for this purpose. For example, 4♠ asks for kings over a response of 4♥, unless spades is the agreed trump suit, in which case 4NT becomes the king-asking bid. The modern tendency is to use 4♦ to show four aces along with 5♣ to ask for kings rather than the next higher bid. This helps remove ambiguity.

There may often be difficulty in distinguishing a conventional 4♣ bid from a natural one. Some players restrict the use of the convention to situations in which no suit has been genuinely bid (e.g., after a 1NT or 2NT opening, or a conventional 2♣ bid followed by 2NT or 3NT).

If 4♣ is to be used more generally, there are three possible rules a partnership can adopt:

(1) 4♣ is conventional unless it is a direct club raise.

(2) 4♣ is conventional unless clubs have been genuinely bid by the partnership.

(3) 4♣ is conventional if it is a jump bid, or if a suit has been specifically agreed. This is perhaps the best of these rules.

A partnership also has to consider how responder should act holding a void, or when there is interference bidding.

Treatment of similar situations is discussed under BLACKWOOD convention.

This convention, invented in 1938 by John Gerber, is sometimes referred to as 4♣ Blackwood. The convention was devised earlier independently by Dr. William Konigsberger and Wim Nye, and published by them in Europe in 1936. See also ACE IDENTIFICATION; BLACK AND RED GERBER; CLARAC SLAM TRY; EXTENDED GERBER; KEY CARD GERBER; RO-MAN GERBER; SUPER GERBER.

GESTURE. A mannerism that suggests a call, lead, play, or plan of play. See LAWS (Law 16).

GET A COUNT. To determine during the play the number of cards held in one or more suits by one of the hidden hands. See COUNTING THE HAND.

GHESTEM. A system of strong two-suited overcalls devised by Pierre Ghestem.
Over one club: 2NT shows the red suits
2♦ shows the major suits
3♣ shows diamonds and spades
(This permits two clubs to be natural).
Over other suit openings:
2NT shows the low-ranking suits
3♣ shows the high-ranking suits
Cuebid shows the top and bottom suits

GHOULIES. See GOULASH.

GIB. A powerful bridge-playing program invented by Matt Ginsberg. GIB stands for Ginsberg's Intelligent Bridge. GIB completely dominated the Orbis World Computer Bridge Championships in Bermuda in 2000, winning the round robin, the bidding competition and the main event. GIB did the same at the Computer Bridge Championships during the world championships in Lille, France, in 1998 and at the Par Contest in 1998. The program has a wide range of bidding systems including Standard American, $^2/_1$ Game Forcing, Kaplan-Sheinwold, Acol and traditional Goren. It also has many individual conventions. It has sophisticated artificial intelligence search algorithms for both bidding and play.

GIN. Colloquialism indicating total certainty of making a contract: "When the heart finesse won, I was gin."

GIVE COUNT. As a defender, to give a LENGTH SIGNAL to one's partner.

GLADIATOR. A method of responding to 1NT, devised in New Zealand, and used in slightly modified forms in the ROMAN and CAB systems.

A response of 2♣ is a relay, requiring the opener to bid 2♦. A minimum suit bid by responder then shows weakness, and the opener passes. Other rebids by the responder are limited.

A response of 2♦ is a Stayman-type inquiry for major suits, and is forcing to game. A response of 2♥ or 2♠ is forcing, and higher suit responses are slam suggestions.

GO DOWN. Synonym for failure to make a contract.

GO FOR A NUMBER. Suffering a heavy penalty, presumably in four figures.

GO OFF. Fail to make a contract.

GO TO BED. Failure to take an obvious winner, usually an ace, and never taking a trick with it: "West went to bed with the ace of spades."

GOLD CUP. The Knockout Team Championship of Great Britain, contested under the auspices of the BRITISH BRIDGE LEAGUE. For results see appendix IV. (See also VON ZEDTWITZ GOLD CUP.)

GOLD LIFE MASTER. An ACBL Life Master who has acquired at least 2500 masterpoints.

GOLD POINT. Points awarded for section firsts and overall awards in regionally-rated or North American Championship events which have no upper masterpoint restrictions such as Open Pairs, Master Pairs, Men's and Women's Pairs, Mixed Pairs, Individual and Team events. One gold point is awarded to section winners in the annual ACBL Instant Matchpoint Game in sections of seven or more tables. Gold points are also awarded at regional events or regionally-rated events of two or more sessions which have a masterpoint limit of 750 or more points. The overall award in some restricted events at certain multiple-session North American Championships may contain a percentage of gold points.

GOLDEN AGE MASTER. A special category set up by ACBL to accommodate older players. There are two ways to qualify — (1) 70 years of age with 300 points

of any color, or (2) 80 years of age with 100 points of any color.

GOLDEN RULE. The Golden Rule of bidding, as laid down by Alan Truscott, is that a suit should not be bid twice unless it has at least six cards. This applies to opener, responder, and the opponents of the opening bidder. Beginners do well to adhere to this rule, which is valid more than 90% of the time. Experienced players will be aware of some exceptions: (1) When a fit has been established, directly or by implication; (2) After a two-over-one response, guaranteeing a rebid in the modern style; (3) In a second suit. A player with 6-5 or 5-5 distribution can bid first suit, second suit and second suit again. See OPENER'S REBID.

GOLDWATER RULE. The satirical suggestion by Tournament Director Harry Goldwater that an opening lead out of turn should generally be accepted (see Laws 54 and 56 for declarer's other options). The rationale is that a player who does not know whose turn it is to lead probably does not know the right lead either.

GOOD. An adjective used to describe a hand which is better than the simple point-count would suggest, as in "a good 18". This may be owing to distributional factors, to the presence of body, to the location of honors in long suits, or to a combination of these items.

GOOD CARDS. Cards which have been established during the play and which are winners that can be cashed. In a wide sense, a player of a partnership holding good cards has more than a fair share of the honor strength. But the term is sometimes used in a more precise technical meaning, referring to honor cards which have improved in value as a result of the auction. In a competitive auction, the improvement may arise because the significant honors are over the opponent who has bid the suit (see POSITIONAL FACTOR).

GOOD FORTUNE. Chance may play an important role at the card table, but fortune can be significant in bridge events away from the table. There are three recorded instances of players achieving international honors as a result of fortuitous circumstances.

In 1937 the United States Women's team at the World Championship in Budapest found itself one player short. An American lady whose name has not been recorded was brought in to complete the team. She was a player with only social bridge experience who happened to be staying in Budapest at the time. In 1961 at the Fall North American Championships in Houston, Robert Stucker and Jack Blair formed an impromptu partnership in order to complete a section in the Open Pairs. They finished second in the event and subsequently represented the United States in the World Open Pairs in Cannes as a result of their success.

Mary Edwards was brought in as a substitute in the 1959 British international women's trials to replace a player who had fallen ill. From an apparently hopeless position, trailing the rest of the field by a substantial margin, she qualified for the British team in partnership with Mrs. G. R. Higginson. Subsequently they became European champions when their team won in Palermo, Italy.

GOOD TWO NOTRUMP. A direct bid of 2NT, the

converse of GOOD-BAD TWO NOTRUMP, to distinguish between competitive and constructive actions. If the opponents have made the last bid at the two-level and it has not been doubled, a player who has not passed after the opponents entered the auction and may have competitive or constructive goals can use this concept. It can apply to any of the four players, in direct or reopening position. Some possible auctions are:

	West	North	East	South
(a)	1♦	1♥	1♠	2♥
	2NT			
(b)	1♥	Dbl	Pass	2♦
	2♥	2NT		
(c)	1♦	Pass	1♥	1♠
	2♣	2♠	2NT	
(d)	1♦	Pass	1♠	2♥
	2♠	2NT		
(e)			Pass	Pass
	1♠	2♦	2NT	

In each case, 2NT bid is an artificial way to show game interest or better. Other actions, such as 3♦ in sequence (a) or (b) are competitive. In most cases there will be other strong actions available, and there will be subtle distinctions to be made. See GOOD-BAD TWO NOTRUMP.

GOOD-BAD TWO NOTRUMP. Described by Jeff Rubens in his articles on the Useful Space Principle. The purpose of this conventional treatment of a 2NT bid in competition is to allow one hand to clarify between purely competitive raises or bids of a new suit, and those showing values. The use of the convention can be extended to cover almost every bid of 2NT in a competitive auction. But the two simplest uses of the bid are by the opening bidder when partner has responded 1NT or made a negative double, and fourth hand has competed with a call of 2♦ or higher. For example consider the three following sequences using standard methods:

West	North	East	South
1♦	1♠	Dbl	2♠
3♣			

The 3♣ bid would be made by opener with a minimum 3-1-5-4 shape and a 12-count; but it would also be made with the same distribution and an extra ace.

West	North	East	South
1♦	Pass	1NT	2♠
3♣			

In standard methods opener could either have a hand with no game interest or a hand close a jump to 3♣ without intervention.

West	North	East	South
1♥	Pass	1NT	2♠
3♥			

Whether 1NT is forcing or not, opener could have a genuine invitation to game or be stretching to compete.

Using 2NT as the equivalent of a transfer to 3♣ lets opener use that sequence as the way to show a purely competitive hand. If he was competing in clubs, opener passes his partner's response. Otherwise he describes his hand appropriately; new suits, or suit rebids after the 2NT call all show purely competitive hands. Direct actions at the three-level therefore show genuine game invitations or better.

Having 2NT available as a puppet to 3♣ allows opener flexibility with strong hands. He can differentiate the

degree of stop in his opponent's suit, since he has two routes to 3NT or the three-level cuebid. In these sequences it makes sense to play that the slower opener gets to 3NT in the opponents' suit, the less confident he is that 3NT is the right spot. Another possibility is to use the direct cue-bid as a single-suited hand, while going via 2NT shows a strong balanced hand, in both cases looking for a stop for 3NT.

Note that responder does not have to bid 3♣ over the 2NT call. If he would prefer to play in opener's first-bid suit rather than clubs, he must break the transfer by reverting directly to opener's suit. With game interest even facing the purely competitive hand, responder makes a cuebid, bids 3NT or jumps, as appropriate. See GOOD TWO NOTRUMP.

GOODWILL COMMITTEE. See ACBL GOODWILL COMMITTEE.

GOREN AWARD. See INTERNATIONAL BRIDGE PRESS ASSOCIATION AWARDS.

GOREN POINT-COUNT. See POINT-COUNT and DISTRIBUTIONAL POINT-COUNT.

GOREN SYSTEM. The bidding methods advocated by Charles H. Goren in many books from 1944 on. The method incorporated the GOREN POINT COUNT. To the basic WORK COUNT, 4-3-2-1, he added a distributional count: a void counts for 3 points, a singleton for 2 and a doubleton for 1. This followed the idea put forward by William Anderson of Toronto. The value of a hand is determined by adding the high card point total to the distributional total. 13-point hands are optional opening bids in the system, but 14-point hands must be opened. A third-hand opening can be made with as few as 11 points if the hand contains a fairly good suit. A fourth-hand opening bid should be made on 13 points, even though no good rebid is available. A different valuation system is used for the hand that figures to be dummy. High cards are counted at face value, and honors in partner's suit are promoted by a point each. One point is added for each doubleton, 3 for a singleton and 5 for a void if a fit has been established. A point should be deducted if dummy holds only three trumps, and another point should be subtracted if the dummy hand has a 4-3-3-3 distribution.

Using these methods, Goren determined that 26 points usually will produce game in a major, 29 game in a minor, 33 a small slam and 37 a grand slam.

The Goren System advocates opening FOUR-CARD MAJORS as long as the suit is biddable–at least Q-x-x-x. When holding biddable touching suits of equal length, the higher-ranking should be the opening bid. When the two biddable suits of equal length are spades and clubs, the opening bid should be 1♣. In other combinations, the suit below the short suit should be the opening bid.

With balanced hands, responder should bid 1NT with 6-10 points, 2NT with 13-15 and 3NT with 16-18. Responder should have the unbid suits stopped for the 2NT and 3NT bids. When responder has trump support, he should raise partner's suit to 2 with 7-10 points, to 3 with 13-16 points. Responder should jump shift with 19 or more points. He should respond in a new suit at the one level with 6 or more points. A two-level response in a new suit requires 10 points. With hands containing 11 or 12 points, responder should find two bids without

forcing partner to game.

Opening two-bids in a suit should be made with a good five-card suit and 25 points, with a good six-card suit and 23 points, and with a good seven-card suit and 21 points.

Openings in notrump should be based on the following: 1NT, 16-18 points; 2NT, 22-24 points; 3NT, 25-27 points. When evaluating for an opening notrump bid, a player should count only his high card values. A 2♣ response to 1NT (also a 3♣ response to 2NT) asks the opening bidder about his biddable major suits. With no four-card major, opener should rebid 2♦; with a four-card heart suit, 2♥; with a four-card spade suit or two four-card majors, 2♠.

GOULASH. A deal in which the cards are not shuffled. They are dealt five to each player for two circuits, and finally three to each player. The name is apparently derived from Hungarian goulash, a highly spiced mixture of meat and vegetables, and is intended to suggest a spicy and unusual mixture.

Players sometimes agree to play goulash when a hand has been passed out, particularly in private or commuter games. Goulashes are standard in CUTTHROAT BRIDGE and TOWIE.

A goulash is sometimes referred to as mayonnaise or hollandaise.

GO UP. To play a high and possibly winning card when faced with a choice of playable cards.

GRAND COUP. A play by which declarer deliberately shortens his trump holding by ruffing a winner in order to achieve a finessing position over an adverse trump holding in an end position.

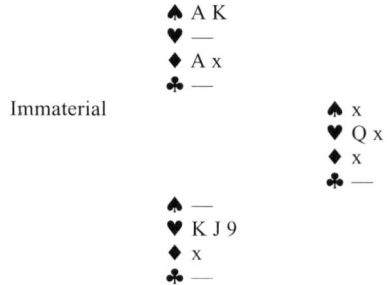

Declarer, in a heart contract, has discovered West to be void of hearts. With the lead in the dummy, declarer leads the ♠A and trumps it. He re-enters dummy with the ♦A to lead any card at trick 12. East must ruff and declarer overruffs.

GRAND LIFE MASTER. Highest rank in ACBL. It requires 10,000 masterpoints and at least one victory in one of the following: North American Championship with no upper masterpoint restriction; Open Team Trials or its equivalent; Women's Team Trials or its equivalent; or any of the following World Bridge Federation events – Bermuda Bowl, Venice Cup, Rosenblum Cup, McConnell Cup, Open Pairs, Women's Pairs, Team Olympiad or Women's Team Olympiad.

GRAND MASTER. See WORLD BRIDGE FEDERATION PLAYER RANKINGS.

GRAND NATIONAL CHAMPIONSHIPS. (1) A series of annual championships first held in 1934 by the UNITED STATES BRIDGE ASSOCIATION and continued annually until 1937. See Appendix I.

(2) See GRAND NATIONAL TEAMS and NORTH AMERICAN OPEN PAIRS. See also CANADIAN NATIONAL TEAMS. See Appendix I.

GRAND NATIONAL FORTY-NINER PAIRS. See NORTH AMERICAN FORTY-NINER PAIRS, FIFTH CHAIR TROPHY and Appendix I.

GRAND NATIONAL PAIRS. See NORTH AMERICAN OPEN PAIRS and Appendix I.

GRAND NATIONAL ROOKIE PAIRS. A major ACBL pair championship 1979-1991. See also NORTH AMERICAN ROOKIE PAIRS and Appendix I.

GRAND NATIONAL TEAMS. A major ACBL team championship, contested since 1973 for the MOREHEAD TROPHY. It is patterned in some respects after the USBA's event of the Thirties. The initial stages of the GNT are conducted over the course of several months in each ACBL district in the United States, Mexico and Bermuda, for members of units within the district to produce a district championship team. Canada originally participated in this event, but in 1980 Canada began conducting its own national team championship parallel to the GNT. Through 1984 the district champions competed within eight Grand National Zones for the Zonal Championship. The final playoffs were contested as knockouts by the eight zonal champions at the Summer North American Bridge Championships. In 1985 the zonal stage was eliminated and the non-Canadian District Champions competed directly for the GNT title. At the same time the North American Teams Flight B was added for players with 0-500 masterpoints. Later the upper limit for Flight B was increased to 1500 points, and a new classification – Flight C – was added. This is a non-Life Master event, but the upper masterpoint limit is 500. Flight A is contested as a strictly United States event, but Flights B and C include teams from all 25 ACBL districts. Through 1991 the GNT champions were entitled to compete against the winners of the VANDERBILT CUP, the SPINGOLD TROPHY and the REISINGER TROPHY for the right to represent North America or the United States in the WORLD CHAMPIONSHIP two years hence. A new method, called the INTERNATIONAL TEAM TRIALS (ITT), was inaugurated in 1994. This event is now known as the United States Bridge Championship (USBC). See ACBL INTERNATIONAL OPEN TEAM SELECTION, NORTH AMERICAN TEAMS. Also see Appendix I.

GRAND OLD MAN OF BRIDGE. A term applied in the Twenties and early Thirties to MILTON C. WORK and in later years to SIDNEY LENZ. If the title belongs to those who have promoted the game at a great age, through writing and in other ways, there are other candidates for the title: R.F.Foster; George Beynon; Oswald Jacoby; B.Jay Becker and Alfred Sheinwold.

GRAND SLAM. The winning of all thirteen tricks by the declarer. The bonus for a grand slam, 1,000 points when not vulnerable and 1,500 when vulnerable, make a grand slam, bid and made, one of the best rewarded accomplishments at rubber bridge, and one of the more effective methods of SHOOTING at duplicate. While the general tendency among rubber bridge players is to avoid bidding grand slams except in ironclad situations, the mathematics of the game suggest rather freer acceptance of the risks involved in view of the large rewards.

See SLAM BIDDING for an explanation of methods of exploration suitable to bidding grand slams, and the percentage or odds that justify such bids. For a brief period (1932-35) the grand slam bonuses were higher than they are now: 1,500 non-vulnerable, 2,250 vulnerable.

GRAND SLAM FORCE. A method of locating the top trump honors when a grand slam is in view. It was devised by Ely Culbertson in 1936. A *Bridge World* article on the subject was given Josephine Culbertson's byline, but it was written by the staff. As a result the convention is often referred to as JOSEPHINE in Europe.

A bid of 5NT asks responder to bid a grand slam if he holds two of the top three trump honors. (This clearly does not apply if 5NT is a natural notrump raise, or if it is used as part of another slam convention.) A jump to 5NT fixes the last bid suit as trump unless another suit has been specifically agreed.

It is sometimes necessary to know whether responder has one of the top three honors. If the agreed trump suit is not clubs, one or more intermediate bids are available at the six-level for this purpose.

If diamonds are agreed, 6♦ should show one top honor. If a major suit has been agreed, several methods are in use, designed to permit a partnership to reach a grand slam missing Q-x-x in the trump suit.

One method is to divide the responses into four steps. The first step would show the weakest trump holding for the previous bidding (three or four small), the second step would show the queen, the third step the ace or king and the fourth step the ace or king with extra length. If hearts are agreed, the first and second steps are combined into one. If diamonds are the agreed suit, the first and second steps and the third and fourth steps are combined. For example:

```
              North
              ♠ K 5 3 2
              ♥ 6 5 4
              ♦ 8 5 3
              ♣ 10 7 2

              South
              ♠ A 10 9 8 6 4
              ♥ A K
              ♦ A K Q 9 7
              ♣ —
```

South	North
2♣	2♦
2♠	4♠
5NT	6♥
7♠	

North's jump raise shows four spades, and his step response to the grand slam force shows the king. Since there is unlikely to be a trump loser, South bids the grand slam.

An alternate expert method, perhaps superior theoretically, is to sign off in the trump suit with the worst trump holding; other responses at the six-level are made inversely, the higher the bid the weaker the trump holding. In order to retain all four steps to show gradation of

trump quality even when a suit other than spades has been agreed, some partnerships use jumps to five of the suit above the agreed trump suit, rather than to 5NT as the Grand Slam Force.

The expert consensus (63% in BWS2001) favored the "cheapest bid is weakest hand" method. If there is ambiguity about the trump suit, the strong expert consensus (88% in the BWS2001) was to use the same rules that apply in a ROMAN KEYCARD BLACKWOOD sequence. If the responder has already shown a strong suit, the responding structure can be modified. This needs partnership agreement.

If there is interference, DOPI and DEPO apply, depending on the space available.

If clubs is the agreed trump suit, several methods are playable.

West	East
♠ A K J 3	♠ 7 2
♥ K 6	♥ A Q J 6
♦ A 5	♦ 9 4 2
♣ K 8 6 4 2	♣ A Q 5 3
1♣	1♥
1♠	3♣
4NT	5♥
5♠	5NT
6♣	7♣

Playing regular Blackwood, West's unexpected bid of 5♠ forces East to bid 5NT. Then East can interpret the belated bid of 6♣, which logically suggests interest in a grand slam, as the Grand Slam Force.

In some systems, such as SCHENKEN, it is possible to agree on a trump suit and cuebid first- and possibly second-round controls before 4NT is reached. Richard Reed suggests that 4NT should then be used to pinpoint trump honors. Partner returns to the agreed trump suit with none of the top three honors, bids the lowest-ranking side suit with the king or queen, the next ranking side suit with the ace, the highest-ranking side suit with two of the top three honors, and 5NT with full control of the trump suit.

The Grand Slam Force remains in the repertory of expert pairs; however, new methods to uncover trump honors, such as ROMAN KEY CARD BLACKWOOD, have increasingly found favor. Furthermore, many expert pairs use a bid of 5NT as a general inquiry: "Partner, pick a slam." See FIVE NOTRUMP BID. See also BYZANTINE BLACKWOOD: TRUMP ASKING BIDS.

GRANO-ASTRO. A two-suited defense to 1NT in which double shows spades and another suit, and a minor-suit bid shows that suit and hearts.

GRASS ROOTS. A term used by the ACBL to describe an event for which qualification begins at the club or unit level. Pairs or teams which qualify must further qualify at the district level in order to compete in the final stages at one of the ACBL major tournaments. The pair events are known as NORTH AMERICAN PAIRS, with three flights – A, B and C. The top event in the teams is the GRAND NATIONAL TEAMS. The second and third flights are known as NORTH AMERICAN TEAMS B and C.

GREEK GIFT. A trick offered to the opponent which, if accepted, leads to disaster. The following example was played about 1930 with Lee Hazen in the East seat.

```
                    ♠ 9 7 4
                    ♥ K Q 5
                    ♦ 8 7 5 4 2
                    ♣ 9 6
♠ —                                ♠ J 8 3
♥ 10 9 8 3                         ♥ J 7 6 4 2
♦ Q J 6 3                          ♦ A K 10 9
♣ J 10 8 7 5                       ♣ 2
                    ♠ A K Q 10 6 5 2
                    ♥ A
                    ♦ —
                    ♣ A K Q 4 3
```

Neither side was vulnerable. The bidding:

West	North	East	South
Pass	Pass	1♥	2♥
4♥	Pass	Pass	6♠
Pass	Pass	Pass	

West led the ♥10 against 6♠ and South took his ace. He then made a tricky play by leading the ♠10. He assumed that somebody would win this, and he would be provided with the dummy-entry he needed to dispose of his club losers.

Hazen was about to take his jack, but paused to consider. Why was South being so generous? Was it a Greek Gift? It was clear from the bidding that South had no more hearts, so he must be trying to create an entry. The ♠10 was allowed to win, and South did not look pleased. His next move was to lead the ace and king of clubs.

Fully alive to the situation, Hazen refused to ruff, dooming South to defeat. If he tried for ruffs he would be overruffed, and if he did not West would score two club tricks.

Since the only danger for South was a bad split in both black suits, a better play would have been to play the top clubs at once. It would now have been more tempting for East to ruff, thus allowing the slam to score. See GAMBIT.

GREEN. A British colloquialism meaning the opponents are vulnerable and we are not. See AMBER, RED, WHITE.

GREEN POINT. A jocular term for tournaments in which the prizes are in dollars and therefore green. In England the equivalent is gold points.

GREEN SUIT. The fifth suit in the American version of FIVE-SUIT BRIDGE, called Eagles. Prior to the introduction of five-suit bridge, the green suit was a nonexistent fifth suit. See HIPPOGRIFFS.

GROSVENOR GAMBIT. A humorous psychological ploy described by Frederick Turner of Los Angeles in *The Bridge World* June 1973. A defender deliberately makes an error, giving the declarer an opportunity refused because he expects rational defense. The hope is that the declaring side will be demoralized on later deals. For example:

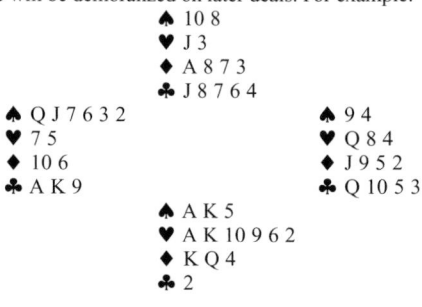

```
                    ♠ 10 8
                    ♥ J 3
                    ♦ A 8 7 3
                    ♣ J 8 7 6 4
♠ Q J 7 6 3 2                      ♠ 9 4
♥ 7 5                              ♥ Q 8 4
♦ 10 6                             ♦ J 9 5 2
♣ A K 9                            ♣ Q 10 5 3
                    ♠ A K 5
                    ♥ A K 10 9 6 2
                    ♦ K Q 4
                    ♣ 2
```

Two top clubs are led against 6 ♥. South ruffs and plays spades, ruffing the third round in dummy. Instead of overruffing East discards. His trick comes back because South plays trumps from the top, sure that West has the queen.

GROUP SCORE. The score made by all the pairs in a group on a set of hands constituting a match. Competition between clubs and cities is sometimes based on a team of eight, twelve, or an even larger number of players. In such a game, each pair from one side meets each of the pairs on the competing side, all playing the same set of boards. The net score (plus and minus) of all pairs is included in the group score.

Also, in total point pair contests, the net score on a set of boards on which two particular pairs are in opposition.

GUARD (or STOPPER). An honor holding in a particular suit which will or may prevent the opponents from running the suit.

A guard may be:

(1) Positive: A, K-Q, Q-J-10, J-10-9-8.
(2) Probable: K-J-x, K-10-x, Q-J-x.
(3) Possible: Q-x-x, J-9-x-x.
(4) Positional: K-x.
(5) Partial: K, Q-x, J-x-x, 10-x-x-x.

GUARD SQUEEZE. A squeeze in three suits, in which an opponent holds guards in two suits, and his holding in a third suit prevents declarer from taking a winning finesse.

There are five basic endings, each of which resembles the basic double squeeze position. By contrast with the double squeeze, the guard squeeze takes place when the same opponent controls both isolated menaces, but as compensation the double menace contains finesse possibilities.

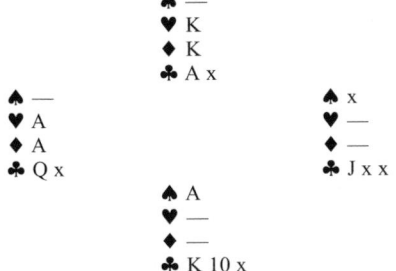

South leads the ♠ A, and West is squeezed in three suits. He must discard a club, but South leads a club to the ace (dropping the queen) and finesses the 10 on the way back.

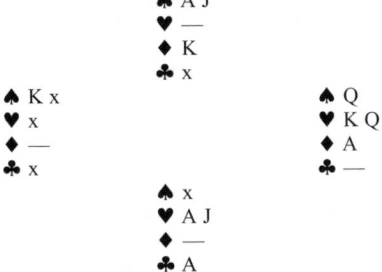

South leads the ♣ A, and East is squeezed in three suits. If he discards a spade, South can lead that suit, and finesse the jack.

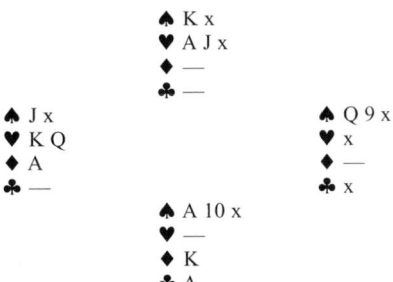

South leads the ♣ A and West is squeezed in three suits. If he discards a spade, South leads a spade to the king (dropping the jack) and finesses the 10 on the way back.

In each of the above positions the squeeze retains its effectiveness even if one of the isolated menaces is guarded by both opponents. This leads to a double guard squeeze whose constituents are a guard squeeze against one opponent and a simple squeeze against the other.

There are two other double guard squeeze positions:

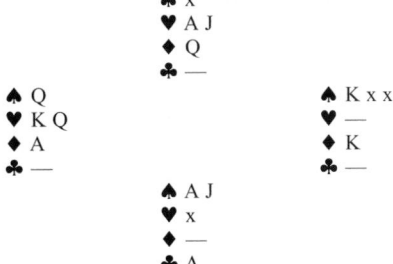

South leads the ♣ A, and West is squeezed in three suits. He must discard a diamond. Now the ♥ A squeezes East in spades and diamonds.

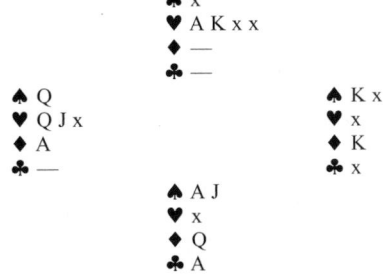

South leads the ♣ A, and West is squeezed in three suits. He is forced to discard a diamond. South takes two top hearts, squeezing East in spades and diamonds. See SQUEEZE.

GUARDED HONOR or GUARDED SUIT. See GUARD.

GUIDE CARD. A card, usually printed, with prearranged instructions to each contestant, telling him which seat to occupy and which boards to play at each round. The guide card may also enable a contestant to check the positions and identities of his opponents.

Guide cards may be in the form of printed instruction cards remaining permanently at each table (suitable only for cyclic movements); or they may be in the form of separate cards to be hand-carried by each contestant (suitable for either cyclic or noncyclic movements).

Guide cards are used for HOWELL MOVEMENT pair games, team games, and individual contests.

H

HACKETT. A defense to a WEAK TWO-BID in which 3 ♣ is a weak takeout request, with fewer than 16 points, and 3 ♦ is stronger, with 16 points or more. Double is for penalties.

HALF TABLES. An extra pair at a duplicate game. To accommodate the pair and still keep the game a fair contest requires a choice of methods by the director. The choice is based on the size of the game, the movement in use, and the time when it becomes known that a half-table situation exists.

If it is known in advance that a half-table situation exists, the director may consider that he has a full table and run the movement with a PHANTOM PAIR. Any pair scheduled to play the phantom pair will have a sitout for that round. However, such a movement should be used only if the game will have a complete movement. Otherwise there are problems with the scoring since pairs will have played different numbers of boards and boards will have different tops. This was a serious problem, but the advent of computers has made handling this type of situation much easier.

A better option, especially when confronted with the problem of adding a late-arriving pair, is to add a pair to the movement already in play. For HOWELL-like movements this pair will be added as an APPENDIX PAIR. For a Mitchell let the extra pair be a ROVER pair or shift into a PIVOT MITCHELL or a BUMP MITCHELL. This shift may be made unless the movement being used is a RELAY MITCHELL (with board sharing). This change in the movement can be effected as late as just before the move for the second round. Note that a Pivot Mitchell and a ROVER MITCHELL can be run in as many rounds as full tables, but a Bump Mitchell must have one fewer rounds than the number of full tables. All three movements may be curtailed at any time with no scoring problem.

The ACBL has guide cards for half-table games which are available upon request. Following are suggestions for half-table movements. No attempt has been made to include all the possibilities. However, it will be pointed out when one movement is clearly superior to the others.

2¹/₂ tables. Use a three-table Howell movement. It is possible to shift to this movement if a two-table game has been begun and a fifth pair arrives late.

3¹/₂ tables. Use a rover pair with this movement: Out, EW2, NS2, EW3, EW1. If there is time to do so, it is better to switch to a four-table Howell.

4¹/₂ tables. A five-table Howell is best if it is known that this will be the size of the game. If the half table comes in during the first round, use an appendix to the four-table Howell at any table other than Table 1. The new pair must be appended to a table that originally had two moving pairs.

5¹/₂ tables. Run a five-table Howell with an appendix pair at any table without a stationary pair. If the size of the game is known early enough, a six-table REDUCED HOWELL can be used. With a Mitchell movement, a Rover

pair will work well. Another reasonable possibility — set up a relay between Tables 1 and 6 with bye boards between Tables 3 and 4. The phantom pair should be North-South 6; East-West pairs will sit out when they reach Table 6.

6¹/₂ tables. The best movement is the seven-table Howell — each pair meets every other pair and the sitout is only two boards long. If the half table comes in late and the movement is a six-table reduced Howell, append the pair to any table where there is no stationary pair. With a Mitchell movement, put out four boards at each table and have the pair at Table 7 sit out the first round. If the phantom pair is North-South, the East-West pairs will sit out when they arrive at Table 7. If the phantom pair is East-West, the North-South pairs will sit out when they are scheduled to meet East-West 7. If the game already has started when the extra pair arrives, use the ROVING PAIR method. (See ROVER.)

7¹/₂ tables. A number of possibilities cover this situation. If the movement is a seven-table Howell, add an appendix pair at any table that does not have a stationary pair. Alternatively an eight-table Reduced Howell may be used. If the movement is a Mitchell, the eight-table movement with a relay between Tables 1 and 8 with bye boards between Tables 4 and 5 will work out well. The phantom pair should be North-South 8 so that effectively there will be no board sharing. If a seven-table Mitchell already is in progress when the late pair arrives, the Rover movement may be used in either of two ways. The Rover may proceed from table to table, replacing either North-South pairs or East-West pairs in the usual progression. The problem here is that each sitout pair must sit out four boards. An alternative is to have the Rover replace first the East-West pair for two boards, then the North-South pair for the other two boards. By doing this every pair sits out two boards instead of half the field sitting out four and the rest playing all the boards. If this movement is used, the game will produce only one winner.

8¹/₂ tables. If you know before the game starts that you have a half table, the best movement is a nine-table Mitchell. Put out boards on all tables and have one of the pairs sit out at Table 9. If the phantom pair is North-South 9 the East-West pairs will sit out when they reach Table 9. If the phantom pair is East-West, the North-South pairs will sit out when they are scheduled to play East-West 9. If the extra pair arrives after the game is under way, use the Roving Pair method. If you are using a Reduced Howell, use the nine-table Reduced Howell or append to any table not having a stationary pair in an eight-table Reduced Howell.

9¹/₂ tables. If the Mitchell movement is used, the best alternative, if time permits playing 10 rounds, is a relay between Tables 1 and 10 with bye boards between Tables 5 and 6. The phantom should be pair 10 North-South. The ACBL has a guide card movement for an East-West Roving Pair movement that works very efficiently — two East-West pairs have unusual progressions. The East-West rover pair progression is given explicitly under Rover. A 10-table Mitchell with the phantom pair at North-South 10 and a skip after the fifth round is a possible alternative, but it is not recommended — both the boards and pairs must be factored, a situation that is difficult to explain to the players' satisfaction. If a Reduced Howell is being used, use the 10-table Reduced Howell with a phantom pair or the nine-table Reduced Howell with an appendix at any table having two moving pairs.

10¹/₂ tables. The Roving Pair movement works very well here. The Bump Mitchell also works well as long

as no more than nine rounds are being played. A Reduced Howell is uncommon with this many tables but it is possible to set up for an 11-table Reduced Howell with a phantom pair or append a 10-table Reduced Howell at any table where there is no stationary pair.

11¹/₂ tables. Best is the Roving Pair or Bump Mitchell. A good alternative is a 12-table game with a relay between Tables 1 and 12. The phantom pair is North-South 12. Put bye boards between Tables 6 and 7. The disadvantage to this game is that approximately half the field play only 22 boards. A Reduced Howell is not recommended, but it is possible to use the 12-table Reduced Howell with a phantom or to append a pair to the 11-table Reduced Howell.

12¹/₂ tables. The best movement is to set up a 13-table Mitchell with a phantom pair at Table 13. If the phantom pair is North-South the East-West pairs sit out when they reach Table 13. If the phantom pair is East-West the North-South pairs sit out when they are scheduled to play against East-West 13. A Roving Pair will work very well and should be used if the half table comes in late. It is possible to append to a 12-table Reduced Howell at any table where there were originally two moving pairs.

13¹/₂ tables. The best movement is a Roving Pair. A Bump Mitchell will work but the game must be curtailed after 12 rounds. It is also possible to play a 14-round game by setting up a relay between Tables 1 and 14 and bye boards between Tables 7 and 8. The phantom pair should be North-South 14. East-West pairs sit out when they reach Table 14.

14¹/₂ tables. The best movement is the Roving Pair or Bump Mitchell. Either will work easily and well.

15¹/₂ tables. The best movement is a Bump Mitchell. The Roving Pair is a reasonable alternative, but it requires special movements after certain rounds.

Olof Hanner recommends a simple method of adding a pair to a SCRAMBLED MITCHELL, whether with an odd number of tables or when using a Skip. Make the N-S Pair at the last table into a moving pair, and have an instruction on the last table as follows: E-W at the last table sits out next, then plays N-S at the last table, then E-W at table 1. This avoids factoring of boards even if the movement is curtailed, since each board is played once in each round. A SKIP MITCHELL with this extra pair can play a full number of rounds without repeating opponents. This technique can be used from the start, or before Round 2 starts.

Another general method is the 1¹/₂-table APPENDIX MITCHELL. 10¹/₂ tables can play nine rounds. Give table 1-9 a set of boards each for a 9-table Mitchell. Table 10 shares boards with table 1 throughout. Moving pairs go to EW 9, then EW 10, then sit out, then EW 1. The basic movement can be a Skip Mitchell. There is no repetition of opponents.

HALF TRICK. An original holding in a suit that will win a trick by virtue of being a high card about half the time. A queen held in company with an ace of the same suit, or a king with a guard, is a half trick on original valuation. The position of adverse bids as the bidding progresses may add to or detract from such a valuation. Situations involving half tricks are usually called FINESSES.

HALL OF FAME. See ACBL HALL OF FAME.

HAMILTON. Also called CAPPELLETTI and, in Great

Britain, POTTAGE. A conventional system of defensive bidding over an opposing opening bid of 1NT. An overcall of 2♣ is a forcing bid showing a one-suiter and demanding a 2♦ response from partner — neither bid says anything about the suit mentioned. However, partner can pass with a long club suit in a weak hand or bid a long major with a good suit. After the 2♦ response, the 2♣ bidder passes or names his suit. Other overcalls in this system show two-suiters. Their meanings: 2♦ — spades and hearts; 2♥ — hearts and a minor; 2♠ — spades and a minor; 2NT — diamonds and clubs. If partner wishes to learn which minor after an overcall of either 2♥ or 2♠, he bids 2NT and the overcaller then names the minor. A double when using this convention is primarily for penalties. See CAPPELLETTI, DEFENSE TO ONE NOTRUMP, DONT, POTTAGE, TRANSFER OVERCALLS OF ONE NOTRUMP.

HAND. (1) A particular deal of 52 cards. The term "deal" is preferred because "hand" is ambiguous. (2) The cards held by one player. The term is also used to indicate the order in bidding rotation, as in "second hand" or "fourth hand."

HAND DISTRIBUTIONS. See HAND PATTERNS for general and specific distributions. See MATHEMATICAL TABLES for percentage frequency and distributions.

HAND HOG. A player who (often mistakenly) feels that he is better qualified than his partner to manage the hands as declarer. The usual method of operation is to pass with minimum opening bids but to respond with jumps in notrump.

HAND PATTERNS. There are 39 possible hand patterns, ranging from the most balanced, 4-3-3-3, to the most unbalanced, 13-0-0-0. A player can hold specifically four spades, three hearts, three diamonds and three clubs $_{13}C_4 \cdot _{13}C_3 \cdot _{13}C_3 \cdot _{13}C_3$ different ways, which computes to 16,726,464,040 or 2.634% of the 635,013,559,600 hands he could hold (see NUMBER OF POSSIBLE HANDS). This, of course, is not the percentage probability that he will have a 4-3-3-3 hand, because the four-card length need not be in spades, but could be in any of the four suits, so the chance of a 4-3-3-3 hand is 10.536%.

A rearrangement of the suits in a particular distributional pattern is termed a PERMUTATION of the pattern; 4-3-4-2 is a permutation of a 4-4-3-2 pattern. If we use the same letter of the alphabet to indicate the same length in a suit, there are three classes of hands: AAAB, such as 4-3-3-3 or 4-4-4-1, etc., which has 4 permutations; AABC, such as 4-4-3-2 or 5-5-2-1, etc., which has 12 permutations; ABCD, such as 5-4-3-1 or 7-3-2-1, etc., which has 24 permutations. Thus, the probability of five spades, four hearts, three diamonds and one club is .539%, but the probability of some 5-4-3-1 distribution is 24 times as great, or 12.931%. For all possible hand patterns, see MATHEMATICAL TABLES, Table 1.

HAND RECORDS. (1) Diagrams set up by the players after a deal in a major match is completed; (2) the sheets on which individual computer-dealt hands are printed for distribution to players for duplication; (3) the sheets distributed to players at the conclusion of a game on which all the hands from that session are printed.

In some tournaments, particularly in Europe, the play-

ers make a record of each hand after they have played it on the first round. This card is then placed with the hand in the pocket, and can be used by succeeding players to check whether the cards they hold are the ones that were originally dealt into that hand. Such hand records are known as CURTAIN CARDS.

HANDBOOK, ACBL. See ACBL HANDBOOK.

HANDICAP KNOCKOUT TEAMS. A handicap is assigned to each team based on a formula that takes experience and ability into consideration. The handicap is in the form of International Matchpoints (IMPs) and is added to the IMP total of the less experienced team. The winner is determined by the score AFTER the handicap has been added in. See BRACKETED KNOCKOUT TEAMS, COMPACT KNOCKOUT TEAMS, DOUBLE ELIMINATION KNOCKOUT TEAMS, MINI-KNOCKOUT TEAMS, MIXED TEAMS, OPEN TEAMS, RANDOM DRAW KNOCKOUT TEAMS, TEAM GAMES, ZIP KNOCKOUT TEAMS.

HANDICAP PAIRS. Conducted like an open pairs game, but the scoring method is different. The game produces two sets of winners, scratch and handicap. The scratch standings are the same as they would be in an open game. However, the handicap standings are based on the scratch score plus handicaps that are awarded to make the event more evenly contested. The handicap can be figured in either of two ways. First, it can be based on the players' ranks (a measure of expertise), with more matchpoints awarded the lower the rank. Second, it can be based on recent performance as compiled either by the director or the computer. A pair eligible for matchpoints both scratch and handicap receives the higher of the two awards, not both.

HANDICAPPED PLAYERS. Many bridge players have overcome serious handicaps to become high-ranking players. Many others have been able to enjoy the game despite severe handicaps. The advent of COMPUTER PLAY has made it possible for persons who cannot take part in club activities to play bridge by computer from their home.

The most accomplished handicapped player is Lynn Deas, who has won many major championships, including world titles, despite being incapacitated by Myasthenia Gravis, a disease similar to Lou Gehrig's Disease. Perhaps the person who made the greatest effort to play bridge was Jay Slotkin, a Potomac MD periodontist. He was almost totally incapacitated by amyotrophic lateral sclerosis, Lou Gehrig's Disease. Even though he could not move or speak, he played three sessions a day at the 1993 North American Championships in Washington DC. Aided by his nurse, Slotkin bid and played by blinking his eyes. He was a regular at club games in the Greater Washington area. Mike Wilson of Vancouver, born armless and with only one leg, played bridge by using his toes.

Here are some of those who successfully conquered their handicaps sufficiently to become Life Masters: Fred Snite – played from an iron lung. Robert Penn – played while attached to a respirator. Morris Ribyat – played for 15 years while suffering from multiple sclerosis. Walter Lewis, paralyzed from the waist down as the result of an auto accident, won four events at an Alabama tournament in 1976. Hermine Baron was always among the leading masterpoint winners despite being forced to

play from a wheelchair. She represented the United States in world play from her wheelchair three times. Roberta Runion became a Life Master while battling a crippling kidney disease and undergoing dialysis three times a week. Ethel Keohane was one of New England's top players for several decades. She continued her top-flight play after being nearly killed in a devastating car crash that killed her partner, Ida Bennett. Her regular partner in later years was Alberta Albersheim, who was legally blind. Hugh Montague continued playing bridge for several years after receiving a heart transplant.

Several blind persons triumphed over their handicap. These include Patrick Dunne, Arthur Dye, Lois Wiley, John Larsen, Anne Cunningham, Sarah Howard and Michael Levinson, all of whom achieved Life Masterhood. Levinson actually won a North American championship – the 1981 Life Master Men's Pairs.

HANDLING CARDS. The handling of cards other than a player's own is improper. At duplicate, a player may ask to see his opponent's (or his partner's) card, and the player involved will turn it for him. There are some players who take a hand belonging to another player out of the board after play has been completed in order to discuss a matter of bidding or play. This practice is officially discouraged and is illegal if the opponents are not present. It is the cause of most fouled boards.

HANNER MOVEMENTS. (1) Individual movements for up to 20 tables devised by Olof Hanner of Sweden, and detailed in his book on Duplicate Organization written in combination with Hans-Olof Hallén and Per Jannersten. See INDIVIDUAL MOVEMENTS. (2) A movement for a team-of-four contest in which each match is completed in two consecutive rounds. This provides for quick results without the board sharing necessary in a twinned movement. The movement may be played with an odd or even number of teams without any sit-out. The boards are either different for different matches, or in each round played with the same boards at half the tables, which requires some duplication.

HEAD-TO-HEAD. A term used to describe any match in bridge of prearranged set opposition; that is, one team of four or more against another of four or more. Use of the term is restricted to two-team contests only.

HEART. The symbol ♥ for the second-ranking suit in bridge. Hearts are between spades and diamonds in ranking order. The suit designation originated in France in the sixteenth century and takes its name from the shape of the pips used in designating card rank.

HEART SUIT. The second-ranking suit, with scarlet pips on each card in the shape of a heart. The suit ranks just below spades in bidding, and above diamonds.

HEARTBREAKER. A term applied to a hand that fails in a big way to live up to one's original expectations of it. It can be a defensive hand where one has, for example, been dealt cards that enable one to double a certain final contract with the assurance of setting the opponents badly. If, because of the distributional situations or highly expert card play by declarer, the contract is made, then surely the "heartbreaker" term would follow.

The following deal was a heartbreaker for West.

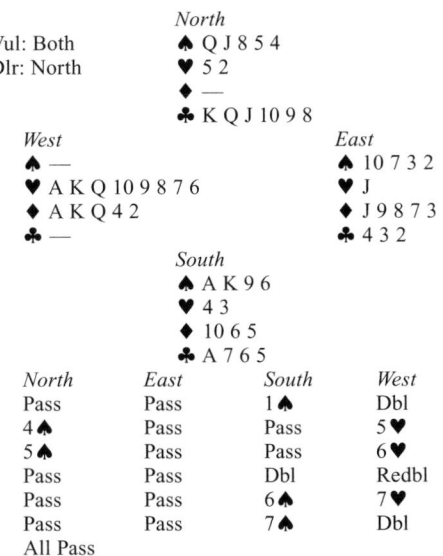

Vul: Both
Dlr: North

```
                North
                ♠ Q J 8 5 4
                ♥ 5 2
                ♦ —
                ♣ K Q J 10 9 8
West                          East
♠ —                           ♠ 10 7 3 2
♥ A K Q 10 9 8 7 6            ♥ J
♦ A K Q 4 2                   ♦ J 9 8 7 3
♣ —                           ♣ 4 3 2
                South
                ♠ A K 9 6
                ♥ 4 3
                ♦ 10 6 5
                ♣ A 7 6 5
```

North	East	South	West
Pass	Pass	1♠	Dbl
4♠	Pass	Pass	5♥
5♠	Pass	Pass	6♥
Pass	Pass	Dbl	Redbl
Pass	Pass	6♠	7♥
Pass	Pass	7♠	Dbl
All Pass			

West could have bid an immediate 7♥, but he did not wish to push his opponents into 7♠. He began with a cunning takeout double, and then bid his hearts gently at the five-level and the six-level. This was good tactical bidding.

But at the six-level West became foolishly greedy. When he was doubled he should have been satisfied to make a doubled slam with an overtrick. Instead he redoubled, and Oswald Jacoby, in the South seat, worked out what was happening. He retreated to 6♠, and to West's considerable disappointment, carried on to 7♠ over 7♥.

West doubled in a bad temper, and could have cashed two heart tricks. But not unnaturally he thought that the ♦ A was a better bet as an opening lead. Jacoby had a good clue to the distribution, and he made no mistake. He made the key play of ruffing with dummy's ♠8, leading the ♠4 and finessing the 6 — a remarkable way to play the first round of trumps in a grand slam.

A diamond was ruffed with the ♠J, and the ♠9 was finessed to reenter the closed hand. The last diamond was ruffed with dummy's last trump, and the closed hand was reentered with the ♣A to draw the missing trumps. Dummy's club winners gave Jacoby his doubled grand slam.

HEDGEHOG SQUEEZE. Hedgehog squeezes were named and analyzed by Hugh Darwen in the (British) *Bridge Magazine*, March 1968 and April 1968. A hedgehog squeeze is a squeeze of one opponent in two or three suits and a squeeze of the other opponent in three suits. These are the basic endings:

I. Single hedgehogs

1. Non-simultaneous guard hedgehog

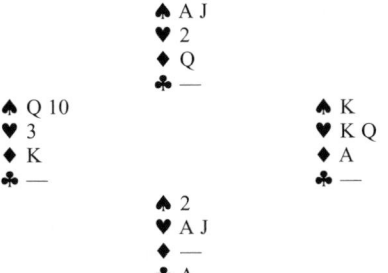

On the lead of the ♣A, West and North discard hearts, and East is squeezed out of the ♦A. Now the lead of the ♥A squeezes West in spades and diamonds.

2. Simultaneous guard hedgehog.

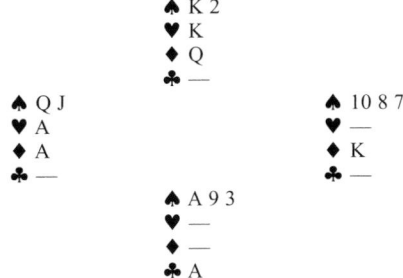

The lead of the ♣ A squeezes West out of the ♦ A, North discards the ♥K, and East is squeezed in spades and diamonds.

3. Blocked guard hedgehog

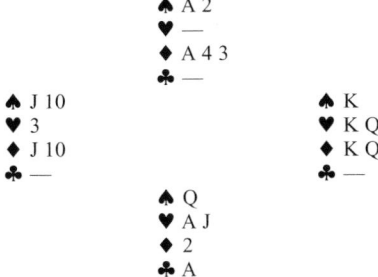

On the ♣A lead, West discards a heart, North discards a diamond, and East is squeezed out of a diamond. Now the lead of the ♥ A squeezes West in spades and diamonds.

4. Automatic clash hedgehog

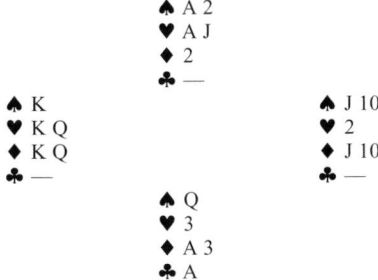

On the ♣A lead, West discards a heart, North discards a diamond, and East is squeezed out of a diamond. Now the lead of the ♥ A squeezes West in spades and diamonds.

5. One-way clash hedgehog

```
                ♠ A 2
                ♥ A J
                ♦ 2
                ♣ —
♠ K                           ♠ J 10
♥ K Q                         ♥ 2
♦ K Q                         ♦ J 10
♣ —                           ♣ —
                ♠ Q
                ♥ 3
                ♦ A 3
                ♣ A
```

The lead of the ♣A squeezes West out of a diamond, while North and East discard hearts. Now a lead to the

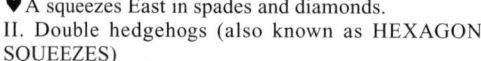

♥A squeezes East in spades and diamonds.

II. Double hedgehogs (also known as HEXAGON SQUEEZES)

1. Double guard hedgehog

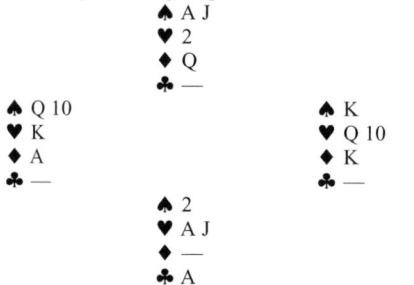

The lead of the ♣A squeezes West out of the ♦A, North discards the ♥2, and East is squeezed in three suits.

2. Double clash hedgehog

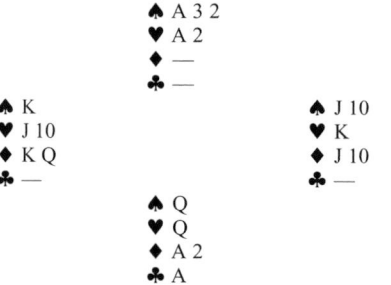

The lead of the ♣A forces West to discard a diamond, North discards the ♠2, and East is squeezed in three suits.

3. Hybrid double hedgehog

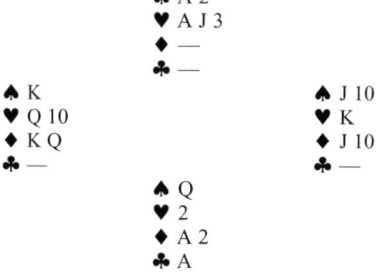

The lead of the ♣A forces West to discard a diamond, North discards the ♥3, and East is squeezed in three suits.

III. Progressive hedgehogs

1. Guard/guard progressive hedgehog

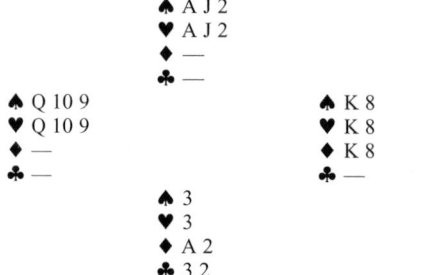

When South cashes his clubs, West, North, and East must discard one card from each major. Now the ♦A squeezes West in the majors.

2. Clash/clash progressive hedgehog

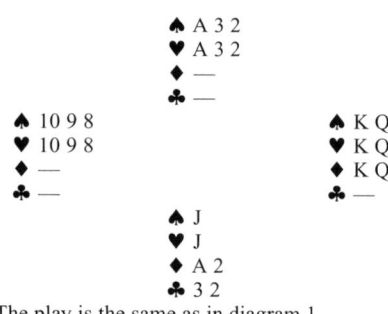

The play is the same as in diagram 1.

3. Clash/guard progressive hedgehog (type 1)

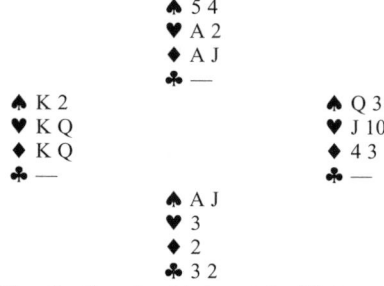

When South cashes his two clubs, West must discard a card in each major, North discards a spade then a diamond (unless West discards a diamond), and East discards two diamonds. Now the lead of a diamond to the ♦A squeezes East in the majors.

4. Clash/guard progressive hedgehog (type 2)

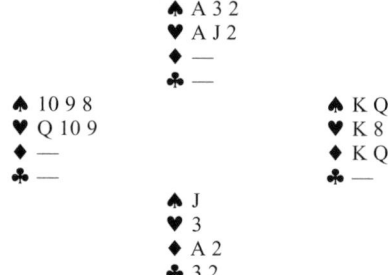

When South cashes his clubs, East is compelled to discard a card in each major. Now the lead of the ♦A squeezes West in the majors. See CLASH SQUEEZE; HEXAGON SQUEEZE; OCTAGON SQUEEZE.

HELP SUIT GAME TRY. See WEAK SUIT GAME TRY.

HERBERT NEGATIVE. The idea that a negative response in a variety of situations can be made by making the cheapest possible suit response. It was advocated by Walter Herbert when he was a member of the Austrian national team in the 30s, and was applied in many ways in the Vienna System. Some of its many possible applications include: response to forcing two-bid; response to takeout double; response to Acol two-bid; as a second negative response or the first or second round to a strong forcing opening.

HERMAN TROPHY. This trophy is awarded to the player with the best overall individual performance record at the American Contract Bridge League Fall North Ameri-

can Championships. It was donated in 1951 by Sally Lipton, formerly Mrs. Lou Herman, of New York, in memory of her husband. For winners see Appendix II.

HESITATION. See HUDDLE.

HESITATION MITCHELL. A way to play one more round, or a few more, than in a Mitchell. The expansion is obtained by decreasing the number of stationary pairs but also letting the moving pairs visit not only E/W places but also the N/S places at some table or tables. See REDUCED HOWELL.

HEXAGON SQUEEZE. A double guard squeeze in which each of the three menaces is protected by both opponents. (Analyzed and named by George Coffin.)

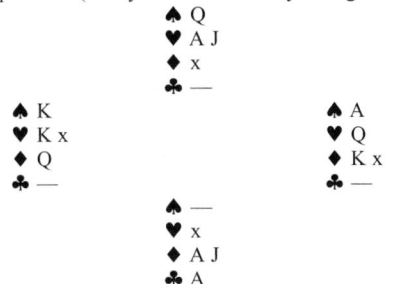

South leads the ♣A, and West must discard a spade. North discards a diamond, and East is squeezed in three suits. Once West discards his spade, East is caught in a standard guard squeeze. See also BARCO SQUEEZE, HEDGEHOG SQUEEZE, HEXAGON TRUMP SQUEEZE, OCTAGON TWO-TRICK SQUEEZE.

HEXAGON TRUMP SQUEEZE. A HEXAGON SQUEEZE in which both opponents are trump squeezed.

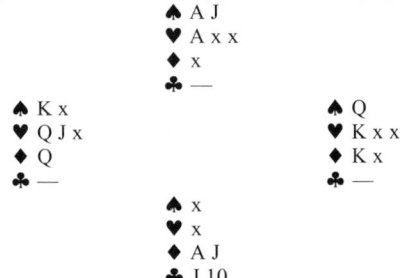

South is on lead needing all the tricks; clubs are trumps. South leads the ♣J. West must discard a heart, dummy can discard a diamond, and East is squeezed in three suits. If East discards a spade, West can be finessed. East obviously cannot discard a diamond, and if he lets go a heart, the ♥A and a heart ruff will establish an extra heart trick.

Alternatively, when West discards a heart on the ♣J, suppose North and East both discard spades. South leads to the ♥A and ruffs a heart. A spade to the ace then squeezes East in hearts and diamonds. In this variation the squeeze of East occurs three tricks later than the squeeze of West.

HIDDEN ENTRY. A low card, usually in the dummy hand, by which an entry may be made, usually established as such through the play of unnecessarily high cards by the declarer. Thus, if dummy has A-Q-10-6 and declarer

K-J-9-5, the 6 may be set up as an entry by playing the king to the same trick as the ace, the jack to the same trick as the queen, and the 9 to the same trick as the ten.

HIGH CARD. A ranking card; an honor card; a card that wins a trick by virtue of its being higher in pip value than the other three cards in the trick. A spot card which becomes the master card in the suit also is said to be high.

HIGH CARD POINT PROBABILITIES. Average High Card Point (HCP) counts are easy to calculate. Before any cards are seen, the average HCP count for any one hand is 10 and the average HCP count for a partnership is 20. (This is based on the popular count of ace = 4, king = 3, queen = 2, jack = 1.)

If a player has seen that his hand has x HCPs but has no information about the strength of any other hand, then on the average the remaining high card points are split equally among the other three hands, giving an average HCP count of $(1/3)$ (40 - x) for each.

However, averages do not mean very much because hands so often vary from the averages. Probabilities can be calculated for the various possible HCP counts, and the appended tables present the results of these calculations.

Table 1 is largely self-explanatory, but it is important to note that its probabilities apply only when there is no information about the strength of any hand. Many bridge players complain that it is hard to get a decent hand. Table 1 shows that the probability of 11 or fewer HCPs is 65.183%, so about $2/3$ of all hands are too weak to open at the one level. Those opening 1NT on 15-17 HCPs can see from Table 1 that the probability of an HCP count in this range is 4.424% + 3.311% + 2.362% = 10.097%.

Table 2 is also largely self-explanatory, but it is important to note that its probabilities apply only when there is no information about the strength of any hand. Table 2 shows that the probability of 26 or more HCP in a partnership's hands is 100%-87.354% = 12.646%, or about one deal in eight. Similarly, the probability of 33 or more HCP in a partnership is 100% - 99.652% = .348%, or about one deal in 300. Also, the probability of 37 or more HCP in a partnership is 100%-99.991% = .009%, or about one deal in 10,000. Readers can calculate the probabilities of other numbers of HCP for game or slam after allowing for their judgments of how many distributional points are present.

Table 1
Probabilities of High Card Point Counts
for One Hand

HCP	Percentage	HCP	Percentage
0*	.364	19	1.036
1	.789	20	.644
2	1.356	21	.378
3	2.462	22	.210
4	3.845	23	.112
5	5.186	24	.056
6	6.554	25	.026
7	8.028	26	.012
8	8.892	27	.0049
9	9.356	28	.0019
10	9.405	29	.00067
11	9.945	30	.00022
12	8.027	31	.00006
13	6.914	32	.00002
14	5.693	33	.000004
15	4.424	34	.0000007

16	3.311	35	.0000001
17	2.362	36	.000000009
18	1.605	37**	.0000000006

Table 2
Probabilities of High Card Point Counts
for a Partnership

HCP	Percentage	HCP	Percentage
0	.00005	21	8.047
1	.0005	22	7.566
2	.002	23	6.831
3	.006	24	5.907
4	.018	25	4.892
5	.043	26	3.883
6	.093	27	2.943
7	.196	28	2.124
8	.341	29	1.463
9	.588	30	.955
10	.955	31	.588
11	1.463	32	.341
12	2.124	33	.186
13	2.943	34	.093
14	3.983	35	.043
15	4.892	36	.018
16	5.907	37	.006
17	6.931	38	.002
19	7.566	39	.0005
19	8.047	40	.00005
20	8.222		

* The probability of a yarborough (no card higher than a 9) is 0.054703%. The probability of a square yarborough (4-3-3-3 suit distribution and no card higher than a 9) is 0.007744%.
** A hand cannot have more than 37 high card points without exceeding 13 cards.

HIGH CARD POINTS. A basis for determining the relative strength of a hand, especially for notrump contracts. The most common method for figuring high card points is as follows: ace = 4, king = 3, queen = 2, jack = 1. Many authorities also count an extra point for holding all four aces and a half a point for each 10. Most of the schemes for opening notrumps are based on this count.

The total of high card points, taking into consideration suit lengths, often is used as a basis for opening the bidding with a suit bid. Usually a hand that contains a total of 13 points in combined high card plus distributional points is considered an opening bid; a 12-point hand usually is considered optional.

Great efforts by Charles Goren, in many books and articles, popularized the point-count method of bidding. Bridge players everywhere suddenly found that they could estimate the strength of their hand reasonably accurately by using this method. Nowhere has this been more apparent than in notrump bidding. Goren told his students that 26 high card points in the partnership hands usually would be enough to produce game, and statistical studies have proved him correct.

The 4-3-2-1 method of evaluating high cards is not the only one that has been promulgated. Since it is acknowledged that the ace is somewhat undervalued using this count, there also have been adherents of a 6-4-2-1 count. Another that has had its share of popularity is the 3-2-1-$\frac{1}{2}$ count. But the method used by the vast majority of players all over the world is the 4-3-2-1. Although it may not be the most accurate, it certainly is

easy to use and is accurate enough to get a partnership to the correct bidding level the vast majority of the time. See POINT-COUNT.

HIGH-CARD TRICK. A term originally used to denote a trick won with an honor. The phrase had some currency in the OFFICIAL SYSTEM.

HIGHER BID. A bid higher in rank at the same level, or lower in rank at the next level, than the last previous bid; a SUFFICIENT BID. Usually a higher bid refers to a bid that is merely sufficient, i. e., does not use as much as a full level of bidding space. Where one or more levels of bidding space are used, it is termed a jump, skip, or preemptive bid.

HIGHEST SCORE. In ACBL competition, several pairs have produced remarkable scores in major North American Championship events. S. Garton Churchill and Cecil Head held the single-session record with a 77.4% game in the 1948 Life Master Pairs until 1963, when Eric Murray and Agnes Gordon scored 77.9% (506$\frac{1}{2}$ match points on a 325 average) in the final session of the Fall NAC Mixed Pairs. This was subsequently beaten by Andrew Bernstein and Gene Neiger, who totaled 244 on a 156 average in the first session of the 1968 Spring NAC Open Pairs for 78.2%. For consistency in scoring, it is unlikely any pair can match the performance of Barry Crane and Dr. John Fisher in the 1970 Spring NAC Open Pairs. They averaged 69.5% in the two qualifying rounds and 63.4% in the two final sessions, the highest set of percentages ever for a four-session pair championship.

In regional competition, Paul Stern and Bob Webber, scored 257 (82.3%) in the Open Pairs at Great Lakes in 1973, only slightly below the 260 (83.3%) — highest on record for a 156 average game — scored by C. C. Wei and Ronald Andersen in a single session at the 1974 New York Winter Regional.

The highest matchpoint score on record is 87.3%, by Bernard and France Marcoux in September 1991 at the Le Club de Bridge St. Adele in the Montreal area of Canada.

The highest score in an international championship scored by victory points occurred in the 1963 European Championships in Baden-Baden, Germany. The British team won with a score of 100 victory points out of a possible 102.

HIGH-LOW SIGNAL. Known also as echo or come-on, the high-low signal is probably the most important single weapon the defenders possess. In its normal, recurring application, the high-low signal in a suit expresses the desire for a continuation of that suit, or an interest in that suit being played when partner obtains the lead. For example:

```
              ♠ Q 8 5
              ♥ K Q 8 2
              ♦ Q 2
              ♣ 7 6 4 3
  ♠ A K 9 4 2              ♠ 10 3
  ♥ 10 3                   ♥ 6 4
  ♦ 8 7                    ♦ A 10 9 6 5 3
  ♣ J 10 9 5               ♣ Q 8 2
              ♠ J 7 6
              ♥ A J 9 7 5
              ♦ K J 4
              ♣ A K
```

Against South's 4♥ contract, West opens the ♠K, dummy plays the 5-spot, and East puts up the 10, South dropping the 6. West then continues with the ♠A, upon which East plays the 3-spot. Observing that East has played high-low, urging the continuation of the spade suit, West plays a third round of spades, East trumping. The ♦A is then cashed for the setting trick.

Unfortunately, as with all conventions, the high-low signal is often applied promiscuously or misapplied, sometimes being given merely because it is the "orthodox" thing to do. One sometimes forgets that the signal is given to get partner to continue the suit led only if it will attain an objective for the defenders. Here is an example of the misuse of the high-low signal.

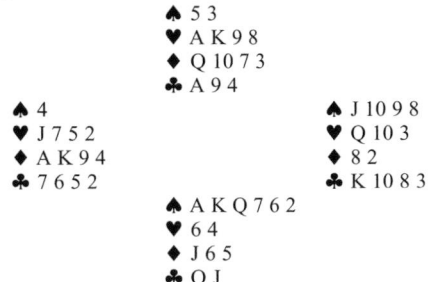

West opened the ♦K against South's 4♠ contract, and East mechanically played the 8-spot. West then continued with the ace, East dropping the 2, after which a third diamond was led, East ruffing. From here in declarer had no problem. He drew trumps, and discarded his ♣J on dummy's high ♦Q.

On the opening lead of the ♦K, East should have played the discouraging 2, not the 8. What did East have to gain by ruffing the third round of diamonds? Not a thing, since he possessed a natural trump trick which could never be taken away. Had he played the ♦2, West, at trick two, would unquestionably have shifted to a club. East would then have made his ♣K, and declarer would have lost his contract.

There is a conventional situation in which a high-low signal is given not to denote an interest in the suit, but to indicate an even number of cards in that suit. This convention is discussed and illustrated in the section entitled LENGTH SIGNALS, but an illustration at this point would not be out of order.

It is a rather simple convention, and is most useful when a defensive holdup play must be employed. The setup to which it is applicable is the following:

When it is obvious that declarer is trying to establish a long suit in dummy (which has no outside entries), and that second hand's partner (or second hand himself) is going to have a problem as to when he should take his ace, second hand (or his partner) gives a high-low signal when holding two or four cards of that suit; where second hand has three cards of that suit (say, 7-4-2), he plays his lowest card (the 2) on the first lead, and then follows up by playing the next highest (the 4).

In this latter case, partner will know that the signaler has exactly three cards in that suit, since with two or four he would have given a high-low signal.

Here is a practical application of this high-low convention:

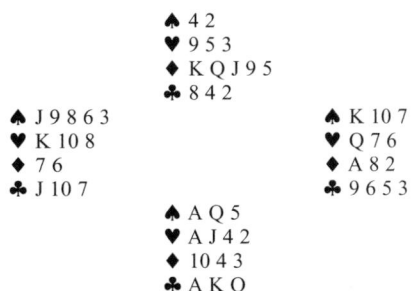

Against South's 3NT contract, West opened the ♠6, East's king falling to declarer's ace. South then led the ♦10, West played the 7-spot, and North and East followed with low diamonds. Declarer then led the ♦4, West played the 6-spot, and dummy's 9 captured the trick when East properly declined to take his ace. Declarer now went down a trick, being unable to establish and cash dummy's diamonds.

West's high-low signal (7, 6) had told East that West had either two or four diamonds. Four became an impossibility when South led a second diamond. Therefore East knew that West originally held precisely two diamonds, and that declarer still had a diamond left after the second diamond lead.

The best policy for the declarer is to "signal" as if he were a defender: Play high to encourage, low to discourage if your opponents play normal signals. This maximizes the chance to scramble the signals and cause the signaler's partner to misread the situation. For alternative methods of signaling, see ODD-EVEN DISCARDS; UPSIDE-DOWN SIGNALS.

HIGH REVERSE. A non-jump bid in a third suit at the level of three in a lower ranking suit than that bid originally. For example, 1♥-2♦-3♣. (This term is English usage, not current in the United States.) See OPENER'S REBID.

HINDSIGHT. Most bridge players are able to find the perfect bid, the correct line of play, and the killing defense after the hand has been misbid, misplayed, or misdefended at the table. Players who regularly indulge in long discussions of this sort are known as RESULT PLAYERS or second-guessers.

HIPPOGRIFFS. Sometime humorous name of a mythical suit; chiefly used in a celebrated anecdote about a man who dreamed he held a perfect notrump hand with 13 sure winners against a stranger (Satan), who was on lead. The Devil then proceeded to run 13 tricks against declarer by cashing all the cards of a weird greenish suit called hippogriffs.

HISTORY OF BRIDGE. Bridge can trace its ancestry at least to the early 16th century in England (first reference 1529 in a published sermon by Bishop Latimer) and through succeeding centuries when prototype forms of whist were played under such names as triumph, trump, ruff, slamm, ruff and honours, whisk and swabbers, whisk, and whist. "Whist" may have referred to the rapid action of sweeping up the cards after winning a trick, or "whist" to a call for silence. The game was popular under its modern name of whist by the middle of the 17th century, but it was not until 1742 that the first

book devoted to whist appeared: EDMOND HOYLE'S famous "Short Treatise on Whist" (see BIBLIOGRA-PHY, A). This rapidly became a best seller, and many pirated editions appeared immediately afterwards.

Whist maintained its popularity as a fashionable amusement, and in 1834 Lord Henry Bentinck invented the first signal. This was the forerunner of much research and writing by authorities on the game such as James Clay, Cavendish, Deschapelles and many others.

The first game of duplicate whist was apparently played in London in 1857 under Cavendish's direction. It was intended to demonstrate the advantage accruing to skillful play, and a team of supposedly good players was deliberately pitted against supposedly poor opposition (there having been no previous criterion for judging them). The "good" players won easily. Cavendish observed that this procedure all but eliminated the luck of the deal, but his pioneering effort was not followed for nearly a quarter of a century.

The United States was slightly ahead of England in extending the duplicate method. A duplicate whist game was played privately in Chicago in 1880 and in a club in New Orleans in 1882. The first interclub match was played in Philadelphia in 1883. The first duplicate match in the Old World was probably in Glasgow, Scotland, in 1888.

Duplicate offered the possibility of replacing private play by public contest. Major steps forward in 1891 were: the foundation of the American Whist League; the invention of the Kalamazoo tray (first duplicate board); and the first book on tournament organization, written by John T. Mitchell who devised the first movement for pair play and described the method of matchpointing which has been used ever since.

Although the American Whist League was to flourish for some 40 years, bridge, the game which eventually led to its decline and fall, had come on the American scene early in the 1890s, at about the time it was also introduced in England. As chronicled by J. B. Elwell and R. F. Foster, the game reached New York in 1893, thanks to Henry Barbey, whose privately printed *Laws of Bridge* are dated 1892. In London, members of the Portland Club began to play bridge in 1894 at the instance of Lord Brougham who had learned it in India from some army officers. (W. Dalton in *Auction Bridge Magazine* of September 1927 states that Lord Brougham brought the game from Cairo.) But, according to a letter published in *Bridge Magazine* in 1932, Frank J. Nathan had played in the "first" English game in 1892 at St. George's Club, Hanover Square. It was introduced by a Colonel Studdy who said it was of Levantine origin and that he had learned it in the trenches at Plevna during the Russo-Turkish War of 1877-1878. (This was probably Col. T.C.J.A. Studdy of the Royal Artillery, who was a Captain in the Crimean War period.)

This earlier dating of the game and the probability that it was of Turkish or Russian origin is strongly supported by evidence uncovered in 1974-1975 by Robert H. True, who quotes from a 1904 issue of *Notes and Queries*, a letter from A. M. Keiley (nationality unknown): "I was in 1886… a member of the Khedival Club in Cairo, and bridge was the principal card game played there at my entry and, as members told me, had long so been." One of the names by which bridge was first known on the Riviera was KHEDIVE, presumably because players had met it in Cairo. Turkey held Egypt almost without interruption from the early 16th century until World War I and "Khedive" was the official title held by the Turkish viceroy.

Further new evidence confirming Levantine origin and earlier dating of the game was presented by Bob van de Velde of The Netherlands in IBPA Bulletin #222. Sources for this evidence are *Daily Telegraph* (England, November 1932), *La revue du bridge* (France, December 1932) and *Bridge* (The Netherlands, February 1933). The primary source, *Daily Telegraph*, carried an article by a Mr. O. H. van Millingen who lived in Constantinople in 1879 or 1880 and remembered "a very interesting game called Britch, a game that became very popular in all clubs and dethroned the game of whist." He included a letter, dated January 7, 1922, of his friend Edouard Graziani who at that time worked for the Italian Embassy as a translator and was one of the best bridge players of the Cercle d'Orient. In August 1873 Graziani played the game of bridge for the first time at the home of Mr. Georges Coronio, manager of the Bank of Constantinople. Also present at that game "in Buyukdere along the bank of the Upper Bosphorus" were Mr. Eustache Eugenidi and a Mr. Serghiadi, "a Rumanian financier" who taught the principles of bridge to the foursome. "After Constantinople," Graziani wrote, "bridge came first to Kairo, from where it conquered the Riviera, Paris, London and then New York."

A claim of even earlier existence of the game appears in the introduction to *Mdern Bridge* by "Slam" published in London in 1901: "Bridge, known in Turkey as 'Britch,'… has been played in South-Eastern Europe… ever since the early sixties."

Now we have, perhaps, a quantum leap backward to the period 1854-56. An Istanbul resident, Metin Demirsar, reports the following: "As part of a course on Ottoman history and architecture… my guide mentioned that British soldiers invented the game bridge while serving in the Crimean War. The card game… got its name from the Galata Bridge, a bridge spanning the Golden Horn and linking the old and new parts of European Istanbul, where they apparently crossed every day to go to a coffeehouse to play cards."

This does suggest a more plausible derivation for the name of the game than any previously offered. It is somewhat puzzling to comprehend why the game did not appear in England earlier than it did. Perhaps its creators were killed at Balaklava or Inkerman but their brainchild continued in action at the "Bridge" club.

Mrs. Marion Harding of the National Army Museum in London confirms that there was a considerable British presence — some 14,000 troops — concentrated around Constantinople in 1854, and a number of officers were there for considerable periods.

There is an even earlier date. Sir James Paget, an English doctor, referred to playing "Bridge" in an 1843 letter, but that is a very faint clue. It is not even clear that he was playing a card game.

The modern authority in this area is Thierry Depaulis of Paris, France. In his comprehensive "Histoire du Bridge" he concluded that bridge developed in the diplomatic community in Istanbul. He connected it with a Serbo-Croatian word 'brc', meaning large quantity, maximum. He subsequently modified his views, connecting the game to Russia where it was called "sibirskii ieralash", or "Siberian mixture". He believes it belonged, like Vint, to the wide family of whist-preference games. It came to Istanbul about 1860-65 and changed its name to something that sounded like britsh, britch or biritch. The British Museum has an 1886 pamphlet entitled "Biritch or Russian Whist". The word itself may be Serbo-Croatian or Ukrainian. The game

is likely to have been spread by wealthy Greeks who traveled to Russia and Turkey and helped introduce it to Western Europe. pick up An important change.

An important change from whist was the exposure of one hand (dealer's partner) as the dummy, following the precedent of Dummy Whist, originated as a game for three players. According to one popular theory, this idea evolved from a game played first in India by three British officers so isolated they were unable to find a fourth. See THREE-HANDED BRIDGE; NEWGATE.

Another innovation was the introduction of the double and redouble. There was no limit to the number of redoubles, and this "gambling" feature of the new game, soon to be eliminated by the change to Auction Bridge, was one of the strong arguments against bridge adduced by whist devotees.

The prototypical game of bridge, or bridge whist, had a short life. A great step forward was taken in 1904, when the auction principle was introduced, traditionally in India, possibly in England. Auction bridge grew steadily in popularity until 1927, though only toward the end of this period were auction bridge tournaments organized. For some reason it was believed that the duplicate principle, long popular among whist players, was not suitable for bridge.

The next major change may have been developed in France, where the game of PLAFOND was played in 1918 and perhaps earlier. A similar game, S.A.C.C., was described by Sir Hugh Clayton as having been "invented" in India in 1912, and similar games had been tried in the United States before 1915. In all such games each side had to bid to its "plafond" or ceiling: only tricks bid and made counted toward game. This variation rapidly became the standard French game, but did not succeed elsewhere in spite of occasional experiments. In his slightly fictionalized memoirs of World War I entitled *Ashenden*, SOMERSET MAUGHAM, who took bridge very seriously, reported a game in Switzerland: "The game was contract, with which I was not very familiar." In the early Twenties, two booklets entitled *Contract Bridge* were published, and an unsuccessful application was made to the Knickerbocker Club to prepare a code of contract rules.

Up to this point whist, bridge, auction, and plafond had simply grown, which is generally the way with card games. No individual can be given credit for inventing the dummy, the idea of bidding, the auction principle, or the ceiling principle of plafond. But in 1925 Harold S. Vanderbilt perfected a new form of the game, embodying the Plafond principle but including the element of vulnerability and producing a scoring table that corrected the major faults in plafond. He succeeded so well that his game of "contract bridge' became the staple diet of card players everywhere. Afterward, he wrote:

"Many years of experience playing games of the Whist family were, I think, a necessary prelude to acquiring the background and knowledge needed to evolve the game of Contract Bridge. Starting as a young boy about 70 years ago, I have played successively over the years Whist, Bridge, Auction Bridge, and Plafond.

"…I compiled in the autumn of 1925 a scoring table for my new game. I called it Contract Bridge and incorporated in it, not only the best features of Auction and Plafond, but also a number of new and exciting features; premiums for slams bid and made, vulnerability, and the decimal system of scoring which by increasing both trick and game values and all premiums and penalties

was destined to add enormously to the popularity of Contract Bridge.

"An ideal opportunity to try out my new game presented itself while I was voyaging shortly after completing my scoring table with three Auction Bridge playing friends on board the steamship Finland from Los Angeles to Havana via the Panama Canal, a nine-day trip.

"…At first, we were at a loss for a term, other than "game in," to describe the status of being subject to higher penalties because of having won a game. Fortunately for us, a young lady on board the Finland solved that problem by suggesting the word "vulnerable.""…

"We enjoyed playing my new game on board the Finland so much that, on my return to New York, I gave typed copies of my scoring table to several of my Auction Bridge playing friends. I made no other effort to popularize or publicize Contract Bridge. Thanks apparently to its excellence, it popularized itself and spread like wildfire."

No world-popular game in history — certainly none in the Whist family — can so accurately pinpoint its conception and the first time it was ever played. Recent research has established that the Finland reached Balboa on October 31, 1925, too late to proceed through the Canal or for passengers to go ashore. Francis Bacon III, in 1975 the then sole surviving member of Vanderbilt's foursome, recalled that on that night the lady who suggested "vulnerable" was allowed to join their game of plafond and attempted to suggest some exotic and impractical changes based on a game she said she had played in China. This so irritated Vanderbilt that the next day, while the Finland passed through the Canal, he worked out the scoring table for contract which, except for notrump tricks then being valued at 35 points each, remained virtually unchanged half a century later. On that night, November 1, the game became Contract Bridge, scored under Vanderbilt's new rules.

Within two years, three codes of laws had been produced for the new game. Those of Robert F. Foster and the Knickerbocker Whist Club (both 1927) were withdrawn in favor of the more authoritative code issued by the Whist Club of New York. In 1928 the game was adopted in the major New York clubs, and late that year the first National Championship was held, with the Vanderbilt Cup as the prize.

In 1929 the American Auction Bridge League dropped the word "Auction" from its title and it became clear that contract had supplanted auction. The established auction authorities struggled to achieve expertise in the field of contract, but for the most part unsuccessfully. Leadership in the new game went to Ely Culbertson, who founded the first contract magazine in 1929. The first issue of *The Bridge World* magazine advocated the promulgation of an international Code of Laws for Contract Bridge. Subsequently, committees representing the United States, England and France were appointed, and the first International Code became effective Nov. 1, 1932. See LAWS OF CONTRACT BRIDGE.

In September 1930, Culbertson published his *Contract Bridge Blue Book*, which became a best seller and which appeared in annual revisions for four years. This revolutionary work set out the principles of approach-forcing bidding which became the nucleus of all modern standard systems. (See BIBLIOGRAPHY). It was Culbertson, through his writings, his personality, his lectures and his organization, who was most responsible for the wide vogue the game quickly attained. The international publicity resulting from the famous CULBERTSON-LENZ

MATCH in 1931 and the ANGLO-AMERICAN MATCHES in 1930, 1933, and 1934 made the new game of Contract Bridge a household word. Thanks to a thriving organization which exploited every phase of bridge activity and to his natural flair for publicity exhibited notably in the Culbertson-Lenz Match, Culbertson retained his leadership throughout the Thirties, untroubled by the tournament successes of the FOUR ACES.

Although Culbertson's was the first widely accepted system of bidding in Contract Bridge, it became outmoded, and numerous other systems of bidding have come to the fore since his day. The GOREN methods, based on POINT-COUNT valuation, which became standard in the United States after 1950, are based firmly on the foundations laid by Culbertson.   The growth of tournament bridge was hampered in the Thirties by the simultaneous activity of three separate organizing bodies, the AMERICAN BRIDGE LEAGUE, the AMERICAN WHIST LEAGUE, and the UNITED STATES BRIDGE ASSOCIATION. But from 1937 onward the AMERICAN CONTRACT BRIDGE LEAGUE had the field to itself, and there followed a period of steady growth stimulated by the masterpoint plan. 1935 became the year of the first recognized World Championship, although several semi-official international matches had been played earlier. Later landmarks on the international scene were the first of the postwar World Championship series in 1950, the foundation of the WORLD BRIDGE FEDERATION in 1958, and the first Team Olympiad in 1960.

The only major innovation in contract bridge during its first 40 years of existence was the development of CHICAGO, the four-deal game which displaced traditional rubber bridge in many clubs during the early Sixties. But this, like contract bridge itself, was a change in scoring rather than in structure. See SCORPION.

HISTORY OF PLAYING CARDS. The earliest known cards were used in China, at least as long ago as 979 A.D. The pack was divided into four suits, 14 cards in each, and was based on representations of coins. This discredits the pleasant story that they were invented in 1120 A.D. to amuse the concubines of the Emperor Suen-ho.

There is a tradition that a Venetian carried cards from China to his native city, the first place in Europe where they were known. This traveler may have been Niccolo Polo, who returned from China about 1269 with his brother Matteo, or it may have been Niccolo's son, the famed Marco, who accompanied his father and uncle on their second trip to that empire.

Some authorities favor India over China as the original source. A tenuous link has been suggested between early European cards and Ardhanari, the goddess of Hindu mythology. She was represented holding in her four hands a wand, a cup, a sword, and a ring (symbolizing money). Similar symbols appeared on some early European playing cards.

Cards were manufactured in many parts of Europe, notably in Nuremberg, Augsburg, and Ulm, in the fourteenth century, and perhaps even earlier. The Italian Tarot cards may have predated the German cards: they are mentioned in an Italian manuscript dated 1299. Johanna, Duchess of Brabant, mentions cards in the Netherlands in 1379, and cards were known in Spain at least as early as 1371. The Moors or Saracens may have brought cards to Spain and Italy, but the attempt to show a resemblance between the Spanish word for cards (naipes) and the

Arabic word (nabi, "a prophet") is not well founded.

In 1392 in France, Charles VI ordered a hand-painted deck to be made by Jacquemin Gringonneur, and this historical fact gave rise to the idea that cards originated in France. However, it seems clear that this order was for cards similar to others already in use. The royal treasurer, accounting for moneys paid out, mentions three packs of cards, painted "in gold and diverse colors, ornamented with many devices, for the diversion of our Lord, the King." Seventeen of these cards are on exhibition at the Bibliotheque Nationale (see COLLECTIONS OF PLAYING CARDS).

Cards probably reached England later than the other European countries. Chaucer, who died in 1400, never mentions cards, although he enumerates the amusements of the day: "They dance and they play at chess and tables." The reference to playing with four kings in the Wardrobe Rolls of Edward I in 1278 ("ad ludendum ad quattuor regis") almost certainly refers to some other game, perhaps a form of chess. The earliest clear-cut reference to playing cards in England dates from 1465, when manufacturers of playing cards petitioned Edward IV for protection against foreign imports, and were favored by an appropriate edict.

"There is a legend telling how the sailors with Columbus," writes Catherine Perry Hargrave in *A History of Playing Cards*, "who were inveterate gamblers, threw their cards overboard in superstitious terror upon encountering storms in these vast and mysterious seas. Later on dry land they regretted their rashness and in the new country made other cards out of the leaves of the copys tree, which greatly interested the Indians." This seems to be more than a legend, for Garcilaso de la Vega (*Historia de la Florida*, Madrid, 1723) tells that the soldiers of Spain played with leather cards in the 1534 expedition. Cards were known to the early Mexicans as amapatolli, from *amatl* meaning paper and *patolli* meaning game.

The present pack of 52 cards, arranged in two black and two red suits, probably derived from the early Italian Tarot packs, in which there were four suits with ten spot cards and four court cards — king, queen, cavalier, and knave. The queen was not included in early packs, and the chevalier still holds her position in some modern packs (see PACK).

The knave has been variously represented by a VALET, and still carries this name, although modern usage changes it to the jack. The chevalier, as apart from the queen, has been dropped from the 52-card pack.

The Chinese playing cards differ considerably from the occidental; they are long and narrow, usually 2 to 2 1/2 inches long and 1/2 to 1 inch wide. Early cards were longer and even narrower. In number of suits and cards, both the Chinese and Hindu decks differ markedly from ours. One Hindu deck includes 144 cards with eight suits of 18 cards, another has 120 cards with 10 suits of 12 cards; one Chinese deck has only 30 cards, three suits of nine cards and three extra cards of supreme value, but four suits were normal.

Long before bridge was heard of, playing cards were used in many forms of gambling and in fortunetelling. Cards acquired an unsavory reputation, being associated with all vices. The DEVIL'S PICTURE BOOK and other names indicate the horror with which they were regarded by the virtuous and religious.

Playing cards, as a luxury, provided a source for much revenue in TAXES, first levied on them in England in 1615.

The modern authority on the history of playing cards is Stuart Kaplan. See MANUFACTURE OF PLAYING CARDS.

HIT. Slang used as two distinct transitive verbs: (1) To double. (2) To ruff.

HOBSON'S COUP. See MERRIMAC COUP.

HOG. A player who attempts to become declarer as often as possible, or the action of one who does so: "to hog the bidding."

HOLD. (1) To possess (a certain card or cards. (2) To win or guarantee the winning of a trick (by the play of a certain card). Thus, if partner plays the king when you hold the ace, and no ruff is impending, the king is said to hold the trick unless you decide to overtake it.

HOLD OFF. To refuse to play a winning card. See DUCK and HOLD UP.

HOLD UP. The refusal to win a trick. The aim of a hold-up play is to keep control of a suit an opponent has led. The purpose is usually to disrupt the opponents' communication.

This section deals only with hold up play by declarer, but the defenders also hold up (as when a defender refuses to take an ace to prevent the use of a long suit in dummy; see LENGTH SIGNALS). The hold up play occurs at both suit and notrump contracts.

The following deal shows the basic hold up play:

```
              ♠ Q 6 5
              ♥ K 8 4
              ♦ A J 9 8 3
              ♣ 8 3
♠ 10 7 2                      ♠ J 9 8 3
♥ Q 10 6 5                    ♥ J 9 3
♦ 7                          ♦ K 6 5
♣ K J 9 5 4                   ♣ Q 10 2
              ♠ A K 4
              ♥ A 7 2
              ♦ Q 10 4 2
              ♣ A 7 6
```

After West has opened 2 ♥ South plays 3NT, and West leads the ♣5. East puts up the queen. South must refuse to take the ace and hold up again when East returns the ♣10. If South wins either the first or second club, East will have a club to lead when he wins the ♦ K, and the defenders will win four clubs and one diamond to defeat the contract. If South waits to win the third club lead, he makes game; the defenders' communication in clubs is broken, and West has no side entry.

Declarer can also hold up a winner other than an ace.

```
              ♠ K 6 4
              ♥ Q 6
              ♦ K 9 7
              ♣ A J 9 5 3
♠ Q 5                         ♠ J 9 7 3 2
♥ A 10 8 7 5 2                ♥ J 9
♦ J 6 5                       ♦ 10 8 4 3
♣ 7 4                         ♣ K 8
              ♠ A 10 8
              ♥ K 4 3
              ♦ A Q 2
              ♣ Q 10 6 2
```

After West has opened 2 ♥, South plays 3NT, and West leads the ♥ 7. If South puts up the ♥ Q to win the first trick, he goes down; East will unblock the jack and return the ♥ 9 when he wins the ♣ K. South should instead play low from both dummy and his own hand at the first trick, safeguarding the contract if West has six hearts and East has the ♣ K.

```
Dlr: North         ♠ 10 8 4 3
Vul: N-S           ♥ K 4
                   ♦ Q J 7 2
                   ♣ A K 2
♠ J 7                           ♠ A K 9 6 5
♥ J 9 8 6 2                     ♥ 10 7 3
♦ K 8 6                         ♦ 5
♣ 10 9 8                        ♣ Q J 7 3
                   ♠ Q 2
                   ♥ A Q 5
                   ♦ A 10 9 4 3
                   ♣ 6 5 4
```

West	North	East	South
	1 ♦	1 ♠	3 ♦
Pass	3 ♠ (1)	Pass	3NT
All Pass			

(1) Partial stopper

West leads the ♠J, 3, 6. South must play low to make the contract.

```
              ♠ 8 5 3
              ♥ A K 3
              ♦ 5 4
              ♣ A 10 9 4 2
♠ A J 9 4 2                    ♠ 10 7
♥ 8 6 4                        ♥ J 9 7 2
♦ J 9 6                        ♦ Q 10 8 7
♣ 8 5                          ♣ K 7 6
              ♠ K Q 6
              ♥ Q 10 5
              ♦ A K 3 2
              ♣ Q J 3
```

West leads the ♠ 4 against South's 3NT, and East plays the 10. To make the contract, South must follow with the 6.

The situation would be similar if the spade suit were:

```
              8 5 3
A 10 7 4 2             Q 9
              K J 6
```

After the lead of the 4 to the 3 and queen, South would need to play the 6.

```
              8
A 10 7 6 4            Q 9 5
              K J 3 2
```

After the lead of the 6 to the 8 and queen, South would follow with the 2 and play the 3 when East next led the 9.

```
              8
A 10 7 6 4            K 9 5
              Q J 3 2
```

If West leads the 6 to the king, and East returns the 9, South must play low. South must also play low if East makes the remarkable play of the 9 at the first trick.

As the examples above demonstrate, hold-up play is

often linked with AVOIDANCE. Change the previous deal to:

```
                    ♠ 8 5 3
                    ♥ A K 3
                    ♦ 5 4
                    ♣ Q 10 9 4 2
    ♠ A J 9 4 2                      ♠ 10 7
    ♥ 8 6 4                          ♥ J 9 7 2
    ♦ J 9 6                          ♦ Q 10 8 7 2
    ♣ K 8                            ♣ 7 5
                    ♠ K Q 6
                    ♥ Q 10 5
                    ♦ A K 3
                    ♣ A J 6 3
```

Since on this layout the club finesse may lose to West, South should win the first spade. He can then reach dummy with the ♥A and finesse in clubs. If West can win, South is safe, since his remaining holding in spades is safe from attack.

Sometimes declarer must guess whether to hold up.

```
Dlr: South          ♠ 8 4 2
Vul: Both           ♥ A J 6 4
                    ♦ K 10 6
                    ♣ Q 8 4
    ♠ A 10 7 6 3                     ♠ Q 9
    ♥ K 3                            ♥ Q 9 8 7 5
    ♦ A 5                            ♦ 8 3
    ♣ J 10 7 5                       ♣ 9 6 3 2
                    ♠ K J 5
                    ♥ 10 2
                    ♦ Q J 9 7 4 2
                    ♣ A K
```

West	North	East	South
			1♦
1♠	Dbl (1)	Pass	2♦
Pass	3♦	Pass	3NT
All Pass			

(1) Negative

N-S bid aggressively to reach 3NT, and West leads the ♠6 to the 2 and queen. If East has the ♦A, South must hold up; if West has it, South should win, preserving a tenace in spades. South must recall the bidding. Since West's vulnerable overcall suggests high-card values, South should play West for the ♦A and win the first trick.

A holdup is often correct with two stoppers:

```
                    ♠ A Q 7
                    ♥ K J 6
                    ♦ 10 9 8 2
                    ♣ K 7 4
    ♠ 9 5                            ♠ 10 8 6 4 3
    ♥ 8 7 4 2                        ♥ Q 10 3
    ♦ K 6                            ♦ A 7 3
    ♣ Q 9 8 6 2                      ♣ J 10
                    ♠ K J 2
                    ♥ A 9 5
                    ♦ Q J 5 4
                    ♣ A 5 3
```

South plays 3NT, and West leads the ♣6. If South wins the first club and attacks diamonds, East will take the ace and lead his second club, establishing the clubs while West still has the ♦K. To make the contract, South must play low from both hands on the first club.

A more testing example:

```
                    ♠ A 6 3
                    ♥ K Q 5
                    ♦ J 10 9 8 2
                    ♣ 10 6
    ♠ K 9 7 4 2                      ♠ J 8
    ♥ 8 6 4                          ♥ J 9 7 3
    ♦ K 7 5                          ♦ A 4 3
    ♣ Q 9                            ♣ J 7 4 2
                    ♠ Q 10 5
                    ♥ A 10 2
                    ♦ Q 6
                    ♣ A K 8 5 3
```

South plays 3NT, and West leads the ♠4 to the 3 and jack. If South impulsively grabs the queen, he is defeated.

A hold-up play may be needed even with three stoppers.

```
                    ♠ Q J 6
                    ♥ 4 2
                    ♦ K 9 3
                    ♣ 9 7 5 4 2
    ♠ 7 5 4 3 2                      ♠ 10 9
    ♥ 9 5                            ♥ J 10 8 7 6
    ♦ Q 8 7 2                        ♦ J 6 4
    ♣ Q 3                            ♣ A K 6
                    ♠ A K 8
                    ♥ A K Q 3
                    ♦ A 10 5
                    ♣ J 10 8
```

South plays 3NT. Since West has few side entries, he leads the ♥9, trying to find East's long suit. To make the contract, South must refuse the first trick.

A hold-up may serve to ruin defenders' communication at a suit contract.

```
                    ♠ Q 3
                    ♥ K 9 8 2
                    ♦ A Q 10 5 4
                    ♣ K 6
    ♠ J 10 9 8 4 2                   ♠ K 7 6
    ♥ 5                              ♥ J 6 4
    ♦ 8 7                            ♦ K 3 2
    ♣ 10 5 3 2                       ♣ A Q 7 4
                    ♠ A 5
                    ♥ A Q 10 7 3
                    ♦ J 9 6
                    ♣ J 9 8
```

South plays 4♥, and West leads the ♠J, covered by the queen and king. South must not take the ace. If South instead wins, draws trumps and tries the diamond finesse, East wins and can put West in with a spade. Then a club shift defeats the contract.

A hold-up play is also proper to keep control.

```
                    ♠ 8
                    ♥ A 7
                    ♦ A 7 6 5 3 2
                    ♣ 9 6 4 2
    ♠ 9 4 2                          ♠ 10 5
    ♥ K Q 10 4                       ♥ J 9 8 3
    ♦ J 9 8 4                        ♦ Q 10
    ♣ A K                            ♣ Q J 7 5 3
                    ♠ A K Q J 7 6 3
                    ♥ 6 5 2
                    ♦ K
                    ♣ 10 8
```

South plays 4♠, and West cashes the ♣A K and shifts to the ♥K. South can safeguard the contract by holding

up dummy's ace. If West shifts to a trump to stop a heart ruff in dummy, South can unblock the ♦ K, reach dummy with the ♥ A and win his tenth trick with the ♦ A; if West leads another heart to force the ace before South unblocks in diamonds, South ruffs a heart in dummy.

In the following deal, timing requires a hold-up play.

```
              ♠ 8 4 3
              ♥ A 6 4
              ♦ A K 7 5 4
              ♣ 5 4
♠ Q 10 5                      ♠ J 9
♥ K 10 8                      ♥ J 9 5 2
♦ J 3                         ♦ Q 10 9 2
♣ K Q 10 9 3                  ♣ J 8 7
              ♠ A K 7 6 2
              ♥ Q 7 3
              ♦ 8 6
              ♣ A 6 2
```

South plays 4♠, and West leads the ♣K. South can expect four trump tricks in his hand, four top cards on the side and a club ruff in dummy. A long card in diamonds must provide the tenth trick, but South must take care with his entries. If he wins the first trick with the ♣A and returns a club, the defense can win and lead a third club, forcing South to use a dummy entry too soon.

South should therefore refuse the first trick. He wins the next club, cashes the ♠A K and proceeds with ♦ A K, diamond ruff, club ruff, diamond ruff. (It makes no difference if West overruffs on one of the diamond leads.) South then goes to the ♥ A to lead the good diamond and is sure of 10 tricks whether or not West ruffs.

Control is also the problem on the deal below.

```
              ♠ 6
              ♥ Q 8 7
              ♦ 7 6 5 4
              ♣ A K Q J 10
♠ K Q 10                      ♠ J 9 8 7 3
♥ 5 3                         ♥ A 6 4 2
♦ K 10 8 3 2                  ♦ J 9
♣ 5 3 2                       ♣ 6 4
              ♠ A 5 4 2
              ♥ K J 10 9
              ♦ A Q
              ♣ 9 8 7
```

South lands in 4♥, and West leads the ♠K. South's best play is to hold up the ace! If West continues spades, South ruffs in dummy and forces out the ♥A. South can win the next trick, draw trumps and take 10 tricks with the help of dummy's clubs. Other lines of play are likely to fail.

A hold-up play may be used in conjunction with avoidance and a LOSER-ON-LOSER play. In the deal below, the purpose is to establish a suit safely.

```
              ♠ Q J 4
              ♥ A 5
              ♦ A K 5 3 2
              ♣ 8 5 2
♠ 7 5                         ♠ 6 3
♥ K Q 10 4 3                  ♥ J 9 8 7 2
♦ 10 8                        ♦ Q J 9
♣ A 10 9 7                    ♣ Q J 3
              ♠ A K 10 9 8 2
              ♥ 6
              ♦ 7 6 4
              ♣ K 6 4
```

South plays 4♠ and West leads the ♥K. If South wins the first trick, draws trumps and leads three rounds of diamonds, East wins and shifts to the ♣Q to defeat the contract. South does better to hold up the ♥A at the first trick. He wins the next heart, discarding a diamond, draws trumps, takes the ♦ A K, ruffs a diamond and returns to dummy with a trump to throw two clubs on winning diamonds.

On some occasions, a hold-up play is ill-judged. Perhaps declarer cannot hold up long enough to accomplish anything; perhaps he cannot stop a dangerous defender from gaining the lead; perhaps a shift to another suit poses a greater threat. In the deal below, a hold-up play would let the defenders untangle their long suit.

```
              ♠ A 5
              ♥ K 6 4
              ♦ J 10 7 5 3
              ♣ J 8 4
♠ K J 8 6 3                   ♠ Q 7
♥ 10 8 2                      ♥ Q J 7 5
♦ A 2                         ♦ 9 8 4
♣ 7 5 3                       ♣ Q 10 9 2
              ♠ 10 9 4 2
              ♥ A 9 3
              ♦ K Q 6
              ♣ A K 6
```

South plays 3NT and West leads the ♠6. South is in no danger if spades split 4-3. If West has five spades, East surely has at least one honor, since West would lead the king from K-Q-J-x-x. Thus, South cannot lose by taking the ♠A at the first trick. As the cards lie, this play blocks the spades; but if South instead plays a low spade, East wins the queen and returns a spade at trick one, and South goes down.

A hold-up play is generally wrong when it costs a winner. Still, the deal below shows an exception.

```
Dlr: East     ♠ 10 5
Vul: E-W      ♥ J 6 4
              ♦ Q J 9 4
              ♣ K J 9 3
♠ Q 9 8 6 2                   ♠ K 7 4
♥ 5                           ♥ Q 10 9 8 7 3
♦ 8 7 6                       ♦ A 2
♣ 8 7 5 2                     ♣ A 6
              ♠ A J 3
              ♥ A K 2
              ♦ K 10 5 3
              ♣ Q 10 4
```

West	North	East	South
		1♥	1NT
Pass	2NT	Pass	3NT
All Pass			

West leads the ♠6, and East plays the king. East's opening bid marks him with most of the missing honors, but West probably has Q-x-x-x-x in spades. South should therefore refuse the first two spade leads and win the third spade. South then loses to the minor-suit aces, but makes his game.

If South takes the ♠A at the first trick (assuring two spade tricks) and leads a diamond, East wins the ace and returns a spade. West lets dummy's 10 win. When East gets back in with the ♣A, he leads his last spade, and West takes three spades.

A common reason to avoid a hold-up play is to preserve an exit card:

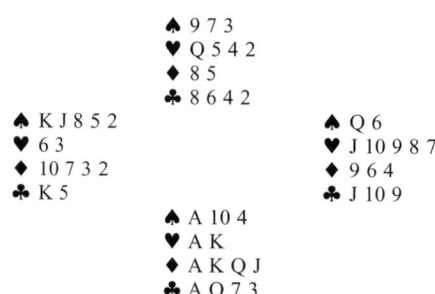

```
                 ♠ 9 7 3
                 ♥ Q 5 4 2
                 ♦ 8 5
                 ♣ 8 6 4 2
  ♠ K J 8 5 2              ♠ Q 6
  ♥ 6 3                    ♥ J 10 9 8 7
  ♦ 10 7 3 2               ♦ 9 6 4
  ♣ K 5                    ♣ J 10 9
                 ♠ A 10 4
                 ♥ A K
                 ♦ A K Q J
                 ♣ A Q 7 3
```

South plays 3NT and West leads the ♠5. South can refuse the first spade, but should win the second. South then cashes his top cards in the red suits and leads his last spade. West can take at most three spade tricks and then must lead a heart or club to South's advantage.

Hold-up play at matchpoint duplicate.

```
                 ♠ 9 7
                 ♥ A 8 3
                 ♦ Q J 10
                 ♣ A J 10 9 5

                 ♠ A 4 3
                 ♥ K 6 5
                 ♦ A K 8 3
                 ♣ Q 8 7
```

South plays 3NT and West leads the ♠6. East plays the queen. At rubber bridge or IMP scoring, South would hold up the ♠A twice before taking the club finesse, almost guaranteeing nine tricks. At matchpoint scoring, South's problem is more difficult; the contract is normal — every N-S pair will reach 3NT — and 12 tricks are available if West has the ♣K. If South gambles by winning the first or second spade, however, he may go minus if East has the ♣K.

Perhaps South's best play is to hold up once and see what spade East leads at the second trick. This play cannot cost, since South can take at most 12 tricks. If East returns the ♠2, South can assume that spades are split 4-4 or 6-2 and win the second trick. If East returns the ♠10 or ♠8, suggesting an original holding of three cards, South must consider holding up again. Obviously, the situation gives the defenders opportunity for deceptive play.

See also BATH COUP, RULE OF SEVEN.

HOLDING. (1) The cards one is dealt in a particular suit, as in the expression, "a club holding of king, queen, and two little." (2) A descriptive term used in reckoning one's entire hand, and often used in the question, "What would you bid holding five spades to the ace-queen, etc.?"

HOLLAND. See NETHERLANDS BRIDGE LEAGUE.

HOLLANDAISE. See GOULASH.

HOME STYLE BRIDGE. In the early 1970s Nate Silverstein of Memphis devised a movement for a one-winner pair game. It is usually called a "Swiss Pair" game. The game gained popularity in some of the country clubs in Memphis. In 1979 the ACBL adopted most of the ideas and converted the game into an experimental Home Style bridge program.

The basic method of scoring is Chicago or "Four-Deal Bridge." Pairs are assigned seats at random by the director. When the game starts, and at the start of each round, the players cut for deal. Each round they play four hands. On the first hand no one is vulnerable, the second and third hands the dealer's side is vulnerable, and the last hand everyone is vulnerable. Partscores carry over, honors are scored. If you complete a hand when your side is vulnerable you score a bonus of 500; if you complete a game on a hand where your side is not vulnerable your bonus is 300 points. If you score a partscore on the last hand, and it does not complete a game, you receive a bonus of 100. All other scoring, overtricks, undertricks, doubles, redoubles, etc., are scored the same as in all other forms of bridge.

The only exception to playing four hands is if you have three or four tables. In this instance the director may opt to play six hands a round. In this instance no one would be vulnerable on the first two hands, the dealer's side vulnerable on the third and fourth hands, and both sides vulnerable on the last two hands.

At the end of the round the players total their points. The pair with the fewer points deducts their total from the greater. The difference is then converted into Victory Points. Following is a Victory Point schedule:

Difference in total points	Victory Points
0-40	10-10
50-140	11-9
150-240	12-8
250-340	13-7
350-540	14-6
550-740	15-5
750-940	16-4
950-1240	17-3
1250-1540	18-2
1550 or more	19-1

This is the ACBL Home Style formula. In the original method 1550-1940 was 19-1, and 1950 or more was 20-0. However, players in this type of game are discouraged by zeros - hence the change.

When the first round is completed and the Victory Point totals have been entered, the director gives each pair their second-round assignment. This is Swiss pairing where each pair plays against a pair with a score as close to theirs as possible. The one exception is that no pair can play another pair more than once. If the two pairs with the most Victory Points could not play because they had already played, the pair with the greatest total would play the pair with the third most points. This continues until all pairs have received a new assignment.

This is usually a fun kind of game and attracts players who are not interested in braving the rigors of duplicate bridge with the attendant restrictions and many conventions. It also appeals to the newcomer to competitive bridge. For these reasons Home Style Bridge is usually limited to the very basic conventions and understandings. Blackwood and Stayman are frequently the only conventions permitted. However, any conventions can be permitted as long as they are determined beforehand.

For more information contact The American Contract Bridge League, P.O. Box 161192, Memphis TN 38116.

HOME TOWN RULING. An action by the director which accepts the credibility of players personally known to him as opposed to others from distant parts; the type of ruling sometimes given by club directors in favor of

regular participants in the games as opposed to occasional drop-ins comes in this category and is even less defensible. Application of the published rules from the rule book for any and all players must in the long run provide the fairest competition and the most enjoyable game.

HONEYMOON BRIDGE. A general name for two-handed bridge games, including the following:

(1) *Double-dummy.* Deal four hands, as in normal bridge, with the players sitting in adjacent seats, not opposite each other. Without seeing the dummies, the players bid, dealer first. A pass following a call ends the auction. The opening lead is made by declarer's opponent and both dummies are then exposed. (In a variant, each player can see his dummy, using a rack, but not his opponent's dummy.) Scoring is normal.

(2) *Semi-exposed dummy.* Players are adjacent. Seven cards of each dummy are exposed, with six of them covering the face-down cards. When the bidding ends, play continues with face-down card exposed when the face-up card above it is played. Scoring is normal.

(3) *Draw bridge.* Players face each other, and receive 13 cards. The remainder form a stock. The non-dealer leads first, and play is in two-card tricks at notrump. After each trick the winner draws a card and then the loser. These tricks do not count in the score. When the stock is exhausted, there is a normal auction. The next 13 tricks are played, and scored in relation to the contract reached. See DUEL and DUOBRIDGE.

HONORARY MEMBER. The title of Honorary Member, awarded by the American Bridge League and the American Contract Bridge League, is bestowed for long and meritorious service to the League.

ABL

1927	Milton C. Work	1964	Jeff Glick
1928	Wilbur C. Whitehead	1965	Sidney B. Fink
1929	Maurice Maschke	1966	Harry J. Fishbein
1930	Eberhard Faber	1967	Oswald Jacoby
1931	Waldemar K. von Zedtwitz	1968	Frank T. Westcott
1932	E.J. Tobin	1969	Samuel M. Stayman
1933	A.E. Manning-Foster	1970	Julius L. Rosenblum
1934	P. Hal Sims	1971	Joseph J. Stedem
1935	Nathan S. Kelly	1972	Phyllis Smith
1936	Nate B. Spingold	1973	Kate Buckman
		1974	Louise Durham
ACBL		1975	Kay Moody
1937	Philip Steiner	1976	Charles S. Landau
1938	Ely Culbertson	1977	Fred B. Ensminger
1939	Henry P. Jaeger	1978	William A. Baldwin
1940	Cmdr. W.A. Corley	1979	Margaret Wagar
1941	Harold S. Vanderbilt	1980	Easley Blackwood
1942	Maj. Clarence Wyatt	1981	Judge Carl B. Rubin
1943	Russell J. Baldwin	1982	Ethel Keohane
1944	Gen. Alfred M. Gruenther	1983	Alfred Sheinwold
1945	Gen. Robert J. Gill	1984	Sol Seidman
1946	Albert H. Morehead	1985	Dave Treadwell
	Maureen O'Brien Bailey	1986	Ernie Rovere
1947	Benjamin M. Golder	1987	Kathie Wei
	Mrs. James C. Baird	1988	Vic Mitchell
1948	Shepard Barclay	1989	Dan Morse
1949	Alexander M. Sobel	1990	George Rosenkranz
1950	Dr. Louis Mark	1991	Bob Hamman
1951	James C. Baird	1992	Percy and Anne Bean
1952	R.L. Miles Jr.	1993	Edgar Kaplan
1953	Curt H. Reisinger	1994	Richard Goldberg
1954	Fred Snite Jr.	1995	Bobby Wolff
1955	George W. Beynon	1996	Aileen Osofsky
1956	George Alderton II	1997	Carol and Tom
1957	Alvin Landy		Sanders

1958	Lee Hazen	1998	Henry Francis
1959	Charles Goren	1999	Bobby Goldman
	Dr. A.M. Dye	2000	Chip Martel
1960	Tom Stoddard	2001	Norman Kay
1961	Charles J. Solomon		Jane Johnson
1962	John E. Simon		
1963	Max M. Manchester		
	Bertram Lebhar Jr.		

HONOR CRASHING PLAYS. See CRASHING HONORS and DECEPTIVE PLAY.

HONOR LEAD. The lead of an honor, usually the top one of a sequence. The lead of an honor conventionally indicates possession of one or more lower touching honors, the exception being the lead of the king, which may be made from an A-K or K-Q holding. The purpose of the honor lead is usually to establish the cards directly beneath it. In the middle game the lead of an unsupported honor card is occasionally correct technically.

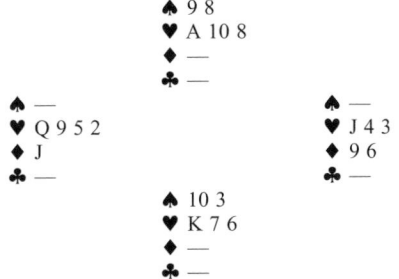

Spades are trump, and West is on lead and forced to open up the hearts. The queen is the proper play, for if he leads a low card, South simply plays the 8 from dummy, forcing the jack from East. On the next round he has a simple finesse position with dummy's A-10 over West's queen.

North (Dummy)
K 9 8

West
J 6 4 3

West is on lead and has no further card of entry. Requiring three tricks from this suit, he must lead the jack, hoping that his partner has A-Q-10. This also guarantees two tricks when partner has A-10-x. See also INTERIOR SEQUENCE; JOURNALIST LEADS; OPENING LEAD; RUSINOW LEAD; ZERO OR TWO HIGHER LEADS.

HONORS. The five highest ranking cards in each suit; specifically, for the purpose of scoring honor premiums, the ace, king, queen, jack, and ten of the trump suit, or the four aces at no trump, are honors.

HONOR SCORE. An extra bonus in rubber bridge and in Chicago scored above the line when claimed by a player (declarer, dummy, or defender) who held during the current deal any of certain honor card holdings as follows: for holding any four of the five top trump honors - 100 points. for all five trump honors - 150 points. for all the aces at notrump - 150 points. Honors are not scored at duplicate.

HONOR STRENGTH. The trick-taking value of a hand in honor tricks. This was of great importance as a basis for calculation of the power of a hand in the CULBERTSON SYSTEM.

HONOR TRICK. A unit of defensive valuation of honor cards and combinations. It is, of course, a combination which may also be expected to win a trick on the offensive. Valuations of combinations were made in accordance with the following table in the CULBERTSON SYSTEM:

2 HT	A-K
1½ HT	A-Q
1 HT	A, K-Q, K-J-10
½ HT	K-x, Q-J-x
plus values	any queen (but not a singleton)
(about ¼ HT)	any jack combined with another honor (but no singleton or doubleton, and not A-K-Q-J)
	any singleton or void (not more than one)

See DEFENSIVE TRICK and QUICK TRICK.

HOOK. Colloquialism for FINESSE.

HORSE AND HORSE. Obsolete slang term for both sides vulnerable.

HOSPITALITY. The general term for efforts by a host unit at a bridge tournament to make the players feel more comfortable and welcome. Among the forms that hospitality takes are souvenir programs and pencils; free juice, coffee, or cokes; after-game refreshments; between-sessions buffets and even dinners; after-session dancing; morning tours to places of local interest; style shows and brunches; panel discussions; daily bulletins, etc.

HOT. Vulnerable.

HOUSE OF COMMONS. See BRITISH PARLIAMENT MATCHES.

HOUSE OF LORDS. See BRITISH PARLIAMENT MATCHES.

HOUSE PLAYER. A player at a bridge club who is available for making up tables and for joining tables when a member wishes to leave. Generally house players receive some compensation for their services to the club, but arrangements vary from club to club regarding winnings or losses at play. Some clubs have a few regular players who make themselves available to help in forming tables in exchange for remission of fees for their play.

HOUSE RULES. Additions or amendments to the Laws as required to meet conditions of play in a club or group. Proper subjects for house rules are the posting of deposits to guarantee losses in rubber bridge games, clothing or dress rules, rules for cutting in to existent games, eligibility to play, pivoting regulations when time for play is limited stakes, termination time of the game, etc.

HOUSTON AFFAIR. The January 1977 North American Team Trials competition that ended when the team captained by John Gerber was forced to forfeit when two members of his five-player team, Larry Cohen and Dr. Richard H. Katz, resigned from both the team and the American Contract Bridge League with 32 deals of the 128-board final still to be played. As a result, the 1976 Grand National Teams victors were declared the Trials champions and became eligible to represent North

America in the 1977 Bermuda Bowl. They eventually won the world title.

The Gerber team, which also included George Rosenkranz, Roger Bates and John Mohan, had a 40-IMP lead, 221-181, after the 96th deal of the final concluded Saturday evening's play. However, the start of the last 32-board set was held up on Sunday because the Tournament Committee was studying some charges concerning irregularities involving Katz and Cohen. Closed-door conferences consumed much of the day until an announcement was made by ACBL President Louis Gurvich that Katz and Cohen had resigned from their team and from the ACBL. This reduced the Gerber team to three members, forcing a forfeit.

In the following days, there was much media conjecture concerning the reasons for the sudden unexpected resignations. Various newspaper articles quoted "reliable sources" as saying that Katz and Cohen had been guilty of serious infractions against the Proprieties of bridge.

Soon after these accusations appeared in print, Katz and Cohen filed a $44 million lawsuit against the ACBL, Gurvich, Lew Mathe and Don Oakie. The suit alleged defamation of character, interference with business interests, false accusations of cheating, coerced withdrawal from the Houston Trials, and forced resignation from the ACBL. The suit demanded that Katz and Cohen be reinstated as ACBL members and that the Trials continue from the point where they were terminated. Gurvich, Mathe and Oakie all were members of the Tournament Committee at Houston, and all three were present during the events that took place on the final day.

Katz and Cohen later filed another suit in which they accused the ACBL of violation of federal antitrust actions.

The action finally was settled on February 23, 1982. The settlement consisted of the following:

1. Dr. Richard H. Katz and Lawrence Cohen are each readmitted, effective immediately, to membership in the ACBL with all privileges of full membership, except that they agree not to play together as a partnership.

2. Should Katz and Cohen desire to play together as a partnership, their request will be submitted to the National Board of the ACBL, to be decided under the rules and regulations of the ACBL. The ACBL will not entertain such an application prior to March 1, 1984.

3. The parties will be compensated by Commercial Union Assurance Company, insurer of the ACBL, for costs and attorneys' fees incurred with respect to this lawsuit: Katz and Cohen will receive the sum of $75,000 and the ACBL will receive an amount yet to be determined.

4. The lawsuit is dismissed. Katz, Cohen and the ACBL shall exchange mutual releases of all claims.

In an explanation of the settlement in the April 1982 *ACBL Bulletin,* ACBL President James Zimmerman wrote:

"This case was unique in that Katz-Cohen resigned from membership in the ACBL rather than face charges of improper communication and certain ejection from the ACBL should those charges be sustained. No matter how one may feel as to whether there was or was not improper communication, the fact remains that because of their resignations no evidentiary presentation of this charge was ever made.

"Those who were of the opinion that Katz and Cohen were guilty of exchanging information improperly have retained that opinion. I doubt that a resolution by a trial

would have changed it, especially since that question would not have been the most relevant issue in the trial. Those who were on the other side were also vehement on behalf of Katz and Cohen — it is equally likely that their opinion would not have been changed by a trial.

"This matter has been before the ACBL Board of Directors for five years. Management has been continually required to furnish information to all lawyers. Katz and Cohen, by their resignations, have not been members of the ACBL nor have they played in ACBL-sanctioned events for five years.

"Estimates were that the trial would take five to eight weeks. A judge in Los Angeles County, therefore, made a most strenuous effort to dispose of this case without a trial.

"The basic position of the ACBL through all negotiations was that Katz and Cohen should not play together as a pair. Katz and Cohen would not accept this restriction. When there was movement by Katz and Cohen toward acceptance of restriction, this basic concession made it possible to find a ground whereby they could be considered for readmission. On February 23, 1982, Katz and Cohen were re-admitted, but they agreed not to play together.

"The Katz-Cohen lawsuit alleged a number of causes of action, all of which were terminated by this settlement. Payment of the plaintiffs' legal fees was made by the insurance company alone, a result of negotiations between the insurance company and the plaintiffs. No payments to the plaintiffs were made by the ACBL. (The amount of remuneration to the ACBL for legal fees is in litigation at this writing.)

"Is this settlement a precedent-setting case for any future lawsuit? Absolutely not! Each case will be dealt with individually."

HOWELL MOVEMENT. A method of producing one winner from a field at duplicate in which all pairs play each of the boards in play, with comparison in direct competition with other pairs on approximately half of the boards, and adverse comparison on the other boards. Because of the requirement that all pairs meet in head-on competition, the movement is not practical for many of the possible number of tables.

The four-table, five-table, and seven-table movements (requiring seven rounds of four boards, nine rounds of three boards, and 13 rounds of two boards, respectively) provide excellent competition. Starting assignments for these movements are given nearby, and positions and boards for each round subsequent can be obtained by applying the following rules: the highest numbered pair remains stationary throughout; each other pair replaces the pair with the next lower number for their next seat, with number 1 replacing the pair with the next to the highest number. Boards progress so that each table plays the boards in ascending order.

There are as many sets of boards in play during the session as there are rounds to be played. The extra sets are on a byestand behind the highest numbered table. From here they are fed into the last table, and the boards at the byestand are replenished from table 1. Note the special byestand layout with four tables.

For six tables, as well as eight to 12 tables, see REDUCED HOWELL.

At the bottom of the page is a chart showing the starting positions for four tables (first line), five tables (second line) and seven tables (third line). The second seven-table movement (fourth line) is a revised schedule created by Olof Hanner. Using it, the balance is preserved if Pair 14 is a phantom in a six-and-a-half table set-up.

See THREE TABLES for the six-pair movement.

HUDDLE. A longer-than-usual pause preceding an action in the bidding (usually) or the play of a hand. Probably no action in bridge produces more appeals at the tournament level than huddles. Even if the huddle is followed by a positive action, some measure of unauthorized information may have been passed. The ethics of the game require the partner of the huddler not to take cognizance of the information that the huddler had a problem. Modern committees tend to look askance at any unusual action taken by the partner of the huddler. Usually the action is compared with what most players of the same expertise would do without benefit of the partner's huddle. The results of such committee actions often find the huddler's side receiving a negative ruling. Therefore it is important that a player set a tempo for his bidding in order to avoid huddling and becoming a target for committee action.

One of the situations that used to cause difficulties was the problem that a player had after a preemptive bid on his right. Many hands seemed too good to pass but did not offer a clear-cut alternative action. A huddle followed by a pass created an ethical problem for the partner. Should he take action on some sort of miscellaneous holding or not? Partner's huddle has reduced the danger that the right-hand opponent holds a powerful defensive hand. This frequently recurring problem was answered in the United States by the "skip-bid warning rule," which puts the player following the preempter under the obligation to take a huddle at all times when a skip bid has been made so that his partner will have no ethical problem in connection with a valid huddle. The requirement to huddle for about 10 seconds occurs when the bidder places the STOP card on the table before pulling the bid card. A similar procedure applies in international competition.

In the play, a hesitation by one defender will often reveal that he holds a key card. His partner is not necessarily barred from making the indicated play, but should satisfy himself before doing so that he would have had sound technical reasons for playing in the same way without any hesitation and that there is no equally reasonable alternative.

Table 1		Table 2		Table 3		Table 4		Table 5		Table 6		Table 7	
Prs.	Bds.	Prs.	Bds.	Prs.	Bds.	Prs.	Bds.	Prs.	Bds.	Prs.	Bds.	Prs.	Bds.
8v1	1	3v6	4	2v7	6	5v4	7						
7v3	1	5v2	2	10v1	3	9v8	4	4v6	5				
5v12	1	2v4	2	9v10	3	14v1	4	8v13	5	7v11	6	6v3	7
8v13	1	2v5	2	9v11	3	14v1	4	6v7	5	4v10	6	3v12	7

A hesitation in the play when there is no possible reason to think (e. g., when playing a singleton, or when following suit with insignificant small cards) is an offense against the Proprieties. In such cases the director may award an adjusted score under Law 73. See RHYTHM and SKIP-BID WARNING.

HUM SYSTEMS. HUM is an acronym for Highly Unusual Methods, which are usually Strong Pass systems.

The World Bridge Federation decided in 1990 to bar HUM Systems from world championship play except in long matches: the Bermuda Bowl, or quarterfinal and subsequent stages of the Rosenblum Cup.

A HUM system was defined as one with one or more of the following elements:

(a) A pass in the opening position may or will show values normally understood to represent an opening bid at the one-level.

(b) An opening bid at the one-level is or may be weaker than a pass, and does not conform with the RULE OF EIGHTEEN. A 1NT opening which shows a balanced hand with a minimum below 9 HCP, or an unbalanced hand with a minimum below 17 HCP.

(c) An opening bid at the one-level with more than one potential meaning. Examples: a bid that shows length or shortage in the suit; a bid that is two-suited, with no suit specified; a bid that does not relate to a single specified suit. This does not restrict players using Strong Club or Strong Diamond systems.

Players using HUM Systems are usually required to give advance notice to their opponents. They also may forfeit seating rights for the entire match.

I

IBM NUMBER. See PLAYER NUMBER.

IBPA. See INTERNATIONAL BRIDGE PRESS ASSOCIATION.

ICY. See COLD.

IDAK (or IDAC). A defensive bidding system against strong artificial club sequences. IDAK stands for Instant Destroyer and Killer, while IDAC means Instant Destruction Against a Club. The system is used when not vulnerable. WONDER BIDS are used when vulnerable.

The system works this way. If RHO opens an artificial club or responds artificially to a 1♣ opening:

1. If you have a long suit, bid the suit immediately below it at whatever level you deem appropriate (notrump shows clubs). This is not a transfer bid per se, for responder can pass the suit you bid. With two suits, "transfer" in one and rebid in the other.

2. 1♠ shows a 4-3-3-3 pattern (any) or a string of spades. Responder assumes you have the first type and bids his best suit at whatever level he wishes. If you really have a string of spades, you can always rescue him.

3. A jump in spades at any level shows the minor suits. Responder can ask for your better minor by bidding notrump.

4. A double shows a three-suited hand (any). If re-

sponder has: (a) a one-suited hand, he responds two suits below his real suit (i.e., spades shows diamonds) at any level. The original doubler bids the suit shown with support, and passes without it. (b) With both majors and an interest in preempting, responder bids 2NT, for the doubler guarantees a major. (c) With both minors and interest in preempting, he bids three or more notrump. (d) With a constructive hand (9 + points) and two suits, responder bids 1NT. The doubler now bids his suits up the line if there is no interference. If there is interference, the doubler should double again if short in the interference suit, and pass otherwise. (e) With specifically spades and diamonds, or hearts and clubs, responder can jump in either suit (which shows the other one), knowing that the doubler will have support for one of the suits.

IDIOT COUP. A defensive play with an indelicate name which works only if the declarer is naive. Consider this position:

```
                A K 10 x x
        J x                 Q x
                x x x x
```

In normal circumstances declarer will play off the top honors. But if South leads from his hand and West plays the jack, South may have to think after winning in dummy. Since it would be bad play for West to split with Q-J-x, South should not be tempted to take a second-round finesse. If he does so his partner may address him by the name of the Coup. If South continued with the ace, as any good player would, and finds that West began with Q-J-x, he has become the victim of a GROSVENOR GAMBIT.

IDLE BIDS. Bids which have little or no natural function in a standard method of bidding, and which are therefore available for specialized use.

Bidding is a language with a limited vocabulary. If more bids can be added to a player's vocabulary without affecting other situations, efficiency tends to be increased. Theoreticians therefore search for idle bids, and try to assign useful meanings to them.

One example is a jump to 2NT when the opener's suit bid has been doubled. This is idle because a player with a strong balanced hand would automatically redouble. Many players therefore use this bid conventionally to show a useful hand, probably 10-11 in high cards, with at least four-card support for the opener's suit. The immediate jump raise over the double can then be reserved for preemptive use. See TWO NOTRUMP RESPONSE (OVER OPPONENT'S TAKEOUT DOUBLE).

Another example is a response of 5NT to a 1NT opening. As 4NT is a natural invitation to 6NT, 5NT is not needed for that purpose. Expert players therefore use it as an invitation to 7NT, guaranteeing six. The same idea would apply to 2NT-5NT. See also IMPOSSIBLE BID.

IDLE CARD. See BUSY CARD.

ILLEGAL CALL. A call out of rotation, insufficient, or otherwise improper, during the bidding period of a hand. See LAWS OF CONTRACT BRIDGE, LAWS OF DUPLICATE BRIDGE.

ILLOGICAL BID. See IMPOSSIBLE BID.

IMP. Abbreviation for INTERNATIONAL MATCH-

POINT. It is frequently used either as the three letters, or as the word imp in conversation.

IMP BRIDGE MAGAZINE. Dutch magazine for the better players, founded in 1990 by Jan van Cleeff. 8 issues annually: PO Box 156, 2394ZH Hazerswoude, Netherlands.

IMPERFECT PACK. A pack of playing cards which is incomplete or in which one or more cards are duplicated. See LAWS (Laws 11, 12), LAWS OF DUPLICATE (Laws 1, 14).

IMPOSSIBLE BID. Legally, an "inadmissible call" (see LAWS 36-39). A bid of eight is one example.

Technically, it is a bid which is inconsistent with previous bidding by the same player, and which therefore reveals that he is ignorant of bidding principles or has made a mistake.

For example, the bidding 1NT - 3NT - 4NT is impossible. If made by a good player, it would imply that the first bid was a mistake: probably there was an ace hidden when he looked at his hand originally.

However, some impossible bids become possible on closer examination. A bid which is forcing but limited can often be employed in a sense which appears impossible. Marshall Miles suggested a response of 2NT to a suit bid (ostensibly 13-15) with a balanced hand counting about 19 points. The idea was to follow with a natural 4NT bid, describing accurately a hand which is difficult to define by normal methods. See also IDLE BID, TRAP BID.

IMPOSSIBLE NEGATIVE. A method of responding over a PRECISION CLUB opening in order to show 4-4-4-1 distribution. Responder first makes the negative response of 1 ♦, then jumps in his short suit in order to show that he did not have a negative hand after all. This was part of original Precision, but has been modified in later versions.

IMPROPER CALL. A bid or double during the auction when the caller is under obligation to pass.

IMPROPER REMARK. Any statement or question by a player during the play or bidding of a hand which refers to a possible holding or interpretation of an action of the current hand. The Proprieties state that any information must be exchanged between partners by proper calls at a steady rhythm, or by the order of play of cards when a choice of possible plays is present. See PROPRIETIES and COFFEEHOUSE BRIDGE.

IMPROPRIETY. A violation or breach of ethical conduct; also the failure to observe proper etiquette. See ETHICS; ETIQUETTE; LAWS (Proprieties, I-III).

IMP PAIR GAMES. The spread of computer scoring has made it practical to employ IMP scoring for pair contests on a regular basis. Since multiple comparisons are involved, scoring such events manually was impractical and slow. There are three types:

(1) The datum method, usually called Butler scoring after Geoffrey Butler. The two extreme scores are put aside and the remainder averaged to produce a datum score, or norm, or mean, against which all results are IMPed. This is unsuitable for a small number of tables.

For a large number of tables, more than 12, it is wiser to eliminate two scores at each end of the spectrum.

(2) The full comparison method, used for example in the CAVENDISH INVITATIONAL CHARITY PAIRS. Each pair receives an IMP score by comparing with every other table, subject to a 17-IMP maximum. This is called cross IMPs.

(3) Two experts play all the deals against each other, and their results constitute the datum, or norm, against which others are IMPed. This produces two sets of winners, one North-South and one East-West.

IMP SCORING. See INTERNATIONAL MATCH-POINTS.

IMP TACTICS. Bidding and play at IMPs is an intermediate stage between matchpoints and rubber bridge. It is important to understand the mathematical factors that influence the bidding of games and slams.
The Odds
Bidding a close, non-vulnerable game can gain a swing of 250 points, 6 IMPS. If you go down, you may lose a swing of 190 points, 5 IMPS. So the odds are only 6 to 5 in your favor, without allowing for the badly-splitting hand on which you get doubled. It is about even money.

Vulnerable games, though, gain 10 IMPs and lose only 6. Here the odds are 5-3, much more favorable. So, bid any vulnerable game that seems faintly possible; but bid a non-vulnerable game only with solid expectation of making it.

For example, suppose you hold:

    ♠ K 8 4
    ♥ A 10 2
    ♦ K 7 3
    ♣ Q J 10 5

After two passes, you open 1♣. Partner jumps to 2NT (11-12 HCP). Push on to 3NT if vulnerable, but pass if you are not.

Small slams are even-money bets at IMPS; you stand to gain or lose the same amount. However, tend to assume that any touch-and-go slam will not be bid at the other table. That is a fact of life. Thus, if you are comfortably ahead in the match, or playing a team you rate to beat easily, hold back; but if you are the underdog, play for the swing and bid. Actually, the best chance a weak team has to beat a stronger one is to bounce into slam whenever there seems to be a possibility of making.

Grand slams appear to have odds against them of only 15 to 11 non-vulnerable, or 17 to 13 vulnerable. These are not nearly so prohibitive as the 2 to 1 total-point odds — IMP scoring always reduces the big swing compared to the little one. But there is a hidden factor: at the other table, your opponents may not bid even a small slam. Then, going down in a grand slam vulnerable costs you 26 IMPS, the 13 you lose, plus the 13 you could have won: and making your grand slam gains only four extra IMPs. Avoid grand slams unless you can count 13 tricks.

How does all this compare to matchpoint duplicate? There it probably pays to bid any game with a 45% chance. (You never get a tremendous score for staying out of a close game even when it should go down, for the defense is too often poor; and, after all, you are trying to get a big score and win the tournament.) This means that a duplicate buff playing at IMP scoring should be less willing than usual to bid a non-vulnerable game, but more ready to bid a vulnerable game.

Slam bidding is much the same at IMPs as at pairs, but you are a little readier to bid a doubtful small slam at pairs, since you are more likely to need points urgently. In pairs, as at IMPS, you steer clear of doubtful grand slams, for a small slam bid and made is usually a good score.

One- and Two-IMP Swings

One major difference between IMPs and pair scoring is the relative insignificance of tiny swings; overtricks, and the extra points for notrump or major suits. Play these North-South hands at 3NT against the lead of the ♦2:

    ♠ 6 4
    ♥ 7 4
    ♦ A 8 3
    ♣ A K Q 7 5 2

    ♠ A K 10 5 2
    ♥ A J
    ♦ J 10 6 5
    ♣ 6 3

At matchpoint play, you should duck; this will probably allow you to make 11 tricks. Of course you will get a heart shift and will go down if clubs do not split, but you must try for the extra tricks. At IMP scoring, you rise with the ♦A and concede a club, playing safe for your contract.

Now, suppose you ducked the diamond. Your heart stopper is knocked out; you test the clubs and they split 4-1. At matchpoints you take a diamond finesse and cash out for down one; it may even be a good score, for everyone is in the same spot. At IMPs, if you neglected to play safe, you would play a spade to your 10, trying desperately to make your contract, because an extra undertrick does not bother you.

Defense is very much simpler at IMPs than at matchpoint pairs, for your objective is always to defeat the contract, never to stop overtricks. For example:

    ♠ A J 4 2
    ♥ 10 6 3
    ♦ 5
    ♣ K Q J 9 5

    ♠ 8 5
    ♥ A Q 2
    ♦ 10 8 6 3
    ♣ A 8 7 2

South opened 1♠, North bid 3♠, South 4♠. You are East, and your partner leads the ♦K, won by declarer. Trumps are drawn and your ♣A is knocked out. At matchpoints, you cash your ♥A, or, if hungry for a good score, you lead the ♥2, hoping that declarer has ♥K-x-x and will duck to ensure his contract.

At IMPs you have no choice; you lead the ♥Q. Clearly, your best chance to defeat 4♠ (not to hold it to four, but to defeat it) is to find declarer with king-third or fourth in hearts and partner with J-9. Declarer is then likely to go wrong, playing you for Q-J. Of course, most of the time you will lose your ace (declarer will hold K-J or K-x, or K-9), but then you never could have defeated the contract.

In bidding, also, you ignore tiny differentials at IMPs. Making your contract is your goal. Suppose you hold:

    ♠ Q 5
    ♥ Q 8 6 3
    ♦ 8 7
    ♣ A 10 7 4 2

Partner opens 1♣, you respond 1♥, partner rebids 1NT. At matchpoints, you might pass, hoping to make 120; at IMPs you bid 2♣. This must be safer, and you simply score 90 or 110 instead of the possible 120 or 150.

Suppose you have the same hand when partner opens 1♠. You bid 1NT; partner rebids 2♣. At matchpoints it is surely right to give a false preference to 2♠; at IMPs, it is surely better to raise clubs. Plus 110 and plus 140 are, in effect, the same at IMPs, and you look for the safest, not the largest, plus. Obviously, this applies even more forcibly to game and slam contracts. You are perfectly willing to play in a minor suit if it is safer; you never strain to play notrump or major suit contracts simply for the few extra points. Of course, whatever the scoring, it is hard to make 5♣ and 5♦, so these are not common contracts. However, they should be played at IMPs much more often than at matchpoint pairs. The answer is: never even consider swings of one or two IMPS. Ignore them in your thinking about dummy play, defense or bidding. Of course, when your contract is secure (or when, on defense, you see that it is impossible to defeat the declarer), you can give yourself the pleasure of battling over the extra trick or tricks. But this is a frill. The business of IMP playing is making or setting contracts. The tiny swings almost always even out over a long match. And if your team goes out to win all the one-IMP and two-IMP swings, you are likely to lose the match.

Competing for Partscores

In many respects the fierce competition over partscore hands which characterizes matchpoint pairs should be carried over into IMPS. That is, you must do a lot of balancing; or, if you prefer, you must get into the auction early and very lightly. One way or the other, you must not let the enemy buy a lot of contracts peacefully at the two-level. The difference between 2♥, making two, and 3♥ down one, is five IMPs, and a few swings like this can cost the match.

Duplicate-oriented players usually do compete or balance at the two-level when playing IMPS. Where they tend to go wrong is in competing at the three-level. Here there is a big difference between the two games. This is a common dilemma in pairs.

West	North	East	South
			1♠
Pass	2♠	Dbl	Pass
3♥	Pass	Pass	

You, South, hold:

    ♠ A Q 8 6 4
    ♥ A 8 5
    ♦ K 10 4
    ♣ J 8

If the cards lie favorably for your side, you might well make 3♠ — you cannot get a good result defending. Likewise, if the lie is unfavorable, the opponents might make 3♥; then you might do better to go down at 3♠. So at matchpoints you should consider bidding.

At IMPs though, you should certainly pass. Whether you are plus 140 or plus 100 is a matter of one IMP; the same is true of minus 100 or minus 140. However, if both 3♥ and 3♠ go down, not at all unlikely, the swing can be five IMPS. If your distribution were unbalanced, so that both contracts might make, then six IMPs might be gained by bidding. But with a flat hand you should expect that only one contract or the other can be made, according to whose finesses work. You cannot lose much

by passing, only by bidding.

The key is to think about plus scores on partscore hands, not how big a plus or how small a minus. If both pairs can be plus on three-quarters of the small hands, the team can win almost any match. See LAW OF TOTAL TRICKS.

Sacrifice Bidding

One area of difference between the matchpoint and the IMP approach is in sacrificing against game contracts. Sacrificing can be very rewarding at matchpoints — it is a triumph to lose 300 rather than 420, or 500 rather than 620. At IMPs, though, for the swing of 120 points you earn three IMPS. This is not a very good return on your for your gamble that the opponents could make their game. If you misjudge slightly, (losing 800 to save 620, for example) this costs only five IMPs. But if you take a PHANTOM SACRIFICE of 500 points against an unmakable game, you lose 12 IMPs. So the odds are not nearly as good as in matchpoint scoring.

The other side of this picture is that you are much more prone at IMPs than you are at duplicate to double an enemy sacrifice rather than push on to five in a major. In a pair game you are reluctant to accept 500 points in exchange for a vulnerable game; it can almost be a zero. Playing IMPs though, you double a sacrifice bid unless you are a cinch for 11 tricks. The odds are greatly against bidding on.

Of course, this refers to the "matchpoint" type of sacrifice. In any game it pays to go for 100 or 300 against a vulnerable game. At any scoring it pays to bid on to five of a major on the chance you will make it when you feel that you may not beat the opponents by more than a trick.

Actually, one type of sacrifice is popular among experienced IMP competitors; this is a premature sacrifice made in the hope of stampeding the opponents to the five-level. Thus, it aims at a 12-IMP gain, not a three-IMP profit.

Suppose partner opens 3 ♥, not vulnerable against vulnerable, right-hand opponent doubles, and you hold:

      ♠ K 6
      ♥ A J 7 4
      ♦ Q 7 2
      ♣ 8 5 4 2

Jump to 5 ♥. You are likely to have to make this bid over 4♠, so bid it immediately. Your left-hand opponent, under pressure, may bid 5♠, down one.

Another time when a sacrifice aims at a large number of IMPs is when you save against a slam. Down five doubled, 1100, can gain eight IMPs if your partners make 1430.

Penalty Doubles

In almost all doubling situations at IMPs, the odds favor the coward, not the hero. Consider the position in which vulnerable opponents have crept up to 4 ♠ on a shaky auction. You can see that they are running into bad breaks and probably will go down, perhaps even two tricks. Then a double stands to gain 300 points for a two-trick set or lose 170 should the contract make; but the IMP odds are only 7 to 5. And if the opponent's contract is a silly one, your partners probably have stopped at a partscore; then a double stands to gain only an IMP or two, for you would have a handsome swing in your favor anyway.

This, actually, is quite similar to matchpoint thinking; why double the opponents if they have overbid when you are getting most of the points anyway? And maybe

they have not overbid; and perhaps your double will allow them to make a contract which otherwise would go down. This is particularly disastrous at IMPS.

An entirely different situation is the one in which you are debating whether to double an enemy overcall or to bid your own game contract. At matchpoints the critical consideration is the vulnerability; can you score in penalties more than the value of your game? For example, suppose you hold as South:

      ♠ A 4 3
      ♥ 7 2
      ♦ 9 5
      ♣ K Q J 8 4 3

North	East	South	West
1NT	Pass	3NT	4♠
Pass	Pass	?	

You are vulnerable and the opponents are not. Your partner is not sure about doubling and is leaving the decision to you. Should you bid 4NT, which will probably score 630, or settle for a double. The double is likely to be worth 500, but might be 200 on a bad day or 800 on a good day.

The scoring should determine. Double at IMPs and make sure of a plus score. Bid 4NT at matchpoints, risking defeat, since 500 will be a poor score if there are many 600s and 630s.

The key question at IMPS, then, is whether or not your game is sure. With the first example, you can feel only that game is probable, so you are anxious to play for penalties. Holding the second example, you can hardly imagine a hand that partner can have which will not produce 10 or 11 tricks at notrump, so you are reluctant to double. In short, at IMPS, go for the surest, not the most sizable, plus score.

One big difference between proper matchpoint and IMP approach is in doubling enemy partscores on competitive auctions. If you have bid up to 3 ♥ in a pair game and vulnerable opponents contest with 3 ♠, you are likely to double any time you feel sure that your contract would make; you must try to get 200 instead of 100. Obviously, this is suicidal at IMPs. If you score 100 when 140 is made at the other table, you lose 1 IMP, and 200 would gain you only 2 IMPs. For this 3-IMP pickup, you are risking a loss of 12 IMPs when the doubled contract is made (and your teammates play it undoubled). At matchpoints, you would gain considerably by doubling such contracts even if one in three is made against you; at IMP scoring you would be a big loser.

Speculative lead-directing doubles (i.e., calling for a lead which does not ensure a set but merely increases your chances) are slightly better bets at IMPs than at total points. For example, suppose you double a non-vulnerable 3NT contract to get a favorable lead. At matchpoints you are gambling a top against a bottom, instead of settling for slightly below average; the odds are a little better than even money. To figure the odds at IMPS, assume that the game is bid and made at the other table. If you beat the contract, you gain 500 while if it makes, you lose 150; these total-point odds become 11 IMPs to 4. The chance of overtricks reduces this to about two to one in your favor. That is, you will break even if the lead you direct beats one game in three.

The odds become most attractive when you double a slam. Superficially, this does not seem to be so. If you double a non-vulnerable 6 ♠ contract you gain 1080 (15

IMPS) when you beat it, while you lose 230 (6 IMPS) if you do not. But this assumes that the contract is the same at the other table, and this is an unwarranted assumption in the case of a close slam (as distinct from a touch-and-go game which probably will be bid). If only game is reached at the other table, your loss from doubling a makable slam is 1 IMP; and when your double was necessary to defeat the slam, your gain is 22 IMPS. (You gain 11 instead of losing 11.) At odds of 22 to 1, it is hard to go wrong.

General Tactics

There is another area of difference, though, caused not so much by the scoring as by the objectives of the two games. At matchpoints, you are trying to beat some huge (and ever increasing) number of competing pairs. At IMPS, you are trying to beat one team (at a time). And, in a pair contest, the huge field usually means that a great number of poor and inexperienced players are your direct or indirect opponents. But in an IMP team game you are not likely to meet any really bad opponents. What this means is that it is probably the winning style at matchpoints to try to beat par, to try for unusually good results. In contrast, at IMP scoring, this is not the winning style (unless you are far behind or a decided underdog).

Par bridge, i.e., taking everything which is yours without trying to steal what belongs to the enemy, will win almost any IMP match. Of course, you and your teammates are bound to make a few errors, but if you play a steady game and make fewer mistakes than your opponents, you will win. A 51% game is good enough. At matchpoints, 51% is a disaster; even 60% games will not win tournaments. You must take more chances (and this means make more bad bids) to win a pair game. One illustration of this is in preemptive bidding.

♠ 6
♥ K Q 10 8 6 4
♦ A J 10 6 3
♣ 2

At matchpoints one might open 4♥ as dealer with neither side vulnerable. At IMPs better heart spots would be desirable, and there is a greater chance that the hand should be played in diamonds, so open 1♥. At IMPS, there is less incentive to "steal."

Another illustration is in balancing in risky positions, i.e., when the opponents have not found a fit. Suppose that the auction goes as follows:

West	North	East	South
1NT	Pass	Pass	?

With neither side vulnerable, you hold, sitting South:

♠ K 10 8 4 3
♥ 5
♦ A 10 6 5
♣ Q 7 4

At matchpoints, bid 2♠. If you pass, you are settling for a normal, under-average score; it would be better to try to beat par with an unsound overcall. At IMPs, you should pass, accepting the fact that it is "wrong" to overcall. The risk of a disastrous result is one you do not have to take when trying to beat one team instead of 200 pairs.

In the bridge world there are quite a few famous players whose great strength is their tactical bidding. (A "tactical" bid is a bad bid which gets a good result.) These experts do very well at matchpoints, winning far more than their share of tournaments, killing the weak fields. But they do poorly in team games.

So, save your bad bids for matchpoints. When you play

IMPS, try a cautious, cowardly style: leave the heroics to your opponents. Then, at the end of the match you can compliment them for some brilliant bid while they are congratulating you for winning.

IN BACK OF. A term describing the relationship of a player to the opponent on his right; i. e., a player who plays after the player on his right is said to be "in back of" that player. An equivalent term is "over."

IN FRONT OF. The phrase used to describe the relationship between a player and his left-hand opponent; i.e., the player who plays before another player is said to be "in front of" that player. An equivalent term is "under."

IN THE RED. A seeming paradox in bridge terminology: in rubber bridge or CHICAGO it would mean being a loser, but in duplicate it describes a score good enough to earn masterpoints, because rankings that qualify for points used to be indicated in red on the recap sheet before computer scoring.

INADMISSIBLE CALLS. See LAWS (Laws 36-39).

INADMISSIBLE DOUBLE OR REDOUBLE. See LAWS (Law 36).

INADVERTENT CALL. See LAWS (Law 25).

INADVERTENT INFRINGEMENT OF LAW. A violation of the proper procedure without deliberate attempt to do so. It is assumed that all infringements of laws are inadvertent, and the penalties prescribed for such infringements are designed to indemnify the non-offenders against potential loss as a result of such inadvertence.

INCOMPLETE HAND. An original holding of fewer than 13 cards with the other three hands correct. The missing cards or cards are deemed to have been part of the original hand providing attention is drawn to the irregularity during the bidding and play. See Law 14.

If the missing card is in one of the other hands and has been looked at, then the normal procedure is to award an artificial adjusted score under Law 13. This Law does, however, give the players an option of playing the board if the information gained is inconsequential.

INCOMPLETE PACK. A pack of cards from which one or more cards are missing. If a deal is made from an incomplete pack, the deal is void, if discovered within the legal time limits, and a new pack is substituted.

INCOMPLETE RUBBER. If a rubber is not completed, bonuses are awarded of 300 for a game already scored and 100 for a partscore already scored.

INCOMPLETE TABLE. (1) In club play, a table of four or five players in which there is room for a newcomer to cut in. Some clubs designate five players, some six, as a full complement of players. (2) In home play, two or three players in search of one or two. (3) In duplicate play, see HALF TABLES.

INCORRECT CARD. Any card played which is improper in that it may become a revoke or is played out of turn.

INDEMNIFY. To give redress to a side that has been injured by an infraction of the laws by the other side. In duplicate bridge it is the duty of the tournament director to impose penalties for infractions. See LAWS OF DUPLICATE (Law 10). In rubber bridge a penalty may be imposed by agreement of the players, or by either member of the nonoffending side (except dummy) so long as he does not consult his partner. See LAWS OF CONTRACT BRIDGE (Law 14).

INDICES. Small identifying marks (numbers or letters) in the corners of playing cards, printed above the suit symbol.

The first use of indices is difficult to determine. Special packs of the seventeenth and eighteenth centuries (educational, heraldic, political, etc.) had so much of the card taken up with pictures and words that the identification consisted of a number or letter beside one pip in an upper corner. No one seems to have adapted this for use with regular playing cards for a long time. In the 1870s three American card makers tried different solutions to the problem. One put miniature cards in two corners (calling the style Triplicate); another used merely a letter or number and a small pip (called Squeezers, because they did not need to be fanned); the third put these in all four corners (Quadruplicate).

The use of double indices permits a hand to be fanned either right or left, and European cards today are usually so made; English and American players chose the single index at each end which is current today. In 1893 some packs were issued with a large corner pip, with a white index within it. Today some Swiss packs use no index pip, but put the index as a white numeral in the pip nearest the corner. Spanish and some Italian (trappola) packs have indices from 1 to 13, including both suit and court cards.

INDIVIDUAL TOURNAMENT. The only form of DUPLICATE BRIDGE in which you do not have a partner chosen by you. The game is set up in such a way that each player is a separate contestant who plays with a multitude of different partners. Sometimes you play only one board with each partner; other times you play two or three, rarely more.

The movement is more complicated than in a pair event. In the RAINBOW MOVEMENT — which nowadays is just about the only one used for games of seven tables or more — it is necessary for the players in each direction to have a different move each round (guide cards are usually used for smaller games). The idea is for each player to partner someone different each round against a brand new set of opponents.

Since each player is playing with so many different partners, it is impractical for partnerships to use complicated systems and conventions. Most players prefer to play some simple form of STANDARD AMERICAN or whatever is the most common method of bidding for the area.

See items under appropriate number of tables. Also see APPENDIX TABLE, INDIVIDUAL MOVEMENT, RAINBOW, SHOMATE.

INDIVIDUAL MOVEMENT. The most popular individual movement is the RAINBOW, described separately.

The SHOMATE MOVEMENT also is possible for some games, but it is not recommended although it does provide for balanced comparisons of a sort. The Shomate involves many movement irregularities and is a major chore to score. Modern-day directors almost never use the Shomate.

Two tables with eight, nine and 10 players can be accommodated in an Individual tournament. The boards of each round are relayed between the two tables. The game can be curtailed at any point, as all boards are completed after each round. In all cases, the players are assigned numbers. They replace the player with the next lower number at the end of each round. (In the eight-player movement, player #8 is stationary, and #1 replaces #7.) Starting assignments are as follows:

	Table 1				Table 2			
	N	S	E	W	N	S	E	W
8 players	8	1	6	2	5	7	3	4
9 players	2	3	4	7	6	8	5	9
10 players	7	8	10	2	5	9	3	6

There is one (and essentially only one) cyclic movement for 12 players with different board sets at the tables. Olof Hanner's variant allows terminating after any round, provided you have one round's warning. The first four rounds are:

N	S	E	W	bd	N	S	E	W	bd	N	S	E	W	bd
12	1	4	5	1	7	11	3	9	2	10	2	8	6	1
12	2	5	6	2	8	1	4	10	3	11	3	9	7	1
12	3	6	7	3	9	2	5	11	4	1	4	10	8	2
12	4	7	8	4	10	3	6	1	5	2	5	11	9	3

Except for the first round, where there is a board sharing between table 1 and 3, the tables play different board sets. In the round that you decide to be the last one, the eleventh or an earlier round if there is not time enough, you do not let table 2 start a new board set, but let this table share with table 1. All boards will then have been played three times and if the movement is played in 11 rounds, 22 boards, all players have met as partners.

The 13-player movement runs 13 rounds, two boards to a round. The tables play the boards in ascending order, the first set starting at table 1, sixth set at table 2 and 12th set at table 3. Seating assignments are as follows: table 1: 1, 3, 5, 6; table 2: 7, 12, 13, 4; table 3: 2, 9, 8, 11. All players replace the next lower numbered player for the next round, player #1 replacing player #13.

Movements for larger numbers of tables have been developed by Olof Hanner, and are set out in his book on Duplicate Organization, written with Hans-Olof Hallén and Per Jannersten.

INFERENCE. A conclusion drawn from a call or play made by partner or an opponent. Though the ability to gather and assimilate the most delicate clues is the hallmark of a fine player, the bidding and play of many hands abound with inferences that can be drawn by the average performer provided that he is alert and knows what to look for. Note that an inference implies uncertainty. An inference leaving no room for doubt would be a deduction.

A declarer's task is frequently lessened when the opponents have been in the auction. Apart from yielding specific information about the enemy suit(s), interference bidding generally assists the declarer to guess better in the play of a critical suit. For example in playing a common combination such as:

K J 10 9

A 8 7 6

Declarer has to catch the queen, and with nothing to guide him, he must sometimes guess wrong. See TWO-

WAY FINESSE. Suppose, however, that in the course of the auction West has made a preemptive bid marking himself with shortages elsewhere; the odds now clearly favor a finesse against his partner.

In taking advantage of the information provided by the bidding, a declarer frequently must resort to unusual plays:

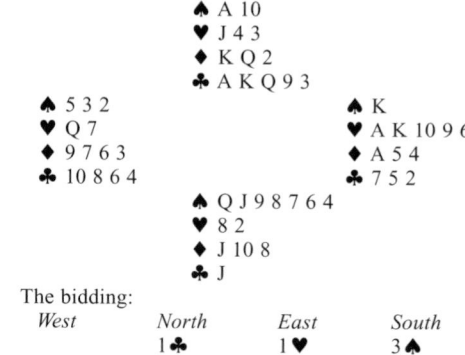

```
              ♠ Q 10 7
              ♥ 10 7 3 2
              ♦ K J 6
              ♣ K Q 10
♠ 5 4                        ♠ A 3
♥ K 8 6 5                    ♥ A Q J 4
♦ 10 5 4                     ♦ Q 7 3 2
♣ 7 5 4 2                    ♣ A 9 3
              ♠ K J 9 8 6 2
              ♥ 9
              ♦ A 9 8
              ♣ J 8 6
```

South is declarer in 4♠ after East has opened the bidding with 1NT. West leads a trump, and South, faced with three certain losers, has to avoid losing a diamond. The standard play of this combination is to finesse the jack, but in this instance declarer is fairly sure that East has the queen from his bid. His best chance is to take a backward finesse, leading the jack through East, and if covered, finessing against West for the 10 on the second round.

Sometimes the defenders find themselves in the unhappy position of guiding declarer's play through not bidding:

```
              ♠ K Q 4
              ♥ Q 6
              ♦ Q J 4 3
              ♣ A J 10 5
♠ 7 5                        ♠ J 9 2
♥ A K 4 3                    ♥ J 9 7 5 2
♦ K 7 6                      ♦ 10 9 8 5
♣ 8 7 4 2                    ♣ K
              ♠ A 10 8 6 3
              ♥ 10 8
              ♦ A 2
              ♣ Q 9 6 3
```

The bidding:

West	North	East	South
Pass	1♣	Pass	1♠
Pass	2♠	Pass	4♠
All Pass			

West cashes two hearts and shifts to a trump, declarer drawing three rounds ending in dummy in order to take the diamond finesse. West wins and exits with a heart, South ruffing. The ♣K is now marked with East, for in the play West has shown up with the ♥A, ♥K and ♦K, and if he also held the ♣K he would have opened the bidding. Declarer's only chance is that the king is singleton. Accordingly, he plays a club to the ace, dropping East's lone king.

Declarer has an even greater scope for making educated guesses based on the play of the opponents' cards. This is particularly true when the defenders are forced to discard on a long suit, the order of their discards being most helpful to declarer. The accuracy of the inferences thus drawn varies with the skill of the opposition, for good players generally plan ahead in these situations, often leaving the declarer with little to go on. Nevertheless, it is the mark of a good player that he guesses the right play more often than not.

On rare occasions, the defenders are helpless to prevent declarer from gaining an inference.

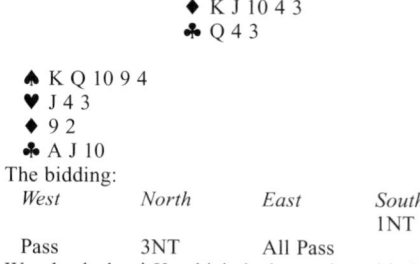

```
              ♠ A 10
              ♥ J 4 3
              ♦ K Q 2
              ♣ A K Q 9 3
♠ 5 3 2                      ♠ K
♥ Q 7                        ♥ A K 10 9 6 5
♦ 9 7 6 3                    ♦ A 5 4
♣ 10 8 6 4                   ♣ 7 5 2
              ♠ Q J 9 8 7 6 4
              ♥ 8 2
              ♦ J 10 8
              ♣ J
```

The bidding:

West	North	East	South
	1♣	1♥	3♠
Pass	4♠	All Pass	

West leads the ♥Q and continues the suit, East winning the king. After cashing the ♦A, East is in a cleft stick: if he returns a third heart, South will ruff high and West's failure to overruff will mark the ♠K. On the other hand, if he does not continue hearts, South's suspicions will be aroused and he is bound to diagnose the position.

The defending side is sometimes better placed to make deductions, for they have the advantage of being able to gather clues from both declarer's and partner's actions.

In a general way, the defenders can make certain assumptions about the nature of declarer's holding by his approach. For example, at a suit contract, if he plays a side-suit before broaching trumps, he probably has a shaky trump suit. On the other hand, if trumps are drawn immediately, it is safe to infer that declarer intends to utilize a side-suit to dispose of his losers. At notrump, when declarer makes no attempt to establish a strong suit, it is reasonably certain that the suit is ready to run.

```
              ♠ 8 7 6
              ♥ A 2
              ♦ K J 10 4 3
              ♣ Q 4 3

              ♠ K Q 10 9 4
              ♥ J 4 3
              ♦ 9 2
              ♣ A J 10
```

The bidding:

West	North	East	South
			1NT
Pass	3NT	All Pass	

West leads the ♠K, which declarer wins with the ace. To the second trick, South leads a club; West plays the ace and then the ♠Q, dropping declarer's jack, and takes three further spade tricks to set the contract. This was declarer's hand:

```
              ♠ A J
              ♥ K 9 7
              ♦ A Q 8 7
              ♣ K 9 5 2
```

West made two unusual plays: he rose with the ♣A in a position where it is customary to play low, and he continued spades at the risk of establishing the jack for declarer. The question is: how did he know? West reasoned that declarer could not have started with A-J-x of spades, for with that holding he would have surely refused the first spade, rendering the defense

helpless. Either partner had the jack or, more likely, declarer had A-J alone. Further, declarer's failure to play on diamonds surely meant that the suit was solid, in which case, if declarer was permitted to steal a club, he would almost certainly have 9 tricks: one spade, five diamonds, one club, and two hearts (he was likely to have the ♥K for his bid).

Defenders are often misled into committing a blunder, basing their defense on the assumption that a declarer has adopted a reasonable line of play. Similarly, in deciding his play at a crucial point in a hand, a defender has to assume that his partner has played well. Terence Reese gives this example:

```
                    ♠ Q 6
                    ♥ A Q J 9 5
                    ♦ J 9 4
                    ♣ Q 7 4
    ♠ 10 5                          ♠ J 9 4
    ♥ 8 6 2                         ♥ 7 3
    ♦ A 5 2                         ♦ K Q 10 7
    ♣ K 10 6 5 3                    ♣ A 9 8 2
                    ♠ A K 8 7 3 2
                    ♥ K 10 4
                    ♦ 8 6 3
                    ♣ J
```

South plays in 4♠ and West leads the ♣5 to his partner's ace. East shifts to the ♦K and continues with the 7, declarer falsecarding with the 8. West is now faced with the problem of guessing whether to attempt to cash the third diamond or the ♣K. From his point of view, declarer might have well dropped the ♣J at trick one from J-x, and with apparently nothing to guide him he played the ♣K, giving declarer the contract. West failed to draw the proper inference from his partner's play: if East had held five diamonds, leaving declarer with two, he would have realized that the defense could take only two diamond tricks and would have played the ♦Q to hold the lead before shifting back to clubs. See also CARD READING and COUNTING THE HAND.

INFERENTIAL PROBLEM. A problem which requires the deduction of the lie of hidden cards through the use of information of a form not found in ordinary play.

Two examples of inferential problems follow. The first problem is of moderate difficulty and provides a good introduction to inferential problems. The second problem is a harder nut to crack with only one clue given as to the makeup of the concealed hands.

Big Casino and Little Casino*
by Jeff Rubens
Reprinted from **The Bridge Journal, Jan.-Feb. 1964.*

```
                    ♠ 3
                    ♥ 9 6 4
                    ♦ A 7 6
                    ♣ K Q 9 5 4 2

                    ♠ A Q 9 5 4
                    ♥ 3 2
                    ♦ K 9 5 3
                    ♣ A 10
```

Contract: 6♦ by South
Clues:
(1) After the lead of any black card, South can make his contract by perfect play. However, after the lead of any red card, perfect defense can defeat the contract.

(2) A "spot card" is any card from 2 through 10. The sum of East's spot cards in hearts subtracted from the sum of his spot cards in diamonds is exactly one third of the sum of all his black spot cards.

(3) Neither defender is void of hearts, and neither defender holds both big casino (♦10) and little casino (♠2).

What are the exact East-West hands and how does South fulfill his contract after a favorable lead?
Solution to "Big Casino and Little Casino"

As neither defender is void of hearts, South must discard all his hearts before losing the lead. Further, he cannot lose a trick to one of the three missing low trumps. If diamonds are 3-3, no discards can be taken. Therefore, diamonds must be 4-2 with West holding two blank honors. In this way, declarer can obtain two discards on the clubs in dummy. These discards must be taken after two trumps are drawn; therefore one ruff must establish the spade suit. This places East with ♠K-J-10 and four clubs. East's four clubs must include the jack as the lead of a black card must help declarer by providing an entry for a black suit finesse. Since the sum of East's black spot cards is divisible by three, East must hold ♣ J-8-6-3. Since West holds the ♠2, East's diamond honor is the 10. Therefore, East holds two hearts with a spot total of 15 and the East-West hands are:

```
    ♠ 8 7 6 2                        ♠ K J 10
    ♥ A K Q J ? ?                    ♥ ? ?
    ♦ Q J                            ♦ 10 8 4 2
    ♣ 7                              ♣ J 8 6 3
```

After a black suit lead, declarer wins easily. He cashes the ♦K and ♦A, takes the remaining black suit finesse, clears all the black-suit tops in the South hand, ruffs a spade in dummy and discards two hearts on good clubs. Clubs are now continued until East ruffs. If East ruffs low, South overruffs and leads good spades. If East ruffs high, South takes the balance easily. If East never ruffs, he is trump couped at trick 12.

East's two hearts must be 10-5, not 8-7, for if East held ♥8-7, the opening lead of ♥5 would not defeat the contract!

Inferential Problem*
By Terence Reese
Reprinted from **The Bridge World. Feb. 1950.*

```
                    ♠ 8 5 2
                    ♥ J 6
                    ♦ K 6 5 3 2
                    ♣ 8 6 5
    ♠ K J 9 6
    ♥ K 7
    ♦ J 9 4
    ♣ Q 9 4 2
```

South played a contract of 3NT. West led the ♠6. East won with the ace and returned the 4. West won with the jack and played the king, on which East played the 3, and all followed. West then cashed the thirteenth spade. The contract was just made.

"Nicely played," said West to declarer at the end of the hand. "There was nothing we could do, was there, partner?"

"Well, yes," said East. "If, at the fourth trick, you had played any card except the thirteenth spade we could have put them one down."

Assuming that East was right, what was South's hand?

Solution to "Inferential Problem"

The key lies in realizing that the last spade, in addition to making the timing right for a squeeze, gives South a chance to unblock in diamonds. The diamond holding is A-Q-8-7, and the suit is blocked unless South can discard one of them. (The diamonds cannot be A-Q-10-8 or A-Q-10-7, for then a diamond lead by West would resolve the difficulty.)

Declarer has, at most, eight tricks on top. The ninth can come only from a squeeze in hearts and clubs. The hearts must be A-Q alone — if A-Q-x, the lead of ♥K would be fatal to the defense — and the clubs A-K-7-3, for if they are as good as A-K-10-x, the lead of ♣Q gives South three tricks in clubs, and enables him to endplay West. So the whole hand is:

♠ Q 10 7 ♥ A Q ♦ A Q 8 7 ♣ A K 7 3

The play, when West leads the last spade, is to discard a heart from dummy and a diamond from declarer's hand. West exits with a diamond; declarer cashes the ♣A-K, and runs off the diamonds. The last diamond squeezes West in hearts and clubs.

INFORMATION, UNAUTHORIZED. See UNAUTHORIZED INFORMATION.

INFORMATORY DOUBLE. An early name for the TAKEOUT DOUBLE.

INFORMATORY PASS. See PENALTY PASS.

INHIBITORY DOUBLE. A psychic maneuver in a competitive auction aimed at intimidating the opponents. It may take the form of a double of a forcing bid after partner has made an overcall. For example:

West	North	East	South
			Pass
1♥	2♣	2♠	Dbl

East's 2♠ bid is forcing in a standard style, and if South held a good hand with spades he would be well advised to wait for better things. The doubler, in fact, usually has a bad hand with support for his partner's suit, to which the latter retreats at his turn.

However, this double is now often used for takeout, showing moderate length in the fourth suit. See SNAPDRAGON and TAKEOUT DOUBLE.

INITIAL BID. The first bid of any deal. See OPENING BID.

INITIAL LEAD. The first lead of any deal. See OPENING LEAD.

INNER SEQUENCE. See INTERIOR SEQUENCE.

INSPECTION OF TRICKS. (1) A trick may be inspected by any player until such player has turned his play to the trick face down. (2) Until play ceases, QUITTED TRICKS may not be inspected except at the director's specific instruction. (3) After play ceases, the played and unplayed cards may be inspected to settle, e.g; a claim of a revoke or of the number of tricks won and lost; but no player should handle cards other than his own. See LAWS OF DUPLICATE, Law 66.

INSTANT MATCHPOINTS. Scoring method used in which the matchpoint scores are predetermined, based on the results in a previous competition in which the same deals were played. The method became known worldwide in 1986 when the first EPSON WORLDWIDE BRIDGE CONTEST was staged. The method was used for the Worldwide Pairs every year thereafter through 1999.

Identical hands are played at all sites of the tournament (often the ACBL or Europe, sometimes the world). Players discovered their score on each board as soon as they opened the TRAVELING SCORESLIP. The ACBL adopted the Instant Matchpoint plan for a game held at clubs throughout ACBL on an annual basis. Usually a good-looking program book is distributed to all players at the conclusion of the game in which each and every hand is thoroughly analyzed by an expert.

In 2000, a new type of contest was inaugurated at the world level in which pairs throughout the world saw their scores matchpointed in the usual way by means of a scoring program devised by Mark Newton of Great Britain. The program made it possible to matchpoint all scores from all over the world. See WORLDWIDE MATCHPOINT GAME.

INSTANT SCORER. A small sheet on which are listed all possible scores for all possible contracts.

INSTINCT (or Intuition). A term loosely applied to one's inherent feeling about the right play, or less often the right bid, to make during a deal of bridge. Some players are said to be totally devoid of instinct or card sense (really sensitivity), and have to make calculations for any play involving percentages. The concept of "instinct" as such has been challenged by many authorities, but those who possess it or claim to possess it maintain its definite existence. See TABLE PRESENCE.

INSTRUCTIONS (director's). The announcements by the director by which a movement in a session of duplicate bridge is completed. At the end of each round, the director instructs the players as to their movement and the movement of the boards in play. At determined times, this movement may vary for one or more rounds. The ARROW SWITCH, skip, and redistribution of boards are examples of such variations. Instructions are also given to the contestants for twinning of boards, methods of qualification, starting times for succeeding sessions, and other conditions of contest.

INSUFFICIENT BID. A bid lower in rank than a bid previously made in the auction. The next bidder has the right to accept the insufficient bid. If the insufficient bid is not conventional and if the next player does not accept it, the player may correct his insufficient bid by making it sufficient in the same suit, without penalty. However, penalties apply even if the player makes his bid sufficient in the same suit if his insufficient bid was conventional. See Law 27 for penalties.

INSULT. The 50-point penalty that the doubling side pays for doubling a contract that the declaring side makes. The insult bonus is 100 if the contract succeeds when redoubled.

INSURANCE BID. A high-level save made in spite of some expectation of defeating the opposing contract. The

insurance bidder is willing to concede a small penalty to guard against the danger of a big minus score.

INTERCITY MATCH. Many intercity matches have been played in various parts of North America. A series of such matches played from 1960 to 1973, usually preceding the Summer North American Championships.

INTERCOLLEGIATE BRIDGE TOURNAMENT. An annual event formerly contested by universities and colleges throughout the United States and Canada, organized by GEOFFREY MOTT-SMITH, 1949-1960, WILLIAM ROOT, 1961-1965, LAWRENCE ROSLER and JEFF RUBENS, 1966-1967, and subsequently by representatives of the Association of College Unions-International and the American Contract Bridge League. When the Charles Goren Foundation offered financial assistance in 1969 the tournament became known as the Charles Goren Intercollegiate Bridge Tournament. One year — in 1974 — the Celanese Corporation assumed full financial responsibility for the tournament.

A feature of the tournament in the early years was the use of par hands. The earliest matches were conducted as a face-to-face contest for 16 finalists, but in 1953 the procedure was changed to a mailing of par hands to each campus with the scorecards rated in New York. Under this plan, titles were awarded to the highest-scoring pair on the North-South hands and on the East-West hands. In 1965, the face-to-face final was restored and par hands were used in the qualifying round. Initially, the final was scored by matchpoints, but international matchpoint scoring was adopted in 1967, and the conversion of IMPs to Victory Points was introduced in 1968. Par hands were eliminated in 1969, and the tournament became a three-stage contest, with an on-campus qualifying round and a regional semifinal in addition to the final. The national final had the reputation of being a showcase tournament and a number of national champions emerged from these contests. The 37th and final contest in this series was held in Memphis in April, 1979 after which the ACBL withdrew technical and financial support. The contest was resumed in 1991 as a joint venture of ACBL and ACU-I. For a list of Intercollegiate winners, see Appendix 1.

INTEREST-SHOWING BID. Bid which can be used as an alternative to a CUEBID when the opener and responder have agreed on a major suit at the level of three or four. The idea was developed in 1948 by some Cambridge University, England, players (E.M.L. and J.R.A. Beale, and H. Peter F. Swinnerton-Dyer), and are an optional part of the ACOL SYSTEM. The bid can be considered an extension of a TRIAL BID at a higher level.

If the bidding goes 1♠-3♠; 1♠-4♠; or similarly in hearts, a change of suit which would normally be a cuebid is made in a suit in which some support is needed. For example:

(a)	(b)
♠ A K 10 5 3	♠ K Q 9 5 4
♥ Q J 7 3	♥ A K J 6
♦ A	♦ Q 7 3
♣ K Q 7	♣ A

The opening bid of 1♠ is raised to 3♠, a limit raise showing about 11 points or the equivalent counting distribution.

On hand (a) the interest-showing bid would be 4♥,

indicating that the opener needs some help in the form of heart honors or a heart shortage.

The interest-showing bid may well be made in a three-card suit. On hand (b) the opener rebids 4♦ to ask for support in that suit.

In each of these cases a normal cuebid would leave the responder in doubt about how to evaluate his hand for slam purposes. For an alternative treatment, see ASKING BIDS.

INTERFERENCE BID. Any defensive overcall which is not attacking or strength-showing, but is designed to obstruct somewhat the path of the opponents. Sometimes interference is made with preemptive or jump-bid tactics. See NUISANCE BID and OVERCALLS.

INTERIM RESPONSE. See WAITING BID.

INTERIOR CARD. An intermediate card; formerly, the second card in sequence, as the jack in a holding of queen, jack, and others.

INTERIOR SEQUENCE. A sequence within a suit such that the top card of the suit is not a part of the sequence, as the Q-J-10 in a holding of A-Q-J-10, or the J-10-9 in a holding of A-J-10-9. Some experts play that the lead of the jack against notrump denies a higher honor, and therefore lead the 10 from A-J-10 and K-J-10. By extension, a lead of the 10 can promise a higher honor by partnership agreement. The 9 would then be led from a holding headed by 10-9. See JOURNALIST LEADS; OPENING LEADS; PLAY FROM EQUALS; RUSINOW LEADS; ZERO OR TWO HIGHER LEADS.

INTERMEDIATE CARDS. See BODY and SPOT CARDS.

INTERMEDIATE JUMP OVERCALL. See JUMP OVERCALL, ROMAN JUMP OVERCALL, WEAK JUMP OVERCALL.

INTERMEDIATE ONE NOTRUMP. An opening bid of 1NT based on a range between weak notrumps and strong notrumps, such as the 13-15 or 14-16 point range used in the Precision Club system.

INTERMEDIATE TWO-BID. An opening bid of two in a suit to show a strong hand somewhat short of game strength. In the original version, introduced about 1930, responder could pass the intermediate two-bid with a worthless hand, and some experts still play it in this fashion. Most, however, play it as a one-round force, with 2NT or a HERBERT NEGATIVE the required weakness response. See ACOL TWO-BID.

INTERNAL BLOCK. See UNBLOCKING.

INTERNATIONAL BRIDGE. There have been international tournaments and challenge matches since the earliest years of bridge. (See ANGLO-AMERICAN MATCHES). The first officially sponsored international tournament was held in Vienna in June 1930 under the auspices of the AUSTRIAN BRIDGE FEDERATION. The first international organization was the INTERNATIONAL BRIDGE LEAGUE, founded in 1932 by a small group of European countries, which conducted

European championships until 1939. After World War II, the EUROPEAN BRIDGE LEAGUE was formed to replace the IBL. Today there are a large number of regional international organizations or tournaments. See AFRICAN BRIDGE FEDERATION, AMERICAN CONTRACT BRIDGE LEAGUE; BRIDGE FEDERATION OF ASIA AND THE MIDDLE EAST; CENTRAL AMERICAN AND CARIBBEAN BRIDGE FEDERATION; EUROPEAN BRIDGE LEAGUE; NORDIC CHAMPIONSHIPS; SOUTH AMERICAN BRIDGE CONFEDERATION; SOUTH PACIFIC BRIDGE FEDERATION.

The first official world championship was held in New York in 1935 between France, reigning European champions, and a team representing the AMERICAN BRIDGE LEAGUE. The only other prewar world championship was held in 1937 in Austria, hosted by the IBL. World championship play resumed in 1950 with the first of a series of contests for the BERMUDA BOWL. Since 1963 the Bermuda Bowl has been conducted by the WORLD BRIDGE FEDERATION, formed in 1958. The WBF also conducts WORLD PAIR CHAMPIONSHIPS, WORLD TEAM OLYMPIADS, VENICE CUP matches, ROSENBLUM CUP matches and McCONNELL CUP matches. For lists of winners, see Appendices III, IV and V.

INTERNATIONAL BRIDGE ACADEMY. Formed in 1965 by Jean Besse and Pierre Collet for the purpose of fostering the study of bridge as a science. The Academy held meetings and published articles on the scientific and technical aspects of bridge. World Bidding Contests were staged for many years. The Academy has been dormant since the mid-1980s.

INTERNATIONAL BRIDGE LEAGUE. A forerunner of the WORLD BRIDGE FEDERATION, founded on June 10, 1932, at Scheveningen, The Netherlands, by a small group of European countries. During the years 1932-39, the IBL organized annual championships, including a World Championship in Budapest in 1937.

INTERNATIONAL BRIDGE PRESS ASSOCIATION (IBPA). A worldwide organization of about 500 bridge writers, mostly professionals, whose reports and articles appear in newspapers and magazines and other periodicals in most countries where tournament bridge is played. Authors and radio and TV lecturers also are eligible for membership. The European Bridge Press Association, the father of the IBPA, was formed at the Oslo 1958 European Championships by the journalists present. At the first Olympiad, played in 1960 in Turin, many non-European bridge writers joined, so the name was changed to International Bridge Press Association.

The presidents have been:

Guy Ramsey	1958-59
Ranik Halle	1960-64
Jack Kelly	1964-70
Richard Frey	1970-81
Alan Truscott	1981-86
Rene Ducheyne	1986-91
Tommy Sandsmark	1991-96
Henry Francis	1996-

Eric Jannersten was executive secretary-treasurer from the foundation of the organization until he resigned that post in 1975. At that time he was named senior vice president for life. He was editor of the IBPA monthly bulletins until 1967, when Rhoda Barrow (Lederer) assumed the editorial duties. Albert Dormer took over the editorship in 1973 and retained that position until he resigned in 1981. He was succeeded by Patrick Jourdain as editor and David Rex-Taylor as managing editor.

Herman Filarski took over as executive vice president in 1975 and was responsible for many promotions in which the IBPA was involved. These included the BOLS TIPS, which bridge writers throughout the world incorporated in their columns; the BOLS BRILLIANCY AWARDS, which were given at World Championships for outstanding articles by bridge writers about outstanding plays by competitors in the World Championships; the Philip Morris tournaments in Europe, which led to a Grand Final in Monte Carlo each year; and the Heineken Fluke Award, which was given to the bridge writer who wrote the best story about a fluke during the 1980 World Team Olympiad in Valkenberg. The Bols Brilliancy Prizes were awarded from 1976-1986, after which the series of Bols Tip contests was resumed.

Others who have made major contributions include Eloene Griggs, Nelson Rice, Evelyn Senn, and Berl Stallard.

The IBPA's functions have embraced negotiations with tournament organizers to improve working conditions and accessibility of information to the press; closer cooperation with national and international bridge organizations; publication of hand collections, such as *Bridge Writer's Choice* (1964 and 1968), *Bols Tips* and *Fit for a King* in 2000; establishment and presentation of annual awards for accomplishments in various fields of bridge; the dissemination of news bulletins to members and associate members, and the sponsorship of bridge promotions. See INTERNATIONAL BRIDGE PRESS ASSOCIATION AWARDS.

INTERNATIONAL BRIDGE PRESS ASSOCIATION AWARDS. Each award is presented at the world championship in the year following the one for which the award is given.

Personality of the Year
(Charles H. Goren Award until 1989; strictly an IBPA award since then)

1973/74	André Lemaitre, Belgium
1974/75	Julius L Rosenblum, USA
1975/76	Rixi Markus, Great Britain
1976/77	Herman Filarski, Netherlands
1977/78	Jaime Ortiz-Patino, Switzerland
1978/79	Edgar Kaplan, USA
1979/80	Amalya L. Kearse, USA
1980/81	Deng Xiaoping, China
1981/82	Albert Dormer, Great Britain
1982/83	Oswald Jacoby, USA
1983/84	Easley Blackwood, USA
1984/85	*Barry Crane, USA
1985/86	José Damiani, France
1986/87	Kathie Wei-Sender, USA
1987/88	Helene Lemaitre, Belgium
1988/89	Not awarded
1989/90	Eloene Griggs, USA
1990/91	André Boekhorst, Netherlands
1991/92	Evelyn Senn-Gorter, Netherlands
1992/93	Hugh Kelsey, Great Britain
1993/94	Ernesto d'Orsi, Brazil
1994/95	Panos Gerontopoulos, Greece

1995/96	Geir Helgemo, Norway
1996/97	Matthew Clegg, USA
1997/98	Paul Chemla, France
1998/99	Marc Hodler, Switzerland
1999/2000	Anna Gudge, Great Britain

* Posthumously

Best Played Hand of the Year
(Charles J. Solomon Award)

1973/74	José le Dentu, France
1974/75	Benito Garozzo, Italy
1975/76	Tim Seres, Australia
1976/77	Harold Ogust, USA
1977/78	Dominique Pilon, France
1978/79	Maurizio Sementa
1979/80	Benito Garozzo, Italy
1980/81	Andrzej Wilkosz, Poland
1981/82	Lajos Linczmayer, Hungary
1982/82	Claude Delmouly, France
1983/84	Zia Mahmood, Pakistan
1984/85	Wan Li, China
1985/86	Henri Svarc, France
1986/87	Jon Andreas Stoevneng, Norway

(Name of winning journalist in parentheses)

1987/88	Trond Rogne, Norway (Knut Kjarnsrod, Norway)
1988/89	Kerri Shuman. USA (Alan Truscott, USA)
1989/90	Miss Raczynska, Poland (Guy Dupont, France)
1990/91	Shmuel Friedman, Israel (Jos Jacobs, Netherlands)
1991/92	Elizabeth McGowan, Great Britain (Barry Rigal, USA)
1992/93	Peter Schaltz, Denmark (Villy Dam, Denmark)
1993/94	Hervé Mouiel, France (Jean-Paul Meyer, France)
1994/95	Philippe Cronier, France (Patrick Jourdain, Great Britain}
1995/96	Wubbo de Boer, Netherlands (Eric Kokish, Canada)
1996/97	Geir Helgemo, Norway (Edgar Kaplan, USA)
1997/98	Jeff Meckstroth. USA (Jean-Paul Meyer, France)
1998/99	Jeff Meckstroth, USA (Omar Sharif, Egypt)
1999/2000	Vincent Ramondt, Netherlands (Jos Jacobs, Netherlands)

Best Bid Hand of the Year
(The Romex Award)

This award is donated annually by George Rosenkranz of Mexico, the author of the Romex system of bidding.

1975/76	Matt Granovetter & Ron Rubin, USA
1976/77	Gabino Cintra & Christiano Fonseca, Brazil
1977/78	Eric Kokish & Peter Nagy, Canada
1978/79	Chip Martel & Lew Stansby, USA
1979/80	Kyle Larsen & Ron von der Porten, USA
1980/81	Knud-Aage Boesgaard & Peter Schaltz, Denmark
1981/82	Not awarded
1982/83	Zia Mahmood & Masood Salim, Pakistan (Pak)
1983/84	Benito Garozzo & Giorgio Belladonna, Italy
1984/85	Steve Cooper & Wayne Timms
1985/86	Hugh Ross & Peter Pender, USA
1986/87	Zia Mahmood, Pakistan

(Name of winning journalist in parentheses)

1987/88	Allan Graves & George Mittelman,Canada

	(Sue Emery, USA)
1988/89	Sven-Akke Bjerregard & Anders Morath, Sweden (Sven-Olov Flodquist, Sweden)
1989/90	Andrew Robson & John Pottage, Great Britain (Patrick Jourdain, Great Britain)
1990/91	Edgar Kaplan & Brian Glubok, USA (Allan Falk, USA)
1991/92	Arma Valta & Juuri-Oja, Finland (Patrick Jourdain, Great Britain
1992/93	Tom Sanders & Bill Pollack, USA (Dick Kaplan, USA)
1993/94	Shakiat & Pobsit, Thailand (Amran Zamzami, Indonesia)
1994/95	Larry Cohen & David Berkowitz, USA (Alfred Sheinwold, USA)
1995/96	Derek Patterson & Pat Collins, Great Britain (Brian Callaghan, Great Britain)
1996/97	Chip Martel & Lew Stansby, USA (Brent Manley, USA)
1997/98	Sylvie Willard & Gerard Tissot, France (Philippe Cronier. France)
1998/99	Geir Helgemo & Tor Helness, Norway (Patrick Jourdain, Great Britain)
1999/2000	David Berkowitz and Larry Cohen, USA (Paul Linxwiler, USA)

Best Article or Series on a System or Convention
(Precision Award)

This award was donated by C.C. Wei and after his death by his widow, Kathie Wei (now Kathie Wei-Sender).

1973/74	Charles H Goren, USA
1974/75	Eric Kokish, Canada
1975/76	George Rosenkranz, Mexico
1976/77	Jeff Rubens, USA
1977/78	Kit Woolsey, USA
1978/79	Jeff Rubens, USA
1979/80	Ed Manfield & Kenneth Lebensold, USA
1980/81	Eddie Kantar, USA
1981/82	Jeff Rubens, USA
1982/82	Ed Manfield, USA
1983/84	Bruce Neill, New Zealand
1984/85	Sven-Olov Flodquist & Anders Morath, Sweden

Renamed Best Defense of the Year
(Sender Award)

The award was changed in 1985 to the best defensive play of the year. Kathie Wei-Sender named the award in honor of her husband, Henry Sender of Nashville TN.

1985/86	Bob Hamman, USA
1986/87	Michel Lebel, France

(Name of winning journalist in parentheses)

1987/88	Primo Levi, Italy (Paolo Frendo, Italy)
1988/89	Dung Duong, Switzerland (Jean-Paul Meyer, France)
1989/90	Vladis Polenieks, Latvia (Uno Viigand, Estonia)
1990/91	Geir Helgemo, Norway (Tommy Sandsmark, Norway)
1991/92	Mike Passell, USA (Phillip Alder, USA)
1992/93	Bob Hamman, USA (Brent Manley, USA)
1993/94	Gabriel Chagas, Brazil (Alan Truscott, USA)
1994/95	Zia Mahmood, USA (AlanTruscott, USA)
1995/96	Larry Cohen/David Berkowitz, USA (Jan van Cleeff, Netherlands)
1996/97	Gunnar Hallberg, Sweden (Robert Sheehan, Great Britain)
1997/98	Geir Helgemo, Norway (Patrick Jourdain,

Great Britain)
1998/99   Andrew Robson. Great Britain (Philip King, Great Britain)

Carey Limousine Award

George Jacobs, representing the Carey Limousine Corporation, took over sponsorship of the Best Defense of the Year Award in 2000.

1999/2000   Roger and Terje Lie, Sweden (Anders Brunzell, Sweden)

Sportsman of the Year

(John E. Simon Award, now in abeyance)

1973	Omar Sharif, France
1974	Alan Sontag, USA
1975	George Rosenkranz, Mexico
1976	Lord Glenkinglas, Sir Timothy Kitson, Rt. Hon. Jarold Lever MP, GB
1977	Maurits Caransa, Netherlands
1979	Steve Landen, USA
1985	Irving Litvack, Joey Silver, Canada

INTERNATIONAL CHAMPIONSHIPS. See INTERNATIONAL BRIDGE. Also see Appendices III, IV and V for results.

INTERNATIONAL CODE. See LAWS OF RUBBER BRIDGE AND LAWS OF DUPLICATE CONTRACT BRIDGE.

INTERNATIONAL COLLEGE TOURNAMENT. The program was cancelled in 1996 and in 1997 became an on-line competition on OKbridge. In 2000, the North American College Bridge Team Championship was reinstated by the ACBL Board, with the finals set for the Summer NABC in Toronto. Both competitions — the North American College Championship and the OKbridge International College Championship – were continued as of 2001.

INTERNATIONAL MATCH. A contest between two (or more) countries. See ANGLO-AMERICAN MATCHES; FRANCO-AMERICAN MATCHES; INTERNATIONAL BRIDGE; WORLD CHAMPIONSHIPS. Also see Appendices III, IV and V for results.

INTERNATIONAL MATCHPOINTS. A method of scoring used frequently in team events, and occasionally in pair events.

The procedure appears to have been invented in Vienna, and was first used at the international level in the 1938 European Championship in Oslo. IMPs were first used in the BERMUDA BOWL in 1951.

The original name was EMP, or European Match Points. The original scale provided for a maximum gain of 12 points, as follows:

Point Diff.	EMP	Point Diff.	EMP
10- 30	1	400-490	7
40- 60	2	500-590	8
70-100	3	600-740	9
110-180	4	750-1490	10
190-290	5	1500-1990	11
300-390	6	2000 and up	12

A revised scale was adopted for the 1948 European Championships in Copenhagen, with a maximum of 15 points. A further revision in 1961, devised by a subcommittee of the World Bridge Federation, brought the maximum to 25 points. This had the effect of increasing the

relative award to large gains, and brought the scale slightly nearer to total-point scoring. A further revision was made effective September 1, 1962. That scale is still in use.

1948 Scale		1961 Scale	
Point Diff.	IMPs	Point Diff.	IMPs
0- 10	0	0-10	0
20-60	1	20-40	1
70-130	2	50-80	2
140-210	3	90-120	3
220-260	4	130-160	4
270-310	5	170-210	5
500-740	6	220-260	6
750-990	7	270-310	7
1000-1240	8	320-360	8
1250-1490	9	370-420	9
1500-1990	10	430-490	10
2000-2490	11	500-590	11
2500-2990	12	600-690	12
3000-3490	13	700-790	13
3500-3990	14	800-890	14
4000 and up	15	900-1040	15
		1050-1190	16
		1200-1340	17
		1350-1490	18
		1500-1740	19
		1750-1990	20
		2000-2240	21
		2250-2490	22
		2500-2990	23
		3000-3490	24
		3500 and up	25

1962 Scale (still in use)

Total Points	Imps	Total Points	Imps
20-40	1	750-990	13
50-80	2	990-1090	14
90-120	3	1100-1290	15
130-160	4	1300-1490	16
170-210	5	1500-1740	17
220-260	6	1750-1990	18
270-310	7	2000-2240	19
320-360	8	2250-2490	20
370-420	9	2500-2990	21
430-490	10	3000-2490	22
500-590	11	3500-3990	23
600-740	12	4000-up	24

The purpose of introducing International Matchpoints was to eliminate the inherent defects of other methods: total-point scoring accentuated one or two big swing boards; board-a-match reduced all boards to equal status. The general effect of the graduated scale of International Matchpoints is to flatten the value of high scores and to heighten the value of partscore contracts.

In team games, the International Matchpoints are awarded after the net score of the team (North-South and East-West) has been computed. Positive points are awarded to the team with a positive net score, negative for the negative net score.

In pair events, each pair is compared with an average score, and the International Matchpoints awarded may be positive (for a score better than average) or negative (for a score below the average). The average score is the arithmetic mean of all scores, except that the best and worst scores are usually omitted in computing the comparison value.

The purpose of this is to prevent one unusual result

from influencing scores at other tables. The best and worst scores, however, are used in computing the difference for those pairs from the average. The net IMP scores on each match may be converted into VICTORY POINTS on a graduated scale.

This use of IMP scoring in pair events was originated by the British Bridge League under the chairmanship of Geoffrey Butler. It is sometimes called the Butler Method.

The most logical use of International Matchpoint scoring in pair competition is in connection with qualifying events for pairs to compete in team events, as it adapts pair play to team scoring results. However, this method of scoring has been used successfully at the club level.

INTERNATIONAL OLYMPIC COMMITTEE. See IOC CUP.

INTERNATIONAL OPEN TEAM SELECTION. The ACBL has employed objective selection processes since 1970. Teams that had the best records in major national events took part in playoffs from 1970 to 1993. Since 1994 a separate International Team Trials has been used for selection. See ACBL INTERNATIONAL OPEN TEAM SELECTION, ACBL WOMEN'S TEAM SELECTION.

Other countries, particularly in Europe, tend to allow the subjective opinions of one or more selectors to determine the team selection. This has usually been the case in Great Britain, although the Premier League has become influential, but not decisive, in recent years.

Hybrid methods are common in many areas. Trials are held, but then selectors make the final decision, taking the results of the trials into consideration.

The Dictator method, where one person makes all the decisions, is used in Sweden. It was used in Italy when Carl Alberto Perroux controlled the Blue Team. In recent years, a playoff among members of the Squadra Azzurra decides the team, but the players must accept certain conditions. France has usually preferred an objective trials method.

INTERNATIONAL POPULAR BRIDGE MONTHLY. A magazine published in Great Britain from 1980-1999.

INTERNATIONAL WOMEN'S TEAM SELECTION. See ACBL INTERNATIONAL WOMEN'S TEAM SELECTION.

INTERNET BRIDGE. Bridge played on computers without cards. Several programs work on this principle. See ACBL ONLINE, E-BRIDGE, MICROSOFT GAME ZONE, OKBRIDGE.

INTERNET WORLD BRIDGE CHAMPIONSHIP. A world-wide knockout team competition in which all hands are bid and played on computers – playing cards are never used. Sponsored by OKbridge, the first championship was staged in 1999. A United States team captained by Marty Seligman defeated Russia in the final, which took place on vugraph in Boston just before the ACBL Fall Championships got under way in November. Romania won the 2000 championship in Birmingham, Alabama, USA, against a primarily American team. Starting in the quarterfinals, each competitor is monitored for security reasons. For results, see Appendix IV.

INTERVENING BID. An overcall.

INTERVENTION, INTERVENOR. Action by a player (intervenor) when the opponents have opened the bidding.

INTERWOVEN HOWELL. Two Howell games of equal size, so arranged that each plays (at each round) the boards which are not in play in the other.

Since a Howell game of x tables requires 2x - 1 sets of boards, x - 1 sets are out of play at a given time. By proper arrangement these boards may be used in a parallel or "interwoven" Howell game; except that there must be one pair of relay tables at which the same set of boards is in play simultaneously in both games.

INTRA-FINESSE. A term introduced by Gabriel Chagas in a Bols Tip to describe certain finessing situations that call for successive finesses against both opponents.

♠ A 9 3

♠ 10 2   ♠ Q J 7 5

♠ K 8 6 4

A finesse of the 9 loses to the jack or queen, and the declarer later cashes the ace and finesses against East's remaining honor. The procedure usually involves crashing an honor (West's 10 here) or setting up a squeeze position.

INVERTED MINOR RAISES. A treatment for showing support for an opening bid of one of a minor devised as part of the KAPLAN-SHEINWOLD SYSTEM. In the original version, a single raise was strong and forcing, with at least 10 HCP, while a double raise was weak and obstructive. The combination allows more room for investigation with good hands and offers a preemptive effect with weak hands.

♠ A 8 4

♥ K 4

♦ 6 4 3

♣ K J 9 5 2

Raise 1♣ to 2♣. The bidding usually goes on to game, although it is possible to stop at 2NT or 3♣. A bid of new suit by opener usually is an attempt to get to a notrump game.

♠ K 6 4

♥ 6 3

♦ 7 5

♣ J 9 8 6 4 2

Raise 1♣ to 3♣.

Experts and many tournament players made changes that covered the three types of raises – forcing, invitational and preemptive. The jump raise retained the same meaning – purely preemptive. However, the single raise became an absolute force to game. Minor suit jump shifts became the method to show invitational values.

♠ 8 6

♥ A 8 5

♦ K 5 2

♣ K 10 9 8 5

Over an opening bid of 1♣ bid 2♦, showing an invitational club raise.

♠ K 7

♥ 5 4

♦ K J 10 9 5

♣ K J 4 3

Over an opening bid of 1 ♦ bid 3 ♣, showing an invitational diamond raise.

If the opponents intervene over the opening bid, it is a matter of partnership understanding whether inverted minors are still in effect.

Inverted Minors was the choice in BWS94.

INVITATION, INVITATIONAL BID.

A bid which encourages the bidder's partner to continue to game or slam, but gives him the option of passing if he has no reserve values in terms of high-card strength or distribution.

In nearly all cases such bids are one level below the game or slam which is being suggested, so bids of 2NT or three of a major suit often come in this category.

West	East	or	West	East
1NT	2NT		1♥	2♣
			2♥	2NT

but a jump by responder (response or rebid) may be an exception, being forcing in old-style methods but invitational in a modern style.

A jump rebid by the opener is invitational:

West	East
1♥	1♠
3♥	

and so is a single raise from two to three in the later stages of the auction:

West	East	or	West	East
1♥	1♠		1♠	1NT
2♥	3♥		2♥	3♥

For other sequences which are invitational in some styles but forcing in others, see JUMP REBIDS BY RESPONDER. See also conventions listed in GAME INVITATION. Also see ENCOURAGING.

IOC CUP.

An annual event played in Lausanne, Switzerland, headquarters of the International Olympic Committee. Adding this event to the bridge calendar was an important step on the road to possible inclusion of bridge in the Olympic Games, provisionally scheduled to take place at the Winter Games in Turin, Italy, in 2006. Progress was made thanks to the efforts of Marc Hodler, vice president of the IOC; José Damiani, president of the World Bridge Federation, and Mazhar Jafri, WBF vice president. The first IOC Cup, in 1998, had a dramatic conclusion. In the final, there was an exact tie between Brazil and China. Earlier, they had tied their round-robin match and shared the lead in that stage. Rather than embark on the expected four-board play-off, the players demonstrated Olympic spirit by linking arms and agreeing to share the honors. "Bridge," said IOC President Juan Antonio Samaranch at the opening ceremony, "is a sport, and as such your place is here with all other sports." For results, see Appendix IV.

IRON DUKE, NOT THROUGH THE.

An expression indicating that the user holds a very strong hand. The remark, an improper one, is usually made when the player splits cards of equal value to prevent a finesse or rises with a high card to prevent a lesser honor from winning the trick.

IRREGULAR LEAD.

A calculated departure from normal procedure occurring in the play of the first card to any trick by a defender. See FISHER DOUBLE, LIGHTNER DOUBLE.

IRREGULAR RAINBOW.

The regular RAINBOW MOVEMENT exists only for prime numbers – 5, 7, 11, 13, 17, etc. tables. For 8 and 9 tables H. Shomate constructed irregular variants. They were presented with stationary boards and completely irregular player progressions. They have been reorganized, however, so that, with one exception, the players and the board sets move regularly. They are therefore easily conducted with table guidecards. A similar 16-table Irregular Rainbow exists and one for 12 tables was constructed by P. Smith. An irregular Rainbow exists also for 15 tables, constructed by O. Hanner.

For 10 tables Shomate showed how to add 4 appendix players to his 9-table movement. Reorganized, this gives a smooth movement for 10 tables in 10 rounds.

Here are the table assignments for each round for the eight-table Irregular Rainbow.

		Table 1					Table 2			
Rd	N	S	E	W	b	N	S	E	W	b
1	1	9	17	25	1	2	10	18	26	2
2	8	14	23	27	1	4	11	21	30	2
3	8	15	17	28	2	5	12	22	31	3
4	8	9	18	29	3	6	13	23	25	4
5	8	10	19	30	4	7	14	17	26	5
6	8	11	20	31	5	1	15	18	27	6
7	8	12	21	25	6	2	9	19	28	7
8	8	13	22	26	7	3	10	20	29	1

		Table 3					Table 4			
Rd	N	S	E	W	b	N	S	E	W	b
1	3	11	19	27	3	4	12	20	28	4
2	7	10	24	25	3	2	15	22	29	4
3	1	11	24	26	4	3	9	23	30	5
4	2	12	24	27	5	4	10	17	31	6
5	3	13	24	28	6	5	11	18	25	7
6	4	14	24	29	7	6	12	19	26	1
7	5	15	24	30	1	7	13	20	27	2
8	6	9	24	31	2	1	14	21	28	3

		Table 5					Table 6			
Rd	N	S	E	W	b	N	S	E	W	b
1	5	13	21	29	5	6	14	22	30	6
2	6	16	18	28	5	5	9	20	26	6
3	7	16	19	29	6	6	10	21	27	7
4	1	16	20	30	7	7	11	22	28	1
5	2	16	21	31	1	1	12	23	29	2
6	3	16	22	25	2	2	13	17	30	3
7	4	16	23	26	3	3	14	18	31	4
8	5	16	17	27	4	4	15	19	25	5

		Table 7					Table 8			
Rd	N	S	E	W	b	N	S	E	W	b
1	7	15	23	31	7	8	16	24	32	8
2	3	12	17	32	7	1	13	19	31	8
3	4	13	18	32	1	2	14	20	25	8
4	5	14	19	32	2	3	15	21	26	8
5	6	15	20	32	3	4	9	22	27	8
6	7	9	21	32	4	5	10	23	28	8
7	1	10	22	32	5	6	11	17	29	8
8	2	11	23	32	6	7	12	18	30	8

Note that the movement is regular except for the first round. From round 2 players 8, 16, 24, and 32 are stationary, as are the boards at table 8.

IRREGULARITY. A deviation from correct procedures set forth in the LAWS and PROPRIETIES.

ISOLATING THE MENACE. A maneuver in SQUEEZE-PLAY technique. A menace may be controlled by both opponents, in which case it is usually advantageous to have the full burden of guarding that suit imposed on one opponent. The term "isolating the menace" refers to declarer's efforts in that direction: he seeks to have the menace isolated so that it is protected by only one opponent.

```
                  A K x x
        Q J x x            10 x x
                  x x
```

If the diagram illustrates the distribution of a side suit at a trump contract, then North's menace can be isolated by playing off the ace and king followed by a ruff on the third round. At any contract a first-round duck would ensure that the menace was isolated. See THREAT CARD.

ITALIAN SYSTEMS. See BLUE TEAM CLUB; LEGHORN DIAMOND; LITTLE ROMAN CLUB; MARMIC SYSTEM; ROMAN SYSTEM; SUPER PRECISION.

J

JACK. The fourth ranking card in a suit. Also called knave. See COAT CARDS; COURT CARDS; VALET.

JACK, TEN, OR NINE SHOWING ZERO OR TWO HIGHER HONORS. See ZERO OR TWO HIGHER LEADS.

JACKPOT. Extra money beyond the entry fee collected from players for special prize purposes. Usually the highest scoring pair or team taking part in the jackpot collects the jackpot money. In calcuttas pairs are sold to the highest bidder and the money goes into a pool that is divided according to the final standings.

JACOBY INDIVIDUAL MOVEMENT. See RAINBOW INDIVIDUAL MOVEMENT.

JACOBY TRANSFER BID. Used in responding at the two-level to 1NT opening bids, or in responding at the three-level to 2NT openings. These transfers were introduced by Oswald Jacoby in a *Bridge World* article in 1956, although they had been used in Sweden as early as 1953-54 as a result of a series of articles in *Bridge Tidningen* written by Olle Willner. 2 ♦ shows hearts and asks opener to bid 2♥. 2♥ shows spades and asks opener to bid 2♠. This convention greatly increases the chance that the strong hand will be the declarer in a suit contract. It also solves the problems created by many hands of intermediate strength:

```
        (a)                   (b)
    ♠ Q 10 8 7 6 4       ♠ 8
    ♥ K Q 3             ♥ A 10 9 5 4
    ♦ 4 3               ♦ 10 5
    ♣ 7 5               ♣ K Q 10 5 3
```

On hand (a) the response is 2♥, and the rebid of 2♠ is raised to 3♠. This is a game invitation which the opener can pass if he wishes.

On hand (b) the response of 2♦ shows the heart suit, and responder continues with 3♣. This shows his two-suited hand, and leaves the next move to the opener. 3♣ is forcing, but might be made on a slightly weaker hand.

There are methods for extending transfers to the minor suits. See FOUR-SUIT TRANSFER BIDS and MINOR SUIT STAYMAN.

If the bidding begins

Opener	Responder
1NT	2♥
2♠	

The normal rebid structure for responder is:

(1) Pass with no game prospects.

(2) 2NT, natural, invitational, balanced.

(3) 3♣ or 3♦, natural, game forcing, possible slam interest.

(4) 3♥ at least 5-5 in the majors if Smolen is in use – otherwise 5-4, game forcing.

(5) 3♠ invitational, 6-card suit.

(6) 3NT balanced, offering a choice of games.

(7) 4♣, 4♦ or 4♥ splinter, slam try setting responder's suit as trump.

(8) 4♠ sign-off, 6-card suit. (But a slam invitation if four-level responses are transfers.)

(9) 4NT. Natural slam invitation, balanced.

Rebids are similar after a transfer to hearts, but the sequence 1NT — 2♦ — 2♥ — 2♠ needs discussion. See PREACCEPTANCE.

Many players break transfers in certain situations. If responder transfers to spades and opener has four trumps and a maximum, he may jump to 3♠. If opener has three trumps and a maximum, he may bid 2NT to get this message across.

For defense see SANDWICH.

JACOBY TROPHY. Awarded to the winners of the NORTH AMERICAN OPEN SWISS TEAMS. Trophy honors Oswald Jacoby, one of the greatest players of all time, and his son Jim, winner of four world championships including two Bermuda Bowls and World Team Olympiad.

JACOBY TWO NOTRUMP RESPONSE. A method of increasing slam-bidding accuracy, developed by Oswald Jacoby and used in conjunction with limit major-suit raises.

After a 1♥ or 1♠ opening, a jump response to 2NT by an unpassed hand is a forcing raise of opener's suit. Responder promises at least four trumps and suggests balanced distribution, but his strength is in theory unlimited. Opener rebids conventionally to clarify his strength and pattern:

New suit at the three level = singleton or void in the suit.

New suit at the four level = five-card suit.

Game in agreed trump suit = minimum hand, no slam interest.

Three of agreed trump suit = 16 or more points, slam interest.

3NT = sound opening, 14-15 points, no singleton or void.

Although many pairs use this schedule of rebids, there are many variations especially in the meaning of the 3NT rebid.

Some structure is desirable when the opener shows a short suit, since his hand has a wide range. One possibility is to use a relay, the next available bid, as a strength inquiry with the following rebids: First step: minimum with a singleton; Second step: maximum with a singleton; Third step: minimum with a void; Fourth step: maximum with a void.

An alternative, more complex, rebid structure:

3♣ = non-minimum, with a singleton or 5332.
3♦ = non-minimum, any 5422.
3♥ = unspecified void, any strength.
3♠ = minimum with a singleton.
3NT = non-minimum 6322 or 7222.
4 of lower-ranking suit = limited 5-5, good second suit.
4 of original major = minimum, no shortness.

After responses below 3NT, a relay inquires further. Then one step shows club shortness, two steps diamond shortness, three steps other major shortness. (Except after 3♦ rebid, when the side length is shown similarly). After 3♣ rebid and 3♦ relay, 4♣, 4♦ and 4♥ show doubletons in 5332 hands. This gives more distributional accuracy, but less definition of the strength of one-suited hands.

Possible variations: (1) Barring use with singletons; (2) restricting 2NT to limited hands or to hands able to take control with a keycard inquiry; (3) using jumps by opening bidder to show voids. See LIMIT RAISE.

JETTISON. The discard of a high-ranking honor, usually an ace or a king, to effect an unblock. The term was originated in England by A.E.Whitelaw in 1921. A typical example is the following:

```
              A 10 8 6 4 3
   Q 2                      J 9 5
              K 7
```

In a notrump contract, South leads the king in a position in which East needs an entry. West must drop the queen, for otherwise South will allow the queen to hold on the next round.

The play may be necessary to effect an unblock for avoidance reasons, to create an entry or to avert a ruff. See also ENTRY SQUEEZE, UNBLOCKING.

JETTISON SQUEEZE. A form of ENTRY SQUEEZE.

JOKER. A fifty-third card in decks of cards, sometimes used as a substitute or "wild" card, but not used in bridge. See TAROT.

JORDAN. See RESPONSES OVER OPPONENT'S TAKEOUT DOUBLE and 2NT RESPONSE (Over opponent's takeout double).

JOSEPHINE. See GRAND SLAM FORCE.

JOURNALIST LEADS. A method of opening leads advocated by the *Bridge Journal* in 1964-1965. The details are as follows:

Against notrump contracts:

A, usually, from A-K-J-x (x-x) or A-K-10-x-(x-x). Third hand is requested to unblock a high honor if he can afford it, otherwise to give a length signal (high with an even number, low with an odd number of cards in the suit).

K from A-K or K-Q (assuming a high honor should be led).

Q from Q-J (or K-Q-10-9; third hand is requested to play the jack if he has it).

J from J-10. The jack denies a higher honor.

10 from A-10-9, K-10-9, Q-10-9, A-J-10, K-J-10. The 10 guarantees a higher honor (Q, K or A).

9 from 10-9. The 9 promises the 10 and no higher honor.

Second highest or highest from lower spot cards to discourage suit continuation.

Usually lowest card from a long suit headed by one or two honors to encourage suit continuation. The purpose of these leads is to make it easier for third hand to know whether to continue the attack on the suit led or to shift. The following hand shows what can happen when Journalist leads are not used.

```
Dir: North           ♠ A J 10 6 3
Vul: Both            ♥ 5
Imps                 ♦ 7 4
                     ♣ A K 10 7 2
                                   ♠ Q 9 5 2
                                   ♥ Q J 10 4
                                   ♦ A 6 3
                                   ♣ Q 5
```

West	North	East	South
	1♣	Pass	1♥
Pass	1♠	Pass	3NT
All Pass			

Using standard leads, West led the ♦10 to East's ace, South playing the 2. Now if South started with a hand like: ♠K-x ♥A-K-x-x-x ♦Q-J-2 ♣x-x-x, East must continue diamonds. But if the 10 was West's highest diamond, a heart shift is called for.

East actually continued diamonds and found South with: ♠K-x ♥K-x-x-x ♦K-Q-J-x ♣ J-x-x. Declarer won the diamond, cashed ♣A-K (because he could hardly afford to lose a finesse to East and get a heart through) and made 10 tricks.

Using Journalist leads, West would have led the ♦9, and East would have shifted to a heart, defeating the contract.

Against suit contracts Journalist Leads follow a different pattern. From two touching honors the second highest is led; from spot cards the highest card below the 9 may be led to indicate a weak holding: otherwise, the third highest is led from an even number of cards or the lowest from an odd number of cards.

JUMP BID. A bid at a level higher than is necessary to raise the previous bid. A bid of two or more than necessary is termed a DOUBLE JUMP, etc. SKIP BID is a more general term, embracing jumps to any level.

JUMP CUEBID. A bid of a suit originally called by an opponent, but made at a higher level than necessary.

A jump cuebid is an unusual action, but modern bidding has found some uses for it. The best known instance is the jump cuebid in response to a simple overcall:

West	North	East	South
1♦	1♠	Pass	3♦

In most partnerships, South promises game-invitational values with spade support and a distributional hand; he has a hand suitable for a limit raise of an opening bid. South may hold:

```
♠ K J 6 4
♥ A J 5 2
♦ 9 7 5 2
♣ 2
```

Another instance is a jump cuebid of an opposing opening bid:

West	North	East	South
		1♠	3♠

South promises a long, solid minor suit and asks North to bid 3NT if he can stop the spades. South may hold:

♠ 8
♥ Q 4
♦ A 10 5
♣ A K Q 9 8 5 3

Other partnerships use a jump cuebid to show specified two- suited hands.

In some circumstances, a jump cuebid may be a SPLINTER RESPONSE.

West	North	East	South
1♦	1♠	Pass	4♦

or

West	North	East	South
	1♠	2♦	4♦

South has a strong hand with an excellent spade fit and a singleton or void in diamonds. Slam is possible. South may hold:

♠ K 9 7 4 2
♥ K J 7 3
♦ —
♣ A J 7 3

JUMP OVERCALL. A suit overcall at a level one higher than necessary:

South	West		South	West
1♦	2♠	or	1♠	3♦

Three types are in common use, all based on good six-card suits, rarely longer.

(1) WEAK JUMP OVERCALL. A hand roughly equivalent to a weak-two opening, normally in the 6-10 point range, below the strength for a normal overcall. The strength requirement declines as vulnerability becomes more favorable.

(2) INTERMEDIATE JUMP OVERCALL. A hand about equivalent to a minimum opening. Frequently used in balancing seat even by those who use weak jump overcalls in other situations.

(3) STRONG JUMP OVERCALL. A hand worth an opening bid followed by a jump. Such a bid is sometimes used over weak two-bids, even by those who use weak jump overcalls in other situations.

The weak jump overcall, also called a preemptive jump overcall, is by far the most popular choice.

Suit responses to all jumps are forcing. A 2NT response can, by agreement, ask for OGUST rebids.

See also separate entries, GHESTEM and ROMAN JUMP OVERCALL.

JUMP PREFERENCE. Returning to partner's original suit at a level one higher than necessary.

West	East
1♥	1♠ or 2♣ or 1NT
2♦	3♥

See JUMP REBIDS BY RESPONDER.

If the opener gives jump preference, it is normally a game force.

West	East
1♣	1♥
2♣	2♦
3♥	

JUMP RAISE. See DOUBLE RAISE.

JUMP RAISE IN RESPONDER'S SUIT. See OPENER'S REBID.

JUMP REBID BY OPENER. See OPENER'S REBID.

JUMP REBID BY RESPONDER. These are jump bids short of game by responder at his second turn. The meanings of such bids vary widely. In traditional STANDARD AMERICAN all such jump bids were considered forcing, whether or not responder rebids his own suit, supports partner's suit or names a new suit. In the modern style all such secondary jumps are non-forcing unless they are in a new suit. Some players treat some as forcing and some as non-forcing. Partnership discussion is essential. See table on the next page.

JUMP SHIFT. A new suit response at a level one higher than necessary:

West	East		West	East
1♥	2♠	or	1♥	3♣

In standard methods this shows a hand of great strength which can almost guarantee a slam (19 points or more including distribution). The hand is usually one of four types: a good fit with opener's suit; a strong single-suiter; a strong two-suiter; or a balanced hand with more than 18 points. However, the last type is not easy to handle with a jump shift, and an alternative method is described under IMPOSSIBLE BIDS.

Many experts have less elevated standards for a jump shift, making the bid with about 17 points including distribution; in ACOL, 16 points or less with a good fit or a good suit. In this last case the response may be made in a three-card suit, either because the hand is balanced or because there is a fit with opener but no side suit.

A theory codified by Paul Soloway is that jump shifts should be limited to three types of hands: (1) one-suiters, (2) semi-balanced hands, and (3) hands with a good fit for opener's suit. Responder clarifies his hand by his rebid. If he has a one-suited hand he rebids his suit. If he has a semi-balanced hand his next bid is in notrump. If he has a good fit for opener, he can make a FRAGMENT bid in a new suit to show a singleton in the fourth suit, or he can return to opener's suit to deny having a singleton.

This method of showing a singleton and support for opener's suit is workable only if it is agreed that the jump shift cannot be made with a two-suited hand; under this agreement responder's bid of a new suit at his second turn cannot show a real suit. A common variation is to bid the singleton on the second round, not the fragment.

Another use proposed by Albert Morehead called for a jump shift with a hand well-provided with controls but lacking suit substance, suggesting that the opening bidder, with a suitable hand, should use Blackwood.

Perhaps the most unusual treatment shows a solid suit in the next higher-ranking suit, opener's suit excepted. For example, after a 1♣ opening, a jump to 2♥ shows a solid spade suit. Opener normally accepts the transfer, which permits responder to cuebid his other controls. If responder is unable to cuebid, he supports the agreed suit, and a subsequent bid of 4NT by opener is not Blackwood, but asks about the length of responder's suit.

Rebids by the opener after a jump shift are not standardized, but the opener should usually make the rebid he was planning after a non-jump response, only, of course, one level higher. There are two exceptions to this principle: a non-jump rebid of 3NT would not prom-

ise extra values, nor would a reverse.

This idea was originated by Ely Culbertson, who called it "jump takeout" or "forcing takeout".

For a preemptive use of this response, see WEAK JUMP SHIFT RESPONSES. See also PASSED HAND.

JUMP SHIFT REBID. See OPENER'S REBID.

JUMP SHIFT TO 3♣. See THREE-CLUB RESPONSE AS MAJOR RAISE.

JUMP TAKEOUT. See JUMP SHIFT.

JUMP TO GAME IN MAJOR SUIT. See OPENER'S REBID for jump to game in responder's major suit or in opener's major suit. See also TRIPLE RAISE.

JUNIOR. In international competition, a player under the age of 26.

JUNIOR CAMPS. The aim of Junior Camps is very simple — to bring together young people with a common interest in the game of bridge and to teach them more about the game and about each other. The camps are aimed at helping the younger generations of bridge players to make new friends and to develop and strengthen the ties already established between older friends, under the umbrella of their common interest.

Junior Camps were first introduced in Europe in 1976 following a suggestion by Dirk Schroeder of Germany. His idea was enthusiastically endorsed and developed by André Boekhorst of The Netherlands, chairman of the EBL Youth Committee at that time. The first camp was in Warmensteinach, Germany. The second was held the following year in Budapest, Hungary. Since then, these events have been organized every two years. EBL camps took place in Ghent, Belgium, 1979; Odense, Denmark, 1981; Porto Hydra, Greece, 1983; Dourdan, France, 1985; Beekbergen. Holland, 1987; Mragowo, Poland, 1989; Fiesch, Switzerland, 1991, and Oberreifenberg, Germany, 1993.

The first WBF Junior Camp was held in 1995 in Ghent, Belgium, incorporating the EBL event. Since then, World Camps have been held in Sportilia, Italy, 1997, and Nymburk, Czech Republic, 1999. The 2001 camp was to be held in Poland. Besides the usual European participants, the World Camps regularly attract many participants from Canada and the United States and lesser numbers from the other WBF zones.

The camps do not exist for expert players. Rather, they are for young players with enthusiasm for the game, youngsters who wish to learn more and improve their standard. Naturally, such players would not normally have the chance to participate internationally, so these camps provide an ideal opportunity for these youngsters to travel to other countries and meet young players from all over the world.

All WBF Junior Bridge Camps have the rule that no player may partner another person of his or her own nationality, and thus a wonderful mixture of language, bidding systems and, as a result, friendship is created.

As a result of special initiatives in this area, the WBF Youth Awards were instituted by the World Bridge Federation in 1989 as part of their general effort to encour-

JUMP REBIDS BY RESPONDER		
2 NT	**Forcing Style**	**Non-forcing Style**
1♣ - 1♥	13-15	10-12. A 13-15 hand bids 3NT, or makes a fourth-
1♠ - 2NT	(An 11-12 point hand remains a problem)	suit bid.
Jump Preference		
1♣ - 1♥	13 or more.	10-12; perhaps only 3-card support if used
1♠ - 3♣		in combination with limit raises.
1♠ - 2♣	13 or more. Probably 3-card support	10-12; 3-card support. But if 2♣ is a virtual
2♥ - 3♠	because of the failure to bid 3♠ originally.	game force, the range is 12+ and forcing with slam interest; the spades are strong.
1♦ - 1♠	12+, 6-card or longer	10-12; 6-card suit
1 NT - 3♠	suit, forcing.	
1♥ - 1♠	12+, usually 3-card support	10-12; 3-card support
1NT - 3♥		
1♦ - 1♠	12+, 4-card support or longer	10-12, probably 4-card or longer support.
1NT - 3♦		
Jump Raise		
1♣ - 1♥	13-15, 4-card support	10-12 and 4-card support. A stronger hand
1♠ - 3♠		bids 4♠, or bids the fourth suit followed by 4♠ as a mild slam suggestion.
Jump Rebid		
1♣ - 1♥	Games values and a	10-11 and a 6-card suit.
1♠ - 3♥	6-card suit – not strong enough for a jump shift	
Jump Shift		
1♣ - 1♥	The standard meaning in either method, is forcing, at least 5-5. Other possible agreements:	
1♠ - 3♦	(a) 5-5 invitational; (b) splinter; (c) mini-splinter.	

age the development of Junior Bridge world-wide. The awards aim at rewarding aptitude, diligence and international spirit shown by the participants at the Junior Camps. The winners do not receive any material prize, but earn the honor of enabling their countries to have a free, ex-quota, place at the next Junior Camp.

JUNIOR PAIRS. Both members of each pair must be at or under the age minimum set for the event, usually 25.

JUNIOR TEAM TRIALS. The method of selection of ACBL teams for the biennial World Junior Bridge Championships which were inaugurated by the World Bridge Federation in 1987.

1987. Representatives of six colleges, who had won their way to the North American Collegiate Bridge Championship final in St. Louis in March, 1987, competed for the right to play in the first World Junior Bridge Championships in Amsterdam, Netherlands. 244 students on 22 campuses participated in first-stage par contests. At St. Louis, two teams were eliminated in a round-robin and, after two knockout rounds, New York University was the victor. After one dropout and two augmentations, a five-person team was fielded at the WJBC. The first three were on the original NYU team. The North American team: Guy Doherty, Jon Heller, Asya Kamsky, Aaron Silverstein, Billy Hsieh, npc Matt Guagliardo.

1989. The selection process for the World Junior Championships was to approve the winning team at the North American College Bridge Championships in Reno, and to augment the four-man team to six at Junior Trials held in Memphis during the last three days of the United States Bridge Championships. The winning team also was to be sponsored to the European Junior Bridge Camp in Poland prior to the World Junior Championships in Nottingham, England, in August. The first four listed are the University of Tennessee champions who won the NACBC, the last two were the top pair at the Junior Trials. The North American team: Michael White, Mike Cappelletti, James Baker, David Williams, Michael Klein, David Rowntree, npc Bill Eisenberg. (When personal reasons forced Michael White to resign from the team he was replaced by Larry Hicks.)

1991. The ACBL was authorized three Junior teams at the World Junior Championships in Ann Arbor MI — two from the United States and one from Canada. U.S. I consisted of the top three pairs at Junior Trials held in Boston in July, 1990. Written examinations reduced the field of 65 candidates to 56 for the first rounds of the trials, conducted as IMP Pairs. Fourteen pairs qualified for the two-session final.

U.S. I: Brad Moss, Leni Holtz, Ravindra Murthy, Mike Cappelletti, David Rowntree, Michael Klein, npc Bobby Wolff.

U.S. II: Jeff Ferro, Wayne Stuart, John Diamond, Brian Platnick, Martha Benson, Tricia Thomas, npc Chip Martel (Tricia Thomas was replaced by Debbie Zuckerberg when employment duties forced Thomas to withdraw from the team).

Canada: Mark Caplan, Eric Sutherland, Fred Gitelman, Geoff Hampson, Bronia Gmach, Mike Roberts, npc John Carruthers.

1993. A pair of Canadians topped the Junior Trials at Toronto in July 1992. The three top U.S. pairs were provisionally named to the team for the NEC World Junior Team Championships in Arhus, Denmark. In February it was announced that two teams would represent the United States and that a third ACBL team would represent Canada.

U.S. I: Eric Greco, Kevin Wilson, Jeff Ferro, Leni Holtz, Debbie Zuckerberg, Rich Pavlicek, npc Chip Martel.

U.S. II: Sam Dinkin, Michael Shuster, Albert Tom, Doug Hsieh, Eric Secan, John Fout, npc Jan Martel.

Canada: Geoff Hampson, Bronia Gmach, Eric Sutherland, Mike Roberts, Jeffrey Blond, Nicholas L'Ecuyer, npc John Carruthers.

1995 - Ten teams participated in the Junior Team Trials that qualified two teams to attend the World Junior Teams Championship in Bali, Indonesia.

U.S. I - Steve Altus, Varis Carey, Eric Greco and Kevin Wilson. Andrew Moss and Leni Holtz were augmented but Moss was unable to attend at last minute. npc was Steve Robinson.

U.S. II - Richard Pavlicek Jr., Eric Secan, Blair Seidler and Michael Shuster. Tom Carmichael and Joel Wooldridge were augmented. Bob Rosen was npc.

Canada - Jeffrey Blond, Darrell Kovacz, David Levey, Fred Pollack, Mike Roberts and Eric Sutherland. John Carruthers was npc.

1997 - In a joint Junior Team Trials, Canada led throughout the trials to qualify to attend the World Junior Teams Championship held in Hamilton, Ontario, Canada. The top two U.S teams also qualified to attend the Championship. Canada was awarded a second team since they were the host country.

U.S I - Varis Carey, Andrew Lewis, Joel Singer, Michael Shuster. Mark Paltrowitz and Sam Hirschman were augmented. Steve Altus was npc.

U.S. II - Tom Carmichael, Shannon Lipscomb, Scott Lewis, Joel Wooldridge. Eric Greco and Chris Willenken were augmented. Bob Rosen was npc.

Canada Red - Jeffrey Blond, David Levy, Frederic Pollack, Mike Roberts, Eric Sutherland and. Darren Wolpert. Fred Gitelman and Sheri Winestock were co-npcs.

Canada White - David Halasi, Colin Lee, Danny Nadler, Mike Nadler, Barry Piafsky and Ben Zeidenberg. John Gowdy was npc.

1999 - Fourteen teams participated in the USA Junior Team Trials during the Chicago NABC. Two teams qualified to attend the World Junior Teams Championship held in Fort Lauderdale, Florida.

U.S I - Kevin Bathurst, Alan Epley, John Hurd, Mike Kitces, Lisa Kow and Brian Meyer. G.S. Jade Barrett was npc and Anne Hoffman was coach.

U.S. II - Chris Carmichael, Tom Carmichael, Eric Greco, David Wiegand, Chris Willenken and Joel Wooldridge. Bob Rosen was npc and Bobby Wolff was coach.

The top three pairs in Canada's Pair Trials qualified to be Canada Red. Canada White earned the right to attend the championship by defeating a USA team in a playoff for the fourth team to represent Zone 2.

Canada Red - David Brower, David Grainger, David Halasi, Mike Nadler, Darren Wolpert and Ben Zeidenberg. Jonathan Steinberg was npc.

Canada White - Erin Anderson, Craig Backhouse, Ian Boyd, Josh Heller, Colin Lee and Gavin Wolpert. Eric Sutherland was npc.

2001- Four teams participated in the USA Junior Team Trials during the 2000 Anaheim NABC. The top two teams qualified to attend the World Junior Teams Cham-

pionship in Rio de Janeiro, Brazil.

USA I - Brad Campbell, Joe Grue, John Hurd, John Kranyak, Kent Mignocchi and Joel Wooldridge. Bob Rosen was npc.

USA II - Kevin Bathurst, Paul Bethe, Jason Feldman, Ari Greenberg and Chris Lubesnik. Todd Wolford was augmented. Henry Bethe was npc.

Three teams participated in the Canadian trials. Representing Canada were Erin Anderson, Ian Boyd, Vincent Demuy and Josh Heller.

JUNIOR TEAMS. All players must be at or under the age limit, which is usually 25.

JUNK. A term used to describe a hand or a holding felt to be particularly valueless by the person describing it. See BAD CARDS.

K

KAMIKAZE NOTRUMP. A bidding system devised by John Kierein of Boulder CO which incorporates a 1NT opener in first and second seat on 9-12 high-card points. Weak two-bids in hearts and spades show 9-11 HCP. A 2♦ opener shows 9-11 with 4-4-4-1 or 5-4-4-0 distribution (any singleton). The system also calls for frequent psychic bids in third seat after two passes.

Because the ACBL does not allow the use of conventions such as Stayman with any opening 1NT with a bottom limit below 10 high-card points, Kierein prepared an insert for his booklet recommending that players who employ the Kamikaze notrump adjust the range to 10-13. In practice 10-12 is a common range.

KANTAR CUEBID. A specialized cuebid after an opponent's overcall suggested by Eddie Kantar. For example:

West	North	East	South
1♠	2♦	3♦	

In this specialized usage, 3♦ shows a 5-4-4-0 or 4-4-4-1 hand with a shortage in the opponent's suit. The strength may be as little as 8-9 high-card points, but there is no limit.

For other uses of the cuebid, see CUEBID IN OPPONENT'S SUIT.

KANTAR THREE NOTRUMP. See THREE NOTRUMP OPENING.

KAPLAN-SHEINWOLD. A system devised by Edgar Kaplan and Alfred Sheinwold, based on the weak notrump and aimed at more precisely limiting the strength shown by all bids. The features of the system are:

(1) Weak notrump with 12-14 points. An 11-point hand may be opened with 2½-3 Quick Tricks, or a 15-point hand with fewer than two quick tricks. Responses of 2♦, 2♥, 2♠, 3♣ and 3♦ are weak signoff bids. A bid of 2♣ followed by a minor-suit rebid is strong and forcing. Other responses are standard, with non-forcing Stayman. A bid of 2♣ followed by a jump to 3♥ or 3♠ is forcing, and shows a more unbalanced pattern than an immediate jump. Whether doubled or not, re-

sponder usually runs from 1NT with fewer than 5 points, often into 2♣ or 2♦.

After an overcall, a double is negative and a new suit bid at the three level is forcing.

(2) Minor-suit openings are sound (but any hand with three quick tricks must be opened). If balanced, 15-20 points and possibly a three-card suit: 1NT rebid shows 15-17; and 2NT rebid shows 18-20. A single raise of responder's major shows 15-17; a double raise shows 18-19; a triple raise shows 20-21 (in each case the requirements are reduced as distribution improves). A maximum unbalanced hand reverses or jump shifts before raising.

Responder bids a major in response whenever possible. Opener's reverse is a one-round force. A 3NT rebid shows a solid minor with outside stoppers.

For single and double raises, see INVERTED MINOR SUIT RAISES. Single raises are forcing and double raises are preemptive. A response of 1NT shows 5-8, and 2NT 12-15. A balanced 9-11 point hand may respond in the other minor.

If the opening is doubled, takeouts retain their meaning, but all raises are preemptive (redouble is the strong raise).

Opener may raise responder's major with three-card support in competition.

(3) NEGATIVE DOUBLE.

(4) Jump shift by responder is preemptive in competition.

(5) FIVE-CARD MAJORS, which can be light: a 9-point hand with quick-trick and playing-trick strength is possible. Exceptionally, a strong four-card suit may be bid, with a balanced minimum with honors concentrated in two suits, or a touching lower-ranking, weak five-card suit. ONE NOTRUMP RESPONSE FORCING, but opener passes with the rare balanced minimum hand.

LIMIT JUMP RAISES are used. The jump raise preceded by 1NT shows three-card support and a more balanced hand. A 3NT response is used instead of the standard (strong) jump raise. A 2NT response is standard. A minor-suit response is 12-13 minimum unless followed by a rebid in the minor, showing only a semi-solid suit headed by the ace; a delayed raise for opener or a 2NT rebid is game-forcing.

After 1♥ - 1♠, opener rebids 1NT, 2♥ or 2♠ with a minimum. A bid of 2♣ or 2♦ would be more constructive. After 1♠ - 2♥ (minimum 10 HCP and a five-card suit), minimum hands bid 2NT, 3♥ or 2♠; maximum hands (18 or more) bid 3♣ or 3♦, which are the only forcing bids; other bids show 15-17.

(6) Opening psychics are lead-directing, containing a legitimate suit with a high honor (2-6 points). A jump shift forces the opener to rebid in his suit or notrump, whichever is cheaper. Psychics are recommended only when non-vulnerable; at IMPs, only non-vulnerable versus vulnerable; at Board-a-Match, never.

(7) WEAK TWO-BIDS need one and one-half to two quick tricks and a semi-solid suit in first and second position. A single raise is preemptive, and other responses by an unpassed hand are forcing: 2NT asks the opener to bid a side honor.

(8) 2♣ is the only forcing opening. After a 2♦ negative response, the bidding can stop short of game if the opener rebids 2NT or bids and rebids one suit.

(9) 3NT opening shows a 2NT hand (20-22) with a long solid minor.

(10) CUEBIDs are used under game to suggest a slam and over game to ask about an unbid suit. A subsequent 4NT bid is a natural slam invitation, as in BLUE TEAM CLUB.

(11) GERBER over notrump bids.

(12) BLACKWOOD in other situations.

(13) GRAND SLAM FORCE.

(14) ROMAN ASKING BIDS.

(15) TAKEOUT DOUBLES emphasize distribution: there should be not fewer than three cards in each unbid suit. A cuebid is the only forcing response.

(16) Overcalls have the same range as an opening bid. Responder should seldom pass if he would have responded to an opening bid.

(17) WEAK JUMP OVERCALLS, usually with a maximum of one and one-half tricks.

(18) 1NT OVERCALL shows 17-19. A two-level takeout is a signoff, and a cuebid is Stayman.

(19) Optional features of the system include: SHORT-SUIT GAME TRIES; FLINT 3♦; UNUSUAL NOTRUMP; LANDY; FRAGMENT BIDS; MICHAELS CUEBID; ROMAN 2♦; WEAK JUMP SHIFT RESPONSES by passed hand; 3♣ as "prelude to signoff" over a jump rebid of 2NT; 2♦ as FORCING STAYMAN; 2NT over opposing takeout double as semi-preemptive raise; 3NT after limit jump raise of major to ask for short suit.

KEEPING SCORE. The process by which a record is kept of the activity during a rubber of bridge or of CHICAGO, and of the result on a board in duplicate. There can be more than one scorekeeper among a group of rubber bridge players, but in duplicate the score is usually kept by North.

KEEPING THE BIDDING OPEN. For the strength needed to make a response, see ONE OVER ONE RESPONSE. For reopening action by the fourth player, see BALANCING.

KENNETH COX AWARD. An adjunct to the American Bridge Association Hall of Fame, named for one of ABA's outstanding players of yesteryear who served in many important positions over the years. The award is similar to the American Contract Bridge League's Blackwood and Von Zedtwitz Awards. There were two recipients in 2000 – Robert Friend and the late Jimmy Lee. Arthur Wills was the 2001 winner.

KEOHANE TROPHY. Awarded to the winners of the North American Swiss Teams. Trophy was donated by Ethel Keohane in honor of her husband Bill, for many years chairman of regional tournaments in New England.

KEYCARD. Each ace and the king of the agreed trump suit when using any of the keycard ace-asking bids.

KEYCARD BLACKWOOD. A form of BLACKWOOD in which the king of trumps is counted as a fifth ace. Responder bids 5♣ with no aces or four aces, 5♦ with one ace or five aces, 5♥ with two aces, and 5♠ with three aces. A subsequent bid of 5NT by the Blackwood bidder may be used in various ways. It may ask for kings in the normal manner, except that the king of trumps would not be shown. Or it may ask for an additional feature in the Blackwood responder's hand.

Although this method of ace-asking still is used in some areas, in general it has been replaced by ROMAN KEYCARD BLACKWOOD. See also BYZANTINE BLACKWOOD; CULBERTSON 4-5NT; EXCLUSION BLACKWOOD; KEYCARD GERBER.

KEYCARD GERBER. A modification of the GERBER CONVENTION in which trump honors may be counted as aces. When only the trump king is to be counted as an ace, responder bids 4♦ with no aces or four aces, 4♥ with one ace or five aces, 4♠ with two aces, and 4NT with three aces. Some partnerships agree to count both the king and queen of trumps as aces. Using this agreement responder's 4♠ bid would show two or six aces. See BYZANTINE BLACKWOOD; KEYCARD BLACKWOOD; ROMAN GERBER.

KHEDIVE. An early name for bridge as played on the French Riviera, which lends support to the belief that the game is of Turkish origin. See HISTORY OF BRIDGE.

KIBITZER. An onlooker at bridge or other games.

KIBITZER'S MAKE. A hand which seems to have sufficient controls, enough high-card winners, and sufficiently few losers to be successful in a contract, but which for reasons of entry problems, duplication of values, or lie of the cards is doomed. The term comes from the habit of some poorly-trained kibitzers to indulge in analyses that careful scrutiny shows to be fallacious.

KIBITZING. The act of watching a game from the sidelines. In serious play at top clubs and at tournaments, the level of play is usually high, so there are unwritten, as well as written, rules concerning the deportment of any onlooker. See LAWS (Law 11 and 76). These onlookers know that it is extremely important for them not to give away any information about the nature of the hand or the holding that they are watching. In ACBL tournaments, kibitzers usually are permitted. However, one kibitzer may be removed at a player's request without cause. Any kibitzer can be removed for cause (failing to observe the proprieties for kibitzers). Numerous stories and legends have sprung up over the years about kibitzers and, although many of them are apocryphal, some are true, and others contain more than a germ of truth. Many of these tales are based on situations where the players are arguing vehemently about a bid or play, and it is decided that the matter be referred to the kibitzer for his opinion, with many varied and humorous endings.

The word "kibitzer" itself derives from the German word for a green plover, a highly inquisitive bird. The role of the kibitzer grew somewhat in stature and story as bridge itself expanded and progressed. In H. T. WEBSTER's regular series of bridge cartoons drawn for the *New York Herald Tribune*, the artist's attention often turned to kibitzers, and the resulting drawings were among his most amusing. Some of the great humorists of the Thirties and Forties occasionally did pieces about kibitzers, and one of the wittiest was George S. Kaufman's *"The Great Kibitzers' Strike."* All the comic and semi-serious articles reflected the general mores and customs of the times regarding kibitzers and attitudes toward them.

A classic story, and one of the few completely true ones, involved the players at a well-known New York

club and their one kibitzer. The five-level contract was doubled, and with the opponents on lead to the tenth trick, declarer spread his hand, claiming the balance, just making the contract. The opposition agreed, and the cards were just about to be thrown in, when the kibitzer pointed out a defensive lead which would have defeated the contract at that point. Bitter harangue and confusion then ensued and the matter was at length referred to the card committee. The final decision was that declarer be credited with making the contract doubled, the defense be credited with defeating the contract one trick, and the kibitzer be ordered to pay the difference.

KICK IT. Colloquial term for "I double." Also a colloquialism for boosting the contract as a preemptive measure.

KICKBACK. A method of using ROMAN KEY CARD BLACKWOOD while saving space. It was proposed by Jeff Rubens in an article in the February 1981 *Bridge World* and has been adopted by many experts. The bid immediately above four of the agreed suit is used to ask for key cards, thus saving space in most cases. 4 ♦ is used with clubs agreed, 4 ♥ with diamonds agreed, and 4 ♠ with hearts agreed. With spades agreed, the normal 4NT bid is used. 4NT, if idle, is a cuebid in the Kickback suits. Kickback followed by five of the Kickback suit suggests a grand slam, promises all the keycards and the trump queen, and asks for specific kings. See MILLER LITE.

KIDNAPPING. Edith Rosenkranz of Mexico City was kidnapped at about midnight on July 19, 1984, at the Hotel Sheraton in Washington DC during the Summer North American Championships. She spent nearly two days in captivity before she was released after the kidnappers picked up the ransom. She came through the ordeal in surprisingly good condition. The FBI and the Washington police captured the five kidnappers within minutes of the time when they released Rosenkranz. The ransom money, which was described as "substantial" by the Washington police, was fully recovered. This was the result of a carefully planned strategy on the part of the FBI. When the FBI was asked if the kidnapping had been the work of amateurs, their reply was, "Not at all. It looks as the abduction was planned two or three months in advance. The FBI won this time, but it could have gone either way."

Here's how the abduction took place, according to Rosenkranz. She escorted a young woman to her car in the Sheraton parking garage when suddenly they were confronted by a man wielding a dark handgun with a six-inch barrel. The women thought they were victims of a robbery, but the man ignored the other woman and took Rosenkranz. He put her into a car and drove off. She said afterward that she was well treated by the kidnappers.

KILLED. (1) Captured, as in "The king was killed by the ace." (2) The fate of a player or pair playing well but scoring badly. At duplicate the term implies that the opponents have played luckily and well on a group of boards. At rubber bridge it would refer to a session of poor cards and bad breaks. The term is always born of frustration and frequently of a desire to avoid admissions of poor play to one's teammates or oneself. (3) Denuded of whatever entries it may have had, as "The spade lead killed the dummy."

KING. The second highest ranking card in a suit in bridge. See COAT CARDS and COURT CARDS.

KING OF CLUBS HAND. See FAMOUS HANDS.

KING OR QUEEN OF BRIDGE. This honorary title is awarded annually to the graduating high school senior in ACBL (U.S., Canada, Mexico and Bermuda) with the best record in bridge. The winner is named by the International Palace of Sports Foundation and ACBL. The title carries with it the $1000 Homer Shoop/International Palace of Sports scholarship award. Earmarked for continuing education or as a career award, the scholarship is presented to the alma mater of the winner to be granted to a deserving student selected by the school from the same class.

Originally the winner was determined by total masterpoints, but over the years the winners have been cited for other bridge achievements and have been commended for deportment, demeanor and sportsmanship at the bridge table and for extra-curricular bridge activities such as teaching, directing, and Unit/District participation.

Past holders of the title are:

1973	J Merrill
1974	Jeff Meckstroth
1975	Bobby Levin
1976	Warren Spector
1977	Marc Franklin
1978	Matt Franklin
1979	Regina Barnes
1980	Tony Marks
1981	Doug Levene and Steve Cochran
1982	Steve Weinstein
1983	Billy Hsieh
1984	James Munday
1985	Adair Gellman
1986	Martha Benson
1987	Richard Pavlicek Jr.
1988	Holly Zulo
1989	Brad Moss
1990	Eric Sutherland
1991	Andrew Moss
1992	Frederic Pollack
1993	Eric Greco
1994	Sam Hirschman
1995	Tony Melucci
1996	Kent Mignocchi
1997	Joel Wooldridge
1998	Josh Heller
1999	Ari Greenberg
2000	Gavin Wolpert
2001	Erin Anderson

KING LEAD. See JOURNALIST LEADS; OPENING LEADS; RUSINOW LEADS.

KISS. An acronym for "Keep it simple, Stupid". It calls for a low-level system with no conventions, also called "momma-poppa".

KISS OF DEATH. A penalty of 200 points on a partscore deal in a pair contest; usually down two vulnerable, or down one doubled vulnerable.

KITCHEN BRIDGE. A social game, perhaps within a family, with little emphasis on technique and skill.

KNAVE. The jack, the fourth highest ranking card of a suit. This term is obsolete in American usage, and obsolescent elsewhere, although it had considerable currency in England and Continental Europe until the Forties. One reason for the quick acceptance of the term "jack" instead of "knave" is that in reporting hands or in any abbreviated diagram or description of play the initial J can be used, whereas previously Kn had to be used, since a plain K would have been ambiguous. See COAT CARDS and COURT CARDS.

KNOCK. (1) An action, of doubtful propriety, consisting of hitting the table lightly instead of speaking the word "pass." While it is true that bridge laws technically condone passes executed in irregular style, provided the offender at least is consistent in passing that way all the time, the best practice and that most approved by top tournament directors remains the spoken word "pass when bid-boxes are not being used." (2) An informal method of ALERTING.

These two meanings create ambiguity: A player who knocks intending an alert may be assumed by the next player to have passed. So knocking is a bad habit no matter what the meaning.

KNOCK TOGETHER. See CRASHING HONORS.

KNOCKOUT SQUEEZE. A squeeze in three suits, one of which is the trump suit. Declarer ruffs the fourth suit in the long trump hand, forcing the threatened defender to choose between establishing declarer's side suit or allowing him to score an extra trump trick. Example:

```
                    ♠ Q J 8
                    ♥ 8 5 4 3
                    ♦ 6 3 2
                    ♣ A 8 4
    ♠ 6 2                           ♠ 7 5 4
    ♥ 9 7 2                         ♥ K J 10 6
    ♦ Q 9                           ♦ A K J 10
    ♣ Q 10 9 7 5 2                  ♣ J 3
                    ♠ A K 10 9 3
                    ♥ A Q
                    ♦ 8 7 5 4
                    ♣ K 6
```

South is declarer in 4♠ after East opened the bidding and West showed club length. West leads a trump won by the ♠8 in dummy. A heart is led for a finesse of the ♥Q, and declarer continues with three rounds of clubs, ruffing the third round with the ♠K. On the third club, East is squeezed in three suits: a spade "discard" allows declarer to score an eventual diamond ruff in dummy, a heart discard allows declarer to establish and cash a long heart in dummy, while a diamond discard enables declarer to score a diamond ruff in dummy or establish and cash a long diamond in his hand, depending on the defense.

KNOCKOUT TEAMS. The name of this event is most apropos — the winners advance to the next round and the losers are knocked out of the competition. There are many kinds of knockout events, but basically they come down to this — two teams face each other in head-to-head competition, and only one survives. The setup is similar to SWISS TEAMS in that two members of a team sit North-South at one table and two others sit East-West at a different table. The opposing team fills the other four seats at the two tables. Knockout matches usually are much longer than Swiss matches — 24 boards is common but sometimes it is as many as 64. In major international competition, matches can last for several days played at the rate of 64 boards a day. After each segment of a match is finished, the East-West pairs return to their home tables to compare scores. Once again INTERNATIONAL MATCHPOINTS are used, just as in Swiss Teams. The team with the greater number of IMPs in the match is the winner and advances to play in the next round. The losers are no longer in the event. Specific conditions of contest may vary. Each team has a responsibility to be aware of the conditions and to conform accordingly.

See also BRACKETED KNOCKOUT TEAMS, COMPACT KNOCKOUT TEAMS, HANDICAP KNOCKOUT TEAMS, MINI-KNOCKOUT TEAMS, RANDOM DRAW KNOCKOUT TEAMS.

KNOCKOUT TOURNAMENT. An event (usually for teams of four) in which one team plays against only one opposing team in a given session. The losers are eliminated. The winners remain in the contest and play new opponents at later sessions until only one team remains.

See BRACKETED KNOCKOUT, DOUBLE ELIMINATION, HANDICAP KNOCKOUT, LOSE AND SNOOZE, ZIP KNOCKOUT.

KO TEAMS. Short for KNOCKOUT TEAMS.

KOCK-WERNER REDOUBLE. A rescue device invented by the Swedish partnership of Rudolf Kock and Einar Werner. When partner's low-level overcall has been doubled, a redouble is for takeout — the redoubler is very short in partner's suit. For example:

West	North	East	South
			1♣
1♥	Dbl	Rdbl	

East has a singleton or void in hearts and requests a takeout into another suit. The possibility of playing in 2♣ is not excluded: the best escape not infrequently is to a suit bid by the opposition.

Such redoubles are almost useless in a natural sense. If East is satisfied to play in 1♥ doubled, he simply passes.

This rarely applies, because in modern play the double is almost alway negative. See also SOS REDOUBLE and ROSENKRANZ DOUBLE.

KOKISH RELAY. A maneuver, devised by Eric Kokish, to facilitate the bidding of very strong balanced hands. In this sequence:

Opener	Responder
2♣	2♦
2♥	2♠

2♥ is semi-artificial, promising either hearts or a strong balanced hand. 2♠ is forced, and opener bids 2NT if he is balanced. Other rebids are natural, showing hearts. This is advantageous with the strong, balanced hands, too strong for an immediate, non-forcing 2NT rebid, because Stayman and transfers can be used conveniently at the three-level. This device loses a little ground when the opener is unbalanced with hearts, since responder loses the chance to use a second negative.

The convention can be enlarged by the following variations suggested by Danny Kleinman:

(1) After 2♥, responder bids 3♣ and 3♦ naturally

over 2 ♥ with a long minor and moderate values.

(2) After 2 ♥, responder bids 2NT with a 6-card spade suit, allowing opener to play spades. Similarly, 3 ♥ shows six spades and three hearts, with opener the declarer in either major.

L

LANCIA TOURNAMENTS. A series of four challenge matches played in 1975, in which an Italian team sponsored by the Lancia division of Fiat opposed four American teams. The nucleus of the Italian team consisted of Walter Avarelli, Giorgio Belladonna, Pietro Forquet, Benito Garozzo and Omar Sharif. They won in Chicago, but were defeated in New York, Los Angeles and Miami.

LANDY. A conventional overcall of 2 ♣ after an opposing 1NT opening as a request for a takeout to a major suit, devised by Alvin Landy. The overcaller promises at least four cards in each major suit and usually has five; some pairs agree that he guarantees five hearts. A Landy bidder is likely to be short in one or both minors, since with balanced distribution he would often double or pass. He seldom has more than 15 high-card points. By agreement, partnerships can use Landy in the direct position, the balancing position or both; over a strong notrump, a weak notrump or both.

Responses to the Landy bid are not standardized but the following scheme had the endorsement of the inventor.

(1) 3 ♣ is a forcing response unrelated to clubs and asks the Landy bidder to describe his hand further. The responder may have equal length in the major suits. This is the **only** forcing response.

(2) 3 ♠ and 3 ♥ are game invitations, often with a 3-card suit.

(3) 2NT and 3 ♦ are natural and encouraging but not forcing.

(4) 2 ♦ shows a weak hand with diamond length.

(5) Pass shows a weak hand with club length.

See DEFENSE TO ONE NOTRUMP and DEFENSE TO TWO-SUITED OVERCALLS.

LANGUAGE. (1) Symbolic: The art of communication between partners as "the language of bidding" and "the language of signals". (2) Verbal: English is the international language of WBF and other international tournaments.

LAST-TRAIN CUEBID. Popularized by Jeff Meckstroth, (although Jeff Rubens had also devised this method 20 years previously), this convention derives its name from the Sixties hit by the Monkees, "The Last Train to Clarksville."

Last-train cuebids were invented because of the problems that frequently arise with space when one hand jumps to the four-level to set a trump suit. For example, a jump to show shortness, via a splinter, often leaves the other hand with no convenient cuebid, despite a desire to try for slam. In such situations the use of the only step available below game neither promises nor denies the ability to cuebid in that suit, but shows the desire to

cooperate in a slam venture. Take the auction:

| 1 ♣ | Pass | 1 ♠ | Pass |
| 4 ♦ | Pass | | |

If responder has some useful values he may well want to cooperate but have no convenient bid. With a hand such as:

♠ Q J 9 5 4
♥ J 5 4
♦ 10 5 4
♣ A 3

The partnership could be in danger at the five-level facing a minimum splinter. But if partner has three key-cards together with the ♣K, slam could be laydown. In such a situation a response of 4 ♥ simply indicates slam interest, and allows opener to determine whether he should make another move to slam. If a player makes a last-train cuebid and then acts again, it confirms that the previous effort was a real cuebid, showing a control in the first bid suit.

The expert consensus (75% in BWS 2001) favored this idea.

LATE PAIR. A pair desiring to enter an event after it has started. An ingenious director can usually add one or more pairs to a game during the first round (or even later) without disrupting play for those who have already started. See APPENDIX TABLE; HALF TABLE.

LATE PLAY. Play, during or after completion of a session, of one or more boards which normally would have been played during an earlier round.

A late play arises when the director observes that a given table has one or more boards to play in a given round when the rest have finished and are ready to move. The director may instruct the contestants not to start another board, but to return at the end of the contest to complete their play.

LATE PLAY PENALTY. A penalty imposed because a pair or a team fails to comply with the time limits set for a contest. In pair games a pair usually is warned after the first transgression and is given a quarter-board penalty for a subsequent offense. The penalties increase for further transgressions within the same session. In team games the penalty usually is in IMPs. In Swiss matches the usual late-play penalty is 3 IMPs. In major knock-out team or round-robin team matches, a schedule of penalties usually is set up within the conditions of contest, with the penalties getting progressively stiffer as the late period increases. The most famous late-play penalty occurred in the 2000 Venice Cup final – the Netherlands won the cup by a margin smaller than the late-play penalty assessed against the United States.

LAVINTHAL SIGNAL. See SUIT PREFERENCE.

LAW OF BALANCED DISTRIBUTION. A general principle relating to suit distributions, proposed by Dr. John A. Tierney in 1959. It applies when the East-West hands contain a given number of cards and two specific divisions of these cards are compared. The principle asserts that:

1. The division in which the cards are more evenly divided is more probable. If East-West hold Q-4-3-2, the specific division 3-2 with West and Q-4 with East is more probable that the specific division Q-3-2 with West and

singleton 4 with East. It is well known that four missing cards are more likely to divide 3-1 than 2-2. This does not apply when comparing two specific divisions.

2. If the missing cards are equally divided, the two divisions are equally probable. If East-West hold Q-J-4-3-2, the specific division Q-2 with East and J-4-3 with West has the same probability as the specific division 4-3-2 with East and Q-J with West.

As an example of the principle, consider the card combination in which South holds A-K-7 opposite Q-10-5-2. South plays the ace and king, then the 7. West follows with 8-4-3 and East with 9-6. South should play the queen since the division 8-4-3 with West and J-9-6 with East is more likely than the division J-8-4-3 with West and 9-6 with East.

LAW OF SYMMETRY. A theory of distribution suggested by Ely Culbertson. His idea was that imperfect shuffles tend to produce a suit pattern equivalent to a hand pattern in the same deal. A player with 5-4-3-1 distribution should expect the outstanding cards in his long suit to be divided 4-3-1 more often than the mathematical odds would suggest. There is no mathematical or empirical basis for this theory.

LAW OF TOTAL TRICKS. The theory that on any given bridge deal the total number of trumps will approximate the total number of tricks available on that deal. The total number of trumps is obtained by adding North-South's longest trump fit to East-West's longest trump fit. The total number of tricks is the sum of the number of tricks North-South would take playing in their best fit and the number of tricks East-West would take playing in their best fit. The Law is a most useful bidding adjunct in competitive auctions. Players often work out how many trumps each partnership has and then use the formula as a guideline. Knowing the number of trumps gives the competitor a good estimate of how many tricks are available. This knowledge often will lead to making the correct bidding decision.

To use the Law to its best effect, certain adjustment factors must be taken into consideration. Extreme distribution, possession of queens and jacks in the opponents' suits and double fits are some of the factors that influence the Law's accuracy.

The Law was first discovered by Jean-René Vernes of France in the Fifties, but the discovery went more or less unnoticed until the Nineties when it was the subject of a book, *To Bid or Not to Bid*, by Larry Cohen.

A simple way to use the LAW is to "always bid to the level of your side's number of trumps" in competitive auctions. For example, compete to the two-level with eight trumps, the three-level with nine trumps, and the four-level with 10 trumps. Most players are taught to raise a weak-two bid (typically a 6-card suit) to the three-level with 3-card support. This is supported by the LAW. Similarly, it is proper to raise one-of-a-major (playing five-card majors) to the four-level with five-card support. Here are a couple of typical Law decisions:

♠ K Q 9 8 7 ♥ A 8 ♦ A 9 2 ♣ 10 7 2

Playing five-card majors, you open 1♠. After a 2♥ overcall, your partner raises to 2♠. RHO bids 3♥, and it is your call. Your opening bid is fine, but you should not bid 3♠ when it is possible that your side has only eight spades – partner of course could have raised with three. If partner has four trumps, giving your side nine, he will

know to bid 3♠. The full deal rates to be something like:

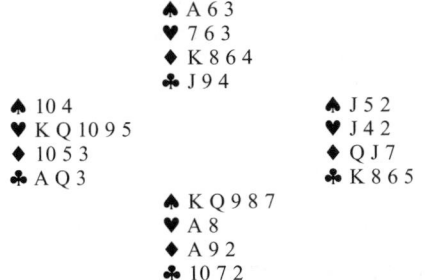

The opponents would fail in 3♥, losing five top tricks. You will also fail if you bid 3♠ as you have five sure losers after the obvious heart lead. Does this full deal contain anything surprising? No, it is a very typical layout for this everyday auction. Both partnerships have an eight-card fit, and both sides can take only eight tricks. Pass stands out over 3♥ on this layout – you score a plus instead of a minus. If you were to give yourself a sixth spade, you would have a clear reason to compete to 3♠. We can even take away some high-card points to illustrate that possession of nine trumps, not possession of an extra jack or queen, is crucial. Holding:
♠ K 9 8 7 5 2 ♥ A 8 ♦ A 9 2 ♣ 10 7, you hear this auction

West	North	East	South
			1♠
2♥	2♠	3♥	?

You are faced with the same auction as in the previous hand. Your partner has raised spades and the opponents have competed to 3♥. This time your side has nine trumps so you bid 3♠, expecting the full deal to be something like:

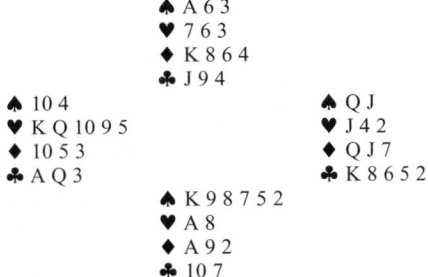

3♥ still goes down one, but now you can make 3♠. Your ninth spade translated into a ninth trick. What if the spades were 3-1? You'd go down – but then 3♥ would make. The *total* number of tricks on a deal is determined by the *total* number of trumps.

LAWS. See LAWS OF CONTRACT BRIDGE and LAWS OF DUPLICATE CONTRACT BRIDGE. In this Encyclopedia, "LAWS" refers to both codes unless otherwise indicated. In general, Law numbers correspond in the two codes.

LAWS OF BRIDGE. In 1743, Edmond Hoyle published *A Short Treatise on the Game of Whist, Containing the Laws of the Game.* The Laws as codified there became so universally accepted that they guided whist players for more than 100 years. The Arlington and Portland clubs revised the code in 1864 and the Portland Club became the recognized authority in the newer game of

bridge. The laws of this newer game appeared under the pen name of Boaz in 1895. Other clubs adopted their own versions, until in 1902 a committee representing many card clubs promulgated an American code. This set of laws was not received with universal acclaim and gradually the laws of the Whist Club (New York) became standardized.

Bridge, which had succeeded in surpassing whist, was itself superseded by auction bridge and in 1909 the Portland and Bath clubs in England framed a Code of Laws of Auction Bridge; The Whist Club followed with its Laws of Auction Bridge in 1910. These were revised in 1911, 1912, 1915, 1917 and 1926.

In the Twenties auction bridge began to be succeeded by the then new game of contract bridge and in 1927 the Whist Club adopted a code based essentially on the 1926 Laws of Auction Bridge. This time the American clubs were ahead of their British counterparts, the Portland and other clubs adopting a code in 1929.

For several years thereafter, the Whist Club, the Portland Club and the Commission Française de Bridge worked through their committees to make a code that would be international in scope, finally agreeing on one on October 19, 1932. This code was revised by equivalent groups in 1935, 1948 and 1963.

Meanwhile, the peculiar requirements of duplicate bridge, which was sweeping the country and most of the world, pointed up the necessity for a code to cover duplicate. The first such code was the result of a committee of the American Bridge League, adopted in November 1928. The 1932 revision of the *Laws of Contract Bridge* necessitated a 1933 revision of the duplicate laws. In America a further revision in 1943 of the laws of duplicate led to an international effort (1948-49 by the Portland Club, the European Bridge League and the National Laws Commission of America) that revised the *Laws of Contract Bridge and the Laws of Duplicate Contract Bridge*. These laws remained in vogue throughout the world until the revision of both, under the same international groups, which became effective July 1, 1963.

The duplicate laws were revised again in 1975 and became a world-wide code with the involvement of the World Bridge Federation. They were revised again in 1986 under the auspices of the ACBL (with major contributions from Edgar Kaplan, Roger Stern, Karen Allison and Amalya Kearse) and the World Bridge Federation. They became effective March 31, 1987.

The contract bridge laws were revised again in 1992, by the same bodies, with major contributions on the American side from Edgar Kaplan, Karen Allison, Roger Stern, Ralph Cohen and Robert Wolff. The new laws became effective January 1, 1993.

Former members who have made substantial contributions include Jean Besse, Geoffrey Butler,. Richard Goldberg, Colin Harding, Robert Howes, Edgar Kaplan and Edgar Theus, all deceased.

LAWS COMMISSION OF THE AMERICAN CONTRACT BRIDGE LEAGUE. A committee of the American Contract Bridge League charged with formulating and promulgating the official Laws of Contract Bridge and Duplicate Contract Bridge.

In the preparation of international codes the Commission collaborates with other bodies. See Laws of Bridge.

Former members of the Commission who have made substantial contributions to the development of the Laws

include: Walter Beinecke, B.Jay Becker, Easley Blackwood, John Gerber, Sam Gold, Charles H.Goren, Lee Hazen, Edward Hymes Jr., Oswald Jacoby, Albert Morehead, William E. McKenney, Geoffrey Mott-Smith, Donald Oakie, George Reith, Harold Richard, Harold Vanderbilt, Waldemar von Zedtwitz and Alfred Sheinwold.

The 2001 commission: Ralph Cohen and Chip Martel, co-chairmen; Karen Allison, Ron Gerard, Amalya Kearse, Sami Kehela, Henry Lortz, Dan Morse, Jeff Polisner, Eric Rodwell, George Rosenkranz, Roger Stern, Peggy Sutherlin, Katie Thorpe and Bobby Wolff.

LAWS OF CONTRACT BRIDGE.

The Scope of the Laws
The Laws are designed to define correct procedure and to provide an adequate remedy whenever a player accidentally, carelessly or inadvertently disturbs the proper course of the game, or gains an unintentional but nevertheless unfair advantage. An offending player should be ready to pay a prescribed penalty graciously.

These Laws do not deal with dishonorable practices; ostracism is the ultimate remedy.

The Proprieties
The object of the Proprieties is to familiarize players with the customs and etiquette of the game, generally accepted over many years, and to enlighten those who might otherwise fail to appreciate when or how they are improperly conveying information to their partners, or are acting on the basis of improper information.

Appendices
Most players will find the Laws and the Proprieties sufficient to their needs. Some, however, may wish to adopt procedures to reduce the risk that, unintentionally, extraneous information is given to partners, or proper information withheld from opponents. Possible procedures, very similar to those successfully used in competitive bridge, are set out in appendices 1, 2 and 3. Note that these appendices are not part of the Laws or the Proprieties of Rubber Bridge.

Part I

DEFINITIONS
Auction — 1. The process of determining the contract by means of successive calls. 2. The aggregate of calls made.

Bid — A declaration to win at least a specified number of odd tricks in a specified denomination.

Call — Any bid, double, redouble or pass.

Contract — The undertaking by declarer's side to win, at the denomination named, the number of odd tricks specified in the final bid, whether undoubled, doubled or redoubled.

Deal — 1. The distribution of the pack to form the hands of the four players. 2. The cards so distributed as a unit, including the auction and play thereof.

Declarer — The player who, for the side that makes the final bid, first bid the denomination named in that final bid. He becomes declarer when a legal opening lead is made and the dummy is faced.

Defender — An opponent of declarer.

Denomination — The suit or notrump specified in a bid.

Double —A call over an opponent's bid increasing the scoring value of fulfilled or defeated contracts (see Law 19).

Dummy — 1. Declarer's partner. 2. Declarer's partner's cards, once they are spread on the table after the opening lead.

Follow suit — Play a card of the suit that has been led.

Game —A unit in scoring denoting 100 or more trick points scored on one deal, or accumulated over two or more deals (see Laws 72 & 73).

Group — A number of players who have agreed to follow the same procedures.

Hand — The cards originally dealt to a player, or the remaining portion thereof.

Honor — Any Ace, King, Queen, Jack or ten.

Irregularity — A deviation from the correct procedures set forth in these Laws.

LHO — Left-hand opponent.

Lead — The first card played to a trick.

Odd trick — Each trick to be won by declarer's side in excess of six.

Opening lead — The card led to the first trick.

Opponent — A member of the partnership to which one is opposed.

Overtrick — Each trick won by declarer's side in excess of the contract.

Pack — The 52 playing cards with which the game of Contract Bridge is played.

Partner — The player with whom one plays as a side against the other two players.

Partscore — 90 or fewer trick points.

Pass — A call specifying that a player does not, at that turn, elect to bid, double or redouble.

Penalty — An obligation or restriction imposed upon a side for violations of these Laws.

Penalty Card — A card prematurely exposed by a defender. It may be a major or minor penalty card (see Law 50).

Play — 1. The contribution of a card from one's hand to a trick, including the first card, which is the lead. 2. The aggregate of plays made. 3. The period during which the cards are played, starting immediately after the final pass.

RHO — Right-hand opponent.

Redeal - A second or subsequent deal to replace a faulty deal.

Redouble — A call over an opponent's double increasing the scoring value of fulfilled or defeated contracts (see Law 19).

Revoke — The play of a card of another suit by a player who is able to follow suit or to comply with a lead penalty.

Rotation — The clockwise order in which the right to deal, to call or to play progresses

Rubber — The scoring period that ends when one side had scored two games.

Side — Two players who constitute a partnership against the other two players.

Slam — A contract to win twelve tricks (called Small Slam) or thirteen tricks (called Grand Slam).

Suit — One of four groups of cards in the pack, each group comprising thirteen cards and having a characteristic symbol: spades (♠), hearts (♥), diamonds (♦), clubs (♣).

Trick — The unit by which the outcome of the contract is determined, regularly consisting of four cards, one contributed by each player in rotation, beginning with the lead.

Trump — Each card of the suit, if any, named in the contract.

Undertrick — Each trick by which declarer's side falls short of fulfilling the contract.

Vulnerable — The status of a side that has won a game and is therefore exposed to greater undertrick penalties and entitled to greater premiums.

Part II

PRELIMINARIES

LAW 1
THE PLAYERS — THE PACK

Contract bridge is played by four players with a pack of 52 cards of identical back design and color, consisting of 13 cards in each of four suits. Two packs should be used, of which only one is in play at any time; and each pack should be clearly distinguishable from the other in back design or color.

LAW 2
RANK OF CARDS

The suits rank downwards in order — Spades (♠), Hearts, (♥), Diamonds (♦), Clubs (♣). The cards of each suit rank in descending order: Ace, King, Queen, Jack, 10, 9, 8, 7, 6, 5, 4, 3, 2.

LAW 3
THE DRAW

Before every rubber, each player draws a card from a pack shuffled and spread face down on the table. A card should not be exposed until all the players have drawn.

Unless it is otherwise agreed, the two players who draw the highest cards play as partners against the other two players. When cards of the same rank are drawn, the rank of suit determines which is higher.

The player with the highest card deals first and has the right to choose his seat and the pack with which he will deal. He may consult his partner, but having announced his decision must abide by it. His partner sits opposite him. The opponents then occupy the two remaining seats as they wish, and having made their selection must abide by it.

A player must draw again if he draws more than one card, or one of the four cards at either end of the pack, or a card adjoining one drawn by another player, or a card from the other pack.

Part III

THE DEAL
LAW 4
THE SHUFFLE

Before the first deal of a rubber, the player to the dealer's left should shuffle the pack thoroughly*, without exposing the face of any card, in full view of the players and to their satisfaction. Thereafter, as each player deals, the dealer's partner shuffles the other pack for the next deal, and places the pack face down on his right.

A pack properly prepared should not be disturbed until the dealer picks it up for his deal, at which time he is entitled to the final shuffle.

No player other than the dealer and the player designated to prepare the pack may shuffle.

It is recommended that the pack be shuffled at least five times.

LAW 5
THE CUT

The pack must be cut immediately before it is dealt.

The dealer presents the pack to his RHO, who lifts off a portion and places it on the table toward the dealer. Each portion must contain at least four cards. The dealer completes the cut by placing what was originally the bottom portion upon the other portion.

No player other than the dealer's RHO may cut the pack.

LAW 6
NEW CUT — NEW SHUFFLE

There must be a new cut if any player demands one before the first card is dealt. In this case, the dealer's RHO cuts again.

There must be a new shuffle, followed by a cut:

(a) If any player demands one before the dealer has picked up the pack for his deal. In this case, the player designated to prepare the pack shuffles again.

(b) If any player demands one after the dealer has picked up the pack but before the first card is dealt. In this case only the dealer shuffles.

(c) If a card is turned face up in shuffling. In this case the player who was shuffling shuffles again.

(d) If a card is turned face up in cutting. In this case only the dealer shuffles.

(e) If there is a redeal (see Law 10).

LAW 7
CHANGE OF PACK

The two packs are used alternately, unless there is a redeal.

A pack containing a card so damaged or marked that it may be identified from its back must be replaced* if attention is drawn to the imperfection before the last card of the current deal has been dealt.

A pack originally belonging to a side must be restored on demand of any player before the last card of the current deal has been dealt.*

*See Law 8.

LAW 8
THE DEAL

The dealer distributes the cards face down, one at a time in rotation into four separate hands of 13 cards each, the first card to the player on his left and the last card to himself. If he deals two cards simultaneously or consecutively to the same player, or fails to deal a card to a player, he may rectify the error, provided he does so immediately and to the satisfaction of the other players. The dealer must not allow the face of any card to be seen while he is dealing.

Players should not look at the face of any card until the deal is completed. A player who violates this provision forfeits those rights to a change of pack (Law 7) or redeal (Law 10).

LAW 9
ROTATION OF THE TURN TO DEAL

The turn to deal passes in rotation, unless there is a redeal. If a player deals out of turn, and attention is not drawn to the error before the last card has been dealt, the deal stands as though it had been in turn, the player who dealt the cards is the dealer (he makes the first call), and the player who missed his turn to deal has no redress; and the rotation continues as though the deal had been in turn, unless a redeal is required under Law 10.

LAW 10
REDEAL

A redeal cancels the faulty deal; the same dealer deals again, unless he was dealing out of turn; the same pack is used, unless it has been replaced as provided in Law 7; and the cards are shuffled and cut anew as provided in Laws 4 and 5.

There must be a redeal:

(a) if, before the last card has been dealt, it is discovered that

(i) a card has been turned face up in dealing or is face up in the pack or elsewhere; or

(ii) the cards have not been dealt correctly;* or

(iii) a player is dealing out of turn or is dealing with a pack that was not shuffled or not cut, provided any player* demands a redeal.

(b) if, before the first call has been made, it is discovered that a player has picked up another player's hand and has seen a card in it.

(c) if, before play has been completed, it is discovered that

(i) the pack did not conform in every respect to the requirements of Law 1, including any case in which a missing card cannot be found after due search; or

(ii) one player has picked up too many cards, another too few; or

(iii) two or more players on opposing sides have allowed any cards from their hands to be mixed together, following a claim that a redeal is in order.

*See Law 8.

LAW 11
MISSING CARD

When a player has too few cards and a redeal is not required by Law 10 (c), the deal stands as correct, and

(a) if he has played more than once to a previous trick, Law 67 applies.

(b) if a missing card is found elsewhere, not in a previous trick, that card is deemed to have belonged continuously to the deficient hand and must be restored to that hand; it may become a penalty card, as provided in Law 23 or Law 49, and failure to have played it may constitute a revoke.

LAW 12
SURPLUS CARD

When a player has too many cards and a redeal is not required by Law 10 (c), the deal stands as correct, and

(a) if the offender has omitted to play to a trick, Law 67 applies.

(b) if the offender has picked up a surplus card from a previous trick, or from dummy's hand, or from the other pack, or elsewhere, such surplus card shall be restored to its proper place; and

(i) if the surplus card is in the offender's hand when it is discovered, there is no penalty.

(ii) if the surplus card has been led or played, or had been played to a previous trick, the offender must substitute for it a card from his hand that he can legally play to the trick, and, if possible, a card of the same suit as the surplus card. The offending side may not thereby win a trick it had lost, but it may lose a trick it had won. When attention is drawn to the offense before the lead to the next trick, either member of the nonoffending side may, without penalty, withdraw a play made subsequent to the offense, and substitute any legal play.

Part IV

GENERAL LAWS
GOVERNING IRREGULARITIES
LAW 13
PROCEDURE FOLLOWING AN IRREGULARITY
(Club Law 13)

When an irregularity has occurred, any player — except dummy as restricted by Law 43 — may draw attention to it and give or obtain information as to the law applicable to it. The fact that a player draws attention to an irregularity committed by his side does not affect the rights of the opponents.

After attention has been drawn to an irregularity, no player should call or play until all questions in regard to the assessment of a penalty have been determined. Premature correction of an irregularity on the part of the offender may subject him to further penalty (see Law 26).

LAW 14
ASSESSMENT OF A PENALTY
(Club Law 14)

A penalty may not be imposed until the nature of the irregularity to be penalized has been determined and the applicable penalty has been clearly stated; but a penalty once paid, or any decision agreed and acted upon by the players, stands and should not, except by agreement of all four players, be corrected even though at some later time it may be judged incorrect.

LAW 15
WAIVER OR FORFEITURE OF PENALTY

The right to penalize an offense is forfeited if

(a) both members of the nonoffending side waive the penalty.

(b) a member of the nonoffending side calls (Law 34) or plays (Law 60) after an irregularity committed by his RHO.

LAW 16
UNAUTHORIZED INFORMATION
(Club Law 16)

A player may be subject to penalty if he conveys information to his partner other than by a legal call or play.

Information conveyed by an illegal call, play or exposure of a card is subject to the applicable law in Part V or Part VI.

If a player conveys information to his partner by means of a remark or question or by an unmistakable hesitation or unwonted speed, special emphasis, tone, gesture, movement, mannerism or any other action that suggests a call, lead or plan of play; and if attention is drawn to the offense immediately, when the offending side has profited through the doubtful call or play so suggested, it should, in conformance with Proprieties 1, redress any damage done to the nonoffending side.

Part V

THE AUCTION
CORRECT PROCEDURE
LAW 17
DURATION OF THE AUCTION

The auction begins when the last card of a correct deal has been placed on the table. The dealer makes the first call, and thereafter each player calls in rotation. When three passes in rotation have followed any call the auction is closed, unless Law 34 applies.

LAW 18
BIDS

Each bid* must name a number of odd tricks, from one to seven, and a denomination. A bid supersedes the previous bid if it names either a greater number of odd tricks or the same number of odd tricks in a higher denomination. A bid that fulfills these requirements is sufficient; one that does not is insufficient. The denominations rank in descending order: notrump, spades, hearts, diamonds, clubs.

* *Pass, double and redouble are calls, not bids.*

LAW 19
DOUBLES AND REDOUBLES

A player may double only the last preceding bid, and then only if it was made by an opponent and no calls other than pass have intervened.

A player may redouble only the last preceding double, and then only if it was made by an opponent and no calls other than pass have intervened.

A player should not, in doubling or redoubling, state the number of tricks or the denomination; but, if he states either or both incorrectly, he is deemed to have doubled or redoubled the bid as it was made. The only correct form is the single word "Double" or "Redouble".

All doubles and redoubles are superseded by a subsequent legal bid. If there is no subsequent bid, scoring values are increased as provided in Law 81.

LAW 20
REVIEW AND EXPLANATION

A player who does not hear a call distinctly may forthwith require that it be repeated.

At his own turn to call during the auction, a player (unless required by law to pass) may require a restatement of the auction in its entirety. After the final pass, declarer before making any play, or either defender at his first turn to play, may require a restatement of the auction in its entirety.

A request to have calls restated should be responded to only by an opponent (dummy, or a player required by law to pass, may so respond).

All players, including dummy, should promptly correct errors in restatement.

A player may require an explanation of the partnership understanding relating to any call made by an opponent, but only at the player's own turn to call or play. A request for an explanation of a call should be responded to by the partner of the player making the call (see Proprieties 4).

LAW 21
CALL BASED ON MISINFORMATION

A player has no recourse if he has made a call on the basis of his own misunderstanding.

Until the auction is closed, a player may, without penalty, change any call he may have made as a result of misinformation given him by an opponent, provided his partner has not subsequently called. If he elects to correct his call, his LHO may then, in turn and without penalty, change any subsequent call he may have made.

LAW 22
PROCEDURE AFTER THE AUCTION IS CLOSED
After the auction is closed:

(a) if no player has bid, the hands are abandoned and the turn to deal passes in rotation.

(b) if any player has bid, the final bid becomes the contract and play begins.

IRREGULARITIES
LAW 23
CARD EXPOSED OR LED DURING THE AUCTION
(Club Law 23)
Whenever, during the auction, a player faces a card on the table or holds a card so that it is possible for his partner to see its face, every such card must be left face up on the table until the auction closes; and (penalty) if the offender subsequently becomes a defender, declarer may treat every such card as a penalty card (Law 50).

In addition:

(a) if it is a single card below the rank of an honor and not prematurely led, there is no further penalty.

(b) if it is a single card of honor rank, or any card prematurely led, or if more than one card is so exposed (penalty), the offender's partner must pass when next it is his turn to call.

(c) when the penalty under this or any other Law compels the offender's partner to pass, and offender could have known at the time of his infraction that the enforced pass would be likely to damage the nonoffending side, the offenders should redress the damage in accordance with Proprieties 1.

LAW 24
IMMEDIATE CORRECTION OF A CALL
A player may substitute his intended call for an inadvertent call, but only if he does so, or attempts to do so, without pause for thought. If legal, his last call stands without penalty; if illegal, it is subject to the applicable law.

LAW 25
CHANGE OF CALL
(Club Law 25)
When a call is substituted for a call made previously at the same turn, and it is too late for correction as provided in Law 24, then:

(a) if the first call was illegal, the substitute call is cancelled and the offender is subject to the applicable law.

(b) if the first call was a legal one, the offender must either

(i) allow his first call to stand and (penalty) his partner must pass when next it is his turn to call; or

(ii) make any other legal call and (penalty) his partner must pass whenever it is his turn to call.

The offender's partner will also be subject to a lead penalty as provided in Law 26 if he becomes a defender. Law 23(c) may apply to (b) (i) and (b) (ii).

LAW 26
CHANGE OF CALL — LEAD PENALTIES
When a player makes a call and subsequently changes it to another legal call (except as permitted under Law 24), then if he becomes a defender:

(a) if the changed call was in a suit, and the substi-

tuted call did not repeat that suit, declarer may* either require the offender's partner to lead, or prohibit him from leading, such suit when first the offender's partner has the lead (including the opening lead). A prohibition continues for as long as offender's partner retains the lead. When the irregular call artificially relates to a denomination other than the one actually named, "such suit" is the suit or suits to which the call relates.

(b) if the changed call was

(i) in notrump, and the player's (or the offender's) final call at that turn was not, or

(ii) pass, double or redouble, other than an out-of-rotation call repeated in turn in accordance with Law 30(a) or Law 32(b)(i), declarer may* prohibit offender's partner from leading any one specified suit when first the offender's partner has the lead (including the opening lead). This prohibition continues for as long as offender's partner retains the lead.

Declarer makes the decision at the time that offender's partner first has the lead.

LAW 27
INSUFFICIENT BID
(Club Law 27)
Any insufficient bid may be accepted (treated as legal) at the option of offender's LHO, and is accepted if that opponent calls.

An insufficient bid made in rotation must be corrected by the substitution of either a sufficient bid (not a double or redouble) or a pass*, unless the irregular bid is accepted.

If the call substituted is

(a) the lowest sufficient bid in the same denomination, the auction proceeds as though the irregularity had not occurred**.

(b) any other sufficient bid, or pass, (penalty) the offender's partner must pass whenever it is his turn to call (Law 23(c) may apply), and the lead penalties of Law 26 will apply if he becomes a defender.

If the offender attempts to substitute a double or redouble, it is cancelled; he must pass at that turn and the offense is subject to the penalty provided in subsection (b) above.

If a player makes an insufficient bid out of rotation, Law 31 applies.

The offender is entitled to select his final call at that turn after the applicable penalties have been stated, and any call he has previously attempted to substitute is cancelled, but the lead penalties of Law 26 will apply if he becomes a defender.

**Offender's partner must not base any subsequent calls or plays on information gained from such a withdrawn bid.*

CALL OUT OF ROTATION
LAW 28
CALLS CONSIDERED TO BE IN ROTATION
A call is considered to be in rotation

(a) when it is made without waiting for the RHO to pass, if that opponent is required by law to pass.

(b) when it is made by the player whose turn it was to call, before a penalty has been imposed for a call out of rotation by an opponent; it waives any penalty for the call out of rotation and the auction proceeds as though that opponent had not called at that turn.

LAW 29
PROCEDURE AFTER A CALL OUT OF ROTA-TION

After a call out of rotation, offender's LHO* may either

(a) make any legal call; if he chooses to do so, the call out of rotation stands as if it were legal (but if it is an inadmissible call, see Law 35), and the auction proceeds without penalty; or,

(b) require that the call out of rotation be cancelled. The auction reverts to the player whose turn it was to call. The offender may make any legal call in proper turn subject to Laws 30, 31 and 32.

He alone exercises the option, although any player may draw attention to the irregularity.

LAW 30
PASS OUT OF ROTATION
(Club Law 30)

When a player has passed out of rotation

(a) before any player has bid or when it was the turn of his RHO* to call, (penalty) the offender must pass when next it is his turn to call.

(b) after any player has bid and when it was the turn of the offender's partner to call, (penalty) the offender must pass whenever it is his turn to call; the offender's partner may make a sufficient bid or may pass, but may not double or redouble at that turn.

After any player has bid, a call at the turn of offender's LHO is a change of call; Law 25 applies and not this section.

LAW 31
BID OUT OF ROTATION
(Club Law 31)

When a player has bid out of rotation

(a) at the turn of offender's partner to call or before any player has called when offender's LHO was the dealer, (penalty) the offender's partner must pass whenever it is his turn to call (Law 23(c) may apply), and the lead penalties of Law 26 will apply if he becomes a defender.

(b) at the turn of the offender's RHO* to call,

(i) if RHO passes, the bid out of rotation must be repeated, and there is no penalty (if the bid out of rotation was insufficient, it must be corrected as provided in Law 27);

(ii) If RHO makes a legal** bid, double or redouble, the offender may in turn make any legal call. If such call repeats the denomination of the bid out of rotation, (penalty) the offender's partner must pass when next it is his turn to call (Law 23(c) may apply). If the substituted call does not repeat the denomination, (penalty) the offender's partner must pass whenever it is his turn to call (Law 23(c) may apply), and the lead penalties of Law 26 will apply if he becomes a defender.

After any player has bid, a call at the turn of offender's LHO is a change of call; Law 25 applies and not this section.

**An illegal call by that opponent may be penalized in the usual way, after which this subsection, (b) (ii), applies.*

LAW 32
DOUBLE OR REDOUBLE OUT OF ROTATION
(Club Law 32)

When a player has doubled or redoubled out of rotation,*

(a) if it was the offender's partner's turn to call, (penalty) the offender's partner must pass whenever it is his turn to call (Law 23(c) may apply); the offender may not thereafter, in turn, double or redouble the same bid he doubled out of turn; and the lead penalties of Law 26(b) will apply if he becomes a defender.

(b) if it was the turn of offender's RHO* to call,

(i) if offender's RHO passes, the double or redouble out of rotation must be repeated and there is no penalty.

(ii) if offender's RHO bids, the offender may in turn make any legal call, and (penalty) the offender's partner must pass when next it is his turn to call (Law 23C may apply), and the lead penalties of Law 26(b) will apply if he becomes a defender.

After any player has called, a call at the turn of offender's LHO is a change of call; Law 25 applies and not this section.

LAW 33
SIMULTANEOUS CALLS

A call made simultaneously with one made by the player whose turn it was to call is deemed to be a subsequent call.

LAW 34
RETENTION OF THE RIGHT TO CALL

When a call has been followed by three passes, the auction does not end when one of those passes was out of rotation, thereby depriving a player of his right to call at that turn. The auction reverts to the player who missed his turn. All subsequent passes are cancelled and the auction proceeds as though there had been no irregularity.

INADMISSIBLE CALLS
LAW 35
INADMISSIBLE CALL CONDONED

When, after an inadmissible call specified below, offender's LHO makes a call before a penalty has been assessed, there is no penalty for the offense (the lead penalties of Law 26 do not apply). If the inadmissible call was

(a) a double or redouble not permitted by Law 19, that call and all subsequent calls are cancelled; the auction reverts to the player whose turn it is to call and proceeds as though there had been no irregularity.

(b) a bid, double or redouble by a player required by law to pass, that call and subsequent legal calls stand; but if the offender was required to pass for the remainder of the auction, he must still pass at subsequent turns.

(c) a bid of more than seven, that call and all subsequent calls are cancelled; the offender must substitute a pass, and the auction proceeds as though there had been no irregularity.

(d) a call after the auction is closed, that call and all subsequent calls are cancelled without penalty.

LAW 36
INADMISSIBLE DOUBLE OR REDOUBLE
(Club Law 36)

Any double or redouble not permitted by Law 19 is cancelled, and the offender must substitute a legal call; and (penalty) the offender's partner must pass whenever it is his turn to call (Law 23(c) may apply), and the lead penalties of Law 26 (b) will apply if he becomes a defender.

If the right of the nonoffending side to penalize is forfeited, Law 35 applies.

LAW 37
BID, DOUBLE OR REDOUBLE IN VIOLATION OF THE OBLIGATION TO PASS

A bid, double or redouble by a player who is required by law to pass is cancelled, and (penalty) both members of the offending side must pass during the remainder of the auction (Law 23(c) may apply), and the lead penalties of Law 26 will apply if they become defenders.

LAW 38
BID OF MORE THAN SEVEN
(Club Law 38)

No contract of more than seven is ever permissible. A bid of more than seven by any player is cancelled, and (penalty) both members of the offending side must pass during the remainder of the auction (Law 23(c) may apply); and the lead penalties of Law 26 will apply if they become defenders.

LAW 39
CALL AFTER THE AUCTION IS CLOSED
(Club Law 39)

A call after the auction is closed is cancelled, and

(a) if it is a pass by a defender or any call by declarer or dummy, there is no penalty.

(b) if it is a bid, double or redouble by a defender, the lead penalties of Law 26 apply, unless the call has been condoned (see Law 35(d)).

LAW 40
PARTNERSHIP AGREEMENTS
(Club Law 40)

A player may make any call or play (including an intentionally misleading call such as a "psychic bid", or a call or play that departs from commonly accepted or previously announced practice) without prior announcement, provided that it is not based on a partnership understanding. But a player may not make use of a bidding or play agreement unless

(a) his side has disclosed its use of such a call or play beforehand, or

(b) it has been agreed beforehand that the use of partnership understandings be disclosed at the time they are used. His partner must then disclose it. In this case, partner's disclosure must be confined to an indication that a partnership understanding has been used; he should not offer any explanation unless requested to do so.

Any group may restrict the use of special partnership understandings in its games.

THE PLAY
CORRECT PROCEDURE
LAW 41
OPENING LEAD, REVIEW, QUESTIONS

After the auction closes* declarer's LHO makes the opening lead. After the opening lead, dummy spreads his hand in front of him on the table, face up, sorted into suits, the cards in order of rank in columns pointing lengthwise towards declarer, with trumps, if any, to dummy's right. Declarer plays both his hand and that of dummy.

Declarer, before making any play, or either defender at his first turn to play, may require a restatement of the auction in its entirety.

After it is too late to have previous calls restated, declarer or either defender is entitled to be informed what the contract is and whether, but not by whom, it was doubled or redoubled.

Either defender may require an explanation of the partnership understanding relating to any call made by an opponent (see Proprieties 4), but only at that defender's own turn to play. Declarer may at any time require an explanation of the partnership understanding relating to any call or play made by a defender.

*After the final pass, either defender has the right to ask if it is his opening lead.

LAW 42
DUMMY'S RIGHTS

Dummy is entitled to give information as to fact or law, but may not initiate the discussion; and provided he has not forfeited his rights (see Law 43) he may also

(a) ask declarer (but not a defender), when he has failed to follow suit, whether he has a card of the suit led.

(b) try to prevent any irregularity* by declarer.

(c) draw attention to any irregularity, but only after play is concluded.

*He may, for example, warn declarer against leading from the wrong hand.

LAW 43
DUMMY'S LIMITATIONS

Dummy may not participate in the play (except to play the cards of dummy's hand as directed by declarer), or make any comment on the bidding, play or score of the current deal; and if he does so, Law 16 may apply. During play, dummy may not call attention to an irregularity once it has occurred.

Dummy forfeits the rights provided in (a), (b) and (c) of Law 42 if he exchanges hands with declarer, leaves his seat to watch declarer play, or, on his own initiative, looks at the face of a card in either defender's hand; and if, thereafter,

(a) he is the first to draw attention to a defender's irregularity, declarer may not enforce any penalty for the offense.

(b) he warns declarer not to lead from the wrong hand, (penalty) either defender may choose the hand from which declarer shall lead.

(c) he is the first to ask declarer if a play from declarer's hand constitutes a revoke, declarer must substitute a correct card if his play was a revoke, and (penalty) unless Law 64(d) applies, one trick is transferred to the defending side.

LAW 44
SEQUENCE AND PROCEDURE OF PLAY

The player who leads to a trick may play any card in his hand.* After the lead, each other player in turn plays a card, and the four cards so played constitute a trick.

In playing to a trick, each player must follow suit if possible. This obligation takes precedence over all other requirements of these Laws. If unable to follow suit, a player may play any card.*

A trick containing a trump is won by the player who has contributed to it the highest trump. A trick that does not contain a trump is won by the player who has contributed to it the highest card of the suit led. The player who has won the trick leads to the next trick.

Unless he is subject to restriction after an irregularity committed by his side.

LAW 45
CARD PLAYED

Each player except dummy should play a card by detaching it from his hand and placing it, face up, on the table where other players can easily reach and see it. Dummy, if instructed by declarer to do so, may play from his hand a card named or designated by declarer.*

A card must be played

(a) if it is a defender's card held so that it is possible for his partner to see its face.

(b) if it is a card from declarer's hand that declarer holds face up, touching or nearly touching the table, or maintains in such a position as to indicate that it has been played.

(c) if it is a card in dummy deliberately touched by declarer except for the purpose of arranging dummy's cards or of reaching a card above or below the card or cards touched.

(d) if the player who holds the card names or otherwise designates it as the card he proposes to play. A player may, without penalty, change an inadvertent designation if he does so without pause for thought; but if an opponent has, in turn, played a card that was legal before the change of designation, that opponent may, without penalty, withdraw any card so played and substitute another.

(e) if it is a penalty card, subject to Law 50.

A card played may not be withdrawn except as provided in Law 47.

If dummy places in played position a card declarer did not name, the card must be withdrawn if attention is drawn to it before each side has played to the next trick, and a defender may withdraw (without penalty) a card played after the error but before attention was drawn to it (see Law 47).

LAW 46
PARTIAL DESIGNATION OF A CARD TO BE PLAYED FROM DUMMY'S HAND

When declarer instructs dummy to play a card from dummy's hand, as permitted by Law 45, but names only a suit or only the rank of a card, or the equivalent, without fully specifying the card to be played, declarer must complete his partial designation. Dummy must not play a card before declarer has completed his partial designation.

LAW 47
RETRACTION OF A CARD PLAYED
(Club Law 47)

A card once played may be withdrawn only

(a) to comply with a penalty, or to correct an illegal play, or to correct the simultaneous play of two or more cards (see Law 58); if a defender's card which has been exposed is withdrawn under this sub-section, it becomes a penalty card (see Law 50); or

(b) after a change of designation as permitted by Law 45(d), or

(c) after an opponent's change of play, to substitute a card for one played*, or

(d) to correct a play* after misinformation by an opponent. A lead out of turn may be retracted without penalty if the leader was mistakenly informed by an opponent that it was his turn to lead.

The offending side must not base any subsequent plays on information gained from such a withdrawn play.

PENALTY CARD
LAW 48
EXPOSURE OF DECLARER'S CARDS

Declarer is not subject to penalty for exposing a card, and no card of declarer's or dummy's ever becomes a penalty card. Declarer is not required to play any card dropped accidentally.

When declarer faces his cards after an opening lead out of turn, Law 54 applies. When declarer faces his cards at any other time, he may be deemed to have made a claim or concession of tricks, in which case Law 68 applies.

LAW 49
EXPOSURE OF A DEFENDER'S CARDS

Whenever a defender faces a card on the table, holds a card so that it is possible for his partner to see its face, or names a card as being in his hand, before he is entitled to do so in the normal course of play or application of the law, (penalty) each such card becomes a penalty card (Law 50).*

Exposure of a card or cards by a defender who is making a claim or concession of trick is subject to Law 70.

LAW 50
DISPOSITION OF A PENALTY CARD

A defender's card is a penalty card when prematurely exposed. It must be left face up on the table until it is played or until an alternate penalty has been selected.

A single card below the rank of an honor and exposed inadvertently (as in playing two cards to a trick, or in dropping a card accidentally) becomes a minor penalty card. Any penalty card of honor rank, or any card exposed through deliberate play (as in leading out of turn, or in revoking and then correcting) becomes a major penalty card; when one defender has two or more penalty cards, all such cards become major penalty cards.

When a defender has a minor penalty card, he may not play any other card of the same suit below the rank of an honor until he has first played the penalty card. (However, he is entitled to play an honor card instead of the minor penalty card.) There is no further penalty, but the offender's partner must not base any subsequent play on information gained through seeing the penalty card.

When a defender has a major penalty card, such card must be played at the first legal opportunity, whether in leading, following suit, discarding or trumping. If a defender has two or more penalty cards that can legally be played, declarer may designate which is to be played. The obligation to follow suit, or to comply with a lead or play penalty, takes precedence over the obligation to play a penalty card, but the penalty card must still be left face up on the table and played at the next legal opportunity.

When a defender has the lead while his partner has a major penalty card, declarer may choose to impose a lead penalty at this point: he may require that defender to lead the suit of the penalty card, or may prohibit that defender from leading that suit (a prohibition continues for as long as he retains the lead). If declarer does not impose a lead penalty, the penalty card is picked up at once. If declarer does not, the defender may lead any card; but the penalty card remains a penalty card. The defender may not lead until declarer has indicated his choice.

LAW 51
TWO OR MORE PENALTY CARDS

When a defender has two or more penalty cards in one suit, and declarer requires or prohibits the lead of that suit, the defender may pick up every penalty card in that suit and may make any legal play to the trick.

When a defender has penalty cards in more than one suit, declarer may prohibit the defender's partner from leading every such suit, or require him to lead one such suit, but the defender may then pick up every penalty card in every suit required or prohibited by declarer and may make any legal play to the trick.

LAW 52
FAILURE TO LEAD OR PLAY A PENALTY CARD

When a defender is required by Law 50 to play a penalty card but instead plays another card, he must leave the illegally played card face up on the table and

(a) declarer may accept the defender's lead or play, and must do so if he has thereafter played from his or dummy's hand, but the unplayed penalty card remains a penalty card; or

(b) declarer may require the defender to substitute the penalty card for the card illegally played, in which case the illegally played card becomes a major penalty card.

LEAD OUT OF TURN
LAW 53
LEAD OUT OF TURN ACCEPTED

Any lead out of turn may be treated by an opponent as a correct lead. It becomes a correct lead if an opponent accepts it by making a statement to that effect, or if that opponent next to play plays a card to the irregular lead.*

However, the player whose turn it was to lead — unless he is the offender's partner — may make his proper lead subsequent to the infraction without his card being treated as played to the irregular lead. The proper lead stands, and all cards played in error to this trick may be withdrawn without penalty.

*When such a play is made by a defender who is not next to play after the irregular lead, Law 57 applies.

LAW 54
OPENING LEAD OUT OF TURN

When a defender makes the opening lead out of turn,

(a) declarer may accept the irregular lead as provided in Law 53. Dummy's hand is spread in accordance with Law 41, and the second card to the trick is played from declarer's hand; but if declarer first plays to the trick from dummy's hand, dummy's card may not be withdrawn except to correct a revoke.

(b) declarer must accept the irregular lead if he could have seen any of dummy's cards (except cards exposed during the auction, subject to Law 23). He is deemed to have accepted the irregular lead if he begins to spread his hand as though he were dummy and in so doing exposes one or more cards; declarer must spread his entire hand, and dummy becomes declarer.*

(c) declarer may accept the irregular lead by spreading his hand and becoming dummy; his partner becomes the declarer.

(d) declarer may require the defender to retract his irregular lead (except as provided in (b) above), and then Law 56 applies.

*If cards are so exposed from both declarer's and dummy's hands, the player who was regularly to become declarer remains declarer.

LAW 55
DECLARER'S LEAD OUT OF TURN

When declarer leads out of turn from his or dummy's hand,

(a) either defender may accept that lead as provided in Law 53.

(b) either defender may require declarer to retract that lead. Then,

(i) if it was a defender's turn to lead, declarer restores the card led in error to his or dummy's hand, without penalty;

(ii) if declarer has led from the wrong hand when it was his turn to lead from his or dummy's hand, he withdraws the card led in error; he must lead a card from the correct hand.

(iii) if declarer adopts a line of play that could have been based on information obtained through his infraction, the offenders should redress the damage in accordance with Proprieties 1.

LAW 56
DEFENDER'S LEAD OUT OF TURN

When a defender leads out of turn,

(a) declarer may accept that lead as provided in Law 53.

(b) declarer may require the defender to retract that lead; the card illegally led becomes a major penalty card (see Law 50 — note that lead penalties are provided).

IRREGULAR LEADS AND PLAYS
LAW 57
PREMATURE LEAD OR PLAY BY A DEFENDER

When a defender leads to the next trick before his partner has played to the current trick, or plays out of turn before his partner has played, (penalty) declarer may

(a) require offender's partner to play his highest card of the suit led; or

(b) require offender's partner to play his lowest card of the suit led; or

(c) prohibit offender's partner from playing any card of one different suit specified by declarer.

Declarer must select one of these options, and if the offender's partner cannot comply with the penalty selected he may play any card, as provided in Law 59.

When, as a result of the application of the penalty, the offender's partner wins the current trick, he leads to the next trick; and any card led or played out of turn by the other defender becomes a major penalty card (Law 50).

A defender is not subject to penalty for playing before his partner if declarer has played from both hands; but a singleton or one of two or more equal cards in dummy is not considered automatically played unless dummy has played the card.

LAW 58
SIMULTANEOUS LEADS OR PLAYS

A lead or play made simultaneously with another player's legal lead or play is deemed to be subsequent to it.

If a defender leads or plays two or more cards simultaneously, and if only one such card is visible, he must play that card; if more than one card is exposed, he must designate the card he proposes to play and each other card exposed becomes a penalty card (Law 50).

If declarer leads or plays two or more cards simulta-

neously from either hand, he must designate the card he proposes to play and must restore any other card to the correct hand. If declarer withdraws a visible card and a defender has already played to that card, such defender may, without penalty, withdraw his card and substitute another (see footnote to Law 47).

If the error remains undiscovered until both sides have played to the next trick, Law 67 applies.

LAW 59
INABILITY TO LEAD OR PLAY AS REQUIRED

A player may play any otherwise legal card if he is unable to lead or play as required to comply with a penalty, whether because he holds no card of the required suit, or because he has only cards of a suit he is prohibited from leading, or because he is obliged to follow suit.

LAW 60
PLAY AFTER AN ILLEGAL PLAY

A play by a member of the nonoffending side after his RHO has played out of turn, and before a penalty has been imposed, forfeits the right to penalize the offense. The illegal play is treated as though it were in turn (but Law 53 applies to the player whose turn it was). If the offending side had a previous obligation to play a penalty card or to comply with a lead or play penalty, the obligation remains at future turns.

When a defender plays after declarer has been required to retract his lead out of turn from either hand, but before declarer has led from the correct hand, the defender's card becomes a penalty card (Law 50).

A play by a member of the offending side before a penalty has been imposed does not affect the rights of the opponents and may itself be subject to penalty.

THE REVOKE
LAW 61
FAILURE TO FOLLOW SUIT —
INQUIRIES CONCERNING A REVOKE

Failure to follow suit in accordance with Law 44, or failure to lead or play, when able, a card or suit required by law or specified by an opponent in accordance with a penalty, constitutes a revoke. Any player may ask a player who has failed to follow suit whether he has a card of the suit led, and may demand that an opponent correct his revoke, except that dummy* may ask of declarer, but not of a defender. (A claim of revoke does not warrant inspection of quitted tricks, except as permitted in Law 66).

*Unless he has forfeited his rights, as specified by Law 43.

LAW 62
CORRECTION OF A REVOKE

A player must correct his revoke if he becomes aware of it before it becomes established (See Law 63). To correct a revoke, the offender withdraws the card he played in revoking and follows suit with any card. A card so withdrawn becomes a major-penalty card (Law 50) if it was played from a defender's unfaced hand. The card may be replaced without penalty if it was played from declarer's or dummy's hand* or if it was a defender's faced card. Each member of the nonoffending side may, without penalty, withdraw any card he may have played after the revoke but before attention was drawn to it (see footnote to Law 47). After a non-offender so withdraws a card,

the hand of the offending side next in rotation may withdraw a played card, which becomes a major-penalty card if played from a defender's hand.

On the twelfth trick, a revoke, even if established, must be corrected if discovered before the cards have been mixed together. If the revoke was committed by a defender before his partner has played to the twelfth trick, and if offender's partner holds cards of more than one suit, (penalty) declarer may then require the offender's partner to play to that trick either of the two cards he could legally have played.

*Subject to Law 43. A claim of revoke does not warrant inspection of quitted tricks except as permitted in Law 67.

LAW 63
ESTABLISHMENT OF A REVOKE

A revoke becomes established when the offender or his partner leads or plays (whether legally or illegally) to the following trick, or names or otherwise designates a card to be so played, or makes a claim or concession of tricks orally or by facing his hand. The revoke may then no longer be corrected (except for a revoke on the 12th trick — see Law 62), and the trick on which the revoke occurred stands as played.

LAW 64
PROCEDURE AFTER ESTABLISHMENT
OF A REVOKE
(Club Law 64)

When a revoke has become established,

(a) if the offending player* won the trick on which the revoke occurred, (penalty) that trick and one of any subsequent tricks won by the offending side are transferred** to the nonoffending side (if no subsequent trick was won by the offending side, only the revoke trick is transferred).

(b) if the offender's partner won the trick on which the revoke occurred, (penalty) that trick is transferred** to the nonoffending side and, if the offending player himself won a subsequent trick with a card that could legally have been played to the revoke trick, one additional trick (but no more) is transferred** to the nonoffending side.

(c) if the nonoffending side won the trick on which the revoke occurred, and if the offending side won any trick after the revoke, (penalty)

(i) the first such trick is transferred** to the nonoffending side, and

(ii) if the offending side won two or more tricks after the revoke, any of which was won by the offending player with a card he could legally have played to the revoke trick, an additional trick is transferred** to the nonoffending side;

(d) there is no trick penalty for the established revoke if

(i) the offending side did not win either the trick on which the revoke occurred or any subsequent trick; or if

(ii) the revoke was a subsequent revoke in the same suit by the same player; or if

(iii) the revoke was made in failing to play any card faced on or belonging to a hand faced on the table, including a card from dummy's hand; or if

(iv) Attention was first drawn to the revoke after all players had abandoned their hands and permitted the cards to be mixed together; or if

(v) the revoke was on the 12th trick (see Law 62).

N.B. When any established revoke, including one not subject to penalty, causes damage to the nonoffending side insufficiently compensated by the law, the offending side should, under Proprieties 1, transfer additional tricks so as to restore equity.

If declarer revokes, but wins the trick on which the revoke occurred in dummy, Section (b) applies.

**For the scoring of transferred tricks, see Law 77.*

TRICKS
LAW 65
COLLECTION AND ARRANGEMENT OF TRICKS

The cards constituting each completed trick are collected by a member of the side that won the trick and are then turned face down on the table. Each trick shall be identifiable as such, and all tricks taken by a side shall be arranged in sequence in front of declarer or of one defender, as the case may be, in such manner that each side can determine the number of tricks it has won and the order in which they were taken.

LAW 66
INSPECTION OF TRICKS

Declarer or either defender may, until a member of his side has led or played to the following trick, inspect a trick and inquire what card each player has played to it. Thereafter, until play ceases, quitted tricks may be inspected only to account for a missing or surplus card. After play ceases, the tricks and unplayed cards may be inspected to settle an allegation of a revoke, of honors, or of the number of tricks won or lost. If, after an allegation has been made, a player on one side makes verification of the allegation impossible, as by mixing the cards or merging the tricks, the issue must be decided in favor of the other side.

LAW 67
TRICK EITHER APPROPRIATED IN ERROR OR DEFECTIVE

A trick appropriated by the wrong side must, upon demand, be restored to the side that has in fact won it*.

A trick containing more or fewer than four cards is defective. When one player is found, during play, to have fewer or more cards than all the other players, the previous tricks should be forthwith examined, face down; if a defective trick is discovered, the player with a correspondingly incorrect number of cards is held responsible. The defective trick is inspected face up and

(a) until the responsible player has played to a subsequent trick, the defective trick is rectified as follows:

(i) if the offender has failed to play a card to the defective trick, he adds to that trick a card he can legally play;

(ii) if the offender has played more than one card to the defective trick, he withdraws all but one card, leaving a card he can legally play;

(iii) the nonoffending side may, without penalty, withdraw any cards played after the irregularity and before attention was drawn to it (see footnote to Law 47); but the offending side may not withdraw cards that constitute legal plays, and any cards they withdraw may become penalty cards (Law 50).

(b) after the responsible player has played to a subsequent trick, the ownership of the defective trick cannot be changed and

(i) if the offender has failed to play a card to the defective trick, he forthwith faces and adds a card to

that trick, if possible one he could legally have played to it.

(ii) if the offender has played more than one card to the defective trick, he withdraws all but one card, leaving the highest card he could legally have played to that trick. A withdrawn card may become a penalty card (Law 50); such a card is deemed to have belonged continuously to the offender's hand and failure to have played it to an earlier trick may constitute a revoke.

If calls have been made on a subsequent deal, see Law 78.

CLAIMS AND CONCESSIONS
LAW 68
DECLARER'S CLAIM OR CONCESSION OF TRICKS

Declarer makes a claim or a concession whenever he announces that he will win or lose one or more of the remaining tricks, or suggests that play be curtailed, or faces his hand. Declarer should not make a claim or concession if there is any doubt as to the number of tricks to be won or lost.

LAW 69
PROCEDURE FOLLOWING DECLARER'S CLAIM OR CONCESSION
(Club Law 69)

When declarer has made a claim or concession, play is temporarily suspended and declarer must place and leave his hand face up on the table and forthwith make a comprehensive statement as to his proposed plan of play, including the order in which he will play the remaining cards.

Declarer's claim or concession is allowed and the deal is scored accordingly if both defenders agree to it. The claim or concession must be allowed if either defender has permitted any of his remaining cards to be mixed with another player's cards; otherwise, if either defender disputes declarer's claim or concession, it is not allowed. Then, play continues.

When his claim or concession is not allowed, declarer must play on, leaving his hand face up on the table. At any time, either defender may face his hand for inspection by his partner, and declarer may not impose a penalty for any irregularity committed by a defender whose hand is so faced.

The objective of subsequent play is to achieve a result as equitable as possible to both sides, but any doubtful point must be resolved in favor of the defenders. Declarer may not make any play inconsistent with the statement he may have made at the time of his claim or concession. And if he failed to make an appropriate statement at that time, his choice of plays is restricted thereby:

(a) if declarer made no relevant statement, he may not finesse* in any suit unless an opponent failed to follow in that suit before the claim or concession, or would subsequently fail to follow in that suit on any conceivable sequence of plays.

(b) if declarer may have been unaware, at the time of his claim or concession, that a trump remained in a defender's hand, either defender may require him to draw or not to draw the outstanding trump.

(c) if declarer did not, in his statement, mention an unusual plan of play, he may adopt only a routine line of play.

If declarer attempts to make a play prohibited under

this law, either defender may accept the play, or, provided neither defender has subsequently played, require declarer to withdraw the card so played and substitute another that conforms to his obligations.

For these purposes, a finesse is a play the success of which depends on finding one defender rather than the other with or without a particular card.

LAW 70
DEFENDER'S CLAIM OR CONCESSION OF TRICKS
(Club Law 70)

A defender makes a concession when he agrees to declarer's claim, or when he announces that he will lose one or more of the remaining tricks.

A defender makes a claim when he announces that he will win one or more of the remaining tricks, or when he shows any or all of his cards for this purpose. If

(a) the claim pertains only to an uncompleted trick currently in progress, play proceeds normally; cards exposed or otherwise revealed by the defender in making his claim do not become penalty cards, but Law 16, Unauthorized Information, may apply to a claimer's partner.

(b) the claim pertains to subsequent tricks, play is temporarily suspended; the claimer must place and leave his hand face up on the table and make a comprehensive statement as to his proposed plan of defense. The claim is allowed and the deal scored accordingly if declarer agrees to it. If declarer disputes the claim, the defenders must play on with the claimer's hand face up on the table. Those cards do not become penalty cards. However, declarer may prohibit claimer's partner from making any play that could be suggested to him by seeing the faced cards.

LAW 71
CONCESSION WITHDRAWN

A concession may be withdrawn

(a) if a player concedes a trick his side has, in fact, won; or if declarer concedes defeat of a contract he has already fulfilled; or if a defender concedes fulfillment of a contract his side has already defeated. (If the score has been entered, see Law 78.)

(b) if a trick that has been conceded cannot be lost by any probable sequence of play of the remaining cards, and if attention is drawn to the fact before the cards have been mixed together.

(c) if a defender concedes one or more tricks and his partner immediately objects, but Law 16 may apply.

THE SCORE
LAW 72
POINTS EARNED

The result of each deal played is recorded in points, which fall into two classes:

1. *Trick Points.* Only declarer's side can earn trick points, and only by winning at least the number of odd tricks specified in the contract. Only the value of odd tricks named in the contract may be scored as trick points (see Law 81). Trick points mark the progression of the rubber towards its completion.

2. *Premium Points.* Either side or both sides may earn premium points. Declarer's side earns premium points by winning one or more overtricks; by fulfilling a doubled or redoubled contract; by bidding and making a slam; by holding scorable honors in declarer's or dummy's hand; or by winning the final game of a rubber.* The defenders earn premium points by defeating the contract (undertrick penalty) or by holding scorable honors in either of their hands (see Law 81).

Each side's premium points are added to its trick points at the conclusion of the rubber.

For incomplete rubber, see Law 80.

LAW 73
PARTSCORE — GAME

The basic units of trick points are partscore and game. A partscore is recorded for declarer's side whenever declarer fulfills a contract for which the trick points are less than 100 points. Game is won by that side which is the first to have scored 100 or more trick points either in a single deal or by addition of two or more partscores made separately. No partscore made by either side in the course of one game is carried forward into the next game.

LAW 74
THE RUBBER

A rubber ends when a side has won two games. At the conclusion of the rubber, the winners of two games are credited with a premium score of 500 points if the other side has won one game or with a premium score of 700 points if the other side has not won a game. The trick and premium points scored by each side in the course of the rubber are then added. The side with the larger combined total wins the rubber, and the difference between the two totals represents the margin of victory computed in points.

LAW 75
METHOD OF SCORING

The score of each deal must be recorded, and it is preferable that a member of each side should keep score.

Scores are entered in two adjacent columns separated by a vertical line. Each scorer enters points earned by his side in the left-hand column, and points earned by his opponents in the right-hand column.

Each side has a trick point score and a premium score, separated by a horizontal line intersecting the vertical line. All trick points are entered, as they are earned, in descending order below the horizontal line (below the line), all premium points in ascending order above the line.

Whenever a game is won, another horizontal line is drawn under all trick point scores recorded for either side, in order to mark completion of the game. Subsequent trick points are entered below that line.

LAW 76
RESPONSIBILITY FOR THE SCORE

When the play of a deal is completed, all four players are equally responsible for ascertaining that the number of tricks won by each side is correctly determined and that all scores are promptly and correctly entered.

LAW 77
TRANSFERRED TRICKS

A trick transferred through a revoke penalty is reckoned for all scoring purposes as though it had been won in play by the side to which it had been awarded.*

Declarer plays in 3 ♥ and makes eight tricks. A revoke by a defender is found to have been established, with

the penalty determined to be two tricks. Two tricks are transferred from the offenders to declarer, who therefore has 10 tricks. Since he bid only 3♥, he scores 90 trick points, which count toward game, and 30 premium points for the overtrick.

LAW 78
CORRECTION OF THE SCORE

When it is acknowledged by a majority of the players that a scoring error was made in recording an agreed-upon result (*e.g.,* failure to enter honors, or incorrect computation of score), the error must be corrected if discovered before the net score of the rubber has been agreed to. However, except with the consent of all four players, an erroneous agreement as to the number of tricks won by each side may not be corrected after all players have called on the next deal.

In case of disagreement between two scores kept, the recollection of the majority of the players as to the facts governs.

LAW 79
DEALS PLAYED WITH AN INCORRECT PACK

Scores recorded for deals played with an incorrect pack are not subject to change by reason of the discovery of the imperfection after the cards have been mixed together.

LAW 80
INCOMPLETE RUBBER

When, for any reason, a rubber is not finished, the score is computed as follows:

If only one game has been completed, the winners of that game are credited with 300 points; if only one side has a partscore or partscores in a game not completed, that side is credited with 100 points; the trick and premium points of each side are then added, and the side with the greater number of points wins the difference between the two totals.

LAW 81
SCORING TABLE
TRICK SCORE

Scored below the line by declarer's side.
RUBBER, GAME, PART-SCORE, CONTRACT FULFILLED

IF TRUMPS ARE

	♣	♦	♥	♠
For each trick over six, bid and made				
Undoubled	20	20	30	30
Doubled	40	40	60	60
Redoubled	80	80	120	120

AT A NOTRUMP CONTRACT

	Undbl	Dbl	Redbl
For the first trick over six, bid and made	40	80	160
For each additional trick over six, bid and made	30	60	120

The first side to score 100 points below the line, in one or more hands, wins a GAME. When a game is won, both sides start without a trick score toward the next game. First side to win two games wins the RUBBER POINTS.

PREMIUM SCORE

Scored above the line by declarer's side.

For winning the RUBBER, if opponents have won no game	700
For winning the RUBBER, if opponents have won one game	500
For having won the only game in an UNFINISHED RUBBER	300
For having the only PARTSCORE in an unfinished game	100
For making any DOUBLED CONTRACT	50
For making any REDOUBLED CONTRACT	100

SLAMS

	Not Vulnerable	Vulnerable
For making a SLAM,		
Small Slam (12 tricks) bid and made	500	750
Grand Slam (all 13 tricks) bid and made	1000	1500

OVERTRICKS

	Not Vulnerable	Vulnerable
For each OVERTRICK (tricks made in excess of contract)		
Undoubled	Trick Value	Trick Value
Doubled	100	200
Redoubled	200	400

HONORS

Scored above the line by either side:

For holding four of the five trump HONORS (A, K, Q, J, 10) in one hand	100
For holding all five trump HONORS (A, K, Q, J, 10) in one hand	150
For holding four ACES in one hand at a notrump contract	150

UNDERTRICK PENALTIES

Tricks by which declarer fails to fulfill the contract: scored above the line by declarer's opponents, if contract is not fulfilled.

	Not Vulnerable		
	Undbl	Dbl	Redbl
For first undertrick	50	100	200
For second and third undertrick	50	200	400
For each additional undertrick	50	300	600

	Vulnerable		
	Undbl	Dbl	Redbl
For first undertrick	100	200	400
For each additional undertrick	100	300	600

PROPRIETIES
1. GENERAL PRINCIPLES

These Laws cannot cover every situation that might arise, nor can they produce equity in every situation covered. Occasionally, the players themselves must redress damage. The guiding principle: The side that commits an irregularity bears an obligation not to gain directly from the infraction itself; however, the offending side is entitled to profit after an infraction, as an indirect result, through subsequent good fortune.*

To infringe a law intentionally is a serious breach of

ethics, even if there is a prescribed penalty that one is willing to pay. The offense may be the more serious when no penalty is prescribed.

There is no obligation to draw attention to an inadvertent infraction of law committed by one's own side. However, a player should not attempt to conceal such an infraction, as by committing a second revoke, concealing a card involved in a revoke or mixing the cards prematurely.

It is proper to warn partner against infringing a law of the game: for example, against revoking, or against calling, leading or playing out of turn.

*Two examples may clarify the distinction between direct gain through an infraction and indirect gain through good luck.

*(a) South, declarer at 3NT, will have nine tricks available if the diamond suit — six cards headed by the ace, king, queen in dummy opposite declarer's singleton — divides favorably; and the six missing diamonds are in fact split evenly, 3–3, between East and West. However, West, who holds three diamonds headed by the jack, shows out on the third round of diamonds, revoking. Thus, declarer wins only three diamond tricks instead of six, for a total of six tricks instead of nine. The established revoke is later discovered, so one penalty trick is transferred after play ends. But declarer is still down two.

Here, East-West gained two tricks as a direct consequence of their infraction. The players should adjudicate this result, scoring the deal as 3NT, making three. (Note, declarer is not given a penalty trick in addition; the object is to restore equity, to restore the result likely to have occurred had the infraction not been committed.)

(b) South, declarer at 4♠, is entitled to require or forbid a diamond opening lead from West, because of an auction-period infraction committed by East. Declarer instructs West to lead a diamond — but West, having no diamonds, leads another suit. East, now aware that partner is void in diamonds, is able to find what would be, under normal circumstances, a most unnatural line of defense to give West two ruffs. Thereby, East-West defeat a contract that would almost certainly have been made but for the infraction.

Here, East-West profited only indirectly through their auction-period infraction; their gain was the direct consequence of declarer's decision to require a diamond lead, and of West's lucky void. So, the players should allow the result to stand. Declarer was damaged not by the infraction itself but by bad luck afterwards — and luck is part of the game of bridge.

2. COMMUNICATION BETWEEN PARTNERS

Communication between partners during the auction and play should be effected only by means of the calls and plays themselves, not through the manner in which they are made, nor through extraneous remarks and gestures, nor through questions asked of the opponents and explanations given to them. Calls should be made in a uniform tone without special emphasis or inflection, and without undue hesitation or haste. Plays should be made without emphasis, gesture or mannerism and so far as possible at a uniform rate.

Inadvertently to vary the tempo or manner in which a call or play is made does not in itself constitute a violation of propriety, but inferences from such variation may

properly be drawn only by an opponent, and at his own risk. It is improper to attempt to mislead an opponent by means of a remark or a gesture, through the haste or hesitancy of a call or play (such as hesitation with a singleton) or by the manner in which the call or play is made.

Any player may properly attempt to deceive an opponent through a call or play (so long as the deception is not protected by concealed partnership understanding). It is entirely proper to make all calls and plays in unvarying tempo and manner in order to avoid giving information to the opponents.

When a player has available to him improper information from his partner's remark, question, explanation, gesture, mannerism, special emphasis, inflection, haste or hesitation, he should carefully avoid taking any advantage that might accrue to his side.

3. CONDUCT AND ETIQUETTE

A player should maintain at all times a courteous attitude toward his partner and opponents. He should carefully avoid any remark or action that might cause annoyance or embarrassment to another player or might interfere with the enjoyment of the game. Every player should follow uniform and correct procedure in calling and playing, since any departure from correct standards may disrupt the orderly progress of the game.

As a matter of courtesy, a player should refrain from,

(a) paying insufficient attention to the game (as when a player obviously takes no interest in his hand, or frequently requests a review of the auction).

(b) making gratuitous comments during the play as to the auction or the adequacy of the contract.

(c) detaching a card from his hand before it is his turn to play.

(d) arranging completed tricks in a disorderly manner, thereby making it difficult to determine the sequence of plays.

(e) making a claim or concession of tricks if there is any doubt as to the outcome of the deal.

(f) prolonging play unnecessarily for the purpose of disconcerting the other players.

Furthermore, the following are considered breaches of propriety:

(a) using different designations for the same call.

(b) indicating approval or disapproval of a call or play.

(c) indicating the expectation or intention of winning or losing a trick that has not been completed.

(d) commenting or behaving during the auction or play so as to call attention to a significant occurrence, or to the state of the score or to the number of tricks still required for success.

(e) showing an obvious lack of further interest in the deal (as by folding one's cards).

(f) looking intently at any other player during the auction or play, or at another player's hand as for the purpose of seeing his cards or of observing the place from which he draws a card (but it is not improper to act on information acquired by inadvertently seeing an opponent's card).

(g) varying the normal tempo of bidding or play for the purpose of disconcerting another player.

(h) mixing the cards before the result of a deal has been agreed upon.

4. PARTNERSHIP AGREEMENTS

It is improper to convey information by means of a

call or play based on special partnership agreement, whether explicit or implicit, unless such information is fully and freely available to the opponents.

It is not improper for a player to violate an announced partnership agreement, so long as his partner is unaware of the violation (but habitual violations within a partnership may create implicit agreements, which must be disclosed). No player has the obligation to disclose to the opponents that he has violated an announced agreement. If the opponents are subsequently damaged, as through drawing a false inference from such violation, they are not entitled to redress.

When explaining the significance of partner's call or play in reply to an opponent's inquiry, a player should disclose all special information conveyed to him through partnership agreement or partnership experience; but he need not disclose inferences drawn from his general bridge knowledge and experience. It is improper for a player whose partner has given a mistaken explanation to correct the error immediately or to indicate in any manner that a mistake has been made. He must not take advantage of the unauthorized information so obtained.

5. SPECTATORS

A spectator, including a member of the table not playing, must not display any reaction to bidding or play while a hand is in progress (as by shifting his attention from one player's hand to another's). He must not in any way disturb a player. During the hand, he must refrain from mannerisms or remarks of any kind (including conversation with a player). He may not call attention to any irregularity or mistake, nor speak on any question of fact or law except by request of the players.

APPENDIX 1

Any group may specify that the Alert procedure be used in its games. Then, the partner of a player who makes a call to which the partnership attaches a special, unusual meaning, one with which the opponents may not be familiar, is required to say, "Alert."

N.B. No explanation should be volunteered. After the Alert, either opponent may, at his own turn to call, inquire as to the special meaning.

A partnership that does not want to be Alerted should so request; and this request should be honored.

APPENDIX 2

Any group may specify that the "Stop" or "Skip Bid" procedure be used in its games. Then, whenever a player opens the bidding at the two level or higher or makes a bid higher than necessary to overcall the last preceding bid, he announces, "Stop," or "Skip Bid" (the group specifies the form to be used) before making the bid.

After this announcement, the opponent next to speak is required to hesitate for approximately 10 seconds before making any call.

APPENDIX 3

Any group may specify that opening leads be made face-down in its games. If this opening lead is determined to be out of turn (before being faced), the leader returns the card to his hand without penalty.

When the face-down lead will be legal, dummy delays spreading his hand. Opening leader's partner asks any questions concerning the auction, including a review. Then, the lead is faced (opening leader may not with-

draw it), dummy is faced, and play proceeds normally.

Part VIII
ALTERNATIVE CLUB LAWS

When bridge is played at a club, it is often practicable to designate an impartial and experienced person as "Arbiter" for the game. The Arbiter interprets and applies the Laws after an irregularity occurs, and generally assumes the role assigned to the "Director" in duplicate bridge. When such an Arbiter is available, certain laws can be modified so as to produce greater equity.

The "Club Laws" prescribe a somewhat different procedure after attention is drawn to an irregularity, and there is a different disposition for disputed claims. The principal changes, however, lie in the authority given to the Arbiter, after specified types of irregularity, to "adjust the score" of a deal once play is over. In adjusting a score, the Arbiter assigns a new result, the result he judges would have been achieved had the irregularity not occurred. The Arbiter should resolve any substantial doubt in favor of the nonoffending side.

The alternative laws are in force only upon advance agreement by the players, or in accordance with the standing and published policy of a club. Any game may play under these Club Laws, so long as an Arbiter is nominated in advance; when there are more than four members of a table, a non-playing member can act as Arbiter.

CLUB LAW 13

The Arbiter must be called as soon as attention is drawn to an irregularity. Calling the Arbiter does not forfeit any rights to which a player may otherwise be entitled. Any player except dummy may draw attention to an irregularity and call the Arbiter. The fact that a player draws attention to an irregularity committed by his side does not affect the rights of the opponents.

After attention has been drawn to an irregularity, no player should call or play until the Arbiter has determined all matters in regard to rectification and to the assessment of a penalty. Premature correction of an irregularity on the part of an offender may subject him to further penalty.

CLUB LAW 14

The Arbiter assesses penalties when applicable. When these Club Laws provide an option among penalties, the Arbiter explains the options available.

The Arbiter may assign an adjusted score, but only when these Club Laws empower him to do so, or when the law provides no indemnity to a nonoffending contestant for the particular type of violation of law or propriety committed by an opponent. He may not assign an adjusted score on the ground that the penalty provided in the law is unduly severe or unduly advantageous to either side.

CLUB LAW 16

If a player conveys information to his partner by means of a remark or question, or by an unmistakable hesitation, special emphasis, tone, gesture, movement, mannerism or any other action that suggests a call, lead or plan of play; and if attention is drawn to the offense and the Arbiter is called, the Arbiter should require that the auction or play continue, reserving the right to assign an adjusted score if he considers that the result could have been affected by the illegal information.

After play ends, he should award an adjusted score to redress damage caused to the innocent side, when an opponent chose from among alternative logical actions one that could reasonably have been suggested by his partner's tempo, manner, remark, etc.

CLUB LAW 23

(Regular Law 23 stands intact but with the following addition, which applies as well to a change of call, an insufficient bid, a call out of rotation and an inadmissible call.)

When the penalty for an irregularity, under this or any other law, would compel the offender's partner to pass at his next turn, and when the Arbiter deems that this enforced pass will necessarily* damage the innocent side, the Arbiter may reserve the right to assign an adjusted score.

*The score should not be adjusted merely because the penalty happened to result in good fortune for the offending side. The word "necessarily" restricts score adjustment to those instances in which the offender could have known, at the time of his infraction, that it would be to his advantage to require partner to pass.

CLUB LAW 25

The penalties in Club Law 23 apply.

CLUB LAW 27

Regular Law 27 stands intact but with the following addition to sub-section (a):

If the insufficient bid conveyed such substantial information as to damage the nonoffending side, the Arbiter may assign an adjusted score.

CLUB LAW 30

The provisions of Club Law 23 may apply.

CLUB LAW 31

The provisions of Club Law 23 may apply.

CLUB LAW 32

The provisions of Club Law 23 may apply.

CLUB LAW 36

The provisions of Club Law 23 may apply.

CLUB LAW 38

The provisions of Club Law 23 may apply.

CLUB LAW 39

The provisions of Club Law 23 may apply.

CLUB LAW 40

If the Arbiter decides that a side has been damaged through its opponents' failure to explain the meaning of a call or play, he may award an adjusted score.

CLUB LAW 47

If a card retracted under sections (c) or (d) above gave substantial information to an opponent, the Arbiter may award an adjusted score.

CLUB LAW 55

Regular Law 55 stands intact, but the Arbiter may assign an adjusted score to redress damage, as authorized in (b)(iii).

CLUB LAW 64

Regular Law 64 stands, except that, when after any established revoke, including those not subject to penalty, the Arbiter deems that the nonoffending side is insufficiently compensated by this law for the damage caused, he should assign an adjusted score.

CLUB LAW 69

When declarer has made a claim or concession, play ceases (all play subsequent to a claim or concession must be voided by the Arbiter). Declarer must place and leave his hand face up on the table and forthwith make a comprehensive statement as to his proposed plan of play, including the order in which he will play his remaining cards.

Declarer's claim or concession is allowed, and the deal is scored accordingly, if both defenders agree to it. The claim or concession must be allowed if either defender has permitted any of his remaining cards to be mixed with another player's cards; otherwise, if either defender disputes declarer's claim or concession, the Arbiter must be called to adjudicate the result of the deal.

The Arbiter should adjudicate the result of the deal as equitably as possible to both sides, but any doubtful point should be resolved in favor of the defenders. He should proceed as follows:

(a) he should require declarer to repeat the statement he made at the time of his claim. The Arbiter should then require all players to put their cards face up on the table and should hear the defenders' objections to the claim.

(b) when a trump is outstanding, he should award a trick to the defenders if

(i) in making his claim declarer made no statement about that trump, and

(ii) it is at all likely that declarer was unaware, at the time of his claim, that a trump remained in a defender's hand, and

(iii) a trick could be lost to that trump by any normal play (an inferior or careless play can be normal, but not an irrational play).

(c) he should not accept from declarer any proposed line of play inconsistent with his statement. If declarer did not make an appropriate announcement at the time of his original claim, the Arbiter should not accept from declarer any unusual line of play, or any proposed play that requires a finesse* in a suit, unless an opponent failed to follow in that suit before the claim or concession, or would subsequently fail to follow in that suit on any conceivable line of play.

*For these purposes, a finesse is a play the success of which depends on finding one defender rather than the other with or without a particular card.

CLUB LAW 70

A defender makes a concession when he agrees to declarer's claim or when he announces that he will lose one or more of the remaining tricks.

A defender makes a claim when he announces that he will win one or more of the remaining tricks, or when he shows any or all of his cards to declarer for this purpose. If:

(a) the claim pertains only to an uncompleted trick currently in progress, play proceeds normally; cards exposed or otherwise revealed by the defender in making his claim do not become penalty cards, but Club Law 16, Unauthorized Information, may apply to claimer's partner.

(b) the claim pertains to subsequent tricks, play ceases (all play subsequent to the claim should be voided by the Arbiter). The defender must place and leave his hand face up on the table and make a comprehensive statement as to his proposed plan of defense. The claim is allowed, and the deal scored accordingly, if declarer agrees to it. If declarer disputes the claim, the Arbiter must be called to adjudicate the result of the deal. He does so as equitably as possible to both sides, but should award to the declarer any trick that the defenders could lose by normal play (an inferior or careless play can be normal, but not an irrational play).

CLUB APPEALS COMMITTEE

Whenever possible, a club should establish an appeals committee to review decisions of the Arbiter; and any game may designate a committee to which appeals may be taken. If such a procedure has been agreed to or published in advance, any player may appeal any decision by the Arbiter. The appeals committee exercises all powers assigned by these Laws to the Arbiter and may overrule any of his decisions.

When an Arbiter's decision is overruled on appeal, only the scoring of the particular deal is affected; subsequent scores stand as recorded. If the committee's decision results in fulfillment of a contract originally recorded as defeated, or defeat of a contract recorded as fulfilled, then,

(a) for a contract now fulfilled: in addition to the other trick score and premium score, declarer's side received a premium of 50 points for a partscore that would not then have increased the below-the-line score to 100; and for any other contract, declarer's side receives a premium score according to vulnerability — 300 points if declarer's side was non-vulnerable, 400 points if declarer's was vulnerable and the defenders not, 500 points if both sides were vulnerable.

(b) for a contract now defeated, when the original scoring resulted in a game: in addition to the other premium score, the defenders receive a premium score of 100 points if they alone had scored a partscore in that game; plus a premium score of 500 points if declarer's side originally won two of two games, or 200 points if the defenders' side originally won two of three games.

RULES FOR CLUB PROCEDURE

The following rules, governing membership in new and existing tables, have proven satisfactory in club use over a long period of years.

A. Definitions

Member — An applicant who has acquired the right to play at a table either immediately or in his turn.

Complete Table — A table with six members.

Incomplete Table — A table with four or five members.

Cut In — Assert the right to become a member of an incomplete table, or to become a member of a complete table at such time as it may become incomplete.

B. Time Limit on Right to Play

An applicant may not play in a rubber unless he has become a member of a table before a card is duly drawn for the selection of players or partners.

C. Newly Formed Tables

Four to six applicants may form a table. If there are more than six applicants, the six highest-ranking ones become members. The four highest-ranking members

play the first rubber. Those who have not played, ranked in their order of entry into the room, take precedence over those who have played; the latter rank equally, except that players leaving existing tables to join the new table rank lowest. Precedence between those of equal rank is determined by drawing cards, the player who draws the highest-ranking card having precedence.

D. Cutting In

An application establishes membership in a table either forthwith or (if the table is complete) as soon as a vacancy occurs, unless applications in excess of the number required to complete a table are made at the same time, in which case precedence between applicants is established by drawing cards, as provided in the preceding rule.

E. Going Out

After each rubber, place must be made for any member who did not play that last rubber by the member who has played the greatest number of consecutive rubbers at that table. Cards are drawn for precedence if necessary. A member who has left another existing table must draw cards, for his first rubber, with the member who would otherwise have played. A player who breaks up a game by leaving three players at a table may not compete against them for entry at another table until each of them has played at least one rubber.

F. Membership Limited to One Table

No one can be a member of more than one table at the same time, unless a member consents, on request, to make a fourth at another table and announces his intention of returning to his former table as soon as his place at the new table can be filled. Failure to announce such intention results in loss of membership at his former table.

FOUR-DEAL BRIDGE

Four-Deal Bridge is a form of rubber bridge much played in clubs and well suited to home play. Long rubbers are avoided; extra players need wait no longer than the time (about twenty minutes) required to complete four deals. The game is also called Club Bridge or Chicago (for the city in which it originated).

A. Basic Rules

The Laws of Contract Bridge and Rules for Club Procedure are followed, except as modified by the following rules.

B. The Rubber

A rubber consists of a series of four deals that have been bid and played. If a deal is passed out, the same player deals again and the deal passed out does not count as one of the four deals.

A fifth deal is void if attention is drawn to it at any time before there has been a new cut for partners or the game has terminated; if the error is not discovered in time for correction, the score stands as recorded. A sixth or subsequent deal is unconditionally void and no score for such a deal is ever permissible.

In case fewer than four deals are played, the score shall stand for the incomplete series and the fourth deal need not be played unless attention is drawn to the error before there has been a new cut for partners or the game has terminated.

When the players are pivoting,* the fact that the players have taken their proper seats for the next rubber shall be considered a cut for partners.

*In a pivot game, partnerships for each rubber follow a

fixed rotation.

C. Vulnerability

Vulnerability is not determined by previous scores but by the following schedule:

First deal: Neither side vulnerable.

Second and third deals: Dealer's side vulnerable, the other side not vulnerable.

Fourth deal: Both sides vulnerable.

D. Premiums

For making or completing a game (100 or more trick points), a side receives a premium score of 300 points if on that deal it is not vulnerable or 500 points if on that deal it is vulnerable. There is no additional premium score for winning two or more games, each game premium score being scored separately.

E. The Score

As a reminder of vulnerability in Four-Deal Bridge, two intersecting diagonal lines should be drawn near the top of the score pad.

The numeral "1" should be inserted in that one of the four angles thus formed that faces the first dealer. After play of the first deal is completed, "2" is inserted in the next angle in clockwise rotation, facing the dealer of the second deal. The numerals "3" and "4" are subsequently inserted at the start of the third and fourth deals, respectively, each in the angle facing the current dealer.

A correctly numbered diagram is conclusive as to vulnerability. There is no redress for a bid influenced by the scorer's failure to draw the diagram or for an error or omission in inserting a numeral or numerals in the diagram. Such error or omission should, upon discovery, be immediately corrected and the deal or deals should be scored or rescored as though the diagram and the number or numbers thereon had been properly inserted.

F. Partscores

A partscore or scores made previously may be combined with a partscore made in the current deal to complete a game of 100 or more trick points. The game premium is determined by the vulnerability, on that deal, of the side that completes the game. When a side makes or completes a game, no previous partscore of either side may thereafter be counted toward game.

A side that makes a partscore in the fourth deal, if the partscore is not sufficient to complete a game, receives a premium of 100 points. This premium is scored whether or not the same side or the other side has an uncompleted partscore. There is no separate premium for making a partscore in any other circumstance.

G. Deal Out of Turn

When a player deals out of turn, and there is no right to a redeal, the player who should have dealt retains his right to call first, but such right is lost if it is not claimed before the actual dealer calls. If the actual dealer calls before attention is drawn to the deal out of turn, each player thereafter calls in rotation. Vulnerability and scoring values are determined by the position of the player who should have dealt, regardless of which players actually dealt or called first. Neither the rotation of the deal nor the scoring should be affected by a deal out of turn. The next dealer is the player who would have dealt next if the deal had been in turn.

H. Optional Rules and Customs

The following practices, not required, have proved acceptable in some clubs and games.

(i) Since the essence of the game is speed, if a deal is passed out, the pack that has been shuffled for the next deal should be used by the same dealer.

(ii) The net score of a rubber should be translated into even hundreds (according to American custom) by crediting as 100 points any fraction thereof amounting to 50 or more points: *e.g.,* 750 points count as 800; 740 points count as 700 points.

(iii) No two players may play a second consecutive rubber as partners at the same table. If two players draw each other again, the player who has drawn the highest card should play with the player who has drawn the third-highest, against the other two players.

(iv) To avoid confusion as to how many deals have been played: Each deal should be scored, even if there is no net advantage to either side (for example, when one side is entitled to 100 points for undertrick penalties and the other side is entitled to 100 points for honors). In a result that completes a game, premiums for overtricks, game, slam, or making a doubled contract should be combined with the trick score to produce one total, which is entered below the line (for example, if a side makes 2♠ doubled and vulnerable with an overtrick, 870 should be scored below the line, not 120 below the line and 50, 500, and 200 above the line).

LAWS OF DUPLICATE CONTRACT BRIDGE.

The first Laws of Duplicate Contract Bridge were published in 1928. There have been successive revisions in 1933, 1935, 1943, 1949, 1963, 1975, 1987 and 1997.

Through the Thirties, the Laws were promulgated by the Portland Club of London and the Whist Club of New York. From the Forties onwards, the American Contract Bridge League Laws Commission has replaced the Whist Club, while the British Bridge League and the European Bridge League supplemented the Portland Club's efforts. The 1975 Laws were also promulgated by the World Bridge Federation Laws Commission, as they have been in 1987 and the current version.

This latest revision supersedes the 1987 Code on September 1, 1997. Zonal authorities may implement the new Code any time after March 1, 1997. In the American Contract Bridge League the revised laws are effective on May 27, 1997.

In the 1975 Laws and prior, words such as may, should, shall and must were used without much discrimination; in 1987 they were rationalized, and the practice is continued in the current Laws. When these Laws say that a player "may" do something ("any player may call attention to an irregularity during the auction"), the failure to do it is in no way wrong. A simple declaration that a player "does" something ("...dummy spreads his hand in front of him...") establishes correct procedure without any suggestion that a violation be penalized. When a player "should" do something ("a claim should be accompanied at once by a statement..."), his failure to do it is an infraction of law, which will jeopardize his rights, but which will incur a procedural penalty only seldom. In contrast, when these Laws say that a player "shall" do something ("No player shall take any action until the Director has explained..."), a violation will be penalized more often than not. The strongest word, "must" ("before making a call, he must inspect the face of his cards"), indicates that violation is regarded as serious indeed. Note that "may" becomes very strong in the negative: "may not" is a stronger injunction than "shall not", just short of "must not."

A great deal of effort has been expended to make these

Laws easy to use. References from one law to another have been made more explicit. The hundreds of headings and sub-headings can help a Director find the section of a law that is applicable to the facts of a case (these headings are for convenience of reference only; headings are not considered to be part of the Laws). The Table of Contents at the front of the book and the alphabetical index at the back should make a Director's task lighter.

The Drafting Committee notes with sorrow the passing of many previous contributors to the Laws whose imprint remains in the new Code — Jean Besse and Colin Harding of the WBF Laws Committee, and B. Jay Becker, Easley Blackwood and Alfred Sheinwold of the ACBL Laws Commission. We also acknowledge the efforts of Stewart Wheeler of the Portland Club for his help and advice.

The Drafting Committee acknowledges with gratitude the work of Rena Hetzer, who acted as secretary and liaison in the preparation of this revision.

The Scope of the Laws

The Laws are designed to define correct procedure, and to provide an adequate remedy when there is a departure from correct procedure. An offending player should be ready to pay any penalty graciously, or to accept any adjusted score awarded by the Tournament Director. The Laws are primarily designed not as punishment for irregularities, but rather as redress for damage.

CHAPTER I
Definitions

Adjusted Score — An arbitrary score awarded by the Director (see Law 12). It is either "artificial" or "assigned". 1. An artificial adjusted score is one awarded in lieu of a result because no result can be obtained or estimated for a particular deal (*e.g.*, when an irregularity prevents play of a deal). 2. An assigned adjusted score is awarded to one side, or to both sides, to be the result of the deal in place of the result actually obtained after an irregularity.

Alert — A notification, whose form may be specified by a sponsoring organization, to the effect that opponents may be in need of an explanation.

Auction — 1. The process of determining the contract by means of successive calls. 2. The aggregate of calls made (see Law 17E).

Bid — An undertaking to win at least a specified number of odd tricks in a specified denomination.

Board — 1. A duplicate board as described in Law 2. 2. The four hands as originally dealt and placed in a duplicate board for play during that session.

Call — Any bid, double, redouble or pass.

Contestant — In an individual event, a player; in a pair event, two players playing as partners throughout the event; in a team event, four or more players playing as teammates.

Contract — The undertaking by declarer's side to win, at the denomination named, the number of odd tricks specified in the final bid, whether undoubled, doubled or redoubled.

Convention — 1. A call that, by partnership agreement, conveys a meaning other than willingness to play in the denomination named (or in the last denomination named), or high-card strength or length (three cards or more) there. However, an agreement as to overall strength does not make a call a conven-

tion. 2. Defender's play that serves to convey a meaning by agreement rather than inference.

Deal — 1. The distribution of the pack to form the hands of the four players. 2. The cards so distributed considered as a unit, including the auction and play thereof.

Declarer — The player who, for the side that makes the final bid, first bid the denomination named in the final bid. He becomes declarer when the opening lead is faced (but see Law 54A when the opening lead is made out of turn).

Defender — An opponent of (presumed) declarer.

Denomination — The suit or notrump specified in a bid.

Director — A person designated to supervise a duplicate bridge contest and to apply these Laws.

Double — A call over an opponent's bid increasing the scoring value of fulfilled or defeated contracts (see Laws 19 and 77).

Dummy — 1. Declarer's partner. He becomes dummy when the opening lead is faced. 2. Declarer's partner's cards, once they are spread on the table after the opening lead.

Event — A contest of one or more sessions.

Follow Suit — Play a card of the suit that has been led.

Game — 100 or more trick points scored on one deal.

Hand — The cards originally dealt to a player, or the remaining portion thereof.

Honor — Any Ace, King, Queen, Jack or 10.

International Matchpoint (IMP) — A unit of scoring awarded according to a schedule established in Law 78B.

Irregularity — A deviation from the correct procedures set forth in the Laws.

Lead — The first card played to a trick.

LHO — Left-hand opponent.

Matchpoint — A unit of scoring awarded to a contestant as a result of comparison with one or more other scores.

Odd Trick — Each trick to be won by declarer's side in excess of six.

Opening Lead — The card led to the first trick.

Opponent — A player of the other side; a member of the partnership to which one is opposed.

Overtrick — Each trick won by declarer's side in excess of the contract.

Pack — The 52 playing cards with which the game of Contract Bridge is played.

Partner — The player with whom one plays as a side against the other two players.

Partscore — 90 or fewer trick points scored on one deal.

Pass — A call specifying that a player does not, at that turn, elect to bid, double or redouble.

Play — 1. The contribution of a card from one's hand to a trick, including the first card, which is the lead. 2. The aggregate of plays made. 3. The period during which the cards are played. 4. The aggregate of the calls and plays on a board.

Premium Points — Any points earned other than trick points (see Law 77).

Psychic Call — A deliberate and gross misstatement of honor strength or suit length.

Rectification — Adjustment made to permit the auction or play to proceed as normally as possible after an irregularity has occurred.

Redouble — A call over an opponent's double, increasing the scoring value of fulfilled or defeated contracts (see Laws 19 and 77).

Revoke — The play of a card of another suit by a player who is able to follow suit or to comply with a lead penalty.

RHO — Right-hand opponent.

Rotation — The clockwise order in which the deal and the right to call or play progress.

Round — A part of a session played without progression of players.

Session — An extended period of play during which a number of boards, specified by the sponsoring organization, is scheduled to be played.

Side — Two players who constitute a partnership against the other two players.

Slam — A contract to win six odd tricks (called Small Slam), or to win seven odd tricks (called Grand Slam).

Suit — One of four groups of cards in the pack, each group comprising thirteen cards and having a characteristic symbol: spades (♠), hearts (♥), diamonds (♦), clubs (♣).

Team — Two or more pairs playing in different directions at different tables, but for a common score (applicable regulations may permit teams of more than four members).

Trick — The unit by which the outcome of the contract is determined, regularly consisting of four cards, one contributed by each player in rotation, beginning with the lead.

Trick Points — Points scored by declarer's side for fulfilling the contract (see Law 77).

Trump — Each card of the suit, if any, named in the contract.

Turn — The correct time at which a player may call or play.

Undertrick — Each trick by which declarer's side falls short of fulfilling the contract (see Law 77).

Vulnerability — The conditions for assigning premiums and undertrick penalties (see Law 77).

CHAPTER II
Preliminaries
LAW 1
THE PACK — RANK OF CARDS AND SUITS

Duplicate Contract Bridge is played with a pack of 52 cards, consisting of 13 cards in each of four suits. The suits rank downward in the order spades (♠), hearts (♥), diamonds (♦), clubs (♣). The Cards of each suit rank downward in the order Ace, King, Queen, Jack, 10, 9, 8, 7, 6, 5, 4, 3, 2.

LAW 2
THE DUPLICATE BOARDS

A duplicate board containing a pack is provided for each deal to be played during a session. Each board is numbered and has four pockets to hold the four hands, designated North, East, South and West. The dealer and vulnerability are designated as follows:

North Dealer	Boards	1	5	9	13
East Dealer	Boards	2	6	10	14
South Dealer	Boards	3	7	11	15
West Dealer	Boards	4	8	12	16
Neither Side Vulnerable	Boards	1	8	11	14

North–South Vulnerable	Boards	2	5	12	15
East–West Vulnerable	Boards	3	6	9	16
Both Sides Vulnerable	Boards	4	7	10	13

The same sequence is repeated for Boards 17–32 and for each subsequent group of 16 boards.

No board that fails to conform to these conditions should be used. If such board is used, however, the conditions marked on it apply for that session.

LAW 3
ARRANGEMENT OF TABLES

Four players play at each table, and tables are numbered in a sequence established by the Director. He designates one direction as North; other compass directions assume the normal relationship to North.

LAW 4
PARTNERSHIPS

The four players at each table constitute two partnerships or sides, North–South against East–West. In pair or team events the contestants enter as pairs or teams and retain the same partnerships throughout a session (except in the case of substitutions authorized by the Director). In individual events each player enters separately, and partnerships change during a session.

LAW 5
ASSIGNMENT OF SEATS

A. Initial Position

The Director assigns an initial position to each contestant (individual, pair or team) at the start of a session. Unless otherwise directed, the members of each pair or team may select seats among those assigned to them by mutual agreement. Having once selected a compass direction, a player may change it within a session only upon instruction or with permission of the Director.

B. Change of Direction or Table

Players change their initial compass direction or proceed to another table in accordance with the Director's instructions. The Director is responsible for clear announcement of instructions; each player is responsible for moving when and as directed and for occupying the correct seat after each change.

CHAPTER III
Preparation and Progression
LAW 6
THE SHUFFLE AND DEAL

A. The Shuffle

Before play starts, each pack is thoroughly shuffled. There is a cut if either opponent so requests.

B. The Deal

The cards must be dealt face down, one card at time, into four hands of thirteen cards each; each hand is then placed face down in one of the four pockets of the board. The recommended procedure is that the cards be dealt in rotation, clockwise.

C. Representation of Both Pairs

A member of each side should be present during the shuffle and deal unless the Director instructs otherwise.

D. New Shuffle and Redeal
1. Cards Incorrectly Dealt or Exposed
There must be a new shuffle and a redeal if it is ascertained before the auction begins for both sides (see Law 17A) that the cards have been incorrectly dealt or that a player could have seen the face of a card belonging to another hand.
2. No Shuffle or No Deal
No result may stand if the cards are dealt without shuffle from a sorted deck or if the deal had previously been played in a different session.
3. At Director's Instruction
Subject to Law 22A, there must be a new shuffle and a redeal when required by the Director for any reason compatible with the Laws (but see Law 86C).

E. Director's Option on Shuffling and Dealing
1. By Players
The Director may instruct that the shuffle and deal be performed at each table immediately before play starts.
2. By Director
The Director may perform the shuffle and deal in advance, himself.
3. By Agents or Assistants
The Director may have his assistants or other appointed agents perform the shuffle and deal in advance.
4. Different Method of Dealing or Pre-dealing
The Director may require a different method of dealing or pre-dealing.

F. Duplication of Board
If required by the conditions of play, one or more exact copies of each original deal may be made under the Director's instructions.

LAW 7
CONTROL OF BOARD AND CARDS
A. Placement of Board
When a board is to be played it is placed in the center of the table until play is completed.

B. Removal of Cards from Board
Each player takes a hand from the pocket corresponding to his compass position.
1. Counting Cards in Hand before Play
Each player counts his cards face down to be sure he has exactly thirteen; after that, and before making a call, he must inspect the face of his cards.
2. Control of Player's Hand
During play each player retains possession of his own cards, not permitting them to be mixed with those of any other player. No player shall touch any cards other than his own (but declarer may play dummy's cards in accordance with Law 45) during or after play except by permission of the Director.

C. Returning Cards to Board
Each player shall restore his original thirteen cards to the pocket corresponding to his compass position. Thereafter no hand shall be removed from the board unless a member of each side, or the Director, is present.

D. Responsibility for Procedures
Any contestant remaining at a table throughout a session is primarily responsible for maintaining proper conditions of play at the table.

LAW 8
SEQUENCE OF ROUNDS
A. Movement of Boards and Players
1. Director's Instructions
The Director instructs the players as to the proper movement of boards and progression of contestants.
2. Responsibility for Moving Boards
The North player at each table is responsible for moving the boards just completed at his table to the proper table for the following round, unless the Director instructs otherwise.

B. End of Round
In general, a round ends when the Director gives the signal for the start of the following round; but if any table has not completed play by that time, the round continues for that table until there has been a progression of players.

C. End of Last Round and End of Session
The last round of a session, and the session itself, ends for each table when play of all boards scheduled at that table has been completed, and when all scores have been entered on the proper scoring forms without objection.

CHAPTER IV
General Laws
Governing Irregularities
LAW 9
PROCEDURE FOLLOWING AN IRREGULARITY
A. Calling Attention to an Irregularity
1. During the Auction Period
Unless prohibited by Law, any player may call attention to an irregularity during the auction, whether or not it is his turn to call.
2. During the Play Period
(a) Unless prohibited by Law, declarer or either defender may call attention to an irregularity that occurs during the play period.
(b) Dummy (dummy's restricted rights are defined in Laws 42 and 43)
(1) Dummy may not call attention to an irregularity during the play but may do so after play of the hand is concluded.
(2) Dummy may attempt to prevent declarer from committing an irregularity (Law 42B2).

B. After Attention Is Called to an Irregularity
1. Summoning the Director
(a) When to Summon
The Director must be summoned at once when attention is drawn to an irregularity.
(b) Who May Summon
Any player, including dummy, may summon the Director after attention has been drawn to an irregularity.

(c) Retention of Rights
Summoning the Director does not cause a player to forfeit any rights to which he might otherwise be entitled.

(d) Opponents' Rights
The fact that a player draws attention to an irregularity committed by his side does not affect the rights of the opponents.

2. Further Bids or Plays
No player shall take any action until the Director has explained all matters in regard to rectification and to the assessment of a penalty.

C. Premature Correction of an Irregularity
Any premature correction of an irregularity by the offender may subject him to a further penalty (see the lead penalties of Law 26).

LAW 10
ASSESSMENT OF A PENALTY

A. Right to Assess Penalty
The Director alone has the right to assess penalties when applicable. Players do not have the right to assess (or waive) penalties on their own initiative.

B Cancellation of Payment or Waiver of Penalty
The Director may allow or cancel any payment or waiver of penalties made by the players without his instructions.

C. Choice after Irregularity
1. Explanation of Options
When these Laws provide an option after an irregularity, the Director shall explain all the options available.
2. Choice among Options
If a player has an option after an irregularity, he must make his selection without consulting partner.

LAW 11
FORFEITURE OF THE RIGHT TO PENALIZE

A. Action by Non-Offending Side
The right to penalize an irregularity may be forfeited if either member of the non-offending side takes any action before summoning the Director. The Director so rules when the non-offending side may have gained through subsequent action taken by an opponent in ignorance of the penalty.

B. Irregularity Called by Spectator
1. Spectator Responsibility of Non-Offending Side
The right to penalize an irregularity may be forfeited if attention is first drawn to the irregularity by a spectator for whose presence at the table the non-offending side is responsible.
2. Spectator Responsibility of Offending Side
The right to correct an irregularity may be forfeited if attention is first drawn to the irregularity by a spectator for whose presence at the table the offending side is responsible.

C. Penalty after Forfeiture of the Right to Penalize
Even after the right to penalize has been forfeited under this Law, the Director may assess a procedural penalty (see Law 90).

LAW 12
DIRECTOR'S DISCRETIONARY POWERS

A. Right to Award an Adjusted Score
The Director may award an adjusted score (or scores), either on his own initiative or on the application of any player, but only when these Laws empower him to do so, or:
1. Laws Provide No Indemnity
The Director may award an assigned adjusted score when he judges that these Laws do not provide indemnity to the non-offending contestant for the particular type of violation of law committed by an opponent.
2. Normal Play of the Board Is Impossible
The Director may award an artificial adjusted score if no rectification can be made that will permit normal play of the board (see Law 88).
3. Incorrect Penalty Has Been Paid
The Director may award an adjusted score if an incorrect penalty has been paid.

B. No Adjustment for Undue Severity of Penalty
The Director may not award an adjusted score on the ground that the penalty provided in these Laws is either unduly severe or advantageous to either side.

C. Awarding an Adjusted Score
1. Artificial Score
When, owing to an irregularity, no result can be obtained, the Director awards an artificial adjusted score according to responsibility for the irregularity: average minus (at most 40% of the available matchpoints in pairs) to a contestant directly at fault; average (50% in pairs) to a contestant only partially at fault; average plus (at least 60% in pairs) to a contestant in no way at fault (see Law 86 for team play or Law 88 for pairs play). The scores awarded to the two sides need not balance.
2. Assigned Score
When the Director awards an assigned adjusted score in place of a result actually obtained after an irregularity, the score is, for a non-offending side, the most favorable result that was likely had the irregularity not occurred or, for an offending side, the most unfavorable result that was at all probable. The scores awarded to the two sides need not balance and may be assigned either in matchpoints or by altering the total-point score prior to matchpointing.
3. Unless Zonal Organizations specify otherwise, an appeals committee may vary an assigned adjusted score in order to do equity.

LAW 13
INCORRECT NUMBER OF CARDS

When the Director determines that one or more pockets of the board contained an incorrect number of cards,* and a player with an incorrect hand has made a call, then when the Director deems that the deal can be corrected and played normally with no change of call, the deal may be so played with the concurrence of all four players. Otherwise, the Director shall award an artificial adjusted score and may penalize an offender. If no such call has been made, then:

A. No Player Has Seen Another's Card
The Director shall correct the discrepancy as follows and, if no player will then have seen another's card, shall require that the board be played normally.
1. Hand Records
When hand records are available, the Director shall distribute the cards in accordance with the records.
2. Consult Previous Players
If hand records are not available, the Director shall correct the board by consulting with players who have previously played it.
3. Require a Redeal
If the board was incorrectly dealt, the Director shall require a redeal (Law 6).

B. A Player Has Seen Another Player's Card(s)
When the Director determines that one or more pockets of the board contained an incorrect number of cards and after restoration of the board to its original condition a player has seen one or more cards of another player's hand, if the Director deems:
1. The Information Gained Is Inconsequential
that such information will not interfere with normal bidding or play, the Director, with the concurrence of all four players, may allow the board to be played and scored normally.
2. The Information Will Interfere with Normal Play
that the information gained thereby is of sufficient importance to interfere with normal bidding or play, or if any player objects to playing the board, the Director shall award an artificial adjusted score and may penalize an offender.

C. Play Completed
When it is determined after play ends that a player's hand originally contained more than 13 cards with another player holding correspondingly fewer, the result must be cancelled (for procedural penalty, see Law 90).
Where three hands are correct and one hand is deficient, Law 14, and not this Law, applies.

LAW 14
MISSING CARD
A. Hand Found Deficient before Play Commences
When three hands are correct and the fourth is found to be deficient before the play period begins, the Director makes a search for any missing card, and:
1. Card Is Found
If a card is found, it is restored to the deficient hand.
2. Card Cannot Be Found
If a card cannot be found, the Director reconstructs the deal, as near to its original form as he can determine, by substituting another pack.

B. Hand Found Deficient Afterwards
When three hands are correct and the fourth is found to be deficient after the play period begins, the Director makes a search for any missing card, and:
1. Card Is Found
(a) If a card is found among the played cards, Law 67 applies.
(b) If a card is found elsewhere, it is restored to the deficient hand, and penalties may apply (see 3., following).

2. Card Cannot Be Found
If a card cannot be found, the deal is reconstructed as nearly as can be determined in its original form by substituting another pack, and penalties may apply (see 3., following).
3. Possible Penalties
A card restored to a hand under the provisions of Section B of this Law is deemed to have belonged continuously to the deficient hand. It may become a penalty card (Law 50), and failure to have played it may constitute a revoke.

LAW 15
PLAY OF A WRONG BOARD
A. Players Have Not Previously Played Board
If players play a board not designated for them to play in the current round:
1. Score Board as Played
The Director normally allows the score to stand if none of the four players have previously played the board.
2. Designate a Late Play
The Director may require both pairs to play the correct board against one another later.

B. One or More Players Have Previously Played Board
If any player plays a board he has previously played, with the correct opponents or otherwise, his second score on the board is cancelled both for his side and his opponents, and the Director shall award an artificial adjusted score to the contestants deprived of the opportunity to earn a valid score.

C. Discovered during Auction
If, during the auction period, the Director discovers that a contestant is playing a board not designated for him to play in the current round, he shall cancel the auction, ensure that the correct contestants are seated and that they are informed of their rights both now and at future rounds. A second auction begins. Players must repeat calls they made previously. If any call differs in any way from the corresponding call in the first auction, the Director shall cancel the board. Otherwise, play continues normally.

LAW 16
UNAUTHORIZED INFORMATION
Players are authorized to base their calls and plays on information from legal calls and or plays, and from mannerisms of opponents. To base a call or play on other extraneous information may be an infraction of law.

A. Extraneous Information from Partner
After a player makes available to his partner extraneous information that may suggest a call or play, as by means of a remark, a question, a reply to a question, or by unmistakable hesitation, unwonted speed, special emphasis, tone, gesture, movement, mannerism or the like, the partner may not choose from among logical alternative actions one that could demonstrably have been suggested over another by the extraneous information.
1. When Such Information Is Given
When a player considers that an opponent has made such information available and that damage could well result, he may, unless the regula-

tions of the sponsoring organization prohibit, immediately announce that he reserves the right to summon the Director later (the opponents should summon the Director immediately if they dispute the fact that unauthorized information might have been conveyed).

2. When Illegal Alternative Is Chosen
When a player has substantial reason to believe* that an opponent who had a logical alternative has chosen an action that could have been suggested by such information, he should summon the Director forthwith. The Director shall require the auction and play to continue, standing ready to assign an adjusted score if he considers that an infraction of law has resulted in damage.

B. Extraneous Information from Other Sources
When a player accidentally receives unauthorized information about a board he is playing or has yet to play, as by looking at the wrong hand; by overhearing calls, results or remarks; by seeing cards at another table; or by seeing a card belonging to another player at his own table before the auction begins, the Director should be notified forthwith, preferably by the recipient of the information. If the Director considers that the information could interfere with normal play, he may:

1. Adjust Positions
if the type of contest and scoring permit, adjust the players' positions at the table, so that the player with information about one hand will hold that hand; or,

2. Appoint Substitute
with the concurrence of all four players, appoint a temporary substitute to replace the player who received the unauthorized information; or,

3. Award an Adjusted Score
forthwith award an artificial adjusted score.

C. Information from Withdrawn Calls and Plays
A call or play may be withdrawn, and another substituted, either by a non-offending side after an opponent's infraction or by an offending side to rectify an infraction.

1. Non-offending Side
For the non-offending side, all information arising from a withdrawn action is authorized, whether the action be its own or its opponents'.

2. Offending Side
For the offending side, information arising from its own withdrawn action and from withdrawn actions of the non-offending side is unauthorized. A player of the offending side may not choose from among logical alternative actions one that could demonstrably have been suggested over another by the unauthorized information.

*When play ends; or, as to dummy's hand, when dummy is exposed.

CHAPTER V
The Auction
PART I
CORRECT PROCEDURE
SECTION ONE
AUCTION PERIOD
LAW 17
DURATION OF THE AUCTION

A. Auction Period Starts
The auction period on a deal begins for a side when either partner looks at the face of his cards.

B. The First Call
The player designated by the board as dealer makes the first call.

C. Successive Calls
The player to dealer's left makes the second call, and thereafter each player calls in turn in a clockwise rotation.

D. Cards from Wrong Board
If a player who has inadvertently picked up the cards from a wrong board makes a call, that call is canceled. If offender's LHO has called over the canceled call, the Director shall assign artificial adjusted scores (see Law 90 for penalty) when offender's substituted call differs in any significant way from his canceled call*. If offender subsequently repeats the canceled call on the board from which he mistakenly drew his cards, the Director may allow that board to be played normally, but the Director shall assign artificial adjusted scores (see Law 90) when offender's call differs in any way from his original canceled call.

E. End of Auction Period
The auction period ends when all four players pass or when after three passes in rotation have followed any call the opening lead is faced (when a pass out of rotation has been accepted, see Law 34).
*Offender's LHO must repeat the previous call.

LAW 18
BIDS
A. Proper Form
A bid names a number of odd tricks, from one to seven, and a denomination. (Pass, double and redouble are calls but not bids.)

B. To Supersede a Bid
A bid supersedes a previous bid if it names either the same number of odd tricks in a higher-ranking denomination or a greater number of odd tricks in any denomination.

C. Sufficient Bid
A bid that supersedes the immediately previous bid is a sufficient bid.

D. Insufficient Bid
A bid that fails to supersede the immediately previous bid is an insufficient bid.

E. Rank of the Denominations
The rank of the denominations in descending order is: notrump, spades, hearts, diamonds, clubs.

F. Different Methods
Zonal Organizations may authorize different methods of making calls.

LAW 19
DOUBLES AND REDOUBLES
A. Doubles
1. Legal Double

A player may double only the last preceding bid. That bid must have been made by an opponent; calls other than pass must not have intervened.

2. Proper Form for Double
In doubling, a player should not state the number of odd tricks or the denomination. The only correct form is the single word "Double".

3. Double of Incorrectly Stated Bid
If a player, in doubling, incorrectly states the bid, or the number of odd tricks or the denomination, he is deemed to have doubled the bid as it was made. (Law 16 — Unauthorized Information — may apply.)

B. Redoubles
1. Legal Redouble
A player may redouble only the last preceding double. That double must have been made by an opponent; calls other than pass must not have intervened.

2. Proper Form for a Redouble
In redoubling, a player should not state the number of odd tricks or the denomination. The only correct form is the single word "Redouble".

3. Redouble of an Incorrectly Stated Bid
If a player, in redoubling, incorrectly states the doubled bid, or the number of odd tricks or the denomination, he is deemed to have redoubled the bid as it was made. (Law 16 — Unauthorized Information — may apply.)

C. Double or Redouble Superseded
Any double or redouble is superseded by a subsequent legal bid.

D. Scoring a Doubled or Redoubled Contract
If after a bid is doubled or redoubled there is no subsequent legal bid, scoring values are increased as provided in Law 77.

LAW 20
REVIEW AND EXPLANATION OF CALLS
A. Call Not Clearly Heard
A player who does not hear a call distinctly may forthwith require that it be repeated.

B. Review of Auction during Auction Period
During the auction period, a player is entitled to have all* previous calls restated when it is his turn to call, unless he is required by law to pass; Alerts should be included in the restatement.

C. Review after Final Pass
1. Opening Lead Inquiry
ß2. Review of Auction
Declarer or either defender may, at his first turn to play, require all* previous calls to be restated (see Law 41B and 41C).

D. Who May Review the Auction
A request to have calls restated shall be responded to only by an opponent.

E. Correction of Error in Review
All players, including dummy or a player required by law to pass, are responsible for prompt correction of errors in restatement (see Law 12C1 when an uncorrected review causes damage).

F. Explanation of Calls
1. During the Auction
During the auction and before the final pass, any player, at his own turn to call, may request** a full explanation of the opponents' auction (questions may be asked about calls actually made or about relevant calls available but not made); replies should normally be given by the partner of a player who made a call in question (see Law 75C).

2. During the Play Period
After the final pass and throughout the play period, either defender at his own turn to play may request** an explanation of opposing auction. At his or dummy's turn to play, the declarer may request an explanation of a defender's call or card play conventions.

*A player may not ask for a partial restatement of previous calls and may not halt the review before it has been completed.

**Law 16 may apply, and sponsoring organizations may establish regulations for written explanation.

LAW 21
CALL BASED ON MISINFORMATION
A. Call Based on Caller's Misunderstanding
A player has no recourse if he has made a call on the basis of his own misunderstanding.

B. Call Based on Misinformation from an Opponent
1. Change of Call
Until the end of the auction period (see Law 17E), a player may, without penalty, change a call when it is probable that he made the call as a result of misinformation given to him by an opponent (failure to alert promptly to a conventional call or special understanding, where such alert is required by the sponsoring organization, is deemed misinformation), provided that his partner has not subsequently called.

2. Change of Call by Opponent Following Correction
When a player elects to change a call because of misinformation (as in 1., preceding), his LHO may then in turn change any subsequent call he may have made, without penalty (unless his withdrawn call conveyed such information as to damage the non-offending side, in which case the Director may assign an adjusted score). (For unauthorized information from withdrawn calls, see Law 16C.)

3. Too Late to Change Call
When it is too late to change a call, the Director may award an adjusted score (Law 40C may apply).

SECTION TWO
AUCTION HAS ENDED
LAW 22
PROCEDURE AFTER THE AUCTION HAS ENDED
After the auction period has ended,
A. No Player Has Bid
if no player has bid, the hands are returned to the board without play. There shall not be a redeal.

B. One or More Players Have Bid
if any player has bid, the final bid becomes the contract, and play begins.

PART II
IRREGULARITIES IN PROCEDURE
LAW 23
DAMAGING ENFORCED PASS

Reference will be made to this Law from many other Laws that prescribe penalties for auction-period infractions.

When the penalty for an irregularity under any Law would compel the offender's partner to pass at his next turn, if the Director deems that the offender, at the time of his irregularity, could have known that the enforced pass would be likely to damage the non-offending side, he shall require the auction and play to continue and consider awarding an adjusted score. (See Law 72B1.)

SECTION ONE
EXPOSED CARD, AUCTION PERIOD
LAW 24
CARD EXPOSED OR LED DURING AUCTION

When the Director determines, during the auction, that because of a player's action one or more cards of that player's hand were in position for the face to be seen by his partner, the Director shall require that every such card be left face up on the table until the auction closes; and (penalty) if the offender subsequently becomes a defender, declarer may treat every such card as a penalty card (Law 50). In addition:

A. Low Card Not Prematurely Led
   If it is a single card below the rank of an honor and not prematurely led, there is no further penalty.

B. Single Card of Honor Rank or Card Prematurely Led
   If it is a single card of honor rank or is any card prematurely led, (penalty) offender's partner must pass when next it is his turn to call (see Law 23 when a pass damages the non-offending side).

C. Two or More Cards Are Exposed
   If two or more cards are so exposed, (penalty) offender's partner must pass when next it is his turn to call (see Law 23 when a pass damages the non-offending side).

SECTION TWO
CHANGES OF CALLS
LAW 25
LEGAL AND ILLEGAL CHANGES OF CALL

A. Immediate Correction of Inadvertency
   Until his partner makes a call, a player may substitute his intended call for an inadvertent call but only if he does so, or attempts to do so, without pause for thought. If legal, his last call stands without penalty; if illegal, it is subject to the applicable Law.

B. Delayed or Purposeful Correction
   Until LHO calls, a call may be substituted when Section A does not apply:
   1. Substitute Call Condoned
      The substituted call may be accepted (treated as legal) at the option of offender's LHO*; then, the second call stands and the auction proceeds without penalty. If offender's LHO has called before attention is drawn to the infraction and the Director determines that LHO intended his call to apply over the offender's original call at that turn, offender's substituted call stands without penalty, and LHO may withdraw his call without penalty (but see Law 16C2).

2. Not Condoned
   If the substituted call is not accepted, it is canceled, and
   (a) First Call Illegal
       if the first call was illegal, the offender is subject to the applicable law (and the lead penalties of Law 26 may apply to the second call).
   (b) First Call Legal
       if the first call was legal, the offender must either
       (1) Let First Call Stand
           allow his first call to stand, in which case (penalty) his partner must pass when next it is his turn to call (see Law 23 when the pass damages the non-offending side), or,
       (2) Substitute Another Call
           make any other legal call, in which case (penalty) the auction proceeds normally (but offender's partner may not base calls on information from withdrawn calls); the offending side** may receive no score greater than average minus (see Law 12C1).
   (c) Lead Penalties
       In either case (b) (1) or (b) (2) above, the offender's partner will be subject to a lead penalty (see Law 26) if he becomes a defender.

*When the original bid was insufficient, apply Law 27.
**The non-offending side receives the score achieved at the table.

LAW 26
CALL WITHDRAWN, LEAD PENALTIES

When an offending player's call is withdrawn, and he chooses a different* final call for that turn, then if he becomes a defender:

A. Call Related to Specific Suit
   if the withdrawn call related to a specified suit or suits and
   1. Suit Specified
      if that suit was specified in the legal auction by the same player, there is no lead penalty, but see Law 16C.
   2. Suit Not Specified
      if that suit was not specified in the legal auction by the same player, then declarer may (penalty) either require the offender's partner to lead the specified suit (or one particular specified suit) at his first turn to lead, including the opening lead, or prohibit offender's partner from leading the specified suit (or one particular specified suit) at his first turn to lead, including the opening lead, such prohibition to continue for as long as offender's partner retains the lead.

B. Other Withdrawn Calls
   For other withdrawn calls, (penalty) declarer may prohibit offender's partner from leading any one suit** at his first turn to lead, including the opening lead, such prohibition to continue for as long as offender's partner retains the lead.

*A call repeated with a much different meaning shall be deemed a different call.

**Declarer specifies the suit when offender's partner first has the lead.*

SECTION THREE
INSUFFICIENT BID
LAW 27
INSUFFICIENT BID

A. Insufficient Bid Accepted

Any insufficient bid may be accepted (treated as legal) at the option of offender's LHO. It is accepted if that player calls.

B. Insufficient Bid Not Accepted

If an insufficient bid made in rotation is not accepted, it must be corrected by the substitution of either a sufficient bid or a pass.

1. Not Conventional and Corrected by Lowest Sufficient Bid in Same Denomination

   (a) No Penalty

   If both the insufficient bid and the bid substituted are incontrovertibly not conventional and if the bid is corrected by the lowest sufficient bid in the same denomination, the auction proceeds as though the irregularity had not occurred (Law 16C2 does not apply to this situation, but see (b) following).

   (b) Award of Adjusted Score

   If the Director judges that the insufficient bid conveyed such information as to damage the non-offending side, he shall assign an adjusted score.

2. Conventional, or Corrected by Any Other Sufficient Bid or Pass

   If either the insufficient bid or the lowest sufficient bid in the same denomination may have been conventional or if the bid is corrected by any other sufficient bid or by a pass, (penalty) the offender's partner must pass whenever it is his turn to call (apply Law 10C1 and see Law 23 when the pass damages the non-offending side; and the lead penalties of Law 26 may apply).

3. Attempt to Correct by a Double or Redouble

   If the offender attempts to substitute a double or redouble for his insufficient bid, the attempted call is cancelled, and (penalty) his partner must pass whenever it is his turn to call (see Law 23 when the pass damages the non-offending side, and the lead penalties of Law 26 may apply).

C. Insufficient Bid Out of Rotation

If a player makes an insufficient bid out of rotation, Law 31 applies.

SECTION FOUR
CALL OUT OF ROTATION
LAW 28
CALLS CONSIDERED TO BE IN ROTATION

A. RHO Required to Pass

A call is considered to be in rotation when it is made by a player at his RHO's turn to call if that opponent is required by law to pass.

B. Call by Correct Player Cancelling Call Out of Rotation

A call is considered to be in rotation when made by a player whose turn it was to call, before a penalty

has been assessed for a call out of rotation by an opponent; making such a call forfeits the right to penalize the call out of rotation, and the auction proceeds as though the opponent had not called at that turn, but Law 16C2 applies.

LAW 29
PROCEDURE AFTER A CALL OUT OF ROTATION

A. Forfeiture of Right to Penalize

Following a call out of rotation, offender's LHO may elect to call, thereby forfeiting the right to penalize.

B. Out-of-Rotation Call Cancelled

Otherwise, a call out of rotation is cancelled (but see A preceding), and the auction reverts to the player whose turn it was to call. Offender may make any legal call in proper rotation, but his side may be subject to penalty under Laws 30, 31 or 32.

C. Call Out of Rotation Is Conventional

If a call out of rotation is conventional, the provisions of Laws 30, 31, and 32 shall apply to the denominations specified, rather than the denominations named.

LAW 30
PASS OUT OF ROTATION

When a player has passed out of rotation (and the call is cancelled, as the option to accept the call has not been exercised — see Law 29):

A. Before Any Player Has Bid

When a player has passed out of rotation before any player has bid, (penalty) the offender must pass when next it is his turn to call and Law 72B1 may apply.

B. After Any Player Has Bid

1. At RHO's Turn to Call

   After any player has bid, when a pass out of rotation is made at offender's RHO's turn to call, (penalty) offender must pass when next it is his turn to call (if the pass out of rotation related by convention to a specific suit, or suits, thereby conveying information, the lead penalties of Law 26 may apply).

2. At Partner's Turn to Call

   (a) Action Required of Offender

   After any player has bid, for a pass out of rotation made at the offender's partner's turn to call, (penalty) the offender must pass whenever it is his turn to call, and Law 72B1 may apply.

   (b) Action Open to Offender's Partner

   Offender's partner may make any sufficient bid, or may pass, but may not double or redouble at that turn, and Law 72B1 may apply.

3. At LHO's Turn to Call

   After any player has bid, a pass out of rotation at offender's LHO's turn to call is treated as a change of call and Law 25 applies.

C. When Pass Is a Convention

When the pass out of rotation is a convention, Law 31, not this Law, will apply. A pass is a convention if, by special agreement, it promises more than a specified amount of strength, or if it artificially promises or denies values other than in the last suit named.

LAW 31
BID OUT OF ROTATION

When a player has bid out of rotation (and the bid is canceled, as the option to accept the bid has not been exercised — see Law 29):

A. RHO's Turn

When the offender has bid (or has passed partner's call when it is a convention, in which case section A2(b) applies) at his RHO's turn to call, then:

1. RHO Passes

If that opponent passes, offender must repeat the call out of rotation, and when that call is legal there is no penalty.

2. RHO Acts

If that opponent makes a legal* bid, double or redouble, offender may make any legal call; when this call

(a) Repeats Denomination

repeats the denomination of his bid out of rotation, (penalty) offender's partner must pass when next it is his turn to call (see Law 23).

(b) Does Not Repeat Denomination

does not repeat the denomination of his bid out of rotation, the lead penalties of Law 26 may apply, and (penalty) offender's partner must pass whenever it is his turn to call (see Law 23).

B. Partner's or LHO's Turn

When the offender has bid at his partner's turn to call, or at his LHO's turn to call if the offender has not previously called,** (penalty) offender's partner must pass whenever it is his turn to call (see Law 23 when the pass damages the non-offending side), and the lead penalties of Law 26 may apply.

*An illegal call by RHO is penalized as usual.

**Later bids at LHO's turn to call are treated as changes of call, and Law 25 applies.

LAW 32
DOUBLE OR REDOUBLE OUT OF ROTATION

A double or redouble out of rotation may be accepted at the option of the opponent next in rotation (see Law 29), except that an inadmissible double or redouble may never be accepted (see Law 35A if the opponent next in rotation nevertheless does call). If the illegal call is not accepted, it is cancelled, the lead penalties of Law 26B may apply, and:

A. Made at Offender's Partner's Turn to Call

If a double or redouble out of rotation has been made when it was the offender's partner's turn to call, (penalty) the offender's partner must pass whenever it is his turn to call (see Law 23 when the pass damages the non-offending side).

B. Made at RHO's Turn to Call

If a double or redouble out of rotation has been made at offender's RHO's turn to call, then:

1. RHO Passes

If offender's RHO passes, offender must repeat his out-of-rotation double or redouble and there is no penalty unless the double or redouble is inadmissible, in which case Law 36 applies.

2. RHO Bids

If offender's RHO bids, the offender may in turn

make any legal call and (penalty) offender's partner must pass whenever it is his turn to call (see Law 23 when the pass damages the non-offending side).

LAW 33
SIMULTANEOUS CALLS

A call made simultaneously with one made by the player whose turn it was to call is deemed to be a subsequent call.

LAW 34
RETENTION OF RIGHT TO CALL

When a call has been followed by three passes, the auction does not end when one of those passes was out of rotation, thereby depriving a player of his right to call at that turn. The auction reverts to the player who missed his turn. All subsequent passes are cancelled, and the auction proceeds as though there had been no irregularity.

LAW 35
INADMISSIBLE CALL CONDONED

When, after any inadmissible call specified below, the offender's LHO makes a call before a penalty has been assessed, there is no penalty for the inadmissible call (the lead penalties of Law 26 do not apply), and:

A. Double or Redouble

If the inadmissible call was a double or redouble not permitted by Law 19, that call and all subsequent calls are cancelled. The auction reverts to the player whose turn it is to call, and proceeds as though there had been no irregularity.

B. Action by Player Required to Pass

If the inadmissible call was a bid, double or redouble by a player required by law to pass, that call and all subsequent legal calls stand, but, if the offender was required to pass for the remainder of the auction, he must still pass at subsequent turns.

C. Bid of More than Seven

If the inadmissible call was a bid of more than seven, that call and all subsequent calls are cancelled; the offender must substitute a pass, and the auction proceeds as though there had been no irregularity.

D. Call after Final Pass

If the inadmissible call was a call after the final pass of the auction, that call and all subsequent calls are cancelled without penalty.

SECTION FIVE
INADMISSIBLE CALLS
LAW 36
INADMISSIBLE DOUBLE OR REDOUBLE

Any double or redouble not permitted by Law 19 is cancelled. The offender must substitute a legal call, and (penalty) the offender's partner must pass whenever it is his turn to call (see Law 23 when the pass damages the non-offending side); the lead penalties of Law 26 may apply. (If the call is out of turn, see Law 32; if offender's LHO calls, see Law 35A.)

LAW 37
ACTION VIOLATING OBLIGATION TO PASS

A bid, double or redouble by a player who is required

by law to pass is cancelled, and (penalty) each member of the offending side must pass whenever it becomes his turn to call (see Law 23 when the pass damages the non-offending side). The lead penalties of Law 26 may apply. (If offender's LHO calls, see Law 35B.)

LAW 38
BID OF MORE THAN SEVEN
No play or score at a contract of more than seven is ever permissible. A bid of more than seven is cancelled, and (penalty) each member of the offending side must pass whenever it becomes his turn to call (see Law 23 when the pass damages the non-offending side). The lead penalties of Law 26 may apply. (If offender's LHO calls, see Law 35C.)

LAW 39
CALL AFTER FINAL PASS
A call made after the final pass of the auction is cancelled, and:

A. Pass or Call by Declaring Side
   If it is a pass by a defender, or any call by the future declarer or dummy, there is no penalty.
B. Other Action by Defender
   If it is a bid, double or redouble by a defender, the lead penalties of Law 26 may apply. (If offender's LHO calls, see Law 35D.)

SECTION SIX
CONVENTIONS AND AGREEMENTS
LAW 40
PARTNERSHIP UNDERSTANDINGS
A. Right to Choose Call or Play
   A player may make any call or play (including an intentionally misleading call — such as a psychic bid — or a call or play that departs from commonly accepted, or previously announced, use of a convention), without prior announcement, provided that such call or play is not based on a partnership understanding.

B. Concealed Partnership Understandings Prohibited
   A player may not make a call or play based on a special partnership understanding unless an opposing pair may reasonably be expected to understand its meaning, or unless his side discloses the use of such call or play in accordance with the regulations of the sponsoring organization.

C. Director's Option
   If the Director decides that a side has been damaged through its opponents' failure to explain the full meaning of a call or play, he may award an adjusted score.

D. Regulation of Conventions
   The sponsoring organization may regulate the use of bidding or play conventions. Zonal organizations may, in addition, regulate partnership understandings (even if not conventional) that permit the partnership's initial actions at the one level to be made with a hand of a King or more below average strength. Zonal organizations may delegate this responsibility.

E. Convention Card

1. Right to Prescribe
   The sponsoring organization may prescribe a convention card on which partners are to list their conventions and other agreements and may establish regulations for its use, including a requirement that both members of a partnership employ the same system (such a regulation must not restrict style and judgment, only method).
2. Referring to Opponents' Convention Card
   During the auction and play, any player except dummy may refer to his opponents' convention card at his own turn to call or play, but not to his own*.

A player is not entitled, during the auction and play periods, to any aids to his memory, calculation or technique. However, sponsoring organizations may designate unusual methods and allow written defenses against opponents' unusual methods to be referred to at the table.

CHAPTER VI
The Play
PART I
PROCEDURE
SECTION ONE
CORRECT PROCEDURE
LAW 41
COMMENCEMENT OF PLAY
A. Face-down Opening Lead
   After a bid, double or redouble has been followed by three passes in rotation, the defender on presumed declarer's left makes the opening lead face down*. The face-down lead may be withdrawn only upon instruction of the Director after an irregularity (see Law 47E2); the withdrawn card must be returned to the defender's hand.

B. Review of Auction and Questions
   Before the opening lead is faced, the leader's partner and the presumed declarer each may require a review of the auction, or request explanation of an opponent's call (see Law 20). Declarer or either defender may, at his first turn to play a card, require a review of the auction; this right expires when he plays a card. The defenders (subject to Law 16) and the declarer retain the right to request explanations throughout the play period, each at his own turn to play.

C. Opening Lead Faced
   Following this question period, the opening lead is faced, the play period begins, and dummy's hand is spread. After it is too late to have previous calls restated (see B, above), declarer or either defender, at his own turn to play, is entitled to be informed as to what the contract is and whether, but not by whom, it was doubled or redoubled.

D. Dummy's Hand
   After the opening lead is faced, dummy spreads his hand in front of him on the table, face up, sorted into suits, the cards in order of rank, in columns pointing lengthwise towards declarer, with trumps to dummy's right. Declarer plays both his hand and that of dummy.

* Sponsoring organizations may specify that opening leads be made face up.

LAW 42
DUMMY'S RIGHTS

A. Absolute Rights

1. Give Information

Dummy is entitled to give information, in the Director's presence, as to fact or law.

2. Keep Track of Tricks

He may keep count of tricks won and lost.

3. Play as Declarer's Agent

He plays the cards of the dummy as declarer's agent as directed (see Law 45F if dummy suggests a play).

B. Qualified Rights

Dummy may exercise other rights subject to the limitations provided in Law 43.

1. Revoke Inquiries

Dummy may ask declarer (but not a defender) when he has failed to follow suit to a trick whether he has a card of the suit led.

2. Attempt to Prevent Irregularity

He may try to prevent any irregularity by declarer.

3. Draw Attention to Irregularity

He may draw attention to any irregularity, but only after play of the hand is concluded.

LAW 43
DUMMY'S LIMITATIONS

Except as specified in Law 42:

A. Limitations on Dummy

1. General Limitations

(a) Calling the Director

Unless attention has been drawn to an irregularity by another player, dummy should not initiate a call for the Director during play.

(b) Calling Attention to Irregularity

Dummy may not call attention to an irregularity during play.

(c) Participate in or Comment on Play

Dummy must not participate in the play, nor may he communicate anything about the play to declarer.

2. Limitations Carrying Specific Penalty

(a) Exchanging Hands

Dummy may not exchange hands with declarer.

(b) Leave Seat to Watch Declarer

Dummy may not leave his seat to watch declarer's play of the hand.

(c) Look at Defender's Hand

Dummy may not, on his own initiative, look at the face of a card in either defender's hand.

B. Penalties for Violation

1. General Penalties

Dummy is liable to penalty under Law 90 for any violation of the limitations listed in A1 or A2 preceding.

2. Specific Penalties

If dummy, after violation of the limitations listed in A2 preceding:

(a) Warns Declarer on Lead

warns declarer not to lead from the wrong hand, (penalty) either defender may choose the hand from which declarer shall lead.

(b) Asks Declarer about Possible Irregularity

is the first to ask declarer if a play from declarer's hand constitutes a revoke, declarer must substitute a correct card if his play was illegal, and the penalty provisions of Law 64 apply as if the revoke had been established.

3. If dummy after violation of the limitations listed in A2 preceding is the first to draw attention to a defender's irregularity, no penalty shall be imposed. If the defenders benefit directly through their irregularity, the director shall award an adjusted score to both sides to restore equity.

LAW 44
SEQUENCE AND PROCEDURE OF PLAY

A. Lead to a Trick

The player who leads to a trick may play any card in his hand (unless he is subject to restriction after an irregularity committed by his side).

B. Subsequent Plays to a Trick

After the lead, each other player in turn plays a card, and the four cards so played constitute a trick. (For the method of playing cards and arranging tricks see Law 65.)

C. Requirement to Follow Suit

In playing to a trick, each player must follow suit if possible. This obligation takes precedence over all other requirements of these Laws.

D. Inability to Follow Suit

If unable to follow suit, a player may play any card (unless he is subject to restriction after an irregularity committed by his side).

E. Tricks Containing Trumps

A trick containing a trump is won by the player who has contributed to it the highest trump.

F. Tricks Not Containing Trumps

A trick that does not contain a trump is won by the player who has contributed to it the highest card of the suit led.

G. Lead to Tricks Subsequent to First Trick

The player who has won the trick leads to the next trick.

LAW 45
CARD PLAYED

A. Play of Card from a Hand

Each player except dummy plays a card by detaching it from his hand and facing* it on the table immediately before him.

B. Play of Card from Dummy

Declarer plays a card from dummy by naming the card, after which dummy picks up the card and faces it on the table. In playing from dummy's hand declarer may, if necessary, pick up the desired card himself.

C. Compulsory Play of Card

1. Defender's Card

A defender's card held so that it is possible for his partner to see its face must be played to the

current trick (if the defender has already made a legal play to the current trick, see Law 45E).

2. Declarer's Card

Declarer must play a card from his hand held face up, touching or nearly touching the table, or maintained in such a position as to indicate that it has been played.

3. Dummy's Card

A card in the dummy must be played if it has been deliberately touched by declarer except for the purpose of arranging dummy's cards, or of reaching a card above or below the card or cards touched.

4. Named or Designated Card

(a) Play of Named Card

A card must be played if a player names or otherwise designates it as the card he proposes to play.

(b) Correction of Inadvertent Designation

A player may, without penalty, change an inadvertent designation if he does so without pause for thought; but if an opponent has, in turn, played a card that was legal before the change in designation, that opponent may withdraw without penalty the card so played and substitute another (see Law 47E).

5. Penalty Card

A penalty card, major or minor, may have to be played, subject to Law 50.

D. Card Misplayed by Dummy

If dummy places in the played position a card that declarer did not name, the card must be withdrawn if attention is drawn to it before each side has played to the next trick, and a defender may withdraw (without penalty) a card played after the error but before attention was drawn to it; if declarer's RHO changes his play, declarer may withdraw a card he had subsequently played to that trick (see Law 16C2).

E. Fifth Card Played to Trick

1. By a Defender

A fifth card contributed to a trick by a defender becomes a penalty card, subject to Law 50, unless the Director deems that it was led, in which case Law 53 or 56 applies.

2. By Declarer

When declarer contributes a fifth card to a trick from his own hand or dummy, there is no penalty unless the Director deems that it was led, in which case Law 55 applies.

F. Dummy Indicates Card

After dummy's hand is faced, dummy may not touch or indicate any card (except for purpose of arrangement) without instruction from declarer. If he does so, the Director should be summoned forthwith. The Director shall rule whether dummy's act did in fact constitute a suggestion to declarer. When the Director judges that it did, he allows play to continue, reserving his right to assign an adjusted score if the defenders were damaged by the play so suggested.

G. Turning the Trick

No player should turn his card face down until all four players have played to the trick.

The opening lead is first made face down (unless the sponsoring organization directs otherwise).

SECTION TWO
IRREGULARITIES IN PROCEDURE
LAW 46
INCOMPLETE OR ERRONEOUS CALL OF CARD FROM DUMMY

A. Proper Form for Designating Dummy's Card

When calling a card to be played from dummy, declarer should clearly state both the suit and the rank of the desired card.

B. Incomplete or Erroneous Call

In case of an incomplete or erroneous call by declarer of the card to be played from dummy, the following restrictions apply (except when declarer's different intention is incontrovertible):

1. Incomplete Designation of Rank

If declarer, in playing from dummy, calls "high", or words of like import, he is deemed to have called the highest card: in fourth seat he may be deemed to have called for the lowest winning card of the suit indicated; if he directs dummy to win the trick, he is deemed to have called the lowest winning card; if he calls "low", or words of like import, he is deemed to have called the lowest.

2. Designates Suit but Not Rank

If declarer designates a suit but not a rank, he is deemed to have called the lowest card of the suit indicated.

3. Designates Rank but Not Suit

If declarer designates a rank but not a suit:

(a) In Leading

Declarer is deemed to have continued the suit in which dummy won the preceding trick, provided there is a card of the designated rank in that suit.

(b) All Other Cases

In all other cases, declarer must play a card from dummy of the designated rank if he can legally do so; but if there are two or more such cards that can be legally played, declarer must designate which is intended.

4. Designates Card Not in Dummy

If declarer calls a card that is not in dummy, the call is void and declarer may designate any legal card.

5. No Suit or Rank Designated

If declarer indicates a play without designating either a suit or rank (as by saying, ""play anything", or words of like import), either defender may designate the play from dummy.

LAW 47
RETRACTION OF CARD PLAYED

A. To Comply with Penalty

A card once played may be withdrawn to comply with a penalty (but a defender's withdrawn card may become a penalty card, see Law 49).

B. To Correct an Illegal Play

A played card may be withdrawn to correct an illegal or simultaneous play (see Law 58 for simultaneous play; and, for defenders, see Law 49, penalty card).

C. To Change an Inadvertent Designation

A played card may be withdrawn without penalty after a change of designation as permitted by Law 45C4(b).

D. Following Opponent's Change of Play
After an opponent's change of play, a played card may be withdrawn without penalty (but see 62C2) to substitute another card for the one played.

E. Change of Play Based on Misinformation
1. Lead Out of Turn
A lead out of turn may be retracted without penalty if the leader was mistakenly informed by an opponent that it was his turn to lead (LHO should not accept the lead).
2. Retraction of Play
(a) No One Has Subsequently Played
A player may retract the card he has played because of a mistaken explanation of an opponent's call or play and before a corrected explanation, but only if no card was subsequently played to that trick. An opening lead may not be retracted after dummy has faced any card.
(b) One or More Subsequent Plays Made
When it is too late to correct a play, under (a) preceding, Law 40C applies.

F. Illegal Retraction
Except as provided in A through E preceding, a card once played may not be withdrawn.

PART II
PENALTY CARD
LAW 48
EXPOSURE OF DECLARER'S CARDS

A. Declarer Exposes a Card
Declarer is not subject to penalty for exposing a card, and no card of declarer's or dummy's hand ever becomes a penalty card. Declarer is not required to play any card dropped accidentally.

B. Declarer Faces Cards
1. After Opening Lead Out of Turn
When declarer faces his cards after an opening lead out of turn, Law 54 applies.
2. At Any Other Time
When declarer faces his cards at any time other than immediately after an opening lead out of turn, he may be deemed to have made a claim or concession of tricks, and Law 68 then applies.

LAW 49
EXPOSURE OF A DEFENDER'S CARDS

Except in the normal course of play or application of law, when a defender's card is in a position in which his partner could possibly see its face, or when a defender names a card as being in his hand, (penalty) each such card becomes a penalty card (Law 50); but see the footnote to Law 68 when a defender has made a statement concerning an uncompleted trick currently in progress.

LAW 50
DISPOSITION OF PENALTY CARD

A card prematurely exposed (but not led, see Law 57) by a defender is a penalty card unless the Director designates otherwise. The Director shall award an adjusted score, in lieu of the rectifications below, when he deems that Law 72B1 applies.

A. Penalty Card Remains Exposed
A penalty card must be left face up on the table immediately before the player to whom it belongs, until an alternate penalty has been selected.

B. Major or Minor Penalty Card?
A single card below the rank of an honor and exposed inadvertently (as in playing two cards to a trick, or in dropping a card accidentally) becomes a minor penalty card. Any card of honor rank, or any card exposed through deliberate play (as in leading out of turn, or in revoking and then correcting), becomes a major penalty card; when one defender has two or more penalty cards, all such cards become major penalty cards.

C. Disposition of Minor Penalty Card
When a defender has a minor penalty card, he may not play any other card of the same suit below the rank of an honor until he has first played the penalty card (however, he is entitled to play an honor card instead). Offender's partner is not subject to lead penalty, but information gained through seeing the penalty card is extraneous, unauthorized (see Law 16A).

D. Disposition of Major Penalty Card
When a defender has a major penalty card, both the offender and his partner may be subject to restriction, the offender whenever he is to play, the partner when he is to lead.
1. Offender to Play
A major penalty card must be played at the first legal opportunity, whether in leading, following suit, discarding or trumping (the requirement that offender must play the card is authorized information for his partner; however, other information arising from facing of the penalty card is unauthorized for partner). If a defender has two or more penalty cards that can legally be played, declarer designates which is to be played. The obligation to follow suit, or to comply with a lead or play penalty, takes precedence over the obligation to play a major penalty card, but the penalty card must still be left face up on the table and played at the next legal opportunity.
2. Offender's Partner to Lead
When a defender has the lead while his partner has a major penalty card, he may not lead until declarer has stated which of the options below is selected (if the defender leads prematurely, he is subject to penalty under Law 49). Declarer may choose:
(a) Require or Forbid Lead of Suit
to require* the defender to lead the suit of the penalty card, or to prohibit* him from leading that suit for as long as he retains the lead (for two or more penalty cards, see Law 51); if declarer exercises this option, the card is no longer a penalty card and is picked up.
(b) No Lead Restriction
not to require or prohibit a lead, in which case the defender may lead any card; the penalty card remains a penalty card.
* *If the player is unable to lead as required, see Law 59.*

LAW 51
TWO OR MORE PENALTY CARDS
A. Offender to Play

If a defender has two or more penalty cards that can legally be played, declarer designates which is to be played at that turn.

B. Offender's Partner to Lead

1. Penalty Cards in Same Suit
    (a) Declarer Requires Lead of That Suit

    When a defender has two or more penalty cards in one suit, and declarer requires the defender's partner to lead that suit, the cards of that suit are no longer penalty cards and are picked up; the defender may make any legal play to the trick.

    (b) Declarer Prohibits Lead of That Suit

    If the declarer prohibits the lead of that suit, the defender picks up every penalty card in that suit and may make any legal play to the trick.

2. Penalty Cards in More Than One Suit
    (a) Declarer Requires Lead of a Specified Suit

    When a defender has penalty cards in more than one suit, declarer may require* the defender's partner to lead any suit in which the defender has a penalty card (but B1(a) preceding then applies).

    (b) Declarer Prohibits Lead of Specified Suits

    When a defender has penalty cards in more than one suit, declarer may prohibit* the defender's partner from leading one or more of such suits; but the defender then picks up every penalty card in every suit prohibited by declarer and makes any legal play to the trick.

* If the player is unable to lead as required, see Law 59.

LAW 52
FAILURE TO LEAD OR PLAY A PENALTY CARD
A. Defender Fails to Play Penalty Card

When a defender fails to lead or play a penalty card as required by Law 50, he may not, on his own initiative, withdraw any other card he has played.

B. Defender Plays Another Card

1. Play of Card Accepted
    (a) Declarer May Accept Play

    If a defender has led or played another card when required by law to play a penalty card, declarer may accept such lead or play.

    (b) Declarer Must Accept Play

    Declarer must accept such lead or play if he has thereafter played from his own hand or dummy.

    (c) Penalty Card Remains Penalty Card

    If the played card is accepted under either (a) or (b) preceding, the unplayed penalty card remains a penalty card.

2. Play of Card Rejected

    Declarer may require the defender to substitute the penalty card for the card illegally played or led. Every card illegally led or played by the defender in the course of committing the irregularity becomes a major penalty card.

PART III
IRREGULAR LEADS AND PLAYS
SECTION ONE
LEAD OUT OF TURN
LAW 53
LEAD OUT OF TURN ACCEPTED
A. Lead Out of Turn Treated as Correct Lead

Any lead faced out of turn may be treated as a correct lead. It becomes a correct lead if declarer or either defender, as the case may be, accepts it (by making a statement to that effect), or if the player next in rotation plays* to the irregular lead, but see Law 47E1. (If no acceptance statement or play is made, the Director will require that the lead be made from the correct hand.)

B. Wrong Defender Plays Card to Declarer's Irregular Lead

If the defender at the right of the hand from which the lead out of turn was made plays* to the irregular lead, the lead stands and Law 57 applies.

C. Proper Lead Made Subsequent to Irregular Lead

If it was properly the turn to lead of an opponent of the player who led out of turn, that opponent may make his proper lead to the trick of the infraction without his card being deemed played to the irregular lead. When this occurs, the proper lead stands, and all cards played in error to this trick may be withdrawn without penalty. (Law 16C2 applies to a defender.)

* But see C below.

LAW 54
FACED OPENING LEAD OUT OF TURN
When an opening lead is faced out of turn, and offender's partner leads face down, the director requires the face down lead to be retracted, and the following sections apply.

A. Declarer Spreads His Hand

After a faced opening lead out of turn, declarer may spread his hand; he becomes dummy, and dummy becomes declarer. If declarer begins to spread his hand, and in doing so exposes one or more cards, he must spread his entire hand.

B. Declarer Accepts Lead

When a defender faces the opening lead out of turn declarer may accept the irregular lead as provided in Law 53, and dummy is spread in accordance with Law 41.

1. Declarer Plays Second Card

    The second card to the trick is played from declarer's hand.

2. Dummy Has Played Second Card

    If declarer plays the second card to the trick from dummy, dummy's card may not be withdrawn except to correct a revoke.

C. Declarer Must Accept Lead

If declarer could have seen any of dummy's cards (except cards that dummy may have exposed during the auction and that were subject to Law 24), he must accept the lead.

D. Declarer Refuses Opening Lead
   When declarer requires the defender to retract his faced opening lead out of turn, Law 56 applies.

LAW 55
DECLARER'S LEAD OUT OF TURN

A. Declarer's Lead Accepted
   If declarer has led out of turn from his or dummy's hand, either defender may accept the lead as provided in Law 53, or require its retraction (after misinformation, see Law 47E1).

B. Declarer Required to Retract Lead
   1. Defender's Turn to Lead
      If declarer has led from his or dummy's hand when it was a defender's turn to lead, and if either defender requires him to retract such lead, declarer restores the card led in error to the proper hand without penalty.
   2. Lead in Declarer's Hand or Dummy's
      If declarer has led from the wrong hand when it was his turn to lead from his hand or dummy's, and if either defender requires him to retract the lead, he withdraws the card led in error. He must lead from the correct hand.

C. Declarer Might Obtain Information
   When declarer adopts a line of play that could have been based on information obtained through the infraction, the Director may award an adjusted score.

LAW 56
DEFENDER'S LEAD OUT OF TURN
When declarer requires a defender to retract his faced lead out of turn, the card illegally led becomes a major penalty card, and Law 50D applies.

SECTION TWO
OTHER IRREGULAR LEADS AND PLAYS
LAW 57
PREMATURE LEAD OR PLAY BY DEFENDER

A. Premature Play or Lead to Next Trick
   When a defender leads to the next trick before his partner has played to the current trick, or plays out of turn before his partner has played, (penalty) the card so led or played becomes a penalty card, and declarer selects one of the following options. He may:
   1. Highest Card
      require offender's partner to play the highest card he holds of the suit led, or
   2. Lowest Card
      require offender's partner to play the lowest card he holds of the suit led, or
   3. Card of Another Suit
      forbid offender's partner to play a card of another suit specified by declarer.

B. Offender's Partner Cannot Comply with Penalty
   When offender's partner is unable to comply with the penalty selected by declarer, he may play any card, as provided in Law 59.

C. Declarer Has Played from Both Hands before Irregularity
   A defender is not subject to penalty for playing before his partner if declarer has played from both

hands, or if dummy has played a card or has illegally suggested that it be played. A singleton in dummy, or one of cards adjacent in rank of the same suit, is not considered to be automatically played.

LAW 58
SIMULTANEOUS LEADS OR PLAYS

A. Simultaneous Plays by Two Players
   A lead or play made simultaneously with another player's legal lead or play is deemed to be subsequent to it.

B. Simultaneous Cards from One Hand
   If a player leads or plays two or more cards simultaneously:
   1. One Card Visible
      If only one card is visible, that card is played; all other cards are picked up without penalty.
   2. More Cards Visible
      If more than one card is visible, the player designates the card he proposes to play; when he is a defender, each other card exposed becomes a penalty card (see Law 50).
   3. After Visible Card Withdrawn
      After a player withdraws a visible card, an opponent who subsequently played to that card may withdraw his play and substitute another without penalty (see Law 16C).
   4. Error Not Discovered
      If the simultaneous play remains undiscovered until both sides have played to the next trick, Law 67 applies.

LAW 59
INABILITY TO LEAD OR PLAY AS REQUIRED
A player may play any otherwise legal card if he is unable to lead or play as required to comply with a penalty, whether because he holds no card of the required suit, or because he has only cards of a suit he is prohibited from leading, or because he is obliged to follow suit.

LAW 60
PLAY AFTER AN ILLEGAL PLAY

A. Play of Card after Irregularity
   1. Forfeiture of Right to Penalize
      A play by a member of the non-offending side after his RHO has led or played out of turn or prematurely, and before a penalty has been assessed, forfeits the right to penalize that offense.
   2. Irregularity Legalized
      Once the right to penalize has been forfeited, the illegal play is treated as though it were in turn (but Law 53C applies to the player whose turn it was).
   3. Other Penalty Obligations Remain
      If the offending side has a previous obligation to play a penalty card, or to comply with a lead or play penalty, the obligation remains at future turns.

B. Defender Plays before Required Lead by Declarer
   When a defender plays a card after declarer has been required to retract his lead out of turn from either hand, but before declarer has led from the correct hand, the defender's card becomes a penalty card (Law 50).

C. Play by Offending Side before Assessment of Penalty

A play by a member of the offending side before a penalty has been assessed does not affect the rights of the opponents, and may itself be subject to penalty.

SECTION THREE
THE REVOKE
LAW 61
FAILURE TO FOLLOW SUIT—
INQUIRIES CONCERNING A REVOKE

A. Definition of Revoke

Failure to follow suit in accordance with Law 44 or failure to lead or play, when able, a card or suit required by law or specified by an opponent in accordance with an agreed penalty, constitutes a revoke (but see Law 59 when unable to comply).

B. Right to Inquire about a Possible Revoke

Declarer may ask a defender who has failed to follow suit whether he has a card of the suit led (but a claim of revoke does not automatically warrant inspection of quitted tricks — see Law 66C). Dummy may ask declarer (but see Law 43B2(b)). Defenders may ask declarer but, unless the zonal organization so authorizes, not one another.

NOTE: *The ACBL Board of Directors under the authority granted in the revised Law 61B, has ruled that in ACBL sanctioned events, a defender may inquire of his partner whether he has a card of the suit led.*

LAW 62
CORRECTION OF A REVOKE

A. Revoke Must Be Corrected

A player must correct his revoke if he becomes aware of the irregularity before it becomes established.

B. Correcting a Revoke

To correct a revoke, the offender withdraws the card he played in revoking and follows suit with any card.

1. Defender's Card

A card so withdrawn becomes a penalty card (Law 50) if it was played from a defender's unfaced hand.

2. Declarer's or Dummy's Card, Defender's Faced Card

The card may be replaced without penalty if it was played from declarer's or dummy's hand*, or if it was a defender's faced card.

C. Subsequent Cards Played to Trick

1. By Non-offending Side

Each member of the non-offending side may, without penalty, withdraw any card he may have played after the revoke but before attention was drawn to it (see Law 16C).

2. By Partner of Offender

After a non-offender so withdraws a card, the hand of the offending side next in rotation may withdraw its played card, which becomes a penalty card if the player is a defender (see Law 16C).

D. Revoke on Trick Twelve

1. Must Be Corrected

On the twelfth trick, a revoke, even if established,

must be corrected if discovered before all four hands have been returned to the board.

2. Offender's Partner Had Not Played to Trick Twelve

If a revoke by a defender occurred before it was the turn of his partner to play to the twelfth trick, and if offender's partner has cards of two suits, (penalty) offender's partner may not choose the play that could possibly have been suggested by seeing the revoke card.

* *Subject to Law 43B2(b), when dummy has forfeited his rights. A claim of revoke does not warrant inspection of quitted tricks except as permitted in Law 66C.*

LAW 63
ESTABLISHMENT OF A REVOKE

A. Revoke Becomes Established

A revoke becomes established:

1. Offending Side Leads or Plays to Next Trick

when the offender or his partner leads or plays to the following trick (any such play, legal or illegal, establishes the revoke).

2. A Member of Offending Side Indicates a Lead or Play

when the offender or his partner names or otherwise designates a card to be played to the following trick.

3. Member of Offending Side Makes a Claim or Concession

when a member of the offending side makes or acquiesces in a claim or concession of tricks orally or by facing his hand (or in any other fashion).

B. Attention Is Illegally Drawn

When there has been a violation of Law 61B, the revoker must substitute a legal card and the penalty provisions of Law 64 apply as if the revoke had been established.

C. Revoke May Not Be Corrected

Once a revoke is established, it may no longer be corrected (except as provided in Law 62D for a revoke on the twelfth trick), and the trick on which the revoke occurred stands as played (but see Law 43B2(b)).

LAW 64
PROCEDURE AFTER ESTABLISHMENT OF A REVOKE

A. Penalty Assessed

When a revoke is established:

1. Offending Player Won Revoke Trick

and the trick on which the revoke occurred was won by the offending player, (penalty) after play ceases, the trick on which the revoke occurred plus one of any subsequent tricks won by the offending side are transferred to the non-offending side.

2. Offending Player Did Not Win Revoke Trick

and the trick on which the revoke occurred was not won by the offending player, then, if the offending side won that or any subsequent trick, (penalty) after play ceases, one trick is transferred to the non-offending side; also, if an additional trick was subsequently won by the offending player with a card that he could legally have played to the revoke trick, one such trick is transferred to the non-offending side.

B. No Penalty Assessed
The penalty for an established revoke does not apply:
1. Offending Side Fails to Win Revoke Trick or Subsequent Trick
if the offending side did not win either the revoke trick or any subsequent trick.
2. Second Revoke in Same Suit by Offender
to a subsequent revoke in the same suit by the same player.
3. Revoke by Failure to Play a Faced Card
if the revoke was made in failing to play any card faced on the table or belonging to a hand faced on the table, including a card from dummy's hand.
4. After Non-offending Side Calls to Next Deal
if attention was first drawn to the revoke after a member of the non-offending side has made a call on the subsequent deal.
5. After Round Has Ended
if attention was first drawn to the revoke after the round has ended.
6. Revoke on Twelfth Trick
to a revoke on the twelfth trick.

C. Director Responsible for Equity
When, after any established revoke, including those not subject to penalty, the Director deems that the non-offending side is insufficiently compensated by this Law for the damage caused, he shall assign an adjusted score.

PART IV
TRICKS
LAW 65
ARRANGEMENT OF TRICKS
A. Completed Trick
When four cards have been played to a trick, each player turns his own card face down near him on the table.

B. Keeping Track of the Ownership of Tricks
1. Tricks Won
If the player's side has won the trick, the card is pointed lengthwise toward his partner.
2. Tricks Lost
If the opponents have won the trick, the card is pointed lengthwise toward the opponents.

C. Orderliness
Each player arranges his own cards in an orderly overlapping row in the sequence played, so as to permit review of the play after its completion, if necessary to determine the number of tricks won by each side or the order in which the cards were played.

D. Agreement on Results of Play
A player should not disturb the order of his played cards until agreement has been reached on the number of tricks won. A player who fails to comply with the provisions of this Law jeopardizes his right to claim ownership of doubtful tricks or to claim a revoke.

LAW 66
INSPECTION OF TRICKS
A. Current Trick
So long as his side has not led or played to the next trick, declarer or either defender may, until he has turned his own card face down on the table, require that all cards just played to the trick be faced.

B. Own Last Card
Until a card is led to the next trick, declarer or either defender may inspect, but not expose, his own last card played.

C. Quitted Tricks
Thereafter, until play ceases, quitted tricks may not be inspected (except at the Director's specific instruction; for example, to verify a claim of a revoke).

D. After the Conclusion of Play
After play ceases, the played and unplayed cards may be inspected to settle a claim of a revoke, or of the number of tricks won or lost; but no player should handle cards other than his own. If, after such a claim has been made, a player mixes his cards in such a manner that the Director can no longer ascertain the facts, the Director shall rule in favor of the other side.

LAW 67
DEFECTIVE TRICK
A. Before Both Sides Play to Next Trick
When a player has omitted to play to a trick, or has played too many cards to a trick, the error must be rectified if attention is drawn to the irregularity before a player on each side has played to the following trick.
1. Player Failed to Play Card
To rectify omission to play to a trick, the offender supplies a card he can legally play.
2. Player Contributed Too Many Cards
To rectify the play of too many cards to a trick, Law 45E (Fifth Card Played to a Trick) or Law 58B (Simultaneous Cards from One Hand) shall be applied.

B. After Both Sides Play to Next Trick
After both sides have played to the following trick, when attention is drawn to a defective trick or when the Director determines that there had been a defective trick (from the fact that one player has too few or too many cards in his hand, and a correspondingly incorrect number of played cards), the Director establishes which trick was defective. To rectify the number of cards, the Director should proceed as follows.
1. Offender Has Too Many Cards
When the offender has failed to play a card to the defective trick, the Director shall require him forth- with to face a card and to place it appropriately among his played cards (this card does not affect ownership of the trick); if
(a) Offender Has Card of Suit Led
the offender has a card of the suit led to the defective trick, he must choose such a card to place among his played cards, and there is no penalty.
(b) Offender Has No Card of Suit Led
the offender has no card of the suit led to the defective trick, he chooses any card to place among his played cards, and (penalty) he is deemed to have revoked on the defective trick — he may be subject to the one-trick penalty of Law 64.

2. Offender Has Too Few Cards
When the offender has played more than one card to the defective trick, the Director inspects the played cards and requires the offender to restore to his hand all extra cards*, leaving among the played cards the one faced in playing to the defective trick (if the Director is unable to determine which card was faced, the offender leaves the highest of the cards that he could legally have played to the trick). A restored card is deemed to have belonged continuously to the offender's hand, and a failure to have played it to an earlier trick may constitute a revoke.

*The Director should avoid, when possible, exposing a defender's played cards, but if an extra card to be restored to a defender's hand has been exposed, it becomes a penalty card (see Law 50).

PART V
CLAIMS AND CONCESSIONS
LAW 68
CLAIM OR CONCESSION OF TRICKS
For a statement or action to constitute a claim or concession of tricks under these Laws, it must refer to tricks other than one currently in progress*. If it does refer to subsequent tricks:

A. Claim Defined
Any statement to the effect that a contestant will win a specific number of tricks is a claim of those tricks. A contestant also claims when he suggests that play be curtailed, or when he shows his cards (unless he demonstrably did not intend to claim).

B. Concession Defined
Any statement to the effect that a contestant will lose a specific number of tricks is a concession of those tricks; a claim of some number of tricks is a concession of the remainder, if any. A player concedes all the remaining tricks when he abandons his hand. Regardless of the foregoing, if a defender attempts to concede one or more tricks and his partner immediately objects, no concession has occurred; Law 16, Unauthorized Information, may apply, so the Director should be summoned forthwith.

C. Clarification Required for Claim
A claim should be accompanied at once by a statement of clarification as to the order in which cards will be played, the line of play or defense through which the claimer proposes to win the tricks claimed.

D. Play Ceases
After any claim or concession, play ceases. All play subsequent to a claim or concession shall be voided by the Director. If the claim or concession is acquiesced in, Law 69 applies; if it is disputed by any player (dummy included), the Director must be summoned immediately to apply Law 70 or Law 71, and no action may be taken pending the Director's arrival.

*If the statement or action pertains only to the winning or losing of an uncompleted trick currently in progress, play proceeds regularly; cards exposed or revealed by a defender do not become penalty cards, but Law 16, Unauthorized Information, may apply, and see Law 57A, Premature Play.

LAW 69
ACQUIESCENCE IN CLAIM OR CONCESSION
A. When Acquiescence Occurs
Acquiescence occurs when a contestant assents to an opponent's claim or concession, and raises no objection to it before his side makes a call on a subsequent board, or before the round ends. The board is scored as though the tricks claimed or conceded had been won or lost in play.

B. Acquiescence in Claim Withdrawn
Within the correction period established in accordance with Law 79C, a contestant may withdraw acquiescence in an opponent's claim, but only if he has acquiesced in the loss of a trick his side has actually won, or in the loss of trick that could not, in the Director's judgment, be lost by any normal* play of the remaining cards. The board is rescored with such trick awarded to the acquiescing side.

*For the purposes of Laws 69, 70 and 71, "normal" includes play that would be careless or inferior for the class of player involved, but not irrational.

LAW 70
CONTESTED CLAIMS
A. General Objective
In ruling on a contested claim, the Director adjudicates the result of the board as equitably as possible to both sides, but any doubtful points shall be resolved against the claimer. The Director proceeds as follows.

B. Clarification Statement Repeated
1. Require Claimer to Repeat Statement
The Director requires claimer to repeat the clarification statement he made at the time of his claim.
2. Require All Hands to Be Faced
Next, the Director requires all players to put their remaining cards face up on the table.
3. Hear Objections
The Director then hears the opponents' objections to the claim.

C. There Is an Outstanding Trump
When a trump remains in one of the opponents' hands, the Director shall award a trick or tricks to the opponents if:
1. Failed to Mention Trump
claimer made no statement about that trump, and
2. Was Probably Unaware of Trump
it is at all likely that claimer at the time of his claim was unaware that a trump remained in an opponent's hand, and
3. Could Lose a Trick to the Trump
a trick could be lost to that trump by any normal* play.

D. Claimer Proposes New Line of Play
The Director shall not accept from claimer any successful line of play not embraced in the original clarification statement if there is an alternative normal* line of play that would be less successful.

E. Unstated Line of Play (Finesse or Drop)
The Director shall not accept from claimer any unstated line of play the success of which depends upon

finding one opponent rather than the other with a particular card, unless an opponent failed to follow to the suit of that card before the claim was made, or would subsequently fail to follow to that suit on any normal* line of play; or unless failure to adopt this line of play would be irrational.

* *For the purposes of Laws 69, 70 and 71, "normal" includes play that would be careless or inferior for the class of player involved, but not irrational.*

LAW 71
CONCESSION CANCELED

A concession must stand, once made, except that within the correction period established in accordance with Law 79C, the Director shall cancel a concession:

A. Trick Cannot Be Lost

if a player has conceded a trick his side had, in fact, won, or a trick his side could not have lost by any legal play of the remaining cards.

B. Contract Already Fulfilled or Defeated

if declarer has conceded defeat of a contract he had already fulfilled, or a defender has conceded fulfillment of a contract his side had already defeated.

C. Implausible Concession

if a player has conceded a trick that cannot be lost by any normal* play of the remaining cards. Until the conceding side makes a call on a subsequent board, or until the round ends, the Director shall cancel the concession of a trick that could not have been lost by any normal* play of the remaining cards.

* *For the purposes of Laws 69, 70 and 71, "normal" includes play that would be careless or inferior for the class of player involved, but not irrational.*

CHAPTER VII
Proprieties
LAW 72
GENERAL PRINCIPLES

A. Observance of Laws

1. General Obligation on Contestants

Duplicate bridge tournaments should be played in strict accordance with the Laws.

2. Scoring of Tricks Won

A player must not knowingly accept either the score for a trick that his side did not win or the concession of a trick that his opponents could not lose.

3. Waiving of Penalties

In duplicate tournaments a player may not, on his own initiative, waive a penalty for an opponent's infraction, even if he feels that he has not been damaged (but he may ask the Director to do so — see Law 81C8).

4. Non-offenders' Exercise of Legal Options

When these Laws provide the innocent side with an option after an irregularity committed by an opponent, it is appropriate to select that action most advantageous.

5. Offenders' Options

Subject to Law 16C2, after the offending side has paid the prescribed penalty for an inadvertent infraction, it is appropriate for the offenders to make any call or play advantageous to their side, even though they thereby appear to profit through their own infraction.

6. Responsibility for Enforcement of Laws

The responsibility for penalizing irregularities and redressing damage rests solely upon the Director and these Laws, not upon the players themselves.

B. Infraction of Law

1. Adjusted Score

Whenever the Director deems that an offender could have known at the time of his irregularity that the irregularity would be likely to damage the non-offending side, he shall require the auction and play to continue, afterwards awarding an adjusted score if he considers that the offending side gained an advantage through the irregularity.

2. Intentional

A player must not infringe a law intentionally, even if there is a prescribed penalty he is willing to pay.

3. Inadvertent Infraction

There is no obligation to draw attention to an inadvertent infraction of law committed by one's own side (but see footnote to Law 75 for a mistaken explanation).

4. Concealing an Infraction

A player may not attempt to conceal an inadvertent infraction, as by committing a second revoke, concealing a card involved in a revoke or mixing the cards prematurely.

LAW 73
COMMUNICATION

A. Proper Communication between Partners

1. How Effected

Communication between partners during the auction and play shall be effected only by means of the calls and plays themselves.

2. Correct Manner for Calls and Plays

Calls and plays should be made without special emphasis, mannerism or inflection, and without undue hesitation or haste (however, sponsoring organizations may require mandatory pauses, as on the first round of auction, or after a skip-bid warning, or on the first trick).

B. Inappropriate Communication Between Partners

1. Gratuitous Information

Partners shall not communicate through the manner in which calls or plays are made, through extraneous remarks or gestures, through questions asked or not asked of the opponents or through alerts and explanations given or not given to them.

2. Prearranged Communication

The gravest possible offense is for a partnership to exchange information through prearranged methods of communication other than those sanctioned by these Laws. A guilty partnership risks expulsion.

C. Player Receives Unauthorized Information from Partner

When a player has available to him unauthorized information from his partner, as from a remark, ques-

tion, explanation, gesture, mannerism, special emphasis, inflection, haste or hesitation, he must carefully avoid taking any advantage that might accrue to his side.

D. Variations in Tempo or Manner
  1. Inadvertent Variations
     It is desirable, though not always required, for players to maintain steady tempo and unvarying manner. However, players should be particularly careful in positions in which variations may work to the benefit of their side. Otherwise, inadvertently to vary the tempo or manner in which a call or play is made does not in itself constitute a violation of propriety, but inferences from such variation may appropriately be drawn only by an opponent, and at his own risk.
  2. Intentional Variations
     A player may not attempt to mislead an opponent by means of remark or gesture, through the haste or hesitancy of a call or play (as in hesitating before playing a singleton), or by the manner in which the call or play is made.

E. Deception
   A player may appropriately attempt to deceive an opponent through a call or play (so long as the deception is not protected by concealed partnership understanding or experience). It is entirely appropriate to avoid giving information to the opponents by making all calls and plays in unvarying tempo and manner.

F. Violation of Proprieties
   When a violation of the Proprieties described in this law results in damage to an innocent opponent,
  1. Player Acts on Unauthorized Information
     if the Director determines that a player chose from among logical alternative actions one that could demonstrably have been suggested over another by his partner's remark, manner, tempo, or the like, he shall award an adjusted score (see Law 16).
  2. Player Injured by Illegal Deception
     if the Director determines that an innocent player has drawn a false inference from a remark, manner, tempo, or the like, of an opponent who has no demonstrable bridge reason for the action, and who could have known, at the time of the action, that the action could work to his benefit, the Director shall award an adjusted score (see Law 12C),

LAW 74
CONDUCT AND ETIQUETTE
A. Proper Attitude
 1. Courtesy
    A player should maintain a courteous attitude at all times .
  2. Etiquette of Word and Action
     A player should carefully avoid any remark or action that might cause annoyance or embarrassment to another player or might interfere with the enjoyment of the game.
  3. Conformity to Correct Procedure
     Every player should follow uniform and correct procedure in calling and playing.

B. Etiquette
   As a matter of courtesy a player should refrain from:
   1. paying insufficient attention to the game.
   2. making gratuitous comments during the auction and play.
   3. detaching a card before it is his turn to play.
   4. prolonging play unnecessarily (as in playing on although he knows that all the tricks are surely his) for the purpose of disconcerting an opponent.
   5. summoning and addressing the Director in a manner discourteous to him or to other contestants.

C. Violations of Procedure
   The following are considered violations of procedure:
   1. using different designations for the same call.
   2. indicating approval or disapproval of a call or play.
   3. indicating the expectation or intention of winning or losing a trick that has not been completed.
   4. commenting or acting during the auction or play so as to call attention to a significant occurrence, or to the number of tricks still required for success.
   5. looking intently at any other player during the auction and play, or at another player's hand as for the purpose of seeing his cards or of observing the place from which he draws a card (but it is appropriate to act on information acquired by inadvertently seeing an opponent's card*).
   6. showing an obvious lack of further interest in a deal (as by folding one's cards).
   7. varying the normal tempo of bidding or play for the purpose of disconcerting an opponent.
   8. leaving the table needlessly before the round is called.

*See Law 73D2 when a player may have shown his cards intentionally.

LAW 75
PARTNERSHIP AGREEMENTS
A. Special Partnership Agreements
   Special partnership agreements, whether explicit or implicit, must be fully and freely available to the opponents (see Law 40). Information conveyed to partner through such agreements must arise from the calls, plays and conditions of the current deal.

B. Violations of Partnership Agreements
   A player may violate an announced partnership agreement, so long as his partner is unaware of the violation (but habitual violations within a partnership may create implicit agreements, which must be disclosed). No player has the obligation to disclose to the opponents that he has violated an announced agreement and if the opponents are subsequently damaged, as through drawing a false inference from such violation, they are not entitled to redress.

C. Answering Questions on Partnership Agreements
   When explaining the significance of partner's call or play in reply to an opponent's inquiry (see Law 20), a player shall disclose all special information conveyed to him through partnership agreement or

partnership experience, but he need not disclose inferences drawn from his general knowledge and experience.

D. Correcting Errors in Explanation
1. Explainer Notices Own Error
   If a player subsequently realizes that his own explanation was erroneous or incomplete, he must immediately call the Director (who will apply Law 21 or Law 40C).
2. Error Noticed by Explainer's Partner
   A player whose partner has given a mistaken explanation may not correct the error before the final pass, nor may he indicate in any manner that a mistake has been made; a defender may not correct the error until play ends. After calling the Director at the earliest legal opportunity (after the final pass, if he is to be declarer or dummy, after play ends, if he is to be a defender), the player must inform the opponents that, in his opinion, his partner's explanation was erroneous.*

* *Two examples may clarify responsibilities of the players (and the Director) after a misleading explanation has been given to the opponents. In both examples following, North has opened 1NT and South, who holds a weak hand with long diamonds, has bid 2♦, intending to sign off; North explains, however, in answer to West's inquiry, that South's bid is strong and artificial, asking for major suits.*

Example 1 — Mistaken Explanation
The actual partnership agreement is that 2♦ is a natural signoff; the mistake was in North's explanation. This explanation is an infraction of Law, since East-West are entitled to an accurate description of the North-South agreement (when this infraction results in damage to East-West, the Director shall award an adjusted score). If North subsequently becomes aware of his mistake, he must immediately notify the Director. South must do nothing to correct the mistaken explanation while the auction continues; after the final pass, South, if he is to be declarer or dummy, should call the Director and must volunteer a correction of the explanation. If South becomes a defender, he calls the Director and corrects the explanation when play ends.

Example 2 — Mistaken Bid
*The partnership agreement is as explained — 2♦ is strong and artificial; the mistake was in South's bid. Here there is no infraction of Law, since East-West did receive an accurate description of the North-South agreement; they have no claim to an accurate description of the North-South hands.
(Regardless of damage, the Director shall allow the result to stand; but the Director is to presume Mistaken Explanation, rather than Mistaken Bid, in the absence of evidence to the contrary.) South must not correct North's explanation (or notify the Director) immediately, and he has no responsibility to do so subsequently.
In both examples, South, having heard North's explanation, knows that his own 2♦ bid has been misinterpreted. This knowledge is "unauthorized information" (see Law 16A), so South must be careful not to base subsequent actions on this information (if he does, the Director shall award an adjusted score). For instance, if North rebids*

two notrump, South has the unauthorized information that this bid merely denies a four-card holding in either major suit; but South's responsibility is to act as though North had made a strong game try opposite a weak response, showing maximum values.

LAW 76
SPECTATORS
A. Conduct During Bidding or Play
1. One Hand Only
   A spectator should not look at the hand of more than one player, except by permission.
2. Personal Reaction
   A spectator must not display any reaction to the bidding or play while a deal is in progress.
3. Mannerisms or Remarks
   During the round, a spectator must refrain from mannerisms or remarks of any kind (including conversation with a player).
4. Consideration for Players
   A spectator must not in any way disturb a player.

B. Spectator Participation
   A spectator may not call attention to any irregularity or mistake, nor speak on any question of fact or law except by request of the Director.

CHAPTER VIII
The Score
LAW 77
DUPLICATE BRIDGE SCORING TABLE

TRICK SCORE
Scored by declarer's side if the contract is fulfilled.

IF TRUMPS ARE:	♣	♦	♥	♠
For each odd trick bid and made				
Undoubled	20	20	30	30
Doubled	40	40	60	60
Redoubled	80	80	120	120

AT A NOTRUMP CONTRACT			
	Undbld	Dbld	Redbld
For first odd trick bid and made	40	80	160
For each additional odd trick	30	60	120

A trick score of 100 points or more, made on one board, is GAME. A trick score of less than 100 points is a PARTSCORE.

PREMIUM SCORE
Scored by declarer's side

SLAMS

	Not Vul.	Vul.
For making a slam		
Small Slam (12 tricks) bid and made	500	750
Grand Slam (all 13 tricks) bid and made	1000	1500

OVERTRICKS

	Not Vul.	Vul.
For each OVERTRICK		
(tricks made in excess of contract)		
Undbld	Trick Value	Trick Value
Doubled	100	200
Redoubled	200	400

PREMIUMS FOR GAME, PARTSCORE, FULFILLING CONTRACT

For making GAME vulnerable	500
For making GAME, not vulnerable	300
For making any PARTSCORE	50
For making any doubled, but not redoubled contract	50
For making any redoubled contract	100

UNDERTRICK PENALTIES
Scored by declarer's opponents if the contract is not fulfilled

UNDERTRICKS
Tricks by which declarer falls short of the contract

	Not Vulnerable			Vulnerable		
	Undbld	Dbld	Rdbld	Undbld	Dbld	Rdbld
For first undertrick	50	100	200	100	200	400
For each additional undertrick	50	200	400	100	300	600
Bonus for the fourth and each subsequent undertrick	0	100	200	0	0	0

LAW 78
METHODS OF SCORING
A. Matchpoint Scoring

In matchpoint scoring each contestant is awarded, for scores made by different contestants who have played the same board and whose scores are compared with his, two scoring units (matchpoints or half matchpoints) for each score inferior to his, one scoring unit for each score equal to his, and zero scoring units for each score superior to his.

B. International Matchpoint Scoring

In international matchpoint scoring, on each board the total point difference between the two scores compared is converted into IMPs according to the following scale.

Difference in points	IMPs	Difference in points	IMPs	Difference in points	IMPs
20–40	1	370–420	9	1500–1740	17
50–80	2	430–490	10	1750–1990	18
90–120	3	500–590	11	2000–2240	19
130–160	4	600–740	12	2250–2490	20
170–210	5	750–890	13	2500–2990	21
220–260	6	900–1090	14	3000–3490	22
270–310	7	1100–1290	15	3500–3990	23
320–360	8	1300–1490	16	4000 & upward	24

C. Total Point Scoring

In total point scoring, the net total point score of all boards played is the score for each contestant.

D. Special Scoring Methods

Special scoring methods are permissible, if approved by the sponsoring organization. In advance of any contest the sponsoring organization should publish conditions of contest detailing conditions of entry, methods of scoring, determination of winners, breaking of ties, and the like.

LAW 79
TRICKS WON
A. Agreement on Tricks Won

The number of tricks won shall be agreed upon before all four hands have been returned to the board.

B. Disagreement on Tricks Won

If a subsequent disagreement arises, the Director must be called. No increase in score need be granted unless the Director is called before the round ends as specified in Law 8 (but Law 69 or Law 71 may supersede this provision when there has been an acquiescence or a concession).

C. Error in Score

An error in computing or tabulating the agreed-upon score, whether made by a player or scorer, may be corrected until the expiration of the period specified by the sponsoring organization. Unless the sponsoring organization specifies a later* time, this correction period expires 30 minutes after the official score has been made available for inspection.

* An earlier time maybe specified when required by the special nature of a contest.

CHAPTER IX
Tournament Sponsorship
LAW 80
SPONSORING ORGANIZATION

A sponsoring organization conducting an event under these Laws has the following duties and powers:

A. Tournament Director

to appoint the tournament Director. If there is no tournament Director, the players should designate one of their own number to perform his functions.

B. Advance Arrangements

to make advance arrangements for the tournament, including playing quarters, accommodations and equipment.

C. Session Times

to establish the date and time of each session.

D. Conditions of Entry

to establish the conditions of entry.

E. Special Conditions

to establish special conditions for bidding and play (such as written bidding, bidding boxes, screens — penalty provisions for actions not transmitted across a screen may be suspended).

F. Supplementary Regulations

to publish or announce regulations supplementary to, but not in conflict with, these Laws.

G. Appeals

To make suitable arrangements for appeals to be heard.

CHAPTER X

Tournament Director
SECTION ONE
RESPONSIBILITIES
LAW 81
DUTIES AND POWERS
A. Official Status

The Director is the official representative of the sponsoring organization.

B. Restrictions and Responsibilities
1. Technical Management

The Director is responsible for the technical management of the tournament.
2. Observance of Laws and Regulations

The Director is bound by these Laws and by supplementary regulations announced by the sponsoring organization.

C. Director's Duties and Powers

The Director's duties and powers normally include the following:

1. Assistants

   to appoint assistants, as required, to perform his duties

2. Entries

   to accept and list entries.

3. Conditions of Play

   to establish suitable conditions of play and to announce them to the contestants.

4. Discipline

   to maintain discipline and to insure the orderly progress of the game.

5. Law

   to administer and interpret these Laws and to advise the players of their rights and responsibilities thereunder.

6. Errors

   to rectify an error or irregularity of which he becomes aware in any manner, within the correction period established in accordance with Law 79C.

7. Penalties

   to assess penalties when applicable.

8. Waiver of Penalties

   to waive penalties for cause, at his discretion, upon the request of the non-offending side.

9. Disputes

   to adjust disputes; to refer a matter to the appropriate committee.

10. Scores

    to collect scores and tabulate results.

11. Reports

    to report results to the sponsoring organization for official record.

D. Delegation of Duties

The Director may delegate any of the duties listed in"C" to assistants, but he is not thereby relieved of responsibility for their correct performance.

LAW 82
RECTIFICATION OF ERRORS OF PROCEDURE

A. Director's Duty

It is the duty of the Director to rectify errors of procedure and to maintain the progress of the game in a manner that is not contrary to these Laws.

B. Rectification of Error

To rectify an error in procedure the Director may:

1. Award of Adjusted Score

   award an adjusted score as permitted by these Laws.

2. Specify Time of Play

   require or postpone the play of a board.

C. Director's Error

If the Director has given a ruling that he or the Chief Director subsequently determines to be incorrect, and if no rectification will allow the board to be scored normally, he shall award an adjusted score, considering both sides as non-offending for that purpose.

LAW 83
NOTIFICATION OF THE RIGHT TO APPEAL

If the Director believes that a review of his decision on a point of fact or exercise of his discretionary power might be in order (as when he awards an adjusted score under Law 12), he shall advise a contestant of his right to appeal or may refer the matter to an appropriate committee.

SECTION TWO
RULINGS
LAW 84
RULINGS ON AGREED FACTS

When the Director is called to rule on a point of law or regulation in which the facts are agreed upon, he shall rule as follows:

A. No Penalty

If no penalty is prescribed by law, and there is no occasion for him to exercise his discretionary powers, he directs the players to proceed with the auction or play.

B. Penalty under Law

If a case is clearly covered by a Law that specifies a penalty for the irregularity, he assesses that penalty and sees that it is paid.

C. Player's Option

If a Law gives a player a choice among penalties, the Director explains the options and sees that a penalty is selected and paid.

D. Director's Option

If a Law gives the Director a choice between a specified penalty and the award of an adjusted score, he attempts to restore equity, resolving any doubtful point in favor of the non-offending side.

E. Discretionary Penalty

If an irregularity has occurred for which no penalty is provided by law, the Director awards an adjusted score if there is even a reasonable possibility that the non-offending side was damaged, notifying the offending side of its right to appeal (see Law 81C9).

LAW 85
RULINGS ON DISPUTED FACTS

When the Director is called upon to rule on a point of law or regulation in which the facts are not agreed upon, he shall proceed as follows:

A. Director's Assessment

If the Director is satisfied that he has ascertained the facts, he rules as in Law 84.

B. Facts Not Determined

If the Director is unable to determine the facts to his satisfaction, he shall make a ruling that will permit play to continue, and notify the players of their right to appeal.

SECTION THREE
CORRECTION OF IRREGULARITIES
LAW 86
IN TEAM PLAY

A. Average Score at IMP Play

When the Director chooses to award an artificial adjusted score of average plus or average minus in IMP

play, that score is plus 3 IMPs or minus 3 IMPs respectively.

B. Non-balancing Adjustments, Knockout Play
When the Director assigns non-balancing adjusted scores (see Law 12C) in knockout play, each contestant's score on the board is calculated separately. The average of the two scores is then assigned to both contestants.

C. Substitute Board
The Director shall not exercise his Law 6 authority to order one board redealt when the final result of a match without that board could be known to a contestant. Instead, he awards an adjusted score.

LAW 87
FOULED BOARD
A. Definition
A board is considered to be "fouled" if the Director determines that one or more cards were misplaced in the board, in such manner that contestants who should have had a direct score comparison did not play the board in identical form.

B. Scoring the Fouled Board
In scoring a fouled board the Director determines as closely as possible which scores were made on the board in its correct form, and which in the changed form. He divides the score on that basis into two groups, and rates each group separately as provided in the regulations of the sponsoring organization.

In some forms of team contests, the sponsoring organization may prescribe a redeal (see Law 6).

SECTION FOUR
PENALTIES
LAW 88
AWARD OF INDEMNITY POINTS
In a pair or individual event, when a non-offending contestant is required to take an artificial adjusted score through no fault or choice of his own, such contestant shall be awarded a minimum of 60% of the matchpoints available to him on that board, or the percentage of matchpoints he earned on boards actually played during the session if that percentage was greater than 60%.

LAW 89
PENALTIES IN INDIVIDUAL EVENTS
In individual events, the Director shall enforce the penalty provisions of these Laws, and the provisions requiring the award of adjusted scores, equally against both members of the offending side, even though only one of them may be responsible for the irregularity. But the Director, in awarding adjusted scores, shall not assess procedural penalty points against the offender's partner, if, in the Director's opinion, he is in no way responsible for the violation.

LAW 90
PROCEDURAL PENALTIES
A. DIRECTOR'S AUTHORITY
The Director, in addition to enforcing the penalty provisions of these Laws, may also assess penalties for any offense that unduly delays or obstructs the game, inconveniences other contestants, violates correct procedure,

or requires the award of an adjusted score at another table.

B. Offenses Subject to Penalty
Offenses subject to penalty include but are not limited to:
1. Tardiness
   arrival of a contestant after the specified starting time.
2. Slow Play
   unduly slow play by a contestant.
3. Loud Discussion
   discussion of the bidding, play or result of a board,
   which may be overheard at another table.
4. Comparing Scores
   unauthorized comparison of scores with another contestant.
5. Touching Another's Cards
   touching or handling of cards belonging to another player (Law 7).
6. Misplacing Cards in Board
   placing one or more cards in an incorrect pocket of the board.
7. Errors in Procedure
   errors in procedure (such as failure to count cards in one's hand, playing the wrong board, etc.) that require an adjusted score for any contestant.
8. Failure to Comply
   failure to comply promptly with tournament regulations or with any instruction of the Director.

LAW 91
PENALIZE OR SUSPEND
A. Director's Power
In performing his duty to maintain order and discipline, the director is specifically empowered to assess disciplinary penalties in points or to suspend a contestant for the current session or any part thereof (the Director's decision under this clause is final).

B. Right to Disqualify
The Director is specifically empowered to disqualify a contestant for cause, subject to approval by the Tournament Committee or sponsoring organization.

CHAPTER XI

APPEALS
LAW 92
RIGHT TO APPEAL
A. Contestant's Right
A contestant or his Captain may appeal for a review of any ruling made at his table by the Director*.

B. Time of Appeal
The right to request or appeal a Director's ruling expires 30 minutes after the official score has been made available for inspection, unless the sponsoring organization has specified a different time period.

C. How to Appeal
All appeals shall be made through the Director.

D. Concurrence of Appellants

An appeal shall not be heard unless both members of a pair (except in an individual contest) or the captain of a team, concur in appealing. An absent member shall be deemed to concur.

* Sponsoring organizations may establish penalties for appeals without merit.

LAW 93
PROCEDURES OF APPEAL

A. No Appeals Committee

The Chief Director shall hear and rule upon all appeals if there is no Tournament or Appeals Committee, or when a committee cannot meet without disturbing the orderly progress of the tournament.

B. Appeals Committee Available

If a committee is available,

1. Appeal Concerns Law

The Chief Director shall hear and rule upon such part of the appeal as deals solely with the Law or regulations. His ruling may be appealed to the committee*.

2. All Other Appeals

The Chief Director shall refer all other appeals to the committee* for adjudication.

3. Adjudication of Appeals

In adjudicating appeals the committee* may exercise all powers assigned by these Laws to the Director, except that the committee may not overrule the Director on a point of law or regulations, or on exercise of his disciplinary powers. The committee may recommend to the Director that he change his ruling.

C. Appeal to National Authority

After the preceding remedies have been exhausted, further appeal may be taken to the national authority (on a point of law, in ACBL the National Laws Commission, 2990 Airways Boulevard, Memphis, TN 38116-3847).

* Zonal organizations may establish differing conditions of appeals for special contests.

ACBL REGULATIONS

The following regulations are in effect in ACBL through actions of the ACBL Board of Directors, under authority granted by the referenced laws.

Law 12 C.3: ACBL elects to specify otherwise. The provisions of this Law do not apply for ACBL (Zone 2) sanctioned contests.

Law 16 A.1: At ACBL sanctioned events, competitors will not be allowed to announce that they reserve the right to summon the Director later. They should summon the Director immediately when they believe there may have been extraneous information available to the opponents resulting in calls or bids which could result in damage to their side.

Law 18 F: The ACBL Board of Directors authorizes sponsoring organizations in Zone 2 to use bidding boxes. Any alternative method which is necessary to enable a person with a disability to compete is authorized subject to the approval of the Chief Director.

Law 40 D: One notrump openings with fewer than eight high-card points are barred in all ACBL sanctioned events.

Law 40 D: An opening one bid in a suit which by partnership agreement could show fewer than eight high-card points is not allowed. This does not apply to an opening bid intended as a psych.

Law 40 E. Both members of a partnership must employ the same system that appears on the convention card.

1. During a session of play, a system may not be varied, except with permission of the tournament Director. (A Director might allow a pair to change a convention but would not allow a pair to change their basic system.)

2. At the outset of a round or session, a pair may review their opponents' convention card and alter their defenses against the opponents' conventional calls and preemptive bids. This must be announced to their opponents. The opponents may not vary their system after being informed of these alterations in defense.

Defenses to methods permitted by the ACBL Mid-Chart and/or SuperChart are designated as "unusual methods" and may be referred to as appropriate during the auction and play of the hand.

Law 41 A & Law 45 A: Face-down opening leads are required at all ACBL sanctioned contests.

Law 61 B: The restriction that otherwise would prohibit defenders from asking one another whether they have a card of the suit led shall not apply, unless otherwise specified by action of the ACBL Board of Directors.

Law 93 B.1 The ACBL Board of Directors authorizes sponsoring organizations in Zone 2 to designate certain contests in which either of the following differing conditions of appeal may apply:

1. The Chief Director shall hear and rule upon all appeals,

or

2. The Chief Director shall hear all appeals but may refer the matter to an appropriate committee.

LAY DOWN. Verb: (1) to put the dummy's cards on the table; (2) to play a (high) card with the assurance of winning that particular trick.

LAYDOWN. A colloquialism for a hand that can virtually be claimed for a successful contract as soon as the dummy is exposed. However, surprising things happen to laydown hands with disconcerting frequency. PIANOLA is a synonym.

LEAD. The first card played to a trick. See LAWS (Law 44). See LEADS.

LEAD OUT OF TURN. An irregularity in play. See Law 54 for opening lead out of turn, Law 55 for declarer's lead out of turn, and Law 56 for defender's lead out of turn.

LEAD OUT OF WRONG HAND (by declarer). A lead out of turn by declarer, leading either from his or dummy's hand incorrectly. See Law 55.

LEAD THROUGH. To lead through a particular opponent is to initiate the lead in the hand to the right of that opponent, forcing that opponent to play to the trick before the leader's partner plays to it. See THROUGH STRENGTH; UP TO WEAKNESS.

LEAD THROUGH STRENGTH. See THROUGH STRENGTH.

LEAD UP TO. To lead, in defense, with the object of enabling partner's hand to win a trick because of weakness in the hand on the leader's right. Occasionally, a strong hand may be led up to, when the object is not necessarily to win the trick. See UP TO WEAKNESS.

LEAD UP TO WEAKNESS. See UP TO WEAKNESS.

LEAD-DIRECTING BID. A bid made primarily for the purpose of indicating a desired suit for partner to lead initially against an impending adverse contract. Sometimes it is clear that the bid is lead-directing:

West	North	East	South
Pass	Pass	3 ♦	Dbl.
4 ♣			

North cannot have a seriously long club suit — he would have bid it originally. He must have a diamond fit and a desire for a club lead against 4 ♥ or 4 ♠. Sometimes it is less clear.

West	North	East	South
		1 ♠	2 ♥
2 ♠	3 ♦		

North may have long diamonds, or may have a heart fit and want a diamond lead against a spade contract. The 3 ♦ bid is relatively safe because a save will have to be at the five-level. In other situations such bids may be less safe. See also FIT-SHOWING JUMP, McCABE ADJUNCT, TRANSFER FOR LEAD, WEAK TWO-BIDS.

LEAD-DIRECTING DOUBLE. The most frequent case is a double of a voluntarily bid contract at 3NT by the player not on lead. In current practice the double requests in order of priority: (a) the lead of the opening leader's suit; (b) the lead of the doubler's bid suit; (c) the lead of the first suit bid by dummy. However, it may not be right to lead dummy's suit if it has been rebid; and some authorities leave to judgment the situation in which both defenders have bid a suit. See also FISHER DOUBLE.

The lead-directing double may occur at the partscore level:

(a)

West	North	East	South
			Pass
Pass	1 ♦	Pass	2NT
Pass	Pass	Dbl	

(b)

West	North	East	South
			1 ♦
Pass	1NT	Pass	Pass
Dbl			

In each case the double is suggesting the lead of a diamond.

A double of 3NT when neither side has bid a suit implies that the doubler has a solid suit or a semi-solid suit with an entry that can be run immediately. The opening leader will tend to lead a short major suit in which he has no honor.

A double of a conventional bid such as a response to Blackwood has obvious lead-directing implications. There is also a negative inference: a player who does not double such a bid is likely to prefer another lead.

See DOUBLES OF ARTIFICIAL BIDS FOR PENALTIES.

LEAD-DIRECTING RAISES. A method of suggesting a lead when partner's preemptive opening is doubled for takeout.

West	North	East	South
	2 ♥	Dbl	3 ♦

This shows, by agreement, heart support and a desire for a diamond lead if East is on lead. This applies in any unbid suit, and operates in the same way if the opening preemptive bid is at the three-level. See McCABE ADJUNCT.

LEAD-INHIBITING BID. A tactical bid, in the nature of a semi-psychic call, which is designed to prevent the opponents from leading a specific suit. For example:

- ♠ K Q 6
- ♥ K J 7
- ♦ 8 5 2
- ♣ A Q 7 5

The normal opening bid should be 1 ♣ followed by a rebid of 1NT. An opening bid of 1 ♦, made with the idea of discouraging a diamond lead against notrump, would be a lead-inhibiting bid.

Another common form of a lead-inhibiting bid:

- ♠ —
- ♥ K 7 6 5 2
- ♦ 9 5
- ♣ A K 8 5 3 2

After an opening bid of 1 ♥ by partner, one immediately thinks in terms of six or seven. A bid of 3 ♦ with this hand might stop the opponents from cashing the first two diamond tricks.

LEADER. The person who first plays to any given trick. The person who leads at trick one is known as the opening leader.

LEADS. See AMERICAN LEADS; ATTACKING LEADS; DESPERATION LEAD OR PLAY; DISCARDING; FORCING LEADS; HONOR LEAD; JOURNALIST LEADS; OPENING LEADS; QUEEN LEAD; ROMAN MUD; RUSINOW LEADS; SHORT-SUIT LEADS; SLAM LEADS; STRONG KINGS AND TENS; THIRD HIGHEST LEAD; THREE SMALL CARDS, LEAD FROM; THROUGH STRENGTH; TRELDE LEADS; TRUMP LEADS; UNDERLEAD; UP TO STRENGTH; UP TO WEAKNESS.

LEAGUE. An organization (also called association, federation or union), which may be on a local, regional, national, or international scale. Members of the league may be individuals, clubs, teams, or other groupings.

LEAPING MICHAELS. A special type of Michaels bid made after an opponent's weak two bid in a major. A jump to four of a minor shows the other major and the bid minor. Over 2 ♠, a bid of 4 ♦ would show hearts and diamonds – probably a 5-5 or better.

LEAVE IN. See PENALTY DOUBLE.

LEAVES. One of the suits in early European PLAYING CARDS (a translation of German and Slavic words). See PACK.

LEBENSOHL. A convention first described by George Boehm of New York and attributed by him, wrongly, to Ken Lebensohl. Sometimes, consequently, called Lebensold. It deals with the problem created for the partner of an opening notrump bidder following an overcall. The mechanism varies depending on whether the overcall shows one suit or two and whether it is made at the two level or three level. Over a natural two-level overcall, a double used to be played for penalties but now is frequently treated as negative. A two-level suit bid is non-forcing, a three-level suit bid is forcing and a 2NT bid forces opener to rebid 3♣. Responder can pass opener's 3♣ bid if he has a weak hand with long clubs or can rebid. If he rebids a suit below the rank of the suit overcalled it is a signoff; if he rebids a suit above the rank of the suit overcalled, it is invitational to game. A cuebid is Stayman while a relay to 3♣ followed by a cuebid is also Stayman. The difference is that one shows a stopper in the opponent's suit and the other denies it. Direct jumps to 3NT and 3NT following a relay to 3♣ are similar raises to game without a four-card major and with or without a stopper. It is up to the individual partnerships to decide which sequence shows the stopper and which denies. The modern tendency is to play SLOW SHOWS, FAST DENIES. Over a two-suited overcall, the double is penalty-oriented in at least one of the suits shown by the overcall. The two-level bid of a suit not shown by the overcall is not forcing, while the three-level bid of such a suit is forcing to game. Cuebids are generally forcing to game, always at least invitational. Only when the overcall shows two specific suits and responder cuebids the cheaper may the partnership stop below game. Over a three-level overcall the double is a takeout for any suits not shown by the overcall. Suit bids at the three-level are forcing to game.

Lebensohl has been modified to extend to other situations. See LEBENSOHL APPLICATIONS; ADVANCED LEBENSOHL; RUBINSOHL.

LEBENSOHL APPLICATIONS. The LEBENSOHL idea can be used, and often is, in two other situations. *Responding to double of weak two-bids:* If a weak 2♠ bid is doubled, a suit response at the three-level has an uncomfortably wide range in standard bidding:

West	North	East	South
2♠	Dbl	Pass	3♥

North cannot tell whether his partner has eight points or none at all. With a good hand he must guess whether to continue to game. Using Lebensohl the responder promises moderate values, perhaps 8-10 points or the equivalent. With a very weak hand he must bid 2NT, forcing a 3♣ bid from opener. Responder can pass 3♣ with length in that suit, or pick another suit. If the doubler is so strong that he hopes for game opposite a very weak South hand, he can disregard the instruction to bid 3♣.

In an alternate method, 2NT in response to the double asks the doubler to select a suit (any suit after 2♠ doubled, a minor after 2♥ doubled). If the 2NT bidder

then bids again (2NT-3♣-3♥), he shows a better hand than he would have if he had bid 3♥ directly. See GOOD-BAD TWO NOTRUMP, RUBINSOHL.

LEBENSOLD. See LEBENSOHL.

LEBHAR TROPHY. Awarded to the winners of the NORTH AMERICAN IMP PAIRS in honor of Bertram Lebhar, sportscaster and former ACBL treasurer. See IMP PAIRS.

LEBOVIC ASKING BID. A convention devised by Wolf Lebovic of Toronto, and publicized by Sami Kehela of Toronto. When two or three suits have been bid and a minor suit has been agreed as trumps, a double jump in an unbid suit asks about control in that suit. The last bid in each of the following auctions would be a Lebovic asking bid.

	(a)			(b)	
South	North		South	North	
1♣	1♥		1♠	2♦	
1♠	3♣		3♦	4♥	
4♦					

The responder to the asking bid answers as follows: with a singleton in the asked suit he bids six of the trump suit, with king doubleton or longer he bids 4NT, with the ace or a void he bids the asked suit, and with none of the above he makes the minimum bid in the trump suit.

This bid conflicts with the popular SPLINTER BID.

LEDGER. See BACK SCORE.

LEFT-HAND PLAYER. The player on declarer's left. In assessing penalties there has been a differentiation between left- and right-hand opponents as respects power or right to invoke penalties. Generally, however, the term is restricted to use in describing situations on play. An alternative term is left-hand opponent, abbreviated to LHO. A colloquialism is "Lefty."

LEG. A colloquial rubber bridge term to indicate a game already won. Partners who have a leg are vulnerable.

LEGAL. Applied to any call or play not in contravention of the mechanics of the game as set forth in the Laws. A legal convention is one that is listed properly on the convention card that is either approved by the tournament committee or by the tournament director for use in that event. See PROPRIETIES.

LEGAL WORDS IN AUCTION. Only 15 words can be legally used in an auction – one, two three, four, five, six, seven, spades, hearts, diamonds, clubs, notrump, double, redouble, pass. Of course the suits can be in the singular and notrump in the plural.

LEGHORN DIAMOND (LIVORNO) SYSTEM. Similar to the ROMAN SYSTEM, developed by Benito Bianchi and Giuseppe Messina and used successfully in many European Championships. The chief features are:

1♣ opening is forcing and may show any of four different types of hand: (1) 12-15 points, balanced distribution and no five-card major; (2) unbalanced with a long minor, 12-20 points, possibly with a side four-card major if the point range is 12 or 13; (3) unbalanced with

a long major and no side four-card major or five-card minor, 16-20 points; or (4) a three-suiter with a singleton or void in a major, 12-13 points.

2♦ *(natural) and 1♦* are both negative responses to 1♣, showing fewer than 8 points. 1♥ and 1♠ responses are positive, 8 points or more, and 1NT and 2NT deny a four-card major and are limited to 8-10 and 11-12 points respectively. Jump suit responses are natural and game forcing, except 3♣, which is forcing for only one round and suggests 3NT. A jump to 2♦ may be made on a four-card suit if responder intends to Canapé into a major.

The auction tends to develop naturally after the initial response. Minimum major-suit rebids by opener usually describe the weak balanced hand, but he may have the minimum major-minor two-suiter or the three-suiter. With either of the unbalanced hands, opener makes a simple rebid in a minor with 12-17, jumps to the two-level in a major with 16-17 or jumps to the three-level in any suit with 18-20. After a positive response, a jump rebid by opener to 2NT shows exactly 15 points. After responding in a major, responder's second suit is his long suit.

1♦ *opening* is forcing and shows either a balanced hand with 19 points or more, or an unbalanced hand that is about a trick short of game, possibly a three-suiter with at least 20 points.

Suit responses show controls by steps (king = 1 control; ace = 2 controls). 1♥ shows no controls; 1♠ shows 1 control, and so on. With no controls but scattered queens and jacks, responder bids 1NT with 5-6 points or 2NT with 7 or more.

A simple notrump rebid by opener describes a balanced hand with 19-21 points and a jump notrump rebid shows 22 points or more. If opener is unbalanced, he usually makes a minimum rebid in a suit, over which responder rebids conventionally by eight steps to show support. A new suit by opener is then a second asking bid, and the responses are on the same scale for that suit. After responder has made his support-showing step response to opener's second suit, a bid of the cheapest denomination by opener is a relay asking responder to choose between opener's suits.

1♥ *and* 1♠ *openings* are natural but show two different types of hand: (1) less than 16 points with a five-card or longer major; or (2) a two-suiter, usually a four-card major and a five-card or longer side suit, with 14-19 points. To distinguish between the two types, opener normally rebids his major with the first type of hand, even if he has a side four-card suit, and bids his second suit (jumping with 17-19 points) with hand type two.

1NT *opening* is standard (16-18) and denies a five-card major.

2♣ *and* 2♦ *openings* show three-suited hands (4-4-4-1 or 5-4-4-0 distribution) with 12-16 and 17-19 points respectively. Responses and rebids are similar to the Roman System.

2♥ *and* 2♠ *openings* show two-suited hands, the bid major and a four- or five-card minor, with 9-12 points.

2NT *opening* shows at least five cards in each minor with 14-16 high card points.

LENGTH. The number of cards held in a particular suit, usually referring to five or more; as opposed to STRENGTH, the high card values held in a suit. See DISTRIBUTIONAL VALUES.

LENGTH SIGNALS. See COUNT SIGNALS.

LESSON HANDS. Bridge teachers regularly offer prepared deals to their pupils, illustrating points in bidding and play covered by their lessons.

LEVANDAAL AWARD. A prize given annually starting in 2001 for the best played hand of the year by the INTERNATIONAL BRIDGE PRESS ASSOCIATION. Prior to 2001 the award was given to an outstanding junior.

LEVEL. The "odd-trick" count in excess of the book, that is, each trick over six. Thus an overcall of 2 is a bid made at the two level and a contract to make eight tricks. A 4 opening bid is said to be made at the four level. See OVERCALLS.

LEVENTRITT TROPHY. Awarded to the winners of the NORTH AMERICAN SILVER RIBBON PAIRS. From 1950 to 1972 awarded to the winners of the Life Master Pairs consolation event. Trophy honors Peter Leventritt, former internationalist for North America.

LHO. Left-hand opponent, or the player on declarer's left.

LIBRARY. See MOREHEAD LIBRARY.

LIFE MASTER. Once the highest rank in the ACBL and in many other NCBOs. In the ACBL, the category was created in 1936. Selection of the early Life Masters was based strictly on successes in national events even though a masterpoint program had been in effect since 1934. Initally the rank was conferred on a group of 10 players ranked in order according to the number and importance of their national victories. There are now six categories of Life Master in the ACBL. See RANKING.

The first 100 players to achieve the rank were:

1. David Bruce	1936
2. Oswald Jacoby	1936
3. Howard Schenken	1936
4. Waldemar von Zedtwitz	1936
5. P. Hal Sims	1936
6. B. Jay Becker	1936
7. Theodore Lightner	1936
8. Richard Frey	1936
9. Michael Gottlieb	1936
10. Sam Fry Jr.	1936
11. Merwin Maier	1936
12. Charles Lochridge	1937
13. Charles Goren	1938
14. Mitchell Barnes	1938
15. Harry Fishbein	1939
16. Charles Solomon	1939
17. Sally Young	1939
18. Fred Kaplan	1939
19. John Crawford	1939
20. Walter Jacobs	1939
21. Morrie Elis	1939
22. Phil Abramsohn	1940
23. Edward Hymes Jr.	1940
24. Alvin Landy	1940
25. Helen Sobel Smith	1941
26. Sherman Stearns	1941

27. Robert McPherran	1941		93. Allen Harvey	1947
28. Jeff Glick	1942		94. Lewis Jaeger	1947
29. Arthur Glatt	1942		95. Mildred Cunningham	1947
30. Dr. Richard Ecker Jr.	1942		96. Elmer Schwartz	1947
31. Albert Weiss	1942		97. Linda Terry	1947
32. Lee Hazen	1942		98. Maurice Levin	1948
33. Peggy Solomon	1942		99. Dave Warner	1948
34. Alvin Roth	1942		100. Ernest Rovere	1948
35. Sidney Silodor	1943			
36. Olive Peterson	1943			
37. Margaret Wagar	1943			
38. Peter Leventritt	1943			
39. Edson Wood	1944			
40. Ralph Kempner	1944			
41. Arthur Goldsmith	1944			
42. Simon Becker	1944			
43. Stanley Fenkel	1944			
44. George Rapee	1944			
45. Ruth Sherman	1944			
46. Robert Appleyard	1945			
47. M. A. Lightman	1945			
48. Samuel Stayman	1945			
49. Edward Marcus	1945			
50. Charles Hall	1945			
51. Emily Folline	1946			
52. Joseph Cain	1946			
53. Harry Feinberg	1946			
54. Ambrose Casner	1946			
55. Samuel Katz	1946			
56. Jack Ehrlenbach	1946			
57. J. Van Brooks	1946			
58. Simon Rossant	1946			
59. Edward Ellenbogen	1946			
60. Sidney Fink	1946			
61. Bertram Lebhar Jr.	1946			
62. Meyer Schleifer	1947			
63. Louis Newman	1947			
64. Elinor Murdoch	1947			
65. Paula Bacher	1947			
66. Florence Stratford	1947			
67. Jules Bank	1947			
68. William McGhee	1947			
69. Maynard Adams	1947			
70. Edith Kemp	1947			
71. David Carter	1947			
72. Jack Cushing	1947			
73. Dr. A. Steinberg	1947			
74. Jane Jaeger	1947			
75. Cecil Head	1947			
76. S. Garton Churchill	1947			
77. Edward Cohn	1947			
78. John Carlin	1947			
79. Lawrence Welch	1947			
80. Frank Weisbach	1947			
81. Charlton Wallace	1947			
82. Dr. Louis Mark	1947			
83. Edward Taylor	1947			
84. Dan Westerfield	1947			
85. Tobias Stone	1947			
86. Mark Hodges	1947			
87. Leo Roet	1947			
88. Sol Mogal	1947			
89. Herbert Gerst	1947			
90. Lewis Mathe	1947			
91. Ludwig Kabakjian	1947			
92. Gratian Goldstein	1947			

LIFE MASTER MEN'S PAIRS, NORTH AMERICAN CHAMPIONSHIP. See APPENDIX I.

LIFE MASTER PAIRS, NORTH AMERICAN CHAMPIONSHIP. See APPENDIX I.

LIFE MASTER WOMEN'S PAIRS, NORTH AMERICAN CHAMPIONSHIP. See APPENDIX I.

LIFT. A term meaning "raise."

LIGHT. (1) Down in a contract – "He was two light." (2) Fewer than standard values, especially in opening the bidding.

LIGHTNER DOUBLE. A lead-directing double of a slam contract. If competent opponents bid a slam voluntarily, it may be expected that they will fulfill their contract or fail by one trick. Thus a normal penalty double is unlikely to gain much. In 1929 Theodore Lightner devised a more useful interpretation of this bid. A double by the hand not on lead is conventional. Partner is requested to choose an unusual lead which may result in the defeat of the slam. A conventional double of this sort excludes the lead of a trump, a suit bid by the defenders, and probably any unbid suit. The player who doubles expects to ruff the lead of a side suit mentioned by the opponents, or else to win two top tricks in that suit. Some experts treat this double quite rigidly. They define the double to mean that partner must lead dummy's first-bid side suit. Other good players, including Lightner, interpret the bid more loosely. An unusual lead is requested and partner must deduce from the context which suit is required.

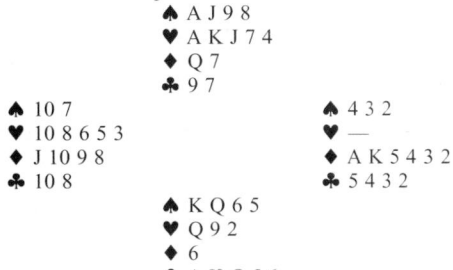

South plays 6♠, after opening 1♣ and getting a response of 1♥. East doubles for an unusual lead. West leads a heart, East ruffs and cashes the ♦ A for the setting trick. Without the double West would have led a diamond which declarer would have covered from dummy. East would be forced to win the only trick the defense could take. See also LEAD-DIRECTING DOUBLES. For an alternative use of the double of a slam when the defenders have bid and raised a suit of their own, see DOUBLE FOR SACRIFICE, MINI-LIGHNER.

LILIES. See ROYAL SPADES.

LIMIT BID. A bid with a limited point-count range. Although a traditional forcing jump raise (1♠ -3♠) is limited in the wide sense of the term, limit is normally applied only to nonforcing bids below the game level. With some exceptions, a bid is limited and nonforcing if it is in notrump, if it is a raise, if it is a preference, or if it is a minimum rebid in a suit previously bid by the same player. Opening notrump bids are invariably limited. Once we have decided that a certain bid is limited the vital question arises: how wide can the limits be? *The nearer the bidding is to game, the closer the limits must be.* When the bidding reaches 2NT with the possibility of 3NT; or when the bidding reaches 3♠, there is no longer any margin for exploration. So to give partner the chance to make an accurate decision, all such bids must have a range of approximately 2 points. Thus 1♥ -2NT by a passed hand shows 11-12, and 1♥ -1NT-2NT shows 17-19; similarly 1♠ -3♠ by a passed hand shows 10-11, or the equivalent, and 1♥ -1♠ -3♠ shows 17-18, or the equivalent. All these are typical encouraging bids, indicating that the partnership has a minimum of 23-24 points and urging partner on to game if he has a little more than his promised minimum.

Conversely, any bid of 1NT and any limited bid of two of a suit can afford a range of 3 or 4 points: there is still time for partner to make an encouraging bid below the game level. So 1♥ -1NT or 1♥ -2♥ are each 6-9 (and may have to stretch a little further at that), and 1♥ -1♠ -2♠ is 13-16, or the distributional equivalent.

LIMIT JUMP RAISE. Originally a feature of the ACOL and KAPLAN-SHEINWOOD systems, this is now common in tournament play.

A raise from 1♥ to 3♥, for example, is nonforcing but strongly encouraging. It shows a hand with about 10 or 11 high-card points or the distributional equivalent.

If the opening bidder has a minimum, he normally passes. If the nine-trick contract fails, it will often turn out that the opponents could have made a partscore or even a game.

Limit jump raises were a part of the original CULBERTSON SYSTEM (to 1934) and were revived for minor suits only in 1948. A few players use limit jump raises in competition only, that is, after a suit overcall by an opponent; and nearly all players ascribe to them quite a low limit over an opponent's takeout double. See FORCING RAISE, LIMIT JUMP RAISE TO SHOW A SINGLETON, WEAK JUMP RAISE.

Rebids by opener

(1) In a major suit, 1♠ -3♠. 3NT makes little sense as a natural rebid. The BWS 1994 expert choice was to use the cheapest action as a request to show a singleton. 1♥ -3♥ -3♠ -3NT shows a spade singleton. 1♥ -3♥ -3NT is a cuebid in spades. See SERIOUS THREE NOTRUMP to see whether a new-suit bid, such as 1♠ -3♠ -4♦ should show length or simply a control requires agreement.

(2) In a minor suit, 1♣ -3♣ or 1♦ -3♦. 3NT is natural. Three of an unbid suit shows strength, not necessarily control, and is a move towards 3NT.

LIMIT JUMP RAISE TO SHOW A SINGLETON. A part of the WALSH SYSTEM, using an immediate jump raise of opener's major suit opening to show three

or four trumps, 10-12 points, and a singleton somewhere in the hand. If opener is interested in locating responder's singleton, he makes the cheapest bid over the limit raise (See MATHE ASKING BID.) This device can be used with other bidding styles if the partnership uses a forcing 1NT response to opening bids of 1♥ or 1♠. The forcing notrump followed by a jump to three of opener's suit can be used to show a balanced limit raise, usually with three-card support.

Rebids by opener.

In a major suit, 1♥ -3♥ or 1♠ -3♠, 3NT makes little sense as a natural rebid. The expert choice in BWS 1994 was to use the cheapest action as a request to show a singleton. 1♥ -3♥ -3♠ -3NT shows a spade singleton. 1♥ -3♥ -3NT is a cuebid in spades. See SERIOUS THREE NOTRUMP. Whether a new-suit bid, such as 1♠ -3♠ -4♦ should show length or simply a control requires agreement.

In a minor suit, 1♣ -3♣ or 1♦ -3♦, 3NT is natural. Three of an unbid suit shows strength, not necessarily control, and is a move toward 3NT.

LIMIT MAJOR RAISE. A response indicating the possibility of game. A single raise usually indicates 6-9 HCP. However, most experts will raise with 5 HCP if they hold an ace. A jump raise usually shows 10-12 points, including distribution. For other methods of making limit major suit raises, see BERGEN RAISES, DOUBLE RAISE, INVITATIONAL BID, LIMIT JUMP RAISE, ONE NOTRUMP RESPONSE, RESPONDER'S REBID, RESPONSE, SINGLE RAISE, SPLINTER BID, THREE NOTRUMP RESPONSE, TRIPLE RAISE, TWO NOTRUMP RESPONSE.

LIMIT RAISE. A raise with closely defined limits of strength. Many such bids are limited in this way in standard methods, such as the single raise of opener's suit. The chief application is the jump raise from one to three (see LIMIT JUMP RAISE). The bid indicates at least four-card trump support with 10-11 points or the distributional equivalent. The corollary is that a jump raise on the second round is invitational but nonforcing:

West	East		West	East
1♣	1♠		1♣	1♥
3♠			1♠	3♠

See JUMP REBIDS BY RESPONDER.

When the opponents overcall, another method of showing a limit raise is available – a cuebid in the opponents' suit.

| 1♥ | 1♠ | 2♠ |

2♠ shows heart support (at least three and usually four) and the strength for a limit raise. The jump raise is preemptive.

A limit raise also is available over an opening 1NT. The bid of 2NT indicates a willingness to go to game if opener has a maximum notrump. When playing four suit transfers, responder wi

1 bid 2♣ Stayman – with or without a four-card ma or – and then rebid 2NT to show the limit raise. Many meth ds of making a limit raise are possible. See BE GEN RAISES, DELAYED GAME RAISE, DOUBLE RAISE, INVERTED MI NOR SUIT RAISE, INVITATIONAL BID, LIMIT JUMP RAISE, NOT UMP OPENING, ONE NOTRUMP RESPONSE, OPENER'

REBID, RESPONDER'S REBID, RESPONSE, SINGLE RAISE, SPLINTER BID, THREE NOTRUMP RESPONSE, TRIPLE RAISE, TWO NOTRUMP RE-

SPONSE, WEAK TWO-BID.

LIMIT RESPONSES. The combination of LIMIT RAISES with limit responses in notrump, so that responses of 2NT and 3♠ to an opening bid of 1♠, for example, are both encouraging but not forcing.

LINE. The dividing horizontal marking on a score pad below which game and partial scores (trick scores) are written. See ABOVE THE LINE and BELOW THE LINE.

LITERATURE AND BRIDGE. Several full-length novels have focused on bridge. *Tickets to the Devil,* by Richard Powell, deals with the activities at a Spring North American Championship, both at the tables and away from them. *Yarborough* by B. H. Friedman outlines the adolescence and young manhood of two precocious heroes. In one Agatha Christie mystery, *Cards on the Table,* the murder takes place during a bridge game and Hercule Poirot solves it by analyzing the scorepad. Another British mystery and suspense writer, Georgette Heyer, also wrote about murder at a bridge game in *Duplicate Death.* A series of paperbacks by Don Von Elsner (*The Ace of Spies, The Jack of Hearts, The Jake of Diamonds, Kona Contract,* etc,) features a fictitious bridge pro, Jake Winkman, in a variety of adventures in tournament settings, in which the quality of the bridge hands is highly professional. Similarly, Frank Thomas, a veteran actor of stage, movies, radio and television, has written two books about *Sherlock Holmes, Bridge Detective,* which combine good storytelling with excellent bridge hands. Author Terry Quinn relates the adventures of a strange foursome caught up in the world of tournament bridge and international intrigue in *The Great Bridge Conspiracy.* In Sinclair Lewis's *Main Street* the local bridge club is a barometer of the characters' accommodation to the social life in Gopher Prairie, MN. In Ian Fleming's *Moonraker,* James Bond rigged a variation of the DUKE OF CUMBERLAND HAND in dealing with the villain of that book. (See DISTRIBUTIONAL VALUES.)

Among famous writers who have used a bridge theme for short story purposes are: Somerset Maugham (*The Three Fat Women of Antibes, The Facts of Life*); Roald Dahl (*My Lady Love, My Dove*); Ring Lardner (*Contract, Who Dealt*); and George S. Kaufman (*The Great Kibitzers' Strike of 1926*). See Cole and Edwards, eds., *Grand Slam,* BIBLIOGRAPHY, I. In his long short story, *The Death of Ivan Illych,* Leo Tolstoi made "vint", a Russian variation of bridge whist, the favorite leisure activity of his central character.

S. J. Simon, a European champion and bridge writer, made some minor references to the game in the delightful series of novels he wrote with Carol Brahms. C. S. Forester made his naval hero, Horatio Hornblower, a whist expert. Jules Vernes' whist expert, Phileas Fogg, begins his incredible journey in *Around the World in Eighty Days* as a result of a wager made with his whist-playing associates.

For Charles Lamb's view of whist players, see BATTLE, SARAH.

LITTLE CUEBID (Petit cuebid). Very popular in France as an alternative treatment to Lebensohl in response to the double by partner of a weak-two opening bid. The normal treatment in North America is to play new-suit bids at the three-level as natural and constructive while 2NT acts as a puppet to 3♣ to show weak

hands. This treatment is reversed in France. The French use 2NT as a constructive, unspecified hand, allowing the doubler to define his hand. Direct action in a new suit by responder is natural and weak.

LITTLE MAJOR SYSTEM. An artificial system of bidding devised by Terence Reese and Jeremy Flint, London, in the early Sixties and now obsolete. In principle, an opening of 1♣ denotes a heart suit and 1♦ denotes a spade suit. Strong hands are opened with 1♥, and minor suit hands with 1♠.

LITTLE OLD LADY. See LOL.

LITTLE ROMAN CLUB (ARNO) SYSTEM. Developed by Camillo Pabis-Ticci and Massimo D'Alelio, and first used successfully in the 1965 Bermuda Bowl. The system is patterned closely on the principles of the ROMAN SYSTEM, especially the opening two-bids and structure of defensive overcalls. Its chief features are:

1♣ opening is forcing and shows either a balanced hand with 12-16 points, or a 17-20 point hand with a club suit or a two-suiter with at least four clubs. After a negative response of 1♦ (less than 10 points), opener rebids on the one-level to show the balanced minimum opening. A response of 1NT is forcing to game, showing 12 points or more, over which opener bids a suit on the two-level with 12-13 points or raises to 2NT with 14-16 points. Jump responses are also forcing to game, and request opener to rebid conventionally by four steps to describe his strength and support for responder's suit.

1♦, 1♥ and 1♠ openings are forcing and natural according to the Canapé principle with 12-20 points. The opening bid may be made in a three-card suit with a minimum of 15 points or if opener's longest suit is clubs. The next higher suit by responder (1NT over 1♠) is the conventional negative, after which opener makes a simple rebid with 12-16 points or a jump rebid with a stronger hand. After a positive response, a normal rebid by opener is forcing for one round, and responder creates a game-force if his rebid is a reverse, a jump in a new suit, a raise of opener's second suit if it is a major, or a jump raise of opener's first suit. A 1NT response, if it is not a negative, shows a balanced hand with at least 12 points and is forcing to game. If opener rebids in notrump after opening 1♦, he has a balanced hand with 17-20 points.

1NT opening is forcing and shows either a balanced hand with 21-24 points, or a powerful distributional hand that is forcing to game. Responder shows the number of aces he holds by steps and opener rebids 2NT with the balanced hand or canapés in a suit with the unbalanced hand.

2♣, 2♦, 2♥ and 2♠ openings are as in the ROMAN SYSTEM. 2NT opening shows a minimum of five cards in both minors with 12-16 points.

LITTLE SLAM. See SMALL SLAM.

LIVORNO SYSTEM. See LEGHORN DIAMOND.

LOCAL TOURNAMENTS. See CHAMPIONSHIP TOURNAMENTS.

LOCK. A colloquial term, used principally in post mortems, to mean a 100% sure play or contract. For example, "4♠ was a lock."

LOCKED (IN OR OUT OF A HAND). To win a trick in a hand from which it is disadvantageous to make the lead to the next (or some later) trick is to be locked in. It usually refers to an endplay against a defender (see THROW IN) or to a declarer who is forced to win a trick in the dummy hand, when he has high cards established in his own hand which he is unable to enter. Locked out refers to situations in which established cards in the dummy cannot be cashed because an entry is not available.

LOL. An acronym with two meanings. (1) Originally LOL was a short form of Little Old Lady, a term used to describe a player of either sex who appeared innocent and vulnerable but who turned out to be a player capable of executing ingenious plays and defenses. The expression also is used to describe a weak player – "All we had to do was beat a bunch of LOLs." (2) In computer bridge shorthand, LOL means Laugh Out Loud.

LONDON SUNDAY TIMES PAIRS. See MACALLAN, SUNDAY TIMES PAIRS. For results see Appendix IV.

LONG CARDS. Cards of a suit remaining in a player's hand after all other cards of that suit have been played.

LONG HAND. The hand of the partnership which has the greater length in the trump suit, or, in notrump play, the hand which has winners that are or may be established. See AVOIDANCE.

LONG SUIT. A suit in which four or more cards are held. Frequently it is used in connection with a hand of little strength but with great length in a particular suit. For bidding on such a hand, see PREEMPTIVE BID.

LONG SUIT GAME TRIES. See WEAK SUIT GAME TRIES.

LONG SUIT LEAD. See FOURTH HIGHEST LEAD, OPENING LEAD and THIRD HIGHEST LEAD.

LONG TRUMP. Any card of the trump suit remaining after all other players' cards of the suit have been played.

LOOSE DIAMOND. See SHORT DIAMOND.

LOSE AND SNOOZE TEAMS. See MINI-KNOCK-OUT TEAMS.

LOSER. A card that must lose a trick to the adversaries if led, or if it must be played when the suit is led by an adversary. At notrump, all cards below the ace and not in sequence with it are possible losers, but may become winners if the play develops favorably. At a suit contract, the same may be said with the exception that losers may possibly be ruffed. A distinction must be made between possible losers and sure losers. The former may be discarded on a setup suit, or ruffed, or perhaps discarded on a setup card cashed by an adversary. If a loser cannot be disposed of, it must, of course, lose a trick to the opponents.

LOSER ON LOSER. The act of playing a card that must be lost on a losing trick in some other suit. This technique can be valuable in many situations, the most common of which are:

(1) *To allow a safe ruff to produce a trick:*

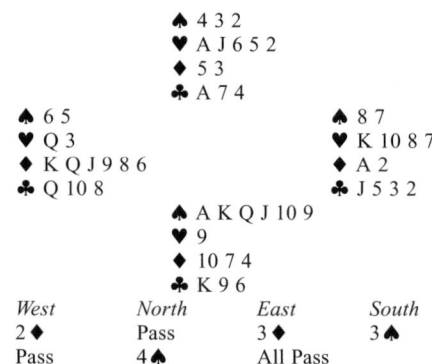

West	North	East	South
2♦	Pass	3♦	3♠
Pass	4♠	All Pass	

West leads the ♦K. East overtakes with the ace, and continues the suit. West wins and plays a third diamond. South realizes that East will be able to overruff dummy. He therefore plays a loser on a loser by discarding a club from dummy. Declarer can later ruff a club in dummy safely.

(2) *To allow a safe re-entry:*

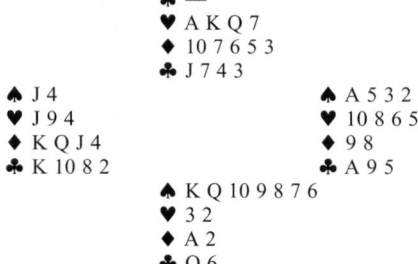

West	North	East	South
1NT	Pass	Pass	2♥
Pass	Pass	2♠	Pass
Pass	3♥	All Pass	

West leads three rounds of spades against 3♥, and declarer ruffs. Two rounds of diamonds are cashed and the third round is trumped in the North hand. After cashing the ♥A, declarer must now re-enter his hand to continue drawing trump. If he leads ace and another club, East will win and his spade continuation will create two trump tricks for the defense. Instead, declarer cashes dummy's ♣A and then leads a fourth round of spades, playing a loser on a loser by discarding his remaining club. The defense is now helpless. Declarer is somewhat fortunate in the distribution of the East-West minor suit cards but has nothing to lose by attempting this play.

(3) *To prevent a later overruff threat:*

      ♠ —
      ♥ A K Q 7
      ♦ 10 7 6 5 3
      ♣ J 7 4 3

♠ J 4   ♠ A 5 3 2
♥ J 9 4   ♥ 10 8 6 5
♦ K Q J 4   ♦ 9 8
♣ K 10 8 2   ♣ A 9 5

      ♠ K Q 10 9 8 7 6
      ♥ 3 2
      ♦ A 2
      ♣ Q 6

With East-West vulnerable, South opens 4♠ and buys the contract. West leads the ♦K, which declarer wins. An immediate discard is necessary, so South takes three rounds of hearts, discarding his losing diamond. If South

now fails to play the last heart, careful defense will obtain two clubs and two trump tricks. East will lead his last heart at a later stage, promoting West's jack of trump (see TRUMP PROMOTION). Instead, South uses the loser-on-loser technique. He leads dummy's remaining heart, discarding a club loser. East wins this trick, but the contract cannot be defeated.

(4) *To prevent a particular opponent from gaining the lead* (see AVOIDANCE):

```
              ♠ K J
              ♥ A K 4
              ♦ A 7 4 3 2
              ♣ J 10 6
♠ A 6 4 2                      ♠ 7
♥ —                            ♥ J 10 9 8 7 6 5
♦ J 10 9 5                     ♦ K Q
♣ A K Q 8 3                    ♣ 5 4 2
              ♠ Q 10 9 8 5 3
              ♥ Q 3 2
              ♦ 8 6
              ♣ 9 7
```

West	North	East	South
		2♥	Pass
Pass	2NT	Pass	3♠
All Pass			

West leads the ♣K and (erroneously) continues with the A-Q. South observes that the bidding suggests West is void of hearts. He therefore plays a loser on a loser by discarding a diamond on the third club. If South ruffs the third club, West will shift to diamond after winning the second round of spades. South will then be unable to enter his hand without surrendering a heart ruff.

After South's discard on the third trick, his contract is safe as the cards lie.

(5) *To establish one or more tricks in the suit played:*

```
West             East
♠ A K J          ♠ 5 4 3
♥ —              ♥ K Q 4
♦ A 3            ♦ 10 7 6 5
♣ A K J 10 9 8 7 3   ♣ Q 6 2
```

Against West's contract of 6♣, North leads the ♦K. West wins and draws two trumps ending in the East hand. He should now lead the ♥K from dummy, throwing a loser on a loser by discarding his diamond if South does not cover. If North wins the ♥A, the ♥Q will provide a discard for the ♠J. (Naturally, West has retained an entry to the East hand in clubs.) If South has the ace, either the ♥K will win or the ace will be ruffed out. Declarer can now try the spade finesse for an overtrick.

(6) *To help establish a side suit* (see AVOIDANCE):

```
              ♠ K Q 3
              ♥ J 9 7
              ♦ A 7 6 3 2
              ♣ 6 4
♠ 10                           ♠ J 9
♥ A K 10 8 5                   ♥ Q 6 4 3
♦ 10 5                         ♦ Q J 9
♣ A Q 10 9 2                   ♣ J 8 7 3
              ♠ A 8 7 6 5 4 2
              ♥ 2
              ♦ K 8 4
              ♣ K 5
```

West	North	East	South
1♥	Pass	2♥	2♠
3♣	3♥	Pass	4♠
All Pass			

West leads the ♥K, and all follow. West realizes that if he leads the ♥A, declarer will play a loser on a loser by discarding a diamond. This will allow the diamond suit to be established by ruffing and prevent East from gaining the lead to annihilate the ♣K.

West therefore shifts to a trump (a diamond has the same effect). Declarer wins in dummy, playing the four from his own hand. Anxious to execute the loser-on-loser play, he leads the ♥9 from dummy. East shakes off a yawn and rises with the queen to prevent the diamond discard. Declarer ruffs with the ♠5, returns to dummy by leading the ♠6 to the remaining honor in dummy. The ♥J is led from dummy. East cannot cover, and declarer sheds a low diamond. West wins and grudgingly cashes the ♣A to prevent an overtrick. Despite the best defense after the opening lead, declarer triumphs by continuing after his loser-on-loser play and careful unblocking in the spade suit (see UNBLOCKING.)

(7) *To avoid a force:*

```
West             East
♠ A K Q J        ♠ 10 8 5
♥ 3              ♥ 9 8 7
♦ A 4 3          ♦ 10 7 5
♣ A K J 9 5      ♣ Q 10 8 2
```

Against West's 4♠ contract, the defense begins with two rounds of hearts. To avoid weakening his trump holding, West should discard losing diamonds on the next two rounds of hearts. A fourth round of hearts can be ruffed in the East hand. If the trumps break 3-3 or 4-2, declarer romps home. If declarer ruffs a heart too early, a 4-2 trump break may defeat him.

(8) *To execute an endplay by creating a throw-in card:*

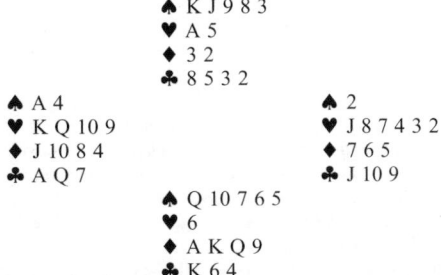

```
              ♠ K J 9 8 3
              ♥ A 5
              ♦ 3 2
              ♣ 8 5 3 2
♠ A 4                          ♠ 2
♥ K Q 10 9                     ♥ J 8 7 4 3 2
♦ J 10 8 4                     ♦ 7 6 5
♣ A Q 7                        ♣ J 10 9
              ♠ Q 10 7 6 5
              ♥ 6
              ♦ A K Q 9
              ♣ K 6 4
```

Against South's 4♠ contract, West leads the ♥K. Declarer wins with the ace, ruffs a heart, and leads a trump. West cautiously rises with the ♠A, and exits with a spade. Declarer wins and tries to drop the ♦ 10. On the third diamond, a club is discarded from dummy. South then leads the fourth round of diamonds. When West covers, declarer makes use of loser-on-loser technique by discarding another club from dummy. West is in, and must give away a trick.

(9) *To execute an endplay by forcing an opponent to remain on lead* (see RUFF AND DISCARD).

```
              ♠ A 3 2
              ♥ A J
              ♦ A 7 6
              ♣ 10 9 6 4 3
♠ 4                            ♠ K Q J 9 8 7
♥ K Q 10 8 7 3 2               ♥ 9 6
♦ J 10                         ♦ Q 9 5 3 2
♣ J 8 2                        ♣ —
              ♠ 10 6 5
              ♥ 5 4
              ♦ K 8 4
              ♣ A K Q 7 5
```

West	North	East	South
			1♣
2♥	3♥	4♠	Pass
Pass	5♣	All Pass	

West leads the ♠4, which is won by North's ace. Declarer draws three rounds of trump and, placing West with seven hearts, cashes the two top diamonds and plays the ♥A and ♥J.

West is stuck on lead with only hearts remaining and must give up a ruff-and-discard. When he leads a heart, a diamond is thrown from dummy. South tosses a loser on a loser by discarding a spade from his own hand. West is forced to remain on lead. On the next heart, declarer ruffs in dummy and discards his last spade. He then crossruffs the balance of the tricks, having turned four losers into only two. West could counter brilliantly by permitting dummy's ♥J to win, after which declarer would have no recourse.

(10) *To rectify the count for a squeeze.* This use of the loser-on-loser technique has many variations. The following hand illustrates the method in a fairly complex setting.

```
              ♠ A K 3
              ♥ 8 4 3 2
              ♦ Q 4 2
              ♣ 6 5 3
♠ Q 10 7 2                  ♠ J 9 5
♥ 6                         ♥ 7
♦ A K 10 8 7 6 3            ♦ J 9 5
♣ 7                         ♣ Q J 10 9 8 4
              ♠ 8 6 4
              ♥ A K Q J 10 9 5
              ♦ —
              ♣ A K 2
```

West	North	East	South
		3♣	4♥
5♦	5♥	Pass	6♥
All Pass			

West leads the ♦K, and South surveys the situation. He realizes that if neither opponent is short of spades (a reasonable assumption on the bidding) an elimination will fail, and the only chance for the contract is a double squeeze. The ♦Q is a menace against West, and declarer's third club threatens East. But the count is wrong. Declarer must lose a trick before the squeeze will operate.

Where can this trick be lost? Certainly not in spades or clubs, for the loss of a trick in either of these suits will destroy the essential menace cards. Therefore, a trick must be lost in diamonds. Furthermore, this trick must be lost *at once*. If declarer attempts to give up a diamond trick later on, the defense will play a third diamond, quashing the diamond menace. Therefore, declarer must throw a loser on a loser on the first trick. He discards a spade.

West has no effective defense. His best play is a spade. Declarer wins and runs winners until this ending is reached.

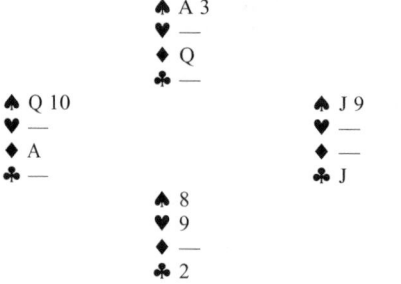

```
              ♠ A 3
              ♥ —
              ♦ Q
              ♣ —
♠ Q 10                     ♠ J 9
♥ —                        ♥ —
♦ A                        ♦ —
♣ —                        ♣ J
              ♠ 8
              ♥ 9
              ♦ —
              ♣ 2
```

When South leads the ♥9, West must surrender a spade. Dummy discards the ♦Q, and East is squeezed in spades and clubs. See DISCARD.

LOSERS. A method of valuation for unbalanced hands used in the ROMAN and ROMEX Systems. Every missing ace, king or queen is counted as a loser unless shortness compensates. A doubleton king is one loser, but a doubleton queen is two losers. See LOSING-TRICK COUNT and COVER CARDS.

LOSING TIE. In WIN-LOSS SWISS TEAMS, a match that is lost by 1 or 2 IMPs. It counts as one-fourth of a win.

LOSING-TRICK COUNT. A method of hand valuation. In 1934 the principle of assessing a hand in terms of "losers" was put forward by F. Dudley Courtenay in his book, *The System the Experts Play.* The general idea was this: when a suit fit came to light, you added the number of worthless cards in your hand to the number of losers revealed by your partner's bidding; the total was subtracted from 18, and the answer would tell you how many odd tricks the combined hands were likely to take.

After years of semi-obscurity the LTC was revived by Maurice Harrison-Gray and is now accepted as a reasonably accurate ready reckoner which pays due regard to the features that really matter.

This method of valuation is no longer treated with disdain by the expert. For instance, it is an integral part of the ROMAN SYSTEM, which helped Italy to win seven world championships.

The Losing-Trick Count applies only to trump contracts. At notrump the standard yardstick is the Milton Work Count.

Basic count of losers. With a void or singleton ace, count no loser in that suit; with any other singleton, or with A-x or K-x, count one loser; with any other doubleton, count two losers. In each suit of three or more cards, including the trump suit, count one loser for each missing high honor (A, K, or Q). Do not count more than three losers in any one suit. Count one loser only in a suit headed by A-J-10. Some distinction must obviously be made between A-x-x, K-x-x, and Q-x-x. The first is a better two-loser holding than K-x-x, and three losers must be counted in a queen-high suit unless: (a) it is the proposed trump suit; (b) the suit has been bid by the partner; (c) the queen is supported by the jack; (d) the queen is "balanced" by an ace in another suit.

The initial count. An opening bid of one is made with: (a) not more than seven losers; (b) adequate high-card values, including two defensive tricks; (c) a sound rebid. A response in a new suit is made with: (a) at the one-level not more than 9 losers (sometimes 10 with compensating values); (b) at the two-level not more than 8 losers (sometimes 9 with compensating values).

The count on the second round. Neutral rebids by opener (e.g., 1♥-1♠-2♥, or 1♠-2♣-2♦ or 1♣-1♠-2♠) do not promise fewer than 7 losers.

A jump rebid by the opener in his original suit (e.g., 1♣-1♠-3♣) shows 7 winners and (in most cases) only 5 losers.

A reverse rebid by the opener at the two-level (e.g., 1♣-1♠-2♦) shows five losers (sometimes six with a high point-count). A reverse at the three-level (e.g., 1♠-

2 ♥ -3 ♣) shows not more than five losers.

A jump rebid by the responder in his original suit (e.g., 1 ♥ -1 ♠ -2 ♣ -3 ♠) shows 6 losers.

A responder's reverse at the two-level (e.g. 1 ♦ -2 ♣ - 2 ♦ -2 ♥) shows 6 to 7 losers. A reverse at the three-level (e.g., 1 ♥ -1 ♠ -2 ♥ -3 ♣) shows not more than 6 losers.

It soon becomes second nature to adjust the original count of losers in the light of the bidding. Trump control is an important factor, and a loser should be deducted whenever the quota of aces and other key features, such as a king or a singleton in the right spot, is better than it might be on the bidding. See COVER CARDS.

LOU HERMAN TROPHY. See HERMAN TROPHY and Appendix II.

LOVE. The state of the game, in rubber bridge, where there is as yet no score.

LOVE, TO PLAY FOR. To play rubber bridge without stakes.

LOVE ALL. A term, borrowed from tennis, used in some countries to describe that situation where neither side has made any score. Used in England at duplicate to indicate that neither side is vulnerable, but not used in the United States.

LOVE SCORE. Zero score; neither side vulnerable and no partscore.

LOW CARD. Not an honor; any card from the 2 to the 9, usually represented by an x in card or hand descriptions.

LOWER MINOR. See DEFENSE TO OPENING THREE-BID; SECOND NEGATIVE RESPONSE AFTER ARTIFICIAL FORCING OPENING.

LOWEST SCORE. The lowest score in major team-of-four play occurred in 1957, in the first Far East Team Championship at Manila. On the third set of eight boards in the match between Hong Kong and the Philippines, not one IMP was scored by either side. On each of the eight hands, both teams arrived at the same contract and made the same number of tricks. In a board-a-match team held at a Greater New York BA sectional tournament in 1975, one of the 74 teams entered scored only one-half board out of 26, a record that is unlikely to be broken. In tournament pair play, the lowest recorded score is 13% (by opera star Lauritz Melchior). In head-to-head team play the record can be claimed for Eddie Kantar, Billy Eisenberg, Alan Sontag, Fred Hamilton and Jim Cayne. In the first 16 deals of the 1983 Vanderbilt Knockout final in Hawaii they were outscored 68-2 by Bill Root, Richard Pavlicek, Edgar Kaplan and Norman Kay and were then penalized 10 IMPs for slow play. So they began the second quarter of the match with a score of minus 8 IMPs.

LUCAS TWO-BID. See MUIDERBERGH TWOS.

LUCK. A basic reason for the success of duplicate bridge is that it incorporates the optimum degree of luck. Although this means that the best players do not invariably win, it adds greatly to the fascination of the game and to the interplay of psychological factors. Par contests, where the luck element is removed, are much less popular.

Individual contests contain by far the largest element of luck and are less highly regarded as a test of skill than other forms of duplicate. The hazardous nature of an individual contest derives partly from the constant change of partners. Good luck may take the form of being teamed with a strong and compatible partner on critical deals which require accurate bidding or play. It would be bad luck to be teamed with an incompatible partner on such deals. Similarly, being teamed against incompatible players on swingy deals could be good luck, and a player might pick up a high matchpoint score without taking an active part.

After individual contests pair events contain the next highest proportion of luck. In a single-session event, a pair who are measurably stronger than the field will probably win less than half the time — but they will nearly always finish in the leading group. The greater the importance of a pair event, the greater the number of boards played, thus reducing the effect of luck.

Another facet of luck in pairs events is that toward the end of a contest an experienced pair who estimate that they have less than a winning score may adopt unusual tactics in an attempt to improve dramatically. Such tactics may take the form of bidding poor slams or games, or declining to bid good slams, in the hope that an improbable distribution of the cards will favor an unusual contract. Thus it is theoretically possible for a pair to have a comfortable lead with a few boards to go, to continue to bid and play perfectly, and yet be passed by a pair who have deliberately bid their way to faulty contracts or made imperfect plays. (See SHOOTING.)

It is in team-of-four games - particularly those where the scoring is by International Match Points - that luck is reduced to a minimum. Consequently these events carry the most prestige and are the accepted medium for international competition.

At the same time, the structure of team games is such that luck, when it does occur, is both more recognizable and more dramatic than in pair contests. This adds greatly to the ways in which skill may be manifested. For example, a player who at a critical stage of a close match is faced with the decision whether to bid an even-money slam may bring into the reckoning such factors as the personal idiosyncrasies of his counterpart at the other table, the bidding systems being played there, whether the players there will be able to judge the score as accurately as he and so on. Dramatic strokes of misfortune can also exert a profound psychological effect on the players and provide a stern test of character in the face of adversity.

Aside from close decisions, luck in team play may result in correct play being penalized by an unfortunate lie of the cards, while less sound play succeeds.

In team play an admitted but small mistake in technique can sometimes be penalized to an extent altogether out of proportion to the degree of error. Following were the cards in the crucial semifinal match between Britain and Italy in the second World Team Olympiad, held in New York City in 1964.

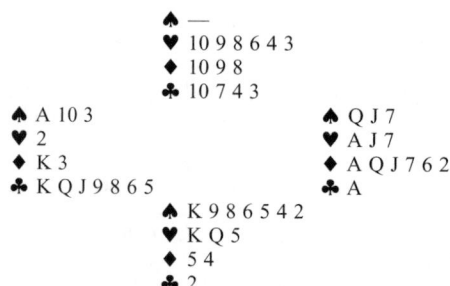

```
              ♠ —
              ♥ 10 9 8 6 4 3
              ♦ 10 9 8
              ♣ 10 7 4 3
♠ A 10 3                    ♠ Q J 7
♥ 2                         ♥ A J 7
♦ K 3                       ♦ A Q J 7 6 2
♣ K Q J 9 8 6 5             ♣ A
              ♠ K 9 8 6 5 4 2
              ♥ K Q 5
              ♦ 5 4
              ♣ 2
```

In the closed room the British bid to the best contract as follows:

West	East
Harrison-Gray	Flint
	2NT
4♣	4NT
7NT	Pass

7NT was a spread, and the British scored 2220. When the deal was replayed on Bridge-O-Rama, the bidding was:

West	North	East	South
Avarelli	Reese	Belladonna	Schapiro
		Pass	1♠
3♣	Pass	4♦	Pass
4NT	Pass	5NT	Pass
6♦	Pass	7♦	All Pass

This contract would be made unless North could ruff the opening lead or unless trumps were divided 5-0, the latter being only a 4% chance. Since 7♦ bid and made gives a score 2140, normal expectation would be a swing of 2 IMPs to the team which had bid 7NT. In fact the British South opened a low spade against 7♦ and his partner ruffed. The swing to Britain was thus 2320, or 20 IMPs. Although the Italian bidding was imperfect, one might say that they suffered ill luck to the extent of perhaps 18 IMPs. See also FORTUNE.

LUNCH-TIME BRIDGE. Popular, especially in large corporations that have teams belonging to the various commercial bridge leagues. In lunchrooms where there is sufficient space, one may find occasional foursomes of a serious or semi-serious nature, and these develop into groups of decent ability from time to time. If a person is willing to take a good chunk of time away from his rest or eating period to play a card game, it stands to reason there must be keen interest. In larger luncheon groups, there are even lunchtime matches, consisting of 6-board contests and lasting about 40 minutes.

M

MAC NAB TROPHY. Awarded to the winners of NORTH AMERICAN PAIRS FLIGHT C. Trophy honors Robin Mac Nab, former ACBL president and long-time member of the ACBL Board of Directors.

MACCABIAH GAMES. Games which celebrate athletic achievement held quadrennially in Israel and sometimes called "Israel Olympics". The Games were named after Judah Maccabeus, a Hebrew religious zealot who fought against the encroaching Hellenization of Jewish life symbolized by the Greek Olympic-style games and the cult of the physical. The Games are open to amateur Jewish participants, all of whom must have Jewish mothers. Since its inception in 1932, the Games have included athletics, gymnastics, football, tennis and cricket. In 1977, for the first time, bridge and chess were accepted as competing sports.

MACGUFFIN. A card that is dangerous to possess but too valuable to discard. The term, coined by Don Kersey, derives from Alfred Hitchcock's word for such an item, perhaps a piece of microfilm or a list of names, that is a key plot element in a movie. Most examples involve elopement, but the following, from Kersey's article in *The Bridge World* (April 2000), is in notrump:

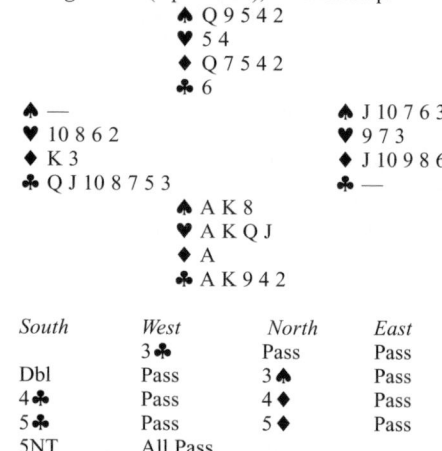

```
              ♠ Q 9 5 4 2
              ♥ 5 4
              ♦ Q 7 5 4 2
              ♣ 6
♠ —                         ♠ J 10 7 6 3
♥ 10 8 6 2                  ♥ 9 7 3
♦ K 3                       ♦ J 10 9 8 6
♣ Q J 10 8 7 5 3            ♣ —
              ♠ A K 8
              ♥ A K Q J
              ♦ A
              ♣ A K 9 4 2
```

South	West	North	East
	3♣	Pass	Pass
Dbl	Pass	3♠	Pass
4♣	Pass	4♠	Pass
5♣	Pass	5♦	Pass
5NT	All Pass		

The normal contract of 6♠ would be defeated by the terrible trump split. However, South lands in the weird contract of 5NT and the ♣Q is led. He wins with the ace and cashes the ♠A. When West discards a club, it seems there are only 10 tricks. But West's doubleton ♦K is a MacGuffin. South cashes the ♠K and red-suit winners reaching this position:

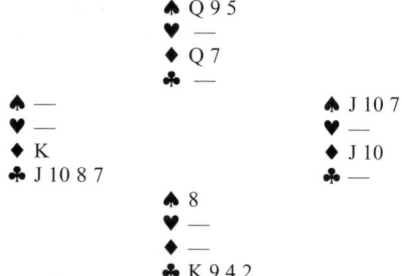

```
              ♠ Q 9 5
              ♥ —
              ♦ Q 7
              ♣ —
♠ —                         ♠ J 10 7
♥ —                         ♥ —
♦ K                         ♦ J 10
♣ J 10 8 7                  ♣ —
              ♠ 8
              ♥ —
              ♦ —
              ♣ K 9 4 2
```

When the ♠8 is led, West will be endplayed if he keeps the ♦K. He will be given the lead in diamonds and allowed to win a club honor. So West throws his MacGuffin and South ducks in dummy. If East wins, he leads a diamond to dummy's queen, and another diamond puts him back in to be endplayed in spades. If he ducks, a low club lead endplays West after all.

MACHINE-PREPARED HANDS. See COMPUTER HANDS.

MACHLIN TROPHY. Awarded to the winners of the NORTH AMERICAN WOMEN'S SWISS TEAMS. Tro-

phy honors Sadie Machlin, North American champion and wife of Tournament Director Jerry Machlin.

MAGAZINES. See BIBLIOGRAPHY.

MAGNETIC CARDS. Cards made from a very thin sheet of metal. Though not themselves magnetic, the cards are attracted to and held onto a magnetized board which is part of the set.

The principal advantage of these cards is that play can take place alongside outdoor pools, on breezy patios, or at the beach.

MAJOR. A major suit, i.e., hearts or spades.

MAJOR PENALTY CARD. Any card of honor rank prematurely exposed, or any card prematurely and deliberately exposed. If more than one card is thus exposed, each is a major penalty card. See Law 50.

MAJOR SUIT. Either of the two highest-ranking suits, hearts and spades, so characterized because they outrank the third and fourth suits in the bidding and scoring.

MAJOR TENACE. An original holding of ace-queen (without the king) of a suit. After one or more rounds of a suit have been played, the highest and third highest remaining cards of the suit in the hand of one player are called a major tenace (when the second highest remaining card is not held by the same player).

MAJORITY CALLING. The principle by which any bid outranks any other bid at a lower level, regardless of scoring value. The opposite principle, numerical calling, was standard in auction bridge, although abandoned in the United States in 1913. In this procedure 4♠, for example, could follow a bid of 5♣ because its scoring value was higher.

MAJORITY RULE. When you hold an eight-card fit missing the jack you usually play for the drop. But if one opponent has a preponderance of cards in two other suits, you might credit him with shortness in this suit and finesse his partner for the jack. The majority rule aids in determining when such a play is warranted.

The rule, first presented by Phillip Martin in *The Bridge World*, January, 1985, advises you to consider the implied lie of the fourth suit. If the hand with suspected length can hold four cards in the problem suit and still hold a majority of cards in the fourth suit, you should assume the bad break.

For example:

```
            ♠ Q 10 9 5
            ♥ A 7 6
            ♦ 9 6 5 3
            ♣ 10 4

            ♠ A 6 4 2
            ♥ K Q 10 9 8
            ♦ —
            ♣ A K 8 5
```

South plays in 6♠ after a diamond overcall by East. West leads a third-best ♦ 2. Declarer ruffs and plays a spade to the nine and king. East returns a diamond. Declarer ruffs with the ace and plays a spade to the jack and queen and cashes the ♠ 10. On the third spade, East follows, declarer

pitches a club and West pitches a diamond. Both opponents follow to the ♣A and ♣K. Since East began with three spades and six diamonds, declarer is tempted to play him for heart shortness and run the ♥ 10. According to the majority rule, declarer should consider the implied lie of the club suit. A 4-1 heart break would leave West with four of the seven clubs, a majority. So declarer should indeed finesse. If West held one more diamond (or had shown up with three spades), a 4-1 break would leave West with three of the seven clubs and declarer should play for the drop. See SUIT COMBINATIONS.

MAKE. Used in bridge in four different senses. As a verb, it may mean (1) to shuffle the deck; (2) to succeed in a contract; (3) to win a trick by the play of a card. As a noun, it means (4) a successful contract but usually a hypothetical one in the postmortem: "5♦ would have been a make."

MAKE UP. To shuffle the cards.

MAKE UP A TABLE. A player who, with at least three others, forms a table for play at rubber bridge or Chicago, is said to make up a table.

MALOWAN SIX CLUBS CONVENTION. A variation of the GRAND SLAM FORCE originated by Walter Malowan. After Blackwood has been used, a 5NT bid is not available as a grand slam force because it would be a conventional bid asking for kings. 6♣ is therefore used as a substitute grand slam force unless clubs is the agreed trump suit.

The responses to 6♣ must be influenced by the fact that the ace of trumps is already known. Marshall Miles suggests that the cheapest available bid should be used at the six level to show the best possible trump holding, with increasingly strong bids showing increasingly worse holdings.

MAMA-PAPA BRIDGE. A term applied to a simple bidding style uncluttered with conventions.

MANUFACTURE OF PLAYING CARDS. After the establishment of papermaking in America, several printers, including Benjamin Franklin, apparently produced packs of cards as a sideline. The first man specifically listed as a manufacturer of playing cards was Jazaniah Ford of Milton MA, about 1800, followed by Thomas Crehore of Dorchester MA.

Modern cardplayers are accustomed to the double-head card, which can be read from either end, and to the INDICES in the two corners, which permit one to recognize the card without seeing its entire face. Cards of this type did not become standard until the late 1870s. Until then a player had to look at a full face of the card, and hold it right-side up, to know what the card was.

Either superstition or habit prevents major changes in playing-card design. Unsuccessful attempts have been made to print the suits in four colors, to redesign the pips, to clothe the face cards in modern dress; and to introduce circular cards. Soviet Russia tried to replace the "anachronistic kings and queens" with revolutionary heroes, but so many packs were smuggled in that the conventional royalty cards were reinstated. (See also FIVE-SUIT BRIDGE.)

A more modest change reintroduced in 1964 and em-

bodied in special decks used in the World Team Olympiad was to use a very pale blue-green tint instead of white for the background of the faces. This has been shown to reduce eyestrain.

For information on early cards and different packs, see HISTORY OF PLAYING CARDS; PACK; TAROT; TAXES. See also PLASTIC CARDS.

MARKED CARD. (1) A card that is known, from the previous play, to be in a particular hand. (2) A damaged card. (3) A card fixed so that it can be read in a cheating situation.

MARKED FINESSE. A finesse that is certain to win because (1) an opponent shows out; (2) the position of an honor has been pinpointed by the bidding; (3) the previous play has indicated the location of a crucial opposing card.

MARMIC SYSTEM. An Italian system, apparently obsolete, whose name is derived from the first names of the inventors (MARio Franco and MIChele Giovine). It is probably the most unusual system ever played in serious international competition by a major bridge country until the advent of HUM SYSTEMS (see WEAK OPENING SYSTEMS.) In some respects it was a forerunner of the ROMAN SYSTEM. The chief feature was that a player was expected to pass in first or second position with balanced distribution and $16^1/_2$-19 points. The same principle applied after an opponent's opening bid, and in each case the passer's partner was expected to balance with 5 points or more. This opened the possibility for trap passing by the opponents, and the system was amended to provide an opening 1NT bid, instead of the strong pass, at unfavorable vulnerability.

MARX TWO CLUBS. An alternate name, especially in England, for the STAYMAN convention. Originated by Jack Marx approximately at the same time as the American counterpart devised by George Rapee. Now obsolete.

MASTER CARD. The highest unplayed card of a suit. It can also be thus characterized while actually being played.

MASTER HAND. The hand which controls the situation—more particularly, the one which controls the trump suit, leading out high trumps to prevent adverse ruffs, and retaining a trump or two to prevent the adverse run of a long side suit. It is usually the declarer's hand, but sometimes, when the declarer's trumps are more valuable as ruffers, the dummy is made the master hand. See DUMMY REVERSAL.

MASTER INDIVIDUAL, NORTH AMERICAN CHAMPIONSHIP. Formerly called World Master Individual or Life Master Individual. See STEINER TROPHY. For results see Appendix I.

MASTER KNOCKOUT TEAMS, NORTH AMERICAN CHAMPIONSHIP. See SPINGOLD TROPHY. For results see Appendix I.

MASTER MIXED TEAMS. See BARCLAY TROPHY, LEBHAR TROPHY, NORTH AMERICAN MASTER MIXED TEAMS CHAMPIONSHIP, NORTH AMERICAN MIXED TEAMS CHAMPIONSHIP.

MASTER PAIRS. Usually run in conjunction with a NON-MASTER PAIRS. An arbitrary lower limit of masterpoints is set, and at least one member of every pair must have at least that number of masterpoints. The game itself is run along the lines of an OPEN PAIRS.

MASTER TEAMS. Usually run in conjunction with a NON-MASTER TEAMS. An arbitrary lower limit of masterpoints is set, and at least one member of each team must have at least that number of masterpoints.

MASTERPOINT. The unit which measures bridge achievement in tournament play.

The term first arose in North America when eligibles for the ABL's 1934 von Zedtwitz Master Pairs (later Life Master Pairs) were chosen from a list of players credited with masterpoints for winning tournaments run by the American Bridge League and the American Whist League, as well as the Vanderbilt and Eastern Championships, which at that time were independent events. In the following year, winners of many smaller tournaments that had applied for ABL sanction became eligible. In 1936, to offset this rapid and somewhat haphazard inflation of masters, the League created the rank of LIFE MASTER, then awarded only to those who had won their points in national championships or the equivalent. These point awards were tiny. At the outset, 10 points was the qualifying minimum, and a scheme for deducting points each year made it necessary for Life Masters to continue successful competition in order to retain their status. Deductions were discontinued in 1944.

Meanwhile, the United States Bridge Association announced its own masterpoint program and appears to have been the first to extend the idea to the club level. Effective Sept. 1, 1935, City Masterpoints were awarded for duplicate games in USBA-affiliated clubs. These were convertible at 10 for 1 into State Masterpoints, awarded for citywide tournaments, which were in turn convertible at 10 for 1 into National Masterpoints, awarded for State tournaments. A legal dispute over the ABL's claim of exclusive right to award masterpoints was not resolved until 1937, when the USBA was merged into the ABL, becoming the American Contract Bridge League. The ACBL introduced Rating Points (later called Fractional Masterpoints and even later Club Masterpoints), worth .01 of a masterpoint, into club games effective Jan. 1, 1938. The result was a rapid acceleration in the growth of ACBL membership, but it also led to the eventual need to distinguish among points won at local, regional and national levels.

Masterpoints are awarded at ACBL tournaments in amounts proportional to the size and classification of the event and the rating of the tournament. The basic point structure is based on open pairs. Since such events as mixed pairs, men's pairs, senior pairs, women's pairs and unmixed pairs are restricted to some extent, point awards for them are lower than for open pairs. Awards for team events are higher than for the same size and kind of pair game. In general, awards at a sectional tournament are higher than those at a local, and awards at a regional tournament are higher than those at a sectional. Awards for most North American Championships are fixed, and they are substantially higher than regional awards.

Masterpoint awards at local, sectional and regional

tournaments are given according to a formula in which the principal ingredients are the size of the event and the rating of the eligible players. In general, awards climb arithmetically up through 60 tables, and thereafter they follow a logarithmic curve which very much slows down the rate of increase.

England adopted a masterpoint scheme in 1956 and many other countries followed suit. In most of these schemes the award scale is less generous, and the achievement of high rank is usually slower. Points won in foreign bridge leagues may be converted to ACBL masterpoints under certain conditions. Many nations also convert ACBL points to the national scale. See BLACK POINTS, GOLD POINTS, MASTERPOINT PLAN, RED POINTS, PLATINUM POINTS, REGIONAL AND NATIONAL POINTS, SILVER POINTS.

MASTERPOINT CERTIFICATE. See RATING POINTS.

MASTERPOINT PLAN. ACBL method of awarding masterpoints in bridge tournaments at club, local, sectional, regional and national levels. Creation of the Masterpoint Plan in 1936 is be credited to William McKenney and Ray Eisenlord, with many others contributing to later developments. The details of the method by which the plan operates at the club level are set out in the ACBL Handbook. The ACBL publishes a directory of clubs, which enables members to find bridge activity in any city they may visit.

Any club or group in the United States, Canada, Bermuda or Mexico may apply for a sanction to issue masterpoints at regularly scheduled duplicate games. The clubs are of four types: Open (to all comers); Invitational (restricted to members of the group and invited guests or restricted by expertise), Novice (restricted to players with not more than 20 masterpoints) and Bridge Plus+ (restricted to new players with not more than 5 masterpoints).

Club masterpoints must be awarded at every duplicate game conducted by a sanctioned club. Club masterpoints are hundredths of a full point. The scale for invitational clubs is slightly lower. Novice and Bridge Plus+ clubs (or games) score at an even lower scale.

Once each calendar quarter a weekly club is entitled to a Club Tournament game with increased awards. Those clubs meeting less frequently are entitled to a Club Tournament for every 12 regularly scheduled sessions.

The scale of awards increases steadily through the various levels: club, local, sectional, regional and national. See also AMERICAN CONTRACT BRIDGE LEAGUE; DUPLICATE BRIDGE; DUPLICATE TOURNAMENT; MASTERPOINT; RANKING OF PLAYERS; SANCTIONED CLUBS.

Many other countries have adopted a masterpoint plan along similar lines. The WORLD BRIDGE FEDERATION also has such a plan, with GRAND MASTER as the premier rank.

Here is how the ACBL masterpoint plan is set up:
CLUB MASTERPOINTS - 100 club masterpoints are the equivalent of one (1) masterpoint.
BLACK POINTS - Points won at club games, unit championships and sectionally rated events.
RED POINTS - Points won at regional tournaments, Grand National Teams, North American Pairs and North American championship events.
GOLD POINTS - Points won for section first and over-

all placing in regional tournament events and North American championship events with an upper limit of not less than 750 masterpoints.
SILVER POINTS - Points won at Sectional Tournaments, STaC's, and progressive sectionals.

Rank	MPs needed	Pigmented points needed
Rookie	0-4.99	None
Junior Master (A)	5	None
Club Master (B)	20	None
Sectional Master (C)	50	5 silver
Regional Master (D)	100	5 red or gold, 15 silver
NABC Master (E)	200	5 gold, 15 red or gold, 25 silver
Life Master (F)	300	25 gold, 25 red or gold, 50 silver

Additional Life Master designations have been established and are available only to players who have achieved LM Rank.

Bronze Life Master (G)	500 masterpoints
Silver Life Master (H)	1,000 masterpoints
Gold Life Master (I)	2,500 masterpoints
Diamond Life Master (J)	5,000 masterpoints
Grand Life Master (K)	10,000 masterpoints and one unlimited NABC championship.

MATCH. A session or event of head-to-head competition between two pairs or two teams.

The shortest matches in international competition were the 18-board qualifying round matches in the 1964 WORLD TEAM OLYMPIAD. The longest matches were played for the BERMUDA BOWL from 1951 to 1957, when there were only two teams in competition, and 224 to 256 boards were played. Even longer matches (300 boards) have been played on semi-official occasions. See ANGLO-AMERICAN MATCHES. The most famous of the nonofficial challenge pair matches of the Thirties were longer still. Both the CULBERTSON-LENZ MATCH (Dec. 1931 - Jan. 1932) and the CULBERTSON-SIMS MATCH (March-April, 1935) were 150 rubbers. In the former, 879 hands were dealt, only 25 of which were passed out.

MATCH PLAY. A team-of-four contest in which two teams are competing for an appreciable number of boards. Tactics at match play are described in IMP TACTICS and STATE OF MATCH.

MATCH RECORDS. See HAND RECORD; BIBLIOGRAPHY.

MATCHPOINT. A credit awarded to a contestant in pair or individual events for a score superior to that of another contestant in direct competition.

In an ACBL event, the number of matchpoints available to a contestant is normally one less than the number of contestants in direct competition. For example, in a game of 13 rounds there are 13 North-South scores in direct competition and 13 East-West scores in direct competition. The highest score in each group beats the other 12 scores in that group and receives 12 matchpoints, the greatest number available to it.

Other pairs receive 11, 10, 9 points, etc., according to the number of pairs beaten in direct competition. The lowest pair in each group beats no pair in direct competition and receives zero matchpoints.

When two or more pairs achieve identical scores, each pair receives $1/2$ matchpoint for each pair with which its score is tied.

When matchpoint scoring is used in team games, the score that is obtained by a team on a board is 1 matchpoint if the combined score is plus, 0 if the score

is minus, and ½ if the team score is neither plus nor minus. (Each board is thus scored as a match in itself, hence "board-a-match" scoring.)

In tournaments in other sections of the world and in WORLD BRIDGE FEDERATION play, matchpoints are doubled to eliminate halves. A pair receives two matchpoints for each pair it beats and one for each pair it ties. Effectively both methods are the same. See also DOUBLE TOP; SCORING ACROSS THE FIELD.

MATCHPOINT BIDDING. If bridge were played double-dummy (if one could see all four hands whenever one had to make a decision), the bidding and play would be exactly the same at matchpoint duplicate as at rubber bridge. A minor exception is caused by the scoring of honors at rubber bridge. If one could see only partner's hand, the bidding would usually be the same. The objective on any one hand is the same for both forms of bridge: to score the maximum number of points or to allow the opponents to score a minimum number. Yet successful matchpoint tactics are quite different from successful rubber bridge tactics. For example, suppose the bidding, with both sides vulnerable, has gone as follows:

West	North	East	South
			1♥
Pass	2♥	Pass	Pass
?			

West holds: ♠ Q 9 8 x x
                   ♥ x
                   ♦ A x x x
                   ♣ Q 10 x

The opponents' lack of enterprise marks East with at least 8 points, perhaps as many as 14. He may or may not fit West's hand. At either rubber or duplicate, West should bid 2♠ when East holds:

                   ♠ K J x x
                   ♥ x x x
                   ♦ K J x
                   ♣ K x x

West should pass when East holds:

                   ♠ x
                   ♥ K J 10 x
                   ♦ J x x x
                   ♣ K x x x

Since West does not know which type of hand his partner has, he must consider what he has to lose or gain by bidding. The best probable result from bidding is that East-West, instead of North-South, will make a partscore. This is equivalent to approximately a 250-point gain. A partscore is worth an additional 50 points at rubber bridge, the same as at duplicate. The worst likely result is a 500- or 800-point penalty. Which is more likely to occur? Surely the former.

A reopening 2♠ bid would probably work out as follows: Four times in ten the opponents would bid and make 3♥, in which case the reopening bid would have neither lost nor gained.

Four times in ten it would gain. Perhaps East-West would be +140 instead of +100, +110 instead of –110, –100 instead of –110, or + 100 instead of –110 (because the opponents bid again).

The other two times the reopening bid would lose, perhaps quite heavily. The net loss from these two occasions would be greater than the gain from the other four.

In rubber bridge or IMP play it would not pay to reopen with a weak suit, because in the long run a reopening bid would lose points. In duplicate, a reopening bid is advisable. This is true whether most of the other West players would bid or not, but it is easier to demonstrate if the potential reopener were a lone wolf. Passing would result in an average score, 6 matchpoints out of 12. Whenever the reopening bid should gain, it would result in a top; whenever it should lose, it would result in a bottom. At rubber bridge, it is necessary to weigh the amount of gain against the amount of loss when considering any action. In duplicate, the main consideration is the frequency of gain or loss. The following hand illustrates a similar principle, except that the mystery is in regard to the opponents' holdings rather than partner's.

West	East
♠ A 10 x	♠ K Q x x
♥ 10 x	♥ x x
♦ A K J x	♦ Q 9 x x x x
♣ Q 10 9 x	♣ A

At rubber bridge, the bidding might well be as follows:

West	North	East	South
			Pass
1♦	Pass	1♠	Pass
2♠	Pass	4♦	Pass
5♦	All Pass		

East has a good enough hand to be almost certain that 5♦ will be safe. Besides, a slam is still possible from his point of view. Consequently, he shows his excellent diamond support while still allowing West to return to spades with four-card spade support.

At duplicate, the bidding should start the same way, but East would probably bid 4♠ over the raise to 2♠. A slam is unlikely, and with such a good four-card-spade suit, East would not want to "risk" a final diamond contract. Perhaps the word "risk" seems unusual here, but at duplicate 5♦ is a much poorer gamble, hence a greater risk, than is 4♠. At least 75% of the time, East-West will do better in spades than in diamonds; they cannot afford to "play safe" when the odds favor the more dangerous contract. This is true despite the fact that the gain in playing spades cannot exceed 20 to 50 points, while the loss, when the spades break badly or the opening diamond lead is ruffed, can be several hundred points.

It has been stated that the same contract usually would be chosen at duplicate as at rubber bridge if one could see partner's hand. The following is an exception. Even the reason for the exception is that bridge is not a double-dummy game.

West	East
♠ A x	♠ x x
♥ A x x	♥ x x
♦ K Q J x x	♦ A x x
♣ 10 8 x	♣ A Q J 9 x x

The ideal contract at rubber bridge is 7♣ — despite the fact that the odds are slightly against making it. To simplify this discussion, assume that the diamonds are not 5-0, and the slam depends merely upon the club finesse. Normally two-to-one odds are needed to justify a grand slam bid at rubber bridge, but these odds are based on the assumption that a small slam is safe. In this case, with a major suit lead, declarer will take either 11 or 13 tricks, never 12. By bidding seven, half the time declarer will score 1440 or 2140 points. At rubber bridge, a nonvulnerable game is worth approxi-

mately 300 points, even though no points are scored till the rubber is completed. When the club finesse fails, he will score -100 or -200. By bidding seven, he will average +670 not vulnerable or +970 vulnerable. This is better than he can score at any other contract.

Why is 7♣ not the ideal contract for duplicate also? The reason is that it will be very difficult, if not impossible, to get to any slam. The best contract is 6♣. Just bidding six, and making seven, will be good for a top board when no one else is in a slam. If the club finesse fails, down one may still be worth some points since the 3NT bidders may also be down one. It is time to move on from theory to some practical applications.

West	North	East	South
			1♥
Pass	1NT	Pass	2♦
Pass	?		

What should North bid with the following?

    ♠ Q 10 x
    ♥ 10 x
    ♦ J 10 x x x
    ♣ Q J x x

At rubber bridge or IMPs the answer is clear cut. Pass, for two reasons. 2♦ should be safer than 2♥. Also, if North bids 2♥, South may bid again, while a pass will prevent him from doing so. Surely 2♦ will be safer than 3♥. Since game is out of the question, one should stop in the safest contract.

At duplicate, a return to 2♥ is advisable. If opener passes he may pick up an extra 10 or 20 points. Quite frequently he will get too high or be defeated by a bad break, but the risk is justifiable because the odds are right.

Dlr.: North   ♠ K J 5
Vul: Both   ♥ A 8 7
              ♦ Q 4
              ♣ J 8 7 4 3

♠ A 10 6   ♠ 3 2
♥ 10 5 4 3   ♥ K Q J 6 2
♦ 10 9 7 2   ♦ K J 6
♣ A 5   ♣ K 9 6

         ♠ Q 9 8 7 4
         ♥ 9
         ♦ A 8 5 3
         ♣ Q 10 2

West	North	East	South
	Pass	1♥	Pass
2♥	Pass	Pass	2♠
3♥	3♠	Pass	Pass
Dbl	All Pass		

East-West must defend carefully to defeat 3♠. As the cards lie, they can make 4♥. There are several interesting features about the bidding. The opening bid and raise were routine. So was the 2♠ bid — at duplicate. West properly bid 3♥ since he had a maximum raise. The first questionable bid was North's raise to 3♠. Usually, when the opponents are pushed one trick higher by a reopening bid, the percentage bid is to pass in all close situations. The reopener has already inferred from the opponents' bidding that his partner has high cards, and his partner has no business bidding again to show these same high cards. He should bid again only with good distribution or cards exceptionally well placed. The result from passing should be no worse than at other tables where someone failed to reopen, and it will be better when the opponents have been pushed beyond their depth. How-

ever, North's questionable bid would have gained him a top if West had not doubled. West knew that he would get a very poor score, perhaps 2 matchpoints out of 12, if North-South should make exactly 3♠. Consequently a double could not cost more than 2 matchpoints. On the other hand, if North-South should make exactly eight tricks, it would be extremely costly not to double. West has a good defensive hand, and is tempted to double anyway; he would double with a poorer hand than he actually has. At rubber bridge a double which could convert a partscore into game would need about seven-to-one odds in its favor.

In duplicate, a double is sometimes the percentage bid even when the odds are *against* defeating the contract. Suppose, for example, that East-West were to bid 4♥ over 3♠. North-South are doomed to get a bottom anyway, since presumably other pairs will not bid game. So a double will not cost them a thing. If the hands were changed slightly so that 4♥ could be defeated, a double would gain a few points, since +200 is better than North-South could do in spades. With nothing to lose and everything to gain, a double must be the right bid. If a double can lose only 2 points and may gain 9 or 10, it is a good gamble, even when one expects the contract to be made.

Another way it pays to be more competitive in duplicate is taking sacrifices, but the attraction of the high-level save has diminished since the scoring table was modified. The more common dilemma is whether or not to take a sacrifice against a game contract. In rubber bridge, it is losing tactics to take deliberate 500-point sacrifice against a vulnerable game when there is any reasonable hope of defeating it. In duplicate, the sacrifice is correct if the contract is a normal one and a favorite to make.

MATCHPOINT DEFENSE. Defense at duplicate is often more difficult than at rubber bridge. In the latter, the objective is clear-cut: try to set the contract. It makes little difference when declarer makes an overtrick as a result of an unsuccessful attempt to defeat him. At duplicate, the overtrick makes a great deal of difference.

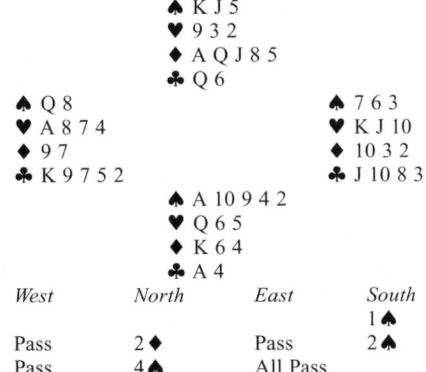

West	North	East	South
			1♠
Pass	2♦	Pass	2♠
Pass	4♠	All Pass	

West leads a small club, won by dummy's queen. Declarer plays the ♠K, then takes a losing trump finesse to West's doubleton queen. What should West do? At rubber bridge, he should lead a low heart. This play will set the contract whenever it can be set — when East has ♥ K-Q-x or K-J-10; also when he has ♥ J-10-x (or Q-10-x) and the ♦K. At duplicate the right play is not clear-cut, but cashing the ace is probably correct. It loses in only two situations, and it gains (a trick) much more frequently whenever declarer has the two red kings.

Suppose that West is on lead with:

♠ Q J 10 9
♥ A 8 7
♦ 9 5 3
♣ 7 5 2

after the following bidding:

West	North	East	South
	1♣	Pass	2♦
Pass	2NT	Pass	3♣
Pass	3♠	Pass	5♦
Pass	6♦	All Pass	

North apparently has the ♥K; South probably has two hearts. The best chance to set the contract is to lead a low heart and hope that East has the queen and that either North or South has the jack. If that situation exists, declarer may misguess. The low heart lead is not correct at duplicate because it stands too good a chance of giving away an overtrick. The opponents may have both the ♥ K-Q, or they may be missing the queen *and* jack (in which case declarer would have to play dummy's king).

The defense against unusual contracts may be just as interesting as the play of unusual contracts.

Another way in which the defense at duplicate varies from the defense at rubber bridge is that the defenders can take advantage of declarer's greed.

```
              ♠ 10 9
              ♥ 9 8 4
              ♦ A Q J 5
              ♣ A K J 7
♠ J 7                        ♠ 8 5 4 2
♥ Q 10 7 6 2                 ♥ A J 5
♦ 8 6                        ♦ K 10 7
♣ 10 8 4 2                   ♣ 6 5 3
              ♠ A K Q 6 3
              ♥ K 3
              ♦ 9 4 3 2
              ♣ Q 9
```

West	North	East	South
			1♠
Pass	2♦	Pass	3♦
Pass	3♠	Pass	4♠
All Pass			

The bidding is not recommended, but that is the way it went. West led the ♣2, won by declarer's 9. He cashed three top spades and took the diamond finesse, which won. Dummy's clubs were now cashed for heart discards; East also discarded a heart on the last club. Declarer then ruffed a heart with his next-to-last trump in order to repeat the diamond finesse. This time the finesse lost. East cashed the good ♠8, and the defenders took the remaining tricks. Down one.

Did East make the right play in refusing the first diamond finesse, or was he just lucky? By playing cautiously, declarer could have made an overtrick after East's duck. However, East had a psychological factor working in his favor. Declarer risked his contract when he took the diamond finesse. If he wanted to play safe, he would have cashed his clubs first for heart discards. He did not play the hand this way because he was afraid of being stuck in the dummy unable to take the diamond finesse. Since declarer has risked his contract to take the diamond finesse, it would be inconsistent for him not to repeat the finesse so as to make his apparently successful gamble pay off.

MATCHPOINT DUPLICATE, MATHEMATICS OF. See MATHEMATICS OF MATCHPOINT PLAY.

MATCHPOINT PLAY. In duplicate play, the test for deciding between various alternatives is not how much (in total points) a given play could gain or lose, but how many matchpoints it could gain or lose. (But see IMP TACTICS for a discussion of this specialized branch of duplicate play.) When the contract is a normal one, this means, "Does the play have better than a 50% chance of success?"

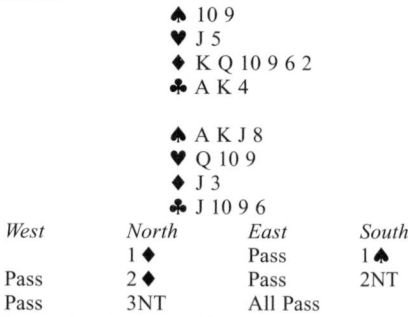

```
              ♠ 10 9
              ♥ J 5
              ♦ K Q 10 9 6 2
              ♣ A K 4

              ♠ A K J 8
              ♥ Q 10 9
              ♦ J 3
              ♣ J 10 9 6
```

West	North	East	South
	1♦	Pass	1♠
Pass	2♦	Pass	2NT
Pass	3NT	All Pass	

The opening lead is the ♥4 to East's king. West ducks the ♥7 return, playing the deuce. It is almost certain that three more heart tricks will be run by the opponents as soon as the lead is lost. Combined with the trick already lost and the ♦A, that is one too many. At rubber bridge, the proper play would be to try for four spade tricks and four club tricks without touching the diamonds. Declarer's chances would not be good, but it would be worth a try with so much to gain, so little to lose. In duplicate there is much more to lose. Down one should be almost an average board, while down two would surely be a cold bottom. The odds are greater than three to one that attacking the black suits will lose a trick rather than gain a trick, which means that playing to make the hand will result in three bottom boards for every top. When the odds are so unfavorable, it is better to play safe for eight tricks. The fact that the contract is for nine tricks is immaterial, since it is the contract everyone will reach.

Following is another example illustrating the same principle. In this case, however, declarer does not deliberately refuse to try to make his contract. He merely adopts a risky line of play which gives him a good opportunity for overtricks.

```
              ♠ 7 5
              ♥ K 4
              ♦ A K 10 9 7 6
              ♣ A J 4

              ♠ A 10 8
              ♥ A 10 7
              ♦ J 5
              ♣ 10 8 7 5 2
```

West	North	East	South
	1♦	1♠	1NT
Pass	3NT	All Pass	

A spade is led, and declarer holds up until the third trick, upon which West discards a heart. The correct rubber bridge play would be to attack the diamonds by cashing the ace and king. If West has the queen, it is unnecessary to finesse, since West has no spade to return, and only five diamond tricks are needed. On the other hand, a losing finesse to East's singleton or doubleton queen would be disastrous. In duplicate, the better play is to take a first-round diamond finesse. This

play will gain (a trick) approximately twice as often as it will lose (several tricks).

The finesse gains if West holds Q-8-4-3, Q-8-4-2, Q-8-3-2, Q-4-3-2, Q-8-4, Q-8-3, Q-8-2, Q-4-3, Q-4-2, Q-3-2 (10 distributions). The finesse loses if East holds Q, Q-8, Q-4, Q-3, Q-2 (5 distributions). Each 3-2 division is slightly more likely than each 4-1 distribution.

Both the contracts shown were quite normal. It is proper to jeopardize one's normal contract when the odds are favorable. When a contract is exceptionally good, it is proper to play safe, just as at rubber bridge.

A hard-to-reach game or slam, or a doubled contract, would be an example of a good contract. When just making the contract will be worth 10 matchpoints out of 12, only exceptionally good odds would justify jeopardizing the contract for an overtrick.

Some of the most interesting problems arise in the play of unusual contracts at duplicate.

```
Dlr: North          ♠ A 10 6 4 2
Vul: N-S            ♥ 8 5
                    ♦ Q 2
                    ♣ Q 5 3 2

                    ♠ K J 9 5
                    ♥ 4 2
                    ♦ A K 10 9 6
                    ♣ 6 4
```

West	North	East	South
	Pass	1♥	1♠
4♥	4♠	Pass	Pass
Dbl	All Pass		

North's 4♠ bid was bold, considering the vulnerability, and surely most South players would not choose to overcall with a four-card suit. It is safe to say that 4♠ doubled will not be played at any other table, and down two will be a bottom, not even a tie for bottom. West leads the ♥Q, followed by the ♥J. Next he plays the ♣A followed by the ♣J to East's king (dummy playing low). East returns the ♦3, and West does not cover the 10. The only problem is how to play the trump suit for no losers. If the spades are split 2-2 and the diamonds no worse than 4-2 the opponents cannot make 4♥; consequently - 200 would be a bottom. Declarer must base his play on the assumption that 4♥ can be made, and a singleton spade is more likely than a singleton diamond. It appears that West has five clubs to his partner's two, so if anyone has a singleton spade, it will be West. The proper play is to lead to the ace and finesse East for the queen. This works, since the four hands are as follows:

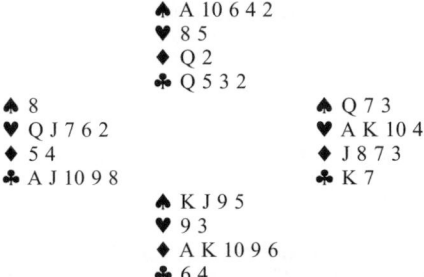

Suppose that the four hands and bidding were changed slightly. The only difference in the bidding is that the 4♠ contract is not doubled.

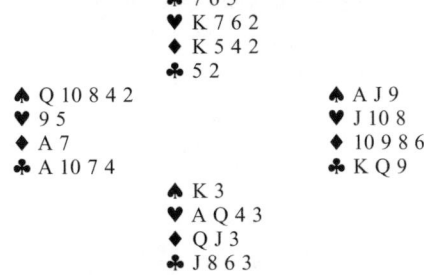

The defenders take the first four tricks in hearts and clubs, then exit with a diamond. Should declarer play the same as before? The fact that he is not doubled enables him to make an unusual type of safety play. He should bang down the ♠A-K. If the queen does not fall, he does not care, because he knows that 4♥ is cold, and -200 will be a good sacrifice. What he does not want to risk is a -200 when, as here, the opponents can make only 3♥. Minus 100 will beat all the -140 scores.

```
Dlr: South          ♠ 7 6 5
Vul: E-W            ♥ K 7 6 2
                    ♦ K 5 4 2
                    ♣ 5 2

                    ♠ K 3
                    ♥ A Q 4 3
                    ♦ Q J 3
                    ♣ J 8 6 3
```

South opens with a weak notrump, and the other players pass. West leads the ♠4 to East's ace. East returns the jack, and West plays the deuce. Before planning the play, declarer should evaluate his contract, and try to determine what other pairs in direct competition will be doing. If they buy the bid, most of them will be playing hearts. They will score 110 or 140, depending upon how the hand breaks. It is impossible to do as well at notrump as at hearts, no matter how badly the opponents defend, so the only hope to salvage the board is that the opponents can make something. Sure enough, North-South have a maximum of five defensive tricks against spades, and perhaps only three or four, depending upon the distribution. Since it is not possible to beat the pairs playing in hearts, the proper attitude is to forget about them and to concentrate on beating the pairs defending against spades. If North-South were vulnerable, it would be necessary to steal a diamond trick somehow — minus 200 would be no good at all. But not vulnerable, North-South can afford a two-trick set. Minus 100 should be just as good as - 50. The proper play is not to try to steal anything, but just to hope that the hearts will break so that five tricks can be cashed. The full deal is:

```
                    ♠ 7 6 5
                    ♥ K 7 6 2
                    ♦ K 5 4 2
                    ♣ 5 2
♠ Q 10 8 4 2                    ♠ A J 9
♥ 9 5                          ♥ J 10 8
♦ A 7                          ♦ 10 9 8 6
♣ A 10 7 4                     ♣ K Q 9
                    ♠ K 3
                    ♥ A Q 4 3
                    ♦ Q J 3
                    ♣ J 8 6 3
```

At most tables, South opens with a suit bid, and West

plays 2♠ or 3♠, after an overcall and a raise by his partner. Minus 100 is an excellent result for East-South, but -150 would be a bottom.

```
              ♠ 5 4 2
              ♥ A Q 6 4 3
              ♦ 10 9 3
              ♣ 4 2

              ♠ A J
              ♥ K J 10 7
              ♦ A K J 7
              ♣ Q 6 5
```

West	North	East	South
			1♥
Pass	2♥	Pass	3NT
All Pass			

West leads the ♠K. How should declarer play this contract? The first question is what will happen at the other tables. It seems quite likely that most of the field will be playing in 4♥. With the same spade lead, the declarers in 4♥ will either make five by discarding a club on the fourth diamond, or be down one if the diamond finesse fails. What are the prospects in notrump? To make 4NT or be down several if the diamond finesse fails. That is, down several if the finesse is attempted and fails. The only chance for a decent board is not to take the diamond finesse, and to hope that it does not work. If it does not work, down at 3NT will tie the field, which will be down one at 4♥. If the queen happens to be doubleton, offside, refusing the finesse will result in an overtrick and a top.

The opening lead can have an important influence upon the play of *normal* contracts.

```
              ♠ J 10 5 2
              ♥ 6 3 2
              ♦ K Q 10 6
              ♣ A 3

              ♠ A Q 7 4 3
              ♥ A 7 4
              ♦ J 3
              ♣ Q 4 2
```

West	North	East	South
			1♠
Pass	2♦	Pass	2♠
Pass	3♠	Pass	4♠
All Pass			

West leads a club, a small card is played from dummy, and when East produces the jack, declarer wins with the queen. How should declarer play the spades? Normally he would take a finesse. However, the lead was very favorable. It gave declarer a trick he could never have won by himself. With a heart lead, declarer would have to be lucky to make four, and he would have no chance for more. Rather than risk a losing spade finesse and a heart return before the diamonds are established, declarer should cash the ♠A and knock out the ♦A. After the favorable lead, declarer should not jeopardize his advantage.

```
              ♠ 8 3 2
              ♥ 7 6 3
              ♦ A J 10 5 4
              ♣ Q 6

              ♠ A 7 6
              ♥ A K
              ♦ Q 9 3
              ♣ A K J 10 5
```

West	North	East	South
			2NT
Pass	3NT	All Pass	

Surely every pair in the room will arrive at 3NT. West goes into a long study, and finally leads the ♠4. Apparently West had no clear-cut lead, but he made a good guess. Without a spade lead, declarer would be cold for 12 or 13 tricks, depending upon the diamond finesse. Should declarer hold up two rounds so as to shut out the thirteenth spade if the diamond finesse loses? Certainly not. If the diamond finesse loses, South is doomed to a poor result by West's fortunate lead. On the other hand, if South wins immediately and if the diamond finesse works, he will still take 13 tricks. For that matter, the correct play at duplicate is probably to win the first trick even when West leads the king. Winning the first trick will always be worth a top or tie for top when the ♦K is onside. Therefore it is clearly the best play half the time. Even when the diamond finesse loses, declarer may tie with pairs who have held up, but not long enough. Holding up one round is best only when the finesse is off and East has a doubleton spade; holding up two rounds will lose to all other lines of play when the diamond finesse works, and it will be worth a top only if East has three spades with the ♦K.

MATCHPOINT SCORING. In duplicate tournaments matchpoint scoring makes each board of equal importance with any other board, whether the hand involved is a partscore competitive bidding situation or a grand slam. Most pair tournaments are scored by matchpoints. Most team contests and, occasionally, important pair events are scored by IMPs, which make larger swings possible on big hands, and approach the tactics of rubber bridge. See DUPLICATE SCORING for the details of scoring procedures. For a fuller discussion of the effect of matchpoint scoring on bidding and play tactics, see MATCHPOINT BIDDING; MATCHPOINT DEFENSE; MATCHPOINT PLAY; SHOOTING. See DUPLICATE BRIDGE for a full listing of the technical aspects of tournament organization. For the origins of the duplicate method, see HISTORY OF BRIDGE. See also LAWS OF DUPLICATE, Laws 77-79.

MATCHPOINT TEAMS. A team-of-four scoring method devised by Allen L. Tan, Philippines, and described in the August 1990 *The Bridge World*. Players play a multiple team movement, and their net score on each board is calculated. These net scores are then matchpointed. If on a partscore deal a pair scores plus 1600 in one room and minus 800 in the other, their net of plus 800 will give them a top score. This removes some of the inequities in IMP scoring, but, unlike board-a-match, rewards a large swing more than a small one.

MATHE. A defense against strong 1♣ openings covered under DEFENSE TO STRONG ARTIFICIAL OPENINGS .

MATHE ASKING BID. A method of locating a singleton in a hand that has responded with a limit jump major raise, devised by Lew Mathe. Used principally by partnerships that use limit jump raises to promise a side singleton, the Mathe Asking Bid is opener's rebid of the

cheapest denomination after responder's limit raise. If the suit that has been established is spades, responder simply bids four of the suit in which he has a singleton. If hearts is the agreed suit, responder rebids 3NT if he has a singleton spade, or bids his minor-suit singleton. Mathe Asking Bids may also be used where the limit raise has not guaranteed a singleton.

MATHEMATICAL APPROXIMATIONS. When we deal with a quantity which can be expressed as a whole number we can express it exactly, – we do not need to approximate. This does not mean that we never approximate. An example of an approximation is when we give the number of possible deals as 5.36×10^{28}. Rather than write out all 29 digits we express the quantity briefly with an error of less than 0.1% (itself an approximation). When we cannot express a quantity as a whole number, we can adopt one of two forms, vulgar fractions or decimal fractions. If we use vulgar fractions, we can always express a quantity (or number) precisely, e.g., $1/2$, $5\,5/13$, $2/3$, etc. We have, however, the disadvantage that when calculating with numbers of which two or more contain vulgar fractions we have to find the common denominator of such fractions, e.g.,

$$5\,^5/_{13} \bullet {}^2/_3 \bullet {}^{70}/_{13} \bullet {}^2/_3 = {}^{140}/_{39} = 3\,^{23}/_{39}$$

Further disadvantages are the space occupied and the greater possibility of error in calculating or writing down the numbers. When we use decimal fractions we frequently are able to express a number precisely, e.g., $1/2$ = 0.5. When we have a recurring decimal the number is still expressed precisely, e.g.,

$$^1/_7 = 0.142857 = {}^{142857}/_{999999} = {}^1/_7$$

However, the great advantage when calculating with decimals is that we have a constant common denominator — the appropriate power of 10. When we have recurring decimals we may lose this advantage and either have to approximate or revert to vulgar fractions.

When our number is one which cannot be expressed precisely in decimal fractions, we are forced to approximate. The most widely-used quantity which can be expressed only as an approximation is the relationship (or ratio) between the circumference of a circle and the diameter of that circle, which is expressed by the Greek letter *pi*. We give this with the first 10 decimal places, i.e.,

$$3.1415926535$$

It is customary to round up the last decimal figure we decide to use by increasing it by 1 if the following figure is 5 or more, e.g., our approximations for *pi* would be

    3.14   3.142   3.1416   3.14159   etc.

Our next problem is to decide how many decimal places we need in order to achieve our required degree of accuracy. If we wish to express a simple number, the choice is easy. We can choose quite arbitrarily and anyone who is given that number knows that it is accurate to within one-half either way of the last digit, e.g., 3.142 must lie between 3.1415 and 3.142499.

Our difficulty arises when we have to perform mathematic operations on one or more approximations. We may not achieve the degree of accuracy we require, e.g., we have

    $3.14 \bullet 4 = 12.56$
    $3.142 \bullet 4 = 12.568$ (or 12.57).

If we wish our answer to be accurate to n places of decimals, it will usually be sufficient if we approximate

to $n + 1$ decimal places. If we want to be extra careful we can use $n + 2$ decimal places — no real problem if we have access to a modern calculator or computer. However, if we multiply by large numbers, any approximation error will be magnified and we should increase our number of decimal places when we make our original approximations.

We should try to use standard methods for similar problems. Failing this, we may find ourselves embarrassed by discrepancies. An instructive example appears in this encyclopedia. Although the articles we mention were first published in the encyclopedia in 1964, it was only in 1982 that the discrepancy was pointed out to the author by his friend, Dott. Ing. Bruno Burian, the well-known Italian bridge mathematician. Under the heading 'Mathematic Assumptions' the defenders hold Q-J-x-x of a suit. A comparison is made between the probabilities of a named defender holding the doubleton Q-J or the singleton J. These are given as

    Q-J   52.17% $_{22}C_{11}$
    J   47.83% $_{22}C_{12}$

Under the heading 'Probabilities a Posteriori' we compare the equivalent holding of a doubleton K-Q or the singleton K when the opponents have a combined holding of K-Q-x-x. The comparison is given as

    K-Q   6.8%
    K   6.2%

The percentages are based on 100% representing all possible divisions of the four cards, but the comparison is K-Q doubleton = 53.31% and singleton K = 47.69%.

In the first case our approximate ratio is 52:48 or 13:12, while in the second case it is 34:31. The discrepancy is shown more clearly if we use a common base

    13:12 = 442:408   34:31 = 442:403

There is a discrepancy of more than 1%. In fact the precise ratio between the holding of the doubleton K-Q (or Q-J) and the holding of the singleton K (or J) is the very simple one of 12:11. A comparatively easy method of making the calculation is given in the heading COMBINATIONS.

MATHEMATICAL ASSUMPTIONS. In all calculations of odds or probabilities, certain assumptions are made. The accuracy of an answer depends upon the validity of the assumptions. A condition that is taken for granted is that the pack has been sufficiently shuffled so that all possible deals are equally probable. Under the heading ODDS GOVERNING SPECIFIED CARDS, paragraph 7(b), is an example of another assumption that is specifically mentioned in the discussion.

Many controversies arise because the parties fail to mention the assumptions they make. By listing these clearly, the cause of dispute is often immediately apparent. An example is the following:

North
5 4 3 2

South
A K 10 9 8

On the play of the ace, West plays the jack, and East the 6. Dummy is entered and the 3 is led, East playing the 7. Should the king be played or the finesse taken? Only two cases have to be considered:
(a) Where West originally held   Q-J   52.17% $_{22}C_{11}$
(b) Where West originally held   J   47.83% $_{22}C_{12}$
(the notation 22C11 can be read: the number of combi-

nations of 22 things taken 11 at a time). We can make any of the following assumptions:

(1) With Q-J, West will always play the jack. In this case, playing for the drop is a 52% chance.

(2) With Q-J, West will always play the queen. In this case, the finesse is a 100% chance (a sure thing).

(3) With Q-J West will play either honor indiscriminately. This means that in the 52.17% of the cases when he held the Q-J, he will have played the queen 26% of the time, and the jack 26% of the time. When he has the singleton jack, he is bound to play it all 48% of the times.

The odds are thus 24 to 13 in favor of the finesse. Assumption (3) is based on a postulate to Bayes's Theorem, published more than two hundred years ago, providing that in the absence of knowledge to the contrary, we assume that all prior probabilities are equal. It is the assumption a player should make in normal circumstances. See OPTIMUM STRATEGY; RESTRICTED CHOICE; SUIT COMBINATIONS.

MATHEMATICAL TABLES. The tables below give a variety of information. When a percentage given is less than .0001th of 1%, the number of zeros before the first significant figure is indicated in parentheses. Thus 0.(6)3 should be read as .0000003.

TABLE 1
*Probable Percentage Frequency of
Distribution Patterns*

This table may be used to determine percentages of various distribution patterns, both for hand patterns and suit patterns. Figures are expressed in percentage of hands. The percentage expectation of a particular pattern with the suits identified is given in the last column. For example, the chance that a given player has four spades, four hearts, three diamonds, and two clubs is 1.796%.

Pattern	Total	Specific
4-4-3-2	21.5512	1.796
4-3-3-3	10.5361	2.634
4-4-4-1	2.9932	0.748
5-3-3-2	15.5168	1.293
5-4-3-1	12.9307	0.539
5-4-2-2	10.5797	0.882
5-5-2-1	3.1739	0.264
5-4-4-0	1.2433	0.104
5-5-3-0	0.8952	0.075
6-3-2-2	5.6425	0.470
6-4-2-1	4.7021	0.196
6-3-3-1	3.4482	0.287
6-4-3-0	1.3262	0.055
6-5-1-1	0.7053	0.059
6-5-2-0	0.6511	0.027
6-6-1-0	0.0723	0.006
7-3-2-1	1.8808	0.078
7-2-2-2	0.5129	0.128
7-4-1-1	0.3918	0.033
7-4-2-0	0.3617	0.015
7-3-3-0	0.2652	0.022
7-5-1-0	0.1085	0.005
7-6-0-0	0.0056	0.0005
8-2-2-1	0.1924	0.016
8-3-1-1	0.1176	0.010
8-3-2-0	0.1085	0.005
8-4-1-0	0.0452	0.002
8-5-0-0	0.0031	0.0003
9-2-1-1	0.0178	0.001
9-3-1-0	0.0100	0.0004
9-2-2-0	0.0082	0.0007
9-4-0-0	0.0010	0.(4)8
10-2-1-0	0.0011	0.(4)4
10-1-1-1	0.0004	0.0001
10-3-0-0	0.00015	0.(4)1
11-1-1-0	0.(4)2	0.(5)2
11-2-0-0	0.(4)1	0.(5)1
12-1-0-0	0.(6)3	0.(7)3
13-0-0-0	0.(9)6	0.(9)2

TABLE 1A
*Probable Frequency of
High Card Content*

This table gives the expectancies of having specific point counts, using the 4-3-2-1 count. Note that the chances of holding exactly one-fourth of the points — 10 — is the most probable, but only by a slight margin over 9. The chart also shows why many players prefer to use a lower range for an opening notrump, say 12-14, rather than the usual 15-17 or 16-18. The chance to use notrump as an opening bid comes up far more often. The chance of holding 12-14 points comes to 20.6345%, or one hand in five. The chance of holding 15-17 is only 10.0963%, or one hand in 10 — only about half as often as 12-14. Of course most of the hands with these counts will not be opened 1NT for one reason or another — usually distribution.

Point Count	%	Point Count	%
0	.3639	16	3.3109
1	.7884	17	2.3617
2	1.3561	18	1.6051
3	2.4624	19	1.0362
4	3.8454	20	.6435
5	5.1862	21	.3779
6	6.5541	22	.2100
7	8.0281	23	.1119
8	8.8922	24	.0559
9	9.3562	25	.0264
10	9.4051	26	.0117
11	8.9447	27	.0049
12	8.0269	28	.0019
13	6.9143	29	.0007
14	5.6933	30	.0002
15	4.4237	31-37	.0001

TABLE 2
*Probability of Holding
an Exact Number of Cards of a Specified Suit*

This table gives the probability (a priori, before dealing) of holding an exact number of cards in a specified suit. The number of times the specified number of cards can be expected in any suit in the course of 100 deals is four times as great.

Number of Cards	%
0	1.279
1	8.006
2	20.587
3	28.633

4	23.861
5	12.469
6	4.156
7	0.882
8	0.117
9	0.009
10	0.0004
11	0.(5)9
12	0.(7)8
13	0.(9)16

TABLE 3

*Probability of Distribution of Cards
in Three Hidden Hands*

This table gives the probability of distribution of the remaining cards in a suit for a one-hand holding in column (a); among the other three hands, column (b); expressed as a percentage, column (c). For brevity, probabilities of less than half of 1% are omitted.

(a)	(b)	(c)	(a)	(b)	(c)
0	6-4-3	25.921		3-3-3	11.039
	5-4-4	24.301		4-4-1	9.408
	5-5-3	17.497		6-2-1	4.927
	6-5-2	12.725		5-4-0	2.605
	7-4-2	7.069		6-3-0	1.390
	7-3-3	5.184	5	3-3-2	31.110
	8-3-2	2.121		4-3-1	25.925
	7-5-1	2.121		4-2-2	21.212
	6-6-1	1.414		5-2-1	12.727
	8-4-1	0.884		5-3-0	3.590
1	5-4-3	40.377		4-4-0	2.493
	6-4-2	14.683		6-1-1	1.414
	6-3-3	10.767		6-2-0	1.305
	5-5-2	9.911	6	3-2-2	33.939
	4-4-4	9.347		4-2-1	28.282
	7-3-2	5.873		3-3-1	20.740
	6-5-1	4.405		4-3-0	7.977
	7-4-1	2.447		5-1-1	4.242
	8-3-1	0.734		5-2-0	3.916
	8-2-2	0.601		6-1-0	0.870
2	4-4-3	26.170	7	3-2-1	53.333
	5-4-2	25.695		2-2-2	14.545
	5-3-3	18.843		4-1-1	11.111
	6-3-2	13.704		4-2-0	10.256
	6-4-1	5.710		3-3-0	7.521
	5-5-1	3.854		5-1-0	3.077
	7-3-1	2.284	8	2-2-1	41.211
	7-2-2	1.869		3-1-1	25.185
	6-5-0	0.791		3-2-0	23.247
3	4-3-3	27.598		4-1-0	9.686
	5-3-2	27.096		5-0-0	0.671
	4-4-2	18.817	9	2-1-1	48.080
	5-4-1	11.290		3-1-0	27.122
	6-3-1	6.021		2-2-0	22.191
	6-2-2	4.927		4-0-0	2.608
	7-2-1	1.642	10	2-1-0	66.572
	6-4-0	1.158		1-1-1	24.040
	5-5-0	0.782		3-0-0	9.388
4	4-3-2	45.160	11	1-1-0	68.421
	5-3-1	13.548		2-0-0	31.579
	5-2-2	11.085			

TABLE 4

*Probability of Distribution of Cards
In Two Hidden Hands*

This table gives the probability of distribution of cards in two given hands. Column (a) shows number of cards in the two known hands; column (b) shows the number of outstanding cards in the two hidden hands; column (c) the ways in which these cards may be divided; column (d) shows the percentage of cases in which the distribution in column (c) occurs, followed by a bracketed figure showing the number of cases applicable. By dividing the percentage in column (d) by the bracketed figure, the probability that one opponent will hold particular specified cards of that remainder can be obtained.

(a)	(b)	(c)	(d)	
11	2	1-1	52	(2)
		2-0	48	(2)
10	3	2-1	78	(6)
		3-0	22	(2)
9	4	3-1	49.74	(8)
		2-2	40.70	(6)
		4-0	9.57	(2)
8	5	3-2	67.83	(20)
		4-1	28.26	(10)
		5-0	3.91	(2)
7	6	4-2	46.88	(30)
		3-3	31.75	(20)
		5-1	18.75	(12)
		6-0	1.49	(2)
6	7	4-3	62.17	(70)
		5-2	30.52	(42)
		6-1	6.78	(14)
		7-0	0.52	(2)
5	8	5-3	47.12	(112)
		4-4	32.72	(70)
		6-2	17.14	(56)
		7-1	2.86	(16)
		8-0	0.16	(2)
4	9	5-4	58.90	(252)
		6-3	31.41	(168)
		7-2	8.57	(72)
		8-1	1.07	(18)
		9-0	0.05	(2)
3	10	6-4	46.20	(420)
		5-5	31.18	(252)
		7-3	18.48	(240)
		8-2	3.78	(90)
		9-1	0.35	(20)
		10-0	0.01	(2)
2	11	6-5	57.17	(924)
		7-4	31.76	(660)
		8-3	9.53	(330)
		9-2	1.44	(110)
		10-1	0.10	(22)
		11-0	0.002	(2)
1	12	7-5	45.74	(1584)
		6-6	30.49	(924)
		8-4	19.06	(990)
		9-3	4.23	(440)
		10-2	0.46	(132)
		11-1	0.02	(24)
		12-0	0.0003	(2)
0	13	7-6	56.62	(3432)
		8-5	31.85	(2574)
		9-4	9.83	(1430)
		10-3	1.57	(572)
		11-2	0.12	(156)
		12-1	0.003	(26)
		13-0	0.00002	(2)

TABLE 4A

*Probability of Distribution of Two
Residues between Two Hidden Hands*

A residue is said to be favorably divided when it is divided as evenly as possible, e.g., 8 cards divided 4-4 or 7 cards divided 4-3. In this table, column (a) shows the number of cards outstanding in each of the two suits in the two hidden hands; column (b) shows the percentage of cases in which both residues will divide as evenly as possible; column (c) shows the percentage of cases in which at least one residue will divide favorably.

(a)	(b)	(c)
8-8	11.87%	53.57%
8-7	21.77	73.13
8-6	12.44	55.81
8-5	23.10	77.45
8-4	13.86	59.56
7-7	40.42	83.93
7-6	23.10	74.60
7-5	43.31	86.69
7-4	25.99	76.88
6-6	13.20	57.86
6-5	24.75	78.61
6-4	14.85	61.37
5-5	46.75	88.90
5-4	28.05	80.47
5-3	53.29	92.53

TABLE 5
Tables of Combinations (Values for nCr)

In making mathematical computations involving bridge (see MATHEMATICS OF BRIDGE), the formula nCr appears frequently. Since the formula involves factorial numbers, the computation is tedious (13! means $13 \cdot 12 \cdot 11 \cdot 10 \cdot 9 \cdot 8 \cdot 7 \cdot 6 \cdot 5 \cdot 4 \cdot 3 \cdot 2 \cdot 1$). Values of nCr appear in the table below.

TOTAL NUMBER FROM WHICH
COMBINATIONS CAN BE TAKEN

r	2	3	4	5	6
2	1				
3	3	1			
4	6	4	1		
5	10	10	5	1	
6	15	20	15	6	1
7	21	35	35	21	7
8	28	56	70	56	28
9	36	84	126	126	84
10	45	120	210	252	210
11	55	165	330	462	462
12	66	220	495	792	924
13	78	286	715	1287	1716
14	91	364	1001	2002	3003
15	105	455	1365	3003	5005
16	120	560	1820	4368	8008
17	136	680	2380	6188	12376
18	153	816	3060	8568	18564
19	171	969	3876	11628	27132
20	190	1140	4845	15504	38760
21	210	1330	5985	20349	54264
22	231	1540	7315	26334	74613
23	253	1771	8855	33649	100947
24	276	2024	10626	42504	134596
25	300	2300	12650	53150	177100
26	325	2600	14950	65780	230230

	7	8	9	10
7	1			
8	8	1		
9	36	9	1	
10	120	45	10	1
11	330	165	55	11
12	792	495	220	66
13	1716	1287	715	286
14	3432	3003	2002	1001
15	6435	6435	5005	3003

16	11440	12870	11440	8008
17	19448	24310	24310	19448
18	31824	43758	48620	43758
19	50388	75582	92378	92378
20	77520	125970	167960	184756
21	116280	203490	293930	352716
22	170544	319770	497420	646646
23	245157	490314	817190	1144066
24	346104	735471	1307504	1961256
25	480700	1081575	2042978	3268760
26	657800	1562275	3124550	5311735

$_{22}C_{11} = 705432$ $_{25}C_{11} = 4457400$
$_{23}C_{11} = 1352078$ $_{25}C_{12} = 5200300$
$_{23}C_{12} = 1352078$ $_{25}C_{13} = 5200300$
$_{24}C_{11} = 2496144$ $_{26}C_{11} = 7726160$
$_{24}C_{12} = 2704156$ $_{26}C_{12} = 9657700$
$_{24}C_{13} = 2496144$ $_{26}C_{13} = 10400600$

TABLE 6
Sundry Odds

Various odds have been of interest to bridge players for many years. Below are a number of different possibilities, with odds computed.

Number of different hands a named player can receive
$$_{52}C_{13} \qquad 635{,}013{,}559{,}600$$

Number of different hands a second named player can receive
$$_{39}C_{13} \qquad 8{,}122{,}425{,}444$$

Number of different hands the third and fourth players can receive
$$_{26}C_{13} \qquad 10{,}400{,}600$$

Number of possible deals
$$52! \div 13!^4$$
53,644,737,765,488,792,839,237,440,000

Number of possible auctions with North as dealer, assuming that East and West pass throughout
$$2^{36} - 1 = 68{,}719{,}476{,}735$$

Number of possible auctions with North as dealer, assuming that East and West do not pass throughout
$(4 \cdot 22^{35} - 1) \rceil 3 = 128{,}745{,}650{,}347{,}030{,}683{,}120{,}231{,}$ 926,111,609,371,363,122,697,557

Odds against each player having a complete suit
2,235,197,406,895,366,368,301,559,999 to 1.

Odds against each player receiving identical hands except for difference of suit

♠ A K Q	♠ J 10 9	♠ 8 7 6	♠ 5 4 3 2
♥ J 10 9	♥ 8 7 6	♥ 5 4 3 2	♥ A K Q
♦ 8 7 6	♦ 5 4 3 2	♦ A K Q	♦ J 10 9
♣ 5 4 3 2	♣ A K Q	♣ J 10 9	♣ 8 7 6

Approximately: 55,976,427,337,829,109,025 to 1.

Odds against receiving a hand
    A K Q   A K Q   A K Q   A K Q J
the jack being in any of the four suits:
   158,753,389,899 to 1

Odds against receiving a perfect hand, a hand that will produce 13 tricks in notrump irrespective of the opening lead or the composition of the other three hands:
   169,066,442 to 1

Odds against a YARBOROUGH
   Approximately 1,827 to 1

Odds against both members of a partnership receiving Yarboroughs
   546,000,000 to 1

Odds against a hand with no card higher than 10
   274 to 1

Odds against a hand with no card higher than jack
   52 to 1

Odds against a hand with no card higher than queen
  11 to 1
Odds against a hand with no aces
  slightly more than 2 to 1
Odds against being dealt four aces
  Approximately 378 to 1
Odds against being dealt four honors in one suit
  Approximately 22 to 1
Odds against being dealt five honors in one suit
  Approximately 500 to 1
Odds against being dealt at least one singleton
  Slightly over 2 to 1
Odds against having at least one void
  Approximately 19 to 1
Odds that two partners will be dealt 26 named cards be-
  tween them, e.g., all the red cards.
  495,918,532,918,103 to 1 against
Odds that no players will be dealt a singleton or void
  Approximately 4 to 1 against
Odds that four specified cards will be cut by the four
  players
  270,724 to 1 against
  See HIGH CARD POINT PROBABILITIES.

MATHEMATICAL VALUE OF GAME. See VALUE
OF GAME.

MATHEMATICAL VALUE OF PARTSCORE. See
PARTSCORE BIDDING.

MATHEMATICS OF BRIDGE. The mathematics of
bridge runs the gamut from simply counting the number of cards in one's hand up to involved problems of
probability theory. Some examples of the application of
mathematics to bridge are:

(1) Bidding systems, methods, and conventions. Use
may be made of the frequency with which various patterns occur (see MATHEMATICAL TABLES, Table 1).

A bidder will also find it valuable to know the ways
in which the outstanding cards are likely to be divided
among the three hidden hands. We may wish to determine the probability that a trick will not be lost in a suit
in which we have a particular holding. It can be determined from Table 3 that with A-K-Q-J-x-x there is a
nearly 94% probability that no trick will be lost, but with
A-K-Q-x-x-x-x, the probability is only 84%.

(2) Sacrifice bidding.

(3) Choice among partscore, game, and slam. These
are dependent on EXPECTATION, and of course, on
correctly estimating the value of the players' hands.

(4) Percentage play. This is shown in MATHEMATI-
CAL TABLES, Table 4.

(5) Safety play. This is governed by expectation. See
SUIT COMBINATIONS.

(6) Countering false cards (see DECEPTION, MATH-
EMATICS OF; FALSECARDING).

To express and solve such mathematic problems, the
ordinary arithmetic symbols are used, and also the following two.

n! (read, n factorial), meaning that one multiplies all
the numerals starting at 1, up to and including the number represented by n.

$_nC_r$ (read, the number of combinations in which n
things can be selected r at a time). Thus $_{52}C_{13}$ is the
number of different hands of 13 cards that can be dealt
to a single player from a pack of 52 cards. The formula

for finding this is:
  $n!/[(n-r)!r!]$ or $52!/(39!13!)$
Applications of this formula are, among others,
  (a) NUMBER OF POSSIBLE HANDS.
  (b) The number of cards held in a suit
  (c) Hand patterns
  (d) ODDS GOVERNING SPECIFIED CARDS
The following headings also cover facets of mathemat-
ics of bridge: CARDS, NEUTRAL AND POSITIVE;
DECEPTION, MATHEMATICS OF; EXPECTATION;
HAND PATTERNS; MATHEMATICAL ASSUMP-
TIONS; BIBLIOGRAPHY, M; MATHEMATICS OF
MATCHPOINT PLAY; NUMBER OF POSSIBLE
HANDS, DEALS; ODDS, IN BRIDGE; OPTIMUM
STRATEGY; PERCENTAGE PLAY; PROBABILITIES,
A POSTERIORI; PROBABILITIES, A PRIORI; PROB-
ABILITY OF SUCCESSIVE EVENTS; SUIT, NUM-
BER OF CARDS IN; VALUE OF GAME.

MATHEMATICS OF DECEPTION. See DECEP-
TION, MATHEMATICS OF.

MATHEMATICS OF MATCHPOINT PLAY. In duplicate, the bonus for making a non-vulnerable game is
always 300 points, and the bonus for making a vulnerable game is always 500 points. The bonus for making a
partial is always 50 points. When a contract is doubled
and made, the bonus is always 50 points — 100 points
when the contract is redoubled.

In rubber bridge, the value of winning a rubber with
two games out of three is 500, of winning a rubber in
two straight games 700, of winning the only game in an
unfinished rubber 350, and of having the only partial in
an unfinished game 100.

This is particularly applicable to SAFETY PLAYS.
In the abstract, a safety play is used in matchpoint duplicate only if the distribution to be guarded against has
a probability of more than 50%. Of course, if the contract is an excellent one that only a few other competitors will arrive at, any safety play that will ensure it is
used; similarly, if the contract is a very bad one, the best
chance to make a good score is that better contracts will
be defeated by unusual distribution, so any possible
safety play is used. For other considerations at
matchpoint play, see MATCHPOINT BIDDING,
MATCHPOINT PLAY and MATCHPOINT DEFENSE.

MAXIMAL DOUBLE. A type of COMPETITIVE
DOUBLE used to invite game when the auction is too
crowded for any other approach. The following situation is typical:

West	North	East	South
			1♠
2♥	2♠	3♥	?

South may have a hand with which he wishes to sign
off in 3♠ or a hand worth a game invitation. Either hand
can be described if the maximal double is used as a
conventional bid inviting game and the 3♠ bid is reserved for use as a sign-off.

If the enemy competition is not in the maximum suit (the
one just below South's), however, maximal doubles are not
needed if the partnership has agreed that opener's bid in
the available side suit constitutes a general game try:

West	North	East	South
			1♠
2♦	2♠	3♦	?

Here South can bid 3 ♥ (conventional, forcing) to invite game in spades and bid 3 ♠ to sign off, so some advocates of maximal doubles prefer to use this double for penalties. In the sequence

| 1 ♥ | 1 ♠ | 2 ♥ | 2 ♠ |
| 3 ♥ | Dbl | | |

the double is maximal and 3 ♠ is a signoff because there is no room to make a bid short of 3 ♠. See also COMPETITIVE DOUBLES.

MAYONNAISE. Variant of GOULASH.

McCABE ADJUNCT. See WEAK TWO-BIDS.

McCONNELL CUP. In 1993, the World Bridge Federation established the McConnell Cup, a knockout team event for women to be played at the World Bridge Championships alongside the competition for the Rosenblum Cup (an open event). The McConnell Cup, first contested at the NEC World Bridge Championships in Albuquerque NM in 1994, is named in honor of Ruth McConnell, WBF treasurer from 1985 to 1990 and ACBL president in 1974.

McCONNELL CUP TEAMS. A team event for women which was inaugurated in 1994 as part of the World Championship that features pair events and the ROSENBLUM CUP TEAMS. The event is held once every four years, and the prize is the McConnell Cup. The event is named in honor of Ruth McConnell of the United States, former treasurer for the WORLD BRIDGE FEDERATION and former president of the AMERICAN CONTRACT BRIDGE LEAGUE. McConnell also was instrumental in inaugurating the VENICE CUP women's team championship in 1974. The McConnell Team now is played opposite the open Rosenblum Teams, just as the Venice Cup is played opposite the open Bermuda Bowl. For winners see Appendix V.

McKENNEY-BALDWIN MOVEMENT. One of a series of pair movements planned by William E. McKenney and worked out by Russell J. Baldwin, then respectively secretary and tournament director of the American Bridge League. The most widely used were two-session pair movements for 16 to 32 pairs, in which each pair played against each of the others in the course of two sessions, with approximately balanced comparisons. One session consisted of a Mitchell Movement using the APPENDIX TABLE concept, and the other of an INTERWOVEN HOWELL.

McKENNEY SIGNAL. Standard term in Great Britain for the SUIT PREFERENCE signal, named for William E. McKenney of the ACBL, who helped popularize it.

McKENNEY TROPHY. This trophy is presented to the ACBL member who has accumulated the most masterpoints during the calendar year. The trophy was put into play on January 1, 1938 by William E. McKenney, ACBL executive secretary. The previous year the AMERICAN BRIDGE LEAGUE awarded a trophy to Charles H. Goren for winning the greatest number of masterpoints in one year. Hence this competition dates back to 1937. Goren dominated the picture in the early

years, winning eight times. The name of the masterpoint race was changed to the BARRY CRANE TOP 500 shortly after Crane was murdered in 1985. For winners see Appendix II.

MEAN SCORE. See IMP PAIR GAMES.

MECHANICS OF BRIDGE. Described in Chapters I, II and III of the LAWS.

MEDIUM CARDS. The lower honor cards and the higher spot cards. They provide BODY in long suit holdings or in support of a partner's bid suit.

MEMBER. (1) Of a table: one of the players constituting a table at rubber bridge, whether actively playing or awaiting re-entry to the table for the next rubber or round of CHICAGO; (2) of a team: a player whose name was listed on the official entry blank whether actively playing or not (see RESERVE PLAYER); BYLAWS OF THE ACBL.

MEMBERSHIP LIMIT. Table membership is limited to six players, unless exactly seven players are present and no player may be a member of two tables simultaneously (LAWS, "Rules for Club Procedure," Section F). In order to make up tables with greater flexibility, many of the larger bridge clubs use HOUSE PLAYERS in order to be able to accommodate members as they arrive. For precedence in play at a table, see CUT IN.

MEMORY DUPLICATE. See REPLAY DUPLICATE.

MENACE. See THREAT CARD.

MEN'S BOARD-A-MATCH TEAMS, NORTH AMERICAN CHAMPIONSHIP. This event is no longer held in the ACBL. See GOREN TROPHY. For results see Appendix I. See BLANCHARD CASE.

MEN'S PAIRS. A pairs event in duplicate competition in which all the competitors are men. The ACBL no longer runs men's events at the North American level. See BLANCHARD CASE. At the Spring NABC, what formerly was the Men's Pairs II, and it is now Open Pairs II, and it is run opposite the nationally-rated Women's Pairs.

MEN'S PAIRS, NORTH AMERICAN CHAMPIONSHIP. This event no longer is held in the ACBL. See WERNHER TROPHY. For results see Appendix I. See BLANCH-ARD CASE.

MEN'S SWISS TEAMS, NORTH AMERICAN CHAMPIONSHIP. This event no longer is held in the ACBL. For results see Appendix I. See BLANCHARD CASE.

MEN'S TEAMS. Team events — Swiss, Knockout or Board-a-Match — in which all competitors are men. The ACBL no longer runs men's events. See BLANCHARD CASE. The former North American Men's Swiss Teams and the former North American's Men's Board-a-Match Teams now are open events. There was no nationally-rated Men's Knockout Teams.

MENTAL PLAY. Hand valuation is mental play. To estimate the trick-winning value of his hand, a player must foresee the conditions that will prevail when the cards are actually played. The better the player, the more accurate his valuation.

MERRIMAC COUP. The deliberate sacrifice of a high card with the object of knocking out a vital entry in an opponent's hand, usually the dummy. Named after the Merrimac, an American coal-carrying ship sunk in 1898 in Santiago Harbor in an attempt to bottle up the Spanish fleet (often misspelled Merrimack, in confusion with the Civil War ironclad that fought the Monitor).

```
                  ♠ 4 3
                  ♥ 5 4 2
                  ♦ A 3
                  ♣ K Q J 10 9 3
♠ J 10 9 8 7                        ♠ A 5 2
♥ K 10 6                            ♥ Q 9 8 7
♦ 10 9 8 4                          ♦ K 7 2
♣ 6                                 ♣ A 5 4
                  ♠ K Q 6
                  ♥ A J 3
                  ♦ Q J 6 5
                  ♣ 8 7 2
```

South is the declarer at a contract of 3NT. West leads the ♠J which East wins with the ace. East at this point sees that the ♦A is dummy's only entry after the ♣A is knocked out, and East, realizing that this entry must be destroyed immediately, effectuates this by playing his ♦K at trick two. This defense holds declarer to eight tricks and defeats the contract. Occasionally called HOBSON'S COUP.

MEXICAN TWO DIAMONDS. A bid showing a balanced hand with 19-21 high-card points and 4-6 losers. A weak five-card major is permitted. Devised by George Rosenkranz as a cornerstone of the ROMEX SYSTEM.

Negative responses (0-4 points) are: pass with diamond length; 2♥ — transfer to 2♠ preparatory to a sign-off in clubs, hearts or spades (2♥ may also be a semi-positive with 5-6 points); 2♠ — transfer to 2NT, planning to pass.

Positive responses (7 points or more and game forcing) include: TEXAS TRANSFERS; 2♠ — transfer to 2NT with 7-9 points, balanced distribution; 2NT — 10 points or more, normally balanced; three of a suit — at least 10 points with a broken six-card suit.

Responder's high-card requirements are reduced by 1 point for each five-card suit and by 2 points for a six-card major. In the modern version (1992) the bid is used differently. If balanced the opener must have 23-24 points, but he may also have an ACOL TWO-BID in a major suit or a strong three-suited hand.

MICHAELS CUEBID. The use of an immediate cuebid in the opponent's suit to show a two-suiter. It was derived from suggestions made by the late Mike Michaels of Miami Beach.

```
♠ J 10 9 4 3          ♠ K Q 6 4 3
♥ A J 10 6 2          ♥ J 10 7 6 4
♦ 6                   ♦ A 4
♣ 8 7                 ♣ 8
```

If an opponent opens with a minor suit, the cuebid is recommended with either of these hands unless the vul-

nerability is unfavorable. Over a minor suit the emphasis is on the major suits; there should be at least nine cards in the major suits and 6-11 points. The strength, however, is a matter of partnership agreement, and some would expect opening values unless the vulnerability is favorable. Greater strength is quite possible, intending further action.

Over a major suit the cuebid shows the unbid major suit and an unspecified minor suit:

```
♠ 7                   ♠ —
♥ Q J 10 9 5          ♥ 10 9 8 7 4
♦ 7 5                 ♦ A K J 6 2
♣ A J 10 6 2          ♣ Q 6 4
```

On each of these hands, 2♠ would be bid over 1♠. If partner does not fit the unbid major, he can bid notrump as a request to the cuebidder to show his minor suit.

The major-suit cuebid is unlimited in point-count: the cuebidder may have a strong hand and plan to take further action. Over either type of cuebid, partner will usually bid the full value of his hand if there is a known fit. In some circumstances he may put pressure on the opponents by making an advance sacrifice. He can also make use of a second cuebid to ask for further definition of the cuebidder's hand.

In BWS 1994 about half the experts favored a split range, so that Michaels is either weak or strong. With hands in the middle range, with values close to an opening bid, simply overcall. This gives more definition when the bid is used, but makes it relatively unlikely that the second suit can be shown when it is not.

As with other devices which are partly obstructive, both the cuebidder and his partner have to watch the vulnerability. At unfavorable vulnerability, more extreme distribution is needed to make the cuebid.

Michaels is often used by agreement in less obvious situations. Some of these are:

(i)	2♥	3♥		
(ii)	3♥	4♥		
(iii)	1♦	Pass	Pass	2♦
(iv)	1♦	Pass	1NT	2♦

At the higher levels, the cuebid promises a sound opening or better. See LEAPING MICHAELS.

For defense to Michaels, see DEFENSE TO TWO-SUITED INTERFERENCE.

MICROSOFT GAMING ZONE. An internet bridge-playing site with a choice between free bridge and the Zone Bridge Club, a paid area. Features include daily special games, masterpoints, ratings. The first player to chieve Net Master, the highest rating, was Jane Eason of Collierville TN.

MIDDLE CARD. The middle card of an original three-card holding. Generally referred to in connection with opening leads. See THREE SMALL CARDS, LEAD FROM.

MIDDLE GAME. The play, usually referring to the declarer's play, after the original lead or first few tricks won by the defenders, during which the plan of the play is developed, frequently leading to END PLAY positions or preparation for them. Aspects of the middle game are discussed in a number of articles listed under DEFENSE and DUMMY PLAY.

MIDDLE SUIT. See DOUBLE MENACE.

MIDNIGHT GAME. A contest staged after the main events of the day have concluded. Usually a midnight game is either an open pairs, a Swiss Teams or a Knockout Teams with abbreviated matches. Usually much shorter time limits on play are imposed so that the game will be finished and scored before 3 a.m. At ACBL sectionals the awards are in silver points. At ACBL regional and North American Championships the awards are in red points.

MIDNIGHT KNOCKOUTS. A knockout event made up of short matches that starts at about midnight after the regular games of the day have finished. This type of event is quite common at ACBL North American Championship tournaments. It is also called Lose and Snooze because any team that loses is through for the night. The event usually takes from two and a half to three hours.

MIDNIGHT SWISS. The most common type of midnight game. The game consists of five matches of five boards played at a rapid-fire pace — only 25 minutes is allowed per round, so that the average time spent on a board is only five minutes instead of the usual seven. ACBL sectional games pay in silver points, regional and North American in red points.

MILES CONVENTION. See TWO NOTRUMP RESPONSE to opening suit bid of one.

MILES RESPONSES TO TWO NOTRUMP OPENING. A method of responding to opening bids of 2NT devised by Marshall Miles to facilitate safe exploration for slams, games, or partscores in any suit. The principal responses are as follows: 3♣ is STAYMAN; following a Stayman sequence, a 4♣ rebid by responder is GERBER, and a 4♦ rebid is a slam try that may be wholly artificial; JACOBY TRANSFER BIDS; jumps to the four level are natural, showing a broken suit with slam interest; 3NT transfers to 4♣ and promises a good suit, after which responder may show a second suit if he has one; 3♠ transfers to 3NT, which responder may pass if he merely wanted to raise to game, or may continue with: (a) 4♣ to show a good diamond suit or a diamond-major two-suiter, (b) four of any other suit to show 4-4-4-1 distribution with shortness in the suit bid, or (c) 4NT to show 5-5 or longer in the minor suits.

MILES TROPHY. Awarded to the winners of the NORTH AMERICAN NON-LIFE MASTER PAIRS. Trophy honors Rufus Miles, ACBL president in 1950 and 1956.

MILLER LITE. A variation of ROMAN KEYCARD BLACKWOOD described by Danny Kleinman in *The Bridge World* March 1997. It is a hybrid of the traditional version, in which a 5♣ response shows 0 or 3 key cards, with 5♦ showing 1 or 4, and the modern version in which these are reversed. A 5♣ response is desirable because it leaves bidding space, and a 5♦ response is undesirable. In Miller Lite, the traditional method is used when the responder has earlier shown substantially more than a minimum opening. In other cases, the modern version is used. This rule tends to maximize the 5♣ response and minimize the 5♦ response.

MILTON WORK COUNT. See WORK POINT COUNT.

MINGLED MOVEMENT. Individual movement, introduced by Olof Hanner, for one session with two or more groups of players, where the groups are mingled so that a player will have most of the other players during the contest either as partner or as opponent. The movements offer an alternative to letting each group play at their own tables with only the boards in common. Two useful examples:

6 tables, 2 groups, 12 rounds & board sets.					10 tables, 3 groups 13 rounds & board sets.				
Starting positions:					Starting positions:				
Table	N	S	E	W	b	Table	N	S	E	W	b
1	1	13	2	4	1	1	40	1	14	27	1
2	7	10	20	17	2	2	16	20	4	35	2
3	11	3	9	15	5	3	10	2	13	19	3
4	23	21	14	6	7	4	12	23	32	33	4
5	5	18	19	12	10	5	39	9	8	37	5
6	24	16	8	22	11	6	31	7	36	30	6

When changing to a new round #1 follows #12 and #13 follows #24. The remaining players follow the next lower numbered player.

7	24	29	15	17	7
8	21	28	3	6	10
9	34	18	26	38	11
10	22	5	25	11	13

#1 follows #13, #14 follows #26, #27 follows #39, #40 is stationary. The remaining players follow the next lower numbered player.

MINI-KNOCKOUT TEAMS. This type of event consists of a series of very short matches. It is designed to produce a winner in just one session of play. It often is played as a midnight game at regionals and NABCs in the American Contract Bridge League. It is often called a Lose and Snooze Teams because the winners play on while the losers can get to bed a little earlier. See BRACKETED KNOCKOUT TEAMS, COMPACT KNOCKOUT TEAMS, DOUBLE ELIMINATION KNOCKOUT TEAMS, HANDICAP KNOCKOUT TEAMS, MIXED TEAMS, OPEN TEAMS, RANDOM DRAW KNOCKOUT TEAMS, TEAM GAMES, ZIP KNOCKOUT TEAMS.

MINI-LIGHTNER. The principle of the LIGHTNER DOUBLE can be applied at the four- or five-level. The following example is from a Grand National Team match in New York.

Dlr: North
Vul: E-W

♠ A K 9 3
♥ A
♦ A K Q 5 3
♣ J 10 8

♠ 10 8
♥ Q J 10
♦ J 10 8 7 4 2
♣ K 2

♠ J 7 6 5 2
♥ 6 4
♦ —
♣ A Q 9 7 6 3

♠ Q 4
♥ K 9 8 7 6 5 2
♦ J 6
♣ 5 4

West	North	East	South
	1♣	3♣	Pass
Pass	3♦	Pass	3♥
Pass	3♠	Pass	4♥
Pass	Pass	Dbl	All Pass

North opened 1♣, artificial and usually strong. East ventured 3♣ in the teeth of the vulnerability. A double would have collected at least 500 for North-South, but it is not easy to penalize such bids and North-South continued to the normal contract of 4♥. The 3♣ bid had been made with the idea of suggesting a club lead, but now East changed his mind. He produced an unexpected double, a mini-Lightner warning West against leading a club. Such doubles are nearly always based on a void somewhere, usually in dummy's original suit.

West had no trouble reading the message and deciding what to do. He carefully led the ♦2, a suit-preference request for a club return. East ruffed and returned the ♣3, giving his partner the entry to provide a second diamond ruff. That was three tricks for the defense, and the ♣A, and an eventual trump trick resulted in a two-trick penalty. In the replay, 4♥ was reached against silent opponents and a passive trump lead permitted South to make two overtricks. See LEAD-DIRECTING DOUBLE, LIGHTNER DOUBLE.

MINI-McKENNEY RACES. See ACBL MINI-McKENNEY RACES.

MINI-NOTRUMP. An opening notrump with 10-12 points. Other very weak ranges are sometimes used, but are often barred by organizing bodies. Lighter notrump openings are allowed by ACBL, but no conventional responses, not even Stayman, may be used.

MINI-SPLINTER. A variation of the SPLINTER bid, in which a jump shift, by opener or responder, shows a fit combined with shortage in the suit named. There are two types:

(1) A jump shift by a passed hand to show near opening values, a fit with opener, and a singleton or void in the named suit. If DRURY is being used, 3♣ will usually be natural since 2♣ is artificial. (Used by a few when responder is unpassed.)

(2) A jump reverse by opener after a one-level response. Example:

Opener	Responder
1♦	1♠
3♥	

If 2♥ is forcing, as it is in the modern style, then 3♥ is meaningless. As a mini-splinter, it shows a raise to 3♠ with a singleton or void in hearts. Responder can sign off in 3♠ if he chooses.

Other possibilities: (1) 3♥ game forcing with a singleton, with 4♥ to show avoid; (2) 3♥ showing a singleton heart, three-card spade support and long diamonds.

MINIMUM. The least possible for a particular action. It can apply to suit length or high card points. Examples (1) 12 HCP to open bidding; (2) 6 HCP for a response to an opening suit bid; (3) 15 HCP for a strong notrump opening bid; (4) 4 HCP for a positive response to an forcing two-bid; (5) a six-card suit for a preemptive bid, etc.

MINOR PENALTY CARD. A single card below honor rank that is exposed inadvertently is a minor penalty card. See Law 50C&D.

MINOR SUIT. Either of the two lower-ranking suits, diamonds or clubs.

MINOR SUIT STAYMAN. A response of 2♠ to 1NT to indicate minor-suit length, used in combination with two-suit transfer responses. Details vary widely from one partnership to another. Most, but not all, require length in both minor suits. Most, but not all, permit weak hands as well as strong ones. It is usual to have at least two meanings. A popular version allows: strong with at least 5-4; weak with 5-5; weak with diamonds. When a weak hand is possible, opener is barred from bidding beyond 3♦. Example hands:

♠ 7	♠ 5
♥ 6 3	♥ 4
♦ K Q 10 6 5	♦ A J 10 5 2
♣ A J 9 8 4	♣ K J 10 9 6 3

See FOUR-SUIT TRANSFER BIDS.

MINOR SUIT SWISS. A method devised by Albert Dormer and Terence Reese for use in conjunction with non-forcing minor suit jump raises, to show a strong hand in support of opener's minor suit without going past 3NT. In response to a 1♣ opening, a jump to 3♥ would show a very good club raise, and a jump to 3♦ would show a moderately good club raise. In response to a 1♦ opening, a jump to 3♠ would show the very good raise and a jump to 3♥ would show the moderately good raise. All these jumps are forcing either to 3NT or to four of opener's minor suit. In determining which jump to make, principal emphasis is placed on the richness of responder's controls.

(a)	(b)
♠ x x	♠ A x
♥ K Q x	♥ x x x x
♦ K Q x x x	♦ K 10 x x x
♣ K x x	♣ A Q

Opposite a 1♦ opening, responder would jump to 3♥ with hand (a), and to 3♠ with hand (b). An alternative recommended by H. W. Kelsey is for responder not to attempt to distinguish between moderate and very good strength, but to choose among all three unbid suits and jump in the suit in which he holds the most secure stopper.

In American methods these jumps to the three level would usually be considered splinter bids. See SWISS CONVENTION.

MINOR SUIT TEXAS. See SOUTH AFRICAN TEXAS.

MINOR TENACE. An original holding of king-jack (without the ace or queen) of a suit. After one or more rounds of a suit have been played, the second and fourth highest remaining cards of the suit in the hand of one player are also called a minor tenace. See TENACE.

MIRROR DISTRIBUTION. Both partners have identical suit distribution. See DUPLICATION OF DISTRIBUTION.

MIRROR MITCHELL. See MIRROR MOVEMENT.

MIRROR MOVEMENT. A movement used in board-a-

match team games that enables teams to play full matches in the same round. The movement requires that the field be broken into an even number of sections. Each section is set up as a Mitchell. The East-West pairs from Section A move to the same table number in Section B, and the Section B pairs move to the same table number in Section A. The same is done in all paired sections. There are no relays. Duplicated boards are distributed in both sections (it is possible to have a duplicating round, but pre-duplicated boards are preferable). Odd number of tables — in one section the movement is the same as in a regular Mitchell – boards move down a table each round while the traveling pairs move up one table each round; in the other section, the pairs move to the next lower table and the boards move lower, skipping a table. Even number of tables – in one section the movement is the same as in a regular Mitchell with boards moving down one table and pairs moving up one table and with a skip at the appropriate time; in the other section the pairs move to the next lower table and the boards move lower skipping a table, except during the skip round when the boards skip an extra table. The regular movement resumes after the skip round.

MISBOARD. Replacement of hands in the wrong slots in duplicate play. If the next table is unable to play the board, the guilty pair or pairs may be penalized. A misboard may also occur during duplication.

MISCUT. An illegal cut; a cut that leaves fewer than four cards in either portion of the deck.

MISDEAL. An imperfect deal, owing to an incorrect number of cards being dealt to any player, a card being exposed during the deal, etc. See LAWS (Laws 8-12); LAWS OF DUPLICATE (Laws 6, 13, 14).

MISERE. A bad line of play that seems guaranteed to fail. The name comes from solo and other card games in which it may be desirable to lose tricks. An alternative term is BUTCHER.

MISFIT. A term used to describe a situation where two hands opposite each other in any given deal are unbalanced, each containing two long suits and extreme shortages in its third and fourth suits, and further, where these lengths are met by shortages in the partner's hand and the short suits correspondingly met by lengths in the reverse hand. Where not even one 4-4 or better trump fit can be found in a set of 26 cards, the deal may be said to be a misfit as respects those two hands.

MISHEARING. For mishearing of a bid or called card there is no recourse. If a player is not sure what a previous bid was, he may and should ask for a review of the auction when it becomes his turn to bid. If left-hand opponent bids 1 ♠, partner passes, and right-hand opponent bids 4 ♠, a call of 3 ♦ is insufficient, even though the caller may have thought that right-hand opponent had bid 2 ♠. The use of BID-BOXES helps to avoid such problems, especially for the hearing impaired.

In the play, dummy should not put a card in the played position until he has ascertained that the card was specifically named by the declarer, and it is the declarer's duty to see that any card he has named is the one actually placed in the played position by the dummy. See ACCIDENTS.

MISINFORMATION. Incorrect information given to opponents. It includes such items as wrong explanations of bids, incorrect rulings by the director and incorrect advisories on signaling methods. Rulings by directors are subject to review if the players feel the director has made a wrong interpretation or has applied the wrong Law. Situations involving misinformation given to opponents frequently are subject to appeal.

MISNOMER. A bid or play improperly called. If a player bids 1 ♥, for instance, when he meant to bid 1 ♠, he may substitute his intended call if he does so without pause for thought; otherwise his call, if legal, stands, and if illegal, is subject to penalty. Should a player change a call after a pause, he is giving information to his partner to which his partner is not entitled, and a penalty under this provision should be enforced. (LAW 25).

If a card is called by declarer from dummy in error, he may change the call if he does so without pause for thought, otherwise the called card, if a legal play, stands as the card played. (LAW 45). Even with BID BOXES, misnomers sometimes occur, although not as often. Sometimes the cards in the bid box stick, sometimes the player has failed to notice what has been bid previously. If the player places a bid on the table that he did not intend, he is allowed to change it if he calls attention to it before his partner makes his next call, but there must be no pause for thought. For instance, a player thinks he is placing the 2 ♠ card on the table, but the cards stick and the 2NT bid card lands on the table. He is allowed to change his call to 2 ♠. See Law 25.

MISPLACED BYESTAND. A byestand in a MITCHELL game with an even number of tables placed at a position other than equidistant from the sharing tables.

Adjustment can be made for a byestand too near the head table or too far from it. If the byestand is too near, the game can proceed without change until the halfway mark; the next round is the correction round, and players should be warned of an unusual move. The first set of boards is placed on the byestand and the byestand is then moved to its proper spot. The highest set of boards does not move, but all other boards move down one table. East-West players make their normal move. The North-South players who have just finished playing the highest numbered boards, and the North-South players at the highest numbered table interchange for this round only (keeping their original table number after the correction round). During the correction round, and all subsequent rounds, the last two tables relay boards instead of the first and last tables. (During the correction round, the two interchanging North-South, pairs play against the pair they met on the first round, unavoidably.)

If the byestand is too far, the adjustment is fairly simple. After half the rounds have been played, Table 1, which has been sharing boards with the highest-numbered table, shares boards with Table 2 for all but the last round. That is the only change during these rounds. The final round is an "adjustment" round. Table 2 and the table just beyond the halfway mark (for instance, Table 5 in an eight-table game) share the lowest-numbered set of boards. There will be two tables at which opponents will meet pairs they have played earlier - this cannot be avoided. For additional information, see Alex Groner's *Duplicate Bridge Direction*.

MISSING CARD. A card which is not in any of the four hands. If three of the four hands have a correct number of cards and the fourth is deficient, and the fact is determined before play ends, a search for the card must take place. If the card is located, it is deemed to have been in the hand which is deficient. In rubber bridge, if the card cannot be found, the hand is thrown out and a new deck of cards substituted. In duplicate, the director consults players who have played the board, and a new deck is used to supply the board. When the missing card has either been found, or its denomination established, it is deemed to have been a member of the deficient hand, and may either be an exposed card or establish a discard or ruff on a previous trick as a revoke. See LAWS (Law 11); LAWS OF DUPLICATE (Law 14).

MISSISSIPPI HEART HAND. A famous trick hand dating from the days of whist:

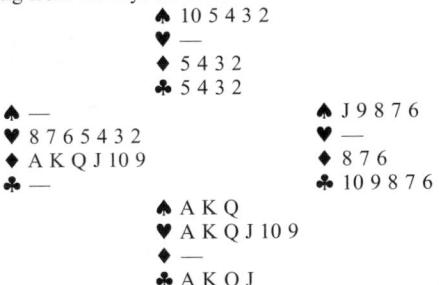

A diamond opening lead holds South to six tricks in a heart contract, and a game cannot be made in any denomination. South can make nine tricks in a spade contract or 10 tricks in a club contract.

An equivalent hand was given by Hoyle in 1747, and the modern version was given by Thomas Matthews in 1804. It was probably used by the cardsharps of the Mississippi River steamboats during the Civil War period, who hoped to persuade South to make a heavy bet on the odd trick with hearts as trumps. It grew in favor among the professional cheaters in the days of BRIDGE WHIST. As doubling and redoubling could continue indefinitely, the odd trick in a low-stake game could become worth $10,000 (or as much as the client was considered good for) with the help of sufficient redoubles. Charles M. Schwab is reported to have paid off not less than $10,000 on this hand.

MISSORTING HAND. See ACCIDENTS.

MR. AND MRS. An event at a bridge tournament in which entries are limited to married couples, playing together. In England such a tournament has the name FLITCH. When held, this event has been quite popular, particularly at tournaments held around St. Valentine's Day.

MITCHELL-HOWELL MOVEMENT. A two-session pair movement, in which one session is played as a SCRAMBLED MITCHELL and the other as a twin or INTERWOVEN HOWELL.

MITCHELL-HOWELL movements are available at the ACBL office for 16 to 38 pairs, and for 42 pairs. Twinned 20's are used for 40.

Mitchell-Howell movements are especially valuable for two-session games of up to 15 tables. For instance, with 10 tables it's fairly simple to run a 10-table Mitchell

in the first session and for the second session to put first-session North-South pairs into one five-table section and the East-West pairs from the first session into another section. Duplicate the boards and run two five-table Howells with combined scoring. Factoring must be done because of the different tops in each session.

Another possibility — use a Relay Mitchell in the first session, producing the same top in both sessions. This also provides a perfect contest — three-board matches against all 19 of the other competing pairs.

The same movement could be used with nine tables. In the first session run a Mitchell movement. In the second session you would have two 4^1/$_2$-table Howells. Let the sitout pairs play each other and avoid a sitout. Top in both sessions is the same so no factoring is involved. The only problem here is each pair plays one pair they played in the first session.

With 16 tables or more it is usually practical to play two Mitchell sections with a crossover for the second session.

MITCHELL MOVEMENT. A method of play for duplicate whist originated by John T. Mitchell which has been continued through auction and contract. In every pairs tournament, the movement has three basic components: boards, tables and pairs. In the Mitchell movement the pairs are in two groups, N-S and E-W, with the aim of having all N-S pairs meeting all E-W pairs and playing all the boards. Except for slight modifications with an even number of tables (SKIP MITCHELL or RELAY MITCHELL), E-W pairs move to the next higher-numbered table, while boards move to the next lower-numbered table. N-S are always stationary. To produce one winning pair, see SCRAMBLED MITCHELL.

For an even number of tables, there are two alternatives: (1) The skip Mitchell, in which E-W pairs skip one table after the half-way round. (2) The relay Mitchell, which is normally used when it is desired to play as many rounds as there are tables. A set of boards is shared throughout between Table 1 and the highest-numbered table. A spare set of boards is left on a byestand at the midpoint: between 4 and 5 for an 8-table game, 5 and 6 for a 10-table game and so on. Boards moving down after each round must include the byestand, so in an 8-table game they go from 5 to byestand to 4. This method has the advantage that all players play all boards and meet all opponents in the other line. It is not necessary that the relay and byestand be located as listed above. The following is the requirement: the byestand must be exactly halfway around the field from the relay. For instance if the relay in an eight-table game is between tables 1 and 2, then the byestand must be between tables 5 and 6.

MITCHELL STAYMAN. This convention applies when a minor suit has been overcalled by a bid of 1NT. Third hand can use partner's minor as artificial, rather than a raise, to show both majors. Thus in the sequence:

        1♣   (1NT)   2♣

the last call acts as Stayman. Some people play that when 1♦ has been overcalled with 1NT, 2♣ rather than 2♦ acts as Stayman.

MITCHELL TROPHY. Awarded to the winners of the NORTH AMERICAN OPEN BOARD-A-MATCH TEAMS. Trophy honors Vic Mitchell, one of the most outstanding players in ACBL history.

MITTELMAN ADJUNCT. A convention used to clarify opener's hand after this sequence:

1♠	1NT
2♥	2NT
?	

3♣ = transfer to 3♦
3♦ = diamond fragment, game force
3♥ = weak 5-5
3♠ = weak 6-4
After 3♣ forces 3♦:
3♥ = 5-5 game force
3♠ = 6-4 game force
3NT = club fragment, game force

MIXED PAIRS. All pairs must consist of one man and one woman.

MIXED RAISE. See CUEBID IN OPPONENT'S SUIT.

MIXED TEAMS. A Mixed Team comprises at least two men and two women. The maximum number of team members is six. During play each pair must consist of one woman and one man. See TEAM GAMES.

MIXING CARDS AFTER PLAY. Illegal if a claim has been made to inspect the cards for a revoke, or to ascertain honors or the number of tricks won or lost. See LAWS (Law 66).

MNEMONIC DUPLICATE. See REPLAY DUPLICATE.

MODIFIED CRASH. While CRASH as a defense to a strong club was first publicized in the USA, the same defense, with minor modifications has been very popular in Great Britain for the past 25 years, particularly when combined with TWERB, Two-Way Exclusion Relay Bidding. The method is based on the idea of maximizing frequency of the obstructive 1♥ and 1♠ overcalls. It operates as follows:

Over a strong 1♣ opening, double shows a heart suit and at least respectable overcalling values, 1♦ shows spades and similarly a respectable overcall. Over these two bids all new suits are natural, jumps in new suits are fit-showing, and 1NT is a relay with genuine game-invitational values. 1♥, 1♠, and 1NT are the two-suited overcalls, (Color, Rank and Shape) which at favorable vulnerability can be 4-4.

In response to these bids, redouble from either side is always for rescue, Responder's actions, including passing a double, are always pass or correct at any level. However, responder can show his own suit by bidding 1NT – that acts as a transfer to 2♣ and passes control to responder. If overcaller redoubles, this is for rescue, but it suggests that his holding in the higher of his known suits is better than his holding in the lower suit.

After a 1NT overcall is doubled, redouble by fourth hand acts as a transfer to 2♣ and passes control to fourth hand. If fourth hand passes, running to the minor by overcaller shows the minor is equal or better than the major. Redouble by overcaller simply shows a better major than a minor; fourth hand will bid 2♣, allowing overcaller to pass or to correct with spades and diamonds.

Immediate two-level bids shows either the suit above the one bid, or the two below it, at least 5-5 distribution. So an overcall of 2♥ shows spades or the minors. 2NT shows the odd suits. In response to these bids, fourth hand will make pass or correct bids, except that the pass of a double implies at least five good cards in the suit doubled. Redouble by fourth hand acts as a transfer to the next higher bid, and passes control to the fourth hand to name his own suit at his next turn.

Similar methods apply after 1♣-P-1♦. Here double is two suits of the same color, 1NT is two suits of the same shape, and 2NT is the minors. 1♥ and 1♠ are natural and two-level actions are two-way exclusion bids again.

MOLE SQUEEZE. A squeeze on one opponent that can lead to an endplay against the other. It was named and analysed by Julian Pottage of Great Britain. The basic position:

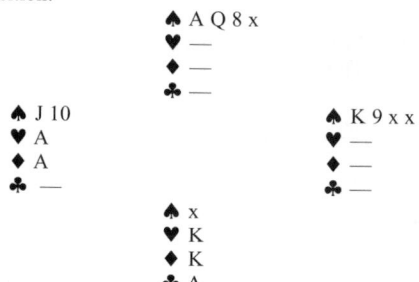

South, playing notrump, is on lead needing three of the last four tricks. South leads the ♣A and West is squeezed in three suits. A discard from either red suit sets up South's king, but watch what happens when a spade is thrown. Next a spade is led and West's remaining honour is covered by the queen and king. Now East has to play from the 9 into dummy's tenace.

Key features: (a) Before the squeeze card is played, West's holding in spades, the mole threat suit, is strong enough to prevent East from being thrown in to damaging effect. West's spades will not take a trick themselves; their value to the defense lies in the way they support East's spades. (b) East has no exit cards. The resulting endplay would not work if East had a red card to lead to one of West' aces. (c) West is squeezed in three suits — in a conventional way in the red suits, but in a subtle, indirect way in spades.

North's low spade is an idle card since it disappears on South's ♣A. That idle card could be in any of the other suits and the squeeze would remain effective. Furthermore, the fact that one of North's cards is spare means one of the simple threats could sit facing the squeeze card. This brings us to the second position:

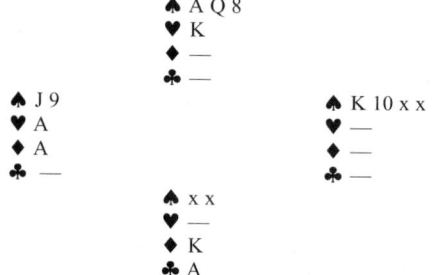

Again South can collect all but one of the remaining tricks by cashing the ♣A. If West discards a heart, North throws a spade; otherwise the ♥K goes on the squeeze trick.

Equally the threat lying with the squeeze card can be the mole threat:

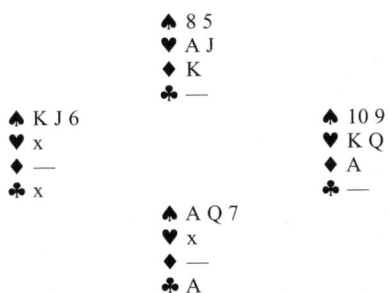

Once more cashing the ♣A executes the mole squeeze. This time East is the victim. The layout has increased to five cards so as to provide North with an entry. If East discards a spade, the ♥A must be cashed before West can be endplayed.

Perhaps you wonder how likely the mole squeeze is to occur in practice. Not that often, but they do serve a useful purpose. In every mole squeeze a trick is lost after the squeeze trick. So, if you are unable to give up the right number of tricks for a simple squeeze (i.e. rectify the count), the mole may come to the rescue. Likewise, as you can see from the first two layouts, the mole can operate even when neither standard threat is accompanied by an entry. Thus the mole can prove useful when you lack the requisite entries for other types of squeeze. Finally, in the first and third layouts the two simple threats are misplaced for a conventional squeeze, sitting as they do under the relevant guards. These are the two layouts you are most likely to encounter at the table.

There are simpler mole endings in which two tricks get lost at the end, for example:

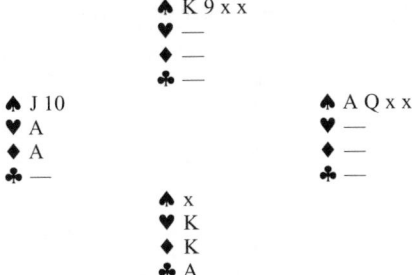

On the ♣A lead West can postpone the fateful moment by discarding a spade. Then a spade to the jack, king and ace lets East win the next two tricks. However North's 9 takes the last trick.

By the same token the mole squeeze can work when the mole threat suit contains two winners:

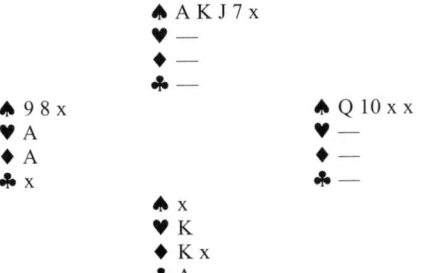

To avoid conceding a trick at once, West discards a spade on the ♣A. After that a spade to the ace followed by the jack gives East no winning option.

The mole threat can be split between two hands:

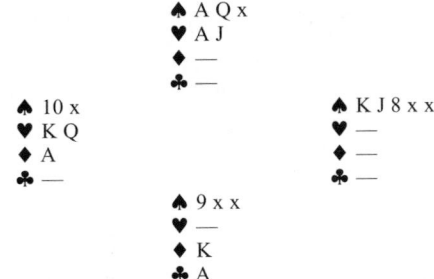

Here North has a winner with the simple heart threat to create space for South to have help in the mole suit. Since that winner scores after the throw-in, it is vital for East to have no hearts. South plays the ♣A and West releases a spade, so North sheds the ♥J. Now a low spade to the queen picks up the 10 on the way and leaves East snookered.

The mole squeeze can function perfectly well even if declarer or dummy has a void in the mole suit:

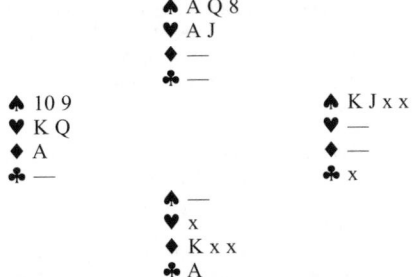

South is on lead needing four of the last five tricks. South leads the ♣A. To avoid instant defeat, West throws a spade, so North discards the ♥J. Now declarer can cross to the ♥A and exit with the ♠Q, squashing West's 10. The squeeze would prove equally effective if West's spades were J-10 or J-9 and if East had a heart instead of a low black card.

Up until now the mole suit itself has provided the throw-in card. This need not be the case:

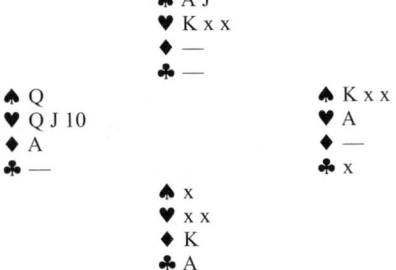

Wanting four of the remaining tricks, South plays the ♣A. If West discards a heart, the ♠J goes from the North hand and ducking a heart leaves dummy high. Releasing a diamond is clearly fatal, but watch happens if West parts with a spade. North throws a heart and declarer concedes a heart. East now has to submit to the jaws of dummy's tenace in spades and the ♥K makes too. Note that East's seemingly idle card has to be a club. Otherwise West could afford to throw a spade since East could jettison the ♥A on the squeeze trick.

Sometimes the player you need to put on play holds

an exit card that will not fall of its own accord. On such occasions you might still be able to effect a throw-in if you can forcibly extract that card by cashing another winner i.e. if a strip squeeze on that opponent follows a mole squeeze on the first one. There are quite a few possible endings for this. Here is an example:

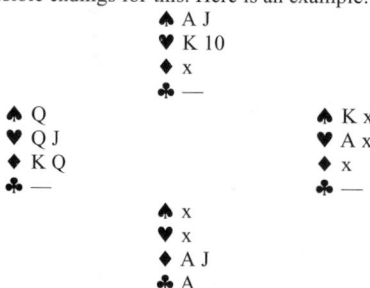

```
              ♠ A J
              ♥ K 10
              ♦ x
              ♣ —
♠ Q                          ♠ K x
♥ Q J                        ♥ A x
♦ K Q                        ♦ x
♣ —                          ♣ —
              ♠ x
              ♥ x
              ♦ A J
              ♣ A
```

If West discards a heart on the ♣A, declarer can play a heart to set up North's 10. So, as releasing a diamond is just as bad, West lets the ♠Q go. East could make life easy by throwing a heart, but suppose he chooses a diamond. South cannot exit with a heart at this point — the defenders would take two tricks in the suit. Instead South cashes the ♦A and North pitches the ♥10. To keep two spades East has to bare the ♥A. Now the endplay works. See VICE SQUEEZE.

MONACO SYSTEM. A prototype relay system devised by Pierre Ghestem of France, and used by him very successfully in world championships in partnership with Rene Bacherich.

The 1♣ opening bid was not necessarily strong. The artificial relay bids available, usually by responder but sometimes by opener, were almost always in diamonds. After major-suit openings the minimum action (1♥ - 1♠, or 1♠ - 1NT) was a relay. Most responses at the two level were transfers. See RELAY SYSTEMS.

MONITORS. Persons assigned to handle specialized chores at the table during high-level team events, occasionally at high-level pair events. Sometimes the monitor keeps track of how long each pair takes to make its bids and plays so that the tournament committee can make an informed decision concerning penalties for slow play. A monitor used to be the liaison between players on either side of the BIDDING SCREEN. The monitor noted the bids made on his side of the table, then called them aloud for the benefit of the players and monitor on the other side of the screen. This use became obsolete when the TRAY was introduced.

The monitor also frequently is called upon to keep complete bidding and play records of the action at his table.

MONSTER. A bridge hand of great trick-taking potential either because of a preponderance of high-card winners or because of concentrated strength in long suits and extreme shortness in weak suits. Also, a very big one-session score — a big game.

MONTREAL RELAY. The idea of playing a major-suit response to a 1♣ opening bid as a five-card suit is not uncommon. In that context playing 1♦ as an artificial response makes sense. Eric Kokish devised a scheme of continuations after the 1♦ response, characterized

by playing 2♦ as reversing values, possibly without real diamonds. Jumps by opener to 3♦/3♥/3♠ are self-agreeing splinters.

MONTY HALL TRAP. A common probability trap treating biased information as random. Whenever the information itself has a direct bearing on whether or not you receive it, care must be taken to take this into account. The name is based on an entertainment show where Monty Hall offers $100,000 if the contestant, given the choice of three doors, chooses the right door.

If you choose door #1, Monty Hall says, "Let's see what's behind door number —No! Wait a minute! Before we look, I'll offer you $20,000 for whatever is behind door #1."

You refuse, of course. Even assuming the booby prizes are worth nothing, the expected value of your choice is $33,333.33 – you have one chance in three at $100,000. Now Monty Hall says, "All right. "But before we see what you've won, let's take a look behind door #2!" Door #2 opens to reveal one of the booby prizes. Monty Hall steps in once more: "I'll give you one last chance. You can have $40,000 for what's behind door #1." You take it because the offer is greater than the expected value.

If Monty Hall had chosen a random door to open, you would calculate that you now had a 50-50 shot at the grand prize and would refuse the $40,000. But he didn't. Showman that he is, he intentionally showed you a booby prize to heighten the suspense. Because you already knew that at least one of the other two doors held a booby prize, you have learned nothing. You still have the same one chance in three you started with.

Here the trap was easy to spot. But the same trap can crop up more subtly in a bridge setting. Let's make up a deal:

```
                North
                ♠ A 5
                ♥ 8 7 5
                ♦ J 5 3
                ♣ K J 7 4 2

                South
                ♠ K 7 2
                ♥ A 6 4 2
                ♦ A 7
                ♣ A 10 5 3
South                        North
1NT                          3NT
```

Problem 1.

West leads a low spade. You duck in both hands; East continues spades. It appears from the carding that spades are 5-3. What is the percentage play to run the club suit?

Problem 2.

What is the percentage play if it appears spades are 4-4?

Problem 3.

Suppose, instead of a spade, West leads from a broken four-card heart suit. Now what is the percentage play in clubs?

Solution 1.

Some players would reason this way: East began with three spades to his partner's five. That leaves East with 10 unknown cards; West, with eight. So East is five to four to hold the ♣Q.

This is falling for the Monty Hall trap. If West had led a random suit and that suit had happened to split 5-3,

the reasoning would be valid. But that's not what happened. West, with malice aforethought, chose to lead his longest suit. Is it any surprise that he has more spades than his partner? Suppose your opponents at the other table somehow reach three notrump from the North hand. East leads a red suit and (surprise!) he has more cards in that suit than West. Is your opponent supposed to finesse against West for the ♣Q, while you finesse against East? No, like the booby prize behind door #2, the relative distribution of the spade suit is biased information. You knew ahead of time that West was apt to be longer in whatever suit he led. "Discovering" what you already knew cannot change the odds.

How then do you determine the percentage play? Given that spades is West's longest suit, the expected spade break is roughly 4.5-3.5. West rates to have one more spade than East. So the actual 5-3 break is only one card away from expectation. It is equivalent to a random suit's breaking 4-3. That means you can counter the bias by pretending that East has only one extra unknown card instead of two. You cash the ♣K and lead toward the ace. East follows. Now he has zero extra unknown cards. So it's a toss-up. The finesse and the drop are equally likely.

Here is the mathematical way to do this. Calculate the frequency of all of West's possible patterns assuming he has one, two or three clubs (4-0 breaks are irrelevant) and no suit longer than five cards. If the pattern includes a second five-card suit, divide that frequency by two, because half the time West would lead the other five-card suit. Then compute the odds for each club play.

West's Pattern	A Priori Frequency	Adjusted Frequency
Singleton Clubs: 31%		
5-5-2-1	672	336
5-4-3-1	3360	3360
5-3-4-1	5600	5600
5-2-5-1	3360	1680
Doubleton Clubs: 47%		
5-5-1-2	288	144
5-4-2-2	2520	2520
5-3-3-2	6720	6720
5-2-4-2	6300	6300
5-1-5-2	2016	1008
Tripleton Clubs: 22%		
5-5-0-3	24	12
5-4-1-3	480	480
5-3-2-3	2240	2240
5-2-3-3	3360	3360
5-1-4-3	1680	1680
5-0-5-3	224	112

Declarer's Play	Frequency of Success
Finesse West	53%
Finesse East	60%
Play for Drop	60%

Solution 2.

With spades 4-4, most players would play for the drop, reasoning that an even split in spades would not change the *a priori* odds. Actually spades are expected to split 4.5 - 3.5, so West's spades are shorter than average. Furthermore, his *diamonds* are shorter than average. A *priori*, West's expected diamond length is four. But, after a spade lead, his *maximum* diamond length is four. His expectation must be something less than four. So West is short in two suits. His expected club length increases accordingly and it becomes right to finesse him for the queen.

North
♠ A 5
♥ 8 7 5
♦ J 5 3
♣ K J 7 4 2

South
♠ K 7 2
♥ A 6 4 2
♦ A 7
♣ A 10 5 3

If you work it out the long way, you find that finessing against East works about 48 percent of the time; playing for the drop, about 61 percent; and finessing against West, about 65 percent.

Solution 3.

After a heart lead. one might finesse against East because he has only two hearts to West's four. But this is by far the *worst* of the three plays. As in problem two, the heart lead reduces West's expected spade and diamond lengths. In theory, he can't have five of either suit and, by restricted choice, he is less likely than normal to have four. So his expected length in spades and diamonds goes down and his expected club length goes up. Despite the fact West has more cards that are specifically known than East, it is right to finesse West for the ♣Q. Finessing against East works 46 percent of the time; the drop, 60 percent; finessing against West, 67 percent.

These arguments assume that West can be relied upon to have led his longest suit. If the auction makes certain leads unattractive or if West has led from a sequence or if West is simply known to be perverse, he might have a longer suit and none of this applies.

Sometimes biased information can come from the auction.

North
♠ K 10 7 6
♥ A 7 4 3
♦ A 5 2
♣ J 6

South
♠ A J 5 3 2
♥ 8 2
♦ Q 9 3
♣ A 5 4

West	North	East	South
		1♣	1♠
Pass	2♣	Pass	2♦
Pass	3♠	Pass	4♠
All Pass			

West leads the ♣2 (third and fifth)—low, 9, ace. You play another club. East wins with the queen and leads the ♣K to tap dummy. West follows to all three clubs. What is the percentage play in spades?

East has five clubs to his partner's three. But, because his club length and his decision to bid clubs were intimately linked, this is biased information.

If East had not opened, you would still know that clubs were 3-5 (he would not have played the 9 at trick one from K-Q-9), and it would be clear to finesse West for the ♠Q. But he did open, so you know more. You know that he cannot have a five-card red suit. This decreases his likelihood of holding a singleton spade. Declarer could test hearts before making a decision, but chances are that once again it will be a toss-up between the two

plays. Both the finesse against West and the drop are about 60 percent.

MOREHEAD TROPHY. Donated by *The New York Times* in memory of its longtime bridge editor Albert H. Morehead. The trophy was originally awarded to the winners of a special knockout team event that followed the Reisinger team contest at the Fall NABC in 1967, but was withdrawn when the event proved unpopular. Since 1973 the trophy has been awarded to the winners of the GRAND NATIONAL TEAMS. For results see Appendix I.

MORNING GAME. Contest played in the morning, usually set up so that it finishes by noon. All ACBL morning games used to be SIDE GAMES, but now many rated games are played in the morning. Some are still morning games, but even these usually are part of a CONTINUOUS PAIRS contest, in which individuals are rated by their best two percentages over a series of games. Daily winners earn red points; overall winners receive gold points. Special pair games also are set up for beginners at North American Championships. In addition most regional and all North American tournaments feature morning knockout team events which are contested over consecutive mornings. These are championship events awarding gold points for overalls and red points for matches won.

Nowadays some two-session games start in the morning and finish in the afternoon. Regionals often feature such Open Pairs games. At the North American level, senior events usually start in mid-morning and finish in the afternoon, giving the players an evening of leisure. Some pair games, such as FAST PAIRS, also stage their first session in the morning.

MORTON'S FORK COUP. A maneuver by which declarer presents a defender with a choice of taking a trick cheaply or ducking to preserve an honor combination, only both decisions cost the defense a trick. If the defender wins the trick, he sets up another high card in the suit for declarer, while if he ducks, his winner disappears because declarer has a discard possibility. The name is derived from an episode in English history. Cardinal Morton, Chancellor under King Henry VII, habitually extracted money from wealthy London merchants for the royal treasury. His approach was that if the merchants lived ostentatiously, it was obvious that they had sufficient income to spare some for the king. Alternatively, if they lived frugally, they must be saving substantially and could therefore afford to contribute to the king's coffers. In either case, they were impaled on Morton's Fork.

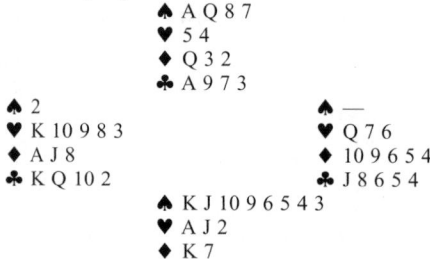

South plays 6 ♠ after West has opened the bidding with 1 ♥ and receives the lead of the ♣K. Since South cannot profitably discard on the ♣A, he ruffs the first round,

draws the outstanding trump and leads a low diamond toward the queen. If West goes up with the ace, declarer subsequently discards two hearts on the ♦Q and ♣A, while if West withholds the ♦A, declarer discards his losing diamond on the ♣A and loses only one heart trick. Alternatively, had declarer judged that East held the ♦A, he could have couped that defender by leading a low diamond toward his king.

MOSCITO. A system devised by Paul Marston and Stephen Burgess. The first four letters are an acronym for Major-Oriented Strong Club. It makes extensive use of the SYMMETRIC RELAY in auctions where the opening side has the balance of power.

It was originally a STRONG-PASS system, but in 1992 it was changed to a strong club system to overcome the restrictions placed on its use in tournament plays. This is the opening-bid structure for the first or second position:
Pass: 0-5 points when not vulnerable; if vulnerable, you may also pass with 6-9 if not at least 5-4 in two suits.

1♣: 15-plus points, any shape
1♦: 4-plus ♥ 9-14 points
1♥: 4-plus ♠ 9-14 points
1♠: 4-plus ♦ 9-14 points. Opener can have a 4-card major if he has 6-plus diamonds.
1NT: 11-14, balanced
2♣: 6-plus clubs may have a 4-card major. Denies 4 diamonds.
2♦: 5-9 with 6 hearts or 6 spades
2♥/♠: 5-card weak twos
2NT: 5-8 with 5-5 in the minors
In the third and four seat,
1♣: 17-plus points, any shape
1♦: Catchall opening
1♥: 4-plus ♥ 11-16 points
1♠: 4-plus ♠ 11-16 points
1NT: 14-16, in third seat, 11-14 in fourth seat, balanced
2♣: 11-16 6-plus clubs may have a 4-card suit
2♦: 11-16 6-plus diamonds denes a four card major
2♥/♠: weak twos
2NT: preemptive with 5-5 in the majors
A symetric relay structure is used in strong auctions.

If the responder has at least game ambitions opposite any of the opening bids, he makes a relay response. Otherwise he tries to consume as much bidding space as possible.

In the third and fourth positions, the point ranges increase because the responder's hand is so limited by virtue of his original pass.

MOSHER. The whimsical name for the "convention" in effect over the opponents' 1NT opening when all overcalls are natural: 2♣ shows clubs, 2♦ shows diamonds and so forth. Named for Robert Mosher.

MOTT-SMITH TROPHY. This trophy is awarded every year to the player with the best overall individual performance record in the American Contract Bridge League Spring North American Bridge Championships. Donated by friends in memory of Geoffrey Mott-Smith in 1961, it was made retroactive to 1958 to include all the winners. For winners see Appendix II.

MOVE. The change of seats in duplicate bridge after a round has been completed.

MOVEMENT. A schedule of progression for players, indicating the seat to be occupied and the boards to be played by each player at each round. The Tournament Director announces the movement to be followed, which is usually arranged to provide each contestant with different opponents at each round.

Specific movements in common use are listed under the following headings: AMERICAN WHIST MOVEMENT, HOWELL MOVEMENT, MIRROR MITCHELL, MITCHELL, RELAY MITCHELL, SCRAMBLED MITCHELL, SHORT HOWELL, SHOMATE, RAINBOW, STANZA HOWELL, STANZA MOVEMENT, STAGGER MOVEMENT, WEB MOVEMENT.

MOVEMENT CARDS. (1) Plastic table cards used usually in Individuals and Howells to indicate the table number, the players or pairs by round number, the boards by round number, and the instructions for the players or pairs to follow next. (2) Small cards issued to players to indicate their pair or player number, the movement they should follow round by round, and the board numbers they should be playing round by round. Such small movement cards are frequently distributed in events with unusual progressions, such as individuals, Howells, Baldwin-McKenneys, and Rover Mitchells.

MOYSIAN FIT. A contract in which declarer's trump suit is divided 4-3, usually thus described when the selection is made deliberately. Named for Alphonse Moyse Jr. whose ardent advocacy of this choice was part of his case in favor of opening four-card majors and raising with three trumps.

MUD. A lead convention in which the original lead from three small cards is the middle one, followed in play by the higher. The name is the acronym of middle, up, down, the order in which the cards are played. See THREE SMALL CARDS, LEAD FROM, OPENING LEAD; ROMAN MUD.

MUIDERBERGH TWOS. (Also called LUCAS TWO-BIDS). Popular in Europe especially in the Netherlands and Great Britain, Muiderbergh Two-bids are named after the village of Muiderbergh where Onno Janssens (the co-inventor with Willem Boegem) lived. Muiderbergh Twos consist of an opening 2♦ to be a Multi, weak in either major, optionally with various strong hand possibilities. Both 2♥ and 2♠ promise at least five cards in the bid major, and a minor suit of at least four cards, with five promised at unfavorable vulnerability. Responses to the 2♥ and 2♠ opening bids are 2NT as a relay promising game invitational values and three of a minor as prepared to play facing length (pass or correct). After the 2NT relay opener rebids his minor with a minimum or bids three of the codified major to show extras (3NT shows a 6/5 maximum and 4♣/4♦ show a 5/6 maximum).

MULTI. The Multi is a 2♦ opening bid showing a weak two-bid in either major, though some pairs tag on stronger types too, such as a big balanced hand, or a big 4-4-4-1, or a strong two-bid in a minor.

This opening made its first appearance at the end of the 1960s. It was devised by Terence Reese and Jeremy Flint, with input from such players as Robert Sheehan, Jonathan Cansino and Irving Rose.

Even if it is possible that the opener may have a strong hand-type, the responder assumes he is opposite a weak two-bid and makes his first bid based on his fit for the majors. His possible actions are:

a. 2♥: The responder wishes to play in 2♥ opposite a weak two-bid in that suit. The responder may be doing anything from passing to bidding a slam if the opener actually has spades. The key aspect is the strength of the responder's hand. If he has a good hand yet bids only 2♥, he must be short in hearts. If he has a weak hand, he might have length in both majors and does not wish to get to the three level.

b. 2♠: The responder wishes to stop in 2♠ opposite spades, but to bid at least 3♥ opposite that suit. Note that this bid strongly suggests shortage in spades and length in hearts. This is important to remember both when devising a defense and when defending if the responder should become the declarer.

c. 2NT: This is the forcing inquiry, similar to a 2NT response opposite a normal weak two-bid, except that the opener must describe not only his strength but also his suit. The bid is made with a hand willing to go to at least the three level opposite a minimum weak two-bid. This is especially true if the 2♦ opening bid cannot contain a strong hand, 2NT might occasionally be a semi-psychic response with length in both majors and a weak hand.

d. 3♣/♦: Either highly invitational or forcing, by partnership agreement.

e. 3♥/♠: Usually these bids are "correctable." In other words, the opener passes with the bid suit or corrects to the other suit at the minimum level (or, perhaps, jumps to 4♠ over 3♥ with a maximum).

f. 3NT: To play (though in the original Reese-Flint version it indicated a very strong minor two-suiter with at most four losers).

g. 4♣: Asking the opener to bid one below his suit: 4♦ with hearts and 4♥ with spades. This allows the responder to play in game in the suit.

h. 4♦: Asking the opener to bid his suit (or both minors).

i. 4♥/♠: To play regardless of the opener's suit.

Note that a pair may have alternative interpretations for some of these bids.

Advantages of the Multi

One of the key pluses of the Multi is that the opponents do not always know the opener's suit. This makes defense more difficult than against a simple weak two-bid, especially when no cuebid is available.

A strong responding hand may be able to become declarer in the major, protecting a side-suit king or tenace from immediate attack.

It is possible to play in 2♦ when this is a better contract than two of the major.

The opening 2♦ bid frees 2♥ and 2♠ openings for other meanings. Perhaps they could be ACOL TWO-BIDS, removing some strain from the overloaded 2♣ opening in Standard; 2♥ could be FLANNERY, or like the PRECISION 2♦ OPENING; 2♠ could describe a minor two-suiter, or a weak preempt either in a minor or in any suit; the other two-bids may be used to show weak two-suiters with at least five cards in each suit.

Disadvantages of the Multi

The major drawback of the Multi is that sometimes the responder cannot make an immediate preemptive

raise. For example, with a weak hand long in one major, the responder could jump to game in that major opposite a normal weak two-bid, but opposite a Multi he must assume his partner holds the other suit. Benito Garozzo says that he will not use the Multi as he is not willing to give up what he considers to be one of the best preempts in bridge: 2♠ - (Pass) -3♠.

By virtue of opening 2♦ rather than 2♥ or 2♠, the opponents have slightly more space to compete. And sometimes they will be able to double the major for penalties when they could not have done so against a normal weak two-bid.

Defenses to the Multi

This is complicated because all possible positions at the table must be considered. First of all:

Second Seat

There are several approaches that work. But there are two important aspects. First, you must act immediately with a decent hand. If you pass initially, waiting for the opener to define his suit, and then bid, your partner will assume you are balancing. Secondly, decide how you wish to play double, 2♥, 2♠ and 2NT; these choices will affect the rest of the structure.

Here are three workable schemes, which we will subhead under the meaning for an immediate double.

1. *Double is a takeout of a weak 2♠ opening*

Dbl: a takeout double of a weak 2♠ opening.
2♥: equivalent to a takeout double of a weak 2♥ opening.
2♠: natural.
2NT: balanced 16-19 points.
3 of a suit: natural (3♠ being stronger than 2♠, of course).
3NT: to play, probably based on a good minor: what is called a "tricks" hand.
4♣/♦: a strong hand with at least 5-5 in hearts and the bid minor.
4♥/♠: natural.
4NT: a big minor two-suiter.

With a minor two-suiter not strong enough to bid 4NT, either bid 3♦, planning to follow up with 4♣; or pass first and try to describe your holding later with an UNUSUAL NOTRUMP.

With a big spade-minor two-suiter, pass and bid four of your minor at your second turn. (If nervous, bid 2♥ immediately and hope to be able to express your two-suiter).

2. *Double shows a strong notrump*

Dbl: balanced 16-18 points, or perhaps a hand too strong for the non-forcing 2♥ and 2♠ bids.
2♥: equivalent to a takeout double of a weak 2♠ opener.
2♠: equivalent to a takeout double of a weak 2♥ opener.
2NT: minor two-suiter.
3 of a suit: natural.
3NT: to play: probably a "tricks" hand.
4♣/♦: a big major-minor two-suiter with the bid minor and either major.

3. *Double is two-way*

Dbl: either a balanced 13-16 points, announcing the values to contest the bidding but making no other guarantees, or a very strong hand: 19-plus points.
2♥/♠: natural.
2NT: balanced 16-18 points.
Rest: as above.

Fourth Seat

After the bidding begins (2♦)-Pass-(2♥/♠), fourth hand should remember that the responder has probably

bid his shorter major. (As we saw above, this is definitely true if the response is 2♠ and probably true if it is 2♥.) The best approach is to make all simple bids including 2NT as natural (and four of a minor as above), except for one little ruse: a double should be two-way: it is either for takeout or for penalties. For example, after (2♦)-Pass-(2♠), fourth hand should double with either of these hands:

	a.		b.
♠	3		♠ K Q J 9 8 7
♥	K J 6 5		♥ 4
♦	A Q 8		♦ A Q 4
♣	K Q 9 8 5		♣ Q 10 9

This might appear to give the doubler's partner an insoluble problem, but it does not. The opener will clarify his suit by passing or correcting, and then the doubler's partner will know which double his partner has from his length in the opener's suit.

For example, it goes (2♦)-Pass-(2♠)-Dbl-(Pass) and the responder holds either of these hands:

	c.		d.
♠	3		♠ K J 9 8 5
♥	9 8 6 5 3		♥ 5
♦	A 7 6		♦ K J 7
♣	Q 9 7 6		♣ J 8 7 3

With hand c, it is obvious that partner has spades. The responder is short in spades and so are you. Just pass.

With d, though, you know partner has a takeout double. However, you are loaded with spades, so you pass, converting the double into one for penalties.

The only time the doubler's partner could have a problem is after (2♦)-Pass-(2♥)-Dbl-(Pass). The responder might have heart length in a weak hand. If unsure, the doubler's partner removes the double. If it was for penalties all along, the final result will probably be 3NT bid and made instead of 2♥ doubled and down some number.

Sixth Seat

You did not act immediately, but the bidding has returned to you, probably after (2♦) - Pass - (2♥/♠) - Pass (Pass). Now you are in a balancing position. Most actions will be natural, but there are two conventional bids you should consider. 2NT shows a minor two-suiter (and a particularly weak one if you could have bid an immediate 2NT as unusual). And three of a minor may be used to show a limited 5-5 in the bid minor and the other major. (Probably you should use these bids only if you could not bid an immediate 2♥ or 2♠ as natural.)

For example:

West	North	East	South
2♦	Pass	2♠	Pass
Pass	2NT: limited minor two-suiter		
	3♣: club-heart two-suiter		
	3♦: diamond-heart two-suiter		

Another defense, devised by Danny Kleinman, is Simpleton. In a second seat, double is Weiss, 2♥ and 2♠ show that suit and a minor, 2NT and 4NT show minors. In a sixth seat double is takeout, 3♣ and 3♦ are natural with a four-card major, 3NT shows a stopper and a running minor, three of other major shows six-card suit and four-card minor, 4♣ or 4♦ is minor-major, too strong for direct 2♥ or 2♠.

Auction Continuations

In general, these are natural, except that over the 2♥ bid that acts as a takeout double of a 2♥ opening, it is logical to use a Lebensohl approach. An immediate response at the three-level promises values, and 3♥, either immediately or via the 2NT puppet, is a cuebid. (There is no need to use Lebensohl over the double show-

ing a takeout of spades because the doubler's partner — the advancer — has a 2♠ cuebid available.)

When the auction goes (2♦) - 3♣ - (Pass), all bids by the advancer must be treated as natural. You have to pay off occasionally against the Multi. See CHICO TWO-DIAMONDS.

MULTIPLICATING BOARDS. See TWINNING.

MURDER. See BENNETT "MURDER."

MURRAY CONVENTION. Devised by Eric R. Murray. See TWO-WAY STAYMAN.

N

NABC. North American Bridge Championships. See NORTH AMERICAN CHAMPIONSHIPS.

NAC. See NORTH AMERICAN CHAMPIONSHIPS.

NAIL TROPHY. Awarded to the winners of the NORTH AMERICAN LIFE MASTER OPEN PAIRS. Trophy honors Robert (Bobby) Nail, an outstanding American player.

NAMYATS. A convention in which an opening bid of 4♣ promises a long heart suit and an opening of 4♦ promises a long spade suit. This was favored by 40% of the experts in BWS2001. As most frequently used, opener promises a hand stronger than the normal direct opening of four of a major suit. Some pairs use the four-of-a-minor opening to show a weaker hand, or a hand with a solid major suit and nothing else.

Responder usually accepts the transfer by bidding four of opener's major. However, the bid of the next higher suit is available without getting the partnership beyond game, and can be used either as a retransfer, making opener the declarer, or as an asking bid.

The convention was devised as part of the Little Major system, and its name is a reversal of Stayman, who introduced the idea in the United States.

To defend against Namyats, players should discuss the meaning of a double, either of the Namyats bid or of a minimum response to it. It can be lead-directing, but it seems slightly better to use the double as take-out of opener's major, promising the other major. The 1994 BWS consensus was that direct doubles of the opening bid or response (relay or natural) is for takeout. Delayed doubles are for penalty.

For an alternative treatment see RUBIN TRANSFERS. Also see SOUTH AFRICAN TEXAS.

NATIONAL APPEALS COMMITTEE. See APPEALS COMMITTEE, ACBL APPEALS COMMITTEE, COMMITTEE.

NATIONAL AUTHORITY. The body which, in each country, has responsibility for sponsoring and promoting bridge in that country. For the names of such organizations, see entry under each country. Most national authorities are members of the WORLD BRIDGE FEDERATION. See NCBO. The national authority has jurisdiction over all competition in that

country and APPEALS on matters of law and fact are taken to the group designated by the national authority to hear them. In the ACBL the national authority on matters of law is the LAWS COMMISSION OF THE ACBL.

NATIONAL LAWS COMMISSION. See ACBL LAWS COMMISSION.

NATIONAL POINTS. See REGIONAL AND NATIONAL POINTS.

NATIONAL TOURNAMENT. A tournament which determines the winners of various events on a nationwide basis. See CHAMPIONSHIP TOURNAMENT; NORTH AMERICAN CHAMPIONSHIP.

NATIONALS. A term formerly used to denote one of the ACBL NORTH AMERICAN CHAMPIONSHIPS. The current designation is NABC (North American Bridge Tournament).

NATIONWIDE CHARITY GAME. See ACBL-WIDE GAMES.

NATURAL CALL. Call that reflects the character of the hand, suggests a suitable final strain, and does not have an artificial or semi-artificial meaning. A bid is not natural if it promises possession of a specific other suit, as in Smolen. A bid may be ambiguously natural or artificial. In the Kokish Relay 2♣-2♦-2♥ is ambiguous. If followed by a suit bid, the hearts are "naturalized."

NATURAL FOUR NOTRUMP. See BLACKWOOD.

NATURALISTS. See SCIENTISTS VS. TRADITIONALISTS.

NAVRATILOVA, Martina. World champion tennis player. On bridge: "Bridge is more than just a card game. It is a cerebral sport. Bridge teaches you logic, reasoning, quick thinking, patience, concentration and partnership skills." On winning: "Whoever said, 'It's not whether you win or lose that counts,' probably lost."

NCBO. National Contract Bridge Organization. A WBF term for any independent or self-governing country, in principle with at least 250 members. The membership of the WBF is 94 NCBOs.

NEAPOLITAN. A system devised principally by Eugenio Chiaradia, and played in many World Championship events by a group of Neapolitan players, which has included Pietro Forquet, Guglielmo Siniscalco, Massimo D'Alelio and Benito Garozzo. Since 1965 Garozzo, as the leading Neapolitan theorist, has gradually revised the system, renaming it the BLUE TEAM CLUB system. It is this version that became increasingly popular in the United States and was adopted as the official system of the SHARIF BRIDGE CIRCUS. See BLUE TEAM CLUB.

NEAPOLITAN FOUR DIAMOND CONVENTION. A form of delayed game raise used in the NEAPOLITAN system. It is a jump bid which applies when a forcing jump in the intended trump suit is not available:

West	East	
1 ♠	2 ♣	
2 ♠	4 ♦	agrees spades

West	East	
1 ♠	2 ♣	
2 ♥	4 ♦	agrees hearts

West	East	
1 ♥	1 ♠	
2 ♣	4 ♦	agrees hearts

See BLUE TEAM FOUR CLUBS-FOUR DIAMONDS CONVENTION.

NEAPOLITAN TWO DIAMONDS. See BLUE TEAM TWO DIAMONDS.

NEAR-SOLID SUIT. See SEMI-SOLID SUIT.

NEBULOUS DIAMOND see SHORT DIAMOND.

NEBULOUS ONE DIAMOND. An opening bid used by some Precision players to indicate no biddable suit. The diamond suit often is as short as two cards, occasionally only one.

NEC SPONSORSHIP. At the 1989 World Championships in Perth, Australia, the World Bridge Federation decided, for the first time, to test corporate sponsorship of world championships in an effort to combat rising costs of staging the events. The Nippon Electric Corporation (NEC) of Japan, an international company specializing in communications and computer technology, was signed on for four years. The contract was later extended for two more years with a one-year option. Therefore in 1989, 1991, 1993 and 1995 the World Championships were designated NEC Bermuda Bowl and NEC Venice Cup World Championships. In 1992 the world championship events in Salsomaggiore, Italy, were named the NEC World Team Olympiad and the NEC World Women's Team Olympiad. In 1994 the world championship events in Albuquerque, New Mexico, were designated the NEC World Championships. NEC sponsorship extended to world junior championships as well. The NEC World Junior Team championships were held in Ann Arbor, Michigan, in 1991 and in Arhus, Denmark, in 1993. NEC sponsorship ended after the 1995 world championship.

NEGATIVE DOUBLE. The original name for a take-out double, in general use from 1915 to 1930, about which time the term INFORMATORY DOUBLE became current, later superseded by the more descriptive take-out double. In 1957 Alvin Roth and Tobias Stone introduced a modern negative double into national championship play; what formerly was a penalty double of a suit overcall became a double for take-out. This feature of the ROTH-STONE SYSTEM was christened SPUTNIK, because the Russian space satellite dated from the same period, and the term is still sometimes used in Europe. The name was new but the idea was not; it had been used by Lou Scharf of the Bronx NY from 1937 on with various partners.

Almost all tournament players employ the negative double. The convention is simple and effective, and chances to use it occur frequently. The cost is negligible;

it is still possible to penalize an opponent's overcall.

North	East	South
1 ♦	1 ♥ or 1 ♠ or 2 ♣	Dbl

South has a hand on which no bid is satisfactory. He may lack the required length, strength or both to bid a suit at the two level.

A negative double can be made at the one level with as few as 6 points — after 1 ♦ -1 ♥, on:

♠ K 6 4 2
♥ 7 4
♦ 7 4
♣ K 9 7 4 2

A negative double may also be appropriate on a hand worth an opening bid:

♠ A J 5 2
♥ 10 7 5 2
♦ K
♣ A Q 8 2

After 1 ♦ -1 ♥, double and bid strongly later; hence, a 1 ♠ response can suggest a suit at least five cards long (i.e., a suit that would welcome a raise on three-card support). Partnership agreement is a factor, however. Some players would bid 1 ♠ because a double would show length in the unbid minor only and deny four spades.

Following are auctions, with possible hands for the negative doubler:

North	East	South
1 ♣	1 ♦	Dbl

♠ K 8 5 2
♥ A 8 5 3
♦ 7 5 4
♣ 7 4

Most pairs expect South to have at least four cards in any unbid major, and some require exactly four cards.

North	East	South
1 ♦	1 ♠	Dbl

♠ 8 6 4
♥ A J 7 5
♦ 8 6
♣ K 10 7 4

♠ 8 6 3
♥ K J 10 5 3
♦ A 8 5
♣ J 4

♠ 9 6
♥ Q 10 8 6 4 2
♦ A 8 4
♣ Q 3

On the second and third hands, if North rebids in a minor, South can show hearts.

Although South promises heart length, not every South would have clubs, the other unbid suit, but South must be able to visualize a place to play whatever North rebids. South might avoid a negative double with:

♠ Q 7 5 4 2
♥ Q 8 5 3 2
♦ K
♣ J 4

because a 2 ♣ or 2 ♦ rebid by North would be uncomfortable.

North	East	South
1♦	2♣	Dbl

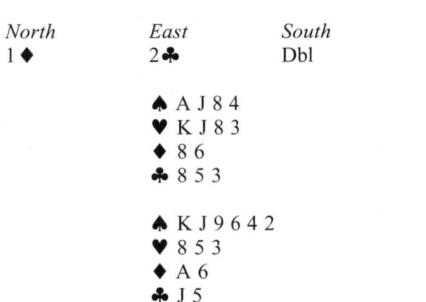

♠ A J 8 4
♥ K J 8 3
♦ 8 6
♣ 8 5 3

♠ K J 9 6 4 2
♥ 8 5 3
♦ A 6
♣ J 5

South promises one or both majors, by partnership agreement. The second hand is an example of a one-suit negative double, but not all Souths would be willing to double with that hand. An opponent's overcall often makes it difficult for responder to handle one-suited hands. (See NEGATIVE FREE BID). But if South were a passed hand, he could comfortably bid 2♠.

North	East	South
1♥	1♠	Dbl

♠ 8 6
♥ 8 5
♦ A J 8 3
♣ K 8 7 4 2

♠ 8 6
♥ 8 3
♦ K J 10 7 5 2
♣ A 7 4

South promises one or both minors, by partnership agreement. On the second hand, he can convert a club rebid by North to diamonds.

North	East	South
1♣	2♥	Dbl

♠ K J 9 4
♥ 7 6
♦ A Q 7 3
♣ 8 6 4

♠ K J 10 6 4
♥ K 7
♦ K 7 5
♣ 9 5 3

North	East	South
1♥	2♠	?

♠ 7 6
♥ 8 5 2
♦ K 6
♣ A J 9 7 5 3

♠ 8 5
♥ 8 6
♦ K Q 8 3
♣ A J 9 5 3

Many Souths would bid 3♥ with the first hand but would double with the second. The difference is the third heart.

North	East	South
1♣	2♠	Dbl

♠ 7 6
♥ K J 9 2
♦ A Q 8 5 2
♣ 8 4

♠ 8 4
♥ A 10 8 5 2
♦ K 5
♣ K 8 4 2

The double stands out on both of these hands. Over a 2♦ rebid by partner on the second, South can bid 2♥ to show a five-card suit with not enough strength to bid 2♥ on his first turn.

Players should avoid a negative double when a good natural bid is available. After North opens 1♣ and East bids 2♠, South should bid 3♦, not double. South should bid 3♦ on:

♠ 7 5
♥ A J 8 5
♦ A K J 8 4 3
♣ 5

Another example of a negative double:

♠ Q 10 8 6 4
♥ 8 5
♦ A J 6 4
♣ K 5

North	East	South
1♥	3♣	Dbl

In KAPLAN-SHEINWOLD, negative doubles are used after non-jump overcalls only and promise four cards in any unbid major. The strength is unlimited.

A few pairs use negative doubles only through the three level. Most use them after overcalls at higher levels, whether strong or preemptive, up to and including 4♦, or even 4♠. In these cases, the doubler is more likely to have general strength and less likely to guarantee length in the unbid suits. After:

West	North	East	South
	1♣	3♠	?

some players would double with:

♠ 7 6 2
♥ A 6
♦ A K 9 4 2
♣ Q J 5

giving North-South a chance to reach 3NT. (See CARD-SHOWING DOUBLE.) Opener is also more likely to pass a high-level negative double for penalty, since accuracy in constructive bidding is difficult. Therefore, if responder has support for opener's suit, he often prefers a shaded raise to a double.

Even at lower levels, experts are increasingly treating a negative double as an all-purpose flexible call rather than a call that promises specific suits.

A penalty double of an overcall is not available to responder if negative doubles are in effect. Responder may pass, however, in the hope that opener will reopen with a double:

West	North	East	South
	1♠	2♣	?

At equal or favorable vulnerability, South would pass with:

♠ 9 2
♥ A J 10
♦ Q 10 6 4
♣ K J 9 2

At unfavorable vulnerability, especially at matchpoint scoring, responder may decline to seek a penalty:

West	North	East	South
	1♠	2♦	?

♠ Q 6
♥ J 8 3
♦ K 10 6 2
♣ A K 3 2

South would bid 3NT, expecting +630; prospects of beating 2♦ doubled four tricks for +800 are unclear.

By the same token, responder must strain to act when he is short in the overcaller's suit:

West	North	East	South
	1♣	1♥	?

♠ K 9 5 3
♥ 8
♦ Q J 8 4 2
♣ 8 6 4

If South passes, West will probably raise hearts, making it harder for North-South to compete. Even if West passes, North may have heart length and hence sell out when North-South have a makable partial. South must tell his story with a double despite the slim values.

Reopening by the opening bidder:

West	North	East	South
	1♠	2♣	Pass
Pass	?		

A common misconception is that North must not pass if North-South use negative doubles. North need not reopen with club length, since the possibility that South has a penalty double of 2♣ is ruled out; nor should North strain to reopen with a double if another action is more descriptive. In these examples, neither side is vulnerable:

♠ A J 9 5 3   Pass. South does not have clubs
♥ K 5   and did not raise spades or make
♦ A 8   a negative double.
♣ Q 10 8 3

♠ A Q 8 5 2   Double. North has minimum
♥ K J 4   high-card values but ideal distri-
♦ Q 9 5 2   bution.
♣ 5

♠ A Q 10 9 5   Double.
♥ A K J 5
♦ K Q 10 5
♣ —

A cuebid is possible, but partner may be waiting for the double. Partner needs little but reasonable clubs to inflict a major penalty.

♠ A K Q 9 6 3   Bid 2♠.
♥ K 5
♦ J 8 5 2
♣ 9

♠ K Q 10 7 2   Bid 2♥.
♥ A Q 9 5 2
♦ K 5
♣ 4

After a negative double, the opening bidder rebids according to the prospects of game. A cuebid is the only absolute force. A jump shift is invitational, not forcing. With strength in overcaller's suit, opener can pass for penalty, but that action is rare, especially at a low level, since doubler's strength and distribution are unclear.

West	North	East	South
	1♥	1♠	Dbl
Pass	?		

♠ 8 4 3   Bid 2♣.
♥ A J 9 5 3
♦ A 6
♣ K Q 5

♠ 8 4   Bid 3♣, invitational.
♥ A K 8 5 3
♦ A 6
♣ K Q 8 3

♠ A J 5   Bid 2NT.
♥ K Q 9 5 3
♦ A 5
♣ K J 9

♠ 6 5   Bid 2♠.
♥ A K J 5 2
♦ A K 7
♣ A J 3

In the following auction, the meaning of North's second bid is open to debate:

West	North	East	South
	1♣	1♠	Dbl
Pass	2♦		

Is North's 2♦ bid similar to a reverse, promising extra strength, or is it a simple placement of the contract? If South's double promises diamonds, North needs no extra strength to bid 2♦; if South promises only hearts, North needs a good hand.

In KAPLAN-SHEINWOLD, opener rebids as though responder had actually bid the indicated major:

West	North	East	South
	1♦	1♥	Dbl
Pass	2♠		

North promises a minimum hand with four spades; to bid 1♠, North might hold only three spades; e.g.:

♠ A J 5
♥ 7 5 3
♦ A K J 3
♣ J 5 3

The negative double can be extended to many situations — for example, after a natural minor-suit overcall at the two or three level after a 1NT opening bid. A double would show support for one or both major suits, but would not be forcing to game (see LEBENSOHL).

In the following auction, most players would treat South's second double as for takeout.

West	North	East	South
	1♥	1♠	Dbl
2♠	Pass	Pass	Dbl

South might hold:

♠ A 8 4
♥ 8 5
♦ A Q 7 3
♣ J 10 7 4

He has a good hand and wants to compete, but lacks a good bid. (See CARD-SHOWING DOUBLE.)

Defense against negative doubles

When right-hand opponent has made a negative double, the situation is similar to a bid over an opposing takeout double. A redouble shows high-card strength

and may expose an opening psychic bid. A jump raise of overcaller's suit is preemptive. See also ROSENKRANZ REDOUBLE and PARKING LOT.

NEGATIVE FREE BID. An obsolescent solution to a common bidding problem. Consider this situation:

West	North	East	South
	1♣	1♠	?

South has:

 ♠ x x
 ♥ A Q x x x x
 ♦ Q x
 ♣ x x x

This is not strong enough in standard methods for a 2♥ bid, so the usual solution is to make a negative double, planning to bid hearts on the next round. But this may be difficult if spades are raised, and the negative double solution is not available if the suit is diamonds rather than hearts.

The alternative is to make a "negative free bid" of 2♥ on this hand, or of 2♦ if that suit is held. This is of course nonforcing. This obviously affects the use of the negative double. It is no longer needed for a hand that can make a negative free bid, but it is required for stronger hands that would normally make a forcing suit-response at a minimum level. Therefore a negative double followed by a new suit becomes forcing, indicating a hand with game values.

The negative free bid is not needed at the one level and is of dubious value at the four level. Many partnerships agree to use negative free bids at the two and three levels only. See FREE BID.

NEGATIVE INFERENCE. Information deduced from a player's failure to take a specific action in the bidding or play. Though this type of inference is frequently available, it is often overlooked, the average player preferring to concentrate on more positive clues.

Here is a deal where the declarer was able to diagnose the location of a critical card based upon negative inferences gleaned from the bidding and play.

Dlr: South
Vul: N-S

    ♠ A 10 8 2
    ♥ 8 4
    ♦ A Q 10 4
    ♣ J 6 4

♠ K Q J 6 4   ♠ 9 7 3
♥ A J 3   ♥ K 10 6 5 2
♦ K 7 6 5   ♦ 9 8 3
♣ K   ♣ 9 3

    ♠ 5
    ♥ Q 9 7
    ♦ J 2
    ♣ A Q 10 8 7 5 2

The bidding:

West	North	East	South
			Pass
1♠	Pass	Pass	2♣
2♦	3♣	3♠	4♣
Pass	5♣	All Pass	

West opened the ♠K, and the declarer won with dummy's ace. With the ♥A K to lose, declarer had to pick up both minor-suit kings. Even though the percentages favor a finesse in the club suit, declarer led a club to his ace at trick two, dropping West's king. A successful diamond finesse gave him 11 tricks.

Declarer *guessed* the club position well. He reasoned that if West had held both top hearts he would surely have led one in order to inspect the dummy and judge the best continuation. The absence of a heart lead therefore marked East with a high heart — if he held the ♣K in addition he would have responded on the first round. The only hope, therefore, was that West held a singleton king. See also INFERENCE.

NEGATIVE RESPONSE. An artificial response that shows weakness. Examples are: a 2NT response to a FORCING TWO or an ACOL TWO; a 1♦ or 2♦ response to an artificial 1♣ or 2♣ opening; or a 2♥ response to an artificial 2♦ opening. See also DOUBLE NEGATIVE; HERBERT NEGATIVE; SECOND NEGATIVE RESPONSE AFTER ARTIFICIAL FORCING OPENING. For natural negative responses, see WEAKNESS RESPONSE.

NEGATIVE SLAM DOUBLE. See DOUBLE FOR SACRIFICE.

NET SCORE. The result of a rubber of bridge or of CHICAGO after the losing side's score is subtracted from the winning side's score. In rounding off to the nearest 100, 50 points counts as an extra 100 in the United States, but is dropped in England.

The term is also used in team matches to designate the difference between the scores of two teams at the end of a session or a match; it can be expressed in total points or in INTERNATIONAL MATCHPOINTS.

NEUTRAL CARD. See CARDS, NEUTRAL AND POSITIVE.

NEUTRAL LEAD. See PASSIVE LEAD.

NEUTRAL SUIT. See ASTRO.

NEWCOMER. See NOVICE.

NEW DEAL. A fresh deal to take the place of a misdeal or to replace a deal voided for any reason.

NEW ENGLAND RELAY. See STAGGER MOVEMENT.

NEW MINOR FORCING (Unbid Minor-Suit Force). After opener's rebid of 1NT, responder often finds it useful to have available a low-level forcing bid, either to inquire about opener's support for responder's suit, or to make responder's description of his own hand flexible. Some pairs thus use a 2♣ rebid by responder as the only force after a 1NT rebid; others use a 2♣ rebid as Stayman on the second round. The most popular modern method, however, is the use of the unbid minor suit as responder's forcing call; when the opening bid was 1♣, this approach allows responder to sign off in his partner's suit.

Suppose the auction is:

West	East
1♣	1♥
1NT	2♦

with 2♦ artificial and forcing. The meaning of West's third bid may depend on partnership agreement. One possible scheme:

2♥ = minimum hand with three hearts.
2♠ = minimum hand with fewer than three hearts, or natural if the 1NT rebid may have concealed a four-card spade suit.
2NT = maximum hand, fewer than three hearts.
3♣ = natural, five-card suit.
3♦ = maximum hand with clubs and diamonds, fewer than three hearts.
3♥ = maximum hand with three hearts.

After a 1♠ response:

West	East
1♦	1♠
1NT	2♣

2♦ = natural, five-card suit.
2♥ = natural, four-card suit.
2♠ = minimum hand with three spades; does not deny a four-card heart suit. (partnership agreement necessary) with diamonds and clubs.
2NT = fewer than three spades, no other attractive rebid.
3♣ = maximum with diamonds and clubs and fewer than three spades.
3♦ = natural, maximum.
3♠ = maximum hand with three spades.

Many pairs use the bid of the other minor on invitational hands; others use it to create a game force, and then all second-round jumps by responder are invitational, not forcing. In the auction 1♦-1♠, 1NT-3♥, responder probably has a five-card suit.

For related devices, see COLE, CROWHURST CONVENTION, FOURTH SUIT FORCING. NEGATIVE FREE BIDS, TWO CLUBS REBID BY OPENER AS ONLY FORCE AFTER ONE NOTRUMP REBID; TWO-WAY STAYMAN AFTER ONE NOTRUMP REBID.

NEW SOUTH WALES SYSTEM. A variation of the VIENNA SYSTEM formerly used by Richard Cummings and Tim Seres and other Australians. The principal features are five-card openings in diamonds, hearts, and spades, strong 1NT openings, weak two-bids in the major suits. The 2♣ opening, which is used sparingly, is game forcing; the 2NT opening shows a strong minor two-suiter, and the 2♦ opening shows a balanced hand with at least 21 HCP. A forcing 1♣ opening is used for all other opening hands, e.g., long club suit, or a balanced hand worth 12-14 or 18-20, or a hand of any strength with 4-4-4-1 distribution. All responses in new suits are forcing, and jump shifts are used as modified CULBERTSON ASKING BIDS.

NEW ZEALAND RELAY SYSTEM. See SYMMETRIC RELAY SYSTEM.

NEWGATE. A prison in London, England, where, prior to 1820, whist was played as a three-handed game with one hand exposed as the dummy.

NEWLY FORMED TABLES. These can be created with four to six players ranking according to precedence, this generally being established by order of entry into the playing room. Players leaving an existing table to cut into the new table have lowest precedence. See RUBBER BRIDGE. Four players can start a new table in the various forms of computer bridge.

NEWPLICATE PAIRS. See NOVICE PAIRS.

NINE or NINE-SPOT. That card ranking sixth highest in a suit, and being between the 10 and 8 in position.

NINE TABLES. At duplicate, nine tables provide for competition among 36 players as individuals, 18 pairs or nine teams-of-four.

As an individual, the IRREGULAR RAINBOW is recommended. It is similar to the movement given under IRREGULAR RAINBOW.

As a pair event, MITCHELL, THREE-QUARTER (Howell) MOVEMENT or SHORT HOWELL movements may be used. However, the Mitchell is strongly recommended because it enables all contestants to play all boards (9-round game) and all contestants in each direction to play a three-board set against all pairs playing in the opposite direction.

A nine-table Mitchell, intending 27 boards, can be cut to 24 late in the play by instructing players to omit the first board on round 7, the second board on round 8, and the third board on round 9.

As a team-of-four event, nine tables provide an excellent movement for meeting each of the other teams in an uninterrupted team-of-four progression, boards going to the next lower numbered table, and players skipping a table toward the lower number. The Swiss Team movement does not work well for nine tables. It requires three-way matches, and bad pairings may become necessary in the late rounds.

For 8½ or 9½ tables, see HALF TABLES.

NO BID or NO. A term meaning "pass", standard in England and some other English-speaking countries such as Australia and New Zealand where there is some likelihood of confusion in the enunciation of pass and hearts. The term has been generally accepted by custom, but does not appear in the official Laws and is subject to the warning (see LAW 74C) against use of different designations for the same call. Regulations for international play may specifically bar the term because it may be mistaken for another call, e.g., double. The problem is no longer significant in serious play because BIDDING BOXES are invariably used.

NO CALL. An obsolete and inaccurate term occasionally used instead of PASS.

NON-FORCING. A bid which does not require a response from partner.

NON-FORCING SEQUENCES. A sequence which permits either member of the partnership to drop the bidding. A sequence starting with a suit bid can be assumed to be nonforcing unless it is listed under FORCING SEQUENCES. A cuebid or a fourth-suit bid makes the sequence forcing.

Before passing a nonforcing sequence, a player should satisfy himself that a game contract is unlikely to be a sound proposition. He should also be sure that he cannot convert safely to a superior partscore. See PARTNERSHIP MISUNDERSTANDINGS.

NON-FORCING STAYMAN. See STAYMAN.

NON-MASTER PAIRS. Usually run in conjunction

with a MASTER PAIRS. An arbitrary upper limit of masterpoints is set, and both members of every pair must have that number of masterpoints or fewer. The game itself is run along the lines of an OPEN PAIRS.

NON-MASTER TEAMS. Usually run in conjunction with a MASTER TEAMS. An arbitrary upper limit of masterpoints is set, and all members of each team must have no more than that number of masterpoints.

NON-MATERIAL SQUEEZE. Nonmaterial squeezes are squeezes against strategic values, rather than material values, such as winners or guards to winners. Nonmaterial squeezes operate against cards that are apparently idle, but actually perform a vital function, such as prevention of a throw-in, or protection of the defender's communications.

```
Dlr: East        ♠ 7 4 2
Vul: None        ♥ A 8 6 5
                 ♦ Q 3
                 ♣ A Q 7 3
♠ 5 3                        ♠ K J 10 8 6
♥ J 9 3                      ♥ Q 10 7 2
♦ K 9 6 5                    ♦ A 4 2
♣ J 6 5 2                    ♣ 9
                 ♠ A Q 9
                 ♥ K 4
                 ♦ J 10 8 7
                 ♣ K 10 8 4
```

West	North	East	South
		Pass	1♦
Pass	1♥	1♠	1NT
Pass	3NT	All Pass	

Lead: ♠5
South wins the first spade, and he unblocks clubs by leading the ♣8 to dummy's ♣A. The ♣3 is returned to the ♣K, as East discards a diamond. Now the ♣10 is led and East is squeezed. If East throws a spade, it is safe to establish diamonds. A heart discard allows declarer to establish a long heart in dummy which can be reached with a fourth round club entry. And another diamond discard allows declarer to establish that suit, since East must take his now singleton ♦A before the spades have been established.

NON-PLAYING CAPTAIN. See CAPTAIN.

NON-VULNERABLE. See NOT VULNERABLE.

NORDIC CHAMPIONSHIPS. Organized in 1946 by delegates from the bridge federations of Denmark, Norway, Sweden and Finland, meeting at Copenhagen. The Nordic Championships represented one of the first postwar efforts to revive international bridge competition in Europe. The initial tournament was staged later the same year in Oslo, and the Championships were held on an annual basis until 1949. Iceland joined the competition in 1949 and has been a regular participant ever since. The Faroe Islands is a recent addition to the field. After the revival of the European Championships, the importance of a separate Nordic competition lessened, so the event became a biennial competition, except for a three-year lapse from 1959-62. The championships rotate among the participating countries. See Appendix IV for results.

NORMAL EXPECTANCY. The holding in either high cards or distribution which a player might expect in partner's hand when he decides whether to open the bidding. For an unpassed partner, this can be roughly approximated as one-third of the missing high cards or high-card points, and one-third of the remaining cards in the suit. Partner's responses and future actions modify this concept as the bidding progresses. See SUIT COMBINATIONS and TRUMP SUPPORT for further treatment.

NORMAN FOUR NOTRUMP. A slam convention in which kings and aces are shown with one bid. An ace is counted as 1 control and a king as ½ control. Responses are according to the following table:

5♣	less than 1½ controls
5♦	1½ controls
5♥	2 controls
5♠	2½ controls
5NT	3 controls, etc.

The 4NT bidder can usually determine which aces and kings are held by responder. This convention once was popular in England, where it is credited to Norman De Villiers Hart and Sir Norman Bennet, and was incorporated into the VIENNA SYSTEM. Several similar methods have been used in America, but only the SAN FRANCISCO convention achieved any substantial following. Similar responding principles are used in the BLUE TEAM CLUB System and by some players after an artificial 2♣ opening.

NORTH. A position in a bridge foursome or in a bridge diagram opposite South and to the left of West. In duplicate games the scoring is usually done by North, a matter designated by the Sponsoring Organization. In newspaper columns North is usually the dummy.

NORTH AMERICAN BLUE RIBBON PAIRS. A six-session premier pair event held at the ACBL Fall Championships. All pairs must qualify by meeting certain criteria set up by the ACBL. Most pairs earn qualification by winning or placing second in a major regional event that is not restricted by masterpoints. Many others qualify by placing in the top 10 in a major North American event. See CAVENDISH TROPHY, BLUE RIBBON PAIRS. For results see Appendix I.

NORTH AMERICAN BRIDGE CHAMPIONSHIP. Name given in 1975 to the three ACBL major championship tournaments. Prior to 1975 these tournaments were known as "Nationals." Results of these championships are reported in Appendix I.

NORTH AMERICAN CHAMPIONSHIPS. See NORTH AMERICAN BRIDGE CHAMPIONSHIPS.

NORTH AMERICAN CHAMPIONSHIP TROPHIES. (Note, not all events have trophies). *Spring:* Women's Swiss Teams, Sadie Machlin; Women's Pairs, Whitehead; Vanderbilt Knockout Teams, Vanderbilt; Silver Ribbon Pairs, Leventritt; Open Pairs I, Silodor; Open Pairs II, Werner; NAOP-A, Baldwin; 49er Pairs, Fifth Chair; Open Swiss Teams, Jacoby; Mixed Pairs, Rockwell; Most masterpoints, Mott-Smith. *Summer:* Grand National Teams-A, Morehead; Grand National Teams-B, Sheinwold; Grand National Teams-C, Mac

Nab; Wagar Women's Knockout Teams, Wagar; Spingold Knockout Teams, Spingold; Red Ribbon Pairs, Bean; Mixed Board-a-Match Teams, Chicago; Life Master Pairs, von Zedtwitz Gold Cup; IMP Pairs, Lebhar; Most masterpoints, Fishbein. *Fall:* Women's Board-a-Match Teams, Coffin; Senior Knockouts, U.S. Playing Card Company; Reisinger Board-a-Match Teams, Reisinger; Open Board-a-Match Teams, Mitchell; Non-Life Master Pairs, Miles; North American Swiss Teams, Keohane; Life Master Women's Pairs, Helen Sobel Smith; Life Master Open Pairs, Nail; Blue Ribbon Pairs, Cavendish; Most masterpoints, Herman.

NORTH AMERICAN FAST PAIRS. A four-session pair event that is very time-sensitive. Players are allowed only five minutes per board instead of the usual 7.5 minutes. The event was first held as a North American championship in 2000. For results see Appendix I.

NORTH AMERICAN FORTY-NINER PAIRS. This event originally was called the GRAND NATIONAL ROOKIE PAIRS when it began in 1979. In 1984 it became the NORTH AMERICAN ROOKIE PAIRS, with competition limited to those with fewer than 20 masterpoints. The initial stage was conducted at the club level, with each district qualifying one pair plus one at-large pair to produce a 26-pair field. A two-session final then was held at the ACBL Fall NABC. In 1991 the event was changed to a 49er championship, open to ACBL members with fewer than 50 masterpoints. The event is conducted as a two-session championship during the ACBL Spring NABC. See FIFTH CHAIR TROPHY.

NORTH AMERICAN GRAND NATIONAL PAIRS. See NORTH AMERICAN PAIRS. For results see Appendix I.

NORTH AMERICAN GRAND NATIONAL ROOKIE PAIRS. See GRAND NATIONAL ROOKIE PAIRS, NORTH AMERICAN FORTY-NINER PAIRS.

NORTH AMERICAN GRAND NATIONAL TEAMS. See GRAND NATIONAL TEAMS, MOREHEAD TROPHY. For results see Appendix I.

NORTH AMERICAN IMP PAIRS. Four-session pair event scored on IMPs rather than matchpoints. See IMP PAIRS, LEBHAR TROPHY. For results, see Appendix I.

NORTH AMERICAN INTERNATIONAL OPEN TEAM SELECTION. Many methods have been tried for selection of the North American team or teams for the Bermuda Bowl or of the United States team for the World Team Olympiad.
1950-60 – Team Performance
From 1950 to 1960, the ACBL selected the winners of the SPINGOLD or the winners of a playoff between the winners of the Spingold and the VANDERBILT. This had the advantage of producing a well-knit team. In 1960 the United States, by virtue of the size of the ACBL membership, was entitled to send four teams to the first World Team Olympiad. The winners of the Vanderbilt and Spingold were chosen. Each of the other teams consisted of three pairs selected from among the contestants remaining in the seventh or eighth round of the Vanderbilt and Spingold respectively.

1961 – Direct Selection
The North American Bermuda Bowl team for 1961 consisted of three pairs selected by the ACBL Board of Directors from among the winners and runners-up in the major national events. This method invited problems because of possible bias on the part of the selectors.
1962-69 – Trials by Pairs
The plan here was to choose pairs currently in effective form. From 1961 to 1966 the top three pairs were nominated as the international representative for the following year. The fourth-place pair became the alternate. Beginning in 1967, the automatic selection method was discontinued, and the non-playing captain was given the right to choose two of the four highest finishing pairs. He then could choose the third pair and the alternate pair from among all the pairs competing in the Trials. Julius Rosenblum exercised this option in 1967 when he named Edgar Kaplan and Norman Kay, who finished fourth. This was the only time in this era when the top three pairs were not chosen.
1970 – Vanderbilt-Spingold Playoff
The Pair-Team trials were discontinued in order to allow selection of an entire team rather than individual pairs to comprise a team. The 1970 International Team was selected by a direct 180-board playoff between the winners of the 1969 Vanderbilt and Spingold. This reduced the prestige of the Fall North American Championships, which previously had two events that qualified pairs for the Trials.
1971-72 Placing-Points Playoffs
Beginning with the 1969 Fall NABC, the ACBL adopted a playoff among the teams with the best records over the course of a year. Teams placing high in the three major team championships (Reisinger, Vanderbilt and Spingold) were awarded points according to the following scale: Vanderbilt and Spingold: 1st 10 points; 2nd 4; 3rd 2. Reisinger: 1st 6 points; 2nd 4; 3rd 2. If a team accumulated 20 points it was to be automatically designated the International Team; otherwise teams with lesser numbers of points were to play off.
Vanderbilt, Spingold, Reisinger, Grand Nationals Winners Playoff
With the introduction of the GRAND NATIONAL TEAM CHAMPIONSHIPS in 1972, the selection of the North American international team became a simple matter of a four-team playoff among the winners of the ACBL's four major team events: the Vanderbilt, Spingold, Reisinger, and Grand Nationals.
Vanderbilt, Spingold, Reisinger, Grand National, Canadian National Winners Playoff
At the request of the CANADIAN BRIDGE FEDERATION, that section of the Grand National Teams that involved Canadian players was separated from the main event and changed into a Canadian National Teams Championship. The Canadian champions became a fifth entry in the Trials in those years when a Bermuda Bowl team was being chosen. The Trials were staged as a round-robin, with one team being eliminated. The usual knockout format was used from that point on, with a carryover formula.
1983- Tri-Country Trials
In 1983, Canada was removed from the Trials by vote of the ACBL Board of Directors. At the same time. it was determined that, for Bermuda Bowl competition. Zone II would select two representatives – one from the United States and one from among Canada, Mexico and

Bermuda. Thus was established the Tri-Country Trials, still in effect in 2001. However, no Trial event was held in 2001 because Canada, Mexico and Bermuda all failed to qualify at the 2000 World Team Olympiad where all three nations placed in the bottom half.

1983- United States Bridge Championship

From 1983. the Bermuda Bowl selection process was known as the United States Bridge Championship and consisted of a four-team playoff among the winning teams in the Vanderbilt., Spingold, Reisinger and Grand National Teams. There were five teams in 1983 because Canada was still a competitor – the Tri-Country Trials did not take place for the first time until 1985. The event was played as a straight knockout. In years when one team won more than one qualifying event, the doubly qualified team had a bye to the final.

In 1983, five teams played off in Minneapolis to determine the two North American teams for the Bermuda Bowl in Stockholm, Sweden. For the first time the top team in Zone II was to be seeded to an automatic berth in the semifinals. In 1985 three teams competed in Memphis for the right to start in the Bermuda Bowl semifinals in Sao Paulo. Brazil. San Francisco went directly into the final as a result of double qualification (Vanderbilt and Grand National). Canada was playing for the first time in tri-country matches with Bermuda and Mexico to determine the second Zone II team. San Francisco defeated Spingold by 5 IMPs over the 128-board final. The winners: Chip Martel, Lew Stansby. Hugh Ross, Peter Pender. Bobby Wolff. Bob Hamman, npc Alfred Sheinwold.

Three ACBL teams were authorized as Zone II representatives for the Bermuda Bowl in Yokohama, Japan, 1991. They were to be the winner of the USBC, the winner of the Tri-Country Trials and the top three pairs from the Pan North American Bridge Championships (PNABC) held in Corpus Christi TX. Twenty pairs qualified in specific NABC and certain regional IMP pair events for the PNABC the PNABC was held in Memphis alongside the USBC and North American Women's Team Bridge Championship. In 1992 the format reverted to the four-team playoff among Vanderbilt, Spingold, Reisinger and Grand National winners. The same plan was followed in 1993.

1994 – International Team Trials

In 1994, the ACBL Board of Directors approved the establishment of the International Team Trials Commission. The commission staged a competition in early 1995 to select two teams to represent Zone II in the 1995 NEC Bermuda Bowl in Beijing, China. A third team was selected in the Tri-Country playoff among Canada, Mexico and Bermuda. Under the ITT Commission, the Trials were open to a much larger field – conceivably as many as 30 teams – and the competition lasted for a week. The commission and new format were the brainchild of Bobby Wolff, World Bridge Federation president during 1993 and 1994. Wolff's idea was to expand the Trials field beyond the usual so as to give more teams the chance to play in top-flight competition, a necessity for success at the world level.

The idea was not universally accepted, so there was some question whether the new trials format would endure beyond the initial competition in 1995. However, just about everyone agreed that the ITT arrangement was a good one after the 1995 competition went off without a hitch. The same format has been used to choose the United States teams for open world competition ever since. Many teams enter each year, and a carefully con-structed screening process is used to decide what teams play which, and when. In Olympiad years (years divisible by four), one team is chosen; in Bermuda Bowl years (odd-numbered years) two teams are selected.

NORTH AMERICAN INTERNATIONAL WOMEN'S TEAM SELECTION. (Now called the United States Women's Bridge Championship). The United States has sent women's teams to each of the World Women's Team Olympiads, each selected by a different method. For the 1960 event, a committee consisting of the five most recent ACBL presidents attending the 1959 Fall Nationals selected the team by choosing three pairs of women who finished first or second in any national championship event during 1959. For 1964, a trial by pairs was held, similar to the trials held during that period for the NORTH AMERICAN INTERNATIONAL OPEN TEAM SELECTION. For 1968 a round-robin was held, for which four pairs qualified. Each pair played a 32-board match in partnership with each of the other pairs, and npc Margaret Wagar was empowered to select any three of the four pairs. For 1972, women's teams were to earn points in the major national team championships and playoff to determine the team. However, one team amassed so many points that it was designated without a playoff. For 1976, women were permitted to earn "selection points," either as teams or as pairs, on all-women teams in the Vanderbilt, Spingold, Reisinger, and Spring National Women's Team events. Available points ranged from 1 point for being runner-up in the Spring Women's teams to 28 for winning the Vanderbilt or Spingold. To be selected intact, a team must have won more qualification points than any individual pair, except that if there were only one higher pair, a four-person team plus the high-ranking pair would form the six-member team.

After 1981 the WBF scheduled Venice Cup contests for odd-numbered years opposite the Bermuda Bowl. After skipping 1983 the new plan took effect beginning in 1985. The selection of women's teams by qualification points was discontinued in 1989, and the North American Women's Bridge Team Championships (NAWBTC) were inaugurated. The 1989 winning team gained a bye to the Venice Cup semifinals in Perth, Australia, while the second-place team (Canada) had to compete in round-robin qualifications. In 1991, three ACBL teams were selected for Yokohama, Japan — first and second in the U.S. Women's Trials and Canada, who won the playoff with Mexico for the third Zone II spot. In 1992 the United States Women's Bridge Championships (USWBC) were held to select a team for the NEC World Team Olympiad in Salsomaggiore, Italy. Zone II once again had three representatives for the Venice Cup in Santiago, Chile, in 1993. All of the trials through 1993 were played in Memphis. There was no women's team trials in 1994. It was held in Washington in 1995, San Francisco in 1996 and Hyannisport MA in 1997. The event was not held in 1998.

Automatic qualifiers for the women's trials included the reigning NEC Venice Cup champions, if the team is intact at the time of the trials; first and second in the Women's Knockout Teams; first in the Women's Swiss Teams; first in the Women's Board-a-Match Teams; any all-woman team reaching the semifinals of the Vanderbilt or Spingold; any all-woman team finishing first through fourth in the Reisinger.

Since 1999, the event has been known as the Women's International Team Trials and has been held in Las Ve-

gas (1999), Raleigh NC (2000) and Las Vegas (2001). The USWBC is open to any women's team approved by the USWBC credentials committee, plus teams that earn byes in qualifying events. See also VENICE CUP, WOMEN'S TEAM OLYMPIAD.

NORTH AMERICAN LIFE MASTER OPEN PAIRS. A four-session pair event open only to ACBL Life Masters and foreigners who are considered on a pair with ACBL Life Masters. See NAIL TROPHY. For results see Appendix I.

NORTH AMERICAN LIFE MASTER PAIRS. A six-session premier pair event open only to ACBL Life Masters and foreigners who are considered on a par with ACBL Life Masters. See VON ZEDTWITZ GOLD CUP. For results see Appendix I.

NORTH AMERICAN LIFE MASTER WOMEN'S PAIRS. A four-session pair event. See SMITH TROPHY. For results see Appendix I.

NORTH AMERICAN MASTER INDIVIDUAL. Formerly called World Master Individual. See STEINER TROPHY. For results see Appendix I.

NORTH AMERICAN MASTER KNOCKOUT TEAMS. One of the two prestigious knockout events staged by the ACBL (the other is the Vanderbilt). This event is known as the Spingold, and each summer it draws outstanding players from all over the world. See SPINGOLD TROPHY. For results see Appendix I.

NORTH AMERICAN MASTER MIXED TEAMS. See NORTH AMERICAN MIXED BOARD-A-MATCH TEAMS.

NORTH AMERICAN MEN'S BOARD-A-MATCH TEAMS. See NORTH AMERICAN OPEN BOARD-A-MATCH TEAMS.

NORTH AMERICAN MEN'S PAIRS. See NORTH AMERICAN OPEN PAIRS II.

NORTH AMERICAN MIXED BOARD-A-MATCH TEAMS. Four-session ACBL championship in which each team must field two mixed pairs at all times. Formerly a masters event, it is now open to all players. See CHICAGO TROPHY. For results see Appendix I.

NORTH AMERICAN MIXED PAIRS. A four-session pair event in which all pairs must consist of one man and one woman. See ROCKWELL TROPHY. For results see Appendix I.

NORTH AMERICAN MIXED TEAMS. See NORTH AMERICAN MIXED BOARD-A-MATCH TEAMS.

NORTH AMERICAN NINETY-NINER PAIRS. An ACBL two-session event limited to players with fewer than 100 masterpoints.

NORTH AMERICAN NON-LIFE MASTER PAIRS. A two-session pair event open only to players who have not achieved Life Master ranking. See MILES TROPHY.

NORTH AMERICAN NON-LIFE MASTER SWISS TEAMS. A two-session team event open only to players who have not achieved Life Master ranking.

NORTH AMERICAN ONE-NINETY-NINER PAIRS. An ACBL two-session event limited to players with fewer than 200 masterpoints.

NORTH AMERICAN OPEN BOARD-A-MATCH TEAMS. Formerly North American Men's Board-A-Match Teams. Four-session event was changed to an open competition when men's events were eliminated from ACBL NABCs. The event trophy formerly was the Goren Trophy but now is the MITCHELL TROPHY. For results, see Appendix I.

NORTH AMERICAN OPEN KNOCKOUT TEAMS. One of the two prestigious knockout events staged by the ACBL (the other is the Spingold). It is known as the Vanderbilt, and each spring it draws outstanding players from all over the world. See VANDERBILT TROPHY. For results see Appendix I.

NORTH AMERICAN OPEN PAIRS. This has been a major ACBL pair championship since 1979. The event originally was known as the Grand National Pairs. Initial stages are conducted at club, unit and district levels. Each district qualifies three or four pairs (determined by the total entry in the district at the club level) to the North American final, which is held at the ACBL Spring NABC. The Grand National Pairs became the North American Open Pairs in 1987, and a special form of the event for non-Life Masters was added. In 1992, Flight A remained the same, but a Flight B was added for players with fewer than 1500 masterpoints. In 1994 a masterpoint limit was placed on the Non-Life Master contest, now called Flight C. If a player had more than 500 masterpoints, he was not eligible to compete in the Non-Life Master category. See BALDWIN TROPHY. For results see Appendix I.

NORTH AMERICAN OPEN PAIRS I. ACBL four-session championship event played at Spring Championships. See SILODOR TROPHY. For results see Appendix I.

NORTH AMERICAN OPEN PAIRS II. ACBL four-session championship event played at the Spring Championships. Once known as North American Men's Pairs, the event was changed to an Open Pairs game when men's events were eliminated from the ACBL championships. See WERNHER TROPHY. For results see Appendix I.

NORTH AMERICAN OPEN SWISS TEAMS. A six-session team competition staged opposite the six-session Reisinger Teams at the ACBL Fall NABC. See JACOBY TROPHY. For results see Appendix I.

NORTH AMERICAN RED RIBBON PAIRS. A four-session pair championship open only to players with fewer than 2000 masterpoints who have earned qualification by winning or placing second in a regional or national championship. For results see Appendix I.

NORTH AMERICAN ROOKIE PAIRS. A two-session event open only to players with fewer than 20 points that is no longer staged by the ACBL. See NORTH AMERICAN FORTY-NINE PAIRS CHAMPIONSHIP.

NORTH AMERICAN RUBBER BRIDGE CHAM-PIONSHIP. A form of nationwide competition conducted in 1962 and 1963 by North American Van Lines in connection with their sponsorship of *Championship Bridge with Charles Goren*. Entrants formed groups for home play, with local winners advancing by stages to a national final.

NORTH AMERICAN SENIOR KNOCKOUT TEAMS. ACBL championship team event in which only players 55 years of age and older are eligible to compete. See U.S. PLAYING CARD COMPANY TROPHY. For results see Appendix I.

NORTH AMERICAN SENIOR MASTERS AND ADVANCED SENIOR MASTERS PAIRS. A nationally-rated pair event no longer staged by the ACBL. See MILES TROPHY. For results see Appendix I.

NORTH AMERICAN SENIOR SWISS TEAMS. An ACBL championship team event for players 55 years of age or older. For results see Appendix I.

NORTH AMERICAN SILVER RIBBON PAIRS. An ACBL four-session pair championship event in which all contestants must be at least 55 years of age. See LEVENTRITT TROPHY, SENIOR PAIRS. For results see Appendix I.

NORTH AMERICAN SWISS TEAMS. A six-session championship event for the KEOHANE TROPHY played at the ACBL Fall Championships. For results see Appendix I.

NORTH AMERICAN TEAMS FLIGHT B. An ACBL grass roots event for teams on which all members have fewer than 1500 points at the start of the event. Championship matches are played at the Summer NABC. See NORTH AMERICAN OPEN PAIRS, SHEINWOLD TROPHY. For results see Appendix I.

NORTH AMERICAN TEAMS FLIGHT C. An ACBL grass roots event for teams on which all members have fewer than 500 points and are not Life Masters at the start of the event. Championship matches are played at the Summer NABC. See MAC NAB TROPHY, NORTHA AMERICAN OPEN PAIRS. For results see Appendix I.

NORTH AMERICAN WOMEN'S BOARD-A-MATCH TEAMS. Four-session event played with board-a-match scoring at the ACBL Fall NABC. See COFFIN TROPHY. For results see Appendix I.

NORTH AMERICAN WOMEN'S KNOCKOUT TEAMS. The premier event on the ACBL women's calendar. Matches are run on a day-long basis. The event is staged during the Summer NABC. See WAGAR TROPHY. For results see Appendix I.

NORTH AMERICAN WOMEN'S PAIRS. A four-session event. See WHITEHEAD TROPHY. For results see Appendix I.

NORTH AMERICAN WOMEN'S SWISS TEAMS. A six-session team event played at the Fall NABC. For results see Appendix I.

NORWEGIAN BRIDGE PRESS ASSOCIATION. (Norsk Bridge Presse (NBP)). The organization was founded in Oslo in 1976 and has reached a membership peak of 130. It deals with press ethics and the working conditions of bridge journalists and nominates receivers of journalist awards in Norway.
Officers 1999:
President: Alf Helge Jensen
Finnmarken, 9800 Vadso
Tel.47-78 95 55 29 / 47-78 92 84 67 / 47-92 04 47 19
Secretary: Arne Thomassen
E-mail: arne.thomassen@c2i.net
Web-site: http://nettvik.no/foreningsgaarden/bridge/NBP/nbp.html

NOT VULNERABLE. A term applied to a side that is subject to smaller rewards and penalties. In rubber bridge, the term covers any side that has not won a game during the rubber. In Chicago, the vulnerability situation is predetermined. Neither side is vulnerable on the first of the four boards. On the second and third, the side that did not deal is not vulnerable while the dealing side is. Both sides are vulnerable on the fourth deal. In duplicate, once again the vulnerability is predetermined. The vulnerability is set up in 16-board segments. Neither side is vulnerable on boards 1, 8, 11 and 16. Only North-South is not vulnerable on boards 3, 6, 9 and 16. Only East-West is not vulnerable on board 2, 5, 12 and 15. Both sides are vulnerable on boards 4, 7, 10 and 13.

NOTRUMP. A denomination in which a player may bid at bridge. Notrump is the ranking denomination during the auction, being just above spades in precedence. Only nine tricks are necessary for game at notrump, since the first trick over book of six counts for 40 points and the subsequent tricks for 30 points each as in a major suit. As the name implies, contracts at notrump are played without a trump suit. The play therefore is entirely different from that of suit contracts, one of the chief differences being that declarer while planning his line of play attempts to count winners rather than losers. At notrump, a primary concern of the side contracting for game or partial is that there be stoppers in the suits bid or held by the opponents. More game contracts are played at notrump than at any other denomination. In Britain it is normal to use two words and pluralize the second: "No trumps". The hyphenated form "no-trump" is a compromise that is in common usage in Great Britain, Australia and New Zealand.

NOTRUMP BIDDING. The standard POINTCOUNT is particularly effective in its application to notrump bidding. A partnership aims to reach 3NT with 26 points in high cards in the combined hands, and is prepared to play in game with 25. Similarly, 6NT will offer a reasonable play with 33 points. For the ranges used in standard methods, see NOTRUMP RANGES. Different aspects of this subject are under: DYNAMIC NOTRUMP; EXPECTED NUMBER OF CONTROLS IN BALANCED HANDS; FIVE NOTRUMP OPENING; FOUR NOTRUMP OPENING; GERBER CONVENTION; GLADIATOR; JACOBY TRANSFER; MINI NOTRUMP; ONE NOTRUMP OPENING; ONE NOTRUMP RESPONSE; OPENER'S REBIDS; QUANTITATIVE 4NT; QUANTITATIVE 5NT; RESPONDER'S REBIDS; SHARPLES; SIX NOTRUMP OPENING; SOUTH AF-

RICAN TEXAS; STAYMAN; TEXAS; THREE NOTRUMP OPENING; THREE NOTRUMP RESPONSE; THREE-QUARTER NOTRUMP; TWO NOTRUMP OPENING; TWO NOTRUMP RESPONSE; TWO-WAY STAYMAN; WEAK NOTRUMP; WEISSBERGER; WOODSON TWO-WAY NOTRUMP.

NOTRUMP DISTRIBUTION. See BALANCED DISTRIBUTION.

NOTRUMP OPENING. See ONE NOTRUMP OPENING; TWO NOTRUMP OPENING; THREE NOTRUMP OPENING; FOUR NOTRUMP OPENING; FIVE NOTRUMP OPENING; SIX NOTRUMP OPENING.

NOTRUMP OVERCALL. See ONE NOTRUMP OVERCALL; TWO NOTRUMP OVERCALL; THREE NOTRUMP OVERCALL; FOUR NOTRUMP OVERCALL; UNUSUAL NOTRUMP.

NOTRUMP PLAY. Play and defense in notrump contracts are discussed in many of the headings listed under DEFENSE and DUMMY PLAY.

NOTRUMP RANGES. The consensus of the expert BWS panel in 2001 favored a slight weakening of notrump ranges. The choices in 2001 (1984 choices in parentheses): suit, then minimum notrump — strong 12 to weak 15 (12-14); 1NT — strong 15 to weak 18 (15-17); suit, then strong notrump bid — strong 18 to weak 20 (18-19), 2NT — strong 20 to weak 22 (same); 2♣ then minimum notrump — strong 22 to weak 24 (same); strong 22 to 24 — 2♣ then strong notrump bid 24-26. See BORDERLINE OPENING BIDS.

NOTRUMP SYSTEM DEFENSES. Method of bidding after an opponent opens the bidding with a notrump bid. See ASPRO, ASPTRO, ASTRO, BECKER, BERGEN OVER NOTRUMP, BROZEL, CANSINO, CAPPELLETTI OVER NOTRUMP, DEFENSE TO ONE NOTRUMP, DOUBLES OF NOTRUMP BIDS, EXCLUSION BID, GRANO-ASTRO, HAMILTON, LANDY, RIPSTRA, SUCTION.

NOTRUMP RESPONSES TO SUIT OPENINGS. See 1NT RESPONSE; 2NT RESPONSE; 2NT RESPONSE OVER OPPONENT'S TAKEOUT DOUBLE; 3NT RESPONSE.

NOTTINGHAM CLUB. A system popular in the English Midlands. It was introduced by Marjorie Burns of Nottingham, England in 1932, and was in many ways a forerunner of the Precision System.
The chief features are:
(1) 1♣ opening bid with 16-21 points. Negative response: 1♦ with fewer than 8 points.
(2) 1♦ with 12-13 points and no four-card major suit. Minimum suit responses are nonforcing and show 0-11 points.
(3) 1♥ and 1♠, 12-15 points with five-card suit.
(4) 1NT, 13-15 points.
(5) 2♣, 12-15 points with club length.
(6) 2♦, forcing opening with 22 or more points.
(7) 2♥ or 2♠, 12-15 points with eight playing tricks.

NOT VULNERABLE. See NONVULNERABLE.

NOVELS. See LITERATURE AND BRIDGE.

NOVICE. A new or inexperienced player.

NOVICE GAME. Game open only to players with a low experience level. Many organizations throughout the world have incorporated novice games into their program in an attempt to get new players more interested in playing. The plan has been quite successful in countries like the Scandinavian nations, France, Italy, the Netherlands and New Zealand In the United States and Canada, many clubs have added novice games to their regular schedule.

NOVICE PAIRS. Only new and inexperienced players are eligible to play.

NOVICE TABLE. An appendix table at a duplicate contest, usually a club game, where inexperienced players remain stationary, getting their boards from a table in the regular competition, relaying with the table to which it is appended. The players at the novice table keep their own scores and can check them later against the actual matchpoint scores. No harm is done if the novice table does not play all the boards, so the regular game is not appreciably slowed up. As players become more familiar with the techniques of duplicate, they join the regular game.

NPC. Nonplaying captain. See CAPTAIN.

NUISANCE BID. A bid made to hinder the opponents by disrupting the flow of their bidding.

NUMBER. Used as in *going for a number*. Number as used here refers to the high numerical value of a set that a competitor sustains (*e.g.*, 500, 800 & 1100). A number usually represents a loss, because it exceeds the value of the score the opponents could have obtained on their own by declaring the contract plus any bonuses that might be connected to the fulfillment of their contract.

NUMBER OF POSSIBLE HANDS, DEALS.
(1) The number of hands any named player can have is
$$\frac{52!}{39! \cdot 13!} = 635,013,559,600$$
(2) The number of hands a second named player can have is:
$$\frac{39!}{26! \cdot 13!} = 8,122,425,444$$
(3) The number of ways the remaining 26 cards can be divided is:
$$\frac{26!}{13! \cdot 13!} = 10,400,600$$
(4) The total number of possible deals is the three above numbers multiplied together, or
$$\frac{52!}{(13!)^4} = 53,644,737,765,488,792,839,237,440,000$$
These rather simple-appearing mathematical formulas for the first three are the number of combinations in which 13 items can be combined from a supply of 52, 39 and 26 respectively. The fourth figure is, as men-

tioned, the product of the other three. In each case the symbol "!" (read "factorial") means that the number preceding it is multiplied successively by each smaller number down to 1. A rather elementary program enables a computer to handle the arithmetic problem in seconds.

NUMERIC PRINCIPLE. In many RELAY systems, relayer's partner bids in steps which relate to distributions in numeric order after already having shown part of his distribution.

Step 1	1-4-4-4
Step 2	4-1-4-4
Step 3	4-4-1-4
Step 4	4-4-4-1

When showing a short suit, this amounts to bidding the high-ranked short suit first. When showing the long suit, on the other hand, this method shows the low-ranked suit first.

Step 1	3-3-3-4
Step 2	3-3-4-3
Step 3	3-4-3-3
Step 4	4-3-3-3

Many relay systems use the alternative idea of actually bidding the short or long suit naturally. In a situation where the relayer has relayed with 2♠, a response of 2NT would show 1-4-4-4, 3♣ 4-4-4-1, 3♦ 4-4-1-4, 3♥ 4-1-4-4. A notrump bid shows the relay suit (spades here). Similarly the long suit is shown the same way — 3♦ 3-3-4-3, 3♥ 3-4-3-3, 3♠ 4-3-3-3, 3NT 3-3-3-4.

O

OBAR BIDS (also known as PREBALANCING). Popularized by Marty Bergen, this acronym stands for after the Opponents Bid And Raise a suit, Bids In the Direct Seat are as if in protective seat. The idea is that once the opponents bid and support a suit, one should act in the direct seat as one would if in the protective position. In other words it is acceptable to act with limited values when very short in the opponents' suit, or with a lead-directing suit. So after the auction goes:

| 1♥ | Pass | 2♥ | Pass |
| Pass | ? | | |

Back to you, you would reopen with a double with

♠ K J 4 3
♥ 4
♦ Q 7 6 5
♣ K 10 9 2

But similarly you should double 2♥ in the direct seat with that hand, to take the pressure off partner. Similarly with AKJxx of a suit you can bid that suit in direct seat if you would have balanced with that hand in protective position.

OBLIGATION TO PASS. When a player bids out of turn, the Laws may require as a penalty that his partner must pass when next it is his turn to call, or for the duration of the auction. This is an "obligation to pass." If a player under such an obligation to pass makes a bid, double or redouble, then both members of the offending side must pass for the entire auction. OBLIGATION TO PASS references may be found in many of the Laws #27 to 40.

OBLIGATORY. A term characterizing a play which cannot lose but may win a trick, when the situation is such that not to make the play will gain nothing.

OBLIGATORY FINESSE. The play of a small card on the second lead of a suit in the hope that the adversary yet to play holds only the commanding card of the suit. The object of the play is to limit the number of losers in the suit when only two of the five honors are held. It is usually made when the position of the master card is marked and the adversaries originally held five cards of the suit. Thus, in the following situation:

```
              ♠ Q 7 4 2
♠ A 5                      ♠ J 10 9
              ♠ K 8 6 3
```

If South leads toward the North hand, and the ace is not played by West, he puts up the queen and wins the first spade trick. When he then leads a low spade from North. East plays one of his equals, South must play a small card in the hope that West originally held only one guard to the ace. This play can lose nothing, since if the cards are otherwise distributed at least two tricks must be lost in spades in any event. Hence, an "obligatory" finesse is a play which cannot lose but may gain a trick.

OCTAGONAL TWO-TRICK SQUEEZE. The ultimate in squeeze complexity is the octagonal two-trick squeeze. The following example, perhaps the only example, was constructed by Eric Mansfield of England. South is playing 7NT, and must succeed against any defense.

```
                   ♠ A Q 8 6
                   ♥ A Q 8 6
                   ♦ A 8 6 4
                   ♣ A
♠ K J 10                           ♠ 7 5 4 2
♥ K J 10                           ♥ 7 5 4 2
♦ K                                ♦ J 9 7 2
♣ 9 8 7 6 4 2                      ♣ K
                   ♠ 9 3
                   ♥ 9 3
                   ♦ Q 10 5 3
                   ♣ Q J 10 5 3
```

The following is Mansfield's analysis:

Whatever the opening lead, declarer's play is essentially the same and it is sufficient to follow the play after the lead of the ♣9. At Trick 2 declarer cashes the ♦A and finesses the ♦10 to reach this position:

```
                   ♠ A Q 8 6
                   ♥ A Q 8 6
                   ♦ 8 6
                   ♣ —
♠ K J 10                           ♠ 7 5 4 2
♥ K J 10                           ♥ 7 5 4 2
♦ —                                ♦ J 9
♣ 8 7 6 4                          ♣ —
                   ♠ 9 3
                   ♥ 9 3
                   ♦ Q 5
                   ♣ Q J 10 5
```

At this point all the opponents' cards are busy: the ♦Q would squeeze West and the ♣Q would squeeze East. The ♦Q lead is superficially the more attractive because West's discard immediately establishes another trick for declarer. However, a closer analysis shows that

the ♦ Q must be preserved a while because it is needed in its role of squeeze card and communication link. In the diagram position declarer therefore leads the ♣Q, discarding the ♦6 from dummy. East is squeezed: a diamond discard would immediately present declarer with an extra trick and enable him to operate a simple positional squeeze against West for his further trick. East therefore discards a major card which, because of their identical distribution, we may as well take to be the ♠2.

From declarer's viewpoint the continued presence of the ♠A-Q in dummy now becomes an encumbrance to his future plans and accordingly his next move is to finesse the ♠Q and cash the ♠A before returning to hand via the ♦Q to squeeze West in this position:

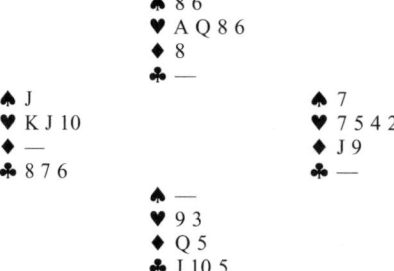

A spade discard by West would immediately present declarer with two extra tricks, while a club discard would enable declarer to squeeze him again in the major suits. West therefore discards a heart, thus promoting the ♥8 in dummy, and declarer continues by cashing his club winners to squeeze East again in this ending.

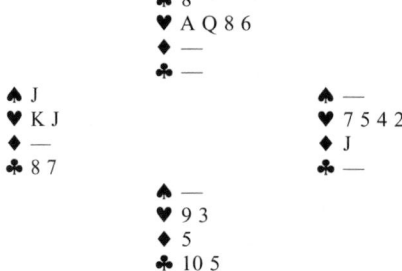

ODD-EVEN DISCARDS AND SIGNALS. A signaling method that assigns different meanings to odd- and even-numbered spot cards. An odd-card discard or signal encourages in that suit; an even-card discard or signal discourages and often doubles as a suit-preference signal (see SUIT-PREFERENCE SIGNALS).

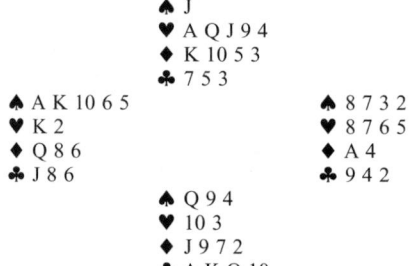

South is in 3NT, and West leads the ♠K. East plays the 8 to discourage and also (suit preference) suggests interest in diamonds instead of clubs.

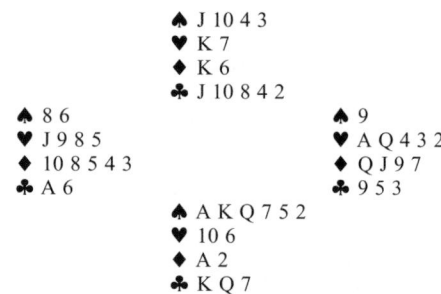

At matchpoint duplicate, South plays 4♠. West leads a trump, and South wins and draws trumps. On the second trump, East discards the ♥3 to encourage, and West will shift to a heart when he takes the ♣A.

Some partnerships use the odd-even concept in only limited circumstances; partnership agreement determines how extensive the use is.

Players using odd-even discards and signals hit a snag when no card is available to give the appropriate signal. The problem may be partially overcome by treating some even cards as more discouraging than others, and some odd cards as more encouraging than others. A 3, for example, may be a more encouraging signal than a 9; a 2 may be more discouraging than a 10.

ODD TRICK. A trick won by the declarer, in excess of the first six tricks. The term is a holdover from WHIST, in which the winning of the odd trick was paramount.

ODDS IN BRIDGE. Odds describe a ratio between two probabilities – the probability that an event (such as a player holding a particular card) will occur to the probability that it will not occur. If such a probability is expressed as a decimal, the alternate probability is the difference between totality (1), and that decimal. MATHEMATICAL TABLES, Table 4, shows the probabilities of distribution of cards between two hidden hands. It shows, for instance, that the probability that three outstanding cards will divide 2-1 is 78%. Expressing this probability in terms of odds on a 2-1 division are 78-22 or 39-11. The odds against a 2-1 division is the opposite (converse) of these figures, or 11-39, (which is the odds on a 3-0 division). Odds represent what would be a fair bet. Odds are often used to express the probability of two events that are mutually exclusive (cannot both happen at the same time, such as two winners in a prizefight). Thus in dealing with the division of four cards in a suit, Table 4 shows that the odds against a 2-2 division are 49.74 to 40.70 (approximately 5-4), provided that it is known that each opponent has at least one card of the suit. It should be noted that in this computation the possibility of a 4-0 split could be eliminated by one lead to test, and therefore odds could be expressed because there were left only two possible a priori divisions, 2-2 and 3-1.

ODEN RULE, (from ODd-evEN). A rule devised by Alex Traub of South Africa to assist a declarer who must make a series of plays, often ruffs, and needs to end in a specific hand. If that is considered the master hand, the first trick must be won in the master hand if an odd number of plays must be made. If an even number of plays must be made, the first trick must be won in the non-master hand. Traub called it the satellite hand, and gave the following example in his book "Trump Technique".

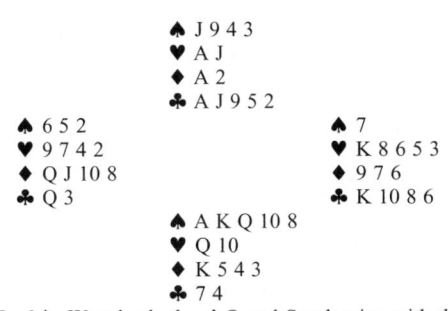

In 6♠, West leads the ♦Q and South wins with the ♦K. He finesses the ♣9, and East wins with the ♣10 and returns a diamond to dummy's ace.

South draws two rounds of trumps, and must then start a minor-suit cross-ruff. He wants to end up in his own hand to remove the missing trump, so the winning sequence of four ruffs must start with a diamond ruff. That conforms to the rule: an even number of plays must start in the non-master hand.

Similarly, if East returns a club at the third trick, South must win with the club ace and cash the diamond ace, enabling him to take the even number of ruffs and end in the master hand.

OFFENDER. The player who commits an irregularity. The laws assume that an offender commits the irregularity without doing so deliberately, and the penalties are devised in order to rectify such an error as equitably as possible. For a player to commit an irregularity, either with the intent of invoking a law to his advantage or with the intent of gaining or giving information improperly, is a violation of the Proprieties of the game. It is unethical conduct and is not acceptable under any conditions. In duplicate bridge, Law 12 or Law 72 may be invoked.

OFFENSE. The attack. An offensive play or bid is an attacking move, as distinguished from a defensive play or bid. This is not to be confused with declarer or defender, since both must take offensive or defensive positions with certain suit holdings. Also, a breach of law.

OFFICIAL LAWS. See LAWS OF CONTRACT BRIDGE and LAWS OF DUPLICATE CONTRACT BRIDGE.

OFFICIAL SCORE. In duplicate bridge, the account prepared by the director (or the official scorer) which sets forth each contestant's score for each board, his score and rank for the session and for the event. The basis for the official score is the set of scoreslips on which all the results for each board are recorded. Team scoreslips or other primary sources also can be used as the base for scoring. These primary sources are recorded on a computer or a recapitulation sheet, from which matchpoints and rankings are computed. It becomes the official score after the expiration of the correction period See LAWS (Law 79); COMPUTER SCORING; PICK-UP SLIPS; RECAPITULATION SHEET; TRAVELING SCORESLIP.

OFFICIAL SYSTEM. A system of contract bridge bidding devised and endorsed by a group of leading American authorities in 1931-32. They opposed themselves to Ely Culbertson, while acknowledging their debt to him in certain areas of theory. Prominent among the group were Milton C. Work, Sidney S. Lenz, Wilbur C. Whitehead, Winfield Liggett Jr., and F. Dudley Courtenay. Other members of the Advisory Council included Shepard Barclay, Fred G. French, Henry P. Jaeger, Madeleine Kerwin and E.V. Shepard. Three of the principles which the Official System advocated in opposition to Culbertson have their place in the modern game: (1) the employment of the 4-3-2-1 count for notrump bidding; (2) the incorporation of an intermediate game invitation (nonforcing) suit bid of two; (3) the employment of an original opening forcing bid — the (artificial) TWO CLUB CONVENTION, designed not only for game but also for slam bidding.

OFFSIDE. A card so placed that a finesse, if taken, will lose: "the king was offside."

OFFSIDE DOUBLE. A penalty double, usually of a game contract in a suit, based on an inference that the doubler's partner has trump length. The bidding may have made it clear that the declaring side is at full stretch, with borderline game values. For an example, see PENALTY DOUBLE.

OGUST REBID. See WEAK TWO-BID.

OKBRIDGE. The first full-scale online bridge-playing program that made it possible to play bridge at home with partners and opponents all over the world. An annual highlight is the Internet World Bridge Championship, in which teams from more than 70 countries compete. Features include complete records, a rating system, chat setups, masterpoints, an online magazine and bridge columns.

OKBRIDGE AWARD. An award given annually starting in 2001 to an outstanding junior by the INTERNATIONAL BRIDGE PRESS ASSOCIATION.

OLDEST CLUBS. The world's oldest clubs go back to the days of whist. The oldest is certainly the PORTLAND CLUB in London, England. It was founded before 1815 as the Stratford Club and reorganized under its present name in 1825. The second-oldest, and the oldest in the Western Hemisphere, appears to be the Hamilton Club in Bala Cynwyd PA, founded in 1887. The third-oldest apparently is the Continental Club in Amsterdam, the Netherlands, founded in 1889.

OLYMPIAD. Worldwide team competition at contract bridge, conducted by the WORLD BRIDGE FEDERATION. Contests have been held every four years since 1960. Two years after each Team Olympiad, beginning in 1962, an Olympiad is played with the main focus on pair play. this is sometimes called the PAIR OLYMPIAD, although many team games also take place.The word "Olympiad" is a misnomer, since in Classical Greek it referred to a four-year period between Olympic Games. It is used in bridge to avoid any suggestion of connection to the modern Olympic Games. For results see Appendix V.

OLYMPIC. A name first applied in bridge in the sense of a contest of skill at contract bridge in which anyone may participate. The first AMERICAN BRIDGE

OLYMPIC and WORLD BRIDGE OLYMPIC were promoted, sponsored and originated by Ely Culbertson in 1932. For results of this and other Olympics, see WORLD PAR CONTESTS and Appendix V. The term was modified to OLYMPIAD to describe WORLD CHAMPIONSHIP events conducted by the WORLD BRIDGE FEDERATION.

OLYMPIC GAMES. World bridge leaders began to consider during the Nineties the possibility that bridge could become an Olympic sport. José Damiani of France, president of the World Bridge Federation, and Mazhar Jafri of Pakistan, WBF vice president, began a years-long investigation that began to pay dividends in 1998 when the first International Olympic Committee Cup event was staged at IOC headquarters in Lausanne, Switzerland. The event has earned world-wide attention each year it has been held. Also instrumental in this development was Marc Hodler of Switzerland, a vice president of the IOC and an avid bridge player who has served for many years as president of the Swiss Bridge Federation.

One of the major problems concerning acceptance of bridge is the fact that bridge is a mind game rather than a physical competition. The argument in favor of bridge is that it is a competition, a sport. Top Olympic officials, including former President Juan Antonio Samaranch, already have declared publicly that bridge is a sport.

A major breakthrough occurred in March, 2001, when the IOC designated bridge as a demonstration sport at the Winter Olympics in Salt Lake City UT in 2002. This was a major step forward in the ongoing effort to have bridge become a full-fledged Olympic sport in time for the 2006 Winter Olympics in Turin, Italy. The word came from Hodler and was released by Damiani, who said, "Bridge has been given the opportunity to demonstrate the competition at the Salt Lake City Olympics before the public and before IOC officials. If the demonstration goes well, the sport will be formally introduced at the Olympic Games four years later."

The event was scheduled to take place two days before the opening ceremony. The WBF planned to field teams in three categories – open, women's and junior. "We must show the IOC the true global reach of our game," said Damiani. However, he also pointed out that one final formality will still exist even if the Salt Lake City demonstration goes off perfectly. "The IOC must amend its regulation that allows only sports contested on ice or snow to participate in the Winter Olympics."

The IOC recognizes only national organizations, so a new bridge organization was formed in the United States in 2001 – the United States Bridge Federation. Effectively this organization is an amalgamation of the American Contract Bridge League and the American Bridge Association. Most other countries already had a national bridge organization.

OLYMPIC PAR EVENTS. See WORLD PAR CONTESTS.

OMAR SHARIF WORLD INDIVIDUAL. One of the largest total purses ($200,000) up to that point in the history of bridge was at stake when the Omar Sharif World Individual bridge tournament was held in Atlantic City NJ May 7-10, 1990. This was the first time the ACBL sanctioned a cash-prize tournament. Winner of the $40,000 first-place prize in the championship division was Zia Mahmood, Pakistani star who makes his home in New York and London. Fred Hamilton was second ($20,000) and P.O. Sundelin of Sweden was third ($12,000).

A swing of $28,000 occurred on this deal when Sundelin's partner pulled a wrong card, blowing a game contract and the first-place prize for Sundelin. Zia was North, Sundelin, West, and Peter Pender, a former world champion, was East.

Dlr: North   ♠ 9 8
Vul: N-S   ♥ K 9 7 5
               ♦ A 3 2
               ♣ A Q 10 2

♠ A K 5 4   ♠ Q 10 6 3
♥ 8 4 3 2   ♥ A J 10
♦ K Q 4   ♦ J 9 8
♣ 9 5   ♣ K 7 6

               ♠ J 7 2
               ♥ Q 6
               ♦ 10 7 6 5
               ♣ J 8 4 3

West	North	East	South
	1♣	Pass	Pass
Dbl	Pass	2♣	Dbl
Pass	Pass	2♠	Pass
3♠	Pass	4♠	All Pass

South led a club and Pender, expecting Zia to win the ace, followed with a low club before he looked down and realized that — to maintain a link with his partner's hand — Zia had played the queen. Pender subsequently lost another club in addition to the expected heart and diamond tricks. Now the cold game, not bid by the majority of the field, was lost. Zia won the tournament and Pender's good friend and former winning NABC Men's Pairs partner, Sundelin, dropped from first place to third.

OMNIUM. A nationwide French tournament with many novel features, first played in 1963. The organizer was Irene Bajos de Heredia. Special decks with perforated edges were distributed to all playing centers, so that the players themselves could select the 13 cards needed for each deal by inserting a metal pin in the appropriate hole. The deals were pre-played but not "prepared". Scoring was on a basis similar to a PAR CONTEST, with awards for good and bad results in bidding and play according to the decisions of an expert panel.

ONE-BID. A bid contracting to win one odd trick, seven tricks in all. Articles appropriate to this heading are: BORDERLINE OPENING BIDS; CHOICE OF SUIT; ONE NOTRUMP OPENING; OPENING SUIT BID.

ONE CLUB ARTIFICIAL AND FORCING. Played in a variety of forms (see ONE CLUB SYSTEMS). The earliest in contract was Harold S. Vanderbilt's "Club Convention," although Robert F. Foster advocated a similar idea in auction.

ONE CLUB SYSTEMS. In an effort to reach the optimum contract, many players use systems which use an artificial opening bid of 1♣. Such systems discussed in this book are BANGKOK CLUB; BLUE TEAM CLUB; CANARY CLUB; CARROT CLUB; FRENCH CLUB; LITTLE ROMAN; MARMIC; ORANGE CLUB; PRECISION; RELAY; ROMAN; SIMPLIFIED CLUB; VANDERBILT; VIENNA.

ONE DIAMOND NEGATIVE RESPONSE TO ONE CLUB. In most bidding systems that use an artificial opening of 1♣ as a forcing bid, a 1♦ response is used to deny certain values. In some systems the 1♦ response denies certain point count; in others it denies a certain number of controls.

ONE DIAMOND STRONG ARTIFICIAL OPENING. See BIG DIAMOND SYSTEM; LEGHORN DIAMOND.

ONE NOTRUMP BIDDING. See DYNAMIC NOTRUMP, EXPECTED NUMBER OF CONTROLS IN BALANCED HANDS, FOUR NOTRUMP OPENING, FIVE NO TRUMP OPENING, GERBER CONVENTION, GLADIATOR, JACOBY TRANSFER BID, MINI NOTRUMP, ONE NOTRUMP OPENING, ONE NOTRUMP REBID, ONE NOTRUMP RESPONSE, ONE NOTRUMP RESPONSE TO MAJOR FORCING, ONE NOTRUMP RESPONSE TO MINOR, OPENER'S REBID, QUANTITATIVE FOUR NOTRUMP, QUANTITATIVE FIVE NOTRUMP, RESPONDER'S REBID, SHARPLES, SIX NOTRUMP OPENING, SOUTH AFRICAN TEXAS, STAYMAN, TEXAS, THREE NOTRUMP OPENING, THREE-QUARTER NOTRUMP, TWO NOTRUMP OPENING, TWO NOTRUMP RESPONSE, TWO-WAY STAYMAN, UNUSUAL NOTRUMP, WEAK NOTRUMP, WEISSBERGER, WOODSON TWO-WAY NOTRUMP.

ONE NOTRUMP OPENING. A bid usually showing a point count within a specified range in a reasonably balanced hand. The development of notrump bidding is discussed under APPROACH PRINCIPLE. Limit bidding and the Stayman Convention have combined to make 1NT a cornerstone of modern bidding methods. In considering an opening notrump bid, three aspects have to be reviewed.

(1) Strength. High-card points only are counted, but a five-card suit is usually worth a point, and the presence of 10s can be taken into account. The standard range in tournament bridge is 15-17. In rubber bridge the range usually is either 15-17 or 16-18. In tournament play, there are many variations. These include:

(a) 17-20, used in the ROMAN SYSTEM.

(b) 15-18, a relaxation of the standard range. — 15+ to 18 is a common compromise;

(c) 14-16, once used in the LITTLE MAJOR SYSTEM, and now used in the modern style of PRECISION.

(d) 13-15, originally used nonvulnerable in the ACOL SYSTEM but now rare; an integral feature of the original version of PRECISION and some other BIG CLUB systems.

(e) 12-15, sometimes used instead of 13-15, offering greater frequency but far less accuracy.

(f) 12-14, the usual range for a WEAK NOTRUMP, employed by many players using standard methods as well as the followers of the KAPLAN-SHEINWOLD and BARON systems. Some partnerships relax the requirements to include 11-point hands.

(g) 10-12, a very weak notrump often called a mini-notrump. Used most often in duplicate pairs tournaments, often played only at favorable vulnerability (also the lower range of WOODSON TWO-WAY NOTRUMP whose upper range is 15-

17). Also the KAMIKAZE NOTRUMP, used by many American experts when vulnerability and/or position are favorable. The original range was 8-10, but this was generally abandoned when the ACBL Board of Directors ruled that the Kamikaze is a conventional bid, and no conventional bids, not even Stayman, could be used in conjunction with it.

(h) 8-10, a super-weak notrump used by some expert partnerships as a preemptive tool.

(i) combinations of two ranges, one weak and one strong, depending on vulnerability and position at the table. The most common is 12-14 not vulnerable and 15-17 vulnerable, used in the Staynran System, the Acol System, and, with a different valuation method, the original CULBERTSON SYSTEM. Some favor a weak notrump at all vulnerabilities in fourth position because a double is virtually impossible. See THREE-QUARTER NOTRUMP; WOODSON TWO-WAY NOTRUMP.

(2) Distribution. An orthodox notrump opening bid has one of the following distributions: 4-3-3-3; 4-4-3-2; or 5-3-3-2 with the five-card suit a minor. The following exceptions occur: (a) 5-3-3-2 with a five-card major-suit, preferably in hearts. This may be tried either because tenace holdings make a notrump contract particularly attractive, or because a 16-point hand is held. The latter is likely to create a rebid problem after a one-level response or a single raise. (b) 5-4-2-2 if 1NT will avoid a rebid problem, which will occur with 2-2-4-5, 2-4-2-5, or 2-4-5-2. Two doubleton major-suit kings and/or queens and a 16-point hand would be typical: An opening bid in a minor suit would lead to a rebid problem after a major-suit response. (c) 6-3-2-2. In this case also the doubletons should preferably be strong, and the strength of the hand is likely to be a minimum or sub- minimum. The expert panel in BWS 2001 determined that the following distributions should all be considered optional 1 NT bids: 5-3-3-2 with a 5-card major; 2-2-4-5 and 2-2-5-4; 2-4-2-5 and 2-4-5-2; 6-3-2-2 with a minor.

(3) Location of strength. There is a tendency to prefer a notrump bid holding tenaces, making it likely that the opening lead will be an advantage to declarer. Conversely, a notrump bid is unattractive with points concentrated in two suits: xxx xxx AKJ AKQx On the other hand, a serious rebid problem would occur after an opening of 1♣ and a one-over-one suit response. There is also a tendency, which some more serious authorities make a rule, to avoid a 1NT bid holding a weak doubleton. The objection to this treatment is that it often creates an impossible rebid problem: .xx .AJx AQ10x KQxx — if the opening bid is 1♦ or 1♣, the rebid will be difficult after any one-level response except 1NT). For reasons of this kind many players open 1NT whenever the point-count and distribution are suitable, regardless of the location of the honor strength.

ONE NOTRUMP OVERCALL. A direct overcall of 1NT is roughly equivalent to a standard strong 1NT opening. The following considerations apply. First, the overcaller promises a stopper in the opener's suit. Second, the range is usually 16-18 or 15-18 rather than 15-17. Other ranges are possible, but rare. A double stopper such as A J x or K J x improves the value of the hand. There may be advantages in making the weak hand declarer so that the opening bidder is on lead. Occasionally, a player may choose to overcall 1NT

with unbalanced distribution:

```
          ♠ 5
          ♥ A Q 5
          ♦ A Q 7 3
          ♣ K J 6 4 2
```

If right-hand opponent opens 1 ♥, a 1NT overcall may be better than 2 ♣ or a trap pass on the hand above.

Since opener has suggested a long suit plus entries, a 1NT overcall is most attractive if overcaller has a source of tricks:

(a)	(b)
♠ J 6 3	♠ 10 6 3
♥ A Q 3	♥ A Q 5
♦ K J 6 3	♦ A 6
♣ A J 3	♣ K Q J 8 3

Hand (b) is a better 1NT overcall of 1 ♥ than hand (a).

Overcaller also prefers secondary strength in opener's suit:

(a)	(b)
♠ K 6 3	♠ K 6 3
♥ A 6 3	♥ Q 10 6 4
♦ Q 10 6 4	♦ A 6 3
♣ A K 4	♣ A K 3

In (a), overcaller's heart stopper may be dislodged immediately, leaving the defenders with winners plus entries; the hand would make a more attractive 1NT overcall if the hearts were A-10-3. In (b), heart leads will actually help overcaller by setting up his secondary honors.

Responses by overcaller's partner. Partnerships should agree on one of the following methods:

(1) The cuebid in opener's suit takes the place of STAYMAN. A response of 2 ♣ is therefore natural and weak unless the opening bid was 1 ♣. A jump response in a suit is invitational to game, not forcing. In the absence of any discussion, these methods can be assumed.

(2) Respond exactly as to an opening 1NT. (Referred to as SYSTEMS ON). This makes slam explorations possible, but these are unlikely and deprive the partnership of the chance to play 2 ♣ or 2 ♦. A transfer into the opener's major suit can be used to show an invitational hand in the other major.

(3) Combining methods (1) and (2), overcaller's partner bids 2 ♣ as non-forcing Stayman and cuebids as forcing Stayman. Overcaller's side cannot play in clubs or in opener's suit, but overcaller has the tools to sign off, invite game or force to game.

(4) Overcaller's partner ignores the opening bid, responding as he would have done to 1NT, except when opener bid clubs. In that case, 2 ♦ is used as Stayman. This method permits overcaller's side to play in the opponent's minor suit, which may be desirable.

(5) Overcaller's partner uses transfer responses. A transfer into opener's suit takes the place of Stayman.

Action by the opening bidder's partner. A bid in a new suit at the two level is weak; responder is likely to have a fair five- or six-card suit with fewer than 9 high-card points. A jump to the three level in a new suit is weak and preemptive with a six- or seven-card suit. With most strong hands (9 or more points), a penalty double is appropriate. The only other strong action is a bid of 2NT (see CUEBID IN OPPONENT'S SUIT), which suggests a freakish hand, probably a two-suiter, unsuitable for defense. A modern tendency is to respond in accordance with HAMILTON.

When a 1NT overcall is doubled, the partnership can employ whatever method it uses when a 1NT opening is doubled. See DEFENSE TO DOUBLE OF 1NT.

Some 1NT overcalls cannot logically be strength-showing. See SANDWICH NOTRUMP, UNUSUAL NOTRUMP and UNUSUAL 1NT OVERCALL. For 1NT overcalls by opener's right-hand opponent, see BALANCING.

ONE NOTRUMP REBID. A 1NT rebid by the opening bidder after a suit bid of one by responder. See OPENER'S REBID. For conventional actions by responder after the 1NT rebid see CROWHURST CONVENTION; NEW MINOR FORCING; STAYMAN ON SECOND ROUND; TWO CLUB REBID BY RESPONDER AS ONLY FORCE AFTER 1NT REBID.

ONE NOTRUMP RESPONSE. A bid of 1NT when partner has opened the bidding with a suit. The normal range for the bid is 6-9, but 10 is possible, particularly by a passed hand which does not wish to bid a four-card suit at the level of two. This assumes that 1NT is not forcing, but the subsequent developments are similar in the modern style. See ONE NOTRUMP RESPONSE TO MAJOR FORCING.

1 ♠-1NT, the most common situation, covers a wide range of hands. The responding hand may be quite unbalanced but unable to respond at the level of two:

```
          ♠ 3
          ♥ K 7 6 4 3
          ♦ K 10 8 7 2
          ♣ J 3
```

If the opener's rebid is 2 ♣, suggesting 5-4 distribution, responder should bid 2 ♦. (But see BART.) This does not exclude a heart contract because the opener will continue to 2 ♥ with 5-3-1-4 distribution. If the opener rebids a lower-ranking suit at the two-level, responder should very rarely go beyond two of the original suit. When he does so, the reason is usually a fine fit for opener's second suit:

(a)	(b)
♠ 5	♠ 5
♥ A 8 5 4 2	♥ A 7 4 3
♦ K 7 4 3	♦ K 8 6 2
♣ 10 7 6	♣ J 8 5 3

After

1 ♠	1NT
2 ♥	

hand (a) can jump to 4 ♥. The five-card trump support, combined with the singleton spade and two useful honors, is enormously powerful. With (b), 3 ♥ is sufficient. Ten tricks may be out of reach if the opener has a minimum with a four-card heart suit.

As the sequence

1 ♠	1NT
2 ♥ (or ♦ or ♣)	

has a very wide range (10-18 in high cards), a very few experts outside the U.S.A. consider a jump rebid of 3 ♥ or 3 ♦ nonforcing. 3 ♣ then becomes an artificial game-force, unrelated to the club suit. The result is that the rebid at the level of two is more limited, and there is less temptation to try for game.

In the U.S.A. other strong rebids available to the opener include:

(1) 2NT:

1 ♠	1NT
2NT	

This shows about 17+-19 points and probably a five-card or even six-card spade suit; the failure to open 1NT is significant. If responder bids a new suit, it is long, weak and nonforcing.

(2) A reverse:

1♥	1NT
2♠	

Traditionally encouraging with about 17-18 points. Shows four spades and five (or six) hearts. The modern style is for the reverse to be forcing, often with a three-card spade suit.

(3) A jump rebid:

1♠	1NT
3♠	

Encouraging but nonforcing, and roughly 16-17 points in high cards.

(4) Jump shift:

1♠	1NT
3♦	

Game-forcing, more than 18 points in high cards. Usually five spades and four or five diamonds, with a singleton or void in an unbid suit. (But see the alternative treatment above.)

(5) 3NT.

1♠	1NT
3NT	

A solid six- or seven-card spade suit.

(6) Jump rebid to game:

1♠	1NT
4♠	

An unbalanced hand with $8\frac{1}{2}$ or more playing tricks, and at least a six-card suit.

An "impossible" sequence can develop:

Opener	Responder
1♥	1NT
2♣ or 2♦ 2♠	

Responder cannot wish to bid spades naturally, so many partnerships use this to show a club or diamond raise stronger than a three-club bid would be. See BART.

The lower the rank of the opening bid, the lower the frequency of the 1NT response. This is because minimum responding hands have alternative possibilities without going to the level of two. Over 1♥, 1NT traditionally denies a four-card spade suit. Some experts are prepared to conceal a weak four-card spade suit, and many who use FLANNERY will conceal any 4-card spade suit. Similarly, the 1NT response to a minor suit denies a four-card major suit in principle and strongly suggests a balanced hand. Over 1♣, 1NT strongly suggests 4-3-3-3 distribution, and the four-card suit is normally a minor (see ONE NOTRUMP RESPONSE TO MINOR SUIT). See also DRURY; ONE NOTRUMP RESPONSE TO MAJOR, FORCING; STRONG NOTRUMP AFTER PASSING.

ONE NOTRUMP RESPONSE TO MAJOR FORCING.
Used in combination with five-card major openings, this bid is intended to handle intermediate hands, in the 10-12 point range, which are not strong enough for a two-over-one response. It is an integral part of many methods, including EASTERN SCIENTIFIC, WALSH, ROTH-STONE and KAPLAN-SHEINWOLD, in which a two-over-one response is virtually or absolutely game-forcing by an unpassed hand. In Roth-Stone it serves to narrow the range for a single raise, which is constructive. Since these systems usually guarantee five cards for a

major-suit opening, it is assumed that the opener can take a further bid without strain. If he has a six-card suit, he rebids it. If not, he makes his rebid in another biddable suit or his lowest-ranking three-card suit. However, some would rebid 2♦ with three strong diamonds and three weak clubs. There are some inconvenient possibilities. If the opener's distribution is 4-5-2-2, the systems do not provide him with a rebid, and he may end up playing with six trumps in the combined hands. (This can also happen, for example, when the opener's distribution is 5-3-3-2 and responder has 1-3-3-6. The final contract may be 2♦.) In this rare situation some players would break the rule and open 1♠ with a 4-5-2-2 if the spade suit was a strong one. This is one of the motivations for using FLANNERY.

A double jump below game:

1♠	1NT
4♦	

This rare action is treated by most experts as a splinter, with a tendency towards a void rather than a singleton. It indicates a powerful one-suiter with slam interest. See BART, MITTELMAN ADJUNCT.

A variation popular with some experts is to invert the meanings of a 1♠ response and a forcing 1NT response. This solves the problem of the opener who has 4-5 in the major suits and is not using Flannery: he rebids 1NT with four spades.

This bid calls for an Alert in most of the world. However, an Announcement, "Forcing," is used instead of an Alert in ACBL countries.

ONE NOTRUMP RESPONSE TO MINOR.
Some systems lay down 8-10 points as the requirement for a response of 1NT to an opening of 1♣; in Goren, 9-11 are needed. This is because a weaker hand can usually find some other bid, perhaps a suit at the level of one, a raise to 2♣ or if inverted minors are not in use, or if need be a response of 1♦ based on a three-card suit. Some players treat a response of 1NT to 1♦ in the same way, but this creates problems when responder has a weak hand including a club suit.

A modern tendency is to relax these requirements and respond 1NT to 1♣ with as few as 6 points. This has some preemptive value because the fourth player cannot bid at the one level; but it loses slightly in constructive efficiency.

In Kaplan-Sheinwold the range is 5-8 points, so that if opener was planning a 1NT rebid with 15-17 points, he may pass and not miss a game.

In BWS 1994 the consensus choice was 8-10 for a response to 1♣ and 6-10 for a response to 1♦. 1♣-1NT does not guarantee four-card club length.

1♣-1NT always shows a balanced hand but 1♦-1NT does not. It strongly suggests club length, usually 4, 5 or 6 cards, since the ability to bid a major or raise diamonds is denied. Those using INVERTED MINORS may be forced to respond 1NT with 4-5 in the minor suits when a diamond raise is not appropriate.

ONE-ODD.
One trick more than six, the book. A bid of one odd is a bid to win seven tricks.

ONE-OVER-ONE RESPONSE.
A suit response at the level of one to an opening suit bid. For example, 1♣-1♥. The usual minimum strength for this response is 6 points, but in some styles a response is permitted with 3 or 4 points

and distributional features. The maximum is just below the level fixed for a JUMP SHIFT, i.e., about 17 points in standard methods and about 15 points in ACOL. For pairs using WEAK JUMP SHIFT responses, the one-over-one has no upper limit. The longest suit is usually chosen for the response, and if two five-card suits are held, the higher-ranking is given preference. However, a four-card suit that can be bid at the one-level is often preferred to a five or six-card suit which has to be bid at the two level when the strength of the hand does not justify a two-over-one response. Many modern players have adopted the Walsh idea that in response to 1♣ a four-card major is bid ahead of longer diamonds unless the hand is invitational values or better. For other aspects of this response, see CHOICE OF SUIT, COURTESY BID, and UP THE LINE.

ONE-SUIT SQUEEZE. A hybrid between a squeeze and a throw-in. Most squeeze situations involve two or more suits.

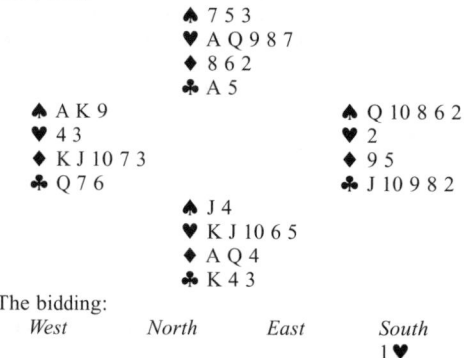

The bidding:

West	North	East	South
			1♥
2♦	3♥	Pass	4♥
All Pass			

Spades are led three times and South ruffs. After ace, king, and a ruff in clubs and three rounds of trumps the position is:

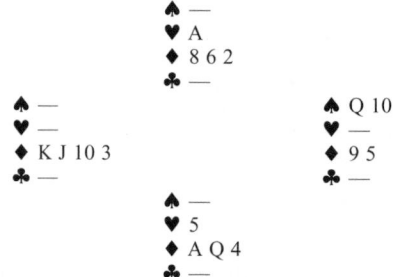

♥ A is led. If West discards the ♦3, South merely ducks a diamond. If West discards the ♦10, South leads the ♦6 from dummy. If East ducks, so does South. If East puts up the ♦9, South covers, creating a tenace position. For a related situation, see RUFF AND RUFF.

ONE-SUITER. A hand with a suit at least six cards long that contains no other suit with more than three cards.

ONE-TWO-THREE STOP. See PREEMPTIVE RE-RAISE.

ONLINE BRIDGE. Bridge played on computers instead of with cards. Several computer programs now make it possible for players in their homes anywhere in

the world to play with and against others who also are using their home computers. See ACBL ONLINE, MICROSOFT GAMING ZONE, OKBRIDGE.

ONSIDE. A card so placed that a finesse, if taken, will win: "the king was onside."

OPEN. (1) To lead to the first trick in the play of the hand. (2) The bidding: to make the first bid in a given auction. (3) Teams, pairs: tournament contests in which any pair, whether mixed (man and woman) or not, or any team of whatever constituency may play. (4) Room: that room in a championship event in which spectators may be present in somewhat substantial numbers as opposed to a CLOSED ROOM that is limited as to both audience and accessibility. (5) Club: a game in which anyone may play.

OPEN BOARD-A-MATCH TEAMS CHAMPION-SHIP, NORTH AMERICAN CHAMPIONSHIP. See REISINGER MEMORIAL TROPHY. For results see Appendix I.

OPEN HAND. The dummy's hand, exposed on the table, as distinguished from the "CLOSED" HAND of the declarer.

OPEN KNOCKOUT TEAMS, NORTH AMERICAN CHAMPIONSHIP. See VANDERBILT CUP. For results see Appendix I.

OPEN PAIR CHAMPIONSHIP, NORTH AMERI-CAN CHAMPIONSHIPS. See CAVENDISH TRO-PHY; SILODOR TROPHY. For results see Appendix I.

OPEN PAIRS. Any two players can compete as partners — no restrictions of any kind. See PAIR EVENTS.

OPEN ROOM. In team-of-four matches, particularly in knockout matches, the two pairs of a team play in different rooms or different areas of the same room. One of these rooms is designated as the Open Room, the other as the CLOSED ROOM. Normally spectators are permitted to watch matches in the Open Room but are barred from the Closed Room. As soon as one of the matches in the Closed Room finishes, the Open Room is closed to any additional spectators.

In important matches where play-by-play arrangements are made for spectators in the VUGRAPH room, the pairs in the Closed Room often play two or three boards before play gets under way in the Open Room. This is done so that comparisons will be possible when the Open Room pairs play on vugraph. See BRIDGE-O-RAMA.

OPEN TEAMS. There are no restrictions on the makeup of the teams — except the numerical limit is six. The event can be run as one of the three basic types. See TEAM GAMES.

OPENER. See OPENING BIDDER.

OPENER'S REBID. The second bid by an opener who began with a suit bid of one is frequently the crucial point in the auction; judgment begins to be a factor. The following summary refers to standard methods (unless otherwise noted) and is limited to auctions in which re-

sponder made a non-jump bid in a new suit. Other rebids are dealt with separately under headings such as JUMP SHIFT, 1NT RESPONSE, 2NT RESPONSE, SINGLE RAISE and DOUBLE RAISE.

(1) After a ONE-OVER-ONE RESPONSE.

(a) 1NT rebid. 13-15 is the standard range using a 16-18 notrump opening, but 12 is possible; if the opening notrump shows 15-17, the 1NT rebid shows 12-14. For users of a weak notrump, the notrump rebid promises a minimum of 15 (15-17 in KAPLAN-SHEINWOLD, 15-16 in ACOL). The sequence 1♥-1♠-1NT is given distinct treatment. In Kaplan-Sheinwold, it shows 12-14, equivalent to a 1NT opening.

A debatable point is whether a 1NT rebid is acceptable with a singleton in partner's major suit. This avoids problems when holding 1-4-4-4, 1-3-4-5, 3-1-4-5 and 1-4-5-3 hands. In BWS94 experts were evenly divided on this.

(b) Rebid in first suit. This suggests minimum strength and usually requires a six-card suit; opener avoids rebidding a five- card suit. A six-card suit is almost a certainty if the response was the most economical:

West	East	West	East
1♥	1♠	1♦	1♦
2♥		2♣	

In each case, West had four other minimum rebids at his disposal, but chose to rebid his first suit. Opener is more likely to rebid a five-card suit if the response consumed bidding space:

West	East
1♣	1♠
2♣	

West may have an unbid four-card suit that he could not show without making a strength-showing REVERSE.

(c) Rebid at the one level. For example, 1♣-1♥-1♠. This is an unrevealing rebid, covering a wide range of hands. Opener has fewer than 19 high-card points; otherwise, he would have made a jump shift. His black-suit lengths remain a mystery: the clubs will often be longer; 5-4 and 6-4 are common distributions, and 6-5 possible. In a FIVE-CARD-MAJOR style, opener could be 4-3-3-3, but some players would prefer to rebid 1NT with that distribution. Even 5-3 and 6-3 are conceivable, since some experts might rebid 1♠ on:

♠ A K J
♥ 5
♦ K 6 4 2
♣ A 9 6 4 2

4-4 distribution is common. Opener could be 5-5, though many experts would then open 1♠ (see CHOICE OF SUIT). In truly exceptional cases, the spades may be longer:

♠ 7 5 4 3 2
♥ 7
♦ A 3 2
♣ A K Q 4

With this awkward hand, the lesser evil may be to open 1♣ and rebid 1♠ over 1♥. Similar considerations apply to the sequences 1♣-1♦-1♠ and 1♣-1♦-1♥, though in the latter case 5-5 distribution is unlikely. 1♦-1♥-1♠ is more precise, since a three-card diamond suit is improbable and so is 5-5 distribution.

(d) Rebid in a lower-ranking suit at the two level. Four sequences are possible, all consisting of a red-suit opening, a major-suit response and a minor-suit rebid.

For example:

West	East
1♥	1♠
2♣	

West's most likely distribution is 5-4, but 5-5, 6-4 and 6-5 are possible. 4-5 and 4-4 are possible in some styles, but this course is risky since responder may wish to give preference on a doubleton. When opener's rebid bypasses 1NT in this way, responder can reasonably assume that opener's distribution is not balanced and his first suit is a five-carder. These sequences have a wide range in standard methods — 10-18 in high cards — and are therefore difficult to handle. (They are strong in ROTH-STONE and KAPLAN-SHEINWOLD, and in the latter system a 2♣ rebid rebid by opener after a 1♦ opening is forcing and virtually artificial.) However, when opener changes suits, he is more likely to hold extra strength. With:

♠ Q 6
♥ A K 7 5 3 2
♦ 5
♣ A Q 6 3

opener would rebid 2♣, since a 2♥ rebid would suggest a minimum hand. Furthermore, with:

♠ Q
♥ A Q 4
♦ A 10 6 3
♣ Q 9 6 4 2

opener might reject the popular notion of opening 1♦ and rebidding 2♣, since he distorts his distribution and leaves the strength of his hand poorly defined. Many players would open 1♣ and rebid 1NT over a 1♠ response (see CHOICE OF SUIT).

(e) Reverse. Opener's second suit is of higher rank than his first. For example:

West	East
1♣	1♠
2♥	

West's most likely distribution is 5-4. His reverse strongly suggests longer clubs than hearts, so alternative distributions are 6-4 and 6-5. A three-card heart suit is possible, especially if opener has spade support in reserve:

♠ K Q 5
♥ A K 4
♦ 5 4
♣ A Q 7 5 3

This atypical reverse is prompted by the weakness in the fourth suit. The same factor may even cause opener to ignore the principle that the first suit must be longer:

♠ K 5 3
♥ A K 4 3
♦ 6 5
♣ A K Q 6

Experts disagree on the high-card requirements for a reverse. One school is willing to reverse with hands worth only a trick more than a minimum; the other treats a reverse as equivalent to a jump shift. Most modern pairs accept a reverse as forcing on any normal response. See REVERSE.

(f) Single raise in responder's suit. For example, 1♦-1♠-2♠. This shows 12-15 points and an expectation of four-card trump support. However, a single raise with three-card support is not uncommon and is desirable unless the hand is completely balanced or the trumps are poor. Expert opinion is divided on the correct rebid when

opener has three-card support and a six-card suit.

       ♠ K 10 3
       ♥ 4
       ♦ A 7 5
       ♣ A J 9 6 4 2

After 1♣-1♠, some experts would raise; others would rebid the clubs, hoping to support spades later.

(g) 2NT rebid. A balanced hand, filling the gap between a 1NT opening and a 2NT opening. A common range for those who use a 15-17 notrump is to rebid 2NT, which is 18-19. A singleton in partner's suit is just possible if there is no other convenient rebid. 1♦-1♠-2NT might have 1-4-4-4 distribution. With this 18-19 range, responder continues unless his values are a dead minimum or sub-minimum. All rebids by responder are forcing, although a rebid of responder's suit is a signoff in Acol. See WOLFF SIGNOFF. The rebid of responder's suit is a sign-off in Acol because 2NT has a slightly lower range.

(h) Jump reverse. For example, 1♣-1♠-3♥. Traditionally, this was simply stronger than a normal reverse. In the modern style, with a simple reverse forcing, the sequence has no obvious meaning. It is often used as a mini-splinter, inviting game with a four-card fit for responder and a singleton in the suit shown. It also is sometimes used as a three-card splinter raise with 6+ cards in the minor.

(i) Jump rebid in opener's suit. For example, 1♣-1♥-3♣. This shows a good six- or seven-card suit and about 15-17 high-card points. The bid is encouraging, not forcing, and responder should go to 3NT with extras. A new-suit bid by responder at the three level may show a stopper for notrump and not necessarily length.

(j) Jump raise in responder's suit. 1♦-1♠-3♠ shows 16-18 high-card points perhaps 15 with a singleton. In standard methods it cannot be a hand suitable for a 1NT opening. A more common action for those using weak no trumps.

(k) Jump shift. For example, 1♦-1♠-3♣. This shows unbalanced distribution and is forcing to game. Opener sometimes has a fit for responder's suit that he plans to show next.

(l) 3NT rebid. A hand with a long, solid suit, usually a minor, and stoppers in the unbid suits. A singleton in responder's suit is likely. The hand is probably worth 8-9 playing tricks.For several reasons, the traditional Goren meaning of 21 balanced points is obsolete.

Open 1♣ and jump to 3NT if the response is 1♠.

(m) Jump to game in responder's major suit. 1♥-1♠-4♠. This shows four-card support and the values to justify game. The most common type of hand is relatively balanced with 18-19 points; a powerful unbalanced hand is likely to prefer a splinter or jump shift (see (k) above and (p) below).

(n) Jump to game in opener's major suit. 1♥-1♠-4♥ is the only possible sequence. Many powerful hands with a seven-card suit or even an eight-card suit would qualify. A six-card suit is possible:

       ♠ Q 5 4
       ♥ A K Q J 10 4
       ♦ A J 3
       ♣ 3

In this case, the partial fit in spades improves opener's hand. (In Acol, the spade fit is indicated because many other hands with enough playing strength would qualify for a 2♥ opening.)

(o) Double jump rebid. This can be a jump to four of opener's suit, or responder's suit:

(a)		(b)	
West	East	West	East
1♣	1♥	1♣	1♦
4♣		4♦	

Sequence (a) is often used to show a hand worth a raise to 4♥ with a long, solid club suit. A typical hand would be:

       ♠ 4
       ♥ K Q 5 4
       ♦ A 5
       ♣ A K Q 8 5 2

An alternative meaning for this sequence is to show a hand with a long minor, probably seven cards, and exactly three cards in partner's major.

Sequence (b) has no natural meaning, but some partnerships use it as a KICKBACK or BLACKWOOD substitute although a freak hand with 5-6 or 5-7 distribution is barely possible.

(p) Double jump shift rebid:

West	East
1♣	1♥
3♠ or 4♦	

This is a SPLINTER for nearly all modern partnerships. In an earlier era it might have been a Culbertson Asking Bid.

For other uses of these jump rebids, see ASKING BID, FRAGMENT BID, SPLINTER BID, VOID-SHOWING BID.

(2) After a TWO-OVER-ONE RESPONSE.

(q) 2NT rebid. For example, 1♥-2♣-2NT. There are two schools among standard players. One school treats the bid as forcing, showing 15-17 points or whatever the opening 1NT range may be; players who adopt this treatment tend to avoid a 1NT opening with a five-card major – very common in France. The other school is willing to rebid 2NT on a minimum balanced hand. In Roth-Stone (13-16) and Kaplan-Sheinwold (15-17), the bid is forcing.

(r) Rebid in first suit. For example, 1♠-2♦-2♠. This shows a minimum opening bid with 10-14 or possibly 15 high-card points (no limit if playing two-over-one game force). The suit will usually be a six-carder, but occasionally may be a good five-card suit. The chance of a five-card suit is greatest when the response is in the suit ranking immediately below opener's: 1♠-2♥-2♠, 1♥-2♦-2♥ or 1♦-2♣-2♦. The sequence 1♠-2♣-2♠ suggests a six-card suit, since if opener had only five spades, he would often find a more descriptive rebid.

Many players would avoid rebidding a weak five-card suit that would play badly opposite a singleton.

       ♠ J 6 4 3 2
       ♥ A 5
       ♦ A Q 6
       ♣ Q 4 2

If the response to 1♠ is 2♣, some experts would rebid 2NT or raise to 3♣ if those actions promised no extra strength (see (s) below). Otherwise, the choice lies between 2♦, which may do no harm, and 2♠.

If the response to 1♠ is 2♥, 2NT is the best rebid if style permits; otherwise, opener must repeat the bad spades or support hearts on the doubleton.

The quality of the suit is more important in a traditional style, since the bidding may die short of game. In

the modern style, the partnership is committed to continue, normally to at least game.

(s) Rebid in a lower-ranking suit. For example, 1♠-2♣-2♦. Although in standard this sequence does not promise a strong hand (opener may have 5-5 with 11 high-card points), neither does it deny extra strength. Hence, responder, having bid at the two level, cannot pass even if the response were not game forcing. A 2♦ rebid after a 2♣ response might occasionally be made with a strong tripleton.

(t) Single raise in responder's suit. For example, 1♥-2♦-3♦. There are three schools of thought. (1) Ambiguous, may or may not have extra values. This applies if two-over-one is game-forcing, but FAST ARRIVAL may affect 1♠-2♥-3♥. (2) Extra values, in traditional standard. Opener will often have to rebid his suit with a minimum. (3) Minimum values, in modern standard.

(u) Reverse at the two level. For example, 1♥-2♣-2♠. All players would regard the sequence as game-forcing. The first suit is strongly suggested to be longer than the second; 5-4 is the expected distribution, with 6-4 or 6-5 possible. Players who raise a two-level response with a minimum may temporize with a reverse in a three-card suit if one is available:

♠ A Q 4
♥ A K 7 5 2
♦ 7 3
♣ K J 3

After 1♥-2♣, a 2♠ rebid is best if a raise to 3♣ would be non-forcing, as it is in Acol.

(v) Second suit at the three level (sometimes called a "high reverse"). For example, 1♥-2♦-3♣. This sequence is game forcing in all methods and game-forcing in most. The distribution is usually 5-5 or 5-4; 5-5 may be less likely if the suits are spades and clubs, since some players would open 1♣. Opener's second suit may be a three-carder:

♠ 5 4
♥ A Q 8 5 2
♦ A J 5
♣ A K 4

After 1♥-2♦, 3♣ would be the expert choice, but only if a raise to 3♦ is non-forcing.

(w) Jump shift to three level. For example, 1♠-2♣-3♦. Game forcing and suggests 5-5 distribution. By partnership agreement this can be a splinter.

(x) Jump rebid in opener's suit. For example, 1♠-2♦-3♠. This is game-forcing in all methods and shows a good six- or seven-card suit with extra high-card strength.

(y) Jump to game in opener's suit. For example, 1♠-2♦-4♠. This shows a strong six-card or longer suit with the values for game, but no interest in a notrump contract. The bid also suggests a hand without controls in the unbid suits; hence, unsuitable for slam. After 1♠-2♦, a typical hand would be:

♠ A K Q 10 5 4 2
♥ J 7
♦ 7
♣ K 6 4

In Acol, the bid implies a moderate fit for responder's suit because of the failure to open with a two-bid.

(z) Jump raise in responder's suit. This is game forcing of course — for example, 1♠-2♦-4♦ — with four-card support. The bid is non-forcing by definition in Acol, but some pairs play it as forcing. 1♠-2♥-4♥ is

a special case; it shows a hand only slightly too good for 3♥ (according to style), but with strong heart support. Some play it as principle of fast arrival if 3♥ is game forcing.

(aa) 3NT rebid. For example, 1♠-2♦-3NT. Equivalent to a 2NT rebid after a one-level response; therefore, 19-20 points. Some experts would make this bid, however, with 18 points or even 17. In a style where a two-over-one response forces to game, the bid may even suggest no extra strength. Another option is to play it as 15-17 with 2NT game forcing and either 12-14 or 18-19.

(ab) Double jump shift. For example, 1♠-2♣-4♦. If 3♦ is a splinter, then 4♦ should be a splinter based on a void rather than a singleton. See GOLDEN RULE.

OPENING BID. The first call in the auction other than a pass. The treatment of opening bids is discussed in the following separate articles: ACOL TWO-BID; BENJAMIN; BIDDABLE SUITS; BIG CLUB; BLUE TEAM TWO DIAMONDS; BORDERLINE OPENING BIDS; CANAPE; CHOICE OF SUIT; DYNAMIC NOTRUMP; FIVE-CARD MAJORS; FIVE OF A MAJOR OPENING; FIVE NOTRUMP OPENING; FLANNERY TWO DIAMONDS; FLANNERY TWO HEARTS; FORCING TWO-BID; FOUR-CARD MAJORS; FOUR NOTRUMP OPENING; GAMBLING THREE NOTRUMP; KAMIKAZE NOTRUMP; MEXICAN TWO DIAMONDS; MULTI TWO DIAMONDS; NAMYATS; ONE NOTRUMP OPENING; OPENING SUIT BID; ORANGE CLUB; PREEMPTIVE BID; REVERSE FLANNERY; ROMAN TWO DIAMONDS; ROMEX TWO DIAMONDS; RUBIN TRANSFERS; SHORT DIAMOND; SIX OF A SUIT OPENING; SIX NOTRUMP OPENING; THREE NOTRUMP OPENING; TRANSFER OPENING PREEMPTS; TWO CLUBS STRONG ARTIFICIAL; TWO NOTRUMP OPENING; TWO NOTRUMP OPENING FOR MINORS; TWO UNDER TRANSFER PREEMPTS; TWO-WAY TWO-BIDS; WALPURGIS DIAMOND; WEAK TWO-BID.

OPENING BIDDER. The player at a deal of contract who makes the first bid of an auction.

OPENING LEAD. After the bidding has been concluded, the play of the hand commences by the declarer's left-hand opponent making an original or opening lead.

Defense is regarded as the most difficult aspect of bridge. Since the opening lead is the only defensive play made while the dummy is concealed, it requires a kind of detective reasoning and considerable analysis of the meaning of every call in the auction, as well as agreed conventional leads. The opening lead is frequently the source of substantial profits and losses.

Choosing the Card

The card chosen for the opening lead should help pave the way for the defeat of the contract, insofar as this is possible, and should convey information to partner about the leader's holding in the suit. Some typical card choices, once the suit has been selected, are summarized in the accompanying table.

The standard approach has a substantial number of critics, and one important controversy concerns the lead from a sequence of honors. With holdings like A-K-Q, K-Q-J, or Q-J-10, any of the honors can be led with equal

trick-taking effect. The main concern is to inform partner about the opening leader's holding. The customary practice is to lead the king from A-K (unless it is doubleton, in which case the ace is led) and the top card from any other honor SEQUENCE. Similarly, the standard lead from holdings such as K-10-9-8 or Q-10-9-8 is the 10, the top of the INTERIOR SEQUENCE. However, standard leads create potentially costly confusion in certain instances. For example, the king is led from both A-K-4 and K-Q-4, so partner may have difficulty deciding whether to signal encouragement with J-8-2; and the 10 is led from both K-10-9-8 and 10-9-8-2, so partner may have difficulty deciding whether to return the suit when he gains the lead. Therefore, conventional nonstandard opening lead methods have become increasingly popular among experts, including ACE FROM ACE-KING; JOURNALIST LEADS; RUSINOW LEADS; and ZERO OR TWO HIGHER LEADS.

A second controversy has to do with the lead from three small cards against a suit contract. The top card is traditional, but all three possibilities have been recommended. See MUD, and THREE SMALL CARDS, LEAD FROM.

A third controversy concerns the standard fourth-best lead from a long suit. Against suit contracts, an increasing number of experts prefer to give count more accurately by leading the third-highest card from an even number, and the lowest card from an odd number. Against notrump contracts, some use a low spot card lead to encourage the return of the suit and lead a high spot card to discourage a return; others object to this because the leader's partner can no longer use the RULE OF ELEVEN. These modifications are an integral part of JOURNALIST LEADS.

Choosing the Suit

Clues from the bidding. Regardless of the carding method that is used, no table or convention can indicate the right suit to lead; judgment and deduction must be applied to each situation. In particular, the auction can provide the astute opening leader with valuable clues:

(1) If the opponents are strong in certain suits, the opening leader should look elsewhere for his selection.

(2) If the opponents are weak in a particular suit, the opening leader should attack it. See ATTACKING LEAD.

(3) If one opponent is likely to be void in a certain suit (as when he bids two suits several times and supports a third suit), the opening leader should not lead that ace if the enemy ends up in a suit contract.

(4) If dummy holds a long and strong side suit that will provide numerous discards (as when he has rebid it several times), the opening leader should be aggressive and try to take tricks in a hurry.

(5) If the opponents have staggered into their contract with little strength to spare, the opening leader should be cautious and avoid giving away the fulfilling trick.

(6) If the opponents have strength to spare, (at rubber bridge or IMPs) an aggressive lead has little to lose save an unimportant overtrick.

(7) If partner has indicated a good suit to attack by bidding it (see LEAD-DIRECTING BID), it is usually safe to lead it.

(8) If partner has denied length and strength in a suit by refusing to make a cheap one-level overcall when given the opportunity, the opening leader should not try to hit him in that suit.

(9) If partner has indicated general high-card strength by making a takeout double, it is relatively safe to lead away from an unsupported honor.

(10) If partner has denied general high-card strength by making a preemptive bid, it is not advisable to lead away from an unsupported honor.

(11) If partner has requested the lead of a specific suit by making a LEAD-DIRECTING DOUBLE or LIGHTNER DOUBLE, it is usually advisable to lead it.

Clues from the strength of the opening leader's hand. If the opponents bid game and the opening leader has 13 or 14 high-card points, he should visualize the near-yarborough in partner's hand and reject any lead that requires substantial high-card help (such as the lead from an unsupported honor). When the opening leader's strength is mediocre, however, it is reasonable to expect some useful aid from partner. The location of the opening leader's strength is also important. If he holds finessable positions such as K-3-2 in front of suits bid by dummy, or a few small cards behind suits bid by declarer, the defenders are likely to be in trouble. Declarer's finesses rate to win, and the suits appear to be breaking well for the opponents. Holding length and weakness in dummy's long suit is also a bad sign, for declarer will probably be able to establish it with little difficulty. In such cases, an aggressive opening lead is often justified. But if the opening leader holds strength behind declarer's bid suits, and if he can see that important suits will be breaking badly for the enemy, a more conservative strategy is preferable.

Clues from the strength of the opening leader's suit. Other things being equal, it is frequently desirable to lead from stronger suits. Leading from Q-10-4-3 is preferable to Q-4-3-2 because less help is needed from partner to build tricks (and avoid a disaster), while Q-J-10-9 is superior to both holdings. However, as the preceding sections indicate, other things are often not equal; and many opening leaders go wrong by using the strength of one suit as their sole guide while ignoring valuable information available from other sources. See FOURTH HIGHEST, RULE OF TWELVE, THIRD AND FIFTH, THIRD HIGHEST, ZERO OR TWO HIGHER LEADS.

Leads against notrump contracts

Since declarer cannot ruff when he runs out of a suit, the defenders should usually try to establish length winners. Assuming that the bidding has not indicated the need for special action, the following guidelines apply:

(1) A five-card or longer holding in an unbid suit is usually an excellent choice, provided that the opening leader has at least one probable entry. For example, leading from A-Q-6-3-2 is ideal; even if declarer gets an undeserved trick with the king, three or four winners are likely to be established while the high cards are retained for use as entries.

(2) From a completely entryless hand, the opening leader should reject his own (weak) long suit and try to build length winners in partner's hand. An unbid major suit containing three cards or a strong doubleton is likely to be a good choice.

(3) From holdings such as J-10-9-x-x, Q-J-10-x-x, K-J-10-x-x, or A-J-10-x-x in a suit bid by the enemy, the fourth-best card may well be led. This avoids blocking the suit when partner has a useful doubleton, and is likely to tempt declarer into a fatal error in situations such as:

```
                    Q 2
      J 10 9 4 3              K 5
                   A 8 7 6
```

After the jack lead, South has two stoppers by covering. If a lower card is led instead, South inevitably plays dummy's queen.

(4) If no five-card or longer suit is held, a solid or nearly solid four-carder (such as Q-J-10-9 or J-10-9-3) is likely to build some winners without giving anything away.

(5) Leading from broken four-card suits is less desirable. Attacking from Q-10-4-2 in an unbid suit is not unreasonable, since the lead has a good chance to pay off if partner has even one of the missing honors. However, a suit like A-Q-3-2 should be avoided because the potential for length winners is too limited to justify giving declarer an undeserved trick.

(6) Against 3NT, leading an honor from A-K-2 in an unbid suit can be every effective (especially at rubber bridge or IMPs). Partner may turn up with five to the queen, or with five small cards and a side entry. Even the lead of an honor from A-Q-2 has at times paid similar dividends.

(7) If no attractive lead exists, a PASSIVE LEAD (as from three or four small cards) has the advantage of being relatively safe. Even the lead of a small doubleton may be advantageous (see SHORT-SUIT LEADS).

(8) In some instances, the opening leader may gain by disguising the length of his long suit. See FALSE-CARDING.

(9) After a 2NT opening bid, a passive lead gains more frequently. Declarer's hand contains most of his side's strength, so he may have entry problems if left to his own devices, and leading an honor from Q-J-x-x may be attractive.

(10) Against notrump partials, a passive lead gains more frequently. The strength is more evenly divided between the two sides, so the defenders are less likely to have to collect tricks in a hurry.

(11) After a GAMBLING 3NT opening bid has been passed out, it is desirable to lead an ace. Declarer is trying to score nine fast tricks with the aid of a solid minor suit, so losing the lead even once may be fatal. See LIGHTNER DOUBLE. The same logic applies to auctions where declarer has preempted.

Leads against suit contracts

Here the defenders are less likely to gain by trying to build length winners, since declarer can simply ruff when he runs out of a suit. Assuming that the bidding has not indicated the need for special action, the following guidelines apply:

(1) Leading from solid or nearly solid honor sequences, such as A-K-J-5, K-Q-J-7-3, Q-J-10-2, or J-10-9-5, is likely to be both constructive and safe. Leading from weaker honor holdings like K-Q-7-3 or Q-J-9-2 can also be effective, but may cost a trick when partner is weak in the suit.

(2) Leads from long suits are safer but less likely to establish several tricks, while leads from short side suits are riskier but more likely to establish several tricks. If the defenders must rush to collect their winners (as when dummy's bidding shows a long side suit that will provide numerous discards), it is better to lead from Q-7-5 in an unbid suit than from Q-8-6-5. When safety considerations are more important, however, leading from length is preferable.

(3) When holding four or more trumps, it is particularly desirable to lead from a long suit. If declarer can be forced to ruff several times, his trumps may run out before the defenders' do and cause him to lose control of the hand. See FORCING LEADS.

(4) When no attractive lead exists, a PASSIVE LEAD (as from three or four small cards) has the advantage of being relatively safe.

(5) A trump lead is desirable in several situations: when the bidding indicates that declarer will try to ruff losers in dummy or crossruff; when the defenders hold substantial strength in all side suits, as when the opponents sacrifice against a contract that the defenders expected to make on power; when a one-level contract is passed out; and when a passive lead is indicated and the opening leader holds a few small trumps. A trump lead is mandatory when a one-level takeout double is passed out. However, a trump lead should be avoided when the opening leader's holding is too precarious to lead from; when the bidding indicates that the defenders must take their tricks in a hurry; when the opening leader is very long in a suit declarer plans to ruff in dummy, indicating that partner will be able to overruff; when the opening leader has a singleton trump; and when the opening leader has four or more trumps, in which case the forcing game is preferable. See TRUMP LEADS.

(6) A side-suit singleton is likely to be effective when the opening leader has some extra low trumps to use for ruffing and a probable entry in trumps, so long as the leader's partner rates to have an entry or two. However, singleton leads should usually be avoided when the opening leader has no excess low trumps to ruff with (as when holding A-Q or Q-J-3); when he has four or more trumps, in which case the forcing game may be preferable; or when the singleton is a king or queen.

(7) Side-suit doubletons are considerably less likely to produce ruffs than are singletons, and should be led for this purpose only when holding a quick entry *in trumps*. However, a small doubleton may be a satisfactory passive lead, however. In some infrequent cases, leading from K-2 or Q-2 may be justified because the opening leader is truly desperate. See DESPERATION LEAD OR PLAY.

(8) With an otherwise worthless hand, leading the king or queen from K-x-x-x-(x) or Q-x-x-x-(x) in partner's bid suit can be effective. If the king holds the trick, the opening leader may now be able to make a profitable attack through dummy in a different suit; while if the opening lead is the normal small card and declarer has a singleton, no further leads through dummy will be possible.

(9) Underleading an ace is normally avoided, but can be a winning choice. The defenders may need tricks in a hurry, and declarer may also be missing the queen and misguess; or it may be urgent to put partner on lead for an attack through declarer's hand or to obtain a ruff. See UNDERLEAD.

Leads against slam contracts

If the opponents reach a small slam and the opening leader holds K-Q and an ace, it is obvious that the king should be led. However, fate usually does not conspire to deal all the defenders' high cards to the opening leader, so he often has to decide whether to lead away from an unsupported king or queen in an unbid suit. Fortunately, slam contracts often involve considerable amounts of bidding, which offer more clues to the opening leader.

OPENING LEADS: SOME TYPICAL CARD
CHOICES ONCE THE SUIT HAS BEEN SELECTED

(In general this table has been set up based on the basic opening lead policy of fourth-best from a holding of four or more cards in a suit. Many tournament players today have switched to leading third and fifth-best. This means that on those leads listed below where a lead is from fourth best in a four-card suit, the third-and-fifth player should lead third best instead of fourth if the usual lead would have been fourth best — otherwise there will be partnership confusion. When the suit chosen for the opening lead is at least five cards long, the lead from a third-and-fifth player should be the fifth best if ordinarily the lead would have been the fourth best.)

Suit Length	Holding in Suit	Lead vs. NT	Lead vs. Suits
Two Cards	Any non-trump doubleton	Top Card	Top Card
	Trumps: honor sequence or ace-any	—	Top Card[1]
	Trumps: any other doubleton	—	Low Card[16]
Three Cards	9-8-7 or worse, not in trumps	Top Card	Low Card[2]
	Trumps: three small	—	2nd best[3]
	10-x-x, J-x-x, Q-x-x, K-x-x	3rd Best	3rd Best
	Q-10-x, K-10-x, K-J-x	3rd Best[4]	3rd Best
	10-9-x, J-10-x, Q-J-x, K-Q-x	Top Card	Top Card
	Trumps: J-10-x	—	3rd Best
	A-x-x, A-10-x	3rd Best[5]	Ace
	A-J-x, A-Q-x	2nd Best[6]	Ace
	A-K-x or better	King	King[17]
Four Cards	9-8-7-6 or worse	4th Best[7]	Top Card
	10-x-x-x, J-x-x-x, Q-x-x-x, K-x-x-x	4th Best	4th Best
	10-9-x-x, J-10-x-x, Q-J-x-x	4th Best	4th best[8]
	Q 10-x-x, K-10-x-x, K-J-x-x	4th Best	4th Best
	Q-10-9-x, J-9-8-x, K-J-10-x	2nd Best	2nd Best
	A-10-9-x, A-J-10-x	2nd Best	Ace[15]
	10-9-7-x, J-10-8-x, Q-J-9-x, K-Q-10-x	Top Card	Top Card
	10-9-8-x, J-10-9-x, Q-J-10-x, K-Q-J-x	Top Card	Top Card
	A-x-x-x, A-10-x-x, A-J-x-x, A-Q-J-x	4th Best	Ace
	K-Q-x-x, K-Q-9-x, A-K-x-x, A-K-10-x	4th Best	King
	K-Q-10-x, A-K-10-9, A-K-J-x, or better	King	King
Five Cards[14]	10-9-7-x-x, 10-9-8-x-x, J-10-8-x-x	4th Best	
	10-9-7-6-x, 10-9-8-6-x, 10-9-8-7-x	Top Card	
	J-10-8-7-x, J-10-9-7-x, J-10-9-8-x	Top Card	
	Q-J-9-x-x, K-Q-9-x-x	4th Best	
	J-10-9-x-x, Q-J-10-x-x, K-Q-10-x-x, K-Q-J-x-x	Top Card or 4th Best[9]	
	Q-J-9-8-x, K-Q-10-9-x	2nd Best[10]	
	Q-J-10-8-x, Q-J-10-9-x, K-Q-J-9-x, K-Q-J-10-x	Top Card	
	Q-10-9-x-x, K-10-9-x-x, A-10-9-x-x	4th Best	
	Q-10-9-7-x, Q-10-9-8-x, K-10-9-7-x, K-10-9-8-x	2nd Best	
	A-10-9-7-x, A-10-9-8-x	2nd Best	
	K-J-10-x-x, A-J-10-x-x	2nd Best or 4th Best[11]	
	K-J-10-8-x, K-J-10-9-x, A-J-10-8-x, A-J-10-9-x	Jack or Ace	
	A-K-10-9-x	King or Ten[12]	
	A-K-J-x-x	King or 4th Best[12]	
	A-K-J-10-x	Ace[13]	

[1] An old chestnut is to lead the jack from Q-J or the nine from 10-9, hoping to induce declarer to misguess on the next round. However, this is unlikely to be necessary against a declarer familiar with RESTRICTED CHOICE.
[2] High and middle are also popular. See THREE SMALL CARDS, LEAD FROM.
[3] Followed by the smallest, thus denying a doubleton.
[4] In some cases, the jack from K-J-x is best in order to unblock.
[5] The ace is preferable if partner does not figure to have a side entry.
[6] The ace is correct is some cases.
[7] The top card or second best may be led to deny an honor; see text above.
[8] The queen from Q-J-x-x is correct in some cases.
[9] Fourth best is preferable when the goal is to establish the whole suit, rather than play safe, and when an opponent is likely to have four cards in the suit.
[10] Partner is expected to play the immediately lower honor if he has it.
[11] King from K-J-10-9-x-x is correct in some cases.
[12] The king is preferable when a sure side entry is held.
[13] Partner is expected to play an honor if he has one, and to signal his count (high-low for even, low-high for odd) if he does not.
[14] The rules for four card suits are frequently correct against suit contracts. Against notrump contracts, however, the degree of solidity of an honor sequence is particularly important.
[15] In general, leading from this holding is not recommended.
[16] There may be suit preference implications.
[17] Depends on type of ace-king leads being used.

Normally, the following guidelines apply:

(1) Against a small slam, an attacking lead is preferable when dummy's bidding indicates a long, establishable suit. A PASSIVE LEAD is more appropriate if both declarer and dummy appear to have balanced hands, whether or not the contract is at notrump.

(2) Against suit small slams, an ace lead is desirable if it is in an unbid suit and the opening leader holds a probable second winner elsewhere, or if the bidding suggests that the opponents might be off two fast tricks. Otherwise the ace lead is more debatable, and should normally be avoided if it is in a suit bid by the enemy.

(3) Against suit small slams, singleton leads are often effective. However, they should be avoided if both opponents have bid the suit, in which case the lead may help them overcome a bad break, or if the opening leader has a sure winner (or a relatively strong hand), in which case the slam will be defeated anyway if partner can take a trick.

(4) Against suit small slams, a trump lead is dangerous; it may pick up partner's queen and save declarer a crucial guess. However, a trump lead may work well if:

(a) the bidding plus the leader's holding indicates that partner has at most a singleton.

(b) the auction strongly suggests that declarer plans to do a great deal of ruffing in one or both hands.

(c) the trump holding is safe to lead from.

(5) Against a grand slam, without an immediate winner to cash, it is usually desirable to make a safe lead. Only one trick is needed to defeat the contract, so building winners unnecessary. Trump leads are frequently desirable against suit grand slams, but should be avoided if partner may have the queen of trumps and a safe selection is available elsewhere.

Board-a-match and matchpoint considerations

At board-a-match scoring, the opening leader must be careful to avoid losing a board that his teammates at the other table have all but won. At matchpoints, there are conflicting considerations. Notrump contracts based on shaky stoppers are more common at this form of scoring, so the opening leader is more likely to gain by trying to run a long suit. Yet conceding even one undeserved trick can result in a bottom score, so care must be taken to avoid presenting declarer with a gift that his counterparts at other tables will not receive. Thus an unusual attempt to defeat a contract, correct at rubber bridge or IMPs, may be wrong at matchpoints because it is too likely to concede the overtrick. See MATCHPOINT DEFENSE. Opening leads at matchpoints are a source of considerable complexity (and headaches). See also JOURNALIST LEADS, RUSINOW LEADS, STRONG KINGS AND TENS, THIRD AND FIFTH.

OPENING ONE NOTRUMP BID. See ONE NOTRUMP OPENING.

OPENING SUIT BID. An opening of 1♣, 1♦, 1♥, or 1♠ has a normal range of 10-20 high-card points. It may sink below 10 in some freak cases — with 6-6 distribution, for example. It may rise above 20 with unbalanced hands, usually 4-4-4-1 or 5-4-3-1 patterns, unsuited to a 2NT opening and not quite strong enough for a forcing opening. For special factors affecting the opening bid, see BIDDABLE SUITS; BORDERLINE OPENING BIDS; CHOICE OF SUIT.

OPPONENT. A member of the adverse team at bridge. An opponent can be a member of an opposing team of two, four, five or six as well as merely a temporary adversary.

OPPONENT'S SUIT. A suit held or bid by one or both adversaries. In judging the bidding, a holding of three small cards in the opponent's suit is generally a danger signal. But if the opponent's suit is bid and supported, a small tripleton may actually be better than a small doubleton because the chance of finding partner with shortages is increased. For bids in the opponent's suit, see CUEBIDS IN OPPONENT'S SUIT.

OPPOSITION. (1) The opponents on a hand, set of hands or rubber; (2) The contestants in DIRECT COMPETITION; (3) The balance of the field; (4) The other team in a head-on team event.

OPTIMUM STRATEGY. Plans of play adopted by declarer or defender in the light of different tactics which may be adopted by the opposing side. The following, from Jean Besse, is one example of the complications which can arise in considering alternative strategies:

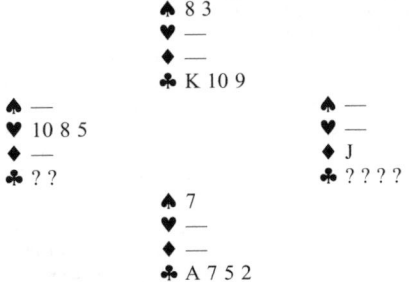

Spades are trumps. East has the lead. Further conditions are that West is marked with three hearts and East with the ♦ J. Declarer knows, therefore, that the critical club suit is divided 2-4, but he doesn't know where the Q and J are. Clubs are therefore designated with question marks on the diagram. Lest he give a ruff and discard, East must obviously lead a club, and, of course, declarer's aim is to make all the tricks. The problem is to analyze the optimum strategy both from declarer's and (more importantly) defender's point of view. The defender's clubs may break:

(1) x-x - Q-J-x-x .... 6 cases

(2) Q-x - J-x-x-x

or

J-x - Q-x-x-x ....8 cases

(3) Q-J - x-x-x-x .... 1 case

TOTAL .... 15 cases

Let us examine East's possible tactics.

(a) The "naive" tactic. East is a weak player. He leads queen or jack in (1). He leads small in (2) and, perforce, in (3). Against such an opponent it is clear that South will lose only in (3). He will win 14 times out of 15.

(b) The "expert" tactic. East is a good player. He leads queen or jack whenever he has one (or both) of these cards.

Now declarer has to reverse his play. As (2) is more likely than (1), South should play for divided honors, i.e., cash the ace in hand and drop West's other honor next. So, South wins in (2) (8 cases) but loses in (1) (6 cases).

Declarer, however, takes a little revenge in case (3) as Terence Reese points out in his *Expert Game*. For South

can easily divine case (3) from the very fact that East had led a small card (having no alternative). So South wins also in case (3) hence, in 9 cases out of 15.

To prevent this, East may lead sometimes small and sometimes high in case (2). Say 50% each. Which leads to:

(c) The shrewd tactic. East always leads an honor in (1), always small in (3), but in case (2) he leads half the time high and the rest small. Against this tactic, South does better to revert to his behavior against tactic (a), playing East for both honors whenever he leads high, and only then.

South thus wins the 6 cases from (1) and 4 of the 8 cases from (2), thus, on balance, 10 cases out of 15.

This shrewd tactic is therefore no improvement, but we may now figure out the correct optimum strategy as follows:

(d) The optimum strategy. East leads, of course, always an honor in (1), but in case (2) he leads exactly, but "at random", a small card $12^{1}/_{2}$% of the time, i.e., once out of 8 times.

It is clear that declarer now has to play for split honors whenever East leads high (7 cases against 6). But if East leads small, declarer may:

(i) play for split honors. He will win in $0 + (7 + 1) + 0 = 8$ cases (out of 15).

(ii) play for Q-J with West. He will win in $0 + (7 + 0) + 1 = 8$ cases (out of 15).

Thus according to whether the opponent's strategy is naive, expert, shrewd, or optimum, the declarer wins a trick in 14, 9, 10, or 8 cases out of 15. And he has no way to improve on those chances. See PERCENTAGE PLAY.

OPTIONAL. A term applied to a bid, play or point of law in which a player may have two or more choices; as distinguished from compulsory action or procedure strictly regulated by law.

OPTIONAL DOUBLE. A COOPERATIVE DOUBLE. shows a balanced hand with enough high cards to defeat the contract in all probability, and with support for any unbid suit, usually used against high-level contracts (at least the three-level). The partner of the doubler need not have a substantial trump holding in order to pass; he is expected to pass unless he has a good suit and unbalanced distribution. For example, the following hand would be appropriate for an optional double of a 3 ♥ opening preempt:

           ♠ A K 7
           ♥ A J 2
           ♦ 7 4 3
           ♣ A Q 6 5

Very few experts use the cooperative double. 3NT would be the normal choice with this hand. See also DEFENSE TO OPENING THREE-BID; PENALTY DOUBLE; TAKEOUT DOUBLE.

OPTIONS. (1) Alternative actions available to a player in certain circumstances after an irregularity by the opposing side. An opening lead by the wrong defender is a case in which the declarer has five options. (See LAWS, Laws 53 and 54). (2) Alternative play possibilities available to a declarer. He should usually adopt a sequence of play which will "preserve options." A play which retains the possibility of trying for other possibilities is usually

better than one which stands or falls on immediate success, even if the second is a better percentage chance. Such a play is known as an echelon play.

ORANGE CLUB. Strong club system used by James Jacoby and Bobby Wolff in the 1970, 1971 and 1972 World Championships, and subsequently by Wolff with Bob Hamman. The 1 ♣ opening promises 17 or more points; responses show controls. Other opening bids are limited and natural according to the CANAPÉ principle. A 1NT opening shows a balanced hand with 13-15 points with a 4- or 5-card club suit or 15-17 with any balanced distribution.

Other features include BLUE TEAM 2 ♦, FLANNERY 2 ♥, weak two-bid in spades only; singleton- and void-showing forcing raises by a passed hand.

ORIGINAL BID. The first bid made in an auction.

ORIGINAL HOLDING. The cards one has in a given suit at the beginning of play or at the beginning of the auction.

ORIGINAL LEAD. See OPENING LEAD.

OUR HAND. A colloquial expression indicating that a player thinks his side can make the highest positive score on a deal in which both sides take part in the auction. See BELONG.

OUT. A player who is a member of a table at rubber bridge, but not actively participating. The order in which players are out is established by cutting, the holder(s) of the lowest card or cards cut sitting out for the first rubber or chukker, other players going out in order.

OUT-OF-THE-BLUE CUEBID. An unusual bid of a new suit which cannot be taken as a suit bid, indicating support for partner's last bid suit, strength in the cuebid suit (often first-round control), and interest in reaching a slam contract. See BLUE TEAM 4 ♣-4 ♦ CONVENTION, SPLINTER BID.

OUT OF TURN. Not in rotation. For a call out of rotation, see LAWS (Laws 30-32). For a lead out of turn, see Laws 53-56. For a play out of turn, see Law 57.

OUT ON A LIMB. A phrase used to describe a player who has taken unusual or precipitate action during an auction and is in great danger of being doubled at a contract that is both risky and untenable. During the play of a hand, one may be said to be out on a limb as respects a situation, for example, when one is "wide open" in a suit at notrump, although the opposition may not be aware of this. Alternatively going out on a limb may occur when one is playing at a trump contract and not only does not have control of the trump suit but is extremely vulnerable to attack in that area.

OVER. A term used to indicate one's position at the table in respect to one's right-hand opponent.

OVERBID. A call offering to undertake a contract for a greater number of tricks than is justified by the bidder's holding. In competitive auctions or auctions that are

likely to become competitive, an apparent overbid may be an ADVANCE SAVE. See SACRIFICE.

OVERBIDDER. A player who consistently bids higher than his high-card and distributional strength justify. Playing with an overbidder, it is clearly necessary to be conservative (but it is important not to let the overbidder find out about your strategy.

OVERBOARD. The state of being (much) too high in a given auction. See SAFETY LEVEL.

OVERCALL. In a broad sense, the term overcall refers to any bid by either partner after an opponent has opened the bidding. The following discussion is limited to non-jump direct overcalls. A direct (or immediate) overcall is a bid at your turn immediately following a bid by your right-hand opponent. The expert consensus (32%) in BWS 2001 was that the following represented a minimum overcall of 1♠ over 1♣ with neither side vulnerable:

> ♠ A Q x x x
> ♥ x x x
> ♦ Q x x x
> ♣ x

One minority (29%) required the ♦ K instead of the ♦ Q, and another minority (24%) would have accepted the ♦ J instead of the ♦ Q.

As many as 10 factors may influence a player's decision to overcall. In roughly descending order of importance, they are:

(1) *Suit length.* An overcall is nearly always based on a suit that is at least five cards long. A strong four-card suit may be sufficient if nonvulnerable at the one level, but obstruction (see [6] below) is a factor. A seven-card or longer suit will often qualify for action at a higher level. A vulnerable overcall at the two level is more likely to be based on a six-card suit. Even non-vulnerable at the two level, a five-card suit would be the exception, not the rule.

(2) *Strength.* An average overcall is perhaps equivalent to a minimum suit opening bid, with about 13 points in high cards. The maximum with a five-card suit is likely to be 18-19 points — a hand just short of the strength required to double and then bid the suit.

Not vulnerable at the one level, a normal minimum is an ace less than an opening bid. Even less strength is possible under some circumstances: if the overcaller passed earlier, he may overcall with little more than a good suit to direct a lead; if the opponents are vulnerable, the overcaller may bid spades on a weakish hand with good distribution, visualizing a 4♠ save against 4♥.

Some successful players practice an aggressive style of light overcalls; this style has advantages and drawbacks. In some circumstances, however — when vulnerable or at the two level — overcaller's partner can assume that overcaller has a sound hand. The BWS consensus (41%) was that overcalls should be "moderate" in strength. A substantial minority (23%) favored "light".

(3) *Vulnerability.* A nonvulnerable bidder can afford to take more risk than a vulnerable player with a marginally sound hand (or a truly "unsound" one). The opponents will be less eager to double for penalties, and when they do so, they may have a poor bargain. This is particularly true at the partscore level with matchpoint scoring. For example, at matchpoint duplicate two down not vulner-able and undoubled is a frequent source of profit compared to partscores of 110 or more in the other direction.

The BWS consensus was that an overcall should be affected by the vulnerability slightly (44%) or moderately (42%).

(4) *Level.* One-level overcalls are safer than two-level overcalls, which are easier to double for penalty. The expert consensus (69%) was that an overcall should be affected by the level by one degree. That is, a player who makes moderate overcalls at the one-level should make conservative overcalls at the two-level.

(5) *Suit quality.* In close cases, the texture of the suit is a factor. Q-J-10-9-8-7 will be worth four tricks, Q-J-5-4-3-2 perhaps only two. An overcall on K-Q-10-9-5-2 can have lead- directing benefits, whereas one on Q-9-5-4-2 may be the prelude to disaster.

(6) *Obstruction.* An overcall that consumes the opponents' bidding space is attractive. 1♠ over 1♣, 2♣ over 1♦, 2♦ over 1♥, and 2♥ over 1♠ all have preemptive value. (In each case, a single raise is the only bid available to the next opponent if he has a minimum responding hand; even if NEGATIVE DOUBLES are in use, the opponent's hand may be unsuitable.) Hence, these overcalls are often based on borderline values. An overcall that consumes little space (e.g. 1♣- 1♦) should imply more strength.

(7) *Opponents' skill.* Doubtful overcalls have less to gain against strong players, who will be quick to punish an indiscretion with a penalty double and defend accurately. Experts will also use inferences from an opposing overcall to judge the bidding and play.

(8) *Holding in opponent's suit.* Experts disagree on whether length in opening bidder's suit makes an overcall desirable. Suppose East opens 1♠, neither vulnerable, and South holds:

> ♠ K 9 5 2
> ♥ K 4
> ♦ A J 9 8 3 2
> ♣ 7

The traditional view is that South's length in spades indicates a misfit deal and dictates caution. Some authorities contend, however, that South's spade length suggests possible spade shortness in North's hand and therefore diamond support; hence, South should be more willing to act. Much may depend on whether the overcaller has weak length (a drawback) or strength, which may represent additional playing strength.

(9) *Opponents' vulnerability.* An overcaller must always be sensitive to the opponent's vulnerability as well as his own. At matchpoint duplicate and favorable vulnerability, an overcaller can show a profit by saving at 4♠, down three, against 4♥. At unfavorable vulnerability, he must exercise discretion. A 2♣ overcaller of 1♠ meets disaster if he is doubled and set two. To overcall in such circumstances requires a solid six playing tricks, and even that may not be sufficient.

(10) *Opponents' methods.* Overcalls can be made slightly more freely if the opponents use NEGATIVE DOUBLES. Overcalls of 1♠ over a minor suit can be made slightly more freely against opponents who play FIVE-CARD MAJORS, since there is a chance to prevent them from finding a heart fit.

Another factor is an overcaller's position at the table:

West	North	East	South
1♣	Pass	1♠	?

After East-West open and respond, an overcall by

South has less to gain and more to lose. The opponents have already exchanged some information (West knows, for instance, that East does not have four hearts and four spades); both opponents have values; South must overcall at the two level.

Most players consider 17 high-card points, or the equivalent, the normal maximum for an overcall.

  ♠ A K Q 10 x
  ♥ A K x
  ♦ J xxx
  ♣ x

The expert consensus (34%) in BWS 2001 was that this hand overcalls 1 ♠, but should double with the ♦ Q instead of the lJ. With a balanced hand, 5-3-3-2, experts overcall with 17 points but double with 18.

Responding to overcalls.

For actions by the opening bidder's partner after an overcall, see FREE BID.

Actions by overcaller's partner come under four headings: (*The Bridge World* magazine has suggested the term "advancer" for the partner of an overcaller to avoid confusion with "responder" of the opening bidder.)

(1) *Raises.* The traditional approach is for a single raise to be mildly encouraging, a double raise to be strongly encouraging (but not forcing), and for a raise to game to be natural and strong. As we shall see later, the traditional approach no longer is the preferred method.

Consider an opening bid of 1 ♣ and a vulnerable overcall of 1 ♠. If advancer has spade support and normal distribution, he raises to 2 ♠ with 7-10 points; to 3 ♠ with 11-12; to 4 ♠ with 13-15. (If the overcall is non-vulnerable, the ranges are raised by about 2 points.) Note that three-card support is enough for any raise, and less support is possible, especially if opener's partner bids. If the bidding, with both sides vulnerable, is:

West	North	East	South
1 ♥	1 ♠	4 ♥	4 ♠

South might hold K-x in spades and considerable strength in the minor suits, although a penalty double might work out well.

A different treatment, proposed in the Sixties by Lawrence Rosler and Roger Stern, influenced modern theory. In this method, all raises of overcalls were preemptive, and cuebids in the opponent's suit were constructive raises at the appropriate level. After 1 ♣-1 ♠, responses of 2 ♣, 3 ♣ and 4 ♣ were sound raises to 2 ♠, 3 ♠ and 4 ♠ respectively.

West	North	East	South
1 ♦	1 ♠	2 ♥	?

South would jump to 3 ♠ on:

  ♠ Q 9 7 4
  ♥ 4
  ♦ 8 5 3
  ♣ K 10 8 5 2

and directly to 4 ♠ on:

  ♠ Q 9 6 5 4
  ♥ 6 5
  ♦ 4
  ♣ A 10 8 4 2

North can hold many other hands that can produce game. Even if 4 ♠ does not make, it may be a fine save against the opponents' possible game.

The modern view of an overcall as a constructive action (as opposed to an obstructive or lead-directing action) has led most pairs to adopt methods that offer greater accuracy after an overcall. Many modern pairs retain preemptive raises, but use a cuebid to start the description of any hand with game interest. In this method, a cuebid is the only forcing response. A strong advancer must therefore be careful to avoid another response, since overcaller may pass. The advancer can clarify with his next bid whether he has a limit raise, a strong raise or perhaps a good suit of his own. (A bid of a new suit after the cuebid is forcing for one round, possibly to game. Such a bid is sometimes used to show an unspecified singleton.)

A jump cuebid (1 ♦ -1 ♠-Pass-3 ♦) is generally used to show a limit raise in overcaller's suit, usually with a singleton somewhere in the hand, or a mixed raise. This leaves the simple cuebid as a general-direction bid seeking further information. However, there is a strong trend toward the mixed raise. See CUEBID IN OPPONENT'S SUIT.After a cuebid, the bidding may end at the two-level if rhe overcaller rebids his suit, or if he bids two of a lower-ranking suit and receives preference. Other rebids by overcaller suggest extra strength and will normally lead to game.

West	North	East	South
1 ♦	1 ♠	Pass	?

South should cuebid 2 ♦ on:

  ♠ J 6 5
  ♥ K 8 4
  ♦ 5 3
  ♣ A K 8 4 2

South has a good offensive hand, but much depends on the strength of North's overcall. If North rebids 2 ♠, chances for game decline and South probably should pass.

(2) *Suit takeouts.* Partnerships should agree whether the suit takeout is constructive, meaning game is possible, or discouraging, meaning game is unlikely.

West	North	East	South
			1 ♣
1 ♥	Pass	1 ♠	

In traditional methods, East has a spade suit (a good five-carder at worst) and is unlikely to have great heart support. East expects West to pass, although game may still be reached if West has spade support. If East had bid 2 ♦, he would suggest a stronger hand.

Since the necessity to cuebid with a strong hand before showing a long suit is uneconomical, many pairs use a new-suit response by an unpassed hand as forcing. Some pairs differentiate between new-suit responses after overcalls at the one level and at the two level; they consider only two-level responses as forcing because a two-level overcall is usually equivalent to an opening bid.

The meaning of a jump shift is also a matter of partnership agreement. It may be forcing to game, forcing for one round, strongly encouraging or preemptive. A popular treatment is the fit-showing jump:

West	North	East	South
1 ♣	1 ♠	Pass	3 ♦

South promises a spade fit with diamond length and strength. This information may help North make an accurate competitive decision if East-West sacrifice against 4 ♠.

(3) *Notrump responses.* These are constructive, but vary in strength with the level and vulnerability of the overcall. After a one-level overcall, the following ranges may apply:

	Not Vulnerable	Vulnerable
1NT	9-11	8-10
2NT	12-14	11-12
3NT	15-16	13-16

The 2NT ranges are reduced somewhat after a two-level overcall.

A 2NT response is non-forcing. After a 3NT response, overcaller seldom insists on game in his suit; advancer could have cuebid to investigate alternative game contracts. A few scientific pairs use a forcing 1NT response to an overcall.

(4) *Cuebid.* In addition to the references under, Raises above, see CUEBID IN OPPONENT'S SUIT.

For other aspects of overcalling see: BARON NOTRUMP OVERCALL; GARDENER NOTRUMP OVERCALL; GHESTEM; JUMP OVERCALL; MICHAELS CUEBID; ONE NOTRUMP OVERCALL; PREEMPTIVE OVERCALL; RESPONDING TO OVERCALLS; ROMAN JUMP OVERCALLS; THREE NOTRUMP OVERCALL; TWO NOTRUMP OVERCALL; UNUSUAL NOTRUMP; WEAK JUMP OVERCALL; WEAK NOTRUMP OVERCALL.

OVERCALL IN OPPONENT'S MAJOR SUIT. 2♥ over 1♥, or 2♠ over 1♠, is most often used as a CUEBID IN OPPONENT'S SUIT, in which case it can have any of a number of agreed-upon meanings. The natural use of an overcall in an opponent's major suit is desirable if, and only if, the opponents use a CANAPÉ style of bidding, in which a major suit opening may frequently be made on a suit of only three cards, and maybe not even then. See MICHAELS CUEBID.

OVERCALL IN OPPONENT'S MINOR SUIT. 2♣ over 1♣, or 2♦ over 1♦, is often used naturally instead of as a cuebid. Such treatment is most useful if the opponents are playing five-card majors, or any other method which requires frequent opening bids with prepared three-card (or shorter) minor suits. If a jump cuebid is natural, then using the cuebid as artificial makes sense. See also CUEBIDS IN OPPONENT'S SUIT, MICHAELS CUEBID.

OVERLEAD. The Australian term for the traditional opening lead: higher of touching honors.

OVERRUFF. To trump higher than the right-hand opponent after a plain-suit lead. An overruff is almost always good policy. The main exceptions occur when there is a possibility of achieving a trump promotion. A player who holds a certain trump trick together with a possibility of a second trick should usually refuse to overruff. This is an obvious position with spades as trumps:

```
                    ♠ 4 3 2
♠ A J                            ♠ 6 5
                ♠ K Q 10 9 8 7
```

If East leads a suit of which South and West are both void, South may elect to ruff with the king or queen. West ensures two trump tricks by refusing to overruff.

OVERTAKE. To play a higher card than the one already played by partner for entry reasons. The objective may be suit establishment:

```
♠ A J 10 9 8 7

♠ K
```

If five tricks are needed from this suit in a notrump contract, and there is only one entry in the North hand, the king must be overtaken by the ace. The same would apply if South held the singleton queen and North's suit was headed by the ace or king. An alternative reason for overtaking would be an urgent need for an entry for finessing purposes.

West	East
♠ A 6	♠ 7 3
♥ K	♥ A J 5 3
♦ A J 8 4	♦ 9 7 3 2
♣ A Q J 6 5 3	♣ 10 9 2

North leads a spade against West's 3NT contract. The only hope is to run the club suit, so West overtakes his ♥K with the ace in order to take the club finesse. This sacrifices a heart trick, but makes the contract if the club finesse succeeds. Another common reason for overtaking is dealt with under UNBLOCKING.

OVERTAKING SQUEEZE. A specialized form of triple squeeze in which the squeeze trick can be won in either hand.

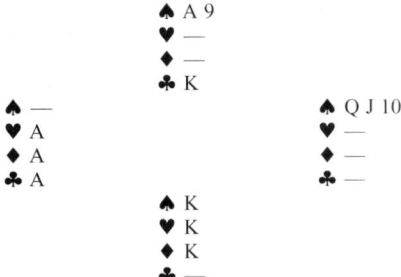

At notrump, South leads the ♠K, and West is squeezed in three suits. If he discards a red ace, North plays low and South cashes the red king. If West discards the ♣A, North overtakes and cashes the ♣K. South thus wins two tricks.

An analogous triple squeeze at a trump contract can give South all the tricks.

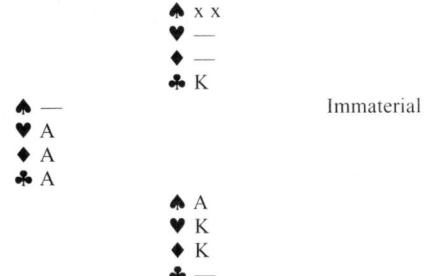

Spades are trump, and South leads the ace of that suit. This squeeze West in three suits, enabling South to win all three tricks.

OVERTRICK. A trick taken by declarer in excess of the number of tricks required for his contract. If a player is in 4♠ and takes 12 tricks, he is said to have made two overtricks. If a contract is doubled or redoubled, and an overtrick or overtricks are taken, the premium accruing to declarer's side can be substantial. Under certain conditions redoubled overtricks can be worth more than the corresponding slam premium. At duplicate, the making of an overtrick can be all-important — it can actually win a board or even an entire tournament.

OVERTRUMP. See OVERRUFF.

P

PACIFIC BRIDGE LEAGUE. An organization founded by Tom Stoddard in 1933 and developed by him through its 15 years of existence. The League included the 11 far-western states plus the territories of Hawaii and Alaska and the Canadian provinces of British Columbia and Alberta.

The League rapidly reached a four-figure membership. It promoted two major tournaments as well as many minor ones. The All-Western tournament was started in Los Angeles in 1935, and Bridge Week in 1936. The latter was held half in Los Angeles and half in San Francisco.

Collaboration between the ACBL and the Pacific BL began in 1940, when uniform masterpoint systems were agreed. A closer affiliation was planned in 1948, when the great services of Tom Stoddard to the Pacific BL were recognized. He was named President Emeritus of ACBL Western Division, with permanent status on the Executive Committee. The final merger between the ACBL and the Western Division became effective Jan. 1, 1956.

PACK. A group of a specific number of cards of consistent composition, sold and used as a unit. The makeup of a pack depends on the date and the country. In the Western world they are composed of four suits, with three FACE CARDS and up to thirteen SPOT CARDS, and have an extra card (JOKER) or cards. The tables below describe some of the many packs that have been in use. When ace is included with the face cards, it ranks high; when included with the spot cards, it ranks low and is called the ONE-SPOT.

(1) Pack with one of each card:

No. of cards	Game or Country	Face Cards	Spot Cards	
62	500	A K Q J	*13 12 11 10 9 8 7 6 5 4 3 2	
60	Fantan	K Q J	12 11 10 9 8 7 6 5 4 3 2 1	
52	Bridge, Poker	A K Q J	10 9 8 7 6 5 4 3 2	
48	Alouette	K C J †	9 8 7 6 5 4 3 2 1	
48	Old German	K O U†	10 9 8 7 6 5 4 3 2	
40	Trappola	K C J	7 6 5 4 3 2 1	
36	Schwerter (Ger.)	K O U	10 9 8 7 6	2
36	Russian	K Q J	10 9 8 7 6	1
36	Sixettes	A K Q J	10 9 8 7 6	
32	Piquet	A K Q J	10 9 8 7	
32	German	K O U	10 9 8 7	2
24	Schnaps	A K Q J	10 9 8	

(2) Packs with two of each suit:

64	Bezique	A K Q J	10 9 8 7	
48	Pinochle	A K Q J	10 9	
48	Gaigel	A K Q J	10	7

(3) With a group of extra cards not a part of the four suits called in various countries, atouts or atutti:

97 Minichiate taroc (Florence) 41 atutti, and each suit has four face cards and ten spot cards.

78 Lombard tarot (Venice) 22 atutti, and each suit has four face cards and ten spot cards.

62 Tarocchino (Bologna) 22 atutti, and each suit has four face cards and six spot cards (10 9 8 7 6 1).

54 Tarok (German) 22 atutti, and each suit had four face cards and four spot cards, black suits 10 9 8 7 and red suits 4 3 2 1.

64 Sicilian 22 atutti, K Q C J 10 9 8 7 6 5 of four suits and the ace and 4 of coins.

*Only two of the 13 spot cards are used.

†C=Cavalier; O=Ober; U=Unter

For the 22 atutti, see TAROT.

For bridge purposes, the pack is a set of 52 standard playing cards divided into four suits (spades, hearts, diamonds and clubs) of 13 cards each, ranking in descending order from the ace to the deuce. See LAWS (Law 1). In the U.S., the term deck is often preferred. See also HISTORY OF PLAYING CARDS; PLAYING CARDS.

PAIR. A twosome or partnership of two players. All games at bridge come down to the basic competitive situation of pair versus pair, bridge being a partnership, or pair, game.

PAIR GAMES. In a pair game, you play with the same partner throughout an event. You play a series of opponents, but your score is determined by how well you do compared to others who played the same deals in the same direction as you.

Several adjustments have been made to pair games to make it possible for new and less experienced players to earn masterpoints in the AMERICAN CONTRACT BRIDGE LEAGUE. In old-fashioned open games, which still are quite common in some clubs, it often was apparent that the same pairs were collecting the masterpoints week after week. The three most common methods used to make pair games more interesting for new and inexperienced plays are called flighting, handicapping, and stratification. First let's consider flighting.

Flighted pairs. When flighting is used, the field is divided into several separate games. Each flight is scored individually, and masterpoint awards are made for each flight. The usual division of flights consists of one game for the experienced and more expert players (Flight A), a second for the intermediate players (Flight B), and a third for the new and inexperienced players (Flight C).

Usually the masterpoint holdings of the players determine the flight in which they play. The flight is always determined by the player with the greater number of masterpoints. If one player is quite expert while his partner is new to the game, the pair must compete in Flight A, the field of the stronger player.

In flighted events, you can play up but not down. That means that you can sign up to play in Flight A or Flight B even if you qualify for Flight C. But conversely you cannot sign up for Flight B or Flight C if you are a Flight A player. The flight method guarantees that many players with B or C rating will earn masterpoints. Of course the awards for A are the highest and for C the lowest to reflect the relative strength of the fields.

Handicap pairs. All the pairs play in the same event — there is no division into different fields. However, the game is ranked twice. How is this done? At the outset, the director assigns a handicap to each pair. Experienced and expert pairs usually get no handicap. Experienced and expert pairs usually get no handicap, and handicap allowance increases as the experience level of the pairs drops.

There are two common methods of handicapping. First, by masterpoints. An arbitrary number of matchpoints is allotted to a player based on his present masterpoint holding. The pair's handicap is the total of the two individual handicaps. Second, by recent performance. Now that we are in the computer age, it is not all that difficult to track every player's record. If two players competing as a pair have had a good recent history, their handicap will be low or non-existent. If they have had bad luck in recent sessions, their handicap will be reasonably high.

At the close of the game, the director scores the game the usual way the first time — strictly by matchpoints earned. The usual matchpoints are distributed to those who place in direct scoring. Then the director scores the game a second time, adding in the handicaps. The awards in the second field are lower, reflecting the less experienced field.

With handicap scoring, there is no guarantee that any less experienced pairs will earn any masterpoints. It is not all that uncommon for the rankings for both the open and the handicap games to be the same. That is why stratification entered the scoring picture.

Stratified pairs. The idea behind stratification is that everyone competes against everyone but is ranked only with his peers. Each pair is assigned a "strat" based on the masterpoint holding of the partner with the most masterpoints. The most experienced players are placed in Strat A, intermediates in Strat B and less experienced players in Strat C. In some events there are four or more strats. Sometimes there are only two strats. Masterpoints are awarded for placings in all strats.

While selling the entries, the director tries to equalize the field as much as possible, putting equal numbers of A, B and C players into each group. The game proceeds normally — the difference comes when the scores are tabulated and ranked.

In a three-strat game, ranking actually is done three times. The first time it is done as in a regular open game. These are the Strat A results. If a B or C player does well in Strat A, he gets full credit for that performance. It is not at all uncommon for a Strat C pair to place first overall, and they get the full masterpoint award for that game. When the ranking is done for the second time, all the scores for Strat A pairs are eliminated — only B and C pairs are compared. Once again, if a C pair does well, they get whatever points are allotted for their finishing position in Strat B. Then the game is ranked for the third time. All the scores for Strats A and B are eliminated — only C scores are compared.

This method of running a pair game guarantees that some B and C pairs will earn masterpoints.

Stratiflighted pairs. Many intermediate and new players don't feel they're qualified to play against the top pros — they feel very uncomfortable when they discover they're playing against some of the biggest names in the game. So what happens here is that the top group plays in a game of their own — Flight A. The rest of the field is divided into strats and plays as in a regular stratified pairs.

This is a win-win solution. The top pairs are happy to get a chance to hone their skills against their peers. Less experienced players compete against their peers without having to worry about the top pros.

PAJAMA GAME. Duplicate session with many tops and bottoms.

PALOOKA. A very poor player.

PAMP PAR CONTEST. A feature of the 1990 World Championships. The following is Alan Truscott's account in the *New York Times*:

Until recently, an expert asked to name the toughest test of cardplaying ability would have hesitated. But now the answer is clear: The Pamp Par Hands contest was the most difficult and challenging event in the history of bridge.

It was played during the World Championships in Geneva in October 1990. Twenty world-famous players were selected as the victims. The torture-master was Pietro Bernasconi of Switzerland, who is highly skilled in both bridge and computers, a rare combination.

The sufferers sat in front of a computer screen and were shown their own hand as declarer, the dummy, the bidding and the opening lead. There were only 12 deals to be played in two days, but such deals. Cover the East-West hands shown in the following diagram, and consider how you would tackle the play in six clubs, given that West has made a weak jump overcall in spades and then led the heart queen.

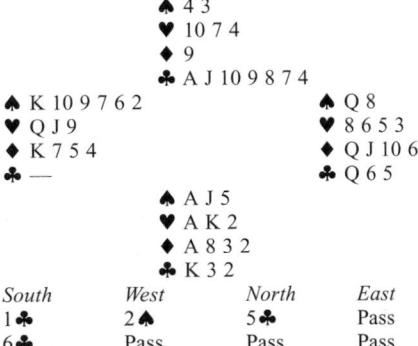

South	West	North	East
1♣	2♠	5♣	Pass
6♣	Pass	Pass	Pass

The computer is keeping track of the time you take, so you are working against the clock. If you make an error the computer will beep at you, charge you 250 points of an initial allowance of 1000, and allow you a second chance. And a third, and even a fourth. Many world champions were unable to solve the deals even with four attempts.

South could look forward to an easy endplay against West if that player began with ♠K-Q and ♥Q-J, but with that hand West might well have led the ♠K. So the declarer must concentrate on finding a way to succeed if the ♠K-Q are in different hands.

The first move after winning the ♥K should be to cash the ♦A and ruff a diamond. Then cash the ♣A, since if anyone has a club void it is no doubt West. That proves to be right, for a spade is discarded. Now the ♣J is led for a marked finesse and the last trump is extracted.

A second diamond is ruffed, and the closed hand is reentered with a spade to the ace to permit the final diamond ruff. The position then is:

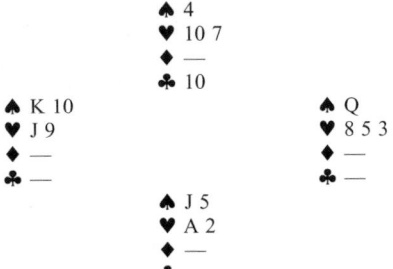

As West has produced the ♦K the chance that he began with ♠K-Q, and would be exposed to a normal squeeze-endplay in the major suits, has vanished. If he had begun with 11 high-card points including a void club, he would have been far too strong for his preemptive jump.

But the lead of the last trump from the dummy succeeds in a more complex fashion. If East throws the ♠Q, West is in trouble as before so East must throw a heart. South throws a heart, and if West throws a spade South can develop his 12th trick in that suit.

So West throws a heart, and South cashes the ace, establishing the 10 in the dummy. Now the ♠5 is led, and West can decide whether to win and concede the last trick to the ♠J, or play low, in which case the ♥10 comes back to life.

The winner was Benito Garozzo, who won many world titles for Italy and now resides in the United States. Following him in the final rankings were Bob Hamman, United States; Pierre Ghestem, France; Chip Martel, United States; and Andrew Robson, Britain. See BESSE PAR CONTEST, PAR CONTEST.

PANAMA. A defensive bidding system against the FORCING CLUB. Bids at the two-level show either a weak jump overcall in the suit bid or a three-suiter with shortage in the bid suit.

PAN AMERICAN BRIDGE CHAMPIONSHIPS. The first-ever Pan American Bridge Championships and Pan American Games, sponsored by the World Bridge Federation and Texas World Bridge, were held in June, 1992, in Corpus Christi TX. Four premier events which required prior qualification were Open Teams, Women's Teams, Open Pairs and Women's Pairs. Every nation in North America, Central America and South America was entitled to field two teams and eight pairs, with the USA as host country allowed a double quota. Five other Pan American events, each four sessions, were open to all comers. In addition there was a full complement of regionally rated two-session games. ACBL and WBF points were awarded in most events of two or more sessions. United States competitors won the gold medals for first place in all four major Pan American championships. For results see Appendix III.

PAN AMERICAN INVITATIONAL CHAMPIONSHIPS. An invitational pair championship first held in 1974 in Mexico City, scored by IMPs. This competition was discontinued after 1977.

PAR. The result on a hand if both sides have done as well as possible.

PAR CONTEST. A tournament using prepared hands, each of which embodies a predetermined optimum (par) result. The players' results are compared with par, rather than with each other. You may not profit by an opponent's blunder if you have already erred. Your skill alone determines the result.

World Championships on a par basis were held in 1961 and 1963 by the World Bridge Federation. Until 1966 the Intercollegiate Bridge Tournament was the only par contest held annually in the United States. The National Industrial Recreational Association Tournament was conducted in 1963 and 1964 as a par contest but then adopted matchpoint scoring.

The following hand (from the 1963 National Industrial Recreation Association Par Tournament) illustrates the fundamental difference between a par contest and an ordinary duplicate contest:

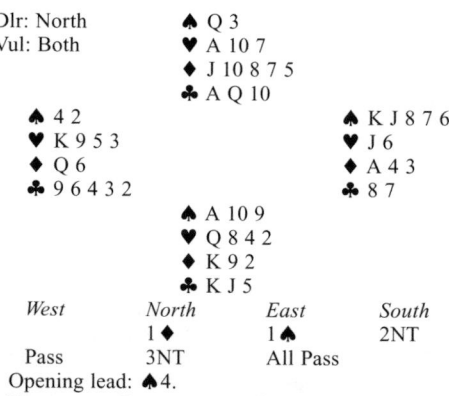

Dlr: North
Vul: Both

	♠ Q 3	
	♥ A 10 7	
	♦ J 10 8 7 5	
	♣ A Q 10	

♠ 4 2		♠ K J 8 7 6 5
♥ K 9 5 3		♥ J 6
♦ Q 6		♦ A 4 3
♣ 9 6 4 3 2		♣ 8 7

	♠ A 10 9	
	♥ Q 8 4 2	
	♦ K 9 2	
	♣ K J 5	

West	North	East	South
	1♦	1♠	2NT
Pass	3NT	All Pass	

Opening lead: ♠4.

To earn par, East must not play an honor on the first trick, no matter what dummy plays. If he does, then when West wins the ♦Q, he can play a spade, establishing East's suit while East still has the ♦A for entry.

In a duplicate tournament, many defenders would defeat the contract after playing an honor on the first trick, because South would play incorrectly and win the trick. In a par contest, these defenders would not be awarded par.

In 1963, the World Bridge Federation adopted an International Par Point Contract Bridge Code, drafted by Michael Sullivan and Robert Williams of Australia. This code deals with irregularities and penalties. The basic decisions about the format of the contest are left to the organizers. Some of the factors to be considered are discussed below.

Par-point scoring may be used for individual, pair, or team contest, (but only pair games are common). For a pair game, the par-setters should strive to ensure that the North-South pairs and East-West pairs will meet problems of equal difficulty. Such judgments are necessarily subjective, however, and it is better to choose the North-South and East-West winners separately.

(1) The Bidding. The bidding problems should be arranged so as not unduly to favor or penalize any common system or convention. As a rule, par points are awarded on the basis of the final contract reached, not on the actual auction. Minor awards may be given to inferior contracts. On some deals, players may be instructed (by a slip accompanying the board) to make specified preemptive bids, so that all pairs holding the other hands will be presented with uniform bidding problems. Furthermore, players are instructed to refrain from psychics or other unwarranted or misleading bids. Nevertheless, all the vagaries of competitive auctions cannot be anticipated. Some players will inevitably face more difficult opposition bidding than others, and the par-setters may be called on to adjudicate. Despite this opportunity for redress, it is here that luck or the skill of one's opponent is most likely to affect one's score.

(2) Before the Play. So that all competitors face the same play or defense problem, it is usual to specify both the contract to be played and the opening lead. A traveling slip, accompanying the board for this purpose, is consulted after the bidding is over. The official contract need not be the same as the contract awarded maximum bidding par points, if a more interesting play problem is presented. The par-setters may also provide a guidance auction, from which the players can derive information needed during the play. They are instructed to ignore the actual bidding at their table (but there again, some luck enters).

(3) The Play. At the discretion of the par-setters, the traveling slip may inform the players before the play begins whether the par is for the declarer or the defenders. This saves time by eliminating long huddles by the non-involved side, but adds another artificial aspect to the event.

In addition to the opening lead, the play to one or more tricks may be directed, and declarer or defenders may receive public or private instructions. The primary purpose is to obviate the awarding of automatic pars, if the opponents should slip in advance of the anticipated problem. These instructions may also ensure the defeat of a misplaced contract or the fulfillment of a misdefended contract. This is of secondary importance, however, as the par would not be awarded in any case if the play at the table deviated from the prescribed line. Minor awards may be given for partially correct or slightly inferior lines of play or defense.

Note that an equitable two-way play par (that is, a separate par both for the declarer and the defenders on one deal) is almost impossible to arrange. For example, in the hand given earlier, South will not have a chance to make a par play (ducking the first trick) if East first makes his par play by ducking. Then that South would have to be awarded an unearned automatic par.

(4) Movements. Every player must play all the boards. No movement is necessary — a pair could well play the entire session against one pair of opponents, sharing the boards with the other tables. This arrangement also saves time, as the faster players need not wait for the slower ones to finish their boards each round. Nevertheless, for social and other reasons, some limited movements of the players is desirable.

It is recommended that a time limit for each group of boards be imposed. In important tournaments, the use of chess clocks should be considered. See BESSE PAR CONTEST, PAMP PAR CONTEST.

PAR HAND. A hand prepared for use in a PAR CONTEST. By extension, a randomly dealt hand suitable for inclusion in such a contest because a single technical aspect of play or defense is dominant.

PAR POINT BRIDGE. See PAR CONTEST.

PARLIAMENTARY MATCHES. An annual bridge contest between Britain's two Houses of Parliament, Lords and Commons. In April, 2000 the Commons won to tie the series at 13 wins each. The match in 2001 was postponed due to the General Election. The contest for the Jack Perry Trophy is held at the Portland Club in London. The Sir Anthony Berry Memorial Trophy goes to the Best Play of the match. Berry, a member of the Commons bridge team, was killed in the Brighton bombing of Margaret Thatcher.

PARTIAL DESIGNATION. An incomplete request for a card to be played from the dummy. If the suit alone is named, the lowest card in the suit must be played. If a card is named but not a suit, and the card is ambiguous, the card must be taken from the suit previously led if possible.

PARTIAL ELIMINATION. A throw-in play depending on ruff-and-discard possibilities in which the strip-

ping process is incomplete. In a perfect elimination the declarer eliminates all the suits which a defender may safely lead and saddles him with the choice of conceding a ruff and sluff or leading into a tenace. A partial elimination, on the other hand, is so called because the declarer only partially eliminates the suits which a defender may safely lead. Whether the defender will have to lead to the declarer's advantage will depend on distributional hazards.

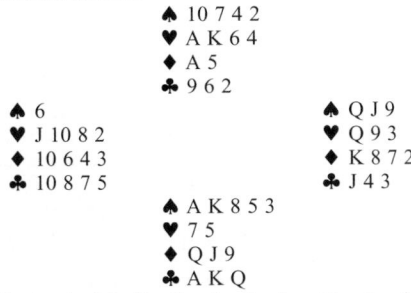

Playing in 6♠, South wins the heart lead and tests trumps. When West fails on the second round, South attempts an endplay to avoid taking the diamond finesse. He plays the second top heart, ruffs the third round in his hand, and takes his three top clubs before throwing the lead to East's master trump. East has no hearts or clubs left, so he must lead away from the king.

South's maneuver is a partial elimination because he could only partially eliminate hearts. He did not have the entries to eliminate the hearts completely. This play had the added advantage that if East did have the 13th club as an exit card he might have been unwilling to give declarer a ruff-sluff and led a diamond anyway. The ruff-sluff could not possibly help South because he had only one trump left and could not ruff both the club return and dummy's last heart.

In the above example the critical suit — hearts — was eliminated from two of the four hands. When the distribution is favorable, a partial elimination may succeed even though the critical suit has been eliminated from only one hand:

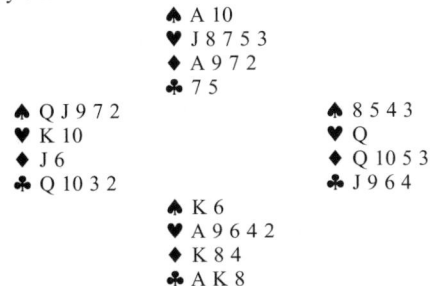

With hearts as trumps, South can make 12 tricks by means of partial elimination. He wins the spade lead, plays off the trump ace, and eliminates the black suits. He cashes the ♦ A-K and exits with a trump. West wins, but he is the only player without a diamond in his hand. He has to return a black suit, and South ruffs on the table, at the same time sluffing a diamond from the closed hand.

A partial elimination can also operate when one of the defenders still has a trump in his hand:

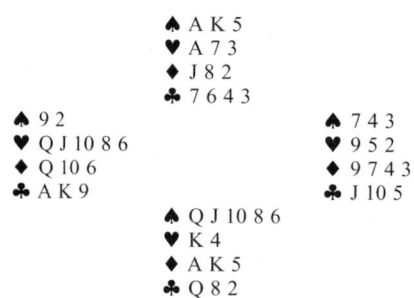

West opens the bidding with 1 ♥, and South reaches a contract of 4 ♠ instead of 3NT. After a heart lead, prospects are poor, but a partial elimination offers the best chance. However, it is essential to keep at least one trump in each hand to profit from a possible ruff and sluff; this means that South can afford to draw only two rounds of trumps, and must therefore rely on West's having no more than two trumps.

South wins the heart lead, plays off the ace and queen of trumps, and continues with a second and third round of hearts, ruffing. He then plays ace, king, and another diamond, throwing West into the lead. As expected, West has the outstanding high cards and has to offer a ruff and discard or concede a trick to the ♣Q.

PARTIAL SCORE. See PARTSCORE.

PARTNER. The player with whom one is paired in a game of bridge.

PARTNER'S SUIT. The suit bid or rebid by the player seated opposite during an auction.

PARTNERSHIP. The two players sitting North-South or the two players sitting East-West. Players who play together frequently are considered to be an ESTAB-LISHED PARTNERSHIP; players who pair up for a particular event, having played together either seldom or never, have a more casual partnership. Most of the bidding and play conventions were established as successful tactics by established partnerships.

PARTNERSHIP LANGUAGE. See BIDDING SYSTEMS.

PARTNERSHIP MISUNDERSTANDING. All partnerships have misunderstandings about the meaning of bids and signals. Bidding misunderstandings fall into four general categories:

(1) *The strength of a bid.* For example, the range for a response of 1NT to 1♣: 5-8, 6-9, 7-10 and 9-11 are all in use.

(2) *The nature of a bid: sign-off, discouraging, encouraging, or forcing (for one round or to game).* A good example is a jump in a new suit over an opposing takeout double (see RESPONSES OVER OPPONENT'S TAKEOUT DOUBLE). According to the partnership understanding, this bid can be preemptive, encouraging, forcing for one round, or fit-showing.

(3) *Artificial or natural quality of a bid.* Confusion can occur when a partnership has not specifically agreed whether a particular artificial device is being employed. Both players may normally use a convention, and be aware that the partner normally uses it, but still be in

doubt about whether it is in use because it has not been discussed. A more common source of difficulty is doubt about whether a convention is applicable to a particular situation. It is sometimes difficult to diagnose, for example, whether 4NT is natural or conventional; or whether a bid in the opponent's suit is a cuebid or an attempt to play in that suit.

(4) *The nature of a double.* There may be doubt about whether a double is for penalty, takeout, lead-direction, support, etc. A failure to agree on the use of RESPONSIVE or NEGATIVE DOUBLES would be an example of this problem. There are also situations, usually after the first round of bidding, in which the intentions of the doubler are not clear.

The nature of a pass may also be crucial, especially if a FORCING PASS is a possibility. No partnership can avoid misunderstandings altogether, but the following suggestions may help to reduce the incidence of disaster.

First, a regular partnership should have a detailed understanding.

Second, a player should avoid making an ambiguous bid when an unambiguous alternative is equally satisfactory.

Third, when an ambiguous bid is made, a partnership should apply some automatic rule. A reasonable rule is to take the weaker interpretation in each case, that is: the lower point range; nonforcing against forcing; natural as against conventional; and takeout rather than penalty double. The opposite rule is also playable, and so are a variety of hybrid rules. In any case, it is advisable to have some rule. This often avoids impending trouble, provided both players are aware of the possibility of trouble.

As for signals, it is easy to mistake a suit preference signal for a count or attitude signal. Partners should always clarify their signaling methods, especially the signal given on the first trick. Misunderstandings involving signals can cause major disasters.

PARTNERSHIP NOTES. Most serious partnerships with prospects of winning national or international titles develop notes on their methods that go far beyond the items on the convention card. These often cover every area of bidding, with a little on defensive play, and may require 50 or more pages. Players will usually re-read these before the start of a major event, but may not, of course, consult them at the table. Sometimes it is permitted to have these notes at the table where a player may consult them between deals or before play. An opponent's convention may require reference to the defensive agreement.

PARTNERSHIP PSYCHOLOGY. The art of keeping partner happy is worth more in terms of results than much advanced technical knowledge; but it is an art which many players, including some at the highest level never learn. At rubber bridge the player who encourages his partner instead of shouting at him, praising the occasional good plays instead of pointing out the obvious bad ones, earns large dividends. His partners then like to play with him and play up to their capabilities. On the other hand, a player who is subjected to a barrage of criticism is likely to play below his best not only for the remainder of the rubber but on subsequent occasions.

In tournament play, two people who have agreed to be

partners ought in theory to be compatible, but this is not always the case, and the same principles are applicable. Though some successful partnerships contain one player whose personality dominates, many long-lived partnerships consist of players who enjoy each other's company and have attained mutual respect. Egotists whose concern is to prove how brilliantly they themselves play and how foolishly their partners perform may have temporary successes, but they must find new partners regularly.

Since distance as well as respect may be a desirable partnership attribute, much has been written about the performance of partnerships — especially those with an emotional attachment. There is no standard; some otherwise affectionate couples seem to let all the tiny frustrations of their relationship surface at the bridge table, while the formidable marital problems of others may vanish. All that is clear is that emotional ties may oblige some partnerships to work harder to be effective.

Perhaps the simplest and best rule for all partners to remember is the "golden" one.

PARTNERSHIP RUBBER BRIDGE. A style of rubber bridge popular in England whereby two players play as partners throughout a session. Players agree in advance to play as partners, as they would in a duplicate event, and there is no game for unpaired individuals. This tends to raise the standard of the game by excluding those who, through inferior ability or character deficiency, find it difficult to get a partner.

PARTNERSHIP UNDERSTANDING. An agreement between partners that enables them to draw information or inferences from the bidding and play. Partnership understandings are of two types: explicit, describing agreements reached through discussion; and implicit, describing those not specifically discussed but arising through experience. The sum of a partnership's understanding comprises not only conventional bids and plays, but STYLE: a player's tendencies in exercising judgment.

In tournament play, pairs have a duty to see that understandings of which the opponents could not reasonably be aware are clearly and accurately stated on the CONVENTION CARD, alerted when required, and explained in response to a query. At rubber bridge, understandings are best announced to the opponents before play begins. In extended team events such as the Bermuda Bowl, pairs are required to provide their competitors with a summary of methods weeks in advance.

Partnership understanding is not to be confused with a PRIVATE CONVENTION, which is illegal and unethical. See ALERTING, EXPLANATION OF CONVENTIONAL CALL OR PLAY, LAW 75.

PARTSCORE. A partial; a trick score of fewer than 100 points. At RUBBER BRIDGE, a successful partscore counts toward game and enables one pair to make game by fulfilling an additional partscore or partscores.

If one side scores a game while the other side has a partscore, that frame ends, and both sides start anew in pursuit of game. But that partscore still is added at the end of the rubber (or, in CHICAGO, after the fourth deal). See PARTSCORE BIDDING, PARTSCORE BONUS.

In duplicate bridge, the score for making a partial is the sum of the trick score and 50.

PARTSCORE BIDDING. Bidding by (or against) a side which possesses a partscore is a subject which is scantily treated by textbooks and produces considerable disagreement among experts. The following treatment is based on the opinion of a number of experts.

Forcing Bids. The most noticeable difference between partscore bidding and normal bidding results from the fact that many bids which would otherwise be forcing are no longer forcing when they complete the game. A new suit by responder, for example, is not forcing if it is sufficient for game. Similarly, a jump from one to three in a suit, or from one of a suit to 2NT, may be passed, through it becomes a slam try if a simple raise would have been enough for game. The jump shift remains forcing, however, regardless of the partscore.

Suit Bids. Because so many bids become nonforcing if they complete a partial, it is difficult for a partnership to conduct any lengthy bidding investigation. It is therefore of primary importance that whenever a partial exists, all suit bids should stress quality. Thus it would be poor policy to open a three-card minor with a partial. With 60 on score, holding ♠ A-K-J-x, ♥ x-x-x, ♦ x-x-x, ♣ A-J-x, a player should open 1♠, and pass partner's response (unless it is a jump shift). Similarly, responder should ignore a suit of doubtful quality. With 70 on score, holding ♠ K-x-x, ♥ Q-9-x-x, ♦ x-x, ♣ A-x-x-x, the response to 1♦ should be 1NT, bypassing the poor heart holding. However, with ♠ K-x-x, ♥ x-x, ♦ x-x, ♣ Q-J-10-9-x-x, the response to 1♦ should be 2♣. This response at the two level does not promise as much high-card strength as at love score. Rather, it stresses the quality of the club suit. The opening bidder is expected to pass unless he has good reason to continue.

Notrump Bids. All notrump bids tend to have a slightly wider range when the bidder has a partscore. Using a 15-17 point notrump range, with 60 on the score, it would be correct tactics to open 1NT holding either the 18-point hand (a) or the 14-point hand (b).

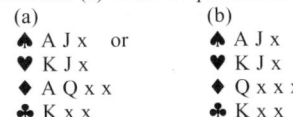

(a)		(b)
♠ A J x	or	♠ A J x
♥ K J x		♥ K J x
♦ A Q x x		♦ Q x x x
♣ K x x		♣ K x x

Some experts allow themselves more latitude than others in the range of their opening notrump, but taking the average approach of the experts consulted, standard expert procedure is to widen the range for an opening 1NT by about a point in either direction when a partscore is held.

There are two reasons for this increase in the notrump range. First, there is always a tremendous tactical advantage in opening with 1NT. Partner is immediately in an excellent position either to place the contract or punish overzealous opponents. The opponents are unable to compete at the one level and may find it too dangerous to begin their search for a fit at the two level. To reopen in fourth seat after an opening notrump by opponents with a 60 partial is particularly dangerous, because opener's partner may pass with up to 13 high-card points, instead of being limited by his pass to seven or less.

Tactical advantages exist for opening 1NT frequently at no score also, but in this case the problem of whether to reach game or settle for a partial is paramount. Widening the range of the notrump would be against the interests of accuracy. With a substantial partial, the question of whether to reach game or not is already solved,

and tactical considerations become more prominent. Naturally the prospect of missing a slam is a deterrent to increasing the upper limit unduly. With 60 on score, and a passed partner, it is surely good tactics to open 1NT with as many as 19 points regardless of the normal range, as slam can hardly be missed.

The second, and less obvious, reason for increasing the range, and thus the frequency of the notrump opening, goes back to the stress on quality for opening suit-bids. If the normal 1NT range is 15 to 17 points, and a partial of 40 is held, it would be proper to open 1NT holding ♠K-x-x, ♥A-x-x-x, ♦A-x x-x, ♣K-x. Ordinarily such a hand would be opened 1♥ or 1♦, depending on partnership attitude toward four-card majors. With the partscore, the suit-bid carries an added implication of quality. Partner will strain to raise the suit-bid, and the safer spot in notrump will be missed. If suit play is better, responder can choose the suit.

Other notrump bids are likewise affected by the partial. Most experts play 20-21 point opening 2NT bids. They increase this range, particularly the upper limit, when a partial exists. By far the most frequently used range (and, therefore, logically, the standard range) for an opening 2NT bid is 21-24 with a partial of 60 or more, and 20-24 with a lesser partial.

The opening strong 3NT bid becomes almost extinct with a partscore of 30 or more. It is better to open with 2♣ and rebid 2NT to a 2♦ response. After any other response a slam can be investigated with impunity.

Of all notrump bids, the simple response of 1NT is most affected by a partscore. Normally this bid shows 6-9 in Standard American, but if 1NT is enough for game the range can be as wide as 4-12. The lower limit is reduced because of the strain to keep the bidding open when game is possible. The upper limit is increased because it keeps the bidding lower but in the game range on a hand where slam appears unlikely. The responses of 2NT and 3NT remain close to their usual ranges. The 13-15 range for a 2NT response increases to 13-16 with a partial, and becomes nonforcing, of course. The 3NT range moves from 16-17 to 17-18. It is a common practice among average players to avoid both these responses on some theory that it is unnecessary to get so high with a partial. This is a fallacy. There should be no danger at this level opposite an opening bid. More important by far is the fact that these bids are extremely useful when the opening bidder has slam aspirations.

Raising Partner's Suit. As responder, when holding a fit with partner, it is imperative to show it immediately. The fact that one side has a fit increases the chances that the opponents have a fit and a profitable sacrifice. With a 90 partscore and an opening 1♠ bid by partner, holding Q-J-x-x, K-x, Q-x-x-x, x-x-x, bid 2♠ immediately. If fourth hand will take some action, and the necessary 2♠ bid on the next round will come after the opponents have found their fit. Immediate action may keep the opponents out altogether. With a partscore, it is standard to give a single raise with 6-12 points. The lower limit may be reduced as far as three points if the raise is necessary to complete the game. With 13-16 points it is still standard to give a jump raise from one to three in a suit. With a stronger hand, a jump shift is in order.

Tactical Considerations. With a partscore, is it wise to open lighter or stronger than usual? What about when the opponents have a partial? Or when both sides are on

score? This is an area of wide disagreement. No standard approach exists, but the various schools of thought are presented so the reader may form his own opinions.

One school holds that as long as fewer tricks are required to make a game, opening bids may be slightly weaker with a partial. A second school recommends using stronger opening bids with a partial. This group reasons: If the bidding is opened with a partial, the opponents are very apt to compete. Responder will fight for the partscore on the strength of the opening bid; if this bid is subminimum, responder may push too high, presenting the opponents with a very attractive double, or, even worse, he may decide to punish competing opponents and double them into game. A third school suggests opening light with spades, but normally or slightly over without spades. Obviously the side with spades has an advantage in any bidding battle. Still a fourth school feels that the advantages and disadvantages of either stronger or lighter bids just about cancel each other out, maintaining that normal bids will work out best in the long run. A majority of the experts consulted recommended normal openings with a partial.

There are also various theories as to the best procedure when the opponents have a partial. A slight majority of the experts suggest opening light, believing that the best defense is an early offense. It is dangerous to overcall or balance against opponents who have a partial as they may have strength in reserve: hence the value of getting in first with the opening bid. Light takeout doubles and overcalls are also favored for the same reason. Many recommend the preemptive opening of 1♠ or 1NT with a slightly lighter range than usual. Ely Culbertson, in his *Contract Bridge Complete*, says "Shade your bids downward if the opponents have a partscore and upward if you have the partscore." Then there are those who like to have stronger openings when the opponents have a partial; they would rather pass out a hand than open a minimum when they are at such a disadvantage in the score. Lastly there are those who stand steadfast for the normal opening.

A further point arising when the opponents have a partial is often overlooked. When in doubt whether to bid game or settle for a partscore, it is better to stretch a bit and bid game. The reason is that the value of success is substantially increased by the fact that the opponent's partial is wiped out.

When both sides have a partscore, the experts are split into roughly two equal camps: those favoring lighter openings and those favoring normal openings. Reasons given are various combinations of those above.

The Value of a Partial. Experts have long been aware that a partscore at rubber bridge is worth far more than the 50 points formerly awarded for a partial in an unfinished rubber. Because of the many imponderable factors involved, including the identity of one's opponents, mathematicians never have been able to agree on the correct way to calculate the value mathematically. However, Jean Besse kept a record or more than 1000 partscore situations. He compared the scores when a partial had just been achieved and again when the partial had been completed. Allowing 300 for any first game, 400 for the second game, and 500 for any third game, his results were as follows:

Values (over and above the trick score) of a
nonvulnerable partial of 40 or more   90

Value of a vulnerable partial (opponents not

vulnerable) of 40 or more   110

  Value of a partial of 40 or more with both

vulnerable   220

  The tremendous value of a partial when both are vulnerable is attributed partly, of course, to the increased value of game but mainly to the increased difficulty encountered by vulnerable opponents in trying to defend.

  In many bridge clubs in the United States, four-deal bridge Chicago has taken the place of rubber bridge. A partial must be worth somewhat less in this form of bridge, due to the limited time in which to capitalize on it. Naturally, a partial on the fourth deal is worth exactly the 100 points awarded for it in the rules.

PARTSCORE BONUS. In duplicate competition, 50 points are scored as a bonus for fulfilling a partscore contract. In CHICAGO, a bonus of 100 points is given for a partscore contract successful on the last hand. For the mathematical value of a partscore see PARTSCORE BIDDING.

PARTY BRIDGE. Private games consisting of at least two tables. The CHICAGO or four-deal method is customary. It is usual to give prizes to the players with the best scores and the player with the worst score may receive a booby prize.

  At the end of each round each player enters on his tally only his net gain or loss — not his total score. At the end of the session these net gains and losses are totaled and the player's final score, plus or minus as the case may be, is entered at the bottom of his tally.

  Some hostesses require players to record only plus scores and ignore minus scores. This compromises the quality of the game for serious bridge players, since it rewards wild doubling and redoubling. See PARTY CONTRACT BRIDGE, LAWS OF.

PARTY CONTRACT BRIDGE, LAWS OF; DUPLICATE FOR HOME PLAY, AND COMPETITION NOT IN DUPLICATE. The forms of Duplicate play described in the Laws are readily adapted to home play. Special games suitable to a small number of tables, or emphasizing the social above the competitive element, are described in the following pages.

  For a single table, the available games are REPLAY DUPLICATE, COMPENSATION and PIVOT BRIDGE (non-duplicate). For two or three tables there are INDIVIDUAL MOVEMENTS, and MITCHELL or HOWELL PAIR MOVEMENTS, and TEAM-OF-FOUR MOVEMENTS. For a larger number of tables, where it is desired to emphasize the social element, the popular game is PROGRESSIVE BRIDGE.

  In general, the Laws of Duplicate Contract Bridge apply to all forms of duplicate and multiple-table play — from the simplest replay contest to the most elaborate championship tournament.

  Even in simple home games, such as Replay Duplicate, it is advisable to appoint one participant as Supervisor and to invest him with all the authority of a Tournament Director. Experience has shown that without a guiding hand even a social game is likely to be delayed or deadlocked by trivial irregularities.

  Replay Duplicate is a contest between two pairs. It is played in two sessions, called the Original Play and the Replay. The players take places, one being designated North. The boards are shuffled, and are played with the arrows pointing North. Any number of boards is feasible. A separate scoreslip is kept for each board. At the close of the session the boards and scoreslips are laid aside where they will be undisturbed.

  At some later time, the same four players take the same relative positions about the table. The boards are replayed with the arrows pointing East. Again a separate scoreslip is kept for each board.

  The scoring may be by matchpoints, total points or IMPs. If the former method is used, each deal is treated as a separate match. The pair having the better net score on a deal is credited with 1 point. The final scores are the totals of these matchpoints. If total point scoring is employed, the two slips for each deal are compared, and the pair having the greater plus or lesser minus is credited with the difference. The net scores for all deals, so determined, are totaled, and the pair having the larger total wins the difference. IMP scoring is similar. Replay Duplicate has some limited popularity as a home game among foursomes that meet weekly for social bridge. It can easily be played in a continuous series of sessions. Half of the time in each session is devoted to the original play of new boards, and half to the replay of old boards.

  The game tends to become a test of memory rather than of bridge skill. To check this tendency the following measures are recommended: 1. Do not play the boards in consecutive order. Choose the boards to be played next at random from the stack. 2. Avoid comment of any sort about the deal after its original play. 3. Allow at least a week to elapse between the original play and the replay.

  It is sometimes desired to make the game a test of skill in play alone. The bidding during the original play is then recorded, and for the replay this bidding is read to fix the contract and declarer.

  Individual Contests. In an individual game, each player plays once with every other as partner, and twice against every other as opponent. The initial seating of the players in games for two or three tables is as follows:

TWO TABLES

THREE TABLES

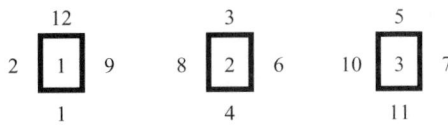

  The game may be conducted without guide cards, as follows:

  (1) Allow the players to take places at random. Reserve the North position at Table 1 for the Supervisor. This player is anchor, retaining his seat throughout the game.

  (2) From this schedule inform each player of his number, and tell him who is the player of next-lower number.

(3) Announce that after each round, all players but the anchor will progress, each player taking the seat vacated by the player of next-lower number. (Player 1 follows Player 7 or 11 in the 2 or 3 table movements, respectively.) A new set of boards is played in each round. The set is played at all tables, the boards being circulated at convenience. The eight-player game requires seven rounds, with a total of 14, 21, or 28 boards. The twelve-player game requires 11 rounds, and the only feasible number of boards is either 22 or 33.

The scoring of individual contests is explained in the Laws of Duplicate Contract Bridge. It is preferable to use IMPs for scoring. With a 3-table movement, give two IMP scores on each deal by comparing with the other tables. See PIVOT BRIDGE.

PASS. A call by which a player indicates that, at that turn, he does not choose to contract for a number of odd tricks at any denomination, nor does he choose, at that turn, to double a contract of the opponents or redouble a contract by his side that opponents have already doubled.

The Proprieties require that only one term be used in passing. NO BID is an acceptable alternative (standard in England), but all calls must be made with uniform usage. See BID, CALL, NO BID, PENALTY PASS.

PASS OUT or THROW IN. A deal in which all four players pass on the first round of bidding. The score is zero. In duplicate, the deal is scored and returned to the board. Some players believe, mistakenly, that the board can be redealt if passed out on the first round. This is illegal. In rubber bridge, the deal passes to the next player, but in CHICAGO a redeal by the same dealer is required. The term "pass out" is also applied to the action of the player who, after two passes, declines to reopen the bidding at a comparatively low level. He is said to be in the "passout seat" or the "passout position."

PASS OUT OF ROTATION. An irregularity in the auction. This can occur in three different circumstances: when it is the turn of LHO, partner or RHO to call. Since damage to the opponents can vary according to the circumstances, the prescribed penalties also vary. See LAWS (Law 30). A conventional pass out of rotation is treated under Law 31, Bid Out Of Rotation.

PASS-DOUBLE INVERSION. A procedure devised by Eric Rodwell for use in strong club methods, but usable by agreement in many standard situations where a partnership is clearly in a forcing auction.

West	North	East	South
1♣ (1)	1♥	1♠	4♥
?			

(1) Strong and artificial.

A pass by West forces East to double unless he has freakish distribution. West then passes with a penalty double or bids with more than one place to play. With 1-0-6-6, for example, he could pass and then bid five clubs. A double by West is a good raise to 4♠. 4♠ directly is a weak raise – perhaps a doubleton honor. Other direct bids show only one place to play. The idea may also apply if responder has doubled and the opponents reach the four-level. In that case the opener's actions are similar, but a double is for takeout.

PASSED HAND. A bid by a previously passed hand usually carries with it the information that the hand is limited to below the requirements for a bid on the earlier round. (Exceptions are unusual passes such as TRAP PASSES and FORCING PASSES.) As a result of the added knowledge partner has about the bidder's lack of strength, the bidder who has passed previously can often safely be somewhat aggressive if his values, vulnerability and other factors warrant it.

When partner has opened the bidding in third or fourth seat, the problems of the responder may be rather special. There are two complicating factors: (1) a change of suit is no longer forcing, so responder must be prepared for a "sudden death" pass of his response; (2) partner may have opened a sub-minimum hand to direct a lead or to try for a small plus score, so he may be annoyed if responder gets too high.

Since any response may be passed, responder must be very wary of responding in anemic suits. In general, the higher the response the greater the chance that it will be dropped. This means that the responder can answer 1♦ to 1♣ with a weakish suit (four to the jack), since someone at the table will likely bail responder out. But if one responds 1♥ or, more particularly, 1♠, one should have a respectable four-card suit (at least four to the queenten). If the response is at the two-level, responder must be prepared to play opposite a doubleton — partner is now even money to pass. So responder should have a six-card suit or at least a husky five-carder. Suppose you had passed this hand:

        ♠ K Q 2
        ♥ J 6 4 3
        ♦ A 9 6 3 2
        ♣ 7

If partner opens 1♣, respond 1♦. If, instead, he opens 1♦, it is arguable that we should respond 3♦ (not 1♥, as one might if it were forcing). If partner opens 1♥, one cannot temporize by answering 2♦, so 3♥ seems best -- perhaps even 4♥. And if partner opens 1♠, one must still avoid the 2♦ response because the partnership belongs in spades, not diamonds — responder may choose between 2♠ or 3♠. The jump raise is better in the long run in the absence of Drury. Suppose you had passed this hand:

        ♠ K 6
        ♥ Q 10 4 2
        ♦ K 10
        ♣ K 9 6 3 2

Again, you must be careful about bidding suits. Should partner open with 1♦ a 1♥ response is preferable to 2♣. True, the hand is strong enough for a two-level response and a rebid; but (1) partner may pass before the second bid, and (2) partner is more likely to find a rebid if he can do so at the one-level, and (3) if partner does pass, you would rather be in the higher scoring major suit. What would be the response with the above hand if partner opened 1♠? Not 2♣, and certainly not 2♥. The best bet is 2NT. This jump response could easily be right over 1♦ or 1♣ as well. The expert consensus (87% in BWS 2001): an action taken by a passed hand should have the same general meaning as the corresponding action taken by an unpassed hand. That applies when it is logically possible, subject to any constraints imposed by the failure to open the bidding, and when there is no explicit understanding to the contrary.

In contrast, if responder passed a hand that contains a

strong suit, he can give himself a little more freedom in bidding at the two-level. For example, holding:

    ♠ Q 7 5 2
    ♥ 7 4
    ♦ 2
    ♣ K Q 10 8 6 3

he would respond 2♣ to a 1♦ opening if he was a passed hand, while 1♠ would be correct if he was not. What makes the difference? Once the responder passed, there is a fighting chance to play in 2♣ when the responder bids it. If partner rebids 2♦, you can carry on with 2♠ without creating a forcing situation. What is more, it is dangerous to respond 1♠ — if partner passes there is no reason to believe that this is either the safest or most productive contract. Since the requirements for a two-over-one suit takeout are shaded down, there is a worry about missing game when holding the normal solid values for this response. Consider these hands:

♠ 8 3	♠ 7 4
♥ K Q 10 8 7 4 2	♥ 6 2
♦ A 10 5	♦ 8 5
♣ 5	♣ A K Q 10 9 6 5

If, for some reason that appealed at the time, either hand has been passed, jump shift over partner's opening. 2♥ or 2♣ in response to 1♠ is no longer nearly enough; you must jump to three. This puts partner on notice that there are game ambitions even opposite the bare minimum opening bid with which partner would pass a simple response.

But since few players would pass either of these hands, the traditional meaning of this jump shift has a very low frequency. The modern tendency is to use the jump shift only with a fit in opener's suit.

Passed hand jump raises and jumps to 2NT entail considerable risk of a minus score. Consider these hands:

♠ K 8 6 2	♠ A Q J 9
♥ J 10 4	♥ 7 5 3
♦ A Q 7 5	♦ 10 2
♣ 7 3	♣ K 10 8 2

West	East
Pass	1♠
3♠	Pass

No one made a terrible bid — East's third-hand opening is irreproachable, and West has the values for a passed-hand jump raise — but the final contract is dangerously high. Unless two finesses succeed, it will go down for a poor score. How do East-West get to 2♠? It is no solution for West to temporize with 2♦, as he might had partner opened in first seat, for he will be left in this unappetizing contract. Some players might bid only 2♠ with the West hand, fearing a light opening. This risks missing game opposite a sound minimum, for the range of the single raise becomes impossibly broad. Note that FIVE-CARD MAJORS bidding avoids the problem (Pass-1♣-1♠-Pass or 2♠). Here is a similar problem:

♠ J 8 7 3	♠ 9 6 2
♥ Q 10 4	♥ A K J 2
♦ K J	♦ Q 10 9 4
♣ A 9 4 2	♣ J 6

West	East
Pass	1♥
2NT	Pass

This contract is not likely to be a success. What went wrong? Surely West had to bid more than 1NT or 2♥; 3♥ is a possible response, but it is almost certainly down one. A response of 1♠ would be passed, and declarer can develop ulcers playing in a trump suit like that, though it is by no means the worst fate on the hand. Perhaps light third- and fourth-hand openings are undesirable.

Not really. You will show a big matchpoint profit in the long run by opening these hands. When partner has a normal minimum count, you will earn a small plus or at least impede the opponents or direct a good lead. The examples above are unlucky, but there is an answer for them.

The REVERSE DRURY Convention solves many problems of this sort. When the bidding is opened in third or fourth seat with one of a major, the response of 2♣ by the passed hand is artificial. It asks opener if he has a normal bid, or if he opened light. If opener has shaded his values, he rebids his suit. If he has a reasonable hand, he makes any other bid, and will often jump to game in his suit.

In the examples cited earlier, West would respond 2♣, Drury. East would rebid his suit and end the bidding. Let us see an auction where opener has his full bid:

♠ K 7 2	♠ A Q 10 8 4
♥ A Q 10 9	♥ K J 6 2
♦ Q 7 6 2	♦ 9 8
♣ 8 6	♣ A 5

West	East
Pass	1♠
2♣	2♥
4♥	Pass

Here, the advantage of Drury is in making it easy to find the essential heart fit; without it, West would likely jump to 3♠. However, the principal use of this convention is in staying at the two-level in case partner's hand is light.

    ♠ A J 9 8 4
    ♥ 6 2
    ♦ 9 8 4
    ♣ A J 5

The bidding then would be:

West	East
Pass	1♠
2♣	2♠

This is called REVERSE DRURY, because the original form of Drury called for a 2♦ rebid when opener is sub-minimum. That method fell out of favor in the Eighties. See also FIT-SHOWING JUMP, RULE OF SIXTEEN, SNAP, STRONG NOTRUMP AFTER PASSING, TWO-WAY DRURY.

PASSIVE DEFENSE. A defense whose principal aim is to avoid establishing tricks for declarer, rather than establishing tricks for the defense. A defender's continuation of a suit already led either by declarer or the defense, rather than attacking a new suit, is a common type of passive defense. See PASSIVE LEAD.

PASSIVE LEAD. An opening lead which is unlikely to hurt the defending side, but is not expected to have a positive value. A lead from three or four small cards is a typical passive lead, but in certain circumstances a trump lead may be passive, or a lead in an opposing suit which is likely to be solid. See ATTACKING LEAD; OPENING LEAD.

PASSOUT SEAT. The position of a player who can end the bidding by passing.

PASTEBOARDS. A name given to playing cards because a coating of black paste between two paper layers gave the stock on which the cards were printed an opacity that made it impossible to see through them. See MANUFACTURE OF PLAYING CARDS.

PATTERN. See HAND PATTERNS.

PATTERN RELAY ORGANIZED SYSTEM. See PRO SYSTEM.

PEARSON POINT COUNT. A guideline for deciding to open the bidding in fourth seat. The general guideline – if the total of high card points plus spades held is 14 or more, the bidding should be opened. The theory is that a holding in spades offers an edge in competitive bidding because spades is the highest ranking suit. However, if the total is less than 14 but the hand includes good distribution plus aces and kings, the hand still should be opened.

(a)	(b)
♠ K 10 9 7 6	♠ —
♥ 4 3	♥ A K 6 4 3 2
♦ A Q 6 5	♦ A J 9 7 4
♣ 8 3	♣ 4 3

The total of HCP (9) and spades (5) in (a) is 14. This qualifies as a fourth-hand opening bid according to the Pearson Count. It is weak in high cards, but the spade holding increases the possibility that your side can buy the hand at a sufficiently low level.

The total of HCP (12) and spades (0) in (b) is only 12, but it is clearly an opening bid. The Pearson Point Count is used as a guideline only when there is a close choice between bidding and passing in fourth chair. As always in bridge, there are many judgment calls. See BORDERLINE OPENING, DRURY, ROSENKRANZ.

PEETERS, MARCEL CHALLENGE CUP. See INTERNATIONAL BRIDGE ACADEMY.

PENAL INSTITUTIONS. See BRIDGE IN PRISONS.

PENALTY. Penalty can refer to rule violations and/or scoring of the hand.

(1) An obligation or restriction imposed upon a side for violation of the Laws of Bridge. In the language of the lawgivers, penalties are designed "... to provide an adequate remedy whenever a player accidentally, carelessly or inadvertently disturbs the proper course of the game. An offending player should be ready to pay graciously any penalty or adjusted score awarded by a Tournament Director."

(2) An amount scored above the line by the declarer's opponents when the declarer fails to make a contract. The penalty provisions of the score table are gauged so as to make competitive bidding a fine art. Many of the great stories in the anecdotage of the game are concerned with penalties. The biggest penalty in a championship tournament was reported from the Men's Pairs at the 1964 Summer North American Championships held at Toronto.

	♠ —	
	♥ A K Q J 9 7 6 4 2	
	♦ 7	
	♣ K Q 5	
♠ 10 8 6 2		♠ A K Q 7 5 4 3
♥ 10 3		♥ —
♦ 5 3		♦ 9 4
♣ J 10 9 8 7		♣ 6 4 3 2
	♠ J 9	
	♥ 8 5	
	♦ A K Q J 10 8 6 2	
	♣ A	

With both sides vulnerable, the par contract is a 7♠ sacrifice by East-West, which costs 1400 as compared with 2220 for the grand slam which North-South can make in hearts. (7♦ by South is defeated if West leads a heart.) At most tables the final contract was in fact 7♠ doubled, but at a number of other tables the North-South pairs refused to be outbid and overcalled 7♠ with 7NT, which was of course doubled and was usually redoubled. The auction at one such table, beginning with a strong two-bid, was:

West	North	East	South
	2♥	2♠	3♦
Pass	4NT	5♠	6♣
Pass	7♥	7♠	7NT
Pass	Pass	Dbl	Redbl
All Pass			

Spades were led, and West did not fail to unblock with the 8 and 10. East thus took the first seven tricks for a penalty of 4000. At another table the bidding was:

West	North	East	South
	2♣	3♠	4NT
Pass	6♥	Pass	7NT
Pass	Pass	Dbl	Redbl
All Pass			

West, doubtless attributing some unusual lead-directing significance to his partner's double, led a club and the contract was made for a score of 2930. The spread between top and bottom score was 6930.

The biggest recorded penalty in tournament play resulted from a hand similar to the following:

Dlr: West	♠ K J 4 3 2	
Vul: N-S	♥ 8	
	♦ 9 7 3 2	
	♣ 8 3 2	
♠ A 8		♠ —
♥ 7 6		♥ K 10 5 3
♦ A K Q J 10 8 5		♦ 6 4
♣ 10 4		♣ A K Q J 9 7 5
	♠ Q 10 9 7 6 5	
	♥ A Q J 9 4 2	
	♦ —	
	♣ 6	

The deal was played at a Baltic Congress, with Andrzej Witkowski and Bogdan Swiatek of Poznan sitting East and West. East could have made 6NT, but this contract was ruled out by the opening bid.

West	North	East	South
3NT	Pass	5♣	5♦
Dbl	Pass	Pass	Redbl
All Pass			

South tried to maneuver into a major, and 5♠ would have succeeded. But North did not realize that the redouble was an SOS. The defense did not score their spade ruff, but they had tricks to spare anyway, taking all 13. The score was 6400, not far short of the maxi-

mum of 7600.

This was exceeded in rubber bridge on the following deal, played in Megve, France, in 1954.

```
Dlr: East           ♠ —
Vul: N-S            ♥ Q 9 6 4
                    ♦ K Q 7 6
                    ♣ K 8 6 4 3
   ♠ A K 10 9 8 7 6 5 4 3 2        ♠ —
   ♥ 3                             ♥ K 10 7 5
   ♦ —                             ♦ 10 9 5 4 2
   ♣ 5                             ♣ J 9 7 2
                    ♠ Q J
                    ♥ A J 8 2
                    ♦ A J 8 3
                    ♣ A Q 10
```

West	North	East	South
		Pass	1NT
4♥!	Dbl	Pass	Pass
5♦!	Dbl	Pass	6NT
Dbl	Redbl	All Pass	

The ♠A was led. The result was down 12 for a penalty of 7000. South should have made two tricks.

One of the biggest penalties conceded by forgetting a convention occurred in Denmark. John Trelde forgot his own COPENHAGEN CONVENTION and went down nine tricks in 3♦ redoubled not vulnerable for a loss of 3400, pre-1987 scoring.

PENALTY CARD. A card that has been prematurely exposed by a defender, and must be left face up on the table until legally played or permitted to be picked up. If it is a LEAD OUT OF TURN, the declarer has several options, some of which permit the penalty card to be picked up; if it remains a penalty card on a lead out of turn, or is prematurely exposed in any other condition, it must be played at the first legal opportunity that the player may have to play it. See LAWS, Laws 24, 49-53, 55, 57, 58, and 62: LAWS OF DUPLICATE (Laws 23, 49-52, 54, 56-58, 62)

The 1987 Duplicate Laws and the 1993 Rubber Bridge Laws introduced a distinction between MAJOR PENALTY CARDS and MINOR PENALTY CARDS, which are explained under those headings.

PENALTY DOUBLE. Length in partner's suit is a deterrent to doubling the opponents. A fair rule of thumb is that the number of cards you have in partner's suit is the minimum level at which a double should be considered. So with a doubleton in partner's suit, you might double at the two-level. If partner pulls your penalty double, you should usually allow him to decide whether to double at the next level.

(1) **Positive doubles.** Suppose an opening bid is overcalled and doubled, and the opener's hand seems unsuited to defense. Should he stand the double or take it out? If the opening bid was of a sort which describes the hand within narrow limits, stand the double. If you open 3♠ with this hand:

```
♠ K J 8 7 6 4 3 2
♥ 3
♦ 2
♣ J 5 4
```

pass a double by partner of an overcall of 4♥. He does not expect you to have defensive strength.

Having opened with a three-bid, a four-bid, a weak two-bid, or any notrump bid, pass partner's double of an overcall. These bids all describe a hand within narrow limits.

Opponents seldom argue with a game-forcing opening, but when they do, retaliation must be swift and sure and there must be no partnership misunderstanding. The responder should beware of doubling on hands which contain a feature outside the enemy suit.

```
♠ A J 6 5
♥ Q 8 7 4
♦ 5 4 3
♣ 7 2
```

After a 2♣ opening by partner, do not double an overcall of 2♠. (2NT is better). Too often the hand will belong in a heart contract. In any event, the hand must be useful in attack, and game must be there. Experience shows that the double is best reserved for hands like:

```
♠ Q 10 7 6 5
♥ 8 7 4
♦ 5 4 3
♣ 7 2
```

If this is the partnership understanding, opener will pass the double with:

```
♠ 4
♥ A K J 5
♦ A K J
♣ K Q J 8 3
```

If the double is made on both hands above, the opener has a very tough decision. He will never know whether he is surrendering game or slam for poor recompense.

Having opened with a game-forcing bid, opener should accept partner's double of an intervening call *unless holding game in hand with fewer than five defensive tricks.*

It is a mistake to double the only contract you can beat.

```
Dlr: East           ♠ A Q 7 5 2
Vul: None           ♥ J 6 2
                    ♦ Q 10 8 4 3
                    ♣ —
   ♠ 8 4                          ♠ K J 9
   ♥ A 9 8 7                      ♥ K Q 10 4
   ♦ J 7                          ♦ K 9 2
   ♣ J 8 7 5 3                    ♣ A 9 2
                    ♠ 10 6 3
                    ♥ 5 3
                    ♦ A 6 5
                    ♣ K Q 10 6 4
```

West	North	East	South
		1NT	Pass
Pass	2♠	Pass	Pass
3♣	Pass	Pass	?

South should pass and take his plus. Even at matchpoint duplicate, a pass is better than a double, since the opponents are too likely to have a better spot. If South doubles, West will be nervous about his ragged suit and may run to hearts, where he can take nine tricks.

(2) **Low-level doubles.** Doubles after a suit opening and a suit overcall are almost invariably NEGATIVE in the modern style. If the double is not negative, the following applies: Stand a low-level double with three quick defensive tricks; pull it with fewer unless there is compensation in trump strength; pull the double nearly always with an unbid five-card suit. In a close decision, decide whether or not a lead of your bid suit will be crucial.

Two other opportunities for penalty doubles occur in these situations:

(a) A double of a 1NT overcall is made with almost any hand with 9 or more high-card points since the partnership is virtually certain to have the balance of strength. However, discretion should be exercised

facing a third-in-hand opening.

(b) A double of an overcall of a 1NT opening depends on the strength of the 1NT opening. It shows that the partnership has the balance of strength and that the doubler has at least three to an honor in the overcaller's suit. The double is more attractive at favorable vulnerability, less attractive at unfavorable. Many now play negative doubles here.

(3) **Game doubles.** Doubles of game contracts in a competitive auction are usually aimed at taking the maximum penalty from opponents who have taken a save. However, the double may also act as a warning to partner not to proceed further. If a pass would be a FORCING PASS, then a double indicates a disinclination to go further. For this reason a player who anticipates disaster if his side bids further may double when his prospects of beating the opposing contract are not better than moderate.

Doubling a game contract which has been reached voluntarily without interference is very seldom good policy (unless the doubler suspects an advance save, for example, after 3♠-4♠), and again that might be construed as takeout.

Doubling a game on the basis of high cards only is a costly exercise. For the double to be worthwhile, both opponents must have limited their hands in such a way that it is clear that neither has any strength in reserve. For example:

West	East
1♣	1♥
2♥	2NT
3NT	

In this auction it is clear that both players are straining to reach game, and either opponent may double if the honor strength, especially in clubs and hearts, seems well placed for the defense

The worst penalty doubles help declarer make a contract that would fail undoubled. Suppose declarer is playing 4♠ with this trump suit:

     ♠ Q 9 7 6 5 2
     ♥ 8
     ♦ A J 10 3
     ♣ K 4

     ♠ K 8
     ♥ A 4 2
     ♦ 9 7 4
     ♣ A Q J 6 5

If East passes, declarer will lead low to the king, intending to duck the next lead and hoping for A-x in East. But if East doubles, declarer may run the 9 through East, saving a trick.

When the deal is a freak and both sides have a double fit, a penalty double may be costly. In the long run, it is better to be declarer.

Dlr: East   ♠ A 10 7 5 3
Vul: E-W   ♥ 2
                ♦ A Q 9 7 6 5 2
                ♣ —

♠ Q 8 6   ♠ —
♥ K Q 5 4 3   ♥ J 10 9 7 6
♦ —   ♦ K 3
♣ A Q 9 8 6   ♣ K 10 5 4 3 2

                ♠ K J 9 4 2
                ♥ A 8
                ♦ J 10 8 4
                ♣ J 7

West	North	East	South
		Pass	Pass
1♥	2♥	4♣ (1)	4♠
Dbl	Pass	5♥	5♠
Pass	Pass	6♥	Dbl
All Pass			

(1) Clubs with heart support

This deal arose in the 1984 Vanderbilt Knockout Teams. In fairness to N-S, they received misinformation. East alerted 4♣ and interpreted the bid correctly for South, his screenmate. Meanwhile, West alerted and told North that 4♣ showed club shortness with a heart fit. Nevertheless, N-S paid dearly for failing to heed the "double-double" fit axiom: "When in doubt, bid one more". 6♥ doubled made for +1660, and 6♠ also would have made.

At the other table, South played 6♠ on a different auction and misguessed the ♠Q to go down one.

If the contract is a suit, a double becomes attractive if the declaring side has run into a bad trump split. It is sometimes possible to double with a void if the other defender is marked by the bidding with five trumps. But it is still necessary for both opponents to be limited, so that all possibility of a redoubled overtrick is excluded. DOUBLES OF NOTRUMP BIDS are listed separately. See also COOPERATIVE DOUBLE, DOUBLE FOR SACRIFICE, LEAD-DIRECTING DOUBLE, LIGHTNER DOUBLE, MAXIMAL DOUBLE, OPTIONAL DOUBLE, SUPPORT DOUBLE.

PENALTY LIMITS. In social or progressive bridge, in order to prevent one hand from assuming overwhelming importance, it is customary to limit the plus score in premium points for doubled and redoubled undertrick penalties. Generally, 1000 points is the limit.

PENALTY PASS. A pass by a player after a TAKEOUT DOUBLE from his partner and a pass by right-hand opponent. For example:

West	North	East	South
1♦	Dbl	Pass	Pass

South's pass indicates considerable length and strength in diamonds; five cards headed by three honors would normally be the minimum diamond holding. Even holding five strong diamonds, a pass would be unwise with a two-suited hand because the declarer would be likely to score ruffs. After such a pass, North has an obligation to lead a trump, because South will wish to draw declarer's trumps.

After a minor-suit opening, a penalty pass may come into consideration with nothing but trump length at unfavorable vulnerability. If the contract succeeds, even with an overtrick, the resulting score may be less than the opener's side could have scored in other ways. This can apply by agreement if opener's partner has redoubled.

A penalty pass becomes more attractive if the doubler was in a balancing position. Q J x x of trumps may be a sufficient trump holding.

PERCENTAGE. A quotient obtained by dividing the actual matchpoint score of a contestant by the possible score of that contestant, which is then expressed as a percentage (of the possible score).

PERCENTAGE PLAY. A play influenced by math-

ematical factors when more than one reasonable line of play is available. See PROBABILITIES A POSTE-RIORI, SUIT COMBINATIONS, and MATHEMATI-CAL TABLES (Tables 4, 4A). The following examples show how the above references can be used in bridge play.

(1) Neither the auction nor the play to the first trick has shown any marked UNBALANCED DISTRIBU-TION in defenders' hands. Dummy has A-K-Q-5-4-3-2, and declarer is void in the suit. There is about 36% probability that the suit will be divided 3-3.

(2)   A K Q 10

              4 3 2

The correct line of play, based solely on PROBABILI-TIES A PRIORI, is to play the A-K-Q unless East shows a singleton or void. From percentage play, probabilities are:

3-3 division	35.53%
J-x (J-9, J-8, J-7, J-6, J-5) either	16.15%
J singleton either	2.42%
J-9-8-7-6-5 with West	.74%
J-x-x-x-x with West	6.05%
Total	60.89%

The alternative play of taking a finesse on the third round, unless the jack has been played, has the follow-ing probabilities:

J in West's hand	50.00%
J-x with East	8.07%
J singleton with East	1.21%
Total	59.28%

To make four tricks in the suit, the odds are slightly less than 61 to 59 on refusing the finesse.

(3)   A Q 10 7 3 2

              9 8 5

Declarer disregards the safety play in favor of trying for the maximum number of tricks. He plans to finesse the queen and make six tricks if West holds both honors doubleton or if East holds the singleton jack. He may also have to decide on his action if West plays low and the finesse loses. Reference to MATHEMATICAL TABLES. Table 4 shows that the distribution

6-4 opposite K-J has a probability of 6.8%
J-6-4 opposite K has a probability of 6.2%

The odds are therefore 34 to 31 on playing the ace on the second round after the finesse has lost, as against taking a second finesse. Percentage play often requires calculations which, though not too difficult, require more involved operations. This may be valuable in subsequent analysis but may not be practical at the table.

In the following, two lines of play present themselves.

              ♠ —
              ♥ Q 3 2
              ♦ A K Q 10 4 3 2
              ♣ 7 5 4

              ♠ K Q J 6 3 2
              ♥ A K J 6 5 4
              ♦ —
              ♣ 3

South plays in 6♥. West leads the ♣Q, then a second club on which East plays the king. South ruffs. As West presumably has the Q-J and East the A-K, the play of this suit has not altered the ratio of the a priori odds, but in our more detailed calculations we must assume that

East and West each originally held at least three clubs. South's best line of play depends upon the probability of the divisions of the two red suits. To determine this accurately it is necessary to calculate the appropriate combinations as explained in SUIT, NUMBER OF CARDS IN. For a satisfactory approximate answer ap-ply the rule of multiplying PROBABILITY OF SUC-CESSIVE EVENTS. (This is an approximation because the distribution of the two suits is interdependent, not independent. We note the discrepancy when we give the result of our detailed calculations later.) To the third trick South leads the ♥A, East and West both following. At trick four South can:

(a) lead the ♥K;
(b) lead a low heart to dummy's queen;
(c) lead the ♥J.

In each case we must consider the position if (i) West follows to the second round of hearts, and (ii) West does not follow.

(a) (♥K) will win whenever

hearts are 2-2	40%	
and diamonds are 3-3		36%
or doubleton J		16%
Total		52%

The probability that both will occur (hearts 2-2 and diamonds come home) is 40% of 52%, which equals 20.8%. If hearts actually divide 2-2, South leads the ♠K, and if this is covered his troubles are over. Assuming that West will cover half the time he holds the ace this gives another 4.8% (50% of 50% of 19.2%), bringing our total to 25.6%.

If West has three hearts (25%), South leads to dummy's ♥Q and makes his contract with the above division of diamonds (52%). This gives another 13%. Similarly, we have a further 13% if East has three hearts and there is the above diamond division.

Our grand approximate total for (a) is thus 51.6%.

(b) (low heart) will win whenever

hearts are 2-2	40%	
diamonds 4-2		48%
diamonds 3-3		36%
singleton J		2%
any other division		
provided West has the ♠A		7%
Total		93%

or

West has 3 hearts or	25%	
four diamonds and		
the ♠A	30%	
East has 3 hearts	25%	
diamonds are 3-3		36%
doubleton ♦J		16%
East has five small diamonds		
and two low spades,		
or		
J-x-x-x and three low spades		2%
Total		54%

Our grand total for (b) is thus (40% of 93%) + (25% of [30% + 54%), or 58.2%.

(c) (♥J) is obviously inferior to (b). If West follows to the second round of hearts and we overtake the ♥J we lose if West has three hearts and three diamonds even if he also has the ♠A, South has to return to his own hand twice — once to take the ruffing finesse in spades and once to draw West's last trump. One entry has to be the ruff of a fourth diamond, and West will overruff. If

the ♥ J is not overtaken, the lead is not in dummy for the diamond suit to be led.

A more detailed calculation which takes account of the interdependence of the suit distributions gives us 48.99% for (a) and 52.62% for (b). We note that there is less difference between these two numbers than between our approximate calculations. This is due to the fact that (b) contains a larger number of unbalanced hands, the type on which approximate calculations give misleadingly high figures. See MARBLES. For a computer program that will make sophisticated percentage calculations, see BASE III. Also see OPTIMUM STRATEGY.

PERCENTAGES. Because chance plays a considerable part in the distribution of cards at a bridge table, it is understandable that expert players are interested in the mathematical percentages applicable to different situations. Among the articles dealing with percentage are: MARBLES, MATHEMATICS OF BRIDGE, PERCENTAGE PLAY, SLAM BIDDING, SUIT COMBINATIONS, VALUE OF GAME, and PARTSCORE. MATHEMATICAL TABLES also deals with various percentage situations. Bridge writers frequently use a variation of percentage, ODDS IN BRIDGE, in discussing situations yielding to mathematical treatment. Many computer bridge programs make sophisticated percentage calculations.

PERFECT BRIDGE HAND. A hand that will produce 13 tricks in notrump irrespective of the opening lead or the composition of the other three hands. A hand containing all 13 cards of a suit, therefore, does not qualify as a perfect hand, since such a hand will not take even a single trick if played in notrump. Although most players think of a hand containing four aces, four kings, four queens and a jack as the perfect hand, actually it is only one of many. Altogether there are 3,756 possible perfect hands, which break down as follows:

Hand Pattern				Number of Possible Hands
AKQJxxxxx	AK	A	A	1,512
AKQJ10xxx	AKQ	A	A	672
AKQJ10xxx	AK	AK	A	672
AKQxxxxxx	A	A	A	480
AKQJ109x	AKQ	AK	A	168
AKQJ109x	AKQJ	A	A	84
AKQJ109x	AK	AK	AK	28
AKQJ109	AKQJ	AK	A	24
AKQJ10	AKQJ	AKQ	A	24
AKQJ109	AKQJ10	A	A	12
AKQJ109	AKQ	AKQ	A	12
AKQJ109	AKQ	AK	AK	12
AKQJ10	AKQJ10	AK	A	12
AKQJ10	AKQJ	AK	AK	12
AKQJ10	AKQ	AKQ	AK	12
AKQJ	AKQJ	AKQ	AK	12
AKQJ	AKQJ	AKQJ	A	4
AKQJ	AKQ	AKQ	AKQ	4
			Total	3,756

As there are 635,013,559,600 possible hands a player can hold, the odds against holding such a "perfect hand" are 169,066,442 to 1

PERIODICALS. See BIBLIOGRAPHY.

PERMANENT TRUMP. At whist, a variation in which club card committees or other governing bodies declared a suit to be trump for all games under their jurisdiction. The rules of whist provided that the trump suit would be the suit of the last card dealt by the dealer to himself.

PERMUTATIONS. All the possible arrangements of the cards, usually the residue of a suit given the cards in two hands. See MATHEMATICAL TABLES.

PERSONALITY OF THE YEAR. An honor conferred annually by the INTERNATIONAL BRIDGE PRESS ASSOCIATION.

PETER. A term used in Great Britain, but rarely elsewhere, to describe a high-low made in discarding, such as high-low in any given suit. Originally, in whist, the use of the term was restricted to a high-low in the trump suit only. See HIGH-LOW SIGNALS and BLUE PETER.

PETIT CUEBID. See LITTLE CUEBID.

PHANTOM PAIR. In a pair contest with an odd number of pairs, the pair which would (if present) complete the last table. The contestants scheduled to play against the phantom pair have a bye round.

PHANTOM SACRIFICE (or phantom save). A sacrifice bid against a contract which would have been defeated. See DEFENSIVE TRICK.

PHENOMENAL HANDS. See FREAK HANDS.

PHILIP MORRIS CHAMPIONSHIPS. The Philip Morris Corp. sponsors European bridge competitions — open pairs in odd-numbered years, mixed pairs and mixed teams in the even-numbered years. The competitions consist of several tournaments, and the overall performance of a pair or team determines its final standing. For results see Appendix IV.

PHONY CLUB. See SHORT CLUB.

PHONY DIAMOND. See SHORT DIAMOND.

PIANOLA. A hand at bridge which presents no problems to declarer, so easily playable that it almost plays itself. The name derives from the old player piano or "pianola" which would "play" itself.

PICK A SLAM. See FIVE NOTRUMP.

PICK UP. To capture or drop an outstanding high card.

PICKUP BOY (GIRL). See CADDY.

PICKUP SLIP. A form devised for the recording of the result of one round. Information contained on the slip includes identifying numbers of the pairs; the board numbers; which pair was the declarer; the final contract and by whom; whether doubled, redoubled, or undoubled; the result; trick-score; extra tricks; game or doubled bonuses; partscore bonus; slam bonus; or undertrick score. Usually the North (or South) player has the responsibility of making out the score. The East-West pair are responsible for checking the entries and verifying the slip. After each round the pick-up slips are collected and results of the round entered in a computer or on a recapitulation sheet by the director or a designated scorer. See SCORESLIP, SCORING FORMS, TRAVELING SCORESLIP.

PIN. The lead of a high card when right-hand oppoient has an unguarded card slightly lower in rank. Either declarer or a defender can make the play.

A 9 8 7 6

Q 10 3 2

Declarer can pick up this suit without loss in two cases. He can lead to the ace, dropping a singleton king from West and then finessing against East for the jack. However, if declarer has reason to think that East is short in the suit, he can lead the queen and pass it, hoping to pin the jack. If this happens, he can pick up the suit by finessing against West for the king:

♥ Q 10 3 2

♥ J 5 4   ♥ A K 8 7 6

♥ 9

South plays in a spade contract after East has bid hearts and West has raised them. If East plays in routine fashion to West's heart lead by winning with the king and shifting to another suit, South can establish a heart trick in the dummy by ruffing a low heart and later leading the queen, or vice versa. But if East wins the first trick with the ace and returns a low heart, South is likely to conclude that West started with K-x-x. Note that the inspired lead of the jack would have pinned the 9 and given South no chance to develop a trick.

PING-PONG. Ping-Pong is a popular method in France of rebidding after opener's 1NT rebid. After the rebid of 1NT, responder can follow one of three courses. The two simple choices are direct action at the two-level or three-level, the second is to start by bidding 2♣ as a puppet to 2♦ to show invitational hands.

The general approach is to put all distributional game-forcing hands through the direct jump to the three-level. All two-level actions except reverses deny game interest. If responder bids 2♣ to force 2♦, he then has a choice of a series of actions which in general show more values and less shape than bidding out the hand directly. So after 1m-1M-1NT responder's actions show:

	Direct actions	via the Puppet 2♣
2M	weak	light invitation
2♠/1♥	5-4 invite	4-4 invitation
2♥/1♠	Weak	5-4 invitation
2NT	invitation	invitation; 4M + 5♣
3♣	5-5 forcing	invitation
3♦	5-5 forcing	invitation; 4M+5 ♦
3♥/1♠	5-5 forcing	invitation: 5-5
3M	forcing	invitation with 6-card suit
3NT	to play	choice of games; 5M.

PINK POINT. An obsolete term for REGIONAL POINT. It was used to distinguish red points won at a Regional tournament from those won at a National tournament.

PINPOINT ASTRO. See ASTRO.

PIP. A small design indicating the suit to which a particular card belongs. The SPADE suit is indicated by a spearhead, the HEART suit by a heart, the DIAMOND suit by a diamond-shaped tile, the CLUB suit by a clover leaf. The spot cards have as many pips as the rank of the card indicates, from 1 to 10 in the standard deck, in addition to two INDICES, the lower half of which is a pip. In German cards, the pips of LEAVES and

ACORNS usually have stems, and are often attached as if on a branch. In the trappola PACK, the pips often vary in size and design, and the SWORDS and CUDGELS are usually interlaced. See SUIT and INDICES.

PITCH. A colloquial term for DISCARD.

PITCH COUNT. An old name for the 4-3-2-1 POINT COUNT.

PITT COUP. A play by which the declarer places himself in a position to lead through his left-hand adversary in a suit in which the dummy holds a major tenace over the left-hand adversary's minor tenace. It frequently involves the unblocking of a trump suit in dummy, and also may include a deliberate higher-than-necessary ruff with an honor in the closed hand so as to be able to lead low through West.

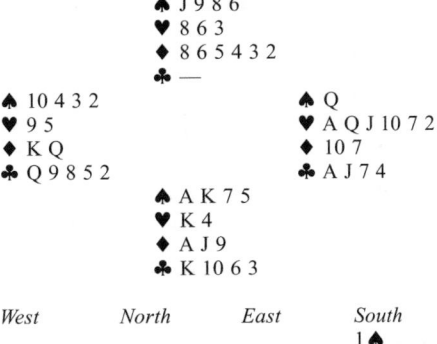

West	North	East	South
			1♠
Pass	2♠	3♥	3NT
Pass	4♠	All Pass	

West opened the ♥9, won by East who returned the suit. South won with the king. The ♠A was led, on which declarer called for the 8 from dummy (maintaining a two-way finesse situation against the 10). East's queen marked West with four spades to the 10. Declarer led ace and another diamond, hoping for and getting the 2-2 split in the suit. West won the second diamond, and returned a club, dummy discarding and East winning the ace. East returned the high heart, which declarer ruffed with the king. The lead of the ♠7 permitted South to take a finesse, playing dummy's 6♠ a further spade lead through West enabled declarer to unblock the high diamond from his hand on the fourth spade lead and win the balance of the tricks in dummy. The name is arbitrary, resulting from the use of Pitt, Chatham, etc., in whist literature to designate particular players.

PIVOT BRIDGE, LAWS OF. (A form of social bridge at home games where, instead of advancing from table to table as in party or progressive bridge, the players change or pivot among themselves at each individual table.) Pivot bridge is played by four (or five and sometimes six) players at a table. This form may be used for a single table or for large gatherings in which it is desirable to have each table play as a separate unit without progression by the players.

The game is so arranged that each player plays with each other player at his table both as partner and opponent. There are two methods of play: first, four deals may be played to a round, one deal by each player, and the players change partners at the end of each four deals.

Second, rubbers may be played, and the players change partners at the end of each rubber.

If four deals to a round are played, the scoring is exactly the same as in Progressive Bridge; if rubbers are played, the scoring is exactly the same as in Rubber Bridge. The laws given below explain only the method of rotation in changing partners, not scoring, vulnerability, etc., which are covered elsewhere

DRAW FOR PARTNERS

1. The players draw cards for partners and deal, and for a choice of seats and pack. The player who draws highest is the first pivot, he deals first and has the choice of seats and packs. The player who draws second highest is the pivot's first partner; the player who draws third highest sits at the pivot's left during the first round; the player who draws fourth sits at the pivot's right; and if a fifth player is present, he does not participate in the first round or rubber.

CHANGING PARTNERS (FOR FOUR PLAYERS)

2. During the first three rounds or rubbers the players change positions as indicated in the following diagram:

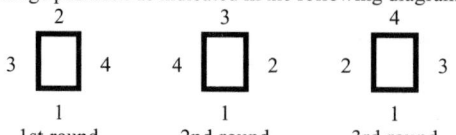

| 1st round | 2nd round | 3rd round |

After the third round or rubber, the players again cut for position and partners.

CHANGING PARTNERS (FOR FIVE PLAYERS)

3. If five players desire to play at the same table, they may be accommodated in this manner: For the first round or rubber, the players take the positions indicated by their draw for position under law No. 1. For rounds one to five, they take the positions indicated in the following diagram:

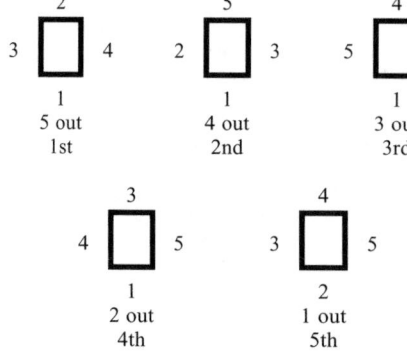

At the end of each five rounds, the players again draw for positions and partners.

This arrangement permits each player to play with each other player once as partner and twice as opponent, and each player sits out one round in turn.

SIX-PLAYER PIVOT

4. With six players at the same table, a complete pivot enabling each player to play once as partner and twice against each combination of opponents other than the player who is cut out at the same time, may be arranged by following this sequence of partnerships:

3-4	1-5	1-3	3-5	1-6	1-4	3-6	1-2
v	v	v	v	v	v	v	v
5-6	2-6	2-4	4-6	2-5	2-3	4-5	5-6

The player numbers correspond to the order in which they are cut out, with 1-2, 3-4 and 5-6 out simultaneously. If more than eight rounds are to be played, the pivot is resumed at round 3, or a new order may be determined by cutting so as to have different players out at the same time.

DETERMINATION OF THE WINNER

5. At the completion of each round or rubber, the player enters on his tally both his own score and that of his opponents. Each player totals his own and his opponents' scores separately and records the difference, plus or minus as the case may be, at the bottom of his tally. The player having the highest plus score is the winner and the others rank in descending order according to their scores.

PIVOT MITCHELL. A method of taking care of a half table in a MITCHELL game, particularly useful in a SCRAMBLED MITCHELL. The last table will have no stationary pair and the moving pairs will pass this table in this way: play East-West, then sit out, then play North-South, then continue to E-W at table one. See BUMP MITCHELL and HALF TABLES.

PIVOT TEAMS. A team event in which each member of a team of four plays equally with each other member. Popular in Britain, and used in New York City in the Betty Kaplan Teams.

PLACE THE CARDS, PLACING CARDS. See ASSUMPTIONS IN PLAY; CARD READING.

PLACING THE LEAD. See AVOIDANCE.

PLAFOND. A French card game which was the immediate predecessor of contract. Harold S. Vanderbilt, the originator of contract bridge, used *plafond* (which means "ceiling") as the basis for his approach to the new game.

PIERRE BELLANGER (*The Bridge World*, Sept. 1931) dates the origin of Plafond to 1918, where it was introduced at the Cercle Litteraire of Paris shortly after the Armistice. Only those tricks bid for and made were scored below the line and counted toward game. Tricks made above the bid scored 50 points above the line for each additional trick. Except for increasing the slam bonuses to 100 for a small slam and 200 for a grand slam, awarded whether the slam was bid or not, the trick scores and penalties were much as in auction. However, a bonus of 50 points was scored for making any contract successfully; the first game for either side received a bonus of 100; winning the rubber was worth an additional 400. Bellanger also claims authorship of the words "Contract Bridge," an appendix to his 1914 edition of *Legislation du Bridge aux Encheres* mentioning *Bridge avec Contrat*. But contract, as it was introduced in 1914 at the Automobile Club de France, was only an embryonic form of Plafond.

GEORGE F. HERVEY, bridge correspondent of *The Field*, cites a letter to that publication, dated February 8, 1941, in which Sir Hugh Clayton records that the contract principle was invented by four players in Poona (India) in 1912. The game was developed out of auction and named S.A.C.C., an acronym of the four men who invented it. On July 15,1914, the rules of this game were published by Sir Hugh in *The Times of India*, and there is evidence that the game was played in various parts of

India from that date until some years after promulgation of the first official code of laws to govern contract bridge (December 1929).

MILTON C. WORK reported that similar games had been tried in the United States before 1914 but failed to become popular. Obviously, none of these games included the vulnerability feature and the scoring table devised by Vanderbilt, but it would appear that the "ceiling" principle of Plafond may have come to France from India or at least have originated there at an earlier date than reported by Bellanger. There was a Franco-American Plafond Match in 1930 which ended about even, and which employed many of the newly established contract bridge methods, but most players essaying both games tended to prefer the more precise and demanding contract.

PLAIN SUIT. A suit other than the trump suit.

PLAN OF PLAY, PLANNING THE PLAY. The mental process by which declarer decides how to use the assets of the combined hands to fulfill the contract and to develop overtricks or minimize penalties. Among the things to be considered is the management of the trump suit, development of long cards in side suits, maintenance of communication between the two hands, if and how to finesse, development of endplays, safety plays against adverse distributions. Declarer should mentally review these and other problems before playing to the first trick, even though such play may be automatic. Original plans should frequently be changed as more information about adverse holdings is developed. See NOTRUMP PLAY.

PLASTIC CARDS. Cards made of acetate cellulose or a vinyl or polyvinyl compound. Most manufacturers no longer make them. See MANUFACTURE OF PLAYING CARDS.

PLASTIC VALUATION. One of the phrases popularized in the writings of Ely Culbertson to describe the mental processes of the bidder as he receives more information regarding the makeup of his partner's hand. REVALUATION, PROMOTION OF TRUMP HONORS, and DISTRIBUTIONAL COUNTS were all covered in the one phrase.

PLATINUM POINTS. Masterpoints awarded by the ACBL in nationally-rated events at North American Championships. The PLAYER OF THE YEAR for the ACBL is determined strictly on platinum points. See BLACK POINTS, GOLD POINTS, MASTERPOINTS, RED POINTS, SILVER POINTS.

PLAY (of the hand). See NOTRUMP PLAY; TRUMP SUIT MANAGEMENT.

PLAY AFTER AN ILLEGAL PLAY. Such action forfeits (waives) any penalty incurred by the illegal play, unless the illegal play constitutes a revoke. This is in accordance with the principle that the non-offending side may "condone" an offense. Such a play may be made only by the player to the left of the hand making the illegal play, and such right is not affected by partner calling attention to the illegality of the play. See LAWS (Law 60).

PLAY FROM EQUALS. When holding cards of equal rank in a suit, it is often very important which card is chosen to be played to a particular trick. A defender's card may provide partner with important information, or it may deceive the declarer. A declarer's card may confuse the defense, or at least avoid giving away information unnecessarily.

Defensive play from equals. On the opening lead, there is a standard table which usually requires that the higher of two equal honors be led. The only exception to this is that the king is sometimes led from ace, king, and others (see OPENING LEADS and RUSINOW). However, when the honor combination is bare (no small cards) the lower honor is sometimes led to inform partner of the situation. For example, the normal lead from A-K-x against a suit contract is the king. From A-K alone, the usual lead is the ace. When this is followed by the king, the partner of the leader will know that the opening leader has exhausted the suit led (otherwise, the normal lead of the king would have been made).

This reversing order of plays can also be used later in the defense. Consider, for example, the deal below:

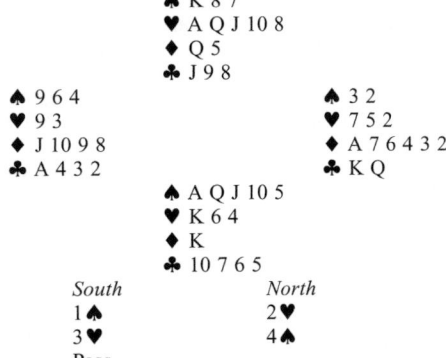

South	North
1♠	2♥
3♥	4♠
Pass	

Against South's 4♠ contract, West leads the ♦J.

East wins the ♦A and sees at once that the defense must look to clubs for the setting tricks. East should shift to the ♣Q, not the king. After the ♣Q wins and East continues with the ♣K, West should overtake to give East a club ruff. In this case, the deliberate play of the wrong honor from equals indicates no other cards in the suit led. If East had started with three clubs to the K-Q, he would have made the normal shift to the ♣K.

Sometimes the lower honor is led from equal cards for the purpose of deceiving the declarer.

In many situations a defender's play from equals should be the card he is known to hold. The most common situation in which this opportunity arises is:

♠ A J 2

♠ Q 10 4   ♠ 8 7 6

♠ K 9 5 3

The declarer, South, leads the ♠3, and finesses dummy's jack. When the ♠A is cashed, West should drop the queen. This card ranks equally with the 10, but the cards are not equivalent, as West is known to hold the queen. If West drops the ♠10 under the ace, South must make four tricks in the suit. If West drops the queen on the second round, South is faced with a guess.

In some situations, the correct play from equals depends on the assumption of a possible distribution of the cards.

♥ A J 3
♥ K Q 4 2   Immaterial
♥ 7 led

When declarer leads the ♥7, if West decides to split his honors, he should play the queen and not the king. It is possible that declarer is missing the 10, and can be put to a difficult guess on the second round of hearts. For example, the suit might be distributed:

♥ A J 3
♥ K Q 4 2   ♥ 10 6 5
♥ 9 8 7

After the queen loses to the ace, declarer will later lead the suit from his own hand once again. If West ducks, declarer must reckon with the possibility that he made a standard falsecard with an original holding of Q-10-4-2. Notice that the initial play of the king would not create this effect, as West could hardly afford to play the king from K-10-4-2, lest declarer hold the queen in the concealed hand.

In other situations, the defense can play from imaginary equal cards:

♣ A K 10 9 7 6
♣ J 8   ♣ Q 2
♣ 5 4 3

The declarer leads the ♣5 and West plays the jack. If the declarer suspects that West has split equals, he may later lose a trick to East's queen.

In choosing a deceptive card to play from equals, the best policy is to make the holding you are representing a believable one.

An opening lead from equal cards is often made in consideration of what dummy is likely to hold in the suit led. On lead against a suit contract with A-K-6-4 of a suit that dummy has bid strongly, the best lead is probably the ace. If the dummy's suit is headed by Q-J without the 10, and the declarer holds a singleton, he may later take a ruffing finesse against third hand's imaginary king instead of choosing a different (possibly successful) line of play.

Another occasion for a deceptive lead from equal cards is when it is desirable to misrepresent the potential entry position. Let us suppose that West is on lead against the auction:

South	North
1NT	3NT

West holds Q-J-10-8-6-2. The best lead might conceivably be the deceptive 10. East's first play will look like a high signal, and declarer may believe that West has hit East's suit. If this plan succeeds, South will probably take losing finesses into the West hand.

Third hand's standard play from equal honors is the lowest of touching cards. Declarer may sometimes be deceived by a change of strategy.

♠ 4 3
♠ 10 8 6 2   ♠ K Q 7 5
♠ A J 9

Against South's notrump contract, West leads the ♠2. If East believes he will obtain the lead first for the defense, he might well play the king as a deceptive move.

When East later leads the ♠5, South may decide his best chance is to hope that East has the 10.

When the declarer must guess which suit to attack, the defense can often mislead him with the play of an apparently unnecessarily high card from equals.

♠ A J 9 8 3
♠ 4 2   ♠ K Q 10 5
♠ 7 6

Declarer plays a spade to dummy's 9. If East wins with the 10 (equal with the king and queen on this trick), the declarer may look elsewhere for his tricks. If East wins with a high honor, however, declarer may continue the suit at his next opportunity, thus losing time (and possibly tricks).

The defense often uses a play from equals as a suit preference signal. This frequently occurs when a defender is establishing a suit against a notrump contract and has a choice of equal cards to use to knock out the declarer's last stopper. The use of a high card shows a possible entry in a high-ranking suit, and the use of a low card shows a possible entry in a low-ranking suit. A similar play from equals involves the play of a high honor from equals to show strength in a high-ranking suit and a low honor from equals to show strength in a low-ranking suit. See SUIT PREFERENCE SIGNAL.

Declarer's play with equals. The selection of declarer's play with equal cards is designed to misguide the defense as much as possible. The selection of which equal to play depends upon declarer's specific objective.

♦ 2

♦ K Q J 10 9

At a suit contract, declarer (South) must avoid a loser in diamonds (a side suit). If dummy holds a few trump cards, his best chance is to lead the ♦9 from his hand. If West holds the ace, he may duck on the assumption that East can win the trick cheaply.

Thus, declarer plays a low equal when he hopes the defense will not use their honor cards. If, in a similar situation, the declarer hopes to remove the ace quickly, he should play the king (or queen) on the first round.

At a notrump contract, the declarer is usually interested in concealing strength or feigning strength so that the defenders will not know whether or not they have hit a weak spot in declarer's armor.

♣ 4 3

♣ K Q 10

Against South's notrump contract, West leads the ♣5 on which East plays the jack. South should win with the king. By so doing, he may deceive West into believing that East holds the queen.

♣ 4 3

♣ A K Q

Declarer has a weak spot elsewhere, and hopes the defense will continue clubs. When West leads the ♣5 and East plays the jack, declarer should play the king. Once again this play may lead West to believe that East holds the ♣Q. If declarer wins with the ace, West will know he has something else in clubs unless the unlikely situation of East holding K-Q-J exists. Thus, West may suspect some trickiness. (On the other hand, against an experienced West, the play of the ace may be a good double cross.)

If the declarer is afraid of a continuation of the suit led, he should put on a mock display of power.

♠ 4 3
♠ A K 8 5 2   ♠ 9 7 6
♠ Q J 10

On West's lead of the ♠5, East plays the 9. South might well gobble this up with the 10, making sure West knows that he holds the queen and jack as well. If South

wins with a higher honor, West may tend to place East with more length because of the chance that the declarer lacks the ♠10.

When the declarer has a very powerful holding in the suit led, he can often paint a very misleading picture.

♥ Q 6 5

♥ 9 7 3 2   ♥ 10 8

♥ A K J 4

Against South's 3NT contract, West leads the ♥2. Dummy plays low and East plays the 10. To encourage the defense to continue the suit, South's best play is probably the king. In addition to concealing the jack, this play suggests to West that East may have started with A-J-10. The play of the ace may present the same type of picture, but if holding the ace, declarer might have played dummy's queen on the first trick to gain a tempo by raking in a fast winner.

In general, declarer's best idea is to keep the defense in the dark as much as possible about his holding. However, he sometimes plays with a specific objective in mind.

♠ 8 6 5

♠ A 2   ♠ 7 3

♠ K Q J 10 9 4

Spades are trumps. In drawing trumps, many declarers think it is amusing to lead the 8 from dummy and let it ride. This is a good way to let the dummy know the hand is not violently overbid, but it also gives away a lot of information. West may feel that declarer has taken a successful finesse and he may adopt an active defense in a desperate attempt to defeat the contract. If this is to declarer's benefit, then this method of playing the trump suit is correct. However, if the declarer fears an active defense, he should play a low spade to his king or queen. West may now hope his partner held J-10-x and that declarer must lose another trick in trumps. He may therefore play safe, assuming that if he does not give away a trick with an aggressive lead, the contract will probably be defeated.

(As with all of these deceptive plays which leave possibilities open, how well declarer knows his opponents is an important factor.)

The purpose of declarer's play from equals is often to locate the defensive honors in a suit.

♣ 4 3 2

♣ K Q 10

The declarer is anxious to discover the location of the ♣A. After he leads the suit from the dummy, his best play against inexperienced players is the king. Against more wary opposition, the queen may be more effective. In the first case, West may fear that the declarer holds the king as his only honor in the suit. However, a more experienced player may decide that the declarer is unlikely to start such a weak suit during the early play.

Declarer is anxious to have West take the ace if he holds it so that he will be able to take informed action on the second round of the suit.

In general, when declarer leads a suit, the play of his highest equal card will conceal his holding in the suit. For example, declarer might lead low to the queen with any of the following holdings:

♦ 4 3 2   ♦ 4 3 2   ♦ 4 3 2

♦ A Q J   ♦ Q J 10 6   ♦ Q 6

In the last example, of course, the declarer is trying to

stop the defense from leading this suit when it gets the lead later in the play.

In a suit contract, the declarer can often conceal a potential ruff from the defense by playing carefully from equal cards.

♥ Q J 10 4 3

♥ 9 8 7 6 5   ♥ 2

♥ A K

West leads the ♥9 against a spade contract. By playing low from dummy and winning with the ace, South may lead West to believe that East holds the K. An alternate form of this deception is to play the queen from the dummy before winning with the ace. This makes it look as if South gave East the opportunity to go wrong.

Declarer can often conceal the possibility of taking a deep finesse by leading low from equals.

♠ Q 5

♠ A 10 9 8

By leading the ♠8 toward dummy's queen, declarer may induce West to pop in with his king, if he holds it. If the ♠10 or ♠9 is led, West may duck smoothly, being more likely to realize the possibility of a finesse against the jack.

♥ Q 3 2

♥ A 9 8 7 6

Declarer has a choice of plays in this situation. By leading the ♥6 toward the dummy, he may conceal from West the possibility of an immediate double finesse on the first round. If West ducks smoothly, declarer should probably let the 6 ride and make a good guess on the next round. In this way, he may avoid two losers when West holds J-x or 10-x in hearts (see SUIT COMBINATIONS).

The following situations are similar:

(a)   ♦ J 5 4

♦ Q 10 2   ♦ K 3

♦ A 9 8 7 6

(b)   ♦ J 5 4

♦ K 3   ♦ Q 10 2

♦ A 9 8 7 6

The declarer intends to lead toward dummy and play West for 10-x (unless he receives information through action at the table). By leading the 6, he can conceal the possibility of a finesse against the 10, and may find West jumping in with his king or queen (much to his subsequent embarrassment).

PLAY OF THE HAND. See NOTRUMP PLAY and TRUMP PLAY.

PLAY OUT OF TURN. A play is considered to be in turn if it is made after the player to the right has led or played, or if it is a lead by a player who has won the preceding trick or is the opening leader. Any other order constitutes a play out of turn, and is covered by the rule for a premature lead or play by a defender, or lead or play from the wrong hand by declarer. See LAWS (Laws 53,54, 55 and 56).

PLAYED CARD. In duplicate each player except dummy plays a card by detaching it from his hand and facing it on the table immediately before him. Declarer plays a card from dummy's hand by naming the card he

proposes to play, after which dummy picks up the card and places it face up on his side of the table. (In playing from dummy's hand, declarer may, if he prefers, pick up the desired card, and place it in such position as to indicate that it has been played. However, this is not correct in duplicate play.)

In addition, a card must be played if it is a defender's card held so that it is possible for his partner to see its face; or if it is a card from declarer's hand that declarer holds face up in front of him with intent to play, and that is touching or near the table. Declarer must play a card in dummy that he touches for purposes other than arranging or in reaching for the card immediately above or below the card touched. Any player also plays a card by naming or otherwise designating it as the card he proposes to play. Also any penalty card must be played if it can be played legally (without revoking). See LAWS (Law 45).

PLAYER. A participant at a table of bridge, one of an active foursome engaged at bridge; one member of either pair playing against each other.

PLAYER NUMBER. A number assigned to a player for identification purposes. This method is used by most NCBOs that have a reasonably large membership.

In the ACBL a seven-digit number assigned to a member. The last digit is a self-checking device by which the computer throws out incorrect numbers. The method by which the checking digit is computed is interesting. Multiply the first six digits by 7, 6, 5, 4, 3, and 2 respectively; then add these products. Divide the total of the products by 11, and note the remainder. This remainder is then subtracted from the divisor, 11, and the resulting difference is the check digit. (If the net result of this work is a remainder of 1, then the number is not used.)

When a player achieves LIFE MASTER status, this is indicated by a change in his player number by the substitution of a letter for the first digit, alphabetically from J for 1 to R for 9. Player numbers were instituted by the ACBL in July, 1961.

PLAYER OF THE YEAR. Each year the ACBL designates one of its members as Player of the Year. The player so designated is the one who earns the most platinum masterpoints (points won in North American championship events with no upper masterpoint limit). For winners see Appendix II.

PLAYING CARDS. The cards, usually pasteboard, used in playing various games. (See also MAGNETIC CARDS, PLASTIC CARDS.) The standard bridge pack (or deck) consists of 52 cards, arranged in four suits of 13 cards each. Among the principal games played in the U.S. are bridge, canasta, casino, chemin-de-fer, cribbage, gin and other rummy games, hearts, piquet, twenty-one (also called blackjack and pontoon), poker, and many varieties of solitaire and patience. Pinochle is played with a special deck, which can be formed from two decks of standard cards. (See PACK for non-standard packs and their makeup, and TAROT for a very special pack.) Each suit is divided into three COURT CARDS and 10 SPOT CARDS. Of the latter, the ACE, or one-spot, ranks highest in bridge (but not necessarily in other games). Below the ace in rank are the court cards — king, queen,

and jack (which has replaced the older term, knave almost completely) — followed by the spot cards — 10, 9, 8, 7, 6, 5, 4, 3 (or trey), and 2 (or deuce). The suits are identified by the symbols for spades, hearts, diamonds and clubs. They rank in descending order in bridge games. Today's cards have corner INDICES showing a letter or numeral above a PIP of the suit to which the card belongs, but this is a modern device. Cards lacked such an index as late as 1870.

For other articles in this book referring to playing cards, see COLLECTIONS OF PLAYING CARDS; DEVIL'S PICTURE BOOK; FACE CARDS; FORTUNETELL- ING; HISTORY OF PLAYING CARDS; MANUFACTURE OF PLAYING CARDS; SUIT; TAXES ON PLAYING CARDS; 10 OR 10 SPOT and other-spot cards; TRANSFORMATION CARDS; and USES OF CARDS.

PLAYING KNOWN CARD. See FALSECARDING.

PLAYING TO THE SCORE. Risk taking in the bidding or play of a hand often is affected by vulnerability. The need to be aggressive or conservative often depends on the current standing of the pair or team involved. Variations from normal play in rubber bridge or CHICAGO are motivated by the pairs involved.

In rubber bridge, the net score is computed at the conclusion of each rubber. In Chicago the net score is computed at the conclusion of each four-board set. In each case the net score is rounded off to the nearest hundred. That means that it makes sense to play the final hand of CHICAGO or the rubber-deciding game in rubber bridge with an eye to the score — if an extra trick means a number rounded off to a higher hundred, then declarer should go for it.

Decisions on whether or not to bid on also depend on the score. Sometimes it is possible in rubber bridge to take a sacrifice that would pay off in duplicate, but the problem is that the opponents still are more likely to get the rubber bonus if they have a game on.

Playing to the score also plays an important role in duplicate. In an event scored by barometer, the pairs know where they stand after each round. In the late rounds, pairs that are close to the leader are likely to take a few more chances in an attempt to get some good scores that will enable them to overtake the leaders. The same is true in Swiss Teams scored by VICTORY POINTS. Teams close to the top going into the last match know that a mere win will not be enough — they will shoot for big scores in their attempt to overtake the leaders. In KNOCKOUT TEAMS, teams that are far behind after the first half will come out shooting in the second half, feeling this is their only chance to win the match.

PLAYING TRICKS. Tricks that a hand may be expected to produce if the holder buys the contract; attacking tricks or winners, as distinguished from defensive tricks or winners when the holder must play against an adverse contract. In estimating the trick-taking strength of a hand, the holder assumes that his long suit (or suits) will break evenly among the other three hands, unless the auction has indicated otherwise, and adds the number of tricks his long suit (or suits) is likely to yield to his quick-trick total of the other suits. For example, the following hand

♠ K 5 ♥ A Q J 8 6 2 ♦ A Q 7 ♣ 9 3

contains about seven playing tricks — five in hearts, $\frac{1}{2}$ quick trick in spades, $1\frac{1}{2}$ quick tricks in diamonds.

When the long suit is not solid or semi-solid, estimation of playing tricks becomes more difficult because a second factor must be considered — the position of the missing honor cards. Thus, this suit

♥ K J 8 6 5 3

is worth approximately $3\frac{1}{2}$ playing tricks. With normal distribution, the declarer might make four tricks if he can lead toward the suit or find the missing honors well placed, but he could be limited to two or three tricks.

Assessment of playing tricks is particularly important when considering a preemptive bid or an overcall. See RULE OF TWO AND THREE.

PLAYS TO CONCEAL STRENGTH. See DECEPTIVE PLAY.

PLAYS TO CONCEAL WEAKNESS. See DECEPTIVE PLAY.

PLUS VALUE. An added feature of a hand or suit that should be weighed when one is planning a bid or series of bids. There are bidding developments which require evaluation of a hand on a fairly precise basis. Therefore, during a subsequent phase of the auction, if a player has been somewhat rigid in describing his holding and does possess plus values such as J-10-9 combinations in suits otherwise protected or strengthened, or a guarded queen, etc., that may be felt to be of help to partner, he may sometimes more liberal in making a final placement of contract than without the aforementioned values.

POCKET. One of four rectangular areas in a duplicate board which hold the four hands, designated North, South, East, and West. See LAWS OF DUPLICATE (Law 2).

PODI. See BLACKWOOD AFTER INTERFERENCE and DEFENSE TO INTERFERENCE WITH BLACKWOOD.

POE, Edgar Allan (1809-1849), writer and poet. He said in 'Murders in the Rue Morgue": "Whist has long been known for its influence upon what is termed the calculating power; and men of the highest order of intellect have been known to take an apparently unaccountable delight in it. Beyond doubt there is nothing of a similar nature so greatly tasking the faculty of analysis — proficiency in whist implies capacity for success in all these more important undertakings where mind struggles with mind."

POINT-A-BOARD. British term for board-a-match.

POINT-COUNT. An almost universally used method of valuation. Many point-counts have become obsolete (see FOUR ACES, REITH and ROBERTSON). In general use is the high-card valuation introduced by Bryant McCampbell in 1915 and publicized by Milton Work after whom it was named:

Ace	4
King	3
Queen	2
Jack	1

This gives a total of 40 points in the pack, and makes an average hand worth 10 points.

The Work count is slightly less accurate mathematically than the Four Aces count, for example, but its simplicity led to its acceptance. It was regularly used by English experts in the Thirties, but did not find favor with American experts until it was adopted and publicized by Fred Karpin and Charles Goren in the late Forties. They supplemented the basic high-card count with valuation for distribution (see DISTRIBUTIONAL COUNTS).

All authorities recognize that the 4-3-2-1 count has some weaknesses and many recommend certain corrections:

(1) Aces are undervalued, so the presence or absence of aces materially affects the strength of a hand. Two methods are: add $\frac{1}{2}$ point for each ace; or deduct a point for an aceless hand, and add a point for holding four aces.

(2) Tens are valuable cards and are sometimes counted as $\frac{1}{2}$ point or a plus value. One expedient is to consider aces and tens as a group, and to count an extra point if the hand contains three or more such cards.

(3) Unguarded or insufficiently guarded honor cards may not be worth their full point value. An extreme case is a singleton king, which some authorities count as 1 point instead of 3, and a singleton queen, which is sometimes counted as worthless. It is more usual to deduct one point from the value of a singleton king, queen or jack. Even the singleton ace is not quite as good as it looks because it has little chance of capturing an opposing honor card and is inflexible in the play.

Stayman went to the extreme of recommending the deduction of a point for each of the following holdings: K-Q; K-J; Q-J; Q-x; J-x; Q-x-x; J-x-x. It is true that these holdings have a reduced value if partner has useless small cards in the suit. But if your side is destined to play the hand, there is a good chance that partner will hold a card which will combine effectively with the short honor holding.

(4) Honor combinations are slightly stronger than the same cards would be in different suits. For example, Q-J-x is more effective than Q-x-x in one suit and J-x-x in another suit. But so much depends on what partner can provide that it is better to make no adjustment in this respect unless there is reason to think that partner's hand will be worthless or nearly worthless; or unless the honor is in a suit bid by partner. For other methods of valuation, see BISSELL SYSTEM, HONOR TRICKS, and LOSING-TRICK COUNT.

(5) Honor combinations not accompanied by a small card are not worth their full weight.

Standard procedure used to be to open balanced hands with a "good" 12 points, but the modern tendency is to weaken that slightly. (See NOTRUMP RANGES). Possession of aces and tens, or lack of them, will usually determine whether to open. Unbalanced hands are often opened with 10 or 11 HCP. An 11-point hand with a singleton is usually an opening bid, as is a 10-point hand with a void. But many other factors come into play.

POINTED. A term coined to describe the combination of the spade and diamond suits (for example a "pointed two-suiter"), since both suits have pips that are pointed at the top. The converse (rounded suits) indicates hearts and clubs.

POINTING CARDS. When four cards have been played to a trick in duplicate, each player turns his own

card face down on the edge of the table immediately before him. If his side won the trick, the card is pointed lengthwise toward his partner; if the opponents won the trick, the card is pointed lengthwise toward his opponents. Each player should arrange his own cards in an orderly overlapping row in the sequence played.

At the completion of the play, each player should have an accurate count of tricks won and lost; should there be a disagreement, the tricks can be inspected in turn, and the disagreement reconciled. Should any alteration of this order of play of the cards occur, the director must assume the possibility that the player whose cards are disarranged is in error. This order of play should never be disturbed until the director has been summoned in event of disagreement.

POINTS. (1) The score earned by a pair as a result of the play of a hand, including TRICK POINTS, PREMIUM SCORES, and BONUS. (2) A unit by which a hand is evaluated. See POINT-COUNT. (3) The holding of masterpoints that have been credited to a player-member in any NCBO that has a masterpoint system.

POKER BRIDGE. A style of bidding that relies heavily on stabbing boldly with bids calculated to produce SWINGS on every hand. Players who use "poker" tactics in bridge are those who constantly overbid or take long chances.

POLITIKEN WORLD PAIRS. A world IMP-pairs event organized by the Danish Bridge Federation, Phoenix Hotel Copenhagen, and the Copenhagen newspaper Politiken, won in 1995 by Zia Mahmood - Peter Weichsel, and in 1997 by Geir Helgemo - Krzyszstof Martens. The 1999 edition actually was played in 2000. For results see Appendix IV.

POLITICIANS. Many persons occupying high political or military offices also have been bridge players. U.S. President Dwight D. Eisenhower enjoyed a few hands of bridge during lulls in World War II, and he even made an appearance at the 1961 Summer North American Championships in Washington DC. He was accompanied by his wartime colleague, General Alfred Gruenther, who was the leading American tournament director prior to World War II. Gruenther's bridge exploits were overshadowed by his wartime services, his appointment as Supreme Allied Commander of NATO and his election to the presidency of the American Red Cross.

Former Secretary of Agriculture Clinton P. Anderson was a prominent tournament player in the Thirties. Lynn Martin, Secretary of Commerce under President George Bush, was a member of the Congress team in its first match against Corporate America. Supreme Court Justice Paul Stevens is an ACBL Life Master. Federal District Court Judge Carl Rubin was a Life Master and a former president of the American Contract Bridge League. Many members of Congress are bridge players, and more than a dozen have competed for Congress in its matches against Corporate America.

Deng Xiaoping, former premier of the People's Republic of China, revived bridge in his country and played regularly. He fostered team tournaments in his country and was instrumental in having his country join the World Bridge Federation. Several other senior members of the Chinese establishment are bridge enthusiasts. One of them

is Wan Li, former Chairman of the People's Congress. He won the International Bridge Press Association's Hand of the Year Award in 1984, and was named the Association's Bridge Personality of the Year in 1989.

In England, Winston Churchill was playing bridge when the news of Germany's 1914 declaration of war on Russia interrupted his game. Iain Macleod had been a top tournament player and was one of the most influential cabinet ministers as Chancellor of the Exchequer at the time of his death in 1970. The House of Lords and the House of Commons have an annual bridge battle that was inaugurated in 1975. See BRITISH PARLIAMENT MATCHES. One regular member of the House of Commons team, Dr. John Marek, has represented Wales in Camrose Trophy matches.

Former Greek Premier Sophocles Venizelos was a member of the French national team during the Thirties and was European champion in 1935. In Argentina, Ricardo Argerich was a player of international class until he retired to concentrate on his diplomatic duties.

Another enthusiast is former President F.W. DeKlerk of South Africa, winner of the 1993 Nobel Peace Prize.

POOL. The total amount of money that is distributed to winning entries at some duplicate games. To create the pool, the competing pairs may be auctioned off, as in a CALCUTTA, or they may contribute a set amount at the beginning of the game. See GAMBLING AT BRIDGE.

The biggest pool annually occurs in the CAVENDISH PAIRS, where a spirited auction builds a pool of more than $1 million.

POPE, Alexander (1688-1744), poet. Wrote perhaps the first poetic description of a pack of cards."Behold, four Kings in majesty revered, With hoary whiskers and a forky beard; And four fair Queens, whose hand sustains a flower, Th'expressive emblem of their softer power; Four Knaves in garbs succinct, a trusty band, And particoloured troops, a shining train, Draw forth to combat on the velvet plain. The skilful Nymph reviews her force with care; Let Spades be trumps! she said, and trumps they were." The Rape of The Lock (1712) He was describing a game of ombre, which was then very popular. It was one of the five games described by Edmund Hoyle in his 1743 "Treatise on Games."

POPULAR BRIDGE MONTHLY. See INTERNATIONAL POPULAR BRIDGE MONTHLY.

PORTLAND CLUB OF LONDON. The principal bridge club of British gentry, nobility, and (at times) royalty; world-famous as promulgator of the Laws used in many countries. Founded before 1815 as the Stratford Club, and reorganized in 1825, according to tradition, in order to be rid of one objectionable member. Bridge, introduced in 1894 by Lord Brougham, was given a code of laws in 1895, and with subsequent revisions at intervals, gave the Portland Club its reputation as a law-making body (see LAWS). Famous members of the Club in its whist days included James Clay, William Pole, William Dalton and HENRY JONES (CAVENDISH).

Stuart Wheeler, following the late Geoffrey Butler and the late Colin Harding, has served since 1993 as the legal link between the Portland Club, the law-making body for Britain, and other law-making bodies, such as the

European Bridge League, the American Contract Bridge League and the World Bridge Federation.

PORTLAND RULES. The laws of WHIST according to the English code, named after the PORTLAND CLUB, which officially issued them.

In the early days of CONTRACT BRIDGE and the later days of AUCTION BRIDGE, the use of bidding calls with conventional meaning (such as the Informatory Double of auction or the Vanderbilt Club Bid of contract) were decried by the card committee of the Portland Club, a staid, conservative, British stronghold, and barred in games held in their clubrooms. These rules were called Portland Rules at that time.

POSITION. The place at a table occupied by a player. The various positions are called by the compass points, i.e., North, South, East, and West. Also, the term "position" can correctly be used to describe one's place in the order of bidding during a given auction. "Second" position means that position directly to the left of the dealer. "Fourth" position is the seat to the dealer's right. See SEAT. Position also can refer to where an individual, pair or team places in a set of standings.

POSITIONAL FACTOR. The value of honor cards during the bidding may improve or decline in accordance with the opposing bidding. A king becomes a much more likely trick when the suit is bid by the right-hand opponent, but is likely to be worthless if the suit is bid on the left, except as a notrump stopper if the holder of the king is declarer. See RIGHT SIDE.

Sidney Silodor gave the following example:

West	North	East	South
	1 ♥	Pass	2 ♥
3 ♦	3 ♥	All Pass	

South holds:

    ♠ A J 7 3
    ♥ 10 6 3 2
    ♦ K 4 2
    ♣ 10 9

Although South has a relatively strong raise to 2 ♥, he should pass, because the ♦ K has been devalued by the bid on the left. The decision to pass would be even clearer if the minor suits were interchanged and West bid 3 ♣. In that case North's failure to make the trial bid of 3 ♦ would imply a lack of interest in game. See COMPETITIVE DOUBLE, FINESSE, TENACE.

POSITIONAL SQUEEZE. A squeeze which is effective against one opponent but not the other. This occurs when the hand opposite the squeeze card has nothing but busy cards; if that hand follows to the squeeze card before the opponent who is menaced, there can be no squeeze.

              ♠ A J
              ♥ K
              ♦ —
              ♣ —
♠ 7   ♠ K Q
♥ 6   ♥ A
♦ 2   ♦ —
♣ —   ♣ —
              ♠ 5
              ♥ 4
              ♦ A
              ♣ —

When the ♦ A is led, the North hand is squeezed before East must play, so that the latter is in no difficulty. However, if the East and West hands were reversed, the squeeze would be effective. Positional squeezes are characterized by the fact that the one-card menaces lie to the left of the opponent threatened. See also AUTOMATIC SQUEEZE and SIMPLE SQUEEZE.

POSITIVE CARD. See CARDS, NEUTRAL AND POSITIVE.

POSITIVE RESPONSE. A natural constructive response in a forcing situation where there is a bid available for an artificial negative or waiting response. See FORCING TWO-BID, TWO CLUBS STRONG ARTIFICIAL OPENING.

POSITIVE SLAM DOUBLE. See DOUBLE FOR SACRIFICE.

POSTING THE SCORE. Among the duties of the tournament director (and his staff) is the posting of the score as rapidly and conspicuously as possible, for the inspection of the players.

Posting of scores has been considerably speeded up, in both tournament and club play, since the introduction of COMPUTER SCORING.

POST-MORTEM. A term applied to discussion of bridge hands after the conclusion of the play or any time thereafter. Generally speaking, post-mortems can be of significant value when engaged in by experts, as points of great interest are sometimes highlighted by this type of discussion, and unusual features of a hand often are brought into better perspective.

POTTAGE. See CAPPELLETTI and HAMILTON.

POWERHOUSE. A descriptive term signifying a very strong hand.

PREACCEPTANCE. This occurs in TRANSFER auctions in two ways.

(1) After a major-suit transfer response:

Opener	Responder
1NT	2 ♦ (=hearts)
3 ♣	

This can be used to show maximum values, four good hearts, and a doubleton club, the suit bid or a source of tricks in clubs with heart support.

This may take the partnership too high if partner is very weak. But in that case the opponents may have been deprived of a partscore.

(2) After a minor-suit transfer, when using four-suit transfers:

Opener	Responder
1NT	2 ♠ (=clubs)
2NT	

The usual practice is similar, using this to show a club fit and strong interest in game. However, the converse, with three clubs to show a fit and 2NT to deny one, has some advantages. It allows the partnership to handle weak minor two-suiters, for if the rebid is 2NT responder can bid 3 ♦ to close the auction.

Sometimes called super-acceptance.

PRE-ALERT. In ACBL tournaments, players are required to explain to the opponents, or pre-Alert, certain aspects of their methods. These are unusual bidding treatments that may require discussion by the defense prior to the play of the deal.

PRECEDENCE IN ENTERING A TABLE. In bridge clubs, precedence is given to that member who first appears in the playing room. The lowest priority belongs to a member leaving an existing table to join the new one. See HOUSE RULES.

PRECISION ASKING BID. The PRECISION CLUB system, in its standard version, allows the 1♣ opener to use asking bids for three purposes: (1) to find out about the length and quality of the trump suit, (2) to find out about responder's control of a particular suit, (3) to find out whether responder can fill in opener's SEMI-SOLID SUIT and what other aces he has.

Trump Asking. The most commonly used is the trump asking bid known as Gamma, which is initiated by the 1♣ opener's single raise of responder's positive suit response. The responses are as follows:

1st step	No top honor
2nd step	Five cards with one top honor
3rd step	Five cards with two top honors
4th step	Six cards with one top honor
5th step	Six cards with two top honors
6th step	Three top honors

These asking bids and responses are used also in the SUPER PRECISION system, which designates them Gamma Trump Asking Bids. For other trump asking devices see TRUMP ASKING BIDS.

Control Asking. (Epsilon). After a trump asking bid has been made and responded to, a bid in a new suit by opener asks about responder's controls in a side suit. The controls shown may be either high card or distributional. The responses are:

1st step	No control
2nd step	Third-round control (Q or doubleton)
3rd step	Second-round control (K or singleton)
4th step	First-round control (A or void)
5th step	First- and second-round control (A-K or A-Q)

Opener may ask whether partner's control is a high card or distributional by rebidding the asked suit. Responder shows a high card by bidding the first step (next suit) and the distributional control by bidding the second step.

Ace Asking. The third type of asking bid asks whether responder has one of the top three honors in a particular suit. It is initiated by a jump shift rebid by the 1♣ opener after a positive response. The responses give information about another suit as well as about the asked suit. The responses are:

Cheapest notrump	No top honor, no aces
Single raise	Top honor in asked suit, no other aces
New suit	Ace of bid suit, no top honor in asked suit
Jump in new suit	Top honor in asked suit, ace in suit jumped in
Jump in notrump	No top honor in asked suit, but two side aces
Jump raise	Top honor in asked suit with two side aces

See also ASKING BIDS; ROMAN ASKING BIDS; ROMEX TRUMP ASKING BIDS; SUPER PRECISION ASKING BIDS.

PRECISION AWARD. Prize given by the INTERNATIONAL BRIDGE PRESS ASSOCIATION for the best article or series on a system of convention during a year. It was donated from 1973-1985 by C.C.Wei and after his death by his widow, Kathie Wei, now Kathie Wei-Sender, through 1999.

PRECISION CLUB. A system developed by C. C. Wei in 1963 with assistance from Alan Truscott. It was used successfully by the Taiwan team in the 1967, 1968, and 1969 Far East Championships, and attracted international attention during the 1969 Bermuda Bowl when Patrick Huang, M. F. Tai, C. S. Shen and Frank Hwang, all using the Precision Club, spearheaded Taiwan's drive into the final. This was the closest a non-European, non-North American team had come to capturing the world team title. The Taiwan team reached the final again in 1970.

In the United States a number of top-level teams were sponsored by Wei to use and popularize the Precision System. One such team won three major ACBL knockout team events within a 19-month period. See PRECISION TEAM.

By 1972, when the Italian BLUE TEAM emerged from retirement to enter the World Team Olympiad, all three of its pairs were using versions of the Precision System. The version used by Giorgio Belladonna and Benito Garozzo was called SUPER PRECISION.

The chief features of the standard Precision System are as follows:

1♣ opening is forcing and artificial, and normally shows a minimum of 16 high-card points. Suit responses other than 1♦, which is the conventional negative, are positive, 8 points or more, guarantee at least a five-card suit and, in principle, are forcing to game. With a positive response and 4-4-4-1 distribution, there are two basic methods of responding. The partnership may agree to use the IMPOSSIBLE NEGATIVE: responder bids 1♦, then jumps in his singleton, or in notrump if his singleton is in opener's suit. Alternatively an UNUSUAL POSITIVE may be used: responder immediately jumps to 2♥, 2♠, 3♣, or 3♦ over 1♣ to show a singleton in the suit he jumps in, and four cards in every other suit. As a variation of the unusual positive, the jump can be made in the suit below the singleton, so that opener can economically cuebid the singleton to obtain additional information. Balanced hands are shown by responding either 1NT (8-10), 2NT (11-13, or 16 on up), or 3NT (14-15). After a negative response and a normal rebid, responder will usually bid again with 4-7 points.

If 1♣ is overcalled, responder passes with fewer than five points; bids a five-card or longer suit, or makes a CARD-SHOWING DOUBLE with 5-8 points; jumps in notrump with the opponents' suit well stopped and 9-11 points; cuebids with a hand too strong for a card-showing double; or bids the cheapest notrump with an unbalanced, game-forcing hand. There are many varieties of this method, however. If 1♣ is doubled, normal responses are used, except that with a weak hand responder passes with clubs, bids 1♦ without clubs or redoubles with both major suits.

After a 1♦ negative response, opener rebids 1NT with

16-18 points, 2NT with 19-21, or 3NT with 25-27. A non-jump rebid in a suit is nonforcing; a jump rebid is forcing to game unless opener rebids his suit at the three level.

After a positive response, the auction develops naturally with one exception. A direct raise of responder's suit is an inquiry about the length of responder's suit and the number of top honors he holds, and subsequent suit bids by opener are asking bids. See PRECISION ASKING BIDS and SUPER PRECISION ASKING BIDS.

STAYMAN is used after all notrump responses and rebids.

1 ♦, 1 ♥, and 1 ♠ openings are natural and limited to a maximum of 15 points. Major-suit openings promise at least a five-card suit.

1NT response to a major-suit opening is forcing; 3NT is a strong balanced raise; double jumps are splinter bids, showing four-card support for opener's major and a singleton or void in the bid suit. Raises are limited and nonforcing, except after 1 ♦ : 2 ♦ is forcing and 3 ♦ is preemptive. A jump response of 2NT shows 16 or more points.

1NT opening is 13-15 points. 2♣ and 2 ♦ are nonforcing and forcing Stayman, respectively. However, many Precision experts prefer a stronger range, 14-16 or 15-17. In this case weaker balanced hands must begin with 1 ♦, which becomes a catchall, sometimes made with a doubleton.

2♣ is a natural opening, showing a six-card club suit (rarely five) and an unbalanced hand. 2 ♦ is a conventional response: with a minimum, opener bids a four-card major; with a maximum, opener jumps in a four-card major, raises to 3♣, or jumps to 3NT with a solid or semi-solid club suit. A rebid of 2NT shows two suits outside of clubs stopped. Responder may ask where the stoppers are by bidding 3 ♦; the responses are 3 ♥ to show hearts and diamonds, 3 ♠ to show spades and diamonds, and 3NT to show both major suits. A rebid of 3♣ by opener over the 2 ♦ response suggests a six-card club suit with one side suit stopped; over a 3 ♦ inquiry opener bids hearts or spades if that is where his stopper is, or bids 3NT if he has diamonds stopped. The standard defense to 2♣ (85% of experts in BWS2001) is that the bid should be treated in the same way as a weak two-bid.

2 ♦ is a specialized opening, describing a three-suited hand (4-4-1-4 or 4-4-0-5) with shortage in diamonds and 11-15 points. (4-3-1-5 and 3-4-1-5 were later included). A 2NT response requests opener to specify the exact distribution and point range of his opening bid. Other responses are limited and nonforcing.

2 ♥ and 2 ♠ openings are weak two-bids.

2NT opening is standard (22-24 points).

3NT opening is gambling, showing a long, solid minor with little side strength.

4♣ and 4 ♦ openings are NAMYATS.

The above describes traditional Precision, as set out in 1964 by C.C.Wei. The many experts who have adopted the system have modified it substantially in a variety of ways. The most important are:

(1) An opening 1NT with 14-16 points (or 15-17). Stronger hands open 1♣ and rebid 1NT (17-19). Weaker hands open 1 ♦ and rebid 1NT (11-13). This means that 1 ♦ becomes a catchall for hands that do not fit elsewhere, and is often made with a doubleton. (Some pairs

permit a singleton). A 2 ♦ response to 1 ♦ is then treated as a forcing two-over-one response with diamond length, rather than a raise.

(2) A rebid of 1 ♥ by a 1♣ opener (1♣ – 1 ♦ – 1 ♥) is forcing, with 1 ♠ as the usual rebid by responder, a waiting move. Notrump bids then show balanced hands, of 20 points or more, and other rebids show that 1 ♥ was natural.

(3) 2 ♦ can have a variety of meanings. A MULTI is one popular choice.

(4) 2 ♥ is sometimes a substitute for Flannery, with four spades and five hearts.

(5) 2NT is sometimes a minimum opening with at least 5-5 in the minor suits.

See SUPER PRECISION.

PRECISION TEAM. A highly successful team of young experts from the New York City area sponsored by C. C. Wei to use his PRECISION CLUB system between 1970 and 1973. While there have been a number of teams using the Precision System and coached by Wei, the designation The Precision Team came to mean the team whose nucleus was Steven Altman, Thomas M. Smith, Joel Stuart and Peter Weichsel, They won three of the four major ACBL knockout team championships held between August 1970 and March 1972.

With David Strasberg as a fifth member in 1970, the Precision Team defeated the world champion ACES to win the Spingold. With Eugene Neiger replacing Strasberg as the fifth member in 1971, the team successfully defended its Spingold title, becoming only the fifth team to do so since the event began in 1934. Adding Alan Sontag as a sixth member, the team won the Vanderbilt in 1972.

In January 1973 four members of the Precision Team entered the SUNDAY TIMES event. Altman-Sontag and Smith-Weichsel finished first and second, respectively, in the select 22-pair field, marking the first time a United States pair had ever finished higher than fourth.

After failing to defend its titles successfully in the 1972 Spingold and 1973 Vanderbilt, the team was disbanded in mid-1973. In the meantime many international stars adopted Precision, including members of the Italian BLUE TEAM, the South American champions from Brazil, and a group of British stars headed by Terence Reese.

PRECISION TWO DIAMONDS. See PRECISION CLUB.

PRE-DEALING. A method of (1) producing duplicated boards for play in more than two sections, or (2) producing deals prior to a match so that duplicates of the hand can be published and furnished to spectators or those who prepare slides or frames for exhibition.

Perhaps the first instance of pre-dealing occurred in Johannesburg, South Africa, in December 1962. The hands were pre-dealt and copies made for the spectators for an exhibition match between South African players and a visiting team from England. In modern times, pre-dealing is done by computer. A program is devised so that a random mathematical setup is instilled in the computer, and the computer then distributes the cards to the four compass corners. Printouts then are made of the deals manufactured by the computer. These printouts are packaged and sealed and placed in storage until they are ready for use. Hand records that are sent to

a tournament are kept intact and sealed until it is time for the game in which they will be used. Then, and only then, the tournament director opens the package and distributes the hand records to his fellow directors for distribution among the players. In addition, a printout of all the hands is provided. If the tournament officials wish, copies may be made of this master sheet for distribution to the players at the end of the session.

The same process makes it possible to have ACBL-wide and worldwide games involving the same deals. The hands are packaged and sealed, then mailed to the various areas where games are going to be held. The games are all held at approximately the same time, reducing the chances that information is passed from one area to another. In recent years, a special dealing machine perfected by Per Jannersten of Sweden produces the random program and then physically distributes the cards to the correct hands. This is made possible by barcoding the cards. See DUPLIMATE.

PREEMPTIVE BID. Sometimes called a shutout bid. A bidding method available to all four players during the course of the auction. For actions by second hand over an opening bid, see PREEMPTIVE OVERCALLS and WEAK JUMP OVERCALLS. For actions by third hand, see PREEMPTIVE RAISES and PREEMPTIVE RESPONSES.

For the opening bidder, a preemptive bid usually occurs at the three level at least. The opener holds a long suit, usually at least seven cards, and limited high-card strength. The bid is defensive in purpose, an attempt to make it difficult for the opponents to find their optimum spot because of the lack of bidding room.

An opening weak two-bid is a form of preemptive bid, although it has a double purpose. In addition to robbing the opponents of bidding room, it also sends a specific message to partner – a six-card suit with most of the limited high-card strength located in the bid suit.

The expert panel in BWS 2001 strongly favored describing preemptive actions as "moderate", or possibly "light", avoiding extremes. The following considerations may influence the preemptive bidder.

(1) Length of suit. An opening three-bid is usually a seven-card suit or a strong six-card suit. An opening four-bid is usually an eight-card suit or a strong seven-card suit. An opening five-bid in a minor is usually a nine-card suit or a strong eight-card suit.

(2) Vulnerability. The traditional rule was to take the playing-trick strength of the hand and add three tricks when not vulnerable or two tricks when vulnerable. This is an over-simplification, and most experts make preemptive bids more freely than the RULE of TWO and THREE would permit.

In the most favorable circumstances, third-hand not vulnerable against vulnerable opponents, some experts would venture 3♠ with a hand as weak as:

> ♠ K J 10 8 6 4
> ♥ 4
> ♦ 3 2
> ♣ 7 6 5 3

A few would preempt without even thinking! When vulnerable against nonvulnerable, on the other hand, the preemptive bidder should be within two tricks of his bid in his own hand, and even then may lose 500 to save 420.

(3) Position at the table. The third player is best placed

to preempt because he knows (1) he cannot preempt his partner, and (2) the fourth player is almost sure to have the best hand at the table. Preemptive bids by the dealer are also attractive. They run the risk of finding partner with a strong hand, and therefore giving him problems, but there are two opponents who may have strength, and the odds are that the hand belongs to them.

Preemptive bids by the second player are less attractive, and should have the full advertised distrubutions. Shaded values and mediocre suits should be excluded. Preempts by the fourth player are very rare, and should indicate a solid or near-solid suit if bid at the three-level. A fourth-hand preempter should be reasonably sure he can score a plus – otherwise he should pass.

(4) Strength of suit, and outside strength. The preemptive bidder prefers to have his honor strength concentrated in his own suit. This automatically increases his playing strength, decreases the danger of suffering a substantial penalty, and decreases the chance of successful defense against an opposing contract. A doubleton queen in a side-suit is unlikely to play a part in attack, but may be an important factor in defense.

Some players make it a practice not to preempt when holding a four-card major side-suit, but this rule is at best doubtful.

(5) Bidding methods. Opening three-bids tend to be weaker, and rarer, when using WEAK TWO-BIDS, which are a form of preemptive bid. The weak two is used with many hands which others players would open with a three-level action. The opponents' defensive methods also have to be taken into account. Opening four-bids tend to be weaker when the partnership is using artificial preemptive bids, which tend to be well-defined in strength and suit texture. More discretion must be exercised in opening three-bids against players who double for penalties than against players who double for takeout. See DEFENSE TO OPENING THREE-BID.

RESPONSES. Responses to opening three-bids are often of a tactical character, intended to reinforce the preemptive effect of the opening bid. If the dealer opens 3♠, for example, and the third player holds three-card spade support or better, he should rarely pass unless he has sufficient defensive honor strength to defend against 4♥. If the third player has a hand so weak that he fears an adverse slam, he may take more positive action by bidding 5♠, or 6♠, or venturing some psychic maneuver. This would have the characteristics of an ADVANCE SAVE.

The following points relate to normal constructive responses to preemptive bids.

(1) Raise to game in a major suit (e.g., 3♠ – 4♠). Responder must take into account the vulnerability and other factors which influenced the opening bid. If vulnerable, he needs three sound playing tricks in the form of trump honors, aces, kings, and more ruffing values. Queens and jacks in side-suits must be discounted. If not vulnerable, he needs at least four playing tricks — more if circumstances favored a light preempt. But this raise is often made on a much weaker hand for the tactical reasons mentioned above.

(2) 3NT. A bid which the opener should almost invariably pass. In response to a minor suit, it shows stoppers in at least two of the unbid suits, and probably a fitting honor in the opener's suit. In response to a major suit, it shows a hand capable of making nine tricks without using the opener's suit. Responder is likely to have

a solid minor suit, and might be void in opener's suit.

(3) Three of a higher-ranking suit (e.g., 3♣ – 3♥). Forcing to game, showing that the preempt has found responder with a strong hand. The responder's suit should be a good five-card suit or better, and the opener should raise with any slight excuse. The opener should bid 3♠ if he has a spade stopper for notrump purposes; a rebid of 3NT in this situation would show a diamond stopper.

(4) Four of a lower-ranking suit (e.g., 3♠ – 4♣; but not 3♠ – 4♥, which would be natural). A slam try, inviting the opener to cooperate. Spades are provisionally, but not definitely, agreed on as the trump suit. (The same applies to five of a lower-ranking suit after an opening four-bid.) These bids can be used as ASKING BIDS.

(5) Five of opener's suit (e.g., 3♠ – 5♠, or 4♠ – 5♠). Traditionally, a natural slam invitation, implying that responder is not worried about two losers in any side suit. The quality of his trumps may decide opener's course of action. The modern style after a three opening is for this bid to be preemptive – the opposition may have a slam.

(6) After a game opening in a major. expert opinion in BWS 1994 strongly favored use of new-suit responses as asking bids. See CHOICE OF SUIT; DEFENSE TO OPENING FOUR-BID, DEFENSE TO OPENING THREE-BID. NAMYATS; PREEMPTIVE ROMAN KEYCARD BLACKWOOD; RUBIN TRANSFERS; THREE NOTRUMP OPENING; TRANSFER OPENING THREE-BIDS; TWO-UNDER TRANSFER PREEMPTIVE OPENINGS.

PREEMPTIVE JUMP OVERCALL. See WEAK JUMP OVERCALL.

PREEMPTIVE OVERCALL. A defensive overcall, usually a double or triple jump in a suit, aimed at obstructing the bidding on the opener's side. After an opening bid of 1♦, a jump to 3♥, 3♠, or 4♣ would be preemptive. Standards would perhaps be slightly higher than for opening preemptive bids at the same level because the chance of seriously inconveniencing the opponents is reduced. A vulnerable jump to 3♠ suggests a hand with 7-8 playing tricks.

A jump to the game level is ambiguous. The overcaller is likely to have a preemptive hand, but may make the same bid with a strong hand, prepared to abandon hopes of slam in view of the opposing opening. See also DOUBLE JUMP OVERCALL and WEAK JUMP OVERCALL.

PREEMPTIVE RAISE. A raise of a suit from the one-level to the four-level, usually in a major, has always been an element of standard preemptive bidding. In recent years there has been a tendency to use jumps to the three-level preemptively even in non-competitive auctions. See BERGEN RAISES, INVERTED MINORS, OVERCALLS.

PREEMPTIVE RE-RAISE. A three-level rebid by opener in his own suit which has been raised by responder, in order to make it more difficult for the opponents to bid. Responder is expected to pass this rebid.

In order to try for game, partnerships using preemptive re-raises must bid notrump or bid a new suit either

naturally or as a SHORT SUIT GAME TRY, a TWO-WAY GAME TRY, or a WEAK SUIT GAME TRY. See also TRIAL BID.

PREEMPTIVE RESPONSE. A new suit response to a suit opening at a higher level than would be required for a jump shift:

South	North
1♥	3♠ or 4♣ or 4♦ or 4♠

North normally holds a seven-card suit or eight-card suit, but the exact playing strength varies with circumstances. He must take the vulnerability into account, and also the likelihood of the opponents entering the auction. The suit will be a broken one; with a solid or near-solid suit a simple response followed by a jump is more appropriate.

As these responses are rarely used, they can be given, and usually are given, conventional meanings. See ASKING BID, SPLINTER BIDS, SWISS, and VOID-SHOWING BID.

Many players today use a single jump response as a preemptive devise (1♣-2♥, 1♥-2♠. 1♠-3♦). This method means the partnership must use some method other than a jump shift to show a powerful hand. See INVERTED MINOR SUIT RAISES and WEAK JUMP SHIFT RESPONSES.

PREEMPTIVE ROMAN KEYCARD BLACKWOOD. After a weak two-bid or a three-level opening, a 4♣ response can be used as a keycard request. (Exception: 3♣-4♦, since 4♣ is natural). Also usable after a weak jump overcall. The responses are: one step, no keycards; two steps, one keycard; three steps, one keycard and trump queen; four steps, two keycards; five steps, two keycards and trump queen.

PREFERENCE. When a player bids two suits, and his partner returns to the original suit at the lowest possible level, he is giving simple preference. This is in no way strength-showing and will very frequently be passed. Preference at an unnecessarily high level is termed jump preference, and is considered under RESPONDER'S REBID.

Simple preference can occur in five common situations:

(1) After three bids at the one level (e.g., 1♣ – 1♥ – 1♠). With a minimum responding hand (5-7 points) and three cards in clubs and spades, it may be best to pass. If the opener has to play a 4-3 spade fit instead of a 5-3 club fit at a higher level, it is no great hardship. A preference to 2♣ would be appropriate with 8-9 points if diamond weakness rules out 1NT and responder wishes to give the opener another chance in case he has 17-18 points.

The most difficult situation arises when the responder has not more than a doubleton in each of the opener's suits, with exactly five cards in his own suit. A preference to 2♣ should never be given with a doubleton, so the choice lies between a pass, leaving the opener to play in a 4-2 fit with the prospect of a club ruff, or 1NT if the partnership method permits this to be weak.

(2) When opener bypasses 1NT (e.g., 1♥–1♠–2♦). Automatic preference to 2♥ is called for if the responder has equal red-suit length (3-3 or 2-2). There is a virtual guarantee that the opener has a five-card heart suit (see OPENER'S REBID). Some authorities suggest a timid

pass when the response is a minimum instead of giving preference, but this is born of fear that the opener may continue bidding without justification. With 8-10 points, two hearts and three diamonds, false preference to 2♥ may be appropriate in case the opener has a maximum rebid.

(3) After a two-over-one response (e.g., 1♠ – 2♣ – 2♥). In traditional style, this was the way to give a strong raise to two spades with about 10 points and three or four spades. The four-card support was ruled out by the general adoption of the LIMIT RAISE. In the modern two over-one style, the sequence is forcing, suggesting three-card support with at least 12 points.

(4) After a 1NT response (e.g., 1♠ – 1NT – 2♥). The responder gives automatic preference, expecting the opener to hold five spades and four or five hearts. (If the opener has chosen this sequence with four spades and five hearts, the wrong contract is reached. But the popularity of FIVE-CARD MAJORS and FLANNERY has made this a rare problem.)

If the opener's two suits are a major and a minor, false preference with two of the original suit and three of the second suit may be appropriate, especially at matchpoints. This applies particularly after the sequence 1♠ - 1NT - 2♣, when the opener is quite likely to have marginal clubs. In the modern style, with a 1NT response forcing, opener may well have five spades and three clubs.

(5) After a 1NT rebid (e.g., 1♥ – 1♠ – 1NT – 2♣). A delicate situation, because the responder may hold a hand with four spades and five or six clubs which was not strong enough for an original response at the two level. The opener should usually refrain from giving preference, even if he holds three spades. (Alternatively, a partnership may agree that with only four spades, responder should pass 1NT, in which contract the minor suit may prove useful.) See NEW MINOR FORCING, RAISE. For preference after a REVERSE, see that heading.

PREMATURE LEAD OR PLAY. A lead or play made before the proper time or before a player's proper turn. This irregularity may occur before or after the auction ends. Declarer incurs no penalty for a premature lead or play. See LAWS (Law 24 for a card led during the auction, Law 54 for a faced opening lead out of turn, and Law 57 for a premature lead or play by a defender); see also LEAD OUT OF TURN.

PREMATURE SAVE. See ADVANCE SAVE.

PREMIUM. A score made above the line in rubber bridge or Chicago. See BONUS.

PREMIUM SCORE. The score ABOVE THE LINE, consisting of extra tricks, making doubled contracts, rubber bonus, slam awards, honors, and premiums for defeating opposition contracts.

PREPARED CLUB. See SHORT CLUB.

PREPARED HANDS. See EPSON; INSTANT MATCHPOINTS; MACHINE-PREPARED HANDS; PAR CONTESTS; PRE-DEALING; TWINNING.

PREPAREDNESS, PRINCIPLE OF. The idea, originally called "Anticipation", of looking forward to the next round of bidding when selecting a bid. It applies regularly to the opening bidder, but may also apply to the responder or to the opponents of the player who opened the bidding. Specific cases are considered under CHOICE OF SUIT.

PRESSURE BID. An overbid made necessary by opposing action. Suppose this bidding has occurred:

West	North	East	South
1♥	3♣	?	

North's 3♣ is a weak jump overcall, and East holds three-card heart support and 8 points in high cards. Although he could not have bid 3♥ in the ordinary way, even using LIMIT JUMP RAISES, he should bid 3♥ at this point under the pressure of the opposing bid. A pass would leave West to consider the possibility that East has a worthless hand. 3♥ is therefore less of an overbid than a pass would be an underbid.

In such circumstances 3♥ shows the upper range of a raise to 2♥ without interference or a marginal limit raise. The opener allows for the pressure, and passes unless he would have considered a game after a single raise.

As a corollary, the responder must overbid similarly with a slightly stronger hand. If he would have made a sound limit raise to 3♥ in normal circumstances, he must jump to 4♥ over the bid of 3♣.

PRETEEN SCHOLARSHIP AWARD. In 1989 Homer Shoop, founder of the International Palace of Sports in North Webster IN, and long-time benefactor of ACBL youth programs, added the Preteen Scholarship to bridge and tennis scholarships previously established. Though Shoop died in 1991, the IPS survives as a public foundation and the scholarships Shoop established endure through the IPS Foundation. The pre-teen award is a 10-year maturity $5000 certificate to be used for academic or career training. Secured by zero coupon government bonds, the certificate can be used as collateral for a student loan or redeemed before maturity at a 10% annual discount.

ACBL members who have not celebrated their 13th birthday before July 1 of the contest year who have at least one full masterpoint on record are eligible for consideration. The winners:

1989 — Lisa Kow, 10, Concord CA
1990 — Joel Wooldridge, 10, Snyder NY
1991 — Vincent Molgat, 11, Red Deer AB
1992 — Bonnie Greco, 12, Annandale VA
1993 — Ari Greenberg, 12, Malibu CA
1994 — Tara Gokavi, 12, North Battleford SK
1995 — Gavin Wolpert, 12, Thornhill ON
1996 — Dan Hirschman, 11, Southfield MI
1997 — Scott Waldron Jr., 12, Hunt Valley MD
1998 — Justin Lall, 11, Tarzana CA
1999 — Roger Lee, 11, Arcada CA

PRIMARY HONORS. Top honors, i.e., aces and kings. The king of a suit may instead be considered a SECONDARY HONOR when it is unaccompanied by the ace or queen and when it is in a suit in which partner is known to be short. Primary honors usually carry more weight in suit contracts than in notrump.

PRIMARY TRICKS. A term first used by P. Hal Sims to describe high cards which will win tricks no matter who eventually plays the hand.

PRIMARY VALUES. Aces and kings, also called Hard Values.

PRISONERS OF WAR. See BRIDGE IN PRISON CAMPS.

PRISONS, PRISONERS. See BRIDGE IN PRISONS.

PRIVATE CONVENTION. A partnership understanding which is not made known to the opponents. The use of such a convention is a violation of the Laws and the Proprieties: "It is improper to convey information to partner by means of a call or play based on special partnership agreement, whether explicit or implicit, unless such information is fully and freely available to the opponents (see Law 40)." LAWS OF DUPLICATE (Law 75). This requirement is not easy to fulfill in tournament play. Many partnerships have elaborate understandings about the precise natural meaning to be allocated to certain bids and sequences. It is difficult to draw a hard-and-fast line to separate convention from style.

ACBL standards require that the opponents automatically be alerted to any conventional bid embodying an understanding that is not classified as a Class A Convention. In other NCBOs, any conventional bid should be alerted. See ALERTING. Other explanations should not be volunteered until the end of the auction. See also EXPLANATION OF CONVENTIONAL CALL OR PLAY.

PRIVATE CONVENTION CHANGE. See LAWS OF DUPLICATE (Law 75).

PRIVATE SCORECARD. Players competing in duplicate events usually keep a written record of their performance. Cards that enable participants to keep such a record usually are given out by the host organization. The inside of the ACBL convention card is a private scorecard. There are spaces for the contract, the declarer and the score, as well as matchpoints or IMPs. The ACBL card also lists an IMP scale and two scales for Victory Point scoring.

PRIZE. Award presented to winner of a bridge contest. The prize can range from a free game at the club to more than $1 million at an event like the Cavendish Pairs. Trophies and small cash prizes are common club prizes as well. Most major events award a major trophy to the winners, but the award stays with the winners only until the next time the event is held, usually the following year. The winners' names are engraved on the permanent trophy.

For many years the ACBL banned cash prizes. The first time a cash prize was permitted occurred in the Omar Sharif Individual in Atlantic City in 1990. The first regional to award a cash prize was the Greater New York Bridge Association at its Green Points events.

Although the ACBL still does not award cash prizes to the victors in major North American championships, many major tournaments in other parts of the world do award cash prizes, some of which are quite large. Most such tournaments are held in Europe, and such events draw competitors from all over the world.

In the late Nineties, the ACBL began offering cash prizes occasionally at one of the regionally-rated open pairs events held during North American Championships. Pairs entering the event have the option of paying an additional fee to become eligible for the cash awards. Those who do not wish to compete for cash pay the usual entry fee and are eligible for the usual masterpoint awards. The general plan is to return in prize money all the cash taken in for prize eligibility.

Strangely enough, the biggest cash prizes are awarded at a tournament in North America – the Cavendish Pairs now held annually in Las Vegas during the second weekend in May. The top prize in 2000 was $293,000, with a prize pool totaling more than $1.1 million. However, the first-place pair gets only a percentage of that award. At an auction preceding the event, individuals and groups bid for the pairs, and those who bid for the winners get the auction pool ($263,000 in 2000) while the winners get $30,000. Each pair has the right to buy a percentage of the money bet on themselves, so the winners always get considerably more than the simple first prize.

PRO. Pattern Relay Organized. Also refers to a professional bridge player. See PRO SYSTEM, PROFESSIONAL PLAYERS.

PRO SYSTEM. A system formerly employed by some West Coast pairs. Many relay sequences allowed the stronger hand to control the auction and inquire about partner's strength and pattern.

The principal features of PRO (Pattern Relay Organized): intermediate (14-16 HCP) notrump opening; forcing 1♣ opening promising either a club suit or a balanced hand with 17-20 points; nonforcing two-over-one responses and jump shifts; four-card major suit openings, with a 1NT response virtually game forcing; reverses based on distribution rather than on high-card strength.

PRO-AM PAIRS. One member of each pair must be a top-flight player – the pro, so to speak — and the other is a new or relatively new player — the amateur. The purpose is to enable the new player to meet and get to know some of the better players in the area. The new player also gets the benefit of good advice and tips from his or her "pro." The game itself is run along the lines of an OPEN PAIRS.

PROBABILITIES. See HIGH CARD POINT PROBABILITIES, MATHEMATICAL TABLES.

PROBABILITIES A POSTERIORI. See PERCENTAGE PLAY; PROBABILITY OF SUCCESSIVE EVENTS.

(1)   A Q 10 7 3 2

                       9 8 5

When dummy's queen is finessed and loses to East's king, there are two events. The first is that East has the K-J, or alternatively, that he has the singleton king. The second is that in both cases, he would play the king. The second is regarded as certain; resultant probabilities are 6.8% and 6.2%. It is assumed is that West has the same choice in both cases, to play either the six or the four. On a second lead, with West following with the other of the small cards, percentage play (slightly) favors the play of the ace.

(2)   A J 10 7 3 2

                       9 8 5

The finesse of the 9 loses to East's king. The a priori

probabilities of relevant distributions are:

6 4 opposite K Q	6.8%	
Q 6 4 opposite K	6.2%	

In the first case there is no certainty that East will win with the king: he can equally well play the queen. If he is a good player the chances are about equal that he will play either honor, as any other method will be likely to help declarer. While the probability of the first event (that East holds the K-Q) is 6.8%, the probability that he will play the king is 50%. Applying the rule for successive events, the probability that East will hold the K-Q, and play the king is 6.8% x 50% or 3.4%. The odds in favor of taking a second finesse are therefore 30 to 17. See RESTRICTED CHOICE.

(3)   A K Q J 4 3 2

                void

Assume that on the ace and king, East plays the 7 and 8, and West the 5 and 6. The only possible distributions are:

West	East	A Priori Probability
5 6 9	7 8 10	1.78%
5 6 10	7 8 9	1.78%
5 6 9 10	7 8	1.61%
5 6	7 8 9 10	1.61%

All the outstanding cards are insignificant (see CARDS, NEUTRAL AND POSITIVE) in that they cannot take a trick. It can be assumed that defenders play insignificant cards at random, avoiding giving declarer information unnecessarily. There are three ways in which each defender can select two cards from both the first two cases. Thus the play of the four cards in question from these cases is 3.56% x 1/9 = .39%. There are only six ways in which the particular played cards could occur from the last two cases in the table, so the probability of the selected play is 3.56% x 1/6 = .54%. The a priori probability of a 4-2 against a 3-3 division is exactly the same as the ratio between these a posteriori probabilities, .54 to .39.

(4) But it is not always apparent to a player that his cards are insignificant.

                4 3 2
J 10 9   Q 8 7
                A K 6 5

West will appreciate that his cards are of equal value, but East will not know that his are. When West plays the 9 on South's ace, East is unlikely to play the queen. The probabilities of the possible distributions can be calculated only on an assessment of how defenders are likely to play from each. Before South attacks the suit (at an early stage, and after a neutral lead) the odds are about 49 to 36 on a 4-2 division as against a 3-3. Declarer's interpretation of the play of the first two rounds may cause him to change his original play. See MATHEMATICAL ASSUMPTIONS.

PROBABILITIES A PRIORI. Basic probabilities of a given distribution of cards is expressed as a fraction where the numerator is the total number of favorable cases, and the denominator the total number of (equally likely) possible cases. MATHEMATICS OF BRIDGE explains how these can be computed. Thus before the cards are seen (a priori), the probability a particular player will hold a 4-3-3-3 hand pattern is

$$\frac{66,905,856,160}{635,013,559,600}.$$

See HAND PATTERNS and NUMBER OF POSSIBLE HANDS.

In bridge, probability is most commonly shown as a percentage (100 times the above fraction). Play based on a priori probabilities is therefore known as PERCENTAGE PLAY.

Probability of any distribution varies at different stages of the game. Before one has seen any cards, there is a probability (see TABLES, MATHEMATICAL, Table 1) of 10.58% that one will hold a 5-4-2-2 hand pattern. There is the same probability that a particular suit will be distributed 5-4-2-2 to the four players. After a player looks at his hand and sees a suit of five cards, the probability that this suit is distributed 5-4-2-2 among the four players is 21.21% (Table 3). Thus 5-4-2-2 is now less than twice as likely as 5-5-2-1 whereas it was more than three times as probable before any cards were seen. (A priori has become a posteriori). The difference is because it is now known that one player does have five of the suit, and concern is only with the distribution of the remaining eight cards.

Subsequently, if partner's hand is seen to contain a doubleton of the five-card suit, the probability of a 5-4-2-2 distribution of the suit rises to 48.45% (Table 4), and 5-4-2-2 is now more probable than 5-3-3-2 although the latter was more probable in the earlier stages. Concern is now with the distribution of the remaining cards of the suit in only the other two hands.

A priori probabilities take no account of INFERENCES in bidding or play. Use should be made of the former only where more accurate probabilities cannot be drawn from such inferences.

When the opening lead has been made, strict a priori probabilities no longer apply; but if the lead gives no material information, they are altered only very slightly or not at all. See CARDS, NEUTRAL AND POSITIVE.

PROBABILITIES OF DISTRIBUTION. See MATHEMATICAL TABLES, Tables 1, 3, 4, and 4A.

PROBABILITY OF SUCCESSIVE EVENTS. The probability that two events will occur is the product of the probability of each, the latter event's probability being calculated on the assumption that the former has taken place. See DECEPTION and PROBABILITIES A POSTERIORI and, for an unscientific but practical application, the last example under PERCENTAGE PLAY.

PROBABLE TRICK. A playing trick that can be reasonably counted on when attempting to forecast the play during the bidding. K-x of a suit bid voluntarily on the right is an example.

PROBLEM. Usually of three types, SINGLE DUMMY PROBLEMS, DOUBLE DUMMY PROBLEMS, and INFERENTIAL PROBLEMS, which are listed in separate articles.

PROFESSIONAL PLAYER (or PRO). Bridge professionalism takes several forms. The most common form consists of experts who are retained to play tournaments in partnership or on teams with lesser players. In addition, many experts teach bridge to pupils of all levels, and some give lessons by playing with the pupil in tournaments. Although bridge may be the full-time profes-

sion of writers, editors and lecturers, they are not considered professional players.

Professionalism in the form of a pro playing with a client is a most controversial subject within the ACBL. Large numbers of members believe professionalism is an evil. They believe it is wrong for some players to hire professional players so that they will have a better chance to win gold points and become Life Masters or so that they can gain prestige by winning events and placing high in the BARRY CRANE TOP 500 race. These members believe that professionalism should not be allowed, that a player should have to earn his way to the top rather than paying a professional to help him along. On the other side of the coin are those that see positive advantages to professionalism. Playing with a professional partner and learning how an expert thinks can help an average player become a good one, their argument goes. They also believe that most persons who engage a professional do so in an attempt to learn more about the game, not to amass masterpoints.

The ACBL Board of Directors has been addressing the issue of professional players for many years. Several committees have made various suggestions concerning regulating professionalism. The first major attempt to come to grips with professionalism came in 1975 when the Board set up regulations for Registered Players. Under these regulations, any player who accepted money or other remuneration, directly or indirectly, in excess of his actual expenses, as consideration for playing in an ACBL-sanctioned event, had to become a Registered Player. This policy was in effect for a time, but it did not work out to the satisfaction of its sponsors, and it finally was repealed. The professionalism committee then attempted to find some other avenue.

It was proposed in 1981 that the ACBL sanction certain professional organizations provided they met a set of strict requirements set down by the ACBL. These organizations were expected to maintain a high degree of responsibility and ethics among their members. At the same time, the Board passed a regulation that any player who accepted payment for playing professionally at a regional or North American Championship must be affiliated with one of these professional organizations. Several such organizations were formed, but were inactive a decade later.

Bridge has had its share of wealthy patrons who have sponsored expert bridge teams. In 1968, Dallas financier Ira Corn organized the ACES, the world's first full-time professional bridge team. This was an eminently successful venture, inasmuch as the Aces won the Bermuda Bowl World Championship in 1970 and 1971. One illustration of a successful sponsor is Malcolm Brachman, who led his team to victory in the International Team Trials of 1979 and thereby qualified to play in the Bermuda Bowl in Rio de Janeiro that year. Brachman and his team won the World Championhship that year, and Brachman played his share of the matches and thereby qualified for full world champion rating. Seymon Deutsch matched this feat by qualifying for, and then winning, the 1988 World Team Olympiad title. Bud Reinhold also led his team to victory in the Team Trials of 1981, and his team went on to win the Bermuda Bowl. However, Reinhold did not play the required number of boards in the final, so did not qualify as a world champion. In 1995 Nick Nickell joined the list of victorious sponsors when his team won the Bermuda Bowl in Beijing, China.

In the Seventies, shipping magnate C. C. Wei sponsored several teams to popularize his Precision System. (See PRECISION TEAM).

In addition, some commercial concerns have sponsored teams in order to promote their products. The Lancia division of Fiat in Italy sponsored a team that made professional appearances in various cities in North America. Rothman's Cigarettes was the sponsor of the 1982 Canadian Team Championships. Philip Morris sponsors a series of tournaments leading to a grand champion in Europe each year.

Some professional players make their living, in whole or in part, by playing bridge for high stakes. This is usually in the form of rubber bridge at clubs, but occasionally it takes place in Calcuttas or tournaments at which substantial money prizes are at stake. Until the coming of accredited professional organizations, money-prize tournaments were extremely rare in North America. However, money tournaments are the rule rather than the exception in Europe.

PROFESSIONAL TOURNAMENT DIRECTORS ASSOCIATION (PTDA). A professional organization of persons who work for the ACBL as tournament directors at the hundreds of tournaments (as distinguished from club and local-rated events) conducted every year in North America. The principal objectives of the PTDA are (1) the development and maintenance of the highest possible standards for the conduct and operation of tournament bridge events, and (2) fair and reasonable working conditions for tournament directors.

The PTDA, officially organized in August 1968 at the Summer NABC in Minneapolis, has a membership of approximately 100. The PTDA is governed by an executive committee consisting of seven regional vice presidents (one of whom is elected president), an executive secretary and a treasurer.

The PTDA conducts general membership meetings three times each year. The PTDA sends, at its own expense, a representative to each of the three yearly meetings of the ACBL Board of Directors for the purpose of representing the interests and opinions of the PTDA, providing technical advice in the area of Tournament Regulations and Direction and continuing an active liaison with the ACBL Board and Management.

Major activities of the PTDA have included a joint venture with ACBL Management to standardize the interpretation and application of the Laws of Duplicate Contract Bridge.

The *Tom Weeks Memorial Award* is presented annually to the PTDA member who demonstrates the greatest improvement in all facets of professional tournament direction. Weeks was an Associate National Director and first treasurer of the PTDA.

Past recipients of the award are: Sol Weinstein, 1972; Roger Putnam, 1973; Brian Moran, 1974; Fran Miller, 1975; Jerry Shakofsky, 1976; Roberta Shipley, 1977; Gary Blaiss, 1978; Thomas Quinlan, 1979; Robert Kitchel, 1980; Eleanor Kipperman, 1981; Jeff Alexander, 1982; Peter Mollemet, 1983; Chris Patrias, 1984; no award presented, 1985; Steve Bates, 1986; Butch Campbell, 1987; Doug Grove, 1988; Patty Johnson, 1989; Millard Nachtwey, 1990; Guillermo Poplawsky, 1991; Betty Bratcher, 1992, Rick Beye, 1993; John Ashton, 1994; Richard Strauss, 1995; Matt Smith, 1996; Jack Mehrens, 1997; Su Doe, 1998; Patty Holmes, 1999; Mike Flader, 2000.

In 1986, the *Fred Friendly Award* was created to honor the director who best exemplified the spirit of the late Paul Stehly, an Associate National Director who was legendary for his warmth and good cheer. Stehly's nickname was Fred Friendly.

Past recipients of the award are: Gus Ducheyne, 1986; Doug Grove, 1987; Margo Putnam, 1988; Betty Bratcher, 1989; Guillermo Poplawsky, 1990; Karl Hicks, 1991; Jack Mehrens, 1992, Jackie Matthews, 1993; Julie Harding, 1994; Louise Sibble, 1995; Priscilla Smith and Nancy Hart, 1996; Ron Johnston, 1997; Charles MacCracken, 1998; Carey Snider, 1999; Alice Kinningham, 2000.

The PTDA has honored two longtime tournament directors by awarding them lifetime membership in the PTDA. They are Phil Wood and Harry Goldwater.

Past presidents of the PTDA include Maury Braunstein, Henry Francis, Dale Egholm, William Weyant, Roger Putnam, William Schoder, Nelson Rowe, Roberta Shipley, Chris Patrias and Peter Mollemet.

2001 officers: Peter Marcus, president; executive committee: Patty Johnson, Pat Jackson, Betty Bratcher, Steve Bates, Jeff Alexander, Tom Whitesides, Ron Johnston. Mike Flader is non-voting treasurer. There is no secretary.

PROGRESSION. (1) The movement of players in duplicate; (2) the movement of the boards in duplicate; (3) the movement of players in PROGRESSIVE BRIDGE.

PROGRESSIVE BRIDGE. A form of competition at Contract Bridge played in the home or among social groups. See PARTY CONTRACT BRIDGE.

PROGRESSIVE SQUEEZE (or Repeated Squeeze or Repeating Triple Squeeze). A sequence of two squeezes which results in a gain of two tricks. In rare instances three or even four tricks may be gained (see #8 and #9 below). It is initiated by a triple squeeze which is followed by a simple squeeze, both against the same player. As in an ordinary triple squeeze, all but two of the remaining tricks must be in hand before pressure can be exerted. There are several types, of which (1) and (2) are the most common.

(1) The requirements for a Type 1 progressive squeeze are:
(a) A one-card threat placed to the left of the opponent threatened.
(b) Two two-card menaces, one in each hand. Example:

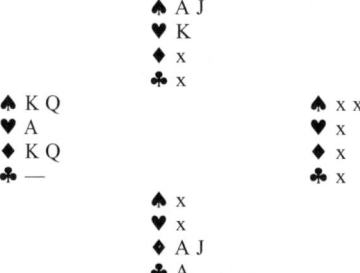

South leads the ♣A, and West is squeezed in three suits. If West discards a spade, South cashes two tricks in that suit which leads to an automatic squeeze against West in hearts and diamonds for the gain of a further trick. If West discards a diamond, South takes two dia-

monds, which results in a positional squeeze in the majors. Finally, if West discards a heart, South crosses to the ♠A in order to play the ♥K, which results in an automatic squeeze against West in spades and diamonds.

(2) The requirements for a Type 2 progressive squeeze are:
(a) A one-card threat placed to the right of the opponent threatened.
(b) The hand with the one-card threat has an entry in each of the other threat suits.
(c) The hand opposite the one-card threat contains the squeeze card, the remaining threat cards and entries in two of the three threat suits.

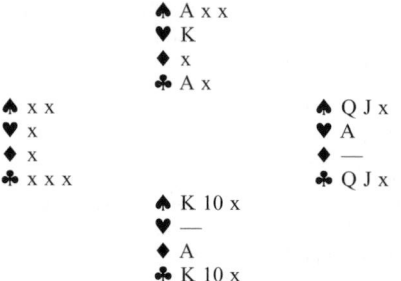

South leads the ♦A, and East is squeezed in three suits. Any discard costs a trick, and leads to a simple squeeze for the loss of another trick by East.

(3) A third form of progressive squeeze may arise, with these requirements:
(a) An extended two-card menace (also called a double threat).
(b) Two one-card menaces opposite the extended threat.

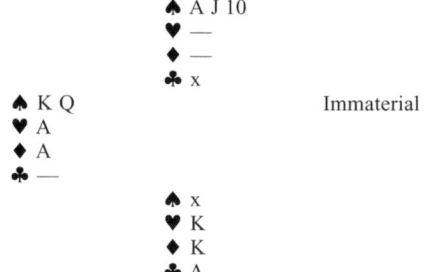

South leads the ♣A, and West is squeezed in three suits. If West discards a spade, it is at the cost of two tricks; if West discards a heart or a diamond, South continues with the king of that suit, effecting an automatic squeeze against West.

This squeeze is equally effective if the East and West cards are interchanged, so that it becomes an automatic squeeze.

(4) (Described by Chien-Hwa Wang)

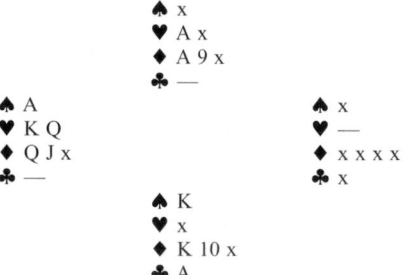

South leads the ♣A, and West is squeezed in three suits. If West discards a spade, then South leads the king of that suit, squeezing West in hearts and diamonds: a heart discard permits North to win his hearts, thereby squeezing West in spades and diamonds; if West discards a diamond, South cashes three diamonds, ending in his hand. The last of these squeezes West in the majors.

This is an automatic squeeze, since North's spade is an idle card. The requirements for this squeeze are as follows:

(a) A one-card menace placed to the right of the opponent threatened.

(b) A two-card menace in the hand opposite the one-card threat.

(c) A twin entry menace, with a menace card accompanying each winner.

The squeeze card lies in the same hand as the one-card menace.

(5)

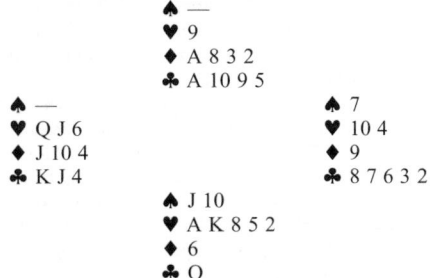

The lead of the ♣A squeezes East in three suits, and South eventually wins all the remaining tricks. (Variation of #2)

(6)

The lead of the ♣A squeezes East in three suits, and South eventually wins all the remaining tricks. (Variation of #2)

(6)
```
              ♠ A J
              ♥ x
              ♦ K
              ♣ x
  ♠ x x                 ♠ K Q
  ♥ x x                 ♥ K Q
  ♦ x                   ♦ A
  ♣ —                   ♣ —
              ♠ x
              ♥ A J x
              ♦ —
              ♣ A
```

South leads the ♣A, and East is squeezed in three suits. The squeeze gains two tricks for South. (Variation of #2)

(7)
```
              ♠ J x x
              ♥ A
              ♦ A J
              ♣ —
  ♠ K Q                 ♠ x x
  ♥ K Q                 ♥ x x
  ♦ K Q                 ♦ x x
  ♣ —                   ♣ —
              ♠ A
              ♥ J x
              ♦ x x
              ♣ A
```

South leads the ♣A, and West is squeezed in three suits. A spade discard gives North two spade tricks; a heart discard enables South to take the ♥A, ♠A, and ♥J squeezing West in spades and diamonds; and a diamond discard leads to a crisscross squeeze.

(8) (Described by Clyde E. Love)
```
              ♠ 2
              ♥ 9 7 3
              ♦ A K 8 3 2
              ♣ A 10 9 5
  ♠ 9 8 4               ♠ 7 6 5 3
  ♥ Q J 6               ♥ 10 4
  ♦ Q J 10 4            ♦ 9 7
  ♣ K J 4               ♣ 8 7 6 3 2
              ♠ A K Q J 10
              ♥ A K 8 5 2
              ♦ 6 5
              ♣ Q
```

South plays in 7♠ doubled by West. West makes his normal lead of the ♦Q. South starts life with only 10 top tricks, but after he has won the diamond lead and cashed three spades this is the position:
```
              ♠ —
              ♥ 9
              ♦ A 8 3 2
              ♣ A 10 9 5
  ♠ —                   ♠ 7
  ♥ Q J 6               ♥ 10 4
  ♦ J 10 4              ♦ 9
  ♣ K J 4               ♣ 8 7 6 3 2
              ♠ J 10
              ♥ A K 8 5 2
              ♦ 6
              ♣ Q
```

When the fourth spade is led West cannot throw a heart or he will set up three tricks immediately. If West discards a diamond, a low club is discarded from dummy. Declarer then leads a diamond to the ace and ruffs a diamond to establish two tricks. After entering dummy with the ♣A, the cashing of these two new winners squeezes West in clubs and hearts to promote a third trick. The result would be the same if West had discarded a club rather than a diamond.

(9) (Constructed by N. Scott Cardell)
```
              ♠ K
              ♥ A 8 7 5 4 2
              ♦ A 9 5 4 3
              ♣ 3
  ♠ 8                   ♠ J 10 9 7 6 5 4 3 2
  ♥ Q 10 9 6            ♥ J
  ♦ K Q 10              ♦ 8 7 2
  ♣ J 9 7 6 5           ♣ —
              ♠ A Q
              ♥ K 3
              ♦ J 6
              ♣ A K Q 10 8 4 2
```

West	North	East	South
		4♠	5♣
Pass	5♠	Pass	5NT
Pass	6NT	Pass	Pass
Dbl	All Pass		

West leads the ♠8 and is happy that dummy has neither red jack. He expects a large penalty, but is disappointed. South is looking at eight top tricks, but makes 12 when he overtakes the ♠K with the ace and leads the queen. Whatever suit West discards will be established for a gain of three tricks, with a squeeze to follow in the other two suits.

Any other play by declarer fails. West finds that he should have led a red card instead of a spade, attacking

South's communications. See also CLASH SQUEEZE; GUARD SQUEEZE; TRIPLE SQUEEZE.

PROMISE. A bidding statement indicating the smallest number of cards in a suit or high card points in a hand. For instance, an opening bid of 1♣ promises a minimum of three cards in standard methods.

PROMOTION. See TRUMP PROMOTION.

PROMOTION OF TRUMP HONORS (in bidding). A higher value is given to a minor honor in a suit bid by partner than to a similar honor in a side suit. See GOOD CARDS.

PROPRIETIES. There are three different kinds of improper conduct: breaches of ethics, breaches of good manners, and cheating. Premeditated cheating is unforgivable; it is not dealt with by the Laws at all, for such a highly civilized game as bridge depends upon the assumption that players will not cheat.

Breaches of ETHICS or ETIQUETTE, however, are dealt with by the Laws. The proper code of behavior is set out in Laws 72-76. In the tournament world breaches of the Proprieties are punishable by the award of an adjusted score and by disciplinary penalties. In rubber bridge there is no way of adjusting the score except by agreement of the players or as provided in Law 16 (see LAWS).

PROTECT. (1) To guard with a small card, as an honor; (2) to make a bid in order that partner may have another opportunity to bid, thus "protecting" him if he has greater strength than his first call has implied (this usage is obsolescent); (3) in England, to balance; see BALANCING.

PROTECTED SUIT. See GUARD.

PROTECTION. An English term for BALANCING.

PROTEST PERIOD. The time specified by the sponsoring organization during which a director's ruling may be appealed. The term is also used, though not quite accurately, to designate the period in which scoring corrections may be accepted. See CORRECTION PERIOD and SCORING CORRECTIONS.

PROTEST. See APPEAL; COMMITTEE.

PROVEN FINESSE. A finesse whose success is guaranteed. For example:

North
♠ A Q J 7

South
♠ 10 9 5 3

The ♠10 is led and wins, while right-hand opponent discards. Subsequent finesses in the suit are proven or established. Also called a MARKED FINESSE, a slightly less absolute circumstance.

PSEUDO ELIMINATION PLAY. See THROW-IN PLAYS.

PSEUDO SQUEEZE. A play intended to induce a wrong discard by a defender who mistakenly believes he has been squeezed.

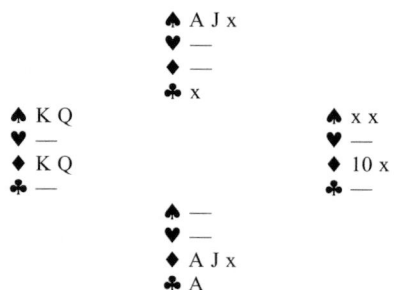

Suppose that West is not aware that South has no spades. South leads the ♣A, and West may discard a diamond hoping that East can protect that suit.

PSYCH. A bid that bears little or no resemblance to a logical choice for the hand in either a natural sense or as a conventional or systemic partnership agreement. Such bids are made primarily to make it more difficult for the opponents to find their optimum spot. The bid has been defined as one which grossly misstates either the high-card count or the suit distribution. See INHIBITORY DOUBLE, PSYCHIC BIDDING; PSYCHIC CONTROLS, SEMI-PSYCHIC. See also LAWS OF DUPLICATE BRIDGE (Law 40).

PSYCHIC BIDDING. A term coined in 1931 by Dorothy Rice Sims, generally meaning bluffing calls to create the illusion of strength or length in a particular suit or to conceal a weakness. From about 1931-34 a wave of blind enthusiasm for psychic bidding swept the country's bridge tables, making it appear that a malignancy was threatening to deform the game that was still in its infancy. Most of these early psychics were hit-or-miss affairs, the bidder never knowing until it was all over whether his ploy had been brilliant or catastrophic.

During this period Ely Culbertson, a keen strategist and psychologist who was not above making an occasional psych himself, was categorically opposed to psychic bidding for the masses. His reasoning was simply that the techniques of the CULBERTSON SYSTEM were designed to create partnership harmony and confidence; any psychic bidding, unquestionably a unilateral and individualistic action, tended to destroy the precision his system was trying to create.

Fortunately the early passion for psychics quickly subsided. Some two decades later, around 1952, psychic openings re-emerged in a more disciplined form as parts of the ROTH-STONE, STAYMAN, KAPLAN-SHEINWOLD, and BULLDOG systems. In the opinions of many experts, however, although the psychic opening had a tendency to force the opponents out of their familiar bidding patterns and into strange and uncomfortable situations, it was never terribly effective against sophisticated opponents, who would act positively when they had good cards in spite of the psych. By 1964, the Roth-Stone system had eliminated the opening psych because the complications it created outweighed the benefits it produced.

Most effective psychs

By and large the most effective psychic bids have been those that misdescribe the bidder's length in a particular suit. Sometimes these psychics promise extreme shortness in the suit; sometimes they promise considerable length in the suit. And when they find gaps in the opponents' defen-

sive bidding conventions, the results can be extremely profitable. The least successful type of psych tends to be one which attempts a bluff as to wholesale strength.

The American Contract Bridge League has taken steps to reduce the usage of psychs. Don Oakie was commissioned by the ACBL Board of Directors to state the League's position in an article in the ACBL *Bulletin*. His article appeared in the February 1978 issue. Here are his conclusions:

"It is high time that we call all of our members' and directors' attention, especially at the club level, to the fact that while a psychic bid is legal, its indiscriminate use is not. People who employ psychic calls against less experienced players may be guilty of unsportsmanlike psyching and thereby be in violation of League regulations. People who psych against their peers may be guilty of frivolous psyching, or of having an unannounced partnership understanding. People who psych against more experienced players will probably get bad boards, and they may lose the few good boards they get by being judged to have indulged in unsportsmanlike psyching, or to have disrupted the game.

"What does this mean to you as a player? If you want to psych any call other than a forcing opening call, go ahead and do it — it's perfectly legal. If you psych on an average of once a month, no player or director is likely to say a word about it. If you can't resist the temptation to do it oftener, sooner or later you're going to run afoul of the Laws or League regulations."

Oakie's definition of a psychic — a bid that deliberately and grossly misstates the bidder's high-card values or suit length — helps to distinguish true psychs from tactical bids.

True psychs and tactical bids

North opens 1♠, and South tries to discourage a club lead by responding 2♣ on:

```
♠ J 8 3
♥ A J 9
♦ A Q J 2
♣ 9 6 2
```

South's 2♣ is a tactical bid. (However, if North never supports clubs with:

```
♠ A 10 7 4 2
♥ K Q 10
♦ 8
♣ A K J 5
```

evidence of an impropriety exists.)

Similarly, a first-hand 1♠ opening on:

```
♠ 8 4 2
♥ 10 7 6 3
♦ J 8 6 4 2
♣ 4
```

is psychic, but a third-hand 1♠ opening on:

```
♠ A K J 8
♥ 8 5
♦ 6 5
♣ 9 7 5 3 2
```

is largely without psychic intent.

In 1991, the ACBL's Board of Directors implemented a new measure to regulate psychs. At the Summer NABC, pairs competing in regional-rated and higher events were required to report their own psych in writing. The requirement was subsequently abandoned. See FIELDING A PSYCH. Following are some examples of various types of psychs:

A psych that has long been almost so standard a part

of the repertoire that it is thought hardly worth using any more is the 1♠ butt-in over an opponent's takeout double of partner's 1♥ opening. Yet it was used to good effect in the final of the 1966 Bermuda Bowl between Italy and North America.

```
Dlr: North        ♠ J 10
Vul: None         ♥ A Q 5 4
                  ♦ A 8 2
                  ♣ 9 8 4 2
♠ K Q 8 6 5                    ♠ A 4 2
♥ J 10                         ♥ K 9 8
♦ 10 6 4 3                     ♦ Q 9
♣ A Q                          ♣ K J 10 7 5
                  ♠ 9 7 3
                  ♥ 7 6 3 2
                  ♦ K J 7 5
                  ♣ 6 3
```

West	North	East	South
Avarelli	Mathe	Belladonna	Hamman
	1♥	Dbl	1♠
1NT	Pass	2♣	Pass
2♦	Pass	2NT	All Pass

Hamman's psychic spade response found a flaw in the ROMAN SYSTEM. A double by Avarelli would have shown spade shortness rather than length. Still, the Italians could have recovered by bidding game in notrump. It was just as well that they did not, however, since after Mathe's opening ♠J was won by dummy's ace, Avarelli led a spade and covered Hamman's 7 with the 8, playing Hamman for a real suit, and lost a trick to Mathe's 10. Mathe wasted no time in shifting to a diamond to collect five tricks in all. In the replay West made 11 tricks in 4♠.

Here is an excellent example of psyching a conventional bid. You hear the following auction and you get all the relevant explanations.

West	North	East	South
			1NT
2♥	2NT (1)	Pass	3♣ (2)
Pass	5♥ (3)	Pass	6♣ (4)
Pass	7♣	All Pass	

(1) Transfer to clubs
(2) Obliged to make this bid
(3) Exclusion Roman Key Card Blackwood, showing a void in the suit bid.
(4) Two Key Cards, not counting the ♥A.

What should West lead? Certainly not the ♥A considering the bidding which announced a heart void in the North hand. This was West's hand:

```
♠ 10 4
♥ A J 10 8 6 5 3
♦ 9 3 2
♣ 3
```

This is the problem Jason Hackett faced in a China Cup match. This was the full deal:

```
Dlr: South        ♠ K Q J 10 8
Vul: N-S          ♥ Q
                  ♦ —
                  ♣ A K Q 8 7 6 5
♠ 10 4                         ♠ 5 3 2
♥ A J 10 8 6 5 2               ♥ J 7 4
♦ 9 3 2                        ♦ K J 10 8 4
♣ 3                            ♣ J 4
                  ♠ A 7 6
                  ♥ K 3
                  ♦ A Q 7 6 5
                  ♣ J 10 2
```

Hackett considered the bidding and finally led . . . a diamond! So declarer scored up his unlikely grand slam.

One of the most spectacularly successful psychs was an opening preemptive psych by Martin Cohn in the Vanderbilt Teams at the 1967 North American Championships in Seattle.

Dlr: North
Vul: E-W

		♠ 10 8 7 6 4 3	
		♥ A 10 6	
		♦ K Q 6	
		♣ 7	
♠ A			♠ K Q 2
♥ K J 9 8 7 5 2			♥ Q 3
♦ A J			♦ 10 8 7 5 4 3 2
♣ A K 4			♣ 2
		♠ J 9 5	
		♥ 4	
		♦ 9	
		♣ Q J 10 9 8 6 5 3	

West	North	East	South
Leventritt	MacCracken	Schenken	Cohn
	Pass	Pass	3♥

All Pass

Holding a weak hand and a shortage of hearts, Cohn opened the bidding with 3♥ and caught LHO Peter Leventritt with a powerful hand including seven hearts. Leventritt could not double for penalties, so he passed, and 3♥ undoubled became the final contract.

Cohn suffered a six-trick penalty (he could have held it to five but would have been down eight on the opening lead of the trump ace followed by a second trump), but that still was a huge gain since this was the auction at the other table:

West	North	East	South
	Pass	Pass	5♣
5♥	Dbl	All Pass	

North did not lead the ♥A and another, so West made an overtrick for 1050 and a 13-IMP gain. See INHIBITORY DOUBLE, PSYCHIC CONTROLS, SEMI-PSYCH.

PSYCHIC CONTROL. Device intended to avert a partnership disaster following a psychic bid.

Controls are usually related to the "disciplined psychic" used in KAPLAN-SHEINWOLD and the original ROTH-STONE. In such cases the opener has 3-6 points, mainly in the suit which he has bid.

Responses of 2NT and 3NT can be used to show powerful balanced hands. 2NT shows a hand with 21-22 points, and therefore shows interest in game even if the opener is psychic. 3NT shows a stronger hand that is sure of game even opposite a psych.

The jump shift remains forcing, and the opener must take care with his rebid. If he has made a psychic opening, he must rebid his suit or rebid in notrump, whichever is the more economical. Conversely, he must avoid these rebids holding a genuine opening.

Psychic controls are disallowed in some countries, notably in England, on the theory that the psychic bidder must be prepared to take his chances along with the opponents.

PSYCHIC LEAD. See OPENING LEAD.

PSYCHIC PLAY. See DECEPTIVE PLAY.

PSYCHOLOGY. See DECEPTIVE PLAY; FALSE-CARDING; PARTNERSHIP PSYCHOLOGY.

PTDA. See PROFESSIONAL TOURNAMENT DIRECTORS ASSOCIATION.

PUDDING RAISE. A balanced major-suit raise based on primarily high-card strength. (British).

PULLING TRUMP. See DRAWING TRUMPS.

PUMP. A colloquialism for FORCE. FORCING DECLARER TO RUFF is frequently referred to as pumping the declarer.

PUNCH. Verb: to cause a player (usually dummy or declarer) to use a trump for ruffing; to shorten; noun: the act of shortening in trumps. See FORCING LEADS.

PUNISH. Double for penalties.

PUPPET STAYMAN. A method of responding to 1NT devised by Kit Woolsey. Responder's 2♣ asks for a five-card major. With no five-card major, opener is forced to bid 2♦. Responder now bids the major he doesn't have, or notrump with both majors. Opener is now in a position to select the right denomination without revealing his distribution to the opponents. Puppet Stayman can also be used over 2NT openers with equal effectiveness.

PUSH. (1) A raise of partner's suit, usually at the partscore level, aimed at pushing the opponents to a level at which they may be defeated. For example:

West	North	East	South
	1♠	2♥	2♠

Neither side is vulnerable and South holds:

♠ 6 5 3
♥ K 9
♦ A 8 4 2
♣ Q 7 3 2

It seems likely to West that both sides will make about eight tricks, so he bids 3♥. East is marked with, at worst, a good five-card heart suit. If North-South continue to 3♠, in which they will have more heart losers than they expect, they may be defeated, and West will have turned a minus score into a plus. The chance of being doubled in 3♥ is slight, and East should be wary of continuing to game.

(2) A board in a team match, in which the result is the same in both rooms (also STAND-OFF).

(3) A rubber in which the net score is zero after ROUNDING OFF.

PUZZLE. In bridge, puzzles are referred to as PROBLEMS, and are usually of three types, DOUBLE DUMMY PROBLEMS, SINGLE DUMMY PROBLEMS and INFERENTIAL PROBLEMS. Examples of each type appear in this book. Crossword puzzles and acrostics using bridge definitions or texts have been published as bridge magazine features.

Q

QUACK. A term to indicate either the queen or the jack in situations where it is of no consequence which of the two cards is held or played. See RESTRICTED CHOICE.

QUALIFYING. Finishing high enough in a QUALIFY-ING SESSION to continue competing in the final session(s) of the event. See CONDITIONS OF CONTEST.

QUALIFYING SESSION. In an event of two or more sessions, one or more of them may be designated as qualifying sessions, to select contestants eligible for continued play in the remaining sessions.

QUALITY. See STRENGTH. Ely Culbertson stressed "quality" and "quantity" in discussing hand valuation. More modern usage concerns control cards, suit strength or the presence of intermediate cards, etc. See also WORKING CARDS.

QUANTITATIVE. A bid is quantitative if it is natural and limited.

QUANTITATIVE FOUR NOTRUMP. A term covering a number of situations where 4NT is a natural bid; usually an invitation to 6NT. See BLACKWOOD .

QUANTITATIVE FIVE NOTRUMP. A raise of 1NT or 2NT, asking partner to bid 6NT with a minimum or 7NT with a maximum.

QUANTITY. See LENGTH.

QUEEN. The third highest card in a suit.

QUEEN ASK.

QUEEN OF BRIDGE. See KING OR QUEEN OF BRIDGE.

QUEEN FROM KING-QUEEN. See RUSINOW LEADS.

QUEEN LEAD. Traditionally, the lead of the queen from a long suit promises the jack and quite frequently the 10 or 9 as well. See OPENING LEADS. In alternative methods the lead of the queen promises the king (see RUSINOW LEADS), or the ace and king. The JOURNALIST system of leads against notrump promises either the traditional holding headed by Q-J-10, or a holding of K-Q-10-9. The latter asks the partner of the opening leader to play the jack if he has it, enabling the opening leader to continue without fear of a BATH COUP by declarer.

QUEEN OVER JACK. The theory, or speculation, that the queen lies over the jack slightly more often than not is credited to Clagett Bowie. The assumption is based on the possibility that the queen may have captured the jack in the previous deal with the same deck, and that the cards may not have been separated in the shuffle. This assumption is valid only if declarer's holding in the suit is A-J opposite K-10. With K-J facing A-10, the chances are just as good that the king was used to capture the queen. However, the manner in which the trick is gathered is an important, and uncertain, influence. The theory has meaning only at rubber bridge, if it has any value at all. See TWO-WAY FINESSE.

QUESTION. For when to ask questions, see ALERTING; EXPLANATION OF ANY CALL OR PLAY; FACE DOWN LEADS.

QUICK TRICK. A high card holding that in usual circumstances will win a trick by virtue of the rank of the cards in either offensive or defensive play. Of course, in some distributional holdings, or FREAK HANDS, such defensive values evaporate. The accepted table of quick tricks is:

2 quick tricks	A-K of same suit
$1^{1}/_{2}$	A-Q of same suit
1	A or K-Q of same suit
$^{1}/_{2}$	K-x

See DEFENSIVE TRICK.

QUITTED TRICK. A trick is quitted, in rubber bridge, when the four cards played to it have been gathered together and turned face down in a packet in front of the side which contributed the winning card. Any player has the right to inspect a quitted trick until either he or his partner has led or played to a subsequent trick. In duplicate, a trick is quitted when all four players have played to it and turned their cards face down. A quitted trick may not be inspected except at the director's specific instruction. If a player wishes to inspect the cards just played to a trick, he may do so only if he has left his own card face up on the table, assuming neither he nor his partner has led or played to the next trick. See LAWS OF DUPLICATE (Law 66).

QUOTIENT. A device used to determine the winner in team competition if a ROUND-ROBIN ends in a tie either in won and lost matches, or in VICTORY POINTS won and lost. The total number of IMPs won by a team against all round-robin opponents is divided by the number lost to determine the quotient. Italy won two European Championships by quotient, over France in 1956 and over Great Britain in 1958.

R

RHO. Right-hand opponent. The opponent to the right of a player.

RABBI'S RULE. "When the king is singleton offside, play the ace." A whimsical rule attributed to Milton Shattner, a New York attorney nicknamed "the Rabbi" because of his authoritative pronouncement of this and other convictions governing play.

RABBIT. An inexperienced player (British).

RACK. (1) A device used by handicapped players for holding a hand of cards. (2) A device to hold traveling scoreslips for inspection by the players after the game has been scored. (3) A device in which to place table assignments for swiss matches; (4) Colloq., (verb) to ruin opponents by holding exceptionally good cards; (noun) a player who holds such cards; also called a cardrack.

RAGS. A holding of only a few high cards, likely to be insignificant in the bidding or play of a hand.

RAINBOW INDIVIDUAL MOVEMENT. A movement for tournaments involving players competing as individuals, in which contestants are divided into groups

corresponding to their original starting directions, with separate instructions for progressing to each group. The guide cards are often printed in different colors to make the groups more easily distinguished — hence the name Rainbow. This movement was devised by Oswald Jacoby and Shepard Barclay.

In a typical set of guide cards (ACBL 52-player Individual, a 13-table game), the North players receive blue cards and sit at the same table throughout. The East players receive yellow guide cards, moving two tables toward the higher number. South players receive white guide cards and move to the next higher-numbered table. West players receive pink guide cards and skip a table toward lower numbers, while the boards go to the next lower-numbered table. For identification purposes, players take a number: North, the table number; West, the table number plus 13; South, the table number plus 26; and East, the table number plus 39.

The movement in its regular form, as given above, will work when the number of tables is not divisible by two or three: 5, 7, 11, 13, 17, 19, 23. For 8, 9, 12 and 16 tables see IRREGULAR RAINBOW. Tournament director Paul Marks devised a variation of this movement for prime number plus one tables (see EIGHT TABLES, TWELVE TABLES, FOURTEEN TABLES), which is based on the Rainbow. Tournament director Maury Braunstein devised a special adaptation of the Rainbow for nine tables and 15 tables. He also devised a stanza movement for 14 tables.

A regular Rainbow can be carried out in any manner as long as it is remembered that there are five different movements for the four groups of players and the boards. As long as the groups and the boards have different progressions, and continue for succeeding rounds as they moved for the second, no difficulty is encountered. The number of rounds is equal to the number of tables, but can be cut short. If it is desired to increase the number of partnerships, the South and West players can interchange after the first boards in a two-board round, or the West player can travel around the table counter-clockwise for three boards to a round. In all cases the North player remains stationary. In no case do balanced comparisons result. Session awards are based on results as achieved in each direction.

RAISE. Noun: an increase of the contract in the denomination named by partner; Verb: to make a bid increasing the contract in the denomination named by partner. See SINGLE RAISE; DOUBLE RAISE; INVERTED MINOR RAISE; OPENERS REBID; TRIPLE RAISE.

RAISE IN RESPONDER'S SUIT. See OPENER'S REBID.

RAISER. The player who bids for a greater number of tricks in a suit first bid by his partner.

RANDOM DRAW KNOCKOUT TEAMS. The teams that win remain in the competition and are paired for their next match by means of a random draw. Typically all the possible positions are written on slips of paper, and the captain of each team draws his next assignment at the time he reports his winning match result. The pairings for the first match also are random. See BRACKETED KNOCKOUT TEAMS, COMPACT KNOCKOUT TEAMS, DOUBLE ELIMINATION KNOCKOUT TEAMS, HANDICAP KNOCKOUT TEAMS, MINI-KNOCKOUT TEAMS, MIXED TEAMS, OPEN TEAMS, TEAM GAMES, ZIP KNOCKOUT TEAMS.

RANDOM FALSECARD. See FALSECARD.

RANK. (1) The priority of suits in bidding and cutting. Starting at the bottom, the suits rank in alphabetical order: clubs, diamonds, hearts and spades, with notrump at the top of the list. (2) The trick-taking power of each card within a suit. The ace, king, queen, jack have priority in that order. The lower cards rank numerically. (3) The status of a player in a masterpoint ranking system.

RANKING. The position of a player, pair or team in the section or in the overall.

RANKING BRIDGE PLAYER. See LIFE MASTER, the highest basic category into which the ACBL ranks players (there are six Life Master ranks). The ranking of players by means of MASTERPOINTS won cannot be construed as definitive as between any two players, because of the difference in time during which points were earned, frequency of competition, ability to attend major regional and NORTH AMERICAN CHAMPIONSHIP TOURNAMENTS. Many other national organizations have set up similar systems to identify their more outstanding players.

RATING POINT CERTIFICATE. Paper certificates once were issued by ACBL clubs that indicated masterpoints earned in club play. Players would accumulate the certificates and mail them to ACBL Headquarters from time to time so that they could be added to their masterpoint record. The advent of the computer spelled the end of the certificates. Other NCBOs also used to use the certificate method, but the computer method is used almost everywhere today.

RATINGS POINTS. Points earned at the club level in games with club rating. The top 40% of competitors earn points on a graduated basis. If the game is stratified or handicapped, additional awards are given to players who place in their strat (if stratified) or in the overall after handicaps are applied (if handicapped). The basic award for first place in an open field is 10/100 of a masterpoint. However, that figure is lowered for handicap and stratified winners. It also is lowered if the event is not open – e.g., an invitational event or a newcomer competition. Points after first place are graduated, with 70% of the first-place award for second, 50% for third, 35% for fourth, etc.

RAZZLE-DAZZLE. A bridge game derived from S.B.Fishburne's CUTTHROAT, which was devised in 1936 and has been played regularly since then at the Peninsular Club in Grand Rapids MI. It includes a nullo bid, which outranks notrump but has the same 40-30 etc. trick score. A bid of six nullos, for example, contracts to lose 12 tricks. The declarer at nullo can choose, before the opening lead, which hand will be exposed. Other rules:

(a) Opening bidder must have three quick tricks: AK = 2; AQ = 1$\frac{1}{2}$; A or KQ = 1; K x = $\frac{1}{2}$ Subsequent bids are unrestricted.

(b) When there are three consecutive passes, the last

bidder becomes declarer. He then selects one player as his partner. That player may accept or reject, but in either case his cards become dummy. Either opponent may then double, and the declarer or an accepting dummy can redouble.

(c) The first game scores a 200 bonus, a second game 500. Other scoring is normal.

(d) Each player has an individual score.

(e) Partscores are not played and redeals are OK.

REBID. See BELATED SUPPORT; CHANGE OF SUIT; CROWHURST; FORCING SEQUENCES; FOURTH SUIT ARTIFICIAL; GOLDEN RULE; JUMP PREFERENCE; JUMP REBIDS BY RESPONDER; NEW MINOR FORCING; ONE NOTRUMP REBID; OPENER'S REBID; PREEMPTIVE RERAISE; PREFERENCE; PUSH; RESPONDER'S REBID; REVERSE; SECOND NEGATIVE RESPONSE; SHORT-SUIT GAME TRIES; STRENGTH-SHOWING BIDS; THIRD-SUIT BID; THREE-CARD SUITS, BIDS IN; TRIAL BID; TWO-WAY GAME TRIES; WEAK-SUIT GAME TRY; WOLFF.

REBIDDABLE SUIT. A suit of six cards or more which can be bid twice. In some cases a five-card suit may be bid twice. See GOLDEN RULE, OPENER'S REBID and RESPONDER'S REBID.

REBID IN ORIGINAL SUIT. See OPENER'S REBID.

RECAP. See RECAPITULATION SHEET.

RECAPITULATION SHEET. A large printed form on which the scores from pickup slips are posted. The scores are posted in such a way that they can be matchpointed, whether the event is pairs or teams. This was the method that was used until computers came on the scene. Nowadays computers score almost all games (some small clubs still use the recapitulation sheet). After the computer finishes calculating the scores, the computer prints out special sheets which resemble recapitulation sheets. The computer printouts show the event, the names, the score on each board, the matchpoints earned, the total scores and placings. If the event is multi-session, it also indicates the seating assignment for the subsequent session.

RECIPROCAL SQUEEZE. A variant of the double squeeze. The squeeze card is not an established card in the fourth suit; rather each opponent is squeezed in turn by a winner in the suit guarded by his partner. These are the basic positions:

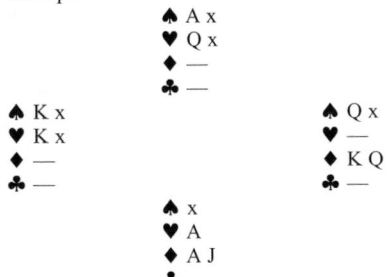

South leads the ♥A, which forces East to discard a spade. Now the lead of the ♦A squeezes West in the majors.

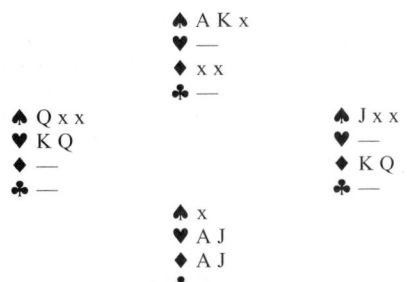

South leads the ♥A, which forces East to discard a spade. Now the lead of the ♦A squeezes West in the majors.

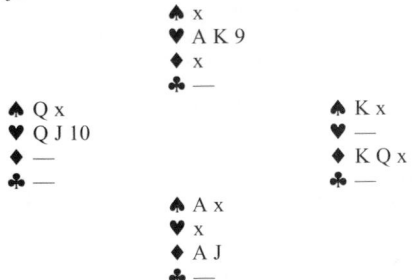

South leads the ♦A, which forces West to unguard spades. Now South leads hearts, and the second winner of that suit squeezes East in spades and diamonds.

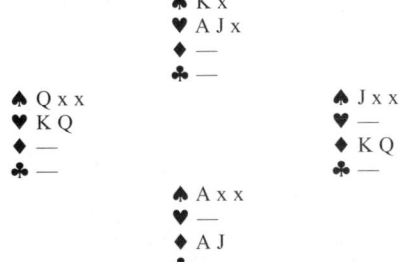

South cashes the ♦A, which forces West to unguard spades. A spade is led to the king followed by the ♥A, which squeezes East in spades and diamonds. A double squeeze may be played as a reciprocal squeeze by running all of declarer's winners in the fourth suit (which is not guarded by either opponent). This has a dual advantage: it allows more room for defensive error, and it enables declarer to obtain additional information regarding the outstanding cards.

RECORDING OF MASTERPOINTS. The results of each MASTERPOINT event are reported by the tournament director to the national organization, and points are recorded to the credit of the winners of club games and to those players placing in local, sectional, or higher rated tournaments.

The ACBL was first to develop a masterpoint plan, but similar plans are now in use by numerous other national bridge governing bodies.

RECORDING OF MATCHES. See BRIDGE-O-RAMA; HAND RECORD; VUGRAPH.

RECTIFICATION. An adjustment made to permit the

auction or play to proceed as normally as possible after an irregularity has occurred. In the bidding stage, irregularities (other than violations of ethical procedure) are covered by specific penalties, as are most of the possible irregularities in the play. However, in the case of a failure to follow suit which is later corrected, it is possible that the offender inadvertently gains information that he is not entitled to under normal play. In this case, rectification is called for.

Occasionally the bidding will have started at a table when it is discovered that the traveling pair has come to the wrong table and should not be playing the board against that opponent. In this case the director may seat the proper pair at the table and have the bidding repeated. If no additional information is gained, the board is permitted to stand; if the bidding progresses differently, then an adjusted score usually is given. See ALCATRAZ COUP and LAWS OF DUPLICATE BRIDGE (Laws 12 and 16).

RECTIFYING THE COUNT. The process of losing a trick or tricks in order to reach a certain number of remaining losers, thus enabling a desired ending to be reached. The most common use of the play is to reduce the number of losers to one, enabling a simple squeeze to be executed.

```
                    ♠ 3 2
                    ♥ A K 6
                    ♦ A Q 7 2
                    ♣ A K Q 5
        ♠ Q J 10 8              ♠ K 9 7 6
        ♥ 3 2                   ♥ J 10 9 8
        ♦ 6 5                   ♦ J 10 9 8
        ♣ 9 8 7 4 3             ♣ 2
                    ♠ A 5 4
                    ♥ Q 7 5 4
                    ♦ K 4 3
                    ♣ J 10 6
```

West leads the ♠Q against South's 6NT contract. South has 11 winners. The contract will succeed if either hearts or diamonds are favorably divided.

Another chance is a squeeze against an opponent holding guards in both red suits. This squeeze will operate only if South has but one loser remaining. If South wins the first trick, he can no longer make his contract. Instead, he should rectify the count by allowing West to hold the first spade. South wins any continuation and runs his black winners, squeezing East between the red suits. For another example, see LOSER-ON-LOSER. Also see CARD READING, COUNTING THE HAND.

RED. Vulnerable. Also a British colloquialism meaning we are vulnerable, they are not. See AMBER, GREEN, WHITE.

RED AND BLACK GERBER. See BLACK AND RED GERBER.

RED POINT. Masterpoints won in regional and NORTH AMERICAN CHAMPIONSHIP TOURNAMENTS are required for the advancement of players to NABC MASTER and LIFE MASTER status in the ACBL. To distinguish points won at these larger and more important events, the ACBL uses the term "red points". One hundred "colored," at least 50 silver and at least 50 red/gold of which at least 25 must be gold, are one of the requirements for promotion to Life Master

status. See also GOLD POINT; PLATINUM POINT; RANKING OF PLAYERS; REGIONAL AND NATIONAL POINTS.

RED RIBBON PAIRS. An ACBL event with national rating open only to players with fewer than 2000 masterpoints who have fulfilled the qualification requirements. A player must win or place second in a qualifying event while he still has 1500 or fewer masterpoints. Red Ribbon qualifying events cannot have an upper limit of more than 1500 masterpoints. A player can qualify for this event with Blue Ribbon, Silver Ribbon or Red Ribbon qualifications. Such qualifications are in effect until used.

REDEAL. A second or subsequent deal by the same dealer to replace his first deal. See LAWS OF CONTRACT BRIDGE, Part III Section 10. Hands are never redealt at duplicate except in special cases on the director's instructions.

REDOUBLE. A call, following an opposing double, that doubles all scores: penalties; trick scores, and overtrick premiums. When the contract succeeds, the bonus for making a doubled contract is also doubled, from 50 to 100.

Although the mathematics of the scoring table favor redoubles at high levels in rubber bridge and IMP play, redoubled contracts are rare when the standard of play is high. Ill-judged doubles of game or slam contracts may attract redoubles.

West	North	East	South
	1♣	Pass	2♥
Pass	2NT	Pass	6♥
Pass	Pass	Dbl	?

```
            ♠ A J 2
            ♥ A K Q 8 6 4 2
            ♦ K 9 5
            ♣ —
```

East's double asks for an unusual lead, usually the lead of North's first-bid suit. East probably has the ♣AK or ♣AQ, since he is unlikely to be void when South is. If North's clubs are only fair, he must have strength in spades and diamonds. South should redouble.

In a high-level competitive auction, an expert may occasionally redouble as a bluff. He may expect his contract to fail by one trick, but he is prepared to sacrifice 100 or 200 points in the hope of inducing the opponents to continue in their own suit and go down.

A special situation arises when an artificial bid is doubled and redoubled. At a high level, when a CUEBID or response to BLACKWOOD is doubled, a redouble is generally regarded as control-showing. Whether the control shown is first- or second-round is usually a matter of partnership agreement.

At a low level, the situation is different:

West	North	East	South
			1NT
Pass	2♣	Dbl	Redbl

South's redouble shows a desire to play at clubs; South may have a five-card club suit or a strong four-card suit.

Prior to 1987, making a redoubled contract was worth 50 extra points for the insult. This brought about some strange situations at high levels: Making 5♦ redoubled with an overtrick vulnerable was worth 1350, less than the value of 6♦ (1370); but making 5♦ redoubled with an overtrick not vulnerable (950) was worth more than

making 6 ♦ (920). A scoring change in the 1987 edition of *The Laws of Duplicate Bridge* increased the bonus for making a redoubled contract to 100 points and overcame this anomaly.

Tactical uses of the redouble

Redoubles are often used to show general strength:

West	North	East	South
			1 ♣
Pass	Pass	Dbl	?

♠ A K 5
♥ A 8 3
♦ 9 3
♣ A K J 10 4

South should redouble to announce considerable extra strength, in this case at least 19 points with real clubs.

West	North	East	South
			1 ♣
Pass	1 ♥	Dbl	?

♠ A 8 3
♥ K 2
♦ Q 9 2
♣ A K Q 10 4

South should redouble. Unless N/S are playing Support Doubles, this call does not promise hearts; indeed, it tends to deny four-card support. It says that North-South have most of the high-card strength.

Another situation:

West	North	East	South
	1 ♥	Pass	2 ♥
Pass	Pass	Dbl	?

♠ A Q 9 4
♥ 10 7 3
♦ Q 5
♣ J 9 8 4

South should redouble to show a maximum single raise and suggest playing for a penalty.

West	North	East	South
			1 ♥
Pass	2 ♥	Dbl	?

♠ 10 5
♥ A K 7 4 2
♦ Q J 5
♣ A K 6

South should redouble, indicating that the deal belongs to North-South. If South later bids 3 ♥, he promises game interest.

For other redoubling situations, see DOUBLES OF NOTRUMP BIDS, KOCK-WERNER REDOUBLE, RESPONSES OVER OPPONENT'S TAKEOUT DOUBLE, ROSENKRANZ REDOUBLE, SOS REDOUBLE, STRIPED-TAIL APE DOUBLE, SUPPORT REDOUBLE.

REDOUBLE OUT OF ROTATION. An improper bid when it is partner's or right-hand opponent's turn to call when the auction is over, or when an oppenent's contract is redoubled. If it is partner's turn to call, he must pass and continue to pass for the balance of the auction. If the partner of the offender has the opening lead, declarer may require or forbid him to lead a specified suit. Also the offender is not permitted to redouble the same bid which he redoubled out of turn.

If it is the turn of the right-hand opponent to bid, the redouble must be repeated if this opponent passes; if the opponent bids, the offender may make any legal call, but his partner must pass at his next opportunity. See Law 32.

REDUCED HOWELL. When a HOWELL has too many rounds a Reduced Howell may be used. It has a reduced number of rounds, compared to the Howell movement for the same number of tables. The reduction comes from increasing the number of stationary pairs, hence decreasing the number of moving pairs, rounds and board sets. The Reduced Howell may replace the play of a Howell with appendix table(s), but it also exists for an even number of rounds. With heavy reduction, when there are stationary pairs at most tables, it can be made very Mitchell-like.

The first movements of this kind were published in 1947 by Sam Gold for 8-12 tables and 13 rounds under the name Three-Quarter Howells. Another sequence, known as the Short Howells, was later constructed for 11 rounds.

With a computer it has been possible to construct Reduced Howells with much better balance than in the original movements and for other numbers of rounds. Note that since the Reduced Howells have several stationary pairs, it is necessary to arrow switch in certain rounds at these tables to get reasonable balance.

These are the starting positions, and the arrow switches, for 6 and 8-12 tables with good balance. In all movements the number of rounds is the same as the number of board sets and of moving pairs. The moving pairs follow the pair with the next lower number, #1 following the highest-numbered moving pair. Tables with stationary pairs switch as indicated.

Table	6 tables, 8 rounds NS EW b			6 tables, 9 rounds NS EW b			8 tables, 11 rounds NS EW b			8 tables, 12 rounds NS EW b			8 tables, 13 rounds NS EW b		
1	9	1	1	10	1	1	12	1	1	13	1	1	14	1	1
2	10	6	2	8	12	2	13	6	2	14	8	2	16	6	2
3	11	4	3	5	11	3	14	8	3	11	6	3	9	5	3
4	12	2	4	7	3	4	16	10	4	15	9	4	2	15	4
5	8	7	5	6	9	5	7	4	5	16	4	5	13	12	5
6	5	3	6	2	4	6	2	3	6	3	7	6	11	3	6
7	9 NS in			10 NS in			15	5	7	2	5	7	10	8	7
8	all rds			all rds			11	9	8	10	12	8	7	4	8
	10 EW in rds 4-7			11 NS in rds 3,6,9			12-16 EW rds 8,10,11			13 NS in all rds;			14 NS in all rds;		
	11 EW in rds 4-8			12 NS in rds 2,5,8						14 EW in rds 2,3,6, 7,10,11			15 NS in rds 9-13		
	12 EW in rds 5-8									15 EW in rds 3,4,7,8,11,12			16 EW in rds 8-12		
										16 EW in rds 2,4,6,8,10,12					

Table	9 tables, 11 rounds NS EW b			9 tables, 12 rounds NS EW b			9 tables, 13 rounds NS EW b			10 tables, 11 rounds NS EW b			10 tables, 13 rounds NS EW b		
1	12	1	1	13	1	1	14	1	1	12	1	1	13	1	1
2	6	4	2	8	4	2	4	10	2	13	11	2	14	7	2
3	13	10	3	14	10	3	9	6	3	14	10	3	15	2	3
4	14	9	4	15	5	4	15	11	4	15	9	4	16	11	4
5	15	2	5	2	9	5	16	2	5	16	8	5	17	8	5
6	16	5	6	16	11	6	17	5	6	17	7	8	18	3	6
7	17	8	7	17	3	7	8	3	7	18	6	9	5	9	7
8	11	3	8	7	6	8	12	13	8	19	5	10	20	12	8
9	18	7	9	18	12	9	18	7	9	20	4	11	19	10	9
10	12-18 EW in rds 8,10,11			13-18 EW in rds 7,8,12			14-18EW in rds 6,7,12,13			2	3	1	4	6	10
										12-20 EW in rds 7,8,11			13-20 EW in rds 7,9,11,12		

Table	10 tables, 13 rounds NS EW b	11 tables, 12 rounds NS EW b	11 tables, 13 rounds NS EW b	12 tables 13 rounds NS EW b
1	14 1 1	13 1 1	14 1 1	14 1 1
2	15 10 2	14 12 2	15 7 2	15 13 2
3	16 5 3	15 11 3	2 10 3	16 12 3
4	17 8 4	16 10 4	16 6 4	17 11 4
5	18 11 5	17 9 5	17 13 5	18 10 5
6	2 3 6	18 8 7	18 4 6	19 9 6
7	19 6 7	19 7 8	19 11 7	20 8 9
8	9 13 8	20 6 9	20 9 8	21 7 10
9	12 7 9	21 5 10	12 5 9	22 6 11
10	20 4 10	22 4 11	22 3 10	23 5 12
11	14-20 EW	2 3 12	21 8 11	24 4 13
12	in rds	13-22 EW	14-22 EW	2 3 1
	5,8,9,13	in rds	in rds	14-24 EW
		7,8,9,12	7,10,12,13	in rds
				6,8,11,13

REDWOOD. A variation of KICKBACK. When a minor suit is agreed as trump in a game-forcing auction, a jump to one above four of that minor acts as Keycard Blackwood. Essentially this corresponds with Kickback except that it applies only to the minors.

A variation of Redwood comes when the minor itself is used as ace-asking. The advantages of that method are that it allows for the use of splinter jumps in all suits (whereas in traditional Redwood one splinter becomes an ace-asking bid).

In the following sequences for example:

1 ♦	2 ♦ (inverted)
4 ♦	

1 ♠	2 ♦
3 ♦	4 ♦

1 ♣	1 ♥
3 ♣	4 ♣

In all three sequences if Redwood or Kickback were in use, making a splinter jump in the kickback suit might be difficult.

RE-ENTRY. A card by which a player who has had the lead (including the opening lead) can regain it.

REFUSE. (1) Deliberate failure to win a trick because of reasons of strategy. (2) Used in the sense of refusing to finesse, i.e., not taking what was previously a winning finesse in order to ensure the contract. (3) An obsolete term formerly used in WHIST and AUCTION BRIDGE, the laws of which defined it as "to fail to follow suit". See DANGER HAND; DISCARD; DUCK; HOLD UP; RENOUNCE; REVOKE.

REGENCY WHIST CLUB (New York City). Formerly Regency Club, founded in 1936 and merged with the WHIST CLUB of New York in 1964. It has remained at 15 East 67th Street since it began its very successful career, with many outstanding bridge personalities among its members.

REGIONAL TOURNAMENT. See CHAMPIONSHIP TOURNAMENT.

REGRES. See WEAK OPENING SYSTEMS.

REID CONVENTION. See RESPONSIVE DOUBLE.

REISINGER MEMORIAL TROPHY. Donated by the Greater New York BA in 1965 in memory of CURT H. REISINGER and awarded to the winners of the Fall Open Teams Championships, better known as the Resinger Board-a-match Teams. It replaced the historic CHICAGO TROPHY. See INTERNATIONAL OPEN TEAM SELECTION.

REISINGER TROPHY. Donated by Curt H. Reisinger in 1930, for the Knockout Teams-of-Four contest in the Eastern States Championships, one of the world's oldest team events.

REITH ONE-OVER-ONE. A system of bidding described by George Reith in a series of five books published 1930-33. Approach bidding was used and four-card suits were bid freely. Responses and bids were kept to minimum levels, and third-hand openings were somewhat shaded. The essence of the system, a forerunner of methods considered as Standard by postwar writers, was the principle of emphasizing distribution in early bidding rounds as opposed to showing strength. The one-over-one response made it incumbent upon the opening bidder to bid at least once more.

REITH POINT COUNT. An appraisal by George Reith of the relative values of high cards, primarily for notrump bidding. The values assigned were ace = 6, king = 4, queen = 3, jack = 2, ten = 1. See REITH ONE-OVER-ONE.

REJECT. When a partnership bids and raises a suit in a non game-forcing auction, one hand typically makes a game-try by bidding a help-suit. This frequently gives useful information to the defense about declarer's hand. To combat this, Eric Kokish devised that once a suit is agreed cheaply, the first step is a relay, to which responder would answer by indicating which is the cheapest game-try that he would reject. Other actions by declarer are short-suit tries. Thus after 1 ♥ -2 ♥ , 2NT is a short suit try in spades; 3 ♣ and 3 ♦ are short suit tries in clubs and diamonds; 3 ♥ shows a source of tricks looking for 3NT; 3NT shows solid hearts. 2 ♠ is a relay (suggesting a long suit somewhere that needs help). After the 2 ♠ relay, responder bids the cheapest strain in which he would reject a help-suit try. So if responder would reject a spade game-try he bids 2NT. That lets opener at his next turn make a game try in clubs or diamonds if that was his intent all along, and responder can accept or reject that now. If responder would accept a try in spades or clubs but not in diamonds, he responds 3 ♦ initially.

Using the reject try and then bidding 3NT offers a choice of games.

The same principle extends to responding to 1NT. A response of 2 ♠ can be set aside to represent a balanced game-try, or a one-suited invitation. It could also be based on the same hands with a slam invitation with more complex continuations.

Responses to the 2 ♠ relay after 1NT - 2 ♠ : 2NT, minimum high cards (which would reject the balanced try); 3 ♣ , non-minimum would decline an invitation in clubs; 3 ♦ , non-minimum would accept a club try, but would decline an invitation in diamonds; 3 ♥ , non-minimum would accept a club or diamond try, but decline an invi-

tation in hearts; 3♠, non-minimum would accept a club, diamond or heart try, but decline an invitation in spades; 3NT, maximum balanced.

RELAY. (1) A minimum bid unrelated to the bidder's hand, aimed simply at keeping the bidding open so that the bidder's partner can describe his hand. The LEBENSOHL response of 3♣ to 2NT is an example – the 3♣ says nothing about clubs, merely keeping the bidding open. Another example is the 2♦ response to the CAPPELLETTI 2♣ overcall of 1NT. 2♦ says nothing about diamonds, merely offering the 2♣ bidder a chance to clarify his hand and his intentions. Some relay bids are asking bids – e.g., the STAYMAN 2♣ bid in response to 1NT. For the full development of the relay principle, see RELAY SYSTEM. (2) The practice of sharing boards in duplicate. This method often is used in a pair game with six, eight or twelve tables. Two pairs share boards while one set of boards sits on a byestand halfway around the room. It also can happen in Howell movements when a late pair is added. And in team events, the boards are relayed between the two teams involved in a match. (3) In Great Britain, a relay is the equivalent of a byestand. See BYESTAND, CAPPELLETTI, DONT, GLADIATOR, KOKISH RELAY, HAMILTON, JACOBY TRANSFER BIDS, RELAYS OVER WEAK TWO-BIDS, RELAY SYSTEMS, ROMAN GERBER, TRANSFER BIDS, WEAK TWO-BIDS

RELAY ASKING BID. An ASKING BID whose distinguishing features are (1) that it is the cheapest possible bid (perhaps skipping trump or other signoff) and (2) that it probably has no relationship to the suit bid. A relay can be used like other asking bids (asking about trump quality, controls, distribution, points), except for asking about a specific non-trump suit (when you would normally have to name that particular suit).

The most common relay asking bid is actually STAYMAN, asking for a 4-card major. A relay is very often used to continue some other kind of asking bid, asking for more information or clarification. An example is ROLLING BLACKWOOD. After a 4NT BLACKWOOD ask for aces, a relay (perhaps skipping trump) is the ask for kings. Another example: in PRECISION, opener has shown an exact 3-4-1-5 distribution and 11-15 high-card points, with 2D-2NT-3C. Responder asks opener to clarify his high-card points by using the relay 3D. Opener responds 3H with a minimum (11-13) and 3S (14-15) with a maximum. See BARON COROLLARY; DENIAL CUEBIDS; JACOBY TWO NOTRUMP RESPONSE; RELAYS OVER WEAK TWO-BIDS; SPIRAL; TWO-WAY STAYMAN, TRUSCOTT 2-DIAMOND; WEAK TWO-BIDS.

RELAY MITCHELL. See MITCHELL MOVEMENT.

RELAY STAND. See BYESTAND.

RELAY SYSTEMS. Systems based on the idea that one player should make a series of minimum bids, or relays, until he has acquired sufficient information about his partner's hand to be able to fix the final contract. The first relay system was developed by Pierre Ghestem of France, about 1950, and was used by him very successfully in world championships, mainly with Rene

Bacherich. In 1963 he played it with Claude Delmouly, using the name Monaco. This encouraged other European theorists to develop relay systems, notably Dr. Bertrand Romanet, with "Alpha", and Pierre Collet, with "Beta". Both these date from 1965.

An important impetus came with work done about 1972 by David Cliff. He can be considered the father of modern relay methods, with Ghestem as the grandfather. Cliff's ideas were adopted and refined by a group of young players including Matt Granovetter, Ron Rubin and Michael Becker. Their successes with the ULTIMATE CLUB attracted new interest in the relay principle and attracted imitators in many parts of the world who developed a series of relay languages. See EFOS, MONACO SYSTEM; MOSCITO, SYMMETRIC RELAY, WEAK OPENING SYSTEMS.

RELAY TABLE. One of the tables at which the players are sharing boards for that round with an adjacent table. See BYESTAND.

RELAYS OVER WEAK TWO-BIDS. There are two ways of using a relay, one concerned with stoppers and the other with distribution.

(1) A method of responding to weak two-bids using the cheapest bid — either notrump if the opening bid was 2♠, or the next higher suit — as a relay bid. The relay asks opener to bid a stopper outside his suit if he has one. If his stopper is in the relay suit, he rebids in notrump. Lacking any stopper, opener rebids his own suit. Using this method, the relay bid is the responder's only forcing bid.

(2) The Symmetric Relay method, usable by any pair employing weak two-bids, uses 2NT to start a relay structure, whether the opening is 2♥ or 2♠. The opener bids 3♣ with a minimum and makes other bids with extras. After 3♣, 3♦ is a relay. The following apply whether the opening bid is minimum or maximum:

(a) 3♥ shows a balanced hand. Then 3♠ asks opener to bid 3NT with two top honors, 4♣ or more with one.

(b) 3♠ shows a singleton in the unbid major.

(c) Four-level bids are void-showing.

Also:

(d) 3♦ shows a singleton in a minor; subsequent 3♠ shows it is diamonds, 3NT that it is clubs.

(e) 3♣ followed by 3NT shows a singleton in a minor. Later 4♦, shows it is diamonds, 4♥ that it is clubs.

(f) 3NT in response to 2NT is normal, showing a solid suit.

See WEAK TWO-BIDS.

REMOVE. To bid on when partner has doubled for penalties or has suggested notrump as a contract.

RENEGE. Failure to follow suit when holding one or more cards of the suit led, a colloquial synonym for REVOKE. The term is borrowed from such games as two-handed pinochle and French whist in which it is permissible to revoke. See REVOKE.

RENOUNCE. A term from AUCTION BRIDGE, meaning to fail to follow suit when able to do so; also (noun), the play involving such failure. See REFUSE, REVOKE.

REOPEN THE BIDDING. See BALANCING.

REPEATED FINESSE. See DOUBLE FINESSE.

REPEATED SQUEEZE. See TRIPLE SQUEEZE.

REPEATING TRIPLE SQUEEZE. See PROGRESSIVE SQUEEZE.

REPECHAGE. A second chance after losing in a knockout competition. A repechage has been used in world championship events: the Rosenblum Cup Teams in 1978, 1982 and 1986. The knockout phase had three brackets. Teams that lost in the knockout moved into a Swiss competition. The five top teams in the Swiss at the time the three knockout survivors were determined joined the three losers of the last knockout round in a mini-knockout. The team winning the mini-knockout joined the knockout winners for the Rosenblum semifinals. In 1978, Poland, losers of an early knockout match, won the mini-knockout and went on to take the Rosenblum Cup. For the 1990 event, the repechage was discarded. See also DOUBLE KNOCKOUT; WORLD CHAMPIONSHIPS.

REPLAY DUPLICATE. A form of duplicate in which just two pairs play against each other, playing the same boards but first in one position (i.e. North-South and then the other, East-West). Although this form of duplicate attained some currency in the Twenties, it quickly became obsolescent simply because a board could so easily be remembered by the players. Even the process of playing the boards one way one week and the other the next did not work well.

REPO. See BLACKWOOD AFTER INTERFERENCE.

RERAISE. A colloquialism for opener's rebid of three of his suit after responder has raised to two:

1♠	2♠
3♠	

Some players use the reraise as a preemptive device; others consider it an invitational bid. See PREEMPTIVE RERAISE.

RESCUE. To bid another suit, or conceivably notrump, when partner has been doubled for penalties.

The most common rescuing situation arises when an overcall has been doubled for penalties, a rarer event than it was before negative doubles became popular.

There are three points for the overcaller's partner to consider:

(1) *His length in the doubled suit.* The more cards he holds, the less desirable a rescue becomes — it is rarely right with a doubleton, and virtually never right with more than two cards.

(2) *The level of the potential rescue.* Rescuing is more likely to be effective at the one-level, and may sometimes be attempted when holding a singleton or void in the doubled suit but no suit of more than five cards. See KOCK-WERNER REDOUBLE, SOS REDOUBLE. There is less reason for rescuing if it must be done at a higher level.

(3) *The quality of the rescuer's suit compared with the likely quality of the doubled suit.* There must be a reasonable expectation that the rescuer's suit is more substantial than the doubled suit. In most circumstances a strong six-card suit or a seven-card suit is necessary.

Another common rescue situation occurs when a 1NT opening has been doubled. Here it is seldom right for responder to sit if he has no high-card strength or if he has a long suit. See DEFENSE TO DOUBLE OF 1NT.

RESCUE BID. A bid, based on a long suit, made with less than normal values because of a misfit with partner's bid suit after it has been doubled.

RESERVE. A back-up line of play.

RESERVE ONE'S RIGHTS. In special circumstances, a player may announce "I reserve my rights." This applies when there is a possibility of an opponent having received unauthorized information. This option is not available in North America. In ACBL territory a player is supposed to call the tournament director immediately.

RESERVE PLAYER. In an event for teams of four or more members, any team member not currently playing. A reserve player is eligible to replace an active member during the current or later sessions, but only under conditions announced by the director or published in advance. In major tournaments reserve players are barred from watching their teammates, and usually they are not permitted to watch play at an adjoining table.

RESOCK, REWIND. To redouble.

RESPOND. To answer in the language of bidding. A pass, however, is not a response.

RESPONDER. The player who responds, normally to an opening bid by his partner.

RESPONDER'S REBID. Many of responder's second bids are covered under separate headings: BART, DELAYED GAME RAISE, DELAYED SUPPORT, FOURTH SUIT FORCING, GOLDEN RULE, JUMP REBIDS BY RESPONDER, NEW MINOR FORCING, 1NT RESPONSE, PREFERENCE, REVERSE, SINGLE RAISE, STAYMAN ON SECOND ROUND, TRIAL BID, 2♣ REBID BY RESPONDER AS ONLY FORCE AFTER 1NT REBID, 2NT RESPONSE.

Other situations are discussed below:

(1) *After three suits at the one level:*

1♣	1♥
1♠	1NT

In most styles, the sequence suggests 6-10 points. Though responder usually has balanced distribution with strength in the unbid suit, exceptions arise.

(a)	(b)
♠ 5	♠ 6 4 2
♥ K 8 7 6 4	♥ A K 10 4
♦ K J 7 4 2	♦ J 4 2
♣ 9 3	♣ J 5 3

1NT is best on both hands: on (a) 2♦ fails to limit responder's strength; on (b) a 2♣ preference is risky, and though pass is an option, game is still possible.

♠ J 7
♥ A J 6 4 2
♦ K J 5
♣ J 8 4

A 2NT rebid is easy if that bid is non-forcing; if it is forcing, responder must underbid with 1NT or improvise a bid of 2♦.

1♣	1♥
1♠	2♠

Usually indicates four-card trump support and 7-10 high-card points. Occasionally, the raise is best with three-card support, even without a ruffing value:

    ♠ K 10 4
    ♥ A K 4 2
    ♦ 7 3 2
    ♣ 10 8 6

Other sequences are listed under FOURTH SUIT FORCING, PREFERENCE and JUMP REBIDS BY RESPONDER.

(2) *After three suits ending at the two level:*

1♦	1♠
2♣	2♠

Normally a six-card suit. If a jump to 3♠ would be forcing or if WEAK JUMP SHIFT RESPONSES are in use, the sequence is mildly encouraging; if 3♠ would be invitational, it is not encouraging.

1♦	1♠
2♣	2NT

1♠	2♣
2♥	2NT

At least one stopper in the unbid suit with 10-12 high-card points.

1♦	1♠
2♣	3♣

1♠	2♣
2♥	3♥

Encouraging but not forcing, showing 10-12 high-card points and four-card support (or, in the first sequence, possibly five-card support). The second sequence is forcing in a style where the 2♣ response forces to game.

The expert panel in BWS 2001 strongly favored describing preemptive actions as "moderate", or possibly "light", avoiding extremes.

Other sequences are listed under FOURTH SUIT FORCING, PREFERENCE and JUMP REBIDS BY RESPONDER.

(3) *After a 1NT rebid:*

1♦	1♥
1NT	2♥

A six-card heart suit (possibly a strong five-card suit) and discouraging. Opener almost invariably passes.

1♦	1♥
1NT	2♦

Discouraging, but game might still be possible even if unlikely if opener can give preference to hearts.

1♦	1♥
1NT	2♣

In the absence of special agreements, non-forcing and neutral. Opener should not rebid 2NT, but may give preference to 2♥ or raise to 3♣, either of which actions might lead to game. Responder is likely to have five hearts and four or five clubs. With only four clubs, he should not automatically retreat from 1NT; with 3-5-1-4 distribution, a pass may be best, especially in a pairs event. This change of suit is forcing in ROTH-STONE. See also NEW MINOR FORCING.

1♦	1♥
1NT	2NT

Invitational to game. The strength depends on the range of opener's 1NT rebid, but responder indicates that the combined hands have a minimum of 23-24 points.

1♦	1♥
1NT	2♠

Usually played as forcing to 2NT, possibly to game. See REVERSE.

1♦	1♥
1NT	3♣

A jump shift, forcing to game, with unbalanced distribution and probable weakness in spades, the unbid suit. (In some styles, the sequence is used to sign off with a weak hand, four hearts and six or more clubs; see NEW MINOR FORCING.)

1♦	1♥
1NT	3♦

Needs agreement if NEW MINOR FORCING is used, the direct jump can be forcing and the slow 3♦ limit (or vice versa).

1♦	1♥
1NT	3♥

At one time generally played as forcing, but the non-forcing treatment is logical and has gained popularity; a game-going hand with a six-card heart suit can jump to 4♥.

1♥	1♠
1NT	2♥

A special sequence that suggests 9-11 points with three-card heart support; with less strength, responder would have raised to 2♥ originally.

1♥	1♠
1NT	3♥

If the meaning of the previous sequence is accepted, this sequence is at least strongly invitational with four-card heart support. Many experts play it as an absolute force with possible slam intentions.

(4) *After a minimum rebid in the original suit:*

1♦	1♠
2♦	2♠

Normally a six-card suit. If a jump to 3♠ would be forcing or if weak jump shifts are in use, the sequence is more likely to be progressive; if 3♠ would be invitational, it is not encouraging. (With an extremely poor hand, responder could pass 2♦; at matchpoint scoring, however, he may wish to play in the higher-scoring strain.)

1♦	1♠
2♠	3♣

Forcing, probably with 5-5 or 5-4 distribution, but a probing rebid in a three-card suit may be necessary:

    ♠ A Q 5 4 3
    ♥ 8 4
    ♦ 8 5 3
    ♣ A K 5

1♦	1♠
2♦	2♥

See HELP SUIT GAME TRY.

Forcing, almost surely with five spades and usually with four or more hearts; rarely, with only three hearts. This is a one-round force, and opener must take clear action. It would be a game force if a reverse (1♦-1♥-2♦-2♠) or made at the three-level (1♦-1♠-2♦-3♣). (BWS1994).

1♦	1♠
2♦	2NT

Encouraging but non-forcing. 10-12 points and presumably guards in both unbid suits.

1♦	1♠
2♦	3♦

Encouraging but non-forcing. Probably 10-12 points

and weak in at least one of the unbid suits.

1 ♦	1 ♠
2 ♦	4 ♦

Forcing or, by partnership agreement, strongly invitational with a distributional hand.

(5) *After a single raise of responder's suit:*

1 ♦	1 ♠
2 ♠	2NT

Encouraging but non-forcing. Stoppers in the unbid suits, 10-12 points, probably a four-card spade suit.

1 ♦	1 ♠
2 ♠	3 ♦

Forcing to game.

1 ♦	1 ♠
2 ♠	3 ♣

Forcing, maybe only a weak three-card club suit. Responder may be aiming for 3NT or trying to learn whether opener has extra strength for a spade game. See TRIAL BID.

1 ♦	1 ♠
2 ♠	3 ♠

Encouraging but not forcing. Responder has a long, strong spade suit without notable features in the unbid suits. Opener will pass or bid on depending on his overall strength and the quality of his trump support.

(6) After a jump rebid by opener:

1 ♣	1 ♠
3 ♣	3 ♠

Forcing.

1 ♣	1 ♠
3 ♣	4 ♣

Forcing. In this situation, any action by responder commits the partnership to game.

RESPONDING HAND. The hand, or player, facing the opening bidder; the partner of the initial bidder.

RESPONSE. Usually bid by a player whose partner has opened the bidding, but may be used to describe a response to an overcall, takeout double, cuebid, conventional bid, etc. See ACE-SHOWING RESPONSES; BERGEN RAISES; CHOICE OF SUIT; COURTESY BID; CRISSCROSS RAISE; DELAYED GAME RAISE; DOUBLE RAISE; DRURY; FLINT; FORCING RAISE; FOUR-SUIT TRANSFER BIDS; FREE BID; GLADIATOR; IMPOSSIBLE NEGATIVE; INVERTED MINOR RAISES; JACOBY TRANSFER BIDS; JACOBY TWO NOTRUMP RESPONSE; JUMP SHIFT; LIMIT JUMP RAISE; LIMIT RAISE; MINISPLINTER; NEGATIVE FREE BID; ONE NOTRUMP RESPONSE; ONE NOTRUMP RESPONSE; ONE NOTRUMP RESPONSE TO MAJOR FORCING; ONE NOTRUMP RESPONSE TO MINOR; ONE-OVER-ONE RESPONSE; PASSED HAND; PREEMPTIVE RESPONSE; RESPONSES OVER OPPONENT'S DOUBLE; REVERSE DRURY; ROMEX STAYMAN; SINGLE RAISE; SINGLE RAISE IN MAJOR CONSTRUCTIVE; STAYMAN; STAYMAN FOR STOPPERS; STAYMAN THREE CLUBS; STEP-SHOWING RESPONSES; STRONG NOTRUMP AFTER PASSING; TEXAS CONVENTION; TRANSFER BIDS; TRIPLE RAISE; TWO NOTRUMP RESPONSE; TWO NOTRUMP OVER OPPONENT'S TAKEOUT DOUBLE; TWO OVER ONE GAME FORCE; TWO OVER ONE RESPONSE; TWO-WAY STAYMAN; UP THE LINE; WEAKNESS RESPONSE; WEAK TAKEOUT.

RESPONSE OVER OPPONENT'S TAKEOUT DOUBLE. Some aspects of bidding over an opponent's TAKEOUT DOUBLE depend on partnership style. Popular treatments are as follows:

(1) A non-jump suit response may be forcing or non-forcing, by agreement. Many pairs use new-suit responses as forcing at the one level only; in that style, a two-level response suggests a six-card suit or strong five-card suit.

Any bid of a new suit logically suggests a fair suit. After 1 ♥ -Dbl, for example, responder has little reason to mention a poor four-card spade suit, since doubler has implied spades. Also, since the auction has become competitive, responder should avoid suggesting a weak suit as trumps. He should instead take the opportunity to make a descriptive bid that will help his partner judge the bidding and defense.

(2) 1NT is mildly constructive, promising about 7-9 points with balanced distribution.

(3) A single raise is preemptive and may be slightly weaker than it would be without the double.

(4) A double raise is preemptive and shows a distributional hand with high-card weakness. After 1 ♠ -Dbl, raise to 3 ♠ (at all but unfavorable vulnerability and perhaps even then) with:

     ♠ K 10 6 4
     ♥ 5
     ♦ J 10 6 5 3
     ♣ 8 5 3

(5) A triple raise is preemptive with extra playing strength.

(6) A redouble may in theory show any hand with about 10 points or more. After a redouble, the doubler's side is seldom allowed to play the hand undoubled. Redoubler will usually have a defensive hand, and opener will not bid at his next turn unless he has a distributional hand unsuited to defense.

With some strong hands, a redouble is tactically unsound. (See REDOUBLE.) If responder has a hand with offensive features, he should begin to describe his hand. To waste a bidding turn on the redouble is shortsighted.

West	North	East	South
	1 ♣	Dbl	?
(a)		(b)	
♠ 7 2		♠ Q 9 2	
♥ A K 10 6 2		♥ J 7 3	
♦ 9 3		♦ K Q 8 2	
♣ K 9 8 2		♣ Q 9 4	

(a) South should bid 1 ♥, planning to support clubs next. South wants to describe a fair hand with a heart suit and club support. If he redoubles, the bidding may continue 1 ♠ on his left, 2 ♠ on his right. Now South will not have room to show his hand below the four level, where he may take a minus.

(b) South's chances of penalizing the opponents are unclear. He should describe his hand with a 1NT response.

Players who use the "omnibus redouble" on every 10-point hand are likely to encounter problems.

West	North	East	South
	1 ♣	Dbl	Redbl
3 ♥	Pass	Pass	?

♠ K J 9 2
♥ 9 6 4
♦ A 10 7
♣ K 6 3

Neither side vulnerable. South is in an impossible situation; he would have done better to bid 1♠ over the double.

A redouble is also unattractive with four-card support or better for opener's suit, since the opponents are given a cheap opportunity to locate a fit for a possible sacrifice. A direct raise may be preferable, and there are also conventional possibilities. In BWS94, exactly half the experts favored redoubling if, and only if, responder has a balanced defensive hand.

(7) 2NT and 3NT have no natural meaning because a strong balanced hand would redouble. Most experienced players use 2NT to show a hand that would have made a LIMIT JUMP RAISE to three of opener's suit if there had been no double. This method, popularly known as JORDAN, was developed by Alan Truscott. 3NT can be used to show a strong raise to game when the opening bid was 1♠ or 1♥. For other methods, see 2NT RESPONSE OVER OPPONENT'S TAKEOUT DOUBLE.

(8) A jump response in a suit by an unpassed hand (for example, 1♦-Dbl-2♠) shows length in the suit — often six or more cards — but the strength is a matter of style. There are four schools: (1) forcing to game; (2) forcing for one round; some pairs use conventional jump responses that indicate a fit for opener's suit as well as length and strength in the bid suit; (3) not forcing, a hand worth about 9 points; (4) preemptive, a hand such as:

♠ K J 10 8 5 2
♥ 7
♦ J 5 3
♣ 9 6 3

(9) Pass shows a hand unsuitable for positive action. But a pass followed by a bid on the next round can show a hand with fair defensive strength:

♠ A 5 3
♥ Q 6 4
♦ K 6 3 2
♣ 7 4 3

If partner's 1♠ opening is doubled, responder may pass and bid 2♠ on the next round to suggest a maximum single raise.

A possible tactic is to trap-pass over a double with a good hand and shortness in opener's suit. After 1♠-Dbl, responder might pass with:

♠ 7
♥ A Q 9 3
♦ K J 3 2
♣ Q J 9 3

The strong expert consensus in BWS1994 was for one-level responses to be forcing, two-level responses nonforcing.

For those who play one-level responses forcing and two-level responses non-forcing, a good arrangement is: weak jumps to the two level, constructive jumps by unpassed hands to the three-level. Also see CODED RAISES.

RESPONSE TO OVERCALL. See OVERCALL.

RESPONSIVE DOUBLE. (Originated by Dr. F. Fielding-Reid). The use of a double for takeout when there has been an immediate raise to the two- or three-level over partner's takeout double. For example:

West	North	East	South
1♦	Dbl	2♦	?

South holds:

♠ J 6 5 2
♥ Q 10 9 5
♦ 3
♣ Q 7 6 3

It would be cowardly to pass, and South is not nearly strong enough to make a cuebid of 3♦. He does not want to guess which suit to bid, so he makes a responsive double. In this situation, it is very seldom that South will wish to make a PENALTY DOUBLE. The double would also be used if East had raised to 3♦ instead of 2♦. The doubler may have a balanced hand if his high-card strength is somewhat improved:

♠ 4 3 2
♥ A Q 9
♦ Q 8 5 2
♣ J 8 6

This would be ideal for a responsive double if an opening spade bid were doubled and raised to 2♠, and would be the most convenient action if the opposition had bid clubs, diamonds or hearts.

The minimum strength required for a responsive double varies slightly with the level of the auction. With a balanced hand, a double of 2♣ might be made with 6 points; a double of 3♣ would need at least 9 points.

The convention normally applies to any bid at the two- or three-level, but a few players use a double of 3♥ or 3♠ for penalties. An extension of the responsive idea can be used in the following situation:

West	North	East	South
	1♥	2♣	2♥
Dbl			

A penalty double of a free raise is very seldom required, so by partnership agreement West's double can show length in spades and diamonds.

An alternative agreement is for the double to show the unbid major when there is only one, together with tolerance for overcaller's suit. Analogous to SNAPDRAGON.

Partnerships need to agree exactly how high this should apply. "Responsive through 4♦" is a common agreement. They must also consider whether it applies after a weak two-bid:

West	North	East	South
2♥	Dbl	3♥	Dbl

or after a minor preempt.

West	North	East	South
3♦	Dbl	4♦	Dbl

See TAKEOUT DOUBLE.

RESTRICTED CHOICE. The play of a card which may have been selected as a choice of equal plays increases the chance that the player started with a holding in which his choice was restricted.

The Rule of Restricted Choice is a rule of card play which can enable the declarer to take the correct action in situations which used to be thought of as guesswork.

The underlying principles were first discussed by Alan Truscott in the *Contract Bridge Journal*. Later, these principles were unified by Terence Reese in his book, *Master Play*.

THE BASIC PRINCIPLE

Following is the sort of card combination which can

call the Rule of Restricted Choice into operation:
Example 1:

> *North* (dummy)
> ♠ Q J 9
> *South* (declarer)
> ♠ 4 3 2

South has to develop a trick in this suit. He leads low to dummy's queen and East wins with the king. Upon regaining the lead, South again leads toward the North hand. Should South play the jack or 9 from dummy? Is one play superior or is South faced with a guess? If either East or West now holds both the ace and 10, South's play is immaterial. The jack will score if West holds the ace and East holds the 10. The 9 is winning play if West holds the 10 and East holds the ace.

It is important to notice that this summary is sufficient, for when it comes time for South to make the final decision, he already knows that East held the king. Thus, South can exclude from the reckoning all distributions in which East does not hold the king.

The two possible distributions of the East-West honors given above are equally likely to occur, but the two plays are not of equal merit. To the statement, "the two crucial defensive holdings are equally likely," should be added, "provided there is no information regarding the distribution of honor cards in the suit."

In fact, there is such information. There is a direct inference to be drawn from the fact that East won the first trick with the king. Consider the first possible honor holding given above. If this is the actual distribution of East-West honor cards, East was forced to play his ♠K on the first round; his choice was restricted. This is not true in the second case, where East had the option of winning the first trick with the ace instead of the king. His choice was not restricted.

It can be presumed that if East started with A-K, he would play the ace some percentage of the time. When East actually plays the king on the first round, the probability that he started with the A-K is diminished because with both honors he might have played the other one.

For the sake of argument, assume that East would play his equal honors with equal frequency, winning with the king 50% of the time and winning with the ace 50% of the time. It can be demonstrated that this is, in fact, East's best strategy.

Under this assumption, imagine that declarer is playing the Example 1 combination 200 times. On 100 of these deals, East starts with the K-10. On the other 100 deals, East starts with the A-K. Since, on the second 100 deals, East wins with the king only 50 times, certain things become clear.

East wins the king from an honor holding of K-10 on 100 occasions. But East wins the king from an honor holding of A-K on only 50 occasions. On the other 50 deals on which East holds A-K, he wins with the ace! From this one may conclude that the jack is the superior play on the second round of spades. In fact, it is exactly twice as good a play as the 9. The position is exactly the same if East wins the first trick with the ace and not the king.

The above conclusions may be checked by examining all possible honor distributions. If either defender holds all three honors, declarer will succeed or fail regardless of his plays, so these combinations can be omitted. This leaves the following possibilities, all equally probable before the suit is played for the first time:

	West holds	East holds
(a)	A K	10
(b)	A 10	K
(c)	K 10	A
(d)	A	K 10
(e)	K	A 10
(f)	10	A K

Each of the above situations is equally probable. Assume that each case occurs 100 times, 600 deals in all. Since East will (it is assumed) play equal honors with equal frequency, he wins a high honor on the first round on the following occasions:

	East wins with ♠ A	East wins with ♠ K
(a)	0	0
(b)	0	100
(c)	100	0
(d)	0	100
(e)	100	0
(f)	50	50
TOTAL	250	250

Thus, East will win with a specified honor 250 times. Of these 250 times, declarer triumphs automatically in cases (b) or (c); a total of 100. Of the remaining 150, the jack is the winning play 100 times in case (d) or (e), but the 9 is right only 50 times in case (f).

Thus declarer's play of a card combination such as Example 1, far from being a blind guess, is subject to very definite analysis.

The logic behind the rule is simple. If the player in question had a choice of plays, he might have elected the other option. Therefore, there is a presumption that he did not have the option. Thus, in Example 1, when East wins with the ♠K, the chances favor the play of the jack on the second round. The jack play caters to the situation in which East started with K-10, where he had no choice of plays on the first round, rather than the situation in which East had a choice of plays from A-K.

Other Card Combinations. The Rule of Restricted Choice can be applied to many more combinations:
Example 2:

> *North* (dummy)
> ♠ J 9 4
> *South* (declarer)
> ♠ Q 3 2

South needs one trick, and is forced to attack the suit himself. He leads low to the queen, and West wins with a high honor. Later, South leads again toward the North hand. If West follows low, what should South do?

Applying the Rule of Restricted Choice, South should reason that if West held both high honors, he might have chosen the other one to capture the queen. But if West started with the high honor and the 10, his choice was restricted. The percentage play is the 9.
Example 3:

> *North* (dummy)
> ♠ K 10 9
> *South* (declarer)
> ♠ 4 3 2

South leads toward the North hand and finesses the 9, losing to a middle honor. On the next lead, South should finesse the 10.

A Mistake to Avoid. Care must be taken to avoid mistaken applications of the Rule of Restricted Choice. Example 4:

North (dummy)
♠ K J 9
South (declarer)
♠ 4 3 2

South requires one trick here. He leads up to the North hand, and decides to play the jack. East wins with the queen. Declarer has gained no information whatsoever concerning the distribution of the outstanding honors. East would win the jack with the queen whenever he held that card. The Rule of Restricted Choice does not apply.

Example 5:

North (dummy)
♠ A Q 10 7 6 5
South (declarer)
♠ 4 3 2

South hopes to take six tricks here, and leads a spade to North's queen, which East wins with the king. Later, South wants to pick up the remainder of the suit. Once again, the Rule of Restricted Choice does not apply.

Lower Odds. In examples 1-3 of the Rule of Restricted Choice, declarer was faced with a choice of plays, one of which was exactly twice as good as the other. Restricted Choice situations do not always give such good odds.

There is a large class of card combinations in which declarer's correct play under the Rule of Restricted Choice gives him less than two-to-one odds.

Example 6:

North (dummy)
K 10 9 8 7 6
South (declarer)
A 3 2

South leads the ace from his hand, West follows with the 4 and East drops the queen or jack.

South leads toward the dummy, and West follows with the 5. Assuming (as always) no important inferences are available from the play of other suits, how should South play? To answer that question, consider the following distributions of East-West cards

(a)   *West*   *East*
            5 4   Q J

is slightly more probable (before the suit is played) than the following distribution:

(b)   *West*   *East*
          Q 5 4   J

Also, the chance of East holding Q-J is slightly more probable than the following distribution:

(c)   *West*   *East*
          J 5 4   Q

But East is less likely to have Q-J doubleton than he is to have a singleton queen or jack. In other words, (b) and (c) together are greater than (a).

Thus, the correct play on the second round is to finesse. The odds favoring this play as opposed to the drop are slightly less than two to one.

Example 7:

North (dummy)
A J 10 9 8 7
South (declarer)
4 3 2

South wishes to take five tricks. The best play is to take two finesses. This fails to bring in the suit (if such was possible) only when East holds K-Q. It is easily seen that all other plays are inferior.

A common argument given about this combination is the following: It is best to take two finesses because it

gains against more distributions than any other play. Once you have finessed the first time, you must follow through and finesse the second time.

This is an unfortunate way to arrive at the right answer. If you finesse the jack and it loses to the king or queen, you have two possible combinations to consider when you lead up to the dummy the second time.

                  West holds   East holds
Case 1   6 5   K Q
Case 2 (a)   K 6 5   Q
        (b)   Q 6 5   K

After the first trick, either Case 2 (a) or Case 2 (b) disappears, so only two relevant combinations remain, and the first is (initially) more probable. Therefore, the argument indicates playing for the drop on the second round.

The correct argument for the second finesse is that if East started with a singleton honor, his choice was restricted on the first round. Thus, the odds on the second finesse are almost two to one.

Another Mistake to Avoid. Some combinations are superficially similar to those in the last section, but the Rule of Restricted Choice, however, does not apply.

Example 8:

North (dummy)
A 2

South (declarer)
K Q 9 8 7 6

Declarer leads the 6 to the ace in dummy, and West plays the 10 or jack. According to the principles developed in the previous section, although an original West holding of doubleton J-10 is more likely than the holding of a particular singleton honor, it is now more likely that West had a singleton honor.

That is true as far as it goes, but declarer should not finesse on the second round. West may well have J-10-3!

Example 9:

North (dummy)
A 2
South (declarer)
K 9 8 7 6

South needs three tricks before the defense makes two. He leads the 6 to the ace, and West plays the jack. If West has the singleton jack, South must finesse coming back. Declarer must avoid a mistaken application of the Rule of Restricted Choice. It is true that a singleton jack is more likely than either Q-J or J-10 doubleton. But the king is the right play if West has either of the two doubleton honor combinations, and these two together exceed the probability of a singleton jack.

Higher Odds. Other types of suit combinations admit application of the Rule of Restricted Choice. Sometimes declarer can obtain even higher odds than two-to-one in favor of the correct play. The odds mount appreciably in the following three examples:

Example 10:

North (dummy)
A K Q 10
South (declarer)
4 3 2

Declarer plays off the A-K, and the jack fails to drop. He later leads toward the tenace in the North hand. If West follows with a small card, the percentage play is the queen. Assuming no relevant information about the side suits, East is a slight favorite to hold the jack.

Example 11:

> *North* (dummy)
> A K Q 9
> *South* (declarer)
> 4 3 2

Dummy's holding is slightly weaker than in the previous example. Declarer cashes the A-K. West follows with two small cards, but East drops an honor. Best play is to enter the South hand and finesse. If West follows to the third round with a small card, it is slightly less than two to one that he holds the missing honor.

Example 12:

> *North* (dummy)
> A K Q 8
> *South* (declarer)
> 4 3 2

Dummy's holding has been further debilitated, but the Rule of Restricted Choice is even more rewarding. When the ace and king are cashed, East drops two of the missing honors. Declarer's best play is to enter the South hand and finesse the 8.

The odds in favor of this play can be computed as follows. If East held J-10-9 originally, there were six ways in which he could have played two honors to the first two tricks. Only one of these ways was chosen; therefore the weight of this combination is only one-sixth its original chance. But if East held two blank honors originally, he still had two ways to play them and chose one of them. Therefore this combination carries only half its original weight. J-10-9 is slightly more likely than any particular doubleton (before any cards are played), but the finesse still has odds of almost three to one in its favor.

Following is an example of such a situation from actual play in a pair tournament:

Example 13:

> *North* (dummy)
> 2
> *South* (declarer)
> Q J 8 7 6 5 4

Declarer entered the North hand, and led the singleton deuce. East followed with the 9. South contributed the jack, and West won with the king. South later regained the lead, and was forced to lead a trump from his own hand. Should he play the queen or the 8?

If the suit originally split 4-1, the card played at this stage is of no significance. Thus a 3-2 division can be assumed. If the doubleton was in the East hand, the 9 could have come from A-9 or 10-9 holdings which initially were equally likely. But if East had 10-9, he would presumably have played the 10 half the time. Furthermore, if East held 10-9, West must have started with A-K-3 and he might have won with the ace instead of the king. The Rule of Restricted Choice can be applied against both opponents in the same suit! Furthermore, the 9 could have come from 10-9-3.

Since the play of a small card on the second round caters to both applications of the Rule of Restricted Choice and guards against the falsecard, it is clearly the superior play.

The odds in favor of this play as opposed to the play of the queen can be computed as follows: Disregarding the falsecard, the odds in favor of the play of a small card are four to one. If East held A-9, the play of both opponents was restricted. There was only one way in which they could have played their cards. If East held 10-9, however, each opponent had a choice of two plays,

giving them four different ways in which their cards could have been played.

Now consider the case in which East may have falsecarded from 10-9-3. This is another specific distribution of cards divided three and two, so it was originally equally likely as all the others. However, the weight of this double application of the Rule of Restricted Choice still applies. Thus, the correct odds are five to one.

Applications. An application of the Rule of Restricted Choice would have saved the United States team several IMPs on this deal from the 1958 Bermuda Bowl match against Italy.

Example 14:

```
              ♠ K 4 2
              ♥ 8 3
              ♦ K 9 3 2
              ♣ A K 8 7

              ♠ A 5
              ♥ Q 10 9
              ♦ A Q J 7 6 5
              ♣ 10 4
```

South	North
1♦	2♣
2♦	2♠
2NT	3NT
Pass	

West led the ♥5 which East won with the king. A low heart was returned and South was faced with a guess. After consideration, he played the queen. This proved to be the wrong move as West had led from A-x-x. The consensus of expert opinion was that South's play was correct. *The Bridge World* commentator wrote: ". . . I think South's play is correct. If the hearts are 4-4, South's play makes relatively little difference; only if the lead was from three is it crucial. And a lead from three to the jack seems a little more attractive than from three to an ace."

This point — and psychological considerations — are important factors in deciding which card to play. But such factors have a lot of ground to make up. On the auction, a heart lead might be expected from any holding of three to an honor. And according to the Rule of Restricted Choice, the 10 is a two-to-one percentage favorite, for if East had started with five hearts to the A-K, he might have played the ace on the first round. With five hearts to the K-J, his choice was restricted to the play of the king. Another way of looking at it is that the combination of A-x-x and K-x-x in West's hand are together twice as likely as J-x-x.

Here is another situation in which the Rule of Restricted Choice should be applied when the defenders attack a suit.

Example 15:

```
              ♠ A K J 3
              ♥ Q
              ♦ 10 8 4
              ♣ A K J 10 5

              ♠ Q 10 9 8 6
              ♥ J 10 5
              ♦ K 3 2
              ♣ Q 9
```

At rubber bridge South is declarer at 4♠ with no East-West bidding. West leads a small heart which East wins with the ace. It is apparent that the contract will be made unless the defense takes three diamond tricks. East shifts

to the queen or jack of diamonds.

South knows that East is a good enough player to have shifted to diamonds from any of these holdings:

(1) ace, queen or jack and small card(s)

(2) queen, jack and small card(s)

(3) queen or jack and small card(s)

Even with restricted choice considerations put aside (which makes (2) less probable), playing low caters only to case (2) so South goes up with the king.

Naturally, West takes the ♦A and continues with a small diamond. Now the 9 becomes important. The only relevant holdings now are:

(4) East started with Q-J and small card(s) but not the 9. (If East led from Q-J-9, the game is over.)

(5) East started with the queen or jack, and possibly small card(s).

(4) and (5) seem to be equally likely possibilities but, as usual, the Rule of Restricted Choice tells us that with (4) East might have selected the other honor to lead. So the correct play is the 10.

Similar considerations can arise when the declarer attacks a suit.

Example 16:

♠ Q 10 9 7 6
♥ 4 2
♦ 5 3
♣ K 6 5 4

♠ A K J 8
♥ A K 3
♦ K 4 2
♣ 10 9 7

South plays in 4♠ at rubber bridge. West leads the ♦Q, East takes the ace, and returns the suit. South wins, ruffs his last diamond in dummy (East discarding a heart), plays a trump to the ace, and plays three rounds of hearts. West discards a diamond on the third round of hearts, which is ruffed in dummy. Now a spade to the king extracts both remaining trumps. Since both defenders have shown with two spades and 6-2 in the red suits, it is clear that both have three clubs, and the position is:

Example 17:

North
♠ 10
♥ —
♦ —
♣ K 6 5 4

South
♠ J 8
♥ —
♦ —
♣ 10 9 7

South needs one club trick (or a ruff and sluff) to make his contract. He leads the 9 (it can be verified that this is a superior play to the 7), and West plays the queen.

This play would be made from any of the holdings of A-Q-x, Q-J-x, or Q-x-x. Even with Restricted Choice set aside, the king is the best play. But East wins and returns a low club.

South must rely on the Rule of Restricted Choice and play the 10.

A little-known safety play shows that the Rule of Restricted Choice can be applied to spot cards as well as honors.

Example 18:

North (dummy)
J 7 6 5
South (declarer)
A Q 9 8

South has adequate entries to both hands and needs three tricks in this suit. The correct play is to lead low from the North hand and finesse the queen. If this loses to the king, South next plays the ace. This play will produce three tricks except when West holds the blank king.

Why, after West wins the king, should declarer play West for the remaining cards rather than East?

Suppose East played the 3 on the first round of the suit. If East started with 10-4-3-2, he had a choice of three low spots to play on the first round. He might equally well have played any of the low cards, therefore this holding can be counted only with a weight of one-third. On the other hand, if East started with the singleton 3, his choice was restricted.

To check this computation, notice that if declarer goes after the suit with the intention of playing the ace on the second round, he loses only when West starts with the singleton king (one distribution) but if he intends to play to the jack on the second round, he loses when East starts with the singleton 4, 3, or 2 (three distributions).

The Rule of Restricted Choice may even be applied to the opening lead.

Example 19:

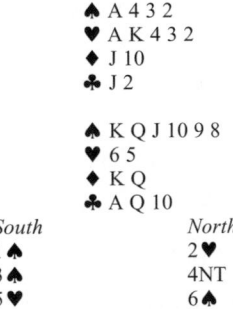

♠ A 4 3 2
♥ A K 4 3 2
♦ J 10
♣ J 2

♠ K Q J 10 9 8
♥ 6 5
♦ K Q
♣ A Q 10

South	North
1♠	2♥
3♠	4NT
5♥	6♠

Against South's 6♠, West leads the ♦7 and East wins with the ace. East shifts to a low club. Should South finesse? There are two plays open to declarer. First, he can duck the club lead, hoping that East has the king. Second, he can rise with the ace, draw trump, and try to ruff out the heart suit. This play depends on a 3-3 heart split.

The chance of an even split in hearts is about 36%. The club finesse appears to offer a 50% chance and therefore seems the better play. However, South must consider West's choice of opening leads. If East holds the ♣K, West started with a collection of small cards in each minor suit. If this was the case, he would have led a club about half the time. Since West did not lead a club, there is some presumption that his club-diamond holdings were not equivalent. If we assume West would lead a club half the time with equal minor suit holdings, the club finesse is only a 33% chance, and should therefore be rejected in favor of the attempt to split the hearts 3-3 (36%).

RESULT PLAYER (or result merchant). A partner (or kibitzer) who suggests a line of play that would have been successful after declarer has failed with a different line of play. Second guesser is a synonym. Often the suggested line is inferior but happens to work this time.

REVALUATION. The reassessment of a hand in light of the bidding. Certain features of a hand may improve or deteriorate in value in the light of the bidding around the table. See DISTRIBUTIONAL COUNTS.

If partner shows a strong two-suited hand, secondary suit honors are of greater significance in those suits, but are probably useless in the other suits. A shortage in partner's side suit, together with a few trumps, is more valuable than a shortage in another suit which is likely to be duplicated.

Kings and queens in a suit bid by an opponent improve if the bid was on the right and deteriorate if the bid was on the left (see POSITIONAL FACTOR).

A holding of three small cards in a suit bid by an opponent at a low level is a liability, but improves if the opponents bid and raise the suit strongly to a high level. It is then reasonable to assume that partner has no more than a singleton. In such circumstances a doubleton is less attractive because there is an increased chance that there will be two losers.

REVERSE. An unforced rebid at the level of two or more in a higher ranking suit than that bid originally — usually a strength-showing bid. The English definition of a reverse by the opener is slightly wider in scope: a bid of a suit in an uncontested auction which prevents responder from returning to the original suit at the level of two. This allows for the situation described in England as a high reverse. The following are standard reversing sequences:

West	East	West	East
1♣	1♠	1♥	2♦
2♥		2♠	

Examples of reverses by responder:

West	East	West	East
1♦	1♥	1♣	1♦
2♦	2♠	1♠	2♥

All reverses, by opener or responder, show strong game possibilities — the combined strength is rarely less than 23 points. In most systems, reverses imply that the first-bid suit consists of at least five cards and the second is shorter. However, see CANAPE.

There has been a change of thinking concerning reverses when the Two-Over-One forcing to game system is used.

West	East
1♥	2♣
2♠	

Since the two-level response to the opening bid already created a situation that called for reaching game under most circumstances, some play that the reverse by opener does not necessarily show any additional strength beyond the opening bid.

In the past reverses were not forcing after a one-level response. However, virtually all experts now treat them as forcing. 1♥-1NT-2♠ is forcing but does not promise a rebid. Other reverses may be played as requiring a rebid.

If all four suits are bid, it is doubtful whether the term reverse should be applied, and the inference that the reverser's original suit is at least five cards in length is less strong. See FOURTH SUIT FORCING and LEBENSOHL CONVENTION.

In the modern style, the forcing quality of the reverse creates problems when the responder is weak. There is a tendency for partnerships to wander on to an unsound game when both players have a minimum. Regular partnerships discuss ways to put on the brakes. A common agreement, the consensus choice in BWS1994, is this:

With a minimum hand, responder (a) rebids his suit with five cards or more; or (b) makes the cheapest available other bid, which is either the fourth suit or 2NT. Although weak, this is forcing.

West	East
1♣	1♠
2♥	2♠

This shows at least five spades and is neutral.
or

West	East
1♣	1♠
2♥	2NT

This shows a weak hand and denies five spades.

West	East
1♣	1♥
2♦	2♠

East denies a five-card heart suit and is likely to be weak. He may be hoping to play in 2NT, or three clubs or three hearts.

The corollary is that other rebids by East, such as 3♣ or 3♥, or in this situation 2NT, are game-forcing.

In some contested auctions, the reverse may not carry full weight.

West	North	East	South
1♣	Pass	1♠	2♦
2♥			

This cannot be a minimum, but it is not as strong as it would be without interference.

REVERSE COUNT. A method of giving count by playing low-high to indicate an even number of cards and playing high-low to indicate an odd number of cards. This was first adopted in Sweden and eventually spread elsewhere. It avoids the disadvantage of the standard signal, which forces a defender to waste a high card, such as 10 from 10-2, that he may not wish to give up. See SIGNALS, SIGNALING.

REVERSE DISCARD. See UPSIDE-DOWN SIGNALS.

REVERSE DRURY. The modern standard version of the DRURY convention used by virtually all tournament players who play Drury. After a third or fourth - seat opening of 1♠ or 1♥, a 2♣ response shows a strong raise of opener's suit, usually in the 9-11 point range. Then opener returns to his suit at the two-level with a minimum or sub-minimum hand. Other rebids are natural and forward-going. Opener will often jump to game in the agreed suit, ending the auction. The 2♦ rebid by opener after the Drury 2♣ bid is sometimes used to show all opening values, not necessarily diamonds. The subsequent auction needs partnership discussion.

REVERSE FLANNERY. An opening bid of 2♦ to show a minimum opening hand with four hearts and five spades. This convention is used almost solely by pairs who use CANAPÉ styles of bidding, e.g., BLUE TEAM CLUB, in which this distribution is difficult to show. Since such pairs usually use a 2♦ opening for some other purpose, the Reverse Flannery bid is usually 2♥.

REVERSE SEQUENCE LEAD. See RUSINOW LEAD.

REVERSE SWISS. The use of unusual jump shift re-

bids by opener to make a game raise of responder's suit, promising a wealth of high cards rather than just suitable distribution. For alternative uses of such jumps see FRAGMENT BIDS and SPLINTER BIDS.

REVERSING THE DUMMY. See DUMMY REVERSAL.

REVIEWING THE BIDDING. A player who does not hear a call distinctly may forthwith require that it be repeated. Any player may, when it is his turn to call, require that all previous calls be restated unless he is required by law to pass. In rubber bridge, after the auction is closed, any player may require such a review before his side has faced any cards. In duplicate, after the auction is closed, the declarer or either defender may require such a review at his own first turn to play. When bidding boxes are in use, the bidding sequence is available to all throughout the bidding process. See LAWS (Law 20); LAWS OF DUPLICATE (Law 20). See also BIDDING BOX, EXPLANATION OF ANY CALL OR PLAY, FACE DOWN LEADS.

REVOKE. The play of a card of a suit other than the suit led, or the play of a card of a suit other than that called for by a lead penalty. A revoke becomes established once either member of the offending side leads or plays to the next trick, or when the revoking side makes a claim or concession. If the player realizes he has misplayed in time, he may replace the illegal card with a legal one. If the offending player is the declarer, he may put the misplayed card back in his hand because there has been no unauthorized information given to partner. However, if the offending player is a defender, the misplayed card becomes a major penalty card, and the appropriate Laws are applied.

Until the last set of Laws of Duplicate Contract Bridge was approved, any player could ask immediately whether a play constituted a revoke and ask that it be corrected. A change in the Laws removed this right – players no long could ask such questions as "No spades, partner?" This Law drew such strong opposition from North America that the Law is now applied in two different ways, depending on where you are playing. In North America, players still have the right to ask the "No spades, partner?" type question, but it is illegal and subject to penalty in the rest of the world. North Americans playing abroad often run into difficulties as a result. Any player except dummy may call attention to a revoke during the play. The dummy gains this right when play is completed.

As a result of changes in the Laws governing duplicate and rubber bridge, the penalties for revokes are the same in both forms of the game. No tricks completed prior to the revoke change hands. If declarer wins the revoke trick and takes at least one more trick subsequent to the revoke, the penalty is two tricks. If declarer wins the revoke trick and takes no more tricks, the penalty is one trick. If declarer loses the revoke trick but wins at least one subsequent trick, the penalty is one trick. If he takes no trick after the revoke trick, there is no penalty. If declarer loses the revoke trick, wins two or more tricks subsequently, and wins, or could have won, a trick with a card he could have played to the revoke trick, the penalty is two tricks. If the defender who wins the revoke trick is the offender and his side wins at least one trick subsequent to the revoke, the penalty is two tricks. If

the defender who wins the revoke trick is the partner of the offender, the penalty is one trick. If the defending side loses the revoke trick but wins at least one trick subsequently, the penalty is one trick. If the defending side loses the revoke trick and fails to win another trick, there is no penalty. If the defender who revoked lost the revoke trick but could have won a later trick with a card he could have legally played to the revoke trick, the penalty becomes two tricks as long as the defending side wins at least two tricks from the revoke trick on.

If a player realizes he has revoked and the opponents fail to call attention to his revoke, the player is not required to call attention to his own mistake. However, any attempt to deliberately conceal the fact that he has revoked is a serious offense against the Proprieties. See LAWS 61-64.

REVOLVING DISCARD. A method of discarding which assigns a suit preference meaning to the first discard on any hand. There are two possible procedures which are similar in effect but vary slightly in execution.

(1) A low card calls for the suit below the suit in which the signal is given, and a high card for the suit above. The suits are considered in a circle with spades below clubs. Thus a low club discard on a heart lead would call for a spade, and a high club would call for a diamond. This version was developed in England, primarily for notrump defense, and is credited to J. Attwood.

(2) A low card calls for the lower-ranking of the other two suits, and a high card for the higher-ranking. This was advocated by Hy Lavinthal, the inventor of suit preference by signaling, who gave this example:

```
              ♠ K 8 5
              ♥ 6
              ♦ K 10 9 8 4
              ♣ Q 7 3 2
♠ Q J 4 2                    ♠ 10 7 3
♥ J 9 7 3 2                  ♥ A Q 5
♦ A 6 5                      ♦ 7 2
♣ 9                          ♣ J 10 8 6 4
              ♠ A 9 6
              ♥ K 10 8 4
              ♦ Q J 3
              ♣ A K 5
```

South plays in 3NT after opening 1NT. West leads the ♥3, and East correctly plays the queen. (After the play of the ace there would be no way to defeat the contract.) South wins the ♥Q with the king, and leads diamonds. West holds up the ace until the third round in order to get a signal from East. Normal signals would not help, because East cannot spare a heart, and a black-suit discard would be unenlightening. Using the Lavinthal discard signal the ♣4 asks for a heart, and the ♠10 would carry the same message. Using the revolving method given in (1), the ♠3 or the ♣J would be appropriate. See SIGNALS. SIGNALING.

REX BRIDGE. A Swedish variation on contract in which any player may introduce a Rex call at any time, ranking between spades and hearts. It is a notrump contract except that the ace of each suit ranks below the deuce, and the king is the high card in each suit, other cards maintaining their rank with respect to the king.

R/H FOUR NOTRUMP CONVENTION. A nonjump bid of FOUR NOTRUMP after a trump suit has been

established to ask about the three top trump honors. Partner responds to 4NT by bidding five of the trump suit with none of the top three trump honors, 5NT with all three honors, or a nontrump suit with one or two honors, as follows:

Lowest side suit = king or queen.
Middle side suit = ace.
Highest side suit = any two of the top three honors.

RHO. Right-hand opponent.

RHYTHM. Bidding and play at a uniform speed. The stress here is on uniformity and not on speed. An expert player attempts to foresee the possible problems that may evolve during the bidding of a hand before choosing his first action so that he may avoid the agony of a later HUDDLE. A good player knows that a huddle followed by a pass, or even a double, places the onus on his partner not to be influenced by the fact that he had a problem. Therefore, he will try to solve his future problems before they occur rather than after.

In the play of the hand, the shrewd declarer will sometimes attempt to cause opponents to be careless in the defense by playing with unusual rapidity, as though the hand was practically a pianola. When confronted by a rapid tempo on declarer's part, a thoughtful defender will deliberately slow his own tempo so that he will have the opportunity to analyze declarer's play to see whether or not he has a problem.

In the play of the hand, too, the necessity for defenders to establish a rhythmic tempo to their play is important. In attempting to locate a particular card, such as an adversely held ace or queen, declarer is frequently put on the right track by applying the old adage "he who hesitates, has it. " While a declarer takes advantage of a hesitation at his own risk (see PROPRIETIES), the opponent who hesitates before making a play with intent to deceive the declarer is guilty of unethical conduct and is subject to penalty.

RICHMOND TROPHY. Awarded annually to the Canadian who wins the most masterpoints during a calendar year. See Appendix 2.

RIDE. (1) To take a finesse with, fail to cover; for example, "dummy's jack was led and declarer let it ride." (2) A large penalty, derived from underworld argot in which a victim is "taken for a ride" by his would-be murderers.

RIFFLE. A light shuffle of the deck; a flexing of the deck with the cards bent and held between the fingers so that a rapid motion ensues as the pack is straightened out.

RIGAL OVER PROTECTIVE NOTRUMPS. When protecting over a one-level suit opening bid, it is now standard practice to bid 1NT with a very wide range of balanced or semi-balanced hands. Accordingly responder may be faced with a problem — sometimes it will not be sufficient to know whether partner is minimum or maximum. If the range for a 1NT bid is 10-16, then that range really needs to be split into three steps — minimum, medium and maximum.

The suggested method, invented by Barry Rigal, continues to employ transfers as over a 1NT opening bid, but the difference from standard methods is that 2♣ acts as both Stayman and a range-finder. Using a 2♣ relay

allows balancer to split his range into three steps.

Responses to the relay are as follows: with all minimum hands balancer bids 2♦. Responder can now pass or bid two of a major to suggest four cards. Balancer passes a two-level action or corrects to a more suitable two-level contract. (2NT by responder after the 2♦ response is a sign-off and three-level action is invitational). With all medium hands, balancer answers at the two-level, bidding a four-card major or 2NT without a major. Now two-level action by responder is a scramble rather than a game-try, and three-level action is again invitational. With all maximum hands, balancer sets up a game-force by bidding his lowest four-card suit at the three-level. Thus in the sequence:

1♦	Pass	Pass	1NT
Pass	2♣	Pass	2♦
Pass	2♠		

After fourth-hand shows any 10-11 HCP, the 2♠ call is non-forcing, suggesting four spades, allowing balancer to pass or bid 2NT. The same principle would apply if fourth-hand's second action was 2♥, suggesting 12-13 with four hearts.

RIGHT-HAND PLAYER. The player who, in rotation, acts before the given player. There are distinctions in the rules between irregular acts committed by the right-hand or left-hand player. The term is generally used, however, to refer to the player on declarer's right, after play commences. See RHO for a similar term.

RIGHT SIDE. The hand of the declaring partnership which can more successfully cope with the opening lead against the chosen contract. For example, assuming all other suits are adequately stopped, the hand holding A-Q-x opposite partner's x-x-x is the *right side* from which to play the hand. Sometimes there is no right or wrong side.

The *rightness* of one side and *wrongness* of the other may relate to factors other than the safety of the declarer's holding in the suit led; for example, the inability of one defender to lead the suit profitably (e.g., from K-x-x-x when the declaring side has the ace and queen), or the inability of one defender to diagnose the most effective lead whereas from his partner's hand the right lead would be obvious.

RIGHTS. A player does not forfeit his rights if a director is called when an irregularity occurs. Neither does an opponent of the violator lose any rights if the violator or his partner is the first to call attention to the irregularity.

RIGHTY. See RHO.

RIPO. See BLACKWOOD AFTER INTERFERENCE.

RIPSTRA. Over 1NT, the use of an overcall in a minor to show a three-suited hand, devised by J. G. Ripstra. The bid guarantees a shortage in the unbid minor:

(a)	(b)
♠ Q 7 4 3	♠ A Q 8 4 3
♥ K J 6 2	♥ K J 6 2
♦ K 10 6 3	♦ 6
♣ 8	♣ Q 6 3

On (a) bid 2♦; on (b) bid 2♣. The strength qualifications for the bid naturally vary according to vulnerability. It can be made freely at favorable vulnerability and

should rarely be made at unfavorable vulnerability.

Some players use the convention with greater emphasis on the major suits, employing it with, for example, a 5-5-2-1 distribution. A disadvantage of the convention is that it has a relatively low frequency. It is more suited to matchpoint events than to rubber bridge or IMP scoring. It is, however, useful in defense against a GAMBLING THREE NOTRUMP OPENING. See DEFENSE TO ONE NOTRUMP for alternatives.

RKCB. See ROMAN KEYCARD BLACKWOOD.

ROBERT COUP. The unnecessary expenditure of a trump in order to preserve a plain suit card to lead later in the play (analyzed and named by Robert Darvas of Hungary).

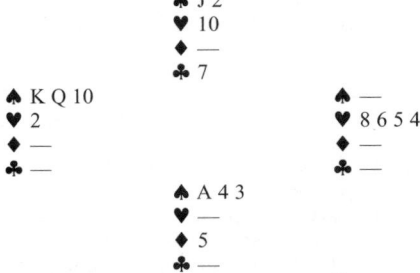

```
                    ♠ J 2
                    ♥ 10
                    ♦ —
                    ♣ 7
  ♠ K Q 10                       ♠ —
  ♥ 2                            ♥ 8 6 5 4
  ♦ —                            ♦ —
  ♣ —                            ♣ —
                    ♠ A 4 3
                    ♥ —
                    ♦ 5
                    ♣ —
```

Spades are trump and East leads the ♥4. If South discards his diamond, his only other trick will be the ♠A. But if South ruffs and leads the ♦5, West will be limited to one trump trick.

The coup may be executed early in the play as in this example given by Jeff Rubens.

```
                    ♠ 10 7 6 2
                    ♥ A K 8 7 6 5
                    ♦ 3
                    ♣ 4 2
  ♠ Q J 9 8                      ♠ —
  ♥ Q 10 9                       ♥ J 4 3
  ♦ Q 10 5                       ♦ J 9 4 2
  ♣ 9 7 3                        ♣ A K Q J 10 6
                    ♠ A K 5 4 3
                    ♥ 2
                    ♦ A K 8 7 6
                    ♣ 8 5
```

Against South's 4♠ contract, West leads the ♣9. East overtakes with the ♣10, cashes the ace and, unwisely, continues with a third round. South ruffs in the closed hand and plays the ♠K ; when the trump situation is revealed, declarer is obliged to play West for completely balanced distribution. The ♦A-K and a diamond ruff, followed by the ♥A-K and a heart ruff, leads to this end position:

```
                    ♠ 10 7
                    ♥ 8
                    ♦ —
                    ♣ —
  ♠ Q J 9
  ♥ —
  ♦ —                           Immaterial
  ♣ —
                    ♠ A 5
                    ♥ —
                    ♦ 8
                    ♣ —
```

South produces his last diamond and West has no reply. The essential feature of the play was for South to reduce his trump holding by accepting the ruff and sluff in the long hand. The fifth spade could not be of use against any distribution but might get in the way if trumps broke badly. See also UNDERRUFF

ROBERTSON POINT-COUNT. A point count published by Edmund Robertson in 1904.

> Ace counts 7 points
> King counts 5 points
> Queen counts 3 points
> Jack counts 2 points
> 10 counts 1 point.

A slight variation of this is the Bamberger point count used by the VIENNA SYSTEM, in which the jack counts one point and the 10 is not counted. In this system, with a total of 64 points in the pack, if both hands are balanced, 39 points should produce a game in notrump or a major suit; and 52 points should produce a small slam.

ROBINSON. A defensive bidding system against the Forcing Club, devised by Kit Woolsey and named after his oft-times partner, Steve Robinson. Double is strong, showing 16+ HCP. A 1♦ overcall shows either a black two-suiter or a red two-suiter. A 1♥ overcall shows either a major two-suiter or a minor two-suiter. 1♠ is natural, but can be very weak. 1NT shows a club-heart two-suiter or a diamond-spade two-suiter. All bids of two of a suit are natural one-suited overcalls

ROBOT BRIDGE PLAYER. A Bendix G-15 computer was built in the shape of a bridge robot, into which Prof. R. F. Jackson of The University of Delaware programmed bridge skills. It was displayed at a Western Regional in 1958, in a hand requiring a VIENNA COUP to make a grand slam. Opponents' plays were typed into Sputternik, as the robot was called, by the operator and Sputternik typed out his and the dummy's plays.

Today this seems a very minor miracle. Several computer programs can work out the double-dummy play of any hand, not just a particular one. See AUTOMATON BRIDGE PLAYER, DEEP FINESSE.

ROCKCRUSHER. A hand with tremendous trick-taking ability.

ROCKWELL TROPHY. For the North American Mixed Pair Championship, donated by Helen Rockwell in 1946; it replaced the Hilliard Trophy contested as a four-session event at the Fall North American Championships. For results see Appendix I.

ROLLING BLACKWOOD. A BLACKWOOD variation in which the cheapest non-trump bid (rather than 5NT) is used to ask for kings. Also called SLIDING BLACKWOOD.

ROLLING BOX. See TRAY.

ROLLING GERBER. A GERBER variation in which the cheapest non-trump bid (rather than 5♣) is used to ask for kings. Also called SLIDING GERBER.

ROMAN ASKING BID. A feature of the ROMAN SYSTEM which, in part, is also included in the 1969

version of the KAPLAN-SHEINWOLD SYSTEM. Both systems limit the use of the asking bids to jump bids that would otherwise be meaningless. If an opening bid of 1 ♠ is raised to 3 ♠, 4 ♣ would be a cuebid and 5 ♣ would be an asking bid. The Roman responses are:

1st step	No control
2nd step	Singleton
3rd step	King
4th step	Ace
5th step	Void
6th step	A-K or A-Q (rare)

If responder cannot be short in the asked suit, the second and fifth steps are dropped.

An older and better known version of Roman asking bids restricts the responses to four steps. First step shows no control; second step shows king or singleton; third step shows ace or void; fourth step shows A-K (rarely A-Q) or perhaps singleton ace. These are called ALPHA ASKING BIDS.

Roman asking bids are also used in certain specialized sequences, the most common of which occur after a 1 ♣ opening bid and a jump in a new suit by opener. Responder bids according to his holding in opener's suit as follows:

1st step	Two or three low cards
2nd step	Singleton or void
3rd step	A, K, or Q singleton or doubleton
4th step	A, K or Q third
5th step	Four low cards
6th step	A, K, or Q fourth
7th step	Two of the top three honors
8th step	Two of the top three honors fourth
9th step	Three top honors

These are called BETA ASKING BIDS. See also ASK-ING BIDS; PRECISION ASKING BIDS; ROMEX TRUMP ASKING BIDS; SPLINTER BIDS; SUPER PRECISION ASKING BIDS; VOID-SHOWING BIDS.

ROMAN BLACKWOOD. A 4NT convention which can help to determine which ace is missing if the partnership holds three. The responses are:

5 ♣	0-3 aces
5 ♦	1-4 aces
5 ♥	2 aces of the same color or rank
5 ♠	2 aces of unlike color and rank

A variation adopted by some BLUE TEAM CLUB users is to reverse the meanings of the traditional Roman responses of 5 ♣ and 5 ♠; the 5 ♣ response is used to show one or four aces in order to facilitate further non-Blackwood exploration of slam on the hands where slam is a more likely proposition.

A subsequent 5NT bid asks for kings in the same way.

The 4NT bidder can easily determine from the previous auction the meaning of a 5 ♣ or 5 ♦ response. 5 ♠ is also unambiguous, but a 5 ♥ response does not pinpoint the aces precisely. If, for example, a player with the ♥A receives the response of 5 ♥, he knows that his partner holds the ♣A and another ace.

A British variation is designed to avoid this ambiguity.:

5 ♥	2 aces of the same color
5 ♠	2 aces of the same rank
5NT	2 aces of unlike color and rank

This may, however, rule out the possibility of asking for kings. The general advantage of the convention is that it may be effective when the 4NT bidder has a void. If his partner has two aces, it is usually possible to tell

whether the void is facing an ace.

When making a decision to go to the six-level, it is usually sufficient to know the number of aces possessed by the partnership. But for grand slam purposes, the identity of a missing king may be vital. For this reason some partnerships abandon the precise identification of the two aces held, using the 5 ♥ response to show two aces with no extra values and the 5 ♠ response to show two aces in a hand with extra values. Alternatively, there can be advantages in using these Roman responses in combination with other conventions. See ACE-SHOWING RESPONSES; BYZANTINE BLACKWOOD; ROMAN GERBER; ROMAN KEY CARD BLACKWOOD.

ROMAN DISCARDS, SIGNALS. Odd-numbered spot cards (3,5,7,9) are encouraging. Even-numbered spot cards (2,4,6,8) are discouraging, with a suit-preference message. This was originated as part of the ROMAN SYSTEM. Usually called ODD-EVEN SIGNALS.

ROMAN GERBER. A modified version of the GERBER FOUR-CLUB slam convention. A response of 4 ♦ shows three aces or none; 4 ♥ shows four aces or one; 4 ♠ shows two aces. If the 4 ♣ bidder continues with the cheapest bid, he asks for kings and subsequently queens in the same way. The next-cheapest bid asks for clarification of the previous response. With one or three of the specified honor cards, responder bids the control he has or does not have. With two honors to be identified, he makes the minimum bid if they are of the same color; the second possible bid if they are unmatched in color and rank; and the third possible bid if both are majors or minors. See ACE IDENTIFICATION.

ROMAN JUMP OVERCALL. The use of a JUMP OVERCALL to show a two-suited hand, specifically the suit bid and the next-higher-ranking suit excluding opener's suit. For example, if the opening bid is 1 ♦, an overcall of

2 ♥	shows ♥ and ♠
2 ♠	shows ♠ and ♣
3 ♣	shows ♣ and ♥

The strength shown is about the minimum for an opening bid or slightly more. Very strong two-suiters are shown by a conventional overcall of 2NT.

ROMAN KEY CARD BLACKWOOD. A form of BLACKWOOD in which the king of trumps is counted as a fifth ace. It has gained in popularity recently among American experts. The responses are similar in nature to ROMAN BLACKWOOD:

5 ♣	0 or 3 aces
5 ♦	1 or 4 aces
5 ♥	2 or 5 aces

In its original version (now obsolete), a response of 5 ♠ was reserved to show two aces with extra values. The modern interpretation uses 5 ♥ to show 2 or 5 aces without the queen of trumps while 5 ♠ shows 2 or 5 aces with the queen of trumps. A minor disadvantage of this method occurs when hearts are the agreed trump suit. If the Blackwood bidder holds only one ace without the queen of trumps he is well advised to not use the convention — a 5 ♠ response would prove most embarrassing.

An extension allows the 4NT bidder to ask for the queen of trumps after a response of 5 ♣ (if spades or hearts are trumps) or 5 ♦ (if spades are trumps). The

bid of the next higher-ranking suit (5 ♦ after 5 ♣) asks for the trump queen. A signoff in the trump suit denies the queen. A bid one higher than the agreed suit shows the queen. A cuebid shows specific second-round controls along with the trump queen.

There is often a danger of ambiguity about the agreed trump suit. The expert consensus in BWS 2001 was that the priority order should be: (1) the only supported suit; (2) the suit most recently shown or raised by the Blackwood bidder; (3) the only shown suit; (4) the most recently shown suit. However, responder's suit is the agreed suit if he has made a strong jump shift. And opener's only bid suit is the agreed suit if he has opened 2 ♣.

There is a strong expert tendency (98% in BWS 2001) to use a six key-card scheme in some auctions, counting two bid-suit kings. The favored method (73% in BWS 2001) of showing a void in responding is 5NT (the cheapest available bid) to show a void with an even number of keycards, almost always two; a bid at the six-level, not above the agreed trump suit, to show an odd number of keycards, almost always one. The actual void is shown where possible. Six of the trump suit shows a higher void.

Partnerships must agree how to respond when the 4NT bidder continues with 5NT. Most experts show specific side-suit kings, starting with the cheapest, but some show the number of side-suit kings on the Blackwood principle.

When responder has a void, the standard arrangement is that 5NT shows two key-cards with a void, and a jump to the six-level shows one key card and a void. The void is bid if below the agreed trump suit, and six of the trump suit shows a higher void.

A modern variation, growing in poularity among experts, is to interchange the meanings of the 5 ♣ and 5 ♦ response. This alternative was favored by 37% of the experts in BWS 2001. When there is no agreed trump suit, RKCB cannot be used. Experts strongly favor (73% in BWS2001) use of a modified responding scheme:

 5 ♣ no ace or three aces
 5 ♦ one ace or four aces
 5 ♥ two aces

See FOURTEEN THIRTY, KICKBACK, PREEMPTIVE ROMAN KEYCARD BLACKWOOD, REDWOOD.

ROMAN LEADS. See RUSINOW LEADS and FOURTH HIGHEST.

ROMAN MUD. A method of leading from four small cards. The opening leader leads the second highest from his four small cards, then he follows with the highest, then with the third highest and finally plays the lowest.

ROMAN SYSTEM. Developed by Walter Avarelli and Giorgio Belladonna, and used successfully in many World Championships The chief features are:

1 ♣ opening is forcing, and may show four distinct types of hands. It usually shows 12-16 points with 4-3-3-3 or 4-4-3-2 distribution. After a negative response of 1 ♦ (usually less than 9 points), the opener bids a major if he can, or 1NT. After a positive response in a suit (minimum of 8-11 points), the opener shows a minimum by a single raise, a rebid of 1NT, or a bid of a new suit on the same level.

Other positive responses are: 1NT, 12-16 points; 2NT, more than 16 points, over which opener rebids conventionally to show his exact point-count.

1 ♣ may also be bid with (1) 21-22 points and balanced distribution, in which case the rebid will be a jump in notrump; or (2) an unbalanced game-going hand, in which case the opener will jump rebid in a suit and responder rebids conventionally by six steps to show his holding in opener's suit; or (3) a two-suited hand with at least a four-card club suit and five cards in another suit and 17-20 points, in which case the opener will rebid in clubs.

If an opponent overcalls a 1 ♣ opening, an immediate cuebid by responder shows 12-16 points without a stopper and suggests a notrump contract.

1 ♦, 1 ♥, and 1 ♠ openings are natural (usually at least a four-card suit) and forcing, and guarantee at least one suit of more than four cards. With two suits, the shorter suit is opened (CANAPÉ principle), unless the shorter suit is clubs. With 5-3-3-2 distribution the opening bid is occasionally in the lower-ranking three-card suit other than clubs. A five-card suit may be opened and rebid with a minimum.

With fewer than 9 points, responder makes a single raise or makes the cheapest possible response, both of which are negative. Rebids are natural except for 1NT, which shows a minimum opening with five cards in the negatively bid suit. Other suit responses are positive, showing 9 points or more. Notrump responses are as over 1 ♣ (except 1 ♠ - 1NT, which is negative).

1NT opening shows a balanced hand with 17-20 points. Responses of 2 ♣ and 2 ♦ are GLADIATOR. Responses of two of a major or three of a minor are forcing to game, and opener rebids by steps to show support and opening-bid strength; the first two steps show minimum openings with poor and good support respectively; the third and fourth steps show maximum openings with poor and good support respectively. Other responses are natural and limited.

2 ♣ and 2 ♦ openings show three-suited hands (4-4-4-1 or 5-4-4-0 distributions) with 12-16 and 17-20 points respectively. A response of 2NT is positive and asks the opener to show his short suit. Minimum suit responses are negative and may sometimes have to be made in a three-card suit. If the suit response strikes opener's shortage, he makes the cheapest possible suit rebid. See also ROMAN TWO DIAMONDS.

2 ♥ and 2 ♠ openings show at least a five-card suit, together with four or five clubs. A 2NT response asks opener to clarify his distribution by bidding a three-card suit with 5-4-3-1 distribution, 3 ♣ with 5-4-2-2, 3NT with 5-5-2-1, four of a minor with 5-5-3-0, or rebidding a six-card suit.

2NT opening shows a balanced hand with 23-24 points. Responses are as over 1NT.

Asking bids are used after a suit has been agreed, usually a jump in a new suit at the level of four or higher. If responder can be short in the asked suit, the responses are by six steps: the first step shows no control, second step shows a singleton, third step shows the king, fourth step shows the ace, fifth step shows a void, and the sixth step shows the ace-king, or occasionally the ace-queen. If responder cannot be short in the asked suit, the second and fifth steps are deleted. Different asking bids are also used in certain special situations. See ROMAN ASKING BIDS.

Overcalls are limited to a maximum of 12 points, and are normally made only on a good suit.

Takeout doubles show 12-16 points. If third hand passes, responder bids his shortest suit if he can do so at

the level of one or two. See EXCLUSION BID. Otherwise, normal responses are given. If third hand bids, a double is for takeout.

1NT overcall is equivalent to a 1NT opening bid, although the distribution might be slightly unbalanced. Responses are as over a 1NT opening.

Jump overcall shows a two-suiter, the bid suit and the next higher-ranking, excluding the opener's suit. The distribution is usually 5-5 or 5-6 with a five- to six-loser hand.

2NT jump overcall shows a strong two-suiter, excluding the opener's suit. Responder bids the lower unbid minor and the overcaller bids an unbid suit, holding the bid suit and partner's conventionally named suit, or 3NT with both unbid suits.

Overcalls in the opponent's suit are natural. A jump cuebid shows a very strong three-suiter with a singleton or void in the opponents' suit and a four-loser hand. See also ROMAN BLACKWOOD

ROMAN TWO DIAMONDS. A bid showing a strong hand with 5-4-4-0 or 4-4-4-1 distribution. This feature of the ROMAN system can be used with standard methods. The original range of 17-20 is sometimes increased by one or two points. A 2NT response is positive, asking opener to bid his short suit. Other responses are natural and negative, but may be in an economical three-card suit. If the response is in opener's shortage he makes the minimum possible rebid.

An alternative method of responding, proposed by Marshall Miles, is to respond 2♥ on all weak hands. Other responses are natural and forcing to game. In all cases the opener bids his shortage on the second round, except that a notrump rebid shows a shortage in the suit bid by responder, whether naturally or artificially.

A version of the Roman 2♦ is also a part of BLUE TEAM CLUB. See BLUE TEAM 2♦.

ROMEX AWARD. A prize given by the INTERNATIONAL BRIDGE PRESS ASSOCIATION for the best bid hand of the year. This award is donated annually by George Rosenkranz of Mexico, the author of the Romex system of bidding.

ROMEX STAYMAN. After an opening 2NT, or after second-round 2NT bids to show similar hands of slightly different strengths (see ROMEX SYSTEM), the Stayman inquiry includes a special rebid of 3NT to show both major suits. 3♠ shows a five-card spade suit; 3♥ shows four or five hearts; and 3♦ denies any of the preceding.

After a 3♦ rebid, 3♥ asks for a four-card spade suit, seeking a 4-4 fit.

After a 3♥ rebid, 3♠ asks for clarification, the opener rebidding 3NT with only a four-card heart suit.

This arrangement allows the partnership to locate 3-5 fits in the major suits.

ROMEX SYSTEM. A 2♣ system devised by George Rosenkranz. The distinguishing feature of the system is the use of the DYNAMIC NOTRUMP opening (showing a balanced hand with 19-20 points and six controls or an unbalanced hand just short of the requirements for a 2♣ opening) and the MEXICAN 2♦ opening (showing a balanced hand with either 21-22 points and seven controls or 27-28 points and 10 controls, or a unbalanced game-force with diamonds the longest suit, or a three-suited game-force).

One-bids and 2♣ (artificial, for all other very strong hands) are normal, except that one-bids are limited by the failure to open 1NT. The lack of a balanced notrump opening is compensated by the special one-bid limitation: opener, with a balanced hand, can make a minimum rebid in notrump with 12-16 points or jump in notrump with 17-18 points. An EASTERN SCIENTIFIC structure is used after major-suit openings.

Special methods include: special asking bids, in preference to cuebidding, after a strength- or weakness-showing opening; the Romex raise to show extra values through an otherwise impossible bid of 4NT by the responder; step responses to many strong bids and asking bids; emphasis on slam-bidding devices. See ROMEX TRUMP ASKING BIDS.

In the latest version of the system (1992), the balanced structure is as follows:

19-20	1NT followed by 2NT
21-22	2♦ followed by 2NT
23-24	2♣ followed by 2NT
25-26	2NT
27-28	2♦ followed by 3NT

On the next round, ROMEX STAYMAN is used, together with transfer bids.

Mexican 2♦ Opening. A bid showing a balanced hand with 21-22 points, or a game-forcing hand with diamonds the longest suit, or a game-force with any 4-4-4-1 distribution.

The responses are:

2♥: 5-10 points, any shape

2NT: 0-4 points.

3♣ and higher: 11-plus points and assuming partner opened 2NT with 21-22 points (viz., 3♣ is Romex Stayman, 3♦ is a transfer to hearts, etc.). See TWO-WAY TRIAL BIDS.

ROMEX TRUMP ASKING BID. This can occur only after a 1NT or 2♣ opening bid. If a trump suit is agreed and the opener either raises the agreed suit below the level of game or bids a minimum number of notrump, it is a Trump Asking Bid (TAB).

Also, if the responder bids a natural 3♥ and 3♠, the opener may jump to 4NT as a TAB agreeing the responder's suit by inference.

The responses to a TAB are:

1st step: could not be worse for the previous bidding

2nd step: one of the top three honors but minimum length

3rd step: no top trump honor but at least one extra trump

4th step: one top honor and at least one extra trump

5th step: two of the top three honors but no extra length

6th step: two top honors and extra length

7th step: three top honors; or the best possible suit

Romex Control Asking Bid. When a trump suit has been agreed, either directly or by inference (perhaps via a splinter bid), following an opening bid of 1NT or 2♣, the opener may make a Control Asking Bid (CAB) to check on his partner's holding in a side suit.

You can make only one CAB that asks about first-round control in a suit. Every subsequent CAB inquires only about third-round control.

If the responder's last bid was a raise of the opener's suit, a bid in a new suit is a CAB. If the responder bids a suit and the opener jumps in another suit, it is a CAB agreeing responder's suit by inference.

Here are the responder's replies to a CAB:
1st step: no control
2nd step: second-round control (king or singleton)
3rd step: first-round control (ace or void)
4th step: ace-king-third or longer
5th step: total control

Romex Special Trump Asking Bid. If a 2♣ opener, after receiving a 2♦ response (at most one control), jumps to 3♥ or 3♠, it is setting the suit as trumps and instigating an asking-bid auction. It is called a Special Trump Asking Bid (STAB).

The responder defines his length in the trump suit thus:
1st step: at most one card in the suit
2nd step: two cards
3rd step: three cards
4th step: four or more cards

If the opener bids the next step after the response, it asks for an honor in the suit.

If the responder made a one-step reply, he bids as follows:
1st step: a void
2nd step: low singleton
3rd step: singleton honor

If the STAB response was higher, the reply to the second inquiry follows this scheme:
1st step: no honor
2nd step: one honor
3rd step: two honors (this is *extremely* unlikely)
See SPIRAL.

RONF. An acronym for Raise Only Non-Force. Used as a response to WEAK TWO-BIDS.

ROPE and ROPI. See BLACKWOOD AFTER INTERFERENCE.

ROSENBLUM CUP TEAMS. A world championship Open Teams event held every four years in conjunction with the Open Pairs and Women's Pairs championships. The event was added to the world championships in New Orleans in 1978 to commemorate Julius Rosenblum, who served as president of WORLD BRIDGE FEDERATION until 1976. The prize is the Rosenblum Cup.

In its early years, the event had an unusual feature – the REPECHAGE. This meant that one team defeated in the early part of the event had a second chance. The teams were divided into three groups, and the winner of each group advanced to the semifinals. The losing teams competed in a Swiss event, with the winner joining the three division winners to decide a champion via knockouts. Poland was beaten in its division but was at the top of the heap in the Swiss, then advancing to the semifinals. Poland won its semifinal match, then defeated Brazil in the final to become the event's first champion despite losing.

The repechage plan was eliminated in the Eighties. Today the event draws a very large field of strong teams. The event starts with a Swiss Teams format, and the top 64 teams advance to the knockout stage. The rest of the event is simply knockouts. Many experts now consider the Rosenblum the key event of what used to be primarily a pairs tournament. A similar event for women, the McCONNELL CUP TEAMS, takes place alongside the Rosenblum. For results, see Appendix V.

ROSENKRANZ AWARD. Endowed by George Rosenkranz, the Romex Award for the Best Bid Hand of

the Year is presented annually by the International Bridge Press Association. It is made to the players who, in partnership, have produced the best bidding sequence. The Award is given only in respect of a hand which occurred in play, whether in a tournament, match or private play. The panel takes into account accuracy, originality and psychological factors. The result in play need not be a determining factor. See INTERNATIONAL BRIDGE PRESS ASSOCIATION AWARDS.

ROSENKRANZ DOUBLE. A convention invented by George Rosenkranz of Mexico to help an overcaller gauge his holding more accurately in light of partner's response. If a player overcalls an opening bid and the next player makes a bid, a double by the partner of the overcaller shows a raise in partner's suit that includes the ace, king or queen of that suit. If the partner of the opening bidder makes a negative double over the overcall, then a redouble by the partner of the overcaller shows a raise with one of the top three honors. Conversely, if the partner of the overcaller, in either situation, merely raises the suit bid by the overcaller, this indicates that he does not hold one of the top three honors in partner's suit. Some players use the Reverse Rosenkranz Double, where the double (or redouble) denies a top honor in the overcaller's suit.

The alternative meaning for the double after three suits have been bid is for takeout, showing five cards in the unbid suit and moderate strength. See SNAPDRAGON.

ROSENKRANZ REDOUBLE. See ROSENKRANZ DOUBLE.

ROTATION. The order in which actions take place at the bridge table. In the bidding stage, the dealer has the first action, followed in turn by the player on his left, his partner, and the right-hand opponent. In the play of the cards, the player to declarer's left has the initial lead. The duty of making the initial lead to each subsequent trick falls on the player whose card was the winning card played to the preceding trick. Any deviation from this clockwise rotation in bidding or play constitutes an irregularity. In tournaments, the director should be summoned when such an irregularity occurs.

ROTH ASKING BID. In response to a preemptive three-level opening, 4♣ asks for the following responses:

    4♦ = bad suit, bad hand
    4♥ = good suit, two of top three honors
    4♠ = good hand, broken suit
    4NT = solid suit
Proposed by Alvin Roth.

ROTH DEFENSE TO ONE NOTRUMP.
    Double = majors
    2♣ = black suits
    2♦ = diamonds and spades
    2♥ = hearts
    2♠ = spades
    2NT = four hearts and a 6-card minor
    3♣ = clubs and hearts
    3♦ = red suits
Proposed by Alvin Roth.

ROTH POINT-COUNT. See DISTRIBUTIONAL COUNTS.

ROTH-STONE ASTRO. See ASTRO.

ROTH-STONE SYSTEM. Developed by Alvin Roth and Tobias Stone. Many of their ideas have been adopted by tournament players using standard methods. Since the publication of the 1953 book on the system, Roth has modified the system considerably, describing his new ideas in a second book published in 1958. Among the features of the revised system are:

(1) Sound opening bids in first and second position. The minimum requirement is 14 points, including at least 10 high card points, which is about one point more than in standard methods.

(2) Five-card majors in first and second position.

(3) ONE NOTRUMP RESPONSE TO A MAJOR, FORCING by an unpassed hand after a major-suit opening.

(4) A single raise in a major suit is constructive. It shows 10-12 points and is never passed by a first- or second-seat opener. With a void or singleton in a side suit and 10-12 points, responder, if he is an unpassed hand, jump raises to show shortness in the other major (e.g., 1♥-3♥ shows a singleton or void in spades), or jumps to 4♣ or 4♦ with shortness in the bid suit. A strong major raise is shown by a conventional jump to 3♣, which guarantees a minimum of four trumps and 13 points. Opener usually rebids conventionally to show whether or not he has a singleton, or, if not, the number of high trump honors he holds, but he may jump in a new suit as an asking bid.

(5) Two-over-one response (e.g., 2♣ in response to 1♠) normally shows at least 11 points. It is forcing for one round and guarantees that responder will bid again.

(6) Opening bids of 1♣ and 1♦ may be prepared with a three-card suit. After a major-suit response, opener jumps to four of his minor with a strong six-card suit and weak four-card support for responder's major, jumps to four of the major with strong four-card support and a weak minor suit, jumps to four of the other minor (or to 4♥ after a 1♠ response) with a singleton in the bid suit and a strong raise, or jumps to three of the other major with a strong, balanced hand and four-card support.

(7) Jump shift responses are weak, except by a passed hand in a non-competitive auction.

(8) Over one of a suit, a jump to 2NT by an unpassed hand is unlimited, at least 13 points, and a jump to 3NT is BABY BLACKWOOD.

(9) After a third- or fourth-seat major-suit opening, responder jumps to 3NT to show a strong, distributional raise, jumps to 4♣ to show a distributional raise with slightly fewer high cards, or jumps to 4♦ to show a strong raise with no singleton or void.

(10) 1NT opening is standard (16-18). Responses of 2♣ and 2♦ are forcing and slam-try STAYMAN respectively. 2NT forces opener to bid a minor; if responder then rebids a major, it shows a singleton. Jump responses to the three-level are weak, but mildly invitational in the major suits. TWO-WAY STAYMAN is also used over 2NT (21-23), except that 3♣ shows slam interest.

(11) TEXAS.

(12) GERBER over notrump openings.

(13) 2♣ opening is forcing to game. 2♥ is the conventional negative response and 2♦ is an artificial positive response, showing the equivalent of an ace and a king. Responses of 2NT and 3NT show balanced hands with 8-9 and 10-12 scattered points respectively.

(14) WEAK TWO-BIDS with 2NT the only forcing response by an unpassed hand. 2NT and a raise of opener's major are invitational by a passed hand.

(15) 3NT opening shows a strong preempt in one of the four suits. If responder bids 4♣, he warns opener not to bid game in a minor.

(16) NEGATIVE DOUBLES.

(17) RESPONSIVE DOUBLES only after an overcall (e.g., 1♣-1♠-2♣-double is responsive).

(18) WEAK JUMP OVERCALLS.

(19) UNUSUAL NOTRUMP.

(20) Bids in the opponents' suit are sometimes natural. After 1♣ - pass - 1♠, an overcall of 2♣ or 2♠ would be natural.

(21) A takeout double may be light, 10 high card points with 4-4-4-1 or 4-4-5-0 distribution. An immediate cuebid of opponent's suit is equivalent to a strong takeout double, 18 points or more.

(22) When an opponent overcalls 1NT, 2♣ is a weak takeout and double is a strong takeout, 8 points or more, but may be passed.

(23) When an opponent opens 1NT, 2♣ and 2♦ show the bid minor and spades, 3♣ and 3♦ show the bid minor and hearts, and double shows the major suits unless the notrump opening is weak, in which case it shows at least 15 high card points.

(24) After 1♥ or 1♠-pass-1NT, 2♣ and 2♦ overcalls show the bid minor and the unbid major.

(25) After 1♣ or 1♦-pass-1NT, 2♣ and 2♠ overcalls show the unbid minor with spades or hearts respectively, and double shows the major suits.

(26) In a competitive auction where a sacrifice may be considered, a double of a slam contract at equal or favorable vulnerability shows no defensive tricks.

(27) A balancing bid of 2♣ is equivalent to a light takeout double.

After briefly experimenting with a Strong Club method, Roth added some new features and modifications to the system in *Picture Bidding* (1991):

(28) 1NT-3♦ promises game in a minor; 1NT-3♥ promises slam in a minor.

(29) 1NT-3♠ Strong 3-suiter, forces 3NT and responder shows short suit.

(30) 1NT-2♠ weak minors.

(31) 2NT-3NT weak with long minor.

(32) 2NT-3♠ weak minors, 4♠ good minors, 5♠ slam in minors.

(33) 1♣-2♠ shows 4-4-1-4 with 13-15.

(34) 1♥/1♠-3♣ strong major-suit raise, slammish.

(35) 2♣-2♠ positive response.

(36) 4♣ good preempt in a major, solid suit plus outside length.

ROUDI. Invented and popularized by Jean-Marc Roudinesco of France, Roudi is a version of Checkback Stayman after a 1NT rebid. In Standard French style the 1NT rebid simply shows 12-14 balanced or semi-balanced. The call is unlikely to have a singleton in partner's suit, but it can conceal semi-balanced hands with good three-card support, as a direct raise by opener guarantees four-card support. Hence opener needs to be able to clarify both range and fit at his second turn. A bid of 2♣ by responder after a 1NT rebid guarantees game-interest and is a relay. In a sequence such as:

1♣	1♥
1NT	2♣

responses are based on the principle that the more you bid the more you have: 2♦, 2-card support minimum; 2♥, 3-card support minimum; 2♠, 3-card support maximum; 2NT, 2-card support maximum. An alternative way to play is to switch the meaning of two of the major and two of the unbid major – such that reversion to partner's suit is always minimum with three-card support.

ROUND. A part of a session of bridge at a tournament during which the players and the boards remain at a table. When two boards are played during a round, its duration should be about 15 minutes. Three-board rounds require about 20 minutes; four-board rounds 25.

In rubber bridge, a round refers to the three or four rubbers (or double rubbers) during which each of the players plays with each of the other players as partners.

ROUND HAND. A colloquialism for a hand with BALANCED DISTRIBUTION, particularly 4-3-3-3. Flat and square are also used to describe such a hand.

ROUNDED. A term used to describe the combination of hearts and clubs, these suits having pips rounded at the tops. The converse is POINTED to indicate spades and diamonds.

ROUNDING OFF. At rubber bridge, it is customary to record the results of a rubber to the nearest 100 points. In America, 50 points are counted as an extra 100, but in Europe it is customary to ignore them. For maintaining a running record of the results of a rubber game, a BACK SCORE sheet is used, showing each player as plus or minus some number of hundreds of points, and this provides the basis of settling the game. Some players use a banker who distributes poker chips at the beginning of a game, and rubbers are settled at the end of each by passing the chips from losers to winners, and they are redeemed by the banker at the end of the session.

ROUND-ROBIN. A form of competition in which each of the contesting groups (usually teams, though occasionally pairs) plays against each of the other groups entered in head-on competition. "League" is used as an equivalent term in England.

Round-robin team contests are increasing in popularity, frequently requiring months to complete. KNOCK-OUT TOURNAMENTS occasionally end up in a round-robin of surviving teams, or start with one. Round-robins frequently are used to determine semifinalists and finalists in WORLD TEAM CHAMPIONSHIPS. See CARRYOVER.

When a round-robin fails to establish a winner some tie-splitting device, such as QUOTIENT, must be used.

ROVER. A method of handling a half table in a MITCHELL MOVEMENT. The Rover is an alternative to the PHANTOM pair and the BUMP MITCHELL. The Rover pair may play in either direction, but North-South is preferable because the movement is easier to administer with a North-South sit-out.

The Rover pair is assigned a number, one higher than the number of full tables in play. After sitting out the first round the Rover pair enters the game by replacing one of the pairs playing in their direction. After playing the round at that table, the Rover pair moves to another table, usually skipping a table up the line. (There are

exceptions when the number of full tables is not a prime.) Meanwhile the pair displaced for the previous round resumes its natural position and progression. This continues for as many rounds as there are in the game.

To start the game, boards are distributed only to full tables, as if there were no half table. This means that the boards never sit out, so all boards have the same top and the game can be curtailed at any point without having to factor boards. However, the pairs that sit out must be factored up.

This movement is good for almost all numbers of tables. In a game with an even number of full tables, there is an East-West skip after the halfway round. Although the usual move for the Rover pair is to skip a table up the line, there are exceptions when the number of full tables is divisible by three. The Rover movement for 9½ tables is especially unusual. Guide cards for Rover pairs in most sizes of half-table games, including the 9½, are available from the AMERICAN CONTRACT BRIDGE LEAGUE. The Rover movement can cause complications, the same as all half-table movements.

Here are suggested Rover movements for various size games:

8½ - Out, 2, 4, 6, 3, 5, 7
10½ - Out, 3, 5, 7, 9 ,4, 6, 8, 10
11½ - Out, 3, 5, 7, 9, 11, 2, 4, 6
12½ - Out, 2, 10, 8, 6, 4, 1, 11, 9, 5, 3
13½- Out, 3, 5, 7, 9, 11, 13, 2, 4, 6, 8, 10, 12
14½ - Out, 3, 5, 7, 9, 11, 13, 4, 6, 8, 10, 12, 14
15½ - Out, 2, 4, 6, 8, 10, 13, 15, 3, 5, 7, 9, 11
16½ - Out, 2, 4, 6, 8, 10, 12, 14, 3, 5, 7, 9, 11

The above are for Skip Mitchells. The following are for Relay Mitchells:

6 tables: Out, 2, 5, 3, 6, 4
8 tables: Out, 1 6 2 7 3 8 4
10 tables: Out, 1 7 2 8 3 9 4 10 5
12 tables: Out, 3 9 4 10 5 11 6 12 7 1 8
14 tables: Out, 1 9 2 10 3 11 4 12 5 13 6 14 7

The movement for 9½ tables involves use of a set of guide cards with East-West 10 as the Rover. Pairs 1 and 7 both have unusual moves. The movement for the Rover pair - Out, 3, 5, 7, 1, 4, 6, 8, 9. The movement for pair 1: 1, 2, 9, 4, 5, 3, 7, Out, 6. The movement for pair 7: 7, 8, 3, 1, 2, 6, 4, 5, Out. All other pairs move normally, going in at their normal table after their sit-out. Other movements are possible with different pairs making the unusual moves.

Both 8½ and 12½ tables lend themselves more satisfactorily to a PHANTOM pair. Pair 9 (or pair 13) in either direction is a phantom.

The Rover movement can be used for another purpose. One or more invited experts can be introduced into the game, using a Rover movement, so that each player plays one board with an expert and sits out one board while his partner does the same.

ROYAL SPADES (popularly LILIES). The spade suit when scored at nine points per trick, in an early phase of bridge whist.

RUBBER. A unit of measurement of games at home or club bridge, hence the expression, "rubber bridge." A rubber must consist of at least two games, but not more than three. The first side to win two games wins the rubber, and a premium is earned on the basis of whether the opponents have won any game. If they have not, the win-

ning side's premium is larger (700 as against 500). If a rubber is stopped before either side has actually won two games, it is called an "unfinished rubber," and there is a somewhat smaller bonus (300) to the side having won one game. If no game has been won by either side but a partial does exist, there is a small premium (50) to the side having the partial.

The word "rubber" is probably borrowed from lawn bowls, which Sir Francis Drake was playing when the Armada was sighted in 1588. "We can finish the rubber and beat the Spaniards too," he is reported to have said. In 1749 Henry Fielding referred to "a rubber at whist" in *Tom Jones*.

RUBBER BRIDGE. The original and once the most popular form of the game. However, DUPLICATE and CHICAGO bridge have increased in popularity. Rubber bridge is played for points, which sometimes may represent a monetary value per point. In a game played for a one cent stake, collecting a penalty of 100 points would be worth one dollar.

Tactics at this type of bridge differ from those used at tournament or duplicate. The premium for winning a rubber of two games where the opponents have not won a game is high, and even in a three-game rubber, the premium is substantial. In rubber bridge, therefore, considerable effort is expended toward winning games, and risks in the bidding are taken to secure that end. (But see VALUE OF GAME.)

Penalties can be inflicted by the opponents if too little regard for safety has been observed by a side. These penalties become more severe when the incurring side has won a game, that is, when they become vulnerable. The competitive features of rubber bridge are sometimes overlooked by players who manifest their principal bridge endeavors in the tournament field. Many club players deplore the tendency toward Chicago and long for the days when rubber was the only game played.

The disadvantage of rubber bridge is that a rubber may last more than an hour, a great inconvenience to players who are waiting to cut in. However, it has some psychological elements that are lost in Chicago: The rubber bridge player will strive to keep a good partner but get rid of a bad one. See PARTNERSHIP RUBBER BRIDGE and RUBBER BRIDGE TACTICS.

RUBBER BRIDGE TACTICS. Should you be willing to go two down at equal vulnerability to save game? At duplicate this is a matter of simple arithmetic. Each time the sacrifice will show a profit, for other things being equal, one concedes 300 to 500 against a game that is worth 400 or 600. At rubber bridge other things are rarely equal, and simple arithmetic is a poor guide. The issue is determined by the personal equation. With a good partner and mediocre opponents, there is always the risk of a phantom sacrifice, of going down to prevent them from going down.

Opponents may have a certain game, one that would be made in the other room. But there is no other room, and mediocre opponents miss a good many certain games.

Conversely, when partner is the weakest player at the table, the cheapest sacrifice may prove expensive, for what attraction can there be in prolonging a rubber when you start every hand at a disadvantage? Broadly speaking, there is little future in sacrificing at rubber bridge. The profit margin is too narrow, and it is generally best to leave this dubious pastime to the other side.

When the best slams are not so good. How about slams? At duplicate, the odds are clearly in favor of bidding a slam which depends on one of two finesses. At rubber bridge, the decision never rests with abstract figures, but always with concrete personalities.

Who will be declarer, you or partner? If it is partner and he goes down playing it his way, it will be poor consolation to know that he would have made it had he played it differently. It will be more painful still if on the next hand he concedes a needless penalty and then, through bad defense, allows opponents to bring home an impossible slam. Of course, when a good partner is in control, and opponents may be expected to slip in defense, you can bid slams with less than an even money chance. Faces alter cases, and it is the people, not the mathematical probabilities, that make the true odds.

Double the player, not the contract. If an overbidder calls 4♠, double him if there seems any reason for doing so. But if the 4♠ call was made by an underbidder, pass. When in doubt, you double the man rather than the contract.

The statistically minded can look at it from another angle. The overbidder's record shows that he often goes down. He is a bad risk actuarially, and doubling him offers favorable odds.

Not so the underbidder, who seldom gives away penalties. The best tactics against him are to open light, to intervene boldly, and to make a general show of strength. You may put him off, but you are not likely to score much above the line. The underbidder's main contribution to your welfare will come from the games and slams he makes but dares not bid.

However, most bad players are neither overbidders or underbidders. Their common error is to bid on with a misfit. Good players sometimes bypass a major to bid notrump, with mixed results.

Confusion - for confusion's sake. Psychic bids can be most rewarding, yet here again everything depends on the uncertain quality of partner and opponents. Each player must be studied separately and treated strictly on his demerits.

In principle it pays to create confusion for confusion's sake, so long as you remain in control. With little defense against opponent's major, but support for partner's minor, you can bid notrump. With support for partner's major you can bid a nonexistent minor. If you are doubled, you have a ready-made escape, and meanwhile you may throw the other side off balance. Sometimes you will steal a hand that does not belong to you. Sometimes you will mislead an opponent in the play of the hand. But you will draw your biggest dividends on all those occasions, the vast majority, when you bid honestly and are unjustly suspected of bluffing. For it is not psyching but the reputation of psyching which creates confusion in the adversary's mind.

Much the same is true of inhibitory bids. If you have decided to bid 6♠ over partner's 3♠, let us say, you may derive a twofold advantage from a spurious cuebid. Holding a worthless doubleton in clubs, call 4♣ on the way. It may discourage a club lead, which you do not want. Better still, it may induce the lead you do want next time, when you make your cuebid, deliberately, on A-K-J or A-Q or K-x. Of course, you must be careful to throw the bait to the same opponent. First develop suspicion, then exploit it. For it is the essence of rubber bridge to play the players as well as the cards. Every

hand forms part of a pattern. In theory every hand must be treated in isolation, but in practice this is not true at all. At roulette red and black have equal chances every time the wheel spins regardless of how many reds or blacks have come up before. This is because the wheel is a purely mechanical device. As soon as the human element is introduced, this no longer applies. Every move is influenced by those that have preceded it, and neither emotion nor superstition can be left out of account.

If you have been doubled into game, you may take certain risks in partscore situations for the next half-hour or so provided that you are up against the same opponents. They will surely hang back, fearful of suffering the same ignominy twice in quick succession.

The partner problem. Handling a weak partner is, per-haps, the most difficult art at rubber bridge. Of course, you want to prevent partner from playing the hand, and of course you do not want him to know that you are trying to prevent him. Fortunately, weak players are sin-gularly unobservant and with a little luck you will get away with it again and again.

On a balanced hand, intending to rebid notrump, there is a good case for opening a weak minor in preference to a strong major. That way you are likely to get the notrump bid in first. At the same time, you may dis-courage an unwelcome lead. Even a 1 ♦ opening on J-x-x may have something to commend it. It is a prepared bid - prepared to steer the contract into your own hand.

In defense, a little cynicism is seldom out of place. Opponents are in 3NT. What do you lead from K-7-6 in a suit bid by partner? The 6? Are you sure that he de-serves the compliment? Perhaps he was brought up to believe that it is sinful not to lead the highest of partner's suit. Humor him. Never hesitate to do the wrong thing with the right partner. There are times when you can take advantage of partner's shortcomings, reversing on the sketchiest of values or falsecarding wantonly. Op-ponents may be misled with impunity when partner is not good enough to be deceived.

When not to concentrate. The key to success at bridge at every level lies in concentration. But whereas at duplicate, concentration can never be relaxed, at rubber bridge the good tactician takes an occasional breather, just as cham-pions do at boxing or at tennis. If declarer can fulfill his contract of 2 ♦ he need not try too hard to make three or four. In terms of money the result will probably be the same, so why waste the effort? An extra ounce of mental energy may be all-important on the next hand or on the one after when the contract is a difficult game or slam. The winning player has his lapses, but he usually knows when he can afford to have them, and is quick to concentrate and to give of his best when the need arises. See also PARTNERSHIP PSYCHOLOGY, PARTSCORE BIDDING.

RUBBER DUPLICATE. A rare form of duplicate with rubber bridge scoring. Identical deals are played at two tables, and if one table scores a rubber the other table terminates, scoring an unfinished rubber. This was for many years played in the Devonshire Club Cup in Lon-don, England. It also is used for the matches between the Lords and the Commons in Great Britain.

RUBENS ADVANCE. A method of using transfer re-sponses to overcalls, advocated by Jeff Rubens in the April 1981 issue of *The Bridge World.* Suit bids below two of the opponent's suit are natural and forcing. There

are no transfers when the overcall has not used any space. Examples:

(1 ♦)   1 ♠   (Pass/double/1NT/2♣)
       1NT natural
       2 ♣ natural (non-forcing but invitational)
       2 ♦ hearts
       2 ♥ spade raise
       2 ♠ natural
       2NT natural
       3 ♣ forcing

Rubens advances can still apply when third hand bids, so long as no artificial bid is taken away. Where advancer can bid a suit in a natural and non-forcing way, a jump is strong and forcing. Where advancer can transfer into a suit, a jump in that suit is fit-showing.

The responder's strength is undefined, as with normal transfer bids. A similar idea can be used by the responder following a weak jump overcall, with 2NT used as a transfer to clubs. See RUBINSOHL.

RUBINSOHL. A transfer method by responder follow-ing an overcall, introduced by Bruce Neill of Australia in a *Bridge World* article in May 1983. His ideas were based on earlier articles by Jeff Rubens, covering dif-ferent situations, so he used the term Rubensohl. How-ever, a similar idea to replace LEBENSOHL had been used much earlier in the United States by Ira Rubin, so Rubinsohl seems the appropriate name.

Examples: (a)

Opener	Overcaller	Responder
1NT	2 ♠	2NT = clubs
		3 ♣ = diamonds
		3 ♦ = hearts
		3 ♥ = 4-card hearts
		3 ♠ = 3NT no stopper, no hearts
		3NT = 3NT stopper

            (b)

Opener	Overcaller	Responder
1 ♦	2 ♠	2NT = clubs
		3 ♣ = diamonds
		3 ♦ = hearts
		3 ♥ = 4-card hearts
		3 ♠ = 3NT no stopper, no hearts
		3NT = 3NT stopper.

The idea can be used similarly after simple overcalls. See LEBENSOHL and RUBENS ADVANCE.

RUBIN TRANSFER BIDS. Devised by Ira Rubin as a method of preventing the opponents from finding a cheap sacrifice against a game or slam, and used in the 1966 BERMUDA BOWL.

4 ♣ opening describes a hand containing either a long, semi-solid major suit with 3½ to 4 honor tricks, or a long minor suit with 2½ to 3 honor tricks and no voids. Responder will usually bid 4 ♦ to allow opener to show his suit. Major-suit responses are slam tries, and minor-suit responses show a solid suit missing the king, queen, or jack, which opener may raise to slam with three first-round controls.

4 ♦ opening shows a strong major suit with 2½ to 3 honor tricks. 4 ♥ is the normal response, while 4 ♠ shows active interest in a heart slam, but only mild in-terest in a spade slam. Responses in the minors are cuebids, agreeing either major as trump, and 4NT is BLACKWOOD .

4NT opening shows a strong minor-suit hand with one

or more voids. Responder bids 5♠ or 5NT with three or four aces respectively.

Game openings in any of the four suits are weak pre-empts, denying much high-card strength. Alternatively, a hand with greater high-card or playing strength can be shown by an opening bid of one followed by a jump to game. See FOUR-CLUB AND FOUR-DIAMOND OPENING TRANSFERS.

RUFF. To trump a lead of a plain suit, winning the trick if no higher trump is played.

RUFF AND DISCARD (or RUFF AND SLUFF). When a defender leads a suit of which both declarer and dummy are void, the declarer gets a ruff and sluff; he can discard a loser from one hand and ruff in the other. This may be declarer's only way of making a contract when too many losers are present. To compel a defender to give a ruff and sluff, he must be placed in the lead after all his safe exit cards have been removed.

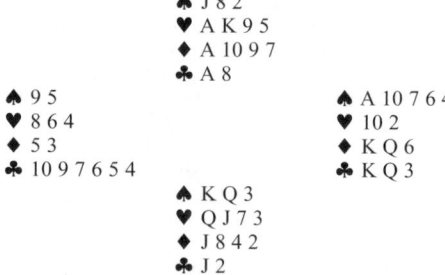

West opens 3♥, North doubles, South jumps to 4♠ and North raises to 6♠. Owing to the unfortunate club break, declarer apparently has a club loser as well as a heart. The two suits are guarded by different opponents, so no squeeze operates, and the only way to make the contract is by compelling a defender to concede a ruff and discard.

The heart lead is won, trumps are drawn and clubs are tested. Finding that he has a club loser, declarer continues by ruffing out diamonds and playing off the remaining clubs, throwing East into the lead. As expected after West's opening three-bid, East has no more hearts and has to return a diamond. South throws the ♥J from his own hand, and ruffs in dummy.

A defensive weapon. It can be winning defense to present declarer with a ruff and sluff even when the defender has safe exit cards in other suits. The usual occasion is when declarer is short of trumps and has to lose the lead before he can develop a side suit:

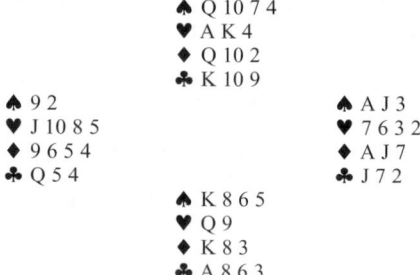

East's 1♣ opening is passed to North, who doubles. South responds 2♥, and passes his partner's raise to three. West, with no clue to the killing spade lead, plays a club, which is won in dummy. After three rounds of

trumps, South leads a spade to dummy's 10, and the queen wins, West starting an echo.

East may cash a club and exit passively with ace and another spade, expecting to beat the hand if West has the ♦Q, for then the declarer would eventually lose two diamonds. If East follows that reasoning, the contract is made because South has the ♦Q.

By forcing declarer with repeated club leads, East succeeds no matter who has the ♦Q and despite giving South a ruff and sluff. After the ♠Q, East plays a second and third round of clubs. It does not matter in which hand declarer ruffs, for when East comes in with the ♠A he plays another club, taking declarer's last trump. South has only eight tricks, East has three, and must make the ♦A and the long club.

The lesser evil. In the first example above the defender had no choice but to concede a ruff and sluff. Sometimes he has an option, albeit an unattractive one, such as leading into a tenace. If the situation does not lend itself to complete analysis, the defender should prefer to give a ruff and sluff rather than concede a trick in a side suit. This is particularly so when both declarer and dummy have four cards in the same side suit.

                    ♠ J 8 2
                    ♥ A K 9 5
                    ♦ A 10 9 7
                    ♣ A 8
    ♠ 9 5   ♠ A 10 7 6 4
    ♥ 8 6 4   ♥ 10 2
    ♦ 5 3   ♦ K Q 6
    ♣ 10 9 7 6 5 4   ♣ K Q 3
                    ♠ K Q 3
                    ♥ Q J 7 3
                    ♦ J 8 4 2
                    ♣ J 2

East's 1♠ opening is passed to North, who doubles. South lands in 4♥, and the defense starts with two rounds of spades. Fearing a ruff, declarer pulls three rounds of trumps before touching the minor suits. South places East with all the missing high cards, and takes out the third round of spades before putting East on play with ace and another club. East counts declarer for four diamonds in his own hand as well as in dummy, so he gives him a ruff and sluff instead of leading a diamond. South still has to lose two diamonds, and is defeated, but had East returned a diamond the contract would have been made.

On the relatively few occasions when it is better to lead into a tenace than to concede a ruff and sluff, the usual reason is that a ruff and a sluff would enable declarer to establish a long card in a side suit. This suit will usually be distributed 4-3 between dummy and the declarer.

                    ♠ Q 10 7 4
                    ♥ A K 4
                    ♦ Q 10 2
                    ♣ K 10 9
    ♠ 9 2   ♠ A J 3
    ♥ J 10 8 5   ♥ 7 6 3 2
    ♦ 9 6 5 4   ♦ A J 7
    ♣ Q 5 4   ♣ J 7 2
                    ♠ K 8 6 5
                    ♥ Q 9
                    ♦ K 8 3
                    ♣ A 8 6 3

South opens 1♣ and after a forcing 2NT response lands in 4♠. West leads the ♥J, and South seeks to improve his chances by taking three rounds of hearts

before leading a trump to the king and a trump back to dummy. East scores two trump tricks, but then has a choice of rotten apples. South had bid clubs, and if East plays the suit, declarer brings it in without loss and makes his contract. He has already discarded a diamond on the third round of hearts and now loses only to the ♦ A. East's choice, therefore, lies between conceding a ruff and discard or playing a diamond.

Declarer had only eight ready tricks, so East willingly gives him a ninth by playing ace and another diamond. South still has to lose a club, and is defeated.

If East concedes a ruff and discard instead, South ruffs in hand and sluffs a club from dummy. The third round of clubs is ruffed on the board, a diamond led to South's king provides a ninth trick, and the long club is the tenth. See DUMMY PLAY.

RUFF AND RUFF. A rare endgame situation described by Jean Besse, Switzerland, in which the declarer is offered a ruff and discard, and the only winning play is to ruff in both declaring hands.

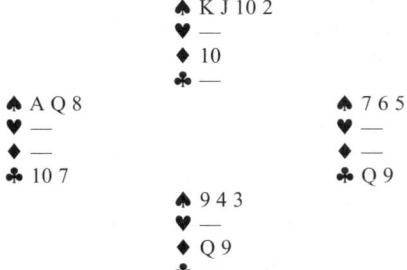

```
                    ♠ K J 10 2
                    ♥ Q J 8
                    ♦ K 10 4 3
                    ♣ K 3
♠ A Q 8                                ♠ 7 6 5
♥ 10 4 2                               ♥ K 7 6 5
♦ A J 6                                ♦ 7
♣ A 10 7 4                             ♣ Q 9 8 6 5
                    ♠ 9 4 3
                    ♥ A 9 3
                    ♦ Q 9 8 5 2
                    ♣ J 2
```

South plays in 3 ♦ after West has opened the bidding with 1♣, and the opening lead is the ♥ 2. Declarer ducks in dummy, and when East does not cover, declarer overtakes with the 9. A diamond is led to dummy's king, and the declarer takes a successful heart finesse, then cashes the third heart. He continues with a trump, and West takes two trump tricks. When West shifts to a low club, South guesses right, putting up dummy's king. He returns a club, and West wins with the ace in this position:

```
                    ♠ K J 10 2
                    ♥ —
                    ♦ 10
                    ♣ —
♠ A Q 8                                ♠ 7 6 5
♥ —                                    ♥ —
♦ —                                    ♦ —
♣ 10 7                                 ♣ Q 9
                    ♠ 9 4 3
                    ♥ —
                    ♦ Q 9
                    ♣ —
```

West returns a club, the best defense, and the only winning play for South is to ruff in dummy and overruff with his queen. He continues with the ♠ 9. If dummy discards any spade on the club lead, West can defend the position. If declarer pitches a low spade from dummy. West plays low and declarer is pinned in dummy. If he sluffs the jack or 10, West covers the 9 with the queen, and declarer again is beaten. For a related situation, see ONE-SUIT SQUEEZE.

RUFF AND SLUFF. See RUFF AND DISCARD.

RUFFING FINESSE. A play by which a finesse is successful if the missing honor lies behind the finesse holding. With a singleton opposite a holding of A-Q-J, a simple finesse may be taken by leading the singleton and playing the jack, thus providing an immediate discard on the ace. The other possibility, granting no problem of entry, is to play for the king to be behind the high card holding. In this case the ace is played at the first trick, and the queen led. If the queen is covered, the trick can be ruffed; if not covered a sluff is taken.

The bidding may give some clue to the missing king's location. When the declarer has no information to guide him, he should choose the ruffing finesse in preference to the simple finesse for the reason that the ruffing finesse will lose one less trick when it fails. If the 10 is missing, the ruffing finesse becomes less attractive:

```
                    A Q J 3 2
                    4
```

The play of the ace followed by the queen cannot produce more than three tricks in all, with the help of two ruffs. Entries permitting, it is slightly better to ruff a low card on the second round and lead the queen later.

The all-out play of finessing the queen on the first round offers the chance of four tricks, with the help of one ruff, if the left-hand opponent began with K-x-x.

Similarly, with a singleton opposite A-K-J-10-x, a first-round finesse must be taken if it is essential to make five tricks in the suit. See FINESSE.

RUFFING SQUEEZE. See TRUMP SQUEEZE.

RUFFING TRICK. A trick won by ruffing. See COUP EN PASSANT; CROSSRUFF; DUMMY REVERSAL; ELOPEMENT. In hand evaluation under the POINT-COUNT system the responding hand, after finding a trump fit with partner, may add substantially for shortness in a side suit. See DISTRIBUTIONAL COUNTS.

RULE OF EIGHTEEN. A rule employed by the World Bridge Federation to define the boundary between light opening bids and HUM (Highly Unusual Methods) methods in which bad hands are regularly opened. Only when the number of high-card points added to the total of the two longest suits totals 18 is the opening bid acceptable. Therefore 11 HCP are needed to open a 4-3-3-3 hand, or 8 HCP to open a 5-5-2-1. In England a similar Rule of 19 applies.

RULE OF ELEVEN. A mathematical calculation applicable when the original lead is construed as FOURTH-HIGHEST. It is sometimes possible to obtain an exact reading of the distribution in all four hands. The discovery of the rule is generally credited to Robert F. Foster, and was published by him in his Whist Manual. First put in writing in a letter from Foster to a friend in 1890, it is said to have been discovered independently by E.M.F. Benecke of Oxford at about the same time. The rule states: "Subtract the pips on the card led from 11; the result gives the number of higher cards than the one led in the other three hands. " Counting such cards in his own hand and in the dummy, both the leader's partner and the declarer can determine the number of such cards in the concealed hand of the other. The application of the rule is easier than stating it. For example:

DUMMY
K 5 2

7 led   A 10 9 3

If the lead of the 7-spot is a fourth-best lead, third hand subtracts 7 from 11 and knows that four cards higher than the 7-spot are held in his, dummy's, and declarer's hands. He has three and dummy one, therefore declarer has no card higher than the 7, which can be permitted to ride.

Frequently only the declarer gains from the application of this rule.

DUMMY
A Q 9 5 4

6 led   3 played

10 7 2

Since declarer sees in his own hand and the dummy five cards higher than the 6-spot, he can bring in the entire suit by successively finessing against the king, jack and 8-spot.

The Rule of Eleven often spots a singleton lead. For example:

DUMMY
A 10 8 7 4

5 led   K 9 3 2

DECLARER
Q J 6

If five is subtracted from 11, the third hand knows that this is the number of cards higher than the 5-spot held by himself, dummy and declarer. He sees six of them so declarer holds none if his partner's lead is a fourth best. Declarer ducks, the king is played, and declarer plays a seventh card higher than the 5. Third hand sees all cards lower than the 5; therefore the opening lead must have been a singleton.

The rule is based on an honest lead of fourth best in a suit. There is a modern tendency to be less revealing on the opening lead, with the lead of a small card indicating a suit whose return is desired and a middle card to indicate a suit to be abandoned. Care must therefore be taken not to apply the rule rigorously when the lead is not certainly a fourth best. See also RULE OF TWELVE, RULE OF FIFTEEN (2).

RULE OF FIFTEEN. A device to help a player remember how many higher cards are outstanding in a suit whether partner leads third, fourth or fifth best, Subtract the rank of the card led from 15 and use that rule. If the card led is fifth best, subtract five from 15 and use the Rule of 10. If it is fourth best, subtract 4 and use the Rule of 11, etc.

RULE OF FOURTEEN. A method proposed by Malcolm Macdonald to determine whether a squeeze play should be considered for winning an extra trick. This is a useful rule to determine whether a squeeze is possible: Count the number of tricks that must be lost, the number of winners that can be run, and the number of cards that must be held in the threat suits by one defender. If the total is 14, a squeeze may be possible. If the total is 13, a squeeze is not possible. Pseudo squeezes always add to 13.

This rule can be applied as early as trick one or whenever declarer determines that he is within one trick of making the contract. The rule is valid for all but the most esoteric squeeze plays. The rule may be applied to each defender separately for double squeezes.

Tricks that can be (or have been or need to be) won in the threat suits may be counted with winners or with cards that must be held by a defender in the threat suit, as long as they are not counted twice.

The rule does not help to determine whether the conditions necessary for the squeeze to succeed exist, nor does it indicate the proper technique for the execution of the squeeze. It merely indicates that a squeeze is possible. The rule is effective because the central concept underlying the squeeze play is that a defender (the potential victim) does not have enough room in his hand to hold all the cards he needs to defend successfully. In other words, he does not have room for more than 13 cards.

Here's an example of how the rule works in practice:

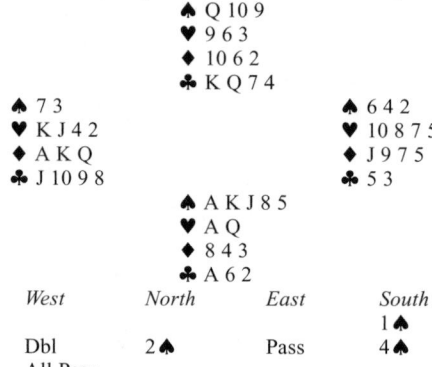

West	North	East	South
			1 ♠
Dbl	2 ♠	Pass	4 ♠
All Pass			

West cashes the top three diamonds and switches to the ♣ J. South is within one trick of his contract. The extra trick could come from the heart finesse, but it is a poor prospect because of West's double. If the clubs split 3-3, another poor prospect, declarer could make it. Is a squeeze possible? Apply the rule of 14. South has three tricks that must be (or have been) lost and has six winners that can be won (five spades and one club already won). West must retain two hearts, namely ♥ K x, and three clubs, ♣ 10 9 8. Thus, 3 + 6 + 2 + 3 = 14. A squeeze is possible and is successful.

RULE OF NINETEEN. See RULE OF EIGHTEEN.

RULE OF N-MINUS-ONE. A rule for squeezes published in the *Red Book on Play* by Ely Culbertson. This is his definition:

Count the number of busy cards in plain suits held by one adversary. This number is represented by the symbol N. N-minus-one equals the number of uninterrupted winners the declarer needs for a squeeze.

This rule is applied at a time when the opponent to be squeezed has been stripped of all idle cards. At that point declarer must be capable of taking all but one of the remaining tricks. See RECTIFYING THE COUNT.

There are exceptions to this rule: see SQUEEZE WITHOUT THE COUNT; SECONDARY SQUEEZE; TRIPLE SQUEEZE.

RULE OF ONE AND TWO. 4NT Blackwood should not be used without at least one ace if diamonds are trumps and without at least two aces if clubs are trumps. In each case you do not want partner's response to be above five of the agreed trumps unless you would then have at least three aces between you. Otherwise you may be forced to bid a slam off two aces.

RULE OF SEVEN. Devised independently by Robert Berthe of France and Gerald Fox of Napa CA. It is a guideline for declarer in holding up an ace. If he subtracts from seven the total number of cards in the suit in his own hand and the dummy, the answer is the number of times he should hold up. So with A x x opposite x x x, he should normally hold up once. Holding up twice may permit an effective shift to another suit.

RULE OF SIXTEEN. With borderline hands in fourth position, the number of spades is crucial. The rule suggests that a bid should be made only if the number of points plus the number of cards in the spade suit totals 16 or more. However, this is on the cautious side. The RULE OF FIFTEEN has merit. Also see PEARSON COUNT.

RULE OF TWELVE. A mathematical calculation applicable when the original lead is construed as a THIRD HIGHEST LEAD, The rule states, "Subtract the pips on the card led from 12; the result gives the number of higher cards than the one led in the other three hands." The application of the rule is similar to the application of the RULE OF ELEVEN. Example:

DUMMY
K 10 7
6 led   A J 8 2

If the lead of the six-spot is a third-best lead, third hand subtracts 6 from 12 and knows that six cards higher than the six-spot are held in his hand, dummy's and declarer's hand. He has three and dummy has three, so if the lead was third highest, he will be able to win cheaply by topping whatever card is played from dummy. See RULE OF FIFTEEN (2).

RULE OF TWENTY. A method of determining whether a hand weak in high cards is strong enough to warrant an opening bid. The total number of cards in the two longest suits is added to the number of high-card points. If the total is 20 or more, the hand may qualify as an opening bid. In general, such a hand qualifies if most of the high cards are in the long suits.

♠ A Q 9 5 4
♥ 6
♦ A 10 9 7 6
♣ 5 3

This hand qualifies – 10 cards in diamonds and spades plus 10 HCP equals 20.

♠ 10 9 7 5 4
♥ A
♦ K 9 7 6 5
♣ K 6

This hand also totals 20, but it does not qualify as an opening bid because most of the high cards are not in the long suits.

RULE OF TWENTY-TWO. This is a way of determining, for players who believe in light opening bids, whether particular hands should be opened. It is based on the WBF RULE OF 18. Add the combined length of the two longest suits to the high-card point count. Always open if the total is 22 or more. Never open with 19 or fewer. Open with 20 or 21 if the hand has two defensive tricks. The disadvantage of this, as with any method that concentrates on long suits, is that 4-4-3-2 is equivalent to 4-4-4-1, 5-5-2-1 is the same as 5-5-3-0, and 5-4-

4-0 is equal to 5-4-2-2. See DISTRIBUTIONAL COUNTS and ASSETS.

RULE OF TWO, THREE AND FOUR. Guides to preemptive opening bids. The number indicates how many tricks you can be set for a favorable sacrifice against a game. Modern expert practice is: Rule of Two (adverse vulnerability); Rule of Three (equal vulnerability); Rule of Four (favorable vulnerability.) Most experts will bid more freely when an opponents has opened with 2♣ or forcing 1♣, strong and artificial. See PREEMPTIVE BID.

RULE OF X-PLUS ONE. A formula conceived by Ely Culbertson as an aid to planning the play at notrump. If it is desired to establish long cards in a suit, estimate the number of losing tricks in the suit before it can be established (X) and add one to this number. This is the number of stoppers in opponents' long suit needed to be able to cash the long cards.

RULING. An adjudication by the director after an irregularity has occurred at a bridge tournament; in rubber bridge, an application of an applicable law by agreement among the players.

RULINGS OUT OF THE BOOK. In all tournament play, whether at the club level or at the level of international competition, the director should carry a Law book (LAWS OF DUPLICATE BRIDGE) to the table where an irregularity occurs and quote the Law that applies directly from the book.

RUN. (1) Bidding: to take partner out into a different suit (or notrump) if he is doubled. (2) Play or run (a suit): to cash all the winning cards of an established or solid suit by playing them one after the other.

RUN OUT OF TRUMPS. To be exhausted of trumps, usually by being forced to ruff. See CONTROL MAINTENANCE.

RUSINOW LEADS. The principle of leading the second-ranking of touching honors, devised by Sydney Rusinow and used by him, Philip Abramsohn, and Simon Rossant in the Thirties. These leads were barred in ACBL tournaments until 1964.

Ever since WHIST was the game, the standard lead from either A-K or K-Q has been the king. This ambiguity often gives third hand an unsolvable problem. Here is only one example of many:

♠ 6 5 2
♠ K   ♠ J 10 4
♠ ?

Against a suit contract by South, West leads the ♠K. If he has K-Q, East wants to play the jack to encourage him to continue. But if he has A-K, East wants to play low to get him to shift. (If East plays the jack, West may try to give East a ruff, and even if he shifts a trick will be lost if South has Q-9-x.) Some players favor the lead of the ace from A-K. Unfortunately this practice substitutes one problem for another. Often an ace should be led against a suit contract without the king. But if this lead convention is used, a guessing situation is created - so much so that one is reluctant to lead an unsupported ace even when it might be right to do so.

A sound solution was proposed about 40 years ago by Rusinow — the lead of the second highest from touching honors (king from A-K, queen from K-Q, etc.). Though endorsed by Ely Culbertson, these leads soon fell out of favor in America. They were adopted by many Europeans, however, notably the users of the ROMAN CLUB. Today many of America's better players have adopted Rusinow leads.The details are:

Ace denies the king (except with A-K doubleton — see next column).

King from A-K. Third hand should encourage with the queen or a doubleton.

Queen from K-Q. Third hand should signal with the ace or jack, but not with a doubleton if dummy has three or four small. (Declarer may duck, and partner may continue into his A-J.)

Jack from Q-J; 10 from J-10, 9 from 10-9. Note that this blends nicely into MUD leads of second highest from three spot cards.

With more than two honors in sequence, the second highest is still led (queen from K-Q-J, etc.), followed by a lower one in most cases. The Romans lead second highest from an interior sequence also (10 from K-J-10, 9 from K-10-9 or Q-10-9).

Rusinow leads are used only on the first trick against a suit contract in a suit which partner has not bid. Later in the hand, or in partner's suit, the highest card should be led from touching honors.

If the touching honors to be led are doubleton, the top card should be led. Then when you play the second honor, partner will know you have no more of the suit. On the following hand, this special feature of the Rusinow leads was crucial. Matchpoints.

```
Dlr: North          ♠ 9 5 2
Vul: E-W            ♥ K J 5
                    ♦ A K J 9 4
                    ♣ Q 3
  ♠ K Q                          ♠ A 8 6 4
  ♥ A 4                          ♥ 8 6
  ♦ 10 5 2                       ♦ 8 7 3
  ♣ K 8 7 6 4 2                  ♣ J 10 9 5
                    ♠ J 10 7 3
                    ♥ Q 10 9 7 3 2
                    ♦ Q 6
                    ♣ A
```

West	North	East	South
	1 ♦	Pass	1 ♥
Pass	2 ♥	Pass	4 ♥
All Pass			

Playing Rusinow leads, West opens the ♠K, which East instantly identifies as a doubleton (if it is a singleton, South has a hidden five-card suit). He plays the 8, then overtakes the queen, and returns a spade for West to ruff, setting the contract.

Playing standard leads, East has to guess. He cannot be sure that West would have led low to the second trick holding K-Q-x, for West might have been afraid East would shift to a club. Nor would it have helped West to have opened the queen, for East would surely have overtaken and tried for a club trick.

Against Notrump Contracts. If Rusinow leads work so well against suit contracts, should they be used against notrump also? Many think not, because the purpose of a lead against notrump is entirely different.

Against a suit, third hand has to know what specific honors the leader has, so the A-K ambiguity must be resolved. Against notrump, third hand has to know whether partner has led his side's best suit - that is, whether he has honors in the suit led, not which specific ones they are. See JOURNALIST LEADS.

S

SAC. Colloquialism for SACRIFICE, as in "We took the sac". See SACRIFICE.

S.A.C.C. A card game that was a forerunner of PLAFOND, named for its originators and reported by Sir Hugh Clayton (probably one of the originators) in *The Times of India,* July 15, 1914, placing it five or six years earlier than Bellanger's dating of the advent of Plafond in Paris. It does not appear to have caught on outside India.

A side received credit toward game only for tricks for which they had bid. Bonuses for slams were of an order that made it worth running the risk of being set: 1,000 for grand slam, 500 for small slam, 250 for five odd. (This idea of a demi-slam bonus, at times suggested for contract bridge, has always been rejected as overrewarding a timid approach to slam bidding.) Tricks not bid for received no score. In addition to scoring game for tricks bid for to a value of 30 points, a game was credited to the side that, since completion of a previous game, scored a total of 500 by honors, penalties and points for slam. The avowed purpose of this rule was to discourage "flag-flying" and allow earlier completion of a rubber. From this distance in time, however, it would seem that the rule exaggerated one of the flaws in the auction scoring base used in S.A.C.C. and in Plafond – the penalties were already severe in ratio to a 250-point rubber bonus. See HISTORY OF BRIDGE.

SACRIFICE (or SAVE). Sacrifices over opponents' games can be much more profitable at matchpoint scoring than at rubber bridge. You'll never see a successful money player chortling in triumph after going down 500 to stop a vulnerable game; he has saved few if any points, and would rather have had whatever small chance there was of defeating the opponents' game. Losing 500 instead of 620 at duplicate, however, can yield a fine result.

Even at matchpoints, a sacrifice can earn a good score only when most of the field is bidding game with the opponents' cards. Suppose South holds this hand, not vulnerable against vulnerable:

```
        ♠ J 8 5
        ♥ 8 6 2
        ♦ J 7
        ♣ K 10 7 6 4
```

West	North	East	South
		1 ♥	Pass
2 ♥	2 ♠	3 ♥	Pass
Pass	3 ♠	Pass	Pass
4 ♥	Pass	Pass	?

4 ♥ may make more often than not; South has too good a spade fit and too little defense to expect a set. Surely, 4 ♠ will go down 500 at most. Nevertheless, South should not sacrifice because the auction suggests that

most East-West pairs will not reach game.

Say the deal is played in a partscore eight times, in 4♥ twice and in 4♠ doubled twice. If 4♥ makes, North-South score ¹/₂ point for letting it play or 2¹/₂ points for saving; if 4♥ goes down, North-South score 10¹/₂ points for letting it play or ¹/₂ point for saving. So a save stands to gain 2 points or lose 10, and the odds are nowhere near 5 to 1 that 4♥ will make.

Suppose South holds the same hand on this auction:

West	North	East	South
		1♥	Pass
3♥	3♠	4♥	?

Now the whole field is likely to be in game. Suppose six pairs are allowed to play 4♥ while the other six double 4♠. A correct decision by South is worth 8 points, an incorrect one is worth 3. At those odds, the price is right for a sacrifice, since 4♥ will make perhaps three-quarters of the time.

The most important factor in sacrificing at matchpoints is the spirit of the enemy bidding. Be reluctant to save when the opponents stagger into game, even if you think. They will make it. Be alert to save against confident auctions when it appears that everyone else will also be in game.

Next in importance is the vulnerability. To be set more than the value of an enemy game is irritating at any scoring, but it is a disaster at matchpoints. Players seldom sacrifice when the vulnerability is unfavorable; if they outbid the opponents, it is with some idea that the contract may make or fail by one trick.

At equal vulnerability, one may loosen up, outbidding the opponents even when going down is certain. Here, there should be some hope of down one; otherwise, too much danger may exist of down three, for a zero. Players cannot be really frisky with sacrifices unless the vulnerability is favorable and down three is affordable. Suppose South holds:

       ♠ 2
       ♥ A Q J 8 4
       ♦ 8 5 2
       ♣ K Q 9 4

West	North	East	South
			1♥
Dbl	2♥	4♠	?

It sounds as if East-West have reached a normal game; should South save?

If the vulnerability is unfavorable, South should pass; he has little chance for ten tricks. At favorable vulnerability, South could consider trying 5♥ East-West can probably make game, but probally cannot defeat 5♥ doubled 800., (though partner's raise to 2♥ suggests only three trumps).

What about at equal vulnerability? The single most probable result is that East-West can make 4♠, while 5♥ is down two. Still, pass is advisable. The combined chance of two events — 4♠ might fail or 5♥ doubled might go for 800 — outweighs the single most likely chance.

A hidden advantage of a sacrifice is that the opponents will push higher and go down. This possibility emphasizes the factor of vulnerability. On unfavorable vulnerability, the defenders are eager to double a save; at equal, they are willing to double; at favorable, they are reluctant and may well be pushed overboard.

At favorable vulnerability, the odds favoring saves are

excellent. Players can consider a sacrifice against a confidently bid game whenever they have a trump suit and a little distribution. It is estimated that a paying non-vulnerable sacrifice exists against a vulnerable suit game between one-third and one-half the time.

Players should avoid unilateral saves — solo flights of fancy. Although a preempt is a relatively descriptive action that makes it easy for partner to sacrifice, other actions are not as well defined:

West	North	East	South
1♦		1♠	?

       ♠ —
       ♥ Q 9 6 4 2
       ♦ K J 9 6 4 2
       ♣ 9 3

Only East-West are vulnerable. Perhaps South should bid 4♦, suggesting a save if East-West reach 4♠, but letting North decide.

West	North	East	South
1♥	2♦	2♠	?

       ♠ A 6 4
       ♥ 8 4
       ♦ Q 10 7
       ♣ J 9 5 3 2

South should raise to 3♦. If East-West bid game, North can save with a shapely hand.

       ♠ 4
       ♥ J 9 8 4
       ♦ K 10 7 5 2
       ♣ J 10 3

Since South will save eventually, he should bid 5♦ *immediately*. If South prevents East-West from exchanging more information, they may land in the wrong major suit at the five level, miss a slam or misjudge by doubling. See ADVANCE SAVE.

       ♠ 8 7
       ♥ J 9 8 4
       ♦ K 10 7 4 2
       ♣ Q 5

South should bid a preemptive 4♦. With a strong hand, South would cuebid. South suggests a save-oriented hand, but with slightly too much defense or too little distribution to save himself. See PHANTOM SACRIFICE.

SAFETY LEVEL. The maximum level a partnership is willing to reach, presumably without undue risk, in order to investigate a higher contract or compete against enemy bids.

At times one partner may wish to suggest a slam. If his hand is not strong enough to guarantee a contract above the level of game, he must make a slam try below game. The game level is then his safety level. If his hand is strong enough to guarantee the safety of an above-game contract (such as 4NT or five of a major suit), he may, if he wishes, make a slam try above game. In this case, the safety level is 4NT, 5♠ or whatever.

When the bidding becomes competitive, the previous bids of a partnership often indicate they hold the strength to reach a certain level. This is their safety level and the contract should not be sold (undoubled) to the opponents below this level. See LAW OF TOTAL TRICKS. For example: South opens with a strong two-bid, forcing to game. If East-West enter the auction, North-South have a safety level at game, implicit in South's bid. North-South will not allow East-West to buy the con-

tract below game unless they feel a satisfactory penalty can be obtained. See also FORCING BID; FORCING SEQUENCES; SLAM BIDDING.

SAFETY PLAY. For the safety play that applies to a specific SUIT COMBINATION, see that heading. This entry emphasizes applications of the safety-play idea.

In a broad sense, a safety play is any play by which declarer tries to reduce the risk of defeat. If the term were so defined, the best play on any hand would amount to a safety play. However, safety play invariably refers to the management of a specific suit; a safety play is the play of a suit to cope with an unfavorable break and minimize the danger of losing the contract.

Most types of safety plays are appropriate only at rubber bridge or IMP play. Since a safety play requires declarer to sacrifice possible overtricks, it is losing tactics at a normal contract at matchpoint duplicate, where overtricks have as much significance as the contract itself. See MATCHPOINT PLAY.

Many plays that are wrongly called "safety plays" only demonstrate good technique and hence are correct at any form of scoring:

(a) K Q 10 9 2   (b) K Q 9 8 3

   A 6 4 3   A 5 4 2

In (a) declarer assures four tricks against any 4-0 break by cashing the king or queen first; in (b) declarer should take the ace first in case the left-hand defender has J-10-7-6. These are NOT safety plays. They are simply correct handling of suit combinations.

A true safety play is like an insurance policy: declarer pays a premium — one or more tricks — for protection against a break that would otherwise be fatal.

```
        ♠ 7 5 4 2
        ♥ K 4
        ♦ A 7 5
        ♣ A Q 7 5

        ♠ A Q 8 6 3
        ♥ 8 3
        ♦ K Q 6
        ♣ K 9 2
```

South plays 4♠, and West leads the ♥J. East takes two heart tricks and shifts to a diamond. South can afford to lose one trump trick, but not two. He therefore starts trumps by cashing the ace, guarding against a singleton king with West. South then reaches dummy to lead a second trump toward his hand. This holds the loss to one trick whenever possible.

At matchpoint scoring, South could not afford to play safe in this normal contract; he would try for an overtrick with a first-round finesse of the ♠Q.

Some safety plays merely improve declarer's chances; others offer him a sure thing.

```
        ♠ 7 6
        ♥ A Q 4
        ♦ 7 6 5 4
        ♣ K J 5 2

        ♠ A K
        ♥ K 3 2
        ♦ A 9 3 2
        ♣ A 9 4 3
```

South plays 3NT, and West leads the ♠Q. South counts eight top tricks; a third club trick will give him game.

South should lead a club to dummy's king and return a club. If East discards, South can take the ace and lead toward the ♣J; if East follows low on the second club, South plays the 9. If West can win the trick, clubs have split 3-2, and South later takes the ♣A and a fourth club.

Suppose the North-South cards are:

```
        ♠ 7 6
        ♥ A Q 4
        ♦ 7 6 5 4
        ♣ K J 5 2

        ♠ A K
        ♥ J 10 3
        ♦ A 9 3 2
        ♣ A 9 4 3
```

Here, South cannot tell immediately whether he should play safe. After winning the first spade, he should lead a heart to the queen. If the queen wins, South can count eight tricks and should employ the safety play in clubs. If East has the ♥K, South needs four club tricks; he should finesse the ♣J.

Some deals offer a chance for a partial safety play.

```
        ♠ 8 4
        ♥ Q 8
        ♦ A K J 7 5 3 2
        ♣ 7 5

        ♠ A Q 3
        ♥ J 9 4 2
        ♦ 6 4
        ♣ A K Q 6
```

South opens 1NT, and North raises to 3NT. West leads the ♠J: 4, king, ace. When South leads a diamond, West plays the 8. The true safety play, which South might consider at rubber bridge, is a low diamond from dummy, winning if West has Q-10-9-8. At matchpoints, South cannot afford this play, but he can compromise by finessing the ♦J. See also EXPECTATION.

SAN FRANCISCO CONVENTION. A 4NT convention, sometimes called the WARREN CONVENTION, with responses showing aces and kings in one bid. Aces are counted as three points and kings as one point, and the responses are:

5♣	less than 3 points
5♦	3 points
5♥	4 points
5♠	5 points
5NT	6 points, etc.

By inspecting his own hand, the 4NT bidder can almost always judge what his partner's response represents in aces and kings. A response of 5♥ must show an ace and a king, or four kings. The convention results in some disadvantage if the responder's hand is strong. If he has three aces, the response of 6♥ may take his side too high. For a similar idea, see NORMAN FOUR NOTRUMP.

SANCTION. The permission given by the ACBL to a club, unit or district to hold a duplicate event within ACBL territory. In general a specific sanction to hold a tournament must be obtained from the ACBL well in advance of the date scheduled for the tournament. The ACBL sends the sponsoring organization a form suitable for use in reporting the results of the tournament and this report is used by the ACBL to record MASTERPOINTS won by the contestants.

SANCTIONED GAMES. Approximately 3500 bridge clubs in North America have been given the right to hold games sanctioned by ACBL. These clubs award masterpoints based on the type of game and the number of participants. Information concerning masterpoints won is relayed to ACBL either on disk or on a monthly report form. Formerly masterpoints were distributed to the players as fractional certificates which had to be bundled by the player and mailed to ACBL. However, the advent of the computer put an end to the need for the fractional certificates.

SANDWICH. A term coined in Europe to describe an overcall or double made in fourth position after both opponents have bid and partner has passed.

West	North	East	South
1 ♦	Pass	1 ♠	?

The expert consensus in BWS 2001 was that 2 ♦ (84%) and 2 ♠ (88%) should both be natural. Jumps to 3 ♦ or 3 ♠ were undefined. 1NT was judged natural (76%) although obviously it is for takeout by a passed hand.

West	North	East	South
1 ♥	Pass	1NT	?

The expert consensus was that double is takeout of opener's suit (96%); 2 ♥ is similar to that bid directly over an opening suit, making it Michaels for most partnerships (90%); 2NT shows the low unbid suits, clubs and diamonds in this case (90%).

West	North	East	South
1 ♥	Pass	2 ♣	?

The expert consensus was that 2 ♥ should be for takeout (59%) and 2NT also (79%). 3 ♣ should be natural (46%) but there was a large minority (39%) favoring a takeout interpretation. The same meanings were judged appropriate after a jump response, weak or strong, such as 1 ♣-Pass-2 ♥.

West	North	East	South
1 ♥	Pass	2 ♥	?

There is considerable disagreement in this situation, and partnership discussion is needed. A large minority (41% in BWS 2001) bid as if acting over a weak-two opening. Many favor "prebalancing", in which South bids as if acting after two passes. 66% favor the use of a 3 ♥ cuebid as Michaels, majors over a minor, major-minor over a major. A minority (27%) use the cuebid to ask for a stopper for 3NT.

Preemptive use of a jump overcall was favored by 55%. Some of this group (13%) made an exception of a jump over a major to four of a minor, using that to show that minor and the unbid major. A minority (30%) preferred the strong jump overcall.

A strong majority (80%) bid similarly after a jump raise, constructive or preemptive, of an opening bid; or a raise of a preemptive opening.

Artificial raises of the opening bid present a variety of problems. If it is a game-force, 74% believe the double should be lead-directing and/or sacrifice-oriented. If it is a limit raise, the double should be for takeout of opener's suit. (42%, but 38% favored lead-directing). If it is a preemptive raise, the double should be takeout of opener's suit (64%, while 30% favored "suit doubled and constructive").

If a preemptive opening receives a new-suit response, forcing or not, a double should show the unbid suits. If a transfer bid is used, the fourth player should double to show the suit bid, and cuebid for takeout of the suit implied (53%).

SANDWICH DEFENSE. See SURROUNDING PLAY.

SANDWICH NOTRUMP. A 1NT bid showing a two-suiter, usually at least 5-5, made between two bidding opponents. Many who employ this convention use double to show a reasonable hand and 1NT to show a weaker hand.

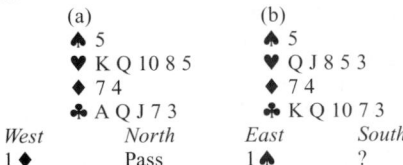

	(a)		(b)
	♠ 5		♠ 5
	♥ K Q 10 8 5		♥ Q J 8 5 3
	♦ 7 4		♦ 7 4
	♣ A Q J 7 3		♣ K Q 10 7 3

West	North	East	South
1 ♦	Pass	1 ♠	?

Both hands qualify as sandwich notrump bids. However, many players would double with (a) and bid 1NT with (b).

SANS ATOUT. Notrump. The term is French.

SAVE. See SACRIFICE.

SCANDINAVIAN CHAMPIONSHIPS. See NORDIC CHAMPIONSHIPS. For results see Appendix IV.

SCANIAN SIGNALS. A combination of standard SIGNALS and UPSIDE-DOWN SIGNALS in an attempt to get the best of both worlds.

Use normal signals unless:
(a) Dummy has a finessable card:

```
            J 7 4 2
  A K 10 5              Q 8 3
            9 6
```

After the lead of the ace or king, according to method, East signals upside-down with the 3 and West can lead the 10.

(b) The opener is known to be short or the signaler is known to be long:

```
          A J
  8 7 3            K Q 10 4
          9 6 5 2
```

The 8 is led, top of nothing, and dummy plays the ace. Signal upside-down with the 4.

Devised by Anders Wirgren.

SCHENKEN SYSTEM (or SCHENKEN CLUB). An artificial 1 ♣ system devised by Howard Schenken and played by him in World Championship competition in partnership with Peter Leventritt. The main features of the system are:

(1) 1 ♣ opening. Forcing, and used on almost all strong hands. It shows a minimum of 17 high-card points or the distributional equivalent. There are three types: balanced notrump type with 19-22; slightly unbalanced hand with 17 or more; strong distribution with 14 or more.

1 ♦ is the conventional negative response, usually 0-6 points. 2 ♣ is also artificial, showing a semi-positive response of 7-8 points, including at least one king or ace, and promising a rebid. Other responses are positive, natural, and forcing to game. After an overcall up to 3 ♦, a double is "positive," for takeout, and shows at least 9 points.

After a 1 ♦ negative response, showing in principle fewer than 7 points but perhaps 7 or 8 without the re-

quirements for a 2♣ response: a non-jump suit rebid may be passed; a jump suit rebid is forcing for one round; a 1NT rebid shows 19-20; a 2NT rebid shows 21-22. STAYMAN is used after a 1NT response or rebid.

(2) One bids in other suits are limited, with a maximum of 16 points. Responder normally passes with less than 8 points.

All raises and notrump responses are limited and nonforcing. A jump to game in a major may be based on high-card strength or distribution because the limited opening has excluded slam chances. 3♣ response to a major is equivalent to a strong raise (16-17 points including distribution) and requests opener to bid a singleton.

(3) 1NT opening is standard (16-18). 2♣ response is non-forcing STAYMAN. 2♦ shows an unbalanced responding hand (with a singleton or void), no four-card major. It is game forcing and requests opener to show major suit stoppers.

(4) 2♣ is a natural opening with at least a good five-card club suit. A response of 2♦ asks opener to show a four-card major.

(5) 2♦. An artificial forcing opening bid used to locate specific honors. A 2♥ response denies an ace; other minimum responses are ace-showing, except that 2NT shows the ♥A . With two aces, responder jumps in the higher ranking ace with touching aces, 3NT with non-touching aces, or 4♣ with the black aces. The opener follows with minimum rebids to locate kings and queens in the same way.

A 2NT rebid over 2♥ shows 23-25, and may be passed. A 3NT rebid shows 26-27.

(6) 2♠ and 2♥ are weak two-bids, 8-12 points and a suit of reasonable strength. 2NT is the only forcing response.

(7) 2NT. Shows a minimum of five cards in each minor suit with 10-12 high card points not vulnerable, 13-16 high card points vulnerable.

(8) 3NT opening is based on a solid minor suit with 8-9 playing tricks and no side suit worse than Q-x.

(9) 3♣. A solid six- or seven-card suit, 10-15 points.

(10) Preemptive jump overcalls depending on the vulnerability.

SCHROEDER SQUEEZE. A triple trump squeeze without the count in a three-card position. This unique ending was executed in play by Dirk Schroeder of Germany.

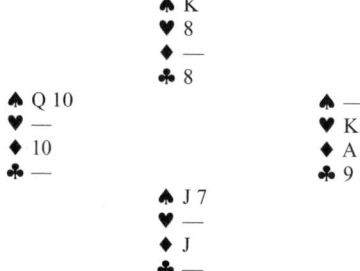

With spades trump, and the lead in North, on the lead of the ♠K East is squeezed. If he throws the winning heart or club South would have a winner to lead from dummy at the twelfth trick. If he sluffs the ♦A, South would ruff something and score his ♦J at the finish. The complete deal was:

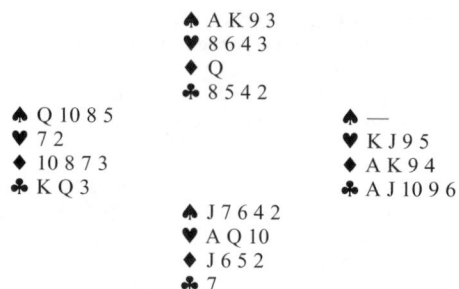

In 3♠ doubled the defense led two rounds of clubs. South ruffed, entered dummy with a high spade, finessed the ♥10, and surrendered a diamond. After a third round of clubs was ruffed in the closed hand South ruffed a diamond, finessed the ♥Q, and led the ♥A. West ruffed and led a diamond which was ruffed in dummy to produce the ending shown.

SCHWAB CUP. For the World Pairs Championship, first contested in Cannes in 1962. Originally presented by Charles M. Schwab in 1933 for a contest between the United States and England (see ANGLO-AMERICAN MATCHES). The trophy was redonated to the WORLD BRIDGE FEDERATION by the heirs of Ely Culbertson. For results of WORLD PAIRS, see Appendix V. For results of Anglo-American matches, see Appendix IV.

SCIENTISTS v. TRADITIONALISTS. Three matches have been played, with somewhat inconclusive results, to test whether players using very few conventions can do as well or better than players using complex, artificial methods.

(1) New York 1965. Scientists (Roth-Stone; Stayman-Mitchell; Jordan-Robinson;) defeated Traditionalists (Murray-Kehela; Becker-Hayden; Mathe-Schleifer) by 53 IMPs over 180 deals.

(2) London 1990. Scientists (Soloway-Goldman; Garozzo-Eisenberg) defeated Traditionalists (Zia, Chagas, Wolff, Forrester, rotating) by two sessions to one, although trailing in IMPs.

(3) London 1992. Scientists (Hamman-Wolff; Rodwell-Meckstroth;) defeated Traditionalists (Chagas-M.Branco; Forrester-Robson) by 70 IMPs over 128 deals, winning a $50,000 prize.

SCISSORS COUP. A play aimed at cutting the opponents' communications, usually in order to prevent a ruff (in the past called, less descriptively, "the coup without a name").

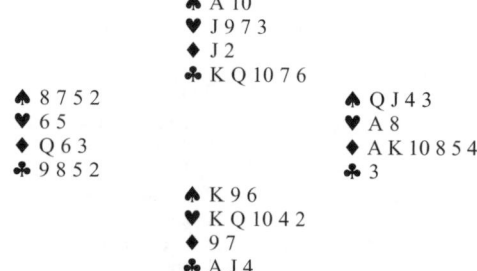

South plays in 4♥ after East has opened the bidding with 1♦. South feels happy when it appears that there are only three losers, but feels much less happy when

East wins the opening diamond lead with the king, and shifts to the ♣3. It is obvious that this is a singleton and that West has a diamond entry to give his partner a ruff.

South must try to cut the diamond communication, so he cashes the ♠ A-K and leads the ♠9. Dummy's diamond is discarded, allowing East to win, and the defense can make only one more trick. South's play succeeds whenever East has both missing spade honors, or if East has a tripleton queen and fails to unblock.

SCORE. (1) Noun: the number of game or premium points earned as a result of the bidding and play of a hand, rubber, or session of bridge. (2) Verb: to record the score.

There are slight differences, due to the nature of the games, between the scoring at rubber bridge, CHICAGO, and tournament bridge. In addition, tournament bridge has different scoring procedures and values, depending on the type of event. See BOARD-A-MATCH SCORING; CUMULATIVE SCORE; INTERNATIONAL MATCH POINTS; LAWS (Laws 75 to 84); LAWS OF DUPLICATE (Laws 73, 74); MATCHPOINT; MATCHPOINT SCORING; TOTAL POINTS; VICTORY POINTS.

SCORECARD. See PICKUP SLIP; SCORE PAD; RECAPITULATION SHEET. A personal (or private) scorecard used in tournaments is called a CONVENTION CARD. When used in PARTY or PROGRESSIVE BRIDGE, it is called a TALLY.

SCORE CORRECTIONS. These are provided for in the regulations concerning tournament bridge.

The correction period for scoring errors is set forth as follows in Law 79C of the LAWS OF DUPLICATE BRIDGE:

"An error in computing or tabulating the agreed-upon score, whether made by a player or scorer, may be corrected until the expiration of the period specified by the sponsoring organization. Unless the sponsoring organization specifies a later time, this correction period expires 30 minutes after the official score has been completed and made available for inspection. An earlier time may be specified when required by the special nature of a contest."

Corrections are made by the scoring staff whenever the scoreslip is clearly in error - i.e., shows incorrect vulnerability, incorrect addition, etc., or when the slip has been incorrectly transcribed. When the correction involves a question of the results themselves — whether a contract was defeated one or two tricks, or whether extra tricks were scored — the correction may be made, within the limits of the correction period, only if there is reasonable proof that a different score was achieved at the table. If both pairs list the same result on their private scorecards, this usually is considered satisfactory proof of the scoring error. See LAWS OF DUPLICATE, Law 75.

ACBL regulations in this area changed radically in 1994. At ACBL events, the score correction period for scorer and player errors expires at the announced starting time of the next session for PLAY-THROUGH events and one hour before the announced starting time of the session following a qualification. For the last (or only) session of an event, the correction period expires 24 hours after the completion of the event or 30 minutes after the completion of the last event of the tournament. Note that this is in effect for scorer errors as well as player errors. Once the correction period expires, no more score corrections can be made. This is a major change from the past — scorer's errors were subject to cor-

rection at any time through the end of the tournament.

At rubber bridge, the rules set a time limit beyond which a correction may not be claimed — in most cases, after the score of the rubber has been determined and agreed upon.

SCORE PAD. A printed tablet of sheets of paper used to keep a record of the scores in a game of rubber or Chicago bridge. Score pads come in various shapes and sizes, and some are imprinted with the name of the club at which they are used, but they are all ruled with printed lines, leaving spaces for entering game and partial score results and extra premiums such as undertrick penalties and slam and rubber bonuses and honors.

In North America each sheet of the pad will have a large cross at the top, like a letter X, so that players can keep track of the deal number at Chicago.

SCORE SHEET. In club games, the summary sheet on which the MATCHPOINTS won by a pair are entered for ease in totaling; in larger tournaments, the RECAPITULATION SHEET, to which the scores are posted from the PICKUP SLIPS. These are seldom used in tournaments any longer because most tournaments are scored by computer programs.

SCORER, OFFICIAL. At many tournaments outside of the ACBL, a person or group is given control of score keeping. In the ACBL, keeping score is one of the duties of the tournament director. See SCORING, TOURNAMENT DIRECTOR.

SCORPION. The site of a remarkable bridge game that occurred in 1917 in the Turkish harbor of Constantinople, now Istanbul. Alan Truscott described it as follows in the *New York Times.*

"An American gunboat, the Scorpion, was attached to the American Embassy. It was boarded by the Turks, who were German allies, when the United States entered World War I. The German Navy, present in force, wanted the Scorpion for use as a decoy, but the crew much preferred to be interned under Turkish control. The ship's fate was to be determined by Talat Pasha, the powerful Minister of the Interior, who happened to be an acquaintance of the ship's captain, Lt. Cdr. Herbert Babbitt.

"Bridge was almost certainly born in the Ottoman Empire, and many of the Turkish magnates were enthusiasts. Babbitt had a happy thought. He challenged Talat to a rubber, with the ship as the stake. If he lost, the Scorpion would go to the Germans. If he won, the vessel would be interned where she was. Talat accepted this remarkably creative suggestion, and play began. Everything hinged on the final deal on which Babbitt had to play 4NT, a contract that was very rare in the auction game. He made the contract, Talat kept his word, and the Scorpion and her crew remained in Turkish waters till the war was over. For the rest of his naval career her captain was known as Four Notrump Babbitt.

SCORESLIP. A printed form on which the results of a round of duplicate play are entered. Caddies collect the scoreslips after each round and give them to the director, who enters the scores either in the computer or on a recap sheet. See PICKUP SLIP, SCORING,SCORING FORMS, TRAVELING SCORESLIP.

SCORING. Tallying the results of a game or event. At

almost all tournaments throughout the world today, scoring is done by computer. Scores are now available to the competitors within only a few minutes of the finish of the game. Whereas high tops on a board were extremely difficult to tally when scoring was done manually, high tops are now common because they are child's play for computers. Today's sophisticated computer programs even allow the director or scorer to rearrange the movement if an irregularity forces changes.

Whether the scoring is done by computer or manually, the system of obtaining the results for each round is the same in general. In games where traveling scoreslips are used, the slips are picked up after the last time the board attached to that slip is played. In games where pickup slips are used, the slips are picked up after each round. With traveling slips, scoring is done during and after the last round. With pickup slips, the scores can be entered either on a recap sheet or on the computer after each round.

Some clubs still use manual scoring. As each board comes out of play, the traveling scoreslip is matchpointed by the director, the scorer or a volunteer. The scores from each board are posted on a recap sheet. When all the scores are posted, each board is matchpointed. When all the boards have been matchpointed, all the scores are added and crosschecked. If the scoresheet is in balance, then the rankings are assigned. Sometimes the starting positions for the next session also are placed on the scoresheet if the event is a multiple-session event. When computers are used, the travelers are collected after the next-to-last round. The scores are entered during the last round, and final-round scores are tallied on pickup slips. If pickup slips are used, the scores can be entered round-by-round, but the matchpointing, adding and ranking still must be done after the last score ticket is entered.

If the game is scored by computer, the scorer merely enters all the scores as they become available. When all the scores are entered, the scorer keys the necessary command and the computer does the rest — matchpointing, adding and ranking. The program is set up so that the computer also can provide printouts of the scoring of the event, including individual scoresheets for the players.

SCORING ACROSS THE FIELD. A method of scoring a multi-section MATCHPOINT event. The score on each board is matchpointed not just against other contestants in the same section but against the contestants in all sections playing in the same direction.Of course this requires that the boards be duplicated across the field. This once was a laborous task, but computers have made it easy.

SCORING FORM. The most common scoring form, used at most clubs in North America and much of the rest of the world, is the traveling scoreslip. One such scoring form is inserted into each board during the first round of play. Each time the board is played, the North player enters the result and the pair numbers on the slip. At the conclusion of play, the slip is matchpointed in preparation for being copied onto the recap sheet or the computer.

The recap sheet, also known as the recapitulation sheet, is used when manual scoring is done. It is a large sheet wide enough to permit the entry of all boards in play and long enough to permit the entry of all pairs — or teams — in play. The recap sheet when a computer is used is printed upon command by the computer.

Another common scoring form is the pickup slip or scoreslip used for entering the scores of a round at tour-

naments and some clubs. The pickup slip has spaces for the two or three board numbers for the round, the key pair numbers, the contracts, the fate of the contracts and the scores. These are collected at the conclusion of each round and immediately copied on the recap sheet or fed into the computer.

In team events of head-on competition, each pair keeps a running score of the results on the boards they play, and verification of these slips at each table makes it possible for each team to determine its own score, either in total point or IMP scoring. See PICKUP SLIP, RECAPITULATION SHEET, TRAVELING SCORE-SLIP.

SCORING TABLE. The current scoring table is set out in LAWS (Law 81) and LAWS OF DUPLICATE (Law 77). See also FRENCH SCORING and SCORING VARIANTS. Today's scoring table includes few deviations from the original developed by Vanderbilt in 1925. It has survived considerable tinkering, especially in the 1932 code. The 1927 Laws provided that each trick in a notrump contract was worth 35 points; that the premium for making a doubled contract was increased from 50 to 100 if vulnerable (if redoubled, the premiums were 100 and 200); and that the penalties for undertricks increased as the tricks won fell farther short of contract, as follows:

PENALTIES (1927)

Undertricks (Scored in Adversaries' honor score):

	Points
If Undoubled (When Declarer is Not Vulnerable)	
per trick	50
If Undoubled (When Declarer is Vulnerable)	
for first trick	100
for subsequent tricks	200
If Doubled (When Declarer is Not Vulnerable)	
for first two tricks, per trick	100
for third and fourth tricks, per trick	200
for subsequent tricks, per trick	400
If Doubled (When Declarer is Vulnerable)	
for the first trick	200
for subsequent tricks, per trick	400

Redoubling doubles the doubled premiums and penalties.

Partly on the theory that the higher scores were largely responsible for the enormous popularity of contract bridge, the 1932 Laws sharply increased slam bonuses and also increased penalties, with nonvulnerable undertricks as well as vulnerable undertricks punished on a rising scale.

Furthermore, the value of tricks made in notrump contracts alternated: first, third, fifth, and seventh trick were worth 30 each; the second, fourth, and sixth, 40 each. Also, the premium for making a doubled contract was dropped.

The distortions imposed by this inflated scoring were corrected within three years – the shortest period ever for the issuance of a new Laws code. In the 40 years following the issuance of the 1935 code, the only change in scoring was the restoration in the 1943 Laws of a bonus for making a doubled contract, 50 points whether or not vulnerable. The current codes, established in 1987 for Duplicate Bridge and in 1993 for Contract Bridge, embody three changes:

(1) Non-vulnerable doubled penalties for defeats by four or more tricks became 800, 1100, 1400, etc. instead of 700, 900, 1100, etc. (Redoubled penalties are twice those numbers.)

(2) The bonus for making a redoubled contract was increased from 50 to 100.

(3) In the Contract Bridge Laws the bonus for having

a partscore in an unfinished rubber was increased from 50 to 100.

SCORING VARIANTS. Several kinds of scoring variants have been introduced that are aimed at making tournament bridge or rubber bridge a better competition. Among the more important are: (1) FRENCH SCORING, to make four of a major and 4NT of equal value. (2) PENALTY LIMITS in TOTAL POINT SCORING and PROGRESSIVE BRIDGE to limit the SWING on one hand. (3) Different TOPS in final competition of multi-session events or all sessions of important tournaments. (4) IMPS FOR PAIR GAMES, to make conditions comparable to INTERNATIONAL MATCH-POINTS. (5) HYBRID SCORING to combine advantages of BOARD-A-MATCH and aggregate scores in team events.

SCRAMBLED MITCHELL MOVEMENT. A modification of the MITCHELL MOVEMENT, used when it is desired to produce one winning pair. Pairs play some boards North-South and the rest East-West. This is accomplished by switching the arrows designating North so that they point to the original East simultaneously in certain rounds. The original East-West pairs, having adopted a moving pattern, continue to move, and the original North-South pairs remain at their tables, even though the arrows have been switched and they are playing the East-West hands.

Arrow-switching arrangements devised by Russell Baldwin, George Beynon, Frank Farrington and Lawrence Rosler may be used but are obsolescent. Modern research by Olof Hanner, using computer analysis, recommends the following:

With odd numbers of tables:

Tables	Arrow East in rounds
7	6, 7
9	6, 8, 9
11	7, 8, 10, 11
13	7, 9, 12, 13
15	7, 10, 12, 14, 15

With even number of tables using relay-and-byestand:

Tables	Arrow East in rounds
6	5, 6
8	4, 7, 8
10	4, 6, 9, 10
12	5, 7, 11, 12
14	7, 9, 10, 11, 14

(But Table 1 does not switch. It is sharing with the last table).

With even number of tables using a skip:

Tables	Arrow East in rounds
6	5
8	2, 3, 5, 6, 7
10	2, 5, 6, 7, 8, 9
12	3, 5, 9, 10
14	4, 5, 10, 12

Frequent arrow-switching is a controversial matter. A mathematical paper by Dr. Ross Moore of Sydney, Australia, asserts that "Too many arrow-switches spoil the balance."

SCRAMBLING. (1) The art of maneuvering into a tolerable contract when the opponents are intent on collecting a low-level penalty. This often calls for the use of an SOS REDOUBLE. One of the commonest situations occurs when 1NT is doubled for penalties.

Here is an example:

	West		East	
	♠ A Q 6 2		♠ J 5 4	
	♥ A K 7 6		♥ 4 3	
	♦ 8 5		♦ J 7 6 4 2	
	♣ J 9 4		♣ 6 5 2	

West	North	East	South
1♣	Dbl	Pass	Pass
Redbl	Pass	1♦	Dbl
Redbl	Pass	1♠	Pass
Pass	Dbl	All Pass	

Both redoubles are SOS, and the best spot is reached. West will probably make six tricks. See DEFENSE TO DOUBLE OF 1NT.

(2) An attempt to score extra trump tricks by ruffing in the long trump hand with trumps that would otherwise be losers.

SCRAMBLING PLAY, SCRAMBLING SIGNAL. See DECEPTIVE PLAY.

SCRAMBLING 2NT. (Also referred to as GROPE). In competitive sequences many partnerships play that 2NT is almost never natural. In particular a non-jump 2NT in response to a takeout double almost always falls into one of two categories — it is either Lebensohl, or a scramble. Scrambling 2NT bids show two or more places to play; typically partner responds assuming the lowest unbid suits. So in an auction such as:

1♠	Pass	2♠	Pass
Pass	Dbl	Pass	2NT

The 2NT bid is best played as artificial, and since both hands have passed at their first turn to speak there can be no suggestion that 2NT would be Lebensohl. Accordingly the takeout doubler responds assuming his partner has the minors, expecting that his partner will remove from an unacceptable suit. Similarly:

1♣	1♥	Pass	1♠
Pass	2♥	Pass	Pass
Dbl	Pass	2NT	

The last call in the auction can be played to show a minor-suit oriented hand – probably 4-3 or 5-3 in the minors.

SCRATCH. (1) In pairs play, to place high enough in a section or overall standings to earn masterpoints (colloq.) (2) In a handicap game, a pair with a zero handicap is said to be a scratch pair. (3) Starting with nothing, as in "starting from scratch."

SCREEN. An opaque barrier placed diagonally across the bridge table so that no player can see his partner. Perforce each player can see only one opponent. The screen has an opening in the center where the board in play is placed. Directly above the board is some sort of curtain arrangement that can be lifted or pulled aside once the bidding is complete and the opening lead has been made. This permits all players to see the cards being played, but the opening is shallow enough that the players still cannot see their partner's face. The screen extends to the floor, blocking partners' feet from each other, the result of a foot-tapping incident in the 1975 Bermuda Bowl (see BERMUDA INCIDENT). The bidding is done by BIDDING BOX.

Bids from one side of the table are revealed to the players on the opposite side by using a TRAY. Since both bids are "trayed" to the other side of the table simulta-

neously, it is usually difficult to discern who huddled if the tray is slow in returning.

Screens were used for the first time by the ACBL during the Vanderbilt Knockout Teams in 1974. The first appearance of screens at a world championship took place at the 1975 Bermuda Bowl in Bermuda. At first there was a great deal of controversy about the use of screens. Those who opposed their use felt that screens would create the public impression that a lot of cheating takes place in high-level bridge. They also felt that screens would be distracting and dehumanizing. Those in favor felt that screens would forestall charges of cheating (see CHEATING ACCUSATIONS).

However, screens received almost unanimous acclaim from the players who used them right from the outset. The players felt it made competing ethically much easier – they no longer had to worry about making facial expressions, they no longer had to bend over backward because of partner's huddle – they no longer knew when partner huddled. Certain rule violations, such as leads out of turn and bids out of turn became very rare because only one side of the table was involved at a time and such violations could be adjusted without any improper information being transmitted to partner. Cheating accusations have been virtually non-existent with screens in use. As a result of these benefits, screens are used in late rounds of almost all major team and some pair championships, and in all world and international championships.

SCREEN-MATE. When screens are in use, the opponent on your side of the screen.

SCRIP. Financial certificates issued by the ACBL for use as prizes at tournaments. The certificates may be used to purchase bridge supplies, pay ACBL dues or pay for tournament entries.

SEAT. The position which a contestant takes at a table; usually designated by one of the four principal points of the compass, North, South, East, or West. The first two and the last two are partners, and each pair is the opponent of the other pair.

SEAT ASSIGNMENTS. See ASSIGNMENT OF SEATS.

SEATING ASSIGNMENTS. At duplicate tournaments in North America, the ENTRIES sold to the players carry a section designation, a table number, and a direction. These are the seating assignments. For subsequent sessions of the same event, players either take their original seating assignments and await DIRECTOR'S INSTRUCTIONS, or pick up a new entry blank or GUIDE CARD for the subsequent session. Sometimes the new assignment is printed on the recap sheet.

SECOND GAME. The second game of a rubber. Two games are required to win a rubber, and at the conclusion of a rubber a side may have won one, two, or no games, during that rubber. The winning of any second game immediately ends the rubber.

SECOND GUESSER. See RESULT PLAYER.

SECOND HAND. (1) The player to the left of the dealer. (2) The player who plays second to a trick.

SECOND-HAND PLAY. The old whist rule of *second hand low* is sound enough as a guide and gains in many positions:

```
            A 4 2
J 6                   K 10 8 3
            Q 9 7 5
```

South, the declarer, leads the 2 from dummy. If East plays the king, South can win three tricks; if East plays low, South wins two tricks.

```
            J 6
A Q 8 3               9 4
            K 10 7 5 2
```

South, playing in notrump, leads the deuce from his hand; West gains by playing low.

In a suit contract, declarer leads a possible singleton toward a suit in dummy headed by K-Q or K-J. Unless the left-hand defender sees an obvious reason to grab the ace (such as having the setting trick to cash in another suit), he should duck promptly. To play the ace may benefit declarer, who avoids a guess if dummy has K-J or sets up two tricks if dummy has K-Q.

```
              ♠ J 9 6 4
              ♥ K Q 5 3
              ♦ 7 5
              ♣ J 6 4
♠ 5                        ♠ K 2
♥ A 10 7 2                 ♥ J 9 6 4
♦ Q 10 8 4 2               ♦ A 9 3
♣ K 9 3                    ♣ Q 10 7 5
              ♠ A Q 10 8 7 3
              ♥ 8
              ♦ K J 6
              ♣ A 8 2
```

West	North	East	South
			1 ♠
Pass	2 ♠	Pass	4 ♠
All Pass			

West leads the ♦ 4, and East wins the ace and returns a diamond to the king. South elects to cash the ♠ A and next leads a heart. Even though declarer has a singleton, West can defeat the contract only by playing low.

A prompt duck is often best in the reverse situation: when declarer leads a singleton from dummy.

Second hand low has many exceptions. Following are the most important reasons to play second hand high:

(1) To win a trick at no cost:
```
            Q 5
K J 9 4 2
```
Declarer leads low toward the Q-5. West should take the king unless he desperately wants East on lead or thinks East may have the singleton ace.
```
            K 6 4 2
A Q J 8
```
Declarer leads low toward the K-6-4-2. A duck by West is unlikely to gain and may lose the ace.

(2) To assure a later trick:
```
            K 7 5
                       Q J 4
```
Declarer leads the 5 from dummy. East should split his honors to assure one trick.

(3) To give partner information:
```
            9 6 3
A 4 2                  J 10 8 7
            K Q 5
```
Declarer leads the 3 from dummy. East should play

the jack, promising a sequence. When West captures an honor with the ace, he can safely return the suit. See PLAY FROM EQUALS.

(4) To prevent a suit establishment:

```
              A J 10 7 5
K 8 3                      Q 9 6
              4 2
```

Dummy has no entry outside this suit. If South leads the deuce, West must play the king, and South can take only one trick. West would also play high from Q-8-3. If West instead plays low, South finesses the jack, and East must duck to stop South from winning four tricks.

(5) To block a suit:

```
              K 9 6 5 3 2
J 8 4                      A 10
              Q 7
```

South leads the 2 from dummy. If East plays low, South wins the queen and plays low from dummy on the next lead to establish the suit. By playing the ace at once, East blocks the suit.

(6) To gain time:

```
              ♠ Q 6
              ♥ K 10 6 3
              ♦ 10 8 5 3
              ♣ K Q 4
♠ K J 8 4 2                 ♠ 10 7 3
♥ A 8 4                     ♥ 9 7 2
♦ J 6                       ♦ A 4 2
♣ 9 5 2                     ♣ J 10 7 3
              ♠ A 9 5
              ♥ Q J 5
              ♦ K Q 9 7
              ♣ A 8 6
```

West	North	East	South
			1NT
Pass	3NT	All Pass	

West leads the ♠4 and dummy's queen wins. When South next leads a diamond, East should put up the ace to return a spade, establishing West's suit while West retains an entry. If East instead plays low, South scores a diamond trick and switches to hearts to establish nine tricks.

(7) To break up an endplay:

```
              ♠ K 10 3 2
              ♥ A 5 2
              ♦ A Q 7
              ♣ K 5 3
♠ 7                        ♠ 8 5
♥ J 10 9 6                 ♥ Q 8 7 3
♦ 10 8 4 2                 ♦ K J 9 6
♣ J 9 7 6                  ♣ Q 8 2
              ♠ A Q J 9 6 4
              ♥ K 4
              ♦ 5 3
              ♣ A 10 4
```

South plays at 6♠. He wins the first trick with the ♥K, draws trumps, takes the ♥A, ruffs a heart and leads a club to the king and another club. East must put up the queen on the second club; otherwise, he is thrown in on the third club to make a losing lead.

```
              8 4 2
A Q 10 5                   J 7 3
              K 9 6
```

At a trump contract, declarer has drawn trumps and eliminated the side suits. He then leads the 2 of this suit from

dummy, planning to play the 9, forcing West to win and endplaying him. East can foil this plan by inserting the jack.

(8) To prevent a later RUFFING FINESSE:

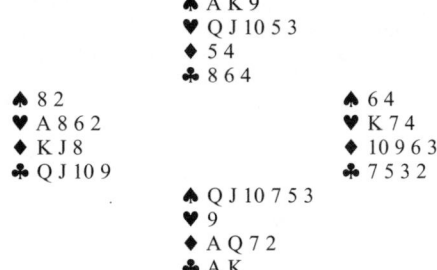

```
              ♠ A K 9
              ♥ Q J 10 5 3
              ♦ 5 4
              ♣ 8 6 4
♠ 8 2                      ♠ 6 4
♥ A 8 6 2                  ♥ K 7 4
♦ K J 8                    ♦ 10 9 6 3
♣ Q J 10 9                 ♣ 7 5 3 2
              ♠ Q J 10 7 5 3
              ♥ 9
              ♦ A Q 7 2
              ♣ A K
```

West leads the ♣Q against South's 6♠. South wins the ace, leads a trump to the ace and returns the ♥3. South is unlikely to play this way with the singleton ace or A-x, so East should put up the ♥K, defeating the contract. See also COVERING HONORS.

SECOND NEGATIVE RESPONSE AFTER ARTIFICIAL FORCING OPENER. A rebid by responder reinforcing an earlier negative or waiting bid and showing 0-3 points. It usually occurs after responder has bid 2♦ showing weakness in response to an artificial forcing 2♣ opening bid. It also occurs when a partnership is using 1♣ as a strong, forcing, artificial bid. Over 2♣ some players use the HERBERT NEGATIVE, the cheapest suit bid available after opener's rebid. After 2♣-2♦-2♥, responder would bid 2♠ to indicate the very weak hand. Others use a rebid in the lower minor after opener's rebid. Over the same sequence, responder would bid 3♣, the cheaper minor, to show the really weak hand – 0-4 and no ace or king. Many modern players use a single bid, 2♥ in response to a 2♣ opener, to show the super-weak hand. Negative bids also are very common in RELAY systems. See DOUBLE NEGATIVE, TWO DIAMOND ARTIFICIAL RESPONSE TO TWO CLUBS, TWO HEARTS RESPONSE TO ARTIFICIAL TWO CLUBS.

SECONDARY EVENT. An event at a North American Championship held concurrently with a championship event. Such events, which are open to players eliminated from the major events and to new players, are usually two sessions long and carry regional rating. See CHAMPIONSHIP TOURNAMENTS, SIDE GAME.

SECONDARY HONORS. The lower honors, i.e., queens and jacks. The king of a suit may also be considered a secondary honor when it is not accompanied by the ace. Secondary honors generally carry their weight better in notrump than in suit contracts, especially when they are not located in partner's long suits. See PRIMARY HONORS.

SECONDARY JUMP. See JUMP REBID BY RESPONDER.

SECONDARY SQUEEZE. A squeeze in which the squeeze card is followed by the loss of one or more tricks to the opponents. (Also called SQUEEZE WITHOUT THE COUNT or STRIP SQUEEZE.

(1) *Squeeze Establishment* (also called delayed duck squeeze by Dr. Clyde E. Love and squeeze suitout by George S. Coffin). A squeeze establishment has these characteris-

tics: one opponent possesses a guard to a long menace and a winner in a suit which declarer seeks to establish. The preliminary squeeze forces him to discard an additional winner or a card which may be led to his partner's winner.

The endings are based on simple squeeze positions except that declarer has two losers with no convenient way to RECTIFY THE COUNT. Thus, in effect, the rectification of the count takes place after the lead of the squeeze card. Some typical positions:

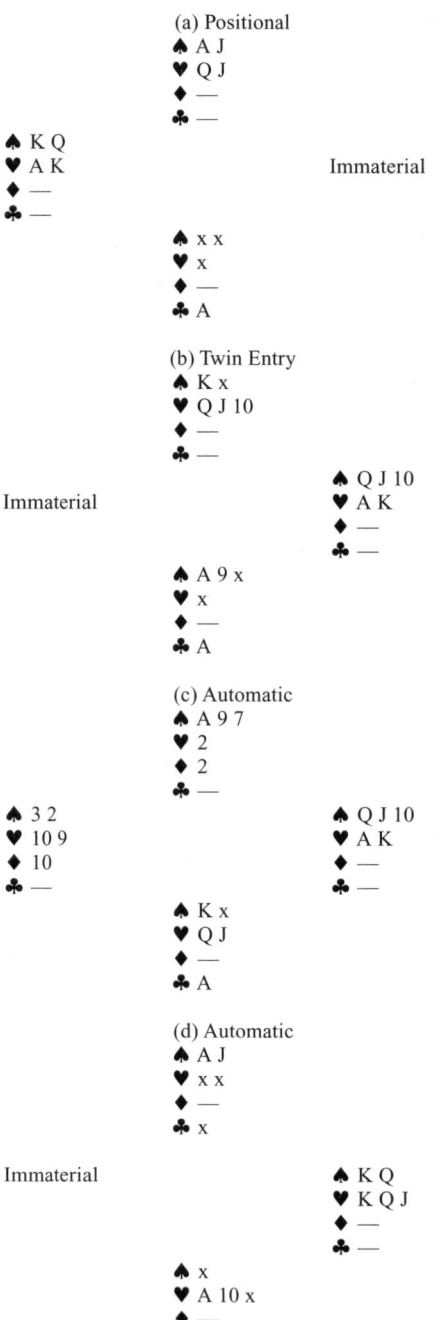

(a) Positional

(b) Twin Entry

(c) Automatic

(d) Automatic

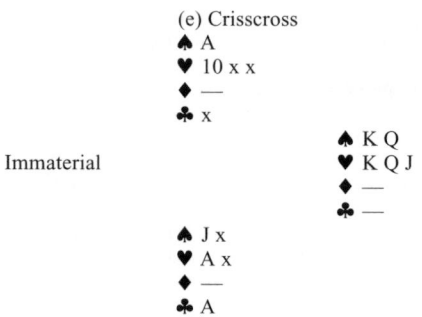

(e) Crisscross

In all the above cases, South leads the ♣A. Defender must discard a heart in order to protect his spade guard. South can then lead a heart in order to establish a trick for himself in that suit.

In (a) through (e) above, a defender was forced to discard a second winner in the suit which declarer sought to establish. In a minor variation (sometimes called a squeeze elimination [Romanet]), the opponent is squeezed out of a side winner or a card which may be led to partner's winner.

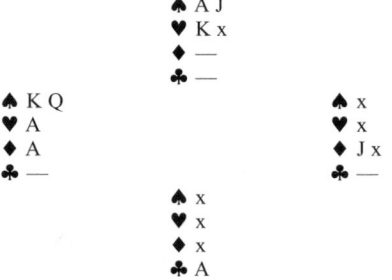

South leads his ♣A, and West is squeezed in three suits. He must discard the diamond winner, and North discards a spade. Now South can concede a heart and establish North's king. Had the diamond winner been with East and a small diamond in the West hand, West would have been forced to part with his exit card to his partner's winner.

(f) It is possible for such a squeeze to gain two tricks. N. Scott Cardell constructed the following example.

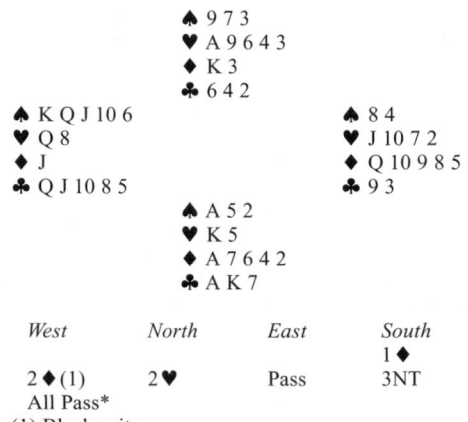

West	North	East	South
			1♦
2♦(1)	2♥	Pass	3NT
All Pass*			
(1) Black suits.			

West is allowed to win the ♠K-Q and shifts to the ♣Q. This wins also, and he shifts back to the ♠J. East discards a club, and the black suits are known. East is probably guarding both red suits, and South cashes the ♣A. East throws a diamond, and the position is:

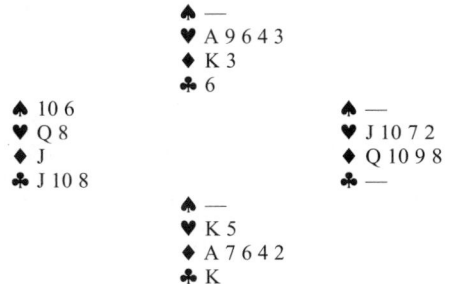

```
              ♠ —
              ♥ A 9 6 4 3
              ♦ K 3
              ♣ 6
  ♠ 10 6                      ♠ —
  ♥ Q 8                       ♥ J 10 7 2
  ♦ J                         ♦ Q 10 9 8
  ♣ J 10 8                    ♣ —
              ♠ —
              ♥ K 5
              ♦ A 7 6 4 2
              ♣ K
```

The ♣K now destroys East. South can develop whichever suit he gives up for two extra tricks.

(2) *Squeeze Throw-In* (also known as a strip squeeze). An opponent guards a two-card menace which is in the form of a tenace combination, and he also holds a winner which corresponds to a low card in that suit held by declarer. Declarer intends to lead the low card, throwing the opponent into the lead to force a play into the tenace.

If the opponent has been stripped of exit cards in all other suits, he still may have too many winners in the throw-in suit. In that case, the preliminary squeeze reduces the number of surplus winners which the defender can hold in the throw-in suit.

A. Declarer has a major tenace, and the throw-in is followed by two tricks for declarer. Declarer may have two or more losers.

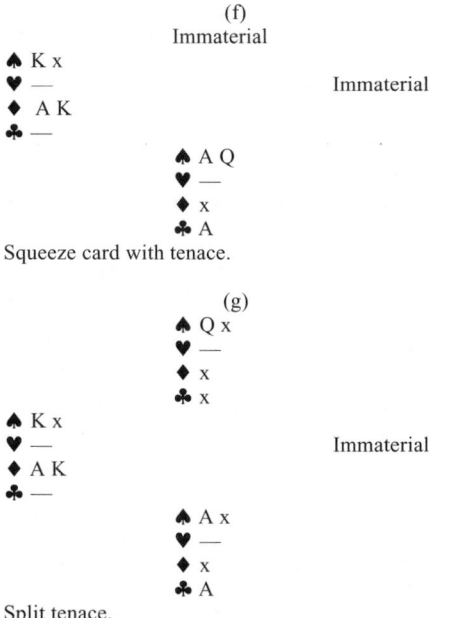

```
                    (f)
                Immaterial
  ♠ K x
  ♥ —                         Immaterial
  ♦ A K
  ♣ —
              ♠ A Q
              ♥ —
              ♦ x
              ♣ A
```
Squeeze card with tenace.

```
                    (g)
              ♠ Q x
              ♥ —
              ♦ x
              ♣ x
  ♠ K x
  ♥ —                         Immaterial
  ♦ A K
  ♣ —
              ♠ A x
              ♥ —
              ♦ x
              ♣ A
```
Split tenace.

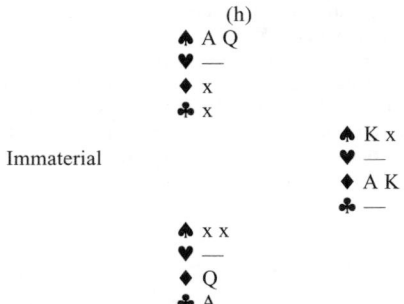

```
                    (h)
              ♠ A Q
              ♥ —
              ♦ x
              ♣ x
                              ♠ K x
  Immaterial                  ♥ —
                              ♦ A K
                              ♣ —
              ♠ x x
              ♥ —
              ♦ Q
              ♣ A
```
Squeeze card opposite tenace.

In (f) through (h), the ♣A is led, forcing the defender to part with a diamond winner. Now South leads the diamond, and the defender is thrown in to lead away from his ♠K. Note that the tenace may be with or opposite the squeeze card, or split between declarer and dummy.

B. Opponent has the major tenace, and the throw-in is followed by one trick for the declarer. Declarer has three or four losers.

```
                    (j)
              ♠ A 10
              ♥ x x
              ♦ —
              ♣ x
  ♠ K Q J
  ♥ A Q                       Immaterial
  ♦ —
  ♣ —
              ♠ x x
              ♥ K x
              ♦ —
              ♣ A
```

```
                    (k)
              ♠ x x x
              ♥ K x
              ♦ —
              ♣ x
                              ♠ K Q J
  Immaterial                  ♥ A Q
                              ♦ A
                              ♣ —
              ♠ A 10 x
              ♥ x x
              ♦ —
              ♣ A
```

```
                    (l)
              ♠ A J
              ♥ x x
              ♦ x x
              ♣ —
  ♠ K Q                       ♠ x x
  ♥ A Q                       ♥ x x
  ♦ x x                       ♦ K Q
  ♣ —                         ♣ —
              ♠ x
              ♥ K x
              ♦ A x
              ♣ A
```

South leads the ♣A, which forces the defender to discard a surplus winner – ♠J in (j), ♠J or ♦A in (k), or a potential exit card, the diamond, in (l). Now South takes

his winner(s) and exits in spades, so that he ends up by taking a trick with his ♥ K.

When a defender cannot afford to lead away from his stopper because declarer has a major tenace, then the endplay is effective when declarer has two losers, as shown in (j). The preliminary squeeze may force the defender to discard a surplus winner (as indicated) or an exit card. In this situation:

(m)

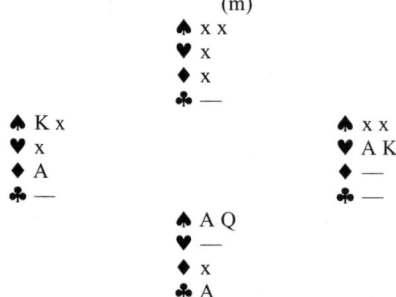

South leads the ♣ A, and West is forced to discard his exit card in hearts. Now he can be thrown in with a diamond and be forced to lead a spade into declarer's tenace.

C. Three-suit variants: in the case where one opponent has guards in three suits, which include at least one vulnerable stopper (i.e., declarer has a major tenace in one of the suits), the squeeze works when declarer has three or more losers. Precisely three losers are required only if the defender has a potential exit card in one of the suits.

(n)

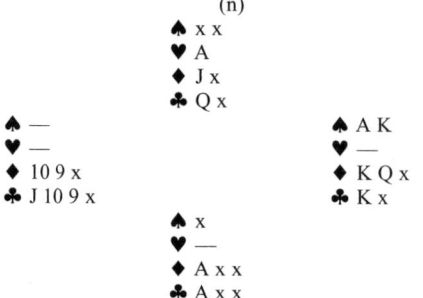

South has four losers, and the squeeze must fail since East has a potential exit card in diamonds. North leads the ♥ A, and East throws a spade. Now East wins the next spade, and plays a high diamond to the ace. He wins the next diamond, but he can now play a low diamond to West's ♦ 10, so the endplay is ineffective.

The squeeze establishment also has a three-suit variant which will gain a trick if declarer has three or more losers. Again, precisely three losers are required only if the defenders can kill one of the menace cards.

(o)

```
            ♠ J x
            ♥ K
            ♦ A
            ♣ x x
                        ♠ K Q
Immaterial              ♥ A
                        ♦ —
                        ♣ K Q J
            ♠ A x x
            ♥ —
            ♦ —
            ♣ A 10 x
```

South has three tricks on top. The ♦ A is led from North and East is squeezed in three suits. He must discard a potential club trick. North leads a club, and declarer ducks in order to establish his 10, which furnishes him with a fourth trick.

In certain squeeze-establishment plays, declarer may duck two or even three times in order to establish a trick for himself; understandably such positions arise rarely in play.

In another rare variant, the secondary squeeze involving three suits may result in the gain of two tricks to declarer. With three losers in hand, a squeeze-establishment play concedes one trick to the opponents and adds one trick to declarer's stock. As a result, the count has been rectified, and declarer may be able to continue with a simple squeeze for the gain of another trick. For related squeeze situations, see STEPPINGSTONE SQUEEZE; VICE SQUEEZE; WINKLE SQUEEZE.

SECONDARY SUIT GAME TRY. See DELAYED GAME RAISE, DOUBLE RAISE, INVERTED MINOR SUIT RAISE, INVITATIONAL BID, LIMIT JUMP RAISE, NOTRUMP OPENING, ONE NOTRUMP RESPONSE, OPENER'S REBID, RESPONDER'S REBID, RESPONSE, SINGLE RAISE, STRONG NOTRUMP AFTER PASSING, THREE NOTRUMP RESPONSE, TRIPLE RAISE, TWO NOTRUMP RESPONSE.

SECONDARY VALUES. Queens and jacks, also called soft values, as distinct from ace and kings, which are primary values or hard values.

SECTION. A group of contestants who constitute a self-contained unit in the competition in one event for one session of a tournament.

SECTIONAL. An ACBL tournament run by a unit or by a club to which the unit has been given the authority to run the tournament. Silver points are awarded in all events at a sectional. Most sectionals run for three days, although some are longer and a few run for only two days. Sectionals draw their competitors mostly from the immediate area. Also see SECTIONAL AT CLUBS.

SECTION MARKERS. Signs at tournaments indicating the location of each group of tables forming a SECTION.

SECTIONAL TOURNAMENT AT CLUBS (STaC). An ACBL tournament with sectional rating staged at many clubs in a geographical area over a period of several days — up to seven days. Events are played at several clubs and results are transmitted to a central office manned by the director-in-charge. The director combines the results to determine the winners and overall placings. Points awarded are silver points.

SEED, SEEDING. The assignment of certain tables to particularly strong contestants when entries are sold so as to assure that there will be no preponderance of strong pairs in direct competition within any one section. It is desirable to seed weak pairs also to prevent an imbalance of weakness in a particular section. In ACBL pair events, tables 3 and 9 are usually reserved for seeded players, at national tournaments, tables 3, 6 and 9 usu-

ally are reserved. In board-a-match team competitions, adjacent pairs of tables such as 1 and 2, 9 and 10, 17 and 18, etc., are used for spotting the strongest teams through the field. In individual tournaments, an effort is made to assure that the North players, at least, are able to keep score. In a Swiss Team event, pairings are random for the opening match.

ACBL North American Championship knockout events (Vanderbilt and Spingold) utilize various formulas for seeding which include not only masterpoint holdings but recent performances by the players. These are called seeding points.

SEEDING POINT. See SEED, SEEDING.

SEESAW SQUEEZE. See ENTRY-SHIFTING SQUEEZE.

SELECTION OF INTERNATIONAL TEAMS. See INTERNATIONAL OPEN TEAM SELECTION; INTERNATIONAL WOMEN'S TEAM SELECTION.

SELF-SUFFICIENT SUIT. See SOLID SUIT.

SEMI-BALANCED. A hand with 5-4-2-2 or 6-3-2-2 distribution.

SEMIFINAL. (1) The round of four or six in a knockout team tournament. (2) In a pair, team or individual tournament, the round immediately following the qualifying round or quarterfinal round and immediately preceding the final round.

SEMI-FORCING 1NT RESPONSE. The main drawback to the forcing 1NT comes from the fact that opener is systemically obliged to remove from 1NT with a completely balanced hand, to cover the possibility that responder has a hand worth an invitation to game – or better. The principle behind the semi-forcing 1NT response, first documented by Marty Bergen, is that responder will not conceal game-forcing hands in this bid, but may at best have a balanced limit-raise or a balanced 10-11 count intending to rebid 2NT. Accordingly opener should pass the 1NT response with all 12-14 balanced hands (in just the same way that opener would pass over a 1NT response with these hands if his partner were already a passed hand).

The corollary is that opener always guarantees an unbalanced hand when he removes 1NT to two of a new suit. This makes it easier for responder to play in a minor suit with knowledge of a fit.

This method works best if opener's range for a 1NT opening bid is 14+ to 17. In other words, if opener has a good 14-count with a five-card major, he may be better off opening 1NT rather than opening one of the major and then feeling obliged to rebid over the non-forcing 1NT response for fear of missing a game.

SEMI-PSYCHIC. A departure from normal bidding methods which is not a complete bluff but is still intended to deceive the opponents. The term usually refers to an opening bid well below minimum values, but LEAD-INHIBITING BIDS belong in the same category.

SEMI-SET GAME. A rubber bridge session involving five or more players in which one pair (sometimes two pairs), such as a husband and wife, play as partners except when one of them is cut out.

SEMI-SOLID SUIT. A suit of at least six cards which appears to contain only one loser, a suit that is one high card short of being a SOLID SUIT, for example, AKJ10xx, AQJ10xx, AKxxxxx, KQJxxxx.

SEND IT BACK. Redouble (colloquialism).

SENDER AWARD. A prize given by the INTERNATIONAL BRIDGE PRESS ASSOCIATION for the best defense of the year from 1985-1999. Kathie Wei-Sender named the award in honor of her husband, Henry Sender of Nashville TN.

SENIOR MOMENT. Humorous expression used to explain an error in play due to a laspe in concentration.

SENIOR PAIRS. Both members of each pair must be at or over the age minimum set for the event, usually 55.

SENIOR PLAYER OF THE YEAR. The ACBL Senior Player of the Year contest recognizes the player 55 years or older who wins the most masterpoints each year. In its inaugural year, only points won at senior regionals counted. Thereafter points won at senior events at other tournaments were counted as well. The George Burns Memorial Trophy is awarded to the winner annually.

SENIOR TEAMS. All members of every team at or over the age limit, which usually is 55.

SENIOR TOURNAMENT. Competitions in which only players older than a specified age, usually 55, may play. The first such event was an ACBL section staged in Sun City FL in 1977. The reaction from participants was so enthusiastic that ACBL tournaments with regional rating are now staged for seniors. The ACBL now features a nationally-rated event for seniors at each of its North American Championships – a knockout, a Swiss and a pair game. There is also a special award – the GEORGE BURNS MEMORIAL TROPHY – for the senior who scores the most points in senior tournaments in a calendar year.

The senior concept has caught on at the world level as well. Secondary championship events for seniors are now a regular part of championships run by the WORLD BRIDGE FEDERATION. The WBF is giving strong consideration to staging a full-fledged senior event at one of its championships, perhaps opposite the BERMUDA BOWL and the VENICE CUP. Other federations also are now staging senior tournaments.

SEQUENCE. Two or more cards in consecutive order of rank, such as A-K-Q, a sequence of three, or Q-J-10-9, a sequence of four. See OPENING LEADS, PLAY FROM EQUALS, RUSINOW LEADS.

SEQUENCE DISCARD. The discard of an honor normally shows an honor sequence, of which the discard is the highest. Therefore the discard of a queen denies the king and guarantees the jack and usually the 10.

The same principle applies in following suit when a top honor has already been played. This follows the more

general principle of discarding the highest card which can be spared in transmitting a signal. See SIGNALS, SIGNALING, DEFENSE, DEFENSIVE PLAY.

SEQUENCE OF ROUNDS. The order set up for the completion of bridge games. For many events the sequence of rounds is orderly and consistent, but on many occasions the circumstances of the movement force irregularities. For instance, if a pair game has an even number of tables, traveling pairs will skip a table about halfway through the game – unless there is a byestand and relay, which is another form of irregularity. Board-a-match team games with an even number of tables also require some unusual movement either twice or three times during a session. Even with an odd number of tables, there often is an irregularity halfway through the game, with both boards and traveling pairs making unusual moves. Most individual movements have various irregularities. See PROGRESSION.

SEQUENCE RE-ENTRY. A type of suit preference signal. After leading a king against notrump from a combination headed by K-Q-J, the defender can follow with the queen or the jack at choice in order to suggest a re-entry in a high- or low-ranking suit. See SUIT PREFERENCE SIGNAL.

SERES SQUEEZE. A rare triple squeeze in a three-card ending discovered by Tim Seres in 1965. Playing in 6♣, he arrived at the following ending with the lead in dummy:

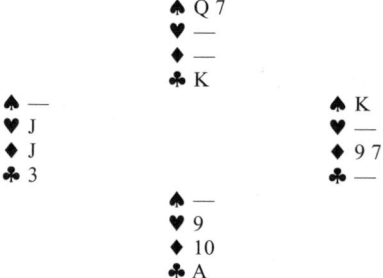

The ♠7 was ruffed, establishing the queen, and West was triple squeezed. An unusual feature is that one of the three cards he is trying to retain is a trump loser. See BACKWASH SQUEEZE.

The complete deal was:

```
              ♠ Q 7 6 4 2
              ♥ 8 6
              ♦ K Q
              ♣ K Q J 10
  ♠ 8 5 3                    ♠ K J 10 9
  ♥ J 10 7 3                 ♥ K 5 4
  ♦ A J 8                    ♦ 9 7 6 5 3
  ♣ 5 4 3                    ♣ 2
              ♠ A
              ♥ A Q 9 2
              ♦ 10 4 2
              ♣ A 9 8 7 6
```

A club was led, and South won in dummy and finessed the ♥Q. He cashed the ♠A and led a diamond. West put up the ♦A and led a second trump. South won in dummy, ruffed a spade, and entered dummy with a diamond for another spade ruff. The ♥A and a heart ruff left the three-card ending shown above.

SERIES GAMES. Formerly duplicate sessions in a club which counted as a unit for points or prizes. As of January 1969, the ACBL discontinued sanctioned series games for point awards. ACBL reinstituted such games in 1993. Four or more sessions of play are required. The masterpoint bonus to the winning player is equal to .02 times the total number of tables in which the winner participated to a maximum of 1.5 points.

SERIOUS 3NT. Invented and popularized by Eric Rodwell, this is one of the most useful extensions of the 2/1 game-forcing style. Serious 3NT depends on the following principle: when one side is in an uncontested game-forcing auction and has discovered an eight-card major fit or better, 3NT is never going to be the final contract. That being the case, one can use the call of 3NT to help differentiate sequences where one hand has real extras, and those where he is prepared to cooperate in a slam try. Consider the two following cases:

1♥	Pass	2♦	Pass
2♥	Pass	3♥	Pass

1♠	Pass	2♥	Pass
3♥			

Playing 2/1 game-forcing, the partnership has agreed a major in a game-forcing auction, and 3NT is sufficiently unlikely to be the right contract that it can be dispensed with as the final resting place. But consider opener's problem in the first sequence; he might hold a hand such as:

```
    ♠ Q 9 4
    ♥ A Q 8 7 6 2
    ♦ 5
    ♣ A 4 3
```

This hand is very suitable for slam, in context, but is absolutely minimum in high cards. Alternatively, opener might have the same hand with an extra ace or king, in which case he would like to make at least one try for slam. It is unsatisfactory to have to bid 4♣ with both hands. The solution would be to use a cuebid of 4♣ as simultaneously implying a willingness to cooperate in a slam venture but not enough extra values to make a serious slam try on one's own. Conversely a call of 3NT would guarantee extra high cards and suggest real slam interest.

There is no especially good reason to play the bids with 3NT as stronger than the direct cuebid. The meanings can be inverted, so that 3NT becomes the weaker slam try. The advantage of this route is that it may conceal information from the defense when the partnership stops at game.

SERPENT'S COUP. When the serpent tempted Eve, she gave in and tried the forbidden fruit and then got Adam to do the same. This coup is similar – it tempts a defender – and the fruit looks very appealing.

```
              ♠ A 8 6
              ♥ K 6
              ♦ A K 5
              ♣ K 10 6 4 2
  ♠ K 10 7 5 2               ♠ Q J 4 3
  ♥ Q 9 8 4 3                ♥ 2
  ♦ 10 2                     ♦ Q J 9 3
  ♣ 9                        ♣ J 8 7 3
              ♠ 9
              ♥ A J 10 7 5
              ♦ 8 7 6 4
              ♣ A Q 5
```

Against 4 ♥, West leads the ♣9 which is won with the ace. A heart to the king is followed by a second heart. East shows out, playing the ♠3 and the 10 loses to West's queen. West returns the ♦ 2, and this is won with dummy's king.

At this point, declarer does not know whether the diamond suit is divided 5-1, 4-2 or 3-3. A club to the queen will lead to defeat if the diamonds are 3-3 and East has a diamond entry: Ace, king and another diamond will lead to immediate defeat if East has four diamonds. The low diamond play at this point makes the contract legitimately if the diamonds are 3-3 and gives far greater temptation to East to give his partner a diamond ruff if they are 4-2 or 5-1. East would be loathe to give West a club ruff since that play establishes the club suit while there are still entries to dummy.

Alternatively, if the diamonds are 4-2, with East having the four diamonds, declarer has two heart losers and two diamond losers. Declarer cannot play the ♦ A and trump a spade – West will have more trumps and be able to force declarer.

One play offers a better chance. At trick five declarer leads a small diamond from the table. East wins the jack and West follows with the 10.

East might hesitate to return a club since that would establish dummy's club suit and leave entries to it as well. But why not return a diamond? The worst that could happen is that West would trump the now bare ♦ A.

East bites the apple and returns a diamond and West does trump it. The Serpent's Coup has worked.

West's spade return is won by the ace in dummy. Declarer trumps a spade back to his hand. The ♥A pulls one of West's trumps and the ♥ J follows in this position:

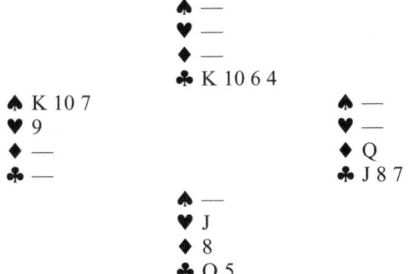

The Serpent's Coup ends with a two-suit squeeze.

SESSION. A period of play during which each contestant is scheduled to play a designated series of boards against one or more opponents. A session may consist of one or more rounds.

SET. (1) The group of duplicate boards to be played in a round; (2) all the boards in play in a section or match; (3) the number of boards in a board case, usually 32 or 36; (4) the defeat of a contract – "Declarer suffered a two-trick set"; (5) to defeat a contract – "The defense set declarer two tricks"; (6) a partnership that plays together regularly – Eric Rodwell and Jeff Meckstroth are a set partnership; (7) a partnership that plays intact through a session of RUBBER BRIDGE or CHICAGO; (8) a game in which both partnerships are set partnerships. See SET GAME, SET PARTNERSHIP.

SET GAME. A pre-arranged match between two part-nerships, with each pair almost always remaining the same for the duration of the contest. There have been set games where one of the players has been spelled for a while by some other player who had been waiting in reserve for such an instance. But generally set games involve only four people and last for several rubbers as previously agreed upon.

The CULBERTSON-LENZ MATCH was the most publicized set game in history. However, there also was wide interest in the match between the SHARIF BRIDGE CIRCUS and English experts Jonathan Cansino and Jeremy Flint (with Claude Rodrigue spelling Flint for part of the match), which was held in London in 1970. The stakes were enormous – 1 pound ($2.40) a point. Over the course of 80 rubbers, of which Sharif had agreed to play a minimum of 52, the Circus won by 5,470 points. See SCIENTISTS vs. TRADITIONALISTS.

SET UP. To establish one or more cards in the hand of the player himself, his partner, or an opponent.

SET-UP SUIT. See ESTABLISHED SUIT.

SEVEN or SEVEN-SPOT. The eighth-ranking card in a suit, located between the 8 and the 6.

SEVEN-ODD. Seven tricks over book, or 13 tricks in all.

SEVEN PLAYERS. See SHUTTLE DUMMY.

SEVEN TABLES. At duplicate, seven tables provide for competition among 28 players as individuals, 14 pairs or seven teams-of-four. This is an ideal number of tables – it provides a basic pattern for all numbers of tables up to 13 for pair contests, and is an excellent base for larger individual tournaments.

Since seven is a prime number, the RAINBOW MOVEMENT is suitable for an individual contest. Three boards to a round, with the West players moving counterclockwise around the table at the end of each board of the round, provides each player with 21 different partners. Six is top and 63 is average in the ACBL; 12 is top and 126 is average elsewhere. See SCORING, TOP, TOP ON BOARD.

Thirteen rounds of two boards each makes the HOWELL MOVEMENT an ideal competition for pair events, each pair meeting every other pair, with almost perfectly BALANCED COMPARISONS throughout the field and at least 10 and no more than 14 direct comparisons between pairs. The MITCHELL MOVEMENT can also be used when two fields are desirable. Six rounds of four boards or seven rounds of three or four boards comprise the usual contest.

As a team event, the regular team-of-four progression, boards going to the next lower and traveling pairs skipping a table to lower numbers, provides six uninterrupted rounds for 24 boards, with no irregularities in the progression. A Swiss Team movement is not recommended. Three-way matches are necessary, and pairings are at best difficult after the second round. For IMP matches, use the team of-four progression and score each match on IMPs.

The following Reduced Howell for seven tables playing nine rounds was devised by Olof Hanner. The starting positions are:

Table	1	2	3	4	5	6	7
NS	1	2	3	4	13	5	14
EW	6	7	8	9	10	11	12
Bd set	1	2	5	6	7	8	9

Pairs 1-5 are stationary. Pairs 6-13 follow next higher number, and 14 follows 6. Boards go to next lower table, with two sets of boards on a byestand between 2 and 3. Short instructions on tables 5 and 7 tell pairs where to go. Use an arrow switch on rounds 6, 8, and 9. In a nine-round game, the best times for arrow switches are rounds 7 and 9.

For 6½ or 7½ tables, see HALF TABLES.

SEXTET BRIDGE. A seldom played bridge game for six players, playing as two partnerships of three each. Two new suits were introduced, called rackets and wheels.

SHADE, SHADED. A bid made on slightly less than technical minimum requirements.

SHAKE. A colloquialism meaning DISCARD.

SHAPE. See DISTRIBUTION.

SHARIF BRIDGE CIRCUS. A touring professional team of world class players, organized and headed by movie star Omar Sharif, to play a series of exhibition matches against leading European and North American teams.

The Circus made its debut late in 1967 when Sharif, Giorgio Belladonna, Claude Delmouly, Benito Garozzo, and Leon Yallouze, all playing the BLUE TEAM CLUB, defeated the Dutch international team in matches sponsored by newspapers and played in three Netherlands cities before enthusiastic audiences who viewed the competition on BRIDGE-O-RAMA. Using this format – a match against a highly-rated team with the play-by-play displayed to the audience accompanied by expert commentary – the Circus made an extended tour in 1968. It defeated teams in Italy and London, lost its first matches to The Netherlands and Belgium in The Hague, and made a swing through six North American cities – Montreal, Toronto, Los Angeles, Dallas, New Orleans and New York – winning the majority of the matches. (Several of the American matches were three-cornered contests involving the Circus, the local team, and the ACES.) A second tour in 1970 received a spectacular sendoff when Jeremy Flint and Jonathan Cansino challenged Sharif and company to a 100-rubber pair game in London (later reduced by time pressure to 80 rubbers). The stakes were an unprecedented British pound ($2.40) per point, plus an additional bonus of $1,000 on the net result of each four rubbers. The match attracted wide newspaper and magazine coverage in the United States as well as in Europe. Sharif won by a margin of 5,470 points and collected more than $18,000. However, this was a comparatively small sum against the expenses of staging the match and taping the highlights for a series of television shows planned for later syndication. The TV shows never took place.

This was immediately followed by a tour of seven North American cities – Chicago, Winnipeg, Los Angeles, St. Paul, Dallas, Detroit and Philadelphia. In addition to matches against powerful teams of local stars, the tour included a marathon 840-deal match against the Aces, who accompanied the Circus throughout the tour. The Circus defeated the all-star teams in Chicago,

Winnipeg and St. Paul, but lost all its other matches, bowing to the Aces by 101 IMPs (1,793-1,692) after the lead had seesawed excitingly from city to city. Pietro Forquet joined the Sharif team in Dallas but could not reverse the effect of the exhausting schedule, which included numerous personal appearances by Sharif.

Despite commercial sponsorship of more than $50,000 in 1970, neither of the American tours proved a financial success, although both resulted in wide publicity for bridge.

SHARING BOARDS. In some movements, it is necessary for two tables, and perhaps more, to "share" by playing the same set of boards in a single round. Boards may be played out of numerical order.

SHARK. An expert player, but more particularly one who specializes in playing for money and is adept at this type of competition.

SHARPLES. (1) A convention devised by James and Robert Sharples – a "natural" extension of the STAYMAN convention.

A responder who sees slam possibilities frequently faces a problem if he uses Stayman and does not find an immediate fit. If the responder has 4-4-3-2 or 4-4-4-1 distribution, he may wish to explore the possibility of a 4-4 fit in a minor suit.

Opposite a 16- to 18-point notrump, responder holds:

♠ K J 7 5
♥ 4
♦ A Q 5 2
♣ A 10 5 3

The Sharples idea is to bid four of a minor suit on the second round, showing specifically a four-card suit and sufficient strength to play in at least 4NT:

Opener	*Responder*
1NT	2♣
2♥	4♣

The opener rebids his hand naturally. If he has four-card club support, he raises to 5♣ or 6♣ in accordance with his estimation of slam prospects. If four-card club support is lacking, opener can make a natural suit bid of 4♦ or 4♠ (although in some styles a four-card spade suit may have been excluded by the 2♥ rebid). 4NT and 5NT would be natural bids announcing that the opener's distribution was 4-3-3-3.

All notrump bids at any stage should be regarded as natural.

Suppose responder holds:

♠ J 3
♥ K J 7 5
♦ A Q 5 2
♣ A 5 3

The bidding goes:

Opener	*Responder*
1NT	2♣
2♠	4♦

By jumping to 4♦, responder denies a four-card club suit, and keeps open the possibility of playing a slam in a red suit.

These sequences need partnership agreement. SPLINTER is the most popular alternative use for the bid.

(2) A defense to 1NT in which: (a) an overcall of 2♣ shows a hand of unspecified shape but with at least four spades; or (b) an overcall of 2♦ shows a weak distributional hand with short clubs.

SHEINWOLD TROPHY. Awarded to the winners of NORTH AMERICAN TEAMS FLIGHT B at the ACBL Summer NABC. Trophy honors Alfred Sheinwold, author, eminent bridge columnist, theoretician, and expert on the Laws.

SHIFT (or switch). To change suit from one originally led on defense; alternatively, a change of suit by declarer in the development of his play. Shift can also be used to describe a bid in a new suit by either the opening bidder, his partner, or an overcaller or his partner. See JUMP SHIFT, ONE-OVER-ONE, WEAK JUMP SHIFT.

SHOMATE MOVEMENT. Used for INDIVIDUAL TOURNAMENTS. These movements are noncyclic and must be conducted with GUIDE CARDS. Since RAINBOW MOVEMENTS are now available for most individuals, the Shomate method is seldom used. See IRREGULAR RAINBOW.

SHOOTING. The art of playing deliberately for an abnormal result. Occasionally near the end of a tournament, a couple of tops are needed in order to have any chance of winning. Two or three average results would be just as fatal to one's chances as bottoms. Under these circumstances, playing for abnormal results is justified. Playing for top or bottom is called shooting.

Many players, quite wrongly, think of shooting as equivalent to overbidding. In fact, good shooting will consist of underbidding as often as overbidding. The aim should be to arrive at a contract which is only slightly wrong.

To bid a game or a slam which has a 30-40% chance of success is an intelligent "shot"; but it is equally sensible to stop short of game or slam which is a 60-70% chance. In each case the shooter is hoping for the less likely result.

But the best chance to shoot intelligently is in the play of the hand.

North
♠ x x
♥ x x x
♦ x x
♣ A 8 x x x x

South
♠ A Q x
♥ A K x x
♦ A Q x
♣ K 9 x

West leads a spade against South's 3NT contract. Declarer wins East's king with the ace, and attacks clubs. Normally he would play the king, and then duck a round. This is the percentage play because the odds are slightly against a 2-2 club break. Obviously if declarer plays the king, then leads the nine to dummy's ace, his contract will be placed in jeopardy. For one who wishes to shoot, this is a wonderful opportunity. By playing the ace on the second round (unless West shows out), he can be almost certain of a top (or bottom).

SHORT CLUB. The short prepared or convenient club is an original opening bid made on a three-card club suit. It was first advocated by the FOUR ACES as a means of providing a comfortable rebid. In principle it requires a minimum of Q-x-x (to support a lead), and failing this, opener may choose instead to open with 1 ♦. It is most often used by the disciples of systems that require five cards for a major suit opening. For example:

♠ A 6 5 4
♥ A Q 3 2
♦ A 8
♣ 9 7 6

When playing FIVE-CARD MAJORS the hand is opened with 1 ♣. When the hand contains two clubs and three diamonds, an opening diamond bid is usually preferred. It is essential in these systems for responder to mention his four-card major holding, if at all feasible, in order to find the all-important major-suit fit. All players, even those who initiate weak major-suit bids, will at times resort to the Short Club.

Some specialized bidding systems use an artificial club opening as an introduction to a very strong hand (see BLUE TEAM CLUB, ONE CLUB SYSTEMS, ORANGE CLUB, PRECISION CLUB, SCHENKEN SYSTEM, VANDERBILT CLUB). However, the short club, per se, is not a system but an opening bid to facilitate future rebids, and may be passed by partner. When otherwise used it is more properly alerted as ONE CLUB ARTIFICIAL AND FORCING. In such cases it does not promise any particular length or strength in the club suit itself.

Inexperienced players often assume that a 1 ♣ bid is likely to be short. Using standard methods it is very unlikely: a four-card or five-card suit is far more likely, and even a six-card suit is more likely than three. See also CHOICE OF SUIT.

SHORT DIAMOND. Many users of strong-club systems, particularly those such as Precision that employ five-card majors, utilize a short diamond as a catch-all for hands that are not suitable for other bids. This must be alerted, and the explanation should include a minimum length: two, one or zero diamonds. A 2 ♦ response is natural and forcing.

It is sometimes called the loose diamond, the nebulous diamond or the phony diamond. The opponents may well choose to agree that against 1 ♦, a bid of 2 ♦ should be natural and not a cuebid.

A short diamond with three cards is a standard part of modern methods. It usually is based on 4-4-3-2 distribution but some players open 1 ♦ with 4-3-3-3 or 3-4-3-3 if the diamonds are better than the clubs. See ONE-CLUB SYSTEMS.

SHORT HAND. A term used to describe the hand of the partnership that contains the fewer cards in the trump suit, such as in the reference, "declarer (or the defenders) took the ruff in the short hand." Occasionally, the term may be applied to a hand that is short in a non-trump suit and therefore expects to ruff.

SHORT HOWELL MOVEMENTS. See REDUCED HOWELL.

SHORT SUIT. In an original hand of 13 cards, a suit containing two or fewer cards. In some contexts, a short suit would be defined as a singleton or a void. See DOUBLETON, SINGLETON, VOID.

SHORT-SUIT GAME TRY. This method was developed as part of the KAPLAN-SHEINWOLD system, but can be used effectively with any standard system. When the opening major-suit bid has been raised to two, the opener tries for game by bidding his shortest suit. For example:

```
                    ♠ A K 6 5 3
                    ♥ A 5 2
                    ♦ 8
                    ♣ K J 7 4
```

The bidding goes:

Opener	Responder
1♠	2♠
3♦	

This asks responder to go to 4♠ if his values are mainly outside diamonds. If responder rebids 3♥, that would also be a short-suit try, expressing doubt about game prospects.

This method gives a partnership a chance to judge whether strength is duplicated. A disadvantage is that it may help the opponents find a cheap save. One defender may double the short-suit try, encouraging his partner to take the save. It may also provide a clue to the most effective lead and subsequent defense.

It is best to restrict these bids to the situations when a major has been raised and there has been no interference.

The specific sequence 1♥ - 2♥ - 2♠ may need special consideration. The 2♠ rebid may be needed as a natural rebid, especially if the opening bidder has not guaranteed a five-card heart suit.

For alternative methods see TWO-WAY GAME TRY. WEAK SUIT GAME TRY.

SHORTEN. To force; to shorten in trumps by forcing to ruff. See FORCING LEADS.

SHORT-SUIT LEAD. An opening lead of a singleton or a doubleton. Such a lead is often indicated when the leader examines his hand in light of the bidding.

Against either notrump or a trump contract, a short-suit lead is normal when partner has bid the suit. Partner's bid suit is less automatic as a lead against a trump contract. It may be necessary to aim quickly for tricks elsewhere.

The short-suit lead is also indicated when there is a bidding inference that this is partner's suit and that he will have the entries to make use of it.

```
                    South
                    ♠ Q 5 3
                    ♥ J 8 6 2
                    ♦ 7 4
                    ♣ Q 7 6 3
```

After the bidding:

West	East
1♠	2♣
2NT	3NT

North should lead a diamond. The hand is too weak to hope to do much with hearts, so a diamond is led in the hope of hitting partner's strength. If South held the ♠A instead of the ♠3, a heart lead would be indicated.

A short-suit lead may be made for passive reasons, usually because other leads seem unattractive. This is most likely to be desirable if the bidding suggests that the declaring side has no long suit, and that therefore there is no urgent need to attack.

In a suit contract a short-suit lead is most desirable if the trump holding suggests that there are real prospects of obtaining a ruff. (A-x, A-x-x and K-x-x are ideal in trumps because they suggest a measure of trump control.) Conversely a short-suit lead, particularly of a singleton, may be a mistake when there is no ruffing

prospect because it may help declarer play a suit which would have presented problems. A singleton trump is usually a bad lead (but see TRUMP LEADS).

Against notrump, a short-suit lead is indicated when the opening leader is very weak and no entries are available to make use of a long weak suit. The leader should try to hit his partner's suit, although this may work out to declarer's advantage. (For this reason the long weak suit may prove best as a passive lead.) A short-suit lead is required when the leader's partner has doubled notrump in an auction where no suit has been bid.

SHOW. Indicate a certain number of HIGH CARD POINTS in a hand. For instance, an opening bid of 1♠ shows a minimum of five spades.

SHOW OUT. To fail to follow suit for the first time during the play of that suit.

SHOW-UP SQUEEZE. A squeeze which permits declarer to avoid a guess between a finesse and a play for a drop.

```
                    K J x x x
        ? x x x                 ? x
                    A x
```

If South can put pressure on West, forcing two discards in the vital suit, the ace and king can be cashed with confidence, knowing the queen will show up on one side or the other.

SHOWING PREFERENCE. See PREFERENCE.

SHUFFLE. Noun: the mixing together of the pack of cards prior to the next, or first deal. Several thorough mixings, or shuffles, are required as it is important that the deck be mixed completely from deal to deal. Verb: to mix the cards.

The most common shuffle is the riffle, in which the deck is divided into two approximate halves and then reunited by a flipping action so that the cards are roughly interleaved. A mathematician has calculated that seven riffles are needed to produce a good result, but few players bother with more than three or four.

SHUTOUT BID. See PREEMPTIVE BID.

SHUTTLE DUMMY. This is a procedure to permit play with seven players at two tables, playing Chicago. One table starts, and dummy moves to the other table. This continues, with an individual score for each player maintained at each table.

S.I.D. See STAYMAN IN DOUBT.

SIDE. A team of two in a rubber game or a CHICAGO game. The term can also describe a pairing in a duplicate contest, or, in team-of-four play, the entire team of whatever number.

SIDE GAME. An event held during a championship tournament that does not have championship rating. The game usually is a pair event, but can be a team competition. Masterpoints awarded usually are one class lower than those given in championship games. At ACBL North American Championships and regionals, side pair events are joined together in groups of three to six to provide

events called CONTINUOUS PAIRS. The usual method to determine an overall winner is to give player credit for his best two scores, and the overall ranking is calculated from these figures. However, occasionally different conditions of contest are set up. Each player may play with as many different partners as there are sessions since the overall standings are determined on an individual basis.

SIDE GAME PAIRS. New name for CONTINUOUS PAIRS. One of a series of side games in which the person with the best total of two percentage scores is declared the winner.

SIDE SUIT. In bidding, a suit of at least four cards held by a player whose first bid is in another suit. In play, a suit of at least four cards other than trumps held by declarer in his own hand or dummy.

SIGNAL, SIGNALING. The language of defensive play by which defenders can legitimately exchange information about the makeup of their hands. Various methods of signaling are discussed under the following titles: BLUE PETERS; COUNT; COUNT SIGNAL; DISCARDING; ENCRYPTED; HIGH-LOW; LENGTH SIGNAL; ODD-EVEN DISCARD; PETER; REVERSE COUNT; REVOLVING DISCARD; ROMAN DISCARDS; SCANIAN SIGNAL; SMITH; SUIT PREFERENCE SIGNAL; TRUMP SIGNAL; UPSIDE-DOWN SIGNAL; VINJE SIGNAL.

SIGNOFF BID. A bid which is intended to close the auction. These sometimes occur in partscore situations:

West	East	West	East	West	East
1♣	1♠	1♠	1NT	1NT	2♠
1NT	2♠	2♠			

In each case the player bidding notrump has limited his hand so partner can place the final contract. In each case, partner is saying that the values of the combined hands are not strong enough for game and that the best place to play probably is spades because the spade bidder has a long suit of spades – probably at least six and maybe more. (Five or more in the third auction, which assumes traditional responses to 1NT.) Other signoff bids occur at the game level. The most common is the raise to 3NT, 4♥ or 4♠ by the partner of a player who opened 1NT. In general signoff bids occur when a player names a contract after partner has severely limited his hand both as to point-count and distribution.

SILENCE. Observed during the play of important events, at least in theory. However, this is honored in the breach more often than in actuality. In the playing rooms of top-level clubs, any noise or disturbance is severely frowned upon. Should a disturbance occur, the officer of the day or other official will usually make the necessary remonstrance.

SILODOR TROPHY. Awarded to the winners of the NORTH AMERICAN OPEN PAIRS I. Trophy honors Sidney Silodor, outstanding American player who was a member of the United States team that won the first Bermuda Bowl. Presented in 1963 and made retroactive to include winners of the event since it started in 1958. For results see Appendix I.

SILVER POINTS. Masterpoints won at ACBL sectional tournaments. A player must earn at least 50 silver points as one of the qualifications for advancing to the rank of Life Master.

SILVER RIBBON PAIRS. An ACBL event with national rating for players 55 years of age or older. Pairs earn qualification by placing first or second in a senior event that is regionally rated or higher. For winners, see Appendix I.

SIMON AWARD. Endowed by John E. Simon, this award for the Bridge Sportsman of the Year was presented annually by the INTERNATIONAL BRIDGE PRESS ASSOCIATION. It has been in abeyance since 1986. It was awarded to the player deemed worthy of special mention for behavior showing a high degree of sportsmanship. For a list of winners, see INTERNATIONAL BRIDGE PRESS ASSOCIATION AWARDS.

SIMPLE. (as applied to an overcall or response). Non-jump; merely sufficient to overcall or respond.

SIMPLE FINESSE. A finesse for a single card held by the adversaries.

SIMPLE HONORS. A term used in auction bridge to denote three honors in the trump suit, for which 30 points were scored.

SIMPLE OVERCALL. An overcall at the minimum level.

SIMPLE SQUEEZE. A squeeze which acts against one opponent in two suits. The minimum requirements are: (1) a two-card menace and a one-card menace, both guarded by the same opponent; (2) all the remaining tricks but one.

The card which forces the defender to discard a busy card is called the squeeze card. The squeeze card must be a winner played from the hand opposite the two-card menace, so that the two menaces and the squeeze card cannot all be in the same hand. The two-card menace contains a master card, which provides an entry to one of the menaces. The following are the basic endings for a simple squeeze:

(1) *Positional (or one-way) squeeze:*

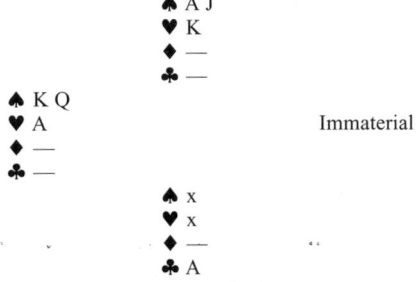

South plays the ♣A, and West is squeezed. When West discards one suit, North discards the other, and so takes the remaining tricks.

In this example, spades are the two-card menace and

hearts the one-card menace. The squeeze card is the ♣A. Declarer has on top two of the remaining three tricks.

In this position both West and North have been reduced to busy cards, but West must discard first so declarer can choose his discard accordingly, resulting in the gain of a trick. If the East and West cards are interchanged, the squeeze is inoperative.

(2) *Split two-card menace:*

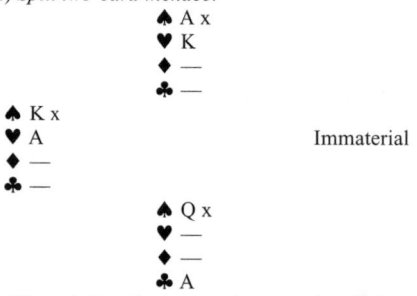

In this variation, the two-card menace is split between North and South. The North hand contains the master card (the ♠A this example), but the South hand contains the menace (here the ♠Q). The (split) two-card menace is still said to be opposite the squeeze card (here the ♣A) provided that a master card of that menace is properly situated, as here.

(3) *Automatic squeeze*

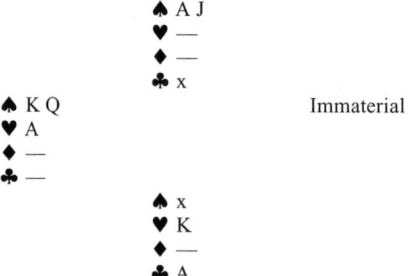

(a) As usual, the two-card menace is opposite the squeeze card, but now the one-card menace accompanies the squeeze card. This means that the North hand has an idle card (see BUSY CARD AND IDLE CARD) which can be played on the ♣A; that is, North's discard does not depend on the opponent's play. As a result, the squeeze is automatic in that it operates against either opponent if the same opponent guards both menace cards.

(b) Twin-entry menace:

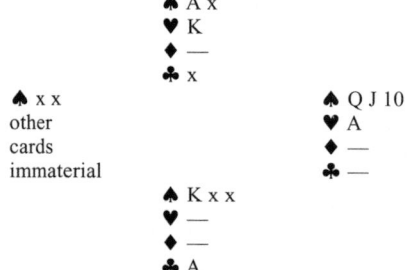

When South plays the ♣A, East is squeezed. The position is automatic. Even though the one-card menace is opposite the squeeze card, there is compensation in the form of an extra winner in the long menace, which is now called a twin-entry two-card menace.

(c) Criss-cross squeeze:

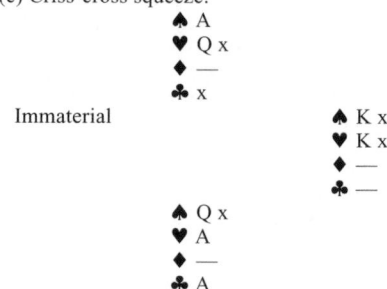

South leads the ♣A, which forces East to unguard one of his major suit kings. Whatever suit East discards, declarer takes the ace of that suit, dropping East's king, plays to his remaining ace and cashes a winning queen. If East can foresee the impending squeeze, he may be able to make a deceptive play, blanking one of his kings early, thereby presenting South with a guess.

SIMPLIFIED CLUB SYSTEM. Originated by Larry Weiss with considerable help from Danny Kleinman. It combines some of the features of the BLUE TEAM CLUB and the ROMAN SYSTEM: (1) 1♣ shows 16 points or more, and responses show controls. A 2♣ rebid shows a stronger hand with game values, and the responses again show controls. A 2♦ rebid shows a strong three-suiter. (2) 1♦, 1♥, and 1♠ guarantee a two-suited hand, at least 5-4, and the shorter suit is bid first unless it is clubs. 1NT is an artificial positive response showing at least 10 points. The suit immediately above the opener's is an artificial negative, but the responder is not required to use it if he has some fit with the opener. (3) 1NT is 12-15 points. (4) 2♣ is 11-16 and three-suited. (5) Other two-bids show single-suited hands with 11-16 points. Club hands are shown by 2NT (14-17) or 3♣ (11-14).

SIMPLIFIED PRECISION. A version of the PRECISION CLUB system that differs from Standard Precision essentially in that (1) it uses no asking bids, (2) its 2♦ opening shows diamond length rather than diamond shortness, and (3) its four-level minor-suit openings are natural preempts. Compare also SUPER PRECISION.

SIMS-CULBERTSON MATCH. See CULBERTSON-SIMS MATCH.

SIMS SYSTEM. A system of contract bidding originated circa 1930-32 by P. Hal Sims. The system stressed strong first- and second-hand opening bids (with corresponding "protection" by third or fourth hand); strong four-card biddable suits, with the opening bid made in the lower ranking. All opening bids of two or three in a suit were forcing, both showing hands strong in honor value, but the three-bid showing length as well. Weak defensive bids were not made when vulnerable. The system also employed forcing overcalls and informatory doubles.

SIMULTANEOUS LEADS, CALLS or PLAYS. If one of the simultaneous acts is legal, that action stands. It the other is out of rotation, it is treated as a call, lead or play out of rotation, and the director applies the appropriate penalty. Many times simultaneous actions take place in which neither is out of rotation. For instance, if

East and South play a card simultaneously when it was East's turn to play, Law 58A clearly states that South's play is subsequent and not out of rotation. Similarly, if East and South bid simultaneously, Law 33 calls South's action subsequent, not out of rotation.

In the bidding situation, South's bid stands and is still subject to penalty if it is insufficient (Law 27) or inadmissible (Law 36).

SIMULTANEOUS PLAY. The play of preduplicated boards at more than one table in a section at the same time, allowing instant scoring. See BAROMETER.

SINGLE COUP. A coup in which declarer shortens his hand or dummy once in trumps by ruffing a card in order to reduce the trump holding to the same number held by the key opponent. See COUP.

SINGLE DUMMY PROBLEM. A solver is given the two hands of a partnership holding, approximating the conditions facing a declarer at the bridge table. Among the foremost inventors of these problems was Paul Lukacs of Israel, who presented these.

    (a)   ♠ 6 3 2
                    ♥ Q J 4
                    ♦ A Q 6 5 4
                    ♣ 6 2

                    ♠ A K 8
                    ♥ 8
                    ♦ K 8 2
                    ♣ A K Q J 10 9

South plays 6♣ against the lead of the ♥5. East takes the first trick with the ♥A, and returns a low heart. Assuming that West holds the ♥K, South can claim the contract. Why?

    (b)   ♠ K 8 5
                    ♥ 8 4 3 2
                    ♦ 6
                    ♣ A 10 9 8 7

                    ♠ A Q 7
                    ♥ K Q J
                    ♦ K 10 9 8 4
                    ♣ K 2

Against South's 3NT contract, West leads the ♣4. East's jack is taken by South's king. Next comes a successful club finesse, East following suit. What is the right continuation?

Solutions. (a) South trumps the heart return; then plays all his trumps (discarding one diamond and two spades from the dummy). The ♦A-K are cashed in that order. If both opponents follow, there is no problem. If West holds the diamond guard and the ♥K, he is squeezed in the two red suits on the second spade lead. If East holds the diamond guard, after the third lead of diamonds, West has the ♥K and East the diamond guard. Neither, then, has three spades, and declarer can claim the last three tricks in that suit. (b) The solution hinges on the continuation of the club suit. If declarer plays the ace and then the 9, he has an impossible discard to make on the second play - discarding either a second diamond or a heart gives the opponents a chance to establish that suit, while a spade discard costs a trick in the suit. Therefore, the potential club loser must be lost immediately, by leading the 9 at trick three, before leading the ace.

SINGLE GRAND COUP. A GRAND COUP in which the declarer shortens his hand in trumps, to reduce his holding to the same number as held by his right hand opponent, by ruffing one winner from the dummy.

SINGLE RAISE. A raise of opener's one-level suit opening to the two-level. The normal range of the bid is 6-9 high-card points; but 10 is possible, and less than 6 is common when there is distributional compensation.

The higher the rank of the opener's suit, the less length is required by responder to raise. 1♠ tends to be a five-card suit in traditional methods and can be raised freely with three-card support. The five-card major-suit bidders might raise with only a doubleton. 1♥ is often raised to two with three-card support, but a raise from 1♦ to 2♦ almost invariably indicates four cards or more. This is a possible exception:

    ♠ 4 3   ♥ 5 2   ♦ A 5 2   ♣ Q 9 7 4 3 2

In reply to 1♣, even four-card support may not be sufficient. With a 3-3-3-4 hand, 1♦ or 1NT might be preferred to 2♣. (See BIDDABLE SUITS.) For some special treatments of single raises see BERGEN RAISES, INVERTED MINOR SUIT RAISES, SINGLE RAISE IN MAJOR, CONSTRUCTIVE.

Rebids by the opener below the game level are almost always game invitations. (See ROMEX, SHORT-SUIT GAME TRY; TRIAL BID; TWO-WAY GAME TRY; WEAK SUIT GAME TRY.) Many partnerships make an exception if opener raises again; this can be regarded as a preemptive measure, especially if the suit is a minor. A rebid of 2NT (1♥ - 2♥ - 2NT) shows 19-20 points, highly invitational but not forcing. If responder then rebids a lower-ranking suit, he is showing a long suit and general weakness.

A raise with a doubleton is possible in competition. If 1♠ is overcalled with 2♥, a 2♠ bid is acceptable with a doubleton honor and 8-10 points.

SINGLE RAISE IN MAJOR, CONSTRUCTIVE. In ROTH-STONE, a raise from 1♠ to 2♠ or 1♥ to 2♥ shows 10-12 points and is very rarely passed.

                ♠ K 5 4
                ♥ A 9 6 3
                ♦ Q J
                ♣ 8 4 3

See ONE NOTRUMP RESPONSE TO MAJOR, FORCING.

SINGLE RAISE IN RESPONDER'S SUIT. See OPENER'S REBID.

SINGLETON. An original holding of exactly one card in a suit. Also called a STIFF. For valuation in a suit contract see DISTRIBUTIONAL COUNTS, DISTRIBUTIONAL VALUES.

SINGLETON-SHOWING BID. See SPLINTER BID; SINGLETON SWISS.

SINGLETON SWISS. In response to a major-suit opening, 4♣ shows good controls, two aces and a singleton. The opener bids 4♦ to ask for the location of the singleton. A 4♦ response shows two aces without a singleton. See SWISS CONVENTION.

SION-COKIN AFFAIR. Steve Sion and Alan Cokin

were expelled from the American Contract Bridge League in July 1979. The action took place after the Appeals and Charges Committee of the Board of Directors determined that this pair had used "prearranged improper communications" during a zonal playoff of the Grand National Teams in Atlanta earlier that year. Some players believed the pair was using illegal signals and worked to discover if this was true, and if so how the system worked. Eventually the code was broken – the pair used pencil placement to pass information about their hands across the table. It is most normal for a player to pick up a pen or pencil after completion of the bidding to record the contract on a scorecard, so such an action would not be suspect as of itself. But the observers found that the angle at which the pencil was placed carried a special message.

The Atlanta tournament appeals committee listened to testimony for 15 hours and heard many witnesses before adjudging the pair guilty. The pair appealed to the national Board, and the case was turned over to the Appeals and Charges Committee. The hearing took place on July 8, 1979, at ACBL Headquarters in Memphis, and many witnesses testified. After 17 hours of deliberation, the committee found the pair guilty of violating Law 80, Part II, Section B. 2 of the Proprieties, which reads as follows:

"Prearranged improper communication. The gravest possible offense against propriety is for a partnership to exchange information through prearranged methods of communication other than those sanctioned by these Laws. The penalty imposed for infractions is normally expulsion from the sponsoring organization." Sion and Cokin attempted to have the ruling overturned by filing a civil suit in which they claimed their ability to earn a living through playing bridge had been taken from them. The courts did not overrule the ACBL's decision.

After five years both players applied for reinstatement. This was granted with certain stipulations, the most important of which was that they would not be allowed to play as a partnership. Since that time Cokin has devoted himself to overcoming this blemish on his record by helping others to become better bridge players and by playing the game strictly according to the rules. However, Sion became involved in another serious proprieties case in 1997 and was once again expelled.

SIT, SIT FOR. To pass partner's PENALTY DOUBLE or TAKEOUT DOUBLE.

SIT OUT. (1) (Verb) To miss a round of play in a duplicate game because there is an odd number of pairs. (2) Waiting to cut in to a Chicago or rubber bridge game.

SITTING. A session of bridge. Also a descriptive term referring to one's position at the table, i.e., North, West, etc. See SEAT, SESSION.

SIX or SIX-SPOT. The ninth highest card in a suit.

SIX NOTRUMP OPENING. A very rare opening bid showing a balanced hand with 12 sure tricks. Responder should raise if he holds an ace or a king. (To raise with a queen is less clear-cut.)

SIX-ODD. Six tricks over book or 12 tricks in all.

SIX OF A SUIT OPENING. The theoretical meaning of this bid is a 12-trick hand which is missing only the ace or king of trumps. Such a hand has such low frequency that the bid is idle. It is perhaps more sensible to reserve it for a freak hand, possibly a complete two-suiter which is likely to offer some play for 12 tricks. This has the required preemptive value and does not encourage the opponents to save, as they would if the opener had guaranteed 12 tricks.

SIX TABLES. At duplicate, six tables provide for competition among 24 players as individuals, 12 pairs or six teams.

In addition, there is available a 25-player individual movement, which can be used for a one-session game using 30 boards, or a two-session game using only 25 boards per session.

As a pair contest, either the MITCHELL or the HOWELL MOVEMENT can be used. If a Mitchell is used, two adjacent tables, such as 1 and 6, share boards by relay, and a byestand is set up halfway around–in this case between tables 3 and 4. The movement is the usual Mitchell, with board sets stopping off at the byestand after being played at table 4. The full six rounds must be played, usually four boards to the round. Top is 5 in the ACBL, 10 elsewhere. If the Howell movement is used, the full 11-round, 22-board movement is desirable for an early finish. For a longer game, the nine-round, three-boards-to-a-round REDUCED HOWELL is excellent. If you lack guide cards for this movement you may play a 5-table Howell with an APPENDIX TABLE.

For a team game the THURNER MOVEMENT is good. As an alternative you may start by having the moving pairs skip a table in the lower direction. After the first round have the moving pairs skip an extra table. After the second round the moving pairs move normally. After the third round the East-West pairs skip an extra table and the boards skip a table. For the last round tables 1 and 4, 2 and 5, 3 and 6 share the boards and relay. East-West Pair 1 follows these moves; 5, 2, 6, 3; then to 4 for the relay. A Swiss Team Movement is not practical for so few teams. For IMP matches use the movement shown for a team-of-four and score each match on IMPs. The STAGGER MOVEMENT has considerable advantages. For 5$\frac{1}{2}$ tables or 6$\frac{1}{2}$ tables, see HALF TABLES. An individual movement for 12 rounds is available; for details, see MINGLED MOVEMENT. There is also a 25-player movement in 25 rounds.

SIXTEEN, RULE OF. See RULE OF SIXTEEN.

SKIP, SKIP MOVEMENT. An irregularity in the progression of the traveling pairs (or the boards) in a MITCHELL MOVEMENT pair game with an even number of tables, where it is not necessary that all contestants play every board in play. Skips also are used in certain forms of team movements, notably board-a-match events with an even number of tables. Skips also are employed in certain individual events, notably the 15-table movement.

SKIP BID. In a wide sense, any bid at a level higher than is required by the previous auction. In practice, a skip bid is used to refer to weak preemptive actions, whether as an opening bid, an overcall or a response. (See PREEMPTIVE BID, WEAK JUMP OVERCALL

and PREEMPTIVE RESPONSE.) To avoid the ethical problems that may arise after preemptive action, the SKIP-BID WARNING is usually used in North America.

SKIP-BID WARNING. A notice given to the opponent by a player who is about to skip at least one level of the bidding. Such a player announces, "I am about to make a skip bid, please wait." The next player to call is expected to hesitate approximately 10 seconds before making his call.

The reason for this warning is that immediate actions by the player on the left of the player who makes a skip bid can give partner information to which he is not entitled. For instance, a quick pass could be construed as showing few if any values. A quick double could mean the player has a very good hand. Long thought before finally making a call or a bid could easily indicate a hand on which no clear-cut action is called for.

All these actions could be perfectly ethical for the player who makes them. However, each one puts a very strong ethical burden on partner. Partner is not supposed to act on the basis that a quick pass shows very little strength, a quick double shows a lot of strength, and a slow pass or bid shows doubt as to whether the pass or the double should have been made. Since the skip-bid warning requires approximately a 10-second hesitation at all times by the next player to call, right-hand opponent will rarely have an ethical problem when left-hand opponent is forced to hesitate under all circumstances. However, if the hesitation is markedly longer than 10 seconds, fourth player may still have an ethical problem.

Sam Fry Jr. was the first to propose such a compulsory pause – he suggested it in 1938. The ACBL adopted this procedure in 1957.

When BIDDING BOXES are used in international matches where SCREENS are not in use, the player who is about to make a skip-bid places a sign saying "Stop!" on the table. He then makes his skip bid, and the next opponent to call must refrain from making his call until the skip bidder has picked up the "Stop" sign. Skip-bid warnings are not necessary when screens are in use because the two calls from one side of the screen come to the attention of the players on the other side at the same time.

SKIP MITCHELL. See MITCHELL MOVEMENT.

SLAM. The winning of 12 tricks (SMALL SLAM, previously called little slam) or all 13 tricks (GRAND SLAM) An original object in the earliest forms of WHIST (some of which were called "Slamm"), these results were rewarded by bonuses in BRIDGE-WHIST and auction bridge regardless of the declaration, so much so that in auction bridge a side that bid seven and won 12 tricks still received the 50-point premium for a small slam although the contract was down one. In contract bridge, however, slam bonuses are paid only when the slam is both bid and made. See SLAM BONUS.

SLAM BIDDING. The methods by which slam contracts are investigated. Accurate slam bidding is vital for a winning player. Successful slams earn large bonuses, and those that fail are severely penalized (the undertrick penalty plus the value of the lost game). Ironically, the history of world championship matches is studded with failures in the slam zone.

The three vital ingredients of a successful slam are trumps, tricks and controls. A partnership must determine that it has a satisfactory suit (STRAIN), that it has the values to take 12 or 13 tricks and that the defense cannot beat the slam at the outset.

The early creation of a game-forcing situation often provides the spark for slam investigation. (See FAST ARRIVAL, PRINCIPLE OF). Conventions have been devised to give slam information simultaneously with the announcement of a trump fit. (See JACOBY 2NT, SPLINTER BID, SUPER SWISS, UNBALANCED SWISS RAISE, VALUE SWISS RAISES.) Once a satisfactory trump fit is established, either player may start the search if he suspects the possibility of slam. Cuebidding may be approached in various ways.

Control bidding, usually an ace, invites partner to cooperate, if his hand is suitable, by cuebidding a control in return or bidding slam. (Good players avoid initial cuebids on singletons and void suits. Doing so may induce partner to attach the wrong value to supporting kings and queens.)

West	East
♠ A K J 10 4	♠ 8
♥ K J 9 8	♥ A Q 10 6 5 2
♦ 6 2	♦ Q 5 4
♣ K 9	♣ A J 3

West	East
1♠	2♥
4♥	5♣
5♥	

By bidding 5♣, East shows the ♣A and asks West his opinion of slam. Having nothing to spare for his bidding, West signs off by returning to the agreed trump suit.

West	East
♠ A K 6 4	♠ 8 2
♥ K 6 5	♥ A Q J 9 2
♦ Q 6	♦ A K 5 3
♣ A 9 6 3	♣ 8 4

West	East
1NT	3♥
4♥	5♦
6♥	

East tries for slam with a 5♦ cuebid; West, with both black aces and fair trumps, accepts.

When a player invites slam with a cuebid, the partnership must clearly be in the slam zone.

West	East
1♥	2♥
3♣	

West does not promise slam interest; he may be trying for game.

Sometimes, however, slam tries are made below game:

West	East
♠ A K J 9 8	♠ Q 10 4 3
♥ 10 6	♥ K Q 9 7
♦ A Q 4	♦ K 10 2
♣ K J 9	♣ Q 2

West	East
1♠	3♠
4♦	4♠

Over East's forcing raise, West shows slam interest with 4♦, a convenient try that does not commit the partner-

ship past game. East lacks controls and declines. When-ever possible, the first slam try should be below game. See LAST TRAIN CUEBID.

West	East
♠ A J 8	♠ K Q 10 6 3
♥ K 10 7 6	♥ A 3
♦ A Q 10 7	♦ 8 3 2
♣ K 9	♣ A 8 6

West	East
1NT	3♠
4♦	4♥
4♠	5♣
6♠	

West's 4♦ does not suggest an alternative trump suit; spades are agreed by implication, since without spade support, West would return to 3NT. The 4♦ bid is a slam try showing the ♦A, a maximum hand and good spade support. With two aces, East cooperates by showing the ♥A. West has nothing more to say, but when East makes a further try, West accepts. (See ADVANCE CUEBID.)

Slam auctions are invariably more accurate when the trump suit is agreed early. Otherwise accidents can hap-pen.

West	East
♠ A K J 8 5 2	♠ 7
♥ A J 5	♥ K 4
♦ K J 4	♦ A Q 10 7 2
♣ 4	♣ K Q 9 5 2

West	East
1♠	2♦
3♠	4♣
4♥	4♠
5♦	6♦
6♠	

East probably thought 4♥ showed a suit and felt obliged to take a 4♠ preference on his singleton. West thought East's 4♣ had been a cuebid, preparatory to showing spade support. 6♠ went down when 6♦ was on. West could have avoided this result if he had set trumps by bidding 4♦ or 5♦ over 4♣.

It is rare, but possible, to involve third-round controls:

West	East
♠ A K 9 8 5 2	♠ Q J 7 6
♥ A K 6 4	♥ 5 3
♦ A K 4	♦ Q 7 3 2
♣ —	♣ J 5 2

West	East
2♣	2♦
2♠	4♠ (1)
5♥	6♦ (2)
7♠	

(1) Good spades, but no side ace, king or singleton.
(2) Since East has denied any first- or second-round control, this bid shows third-round diamond control and, since it accepts West's slam try, implies third-round heart control. (See CUEBIDS TO SHOW CONTROLS.)

A Voluntary Bid Beyond Game is a slam try that usu-ally asks about control of a specific suit.

West	East
♠ A K J 10 8 7	♠ Q 9
♥ Q 4	♥ 7 6
♦ A 10 7	♦ K Q 9 8 4
♣ K 6	♣ A Q 10 7

West	East
1♠	2♣
3♠	4♣
4♦	4♠
5♠	

West interprets East's sequence as a mild slam try. Since West has the minor suits under control, his 5♠ bid compels East to bid slam with as much as second-round control in hearts, the unbid suit. Though East holds a useful hand, he must pass.

West	East
♠ Q 7 6 4	♠ A K J 5 3
♥ A 6 5 4	♥ 8 7
♦ A 10 4	♦ 7
♣ 5 4	♣ A K Q J 2

West	East
Pass	1♠
3♠	4♣
4♦	5♠
6♥	7♣
7♠	

East's 5♠ bid asks West to bid slam with a control in hearts. Since West has the ♥A, he cuebids 6♥, and East-West reach the grand slam.

If the opponents have bid, a bid of five of the agreed trump suit asks partner to bid a slam if he controls the enemy suit, unless one member of the partnership has cuebid the suit.

West	North	East	South
			1♥
2♠	3♥	Pass	5♥

South has a powerful hand, but losing spades.

West	North	East	South
			1♥
1♠	3♥	Pass	3♠
Pass	4♥	Pass	5♥

South has spades controlled, but poor trumps. South probably has both minor-suit aces, since he would cuebid if he had one or the other.

The situation changes when the opponents' bidding *forces* the auction to the five level.

West	North	East	South
			1♥
1♠	3♥	4♠	5♥

South has no slam aspirations. He feels that doubling 4♠ will not produce a satisfactory penalty and prefers to try for 11 tricks at 5♥.

Even a bid of 5♣ or 5♦ by South would not clearly be a try for slam. In a competitive auction, it is more practical to use new-suit bids to assist partner's judg-ment. South might bid 5♦ on:

♠ —
♥ A K J 6 5
♦ A J 10 5 4
♣ 6 5 2

to help North decide what to do if East-West go on to 5♠.

Cuebidding Style. One important cuebidding ques-tion a pair must answer is whether return cuebids below game are *cooperative* or *constructive*.

West	North	East	South
			1♣
1♠	2♦	Pass	2♥
Pass	4♦	Pass	?

South holds:

♠ A J
♥ Q J 10 7
♦ A 3
♣ J 8 7 6 3

Although South has a minimum hand, some players would consider a 4♠ cuebid mandatory; others would exercise judgment and bid 5♦.

The sequence;

West	East
1♠	3♠
4♦	5♣
5♥	

sounds as if it is asking about trump quality.

Few players are willing to go *past game* to make a doubtful cuebid.

West	East
♠ K 3	♠ A Q 4 2
♥ A J 10 5 4	♥ K Q 3 2
♦ A K J	♦ 7 6 5
♣ J 4 3	♣ Q 6

West	East
1♥	3♥
4♦	4♥

Since East has a minimum, he refuses to cuebid 4♠. With a choice of aces to cuebid, the usual choice is the cheapest ace to save bidding room.

West	East
♠ Q J 8 5 2	♠ A K 9 4
♥ A K 7 3	♥ 8 2
♦ 5	♦ A J 8 3
♣ A J 5	♣ K 4 3

West	East
1♠	3♠
4♣	4♦
4♥	5♣
5♥	6♠

Positional Slams. Occasionally slam can be made only from one side of the table. Thus, a player with a vulnerable holding tries to become declarer for protection from the opening lead.

♠ A K Q 9 7 6 5 2
♥ 8 5
♦ K
♣ J 2

♠ J 4 3	♠ 10
♥ J 6 2	♥ K 7 4 3
♦ J 8 4	♦ 9 7 3 2
♣ A Q 10 7	♣ 8 6 5 4

♠ 8
♥ A Q 10 9
♦ A Q 10 6 5
♣ K 9 3

This deal is from the 1962 Bermuda Bowl match between Great Britain and North America. In one room North America played 4♠, taking 11 tricks after a club lead. The British bidding was:

South	North
1♦	2♠
3♥	4♠
4NT	5♦
6NT	

North's bidding showed a solid spade suit. Learning through BLACKWOOD that the ♣A was missing, South

bid slam in notrump to protect his ♣K.

West	East
♠ A J 10 8	♠ K Q 7 3 2
♥ K	♥ A 10 8 3
♦ A Q 10	♦ J 8 7
♣ K Q J 10 2	♣ 6

West	East
1♣	1♠
4♠	5♥
6NT	

West accepts his partner's slam try, but bids 6NT; at 6♠, a diamond opening lead might break the contract. (See RIGHT SIDE.)

Asking About Controls. Since controls are a necessary feature of successful slams, conventions have been devised to determine how many aces and kings a partnership holds. The most prevalent is BLACKWOOD.

West	East
♠ A	♠ K 8
♥ K 10 8 7	♥ A Q 9 6 3 2
♦ A 5	♦ K Q 10
♣ A Q 9 8 7 6	♣ 10 3

West	East
1♣	1♥
4♥	4NT
5♠	5NT
6♦	6♥

The 4NT and 5NT bids are conventional, and West responds by showing aces and kings (5♠ = three aces, 6♦ = one king). Though East has a powerful hand, he must not venture beyond six, because he knows a critical king is missing.

Although Blackwood determines the total number of aces and kings a pair holds, it reveals nothing about power, trump quality or the fit in a key side suit; nor should a player use Blackwood if he must identify *specific* controls. West holds:

♠ A K Q 10 7 4 2
♥ 7
♦ 8 3
♣ A Q 4

West opens 1♠ and jumps to 3♠ over a 2♣ response by East. East raises to 4♠. West wants to be in slam if East has the ♦A, but if East instead has the ♥A, the defense may take the first two diamond tricks. Since a 5♦ response to Blackwood will leave West no wiser, he should cuebid 5♣, inviting East to cuebid an ace. If East then bids 5♦, West can jump to 6♠.

Variations of Blackwood are popular. See BABY BLACKWOOD, EXCLUSION BLACKWOOD, KEY CARD BLACKWOOD, REDWOOD, ROMAN BLACKWOOD, ROMAN KEY CARD BLACKWOOD.

ASKING BIDS inquire about controls in a specific suit.

West	East
1♠	3♠
5♣	

If asking bids are in use, West's 5♣ bid may conventionally ask East about his holding in clubs. East's responses would be conventional and confirm or deny controls.

West	East
4♥	5♣

East asks West whether he has a control in clubs (or even in diamonds). East might hold:

```
♠ A 5
♥ A 7
♦ A K Q 8 3
♣ 9 6 4 2
```

For details see ASKING BIDS.

Among the more scientific slam-bidding methods, RELAY SYSTEMS are renowned for their accuracy.

Distributional Slams. Well-fitting hands may produce slam with far fewer than 33 high-card points. If a player shows his distribution while committing to game, he suggests slam and lets partner judge the fit.

West	East
♠ K Q 10 8 4	♠ A J 6
♥ A 7 4 2	♥ 5
♦ 7 4	♦ K Q 8 3
♣ K Q	♣ A J 8 6 2

West	East
1 ♠	2 ♣
2 ♥	3 ♦
3NT	4 ♠
6 ♠	

If East were interested in game, he would bid 3 ♠ at his second turn. Since East stops to bid diamonds before supporting spades, he promises extra strength and heart shortness. If West had an unsuitable heart holding (such as K-J-4-2) or no help in clubs, he would avoid slam.

SPLINTER BIDS are a popular slam-bidding tool with wide application. A splinter bid is an unusual jump to show support for partner's suit with shortness in the suit in which the jump is made. Partner can judge how well the hands fit.

Trump Suit Quality. If a grand slam is on the horizon, trump solidity is a critical factor. When a trump suit is agreed, a 5NT bid is available. This is the GRAND SLAM FORCE, asking responder to bid seven if he holds two of the top three trump honors. West holds:

```
♠ Q J 8 4
♥ A K Q 6 4 2
♦ —
♣ A K 6
```

West opens 2♣, strong and artificial, and East responds 2♠, natural and positive. West's only concern is the spade suit, and a bid of 5NT, agreeing spades by inference, will let East bid seven if he holds the A-K; otherwise, East will settle for a small slam.

Blasting. The success of slam contracts often depends on the opening lead. A player may resort to an adventurous approach when either he despairs of locating key cards in his partner's hand or feels that the opponents are more likely to profit from scientific investigation. South holds:

```
♠ K 7 4 3
♥ A K J 10 6 2
♦ —
♣ 6 4 2
```

North opens 1♠ and rebids 2♠ over South's 2♥ response. 6♠ must have an excellent chance without a club lead, and rather than tip off the opponents, South might blast into 6♠. In the same vein, a player may bid a nonexistent suit en route to a slam to discourage a possibly lethal lead. South holds:

```
♠ Q J 6 4 2
♥ —
♦ A K 10 6 4 2
♣ 3 2
```

If North opens 1♠, South might jump to 6♠ directly. However, against ingenuous opponents, it may pay to bid a tactical 2♣ first in an effort to get a favorable lead. However, this tactic may induce a LIGHTNER DOUBLE. (See PSYCHIC BIDDING.)

West	East
♠ K J 7	♠ A Q 10 8 5 2
♥ A K J 4	♥ 3
♦ Q 8 6 3	♦ J 4
♣ Q 8	♣ A K J 4

West	East
1NT	3 ♠
4 ♠	5 ♣
5 ♥	5 ♠

This would be the auction if East-West used cuebidding. They would discover the lack of a diamond control and stop at 5 ♠. In real life, East might bash into 6 ♠ over 1NT. South must find the diamond lead to beat the contract.

Bidding slams at notrump is often easier, especially after an opening bid in notrump. Point count can evaluate balanced hands and reduce the matter to simple arithmetic: responder can add his points to opener's and place the contract. East holds:

```
♠ Q J 8
♥ A J
♦ K Q 3
♣ K J 8 4 2
```

If West opens 1NT, showing at least 16 points, East can leap to 6NT, counting at least 33 points in the combined hands.

With an in-between hand, responder needs his partner's cooperation and bids 4NT as an invitation. By going past game, East shows slam interest and asks West to continue with a maximum. (See EXPECTED NUMBER OF CONTROLS IN BALANCED HANDS.)

West	East
♠ A 8 4	♠ K 6 3
♥ J 6 4	♥ A K
♦ K J 3	♦ A Q 7 4
♣ A K 8 3	♣ Q J 6 4

West	East
1NT	5NT
6 ♣	7 ♣

East's 5NT bid forces to 6NT and invites a grand slam. West shows his strong four-card club suit on the way, and East-West reach a good grand slam.

Since in notrump sequences a 4NT bid has a quantitative meaning, Blackwood is unavailable. A bid of 4♣, the GERBER convention, is used instead to check on aces and kings.

Power slam auctions are also available when a trump suit is agreed. If South opens 1♠ on:

```
♠ A Q 9 6 4
♥ K 5
♦ A J 4
♣ A Q 7
```

and North raises to 3♠ (forcing), South can try 6♠. The power for slam is there, and controls are no problem.

Jump shifts. An immediate jump shift by responder suggests slam and implies that responder knows in what STRAIN the hand should play. Hence, responder may

have great high-card strength for notrump, a solid suit or a fit for opener's suit. South has:

      ♠ 7
      ♥ K Q 5 4 3
      ♦ A K J 4 3 2
      ♣ 3

If North opens 1 ♥, South should jump to 3 ♦, intending to support hearts next.

On some strong hands, a jump shift is ill-prepared. South holds:

      ♠ A Q 10 5
      ♥ 5
      ♦ A K 5 4
      ♣ A Q 4 3

If North opens 1 ♥, South should respond 1 ♠. South needs bidding space to look for the best strain.

Slams at Duplicate. Because a minus score usually produces a poor result, matchpoint duplicate players tend to be conservative slam bidders. If good play is required to take 12 tricks, a good matchpoint score is available for +480 or +680. If most pairs in the field will bid a slam, however, players may prefer a higher-scoring strain even though a slightly superior slam is available in a minor suit.

Five-or-Seven Deals.

Dlr: North
Vul: None

      ♠ 8
      ♥ Q 5 2
      ♦ A Q 8 7 6 5 2
      ♣ K 9

♠ Q J 9 7 5 3   ♠ A K 10 4
♥ 10 8 4   ♥ A 9 3
♦ 10   ♦ —
♣ 6 3 2   ♣ A Q J 10 8 4

      ♠ 6 2
      ♥ K J 7 6
      ♦ K J 9 4 3
      ♣ 7 5

Table 1

West	North	East	South
	1 ♦	Dbl	1 ♥
1 ♠	2 ♥	5NT	Pass
6 ♠ (1)	Pass	7 ♠	All Pass

(1) One top honor, extra length

Table 2

West	North	East	South
	1 ♦	Dbl	1 ♥
1 ♠	2 ♦	3 ♦	4 ♦
Pass	5 ♦	6 ♠	All Pass

This deal arose in the 1986 Vanderbilt Teams. At table 1 East (Edgar Kaplan) thought he might as well bid seven. If South had held the ♣K, a heart lead would have beaten 5 ♠; as it was, 7 ♠ was cold.

Since East-West stopped in a small slam at the other table, Kaplan was getting excellent odds; he would gain 11 IMPs if the ♣K was right and lose 2 if it was wrong.

SLAM BONUS. The amount of points awarded for bidding and making a slam. The grand slam bonus is 1500 if vulnerable, 1000 if not. The small slam bonus is 750 if vulnerable, 500 if not. These bonuses are in addition to trick points, honors, game bonuses and awards for making doubled or redoubled contracts.

SLAM CONVENTIONS. Specialized methods adopted for slam exploration include the following conventions which are listed separately: ACOL DIRECT KING;

ACOL FOUR NOTRUMP OPENING; ALPHA ASKING BIDS; ANTISPLINTER; ASKING BIDS; BABY BLACKWOOD; BARON SLAM TRY; BETA ASKING BIDS; BLACK AND RED GERBER; BLACKWOOD; BLACKWOOD AFTER INTERFERENCE; BLUE TEAM FOUR CLUB AND FOUR DIAMOND; BYZANTINE BLACKWOOD; CULBERTSON FOUR-FIVE NOTRUMP; DECLARATIVE-INTERROGATIVE FOUR NOTRUMP; DENIAL CUEBID; EXTENDED GERBER; FRAGMENT BID; GAMMA TRUMP ASKING BID; GENERAL PURPOSE CUEBID; GERBER; GRAND SLAM FORCE; KEYCARD BLACKWOOD; KEYCARD GERBER; KICKBACK; LAST TRAIN CUEBID; LIGHTNER DOUBLE; MINOR-SUIT SWISS; NORMAN FOUR NOTRUMP; PRECISION ASKING BIDS; PREEMPTIVE ROMAN KEYCARD BLACKWOOD; REVERSE SWISS; R/H 4NT CONVENTION; ROMAN ASKING BIDS; ROMAN BLACKWOOD; ROMAN GERBER; ROMAN KEYCARD BLACKWOOD; ROMEX TRUMP ASKING BIDS; SAN FRANCISCO; SERIOUS THREE NOTRUMP; SHARPLES; SINGLETON SWISS; SIX NOTRUMP OPENING; SIX OF A SUIT OPENING; SLIVER BID; SMITH CONVENTION; SPLINTER; SUCKER DOUBLE; SUPER BLACK-WOOD; SUPER GERBER; SUPER PRECISION ASKING BIDS; SUPER SWISS; SWISS; TRUMP ASKING BID; VALUE OF SLAM; See also topics such as EXPECTED NUMBER OF CONTROLS IN BALANCED HANDS; FAST ARRIVAL, PRINCIPLE OF; RIGHT SIDE; SAFETY LEVEL.

SLAM DOUBLE CONVENTIONS. See DOUBLE FOR SACRIFICE; LIGHTNER DOUBLE.

SLAM LEADS. Opening leads against slam contracts frequently involve some special considerations. The general principle is to make passive leads against grand slams and active leads against small slams, but there are many exceptions to this.

An attacking lead against a small slam is often necessary when the bidding indicates a long, establishable suit in the dummy. It may then be necessary for the defense to lead from a king or a queen, in the hope of establishing a trick in the suit led before dummy's suit can be established for discards. But if declarer and dummy both seem likely to have balanced hands, whether or not the contract is notrump, a passive lead is indicated. A deceptive lead is often appropriate, such as a third-best, a fifth-best, or the lower of touching honors. Misinforming the leader's partner is usually less important than misleading the declarer. Assessing the safety of a lead depends on the bidding as well as the suit holding. A low trump is safe from three small if the declaring side can be credited with at least nine trumps, but it would be unsafe against a likely eight-card trump fit, because partner may have Q-x.

The lead of an ace is right more often than some authorities indicate. Apart from the obvious advantage at matchpoint of preventing an overtrick, the ace lead is desirable if the opposing bidding has been crowded or rushed in such a way that two top losers are likely. See also LEADS; LIGHTNER DOUBLE.

SLIDING BLACKWOOD. See ROLLING BLACKWOOD.

SLIDING BOX. See TRAY.

SLIDING GERBER. See ROLLING GERBER.

SLIVER BID. An extension of the SPLINTER BID principle, devised by George Rosenkranz for use with weaker responding hands. With four- or preferably, five-card trump support for a major suit opening and fewer than 10 HCP, the standard response would be a jump to game. When such a hand includes a singleton or void and a minimum of three controls including at least one king (2 controls – ace or void; 1 control – king or single-ton) possession of a "sliver" is indicated by a response of 3NT. Opener's rebids: Sign off in the major with more than five losers and a hand poor in HCP and controls. With at least six high-card controls, or five controls and a singleton, 15 or more HCP and fewer than six losers, opener explores slam possibilities by bidding the suit where responder's singleton or void will represent du-plication and be of least value.

Responder's rebids: Sign off by bidding game in agreed suit if singleton or void is opposite partner's "exclusion" rebid. With shortage elsewhere, rebid by steps: 1st step: Singleton in lower unbid side suit. 2nd step: Singleton in higher suit. 3rd step: Void in lower unbid suit. 4th step: Void in higher unbid suit. In count-ing steps, a game bid in the agreed trump suit – the sign-off – is omitted.

SLOW ARRIVAL. Players using two-over-one game-forcing often have a choice about whether to bid game quickly or slowly.

	(a)		(b)
West	East	West	East
1♠	2♥	1♠	2♣
3♥ or 4♥		2♥	3♥ or 4♥

Many favor FAST ARRIVAL, with the immediate jump to game showing minimum values. However, the expert consensus in BWS 2001 was against this. The majority view is that 4♥ in sequence (a) should be stronger than 3♥, and that 4♥ in (b) should show strong trumps. In each case, the single raise is non-descriptive.

SLOW PASS. A pass made with enough of a pause to indicate that the passer also was considering an alterna-tive action. Since it is very possible that such action could convey unauthorized information to partner, the slow pass often results in director calls and appeals. The part-ner of the slow passer often finds himself in an impos-sible situation where any action he takes could be ap-pealed as being a result of the unauthorized information provided by the slow pass. In recent years appeals com-mittees both at the world level and the national level have frequently adjusted results as a result of slow pass situations. Here are four situations that arise as a result of a slow pass.

(1) If the opening bidder takes some time before pass-ing, he probably was considering opening the bidding and then decided against it. Of course it is possible he was considering some other action, such as a weak two-bid or a preempt, but the likelihood is that he was con-sidering opening the bidding with a one-bid. His part-ner must be careful not to take advantage of the implied message.

(2) A slow pass could indicate a willingness to go to a higher level if the opponents compete. If opener starts

with 1♠ and thinks for some time before passing partner's raise to 2♠, it is clear that he considered his hand almost good enough to bid again. If the oppo-nents compete, partner is not allowed to use this infer-ence.

(3) A slow pass often is extremely revealing in com-petitive situations, and this is the area where most of the director calls and appeals occur. Some of the prob-lems are avoided by the SKIP BID WARNING. Nev-ertheless many situations arise where it is next to im-possible for the partner of the slow passer not to be influenced, at least subconsciously. Appeals commit-tees take this into consideration when ruling on slow pass situations.

(4) Even a slow final pass can send unauthorized information. In a slam auction, for instance, the slow pass could indicate that the passer was thinking of making a Lightner double and then thought better of it. If partner makes an opening lead that fits the Lightner double, the opponents certainly will have grounds for appeal.

SLOW PLAY. As opposed to careful or thoughtful play, slow play is discourteous not only to the opponents of the moment, but to all other competitors as well. In rubber bridge, it decreases the number of hands that can be played in a session; in duplicate tournaments, a con-sistently slow pair can delay the entire game by many minutes.

Contributing to slow play as defined here are some or all of these violations of the Proprieties of duplicate play: (1) delay in coming to the table after the round has been called; (2) discussion of boards previously played; (3) failure to pass at least one completed board promptly; (4) inattention during the bidding necessi-tating frequent reviews of the auction; (5) post-mortems, particularly those involving the player whose duty it is to score the board just played; (6) failure to accept a ruling from the director pleasantly and promptly in the event of an infraction; (7) blaming pre-vious opponents for present tardiness instead of con-centrating on finishing the present hand; (8) waiting for a miracle to change the opponents' aces to deuces so that a bad contract will not receive its deserved re-sult. The LAWS OF DUPLICATE specifically provide that as a matter of courtesy a player should avoid "Pro-longing play unnecessarily for the purpose of discon-certing the other players." (Proprieties III.)

In national and international championships a team which repeatedly exceeds the time limit allowed for play is subject to penalties. The penalty may take the form of a matchpoint or victory-point "fine." It may be as ex-treme as exclusion of a team from an event. In team events, the penalty sometimes takes the form of barring offending pairs from playing as partners in later rounds. Sometimes SEEDING POINTS are subtracted from a pair's total.

There is a recurring problem in controlling slow play in major national and international team play. If a table is slow, players may ask for a monitor to keep track of the time use, but there is no record of the period during which the problem arose.

The use of chess clocks has been proposed as a means of monitoring slow play. However, experiments with chess clocks have not been fruitful.

In the final of the 2000 Venice Cup in Bermuda, the

Dutch team won by one-half an IMP after profiting from the imposition of a slow play penalty against the American team. This caused considerable controversy, with many believing that such a penalty should not change the result of a match. Others feel there is no way to control persistently slow players without the imposition of meaningful penalties.

SLOW SHOWS, FAST DENIES. The idea that a Lebensohl bid followed by a cuebid or 3NT promises a stopper in the opponent's suit:

West	North	East	South
1NT	2♥	2NT	Pass
3♣	Pass	3♥ or 3NT	

These bids show a heart stopper. Conversely, such bids made on the first round deny a heart stopper.

Some players prefer the converse: Slow denies, direct shows.

The same idea applies when Lebensohl is used in response to a double of a Weak Two-bid.

SLUFF. To dispose of a loser by throwing it off on the lead of a suit not held by the sluffer. The word derives from slough, to cast off.

SMALL CARD. A card in a suit lower than the 6, although the 6 itself on occasion is considered a small card.

SMALL SLAM. The bidding and making of six-odd, or 12 tricks in all. The premium, scored above the line in rubber bridge, but in regular fashion in Chicago or Duplicate, is 500 points when not vulnerable and 750 points when vulnerable. See SLAM BIDDING for a mathematical treatment of percentage expectation of success for the bid. See also MATHEMATICAL VALUE OF GAME.

SMITH CONVENTION. (1) A club takeout as a DEFENSE TO OPENING THREE-BID, devised by Curtis Smith. (2) A 4NT slam convention devised by William S. Smith and Gertrude Smith of Waterbury CT, in 1935 and which was popular for many years. Identical in principle to the NORMAN 4NT, it is different in one detail - a response of 5♠ showed specifically one ace and three kings, while 5NT was used to show two aces and one king.

SMITH SIGNAL. An ATTITUDE signal given at the first opportunity by the partner of the opening leader against a notrump contract to indicate the degree of enthusiasm for the opening leader's suit. If defender's first spot card is low, this indicates he cannot stand a continuation in the opening leader's suit should opening leader regain the lead. Conversely, following with a high spot card pinpoints the desirability of a second lead in the original suit led. The opening leader can give the same kind of signal – a high spot card indicates a desire to have the opening suit continued should partner gain the lead; a low spot card suggests trying something else. The signal is sometimes attributed to T.R.H. Lyons of Great Britain, but I.G.Smith of Great Britain suggested virtually the same signal as early as the December 1963 issue of *British Bridge World*. Here is how the signal works:

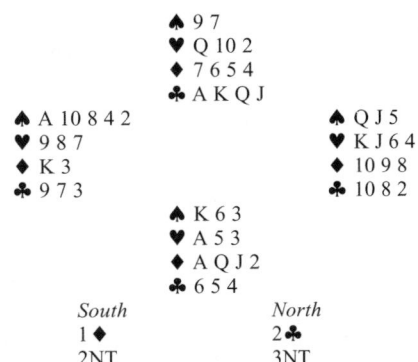

South	North
1♦	2♣
2NT	3NT

West leads the ♠4 against 3NT. Declarer wins East's jack with the king and leads a club to dummy. East should play the ♣10 on this trick, meaning please continue. Declarer takes the diamond finesse, and when West wins the king he cashes four spade tricks for one down. Now suppose the East and South cards had been slightly different:

```
              ♠ 9 7
              ♥ Q 10 2
              ♦ 7 6 5 4
              ♣ A K Q J
♠ A 10 8 4 2            ♠ J 6 5
♥ 9 8 7                 ♥ A J 6 4
♦ K 3                   ♦ 10 9 8
♣ 9 7 3                 ♣ 10 8 2
              ♠ K Q 3
              ♥ K 5 3
              ♦ A Q J 2
              ♣ 6 5 4
```

The bidding is the same and West, who has the same hand as before, makes the same opening lead and sees the same dummy. Again declarer wins the ♠J with the king and leads a club. This time, however, East cannot stand a spade continuation from partner, so he contributes the ♣2. Declarer takes a diamond finesse, losing to the king. West now knows he cannot afford to continue spades from his side of the table, and he exits with the ♥9. East grabs the trick, returns the ♠6, and the contract fails by two tricks. Some use the reverse procedure. Leader's echo says "shift" as written by Smith. See SIGNALS; SIGNALING.

SMITH TROPHY. Awarded to the winners of the Life Master Women's Pairs contested at the Fall North American Championships, under which heading past results are listed. Donated by Charles H. Goren in 1969 in memory of his longtime partner Helen Sobel Smith. For results see Appendix I.

SMOLEN TRANSFER. An adjunct to Stayman and Jacoby Transfer Bids for game-going hands. It was devised by Mike Smolen of Los Angeles to allow the notrump opener to become the declarer in responder's long suit after responder has used Stayman with 5-4 or 6-4 in the major suits. Using Smolen Transfers, after the auction has started

North	South
1NT	2♣
2♦	

South jumps to three of his four-card major suit, showing that he has more than four cards in the other major.

If opener has three cards in the unbid major, he bids game in that major. If opener has only a doubleton he bids 3NT and, if responder has six cards in the unbid major, he continues by bidding four of the suit just below his unbid major, as a transfer bid.

After an opening 2NT bid, Stayman followed by 3 ♥ or 3 ♠ can be used similarly.

The convention can be used at the two level. 1NT-2♣ -2 ♦ -2 ♥ shows four hearts and five spades with invitational strength.

This was adopted as the consensus choice in BWS94, with two-thirds approving.

SMOTHER PLAY. A rare end position that permits capture of a defender's virtually certain trump winner.

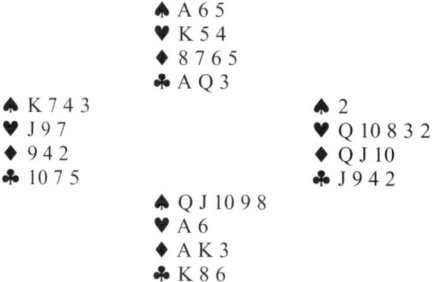

South plays 6♠. The contract appears doomed, for declarer must lose a diamond trick and West's trump king is sufficiently protected to elude capture by normal finessing. However, the opening lead of a diamond is won, and the ♠10 and ♠9 are finessed, West declining to cover. South continues with three rounds of clubs, and follows with the ace, king, and a heart ruff in his own hand. The ♦ A is taken, leaving the following ending:

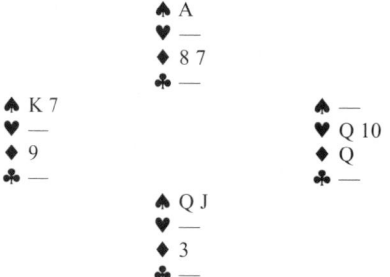

East is thrown in with a diamond and has nothing but hearts to return. South ruffs with the queen, and West is helpless. Also known as the "disappearing trump trick." See also DEVIL'S COUP; ENDPLAY.

SNAP. Abbreviation for STRONG NOTRUMP AFTER PASSING. Frequently the initials are used as a word.

SNAPDRAGON. A double by fourth hand when the first three players have each bid a different suit.

West	North	East	South
1♣	1♥	2♦	Dbl

The double shows a five-card suit and moderate values, probably with a doubleton heart. Players should discuss the levels at which this applies. The convention is also known as competitive double and fourth-suit double.

SOCIAL BRIDGE. Played in a home for moderate or no stakes. For larger gatherings, see PARTY BRIDGE

and PROGRESSIVE BRIDGE. In expert circles, social bridge increasingly is taking the form of team-of-four competition, with a stake based on IMPs.

SOCK, SOCK IT. Obsolete slang for "double."

SOFT VALUES. Queens and jacks, which may well have no role in the play, as distinct from "hard values" which are aces and kings.

SOLID SUIT. A holding which is expected, at a trump or notrump contract, to win as many tricks as there are cards in the suit. Theoretically it should contain as many high cards as there are outstanding cards in the suit: A-K-Q-x-x-x-x-x might lose a trick if all four cards are in the same hand. Culbertson gave as his definition of reasonable expectancy of the solidity of a suit the rule of thumb that a suit was solid if half the outstanding cards were in one hand the entire suit could still be picked up by successive leads.

An alternative definition, similar in effect, is "a suit which can be expected to lose no tricks with a singleton in dummy, and may lose no tricks opposite a void." By this standard, A-K-Q-x-x-x-x, A-K-Q-10-x-x qualify, but A-K-Q-x-x-x does not. See SEMI-SOLID SUIT.

SOLOMON AWARD. A prize formerly awarded by the INTERNATIONAL BRIDGE PRESS ASSOCIATION to the player who makes the best play of the year. Now known as LEVANDAAL AWARD.

SOLOWAY JUMP SHIFT. See JUMP SHIFT.

SORTING THE HAND. The act of arranging the cards of a hand into suits and by order within suit after the cards have been dealt. Many fine players, after arranging their hand, then remove a couple of cards from a long suit and put them apart from the rest of the cards in the suit as a protection against an inadvertent glance of an opponent. Among the habits that experienced players develop are the placing of a singleton in the middle, rather than at an end of the hand, and the avoidance of rearranging a hand when a suit has been exhausted therefrom. It is a violation of the Proprieties to note from what part of a hand an opponent or partner draws a card in order to get a clue as to his holding or distribution.

SOS REDOUBLE. A redouble calling on partner to select another denomination. It applies whenever there is no possibility of the redouble being applied in a natural sense.

West	North	East	South
			1♣
Dbl	Pass	Pass	Redbl

South may have opened on a short club suit. His redouble requests North to bid his best suit outside of clubs as a rescue. However, in a major suit such a redouble would be strength-showing, not an SOS. A double of an opening weak notrump bid often prompts an SOS redouble. For example:

West	North	East	South
			1NT
Dbl	2♣	Dbl	Pass
Pass	Redbl		

This sequence implies that North is planning to play in some other suit, and does not hold clubs. South should

bid his lowest-ranking four-card suit, and if his only suit is clubs he should bid his lowest-ranking three-card suit. If South retreats to 2 ♦ and an opponent doubles, North might redouble again to ask South to select a major suit. Similar situations arise when the opening notrump bid is doubled and redoubled. It is the doubling side which is then on the run, perhaps using SOS redoubles in an attempt to find the best part-score fit at the level of two. In rare circumstances a player may redouble his partner's bid as an SOS instead of his own bid.

West	North	East	South
			1 ♣
Pass	Pass	Dbl	Pass
Pass	Redbl		

If North could not respond to 1 ♣ he cannot wish to redouble naturally. The redouble therefore shows extreme shortage in clubs and begs South to pick another denomination. See also DEFENSE TO DOUBLE OF ONE NOTRUMP, KOCK-WERNER REDOUBLE, SCRAMBLING and WRIGGLE.

SOUND BIDDING. A bidding system stressing elevated standards for some opening bids and overcalls. ROTHSTONE opening bids in first or second position are examples of sound bids. A sound bidder refers to one whose bids, rebids and responses are fully justified by his holding, and who, when choices of bids are available, will choose the more conservative action.

SOUTH. One of the compass points used in describing the players at the table. South is partnered by North, and is OVER the East hand but UNDER the West hand.

SOUTH AFRICAN TEXAS. A special method of TRANSFER BIDS at the level of four, now obsolescent. After an opening bid of 1NT or 2NT, a jump to 4 ♣ requires the opener to bid 4 ♥, and 4 ♦ asks for 4 ♠. This was the original form of David Carter's TEXAS convention, and was developed independently in South Africa. It was quickly abandoned in the U.S. in favor of red-suit transfer bids which permit the use of 4 ♣ as GERBER. However, 4 ♣ and 4 ♦ opening bids to show hearts and spades respectively are still very common. The South African version has the psychological advantage that the responses do not sound natural, and the opener is protected from a lapse of memory.

SPADES. The highest ranking of the four suits at bridge. The 13 cards of the suit are indicated with a black symbol, ♠. In American and British decks, and some made for export to North America, the ace of spades usually carries a special design, trademarked by the manufacturer, on its face. The word "spade" is not agricultural. It designates a broadsword, derived from "spatha" in Greek and Latin. It is the point of a spear in French — "pique", and German — "pic".

SPECIFIED CARDS, ODDS GOVERNING. See ODDS GOVERNING SPECIFIED CARDS.

SPECIFIED SUIT. A suit of which the lead may be required or forbidden because of an irregularity earlier in the auction or play.

SPEEDBALL. An event with an unusually fast time-limit, often a ZIP SWISS played at midnight or a day-time FAST PAIRS game that leaves the evening open for the competitors. Only about five minutes per hand is allowed instead of the usual seven minutes.

SPEEDBALL PAIRS. See FAST PAIRS.

SPEEDBALL SWISS TEAMS. Speed of play is a major factor. Each match consists of five boards, and an average of only five minutes per board is allowed for play — 25 minutes per round. Usually five rounds are played, and the event sometimes is called a five-five-five Swiss. This event frequently is a late-night game during an American Contract Bridge League sectional, regional or NABC. It is sometimes flighted or stratified. See FLIGHTED TEAMS, MIXED TEAMS, OPEN TEAMS, ROUND-ROBIN TEAMS, BOARD-A-MATCH SWISS TEAMS, STRATIFIED TEAMS, STRATIFLIGHTED TEAMS, TEAM GAMES, VICTORY POINT SWISS TEAMS, WIN-LOSS SWISS TEAMS, ZIP SWISS TEAMS.

SPIDER MOVEMENT. See WEB MOVEMENT.

SPINGOLD TROPHY. For the NABC Master Teams Championship, donated by Nathan Spingold in 1934 for what was then called the World Championship Masters Team-of-Four and played originally as a separate knock-out event. In 1938 this event became a part of the Summer NABC (under which results are listed in Appendix I), superseding the CITY OF ASBURY PARK TROPHY event. In the Fifties and Seventies the Spingold helped select a number of U.S. international teams. The trophy ranks with the Vanderbilt as the most highly prized trophy in the ACBL. The Spingold often has been a major factor in selecting the American representatives in world championship play. See INTERNATIONAL OPEN TEAM SELECTION. For results see Appendix I.

SPIRAL. (Also known as Spiral Scan Cuebids.) An idea introduced in SYMMETRIC RELAY and now used in other contexts. A player whose hand is already well-defined is asked to scan through the suits looking for high cards in a set order. A minimum step denies a top card in the longest suit. An extension of this idea is for the first step to show either the lack of the highest card or all three (A-K-Q) top cards. The rest of the auction usually indicates which. Minimum plus one shows a top card in the longest suit but denies one in the second-longest, and so on. When suits are of equal length the higher is scanned first. Used in the ROMEX SYSTEM following Blackwood and in other situations. See DENIAL CUEBIDS.

SPLINTER BID. An unusual jump guaranteeing a fit for partner's last-named suit and showing a singleton or void in the suit in which the jump is made. It often suggests a slam. The idea was developed independently in 1963 by David Cliff, who was the first to write about it, and Dorothy Hayden, now Truscott. It grew out of two earlier bidding tools, the FRAGMENT BID and the VOID-SHOWING BID.

The device can be used in a variety of situations. The most common are:

West	East
1 ♠	4 ♣

East shows a forcing raise that includes club shortage.

West	East
1♣	1♠
4♦	

Here West shows a powerful opening bid (willing to play 4♠ opposite what may be only 6 points) with 4-card support and diamond shortage.

Splinters bids suggest slam on the basis of fit and distribution rather than high cards. Over a 1♠ opening, responder would try 4♣ on as little as:

♠ Q J 7 4 2
♥ A 8 4
♦ A 10 5 2
♣ 8

Even if opener has a minimum hand, slam may have a good chance if he has no wasted strength in clubs: e.g.,

♠ A 9 8 5 3
♥ K Q 2
♦ K 4
♣ 9 5 2

Most experts also use splinters in the majors:

West	East
1♠	4♥

If East really had hearts he could bid 2♥ then 4♥.

West	East
1♥	3♠

If East really had a preempt in spades, he could bid 1♠ then 2♠ then 3♠.

Other splinter sequences include:

West	East
1NT	2♣
2♥	4♦

1♠	2♦
2♥	4♣

1♥	1♠
2♥	4♣

This time East is suggesting only three trumps.

West	East
2♣ (1)	2♦ (2)
2♠	4♦ (3)

(1) Strong, artificial
(2) Negative, artificial
(3) Splinter

West	North	East	South
1♥	1♠	3♠	

East's 3♠ is a splinter, not a cuebid.

Splinters are very useful over a minor suit opening bid.

West	East
1♦	3♥

East denies a four-card major but shows excellent diamond support (usually at least five cards), opening bid values and heart shortage. Perhaps

♠ A 5 3
♥ 5
♦ A 9 8 5 2
♣ K J 9 7

If West holds

♠ J 10 8
♥ K Q 10
♦ K J 7 6 3
♣ A 2

he will bid 3NT. Reverse his major-suit holdings and he should get to 6♦.

Be careful of this sequence:

West	East
1♠	2♣
3♦	

Is this a splinter agreeing clubs or a jump shift in a new suit? Since 2♦ is forcing, it is more flexible to use the jump to show shortness.

If the splinter bidder follows with a cuebid in the splinter suit, he is showing a void (or a singleton ace).

West	East
1♥	4♦
4♠	5♦

A splinter at the five level which deprives the partnership of Blackwood should be used only with a void.

West	East
1♥	3♥
5♣	

East is being asked to evaluate his hand for slam in the light of partner's club void.

West	East
1♣	1♠
3♥ or 4♥	

As 2♥ would be forcing in the modern style, both 3♥ and 4♥ are available as splinters. Some play that 3♥ shows a singleton and 4♥ a void. Others play 3♥ as a mini-splinter (highly invitational but not forcing to game) and 4♥ as a game force.

Splinters are available when the opponents have opened, provided the bid is made below game.

West	North	East	South
1♣	1♠	Pass	4♣ or 4♦

but NOT 4♥.

In one situation, the splinter can be in partner's suit:

West	East
1♣	1♥
1♠	4♣

Shows at least 4-card spade support and club shortage.

The splinter may occur in competition:

West	North	East	South
1♣	Pass	1♥	1♠
3♠			

Shows at least 4-card heart support and spade shortage.

In one situation, the splinter can be in partner's suit:

West	East
1♣	1♥
1♠	4♣

Defense to Splinters

The defensive agreement varies with vulnerability. If the vulnerability is favorable, the double shows length and suggests a save. At other vulnerability the double is lead-directing. Some experts play that the double calls for the lead of the lower side suit. For alternative treatments, see ASKING BIDS, SWISS CONVENTION, VALUE SWISS RAISE, VOID-SHOWING BID, MINI-SPLINTER.

SPLINTER RAISE. See SPLINTER BID.

SPLIT. See BREAK.

SPLIT EQUALS. See PLAY FROM EQUALS.

SPLIT REGIONAL. An ACBL tournament with regional rating held at two widely separated sites within

an ACBL district. Scores are compared between the two sites to determine winners of regionally-rated pair games. Swiss teams and knockout teams are separate events with different winners at each site.

SPLITTING HONORS. The play of an honor in second position from two or more sequential cards. A common position is:

```
                A J 9
    K Q 4                   10 8 7 3
                6 5 2
```

When South leads low, second-hand low by West would work well since South will probably finesse the 9. But if West plays high, the queen is slightly better than the king. If South takes the ace he may go wrong later: the queen is a plausible second-hand play from Q-10-x, but second-hand play of the king is much less plausible from K-10-x since South could have the queen.

Most partnerships make rules about whether to split high or low in such situations.

SPONSORING ORGANIZATION. The group which sponsors bridge tournaments conducted under the LAWS OF DUPLICATE (Law 80). Generally, this is a club or clubs for tournaments of local rating; a unit of the American Contract Bridge League for sectionally rated tournaments; a conference of units or a very large unit for regionally rated tournaments; and the American Contract Bridge League itself for the North American tournaments. See COMMITTEE. Outside North America, the sponsoring organization is usually an NCBO or a local organization delegated by the NCBO. In a wider sense, the sponsor may be a corporation or individual who is paying the expenses of the tournament in return for a public relations benefit.

SPONSOR. See PROFESSIONAL PLAYER.

SPOT CARD. Cards ranking below the jack, from the 10 down to the 2. Of the 13 tricks which are won on each deal, approximately eight are won with aces, kings, queens, and jacks; the remaining five tricks are won with spot cards. A fraction more than five tricks is won by the lower cards in trump contracts, since low trumps win tricks which are not available in notrump contracts. Through the years, all the emphasis on winning tricks has been on aces, kings, queens, and jacks (HONOR TRICKS, POINT-COUNT) and quite naturally so, since these cards are the leaders in the area of winning tricks. However, as can be observed from the above, the lower cards are not merely pawns in the trick-taking field.

SPOT CARD LEAD. See JOURNALIST LEAD; OPENING LEAD; THREE SMALL CARDS, LEAD FROM.

SPREAD. (1) Verb: to spread the hand, either as a claim or as a concession of the remaining tricks. See CLAIM OR CONCESSION for the proper method of making such a claim. (2) Noun: the difference between the minimum and maximum values shown by a particular bid; in STANDARD AMERICAN, the range of values for an opening bid of 1NT is 15 to 17 high-card points, a spread of three, while an opening bid of one in a suit may have a high-card point-count spread of 10 to 24, or 15 points.

SPRING NORTH AMERICAN BRIDGE CHAMPI-ONSHIPS. Formerly called the Spring Nationals, this annual tournament of the American Contract Bridge League is held in March and was first convened in 1958. The most important event is the Vanderbilt Knockout Teams. In 1968 the tournament held in New York attracted a total of 13,535 tables, a record for the series until the Spring of 1989 when 13,808 were registered in Reno. For past results of Spring North American Bridge Championships, see Appendix I.

Spring North American Championships Attendance (an asterisk indicates the record was broken that year)

Year	Site	Tables
1958	Atlantic City	3,076
1959	Seattle	4,124
1960	Jackson MS	3,485
1961	Denver	4,910*
1962	Lexington KY	4,703
1963	St. Louis	6,556*
1964	Portland OR	6,950*
1965	Cleveland	8,128*
1966	Louisville KY	7,929
1967	Seattle	7,098
1968	New York City	13,535*
1969	Cleveland	8,958
1970	Portland OR	7,025
1971	Atlanta	9,706
1972	Cincinnati	9,495
1973	St. Louis	8,418
1974	Vancouver BC	8,329
1975	Honolulu	10,234
1976	Kansdas City	8,790
1977	Pasadena	12,713
1978	Houston	9,388
1979	Norfolk VA	8,273
1980	Fresno CA	9,669
1981	Detroit	8,221
1982	Niagara Falls	9,021
1983	Honolulu	11,698
1984	San Antonio	8,829
1985	Montreal	10,184
1986	Portland OR	9,222
1987	St. Louis	10,829
1988	Buffalo	9,157
1989	Reno	13,808*
1990	Fort Worth	11,303
1991	Atlantic City	11,279
1992	Pasadena	12,502
1993	Kansas City	10,132
1994	Cincinnati	11,003
1995	Phoenix	11,945
1996	Philadelphia	10,995
1997	Dallas	11,101
1998	Reno	13,967*
1999	Vancouver	13,180
2000	Cincinnati	10,830
2001	Kansas City	9370.5

SPUTNIK. See NEGATIVE DOUBLE.

SQUARE HAND. Bridge geometry is peculiar; square hand, flat hand, and round hand all describe 4-3-3-3 distribution. Another colloquialism is pancake.

SQUEEZE. A play which forces an opponent to discard at a time when he would prefer not to. The forced discard

will cost the opponent at least one trick sooner or later. In most cases, a squeeze compels an opponent to discard a winner, a potential winner, or a guard to a winner. The most familiar squeezes have the following requirements: a. Two Threat (or menace) Cards, at least one of which is accompanied by a winner in that suit. A threat card is any card that will take a trick provided the opponents unguard that suit. (When a threat card is accompanied by a winner in that suit, it is called a two-card threat.) b. The hand opposite at least one of the two-card threats contains a card in the suit of the threat card. This card provides a means of reaching the two-card threat in the opposite hand. c. The opponent to be squeezed holds no idle cards. This usually requires that the squeeze player can win all but one of the remaining tricks. (See RECTIFYING THE COUNT) When these conditions have been satisfied, the card played to the next trick forces an unwanted discard from at least one opponent. This card is called the squeeze card. It is usually a winner played from the hand opposite the two-card threat. If both menaces are in the same hand, only the opponent who is to the left of the squeeze card is affected. These are called positional (or one-way) squeezes. In an automatic squeeze, either opponent can be subjected to pressure. This occurs when the squeeze card is accompanied by a menace card, so that the hand opposite has one card which is immaterial and furnishes an automatic discard.

The term "squeeze" was coined by Sidney Lenz well after the operation of a squeeze had been recognized and analyzed. Originally a squeeze was simply called a coup. In the heyday of American whist it was known as "putting the opponent to the discard." Circa 1910 J. B. Elwell called squeeze play "forcing discards," and this term was in general use until Lenz in the middle Twenties, inspired by a squeeze play in a professional baseball game, introduced his new term. For various types of squeeze and aspects of squeeze play see ALTERNATE SQUEEZE; AUTOMATIC SQUEEZE; BACKWASH SQUEEZE; BARCO SQUEEZE; BONNEY'S SQUEEZE; BUSY CARD; CLASH SQUEEZE; COMPOUND SQUEEZE; COMPOUND TRUMP SQUEEZE; COUNT SQUEEZE; DEFENSE TO A SQUEEZE; DOUBLE SQUEEZE; ENTRY-SHIFTING SQUEEZE; ENTRY SQUEEZE; GUARD SQUEEZE; HEDGEHOG SQUEEZE; HEXAGON SQUEEZE; HEXAGON TRUMP SQUEEZE; KNOCKOUT SQUEEZE; MOLE SQUEEZE; NONMATERIAL SQUEEZE; OCTAGONAL TWO-TRICK SQUEEZE; ONE-SUIT SQUEEZE; OVERTAKING SQUEEZE; POSITIONAL SQUEEZE; PROGRESSIVE SQUEEZE; PSEUDO-SQUEEZE; RECIPROCAL SQUEEZE; RECTIFYING THE COUNT; SCHROEDER SQUEEZE; SECONDARY SQUEEZE; SERES SQUEEZE; SHOW-UP SQUEEZE; SIMPLE SQUEEZE; SQUEEZE FINESSE; SQUEEZE MNEMONICS; SQUEEZE WITHOUT THE COUNT; SQUEEZED POSITION; SUICIDE SQUEEZE; THREAT CARD; THROW-IN SQUEEZE; TRANSFER SQUEEZE; TRANSFERRING THE MENACE; TRIPLE SQUEEZE; TRUMP SQUEEZE; UNBLOCKING SQUEEZE; VICE SQUEEZE; WINKLE SQUEEZE.

SQUEEZE CARD. The card played that forces an opponent to give up a key card. See SQUEEZE.

SQUEEZE FINESSE. Closely related to the GUARD SQUEEZE. In each case, declarer threatens to take a

successful finesse. In a guard squeeze, the opponents are not equally threatened, whereas the squeeze finesse is characterized by the presence of a symmetric menace which must be guarded with an equal number of cards by both opponents.

(1) *Four-card squeeze finesse menaces:*

Triple tenaces

	K 9			K 2	
Q 8		10 5	or Q 8		10 5
	J 2			J 9	

These positions may lead to a squeeze or throw-in of either opponent.

Quadruple tenaces

	K 8			K 2	
Q 7		10 9	or Q 7		10 9
	J 2			J 8	

In these positions, only West can be thrown in successfully.

(2) *Six-card squeeze finesse menaces:*

Triple tenaces

	K 9 x			K 3 2	
Q 8 x		10 5 x	or Q 8 x		10 5 x
	A J 2			A J 9	

Either opponent may be thrown in.

Quadruple tenaces

	K 8 x			K 3 2	
Q 7 x		10 9 x	or Q 7 x		10 9 x
	A J 2			A J 8	

Only West can be thrown in.

(3) *Squeeze-finesse positions (at notrump):*

(a)

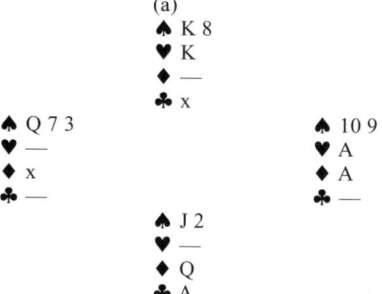

South has two of the remaining tricks. The ♣A is led and East is squeezed in three suits. He must discard a spade, and now South leads the ♠J to smother the 10. If West's small diamond is exchanged for the king, this merely opens up the possibility of a squeeze throw-in against West.

(b)

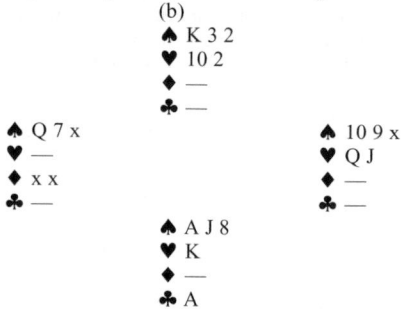

South has four of the remaining five tricks. The ♣A squeezes East in two suits. He must discard a spade, but declarer can now pick up three tricks in spades by leading the jack through West. The squeeze fails if the ♠8 and ♠2 are interchanged.

(c)

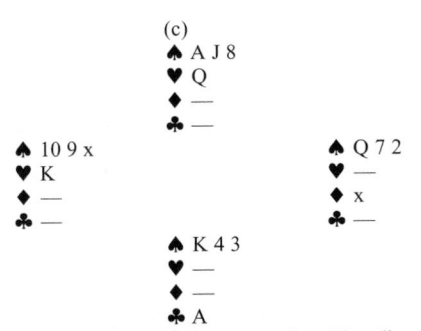

```
              ♠ A J 8
              ♥ Q
              ♦ —
              ♣ —
♠ 10 9 x                    ♠ Q 7 2
♥ K                         ♥ —
♦ —                         ♦ x
♣ —                         ♣ —
              ♠ K 4 3
              ♥ —
              ♦ —
              ♣ A
```

The ♣A squeezes West in two suits. West discards a spade, and declarer leads to the ♠A, then runs the jack through East to pick up the suit.

The ♠8 and ♠2 may be interchanged without affecting the squeeze. East's small diamond may be exchanged for the ♥A, but the squeeze still works.

(4) *Squeeze Finesse at Trumps (also called simply TRUMP SQUEEZE).*

Simple

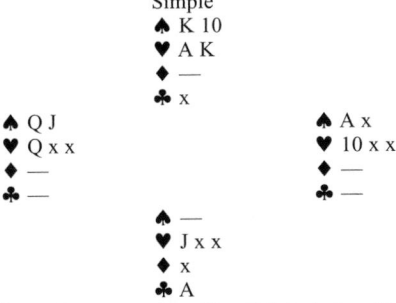

```
              ♠ K 10
              ♥ A K
              ♦ —
              ♣ x
♠ Q J                       ♠ A x
♥ Q x x                     ♥ 10 x x
♦ —                         ♦ —
♣ —                         ♣ —
              ♠ —
              ♥ J x x
              ♦ x
              ♣ A
```

Diamonds are trumps. The ♣A is led, putting the squeeze on West. If he discards a heart, declarer cashes the two top hearts and re-enters his hand by ruffing a spade to cash the ♥J. If West discards a spade, declarer can go to dummy with a heart and lead the ♠K to ruff out the ace and smother the queen, establishing North's 10.

Double

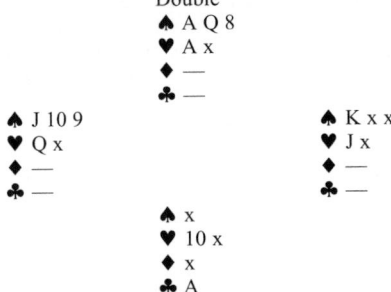

```
              ♠ A Q 8
              ♥ A x
              ♦ —
              ♣ —
♠ J 10 9                    ♠ K x x
♥ Q x                       ♥ J x
♦ —                         ♦ —
♣ —                         ♣ —
              ♠ x
              ♥ 10 x
              ♦ x
              ♣ A
```

Diamonds are trumps. The ♣A is led and West is squeezed. If he discards a spade, the ace and the queen of that suit are led, ruffing out the king and smothering West's honors. If West discards a heart, then North throws a heart and East is caught in a standard trump squeeze.

SQUEEZE MNEMONICS. An acronym or other set of initials used as a reminder of the ingredients necessary for the operation of a squeeze. Among the more well-known mnemonics are:

(1) Clyde Love's BLUE:

  B = Busy (one defender Busy in two suits)
  L = Loser (one Loser remaining)
  U = Upper (at least one threat in Upper hand)
  E = Entry (to the threat card)

(2) George Coffins's EFG (to Enter freedom, Force the Guards):

  E = Entry (to the threat card)
  F = Forcing card
  G = Guards (in one defender's hand)

(3) John Brown's STEM:

  S = Share-out or Substance
  T = Timing (count has been rectified)
  E = Entries (to the threat card)
  M = Menaces

SQUEEZE SUIT-OUT. A particular form of SECONDARY SQUEEZE.

SQUEEZE WITHOUT THE COUNT. An unusual variation of the squeeze. In order for a squeeze to be effective, declarer ordinarily must have all but one of the remaining tricks (see Rule of N-Minus-One). However, this is not invariably the case. In certain squeeze positions declarer gives up a trick after the squeeze. This is called "squeeze without the count" (see SECONDARY SQUEEZE).

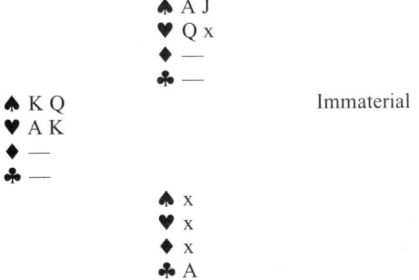

```
              ♠ A J
              ♥ Q x
              ♦ —
              ♣ —
♠ K Q                                     Immaterial
♥ A K
♦ —
♣ —
              ♠ x
              ♥ x
              ♦ x
              ♣ A
```

South leads the ♣ A which squeezes West, despite the fact that South has only two of the last four tricks. West must discard a heart; now South leads a heart to establish the queen.

SQUEEZED POSITION (PLAYING TO). In the development of the understanding of squeezes, Sidney Lenz invented the idea of a squeeze card, and this concept has dominated the analysis of squeeze play ever since. Indeed, some writers have even given special names, for example "reciprocal squeeze," where the actual squeeze card could not be identified.

(1)

```
              ♠ A K x
              ♥ x
              ♦ x
              ♣ —
♠ Q x x                     ♠ J x x
♥ K x                       ♥ —
♦ —                         ♦ K x
♣ —                         ♣ —
              ♠ x
              ♥ A x
              ♦ A x
              ♣ —
```

In this double automatic position, for instance, there is no separate and identifiable squeeze card. The two red aces are led, and each opponent is squeezed by the ace of his partner's suit. As more and more squeeze po-

sitions have been identified, the burden of remembering them for use in play has become impossible except for the most expert. In trying to simplify the rules for the less expert players it has been found that, by abandoning the concept of a squeeze card, the number of end positions can be reduced, and, in particular, the more complex ones can be forgotten. This has probably always been the practice in expert circles, and was almost implied by Ely Culbertson in his *Red Book*.

When South leads the second ace, West must keep his ♥ K, so must pitch a spade. East must keep the ♦ K, so must sluff a spade. So dummy's spades take the last three tricks.

This position is true of all automatic double squeezes: squeeze cards, reciprocal squeeze, simultaneous and interrupted automatic double squeezes can all be forgotten.

The following are simple automatic squeezes:

(2)
```
            ♠ A 10
            ♥ x
            ♦ —
            ♣ —
♠ 3 2                   ♠ Q J
♥ 2                     ♥ K
♦ —                     ♦ —
♣ —                     ♣ —
            ♠ x
            ♥ Q
            ♦ —
            ♣ A
```

(3)
```
            ♠ A 10
            ♥ A
            ♦ —
            ♣ 2
♠ 3 2                   ♠ Q J
♥ 3 2                   ♥ K x
♦ —                     ♦ —
♣ —                     ♣ —
            ♠ x
            ♥ Q x
            ♦ —
            ♣ A
```

(4)
```
            ♠ K 9 x
            ♥ Q
            ♦ —
            ♣ —
♠ 4 3 2                 ♠ Q J x
♥ 2                     ♥ K
♦ —                     ♦ —
♣ —                     ♣ —
            ♠ A 10 x
            ♥ —
            ♦ —
            ♣ A
```

These three endings, Nos. 2, 3, and 4, can all be represented by one squeeze position, No. 5, with South on lead. North and South have both played, but the opponent with the high cards, either East or West, must now play and is squeezed. In No. 2 the ♣A squeezes either East or West, the ♥x being thrown from North. In No. 3 we first Vienna-Coup with the ♥A, and then the ♣A squeezes whichever opponent holds the high cards. In No. 4 we have to imagine North as South in No. 5.

(5)
```
            ♠ A 10
            ♥ —
            ♦ —
            ♣ —
♠ 3 2                   ♠ Q J
♥ 2                     ♥ K
♦ —                     ♦ —
♣ —                     ♣ —
            ♠ x
            ♥ Q
            ♦ —
            ♣ —
```

Examples could be given for all varieties of squeezes. However, this would be tedious, so let the following suffice:

(6)
```
            ♠ A 10 9
            ♥ —
            ♦ x
            ♣ —
♠ Q J                   ♠ 2
♥ A                     ♥ x
♦ A                     ♦ x
♣ —                     ♣ x
            ♠ x
            ♥ K
            ♦ K
            ♣ A
```

(7)
```
            ♠ K x
            ♥ K
            ♦ K x
            ♣ —
♠ Q J x                 ♠ x x
♥ A                     ♥ —
♦ A                     ♦ x x
♣ —                     ♣ x
            ♠ A 10 9 8
            ♥ —
            ♦ —
            ♣ A
```

Examples Nos. 6 and 7 are two triple squeeze positions, both automatic, in which the lead of the ♣A squeezes an opponent into promoting one of declarer's kings, then squeezes him a second time when that king is played— the other ace or the guard to declarer's long suit must be given up. Example No. 8 is either of these reduced to the squeezed position, with South on lead. No. 7 has to be turned upside down to get to No. 8, but as the position is automatic, this is of no consequence.

(8)
```
            ♠ A 10 9
            ♥ —
            ♦ —
            ♣ —
♠ Q J                   ♠ 2
♥ A                     ♥ x
♦ A                     ♦ x x
♣ —                     ♣ —
            ♠ x
            ♥ K
            ♦ K
            ♣ —
```

Finally, the simple trump squeeze. Although the three examples, Nos. 9, 10, and 11, all appear to be different, once one plays down to the squeezed position they all become the same.

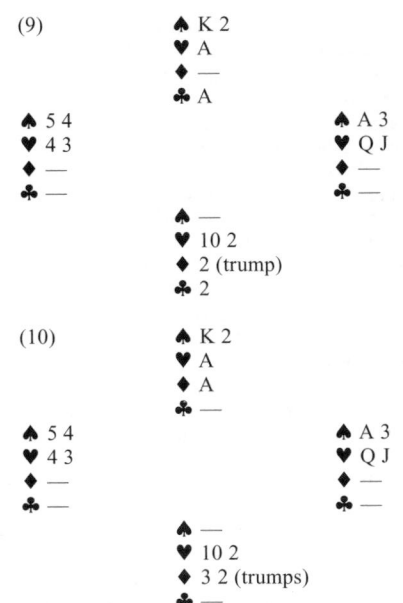

(9)

(10)

Trump squeezes are always automatic. In No. 9 the lead of the ♣2, or in No. 10 the lead of a trump, squeezes the opponent (in this case East) who holds the high cards. If he throws a spade the ♠2 is led and trumped, North is re-entered and the ♠K is cashed. If he throws a heart the ♥A is cashed, a spade is ruffed, and the last heart made.

(11)

     ♠ K 2
     ♥ A K 2
     ♦ —
     ♣ —

♠ 5 4   ♠ A 3
♥ 4 3   ♥ Q 8 5
♦ —   ♦ —
♣ 3   ♣ —

     ♠ —
     ♥ 10 4 3
     ♦ 2 (trump)
     ♣ A

In No. 11 the ♣A is led and North's ♥2 discarded. If East throws a spade North is entered with a heart, the ♠2 is ruffed, and North re-entered to make the ♠K. If East throws a heart, North's ♥A-K are cashed and a spade ruff puts South in again to make the ♥10.

(12)

     ♠ K 2
     ♥ A
     ♦ —
     ♣ —

♠ 5 4   ♠ A 3
♥ 4 3   ♥ Q J
♦ —   ♦ —
♣ —   ♣ —

     ♠ —
     ♥ 10 2
     ♦ 2 (trump)
     ♣ —

Each of the above three cases reduces to the squeezed position, No. 12, with East to discard and then North to lead. This is a much simpler position to remember – in fact it is all simple trump squeezes, and is one position instead of three.

STACK, STACKED. (1) The cards are said to be stacked against one when a single opponent holds all or nearly all of the cards in a crucial suit. (2) To stack a deck is to arrange cards in an undealt deck in order to put predetermined holdings into one or more hands. See CHEATING.

STAGGER MOVEMENT. A movement for an even number of teams which permits scoring to start at the halfway mark. It is particularly useful for a two-session game.

Two parallel rows of tables are set up so that board-sharing is possible. The movement is the same as in an American Whist movement: boards down one table, sharing with the adjacent table (1&5, 2&6, 3&7, 4&8); East-West pairs down two tables. On reaching the end of a row, pairs must go to the start of the opposite line.

When all the boards have been played, i.e. after n/2 rounds, they are removed. E-W pairs move down one and start on a new set of boards for the start of the second half. This movement works for any even number of tables, and like the American Whist movement, can be shortened by eliminating the first and last rounds of either or both halves. A reduced number of boards can be played in the second half. See EIGHT TABLES and TEAM-OF-FOUR MOVEMENTS.

The two stanzas in the Stagger movement may be played intermingled, with half the board sets idle in each round. This method is known as the NEW ENGLAND RELAY.

STAKES. Rubber bridge is frequently played for stakes. In major North American bridge clubs, where membership and card fees are considerable, stakes usually range from one-half cent to three cents per point, but higher stakes do occur, ranging up to 50 cents or even a dollar. In home and social games, stakes are usually much more modest and may be as little as one-tenth of a cent.

In Britain and other parts of the world stakes are expressed on a "per hundred" basis. Therefore scoring 100 honors is worth the announced stake in Britain, but 100 times the announced stake in North America.

STAND, STAND FOR. To pass partner's PENALTY DOUBLE or TAKEOUT DOUBLE.

STANDARD AMERICAN. A nebulous term applied to the methods of bidding most commonly used in the United States. It approximates closely the methods formerly advocated by Charles Goren. Among serious tournament players the weak two-bid is standard, while some rubber bridge players continue to use the forcing two. Another debatable issue is the idea that jump bids by responder are always forcing. This is implicit in Goren's methods, but in North America the trend has been toward expert methods which include limit bids, signoff bids and nonforcing jumps.

In the Eighties the Goren methods gradually fell out of favor in tournament play. A majority adopted methods which may be called EASTERN SCIENTIFIC or TWO- OVER-ONE GAME FORCE. The shift is continuing in the Nineties, and traditional Goren, with four-card major openings and a 1NT response to a major opening non-forcing, is no longer the norm. But players continue to describe their methods as "standard" when they use a modern style which is far removed from traditional Goren.

STANDOFF. A colloquialism for either a rubber with no net score (after ROUNDING OFF); a hand in which HONOR SCORE balances undertrick penalties: or a deal in a team game (BOARD-A-MATCH, IMP or TOTAL POINTS) on which neither team gains.

STAND UP. In defensive play, a high card that wins a trick. A suit is said to stand up until it is trumped by the declarer. On the offense or on the defense, too, a high card is said to stand up if it wins the trick, even though a higher card may be outstanding in the suit.

STANZA HOWELL. A Howell-type movement for pairs or individuals which is split into several stanzas (or segments) usually played in several sessions with one stanza per session. When all sessions are played in a Stanza Howell for pairs, all pairs have met once. In a Stanza Howell for individuals, each player will have each other player as a partner once and an opponent twice.

STANZA MOVEMENT. A method of conducting a combined-section pairs game whereby the scoring of the first half of the game could be completed while the second half was taking place. The method, devised by Maury Braunstein, is now obsolete as a result of computer scoring.

STAR TEACHER. The designation was initiated in 1988 for those who use ACBL teaching materials — the *Club, Heart, Diamond* and *Spade Series* books. Any ACBL-accredited teacher who teaches 100 students using one or more of the ACBL manuals earns the designation of Star Teacher.

STARTING TIME. (1) The time designated for the start of the session; (2) the time the session actually gets under way. At or near the end of each session, the director clearly announces the starting time for the next session. If it is a continuation of an event, the director may assess penalties for tardiness. After the scheduled starting time, late players may be added to the event if the director can do so without restarting or unduly delaying the game.

STATEN BANK. See CAP GEMINI WORLD TOP TOURNAMENT. For results see Appendix IV.

STAYMAN. The response of 2♣ to 1NT, or 3♣ to 2NT. asking opener to bid a four-card major suit. The Stayman convention was invented by George Rapee, but the first article on the convention (*The Bridge World*, June 1945) was authored by Sam Stayman, and the convention was named for the writer rather than the inventor. The device quickly became standard practice throughout the world, vying with the BLACKWOOD CONVENTION as the most popular. Rapee and Stayman were a strong, established partnership at that time. A similar convention was played in the early Thirties by Ewart Kempson in England and a group of Boston players headed by Lawrence Weiss. J.C.H. Marx of London, England, devised a similar 2♣ convention in 1939, but publication was delayed by World War II. It appeared in 1946, in the first issue of the *Contract Bridge Journal*. The Rapee and Marx ideas, independently generated, were identical. The original convention provided for opener to rebid 2♦ with a minimum hand and 2NT with a maximum. S.J. Simon suggested the simplification which became generally adopted: opener automatically rebids 2♦ if he does not have a major suit. The authorities are divided on the correct rebid

for the opener holding both majors. Partnership agreement is necessary if 2♣ does not promise a major. However, if 2♣ does promise a major, opener can bid the other major if responder bids 2NT or 3NT.

Responder has a wide range of possible rebids, many of which are subject to varying interpretations.

(1) *Two of a major suit.* This can be treated in four ways: (a) Forcing. The bidding must continue at least as far as 2NT. Most experts reject this treatment because strong hands can be bid satisfactorily by bidding the suit at the three-level on the first or second round, using a transfer bid. (b) Encouraging. The use of transfer bids has diminished the need for this usage, since responder can transfer and then invite with a 2NT bid. (c) Weak. (d) Modern. Use 2♥ as weak, inviting preference to 2♠, and 2♠ as invitational with a 4-card spade suit. In this treatment, opener must bid 2 ♥ with both majors, and 1NT 2♣ - 2♥ -2NT denies four spades. This is useful for partnerships using a direct 2NT artificially.

(2) *2NT.* This is encouraging, showing the same strength as an immediate raise to 2NT. If the opener showed a major, responder now implies that he holds the other major unless 2♣ does not promise a four-card major. If the opener rebids 2 ♦, responder simply indicates he has one or both majors. However, in many modern styles a direct raise to 2NT has an artificial meaning. Therefore a delayed 2NT, via Stayman, carries limited information about major suits. If the rebid was 2 ♦, it gives no information. If it was a major, 2NT denies a fit and may deny the other major, depending on the rebid agreement when opener has both majors. See FOUR-SUIT TRANSFER BIDS. Also see (1)(d) above.

(3) *Three of a minor suit.* The traditional treatment is for 3♣ to be weak, with a six-card or seven-card club suit and no game interest. 3 ♦ is forcing. (But see WEISSBERGER convention.) However, most experts use immediate jumps to 3♣ and 3 ♦ as preemptive (as in ROTH-STONE and KAPLAN-SHEINWOLD) in which case the delayed bid of 3♣ or 3 ♦ is forcing to game: responder is exploring the possibility of a minor-suit game or slam. These bids are usually encouraging when using FOUR-SUIT TRANSFER BIDS, since the transfer is employed with weak hands and strong hands.

(4) *Three of an unbid major suit (always a jump unless opener bid spades).* Forcing, showing a five-card or longer suit, with an implication of four cards in the other major. See SMOLEN.

(5) *Raise to three of a major.* A natural invitation to game, showing four-card support for the major suit.

(6) *3NT.* A natural bid.

(7) *Four of a minor suit.* When opener shows a major, 4♣ can be Gerber by partnership agreement. Many use such a bid as a SPLINTER. Another possible meaning is natural: a long, strong suit with a void and slam interest. Opener relays to ask for the void. See SHARPLES.

(8) *4NT.* Quantitative. A 4-3-3-3 hand would make an immediate raise to 4NT. (And a 4-4-3-2 hand could use SHARPLES .) Other rebids by the responder are natural.

The above sequences apply to 1NT opening bids of any range. However, the employment of a weak notrump strengthens the argument for using nonforcing Stayman.

Some players use both 2♣ and 2 ♦ as Stayman bids. 2♣ is the same as explained above and opens a sequence that is not forcing to game. A Stayman response of 2 ♦, however, is forcing to game. Opener bids 2NT if he holds neither major.

See also ANTI-LEMMING; GLADIATOR; ONE NOTRUMP OPENING; SMOLEN; TWO-WAY STAYMAN; STAYMAN IN DOUBT.

STAYMAN FOR STOPPERS. TWO-WAY STAYMAN may also be used in a way in which only the 2♣ bid searches for a 4-4 major suit fit. The 2♦ bid would then be used to discover whether the partnership has all suits sufficiently well-stopped to play in notrump. Responder normally reserves his 2♦ bid for a hand containing a singleton or a void. The bid asks opener to bid whichever major suit he has guarded. Suits containing four cards headed by the queen, or three headed by the queen and 10, are considered minimum sufficient stoppers. With both major suits guarded opener should bid 2NT. If opener does not have the responder's short suit stopped, responder can explore other game or slam possibilities.

STAYMAN IN DOUBT (S.I.D.) A British idea intended to deal with the difficulty presented by two hands with a 4-4 major-suit fit and identical 4-3-3-3 distributions. A 3♦ rebid by the Stayman bidder suggests this possibility, asking the opener to decide between 3NT and a game in the major suit.

STAYMAN ON SECOND ROUND. This is standard in one situation:

South	North
2♣ (artificial)	2♦
2NT	3♣

As no suit has been naturally bid, the responder can bid as he would opposite a 2NT opening, with the knowledge that the opener is slightly stronger. By partnership agreement this can be extended to other notrump rebids:

South	North
1♣	1♥
1NT	2♣ (asking for a spade suit)

This checkback procedure permits the opener to conceal a four-card major suit on the second round if he wishes, but deprives the responder of some natural rebids. If the rebid is 2NT, 3♣ is not available for players who use it as preparation for a signoff at the three level (see WOLFF CONVENTION). See CROWHURST CONVENTION; TWO CLUB REBID BY RESPONDER AS ONLY FORCE AFTER ONE NOTRUMP REBID; NEW MINOR FORCING, CHECKBACK STAYMAN.

STAYMAN THREE CLUBS. See TWO NOTRUMP OPENING.

STEP RESPONSES TO STRONG ARTIFICIAL TWO-BIDS. Responses to a TWO-CLUB STRONG ARTIFICIAL OPENING that show, by steps, how many controls responder holds, counting a king as one control and an ace as two. As described in *The Bridge Journal*, a 2♦ response shows 0-1 control, 2♥ shows 2 controls, 2♠ shows an ace and a king (3 controls), 2NT shows three kings (3 controls), 3♣ shows 4 controls and so on. The theory underlying using the 2NT response to show three kings is that if the hand is to be played in notrump it will more likely be played from the RIGHT SIDE. This method of responding is similar to that used in BLUE TEAM CLUB. See also NORMAN 4NT. A modification proposed by Edgar Kaplan requires responder to bid 2♦ with 0-6 points and 2♥ shows more than 6 points; both bids,

however, show fewer than two controls. Most other responses are amended accordingly: a 2♠ response shows two controls, 2NT still shows three kings, 3♣ shows one ace and one king, 3♦ shows four controls, and so forth. See ACE-SHOWING RESPONSES.

STEPPINGSTONE SQUEEZE. A secondary squeeze in which the opponents must choose between a throw-in and a suit establishment play, each of which enables declarer to gain a trick. (Analyzed and named by Terence Reese).

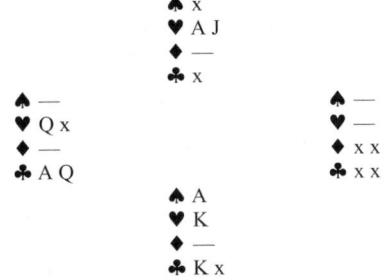

South leads the ♠A, and West is squeezed in two suits. In order to retain his guard in hearts, he must throw a club. If West discards the ♣Q, South takes the ♥K, and exits with a club, forcing West to lead a heart to North's ace; if West discards the ♣A, South's king is established. The blocked suit must include two winners, one in each hand, but the higher must be in dummy. South must have a one-card menace against the same player who protects the blocked suit. In the diagram position, if the East and West cards were reversed the squeeze would still be effective. See also ENTRY SQUEEZE and WINKLE SQUEEZE.

STERN SYSTEM. See VIENNA SYSTEM.

STIFF. (1) Adjective or noun: Colloquialism for SINGLETON, frequently used in reference to a major honor (ace, king, or queen) without guards. (2) Verb: Colloquially, to blank; to discard the guards.

STOP. See SKIP-BID WARNING.

STOP BID. A bid which fixes the final contract and commands partner to pass. Responses of 4♠ or 3NT to an opening notrump bid are examples. SIGNOFF BIDS are virtually stop bids, but in some cases the partner may have a reason to violate and continue with the auction. See PREEMPTIVE RERAISE.

STOPPER. A card which may reasonably be expected to or actually does stop the run of a suit. To be counted in the auction as a stopper, a high card, except an ace, must usually be accompanied by lower cards so that it will not have to be played on a higher one if the holder of the higher card decides to play for the drop. The number of low cards, or guards, needed is in inverse proportion to the rank of the honor. Thus, the king must ordinarily be accompanied by at least one guard, and the queen by at least two unless the bidding indicates that a higher ranking card is held by partner. Stoppers are particularly important at notrump contracts. Holdings such as Q-x and J-x-x are partial stoppers, needing help from partner to build a full stopper. For instance, if you have Q-x and partner has J-x-x, you have a full stopper. See GUARD; NOTRUMP BIDDING.

STOPPING ON A DIME. Stopping one trick short of game (or perhaps slam) and making exactly the right number of tricks.

STRAIN. A term encompassing all four suits plus notrump. See DENOMINATION.

STRAT. A group of players within a game that is differentiated by an upper and lower level of masterpoints. Many North American events are stratified, with top finishers in each strat winning masterpoints. Stratification usually is divided into three groups, e.g., 0–300, 300–1000, 1000 plus. Many other configurations are used.

STRATIFIED PAIRS. A pair event that produces more than one set of winners. The field is divided into a number of strata – at least two, each with a predetermined masterpoint limitation. Tournament officials attempt to seed the field in such a manner that approximately equal numbers of players from each strat are in each direction in each section. The event is played like a regular pair game. When it comes time for the scoring, all pairs are ranked in the top strat for Strat A rankings. Then all Start A scores are eliminated to determine the Strat B standings. Then all A and B scores are eliminated to determine the Strat C standings. A pair is stratted according to the number of masterpoints held by the higher ranking player.

Late in the Nineties events known as STRATI-FLIGHTED PAIRS were tried which received a favorable response from the players. The A players play in a game of their own – Flight A, while the remaining players compete in a strat game with two or three strats. An additional element was added after this type of event became popular. Flight A was divided into two strats. So the game being played consisted of two events – Flight A with two strats and Stratified Pairs with three strats. This of course produced a total of five winners. See STRATIFLIGHTED PAIRS.

STRATIFIED TEAMS. A Swiss Team event that produces more than one set of winners. The event is run along exactly the same lines as an Open Swiss Teams — the only difference comes in the ranking. First overall rankings are determined for Stratum A by comparing all scores. Then Stratum A scores are eliminated to determine the placings in Stratum B. Then Stratum A and Stratum B scores are eliminated to determine the placings in Stratum C. It is possible for Stratum B and C pairs to place in higher strata, but Stratum A pairs are eligible only for Stratum A awards. The stratum in which a team plays is determined by the player who has the most masterpoints. This event has become quite unpopular because B and C teams that do well early find themselves playing strong A teams in later rounds. As a result Flighted Teams are held whenever the fields are large enough to accommodate flights. Another method that has become popular: form a flight for the A players and run a second event (stratified) for the B and C players. Sometimes the strat part of the event is divided into three strats (B, C, and D). See STRATIFLIGHTED TEAMS.

STRATIFLIGHTED PAIRS. See STRATIFIED PAIRS.

STRATIFLIGHTED TEAMS. See STRATIFIED TEAMS.

STRATUM. See STRAT.

STRENGTH. The top-card holding in a suit, either as stoppers in notrump, for drawing adversely held trumps, for trick-taking potential, or to set up LONG CARDS as winners.

STRENGTH-CONCEALING PLAY. See DECEPTIVE PLAY.

STRENGTH-SHOWING BID. In some special situations a suit bid can be used to show strength rather than length or control. This applies particularly when exploring for a 3NT contract as an alternative to an obvious minor-suit possibility. The following are typical cases. The suit bid might conceivably be as weak as Q-J-x, but would usually contain at least 4 points.

(a) West   East
     1♦   2♣
     3♣   3♥

East can bid a strong three-card suit because West is unlikely to be interested in a major suit.

(b) West   East
     1NT   3♦ (forcing)
     3♥

West can bid a strong three-card suit because East is unlikely to be interested in a major suit. This may reveal duplication if East is short in hearts, permitting a final contract of 3NT.

(c) West   East
     1♦   3♦
     3♥

(d) West   East
     3♣   3♦
     3♥

In (c) and (d) the suit is unlikely to be raised. If it is, the choice lies between playing in a 3-4 fit and retreating to a minor suit.

STRIP PLAY. A method of play by which a chosen opponent is stripped of his cards in a certain suit with the purpose of later throwing the lead to that player and thus compelling him to lead a suit desired by the declarer. The term is also used for a method of play by which declarer exhausts the cards in a suit or suits in both his and the dummy's hands so that a later lead by a defender will give him a ruff-sluff. Often combined with endplay as in "strip and endplay". See ELIMINATION; ENDPLAY; SQUEEZE; THROW-IN.

STRIPED-TAILED APE DOUBLE. An inhibitory double of an opposing game contract made by a player who feels sure his opponents can make a slam. The doubled contract with overtricks scores less than the score for bidding and making the slam. So named by John Lowenthal and Samuel Scaffidi in a *Bridge Journal* article because the doubler flees like a striped-tailed ape in the face of a redouble. The same tactics can be applied at the small slam level if a grand slam can be made. This double is very rare, but not as rare as a striped–tailed ape – apes do not have tails!

STRONG JUMP OVERCALL. See JUMP OVERCALL.

STRONG KINGS AND TENS. A British system of honor leads against a notrump contract whereby the lead

of a king or 10 suggests a strong holding and the lead of any other high card suggests a relatively weak holding. Therefore:

Ace from: A K x
King from: A K Q, A K J, A K 10, K Q J, K Q 10
Queen from: K Q x, K Q 9, Q J 10
Jack from: J 10 x
Ten from: A J 10, A 10 9, K J 10, K 10 9, Q 10 9
Nine from: 10 9 x

See LEADS

STRONG MINOR RAISE. See INVERTED MINOR RAISE.

STRONG NOTRUMP. The traditional range for an opening bid of 1 NT was 16-18 for many years, but that fell out of favor in the Eighties. In tournament play 15-17 became standard, although 16-18 still is often used in rubber bridge. Some players straddle, using a range of 15-18, or $15^{1}/_{2}$ to $17^{1}/_{2}$. Sub-minimum hands in point-count may be opened 1NT if there is a five-card suit or a wealth of aces and tens. See ONE NOTRUMP OPENING.

Even stronger 1 NT opening bids are advocated in some systems, notably ROMAN, SIMS, and VANDERBILT. For strong notrump openings that are forcing for one round, see DYNAMIC NOTRUMP, LITTLE ROMAN CLUB SYSTEM, ROMEX SYSTEM.

STRONG NOTRUMP AFTER PASSING (abbreviated to SNAP). A response of 1NT by a PASSED HAND as a strong bid, showing 9-12 points. This permits the bidding to stay in a comfortable low-level contract when the opener has a minimum or sub-minimum hand. The notrump bidder promises a relatively balanced hand and denies holding a five-card major suit which could have been bid at the level of one. The idea often gives an advantage in a partscore deal, and is therefore of most value in a matchpoint event. This sometimes forces a pass with 6-8 points which has some risks. For a device with similar objectives, see DRURY.

STRONG PASS. Any of several systems used in various parts of the world whereby an opening pass indicates the values for an opening bid, while various opening bids indicate values less than sufficient for an opening bid in most other systems. Partner of the opening passer is usually required to open the bidding, and the process puts strong pressure on the opposition. Since the meaning of many ordinary sequences is reversed, the opposition must work out entirely new defensive bidding systems. The first strong pass system was MARMIC in Italy. The idea later became popular in Poland and spread to other parts of the world. Such systems have largely been abandoned because sponsoring organizations place heavy restrictions on their use. See FERT, FORCING PASS, MARMIC SYSTEM, WEAK OPENING SYSTEMS.

STRONG SUIT. A suit of four or more cards containing a minimum of six points.

STRONG TWO-BID. See FORCING TWO-BID.

SUBMARINE SQUEEZE. The concession of a trick by declarer in order to correct the count for a squeeze. If declarer gives up the trick on a lead by the opponents, he

is said to be RECTIFYING THE COUNT; however, if the trick is conceded at a time when declarer holds the lead, some writers call this move a submarine squeeze.

SUBSTITUTE. (1) Call. When a player makes an illegal call, he may be required to substitute a legal call, with appropriate penalties against his partner. (2) Player. A player who, in rubber bridge, replaces a member of the table who is called away or must leave during or before the finish of a rubber. Such a substitute must be acceptable to all members playing at the table; and he would be assumed to have no financial responsibility unless agreed otherwise. (3) Player. In duplicate play, a player who is permitted by the director to replace a player who is unable to finish a session or play in a second or later session. (4) Board. In team play, a board is introduced by the director at a table when an irregularity has occurred that makes a normal result impossible. Such a board is withdrawn after play, but reinstated when the teammates of the pairs who played it are scheduled to play that board. If the substitute board is needed on the replay (after the teammates have recorded a result), an offending side causing the substitution may be playing for at best a halved board.

SUCCESSIVE EVENTS, PROBABILITY OF. See PROBABILITY OF SUCCESSIVE EVENTS.

SUCKER DOUBLE. A double of a freely bid game or slam contract by a player who is relying solely on defensive high-card strength. Against good opponents such doubles rarely show more than a small profit. They can, however, show a disastrous loss, especially when the double helps declarer to make his contract. The probability is that the declaring side has distributional strength to compensate for the relative lack of high-card strength.

SUCTION. A defense to a 1NT opening. The overcall of any suit shows the next-higher suit, or the other two suits.

2♣ = diamonds, or hearts and spades
2♦ = hearts, or spades and clubs
2♥ = spades, or clubs and diamonds
2♠ = clubs, or diamonds and hearts

Partner of the suction bidder assumes the next-higher suit until he hears otherwise. He bids as high as he can afford. For instance, 1NT-2♣-Pass-3♦ implies a willingness to play 3♦ or three of a major, depending on partner's hand.

SUFFICIENT BID. A bid of the same number of a higher ranking denomination or of a greater number in a lower ranking suit or the same denomination. If the enforcement of a penalty permits a player to substitute a sufficient bid for an incorrect call, a double of an opponent's bid may not be substituted, even though such double is a legal call. See INSUFFICIENT BID.

SUICIDE SQUEEZE. A squeeze inflicted by a defender on his partner. It also can be a defender squeezing himself or a declarer squeezing his dummy. (But as this name is hardly accurate, it is called by some the Cannibal Squeeze.) Inaccurate defense may lead to this position, but there are times when the opponents have no recourse.

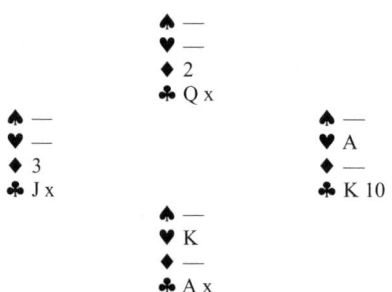

West, on lead, produces a suicide squeeze on his partner if he cashes the high diamond. If East discards the ♥A, South discards the low club, winning two tricks. If East discards the ♣10, South discards the ♥K. Proper defense calls for a club lead. If North were on lead, the small diamond lead would produce the simple squeeze against East. This is a simple squeeze position, with North on lead, but the squeeze card is a loser. Thus declarer must have all but two of the remaining tricks. In addition, the player who wins the squeeze card must have no other winner which he can cash. When these additional requirements are met, any simple squeeze ending may lead to a suicide squeeze, as can other squeeze positions.

SUIT. The group to which each card in a pack belongs. Modern packs have four suits. Until the 16th century, there was no agreement as to number; Hindu cards had 10, and packs of 5-11 suits were used in various areas. In the Thirties there was a brief flurry of interest in a fifth suit, but it faded. Three different sets of symbols have been developed which are in use today: International (British, American, French); spades, hearts, diamonds and clubs.

Trappola (Italy, Spain, Latin countries); cups, coins, swords and cudgels.

German (Germany, Austria, Bohemia, Poland, Hungary); hearts, leaves, bells and acorns, with the Swiss modification of blossoms and shields for the latter two.

The club design is the cloverleaf of the French but the name is from the trappola deck. The diamond design is also French, but the name is an English descriptive term. The heart design is from the German pack. The spade design is the French pikehead, but the name is from the trappola deck. The suit names reflect the four orders of society — hearts for the church, spades for the military, clubs for the peasantry, and diamonds (tiles) for the merchants — was made long after the development of the suit names and symbols. See PLAYING CARDS.

SUIT, NUMBER OF CARDS IN. For notations used, see MATHEMATICS OF BRIDGE.

(1) A player can have x cards of a given suit in $_{13}C_x \leftrightarrow {}_{39}C_{(13-x)}$ ways. The percentage probability is found by multiplying this by 100 and dividing by $_{52}C_{13}$. A player can have exactly five spades, then, in $_{13}C_5 \leftrightarrow {}_{39}C_8 = 79,181,063,676$ ways. The percentage is

$$\frac{7,918,106,367,600}{635,013,559,600} = 12.469\%$$

(2) A player can have x cards of one suit and y cards of another suit in $_{13}C_x \leftrightarrow {}_{13}C_y \leftrightarrow {}_{26}C_{(13-x-y)}$ ways. He can have five spades and four hearts, then, in $_{13}C_5 \leftrightarrow {}_{13}C_4 \leftrightarrow {}_{26}C_4 = 13,757,064,750$ ways. The percentage is 2.166%.

(3) If 26 cards are known (such as after the dummy is exposed), of which y are the cards of the suit in question, a player can have x cards in that suit in $_{(13-y)}C_x \leftrightarrow {}_{(26-13+y)}C_{(13-x)}$ ways. If four spades are seen (y), he can have five spades in $_9C_5 \leftrightarrow {}_{17}C_8$ ways This computes to 3,063,060 ways, or a percentage of 29.451%.

SUIT COMBINATIONS. The correct treatment of particular suit combinations by declarer is a highly complex subject. The analysis on the following pages is the first attempt in bridge literature at a comprehensive coverage. To find any particular combination, first count the number of high-card points held by the defense in the crucial suit. Then find the appropriate section, which is subdivided according to the number of cards held by the declaring side. The play of each combination is considered in two ways. (1) from the angle of safety plays, the number of tricks required is given together with the appropriate play and the percentage prospects, and (2) where no particular number of tricks is required, but declarer simply wants to do as well as possible, the indicated maximum play (abbreviated to MAX) is given, with the expectation of tricks if this line is followed. Whenever the symbol x is used, it should be assumed to be a completely insignificant spot card. In many cases the replacement of an x by an 8 or a 7 would affect the play or the percentages. Dummy is always assumed to have the greater length. When the same holding occurs the other way up, with the length in declarer's hand, the analysis and percentages are identical (except in very rare cases when psychological considerations apply). See suit combinations on pages 447-502.

SUIT DISTRIBUTION. There are 39 possible suit distributions. For the percentage play in handling any combination, see SUIT COMBINATIONS. For relative frequency of the occurrence of each pattern, see MATHEMATICAL TABLES, Table 1.

SUIT OPENING BID. See OPENING SUIT BID.

SUIT PATTERNS. For the 39 suit patterns, ranging from a balanced 4-3-3-3 to an outlandish 13-0-0-0, and the percentage frequency of each, see MATHEMATICAL TABLES, Table 1.

SUIT PLACING. The process of marking during the bidding the suit lengths around the table. See CARD READING; COUNTING THE HAND.

SUIT-PREFERENCE SIGNAL. A device whereby a defender may direct his partner to lead a specific suit. This method, devised by Hy Lavinthal in 1934, has had a greater effect on defensive play than any other development of this century and ranks with the distributional echo and HIGH-LOW SIGNAL of the 19th century. In various countries the suit-preference signal is known by the names of bridge writers, especially William E. McKenney and B. Jay Becker, who adopted and publicized it but did not otherwise contribute to it.

The signal never applies to the suit led, and never to the trump suit. The essence of the suit-preference signal is this: When a player has the lead and seems likely to switch suits, or when he may have a choice of suits when he next obtains the lead, the play of a conspicuously high card calls for a lead in the higher-ranking suit in question, the

play of a conspicuously low card calls for a lead of the lower-ranking suit.

Properly used, the suit-preference signal does not interfere with signals that show ATTITUDE and LENGTH.

A common suit-preference application is seen in this deal:

```
                    ♠ K 9 6
                    ♥ 8 7
                    ♦ K 4 3 2
                    ♣ K 4 3 2
  ♠ 2
  ♥ 5 4 3 2
  ♦ J 10 9 8
  ♣ J 10 9 8
```

West	North	East	South
			1♥
Pass	1NT	Pass	3♥
Pass	4 ♥	All Pass	

West leads the ♠2. East wins the ace and returns a spade. Which suit does West lead after he ruffs?

To help West, East signals with the rank of the spade he leads at the second trick. If East holds:

```
                    ♠ A 10 7 4 2
                    ♥ 9
                    ♦ Q 7 6 5
                    ♣ A Q 7
```

he returns the ♠2, his lowest, showing a desire for clubs, the lower ranking side suit. But if East holds:

```
                    ♠ A 10 7 4 2
                    ♥ 9
                    ♦ A Q 7
                    ♣ Q 7 6 5
```

he returns the ♠10, suggesting strength in diamonds, the higher-ranking suit.

Suit preference can also indicate the location of an entry.

```
                    ♠ J 5
                    ♥ 6 5 3
                    ♦ A Q 10 7 6
                    ♣ J 6 5
  ♠ A 4
  ♥ Q 10 8 7 4 2
  ♦ 5 3
  ♣ 8 7 4
```

West leads the ♥7 against South's 3NT. East plays the king, ducked by South, and returns the ♥J to South's ace.

On the second heart West should follow with the queen. If East gets in with, say, the ♦ K, he may be unsure which black suit to lead. A spade may look risky if he has the queen. West's striking play of the ♥Q must suggest an entry in the highest-ranking suit.

Suit preference is sometimes available on the opening lead:

West	North	East	South
3♦	Dbl	4♦	4♠
All Pass			

West holds:

```
                    ♠ 5 3
                    ♥ J 8 4 2
                    ♦ K J 10 8 7 4 2
                    ♣ —
```

West would like East to win the first trick and return a club. East's most likely fast entry is the ♦ A, but if West leads normally, he cannot expect East to shift to clubs. West should lead the ♦ 2. Since on the bidding this lead cannot be fourth highest, East should get the message.

Dlr: West
Vul: N-S

```
                    ♠ K
                    ♥ A J 7 6
                    ♦ Q 10 6 4
                    ♣ K Q 7 6
                                        ♠ Q 9 5 2
                                        ♥ 4
                                        ♦ A 7 5 3
                                        ♣ J 9 4 2
```

West	North	East	South
3♠	Dbl	5♠	6♥
All Pass			

West leads the ♠A; East should jar partner by dropping the queen.

Suit preference is often abused and overused. Most authorities agree that attitude and length signals take priority over suit preference. A defender must not interpret a signal as suit preference if his partner may have sent a simpler message. A suit-preference signal is an unusual play of unmistakable significance.

```
                    ♠ K 4
                    ♥ Q 8 5 3
                    ♦ 7 4 2
                    ♣ A K Q 4
                                        ♠ J 9 5 2
                                        ♥ 7 4
                                        ♦ A Q 6
                                        ♣ 10 7 5 3
```

West	North	East	South
1♠	Dbl	3♠	4♥
All Pass			

West leads the ♠ A. East's play should show attitude as long as that is a conceivable message to send. East can get a shift (to diamonds) simply by following with the ♠2. West can look at dummy and see that diamonds is the logical switch.

East's play cannot ask for a club shift (especially since dummy has strong clubs). As long as East might merely want to signal for a spade continuation or a switch, West must interpret his play as attitude.

```
                    ♠ K 4
                    ♥ Q 8 5 3
                    ♦ 7 4 2
                    ♣ A K Q 4
                                        ♠ J 9 5 2
                                        ♥ A 4
                                        ♦ 9 5 3
                                        ♣ 10 7 5 3
```

The bidding and opening lead are the same. This time East should play the 9 to ask West to *continue spades*. (There is nothing illogical about a spade continuation although dummy can win. East may prefer a passive defense.) If East plays the ♠2, West will shift to a diamond, which may cost a trick.

```
                    ♠ K 5 3
                    ♥ 8 6 5 3
                    ♦ Q 3 2
                    ♣ Q 3 2
                                        ♠ J 9 5 2
                                        ♥ Q 4
                                        ♦ K J 10
                                        ♣ 8 6 5 4
```

West	North	East	South
			1♥
1♠	2♥	2♠	4♥
All Pass			

West leads the ♠A, and East should play the jack. This

is suit preference for several reasons. First, the jack is an unusually high spade when East clearly has a choice of plays. Also, a suit-preference signal is *needed*; since South is about to take a discard on the ♠ K, the defenders need to cash out. But West has no obvious shift (as he would if dummy held good clubs and weak diamonds). An attitude signal is not enough.

```
                    ♠ A K
                    ♥ A 9 6 5 3
                    ♦ 9
                    ♣ A K J 8 3
♠ 7
♥ J 10 4
♦ A K 10 4 2
♣ 7 6 5 4
```

West	North	East	South
	1♥	Pass	1♠
Pass	3♣	Pass	3♠
Pass	4♠	Pass	5♥
Pass	6♠	All Pass	

West leads the ♦ A. East plays the 8, South the 3. West should continue with the ♦ K. This is not a suit-preference situation, since there is no suit East can want led. A diamond continuation is possible, and East might want to use attitude to ask for it. In fact, East has ♠ J 10 5 and wins a trump trick when dummy must ruff the second diamond.

Here are other applications of the suit-preference signal:

```
                    ♠ A K Q 5
                    ♥ Q 10 6 5
                    ♦ 5 4
                    ♣ 6 5 4
                              ♠ J 10 7 4 2
                              ♥ 4 3
                              ♦ A 9 3
                              ♣ J 3 2
```

West	North	East	South
			1NT
Pass	2♣	Pass	2♥
Pass	4♥	All Pass	

West leads the ♠ 3, won in dummy. East should follow with the jack. West has led an obvious singleton and may have a reentry in trumps. The ♠ J suggests an entry in diamonds. If East had an entry in clubs, he would play his lowest spade.

```
Dlr: West           ♠ Q J 7 5
Vul: None           ♥ A 8 5 2
                    ♦ A 7 3
                    ♣ 5 4
♠ A K 2                       ♠ 9 6 4 3
♥ K J 9 3                     ♥ Q 6
♦ Q 6                         ♦ 10 5 4
♣ A J 10 6                    ♣ Q 7 3 2
                    ♠ 10 8
                    ♥ 10 7 4
                    ♦ K J 9 8 2
                    ♣ K 9 8
```

West	North	East	South
1♣	Dbl	Pass	1♦
Dbl	Pass	1♠	2♦
All Pass			

West leads the ♠ A, and East plays the 9. This can't be attitude or length — West cannot be eager to cash his second spade. West should interpret East's play as suit

preference and shift to a low heart.

```
Dlr: East           ♠ 6 5
Vul: N-S            ♥ K J 9 5
                    ♦ 10 6 5
                    ♣ K 10 9 5
♠ Q 9 3                       ♠ J 8
♥ 10 6 4 2                    ♥ A 8 7
♦ K J                         ♦ A Q 8 7 3 2
♣ J 8 6 2                     ♣ Q 4
                    ♠ A K 10 7 4 2
                    ♥ Q 3
                    ♦ 9 4
                    ♣ A 7 3
```

West	North	East	South
		1♦	1♠
Dbl	Pass	2♦	2♠
3♦	3♠	All Pass	

West leads the ♦ K and continues with the ♦ J. East wins the ace and leads the ♦ Q, ruffed low by South and overruffed. East had no chance for a suit-preference signal on the third diamond; he had to lead the queen to beat dummy's ten. However, East's play at the second trick was meaningful; when he won the ♦ A instead of the queen, he suggested heart strength. West should lead a heart at the fourth trick, and East will win and lead another diamond, promoting a second trump trick for the defense.

In an expert partnership, suit-preference signals extend to many subtle situations; for example, a defender may signal as he discards in a side suit.

```
Dlr: East           ♠ K J 5 3
Vul: Both           ♥ J 7 3
                    ♦ A 7 4
                    ♣ A 8 3
♠ A 6 2                       ♠ 10
♥ K Q 9 5 2                   ♥ 10 8 6 4
♦ J 2                         ♦ K Q 10 6
♣ Q 9 6                       ♣ 10 7 5 4
                    ♠ Q 9 8 7 4
                    ♥ A
                    ♦ 9 8 5 3
                    ♣ K J 2
```

West	North	East	South
		Pass	Pass
1♥	Dbl	2♥	4♠
All Pass			

West leads the ♥ K, and East signals with the 8 (length). South wins the ace, leads a trump to the king and another trump. East would prefer not to discard a high diamond or low club, either of which could be costly; he can discard the ♥ 10 to suggest diamond strength.

```
                    ♠ 7 5 3
                    ♥ Q 8 5
                    ♦ K Q J 8
                    ♣ Q 7 6
                              ♠ 9 2
                              ♥ A K J 10
                              ♦ 10 5 2
                              ♣ 9 8 4 3
```

South opens 1NT, raised to 3NT. West leads the ♠ J, and East plays the 2, discouraging. South wins the queen and leads a diamond to the king. East follows with the 2, length. South comes back to the ♠ K and leads a second diamond. West's ace wins and East plays the ten (suit preference), suggesting a preference for hearts over clubs.

(continued on page 503)

Dummy Declarer	Tricks Required		% Chance of Success	Tricks per Deal

I. THE DEFENSE HAS NO POINTS

(a) Declarer Has Six Cards

1.	A K Q J 9 x	5	Cash top honors in the hope of dropping the ten	72

(b) Declarer Has Seven Cards

2.	A K Q J 9 x x	6 5	Cash top honors Finesse the nine, in case East is void	86 99
3.	A K Q J 9 x x	5	Cash top honors in the hope of dropping the ten	87
4.	A K Q 9 x J x	5	Cash top honors in the hope of dropping the ten	87
5.	A K Q J 8 x x	5	Cash top honors* (*But against defenders who would not false- card from 109x or 109xx, cash the jack and finesse the eight if the nine or ten appears from East)	84 85
6.	A K Q 8 x J x	5	See (5) above	84

(c) Declarer Has Eight Cards

7.	A K Q 8 x J x x	5	Cash the jack first in case East is void	98

II. THE DEFENSE HAS ONE POINT

(a) Declarer Has Five Cards

8.	A K Q 10 x	4	Finesse the ten	50

(b) Declarer Has Six Cards

9.	A K Q 10 9 x	5	Play off the top honors. This is fractionally better than the immediate finesse	36	
10.	A K Q 10 x x	5 4 Max	Finesse the ten Finesse the ten Finesse the ten	31 81	 4.12
11.	A K Q 10 x x	4	Cash the queen, and then finesse the ten	50	
12.	A K Q 9 x x	4	Finesse the nine; hope that West has both the jack and ten	24	
13.	A K 10 x Q x	4	Cash the queen, and then finesse the ten	50	
14.	A K 9 x Q x	4	Play off the queen, king, and ace, hoping that the jack and ten fall in three rounds* (*But against defenders who would not false- card from J10x, cash the queen and finesse the nine if East drops an honor)	 11	

(c) Declarer Has Seven Cards

15.	A K Q 10 9 x x	6	Cash the top honors	54

	Dummy Declarer	Tricks Required		% Chance of Success	Tricks per Deal

II. THE DEFENSE HAS ONE POINT (cont'd)

	Dummy / Declarer	Tricks Required		% Chance of Success	Tricks per Deal
16.	A K Q 10 x x	6	Cash the top honors	52	
	x	5	Finesse the ten	91	
		4	Finesse the ten, in case East is void	99	
		Max	Cash the top honors		5.37
17.	A K Q 10 9	5	Play off the top honors	54	
	x x				
18.	A K Q 10 x	5	Play off the top honors	52	
	x x	4	Cash the ace, and finesse the ten	93	
		Max	Play off the top honors		4.39
19.	A K Q 9 x	5	Play off the top honors, hoping that the jack and ten drop in three rounds	39	
	x x	4	Lead small to the nine, in case East has a void or small singleton	90	
		Max	Play off the top honors*		4.23
			(*But against defenders who would not false-card from J 10 x, cash the ace and finesse the nine if East drops an honor)		4.24
20.	A K10 9 x	5	Play off the top honors	54	
	Q x				
21.	A K 10 x x	5	Play off the top honors	52	
	Q x	4	Cash the queen and finesse the ten	93	
		Max	Play off the top honors		4.39
22.	A K 9 x x	5	Cash the queen, king, and ace	54	
	Q 10	4	Cash the queen, and run the ten	100	
		Max	Cash the queen, and run the ten		4.44
23.	A K x x x	5	Finesse the ten	42	
	Q 10	4	Finesse the ten	92	
		Max	Finesse the ten		4.34
24.	A K 9 x x	5	Play off the top honors	39	
	Q x	4	Cash the queen, and finesse the nine if an honor drops from East	86	
		Max	Play off the top honors*		4.23
			(*But against defenders who would not false-card from J10x, cash the queen, and finesse the nine if an honor drops from East)		4.24
25.	A K Q 10	4	Cash the king and queen; if both follow, play the ace. This is 2% better than a third-round finesse	61	
	x x x				
26.	A K Q 9	4	Cash the queen and king; if an honor drops from East, finesse the nine next. This is 6% better than cashing the three top honors regardless	48	
	x x x				
27.	A K 10 x	4	See (25) above	61	
	Q x x				
28.	A K 9 x	4	See (26) above	48	
	Q x x				
29.	A K x x	4	Cash the ace, queen, and king, This is 4% better than a second-round finesse	55	
	Q 10 x				
30.	A 10 x x	4	See (25) above	61	
	K Q x				
31.	A 9 x x	4	See (26) above	48	
	K Q x				
32.	A x x x	4	Cash the king, queen, and ace. This is 4% better than a second-round finesse.	55	
	K Q 10				

(d) Declarer Has Eight Cards

	Dummy / Declarer	Tricks Required		% Chance of Success	Tricks per Deal
33.	A K Q 10 x x x	7	Play off the top honors	73	
	x	6	Finesse the ten, in case East is void	98	
		Max	Play off the top honors		6.70

	Dummy Declarer	Tricks Required		% Chance of Success	Tricks per Deal
			II. THE DEFENSE HAS ONE POINT (cont'd)		
34.	A K Q 9 x x x x	6	Play off the top honors* (*But against defenders who would not false- card from J10x, cash the ace and finesse the nine if an honor appears from East)	68 70	
		5	Lead small to the nine, in case East is void	98	
35.	A K Q 8 x x 10 x	6	Play off the top honors	73	
		5	Lead small to the ten	100	
		Max	Play off the top honors		5.70
36.	K Q 9 x x x A x	6	Play off the top honors* (*But against defenders who would not false- card from J10x, cash the ace and finesse the nine if an honor appears from East)	68 70	
37.	A K 9 x x Q 8 x	5	Cash the ace and queen (or the queen and ace) hoping for a 3-2 break or a singleton honor with East* (*But against defenders who would not false- card with J10x, cash the ace, and finesse the eight if West drops an honor)	 73 76	
		4	Lead small to the eight or nine	100	
38.	A K 10 x Q 9 x x	4	Cash the ace. If the eight falls, play the next top honor from the hand on the left of the eight. Otherwise guess which honor to play next (*Assuming that the eight is not a false-card from J8xx)	 92*	
39.	A K 9 x Q 8 x x	4	Cash the ace. If an honor appears, cash the next top honor from the hand on the left of the J or 10	 79	
40.	A K 9 x Q x x x	4	Cash the queen, in case West has J10xxx	75	

(c) Declarer Has Nine Cards

	Dummy Declarer	Tricks Required		% Chance of Success	
41.	A K Q 8 x x x 9 x	7	Lead the nine, and play the ace whatever hap- pens. This saves a trick if West covers with J10xxx	 90+	
42.	A K Q 7 x x 8 x x	6	Lead the eight, and play the ace whatever hap- pens. This saves a trick if West is lulled into covering with J109x	 90+	
43.	A K 10 x x x Q 9 x	6	Lead the ace first in case either opponent is void	100	
44.	A K 9 x x x Q x x	6	Play the queen first, in case East is void	95	
45.	A K Q 7 x 8 x x x	5	Lead the eight, and play the ace whatever hap- pens. This saves a trick if West is lulled into covering with J109x	 90+	
46.	A K 10 x x Q 9 x x	5	Cash the ace first, in case either opponent is void	100	
47.	A K 9 x x Q x x x	5	Cash the queen first, in case East is void	95	

III. THE DEFENSE HAS TWO POINTS

(a) Declarer Has Five Cards

	Dummy Declarer	Tricks Required		% Chance of Success	
48.	A K J 10 x	4	Finesse the jack. This line is 6% better than try- ing to drop the queen	 11	

(b) Declarer Has Six Cards

	Dummy Declarer	Tricks Required		% Chance of Success	Tricks per Deal
			III. THE DEFENSE HAS TWO POINTS (cont'd)		
49.	A K J 10 9 x	5	Finesse the jack	18	
50.	A K J 9 8 x	5	Lead small to the jack or nine, playing West for Q10x or Q10	5	
		4	Lead small to the jack	58	
		Max	Lead small to the jack		3.63
51.	A K J 9 x x	4	Finesse the nine; if this loses to the ten, finesse the jack	24	
		3	Finesse the jack and then the nine, *or* finesse the nine and then the jack	76	
52.	A K 9 8 J x	4	Run the jack; if it is covered, finesse the nine next. West must have Q10, Q10x or Qxxxx	6	
		3	Lead the jack; if it loses, finesse the nine next	76	
53.	A K 9 x J x	3	Lead small to the jack. If this loses, finesse the nine	74	
54.	A J 9 8 K x	4	Cash the king and, unless an honor appears from East, finesse the jack	6	
		3	Cash the king, and unless an honor appears from East, finesse the jack or nine*	69	
		Max	Cash the king and, unless an honor appears from East, finesse the jack or nine* (*This line is only fractionally better than running the nine, which will be superior if West is likely to have fewer cards in the suit than East)		2.75
55.	A J x x K 9	3	Finesse the nine; if this loses to the ten, cash the king and ace	68	
56.	A K 9 J x x	3	Lead small to the nine, hoping that West has both the queen and ten	24	

57.	A K x
	J 9 8
		3	*Either* run the nine *or* run the jack. Guess
			   whether West has the bare queen or East the
			   bare ten*
			(*But against defenders who can be relied
			upon to cover the nine with the ten, lead the
			nine, and play the ace and king if it is not
			covered; if the nine is covered, run the jack
			next)
				24
				
				29	

(c) Declarer Has Seven Cards

	Dummy Declarer	Tricks Required		% Chance of Success	Tricks per Deal
58.	A K J 10 9 x x	6	Finesse the jack. This line is 8% better than try- ing to drop the queen	27	
59.	A K J 9 8 7 x	6	Finesse the jack	19	

		5	Finesse the jack. This line is 2% better than
			   cashing the ace and king, and 1% better than
			   finessing the nine
				71	

60.	A K J 10 9 x x	5	Finesse the jack. Do not cash the ace first; Qxxx with West is more likely than Q with East	43	
61.	A K J 9 x x x	5	Finesse the jack, alternatively cashing the ace first	19	
		4	Finesse the nine; if this loses to the ten, cash the ace and king	73	

		3	Finesse the nine, and then the jack *or* finesse the
			   jack and then the nine, *or* cash the ace, and
			   then finesse the jack or nine
				94	

		Max	Finesse the nine; if this loses to the ten, cash the ace and king		3.85
62.	A K 9 8 x J x	5	Run the jack *or* lead small to the nine	9	
		4	Cash the ace and then run the jack	73	
		Max	Run the jack. If it is covered, finesse the nine; if it loses, cash the ace; if it holds, cash the ace		3.79

	Dummy Declarer	Tricks Required		% Chance of Success	Tricks per Deal
			III. THE DEFENSE HAS TWO POINTS (cont'd)		
63.	A K 9 x x J x	5	Run the jack *or* lead small to the nine. West must hold Q10x	7	
		4	Lead small to the jack; if it loses, cash the ace and king	68	
		3	Lead small to the jack; if it loses, finesse the nine	99	
		Max	Lead small to the jack; if it loses, cash the ace and king		3.62
64.	A J x x x K 9	5	Cash the king, and then finesse the jack	18	
		4	Lead small to the nine	68	
		3	Cash the king, and then finesse the jack	94	
		Max	Cash the king, and then finesse the jack		3.74
64A.	K J 9 x x A x	5	Cash the ace and then finesse the jack. (If East plays the ten, play for the queen to drop unless East is capable of a falsecard from 10 x x.)	20.99	
'		4	Cash the ace and then finesse the jack or the nine. If East plays the queen, finesse the nine	69.04	
		Max	Cash the ace and then finesse the jack.		3.84
65.	A K J 10 x x x	4	Cash the ace, and finesse the ten	51	
66.	A K J 9 x x x	4	Cash the ace, and finesse the jack	29	
		3	Cash the ace. Then lead toward dummy, and play the king if the ten fails to appear. Then lead up to the jack	85	
		Max	Cash the ace, and finesse the jack		3.07
67.	A K J x x x x	4	Cash the ace, and finesse the jack	18	
		3	Play off the ace and king, and then lead up to the jack	77	
		Max	Cash the ace, and finesse the jack		2.87
68.	A K 10 x J x x	4	Cash the ace, and then lead small to the ten. Don't lead the jack for the finesse; West may have Qx	28	
69.	A K 9 8 J x x	4	Run the jack; if this is covered, finesse the nine	25	
		3	Play the ace, and if no honor appears, run the nine; if it loses, run the jack through next* (*Assuming East would not duck with Qxx, this line only loses when West has 10x. If East is a very good defender, play the king if the nine loses to the ten)	94 84	
		Max	Run the jack; if this is covered, finesse the nine; if the jack loses, cash the ace and king		3.01
70.	A K 9 x J x x	4	Lead small to the nine, hoping that West has Q10 or Q10x	9	
		3 } Max }	Cash the ace and, unless the ten appears, lead small to the jack; if the jack loses, cash the king	84	2.88
71.	A K x x J 10 9	4	Finesse the jack	50	
		3	Finesse the jack *or* play the ace, and then finesse the jack	100	
72.	A K x x J 9 8	4	Run the nine and then the jack *or* run the jack and then the nine, hoping that West has Q10x or either Q or Qxxxx	8	
		3	Play the ace, and lead small to the jack	78	
		Max	Run the nine; if it loses to the ten, run the jack next		2.85

	Dummy Declarer	Tricks Required		% Chance of Success	Tricks per Deal

III. THE DEFENSE HAS TWO POINTS (cont'd)

	Dummy Declarer	Tricks Required		% Chance of Success	Tricks per Deal
73.	A K x x J 9 x	4	Play the ace, hoping that West has the singleton queen	1	
		3 } Max }	Play the ace, and then lead small to the jack or nine	78	2.79
74.	A K x x J x x	3 } Max }	Play the ace, and lead to the jack	69	2.69
75.	A J 9 8 K x x	4	Cash the king, and finesse the jack	29	
		3	Cash the king, and lead toward dummy, playing the ace unless the ten appears	85	
		Max	Cash the king, and finesse the jack		3.07
76.	A J 9 x K x x	4	Cash the king, and finesse the jack	29	
		3	Cash the king and ace; then lead to the jack	85	
		Max	Cash the king, and finesse the jack. If it loses, cash the ace		3.07
77.	A J x x K 9 x	4	Cash the king, and finesse the jack	19	
		3	Cash the king and ace; then lead to the jack	85	
		Max	Cash the king, and finesse the jack		2.98
78.	A J x x K x x	4	Cash the king, and finesse the jack	18	
		3	Cash the king and ace; then lead to the jack	77	
		Max	Cash the king, and finesse the jack		2.87
79.	K 9 x x A J x	4	Finesse the jack; then play the ace and king* (*Against defenders who would not falsecard from Q10x, finesse the nine if East drops the queen under the ace)	21 27	
		3	Lead small from dummy, and play the ace unless the ten appears. Then, unless West drops the ten, lead small to the jack	84	
		Max	Finesse the jack; then play the ace and king		3.03
80.	J 10 x x A K x	4	Cash the ace, and then run the jack. This line is only 1% better than cashing the two top honors	20	
81.	J 9 8 x A K x	4	Cash the ace and king, unless the queen drops from West* (*But if West is good enough to falsecard from Q10, we have to play the king, even if the queen falls under the ace)	12 11	
		3	Cash the ace and king; then lead to the jack	85	
82.	J x x x A K 9	4	Lead small to the nine, hoping that East has Q10 or Q10x	9	
		3 } Max }	Cash the ace and king; then lead to the jack	85	2.90

(d) Declarer Has Eight Cards

	Dummy Declarer	Tricks Required		% Chance of Success	Tricks per Deal
83.	A K J 10 9 x x x	7	Finesse the jack. This line is 4% better than playing off the ace and king	37	
84.	A K J 9 8 7 x x	7	Finesse the jack	34	
		6	Finesse the nine or, more profitably, finesse the jack	85	
85.	A K J 10 x x x x	6	Finesse the jack. Don't cash the ace first: Qxxx West is more likely than Q with East	48	
		5	Finesse the jack	98	
		Max	Finesse the jack		5.46

	Dummy Declarer	Tricks Required		% Chance of Success	Tricks per Deal
			III. THE DEFENSE HAS TWO POINTS (cont'd)		
86.	A K J 9 x x x x	6	Finesse the jack, alternatively cashing the ace first*	37	
			(*Against defenders who would not falsecard from 10x, cash the ace, and play the king if the ten falls from East)	40	
		5 } Max	Cash the ace, and finesse the jack	88	5.22
87.	A K J x x x x x	6	Finesse the jack, alternatively cashing the ace first	34	
		5 } Max	Cash the ace, and then finesse the jack	85	5.17
88.	A K 9 8 7 x J x	6	Run the jack. If it is covered, guess whether to finesse for or drop the ten next	16	
		5 } Max	Run the jack. If it loses, cash the ace and king; if it is covered, guess as above	87	5.03
89.	A K 9 8 x x J x	6	Run the jack. If it is covered, guess whether to finesse or cash the ace next	16	
		5	Lead small to the jack, and then cash the ace and king (which will be best if West is likely to be short in the suit) *or* Run the jack, cashing the ace and king if it loses, and guessing if it is covered (which will be best if East is likely to be short in the suit)	85	
		Max	Run the jack, guessing what to do next if it is covered		5.01
90.	A K 9 x x x J x	6	Run the jack. If it is covered, finesse the nine *or* cash the ace	14	
		5	Lead small to the jack; then cash the ace and king	85	
		4	Lead small to the jack	100	
		Max	Lead the jack. If it is covered, finesse the nine next		4.94
91.	A J 8 x x x K 9	6	Play the king. If the queen drops from East, run the nine; otherwise finesse the jack	37	
		5	Cash the king, and then lead the nine, and finesse the jack	88	
		4	Lead small to the nine	100	
92.	A J x x x x K 9	6	Cash the king, and finesse the jack	34	
		5	Cash the king, and lead the nine, intending to finesse the jack	88	
		4	Lead small to the nine	100	
		Max	Cash the king, and finesse the jack		5.20
93.	A K 9 8 x J x x	5	Play the ace. Then play the king unless the queen has appeared from East	30	
		4	Play the ace, and unless an honor appears, lead low to the jack	96	
		Max	Lead the jack. If it is covered, finesse the nine; if it loses, cash the ace		4.14
94.	A K 9 x x J x x	5 ·	Play the ace and king (unless the queen drops from East)	30	
		4	Play the ace, and if the ten fails to appear, lead small to the jack	96	
		Max	Play the ace and king		4.09

	Dummy Declarer	Tricks Required		% Chance of Success	Tricks per Deal

III. THE DEFENSE HAS TWO POINTS (cont'd)

	Dummy Declarer	Tricks Required		% Chance of Success	Tricks per Deal
95.	A K 7 6 x J 9 8	5	Lead the nine to the ace. (This makes it harder for West to falsecard with queen from Q10, as it would help a declarer with J9.) If the queen falls, finesse accordingly; if not, cash the king Assuming no falsecard:	33	
		4	Play the ace, and if no honor appears, lead low to the jack	98	
		Max	Cash the ace and king*		4.11
			(*If West would not falsecard from Q10)		4.14
96.	A K x x x J 10 9	5	Finesse the jack. Don't cash the ace first: Qxxx with West is more likely than queen with East	48	
		4	Finesse the jack	100	
97.	A K x x x J 9 8	5	Cash the ace and king*	27	
			(*But against defenders who would not false-card with Q10, finesse the nine if West drops the queen on the first round)	30	
		4	Play the ace, and lead small to the jack	88	
		3	Run the jack *or* lead small to the jack	100	
		Max	Cash the ace, and unless West is void, lead small to the king*		4.01
			(*If West would not falsecard with Q10)		4.04
98.	A K x x x J 9 x	5	Play the ace and king*	27	
			(*But against defenders who would not false-card with Q10, finesse the nine if West drops the queen on the first round)	30	
		4	Play the ace, and lead small to the jack	88	
		Max	Play the ace and king		3.99
99.	A J 9 x x K x x	5 }	Cash the king, and finesse the jack*	40	4.27
		Max ∫	(*But against defenders who would not false-card, it is fractionally better to play the ace if East drops the ten on the first round.)		
100.	A J x x x K 9 x	5	Lead low to the jack*	34	
			(*Against defenders who would not falsecard from Q10, finesse the nine next if the queen appears from West)	37	
		4	Play the ace, and unless an honor appears from West, lead low to the nine	96	
		3	Play either top honor	100	
		Max	Play the king, and finesse the jack		4.22
101.	A 9 x x x K J x	5	Finesse the jack. Don't cash the ace first, for East may have the singleton queen	37	
		4	Play the king, and unless the ten appears, lead low to the jack	96	
		3	Finesse the jack, and cash the king *or* play the king and lead small to the jack	100	
		Max	Finesse the jack		4.30
102.	J 9 8 x x A K x	4	Cash the ace, cross to dummy in another suit and lead the nine. If East shows out or covers, play the king. If not, run the jack.	96	
103.	A K J 10 x x x x	4	Play the ace, and finesse the jack	53	
104.	A K 9 x J x x x	4	Play the ace and king	30	
		3	Play the ace, and then lead small to the nine or jack	100	
		Max	Play the ace and king		3.21

Dummy Declarer	Tricks Required		% Chance of Success	Tricks per Deal

III. THE DEFENSE HAS TWO POINTS (cont'd)

Dummy Declarer	Tricks Required		% Chance of Success	Tricks per Deal
105. A K 8 x	4	Play the ace and king	27	
J x x x	3	Play the ace; if the ten or nine appears from East, lead small to the jack	92	
	Max	Play the ace and king		3.14
106. A K x x	4	Play the ace and king	33	
J 9 8 x	3	Play the ace, and unless the ten appears from East, run the nine	100	
	Max	Play the ace and king		3.24
107. A J x x	4	Finesse the jack	37	
K 9 x x	3	Play the ace, and lead small to the nine	100	
	Max	Finesse the jack; if it loses, play the ace next		3.34
108. A 10 8 x	4	Lead the jack to the ace *or* the ten to the king, and then take a second-round finesse. This gives		
K J 9 x		the extra chance of a defender covering with Qx and Qxx	53+	

(c) Declarer Has Nine Cards

Dummy Declarer	Tricks Required		% Chance of Success	Tricks per Deal
109. A K J x x x x x 8		Play the ace and king. This line is 8% better than		
x		a first-round finesse	53	
	7	Finesse the jack, in case East is void	95	
	Max	Play the ace and king		7.44
110. A K J x x x x	7	Play the ace and king. This line is 2% better than		
x x		a second-round finesse.	53	
111. A K 9 x x x x	7	Play the ace and king	53	
J x	6	Lead low to the jack	100	
	Max	Play the ace and king*		6.44
		(*But againsst defenders who would always cover the jack, and would not falsecard with Q10, lead the jack, and play the ace whatever happens, finessing the nine next if East plays the queen)		6.48
112. A J x x x x x	7	Play the king and ace	53	
K 9	6	Lead small to the nine, in case West is void	100	
	Max	Play the king and ace		6.48
113. A K J 10 x x	6	Play the ace and king	58	
x x x				
114. A K 9 x x x	6	Play the ace and king	53	
J x x	5	Play the ace	100	
115. A K 8 x x x	6	Play the ace and king	53	
J x x	5	Lead small toward dummy, and cover whatever West plays	100	
	Max	Play the ace and king		5.48
116. A K x x x x	6	Lead the jack to the ace; then cash the king	53	
J 10 9				
117. A K x x x x	6	Play the ace and king	53	
J 9 8	5	Lead small to the jack *or* (best) run the nine	100	
	Max	Play the ace and king		5.48
118. A J x x x x	6	Play the ace and king	53	
K 9 x	5	Play the ace	100	
	Max	Play the ace and king		5.53
119. A 9 x x x x	6	Play the ace and king	53	
K J x	5	Play the king	100	
	Max	Play the king and ace		5.53

	Dummy Declarer	Tricks Required		% Chance of Success	Tricks per Deal

III.   THE DEFENSE HAS TWO POINTS (cont'd)

	Dummy Declarer	Tricks Required		% Chance of Success	Tricks per Deal
120.	A K 8 x x J x x x	5	Play the ace and king*	53	
			(*Against defenders who would always cover the jack, lead the jack, and play the ace whatever happens. If West covers and the ten or nine drops from East, finesse the eight next. This line will be better if East is likely to be short in the suit)	53	
		4	Lead small to the eight *or* small to the jack	100	
		Max	Play the ace and king		4.48
121.	A K x x x J 10 9 x	5	Play the ace and king. This line is 2% better than a second-round finesse	58	
122.	A J 9 x x K 10 8 x	5	Lead the jack to the king *or* lead the ten to the ace, and play for the drop on the second round. This gives the extra chance of a defender covering with Qxx	58	
123.	A J x x x K 9 8 7	5 4	Play the king and ace, in case East is void Play the ace, in case West is void	58 100	
124.	A J x x x K 9 x x	5 4	Cash the ace and king, preferably in that order Play the ace (best) *or* finesse the jack or nine	53 100	
125.	A 9 x x x K J x x	5 4	Play the ace and king in either order Play the king (best), *or* finesse the jack	53 100	
126.	A x x x x K J 9 8	5 4	Play the ace and king, in case West is void Play the king, in case East is void	58 100	
127.	J 10 9 x x A K x x	5	Play the ace and king; this line is 2% better than a second-round finesse	58	
128.	J x x x x A K 8 x	5 4	Play the ace and king Lead small to the eight, in case West is void	53 100	
		Max	Play the ace and king		4.48

(f)   Declarer Has Ten Cards

	Dummy Declarer	Tricks Required		% Chance of Success	Tricks per Deal
129.	A K 9 x x x x x 8 J x		Lead the jack, and play the ace whatever happens. This line succeeds against all 2-1 breaks and when West is lulled into covering with Q10x	78+	
130.	A K 9 x x x x J x x	7	See (129) above	78+	
131.	A J x x x x x K x x	7	Lead the king, in case East is void	89	
132.	A K 9 x x x J x x x	6	See (129) above	78+	
133.	A J x x x x K x x x	6	See (131) above	89	
133A.	K x x x x x A J 9 8	6	Play the king, in case West is void* (*But if there is no side entry to dummy, play the ace, as the only way to avoid a suit block is to find a singleton queen)	26	
134.	A K 9 x x J x x x x	5	See (129) above	78+	
135.	A J 9 x x K 10 x x x	5	Lead the ten to the ace, *or* lead the jack to the king. Guess who is most likely to be void	89	
136.	A J x x x K x x x x	5	See (131) above	89	

Dummy Declarer	Tricks Required		% Chance of Success	Tricks per Deal

IV.   THE DEFENSE HAS THREE POINTS
A.   THE KING

(a)   Declarer Has Five Cards

137. A Q J 9   4   The only hope is that West has K10 doubleton   0.3
         x   3   Lead small to the nine   52
                  Max   Lead small to the nine   2.53

(b)   Declarer Has Six Cards

138. A Q J 9 8   5   Finesse the queen. The only hope is that West has
         x   K10 doubleton   1
                   4   Finesse the nine*   41
                  Max   Finesse the nine*   3.42
                         (*The nine finesse is only 0.36% better than
                         the queen finesse)

139. A Q J 9   4   Finesse the queen, hoping that West has K10 or
         x x   K10x   5
                   3 ⎱   Finesse the queen. If it holds, finesse the jack; if it   2.73
                  Max ⎰ loses, cash the ace and jack*   68
                         (*This assumes that East will duck the queen
                         with Kx or Kxx. If not, it is better to finesse
                         the nine if the queen loses)   76

140. A Q 9 8   4   Run the jack. If it is covered, finesse the nine
         J x   next   5
                   3 ⎱   Run the jack. If it losses, finesse the nine; if it
                  Max ⎰ holds, finesse the queen*   76   2.81
                         (*This assumes that West will cover the jack
                         with Kxxxx or Kxxx, and that East will win
                         with Kx or Kxx. If they would withhold the
                         king in such circumstances, it is better to cash
                         the ace and queen if the jack loses)   68

141. A Q 9 x   3   Lead small to the jack and finesse the nine next
         J x   whatever happens   56

142. A Q 8 x   3   Lead the jack. If it holds, finesse the queen; if it
         J 9   loses, cash the ace; if it is covered, run the
                           nine*   68
                         (*The best defense is for East not to win with
                         Kx or Kxx, and for West not to cover with
                         Kxxxx or Kxxx)

143. A Q x x   3   Lead small to the nine, hoping that East has the
         J 9   singleton ten or king*   50
                         (*Or that he will mistakenly play the king from
                         Kx)   54

144. A Q 9   3   Lead small to the nine *or* (best) run the jack; if
         J x x   it is covered, finesse the nine   24
                  Max   Run the jack; if it is covered, finesse the nine next   2.24

145. A Q x   3   Run the nine *or* (best) run the jack; if it is cov-
         J 9 8   ered, run the nine next   24
                  Max   Run the jack; if it is covered, run the nine next   2.24

146. A x x   3   Lead the queen. If it is covered, play the jack, if
         Q J 9   the queen holds, guess*   5
                         (*But against defenders who might cover un-
                         necessarily—let us assume half the time—
                         finesse the nine if the queen is covered and lead
                         the jack next if the queen holds)   15

Dummy Declarer	Tricks Required		% Chance of Success	Tricks per Deal

IV. THE DEFENSE HAS THREE POINTS (cont'd)
A. THE KING (cont'd)

(c) Declarer Has Seven Cards

147.	A Q J 9 8 7	6	Finesse the queen. The only hope is that West has K10 doubleton	2	
	x	5 Max }	Finesse the queen; then cash the ace	62	4.63
148.	A Q J 9 x x	6	Finesse the queen, hoping that West has K10 doubleton	2	
	x	5	Finesse the queen; then cash the ace	58	
		4	Finesse the nine; then cash the ace	92	
		3	Finesse the nine; then cash the ace	99	
		Max	Finesse the queen; then cash the ace		4.46
149.	A Q J 9 8	5	Finesse the queen; if it loses, cash the ace and jack	19	
	x x	4 Max }	Finesse the queen; if it loses, cash the ace and jack	71	3.91
150.	A Q 9 8 x	5	Lead small to the nine *or* (best) run the jack, finessing the nine next if it is covered	9	
	J x	4 Max }	Run the jack. If it loses, cash the ace; if it is covered, finesse the nine; if it holds, finesse the queen.	70	3.79
151.	A Q 9 x x	5	Lead small to the nine *or* (best) run the jack, finessing the nine next if it is covered	7	
	J x	4	Lead small to the jack. If it holds, play the ace; if it loses, play the ace	58	
		3	Finesse the nine on the first or second round	93	
		Max	Run the jack. If it holds, finesse the nine; if it loses, cash the ace and queen; if it is covered, finesse the nine		3.54
152.	A Q x x x	4	Lead small to the nine; if it loses, run the jack next*	49	
	J 9	3 Max }	Lead small to the nine; if it loses, run the jack next*	93	3.42
			(*This line will also produce four tricks if East is tempted to play the king from Kx)	56	
153.	A Q x x x	4	Lead small to the jack, hoping that the suit divides 3-3 or that East has Kx	44	
	J x	3	Play the ace, and lead small to the jack, in case West has the singleton king	86	
		Max	Lead small to the jack		3.29
154.	Q J 9 8 7	5	Run the queen, cashing the jack next if it is covered	2	
	A x	4	Play the ace, and lead to the queen	63	
		Max	Run the queen, cashing the jack next if it is covered*		3.63
			(*Playing the ace and leading to the queen makes only .004 tricks fewer, and will be the best line if West is more likely to be short in the suit)		
155.	Q J 9 x x	4	Play the ace, and lead to the queen	59	
	A x	3	Play the ace, and lead to the nine	94	
		Max	Play the ace, and lead to the queen		3.49
156.	Q J x x x	4	Lead small to the nine	50	
	A 9	3	Lead small to the nine	93	
		Max	Lead small to the nine		3.43

	Dummy Declarer	Tricks Required		% Chance of Success	Tricks per Deal
			IV. THE DEFENSE HAS THREE POINTS (cont;d)		
			A. THE KING (cont'd)		
157.	A Q J x	4	Finesse the queen, hoping that West has Kxx	18	
	x x x	3	Play the ace, and lead to the queen, in case East has the singleton king	69	
		Max	Finesse the queen		2.86
158.	A Q 10 x	4	Lead small to the ten, and then small to the queen. Do not lead the jack in case West has K or Kx	27	
	J x x				
159.	A Q 9 8	4 } Max }	Run the jack. If it is covered, finesse the nine; if it holds, leads to the nine; if it loses, cash the ace and queen	25	3.03
	J x x				
		3	Finesse the queen. If it holds, run the jack; if it loses, cash the jack and ace	79	
160.	A Q 9 x	4	Lead low to the nine, hoping that West has K10 or K10x	9	
	J x x	3	Finesse the queen. If it loses, cash the jack and ace; if it holds, lead low to the nine	72	
		Max	Run the jack. If it is covered, finesse the nine; if it loses, cash the ace and queen		2.78
161.	A Q 8 7	4	Run the jack, hoping that East has the singleton nine or ten	2	
	J x x	3 } Max }	Lead the jack. If it loses, cash the ace, and finesse East; if it holds, finesse the queen; if it is covered, finesse the eight and then the seven next* (*Assuming that West will not cover with Kxxx, K10xxx, or K9xxx)	59	2.61
162.	A Q 8 x	3	Lead small to the ace, then small to the jack. Then finesse the eight if possible. But if West plays the nine or ten, finesse the queen. (This assumes that West will play low with K 10 9 x or 10 9 x x. It is fractionally superior to the alternatives: Finesse the queen, and if it wins lead the jack (57%); small toward the jack (56%); or running the jack (53%).	59	
	J x x				
163.	A Q x x	4	Run the jack, and then the nine (best) or run the nine. Hope that West has K10x or either Kxxxx or K	8	
	J 9 8	3 } Max }	Lead the jack. If it loses, cash the ace; if it is covered, run the nine next	77	2.85
164.	A Q x x	4	Play the ace, hoping that West has the singleton king	1	
	J 9 x	3 } Max }	Play the ace, and lead small to the jack	64	2.65
165.	A 9 8 7	4	Lead the queen. If it holds or is covered, lead the jack next	9	
	Q J x	3	Lead small to the queen. If it holds, lead small to the jack; if it loses, cash the jack and ace	83	
		Max	Lead the queen. If it loses, cash the jack and ace; if it holds or is covered, lead the jack next		2.88
166.	A 9 x x	3 } Max }	Lead small to the queen. If it holds, lead small to the jack; if it loses, cash the jack and ace	83	2.83
	Q J x				
167.	Q J 9 x	4	Play the ace, hoping East has the singleton king	1	
	A x x	3 } Max }	Play the ace and then lead to the queen and jack	78	2.79

	Dummy Declarer	Tricks Required		% Chance of Success	Tricks per Deal
			IV. THE DEFENSE HAS THREE POINTS (cont'd)		
			A. THE KING (cont'd)		
168.	Q J x x A x x	3	Play the ace, and lead low to the queen; then lead low to the jack	69	
169.	J 9 8 7 A Q x	4	Run the nine. If it is covered, run the jack	10	
		3	Finesse the queen. If it holds, run the jack; if it loses, cash the ace and jack* (*This line offers extra chances if West is tempted to win the queen with K10xxx)	78 83	
		Max	Run the jack. If it is covered, run the nine next		2.86
170.	J 9 8 x A Q x	4	Finesse the queen. If it holds, run the nine, hoping that East has K10, Kx, or K	9	
		3	Finesse the queen. If it holds, lead the jack; if it loses, cash the ace and jack* (*This line offers extra chances if West is tempted to win the queen with K10xxx)	78 83	
		Max	Finesse the queen. If it holds, run the nine; if it loses, cash the ace and jack		2.85
171.	J 9 x x A Q x	4	Finesse the queen, and then cash the ace, hoping that East has K, Kx, or K10	9	
		3	Lead small to the ace, unless the ten appears from East; then lead to the queen and jack	69	
		Max	Finesse the queen, and then cash the ace		2.77
172.	J x x x A Q 9	4	Lead small to the nine, hoping that East has K10 or K10x	9	
		3	Lead small to the queen. If it holds, finesse the nine; if it loses, cash the ace	71	
		Max	Lead small to the nine. If it loses, finesse the queen		2.77

(d) Declarer Has Eight Cards

	Dummy Declarer	Tricks Required		% Chance of Success	Tricks per Deal
173.	A Q J 9 x x x x	7	Finesse the queen, hoping that West has Kx or K10	14	
		6	Play the ace, and lead the queen	79	
		5	Finesse the nine, in case East is void	98	
		Max	Finesse the queen		5.86
174.	A Q J 9 x x x x	6	Finesse the queen	34	
		5	Finesse the queen; if it loses, cash the ace	85	
175.	A Q 9 8 x x J x	6	Finesse the queen, and run the jack if it holds *or* run the jack; if it loses, cash the ace; if it holds finesse the queen; if it is covered, guess	14	
		5	As above	85	
176.	A Q 9 x x x J x	6	Finesse the nine *or* finesse the queen *or* lead the jack and guess next time	14	
		5	Run the jack. If it is covered, finesse the nine next	82	
		4	Safeguard against East being void by leading the jack, leading to the jack or finessing the nine	98	
		Max	Run the jack. If it is covered, finesse the nine next		4.94
177.	A Q x x x x J 9	5	Lead small to the jack	76	
		4	Lead small to the nine, in case West is void	98	
		Max	Lead small to the jack* (*But against defenders who would play the king from Kx as East, lead small to the nine and run the jack next)		4.72 4.73

	Dummy Declarer	Tricks Required		% Chance of Success	Tricks per Deal

IV.   THE DEFENSE HAS THREE POINTS (cont'd)
A.   THE KING (cont'd)

	Dummy Declarer	Tricks Required		% Chance of Success	Tricks per Deal
177a	A Q 6 5 x x J 9	5	Run the jack. If West covers and East drops the seven, eight or ten, take the ace, return to hand and run the nine.	79	
178.	A Q x x x x J x	5 } Max }	Play the ace. This succeeds if the suit divides 3-2 or there is a singleton king somewhere	73	4.70
179.	Q J 9 x x x A x	6	Lead the queen. If it is covered, finesse the nine, hoping East has Kx	10	
		5	Play the ace, and lead to queen	79	
		4	Play the ace; fails only if West is void	98	
		Max	Lead the queen, finessing the nine next if it is covered		4.83
180.	A Q 10 x x J x x	5 } Max }	Finesse the queen. Don't lead the jack in case West has the singleton king	37	4.33
181.	A Q 9 7 6 J 8 x	5	Run the jack. If it is covered, finesse the nine next	25	
		4	Run the jack *or* finesse the queen	90	
		Max	Run the jack. If it is covered, finesse the nine next		4.14
182.	A Q 9 x x J 8 x	5	Finesse the queen. If it holds, guess whether to play the ace or the jack next*	16	
			(*If West would not falsecard with K10, finesse the eight if the king appears on the first round)	19	
		4	Finesse the queen *or* run the jack *or* play the ace and lead small to the jack	88	
183.	A Q 9 x x J x x	5	Finesse the queen *or* run the jack. Guess whether West has K10x, Kxx, or Kx	14	
		4	Finesse the queen, and lead to the nine if it holds *or* play the ace, and lead to the jack	88	
		3	Finesse the queen	98	
		Max	Finesse the queen. If it loses, cash the jack; if it holds, lead to the nine		3.99
184.	A Q 8 x x J x x	5	Finesse the queen; if it holds, lead small to the eight*	14	
			(*If East would not falsecard from 109x, lead the jack if the nine or ten appears on the first round)	17	
		4	Lead small to the ace, unless the nine or ten appears from West; then lead low to the jack (best) *or* run the jack; if it is covered, lead low to the eight unless the nine or ten has dropped	79	
		3	Run the jack. If it is covered, lead low to the eight unless the nine or ten has dropped from East (best)	98	
		Max	Finesse the queen. If it holds, lead small to the eight		3.86
185.	A Q x x x J 9 8	5	Lead the jack. If it holds, finesse the queen; if it is covered, guess whether to run the nine or play the ace next	16	
		4 } Max }	Lead the jack. If it loses, cash the ace; if it holds, finesse the queen; if it is covered, run the nine	85	4.01
		3	Lead the jack (best) or lead small to the jack	100	
186.	A Q x x x J 9 x	5	Finesse the queen. If it holds, guess whether to lead the nine or the jack next*	14	
			(*If West would not falsecard from K10, finesse the nine if the king appears from West)	16	
		4	Play the ace, and lead small to the jack	79	
		3	Play the ace, or finesse the queen	98	
		Max	Finesse the queen, and cash the ace next		3.88

Dummy Declarer	Tricks Required		% Chance of Success	Tricks per Deal

IV. THE DEFENSE HAS THREE POINTS (cont'd)
A. THE KING (cont'd)

	Dummy Declarer	Tricks Required		% Chance of Success	Tricks per Deal
186a	A Q 6 x x J 9 x	4	Run the jack. If West covers with the king, win the ace and lead to the nine.	85	
187.	A Q x x x J x x	5	Finesse the queen, and then play the ace	14	
		4	Play the ace, and lead toward the jack, in case East has the singleton king	73	
		Max	Finesse the queen		3.80
187a	A Q 7 x x J x x	4	Run the jack. If West covers and East drops the eight, nine or ten, win the ace, return to hand for the next lead.	76	
188.	A 9 x x x Q J x	5	Lead the queen. If it holds, lead the jack, hoping that West has Kxx or K10	14	
		4	Lead small to the queen. If it holds, lead to the jack	93	
		3	Lead small to the queen	100	
		Max	Run the queen. If it holds, lead the jack		3.96
189.	A x x x x Q J 9	5	Lead the queen. If it is covered, play the jack next; if it holds, lead the jack next* (*This assumes that West will cover with Kx about once in four times—best defense)	14	
		4	Lead small to the queen, and then small to the jack	85	
		3	Lead the queen *or* lead small to the queen	98	
		Max	Lead the queen. If it is covered, play the jack; if it holds, lead the jack next* (*The best defense is now for West never to cover with Kx		3.85
190.	Q J 9 x x A x x	5	Lead the Queen. If it holds, lead the jack; if it is covered, finesse the nine* (*This assumes that East will cover with Kx half the time; if he always covers, this line will produce five tricks)	15 20	
		4	Play the ace, and lead toward the queen	88	
		Max	Lead the queen. If it loses, play the ace; if it holds, play the ace; if it is covered, finesse the nine* (*But if West would not duck the queen with K10xx, lead the jack if the queen holds; and if East would always cover with Kx, lead the jack if the queen holds)		3.93 3.98 4.03
191.	J 9 8 x x A Q x	5	Finesse the queen. If it holds, guess whether East has Kx or Kxx	16	
		4 ⎱ Max ⎰	Finesse the queen. If it loses, cash the ace; if it holds, run the nine	93	4.10
192.	J x x x x A Q 9	5	Finesse the queen *or* finesse the nine	14	
		4 ⎱ Max ⎰	Finesse the queen. If it holds, lead small to the nine; if it loses, cash the ace	85	3.96
192a	J 7 x x x A Q 6	4	Run the jack. If West covers and East drops the eight, nine or ten. win and return to hand for next lead.	76	
193.	A Q J x x x x x	4	Finesse the queen	34	
		3	Play the ace, and lead to the queen	87	
		Max	Finesse the queen		3.18
194.	A Q 10 x J x x x	4	Finesse the ten. Don't lead the jack in case West has the singleton king	37	
195.	A Q 9 8 J x x x	4	Lead the jack. If it is covered, finesse the nine; if it holds, lead small to the nine	27	
		3	Lead small to the queen. If it loses, cash the ace; if it holds, lead to the nine	97	
		Max	Both the above lines produce		3.16

	Dummy Declarer	Tricks Required		% Chance of Success	Tricks per Deal

IV.   THE DEFENSE HAS THREE POINTS (cont'd)
A.   THE KING (cont'd)

	Dummy Declarer	Tricks Required		% Chance of Success	Tricks per Deal
196.	A Q 9 x J x x x	4	Finesse the queen *or* run the jack, guessing whether West has Kx or K10x	14	
		3 ⎫ Max ⎭	Finesse the queen. If it loses, cash the jack; if it holds, finesse the nine	90	3.03
197.	A Q 8 x J x x x	4	Finesse the queen; if it holds, lead small to the eight* (*If East would not falsecard from 109x, lead the jack next if the nine or ten drops)	14 17	
		3	Lead the jack. If it is covered, lead small to the eight unless the nine or ten has appeared from East	81	
		Max	Finesse the queen; if it holds, lead small to the eight		2.90
198.	A Q x x J 9 8 x	4	Finesse the queen, hoping that West has K, Kxxx, K10, or Kx	19	
		3 ⎫ Max ⎭	Finesse the queen. If it loses, play the ace; if it holds, run the nine	97	3.16
199.	A Q x x J 9 x x	4	Finesse the queen. If it holds, guess whether to lead the jack or play the ace	16	
		3	Play the ace, and lead small to the queen	90	
		Max	Finesse the queen, then play the ace		3.03
200.	A Q x x J x x x	4	Finesse the queen; then play the ace, hoping West has Kx	14	
		3	Play the ace, and lead small to either honor	73	
		Max	Finesse the queen, then play ace		2.84
200a	A Q 7 x J x x x	3	Run the jack. If West covers and East drops the eight, nine or ten, win with the ace and return to hand for the next lead.	76	
201.	A 9 8 x Q J x x	4	Lead the queen. If it is covered, cash the jack; if it holds, lead the jack. Hope that West has Kxx, K10, or Kxxx* (*It has been assumed that, if the queen is led, West will cover 1/3 of the time with Kx, and East will win 1/3 of the time with K10xx. This is the best defense)	16	
		3	Lead the queen (best). If it loses, cash the ace; if it holds, lead small to the nine *or* lead small to the queen. If it loses, cash the jack; if it holds, lead small to the nine	97	
		Max	Lead the queen. If it loses, cash the ace; if it is covered, run the nine; if it holds, lead small to the nine* (*It has been assumed that, if the queen is led, West will cover 1/3 of the time with Kx, and East will win 1/3 of the time with K10xx. This is the best defense)		3.10
202.	A x x x Q J x x	3	Play the ace, and lead to the queen. This fails only if East has a void or a small singleton	87	
203.	Q J 9 x A x x x	4	Lead the queen. If it holds, lead the jack; if it is covered, finesse the nine next* (*This assumes that East will cover 1/2 the time with Kx; if he always covers, this line will produce four tricks)	15 20	
		3	Play the ace and lead to the queen	90	
		Max	Lead the queen. If it holds, play the ace; if it is covered, finesse the nine* (*But if West would not duck the queen with K10xx, lead the jack next if the queen holds)		2.97 3.02

Dummy Declarer	Tricks Required		% Chance of Success	Tricks per Deal

IV.   THE DEFENSE HAS THREE POINTS (cont'd)
A.   THE KING (cont'd)

(c) Declarer Has Nine Cards

Dummy Declarer	Tricks Required		% Chance of Success	Tricks per Deal
204.	Q J x x	4	Lead the queen. If it holds, lead the jack; if it		
	A 9 x x		loses or is covered, cash the jack	14	
		3	Lead small to the queen. If it loses, cash the		
			jack; if it holds, lead small to the nine	97	
		Max	Lead the queen, and play the jack next whatever		
			happens		3.00
205.	A Q J 10 x x x x	8	Finesse the queen; Kx with West is more likely		
	x		than K with East	27	
206.	A Q 9 x x x x	7	Finesse the queen	33	
	J x	6	Run the jack *or* lead small to the jack	95	
		Max	Finesse the queen		6.23
207.	Q J x x x x x	7	Run the queen, hoping West has Kx	20	
	A x	Max	Run the queen		6.11
208.	A Q 9 x x x	6 }	Finesse the queen, hoping that West has Kxx,		
	J x x	Max }	K10, Kx, or K	33	5.28
209.	A Q 8 x x x	6	Finesse the queen	27	
	J x x	5	Lead the jack, in case East is void	95	
		Max	Finesse the queen		5.17
210.	A Q 7 x x x	6	Finesse the queen	33	
	J 9 8	5	Play the ace *or* finesse the queen	100	
		Max	Finesse the queen		5.33
211.	A Q x x x x	6	Finesse the queen, hoping that West has Kxx,		
	J 9 8		K10, Kx, or K	33	
		5	If West is more likely to be void, play the ace or		
			finesse the queen; if East is more likely to be		
			void, run the jack or lead small to the jack	95	
		Max	Finesse the queen		5.28
212.	A x x x x x	6	Run the queen	27	
	Q J 9	5	Run the queen (best) *or* lead small to the queen	95	
		Max	Run the queen		5.22
213.	A x x x x x	6	Run the queen	20	
	Q J x	5	Lead small to the queen, in case West is void	95	
		Max	Run the queen		5.11
214.	Q J 9 x x x	6 }	Lead the queen. If it is covered, cash the jack	27	5.22
	A x x	Max }			
215.	Q J x x x x	6	Run the queen	20	
	A x x	5	Play the ace, and lead to the queen	95	
		Max	Run the queen		5.11
216.	J 9 8 x x x	6	Finesse the queen	33	
	A Q x	5	Finesse the queen *or* play the ace	100	
		Max	Finesse the queen		5.33
217.	A Q J x x	5	Finesse the queen	45	
	x x x x	Max	Finesse the queen		4.40
218.	A Q 9 7 x	5	Finesse the queen. A singleton king with West is		
	J 8 x x		more likely than K10xx	33	
		4	Finesse the queen, in case West is void	100	
219.	A Q 9 x x	5	Finesse the queen	33	
	J x x x	Max	Finesse the queen		4.28
220.	A Q 8 x x	5	Finesse the queen	27	
	J x x x	4	Run the jack, in case East is void	95	
		Max	Run the jack. If it is covered, and the nine or		
			ten drops from East, finesse the eight next		4.21
221.	A 9 8 x x	5	Run the queen. If it is covered, cash the jack	27	
	Q J x x	4	Run teh queen (best) *or* lead small to the queen	100	
		Max	Run the queen. If it is covered, cash the jack		
			next		4.27

Dummy Declarer	Tricks Required		% Chance of Success	Tricks per Deal

IV.   THE DEFENSE HAS THREE POINTS (cont'd)
A.   THE KING (cont'd)

222.	A 9 x x x Q J x x	5	Run the queen, hoping that West has Kxx, K10, or Kx	27	
		4	Lead small to the queen	100	
		Max	Run the queen		4.22
223.	A x x x x Q J 9 x	5 ⎫ Max ⎭	Run the queen. If it is covered, cash the jack	27	4.22
224.	A x x x x Q J x x	5	Run the queen, hoping that West has Kx	20	
		4	Play the ace, and lead to the queen	95	
		Max	Run the queen		4.11
225.	Q J 9 x x A x x x	5 ⎫ Max ⎭	Run the queen. If it is covered, cash the jack	27	4.22
226.	Q J x x x A x x x	5	20		
		4 ⎫ Max ⎭	See (224) above	95	4.11
227.	J 9 8 x x A Q x x	5	Finesse the queen; then cash the ace. Unless West plays the ten	33	
		4	Finesse the queen (best) *or* cash the ace	100	
		Max	Finesse the queen, then cash the ace		4.33

(f)   Declarer Has Ten Cards

228.	A J 9 x x x x x Q x	8 ⎫ Max ⎭	Run the queen	50	7.50
229.	A Q J x x x x x x x	7 ⎫ Max ⎭	Finesse the queen	50	6.50
230.	A J 9 x x x x Q x x	7 ⎫ Max ⎭	Run the queen. Don't finesse the jack in case East is void	50	6.50
231.	Q J x x x x x A x x	7 ⎫ Max ⎭	Run the queen	39	6.39
232.	A Q J x x x x x x x	6 ⎫ Max ⎭	Finesse the queen	50	5.50
233.	A J 9 x x x Q x x x	6 ⎫ Max ⎭	See (230) above	50	5.50
234.	Q J x x x x A x x x	6 ⎫ Max ⎭	Run the queen	39	5.39
235.	A Q J x x x x x x x	5 ⎫ Max ⎭	Finesse the queen	50	4.50
236.	A J 9 x x Q x x x x	5 ⎫ Max ⎭	See (230) above	50	4.50
237.	A x x x x Q J x x x	5 ⎫ Max ⎭	Run the queen	39	4.39

(g)   Declarer Has Eleven Cards

238.	A Q J x x x x x x x x	6	Play the ace. The singleton king with East is 2% more likely than Kx with West	52	

B.   THE QUEEN-JACK

(a)   Declarer Has Six Cards

239.	A K 10 9 8 x	5	Play the ace and king, hoping that the queen- jack are bare	1	
		4	Lead small to the ten	45	
		Max	Lead small to the ten		3.46

Dummy Declarer	Tricks Required		% Chance of Success	Tricks per Deal

IV.   THE DEFENSE HAS THREE POINTS (cont'd)
B.   THE QUEEN-JACK (cont'd)

	Dummy Declarer	Tricks Required		% Chance of Success	Tricks per Deal
240.	A K 10 9	4	Lead small to the ten, hoping that West has		
	x x		QJx or QJ	5	
		3 ⎱	Finesse the ten; if this loses, finesse the nine		
		Max ⎰	next	76	2.81
241.	A 9 x x	3	Lead small to the ten; then cash the king and		
	K 10		ace	55	
(b)	**Declarer Has Seven Cards**				
242.	A K 10 9 x	5	Finesse the ten, hoping that West has QJx or QJ	9	
	x x	4	Finesse the ten; then finesse the nine	66	
		3	Play the ace, and then finesse the ten *or* finesse		
			the ten and then the nine	94	
		Max	Finesse the ten; then finesse the nine		3.69
243.	A 10 x x x	4	Lead small to the nine	61	
	K 9	3	Lead small to the nine	92	
243A.	A 10 9 x x	5	Play the king, then the ace	3	
	K x	4	Play the king, then the ace (unless East shows out)	61	3.54
		Max			
		3	Play the king, then finesse the nine or ten	93	
244.	A K 10 9	4	Finesse the ten, hoping that West has both the		
	x x x		queen and jack	24	
		3	Finesse the ten; if it loses, cash the ace, and		
			finesse the nine (best) *or* play the ace, and		
			then finesse the ten and nine	78	
		Max	Finesse the ten; if it loses, cash the ace, and		
			finesse the nine		3.00
245.	A K 9 x	4	Finesse the nine, hoping that West has QJx or QJ	9	
	10 x x	3	Play the ace. If no honor drops from East, lead		
			small to the nine next	72	
		Max	Finesse the nine		2.78
246.	A 10 9 x	4	Play the king. If an honor drops from East,		
	K 8 x		finesse the nine	4	
		3 ⎱	Lead small to the eight. If it loses, run the ten		
		Max ⎰	next*	82	2.84
			(*This line fails only when West has QJ, QJx,		
			or QJxx. In practical play, however, it might		
			be better to lead small to the king, and then		
			finesse the ten and nine: for East may split		
			his honors with QJx, QJxx, etc.)		
247.	A 10 x x	4	Play the ace anbd king, hoping that the queen		
	K 9 x		and jack are doubleton	3	
		3 ⎱	Lead low to the nine; then cash the king and		
		Max ⎰	ace*	75	2.77
			(*This assumes that East would never split his		
			honors from QJxx and longer; if this is not		
			so, lead low to the king and then finesse the		
			ten)		
248.	A 10 x x	3 ⎱	Play the king, and unless an honor appears from		
	K x x	Max ⎰	East, lead small to the ten*	56	2.56
			(*But if West might be tempted to split his		
			honors, it might be better to play the king and		
			ace and lead to the ten)		
(c)	**Declarer Has Eight Cards**				
249.	A K 10 9 x x	6	Finesse the ten, hoping that West has QJ or QJx	14	
	x x	5	Play the ace. If an honor drops from East, play		
			the king; otherwise finesse the ten	88	
		Max	Finesse the ten. If it loses, play the ace and king		4.94

	Dummy Declarer	Tricks Required		% Chance of Success	Tricks per Deal
			IV. THE DEFENSE HAS THREE POINTS (cont'd)		
			B. THE QUEEN-JACK (cont'd)		
250.	A 10 9 x x x K x	6	Play the ace and king, hoping that the queen-jack are doubleton	7	
		5 Max	Play the king, and unless an honor drops from East, lead small to the ten	88	4.92
251.	A 10 x x x x K 9	6	Play the king and ace, hoping that the queen-jack are doubleton	7	
		5	Lead small to the nine	82	
		4	Lead small to the nine	98	
		Max	Lead small to the nine		4.83
252.	A K 10 9 x x x x	5	Finesse the tne, hoping that West has QJxx, QJx, or QJ	22	
		4 Max	Finesse the ten. If it loses, cash the ace next	90	4.10
253.	A K9 x x 10 x x	5	Run the ten, hoping that West has QJ or QJx* (*Or will cover with Qxx or Jxx)	14	
		4	Play the ace. Unless an honor appears, run the ten next	88	
		3	Play the ace	100	
		Max	Lead small to the nine		3.96
254.	A K 8 x x 10 x x	5	Play the ace and king, hoping that the queen-jack are doubleton	7	
		4	Play the ace, and lead small to the ten	82	
		3	Lead small to the ten	100	
		Max	Play the ace, and lead small to the ten		3.78
255.	A 10 9 x x K x x	5	Play the king. If an honor falls from East, finesse the ten	9	
		4	Play the king, and finesse the ten	88	
		3	Play the king, and finesse the ten	98	
		Max	Play the king, and finesse the ten		3.95
256.	A 10 x x x K 9 x	5	Play the king and ace, hoping that the queen-jack are doubleton	7	
		4	Lead low to the nine; then cash the king	90	
		3	Play the king, or lead small to the nine	100	
		Max	Play the king, and unless an honor appears, lead low to the ten		3.94
257.	A 10 x x x K 8 x	5	Play the king and ace, hoping that the queen-jack are doubleton	7	
		4	Play the king, and unless an honor drops from East, lead small to the ten (best), *or* lead small to the ten; if an honor appears from West, lead small to the eight next. The latter method might be better if West is more likely to be short in the suit	82	
		Max	Play the king, and unless an honor appears from East, lead small to the ten		3.87
258.	A 10 x x x K x x	5	Play the king and ace, hoping that the queen-jack are doubleton	7	
		4	Play the king, and unless an honor appears from East, lead small to the ten	82	
		3	Play the king, in case East is void	98	
		Max	Play the king, and unless an honor appears from East, lead small to the ten		3.87
259.	A K 10 9 x x x x	4	Finesse the ten	24	
		3 Max	Finesse the ten; if it loses, cash the ace	90	3.14
260.	A K 8 x 10 x x x	4	Play the ace and king, hoping that the queen-jack are doubleton	7	
		3	Play the ace. Then either lead small to the		

Dummy Declarer	Tricks Required		% Chance of Success	Tricks per Deal

IV. THE DEFENSE HAS THREE POINTS (cont'd)
B. THE QUEEN-JACK (cont'd)

Dummy Declarer	Tricks Required		% Chance of Success	Tricks per Deal
		eight, *or* if an honor has appeared from West, small to the ten	82	
	Max	Play the ace. Unless an honor appears from West, lead small to the ten next		2.85
261.	A 10 9 8	4	Play the ace, and run the ten if an honor appears, *or* cash the king and finesse the ten if an honor appears	9	
	K x x x				
		3 ⎫	Run the ten. If an honor appears from East,		
		Max ⎬	finesse the eight next; if the ten loses, cash the king. Alternatively, if East is more likely to be short in the suit, finesse the ten first and cash the ace if it loses	94	3.00
262.	A 10 x x	4	Play the ace and king, hoping that the queen and jack will be doubleton	7	
	K 9 x x				
		3 ⎫	Lead small to the ten, and then cash the ace, *or*		
		Max ⎬	lead small to the nine, and then cash the king; the latter line will be better if West is likely to be short in the suit	94	2.98
263.	A 10 x x	4	Play the ace and king, hoping that the queen-jack will be doubleton	7	
	K 8 x x				
		3	Lead small to the ten. If it loses, cash the ace; if West plays the jack or queen on the first round, lead small to the eight next	87	
		Max	Play the king, and unless an honor appears from East, lead small to the ten		2.91
264.	A 10 x x	4	Play the ace and king, hoping that the queen-jack will be bare	7	
	K x x x				
		3 ⎫	Play the king, and unless an honor appears from		
		Max ⎬	East, lead small to the ten	84	2.91

(d) Declarer has Nine Cards

Dummy Declarer	Tricks Required		% Chance of Success	Tricks per Deal
265.	A K 10 9 x x	6 ⎫	Play the ace. If an honor drops from East, finesse		
	x x x	Max ⎬	the ten	46	5.42
266.	A K 8 x x x	6	Play the ace and king	41	
	10 x x	5	Lead small to the eight, *or* run the ten, *or* lead small to the ten	95	
		Max	Lead the ten, and play the ace whatever happens; then play the king		5.36
267.	A 10 x x x x	6	Play the ace, and finesse the nine if an honor appears from West, *or* play the king, and finesse the ten if an honor appears from East	46	
	K 9 x				
		5	Lead small to the nine or ten	100	
		Max	Play the ace, and finesse the nine, *or* play the king and finesse the ten		5.42
268.	9 8 7 6 x x	6	Play the ace and king	41	
	A K 5	5	Lead small to the five	95	
		Max	Play the ace and king		5.31
269.	A K 10 9 x	5 ⎫	Play the ace. If an honor drops from East,		
	x x x x	Max ⎬	finesse the ten next; otherwise play the king	46	4.42
270.	A K 9 x x	5 ⎫	Play the ace. If an honor drops from East,		
	10 x x x	Max ⎬	finesse the nine.	46	4.42
271.	A K 8 x x	5	Play the ace and king	41	
	10 x x x	4	Lead small to the eight, *or* run the ten, *or* lead small to the ten	95	
		Max	Lead the ten, and play the ace whatever happens; then play the king. This line saves a trick if West is tempted to cover with QJ9x.		4.31+

	Dummy Declarer	Tricks Required		% Chance of Success	Tricks per Deal
			IV. **THE DEFENSE HAS THREE POINTS (cont'd)**		
			B. **THE QUEEN-JACK (cont'd)**		
272.	A 10 x x x K 9 x x	5	Play the ace (or king). If an honor falls, finesse the nine (or ten)	46	
		4	Lead small to the nine or ten	100	
		Max	Play the ace (or king). If an honor falls, finesse the nine (or ten)		4.42
(c)	**Declarer Has Ten Cards**				
273.	A K x x x 10 9 8 x x etc.	5	Lead the ten, and play the ace whatever happens; this saves a trick when West is lulled into covering with QJx	78+	

V.   **THE DEFENSE HAS FOUR POINTS**

A.   **THE ACE**

	Dummy Declarer	Tricks Required		% Chance of Success	Tricks per Deal
(a)	**Declarer Has Five Cards**				
274.	K Q J 9 x	3	Finesse the nine	50	
(b)	**Declarer Has Six Cards**				
275.	K Q J 9 8 x	4	Play the king, queen, and jack	36	
		Max	Play the king, queen, and jack		3.36
276.	K Q J9 x x	4	Finesse the nine	31	
		3	Finesse the nine	82	
		Max	Finesse the nine		3.13
277.	K Q J 9 x x	3 Max	Lead to the king; then finesse the nine	55	2.55
278.	K Q 9 x J 8	3	Lead to the jack, and run the eight next	51	
279.	K Q 9 x J x	3	Lead to the jack; then finesse the nine	51	
280.	K Q x x J 9	3	Finesse the nine	50	
(c)	**Declarer Has Seven Cards**				
281.	K Q J 9 x x x	5	Lead to the king; then play the queen and jack	52	
		4	Finesse the nine	92	
		3	Finesse the nine, in case East is void	99	
		Max	Lead to the king; then play the queen and jack		4.38
282.	K Q J 9 8 x x	4 Max	Lead to the king; then lead to the queen	61	3.61
283.	K Q J 9 x x x	4	Lead to the king; then lead to the queen	58	
		3	Lead to the king; then finesse the nine	94	
		Max	Lead to the king; then lead to the queen		3.46
284.	K Q J x x 9 x	4	Lead to the king; then lead to the queen	44	
		3	Lead small to the nine, in case West has a void or small singleton	93	
		Max	Lead to the king; then lead to the queen		3.31
285.	K Q 9 x x J 8	4	Lead to the jack; then play to the king and queen	54	
		3	Lead small to the eight, *or* (best) lead to the jack and then run the eight	100	
		Max	Lead to the jack; then play the king and queen		3.49
286.	K Q 9 x x J x	4	Lead to the jack, and then lead to the king	52	
		3	Lead to the jack, and then finesse the nine	93	
		Max	Lead to the jack, and then lead to the king		3.40

	Dummy Declarer	Tricks Required		% Chance of Success	Tricks per Deal
		V.	**THE DEFENSE HAS FOUR POINTS (cont'd)**		
			A. THE ACE (cont'd)		
287.	K Q x x x	4	Finesse the nine. This offers a 5% better chance		
	J 9		than hoping for a 3-3 break	42	
		3	Finesse the nine	93	
		Max	Finesse the nine		3.25
288.	K Q J 9	3	Lead to the king, to the queen, and to the jack.		
	x x x		This is fractionally better than the third-round		
			finesse	78	
289.	K Q 9 x	3	Lead to the queen. If it loses, cash the jack and		
	J xx		then the king. If it wins, lead to the king	62	
290.	K Q x x	3	Lead to the king; then lead to the jack	56	
	J 9 x				
291.	KQ x x	3	Lead to the king, and then to the queen. This is		
	J x x		8% better than leading to honors at randmon		
			nad hoping for a 3-3 break	45	
292.	K 9 x x	3	Lead to the queen and then to the jack; play the		
	Q J x		king on the third round. This is 1% better than		
			the third-round finesse of the nine	67	
293.	K x x x	3	Lead to the queen and then to the jack	63	
	Q J 9				
(d)	**Declarer Has Eight Cards**				
294.	K Q J 9 x x x	6	Lead to the king; then play the queen and jack	76	
	x	5	Finesse the nine, in case East is void	98	
		Max	Lead to the king; then play the queen and jack		5.72
295.	K Q J x x x	5	Lead to the king; then play the queen and jack	76	
	9 x	4	Lead small to the nine, in case West is void	98	
		Max	Lead to the king, and then play the queen and		
			jack		4.72
296.	K Q x x x x	5	Lead to the jack, and then to the king	76	
	J 9	4	Finesse the nine, in case West is void	98	
		Max	Lead to the jack, and then to the king		4.72
297.	K Q 10 7 x	4 ⎫	Lead to the jack first; this fails only if West is		
	J x x	Max ⎬	void	98	3.98
298.	K Q 9 x x	4	Lead to the king, and then to the jack	88	
	J 8 x				
299.	K Q 9 x x	4 ⎫	Lead to the king, and then to the jack	88	3.86
	J x x	Max ⎬			
300.	K Q 8 x x	4	Play to a high honor, and play the jack on the		
	J x x		first or second round	76	
		3 ⎫	Lead small to the jack. This fails only when		
		Max ⎬	West is void	98	3.74
301.	K Q x x x	4 ⎫	Lead to the king, and then to the jack, *or* lead		
	J 9 x	Max ⎬	to the jack and then to the king. The latter		
			line is better if East is likely to be short in		
			the suit	76	3.74
302.	K Q J 9	3	Lead to the king first, in case West has the		
	x x x x		singleton ace	90	
303.	K Q 9 x	3	Lead to the king, and then to the jack. This fails		
	J 8 x x		only when West has a smal singleton	92	
304.	K Q 9 x	3	Lead to the king, and then to the jack. This fails		
	J x x x		only when West has a void or a small singleton	90	

Dummy Declarer	Tricks Required		% Chance of Success	Tricks per Deal

V. THE DEFENSE HAS FOUR POINTS (cont'd)
A. THE ACE (cont'd)

#	Dummy / Declarer	Tricks Required	Action	% Chance	Tricks per Deal
305.	K Q 8 x J x x x	3	Lead low to the jack first, in case East is void	78	
306.	K Q 7 x J 9 x x	3	Lead to the king and then to the queen* (*But if East would not falsecard from A108x, lead to the king, and if the eight drops from East, lead to the jack next; otherwise lead to the queen)	87 90	
307.	K Q x x J 9 x x	3	Lead to the king, and then to the queen	87	

(e) Declarer Has Nine Cards

#	Dummy / Declarer	Tricks Required	Action	% Chance	Tricks per Deal
308.	K Q 9 x x x J 8 x	5	Lead to the king	100	
309.	K Q 8 x x x J x x	5	Lead small to the jack. This fails only when West is void	95	
310.	K Q 9 x x J 8 x x	4	Lead small to the king	100	
311.	K Q 8 x x J x x x	4	Lead small to the jack, in case East is void	95	

B. THE KING-JACK

(a) Declarer Has Five Cards

#	Dummy / Declarer	Tricks Required	Action	% Chance	Tricks per Deal
312.	A Q 10 9 x	4	Finesse the queen, hoping that West has king-jack doubleton	0.3	
		3 } Max }	Finesse the ten. If it holds, play the ace and queen	13	2.14
313.	A Q 10 x x	3	Finesse the ten, hoping that West has both the king and jack	24	
		2	Finesse the queen and then the ten, *or* (best) finesse the ten and then the queen	76	
		Max	Finesse the ten; if it loses, finesse the queen		2.00
314.	A Q 9 x x	2	Finesse the nine, and then finesse the queen	63	
315.	A 10 9 Q x	3	Lead the queen, hoping that East has the singleton jack	0.2	
		2 } Max }	Run the queen, finessing the ten next if it loses	76	1.76
316.	A 10 x Q x	2	Lead small to the queen. If it loses, finesse the ten	74	
317.	Q 10 9 A x	3	Play the ace, hoping that East has the singleton king	0.2	
		2 } Max }	Play the ace, and guess whether to play the queen or ten next	53	1.53
318.	Q x x A 10	2	Finesse the ten	52	

(b) Declarer Has Six Cards

#	Dummy / Declarer	Tricks Required	Action	% Chance	Tricks per Deal
319.	A Q 10 9 8 x	5	Finesse the queen, hoping that West has the king-jack doubleton	1	
		4	Finesse the ten. If it holds, play the ace and queen	23	
		Max	Finesse the ten; then play the ace and queen		3.24

	Dummy Declarer	Tricks Required		% Chance of Success	Tricks per Deal
		V.	**THE DEFENSE HAS FOUR POINTS (cont'd)**		
		B.	**THE KING-JACK (cont'd)**		
320.	A Q 10 9 x x	4 3 ⎰ Max ⎱	Finesse the ten, hoping that West has KJ or KJx Finesse the ten; if it loses, finesse the nine	5 63	2.68
321.	A Q 10 8 x x	4 3 ⎰ Max ⎱ 2	Finesse the ten, hoping West has KJ9 only Finesse the eight, and guess whether to finesse the ten or queen next, *or* finesse the ten and guess whether to finesse the queen or eight next Finesse the eight, ten, or queen, and guess which finesse to take next	1 33 86	2.19
322.	A Q 9 8 x x	3 2 ⎰ Max ⎱	Finesse the eight, and guess whether to finesse the nine or queen next Finesse the eight; if it loses, finesse the nine	24 86	2.09
323.	A 10 9 x Q x	3 ⎰ Max ⎱	Lead small to the queen, and finesse the nine next	24	2.24
324.	Q 10 9 8 A x	3	Run the ten. Then play the ace and queen* (*But if East might be tempted to cover with Kxx, the best practical chance is to lead the queen first)	23 27	
325.	Q 9 x x A 10	3 ⎰ Max ⎱ 2	Finesse the ten, and then play the ace and queen Finesse the ten, *or* play the ace and run the ten	23 100	2.23
326.	Q x x x A 10	2 ⎰ Max ⎱	Finesse the ten. If it loses to the jack, cash the ace, and if the king fails to appear, play small from the queen	68	1.68
327.	A Q 10 x x x	3 2 Max	Finesse the ten Finesse the queen and then the ten, *or* (best) finesse the ten and then the queen Finesse the ten; if it loses, finesse the queen	24 76	 2.00
328.	A Q 9 x x x	2 ⎰ Max ⎱	Finesse the nine, and then finesse the queen	63	1.63
329.	A Q x 10 x x	3 2 Max	Finesse the queen, hoping that West has king- jack doubleton Play the ace, and lead low to the queen Lead toward the ace-queen, and play the ace, unless the jack appears from West; then lead low to the queen	1 55	 1.56
330.	A Q x x x x	2 ⎰ Max ⎱	Lead small from the ace-queen, in case East has the singleton king; then finesse the queen* (*And if East panics into playing the king from Kx)	50 54	1.50
331.	A 10 9 Q x x	3 2 ⎰ Max ⎱	Lead the queen, hoping that East has the single- ton jack, *or* play the ace, hoping that West has the singleton king Lead small to the ten; if it loses to the jack, finesse the nine* (*But if East would play the king from Kx, run the ten first; if this loses to the jack, finesse the nine next)	0.5 76 78	1.77
332.	A 10 x Q x x	2	Lead small to the queen; if it loses, finesse the ten next	74	
333.	A x x Q 10 9	3 2 ⎰ Max ⎱	Lead the queen, hoping that East has the single- ton jack, *or* play the ace, hoping that West has the singleton king Run the ten; if it loses, run the queen* (*But if East would play the king from Kx, lead small to the ten; if this loses to the jack, run the queen next)	0.5 76 78	1.77

Dummy Declarer	Tricks Required		% Chance of Success	Tricks per Deal

V. THE DEFENSE HAS FOUR POINTS (cont'd)
B. THE KING-JACK (cont'd)

(c) Declarer Has Seven Cards

Dummy Declarer	Tricks Required		% Chance of Success	Tricks per Deal
334. A Q 10 9 x x x	6	Finesse the queen, hoping that West has king- jack doubleton	2	
	5	Finesse the queen; then play the ace	40	
	4	Lead toward the dummy, and play the ace unless the jack appears from West; then lead the queen	89	
	Max	Finesse the queen; then play the ace		4.28
335. AQ 10 9 x x x	5	Finesse the ten	9	
	4	Finesse the ten; if it loses, finesse the nine next	59	
	3	Finesse the queen, and lead to the ten if it holds *or* (best) finesse the ten	93	
	Max	Finesse the ten; if it loses, finesse the nine next		3.61
336. A Q 9 8 x x x	4 ⎱ Max ⎰	Finesse the nine, and finesse the queen next if it loses	33	3.09
	3	Finesse the nine, and finesse the eight next if it loses	82	
337. AQ x x x 10 x	4	Play the ace, and lead to the queen, *or* finesse the queen and then cash the ace, *or* (best) lead small to the ten, and then finesse the queen	18	
	3	Lead small to the ten, and then finesse the queen* (*And there is the additional chance of East playing the king from Kx)	71 78	
	2 ⎱ Max ⎰	Lead small to the ten, and then finesse the queen. This fails only when West has the singleton jack	99	2.88
338. A 10 9 x x Q x	4 ⎱ Max ⎰	Run the queen, and finesse the ten next if it loses, *or* lead small to the ten and run the queen next	36	3.23
	3	Play the ace	89	
	Max	Run the queen, and finesse the ten next if it loses, *or* lead small to the ten, and run the queen next		3.23
339. Q x x x x A 10	4	Play the ace, and lead to the queen, *or* (best) finesse the ten	18	
	3	Lead small to the ten	68	
	2	Play the ace, and lead to the queen. This fails only when West has a void or a small single- ton	94	
	Max	Lead small to the ten		2.86
340. A Q 10 9 x x x	4	Finesse the ten, hoping that West has both the king and jack	24	
	3	Finesse the queen, and then the ten, *or* (best) finesse the ten and then the nine	76	
	Max	Finesse the ten and then the nine		3.00
341. A Q 10 8 x x x	4	Finesse the eight	11	
	3	Finesse the queen; then finesse the ten	53	
	2	Cash the ace, *or* (best) lead to the ten, and if it loses and the nine fails to appear on the second round, cash the ace next	91	
	Max	Finesse the eight. If it loses, finesse the queen. If that loses, cash the ace		2.51
342. A Q 10 x x x x	4	Finesse the ten, hoping that West has KJx	7	
	3	Finesse the queen, and finesse the ten next	47	
	2	Play the ace on the first or second round. The best line is to finesse the ten and cash the ace next if it loses	85	
	Max	Finesse the ten, and finesse the queen next if it loses		2.36

Dummy Declarer	Tricks Required		% Chance of Success	Tricks per Deal

V. THE DEFENSE HAS FOUR POINTS (cont'd)
B. THE KING-JACK (cont'd)

343. A Q 9 8 / x x x

- 3 — Finesse the eight, and finesse the nine next if it loses — 50
- 2 — Finesse the eight. If it loses, (best) lead toward dummy and play the ace unless the jack or ten appears from West — 91
- Max — Finesse the eight. If it loses, finesse the nine. If that loses, cash the ace — — 2.39

344. A Q 9 x / x x x

- 3 } Finesse the nine, and finesse the queen next if
- Max } it loses — 32 — 2.08
- 2 — Play the ace, and lead to the nine, *or* (best) finesse the nine, and play the ace next — 79

345. A Q x x / 10 x x

- 3 — Play the ace, and unless the jack appears from East lead small to the queen* — 21
  - (*And if West would not falsecard from KJ, lead to the ten if the king appears from West on the first round) — 22
- 2 — Play the ace, and then lead low to the ten; then lead to the queen. This fails only when West has Jx — 94
- Max — Finesse the queen; if it loses, lead small to the ten. If the queen holds, play the ace* — — 2.05
  - (*And if West would not falsecard from KJ, lead to the ten if the king appears from West on the first round. But if East would play the king from Kx, the best practical play is to lead low to the ten; if this loses, finesse the queen) — 21.0 — 2.06

346. A Q x x / x x x

- 3 — Play the ace, and lead to the queen, *or* finesse the queen — 18
- 2 — Lead low from dummy, then play the ace, and then lead to the queen — 77
- Max — Play the ace, and lead to the queen — — 1.87

347. A 10 9 8 / Q x x

- 4 — Run the queen, hoping that East has the singleton jack — 1
- 3 } Finesse the ten and then the nine, *or* (best) run
- Max } the queen, and finesse the ten next if it loses — 76 — 2.77

348. A 10 9 x / Q 8 x

- 4 — Run the queen, hoping that East has the singleton jack — 1
- 3 — Run the eight, and then run the queen, *or* (best) run the queen, and then finesse the ten — 76
- Max — Run the queen, and finesse the ten next if it loses — — 2.77

349. A 10 9 x / Q x x

- 3 } Lead small to the ten. If it loses to the jack, lead
- Max } small to the nine. If the ten loses to the king, cash the queen, and finesse the nine — 68 — 2.68

350. A 10 x x / Q 9 x

- 3 } Lead small to the nine, and finesse the ten next if
- Max } it loses to the jack. If East plays the king on the first round, finesse the nine next — 52 — 2.52

351. A 10 x x / Q x x

- 3 — Lead small to the queen, and finesse the ten next if it loses. If East plays the king on the first round, cash the queen and ace — 28
- 2 } Play the ace, and unless the jack appears from
- Max } West, lead small to the queen — 94 — 2.16

352. A x x x / Q 10 9

- 3 — Finesse the ten. If it loses to the king, finesse the nine. If the ten loses to the jack, run the queen next. If East plays the king on the first round, finesse the ten next* — 50
  - (*And if West omits to falsecard with KJx) — 57

353. Q 10 9 8 / A x x

- 4 — Play the ace, hoping that East has the singleton king — 1
- 3 } Run the ten, and run the nine next if it loses — 69 — 2.69
- Max }

Dummy Declarer	Tricks Required		% Chance of Success	Tricks per Deal
	V.	**THE DEFENSE HAS FOUR POINTS (cont'd)**		
	B.	**THE KING-JACK (cont'd)**		
354. Q x x x A 10 9	3 ⎱ Max ⎰	Finesse the ten, and finesse the nine next if it loses	68	2.68
	2	Finesse the ten and then the nine (best), *or* play the ace and run the ten	100	
355. Q x x x A 10 x	3 ⎱ Max ⎰	Lead small to the queen, and finesse the ten next if it loses. If West plays the king on the first round, play the ace next	26	2.12
	2	Play the ace, and unless the jack appears from West, lead small to the ten. This fails only when West has J x	94	
356. 10 9 8 7 A Q x	4	Run the ten, hoping that East has KJ or KJx	9	
	3	Finesse the queen. If it loses, run the ten; if the queen holds, run the ten	62	
	Max	Run the ten, and finesse the queen next		2.69
357. 10 9 x x A Q x	4	Finesse the queen, hoping that East has king-jack doubleton	2	
	3 ⎱ Max ⎰	Finesse the queen. If it holds, play the ace; if the queen loses, run the ten next	47	2.48
(d) **Declarer Has Eight Cards**				
358. A Q 10 9 x x x x	7	Finesse the queen, hoping that West has king-jack doubleton	3	
	6 ⎱ Max ⎰	Finesse the queen, in case East has the singleton jack	56	5.55
359. A Q 10 9 x x x x	6	Finesse the ten	14	
	5	Finesse the queen, and then the ten, *or* (best) finesse the ten and then the queen	71	
	4	Finesse the queen, *or* (best) finesse the ten	98	
	Max	Finesse the ten, and if it loses, finesse the nine		4.83
360. A Q x x x x 10 x	5	Play the ace, and then lead to the queen* (*But if East would play the king from Kx, lead to the ten, and then finesse the queen)	37 44	
	4	Lead small to the ten, and then finesse the queen	93	
	3	Lead small to the ten, in case either opponent is void	100	
	Max	Lead small to the ten, and then finesse the queen		4.27
361. A 10 9 x x x Q x	5 ⎱ Max ⎰	Run the queen. If it loses, finesse the jack next	60	4.53
362. Q 9 x x x x A 10	5	Play the ace, and then either run the ten or lead the ten to the queen	59	
	Max	Play the ace, and then either run the ten or lead the ten to the queen* (*The latter line is better against defenders who might cover the ten with Jxx)		4.55
363. Q x x x x x A 10	5	Finesse the ten	47	
	4	Play the ace, and lead to the queen	88	
	3	Finesse the ten	100	
	Max	Finesse the ten		4.32
364. A Q 10 9 x x x x	5	Finesse the ten and then the nine	22	
	4 ⎱ Max ⎰	Finesse the ten and then the nine	76	3.96
365. A Q 10 8 x x x x	5	Finesse the ten	16	
	4	Finesse the queen; if it loses, finesse the ten	66	
	Max	Finesse the ten; if it loses, finesse the queen		3.70
366. A Q 10 x x x x x	5	Finesse the ten	14	
	4	Finesse the queen; if it loses, finesse the ten	66	
	Max	Finesse the ten and then the queen		3.64

	Dummy Declarer	Tricks Required		% Chance of Success	Tricks per Deal
		V.	**THE DEFENSE HAS FOUR POINTS (cont'd)**		
		B.	**THE KING-JACK (cont'd)**		
367.	A Q 9 x x	5	Lead small to the nine, *or* run the ten	14	
	10 x x	4	Finesse the queen, in case East has the singleton jack	71	
		Max	Finesse the nine and then the queen, *or* run the ten, and finesse the nine if it loses. The latter line will be better if East is likely to be short in the suit		3.80
368.	A Q 9 x x	4	Finesse the nine and then the queen	50	
	x x x	3	Finesse the nine. If it loses, finesse the queen (best), *or* play the ace	87	
		Max	Finesse the nine and then the queen		3.35
369.	A Q x x x	5	Finesse the queen, hoping that West has king-jack doubleton	3	
	10 x x	4	Play the ace, and unless the king appears from West, lead small to the queen	50	
		3	Play the ace, and lead small to the ten; this fails only if either opponent is void	96	
		Max	Lead to the ace, and unless West plays the king lead small to the queen* (*If West plays the jack on the first round, finesse the queen immediately; a good defender, however, will play the king from king-jack doubleton)		3.41
370.	A Q x x x	4	Finesse the queen, *or* (best) play the ace, and lead small to the queen	34	
	x x x	3 } Max }	Play the ace, and lead small to the queen	85	3.17
371.	A 10 9 x x	4 } Max }	Finesse the ten and then the nine, *or* run the queen, and finesse the ten next if it loses. The latter line is better if East is likely to be short in the suit	71	3.69
	Q x x				
372.	A 10 x x x	4	Play the ace, and lead small to the queen, *or* lead small to the queen, and if it loses, finesse the ten next	50	
	Q x x	3 } Max }	Play the ace, and lead small to the queen. This fails only if either opponent is void	96	3.46
373.	A 9 7 x x	5	Lead the queen, hoping that East has the singleton jack	3	
	Q 10 8	4 } Max }	Lead the queen; if it loses, run the ten next* (*But if East would play the king from Kx, and West would not falsecard with KJ, lead low to the ten; if this loses to the jack, run the queen next)	76 83	3.79 3.83
374.	A 9 x x x	5	Lead the queen, hoping that East has the singleton jack	3	
	Q 10 8	4	Lead the queen; if it loses, run the ten next* (*But if East would play the king from Kx and West would not falsecard with KJ, lead low to the ten; if this loses to the jack, run the queen)	74 83	3.77 3.83
		3	Lead the queen, *or* lead small to the ten, in case either opponent is void	100	
375.	A 9 x x x	4 } Max }	Lead small to the ten; if it loses to the jack, run the queen next* (*And there is the extra chance that East will play the king from Kx)	62 72	3.60
	Q 10 x	3	Lead small to the ten. This fails only if East is void	98	

	Dummy Declarer	Tricks Required		% Chance of Success	Tricks per Deal
		V.	**THE DEFENSE HAS FOUR POINTS(cont'd)**		
		B.	**THE KING-JACK (cont'd)**		
376.	A x x x x Q 10 9	4	Run the queen; if it loses, run the ten* (*But if West would not falsecard with KJ or KJx, lead small to the nine. If this loses to the jack, run the queen; if the nine loses to the king, finesse the ten And if East would play the king from Kx:)	60 62 72	
		3	Lead small to the nine	98	
		Max	Lead small to the nine; if it loses to the jack, run the queen through next* (*And if West would not falsecard with KJ or KJx, finesse the ten if the nine loses to the king)		3.57 3.60
377.	A x x x x Q 10 x	4 ⎫ Max ⎭	Play the ace, and then guess whether to lead to the queen or the ten	50	3.36
		3	Lead small to the ten. If it loses or holds, lead small to the queen next	90	
378.	Q 10 9 x x A 8 x	5	Lead small to to the ace, hoping that East has the singleton king	3	
		4 ⎫ Max ⎭	Finesse the eight. If it loses to the jack, run the queen next; if the eight loses to the king, run the ten next* (*But if West would play the king from Kx, lead low to the ten; if this loses to the jack, finesse the eight next)	71 72	3.74
379.	Q 10 9 x x A x x	5	Play the ace, hoping that East has the singleton king	3	
		4 ⎫ Max ⎭	Play the ace and lead small to the ten* (*But if West would play the king from Kx, lead small to the ten; if it loses to the jack, run the queen next)	67 72	3.68 3.70
380.	Q x x x x A 10 x	4	Play the ace, and unless the king appears from West, lead small to the queen	50	
		3	Play the ace, and lead small to the ten. This fails only if either opponent is void	96	
		Max	Lead small to the ten, and then cash the ace, *or* lead small to the queen, and finesse the ten next if it loses		3.41
381.	10 x x x x A Q x	5	Finesse the queen, hoping that East has king-jack only	3	
		4	Play the ace, and lead small to the queen, *or* finesse the queen, and then cash the ace	50	
		3	Play the ace, and lead small to the queen. This fails only if either opponent is void	96	
		Max	Finesse the queen, and then cash the ace		3.47
382.	A Q 10 9 x x x x	4	Finesse the ten	24	
		3	Either finesse the ten *or* finesse the queen; if it loses, finesse again	76	
		Max	Finesse the ten; if it loses, finesse the nine		3.00
383.	A Q 10 8 x x x x	4	Finesse the ten	16	
		3	Finesse the queen; if it loses, finesse the ten	68	
		Max	Finesse the ten; if it loses, finesse the queen		2.73
384.	A Q 9 x x x x x	3 ⎫ Max ⎭	Finesse the nine, and then finesse the queen	52	2.38

	Dummy Declarer	Tricks Required		% Chance of Success	Tricks per Deal

V.   THE DEFENSE HAS FOUR POINTS (cont'd)
B.   THE KING-JACK (cont'd)

385. A Q x x / 10 x x x

Tricks	Line	%	Tricks/Deal
4	Finesse the queen, hoping that West has king-jack doubleton	3	
3	Finesse the queen, *or* play the ace, and lead small to the queen	50	
2	Play the ace, and lead small to the queen	100	
Max	Lead small from the ten, and unless the jack appears, play the ace; then lead small to the queen		2.54

386. A Q x x / x x x x

Tricks	Line	%	Tricks/Deal
3	Finesse the queen, *or* play the ace, and lead small to the queen*	34	
	(*But if East would not falsecard from Jx, play the ace, and duck on the second round if the jack appears from East)	37	
2 } Max	Play the ace, and lead small to the queen	87	2.21

387. A 10 9 8 / Q x x x

Tricks	Line	%	Tricks/Deal
4	Lead the queen, hoping that East has the singleton jack, *or* play the ace, hoping that West has the singleton king	3	
3 } Max	Finesse the ten; if it loses to the jack, finesse the nine*	78	2.81
	(*But if West would not falsecard with KJxx, and East would play the king from Kx, run the ten. If the ten loses to the jack, finesse the nine; if the king appears on the first round, play the ace next)	84	2.84

388. A 10 9 x / Q 8 x x

Tricks	Line	%	Tricks/Deal
4	See 387 above	3	
3	See 387 above	78	

389. A 10 9 x / Q x x x

Tricks	Line	%	Tricks/Deal
3	Finesse the ten, and then finesse the nine, *or* lead the queen, and finesse the ten next if it loses. The latter line is better if East is likely to be short in the suit	73	

390. A 10 x x / Q 9 x x

Tricks	Line	%	Tricks/Deal
3 } Max	Play the ace, and lead small to the nine*	69	2.69
	(*But if East would play the king from Kx, lead small to the nine. If this loses to the jack, finesse the ten next; if East plays the king on the first round, play the ace next)	71	2.71

391. A 10 x x / Q x x x

Tricks	Line	%	Tricks/Deal
3	Play the ace, and lead small to the queen (best), *or* lead small to the queen, and finesse the ten next if it loses, *or* lead small to the queen, and cash the ace next if it loses	50	
2	Play the ace, and either lead to the queen (best) or to the ten	100	
Max	Play the ace, and lead small to the queen		2.50

391A. Q x x x / A 10 8 7

Tricks	Line	%	Tricks/Deal
4	Lead the queen, hoping that East has the singleton jack	2.83	
3 } Max	Lead the ace, followed by the seven or eight and guess whether to play the queen or duck in dummy. If East's first play is the nine, jack, or king, lead the ten on the second round intending to play low from dummy	61.62	2.62
2	Play the ace	100	

Dummy Declarer	Tricks Required		% Chance of Success	Tricks per Deal

V.   THE DEFENSE HAS FOUR POINTS (cont'd)
B.   THE KING-JACK (cont'd)

392. A x x x Q 10 9 x	4	Play the ace, hoping that West has the singleton king	3	
	3 ⎱ Max ⎰	Play the ace, and lead low to the ten* (*But if East would play the king from Kx, lead small to the ten. If it lsoes to the jack, run the queen next; if the king appears on the first round, play the ace next)	69 74	2.72 2.74
393. A x x x Q 10 x x	3 ⎱ Max ⎰	Play the ace, and lead small to the ten	64	2.53
	2	Play the ace, and then lead low to the ten (best) or low to the queen	90	

(c) Declarer Has Nine Cards

394. A Q 10 9 x x x x x	8	Finesse the queen	20	
	7	Finesse the queen (best), *or* finesse the ten	72	
	Max	Finesse the queen		6.92
395. A Q 10 x x x x x x	7	Finesse the queen, hoping that West has Kxx, KJ, or Kx	27	
	6	Play the ace, and lead small to the queen	78	
	Max	Finesse the queen; if it loses, cash the ace next		5.94
396. A Q x x x x x 10 x	7	Finesse the queen	20	
	6	Lead small from the ten, and play the ace unless the jack appears; then lead to the queen	78	
	5	Lead small to the ten	100	
	Max	Finesse the queen		5.87
397. A 10 9 8 x x x Q x	7	Run the queen, hoping that East has the singleton jack	6	
	6 ⎱ Max ⎰	Run the queen; if it loses, play the ace next	77	5.83
398. A 10 9 x x x x Q x	7	Run the queen, hoping that East has the singleton jack	6	
	6	Run the queen, and play the ace next if it loses, *or* lead small to the queen, and play the ace next if it loses. The latter line is better if West is more likely to be short in the suit	72	
	Max	Run the queen; if it loses, play the ace next		5.78
399. Q 10 9 x x x x A x	7	Play the ace, hoping that East has the singleton king	6	
	6 ⎱ Max ⎰	Play the ace, and lead to the queen	78	5.84
400. Q x x x x x x A 10	6 ⎱ Max ⎰	Play the ace, and lead to the queen	78	5.73
	5	Finesse the ten	100	
401. A Q 10 x x x x x x	6	Finesse the queen	27	
	5	Play the ace, and lead small to the queen	83	
	Max	Finesse the queen; if it loses, play the ace next		4.98
401 A Q 10 x x x x x x	5	Lead to the ace, then lead small to the queen. But finesse the queen if the jack appears originally.	83	
402. A Q x x x x 10 x x	6	Finesse the queen	20	
	5	Play the ace, and lead small to the queen	78	
	Max	Finesse the queen		4.92
403. A Q x x x x x x x	6	Finesse the queen	20	
	5	Play the ace, and lead small to the queen	72	
	Max	Finesse the queen		4.81
404. A 10 9 x x x Q x x	6	Lead the queen, hoping that East has the single-ton jack, *or* play the ace, hoping that West has the singleton king	6	
	5 ⎱ Max ⎰	Play the ace, and lead small to the queen	78	4.84

V. THE DEFENSE HAS FOUR POINTS (cont'd)
B. THE KING-JACK (cont'd)

	Dummy Declarer	Tricks Required		% Chance of Success	Tricks per Deal
405.	A 10 x x x x Q x x	5 Max	Play the ace, and lead small to the queen	78	4.78
406.	A x x x x x Q 10 9	6	Lead the queen, hoping that East has the singleton jack, *or* play the ace, hoping that West has the singleton king	6	
		5	Play the ace and lead small to the queen* (*But if East would play the king from Kx, lead small to the ten; if it loses to the jack, run the queen next)	78 89	
		4	Run the ten, *or* lead small to the ten, *or* run the queen, and play the ace if it lsoes	100	
		Max	Play the ace, and lead small to the queen		4.79
407.	A x x x x x Q 10 x	6	Play the ace, hoping that West has the singleton king	6	
		5 Max	Play the ace, and lead small to the queen	78	4.79
408.	Q 10 9 x x x A x x	6	Lead the queen, hoping that West has the singleton jack, *or* play the ace, hoping that East has the singleton king	6	
		5 Max	Play the ace, and lead to the queen* (*But if West would play the king from Kx, lead small to the ten; if it loses to the jack, run the queen next	83 89	4.89
409.	Q 8 x x x x A 10 9	6	Play the ace, hoping that East has the singleton king, *or* lead the queen, hoping that West has the singleton jack	6	
		5 Max	Play the ace, and lead to the queen	83	4.89
410.	Q x x x x x A 10 x	5 Max	Play the ace, and lead small to the queen	78	4.78
411.	10 x x x x x A Q x	6	Finesse the queen	20	
		5	Play the ace, and lead small to the queen	78	
		Max	Finesse the queen		4.92
412.	A Q 10 x x x x x x	5	Finesse the queen	27	
		4	Play the ace, and lead to the queen	83	
		Max	Finesse the queen; if it loses, play the ace next		3.98
413.	A Q x x x 10 x x x	5	Finesse the queen	20	
		4	Play the ace, and lead to the queen	78	
		Max	Finesse the queen		3.92
414.	A Q x x x x x x x	5	Finesse the queen	20	
		4	Play the ace, and lead to the queen	72	
		Max	Finesse the queen		3.81
415.	A 10 9 x x Q 8 x x	5	Lead the queen, hoping that East has the singleton jack, *or* play the ace, hoping that West has the singleton king	6	
		4 Max	Play the ace, and lead small to the queen* (*But if East would play the king from Kx, lead small to the eight; if this loses to the jack, run the queen next)	83 94	3.89
416.	A 10 9 x x Q x x x	5	Lead the queen, hoping that East has the singleton jack, *or* play the ace, hoping that West has the singleton king	6	
		4 Max	Play the ace and lead small to the queen* (*But if East would play the king from Kx, run the ten; if this loses to the jack, run the queen next)	78 84	3.84

	Dummy Declarer	Tricks Required		% Chance of Success	Tricks per Deal

V. THE DEFENSE HAS FOUR POINTS (cont'd)
B. THE KING-JACK (cont'd)

417.	A 10 x x x Q 9 x x	5	Lead the queen, hoping that East has the single- ton jack, *or* play the ace, hoping that West has the singleton king	6	
		4 } Max }	Play the ace, and lead to the queen* (*But if East would play the king from Kx, lead small to the nine; if this loses to the jack, run the queen next)	83 89	3.89
418.	A 10 x x x Q x x x	4	Play the ace, and lead small to the queen	78	
419.	A x x x x Q 10 9 8	5	Lead the queen, hoping that East has the single- ton jack, *or* play the ace, hoping that West has the singleton king	6	
		4 } Max }	Play the ace, and lead to the queen* (*But if East would play the king from Kx, lead small to the ten, and run the queen next if it loses to the jack)	83 94	3.89
420.	A x x x x Q 10 9 x	5	Lead the queen, hoping that East has the single- ton jack, *or* play the ace, hoping that West has the singleton king	6	
		4 } Max }	Play the ace, and lead to the queen* (*But if East would play the king from Kx, lead small to the ten, and run the queen next if it loses to the jack)	83 89	3.89

(f) Declarer Has Ten Cards

421.	A Q 10 x x x x x x x etc.*	5 Max	Finesse the queen Finesse the queen	39	 4.28
422.	A Q x x x 10 9 8 x x etc.*	5 } Max }	Lead the ten, and play the queen, giving an extra chance if West is tempted to cover with KJx	 39	 4.28
423.	A 10 9 x x Q x x x x etc.*	5 4 Max	Play the ace, hoping to drop the singleton king Lead small to the queen, *or* (best) lead small to the ten Play the ace	26 100	 4.15

(g) Declarer Has Eleven Cards

424.	A Q 10 x x x x x x x x etc.*	6	Play the ace. This line is fractionally better than the queen finesse	52	

*N.B. Similar principles apply if declarer's ten or
eleven cards are distributed differently between
his hand and dummy

VI. THE DEFENSE HAS FIVE POINTS
A. THE ACE-JACK

(a) Declarer Has Five Cards

425.	K Q 10 9 x	3	Finesse the ten	11	
426.	K Q 10 x x	2	Lead to the king, and whether it holds or loses, lead to the queen next* (*But this assumes that East will duck the king if he holds Ax (xxx), which is best defense. If he always wins with these holdings, lead to the king; if it holds, lead to the queen; if the king loses, finesse the ten next)	52 76	

	Dummy Declarer	Tricks Required		% Chance of Success	Tricks per Deal

VI. THE DEFENSE HAS FIVE POINTS (cont'd)
A.   THE ACE-JACK (cont'd)

	Dummy Declarer	Tricks Required		% Chance of Success	Tricks per Deal
427.	K 10 x Q x	2	Lead to the queen, and then finesse the ten	50	
428.	K x x Q 10	2	Finesse the ten	50	

(b) Declarer Has Six Cards

	Dummy Declarer	Tricks Required		% Chance of Success	Tricks per Deal
429.	K Q 10 9 8 x	4	Finesse the ten, hoping that West has AJx, Jxx, AJ, Jx, or J	18	
430.	K Q 10 9 x x	4	Finesse the ten	14	
		3	Lead to the king; then play the queen. This line gains a trick when East has AJ, Jx, or J	72	
		Max	Finesse the ten		2.82
431.	K Q 10 9 x x	3	Finesse the ten	50	
432.	K Q 9 8 x x	3	Finesse the nine, hoping that West has AJ10, J10x, or J10	5	
		2 } Max }	Finesse the nine. If this loses to the jack or ten, finesse the eight next*	79	1.85
			(*But if East would not duck with Ax, Axx, A10xx, or AJxx, lead to the king; if it holds, lead to the queen; if the king loses, finesse the nine)	81	
433.	K Q x x 10 x	2	Lead small to the ten. If the ten loses, play to the king; if the king holds, play small from the queen	56	
434.	K Q 10 x x x	2	Lead to the king and whether it holds or loses, lead to the queen next*	55	
			(*But if East would not duck the king if he holds the ace, lead to the king: if it loses, finesse the ten; if the king holds, lead to the queen)	76	
435.	K 10 x Q x x	2	Lead small to the queen, and then finesse the ten	51	

(c) Delcarer Has Seven Cards

	Dummy Declarer	Tricks Required		% Chance of Success	Tricks per Deal
436.	K Q x x x x x —	5	Duck one round, and then play the king (best), *or* lead the king	36	
		4	Duck one round; then either duck again or lead the king	86	
		Max	Duck one round, and then lead the king		4.20
437.	K Q 10 8 x x x	5	Finesse the ten. If the jack appears from West, duck the next round	21	
		4	Finesse the ten or the eight	68	
		3	Finesse the ten or the eight	94	
		2	Finesse the ten or the eight	99	
		Max	Finesse the ten		3.82
438.	K Q 10 9 x x x	4	Finesse the ten*	42	
			(*But if East would not duck with Axx, lead to the king; if it holds, lead to the queen; if the king loses, finesse the ten)	43	
		3	Finesse the ten	93	
		Max	Finesse the ten		3.35

	Dummy Declarer	Tricks Required		% Chance of Success	Tricks per Deal

VI. THE DEFENSE HAS FIVE POINTS (cont'd)
A. THE ACE-JACK (cont'd)

	Dummy Declarer	Tricks Required		% Chance of Success	Tricks per Deal
439.	K Q 9 8 x x x	4	Lead to the king; if it holds, lead to the queen	21	
		3	Lead to the king, and whether it holds or loses, lead to the queen next*	74	
			(*But if East would not duck with Ax, lead to the king; if it holds, lead to the queen; if the king loses, lead to the nine)	76	
		2	Lead to the king. If it loses, lead to the nine; if the king holds, lead to the queen or nine; *or* finesse the nine, and if it loses, finesse the eight	96	
		Max	Lead to the king, and whether it holds or loses, lead to the queen next*		2.90
			(*But if East would not duck with Ax, play to the nine if the king loses and to the queen if the king holds)		2.92
440.	KQ x x x 10 x	4	Lead small to the king; then lead to the queen	18	
		3	Lead small to the ten, and then lead to the king. This saves a trick when East has AJonly	61	
		2	Lead to the king and then to the queen, *or* lead small to the ten and then to the king. The latter line will be better if West is more likely to be short in the suit	93	
		Max	Lead to the king and then to the queen		2.71
441.	K Q 10 9 x x x	3	Lead to the king, and whether it holds or loses, finesse the ten next*	51	
			(*This assumes that East will duck about half the time with Ax and Axx, which is the best de- fense. If he always wins with these holdings, play to the queen if the king holds, and finesse the ten if the king loses.	54	
			Similarly, if East always ducks with Ax and Axx, play the queen if the king loses, and finesse the ten if the king holds)	52	
442.	K Q 9 8 x x x	3	Finesse the nine	24	
		2	Finesse the nine. If it loses, play to the king; if that loses, finesse the eight (best), *or* play to the king. If it loses, finesse the nine and, if necessary, the eight; if the king holds, play to the queen (best), or finesse the nine	89	
		Max	Finesse the nine. If it loses, lead to the king; if that loses, finesse the eight		2.13
443.	K 10 9 x Q x x	3	Lead small to the queen; then finesse the ten	53	
444.	K 10 x x Q 9 x	3 } Max }	Lead small to the queen; then finesse the ten. This is better than leading to the king first, for there is time to discover whether the insertion of the ace by East is from AJdoubleton or A single- ton	31	2.31
445.	K x x x Q 10 9	3	Finesse the ten	50	
446.	K x x x Q 10 x	3 } Max }	Lead small to the ten and then small to the queen, hoping that East has AJ, AJx or Jxx	19	1.95
		2	Lead small to the queen and then small to the ten	77	
447.	10 9 8 7 K Q x	3	Lead to the king. If it holds, lead to the queen; if the king loses, cash the queen*	36	
			(*This assumes that West will duck with Axx, which is the best defense. If he always wins with this holding, lead to the king; if it holds, lead to the queen; if the king loses, run the ten next)	45	

Dummy Declarer	Tricks Required		% Chance of Success	Tricks per Deal

VI.   THE DEFENSE HAS FIVE POINTS (cont'd)
A.   THE ACE-JACK (cont'd)

(d)   Declarer Has Eight Cards

448.	K Q x x x x x x	6 ⎫	Duck the first round, in case the ace is singleton;		
	—	Max ⎭	then play the king and queen	73	5.70
449.	K Q 10 x x x x	6	Finesse the ten	34	
	x	5	Finesse the ten	85	
		4	Finesse the ten	98	
		Max	Finesse the ten		5.17
450.	K Q x x x x x	6 ⎫	Lead to the king, hoping that West has the double-		
	x	Max ⎭	ton ace	14	4.80
		5	Play small from both hands, in case the ace is in-		
			gleton; then play the king and queen	73	
451.	K Q 10 x x x	5 ⎫	Lead to the king. If it holds, lead to the queen; if		
	x x	Max ⎭	the king loses, cash the queen next*	47	4.30
			(*But if East would not duck with Ax, finesse		
			the ten if the king loses and lead to the queen		
			if the king holds)	54	4.40
		4	Lead to the king. If it loses, finesse the ten; if the		
			king holds, guess which honor to play next	88	
452.	K Q x x x x	5 ⎫	Lead to the king and then to the queen	34	4.17
	10 x	Max ⎭			
		4	Lead to the king and then to the queen (best) *or*		
			lead small to the ten	85	
		3	Lead to the king *or* lead small to the ten. The latter		
			line will be better if West is more likely to be		
			short in the suit	98	
453.	K Q 10 x x	4 ⎫	Lead to the king, and whether it holds or loses		
	x x x	Max ⎭	finesse the ten next*	55	3.43
			(*This assumes that East will duck about half		
			the time with Ax. If he always ducks with this		
			holding, finesse the ten if the king holds, and		
			play the queen if the king loses.	59	
			Similarly, if East always wins with Ax, finesse		
			the ten if the king loses, and lead to the queen		
			if the king holds)	57	
454.	K 9 x x x	4	Lead small to the queen. If it holds, finesse the		
	Q 10 x		nine; if the queen loses, either play the king or		
			finesse the nine	46	
		Max	Lead small to the queen, and then finesse the		
			nine		3.42
455.	K x x x x	4	Finesse the ten	48	
	Q 10 9	3	Finesse the ten	98	
		2	Finesse the ten (best), *or* lead to the queen	100	
		Max	Finesse the ten		3.46
456.	K x x x x	4 ⎫	Lead small to the king, and then finesse the ten*	37	3.20
	Q 10 x	Max ⎭	(*The alternative is to lead small to the king or		
			queen, playing the other top honor if it loses		
			and ducking the next round if it holds, but this		
			line is inferior against defenders who would not		
			take the ace immediately)		
		3	Lead small to the queen, and then lead small to		
			the ten	88	

Dummy Declarer	Tricks Required		% Chance of Success	Tricks per Deal

VI. THE DEFENSE HAS FIVE POINTS (cont'd)
A. THE ACE-JACK (cont'd)

	Dummy Declarer	Tricks Required		% Chance of Success	Tricks per Deal
457.	K Q 10 x x x x x	3 Max	Lead to the king, and whether it holds or loses, finesse the ten next* (*This assumes that East will duck about half the time with Ax. If he always ducks with this holding, finesse the ten if the king holds, and play the queen if it loses. Similarly, if East always wins with Ax, play to the queen if the king holds, and finesse the ten if the king loses)	57 61 59	2.47
458.	K 10 x x Q x x x	3 ⎫ Max ⎭ 2	Lead to the queen, and then finesse the ten Play small from both hands; then lead to the queen	40 90	2.27
459.	K 9 8 7 Q x x x	3 ⎫ Max ⎭ 2	Lead to the queen, and then finesse the nine, hoping that East has 10, J, Ax, A10, AJ, or Axx; or lead to the king, and then run the nine. The latter line will be better if West is more likley to be short in the suit Finesse the nine. If this loses to the jack or ten. guess which honor to lead to next; if the jack or ten appears from West, run the eight, or run the nine. If this loses to the jack or ten, guess which honor to lead to next; if the jack or ten appears from East, finesse the eight	23 94	2.12
460.	K x x x Q 10 9 8	3	Lead to the queen, and then run the ten, or lead to the king, and then finesse the ten	56	
461.	K x x x Q x x x	3 ⎫ Max ⎭ 2	Lead to either honor, and duck on the next round, hoping to find the right opponent with the doubleton ace Play low from both hands, in case the ace is singleton, and then lead to either honor	14 73	1.84

(e) Declarer Has Nine Cards

	Dummy Declarer	Tricks Required		% Chance of Success	Tricks per Deal
462.	K Q 8 x x x x 10 x	6 ⎫ Max ⎭ 5	Lead small to the king, and then small to the queen Lead small to the ten	72 100	5.67
463.	K Q 10 9 x x x x x etc.*	4	Lead to the king; if it loses to the ace, lead to the queen next	77	
464.	K 9 x x x Q 10 x x etc.*	4	Lead to the king, and play the queen next if it loses, or lead to the queen, and play the king next if it loses	59	
465.	K 9 x x x Q x x x etc.*	4 ⎫ Max ⎭ 3	Lead small to the queen; if an honor appears from East, finesse the nine next Lead small to the queen, in case East is void *N.B. Similar principles apply, if declarer's nine cards are distributed differently between his hand and dummy	53 95	3.48

(f) Declarer Has Ten Cards

	Dummy Declarer	Tricks Required		% Chance of Success	Tricks per Deal
466.	K 8 x x x x Q 10 x x etc.*	5	Lead small to the king. This fails only if East is void *N.B. Similar principles apply if declarer's ten cards are distributed differently between his hand and dummy	89	

	Dummy Declarer	Tricks Required		% Chance of Success	Tricks per Deal

VI. THE DEFENSE HAS FIVE POINTS (cont'd)
B. THE KING-QUEEN

(a) Declarer Has Five Cards

	Dummy Declarer	Tricks Required		% Chance of Success	Tricks per Deal
467.	A J 10 9 x	3	Finesse the jack; then play the ace	7	
468.	A J 10 x x	2	Finesse the jack; then finesse the ten	76	
469.	A J 9 x x	2	Finesse the nine; if it loses to an honor, finesse the jack next* (*If West inserts a high honor on the first round, still finesse the nine next, for West should falsecard with holdings like K10x, Q10x, etc. If he would not falsecard in this way, and would split high honors on the first round, finesse the jack next if the king or queen appears from West)	37 50	

(b) Declarer Has Six Cards

	Dummy Declarer	Tricks Required		% Chance of Success	Tricks per Deal
470.	A J 10 x x x —	4	Play the ace, and then lead small from the jack-ten, hoping that the king-queen are doubleton or tripleton	10	
		3 Max	Play the ace, and then lead small from the jack-ten, in case there is a doubleton honor	78	2.83
471.	A J 10 9 8 x	4	Finesse the jack, and then play the ace, hoping that West has xxxxx, KQx, KQ, Kx, Qx, K, or Q	14	
472.	A J 10 9 x x	3	Finesse the jack, and then finesse the ten	50	
473.	A J 9 x xx	3	Finesse the jack, hoping that West has KQ10 only	1	
		2 Max	Finesse the nine. If it loses to the ten, play the ace and a small card; if the nine loses to a high honor, finesse the jack next* (*And if East omits to falsecard with KQ10)	41 42	1.42
474.	A J x x 10 x	2	Lead small to the ten; if it loses, play the ace, and lead small from the jack* (*But if East would play an honor from Qx, Kx, or Qxx, lead small to the ten, and finesse the jack next if it loses)	55 65	
475.	A J 10 x x x	2	Finesse the jack, and then finesse the ten	76	
476.	A J 9 x x x	2	Finesse the nine, and then finesse the jack. If West inserts a high honor on the first round, still finesse the nine next; West should falsecard with K10x, etc.* (*But if West would split high honors and would not falsecard, finesse the jack next if West plays the king or queen on the first round)	38 50	
477.	A J 8 10 x x	2	Run the ten. If it loses, finesse the jack. If the ten is covered, win the ace and finesse the eight.	39 51	
478.	A J x 10 x x	2	Lead small to the jack; then play the ace* (*But if East might be tempted to play an honor from Kx, Qx, or Qxx, lead small to the ten, and then finesse the jack)	33 41	
479.	A x x J 10 9	2	Run the jack, and then run the ten	76	

	Dummy Declarer	Tricks Required		% Chance of Success	Tricks per Deal

VI. THE DEFENSE HAS FIVE POINTS (cont'd)
B. THE KING-QUEEN (cont'd)

(c) Declarer Has Seven Cards

	Dummy Declarer	Tricks Required		% Chance of Success	Tricks per Deal
480.	J 10 x x x x A	5	Play the ace, and then lead small from the jack-ten, hoping that the king-queen are doubleton	3	
		4	Play the ace, and then lead small from the jack-ten, in case there is a doubleton honor	65	
481.	A J 10 9 x x x	5 } Max }	Finesse the jack, and then cash the ace	23	4.08
		4	Play the ace, and then lead the jack, in case East has a singleton honor	89	
482.	A J 10 9 x x x	4 } Max }	Finesse the jack, and then finesse the ten	53	3.45
		3	Finesse the jack	92	
483.	A J 9 x x x x	4 } Max }	Finesse the nine, and then finesse the jack	12	2.58
		3	Finesse the nine, and the jack	55	
		2	Finesse the nine, and the jack This fails only when West has a void or a singleton, or when East has a singleton ten	91	
484.	A J 10 9 x x x	3	Finesse the jack, and then finesse the ten	76	
485.	A J 10 x x x x	3 } Max }	Finesse the jack, and then finesse the ten	45	2.28
		2	Play the ace, and lead small to the jack, or finesse the jack, and then play the ace	85	
486.	A J 9 8 x x x	3	Finesse the eight, and then finesse the nine	37	
		2	Finesse the eight, the nine, and, if necessary, the jack (best), or finesse the jack, the eight, and then the nine	89	
		Max	Finesse the eight, the nine, and, if necessary, the jack		2.26
487.	A J 9 x x x x	3 } Max }	Finesse the nine, and then finesse the jack, hoping that East has x, xx, xxx, Qxx, Kxx, or void	22	1.89
		2	Play the ace, and lead to the nine, or finesse the nine and the jack, or finesse the jack and the nine	68	
488.	AJ 8 x 10 x x	3	Lead small to the eight. If this loses to the king or queen, lead from the ten, and play the ace unless the nine appears from West* (*And if West omits to falsecard with 9xx And if West is tempted to split his honors with KQx)	26 28 33	
		2	Play the ace, and unless an honor appears from West, lead small to the ten. This fails only when West has Kx or Qx	90	
		Max	Lead small to the eight. If this loses to the king or queen, lead from the ten, and play the ace unless the nine appears from West. If the eight loses to the nine, lead small to the jack next* (*And if West omits to falsecard with 9xxx And if West splits his honors with KQx)		2.15 2.16 2.22
489.	A J x x 10 x x	3	Lead small to the jack, hoping that West has KQ or KQx	9	
		2	Lead small to the ace, and unless an honor appears from West, lead small to the ten next. This fails only when West has Kx or Qx	87	

	Dummy Declarer	Tricks Required		% Chance of Success	Tricks per Deal

VI. THE DEFENSE HAS FIVE POINTS (cont'd)
B. THE KING-QUEEN (cont'd)

		Max	Lead small to the ace, and unelss and honor appears from West, lead small to the ten*		1.90
			(*But if East would play an honor from Kx or Qx, lead small to the ten, and finesse the jack next if it loses to West)		1.93
490.	A 9 8 7	3	Run the nine. If this loses to the king or queen from West, run the jack next, hoping that East has 10 or 10x*		
	J x x			6	
			(*But if East would not falsecard with 10x, run the nine; if the ten appears from East, play the ace next; if the king or queen appears from East or the nine loses to the king or queen from West, run the jack next.	8	
			And if East would play a higher honor from K10 or Q10, run the nine; if the king or queen appears from East, or the nine loses to the king or queen from West, run the jack next. This succeeds when East has 10, 10x, Q10 or K10)	9	
		2 ⎱ Max ⎰	Run the jack. If it loses, finesse the nine next; if that loses, finesse the eight	89	1.90
491.	A x x x	3	Run the jack and then the ten	28	
	J 10 9	2	Run the jack and then the ten	100	
492.	J x x x	3 ⎱ Max ⎰	Lead small to the ten, and then play the ace, hoping that East has KQ or KQx	9	1.93
	A 10 x	2	Play the ace, and unless an honor appears from West, lead small to the ten	87	

(d) Declarer Has Eight Cards

493.	A J 10 9 x x x	6 ⎱ Max ⎰	Finesse the jack, and then play the ace	43	5.39
	x				
494.	A J 10 x x x	5 ⎱ Max ⎰	Lead small to the ten; then run the nine. Do not lead the nine for the first finesse: West may have a singleton honor	60	4.56
	9 x				
495.	A J 9 x x x	5	Finesse the nine, and then finesse the jack*	27	
	x x		(*If West would not falsecard with 10xx, play the ace if the nine loses to a high honor, and the ten fails to appear on the second round)	31	
		4 ⎱ Max ⎰	Finesse the nine, and then finesse the jack	79	4.04
		3	Finesse the jack or the nine in case East is void	98	
496.	A J x x x x	5	Lead small to the ten, and finesse the jack next, or run the ten and lead up to the jack next	24	
	10 x	4 ⎱ Max ⎰	Lead small to the ten, and finesse the jack next	90	4.14
		3	Lead small to the ten	100	
497.	A 9 8 x x x	5	Lead small to the jack, hoping that East has K10 or Q10	7	
	J x	4	Lead small to the jack and then to the nine, or play the ace, or run the jack, and finesse the nine next, or lead toward the ace, and play small unless an honor appears from West	85	
		3	Lead small to the jack	100	
		Max	Lead small to the jack. If an honor wins from East, run the jack next; if East plays the ten on the first round, cash the ace next		3.92

	Dummy Declarer	Tricks Required		% Chance of Success	Tricks per Deal

VI. THE DEFENSE HAS FIVE POINTS (cont'd)
B. THE KING-QUEEN (cont'd)

	Dummy / Declarer	Tricks Req.	Description	% Chance	Tricks/Deal
498.	A 9 x x x x J x	5	Lead small to the jack, hoping that East has K10 or Q10	7	
		4	Lead small to the jack; if the ten appears from East, finesse the nine next	73	
		Max	Lead small to the jack. If an honor wins from East, run the jack next; if East plays the ten on the first round, finesse the nine		3.76
499.	A J 10 x x x x x	4 } Max }	Finesse the jack, and then finesse the ten	63	3.50
		3	Finesse the jack, and then play the ace, *or* finesse the jack and then the ten (best)	90	
500.	A J 9 x x x x x	4 } Max }	Finesse the nine, and then finesse the jack* (*If West would not falsecard from 10xx, play the ace if the nine loses to a high honor, and the ten fails to appear on the second round)	33 36	3.15
		3	Finesse the nine, and then finesse the jack	84	
501.	A J 8 7 x 10 x x	4 } Max }	Run the ten. If it is covered, lead to the eight next; if the ten loses to East, finesse the jack next* (*But if West would not falsecard with K9 or Q9, and would not split his honors with KQ9, lead small to the eight. If this loses to the nine, lead to the ten next; if the eight loses to a high honor, finesse the seven next; and if the king or queen appears from West on the first round, run the eight next. And if West would split his honors with KQx or KQ9)	42 44 47	3.35 3.37 3.40
		3	Lead small to the jack. If it loses, lead small to the ten next. This fails only if West is void.	98	
502.	A J x x x 10 x x	4	Lead small to the jack, and then cash the ace	37	
		3	Play the ace, and lead small to the ten. This fails only to a 5-0 break	96	
		Max	Lead small to the jack, and then cash the ace* (*But if East would play an honor from Kx or Qx, lead small to the ten, and then finesse the jack)		3.19 3.24
503.	A 9 8 7 x J x x	4	Run the nine. If it loses to the king or queen from West, run the jack; if the king or queen appears from East, either run the jack or cash the ace* (*This assumes that East will play an honor from K10 or Q10 about half the time, which is the best defense. If he would always play the high honor from these holdings, run the nine, and run the jack next if it loses to the king or queen on either side)	13 16	
		3	Run the nine. If this loses to the ten, run the jack next; if the nine loses to the king or queen on either side, lead small to the jack. This fails only when either opponent is void, or West has the singleton ten	93	
		Max	Run the nine. If this loses to the ten, run the jack next; if the nine loses to the king or queen from West, run the jack next; if the king or queen appears from East on the first round, lead small to the jack next		2.97

Dummy Declarer	Tricks Required		% Chance of Success	Tricks per Deal

VI. THE DEFENSE HAS FIVE POINTS (cont'd)
B. THE KING-QUEEN (cont'd)

Dummy Declarer	Tricks Required		% Chance of Success	Tricks per Deal
504. A x x x x	4	Run the jack and then the ten	54	
J 10 9	3	Run the jack and then the ten	96	
	2	Run the jack	100	
	Max	Run the jack and then the ten		3.50
505. J 10 9 x x	4	Run the jack and then the ten	60	
A x x	3	Play the ace, *or* lead low to the jack. This fails only if West is void	98	
	Max	Run the jack and then the ten		3.56
506. A J 10 9	3	Finesse the jack and then the ten	76	
x x x x				
507. A J 10 x	3 }	Finesse the jack and then the ten	65	2.54
x x x x	Max }			
508. A J 9 x	3 }	Lead small to the nine; then finesse the jack*	35	2.19
x x x x	Max }	(*And if West would not falsecard with 10xx, play the ace if the nine loses to a high honor, and the ten fails to appear on the second round)	38	
	2	Play the ace, *or* take two finesses	84	
509. A J8 x	3	Run the ten. If it loses to East, finesse the jack next; if the ten is covered, finesse the eight next	44	
10 x x x	2	Lead small to the jack, and finesse the eight next if it loses (best), *or* play the ace, and lead small to the ten	100	
	Max	Finesse the jack; if it loses, finesse the eight next		2.37
510. A J x x	3 }	Finesse the jack; then cash the ace	37	2.32
10 x x x	Max }			
	2	Play the ace, and lead small to either honor	100	
511. A 9 8 7	3	Run the nine. If it loses to the king or queen from West, run the jack; if East plays an honor on the first round, cash the ace next* (*But if East would play an honor from K10 or Q10, run the nine, and run the jack next if it loses to the king or queen on either side)	13, 16	
J x x x	2	Run the nine. If this loses, lead small to the eight next. This fails only when West has the singleton ten	97	
	Max	Play the ace, and then run the nine		2.05

(e) Declarer Has Nine Cards

Dummy Declarer	Tricks Required		% Chance of Success	Tricks per Deal
512. A J 10 9 x x x x	7 }	Play the ace, *or* finesse the jack, and then play the ace	66	6.66
x	Max }			
513. A J 10 9 x x x	6 }	Finesse the jack and then the ten	76	5.76
x x	Max }			
514. A J 9 x x x x	6	Play the ace, and lead to the jack, *or* finesse the jack* (*But if West would not falsecard with K10x, Q10x, or 10x, lead toward dummy, and play the ace unless the ten appears from West. And if West splits his honors with KQx)	53, 59, 66	
x x	5	Finesse the jack or the nine, in case East is void	95	
	Max	Finesse the jack* (*But if West would not falsecard with K10x, Q10x, or 10x, lead toward dummy, and play the ace if the ten fails to appear)		5.48, 5.50

Dummy Declarer	Tricks Required		% Chance of Success	Tricks per Deal

VI.   THE DEFENSE HAS FIVE POINTS (cont'd)
B.   THE KING-QUEEN (cont'd)

Dummy Declarer	Tricks Required		% Chance of Success	Tricks per Deal
515. A 8 7 x x x x J 10	6 Max	Run the jack, and then play the ace; this gains a trick when East has the singleton nine	47	5.42
	5	Run the jack, in case East is void	95	
516. A J 10 x x x x x x	5 Max	Finesse the jack and then the ten	76	4.71
517. A J 9 x x x x x x	5 Max	Finesse the nine. If this loses to the king or queen, finesse the jack next*	57	4.53
		(*But if West would not falsecard with K10x, Q10x, or 10x, lead toward dummy, and play the ace if the ten fails to appear.	59	4.55
		And if West splits his honors with KQx	66	4.61
518. A J x x x x 10 x x	5 Max	Lead small to the jack, *or* play the ace, and lead small to either honor	66	4.66
519. A 9 x x x x J x x	5	Play the ace, and lead small to the jack	53	
	4	Lead small to the jack	100	
	Max	Lead toward dummy, and play the nine if West follows small; otherwise play the ace, and lead small to the jack		3.48
520. A x x x x x J 10 9	5 Max	Run the jack and then the ten	71	4.71
	4	Run the jack	100	
521. A J 10 9 x x x x x	4	Finesse the jack and then the ten	76	
522. A J 9 x x x x x x	4 Max	Finesse the nine; if this loses to the king or queen, finesse the jack next*	57	3.53
		(*But if West would not falsecard with K10x, Q10x, or 10x, lead toward dummy, and play the ace if the ten fails to appear from West	59	3.55
		And if West splits hs honors with KQx)	66	3.61
523. A J x x x 10 x x x	4 Max	Finesse the jack, *or* play the ace, and lead small to either honor	66	3.66
524. A 9 x x x J x x x	4	Play the ace, and lead small to the jack	53	
	3	Lead small to the jack, *or* lead small to the nine	100	
	Max	Lead toward dummy, and play the nine if West follows small; otherwise play the ace, and lead to the jack		3.53
525. A x x x x J 10 9 8	4	Run the jack and then the ten	76	

(f) Declarer Has Ten Cards

Dummy Declarer	Tricks Required		% Chance of Success	Tricks per Deal
526. A J 10 x x x x x x x	4 Max	Lead to the jack, in case East is void	89	3.89
etc.*		*N.B. Similar principles apply if declarer's cards are distributed differently between his hand and dummy.		

VII.   THE DEFENSE HAS SIX POINTS
A.   THE ACE-QUEEN

(a) Declarer Has Five Cards

Dummy Declarer	Tricks Required		% Chance of Success	Tricks per Deal
527. K J 9 x x	2 Max	Finesse the nine and then the jack, *or* finesse the jack and then the nine	24	1.02
	1	Immaterial: take two finesses	78	

Dummy Declarer	Tricks Required		% Chance of Success	Tricks per Deal

VII. THE DEFENSE HAS SIX POINTS (cont'd)
A. THE ACE-QUEEN (cont'd)

(b) Declarer Has Six Cards

Dummy Declarer	Tricks Required		% Chance of Success	Tricks per Deal
528. K J 10 9 x x	3	Finesse the jack and then the ten	18	

529. A J 9 8
    x x
	3	Finesse the eight, hoping that West has AQ10,
		   Q10x, or Q10
			5	

	2 ⎱ Max ⎰	Finesse the eight:if this loses, finesse the nine next	63	1.68

530. K x x x
    J 9
	1	Lead small to the nine or jack; if this loses, lead
		   to the king. Finessing the nine first will be
		   better against East, who might be tempted to
		   play an honor from AQ and others
			75	

531. K J 9 x x x	2	Finesse the jack or the nine	25	
	1	Immaterial:take two finesses	79	

	Max	Finesse the jack, and guess which to play next
		   if the queen wins, *or* finesse the nine, and
		   guess which to play next if the ten wins
				1.04

532. K J x
    x x x
	2 ⎱
	Max ⎰
		Lead to the jack, hoping that West has both the
		   ace and queen
			24	1.00

	1	Lead to the jack and then to the king (best), *or* lead to the king and then to the jack	76	

533. K 9 8
    J x x
	2	Lead small to the king, hoping that West has
		   AQ doubleton or the singleton queen
			1	

	1 ⎱
	Max ⎰
		Finesse the eight; if this loses to the ten, guess
		   whether to play the nine or king next*
		   (*But if East would play a high honor from
		   AQ and others, run the nine first; if this loses
		   to the ten, lead to the king next)
			80
			
			88
				0.81

534. K x x
    J 9 x
	2	Lead small to the king, hoping that West has the
		   ace-queen doubleton or the queen singleton
			1	

	1	Lead small to the king, and then back to the jack
		   or nine (best), *or* lead to the nine and then
		   to the king, *or* lead to the jack and then to the
		   king. The last two lines will be better if East is
		   more likely to be short in the suit
			76	

	Max	Lead small to the king and then back to the jack or nine		0.77

535. K x x
    J x x
	2	Lead small to the king, hoping that West has
		   the ace-queen doubleton
			1	

	1	Lead small to the king and then small to the
		   jack (best), *or* lead small to the jack and then
		   small to the king. The latter line will be better
		   if East is more likely to be short in the suit*
		   (*But if East would play an honor from AQ
		   and others, lead small toward the jack, and
		   duck whatever happens, then lead small to the
		   king)
			74
			
			79	

	Max	Lead small to the king and then small to the jack		0.75

(c) Declarer Has Seven Cards

Dummy Declarer	Tricks Required		% Chance of Success	Tricks per Deal

536. K J 9 8
    x x x
	3	Finesse the eight, hoping that the queen and ten
		   are both with West
			24	

	2	Finesse the eight; if this loses to the ten, finesse
		   the nine next (best), *or* finesse the jack, and
		   then finesse the eight
			76	

	Max	Finesse the eight and then the nine		2.00

	Dummy Declarer	Tricks Required		% Chance of Success	Tricks per Deal
			VII. THE DEFENSE HAS SIX POINTS (cont'd)		
			A. THE ACE-QUEEN (cont'd)		
537.	K 10 8 x	3	Finesse the eight	20	
	J x x	2	Finesse the ten. If it loses to the queen, lead small to the jack and then to the king; if the ten loses to the ace, finesse the eight next	79	
		Max	Finesse the eight. If this loses to the nine, finesse the ten next		1.95
538.	K 10 x x	3	Finesse the ten, hoping that West has AQ or AQx	9	
	J x x	2	Lead small to the king; then lead small to the ten	69	
		Max	Finesse the ten. If this loses to the queen, lead small to the king next		1.76
539.	K 9 8 7	3	Run the jack, hoping that East has the singleton ten	1	
	J x x	2	Run the jack, and then finesse the nine. If the ace appears from West on the first round, finesse the nine, and if necessary, the eight (best) *or* finesse the nine. If this loses to this queen, lead to the jack next; if the ace appears from West, finesse the nine next; if the nine loses to the ten, finesse the eight next* (*But if West would not falsecard with AQ10 or AQ10x, run the nine. If this loses to the ten, finesse the seven next; otherwise run the eight.	76 77	
			And if East is tempted to play an honor from AQxxx)	78	
		Max	Run the jack. If it loses to the ace or queen from East, lead small to the nine next; if the ace appears from West on the first round, finesse the nine, and, if necessary, the eight		1.77
540.	Kx x x	2	Lead small to the jack, and then small to the ten. This fails only when West has AQ doubleton, AQ and at least two others, or the singleton or doubleton queen	75	
	J 10 x				
541.	K x x x	2	Lead small to the nine. If the ten or queen appears from East, lead small from the king next; otherwise lead small to the king	47	
	J 9 x	1 } Max }	Lead small to the nine, then small to the jack, and then small to the king. This fails only when West has the Q10 doubleton	98	1.36
542.	K x x x	2 } Max }	Lead to the jack, and then, unless the queen appears from East, lead to the king, *or* lead to the king and then to the jack. The latter line will be better if West is more likely to be short in the suit	26	1.12
	J x x	1	Lead small from both hands; then, unless the queen has appeared from West, lead to the jack; then lead to the king. This fails only when West has Qx	94	
(d)	**Declarer Has Eight Cards**				
543.	K 10 8 x x	4	Lead small to the ten (and repeat if West takes the ace). If it holds, lead to the king. If the ten loses to the queen, play the jack. If the ten loses to the ace or if East follows with the nine, finesse the eight	25	
	J x x	3	Finesse the ten, and run the jack if it loses to the ace (best), *or* lead small to the king, and then small to the jack	90	
		Max	Finesse the ten; if this loses to the ace, run the jack		3.12

Dummy Declarer	Tricks Required		% Chance of Success	Tricks per Deal

VII. THE DEFENSE HAS SIX POINTS (cont'd)
A. THE ACE-QUEEN (cont'd)

544. K 9 8 x x J x x	4	Lead small the king, hoping that West has the AQ only	3	
	3	Lead small to the eight. If it loses to the ten, finesse the nine next; if the ace appears from West on the first round, lead small to the jack	84	
	Max	Finesse the eight. If it loses to the ten, finesse the nine next; if the ace appears from West on the first round, lead small to the king		2.82
545. K x x x x J 10 x	4	Lead small to the king, hoping that West has the AQ only	3	
	3 ⎱ Max ⎰	Lead small to the jack, and then small to the ten	85	2.83
	2	Lead small to the jack. This fails only when East is void	98	
546. K x x x x J 9 x	4	Lead small the king, hoping that West has the AQ doubleton	3	
	3 ⎱ Max ⎰	Lead small to the nine, and then small to the king	63	2.58
	2	Lead small to the nine, and then small to the jack. This fails only if East is void	98	
547. K J 9 8 x x x x	3	Finesse the eight	27	
	2	Finesse the eight and then the jack (best), *or* finesse the jack and then the eight, *or* lead small to the king	83	
	Max	Finesse the eight; if it loses to the ten, finesse the jack		2.10
548. K 10 8 x J x x	3	Run the jack. If this is covered, finesse the eight next	27	
	2	Finesse the ten. If this loses to the queen, lead small to the jack; if the ten loses to the ace, run the jack (best), *or* lead small to the king, and then small to the jack	92	
	Max	Finesse the ten. If this loses to the queen, lead small to the jack; if the ten loses to the ace, run the jack		2.16
549. K 9 8 7 J x x x	3	Lead small to the king, hoping that West has the ace-queen doubleton or the queen singleton	6	
	2 ⎱ Max ⎰	Finesse the nine. If this loses to the queen, lead small to the jack; if the nine loses to the ten, finesse the eight	88	1.94
550. K x x x J 10 8 x	3 ⎱ Max ⎰	Run the jack. If the ace appears from West, run the ten next; if the jack loses to the ace from East, guess whether to lead small or run the ten next; if the jack is covered, guess whether to lead to the ten or to the eight next*	14	
		(*This assumes that West will always play the ace from ace-queen doubleton and will cover with Qx about half the time, which is the best defense. If he always covers with Qx, lead to the eight if the jack is covered, lead the ten if the jack loses to the ace from East, and run the ten if the ace appears from West on the first round.	17	2.01
		Similarly, if West never covers with Qx, lead small to the king if the jack loses to the ace from East, lead to the ten if the jack is covered, and run the ten if the ace appears from West on the first round)	17	2.01

	Dummy Declarer	Tricks Required		% Chance of Success	Tricks per Deal
			VII. THE DEFENSE HAS SIX POINTS (cont'd)		
			A. THE ACE-QUEEN (cont'd)		
		2	Lead small to the jack, and then small to the king. This fails only when East has a void or a small singleton	92	
551.	K x x x J 10 x x	3	Lead small to the king, hoping that West has AQ doubleton	3	
		2	Lead small to the king and then small to the jack, *or* lead small to the jack. The latter line will be better if East is more likely to be short in the suit	87	
		Max	Lead small to the king, and then small to the jack		1.90
552.	K x x x J 9 x x	3	Lead small to the king, hoping that West has AQ doubleton	3	
		2 } Max }	Lead small to the king and then small to the nine	70	1.71
		1	Lead small to the nine (best), *or* lead toward the king, and duck if West fails to play an honor, *or* lead small to the jack	100	
553.	K x x x J x x x	3	Lead small to the king, hoping that West has AQ doubleton	3	
		2	Lead toward the king, and duck if the queen fails to appear; then lead to the king (best), *or* lead to the king and then to the jack	50	
		1 } Max }	Lead toward the king, and duck if the queen fails to appear; then lead to the king and finally to the jack	100	1.54
(e)	**Declarer Has Nine Cards**				
554.	K J 9 x x x x x x*	4 Max	Lead small to the jack Lead small to the jack	33	3.17
555.	K J x x x x x x x*	4 Max	Lead small to the jack Lead small to the jack	33	3.11
556.	K 9 8 7 x J x x x*	4 3 Max	Lead small to the king Lead small to the nine (best), *or* run the nine Lead small to the king	27 94	3.16
557.	K x x x x J 10 9 8*	4	Run the jack	50	
558.	K x x x x J 10 x x*	4 3 Max	Lead small to the king Lead small to the king, in case West is void Lead small to the king	33 95	3.28
			*N.B. Similar principles apply if declarer's nine cards are distributed differently between this hand and dummy		
(f)	**Declarer Has Ten Cards**				
559.	K J x x x x 10 x x x*	5	Finesse the jack	63	
560.	K x x x x x J 10 9 x *	5	Run the jack	63	
			*N.B. Similar principles apply if declarer's ten cards are distributed differently between this hand and dummy		

Dummy Declarer	Tricks Required		% Chance of Success	Tricks per Deal

VII.   THE DEFENSE HAS SIX POINTS (cont'd)
B.   THE KING-QUEEN-JACK

(a)   Declarer Has Five Cards

561.   A 10 9 8   2   Finesse the ten, and then play the ace   25
       x

(b)   Declarer Has Six Cards

562.   A 10 9 8 x   3 ⎫ Finesse the ten, and then play the ace   16   1.99
       x   Max ⎭

              2   Play the ace, and then lead low from the 1098;
                   this gains a trick when East has a singleton
                   or doubleton honor   87

563.   A 10 9 8   2   Finesse the ten and then the nine   77
       x x

(c)   Declarer Has Seven Cards

564.   A 10 9 8 x x   4 ⎫ Finesse the ten, and then cash the ace   65   3.55
       x   Max ⎭

              3   Finesse the ten, and then play the ace (best),
                   or play the ace   91

              2   Finesse the ten, in case East is void   99

565.   A 10 9 8 x   3 ⎫ Finesse the ten and then the nine; then play the
       x x   Max ⎭ ace   74   2.70

              2   Finesse the ten and then the nine (best), *or*
                   play the ace   96

566.   A 10 9 8   2   Finesse the eight, nine, and, if necessary, ten   89
       x x x

567.   A 10 9 x   2   Finesse the ten and then the nine; then play the
       x x x   ace   68

568.   A 10 x x   2   Lead small to the nine. If this loses to West,
       9 x x   cash the ace next. If an honor appears from
                 East on the first round, run the nine
                 and then finesse the ten next.   51

(d)   Declarer Has Eight Cards

569.   A 10 9 8 x x x   5 ⎫ Play the ace, in case East has a singleton honor   85   4.81
       x   Max ⎭

              4   Finesse the ten, in case East is void   98

570.   A 10 9 8 x x   4 ⎫ Finesse the ten and then the nine   90   3.88
       x x   Max ⎭

              3   Finesse the ten and then the nine   98

571.   A 10 9 8 x   3 ⎫ Finesse the ten and then the nine   92   2.90
       x x x   Max ⎭

              2   Finesse the ten and then the nine   98

572.   A 10 x x x   3   Play the ace, and lead small to the nine   85
       9 x x   2 ⎫ Lead small to the nine and then small to the ten   100   2.82
              Max ⎭

573.   A 8 7 x x   3 ⎫ Run the ten, *or* lead small to the ten, in case
       10 x x   Max ⎭ East has the singleton nine   71   2.69

              2   Run the ten, *or* lead small to the ten, in case
                 East is void   98

Dummy Declarer	Tricks Required		% Chance of Success	Tricks per Deal

VII.   THE DEFENSE HAS SIX POINTS (cont'd)
B.   THE KING-QUEEN-JACK (cont'd)

574.	A 10 9 8	2	Finesse the ten and then the nine; this fails only	
	x x x x		when West has a void or a small singleton	92

(c)   Declarer Has Nine Cards

575.	A 10 9 8 x x x x	7	Play the ace, hoping for a 2-2 division	41	
	x	6 ⎱	Finesse the ten, and then play the ace	95	6.36
		Max ⎰			
576.	A 10 9 x x x x	6	Play the ace, hoping for a 2-2 division	41	
	x x	5 ⎱	Finesse the ten, and then play the ace	95	5.36
		Max ⎰			
577.	A 10 x x x x	5	Play the ace	41	
	9 x x	4	Lead small to the ten, *or* lead small to the nine	95	
		Max	Lead small to the ten or nine; then play the ace		4.36
578.	A 10 x x x	4	Play the ace, hopin g for a 2-2 division	41	
	9 x x x	3	Lead small to the ten or nine	95	
		Max	Lead small to the ten or nine; then play the ace		3.36

VIIII.   THE DEFENSE HAS SEVEN POINTS
A.   THE ACE-KING

(a)   Declarer Has Five Cards

579.	Q J 9 8	2	Finesse the eight. If it loses to the ace or king	
	x		on either side, lead the queen and jack next	11
580.	Q J 9	1	Lead to the queen and then to the jack	78
	x x			
581.	Q 9 x	1	Lead small to the jack. If it loses to West,	
	J x		finesse the nine next	62
582.	Q x x	1	Finesse the nine	51
	J 9			

(b)   Declarer Has Six Cards

583.	Q J 9 8	2	Finesse the nine	51
	x x			
584.	Q x x x	1	Finesse the nine. If it loses to the ten, play the	
	J 9		jack and then low from the queen*	56
			(*This is only fractionally better than leading	
			small to the jack and then ducking two rounds,	
			and the latter line might be better if East is	
			more likely to be short in the suit)	
585.	Q J 9	1	Lead to the queen and then to the jack	79
	x x x			
586.	Q 9 x	1	Lead small to the jack. If it loses to West, finesse	
	J x x		the nine next	64
587.	Q x x	1	Lead to either honor and then back to the other	49
	J x x			

(c)   Declarer Has Seven Cards

588.	Q J 9 x x	3 ⎱	Lead to the queen and then to the jack	38	2.12
	x x	Max ⎰			
		2	Finesse the nine, and then lead to the queen	80	
		1	Lead to the queen and then to the nine or jack		
			(best), *or* finesse the nine, and then lead to		
			the queen	96	

Dummy / Declarer	Tricks Required		% Chance of Success	Tricks per Deal

VIII.   THE DEFENSE HAS SEVEN POINTS (cont'd)
A.   THE ACE-KING (cont'd)

589. Q J x x x / 9 x   3 } Max }   Lead to the queen and then to the jack   30   1.98

   2   Lead to the queen and then to the jack   73

   1   Lead small to the nine. This fails only when West has the singleton ten   99

590. Q J 9 8 / x x x   2 } Max }   Lead small to the queen. If it loses, finesse the nine next   63   1.63

591. Q J 9 x / x x x   2 } Max }   Lead small to the queen. If it loses, finesse the nine next   55   1.46

592. Q J x x / 9 x x   2 } Max }   Lead to the queen and then to the jack   49   1.38

   1   Lead small to the queen. If it loses, lead small to the nine and then small to the jack. This fails only when West has the doubleton ten   95

593. Q J x x / x x x   2 } Max }   Lead to the queen and then to the jack   45   1.28

   1   Lead to the queen; if it loses, duck one round, and then lead to the jack (best) *or* duck one round, and then lead to the queen and jack   85

594. Q 9 8 x / J x x   2   Lead small to the jack. If it loses to West, finesse the nine next; if an honor appears from East on the first round, lead to the jack again   56

595. Q x x x / J 9 x   2 } Max }   Lead small to the nine. If it loses to a high honor from West, lead small to the queen; otherwise lead small to the jack   33   1.30

   1   Lead small to the nine and then small to the jack. This fails only if West has A10 or K10   97

596. Q x x x / J x x   2   Lead small to the queen or jack, and then back to the other honor, hoping to find either opponent with AKx or the right opponent with AK doubleton   16

   1   Lead toward the jack and duck; then lead to the jack and to the queen. This fails only when West has Kx or Ax   87

   Max   Lead small to the jack. If it loses, duck the next round, and then lead to the queen   0.93

(d)   Declarer Has Eight Cards

597. Q J 10 6 x x / 8 x   4 } Max }   Lead to the queen and then to the jack   85   3.83

   3   Lead small to the eight, in case West is void   100

598. Q J 9 8 7 / x x x   3   Lead small to the queen. If it loses, finesse the nine   75

599. Q J x x x / x x x   3 } Max }   Lead to the queen and then to the jack   63   2.50

600. Q 10 9 6 x / J x x   3 } Max }   Lead the jack, in case East is void   98   2.98

601. Q x x x x / J 9 x   3   Finesse the nine. If it holds, lead to the jack. If East inserts an honor, finesse the nine next.   48

   2 } Max }   Lead low to the jack. If West wins, lead low from South and play low from North unless the ten appears. If West plays the 10 under the jack, lead low to the nine. If East plays an honor, lead to the jack.   98   241

602. Q J 9 8 / x x x x   2   Lead small to the queen. If it loses, finesse the nine   77

Dummy Declarer	Tricks Required		% Chance of Success	Tricks per Deal

VIII.   THE DEFENSE HAS SEVEN POINTS (cont'd)
A.   THE ACE-KING (cont'd)

603.	Q 9 8 7	2	Lead small to the jack. If it loses to West, finesse	
	J x x x		the nine next	66
604.	Q 9 x x	2 ⎫	Lead small to the jack. If it loses to West, finesse	
	J x x x	Max ⎭	the nine next	64 1.58
		1	Finesse the nine (best), *or* lead small to the queen and them small to the jack, in case West has a bare honor	100
605.	Q x x x	2 ⎫	Lead to the queen (or jack); if it loses, duck the	
	J x x x	Max ⎭	next round	37 1.32
		1	Duck the first round, and then lead small to either honor	100

(e)   Declarer Has Nine Cards

606.	Q J 7 x x x x	5 ⎫	Lead small to the queen and then to the jack	84 4.79
	9 x	Max ⎭		
		4	Led small to the nine, in case West is void	100
607.	Q x x x x x	4	Finesse the nine. This only fails when West has	
	J 9 x		AK10x, AK10, or 10	83
608.	Q J 8 x x	3 ⎫	Lead small to the queen, in case either opponent	
	10 7 x x	Max ⎭	is void	100 3.00
609.	Q J x x x	3 ⎫	Lead small to the queen and then small to the	
	x x x x	Max ⎭	jack	83 2.78
610.	Q 9 x x x	3	Lead small to the jack and then small to the queen, *or* finesse the nine. The latter line will be better if West is more likely to be short in the suit	
	J x x x			83

B.   THE ACE-QUEEN-JACK

(a)   Declarer Has Five Cards

611.	K 10 9	1	Finesse the ten and then the nine	78
	x x			
612.	K 10 x	1	Finesse the ten and then lead to the king	63
	x x			

(b)   Declarer Has Six Cards

613.	K 10 9 8	2	Finesse the ten and then the nine	50
	x x			
614.	K 10 9	1	Finesse the ten and then the nine	79
	x x x			

(c)   Declarer Has Seven Cards

615.	K 10 9 8	2	Finesse the eight and then the nine	76
	x x x			
616.	K 10 9 x	2 ⎫	Finesse the nine and then the ten	61 1.51
	x x x	Max ⎭		
617.	K 10 x x	2 ⎫	Lead small to the ten and then small to the king	37 1.25
	9 x x	Max ⎭		
		1	Lead small to the king, and then, unless an honor appears from West, small to the nine (best), *or* lead to the ten and then to the nine	90

Dummy / Declarer	Tricks Required		% Chance of Success	Tricks per Deal

VIII. THE DEFENSE HAS SEVEN POINTS (cont'd)
B. THE ACE-QUEEN-JACK (cont'd)

	Dummy / Declarer	Tricks Required		% Chance of Success	Tricks per Deal
618.	K 10 x x / x x x	2 / Max	Lead small to the ten and then small to the king	32	1.08
		1	Duck one round; then lead to the ten, and lead to the king	79	
619.	K 9 8 7 / x x x	2	Lead to the nine and then to the king (best), *or* lead to the king, hoping that West has the ace and two other cards	18	
		1 / Max	Finesse the seven and then the eight. This fails only if West has xx, x, or a void	95	1.11
620.	K x x x / x x x	2	Duck one round, and then lead to the king (best) *or* lead to the king, hoping that West has the ace and two other cards	18	
		1	Duck two rounds, and then lead to the king	77	
		Max	Duck one round, and then lead to the king		0.87

(d) Declarer Has Eight Cards

	Dummy / Declarer	Tricks Required		% Chance of Success	Tricks per Deal
621.	K 10 9 x x / x x x	3 / Max	Finesse the ten and then the nine	75	2.66
		2	Finesse the ten and nine (best), *or* lead to the king	92	
622.	K 10 x x x / 9 x x	3 / Max	Finesse the ten, and then lead small to the king	63	2.56
		2	Finesse the ten. If it loses to the jack or queen, lead small to the nine next. This fails only if West is void	98	
623.	K 10 9 8 / x x x x	2	Finesse the eight and then the nine	83	
624.	K 10 x x / x x x x	2 / Max	Finesse the ten, and then lead to the king	52	1.38
625.	K x x x / x x x x	2	Lead small to the king, preferably ducking one round first	34	
		1	Duck one round. Then either lead small to the king (best), *or* duck a second round	87	
		Max	Duck one round, and then lead small to the king		1.21

(e) Declarer Has Nine Cards

	Dummy / Declarer	Tricks Required		% Chance of Success	Tricks per Deal
626.	K 10 9 x x x / x x x	5	Lead small to the king, hoping that West has the doubleton ace	20	
		4 / Max	Finesse the ten. This gains a trick when East is void or has the singleton ace	89	3.98
627.	K 10 x x x x / 9 x x	5	Lead small to the king, hoping that West has the doubleton ace	20	
		4 / Max	Finesse the ten, and then lead small to the king	89	4.03
628.	K 8 x x x x / 10 x x	5 / Max	Lead small to the king, hoping that West has the doubleton ace	20	3.94
		4	Lead toward the king, and play the king if the nine fails to appear from West*	84	
			(*But West should falsecard from QJ9)	78	
		3	Lead small to the ten	100	
629.	K x x x x x / x x x	5 / Max	Lead small to the king, hoping that West has the doubleton ace	20	3.81
		4	Duck one round, and then lead small to the king	72	

	Dummy Declarer	Tricks Required		% Chance of Success	Tricks per Deal

VIII.   THE DEFENSE HAS SEVEN POINTS (cont'd)
B.   THE ACE-QUEEN-JACK (cont'd)

	Dummy Declarer	Tricks Required		% Chance of Success	Tricks per Deal
630.	K 9 x x x x x x x	4 } Max }	Lead small to the king, hoping that West has the doubleton ace	20	2.81
		3	Duck one round, and then lead small to the king	72	
631.	K 8 x x x 10 x x x	4 } Max }	Lead small to the king, hoping West has the doubleton ace	20	2.98
		3	Lead toward the king, and play the king if the nine fails to appear from West* (*But West should falsecard from QJ9)	84 78	

IX. THE DEFENSE HAS EIGHT POINTS

(a)   Declarer Has Five Cards

	Dummy Declarer	Tricks Required		% Chance of Success	Tricks per Deal
632.	Q 10 9 8 x	2	Finesse the ten, hoping that West has J, AJ, KJ, or Jx	2	
633.	Q 10 x x x	1	Finesse the ten, and then lead to the queen	37	

(b)   Declarer Has Six Cards

	Dummy Declarer	Tricks Required		% Chance of Success	Tricks per Deal
634.	Q 10 9 8 x x	2	Finesse the ten and then the nine	18	
635.	Q 10 x x x x	2	Lead to the queen, hoping that West has the AKJ only	1	
		1 } Max }	Lead to the ten and then to the queen	41	0.42
636.	Q 10 9 x x x	1	Finesse the ten and then the nine	51	
637.	Q 10 x x x x	1	Finesse the ten, and then lead to the queen	38	

(c)   Declarer Has Seven Cards

	Dummy Declarer	Tricks Required		% Chance of Success	Tricks per Deal
638.	Q 10 x x x x x	3 } Max }	Lead to the ten and then to the queen	12	1.58
		2	Lead to the ten and queen	55	
		1	Lead to the ten and queen	91	
639.	Q 10 x x x x x	2 } Max }	Lead to the ten and then to the queen	22	0.89
		1	Lead to the ten and queen (best), *or* duck one round and then lead to the ten and queen, *or* lead to the queen and then to the ten	68	
640.	Q 9 8 7 x x x	2	Lead small to the queen	7	
		1 } Max }	Finesse the seven and then the eight	85	0.88
641.	Q x x x 10 9 x	2	Lead small to the queen, hoping that West has AKx or AKJ	7	
		1 } Max }	Lead small to the ten and then small to the nine. This fails only when West has AJor KJ	97	0.97
642.	Q x x x 10 x x	2	Lead small to the queen, hoping that West has AKx or AKJ	7	
		1 } Max }	Lead small to the ten. If an honor appears from East, lead small to the ten again; if the ten loses to West on the first round, duck one round, and then lead to the queen	70	0.70

(d)   Declarer Has Eight Cards

	Dummy Declarer	Tricks Required		% Chance of Success	Tricks per Deal
643.	Q 10 x x x x x x	3 } Max }	Finesse the ten, and then lead to the queen	33	2.15
		2	Finesse the ten, and then lead to the queen, in case East is void	84	

	Dummy Declarer	Tricks Required		% Chance of Success	Tricks per Deal

IX. THE DEFENSE HAS EIGHT POINTS (cont'd)

	Dummy / Declarer	Tricks Required		% Chance	Tricks/Deal
644.	Q x x x x 10 x x	3	Lead small to the queen. If the jack appears from West, cover with the queen, and duck the next round; if the ace or king appears on the first round, lead to the queen again	20	
		2 ⎱ Max ⎰	Lead toward the queen, and duck the trick. If an honor appears on the first round, lead small to the ten next; otherwise lead to the queen	90	1.95
		1	Lead small to the ten, in case West is void	100	
645.	Q x x x x x x x	3 ⎱ Max ⎰	Lead small to the queen	14	1.88
		2	Duck one round, and then, unless the ace or king appears from East, lead small to the queen	82	
646.	Q 10 x x x x x x	2 ⎱ Max ⎰	Finesse the ten, and then lead to the queen	35	1.19
647.	Q x x x 10 x x x	2 ⎱ Max ⎰	Lead small to the queen, and then, unless the jack appears from West, lead small to the ten	20	1.15
		1	Lead small to the queen and then small to the ten, *or* lead from the ten, and duck unless the jack appears from West; then, unless the ace or king appears from East, lead small to the queen. The latter line will be better if East is more likely to be short in the suit	94	
648.	Q x x x x x x x	2	Lead small to the queen	14	
		1	Duck one round, and then lead small to the queen	84	
		Max	Lead small to the queen		0.92

(e) Declarer Has Nine Cards

	Dummy / Declarer	Tricks Required		% Chance	Tricks/Deal
649.	Q 10 9 x x x x x x*	3	Finesse the ten	70	
		Max	Finesse the ten		2.66
650.	Q x x x x x x x x*	3 ⎱ Max ⎰	Lead small to the queen, *or* duck one round, and then lead small to the queen	53	2.48
			*N.B. Similar principles apply if declarer's nine cards are distributed differently between his hand and dummy		

X. THE DEFENSE HAS NINE POINTS

(a) Declarer Has Seven Cards

	Dummy / Declarer	Tricks Required		% Chance	Tricks/Deal
651.	J 10 8 x x x x	1	Lead to the jack, and then either lead to the ten or finesse the eight	73	
652.	J 10 x x x x x	1	Lead to the jack and then to the ten	68	
653.	J x x x 10 x x	1	Lead small to the ten. If it loses to West, duck the next round, and then lead small to the jack	69	

(b) Declarer Has Eight Cards

	Dummy / Declarer	Tricks Required		% Chance	Tricks/Deal
654.	J x x x x 10 x x	2 ⎱ Max ⎰	Lead small to the ten. If it loses to West, lead small to the jack	88	1.88
		1	Lead small to the ten	100	
655.	J 10 x x x x x x	1	Lead small to the jack and then small to the ten	84	
656.	J x x x 10 x x x	1	Lead small to the jack (or ten). If it loses, lead small to the other honor	92	

E.C.

(continued from page 446)

```
                ♠ 7 6
                ♥ Q 7 3
                ♦ J 6 3
                ♣ Q 10 8 4 2
  ♠ 5 4 3 2                      ♠ 10
  ♥ K 10 6 4                     ♥ A J 9 5
  ♦ 7 4 2                        ♦ Q 9 8 5
  ♣ 7 3                          ♣ K J 6 5
                ♠ A K Q J 9 8
                ♥ 8 2
                ♦ A K 10
                ♣ A 9
```

West	North	East	South
Pass	Pass	Pass	2♠
Pass	2NT	Pass	4♠

West leads the ♣7: 2, jack, ace. South draws trumps, and West follows with the 5, 4, 3 and 2. South then leads a club. When East takes the king, he should shift to a low heart. West's trump plays can have no significance other than suit preference. See SIGNAL; SIGNALING.

SUIT SIGNAL. See COUNT SIGNAL.

SUIT TAKEOUT. See RESPONSE.

SUMMARY SHEET. See RECAPITULATION SHEET.

SUMMER NORTH AMERICAN BRIDGE CHAM-PIONSHIPS. Formerly called the Summer Nationals, this annual American Contract Bridge League tournament held since 1929 takes place in July or early August. These championships, usually the largest of the three North American Championships, were originally under the auspices of the American Bridge League, and since 1938 have been controlled by the ACBL. In the Thirties they were played at Asbury Park NJ and lasted eight days. In post-war years the program was gradually enlarged to nine days. In 1969 it became a ten-day tournament and in 1979 a pre-tournament Charity Gala was added. By 1991 this was a substantial bridge event with 156 tables in play on Thursday evening in the Charity Pairs and Charity Knockout Teams.

In 1930 the Knockout Team event (now the Spingold Master Knockout Teams) attracted an entry of 16 teams, and 22 pairs were entered in the Master Pairs for the von Zedtwitz Gold Cup (now the six-session Life Master Pairs). In the postwar years the size of the tournament expanded rapidly, partly as a result of the impetus given by the masterpoint scheme. A peak was reached in 1991 in Las Vegas with 24,221 tables, an all-time world record. For past results of Summer North American Bridge Championships, see Appendix I.

Summer North American Championships Attendance (an asterisk indicates the record was broken that year; table counts not available prior to 1952)

Year	Site	Tables
1929	Chicago	
1930-41	Asbury Park NJ	
1942-47	New York City	
1948-49	Chicago	
1950	Columbus	
1951	Washington	
1952	Cincinnati	3,093
1953	St. Louis	3,054
1954	Washington	4,496*
1955	Chicago	4,619*
1956	New York City	5,679*
1957	Pittsburgh	5,625
1958	Miami	4,068
1959	Chicago	6,939*
1960	Los Angeles	8,462*
1961	Washington	7,989
1962	Minneapolis	5,820
1963	Los Angeles	12,486*
1964	Toronto	11,150
1965	Chicago	14,511*
1966	Denver	10,112
1967	Montreal	10,926
1968	Minneapolis	9,857
1969	Los Angeles	11,470
1970	Boston	12,584
1971	Chicago	13,566
1972	Denver	11,449
1973	Washington D.C.	16,043*
1974	New York City	15,310
1975	Miami Beach	10,368
1976	Salt Lake City	10,722
1977	Chicago	13,170
1978	Toronto	18,408*
1979	Las Vegas	18,517*
1980	Chicago	11,889
1981	Boston	14,079
1982	Albuquerque	9,776
1983	New Orleans	10,520
1984	Washington D.C.	15,228
1985	Las Vegas	19,828*
1986	Toronto	21,075*
1987	Baltimore	17,052
1988	Salt Lake City	11,501
1989	Chicago	14,902
1990	Boston	15,325
1991	Las Vegas	24,221*
1992	Toronto	16,680
1993	Washington D.C.	18,270
1994	San Diego	15,879
1995	New Orleans	12,840
1996	Miami Beach	9,395
1997	Albuquerque	11,355
1998	Chicago	13,022
1999	San Antonio	12,281
2000	Anaheim	13,712

SUNDAY TIMES PAIRS. An invitational pair event that until January 1981 was sponsored by the *London Sunday Times*. The field is usually limited to 16-22 leading pairs from many countries. The competition was in abeyance from 1982 to 1989. It was revived in 1990 with the *Sunday Times* and Macallan Malt Whisky as the primary sponsor until 1999. There was no contest in 2000 or 2001. For winners, see Appendix IV.

SUPER BLACKWOOD. A method of asking for aces when 4NT would be a natural bid. Easley Blackwood listed three situations in which 4NT would be natural. (a) when the partnership has not bid a suit; (b) when no suit has been agreed, and the 4NT bidder has previously bid notrump; (c) when no suit has been agreed, and a notrump bid immediately preceded 4NT. In each of these situations Blackwood suggests that a bid of four in the lowest-ranking unbid suit should ask for aces with step responses. A subsequent 5NT bid asks for kings in the

same way. The Super Blackwood bid will usually be 4♣ which lines it up with the GERBER convention. See BLACKWOOD.

SUPER GERBER. An ace-asking convention devised by Robert Goldman for use when a minor suit fit has been established, or when the last bid was 3NT, so that a 4NT call would be natural. The Super Gerber bid is the lowest possible bid in an unbid suit or in a suit that cannot be deemed trumps; if all suits are unavailable or ambiguous, the Super Gerber bid is a jump to 5♣. Over establishment of a minor suit fit, either expressly or by implication, the Super Gerber bid is a jump to four of the cheapest unbid suit:

(a)	(b)	(c)	(d)
1♦ 3♦	1♣ 3♣	1♦ 2♦	1♦ 1♥
4♥	4♦	4♣	3♦ 4♠

The last bid in each auction is Super Gerber. The use of Super Gerber in minor suit auctions is designed to allow 4NT to be used as a balanced general strength slam try, and to provide an ace-asking bid that does not risk getting the partnership beyond the game level with too few aces.

Responses as used by the ACES TEAM are in steps as follows:

1st step	0 or 3 aces
2nd step	1 or 4 aces
3rd step	2 aces
4th step	2 aces with extra value outside the trump suit
5th step	2 aces and a useful void
higher step	1 ace and a useful void

In showing one ace and a void, the void suit is bid if it ranks lower than the trump suit; the trump suit is bid if the void suit is higher ranking. This is sometimes called High Gerber, particularly when the bid is restricted to a five-club bid. See GERBER.

SUPER PRECISION. A version of the PRECISION CLUB system used by Giorgio Belladonna and Benito Garozzo in which there are many specialized bids and asking sequences. It differs from standard Precision in the following essential respects:

Notrump responses to 1♣ are revised: 1NT is enlarged to encompass hands worth 8-13 points. A 2NT response shows 14 or more points, with no upper limit. A 3NT response shows a solid seven-card suit, with or without a side suit stopper. Opener's rebids over 3NT ask about high card controls, or identification of responder's suit.

Over interference with 1♣, controls are shown (A = 2, K = 1). After a one-level overcall, a double shows 6 or more points with 0-2 controls, 1NT shows 3 controls and a stopper, 2♣ shows 3 controls without a stopper, 2♦ shows 4 controls, 2NT shows 5 or more controls; bids of 3♣, 3♦, and one, two, or three of a major are all natural, showing 0-2 controls.

Over a two-level overcall the double shows a balanced hand with as many as 3 controls; 2NT shows 3 or 4 controls with a stopper; a cuebid shows 5 or more controls; suit bids are natural, showing unbalanced hands with 0-3 controls. Over a three-level overcall the responses are similar.

2♦ *opening* may be 4-3-1-5 or 3-4-1-5 as well as 4-4-0-5 and 4-4-1-4. A 2NT response asks for clarification of distribution and strength. 3♣ and 3♦ rebids show the hands with three spades and three hearts respectively; 3♥

and 3♠ rebids show 4-4-1-4 distribution of minimum and maximum strength; 4♣ and 4♦ rebids shows 4-4-0-5 distribution of minimum and maximum strength.

Super Unusual Positive is used in responding to 1♣ with 4-4-4-1 hands. An immediate jump to 3♣ shows a singleton in a black suit, a jump to 3♦ shows a singleton in a red suit; both show minimum high card values. Opener's bid of the next suit asks where responder's singleton is: responder bids the first step with the minor suit singleton, or the second step with the major suit singleton. Immediate jump responses of 3♥, 3♠, 4♣ and 4♦ over 1♣ show maximum values and a singleton in the next higher suit. Opener's bid of the next suit (responder's short suit) asks for controls — first step 4, second step 5, etc.

Three-level minor suit openings are offensive rather than purely preemptive. 3♣ shows a seven playing-trick hand with a semi-solid club suit and an outside entry. 3♦ shows any solid seven-card suit with an outside entry. In response to 3♦, 3♥ is a signoff to play in opener's suit; 3♠ is a general constructive bid. Over 3♠ opener bids 3NT if he has a minor suit, 4♣ if his suit is hearts and he has a side void or singleton, 4♦ if his suit is spades and he has a side void or singleton; 4♥ and 4♠ are natural and deny a side void or singleton. Responder may ask opener where his shortness lies.

3NT opening shows a preemptive minor suit opening similar to standard openings of 4♣ or 4♦. Responder retreats with a weak hand by bidding 4♣ which opener passes if his suit is clubs, or corrects to 4♦.

Asking bids of several kinds are used after a 1♣ opening, each with its own series of responses. These include bids designated Alpha, in which opener asks about responder's support for opener's suit; Beta, in which opener asks about responder's length and strength in a particular suit; Gamma which asks about trump honors; Delta, which asks about length and strength in a specific suit after a notrump bid or STAYMAN response. See SUPER PRECISION ASKING BIDS.

SUPER PRECISION ASKING BID. Any of a number of types of asking bids in the SUPER PRECISION system as played by Giorgio Belladonna and Benito Garozzo, used by the 1♣ opener to ask a variety of questions, such as trump suit quality, high card or distributional controls, and responder's support for opener's suit.

Alpha Support Asking Bids. After a positive response in a suit, a new suit bid by opener asks about responder's support for opener's suit and his overall controls. Support is defined as Q-x-x or better. A hand with 0-2 controls is considered minimum, four or more controls is maximum, and three controls can be considered in either category. The responses are in five steps:

1st step	no support, minimum
2nd step	no support, maximum
3rd step	support, minimum
4th step	support, maximum
5th step	four cards, maximum

Further definition of responder's support may follow.

Beta Suit Asking Bids. After a negative 1♦ response to 1♣, a jump to 2♥ or 2♠ by opener is a Roman-style asking bid inquiring about responder's strength and length in that suit. The responses are the first eight steps set out in ROMAN ASKING BIDS. See also Delta Suit Asking Bids below.

Gamma Trump Asking Bids. Initiated by the 1♣ opener's single raise of responder's positive suit response.

The responses show trump quality and length as set forth in PRECISION ASKING BIDS. Delayed trump asking bids are also available.

Delta Suit Asking Bids. After a positive response in notrump, a jump in a suit by opener is used to determine the number of cards and honors held by responder in that suit. The responses are: 1st step, no honors, doubleton or tripleton; 2nd step, doubleton honor; 3rd step tripleton honor; 4th step, four headed by an honor; 5th step, two honors doubleton or tripleton; 6th step four headed by two honors.

Control Asking Bids. After a suit fit has been established, a direct bid of 4♣ is control asking. If cuebidding has begun, 4♣ is a cuebid. There is one exception: if responder's first bid suit was clubs, then 4♦ is the control asking bid. Responses are in steps, with the first step showing none or one. See PRECISION ASKING BIDS. However, it may be agreed to vary the first step according to responder's previously shown strength.

Special Suit Asking Bids. After a Control Asking Bid, a new suit by opener asks responder to show his length and strength in the new suit as follows:

1st step, void or singleton; 2nd step, doubleton; 3rd step, tripleton; 4th step, one of top three honors, any length; 5th step, two of top three honors, any length; 6th step, three top honors, any length.

SUPER SWISS. An expansion of the SWISS CON-VENTION recommended by Hugh W. Kelsey that allows responder to make a forcing raise of opener's major suit while announcing immediately whether he has a singleton, a void, or neither, showing whether he has good controls. Responder bids one of four steps, the first step being the bid next above a single jump raise (3♠ over 1♥, 3NT over 1♠):

1st step, void (unidentified) ; 2nd step, singleton (unidentified); 3rd step, two or three aces, denies a singleton or void; 4th step, fewer than two aces, denies a singleton or void.

After responder has shown a singleton or void, opener makes the cheapest bid to ask where responder's shortness lies. After the response, opener will usually be able to use Blackwood to ask about aces.

For alternative methods see UNBALANCED SWISS RAISE, VALUE SWISS RAISE.

SUPERFLAGS. Devised by Eric Kokish, this is a method of transfer breaks over 2NT to describe various sorts of strong side suits to enable responder to gauge the degree of slam potential once a fit has been established. The general principle is that opener will complete the transfer with fewer than four cards in support of partner. With four-card support and good controls on otherwise unremarkable hands, opener will jump to four of the major (the control superflag). However, with hands with a decent or a very good side suit, opener can describe his hand precisely.

A very good side suit (a concentration superflag) is one that will play for four or more tricks facing any honor in partner's hand, so the bid essentially requires a good five-card suit or a four-card suit to three of the top four cards. With such a holding opener 'bids' his suit directly. If opener has support together with a good four-card suit (defined as being two of the top three honors at least) he makes an artificial bid (the general superflag), allowing responder to clarify his hand type. Thus over 2NT - 3♥:

3♠, normal; 3NT, fit plus unspecified good suit (responder can relay with 4♣ to find out where the suit is, or retransfer with 4♥ to play 4♠ the right way up, or bid 4♠ as a slam-invitation based on high cards); 4♣, very good suit in clubs; 4♦, very good suit in diamonds; 4♥, very good suit in hearts; 4♠, transfer break meeting none of the above requirements. After all transfer breaks responder can retransfer at the four-level to play four of the major the right way up, or he can bid four of the major as a slam invitation relating to whether his partner is minimum or maximum.

SUPERSTITION. Common as regards cards ever since games were first played. Some persons have the reputation of being good or bad cardholders, but if you collate records on a series of several hundred hands held, you will find that the point-count holdings over the course will average about 10 points.

Numerous superstitions occur at or apply to bridge games, such as shuffling the cards in a certain way, or positioning the deck after the cut, or using a certain pencil for scoring but for no other purpose, or getting up from one's seat and walking around one's chair or around the entire table "for luck" after a bad hand or a bad run of cards. A common superstition involves choices of seats or decks of cards after the cut for partners. Other players believe their luck will desert them if attention is drawn to it by calling them "lucky" or "the big winner," and so on, ad infinitum.

SUPER-UNUSUAL NOTRUMP. Popularized by Marty Bergen, the idea is based on the fact that when the opponents open and raise a suit it can be awkward to act with certain two-suiters. The problem is especially thorny over a sequence like 1♠-2♠, with a moderate hand with hearts and a minor a player will not want to use a Michaels Cuebid and drive to the four-level, nor would he want to bid one suit and risk losing a far better fit in the other suit. Therefore the idea is that a bid of 2NT shows an unspecified two-suiter rather than the minors.

SUPPORT. Verb: to raise. Noun: (1) a raise; (2) whatever strength partner has in support of one's bid. See TRUMP SUPPORT.

SUPPORT DOUBLE. A method invented by Eric Rodwell that enables the opening bidder to clarify more precisely the degree of support for partner's suit in a competitive auction. If partner responds in a suit to the opening bid and the next player overcalls or doubles, the support double comes into play as long as the overcall does not raise the level above two of responder's suit. If opener raises responder's suit, he is showing at least four-card support. If he doubles or redoubles, he is showing precisely three-card support for partner's major. When opener passes, rebids his suit or bids another suit at his second turn, the implication is strong that (1) he does not have three or more cards in partner's suit, or (2) he will show support later. Partnerships using support doubles lose the option of doubling the opponent's overcall for penalties.

Examples of the support double:

(a) 1♣   1♥   1♠   2♥
    Dbl
(b) 1♣   Pass   1♥   2♦
    Dbl

(c) 1♣	Pass	1♥	Dbl
Redbl			
(d) 1♣	Pass	1♥	2♦
2♥			
(e) 1♣	Pass	1♥	Dbl
2♥			
(f) 1♦	Pass	1♥	1♠
2♣			
(g) 1♦	Pass	1♥	1♠
Pass			
(h) 1♥	Pass	1♠	2♣
2♥			

Opener is showing precisely three-card support for partner's heart suit in the first three examples by using the support double or redouble. In (d) and (e) he is guaranteeing at least four-card support for partner's suit. In (f), (g) and (h), the primary message is that opener has fewer than three cards in partner's suit because he has (f) bid a new suit, (g) passed, and (h) rebid his suit.

The support double can be used even when the overcall is in notrump.

1♣	Pass	1♠	1NT
Dbl			

The double can be for penalties by agreement, but it probably is better to use it as a support double since there are few times when opener can double for penalties in such a sequence.

Even playing support doubles, many players use the double for a different purpose in this sequence:

1♣	Pass	1♦	1♠
Dbl			

By agreement this double can be used to show four hearts even if the partnership is playing support doubles.

SUPPRESSING THE BID ACE. Ace-asking conventions such as BLACKWOOD are occasionally used when the responding hand is already known to have a particular ace. The holder may have made a cuebid or shown a solid suit. In such cases the partnership should agree whether the ace already identified should be shown when responding to the conventional bid. Similar questions arise when the partnership has used a VOID-SHOWING BID. It is preferable to agree that the ace of a suit in which partner is known to be void should not be shown. Lacking any agreement, however, the previous bidding should be disregarded and the number of aces shown in the normal way. See EXCLUSION BLACKWOOD.

SURE TRICK. A trick that a player must win. For example: the ace of trumps, the guarded king of trumps when it is behind the ace, the ace of a suit you intend to lead against notrump. The lead of an ace against a suit contract, even though it be from a short suit not mentioned in the bidding, is not necessarily a sure trick, as declarer or dummy may be void. See HONOR TRICK, QUICK TRICK. The term is also used by George Coffin to describe single-dummy problems in which correct play will ensure the making of a specific number of tricks.

SURPLUS CARDS. A card in excess of 13 in a bridge hand before the play begins, or a card in excess of the number of tricks remaining to be played after play has commenced. See LAWS (Laws 12, 67), LAWS OF DUPLICATE (Laws 13, 67). See MISSING CARD.

SURROUND, SURROUNDING DEFENSE. See SANDWICH DEFENSE., SURROUNDING PLAY.

SURROUNDING PLAY. (Also called a SURROUNDING DEFENSE.) A group of defensive suit combination plays calling for the play of the second-highest card from particular broken holdings.

North
J x x

East
A Q 10

North
10 x x

East
A J 9 or K J 9

North
9 x x

East
K 10 8 or Q 10 8

In each case dummy's highest card is "sandwiched" by the second and third cards held by East. East must lead his second card, the top of the sandwich, to neutralize dummy's card. The importance of the play can be seen by putting appropriate combinations in declarer's hand: in (1) K-x-x; in (2) Q-x-x (or A-Q-x), in (3) A-J-x.

The same plays must be made if these positions are turned 180 degrees, with the lead in the West hand and the card to be sandwiched hidden. In such cases the play is less obvious.

For a similar play by the declarer, see BACKWARD FINESSE.

SUSPENSION. See DISCIPLINARY CODE; EXCLUSION.

SWIFT, Jonathan (1667-1745), author of Gulliver's Travels. His comment on luck: "I must complain the cards are ill-shuffled til I have a good hand."

SWINDLE, SWINDLING. Legitimate methods of attempting to get better than deserved results are discussed under DECEPTIVE PLAY, FALSECARDING, LEAD-INHIBITING BID, and PSYCHIC BIDDING. Also see CHEATING and CHEATING ACCUSATIONS.

SWINE (Sebesfi-Woods-1-Notrump-Escape). Developed in Australia. If 1NT is doubled, pass forces opener to redouble. Then responder may pass for penalties or bid the cheaper of touching suits. With a weak single-suited hand responder redoubles, requiring a 2♣ bid. A direct 2♣ shows clubs and hearts, 2♦ shows diamonds and spades. Direct 2♥ and 2♠ show moderate values; direct 2NT is strong and unbalanced.

SWING. (1)The difference between the actual score made on a deal and "what might have been" were the bidding, play or defense different. Thus if poor dummy play by declarer results in down one on a vulnerable 6♠ contract, the swing is said to be 1,530 points. (2)The term frequently used in team matches to name the actual gain or loss on a single hand. The term may be in total points or in IMPs. If North-South of a team make 3♠ for 140 points and their teammates defeat 4♠ by 50 points, the swing is 190 points or 5 IMPs. See SWING HAND.

SWING HAND. A term used to denote a hand on which a successful or unsuccessful result by a partnership produces a very decisive change in overall results of a rubber or a match. Consider this hand from a European championship:

Vul: N-S	♠ Q 5 3		
Dlr: South	♥ A Q J		
	♦ K		
	♣ A Q J 9 4 3		

♠ A 7 4		♠ K 10 9
♥ 10 8 5 2		♥ K 9 7 6 4 3
♦ 10 8 7 3		♦ 4
♣ 6 5		♣ 10 8 2

	♠ J 8 6 2
	♥ —
	♦ A Q J 9 6 5 2
	♣ K 7

West	North	East	South
			1♦
Pass	3♣	3♥	4♦
4♥	4NT	6♥	Pass
Pass	6NT	Pass	7♦
Dbl	7NT	Dbl	Pass
Pass	Redbl	All Pass	

On the bidding above, East led a diamond, and North-South were plus 2,930 points. In the other room, North-South reached a contract of 6♣, down one, for a score of -100, a swing of more than 3,000 points on a single hand. See PENALTY.

SWISH. A colloquialism indicating that a bid is followed by three passes. A similar term is FLOAT.

SWISS CONVENTION. A response of four in a minor suit to an opening of one in a major suit shows a standard forcing raise to the three-level. This is a strength-showing substitute used by players employing limit jump raises. (3NT is sometimes used for the same purpose, for example in KAPLAN-SHEINWOLD) . The usual high-card strength would be 13-15.

	♠ A Q x x
	♥ K J x x
	♦ A x x
	♣ x x

Over 1♥ or 1♠, the response is 4♣ or 4♦ to show a hand too strong in high cards to raise directly to game. It also suggests a relatively balanced hand because responder would bid a side suit and raise to game on the second round with a two-suiter. The distinction between 4♣ and 4♦ is a matter of partnership agreement, but the trend is toward using 4♣ as the more forward-going bid. When 4♣ and 4♦ are the only forcing raises employed, one of the following treatments is usual:

(1) Trump quality: 4♣ shows (and 4♦ denies) four trumps headed by at least two of the top three honors, or five or more trumps headed by at least the ace or king.

(2) Controls: 4♣ shows (and 4♦ denies) three aces, or two aces and the king of trumps.

(3) Controls or Trumps: 4♣ emphasizes good controls, and 4♦ emphasizes strong trumps. Several methods have been developed which combine the jumps to four of a minor with other jump responses in order to allow for a finer distinction among types of strong raises. See CONGLOMERATE MAJOR RAISES, FRUIT-MACHINE SWISS, SINGLETON SWISS, SUPER SWISS, UNBALANCED SWISS RAISE, VALUE SWISS RAISES.

For other conventional uses of four of a minor in response to one of a major, see ASKING BID, FRAGMENT BID, SPLINTER BID and VOID-SHOWING BID.

SWISS MOVEMENT. A partial round-robin movement similar to the method used for many years in major chess tournaments when insufficient time is available for a complete round-robin. It was first used for chess in Switzerland; hence the name.

The basic feature of a Swiss movement is that after the first round, winning teams (or pairs) are pitted against each other for the second round, and losers face each other. For each succeeding round, new pairings are made on the basis of the records of the matched teams (or pairs) with the added proviso that no two teams (or pairs) may play a second match against each other. Scoring is usually by international matchpoints, although BOARD-A-MATCH and HYBRID SCORING are feasible.

Team events: Although many attempts at adapting the Swiss method to team contests had been made in the past, it was not until 1967 when John Hamilton and Marc Low developed the present method that Swiss team contests became popluar. The method was first tried and proved successful at a Cincinnati Sectional. The idea caught on quickly throughout the ACBL and resulted in a spectacular increase in team attendance at sectional and regional tournaments, more than doubling the size of the previous board-a-match team events in many cases. The first North American Swiss team was held at the 1970 Spring North American Championships in Portland OR.

The team event is divided into a series of short, IMP-scored matches. Pairings for the first round are random. Pairings for each succeeding round are determined by the won-loss or the Victory Point records of the teams. Since sufficient matches must be scheduled to produce a significant won-loss record, a minimum of two sessions of play usually is required. When possible, more matches are scheduled than needed to reduce the field to one undefeated team so that a team is not necessarily eliminated from a chance to win the event by a single loss.

An odd number of entries creates difficulties, but can be handled in various ways. The most common are short round-robins, lasting as long as one regular match, in which each winning team is given credit for half a match. The other common method is a three-team round-robin playing the full number of boards, so that a round lasts as long as two full matches. In either case, there is no comparison of scores until the round-robin is completed.

An alternate method of scoring Swiss Teams is to convert IMP results into Victory Points. Pairings are then based on Victory Point totals, not wins and losses. The team with the most Victory Points is declared the winner.

Board-a-match provides a third method of scoring. Using this method, a team scores a point for each board on which they score better than their opponents and half a point for each board they tie.

In recent years a second method of pairing has evolved, aimed at speeding up the game by cutting down the time between rounds. Pairings for the first and second rounds are assigned at the start of the game. The results of the first round determine the pairing for the third round, the standings after two matches determine the pairings for the fourth round, etc. If there is a lunch or dinner break, pairings for the following round are based on the standings at the time of the break. The pairings for the last round, and sometimes for the last two, are based on the present standings.

Pair events: The ACBL introduced Swiss pair contests in 1970. As in the team event, the pairs play a series of short matches against each other, with each board IMPed against a computed average for the field. Pairings may be based on wins and losses or on VICTORY POINTS. Some of the difficulties encountered are:

(1) the boards must be duplicated for each round and

(2) since pair events attract larger fields than team contests, it may be difficult to determine an overall winner in two sessions.

SWISS PAIRS. Similar to Swiss Teams. After each short match pairs face those with similar scores.

SWISS TEAMS. For many years Swiss Teams has been the most popular form of team event, but in recent years it is being overtaken by KNOCKOUT TEAMS. A Swiss event is a partial ROUND-ROBIN set up in such a way that winners play winners and losers play losers. It is based on the Swiss concept that governs play in most chess tournaments. After each round, the game directors sort the team records and set up new matches between teams of approximately equal records. Sometimes matches are set from the previous round's results to speed up the game. In general, teams are not permitted to play against each other more than once. The length of matches is determined by the size of the field and the number of sessions. The most common match length is seven boards, but five, six, eight and nine are not uncommon.

At the end of a match, the East-West pair return to their home table where they compare scores with their teammates. The event usually is scored on INTERNA-TIONAL MATCHPOINTS (IMPs). This is a special conversion system designed to translate totals into a scoring system that gives fairer comparisons. To figure the score, the algebraic difference is taken on each board and then translated into IMPs. When all the boards have been scored, the pluses and minuses are added. If the total is a plus, that team is the winner; if the total is a minus, that team is a loser.

There are three different ways to compute the final score of a match. See BOARD-A-MATCH SWISS TEAMS, VICTORY POINT SWISS TEAMS and WIN-LOSS SWISS TEAMS.

Sometimes the field for a Swiss teams is very small. Quite often in such a situation the game is changed into a full round-robin. Each team plays every other team in a short match. The winner is determined in the same manner as in a Swiss teams. The same types of scoring used in Swiss teams are used in a round-robin event.

SWISS TEAMS, NORTH AMERICAN CHAM-PIONSHIP. See Appendix I.

SWITCH. See SHIFT and ARROW SWITCH.

SWORDS. One of the suits in early PLAYING CARDS. Still used in the trappola deck (see SUIT).

SYMMETRIC RELAY. A modern relay system developed by a group of New Zealand players. It was first described by Roy Kerr and first played successfully in international championships by Paul Marston and Malcolm Sims. A major difference between Symmetric and the ULTIMATE CLUB is that almost all Symmetric responses to the strong club opening, other than the

1 ♦ negative, are natural. (This makes the system somewhat more acceptable to tournament committees and directors.) The responder describes his distribution, with sequences which usually end at the three-level. The opener can then relay to find the number of controls and the location of high cards. If the response is a negative 1 ♦ a relay of 1 ♥ asks responder to use the normal descriptive sequences but two steps higher than they would otherwise be. The general structure is based on five-card major openings (as opposed to Ultimate, which uses four-card majors.) In response to 1 ♦, 1 ♥ and 1 ♠, 1NT is used as a strong relay.

These relays have been developed by Alan Truscott for use after other opening bids, as follows:

(1) After 1 ♦, 1 ♥ or 1 ♠, 1NT starts similar relays. 1 ♠-1NT-2 ♥ shows four hearts and long spades. 1 ♥-1NT-2 ♥ shows four spades and long hearts. 1 ♦-1NT-2 ♦ shows four spades unless followed by 2 ♠, which shows three suits with a singleton. 1 ♦-1NT-3 ♦, directly or indirectly, shows three suits with a void.

(2) 1NT is 12-15, may be 2-4-2-5 or 4-2-2-5, with 2 ♦ relays described under TWO-WAY STAYMAN.

(3) 2 ♣ is a 6-card suit. 2 ♦ relay may lead to: 2 ♥-2 ♠ natural; 2NT balanced, with 3 ♦ relay; 3 ♣ unbalanced minimum; 3 ♥-3 ♠-3NT unbalanced maximum with high, middle, low singleton. Higher shows void, similarly.

(4) 2 ♦ shows short diamonds, 2NT relay.

(5) 2 ♥ shows both majors, 2NT relay.

(6) 2 ♠ is a weak two-bid. See RELAYS OVER WEAK TWO-BIDS.

(7) 2NT is 10-13 HCP with both minors, with 3 ♥ relay.

SYMMETRY. See LAW OF SYMMETRY.

SYNDICATED ARTICLES. See BRIDGE COLUMNS.

SYSTEM FIX. A bad result caused by one's own bidding methods.

SYSTEM ON (or system off). An agreement to apply (or not to apply) certain artificial methods in slightly changed circumstances. The commonest example occurs after a 1NT overcall. The partnership may agree to respond exactly as if the opening bid had been 1NT.

SYSTEM. See BIDDING SYSTEM.

T

TAB. See ROMEX SYSTEM.

TABLE. Four players, two pairs, or one team, in duplicate play, for individual, pair, and team movements suitable to a particular number of tables. See TWO, THREE, FOUR, etc., to FIFTEEN TABLES. The table most frequently used for bridge is a folding square table, about 30 inches on a side, and from 26 to 27 inches in height. The accoutrements should include two scorepads, two decks of bridge cards, two sharp pencils, ashtrays, coasters and four chairs.

Other meanings are:
  (1) The dummy. "The lead is on the table."
  (2) To face one's cards, either as dummy or in making a claim.

TABLE CARD. See TABLE GUIDE CARD.

TABLE FEEL. See TABLE PRESENCE.

TABLE GUIDE CARD. A large card placed under the boards in the center of a table, containing instructions for the players. See GUIDE CARD.

TABLE MANNERS. Bridge is a social game, and good manners at the bridge table are as necessary for full enjoyment of the game as in any other form of sociability. See ETIQUETTE, PROPRIETIES.

TABLE NUMBERS. Rectangular, large cards in the center of the table identifying the section and the numbers of the table. Sections are distinguished by the color of the table card as well as by letter.

TABLE PRESENCE. One of the features that enable a good bridge player is become an expert is the undefinable something that is referred to as table presence. It is a combination of INSTINCT; the drawing of correct inferences from any departure from RHYTHM by the opponents; the exercise of DISCIPLINE in bidding; the ability to coax maximum performance from partner, and the ability to make the opponents feel that they are facing a player of a higher order. Includes TABLE FEEL and also a poised demeanor that does not give clues.

TABLE SPACING. The arrangement of tables for a tournament. For comfortable play tables should be spaced with nine-foot (2.7 meters) centers. When the available space does not permit the ideal arrangement, reduction to eight feet (2.44 meters) between centers is practicable. The minimum spacing permitting any degree of comfort is a trifle over seven feet (2.14 meters) between centers in a row. When the rows cannot be spaced at least eight feet apart, tables can be staggered in adjoining rows. If possible, the setup of tables within the section should put the last table in the section near the first so that boards and players have a minimum of movement. This can be done with a hairpin arrangement, utilizing two rows of seven, eight or nine tables.

TABLES, MATHEMATICAL. See MATHEMATICAL TABLES .

TACTICS. Various maneuvers in the play of the hand, bidding nuances and choices of action, taking into consideration the methods of scoring, quality of the competition and conditions of contests.

TAKEOUT. A bid at a denomination other than one previously named by partner, as distinguished from a raise. See JUMP SHIFT and RESPONSE.

TAKEOUT DOUBLE. The use of a low-level double in certain circumstances as a request to partner to bid an unbid suit. This is a "natural" convention because the possibility of a penalty double of an opening suit bid. is so low. A player with great strength in the opponent's suit prefers to lie in wait (see TRAP PASS). The idea of doubling for a takeout appears to have been devised independently by Major Charles Patton in New York and Bryant McCampbell in St. Louis in 1912-13 and probably by others. For the problems involved in distinguishing a takeout double from a penalty double, see DOUBLE. By far the most common takeout double occurs when it immediately follows an opening bid of one in a suit. The doubler normally indicates a hand worth an opening bid with at least three-card support for all unbid suits. However, the respective vulnerability and the rank of the opener's suit may play a part in the decision.

  ♠ A Q x x
  ♥ x
  ♦ K x x
  ♣ J 10 x x x

At favorable vulnerability, a double of 1♥ could be profitable. If the doubler's partner can fit spades, a cheap save in 4♠ over 4♥ is likely to materialize. A player who doubles a major-suit opening tends to hold four cards in the unbid major, and this may be a factor in deciding to double. The high-card strength required for the double increases: (a) as the distribution becomes less suitable; (b) if the doubler is vulnerable; (c) if the opener's suit is spades, which will force a response at the two-level.

Experts now tend to make takeout doubles quite freely.

  ♠ Axxx
  ♥ Axxx
  ♦ Qxxx
  ♣ x

With neither side vunerable, the expert consensus in BWS.2000 (60%) was that this would be a minimum double of 1♣. The experts would be slightly more cautious if vunerable, and slightly more cautious with more balanced distribution. With a doubleton in the suit bid, opening values represents a resonable rule of thumb.

The doubler should seldom ignore the requirement of at least three cards in each unbid suit unless his hand contains at least 17 high-card points.

  ♠ 7 5
  ♥ A Q 10 6 4
  ♦ A K 6
  ♣ K Q 4

Over 1♣, 1♦ or 1♠, a double followed by a minimum bid in hearts is appropriate. The hand is too strong for a simple heart overcall.

A takeout double is made with strong hands unsuitable for a 1NT overcall or a strength-showing suit overcall. The maximum for a double was once a hand just short of the requirements for a direct cuebid. However, many pairs have abandoned the direct cuebid as a strength-showing action because opportunities were rare. These pairs use conventional cuebids such as MICHAELS, in which case a takeout double has no upper limit. Most players would double a 1♠ opening, planning to cuebid next, with:

  ♠ A 5
  ♥ A K Q 9 6 2
  ♦ 7
  ♣ A Q J 4

Equal level conversion
There has long been debate about whether in certain circumstances the doubler can continue bidding with minimum values.

♠ x x
♥ A Q x x
♦ A Q J x x
♣ x x

If the opening bid is 1♠, should this hand double and then bid 2♦ after a 2♣ response? Or would this show substantial extra values? The expert consensus in BWS 2001 is that this is acceptable if, and only if, the response is 2♣ and the conversion is to 2♦. So it applies to the hand shown and also to hands containing four spades and diamond length.

Subsequent bidding

For action by the opener's partner, see RESPONSES OVER OPPONENT'S TAKEOUT DOUBLE. The following summarizes possible actions by the doubler's partner if the bidding starts:

1♦   Dbl   Pass   ?

(1) *Minimum suit response* (1♥ or 1♠ or 2♣). A forced response which may have no high-card points. The normal maximum is 8 points, but see (3) following. Responder prefers a major suit to a minor, so 2♣ is more likely to be five cards than four. 1♥ is sometimes bid with a three-card suit because there is no alternative: if responder's only suit is diamonds he has to invent an economical bid. Even 1♠ might be a three-card suit, with 3-2-5-3 distribution for example.

The doubler passes these responses automatically if he has a minimum or near-minimum double. Further action shows that game is still possible in the face of responder's announced weakness. A raise of responder's suit or a bid in a new suit should show at least 17 points in high cards. However, a raise in competition promises only minimal extras. A minimum rebid in notrump is very constructive, suggesting a hand too strong to overcall 1NT (i.e., 18-20 points). In one case responder may make an uneconomical response.

♠ A x x x
♥ K x x x
♦ x x x
♣ x x

After 1♦-Dbl-Pass, 1♠ is a better response than 1♥, as responder can then continue readily to 2♥ if, as is likely, the opponents contest with 2♣ or 2♦.

(2) *1NT response*. Indicates a relatively balanced hand with moderate strength and a stopper in opener's suit. The exact strength is a matter of style, and expert opinions vary. The conservative view is to use the bid for hands with 8-10 or perhaps 11 points, but this sets a problem when responder has a hand such as:

♠ K 9 4
♥ J 7 3
♦ Q 10 6 3
♣ 8 5 3

Many authorities recommend a range of 6-9. (Another factor is the rank of opening bidder's suit. If the opening was 1♣, responder has more options; hence, a 1NT response is more likely to show fair values; if the opening was 1♠, 1NT may be responder's indicated action with 6 points.)

(3) *Jump shift* (2♥, 2♠ or 3♣). Encouraging but not forcing. The high-card strength is likely to be 9-11, but might be eight with a five-card suit. (Playing this as forcing is an obsolete idea.) The jump in a major suit is often a four-card suit: in a minor at least five cards are desirable.

(4) *Cuebid* (2♦). Shows any hand which can guarantee

game but cannot be sure of the final resting place. The bid is totally unrelated to the opener's suit. The modern tendency is to use the cuebid slightly more freely:

♠ A Q x x
♥ K J x x
♦ J x x
♣ x x

Rather than make a nonforcing jump in one of the major suits, and perhaps pick the wrong suit, a possible treatment is to cuebid 2♦, intending to raise either major to the three-level. The doubler then passes with a minimum, because the responder would have bid game himself if he could.

(5) *2NT response*. Shows 11-12 points and at least a single stopper in the opener's suit. The strength will depend slightly on the range adopted for the 1NT response, in (3) preceding. If that is 6-9 the 2NT bid may be made with 10; if 1NT is 8-11, 2NT is likely to be 12.

(6) *3NT response*. Usually a double stopper in the opener's suit and 13-16 points. Alternatively, responder may have a single stopper and a long minor suit which he expects to run with the help of doubler's expected fit. With more than 16 points, responder may suspect that the opener or the doubler has psyched. Responder should proceed more slowly with a cuebid.

(7) *Higher suit responses*. (3♥, 3♠, 4♣, 4♥, 4♠, 5♣). Natural limited bids based on a long suit (usually six cards or longer). Responder expects to make his contract if doubler has a minimum.

(8) *Pass*. Great length and strength in diamonds (see PENALTY PASS).

(9) After action by opener's partner

Action by third hand relieves the doubler's partner of his obligation to bid, but he should still make a "free" response if he has moderate values and can do so at a convenient level. A five-card suit and 5+ points is adequate.

(10) *After a redouble*. A pass denies any opinion about a possible trump suit. (The idea that responder should ignore the redouble and therefore pass for penalty is virtually obsolete. But a few experts play that a pass after a minor-suit opening shows at least five cards in opener's suit. 1♣ or 1♦ redoubled may be the least evil for the doubling side, which may be in trouble otherwise.) Since responder is likely to have little strength — probably fewer than six points — doubler should not construe a suit bid as strength-showing. Responder should usually show a four-card suit if he can do so at the one level, and a five-card suit at the two level. Responder should always bid the cheapest suit if he can, for fear that the doubler may run to a suit he cannot support. A jump response is weak and preemptive.

(11) *After a change of suit by opener's partner*. If responder can bid a suit of his own at the one-level, he should usually do so with five points. He should make the normal encouraging jump with nine. Slightly more is needed to bid at the two-level, but the free two-level response (1♦-Dbl-2♣-2♠) should be made more freely than the jump shift when third hand has passed.

(12) *After a raise by opener's partner*. The opener's partner is trying to shut out the doubler's partner, who must often strain his resources to avoid being shut out. For a treatment of hands which do not offer an obvious bid, see RESPONSIVE DOUBLE.

Other takeout doubles

These can usually be identified by the general rule

that a double of a suit bid below game is for a takeout when partner has not bid. The most important cases are as follows:

(13) *The balancing double.* See BALANCING.

(14) In standard practice, *the double of two suits* (1♣-Pass-1♥-Dbl) may range from a relatively weak distributional two-suiter to a strong, relatively balanced hand. However, when both opponents are bidding and partner is silent, there are obvious dangers in entering the auction. Many tournament players therefore dispense with a natural 1NT overcall in this position (or 2NT if the bidding is at the two-level) and treat a notrump bid as UNUSUAL. This takes care of the distributional two-suited hands, and the double can be reserved for relatively balanced hands, strong in high cards.

If the doubler's partner bids opener's suit (1♣-Pass-1♥-Dbl-Pass-2♣), the expert consensus (BWS 1994) is that the bid is natural.

(15) *The double of a 1NT response* (1♥-Pass-1NT-Dbl). This is one of the few situations in which a double of a notrump bid is for takeout, but the takeout aspect is not very pronounced; partner will pass more often than he will pass any other takeout double. The double may have to be made with a strong balanced hand which would have overcalled 1NT if opportunity had offered.

(16) *The double of a raise* (1♥-Pass-2♥-Dbl). Vulnerability and the rank of opener's suit are important considerations here. At favorable vulnerability a double of 2♥ may be made lightly with suitable distribution because a save in 4♠ seems possible. A double of 2♠ in a similar sequence commits the doubler's side to the three-level, and does not offer such good prospects of a save, so solid values are needed by the doubler. The double of a minor-suit raise emphasizes the major suits and may be made freely. The probability that the doubling side has a fit is increased by the opening side's established fit.

(17) *The double of a suit response to a 1NT opening* (1 NT-Pass-2♥-Dbl). Here again vulnerability and the rank of the suit are important factors. If the double of 2♦ or 2♥ offers the possibility of play at the two-level, a nonvulnerable player may double with as little as 10 points and favorable distribution. He can rely on strength in his partner's hand because the opener's side has announced its intention of stopping at the two-level.

(18) *Doubles of weak two-bids and weak three-bids can be regarded as takeout.* See DEFENSE TO OPENING THREE-BIDS.

(19) When three suits have been bid around the table, a double by fourth-hand needs agreement:

West	North	East	South
1♣	1♥	1♠	Dbl

It makes no sense for this to be penalty, as it would be on general principles since partner has bid. A common agreement is for it be takeout for the fourth suit. In this case the fourth player would have five diamonds and probably some tolerance for hearts. See SNAPDRAGON.

TALLIES. Prepared cards for the recording of results at the end of each round (four deals) in PROGRESSIVE or PARTY BRIDGE. These can be purchased at most gift and stationery stores.

TANK. A colloquialism in the phrase "go into the tank" or "to tank", meaning to fall into a protracted HUDDLE.

TAP. (1) Shortening a hand in trumps by forcing it to (ruff colloquial). See FORCE. (2) The Teacher Accreditation Program used by the Education Depatment of the ACBL.

TAP THE TABLE. (1) Give an informal ALERT. (2) Make an informal PASS. Both practices are undesirable, since they can be confused with each other and create problems.

TARDINESS. Late arrival at rubber bridge games curtails the length of time available for play and is inconsiderate of the host or hostess. At duplicate tournaments far more people may be inconvenienced when the start of a second session is delayed while the director seeks substitutes for no-shows. Purchase of an entry into an event obligates the players to abide by the conditions of play, including reporting on time for all following sessions of the same event. See TIME LIMIT ON RIGHT TO PLAY.

TAROT. The pack of 22 numbered cards without suit signs that were part of the first pack known to be used in Europe; or a pack containing these 22 atouts (atutti, trumps) plus 56 other cards divided into four suits, each with ten SPOT CARDS and four COURT CARDS. Not all packs are alike, but the basic cards were:

0   The fool (Il Pazzo or Il Matto), like a jester (most packs omit the numeral)
1   The juggler (Bagatto), wand or cup in hand, items of legerdermain on the table in front of him
2   The papess (La Papessa), double crowned, seated, book in hand
3   The empress (L'Imperatrice), singly crowned, scepter and shield
4   The emperor (L'Imperator), perhaps Charlemagne, scepter in hand
5   The Pope (Il Papa), crowned, carrying staff, seated before two columns
6   Love (Amore), Cupid aiming a double arrow at two of three persons
7   The chariot (La Carrozza), shows one driver and two horses
8   Justice (La Giustizia), a woman, sword in one hand, scales in other
9   The hermit (L'Eremita), an old man, lantern in right hand
10 Wheel of fortune (La Ruota della Fortuna), a crowned figure with sword above a wheel with one figure going up and another down
11 Force (La Forza), either a man opening the jaws of a lion, or a woman breaking a pillar
12 The hanged man (Il Penduto), suspended upside down by one foot
13 Untitled, picturing Death, a skeleton wielding a scythe over fragments of people
14 Temperance (La Temperanza), an angel pouring water from one jug into another
15 The devil (Il Diavolo), winged, with pitchfork and forked tail, threatening one or more figures
16 The tower (La Torre) being struck by lightning as two men fall
17 The star (La Stella), a nude woman pouring water from two jugs into a stream
18 The moon (La Luna), a profile face, riding over rooftops, with dogs baying below
19 The sun (Il Sole), full-face, shining on two boys in breechcloths
20 The angel (L'Angelo), blowing a trumpet over people rising from the grave
21 The world (Il Mondo), a female in a wreath; an angel, a winged beast, a cow, and a lion are in each corner

The first tarot cards appeared in Italy, probably in the fourteenth century, and the original suits were cups, coins, swords and cudgels: the court cards king, queen, cavalier and knave.

TARTAN TWO-BID. Devised by Hugh Kelsey and Tom Culbertson. 2 ♥ and 2 ♠ are multi openings, with clarification after a relay response. After a 2 ♥ opening and 2 ♠ relay: 2NT is 21-22 balanced; 3 ♣ is hearts and clubs, 3 ♦ is hearts and diamonds, 5-5 distribution with 6-10; 3 ♥ and higher are ACOL TWO-BIDS with hearts. After a 2 ♠ opening and a 2NT relay, 3 ♠ and higher shows an Acol Two, lower bids show the suits bid, 5-5 with 6-10. 2 ♦ may be ROMAN TWO DIAMONDS, a strong three-suiter. See TWO-WAY TWO-BIDS.

TAXES ON PLAYING CARDS. The first tax on playing cards in the United States was levied in 1862 to raise money for the Civil War. The tax varied from 1 to 15 cents (or 15% of the cost, whichever was greater), until 1866 when it became 6 cents per pack. This tax was repealed in 1883 and not reinstated until the depression of Cleveland's second administration, when a 2-cents-a-pack tax was imposed under the Act of August 27, 1894. Since that time it has been retained by the Federal Government as a constant source of revenue. The levy remained constant until the necessity of increased revenue following World War I caused an increase in 1920 to 8 cents a pack, increased to 10 cents in 1925, and to 13 cents in 1961. Revenues exceeded $5 million dollars in 1929, and more than $8 million in 1962. This tax was lifted on July 1, 1965. The first tax levied on playing cards, so far as the records show, was imposed in England in the reign of James I (1615).

TEACHING IN BRIDGE. The first teacher of games in the bridge family was also one of the most successful. The ladies of good family to whom EDMUND HOYLE taught whist were charged at the rate of one guinea an hour, equivalent to at least $100 an hour in modern terms. His celebrated *Short Treatise*, published in 1743, which became a best-seller for more than a century, was intended as a textbook for his students.

The first professional teacher of whist in America was Miss Kate Wheelock, who began teaching in Milwaukee in 1886. She achieved immediate success, touring the continent to lecture in all the principal cities. The whistograph which she invented for use in her classes was the forerunner of the VUGRAPH used by the ACBL in modern times. She was the first woman to be made an associate member of the American Whist League, and Cavendish called her, "The Whist Queen."

Whist teaching was a highly suitable occupation for ladies of some status and education who needed to supplement their incomes, and many others followed Miss Wheelock's example.

The first prominent male teacher was Charles Stuart Street of New York City, who began in 1890. The most successful teacher of BRIDGE WHIST and AUCTION BRIDGE was Joseph B. Elwell. Among his most prominent successors was Josephine Culbertson.

In the Twenties Milton Work and Wilbur Whitehead organized conventions for teachers, issuing certificates to those who had completed courses. A similar procedure was followed later by Ely Culbertson, and later still by Charles Goren, who was one of the highest-paid teach-

ers of all time before he decided to concentrate on writing. The AMERICAN BRIDGE TEACHERS ASSOCIATION (ABTA), founded in 1957, holds an annual convention immediately preceding the ACBL's Summer North American Bridge Championships.

Many persons turned to bridge teaching as a temporary occupation during the Depression years, and at its peak the membership of the Culbertson National Studios totaled some 6,000. The number of bridge teachers dwindled markedly when prosperity returned, but increased again in the postwar years, particularly after Goren's point-count methods gained general currency.

In the Sixties and Seventies, the number of teachers continued to grow. Their ranks included many players of the highest quality. These teachers popularized the playing lesson for students with tournament ambitions. ABTA activities for bridge teachers flourished and certification by this organization was thought by many to be a prerequisite for professional bridge teachers.

In the late Eighties, ACBL contracted with Audrey Grant to write a series of beginning bridge textbooks and teacher manuals. Through a program known as the TAP, new bridge teachers were recruited and taught to teach bridge effectively using the ACBL materials. These teachers became known as ACCREDITED TEACHERS and numbered more than 4,500 by the mid-Nineties. See also ACBL TEACHING SERIES, AUTOBRIDGE, LESSON HANDS and E-Z DEAL CARDS.

In Europe, as in the United States, major steps have been taken to put major teaching programs to work. According to José Damiani, president of the World Bridge Federation, the French Bridge Federation is among the leaders in bridge education. Damiani wrote as follows in the *European Bridge League Review*: "To make a success of such a challenge, a definite consistency between the mini-bridge taught to students and a complete teaching system of training for instructors was needed. Rigorous methods were used to obtain the magnificent results achieved by the French Bridge Federation."

In the Netherlands, a similar approach has produced excellent results. A high percentage of the population of the Netherlands play bridge as a result of the Dutch teaching program.

Some years ago, bridge leaders in Poland succeeded in setting up a school championship with more than 3000 finalists.

Many other countries have outstanding teaching programs, and bridge is thriving in those countries — New Zealand, Norway, Denmark, Italy, Iceland, Sweden and Australia to name a few.

TEAM. Four, five or six players competing as a unit in bridge tournaments.

TEAM GAME. This type of event has become very popular since the advent of bracketed knockout teams. A team can consist of four, five or six players, but only four team members ever play at the same time. Here is how a team game works. Two members of one team, playing as a partnership, sit North-South at one table. Two other members of the same team, also playing as a partnership, sit East-West at a different table. The two pairs from the opposing team fill the empty spots at the two tables. During the course of a match, exactly the same boards are played at both tables. Since results are achieved at both tables on exactly the same boards, a

comparison of results is possible. Scoring is done by comparing the results, but the methods of scoring vary according to the type of team game being played.

The three basic types of team games are Swiss, knockout and board-a-match. A fourth type, a round-robin teams, also is sometimes held. A round-robin, however, really is a special case of Swiss teams.

Swiss Teams. For many years Swiss Teams was the most popular form of team event, but in recent years it has been overtaken by Knockout Teams. A Swiss event is a partial round-robin set up in such a way that winners play winners and losers play losers. It is based on the Swiss concept that governs play in most chess tournaments. After each round, the game directors sort the team records and set up new matches between teams with approximately equal records. In general, teams are not permitted to play against each other more than once. The length of matches is determined by the size of the field and the number of sessions. The most common match length is seven boards, but five, six, eight and nine are not uncommon.

At the end of a match, the East-West pair return to their home table where they compare their scores with their teammates. Such events usually are scored on INTERNATIONAL MATCHPOINTS (IMPs). This is a special conversion system designed to translate totals into a scoring system that offers fairer comparisons. The IMP scale usually is printed on whatever convention card is being used. To figure the score, the algebraic difference is taken on each board and then translated into IMPs. When all the boards have been scored, the pluses and minuses are added. If the total is a plus, that team is the winner; if the total is a minus, that team is a loser. There are three different ways to compute the final score of a match. See also BOARD-A-MATCH SWISS TEAMS, SPEEDBALL SWISS TEAMS, VICTORY POINT SWISS TEAMS, WIN-LOSS SWISS TEAMS, ZIP SWISS TEAMS.

Sometimes the field for a Swiss teams is very small. Quite often in such a situation the game is changed into a full ROUND-ROBIN TEAMS event. Each team plays every other team in a short match. The winner is determined in the same manner as in a Swiss teams. The same types of scoring used in Swiss teams are used in a round-robin event.

Knockout Teams. The name of this event is most apropos — the winners advance to the next round and the losers are knocked out of the competition. There are many kinds of knockout events, but basically they come down to this — two teams face each other in head-to-head competition, and only one survives. There are variations on this theme, but the above explanation fits the vast majority of knockout situations.

The setup is similar to Swiss Teams in that two members of one team sit North-South at one table and the other two sit East-West at a different table. The opposition team fills the other four seats at the two tables.

Knockout matches usually are much longer than Swiss matches — 24 boards is common but sometimes there are as many as 64 — even more in major events such as world championships. After the match is finished, the East-West pairs return to their home table to compare scores. Once again the International Matchpoint Scale is used, just as in Swiss Teams. The team with the greater number of IMPs is the winner and advances to play in the next round. The losers are no longer in the event

unless the event is a DOUBLE ELIMINATION KNOCKOUT TEAMS.

Specific conditions of contest may vary. Each team has a responsibility to be aware of the conditions and to conform accordingly. See also BRACKETED KNOCKOUT TEAMS, COMPACT KNOCKOUT TEAMS, HANDICAP KNOCKOUT TEAMS, MINI-KNOCKOUT TEAMS, MIXED TEAMS, OPEN TEAMS, RANDOM DRAW KNOCKOUT TEAMS, ZIP KNOCKOUT TEAMS.

Board-a-Match Teams. Many experts consider this to be the toughest type of event in tournament bridge, which may account for its lack of popularity. A team plays a small number of boards against one opponent — usually two, three or four — then moves on to take on another opponent. The movement is set up in such a way that a team always plays any given board against two opposition pairs of the same team. Often the movement is similar to the Mitchell movement used in pair games, but with some major differences that are always explained by the tournament director. At the end of a session, the members of a team gather to compare scores. Each board is scored separately as a win, a tie or a loss.

The reason why the game is so tough is that *every* board is equally important. Some boards in Swiss and knockout events are not all that important — very little may be at stake. But every board in a board-a-match game is worth one full matchpoint, and a high degree of concentration is necessary throughout every board of a session.

TEAMMATES. A term applied to the other members of a team of four (five or six). During the play of an event, the term is usually used to refer to the other pair, rather than including one's partner in the term.

TEAM-OF-EIGHT MATCH. A four-table team contest in which each team has eight active players.

TEAM-OF-FOUR MOVEMENTS FOR KNOCKOUT TEAMS. Usually knockout matches are head-to-head affairs, with the winner advancing to the next round and the loser eliminated. However, special arrangements have to be made when the number of teams entered is not a power of 2.

Three-team matches have become quite common, with two outcomes possible. If the purpose is to eliminate one of the three, then the two with the better records advance. If each team wins one match, then the QUOTIENT method is used to determine which teams advance. If the purpose is to eliminate two of the three, then only the team with the best record advances. Once again the quotient method is used if each team wins one match. Three-way matches provide a good way to reduce the field to a power of 2. For instance, if the field consists of 26 teams, the game could be set up with four head-to-head matches and six three-ways, with the top two advancing to the next round. The three-ways would provide 12 teams and the head-to-heads four — a total of 16, which is a power of 2.

Quotient works as follows: each team adds ALL its IMPS for and against, then divides the IMPS won by the IMPS lost. This provides the quotient with which to compare with the other teams.

Frequently when large fields enter a knockout event, the teams are bracketed. The top 16 teams, usually determined by masterpoints but sometimes by other seed-

ing methods, are placed in the first bracket, the next 16 in the second, etc.

Head-to-head matches usually are staged in halves. In a 28-deal match, boards 1-7 are given to one table and boards 8-14 to the other. When these boards are finished, the two tables exchange boards. After both tables finish 14 boards, the teams compare scores. Then they return to the tables to play boards 15-28 in the same fashion.

In major matches, the boards often are preduplicated, with one full set for each table. This means there is no board exchange.

Three-way matches are somewhat more complicated. In a 28-board session, boards 1-7 are given to Table 1, boards 8-14 to Table 2 and boards 15-21 to Table 3. Upon completion of these boards, the East-West pairs bring the boards just played to their home table, then proceed to the table where they have not played. After 14 boards have been completed, the teams compare. They will have played seven boards against each of the other two teams. The same method is used for the second half, and at the end of the session each team will have 14-board match results against each of the other teams.

TEAM-OF-FOUR MOVEMENTS FOR SWISS TEAMS. The pairings for the first round usually are random. Various methods are used for subsequent pairings. The basic idea, however, is to set up matches between teams with approximately equal records.

The most commonly used method works like this. All the results are tabulated at the close of each round. Pairings are then made based on team records, with the proviso that no team may play another a second time. This method provides the fairest pairings, but its major disadvantage is the time problem – in general, pairings cannot be made until just about all the results are tabulated.

Because of this factor, pairings for an upcoming round are sometimes based on the records for one less than the number of rounds played. For the second round, the pairings again would be random since the teams do not yet have a record. For the third round, the pairings would be made based on the results from the first round. For the fourth round, the pairings would be based on the results of the first two rounds, etc. If there is a break during the event, up-to-date pairings can be made since the tournament staff would have the necessary time.

Sometimes all pairings are done two at a time. The first two pairings are random. The pairings for the third and fourth rounds are made based on the first-round results, etc.

TEAM OLYMPIAD. See WORLD TEAM OLYMPIAD. For results see Appendix V.

TEAM-OF-TWO PAIRS. An event in which both of a team's two pairs sit in the same direction in two different sections. Both pairs of the opposing team sit in the opposite direction. Everyone plays a session of matchpoint duplicate — just like a pair game.

Of each team's two results on every board, only the better of the two is entered to determine the matchpoint score. Naturally, the score not used for your team is the "better" score for your opponent. This means it is possible to get a cold bottom on a board but still score a top because of your teammates' result on the same deal.

Strategy is necessary to maximize potential matchpoints. A team should not play or defend the same

contract or make the same play at both tables. Here are some ways that teams use to maximize their results.

Bidding: Weak notrump at one table, strong at the other. Science at one table, natural at the other. Strong two-bids at one table, weak two-bids at the other. Sound opening bids at one table, open all 11-pointers at the other. Five-card major style at one table, four-card major style at the other.

Play: Agree in advance that, with a two-way guess for a queen, one pair always takes it one direction while the other takes it in the opposite direction. One pair should go all out for overtricks, the other should play safe for the contract. One pair should play for even splits, the other for unusual distributions.

TEAM-OF-TWELVE (or more) MATCH. A team contest in which each team has 12 (or more) active players.

TEAM TRIALS. See INTERNATIONAL OPEN TEAM SELECTION. For results see Appendix III.

TELEVISION. Bridge has had a great deal of exposure on television. *Championship Bridge with Charles Goren* ran for three seasons on primetime TV (1959-1962). In its first year, Goren's series won the TV Critics Award as one of the five most outstanding programs of the year. The show, one of the most popular sports shows on TV, was sponsored by Sara Lee, North American Van Lines and Samsonite. The series was broadcast weekly on ABC either before or after Sunday football. Bridge's network debut on the small screen featured matches between well-known bridge-playing celebrities and bridge experts of the day. Goren, the man who made bridge a household word with the introduction of his point-count system, and Alex Dreier, veteran newscaster and analyst, were the hosts.

Earlier TV bridge shows always generated lots of calls and letters, but most of these programs were one-shot deals. Bridge enthusiasts agreed that peering over the shoulder of a player, especially an expert, was fun. Watching bridge on TV, kibitzers could be vocal and active without disturbing the players. This interest in watching good bridge competition motivated a number of television stations during the late Fifties and early Sixties to present live bridge telecasts.

Manhattan's WOR-TV is generally credited with starting the trend by filming players battling for the Manhattan Championship. Billy Seamon was the commentator. NBC's *Tonight* cameras aired segments of the final of the Eastern States Championship in New York with commentary by Goren and by syndicated bridge columnist and author Alfred Sheinwold. In 1957 the final of the Iowa State Team Championship was televised live, with commentary from Dr. John Gustafson of Des Moines. WCCO in Minneapolis televised the Twin City Team final, importing Goren for the show. In 1958 KTTV aired live a portion of Los Angeles Bridge Week, which was acclaimed technically as the best bridge shown yet.

Local programs were appearing regularly in other markets and bridge was a hot ticket. Billy Seamon's *Bridge Clinic* was one of the first regularly scheduled TV bridge series. Produced by WITV in Miami, Seamon monitored a game from a soundproof booth while an assistant marked the play on a chart. The program ran for more than a year. Another early TV series came from WOAI-TV in San

Antonio. *What's Your Bid?* was produced in 1957 by Bobby Wolff, his brother Walter and Oswald Jacoby. KPTV in Portland OR featured Sam Gordon's *Horse Sense Bridge.* This was the first recorded effort to give formal bridge lessons on television. Sam taught a beginner's lesson for the first half, and this was followed by actual play. In Los Angeles many Hollywood celebrities played on KTLA's *What's the Bid?* with Robert Lee Johnson as commentator. KQED, Channel 9 San Francisco, in combination with KVIE, Channel 6 Sacramento, ran a TV bridge program designed by Ernest Rovere on Thursdays for 26 weeks. This was done in combination with the *San Francisco Chronicle*, which published a quiz based on the preceding night's program. Viewers were invited to mail their answers to the quiz show.

Bridge found its first home on public television in 1974. Duplicate bridge was welcomed to the small screen when the Charlotte NC Bridge Association staged their own show on KTVI, an educational channel. The program was geared toward rubber bridge and social bridge players who had never tried duplicate. In 1975 *Play Bridge with the Experts*" ran on KUHT in Houston. John Gerber was the expert consultant. Each of the 26 shows featured a different guest expert. Ed Allen of Beaumont, head of Educational Television Productions, created the series.

Eddie Kantar was the host-narrator of *Master Bridge*, which was developed in 1978 by Barbara Warner, executive producer of Jack Warner Productions. Celebrity guests such as Jim Backus, Jayne Meadows, MacDonald Carey and Carol Lawrence appeared. In 1983 Mary McVey, a bridge teacher from Lexington KY, filmed seven half-hour instructional shows called *Basic Bridge* for KET-Kentucky Educational Television. McVey hosted an additional 14 shows in 1984 called *Play Bridge*. Both shows were carried by more than 100 public television stations and later appeared on The Learning Channel.

In 1986 ACBL funded McVey's third show, *Play More Bridge*, a 13-installment series of bridge lessons for intermediate players. In 1989 ACBL began a campaign to develop new players through television bridge lessons. This time the audience was people who had never played bridge and social/rubber bridge players looking for a review of the basics. *The Bridge Class*, 13 half-hour shows based on the material from ACBL's first beginning bridge text, *The Club Series*, was produced by Audrey Grant. The series, which presented bridge as fun and easy-to-learn in an upbeat setting, found its first audience on The Learning Channel. In 1991 it was picked up by the PBS affiliate SECA, the Southern Educational Communications Association and currently known as NETA. It enjoyed an impressive reception on public television stations. Using the material from ACBL's second and third beginning bridge texts, *The Diamond Series* and *The Heart Series*, 26 half-hour shows known as *Play Bridge with Audrey Grant* hit the airways in 1993 and 1994 with the help of WITV, Harrisburg PA. In 1996 ACBL in association with Audrey Grant and independent film and video producer Jeff Drzycimski produced a fourth television series entitled *Bridge Brush-Up*. It was a 13-part series of half-hour shows which offered viewers an opportunity to review the basics while learning new techniques. The program also featured the ACBL Bridge Hall of Fame. A fifth series followed in 1998 – *Bridge at Sea with Audrey Grant* was produced by Audrey Grant and Jeff Drzycimski.

Perhaps the biggest TV bridge show ever produced occurred during the Bermuda Bowl World Championship in Beijing, China, in 1995. Play-by-play shows were sent out over the national network on several days, and it was estimated that more than 8 million Chinese bridge players watched the show. China Cup matches in later years also were featured on national television.

Many other countries also have televised either lessons or actual matches. France has been in the forefront of TV productions. The Scandinavian countries and the Netherlands also have been very active in airing bridge on TV.

With the help of major bridge web sites, major competitions now are televised for computer fans. The ACBL featured the 2000 Vanderbilt Teams on its website. Other live presentations include such events as the Cavendish Pairs in Las Vegas, the Bermuda Bowl and Venice Cup in Bermuda, the Cap Gemini, and others.

TEMPO. (1) The element of timing in card play, with special reference to the use of opportunities to make an attacking lead.

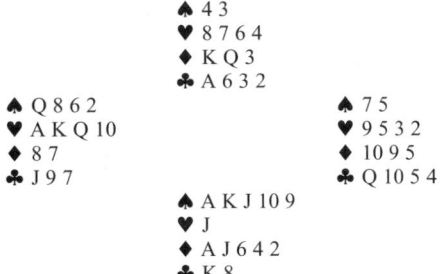

West leads two rounds of hearts against South's 4♠ contract. South should avoid losing a tempo in drawing trumps by cashing the ♠ A-K immediately and then starting his diamonds. The defenders can score the two remaining trumps but cannot damage the contract. If South loses a tempo by taking a spade finesse, the defense will continue hearts, reducing South's trumps to one fewer than West's. Should South allow this to happen, the defense will score a trick with a long heart and defeat the contract.

(2) The speed with which a bid or a play is made. Experienced players attempt to adjust the speed of their own bidding and play so as always to use the same tempo and thus not convey information to partner or the opponents. Players sometimes seek to force a rapid tempo of play, hoping to gain an advantage by encouraging an error by the opponents or by obtaining information from the opponents' pauses to think. The best defense against this somewhat unsporting tactic is to refuse to alter the tempo of one's own play, or even to slow the tempo down so as to protect one's partner. The term tempo, however, does not stretch to include deliberate hesitation when in fact a player has no problem.

TEMPORIZING BID. See WAITING BID.

TEN or TEN-SPOT. The fifth ranking card in each suit; at trump it is the lowest ranking honor card.

TEN TABLES. At duplicate, 10 tables provide for competition among 40 players as individuals, 20 pairs or 10 teams-of-four.

As an individual, use either the 13-round MINGLED MOVEMENT or the 10-round IRREGULAR RAINBOW.

As a pair game, the best contest is a MITCHELL. Three boards are given to each table, and a skip is called after the fifth round. This permits all pairs to play 27 boards — or fewer if desired since all boards are in play every round. If it is desired that all 30 boards be played, a byestand and relay setup can be employed. Boards should be relayed between tables 1 and 10, with the byestand between tables 5 and 6. The relay and byestand actually can be placed anywhere as long as they are exactly halfway around the game from each other.

The best movement for a one-winner game is the 10-table REDUCED HOWELL. For an interesting variation, see BLACKPOOL MOVEMENT. Also see EXPANDED MITCHELL. For $9\frac{1}{2}$ tables and $10\frac{1}{2}$ tables, see HALF TABLES.

As a team contest you may use the INTERWOVEN HOWELL or play a Swiss Team movement. As an alternative play the standard team-of-four movement with two modifications. The East-West, or moving, pairs skip a table in the lower direction, while the boards move to the next lower table. After the second round the East-West pairs skip an extra table. After the sixth round the East-West pairs skip an extra table and the boards skip a table. East-West pair 1 moves, 9, 7, 4, 2, 10, 8, 5 and 3. If it is desirable to play a ninth round, East-West pairs 1 to 5 add five to their number and go to that table. East-West pairs 6 to 10 subtract five from their number and go to that table. 1 and 6, 2 and 7, 3 and 8, 4 and 9, and 5 and 10 relay newly shuffled boards during this final round. An important alternative is the STAGGER MOVEMENT.

TENACE. Two cards in the same suit of which one ranks two degrees lower than the other; the major tenace is A-Q; the minor tenace is K-J; more broadly, any holding of cards not quite in sequence in a suit.

TEXAS TRANSFER. A transfer bid, originated independently by David Carter of St. Louis and Olle Willner of Sweden. It is used after an opening 1NT or 2NT bid to make the strong hand declarer in a high suit contract. With a hand justifying a game contract, the responder jumps to 4♥ holding a six-card or longer spade suit; the opener is required to bid 4♠. Similarly, 4♦ requires the opener to bid 4♥. The convention is usually limited to those sequences in which the responder has a major suit. 4♣ can be used in the same way to show diamonds, and 4♠ to show clubs. A South African variation uses 4♣ to ask for hearts and 4♦ to ask for spades. This has a psychological advantage, alerting an absent-minded partner who might otherwise pass a 4♥ bid that asked for spades, but it has the disadvantage of ruling out the use of the GERBER convention. The standard defense is: double is one-suited and lead-directing, 4NT is for the minors, four of responder's suit is a MICHAELS CUEBID. A delayed double after opener accepts the transfer is a three-suited takeout.

THEIR HAND. Term used by player who believes his opponents can make the highest positive score.

THIN. An adjective used to describe (1) a hand without BODY; "a thin 15-count" indicates a hand with 15 high card points that lacks intermediates; (2) a makable contract with fewer than the expected HCP between the two hands.

THIRD. (Similarly fourth, fifth, sixth, etc.). An adjective that, when used after naming a specific card, counts the number of cards held in the suit, e.g., ace-third denotes the holding of A-x-x.

THIRD AND FIFTH. During the Seventies and Eighties a majority of North American experts, and many in other parts of the world, abandoned the traditional fourth-best lead and adopted "third and fifth" leads. The idea is to lead the third card from a three or four-card suit, and fifth from five-card or longer suits. However, there has been a trend toward third from even, low from odd. This helps distinguish a six-card suit from a five-or seven-card suit.

If your partner leads, for example, the 2 from a presumed long suit, he is known to have three or five. This is easier for partner to judge than when using normal fourth-best leads when the 2 could be from a three-card or a four-card length. There is a corresponding disadvantage, however: The third-best card from a four-card suit may mean the wasting of a significant spot card. The lead of the 9 from K J 9 2 may work out badly. The fifth best lead is often less clear to partner than a fourth-best lead from a five-card holding. See THIRD-HAND PLAY, section VII.

If the lead is third-best, the RULE OF TWELVE applies instead of the RULE OF ELEVEN. See also THIRD HIGHEST LEADS.

THIRD BEST. See THIRD HIGHEST LEAD.

THIRD HAND. In the bidding, the partner of the dealer; in the play, the partner of the leader to a trick. For considerations affecting the third hand in the bidding after two passes, see BORDERLINE OPENING BIDS and PASSED HAND. Also See THIRD-HAND PLAY.

THIRD-HAND BID. See BORDERLINE OPENING BIDS and PASSED HAND.

THIRD-HAND PLAY. The outcome of many deals is determined at the first trick, and correct play by the partner of the opening leader is often the key to a successful defense. Players should be familiar with the following elements of third-hand play. (If no mention is made whether the contract is at a suit or notrump, assume that third hand plays identically.)

I. When partner leads low and dummy has low cards, the old whist rule of "third hand high" is usually right:

	North (dummy)	
	9 4 3	
West		East
A 10 8 2		K J 5
	South	
	Q 7 6	

Against notrump, West leads low. East must play the king.

If third hand has equal high cards, he plays the lower or lowest equal.

	9 4 3	
K 8 7 2		Q J 6
	A 10 5	

West leads low, and East plays the jack. The play of the jack denies the 10, but East may hold the queen.

II. When not to play high when dummy has low cards.

(1) With A-Q-x against notrump:

```
              9 3
J 8 7 6 2              A Q 5
             K 10 4
```

West leads low, and East plays the queen. If West has the king, no matter; if declarer has the king, the play of the queen prevents him from making a holdup play. This play works far better when East expects to regain the lead before West; if West gets in first, he may think East lacks the ace and shift. A similar play is available with A-J-x, but it is dangerous since West may have K-10-x-x-x.

(2) To maintain communication with partner's hand at notrump:

```
              7 5 4
8 3                   A K 10 9 2
             Q J 6
```

West leads the 8, and East does best to cover with the 9. If West has an outside entry, the defense can run the suit later.

```
              5
A 9 6 4 2             K J 3
             Q 10 8 7
```

West leads the 4. If East's hand is entryless, his winning play is the jack.

```
                 ♠ A J
                 ♥ A Q 5
                 ♦ Q J 10 7 6
                 ♣ A 7 6
♠ 9 4                          ♠ K Q 8 7 6
♥ 10 9 6 2                     ♥ J 8 7
♦ A 5 4                        ♦ K 3 2
♣ Q 10 8 3                     ♣ 9 5
                 ♠ 10 5 3 2
                 ♥ K 4 3
                 ♦ 9 8
                 ♣ K J 4 2
```

West	North	East	South
	1♦	1♠	Pass
Pass	Dbl	Pass	1NT
Pass	2NT	Pass	3NT
All Pass			

West leads the ♠9, and dummy plays the jack. To defeat 3NT, East must follow with the 8, letting South win one of his two spade tricks while West still has a spade to lead.

(3) When declarer is known to have all the missing honors:

```
              4 3 2
9 8                   K 10 6 5
             A Q J 7
```

Against a suit or notrump contract, West leads the 9. East should play low. Since the lead marks declarer with A-Q-J, East has no reason to play the king. Indeed, the play of the king lets declarer win four tricks.

(4) At a suit contract to make a discovery play:

```
              7 6
10 8 3 2              K J 5 4
             A Q 9
```

West leads low, and East knows that South has the ace (West will seldom lead low from the ace against a suit contract). To discover who has the queen, East plays the jack. If declarer wins the queen, East knows there is no future in the suit.

III. When dummy has an honor and third hand has a higher honor.

```
              Q 7 4
10 8 6 2              K 9 3
             A J 5
```

West leads the 2. If dummy plays low, East inserts the 9. The rule is that when third hand has an honor higher than dummy's honor, plus a middle card higher than the 8, he plays the middle card. With K-8-3, East should play the king if dummy plays low.

At suit play, this rule has exceptions when third hand has the ace and dummy has the queen.

```
              Q 7 5
             A 10 9
```

Against a suit contract West leads low and dummy plays low. East has a problem. If West is leading from the jack, it is usually right to play the 9 to deny declarer two tricks. If West is leading from the king, and declarer has the jack, it is usually right to play the ace.

If West is leading from K-J-x-(x), the play of the 9 saves a trick. There is no 100% answer. Third hand must judge from the dummy and the bidding.

```
                 ♠ K 7 4
                 ♥ 10 6 3
                 ♦ A J 10 6 5 4
                 ♣ 9
♠ 10 8 6 5 2                   ♠ A J 3
♥ 5 2                          ♥ K Q J 9
♦ 8 7                          ♦ K 3
♣ 10 7 4 2                     ♣ J 8 6 5
                 ♠ Q 9
                 ♥ A 8 7 4
                 ♦ Q 9 2
                 ♣ A K Q 3
```

South plays at 3NT, West leads a low spade and dummy plays low. Clearly, in this case East must take the ♠A and shift to the ♥K.

Sometimes third hand can make no effort to win the trick:

```
              Q 10 2
J 9 7 3               K 6 4
             A 8 5
```

If West leads the 3 and dummy plays low, East must play low. If East plays the king, South takes three easy tricks; after East ducks, the third trick remains in contention.

The correct play may depend on entry considerations:

```
              Q 7 2
J 9 5 3               K 8 4
             A 10 6
```

West leads the 3, and dummy plays low. If East has no entry, he should play the 8 (West can then continue the suit safely). However, if East has an entry, he must play the king; later, he can continue the suit safely.

```
                 ♠ J 9 3
                 ♥ J 4
                 ♦ K Q 10 6 4
                 ♣ 7 6 5
♠ Q 10 6 5 2                   ♠ K 8
♥ Q 6 5                        ♥ K 9 8 7
♦ 8 7 2                        ♦ A 5 3
♣ 4 3                          ♣ J 10 9 8
                 ♠ A 7 4
                 ♥ A 10 3 2
                 ♦ J 9
                 ♣ A K Q 2
```

South plays 3NT, West leads the ♠5 and declarer plays the 9 from dummy. East should play low to deny declarer a later entry to dummy's diamonds with the ♠J.

When third hand has one or two honors, and dummy has a higher honor, third hand often plays as if dummy had only low cards:

```
            A 8 4
J 7 3 2              Q 9 6
            K 10 5
```

West leads low, and dummy plays low. East should play the queen.

IV. Against a suit contract, when declarer is known to hold the ace.

(1) When third hand has the Q-9 with or without lower cards:

```
            K J 5
10 8 6 2              Q 9 3
            A 7 4
```

West leads low and dummy plays low. East, knowing that South has the ace, plays the 9. (If West leads low in the middle game or end game, he may be underleading the ace; East must make an informed decision.)

(2) When third hand has J-8-x or J-7-x, and dummy has K-10-x or A-10-x.

```
            K 10 4
Q 9 8 2              J 7 3
            A 6 5
```

West leads low and dummy plays low. East does best to play the middle card and hope it drives out the ace. With a weaker holding including the jack, East plays the jack and hopes declarer thinks he also has the queen. (Note that if West leads in this position after the first trick, it is usually right to attack with the 9.)

V. More on third-hand play from equals.

(1) When third hand has three or more equal honors, the proper order of plays is the lowest equal first, then the highest.

```
            7 6 3
8 4                  K Q J 10
            A 9 5 2
```

West leads the 8, and East plays the 10. East's second play in the suit is the king.

(2) Against notrump, with Q-J-10:

```
            5 4
A 9 8 7 6            Q J 10
            K 3 2
```

West leads low, and East should play the jack. If East plays the 10, West may think East started with J-10-x and South remains with Q-x; then West must wait for East to lead the suit.

However, if East plays the jack, West can safely continue the suit: either East has the queen, or South has K-Q-10, in which case it does not cost a trick to lead the suit again.

(3) Against notrump, with J-10-9:

```
            5 4
K 8 7 3 2            J 10 9
            A Q 6
```

West leads low, East plays the 10 and South wins the queen. West can safely continue the suit. Either East has the jack, or South has A-Q-J-9, in which case a tempo has been lost, but not a trick.

(4) With A-K-Q or A-K-Q-J to conceal strength:

```
            9 8
10 5 4 2             A K Q J 3
            7 6
```

If East wins the first trick with the ace and returns the queen, declarer may place West with the king. If East makes the normal play of the jack, South will know that East has 100 honors in the suit.

(5) With equal spot cards:

```
            Q 9 7 5
2                    K 10 8 6
            A J 4 3
```

West leads low and dummy plays low. East plays the 6 to limit South to two tricks.

(6) Third hand plays equal honors out of order to show a doubleton:

```
            J 8 6
Q 9 4 3 2            A K
            10 7 5
```

West leads low, and East wins the ace and cashes the king to show a doubleton.

```
            A 9 4
J 8 7 3 2            K Q
            10 6 5
```

West leads low and dummy plays low. East wins the king and returns the queen to show a doubleton. If East won the queen and led the king, West would assume that East had another card. (With equal doubleton honors, third hand should play them out of order only when he knows that he, not declarer, will win the trick.)

(7) At notrump, to ask for an unblock:

```
            7 6
Q 5 2                A K J 8 3
            10 9 4
```

West makes the inspired lead of the 2 in an unbid suit. East wins the ace and leads the king, asking West to unblock the queen if he has it.

```
            J 10
9 8 2                K Q 7 6 5
            A 4 3
```

West leads the 9, and East plays the king! When East leads the queen later, West unblocks the 8. Had East not wished an unblock, he would have played the queen first.

VI. Deceptive plays.

(1) At notrump, holding A-K-x-x:

```
            4 3
J 9 6 2              A K 7 5
            Q 10 8
```

West leads the 2, and East places South with three cards in the suit. If South has both the queen and ten, a swindle looms. East wins the first trick with the ace and returns a low card, giving declarer a chance to misguess.

(2) At a suit contract, holding A-K-x-(x):

```
            10 6 3
J 9 7 2              A K 5
            Q 8 4
```

West leads the 2, and East wins the ace and returns the 5. South may well play low and win no tricks.

(3) To feign a doubleton to encourage partner to continue a suit:

```
                    ♠ Q J 4
                    ♥ 6 4 2
                    ♦ A Q J
                    ♣ A Q J 6
♠ A K 9 5 3                      ♠ 10 7 6
♥ 9                              ♥ A K
♦ 9 7 5 3                        ♦ 10 8 6 4 2
♣ 9 8 3                          ♣ 10 7 5
                    ♠ 8 2
                    ♥ Q J 10 8 7 5 3
                    ♦ K
                    ♣ K 4 2
```

South opens a vulnerable 3 ♥, and North raises to 4 ♥. West leads the ♠ K. East can see that the only chance

for the defense is to cash two spades. Accordingly, he plays the ♠10 to feign shortness. West continues with the ♠A, and the contract is defeated. If East plays his lowest spade at the first trick, West may shift to a minor suit and lose the setting trick.

(4) To feign a doubleton in the hope of conning declarer into trumping high in dummy unnecessarily:

```
                ♠ 3 2
                ♥ K Q 6 4
                ♦ A Q 10 6
                ♣ Q 8 3
♠ A K Q 7 6              ♠ 9 8 5
♥ 10 7 5 3              ♥ J 9 8
♦ J 8 4 2              ♦ 9 7 5 3
♣ —                    ♣ J 10 9
                ♠ J 10 4
                ♥ A 2
                ♦ K
                ♣ A K 7 6 5 4 2
```

After South opens 1♣ and West overcalls 1♠, South shows a strong hand and becomes declarer at 5♣. West leads two high spades, and East signals high-low to try to convince declarer that he has a doubleton. If West continues with a third spade, South may trump with the ♣Q and lose a trump trick.

VII. Using the RULE OF ELEVEN.

(1) To save a trick:

```
                ♠ A J 7
                ♥ K 5 3
                ♦ 7 3 2
                ♣ 7 5 4 2
♠ Q 10 8 6 3            ♠ K 9 2
♥ 10 7                  ♥ 8 4
♦ J 9 5                ♦ Q 10 8 6
♣ A 8 3                ♣ Q J 10 9
                ♠ 5 4
                ♥ A Q J 9 6 2
                ♦ A K 4
                ♣ K 6
```

South plays 4♥, and West leads the ♠6. If declarer plays low from dummy, the Rule of Eleven tells East that South has no spades higher than the 7. East can safely play the 9. If East incorrectly wins the king, South can finesse dummy's ♠J later for his tenth trick.

(2) To avoid an endplay:

```
                ♠ 10 4 3
                ♥ A K 4 2
                ♦ 6 4 3 2
                ♣ 7 4
♠ A Q 9 6 2            ♠ J 8 7
♥ 7 5 3                ♥ 10 9 8
♦ 9 7                  ♦ Q J 10 8
♣ K J 8                ♣ 10 5 2
                ♠ K 5
                ♥ Q J 6
                ♦ A K 5
                ♣ A Q 9 6 3
```

South plays 3NT, West leads the ♠6 and dummy plays low. East can tell that South has one spade higher than the 6; since it must be an honor, East does best to play the 7.

South runs his red-suit winners and exits with a spade, hoping West must win and lead a club. Because East remains with the ♠J, however, no endplay is possible. Had East played the ♠J at the first trick, South could make his contract. (See RULE OF ELEVEN.) The situation is less clear if the defenders are using third-and-fifth leads. The 3 is led, and East cannot tell whether partner's lead is from Q10863, Q10853, Q10843, Q10543, Q8543 or 108543. The lead might be from a three-card holding. The play of the 9 is still appropriate, but could be wrong with a different layout of the whole deal.

VIII. With the Q-J when partner leads from A-K-x-(x).

When third hand plays the queen under the lead of the ace or king, he promises the jack or a singleton (unless the jack is in dummy; see subsequent example). Opening leader can underlead his remaining honor if he wants his partner on lead. The play of the queen is not a command to underlead; it simply shows the ability to win the next lead.

```
                ♠ 6 4
                ♥ A J 6
                ♦ 8 3
                ♣ A K Q 10 7 4
♠ A K 9 3              ♠ Q J 7
♥ 8 5                  ♥ 7 2
♦ A Q 9 2              ♦ 10 7 5 4
♣ 6 3 2                ♣ J 9 8 5
                ♠ 10 8 5 2
                ♥ K Q 10 9 4 3
                ♦ K J 6
                ♣ —
```

South plays 4♥ after West opens 1♦. West leads the ♠K, and East plays the queen, promising the jack. West has no trouble leading a low spade next, and East wins and returns a diamond. Down one.

If third hand has the Q-J doubleton and wants a ruff rather than a possible underlead, he plays the jack first.

IX. With Q-x when partner leads from A-K-x-(x) against a suit contract.

(1) Dummy does not have the jack:

```
                10 6 5
A K 8 7                      Q 2
                J 9 4 3
```

West leads a high honor, and East must play the 2. The play of the queen might induce West to underlead next.

(2) Dummy has the jack:

```
                J 6 5
A K 10 4                     Q 3
                9 8 7 2
```

West leads a high honor; East can play the queen to show a doubleton, and West cannot be misled.

X. When partner leads a short suit against a suit contract.

(1) Third hand has the ace and reads the lead as a doubleton:

```
                10 7 6
9 5                         A 8 4 3 2
                K Q J
```

West leads the 9, and East judges from the bidding that the lead is top of a doubleton. If East has no side entry, he must signal with the 8 and hope West has an early entry. Then West can continue with the 5 and get a ruff.

(2) Third hand reads the lead as a singleton but cannot win the trick:

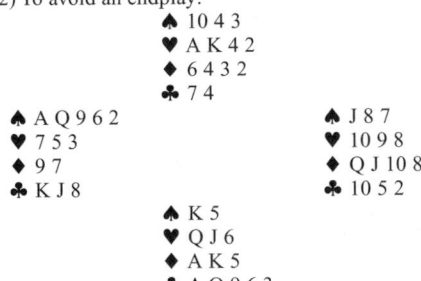

```
                ♠ Q J 5 4
♠ 6                         ♠ 10 9 8 3 2
                ♠ A K 7
```

Assume hearts are trumps, and West leads the ♠6, which East reads as a singleton. East's play should be a suit-preference signal to tell West where East's side-suit strength lies. If East has diamond strength, for example,

he plays the ♠10 at the first trick; with club strength, East plays the ♠2. With equal strength in the minor suits, East plays a middle spade.

XI. Other suit-preference plays at the first trick.

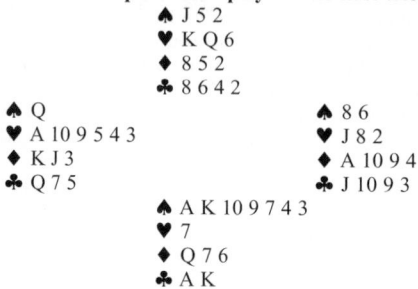

South plays 4♠ after West opened 1♥ and East raised to 2♥. West leads the ♥A, and both defenders know that a heart continuation cannot be right. East signals suit preference by playing the ♥J to show diamond strength. Had East not supported hearts, his first play would be count. See also SUIT-PREFERENCE SIGNALS.

```
          653
A 9                   K Q J 10 2
          874
```

At a suit contract or notrump, East has bid this suit, and West leads the ace. If East plays the king, he shows a solid suit. This is not a suit-preference play.

XII. When partner leads a trump.

(1) Third hand high may apply:

```
          6 2
J 9 3                 K 5 4
          A Q 10 8 7
```

West leads a low trump. If the bidding marks West with as many as three trumps, East should play the king, hoping to promote a lower honor.

(2) Third hand has A-x-x:

```
          J 5 4
3 2                   A 7 6
          K Q 10 9 8
```

If it is best to play two rounds of trumps quickly, third hand wins the ace and returns a trump. If it is best to play three rounds of trumps eventually, and third hand has no outside entry, he ducks the first trump. If opening leader has an early entry, he can lead a second trump, and third hand can win and lead a third trump.

(3) Third hand has an honor and wants to prevent dummy from gaining an entry:

```
          J 9 3
5 4                   K 7 6
          A Q 10 8 2
```

If East wants to deny declarer a later trump entry to dummy, he plays low regardless of which trump dummy plays at the first trick.

(4) When third hand has an honor he may use to overruff dummy:

```
          ♠ J 10 4
♠ 8 5                 ♠ K 2
          ♠ A Q 9 7 6
```

Assume spades is trumps, and both East and dummy have a doubleton heart. If West leads a trump, East plays low, saving the king for a possible overruff of dummy later.

XIII. Overtaking. Third hand usually overtakes partner's honor lead with a higher doubleton honor:

(1) When the queen is led, and third hand has K-x or A-x:

```
          9 4 3
Q J 10 8 7            K 5
          A 6 2
```

Against a suit or notrump contract, East overtakes the lead of the queen to unblock the suit. If dummy has 10-x-x, however, East establishes the 10 if he overtakes.

(2) When the jack is led against notrump, and third hand has Q-x, K-x or A-x:

```
          7 4 2
J 10 9 6 3           Q 5
          A K 8
```

West leads the jack, and East plays the queen to unblock. (At a suit contract, East need not unblock with Q-x or K-x.)

```
              ♠ Q 7 5 2
              ♥ K J 4
              ♦ A 7 6
              ♣ 10 6 4
♠ J 10 9 8 4              ♠ K 3
♥ A 10 9                 ♥ 8 7 6
♦ 10 3                   ♦ Q 9 5 4 2
♣ A 9 2                  ♣ 7 5 3
              ♠ A 6
              ♥ Q 5 3 2
              ♦ K J 8
              ♣ K Q J 8
```

South plays at 3NT, and West leads the ♠J. If dummy plays low, East must play the king to defeat the contract.

(3) When third hand has dazzling spot cards:

```
          9 4 3
J                     K Q 10 8 2
          A 7 6 5
```

West leads the jack, and East overtakes with the queen to prevent declarer from holding up. If the 9 were not in dummy, East could not afford this play. When partner leads an honor card from shortness, an encouraging signal indicates the inability to overtake.

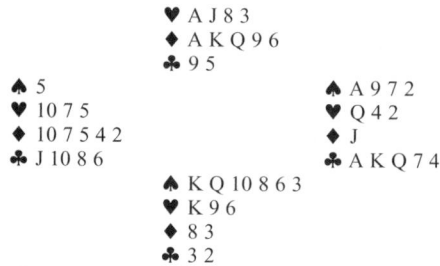

In the 1967 Bermuda Bowl final, South played 4♠ at both tables, and West led the ♣J. Both Easts overtook with the queen to return the ♦J. When East won the ♠A, he underled his remaining club honors to West's ♠10 and got a diamond ruff to defeat the contract.

XIV. Unblocking.

(1) When partner leads the king against notrump, and third hand has J-x:

```
          8 4 3
K Q 10 7 6            J 2
          A 9 5
```

West leads the king, and East plays the jack. To play low denies a significant honor. Some partnerships lead the queen from K-Q-10-9 combinations and perhaps from K-Q-10; in this case, the lead of the queen compels third hand to unblock the jack if he has it.

When the king is led against a suit contract, East can

afford to signal encouragement with J-x only if he knows that West has A-K.

(2) When partner leads the queen against notrump, and third hand has 10-x or 10-x-x:

```
                 A 4 3
    Q J 9 7 2             10 6
                 K 8 5
```

West leads the queen, and regardless of dummy's play, East unblocks the 10. Unblocking is also safe from 10-x-x, provided West is not leading from Q-J-x. (Usually West will have Q-J-9; with Q-J-x-x, he would lead low.)

(3) When partner leads the ace against notrump, and third hand has the jack or high, he unblocks the honor:

```
                 7 2
    A K J 10             Q 5 4
                 9 8 6 3
```

West leads the ace, and East unblocks the queen. (Some play that the lead of the king asks for an unblock, and the lead of the ace shows A-K-x or A-K-x-x.)

When third hand has no honor to unblock, he gives count.

```
                 7 2
    A K Q 10 9            8 3
                 J 6 5 4
```

West leads the ace, and East plays the 8, count. West can deduce that South has the guarded jack.

(4) Miscellaneous positions:

```
                 6 4
    A J 9 8              Q 7 5 3 2
                 K 10
```

Against notrump, West leads the 8. If East plays the queen, he blocks the suit.

```
                 A 7
    K J 9 6 4             Q 2
                 10 8 5 3
```

Against notrump, West leads the 6, and declarer puts up the ace. If East unblocks the queen, he can lead the 2 later for the defense to run the suit.

XV. Third hand middle.

Third hand should be familiar with some seemingly strange plays with honor-9-x or honor-8-x.

```
                 10 5
    K 8 3 2              A 9 4
                 Q J 7 6
```

West leads the 2 against notrump, amd dummy plays low. If East plays the 9, declarer takes one trick; if East plays the ace, declarer takes two tricks.

These plays do not come with a guarantee; they work most often when both leader and declarer have four cards and dummy has 10-x or J-x.

```
                 10 2
    K 7 6 3              Q 8 4
                 A J 9 5
```

Against notrump, West leads the 3, dummy plays low and East saves a trick by playing the 8.

```
                 9 2
    A 7 4 3              J 8 5
                 K Q 10 6
```

West leads low and dummy plays low. East saves a trick by playing the 8.

The play of the middle card also gains in this relatively common position:

```
                 10 2
    A 9 7 5 3             Q 8 4
                 K J 6
```

West leads the 5 (fourth best), dummy plays low and East saves a trick by inserting the 8 (similarly from Q-

9-x). However, if West started with K-J-7-5-3, East must play the queen.

```
                 10 5
    A 8 4 2             J 7 6
                 K Q 9 3

                 10 3 2
    A 9 7 5 4           J 7 6
                 K Q
```

In both cases, West leads low, and dummy plays low. East can play the 6 to save a trick.

```
                 10 5 2
    Q 9 8 7 3            J 6 4
                 A K
```

Against notrump, West leads the 7 and dummy plays low. If West will be first to regain the lead, it makes things easier if East plays low to the first trick. However, if East is first to regain the lead, his play at the first trick may not matter. And if the suit is:

```
                 10 5 2
    K Q 9 7             J 6 4
                 A 8
```

to play low is disastrous.

```
                 10 6 4
    Q 9 8 7 2             J 3
    (K 9 8 7 2)
                 A K 5
                 (A Q 5)
```

Against notrump, West leads the 7 and dummy plays low. If East has no entries and West is likely to get the lead first, East does best to play low.

XVI. Spot-card signaling.

(1) Third hand must not waste a valuable spot card to signal:

```
                 J 8 7 6
    A K 2              Q 9 5 3
                 10 4
```

West leads a high honor, and East must content himself with the 5. To play the 9 sets up a fourth-round winner in dummy. Many partnerships use UPSIDE-DOWN ATTITUDE SIGNALS to overcome this problem.

```
                 K 4 3
    Q J 7              A 9 8 2
                 10 6 5
```

Against a suit or notrump contract, West leads the queen, and dummy plays low. East signals with the 9, the higher equal, denying the 10. If West suspects the distribution, he does best to switch rather than continue and establish declarer's 10.

When third hand has three low cards, he should give count rather than play third hand high.

```
                          ♠ A 10 3
                          ♥ 7 6 5
                          ♦ Q 9 2
                          ♣ K J 4 3
    ♠ K J 7 5 4                        ♠ 8 6 2
    ♥ J 9 3                            ♥ Q 10 8 2
    ♦ A 8 6                            ♦ 4 3
    ♣ A 7                              ♣ 10 8 6 5
                          ♠ Q 9
                          ♥ A K 4
                          ♦ K J 10 7 5
                          ♣ Q 9 2
```

South opens 1NT and North raises to 3NT. West leads the ♠5, and dummy plays low. East should play the 2, giving count. South wins and knocks out the ♦ A, but

West will know to lead the ♠ K next.

The same play may be made with 9-x-x (usually against a suit contract) when it is clear the 9 cannot drive out a significant card.

THIRD HIGHEST LEAD. The lead of the highest card but two. This is standard when holding three cards headed by an honor. When the suit is longer, the third highest is led as a matter of system by some players. In fact, more and more players are leading THIRD AND FIFTH. This type also may be used as a deceptive lead. A player who holds 10-5-4-2 and a weak hand may choose to lead the 4 followed by the 2. His purpose is to suggest a five-card suit in the hope that declarer will make losing avoidance plays which are unnecessary, and which he would not have made if he had known that the opening leader's suit was a four-carder. For third-hand play when third highest leads are used, see RULE OF TWELVE. See also THREE SMALL CARDS, LEAD FROM; JOURNALIST LEADS.

THIRD-SUIT BID. A bid in a third suit at the one-level, is non-forcing except in the obsolete Baron System. If two suits are bid at the one level and a third at the two level, the situation is not forcing except when the second bid by opener is of higher rank than the first—e.g., 1 ♦ -1 ♠ -2 ♥ . There is an exception in KAPLAN-SHEINWOLD: 1 ♦ followed by 2 ♣ is forcing. After a response at the two-level, a third-suit bid is forcing in any standard method.

THIRTEEN TABLES. At duplicate, 13 tables provide competition among 52 players as individuals, 26 pairs, or 13 teams-of-four. In the development of bridge tournament movements, it was early recognized that 13 rounds of two boards each, 3 1/2 hours of play approximately, came close to being the ideal game. For this reason, 13 tables is considered to be the ideal for section size because every player plays each of the boards in play.

For 13 teams it would be normal to use the AMERICAN WHIST MOVEMENT. See TEAM-OF-FOUR MOVEMENTS.

Since 13 is a prime number, the RAINBOW MOVEMENT is practical and is generally used for individual tournaments. This can be cut to 11 or 12 rounds for a shorter game without introducing any complications. To maximize the number of partnerships, South and West can exchange positions after the first board of each round.

For a pair game, the simple MITCHELL MOVEMENT is used.

For 12 1/2 and 13 1/2, see HALF TABLES.

THIRTEENER. The card remaining in a suit when all other cards in that suit have been played on the first three tricks of the suit.

THREAT CARD (or menace). A threat card is a potential winner. It will take a trick provided that the opponent's holding in that suit can be weakened sufficiently. The term "menace" (or "threat card") may be used in one of the following specialized senses:

(1) Isolated menace: A menace consisting of one card, as the queen in the diagram.

```
              Q
  A                      K
              x
```

(2) Two-card menace: A two-card holding, consisting of a winner in the suit accompanied by a menace, as in the diagram.

```
              A J
  K Q                    x x
              x x
```

(3) Split two-card menace: A two-card menace in which the winner and the threat card are in opposite hands, as in this diagram:

```
              A x
  K J                    x x
              Q x
```

(4) Double menace: A threat card against both opponents (the diagram for a one-card menace, preceding, shows a double menace).

(5) Extended two-card menace: A two-card menace accompanied by one or more cards in that suit with the property that if the two-card menace is established, then the whole suit will run, e.g.:

```
              A J 10
  K Q                    x x x
              x x
```

In this diagram if West discards the queen (or king) he permits South to cash two additional tricks in the suit.

(6) Recessed menace: A menace card is accompanied by two (or more) winners in that suit, e.g.:

```
              A K 9
  Q J 10                 x x x
              x
```

North's holding is a recessed menace against West.

(7) Twin entry menace: One hand contains a winner and one (or more) small card(s) while the opposite hands holds a winner, a menace, and one (or more) small card(s) in that suit, e.g.:

```
              K x
  Q J x
              A 10 x
```

This suit is a twin-entry menace against West.

THREE or THREE-SPOT. The second-lowest card in a given suit, ranking between the 2 and the 4, sometimes called "trey."

THREE BID. See PREEMPTIVE BID.

THREE CLUB RESPONSE AS MAJOR-SUIT RAISE. A convention devised by Alvin Roth to make a strong major suit raise while conserving space for exchange of information as to trump suit texture, singletons and controls below the game level. Over the 3 ♣ response, opener rebids 3 ♦ if he has any singleton; without a singleton he rebids 3 ♥ , 3 ♠ or 3NT with two, one, or none of the top three trump honors, respectively. If opener has bid 3 ♦ , responder can show his own trump texture in the same way. Four-level bids show high card or distributional controls. See BERGEN RAISES, FORCING RAISES.

THREE NOTRUMP. The lowest, quantitatively, bid that produces a game from a zero score; nine tricks without benefit of a trump suit.

THREE SMALL CARDS, LEAD FROM. There are

three distinct schools of thought.

(1) *Top of nothing.* The traditional lead of the 8, for example, from 8-5-2, is advocated in many textbooks. This has the advantage of advising partner immediately that no high honor is held, but it has some disadvantages. It clarifies the suit distribution for the declarer also; it leads to ambiguity on the second round because partner cannot be sure whether the lead was from three cards or two; and it may waste a significant card, especially if the lead is an unsupported 9. Partners using this treatment must agree which card should be played on the second round of the suit. Most experts believe in following with the middle card, whether leading or following suit. This identifies a doubleton with certainty if the second card is the lowest possible. There is no technical objection to the alternative of following with the lowest card, in which case a doubleton is identified if the second card played is the highest possible. Whether or not there is any partnership agreement, it is important to play in tempo. Hesitation clearly shows the three-card holding and is unethical.

(2) *Low Lead.* Most American experts now favor this, following the trend to THIRD AND FIFTH leads. This avoids the disadvantages of the top of nothing lead, but leaves partner in doubt whether the lead is from an honor. (An obvious exception occurs when the highest card is led in the suit that has been bid by partner and raised by the leader.)

(3) *Mud.* The lead of the middle card, usually to be followed by the top card. The term is derived from the initial letters of middle-up-down. This lead is used by fewer and fewer pairs. Ambiguity is possible on the second round. Partner may be unsure whether the leader has an honor.

A few expert partnerships have no clear-cut agreement, but use the method which seems best adapted to the particular situation. The top card is led if partner is likely to need to know about honors rather than length. The bottom card is led if length is the vital factor. And the middle card is chosen if it is desired to keep declarer in doubt. See LEADS, OPENING LEADS.

THREE TABLES. At duplicate, three tables provide for competition among 12 (or 13) players as individuals, five or six pairs, or three teams-of-four.

As an individual tournament, 11 rounds are required for 12 players, 13 for 13 players. Conduct of such a game is described under INDIVIDUAL MOVEMENT for 12 or 13 players.

As a pair contest, the HOWELL MOVEMENT is far superior to the MITCHELL, as it provides that each pair of players will meet with each other pair as opponents.

	Board			Board			Board	
Round	NS	EW	Sets	NS	EW	Sets	NS	EW	Sets
1	6	1	1	5	2	4	4	3	2
2	6	2	2	1	3	4	5	4	3
3	6	3	3	2	4	1	1	5	2
4	6	4	4	3	5	1	2	1	3
5	6	5	5	4	1	5	3	2	5

The usual method of handling this movement is to put five boards in a set. The first four sets will have been played by all six pairs by the end of the fourth round. During the fifth round the fifth set of boards is relayed among all three tables. In this manner every pair plays 25 boards — five against each other pair. It is also possible to have the pairs share five boards each round.

A third possibility divides the game into 10 rounds.

Each pair makes the circuit of all other pairs twice. If there are two boards per set, the game consists of 20 boards. With three boards per round, the game consists of 30 boards. By making sets 1 through 5 consist of two boards and sets 6 through 10 consist of three boards, each pair would play 25 boards. Here is how the movement would work:

	Board			Board			Board	
Round	NS	EW	Sets	NS	EW	Sets	NS	EW	Sets
1, 6	6	1	1, 6	5	2	4, 8	4	3	2, 10
2, 7	6	2	2, 7	1	3	4, 5	5	4	3, 6
3, 8	6	3	3, 8	2	4	1, 5	1	5	2, 9
4, 9	6	4	4, 9	3	5	1, 7	2	1	3, 10
5, 10	6	5	5, 10	4	1	7, 8	3	2	6, 9

The main advantage of this movement is that it offers nearly perfect balance whereas the prior two do not. The main disadvantage is the extra time made necessary by the five extra moves.

A way for pairs to play three tables without board sharing and with good balance is to play two sets of boards in each round:

Round	NS	EW	b	NS	EW	b	NS	EW	b
1,	6	1	1+2	5	2	7+6	4	3	3+9
2,	6	2	3+4	1	3	7+10	5	4	5+2
3,	6	3	5+6	2	4	1+10	1	5	3+8
4,	6	4	7+8	3	5	1+4	2	1	5+9
5,	6	5	9+10	4	1	4+6	3	2	2+8

Two boards a set gives four boards a round, in total 20 boards, and three boards gives six per round and 30 in total. If 25 boards are desired, let board sets 1,3,5,7 consist of three boards and the remaining sets of two boards. You will then have 5 boards a round in all rounds except the last round. Add one board in the last round, for instance played as the first board at table 3, as the third at table 2 and as the last board at table 1.

If the game consists of 2 1/2 tables, the easiest method to use is to eliminate the stationary pair. That way each pair sits out the round that matches their pair number.

A movement for three tables of players works out well as a team event. The following movement is used. If the plan is to play 24 boards, then 12 boards are placed at each table. The East-West pairs move to the next higher table (1 to 2, 2 to 3 and 3 to 1) and play those boards. The East-West pairs then return their boards to their home table and go back one table from their home table (3 to 2, 2 to 1 and 1 to 3). Without shuffling, the players play the boards at their table. At the finish each team will have played a 12-board match against each of the other teams. For 3 1/2 tables see HALF TABLES.

THREE-CARD SUIT, BID IN. In many situations the most convenient bid available may be in a three-card suit. Some of the more common examples are:

(1) *In opening the bidding.* Most frequent is an opening bid of 1♣ , to keep the bidding at a low level and avoid an opening in a poor four-card major suit. Less common is an opening of 1♦ with a three-card suit, although this is standard practice with five-card majors. (Some bid 1♦ with 4-3-3-3 or 3-4-3-3 to avoid 1♣ with three small). Semi-psychic opening bids of 1♠ with a three-card suit are sometimes made, especially third-hand, nonvulnerable, with a subminimum opening. Opening bids in a three-card suit, of any rank, are often required in the ROMAN SYSTEM. See SHORT CLUB.

(2) *In responding.* A response in the lowest possible suit

is sometimes made with a three-card suit, especially if the suit is strong, because no good alternative presents itself:

(a)

♠ J x x
♥ x x x
♦ A K x
♣ x x x x

(b)

♠ A K x
♥ x x x x
♦ x x x
♣ A Q x

(a) A response of 1 ♦ to 1 ♣ is slightly preferable to 1NT or 2♣.

(b) In response to 1 ♠, 2♣ is the least of evils unless 1NT forcing is available.

(3) *In rebidding.* See OPENER'S REBID.

(4) *In responding to a takeout double.* See also FOURTH SUIT FORCING, FRAGMENT BID, INTEREST-SHOWING BID, TRIAL BID.

THREE-CLUB RESPONSE TO ONE NOTRUMP. Possibilities include (1) strong and forcing, showing slam interest; (2) preemptive; (3) invitational – normal with four-suit transfers since weak and strong hands can transfer vi 2♠; (4) transfer to diamonds; (5) 5-5 in the minors, invitational or weak; (6) a prototype Stayman asking for a major also nowadays played as asking for a five-card major or a good 4-card major. (7) short club 3-suiter. (8) diamond slam try.

THREE-CLUB STAYMAN. See TWO NOTRUMP OPENING.

THREE-DIAMOND RESPONSE AS MAJOR RAISE. See BERGEN RAISES.

THREE-DIAMOND RESPONSE TO ONE NOTRUMP. Possible meanings: (1) Strong and forcing, suggests slam interest; (2) Preemptive; (3) 5-5 in the minors, forcing to game. (4) short diamond 3-suiter; (5) heart slam try.

THREE-HANDED BRIDGE. Many three-handed versions of bridge have been devised. Apart from TOWIE, described separately, two games deserve consideration.

In the traditional cutthroat game, the players bid for a hidden dummy. The bidding continues until a bid, doubled or redoubled, is followed by two passes. The player on declarer's left leads, and the dummy is spread between the two opponents. The scoring is normal, declarer scoring a 700 rubber bonus only if neither defender has a game. Plus scores only are recorded for each player, and settlement is made on the net difference in scores. See CUTTHROAT.

An alternative game with a pre-exposed dummy was devised by George S. Coffin in 1932. It is sometimes called triangle contract or trio bridge. The laws are as follows:

(1) The three players are designated as North, South, and East. North and South bid as well as play as partners against East and his exposed dummy. There is no West player. Nor is there a second dummy, because North and South always play with closed hands, even if one or the other is declarer.

(2) To begin a game, the three players draw cards; the two players who draw the highest cards play as partners as North and South against East, who has the dummy for the entire rubber.

(3) For the first deal only, South shuffles either pack. Then East cuts and South deals while North shuffles the still pack. For the next hand, East cuts and North deals

while South shuffles the still pack. Thereafter, North and South continue to deal alternately.

(4) East never deals or shuffles, but always cuts.

(5) Dummy is exposed before there is any bidding. Hence, if any dummy card is faced up during the deal, it is not treated as an exposed card. If a card is turned up in any other hand, there must, of course be a new deal.

(6) South always calls first regardless of who dealt; North bids second. Dummy never bids, for East bids on the combined 26 East-West cards. If any player makes a bid, the auction continues indefinitely until two consecutive passes close it.

(7) As in four-handed bridge, the left-hand opponent (LHO) of declarer makes the opening lead. If South is declarer, dummy leads first; if North is declarer, East leads; or if East is declarer, South leads.

(8) If the revoke is established against East, he cannot be penalized for it unless South or North has called attention to East's failure to follow suit on the revoke trick. This special rule for three-handed bridge is called the courtesy of the table, and it is due to the fact that East has no partner to say "having none?" This service is rendered by North and/or South.

(9) Regular contract bridge scoring is used. After the net amount of a finished rubber has been computed, East wins or loses twice the net amount because he collects dummy's gain or suffers dummy's loss.

(10) At the end of each rubber, North shifts into the vacant chair on his right and becomes redesignated as South and his former partner as East. A weird variety calls for the dealer to play automatically in 2NT redoubled. See DUMMY BRIDGE.

THREE-HEART RESPONSE TO ONE NOTRUMP. (1) Forcing to game, showing at least a five-card suit, slam oriented; (2) 5-5 in majors, invitational; (3) shortage, at least 5-4 in the minors. (4) spade slam try.

THREE-NOTRUMP OPENING. Traditionally this shows a balanced hand with 25-27 points. But with such hands most experts bid 2♣ followed by 3NT, or use KOKISH RELAY, and therefore prefer to use the 3NT opening for some other purpose, such as:

(1) GAMBLING 3 NT. Usually this shows a solid suit with no ace or king outside.

(2) Weak minor suit preempt, comparable to a standard 4♣ or 4 ♦ opening. This method is useful for those who use NAMYATS to show strong major suit hands.

(3) Solid major suit preempt with no side suit aces and at most one side king. This use, suggested by Edwin Kantar, is designed to ease responder's task of judging his side's game or slam prospects. The recommended responses are as follows: 4♣ asks opener to bid a side king if he has one; 4 ♦ transfers to opener's suit; 4 ♥ or 4 ♠ indicates that responder wants to be declarer and has tried to guess opener's suit (if he misguesses, opener should correct); 4NT asks about queens; 5NT asks opener to bid a grand slam if he can play opposite a void.

THREE-NOTRUMP OVERCALL. An overcall at the game level, usually made on a strong balanced hand or one of a preemptive nature.

North	East
3 ♠	3NT

In the above example East's hand might be:

♠ A J 9
♥ K 2
♦ A J 10 6 4
♣ K Q 2

East should not double 3♠ since he has poor support for the "other major." Normally, the double of one major suit invites partner to bid the other if he can. East therefore "gambles" on 3 NT. In these awkward situations it is generally a good idea arbitrarily to place 8 points in your partner's hand and proceed accordingly. An opponent's double or raise from partner will clarify the situation. In many situations the 3NT overcall is gambling and semi-preemptive in nature.

For example:

South	West
1♥	3NT

West is trying to "steal" 3NT. His holding might be:

♠ 6
♥ K 5
♦ A K Q 7 6 3 2
♣ 8 7 6

If an opponent doubles, it usually is incumbent upon partner of overcaller to run out to 4♣ if he has nothing of great value. A pass by partner would indicate a desire to play 3NT. This bid is usually made when not vulnerable. However, many experts would require two side suits to be stopped, with a hand similar to a 3NT rebid after a one-level response.

THREE-NOTRUMP REBID. See OPENER'S REBID.

THREE-NOTRUMP RESPONSE. to an opening suit bid of one. There are a number of treatments which can be adopted:

(1) *Standard*, traditional. Shows 16-18 points and any 4-3-3-3 distribution. Stoppers in the unbid suits, and the four-card suit usually is a minor.

(2) *Limit*. Shows 13-15 points and any 4-3-3-3 distribution (ACOL SYSTEM).

(3) *Conventional*. Used with limit raises to show a standard forcing jump raise of 13-15 points when the opening bid was in a major (invented by Monroe Ingberman.) For alternative methods of solving this problem see DELAYED GAME RAISE and SWISS CONVENTION .

(4) *Distributional*. Shows a 13-15 point raise with a side suit singleton when the opening bid was in a major (ACES SCIENTIFIC SYSTEM).

(5) *Extra Strong or Distributional*. Shows one of a series of CONGLOMERATE MAJOR RAISES. In response to a 1♥ opening, 3 NT would show 17-18 points. In response to a 1♠ opening, 3NT would be as in (4) above.

(6) *Ace-asking*. See BABY BLACKWOOD.

(7) *Psychic Control*. Showing 23 points or more — a hand which offers a play for game opposite a psychic opening bid. This assumes a ROTH-STONE psychic with 3-6 points concentrated mainly in the bid suit. If the opening bidder has a normal opening he proceeds to a slam. The combined strength already suggests a grand slam.

(8) *Preemptive Major Suit Raise*. Similar to a direct raise to four of a major, but with some defensive value.

(9) A splinter in the unbid major suit.

THREE-ODD. Three tricks over book or nine tricks.

THREE-QUARTER MOVEMENT. See REDUCED HOWELL.

THREE-QUARTER NOTRUMP. The use of a weak notrump in all situations except vulnerable against non-vulnerable. Players who combine this with a fourth-hand weak notrump at all vulnerabilities (safe because neither opponent can double and dummy must have some values) can be said to play 13/16ths.

THREE-SPADE RESPONSE TO ONE NOTRUMP. (1) forcing to game, showing at least a five-card suit, slam oriented; (2) 5-5 in majors, forcing to game; (3) singleton spade, 5-4 in the minors, game-forcing values.

THREE-SUITER. A hand with at least four cards in each of three suits, and therefore distributed 4-4-4-1 or 5-4-4-0. For opening the bidding with a three-suiter see BIDDABLE SUITS, BORDERLINE OPENING BIDS, and CHOICE OF SUIT. For specialized three-suiter conventions see BLUE TEAM TWO DIAMONDS, KANTAR CUEBID, PRECISION CLUB (2♦ opening), ROMAN SYSTEM (2♣ and 2♦ opening), SPLINTER BID, VOID-SHOWING BIDS.

THROUGH STRENGTH. The old whist idea that a defender should lead "through strength" is one of the least valuable rules of thumb. The implication is that a player on declarer's left should lead a suit in which dummy is strong. The rationale is that partner may hold any missing honors behind dummy; the defenders can profit by leading suits in which declarer's finesses will fail.

♠ 10 7 5 2
♥ J 9 3 2
♦ A Q 3
♣ J 2

♠ K J 6		♠ 9 8 3
♥ 8 4		♥ K 5
♦ 9 7 5		♦ K J 8 4
♣ K Q 10 7 5		♣ 9 8 6 4

♠ A Q 4
♥ A Q 10 7 6
♦ 10 6 2
♣ A 3

South plays at 3♥; he wins the ♣K opening lead and leads a club back. When West takes the queen, he shifts to the ♦9 through dummy, since if East has diamond honors, they are well placed. If South ducks, East wins the jack and leads the ♠9 in turn through declarer. Best defense defeats the contract.

Sometimes a lead through strength merely gives declarer time to establish the suit for discards. When dummy has a strong side suit, the defenders must often hasten to establish tricks elsewhere while they can. Even when a safe exit is a defender's goal, however, it may be safer to lead a suit in which dummy is weak.

In the following examples it is assumed that dummy is on the leader's left, and that declarer is unlikely to have a singleton or to be able to discard all of his holding on one of dummy's suits.

To lead from a worthless suit rarely costs a trick, though it may avoid a guess for declarer, but a defender must consider carefully before he leads from an honor. If dummy has A-K-x, for example, a lead from a queen is dangerous, but most other leads are safe. Other cases:

Dummy has A-x-x: A lead from J-9-x is safe; from J-x-x or Q-x-x more risky; from K-x-x, dangerous.

Dummy has A-Q-x or A-J-x: A lead from a king is dangerous; from the jack or queen, less dangerous. From

K-J-9 or K-10-8, lead the middle card.

Dummy has K-Q-x: A lead from the jack is dangerous; from the ace or x-x-x, safer.

Dummy has K-J-x: A lead from the ace is safe; from the queen, dangerous, but for this reason declarer may be induced to misguess if he holds a low doubleton.

Dummy has K-x-x: All leads from single honors are risky.

Dummy has Q-x-x: A lead from the king is safest, since the king may win a later trick even if declarer has the ace; from the ace, dangerous.

Dummy has J-x-x: A lead from the ace is worst; it is better to lead from the king or queen.

Dummy has x-x-x: The lower the honor to be led from, the safer the lead. A lead from the jack is almost completely safe; from the queen loses only if declarer has A-K-J.

For a related situation, see UP TO WEAKNESS. Also see LEADS.

THROW AWAY. (1) To discard. (2) To defend or play so badly that a very poor score results.

THROW IN. (1) To make a THROW-IN PLAY. (2) In rubber bridge, to toss the cards into the center of the table, after four passes. Used in Great Britain as a synonym for PASS OUT.

THROW-IN PLAY. When an opponent is given the trick, gaining the lead costs him a trick or more. There are three types of throw-in play, based on the way the throw-in costs the defender his tricks.

(1) Tenace Throw-in (usually shortened to throw-in). An opponent is thrown in and forced to lead from a broken honor holding at the cost of a trick.

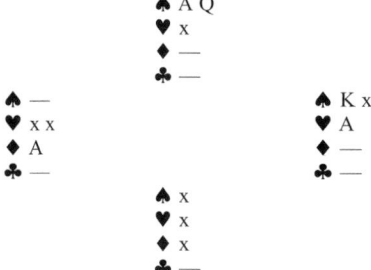

South has placed East with the ♠K. In order to avoid a losing finesse, a heart is led and East is forced into the lead. He must lead into North's spade tenace.

(2) Trump Throw-in (also known as an elimination play). An opponent is thrown in and forced to concede a ruff and discard.

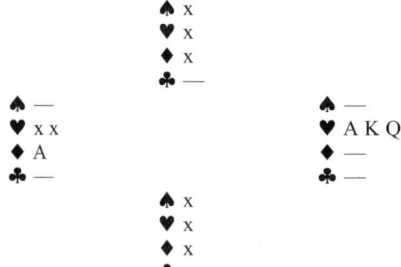

Spades are trumps, and South apparently has two unavoidable losers in hearts and diamonds. However, he

leads a heart, forcing East into the lead. East must continue a heart, permitting South to discard the losing diamond while ruffing the heart in dummy. The distinction between these two types of throw-in does not rest on the contract, trump or notrump, but on the mechanism involved. Both types may occur at a trump contract. At a trump contract, the opponent who is thrown in may be faced with a choice of plays, each of which costs a trick; thus the various categories of throw-in may overlap.

(3) Entry Throw-in. The opponent who gains the lead must play a suit in which declarer has established tricks to which there is no entry.

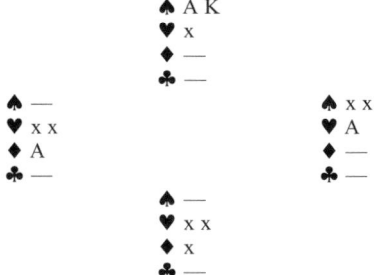

South has the lead in a notrump contract. North's two spade tricks are inaccessible. However, a heart lead saddles East with the necessity of leading a spade to the next trick, providing the entry to dummy's hand.

Proper execution of a throw-in play requires declarer to consider two factors: (a) the stripping, or elimination, process: this means that declarer must assure himself that, once thrown in, the defender has no safe lead; and (b) the throw-in card: at the judicious moment, declarer must be able to lose the lead to that opponent whose hand has been stripped of safe exit cards. Declarer may strip an opponent's hand by plain suit leads, by ruffing, or by a preliminary squeeze (see SECONDARY SQUEEZE). Sometimes a perfect elimination is not possible, and declarer must hope for favorable distribution.

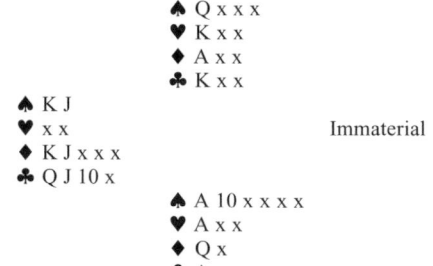

South has become declarer at a 5♠ contract reached by trying for a slam. A club was led by West, won by the ace. The A♠ was cashed, followed by a club to the king and a club ruff, (stripping both hands of clubs). Declarer played two top hearts, hoping to strip West of exit cards in that suit, followed by a spade, throwing West into the lead. Since West in fact had no more hearts, his choice was between a club or diamond, either of which would forfeit a trick.

Certain suit combinations lend themselves to a throw-in. In the following combinations, the throw-in card is in the critical suit, which the defenders must return at the cost of a trick:

A Q 9	A J 10	K 10 x	Q J x	K 9 x	A 10 x
x x x	x x x	x x x	x x x	J x x	J 9 x

In each case, South leads low, and then simply covers the card played by West. Provided East has been stripped of all other exit cards, he will have to return this suit; in this way declarer can hold his losses in the suit to a minimum. There are other combinations in which an extra trick is guaranteed, provided the opponents must open the suit. The throw-in card must be in some other suit.

A 10 x	K x x	K 9 x	Q x x
J x x	J x x	Q 10 x	J x x

There are certain combinations in which declarer's prospects are improved if the opponents can be forced to lead the suit. The throw-in card must be in some other suit:

A 10 x	A x	A x x
K 9 x	Q x	J 9 x

There are many suit combinations which can provide the means for a throw-in play. The most common is an eight-card holding, missing the king and queen, A-x-x opposite J-x-x-x-x. Declarer leads the ace, and then plays a small card in the suit after the elimination is complete. If either player holds K-Q, he can be thrown in; even if he holds K-x or Q-x, he may neglect to unblock, or else it may cost him a trick to do so. Many throw-in plays are named after the means employed to strip the hand or throw-in the opponents. One such would be a crossruff strip, and another a loser-on-loser elimination. The latter is commonly available, although often missed.

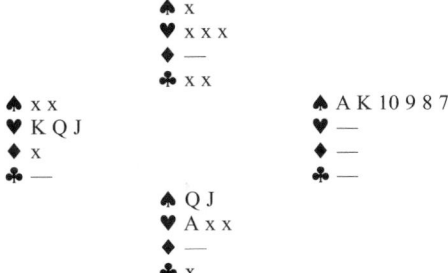

```
               ♠ 8 6 4 2
               ♥ K Q 7 3
               ♦ A 7
               ♣ Q 5 4
  ♠ 10 5                      ♠ A K Q 9 3
  ♥ 9 5                       ♥ 8 4
  ♦ Q J 8 4 2                 ♦ 10 6 3
  ♣ 10 8 6 2                  ♣ K J 9
               ♠ J 7
               ♥ A J 10 6 2
               ♦ K 9 5
               ♣ A 7 3
```

After East opened the bidding with 1♠, South became declarer at 4♥. Spades are led and declarer ruffs high on the third round. Placing East with the ♣K for his opening bid, South draws trumps in two rounds, plays the A-K of diamonds followed by a diamond ruff, ending in dummy. So dummy's last spade is led, on which South discards a losing club, throwing East into the lead. East must concede a ruff and sluff or lead from his club tenace.

The throw-in usually follows the elimination, but this is not invariably the case.

```
               ♠ x
               ♥ x x x
               ♦ —
               ♣ x x
  ♠ x x                       ♠ A K 10 9 8 7
  ♥ K Q J                     ♥ —
  ♦ x                         ♦ —
  ♣ —                         ♣ —
               ♠ Q J
               ♥ A x x
               ♦ —
               ♣ x
```

Clubs are trumps and South requires four of the remaining tricks, with only three in sight. A spade is led, won by East. On the spade continuation, North discards a heart. On the next spade, North discards another heart, while South ruffs. South can now lead the ♥A and win

both of dummy's trumps for three more tricks. In a double elimination, either opponent may win the throw-in card, but the declarer gains a trick in either case.

(4) Double Elimination.

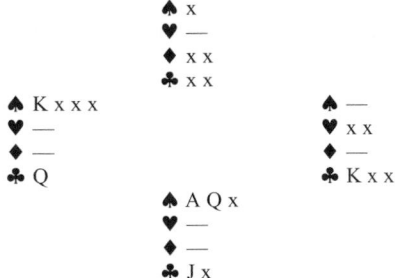

```
               ♠ x
               ♥ —
               ♦ x x
               ♣ x x
  ♠ K x x x                   ♠ —
  ♥ —                         ♥ x x
  ♦ —                         ♦ —
  ♣ Q                         ♣ K x x
               ♠ A Q x
               ♥ —
               ♦ —
               ♣ J x
```

Diamonds are trumps, and South requires four of the remaining tricks. A club is led which may be won by either opponent. If West's queen holds, he must lead into South's spade tenace; if East overtakes with the ♣K, South's jack is established. There are certain rare positions in which the declarer can bring off a repeating elimination. The same defender can be thrown in several times to make a losing lead.

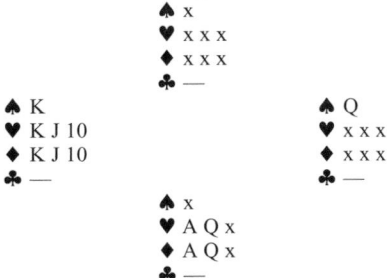

```
               ♠ x
               ♥ x x x
               ♦ x x x
               ♣ —
  ♠ K                         ♠ Q
  ♥ K J 10                    ♥ x x x
  ♦ K J 10                    ♦ x x x
  ♣ —                         ♣ —
               ♠ x
               ♥ A Q x
               ♦ A Q x
               ♣ —
```

Spades are trump. South leads a spade and West is thrown in. Whatever card he returns, South wins two tricks in that suit and throws West in again with the third round of the suit. West must now give declarer two tricks in the second suit. South, starting with two tricks, ends up with four.

(5) Pseudo Elimination. A defender may believe that he has been thrown in and must concede a trick, although this may not be the case. Usually this occurs when the defender fears to give declarer a ruff and sluff. This may not benefit declarer for either of two reasons: he may have concealed another card of that suit in his hand, or the ruff and discard permits declarer to discard a card which was not a loser in any case.

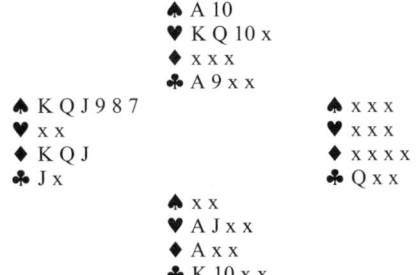

```
               ♠ A 10
               ♥ K Q 10 x
               ♦ x x x
               ♣ A 9 x x
  ♠ K Q J 9 8 7               ♠ x x x
  ♥ x x                       ♥ x x x
  ♦ K Q J                     ♦ x x x x
  ♣ J x                       ♣ Q x x
               ♠ x x
               ♥ A J x x
               ♦ A x x
               ♣ K 10 x x
```

South is declarer at 4♥. A spade is led, won by the ace. Trumps are drawn, the ♦A is taken, and the suit continued. West wins two diamonds and a spade. The only correct defense is a spade continuation, although

South can discard a club in one hand while ruffing the spade in the other. South still has a club loser. However, if West is reluctant to give the ruff and sluff, he will lead a club, permitting South to avoid a loser in that suit.

(6) Defense Against a Throw-in. Often the defenders can foresee an impending throw-in. They have several ways of escaping the endplay.

(a) By retaining an Exit Card.

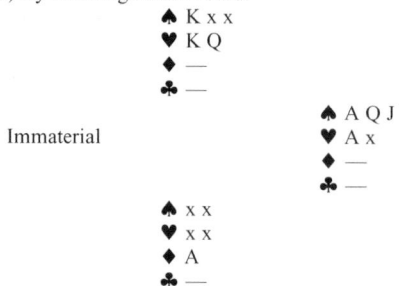

At notrump, South leads the ♦ A, throwing a spade from dummy. East must discard a spade, not the small heart. If he discards the heart, South can throw him in the lead with a heart, and East is forced to lead the spade. If he holds the small heart, he can exit with it after winning the ♥ A, forcing the spade lead to come to him from North.

(b) By Unblocking.

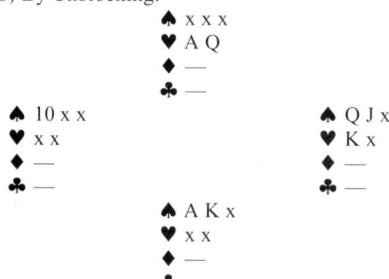

South cashes the ♠ A-K on which East must unblock by playing his queen and jack, so that West can win the third round of spades with the 10, returning a heart, to ensure a trick for East's king.

(c) By Playing Second Hand High.

South leads small, intending to insert the 8. East can win with the 9, but then must lead into North's tenace. When South plays small, West must rise with the 10 to protect his partner from the endplay.

(d) By Refusing to Assist in the Elimination.

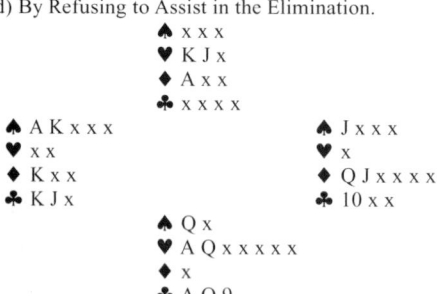

After West opened 1 ♠, South became the declarer at 4 ♥. West took two top spades. West must switch to hearts or diamonds. South does not have enough entries to dummy to ruff out spades and diamonds to strip the West hand before leading a club. See also ENDPLAY and PARTIAL ELIMINATION.

THROW-IN SQUEEZE. A squeeze which operates as a trick is surrendered.

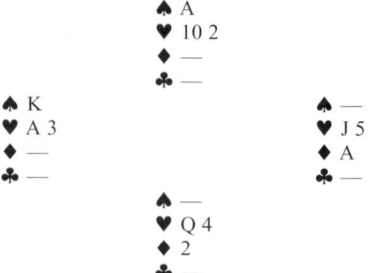

In notrump, South leads his diamond. If West discards a heart, dummy also throws a heart and scores the last trick with the ♠ A. If West discards the ♠ K, dummy pitches the ♠ A and declarer wins a heart trick by guessing the position

THROWING THE LEAD. (into a desired defender's hand). See THROW-IN PLAYS.

THURNER MOVEMENT. A team movement for a round-robin among an even number of teams. In each round there are two tables sharing boards. The movement exists for 6, 8, 12 and 14 tables. It is Mitchell-based with an appendix table.

Six teams. Tables 6 shares with each other table in turn, so it should be centrally situated.

Table	1	2	3	4	5	6
Rnd	NSEW BD	NSEW BD	NS EW BD	NSEW BD	NSEW BD	NSEW BD
1	1 6 1	2 3 2	3 5 3	4 2 4	5 4 5	6 1 1
2	1 4 2	2 1 3	3 6 4	4 5 5	5 2 1	6 3 4
3	1 2 3	2 4 4	3 1 5	4 3 1	5 6 2	6 5 2
4	1 5 4	2 6 5	3 4 1	4 1 2	5 3 3	6 2 5
5	1 3 5	2 5 1	3 2 2	4 6 3	5 1 4	6 4 3

Eight teams.

Table and NS #	1	2	3	4	5	6	7	8
E-W #	8	4	7	3	6	2	5	1
Boards	1	2	3	4	5	6	7	1

N-S pairs remain stationary. E-W 1-7 move one table up, boards one table down. E-W 8 move two tables down: 1-6-4-2-7-5-3.

Twelve teams.

Table and NS #	1	2	3	4	5	6	7	8	9	10	11	12
E-W #	12	6	11	5	10	4	9	3	8	2	7	1
Boards	1	2	3	4	5	6	7	8	9	10	11	1

N-S pairs remain stationary. E-W 1-11 move one table up, boards one table down. E-W 12 move four tables up (five tables if home table 12 is encountered): 1-5-9-2-6-10-3-7-11-4-8

Fourteen teams.

Table and NS #	1	2	3	4	5	6	7	8	9	10	11	12	13	14
E-W #	14	7	13	6	12	5	11	4	10	3	9	2	8	1
Boards	1	2	3	4	5	6	7	8	9	10	11	12	13	1

N-S pairs remain stationary. E-W 1-13 move one table up, boards one table down. E-W 14 move four tables down (five tables if home table 14 is encountered): 1-10-6-2-11-7-3-12-8-4-13-9-5. See TEAM OF FOUR MOVEMENTS.

TICKETS. A colloquialism used to refer to (1) pick-up slips, (2) the right high cards for a particular action — "He had the tickets."

TIE. Equality of result in a competition. (1) On a board; (2) In a knockout match. Additional boards must be played, in accordance with the conditions of contest, to determine a winner; (3) In overall standings or section standings. In ACBL contests, since 1992, any margin is a win.

TIERCE. A term, obsolete in bridge, used to describe a sequence of three cards, one or more of which usually has honor rank.

TIGHT. A colloquialism for SINGLETON or STIFF, particularly in describing a singleton high honor. Refers also to doubleton honors as in A-K or K-Q tight.

TIME LIMIT ON RIGHT TO PLAY. This is usually at the discretion of the director. In some tournaments the sponsoring organization sets a deadline beyond which purchase of additional entries depends on the need to fill in sections. In second and later sessions of multi-session events, the director must seek substitutes for pairs who are late to report.

TIME VALUATION. See TEMPO.

TIMING. An element in the play of a hand. The order in which trumps are pulled, losers are trumped, and side suits are developed is an element that enters into both declarer's and defenders' play.

The following example is given by Terence Reese:

```
              ♠ 10 8 7 6 2
              ♥ 7 6
              ♦ 9 8 5 2
              ♣ A K
  ♠ K 3                      ♠ A Q J 9 5
  ♥ J 10 3 2                 ♥ K Q 9 8 4
  ♦ J 6 4                    ♦ —
  ♣ Q 10 9 5                 ♣ 8 7 3
              ♠ 4
              ♥ A 5
              ♦ A K Q 10 7 3
              ♣ J 6 4 2
```

Spades are led against 5 ♦ and South ruffs the second round. If South makes the obvious play of drawing one round of trumps he will fail. He plays top clubs, returns to his hand with a diamond lead and ruffs a club. He returns to his hand with a heart and ruffs his last club. But he then lacks an entry to his hand and cannot prevent the defense from scoring a heart trick and also the ♦ J, promoted by a spade play from East.

If South considers the danger of a 3-0 trump split, he can take precautions. He must take the slight risk of playing dummy's club winners before leading a round of trumps. Then he can maneuver the club ruffs and eventually draw West's last trump.

TONTO. A method of responding to a 3NT overcall of an opening three-bid, devised by Robert Stone. The name is an acronym for Transfers Over 3NT Overcalls. The transfer always consists of two or more steps. (1) 4NT is quantitative ; (2) 4 ♠ is regular Blackwood; (3) 4 ♥ is a high transfer to diamonds unless that is the bid suit (then it is clubs); (4) 4 ♣ is a low transfer to hearts unless is the bid suit (then it is spades); (5) 4 ♦ is a middle transfer to the remaining suit. After a transfer response, opener bids cheaply to show a fit and accept the transfer to discourage. (But if the transfer shows a minor, 4NT discourages.) See *The Bridge World,* December 1995.

TOP. (1) On a board: the best score made in the play of a particular hand in a duplicate tournament. If one pair earns a top, their opponents must score zero points or a BOTTOM. (2) Score: the best score for a session of play among the contestants in direct competition (3) A card: to play a card higher in rank than the ones previously played by the second or third player to play to the trick; (4) The highest card in dummy's suit, as, declarer called for the top heart.

TOP AND BOTTOM CUEBID. An immediate overcall in the opponent's major suit to show the highest and lowest ranking unbid suits. See also MICHAELS CUE-BID.

TOP HONOR. See PRIMARY HONOR.

TOP OF INTERIOR SEQUENCE. See INTERIOR SEQUENCE.

TOP OF NOTHING. See THREE SMALL CARDS, LEAD FROM .

TOP ON A BOARD. The maximum number of matchpoint possible on a board. Two different methods are used, one by the ACBL and the other by the rest of the world. In the ACBL, top on a board is the number of times the board is played minus one. In the rest of the world, top on a board in the number of time the board is played multiplied by two, minus two. In the ACBL, a board played 13 times would have a top of 12 (13 times played minus 1), In the rest of the world, a board played 13 times would have a top of 24 (13 times 2 = 26, minus 2 = 24). Effectively all matchpoint scores in the rest of the world are double those in the ACBL, but this in no way ever effects the outcome. The difference in scoring methods is one of the major reasons why most final scores are now posted as percentages.

TOP SCORE. The highest number of matchpoints available to any contestant in direct competition. See MATCHPOINT; SCORING ACROSS THE FIELD; BAROMETER SCORING. In North America and some other areas of the world, top is one less than the number of times a board is in play. In Europe and some other areas, it is more common to make top two less than double the number of times a board is in play. The second method results in scores exactly twice as large as the first method, the major difference being that halves are eliminated. In American tournaments, fields are divided into sections and tops usually are figured within each section or, in some major events, combinations of sections. It is common in other parts of the world to score across the entire field, making for much larger tops. This has been easier to arrange since the advent of computers.

TORINO BULL. The trophy for the World Women's Team Olympiad, presented by the City of Turin, Italy,

on the occasion of the 1960 Olympiad. See Appendix V for winners.

TOTAL POINT SCORING. (British term is aggregate scoring.) Computation of scores based on points earned minus points lost, from the scoring table of contract bridge (see LAWS OF CONTRACT BRIDGE (Law 81), LAWS OF DUPLICATE (Law 77)); the scoring used at rubber bridge or CHICAGO. As a form of scoring in pair tournaments, total point scoring was complicated by the imposition of PENALTY LIMITS and the resulting EXCESS POINTS. It has been almost wholly eliminated, generally in favor of MATCHPOINT SCORING, but occasionally, in important matches, by IMPS FOR PAIR GAMES or scoring in team games by VICTORY POINTS. As a form of scoring in team games, it is adaptable particularly for match play in head-on contests. IMP scoring has largely replaced total point scoring. The Reisinger Trophy knockout teams in the Eastern States Regional was the last important knockout event in the United States to replace total point scoring with IMP scoring, doing so in 1965.

TOTAL TRICKS, LAW OF. See LAW OF TOTAL TRICKS.

TOUCHING CARDS. (1) Cards that are in sequence in the same suit, as the 10 and 9 in a holding of K-10-9-6. See SEQUENCE and PLAY FROM EQUALS. (2) With fingers: in duplicate bridge, it is illegal for any player to touch any cards other than his own, unless he is arranging the dummy's cards and so declares. See LAWS OF CONTRACT BRIDGE (Law 7).

TOUCHING HONORS. A holding of two or more honors that are in sequence. In a holding of Q-J-10-7 of a suit, the first three are touching honors.

TOUCHING SUITS. Suits that, within the order of ranking, are next to each other; spades and hearts, hearts and diamonds, and diamonds and clubs are touching suits. For some purposes, such as selecting the suit for an opening bid, clubs and spades are regarded as touching, with the clubs the "higher" suit.

TOURNAMENT. In the days of WHIST, gatherings of players for the purpose of competing at the game were termed "congresses", a term still current in Britain and Australia. As auction bridge replaced whist, the term "congress" gave way to "tournament", as the accent shifted from sociability to competition. Club games among local groups up to competition at national and international level are all so described. The essentials of a tournament are the planning thereof by a SPONSORING ORGANIZATION, publicity and promotion, the programming of events, the competition itself, the SCORING and determination of winners, and the HOSPITALITY in connection therewith. Various aspects of tournament play and references to the results of important tournaments are treated in special articles in this book. See DUPLICATE BRIDGE and CHAMPIONSHIP TOURNAMENTS.

TOURNAMENT COMMITTEE. See COMMITTEE.

TOURNAMENT DIRECTOR. The official represen-

tative of the sponsoring organization responsible for the technical management of the tournament, subject to the LAWS OF DUPLICATE BRIDGE to supplementary regulations announced by the sponsor.

Classification of directors. ACBL tournament directors are ACBL employees. As such, ACBL hires, trains and assigns (as needed and required) TDs to officiate at ACBL sanctioned tournaments. Occasionally they will be assigned to direct at non-ACBL tournaments (such as World Bridge Federation Championships). They are ranked according to ability and experience. There were 27 tournament directors listed by ACBL in 1994 in its two top categories, National and Associate National tournament directors. Exclusive of club and local directors authorized to conduct games at affiliated duplicate clubs, there were approximately 200 more lower rated TDs.

ACBL directors are designated as follows in descending order of rank: National Director, Associate National Director, Tournament Director (formerly Regional Director), Associate Tournament Director (formerly Sectional Director), and Local Tournament Director (formerly Local Director). Trainee is no longer a rank. As of 1995 only full-time or salaried directors are assigned as directors-in-charge at regional tournaments.

Field Representatives. There are six National tournament directors who supervise the tournament directors residing in their geographical area. Each field representative is responsible for training and promotions of TDs, staffing of tournaments, communication with his area units and districts and members, and helping solve any problems which may develop.

Field representatives: Betty Bratcher, Charles MacCracken, Peter Mollemet, Millard Nachtwey, Chris Patrias, Roger Putnam, Sol Weinstein, Tom Whitesides.

Other National Tournament Directors. Some are full-time salaried employees of the ACBL while the others, retired from the salaried staff, work various numbers of tournaments each year. All are qualified to provide top-flight direction at international, national and regional tournaments. When schedules permit, their services are also available as chief directors of sectionals, ensuring smooth conduct of these events as well as trained supervision of other directors of the staff.

National directors: Henry Cukoff, Charles MacCracken, Peter Mollemet, Millard Nachtwey, Chris Patrias, Roger Putnam, Thomas Quinlan, Bill Schoder (retired), Bobbie Shipley (retired), Sol Weinstein, Tom Whitesides.

Associate National directors. Some, but not all, are full-time salaried ACBL employees. Members of this group are fully qualified to serve as chief directors at regional and national events.

Associate National directors: Jeff Alexander, John Ashton, Steve Bates, Richard Beye, Betty Bratcher, Doug Grove, Olin Hubert, Pat Jackson, Patty Johnson, Ron Johnston, Bob Katz, Eleanor Kipperman, Guillermo Poplawsky, Matt Smith, Richard Strauss, Stan Tench.

World tournament directors. Since the beginning of the Eighties the EBL has organized a training course once every couple of years for tournament directors. It is attended by 50 to 60 tournament directors from all over Europe. All participants take an examination at the conclusion of the course. The purpose is to recognize the EBL's best directors and to develop a higher

standard of tournament directing.

Note: Throughout this book, "Director," when capitalized, refers to a member of the Board of Directors of a governing body and not to a tournament director.

TOWIE. A form of bridge devised for three players but intended to be played usually by four, five or more players, of whom only three play at one time but the others participate in the defenders' score against the declarer. The game was originated in Paris in 1931 by two Americans, J. Leonard Replogle and Paulding Fosdick, who were then living abroad. In 1935 Replogle, with the assistance of William Huske, sought to make Towie a popular game in the United States, with only moderate success, though it is still played. The principal books on the game were written by Huske and by Stuyvesant Wainwright Jr.

The deal in Towie conforms to that of certain earlier three-hand bridge games: After dealing four hands, the dealer turns up six cards of the dummy, after which the auction proceeds as in any three-handed game. Scoring is based on the 1932 INTERNATIONAL CODE, which differs from later codes in undertrick penalties and in the fact that notrump tricks count 35 each.

The three active players bid for the dummy. The high bidder becomes declarer. If he fulfills his contract, he collects from every other player, active or inactive; if he loses, he pays every such player. After each deal, one player is replaced by an inactive player, in order of precedence except that a player who is not vulnerable takes precedence over a vulnerable player.

If a game contract is not reached, the hands are thrown in, and a GOULASH follows. See also THREE-HANDED BRIDGE.

TRADITIONALISTS. See SCIENTISTS.

TRAIN BRIDGE. See COMMUTER BRIDGE.

TRAM TICKETS. Very poor cards. (British colloquialism).

TRANCE. A protracted break in the tempo of bidding or play during which a player attempts to solve a problem. Trances and huddles are frequent causes of ethical difficulties and disputes. See HUDDLE and SLOW PLAY .

TRANSFER BID. A bid that shows, by agreement, length in the next higher suit (1) to transfer the contract into the stronger hand and (2) to provide flexible bidding. Transfer bids were first used in the United States by David Carter (see TEXAS CONVENTION) and subsequently developed by Oswald Jacoby (see JACOBY TRANSFER BIDS). These bids were independently devised by Olle Willner of Stockholm, Sweden, who discussed the use of transfers in a series of articles in *Bridge Tidningen* in 1953-54. See also FOUR-SUIT TRANSFER BIDS. The original form of transfer bid was the Texas Convention, and SOUTH AFRICAN TEXAS is a revised form. Another purpose of transfer bids is to distinguish between weak and strong opening preempts, to enable responder to judge whether to try for slam. See BLACKWOOD AFTER INTERFERENCE; FOUR NOTRUMP OPENING AS MINOR PREEMPT; FOUR-SUIT TRANSFER BIDS; NAMYATS; RUBIN TRANSFERS, SMOLEN TRANS-

FER, TWO-UNDER TRANSFER PREEMPTS. For defense, see SANDWICH.

TRANSFER BREAKS. After a 1NT opening bid and a transfer into a major, opener is not obliged to complete the transfer. There are two good reasons why opener, with a good fit, should take stronger action than completion of the transfer: (1) his side may miss a game if he does not do so; (2) simply making the transfer may well make it easier for the opponents to come into the auction if responder has a very weak hand with nothing but length in the transfer suit.

After a JACOBY TRANSFER BID there are two common methods that allow opener to define his hand with a greater or lesser degree of precision. The first and simpler method is to use a new suit by opener as showing a four-card fit plus a source of tricks in the bid suit. 2NT shows a maximum and good three-card support, and a jump to three of the major shows fit and a maximum with a hand that does not fall into any of the other categories. In this method Marty Bergen has suggested that opener should break the transfer into two parts rather than show a source of tricks, with 2NT showing a 4-3-3-3 maximum and three of the major showing a 4-3-3-3 minimum.

The more complex method of transfer breaks focuses on describing shortage (and is particularly appropriate when playing a weak notrump, since the likelihood of not having a source of tricks is clearly higher). Playing this method, opener simply completes the transfer with a 4-3-3-3 minimum, and jumps to three of the major with a 4-3-3-3 maximum. Opener bids a strong doubleton (Ax or Kx) if he has one, or bids the second step with a weak doubleton. Thus after 1NT - 2◆, 2♥ is normal; 2♠ shows a fit plus an unspecified weak doubleton (responder can relay with 2NT to find out where the doubleton is, or retransfer with 3◆ to play 3♥ or 4♥ the right way up, or he can bid 3♥ as an invitation); 2NT shows Ax or Kx of spades; 3♣ shows Ax or Kx of clubs; 3◆ shows Ax or Kx of diamonds; 3♥ is a transfer break with a 4-3-3-3 maximum or five trumps.

After virtually all transfer breaks responder can retransfer at the three-level to play three or four of the major the right way up. Alternatively, he can bid three of the major as an invitation relating to whether his partner is minimum or maximum. Direct actions above three of the major are cuebids, while 3NT can be played as a serious slam try. A retransfer followed by a new suit can be played as a help-suit slam try.

TRANSFER FOR LEAD. A device used by some experts in the following situations:

(a) *West*	*North*	*East*	*South*
1♠	Dbl	2♣	
(b) *West*	*North*	*East*	*South*
1♥	1♠	Dbl	2♣

In each case, 2♣ is a transfer to diamonds. It may be based on diamond length, but it may show diamond strength, for lead-directing reasons, with spade support. Perhaps:

$$♠ \ J \ x \ x$$
$$♥ \ x \ x$$
$$◆ \ K \ Q \ J \ x$$
$$♣ \ x \ x \ x \ x$$

Invented by Eric Rodwell. See BROMAD, RUBENS ADVANCES.

TRANSFER OPENING PREEMPT. See NAMYATS; FOUR NOTRUMP OPENING AS MINOR PREEMPT; RUBIN TRANSFER; TRANSFER OPENING THREE-BID; TWO-UNDER OPENING PREEMPT.

TRANSFER OPENING THREE-BID. A development of the TEXAS principle. The bid has three technical advantages. First, the lead comes up to the hand which is likely to be strong in the side suits. Second, the defense is more difficult because little is known about declarer's strength and distribution. Third, the opening bidder may be able to show a freak two-suited hand by bidding his second suit on the second round. A technical disadvantage is that it is easier for the opponents to take action than it would be after a normal three-bid: a double and a cuebid in the opener's genuine suit are available as takeout bids of varying strength. Also, a preemptive bid in clubs cannot be made at the level of three. A practical disadvantage is that an absentminded partner may forget that the convention is being used. Also, it may gain an unfair advantage against opponents unfamiliar with the convention. Used in the world championships by Pierre Ghestem and René Bacherich of France.

A complete method was devised in 1968 by Svend Novrup and Anders Laustsen of Denmark. It is called Verdi because the players make beautiful music with it. 3♣, 3♦ and 3♥ are transfers to the next-higher suit, with normal preemptive strength. 3♠ shows a solid minor, allowing 3NT to be played from the correct side (unlike the gambling 3NT). 3NT opening shows a semi-solid minor suit. NAMYATS is used with this structure. See TWO-UNDER OPENING PREEMPT. The consensus defense (BWS1994) is that a double of the artificial opening shows strength but does not create a force.

TRANSFER OVER DOUBLES OF A PREEMPTIVE BID. When a preemptive action is doubled, minimum actions can be used to show length in the next-higher strain, with or without a fit with opener. A transfer to opener's suit shows a fitting top honor.

TRANSFER OVER DOUBLES OF ONE NOTRUMP. A four-suit escape method. A redouble is a transfer to clubs, 2♣ transfers to diamonds, 2♦ to hearts and 2♥ to spades. If responder redoubles and then bids 2♦ over the forced 2♣, he is asking opener to bid his better major.

TRANSFER OVERCALLS OF ONE NOTRUMP.
Over 1NT:
2♣ = diamonds
2♦ = hearts
2♥ = spades
2♠ = clubs.
Responder normally accepts the transfer if he would have passed an overcall. Other actions are those he would have made in response to a normal overcall.

This idea was introduced as part of the BLUE TEAM CLUB and has gained favor in Europe.

TRANSFER SQUEEZE. A squeeze play which results from TRANSFERRING THE MENACE. The following hand was played by Alan Truscott in the 1958 European Championships:

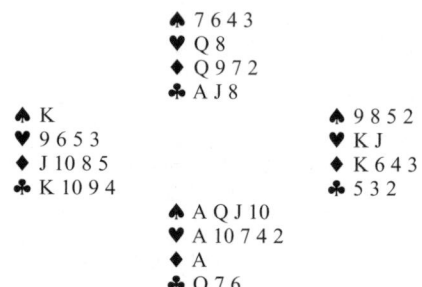

West led the ♦J against 4♠, which was ducked around to the ace. A heart to the queen and king brought a spade return, and the finesse of the queen lost to the king. A heart was returned and won by South, who led a second round of trumps, revealing the bad split. A low heart was ruffed and overruffed, and East exited with his last trump. The ♣J was finessed, and the ♦Q was led to transfer the diamond menace. East covered, South ruffed, and two winning hearts squeezed West in the minor suits.

TRANSFERRED TRICK. A trick transferred to the non-offending side after a revoke has been established. See LAWS OF DUPLICATE (Law 64).

TRANSFERRING THE MENACE. The process whereby control of a suit is transferred from one opponent to the other.

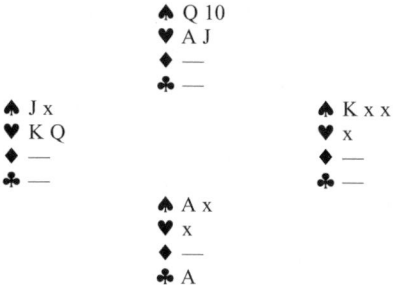

South has menaces in two suits, so the material for a squeeze is present, but each opponent controls one menace, and neither can be squeezed. If the lead is in the North hand, the ♠Q is led forcing East to play the king which is taken by the ace. The spade menace is no longer the queen guarded by East's king but the ♠10 guarded by West's jack, so West has BUSY CARDS in two suits, and he is squeezed by the lead of the ♣A. But if the lead had been in the South hand, the lead of the ♣A would have effected a GUARD SQUEEZE against West.

TRANSFORMATION CARDS. These are specially designed packs whose faces include the various pips on the suit cards as part of an overall design. During the last century, a number of artists tried their hands at creating pictures that would incorporate all of the pips, in their usual locations, into larger designs, generally of human or animal figures. The first such cards seem to have been made by J. G. Cotta, in Tubingen, Germany, in 1805, with several different packs produced by him in the next few years. English transformation cards appeared first in Ackerman's Repository in 1818, and several other packs soon followed. About 1850, sets of cards appeared in London, New York, Munich, Vienna and Paris, partially duplicates in design, some cards being

different while others appear in three or four of the packs. Because of the widespread copying, it is difficult to know which versions were original. Grimaud and Hart put their names on packs, and some artists' initials can be found, but precise dating appears impossible. The Eclipse Comic cards issued in New York were designed by F. H. Lowerre in 1876, Tiffany & Company issued their Harlequin cards three years later. These same designs were used for the first series of Kinney Brothers Cigarette cards. A second Kinney series followed with all new designs. In 1895, the United States Playing Card Company published its own packs, called "Hustling Joe" and "Vanity Fair."

For more information, see "Transformation Cards" by Albert Field, published by U.S. Games Systems, Stamford CT.

TRANSNATIONAL MIXED TEAMS. Major side event sometimes staged during the late stages of world championship events involving the Bermuda Bowl, the Venice Cup, the Olympiad Open Teams and the Olympiad Women's Teams. Teams that failed to qualify in the main event as well as new teams may enter. It is not necessary that all team members be from the same country – hence the transnational. A series of Swiss matches leads to the qualification of the top four teams for knockout semifinals and finals.

TRANSNATIONAL OPEN TEAMS. Major side event sometimes staged during the late stages of world championship events involving the Bermuda Bowl, the Venice Cup, the Olympiad Open Teams and the Olympiad Women's Teams. Teams that failed to qualify in the main event as well as new teams may enter. It is not necessary that all team members be from the same country – hence the transnational. A series of Swiss matches leads to the qualification of the top four teams for knockout semifinals and finals.

TRANSPORTATION. A synonym for COMMUNICATION.

TRAP. A defensive bidding system against the FORCING CLUB. Double indicates a heart suit and 1 ◆ shows a spade suit. 1 ♥ shows either a black two-suiter or a red two-suiter. 1 ♠ shows either both minors or both majors. 1 NT shows either a club-heart two-suiter or a diamond-spade two-suiter. All bids at the two level show either the suit bid or a three-suiter short in the suit bid. A modification to the two-level structure is to play that those bids show the suit above, or the two suits above. For example, 2 ◆ is either hearts or spades and clubs. See CRASH.

TRAP BID (or trap bidding). An inconsistent sequence of bids which traps partner by showing strength denied by an earlier bid. For example:

South	North
1 ♣	1 ♠
3 ♠	4 ♠
5 ♥	

South's raise to 3 ♠ was encouraging but nonforcing. North accepted the invitation to bid game, perhaps straining his values to do so, and is now faced by a slam invitation. South's bidding cannot be correct. If he is strong enough to bid 5 ♥, he must have been too strong to make

the invitational bid of 3 ♠. His bidding means that his side must play below game or above game, but cannot stop in 4 ♠. See also IMPOSSIBLE BID and PRESSURE BID.

TRAP PASS. A pass by a player holding a strong defensive hand, hoping the opposition will bid themselves into difficulties. It is usually made by a player holding length and strength in the suit bid by the opener on his right:

> ♠ 6
> ♥ A Q 10 7 4
> ◆ K J 7
> ♣ A K 5 3

If the right-hand opponent opens the bidding with 1 ♥, there is no good alternative to a pass. There is strong evidence that the hand is a misfit and that it will pay to defend. If 1 ♥ is passed out, the result should be reasonable. The same principle applies, only less forcefully, in a balancing position. A player with the above hand may consider passing if an opening bid of 1 ♥ is followed by two passes. This would certainly be sound tactics at matchpoint scoring against vulnerable opponents, as a score of 200 for the defense would beat all partscore results. A trap pass becomes a doubtful proposition when holding 18 or 19 high-card points, and is usually unwise with 20 or more. The danger of passing up a game in favor of a small penalty becomes too great.

Passes with strong hands by the player on dealer's right after an opening suit bid and a suit response are similar in principle, although the motive is slightly different: the prospect of a penalty is reduced, but the danger of taking action is greater. With a hand of exceptional strength, the fourth player should not necessarily rely on the fact that responder's bid is technically forcing. It is not at all unlikely that the dealer has made a psychic bid, and if he passes, the other defender cannot be expected to balance with a very weak hand. An unusual, and experimental, type of trap pass may sometimes be ventured by the partner of the opening bidder:

> ♠ 6
> ♥ K 8 5 3
> ◆ A J 4 2
> ♣ Q 10 5 4

If partner opens 1 ♠ and the next player passes, there is something to be said for a prompt pass if not vulnerable against vulnerable opponents. There is no certainty of a game, and if 1 ♠ is passed out the loss as a result of missing a game is unlikely to exceed 300. On the other hand, the fourth player may balance, in which case the penalty should be not less than 500 and might be 1,400. Such experiments should not be tried in matchpointed events (except when SHOOTING). See also MARMIC SYSTEM.

TRAP PLAY. See DECEPTIVE PLAY.

TRAVEL WITH GOREN. Returning by ship from the 1958 Bermuda Bowl competition, Charles Goren gave some on-board lectures. They drew full houses. Harold Ogust realized the potential of this and, together with Goren and Horace Craddock, founded Travel with Goren. In 1966, the business was incorporated and became a full-service travel agency specializing in bridge cruises.

TRAVELING SCORESLIP (or TRAVELER). The official score of each deal in a pair duplicate game may be

recorded either of two ways: on a traveling scoreslip or an individual pick-up card. A majority of clubs and lesser championship events use the traveling scoreslip. This slip travels with the board, folded and inserted in a pocket so that the scores for the tables which have played it earlier are not visible until the slip is opened after the board has been played. The score at the new table is then entered. At the end of the session, when the board has been played at each table in the game, all the results will have been entered on the slip. The tournament director will then either enter the scores on his computer or matchpoint the scores if he is scoring manually. See CALIFORNIA SCORING, COMPARING SCORES, ESTIMATION, PICKUP SLIPS, SCORING FORMS.

TRAY. (1) An obsolete term for a board. (2) The tray which slides under the SCREEN in major championships, carrying the bidding-box cards from one pair of opponents to the other pair. It was invented by Henny Dorsman of Aruba and introduced at the Central American and Caribbean Championships at Aruba in 1977.

TREASURER. Those who have held this position in the AMERICAN BRIDGE LEAGUE and the AMERICAN CONTRACT BRIDGE LEAGUE are:

1927-28	Clayton W. Aldrich
1929	E. J. Tobin
1930-31	J. J. Laffeny
1932-34	Russell Baldwin
1935	David Burnstine (Burns)
1936	Gordon M. Gibbs
1937	J. N. S. Brewster, Jr.
1938-40	Gordon M. Gibbs
1941-42	J. H. Block
1943-44	Ralph W. Gresham
1945-47	Bertram Lebhar, Jr.
1949-51	Ralph W. Gresham
1952-66	Harry J. Fishbein
1966-69	Samuel Stayman
1969-70	Percy X. Bean
1970-72	Jerome Silverman
1973-74	Walter O'Loughlin
1975-76	Donald A. Moeller
1976-78	Lawrence Jolma
1979-80	Sydney A. Levey
1981	Lawrence Jolma
1982-83	Donald A. Moeller
1984	George Retek
1985-87	Herbert L. Smith
1988-95	Donald A. Moeller
1995-99	Glenn Smith
1999-	Bob Lix

TREATMENT. A natural bid that indicates a desire to play in the denomination named (or promises or requests values in that denomination), but that also, by agreement, gives or requests additional information on which further action could be based. A treatment thus differs from a CONVENTION, which is a bid that gives or requests information unrelated to the denomination named. For example, a LIMIT JUMP RAISE is a treatment; but a LIMIT JUMP RAISE TO SHOW A SINGLETON in a side suit is a convention. INVERTED MINOR SUIT RAISES and PREEMPTIVE RE-RAISES are other examples of treatments.

TRELDE LEAD (developed by John Trelde of the Neth-

erlands). A method of leading from honor sequences to distinguish between a genuine sequence of three touching honors and a false sequence of only two touching honors. The principle is that from a genuine sequence the highest card is led and from a false sequence the second highest card is led. Partner should be able to determine which combination the lead is from by his and dummy's holding in the suit. Leads from A-K doubleton, a suit headed by A-K-Q and internal sequences follow accepted practices. See LEADS.

TREY. The 3 or three-spot of each suit.

TRIAL BID. A game suggestion made by bidding a new suit after a major suit fit has been located:

South	North
1♥	2♥
3♣	

North-South have provisionally agreed to play a heart contract, although a final contract of 3NT is not completely excluded. However, it is completely impossible that the right contract could be clubs, except at the six-level so the club bid can only be an exploring maneuver. If North has no interest in game, he signs off with 3♥. If he wants to accept the invitation, he bids 4♥ or 3NT. As a rare alternative, he may bid an unbid suit in which he has strength, as a move toward 3NT or as a way to show his honor location. The usual practice is for South to make his trial bid in a suit in which he needs support, so it will generally contain at least three cards and at least two losers. Possible holdings would be: x-x-x, A-x-x, K-10-x-x, J-x-x-x, and many others.

The responder therefore takes his holding in the trial bid suit into account when making the decision whether to bid game. If his holding is neither maximum nor minimum in strength, he allows himself to be encouraged if he has honor strength or a shortage in the trial bid suit. Conversely, he should tend to reject the invitation if he has three or four small cards in the suit; a holding headed by the jack is only a slight improvement. In one special case, the final contract may be in a suit other than the one originally agreed on:

South	North
1♠	2♠
3♥	4♥

4♥ may easily prove a superior contract to 4♠. If South holds four hearts, and North holds four, five, or six, spades will be an inferior landing place if the spade fit is 5-3.

There are two other situations in which bids of similar types are made.

South	North
1♣	1♠
2♠	3♥

North's bid invites 4♠ and suggests some length in hearts, in which he would welcome support.

South	North
1♣	2♣
2♥	

This is not a trial bid because no major suit has been agreed on. A heart fit is still possible, but it is very likely that the partnership will head for 3NT. South will tend to bid a suit in which he is strong, rather than a suit in which he is weak. His heart suit might be A-Q-x, but in no circumstances could it be x-x-x unless he was making a psychic effort to inhibit a lead.

Similarly:

South	North
1 ♥	2 ♥
2 ♠	3 ♠

With three hearts and four spades in North, or with five hearts and four spades in South, the spade contract may be superior. However, restraint must be exercised. South's spade bid may be a three-card suit; hence a jump in spades by responder is unwise and unnecessary. See also INTEREST-SHOWING BID; PREEMPTIVE RERAISE; SHORT-SUIT GAME TRY; SINGLE RAISE; TWO-WAY GAME TRY; WEAK SUIT GAME TRY .

TRIATHLON. A three-event tournament, usually conducted over three days. The first event is a team of-four. Then the teams break down into pairs for a pairs contest. The final event is an individual. The winner is the player who has the best aggregate score. Since team events are scored differently from pair and individual events, the sponsoring organization has to set up a conversion scale that gives each event a proportional weight in the final standings.

TRICK. Consists of four cards played in rotation after an initial lead of one of the cards by the player whose turn it was to lead or to play first to the trick. A trick of four cards can be won by virtue of the winning card being highest in rank (number) of the four played; or because the card led is "long," that is, a remaining card in one's hand of a suit not held by any other player; or by having a trump card played to it either by declarer or dummy or either defender.

TRICK APPROPRIATED IN ERROR. A packet of the four cards played to a trick that has been gathered in by the pair of which neither contributed the winning card. Such a trick must be restored to the side that contributed the winning card if discovered in time.

TRICK POINTS. Points scored for fulfilled contracts toward the game. See BELOW THE LINE.

TRICK-SCORE. The value of the odd tricks of fulfilled contracts toward the winning of the game; in clubs or diamonds, 20 points each; in hearts or spades, 30 points each; at notrump, 40 points for the first and 30 for each subsequent trick. In French tournament play the fourth trick at notrump was reduced to 20 points for a while so that 4 ♥, 4 ♠, and 4NT each scored 120 points. See FRENCH SCORING. Different trick scores operate in auction bridge and plafond.

TRI-COUNTRY TRIALS. Since 1985, a three-way playoff among Bermuda, Canada and Mexico has determined one of the Zone II teams for the Bermuda Bowl and Venice Cup world championships. The tri-country trials are held every other year in odd-numbered years. (In even-numbered years, the three countries send their national champions to the World Team Olympiad or the World Pairs/Rosenblum Teams/McConnell Teams championships.) In the tri-country trials, each team plays a match against the others. The team with the poorest record is dropped, while the other two play to determine the representative. Canada, which had never participated in the Bermuda Bowl world championships before, won the first four tri-country trials to become one of the North American teams in the

Bermuda Bowl. In 1993 Mexico won its first trip to the Bermuda Bowl by defeating Canada and Bermuda in the tri-country trials. In 2001 there was no trial event because all three nation failed to qualify because they finished in the bottom half of the 2000 World Team Olympiad. Canada qualified for the Venice Cup because the Canadian women finished in the top half of 2000 Women's Olympiad. See INTERNATIONAL OPEN TEAM SELECTION. For results see Appendix III.

TRIPLE COUP. A series of plays by the declarer in which he trumps three cards from the dummy's hand in order to shorten his own trump suit to the number held by his right-hand opponent. The purpose is to lead a card from the dummy at the 11th or 12th trick which the right-hand opponent must trump (being void of all other suits), and thus permit declarer to win the last two or three tricks by virtue of his own trumps being over those of his opponent. If the cards deliberately trumped by the declarer are side suit winners in their own right the coup is termed a grand coup. See COUP, GRAND COUP, TRIPLE GRAND COUP.

TRIPLE CROWN. This consists of the World Team Olympiad, the Bermuda Bowl and the World Pairs. It has been won by: Pierre Jais and Roger Trezel of France; Bobby Wolff and Bob Hamman of the United States; Jeff Meckstroth and Eric Rodwell of the United States; Gabriel Chagas and Marcelo Branco of Brazil.

TRIPLE GRAND COUP. A grand coup in which the declarer shortens his hand three times in trumps, to reduce his holding to the same number as held by his right-hand opponent, by ruffing three winners from the dummy.

TRIPLE RAISE. A raise of partner's opening suit bid to the four-level. In a major suit the bid indicates that a fine distributional fit has been found, but that slam prospects are remote. A typical hand for responder would include an ace, a singleton, five trumps, and 0-10 points in high cards. None of these requirements is essential, but the hand should give promise of nine tricks opposite a minimum opening bid. The opener can assume that responder does not hold two aces, for he would then be likely to bid more slowly in case slam possibilities exist. See FAST ARRIVAL; THREE NOTRUMP RESPONSE. In a minor suit the bid is rarer, indicating an even more distributional hand. It is markedly preemptive in character and weaker in high cards than the major suit raise. A typical distribution would be 6-5-2-0 with length in both minor suits. The raise of the major-suit opening to game can have a much wider range, up to perhaps 14 points in high cards, if the opening bid is limited as in the PRECISION, SCHENKEN and BLUE TEAM CLUB systems. See also DOUBLE RAISE and DELAYED GAME RAISE.

TRIPLE SQUEEZE. A squeeze against one opponent in three suits. It is a combination of three simple squeezes against the same opponent, which justifies the term. The term triple squeeze is often used to encompass squeezes which produce one trick and squeezes which produce two tricks. The latter is described under PROGRESSIVE SQUEEZE. See also BARCO SQUEEZE; CLASH SQUEEZE; COMPOUND SQUEEZE; GUARD SQUEEZE; HEXAGON SQUEEZE. The minimum requirements for a triple squeeze are two one-card menaces and a two-card menace with an entry opposite the

squeeze card. These are the basic end positions:

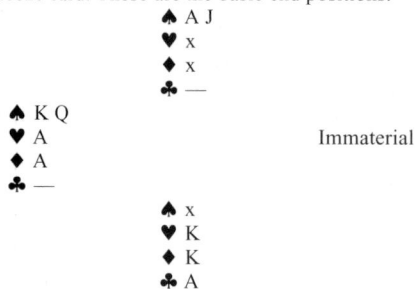

South leads the ♣ A, and West must surrender a spade, establishing a trick for South in that suit. (Any other discard permits South to win all four tricks.) In this position the hand opposite the squeeze card has one menace. Since North has two idle cards, the position is automatic and either opponent may be squeezed.

♠ A J
♥ x
♦ —
♣ K

Immaterial   ♠ K Q
                    ♥ A
                    ♦ —
                    ♣ A

♠ x
♥ K
♦ A
♣ x

In notrump, South needs three tricks. He leads the ♦ A, throwing a heart from the dummy, and East is squeezed in three suits.

In this position the hand opposite the squeeze card has two menaces. The ending shown is automatic and works equally well against either opponent.

♠ K
♥ A x
♦ K
♣ —

♠ A
♥ K J   Immaterial
♦ A
♣ —

♠ —
♥ Q x
♦ x
♣ A

This is a variation of the above position, which is positional. If the East and West cards are transposed, the squeeze is ineffective. South leads the ♣ A, and West is squeezed in three suits.

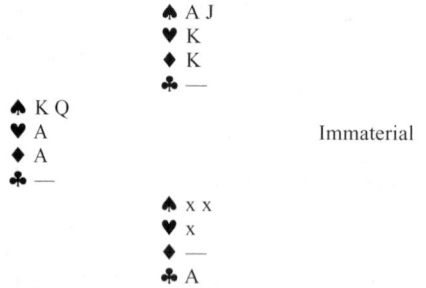

South leads the ♣ A, and West is squeezed, permitting

South to win two more tricks. In all these squeezes South has all but two of the remaining tricks. This is a characteristic of triple squeezes.

Fook H. Eng describes a situation where a gain of four tricks can be had in a progressive triple squeeze.

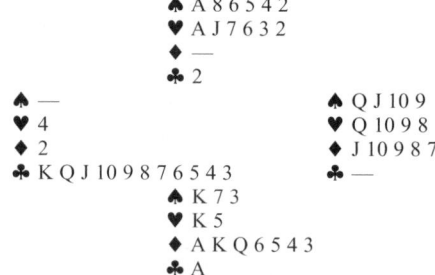

West leads the ♣ K against an outrageous 6NT contract which has only eight top winners. However, on the very first trick East is already squeezed. No matter which suit he discards, a trick in that suit will immediately be conceded. It is not without complications, so let us examine the different cases.

If East discards a spade, a low spade is immediately conceded. If East returns a heart the free finesse provides us the balance already. Because of our immediate concession in the spade suit we have sufficient entries to pick them off in the right order. If East returns either a diamond or a spade, we simply win the trick and run the rest of the spades for a heart-diamond squeeze.

If East discards a heart, the A and K are taken and East is given his heart winner. If he returns a spade, the trick rides to the ace. The hearts are run and East is caught in a positional spade-diamond squeeze. If he returns a diamond, the three diamonds are cashed first just to tighten the hand. Then the ♠ A is cashed and the hearts are run for the same spade-diamond squeeze.

If East discards a diamond, a diamond is conceded. If a spade is returned, the ace is won and either of the kings provide entry to run the diamond suit to squeeze East in hearts and spades. If a heart is returned, the free finesse provides the additional trick. If a diamond is returned, we simply run the suit to affect the spade-heart squeeze.

Another deal leading to a four-trick gain was constructed by N. Scott Cardell

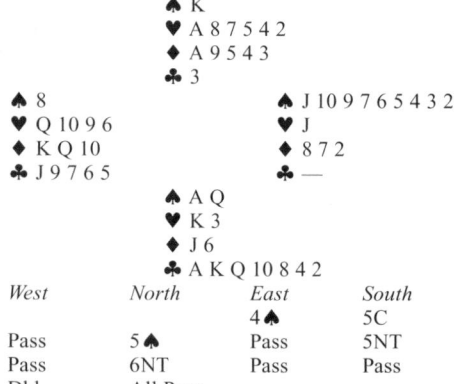

West	North	East	South
		4♠	5C
Pass	5♠	Pass	5NT
Pass	6NT	Pass	Pass
Dbl	All Pass		

West leads the ♠ 8, and is pleased to see that dummy has neither red jack. He correctly counts that declarer has at most eight top tricks, and he judges that South will have to duck twice to establish any suit. But he is

ruined when South overtakes the ♠K with the ace and cashes the ♠Q. South will play whichever suit West discards, cashing winners and conceding a trick. That will establish three tricks, and there will be a squeeze for one more in the other two suits. The play of the ♠Q is worth 2780 points.

In rare situations the triple squeeze may win two tricks immediately. In the following position there are three two-trick threats:

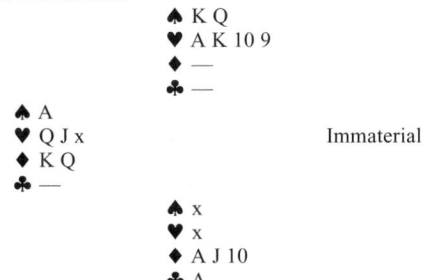

South has only four tricks on top, but the ♣A squeezes West in three suits, and any discard costs him two tricks.

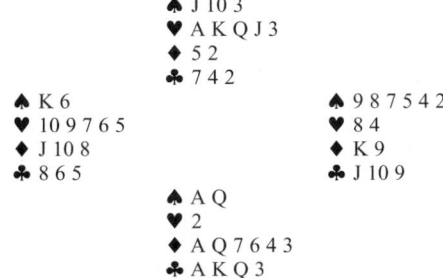

Clubs are led and South must take all the tricks in a notrump contract. South takes four club tricks, and West is squeezed in three suits. A discard of a spade or diamond costs two tricks, so West must throw a heart. South cashes the ♠A, and then runs the hearts, squeezing West in spades and diamonds. See also PROGRESSIVE SQUEEZE. For repeating triple squeezes, see BONNEY'S SQUEEZE; CLASH SQUEEZE; GUARD SQUEEZE; OVERTAKING SQUEEZE.

TRIPLETON. A holding of three cards in a given suit in a particular hand. The term is usually used to describe an original, or dealt, combination; as, an ace-king tripleton in diamonds. For an opening lead from a small tripleton, see THREE SMALL CARDS, LEAD FROM.

TROPHIES. Those trophies competed for in International events are listed under the following headings: BERMUDA BOWL; CROWNINSHIELD TROPHY; CULBERTSON TROPHY; LENZ TROPHY; McCONNELL CUP; ROSENBLUM CUP; SCHWAB CUP; SOLOMON TROPHY; TORINO BULL; VANDERBILT CUP (2); VENICE CUP; WORLD BRIDGE FEDERATION TROPHY. ACBL Trophies are listed separately: CHICAGO TROPHY; FISHBEIN TROPHY; HERMAN TROPHY; MCKENNEY TROPHY; MOREHEAD TROPHY; MOTT-SMITH TROPHY; REISINGER MEMORIAL TROPHY; SPINGOLD TROPHY; VANDERBILT CUP (1); VON ZEDTWITZ GOLD CUP.

TRUMP. The suit named in the final bid, other than notrump. Such suit is the trump suit. and a card of the trump suit, when played, is a winner over any card of a plain (not trump) suit. If two or more trumps are played on the same trick, the highest trump card played wins the trick. As a verb, See RUFF.

TRUMP ASKING BID. A convention used to inquire about key cards in the trump suit. As used in conjunction with ASKING BIDS as developed by Ely Culbertson, 4NT asked partner to describe his holding in the trump suit, as follows: 5♣ no ace, king, or queen; 5♦ one of three top honors; 5♥ two of three top honors 5♠ all three top honors. If the 4NT bidder now bids 5NT, partner must show his trump length by a series of artificial responses. If the response to an asking bid is at the five level, 5NT can be used as a trump asking bid for honor cards but it is not possible to follow up by asking for trump length. See also BARON SLAM TRY; BYZANTINE BLACKWOOD; GRAND SLAM FORCE; KEY CARD BLACKWOOD; KEY CARD GERBER; MALOWAN SIX CLUBS CONVENTION; PRECISION ASKING BIDS; ROMAN KEY CARD BLACKWOOD; ROMEX ASKING BIDS. WANG TRUMP ASKING BID.

TRUMP CONTROL. See CONTROL MAINTENANCE and TRUMP SUIT MANAGEMENT.

TRUMP COUP. See COUP.

TRUMP ECHO. See TRUMP SIGNAL

TRUMP INDICATOR. Small table-top items used to indicate the trump suit on each deal. They were used primarily in the game of whist where the trump suit was arbitrary and there was no dummy to indicate the trump suit. Trump indicators were used to show the trump suit as there was no bidding in whist and trump was arbitrarily selected by the cut of the cards or by turning up the 52nd card. This card then became concealed. As trump was not designated by either length or strength, it was easy to forget what trump was. The trump indicator was placed on the table as a Trump Reminder for all to see. Many trump indicators were double faced so they could be seen by both sides of the table, and some even had an arrow to designate who was the next dealer. "Trump indicators are whimsical and colorful, and they all move in some way to indicate the trump suit," according to Joan Schepps of Holyoke MA, who has been an avid collector of trump indicators for more than 15 years. Interest in trump indicators has exploded in the "collectibles" world. The computer and ebay auctions have made a major impact on the availability of trump indicators (also called trump markers), and they now command impressive prices and spirited bidding. Many originated in England, so Europeans knew about and appreciated trump indicators long before Americans did. Many trump indicators show ingenious imagination with all kinds of motifs ranging from the ordinary to the fanciful and exotic. Schepps has perhaps the largest collection in the world – more than 600 – which are displayed in a specially-built glass wall in Holyoke. Her collection has been highlighted in feature articles in the *ACBL Bridge Bulletin* and *Better Bridge*. Two other major collections are located in England and Italy.

TRUMP KING. See conventions listed under TRUMP ASKING BID.

TRUMP LEAD. The opening lead of a trump is not a first-line lead, and it may prove costly if the particular deal happens to be one where it was necessary for the defenders to cash tricks in a hurry. Nevertheless, there are circumstances when an opening trump lead figures to be eminently proper. (Trump leads should not be made merely because one does not know what else to lead.)

Here are the major situations: (1) where the bidding has indicated that dummy will be able to trump some of declarer's losing tricks; (2) where the leader has reason to fear an aggressive lead in some other suit, lest it be beneficial to declarer; (3) where there is a desire to mislead declarer as to the true state of affairs in the trump suit, as, for example, talking him out of taking a finesse that he figures to take if left to his own resources.

The following hands illustrate some of the situations in which a trump opening should be made. Where the bidding has indicated that dummy will be able to trump some of declarer's losing tricks, a trump should be seriously considered.

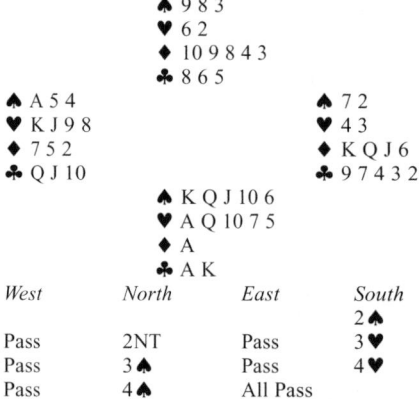

```
              ♠ 9 8 3
              ♥ 6 2
              ♦ 10 9 8 4 3
              ♣ 8 6 5
 ♠ A 5 4                    ♠ 7 2
 ♥ K J 9 8                  ♥ 4 3
 ♦ 7 5 2                    ♦ K Q J 6
 ♣ Q J 10                   ♣ 9 7 4 3 2
              ♠ K Q J 10 6
              ♥ A Q 10 7 5
              ♦ A
              ♣ A K
```

West	North	East	South
			2♠
Pass	2NT	Pass	3♥
Pass	3♠	Pass	4♥
Pass	4♠	All Pass	

What could be more "normal" than to open the ♣Q? If made, this will be won by declarer and he will promptly bang down the ace and another heart. A belated shift by West to the ace and another trump permits South to trump one of his losing hearts with dummy's last trump; the closed hand is entered with the ♦ A, picking up the last outstanding trump and conceding a further heart trick. Declarer makes 4♠. Based on the bidding, West should open the ace and follow with another trump. From the bidding it is apparent that South has a minimum of five spades and five hearts. It is clear that North prefers spades (however mildly) to hearts as the trump suit. West should immediately make every effort to reduce dummy's ruffing power and prevent dummy from ruffing hearts, especially since West has the ♥ K-J-9-8 behind South's rebid suit. With the ace of trumps lead, followed by another trump (and a third trump when West regains the lead in hearts), declarer will be defeated, losing three heart tricks and a trump trick.

When you want to mislead declarer as to the true state of affairs in the trump suit; as, for example, talking him out of taking a finesse which he figures to take if left to his own resources, a trump lead may turn out to be the winning lead. A deal which illustrates this point arose in the Men's Pair Championship of 1956. The West defender was Dr. Richard Greene.

```
              ♠ K 9 8 3
              ♥ A 5 4
              ♦ A Q 9
              ♣ K J 7
 ♠ A Q 6 2                  ♠ J 10 5 4
 ♥ K 10                     ♥ 9
 ♦ J 7 5 2                  ♦ 10 8 3
 ♣ 8 6 5                    ♣ A Q 9 4 2
              ♠ 7
              ♥ Q J 8 7 6 3 2
              ♦ K 6 4
              ♣ 10 3
```

North-South vulnerable, North deals. The bidding:

West	North	East	South
	1NT	Pass	4♥
Pass	Pass	Pass	

West opened the 10 of trumps on the reasoning: (a) On the bidding, North figured to have the ♥A, and South figured to have a long heart suit. (b) Even if South had something like an A-Q-J-x-x-x and dummy the x-x-x of hearts, West would still make his king, since declarer couldn't possibly diagnose the situation. (Upon winning the opening lead with the jack, declarer would enter dummy, and lead a low heart, finessing East for the king.)

What would you, as declarer, have played to the first trick? Probably the same as our declarer did: he went up with the ace in the hope that West was leading from the doubleton 10-9 and, hence, East had the singleton king. Had Dr. Greene not opened a trump, declarer, upon obtaining the lead, probably would have made the standard PERCENTAGE PLAY of leading the queen of trumps and finessing. As it was, he was talked out of finessing, and thus went down, losing two clubs, one spade, and, of course, the king of trumps.

The following specific situations suggest a trump lead, although circumstances may indicate another selection:

(1) The opponents have bid three suits and ended up in a fourth.

(2) Declarer, raised in his suit, has bid notrump, and been put back to his suit.

(3) The declaring side appears to have a good fit (5-4 or 4-4) in one suit and a misfit in the other suits. For example:

West	East
1♠	2♦
2♥	4♥

(4) The bidding indicates that dummy has exactly three trumps and a short suit.

(5) A takeout double has been passed for penalties.

(6) An opening suit bid of one has been passed out, and the opening leader has a weak hand. Partner's failure to balance suggests long, strong trumps.

(7) Your side has been doubled for penalties, and one opponent has removed the double.

(8) Your side has opened the bidding with a notrump bid.

(9) Against a high-level sacrifice bid, when the declaring side appears to have little high-card strength. Note also that a small trump is usually the desirable lead from holdings which would call for the highest in a plain suit: x-x-x, x-x; or J-10-x. See LEADS, VINJE SIGNALS.

TRUMP PETER. See TRUMP SIGNAL.

TRUMP PICK-UP. A play that reduces trump loss by

plain suit leads. It usually involves the lead of a side suit through an opponent in order to pick up his seemingly impregnable trump holding.

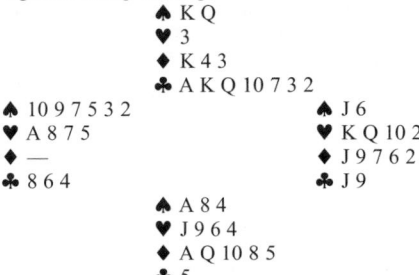

```
                    ♠ K Q
                    ♥ 3
                    ♦ K 4 3
                    ♣ A K Q 10 7 3 2
♠ 10 9 7 5 3 2                          ♠ J 6
♥ A 8 7 5                               ♥ K Q 10 2
♦ —                                     ♦ J 9 7 6 2
♣ 8 6 4                                 ♣ J 9
                    ♠ A 8 4
                    ♥ J 9 6 4
                    ♦ A Q 10 8 5
                    ♣ 5
```

Against South's 6 ♦ contract, West leads the ♥ A and continues the suit in response to his partner's violent signal. Dummy ruffs and leads the ♦ K, revealing the trump break. Declarer would have had no difficulty in finessing East out of his jack of trumps if dummy had not been forced to ruff; as it is, however, he has to utilize the club suit for that purpose. At trick three declarer leads a diamond to his 8 and then starts the clubs. If East ruffs, declarer overruffs, draws trumps, and enters dummy with a spade to make the good clubs. If East refuses to ruff, South discards his spades and hearts until the following position is reached:

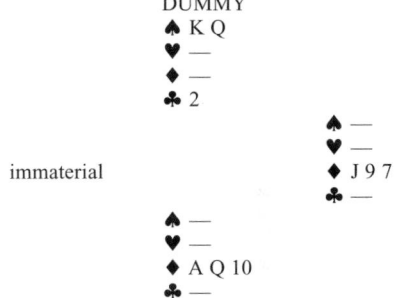

```
                    DUMMY
                    ♠ K Q
                    ♥ —
                    ♦ —
                    ♣ 2
                                        ♠ —
                                        ♥ —
immaterial                              ♦ J 9 7
                                        ♣ —
                    ♠ —
                    ♥ —
                    ♦ A Q 10
                    ♣ —
```

Dummy is on lead, and East is helpless to prevent declarer from taking the balance. See COUP; DEVIL'S COUP; GRAND COUP; SMOTHER PLAY.

TRUMP PLAY. See the following headings: CONTROL MAINTENANCE; COUNTING TRUMPS; CROSSRUFF; DRAWING TRUMPS; DUMMY REVERSAL; ELIMINATION; ELOPEMENT; ODEN RULE; PARTIAL ELIMINATION; RUFF AND DISCARD; RUFF AND RUFF; SMOTHER PLAY; TRUMP PICK-UP; TRUMP PROMOTIONS; TRUMP SUIT MANAGEMENT; UNDERRUFF.

TRUMP PROMOTION. The creation of trump tricks by forcing the premature use of trump cards by the opposition. There are several ways in which trump tricks can be promoted: (1) forcing ruffs (see FORCING DECLARER TO RUFF) so as to make trump tricks by length or by strength, when declarer is forced to ruff in one hand or the other with high trumps. (2) COUP EN PASSANT so as to make trump tricks by position (see also ELOPEMENT); (3) ruffing so as to make trump tricks by force of cards (See UPPERCUT); (4) threatening an overruff so as to make trump tricks by force of cards. In the following examples, spades are trump, and East has led a plain suit of which both South and West

are void. The best technique to promote trump tricks is to discard behind a player who has wasted a valuable card attempting to stop an overruff.

```
West
♠ A J
                    South
                    ♠ K Q 10 9 8 7 6 3
```

South must ruff with the king or queen to shut out West's jack. West discards and now has promoted a second trump trick. Notice that West must not overruff.

```
West
♠ K 10 2
                    South
                    ♠ A Q J 9 8 7 3
```

South must ruff with queen or jack to prevent West's 10 from winning. West discards and now makes two trump tricks.

```
West
♠ J 3 2
                    South
                    ♠ A K Q 10 9 8 7
```

A trick is promoted for West's jack.

TRUMP-REDUCING PLAY. A play designed to reduce the number of trumps in a hand, usually as a preparation for the trump pick-up. The principal trump-reducing plays are the simple and grand coup, the preliminary throw-in to force the lead of a ruffable suit, and the play of a trump on a trick taken by a higher trump.

TRUMP SIGNAL. A play by defenders to indicate length of trump holding. The play of an intermediate card followed by a lower card in the trump suit (HIGH-LOW SIGNAL) says a third trump is held. Such a signal is important if the player has a potential RUFFING TRICK. Note that the high-low trump signal to show a third card in the suit is the reverse of the meaning of an echo in a nontrump suit. Some players use the trump signal whenever they hold three trumps. But as the defenders can count declarer's trumps from the bidding far more often than vice versa, it is better to confine its use to situations in which there is a real prospect of a ruff. Many players these days sensibly use the trump echo as a suit-preference signal, which is a far more potent signal. See also SIGNAL, SIGNALING; VINJE SIGNALS.

TRUMP SQUEEZE. A squeeze in which the ruffing power of the trump suit plays an essential part. Here is an example of the most common form of simple trump squeeze:

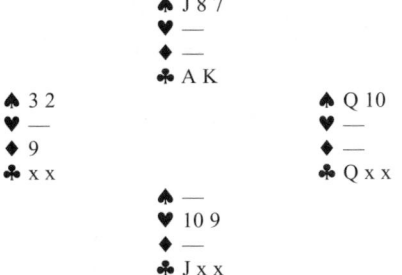

```
                    ♠ J 8 7
                    ♥ —
                    ♦ —
                    ♣ A K
♠ 3 2                                   ♠ Q 10
♥ —                                     ♥ —
♦ 9                                     ♦ —
♣ x x                                   ♣ Q x x
                    ♠ —
                    ♥ 10 9
                    ♦ —
                    ♣ J x x
```

Hearts are trumps, and South leads a trump, discarding a spade from dummy. East is squeezed. If he discards a spade, declarer enters dummy with a club and ruffs the ♠ Q. If East discards a club, South cashes his winners in

that suit, dropping the queen, and returns to hand by ruffing a spade in order to cash the established ♣J. This squeeze is automatic, and it has a distinct resemblance to the CRISSCROSS SQUEEZE with a trump taking the place of an isolated master card in the other position.

These are the characteristic elements of the trump squeeze:

(1) A split menace. But see BACKWASH SQUEEZE.

(2) A ruffing menace (this consists of two low cards in dummy, and a trick that can be established by ruffing provided RHO weakens his guard in that suit).

(3) Dummy must have two entries either in the split menace (as above) or by means of an additional entry in a third suit. If both menaces are guarded on the left the trump factor is not essential and we have an ordinary simple squeeze against LHO. It is worth noting that the squeeze takes place while declarer retains a trump; in most squeeze positions the last trump must be played before the pressure is felt.

There are two more simple trump squeeze positions:

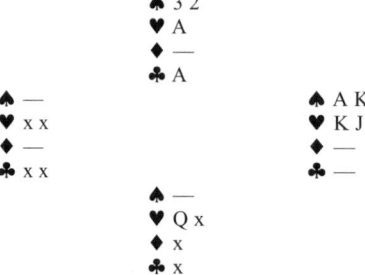

Diamonds are trumps. A club is led to the ace and East is squeezed. A spade discard enables South to ruff out East's spade guard and a heart discard permits North to cash the ace of that suit. The South hand is re-entered with a spade ruff and the ♥Q is cashed.

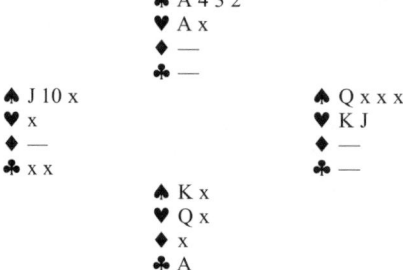

Diamonds are trumps. The ♣A is led and East is squeezed. A spade discard unguards his stopper, which can be ruffed out; a heart discard establishes the queen once the ace is cashed.

Squeeze-Finesse at Trumps
Simple

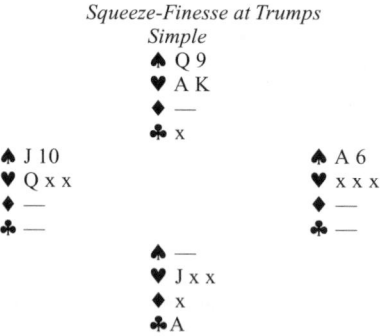

Diamonds are trumps. The ♣A squeezes West. If he discards a heart, the ace and king of that suit are cashed, South re-enters his hand by ruffing a spade in order to cash the ♥J. If West discards a spade, a heart to North, and leads the ♠Q declarer leads to ruff out the ace and establish the 9.

Double

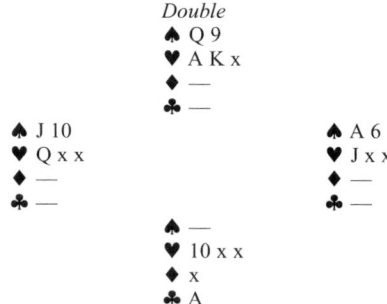

Diamonds are trumps. South leads the ♣A, and West is squeezed. A spade discard enables South to ruff out East's stopper. If a heart is discarded, East is subjected to a simple trump squeeze.

Double

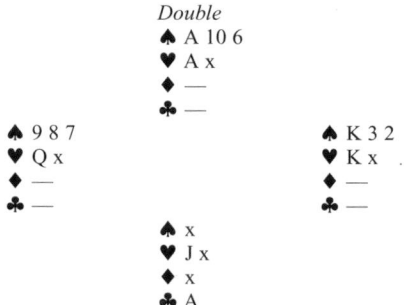

Diamonds are trumps. South leads the ♣A, and West is squeezed. A spade discard enables South to establish a spade by leading to the ace, and returning the 10. A heart discard places East in a simple trump squeeze.

Trump Guard Squeeze
Simple

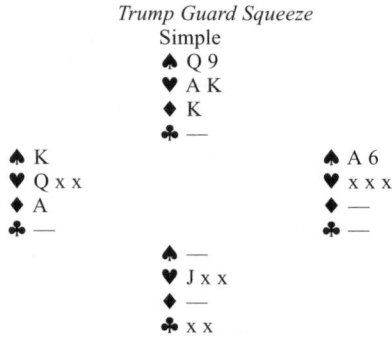

Clubs are trumps. A trump is led, and West is squeezed in three suits. A diamond discard establishes the king; a heart discard permits South to play ace and king of that suit, establishing the jack, with a spade ruff as re-entry; a spade discard allows South to lead a heart to the king and lead a spade to ruff out East's ace.

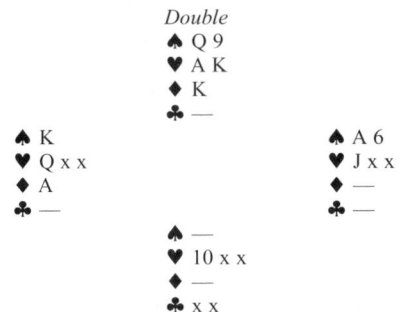

Double

Clubs are trumps. A trump is led, and West is squeezed in three suits. A diamond discard establishes the king; a heart discard places East in a simple trump squeeze; a spade discard permits South to lead a heart to the king, and lead a spade to ruff out East's ace.

TRUMP SUIT. The principles governing the choice of a trump suit are well established. The following are basic rules, subject to certain exceptions.

(1) Eight cards or more between the partnership constitute a satisfactory trump suit.

(2) If the partnership can find an eight-card (or longer) fit in a major suit, the contract should usually be played in that suit.

(3) If the partnership has values for game (i.e., 25-26 points), the contract should be 3NT if no major suit is available.

The following discussion centers on some of the exceptions.

When to play with fewer than eight trumps. Occasionally a trump suit in which the partnership has only seven cards may be the best bet, especially if the suit is strong (at least three of the top four honors) and one of the other suits appears to be weak. This type of hand is not uncommon:

```
♠ A Q 10 8 4        ♠ K 6
♥ 8 7               ♥ 9 3
♦ K 6 2             ♦ A Q J 10 7
♣ K Q 3             ♣ 10 8 6 4
```

These hands are on the borderline between partscore and game as far as values go. Clearly the only sound game contract is 4♠, which needs a 3-3 break in spades or the ♠J falling doubleton. Notice the symptoms which point to this seven-card trump suit: a strong trump suit and a marked weakness in another suit.

When the seven-card trump suit is split 4-3, a strong trump suit and a weak side suit are still the signs to look for, but there is a further and most important complication. For the contract to be a good one, it is usually necessary for the hand which is shorter in the trump suit to be able to ruff the weak suit.

```
♠ A K J 5           ♠ Q 6 2
♥ 9 8 5             ♥ 3
♦ K 10 5            ♦ A Q J 9 2
♣ A 7 3             ♣ 10 8 6 4
```

4♠ is laydown, barring very bad breaks, and on a heart lead West can certainly make 11 tricks and perhaps 12. Although the 5-3 fit in diamonds looks like a better bet than spades, 5♦ has no chance whatever. As the heart ruffs come in the long trump hand, 10 tricks are the limit. The fact that the heart shortage is with the spade shortage is doubly advantageous; there is a positive profit, in that the heart ruffs score extra tricks, and a negative profit

in that heart ruffs do not weaken control of the trump suit. The converse position is much less attractive:

```
♠ A K J 5           ♠ Q 6 2
♥ 3                 ♥ 9 8 5
♦ K 10 9 5 2        ♦ A Q J
♣ A 7 3             ♣ 10 8 6 4
```

If you play this hand in 4♠ and ruff the second heart lead, you are uncomfortably placed. It looks as though a 4-2 spade break will be fatal, but the play is interesting. West should cash his ♠ K-J, leaving two trumps at large, and then play diamonds. A defender ruffs and plays another heart, and now West can please himself whether he ruffs and continues diamonds, or simply discards a club loser. Is there a simpler way of dealing with West's problems? He should, of course, quietly discard his two club losers on the second and third rounds of hearts. Then a fourth heart can be ruffed in dummy.

So in this situation declarer has made 10 tricks by skillful play, and can never make more; while in the previous case, with the heart and spade shortages in the same hand, he makes 10 tricks without effort, and will often make more.

The moral is that a 4-3 fit in a strong suit will be satisfactory if the hand with three trumps has a shortage in the enemy suit. But if the hand with four trumps is going to be forced to ruff, the bidding should be more cautious: there will certainly be problems of control which may be difficult to solve.

Seven trumps divided 6-1 or 7-0, on the other hand, will usually prove adequate because declarer can accept ruffs without losing control. But here also it is better for the suit to be fairly robust, and if a six-card suit has only one high honor, there may well be a better spot to play the hand.

To play with six trumps is nearly always a mistake. It is true that a strong 6-0 fit will play well, and occasionally a strong 5-1 fit may be the best spot; it is even possible to construct hands on which the only game to be made is in a strong 4-2 fit. But for practical purposes we can rule out any deliberate intention of playing in a trump suit in which the opposition have the majority of cards.

When to reject an eight-card fit. There are three situations in which 3NT should be preferred to four of a major suit.

Type 1:

```
♠ K J 7             ♠ A 4
♥ 9 7 6 3 2         ♥ K 8 4
♦ Q 10 7            ♦ K J 9
♣ A 3               ♣ K Q J 9 6
```

Although there is a ruff to be had in dummy, both hands are balanced and the heart suit is very feeble. If East opens 1NT (strong), West can simply raise to 3NT, making no effort to play in hearts, or he can use Stayman and bid 3NT over the 2♦ response. If East has good hearts, the suit will pull its weight in notrump. It is easy to see that 3NT is a virtual certainty, while 4♥ needs a 3-2 heart break with the ace well placed.

Type 2:

```
♠ A 4               ♠ 8 6
♥ A K Q J 8 3       ♥ 10 6 2
♦ A 5               ♦ J 7 4
♣ A 7 6             ♣ J 9 8 4 3
```

Here the possible trump suit, far from being weak, is absolutely solid. But there are nine sure tricks in notrump and little chance of 10 in hearts — the East hand has no usable ruffing value. This is, of course, easy for West to

spot, because he can count nine tricks in his own hand; but the position will be difficult and perhaps impossible to diagnose if some of West's strength is transferred to East. If West has eight tricks in his hand, he can sometimes take the gamble that East will produce the ninth and that the opponents will not manage to cash five tricks first.

To land this sort of contract the tricks have to be quick ones; aces in the side suits are essential, and the presence of minor honors will suggest that the suit contract is preferable. There is a paradoxical element in this: in a general way, the presence of aces normally suggests a suit contract, and the presence of minor honors suggests notrump.

Failure to recognize type 3 often does not show on the scoresheet, so it usually stays unrecognized.
Type 3:

♠ J 5 3 2	♠ A Q
♥ K J 7 5	♥ Q 6 3 2
♦ A Q	♦ K J 7 5
♣ Q J 4	♣ K 8 7

Suppose East opens 1NT (15-17). West should now reason along these lines: our combined count is about 30, so game is very easy, but there is no slam; even if there is a major-suit fit, the suit game may fail through a bad break, while 3NT is surely ironclad. So West raises to 3NT, which is impregnable, while 4♥ would fail with a little bad luck— a 4-1 trump break and the ♠K with South. These tactics may cost 20 or 50 points aggregate, but this is good insurance except at matchpoint pairs.

In the slam zone there are other considerations that may cause us to reject a combined eight-card major suit holding. The most common symptom is a weak trump suit:

♠ A 8 6 3	♠ J 7 4 2
♥ A Q J 7	♥ K 3
♦ A K 6	♦ 4 2
♣ J 7	♣ A K Q 10 8

Twelve tricks are obviously laydown in clubs or notrump, but many players would arrive disastrously in 6♠, which needs the 7% miracle of doubleton K-Q. To avoid this type of trap often requires fine bidding judgment.

This is another example in which the major suit has one loser only, but that denomination is still wrong:

♠ A 10 8 7 6 3	♠ K 5
♥ K Q 2	♥ 9 7 6
♦ A Q	♦ K 8 4
♣ J 6	♣ A K Q 10 8

6♠ again needs a miracle. 6NT is a good contract, with slightly better than an even chance: as well as the ♥A with South, we can hope for a lucky spade position or a squeeze against North if he holds all the major-suit honors. But far and away the best contract is 6♣, in which the 12th trick may come from hearts or from ruffing out the spade suit. Again the strength of the trump suit proves more important than the length.

It may sometimes be advisable to reject an eight-card fit headed by the three trump top honors:

♠ A Q 7 5 4	♠ K 8 3
♥ K	♥ Q J 6 5
♦ A Q 9 3	♦ K
♣ K 9 4	♣ A Q 7 5 2

6♠ and 6♣ are obviously both sound contracts, depending on a 3-2 trump break. But with a lot of general strength, 6NT will often offer more chances. Here the notrump slam makes if either black suit breaks, or if a squeeze develops.

When to play in five of a minor. As it is much easier to make nine tricks than 11, contracts of five in a minor suit are rare. It is nearly always possible to play in 3NT, or in a seven-card major-suit fit.

This is particularly true in matchpoint duplicate events, when a successful contract of 5♣ or 5♦ usually scores badly. Other pairs are likely to score slightly more by making 10 tricks in notrump or a major. To play in a minor-suit game with a 4-4 or 5-3 fit is very rare indeed. When it does happen, it is usually because *both* minor suits are held, and there is no seven-card fit in a major:

♠ x	♠ x x x x
♥ A x	♥ K x x
♦ A x x x	♦ K x x x
♣ A K x x x x	♣ x x

5♦ is the only possible game. It requires 3-2 breaks in both minor suits, representing a 46% chance.

This demonstrates two common symptoms of minor-suit games; a completely exposed suit, and obvious ruffing values (singleton or void) in each hand.

If a solid six-card minor suit is held opposite a balanced hand, 3 NT is usually right. But in some cases it may be possible to diagnose a serious weakness and play in the minor suit:

West	*East*
♠ x x x	♠ A K x
♥ x	♥ x x x
♦ A Q x x x x	♦ K x x x
♣ A K x	♣ Q J x

The bidding may start:

West	*East*
1 ♦	2NT
3 ♣	3 ♠

after which the heart weakness is identified and the diamond game is reached. As is often the case when the choice lies between 3 NT and a minor suit, the players bid suits in which they have strength but not necessarily length (see STRENGTH-SHOWING BIDS). Interchanging East's rounded suits would produce a different contract:

West	*East*
♠ x x x	♠ A K x
♥ x	♥ Q J x
♦ A Q x x x x	♦ K x x x
♣ A K x	♣ x x x

In this case the first three bids would be the same, but East's second bid would be 3NT, showing stoppers in both major suits, and West would subside. Ten tricks in notrump are certain, and 11 are likely, while 5♦ needs a high heart lead or an endplay to succeed.

TRUMP SUIT MANAGEMENT. The way in which declarer utilizes the trump suit in the play of the hand.

The proper technique in handling the trump suit varies, depending first upon the length and the division of the trump suit in the combined hands, i.e., declarer and dummy, and secondly the manner in which the outstanding trumps are distributed in the defenders' hands. Generally speaking, the minimum number of trumps required for a game contract is eight, and the most favorable distribution is four in the dummy and four in the declarer's hand, referred to as:

The 4-4 Fit: The main advantage of this division is that declarer can stand being forced to ruff twice in either hand, reserving the other for purposes of drawing trump. If one opponent holds four trumps, the situation will be much more satisfactory with a 4-4 than a 5-3 distribution; declarer must then take the precaution of

looking to his side suits before tackling trumps:

```
              ♠ K J 10 4
              ♥ 8 7 6 3
              ♦ A K 2
              ♣ 4 3
♠ 8                        ♠ 9 7 6 5
♥ A K 5                    ♥ Q J 9 2
♦ J 9 8 7                  ♦ 6 5 3
♣ 9 8 7 5 2                ♣ A 10
              ♠ A Q 3 2
              ♥ 10 4
              ♦ Q 10 4
              ♣ K Q J 6
```

Against 4♠, West opens the ♥K. If the defense continues hearts, declarer ruffs the third round and knocks out the ♣A. East leads his last heart and South ruffs with the ace, draws trump, and takes the rest. On any other defense, declarer makes 10 tricks by ruffing his losing club high in the dummy before drawing East's trumps.

The 4-4 distribution lends itself ideally to crossruffing. Declarer must be careful to cash his side-suit winners before attempting to score his trumps separately.

```
              ♠ A 7 6 2
              ♥ A Q J 5
              ♦ —
              ♣ Q 10 6 3 2
♠ J 9 5 3                  ♠ Q 4
♥ —                        ♥ 9 8 4 3 2
♦ 10 7 6                   ♦ A J 5 4
♣ A K J 8 5 4              ♣ 9 7
              ♠ K 10 8
              ♥ K 10 7 6
              ♦ K Q 9 8 3 2
              ♣ —
```

The contract is 4♥, against which West leads the ♣K. Declarer ruffs and is in a position to make 10 tricks in spite of the vile distribution, provided he makes the ♠A-K before he ruffs the third club. Failure to do so would give East an opportunity to discard a spade, and declarer would then be unable to enjoy both of his spade winners.

The 4-3 Fit: When the dummy holds only three trumps, facing four in declarer's hand, the play is unlikely to proceed favorably. These hands normally play better in notrump, especially at the higher levels; exceptionally (e.g., when the opponents have an established suit), 4-3 fits are the only ones available. These contracts frequently call for delicate handling.

The problem of control is critical, and declarer must often establish his side winners before embarking on drawing trumps.

```
              ♠ K 4 3
              ♥ Q 10
              ♦ Q J 9 7 4
              ♣ K 3 2
♠ 6 5 2                    ♠ 10 8 7
♥ A K 7 4 3                ♥ J 9 8 6 2
♦ A 3                      ♦ 6 2
♣ 10 5 4                   ♣ A 7 6
              ♠ A Q J 9
              ♥ 5
              ♦ K 10 8 5
              ♣ Q J 9 8
```

4♠ is the only possible game contract, and, as the cards lie, cannot be defeated. The defense does best to play hearts at every opportunity, and South ruffs the second round and plays diamonds. West plays a third round

of hearts which is ruffed in dummy. Declarer now knocks out the ♣A and ruffs a further heart in dummy. Only now can he afford to draw trumps, and when they break he claims the balance with good diamonds and clubs.

Sometimes declarer can retain control of a shaky trump suit by refusing to ruff.

```
              ♠ K Q 10
              ♥ 4 3 2
              ♦ Q J 9 7
              ♣ A 10 4
♠ 8 7 6 4                  ♠ 9 5
♥ A K Q 8 5                ♥ J 9 7
♦ 10                       ♦ 8 6 5 2
♣ Q 6 5                    ♣ J 9 8 7
              ♠ A J 3 2
              ♥ 10 6
              ♦ A K 4 3
              ♣ K 3 2
```

Against 4♠, West leads three top hearts. If declarer ruffs and draws trump, West will be left with a long spade which he will use to interrupt the run of the diamonds to cash his remaining heart winners. South can ensure the contract against all reasonable distributions by discarding his losing club on the third round of hearts. If the defense persists with a fourth round, he is able to ruff in dummy, preserving his own trump length, and is in a position to draw all West's trumps and take the rest of the tricks with minor-suit winners. A less obvious example from the same family:

```
              ♠ 4
              ♥ K Q 3
              ♦ A Q 4 3
              ♣ K J 8 6 2
♠ 10 6 5 2                 ♠ K Q J 9 7
♥ 10 5 4 2                 ♥ 8 7
♦ 10 5 2                   ♦ K J 9
♣ 7 4                      ♣ A 5 3
              ♠ A 8 3
              ♥ A J 9 6
              ♦ 8 7 6
              ♣ Q 10 9
```

South plays in 4♥ after East has bid spades, and West leads the ♠2, East playing the jack. Declarer's best play is to let East hold the trick, ruffing in dummy if spades are continued. Declarer is now in a position to draw trumps and give up a club trick while still maintaining control of the enemy suit. Attacking the trump suit by forcing declarer to ruff is by far the most effective form of defense against 4-3 trump contracts. Curiously enough, declarer can often turn this to his advantage and succeed in an otherwise impossible contract.

```
              ♠ Q 10 9
              ♥ 9 8 5 4
              ♦ J 5 2
              ♣ 7 5 3
♠ 8 4 3                    ♠ 6 5 2
♥ A K J 10                 ♥ Q 7 3
♦ 10 9 8                   ♦ K Q 7 6
♣ 10 6 2                   ♣ 9 8 4
              ♠ A K J 7
              ♥ 6 2
              ♦ A 4 3
              ♣ A K Q J
```

3NT is safe as the cards lie but, unsure of the heart

suit holding, North-South settled reasonably enough in 4♠, West leading the ♥K. If West shifts at trick two, South has four inescapable losers — two hearts and two diamonds — and must go one down. A heart continuation looks tempting however, and South ruffs the third round with the ace, leads the ♠7 to dummy's 9, and ruffs the fourth round of hearts with the king. He now overtakes the ♠J to draw trump in dummy, discarding his losing diamond. Four club tricks plus the ♦A (in addition to the five trump tricks) round out the contract.

It is sometimes possible for declarer to counter the forcing game, utilizing a strong side-suit for the purpose of weakening the defender's trump holding.

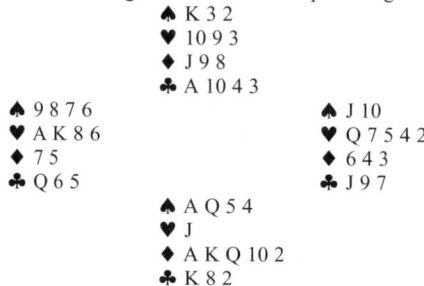

Against 4 ♠, West leads two top hearts, declarer ruffing the second round. If South attempts to draw all the outstanding trumps, the hand collapses. In order to succeed, he must draw only two rounds of trumps with the ace and queen, and then start the diamonds. If West ruffs the third diamond to lead a heart, South ruffs with his last trump, crosses to dummy's ♣A, and draws West's last trump with the king, making 11 tricks. After ruffing the diamond, West does better to lead his last trump, but declarer still makes 10 tricks.

TRUMP SUPPORT. A variable factor, depending on the nature of the bid which is being supported. (See BIDDABLE SUITS) In general, a player will be very ready to give support if he knows that his side has eight cards in the suit and may give a single raise when a combined seven-card holding is guaranteed and there are reasonable prospects of eight. In most situations in constructive bidding, a suit bid promises four cards, and therefore four cards are needed for any kind of raise. But many special cases should be noted.

(1) Five-card support may be desirable if there is a fair chance that the suit being raised consists of three cards only. This applies particularly to minor-suit raises when the five-card major rule is being used and the incidence of prepared minors is therefore high. KAPLAN-SHEINWOLD, for example, insists on five-card support for a preemptive jump raise of a minor suit, and a single raise in a minor may be avoided with four-card support if there is any convenient alternative. In standard methods, there is a tendency to avoid raising 1♣ with four-card support. With 3-3-3-4 distribution, an expert would often choose a response of 1♦ in preference to a raise to 2♣.

However, many players are too reluctant to raise 1♣ or 2♣ with four-card support using standard methods. Such raises limit the hand, preempt the opponents, and allow the opener to compete to the three level in some cases. Remember that a three-card opening is unlikely. See SHORT CLUB.

(2) Three-card support may be given to any suit which

is known or expected to be of at least five cards (e.g., a five-card major opening; a response of 2♥ to 1♠; or an overcall).

Three-card support is normally considered adequate for a single raise of a major suit bid by opener or responder at the first opportunity. Many players prefer the three-card holding to be headed by a high honor, but consider the following cases:

(a)	(b)
♠ 4 3 2	♠ 4 3 2
♥ 3 2	♥ 3 2
♦ 4 3 2	♦ A Q 2
♣ A Q 4 3 2	♣ A Q 4 3 2

In (a) an opening bid of 1♠ should be raised to 2♠, unless a forcing 1NT response is available. Even if 4-card majors are in use, much more often than not the opener will hold more than four spades. The raise is a lesser evil than 1NT because of the weakness in hearts. The responder does not wish to play notrump, nor to allow a heart bid by the opposition at the level of two. Hand (b) opens the bidding with 1♣ and gets a response of 1♠. A raise to 2♠ may again be a lesser evil than a rebid of 1NT, for similar reasons. A jump raise or a raise of a secondary suit requires at least four-card support, but there are occasional exceptions on a least-evil basis:

(c)	(d)
♠ A Q 3	♠ K 6 4
♥ 10 8 5 4 2	♥ 4 2
♦ A 5 3 2	♦ A Q 6 4 3
♣ 2	♣ 5 4 2

Hand (c) has to respond to a fourth-hand opening bid of 1♠ and a jump to 3♠ is superior to a nonforcing bid of 2♥. (Better still, however, is DRURY.) Hand (d) has responded 1♦ to an opening bid of 1♣ and the opener has rebid 1♠. With the prospect of a ruffing value in hearts, responder is not unwilling to play in a 4-3 fit, and the mildly constructive raise to 2♠ is much better than the rather negative preference bid of 2♣ at pairs especially.

(3) Two-card support may be given to any suit which is known or expected to be of at least six cards (e.g., any opening preemptive bid; a vulnerable overcall at the level of two; and almost any suit which has been bid twice (see OPENER'S REBID). In an emergency, a doubleton may be sufficient to raise a suit which is known to be of at least five cards.

(4) One-card support is usually adequate only when the suit has been bid so strongly as to indicate that support is not needed. An exceptional case is suggested by Terence Reese: South holds:

♠ Q J 6 2
♥ 8 6 5 4
♦ A K 4 3
♣ Q

Vul: None

West	North	East	South
1 ♥	2 ♣	2 ♥	?

Reese's suggestion, endorsed by an expert panel, was to bid 3♣ (See RESPONSIVE DOUBLE). With bidding all round the table, North's overcall is likely to be distributional based on a good six-card suit; 3♣ is likely to be the best contract for North-South; and East-West may be tempted to bid 3♥, which South can double effectively, and be surprised by the club situation. This is one case of a useful general rule: in competitive situations raises should be given more freely.

TRUMP SWISS CONVENTION. See SWISS CONVENTION .

TRUMP TRICK. A playing trick in the trump suit.

TRUNCATED HOWELL MOVEMENT. A shortening of the HOWELL MOVEMENT. Since this does not give balanced comparison, it is no longer used but has been replaced by the REDUCED HOWELL.

TRUSCOTT CARD. A card placed in the first board played in a session of team play. The players record their names, positions and table number. When the boards are exchanged, the new recipients can check, allowing for corrective action by the director if an error is discovered. Originated by Alan Truscott in 1976, following an episode at the World Team Olympiad: Because of an error in seating, a match between Brazil and Italy, the eventual gold and silver medal winners, was canceled and not replayed.

TRUSCOTT DEFENSE. A system of two-suited takeouts that can be used over strong artificial openings of 1♣, 2♣, 1♦ or 2♦ . See DEFENSE TO STRONG ARTIFICIAL OPENINGS.

TRUSCOTT TWO DIAMONDS. See TWO-WAY STAYMAN.

TTASL. English colloquial acronym standing for "Teach Them A Sharp Lesson." The usual example occurs when the opponents reopen the bidding at the partscore level and allow a game to be bid and made.

TURGENEV. The Russian novelist, Ivan Turgenev, found playing cards useful. "You don't like walking, but you should force yourself to do it. I was once in prison — in solitary confinement — for more than a month: the room was small, the heat stifling. Twice a day I carried 104 cards (two packs), one by one, from one end of the room to the other ... that made 208 round trips; 416 a day, the round trip was eight paces, that made 3,300, nearly two kilometers! Let this ingenious calculation give you courage! The day I didn't take my walk all the blood went to my head!" (Letter to Gustave Flaubert 1879).

TURKEY (TURKEY GAME, TURKEY SHOOT). A colloquial term used to describe events in a tournament other than major championships, such as secondary events, consolation events and side games. Also sometimes used to describe a weak player.

TURN. (1) Noun: the appropriate moment for a player to make a bid or play; (2) verb: to quit a card at duplicate or a trick at rubber bridge after all four players have played; (3) verb: to take a trick, as "We turned six tricks against 3♠".

TWELVE, RULE OF. See RULE OF TWELVE.

TWELVE TABLES. At duplicate, 12 tables provide for competition among 48 players as individuals, 24 pairs or 12 teams-of-four.

As an individual, the obvious choice is the IRREGULAR RAINBOW. The alternative is the Appendix Rainbow devised by Paul Marks. Four stationary player seats are assigned: 45, North at table 1; 46, East at table 2; 47, South at table 3; and 48, West at table 4. Players numbered 1 to 11 sit North at the corresponding tables; numbers 12 to 22 sit East at tables 1 to 11; numbers 23 to 33 sit South at tables 1 to 11; and numbers 34 to 44 sit West at tables 1 to 11. However, four of these players, one from each group, find their new seats occupied by the stationary players, 45 to 48. These players for the first round and their counterparts at every successive round play boards 23 and 24 at table 12. Otherwise, at the end of each round, North players skip a table to lower numbers, South players skip a table to higher numbers, East players go to the next higher number table, and West players skip two tables to higher numbers, boards going to next lower numbered tables. For purposes of progression and board numbers, table 12 is ignored, and is filled each round with players who find stationary players in the seats to which they are assigned. Each player thus plays 22 of the 24 boards in the 11 rounds. Ten is top and 110 average.

As a pair game, 22 boards can be played in 11 rounds, traveling players skipping a table after round 6. By inserting a byestand between tables 6 and 7, and relaying boards between 1 and 12, 24 boards can be played. The byestand and relay tables can be placed elsewhere, but they must always be halfway around the room from each other. It is also possible to give three boards to each table, skip after the sixth round and play nine rounds (27 boards) with an average of 108. The disadvantage is that all pairs will miss nine boards that most of the other competitors will play.

For team-of-four games a Swiss Team movement is a possibility. You can play an 11-round THURNER MOVEMENT. Alternatively you may start by letting the East-West pairs skip a table in the lower direction. After the first round you follow the normal team progression of the moving pairs skipping a table in the lower direction with the boards moving to the next lower table. After the second round the moving pairs skip an extra table. For the next six rounds the moving pairs follow the normal progression of skipping a table in the lower direction. After the eighth round the moving pairs skip an extra table and the boards skip a table. Following the 10th round, East-West pairs 1 through 6 add six to their number and go to that table number, and East-West pairs 7-12 subtract six from their number and go to that table. New boards are given out at tables 1 through 6 and, after being shuffled and dealt, are relayed with the table six numbers higher (1 and 7, 2 and 8, etc.)

The problem with an 11-round movement is that you will have 22 or 33 boards. By putting out three boards to a table and eliminating the relay round, 30 boards can be played in a session. The movement can be curtailed to 24 boards by eliminating the first and 10th rounds. At the start of the game East-West pairs 1 through 4 add eight to their number and go to that table; pairs 5-12 subtract four from their number and go to that table. After the first round, the moving pairs skip an extra table. After the seventh round , the moving pairs skip an extra table and the boards skip a table. For 11½ and 12½ tables, see HALF TABLES.

TWERB. Two-Way Exclusion Relay Bidding. See CRASH, MODIFIED CRASH.

TWINNED MOVEMENT. To twin a movement is to set up two parallel rows, each playing the same move-

ment with the same boards. If the boards are not duplicated, parallel tables share boards.

For a team contest you may twin any pair movement and reverse the compass direction in one of the rows. In each round each team will sit at parallel tables in different directions. See MIRROR MOVEMENT.

TWINNING. The process used to produce identical boards to be played in two (or more) sections. To twin the boards in a two-board movement (either for social purposes or for scoring with a multiple top), the odd-numbered boards are passed out, one to a table, in one section and the even-numbered boards are passed out in the other. As the boards are being shuffled and played, a second board of the same number is put on the table. After play is complete and the score is recorded, the twinning is done. There are several methods but this one works best. The cards in the second board are divided into suits, and each player picks up one suit. Each player faces the hand just played in front of him. Then each player distributes his suit to the four players to match the cards in front of them. Once all the cards from the second board are distributed, each player puts the hand actually played back in its original board, then puts the twinned hand in the second board. The director then picks up the twinned board and brings it to the correct table in the other section, where the board is played "as is", that is without being shuffled.

When boards are being twinned over three sections, one section is given the odd boards and another the even boards. The director then gives each table an additional two boards of the same number to duplicate. Meanwhile, the third section is patiently waiting. However, the first twinned board at each table is brought to the third section, so that the third section finishes first-round play at approximately the same time as the two sections where twinning took place.

Sometimes boards are twinned when three boards are being played per round.

In multi-section events, when it is desirable to have the same hands in play in all sections, computer-dealt hands usually are used. These are available in groupings of even numbers starting with two sections and going as high as needed. See COMPUTER-DEALT HANDS.

TWO or TWO-SPOT. The lowest-ranking card in any given suit. Sometimes referred to as the deuce.

TWO CLUBS ARTIFICIAL, BALANCING TAKE-OUT. See BALANCING TWO CLUBS FOR TAKE-OUT.

TWO CLUBS CONVENTION. *OPENINGS*: See TWO CLUBS OPENING AS MULTI-SUITER; TWO CLUBS SYSTEMS; TWO CLUBS STRONG ARTIFICIAL OPENING. *RESPONSES AND OTHERS:* See DRURY; GLADIATOR; STAYMAN CONVENTION; STAYMAN ON SECOND ROUND; TWO CLUBS REBID BY RESPONDER AS ONLY FORCE AFTER ONE NOTRUMP REBID. *TAKEOUTS: SEE* TWO-SUITER CONVENTIONS. TWO CLUBS OPENING AS MULTI-SUITER.

TWO CLUB REBID BY RESPONDER AS ONLY FORCE AFTER ONE NOTRUMP REBID. A convention devised by Edwin Kantar to provide a full range

of rebids by responder over a 1NT rebid by opener. Using 2♣ as the only forcing rebid by responder, all other two-level suit bids are discouraging and jump bids at the three level invite game. For example:

(a)	(b)
1♣ 1♥	1♣ 1♥
1NT 3♥	1NT 3♦

The last bid in each of the above sequences is nonforcing but invitational. See also CROWHURST CONVENTION; STAYMAN ON SECOND ROUND; UNBID MINOR SUIT FORCE.

TWO CLUB STRONG ARTIFICIAL OPENING. An artificial opening bid on powerful hands which is a feature of many standard systems. It permits the use of other two-level actions as weak two-bids. A response of 2♦ is usually either negative or waiting. See TWO DIAMONDS ARTIFICIAL RESPONSE TO FORCING TWO CLUBS OPENING. See also SECOND NEGATIVE RESPONSE AFTER ARTIFICIAL FORCING OPENING.

Many experts now use 2♥ as the negative response with 2♦ showing values. See TWO HEARTS ARTIFICIAL RESPONSE TO FORCING TWO CLUBS OPENING. The first use of the bid of 2♣ in this way is credited to David Burnstine at the Raymond Club, New York City, in 1929, but some experts soon used 2♣ for all strong hands, and this concept gradually superseded the FORCING TWO-BID in serious tournament play. It was part of the OFFICIAL SYSTEM which, although theoretically sounder, lost the public relations war with Ely Culbertson. It is often used in combination with WEAK TWO-BIDS, but may be combined with INTERMEDIATE TWO-BIDS of various types. The expert panel in BWS 2001 determined that the following hand represents a minimum 2♣ opening:

    ♠ A K Q J 10
    ♥ A K Q
    ♦ K 10 9 x
    ♣ x

However, substantial minorities found slightly weaker hands acceptable, with the ♦ K replaced by the queen or jack.

Originally the 2♣ bid was forcing to game. In modern practice many experts announce it as forcing to 2NT or three of a major (after a negative response), to cover two common exceptions;

South	North
2♣	2♦
2♥	2NT or 3♣
3♥	

North may pass. This widens the use of the 2♣ opening to include a powerful one-suited hand where game may be missed if partner passes with 4-5 points, or slam may be missed because it becomes difficult for opener to show his strength clearly if he commences with a bid of one.

Another exception tightens the gaps in the structure of notrump bids:

South	North
2♣	2♦
2NT	

North may pass. Under this method, instead of the traditional standard of 22-24 (or 21-23), a 2NT opener shows 21-22 (or 20-22) while 2♣ followed by 2NT shows 23-24 (or 22-24).

A semi-artificial rebid, the KOKISH RELAY, has become very popular.

South	North
2♣	2♦
2♥	

This can be used to require a 2♠ rebid. Then opener can bid 2NT forcing with 25 points or more. Any other rebid shows that the 2♥ bid was natural. This gains on strong balanced hands, but deprives the responder of the chance to make a second negative. BWS2000 voted, by a small margin, to adopt the Kokish Relay.

Standard for a positive response to 2♣ varies, but most authorities insist on 1¹/₂ quick tricks (an ace and a king, or three kings). Others are satisfied with an ace, or a good suit headed by king and queen with some plus values; these treatments have the advantage that positive responses can be given more frequently. 2NT can be regarded as an exception. Some players make this response with 8 points or more, irrespective of quick trick strength. Since this response often results in the weak hand becoming declarer, some avoid the bid altogether. It can be used artificially to show a weak minor two-suiter or hearts if 2♥ is a double negative.

After a positive response, the opener will usually rebid as though the response had been negative. Therefore, 2♣-2♥-2NT, or 2♣-3♣-3NT, shows the balanced minimum hand with 23-24 points. Similarly, 2♣-2♥-3NT would show a balanced hand with 25-27. See TWO DIAMONDS.

In systems employing an artificial strength-showing bid of 1♣, a bid of 2♣ may be the equivalent of a standard 1♣ opening, including a long club suit and limited values. See also ACE-SHOWING RESPONSES, FORCING TWO-BID, KOKISH RELAY; STEP RESPONSES TO STRONG ARTIFICIAL TWO-BIDS. TWO DIAMONDS ARTIFICIAL RESPONSE TO TWO CLUBS OPENING. See also ACE-SHOWING RESPONSES; ACOL; BARON; BENJAMIN; BULLDOG; CAB; KAPLAN-SHEINWOLD; OFFICIAL; ROMEX; ROTH-STONE; TWO CLUBS STRONG ARTIFICIAL OPENING.

TWO CLUBS FOR MINORS, TWO DIAMONDS FOR MAJORS. See BECKER.

TWO CLUBS RESPONSE TO ONE NOTRUMP. See GLADIATOR; STAYMAN CONVENTION.

TWO DIAMOND ARTIFICIAL OPENING. As a strong forcing opening bid, see BENJAMIN CONVENTION, ROMEX SYSTEM and SCHENKEN SYSTEM. As a two-suited or three-suited opening bid, see conventions listed in TWO DIAMONDS OPENING AS MULTI-SUITER.

TWO DIAMOND ARTIFICIAL RESPONSE TO FORCING TWO CLUBS OPENING. In response to a TWO CLUBS STRONG ARTIFICIAL OPENING a 2♦ response is often played as negative, showing about 0-7 points but lacking the partnership requirements for a positive response. Alternatives are to use this response as:

(1) Automatic. The 2♦ bid is nondescriptive, but gives opener room to describe his hand.

(2) Positive. Responder's 2♦ shows 8 or more points, but says nothing about his distribution. All other responses are negative, showing 0-7 points with length in the suit bid. (2NT should show minor suits.)

(3) Double Negative. Responder's bid shows 0-3 points. With this treatment it is possible to use a 2♥ response artificially either to show specifically 4-7 points (see STEP RESPONSES TO STRONG ARTIFICIAL TWO-BIDS), or as a neutral bid showing at least 4 high-card points and allowing opener to describe his hand.

(4) ACE-SHOWING RESPONSE.

Also See TWO HEARTS ARTIFICIAL RESPONSE TO FORCING TWO CLUB OPENING.

TWO DIAMOND ARTIFICIAL RESPONSE TO ONE NOTRUMP OPENING. Conventions used in response to 1NT opening bids designed to solve particular notrump bidding problems. In conjunction with the various conventions so used, a substitute sequence may be required to show a weak hand with a long diamond suit: an immediate 3♦; or 2♣ followed by 3♦; or 2♦ followed by 3♦; or 2NT followed by 3♦. See FLINT 2♦; FOUR-SUIT TRANSFERS; GLADIATOR; JACOBY TRANSFER BID; TWO-WAY STAYMAN.

TWO DIAMONDS AS MULTI-SUITER. There are several conventions that use a 2♦ opening to show a two-suited or three-suited hand. The principal ones are BLUE TEAM TWO DIAMONDS, FLANNERY TWO DIAMONDS and ROMAN TWO DIAMONDS. In addition, a 2♦ opening shows a three-suited hand in the PRECISION CLUB system and a hand with both major suits in the BIG DIAMOND SYSTEM. See also MULTI.

TWO HEARTS RESPONSE TO STRONG ARTIFICIAL TWO CLUBS. Many experts now use this bid as a negative showing a maximum of 4 HCP. 2NT is used as the positive bid showing a good heart suit. This frees 2♦ to be a positive bid showing enough strength to force to game.

TWO NOTRUMP (AS A NEGATIVE RESPONSE TO TWO-BIDS). The traditional negative response to a strong opening two-bid, showing fewer than 7 or 8 points, counting high cards plus distribution.

TWO NOTRUMP OPENING. This shows a balanced hand, usually with 20-21 or 20-22 points. The traditional range of 22-24, which was used in combination with the FORCING TWO-BID, is obsolescent. See also TWO NOTRUMP OPENING FOR MINORS.

Theoretically the distribution should be the same as for an opening notrump bid: 4-3-3-3, 4-4-3-2, or 5-3-3-2 with the five-card suit a minor. However, the 2NT opening often has to serve as a least evil choice with hands too strong to open with one of a suit and not strong enough for a forcing opening. 5-3-3-2 with a major suit is frequently opened with 2NT, and occasional departures such as 6-3-2-2 or 5-4-2-2 are permissible.

The BWS2000 panel found it acceptable to have any of the following when opening 2NT or when opening 2♣ intending to rebid 2NT: an unstopped doubleton, a five-card major, a six-card minor and a 5-4-2-2 hand with a five-card minor. A small doubleton is acceptable.

Responses are as follows:

(1) 3♣. Stayman, asking opener to bid a major suit. With no major he bids 3♦, and if responder then bids a major, he shows a five-card suit. Holding both majors,

either suit may be bid by partnership agreement, and agreement is not essential. If responder then bids 3NT, the opener bids his second major.

A rebid of 3NT by the opener virtually does not exist in standard methods. It can be used by partnership agreement to show a hand with no interest in a major-suit contract, perhaps a doubleton in each. (An alternative is to show a 5-card heart suit with this bid.) A variation popular in England (due to the BARON SYSTEM) is for the opener to bid all his suits up the line. 3 ♦ would show a diamond suit but would not deny a major. 3NT would show that the opener's only suit was clubs. This method facilitates minor-suit slam bidding but is somewhat inefficient when responder is 5-4 or 4-5 in the major suits.

For a more sophisticated structure, see ROMEX STAYMAN. See also SMOLEN.

(2) 3 ♦. Most tournament players use this as a JACOBY TRANSFER, showing heart length, and 3 ♥ similarly to show spade length. See TWO NOTRUMP OPENING WITH TRANSFER RESPONSES.

A few use this as the FLINT convention. In a natural sense the bid shows at least five diamonds, and is a slam suggestion.

(3) 3 ♥ or 3 ♠. For 3 ♥, see TWO NOTRUMP OPENING WITH TRANSFER RESPONSES. Used naturally, these bids are forcing and show at least a five-card suit . The suit may be longer [see (6) below]. Responder is asking the opener to choose between the major-suit game (with three-card support) or 3NT (with a doubleton in responder's suit). However, the responder may have slam interests, so the opener makes a cuebid (2NT-3 ♥ -4 ♦) if he has good support and a suitable hand for slam purposes. See also AUTOMATIC ACES; EXPECTED NUMBER OF CONTROLS IN BALANCED HANDS; ROMEX STAYMAN.

(4) 3NT. A range of 4-10, although a thin 4-point hand may be passed. An occasional 3-point hand (K-x-x-x-x) may be worth a raise.

(5) 4 ♣ or 4 ♦. These bids are usually conventional (GERBER, TEXAS, or SOUTH AFRICAN TEXAS). In a natural sense they would show a strong suit, but this method is rarely used. If 4 ♦ is Texas for hearts, it must be at least a 6-card suit with either no slam interest or strong slam interest intending to head for slam subsequently. Some play Texas itself as a slam try.

(6) 4 ♥ or 4 ♠. In standard methods this shows a six-card suit with no slam interest. With mild slam interest, responder bids at the three level and then bids game. The traditional treatment, reversing these sequences, is obsolescent.

(7) 4NT. A natural invitation to 6NT, holding about 11 points. Responder's distribution is likely to be 4-3-3-3, but might be 4-4-3-2 or 5-3-3-2 if no major suit is held.

(8) 5 ♣ or 5 ♦. A very unbalanced weak hand. A seven-card suit and a void would be typical. The opener is expected to pass, but might bid six with a fine fit and excellent controls.

(9) 5 ♥ or 5 ♠. A strong invitation to bid six, based on a six-card suit.

(10) 5NT. An invitation to 7NT. With no interest in a grand slam, the opener bids 6NT.

(11) 6NT. A balanced hand, probably 4-3-3-3, with 12-14 points. For an alternative system of responding, see MILES RESPONSES TO TWO NOTRUMP OPENINGS.

TWO NOTRUMP OPENING FOR MINORS. A convention using a 2NT opening bid to show a hand with at least five cards in each minor suit. The strength and the meaning of responses in a major require agreement. This is often part of a Strong Club system in which 2NT is not needed as a natural bid.

TWO NOTRUMP OPENING WITH TRANSFER RESPONSES. The vast majority of American tournament players, and many others around the world, use JACOBY TRANSFER responses to a 2NT opening, with 3 ♦ to show heart length and 3 ♥ to show spade length, at least five cards. The opener usually bids the next step, ending the bidding if responder has a weak hand with no game interest. Possible rebids by responder are:

(a) 3 ♠ (2NT-3 ♦ -3 ♥ -3 ♠). Four spades, heart length, forcing. May have slam interest. Other artificial meanings are possible, especially if SMOLEN is in use.

(b) 3NT. Asks opener to choose between this contract and game in the major. Opener will almost always select the major when holding three-card or four-card support.

(c) New suit at four-level. Forcing, natural, and slam interest. (Now four of a major and 4NT discourage).

(d) Four of anchor suit. A mild slam invitation, since hands with no slam interest would bid game directly, or make a four-level Texas transfer with the same effect.

(e) 4NT is natural and invitational, usually 5-3-3-2 with borderline slam values.

(f) 5NT. Pick a slam.

(g) 6NT. Pass or bid seven of a major.

A corollary is that 3 ♠ is used to show a minor-suit hand, usually at least 5-4 or 4-5, with slam interest. The opener bids 3NT with a fit in neither.

TWO NOTRUMP OVERCALL. Can be used in six different ways:

(1) *Natural.* To show a 2NT opening bid with about 22 points. The bid might be based on a slightly weaker hand with a long, strong minor. This helps to define the range of a minimum notrump bid preceded by a takeout double, which would indicate 19-20. These two procedures can be interchanged by partnership agreement. STAYMAN would apply with partnerships that use it after a ONE NOTRUMP OVERCALL.

(2) *Unusual.* To show a specific two-suiter. The minimum strength would vary according to vulnerability. At favorable vulnerability, a 6-5 distribution with 6 points in the suits would usually be considered adequate. At unfavorable vulnerability both the hand and the suits should be distinctly stronger.

The suits are always clubs and diamonds if the opening is a major. If the opening is a minor, it is usual to play "Two Lower Unbid", and therefore it is red suits over 1 ♣ and rounded suits over 1 ♦ .This treatment is now standard among American experts.

In BWS94 about half the experts favored a split range, so that 2NT is either weak or strong. Hands in the middle range, with values close to an opening bid, simply overcall. This gives more definition when the bid is used, but makes it relatively less likely that the second suit can be shown when it is not.

(3) *Preemptive.* To indicate a long broken suit lower in rank than the opening bid, justifying a preemptive bid at the level of three. Partner is expected to bid 3 ♣ if third hand passes, to permit his side to reach the appro-

priate suit; but third hand seldom passes. This is not needed playing WEAK JUMP OVERCALLS and has dubious value in any event, since partner may be left in doubt when a save is possible.

(4) *Roman*. To show a strong two-suited hand in which the suits are not specified. Responder bids the lowest unbid suit, and if the 2NT bidder shows a suit, he holds that suit and the suit in which responder made his artificial response. 3NT would show the two unbid suits. (For weaker two-suited hands, see JUMP OVERCALL.)

(5) *Constructive*. To show a strong hand with a near-solid minor suit, for example:

♠ A 2
♥ K 5
♦ J 4 2
♣ A Q J 9 6 2

Responder may raise to 3NT, or bid 3♣ with no interest in game. In the latter case the overcaller passes or converts to 3♦. In borderline cases, responder is guided by possession of a key card in his partner's minor. With a diamond honor he bids 3♣, and converts a 3♦ rebid to 3NT. With a club honor he responds 3♦, giving the overcaller the choice between 3♦ and 3NT.

(6) *Artificial*. When an immediate cuebid in the opener's suit is given a specialized meaning (as in MICHAELS CUEBID), 2NT can be used to show a hand of game-going strength, with 3♣ as a conventional negative response.

TWO NOTRUMP REBID. See OPENER'S REBID.

TWO NOTRUMP RESPONSE (AS A PUPPET TO 3♣). A convention whereby a response of 2NT to a 1NT opening forces the opener to rebid 3♣. If the responder has a weak hand with a long club suit, he passes. If he has instead a weak hand with a long diamond suit, he bids 3♦, which opener is required to pass.

Some partnerships also use the relay when responder has a three-suited game-going hand with a singleton in one of the major suits. The responder shows this type of hand over opener's forced 3♣ bid by bidding the suit of his singleton. If the singleton is clubs, responder bids 3NT or 4♣ depending on strength.

TWO NOTRUMP RESPONSE (OVER OPPONENT'S TAKEOUT DOUBLE). An artificial response of 2NT to an opening suit bid, devised by Alan Truscott.

The bid shows a LIMIT RAISE in opener's suit, allowing the raise to the three-level to be preemptive. The 2NT bid is usually in the 9-11 point range, with some allowance for distribution. Stronger hands need partnership agreement: either 3NT to show 12-15, or 2NT, intending to continue following a signoff, are possible.

If the opening bid is a minor, some partnerships reverse the meanings of 2NT and the jump raise. See FLIP FLOP.

This convention is popularly called Jordan, in the mistaken belief that Robert Jordan originated it.

TWO NOTRUMP RESPONSE TO OPENING SUIT BID OF ONE. There are at least five treatments that can be adopted.

(1) *Standard*. 13-15 points and game forcing. The opener raises with any balanced distribution. If he rebids at the three-level in a suit, it will usually show an aversion to notrump: he is likely to have a singleton or void. The responder must then move cautiously:

♠ Q 3
♥ A 8 6 2
♦ A Q J
♣ J 8 5 3

The bidding:

North	South
1 ♠	2NT
3 ♣	3 ♦

The most useful bid South can make is a call at the three-level in a suit in which he holds considerable strength. If this corresponds to North's shortage, he will know that 3NT will be safe and that there would be duplicated values in a high suit contract. But if North's shortage is in an unbid suit, he will know that a suit contract will be preferable to notrump. Responder should avoid raising opener's secondary minor suit, although he may do so at a later stage if circumstances warrant it.

2NT usually denies a four-card major. Some systems have a rebid structure that covers this. A possible additional use for the 2NT response, suggested by Marshall Miles, is for balanced hands with about 19 points. Whatever the opener rebids, the responder then suggests a slam, usually by rebidding 4NT. This makes it clear that responder cannot have the normal 2NT response. This traditional treatment was chosen by a slight majority in BWS94.

(2) *Limit*. 11-12 points, encouraging but not forcing. The bidding can stop short of game in three ways: (a) an immediate pass by the opener, holding a minimum balanced hand; (b) after a rebid of his own suit by opener, showing a subminimum opening and, usually, a six-card suit (a typical ACOL signoff bid); (c) after a bid of a new suit by the opener and a preference bid at the three level by responder. The responder must give jump preference to 4♥ or 4♠ if his hand is particularly suitable for the game suit.

In choosing a rebid at the three-level, responder should consider the possibility of bidding a strong suit, as in (1) above. The Miles variation for balanced hands with about 19 points is not available since 2NT is not forcing.

The limit 2NT response after minor suit openings became popular in the Eighties with players using modern methods. This solves some of the problems involved in a game-forcing 2♣ response to 1♦. If 1♦ -2♣ is game forcing, the limit 2NT is needed by a responder with about 11 points and clubs the only suit.

If responder has passed originally, a response of 2NT is generally a limit bid (unless DRURY or SNAP is being used). This is the modern treatment, chosen by nearly half the experts in BWS94.

(3) *Baron*. 16+ points and game forcing. In this system the responses of 2NT and 3NT are inverted. After 3NT (12-14) it is usually easy for the opener to select a suitable game; and the 2NT response leaves more room for exploration on hands on which a slam is likely.

The 2NT response routinely conceals one or two four-card majors. 3♣ asks responder to bid his suits up the line, with 3NT showing clubs.

(4) *Psychic Control*. 21-22 points, and therefore offering prospects of game if the opening bidder has a systemic ROTH-STONE psychic.

In all the cases listed, with the possible exception of (4), the 2NT response normally has a 4-3-3-3 distribution, or 4-4-3-2 with the doubleton in the opener's suit.

(5) *Conventional*. Used with limit raises to show a stan-

dard forcing jump raise when the opening bid was in a major (invented by Oswald Jacoby). See JACOBY TWO NOTRUMP RESPONSE.

TWO TABLES. At duplicate, two tables provide for competition among eight (or nine) players as individuals, four pairs of players, or two teams of four. As an individual tournament among eight players, seven rounds are required so that each player will play with each other player as a partner. Conduct of this game is described under INDIVIDUAL MOVEMENTS for eight or nine players.

As a pair tournament, three rounds are required. In each round the boards are relayed between the two tables, and scores can be determined almost instantly by direct comparison. Pair 4 is North-South at table 1, facing pair 1 as East-West; at table 2, pair 2 is North-South, and pair 3 is East-West. The better score between the North-South pairs is awarded 1 point, the East-West players at the other table (having the better East-West score) also receiving a point.

New boards are brought in (or the same boards are reshuffled) for round 2, pair 3 replacing 2, 2 replacing 1 and 1 replacing 3 for positions. This is repeated for the third round with a third set of boards. Eight boards to a round give about a three-hour game. (This game also can be scored by IMPs.)

As a contest between two teams of four, the game may be divided into halves, if it is desired to have each pair of one team in head-on competition with both pairs of the other team. Otherwise it may be played straight through. In each half, one-quarter of the total number of boards to be played are shuffled at each table and played; the boards are then exchanged between tables. Scoring may be BOARD-A-MATCH, AGGREGATE (or total points), or scored by IMPs. The last is preferred by most top players.

TWO-BID. The bid of two in a suit as an opening bid is used in many different ways by various players. Specialized uses are referred to in the following articles: ACOL TWO-BID; BENJAMIN; BLUE TEAM TWO DIAMONDS; FLANNERY TWO DIAMONDS; FLANNERY TWO HEARTS; MEXICAN TWO DIAMONDS; ROMAN SYSTEM; ROMAN TWO DIAMONDS; TARTAN TWO-BID; TWO CLUBS STRONG ARTIFICIAL OPENING; TWO-WAY TWO-BID; WEAK TWO -BID.

TWO-DEMAND BID. See FORCING TWO-BID.

TWO-HANDED BRIDGE. See BRIDGETTE, DUEL, DUOBRIDGE and HONEYMOON BRIDGE.

TWO-ODD. Two tricks over book or eight tricks in all.

TWO-OVER-ONE GAME FORCE. A method of bidding in which a two-level simple new-suit response by an unpassed hand to an opening suit bid is forcing to game, e.g., 1♠ - 2♣ or 1♥ - 2♦. When using this system, it is necessary to use the FORCING 1NT response or the smi-forcing 1NT to a major to handle certain types of intermediate hands. The method is used primarily in conjunction with FIVE-CARD MAJORS. The two-over-one forcing response allows the partnership to test slam possibilities while the bidding level is still low.

A very few partnerships allow one exception: If the responder bids and rebids a minor suit at a minimum level, he cancels the game-forcing message and opener may pass.

Many additionally allow a second exception: The bidding may end at four of a minor suit, although that introduces some ambiguity.

If there is interference the situation changes completely. The majority view is that new suits are forcing but not to game. A minority still consider the new suit forcing to game, using jump shifts non-forcing. See NEGATIVE FREE BIDS.

A very few partnerships restrict the game-forcing meaning to major-to-minor auctions, The opener will frequently have a rebid problem. The BWS94 consensus was that opener, in difficulty, may rebid a five-card suit or rebid 2NT with an unstopped suit. He may not bid a new suit at the three-level without extra shape or extra values. A raise of the responder's suit does not guarantee additional strength but is forcing. A single raise of the opener's second suit is forcing but does not show extra values. (Some, by agreement, play that it does.) Experts using two-over-one in response to a major were in a slight minority, just, in BWS94. Only one-third of experts favored making 1♦ -2♣ a game force. See BRIDGE WORLD STANDARD, EASTERN SCIENTIFIC, TWO-OVER-ONE RESPONSE, WESTERN SCIENTIFIC.

TWO-OVER-ONE RESPONSE. A minimum response in a lower-ranking suit to an opening suit bid. For example, 1♥ -2♣. Most experts now play that this type of response is forcing to game. See TWO-OVER-ONE GAME FORCE.

Traditionally the minimum strength required for this response is 10 points in standard methods. Rather more is required in ROTH-STONE and KAPLAN-SHEINWOLD, when responder guarantees a second bid; rather less in traditional ACOL, although that system is now more conservative. The maximum strength tends to be just short of a JUMP SHIFT, i.e., about 17 points in standard methods or about 15 points in Acol. But many strong hands are unsuitable for a jump shift, so there is effectively no upper limit.

The longest suit is usually chosen for the response, and if two five-card suits are held, the higher-ranking is given preference. If the sequence is specifically 1♠ - 2♥, the responder virtually guarantees a five-card suit, and the opener can raise confidently with three-card support or conceivably with a doubleton. Any response in the suit immediately lower in rank is likely to be at least five cards (1♥ - 2♦, or 1♦ - 2♣).

How far the two-over-one response is forcing is a debatable point for those who do not use the game-forcing treatment. Most experts play that the bid guarantees a rebid. The exception is 1♦ -2♣, which some play as not guaranteeing a rebid. For other aspects of this response, see CHOICE OF SUIT and UP THE LINE.

TWO-SUITER. A hand with one suit of more than four cards and another suit of more than three cards. The term used to be confined to hands with at least five cards in each of two suits. A 5-4 distribution was called a semi-two-suiter. For opening the bidding with a two-suiter, see BORDERLINE OPENING BIDS and CHOICE OF SUIT.

TWO-SUITER CONVENTIONS. Several defensive two-suiter conventions are listed under the following headings: ASTRO, ASTRO CUEBIDS, BROZEL, COLORFUL CUEBIDS, COPENHAGEN, CRASH, DEFENSE TO STRONG ARTIFICIAL OPENINGS, GENEVA, GHESTEM, LANDY, MICHAELS, PANAMA, ROBINSON, ROMAN JUMP OVER-CALLS, TOP AND BOTTOM CUEBID, TRAP, TRAP WITH TWO-LEVEL TRANSFERS, TRUSCOTT, UNUSUAL NOTRUMP, UPPER SUITS CUEBID. Offensive-type two-suited conventions include BIG DIAMOND SYSTEM (2♣ and 2♦ openings); FLANNERY TWO DIAMONDS; FLANNERY TWO HEARTS; ROMAN SYSTEM (2♠ and 2♥ openings).

TWO-UNDER TRANSFER PREEMPT. A preemptive opening of 3♣ and higher can be used to show the suit two steps higher than the suit bid. For example:

(a)	(b)
♠ 6	♠ 6 5
♥ Q J 10 8 6 3 2	♥ K Q 10 8 6 3 2
♦ 8 7	♦ K 8 7
♣ 9 7 3	♣ 3

These are possible 3♥ bids, but are substantially different in playing strength. If 3♥ is bid with both hands, the responder will often have to guess. Bidding 3♣ to show a 3♥ opening allows the responder to bid 3♦ if he wishes to invite 4♥.

This has the usual advantage of transfer bids, in that partner becomes the declarer and the lead comes up to his possible tenace positions. A disadvantage is that it places less pressure on the opponents in the bidding: Second hand will have two opportunities to act. (Devised by Marty Bergen.) See TRANSFER OPENING THREE BIDS.

TWO-WAY FINESSE. A recurring type of situation in which a FINESSE may be taken through either opponent. For example:

(a)	(b)
North	*North*
A 10 3 2	K 10 2
South	*South*
K J 5 4	A J 3

The question, of course, is whom to play for the queen: East or West? In many cases, in the absence of any clues revealed during the bidding or the play, it becomes a pure guess. Quite a few players, in these circumstances, will finesse West for the queen, on the theory that the queen lies over the jack. This method is unscientific. In the absence of any external clues, a queen can frequently be located without resorting to guesswork. Here is such a case.

```
              ♠ K Q 3
              ♥ K Q 7 5
              ♦ K 10 9
              ♣ Q J 4
♠ 8 4 2                    ♠ 9 7 6 5
♥ 6 4 3                    ♥ 10 8
♦ 7                        ♦ Q 8 6 5 3 2
♣ 10 9 8 6 5 2             ♣ 7
              ♠ A J 10
              ♥ A J 9 2
              ♦ A J 4
              ♣ A K 3
```

South arrived at 7NT, against which West opened a club, dummy's jack winning. Declarer counted 12 tricks, and perceived that the 13th trick would be obtained only in the diamond suit. Whom to finesse for the ♦ Q, East or West?

At trick two South cashed the ♣K, East discarding a diamond. Three rounds of spades were then taken, everybody following suit. Next, three rounds of hearts were played and declarer paused to take inventory.

West was known to have started with six clubs, three spades and three hearts. Hence he had, at most, one diamond. Dummy's ♦ K was then played, and when West followed suit, all 13 of his cards were accounted for. The ♦ J was finessed successfully for declarer's 13th trick.

On occasion, when declarer is confronted with a two-way finesse, he can maneuver his play so that an opponent will lead that suit to him, thereby giving declarer a "free finesse." This deal illustrates this point.

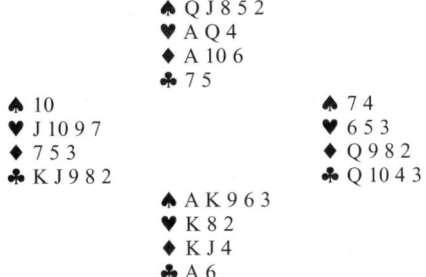

South arrived at a 6♠ contract. West opened the ♥ J, dummy's queen winning. The opponents' trumps were picked up in two rounds, after which the ♥ A-K were cashed. Next came the ♣A, followed by another club, and this position was reached:

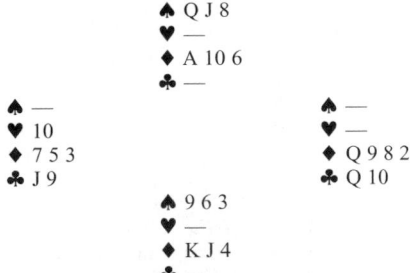

It did not matter which opponent won the trick. On a heart or a club return, declarer would ruff in dummy while simultaneously discarding the ♦4 from his own hand. If the winner of the club lead led a diamond, declarer would surely make three diamond tricks.

The rules of thumb for taking two-way finesses for the queen fall under four headings. They all assume that other things are equal, which they very seldom are. In almost all cases, one defender will appear more likely to have missing honor cards or to have greater length in the crucial suit.

(1) *Technical.* Play the left-hand opponent for the missing honor. Without the honor, he might have selected a passive opening lead in that suit. His selection of another opening lead is a slight indication that he may hold the missing queen.

(2) *Practical.* Declarer can often take advantage of the fact that the defenders are human.

DUMMY
♥ A 10 8 4
DECLARER
♥ K J 9 3

By leading the jack, South may induce West to cover with the queen (or think revealingly about covering). The cover would be necessary if South started with a doubleton jack (or with a tripleton jack, but in that case he would be unlikely to lead the jack). West has no temptation to cover if South has bid the suit, or if the 9 is visible in dummy as well as the 10. If West plays low without thought, South plans to put up dummy's ace and finesse on the way back. Note that this would be risky technically if dummy did not hold the 8. East would be able to make a trick from an original holding of Q-8-7-x.

(3) *Superstitious*. The QUEEN OVER JACK rule is such a slight indication that it virtually ranks with the Belgian rule-of-thumb that the younger player always has the queen. If it has any value, the king-over-queen and ace-over-king must be very slightly superior rules, because more significant cards are involved. Such rules normally have no applicability at tournament play, where the cards played to a trick are not gathered together. In England, however, it is not uncommon to sort the hand into suits at the end of each duplicate deal. If two adjacent honor cards were in the same hand on the previous deal and were not separated in the shuffle, the tendency will be for the jack to lie over the queen and the queen to lie over the king.

(4) *Psychological*. P. Hal Sims claimed that the first defender to speak, light a cigarette, order a drink or react in similar fashion could be expected to hold the queen. This would be an attempt to show nonchalant disinterest, but in fact betray nervousness.

Other two-way finesses:

(a)	(b)
DUMMY	DUMMY
♠ Q 10 5	♠ J 9 5
DECLARER	DECLARER
♠ K 9 7	♠ Q 8 4

(a) is a two-way finesse for the jack. (b) is a two-way finesse for the 10. For other specific situations, see SUIT COMBINATIONS .

TWO-WAY GAME TRY (devised by Robert Ewen). A method that combines both the LONG SUIT GAME TRY and SHORT SUIT GAME TRY after a major-suit raise. If the auction starts 1♥-2♥, opener bids 2NT, 3♣ or 3♦ to make a short-suit try in spades, clubs or diamonds respectively. A 2♠ rebid by opener forces responder to bid 2NT, after which opener bids 3♣, 3♦ or 3♥ to make a long-suit try in clubs, diamonds or spades respectively. If the auction begins 1♠-2♠, a new suit by opener on the three-level is a short-suit try with the named shortage. A 2NT rebid by opener forces responder to bid 3♣, after which opener bids 3♦, 3♥ or 3♠ to make a long-suit try in diamonds, hearts or clubs respectively. Reraises of the major (1♥-2♥-3♥) are general-strength game tries. This method may be expanded to include raises of overcalls, or as a slam try after a forcing double raise. A similar procedure, Reverse Romex, is recommended by George Rosenkranz. The converse procedure is possible – delayed tries with short suits, direct tries with long suits.

TWO-WAY NOTRUMP. The use of two different point-count ranges for a 1NT opening bid. A popular treatment, especially in Britain, is the use of a WEAK NOTRUMP not vulnerable with a standard notrump vulnerable, and an alternative is the THREE-QUARTER NOTRUMP. WOODSON TWO-WAY NOTRUMP combines a strong notrump and a kamikaze notrump in one bid.

TWO-WAY REVERSE DRURY. Two-way Drury, based on an idea from Marty Bergen, uses the responses of both 2♣ and 2♦ by a passed hand to show raises of partner's major suit. 2♣ shows a three-card raise, and 2♦ shows a four-card raise. Continuations are as for Reverse Drury.

TWO-WAY STAYMAN. Any of a variety of conventions that use a 2♣ response to a 1NT opening as STAYMAN and use a 2♦ response to 1NT as a supplement to Stayman. The following describe the principal uses of the 2♦ responses.

(1) *Double-barreled Stayman*. 2♣ is used for hands which cannot guarantee game, and 2♦ for hands which wish to force to game. After 2♣, the opener's rebids are normal, and the responder's rebids are all nonforcing. Since responder's second-round jump to 3♠, for example, would not be forcing, a two-level rebid can be regarded as weak. (See Stayman convention.) The meaning of 2♣ followed by a jump to the four-level is a matter of partnership agreement .

Over 2♦, the opener normally shows a major suit or rebids 2NT; but he can rebid at the three-level in a suit or in notrump if he wishes, showing a five-card suit, or a maximum 4-3-3-3 hand without a major. Those who insist that the rebid be at the two-level have the advantage that responder can show his suit at the three level. When there is a possibility of a minor-suit slam, a fit can be explored at the level of three because a forcing situation exists.

(2) *Stayman 2♦*. A forcing to game response showing an unbalanced minor-suit hand: no four-card major suit, and a singleton or a void is a necessary requirement. The opener rebids in a suit to show concentrated strength (e.g., A-K-J, not necessarily a four-card suit) and 2NT to show scattered strength. If the concentrated strength proves to be opposite responder's shortage, he will know that 3NT is playable and that there is duplication of values for a suit contract. The subsequent bidding is also aimed at determining whether there is a serious notrump weakness.

(3) *Roth 2♦*. A response that is forcing to game and invitation to slam. This convention allows slam exploration without getting past the game level.

Like doubled-barreled Stayman, the 2♦ response asks opener about his four-card majors; unlike double-barreled Stayman, the 2♣ response can be followed by rebids that are game-forcing as in simple STAYMAN. Opener's rebids show whether he has one or both four-card majors, or if he has none, whether he has a minimum or maximum notrump.

(4) *Murray 2♦* asks the opener to bid his longer major suit, bidding a three-card suit if necessary. With equal length (4-4 or 3-3) in the majors the opener bids 2♥. One advantage of the convention is that it permits responder to bid weak unbalanced hands with 5-5 or 4-4 in the major suits. The responder does not promise any

strength whatever, although he can have a strong hand. A rebid of 2NT by the responder asks the opener to bid four-card suits up the line.

The opener's rebid must be in a major suit unless he has two major-suit doubletons, in which case he bids a six-card minor suit or 2NT.

(5) *August 2♦*, developed concurrently with Murray 2♦ and patterned on similar principles, is also a take-out for the majors with the added proviso that any suit rebid by responder is a signoff. This permits responder to use the convention with a weak 4-5 major-minor two-suiter. If the opener rebids the wrong major, responder retreats to his minor. With a weak minor two-suiter, responder first bids 2♣ (Stayman), then rebids 3♣.

(6) *Truscott 2♦*, a relay method devised by Alan Truscott and used widely in Israel. After the 2♦ response, opener defines his distribution and responder uses relay bids, as follows: With 4-3-3-3 hands opener rebids 2NT and shows his suit after a 3♣ relay; with 4-4-3-2 hands, opener bids 3♦ with both minors; with a major and a minor, he bids the suits in that order; with both majors he bids 2♥ and then 2NT. In all cases after opener's two suits have been identified, the next relay by responder asks for a two-step clarification of opener's distribution; the first step shows that the doubleton ranks below the tripleton. With five hearts, spades, or clubs, opener bids the suit, and after a relay he rebids 3♥, 3♠, or 3NT to show the low, middle, or high ranking doubleton, respectively. If opener has a five-card diamond suit, he shows it and simultaneously identifies his doubleton by bidding 3♥, 3♠, or 3NT directly over 2♦. Responder can use a meaningless bid just below the 3NT level to ask whether opener is minimum or maximum. This structure was later modified to make the remainder bids "numeric": 23 is shown before 32; 233, 323 and 332 in that order. See also BARON COROLLARY.

TWO-WAY TWO-BID. A method devised by Ira Rubin to open the bidding with a two-level bid with a strong ACOL two-bid or better or weak hand. An opening bid of two in any suit usually is weak, showing a weak two-bid type hand in the suit just above the bid suit (2♣=2♦, 2♦=2♥, 2♥=2♠, 2♠=3♣). Both partner and the opponents assume at the start that the opening bid is weak, and partner is expected to make responses in line with a weak two-bid opener — opener's suit with a non-game hand, 2NT asking for a feature, etc. However, opener may have a *strong* hand, in which case his opening bid is either his suit in a one-suiter or one of his suits in a two-suiter. Here are typical rebids after opener bids 2♥ and responder, with a weakish hand, bids 2♠, the suit opener holds if his hand is weak:

Opener	Responder
2♥	2♠

3♥ - an excellent one-suiter, not enough for game, with values in the side suits; not forcing but highly invitational. 3♣/3♦ - a second suit; a one-round force. See TARTAN TWO-BIDS.

U

USBA. Abbreviation for UNITED STATES BRIDGE ASSOCIATION, one of the predecessor organizations from

which AMERICAN CONTRACT BRIDGE LEAGUE emerged. For tournament results see Appendix I.

USBA GRAND NATIONALS. For tournament results see Appendix I.

ULTIMATE CLUB. The first totally integrated relay system to be substantially successful in tournament play. It is based on ideas propounded by Dave Cliff of Basking Ridge NJ, and was developed and refined by Matthew Granovetter, Ron Rubin and Mike Becker.

The advantage of this system, and of other relay methods, is that it greatly increases the number of meaningful auctions. The relay is a meaningless bid (usually but not invariably a minimum action) that asks partner to describe his hand further.

After a strong 1♣ opening, the responder describes his hand in three stages: the number of aces, kings and queens; the exact distribution; and the location of the high cards. In response to 1♦, 1♥ or 1♠, 2♣ by the responder is a relay, an artificial game force requiring a description by the opener. 2♦ in response to one of a major is an artificial invitation.

In response to 1NT, 2♣ is a relay requiring an exact description. See RELAY SYSTEMS.

UNASSUMING CUEBID. The use of a cuebid in response to an overcall to show a sound raise to the two-level. This may make it difficult to bid some strong hands, so it can be combined with the style in which new suits are forcing in response to an overcall. See CUEBID IN OPPONENT'S SUIT.

UNAUTHORIZED INFORMATION. Information which is given to a partner by means other than a legal call or play. Such information may be conveyed by questions, tone of voice, special emphasis, mannerisms, grimaces, remarks, squirms or huddles. If such information is received, a player should be governed by Law 16 of either rubber or duplicate bridge. See ALERTING; EXPLANATION OF ANY CALL OR PLAY .

At times in duplicate games a player may inadvertently overhear a remark by a contestant about a particular board which he has not as yet played. Such a fact should be reported to the director who will act in a manner as fair as possible to the player so reporting. See LAWS (Law 16).

UNBALANCED DISTRIBUTION. Referring to either the distribution of the suits in a hand or the distribution of one suit among the four hands. Unbalanced is the opposite of BALANCED DISTRIBUTION. Among the requirements for unbalanced distribution is the combination of one or more long suits and one or more singletons or voids.

UNBALANCED SWISS RAISE. Part of the ACES SCIENTIFIC SYSTEM, used in combination with VALUE SWISS RAISES to provide a full range of game-forcing raises in response to a major-suit opening. A jump response of three of the other major is used to show 10-12 with a singleton somewhere in the hand; a jump to 3NT shows 13-15 with a singleton.

Opener makes the cheapest bid to locate opener's singleton. Responder answers by bidding one of the next three steps; two of the steps will be natural and will show a singleton in the suit bid; the other step, either 3NT or

four of the anchor suit, will show a singleton in the remaining suit. See also CONGLOMERATE MAJOR RAISES, SUPER SWISS.

UNBEATABLE. See COLD.

UNBID MINOR FORCING. See NEW MINOR FORCING.

UNBID SUIT. Suit which has not been bid by declarer or his partner during the auction. Frequently, without any attractive opening lead, a player will select a lead on the basis that the suit has not been bid. This applies particularly to a major suit against a notrump contract.

Bidding an unbid suit may be a useful waiting move in the auction. See FOURTH SUIT FORCING AND ARTIFICIAL.

UNBLOCKING. Throwing a high card in play in order to gain some advantage for the hand opposite.

```
                A 10 6 2
    J 9 8 3                 K 7 5
                Q 4
```

Dummy has no side entry. West leads the 3, won by East's king. South unblocks with his queen, permitting a later finesse of the 10 so that South makes two tricks. Similarly:

```
                A 9 5 3
    J 10 8 7               K 6 2
                Q 4
```

Dummy has no side entry. West leads the jack, won by East's king. South unblocks the queen, and makes two tricks by a later finesse of the 9.

```
                Q 10 5 3
    K 8 7 2                 6 4
                A J 9
```

If South needs a later entry to dummy in this suit, he must be careful to win the opening lead with the ace.

A blind spot for many players is the internal block:

```
        A K Q 4 3              A 7 6 4 2
                 or
        10 8 7 6              K Q 9 8
```

If one defender holds J x x, five tricks cannot be run without a side entry to dummy. Similarly:

```
                A 5 4 3 2


                Q J 10 9
```

If there is no side entry to dummy, this is never worth five tricks.

There are numerous unblocking situations for the defense.

```
                A 3 2
    Q 10 6 5 4               K 7
                J 9 8
```

If the 5 is led against 3NT and dummy plays the ace, East must unblock the king. If East has an entry, the defense will take four tricks. The declarer's play would be right if opening leader held the entry.

See BLOCK, BLOCKING.

UNBLOCKING SQUEEZE. See JETTISON SQUEEZE.

UNCONSTRUCTIVE. A bid which is distinctly discouraging, but does not bar partner from making a further non-constructive move.

UNDER THE GUN. A term borrowed from poker in which game the phrase refers to the hand betting immediately after the dealer. In bridge there are various meanings, both in bidding and play. The term can be used in bidding situations to cover the position where a hand or player can be said to be "under the gun" if he is bidding directly after a preemptive bidder and before a hand which has not yet been heard from. The term also can describe a position where a player has to meet a bid-or-double situation at the slam level. In play, it is used to describe the hand between dummy and declarer that has a high card or high cards that are finessable and are in a vulnerable position as a result.

UNDERBID. A bid lower than the value of the hand warrants. Sometimes such bids are made because of inferior judgment, sometimes they are made consciously and deliberately because the value of some cards has been devalued because of the way the auction has progressed. One justification would be a tactical situation in which the opponents seem likely to save if the full value of the hand is bid. If the final contract is reached with apparently less assurance, the opponents may be deterred from saving. An underbid may also be made as an upside-down type of SHOOTING.

UNDERBIDDER. A player who regularly bids slightly less than the value his hand warrants. He is rarer, and easier to play with, than the overbidder. His psychological motivation is usually a reluctance to be set in any contract.

UNDERLEAD. The lead of a low card in a suit in which the master card or cards is held. This is routine in notrump contracts, but is unusual in trump contracts.

```
                K 7 2
    A 10 8 3               Q 9 6 5
                J 4
```

If West gains the lead early in the play and leads a low card, South should guess right. West would be unlikely to lead from the queen, giving South the chance for a trick he could not otherwise make. As the cards lie, one trick is all the defenders can make if they play passively.

But if West can find the lead of a low card originally, South is almost sure to go wrong and play low from dummy. Underleads of aces as the opening lead are distinctly daring, but may sometimes be risked if the bidding suggests strongly that dummy will have the king of the suit.

Another motive for an underlead is an urgent desire to get a particular lead from partner, perhaps for a ruff. The following celebrated example occurred in the 1958 Bermuda Bowl.

```
                    ♠ A K 8 4
                    ♥ A 7 6 3 2
                    ♦ 5
                    ♣ A J 8
    ♠ 10 6 5 3 2                    ♠ Q J 9
    ♥ 9                             ♥ 10 5
    ♦ A J 10 8 7 4 3                ♦ K Q 2
    ♣ —                             ♣ K Q 6 5 4
                    ♠ 7
                    ♥ K Q J 8 4
                    ♦ 9 6
                    ♣ 10 9 7 3 2
```

Neither side was vulnerable.

West	North	East	South
		1NT	2 ♥
2 ♠	3 ♠	Pass	3NT
5 ♦	5 ♥	Pass	Pass
Dbl	All Pass		

Pietro Forquet, West for Italy, judged that his partner's most likely entry was ♦ K. He therefore led ♦ 3, a suit preference signal. East duly won and returned ♣K. West ruffed, and East had to make a club trick to defeat the contract.

In the other room the ♦ A was led against 5 ♥. The contract could not then be defeated. South was able to strip the hand and endplay East. See LEADS, OVERLEAD.

UNDERRUFF, or undertrump. To play a low trump when a trick has already been ruffed with a higher trump. It can be the right play whether the previous ruff was by an opponent or by partner. The underruff, though unusual, is necessary in many situations.

(1) *To avoid a trump surplus (simple trump coup).* It is on occasion a disadvantage to hold too many trumps. When reduced to only trump cards you may be forced to ruff a trick belonging to your partner, and then lead away from or into a tenace position.

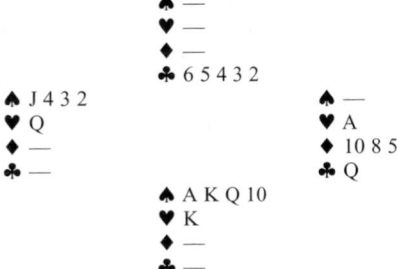

South is declarer at a spade contract and needs four tricks to make it. The lead is in North's hand. A club is led which East covers. South, knowing the trump position, realizes his only chance is to ruff high. West must undertrump to avoid a trump endplay. If West discards, South will lead his losing heart. West must ruff and lead into a spade tenace. When West undertrumps, declarer is helpless. If he leads a heart, East will win and play a diamond through South's trump holding. (If South ruffs this high, West must undertrump perforce.)

(2) *To avoid a fatal discard in a plain suit.* In the following deal an underruff was necessary at the third trick because East could not spare any cards in the side suits.

```
                ♠ 9 5
                ♥ 7 2
                ♦ J 10 9 4
                ♣ A K 10 9 6
  ♠ 10 6 4                    ♠ Q J 7 3
  ♥ A K J 9 5 4               ♥ 10 3
  ♦ Q 7                       ♦ 6 5 2
  ♣ 4 2                       ♣ Q J 8 3
                ♠ A K 8 2
                ♥ Q 8 6
                ♦ A K 8 3
                ♣ 7
```

South played in 5 ♦ , and West led two high hearts. East played high-low, perhaps wrongly, and when the ♦ J could not be overruffed at the third trick West was marked with the ♦ Q. East had a discard problem which he solved by underruffing with the ♦ 2; any black suit discard would have made the play easy for South. The contract failed,

although South could have succeeded by very accurate play. Two high spades, a spade ruff and four rounds of trumps would have squeezed East in the black suits.

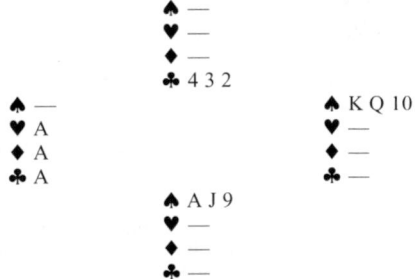

Again North is on lead with South the declarer at a spade contract. South needs two more tricks for the contract. When a club is led from dummy, East must ruff high to prevent South from scoring the ♠ J.

South can now undertrump with the ♠ 9, leaving East to lead into an established tenace. If South overruffs, he must concede two spade tricks to East.

(3) *To be able to lead a plain suit card at a later time (ROBERT COUP).* In certain positions, it is profitable to be able to lead a plain suit card rather than a trump.

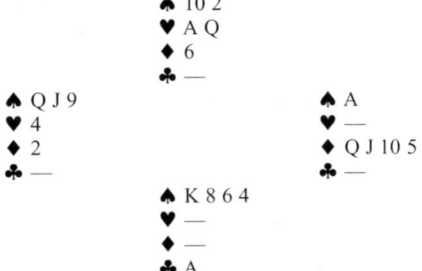

West leads against South's spade contract. South needs three tricks to make the contract.

West leads the ♥ 4 which East ruffs with the ♠ A. This appears to give West two natural trump tricks, but South underruffs! East returns a diamond and South ruffs again. South now leads the ♣ A. West must ruff with a high honor to prevent dummy's ♠ 10 from winning this trick. Dummy discards and West must now lead away from his remaining spade honor.

If South does not preserve the ♣ A to lead toward dummy, he will be defeated. When a low trump is led from the South hand, West wins with the jack and dummy must follow suit. West can now lead the ♠ Q, smothering North's 10 and setting up the ♠ 9 for the setting trick.

(4) *To avoid a premature squeeze (anti-positional squeeze).* It is sometimes possible to avoid making a premature discard by undertrumping.

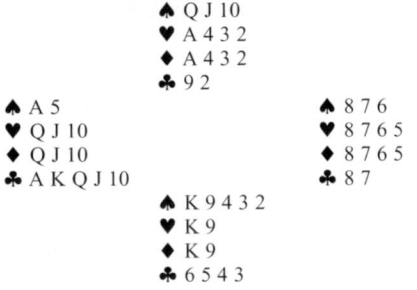

West	North	East	South
2NT	Pass	Pass	3 ♠
Pass	4 ♠	All Pass	

South's 3 ♠ bid had nothing to recommend it, but it happened that the contract was difficult to defeat. East had a poor hand but he played the star role. West led the ♣ K and promptly shifted to ace and another trump. Dummy won and another club was won by West. West now shifted to the ♥ Q which declarer won with the king.

When declarer ruffed a club in dummy, East had to undertrump to defeat the contract. If he discarded from a red suit, South would have been able to establish a trick in that suit in dummy by ruffing, and the contract would have been made. After East underruffed, declarer was helpless. See TRUMP PLAY.

UNDERTRICK. Each trick by which declarer's side fails to fulfill its contract.

UNDERTRUMP. See UNDERRUFF.

UNDOUBLE. See DOUBLE FOR SACRIFICE.

UNFACED HAND. During the play, the hands of the declarer and both defenders. After the opening lead, the declarer's partner's hand is faced up on the table so that all players may see the cards (dummy's hand). Prior to the play, none of the hands is faced. A player in claiming or conceding tricks faces his hand in properly presenting his claim. See CLAIM OR CONCESSION; DEFENDING HAND; DUMMY.

UNFAVORABLE VULNERABILITY. Your side is vulnerable and your opponents are not. Preempts must be stronger at this vulnerability because penalties mount much faster at this vulnerability. Balancing and sacrifices also need very careful evaluation. See EQUAL VULNERABILITY, FAVORABLE VULNERABILITY.

UNFINISHED RUBBER. A rubber ended by agreement before either side has won two games. A side which has won one game is credited with a bonus of 300 points; a side which has the only partial is credited with a bonus of 100 points. (This was 50 until a change in the 1993 Code.)

UNINTENTIONAL. A violation of rules, ethics or proprieties is assumed in bridge circles to be unintentional, not deliberate. It is the purpose of the LAWS to provide indemnities for the non-offending side to permit an accurate or fairly accurate result on the board or a hand. Any intentional violation contravenes the philosophy of the game. An assumption that such an act by an opponent is intentional is as much a violation of ethics as such an intentional act itself would be.

UNIT. See UNITS OF THE ACBL.

UNITED STATES BRIDGE ASSOCIATION. One of the predecessor organizations which merged to form the AMERICAN CONTRACT BRIDGE LEAGUE. The purpose of this association was to organize a national tournament in which participation would be based on skill alone, and which would be a thorough enough test so that its winners could be clearly recognized as national champions.

The grand national plan which this organization evolved was a pyramiding series of qualifying tournaments starting with open local tournaments, proceeding to city, state, and regional tournaments, and culminating in the Grand National.

In addition to the organization of tournaments truly national in scope, the United States Bridge Association was a charter member of the International Contract Bridge Union which was organized in 1934 under the joint sponsorship of the United States Bridge Association, the National Bridge Association of Great Britain, and the French Contract Bridge Association.

The American Bridge League (organized 1927) and the International Bridge League (headquarters at The Hague, Holland) existed concurrently, and some short-lived rivalry between the two organizations was eliminated in 1937 when the American Contract Bridge League resulted from the amalgamation of the two United States organizations.

For results see Appendix I.

UNITED STATES BRIDGE FEDERATION. An organization formed in 2000 incorporating both the American Contract Bridge League and the American Bridge Association, the two organized bridge associations in the United States. One of the main goals is to convince the U.S. Olympic Committee, and later the International Olympic Committee, of bridge's worth as an Olympic sport. The new organization was formed because it is necessary to approach the IOC as an organization representing the entire country.

The following were named as USBF directors by the ACBL in 2001: Dan Morse, Bruce Reeve, Nick Nickell, Shawn Quinn, Alan Popkin and Michael Becker. David Silber, CEO of ACBL, was named an ex-officio member and has a vote. Two more directors were to be named by the American Bridge Association.

UNITED STATES INTERNATIONAL REPRESENTATIVES. The names of players who have represented the U. S. or North America in international team events may be found under ANGLO-AMERICAN MATCHES, BERMUDA BOWL, FRANCO-AMERICAN MATCHES, INTERNATIONAL OPEN TEAM SELECTION, WORLD TEAM OLYMPIAD, INTERNATIONAL WOMEN'S TEAM SELECTION, VENICE CUP, ROSENBLUM CUP and WORLD CHAMPIONSHIPS.

UNITS OF THE ACBL. Units of the ACBL have been formed at different times and under different conditions, and they differ widely in background, scope, and membership. Some limit their activity to a given town or city, others comprise states.

The jurisdiction of a unit consists of a geographical area, bounded in its application and charter, and each unit has jurisdiction over its own members, while participating in the management of ACBL.

A new unit may be formed in any area where no unit exists, provided there are 100 or more members in the area to be organized. In the process of formation, a provisional charter may be granted with more than 50 members if a reasonable prospect of reaching the 100-member status exists.

The unit is expected to perform certain functions:
(1) Establish and maintain a membership of at least 100.

(2) Promote and stimulate interest in duplicate bridge among members and prospective members by providing an attractive program of bridge events.

(3) Expand and increase membership.

(4) Conduct or supervise tournament events at which masterpoints and rating points are awarded under ACBL regulations.

(5) Establish and maintain contact with neighboring units, supporting each other's activities.

(6) Conduct annual elections by popular vote for officers and/or Directors.

(7) Elect, in collaboration with other units in the district, a member of the National Board of Directors, a first and a second Alternate Director, and three representatives to the National Board of Governors.

(8) Adopt bylaws consistent with those of the ACBL, which must be filed with ACBL.

(9) Assume fiscal responsibility for funds collected on behalf of the ACBL and membership dues collected from its members; submit semi-annual financial reports to its officers; maintain accurate records.

UNLAWFUL. An action not in accordance with the mechanics of the game, as described in Parts I to III of LAWS.

UNLIMITED BID. A bid with wide limits in valuation. The bid with the widest limit of all is a STAYMAN response to a weak notrump, which could range from a worthless hand to a hand worth a forcing opening bid. Other unlimited bids are discussed under ONE OVER ONE, OPENING SUIT BID and TAKEOUT DOUBLE.

See TWO-OVER-ONE RESPONSE.

UNMAKABLE. A contract which cannot succeed unless the defense slips.

UNMIXED PAIRS. An event in which all pairs must consist of either two women or two men.

UNMIXED TEAMS. Each pair must consist of either two men or two women.

UNPENALTY DOUBLE. See DOUBLE FOR SACRIFICE.

UNSEEDED KNOCKOUT TEAMS. A method first tried in 1982 for improving the attendance at knockout team events. Random draws determine the pairings for all rounds leading up to the final. It is theoretically possible, but not too likely, that the two best teams in the field would meet each other in the first round. The event has proved quite popular.

UNUSUAL JUMP. See ASKING BIDS; FRAGMENT BID; GRAND SLAM FORCE; LEBOVIC ASKING BID; ROMEX TRUMP ASKING BIDS; SPLINTER BID; SUPER GERBER; SUPER SWISS; VOID SHOWING BIDS.

UNUSUAL NOTRUMP. A method of showing two-suited hands in competitive situations. The convention, which normally indicates length in the minor suits, was devised by Alvin Roth in 1948 and developed by him with Tobias Stone.

An overcall of 2NT after an opening bid of one of a major is normally used to show the minor suits. The overcaller may well be suggesting a sacrifice:

♠ 5
♥ 4
♦ K Q 9 5 2
♣ Q J 9 7 6 3

Overcaller might also have an extremely strong hand and be intending to take further action.

♠ A Q
♥ 2
♦ A Q 7 5 3
♣ A K J 8 4

With this, bid 2NT over 1♥ and follow with a cuebid of 3♥. Bid 2NT over 1♠ and follow with a bid of 3NT, implying that you are assuming a heart stopper with partner. Any voluntary rebid by the 2NT bidder, including a double, shows an extremely strong hand.

In many situations the unusual notrump is a balancing move:

(a)

West	North	East	South
			1♠
Pass	1NT	Pass	2♠
Pass	Pass	2NT	

(b)

West	North	East	South
			1♠
Pass	2♠	Pass	Pass
2NT			

In both cases the unusual notrump bidder wishes to contest the partscore and invites his partner to pick a minor. Case (b) is slightly safer than (a) because the known fit for North-South in spades increases the chance that East-West have a fit. The Unusual Notrump may be used when the auction is still very much alive:

(c)

West	North	East	South
			1♠
Pass	1NT	Pass	2♠ or 2♥
2NT			

(d)

West	North	East	South
			1♥
Pass	1♠	Pass	2♠
2NT			

In (c) both North and South are limited and are unlikely to go beyond the level of two. West can rely on some strength from East, who should not entertain any hopes of game. In (d), North is not limited, but the North-South fit gives West some assurance of an East-West fit. If the vulnerability is favorable for East-West, 5♣ or 5♦ may prove a cheap save if North-South go to 4♠.

An original pass may serve to identify the unusual notrump, as when the dealer overcalls 1NT after a fourth-hand major-suit opening bid. See SANDWICH NOTRUMP. Many players apply the convention whenever the opponents have bid two suits:

(e)

West	North	East	South
			1♣
Pass	1♥	1NT	

(f)

West	North	East	South
			1♠
Pass	2♦	2NT	

It would seldom be right for East to make a notrump bid in a natural sense because he would be laying himself open to a heavy penalty opposite a probably worthless dummy. With a strong defensive hand he would prefer to stay out of the auction, expecting to defeat any game contract.

So in this case, East's bid shows great length (at least 5-5) in the unbid suits. This is one extension of the convention (optional by partnership agreement) to situations not limited to minor suits. Another is a direct 2NT overcall of a minor-suit opening, which many pairs use to show length in the two lower-ranking unbid suits. (However, since 1♣ openings are sometimes based on a three-card suit, some pairs use a 2NT overcall of 1♣ to show both minors.)

The unusual meaning is clearer when the bidder is a passed hand.

West	North	East	South
Pass	1♣	Pass	1♠
1NT			

This shows at least 5-5 in the unbid suits and is thus more distributional than a takeout double. A jump to 2NT would be similar with more distribution.

West	North	East	South
Pass	Pass	Pass	1♠
1NT			

This shows the minor suits. A jump to 2NT would be similar but with more distribution. This was the expert consensus in BWS 200 (77%), but more complex arrangements are possible by agreement.

Balancing 1NT by a passed hand is natural but is obviously limited by the failure to open. Similarly, a jump in a suit by a passed hnd shows strong a one-suiter as is possible in the circumstances. It is improbable action in view of the failure to open with a weak two-bit or a preemptive three-bid.

A takeout double by a passed hand can be off shape, intending an equal-level conversion to a long suit if necessary. For example, a double of 1♥ could have 4-2-5-2 distribution (64% of experts in BWS 2001).

The unusual notrump can be used when your side has already bid, and even when your side has opened the bidding:

(g)

West	North	East	South
			Pass
3♥	Dbl	Pass	4NT

(h)

West	North	East	South
			1♣
4♠	4NT		

In (g) South shows a good minor two-suiter, probably not far short of an opening bid. North may be able to jump to 6♣ or 6♦. In this case the Unusual notrump is an attacking weapon.

When the bidding has been seriously crowded by an opponent's preemptive action, 4NT is usually a takeout bid rather than BLACKWOOD. In (h) Sidney Silodor suggested the 4NT bid on this hand:

♠ —
♥ K Q 6 5 3
♦ A J 9 8 3
♣ 9 7 2

The bid indicates a desire to play at the five-level, with a free choice left to partner.

Partnerships must define the meaning of a 4NT overcall after a 4♠ or 4♥ opening. Most play that over 4♥,

a double is a three-suit takeout and 4NT is for minors; over 4♠, a double is for penalties and 4NT is a takeout for all three suits.

The unusual notrump can operate when the user has already bid a minor suit:

(i)

West	North	East	South
			1♠
2♣	2♠	Pass	Pass
2NT			

(j)

West	North	East	South
			1♣
1♥	Pass	4♥	4NT

In (i), West wishes to contest the partscore and is likely to have five or six clubs and four diamonds. If his second suit were hearts he would double. In (j), South is likely to have five diamonds and six clubs: 4NT is his only way to indicate this distribution.

The unusual notrump is usually made by the side which did not open the bidding. In (h) and (j) above, its use by the opener's side is shown, and here are two further examples:

(k)

West	North	East	South
			1♦
1♠	Pass	4♠	4NT

(l)

West	North	East	South
			1♥
1♠	Pass	2♠	Pass
Pass	2NT		

In (k) South must have a second suit but opinions would differ. Possible interpretations are: (1) hearts; (2) 6-4 in diamonds and clubs; (3) ambiguous, intending to correct to 5♣ to 5♦ holding hearts.

If a player bypasses a natural notrump bid, makes a non-forcing bid, and later, uninvited, bids notrump competitively, he shows extra distribution with no intention of playing notrump. Example:

West	North	East	South
1♦	Dbl	1♠	2♣
2♠	Pass	Pass	2NT

South did not bid 1NT, so he cannot wish to play 2NT. See GENEVA CONVENTION.

UNUSUAL POSITIVE. A set of artificial jump responses to a Precision Club opening to describe 4-4-4-1 distribution. However, on this auction, 1♦-Pass-Pass-2NT, 2NT is natural showing 19-20 HCP

UNUSUAL OVER UNUSUAL. See DEFENSE TO TWO-SUITED INTERFERENCE.

UPPER SUITS CUEBID. An immediate overcall in the opponent's suit to show the two highest ranking unbid suits. See also MICHAELS CUEBID.

UPPERCUT. A ruff, usually by a defender, aimed at promoting a trump trick for partner.

```
            ♠ 4 3 2
♠ J 5                 ♠ Q 6
            ♠ A K 10 9 8 7
```

In a spade contract, West leads a suit of which East and South are void. East ruffs with his ♠Q, ensuring a trump trick for the defense. If South overruffs, the jack wins a trick.

A defender with a completely useless trump holding should usually ruff with his highest trump if he gets the opportunity. A ruff with a card as low as the 3 can possibly effect an uppercut and promote a trump trick for the defense.

```
                    8 7
10 9 6 5                           4 3
                  A K Q J 2
```

If both East and South are void in the suit led, East can set up a trump trick for partner by ruffing with the 3 and forcing an honor.

UPSIDE-DOWN SIGNAL. The use of a low card in defense to encourage a continuation of a suit, or a shift to a suit, and a high card to discourage. The method is credited to Karl Schneider, but seems to have been first published by E.K. O'Brien in a *Bridge World* article in 1937.

The chief theoretical advantage of this procedure is that a player may not be able to spare a high card from a strong holding:

```
                  ♠ 10 7 6 3
♠ J 5                           ♠ K Q 9 2
                  ♠ A 8 4
```

West leads the ♠J against 3NT because his own suit has been bid by declarer. East has to drop the deuce because he cannot spare the 9. Using normal methods, it is now difficult for West to continue the suit when he gains the lead. But he continues happily using upside-down signals.

Other advantages claimed for this method are that it is harder for declarer to falsecard effectively, and that a single discard signal during the defense may be clearer than with normal methods.

As with standard signals, the appropriate counter for the declarer is to signal as if he were a defender: Play low to encourage, high to discourage. This gives the best chance to scramble the signals and confuse the signaler's partner.

For a different upside-down signal, which grew in popularity in the 80s, see COUNT SIGNALS. For a combination of standard and upside-down attitude signals, see SCANIAN SIGNAL; SIGNAL, SIGNALING.

UP THE LINE. The practice of making the cheapest bid when responding or rebidding with two or three four-card suits, laid down as a principle by the BARON SYSTEM. The idea is employed in many bidding styles, with some reservations.

```
♠ K 8 4 3
♥ K 8 4 3
♦ A J
♣ K 10 5
```

A 1♥ response to an opening bid in either minor suit gives the opener the opportunity to rebid in spades. If he fails to do so, responder can assume there is no spade fit and bid 3NT.

This idea has validity but there are many circumstances in which expert players would depart from the principle.

(1) If there is a great disparity in the strength of the suits:

```
♠ A Q J 3
♥ 8 4 3 2
♦ A J
♣ Q 10 5
```

The chief arguments in favor of bidding 1♠ in re-

sponse to a minor-suit opening are that a heart response might lead to a notrump contract with an unguarded heart suit, and that a high heart contract might result in a weak trump holding. The opposing view is that 1♥ may inhibit a heart lead in notrump, and that a 1♠ response may exclude a 4-4 fit in hearts.

(2) With two strong major suits:

```
♠ K Q J 3
♥ A Q 5 2
♦ 8 3
♣ 9 4 2
```

Some authorities used to recommend a response of 1♠ to an opening bid in a minor, with the intention of bidding hearts on the next round.

The choice of response is closely connected with the treatment of BIDDABLE SUITS. If the opener is not expected to rebid 1♠ with a bad four-card suit, the spade response is necessary to avoid missing a possible fit.

A disadvantage is that 1♠ followed by a heart bid strongly suggests a five-card spade suit. The "up the line" response of 1♥, used by players who do not impose standards for biddable suits, leads to a problem if the opener rebids his suit. In that case an eccentric reverse bid of 2♠ may be tried.

(3) With one major suit and one minor suit:

```
(a)                    (b)
♠ Q J 7 3              ♠ 8 2
♥ 8 2                  ♥ Q J 7 3
♦ Q J 7 3              ♦ Q J 7 3
♣ J 7 2                ♣ J 7 2
```

In each of these cases there is a good argument for rejecting the 1♦ response to 1♣ in favor of the major suit. The danger of 1♦ is that opposing intervention may shut out the major suit, which is a serious possibility in case (b). In case (a), 1♠ may work well by shutting out an opposing heart contract. But if the responding hand is stronger, there is less likelihood of intervention, and therefore less reason to prefer the major-suit response. The case for ignoring "up the line" is greater with diamonds and hearts than with diamonds and spades. Spades are less likely to be shut out by interference. Suit quality affects the decision. A strong suit may be playable in a 4-3 fit. There also could be lead-directing reasons.

If the response is at the two-level, the minor-suit response is preferable. The chance of interference is slight, and a response of 2♥ to 1♠ is generally expected to show a five-card or longer suit. See CHOICE OF SUIT.

UP TO. (1) Toward the hand that will play last to a particular trick, as in UP TO WEAKNESS. (2) Toward a vulnerable third-hand holding such as K-x-x or K-Q-x, as opposed to leading away from such a holding.

UP TO STRENGTH. Traditional wisdom advises leading up to weakness but is silent about leading up to strength. If dummy is on your right, it is sometimes appropriate to lead a suit in which dummy is strong.

You should tend to avoid leading a suit in which you have an honor poised over an honor in dummy: ace over king or queen; king over queen or jack; queen over jack or ten. Leading in such circumstances will often give away a trick.

If dummy on your right has two high honors, leading from a jack tends to be safer than leading from another honor:

♣ A K 2	♣ A Q 2
Dummy	Dummy
♣ J 4 3	♣ J 4 3
You	You
(a)	(b)

Leading from the jack can do no harm, but leading from any other honor could cost a trick. See LEADS.

UP TO WEAKNESS. The old whist maxim recommending a lead "up to weakness" is valid but not very helpful. It is quite true that a lead by declarer's right-hand opponent up to a completely worthless holding in dummy will never give away a trick, although it may help the declarer if he is short of entries to dummy.

The following discussion will consider defender's problems in this situation on the assumption that the suit in question is distributed evenly around the table. If one player is known to be short or is likely to be short, the prospects are of course altered. Crucial situations are classified in increasing order of dummy strength.

(1) Dummy has 9-x-x. Almost invariably a safe lead, but the defender should be careful to lead the 10 from holdings headed by K-10 or Q-10.

(2) Dummy has 10-x-x. The defender must lead the jack from holdings headed by A-J or K-J. If leading from a single honor, the higher the honor the safer the lead. A-x-x is completely safe, while J-x-x is the most dangerous.

(3) Dummy has J-x-x. Again, the higher the honor the safer the lead. A-x-x is relatively safe, while Q-x-x is very dangerous.

(4) Dummy has Q-x-x. A lead from the jack is virtually safe. A lead from the ace or king is very dangerous.

(5) Dummy has K-x-x. The lead from the ace is very dangerous. The lead from the jack or queen is safer.

(6) Dummy has A-x-x. All leads are relatively safe, with J-x-x slightly the safest and Q-x-x the least safe.

The general principle applying in all the above cases is also applicable when leading through dummy. The defender should avoid breaking a suit in which an honor is poised over the honor ranking immediately below it. In other words, one should avoid leading from a jack up to a 10, a queen up to a jack, a king up to a queen, or an ace up to a king. Similarly, one should avoid leading from a jack through a queen, a queen through a king, or a king through an ace.

This applies also if dummy has two honors. It is obviously dangerous to lead from a king up to A-Q, or a queen up to A-J or K-J. See also LEADS, THROUGH STRENGTH.

USEFUL SPACE PRINCIPLE. When allocating bidding space under partnership agreements, assign it where it is most useful without reference to natural or traditional meanings of calls. This may involve deciding which tasks are most important to accomplish and arranging adequate space to perform those tasks efficiently. Techniques for allocating space include "lumping" (giving over all extra space to one function), "spreading" (giving increments of space to each of several functions, usually by removing most or all space from one task deemed less important), and making compromises (not making use of all available space in order to achieve some or all of a transcending objective).

According to Jeff Rubens in a series of articles in *The Bridge World*, several popular conventions and many standard methods are based on a misguided idea of simplicity. "They are not well-designed because they ignore the Useful Space Principle," he wrote. Rubens studied the BLACKWOOD convention, among others, to illustrate the principle. He pointed out that bidding the suit immediately above the agreed trump at the four-level (see KICKBACK) allows more room for control asking and trump length asking, while 4NT works perfectly well as the cuebid in the suit that initiates a Blackwood sequence. For example, if the auction has begun 1♥-3♥, then 4♠ would be Blackwood and 4 NT would be a spade cuebid. If the agreed suit is clubs, then 4♦ would be Blackwood and 4NT would be a diamond cuebid. However, if the agreed suit is spades, then 4NT is Blackwood. Specialized responses allow much more specific exploration of slam possibilities. Rubens also offered new structures for new-suit responses to overcalls and new methods for using the GRAND SLAM FORCE, while pointing out that many other applications also are possible.

USES OF CARDS. Although playing cards are made for the playing of games, individual cards have been used for other purposes. Since the backs were (until about 120 years ago) blank and unmarked, paper was scarce and expensive, and playing cards used the very finest quality paper obtainable, cards were practical to use for purposes where standardization was an asset.

Both handwritten and printed visiting cards were made on card backs, as were tickets and identifying passes. Workmen dismantling the Bastille carried such passes to distinguish them from the crowds of curious visitors who interfered with their work.

In France and Canada, cards were used in emergencies as money. Several libraries used them for their original index cards. At one time it was fashionable to write social invitations on them. Advertisements were printed and written on them.

Old cards and sheets of cards were used to stiffen the covers of books, and some of our knowledge of early cards comes from discoveries of these fragments. And, of course, they are the building blocks for constructing a house of cards. See TURGENEV.

UTILITY. A British expression which summarizes the straightforward bidding methods used there in many rubber bridge clubs: strong notrump (16-18); 2♣ as the forcing opening; intermediate two bids; and 3NT for takeout over opposing three-bids.

UTILITY NOTRUMP RESPONSE. See CHURCHILL.

V

VALET. One of the court cards in decks of cards used centuries ago, decks that were ancestors of present-day cards. The term survives in French, meaning the equivalent of English jack or knave. A knave, like a valet, is a male servant.

VALIDATION. In duplicate bridge, the certifying by the director of the correctness of an auction; the approval

of the opponents to a correction of the scoring of the results of a board of duplicate play; the initialing of a pair score in team play by the opponents of this pair on a set of boards.

VALUATION. Valuation of a hand is covered under particular types of valuation in the following articles: ACE VALUES; ASSETS; BISSELL; BORDERLINE OPENING BIDS; DEATH HOLDING; FOUR ACES SYSTEM; LAW OF TOTAL TRICKS; LOSING TRICK COUNT; POINT COUNT; REITH POINT COUNT; REVALUATION; ROBERTSON POINT COUNT; RULE OF EIGHTEEN; RULE OF FIFTEEN; TRUMP SUPPORT; VALUE OF GAME; VALUE OF SLAM; WORK POINT COUNT.

VALUE OF GAME. At matchpoint play, a game bonus of 300 points is added to the trick score for non-vulnerable games and a bonus of 500 points is added to the trick score for vulnerable games. These values determine the mathematics of sacrificing against an opponent's game. For example, a better score results from going down three, doubled, non-vulnerable rather than letting an opponent make a vulnerable game. At matchpoints, any game should be bid with a 50% chance, all other things being equal.

In IMP play, the values of the game and slam bonus are used to determine the probability of success needed to abandon a safe game for a risky small slam. For example, in a close team match with IMP scoring, a 50% chance of success is needed to bid a vulnerable small slam vs. a sure game. At IMPS, games should be bid with a 37% chance vulnerable and a 45% chance non-vulnerable.

In rubber bridge, it has been shown that a game bonus of 500 points is appropriate for scoring the rubber game when both sides are vulnerable and a game bonus of 350 points is the correct value in all other combinations of vulnerability. This leads to the following decisions on the probability of success needed to bid a small slam in rubber bridge:

	Opponents vulnerable	Opponents non-vulnerable
Declarer vulnerable	50%	38%
Declarer non-vulnerable	55%	55%

Safety factors required for bidding grand slams in rubber bridge are 65% when declarer is vulnerable and the opponents are non-vulnerable and 68% in all other combinations of vulnerability.

The safety factor required for bidding a game can be shown to be 54% when declarer is vulnerable and the opponents are non-vulnerable and 49% in all other combinations of vulnerability. These factors are calculated using the values of the game bonus and the values of the partscore bonus of 100 or 150 points, depending upon vulnerability. See VALUE OF PARTSCORE.

Safety factors required for doubling an opponent's game bid are 63% to 77%, depending upon vulnerability. Safety factors required for doubling an opponent's partscore into game are 77% to 87%, depending upon vulnerability.

VALUE OF PARTSCORE. In matchpoint play, a bonus of 50 points if awarded for successful less-than-game contracts. In CHICAGO, a partscore remaining at the end of four deals is not rewarded except on the last deal where a partscore earned is worth 100 points. In rubber bridge, a partscore bonus has been shown to be worth 150 points when both sides are vulnerable and 100 points in all other combinations of vulnerability. For safety factors required to abandon a safe partscore and bid a game, see VALUE OF GAME.

VALUE OF SLAM. It is assumed that 11 tricks are a certainty for computing small slam percentages and that 12 tricks are certain for computation of grand slam percentages. At matchpoint play, a 50% chance of success justifies bidding a small slam, and a 67% chance justifies bidding a grand slam. Expert players will frequently take into account intangible factors such as the quality of the field.

VALUES. Strength in high cards or in distribution.

VALUE SWISS RAISES. An expansion of the SWISS CONVENTION used in the ACES SCIENTIFIC SYSTEM to show a range of forcing balanced raises in response to an opening bid of 1♥ or 1♠. They deny a singleton or a good 5-card suit, and promise 4-card support or a tripleton with two top honors. The ranges shown, assuming a 1♠ opening, are as follows:

1NT forcing, then 4	
of opener's major	12-13 points
4♦	13-14
4♣	14-16
2NT then strong support	16-18

VANDERBILT CLUB SYSTEM. Harold S. Vanderbilt, who codified the game of contract bridge in 1925, was the first to advocate use of a 1♣ opening bid as an artificial bid to show a strong hand, and of a 1♦ artificial negative response to show a weak hand. He wrote three books, now long since out of print, on his Club Convention prior to 1934.

After a lapse of about 30 years, interest in 1♣ systems revived. The BLUE TEAM CLUB, which helped to win many World Championships for Italy, uses an opening 1♣ convention very like the Vanderbilt Club, and the SCHENKEN SYSTEM, used in two World Championships, is an even closer relation.

In 1964, Vanderbilt wrote a modernized version of his system entitled *The Club Convention Modernized*, which may be summarized as follows:

(1) Opening bids of 1♦ (perhaps 3 cards), 1♥ or 1♠, (both perhaps 4 cards), 2♣ (good 5-card suit or better) are limited, usually fewer than 16 points.

(2) Opening bids of 1♣ show hands with 16 or more points. 1♦ is the negative response. Other minimum responses show two aces or their equivalent. 2♥ and other single jumps show solid 5-card suits. 3♥ and other double jumps show one-loser six-card suits. 1NT response is strong, with an honor in every suit.

(3) Opening notrump bids are: 1NT 16-18; 1♣ followed by 1NT with 19-20; 2NT with 21-22; 1♣ then 2NT with 23-24; 1♣ then 3NT with 9 tricks and all suits stopped.

(4) After interference over 1♣, double, redouble, and jump bids are positive and forcing. Minimum actions are encouraging but non-forcing.

(5) Other opening bids include weak two-bids, solid 3♣ and 3♦, sound 3♥ and 3♠.

VANDERBILT CUP. (1) For the National Knockout Team Championships presented by Harold S. Vanderbilt in 1928. The organizing body 1928-57 was the Vanderbilt Cup Committee. It was contested annually in New York until 1958 when it became part of the Spring North American Championships, under which heading past results are listed. The Vanderbilt often is used to help select United States and North American international teams. It ranks with the Spingold as the most highly prized trophy in the ACBL calendar. See INTERNATIONAL OPEN TEAM SELECTION. For results see Appendix I.

(2) For the World Olympiad Team Championship, presented by Harold S. Vanderbilt on the occasion of the first World Team Olympiad held in Turin, Italy, in 1960. For results see Appendix V.

The two events are among the few for which the winners receive individual replicas of the trophy, a practice initiated by the donor from the first running of the events, and perpetuated by a $100,000 trust fund administered by the ACBL under the terms of Vanderbilt's will.

VANIVA PROBLEM. One of the most famous of all DOUBLE-DUMMY PROBLEMS; composed by Sidney Lenz in 1928 in a contest promoted by Vaniva Shaving Cream.

```
              ♠ 5
              ♥ 8 5
              ♦ A K 7
              ♣ A K 8 6 5 4 2
♠ K 10 7                      ♠ 8 6 4 3 2
♥ 9                           ♥ Q 6 3 2
♦ Q 10 8 3                    ♦ J 6 2
♣ Q J 10 9 7                  ♣ 3
              ♠ A Q J 9
              ♥ A K J 10 7 4
              ♦ 9 5 4
              ♣ —
```

South to make 7♥ after the lead of the ♣Q.

North wins the club opening, South discarding a diamond, and leads the other top club. Now:

(1) If East ruffs, South overruffs and takes a ruffing finesse in spades to kill West's king. A trump finesse gives South the balance.

(2) If East sheds a spade, South ruffs in hand and ruffs out the king of spades as before. He takes a trump finesse, cashes his spades, crosses to a diamond and ruffs a club. Then he crosses to another diamond and takes the last three tricks with the A-K-J of trumps over the queen.

(3) If East throws a diamond, South throws a spade and finesses in trumps. He crosses to a diamond, repeats the trump finesse, and runs all the trumps for a repeating squeeze against West in three suits.

VARIABLE NOTRUMP. An opening of 1NT which is weak or strong depending on vulnerability and/or seat (1st, 2nd, 3rd, or 4th). See TWO -WAY NOTRUMP.

VENICE CUP (or Venice Trophy). A world competition for women based on the same parameters as the BERMUDA BOWL. It is staged every two years simultaneously with the Bermuda Bowl. The competition started as a challenge battle between Italy and the United States. Venice was the host to the 1974 Bermuda Bowl, and Italy invited the United States to

send a women's team to play in an exhibition match for a new trophy – the Venice Cup. Ruth McConnell, an official of both the ACBL and the WBF, responded to the challenge by putting together a team of American all-stars. The United States won the match handily.

In 1976, Italy and the United States played another challenge match in Monte Carlo alongside the Bermuda Bowl. Once again the Americans were victors. Meanwhile McConnell had convinced the WBF that there was considerable interest in this event, and plans were begun to set up a full-fledged women's competition involving zone champions in 1978. Five teams – United States, Italy, the Philippines, Argentina and Australia – competed, with the United States once again the victor. Similar events were staged in 1981, 1985, 1987 and 1989.

The WBF introduced a new format in 1991, radically increasing the size of the event. The field consisted of four teams from Europe, three from North America, one from the South Pacific, one from Japan, the host country, and two from each of the other WBF zones. Two groups of eight played round-robins with four teams from each advancing to the quarterfinals. Since that time a similar plan has been in effect, but the number of qualifying teams has been increased to 20. As of 2001, the event was being staged every two years simultaneously with the Bermuda Bowl. For results see Appendix V.

VERDI. See TRANSFER OPENING THREE - BIDS.

VERIFY (a score). In pair play, it is the duty of the North player to fill out the pickup slip or traveling score and of the traveling pair or one of its members to verify (by initialing in a box provided on pickup slips) the score as correct. In match play at teams-of-four, both pairs keep a record of their scores at each table, and each pair must verify the scoreslip of its opponents, from which the results of the match can be determined.

VICE SQUEEZE. A secondary squeeze that leads to a suit establishment play (analyzed and named by Terence Reese; the American spelling would be vise.)

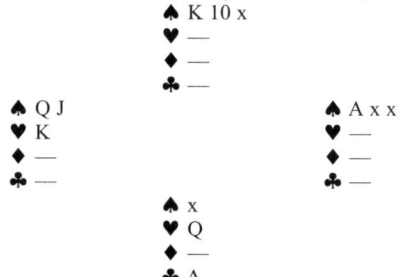

```
              ♠ K 10 x
              ♥ —
              ♦ —
              ♣ —
♠ Q J                         ♠ A x x
♥ K                           ♥ —
♦ —                           ♦ —
♣ —                           ♣ —
              ♠ x
              ♥ Q
              ♦ —
              ♣ A
```

South leads the ♣A, and West is squeezed in two suits. If he discards the ♥K, then South's queen will take a trick; if he discards a spade, South can establish a trick in that suit.

The position looks like an automatic squeeze against West which has been modified in a particular way: instead of a two-card menace we have a vice menace consisting of the second-best card of the suit accompanied by a card which can be established if West weakens his second-round stopper.

```
                ♠ K 10
                ♥ A J
                ♦ —
                ♣ —
  ♠ Q J                        ♠ A x x
  ♥ K Q                        ♥ x
  ♦ —                          ♦ —
  ♣ —                          ♣ —
                ♠ x x
                ♥ x
                ♦ A
                ♣ —
```

South leads the ♦ A, which forces West to unguard hearts or to discard his second-round trick in spades.

This position is a modification of the simple positional squeeze. The vice menace does not provide an entry, so North's threat must be accompanied by a master card in the suit, which makes it a two-card threat.

In addition to the requirements stated above, East must have no trick to cash besides his stopper in the doubly-guarded suit.

VICTORY POINTS. In a contest among a great number of teams with a limited number of sessions, each team plays a relatively small number of deals against each of the other teams, ranging from 32 in the round-robin of the WORLD CHAMPIONSHIPS to as few as two deals in some smaller events. Various methods have been devised to counteract the excessive rewards to a 10- or 20-point swing in BOARD-A-MATCH SCORING, and to the slam contract made at one table and defeated at the other in IMP or TOTAL POINT SCORING.

The scoring method favored by many experts awards the IMP score on each board. The total IMP score on the boards of the match are then converted to victory points in accordance with a predetermined scale. This is the method most used in major championships throughout the world. It is also used in the round-robin portions of the Bermuda Bowl, the World Team Olympiad, the World Women's Team Olympiad and the Venice Cup and the Open and Mixed Transnational Teams.

The following scales have been used in recent world championships:

IMP DIFFERENCE	VICTORY POINTS
0 - 3	10 - 10
4 - 10	11 - 9
11 - 16	12 - 8
17 - 22	13 - 7
23 - 28	14 - 6
29 - 34	15 - 5
35 - 40	16 - 4
41 - 46	17 - 3
47 - 52	18 - 2
53 - 58	19 - 1
59 - 64	20 - 0
65 - 73	20 - (-1)
74 - 82	20 - (-2)
83 - 91	20 - (-3)
92 - 100	20 - (-4)
101 and more	20 - (-5)

VPs are used frequently in Swiss Team competitions and in round-robins with short matches. Here are the VP scales most often used in such competitions when matches consist of seven boards:

20-POINT VP SCALE			
IMPs	VPs	IMPs	VPs
0	10-10	14-6	16-4
1-2	11-9	17-19	17-3
3-4	12-8	20-23	18-2
5-7	13-7	24-27	19-1
8-10	14-6	28 +	20-0

30-POINT VP SCALE			
IMPs	VPs	IMPs	VPs
0	15-15	9-10	24-6
1	18-12	11-13	25-5
2	19-11	14-16	26-4
3	20-10	17-19	27-3
4	21-9	20-23	28-2
5-6	22-8	24-27	29-1
7-8	23-7	28 +	30-0

Even in win-loss type Swiss events, a form of victory points often is used in the ACBL. To receive credit for a full win, a team must win by 3 or more IMPs. A win by 1 or 2 IMPs constitutes a 3/4 win, with the losing team getting the other quarter of a point. However, the team winning the match receives the entire match masterpoint award. See ZIRINSKY FORMULA.

VICTORY POINT SWISS TEAMS. The difference between this type of SWISS TEAMS and others is the method of scoring (see TEAM GAMES). The boards are IMPed and an algebraic sum is arrived at. However, this figure is then translated into Victory Points according to a formula worked out in advance. Subsequent matches are paired according to a team's Victory Point total, not according to its win-loss record. Overall rankings are based on Victory Point totals. The 20-point and 30-point Victory Point scales are printed on the ACBL convention card. Other scales are used in other areas, including WORLD CHAMPIONSHIPS. See FLIGHTED TEAMS, MIXED TEAMS, OPEN TEAMS, ROUND-ROBIN TEAMS, BOARD-A-MATCH SWISS TEAMS, STRATIFIED TEAMS, STRATIFLIGHTED TEAMS, TEAM GAMES, SPEEDBALL SWISS TEAMS, WIN-LOSS SWISS TEAMS, ZIP SWISS TEAMS.

VIENNA COUP. An unblocking play made in preparation for a squeeze. Declarer plays off a master card which establishes a high card for an opponent. This clears the way for an automatic squeeze. Here is an example:

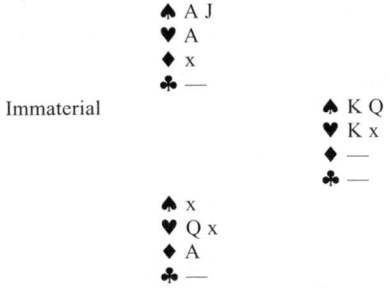

The menaces are correctly positioned for an automatic squeeze against East. Hearts should be a one-card menace, and spades the two-card menace. Therefore the ♥ A should be played before the squeeze card, which is the ♦ A.

If the ♦ A is played prematurely in the diagrammed position East can discard a heart with impunity. Declarer can establish the ♥ Q by crossing to the ace, but he cannot return to his hand to cash the queen.

VIENNA SYSTEM. Based on an artificial 1♣ bid for hands of normal strength and an artificial 1NT bid for strong hands. Devised in 1935 by Dr. Paul Stern, this was the first highly conventional system to achieve international success. (See WORLD CHAMPIONSHIPS.) Also known as the Austrian System, it has been played in many countries. In postwar years its main adherents have been in Iceland and Australia.

The Bamberger point count (7-5-3-1) was originally used, but many Vienna players have preferred the standard 4-3-2-1 point-count which is employed in the following system summary.

(1) 1♣ shows 11-17 points and no suit except clubs longer than four cards. 1♦ is the negative, or Herbert, response showing 0-7 points. With a six-card or longer suit, an alternative negative response is available: a negative jump to two of a major or three of a minor suit. Over 1♦ the opener rebids cheaply, as in the ROMAN SYSTEM.

Responses of one in a major or two in a minor are positive but limited, showing 8-11 points. The opener can pass or make a natural rebid: any jump rebid would be encouraging but not forcing.

The strongest response to 1♣ is 1NT, artificial, showing 12 points or more. This almost always leads to game, but the responder can pass if the opener rebids 2NT at any stage.

(2) 1♦, 1♥ and 1♠ shows a five-card suit with 11-17 points. Responses are standard except that 2NT is limit and nonforcing.

(3) 1NT shows 18 points at least, and is unlimited; any distribution is possible. With 0-7 points, the responder gives a negative response of 2♣ or a negative jump to 3♦, 3♥, or 3♠.

With 8 points or more, responder bids a five-card suit; but the jump to 3♣ is made only if the suit is very strong. With a broken five-card club suit, the response is sometimes 2NT, which denies a five-card diamond suit and also a total of five cards in the major suits. For other hands containing between five and eight cards in the major suits the response is 2♠, which is therefore a two-way bid.

After a negative response of 2♣, a rebid of 2♦ asks for a major suit. (A forerunner of the DYNAMIC NOTRUMP.)

(4) Two-bids were designed to be specialized asking bids, but most adherents of the system prefer standard methods.

(5) Three-bids in a minor are strong, with a powerful suit and an outside trick.

(6) Other opening bids are standard.

VIEW, TO TAKE A. To make a decision in the bidding or play.

VINJE SIGNAL. A method of signaling devised by Helge Vinje which pinpoints many distributions and situations that are ambiguous in standard signaling.
Distribution Signal: The length of a suit is shown by leading (counting lead) or by following suit or by discarding (counting signal) in this manner:

2-card suit:	high-low	} even number
4-card suit:	next lowest - lowest	
6-card suit:	third lowest - lowest	
3-card suit:	lowest - next lowest	} odd number
5-card suit:	lowest - next lowest	
7-card suit:	lowest- third lowest	

The New Third-Hand Rule: On a counting lead from a long suit against a notrump contract, third hand should play high except in the following case: If dummy and third hand hold only spot cards in the suit, and the sum of leader's, dummy's and third hand's cards totals 11, third hand should play his lowest card.
The New Trump Signal: The new trump signal indicates the distribution type. High-low shows the hand has the distribution pattern of one suit with an even number of cards, three odd. Low-high shows the hand has the distribution pattern of one suit with an odd number of cards, three even.
Positive and Negative Signal: Positive or negative signals to show strength or weakness should be used generally on ace leads in situations where the defenders are obviously compelled to take their quick tricks immediately.

They should be used particularly on ace leads against slam contracts. The lead denies the king and asks primarily for the king in partner's hand. They should also be used on honor leads, in accordance with the rules for signaling on sequence leads against notrump contracts and against trump contracts. A positive signal is given by playing the lowest card in the suit. A negative signal is given by playing the third lowest card in the suit but the next lowest if the third lowest is an active card.
Suit Preference Signal: The suit preference signal should be used in situations where the defender in the lead is *obviously* compelled to switch to a suit other than the one played, and needs guidance from his partner. When partner plays an unusually high card he wants the higher ranking of the possible suits in return. When partner plays a low card he wants the lower ranking of the possible suits in return.
Combined Signaling: The use of a positive or a negative or a suit preference signal should be combined with a delayed distributional signal according to the following rules: The first signaling card indicates a positive or a negative or a suit preference signal, according to the respective rules. The second signaling card in the same suit is a delayed distributional signal indicating the remaining length in that suit.

New Table for Opening Sequence Leads Against Notrump Contracts:

Holding in suit	Lead	Reading
A K x (x-)	Ace	Partial sequence without other honors in the suit.
A K J (x-) K Q 10 (x-)	King	Incomplete sequence lacking the queen or the jack
A K Q (x-) Q J 10 (x-) A-Q J 9 (x-)	Queen	Two or no higher honors than the queen. Holding K-Q the second lead indicates the original suit length: king (13) shows an odd number; ace (14) shows an even number.

A Q J (x-)	Jack	Two or no higher honors than the jack. Holding K-Q-J the second lead or play indicates the original suit length: queen (12) shows an even number; king (13) shows an odd number.
K Q J (x-)		
J 10 9 (x-)		
J 10 8 (x-)		
A Q 10 (9-)	10	Two or no higher honors than the 10. With two higher cards the sequence is an interior one.
A J 10 (x-)		
K J 10 (x-)		
10 9 x		
A 10 9 (x-)	9	Two or no higher cards than the 9. With two higher cards the sequence is an interior one.
K 10 9 (x-)		
Q 10 9 (x-)		
9 8 x		

Appropriate signaling: Unblock with an honor second, unless this is likely to result in the loss of a trick. Use a counting signal when dummy holds at least three cards in the suit. Use any complementing card, followed by the next-lowest card, when the lead shows an incomplete sequence and dummy as well as partner holds exactly three cards in the suit. Use a positive or negative signal to show the existence or non-existence of a card touching the actual sequence, followed by a distributional signal on the next round, when dummy holds at most two cards in the suit.

New Table for Opening Sequence Leads Against Trump Contracts

Holding in suit	Lead	Reading
A K (x-)	Ace	When holding an even number (A = 14).
	King	When holding an odd number (K= 13). Exception: Against slam contracts the lead from A K (x) should always be the king, partner using counting signal.
K Q J (x-)	King	Ambiguous: partner should read the lead as a counting lead from A-K with an odd number, unless dummy or partner has the ace. The second lead or play indicates the original suit length: queen (12) shows an even number; jack (11) shows an odd number.
K Q (alone)		
A K Q (x-)	Queen	Ambiguous: partner should read the lead as K-Q-x. Holding A-K-Q the second lead or play indicates the original suit length: king (13) shows an odd number; ace (14) shows an even number.
Q J x (x-)	Jack	Unambiguous.
J 10 x (x-)	10	Generally unambiguous.
A J 10 (x-)		
K J 10 (x-)		
10 9 x (x-)	9	Generally unambiguous.
A 10 9 (x-)		
K 10 9 (x-)		
Q 10 9 (x-)		

9 8 x (x-)	8	Generally unambiguous.
K 9 8 (x-)		
Q 9 8 (x-)		
J 9 8 (x-)		

Note: The lead from A-K-Q-(x) may alternatively be the ace or the king according to the rules for a counting lead from A-K-(x-).

Appropriate signaling:

1. On a counting lead from A-K-(x-) partner should: Use a counting signal if dummy has at least three cards, including the queen, in the suit. Use a trick counting signal on all other occasions by signaling as follows:

   (a) Playing the lowest card (low-high) indicates that the defenders can make either one or three tricks in relation to declarer's closed hand. The three tricks may arise from a ruff or from the queen or from J-10-x.

   (b) Playing the third lowest card, but the next lowest if the third lowest is an active card, means that the defenders can make two tricks in the suit, either because declarer has only two cards in the suit, or because partner cannot assist in making a third trick.

2. On a sequence lead showing K-Q-(J), with dummy or partner holding the ace, partner should use a counting signal if dummy holds the ace; use a counting signal or overtake when he himself holds the ace.

3. On a sequence lead showing K-Q-x or A-K-Q partner should use a positive or negative signal to show whether or not he holds the ace or jack; use a counting signal if dummy holds at least three cards, including the jack, or if dummy holds A-J.

Indicating a Sequence When Following Suit or When Discarding: A sequence is indicated by playing the lowest card in the sequence when the card has a possibility of influencing the trick; a sequence is indicated by playing the highest card in the sequence when the card will not influence the trick; a sequence is indicated by discarding the highest card in the sequence.

When holding a complete sequence, the sequence as well as the suit length may be indicated.

A K Q (x-) The queen indicates the complete sequence. The next play may now indicate the length of the suit (original length): The king (13) indicates an odd number; the ace (14) indicates an even number.

K Q J (x-) The jack indicates the complete sequence. The next play may now indicate the suit length (original length): The queen (12) indicates an even number; the king (13) indicates an odd number.

When holding A-K, the sequence as well as the suit length may be indicated:

A K (x-) The ace followed by the king indicates an even number in the suit; the king followed by the ace indicates an odd number in the suit.

VIOLATION. (1) The disregard of a law or propriety. It is assumed that any violation that occurs is either through carelessness or ignorance. A penalty for a violation is enforced in an attempt to indemnify the nonoffending side, not to punish the offender. (2) A deliberate breach of a system agreement. Judgment may

occasionally lead an expert player to pass a forcing bid or to continue bidding after a signoff bid, but such violations should be very rare for the sake of partnership confidence.

VIOLATION OF ETHICAL CONDUCT. An act of a player that deviates from the spirit or the form as described in the PROPRIETIES.

VIOLATION OF SYSTEM. A player is at any time entitled to violate his partnership agreement, and most players do so from time to time in minor ways. Major violations, such as passing a forcing bid, are very rare indeed among good players.

VISE SQUEEZE. See VICE SQUEEZE.

VOID. An original holding of no cards in a suit. "Chicane" is a much older term; "blank" is a synonym in current use.

VOID-SHOWING BID. The use of a jump bid which has no natural meaning to show a void suit. The idea was revived by E. M. L. Beale of Cambridge University, England, about 1948, following a prototype idea once adopted briefly by Ely Culbertson.

According to this idea, the last bid in each of the following sequences would show specifically a void in the suit bid, and, by inference, a good suit fit with partner.

West	North	East	South
(a)			1 ♥
Pass	4 ♣		
(b)			1 ♣
Pass	1 ♥	Pass	3 ♠ or 4 ♦
(c)			1 ♦
1 ♠	3 ♠		

The following are examples of opportunities for using the bid at later stages in the auction:

Dlr. South
Vul: Both

        ♠ 10 6 2
        ♥ Q 8 7 5 4
        ♦ 4
        ♣ K 8 3 2

♠ A K J 9 5 3   ♠ 7
♥ J 2   ♥ A 6 3
♦ A 10 9 6 5   ♦ K J 8 3 2
♣ —   ♣ 10 6 5 4

        ♠ Q 8 4
        ♥ K 10 9
        ♦ Q 7
        ♣ A Q J 9 7

This deal was reported in *The Bridge World*, August 1951. Both teams reached 5 ♦ played by East after this bidding:

West	North	East	South
			1 ♣
2 ♠	Pass	3 ♦	Pass
5 ♦	Pass	Pass	Pass

If East-West had been using void-showing bids, West could have used one over 3 ♦ by jumping to 5 ♣ and the grand slam would have been reached after a 5 ♥ cuebid by East. From West's angle, East's diamonds might be headed by queen-jack, but the finesse for the king would surely succeed.

Void-showing bids will sometimes make it possible to apply the brakes when duplication of values is present:

Dlr: South
Vul: E-W

        ♠ K Q 10 7 4
        ♥ 10 6 5 3
        ♦ —
        ♣ K Q J 2

♠ 9 5   ♠ A 8 3 2
♥ 8 4 2   ♥ 9
♦ 8 5 4 2   ♦ 10 9 7 3
♣ A 9 7 3   ♣ 10 6 5 4

        ♠ J 6
        ♥ A K Q J 7
        ♦ A K Q J 6
        ♣ 8

In the 1953 Bermuda Bowl both the American and Swedish teams bid to 6 ♥ missing two aces. This is an not uncommon disaster when one side holds everything else in the pack except two aces. Ace-showing conventions are of limited value when a void is present, although Blackwood has some void-showing possibilities. (See also SUPRESSING THE BID ACE.)

Using a void-showing bid, the final contract should be 5 ♥.

South	North
2 ♣	2 ♠
3 ♥	5 ♦
5 ♥	Pass

When North shows a diamond void, South puts on the brakes and North reluctantly accepts this decision.

In response to an opening of 1 ♥ or 1 ♠, there are several complicated schemes to show both singletons and voids. For example: Bid one step above three of opener's suit to show an unspecified void. 1 ♥-3 ♠ shows a void, and which suit is void is shown after 3NT relay. (Then 4 ♥ shows spade void.) 1 ♥-4 ♣/4 ♦ are singleton splinters. 1 ♥-3NT is a spade singleton. Similarly after 1 ♠, with 3NT showing a void.

The void-showing bid is an ancestor of the SPLINTER. For alternative treatments, see conventions listed under UNUSUAL JUMP.

VOLMAC. See CAP GEMINI WORLD TOP TOURNAMENT.

VOLMAC PRECISION. Strong club system developed by Benito Garozzo for the training of the Dutch Volmac group. A computer program of the system was demonstrated during the 1980 Olympiad in Valkenburg.

VOLUNTARY BID. See FREE BID.

VON ZEDTWITZ GOLD CUP. The trophy for the Life Master Pairs Championship, donated by Waldemar von Zedtwitz in 1930 for one of the most highly regarded pair events on the ACBL calendar. It is contested at the Summer North American Championships, under which heading past results are listed. Until Life Masters became numerous, the trophy was contested by master players who had qualified by winning a previous national championship. It was then a four-session event, and the field was limited to 64 pairs so that a complete movement could be played.

The trophy was originally presented on the basis that three wins by one player would secure him outright possession of the trophy, and this feat was achieved by Howard Schenken in 1934. The cup was subsequently put back into competition by the donor.

The cup was stolen in 1954 while in the possession of John Hubbell, who at that time held the Life Master Pairs title. The theft immediately followed a television appearance during which he had exhibited the trophy and given the address of his bridge club at which the cup was normally displayed. The trophy was not recovered and the present cup is an exact replica. For results see Appendix I.

VUGRAPH. (Often spelled viewgraph outside the United States.) A method of presenting an important match to an audience larger than can be accommodated around a bridge table. Until the computer was brought into the vugraph picture in the Eighties, a board was dealt, bid and played in the closed room, with a recorder at the table noting the bidding, opening lead and result obtained. The board and record were sent to a copier, who wrote the hands, bidding, and play with wax pencil on a framed cellulose sheet, a form of hand record. The board was then sent to the open room where a microphone connected to the exhibition hall was used by a director in charge to relay the calls, leads, plays and results to an operator in the exhibition hall. The frame was sent to the exhibition hall where an operator, with a wax pencil, recorded the bids, plays, and results as announced from the open room on the frame which was put into an over-head projector.This was visible to the audience in greatly enlarged form on a screen. Bidding was recorded in boxes on the printed frame, cards as played were crossed out from the hands, and results tabulated for further reference on the side of the screen.

Required for vugraph presentation were a recorder in the closed room, a runner to transport results to the vugraph area from the closed room, a scribe, a director and commentator in the open room, and an operator at the projector who doubles as or is assisted by a commentator.

A more elaborate setup, used for many years in world championships and other major events was BRIDGE-O-RAMA. In the Eighties various electronic vugraphs of considerable sophistication were introduced in Italy, Netherlands and elsewhere, with all the entries on the projected image controlled by a computer. These are regularly accompanied by closed circuit television, showing the players at work, and often by a screen showing the progress of the scores, perhaps in several matches.

In 1991, the ACBL commissioned Fred Gitelman, a Toronto programmer, to develop a computer vugraph program with a grant from the estate of Peter Pender. The vugraph was subsequently named the PenderGraph.

The PenderGraph debuted at the 1991 Summer NABC in Las Vegas, where the final of the Spingold Knockout Teams was shown to a huge audience. In 1993, Gitelman wrote a new PenderGraph program to work under the Windows operating system, enhancing and enlarging the graphics and adding features that distinguished the PenderGraph as the top program of its kind.

VULNERABILITY. The condition of being subject to greater undertrick penalties and eligible to receive greater premiums as provided by the scoring table. In rubber bridge, vulnerability comes about by having won one game toward rubber. In duplicate bridge, vulnerability is arbitrarily assigned by board numbers. Vulnerability in duplicate is on a 16-board cycle, repeating for each succeeding 16 boards; boards 1, 8, 11 and 14 have no vulnerability; boards 2, 5, 12, and 15 have North-

South vulnerable, East-West not vulnerable; boards 3, 6, 9 and 16 have East-West vulnerable, North-South not vulnerable; boards 4, 7, 10 and 13 have both sides vulnerable. This can be remembered fairly easily by the 16 letters forming this arrangement:

O N E B

N E B O

E B O N

B O N E

where O stands for no vulnerability, N for North-South, E for East-West and B for both.

In CHICAGO, a four-hand variation of rubber bridge, the vulnerability also is arbitrarily assigned in similar fashion; no vulnerability on the first hand; dealer vulnerable on the second and third hands; and everyone vulnerable on the last hand. A variation in a few clubs that is technically perhaps a slight improvement assigns the vulnerability on the second and third hands to the opponents of the dealer. The purpose is to allow opener more latitude in preempting.

The feature of vulnerability gives rise to many variations in the strategy of bidding and play. These variations probably are foremost among the reasons for the great interest which contract bridge has stimulated. Some strategies: (1) bidding low-point games when vulnerable, (2) preempting with minimum values when not vulnerable, (3) taking saves when not vulnerable, etc. See EQUAL VULNERABILITY, FAVORABLE VULNERABILITY, PREEMPTIVE BID, SCORING TABLE, UNFAVORABLE VULNERABILITY, VARIABLE NOTRUMP.

VULNERABLE. A term indicating that the values of premiums and the severity of penalties are greatly increased. In rubber bridge, a pair becomes vulnerable when they win their first game of a rubber. In duplicate and Chicago, vulnerability is arbitrarily assigned. Premiums for bidding and making slam or game are larger, but penalties when set, especially when doubled, are much greater than when not vulnerable. The term was coined by a woman aboard the ship on which Cornelius Vanderbilt codified contract bridge. See EQUAL VULNERABILITY, FAVORABLE VULNERABILITY, UNFAVORABLE VULNERABILITY.

W

WAGAR TROPHY. Awarded to the winners of the North American Women's Knockout Teams. The trophy honors Margaret Wagar, a member of the ACBL Hall of Fame.

WAITING BID. A temporizing bid by a player who aims to extract information from partner rather than give information about his own holding. This is usually made in a minor suit. See ASKING BID; FOURTH SUIT FORCING; IMPOSSIBLE BIDS; LAST TRAIN CUEBIDS; NEW MINOR FORCING; RELAYS; THREE-CARD SUITS, BIDS IN.

WAIVE A PENALTY. In rubber bridge, either member of a partnership, without consulting the other member, may waive a penalty (condone an irregularity). If either

member so elects, the right to enforce a penalty is forfeited. In duplicate, players do not have the right to waive penalties on their own initiative, and the director may allow or cancel any waiver of penalties made by the players without his instructions. However, the right to penalize an irregularity may be forfeited. See LAWS (Law 15), LAWS OF DUPLICATE (Laws 10, 11).

WALLET. British name for a form of DUPLICATE BOARD in which each pocket is formed in the fold of a wallet-shaped receptacle. The board can be folded into one-half size for ease in carrying. Plastic wallet boards are popular in Europe. They date back to the 1932 World Bridge Olympics.

WALPURGIS DIAMOND. A convention used by John Collings and Paul Hackett of Great Britain in the 1981 European Championships and Bermuda Bowl. As an opening bid, 1 ♦ showed either 0-8 high card points with any distribution, or 12-20 points with at least four diamonds, or any 4-3-3-3 with 20-22 points. It was used in conjunction with their specialized opening pass which showed 9-12 points and any distribution.

WALSH SYSTEM. A style of bidding popular in the West, sometimes known as WESTERN ROTH-STONE, WEST COAST SCIENTIFIC or WESTERN SCIENTIFIC. Its chief architect was Richard Walsh.

The main features are: (1) five-card majors; (2) 1NT response forcing; (3) limit major raises; (4) negative doubles; (5) two-over-one game forcing; (6) after 1♣, routine bypassing of diamonds to bid a major without game-forcing strength; (7) inverted minors; (8) limit 2NT and 3♣ response to 1♦, other jump shifts weak; (9) unbid minor forcing after 1NT rebids, and weak canapé jumps in unbid minor; (10) after 1♦-2♣, 2♥ or 2♠ can be minimum balanced; (11) Stayman, Jacoby and Texas; (12) 1NT-2; either Minor Suit Stayman, or weak diamonds, or weak both minors; (13) TWO NOTRUMP RESPONSE as a puppet to 3♣, with weak clubs or strong three-suiter; (14) 1NT- 3♣ or 3 ♦ invitational.

Two-over-one responses are game forcing. Over a 2♣ response to 1 ♦, opener has specialized responses: 2♥ or 2♠ shows a four-card suit and no extra values; 2NT shows 4-4-3-2 distribution and no extra values, and 2 ♦ usually shows five or more diamonds, but may be forced with 3-3-4-3 distribution and poor clubs.

Other methods include MATHE ASKING BID; COMPETITIVE DOUBLE; NEW MINOR FORCING; NAMYATS; NEGATIVE DOUBLE, RESPONSIVE DOUBLE, TWO OVER ONE GAME FORCE; WANG TRUMP ASKING BID.

WANG TRUMP ASKING BID. Bids at relatively low levels to ask about trump honors. The responses are given in three steps as follows:

First step = none of the top three honors.
Second step = one of the top three honors.
Third step = two of the top three honors.

WARNING PARTNER. A privilege of all players (including a dummy who has not intentionally looked at another hand) if the player feels that his partner is about to commit an irregularity. Examples: "It's not your lead, partner." "No hearts, partner?" "The lead is in the dummy, partner." It is not permitted during the auction to warn

partner about a convention you or an opponent may be using, or to review the auction to apprise partner of a previous bid you think he may have misunderstood.

Defenders' questions to draw attention to a possible revoke ("having no hearts, partner?") can be controversial, since they can convey information. Such questions were barred by the 1987 Duplicate Code, but zonal bodies were later given authority to permit such questions. They are permitted in Zone 2 (North America) and Zone 7 (South Pacific) but not elsewhere. When questions are barred, an illegal question creates an automatic revoke penalty if partner has a card of the suit. See Law 61B and ALERTING.

WARREN. See SAN FRANCISCO.

WASHING LIST. See BACK SCORE.

WBF. See WORLD BRIDGE FEDERATION.

WEAK JUMP OVERCALL. The use of a jump overcall in a suit as preemptive. A FOUR ACES innovation of the Thirties, credited to OSWALD JACOBY and embodied in ROTH-STONE and later systems.

Over a 1 ♦ opening, 2♥, 2♠ or 3♣ would show the equivalent of a WEAK TWO-BID — 6-12 points and a six-card or perhaps a seven-card suit. For many years, strong jump overcalls were a basic part of the Goren bidding system, which was the system used by the vast majority of players. However, the twin values of the weak jump overcall — telling the whole story about a hand in one bid while throwing up a blockade against the opponents' bidding — caused Goren to incorporate the weak jump overcall into his standard bidding system.

The weak jump overcall must always take the vulnerability into account. Not vulnerable against vulnerable, a weak jump to the level of two could be made on a really good five-card suit and little else. A vulnerable jump to the three-level against nonvulnerable would almost always be too dangerous with a weak hand. For this reason, Sam Stayman advised a strong jump overcall at unfavorable vulnerability.

The opening bidder's partner often faces a bidding problem after a weak jump overcall. If he makes his normal bid, but one level higher, he may easily be giving a wrong impression of the strength of his hand. If he passes, this could mean that the overcaller has achieved his objective — to buy the contract cheaply. Many players use the NEGATIVE DOUBLE against weak jump overcalls. The usual agreement is that the negative double shows a hand that would have responded with a natural bid at a lower level, but is not strong enough to make that natural bid at this higher level. The negative double can also show other types of holding. The next call by the negative doubler should make clear the type of hand he holds. Another possible solution is for minimum bids in a new suit to be nonforcing (NEGATIVE FREE BID). However, if this method is used, it becomes necessary to consider the use of a pass as a forcing call, in addition to a cuebid and a jump shift.

The partner of a weak jump overcaller may have sufficient values to be interested in game. A good agreement is to respond as to a weak two-bid. Thus those who use 2NT to ask for OGUST rebids can do so similarly after a weak jump overcall. 2NT also could be used to ask the preemptor to indicate a singleton.

The weak jump overcall would not apply in the pass-out position, for there would be no object in preempting. In that situation a jump would be made with slightly less than the values needed for a strong jump. But if the opponents bid two suits, the jump retains its preemptive character. See also DOUBLE JUMP OVERCALL.

WEAK JUMP RAISE. Many players now use a jump raise in partner's suit as a preemptive action showing weakness rather than strength. If opener starts with 1 ♥ and responder bids 3 ♥, responder is showing at least four-card trump support with limited high-card values – often only a king or a queen. Opener will carry on to game in two circumstances – when he has the necessary values and when he has a distributional hand that makes it appear that further preemptive action is warranted. If responder leaps to 4 ♥ in response to 1 ♥, he has at least five trumps and minimal values.

WEAK JUMP SHIFT RESPONSE. The use of a jump response in a new suit as a preemptive bid. After an opening 1 ♣, a response of 2 ♠ would be made by a player whose only asset was K-J-6-5-4-2. This works for the subminimum responding hands with a six-card or seven-card suit, but greatly increases the problem of bidding strong hands which would normally make a jump shift. The simple suit response becomes overloaded because it may be made with a hand of any strength from 6 points upwards.

Nevertheless, the weak jump shift response has merit in that it enables a player to describe his hand in just one bid while stealing a level of bidding from the opponents. The bid also makes it much easier for the opening bidder to assess his hand. He knows, as a result of a single bid, that his partner has a hand that probably will play best in his suit, and the opener also knows there is little hope for game unless he holds close to an opening force.

Like all preemptive bids, the weak jump shift response exerts pressure on an opponent with a good hand. The fourth player should bid as he would over an opening one-bid: double for a takeout, and bid 2NT on a hand which would open a strong 1NT, but with some flexibility, perhaps 15-19. See ROTH-STONE SYSTEM and OGUST REBIDS.

Weak jump shift responses are popular in competition:

West	North	East	South
	1 ♣	1 ♠	3 ♦

They are the expert consensus in BWS if the opening is in a minor. Jump shifts by passed hand indicate a fit.

WEAK NOTRUMP. An opening 1NT with a minimum hand is an integral part of many systems. The usual range of the bid is 12-14 points, although 13-15, 14-16 and 12-15 are in use, particularly in PRECISION. The usual corollary is that a rebid of 1NT shows a hand too strong to open with 1NT (15-17 in KAPLAN-SHEINWOLD, 15-16 in English systems).

Many modern tournament players have lowered the range to 10-12 points, in keeping with the philosophy that the side to strike first has the advantage in competitive auctions. Most players use the 10-12 1NT opener in the first three seats when not vulnerable, but some employ it at all vulnerabilities and in all positions with the rationale that the preemptive value of the bid is worth the risk of an occasional large penalty. Some experts recommend that a 10-12 notrump opener be a hand most

other players would not open. This helps responder decide what to do with invitational values.

The 10-12 notrump works best in conjunction with a strong club system, but can be used by partnerships playing standard. Standard bidders employing the 10-12 notrump usually use semi-artificial minor-suit openings to distinguish between balanced hands of 13-14 points (1 ♣ followed by a notrump rebid) and 15-17 points (1 ♦ followed by notrump). See KAMIKAZE NOTRUMP.

Each of these systems has some special features in response, but with a suitable adjustment of range, any normal principles of responding to a strong notrump can be followed.

Some special tactical situations arise when 1NT by the dealer has been passed and the responder is very weak. The fourth player is almost certain to have a strong hand, and there is a danger of conceding a heavy penalty, so third hand may have to take evasive action:

♠ 6 2
♥ 9 7 4 3
♦ J 10 7 3
♣ 9 5 3

What the action should be depends on the methods in use. In a traditional style, natural weak 2 ♦ or 2 ♥ bids, purporting to show a 5-card suit, are possible since it will be difficult for the opposition to double for penalties. In a modern style, the least evil may be a 2 ♦ transfer to hearts with the probability of finding at least a 7-card fit. Stayman is not recommended, because a 2 ♠ rebid will leave the partnership in serious jeopardy. However, this would be a sensible choice if the black suits were reversed.

Some partnerships agree that a very weak hand must bid in response to 1NT, in which case a pass should be Alerted as denying a very weak hand.

Competitive bidding is much more common and much more critical when the weak notrump is being used. The opponents frequently need some conventional defensive arrangement such as ASTRO, BROZEL, CAPPELLETTI, DEFENSE TO ONE NOTRUMP, DONT, EXCLUSION BIDS, HAMILTON, LANDY or RIPSTRA. A double of a weak notrump should be for penalties, and partner should rarely remove the double. Only a weak hand with a long suit would justify a takeout. The doubler should have a better hand than the notrump bidder, whether the double is made immediately or in the pass-out position. See also SWINE.

The action by fourth hand after a two-level response needs consideration. A double of a STAYMAN 2 ♣ response is usually taken to be an indication of a good club suit for lead-directing purposes. The modern tendency among some experts is to double 2 ♣ or any suit takeout at the level of two with a hand which would have doubled if responder had passed 1NT.

For other details about notrump bidding, see DEFENSE TO DOUBLE OF ONE NOTRUMP; MINI-NOTRUMP; ONE NOTRUMP OPENING; STAYMAN; TEXAS.

WEAK NOTRUMP OVERCALL. The use of an overcall of 1NT as the equivalent of a weak notrump opening. This permits a defender to enter the auction on many hands which he would normally pass, but the value is doubtful because the overcaller will often be doubled for penalties with no escape. The bid is sometimes confined to nonvulnerable situations. For matchpoint play,

a 13-16 range has achieved some popularity.

The opener's partner follows the procedure for bidding over a normal strong notrump overcall. He usually doubles with 9 points or more because his side is almost sure to have the balance of strength. With a weaker hand he can bid a five-card or longer suit at the two-level, which is not constructive. He can make a cuebid of 2NT with a strong unbalanced hand. See also BARON NOTRUMP OVERCALL.

WEAK OPENING SYSTEMS. The original work on Weak Opening Systems (WOS; also known as Forcing Pass) was done in Poland, primarily by Lukosz Slawinski. It took the theory behind a strong-club system one step further. The major difference is that if you pass with a good hand, you must open even with a yarborough. This weak bid, also called a FERT because of its affinity to fertilizer, normally shows 0-7 points. With 8-12 points, the most common point range, you open with a different set of agreed-upon bids. With 13 or more points, you pass.

These systems are known as *dominant* because they force the opponents into a defensive position on most deals. The opponents use their own bidding system only when they deal *and* the dealer opens. At all other times, the WOS pair dictates the form of the auction.

There are many weak opening systems. Here are three from Poland, with the initial actions listed.

Regres
Pass: 13-plus points
1♣: 8-12 points and a catch-all opening for any hand that doesn't fit anywhere else
1♦: 0-7 points
1♥/♠: 8-12 with three or four cards in the bid suit; perhaps a five-card minor on the side
1NT: 8-12 with at least five cards in one of the majors
2♣/♦: 8-12 with at least five cards in the bid suit; no major
2♥/♠/NT/3♣: 8-12 with a 5-5 or 6-4 shape

No Name
Pass: 13-plus points
1♣: 8-12 points with at least 3-3 in the majors (at most 5-4 but not 5-3)
1♦: 0-7 points
1♥/♠: 8-12 with at most two cards or at least six cards in the bid suit
1NT: 8-12 with five hearts and four clubs or five spades and four diamonds
2♣: 8-12 with five hearts and four diamonds or five spades and four clubs
2♦: 8-12 with 5-3-3-2 shape and either five-card major
2♥/♠/NT/3♣: 8-12 with a 5-5 or 6-4 shape

Delta
In this unusual system, the opener shows his shortage before his long suit. This helps the responder to decide immediately how well the hands are fitting.
Pass: 13-plus points
1♣: 8-12 points and any hand with no singleton or void
1♦: 0-7 points
1♥: 8-12 and any hand with a singleton or void in hearts, or a singleton or void in clubs and either a long major or a 5-5 shape
1♠: 8-12 and any hand with a spade shortage
1NT: 8-12 with diamond shortage and either a long major or a 5-5 shape
2♣: 8-12 and all other hands with a diamond shortage

2♦: 8-12 with a club shortage and long diamonds
2♥: 8-12 and all other hands with a club shortage

It is possible to modify this system to avoid the forcing pass. Then pass shows 0-11 points, 1♦ is any 17-plus pointer and the other bids are as above but with 12-16 points.

In all these systems, if the responder has a good hand, he continues the auction with a relay, the opener describing the complete shape of his hand. Then the responder has two choices: continue the relay with asking bids or employ the End Signal. The End Signal is a bid of 4♦. It asks the opener to puppet with 4♥, whereupon the responder names the final contract.

In Australia and New Zealand some modifications were introduced. The "bid of misery" varied with the vulnerability, going as high as 1♠ when non-vulnerable against vulnerable. And the systems all employed the SYMMETRIC RELAY rather than the Polish structures.

One of the earliest possibilities included using one-under opening bids: 1♦ was equivalent to a normal one-heart opening and 1♥ was equivalent to 1♠.

Whenever a relay system is employed, the ideal is that the known hand, the one that has been described, becomes the dummy, keeping the unknown hand hidden. This scheme tries to increase the chance that this will happen.

In the original form of MOSCITO, a 1♦ opening showed at least 4-4 in the majors. A opening of one of a major showed at least four cards in that suit, fewer than four cards in the other major, and maybe a longer minor. A 1NT opening showed a balanced hand without a four-card major (so Stayman asked for three-card majors!)

The above only scratches the surface of the subject. However, as these systems are dominant, they have been unpopular with officialdom. Nowadays, these methods are permitted in so few events that many pairs, unable to practice to their satisfaction, have abandoned them. See FORCING PASS, HUM SYSTEMS, RULE OF EIGHTEEN. STRONG PASS.

WEAK SUIT. A suit which the opponents are likely to lead and in which they can probably cash several tricks. Sometimes the term refers to an unstopped suit, but if a notrump contract is being considered it could also apply to a suit in which the opponents hold nine or more cards and in which declarer has only one stopper.

The weakness of a suit is relative to the auction. A small doubleton used to be regarded as a weak suit for the purposes of a 1NT opening, although there are two schools of thought, and few modern players would allow themselves to be deterred. For the purposes of a notrump rebid, a small doubleton in an unbid suit is undesirable, and a small tripleton is unattractive. The chance that the opponents will lead the suit is increased, and the chance that partner can guard it is decreased.

If a side has bid three suits, a notrump bid requires at least one positive stopper and preferably two in the fourth suit.

Sometimes anything less than a double stopper would certainly represent a weak suit:

West	North	East	South
			1♦
Dbl	Pass	3NT	

As West is likely to have a diamond shortage, the jump

to 3NT shows a double diamond stopper. Anything less would constitute a weak suit, unless perhaps East held a single stopper with a long strong club suit.

WEAK SUIT GAME TRY. A rebid by opener in his weakest suit to try for game after responder has raised the major suit opening bid to two. Sometimes called a "help suit game try." For example if opener holds:

♠ A K x x x   ♥ x x x   ♦ x   ♣ A Q J x

the bidding goes

Opener	Responder
1 ♠	2 ♠
3 ♥	

Opener's 3 ♥ bid asks responder to bid game in spades if he has either strength or shortness in hearts. Responder might hold any of the following hands:

(a)	(b)	(c)
♠ Q x x	♠ Q x x	♠ Q x x
♥ J x x x	♥ A x x x x	♥ x
♦ A x x x x	♦ J x x x	♦ A J x x x
♣ x	♣ x	♣ x x x x

With hand (a) responder would sign off in 3 ♠ since he has no help for opener's anemic hearts. With hand (b) or hand (c), however, responder would bid game in spades since his strength in (b) and his singleton in (c) can take care of the heart situation.

A disadvantage of weak suit game tries is that they usually reveal to the opponents the vulnerable spot of opener's hand, and therefore the defenders' most advantageous point of attack.

Another disadvantage is that the partnership may wish to shift to a different suit.

West	East
♠ K Q x x x	♠ A J x
♥ A Q J x	♥ K x x x x
♦ A x x	♦ x x
♣ x	♣ x x x

West	East
1 ♠	2 ♠
?	

3 ♥ may enable E/W to reach 6 ♥. 3 ♦, the weak suit, will not. See SHORT-SUIT GAME TRIES and TWO-WAY GAME TRIES.

WEAK TAKEOUT. An English term for a natural unconstructive suit response to 1NT. The American colloquialism is "drop-dead bid". See WEAKNESS RESPONSE.

WEAK TWO-BID. The use of suit openings of 2 ♦, 2 ♥ and 2 ♠ as PREEMPTIVE BIDS, in combination with TWO CLUBS STRONG ARTIFICIAL OPENING. A prototype of the weak two was used in auction bridge and adopted in the VANDERBILT CLUB SYSTEM. Subsequently Charles Van Vleck, New York, was responsible for an ultra-weak two-bid. Howard Schenken developed the modern weak two-bid along lines similar to Vanderbilt's. It was later incorporated into most modern American systems and into the NEAPOLITAN and BLUE TEAM CLUB systems.

In modern tournament play the announced range for a weak two-bid is usually 5-10, 5-11, 6-10 or 6-11. Vulnerability and position at the table may be a factor in deciding whether to make a weak two-bid. Usually there is little side strength with a weak two-bid.

In BWS 2001, the expert panel considered which of the following should be considered flaws in making a normal weak two-bid in first or second position: (1) a five-card suit; (2) a seven-card suit; (3) a flimsy suit, in light of the vulnerability; (4) a side void; (5) a side four-card major; (6) a side four-card minor; (7) a side five-card suit; (8) any two of the above; (9) any three of the above. No one objected to (5). All the other items, (1) to (8), were found acceptable, although substantial minorities objected to (3), (5), (7) and (8). 75% objected to (9).

Responses. There are many schools of thought. The responses and rebids need precise partnership agreement.

(1) *Raise to four.* A two-way bid: perhaps a hand which expects to make game, or perhaps a preemptive action of the ADVANCE SAVE variety. The left-hand opponent may have a difficult decision with a strong hand.

(2) *Raise to three.* Originally a constructive invitation to opener to bid game, but modern players use the raise preemptively. Frequently the single raise is the only non-forcing response, leading to the expression RONF (raise only non-force).

(3) *Suit takeout.* Normally natural and forcing. Psychic responses once were common, especially at the level of two, but such psychs are rare in modern play. An alternative treatment which has decreased in popularity is to play suit takeouts as nonforcing and unconstructive, indicating that the responder has a misfit and expects a better result playing in his long strong suit. Responder must bid 2NT whenever he wishes to make a forcing bid when using this method. Some play non-forcing (corrective) at the two level and forcing at the three level.

(4) *2NT.* A one-round force with at least game interest. A rebid by opener in his own suit can be used to show a minimum; some players prefer to show a minimum by a 3 ♣ rebid. Using either agreement, a rebid in another suit shows a high-card feature (usually an ace or king, but a queen is possible) and better than a minimum hand. If responder then gives a mere preference to opener's original suit on the second round, the defenders should find out whether the opener is encouraged or permitted to continue: if not, a psychic should be suspected. Similarly, it is important for both the opener's side and the defenders to know whether the opener is permitted to rebid above the level of three in his original suit. A raise of 2NT to 3NT, if permitted, should show a solid suit. In recent years, some experts have used the 2NT response to ask opener to bid a singleton (or void) if he has one - otherwise opener must rebid his suit. Often when this method is used, a 3 ♣ response to the weak two-bid asks for a feature (usually an ace or king). Some experts reverse the meaning of 2NT (asking for feature) and 3 ♣ (asking for singleton or void).

(5) *Ogust.* A system of rebidding after a 2 NT response devised by Harold Ogust that requires opener to describe the strength of his hand and the quality of his suit by a series of artificial bids. They are as follows:

3 ♣ minimum strength, poor suit
3 ♦ minimum strength, good suit
3 ♥ maximum strength, poor suit
3 ♠ maximum strength, good suit.

A good suit is usually defined as one with two of the three top honors. (A solid suit would call for a 3NT rebid). In the original version devised by Ogust the meanings of the red-suit responses were reversed.

(6) *McCabe Adjunct.* Described by J.I. McCabe, Columbia SC, in *The Bridge World*, January 1955. This is a method of playing at the three-level in a new suit. After

the 2NT response, the opener is required to rebid 3♣, irrespective of his holding. The responder can now play in his long suit at the three-level, either by bidding it or by passing 3♣. A preference to three of opener's suit is invitational.

(7) *Relays.* The cheapest response — either 2NT if the opening bid was 2♠, or the next higher suit. The relay asks opener to bid a stopper outside his suit if he has one. If his stopper is in the relay suit, he rebids in notrump. Lacking any outside stopper, opener rebids his own suit. Using this method, the relay is responder's only forcing bid. Another style is for the relay to ask for a singleton.

(8) *Two Relays and a Transfer.* A single raise is constructive. 2NT is natural and not forcing. Almost all other responses are artificial and forcing for at least one round. The bid of the cheapest suit is a relay, forcing to game and asking opener to bid his lowest ranking feature (ace, king, singleton or void). Without a feature, opener rebids his suit. The bid of the second higher ranking suit, i.e., 2♠ over 2♦ or 3♣ over 2♠, is forcing and game invitational. This relay asks partner to show his point count. With a minimum (5-8), opener rebids his suit. With a maximum (9-11), opener makes the cheapest suit rebid. Since the direct raise is constructive, a transfer bid is used to make a preemptive raise. The bid of the suit just below the suit of the weak two-bid forces opener to rebid his suit.

(9) *Asking for singleton.* Many players now use the 2NT response to the weak two-bid as a request to show a singleton and 3♣ to ask for a feature. After 2NT opener either bids a singleton or returns to his suit. Opener bids 3NT with a club feature. Some partnerships reverse this by using 2NT to ask for a feature and 3♣ for a singleton. In this case 3NT shows singleton club.

For a more advanced responding method involving relays, see RELAYS OVER WEAK TWO-BIDS.

Defense. Standard procedure is to bid as over a one-bid: double for takeout, and bid 2NT on a hand which would qualify, loosely, for a strong notrump opening bid. But many other defensive arrangements are possible.

Nearly all American experts use a 2NT response to a double as Lebensohl, forcing 3♣. The French invert this treatment. See LEBENSOHL APPLICATIONS

To combat players addicted to psychic suit responses to a weak two-bid, some players use a double of the response for penalty. But if the suit response is natural and nonforcing, the double should be a normal takeout action. The expert consensus (63% in BWS2000) is that a jump in a minor suit is Leaping Michaels. It shows a two-suiter with the other major and the minor-suit bid. Thus 2♥ - 4♣ shows clubs and spades. It should show a strong hand, but how strong is a matter of agreement. Vulnerability will be a factor. The bid may lead to a profitable save at favorable vulnerability.

If the weak two-bid receives a 2NT response, fourth-hand should bid in much the same way as he would in the direct seat. See HACKETT, RONF.

WEAKNESS RESPONSE. A natural response which indicates a strong desire to close the auction at that point.

The most common case is the response of 2♠, 2♥, or perhaps 2♦ to an opening 1NT bid. Using traditional methods, with the STAYMAN 2♣ convention, responder shows at least a five-card suit and no desire to progress toward game.

In very rare circumstances the opener may make one further bid if he has a fine fit with responder, presum-

ably four cards and a maximum notrump opening consisting largely of top honors, usually including two of the three top honors in responder's suit. If opener raises to the three level and the contract fails, it may prove that the raise has forestalled a successful balancing action by the opponents.

If the opener bids a new suit 1NT-2♥-3♣ he implies a maximum with a fine fit for responder's suit. The clubs may be, by agreement, either a doubleton or concentrated strength.

Another example of a weakness response:

West	North	East	South
			1 ♣
1NT	2 ♥		

North's failure to double 1NT marks him with a weak hand (less than 8 or 9 points) and heart length. South will rarely be strong enough to attempt a game, and should rarely rescue relatively.

Weakness responses, which are natural, are sometimes confused with negative responses, which are conventional. Examples of these would be a negative 2♦ response to a conventional 2♣ bid, or a HERBERT NEGATIVE .

WEAKNESS-CONCEALING PLAY. See DECEPTIVE PLAY.

WEB MOVEMENT. The Web Movement was devised by National Tournament Director John "Spider" Harris in 1977 and was described by him as follows:

It is not uncommon to have, at least in small tournaments, sessions of from 16 to 22 tables in which a movement of reasonable technical adequacy is required, such as in a Master Pairs or an Open Pairs final. In the past the standard procedure has been to use twinned three-quarter movements and combined matchpointing.

Three-quarter movements are universally disliked by players. They do have the purported advantage provided by rotating comparisons, but this is the subject of some disagreement. In all other respects the web movements are superior.

In effect, these movements consist of two subsections in which the boards circulate independently, while the moving pairs progress to the other subsection after playing at the highest numbered table in one. In all cases, the traveling pairs move each round to the next higher numbered table with the boards moving next lower within each sub-section. The 18-table game will be described in detail; the others will be understood by simply glancing at the Master Sheet and remembering what happened in the 18-table progression. (Master sheets are available on request from ACBL Tournament Division.)

Basic Distribution of Boards. Tables 1-9 play one set ("A"), tables 10-18 another ("B"). Stationary pairs at 1-9 play the boards in ascending sequence, those at 10-18 in descending. Boards 1-2 start at Table 1, 3-4 at 2, etc. up to 17-18 at 9. The board order is inverted and displaced in the other sub-section: 25-26 start at Table 18, 1-2 at 17, 3-4 at 16, etc. to 15-16 at 10. Note that on round one, Boards 1-16 may be duplicated in the two sub-sections, 17-18 and 25-26 may either be duplicated at tables 9 and 18 respectively, or pre-duplicated (preferred). Boards 19-24 must be duplicated by the staff.

Movement of Boards and Players. Traveling pairs always move to the next higher numbered table. There is no skip. "A" boards move down until they reach Table 1

at which point they go to a bye-stand to re-enter at Table 9. "B" boards move down until they reach Table 10 at which point they go to the other bye-stand to re-enter at Table 18.

Seeded Tables. Assuming that Table 1 is to be seeded, the only suitable tables are:

Sixteen tables - 1, 5, 9, 13. Eighteen tables - 1, 7, 13. Twenty tables - 1, 9. Twenty-two tables - 1, 12.

Seating Assignments. In Open Pairs finals, two qualifying sections, the A qualifiers are simply made N-S, the B's E-W. For three qualifying sections, a schedule accompanies each Master Sheet for assigning pair numbers.

WEI AWARD. See SENDER AWARD.

WEISS CONVENTION. See DEFENSE TO OPENING THREE BIDS.

WEISSBERGER. A conventional extension of the STAYMAN convention to ask for three-card major suits, suggested by John Pressburger and developed by Alan Truscott and Maurice Weissberger. It is intended for use with English-style Stayman in which a secondary jump to 3♠ or 3♥ is invitational and not forcing. This is an optional feature of the ACOL system. Suppose the bidding proceeds:

Opener	Responder
1NT	2♣
2♦	3♦

The bid of 3♦ has little or no natural meaning in Acol. The Weissberger idea is to use it to inquire for three-card major suits. This helps the responder to solve three types of bidding problems:

(1) A game-going hand with five spades and four hearts.

(2) A game-going hand with five spades and five hearts.

(3) A hand with five spades and five hearts on which game is doubtful. As the responder is certain to have five spades, the opener, holding three spades, bids 3♠ with a minimum hand; 4♠ holding a maximum.

With only a doubleton spade, the opener bids 3♥ holding a minimum hand and 3NT holding a maximum. In all cases the responder has no problem in selecting the best final contract.

Notice that there are two other cases in which the convention is not needed:

(4) A game-going hand with four spades and five hearts. In this case the responder bids 3♥ immediately over 1NT, relying on the opener to show a four-card spade suit if he can.

(5) A hand with four in one major and five in the other on which game is doubtful. In this case the responder bids three of the five-card major suit over the opener's 2♦ rebid. This sequence is strictly non-forcing in Acol.

WERNHER TROPHY. Awarded to the winners of the NORTH AMERICAN OPEN PAIRS II, formerly the NORTH AMERICAN MEN'S PAIRS.

WEST. The player who sits to the left of South. South is to his right and North to his left. He is the partner of East.

WEST COAST SCIENTIFIC. See WALSH SYSTEM.

WESTERN CONFERENCE. Originally PACIFIC

BRIDGE LEAGUE, founded by Tom Stoddard, it became known as the Western Division in 1948, and the Western Conference in 1956 when it merged with ACBL. Current member districts are 17, 20, 21 and 22. *Functions of Western Conference.* (1) Publishes *The Contract Bridge Forum.* (2) Assists member units in promotion of Novice and Junior games at regionals; (3) Schedules regionals, handled by the Conference coordinator.

The last president of the Western Division, the late Winslow Randall, was the first president of the Western Conference. Other presidents:

1956	Lewis Mathe
1957	Robin MacNab
1958	Hugh Edwards
1959	C.F. Crossley
1960	Roy Hislop
1961	Tom Bussey
1962	Lewis Mathe
1963	Kelsey Petterson
1964	Lewis Mathe
1965	Max Manchester
1965	Donald Oakie
1966	Robin MacNab
1967	Eilif Andersen
1969	Paul Rhodes
1970	Percy Bean
1971-72	Maurice Hole
1973-74	Alfred Gilpin
1975-76	David Tuell
1977-78	George Clemens
1979-80	Herbert Smith
1981-82	Chris Wilson
1983-84	Robert Wingeard
1986-86	Syd Levey
1987-88	Roger Smith
1989-90	Chris Wilson
1991	Frank Sweeney
1992	Mike Jones
1993	Mike Jones and Frank Sweeney
1994-95	Bob Mackintosh
1996-97	John Van Ness
1998-99	Sally Lix
2000-2001	Jerry Fleming

WESTERN CUEBID. Generally, a cuebid of a suit bid by an opponent to ask about stoppers for notrump play, rather than promising such stoppers. See EASTERN CUEBIDS, CUEBIDS IN OPPONENT'S SUIT, DIRECTIONAL ASKING BID .

WESTERN ROTH-STONE. See WESTERN SCIENTIFIC.

WESTERN SCIENTIFIC. Also called WEST COAST SCIENTIFIC, or WESTERN ROTH-STONE, or WALSH. Originally devised by Richard Walsh in the 1960s and described in books by Max Hardy.

Many of the elements are identical with those listed under Eastern Scientific. Distinctive features are:

(1) 1♦ response to 1♣ denies a 4-card major unless responder is strong.

(2) Limit raise promises a singleton.

(3) Swiss raises instead of splinters.

(4) After 1♦ - 2♣: (i) 2♦ may be 3-3-4-3 with poor clubs; (ii) 2♥ and 2♠ show minimum hands with a 4-card suit, denying the other major; (iii) 2NT shows 4-4-3-2 with minimum values.

(5) Mathe asking bids.

See WALSH SYSTEM.

WETZLAR TROPHY. Awarded for distinguished services to bridge, this trophy was presented in memory of Edwin A. Wetzlar in 1935. The first winners were:

1935	H. Huber Boscowitz	1938	Alfred Gruenther
1936	Waldemar von Zedtwitz	1939	Nate Spingold
1937	Gordon Gibbs	1940	Harold S. Vanderbilt

After 1940 the Wetzlar was presented to ACBL HONORARY MEMBERS, under which heading the recipients are listed.

WHEEL. See CHUKKER.

WHISK. An alternative name for whist. It was an English lower-class term, according to Dr. Samuel Johnson, used until about the end of the eighteenth century.

WHIST. A game of cards of English origin gradually evolved from several older games such as triumph, trump, ruff and honors, swabbers, and whisk. Whist is played by four persons, two partners against two partners. A regular pack of 52 cards is dealt, 13 to each player. The last card dealt is turned face up on the table. Its suit becomes the trump suit. This card remains on the table until it is the dealer's turn to play to the first trick, when he may return it to his hand. The player at the left of the dealer makes the first lead, and the play proceeds as in bridge except that all four hands are concealed; there is no dummy. Six tricks taken make the BOOK. Each trick won over the book scores one point for the partners winning that trick. The range of possible scores for either set of partners is from one to seven. Any number of deals may be played. Scoring is by games. The English code of laws provides for rubber bonuses and honor bonuses. At the conclusion of play the side having the greatest number of points is the winner. The game of whist has, in general, been superseded in the United States by changing versions of the basic game — by BRIDGE, AUCTION BRIDGE and CONTRACT BRIDGE. It is still played in Great Britain and the U.S. See also AMERICAN WHIST LEAGUE; BIBLIOGRAPHY; CONTRACT WHIST; HISTORY OF BRIDGE.

WHIST CLUB. A club of men interested in whist and later in all successive forms of bridge, founded in New York 1893, merged with the REGENCY CLUB of New York 1964. Because nearly all of its members were men of great wealth and prominence (including bridge prominence, such as Harold S. Vanderbilt, J. B. Elwell, Milton Work, Ely Culbertson), unquestioned authority in the making of bridge laws for the U.S. was accorded to the Whist Club for more than 40 years. Two earlier codes of contract bridge laws were voluntarily withdrawn when in 1927 the Whist Club produced a code for contract bridge (formulated by a committee composed of Vanderbilt, H. C. Richard, Charles Cadley, Raymond Little and William Talcott).

Later the Whist Club's committees collaborated with the Portland Club of London and French Bridge Federation in producing the first and second international codes (1932, 1935), and Whist Club representatives served continuously on the NATIONAL LAWS COMMISSION for the laws of 1943, 1948, 1949, and 1963.

WHITE. Not vulnerable. Also British colloquialism meaning neither side vulnerable. See AMBER, GREEN, RED.

WHITEHEAD TROPHY. For the North American Championship Women's Pairs, donated by Wilbur Whitehead in 1930; contested at the Summer NABC until 1962 and subsequently at the Spring NABC, under which heading results are listed.

WHITFELD SIX. The father of all end-game problems, devised and published on January 31, 1885, by W. H. Whitfeld, mathematical tutor at Cambridge, England, who was Cavendish's successor as card editor of the *London Field*. (Sometimes known as the "Whitfield Six" through a common mispronunciation of the inventor's name.) Hearts are trumps. South must lead and make all the tricks.

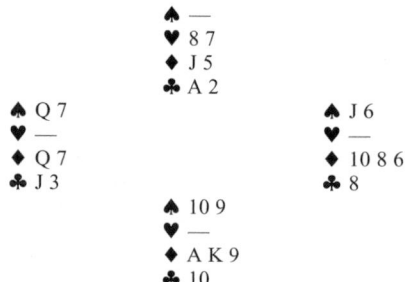

Solution. South cashes the ♦ A, unblocking the jack from dummy. to prepare for a possible finesse. A spade is ruffed and the last trump from dummy is cashed, on which South discards the ♣ 10. The only temporary defense is for East to keep diamonds and the high spade, and for West to keep clubs and the ♦ Q. The ♣ A from dummy then squeezes East. The Whitfeld Six is a type of double guard squeeze.

WIDE OPEN. A phrase describing a suit in which declarer has no stopper or is extremely vulnerable to attack. For example, "Declarer was wide open in spades."

WIN-LOSS SWISS TEAMS. The difference between this type of SWISS TEAMS and others is the method of scoring (see TEAM GAMES). A team compiles its results and determines whether the total is plus or minus. If the total is plus 3 or more, the match is deemed won and the team receives one matchpoint. If the total is plus 1 or plus 2, the team receives three-quarters of a matchpoint — this result is termed a WINNING TIE. If both teams score exactly the same number of IMPs, each team gets half a matchpoint. The team that loses by 1 or 2 is said to have suffered a LOSING TIE and is awarded one-fourth of a matchpoint. A team that loses by 3 or more IMPs gets no matchpoints. No losing team receives masterpoints for the match, even if they lose by only 1 or 2 IMPs. Winning teams receive full match masterpoints even if they win by only 1 or 2 IMPs. See FLIGHTED TEAMS, MIXED TEAMS, OPEN TEAMS, ROUND-ROBIN TEAMS, BOARD-A-MATCH SWISS TEAMS, STRATIFIED TEAMS, STRATIFLIGHTED TEAMS, TEAM GAMES, SPEEDBALL SWISS TEAMS, VICTORY POINT SWISS TEAMS, ZIP SWISS TEAMS.

WINKLE SQUEEZE. A secondary squeeze that forces the opponents to choose between a throw-in and an unblock, each of which costs a trick (analyzed and named by Terence Reese.) Declarer has enough winners for all

but one of the remaining tricks, but he cannot take all his tricks because of entry problems.

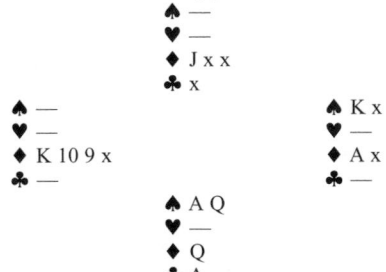

```
                    ♠ —
                    ♥ —
                    ♦ J x x
                    ♣ x
♠ —                              ♠ K x
♥ —                              ♥ —
♦ K 10 9 x                       ♦ A x
♣ —                              ♣ —
                    ♠ A Q
                    ♥ —
                    ♦ Q
                    ♣ A
```

South leads the ♣A, and East is squeezed in two suits. He must discard a diamond in order to protect the ♠K. If East discards a low diamond he will be thrown in to lead from his ♠K; if he discards the ♦A, South takes the ♣A and then leads a diamond, eventually winning a trick with the ♦J.

The French name for a winkle is "crochet". The most famous example occurred in the 1963 International Team Trials in Miami Beach FL.

Vul: None
```
                    ♠ Q 8
                    ♥ 10 6 3
                    ♦ A Q J 9 6
                    ♣ A Q 4
♠ 5 4 3                          ♠ J 10 7 2
♥ A 8 5                          ♥ K Q 7 4
♦ K 5 3 2                        ♦ 10 8 7
♣ 10 5 2                         ♣ 7 6
                    ♠ A K 9 6
                    ♥ J 9 2
                    ♦ 4
                    ♣ K J 9 8 3
```

South	West	North	East
(Becker)	(Stayman)	(Hayden)	(Mitchell)
1♣	Pass	1♦	Pass
1♠	Pass	3♣	Pass
4♣	Pass	4♠	Pass
6♣	Pass	Pass	Pass

3NT was the only good game, but was hard to reach with no heart stopper. A slight misunderstanding led to 6♣: South had forgotten a partnership agreement that 4♣ would always be Gerber after a minor-suit opening. South assumed that 4♠ indicated a singleton heart, and bid the slam.

West was also misled and chose a diamond lead. South, apparently calm, finessed the ♦J successfully. He threw a heart on the ♦A and ruffed a diamond. He crossed to the ♣A, ruffed another diamond to remove the king, and cashed the ♣K-Q.

The lead was in dummy in this position:
```
                    ♠ Q 8
                    ♥ 10 6 3
                    ♦ Q
                    ♣ —
♠ 5 4 3                          ♠ J 10 7 2
♥ A 8 5                          ♥ K Q
♦ —                              ♦ —
♣ —                              ♣ —
                    ♠ A K 9 6
                    ♥ J 9
                    ♦ —
                    ♣ —
```

On the ♦Q East perforce threw the ♥Q. South threw the ♥9, and West a spade. The ♠Q was cashed, and when the 8 was played East covered with the 10. Now the ♥J was led and the defense was helpless. West chose to win and endplay himself, giving dummy two heart tricks. If he had played low, East would have been endplayed to give South two spade tricks. Interchange the ♥6 and ♥5 and the slam cannot be made, even with the favorable opening lead. See also ENTRY SQUEEZE and STEPPING-STONE SQUEEZE.

WINNER. (1) A card that may reasonably be expected to win a trick in dummy or declarer's hand. On defense, a card that will win a trick during the play of a given hand may be termed a winner as well. (2) The player, the pair or team with the highest score in an event at a duplicate tournament.

WINNING CARD. The card that takes the trick. In a notrump declaration this is always the highest card played in the suit that has been led; it may be a LONG CARD, led in a suit to which the other players cannot follow. In suit declarations, the above will apply, except that on a trick where more than one trump is played it is the highest trump that will win the trick.

WINNING TIE. In WIN-LOSS SWISS TEAMS, a match that is won by 1 or 2 IMPs. It counts as three-fourths of a win.

WINSLOW SYSTEM. See WINSLOW, Thomas Newby.

WITHDRAWN CARD. It is not permitted to withdraw a card previously played except to correct a revoke, or a card played by an opponent after such a card was withdrawn. Declarer may insist that a card he had called to be played from dummy be substituted for a card actually put into the playing position by the dummy. In this case, too, the opponent may without penalty withdraw his card and substitute a different proper card. See, however, ALCATRAZ COUP for a possible situation that calls for a redress under the general powers of the director.

WOLFF SIGNOFF. Devised by Bobby Wolff to allow responder to sign off at the three-level after opener has made a jump rebid of 2NT. It can also apply if the auction goes one of a major-1NT-2NT-3♣. Responder's rebid of 3♣ asks opener to bid three of responder's suit if he has three-card support, and otherwise to bid 3♦. Responder can then sign off by passing, by bidding 4♣, or by introducing a new suit of lower rank than his first suit; a rebid of 3NT by responder would be a mild slam try in clubs.

This was the consensus choice of the experts in BWS1984.

WOMEN'S INTERNATIONAL TEAM TRIALS. See INTERNATIONAL WOMEN'S TEAM SELECTION. For results see Appendix III.

WOMEN'S KNOCKOUT TEAMS, NORTH AMERICAN CHAMPIONSHIP, for the Coffin Trophy. Initiated in 1976 the event was played in the Spring NABC 1976-85 after which it was transferred to the Summer NABC. For results see Appendix I.

WOMEN'S PAIRS. All pairs must consist of two women.

WOMEN'S PAIRS, NORTH AMERICAN CHAMPIONSHIP, for the Whitehead Trophy. Played at the Summer NABC 1930-62 and subsequently at the Spring NABC. For results see Appendix I.

WOMEN'S SWISS TEAMS, NORTH AMERICAN CHAMPIONSHIP. Played in the Spring NABC. For results see Appendix I.

WOMEN'S TEAMS. All members of every team must be women.

WONDER BID. A defensive bidding system against strong artificial club sequences. They are used when vulnerable; IDAK (or IDAC) is commonly used when not vulnerable. If RHO opens an artificial club or responds artificially to a 1♣ opening:

1. Any nonjump suit bid shows that suit or the other three (let partner guess). Responder obviously cannot raise blindly, but can: (a) bid 1NT with four or more cards in the Wonder suit (not forcing if the Wonder bidder has the three-suited hand); (b) bid two of any suit with four or more cards if he also has tolerance for the Wonder suit. The overcaller passes or returns to his real Wonder suit. The Wonder bidder redoubles for takeout if doubled in his short suit.

2. Double shows the major suits.

3. Notrump shows the minor suits.

4. A jump in diamonds shows diamonds and hearts, a jump in hearts shows hearts and clubs, a jump in spades shows spades and a minor (notrump asks which minor).

WOODSON TWO-WAY NOTRUMP. An opening notrump bid holding a balanced hand with 10-12 points or 16-18 points. A 2♣ bid asks for clarification. It was devised by the late William Woodson. See TWO-WAY NOTRUMP.

WOOLSEY. Devised by Kit Woolsey, this method of interfering over 1NT gives up on a penalty double of 1NT in order to provide a way to show all the two-suited hands while emphasizing the relative lengths of the two suits.

After a 1NT opening bid, Double shows a major-minor two-suiter, with the minor being five or more cards long, and the major being a four-carder. 2♣ shows the majors, 2♦ shows one major, 2♥/2♠ are the bid major and a minor, at least 5/4 respectively. It is permissible to double 1NT with a single-suited minor in the hope of being able to get out in the minor.

After the double, responder bids 2♣ to play in partner's minor, 2♦ to play in partner's major, and 2♥/2♠ are natural. After 2NT, which is a game-try, overcaller bids his minor with a minimum and his major with a maximum.

After the 2♣ overcall, 2♦ asks partner to bid his better major, 2NT is natural, and 3♣ can be used as a game-try. Overcaller bids 3♦ with a minimum and his better major with a maximum.

After the 2♦ overcall, 2♥/2♠ are both pass or correct, 2NT is a relay showing game interest. Overcaller bids 3♣ with a minimum and one under his major with a maximum.

After the 2♥ or 2♠ overcall, 2NT asks for the minor, and 3♣ and 3♦ are natural.

If the opposition continue bidding after an ambiguous action by overcaller, fourth hand's bids are natural rather than pass/correct while his doubles are always takeout, as indeed are further doubles by the overcaller. All actions are unchanged by a passed hand.

This defense also can be used against weak notrumps, perhaps incorporating various strong balanced options into the double.

WORK POINT-COUNT. A 4-3-2-1 point-count based on the Bryant McCampbell count of 1915, publicized and advocated by MILTON WORK, circa 1923. See POINT-COUNT.

WORKING CARD. High card which, on the basis of the auction, rates to mesh well with partner's hand for suit play. For example, a secondary honor or an unsupported king is usually discounted opposite a known singleton, whereas any top honor is likely to be "working" if it is in one of partner's suits. See also GOOD CARDS.

WORLD BIDDING CONTEST. See INTERNATIONAL BRIDGE ACADEMY.

WORLD BRIDGE FEDERATION (WBF). The World Bridge Federation was founded in August 1958 in Oslo, Norway, by delegates from Europe, the United States and South America. In 1977 it was incorporated in New York State as a not-for-profit organization and new by-laws were adopted. A new set of bylaws and a new constitution were adopted in 2000.

In 2000 the membership consisted of 113 National Contract Bridge Organizations (NCBOs) with a total of about 1.5 million individual members. The Executive Council, meeting annually at world championships, consists of five delegates each from Europe (Zone 1) and North America (Zone 2), plus one delegate each from five other zones (South America; Asia and Middle East; Central American and Caribbean; Pacific Asia; South Pacific:) plus the president. A Management Committee transacts necessary business between meetings. A Congress, with one representative from each NCBO, meets biennially.

Major activities of the WBF include: promoting bridge throughout the world; coordinating periodic revision of the Laws; conducting world championships; preparing for possible inclusion in the Olympics, publishing *World Bridge News*; maintaining WBF masterpoint records and maintaining the WBF Educational Foundation.

The zones of the WBF are: (1) Europe, (2) North America, including Bermuda, (3) South America, (4) Asia and the Middle East, (5) Central America and the Caribbean, (6) Far East, (7) South Pacific, (8) Africa.

The major world events are: NEC World Team Olympiad (held years divisible by four); World Championships (held in even-numbered years); NEC Bermuda Bowl and NEC Venice Cup (held in odd-numbered years); and NEC World Junior Team Championships (held in odd-numbered years).

For a predecessor organization, see INTERNATIONAL BRIDGE LEAGUE. Also see BERMUDA BOWL, McCONNELL TEAMS, ROSENBLUM TEAMS, TRANSNATIONAL MIXED TEAMS, TRANSNATIONAL OPEN TEAMS, VENICE CUP, WORLD BRIDGE ALERTING POLICY, WORLD BRIDGE FEDERATION COMMITTEE OF HONOR, WORLD

BRIDGE FEDERATION CLASSIFICATION OF SYSTEMS AND CONVENTIONS, WORLD BRIDGE FEDERATION COUNCIL, WORLD BRIDGE FEDERATION MASTERPOINT PLAN, WORLD BRIDGE FEDERATION MEMBER NATIONS, WORLD BRIDGE FEDERATION PLACING POINTS, WORLD BRIDGE FEDERATION PLAYER RANKINGS, WORLD BRIDGE FEDERATION PRESIDENTS, WORLD JUNIOR TEAM CHAMPIONSHIP, WORLD OLYMPICS, WORLD PAR CONTESTS, WORLD TEAM OLYMPIAD. For World Championship results, see Appendix V.

WORLD BRIDGE FEDERATION ALERTING POLICY. The WBF Alerting poicy applies to all events sponsored by the WBF. The following classes of calls should be Alerted: (1) Conventional bids (conventional is defined to mean a call that serves by partnership agreement to convey a meaning not necessarily related to the denomination named). (2) Bids that have special meanings or which are based on a special partnership understanding. (3) Non-forcing jump changes of suit responses to opening bids or overcalls, and non-forcing new suit responses by an unpassed hand to opening bids of one of a suit. The following calls should not be Alerted unless screens are in use: (1) All doubles; (2) Any notrump which suggests a balanced or semi-balanced hand or suggests a notrump contract; (3) All bids, with the exception of conventional opening suit bids, at the four level or higher.

WORLD BRIDGE FEDERATION CLASSIFICATION OF SYSTEMS AND CONVENTIONS. The WBF has divided systems into three classifications: Green – natural; Blue –strong club/strong diamond; Red – artificial – includes all artificial systems that do not fall under the definition of Highly Unusual Methods (HUM) systems, other than strong club and strong diamond systems; Yellow –Highly Unusual Methods.

The following conventions or treatments are categorized as Brown Sticker Conventions:

(1) Any opening bid of 1 ♣ through 3 ♠ that (a) could be weak, and (b) does not promise at least four cards in a known suit.

(2) A two-level opening bid in a minor showing a weak two in either major, whether with or without the option of strong hand types.

(3) An overcall of a natural opening bid of one of a suit that does not promise at least four cards in a known suit (exception – a natural overcall in notrump).

(4) Any weak two-suited bids at the two or three level that may by agreement be made with three cards or fewer in one of the suits.

(5) Psychic bids protected by system or required by system.

None of the foregoing restrictions pertain to conventional defenses against strong, artificial opening bids or defenses against Brown Sticker or HUM conventions. Any partnership using one or more Brown Sticker conventions must indicate this alongside the system classification. HUM conventions can be used only in the Bermuda Bowl and the Venice Cup. Brown Sticker conventions can be used in the Bermuda Bowl, the Venice Cup and the knockout matches of the Rosenblum Teams, McConnell Teams, Open Olympiad and Women's Olympiad.

WORLD BRIDGE FEDERATION COMMITTEE OF HONOR. Formed in 1972 to recognize the unselfish efforts of individuals making significant contributions to the enhancement and growth of bridge throughout the world. The three so honored in 1972 were Geoffrey Butler, Great Britain; Waldemar Von Zedtwitz, United States, and Charles Solomon, United States. Other honorees since then:

1974 – Julius Rosenblum, United States; Albert Morehead, United States; Baron Robert de Nexon, France. 1976 – Ben Johnson, United States, and Andre LeMaitre, Belgium. 1978 – Alfred Gruenther, United States, and Jaime Ortiz-Patino, Switzerland. 1984 – Richard Goldberg, United States; Nils Jensen, Sweden, and Edgar Kaplan, United States. 1986 – Robert Howes, United States, and Ernesto d'Orsi, Brazil. 1988 – José Damiani, France. 1994 – Bobby Wolff, United States. 1998 – Jean-Claude Beneix, France; Mazhar Jafri, Pakistan, and John Wignall, New Zealand. See WORLD BRIDGE FEDERATION.

WORLD BRIDGE FEDERATION EXECUTIVE COUNCIL. The WBF is governed by an executive council made up of representatives from the WBF's eight zones. The Council meets several times at each world championship. The 2001 Council officers:

José Damiani, France, president; Jaime Ortiz-Patino, Spain, president emeritus (former president); Jens Auken, Denmark, vice president; Patrick Choy, Singapore, vice president; Joan Gerard, United States, vice president; Panos Gerontopoulos, Greece, vice president; Mazhar, Jafri, Pakistan, vice president; George Retek, Canada, vice president and treasurer; John Wignall, New Zealand, vice president; Jean Louis Derivery, Guadeloupe, secretary; Jeff Polisner, general counsel. Other members of the 2001 Council: Jean-Claude Beneix, France; Bharat Bhardwaj, Kenya; Alan LeBendig, United States; Dan Morse, United States; Ernesto d'Orsi, Brazil (former president); Gianarrigo Rona, Italy; Anna Maria Torlontano, Italy; Nadine Wood, United States; Bobby Wolff, United States (ex-officio, former president). Consultants: Pietro Bernasconi, masterpoint plan; Eric Kokish, *World Bridge News* editor; Ton Kooijman, director of operations; Bill Schoder, chief tournament director; Kathie Wei-Sender, ambassador of bridge. See WORLD BRIDGE FEDERATION, WORLD BRIDGE FEDERATION PRESIDENTS.

WORLD BRIDGE FEDERATION MASTERPOINT PLAN. The WBF looks upon masterpoints as an attempt to indicate the true present worth of a player. Therefore points won years ago are not worth as much as points won recently. The masterpoint system has been set up so that points will disappear if not fortified by new successes. On the other hand, PLACING POINTS (PPs) represent the career of a WBF player. This means that Placing Points won years ago count just as much as Placing Points won today.

The WBF has three categories: World Grand Master (WGM), (10 PPs and at least one world championship title); World Life Master (WLM), (5 PPs); World Master (WM) (150 masterpoints). WGMs and WLMs keep their title for life. WMs lose their title when their masterpoint total falls below 150.

The masterpoints won on Open and Women's events are subject to different rankings. If a woman wins points in both types of events, her name could appear on both lists. Under the new system, inaugurated in 1992, the masterpoint totals took into account only those points won in the previous 12 years (1981-1992). All totals were multiplied by 10 to reduce the number of decimals necessary. At the end of

each year, the total masterpoints are reduced by 15% (the points won in that year remain untouched). The end of a masterpoint year coincides with the start of that year's world championship. If a player's masterpoint total drops below 3, he or she is dropped from the list.

Masterpoint awards by event: Open Olympiad – 1000 and 5 PPs for first down to 200 1 PP for eighth; Women's Olympiad – 700 and 5 for first down to 90 and 1 for eighth; Bermuda Bowl and Venice Cup – 800 and 5 for first down to 60 for eight and 1 PP for fourth; Rosenblum Teams – 600 and 4 for first down to 40 die 33rd through 64th and 1 PP for fourth; McConnell Teams – 450 and 4 for first down to 40 for 33rd through 64th and 1 PP for fourth; Open Pairs – 800 and 4 for first down to 100 for 31st and 1 PP for fourth; Women's Pairs – 600 and 4 for first down to 100 for 19th and 1 for fourth; Mixed Pairs – 200 and 2 for first down to 30 for 10th and 1 for second; World Junior Teams – 300 for first down to 100 for third (no PPs); World Junior Pairs – 150 for first down to 100 for third (no PPs).

Lesser masterpoints and PPs also are awarded for Transnational Open, Women's and Senior Teams, Senior Pairs, Simultaneous Pairs, approved Zonal Open and Women's championships, Junior Teams, Junior Pairs, Junior Individual and Junior Triathlon

Masterpoints won in events sponsored by the WBF are called WMPs (WBF masterpoints). Those won in other competitions are called WYPs (WBF Year Points). At the end of a year's competition, a ranking is established that takes into account both types of points won during that year. This makes it possible to name a Champion of the Year. See WORLD BRIDGE FEDERATION, WORLD BRIDGE FEDERATION PLAYER RANKINGS, WORLD GRAND MASTER, WORLD LIFE MASTER, WORLD MASTER.

WORLD BRIDGE FEDERATION MEMBER COUNTRIES.
Antigua, Argentina, Aruba, Australia, Austria, Bahamas, Bangladesh, Barbados, Belarus, Belgium, Bermuda, Bolivia, Botswana, Brazil, Bulgaria, Canada, Chile, China, Chinese Taipei, Colombia, Costa Rice, Cote d'Ivoire, Croatia, Cyprus, Czech Republic, Denmark, Dominica, Ecuador, Egypt, England, Estonia, Finland, France, French Guyana, French Polynesia, Germany, Greece, Guadeloupe, Guatemala, Haiti, Hong Kong, Hungary, Iceland, India, Indonesia, Ireland, Israel, Italy, Jamaica, Japan, Jordan, Kenya, Korea, Kuwait, Latvia, Lebanon, Liechtenstein, Lithuania, Luxembourg, Macao, Madagascar, Malaysia, Malta, Martinique, Mauritius, Mexico, Monaco, Morocco, Netherlands Antilles, Netherlands, New Caledonia, New Zealand, Norway, Pakistan, Palestine, Panama, Paraguay, Peru, Philippines, Poland, Portugal, Qatar, Reunion, Romania, Russia, Saint Kitts, San Marino, Saudi Arabia, Scotland, Singapore, Slovenia, South Africa, Spain, Sri Lanka, Surinam, Sweden, Switzerland, Syria, Tanzania, Thailand, Trinidad and Tobago, Tunisia, Turkey, Ukraine, Uruguay, United States of America, Uzbekistan, Venezuela, Virgin Islands, Wales, Yugoslavia, Zimbabwe. See WORLD BRIDGE FEDERATION.

WORLD BRIDGE FEDERATION PLACING POINTS.
Points, other than WBF MASTERPOINTS, awarded by the WORLD BRIDGE FEDERATION to winners and very high finishers in WBF tournaments and Zonal team championships. A certain number of placing points are needed to achieve the WBF rankings of Grand Master and World Life Master. See WORLD BRIDGE FEDERATION MASTERPOINT PLAN, WORLD BRIDGE FEDERATION PLAYER RANKINGS.

WORLD BRIDGE FEDERATION PLAYER RANKINGS.
The ranking of players according to the world masterpoint plan of the World Bridge Federation. The three ranks, in descending order, are World Grand Master, World Life Master, and World Master.

The rank of World Grand Master is achieved by accumulating 10 or more WBF Placing Points and winning at least one World Champion title. The rank of World Life Master is achieved by winning 5 or more Placing Points. These titles are lifetime. A player who wins 150 WBF masterpoints becomes a World Master, but loses this rank if his total falls below 150 as a result of the annual percentage cut of 15%.

For listings, see Appendix II.

WORLD BRIDGE FEDERATION PRESIDENTS.

1958-1964	Robert de Nexon
1964-1968	Charles J. Solomon
1968-1970	Carl Bonde
1970 1976	Julius Rosenblum
1976-1986	Jaime Ortiz-Patino
1986-1991	Denis Howard
1991-1992	Ernesto d'Orsi
1992-1994	Robert Wolff
1994-	José Damiani

WORLD BRIDGE FEDERATION TROPHY.
This trophy, for the World Women's Pairs Championship, first was contested in Cannes, France, in 1962. See Appendix V for results.

WORLD BRIDGE OLYMPIC.
See WORLD PAR CONTESTS. For results, see Appendix IV.

WORLD COMPUTER CHAMPIONSHIPS.
See COMPUTER CHAMPIONSHIPS.

WORLD GRAND MASTER.
Highest rank in the World Bridge Federation. A player must have 10 PLACING POINTS and at least one world championship title. Once earned, the title is for life. See WORLD BRIDGE FEDERATION MASTERPOINT PLAN, WORLD BRIDGE FEDERATION PLAYER RANKINGS.

WORLD JUNIOR TEAM CHAMPIONSHIP.
This contest, is for players 25 years or younger, and is played along Bermuda Bowl lines. For results, see Appendix V.

WORLD LIFE MASTER.
Second highest ranking in the World Bridge Federation. Player must earn 5 PLACING POINTS. Once earned, the title is for life. See WORLD BRIDGE FEDERATION MASTERPOINT PLAN, WORLD BRIDGE FEDERATION PLAYER RANKINGS.

WORLD MASTER.
The third highest ranking in the World Bridge Federation. The player must have 150 masterpoints. Since masterpoints are reassessed each year, it is possible for a player who is a World Master to lose that title because his or her masterpoint total drops below 150 as a result of a reassessment. See WORLD BRIDGE FEDERATION MASTERPOINT PLAN, WORLD BRIDGE FEDERATION PLAYER RANKINGS.

WORLD OLYMPICS. See WORLD PAR CONTESTS and WORLD TEAM OLYMPIAD.

WORLD PAR CONTESTS. International events using prepared deals (see PAR CONTESTS). The idea of a series of par tournaments conducted throughout the world was conceived by Ely Culbertson, and in 1932 the first World Bridge Olympic, using the par hand format, was held. Culbertson founded the National Bridge Association, a nonprofit corporation, in the same year, to conduct the tournaments. The bridge world's principal experts, regardless of their affiliation in the bridge politics of those times, constructed the prepared deals, and Culbertson's staff did the central management and scoring. Each contestant paid a fee of one dollar, of which half went to the game captain (who pre-arranged the hands and directed his game), and half was retained by the NBA. In 1932, and 1933, both American and World Olympics were conducted: from 1934 on, only the World Olympics. In 1934 self-dealing cards (marked on their backs to show which player should receive each card for the bridge WALLETS) were supplied without extra charge by the NBA. The World Bridge Olympic reached its peak in 1934 with 70 countries and nearly 90,000 players entered, but even in that year the NBA lost money. In 1938 the ACBL took over the management, with William McKenney in charge and Geoffrey Mott-Smith constructing the hands, but there were problems of foreign exchange, and World War II forced the abandonment after 1941.

The Olympic trophies were famous. For the American event, the two largest silver trophies in bridge history were provided. One of them is the McKenney Trophy; the other was lost in circumstances that had a lasting effect on insurance law. A winner, entitled to one year's possession only, pawned the trophy. A court ruled that since it was his honest intention to redeem it within the year, he was not liable although he found himself later without funds to redeem it, nor was the pawnbroker responsible for having sold it when the time for redemption had passed. The insurance underwriter paid its value to the NBA. The two World trophies each contained $5,000 worth of pure platinum but Culbertson, who donated them, never relinquished personal title to them and sold them for their value in platinum when the tournament was discontinued.

Individual prizes were given to all international and national winners and to state winners in the United States and provincial winners in Canada, both North-South and East-West, so the list of winners for each year was long indeed.

In 1951, the World Par Contest was revived by Australia and won by Dr. J. L. Thwaites and Dr. E.L. Field of Melbourne, Australia, in that year. It was held in 1961 and 1963 under the auspices of the World Bridge Federation. The WBF intended to hold this event biennially, but it has not been held since 1963. The organizers in 1961 and 1963 were Michael J. Sullivan and Robert E. Williams (Australia).

For winners, see Appendix IV.

WORLD SENIOR PAIRS. A secondary world championship open only to players who are 55 or older. This is a transnational event. For results see Appendix IV.

WORLD TEAM OLYMPIAD. A WBF tournament conducted quadrennially starting in 1960, consisting of an open team event and a women's team event. In 1960 NCBOs having a very large number of members were allowed to enter more than one team. On this basis Sweden entered two teams and the United States entered four in the open event. Since 1960 each NCBO has been allowed to enter only one team in each event of the Olympiad. For results see Appendix. See INTERNATIONAL OPEN TEAM SELECTION and INTERNATIONAL WOMEN'S TEAM SELECTION. For results, see Appendix V.

WORLD TOP TOURNAMENT. See CAP GEMINI WORLD TOP tournament. For results, see Appendix IV.

WORLDWIDE BRIDGE CONTEST. The first worldwide bridge contest, a simultaneous pairs event, took place in June 1986, sponsored by the Seiko Epson Corporation of Japan. The event became known as the Epson Pairs as a result of this sponsorship. Organized by José Damiani of France, who was about to become president of the World Bridge Federation, the format was a single session 24-board game conducted throughout the world on the same day at approximately the same time everywhere. This meant, of course, that some areas of the world, mostly in Asia and the South Pacific, the game was being played in the early morning hours. All contestants played the same hands, and everyone received a booklet containing analyses by Omar Sharif at the conclusion of the session. The game was scored by Instant Matchpoints with 100 as top and 1200 as average. The matchpoints were instant because they were predetermined based on play at an earlier tournament. Players from 80 countries participated in the first contest.

The following year more than 75,000 players participated in 85 countries, a fact that that made the *Guinness Book of Records 1988* as the biggest tournament ever held. Beginning in 1990 an association with the World Federation of Great Towers added interest when games were presented live by satellite from famous towers around the world. In 1991 about 90,000 players from 95 countries competed. A major change occurred in 1992 when the game was conducted in two separate sessions. Players could compete on Friday night, Saturday afternoon or both. Attendance grew to 100,000 in 1993, a record that still stands. Epson withdrew as a sponsor after the 1994 event which was co-sponsored by France Telecom, but the contest continued in the two-day form with and without sponsors.

A monumental change occurred in 2000 when the Instant Matchpoint method was dropped and matchpointing across the whole world was tried for the first time. A computer program developed by Mark Newton of Great Britain and administered by Anna Gudge, also of Great Britain, did the matchpointing. Clubs all over the world sent their results to England either by e-mail or by disc, and the information was fed to the program which immediately assimilated the results.

WRIGGLE. An intermediate step when escaping from an opposing penalty attempt at a low level.

       ♠ A 3 2
       ♥ A 3 2
       ♦ A 2
       ♣ J 5 4 3 2

You deal as South and the bidding is:

South	West	North	East
1 ♣	Pass	Pass	Dbl.
Pass	Pass	Redbl.	Pass
?			

West has the clubs stacked over you. Your partner's

SOS redouble shows that he is short in clubs and prepared for any other suit. The least evil will be to play in one of a major suit, but which? You should wriggle by bidding 1 ♦ and then make an SOS redouble to force your partner to choose a major suit. See also DEFENSE TO DOUBLE OF ONE NOTRUMP, SOS REDOUBLE.

WRITTEN BIDDING. A variation in the bidding technique such that each bidder writes his bid on a sheet (designed to facilitate the placing of each bid in a proper box) which is passed to him as it becomes his turn to bid. The theory is that any extra time a player might take in a huddle can be construed as a review of previous bidding, as shown on the sheet, and no information can be conveyed to the partner by mannerism, gesture, or inflection, and the need for a review of the bidding at any time is removed. Another advantage is that it provides a written record for directors, journalists or others involved.

Written bidding is standard in Australia, New Zealand and China, has been used in Far East Championships and some other international events. See BIDDING BOXES.

WRONG BOARD. Occasionally the play of a wrong board is commenced before it is discovered that it is a wrong board. If this occurs, the director should be summoned and he will act under LAWS OF DUPLICATE, Law 15.

WRONG SIDE. The hand of the declaring partnership which is less well equipped to cope with the opening lead. See RIGHT SIDE.

X

X. (1) A symbol used in lower case in bridge literature to signify an insignificant small card in any suit, a card lower than a 10. Thus, K-x-x means the king and two low cards in that suit. (2) A capital X indicates a double, and is used in recording bidding, and in WRITTEN BIDDING, by hand in important matches. Similarly, XX means "redouble."

X PLUS ONE, RULE OF. See RULE OF X PLUS ONE.

Y

YARBOROUGH. Any hand containing no card higher than a 9, named after an English lord who customarily would offer to wager 1,000 pounds to one against the chance of such a hand being held by a player. The odds against holding a Yarborough are 1,827 to one, so he was giving himself a substantial edge. In post-mortem discussions the term "yarborough" has gained currency to describe bad hands even if they do not meet the strict requirements. In some circles any hand with no card higher than a 10 is considered a yarborough.

YOUNGEST LIFE MASTER. The following players were the Youngest Life Masters at the time they achieved that status:

1952	Richard Freeman	18 yrs. 10 mos. 7 days
1961	Diane Barton-Paine	18 yrs. 12 days
1965	Kyle Larsen	15 yrs. 11 mos.
1968	Joseph Livezey	15 yrs. 5 mos.
1973	Bobby Levin	15 yrs. 4 mos.
1975	Michael Freed	15 yrs. 20 days
1976	Regina Barnes	14 yrs. 11 mos.
1977	Steve Cochran	14 yrs. 5 mos. 20 days
1980	Billy Hsieh	13 yrs. 7 mos. 15 days
1981	Andrew Kaufman	13 yrs. 4 mos. 15 days (June)
1981	Doug Hsieh	11 yrs. 10 mos. 4 days (Sept.)
1988	Sam Hirschman	11 yrs. 9 mos. 5 days
1990	Joel Wooldridge	11 yrs. 4 mos. 13 days
1994	Dan Hirschman	10 yrs. 2 mos. 20 days

To become a Life Master is the dream of all serious bridge players. Some never make it in their lifetime; others seem to have a special gift for the game and become Life Masters within a very short time. To become a Life Master a player must win a specified number of masterpoints at different levels of play, including major bridge tournaments, and accumulate 300 of these "colored" masterpoints. A masterpoint is the unit which measures bridge achievement in tournament play.

The first person to be recognized in the *Official Encyclopedia of Bridge* as the youngest Life Master, was John R. Crawford. He earned the title in 1939 when he was 23 years old and held this honored position for nearly 13 years. Crawford went on to become one of the most famous bridge stars, winning many titles and championships during his career.

In 1952 Richard Freeman, a former "Quiz Kid" of radio fame, became a Life Master at the age of 18. He once challenged and defeated a computer in a race to score a bridge event. Freeman was unquestionably "The Fastest Pencil" in the days of manual tournament scorekeeping.

The first female to achieve the distinction of being the youngest Life Master was Diane Barton-Paine in 1961, just 12 days after her 18th birthday. The same year she became one of ACBL's youngest tournament directors.

Diane held the title of youngest female Life Master for 12 years, until Connie McGinley became a Life Master in 1973 at the age of 17 years, 5 months.

As more and more young players became seriously involved with the game of bridge, the age limit was quickly lowered. For example, the first female Life Master under the age of 17 was Regina Barnes. At 14 years and 11 months, she broke the record for both sexes in 1976. Six years later she was still the youngest female Life Master when her record was broken in 1982 by both Adair Gellman and Tricia Thomas. Adair was 14 years, 6 months and 4 days old, and Tricia was 14 years, and 26 days old. Tricia still holds the Youngest Female Life Master title and is listed as such in *Guinness Book of World Records*.

In 1965 Kyle Larsen became the first 15-year-old to become a Life Master. He was 15 years, 11 months. In 1968 he won the Reisinger Team trophy, thus becoming at 18 the youngest player ever to win a major NABC team title. In the years that followed he won half a dozen major championships.

Another 15-year-old, Bobby Levin, became the youngest Life Master in 1973. When he graduated from high school two years later he was named the *King of Bridge* by ACBL and the International Palace of Sports. In 1979 he won the Reisinger, Blue Ribbon and Lou Herman Trophies. In 1980 he won the Vanderbilt Knockout Team title. In 1981 he was a key member of the winning Ber-

muda Bowl team — the youngest player ever to capture that championship.

The players who became youngest Life Master in the Eighties have yet to make a substantial mark on the national and international scene — but they are younger than ever — with two preteens completing the prestigious list of a dozen Youngest Life Masters.

In 1980 Billy Hsieh became a Life Master at the age of 13 years, 7 months old. Then in 1981, Andrew Kaufman broke the record when he was 13 years, 4 months and 15 days old.

In 1981 Doug Hsieh astounded the bridge world by becoming a Life Master at the age of 11 years, 10 months and 4 days. Doug, younger brother of Billy Hsieh, is a member of a well-known bridge playing family of four ACBL Life Masters. When his achievement was announced by the ACBL one writer predicted that his record "is likely to stand well into the next century."

Doug held the title for almost seven years until Sam Hirschman came along in 1988. (Incidentally Sam's father Martin became a Life Master when he was 26.) Sam was 11 years, 9 months and 5 days old. His achievement received national recognition and was recorded in the *Guinness Book of World Records.*

It was felt that the record set by Sam Hirschman would never be broken, but on the final day of the 1990 Fall NABC in San Francisco, Joel Wooldridge of the Buffalo NY area assumed Hirschman's spot in the annals of bridge.

Wooldridge became a Life Master at the age of 11 years, 4 months and 13 days, breaking Hirschman's record by nearly five months. Wooldridge's accomplishment culminated a remarkable run for the precocious youngster. He had not seriously contemplated going for the Youngest Life Master crown until he and his mother, Jill, won the Mixed Pairs at the Toronto regional April 10, 1990.

Going from there and playing mostly with his mother, Joel earned his gold card in a breeze. Along the way, he was encouraged to go for the record by Martin Hirschman, Sam's father.

Wooldridge's record seemed virtually impregnable, but only four years later his mark was surpassed by more than a year. Dan Hirschman, brother of Sam, won enough points in the Midnight Knockouts at the 1994 Fall NABC in Minneapolis to go over the top at the age of 10 years, two months and 20 days. He collected all his gold (more than 100), red, silver and black points in only 15 events. As was the case with his older brother Sam, his mentor and frequent partner was his father Marty.

Marty introduced Dan to bridge when he was 4, but Dan wasn't interested. It wasn't until he was 9 that he decided to try duplicate. On his way to his gold card, Dan won two major regional events. And just as the Hirschmans helped Wooldridge to become the youngest LM, the Wooldridges in turn helped Dan to beat Wooldridge's record by joining the Hirschmans in a team game. In speaking of Dan's game, his father said he felt that defense was his strongest point.

Several other young players have become Life Masters while in their early teens in recent years, but none have come close to Hirschman's record. See KING OR QUEEN OF BRIDGE.

YOUTH PLAYER OF THE YEAR. The Youth Player of the Year award was established in 1990 by the American Contract Bridge League. The competition to determine the youth who wins the most masterpoints in a single year is restricted to contestants 19 or younger who had not reached their 20th birthday as of Dec. 31 of the previous year. For winners see Appendix II.

Z

ZERO. The lowest score possible on a duplicate board, hence loosely, a very bad score. It also refers to a lost board in a team-of-four contest. Note that a score on a board of zero points (all four hands pass) may be any matchpoint score from none to top.

ZERO OR TWO HIGHER LEAD. An opening lead convention designed to eliminate the ambiguity of standard honor leads. The lead of the 10 or 9 promises either zero or two higher honors in the suit, while the lead of the jack denies any higher honors. Leads of the ace, king, and queen retain their standard meanings. These leads may be used against any contract or only against notrump, and may also be used throughout the deal. Proponents claim that the opening leader's partner usually has no trouble deducing the true situation, and that it keeps declarer in the dark better than do JOURNALIST LEADS or RUSINOW LEADS. Opponents consider that they give too much away to the declarer.

ZIP KNOCKOUT TEAMS. Another name for COMPACT KNOCKOUT TEAMS. This type of event often is staged as a midnight game at regionals and North American Championships in the American Contract Bridge League. See BRACKETED KNOCKOUT TEAMS, COMPACT KNOCKOUT TEAMS, DOUBLE ELIMINATION KNOCKOUT TEAMS, HANDICAP KNOCKOUT TEAMS, MINI-KNOCKOUT TEAMS, MIXED TEAMS, OPEN TEAMS, RANDOM DRAW KNOCKOUT TEAMS, TEAM GAMES.

ZIP SWISS. A special version of Swiss Teams designed to be finished in a short time, usually as a one-session event at the end of a day's championship play. The usual format is to conduct the game with five-board matches, five minutes per board, and five matches per game. These events are sometimes played in Australia, with even shorter time limits.

ZIRINSKY FORMULA. A method of determining victory points long used in Far East Championships. All "push" boards (with zero IMPs) are scored as one to each team. Then the winning score is multiplied by four and divided by the losing score, with a maximum of eight VPs. The losing team receives the balance of the eight points at stake. The "push board" provision was introduced by the inventor, Victor Zirinsky of Hong Kong, as a modification to the original idea which gave inequitable results in low-scoring matches.

ZONAL. A championship of one of the World Bridge Federation's geographical zones, such as the European Championship.

AFRICAN BRIDGE FEDERATION. Recognized in 2000 as Zone 8 of the World Bridge Federation. For the four previous years, it was a sub-zone of The Bridge Federation of Asia and the Middle East. It has nine member countries: Botswana, Egypt, Kenya, Mauritius, Morocco, Reunion, South Africa, Tanzania, and Zimbabwe. Membership in 2000 was 3,978.

> President 2000:
> Bharat Bhardwaj
> P.O.Box 41625
> Nairobi, Kenya.
> Tel: 254 2 211 454
> Fax: 254 2 221 219

AMERICAN BRIDGE ASSOCIATION. Founded in 1932 as an organization in which American black players could play bridge. For details, see AMERICAN BRIDGE ASSOCIATION in Section I.

> ABA Headquarters
> 2828 Lakewood Drive SW, Atlanta GA 30315
> President: Cleo Terrell
> 8030 S. Indiana Rd., Chicago IL 60619
> 773-483-1348
> Vice President: Richard Bowling
> 1806 Sharpe Rd., Greensboro NC 27406
> 336-272-246
> Executive Secretary: Gloria Christler
> 2828 Lakewood Ave. SW, Atlanta GA 30315
> 404-768-5517
> Treasurer: Edward High
> 1709 Patton Ave., Charlotte NC 28216
> 704-375-3176
> Elise Gilman, Headquarters Keeper
> Gloria Christler, National Secretary

AMERICAN CONTRACT BRIDGE LEAGUE. Founded in 1937 as the result of a consolidation of the AMERICAN BRIDGE LEAGUE and the UNITED STATES BRIDGE ASSOCIATION. For details see UNITED STATES in this section and AMERICAN CONTRACT BRIDGE LEAGUE in Section I.

> ACBL Headquarters
> 2990 Airways Blvd., Memphis TN 38116

ANTIGUA CONTRACT BRIDGE ASSOCIATION. Membership in 2001 was 77.

> 1999 officers.
> President: Errol James
> Secretary: Merna Norde
> P.O.Box 384
> St. Johns, Antigua
> Tel: (268) 461 1208
> Fax: (268) 462 1444
> E-mail: jamesp@candw.ag

ARABIA. See SAUDI ARABIA.

ARGENTINE BRIDGE ASSOCIATION. (Asociacion del Bridge Argentino). Founded in 1934, the first association formed in South America. Member of the South American Bridge Confederation with 1,196 members in 2001. Sponsored teams that won the South American championship 18 times. Until Venezuela triumphed in 1965 was the only country to represent South America in the Bermuda Bowl. Represented South America in the Bermuda Bowl 11 times starting in 1958. GABARRET

CUP given to player who earns the most points in a year. Officers 2000:

> President: Ana V. de del Carril
> Secretary: Ana Maria Marchese
> Maipu 934 1006
> Buenos Aires, Argentina
> tel: 54 1 315 4544
> fax: 54 1 314 2238
> Web Site: www.bridgeargentino.org.ar

ARUBA BRIDGE FEDERATION. Founded in 1986 after separating from the Netherlands Antilles Bridge Association. Its Aruba Ariba club organized CAAC Championships in 1977 and 1988. 2001 membership was 58.

> Secretary: Adeline Eilers
> 17 Beaujonstraat, Oranjestad,
> Aruba, Dutch Caribbean
> Tel. (297) 8 24953
> Fax: 297 24 953

AUSTRALIAN BRIDGE FEDERATION. The Federation was founded in 1934 as the Australian Bridge Council, with New South Wales, Victoria and South Australia as members. It now covers all of Australia, and membership has risen from 2,000 in 1970 to more than 31,000 in 2000. Australia competes in championships of the Pacific Asia Bridge Federation and hosted the event in 1971, 1985 and 1995. Its teams have won the open title twice and the women's title eight times. Australia is a member of the South Pacific zone and has represented it in many world championships, finishing third in two Bermuda Bowls. Major Australian tournaments are played throughout the year, and the 2001 National Open Teams attracted an entry of about 300.

> Officers 2001:
> President: Keith McDonald
> Secretary: Dennis Yovich
> P.O. Box 397
> Fyshwick,
> ACT 2603 Australia
> Tel: 61 026 239 1816
> Fax: 61 026 239 1816
> E-mail: valbrockwell@ozemail.com.au

AUSTRIAN BRIDGE FEDERATION. (Austerreichischer Bridgesportverband). Founded in 1929 by Dr. Paul Stern, inventor of the Vienna (Austrian) System. He became its first president. 2,109 members in 1999. Austrian teams were extremely successful before World War II with these victories: European Open Teams 1932, 1933 and 1936, European Women's Teams 1935 and 1936, both titles World Championships 1937. Austrians have had several victories since World War II: World Pairs 1970, European Junior Teams 1976, European Open Pairs 1981, European Open Teams 1985, European Team Cup 1988, European Women's Teams 1991, European Junior Pairs 1991, European Women's Individual 1992, Women's Team Olympiad 1992, McConnell Cup 1998. The Federation organizes Open Team, Open Pair and Mixed Pair Championships, and numerous tournaments.

> 2001 contacts:
> Reischachstrasse 3, A-1010 Vienna, Austria
> Tel and Fax 43 1 713 1017

BAHAMAS BRIDGE LEAGUE. Organized under an-

other name in 1965 by the late Fred Rubbra. 24 members in 2001.

> Officers 1999
> President: Matthew Willian
> Secretary: Bill Weeks
> P.O. Box N1184
> Nassau, Bahamas
> Tel: (242) 323 6593
> Fax: (242) 328 0622
> E-mail: dcsands@bahamas.net.bs

BANGLADESH BRIDGE FEDERATION.
Membership in 2001 was 88.

> Dhaka Club
> Ramna Dhaka 2
> Bangladesh
> Fax: (880) 2 863 625

BARBADOS BRIDGE LEAGUE. Founded in 1966 by the late E.L. "Jimmy" Cozier. Hosts an annual international tournament at the end of October. Membership in 2001 was 65.

> Officers 1999:
> President: Hyacinth, Lady Burton
> Secretary: Adelie Springer
> 23 Pine Road, St. Michael, Barbados
> Tel: (246) 427 4839
> Fax: (246) 431 0510
> E-mail: tonyw@caribsurf.com

BELARUS. (Byelorussian Bridge Union). 2001 membership was 120.

> P.O. Box 133
> 220088 Minsk
> Belarus
> Tel and Fax: (375) 017 227 4854

BELGIAN BRIDGE FEDERATION. (Belgische Bridge Federatie, Federation Belge de Bridge - BBF-FBB). Founded in 1932 by a group of 13 clubs. In 1978 it divided into two leagues, the FLEMISH BRIDGE LEAGUE (VBL - Vlaamse Bridge Liga) and the LEAGUE OF THE BRIDGE CLUBS OF THE (BELGIAN) FRENCH COMMUNITY (LBF - Ligue des Cercles de Bridge de la Communaute Culturelle Francaise). The Belgian Federation hosted European Championships in 1935, 1965 and 1973, six Common Market (later European Union) Championships and one mixed European Championship, as well as numerous international events for Juniors such as the First World Junior Pairs in 1995 and the first University Teams in 1993. In 2001 there were 8,417 members in 200 clubs, and 8,147 individual members.

> President 1999: Francois Kilian
> Rue N.D. du Sommeil, 28/1, 1000 Brussels
> Belgium
> tel: 32.2.514.54.57
> fax +32.2.514.17.27

BELGISCHE BRIDGE FEDERATIE. (BBF-FBB). See BELGIAN BRIDGE FEDERATION.

BERMUDA BRIDGE ASSOCIATION. Unit 198 of ACBL and part of District 2. 160 members in 2000.
President: John Hoskins

> P.O.Box Hm 1345
> Hamilton Hm Hx, Bermuda

> (H) 441-234-7814
> Secretary: Stephanie Kyme
> Weeholme, 3 Old Slip Lane
> Pembroke HM 06, Bermuda
> (H) 809-295-4949
> (W) 809-296-2000
> All Correspondence to
> Bermuda Bridge Club
> 7 Pomander Road
> Paget PG 05, Bermuda

BFAME. See BRIDGE FEDERATION OF ASIA AND THE MIDDLE EAST.

BOLIVIAN BRIDGE ASSOCIATION. (Asociacion Boliviana de Bridge). Founded in 1968, and in 2001 had 115 members in three clubs. Conducts 5 national championships. Hosted 1989 South American Championships in Santa Cruz de la Sierra. Its players have won 2 South American Pairs titles.

> P.O. Box 635
> La Paz, Bolivia
> Tel: (591) 278 20 50
> Fax: 591 277 1656

BOTSWANA BRIDGE FEDERATION. Founded 1989. 2001 membership was 99.

> Officers 1999:
> Chairman: Walter Grisdale
> Public Relations Officer: Janet Pinard
> P.O. Box 802, Gaborone, Botswana
> Fax: 267 352 490
> E-mail: janetmp@global.bw

BRAZILIAN BRIDGE CONFEDERATION (CONFEDERACAO BRASILEIRA DE BRIDGE).
Founded in 1955, joining the bridge leagues of 7 states. By 2001 it had a membership of 2,978. Brazilian players have won the Bermuda Bowl, the World Teams, and the World Pairs twice. They have won the South American Teams 22 times and the South American Women's Teams 17 times.

> Officers 2001:
> President: Ernesto D'Orsi
> Avenida Brigadeiro Faria Lima 1685 Conj. 1B
> 01452-001 Sao Paulo S.P. Brazil.
> Phone 55 11 212 7904
> Fax 55 11 814 1518

BRIDGE FEDERATION OF ASIA AND THE MIDDLE EAST (BFAME). Approved by the WBF in 1979 and commissioned in 1980 as Zone 4 of the WBF, representing Asia and the Middle East. (Africa was added later, but became Zone 8 in 2000). Founded by P.C.Goenka of India and Mazhar Jafri of Pakistan who served as president and secretary - CEO for 16 years. Jafri became president in 1995. Federation has 11 NCBOs: Bangladesh, India, Jordan, Kuwait, Nepal, Pakistan, Palestine, Saudi Arabia, Sri Lanka, Syria, and Uzbekistan. They are divided into two sub-zones. Pakistan teams representing the zone finished second in world team championships in 1981 and 1986.

> Officers 2000:
> President: Mazhar Jafri
> President Emeritus: P.C. Goenka
> Secretary: Mukul Chatterjee, India

217-218 Central Hotel Annexe
Abdullah Haroon Road, Karachi
Pakistan.
Tel: (92-21) 568 1495 or 568 7102
Fax: (92-21) 568 6223

BRIDGE GREAT BRITAIN. Created on Jan. 1 2000 to fill a gap left by the closure of the British Bridge League when the Bridge Unions of England, Scotland and Wales were upgraded to National Federations within the European Bridge League and the World Bridge Federation. BGB has a core committee of one delegate each from England, Scotland and Wales to run the Gold Cup (knock-out championship of Britain) and the BGB Simultaneous Pairs. Money raised in the pair event is use to send teams from the three Federations to the European and World Championships. The Committee is expanded by delegates from the Northern Ireland Bridge Union and the CBAI (Contract Bridge Association of Ireland) to run the four Home Internationals series: the Camrose, Lady Milne (women), Junior Camrose (under 25s) and Peggy Bayer (under 20s). Sandra Claridge (brian.sandra@tesco.net) is secretary, and the first chairman was Gerard Faulkner. The chairman for 2001 is Patrick Jourdain
E-mail: PatrickJourdain@compuserve.com

BRITISH BRIDGE LEAGUE. Founded in 1931 by A.E. Manning-Foster, and reorganized in 1938 as a federal body. The members were English Bridge Union, Northern Ireland Bridge Union, Scottish Bridge Union, and Welsh Bridge Union, with a combined membership of 30,000. India, New Zealand and South Africa were formerly affiliated.

Until 1999, the League selected British teams for European Championships and world events. Their successes include wins in the 1955 Bermuda Bowl, 1981 and 1985 Venice Trophy, 1989 and 1995 World Junior Championship, and many European titles. In 1999, the European Bridge League decided, following a request by the English Bridge Union, that England, Northern Ireland, Scotland and Wales would be separately represented in international events. The British Bridge League then ceased to be an NCBO.

The League was host to the 1989 World Junior Championships in Nottingham and has staged many European Championships.

The League organizes the CAMROSE TROPHY for home international competition, together with under 25s and under 20s events, the GOLD CUP for open teams, the Portland Cup for Mixed Pairs, and the Lady Milne Cup for Women's Teams.

Officers 1999:
President: Russell McClymont
Secretary, Anna Gudge
The Old Railway Station
Long Melford, Sudbury,
Suffolk CO1O 9HN England
Tel. 44 (1) 787 881920
Fax: 44 (1) 787 881339
E-mail: anna@ecats.co.uk

BULGARIAN BRIDGE FEDERATION. Founded in 1980 and had 450 members in 1999. Organizes annual team, pair and mixed championships. Hosted 1988 European Junior Championships. Bulgarian women players have won the European Women's Pairs and bronze medals in 1988 World Team Olympiad. 2001 membership was 550.

Officers 1999:
President: Christo Drumev
Address: 18 Vassil Aprilov Str.
1504, Sofia, Bulgaria
Tel 00359 2 543 121
Fax 00359 2 902 042
E-mail: drumev@tusk.icn.bg

CAAC. See CENTRAL AMERICAN AND CARIBBEAN BRIDGE FEDERATION.

CAC. See CENTRAL AMERICAN AND CARIBBEAN BRIDGE FEDERATION.

CANADIAN BRIDGE FEDERATION. An organization within the ACBL that handles Canada's national tournaments – Open Teams, Women's Teams, Open Pairs. It also handles other matters of a strictly Canadian nature, such as selection of teams to represent Canada in world championship events. Headquarters are located at
279 Jolly Place, Regina SK, Canada
Phone 306-761-1677;
Fax 306-789-4919;
E-mail: can.bridge.fed@sk.sympatico.ca

The history of organized bridge in Canada is linked inextricably with the evolution of the American Contract Bridge League. After the invention of contract, players in Canada organized themselves into regional entities which eventually coalesced with larger organizations centered south of the border. Eastern-Central and Western Canada followed different paths. The former was always aligned with the ACBL, even before that organization became predominant in North America. Western Canada, on the other hand, was originally a part of the Pacific Bridge League which amalgamated with the ACBL in 1955. These two separate histories are reflected today in the size difference between eastern-central and western Canadian units: the latter usually are smaller geographically.

By the 1960s Canadian membership in the ACBL had surpassed 10,000, due mainly to the stimulus provided by the ACBL's club and tournament programs. As much as Canadians enjoyed ACBL bridge, they still lacked an organization that linked them directly. The Canadian Bridge Federation (CBF) came to fill this void.

The impetus for creating the CBF was the 1960 World Team Olympiad, a new opportunity for international competition created by the fledgling World Bridge Federation. This was a competition where each country would be represented by its own national team. By then, Canadian experts such as Eric Murray, Sami Kehela, Bruce Elliott and Pearcy Sheardown had made their mark on the North American scene. They, and a younger phalanx of budding Canadian superstars, took up the challenge of playing for Canada. Canada's effort at the first Olympiad was moderately successful. Things improved in 1964 when Canada finished an impressive fourth.

It soon became obvious that some sort of entity was needed to organize national competition for selection of international teams, and, if possible, to provide them with both moral and financial support. Murray was the prime instigator of the new, as yet unnamed, organization. The organization began as an informal coast-to-coast network of supporters which gradually evolved into a more concrete structure.

At the 1965 Nationals in Chicago, a group of Canadian organizers and enthusiasts, led by Murray, made the historic decision to create the Canadian Bridge Federation. This would be a voluntary association of Canadian ACBL units where each member unit would decide the level of its financial contribution. Besides Murray, the Chicago group included: Henry Smilie, Vancouver; Doug Cannell, Winnipeg; Chuck Jane, Woodstock; Bill Robinson, Al Lando, and Doug Drew, Toronto; Aaron Goodman, Montreal; and Don Dobson, Halifax. Together, these individuals represented more than 80% of Canadian ACBL members.

Chuck Jane undertook the mammoth task of devising the first trials format and organizing a nationwide group of volunteers to conduct local events for qualification to a national final. The CBFs first playdown culminated in a national final held in Winnipeg in September, 1967.

The CBF has grown and changed since those early years. The current constitution provides for six zones, each represented by a Zone Director. The zones comprise units which are grouped more or less according to geography.

Units remain the cornerstone of the CBF since they elect the Zone Directors and continue to contribute financially on a voluntary basis. A historic event occurred in 1990 when the ACBL agreed to levy CBF membership fees from individual Canadian ACBL members and turn these funds over to the CBF. The CBF now represents all players, not just champions vying for international competition. This has required a rethinking of the aims of the organization, and the CBF is now in the process of developing programs having broad appeal including, for example: flighted national championships; a magazine tailored to a wider readership; various educational initiatives, and promoting bridge in a broader spectrum of Canadian institutions.

President: Nicholas Gartaganis
1816 Braeside Place SW
Calgary AB T2W 0Z5
403-253-2767
Nick.Gartaganis@gov.ab.ca
gartagan@cadvision.com
Vice President: Ray Lee
331 Douglas Avenue, Toronto ON
416 -781-9327 (p)
416 781-1831 (f)
416-781-0351 (MPP phone)
masterpointpress@home.com
Executive Secretary/Treasurer: Jan Anderson
2719 East Jolly Place, Regina SK S4V 0X8
CBF HOTLINE
306-761-1677 (p)
306-789-4919(f)
can.bridge.fed@sk.sympatico.ca
Editor: Jude Goodwin-Hanson,
604-898-1013 (H&W),
604-898-1023 (F)
P.O. Box 3104
Garibaldi Highlands, BC V0N 1T0;
E-mail: jude@cbf.ca

CENTRAL AMERICAN AND CARIBBEAN BRIDGE FEDERATION (CACBF). Founded in 1971 with E.L.Cozier as president. Recognized in 1976 as Zone 5 of the World Bridge Federation. Member countries in 1999 were: Antigua, Aruba, Bahamas, Barbados, Colombia, Costa Rica, Dominica, Dominican Republic, French Guyana, Grenada, Guadeloupe, Guatemala, Guyana, Haiti, Jamaica, Martinique, Netherlands Antilles, Panama, St. Kitts and Nevis, St. Lucia, Suriname, Trinidad and Tobago, Venezuela, Virgin Islands. Total membership in 2000 was 2,298.

Officers 1999:
President: Felicity Reid
32 Markway Manor
Kingston 8, Jamaica
Tel: (876) 925 4208
Secretary: Lillian Morganti
Centro de Bridge de Caracas
Quinto Ekeko, 2a Calle de Campo
Alegre, Caracas, Venezuela
Tel: (582) 262 1160
Fax: (571) 312 2649

CHILEAN BRIDGE FEDERATION (Federacion Chilena de Bridge). Founded in 1951, it had a membership in 2001 of 968. Chile hosted the 1993 world team championships in Santiago and the South American Championships in 1951, 1957, 1965, 1972, 1979, 1984 and 1987.

Officers 1999:
President: Horacio Valdes
Av. Escriva de Balaguer 5428
Vitacura, Santiago, Chile
Tel: 52 206 4030
Fax: 52 22 336 516

CHINESE BRIDGE ASSOCIATION. Founded in 1980. In 1999, there were 73 groups, organized by province and city. 2001 membership was 55,000.

Officers 1999:
President Emeritus: Wan Li
President: Rong Gaotang
Executive Vice President &
Secretary General: Liu Gang
9 Tiyuguan Road, Beijing, China 100763
Tel: 8610 6504 4062, 65044062
Fax: 86-10-65043842, 65044062
E-mail: ccba@ccba.org.cn
Web Site: www.ccba.org.cn

CHINESE TAIPEI. See TAIWAN.

COLOMBIAN BRIDGE FEDERATION (Federacion Colombiana de Bridge). Founded in 1963 by clubs in Bogota, Medelin, Barranquilla, Cali and Pereira. Hosted the South American Championships in 1968 and 1975, winning the Women's Team title in 1968, 1970 and 1976. Hosted the Central American and Caribbean Championships in 1980 and 1989, and won both CACC titles in 1989. Membership in 2001 was 398.

Tel. (57) 2 558054
Fax: (57) 404483
E-mail: romanlee@axesnet.com

COSTA RICA NATIONAL BRIDGE ASSOCIATION (Asociacion Nacional de Bridge de Costa Rica). 2001 membership was 94.

Officers 1999
President: Amalia Meltzer
Secretary: Pilar Vitoria
Apartado Postal 3075-1000
San Jose, Costa Rica

Tel: 506 232 9154
Fax: 506 220 1741
E-mail: amelsa@sol.recsa.co.cr

CROATIAN BRIDGE FEDERATION. In 2001, the memberships was 410.
Aleksandar Ivancic
Kraiska 19
41000, Zagreb, Croatia
Tel: 385 1 610 2608
Fax: 385 1 611 5741
Web Site: www.bridge.hr

CYPRUS BRIDGE ASSOCIATION. In 2001, the membership was 153.
64 John Kennedy Avenue,
P.O. Box 25467. 1076 Nicosia, Cyprus
Tel and Fax: 357 2 516 221

CZECH BRIDGE ASSOCIATION. Founded in 1932 but closed by the Communist government in 1941. Revived in 1965, about 500 members in 2001.
President: Lubosh Batela
PS 1063, 11121 Praha 1
Czech Republic
Tel: 420 2 231 9719
Fax: 420 2 7211 2410
E-mail: bahnikp@ms.anet.cz

DANISH BRIDGE LEAGUE (Danmarks Bridge-forbund). Founded in 1939 when Dansk Bridge Liga and Dansk Bridge Union, both founded in 1933, were unified. The first international event in Denmark was a match against Great Britain in 1932, won by Denmark. In 1933 Denmark joined the EBL, came third in its first European Championship, and since has participated regularly. After World War II Denmark restarted the European Championships in Copenhagen. Danish women were the most successful, from 1938 to 1959, winning six European Championships.

In the 80s a new generation made its way to the top and won Olympiad gold in Venice 1988. One of the pairs, Bettina Kalkerup - Charlotte Palmund, is the most successful Danish pair ever, also taking silver in the World Women's Pairs 1984. Danish open teams have won three bronze medals in world competition and four medals, two silver and two bronze, in zonal play. The Danish Junior team won the world title in 1997 and the European title in 1970.

In the 70s, the League began a period of expansion under Gunnar Zabel as chairman, ending with a masterpoint scheme, a publishing firm, a book store, a secretariat, and a full-time general secretary. Membership grew rapidly with 29,980 in 2001. All towns of a moderate size have bridge clubs and/or bridge schools, and they participate actively in League activities.

The most common systems in Denmark are inspired by Standard American and Acol, very often mixed to some extent. Five Card Majors is a more and more common approach among the top pairs. The official magazine of the bridge league, *Dansk Bridge*, founded in 1941, goes to all members. See BRIDGE TOURNAMENT FOR CLUBS IN COPENHAGEN.
Address: Asmindereodgade 53
DK-3480 Fredensborg
Denmark
Tel: (45) 48 47 52 13

Fax: (45) 48 47 62 13
Web Site: www.bridge.dk

DOMINICA (Commonwealth of Dominica Bridge Association). Membership in 2001 was 22.
Officers 2001:
President: Dorian Shillingford
Secretary: Peter Israel
37 King George V Street,
Roseau, Dominica
Tel: (1809) 448 4839
Fax: (1809) 448 1762
E-mail: to: shillingfordd@cwdom.dm

EBL. See EUROPEAN BRIDGE LEAGUE.

ECUADOR BRIDGE FEDERATION (Federacion Ecuadoriana de Bridge). Founded in 1952. In 2001 had a membership of 92. Hosted 1998 South American Championships.
Casilla 17.21.01260
Edificio Albatros, 6to Piso, Suite 603
Av de los Shyris 1240 y Portugal
Quito. Ecuador
Fax: 593 2 432 997

EGYPTIAN BRIDGE FEDERATION. Founded in 1934 as the Association Egyptienne de Bridge. Its women's team won the 1960 world title (as United Arab Republics) and BFAAME titles in 1987 and 1991. Its open team won the BFAAME title in 1989. Membership in 2001 was 440.
P.O.Box 11361
15 El-Zohour St. - Hediko Buildings
El-Oroba Way
Cairo, Egypt
Tel: 20 2 267 3587
Tel: 20 2 268 1032
Web Site: www.egybf.com

ENGLISH BRIDGE UNION. Founded in 1938 as the successor to the Duplicate Bridge Control Board. Once a member of the British Bridge League, where its players achieved many international successes representing Great Britain, but from 2000 an independent NCBO. The EBU was host to European Championships in 1950, 1961, 1975, 1981 and 1987. In 2001 it had a membership of about 28,000 in more than 1000 clubs.
Officers, 2000:
Chairman, David Harris
General Manager, Phil Lloyd
Broadfields, Bicester Road
Aylesbury, Bucks. HP19 8AZ England
Tel: (44) 01296 317200
E-mail: Postmaster@ebu.co.uk
Web Site: www.ebu.co.uk

ESTONIAN TOURNAMENT BRIDGE LEAGUE (Eesti Turniiribridzgiliit). 1999 memberships was 485.
Officers 1999:
President: Kalle Pedak
Vice President: Aavo Heinlo
10502 PO BOX 14, Tallinn, Estonia
Phone: (+372-2) 53 22 05
Fax (+372-2) 43 41 72
E-mail: aavo.heinlo@stat.ee

EUROPEAN BRIDGE LEAGUE. Founded in 1947 at Copenhagen by delegates from the bridge federations of eight countries (Belgium, Denmark, Finland, France, Great Britain, The Netherlands, Norway, and Sweden). All were members of the INTERNATIONAL BRIDGE LEAGUE, which they voted to dissolve to form a new league, in a new setting, Denmark. A. I. E. Lucardie was elected president, and Herman Dedichen (at whose instigation the meeting was called) was named honorary secretary. EBL congresses have always been combined with the European Championships. In 1948 the League was a member of the group of three, with the Portland Club and ACBL, that issued the International Laws of Bridge.

In 2000, the EBL was the largest WBF zone, both in terms of NCBOs (44) and individuals membership (366,852). Member countries are: Andorra, Armenia, Austria, Belarus, Belgium, Bulgaria, Croatia, Cyprus, Czech Republic, Denmark, England, Estonia, Faroe Islands, Finland, France, Germany, Greece, Hungary, Iceland, Ireland, Israel, Italy, Lebanon, Liechtenstein, Lithuania, Luxembourg, Malta, Monaco, Netherlands, Norway, Poland, Portugal, Romania, Russia, San Marino, Scotland, Slovenia, Spain, Sweden, Switzerland, Turkey, Ukraine, Wales, Yugoslavia.

The European Championship results, listed in Appendix III, include the prewar events held under the auspices of the International Bridge League. Similarly, there were no European Championships in 1960, 1964, 1968, 1972 and 1976 because World Team Olympiads took place in those years. When the WBF decided to hold the BERMUDA BOWL competition in the odd-numbered years only, starting in 1977, the European Championships also became a biennial event, to be held shortly prior to each Bermuda Bowl.

Some of the many contributions of the European Bridge League and its constituent bodies to bridge on the international level include: European Match Points (later called INTERNATIONAL MATCHPOINTS); procedures for recording in detail a large number of matches played simultaneously; the development of BRIDGE-O-RAMA; and the custom of using English as the international bridge language.

Considerable contributions to the development of international bridge in Europe have been made by: A. J. E. Lucardie (IBL president 1933-34 and 1938- 39); Sir A. Noel Mobbs of England (EBL president 1948- 50); Baron Robert de Nexon (EBL president 1950-65); Count Carl Bonde (EBL president 1965-69); Marchese Silvio Carini-Mazzaccara EBL president 1970-73); André Lemaitre (EBL president 1974-80); Nils Jensen (president 1981-87); Herman Dedichen (EBL secretary 1947 -58); Ernst Heldring (EBL secretary 1958-71); Wolf Achterberg (EBL secretary 1971-79); David Bardach (EBL secretary 1979-1993). Because of their impressive contributions to the EBL, the following have been elected President Emeritus: Baron de Nexon (1965); Geoffrey Butler (1974); Nils Jensen (1987).

> President 2000:
> Gianarrigo Rona
> Via Ciro Menotti 11/C
> I-20129 Milano, Italy
> Tel: 39 02 7000 0483
> Fax: 39 02 7000 1398

For results of EBL Championships, see Appendix III.

FAR EAST BRIDGE FEDERATION. See PACIFIC ASIA BRIDGE FEDERATION.

FEDERATION BELGE DE BRIDGE (FBB-BBF). See BELGIAN BRIDGE FEDERATION.

FINLAND, BRIDGE LEAGUE OF (Suomen Bridgeliitto - Finlands Bridgeforbund). Founded in 1936 by the Helsingfors Bridge Club and Bridge Club Spades, the two clubs then in existence. In 1999 it had 1782 members and 52 clubs. Hosted European Championships in 1953 and 1989, the Nordic Championships in 1957, 1971, 1982 and 1994.

> Executive Officer: Kauko Kostinen
> Perttulantie 6
> 00210 Helsinki, Finland
> Tel 358 9 6848168
> Fax: 358 9 6871 4110
> E-mail: kaukokostinen@bridge.pp.fi
> Web Site: personal.eunet.fi/pp.Ineimo

FLEMISH BRIDGE LEAGUE (Vlaamse Bridge Liga - VBL). Founded in 1978 as a result of a Belgian law change that would henceforth provide support to only sporting organizations that would split into regional organisations. In 1999 there were 6,333 members in 137 clubs.

> Officers 1999:
> President: Jules Hendrickx
> Director: Eric Smets
> Boomgaardstraat 22/45, 2600 Antwerpen
> tel: +32.3.286.07.58, fax +32.3.286.58.10
> web-site: www.vbl.be,
> E-mail: carine@vbl.skynet.be
> bi-monthly publication : Bridge Kontakt

See BELGIAN BRIDGE FEDERATION.

FRANCE. See FRENCH BRIDGE FEDERATION.

FRENCH BRIDGE FEDERATION (Federation Francaise de bridge). Founded in 1933. Membership in 2001 was 81,420. Victories in international events include 6 world team championships, one world pairs, 7 European teams and 10 European women's teams. Has hosted 5 world championships and 1 European Championship.

> Officers 1999:
> President: Bernard Liochon
> 73 Avenue Charles de Gaulle,
> 92200 Neuilly sur Seine, France
> Tel. 33-1 41 43 7700
> Fax: 33-1 47 38 66 74

FRENCH GUYANA BRIDGE LEAGUE (Comite de Bridge de Guyane). 2001 membership was 77.

> Officers 1999:
> President: Jean Jacques Leothaud
> P.O. Box 599
> Cayenne, French Guiana
> Tel. (594) 31-32-71
> Fax: 594 316 368
> E-mail: ffbguyan@citeweb.net

FRENCH POLYNESIA. 2001 membership was 142.

> BP 524, 98713 Papeete
> Tahiti, French Polynesia

GERMAN BRIDGE LEAGUE (Deutscher Bridge-Verbund). Founded in 1932, disbanded in World War II, refounded in 1949 and by 2001 had approximately 24,536

members. Hosted European Championships in 1963 in Baden-Baden and 1983 in Wiesbaden, and the European Mixed Championships in 1998 in Aachen. Its Open Team won the Rosenblum Cup in 1990, and its Women's Team won the Venice Cup in 1995 and the European Women's Teams in 1989. Germany's team won the World Junior Teams in 1993.

> President 2001:
> Dr. Walter Hoeger
> Wolframs-Eschenbacher-Strasse 60
> D-90449 Nurnberg, Germany
> Tel: 49 911 67 31 14
> Fax: 49 911 672 2125
> Web Site: www.bridge-verband.de/index.htm

GREAT BRITAIN. See BRITISH BRIDGE LEAGUE.

GREEK BRIDGE FEDERATION (HELLENIC BRIDGE FEDERATION). Founded in 1965 by two clubs with about 320 members. By 2001 it had a membership of 2,550 with 27 affiliated clubs. Organized the 1971 European Championships and the 2000 Generali Masters Individual in Athens; sends representatives to European Championships and World Olympiads. National championships include Open Teams and Open Pairs. Publishes a bimonthly magazine and distributes it free of charge to members.

> Officers 2001:
> President: George Karlaftis
> Secretary-General: Spiros Koutroumbas
> 30, Phidipidou Str., Athens 115 27 Greece
> Tel: 30 1 74 80 400-2
> Fax: 31 1 74 80 403
> E-mail: press@bridge.org.gr

GRENADA.

> Secretary: Brenda Williams
> Grenada Bridge Club,
> P.O. Box 221
> St. George's, Grenada W.I.
> Tel: (473) 4435328
> Fax: (473) 4404113
> E-mail: brenwil@caribsurf.com

GUADELOUPE BRIDGE ASSOCIATION. 145 members in 2001.

GUATEMALA BRIDGE ASSOCIATION. 2001 membership was 55.

> Fax: 502 369 6850

GUYANA BRIDGE LEAGUE. Founded before 1975, participates in the Inter-Guyanas Team Championship, the oldest annual tournament in the CACBF area. 2001 membership was 20.

> Officers 1999
> President: Andrew Kartick
> Secretary: Marilyne Trotz
> 100-101 Regent Street
> Lacytown, Georgetown, Guyana
> Tel: 592 2 60 543
> Fax: (592) 2-61939
> E-mail: mbeepat@networksgy.com

HAITI BRIDGE ASSOCIATION (Association de Bridge de Haiti). 2000 membership was 55.

> President 1999:
> Dr. Raymond Hyppolyte,
> Cercle Bellevue, Port-au-Prince, Haiti
> Tel: (509) 463558
> Fax: (509) 460699

HONG KONG CONTRACT BRIDGE ASSOCIATION. Founded in 1951 by J.M. Remedios, E.M. Marchetti and Victor Zirinsky, with a nucleus of Hong Kong social clubs. Membership in 2001 was 274. Won Far East Open (PABF) Teams titles in 1960, 1965, 1973 and 1983, and hosted the Championships in 1959, 1960, 1976 and 1987.

> 1999 officers:
> Chairman: Derek Zen
> Vice-Chairman: Anthony Ching
> G.P.O Box 1445, Hong Kong
> Tel: 813 33 573 741
> Fax: 813 33 577 444
> Web Site: home.netvigator.com/~hkcba/

HUNGARIAN BRIDGE FEDERATION. In 2001 the membership was 968.

> Geza Stepanos
> Bajza-u 52, H-1062 Budapest, Hungary
> Tel: 36 1 269 5181
> Fax: 36 1 269 5184
> Web Site: www.ecosoft.hu/bridge

ICELANDIC BRIDGE FEDERATION. (Bridgesamband Islands). Founded in 1948 by 6 leading clubs. By 2001 there were 3,343 members in 46 clubs. Won Bermuda Bowl 1991, Transnational Mixed Teams 1996, Nordic Open Championship 1988, 1992, 1994, Nordic Women's Championship 1990, Nordic Junior Championship 1997.

> Officers 2000:
> President: Gudmundur Agustsson
> Secretary: Stefania Skarphedinsdottir
> Thonglabakki 1, P.O.box 9238
> IS-129 Reykjavik, Iceland
> Tel: +354 587 9360
> Fax: +354 587 9361
> E-mail: bridge@bridge.is
> website: www.bridge.is

INDIAN BRIDGE FEDERATION (Bridge Federation of India). Founded in 1958 by 4 state bridge associations: Andhra Pradesh, Maharashtra, South India and West Bengal. Its founder-president was Ramniwas Ramnarain Ruia of Bombay, who held the office until 1970 and died in 1978. There are now 34 member associations, some geographical entities and some government bodies such as the railways. There were about 16,000 registered players in 1999.

Indian teams have had many successes at the international level. The open team was a semifinalist in the 1988 World Teams and won the 1977 Far East Teams. It won the BFAAME Open Teams 1997 and finished second five times. The Indian women's team won the BFAAME title in 1981, 1983, 1985, 1989, 1993, and was second three times.

> Officers 1999:
> President Emeritus: P.C.Goenka
> President: Y. Kamalakara Rao
> Hon. Secretary: Mukul Chatterjee

23, V.P.R. Road
625 014 Madurai, India
Tel: 91 452 532 397
Fax: 91 452 531 737

INDONESIAN CONTRACT BRIDGE ASSOCIATION (GABUNGAN BRIDGE SELURUH INDONESIA). Founded in 1953, and by 2001 had a membership of 5,063. It hosted the 1995 World Junior Teams. Its players have won the PABF (Far East) Team title 12 times, and represented the zone in the Bermuda Bowl eight times and the Venice Cup once. Indonesia was second in the 1996 World Open Teams.

Jl Jend Urip Sumohardjo 31E
13310 Jakarta, Indonesia
Tel: 62 21 819 4409
Fax: 62 21 856 9118
Web Site: www.bridgeindonesia.com

IRELAND, CONTRACT BRIDGE ASSOCIATION OF. Founded in 1932 in Dublin to control the game in the Republic of Ireland. In 2001 there were about 27,000 members organized through 520 clubs. The organization hosted the European Championships in 1952, 1967 and 1991. For international participation, see IRISH BRIDGE UNION. See also NORTHERN IRELAND BRIDGE UNION.

Officers 2001
President: Seamus Dowling
General Secretary: Paul Porteous
C.B.A.I.
Templeogue House,
Dublin 6W, Ireland
Tel: 353 1 492 9666
Fax: 353 1 492 9751
E-mail: irebridge@indigo.ie

IRISH BRIDGE UNION. Founded in 1955, the union consists of representatives from the CONTRACT BRIDGE ASSOCIATION OF IRELAND and the NORTHERN IRELAND BRIDGE UNION. It is responsible for selecting teams to represent the whole of Ireland in World Olympiads and European Championships (but not for CAMROSE TROPHY matches), and for organizing all-Ireland events for teams and pairs. Registered membership was 1367 in 2001.

2001 officers:
President: Mrs. Kay Murphy
Joint Honorary Secretaries
Mrs Kay Downes
8 Orchardstown Park
Dublin 14, Ireland
Tel. 353 1 4947726
E-mail: kaydownes@eircom.net
Dr. Alan Hill
161 Moss Road, Lambeg,
Lisburn, Co. Antrim, Ireland
Tel. 028 92 601882
E-mail: alan.hill@qub.ac.uk

ISRAEL BRIDGE FEDERATION Founded in 1940 as the Palestine Bridge Federation. Present name was adopted in 1948. It had 6,536 members in 1992, in more than 40 branches. It hosted the 1974 European Championships in Herzlia and the 1980 European Team Championship in Tel Aviv. Israel teams have twice been second in the European Championships, and placed third in the 1985 Bermuda

Bowl. The Federation sponsors an International Bridge Festival, held in Tel Aviv in February annually since 1966.

Officers 2001:
President: Zvi Ben Tovim
General Manager: Noah Tymianker
P.O. Box 9671, Haifa, Israel 31096
Tel: 972 4 833 5333
Fax: 972 4 833 6343
E-mail: zbt@zahav.net.il

ITALIAN BRIDGE FEDERATION (FEDERAZIONE ITALIANA GIOCO BRIDGE). Founded in 1937 by Paolo Baroni, Federico Rosa and Enzo Pontremoli. Reactivated after World War II with Carl'Alberto Perroux as president, and became an official body organizing regular national events. In 2001 there were 28,825 members in 350 affiliated bodies. In February 1993 FIGB was recognized by the Italian Olympic Committee (CONI) as an associated discipline. More than 15 national championships involving 8,000-9,000 players are organized annually. The knockout teams contest for the Italian Cup attracts annually more than 900 teams. In 1994 FIGB signed an agreement with the Italian Ministry of Education to make bridge an optional school subject and from 1994 to 1998 more than 7,000 students between the ages of 12 and 18 were involved in the project.

The record of the Italian BLUE TEAM is extraordinary and is unlikely to be equaled. The first Italian team to compete in the European Championships in 1938 was the predecessor of the invincibles who became European champions 1951, 1956, 1957, 1958, 1959, 1965, 1967, 1969, 1971, 1973, 1975, 1976, 1979. They won 16 world team titles: Bermuda Bowl 1957-69 and 1973-75, World Team Olympiad 1964, 1968, 1972.

Italy won Rosenblum Cup 1998, European Teams 1995 and 1997, World Mixed Pairs 1998. The FIGB has been host to eight world championships, second only to the United States, from 1951 to 1992.

Officers, 1999:
President, Gianarrigo Rona
Secretary, Niki Di Fabio
Via Ciro Menotti, 11/C
20129 Milan, Italy
Tel. (39) 2 7000 483
Fax (39) 2 7001 398
E-mail: fedbridge@galactica.it
Web Site: www.federbridge.it

JAMAICA BRIDGE ASSOCIATION. Founded in Kingston in 1944 and in 2001 had a membership of 68. Hosted 1987 Bermuda Bowl, Venice Cup in Ocho Rios, hosted CACBF Championships in 1972, 82, 95. Represented Zone 5 in the 1983 Bermuda Bowl.

Officers 2001:
President: Charles Williams
Secretary: Elizabeth Hall
29 The Pines, 15 Millsborough Avenue
Kingston 6, Jamaica
Tel: (876) 927-7650
E-mail: com" halls@cwjamaica.com

JAPAN CONTRACT BRIDGE LEAGUE. Founded in Tokyo in 1953 with 11 members. By 2001 the membership had grown to 5,897 with 124 affiliated clubs. Hosted 1991 Bermuda Bowl and Venice Cup in Yokohama, and the Far East Championships in 1958, 1964, 1979 and 1998.

Hosted 3 Epson international tournaments 1983-4-5 and 3 NEC Bridge Festivals 1995,1997, 1998.
> Officers 1999:
> President: Kensuke Yanagiya
> Secretary: Tadayoshi Nakatani
> Address: 4th Floor, TJK Yotsuya Bldg.,
> 1-13 Yotsuya,
> Shinjuku-ku, Tokyo 160-0004, Japan
> Telephone: 81-3-3357-3741
> Fax: 81-3-3357-7444

Web Site: www2h.meshnet.or.jp/~jcbl/index.html

JORDANIAN BRIDGE ASSOCIATION. 2001 membership 220.
> Tel: (962) 655 26 990
> Fax: (962) 655 25 340

KENYA BRIDGE ASSOCIATION. 2001 membership 110.
> P.O.BOX 42914
> Nairobi, Kenya
> Tel: (254) 2 228 944
> Fax: (254) 2 318 931

KUWAIT BRIDGE COMMITTEE. The game was introduced to Kuwait in 1950 and played in private clubs until 1957 when a national organization was founded. Joined BFAME in 1981. There were 80 members playing in one club in 2001.
> 1999: President: Sa'id Sulaiman Al-Saleh
> P.O. Box 9226
> 61003 Ahmadi, Kuwait
> Tel: 965 361 2101
> Fax: 965 398 1585

LEAGUE OF THE BRIDGE CLUBS OF THE (BELGIAN) FRENCH COMMUNITY (Ligue des cercles de Bridge de la communaute culturelle Francaise - LBF). Founded in 1978 as a result of a Belgian law change that would henceforth provide support only to sporting organizations that would split into regional organizations. In 1999 there were 2,800 members in 60 clubs.
> Officers 1999:
> President: Albert Vanescote
> Rue des Deux Eglises, 133/6, 1210 Bruxelles
> Belgium
> tel: +32.2.514.53.82, fax +32.2.230.68.95
> bi-monthly publication : Bridge Info

See BELGIAN BRIDGE FEDERATION

LEBANESE BRIDGE FEDERATION (Federation Libanaise de Bridge). Founded in 1949 by 3 Beirut clubs and hosted the 1962 European Championships in Beirut. Lebanon was represented in most European Championships and World Olympiads in spite of the Civil War between 1975 and 1991. Membership in 2001 was 200.
> President: Georges Fayad
> Secretary: Gaby Merhy
> P.O. Box 54 Beirut, Lebanon
> Tel: 961 1 201 023
> Fax: 961 1 647 947

Web Site: www.cyberia.net.lb/BRIDGE/flb.htm

LIECHTENSTEIN BRIDGE UNION (Liechtensteinische Bridge Vereinigung). 2001 membership was 103.
> President 1999: P. Sprenger

> Postfach 183
> FL-9490 Vaduz, Liechtenstein
> Tel: (41) 75 237 0607
> Fax: (41) 75 237 0666

LIGUE DES CERCLES DE BRIDGE DE LA COMMUNAUTE CULTURELLE FRANCAISE (LBF). see LEAGUE OF THE BRIDGE CLUBS OF THE (BELGIAN) FRENCH COMMUNITY.

LITHUANIA BRIDGE ASSOCIATION (Lietuvos Sportinio Bridzo Asociacija). 2001 membership was 80.
> Pamelkanio Street 14
> 2001 Vilnius, Lithuania
> Tel: (370) 2 627 015
> Fax: (370) 2 628 281

LUXEMBOURG BRIDGE FEDERATION (Federation Luxembourgeoise de Bridge). Founded in 1979 and in 2001 had 155 members, comprising 17 nationalities.
> Secretary: David Thompson
> 12 Rue Massarett
> L-2137 Luxembourg
> Tel: (352) 432 962

MACAU BRIDGE ASSOCIATION (Associacao de Bridge de Macau). Founded 1944. 2001 membership was 70.
> Officers 1999:
> President: Dr. Francisco M. Dias
> Secretary: Nuno S. Mata
> Apta. 13A, Edif. Ka Vo, No. 30
> Praca Lobo d'Avila, Macau via Hong Kong
> Tel: 853 312 085
> Fax: 853 312 180

MALAYSIAN CONTRACT BRIDGE ASSOCIATION. Founded in 1961. 93 members in three branches in 2001. Hosted Far East Championships (PABF) in 1968, 1986, and Asean Bridge Club Championships in 1982, 1987, 1990 and 1994.
> 9.06 Wisma Inai, 241 Jalan Tun Razah
> 50400 Kuala Lumpur, Malaysia
> Tel: 60 3 245 4882
> Fax: 60 3 248 7868.
> E-mail: trumps@pop.myweb.com.my

MALTA BRIDGE ASSOCIATION. 2001 membership was about 100.
> "Zia"
> Palm Street, The Gardens
> St. Julians STJ 12, Malta
> Tel: 356 380 333
> Fax: 356 380 555
> Web Site: www.bridge.org.mt

MARTINIQUE BRIDGE COMMITTEE (Comité de Bridge de la Martinique). 2001 officers
> President: Jean Yves Dabreteau
> c/o Bamex, 97292 Lamentin
> Cedex 2, Martinique
> Tel: (596) 640011
> Fax: (596) 502071
> E-mail: bamex@cgit.com

MAURITIUS BRIDGE LEAGUE. Founded in 1960, and in 2001 had 100 members organized in 7 clubs. Hosted the 1983 BFAME Championships, and its open team finished second in 1987.

> President 1999: Pierre Philogene
> Alpha Bridge Club
> Old Moka Road,
> St. Jean, Quatre Bornes
> Mauritius
> Tel: (230) 454 3810
> Fax: (230) 636 8695

MEXICO. Two ACBL units with 315 members in 2000. Part of ACBL District 16.

> Unit 173 president : Moises J Ades
> 418 Hegel St Apt 401
> Polanco 11570, Mexico
> (H) 525-510-1749
> Secretary: Miriam Rosenberg
> Lopez Cotilla 719, Mexico DF 02100

All Correspondence to:

> Asoc Mex de Br Cultural y Dep AC
> 1605-B Pacific Rim Road
> PMB MX 34-527/439015
> San Diego CA 92143-9015
> Unit 205 president: E G Pete Schaefer
> P.O. Box 1176, Chapala, Mexico
> Secretary: Herman Arbitter
> c/o Verduzzo
> Antonio Valeriano #3373
> Guadalajara, Jalisco 45040, Mexico
> (H) 523-682-0208

MONACO BRIDGE FEDERATION (Federation Monagesque de Bridge). 2001 membership was 116.

> Centre de Congress
> Auditorium de Monaco
> Monte Carlo
> Tel: (33) (93) 300 4030

MOROCCO BRIDGE FEDERATION (Federation Royale Marocaine de Bridge). 2001 membership was 200.

> 10, rue Bendahan,
> Casablanca, Morocco
> Tel and Fax: (212) 222 3875

NATIONAL CONTRACT BRIDGE LEAGUE OF. See country name.

NEPAL BRIDGE ASSOCIATION. 2001 memberships was 99.

> Dasarath Sport Complex
> Trepwreswore, Nepal
> Tel: 977 1 521 283
> Fax: 977 1 526 283

NETHERLANDS BRIDGE LEAGUE (Nederlandse Bridge Bond). Founded in 1930 by the late A.J.E. Lucardie. Located in Utrecht, where it founded the National Bridge Centre. Hosted World Pair Olympiad 1966, World Team Olympiad 1980, 2000, European Championships 1932, 1939, 1955, European Junior Championships 1972, World Junior Championships 1987. Dutch players have won 2 world titles, 1 European title, and medals on 11 other occasions. Due largely to a beginners course based on a sound bidding system, the League doubled its membership from 40,000 to 80,000 in the 80s, and in 2001 had 102,524 members, second largest in the world. It organizes bi-annual courses for tournament directors and bridge teachers. Most international championships are under the technical control of Dutch supervisors. Its monthly magazine is named *Bridge*.

> Officers, 2000:
> President: Laurens Hoedemaker
> Secretary: Gijs v.d. Scheer
> Willem Dreeslaan 55, 3515 GB Utrecht,
> The Netherlands
> Telephone: 31-30-275 9999.
> Fax 31-30-275 9900.
> Web Site: www.bridge.nl

NETHERLANDS ANTILLES BRIDGE LEAGUE (Bridge Bond Nederlandse Antillen). 2001 membership was 100.

> Officers 1999:
> President: Ad van der Pol
> Secretary: Peter Hendriks
> Kaya Roi Katochi 923
> Curacao, Netherlands Antilles
> Tel: (599) 9 73770130
> Fax: (599) same

NEW CALEDONIA. 2001 membership was 115.

> PB 9615, Noumea
> New Caledonia
> Tel: 687 269 249
> Fax: 687 252 570

NEW ZEALAND CONTRACT BRIDGE ASSOCIATION. Founded by four clubs in 1936, and had 463 members by 1949. In 2001 had 113 clubs with a total membership of 17,878. New Zealand has won Far East Teams 1990, 1995; Far East Women's Teams 1976, 1981, 1983.

> Officers 2001
> President Charlie Cahn
> Secretary: Fran Jenkins
> P.O. Box 12116, Wellington, New Zealand
> Tel and Fax: 04 473 7748
> E-mail: fran@nzcba.co.nz

NORTHERN IRELAND BRIDGE UNION. Founded in 1932, controlling body of bridge in Northern Ireland. By 2001 there were about 40 clubs affiliated with a total membership of about 2000. The Union participates in the Camrose Trophy. For international participation, see IRISH BRIDGE UNION.

> Officers 2001:
> President: C. Richey
> Secretary: Anne Hassan
> 1 Lenamore Drive, Jordanstown,
> Co. Antrim, BT37 0PQ, Northern Ireland
> Tel: (02890) 862179
> E-mail: anne.hassan@talk21.com

NORWEGIAN BRIDGE FEDERATION (NORSK BRIDGEFORBUND (NBF)). Founded in 1932, and by 2001 had a membership of about 12,847 organized in 600 clubs in 25 districts. The National Open Teams attracts an entry of about 450 teams, and the National Open Pairs has had an entry exceeding 2,000. Norway has a national teams series with 600 participating teams, divided into a

pyramid of 5 divisions. Norway was second in the European Championship in 1938 and 1969, third in the 1970 Bermuda Bowl, 2nd in 1993 and 3rd in 1997. Norway also came 3rd in the 1980 Olympiad and won the Nordic Championship 10 times. Norwegian women won the Nordic Championship twice, but have seldom competed in European Championships because of the opinion that women's bridge represents an unnatural segregation. Norwegian juniors won the European Junior Teams in 1980, 1990 and 1996, and were second in the World Junior teams in 1993 and 1997. Norway hosted the 1938, 1958 and 1969 European Championships in Oslo. The NBF issues a bridge periodical *Norsk Bridge* every 2 months.

       Officers 1999:
       President: Jan Aasen
       Secretary General: Rune B. Anderssen
       Enebakkveien 133, 0680 Oslo, Norway
       Tel.47-22 08 17 82
       Fax: 47-22 08 17 85
       E-mail: nbf@bridgefederation.no
       Web-site: www.bridgefederation.no

NORDIC BRIDGE UNION (Nordisk Bridge Union (NBU)). Founded in 1969. Nordic top bridge politicians meet every 2nd year to discuss and decide upon Nordic topics and policy. It is the responsibility of the NBU to stage a biennial Nordic Team Championship in 3 classes: Open, Women and Juniors.

       Officers 1999:
       President: Jan Aasen
       Secretary: Rune B. Anderssen
       Enebakkveien 133, 0680 Oslo, Norway
       Tel.47-22 08 17 80
       Fax: 47-22 08 17 85
       E-mail: nbf@bridgefederation.no
       Web-site: www.bridgefederation.no

PACIFIC ASIA BRIDGE FEDERATION (PABF). Zone 6 of the World Bridge Federation. Until 1995, when it was renamed, it was the Far East Bridge Federation. Founded in 1957 and began regular zonal championships in that year. Members in 1999 were: China, Chinese Taipei (Taiwan), Hong Kong, Indonesia, Japan, Macau, Malaysia, Philippines, Singapore, Thailand. Australia and New Zealand are also members, but are not eligible to represent the zone in world competition.

       Officials as of 1999:
       President: Khunying Esther C.
           Sophonpanich (Thailand)
       Executive Vice President: Liu Gang (China)
       Honorary Secretary: Takeshi Nozaki (Japan)
       c/o Japan Contract Bridge League
       Attention: Nakatani Tadayoshi
       4th Floor, TJK Yotsuya Bldg., 1-13 Yotsuya,
       Shinjuku-ku 160-0004 Tokyo, Japan
       Tel. +81 3 3357 3741
       Fax +81 3 3357 7444
       E-mail:nakatani@jcbl.org.jp

PAKISTAN BRIDGE ASSOCIATION. Founded 1972, competed in Far East (PABF) Championships through 1979. Won 5 out of a possible 9 BFAAME Championships from 1981. Pakistan has twice reached world team championship finals, in the 1981 Bermuda Bowl and the Rosenblum Teams 1986. Pakistan hosted 1985 BFAME Championships. In 2001 membership was 1300.

       Officer 1999:
       President: Khurshid Hadi
       Secretary: M. Azwerul Haq
       Citizens Enclosure-2
       Block-M National Stadium
       Karachi, Pakistan
       Tel: 92 21 476 247
       Fax. (92-21) 5685329
       E-mail: azwer@khi.comsats.net.pk
       Web Site: www.pbf.port5.com

PALESTINE BRIDGE FEDERATION. 2001 membership was 110.
       P.O. Box 3598
       Al-Bireh, Ramallah, Palestine
       Tel: 972 2 995 1285
       Fax: 972 2 627 1285

PANAMA BRIDGE ASSOCIATION (Association Panamena de Bridge). Founded in 1968. Open Team finished second in the CAAC Zonal Teams in 1971, 1972 and 1974. 101 members in 2001.
       President 1999: Manuel Hernandez
       P.O. Box 10520
       Panama 4, Panama
       Tel: (507) 263 2558
       Fax: (507) 263 2059
       E-mail: mhc@sinfo.net

PARAGUAY BRIDGE ASSOCIATION (Asociation Paraguaya de Bridge). 2001 membership was 54.
       Chaco Boreal 381
       Asuncion, Paraguay
       Tel: 595 21 611 302
       Fax: 595 21 601 168

PERUVIAN BRIDGE COMMISSION (Comision Nacional de Bridge de Peru). Founded in 1957. In 2001 the membership was 242. Hosted South American Championships in 1956, 1961, 1974, 1981, 1991. Its women players won the South American women's team title 1963, 1969.
       Av. Jorge Basadre 475
       27 Lima, Peru
       Tel: (51) 14 419 995
       Fax: (51) 14 423 138

PHILIPPINE CONTRACT BRIDGE LEAGUE. Organized in 1954. By 2001 the membership was about 168. Hosted the 1977 Bermuda Bowl, the 1957, 1962, 1967, 1974 and 1977 Far East (PABF) Championships, and the 1980, 1988 and 1995 Asean Championships.
       Officers:
       President: Daniel Lulu
       Secretary: Mario Padua
       5338 Amorsolo St.,
       Dasmarinas Village,
       Makati City, Philippines
       Tel/Fax: (632) 844 2337.
       E-mail: altan@ginet.net
Web Site: www.qinet.net/user/altan/index.html

POLISH BRIDGE UNION. Founded in 1956, known as the Contract Bridge Association in Poland 1962-91. Since 1963, bridge has been regarded as a sport discipline and the PBU is subordinated to the Office of Sport. Since 1998, the PBU has been a member of the Polish

Olympic Committee. In 2001 had about 7,814 full members and about 1,700 junior and associate members, organized in 850 clubs. Its players have won 7 world championships and 15 European championships. The Union publishes *Swiat Brydza* and *Przeglad Brydzowy*. Bridge courses are organized at schools for children of 12 and more, for more than 700 children.

> Officers 1999:
> President: Piotr Zak
> Honorary President: Jan Prochowski
> Address: Zlota 9/4, Warsaw, Poland
> Tel. (+48 22) 827 24 29
> Fax (+48 22) 827 34 88
> E-mail: biuro@polbridge.pl
> Web Site: www.polbridge.pl

PORTUGUESE BRIDGE FEDERATION (FEDERACAO PORTUGUESA DE BRIDGE). Founded in 1960, and in 2001 had a membership of 948 in 7 regional circles. Hosted the 1970 (Estoril) and 1995 (Vilamoura) European Championships and the 1993 (Montechoro) European Union Championships. Won European Union Open Teams 1998, was second in the European Junior Teams 1968, 4th in the European Union Mixed Teams 1993, 5th in the European Open Teams 1966 and in the European Women's Teams 1970 and 9th in the Rosenblum Cup Teams 1994.

> 2001 President : Jos, Antonio Debonnaire
> Av. Ant¢nio Augusto de Aguiar, 163-4§ Esq.
> 1050-014 Lisbon, Portugal
> Tel. 351 21 3884844
> Fax 351 21 3832156
> E-mail: np43je@mail.telepac.pt
> Net: www.fpbridge.pt

REUNION BRIDGE COMMITTEE (Comite de Bridge de la Reunion). 2001 membership was 308.

> 1, rue Rico Carpaye,
> 97420 Le Port, Reunion
> Tel: (262) 298 380
> Fax: (262) 211 425

ROMANIAN BRIDGE FEDERATION (Federatio Romana de Bridge). Founded in 1990 following the Romanian Revolution. There are 41 clubs in 32 towns, and 32 championships are conducted. Membership in 1999 was 997. Won 2000 OKbridge Internet World Championship.

> 1999 Officers:
> President: Tania Tomescu
> General Secretary: Marius Georgescu
> 16 Vasile Conta
> P.O. Box 37
> 70139 Bucharest 2, Romania
> Tel/Fax: (401) 222 76 75

RUSSIAN BRIDGE LEAGUE (ROSSIJSKAYA LIGA SPORTIVNOGO BRIDJA). Founded in 1989 after the break-up of the Soviet Union. By 2001, it had a membership of 1067 members organized in about 50 clubs.

> Officers 2000:
> President: Valery Khanykov
> Vice President & International contact:
> Michael Rosenblum
> Starokoniushennyj 19 - 64 121002
> Moscow, Russia

> Tel. 7 095 205 01 15
> Fax: 7 095 241 7300
> E-mail: blum@iitp.ru

ST. CROIX. See Virgin Islands.

ST. KITTS AND NEVIS (St. Kitts Bridge Association). Membership in 2001 was 47.

> President 1999: David Rawlins
> c/o Ian Slack,
> Coca Cola, Basseterre, St. Kitts
> Tel: (869) 465 2074
> Fax: (869) 465 1201

SAN MARINO, THE BRIDGE FEDERATION OF. In 2001, had a membership of 60.

> Fiorenzo Fiorini,
> Via G.Giacomoni 73
> I-47031 San Marino, Italy
> Tel: 378 992 114
> Fax: 378 990 434

SAUDI ARABIA (Arabian Bridge Federation). 2001 membership 107.

> Box 5660
> 31311 Dhahran, Saudi Arabia
> Tel: (966) 3 874 3617
> Fax: (966) 3 878 4783

SCOTTISH BRIDGE UNION. divided into 7 regional districts, and had a membership in 2000 of about 8,000. Independent NCBO since 2000 when the British Bridge League was dissolved. Its players have often represented Britain in international events. Scottish victories in the CAMROSE TROPHY are listed under that heading. The equivalent event for women's teams, the Lady Milne Cup, was won by Scotland in 1980, 1984, 1986 and 1992. Officers:

> President: James P. Wilcox
> Secretary: Tom Workman,
> 32, Whitehaugh Drive
> Paisley PA1 3PG, Scotland
> Tel. 44 41 887 1903.

SINGAPORE CONTRACT BRIDGE ASSOCIATION. Founded in 1965, when Singapore left the Malaysian Federation. Hosted Far East (PABF) Championships, 1972, 1986, 1990. Membership in 2001 was 175.

> 51 Bishan Street 3
> #01-01 Singapore 579799, Singapore
> Tel: 65 356 8540
> Fax: 64 259 7832
> Web Site: www.come.to/scba

SLOVENIAN BRIDGE ASSOCIATION (Bridge Zveza Slovenije). Founded in 1972, joined WBF in 1992 when Slovenia became independent. In 2001 there were 129 members.

> PP 1638, SLO-1101 Ljubljana, Slovenia
> Tel: (386) 61 123 1393

SOUTH AFRICAN BRIDGE FEDERATION. Formed in 1954 and participated in all Olympiads 1960-80. It voluntarily withdrew from international competition 1983-93 because of international sanctions imposed on the country as a result of the apartheid policies of the

goverment in power. International play resumed in 1992. Membership reached 5,000 in 1980, declined to 2,000 in 1991 because of sanctions, then stagnated because of emigration. 2001 membership was 2,433. There are 48 clubs, with Johannesburg the focal point. The SABF sponsors an 8-day national tournament in May and other events. The South African women players won silver medals in the 1968 and 1972 Team Olympiads and the 1974 Pairs Olympiad. The organization's magazine is *Showcase*, formerly *S.A.Bulletin*.

    Officers 1999:
    President: Julius Butkow
    Secretary: Glenda Schwartz
    P.O. Box 890347
    Lyndhurst 2106 South Africa
    Tel: 27 11 440 6435
    Fax: 011 333 6698
    Web Site: www.sabf.port.com

SOUTH AMERICAN BRIDGE CONFEDERATION (Confederacion Sudamericana de Bridge). founded in 1948. Representatives have competed in world championships since 1958. Zonal championships were originally played annually, but are now staged in odd-numbered years. The winners represent the zone in the Bermuda Bowl. 8 member countries: Argentina, Bolivia, Brazil, Chile, Ecuador, Paraguay, Peru, Uruguay.

    President 2000:
    Pascal Burro
    Estados Unidos 951
    Asuncion, Paraguay
    Tel: (595) 21 444 557
    Fax: (595) 21 213 813
    WBF Delegate: Ernest d'Orsi (Brazil)

SOUTH PACIFIC ZONE. Zone 7 of the World Bridge Federation is the third largest zone measured by registered players. There are six member countries: Australia, Cook Islands, French Polynesia, New Caledonia, New Zealand, Vanuatu. An annual championship is held for the island countries, beginning in 1991. The first two were won by Tahiti. Qualification for world championships (Bermuda Bowl and Venice Cup) was regularly by a "Test Match" between Australia and New Zealand. This was replaced in 1991 by a South Pacific Championship.

SOVIET UNION. Bridge was an "unofficial" game in the Soviet Union until 1986, but some internal tournaments were played, mainly in the Baltic states. International contacts began in Estonia about 1980, but full international participation did not begin until 1989. See RUSSIA, ESTONIA, LATVIA, UKRAINE, UZBEKISTAN.

SPANISH BRIDGE FEDERATION (FEDERACION ESPANOLA DE BRIDGE). Recognized by the Consejo Superior de Deportes Espanol. Founded in 1941, in 2001 the Federation had about 3,238 members. The Federation hosted the 1974 World Pair Olympiad in Las Palmas, the 1994 European Mixed Pairs Championship in Barcelona, and the 2001 European Championships in Tenerife.

    Officers 2000:
    President: Miguel Mestanza Fragero
    Secretary: Javier Valmaseda
    c/ Juan Hurtado de Mendoza, 17
    28036 Madrid, Spain

    Tel: 34 91 350 47 00
    Fax: 39 91 350 54 53
    E-mail: javalma@avrakis.es
    Web Site: www.aebridge.com

SRI LANKA (Bridge Federation of Sri Lanka). 2001 membership was 100.
    97 Castle St., 8 Colombo, Sri Lanka
    Tel: (94) 1 691 823
    Fax: (94) 1 686 670

SURINAME BRIDGE BOND. Membership in 2001 was 76.
    President 1999: Robert de Boer
    c/o Mrs. G. Treurniet
    P.O.Box 635
    Paramaribo, Suriname
    Tel: 597 476 810
    Fax: 597 410 344
    E-mail: doesje@cg-link.sr

SWEDISH BRIDGE LEAGUE (Sveriges Bridgeforbund). Founded in 1933. In 2001 had 15,000 members. Won World Women's Teams 1968, European Teams 1939, 1952, 1977, 1987, European Women's Teams 1962, 1967, 1993. Hosted Bermuda Bowl 1970, 1983, World Pairs Olympiad 1970, European Championships 1936, 1956. National open team championships attract 650 teams, and national open pairs attract 1,600 pairs.

    President: Mats Qviberg
    Secretary: Bjorn Gustafsson
    Kungsgatan 36
    111 35 Stockholm, Sweden
    Tel: 08 22 00 56
    Fax: 46 8 220 057
    Web Site: www.bridgefederation.se

SWISS BRIDGE FEDERATION (Federation Suisse de Bridge). Founded in Geneva in 1950, and by 2001 had about 3611 members in 66 affiliated clubs. Host to 2 European Championships, in Montreux in 1954 and in Lausanne in 1979, and 1 World Championship, the Pairs Olympiad in Geneva in 1990.

    Officers 1999:
    President: Roberto Valsargiacomo
    Secretary: Rita Mucha
    Klarastrasse . 3
    8008 Zurich, Switzerland
    Tel. 41 1 262 5655
    Fax 41 1 262 5645
    Web Site: www.home.worldcom.ch/-fsb

SYRIAN BRIDGE ASSOCIATION. 2001 membership was 99.
    Al Assad Village area
    Dimas-Damascus, Syria
    Fax: (963) 11 224 9507

TAIWAN CONTRACT BRIDGE LEAGUE. (National Contract Bridge League of Republic of China; designated by the WBF for international purposes as Chinese Taipei). Founded in 1950 in Taipei, Taiwan and by 2001 had a membership of about 3000. Taiwan hosted the 1971 Bermuda Bowl in Taipei, and has also hosted three Far East Championships. Its teams have twice finished second in the Bermuda Bowl, the best performance by any Far East

country, and have won 10 Far East Open Team titles and two Far East Women's Team titles. Its magazine, *Chinese Bridge*, has been published for more than 40 years.

P.O. Box 24-20 Taipei, Taiwan R.O.C.
Tel: 886-2-2772 4510
Fax: 886-2-2771 4493
E-mail: dvc11@hotmail.com

TANZANIA BRIDGE ASSOCIATION. 2001 membership 24

P.O. Box 5104
Dar-Es-Salaam, Tanzania
Tel: (255) 51 38 375
Fax: (255) 51 112 949

THAILAND, CONTRACT BRIDGE LEAGUE OF. Founded in 1947 by Lt. William Howard Hunter, and in 2001 had 283 members in 13 clubs. Won Far East (PABF) Teams in 1961, 1963, 1965 and 1966, and became the first representatives of their zone in the Bermuda Bowl, 1966 and 1967. Won Far East (PABF) Women's Teams in 1964 and 1966, and 21 titles in the Asean Championships. Hosted PABF (Far East) Championships in 1961, 1966, 1975 and 1982.

Officers 1999:
President: Kunying Chodchoy Esther
 Sophonpanich
Secretary: Pimpraphai Bisalputra
319/1 Sukhumvit 31
Bangkok 10110, Thailand
Tel: 66 2 230 1884
Fax: 66 2 236 8984
E-mail: stmsadv@kscl5.th.com

TRINIDAD AND TOBAGO CONTRACT BRIDGE LEAGUE. Membership in 2001 was 90.

President 1999: Nicky Inniss
P.O.Box 1328
Port of Spain
Trinidad (Attn. Roger Vieira)
Tel: 868 674 6720
Fax: (868) 674 0145
E-mail: aml@trinidad.net

TUNISIAN BRIDGE FEDERATION (Federation Tunisienne de Bridge). 2001 membership was 198. Host to Bermuda Bowl, Venice Cup 1997.

Laboratoire Medicale
Centre Cial Jemil
El Menzah 6
1002 Tunis, Tunisia
Tel: (216) 1 751 050
Fax: (216) 1 750 858

TURKISH BRIDGE FEDERATION. (TURKIYE BRIC FEDERASYONU). Founded in 1964, and in 2001 had a membership of 1,500 players.

Ulus is hani, A blok, 7.
kat Ulus/ Ankara, Turkey
Tel: 90 312 324 0825
Fax: 90 312 324 0926
Web Site: www.tbricfed.org.tr

UKRAINIAN BRIDGE FEDERATION. Founded in 1991 following the break-up of the Soviet Union, and had 113 players in 2001.

1999 Officers:
President: Dmytro Shklyar
Ukrainian Bridge Federation
M.Mikhailivska 1/3, office 801
252001 Kiev, Ukraine
Tel: 380 44 229 2510
Fax: 380 44 265 0034
E-mail: di_ksi@sabbo.net

UNITED STATES. Two organizations, the AMERICAN CONTRACT BRIDGE LEAGUE (ACBL) and the AMERICAN BRIDGE ASSOCIATION (ABA), are the primary operatives of club and tournament bridge in the United States. The ACBL, with about 170,000 members, governs bridge throughout North America – Canada, Mexico and Bermuda as well as the United States. The ABA operates strictly within the United States.

Principal ACBL Headquarters personnel:
Chief Executive Officer – Wayne Hascall
Controller – Jack Zdancewicz
Bridge Administration – Gary Blaiss
Bridge Bulletin editor – Brent Manley
Sales – Jim Miller
Education – Julie Greenberg
Membership – Carol Robertson
Important ACBL e-mail addresses:
Chief Executive Officer – ceo@acbl.org
Bridge Bulletin – editor@acbl.org
Masterpoints – masterpoints@acbl.org
Tournaments – tournaments@acbl.org
Education – education@acbl.org
Club Department – club@acbl.org
Membership – membership@acbl.org
ACBLscore – acblscore@acbl.org
North American Bridge Championships –
 nabc@acbl.org
International events –
 internationalevents@acbl.org
See ACBL BOARD OF DIRECTORS, ACBL BOARD OF GOVERNORS, ACBL BULLETIN, ACBL CHARITY FOUNDATION, ACBL EDUCATIONAL FOUNDATION, ACBL GOODWILL COMMITTEE, ACBL HALL OF FAME, ACBL HANDBOOK, ACBL HEADQUARTERS, ACBL LIBRARY, ACBL ONLINE, ACBLSCORE, ACBL-WIDE GAMES.

URUGUAY BRIDGE ASSOCIATION (Asociacion Uruguaya de Bridge). Founded in 1948 and has 225 members. Won 1 South American Open Teams and 4 Women's Teams. Hosted the South American Championships 7 times.

Sarandi 584
1100 Montevideo, Uruguay
Tel: 598 2 957 820
Fax: 598 2 951 247

UZBEKISTAN BRIDGE FEDERATION. 2001 membership was 99.

P.O. Box 4501
Tashkent 700000, Uzbekistan
Tel: (7 371) 162 6360

VENEZUELAN BRIDGE FEDERATION (Federacion Venezolana de Bridge). Founded in 1958, and in 2001 had 281 members playing in 12 clubs. Competed in the South American Championships 1955-1978, winning

the Open title 1963, 1965 and 1966 and representing the zone in the 1966 and 1967 world championships. Hosted the championship 1963, 1970 and 1978. Hosted the CAAC Championships in 1975, 1984, 1987 and 1991 events, and its players won the open team title 1973, 1977, 1984, 1985, 1986, 1987, 1991, 1993 and 1997, and the women's team title 1978-1987 inclusive, and in 1991, 1993 and 1995.

> Quinta Ekeko
> 2ø Calle de Campo Alegre
> Caracas, Venezuela
> Tel: 58 2 262 1160
> Fax: 58 2 241 3076
> E-mail: fvbridge@ven.net

VIRGIN ISLANDS BRIDGE FEDERATION. 148 members in 2001.

> Officers 1999:
> President: Alan J. Bronstein
> Secretary: Jeffrey L. Resnick
> P.O.Box 3485 Christianstedt
> St. Croix, Virgin Islands 00820
> Tel. (809) 773 0096
> Fax (809) 778 8640

VLAAMSE BRIDGE LIGA (VBL). See FLEMISH BRIDGE LEAGUE.

WALES. See WELSH BRIDGE UNION.

WELSH BRIDGE UNION. Founded about 1934, combining three areas, North, West and East, and was affiliated to the British Bridge League. Conducts 5 national events and a masterpoint program. In 2001 had 2000 members and 50 affiliated clubs. In 2000, Wales became a separate NCBO, entitled to separate representation in international events.
Officers 1999:

> President: Jo Davies
> Treasurer: Linda Greenland
> 31 Deri Road, Penylan, Cardiff CF2 5AH
> Wales, Great Britain
> Tel: 44 2920 223 100
> Fax: 44 2920 255 162
> Web Site: www.ukonline.co.uk/wbu
> E-mail: deri31@ntlworld.com
> Secretary: Michael Brunt
> E-mail: mikepbrunt@tesco.net

WORLD BRIDGE FEDERATION (WBF). Founded in 1958 in Oslo, Norway. Had 1.5 million members in 113 nations in 2001. Stages at least one world championship each year. Governed by an Executive Council made up representatives from the eight WBF zones. For major activities, zone listing and major championship events, see WORLD BRIDGE FEDERATION. For makeup of Executive Council, see WORLD BRIDGE FEDERATION EXECUTIVE COUNCIL. For information about the masterpoint plan see WORLD BRIDGE FEDERATION MASTERPOINT PLAN, WORLD BRIDGE FEDERATION PLACING POINTS, WORLD BRIDGE FEDERATION PLAYER RANKINGS, WORLD GRAND MASTER, WORLD LIFE MASTER, WORLD MASTER. For the country membership list see WORLD BRIDGE FEDERATION MEMBER NATIONS.
President: José Damiani

> 40 , rue Francois 1ᵉʳ
> 75008, Paris, France
> Tel. : 33 1 5323 0315
> Fax : 33 1 4070 1451
> E-mail : cfrancin@worldbridgefed.com

Treasurer: George Retek

> 1650 de Maisonneuve Blvd West, Suite 202
> Montreal PQ H3H 3PS, Canada
> Tel: 1 514 937 9907
> FaX: 1 514 931 2205

Secretariat: Carol von Linstow

> 29 bis, res Les Roussets
> 01210 Omex, France
> Tel : 33 4 5040 5131
> Fax : 33 3 5040 4257
> E-mail : carolwbf1@aol.com

General Liaison and Simultaneous Pairs Organizer: Anna Gudge

> The Old Railway Station
> Long Melford, Sudbury
> CO10 9HN Suffolk, Great Britain
> Tel: 44 1787 88 19 20
> Fax 33 1787 88 13 39
> E-mail: wbf@ecats.co.uk

YUGOSLAVIA.

> Ranko Grba
> Tel/fax: 381 11 439 904
> Web Site: www.bss.cjb.net

ZIMBABWE BRIDGE UNION. Founded in 1967, a successor to the Central Africa Bridge Union. In 2001 there were six clubs and 489 members.
Officers 1999:

> Chairman: Cyril Gordon
> 11 Bookless Road
> Khumalo-Bulawayo, Zimbabwe
> Tel: 263 9 631 45
> Fax: 263 9 784 25

LEADING BRIDGE PERSONALITIES

A

AA, Terje (b. 1961) of Norway, post office employee. WBF World Life Master. 2nd Bermuda Bowl 1993, 3rd European Teams 1993, 97. Many national titles.

AABYE, Jon (b. 1952) of Oslo Norway, accountant. Was 3rd World Team Olympiad 1980. One Nordic team title. Represented Norway in 2 European championships. Many national titles.

AARONS, Stephen H. (b. 1937) of Toronto ON, attorney, appointed Queen's Counsel 1978. Owner of thoroughbred race horses. Served on Unit 166 Board of Directors 1965-80, chairman Unit Ethics Committee 1968-78, Chairman District 2 Ethics Committee 1979-85, served on ACBL Appeals Committee 1975-83, District 2 director 1972-75. Represented Canada in WBF events New Orleans 1978 (placed 10th World Mixed Pairs) and Bal Harbor 1986. Was npc Canadian team Seattle 1984, placed 2nd 1989 Maccabia Games. Won numerous regionals.

AASEN, Jan (b. 1967) of Gjovik, Norway, municipal department manager. President Norwegian Bridge Federation and Nordic Bridge Union.

ABDEL BARI, Mohamed (b. 1954) of Cairo Egypt, engineer. Won BFAAME Open Teams 1989, runner-up 1991. Won 5 national titles. Author of a series of magazine articles on relay structures.

ABDEL RAOUF, Walid El Ahmady (b. 1961) of Cairo, Egypt, engineer. Won BFAAME Open Teams 1989. Won 5 national team titles.

ABDOU, Wafik A. (b. 1962) of Bakersfield CA, born in Cairo, Egypt; physician, anesthesiologist, Chief of Anesthesiology; listed in *Who's Who Among Notable Young Americans*. Won Open BAM Teams 1992, Mixed Pairs 1997 and more than 30 regionals.

ABE, Hiroya (b. 1945) of Tokyo, Japan, bridge club director. Represented Japan in one world championship and 5 Far East Championships. Won National Open Teams 14 times and National Open Pairs 10 times. Expert in Shogi (Japanese chess).

ABECASSIS, Michel (b. 1952) of Paris, France. WBF World Master. Won European Pairs 1991, 93. Represented France in one zonal championship. Editor of *Le Bridgeur* from 2001.

ABEDI, Nishat M.H. (b. 1939) of Karachi, Pakistan, born in India, accountant. WBF World Master. Pakistan's top masterpoint winner. Placed 2nd Bermuda Bowl 1981 and Rosenblum Teams 1986. Won BFAAME Open Teams 1983, 85. Many national titles.

ABRAHAMS, Stanley J. (b. 1940) commercial manager, born in Scotland. Represented New Zealand in 2 world championships and 3 Far East Championships. 3rd Far East Pairs 1981. National wins include Open Teams 3 times.

ABRAMIAN, Vikenti (b. 1969) of Moscow, Russia, journalist. Chief editor *The Bridge Review* magazine. Director of Moscow Invitational international tournament.

ABRAMS, Elsie (d. 1993) of Pompano Beach FL, registered nurse and certified director. Won Mixed Pairs 1960; placed 2nd Women's Teams 1963. Had many regional wins.

ABRAMS, Susan (b. 1942) of Elkins Park PA, illustrator, jewelry and graphic designer. Originator of left-handed bidding boxes; designer of bridge-related greeting cards. Has won many regionals.

ACH, Jacques L., Sr. (1903-1971) of Cincinnati Ohio, attorney and accountant. Co-invented Ach-Kennedy schedules (1935) which were the first Howell Movements with perfectly balanced comparisons. Contributor to *The Bridge World* in the Thirties.

ACKERMAN, Gerald W. (Jerry) (b. 1925) of Fair Lawn NJ, retired CPA and manager Price Waterhouse Coopers. Served North Jersey B.A. as Board member, vice president, auditor, and chairman of Conduct and Ethics Committee. Won Marcus Cup 1954, placed 2nd 1956.

ADAMCZYK, Wesley (Wes) H. (b. 1933) of Deerfield Il, born in Warsaw, Poland, senior chemist and senior tax consultant. At age 10 he and his family were deported to Russia - they escaped 2 years later. He lost both parents during this period - his father was murdered in the Katyn Forest massacre. Moved from camp to camp for displaced persons before finally arriving in Chicago in 1950. He has appeared on BBC radio and on television documentaries concerning the massacre. Currently finishing a book on the subject of his deportation and survival and has been on a 50-year search for his father's grave site. Diamond Life Master, a contributor to District 8 *Advocate* and has more than 25 regional wins.

ADAMS, Bill R. (Tornado) (b. 1930) of Wichita KS, retired ACBL employee. Formerly a national tournament director.

ADAMS, Charles True (1900-1942) of Chicago, utilities attorney. Was a valuable contributor to the Official System. One of first widely read authors on contract bridge, his *Contract Bridge Standardized* was published in 1928. Adams was co-editor-in-chief (with Milton Work) of *The Bridge Magazine* and Director of American Auction Bridge League 1927.

ADAMS, Peggy (1900-1974) of New York City, ACBL staff member who worked in masterpoint department from 1948 to 1966. Wrote the feature *Club Corner* for *The Bridge Bulletin*. Vaudevillian in her youth, playing the Keith Circuit and picture theaters, under stage name of Peggy Hart. In 1950 she became Life Master #300 and at that time was 2nd Life Master in ACBL headquarters, the first being the late Alvin Landy. Won Women's Teams 1955, placed 2nd 1952.

ADAMS, Dr. Robert T. (Bob) (b. 1923) of Lafayette CA, born in Japan, retired manager and research chemist. Roller skate dance champion 1968-69. Served on Oakland and Richmond Unit Board of Directors. Authored a bridge column for American Chemical Society magazine, *The Vortex*, 1967-78. Won Mixed Pairs 1957 and many regionals.

ADAMS, William E. (b. 1917) of North Branford CT. Retired aeronautical, mechanical engineer; product engineer for U.S. Steel Corp. Served on ACBL Board of Directors in the Sixties; Connecticut Unit Board of Directors 1952-78 (past president); District Board of Directors 1955-78. Winner National Senior Master Individual 1953 and several regionals.

ADLER, Betty (Mrs. Julian) (1927-2000) of Baltimore MD, bridge teacher since 1959, social worker 1949-51, did birth control surveys for Sinai Hospital. Maryland B.A. board member for 15 years, president twice, tournament chairman 1970-80. Director on bridge cruises. National wins include Women's Pairs 1959, Women's KO Teams 1977, 79. Placed 2nd Women's KO Teams 1980; Master Mixed Teams 1970, 74, 78. Diamond Life Master.

ADLER, Julian (b. 1918) of Baltimore MD, retired CEO and Board chairman. Recipient of 3 Battle Stars in WW II. Competed in Maryland Senior Olympics from 1980 to 1991 winning several medals. Placed 2nd in Non-Master Pairs 1961, Master Mixed Teams 1970, 74, 78. Won many regionals including District 6 GNOT 1975.

ADLER, Patricia. See SHEINWOLD, Patricia Fox.

AFDAHL, Darwin (Dar) (b.1940) of Virginia Beach VA, retired U.S. Naval aviator, insurance/financial consultant. President on Unit and District level, past member ACBL Appeals Committee; columnist for unit newsletter. Diamond Life Master, won more than 25 regionals.

AFSAR, Tugrul (b. 1949) of Ankara, Turkey, bridge teacher. Represented Turkey in 2 zonal championships. 4 national wins.

AGRAN, Nathan (Nat) (1908-1993) of Sarasota FL, Philadelphia attorney. As general counsel of the Commonwealth of Pennsylvania Commission on Human Relations (1960-73) he won landmark decisions before Supreme Court of Pennsylvania on de facto school segregation. Taught bridge during WW II to GIs and officers and later to disabled veterans with his late wife, Violet. Life Master #148. After retirement to Florida he became active in local bridge and community activities. Won the Beynon Trophy 1948 and several regionals.

AGUW, Maximiliaan (b.1951) of Manado, Indonesia, police office. Former regional chess champion. Represented Indonesia in Bermuda Bowl 1973, 74, 81; World Team Olympiad 1976, 80. Won PABF (Far East) Teams 1972, 73, 79, 81. Won many national titles.

AHMED, Javed (b. 1947) of Karachi, Pakistan, business executive. Won BFAAME Open Teams 1991 and represented Pakistan - Bermuda Bowl 1991. Many national titles.

AHMED, Nisar (b. 1936) of Karachi, Pakistan, accountant. WBF World Master. Placed 2nd Bermuda Bowl 1981 and Rosenblum Teams 1986. Won BFAAME zonal championship 1981, 83, 85, 87. 2nd Far East Championship 1979. Many national titles.

AKCA, Necmi (b. 1915) of Istanbul, Turkey, businessman. Represented Turkey in 5 world championships and 7 zonal championships. 5 national wins.

AKTURK, Hans (b.1932) of Tallahassee FL, born in Turkey, manager systems programmer. Has more than 20 regional wins.

ALBANO, Helen D. of Newark NJ, was a charter member of the ABTA and its president in 1967. She was president and founder of Bridge for the Blind, a non-profit organization of some 118 volunteers who teach bridge to the blind throughout the United States, Canada, South Africa, Iran and Israel. Albano formerly wrote a column titled *Chuckles* for the ABTA *Quarterly* and is author of the textbook, *Analysis and Practical Application of the Goren Method*. Her textbook was translated into Braille, together with her program of lessons and techniques.

ALBARRAN, Pierre (1894-1960) of Paris, France, born in West Indies. Leading figure in French bridge until his death. Won European Teams 1935, represented France

that year in first World Championship in New York. Represented France on 30 other occasions. Won 19 national titles, mainly in the Thirties. Developed the canape principle, short suit before long, which influenced many European players including Jais-Trezel and the Italian world champions. Also developed ace-showing responses to 2♣, and a distributional point count. Author or co-author of 9 books, 5 of them in collaboration with Jose Le Dentu. The most influential for theory of bridge were *Notre Methode de Bridge* with Robert De Nexon (1935) and *Le Canape* (1946). Twice a member of the French Davis Cup tennis team.

ALBERSHEIM, Alberta G. (1906-1996) of Waban MA, former attorney. Became virtually blind and had to carry her own boards with giant cards. These enabled her to continue to attend tournaments. Served as board member Eastern Massachusetts B.A. for 10 years and was treasurer of Summer NABC 1970; chaired a committee for Summer NABCs 1980, 90. Diamond Life Master, placed 2nd Women's Pairs 1958 and won numerous regionals.

ALBERT, Mary (b. 1947) of Omaha NE, office manager for family owned food brokerage business. Competes in ballroom dancing Pro-Am tournaments, does demonstrations and exhibitions of partnership dancing. Has won several dance awards. Placed 2nd Life Master Women's Pairs 1982 and Women's Swiss Teams 1983. Has won several regionals.

ALBERT, Michael L. (Mike) (b. 1938) of Omaha NE, consultant, former owner/CEO Michael Albert Inc. Has served in local politics. Grand Life Master with 11,229 MPs as of 3/2001. Won Open Swiss Teams 1983, IMP Pairs 1996, Senior KO Teams 1997.

ALBUENA, Lydia (b. 1923) of Long Island NY, formerly of the Philippines, secretary. Won Far East Women's Teams 1982. Represented Philippines in 4 world championships and 11 other zonal championships.

ALCORN, Margaret. See Gaer, Margaret.

ALDER, Phillip D. (b. 1951) of Hobe Sound FL, formerly of London, England, self-employed bridge journalist. Succeeded Jim Jacoby as bridge columnist with Newspaper Enterprise Association. Served as member of GNYBA Board of Directors, former member of ACBL Appeals Committee, member of conventions working party of English Bridge Union. A Life Master both in England and U.S. At the time he became a Life Master (in England) he was 2nd youngest ever to attain that rank. Authored *You Can Play Bridge* and *Get Smarter at Bridge*. Was a principal analyst for the World Championship books for 1986, 87, 88. Has written and/or edited with Alan Truscott, Dr. George Rosenkranz, Bill Root, Zia Mahmood and Kathie Wei-Sender. Regular contributor to ACBL *Bulletin, New Zealand Bridge, Bridge d'Italia, Bridge World, Australian Bridge* and *International Bridge Press Association Bulletin*. Was editor of *Bridge Magazine* 1980-85. Has been *Daily Bulletin* editor at many World, European, Common Market and Zone 4 Championships and is a contributing editor *Official Encyclopedia of Bridge*.

Winner of Bols Brilliancy Prize 1979, Royal Viking Line Player of the Year (1986), and Precision Defense of the Year (1992). Invented Alder Transfer Preempts. Has acted as a vugraph commentator at international events and coached teams from Egypt, Pakistan and Mauritius to prepare them for international competition. Represented England in Camrose Trophy 1980, the Junior Camrose 1971, 72. Represented Great Britain in Junior

European Championship 1972, Common Market Championships 1974, Junior Common Market Championships 1976. British national victories include Junior Pairs Championship and Anglo-American Junior Pairs Championship 1971, Junior Team Championship 1972, Two Star Pairs 1973, Crockford's Cup 1984. In the U.S. he has won several regional events.

ALDERTON, George A., II (1904-1982) of Detroit MI, born in Saginaw MI, was a probate and tax attorney in private practice until his death. Was ACBL president 1945, ACBL vice-president 1944, ACBL Honorary Member 1956 and former president of the Midwest Conference and Michigan B.A. .

ALDRICH, Clarence (Clayton) W. (1871-1961) Cleveland furniture store owner. Was active in forming the American Bridge League in 1927. Was president of ABL in 1930 and member of the executive committee 1933.

ALIOTTA, Mike (b.1943) of Detroit MI, bridge professional. Has served as vice chairman ACBL Appeals Committee, president Ethical Oversight Committee. 2nd Men's BAM Teams 1981. Diamond Life Master with more than 13,100 MPs as of 3/2001. Won 40+ regional titles.

ALLAN, Thomas W. (Tom) (b.1951) of Broken Arrow OK, regional sales manager. Won Intercollegiate Championship 1975, several regionals.

ALLANA, A.R. (b. 1944) of Karachi, Pakistan, industrialist. Won BFAAME Open Teams 1991, represented Pakistan in 4 world championships.

ALLEN, Alexander (Alex) (b. 1953) of Metulhen NJ, research chemist. Served on Unit 140 and District 3 boards. Won 16 regionals.

ALLEN, Charles L. (b. 1943) of Morrill KS, retired. Won more than 15 regionals.

ALLENSPACH, Frederick R., II (b. 1956) of Potomac MD, self employed accountant. Has won more than 35 regionals.

ALLINGER, Paul (1929-1988) of Alameda CA, accountant. Won Men's Pairs 1956, Men's Teams 1962, Chicago (since 1965 the Reisinger) 1962, Spingold 1958. Placed 2nd Open Pairs 1957, Men's Teams 1956, Men's Pairs 1961. He won numerous regional titles and was co-inventor of Astro. Represented U.S. in World Team Olympiad 1960.

ALLISON, Karen R. of Jersey City NJ, formerly of Toronto. Served on drafting committee for duplicate and rubber bridge laws revisions, ACBL Appeals Committee vice-chairman and past chairman GNYBA. Elected to ACBL Laws Commission in 1982. Represented Canada in world competition - New Orleans 1978, Valkenburg 1980. WBF World Master, first woman ever to represent Canada in Open Teams - Monte Carlo 1976, where her team placed 13th in Olympiad Open Teams. Placed 2nd McConnell Cup 1994, 7th Women's Pairs 1990. Won Women's Teams 1968, Women's KO Teams 1969, Master Mixed Teams 1983. Placed 2nd Life Master Women's Pairs 1969, Women's BAM Teams 1986, 92; North American Swiss Teams 1995.

ALLOUCHE, Danielle (b. 1956) of Paris, France. WBF World Life Master. 2nd World Women's Teams 1987, 3rd 1985. Won European Women's Teams 1983, 85, 87. Represented France in 2 other world championships, won many national titles.

ALPAUGH, Nancy T. (formerly Mrs. Ray Zoller) of New Orleans, former bridge teacher, Diamond Life Master. Won World Mixed Teams 1972. Won Women's KO Teams 1978, 84; Women's Swiss Teams 1988, Women's Pairs 1986, Master Mixed Teams 1977, 78, 79; North

American Women's Swiss Teams 1982. Placed 2nd Women's KO Teams 1991, Women's BAM Teams 1990.

ALPERN, Steven R. (The Dragon) (b. 1943) of San Diego CA, real estate investor, bridge professional, genealogist. National Merit Scholar. Represented college in chess and table tennis. Certified director since 1972. Has written several pamphlets on bridge for Allen Publications. Won 18 regionals.

ALTAY, Andrew J. (Andy) (b.1947) of Toronto ON, born in Hungary, data processing manager. Served on Unit 166 Board of Directors and Board of Directors of Canadian Bridge Federation, was national coordinator of Canadian National Team Championships (CNTC) first 3 years of its existence. Represented Canada in international competition New Orleans 1978. Won several regional events.

ALTER, William N. (Bill) (b. 1940) of Farmingdale NY, ACBL accredited teacher. Pioneered in the field of teaching bridge to the hearing impaired.

ALTMAN, Steven B. (b.1943) of Tenafly NJ, options trader. An original member of the Precision Team. Coached U.S. winning Bermuda Bowl team 1973, 77. Won Spingold 1970, 71; Vanderbilt 1972, Morehead Trophy 1967, London Sunday Times Pairs 1973. Placed 2nd Reisinger 1967, Spingold 1968, 78. Won numerous regionals, retired from tournament play 1981.

ALTUS, Philip (b.1945) of Tampa Fl, physician, professor of medicine University of Southern Florida. Former Governor of the American College of Physicians (FL. Chapter). Has served as District Director from 1998 to present, past president District 9 and board member Unit 128. Certified club director. Won several regionals.

ALTUS, Stephen S. (b.1969) of Stanford CA, graduate student, collector of more than 3000 airline schedules. Member ACBL Junior Corps, collegiate coordinator of Youth Bridge Federation 1988-90 and a certified director. Winner Junior Pairs 1990, Red Ribbon Pairs 1994, Junior Team Trials 1995. Also won many regionals.

ALUJAS, Gustavo (b. 1952) of Buenos Aires, Argentina, bridge teacher. South American champion 1981; represented Argentina Bermuda Bowl 1981. 9 national titles.

ALVAREZ, Jaime Carrera (b. 1956) of Girardot, Colombia, teacher and computer programmer. Won CAC Open Teams 1980, 89, runner-up 1987. Runner-up South American Open Teams and Open Pairs 1985, Junior Teams 1979, 80. Represented Colombia in one world championship and is its top-ranked player, with wins in all national events.

AMANO, Ayako (b. 1959) of Tokyo, executive assistant to the President of medical device import company. Won CAC Women's Teams 1993, 2nd ACBL Women's Pairs 1995. Represented Venezuela in 2 Venice Cups and Japan in one Women's Team Olympiad. Won national championships in both Japan and Venezuela.

AMARAL, Marcelo (b. 1949) of Sao Paulo, Brazil, engineer. WBF World Master. Won South American Teams 1974, 88, 93; represented Brazil in 4 world championships.

AMES, Anthony C. (Tony) (b. 1948) of Minnetonka MN, management, CPA. Vice president Unit 178 Board of Directors 1997-present; certified club director and teacher, contributor to Units 178 & 103 newsletters. Has more than 30 regional wins.

ANDERSEN, Eilif B. (1907-1977) of Los Angeles CA, was president of the ACBL in 1966. A vital member of the Board of Directors from 1956-58 and 1961-67, Andersen chaired the finance, building fund, headquarters site and other important committees. He sponsored

ACBL's acceptance of district organization plan. In the early Sixties Andersen founded and presided over Association of Los Angeles County Bridge Units (ALACBU). In 1967 he was elected president of the Western Conference. He also founded and edited *Southern California Bridge News*.

ANDERSEN, Morten (Duck) (b. 1958) of Copenhagen, Denmark, travel organizer. World Master. 3rd World Team Olympiad 1996. Also represented Denmark in one world championship and 2 zonal championships. Won Icelandair Teams 1998 and China Cup 1999. 3 national titles include 2 Danish Cups.

ANDERSEN, Ronald E. (Ron) (1941-1997) of Chicago IL, options trader and professional bridge writer, player and teacher. Was one of the most successful American players. World Master, ACBL Grand Life Master with 38,338 MPs; was #3 on list of members with greatest total points at the time of his death. Lectured, hosted panel shows and emceed bridge programs at NABCs and regionals all over North America and at international bridge tournaments throughout the world. For several years he hosted and coordinated vugraph presentations at NABCs and was chief commentator at many European Championships.

Placed 6th in World Championship Open Pairs 1978, 8th 1982, tied for 5th 1984 World Team Olympiad in Seattle. Also represented ACBL in WBF competition Las Palmas 1974, New Orleans 1978, Bal Harbour 1986, Geneva 1990. Finished 3rd in 1990 resumption of the London Times Invitational, won London Times Charity Pro-Am event 1991, won Proton Invitational Teams in Taipei 1990. In 1981 played in first international bridge tournament ever held in mainland China (Shanghai). Delivered a lecture at Chinese University in Shanghai with the aid of Kathie Wei (now Wei-Sender) as translator. Developer of DOOP and contributed to the development of the Precision System. Editor-in-chief of Devyn Press's *Championship Bridge Series* and author of 2 pamphlets in the series titled *Killing Their Notrump* and *Matchpoint Tactics*. Edited 4 books on Precision, was associate editor of *International Precision Newsletter*, wrote articles for the ACBL *Bulletin* and several other bridge periodicals throughout the world. Authored *Where and How High*, *Lebensold* and co-authored *Matchpoint Precision*, *Bridge from A to Z*, *Making the Most of Your Limited Opening Bids*, *Profits From Preempts*, *Perfect Your Notrump Bidding* and *Action for the Defense*. Coach and acting captain U.S. Venice Cup team that placed 2nd 1981. Was captain of Venice Cup team that reached semifinals in Yokohama 1991.

Won Mott-Smith Trophy with a record 250 masterpoints 1974. Four-time winner McKenney Top 500 (more than any other living player). Was first to win more than 2000 MPs in one year (2009 MPs 1977, 2725 MPs 1980, 2994 MPs 1983). Won Life Master Men's Pairs 1970, Master Mixed Teams 1971, Men's Teams 1974, Blue Ribbon Pairs 1978, Reisinger 1980, 92; Life Master Pairs 1982, Spingold 1983, 88, 86; Men's Swiss Teams 1989. He placed 2nd Vanderbilt 1974, 77, 79, 80; Open Pairs 1974, Blue Ribbon Pairs 1975, Spingold 1990, Reisinger 1992, Mixed Pairs 1993. Won hundreds of regionals. He died at the European Championships while commentating on vugraph.

ANDERSON, A.T. Rex (b. 1945) of Coleraine, Northern Ireland, solicitor. 3rd European Team Championship 1979, represented Ireland on 3 other occasions and 2 world championships. Represented Northern Ireland regularly in Camrose Trophy matches since 1971. National titles

include Open Teams 11 times and Open Pairs 8 times.

ANDERSON, Janice (Jan) (b.1952) of Regina SK, executive secretary Canadian Bridge Federation, former parent aide with Social Services and chemistry teacher. Has been Unit 573 Secretary/Treasurer since 1978, CBF Coordinator since 1989, District 18 election officer since 1994; certified director since 1979 and became manager of Regina DBC 1991. Daughter Erin was Canada's youngest female Life Master and member of Canada's World Junior Team 1999.

ANDERSON, John C. (Big John) (1942-1998) of Sixes River OR, bridge professional, formerly taught school. One of the leading bridge personalities of the Northwest, a Grand Life Master with more than 14,600 MP. Won Master Mixed Teams 1971, won dozens of regionals.

ANDERSON, Joyce (formerly Miller) (b.1946) of Moline IL, bridge club owner, teacher. Past president Unit 163. Won approximately 15 regionals.

ANDERSON, Merrell R. (b.1931) of Littleton CO, retired mechanical engineer, bridge teacher. Diamond Life Master, co-authored *The Subtle Club*. Placed 15th World Senior Teams in 1994; won approximately 20 regionals.

ANDERSON, Richard G. (Dick) (b. 1940) of Regina SK, teacher. Recipient of Wilma Downing Award for coaching high-school athletics. Has served as unit treasurer, unit president, Canadian Bridge Federation Board member, CBF president and treasurer. Became member of ACBL Board of Directors in 1992 and served as ACBL president 1998 and Chairman of the Board 1999. Has chaired many regionals and numerous sectionals. Contributor to *Wasumi*. Diamond Life Master with many regional wins.

ANDERSON, Virgil V., Jr. (b.1924) of Springfield MO, retired attorney and president of Anderson and Son, Inc. Has acted in some 75 plays (college, community theater and professionally), is active in Springfield area Arts Council, former president Springfield Little Theatre, former member of Missouri House of Representatives, and Springfield Chamber of Commerce. Directed summer camps for boys and served on Board of Directors of the Gus Giordano Dancers. Served as president of ACBL 1994, Chairman of the Board 1995. Member of ACBL Board of Directors since 1989, has served on District 15 Board of Directors, Unit 101 Board of Directors, member WBF Executive Council 1994 to 2000. Diamond Life Master, won Silver Ribbon Pairs 1994 and numerous regionals.

ANDERSSEN, Rune Brendeford (b. 1953) of Oslo, Norway. Secretary General Norwegian Bridge Federation and Nordic Bridge Union. Represented Norway in Nordic Championship. Several national titles.

ANDERSSON, Lars (b. 1962) of Stockholm, Sweden, computer consultant. World Master. 2nd World Mixed Pairs 1990, 2nd European Teams 1999. Won 2 Swedish titles.

ANDRESS, Patricia (Tricia) (b. 1968) of Nashville TN. Won New Mexico NATS competition 1990 (for singing). Has played tournament bridge since she was 9. Became youngest Life Master 1982 at age 14. While living in Scotland reached semifinals of Scottish National Pairs at age 12. Qualified to be on Junior Team to play in World Junior Championships in 1991 but was unable to play. Has won many regionals.

ANDREW, Mollie (b. 1936) of Belfast, Northern Ireland. Won Lady Milne Cup twice, represented Northern Ireland more than 20 times in the contest against England, Scotland and Wales. Also represented N. Ireland

in Camrose Trophy and Ireland in Europa Cup. Has won all N. Ireland national titles.

ANDREWS, Lowell (b. 1929) of Huntington Beach CA, bridge professional. Created and hosted TV show *Pets on Parade* in Phoenix AZ. Certified director, directed on 70 cruises. Member ACBL Appeals Committee. Diamond Life Master, placed 2nd Mixed Pairs 1963, Senior Player of Year 2000, has won more than 75 regionals.

ANSAY, Nadine. See LIECHTENSTEIN, Princess Nadine von.

ANTHONISEN, Robert (Rob) (b.1941) of Altadena CA, sales representative. Was editor of Diablo Valley District Newsletter for 2 years. Has dubious record of highest score on a board +4600 and lowest score -5800. A Diamond Life Master, has won more than 20 regionals.

ANTUNE, Hugo Carve (b. 1943) of Montevideo, Uruguay, Procurator. 2nd South American Teams 1980, represented Uruguay regularly in zonal championships since then. Won 30 national titles.

ANTUNES, Manuel Costa (b. 1930) of Lisbon, Portugal, civil engineer. Represented Portugal in 6 European championships. 5th European Teams 1966, 6th 1974. Won many national titles.

APFEL, Dr. Kalman (1907-1988) of West Palm Beach FL. Won Vanderbilt 1954, Spingold 1956 and several regionals.

APFELBAUM, Jay M. (b. 1951) of Pittsburgh PA, Regional one director. Served 3 years as member ACBL Board of Directors. Edited ACBL appeals books. Won Blue Ribbon Pairs 1976 and has won several regionals.

APPLEYARD, Robert (1909-1984) of New York City, bridge teacher and club director. Won the Chicago (since 1965 the Reisinger) 1947; Vanderbilt 1948; Life Master Pairs 1939, 45; placed 2nd Life Master Pairs 1936, Master Individual 1950, 56; Men's Teams 1950.

ARIMA, Keiichi (b. 1916) of Tokyo, Japan, company director. Flying officer Japanese Navy 1936-45. Chairman JCBL Board of Directors, manager 1964 Far East Championships. Recipient Fourth Class Order of the Sacred Treasure.

ARLINGHAUS, Dr. William Charles (b. 1944) of Ann Arbor MI, professor of mathematics and computer science Lawrence Technological University. Golfer with 2 holes-in-one. Listed in *Who's Who in the Midwest*. Served on Michigan B.A. Board of Directors as president 1975, 88, 95; Chairman of Board 1976, 89, 96, and tournament chairman. Chief Scorer and co-chairman for hospitality WBF World Junior Championship 1991. Contributor to MBA newsletter, *Table Talk*. Won more than 30 regionals.

ARMANNSSON, Sverrir G. (b. 1953) of Kopavogur, Iceland, financial adviser. World Master. Won Nordic Championship 1992. Represented Iceland in one other Nordic Championship, one European Junior Teams and one Nordic Junior Teams. 14 national wins.

ARMSTRONG, John (b. 1952) of Formby, England, systems analyst. WBF World Master. 2nd Bermuda Bowl 1987. Won European Teams 1991, 2nd 1987. Represented Britain in 3 other world championships, 5 other zonal championships, and England in 30 Camrose Trophy matches. Many national wins include 6 Gold Cups.

ARMSTRONG, John of Toronto. Editor *Kibitzer* 1984-1999.

ARNARSON, Gudmundur Pall (b. 1954) of Kopavogur, Iceland, publisher, bridge teacher and writer. WBF World Life Master. Won Bermuda Bowl 1991. Represented Iceland in 3 other world championships, 6 European Cham-

pionships, 3 Nordic Championships, one European Junior Teams and 2 Nordic Junior Teams. 8 national wins. Publisher and editor of *Icelandic Bridge Magazine*. Writer of daily column for *Morgunbladid* and author of numerous bridge books. Owner of Iceland's only bridge school.

ARNDT, Patsy L. (b. 1935) of Houston TX, teacher, classical piano player. Diamond Life Master, placed 2nd Women's KO Teams 1983; has won more than 30 regionals.

ARNIM, Daniela von (b. 1964) of Wiesbaden, Germany. WBF World Grand Master, #5 on WBF Women's world ranking list. Won Venice Cup 1995, 2nd 1993; 2nd McConnell Cup 1998, 2nd World Women's Pairs 1998, 3rd World Women's Team Olympiad 2000. Represented Germany in almost every world championship since 1986. Won European Women's Teams 1989, 2nd 1991, 95; 2nd European Mixed Teams 1996. Won European Women's Pairs 1995, 97. Also 3rd Macallan (best ever performance by a woman to that time), 4th Cap Gemini

ARNOLD, Rodger S. (b.1947) of Aurora CO, poker dealer. Playing with a variety of partners he once had a streak of 28 consecutive Swiss Team match wins. In one of his Swiss victories his team gave up IMPs on only 4 of 40 boards. He has won 20 regional events.

ARNOLD, Russell D. (Russ) (b. 1927) of Miami FL, accountant and partner in a major appliance company. World Life Master. Won Bermuda Bowl 1981; placed 2nd World Senior Teams 1994. Grand Life Master with 13,774 MPs as of 3/2001; World Life Master. NABC wins include Spingold 1963, 85; GNOT 1973, Reisinger 1979, Vanderbilt 1980, 93, Senior KO Teams 1994, 95, 96. Placed 2nd in Vanderbilt 1960, GNOT 1980, Spingold 1987, Senior KO Teams 1997. Has won well over 100 regional events.

ARNOLDS, Carla (b. 1960), of Tilburg, The Netherlands, bridge teacher and journalist. WBF World Master. Won Women's Pairs 1994; 2nd Venice Cup 1989, 3rd World Women's Pairs 1990. Represented the Netherlands in 3 other world championships and 2 European Championships. National titles include Women's Pairs 1991.

ARNTHORSSON, Orn (b. 1945) of Reykjavik, Iceland, pension funds manager. WBF World Master. Won Bermuda Bowl 1991. Represented Iceland in 6 other world championships, 6 European Championships and one Nordic Championship. 11 national wins.

ARON, Adrien (1902-c.1970) of Paris, France, bridge writer. European Champion 1935. Represented France at Plafond against Ely Culbertson in 1933. Author of 2 books and many articles.

ARONSON, Sidney (b. 1911) of Pompano Beach FL, retired attorney and deputy assistant inspector general, U.S. Department of Agriculture. Served as president and tournament chairman of New England B.A. Authored articles for *The Bridge World* in the Forties. Aronson won the Chicago (since 1965 the Reisinger) 1949, placed 2nd in Life Master Pairs 1959, had many regional wins.

AROSEMENA, Carlos (b. 1924) of Lima, Peru, businessman and bridge teacher. Represented Peru in one world championship and several zonal championships. Won several national titles.

AROSEMENA, Teresa (b. 1933) of Lima, Peru, bridge teacher. Represented Peru in 2 world championships and many zonal championships. Won many national titles. President of Peruvian Bridge Commission.

ARST, Frieda (1906-1985) of Chicago IL, bridge teacher. Won Women's Teams 1966, Life Master Women's Pairs 1973; placed 2nd Women's Teams 1972. Numerous regional wins.

ARVEDON, Lloyd B. (b. 1953) of Medford MA, school fund- raising representative. Grand Life Master with 13,027 MPs as of 3/2001. Won Open Pairs I 1994, Open Pairs II 1997; has more than 40 regional wins including District 25 GNOP 3 times.

ASHBACHER, Ronald W. (Ash) (b. 1946) of Topeka KS, Goodyear area manager. Contributor to *Bridge Bulletin*; authored the convention Suction, and has won more than 30 regionals.

ASHBURN, (formerly Hyder) Laurel (b. 1941) of Colorado Springs CO, administrative assistant. Diamond Life Master with more than 15 regional wins.

ASHLEY, David D. (b. 1941) of Las Vegas NV, expert bridge, backgammon and poker player, backgammon champion. Served on ACBL Conduct and Ethics Committee, directs on cruises. Grand Life Master with 14,299 MPs as of 3/2001. Won Men's BAM Teams 1976, North American Swiss Teams 1982. Placed 2nd Life Master Men's Pairs 1987. More than 100 regional wins.

ASHWORTH, John W. (b. 1933) of Perth, Australia. Represented Australia in 1984 Bermuda Bowl. 7 national wins include Victor Champion Cup 3 times and Interstate Open Teams. Has won 39 Western Australia titles.

ASMENIADIS, Nikos (b. 1931) of Thessaloniki, Greece, civil engineer. Honorary vice-president of Hellenic Bridge Federation and member of its Board for nearly 20 years. International tournament director, with involvement in computerizing various bridge events. Founded the 1st club in Thessaloniki. Translated Edgar Kaplan's *Winning Contract Bridge* into Greek. Won several national events.

ASSAEL, Salvador (b. 1954) of Manisa, Turkey, economist. Represented Turkey in 4 world and 3 zonal championships. Several national wins.

ASSINI, Jan L. (b. 1945) of Aurora OH, administrative assistant. Served as Unit 125 Secretary 1973-1982. Placed 2nd Women's KO Teams 1998.

ASSOUAD-DOCHE, Marie Lucette (b. 1947) of Cairo, Egypt. Won BFAAME Women's Teams 1991, runner-up 1989. Represented Egypt several other times.

ASSUMPCAO, Pedro Paulo Puglisi de (P.P.) (b. 1935) of Sao Paulo, Brazil, retired company director. WBF Grand Master. Won World Olympiad Teams 1976. 2nd Rosenblum Teams 1978. Represented Brazil in 13 other world championships. Won South American Teams 1967, 68, 69, 70, 71, 72, 73, 74, 75, 77, 78, 82, 84, 86, 90, 96, 98. Won many national titles.

ASTROM, Lisbeth (Lisa) (b. 1955) of Sweden, immigration camp manager. World Master. 3rd Venice Cup 1993, won European Women's Teams 1993, Nordic Women's Teams 1982. Represented Sweden in 2 other zonal championships, won 3 national titles.

ATA-ULLAH, Munir Ahmed (b. 1940) of London, England, (born in Pakistan) formerly of Pakistan and Dubai, attorney and managing director. WBF World Master. 2nd Bermuda Bowl 1981. Won BFAAME zonal championship 1983, 85, 87. Won many national titles. Inventor of *Stoneage Acol with Paki Preempts* system. Bridge theoretician who contributes to newspapers and magazines.

ATHANASSIADIS, Alexandros (b. 1954) of Thessaloniki, Greece, bridge teacher and journalist. National wins include Open Pairs 1986. Writes a daily newspaper column in Thessaloniki and a weekly one in Macedonia. Former vice-president of Hellenic Bridge Federation, represents Northern Greece on its Board. Offers free classes for beginners, and occasionally promotes bridge on national television.

ATTAGUILE, Luis (b. 1926) of Buenos Aires, Argentina, clerk. World Life Master. South American champion 1961, 62, 64, 76, 79, 80, 81, 85. Represented Argentina in Bermuda Bowl 1962, 63, 65, 77, 85; in World Team Olympiad 1964, 80. 15 national wins. Gabarret Cup 1961.

AUBY, Daniel (b. 1955) of Vallentuna, Sweden, computer consultant. WBF World Master. 3rd Rosenblum Teams 1994. Npc Swedish international teams 1997-2000. Regular contributor to Swedish bridge magazines.

AUGUST, William J. (Bill) (b. 1926) of Palm Beach FL, bridge teacher, author, columnist, certified director and former bridge club owner. Was affiliated with Goren International 1962-76 lecturing on cruises and teaching classes for training teachers. Has authored several pamphlets on bidding and directing, teaching texts, and duplicate bridge instructional club director's manual. Devised August 2♦ Convention (see 2-Way Stayman). Former president and vice president of New England Bridge Conference and vice-president of ABTA. During the administration of Easley Blackwood he was special consultant to ACBL regarding club matters, membership and club/unit/league relations. Has won more than 20 regional titles.

AUKEN, Jens (b. 1949) of Copenhagen, Denmark, lawyer. World Life Master, placed 3rd World Teams 1984, 86, World Mixed Pairs 1998. Represented Denmark in 3 other world championships, 7 zonals and many Nordic championships. 25 Danish titles. Top Danish masterpoint winner 5 times. Won Rottneros Cup 1990, European Club Cup 1990. WBF vice-president. Legal consultant for Danish Federation and member of its Appeals Committee.

AUKEN, Sabine (nee Zenkel) (b. 1965) of Copenhagen, Denmark. Formerly of Bamberg, Germany; represents Germany in international events. WBF World Grand Master, #2 on WBF Women's world ranking list. Won Venice Cup 1995, 2nd 1993. Placed 2nd McConnell Cup 1998, World Women's Pairs 1998, World Mixed Pairs 1994; 3rd Mixed Pairs 1998, World Women's Team Olympiad 1996, 2000. Represented Germany in almost every world championship since 1986. Won European Women's Teams 1989, 2nd 1991, 95. Won European Mixed Pairs 1994. 2nd European Mixed Teams 1996. Won European Women's Pairs 1995, 97. Placed 2nd Macallan 1995. ACBL titles include Life Master Women's Pairs 1989, 93, Women's Swiss Teams 1990. Became ACBL Life Master in 6 weeks in 1989, setting a record. Co-author of *Bridge from A to Z*.

AVARELLI, Walter (1912-1987) of Rome, Italy, judge. WBF Grand Master, one of the all-time greats of the game. Was 5th in world career rankings at the time of his death. Won World Team Olympiad 1964, 68, 72; Bermuda Bowl 1957, 58, 59, 61, 62, 65, 66, 67, 69; European Teams 1956, 57, 58, 59.

AVELINO, Ronaldo (b. 1949) of Rio de Janeiro, Brazil, engineer. Won South American Teams 1986, 1987. Represented Brazil in 2 world championships.

AYDIN, Ata (b. 1957) of Istanbul, Turkey, business administrator. Represented Turkey in one world and 2 zonal championships. 7 national wins.

B

BABIN, Elmer J. (1902-1990) of Shaker Heights OH, attorney, president of ACBL 1940. Played first duplicate in March 1930. Won Open State Pairs championship in

May and the AWL Open Pairs in June. Also won other events before retiring from tournament play in 1951.

BABSCH, Andreas (b. 1961) of Vienna, Austria, bridge teacher. WBF World Life Master. Represented Austria in 4 world championships, 2 European open championships and 7 other European events. Won 2 national Open Teams, 2 Life Master Individuals, 2 Open Pairs. Youngest ever Austrian Life Master.

BABSCH, Fritz (b. 1933) of Vienna, Austria, retired civil engineer, bridge journalist and tournament director. WBF World Life Master. World Pair champion 1970. Represented Austria in one World Team Olympiad and 6 European Championships. Won Caransa Tournament (Amsterdam). Won 7 national teams and one pairs. Chief organizer most Austrian tournaments since late Seventies. Tournament Director several European Championships. Editor *Austrian Bridge Magazine* 1971-90.

BACH, Norman (1913-1971) accountant from Paget East, Bermuda. Best remembered for initiating and organizing first post-World War II World Championships — the Bermuda Bowl — in Bermuda - 1950. Enjoyed several bridge exploits, including capturing Gold Cup for Great Britain 1938 and acting as playing captain of British team in European Championships 1938, 39.

BACHERICH, Rene (d. 1997) of Lille, France, retired merchant. WBF World Grand Master. Won Bermuda Bowl 1956, World Team Olympiad 1960. Won European Teams 1953, 55, 62. 2nd 1956, 1961. Represented France in 4 other world championships. Many national wins include Open Teams once. (see RELAY SYSTEM.)

BACON, Francis M., III (1899-1983) of New York City, stockbroker. Played in first game of contract bridge played aboard the S.S. FINLAND on Nov. 1, 1925. Contributed much new information regarding background of origin of contract bridge and helped to pinpoint date of its inception. At that time he was the only surviving player of that game.

BAER, Henry (1930-1999) of Dallas TX, born in Germany, attorney. Served as executive secretary for District 16 for many years. District GNOT and tournament coordinator. Received ACBL Presidential Citation for service 1992. Several regional wins.

BAFF, Martin (Marty) (b. 1927) of Beachwood OH, founder and retired president of wholesale plumbing supply firm. In 1985 won all events at a sectional tournament. Diamond Life Master with more than 15,600 MPs as of 3/2001. Placed 2nd Senior KO Teams 1996, more than 50 regional wins.

BAGCHI, Ritobrata (Khokan) (b. 1961) of Sydney, Australia, born in India; environmental scientist. Won South Pacific playoff 1997. Represented Australia in 2 Bermuda Bowls, 2 other world championships and 3 zonals. Many national wins include Butler Trials 4 straight years, 1995-98.

BAINS, Kenneth (Ken) (b. 1944), of Austin TX, mortgage banker, soccer referee. On Top 500 list 1974-1981. More than 15 regional wins.

BAIRD, James C. (1878-1963) a widely traveled bridge player, he lived in a town named after him, Baird MS. Twice headed Mississippi Unit. ACBL feted him by naming him Honorary Member in 1951. His wife, Mary Elizabeth Baird, was ACBL Honorary Member 1947, the year she died. In her memory, Baird donated Baird Trophy for Open Individual.

BAKALISH, Robert (Bob) (b. 1947) of Eureka CA, salesman. Founder and former president 5th Chair Foun-

dation. Won more than 20 regionals.

BAKER, Lynn (b. 1957) of Austin TX, law professor, author, consultant on issues of legal ethics in mass tort settlements, former law clerk to Judge Amalya Kearse of U.S. Court of Appeals. Won Women's Swiss Teams 1998, 2001; Mixed BAM Teams 1999, Women's BAM Teams 1999; placed 2nd Women's Swiss Teams 1999. Member of Women's International Team Trials Committee (2001-04).

BAKKER, Ellen (b. 1958) of Amsterdam, The Netherlands, systems analyst. WBF World Master. 2nd Venice Cup 1989. Represented The Netherlands in 2 other world championships and 2 European Championships. National titles include Women's Pairs 1991.

BALDURSSON, Jon (b. 1954) of Reykjavik, Iceland, airline manager. One of Iceland's most succesful players. WBF World Master. Won Bermuda Bowl 1991, Nordic Teams 1988, Generali Individual 1994; 2nd Cavendish Invitational 1990. Represented Iceland in many other world, European and Nordic championships. Many national titles.

BALDWIN, Col. Russell J. (1889-1969) of Norwalk CT, Army officer and expert on tournament procedure. One of the leading American bridge personalities. Was active as an organizer from the earliest days of contract bridge. Became a director of the American Bridge League and its treasurer shortly after its foundation in 1927. A member of ACBL Laws Commission (originally Committee) since its foundation 1933. Baldwin was primarily responsible for the first Duplicate Code issued in 1935 and played a considerable part in formulating subsequent codes. Author of McKenney-Baldwin schedules for Howell Movements and constructed other movements. His many contributions to tournament procedure included ACBL's former method of dealing with fouled boards. Tournament director 1927-41 and after war service became ABCL business manager, 1946-51. Recalled to military service at outbreak of Korean War and returned to ACBL in charge of tournament scheduling 1958-63. ACBL Honorary Member 1943. His writings included many magazine contributions. Contributing editor to *Encyclopedia of Bridge*.

BALDWIN, William A. (1907-1978) of Albuquerque NM. As 1970 ACBL president was person most instrumental in relocating national headquarters to Memphis. His interest in this project grew naturally from his career as a building and land developer. Was also president of Western Conference, trustee of the Charity Foundation and chairman of ACBL Board of Directors (1971). ACBL Honorary Member 1978. Baldwin was ACBL representative to WBF and treasurer of that body.

BALFE, Raymond A. (1895-1969) of New York City, enjoyed distinction of winning national championships in both auction and contract bridge, taking the 1926 All-American Open Pairs (auction) title with Waldemar von Zedtwitz as well as 1936 USBA Grand National Mixed Teams (contract).

BALICKI, Cezary (b. 1958) of Wroclaw, Poland, bridge professional and chess instructor. WBF World Life Master. Winner World Transnational Open Teams Bermuda 2000. 2nd Bermuda Bowl 1991, 2nd Rosenblum Teams 1994, 3rd World Open Pairs 1990, 3rd Bermuda Bowl 1989. Winner European Open Teams 1989, 93; 2nd 1997, 3rd 1992. 4th 1998 Par Contest in Lille. Won ACBL Spingold 1997, Vanderbilt 2001; placed 2nd Spingold 1998, Reisinger 1997. Represented Poland in many World and European Championships. Del Duca winner. Winner of many titles in Polish championships.

BALLANTYNE, Aidan (b. 1951) of Vancouver BC, born

in Switzerland, consultant in environmental planning and private bridge teacher. Member Canadian World Cup Ski Team (Alpine) 1969-73. Past president Canadian Bridge Federation. Has been member of CBF Board of Directors since 1985. Member Unit 430 Conduct and Ethics Committee since 1983. Co-chaired 1999 Vancouver NABC. 1991 he won Calgary Calcutta. Was npc of Canadian team, 1991 Bermuda Bowl in Yokohama, Japan. Does hand analyses for CBF-sponsored events, contributor to several bridge magazines. Diamond Life Master, won GNOP 1997 and more than 50 regional events.

BALLAS, Dimitris (b. 1959) of Athens, Greece, bridge teacher. International Director holding EBL degree since 1993 and has directed many tournaments in Greece as well as other countries. Was technical director EBU Championships 1991, WBF Junior Championships Indonesia 1995 and Generali Masters 2000. Tournament manager of European and World Junior Championships since 1996. Represented Greece in European Junior Championship 1984.

BAMBERGER, Gabriele (b. 1953) of Vienna, Austria, bridge teacher. WBF World Life Master. Won European Women's Teams 1991, runner-up Venice Cup 1991. Represented Austria in 2 World Team Olympiads and 5 other European events. Won 5 National Open Teams, one Open Pairs and 5 Mixed Pairs.

BAMBERGER, Johannes (b. 1946) of Vienna, Austria, publishing company employee. WBF World Life Master. Represented Austria in one World Team Olympiad and 3 European Championships. Won Caransa Tournament (Amsterdam). Won 8 National Open Teams and 5 Mixed Pairs.

BANDLER, Michael L. (Mike) (b.1938) of Alamo CA., retired vice president of Pacific Bell. Served as president of Unit (1991-1994). Has won more than 15 regional events.

BANK, Julius (b. 1913) of Chicago, CPA. Became Life Master #63 in 1946 and was among the Top Ten players that year. Won Spring Men's Teams 1946, placed 2nd Spingold 1948, had several regional wins.

BAQAI, Iftikhar (Ifti) (b. 1946) of Los Angeles CA, born in India. Won BFAAME Open Teams 1987 and played in 1987 Bermuda Bowl.

BARAN, Boris (b. 1945) of Montreal, born in Switzerland, professor of computer information systems. Was a nationally rated swimmer. One of Canada's leading players and a 3-time runner-up for Richmond Trophy. WBF World Master and ACBL Grand Life Master with 11,768 MP as of 3/2001. Represented Canada in world championship competition 1978, 84, 86, 88, 1990 (3rd Rosenblum Teams), 92, 1995 (2nd Bermuda Bowl), 1992 (2nd Pan American Teams). Won Epson World Towers competition (E-W) 1990 and Icelandic Invitational Pairs 1991. Won ACBL GNOP 1991, North American Swiss Teams 1992, 94, 95; placed 2nd GNOP 1990. Won Canadian National Team Championship 1983, 85, 87, 89, 91; placed 2nd in CNTC 1986, 88, 90 and won Canadian Open Pairs 1985. Numerous regional credits include District one GNOP at least 8 times.

BARATTA, Franz (b. 1935) of Vienna, Austria, born in Czechoslovakia born in Czechoslovakia; managing director. Represented Austria in 2 World Team Olympiads and 4 European Championships. Won National Open Team title, npc winning Austrian team 1985 European Championship, and on many other occasions.

BARBER, Diana L. (b. 1940) of Bozeman MT, teacher and financial advisor. #1 masterpoint holder in Montana, has won 15 regionals.

BARBEY, Henry I. (1832-1906) of New York City, a cosmopolitan who spent many years in Europe. Is credited by Joseph B. Elwell and Robert R. Foster with introducing bridge to New York in 1893. A yachtsman, banker and company director, the colorful Barbey is best remembered for writing the first code of laws for the new game, dated 1892.

BARBONE, Guido (1925-1995) of Italy, columnist and bridge writer, was npc of Italian Team Bermuda Bowl 1967, npc winning Women's Team in European Championships 1977, 2nd-place Women's Team Venice Cup 1978. Former president Italian Bridge Federation, member of executive committee of EBL, vice president of IBPA 1981-85. Writings include The *Complete Book of Bridge, Funny Bridge* and *Complete Book of Duplicate Bridge.*

BARBOSA, Jose (b. 1936) of Rio de Janeiro, Brazil, engineer. WBF World Life Master. Won South American Teams 1977, 78, 86, 87, 93. Represented Brazil in 3 world championships.

BARBOSA, Juliano (b. 1949) of Oporto, Portugal, civil engineer. Represented Portugal in one World and 4 European championships. Won many national titles.

BARBOSA, Maria de Lourdes (b. 1928) of Lisbon, Portugal. Represented Portugal in 2 European championships. 5th European Women's Teams 1970. Won many national titles.

BARBOSA, Sergio Marinho (b. 1942) of Rio de Janeiro, Brazil, engineer and economist. Educational insurance executive. WBF World Life Master. Won World Olympiad Teams 1976. 2nd Rosenblum Teams 1978. Won South American Teams 1971, 83, 84. Represented Brazil in 6 other world championships. National wins include 7 open teams.

BARBOUR, Kenneth R. (b. 1938) of Scottsdale AZ, born in Scotland, retired computer executive. Represented Great Britain in European Championships 1963 and was one of its first Life Masters. Won British Team Trials 1962, Crockford's Cup, Gold Cup 1963, and placed 2nd in Sunday Times Pairs (now the Macallan), Master Mixed Teams 1970. Contributor to *The Bridge World, British Bridge World* and *Bridge Journal.* More than 30 regional wins.

BARCINSKI, Jack H. (b. 1929) of Dallas TX, executive, contributor to *Bridge World,* father was member of Polish National team in the Thirties. Won 17 regional events.

BARCLAY, Shepard (1889-1955) of New York City, was a bridge writer, publisher, lecturer and club director. In 1927 he bought *Auction Bridge Magazine* and sought to make it a mass magazine, featuring the editorship of Milton Work and Wilbur Whitehead. The magazine failed (1929) and its mailing list was used by Ely Culbertson to start *The Bridge World.* Barclay conducted a bridge page, with doggerel pertaining to bridge as a regular feature, in the *New York Herald Tribune* 1929-34. During those years also ranked the ten best (or most successful) players each year for *Collier's* magazine. He conducted bridge clubs and duplicate games. Wrote many books on bridge and from 1932 until his death he wrote a daily newspaper feature on bridge for King Features Syndicate. Member of executive committees of ABL and ACBL 1936-49. ACBL Honorary Member 1948.

BARDACH, David (1916-1993) born in Poland, book publishing executive and controller. Represented Israel in one world championship and one European Championship. Won Tel Aviv Teams 1977, runner-up in 4 national events. EBL Honorary Secretary 1979-93, and member EBL Management Committee. Member WBF

Executive Council 1981-93. President of Israel Bridge Federation 1988-92 and formerly its secretary, treasurer and chairman of Executive Committee.

BARDOLA, Marcello (b. 1925) of Zurich, Switzerland, mathematician. Represented Switzerland in 4 European Championships. Many national wins. Former president of Swiss Bridge Federation.

BARE, Dorothy O. (Mrs. Gerald) (1923-1996) of Pacific Palisades CA, travel agency owner since 1967. Won Master Mixed Teams 1970, also won several regionals.

BARE, Gerald W. (b. 1933) of Pacific Palisades CA, civil engineer, owner of travel agency. Was District 23 Chairman of Conduct, Ethics and Deportment Committee 1973-77. Placed 9th Rosenblum Teams 1990. ACBL Grand Life Master with 13,217 MPs as of 3/2001. Won Master Mixed Teams 1970; placed 2nd in Reisinger 1966, Senior Swiss Teams 2000. Has won more than 100 regional events.

BARKER, Michele V. (formerly Handley) (b. 1964) of Chobham, England, bridge teacher. WBF World Life Master. 2nd World Women's Teams 1992. Won European Women's Teams 1997; Common Market Women's Pairs 1991, Teams 1993. Won ACBL Women's Swiss Teams 1992. Won 2 national titles. Co-presenter, with Zia Mahmood, of 1991 British TV program *Play Bridge with Zia*.

BARNES, A. Mitchell (Mitch) (1906-1985) of New York City, former executive vice president of Travel With Goren. Was one of the leading East Coast players in early years of bridge. Became Life Master #14 in 1938. Won many USBA and AWL titles including USBA Grand National Open Teams 1936, AWL All-American Open Teams 1934, 1935. Won Open Pairs 1937, Spingold 1941, Chicago (now the Reisinger) 1946 and placed 2nd in Vanderbilt 1933, Spingold 1938, Chicago 1938, 41; Mixed Teams 1934, Men's Teams 1946, USBA Grand National Open Pairs 1934, Mixed Teams 1936.

BARNETT, Patricia (Patty) (b. 1951) of Gainesville Fl, teacher. Won Mixed Pairs 1980.

BARNICLE, John F. (b. 1925) of Baltimore MD, retired management consultant for computer systems. Active in bridge administration for more than 30 years. Served as president of New Jersey B.L., Delaware State B.A. and Maryland B.A. Former co-owner of bridge club. Certified director since 1968. Teaches and directs on cruises. Has won more than 30 regionals.

BARON, Hermine (Mrs. Arthur) (1912-1996) of Los Angeles, was one of the leading American women players, Grand Life Master. Won more masterpoints than any other woman (more than 22,600) in this country. Won McKenney Trophy 1964, 70. Her winning total of 1370 masterpoints in the 1964 competition stood as all-time record until 1969. Represented United States in world competition 1968, 78. Won Women's Teams 1964, 68, Women's Pairs 1968, 82; Life Master Women's Pairs 1963; Life Master Pairs 1966, placed 2nd Women's Teams 1967, 74; Women's Pairs 1967, 75, 77, 80; Blue Ribbon Pairs 1971. Won more than 100 regional events. (see also HANDICAPPED PLAYERS.)

BARON, Leo (d. 1985) of Harare, Zimbabwe, born in England; attorney. Invented Baron System. Made many important contributions to bidding theory. British wins included Gold Cup twice. Co-author of a book on his system. Retired from bridge after emigrating to Rhodesia (now Zimbabwe) in 1952. Became chief justice of Zimbabwe and later Zambia.

BARON, Randall S. (Randy) (b. 1949) of Louisville KY, writer and publisher, owner and president of Baron Barclay Bridge Supplies, owner of Devyn Press, a certified director, served as secretary of District 11 for 5 years and as chairman of Unit Ethics Committee. Has authored more than 20 books and pamphlets on bridge, including ABTA Book of the Year, *The Bridge Book* with Frank Stewart. Also authored eight books on the history of baseball, basketball and horse racing. Was chairman and npc of 1993 U.S. Maccabiah bridge team. Has won several regionals.

BARRETT, Annette C. (b. 1934) of Miami FL, secretary and salesperson, Diamond Life Master, has won more than 15 regional titles.

BARRETT, Geoffrey S. Jade, (the Chairman) (b. 1960) of Vancouver WA, former chef and musician, now bridge club director/operator. Won silver medal in Junior Olympics in long jump and triple jump. Coach Junior USA II 1997, 1st alternate District 20, North American Youth Bridge Foundation chairman 1997, npc USA Junior I 1999, Junior Team for Lille 1998, has served on Board of Appeals European Youth Bridge Festival 1997-99, World Junior Pair Championships 1999. Authored *It's All in Your Head*, several conventions, unique treatments and concepts; contributes to District 20 *Forum*. Founder North American Youth Bridge Foundation 1997. An ACBL and ABA Diamond LM, with more than 130 regional wins.

BARRETT, (formerly Singer) Karen Lee (b. 1949) of Vancouver WA, computer programmer. She and her husband, G.S. Jade Barrett, met while playing bridge on the internet. Won Life Master Women's Pairs 1984, Women's KO Teams, Women's BAM Teams 1998, Women's Swiss Teams 2000; placed 2nd Women's BAM Teams 1992, 98 and has won more than 30 regionals.

BARRETT, William K. (Billy) (1909-1981) of Atlanta GA, became one of the youngest players to win a national championship when he and the late Johnny Rau captured the Chicago Trophy (now the Reisinger) in 1930. The two were credited in *Watson's Play of the Hand* and other sources as being the first to use psychic bids in a national tournament. A lawyer, Barrett served 2 terms in the Georgia House of Representatives.

BARROW, James M. (Jim) (b.1942) of Phoenix AZ. Won Barry Crane Top 500 in 1999 with record total of 3584.26 MPs, crushing the old record - 3270 MPs by Grant Baze. Diamond Life Master with 15,238 MPs as of 3/2001. Placed 2nd Senior KO Teams 1998, 99; won McKenney Trophy 1980. Has won more than 50 regional events. Author of *Record Run*.

BARROW, Rhoda See LEDERER, Rhoda.

BART, Leslie C. (Les) (b. 1947) of Olney MD, accountant for Marriott Corp. Competes in backgammon tournaments. Won Life Master Men's Pairs 1972. Invented Bart convention. Has won dozens of regionals.

BARTON, Lionel Oscar (b. 1942) of Missouri City TX, born in Guyana, retired senior geophysicist with Chevron. The Southwest section sectional vice president and one of the leading players of the ABA. #2 in ABA masterpoints with more than 18,000 points. He is also an ACBL Life Master and a bridge teacher. Has won more than 200 regional ABA titles and more than 40 national ABA titles (including 15+ KOs), Summer Open Pairs 1980, Summer Open Teams 1981, Spring Open Teams 1982. Was Spring National Player of the Year 1976, 86; Summer National Player of the Year 1981, 85, 92; won William A. Friend award (Player of the Year) 6 times 1978, 1982-85, 1992.

BARTON-PAYNE, Diane (Peanut) (b. 1943) of San Francisco CA, R-3 certified ACBL director, former computer systems project manager. At age 6 taught herself to play chess and set a world's record at 8 when she played 20 games simultaneously in an exhibition match. Both parents were directors and opened the first duplicate bridge club in San Francisco. Self-taught bridge at age 8 but didn't play seriously until 11. Became the youngest Life Master in 1961, also one of the ACBL's youngest tournament directors. She has been the subject of national magazine, radio and TV interviews including an article in *The Saturday Evening Post* and made a guest appearance on *To Tell the Truth*. Has won several regionals.

BARTUSEK, Mark J. (b. 1955) of Santa Barbara CA, software engineer for Hughes Aircraft, now at Raytheon. Won his high school chess conference 1973 74, was on intercollegiate chess, table tennis and bridge teams 1974 75. Mini-McKenney National Master of the Year for 1978. Has won more than 15 regionals.

BASARSKY, Dr. Peter R. (b. 1943) of Moose Jaw SK, dentist. Won Canadian National Open Pairs 1994.

BASEGGIO, Franco (b. 1970) of New York City, portfolio manager. President of Harvard Bridge Club 1991-92 and a certified director. Won North American College Bridge Championship 1990, 2nd 1989.

BATCHELLER, John (b.1941) of St. Petersburg FL, bridge club owner, certified director and teacher. Served as member of Western Massachusetts Board for more than 20 years in several capacities including president Unit 196. Diamond Life Master, has won more than 15 regionals.

BATES, Roger W. (b. 1947) of Mesa AZ, professional player, one of the leading American players; WBF World Life Master and ACBL Grand Life Master with 17,407 MPs as of 3/2001.Won Rosenblum Teams 1994, placed 3rd World Open Pairs 1978, won 1980 Cavendish Invitational Pairs; won Mott-Smith Trophy 1975, 88, 92; Vanderbilt 1975, 76, 88, 92; Spingold 1976, Blue Ribbon Pairs 1971, Spring Men's Swiss Teams 1986, North American Men's Swiss Teams 1985, Life Master Men's Pairs 1985, North American Swiss Teams 1982, 90; placed 2nd Blue Ribbon Pairs 1974, 89, Men's Teams 1975, Men's BAM Teams 1985; GNOT 1989.

BAUER, Robert E. (Bob) (b. 1943) of Lauderhill FL, bridge professional, certified director since 1975 and bridge teacher since 1983, member ACBL Appeals Committee 1983-1993. Has won more than 20 regionals.

BAUM, Jay A. (1947) of Omaha NE, executive director Greater Omaha Convention & Visitors Bureau, vice president Unit 241, certified director, won 32 regional events including District 14 GNOP and GNOT both twice.

BAUM, Kathy J. (b. 1946) of Omaha NE, vendor managed inventory specialist with ConAgra Grocery Products. Has won 23 regional events including District 14 GNOT and GNOP 2 times each.

BAVIN, Max (b. 1954) of Aylesbury, England, tournament director. Assistant chief tournament director of both WBF and EBL. Chief tournament director of England. Full-time employee of English Bridge Union at its headquarters in Aylesbury since 1984.

BAXTER, Donald E. (Don) (b. 1931) of Cerritos CA, retired certified public accountant. Has served in many capacities in Dallas and New Orleans Units including president of both. Has been tournament chairman for 12 regionals and 2 nationals. Won about 40 regional events.

BAXTER, Ken (b. 1939) of Edinburgh, Scotland, computer consultant. Won Gold Cup 1980. Represented Scotland 9 times in Camrose matches. Many Scottish wins including Scottish Cup.

BAZE, Diane (see HAYWARD, Diane).

BAZE, Grant Sheridan (b. 1943) of San Diego CA, one of the leading professional players. Also an expert rubber bridge player — from 1965-79 was a rubber bridge professional. Won Pan American Games the first 2 years of event. Represented ACBL in 1986 and 1990 in world championships. Captained Women's team that played in Venice Cup 1988. Placed 9th in World Championship Mixed Pairs 1986 and 11th in Rosenblum Teams 1986. First player to win 3000 MPs (3270) in one year (1984). Won Barry Crane Top 500 - 1984, 85, 87; Fishbein Trophy 1975, Lou Herman Trophy 1984. North American titles include Reisinger 1970, 2nd 1971; Spingold 1975, 97, 2nd 1998; BAM Teams 1983, 98, 2nd 1972; North American Swiss Teams 1984; Open Swiss Teams 1983, 2nd 1990, 94, 99. WBF World Master and an ACBL Grand Life Master with 33,111 MPs as of 3/2001. Ranked #6 in total masterpoints in ACBL as of 3/2001. Contributor ACBL *Bridge Bulletin*. More than 500 regional wins.

BAZE, Shaleen Notaro (b. 1948) of Atlanta GA, legal assistant, former statistical analyst. Served Unit 114 as president, vice-president, secretary; served as secretary of Unit 506. Worked actively organizing NABC-Atlanta and was editor of District 7's *Pips 'n' Tips* 1980-86 and Unit 114's *Pips 'n Tips* 1986-1989. More than 30 regional wins.

BEALE, Felicity of Melbourne, Australia, born in Yugoslavia. WBF World Master. Won PABF (Far East) Women's Teams 1973, 84, 90. Represented Australia in several world championships and several other zonal championships. Won many national titles.

BEALL, Ron (b. 1944) of Walnut Creek CA, professor of market research, computer consultant, art broker, dot.com consultant. Won North American Swiss Teams 1981 and a few regionals.

BEAN, Anne Z. (Mrs. Percy X.) (1915-2000) of Olympia WA, born in Poland. Past president Unit 441, assisted husband on bridge cruises. Only husband/wife to receive Honorary Member, it was awarded shortly before his death in 1992. Won several regional events.

BEAN, Percy X. (1916-1992) of Olympia WA, owned wholesale hardware business, was very active in his community where he was known as a businessman, fund raiser and civic leader. First recipient of Olympia's Man of the Year award 1968. Served ACBL for many years in almost every capacity including being on ACBL board for 24 years 1964-1988, president 1972, chairman of Board 1973, president of Charity Foundation 1974-81, past president of his unit and general chairman of arrangements for World Bridge Team Olympiad in Seattle 1984. Did bridge cruises from 1975-1991. Bean and his wife Anne were named ACBL Honorary Members for 1992, the only time that honor has been bestowed on a husband-wife combination. Editor of *Mad, Mad World of Bridge*, a publication strongly championing players of less than expert class. Also an accomplished player with many regional championships.

BEARD, Fran (b. 1929) of Dallas TX, owner for 25 years of a travel agency, twice voted "best" by *D Magazine*. Considered an expert in European travel, was commissioned to write a book on great resort hotels in Europe. Competed in world championships 1970, 1978, 1982, 1986, 1990. In 1978 in New Orleans she became a World

Master by placing 4th World Mixed Pairs. Diamond Life Master, was 2nd Women's BAM Teams 1973. Won more than 20 regional events.

BEATTY, R. Stephen (Steve) (b. 1949) of Birmingham AL, manages software development for Bell-South. Served as District 10 recorder, past president of Birmingham BA. A Diamond Life Master, Beatty has won ACBL-wide Royal Viking Instant Matchpoint Pairs (E-W) 1992, North American Swiss 1998; placed 2nd Open Pairs II 1994, IMP Pairs 1996, 2000, GNOT 1997, Spingold 1999 and won more than 20 regional events.

BECHER, David S. (Dave) (b. 1952) of Swampscott MA, insurance agent, won more than 30 regionals.

BECKER, B. Jay (1904-1987) of New York City, attorney, bridge columnist and bridge teacher, born in Philadelphia where he trained as a lawyer at Temple Law School. One of greatest players of all time. Life Master #6, WBF Grand Master, member ACBL Hall of Fame. Has rare distinction of winning a North American championship in his first year of tournament play. His introduction to duplicate play was early in 1932. He entered and won a special pair contest organized by Gen. Alfred Gruenther, using unpublished hands from the just-concluded Culbertson-Lenz Match. In 1932 Summer NABC placed 2nd in Challenge Teams of Four (now the Spingold) and Mixed Pairs (Hilliard Trophy). At Fall NABC he won his first major title, the Chicago Trophy (since 1965 the Reisinger), an event he was to win on 7 subsequent occasions, 1939, 42, 43, 50, 53, 54, 56.

Becker had equal success in the other major team championships, winning the Spingold 7 times, 1936, 38, 44, 47 52, 57, 72, and Vanderbilt 8 times 1944, 45, 51, 55, 56, 57, 59, 81. His win in 1981 came at age of 76. At that time no one had ever won a major championship at a greater age. Becker had the best record of any player in the Master Individual Championship, winning in 1937 and 1948 and placing 2nd 1934, 41, 49, 55. Never won an NABC mixed pairs or mixed team event, although his chief successes in the early Sixties were with Dorothy Hayden Truscott. From 1962-64, they won 3 most important NABC pair championships — Open Pairs 1962, Blue Ribbon Pairs 1963 and Life Master Pairs 1964. Becker's other wins include AWL All-American Open Pairs, Open Teams 1935 and Fishbein Trophy 1972. He was 2nd in 27 NABC events, and had numerous regional victories.

Considered to be perhaps the most conservative of leading experts. Becker adopted very few bidding conventions, declining to play even the almost universally used Stayman convention. He was, however, among the first to adopt and recommend suit-preference signals. Becker managed 3 New York clubs: the Cavendish 1942-47, The New York Bridge Whist Club 1948-50 and the Regency 1951-56. Was associated with Card School of New York 1952-57. Became the bridge columnist for King Features Syndicate in 1956. Was a member of ACBL Laws Commission in 1954. A regular contributor to *The Bridge World* and ACBL *Bridge Bulletin*. Becker was a member of the Editorial Advisory Board of *Encyclopedia of Bridge*. (see JACOBY, Oswald) (see also BUENOS AIRES AFFAIR, FAMILY.)

BECKER, James W. (Jim) (1937-1994) of New York City, was owner and manager of Beverly Bridge Club, formerly an electrical engineer. Certified director since 1970, member District Board since 1988, Unit Board since 1980, vice chairman ACBL Appeals Committee from 1985, first alternate to District director from 1986.

Authored *Biggest Little Bridge Book in the World*. Grand Life Master with more than 18,000 MPs. Placed 5th World Mixed Pairs 1978, 9th World Mixed Pairs 1986; also competed in world competition 1982, 1990. Won Barry Crane Top 500 in 1991 with 3rd highest total—2916 points for one year. Won 39 regional events that year and had a lifetime total of more than 200. Won Intercollegiate Championship teams 1959, 60; placed 2nd in Men's Pairs 1984, Vanderbilt 1987, Master Mixed Teams 1990, Mixed Pairs 1991.

BECKER, Judith (b. 1947) of Boca Raton FL. Won North American Swiss Teams 1980, the same year she was winner of Harter Cup (New York City KOs for non-Life Masters).

Won Von Zedtwitz Teams, a New York City year-long KO event. (see FAMILY.)

BECKER, Michael M. (b. 1943) of Boca Raton FL, former options trader, associated with American Stock Exchange as Exchange official, arbitrator, disciplinary hearing panelist, chairman of Option Market Makers Association 1991, 92 and member executive committee 1987-94. Trainer, supervisor, investor and partner of 100 AMEX traders, including 50 ACBL members, 15 of whom are world or national champions. Generated net aggregate profits of $100 million.

One of leading players in world. Member Board of Directors U.S. Bridge Federation. Has served on numerous committees of the Greater New York BA, including president and vice president. Chairman of the International Team Trials Committee from 1996 to present; ACBL Hall of Fame Committee; treasurer Cavendish Club of New York 1979. A *Bridge World* Master Solvers panelist since 1981 and co-author of *Ultimate Club*. He and father, B.J. Becker, are the only father-son to play as partners in a world championship, (Guaruja, Brazil 1973). Awarded GNYBA player of year twice, team player of year twice, Fishbein Trophy winner 1990. Becker and Ron Rubin, partner of many years, formed a formidable partnership that became world renowned. Member of a famous bridge-playing family which boasts many Life Masters. Introduced to game at early age. Won Teenyear Pairs 1961 and 2 years later became Life Master at age 19. From 1981-82 was a member of the Aces Team.

WBF Life Master, won Bermuda Bowl 1983. Placed 4th in the Bermuda Bowl 1973, 5th 1993; 5th Rosenblum Teams 1986, 10th in 1982. Was captain of USA II Bermuda Bowl Team 2000. An ACBL Diamond Life Master and national champion many times over. Has won Morehead Trophy 1967, Spingold 1972, 80, 82, 92; Vanderbilt 1977, 81, 85, 89; USBC (Team Trials) 1972, 82, 93; Life Master Pairs 1990, Open Pairs 1988. Placed 2nd Men's BAM Teams 1968, Spingold 1968, 88; Vanderbilt 1978, 88, 99; Reisinger 1967, 83; USBC (team trials) 1980, GNOT 1981, 92; Open Pairs I 1998. (see FAMILY)

BECKER, Phillip (b. 1949) of Cleveland Ohio, bridge teacher. Three-time president Cleveland Whist Club, Diamond Life Master. Won Swiss Teams 1970, placed 2nd Mixed Pairs 1986, won dozens of regionals.

BECKER, R. Jay (Bob) (b. 1944) of New York City, actuary and stock options trader, presently a bridge teacher. Won North American Swiss Teams 1979. One of the youngest seniors to win a senior event, winning 2 days after his birthday. More than 15 regional wins.

BECKER, Simon (Skippy) (1899-1987) of Philadelphia PA, born in Poland, retired court stenographer. A top checker player, 1923 Pennsylvania champion. Won the

Chicago (now the Reisinger) in 1944 and became Life Master #42 the same year. Placed 2nd Spingold 1944, Chicago 1946, Open Pairs 1949, 60. Member of the Board of Directors and the Conduct and Ethics Committee of the Philadelphia CBA for 30 years, he was also president of Cavendish Club (Philadelphia) in 1973. His win in 1964 Goldman Open Pairs at the Eastern Regional set a record — he and Eli Jaye had a 72% score. Was npc of American team in 1976 match with England held in Philadelphia. (see FAMILY)

BECKER, Steve (b. 1937) of Old Greenwich CT, syndicated bridge columnist for King Features, bridge teacher and certified director. Frequent contributor to ACBL *Bridge Bulletin* and was its executive editor 1970-72, advertising manager and assistant editor from 1964-70. Won North American Swiss Teams 1980. More than 20 regional wins including District GNOP 6 times and several GNOTs. (see FAMILY)

BEECH, Lidia of Melbourne, Australia, physician. WBF World Master. Won Pacific Asia Teams 1995, South Pacific Teams 1995, 97, 99. Represented Australia in 9 world championships 1988-2000. Since 1976, a multiple winner of all Australian Women's titles including Interstate Teams and Butler Trials.

BEECHER, Martha (b. 1942) of Las Vegas NV, real estate salesperson. Member Board of Governors since 1986, on Unit 373 Board of Directors 1976 to 1998. Directs and teaches on cruises and writes column for local newsletter. Co-chairman for largest NABC held in Las Vegas 1991. Was co-chairman for Las Vegas regionals and sectionals from 1984-98 and holds record for largest of both. Diamond Life Master, won North American Swiss Teams 1982 and more than 50 regional titles.

BEERS, Dale G. (Captain) (b. 1950) of Media PA, analyst/programmer. A former semi-pro baseball player. Won Senior/Advanced Senior Master Pairs 1974, Swiss Teams 1980 and several regionals.

BEERY, James L., Jr. (b. 1938) of Huntington NY, radio engineer. Won GNOT 1973.

BEEZLEY, Britrin A. (b. 1932) of Oklahoma City OK, retired. Diamond Life Master with more than 60 regional wins.

BEGIN, Jackie (b. 1917) of Montreal PQ, retired stock broker and travel agent, professional football handicapper and poker player, Life Master #234, and in 1947 became the first woman Life Master in Canada. Represented Canada in international competition 1968, 70, 72. Before retiring from tournament play she won Women's Teams 1952, Canadian National Open Teams 1963 and many regional events.

BEGUIN, Pierre (1911-1992) of Geneva, Switzerland, architect. Playing captain of Swiss team in 6 consecutive European Championships 1951-56. 11 national wins. Founder of Swiss Bridge Federation.

BEILES, Roger (b. 1949) of El Cerrito CA, actuary for corporate pension plans and overseas compensation studies, awarded Fellowship in Society of Actuaries 1986. Placed 2nd Men's Pairs 1989; won several regionals.

BEINECKE, Walter (1888-1961) of New York City, corporate executive, was a leading figure in bridge administration. Was vice president of Whist Club in New York and the U.S. Bridge Association. A member of Laws Commission from its formation in 1933. Beinecke assisted in preparation of all codes issued from that time until his death. In 1942 and 1943 he served as an ACBL director. Placed 2nd 1936 Vanderbilt.

BELL, Alan C. (b. 1925) of Anaheim CA. Formerly electrical engineer, bridge teacher and owner of harness race horses, currently a bridge professional. Was member Board of Directors Chicago B.A. 1955-63. Founded Emporium B.C. in Pennsylvania. Has been a contributor to ACBL *Bridge Bulletin* and *Bridge World* and a long-time panelist for *Bridge World*. Co-author and inventor of many currently popular conventions — the Support Pass was printed with his name. Others were developed independently by several players, e.g. Landy, Checkback Stayman and Unusual Vs. Unusual. A regular on the Barry Crane Top 500 and placed 2nd in McKenney 1958. Diamond Life Master with 21,246 MPs as of 3/2001, #27 in ACBL. Has won more than 150 regionals.

BELL, Frank A. (b. 1950) of Wayland MA, trader and software engineer. Placed 2nd GNOT 1982; has many regional wins.

BELL, Gail (b. 1942) of Laverock PA, president of cosmetic company. Certified star bridge teacher, contributor to *The Bridge World*, has won 16 regional events.

BELL, Leo A. (b. 1948) of Los Angeles CA, financial manager, and administrator for California State Universiy at Northridge, certified director and bridge teacher. Co-authored *Two-Over-One Game Forcing* with Tom Oakley. Winner of several regional events. Won Las Vegas Pro-Am Money Tournament 1985.

BELL, Linda (d. 1999) of Montgomery AL. Regional tournament director, head of Special Events department at ACBL.

BELLADONNA, Giorgio (1923-1995) of Rome, Italy, retired public official. WBF World Grand Master and at one time ranked #1 in the world. Won World Team Olympiad 1964, 68, 72; Bermuda Bowl 1957, 58, 59, 61, 62, 63, 65, 66, 67, 69, 73, 74, 75, 2nd 1979, 83. Only player to be a member of every Italian team throughout that 16-victory stretch. Won European Teams 1956, 57, 58, 59, 65, 67, 69, 71, 73, 79. Won ACBL Men's Pairs 1971, many national titles. Primary inventor of Roman System and collaborated in the invention of Super Precision.

BELLANGER, Pierre (1877-c.1938) of Paris, France. Captain of first French team to play international match against America (1932). Theorist, wrote *Les Impasses au Bridge*. Formulated idea that Probabilities a Priori reliable guide to play after a few tricks have been played. Also analyzed correctly a number of situations that were not generally understood until the principle of Restricted Choice was formulated 20 years later. Took an active part in formulating the 1935 Laws.

BEN TOVIM, Zvi (b. 1930) of Haifa, Israel, civil engineer, tournament director and bridge teacher. General manager of Israel Bridge Federation 1989-99, president since 2000. Earlier National Sports Captain. Edits IBF section in Israel's *Bridge Magazine*. Frequent npc of Israel teams.

BENDERSKY, Marion F. (Mrs. Lewis) (1928-1992) of Memphis TN, ACBL executive administrator. Earlier ACBL affiliations — director of Board communications, director of elections, club department supervisor. Former bridge teacher, director and club owner.

BENEDICT, Commander J. Frederic (Fred) (1910-1993) of West Des Moines IA, past president Central New York BA. Served as an ACBL Director 1945-55 and as a member of Board of Governors. Held several civic positions including mayor of Norwich NY 1948-52. Diamond Life Master, won World Olympic and USBA Open Teams 1933 and a few regionals.

BENEDICT, Gene F. (b. 1953) of Toledo OH, safety director and truck driver. Former member District 12 Board of Governors, has served Unit 105 in various positions. Bridge columnist for *Toledo Blade* since 1993. Diamond Life Master, won more than 20 regional events.

BENEDICT, Paul (b. 1952) of Baltimore MD, information technology. Has won 15 regional events.

BENJAMIN, Albert (b. 1909) of Glasgow, Scotland, company director and bridge writer. Represented Scotland 17 times in Camrose matches, and member of first Scottish winning team in 1964. Co-author of *Bridge for Everyone*. Wrote daily bridge column 1937-76, some of which were collected in *Albert Benjamin, the Lion of the North*. Regular contributor to *Bridge Magazine*. Club owner.

BENJAMIN, Peter E. (b. 1939) of Culver City CA, retired budget analyst, part owner print store, bridge teacher, tournament director. Won Jan Cohen Award for outstanding service to bridge, won Silver Ribbon Pairs 1995. Won 15+ regionals.

BENNETT, Deborah (b. 1951) of Toronto ON, data entry worker. Won Silver and Gold Life Master masterpoint race Unit 166 in 1996, 97, 98, respectively. Was 2nd Richmond Trophy 1997, the highest achievement for a Canadian woman - with more than 900 MPs in one year. Has won approximately 40 regionals.

BENNETT, Hamish (b. 1932) of Menlo Park CA, born in Scotland, retired financial executive. Captain winning Oxford bridge team 1955-56. Served on Unit Board 1974-76, served as Unit recorder and chairman ethics committee 1988-94. Certified director, former bridge correspondent for *San Mateo Times*. Won WBF World Senior Pairs 1994. ACBL Grand Life Master with 13,641 MPs as of 3/2001. Won Senior Swiss Teams 2000, placed 2nd Men's Swiss 1982, North American Swiss 1984, Senior KO Teams 1994. Has won more than 100 regional titles.

BENNETT, James E., Jr. (1936-1992) of Staten Island NY, insurance company supervisor. Diamond Life Master, won Amateur Swiss Teams 1976, 2nd Blue Ribbon Pairs 1979. Numerous regional wins.

BENNETT, John G. (see BENNETT MURDER)

BENNETT, Randy (b. 1952) of St. John's NFLD, environmental health officer with Health and Welfare Canada. Won Canadian National Teams 1989, Royal Viking Pairs. Represented Canada in world play 1974, 1990 1991. Several regional wins.

BENNETT, Roy (b. 1940) of Falkirk, Scotland, teacher. Represented Britain in one world championship and Scotland in 22 Camrose matches. National wins include Gold Cup once and Scottish Cup once.

BENSON, Kirk W. (b. 1949) of Atlanta GA, computer programming manager. Contributor to *The Kibitzer* and *"Pips' n Tips"*, certified director, Diamond Life Master, won ACBL-wide International Fund Game 1975 and several regionals.

BENSON, Leo O. (1907-1979) of Chicago, bridge columnist, teacher and ABCL regional tournament director. Was 1st person to become both ABA Life Master and ACBL Life Master.

BERGEN, Marty A. (b. 1948) of Farmingdale NY, bridge teacher, writer and bridge professional since 1976. Won tennis championships in high school and college. Former member ACBL Appeals Committee. Has had regular column in Master Pointers section of ACBL *Bridge Bulletin* since 1976 and *Bridge Today* since 1988. Author of 4 books, including *Points Schmoints* and *More Points Schmoints*. Well-known for his development of

new conventions and treatments, many of which are in common use. He also assisted with development of *Law of Total Tricks*, Support Doubles and 1NT Semi-Forcing. Bergen's aggressive preemptive bidding style prompted ABCL to pass the 5-5 rule in 1984. WBF World Master, placed 9th Rosenblum Teams 1986, 90. ACBL Grand Life Master with 12,644 MPs as of 3/2001, won BAM Teams 1981, 84; Blue Ribbon Pairs 1983, 88; Men's Pairs, Life Master Men's Pairs 1983; Spingold 1984, Reisinger Teams 1985, 91; Life Master Pairs 1988. Some of his 2nd places are GNOT 1979, 91; Vanderbilt 1983, 90; Spingold, GNOP 1984; Men's Pairs 1986. Has won more than 60 regionals. Won Cavendish Invitational twice, has played in other international invitational tournaments.

BERGER, Heinrich (b. 1952) of Vienna, Austria, merchant. WBF World Life Master. Placed 2nd in Bermuda Bowl 1985, World Teams 1988, World Pairs 1986. Won European Teams 1985, European Pairs 1981, European Team Cup 1988. Won 10 National Open Teams and 4 Open Pairs.

BERGER, Mark A. (b. 1927) of Fort Lee NJ, sales representative. Used to fly to tournaments in his Cherokee 180. He plays oboe and piano and was oboist with the Queens Symphony Orchestra. Placed 2nd Men's Pairs early Sixties and Master Mixed Teams 1973.

BERGOVOY, Bernie (b. 1930) of Oakland CA, president of data processing company. Won Men's Teams 1970 and several regionals.

BERISSO, Alberto (b. 1923) of Buenos Aires, Argentina, Doctor of Economics. WBF World Life Master. South American champion 1958, 59, 61, 62. Represented Argentina in Bermuda Bowl 1959, 62, 65; in World Team Olympiad 1972. 28 national wins. Won Gabarret Cup 1958, 62, 68, 71.

BERKLEY, Lawrence (b. 1924) of New York City, editor. Ranked 10th in ABA rankings. Production editor of *The Bridge World*.

BERKOWITZ, David (b. 1949) of Old Tappan NJ, certified public accountant, one of the leading American players. Past president Greater New York B.A. and longtime member of its board. WBF World Life Master, placed 2nd World Open Pairs 1998, 8th in 1982; 5th World Mixed Pairs 1986; 6th Rosenblum Teams 1986, 9th in 1990. In 1992 Pan American Championships won Open Teams and placed 3rd in Open Pairs. ACBL Grand Life Master with more than 19,229 MPs as of 3/2001. Won Blue Ribbon Pairs 1978, 95; Men's Teams, Men's Pairs, Mott-Smith Trophy 1982; Mixed Pairs 1986, 87; Life Master Pairs 1986, 96; Master Mixed Teams 1986, 93, 95, Mixed BAM Teams 1998; Reisinger, Open BAM Teams, Herman Trophy 1991; GNOT 1994; Open Pairs II 1998; North American Swiss Teams 1998. Placed 2nd in Spingold 1976; Blue Ribbon Pairs 1977, 96; Vanderbilt 1980, 84, 88, 90, 93, 98; Open Pairs 1983, 85; Life Master Pairs 1991.

BERKOWITZ, Lisa H. (Mrs. David) (b. 1952) of Old Tappan NJ, currently full-time mother and homemaker, former CPA for "Big 8" firm. Won Venice Cup 1987, 5th World Mixed Pairs 1986, 14th World Women's Pairs 1990. In 1992 Pan American Championships won Women's Teams and placed 3rd Women's Pairs. Also represented ACBL in international competition 1982. WBF World Master, #48 in world rankings. Won Mixed Pairs 1986, 87; Master Mixed Teams 1986, 93, 95, Mixed BAM Teams 1998; Women's BAM Teams 1986, 88, 97;

Women's KO Teams 1990, 99 (2nd 1994); North American Women's Swiss Teams 1992; GNOP 1995.

BERNASCONI, Pietro (b. 1932) of Geneva, Switzerland, data manager. WBF World Life Master. Represented Switzerland in 5 world championships and 15 European Championships. Many national successes. Created the Par contest at 1990 world championships, an electronic test for world class players. It was generally thought to be the most difficult playing challenge ever devised. This was repeated at 1998 world championships. He is in charge of recording WBF masterpoints.

BERNING, Dorothy E. (b. 1905) of Lake Worth FL, retired advertising traffic manager. Active for many years in GNYBA and in organization of 2 New York nationals. Was production manager for 13 years of *Post Mortem*. Placed 2nd Senior/Advanced Senior Master Pairs 1950, won Marcus Cup 1951.

BERNSTEIN, Andrew J. (Andy) (b. 1942) of Memphis TN, clinical psychologist, publisher and editor of bridge books with Devyn Press 1979-87 and Pando Publications since 1988. Has served as District 7 Judiciary Committee chairman and on ACBL Appeals Committee. Developed 2-way Exclusion Bid overcall convention. Co-authored *Do You Know Your Partner*. Edited more than 50 bridge books. Represented ACBL in Guaruja, Brazil 1973 in Bermuda Bowl, placing 4th. ACBL Diamond Life Master, won Spingold 1972. Numerous regional wins.

BERNSTEIN, Dr. Cynthia G. (Cindy) (b. 1947) of Memphis TN, professor of English linguistics. Research interest is in Southern American dialects. A certified director, has been directing since 1968 and on cruise ships with her husband Robert since 1986. Placed 4th in Venice Cup 1987. Won Women's KO Teams 1986, Mixed Pairs 1995 and was 2nd Women's KO Teams 1984, 88, 89; Women's Swiss Teams 1985. Many regional wins.

BERNSTEIN, Robert A. (Bob) (b. 1958) of Albuquerque NM, attorney. Winner of Worldwide Viking Pairs 1990 and 18 regional events.

BERRY, Dolores (Dee) (b. 1934) of Kirkland WA, bridge teacher since 1959. Wrote for *Denver Post* in the Sixties. Very active in American Bridge Teachers Association; has held several executive positions. District 19 Education Liaison since 1989. Initiated college and high school teaching programs in District 19. Has written more than 200 original lesson sheets and is a contributor to *ABTA Quarterly*. Named 1991 Bridge Citizen of the Year by the Seattle Unit. Diamond Life Master, has several regional wins.

BERT, Marylou of Ferndale WA, born in Darjeeling India. President Fresno Unit, treasurer District 22. Diamond Life Master, won Canadian Women's Teams 1997 and 15 regional events.

BESSE, Jean (1914-1994) of Geneva, Switzerland, program director and bridge writer. WBF World Life Master, one of world's top players and commentators. Placed 2nd 1954 Bermuda Bowl, representing Europe. Represented Switzerland in 10 world championships and 17 European Championships. Won London Sunday Times Invitational 1969. Many national wins include Open Teams in both France and Switzerland. Won 1976 Bols Bridge Tips contest. Bridge columnist *Journal de Geneve* and author of many magazine articles. First vice-president of IBPA. Originator of Swiss Acol System.

BESSIS, Michel (b. 1952) of Paris, France, bridge pro-

fessional. World WBF Master. Won European Mixed Teams 1996, 98. Author of 5 bridge books. The Bessis family team includes wife Veronique and 2 sons who are members of French schools team.

BESSIS, Veronique (b. 1950) of Paris, France, mathematics teacher. WBF World Life Master. In 2000, #6 in world Women's ranking. Placed 2nd World Women's Team Olympiad 1987, 3rd 1985. 3rd Venice Cup 1995. Won European Women's Teams 1983, 85, 87, 95; 2nd 1997. Won European Mixed Pairs.

BETHE, Henry (b. 1944) of New York City, senior financial strategy and planning officer for Chase Manhattan Bank. Won New York Triathlon Championship 1979, 80. Wrote a computer program for scoring IMP Pairs. Has served as vice chairman ACBL Appeals Committee, GNYBA president, associate editor of *Post Mortem*. Contributor to *Encyclopedia of Bridge*, *International Popular Bridge Monthly, Bridge Today, Bridge World* and ACBL *Bridge Bulletin*. Represented Great Britain 1986 world championships and European Pairs 1987, ACBL in 1990. In 1989 coached winning Venice Cup team in Perth. Diamond Life Master, won Life Master Men's Pairs, Herman Trophy 1968; Swiss Teams 1987, Open Pairs 1991; placed 2nd Open Pairs I 2001. Has won more than 40 regionals.

BETHE, Kitty. See MUNSON-COOPER, Kitty.

BETTER, David S. (b. 1964) of Holland PA, stock options trader. Won GNOT Flt B. 1992. Has 35 regional wins.

BETTS, Laurence (b. 1950) of Burnaby BC, born in London, England. Diamond Life Master, has won 24 regionals.

BEYNON, George W. (1864-1965) born in Portage La Prairie MB; lived in St. Petersburg FL. An authority on tournament directing, and one of the leading personalities in the world of bridge. First career was as professional hockey player. He made music his major occupation, studying at La Scala in Milan and later directing orchestras in Europe and America. After becoming an American citizen in 1904, Beynon developed a successful plan for synchronizing music with silent films. He was musical director of *Birth of a Nation* (1915) and other early successes before retiring to East Orange NY in 1917. Forced out of retirement by 1929 crash, Beynon made a new career in bridge. After directing games in New Jersey and writing a Newark bridge column, he joined the Culbertson organization in 1935 as office manager and became secretary general for USBA. He rapidly became an authority on movements and continued to report on tournaments. After moving from New York to St. Petersburg in 1955, Beynon founded a successful correspondence school for directors and began writing a weekly bridge column for *St. Petersburg Times*. When he celebrated his 100th birthday - September 1964- he was probably the oldest working newspaperman in America. His writings include *Bridge Directors Manual*, the standard work on duplicate organization, as well as many magazine articles. He was a contributing editor of *Encyclopedia of Bridge*.

BHATIA, Gena (Mrs. Kumar) of Pepper Pike OH, pharmaceutical sales representative. Won 15 regional titles.

BHATIA, Kumar (b. 1942) of Pepper Pike OH, grew up in India, pharmaceutical sales representative. Has served as president of Unit 125 and District 5. Co-chaired All-America Regional 1974-1990. Has won more than 25 regionals.

BHAVNANI, Krishin H. (Kris) (b. 1930) of Carlisle MA,

born in India, CEO of small software-based aerospace research company. Co-inventor of American Relay and Super-Canape systems. Proponent of active defensive overcalls and balloon bids. Has won several regionals.

BIANCHI, Benito (1924-1979) of Leghorn, Italy, furrier. WBF Grand Master. Won Bermuda Bowl 1973, 74, European Teams 1965, 67, 69, 71. Represented Italy in 5 other zonal championships, and won 7 Italian national titles. Co- developer of Leghorn Diamond.

BIANCHI, Marisa (Mrs. Benito) (b. 1928) of Leghorn, Italy. Won World Women's Teams 1972, 76. Represented Italy in 7 European Women's Championships, winning in 1970, 71, 73, 74, 77. WBF Grand Master. Won European Common Market Women's Teams 1971, 73; Italian Mixed Teams twice and British Women's Teams 1973.

BIDDLE, John R. (b. 1928) Columbus OH. Won Open Pairs 1965 and had many regional wins.

BIRD, David (b. 1946) of Chandlers Ford, England, bridge writer. Author of 54 books, 20 co-authored by Terence Reese. Best known for his humorous fiction, including tales of the monks of St. Titus. Contributor to many magazines worldwide, including ACBL *Bridge Bulletin*. Bridge columnist of *Mail on Sunday, London Evening Standard* and the *Glasgow Times*. Winner of 9 national titles.

BIRMAN, Daniela (b. 1949) of Tel Aviv, Israel, born in Poland, publishing and public relations executive. WBF World Master. 5th World Women's Teams 1994, 96, 2000. 3rd European Teams 1997. Won European Union Teams 1991. Many national titles.

BIRMAN, David (b. 1948) of Tel Aviv, Israel, born in Poland; engineer-consultant in logistics and transportation. WBF World Master. 3rd Bermuda Bowl 1985, 2nd European Teams 1985, 2nd European Junior Teams 1972. Represented Israel regularly in world and European championships since 1977. Won Cavendish Teams 1991. Many national wins include Open Pairs 3 times and Open Teams 8 times. Coach of Junior and Women's National team. Editor of Israel's Bridge Magazine since 1983. Chairman of organizing committee of Israel's International Bridge Festival since 1995.

BISHOP, Clifford W. (1921-1986) of Detroit MI, advertising executive, was one of the leading players of the Midwest. Bermuda Bowl champion 1954, also represented United States in Bermuda Bowl 1955. Won Spingold 1953, 54 and placed 2nd in Men's Pairs 1951, Men's Teams 1953. Won numerous regionals.

BITMAN, Jack (b. 1922) of Denver. Won GNOT 1980 and several regionals.

BITSCHENE, Jochen (b. 1958) of Heidelberg, Germany, computer programmer. WBF World Master. Won World Teams 1990 and 4 national titles.

BJERKAN, Cheri of Elmhurst IL, former pension consultant and owner of folk art gallery. Her very active outside life, including antiquing, spectator sports and her children's activities combined with her job led her to restrict her bridge life to NABCs and WBF events. WBF World Master, won Venice Cup 1987. She was 4th Venice Cup 1991 and 10th World Women's Pairs. Placed 3rd in Women's Teams in Pan American Games 1992. Represented ACBL in 1986 world championships. Diamond Life Master, has won several national titles - Women's Swiss Teams 1984, 88, 91, 97; Women's KO Teams 1989, 92, 96; Women's BAM Teams 1991; Women's Pairs 1992; Mixed BAM Teams 1998. 2nd Women's KO Teams 1978, 79, 81, 86, 90, 93; Women's Pairs 1991.

BJERREGARD, Sven-Ake (b. 1948) of Eskiltuna, Swe-

den, computer system administrator. WBF World Master. 3rd Bermuda Bowl 1991, 4th in 1995. 4th World Team Olympiad 1992, 2nd European Teams 1991, 4th 1995. Won Nordic Teams twice and several national titles.

BLACK, Robert A. (Bob) (b. 1954) of Beaumont TX, attorney, listed in *Who's Who in American Law* since 1987. Became certified director (1972) at age of 17, youngest in country. Member ACBL Board of Governors and has served Unit 201 in various capacities including president. Author of bridge column since 1989. Has won several regionals.

BLACKSTOCK, Dr. Stephen (b. 1951) of Wellington, New Zealand, public servant. WBF World Master. Far East champion 1990. National wins include 2 Open Teams, KO Teams once, Open Pairs 4 straight times. Member N.Z. Management Committee 1986-90. Bridge columnist *Wellington Evening Post*.

BLACKWOOD, Easley R. (1903-1992) of Indianapolis IN, one of the most famous bridge personalities in the world. Most notable for his invention of Blackwood 4NT convention. When he submitted his convention idea to *The Bridge* World the article was turned down - saying it would never catch on. A former insurance manager. From 1964 presided over Blackwood Enterprises which included a bridge club and bridge activities on 32 luxury ship cruises. Served as ACBL executive secretary 1968-71 and put the ACBL back on a sound financial basis. President of Midwest Conference and Central Indiana Unit. History buff and enjoyed chess and music, singer and string player.

Member ACBL Hall of Fame, ACBL Honorary Member 1980. Awarded Honorary Membership in American Bridge Teachers Association 1978. Longtime member ACBL Laws Commission. International Bridge Press Association Personality of the Year 1984. Honored by Indianapolis mayor who proclaimed October 28, 1977 Easley Blackwood Day. Writings include *Bridge Humanics, Blackwood on Slams, Winning Bridge with Blackwood, Play of the Hand with Blackwood*, articles for many magazines including the ACBL *Bridge Bulletin* and a syndicated newspaper column.

BLAIR, Jack (1933) of Tulsa OK, oil executive. One of the leading Southwest players. Represented U.S. in world competition Cannes 1962. Won Men's Pairs 1960, Men's Teams 1972, Life Master Pairs 1973, Mott-Smith Trophy 1972; placed 2nd Open Pairs 1961, 64; Reisinger 1973, Vanderbilt 1972. Diamond Life Master, has won numerous regionals.

BLAISS, Charlotte (Mrs. Gary) of Memphis TN, ACBL director of youth/junior programs and assistant manager of Education Department, formerly taught school in Texas for 27 years. Came to ACBL June 1994. Responsible for School Bridge Lesson program; planning and organizing a Junior Trials; a training program and travel arrangements for teams participating in World Junior Teams Championships; selecting Juniors to attend WBF's World Junior Pairs and World Bridge Camp; planning and directing ACBL's Junior Bridge Camp (1996, 98 and 2000); organizing and conducting North American College Bridge Team Championships; coordinating all aspects of Youth/Junior Program. Blaiss was awarded WBF Bronze Medal of Distinction, given for devotion and dedication to working for bridge, in 1999 during the World Junior Teams Championship in Fort Lauderdale FL.

BLAISS, Gary of Memphis TN, ACBL bridge administrator and former national tournament director. Worked

first tournament in 1971 under Paul Herndon. First NABC was Denver 1972, and has missed only 3 since Vancouver 1974 (working at a Florida regional), Albuquerque 1982 (Mother's health) and Chicago 1998 (heart bypass operation). Sometimes taught director's course after NABCs. Was salaried employee in May of 1977 as an Associate National Director. Became National Director January 1979. Became bridge administrator August 1993 and moved to Memphis October 1993.

BLAKEY, Helen Margaret (b. 1945) of Baltimore MD, technical editor specializing in software manuals, test documents. Certified director, has served Maryland B.A. as president, secretary and tournament chairman. Won GNOP 1981, has several regional wins.

BLAKEY, Robert C. (b. 1946) of Columbia MD, senior software engineer. Won GNOP 1981 and many regionals.

BLAKSET, Knut (b. 1960) of Copenhagen, Denmark, born in Norway; bridge club manager. WBF World Master. Won World Junior Pairs 1983, Nordic Teams 1986 and Nordic Junior Teams. 5th World Team Olympiad 1992. Usually with brother Lars, represented Denmark on many occasions Olympiad 1992 starting at age 21. 15 Danish titles. Co-author of a bridge primer.

BLAKSET, Lars (b. 1961) of Copenhagen, Denmark, born in Norway; bridge writer and club manager. Placed 3rd World Team Olympiad 1988, 96; 5th 1992. Won World Junior Pairs 1983 and Nordic Junior Teams. Represented Denmark in 2 other world championship and 5 zonals. Won Hoechst 1991, Rottneros (Nordic) Cup and Icelandair Open. 24 Danish titles. Columnist for *Berlingske Tidende* and author of the official Danish book of systems and conventions. Inventor of several conventions.

BLANCHARD, Jillian Shane See LEVIN, JILLIAN SHANE.

BLANCHARD, Robert W. (b. 1951) of New York City, manufacturer of electromechanical devices. Chairman of Unit 128 and District 24 1992. ACBL Rookie of the Year 1975 .13th Rosenblum Teams 1986, 17th 1990. In Cavendish Invitational Pairs placed 6th 1981, 4th 1982, 3rd 1984. Won Blue Ribbon Pairs 1996, Open BAM Teams 1997; placed 2nd Blue Ribbon Pairs, Men's BAM 1982; Reisinger 1989. Qualified to play in USBC in 1991. Has won many regionals. Blanchard was involved in fight for Women's rights in bridge (see BLANCHARD CASE; LEVIN, JILLIAN; FAMILY.)

BLESSING, Leonard C. (b. 1920) of New Providence NJ, retired supervisor of science with Millburn N.J. Board of Education. Fellow of American Association for Advancement of Science. Has won several teaching awards, successful track coach. For 20 years ran student bridge club with more than 100 members, started directing 1941. Wrote bridge column for *The Montclarion, The Hills-Bedminster Press* and *Independent Press*; author of *Crossing Your Bidding Bridges.* Authored *Blackwood with Void* - using Blackwood to show one ace and a void in lower ranking suit (other than trump suit) by jumping to 6 in the void. Introduced in 1948, published in 1959.

BLOM, Britt See NORDENSON, Britt.

BLOOM, Betty of Duanesburg NY, Diamond Life Master, won Master Mixed Teams 1979, 2nd 2000; won North American Swiss Teams 2000.

BLOOM, Steven H. of Duanesburg NY, professor of math, Diamond Life Master. Won Master Mixed Teams 1979, 2nd 2000; won North American Swiss Teams 2000.

BLOOM, Valerie (b. 1949) of Johannesburg, South Africa, company director and bridge teacher. WBF World Master. Represented South Africa in 2 world championships and won several national titles.

BLOOMER, George Beale, Jr. (b. 1930) of Pittsboro NC, retired comptroller. Board member Northern Virginia B.A. 1972-82, board member Unit 119 1991-to date. Diamond Life Master with more than 16,900 MPs as of 3/2001. Won more than 50 regional events.

BLOOMER, Judith P. (b. 1936) born in Australia, of Pittsboro NC, retired production manager. Served as District 7 secretary 1992-96 and Mid-Atlantic Conference secretary since 1996. A Diamond Life Master with more than 15 regional wins.

BLOOMFIELD, Ruth (1925-1993) of Chicago IL, bridge teacher, certified director, ceramic jewelry maker. Winner Life Master Women's Pairs 1971 and a few regionals.

BLOUSSON, Alberto (1908-1967) of Buenos Aires, Argentina. Won South American Teams 1948, 57, 58. Represented Argentina in Bermuda Bowl 1958. 7 national wins.

BLUBAUGH, John E. (b. 1950) of Indianapolis IN. Full-time bridge professional. ACBL Rookie of the Year 1987, Regional Master of the Year 1988. Has won more than 50 regionals., Has written more than 20 books on various bridge topics. Former member NABC Appeals Committee, former member Board of Governors. Won 50+ regionals. Disciplined for card manipulation 2001.

BLUHM, Louis E. (Lou) (1940-1990) of Atlanta, bridge professional, expert at poker and gin. One of the leading American players, well-known for his high standard of ethics and deportment. Member ACBL Hall of Fame. Placed 3rd in World Mixed Pairs 1978, won Cavendish Invitational Pairs 1981. Grand Life Master with 13,000 MPs. Received ACBL's Distinguished Player Award (an award that was originated for him). Won Reisinger 1972, Spingold 1974, 77; Vanderbilt 1979, 89; Blue Ribbon Pairs, Men's Teams 1977; Open Pairs 1984, Life Master Men's Pairs 1987. Placed 2nd Vanderbilt 1978, 86; Spingold 1988, Men's Teams 1973, GNOT, Men's BAM Teams 1983; Men's BAM Teams 1987. Won more than 50 regionals.

BLUM, Desiderio (1906-1966) of Buenos Aires, Argentina, businessman. Won South American Teams 1959, 62, 64. 3 national titles. President Argentine Bridge Federation 1957-59.

BLUM, Robert (b. 1927) of Marco Island FL, bridge columnist for *Scripps Daily News* (Naples FL). Won 16 regional events.

BLUM, Shirley (Pepi) (b. 1930) of Fresno CA, businesswoman, Diamond Life Master, placed 2nd Mixed Pairs 1997, has won more than 15 regionals.

BLUMENTHAL, Lynn (1946-1994) of Bellevue WA, special education teacher, company manager and tax consultant. Was an avid tennis player and had won various trophies in ballroom dancing contests. Was Woman of the Year - Toast Mistress 1986, and was national winner in American Apple Pie bake-off. Placed 2nd Women's Team Trials 1988; won Women's BAM Teams 1987, placed 2nd North American Swiss Teams 1993. Many regional wins.

BLUMENTHAL, Mark E. (b. 1942) of Chicago, one of the leading American players until 1977 when complications arising from open heart surgery caused his retirement from active participation in tournament bridge.

Member Aces Team 1972-74. WBF Life Master, he placed 2nd in Bermuda Bowl 1973, 74; won Vanderbilt 1973, 77; Mott-Smith Trophy 1977; placed 2nd Spingold 1976. Grand Life Master with more than 11,692 MPs as of 3/2001.

BOBOLAKIS, Stavros (b. 1957) of Athens, Greece, mathematician. Top bridge teacher for past 20 years. Non-playing captain 1988 World Team Olympiad, finishing 5th, the best performance ever by a Greek team. Many national wins include open teams.

BOBORICKEN, Anne (b. 1937) of Campbell CA, won more than 20 regional events.

BOCCHI, Norberto (b. 1961) of Milan, Italy, professional player. Partnership with Giorgio Duboin one of best in world. Won World Team Olympiad 2000. Placed 2nd 1984 European Junior Championships. Won European Union Pairs 1989, European Teams 1997 (Italy's first win in 18 years), 1999, 2nd European Pairs 1999. Won Schiphol International Teams 1992, Forbo Teams 1999, Politiken Pairs, 1999. Many national titles.

BOEDER, John (1943-2000) of Roseville MN, data network architect. 20-year member Amnesty International. Authored *Thinking About IMPs,* contributor to *Gopher Bridge News.* Has won 19 regionals.

BOEHM, George A. W. (1922-1993) of New York City, retired writer, editor, mathematician. Was on staff of *Fortune, Newsweek* and *Scientific American.* Editor of *Post-Mortem* in the Sixties. Wrote several articles for *The Bridge World* including a 2-part exposition of Lebensohl which he popularized.

BOEKHORST, Andre (b. 1934-1992) of Utrecht, The Netherlands, chemistry teacher. Won National Pairs 1969 and represented The Netherlands in one zonal championship 1969. President Netherlands Bridge League; vice-president European Bridge League; member WBF Executive. Secretary Netherlands Bridge League 1978-90; chief editor of its magazine *Bridge* 1971-90. Columnist until 1990; author of one book and translator of others.

BOER, Wubbo de (b. 1963) of Amsterdam, The Netherlands, application manager computer systems. WBF World Life Master. Won Bermuda Bowl 1993; 3rd World Team Olympiad 1992. World Junior champion 1987, European Junior champion 1986. Many national wins.

BOESGAARD, Knud-Aage (b. 1950) of Copenhagen, Denmark, accountant. WBF World Master, 3rd World Team Olympiad 1984, 2nd European Teams 1979. Won European Junior Teams 1970, Nordic Teams 1986. Also represented Denmark in 2 other world championships and 4 other zonals, all in partnership with his cousin, Peter Schaltz. 20 Danish titles. Treasurer Danish Bridge Federation. See FAMILY.

BOIVIN, Anna K. (b. 1932) of Victoria BC, ACBL director and teacher for more than 15 years. Club owner since 1972. Zone 2 Director for Canadian Bridge Federation for 3 years. Represented Canada in World Olympiad 1978, & 86. Diamond Life Master. In Canada Women's Teams Championship has won once and finished 2nd once. Several regional wins.

BOLLE, Michel (b. 1950) of Brussels, Belgium, full-time bridge teacher and journalist. Represented Belgium in 3 World Championships and 7 European Championships. Several national wins.

BOLLS, Col. (ret) Larry R. (b. 1939) of Walnut CA, Air Force officer. Won Amateur Swiss Teams 1977 and several regionals.

BONDE, Count Carl (1897-1990) of Moerkoe, Sweden, landed estates owner. Npc Swedish open and Women's team on many occasions. President Swedish Bridge League 1960-65, president European Bridge League 1965-69, president World Bridge Federation 1968-70. Honorary member of WBF, EBL and Swedish Bridge League.

BONNEY, C. Jack (1904-1982) of Ozona FL, accountant and bridge teacher. Organized formation of Westchester Contract B.A. and was its first president. Served as president of Miami Bridge Club in late Thirties. A bridge teacher and director in Westchester County NY from Forties until 1975. He wrote several bridge teaching handbooks including *Master Bridge Teaching Guide.*

BOOLKIN, Leon Marc (b. 1957) of Johannesburg, South Africa, radiologist. WBF World Master. Won BFAME Open Teams 1995; represented South Africa in 2 world championships. Won several national titles.

BOONSUPA, Ananta (b. 1934) of Bangkok, Thailand, marketing manager. Won PABF (Far East) Teams 1965. Represented Thailand in 3 world championships and 6 zonal championships. Won 6 national titles.

BOREWICZ, Marek (b. 1947) of Warsaw, Poland, bridge professional. 2nd Rosenblum Teams 1994. Won European Junior Teams 1972.

BORIN, Jim (b. 1935) of Australia, born in England, bridge club-owner and teacher. World Life Master. Placed 3rd Bermuda Bowl 1971, 79. Won PABF (Far East) Teams 1970, 1971. Represented Australia in 2 other world championships and other zonal championships. Won many national titles. Bridge columnist *Melbourne Age.* Co-author of one book.

BORIN, Norma of Melbourne, Australia, bridge teacher. Placed 3rd Bermuda Bowl 1971, 1979. Won PABF (Far East) Open Teams 1970, 71, PABF (Far East) Women's Teams 1990. Represented Australia in 2 other world championships and other zonal championships. Won many national titles. Co-author of one book.

BOSCOWITZ, Herbert (Hubie) (b. 1902) of New York City, first recipient of Wetzlar Trophy. Was president of American Bridge League in 1935. Was responsible for introducing the masterpoint plan, which became the basis of the ACBL's subsequent prosperity. Won AWL All-American Open Teams 1933, Master Mixed Teams 1932; placed 2nd Vanderbilt 1934.

BOTELER, Charles M. Jr. (Chuck) (b. 1923) of Rockville MD, retired insurance executive. Has more than 15 regional wins.

BOULENGER, Jean-Michel (1934-1985) of Paris, France. Represented France in World Team Olympiad 1964, 76; Bermuda Bowl 1967, 69, 73. European champion 1966, 1970, 1974; 2nd 1967. Won London Sunday Times Invitational 1977, many French titles.

BOURBON, Philippe de (b. 1921) of Punta del Este, Uruguay, born in U.S.A., engineer. Regularly represented Paraguay 1980-87 and Uruguay from 1988 in zonal championships. Won 5 Uruguay national championships and several ACBL regional titles.

BOURCHTOFF, Andree (Mrs. Gerard) (b. 1923) of Paris, France. European Women's champion 1953, 1954.

BOURCHTOFF, Gerard (b. 1923) of Paris, France, retired company director, Grand Master. Won World Team Olympiad 1960; represented France in Olympiad 1968, 1972; won European Championship 1952, 56, 59. 2nd 1956. Many national titles.

BOURKE, Margaret of Canberra, Australia, finance officer. WBF World Master. Won Far East Teams 1985, Pacific Asia Teams 1995, South Pacific Teams 1995, 97,

99. Represented Australia in 14 world championships 1979-2000. Since 1976, a multiple winner of all Australian Women's titles including Interstate Teams and Butler Trials.

BOURKE, Timothy (Tim) (b. 1947) of Canberra, Australia, executive in a government-owned enterprise. Won 10 national titles including open teams twice. Inventor of Bourke Relay. Co-author of 5 books. Bridge book collector, valuer and bibliographer. Regular magazine contributor, including more than 30 reports of Australian Team finals. Quiz and hand composer. Bibliography editor for *Encyclopedia of Bridge, Sixth Edition*. Reorganized library at ACBL Headquarters.

BOWIE, Clagett (Clag) (1907-1989) of Falls Church VA, mathematician, discovered and published a theorem in matrix algebra 1971. Credited with queen-over-jack rubber bridge theory. Won several regional events. (see QUEEN OVER JACK and TWO-WAY FINESSE)

BOYD, Lorraine of Auckland, New Zealand. Represented New Zealand in 2 world championships and 5 zonal championships.

BOYD, Peter A. (b. 1950) of Silver Spring MD, systems analyst, bridge professional. Overcame non-Hodgkins lymphoma, a form of cancer. Has served as president for District 6 and Washington Bridge League. Won Rosenblum Teams 1986 and is WBF World Master. ACBL Grand Life Master with 18,975 MPs as of 3/2001. Won GNOT 1984, 88, 92; GNOP 1985, Reisinger, Men's Swiss Teams 1986; Vanderbilt 1987, 91, 97, 98; Men's BAM Teams 1989; Open BAM Teams 1994. Placed 2nd Blue Ribbon Pairs 1982, GNOT 1985, Life Master Pairs 1987, Life Master Men's Pairs 1988, Vanderbilt 1992, 99, Spingold 1992.

BRACHMAN, Malcolm (b. 1926) of Dallas TX, independent oilman and company president, former physicist and life insurance executive. Grand Life Master with 15,229 MPs as of 3/2001, WBF World Master. Won Bermuda Bowl 1979, competed internationally 1978 (9th Rosenblum Teams), 1984, 86, 1990 (9th Rosenblum Teams). Won Reisinger 1976, 80; Men's Teams 1976, Vanderbilt 1978, Spingold 1978, 83, 86. Placed 2nd Spingold 1973, Vanderbilt 1976, Men's BAM Teams 1984, Reisinger 1990, GNOT 1998. Has won considerably more than 100 regional events.

BRACHMAN, Minda (Mrs. Malcolm) (b. 1931) of Dallas TX, racehorse owner, president of Master Point Farm. Diamond Life Master, won Master Mixed Teams 1968, placed 2nd Life Masters Pairs 1971. Has won more than 45 regionals.

BRADLEY, Kenn (b. 1933) of Tulsa OK, retired attorney. Unit president, member of District 15 board. Won 15+ regionals.

BRADY, Joseph L. (Joe) (b. 1926) of Upper Saint Clair PA, retired financial consultant. Won Mixed Pairs 1996 and about 35 regionals.

BRADY, Phil of Philadelphia PA, business systems analyst, member ACBL Appeals Committee since 1983. Diamond Life Master with more than 10,900 MPs as of 3/2001. Won more than 70 regionals.

BRAHMACHARI, Ajoy (b. 1939) of Calcutta, India, engineer. Won Far East Open Teams 1977, 3rd Far East Open Pairs 1978. Won 3 national titles.

BRALL, Carlyn (Mrs. Ira) (b. 1911) of New York City, editorial consultant, former editor of *Post Mortem* and editorial assistant to Waldemar Von Zedtwitz and Albert Morehead. Has edited several bridge books including *Goren Answers the Bridge Problems*. Won Women's

Teams 1955, 58.

BRAMLEY, Bart (b. 1948) of Chicago IL, stock options trader, has written articles for *The Bridge World*. Once played 10 consecutive days of national KO events at one tournament, placing 2nd in both. Represented ACBL in international play 1986, 90, 91. Captained 1996 Olympiad team. WBF World Master, placed 11th Rosenblum Teams, 20th World Open Pairs 1986; 9th Rosenblum Teams 1990, 5th Bermuda Bowl 1991, 3rd Rosenblum Teams 1998. Also won Icelandic Open Teams 1994, placed 2nd World Par Contest 1998. Grand Life Master with 13,107 MPs as of 3/2001. 1997 ACBL Player of the Year. Won both Herman Trophy and Mott-Smith Trophy 1997. National wins include Men's BAM 1980, Open Pairs, Men's Swiss Teams 1984; Life Master Men's Pairs 1987, Vanderbilt 1989, Open Swiss Teams 1990, 97; Life Master Open Pairs 1995, Reisinger 1997. Placed 2nd Men's BAM Teams 1976, 87; Spingold 1981, 88; Mixed Pairs 1981, Vanderbilt 1986, GNOT 1988, Open Swiss Teams 1991, 94; Open Pairs II 1997.

BRANCO, Marcelo Castello (b. 1945) of Rio de Janeiro, Brazil, computer engineer and government official. WBF Grand Master. In 2000, 6th in WBF world rankings. Won World Olympiad Teams 1976, World Pairs 1978, 90; Bermuda Bowl 1989. He is the only player to have won the World Pairs twice, and one of 8 to have won the Triple Crown — World Olympiad Teams, World Pairs and Bermuda Bowl. 2nd Rosenblum Teams 1978, 98; 2nd Bermuda Bowl 2000. Represented Brazil in many other world championships. Won South American Teams 1968, 71, 72, 73, 75, 77, 78, 83, 86, 89, 91, 93, 97. National wins include 10 open teams. Won Reisinger 1992, London Sunday Times Invitational 1992, Cap Gemini 1993, 97.

BRANCO, Pedro Paulo Castello (b.1940) of Rio de Janeiro, Brazil, insurance executive. WBF Grand Master. Won Bermuda Bowl 1989, South American Teams 1969, 72, 73, 82, 89, 93, 96, 97, 98. Represented Brazil in 12 other world championships. National wins include 20 open teams and 3 open pairs.

BRASHLER, Ted H. (b. 1921) of Lockport IL, retired general contractor. Authored *Sweep Q-Bids* and *The Meaning of Bids* and has contributed to *The Bridge World*. Won more than 35 regionals.

BRATCHER, Betty (b. 1950) of Vista CA. Became tournament director 1980, advanced to National Tournament Director and Field Supervisor 2000, Intermediate/Novice coordinator 1992-99. Winner of Fred Friendly and Tom Weeks awards.

BRATCHER, Robert (Bob, Rapid) (b. 1930) of Vista CA. Became tournament director 1957, owned and operated full-time club in Montrose CA in Sixties, in Vista 1976-90. Introduced Swiss Teams to West, made first poles for identifying sections, began use of clocks for timing rounds and matches. Won Fall NABC Commercial and Industrial Pairs 1962, several regionals.

BRATTON, Paul Edward (b. 1943) of Indianapolis IN, buyer for General Motors. Won Non-Life Masters Pairs, placed 2nd Red Ribbon Pairs 1987.

BRAUNSTEIN, Marion (Mrs. Maurice) (b. 1930) of Schenectady NY, auditor and regional tournament director. Won Sub-Senior Master Teams 1956.

BRAUNSTEIN, Maurice (Maury) (1914-1997) of Schenectady NY, national tournament director, formerly a computer processing director for State of New York. Began his career as a tournament director in 1954 and soon found directing more of a challenge than playing.

Became a national director in 1968 when he retired from his New York work. He was in charge of all nationally-rated events at North American Championships from 1973-1990. Made his debut as World Bridge Federation director in 1972 and was director-in-charge at 1973 Bermuda Bowl in Guaruja, Brazil. He was also chief director for the world championships in Bermuda 1975, Bal Harbour 1986, Jamaica 1987, Venice 1988. Assistant chief director at the world championships in 1974 and for all other championships 1976-1985. He originated several duplicate movements, including the Stanza Movement. Known worldwide for his bow ties which became his trademark at tournaments everywhere.

BRECHNER, Dora (Dosha) (b. 1920) of Tel Aviv, Israel, formerly of New York, born in Poland, former owner/operator of nursing home. A survivor of Auschwitz and Bergen Belsen, her weight was down to 76 pounds at the time of her liberation by the British in 1945. Represented Israel in European Championships, World Women's Teams and World Women's Pairs for many years. After retiring from tournament bridge she hired teachers to help teach the Israeli Women. She was rewarded when her protegees won European Community Championship in Athens.

BRECK, Per (b. 1931) of Bergen, Norway, medical doctor. Won Nordic Teams 1975, 78, 82. Represented Norway in several European Championships. Many national wins.

BREED, Mildred (b. 1947) of Austin TX, purchasing agent. WBF Grand Master, #30 all time, ranked 12th in recent years. Master, placed 2nd Venice Cup 2000, represented ACBL 1992. Diamond Life Master. Won Women's Pairs 1980; Women's Swiss Teams 1999; Women's BAM Teams 1994, 98; Women's KO Teams 1997; Life Master Women's Pairs 1999, 2000; placed 2nd in Women's Teams 1975, Women's Pairs 1984, 99; Women's KO Teams 2000. Won many regional events.

BRIDSON, Edward W. (Edson) (b. 1951) of Unionville ON, born on Isle of Man, Great Britain, vice principal, former mathematics teacher. Winner Canadian National Team Championship 1991; placed 2nd 1985, 93. Bridson competed for Canada in world championships 1978, 86, 92. Placed 2nd Pan American Championship Open Teams 1992. Has won 20 regionals.

BRIER, Barbara S. (1923- deceased) of Miami FL, bridge teacher, was one of the leading American Women players. Frequent partner of Waldemar Von Zedtwitz. They won World Mixed Pairs in 1970. She also had high placings in World Women's Pairs and World Mixed Teams twice. Her national titles included Open Pairs 1955, Mixed Teams 1965. Placed 2nd Mixed Teams 1956, Mixed Pairs 1963, Women's Pairs 1971.

BRIGHTLING, Richard John (b. 1949) of Canberra, Australia, born in New Zealand, bridge shop owner. Represented New Zealand in one world championship and one PABF (Far East) Championship. Former publisher of *Australian Bridge*. Won national titles in New Zealand and Australia. Co-author of one book.

BRILL, Laura (b. 1943) of White Plains NY, English teacher, communications instructor, co-owner The Bridge Deck bridge club. Served on Unit 188 Board of Directors for past 10 years. Diamond Life Master, about 65 regional wins.

BRISSMAN, Jon C. (b. 1944) of San Bernardino CA, attorney, former elementary school principal, bridge professional and teacher. Has competed in more than 70

10K runs. Served as co-chairman ACBL Goodwill Committee 1983-88 and 1996-present, chairman Conventions Committee 1986-87, coordinator of President's Advisory Committee 1986-87, ACBL National Recorder 1985-88. Was actively involved in setting up recorder program presently in effect at NABCs. Responsible for revision of ACBL Convention Chart, created or implemented many of the policies and procedures in effect at ACBL Goodwill Committee hearings and helped to create ACBL Standard. Has written for ACBL *Bridge Bulletin.* Also contributed to *Contract Bridge Forum* and *Southern California Bridge News*. Retired from active bridge in 1988. Diamond Life Master with 50+ regional titles.

BRITTON, Sonya of Marbella, Spain, formerly of Dublin, Ireland. Represented Ireland in 3 world championships and one zonal championship. 7 national titles include National Teams once. Former president Contract Bridge Association of Ireland, Vice-president of Irish Bridge Union, and Irish delegate to EBL. Donor of Sonya Britton Trophy for annual competition between CBAI and NIBU.

BROCK, Raymond (b. 1940) of High Wycombe, England, computer consultant. WBF World Master. Runner-up 1987 Bermuda Bowl and European Teams. Played in more than 30 Camrose matches. Many national wins include Gold Cup 7 times. Npc winning British Junior Team 1989 and 1995. Technical director and planner of 1989 World Junior Championships and many other events, primarily for juniors. Chairman of Trustees of Charity Educational Trust for British Bridge 1989-94. President British Bridge League 1986-88 and 1990-92. Member of Portland Club Card Committee which, as joint copyright holders, are responsible for drafting changes to the Laws. Author of 4 books.

BROCK, Sally (formerly Sowter, later Horton) (b. 1953) of High Wycombe, England, bridge writer and editor. WBF World Grand Master. Won Venice Cup 1981, 85. 2nd World Women's Teams 1984. Won European Women's Teams 1979, 1981, Common Market Women's Teams 1979, 81, 93. Won Gold Cup 1984, 89, 90. Author of 7 books, and co-author with Raymond Brock. Former executive editor of *International Popular Bridge Monthly*. Active as publisher, author and typesetter.

BROCKMAN, Elaine B. (Mrs. Charles C.) (b. 1914) of Issaquah WA, housewife, former dance teacher. Ran lectures and bridge games on cruise ships for 15 years. Placed 2nd Women's Teams 1965. Won several regionals.

BROCKWELL, John (b.1929) of Canberra, Australia, agricultural scientist. President of Australian Bridge Federation 1990-94. Winner of 3 national titles. Organizer of many Australian championships. Named Member of Order of Australia for services to bridge and agricultural science.

BRODY, Harvey D. (b. 1939) of San Francisco CA, bridge professional, retired accountant, collector of paperback books. Has served as treasurer (1988-90) and disciplinary chairman (since 1999) of District 21. Was treasurer of 1990 and 1996 NABCs. Grand Life Master with 12,026 MPs as of 3/2001, won IMP Pairs 1992, has won more than 100 regional events.

BROER, Lawrence (Bertie) (b. 1923) of Johannesburg, South Africa, chartered accountant. Represented South Africa in World Team Olympiad 1968, 72. 80, Maccabiah Games 1977, 81, 85. Many national wins.

BROGELAND, Boye (b. 1973) of Bergen, Norway. WBF World Master. Junior World Pair champion 1995. 3rd Bermuda Bowl 1998, 4th 2000. 3rd World Junior Pairs

1997. Won European Junior Teams 1996. Won 2 European (1990 and 1996) and 2 Nordic (1993 and 1995) Junior team titles. Nordic Team champion 1998. 3rd European Teams 1997 and 1999. 2nd World Junior Teams 1997. Was rated as world's most prominent Junior player from 1996 to 1999. Several national titles. Publisher and editor of *Bridge i Norge*.

BRONDUM, Freddi (b. 1974) of Copenhagen, Denmark, floorer. Won World Junior teams 1997, 3rd 1995. 3rd European Junior Teams 1996. Won European Junior Teams. Won 5 Danish Junior Teams, starting at age 15, and 2 Junior Pairs.

BRONSTEIN, Alan J. (b.1941) of Christiansted, St. Croix, Virgin Islands, born in U.S. certified public accountant. Represented Virgin Islands in 3 world championships and 14 CAAC zonal championships. President of Virgin Islands B.F. Bridge columnist of *St. Croix Avis*.

BRONSTEIN, Saul (The Pup) (b. 1949) of Bradenton FL, formerly New York City, comptroller, former bridge director and teacher. 4-time scrabble champion. Chief bridge lecturer on Royal Viking Sun 1992-1997. General secretary Unit 155 (GNYBA) 1979-1991, former associate editor GNYBA's *Post Mortem*. Won GNYBA Player of the Year and Team Player of the Year 1987, co-founder (with wife Janie) Academy of Bridge (New York City). WBF World Master, placed 8th Rosenblum Teams 1986. Won Reisinger 1984, Cavendish Teams 1989, District 24 G NOT 1987.

BROOKS, Dorsey W. (b. 1926) of Stanwood MI, retired General Motors senior administrator. Played exhibition matches on team with Charles Goren and Harold Ogust. Placed 2nd Mixed Teams 1971, was Intercollegiate champion 1949. Has won many regionals and 2 National Industrial League Par Contests.

BROOKS, Zerrene (Mrs. Dorsey Brooks) of Stanwood MI, bridge teacher and recreational consultant. Placed 2nd Mixed Teams 1971, 2nd Intercollegiates 1950. Won several regionals and 2 National Industrial League Par Contests.

BROTMAN, Oscar J. (b. 1911) of Bayside NY, retired controller. Won Spingold 1940, Eastern States KO Teams (Reisinger) 1946. As a partner of Alvin Roth, he contributed to the early development of the Roth-Stone System.

BROWN, Claude (b. 1930) of Kuala Lumpur, Malaysia, company director. Represented Malaysia in 5 zonal championships. Won many national titles.

BROWN, Dudley B. (b. 1935) of Grandview WA, Army Reserve technician. Member ACBL Board of Directors since 1989, ACBL president 1996, Chairman of the Board 1997. Has served District 19 as president, board member and chairman of various committees. Unit 450 Manager for more than 20 years. Former executive editor of *The Dino Bridge Buff*. Diamond Life Master, placed 2nd Silver Ribbon Pairs 1998, won several regionals.

BROWN, Gloria of Virginia Beach VA, worked in public relations and modeling, highly involved in community and charity work. Served as Unit Board member 1980-94, including as president, member Board of Governors 1991-97 and 1998 to present. Served as vice president and president District 6, also Charity Chairman since 1995. Unit Recorder since 1995. Has won more than 15 regionals.

BROWN, H. Sanborn (b. 1906) of Grosse Pointe Farms MI, architect. Won Life Master Pairs 1957, placed 2nd in De La Rue International Pair Championship, London, England 1957. Also won Marcus Cup 1949 and a few regionals. Served as ACBL Board of Governors member 1942-66, Michigan B.A. board member 1942-66, Michigan B.A. president 1964-66.

BROWN, Jeffrey C. (b. 1955) of Albuquerque NM, attorney. Won Non-Life Masters Pairs 1989.

BROWNE, Seamus John Charles (b. 1952) of Sydney, Australia, born in New Zealand, bridge teacher, journalist and director. Represented Australia in 4 world championships and 3 zonal championships. Won many national titles.

BROWNSTEIN, Sidney Dr. (Sid) (b. 1947) of Santa Monica CA, dentist in private practice and on faculty at UCLA School of Dentistry. District 23 Recorder. Diamond Life Master, placed 2nd Men's Teams 1988. Won more than 25 regionals.

BRUCE, David (formerly Burnstine) (1900-1965) of Los Angeles, Life Master #1, member ACBL Hall of Fame. A tremendously successful player in early Thirties. He headed a group that made the Contract Bridge Club in New York the center of the most expert game of the times. Burnstine, the name he went by during his bridge career, introduced the artificial 2♣ opening bid to show a strong hand (including A-K, A-K, A). Other 2 bids were not game forcing, a method which became the most widely used among experts of the day. It later developed into the cornerstone of ACOL. Known as a soothing partner but an unsettling opponent. Burnstine played with Oswald Jacoby and Howard Schenken on the first of the outstanding teams, the Four Horsemen, captained by P. Hal Sims. He authored the first book on that team's system B *Four Horsemen's One Over One*, 1932.

In 1933, with Schenken, Jacoby and Dick Frey, (joined shortly afterward by Michael T. Gottlieb) he organized the Four Aces. This team took the leadership in the field and held it, (with several amendments in personnel) for the next decade. With his teammates he wrote *Four Aces System of Contract Bridge*, 1935. In the brief interlude between the reigns of the Four Horsemen and the Four Aces, Burnstine helped to organize and played on the Bid-Rite Team. An all-round star, Burnstine was rated by many of his teammates as the best bidder in the game. Brashly self-confident, he frequently locked horns with Ely Culbertson and rarely came out second best. His impressive tournament record includes a victory in the first official World Championship in 1935 and many national championships including AWL All-American Open Teams (Contract) 1932, (Auction) 1931, 32, 33; USBA Open Teams 1934, 37; Open Pairs 1936, ABL Challenge Teams 1931, 33, 37; Spingold 1934, 36, 38; Vanderbilt 1931, 34, 35, 37, 38; Master Mixed Teams 1931, 33; Life Master Pairs 1931, 33, 36; Men's Pairs 1934, Master Individual 1933. Also won Eastern States Open Teams (Reisinger) 1931- 34.

BRUELHEIDE, Frank E. (1884-1943) of Minneapolis, bridge book publisher, writer and lecturer. First became an associate of Ely Culbertson and later became a Director of ACBL and organized the Bridge League of the Northwest. Traveled throughout U.S. lecturing, teaching and broadcasting over radio in the interests of bridge promotion. Published and edited his own magazine, *Bridge Digest*, 1936-39. His writings include several articles for *The Bridge World* and other publications, pamphlets on bridge such as *Duplicate Bridge Guide* and the book *Party Bridge*.

BRUN, Johannes (1891-1977) of Oslo, Norway, Army officer and bridge writer. Founding member Norwegian Bridge Association 1932, president 1934. President of

International Bridge League, forerunner of World Bridge Federation, 1937. Founding member of European Bridge League 1947, elected Honorary Member 1957. Represented Norway in European Championships 6 consecutive years, placed 2nd in both pairs and teams 1933. Awarded IBL prize for most distinguished player 1934. Editor of *Aftenposten*, contributor to several bridge magazines. National teams champion 1936, 37.

BRUNNER, Michelle (b. 1953) of Manchester, England, bridge professional and teacher. WBF World Master. Won Venice Cup 1985. 2nd World Women's Teams 1988. Won European Women Teams 1979, 2nd 1977. Won many national titles. Represented Great Britain twice and England 6 times in zonal championships

BRUNO, Steve (b. 1947) of Bellevue WA, retired state unemployment insurance adjudicator. Captain and coach for 1988 Women's Team runner-up USBC. Promoter of Women's teams in Pacific Northwest and originator of N.W. Women's Intercity Team Challenge. Co-authored *Two-over-one Game Force - An Introduction*. Placed 2nd North American Swiss Teams 1993. Won 22 regionals. Bruno with partner Darrell Keel posted highest score reported to ACBL on two-session play-through on 156 average for each session. Their combined scores came to 452 2 .

BRUNZELL, Anders (b. 1938) of Gothenburg, Sweden, mathematics and physics teacher. WBF World Master. 3rd Bermuda Bowl 1977, represented Sweden in 4 other world championships. European champion 1977, represented Sweden many other times. Nordic champion 1968.

BRUSTUNOV, Witold (b. 1944) of St. Petersburg, Russia, physicist and engineer. Chief organizer of tournaments in St. Petersburg (formerly Leningrad). Winner of several national titles.

BRYANT, Brenda D. Dr. (b. 1956) of Ferndale MI, dean of associate graduate studies Mary Grave College, consultant for executives. Has won 16 regionals.

BRYANT, Jack N. (b. 1934) of St. Louis MO, retired manager, systems development, Dept. of Agriculture. Served as Unit 143 president 1994-95, member District 8 Board of Directors 1982-83, 1994-95. Diamond Life Master, has won 25 regionals.

BUCHALTER, Ralph (b. 1958) of Berkeley CA, technical writer. Won IMP Pairs 1991 and a few regionals.

BUCHANAN, Dorothy (Mrs. Robert, formerly Kantor) of Minneapolis, retired, former owner/operator of full-time bridge studio, former office manager construction union. Has been active in all phases of bridge at unit level including president. Chairman 1982 Fall NABC and of many regionals and sectionals. Served on ACBL Board of Directors 1972-81 and Board of Governors. Wrote *Basic Bridge, New and Easy*. Diamond Life Master, won Life Master Women's Pairs 1982 and many regionals.

BUCHNER, Robert (Bob) (b. 1960) of Wheaton IL, software engineer, certified director. Placed 2nd Flt B. GNOT 1985 and won several regionals.

BUCKMAN, Harriett (b. 1935) of Lincolnwood IL, until 1984 a language arts and social studies teacher, currently teaches bridge. Former Girl Scout community administrator. Representative of District 13 on ACBL Board of Directors, member National Education Foundation, Charity Foundation, past president Chicago Contract B.A., CCBA Board member since 1984. directs on bridge cruises, has written articles for newcomers for CCBA *Kibitzer*. She once played a round with Charles Goren when she was a caddy. Has won more than 30 regionals.

BUCKMAN, Kate (1902-1997) of Toronto ON, bridge teacher, director and bridge club owner. Introduced duplicate bridge to Vancouver BC shortly after World War II. She opened her studio in Toronto in 1959. It developed into the largest bridge club in Canada averaging 300 tables a week and 750 students a year. Many bridge stars and personalities such as Sami Kehela, Eric Murray, George Mittelman, Percy Sheardown, Bruce Elliott and Bruce Gowdy developed at this studio. She had certain ideals and traditions upon which she was insistent and these remain in effect today. In 1973 she received the Edwin A. Wetzlar Memorial Award and was made ACBL Honorary Member. In 1983 she suffered a stroke and in 1990 sold her studio, but continued to visit and play occasionally. In 1982 the Metropolitan Toronto B.A. donated a trophy to Unit 166 to honor Kate. Kate Buckman Award recognizes special qualities, not solely bridge ability. She was its first recipient.

BUDD, Richard (The Bear) (b. 1937) of Portland ME, retired physicist and computer system designer. Member Board of Governors. Diamond Life Master, won Senior KO Teams 2000, placed 2nd Silver Ribbon Pairs 1998. Has won approximately 50 regionals.

BUDIN, Barnett (d. 1964) of Philadelphia, printer. ACBL Director 1963-64 and past president of Keystone Conference and Philadelphia Unit. Co-authored *Bridge Players Digest of Conventions.*

BUDKIN, Diana (b. 1943) of Buenos Aires, Argentina, bridge teacher. South American Women's Team champion 1983, 84, 85, 87, 88. Represented Argentina in Venice Cup 1985, 87. Has 3 national wins.

BULLER, Walter (1887-1938) of London, England, author and leading personality in Britain in the Thirties. Organized first Anglo-American match 1930 and captained English team. Leading protagonist for *British Bridge,* for direct methods of bidding without forcing bids. Bridge columnist, authored several books.

BURGER, Charles F. (Chuck) (b. 1936) of West Bloomfield MI, attorney. One of the leading American players. WBF World Master, ACBL Grand Life Master with 11,861 MPs as of 3/2001. Placed 9th Rosenblum Teams 1990, also represented United States 1970, 1986. Won Life Master Men's Pairs 1969, Blue Ribbon Pairs 1970, Spingold 1985, 89, 90; Reisinger 1988, 92; Men's BAM Teams 1988, Open Swiss Teams 1997; placed 2nd Reisinger 1981, 96, GNOT 1982, 96, Men's BAM Teams 1989, Master Pairs 1969, 1973, Spingold 1994, 97, Master Mixed Teams 1994, Open BAM Teams 1995, Vanderbilt 1997, 98, Life Master Open Pairs, Senior KO Teams 2000. Co-winner Herman Trophy 1970.

BURGER, Suzanne (Suzy) of West Bloomfield MI, former social worker presently part time in law office and homemaker. Won Women's BAM Teams 1989, Life Master Women's Pairs 1996; 2nd Mixed BAM Teams 1996, Women's Pairs 1997, Women's Swiss Teams 1998. Competed internationally 1986 and 1990. Won District 12 GNOT 1991 and several regionals.

BURGESS, Stephen (b. 1956) of Sydney, Australia, born in New Zealand. Options trader and bridge professional. WBF World Master. Placed 3rd World Pairs 1986. Represented Australia in 4 other world championships and 4 zonal championships. Won many national titles in Australia since 1982 and before that in New Zealand. A leading practitioner of relay methods. (see MOSCITO.)

BURKA, Paul J. (b. 1942) of Austin TX, former attorney. Senior editor of *Texas Monthly* and editor of *Scorecard.*

BURKE, Phyllis (Phyl, Mrs. Wayne) (d.1998) of Pocatello ID, former supervisor with state of Idaho Dept. of Employment, beauty salon owner, operator, owner/operater of a number of bridge clubs. Member of ACBL Board of Directors for 10 years, ACBL president 1989 and chairman of the board 1990. Member District 18 Board of Directors for 18 years, including serving as president for 3 consecutive terms (1979-84), past president of her Unit. Also served as chairman of many District 18 regionals and local sectionals. Played with 8 novices until they achieved rank of Life Master. Established ACBL Education Program.

BURN, David (b. 1956) of London England, business analyst. Coach to 10 British teams, captain of 1. Played on 6 England teams. WBF World Master. 4th Olympiad 2000, won Bonn Cup 2000. Contributor to many bridge magazines.

BURNHAM, Dr. Charles (Charlie) (b. 1919) of Birmingham AL, physician, opthalmologist, Fellow in American College of Surgeons, American Academy of Ophthalmology and Pan-Am Society of Ophthalmology. Held executive positions in Alabama B.A. in early Sixties. Was partner for many years to Elinor Murdoch, one of the top Women players of the Thirties. Burnham won Open Teams 1960 and several regional events.

BURNS, George of Hollywood CA, all-time great comedian and actor. Played bridge regularly at his country club almost to the time of his death. Daughter placed cigar, lighter and $20 in his casket so he could smoke cigars and buy bridge entries when he got to heaven. Donated George Burns Trophy which is given annually to ACBL senior who earns the most masterpoints in Senior events.

BURNS, Sanford R. (Sandy) (b. 1928) of Sarasota FL, retired real estate developer, former furniture manufacturer and owner of a chain of stores. Awarded Governor's Medal of the State of Florida for his bridge activities in 1983. Won 15 regionals.

BURNSTEIN, Anne (Mrs. Robert) (d. 1988) of Las Vegas, one of the leading players of the Western States, won Life Master Women's Pairs 1963, Women's Teams 1951, 62, 79, Women's Pairs 1979, Master Mixed Teams 1952, 53; Mixed Pairs 1946, 52; placed 2nd Life Master Women's Pairs 1962, Women's Teams 1955 and had numerous regional wins. Sister of Edith Kemp-Freilich and William Seamon. (See FAMILY.)

BURNSTINE, David. See BRUCE, DAVID.

BURTON, Charles G. (Chuck) (b. 1950) of Steilacoon WA, tax preparer, substitute teacher and tournament director. Won 26 regionals.

BUSTROS, Fady (1905-78) of Beirut, Lebanon, newspaper manager and bridge columnist. Represented Lebanon World Team Olympiad 1960, 64; European Championships 1954, 56, 57, 61, 62. Had many national successes.

BUTCHER, Thomas D. (b. 1932) of Tokyo, Japan, born in Defiance, Ohio; securities news editor and analyst. Represented Japan in 8 Far East Championships, twice as playing captain. Won Far East Pairs 1964. Won many national team titles. Former editor JCBL *Bulletin*. Bridge columnist *Mainichi Daily News*. Chief director Far East Championships 1964, 79. He is a war-gamer, bridge system theorist, and advocate of total-point bridge.

BUTKOW, Hyman (b. 1927) of Johannesburg, South Africa, accountant. Represented South Africa in World Team Olympiad 1968, 72, 76. 20 national wins.

BUTKOW, Julius (Big Julie) (b. 1933) of Johannesburg, South Africa, chartered accountant. Represented South

Africa in 2 world championships 1968, 76. Many national wins. Member WBF Executive Council 1976, 80. President South African Bridge League since 1969 and organizer of all its national events. Secretary of Africa Bridge Federation 1998. Tournament director World Championships 1995, 96; Maccabiah Games 1981, 92. Editor of *Showcase*; Bridge columnist for *Prime Talk* and *Finance Week*.

BUTLER, David C. (b. 1949) of Keswick VA, comptroller. Has won approximately 25 regionals.

BUTLER, Geoffrey (1898-1985) of London, England, journalist. Former member WBF Executive and EBL Executive, then President Emeritus. Former president of BBL, vice-president of EBU. Represented EBL and Portland Club in preparation of 1963 Codes of Laws. (see BUENOS AIRES AFFAIR.)

BUTLER, John (b. 1921) of Cardiff, Wales. Represented Wales in 50 Camrose Trophy matches between 1955 and 1982. 15 national wins. Former president WBU and vice-chairman BBL.

C

CABANNE, Carlos (b. 1917) of Buenos Aires, Argentina, dentist. WBF World Life Master. Won South American Teams 1948, 50, 51, 54, 57, 59, 61, 62, 64, 76. Represented Argentina Bermuda Bowl 1958, 62, 65, 77; World Team Olympiad 1964, 68, 72, 76, 80. 43 national wins. Won Gabarret Cup 1972, 83. Secretary, then president of the South American Bridge Confederation and named Honorary Member 1980. President Argentine Bridge Association. Member WBF Executive Committee 1961, 62, 64 and 1969-77, and member of its Laws Commission since 1970. Author of four books: *Bridge Razonada de A hasta Q; Bridge despu_s de la Q; Cuentos de Bridge; El Carteo in Bridge Contrato*. Frequent contributor to bridge publications. Member Editorial Board, *Bridge Encyclopedia*.

CABOT, Antonio (b. 1933) of Barcelona, Spain, bridge teacher. Represented Spain in 4 world championships and 7 zonal championships. Won many national titles.

CABRAL, Francisco Costa (b. 1943), of Lisbon, Portugal, leasing company executive. Represented Portugal in 3 world and 2 European championships. Won many national titles.

CAESAR, Karin of Germany. WBF World Life Master. 2nd Venice Cup 1993. Won European Women's Teams 1989, 2nd 1991. 2nd European Women's Pairs 1993, has won 6 national titles. Represented Germany other world championships. Member of German team winning Venice Cup 1995, ofter plays with sister, Marianne Moegel.

CAFFERATA, Mike (b. 1948) of Scarborough ON, high school math teacher. Npc of two Canadian Women's International Teams. Won CNTC 1993 and Canadian Open Pairs three times; has won more than 50 regionals.

CAHN, Nell Bridge (b. 1935) of Shreveport LA, bridge teacher, accomplished oil painter, has an extensive collection of bridge memorabilia. Served on Board of Governors, National Appeals Committee, president and VP of Unit 170. WBF World Master, Grand Life Master, has been included in the Shreveport Sports Museum. Won Venice Cup 1991. Won Life Master Women's Pairs, Women's KO Teams 1991, placed 2nd Women's KO Teams

1983, Women's Swiss Teams 1986, 90, Women's BAM Teams 1988; Silver Ribbon Pairs, 1997 and Life Master Women's Pairs 1999. Has won 75+ regional titles.

CAHN-SPEYER, Anton (b. 1918 in Austria) of Bogota, Colombia, public accountant. Won CAAC Teams 1968, represented Colombia in 6 other zonal championships. Won 8 national titles.

CALE, Helen (1912-1990) of Glendale CA, bridge teacher and writer, served as president of ABTA and ACBL Western Division and as chairman of the Los Angeles Unit. Won Mixed Pairs 1957.

CALLAGHAN, Brian (b. 1952) of London, England, computer consultant. WBF World Master. 4th Olympiad 2000, won Bonn Cup 2000. Represented England in 4 Camrose matches. National wins include Crockfords and Spring Fours.

CALLAHAM, Thomas M. (b. 1934) of Covington VA, retired pharmacist and research chemist, won 25-30 regionals.

CALVENTE, Ricardo (b. 1918 in Argentina, deceased) of Madrid, Spain, trader. WBF World Life Master. 3rd Bermuda Bowl 1958, 59. Won South American Teams 1959, 61, second 1963, 67. Represented Argentina in 3 other world championships. In Spain since 1969, represented Spain in one zonal championship.

CAMACHO, Carlos (b. 1946) of Rio de Janeiro, Brazil, engineer. WBF World Life Master. Won Bermuda Bowl 1989, South American Teams 1987, 88, 89, 91, 93. Represented Brazil in 4 other world championships.

CAMARA, Helen (Ninny) (b. 1907 in Greece) formerly of Cairo, Egypt. WBF World Life Master. Won World Women's Teams 1960, and represented Egypt many other times. National wins include 5 open teams. Contributor to bridge periodicals.

CAMBEROS, Hector R. (b. 1948) of Buenos Aires, Argentina, chemical engineer. WBF World Master. South American champion 1979, 80, 81, 85, 94 and represented Argentina in Bermuda Bowl 1977, 81, 85, 92, World Team Olympiad 1984, 1988, 2000. 8 national wins. Won Gabarret Cup 1979. Editor *Bridge Para Todos* 1977-79.

CAMPBELL, Andrew (b. 1942) of Manhattan Beach CA, research scientist, has worked in orbit determination, kalman filtering, artificial intelligence scientific simulation. Diamond Life Master, placed 2nd Reisinger 1982, has won 16 regionals.

CAMPBELL, Clifford V. (Cliff) (b. 1949) of Thunder Bay ON, store owner and bridge professional, placed 2nd in Canadian Curling Championship 1979. Past president Unit 228. Diamond Life Master, one of Canada's leading masterpoint holders and winner of Richmond Trophy 1985, 86, 92. He set a Canadian record by winning more than 1500 masterpoints in one year. Has won more than 60 regionals.

CAMPBELL, Dr. Donald Keith (b. 1957) of Saskatoon SK, dentist, bridge teacher, club director. Has held several executive positions on local and Unit level including president and vice-president. Won Open Pairs 1990. Has won more than 15 regionals.

CAMPBELL, Gordon (b. 1951) of Calgary AB, computer systems analyst. British Junior chess champion 1966, Alberta chess champion 1976. Past president Edmonton Unit 391 1981-83, served as tournament chairman 1979-81. Won CNTC 1984, represented Canada Bermuda Bowl 1985.

CAMPBELL, Hastings (b. 1949) of Belfast, Northern Ireland, property company director and lecturer in business and management. Represented Ireland once in the European Championship and Northern Ireland 48 times in Camrose Trophy matches.

CAMPOS, Joao Paulo of Rio de Janeiro, Brazil. WBF World Life Master. 2nd Rosenblum Teams 1998, Bermuda Bowl 2000. Won IOC Lausanne 1998. Won 2 national titles. Finalist 2000 Internet World Championship.

CAMPOS, Orlando (b. 1925) of Bombay, India, retired executive. Represented India in 7 world championships and 2 zonal championships. Formerly India's top masterpoint holder. 22 national wins. BFI Treasurer 1970-85. Chief tournament director Far East Championships 1978.

CANESSA, Luciana of Rome, Italy. WBF World Life Master. Won World Women's Team Olympiad 1972, European Women's Teams 1970, 71, 73.

CANNELL, Douglas L. (b. 1924) of Winnipeg MB, archaeology architect Rio Azul Archaological Project Guatemala for three field seasons. First president and founding member Canadian Bridge Federation, past president Unit 181, chairman Canadian Charitable Foundation, chairman 1985 Fall NABC. Has written bridge articles for newspapers.

CANNELL, Drew (Panama) (b. 1952) of Hampstead PQ, computer operations manager, bridge club general manager and bridge teacher. Developed own bidding system - Panama Relay System, authored Crashdak defense to Strong Club and Central American and Caribbean Bridge Federation Grand Master. Was Canadian coach 1984 and npc for Panama Venice Cup team 1988. Has competed in world championships since the Seventies; at Las Palmas 1974 was the youngest player). Has won tournaments on 5 continents. First Canadian (with partner G. Sekhar) to win GNOP 1986, npc of winning team 1985; placed 2nd Reisinger 1982. Won CNTC Teams 1985, 99, 2nd in 1986, 2nd CAC Open Teams 1987. Pairs; 1991 2nd Open Board-a-Match NABC; won North American Swiss Teams 1994, 95.

CANSINO, Jonathan (b. 1939) of London, England, former stockbroker. Represented Britain in 2 zonal championships and England in Camrose matches. 8 national wins. Inventor of Cansino Defense to Notrump.

CAPLAN, Jo Anne (See CASEN, Jo Anne)

CAPLAN, Mark E. (b. 1965) of Toronto ON, interest rate swap trader at Bank of Montreal, contributor to *Canadian Masterpoint*. Won Junior Collegiate Par Contest 1987, 2nd ACBL Intercollegiate Championships 1987. Placed 2nd World Jr. Championships 1991.

CAPODANNO, Luciana (b.1934) of Naples, Italy, WBF World Grand Master. Won World Women's Team Olympiad 1976, 2nd Venice Cup 1978. European Women's champion 1974, 77.

CAPPELLETTI, Katherine H. (Cathy) See WALVICK, Katherine H.

CAPPELLETTI, Michael (b. 1942) of Alexandria VA, lawyer, poker columnist. One of world's leading authorities on Omaha poker, and has written a bi-weekly column, *Cappelletti on Omaha*, for The Card Player since 1989. Has served on ACBL Board of Governors, National Appeals Committee, president of the Mid-Atlantic Bridge Conference and Washington Bridge League. Authored Cappelletti over Notrump, Cappelletti Over One-of-a-Major Doubled, Cappelletti Two-Suited Cuebids. Grand Life Master with 16,752 MPs as of 3/2001, placed 3rd World Mixed Teams 1974, 6th World Open Pairs 1978. Won Master Mixed Teams 1967, placed 2nd

in Mixed Pairs 1967, 1988, Blue Ribbon Pairs 1973, 77; Spring Men's Teams 1979, North American Swiss 1985, Reisinger 1991.

CAPPELLETTI, Michael D. (Mike Jr.) (b. 1965) of Knoxville TN, student and professional player, was National Merit Scholar finalist. Active in Junior Bridge, became Life Master just prior to 16th birthday. Had highest pair score in Intercollegiates (Instant Matchpoints) 1990, won District 7 Flight A GNOP 1991 and in 1989 was first in NACBC (Inter-Collegiates). Grand Life Master with 13,750 MPs as of 3/2001. Won Mixed Pairs 1999; Open Pairs I 2000, Open Swiss Teams 2000. Placed 2nd Reisinger 1991, 2000.

CAPPS, Richard Aaron (b. 1944) of Baton Rouge LA, elementary school principal, Served as president and secretary-treasurer for Unit 182. Placed 2nd North American Swiss 1983, won several regionals.

CARACCI, Marcelo (b. 1949), of Santiago, Chile, civil engineer. Represented Chile in 10 zonal championships.

CARANSA, Maurits of The Netherlands. Founded tournament named for him. Kidnapped 1978 after a visit to Continental Club of Amsterdam and released after payment of 8 million guilders. See CONTINENTAL CLUB.

CARAVELLI, Gerald A. (Gerry) (b. 1943) of Des Plaines IL, retired accountant, financial analyst; regular partner of Barry Crane for many years. Has served as tournament chairman, president and vice president of Chicago CBA. Long-time panelist on *Bridge World* Master Solvers Club. Grand Life Master with 16,664 MPs as of 3/2001. Won Mixed Pairs 1974, Master Mixed Teams 1975, Men's Pairs 1976, GNOT 1978, 95; Open Pairs 1982, North American Swiss 1996. Won International Team Trials 1996. Was 2nd Senior and Advanced Master Pairs 1964, Men's Teams 1971, Mixed Teams 1980, GNOT 1984, 88; North American Swiss 1979, 88, 89; Vanderbilt 1977, Open Pairs 1984, Silver Ribbon Pairs 1999, 2000, 2001. Was first in Central American and Caribbean Championships Open Teams 1991 Has won more than 100 regionals.

CARCASSONNE, Valerie (b. 1961) of Brussels, Belgium. WBF World Master. Used to play under her married name of Polet. Represented Belgium in open category in one European Championships, as well as numerous times in the Women's Teams. Won Common Market Mixed Teams 1991. National wins include 3 open teams.

CARGILE, Charles A. (Charlie) (b. 1940) of Toney AL, professional gambler and card player since 1970. Cargile won his division in Mini McKinney 2 years in a row, Master in 1985 and Advanced Senior Master 200-Life Master in 1986. Placed 2nd Red Ribbon Pairs 1986, 89.

CARINI-MAZZACCARA, Silvio (1907-1990) of Florence, Italy. Former member of executive committees of World Bridge Federation, European Bridge League and Italian Bridge Federation; contributor to *Bridge Encyclopedia*.

CARLSON, Isabella S. (Mrs E. N.) (d. 1990) of Webster Groves MO, former bridge teacher, cruise conductor, club director, pioneers of bridge in St. Louis area, helped organize St. Louis Unit in the Thirties and the St. Louis Women's Bridge League, of which she was president for many years. Past president of St. Louis Unit and former member ACBL Board of Directors.

CARMICHAEL, Thomas A. (Tom) (b.1974) of Iselin NJ, network engineer, member of Junior Corps. Learned bridge at age 4. In 1997 he and Joel Wooldridge became

the youngest pair to win an NABC event when they placed first in IMP Pairs. Placed 2nd 7th World Junior Team Championships.

CARNS, Dr. Gail (b. 1941) of Export PA, systems analyst. President Unit 142 1976, 77 and 1983,84. Diamond Life Master, has won 16 regionals.

CARRAGHER, Marie (b 1929) of Charlottetown PEI, retired. Served Unit 230 as secretary; certified club director and club manager. Won 15 regionals.

CARRUTHERS, John (JC) (b. 1947) of Toronto ON, born in England, project manager, systems analyst, writer. Editor of Ontario *Kibitzer* for 5 years, has had articles published in many bridge magazines. Served on Unit 166 Board of Directors and Canadian Bridge Federation Board of Directors. Carruthers, a WBF World Master, was npc of Canadian Bermuda Bowl team 1985; Venice Cup team 1989 (placed third), 1991; Women's Olympiad Teams 1992; also World Junior Championship 1991 (placed 2nd), Denmark 1993. Diamond Life Master, was the first winner of the Richmond Trophy (Canadian Top 500) 1974. Won Master Mixed Teams 1991, 2nd Life Master Pairs 1988. Has won CNTC 3 times and placed 2nd 3 times, won Canadian Open Pairs Championship. Placed 4th Cavendish Teams 1997.

CARSTENSEN, Svend (1899-1997) of Copenhagen, Denmark, bridge writer and journalist. Pioneered electronic scoring system.

CARTEAUX, Robert W. (Bob) (b. 1934) of Fort Wayne IN, president and CEO of CTD Inc. Bowled first 800 series (823) in the nation by a left-handed bowler in 1955. Served as Unit 154 Area Director 1991-98, Vice President 1999; District 8 Board of Directors 1995-99, ACBL Board of Governors 1995-99. Diamond Life Master, won Senior KO Teams 1997 and has won 20-25 regionals.

CARTER, David C. (1906-1989) of St. Louis MO, building and loan executive, past president Missouri Valley Conference and former vice president Midwest Conference. Originator of transfer bids in form now known as South African Texas (see also Texas). Originated the double-barreled variety of Two-Way Stayman, in which 2♣ is a one-round force and 2♦ is forcing to game. Won McKenney Trophy 1954, Life Master Pairs 1954, Men's Teams 1950, Men's Pairs 1957. Placed 2nd Spingold 1953, 62; Open Pairs 1946, 53, 54; Men's Pairs 1960.

CARTER, Kay (b. 1921) of Seminole FL, insurance agency secretary/treasurer, placed 2nd Women's Pairs 1962, Mixed Pairs 1965.

CASABAL, Leon (1892-1965) of Buenos Aires, Argentina. A pioneer of Argentine bridge. Played in radio match against Culbertson team in 1936. Columnist for *La Nacion* in early 30s. Author *Bridge de Hoy*.

CASE, Leonard L. (Len) (b.1951) of Charlotte NC, manager computer programming; served District 7 as president 1999-present, vice president 1997-1999, Treasurer 1993-97; served as Unit 153 president and vice president.

CASEN, Drew (b. 1950) of Boca Raton FL, bridge professional, former accountant, 9 handicap golfer and expert holdem (poker) player. WBF World Master, placed 2nd Rosenblum Teams 1990, in Rosenblum Teams and 17th i0n World Open Pairs 1986. Diamond Life Master. Won Cavendish Invitational Pairs 1987. Won Master Mixed Teams 1983, Open Swiss Teams 1992. Placed 2nd Men's BAM 1982, 88; Blue Ribbon Pairs 1982, Men's Swiss Teams 1986, Vanderbilt 1987, 2000, Open Swiss Teams, IMP Pairs 1990; Open Pairs II 1993.

CASEN, Jo Anne (b. 1954) of Boca Raton FL, accountant. Placed 2nd McConnell Teams 1994, won International

Invitational Shanghai Bridge tournament 1981. Won Women's Pairs 1985, Women's KO Teams 1994, was 2nd Women's BAM Teams 1996, Mixed BAM Teams 1997.

CASEY, Jill (b. 1948) of Newport, Wales, teacher. Represented Britain in one Venice Cup, one zonal and 3 Common Market Championships. Represented Wales in Camrose Trophy. Won Lady Milne Cup and 4 Welsh titles.

CASH, Ralph A. (b. 1904) of Phoenix, insurance agent, was U.S. winner World Olympic 1936. President Western Division 1954, member of Western Conference and ACBL executive committee, chairman of Phoenix Unit, general chairman Fall NABC in Phoenix 1962.

CASIAN, Esteban (b. 1932 in Chile) of Madrid, Spain, bridge teacher. Won South American Teams 1964. Represented Chile in 3 world championships and 4 other zonal championships. In Spain since 1978.

CASLAN, Dr. David F. (b.1948) of Columbus IN, college professor, formerly an attorney. Has done mountain climbing in the Himalayas, Europe and U.S. Won the GNOP in 1989, more than 30 regionals.

CASTRO, Alejandro (1916-1989), of Lima, Peru, formerly of Buenos Aires, Argentina. World Life Master. Founder of the South American Championships. Secretary South American Bridge Confederation 1955-63. South American champion, for Argentina, 1948, 53, 54, 57, 58, and represented Argentina 1958, 1959, 1961 Bermuda Bowl. Later competed for Peru 1976-1981. President of Argentine Bridge Association 1948-50 and 1952-56. Won Gabarret Cup 1957 and many national titles. Author of *Rebland System*.

CATON, Don J. (b. 1941) of Pensacola FL, attorney for city of Pensacola, Florida junior tennis champion and ranked 5th in the US in singles and 2nd in doubles, boys division, in the mid-Fifties; also a table tennis champion. Placed 2nd Life Masters Pairs 1980, Men's BAM Teams 1986.

CATZEFLIS, Georges (b.1931) of Lausanne, Switzerland, engineer. WBF World Life Master. Represented Switzerland in 5 world championships and 7 European Championships. Won 9 National Open Teams and 10 Open Pairs.

CAVENDISH, pseudonym of Henry James 1831-1899), a famous London whist authority. Cavendish was the name of the club to which James belonged and the name under which he chose to publish his first book on whist in 1863. This book, *The Laws and Principles of Whist Stated and Explained, and Its Practice Illustrated on an Original System, by Means of Hands Played Completely Through*, became the most popular guide to the game of whist since Hoyle's *Short Treatise. Cavendish on Whist* (book spine title) went through many editions and revisions, incorporating Jones's latest and best theories. He was the author of a number of other books on whist, among them *Whist Developments, American Leads and The Plain-Suit Echo, Card Essays, Clay's Decisions and Card Table Talk, American Leads Simplified*. With Nicholas Browse Trist he developed the system of whist play named by him the "American Leads", which encountered rather violent opposition in some quarters, but nevertheless enjoyed great popularity in England and even greater in America. Honorary member American Whist League.

CAYLEY, Henry Francis (Frank) (1910-1981) of Sydney, Australia, broadcaster, historian, bridge writer and teacher. 4th World Par Contest 1951. Won 4 Australian Par Contests. 6 national wins included 3 Open Teams.

Chairman Australian Bridge Federation. Columnist *Sydney Morning Herald*. Conducted bridge cruises. Author of 3 books.

CAYNE, James (Jimmy) (b. 1934) of New York City, investment banker. Placed 2nd World Mixed Pairs and World Mixed Teams 1974, WBF World Master. Won International Team Trials 1993, Master Mixed Teams 1966, Life Master Men's Pairs 1969, Reisinger Teams (playing captain) 1977, 88, 92; Men's Teams 1969, Men's BAM Teams 1988, Spingold 1989, 90; npc Open BAM 1993; placed 2nd Life Master Pairs 1969, 73; Reisinger 1981, 93, 94; Men's BAM Teams 1989; Spingold 1994; Mixed Teams 1996; Open BAM Teams 1997. Diamond Life Master, was playing captain of the gold medalist team in the 1981 Maccabiah Games, has been on the winning team in all Corporate America vs Congress matches. Participant in Corporate America vs Hollywood Celebrities match.

CAYNE, Patricia (Pat) (b. 1939) of New York City, educational neuropsychologist. Non-playing captain Chinese Women's team 1993; started bridge program for New York League for Hard of Hearing 1989; authored *Hear I Am* for hearing impaired; member ACBL Educational Foundation; chairman Congress vs. Corporate America and Congress vs. Parliament matches; author of *Language Through Play*, a book for teaching language to language-impaired children.

CHAGAS, Gabriel P. (b. 1944) of Rio de Janeiro, Brazil, financier, investment consultant, Grand Master ranked #6 in world. In 2001, 4th in WBF recent world rankings. Won World Olympiad Teams 1976, Bermuda Bowl 1989, World Pairs 1990. One of just 8 players to have won the Triple Crown of World Olympiad Teams, World Pairs and Bermuda Bowl. 2nd Rosenblum Teams 1978, 98. Represented Brazil in 26 other world championships, apparently a record. 2nd Bermuda Bowl 2000. Won South American Teams a record 22 times in the period 1967-98, in 28 attempts. Won 28 national titles, and is the top-ranked South American player. Won Reisinger 1992, London Sunday Times Invitational 1979, 92; Cap Gemini 1993, 1997. Magazine contributor. Created the term Intra-Finesse.

CHAIKIN, Marla (b. 1944) of Sea Bright NJ, needlepoint shop owner, former interior designer, GNYBA board member 1976-80. Placed 2nd Life Master Women's Pairs 1990.

CHAITT, Ellasue of Palm Beach Gardens FL. ACBL Grand Life Master with 13,365 MPs as of 3/2001. Placed 2nd Women's BAM Teams 1987, North American Women's Swiss Teams 1992, Women's Pairs 1994. Won scores of regionals.

CHAITT, Martin C. (Marty) (b. 1929) of Palm Beach Gardens FL. retired tournament director; computer system specialist. Served as 1st/2nd alternate for District 6 1962. Won more than 18 regional events.

CHAMBERS, Jim of Denver, one of the early national tournament directors. Was considered to be the fastest adder in the directing field.

CHAMBERS, Juanita of Schenectady NY, bridge professional. World Grand Master ranked #19 among women, won Venice Cup 1987, World Mixed Pairs 1990. Won first Pan-American Women's Pairs, placed 3rd Women's Teams. Grand Life Master with 12,251 MPs as of 3/2001, won Women's KO Teams 1985, North American Women's Swiss Teams 1987, 91, 94, 96; Master Mixed Teams 1984, 89, 92, Women's KO Teams 1989, 92, 95, 2000; Mixed Pairs 1979, Women's BAM Teams

1991, 93; Women's Pairs 1995; placed 2nd Mixed Pairs 1987, Women's KO Teams 1986, 90, 97, 98; Life Master Women's Pairs 1995, Women's Swiss Teams 2000.

CHAMBERS, Neil J. (b. 1946) of Schenectady NY, born in Regina SK, tax accountant, bridge professional. Coach for Canadian team World Team Olympiad 1980. Created the Chico 2♦ bid, an early form of Multi. Won North American Swiss Teams 1977, Men's Teams 1978, 81; Vanderbilt 1992; placed 2nd Spingold 1986. Diamond Life Master, was 2nd Cavendish Pairs, 3rd Pan American Open Teams.

CHAN, David Y.K. (b.1951) of Hong Kong, banking executive. Won Far East Team 1987, represented Hong Kong in 3 world championships and 2 other Far East Championships.

CHAN, Lapt H. (b. 1963) of Forest Hills NY, webmaster, former manager of Manhattan Bridge Club. Rookie of Year in Ace of Clubs competition 1985. Won 15 regionals.

CHANDROSS, Howard (1946-1996) of Long Beach NY, tax accountant and bridge professional. Served on Board of Directors GNYBA and NSBA 1975-88; was member of Board of Governors and Goodwill Committee, past president and treasurer of NSBA. Placed 15th Rosenblum Cup Teams 1986. Grand Life Master with 17,933 masterpoints. Placed 2nd Vanderbilt 1987, Life Master Men's Pairs 1984, Master Mixed Teams 1990; placed 13th Rosenblum Teams 1986. Had severe physical problems as a result of birth defect that affected his feet and hands, played bridge in wheelchair.

CHANFRAY, Annie (d. 1981) of Lyons, France. World Life Master, 2nd World Women's Team Olympiad 1960, 3rd 1964.

CHANG, Godfrey (b. 1937) of Honolulu HI, supervisory telecommunications/computer. Diamond Life Master, placed 2nd Silver Ribbon Pairs and Mixed Pairs 1999. Has won 30 regionals.

CHANG, Morris (b. 1931) of Santa Clara CA, born in China; chairman, Taiwan Semiconductor; president, General Instrument; Senior VP Texas Instruments. Placed 2nd North American Swiss Teams 1992, won about 100 regionals.

CHARNEY, Gerald (Gerry) (b. 1933) of Toronto, barrister and solicitor. Placed 3rd World Olympiad Teams 1968, 72; 5th Rosenblum Cup Teams 1978; captained Canada in World Team Olympiad Seattle 1980. WBF World Life Master.

CHATTA, Patricia J.(Pat) (b. 1936) of Watertown MA, financial planner, cost analyst, technical writer. Won North American Rookie Pairs 1981, several regionals.

CHATTERJEE, Mukul (b.1938) of Calcutta, India, bridge organizer. Secretary of BFAAME since 1993 and secretary of Bridge Federation of India since 1998.

CHATZINOFF, Kenneth (b. 1945) of Cinnaminson NJ, psychologist working in correctional institutions. Won National Amateur Men's Pairs 1976 and a few regionals.

CHAZEN, Bernard (Bernie) (b. 1942) of Tamarac FL, professional bridge player, former math teacher and systems analyst. Chairman District 9 Appelate Committee 1996-present, chairman Unit 243 Conduct and Ethics Committee. Head writer and publisher of *Club Letter Standard, Avoiding the Traps, 2/1 Series Parts I,II,III, Bid-Em-Ups.* Regular contributor to *Bridge Sense, Aces' Bridge Monthly.* Grand Life Master with 17,098 MPs as of 3/2001, won Men's Teams 1971, Mixed Pairs 1973, 2000, Mixed Teams 1984, Senior KO Teams 1999; placed 2nd Spingold 1984, 87, Senior KO Teams 2000, and has

won several hundred regional events.

CHEEK, Curtis (b. 1958) of Huntsville AL, bridge professionl, formerly aerospace engineer, active in bridge teaching and administration in Unit 232, president 1988, 94. WBF World Master. Diamond Life Master with more than 15,200 MPs as of 3/2001. Placed 2nd Open Pairs II 1994, Open Swiss Teams 1994, Life Master 4-Session Open Pairs 1996, GNOT 1997, North American Swiss Teams 1999. Won more than 300 regional titles.

CHEMLA, Paul (b. 1944 in Tunis) of Paris, France, bridge professional, former literature lecturer. WBF World Grand Master. In 2001, 14th in WBF world rankings. Won World Team Olympiad 1980, 1992, Bermuda Bowl 1997. 2nd World Team Olympiad 1984. 3rd Bermuda Bowl 1995. Won European Pairs 1976 and 1985, European Mixed Teams 1998, 2nd European Teams 1995, 3rd 1997. Represented France in many other world and zonal championships. Won London Sunday Times Invitational 1991, Generali Individual 1998. IBPA Personality of Year 1998.

CHEN, Amy (b. 1949) of Taipei, Taiwan. Won Far East Women's Teams 1988, 89. Represented Taiwan in 5 zonal championships and 3 world championships.

CHEN, Chuan-Cheng (b. 1952) of Hsinchu, Taiwan, mechanical engineer. Won Far East Teams 1987, 89, 94, Far East Pairs 1989. Represented Taiwan in 5 world championships and 6 Far East Championships.

CHEN, Kuo-Yong (b. 1944 in China) of Taipei, Taiwan, insurance manager. Far East Champion 1981, 1988, represented Taiwan in 4 zonal championships and 2 world championships.

CHEN, Rongchang of Shanghai, China, technical employee. WBF World Master. Won Far East Teams 1991, 2nd 1993. Represented China in 6 World championships and 4 zonal championships. Won many national titles.

CHEN, Zelan (b. 1959) of Beijing, China. Winner of many national championships, treasurer and deputy secretary of Chinese Bridge Association. Organizer for 1995 Bermuda Bowl and Venice Cup in Beijing.

CHENG, Kuen Renor Conrad (b. 1934) of Hsinchu, Taiwan. WBF World Life Master. Runner-up Bermuda Bowl 1970 and represented Taiwan in 2 other Bermuda Bowls. Won Far East Open Team 4 times and Open Pair 3 times. Author of *Modern Bidding System* and other works.

CHERNOFF, Victor B. (b. 1937) of Los Angeles CA, consulting actuary, former principal actuary with IRS. College table tennis champion. Won Eastern States Open Pairs (Goldman) 1970 as non Life Master. Diamond Life Master with approximately 40 regional wins. Represented Dist. 23 in GNOT 1980, 82, 89 and 97.

CHEVALLEY, Ginette (b. 1933) of Paris, France. World Life Master, 2nd Venice Cup 1987, 3rd 1985. Won European Women's Teams 1983, 85, 87; European Women's Pairs 1991. Represented France in 6 other world championships and won many national titles.

CHIARADIA, Eugenio (The Professor) (1917-1977) of Naples, Italy, professor of philosophy. World Grand Master, won Bermuda Bowl 1957, 58, 59, 61, 62, 63; won European Teams 1951, 56-59, 2nd 1952. Many national titles. Devised Neapolitan system, a cornerstone of Italy's rise to the top in world bridge, leader of Italian team in its early days. After retirement moved to Sao Paulo, Brazil, where he coached the Brazilian team. Author of one book.

CHILCOTE, Mary J. (b. 1926) of Cleveland OH. Mother was survivor of Titanic. Board of Governors (1970-78) and Unit 125 Board (1975-80). Placed 15th

World Mixed Pairs 1974. Grand Life Master with 12,948 MPs as of 3/2001, won Senior KO Teams 1996, placed 2nd Mixed Pairs 1970. Won more than 75 regionals.

CHILDS, Allen Jr. (Al) (b. 1934) of Little Rock AR, bridge professional and glass shop owner, lives in a converted 100-year-old livery stable. National champion dairy cattle judge. Has served Unit 161 and Dist. 10 in various executive positions and as member of the Board of Governors. Editor of *Mid-South Bridge Forum* since its inception. Grand Life Master with 11,956 MPs as of 3/2001, won Senior KO Teams 1997.

CHILDS, Derrell W. (b. 1934) of Garland TX, CPA. Served Dallas BA as president, treasurer, Board member. Diamond Life Master with more than 7000 masterpoints, won 35-40 regionals.

CHING, Anthony W. (Tony) (b. 1948) of Hong Kong, vice president Hong Kong BA, HON treasurer, Hong Kong Grand Master, tournament director since 1967. Directs in zonal competitions.

CHIU, Karic P.K. (b. 1954) of Hong Kong, computer operations manager. WBF World Master. Far East champion 1987. Represented Hong Kong in 4 world championships and 4 other Far East Championships.

CHMIELOWIEC, John (Big John) Michigan City IN, retired draftsman, restores 1964 Pontiac GTOs. Won 16 regionals.

CHOKSI, Rita (b. 1938) of Delhi, India, export company director. WBF World Master. Won Far East Women's Teams 1978, BFAAME Women's Teams 1983, 85, 2nd 1991. 2nd BFAAME Open Pairs 1983. Represented India in 3 other zonal championships and 4 world championships. Won more than 11 national titles. Only woman to qualify for Indian Open Team.

CHONG, Antonio T. (Tony) (1927-1998) U.S. citizen of China origin, worked in Taiwan 35 years as chairman and CEO of petrochemical company. Far East Champion 1989 and played in 2 world championships. Npc Taiwan team in 7 world championships and 15 Far East Championships. Won Hong Kong Inter-City tournament 1989, 90. National titles include teams and pairs many times. Chief organizer of major events in Taiwan including Far East Championship and Proton International tournaments.

CHOY, Patrick of Singapore, corporate vice president of Motorola Inc, WBF vice president, WBF Executive Council member since 1991, member of WBF committees including masterpoints, finance, youth, infrastructure, zonal structure. Honorary president Hong Kong Contract Bridge Association. Organized historic 1981 Hong Kong Inter-City Tournament when the Chinese from mainland and Taiwan officially met for the first time since their separation in 1949. Numerous Hong Kong and Singapore national titles, represented Hong Kong and Singapore in various Zonal and World Championship events including 1992 and 2000 Olympiads; 1994 and 1998 World Championship; 1996, 98, 99, 2000 Zone 6 Championships.

CHRISTIAN, Col. William (1914-1986) of Chipley FL, retired Army officer. In 1946 shared distinction with teammate Capt. Mark Hodges in being first members of military service on active duty to win North American Championship. Awarded Bronze Star, Silver Star 1944; French Croix de Guerre 1945, 1st OLC Bronze Star 1951, Legion of Merit 1967, Air Medal 1967. Won Spingold 1946, Men's Pairs 1960, placed 2nd Life Master Men's Pairs 1964.

CHRISTIANSEN, Leif (1914-1989) of Oslo, Norway.

Actuary. Won Nordic Teams 1946 and 1949. Represented Norway in 7 European Championships. Many national wins.

CHRISTIANSEN, Soren (b 1955) of Copenhagen, Denmark, bridge teacher and theorist. WBF World Master. 3rd World Team Olympiad 1996. Also represented Denmark in one other world championship and 3 zonal championship. 6 Danish titles.

CHRISTIE, Agatha (1890-1976), pre-eminent British writer, wrote more than 100 works, among them 60 detective novels and 19 volumes of short mystery stories. One of them, *Cards on the Table*, concerns a murder committed during a bridge game. Poirot solves the mystery by ascertaining the abilities and bidding styles of each player and the contracts they reached.

CHU, Nytt (b. 1944) of Singapore, chemical engineer. Represented Singapore in 4 zonal championships. Several national wins.

CHU, Yung-Ming (b. 1922) of Irvine CA, formerly of Hong Kong, born in Shanghai, retired accountant. Was Far East Open Team champion 1959, placed 2nd Open Teams 1963, 65, 69, Open Pairs 1971; represented Hong Kong in Far East Championships 1963-71. National wins include Master Teams 1960, 63, 68; Open Teams 1958, 62, 69, 70; Master Pairs 1959, 71; Open Pairs 1966, Mixed Pairs 1968, 72; Individual 1958. Emigrated to U.S. 1973, has won 33 regionals.

CHUA, Chee Peng (b. 1945) of Singapore, chemist. Represented Singapore in one world and 2 zonal championships.

CHUA, Stephen (b. 1919-81) of Paranaque, Philippines, businessman. Won Far East Teams 1957, 58, Far East Pairs 1970. Represented Philippines in 3 world championships and in Far East Championships regularly from 1958. Won more than 50 nationals titles.

CHUCK, Cecil (b. 1928) of Kingston, Jamaica, business executive, WBF World Master. Former President of the Jamaica Bridge Association. CACBF National Team champion 1983. Represented Jamaica in 1987 Bermuda Bowl. Numerous national titles.

CHUN, Peter H.L. (b. 1949) of Hong Kong, computer systems manager. WBF World Master. Won Far East Open Teams 1987, 2nd Open Pairs 1984, 1988. Represented Hong Kong in 3 world championships and 4 other Far East Championships.

CHURCHILL, S. Garton (Church) (1900-1992) of Great Neck NY, attorney, great American bridge player and personality. Bridge-playing activities somewhat curtailed after 1944 due to law practice and his desire to spend time with family, but his interest in bridge never diminished. Originator of Churchill System, advocated ideas often scoffed at in early Thirties but generally adopted some 20 years later. These original theoretical ideas were set out in *Contract Bidding Tactics at Matchpoint Play* and articles in *The Bridge World*. Won Life Master Pairs 1937, 48, setting two records in partnership with Cecil Head. They scored 65% as an average for four sessions and 77.4% in a single session. Churchill won the Chicago (now the Reisinger) 1932, placed 2nd in 1933, 39, 41, 42; Master Mixed Teams 1937, Asbury Challenge Teams 1931.

CIMON, Francine A. (b. 1950) of Montreal PQ, high school teacher in charge of computer lab, former bridge club owner/manager, taught bridge on national television in Canada 1974-75. WBF World Life Master, represented Canada in World Team Olympiads 1976, 80, 84, 88. Placed

3rd Venice Trophy 1989, 4th World Women's Olympiad Teams 1976, 88, 7th 1980, 9th 1984; 5th Swiss Plate 1984. Also represented ACBL Venice Cup 1991. Won Canadian Open Pairs 1981, Canadian Women's Teams 1979, 83, 84, 86, 87, 88, 89, 90, 91; was 2nd CNTC 1988.

CINTRA, Gabino (b. 1942) of Rio de Janeiro, Brazil, IBM executive. WBF Grand Master, #26 in world. Won World Olympiad Teams 1976, World Pairs 1978, a very rare double. 2nd Rosenblum Teams 1978, represented Brazil in 11 other world championships. Won South American Teams 1970, 72, 73, 75, 77, 78, 82, 84, 91. National wins include 7 open teams.

CINTRA, Lia of Rio de Janeiro, Brazil. Won South American Women's Teams 1971, 72, 73, 81, 89, 91, 93, 95. Represented Brazil in 3 world championships.

CLARK, Harry (b. 1932) of Sebring FL, retired, became ACBL national tournament director 1978.

CLARK, Sandi (b. 1944) of Sebring FL, former assistant manager of ACBL Education Dept. Assisted with first ACBL Junior Camp. Former tournament director.

CLARKE, Angela (Gale) of McLean VA, bridge teacher, won Women's Pairs 1969. Placed 15th World Women's Pairs 1970.

CLARKE, Thomas (Tom) (b. 1946) of Lake Charles LA, insurance and financial services executive, Navy veteran. Has served Unit 221 and Dist. 10 in various executive positions. Won North American Swiss Teams 1993; placed 2nd Life Master Pairs 1993. Has approximately 25 regional wins.

CLARREN, David B. (1918-1989) of Minneapolis, insurance agent, pioneer of bridge development in Minnesota, taught bridge for many years and lectured on TV for 52 weeks in 1960. Won Vanderbilt 1947, placed 2nd Spingold 1949, 53.

CLAY, Ann S. ((b. 1929) of Little Rock AR; high school teacher, placed 2nd Women's Pairs 1957, has won 15+ regionals.

CLAY, Dane (b. 1928) of Little Rock AR; senior member law firm; served as president Arkansas Bridge Association and Little Rock BC. Diamond Life Master.

CLAY, James (1805-1873) of London, was leading British whist authority between Hoyle and Cavendish. Chief work was *Treatise on the Game of Whist* (1864).

CLAYTON, Sir Hugh Bayard (1877-1947) of India, one of inventors of SACC system, the initials of 4 players from India who developed an earlier form of plafond in 1912.

CLEGG, Matt of San Diego, founder and proprietor of OKbridge, the first online bridge game to make a serious impact. Almost 20,000 members as of 3/2001. Sponsors annual Internet World Bridge Championship, with teams from all over the world competing. Also sponsors OKbridge University, an online teaching program.

CLERKIN, Dennis E. (b. 1950) of Bloomington IN, professional bridge player and instructor, Grand Life Master with 16,984 MPs as of 3/2001, has won NAOP 1989, NAOT 1990, Master Mixed Teams 1992, placed 2nd Swiss Teams 1977, Master Mixed Teams 1992. Numerous regional wins.

CLERKIN, Gerald P. (Jerry) (b. 1952) of North Vernon IN, professional bridge teacher and player. Placed 2nd Swiss Teams 1977, Diamond Life Master with more than 14,100 MPs as of 3/2001.

CLIFF, David (Dave) (1932-1999) of Branchburg NJ, retired school teacher, principal and associate professor, a leading bridge theorist. Developed comprehensive relay system in which one player uses bids to ask questions and the partner describes his hand with specialized responses. Relay systems of various kinds, including the Ultimate Club, now are commonly used by ranking experts throughout the world. Also invented Splinter Bid and Denial Cuebid. Other contributions include specialized responses to both strong 2♣ opening bids and weak two-bids, transfer overcalls of a natural 1♣ opening bid, a specialized defense against 1NT, and rebids after a Stayman response to an opening 1NT bid.

COBB, Bruce (BC) (1931) of Denver CO, retired engineer, professional bridge player; served as VP and tournament chairman Unit 361 6 years; Mini-McKenney Silver Life Master of the Year 1995, 96, 97; Gold Life Master of the Year 1998, 99; Has won 20 regionals.

COCHINWALA, A. Ghaffar (b. 1931) of Karachi, Pakistan, businessman. Won BFAAME Open Teams 1981. 2nd Far East Open Teams 1978.

CODY, Judi L. (b. 1949) of Annandale VA, court reporter. Past president Unit 195, member Board of Governors 1976-88. Placed 16th World Women's Pairs 1990. Won Life Master Women's Pairs 1986, placed 2nd GNOP 1987, Women's BAM 1987, Women's Swiss Teams 1992. Diamond Life Master with many regional wins.

COENRAETS, Philippe (b. 1951) of Huy, Belgium, engineer. Represented Belgium in 4 World Championships and 6 European Championships. Won Common Market Mixed Teams 1991. National wins include 5 open teams and 4 open pairs.

COFFIN, George S. (1903-1994) of Waltham MA, author, publisher and distributor of bridge books and supplies. Won *The Bridge World* international problem-solving contest 1930. Principal bridge work is *Bridge Play Four Classics*, a 960-page compilation of his earlier works — *Endplays, Bridge Perfect Plays and Matchpoint Ways* appended by *The Bridge Writer's Manual*. Wrote many volumes on games other than bridge (poker, pinochle, cribbage, etc.). Co-founder of ABTA and first editor of its quarterly magazine; developer of Three-handed Bridge; creator of many items of bridge equipment; publisher of many bridge books, including Beynon's *Bridge Director's Manual*, his own *Bridge Director's Logistics*, books by British writers; author of magazine and newspaper articles and of *Instant Bridge Bidding*; contributing editor, *Bridge Encyclopedia*.

COGAN, Evie (b. 1948) of Penn Valley PA, attorney and professor of law La Salle University, formerly a trial attorney with the Dept. of Navy and EEOC. Won Master Mixed Teams 1988.

COHAN, Joseph (1899-1958) of Wooster OH, born in Canada, businessman, ACBL president 1952. Placed 2nd Men's Teams 1947, 49.

COHEN, Barry See CRANE, BARRY.

COHEN, Ben (1907-71) of Hove, England, bridge entrepreneur. Early pioneer of duplicate bridge, published the first book on the Acol System. Wrote and published many others, including European edition of *Official Encyclopedia of Bridge*, often in collaboration with Rhoda Barrow Lederer.

COHEN, David (1897-1982) of Belfast, Northern Ireland. WBF World Master, Represented Ireland European Championships 1956, Northern Ireland in more than 70 Camrose Trophy matches, a record. President Irish Bridge Union 1962-63, chairman North of Ireland Bridge Union 1956.

COHEN, Harvey C. (b. 1935) of Encino CA, attorney,

won Open Pairs 1967. Member of Los Angeles team that defeated the Sharif Bridge Circus 1970.

COHEN, Israel (1913-1996) of Washington, merchant. Won Open Pairs 1952, placed 2nd Chicago (since 1965 the Reisinger), Master Mixed Teams 1963, Open Individual 1956.

COHEN, Janet (Jan) (1934-1997) of Los Angeles CA, accountant and business manager. Unit 552 treasurer, Dist. 23 president, Board of Governors, member Ethical Oversight Committee, President's Advisory Committee on Policy and Procedures from its inception. Placed 20th World Women's Pairs 1990, Pan American Women's Pairs 1992. Won Life Master Women's Pairs 1992, Women's BAM 1993, Women's Swiss Teams 1994; placed 2nd Women's Pairs 1993.

COHEN, Kenneth L. (Ken) (b.1948) of Philadelphia PA, bridge professional. Won Master Mixed Teams 1988, Mixed Pairs 1990, Open Pairs 1991; placed 2nd Mixed Pairs 1972, Life Master Pairs, Spingold 1977. Won Fishbein Trophy 1977. Diamond Life Master.

COHEN, Larry Neil (b. 1959) of Boca Raton FL, options trader, author of *To Bid or Not to Bid*, best-selling bridge book of 1992-1993. His other books include *The Law of Total Tricks*. Also contributor to *The Bridge World*. World Life Master. Placed 2nd World Open Pairs 1998, 9th Rosenblum Teams 1990, 13th 1982. Won Pan American Open Teams 1992, placed 8th World Simultaneous Pairs 1986. Grand Life Master with 14,807 MPs as of 3/2001. Won Spingold 1981, 84; Blue Ribbon Pairs 1981, 83, 88, 95; Reisinger 1985, 1991; Life Master Men's Pairs 1983; Men's BAM 1984; Open BAM 1991; Life Master Pairs 1987, 88, 96; GNOT 1994; Open Pairs II 1996; North American Swiss Teams 1999. Placed 2nd Open Pairs 1979; NAOP 1980, 84; Spingold 1983; Life Master Men's Pairs 1986, 91; Vanderbilt 1990, 93, 98; Open BAM Teams 1990; North American Open Teams 1991; Mixed Teams 1994; Blue Ribbon Pairs 1996. Winner of the Cavendish Invitational Pairs 1983, 88. At 1991 Fall NABC in Indianapolis he won 356 masterpoints.

COHEN, Lawrence (Larry) (b. 1943) of Las Vegas NV, pharmacist. Co-author of *Breakthrough in Bridge*. Grand Life Master with 11,542 MPs as of 3/2001, won Spingold 1973, 76; Reisinger 1973, GNT 1974, Vanderbilt 1975,76; Blue Ribbon Pairs 1968, Men's Pairs 1976, Life Master Men's Pairs 1989, Herman Trophy 1973, Mott-Smith Trophy 1976. Placed 2nd Blue Ribbon Pairs 1968, Men's Teams 1971, Vanderbilt 1973, 89; North American Swiss Teams 1992. See HOUSTON AFFAIR.

COHEN, Mark Allen (b. 1954) of New York City, elementary school teacher, bridge club owner, bridge teacher and director, theatrical producer. Vice-Chairman ACBL Board of Governors 1990-93 and served on Greater NYBA Board and ACBL Board of Governors 1984-93. Has won about 18 regionals.

COHEN, Mark D. (b. 1951) of Glen Ridge NJ, stock options trader, regular member of expert panel *Bridge World* Master Solvers Club since 1983. Placed 5th Rosenblum Teams 1990. Won Master Mixed Teams 1979, 86; Men's Swiss Teams 1984, 86. Placed 2nd in North American Swiss Teams 1979, Vanderbilt 1982, Spingold 1983, 89; Reisinger 1987, GNOP 1988, USBC (Team Trials) 1989. Cohen and wife Stasha Cohen are one of the more successful husband-wife partnerships. Diamond Life Master with more than 30 regionals.

COHEN, Nathan (Mr. Money Bags, Nat) (1915-1995) of Memphis, ACBL assistant treasurer and finance of-

ficer at North American Championships 1948-1984, worked with Ely Culbertson as production manager of Autobridge sets 1936-46. In 1931 Cohen won 56 medals in various track events.

COHEN, Ralph (b. 1926) of Memphis TN, born in Montreal PQ, retired, CEO of ACBL 1984-86, assistant executive secretary ACBL 1971-84, consultant to ACBL 1986-91. Retired from ACBL 1991 and was manager of MA Lightman Bridge Club in Memphis for 3 years. Member ACBL Laws Commission since 1984, is currently serving as co-chairman and as vice-chairman of WBF Laws Committee. Served on ACBL Laws Commission Drafting Committee for revision of rubber bridge Laws. Wrote *Ruling the Game* column for two years along with other contributions to ACBL *Bridge Bulletin* and was a contributor to the Fourth Edition, *Official Encyclopedia of Bridge*. WBF International Master and Diamond Life Master. Represented Canada and placed 4th World Team Olympiad 1964, 5th Rosenblum Teams 1990. Won IMP Pairs 1990, Senior KO Teams 1997, Open Swiss Teams 1998. Placed 2nd Amateur Swiss 1977, North American Open Pairs 1994; was member of Montreal's winning Intercity Team 1967, 68. See FAMILY.

COHEN, Stasha (Mrs Mark D., formerly Wroblewski) (b. 1954) of Glen Ridge NJ, civil trial attorney, formerly a computer programmer analyst with IBM. Student of Japanese flower arranging, enjoys gourmet cooking. Has served on Board of Directors of GNYBA and New Jersey BA. WBF World Master, won Venice Cup 1991. National Master of the Year 1976. Won Women's KO Teams 1982, 91, 93; Women's Swiss Teams 1982; Master Mixed Teams 1986. Was 2nd in GNOP 1988, Women's BAM in 1986, 87. Won first regional she ever played in, Fun City Swiss Teams 1975.

COHEN, William E. (Billy) (b. 1958) of Las Vegas, born in Montreal, professional bridge player, Diamond Life Master, won Swiss Teams 1978, 95; Reisinger 1987, Open Swiss Teams 1993; placed 2nd Spingold 1982, 86; Vanderbilt 1988; GNOT 1995. See FAMILY.

COHLER, Dean (b. 1927) of Northbrook IL, retired CPA. Won Swiss Teams 1979.

COHN, Bette L. of Sarasota FL, tax consultant, bridge director and teacher. Won Venice Cup 1974, placed 10th World Mixed Pairs 1974. Won Mixed Pairs 1966, Women's Teams 1967, Life Master Women's Pairs 1970. Many regional

COHN, Janice See HORWITZ, Janice.

COHN, Judith (Judy) (nee Orr) (b. 1942) of Ft. Thomas KY, aerodynamics engineering specialist, member Unit 124 Board 1976-1991, co-chairman 1979 Fall NABC and past president Unit 124 and Dist. 11, editor Unit 124 newsletter. Co-authored *Cincinnati Power Defensive Carding*.

COHN, Martin J. (Marty) (1923-2000) of Sarasota FL, retired business executive. Was one of game's most colorful players. Retired from tournament bridge in 1985 as a protest against the cheating scandals. Won Life Master Pairs 1957, Mixed Pairs 1966, placed 2nd Men's Pairs 1961, Master Mixed Teams 1964, Men's Teams 1969.

COLATOSTI, Daniel (b. 1936) of Waltham MA, printing executive. Won North American Swiss Teams 1997, won more than 25 regionals.

COLCHAMIRO, Janet of Merrick NY. Won North American Swiss Teams 2000, placed 2nd Mixed BAM Teams 2000.

COLCHAMIRO, Mel Alan (b. 1945) of Merrick NY, bridge teacher, writer, professional player and director, former Wall Street economist and stock options trader. Past president Nassau-Suffolk BA, member Board. Won North American Swiss Teams 2000, placed 2nd Mixed BAM Teams 2000.

COLE, Dr. William D. (Bill) (b. 1963) of Sitges, Barcelona, Spain, teaches art connoisseurship and medieval literature at the Universitat Ramon Llull and the Universitat Pompeu Fabra, has played bridge professionally in U.S. and Spain, has written articles for *The Bridge World, ACBL Bridge Bulletin* and *Popular Bridge*; described Fishhead Coup in *Fishheads* (1991). Founded Harvard bridge team 1985, served as coach and captain until 1994. Won North American Collegiate Bridge Championship 1990, second 1988. Has had many tournament wins in U.S. and Spain.

COLE, William P. (Bill) (b. 1950) of Silver Spring MD, engineer for Bell Atlantic. Developed Cole 2♣ Bid and Deas Over Notrump with Lynn Deas. Won Master Mixed Teams 1982, placed 2nd Master Mixed Teams 1981. Grand Life Master with 11,011 MPs as of 3/2001.

COLEMAN, John (Jack) (b.1933) of San Francisco, real estate insurance. Grand Life Master, won 3 and placed second 4 times in North American Championships. Rookie of the Year 1984. Contributor to *The Bridge World, Bridge Bulletin, Bridge Today*.

COLKER, Dr. Richard E. (b. 1946) of Wheaton MD, psychology professor, psychology research investigator. Recorder for ACBL Dist. 6, Appeals chair for Washington Bridge League, vice chair for National Appeals Committee, member National Ethical Oversight Committee, columnist for Washington BL *Bulletin* since 1988, ACBL recorder 1996-, member WBF Appeals Committee 1995-, member ACBL Conventions and Competition Committee 1999-, member ACBL International Team Trials Committee 1995-, Cavendish appeals chief 1998-. Diamond Life Master.

COLLIER, Gladys W. (b. 1922) of East Hampton NY, mathematician. Won Master Mixed Teams 1989, placed 2nd Life Master Women's Pairs 1969.

COLLINGS, John D.R. (b. 1933) of London, England, retired bank officer. 2nd European Teams 1981. Represented Britain in one world championship and one other zonal championship. Also represented Switzerland in one world and one zonal championship, and England in Camrose Trophy over 6 decades. National wins include 6 Gold Cups. Won London Sunday Times Pairs 1969.

COLLYER, Barbara. See KACHMAR, Barbara.

COLSON, Sharon M. (b. 1946) of Kirkland WA, compliance manager, formerly CPA, controller. Placed 2nd Women's Swiss Teams 1993, Women's BAM Teams 1993; 3rd Women's Team Trials 1995, Mixed Pairs 1998.

COMPTON, Dane Christopher (Chris) (b. 1961) of Austin TX, bridge professional, certified director. Handles vugraph for North American Championships. WBF World Master. Placed 4th World Open Pairs 1986. Grand Life Master with 14,771 MPs as of 3/2001, won Reisinger 1989, placed 2nd Vanderbilt 1986, Men's Pairs 1987, Open BAM Teams 1994.

CONILL, Buenaventura (b. 1927) of Barcelona, Spain, engineer. Represented Spain in 3 zonal championships. Won many national titles.

CONWAY, Kevin M. (b. 1945) of Kirkland Lake ON, high school teacher. Won 25 regionals.

COOK, Bill Jr. of Madison MS, commercial real estate

broker. President District 10 for 2 terms, member District Board 10 years; president of Jackson Bridge Association; president of Mississippi Bridge Association; first alternate director to ACBL Board from District 10; member Board of Governors. Won Men's BAM Teams, 25+ regionals.

COOK, Cecil Q. (b. 1932) of Long Beach CA, aerospace consultant. Won Volare Award for outstanding achievements in aircraft avionics, RTCA Citation for contribution to advancement of aeronautics. In 1958 started duplicate game in Guam. ACBL president 1995, chairman of Board 1996, ACBL representative to WBF. President Dist 23 1975, Unit 554 president 1961, 63, helped organize District 23 (ALACBU) and was its first VP, president 1975, District tournament manager 1976, 77, first alternate Director Dist. 23 1983-90, Dist. 23 representative to ACBL Board 1990-97.

COOK, Dorothy Jane (D.J.) of Asheville NC, bridge teacher and writer, former president and executive VP of ABTA. Authored *Learn to Play Winning Bridge, Cook and Deal, Cook and Deal II, Cook and Deal III*.

COOK, Edward M. (Ed) (b. 1901) of Palo Alto CA, commercial real estate developer, physicist. Won Men's Pairs 1935, 37.

COOLIK, J. Samuel (b. 1943) of Atlanta GA, stockbroker. Has served on Unit 181 Board, has been member Board of Governors and National Appeals Committee. Won Men's Teams 1972, more than 25 regionals.

COOMBS, Norman D. (Norm, Stormin Norman) (b. 1934) of Brookville IN, financial agent, bridge professional, writer and teacher. Invented Coombs Gambit—a defense to artificial club and diamond opening bids — and Nebulous Diamond Openings. Grand Life Master with 14,801 MPs as of 3/2001. Won Life Master Men's Pairs 1978, placed 2nd Senior KOs 1995.

COON, Charles (b. 1931) of Marshfield MA, bridge director and teacher, real estate broker, taxi driver. WBF World Master, placed 2nd Bermuda Bowl 1962, Rosenblum Teams 1990. Won Team Trials 1961, Vanderbilt 1961, Master Mixed Teams 1962, Life Master Mens Pairs 1964, Blue Ribbon Pairs 1966, Men's Pairs 1989, Silver Ribbon Pairs 2000; placed 2nd Men's Teams 1964, 68; Reisinger 1961. Grand Life Master with 14,190 MPs as of 3/2001.

COOPER, Kitty See MUNSON-COOPER, Kitty.

CORBIN, Helen (Mrs. Warren) of Menlo Park CA, born in Tokyo. Won Takamatsu KO Teams 1963,64, represented Japan in Far East Women's Teams. Won 16 ACBL regionals.

CORDOEIRO, Jos Antonio (1946-1991), of Lisbon, Portugal. Represented Portugal in 5 European championships. 2nd European Junior Teams 1968, 6th European Teams 1974. Won many national titles.

CORMACK, Janas C. (Jan) (b.1941) of Auckland, New Zealand, legal executive and journalist. WBF World Master. Won Far East Women's Teams 1981, placed 2nd 1978. Represented New Zealand in many world, zonal and national championships *New Zealand Women's Weekly*.

CORN, Ira G., Jr. (1921-1982) of Dallas, co-founder, executive and director of Micgan General Corp., former assistant professor SMU. Organizer, financier and captain of the Aces (the world's first professional bridge team), administrator for the Dallas BA and successful tournament player. President Dallas BA 1968, tournament chairman 1966-67, Board member from 1965. Member ACBL Board of Directors, ACBL president

1980, chairman of Board 1981. Won Mixed Pairs 1963, Men's Teams 1968, Vanderbilt 1973. Listed in *Who's Who In America*, wrote *The Story of the Declaration of Independence* 1977. See also ACES TEAM.

CORNELL, Michael (b. 1947) of Auckland, accountant. WBF World Master. Second FarEast Teams 1982, 1991; also represented New Zealand in 8 world championships and 5 other zonal championships. National wins include 4 open teams and 2 open teams.

COTTER, E. Patrick (1904-1997) of London, England, bridge writer, school teacher. 2nd European Teams 1938, represented Britain in one other zonal championship. Represented England in several Camrose matches. Won Gold Cup twice and other national titles. Bridge columnist of *Financial Times* and *Country Life*. Author of one book. Croquet champion.

COTTON, Cameron R. (b. 1956) of Chula Vista CA, bridge teacher. ACBL Rookie of Year 1979, has won 24 regionals.

COURT, Russell Asher (Rusty) (b. 1928) of Johannesburg, South Africa, pharmacist and clinic manager. Won Namibian Teams 1991. Chief tournament director of South African Bridge Federation since 1982. Contributor to *Showcase*.

COURTENAY, F. Dudley (deceased) of South Dennis MA, manufacturer of the first metal duplicate boards, major figure in the bridge battles of the early Thirties. Founded Bridge Headquarters, member of group that produced the Official System in opposition to Ely Culbertson. Chief contribution to theory was development of Losing Trick Count, an unusual and important method of hand valuation, which he described in his book *The System the Experts Play*. His other writings include *Standardized Code Of Contract Bridge Bidding, The Losing Trick Count, The Standard Manual on Play, Standardized Contract Bridge Complete.*

COVALCIUC, Richard (b. 1945) of Fort Myers FL, lithographer, pre-press printer. Board of Governors 1999. Won 15+ regionals.

COVALCIUC, Valerie A. (Val) (b. 1946) of Fort Myers FL, bridge teacher (since 1972), teacher-trainer (1987-93), former newspaper copy editor. Former member ACBL Board of Directors for District 14, ACBL president 1999, chairman of Board 2000, member ACBL Goodwill Committee. Served in various executive positions on the Unit and District level, including president Unit 241 1986-87, District 14 president 1992. Trustee ACBL Educational Foundation, named first Area Manager for ACBL Education Program. Diamond Life Master, many regional wins.

COWAN, Donald (Moo Cow) (b. 1931) of Toronto ON, entertainment booker. 15+ regional wins.

COWAN, Philip (Flip) (b. 1943) of New York City, lawyer. Won Swiss Teams 1980, placed 2nd Swiss Teams 1984, won many regionals.

COX, Marge (b. 1927) of Willowick OH, retired real estate broker. Placed 2nd Silver Ribbon Pairs 1995, won 15+ regionals.

COYLE, William (Willie) (b. 1937) of Renfrew, Scotland, science and mathematics teacher. Won Camrose Trophy once and represented Scotland in 14 Camrose Trophy matches. Won Gold Cup 1969, 73. National wins include 2 open teams.

CRABBS, Terry (b. 1945) of Kansas City MO, postmaster. Won Golder Pairs 1963 with mother, Beth Crabbs, and became Life Master at age 18. Both mother

and father (Gordon) were rated tournament directors.

CRAMER, Hector (1901-1974) of Buenos Aires, Argentina. South American champion 1954, 1957. Represented Argentina in Bermuda Bowl 1961. Many national wins.

CRANE, Barry (d. 1985) of Studio City CA, television producer and director, considered by many to be the top matchpoint player of all time. Member ACBL Hall of Fame. He became the ACBL's top masterpoint holder (see LIFE MASTER) in 1968 when he replaced Oswald Jacoby who had held the record since 1962. Crane's hold on the top spot was not broken until six years after his death. Paul Soloway, who was 11,359 MPs behind at Crane's demise, took the lead in 1991.

Victim of brutal murder in 1985 that has never been solved. In a poignant aftermath, Crane's knockout squad was allowed to substitute Kerri Shuman (now Sanborn), one of his longtime partners, and they went on to win the event. Crane was Life Master # 325, won McKenney Trophy (now the Barry Crane Top 500) six times 1952, 67, 71, 73, 75, 78 and finished second on five other occasions 1961, 62, 63, 64, 81. Won World Mixed Pairs 1978 (by five boards), Master Mixed Teams 1953, 54, 80; Open Pairs 1964, 70, 71, 72, 74, 77, 83; Men's Pairs 1966, Mixed Pairs 1975, 77, Open Swiss Teams 1978; Men's Swiss Teams 1983; placed second Master Mixed Teams 1969, Mixed Pairs 1971, 74; Men's Teams 1971, Open Pairs 1976, 84; Vanderbilt 1985. Won Mott-Smith Trophy 1970, 71; the Oeschger Trophy (West Coast McKenney) 1961, 62, 63, 67 and the Stoddard Memorial Trophy 1980. It was once estimated that Crane had won more than 700 pairs titles at the regional or higher level.

CRAWFORD, Carol (Mrs. John) (1934-1982) of New York City, won Mixed Pairs 1958, Women's Teams 1966, placed 2nd Women's Teams 1972, Master Mixed Teams 1974, 75; Life Master Women's Pairs 1976. World backgammon champion in 1973, she was one of only three women ever to win the title.

CRAWFORD, John R. (1915-1976) of New York City, bridge teacher and writer, one of the world's great players, member ACBL Hall of Fame. His total of 37 ACBL national titles up to 1964 exceeded any other player's record at that time. By winning 3 consecutive Bermuda Bowls 1950, 51, 53 and by other performances abroad, he established a solid international reputation. Represented United States in the Bermuda Bowl 1958, World Team Olympiad 1960. His 10 wins in the Chicago Trophy (since 1965 the Reisinger), 1937, 38, 39, 42, 46, 47, 53, 54, 56, 61, set a record. The first of these wins, at the age of 22, gave him his first national title at a younger age than any of the other great American players. Two years later he became Life Master #19, at that time much the youngest of a select group. His other national wins include Spingold 1943, 48, 50, 52, 57; Vanderbilt 1941, 46, 50, 51, 55, 56, 57, 59, 60; Men's Teams 1956, 61, Master Mixed Teams 1942, 45, 48, 57; Life Master Pairs 1943, Men's Pairs 1939, Mixed Pairs 1945, 48, 49, 59; Master Individual 1956. His 23 seconds in national events include 5 in Life Master Pairs.

In 1957 he achieved a unique grand slam of national team titles by holding simultaneously the Vanderbilt, Spingold, Chicago, Men's and Mixed Team championships. He demonstrated his adaptability by achieving national successes with many different partners and earned a reputation for competitive repartee, table presence and psychological awareness. An expert on many card games and forms of gambling, Crawford lectured

extensively during his war-time Army service in an attempt to help servicemen avoid being cheated. He helped to found the New York Card School in 1950 and moved to New York from Philadelphia in 1959. His writings include *Crawford's Contract Bridge, How to Be a Consistent Winner in the Most Popular Card Games*, books on canasta, samba.

CROCKER, Anthony F. (b. 1952) of Glendale CA, actuary. Won Amateur Swiss 1977.

CROMBIE, Dr. Dwayne Edward (b. 1960) of Auckland, New Zealand, consultant in community medicine. WBF World Master. Far East Champion 1990, and represented New Zealand in 2 world championships and one other Far East Championship. Five national wins include open teams.

CRONIER, Benedicte of Paris, France, (b. 1961) bridge professional. WBF World Life Master. 2nd Venice Cup 1987, 3rd 1995 Won European Women's Teams 1985, 95, 2nd 1993. Won European Junior Teams 1984, China Cup 1999. Won Generali World Women's Individual 2000, 2nd 1996.

CRONIER, Philippe (b. 1953) of Paris, France, bridge teacher and writer. WBF World Master. 3rd Bermuda Bowl 1983, 95. Won European Teams 1983, 2nd European Pairs 1987.

CROSSLEY, Brian (b. 1946) of Minneapolis MN, network administrator/PC specialist, formerly network and PC administrator for ACBL. Won 18+ regionals. Won national aerobatics championship 1979.

CROSSLEY, C(larence) F. Jr. (Cap) (b. 1924) of Henderson NV, retired physician and anesthesiologist, former president of District 17, the Western Conference, Marin County CA and Nevada Units. Diamond LM See FAMILY.

CROSSLEY, David M. (b. 1948) of Las Vegas, anesthesiologist, won Vanderbilt 1974, many regional titles. See FAMILY.

CROSSLEY, Robert E. (Bob) (b. 1951) of Corte Madera CA, bridge professional, juggler, film maker. In the Seventies traveled extensively for "Travel with Goren", teaching and directing bridge cruises. Started playing at age 7 and became a LM at age 16. Won 1974 Vanderbilt at age 23. Has written two books, *Learn and Enjoy Bridge, Advanced Concepts in Bridge*, and numerous articles for the *Bridge World*. Developed Crossley 2NT which was in use in the early '70s before Jacoby 2NT became popular, also IDAK and Wonder Bids. See FAMILY.

CROUNSE, Eleanor B. of Paducah KY, won Women's Teams 1962, Mixed Pairs 1964. Diamond Life Master with more than 50 regional wins.

CROWHURST, Eric (b. 1935) of Reading, England. Supplied the Suit Combinations section for the *Bridge Encyclopedia*, inventor of the Crowhurst Convention, contributor to many bridge magazines, author several bridge books.

CRUZ, Joao Nuno Moreira da (1936-1989), of Lisbon, Portugal, lawyer. Represented Portugal in one world and 5 European championships. Placed 5th in European Teams 1966, 7th 1971. Won many national titles.

CUKOFF, Henry (b. 1949) of Montreal PQ, National Tournament Director. Has attended games at all major league baseball stadiums. Began directing in 1973, director in charge of the NABC events since 1990. Directs mainly in Northeastern U.S. and Eastern Canada. Several regional wins.

CULBERTSON, Ely (July 22, 1891-December 27, 1955) stood for many years as America's foremost authority on contract bridge, member ACBL Hall of Fame. Generally credited with making the game an internationally popular pastime, Culbertson was also an author and lecturer on mass psychology and political science. He was born in Romania but was an American citizen from birth by registration with the U.S. consul, being the son of Almon Culbertson, an American mining engineer who had been retained by the Russian government to develop the Caucasian oilfields and who had married a Russian woman, Xenia Rogoznaya, daughter of a Cossack atamon or chief. Culbertson belonged to a pioneer American family settled about Titusville and Oil City PA, and later joined the Sons of the American Revolution to refute rumors that he had changed his name or falsified his ancestry. He attended gymnasia in Russia and matriculated at Yale (1908) and Cornell (1910), but in each case remained only a few months.

Later (1913-14) he studied political science at l'Ecole des Sciences Economiques et Politiques at the University of Paris (Sorbonne) and in 1915 at the University of Geneva in Switzerland, but he was largely self-educated, and the erudition for which he was admired can principally be attributed to a self-imposed and invariable regimen of reading a book designed to improve his knowledge at least one hour before going to sleep each night. In this he was aided by an aptitude for languages. He conversed fluently in Russian, English, French, German, Czech, Spanish and Italian, had a reading knowledge of Slavonic, Polish, Swedish, and Danish-Norwegian, and a knowledge of classical Latin and Greek. In 1907 Culbertson participated as a student in one of the abortive Russian revolutions. He pursued his revolutionary ideas in labor disputes in the American Northwest and in Mexico and Spain (1911-1912), serving as an agitator for the union and syndicalist sides.

The foregoing biographical data, all of which is a matter of official record, is here given in detail because it has been disputed in various writings about Culbertson. After the Russian Revolution of 1917 wiped out his family's large fortune there, Culbertson lived for four years in Paris and other Europeans cities by exploiting his skill as a card player. In 1921 he returned to the U.S., almost penniless, and continued to derive his chief living from winnings in card games. In 1923, having acquired some reputation as a bridge player, he married Mrs. Josephine Murphy Dillon (See Culbertson, Josephine), one of the highly reputed bridge teachers in New York City. Together they became a successful pair as tournament players and bridge authorities. Between 1926 and 1929, the then new game of contract bridge began to replace auction bridge, and Culbertson saw in this development an opportunity to overtake the firmly entrenched authorities on auction bridge. Culbertson planned a long-range campaign that included the construction of a dogmatic system; publication of a magazine to appeal to group leaders in bridge; authorship of a bridge textbook to serve as a "bible"; organization of professional bridge teachers; dramatization of himself and his wife as largely fictitious personalities; and expansion of the appeal of bridge by breaking down religious opposition to card playing. The plan proved conspicuously successful.

Culbertson founded his magazine, *The Bridge World*, in 1929, and through the same corporation published his earliest bridge books, all of which were best sellers; manu-

factured and sold bridge players' supplies including the introduction of Kem playing cards; maintained an organization of bridge teachers (Culbertson National Studios) which at its peak had 6000 members; and conducted bridge competitions through the United States Bridge Association and the World Bridge Olympics and American Bridge Olympics. In its best year, 1937, The Bridge World, Inc., grossed more than $1,000,000, of which $220,000 were royalties payable to Culbertson before profits were calculated. As a regular tournament competitor Culbertson had the best record in the earliest years of contract bridge. In 1930 he won the Vanderbilt and American Bridge League Knockout Team events, also the ABL Board-a-Match Team event, and finished second in the Master Pairs. That year he led a team that played the first international match, in England, and defeated several teams there. In 1933 and 1934 his teams won the Schwab Cup.

After 1934 Culbertson seldom played tournament bridge, but he was second in the ABL's 1935 matchpoint team contest and in the International Bridge League's first intercontinental tournament in 1937. Culbertson continued to play high-stake rubber bridge until about two years before his death. The success of Culbertson's *Blue Book* in 1930 caused the established auction bridge authorities to join forces to combat his threatened domination of contract bridge. Culbertson countered by challenging the leading player among his opposition, Sidney Lenz, to a test match, offering 5-1 odds. Culbertson's victory in this match, played in the winter of 1931-32, fortified his leading position (see Culbertson-Lenz Match). The great publicity accorded the match enriched Culbertson; he and his wife both acquired contracts for widely syndicated newspaper articles, he made a series of movie shorts for $360,000, and he received $10,000 a week for network radio broadcasts. In 1935 Culbertson tried to recapture the magic of his match against Lenz by playing a similar match against P. Hal and Dorothy Sims (See Culbertson-Sims Match), but although the Culbertsons won this match also, there was no such publicity advantage as accrued from the Lenz match.

The publicity accorded Culbertson throughout his professional career can be attributed equally to his unquestioned abilities, his colorful personality and his flamboyant way of life. Culbertson lived in the grand manner, with total disregard of expense whether at the moment he happened to be rich or penniless. Once he strolled into Sulka's (then) on Fifth Avenue in New York and bought $5,000 worth of shirts. He smoked a private blend of cigarettes that cost him $7 a day. When he decided to buy a Duesenberg automobile in 1934 he did not sell his Rolls Royce but gave it away. His home for years was an estate in Ridgefield CT, with a 45-room house, several miles of paved and lighted roads, greenhouses, cottages, lakes, and an enclosed swimming pool with orchids growing along its periphery. He always had caviar with his tea and made special trips to Italy to buy his neckties. When he died in 1955, he owned five houses for his own use - four of them with swimming pools. But Culbertson rationalized these extravagances as publicity devices. He actually lived in one small room with a cot and a table, and he spent most of his time pacing the floor and thinking.

In 1933, when a newspaper reporter asked him, "Mr. Culbertson, how did you get ahead of those other bridge authorities?" he answered, "I got up in the morning and went to work." Culbertson's contributions to the science of contract bridge, both practical and theoretical, were basic and timeless. He devised the markings on duplicate boards for vulnerability and the bonuses for games and partscores. He was the first authority to treat distribution as equal or superior to high cards in formulating the requirements for bids. Forcing bids, including the one-over-one, were original Culbertson concepts, as were four-card suit bids, limited notrump bids, the strong two-bid, and wholesale ace-showing including the 4NT slam try. These were presented in the historic Lesson Sheets on the Approach-Forcing System (1927) and in numerous magazine articles written by Culbertson in the Twenties and early Thirties. Specific bridge principles attributable to Culbertson, separately described, include among others Asking Bids, the Grand Slam Force, Jump Bids, and the New-Suit Forcing principle, which Culbertson first introduced and later repudiated. In 1938, with war imminent in Europe, Culbertson lost interest in bridge and thereafter devoted his time to seeking some grand achievement in political science.

To effect world peace he proposed international control of decisive weapons and a quota for each major nation in tactical forces. After formation of the United Nations, to which Culbertson's ideas made a discernible contribution, he persisted in a campaign to give it adequate police power. At one time 17 U.S. Senators and 42 U.S. Congressmen subscribed to a proposed joint resolution of Congress advocating Culbertson's proposals. But in the course of these activities Culbertson lost his position as the leading bridge authority; by 1950 or earlier, Charles Goren had surpassed him in the sale of books and other bridge writings and in the adherence of bridge teachers and players. However, when a bridge Hall of Fame was inaugurated in 1964, nine years after his death, Culbertson was the first person elected. Though never an ACBL Life Master, he was named Honorary Member in 1938. Ely and Josephine Culbertson were divorced in 1938 and in 1947 Culbertson married Dorothy Renata Baehne, who was 35 years younger than he. There were two children by each of his marriages. Culbertson suffered in late years from a lung congestion (emphysema) and died at his last home, in Bratttleboro VT, of a common cold that proved fatal because of the lung condition.

Minor works by Ely Culbertson, such as paperbound books and pamphlets, are literally too numerous to mention, and all or nearly all were written by members of Culbertson's staff, as also were most of the newspaper and magazine articles published under Culbertson's name from 1932 on. Earlier articles in bridge periodicals were written by Culbertson, as were the following of his major books, each of which was published in many editions: *Contact Bridge Blue Book*, 1930; *Culbertson's Self-Teacher*, 1933; *Red Book on Play*, 1934; *The Gold Book*, or, *Contract Bridge Complete*, 1936; and *Point-Count Bidding*, 1952. Culbertson's autobiography, *The Strange Lives of One Man*, was published in 1940. His principal works on political science were *Total Peace*, 1943, and *Must We Fight Russia?* 1947.

CULBERTSON, Josephine (Mrs. Ely) (February 2, 1898-March 23, 1956) stood in her own right as a renowned bridge teacher, player and writer, member ACBL Hall of Fame. She was born Josephine Murphy in Bayside NY (now part of New York City). In 1919 she married James Dillon, and was widowed by his suicide shortly thereafter. Her interest in bridge commenced when she became secretary to Wilber C. Whitehead. On June 11, 1923 she married Ely Culbertson and collaborated with him in the development and teaching of the Culbertson

or Approach-Forcing systems of auction and contract bridge. Through the Twenties and into the Thirties, Culbertson was known as "the modern miracle - the woman who can play on even terms with the best men." She was the first woman to achieve highest championship caliber, and as such was unique in her times, before the advent of Helen Sobel Smith and others. As a member of the Bridge World team, with Waldemar Von Zedtwitz as her partner and later Michael Gottlieb and Albert Morehead, Culbertson won several national and international championships including the Schwab Cup 1933, 1934. Paired with her husband she played many high-stake set games, won international matches in England and France, and achieved national fame in the Culbertson-Lenz Match, 1931-1932.

She was co-founder of *The Bridge World*, 1929, and inaugurated its "Pro et Contra" department, which appeared under her name until her death. She was often on radio bridge shows, including two long series with her husband. She participated briefly in motion pictures made by her husband. Jo, as she insisted she be called by her close friends, was as glamorous as a movie star - the world of bridge was at her feet as was the world of fashion. Every paper, every smart magazine sang her praises and quoted not only her success at the bridge table, but also her beautiful clothes and the chic with which she wore them. Josephine and Ely Culbertson were divorced in an uncontested action brought by Culbertson in Reno NV in 1938, though they continued as business partners and co-editors.

She died March 23, 1956, of a cerebral stroke, 87 days after Ely's death. Culbertson won ABL Open Challenge Team 1930, Vanderbilt 1930, and placed second in the Life Master Pairs 1930, Open Pairs 1928 (both of these events played for the first time on these dates), Chicago 1935, Women's Pairs 1930. She was an active editor of all books on the Culbertson System. She was coauthor of the historic Lesson Sheets on the Approach System (1927) and made the first arrangement of material for Culbertson's Summary (1932), the largest-selling bridge book. However, her widely syndicated newspaper column, 1931-56, her department in *The Bridge World*, and the several books published under her name were largely prepared by *The Bridge World* technical staff; the best-known of these is *Contract Bridge for Beginners*, 1937.

CULP-BRANDL, Mrs. Maureen A. (b. 1934) of Pickering ON, school teacher, travel agent. Served as president Trent Valley B.A. 1966-73, Oshawa Duplicate Bridge in the Sixties. Placed second CWTC 1985-88. Won 24 regionals.

CUMMINGS, Richard John (1932-1999) of Sydney, Australia, bridge writer, teacher. WBF World Life Master. One of Australia's greatest players, Cummings had a long and successful partnership with Tim Seres. They helped Australia finish 3rd in Bermuda Bowl 1971 and 1979. Represented Australia on many other international occasions. Won more than 20 national titles, in teams and pairs. Bridge columnist *Sydney Morning Herald* and *Sydney Sun-Herald*. Former editor *World Bridge Federation News*. Former member WBF Appeals Committee. Won Bols Brilliancy player prize 1980. Contributor to *Bols Tip* series.

CUTLER, Sue S. (B. 1939, of New York City,. Won 15+ regionals.

CYMERMAN, Frank R. (b. 1953) of Pittsburgh PA, physician. Won 17 regionals.

CYPRES, Suzanne (b. 1946) of Brussels, Belgium. Won Common Market Mixed Teams 1991, and several national titles. Represented Belgium in Women's teams several times.

D

DACOSTA, Donald (b. 1927. in United States) of Kingston, Jamaica, bridge teacher. Represented Jamaica in 1983 Bermuda Bowl and 6 CACBF Zonal championships. Won CACBF Open Pairs and Open Pairs and numerous national titles. Former owner, St Clair Bridge Club, Toronto, Canada.

DAHL, Mark W. (b. 1950) of Richmond VA, stock and commodities broker. Has won approximately 25 regionals.

DAHL, Trine (b.1954) of Copenhagen, Denmark. WBF World Master. Won World Women's Team Olympiad 1988, 3rd 2000. Represented Denmark on many occasions including 2 other world championships and 4 zonals. 11 national wins.

DAHLER, Ivy Charlotte Marjorie (b. 1923) of Toowoomba, Australia, born in England. Won PABF (Far East) Women's Teams 1974, 1977, 1984 and represented Australia in 3 world championships. Won 4 national titles.

DAI, Jianming (b. 1963) of Shanghai, China. WBF World Master. Won Far East Open Teams 1998, IOC Grand Prix 1998. Won many national titles.

DALAL, Rajesh (b. 1953) of Bombay, India, chartered accountant and director of export company. 4th World Open Teams 1988. Represented India in 8 other world championships. Won BFAAME Open Teams 1997, 2nd 1985, 1989, 1993. 2nd BFAAME Open Pairs 1985. 15 national wins.

DALATI, Henri (d. 1971) of Beirut, Lebanon. Represented Lebanon in World Team Olympiad 1960, 64; European Championships 1954, 1956, 57, 61, 62, 63. Won many national titles. Former secretary of Lebanese Bridge Federation.

D'ALELIO Massimo (Mimmo) (1916-1998) of Rome, Italy, retired lawyer and advertising man. World Grand Master. Won World Team Olympiad 1963, 68, 72. Bermuda Bowl 1957, 58, 59, 61, 62, 83, 65, 66, 67, 69. Won European Teams 1956, 57, 58; 2nd 1955, 62, 63. Many national titles.

DALING, Dr. Janet R. (b. 1934) of Seattle WA, professor, University of Washington where she does cancer research. Placed 2nd Women's Pairs 1987, 1993; Diamond Life Master with more than 11,500 MPs as of 3/2001, won 25 regionals.

DALLAS, Richard N. (b. 1916) of Studio City, CA, retired chemical engineer. Diamond Life Master, won more than 15 regionals.

DALTON, Roy S. (b. 1955) of Mississauga ON, chartered accountant, and financial consultant. At age 18 (1974) was Canada's youngest Life Master. 11th Rosenblum Teams 1978. Represented Canada Geneva 1990. Placed 2nd CNTC 1993. Has won several regionals.

DALY, Victor R. (1895-1986) of Washington DC, retired government deputy director and travel consultant. Was one of the 36 founders of American Bridge Association at Hampton VA in 1932. For many years he was a prominent figure in the ABA, serving as its president from 1950-65, vice president 1941-49. He was President Emeritus for many years. Contributing editor, *Bridge*

Encyclopedia. Daly received The Distinguished Service Award from the U.S. Dept. of Labor 1955, had 2 articles on labor problems entered into the Congressional Record. Was listed in *Who's Who in America,* 1976.

DAM, Villy (b. 1945) of Vejle, Denmark, bridge writer and organizer. Represented Denmark in one world championship and one zonal. Many national wins. Won Hoechst 1991. Promoter of bridge in schools, and organizer of Danish school championships. Author of Acol system book for Danish bridge teachers.

DAMIANI, José (b. 1939) of Paris, France, marketing and public relations consultant. President French Bridge Federation 1978-83, doubling the membership, then President d'Honneur. President European Bridge League 1987-95, then President Emeritus. WBF vice-president 1986-94. Elected president 1994, re-elected 1998. Chairman of several committees. His initiatives 1987-90 brought the former Soviet Union into the international bridge community. Originator and organizer of Epson World Wide Bridge Contest since 1986. Originator of Philip Morris Mixed Teams and Pairs, and Generali World Masters Individual. Chief organizer of world championships in Biarritz 1982, Lille 1998, greatly enlarging the role of sponsorship, computers and television. Originated the World Trans-National Mixed Championship in 1996, the World Transnational Open Teams in 1997, and the IOC Grand Prix in the Olympic Museum - Lausanne in 1998. In 1999 obtained recognition of bridge as a sport and of the WBF as an International Sports Organization. As a player in 1994 world championships, reached final 16 in Rosenblum Teams.

Currently working to include bridge in Olympic Games. IBPA Personality of the Year 1986. Chevalier de la Legion d'Honneur. Gold medal French Ministry of Sport and Youth. WBF World Master. Won many national titles and international medals. Npc French world champion team in Olympiad 1992.

DAMM, Otti (1918-1984) of Copenhagen, Denmark, bridge teacher. 3rd Women's Team Olympiad 1960. Won European Women's Teams 1949, 55, 57, 58; 2nd 1951. Represented Denmark internationally several other times. Many national titles.

DANAS, Linda See GORDON, Linda.

D'ANDREA, Baffi Marisa (b. 1932) of Naples, Italy. WBF World Grand Master. Won World Women's Teams 1976, 2nd Venice Cup 1978. Won European Women's Teams 1976, 1977. Represented Italy on other occasions and won several national titles.

DANG, Douglas (b. 1942) of San Mateo CA, attorney. Won 40+ regional events.

DANIEL, Jim (b. 1948) of Shrewsbury NJ, registered investment advisor. Won more than 18 regionals.

DARLING, Dean A. (1927-1991) of Eureka KS, retired chemical engineer. Diamond Life Master. Passed away in his sleep at a tournament while sitting out first half of afternoon session of KO Teams. His team went on to win the event. He had numerous regional wins.

DARWEN, Hugh (b. 1943) of Warwick, England, computer database specialist. World's leading authority on double dummy problems. Conductor of double dummy column in *Bridge Magazine* and successors, 1962-1990, *International Popular Bridge Monthly,* 1990-1999, and *Bridge Magazine* again 1999-2001. Author of *Bridge Magic.* Internationally recognized expert and writer in the field of relational databases.

DAS, Salil K. (b. 1940) of Antioch TN, professor of bio-

chemistry. Das has been the recipient of numerous research grants and awards from federal and non-federal agencies. Won more than 15 regionals.

DAUTELL, Eugene G. (Duke) (1921-1996) of Los Angeles, bridge teacher, former insurance underwriter. Past president Toledo Bridge Unit. Ran 10-15 bridge classes weekly from 1964. Won Men's Teams 1951 and several regionals.

D'AVE, Adelstano P. (b. 1928) of Rio de Janeiro, Brazil, insurance broker. Won South American Teams 1967, 68, 71, 82, 84. Represented Brazil in 4 world championships. 16 national wins.

DAVID, Sharon H. (b. 1933) of Valley Village CA, retired accountant, now teaches bridge. Served on San Fernando Unit 561 Board and as Assistant Chairperson ACBL Goodwill Committee. Placed 2nd Women's Pairs 1993 and has won several regionals.

DAVIDSON, Sidney L. (1918-1996) of San Francisco, ACBL national director, formerly a dentist. Began his bridge career in 1956 and became national director 1972. He contributed to the simplification of fouled board calculations and carryover computations, evolved and modified various movements including the Mirror Mitchell.

DAVIES, Pat (b. 1947) of Bath, England, computer software company director. WBF Grand Master, #13 among women in world. Won Venice Cup 1981, 85; European Women's Teams 1981, 97, 99. 2nd World Women's Teams 1984, 1988, 1992. Won Common Market Women's Teams 1977, 81. 2nd Macallan 1997, 98 with Nicola Smith — best ever performance by women's pair. National wins include Gold Cup.

DAVIS, Anita (Pidgeon) (1924-deceased) of Beaumont TX, served Unit 201 on various committees; as alternate for ACBL Board of Governors; served on ACBL Rules and Ethics Committee. Wrote weekly bridge column for *Beaumont Enterprise* for more than 30 years. A Diamond Life Master she placed 2nd in Women's Teams 1975.

DAVIS, Charles M. (b. 1936) of Lilburn GA, chemical engineer, attorney, systems analyst. Has won 20 regionals

DAVIS, Chester P. Jr. (Chet) (b. 1922) of Vero Beach FL, retired attorney and company president. Served Eastern MA Bridge Association as president and on various committees. Served for more than 20 years on ACBL Appeals Committee. Diamond Life Master with more than 10,300 MPs. Placed 2nd Blue Ribbon Pairs 1979. Won more than 60 regionals.

DAVIS, Edgar F., Jr. (Ed) (b. 1942) of Seal Beach CA, systems analyst. Author of various ideas and methods including Octopus preempts, contributor to *Southern California Bridge News, Problem Solvers Panel.* Diamond Life Master with more than 11,600 MPs as of 3/ 2001. Placed 2nd Men's Swiss 1985, GNOT 1999, NAOP 2001. Numerous regionals wins.

DAWKINS, George S. (Dr. Doom) (1931-2000) of Austin TX, professor of business, bridge professional. Dawkins and his wife Carole were killed in an automobile accident while traveling in Spain. Had 2 books of poetry published. Served on Houston and Austin Boards, directed on bridge cruises. Diamond Life Master with 13,333 MPs, won Mixed Pairs 1970 and more than 60 regionals.

DAWSON, Dennis L. (b. 1946) of Reading MA, owner Dawson's Get Away Bridge Weekends since 1987, former bridge club owner and teacher, editor *Northeast Bridge* 1973-76. Won more than 15 regionals.

DE FALCO, Dano (b. 1943) of Padua, Italy. WBF World Life Master. Won Bermuda Bowl 1974; placed 2nd 1979,

1983. Won 1ˢᵗ World Transnational Team Championships 1997, European Team Championships 1973, 1979; Common Market 1977, 1979. Played in Burgay challenge match. Represented Italy on many other occasions.

DE MIGUEL, Carlos (b.1949) of Buenos Aires, Argentina, industrialist. Won South American Teams 1985, and then represented Argentina in Bermuda Bowl. 8 national titles include 2 open teams.

DENEXON, Baron Rebert. See NEXON, Baron Rebert de.

DE PAUW, Marc (b. 1953) of Destelbergen, Belgium, Mayor. Treasurer of European Bridge League from 1999.

DE SCHRIJVER, Herman (b. 1938) of Ostend, Belgium, retired language teacher. EBL tournament director since 1980. Director in charge at several European Mixed and University Championships.

DE WAEL, Herman (b. 1961) of Antwerp, Belgium, insurance broker. EBL tournament director since 1993. Member (scribe) of the EBL Appeals Committee. Developer of 2 new forms of calculation of bridge tournaments: Ascherman and Bastille.

DEAL, Henry (b. 1922) of Charlotte NC, won 16 regionals.

DEAS, Lynn (b. 1953) of Newport News VA, professional bridge player and teacher. Served as Conduct and Ethics chairman Unit 115. One of the leading women players in the world. WBF Grand Master, ranks #1 in world among women Grand Masters, ranks 13ᵗʰ in world among women for achievements over past 10 years. Three-time winner of Venice Cup 1987, 89, 91; 3ʳᵈ 1997; 5ᵗʰ 1993. Also won Women's Team Olympiad 1996. Placed 2ⁿᵈ World Women's Pairs 1982, 3ʳᵈ 1994; 4ᵗʰ World Women's Pairs and World Mixed Pairs 1990. Placed 3ʳᵈ in Pan American Women's Teams Championship 1992. Won China Cup Teams 1995, 96, Pairs 1995. Deas, suffering from a debilitating disease that severely restricts her movement and forces her to play from a wheelchair, has continued her winning ways despite her iullness. ACBL Grand Life Master with 22,501 MPs as of 3/2001, ranks #23 in ACBL. Won Master Mixed Teams 1982, Life Master Women's Pairs 1983, 85, 94; BAM Teams 1992, 95. She was 2ⁿᵈ Master Mixed Teams 1984, 1990; Women's KO Teams 1986, 92, 94, 97; Life Master Women's Pairs 1989, Women's BAM Teams 1991, Women's Swiss Teams 1994.

DEBONNAIRE, Carlos Augusto (b. 1940) of Lisbon, Portugal, attorney. Represented Portugal in one world and 6 European championships. 2ⁿᵈ European Junior Teams 1968. 5ᵗʰ European Teams 1966, 6ᵗʰ 1974. Won many national titles.

DEBONNAIRE, Jos Antonio (b. 1943) of Lisbon, Portugal, technician. Represented Portugal in one world championship and 9 European championships. Won International Pairs Tournament of Estoril (Portugal) 1974, 5ᵗʰ Sunday Times Invitational Pairs 1990, 5ᵗʰ European Open Teams 1966, 6ᵗʰ European Teams 1974, 6ᵗʰ European Union Open Pairs 1993. President of Portuguese Bridge Federation since 1998.

DEDICHEN, Herman (d. 1958) of Copenhagen, Denmark; born in Norway. Lived in France 17 years before settling in Denmark. Reactivated European Championship 1948, honorary EBL secretary 1947-1958. Wrote newspaper column on bridge for 30 years.

DEERY, Desmond (b. 1939) of Marbella, Spain, formerly of Belfast, N. Ireland, solicitor, and club owner. Represented Ireland in one world championship and 2 European Championships. Represented Spain in one Eu-

ropean Championship. National titles include open teams once and open pairs 3 times in Northern Ireland and open teams twice in Spain. Former Secretary of Irish Bridge Union and Northern Ireland Bridge Union.

DEIK, Adriana (b. 1941) of Santiago, Chile, English and bridge teacher. Won South American Women's Teams 1978, 1994. Represented Chile in 3 world championships and 6 other zonal championships. Top-ranked Chilean woman player.

DELEVA-SENIOR, Nevena See SENIOR, Nevena.

DEL GALLEGO, Tina (b.1949) of Long Island, N.Y., formerly of the Philippines, secretary. Won Far East Women's Teams 1979, 1982. Represented Philippines in one world championship and one other zonal championship.

DELMOULY, Claude (b. 1927) of Paris, France, bridge teacher and writer. Grand Master, won World Team Olympiad 1960, represented France 1968, 72. Represented France European Championships 1957, 59, 65. Won London Sunday Times Invitational 1968, many national titles. Authored 6 books including *Tous les Secrets de Bridge.*

DELOGU, Richard (Rick, The Professor) (b.1954) of Waterloo ON, chartered accountant and business executive. Won Tri-Country Playoff for Bermuda Bowl qualification 1997. Placed 4ᵗʰ in inaugural World Transnational Teams. Won Canadian National Teams Championship 1996. Has 35 regional wins.

DELOR, Elisabeth (b. 1945) of Paris, France, World Life Master. 3ʳᵈ World Women's Pairs 1978, 2ⁿᵈ European Women's Team 1974. Won Women's Generali Individual 1996. Represented France in 8 other world championships and won many national titles.

DEMARTINO Richard A. (Rich) (b. 1939) of Riverside CT, insurance company executive, bridge teacher since 1993. Has served as president of NY Metropolitan Commercial Bridge League and Stamford Bridge Club; treasurer District 25 since 1997, president 1996, current member ACBL Board of Directors from District 25. Grand Life Master with 11,646 MPs as of 3/2001. Won North American Swiss Teams 1980, Senior KO Teams 2000. His regional wins number 86.

DENBY, Charles W. D. (b. 1930) of Huntington NY, accountant, teaches adult education bridge courses. Won Men's Teams 1960.

DENG, Xiaoping (1904-1997) of Beijing, China. Former premier of the People's Republic of China, the chief architect of Chinese economic reform and modernization. Former honorary president of Chinese Bridge Association. Awarded IBPA *Man of the Year* title in 1980. WBF Golden Award 1989. Gold Medal winner 1993 from WBF. Winner of ACBL Presidential Citation 1993. Responsible for the rapid growth of bridge in China.

DENNEHY, Daniel T. (b. 1949) of River Hills WI, attorney, gives employment and personnel seminars. Member ACBL Board of Governors, 2ⁿᵈ alternate director District 13. Served in various positions on Unit and District level and was Unit 222 Player of the Year 1989. Won North American Non-Life Master Swiss Teams 1983 and a few regionals.

DENNINGER, Tracy (1924-1995) of Altamonte Springs FL, formerly of Bermuda, retired condominium manager and consultant. Florida State cribbage champion 1986. Represented Bermuda in world championship competition in 1968, 72, 74, 76. Won a few regionals. Denninger monitored alleged cheating by two members of the Ital-

ian team during 25th anniversary Bermuda Bowl in Bermuda 1975. He played his first game of bridge at age 5.

DENNIS, Paul W. (b. 1952) of Winter Springs FL, claims adjuster, CPCU, accredited teacher, editor Unit 240 *Trumpet* 10+ years. Contributor to *Bridge Buffs Bulletin* and other publications. Chairman Fall NABC 1992. Diamond Life Master. Was co-winner of ACBL-Wide Millenium II Game (N/S). Won several regionals.

DENNISON, Maureen of Isleworth, England, sales representative. Played on winning Venice Cup team 1981, won European Women's Teams 1981, Common Market Women's Teams 1979, 1981. Magazine contributor. Secretary of IBPA.

DENNY, Jill (Mrs. Jack) (d. 1993) of Bradenton FL, bridge club owner, certified director and teacher. Won more than 15 regionals.

DENNY, John W. (Jack) (1911-1993) of Bradenton FL, sales representative for Mahaffey Corp, bridge teacher and club owner (for 30 years), worked until his death. Lectured and ran bridge games on cruises. Formerly one of the leading players of the Midwest. Won Men's Teams 1951, Spingold 1985 and was 2nd in Open Pairs 1961, Spingold 1987. Competed in USBC in 1987 and represented ACBL 1962. A Diamond Life Master with numerous regional wins.

DERBLAY, Paul, physician, of Mauritius. 2nd BFAME Teams 1987. Represented Mauritius in one world championship and 3 other zonal championships.

DERMER, Dale (b. 1935) of Richmond VA, tax preparer, bookkeeper, bridge teacher and homemaker, member Unit Board. Won Women's Pairs 1985. Diamond Life Master.

DERUY, Claude (b. 1927) of Vimy, Pas de Calais, France. Represented France Bermuda Bowl 1961, World Team Olympiad 1964 ; 2nd European Championship 1961. Author of *Bien Jouer au Bridge*

DESCHAPELLES, Alexandre Louis Honore Lebreton sometimes referred to as **Guillaume le Breton** (1780-1847). Described by his contemporary James Clay, English whist authority, as the finest whist player, beyond any comparison, the world has ever seen. Also excelled at billiards, Polish draughts and chess. Invented the Deschapelles Coup and a number of other coups.

DeSERPA, Dr. Allan C. (b. 1945) of Tempe AZ, professor of economics. Wrote *Mexican Contract* and *Principles of Logical Bidding*. Won about 15 regionals.

DESHPANDE, Dr. Aniruddha (b. 1961) of Glendale WI, born in India, physician of emergency medicine. Won Non-Life Master Swiss 1983.

DESPAIN, Elizabeth, Patricia (Pat) of Los Angeles CA, retired. Former ABA Western Section vice president, member ABA Board of Directors 1974-77, western Section coordinator 1990-91. Won many ABA national, sectional and regional events.

DESROUSSEAUX, Gerard (1927-1985) of Paris, France, bridge teacher and writer. Won World Par Contest 1963, represented France in Bermuda Bowl 1963, 69; World Team Olympiad 1964, 68; European Championships 1965, 67, 79. Won London Sunday Times Invitational 1966. Contributor to French bridge periodicals. Won many national titles.

DEUTSCH, June A. of Aventura FL, homemaker. Represented ACBL internationally New Orleans 1978, Miami 1986. Placed 2nd Pan American Championships Women's Pairs 1992. She has won each of the 5 Women's national titles at least once — Women's Teams 1966, Life Master Women's Pairs 1973, Women's Swiss Teams 1984,

85; Women's KO Teams 1981, Women's Pairs 1990. She was 2nd Women's Teams 1972, Life Master Women's Pairs 1979, Women's KO Teams 1979, 96; Women's BAM Teams 1994. Diamond Life Master, has won more than 50 regionals.

DEUTSCH, Seymon (b. 1935) of Laredo TX, rancher and merchant specializing in fine men's and women's items. He quit bridge for 22 years to devote his time and energy to home and business. After his layoff he won Rosenblum Teams 1994, World Team Olympiad 1988 and placed 2nd in World Team Olympiad 1992. He won GNOT 1986, Spingold 1991, Vanderbilt 1994, 96; placed 2nd in Vanderbilt 1990, 91; Spingold 1993, Open Pairs I 1995.

DEUTSCH, Tobi. See SOKOLOW, Tobi.

DE WITT, Joan See McKEAN, Joan M.

DEWITZ, Egmont von (1907-1987), of Cologne, Germany, judge. Represented Germany in 2 world championships, and most European championships 1938-65. National wins included 15 open teams.

DeYOUNG, Bernace A. (Bernie) (b. 1947) of Aventura FL, bridge teacher/professional, former attorney. Was 1952 March of Dimes Poster Child. A Diamond Life Master, she placed 2nd Women's Pairs 1994 and has won 86 regional events.

DHERS, Alberto (b. 1932) of Caracas, Venezuela, professor of chemistry and mathematics. Won CAC Teams 1973, 86, 91, 93. Represented Venezuela in 5 world championships and won more than 30 national titles. Bridge teacher.

DHONDY, Heather J. (b. 1966) of London, England, certified accountant. WBF World Life Master. Won European Women's Teams 1997, 1999; World Transnational Mixed Teams 1996. Represented Britain in 3 world championships. Represented England in 9 Lady Milne matches, winning 8 times.

DIAMOND, John (b. 1966) of New York City, formerly of College Park MD, options trader. Was a member of the Junior Corps. He was a member of the winning World Junior Championship team in Ann Arbor Michigan 1991.

DIBBLEE, Carol of Salt Lake City UT, director of Downtown Retail Merchants Association, former school teacher. Served on District 18 Board of Directors and is past president Salt Lake Unit, chairperson Salt Lake NABCs 1976, 88. Contributor to District 18 *WASUMI*, bridge reporter to *Salt Lake Tribune*, originated and edited Salt Lake Unit newsletter.

DICKENS, Charles (1812-1870) famed English novelist, describes Mr. Pickwick's anguish after being inveigled into a whist game with 3 imposing women in Chapter 46 of *The Pickwick Papers.*

DIMLER, William A. (Bill) (b. 1930) of Phoenix AZ, retired business planner. Past president New Jersey B.L. 1970,71; vice president District 3 1969-74; District 3 tournament coordinator 1969-74. Won more than 15 regionals and was 2nd in Lancia Teams (New York City).

DIONISI, Antonio H. (Tony) (b. 1934) of New York City, formerly of Tokyo, banker. Won the Reisinger 1970; placed 2nd Men's Teams 1966, Reisinger 1971.

DISCHNER, Robert J. (Dish, Bob) (1920-1998) of Santa Ana CA, ACBL national tournament director since 1972. Began his directing career in 1950.

DI STEFANO, Franco (b. 1942) of Milan, Italy, journalist and director of bridge school. Won European Teams 1975. Bridge columnist. Chairman of Board of Italian Bridge Teachers.

DIXON, Christopher P. (b. 1944) of Bath, England,

computer software company chairman. 2nd European Teams 1971. Won Common Market Open Teams 1981, represented Great Britain as npc World Team Olympiad 1992. Represented England in 6 Camrose Trophy matches. Won Gold Cup 3 times.

DODDS, Leslie (1903-1975) of London, England, import-export merchant. Won Bermuda Bowl 1955, European Teams 1948, 49, 50, 54. Represented Britain in 3 other zonals. Many national wins include 4 Gold Cups.

DOMBU, Sivert R. (Si) (b. 1938) of Las Vegas NV, printer, quality control chemist, poker dealer. Served as Unit 373 president and vice president. Contributes to Unit 373 newsletter *Password* and authored *The Rules of Poker*.

DONAGHY, Ernest C. (1897-1986) of Mexico Beach FL, retired statistician. Was one of the first 6 to be named ACBL associate national director when that rating was created in 1963.

DONAGHY, George (1928-1995) of Memphis TN, ACBL employee since 1968, retired 1993. Was assistant manager Tournament Division, in charge of sanctioning regional and sectional tournaments, assigning tournament directors, assisting DICs with staffing. Before joining the ACBL staff he was a regional tournament director. Contributing editor *Bridge Encyclopedia*.

DONATH, Andres (b.1953) of Montevideo, Uruguay, born in Argentina; industrialist. 2nd South American Teams 1979. Represented Uruguay regularly in zonal championships since 1978, won 43 national titles.

DONER, Cameron P. (b. 1954) of Richmond BC, professional bridge player, in real estate and construction. Past member ACBL Appeals Committee. A Diamond Life Master, Doner has won Richmond Trophy twice and is currently #7 all-time masterpoint holder in Canada. Placed 2nd North American Swiss Teams 1997, Open Swiss Teams 1995. He has more than 65 regional wins.

DORMER, Albert (b. 1925) of Scotland, bridge journalist and retired surveyor. Won World Senior Pairs 1990, British Gold Cup twice. Bridge Editor of *London Times* 1990-94. Editor *British Bridge World* 1962-64. Associate Editor *ACBL Bridge Bulletin* 1964-65. Editor *IBPA Bulletin* 1972-82. Editor *World Bridge News* 1971-87. Contributing editor *Encyclopedia of Bridge*. Executive Assistant to WBF President 1982-1986. IBPA Personality of the Year 1981. Author and co-author of 10 other books including *The Complete Book of Bridge*.

DORN, H. Charlie (b. 1919) of San Jose CA, retired naval aviator. Placed 2nd Mixed Pairs 1981. Diamond Life Master.

D'ORSI, Ernesto (b. 1936) of Sao Paulo, Brazil, business consultant. Represented Brazil in 7 world championships. National wins include one open teams. WBF president 1990-92, vice-president 1986-90, member WBF Executive from 1980, member of Committee of Honor 1986. Chief Organizer of world championships in 1979 and 1985, and member of organizing committee in 1973. CBB president since 1984, and member of South American Executive Council since 1978. Author of 2 books as well as the specifications for Bermuda Bowl and Venice Cup organization. Magazine contributor.

DORSMAN, Henny B. (b. 1927) of Staunton VA, born in the Netherlands, formerly of Aruba, educator and retired director of technical/vocational school, writes weekly bridge column. Honored by the Queen of Holland for the social and educational accomplishments he made in Aruba. Was technical director of the Central American and Caribbean Bridge Federation (CAC)

1977-83. Organizer of 1st official CAC bridge tournament in 1977. Represented Netherland Antilles in Miami 1972, New Orleans 1978, Valkenburg 1980, Biarritz 1982. Also represented Netherland Antilles in numerous CAC championships. Inventor of the Dorsman-tray, a sliding bidding card-tray used in international play.

DOUGHMAN, Roger A. (b. 1931) of San Diego CA, retired engineer. Diamond Life Master with more than 15 regional wins.

DOUGHTY, Richard E. (b. 1943) of Baton Rouge LA, businessman. Won Men's Teams 1977; placed 2nd Reisinger 1975. Was 2nd in international Calcutta in Guadaloupe 1977.

D'OVIDIO, Catherine (formerly Saul) (b. 1959) of Paris, France, bridge administrator. In 2000, 11th World Women's rankings. 3rd Venice Cup 1985, 95. 2nd World Women's Pairs 1994, 3rd 1998. Won European Women's Teams 1985, 95, 2nd 1997. Won European Mixed Teams 1996, 1998. Won European Mixed Pairs 1990, 2nd 1998.

DOWNES, E(dwin) Hall (1897-1976) of Dover DE, was bridge teacher, writer and educator. A graduate of the Naval Academy, Downes remained at Annapolis for 3 years as instructor to midshipmen. He later received a Master's degree in Education from Columbia University and served in that field for the rest of his life. In the early Thirties Downes promoted bridge through his books, radio and lectures. He was called "ace of contract teachers". His writings included self-teachers and he was *Town and Country* editor for *The Bridge Magazine* (1931-33). A book by him on the Culbertson system provoked a lawsuit by Ely Culbertson, who had warned booksellers not to sell Downes' books on pain of legal action. Downes won both suits, the courts holding that the name of a system was public property. The case had permanent importance in legal history, both in respect of plagiarism and of unfair practices.

DREW, Douglas A. (b. 1930) of Toronto ON, retired company vice-president and general manager. Has continuously served the interest of tournament bridge in elected office since 1958. Past president of Ontario Unit 166 and District 2. Member ACBL Board of Directors 1969-78 and 1981-93, member ACBL Board of Governors, served as president of ACBL 1984, ACBL Chairman of the Board 1985, chairman of various standing committees of the ACBL since 1969, member WBF Executive Council 1984-88. Drew initiated action to create the ACBL Education Program, was founding member of the Canadian Bridge Federation, originator of proposal creating all Canadian Districts within the ACBL.

DREYFUS, Jack (b. 1913) of New York City, founder of the Dreyfus Fund and "Wizard of Wall Street", formerly a leading bridge player. Reputed also to be the best American player of gin rummy. He won AWL Southern New England Open Teams 1937. Dreyfus has played on the Corporate America bridge team and participated in the charity matches against Congress, Hollywood celebrities and Los Angeles Business. He is the author of *A Remarkable Medicine Has Been Overlooked,* a book about the drug Dilantin.

DRUCKER, Ned (1916-1983) of New York City, salesman, won the Vanderbilt 1952, 54; placed 2nd Life Master Pairs 1951, Open Pairs 1943.

DRUMEV, Christo (b. 1932) of Sofia, Bulgaria, President Director General of National Palace Culture; President of the Union "Made in Bulgaria", and of the Bulgarian Convention Bureau. Formerly Deputy Cultural Minister. Order of Merit of the Republic of France. Won

World Senior Teams 1998. Won 16 Bulgarian teams and pairs titles, a record. Won Austrian Team Championship 1984, 85; and several Open Pairs at Philip Morris grand prix tournaments including Athens 1982 and Vienna 1987. Npc bronze-medal Bulgarian Women's Team 1988, World Team Olympiad. Vice-president Bulgarian Bridge Federation 1982-89, president since 1989. Author, columnist and translator of books into Bulgarian. President of Bulgarian Bridge Federation since 1988.

DRURY, Douglas A. (Doug) (1914-1967) of Sebastopol CA, stockbroker, bridge teacher and club owner. Was best known for his invention of Drury Convention. A capable and popular bridge administrator, he served as a member of the ACBL Board of Governors; Systems and Conventions Committee. He made his mark early as a tournament player while living in Toronto. He won Men's Pairs 1954, 55; Master Mixed Teams 1956.

DUBOIN, Giorgio (b.1959) of Turin, Italy, computer programmer and bridge teacher. WBF World Life Master. Won World Team Olympiad 2000. Won European Teams 1997, European Junior Pairs 1980, Common Market Teams 1985, 87; Common Market Pairs 1987, NABC Swiss Teams 2001.

DUBRAU, Kenneth B. (b. 1943) of Surprise AZ, former program expediter with city of Chicago, Department of Human Services. Has taught bridge for 20 years, certified director and member ABTA. Has won more than 15 regionals.

DUCHEYNE, Elly of The Hague, The Netherlands, bridge organizer. In charge of press room at nearly all world and European Championships from 1974. Public relations officer and organizer of Hoechst and Forbo tournaments. Honor Member of IBPA.

DUCHEYNE, Rene (1938-1991), of The Hague, The Netherlands, patent office employee. Head of press room at nearly all world and European Championships 1974-1991, assisted by his wife Elly. President IBPA 1986-1991.

DUDKA, Bette of Alexandria VA, Professor Emeritus in psychology and bridge teacher for 20 years. District 6 first alternate to Board of Directors. Past president of Mid-Atlantic BC, Unit Recorder, served on ACBL and District 6 Board of Governors. Co-chairman of 1984 Summer NABC, entertainment chairman Summer NABC 1973, 1993. Served in various other executive positions on Unit and District level. Some of her 11 books include *Comprehensive American Bidding, One* and *Two, Conventions in Vogue, Two over One Sequences, Play of the Hand I, II,* and *III, Defensive Play of the Hand I* and *II.* Founded Land Cruise Bridge Festival seminars starting 1985, now called The Bridge School. Gives weeklong instructional programs in South Carolina, Florida, Texas, North Carolina and Louisiana.

DUNAWAY, Suzanne (Sue) (b. 1947) of Oak Park IL, elementary school principal. Has won more than 18 regionals.

DUNCAN, Alexander H. (Sandy) of Dunfermline, Scotland, computer consultant. Represented Britain in 2 world championships and the Common Market Championships. Represented Scotland in 22 Camrose Trophy matches. Many national wins include 3 Scottish Cups.

D'UNIENVILLE, M. V. Robert M. (1927-1996) of Phoenix, Mauritius, mathematics teacher. 3rd European Teams 1951, representing Britain. Represented Mauritius in one world championship and 3 zonal championships. Won ACBL Senior Knockout Teams 1988.

DUNITZ, Mitch (b. 1956) of Sherman Oaks CA, owner

real estate investment company. A Diamond Life Master. Placed 2nd GNOP 1987, GNOT 1999. With 30-40 regional wins.

DUNLAP, Jim (b. 1925) of Yuma AZ, retired, past president Portland OR Unit. Won Men's BAM Teams 1967.

DUNN, Suzanne E. (b. 1935) of Crystal Lake IL, bank director, former teacher. Member ACBL Board of Governors. Diamond Life Master with more than 75 regional wins.

DUPONT, Lea C. (b. 1939) of Wilmington DE. WBF World Master. Placed 2nd World Senior Pairs 1998; 5th World Olympiad Women's Teams 1984. Won North American Swiss Teams 1984 and placed 2nd Swiss Teams 1981, Mixed Pairs 1983, Open Swiss Teams 1993, North American Swiss Teams 1995, 2000. Regularly plays in major European championships and has won Coppa Italia 1977, Venice Open Pairs 1978, Deauville Open Pairs 1980.

DURHAM, Louise (Honeychile) (d. 1999) of Durant MS. Life Master # 358 and the first Life Master in Mississippi. Served as ACBL director and secretary, co-chairman of Goodwill Committee and WBF Friendship Committee. Past president of Mississippi BA. Durham was named ACBL Honorary Member 1974.

DURRAN, Joan of Brighton, England. WBF World Life Master. Won World Women's Pairs 1966, 2nd World Mixed Pairs 1966. Won European Women's Teams 1961, 66. Represented Britain in 2 other world championships and 3 other zonal championships. Won several national titles.

DYE, Dr. Arthur M. (1896-1980) of Charlotte NC, was the first blind bridge player to become an ACBL Life Master. A perfect sportsman, Dye never took advantage of his affliction. When he pulled wrong cards, he refused to allow opponents to let him retract his plays. When Dye made Life Master at New Orleans Winter Nationals 1956, he received a standing ovation. A charter member and long-time president of the Charlotte BA, he served as president of the Mid-Atlantic BC. He shared with Charles Goren in 1959 the ACBL Honorary Member award. (see HANDICAPPED PLAYERS.)

E

EARLY, Richard (b.1942) of Cuyahoga Falls Ohio, insurance agency owner and bridge teacher. Treasurer of District 5 for 20 years. Winner of District 5 Ann McGilvery Sportsmanship award. A Diamond Life Master, has won more than 20 regional events. Early invented a game he has dubbed "The Olympiad" for players 0-300 MPs where they play a duplicate game which is followed by instruction and transparencies of the hands. (see Dec. 1999 *Bridge Bulletin)*

EBER, Neville (b. 1944) of Johannesburg, South Africa, investment manager. WBF World Master. Represented South Africa in 4 World Team Olympiads and 2 Bermuda Bowls. 23 national wins. Top South African masterpoint winner. Co-author *You Too Can Play Bridge Well* (1978). Winner of numerous international backgammon events, and competes in world series of poker.

EBERSON, Gertrude L. (d. 1992) of St. Petersburg FL. Won Women's Teams 1949; placed 2nd in Master Mixed Teams 1954, Women's Pairs 1960.

ECCLES, Bert (b. 1951) of Montreal PQ, document controller, former teacher. Represented Canada in

Biarritz 1982. Won 17 regionals.

ECKER, Wynne (Mrs. Richard H.) of NYC. Won Women's Teams 1954, placed 2nd Women's Pairs 1956.

ECONOMIDY, Ann (Mrs. Byron) of Tucson AZ, won Women's Pairs 1973 (with her mother Vivian Williamson), placed 2nd in Life Master Women's Pairs 1978.

EDELSON, Shirley M. (d. 2000) of Redmond WA, bridge professional, teacher and lecturer, certified director since 1965. She guided bridge groups in Soviet Union in 1989-90 for three Friendship tournaments. Diamond Life Master, placed 2nd USBC 1988 and won Women's BAM Teams 1987. She won more than 24 regionals.

EDWARDS, J. Michael (b.1940) of Rock Island IL.,accountant. Served on Unit 163 Board of Directors in several capacities, on ACBL Board of Governors 1968 and 1993. A Diamond Life Master with between more than 40 regional wins.

EGAN, Victoria Zablan of Quezon City, Philippines, businesswoman. Won Asean Mixed Teams 1995, 1997. Frequent member of Philippines women's teams.

EGHOLM, Dale (1928-1998) of St. Paul MN, ACBL associate national tournament director, had been in the field of tournament directing since 1968.

EHRLENBACH, Julius (Jack) (1894-1979) of Los Angeles was Life Master #56, a designation he earned in 1946 to become the first Life Master on the West Coast and the first one west of Chicago. A well-known teacher and a bridge player with very few peers, he taught the game to hundreds of players. He won the Barclay Trophy 1949, 1950 and scores of regional championships. He had a lifetime total of 5753 MPs and was on the list of the "Top 100" MPs holders from its inception through November 1977.

EICHENBAUM, Kenneth J. (b. 1947) of Columbus Ohio, bridge teacher, lecturer and professional player. Authored *Bridge Without a Partner, What Do I Bid Now?* and *Keys to Winning Defense*. Won more than 30 regionals.

EINHORN, Bolo of Amsterdam, The Netherlands, was deported by the Germans and died in a concentration camp during World War II. Regarded as the most brilliant Dutch player of the pre-war era. Second European Championship 1932, 1933, 1934 and represented The Netherlands 1935-39. Member of the Continental Club team that drew a 232-board challenge match in 1937 against the Austrian team that won the first world championship later that year.

EISENBERG, William (Billy) (b. 1937) of Boca Raton FL, bridge professional, teacher, coach and vugraph commentator, former professional backgammon player. WBF Grand Master, ACBL Diamond Life Master, member ACBL Hall of Fame, one of world's leading players. Won World Backgammon Championship 1974. Vugraph commentator for the WBF and was coach to first ACBL Junior team to attend Junior Camp in Poland 1987. Has coached and been teacher to many players in countries such as Israel, Panama, Venezuela and Holland. Eisenberg has won 5 Bermuda Bowls 1970, 71, 76, 77, 79 (with four different partners) and represented ACBL in three others 1969 (placed 3rd), 73, 75 (placed 2nd). Placed 2nd World Senior Teams 1994, 7th in World Olympiad Teams 1976, 9th in Rosenblum Cup Teams 1978 and 17th in 1990. Has won numerous European tournaments including the London Sunday Times Pairs, Top 16-Italy, Mixed Pairs and Teams-Israel, Paris 600-Paris and Staten Bank-Holland. Won Spingold 1969, 73; Vanderbilt 1971,

78; Reisinger 1970, 74, 76; GNOT 1974, 76; Life Master Pairs, Men's Teams 1968, Senior KO Teams 1995, 96. He has placed 2nd many times including Spingold 1970, 99; Vanderbilt 1966, 70, 73, 76, 83, 89; Reisinger 1968, 81, 83; Men's Teams 1969, Men's Pairs 1981, Open Swiss Teams 1993. See ACES TEAM.

EISENHOWER, Dwight D. (1890-1969) had a keen interest in bridge from the time he was a captain in the U. S. Army through his Presidency of the United States (1953-1961), and even after retirement. Nov. 7, 1942, was the day of the landing at Casablanca which constituted the first Allied invasion after the fall of France. During the nerve-racking period when the landing had begun and the first news had not yet come back to his headquarters, he relaxed in a celebrated bridge game with Mark Clark, Alfred M. Gruenther and Harry C. Butcher. Bridge was his regular recreation before the Normandy invasion when he was Supreme Allied Commander, while he was NATO chief in Paris, and during his term of office in the White House. After his retirement he hosted occasional games at his homes at Gettysburg PA and Palm Springs CA. Oswald Jacoby characterized his skill as "superior." Jacoby said Eisenhower was capable of holding his own in all but the most expert club games. When Eisenhower was asked whom he would choose as his NATO deputy in 1950 he said, "Al Gruenther - he's the best bridge player" (among the generals). Gruenther called him from Chicago at 7 a.m. one day in 1960 to tell him to read the New York Times bridge column of that morning. It was a report on one of his hands, Eisenhower's reply was, "I've already read it."

EISENLORD, Ray H. (1884-1965) from Erie PA, accountant, was ABL president in 1934 and one of the originators of the masterpoint plan.

EISENSTEIN, Lilyan P. (1940-1999) of Beverly Hills CA, bank founder, real estate and travel agent. Served as trustee of ACBL Charity Foundation 1987-91. Served as Unit 566 president and Board of Directors member. Won several regionals.

EISENSTEIN, Robert A. (1933-1990) of Beverly Hills CA, film producer, attorney, president of property management company. He served on ACBL Board of Directors 1982-90, was president of District 23, and served several terms as Unit president. He served on the ACBL Board of Governors.

EKEBLAD, Russell A. (Russ) (b. 1946) of Providence RI, co-owner (with wife) of jewelry distrbuting firm. WBF World Master, 3rd Rosenblum Teams 1990. Grand Life Master with 11,544 MPs as of 3/2001, won Spingold 1992; Vanderbilt, Open Pairs II 1993; placed 2nd Blue Ribbon Pairs 1999. Won Canadian Invitational Pairs Calcutta 1990, 2nd in 1991; placed 3rd in the Cavendish Invitational Pairs 1991. Placed 2nd Blue Ribbon Pairs 1999, Open BAM Teams 1997. Contributor to *Bridge World*.

ELIAS, Enrique (Quique) (b. 1937) of Lima, Peru, professor of law. Former Peruvian Minister of Justice. Congress deputy. Represented Peru in 2 world championships and 10 zonal championships. Won many national titles.

ELIASSON, Hjalti (b. 1929) of Kopavogur, Iceland, electrician. Represented Iceland in 4 world championships, 8 European Championships and 2 Nordic Championships. 17 national wins. Frequently an Npc. Built bridge-o-rama used to display major Icelandic events 1961.

ELIS, Morrie (1907-1992) of Lauderhill FL, company president. For many years was one of the leading American players. He assisted William E. McKenney in for-

mulating and establishing the ACBL Charity Foundation from 1933-37. He constructed hands for Autobridge and wrote a column for *Bridge World* from 1936-40. In 1934 he represented the United States in a match against the Bermuda team which the US won. He won the McKenney Trophy 1938, 40; Vanderbilt 1949, Master Mixed Teams 1937, Life Master Pairs 1938, 40; Master Individual 1940, 50; placed 2nd in Asbury Challenge Teams 1937, Spingold 1937, 38; Vanderbilt 1943, 54; Open Pairs 1939, Master Individual 1946, Men's Pairs 1934, 37, 38, 39, 40, 47. Was semifinalist in the National Table Tennis Championship 1932.

ELKNER, Jeanne (b. 1940) of Clementon NJ, investigator for New Jersey Division of Public Welfare, bridge professional, founder and former manager South Jersey BC. Elkner won Women's Pairs 1989. Diamond Life Master with 30-40 regional wins.

ELLENBY, Milton Q. (b. 1923) of Skokie IL, actuary and physicist. Was a physicist on the Manhattan Project for three years. In the mid-Forties he was a state and regional chess champion. One of the leading players of the postwar period, Ellenby is a WBF Life Master and was Bermuda Bowl champion 1954 and came 2nd in 1955. He won the Men's Pairs 1951 (2nd in 1954), Spingold 1953, 54; Life Master Pairs 1953, Open Pairs 1955, Master Mixed Teams 1957, Fishbein Trophy 1953, Lou Herman Trophy 1955.

ELLIOTT, C. Bruce (b. 1922) of Weston ON, estimator. Formerly one of the outstanding Canadian players, a WBF Life Master. He represented Canada in the World Team Olympiad 1960 and 1968. Won Spingold 1964, 65 and placed 2nd in Life Master Pairs 1964. Diamond Life Master.

ELLIOTT, Loren S. (b. 1923) of Mesa AZ, retired resource planning engineer for state of Iowa. Formerly with the USDA-Soil Conservation Service. A certified director for 25 years, past president of Hawkeye Bridge Unit and former Board member. A Diamond Life Master, won more than 20 regionals.

ELLIS, Brian (b. 1945) of Cleveland Heights, Ohio, attorney, Chairman District 5 Judiciary Committee. Diamond Life Master, placed 2nd GNOT 1993, Master Mixed Teams 1993, Mixed BAM Teams 1999. He has more than 25 regional wins.

ELLISON, Donald McLaren (b. 1949) of Rossland BC, residential designer and partner in planning and design firm. Involved in local Chamber of Commerce, past president Unit 574, sectional chairman since 1981, editor, *Trump-It*. Co-authored with Jude Goodwin *Teach Me to Play"*, *"Teach Me to Play the Cards"* and *"Teach Me to Play Defense"*, also beginner's and intermediate bidding manuals *Elwin: Module One and Two*. Won Zone VI Canadian National Team Championship 1987.

ELSTON, A. Roger (b. 1933) of Commack NY, attorney, won 50 regionals.

ELWELL, Joseph Bowne (1873-1920) was the principal American authority on the original game of bridge (bridge-whist) and the early form of auction bridge. However, he is remembered chiefly as the victim of one of the most celebrated murder cases of the century. Born in Cranford NJ, Elwell began his bridge career about 1900 as a bridge teacher and quickly became a favorite of high society in New York City and Newport RI. He was a regular high-stake player at the Whist Club of New York and other clubs. He and his regular partner, Harold S. Vanderbilt, were considered the strongest American pair from about 1910 to 1920. Elwell amassed a considerable fortune, chiefly through speculation in Wall Street and at the time of his death owned more than 20 race horses. His books, most of which went through several editions and sold in large quantities, included *Elwell on Bridge, Advanced Bridge, Practical Bridge, Bridge Axioms* and *Laws, Elwell on Auction Bridge,* and *Elwell's New Auction Bridge*.

He also showed great skill at hand analysis. On the morning of June 11, 1920, he was found in his home by his housekeeper. He had been fatally shot only about an hour earlier. Because none of the considerable amount of money or jewelry was touched, the motive could not have been robbery. At that time he was separated from his wife and several women had keys to his home. The case received wide publicity and has been the subject of several books and hundreds of articles. Officially the murder was never solved, though it is generally believed that the police knew the murderer but had insufficient evidence. Several novelists used the setting of the case for mystery novels in which they supplied their own solutions.

EMERY, Sue (b. 1920) of Wichita Falls TX, formerly of Memphis TN, bridge club owner/operator; editor of ACBL *Bulletin* 1972-96, co-editor of the ACBL *Daily Bulletin* at North American Bridge Championships 1961-93 (attended 95 consecutive tournaments in 32 years) and co-editor of the World Championships *Daily Bulletin* 1972, 75, 78. She is a former school teacher, newspaper reporter, bridge teacher and bridge club owner/operator. She has been a tournament director since the early Sixties and directed in many Texas tournaments with her late husband, John W. "Big John" Emery (1926-72), a well-known ACBL associate national tournament director. She authored ACBL publication *No Passing Fancy* 1977. Is a contributing editor of *Bridge Encyclopedia* and was associate editor of *Texas Bridge*. She won the International Bridge Press Association Romex Award in 1988 and WBF Epson Award for journalists in 1989. She has won several regionals.

ENDICOTT, Grattan (b. 1924) of Liverpool, England, executive. secretary to the trustees & chief executive of Foundation for Sport & the Arts. Secretary, WBF Laws Committee. Member EBL Executive Council. Former positions include: Vice Chairman, WBF Laws Committee; Chairman, European Laws Committee, English Laws & Ethics Committee; EBU Treasurer. Joint author, EBL Commentary (1992) on the Laws of Duplicate Contract Bridge and WBF Code of Practice for Appeals Committees. NPC winning British team Venice Cup 1985. Invested Order of the British Empire 1998.

ENG, Fook (b. 1925) of Monterey Park CA, retired astronautical guidance engineer with Rockwell International. He worked on the space shuttle program, orbital tracking and analysis and on manned orbital lab missions. Author of what is considered to be one of the best books on squeezes, *Bridge Squeezes Illustrated*. He has also been a contributor to the *Bridge World*.

ENGEL, Michael (b.1935) of New York City, stock trader. Placed 2nd in Reisinger 1965 and 4th in Cavendish Invitational Pairs 1965.

ENGEL, Zvi (b. 1952 in Israel) of Brussels, Belgium, company manager. WBF World Master. Represented Belgium in 2 World Championships and 4 European Championships. National wins include 4 open pairs and 7 open teams.

EPPERSON, William E. (Bill) (b. 1931) of Sarasota

FL, retired commercial airline pilot, former USAF officer, member Hole in One Club, docent at Mote Marine Aquarium. Won North American Swiss Teams 1980, has many regional wins.

EPSTEIN, Isadore (Eppy or Izzy) (1908-1992) of Tacoma WA, born in Grodno Russia, retired teacher. Developed a one-handed typewriter keyboard for either hand for handicapped students, he could type 150 WPM. In 1932 Epstein beat a renowned chess champion in both his games. He devised a movement that allowed for one winner in a 16-plus table game. It was replaced by the Mitchell movement in 1945. Won several regionals.

EPSTEIN, Roberta E. (b. 1936) of South Orange NJ, computer science teacher. Won Women's Teams 1960, 61; North American Women's Swiss 1986, Womens KO Teams 1990. Epstein has placed 2nd in Women's Teams 1971, Women's Pairs 1981, Women's KO Teams 1985, 87; Women's BAM Teams 1986, 88.

ERB, Paul W. (b. 1951) of Austin TX, retired. Has won 15 regionals.

ERDOS, Ivan (1924-1967) edited the popular "Dupliquiz" column for the ACBL *"Bulletin*. A leading player, teacher and writer, Erdos also contributed to *American Bridge Digest* and wrote *Bridge A La Carte*. He was bridge editor of *San Diego* magazine and several Southern California newspapers. Born in Budapest, Erdos lived in England from 1939 to 1951 before moving to Los Angeles, where he worked as a travel agent. He won the World Mixed Pairs 1966 and represented North America in the Bermuda Bowl in Buenos Aires 1965. He won Men's Teams 1959, Men's Pairs 1962.

ERGUDEN, Garland I. (b. 1951) of Memphis TN, attorney, former database administrator in a technical support group with "Fortune 500" company. Has served as vice-chair ACBL Appeals Committee, secretary District 7. Has more than 30 regional wins.

ERHART, Maria (nee Kirner) (b. 1944) of Vienna, Austria. WBF World Grand Master. Won World Women's Team Olympiad 1992; McConnell Cup 1998; European Women's Teams 1991; European Mixed Pairs 1996; Women's Generali Individual 1992. Runner-up Venice Cup 1991. Represented Austria in four other world championships, twice in European Open Championship, and on many other occasions. 13 national victories include Open Teams 8 times. Won Caransa tournament (Amsterdam). Oriental carpet expert.

ERNST, Leonard (Len) (b. 1935) retired, was bridge columnist for *Chicago Tribune* 1970-79; associate editor *Kibitzer* for the Chicago Contract BA. Diamond Life Master with more than 15 regional wins.

ESBERG, William (b. 1935) of Elberon NJ, retired English teacher, currently bridge teacher, learned bridge at age 9. Placed 2nd Senior KO Teams 1994, 96. Diamond Life Master with several regional wins.

ESCUDE, Manuel (b. 1938) of Barcelona, Spain, businessman. Represented Spain in 2 world championships and 6 zonal championships. Won many national titles.

ETTER, Bob G. (b. 1954) of Sacramento CA, assistant math professor. He was placekicker for the Atlanta Falcons 1968-69 and All SEC football and baseball 1964-67. Won North American Swiss Teams 1981, placed 2nd North American Men's Swiss Teams 1982, Master Mixed Teams 1986. Grand Life Master with 11,590 MPs as of 3/2001.

ETTLINGER, Douglas M. (Duggie) (b. 1931) of Johannesburg, South Africa, retired trial lawyer. Represented South Africa in World Team Olympiad 1980,

Maccabi Games 1977. 19 national wins. Member WBF Executive Council 1970, 1974. Bridge columnist *Finance Week*. Scorer at international cricket matches, and a world authority on cricket history and statistics.

EVANS, Claire (b. 1989) of Bristol, England. The youngest player ever to represent a country internationally. In January 1999, at the age of 9 years and 8 months, represented Wales in Under-20 international competition against England, Scotland and Northern Ireland, partnered by her 13-year-old sister Catherine.

EVANS, Norah (Penguin) (1906-1977) of Bournemouth, England, bridge club proprietor. Won European Women's Teams 1950, 1951, 1952, 2nd 1939.

EVITT, Jane. See SKIPPER, Jane.

EVITT, John (b. 1946) of Auckland, New Zealand, sales director. Represented New Zealand in one world championship and 2 zonal championships. National wins include 2 team events. Former President of New Zealand CBA.

EWEN, Robert (Bob) (b. 1940) of Miami FL, self-employed author, former psychology professor, NYU. Ewen has written one book on psychology for the general public and two college psychology textbooks. He is the creator of Two-Way Game Tries and the author of articles for the *Bridge World*, contributor to ACBL *Bulletin*. Former associate editor of *Bridge Journal*, contributor to *Bridge Encyclopedia* and other publications. Has authored six bridge books including *Opening Leads, Doubles For Takeout, Penalties* and *Profit in Contract Bridge, Preemptive Bidding, Contract Bridge: A Concise Guide, The Teenager's Guide to Bridge and The Defensive Bidding Quiz Book.* He edited *Charles Goren Presents the Precision System* and *The Simplified Precision System.*

EYSTEINSSON, Bjorn (b. 1948) of Hafnarfjordur, Iceland, bank manager. WBF world master. Npc and coach of Iceland's Bermuda Bowl champions 1991. Won Transnational Mixed Teams 1996, Nordic Teams 1992. Represented Iceland in 3 other world championships and 2 European Championships. 9 national wins.

EYTHORSDOTTIR, Hjordis (Disa) (b. 1965) of Huntsville AL, born in Iceland, bridge professional. WBF World Master. ACBL Diamond Life Master, won the Nordic Women's Teams 1990, bronze medal in European Women's Pairs 1993. Represented Iceland in two World Championships, one European Championship and two other Nordic Championships. Eythorsdottir has also won several ACBL national titles including Women's Swiss 1994, 98, 2000; Women's BAM Teams 1994; 2nd GNOT 1997, Life Master Women's Pairs 1997.

EZEKIEL, David (b. 1948) of Paget Bermuda, born in Darjeeling, India, company president, former partner in international accounting firm. Two-time Bermuda backgammon champion. Has served as chairman of Bermuda regional twice, president Unit 198 and president of Bermuda BC for five years, received ACBL Presidential Citation for services to bridge. Bridge columnist *Mid-Ocean News* since 1980. Ezekiel's quick wit and wry sense of humor earned him the opportunity to be the Master of Ceremonies at all ACBL Hall of Fame dinners to date. Representing Bermuda he has competed in international play New Orleans 1978, Valkenburg 1980, Biarritz 1982, Seattle 1984, Bal Harbour 1986, Tri-Country playoff 1987. Won ACBL-wide Charity Game 1987. Has won several regionals. Winner of Norman Bach Trophy 5 times (top local masterpoint winner at annual Bermuda Regional).

F

FACCHINI, Gianfranco (b. 1937) of Bologna, Italy, attorney. Won Bermuda Bowl 1975, London Sunday Times Pairs 1974. During 1975 Bermuda Bowl was accused of illicit communication through foot signals. (see BERMUDA INCIDENT.)

FAHS, Baha (b. 1938) of Saida, Lebanon. Represented Lebanon in 8 international championships. Won Gold Cup, Lebanese Festival 1971 and many national titles.

FAIGENBAUM, Albert (b. 1946) of Paris, France, public relations executive. WBF World Master. Won Rosenblum Teams 1982, represented France in one other world championship.

FALK, Allan (the Zookeeper, Curmudgeon) (b. 1947) of Okemos MI, attorney. Has served as commissioner of Michigan Court of Appeals and state director of Common Cause of Michigan, legislative draftsman and founder Opera Guild of Greater Lansing. Falk fought a 14-year legal battle with State Bar of Michigan that led to nationwide reforms in lobbying and other activities of state organizations for attorneys. Named to Outstanding Young Men of America 1975. He served on ACBL Board of Governors 1982-88; president Unit 195 1982-86 on their Board 1978-96; District 12 Board member 1982-86 and recorder 1992-94, and was chairperson Bridge Center of Greater Lansing. He served on President's Advisory Committee and Committee to Revise Appeals Procedures. Winner of Rosenkranz Journalist Award. He has been on *Bridge World* Master Solvers Panel several times, has contributed to *IBPA Bulletin* and is 2-time winner World Bidding Contest. Co-inventor of Supersplinter, extended Lebensohl and transfer responses to preempts. Authored *Spingold Challenge 1988*, *Team Trial 1992*, *The Bridge Player's Toolkit* (with the late Jim Jacoby), *Bermuda Bowl Challenge Team Trial,* and *Short Tall Bridge Tales.* Diamond Life Master, won Open Pairs I 1994, Blue Ribbon Pairs 1997, Open Pairs II 1997; placed 2nd GNOT Flt A 1996.

FALLENIUS, Bjorn (b. 1957) of Manhattan NY, formerly of Malmo, Sweden, bridge professional and former controller. WBF World Life Master. Representing Sweden, 3rd Bermuda Bowl 1987, 91; Rosenblum Teams 1986, 98; World Team Olympiad 1988. Won European Teams 1987, 2nd 1999. Won Reisinger 1991, Open BAM Teams 1991, Master Mixed Teams 1992. 2nd Vanderbilt 1993. Won Cavendish 1988.

FANG, Hien-Chee (b. 1991) of Fu-chien, China, telecommunications expert. Former Taiwanese director-general of telecommunications, vice minister transportation. Founder of Taiwan Bridge League. Npc of Taiwan team in 2 world championships and many Far East Championships. Chief organizer 1969 Far East Championship and 1971 Bermuda Bowl. Associated with Charles Wei in promotion of Precision System in Taiwan.

FARELL, Mary Jane (Mrs. Jules) of Los Angeles CA, bridge teacher, one of the world's leading women players. WBF Grand Master. Ranked #25 among women Grand Masters, member ACBL Hall of Fame -1998. Grand Life Master with 23,321 MPs as of 3/2001, ranked #18 in ACBL. *Los Angles Times* "Woman of the Year" 1964 in recognition of gaining first place among women in all-time masterpoint rankings of the ACBL, displacing Helen Sobel Smith. Farell went over 20,000 MPs in July of 1989 by winning a Women's Swiss Teams in Pasa-

dena. Won World Mixed Pairs 1966, World Women's Pairs 1970, Venice Cup 1978, World Women's Teams 1980. She won Women's Teams 1968, 70, 72, 74, 75, 76 (2nd 1967, 73); Women's Pairs 1960, Master Mixed Teams 1949, 50, 55 (2nd 1969, 89); Life Master Pairs 1978, Women's KO Teams 1984, 90; North American Women's Swiss Teams 1982. She placed 2nd Life Master Women's Pairs 1965, 66, 67, 68; Women's KO Teams 1987, Women's BAM Teams 1988, Women's Teams 1990. She has won more than 100 regional events.

FARIA, Octavio (b. 1920) of Rio de Janeiro, Brazil, business executive. Won South American Teams 1971, represented Brazil in 6 world championships. National wins include 4 open teams.

FARWIG, Katrin (nee Reps) (b. 1968) of Berlin, Germany. WBF World Master. 2nd 1998 McConnell Teams, 3rd Women's Team Olympiad 2000.

FASKOW, Donald (Don) (b. 1934) of McMurray PA, financial consultant. Placed 2nd Chicago (now the Reisinger) 1963, Life Master Men's Pairs 1967. Won approximately 30 regional events.

FAUCONNIER, Paul (b. 1943) of Liege, Belgium, teacher. Represented Belgium in 4 World Championships and 7 European Championships. National wins include 7 Open Teams and 2 Open Pairs.

FAZLI, Jan-e-Alam (b. 1939) of Karachi, Pakistan, tax consultant. WBF World Life Master. Placed 2nd in 2 world championships: Bermuda Bowl 1981 and Rosenblum Teams 1986. Played in several other world championships. Won BFAAME Open Teams 1983, 85, 87 and many national titles.

FEAGIN, Claudia (b. 1947) of Atlanta GA, teacher. First to win 2 Mini-McKenney categories – Sectional Master 1975, NABC Master 1976. Diamond Life Master, has won many regional titles.

FEAGIN, Jack (b. 1948) of Atlanta GA, attorney. Has served in many capacities including president of Unit 114, District 7, Mid-Atlantic Conference and COI (Committee for an Open and Improved ACBL). On ACBL President's Committee on Policies and Procedures. Was chairman of Atlanta NABCs 1986 and 1995. Co-editor COI newsletter. A Diamond Life Master, he has numerous regional credits.

FEATHERSTON, Norman D. (Norm) (b. 1934) of Redmond WA, retired electrical engineer, bridge teacher and bridge administrator. District 19 recorder since 1992 and 2-time president Seattle Unit. Diamond Life Master, has won more than 50 regionals.

FEICHTINGER, Andrea (b. 1959) of Linz, Austria, entrepreneur. Placed 2nd European Mixed Pairs 1993. Represented Austria in 8 European Championships. Won National Open Teams and Mixed Pairs.

FEICHTINGER, Kurt (b. 1954) of Linz, Austria, industrial manager. WBF World Master. Placed 2nd Bermuda Bowl 1985. Won European Open Teams 1985, European Team Cup 1988. 2nd European Mixed Pairs 1993. Represented Austria in 6 other world championships and 10 European Team and Pair Championships. Won Coppo D'Oro (Paris) and CAC Open Pairs. Won 5 National Open Teams and 2 Open Pairs.

FEIGUS, Jay T. (1892-1990) retired labor relations mediator. Won the Vanderbilt 1948 and placed 2nd Spingold 1942. He had a few regional wins.

FEIN, Phyllis M. (now Denton) (b. 1930) of Fourways, South Africa, formerly of Boynton Beach FL, owner/operator of executive search firm 1978-92. Former advertis-

ing director for New York Nets; was in the Peace Corps in Ukraine 1994-96. Past president Unit 566, contributing editor *The Southern California Bridge News*. Author of *The Lighter Side of Bridge*. Wrote, directed and scored 4 bridge musicals plus scored 2 musicals for Unit 566.

FELDESMAN, Phillip (1919-1986) of New York City, diamond merchant. One of the leading American players, represented United States in World championships 1962, 66. He won Herman Trophy 1962, Mott-Smith Trophy 1965, 66; Vanderbilt 1965, 66; Reisinger 1969, Life Master Pairs 1961, 62, 67; Master Mixed Teams 1973, Senior/Advanced Senior Master Individual 1957, Open Pairs 1961, Men's Pairs 1961, 62; Men's Teams 1962, 63, 66; placed 2nd Chicago (now the Reisinger) 1965; Spingold, Vanderbilt 1969; Men's Teams 1965, Open Pairs, Blue Ribbon Pairs 1967.

FELDHEIM, Harold (b. 1936) of Hamden CT, author, bridge professional, owned and operated bridge club 1975-86. Authored *The Weak Two-Bid in Bridge, Winning Swiss Team Tactics in Bridge, Negative and Responsive Doubles in Bridge, Five-Card Majors, Tactical Bridge,* a chapter on Pressure Bidding in *Expert Bridge,* and *Charles Goren Teaches Bridge* (a computer program). Contributor to ACBL *Bulletin* and *Popular Bridge*. A Diamond Life Master with more than 11,400 MPs as of 3/2001, won 60 regional titles.

FELDMAN, Lynne of Champaign IL, immigration and naturalization attorney. Former municipal attorney in California. Won Master Mixed Teams 1979, Women's Swiss Teams 1986, Women's BAM Teams 1988, placed 2nd Women's KO Teams 1985, Women's BAM Teams 1987, 94.

FELDMAN, Mark David (b. 1951) of New York City, former professor, now with Bear-Stearnes. In 1971 devised defenses to strong club and 1NT openings (SCREW) which later became known as CRASH. In 1975 invented the treatment of a jump to 4 of a minor over an opposing major suit weak 2-bid to show the bid minor and the other major. 2nd World Transnational Mixed Teams 1996. Won Men's Teams 1974, Master Mixed Teams 1979, placed 2nd Vanderbilt 1974, 1980, 97; GNOP 1981, Spingold 1989, 97; Open Swiss Teams, Master Mixed Teams 1995, Reisinger 1996. Feldman placed 5th-8th Bermuda Bowl 1991, WBF World Master. Diamond Life Master with many regional wins.

FELDMAN, Ron L. (The Godfather, BARF) (b. 1950) of Petaluma CA, president, World Business Services, Inc., inventor, entrepreneur and professional bridge player. Listed in *Who's Who in California* 1988; was Entrepreneur of the Year 1991. A former elementary school counselor, he received Congressional recognition for his work with children. Has directed more than 35 performances of his popular "Bidding Contest", a vugraph show sponsored by entertainment committees of regionals and NABC's. Founder and president of Association of Professional Bridge Players, Inc. (APBP Inc.), the first professional organization recognized by the ACBL-1981. Organized the "Marquette Hotel Bridge Carnival" (the largest cash prize corporate sponsored tournament) and "The Stars of Tournament Bridge". Was on ACBL Appeals Committee more than 10 years. Major contributor to 2/1 Game Forcing and invented Ron Feldman 2♦ response to 1♣ and 4-level agreed minor is Roman Key Card Blackwood. Placed 2nd Life Masters Pairs 1978, Men's Teams 1979. Diamond Life Master with more than 40 regional wins. To distinguish between

the 2 California Ron Feldmans, bridge players named them for their area - Bay Area Ron Feldman (BARF) and Los Angeles Ron Feldman (LARF).

FELDMAN, Ronald W. (Ron, LARF) (b. 1948) of Torrance CA, CPA, controller for McDonald's Franchises. Feldman was 2nd in IMP Pairs 1991. Has won more than 25 regionals. To distinguish between the 2 California Ron Feldmans, bridge players named them for their area - Bay Area Ron Feldman (BARF) and Los Angeles Ron Feldman (LARF).

FELDSTEIN, Gretchen S. (Mrs. Harold) of Melbourne FL. Won Women's Teams 1953, Women's Pairs 1960; placed 2nd Women's Pairs 1953.

FELDSTEIN, Harold F. (b. 1919) of Melbourne FL, retired computer systems analyst and ACBL national tournament director. Placed 2nd Men's Pairs 1948 and won several regional events.

FELLER, Robert H. (Bob) (b. 1952) of Albany NY, attorney. Won GNOP 1980 and has several regional wins.

FELLOWS, Barbara A. (Mrs. James E.) (b. 1938) of Omaha NB, ACBL accredited bridge teacher and director. Unit 241 Board member and Unit Education Liason. Won Women's Pairs 1976 and several regional titles.

FELLOWS, James E. (b. 1932) of Omaha NE, retired attorney. Member of Unit and District Boards (was president of both), editor of unit publication 1975-85. Nebraska's 1st Certified Director and Gold Life Master. Diamond Life Master with more than 10,800 MPs as of 3/2001. Won almost 200 regionals.

FELTON, Ronald L. (1938) of New York City, bridge professional. Diamond Life Master, Felton has won at least 20 regionals.

FENKEL, Stanley O. (1902-1986) of Deerfield Beach FL, company vice president, former plastics manufacturer, Life Master #43. Placed 2nd in Spingold 1944, Chicago (now the Reisinger) 1946, Vanderbilt 1954. Fenkel was founder and former secretary/treasurer of Cavendish Club of Philadelphia.

FENWICK, Thomas (b. 1928) of Geneva, Switzerland, company director. Represented Switzerland in 4 world championships and 7 European Championships. Many national titles.

FERER, Leland E. (b. 1927) of Miami Beach FL, import manager and bridge writer. Former vice president of the Florida Unit and editor of its *Bridge News*. Won Master Mixed Teams 1958, placed 2nd Master Mixed Teams 1967, Mixed Pairs 1972, Blue Ribbon Pairs 1966.

FERGUSON, James P. (1907-1981) of North Palm Beach FL, candy manufacturer. Was ACBL president in 1961 when the League was converting to a data processing system for MPs and memberships. As president, Ferguson worked on establishing bridge as a spectator sport, promoting such bridge exhibitions as vugraph and Bridge-O-Rama. Served 3 terms on the ACBL Board of Directors.

FERNANDEZ, Carlos (b. 1958) of Barcelona, Spain, economist and enterprise manager. 2nd European Junior Teams 1980 and represented Spain in 8 other zonal championships and 3 world championships. Won 5 national titles.

FERNANDO, Violet (b. 1926) of Kuala Lumpur, Malaysia, secretary. Represented Malaysia in 2 world championships and 10 zonal championships. Won 1989 Asean Women's Teams. 2 national wins.

FERRO, Jeffrey (Jeff) (b. 1968) of San Francisco CA, vice president, executive producer at ad agency produc-

ing TV and radio commercials. Appointed Junior Liaison 1991. At age 15 he became a Life Master and won his 1st regional. He won 458 points in 1989 (more than any other junior for that year). He was on the winning team at the World Junior Championships 1991. Playing on the USA II open team he competed in Bermuda Bowl Yokohama 1991 - tying 5th/8th. Won NABC Junior Pairs 1991, GNOT 1993. Was 2nd in First Annual "Expert Calcutta" in 1991. Won Mixed BAM Teams 2000.

FIELD, Albert (b. 1916) of Astoria NY, teacher, contributing editor, *Bridge Encyclopedia*. A collector of playing cards with the largest collection in the world. Field has been the official cataloguer for Salvador Dali.

FIELD, Myron (formerly Fuchs) (1912-1974) New York stockbroker. Won Vanderbilt 1941, 53; Reisinger 1950, Spingold 1951, 55; placed 2nd Spingold 1939, 40; Life Master Pairs 1940, Master Individual 1948, Vanderbilt 1949, 50; Reisinger 1951, Master Mixed Teams 1951. Field represented USA in 1956 Bermuda Bowl.

FILARSKI, Herman W. (1913-1982) of Deil, The Netherlands, wine merchant, bridge teacher and journalist. Learned to play bridge while in a German prison camp during World War II. Placed 2nd World Mixed Pairs, represented Netherlands World Open Pairs 1962, in many European championships 1947 thru 1962. Many national wins. Served several terms as executive vice president International Bridge Press Association. Originated idea of Daily Bulletins for major championships. Founder of Bols Tips and Bols Brilliancy competitions. Authored several books and was editor for Netherlands bridge publication. IBPA Personality of Year 1977.

FINCH, Curtis of Little Rock AR, owner retail furniture and appliance. Was very active in local bridge and was considered "Mr. Bridge" of Arkansas. Won more than 20 regional events and was an early Life Master.

FINK, Jerold (Jerry) (b. 1941) of Cincinnati OH, tax attorney. Listed in *The Best Lawyers in America* and *Who's Who in American Law*. A chess master, has won chess championships in Ohio and North Carolina. Co-authored *Power Defensive Carding*. Introduced several bidding and defensive signaling innovations through articles published in the *Bridge World*. Developed and organized 1st intercity match between Cincinnati and Indianapolis 1988. Won several regionals.

FINKEL, Lewis M. (Lew) (b. 1946) of Jupiter FL, retired attorney and CPA. Served as District 25 judiciary chairman. Intercity champion (representing Boston) 1972. Has won significantly more than 15 regionals.

FISCHER, Doris (b. 1959) of Vienna, Austria, teacher of history and German. WBF World Grand Master. In 2000, ranked 20th Women's World rankings. Won World Women's Team Olympiad 1992, McConnell Cup 1998, European Women's Teams 1991. Placed 2nd Venice Cup 1991. Represented Austria in one other world championship and 2 other European events. Won National Open Teams.

FISCHER, Norman H. (b. 1941) of Columbus OH, research mathematician, space systems analysis for DOD and NASA. Served Unit 122 as president and District 11 as president and vice-president. Placed 2nd Life Master Men's Pairs, Men's Teams 1969. Diamond Life Master with numerous regional wins.

FISHBEIN, Harry J. (1898-1976) of New York City, pro basketball player, president of the famous Mayfair Club, proprietor 1940-70. Authored Fishbein Convention. An outstanding player who wore a beret as his trademark. Won 12 North American titles: Vanderbilt 1936, 43, 47, 49, 58; Life Master Pairs 1939, 40; Master Individual 1942, 52; Master Mixed Teams 1947; Men's Pairs 1959; Men's BAM Teams 1965. Placed 2nd 18 times - Spingold 1937, 43, 45, 58; Master Individual 1938; Men's Pairs 1940; the Chicago (since 1965 the Reisinger) 1942, 53, 57, 59; Master Mixed Teams 1945, 48; Men's BAM Teams 1952, 53, 60; Open Pairs 1959, 68; Life Master Men's Pairs 1963. Represented U.S. in Bermuda Bowl 1959 and served as npc of 1960 U.S. World Olympiad Team. ACBL treasurer for 14 years (1952-1966), Honorary Member 1966, member ACBL Hall of Fame.

FISHER, Arnold H. (Arnie) (b. 1938) of Clementon NJ, university instructor in German and Russian, owner foreign language typesetting company and bridge professional. Served as vice-chairman ACBL Appeals Committee 1985-1990. Wrote *Solobridge* and *Bridge for Four*. Fisher competed internationally Bal Harbour 1986 (placed 15th Rosenblum Teams) and Geneva 1990 . Won North American Swiss Teams 1996, Senior KO Teams 1999; 2nd Senior KO Teams 1997, Mixed Pairs 1996. Grand Life Master with 13,329 MPs as of 3/2001, more than 100 regional wins.

FISHER, Dr. John W. (b. 1925) of Dallas TX, physician, LSU School of Medicine (MD). Past president Dallas BA. Inventor of Fisher Double. Winner McKenney Trophy (now Barry Crane Top 500) 1972, a Grand Life Master with more than 17,896 MPs as of 3/2001. WBF World Life Master, placed 2nd World Open Pairs 1966, 5th Olympiad Mixed Teams 1972. Won McKenney Trophy 1972, Open Pairs 1958, Master Mixed Teams 1964, Vanderbilt 1965, Open Pairs 1970, 71, 72, 74; GNOT 1975. Placed 2nd Men's Teams 1954, 56, 71; Master Mixed Teams 1961, 67, 72; Open Pairs 1976. Won well over 100 regionals. Was a frequent partner of Barry Crane.

FISHER, Margaret L. (1912-1987) of Washington DC, technical writer. Won Senior/Advanced Senior Master Pairs 1953 and a few regionals. Fisher was a bridge columnist for Washington *Evening Star* 1948-1960. Founder and secretary of Northern Virginia B.A.

FISHER, Richard C. (Dick) (1921-82) of Tokyo, Japan, business manager. Won North-Eastern Open Teams 1943 and became a permanent Japanese resident 1945. Represented Japan in several Far East Championships and won many national titles. Founded and directed 2 clubs and a team event which led to the formation of the JCBL. Bridge columnist *Japan Times*.

FITZGIBBON, Nicholas (b. 1948) of Dun Laoghaire, Ireland, telecommunications engineer. 3rd European Teams 1979. 2nd Mixed Teams, European Championships 1989, Common Market Teams 1975. Represented Ireland in many world and zonal championships. 53 national wins.

FLADER, Michael F. (Mike) (b. 1947) of Hopkins MN, ACBL tournament director since 1989, former bridge club manager. Has served as a tournament coordinator, Education Liaison, representative Unit 103 Board of Governors. Won several regionals.

FLANAGAN, Barbara J. (b. 1933) of Westlake Village CA, bridge teacher. A Diamond Life Master she has won 67 regional titles.

FLANAGAN, Michael L. (b. 1939) of Westlake CA, statistician. Was U.S. Intercollegiate bowling champion in 3 events 1961. Flanagan is a Diamond Life Master with more than 70 regional wins.

FLANNERY, William L. (1932-2000) of Sacramento CA,

retired steamfitter, was a specialist in installing sectional boilers. Originator of the Flannery 2♦ convention. Placed 2nd in the Chicago (since 1965 the Reisinger) 1963, Life Master Men's Pairs 1967, Mixed Pairs 1968. Placed 2nd Chicago (now the Reisinger) 1963 and Life Master Men's Pairs 1967. Had approximately 30 regional wins.

FLATOWICZ, Pierre D. (b. 1950) of Omaha NE, resource management flight chief. Has written for quarterly bridge newsletters and monthly articles for the Lompoc California newspaper. Has personally recruited more than 50 new duplicate players. Has won 41 regional events.

FLEISCHMAN, Dr. Richard K. (Dick) (b. 1941) of Shaker Heights OH, professor and chairman-Dept. of Accountancy, former professor of history. Recipient of "Excellence in Teaching Award". Past president Buffalo and Hilo HI Units, Treasurer Unit 125 1990-to date. Diamond Life Master with more than 50 regional wins.

FLEISHER, Martin E. (b. 1958) of New York City, employee benefits attorney. Placed 2nd GNOT 1976, earning him the distinction of being the youngest (17 years, 10 months) ever to compete in the finals of an NABC KO championship. He was Intercollegiate champion in 1977 and runner-up in 78. Won Cavendish Pairs 2000. Won 20 regional events.

FLEMING, Ian (1908-1964), famous British novelist and creator of James Bond, pits 007 agent against the diabolical Drax in a high-stake bridge game in his short story *Bridge at Blades* which has been anthologized in *Grand Slam*. Bridge plays an important part in the plot of *Moonraker*, another 007 novel. (see DISTRIBUTIONAL VALUES.)

FLEMING, Irene (Dimmie) (1911-1996) of Heron's Ghyll, England, bridge supplies distributor. WBF World Life Master. Won World Women's Teams 1964, European Women's Teams 1951, 52, 59, 63. 2nd European Open Teams 1953, the best performance ever by a woman and the only time a woman has represented Britain in European open competition. Represented Britain in 4 other world championships, 11 national wins include Gold Cup once. Secretary of EBU 1956-75, then vice-president and honorary life member. Magazine contributor.

FLINT, Honor of London, England. Represented Britain in 3 world championships and 2 zonal championships. Won 5 national titles and 3 ACBL regional titles.

FLINT, Jeremy M. (1928-1990) of London, England, bridge writer. WBF World Life Master. 2nd World Olympiad Teams 1960 and Bermuda Bowl 1987. Won European Teams 1963, 2nd 1987. Won Far East Open Pairs 1973. Represented Britain in 7 other world championships and 5 other zonal championships. Won more than 10 British titles including 2 Gold Cups. During a 1966 tour of the United States he won 13 regional titles and was runner-up in the McKenney Trophy race. Became an ACBL Life Master in 11 weeks, a record that stood until 1989. Co-inventor of Multi 2♦ convention, Little Major system and Flint-Pender system. Bridge columnist *London Times* 1980-1990. Author of more than 6 books on bridge, as well as a book about horse racing. Chief presenter of several televised series on bridge.

FLODQVIST, Ann-Margreth (Pyttsi) (b. 1948) of Stockholm, Sweden, chemical dependency counselor. WBF World Master. Placed 3rd Venice Cup 1993. Won European Women's Teams 1993, Nordic Women's Teams 1992. Represented Sweden in one other world championship and 2 other zonal championships.

FLODQVIST, Sven-Olov (Tjolpe) of Stockholm, Sweden, computer analyst and bridge editor. WBF World Life Master. Placed 3rd Bermuda Bowl 1977, 87; Olympiad Teams 1988. Represented Sweden in 5 other world championships. European champion 1977, 1987, 3rd 1989. Played on 6 other occasions. Won London Sunday Times 1978, 81. Placed 2nd Generali Individual 1993. Several national wins. Bridge editor *Dagens Nyheter*. Author of book on Carrot Club System.

FLOURNOY, Carolyn Clay (b. 1924) of Shreveport LA, food columnist and cooking teacher. Delegate to Republican party convention for 3 Presidential elections. Named to Sports Museum of Champions of Louisiana. Served on local Board of Directors for many years, was tournament publicity chairman for more than 25 years. Won Mixed Pairs 1970 and many regionals.

FLOYD, Jason H. (b. 1908) of Gulfport MS. A representative in Mississippi State Legislature 1936-40. Past president of Unit 180, Life Master #471. Won several regionals.

FOLLINE, Emily (1907-1984) of Columbia SC, bridge studio owner. Won the Chicago (now the Reisinger) 1949, Women's Teams 1943, 44, 45, 46. She placed 2nd Women's Teams 1942, Master Mixed Teams 1946.

FONSECA, Christiano (b. 1940) of Rio de Janeiro, Brazil, financial executive. WBF Grand Master. Won World Olympiad Teams 1976, South American Teams 1970, 71, 72, 73, 75, 97. Represented Brazil in 3 other world championships. National wins include 6 open teams.

FONTAINE, Walter J. (b. 1944) of North Providence RI, produces statistics and publications for the adult prison system for Rhode Island Department of Corrections. Served as president RI Bridge Association and chairman of Judiciary Committee District 25. Authored *Use Your Imagination and Win at Bridge.* Diamond Life Master, won 23 regionals.

FORQUET, Pietro (b. 1925) of Naples, Italy. World Grand Master, one of the greatest players of all time. Won World Olympiad Teams 1964, 68, 72; Bermuda Bowl 1957, 58, 59, 61, 62, 63, 65, 66, 67, 69, 73, 74. Known for calm, unruffled appearance , apparently immune to the nervousness that afflicted many other top stars. Employed Blue Team Club and Neapolitan Club with 3 regular partners B Guglielmo Siniscalco, Eugenio Chiaradia and Benito Garozzo. He shifted to the Precision Club 1972-1974, playing with Garozzo and Benito Bianchi. He won European Championship 1951, 56, 57, 58, 59. Author of one book, columnist.

FORRESTER, Anthony R. (Tony) (b. 1953) of Upton Bishop, England, chartered accountant and bridge writer. WBF World Master. Placed 2nd Bermuda Bowl 1987. Won European Teams 1991, 2nd 1987. Won European Junior Teams 1978, Common Market Teams 1981, 1983. Represented Britain in 7 other world championships and 4 other zonal championships and England in 41 Camrose Trophy matches, a record. Won Sunday Times 1990, Cap Gemini 1990, 98; Reisinger 1998, 99. Numerous national titles including 7 Gold Cups. Author of 9 books, including best seller *Secrets of Success* and *Bridge Masterclass* tutorial videos. Bridge columnist of *London Daily Telegraph* from 1993 and *Sunday Telegraph* from 1996.

FORSTER, Dale E. (b. 1942) of Eugene OR, real estate broker. Won the Intercollegiate Championship 1964 and several regional events.

FORTIN, Raymond (b. 1945) of Montmagny PQ, physician. Won Canadian National Championship 1988. Played for Canada in 1989 Bermuda Bowl in Australia. Won more than 15 regionals.

FOSTER, Robert Fredrick (1853-1945) world famous authority on card games, invented the Rule of Eleven. Born in Scotland, Foster was a surveyor and prospector for gold and in this capacity traveled the globe. After making and losing two fortunes, he established himself as the world's leading authority on cards by writing *Foster's Complete Hoyle* (1897), a copy of which was inserted into the time capsule at the 1939 New York World's Fair. Although the Rule of Eleven is his chief theoretical contribution, he promoted numerous ideas in his *Vanity Fair* magazine column and in the *New York Sun*. His various writings traced the successive developments of bridge — auction and contract. Foster was an AWL Director and he later wrote the first set of laws for contract bridge. Up to age 85 he continued to lecture on games throughout the world and to teach and conduct games in New York. In addition to writing on various subjects, he wrote at least 50 books on card games.

FOUT, John (b.1967) of New York City, options trader. Member of USA II World Junior team in Denmark. A Diamond Life Master with more than 100 regional wins.

FOWLER, Candace (Candy) See GRIFFEY, Candace.

FOX, Betty (1903-1995) of Hove, England, bridge teacher and club owner. Won European Women's Teams 1966 and represented Britain in 2 other zonal championships. Many national wins included a sweep of all major women's events 1964. Former training officer of EBU.

FOX, G.C.H. (Foxy) (1914-1997) of Hove, England, bridge writer, teacher. Won 5 national titles and represented England in a Camrose Trophy match. Bridge columnist *Daily Telegraph* 1957-93, frequent magazine contributor and author of more than 8 books.

FOX, Gerry of Napa CA, bridge cruise director, bridge teacher, author. Instructor on 131 cruises over the past 30 years, has taught about 500 students per year for 30 years, author of four bridge teaching books.

FOX, John H. (b. 1933) of Cathedral City CA, physicist and mathematician. Served as consultant to U.S. and West German aerospace industries, owner Bacchus Press. Has authored best selling poker book *Play Poker, Quit Work and Sleep 'Til Noon*, authored other books on philosophy, humor and card play. Was handball champion, directs bridge cruises, contributed to *British Popular Bridge*. Diamond Life Master with more than 12,200 MPs as of 3/2001, placed 2nd North American Swiss Teams 1987, won more than 80 regionals.

FOX, Joseph L. (Joe) (b. 1937) of Mariposa CA, retired insurance company executive, partner in a winery. Won Men's Pairs 1977. More than 20 regional titles.

FOY, Nancy W. (b. 1956) of Memphis TN, meeting planner on staff of ACBL, graduate of Memphis State University, listed in *Who's Who Among Students in American Colleges and Universities*. Joined ABCL staff 1991.

FRAENCKEL, Rigmor (1909-1983) of Copenhagen, Denmark, bridge teacher. 3rd World Women's Team Olympiad 1960, won European Teams 1948, 49, 55, 57, 58; 2nd 1951. Many national titles.

FRANCES, Antonio de Velasco (b. 1962) of Madrid, Spain, lawyer notary. WBF World Master. 3rd European Community Pairs 1998. Represented Spain in 4 zonals and 2 European Junior Teams. National titles include Open Teams and Open Pairs several times.

FRANCIS, Dorthy A. (b. 1940) of Memphis TN, bridge writer, professional player, with gardening and handicrafts as hobbies. Co-editor of World Championship Daily Bulletins 1979-1987; co-editor of Junior World Championship Daily Bulletins 1995 and 1999; editor of the Fifth and Sixth Editions of the *Official Encyclopedia of Bridge*; contributor to ACBL *Bridge Bulletin,* edited several World Championship books. Won BOLS prize for best article on 1978 World Championships and several other IBPA bridge writing awards. Won her first Senior event on the first day she was eligible. Won WBF Transnational Women's Teams 2000, many regional wins.

FRANCIS, Henry G. (b. 1926) of Memphis TN, formerly of Nahant MA; editor, bridge columnist and former ACBL associate national tournament director. ACBL Honorary Member 1998, president International Bridge Press Association since 1996. Executive editor and publishing manager of ACBL publications 1973-97. Publications include ACBL *Contract Bridge Bulletin*, annual *World Championship Book* (1973-89 and 1995), Daily Bulletins at all North American Championships since 1972; *Laws of Contract Bridge* and *Laws of Duplicate Contract Bridge*. Executive Editor of editions IV, V and VI of the *Official Encyclopedia of Bridge*; editor of OKbridge's *The Spectator* 1999-2001; co-author of *The History of the Bermuda Bowl*; editor-in-chief of Daily Bulletins at world championships 1977-98; editor-in-chief of Junior World Championship Daily Bulletins 1991, 95, 99; weekly bridge columnist for *Boston Herald* and *Boston Herald-American* 1965-1990. President of Professional Tournament Directors Association 1968-72. Sportswriter for *Boston Traveler* starting in 1947, later served as copy, layout, sports and news editor for both the *Boston Traveler* and the *Boston Herald* until those papers closed shop in 1972. Tournament director 1958-72, assisting at and running tournaments mostly in Northeast and Maritime provinces of Canada. Founder and 1st editor of *New England Bridge Bulletin* 1955-64 and 1967-72. Won several bridge-writing prizes for articles in ACBL *Bridge Bulletin* and World Championships *Daily Bulletins*. Many regional wins.

FRANCO, Arturo (b. 1946) of Milan, Italy, World Grand Master. Won Bermuda Bowl 1974, 75, 2nd 1976, 79, 83 – lost in last 2 finals by only 5 IMPs in each case. Won European Teams 1973, 75, 79, 2nd 1977, 83. Many national wins.

FRANKEL, Jean (b. 1926) of New Orleans LA, bridge teacher and director, secretary of Unit 134 and District 10 for many years, certified director. Frankel placed 2nd Master Mixed Teams 1961, Women's Pairs 1965; Women's Teams 1968.

FRANKLIN, Harold (1915-1998) of Leeds, England, tournament director and bridge writer. Represented Britain in 2 zonal championships. National wins include Gold Cup twice. Former chief tournament director WBF and EBU. Former member EBL Laws Commission and WBF Tournament planning committee. Franklin represented Great Britain in international play in Europe, won British national team event, the Spring Fours. Broadcaster, magazine contributor and bridge columnist *Yorkshire Post*. Organizer of crossword solving competitions.

FRANKLIN, Marc S. (b. 1959) of Sherman Oaks CA. Manages policy issue and financial analysis in insurance, former banker. Organized and directed a duplicate bridge club for the 5 Claremont colleges during his education. National Merit Scholar, King of Bridge 1977. He and his brother (Matthew, King of Bridge - 1978) are the first siblings to have attained that title. All regional wins have been partnered by his brother; they won their first one at ages 12 and 14. (see MOSS, Andrew and Brad)

FRANKLIN, Matthew (b. 1961) of Palo Alto CA, research scientist. Collector of old bridge and whist books; AT&T Bell Labs PhD scholar 1989-93; has published numerous articles on cryptography. King of Bridge 1978, he and his brother Marc were the first siblings to attain that title. He and his brother, at ages 15 and 17, had several regional wins. (see MOSS, Andrew and Brad)

FRASER, A. A. Douglas (b. 1940) of Mount Royal PQ, retired bridge professional and bridge club owner, has served on Canadian Bridge Federation Board. WBF World Master. Fraser represented Canada in Rosenblum Teams 1978, 82, 86, 90; won CNTC 1992. Diamond Life Master, won Master Mixed Teams 1981, Men's Swiss Teams 1988, placed 2nd Master Mixed Teams 1974.

FRASER, Renate (b.1951), psychologist. European Women's Champion 1991, represented Austria in 3 other European events.

FRASER, Sandra E. (b. 1944) of Mount Royal PQ, born in New Zealand, Vice president financial administration. Has served as vice chairman for Eastern Canada of the ACBL Goodwill Committee. Former president Montreal B.L . Unit 151. Represented Canada in Rosenblum Teams 1982, 86, 90 and Women's Team Olympiad 1984, (placed 9th) and 5th in Swiss Plate. A Diamond Life Master, she won CNTC 1992, Master Mixed Teams 1981, placed 2nd Master Mixed Teams 1974, North American Women's Swiss Teams 1983, 88.

FRED, James David (Dave) (b. 1947) of Granger IN, associate professor of accounting-Indiana University. A certified director, treasurer of St. Joe Valley B.A. 1992-to date. Diamond Life Master, won 50+ regional events.

FREDD, Claudius G. (b. 1921) of College Park GA, retail liquor distributor. Won more than 300 American Bridge Association tournaments over 4 decades including ABA National Open Teams 1974. He is a former member of ABA Board, editor of ABA *Bulletin* and chairman of ABA Tournament Authority. Fredd is a former chess master.

FREDIN, Peter (b. 1969) of Malmo, Sweden. WBF World Master. 3rd World Teams 1998, World Pairs 1998. 2nd European Teams 1999, 3rd European Pairs 1997. Won Nordic Teams 1996, China Cup 1999. Also won Nordic Junior Teams and 7 Swedish titles.

FREED, Dr. Eugene (Gene) (b. 1930) of Los Angeles CA, plastic surgeon, specializing in ears, nose and throat. Treated such Hollywood personalities as Mario Lanza, Marie Callas, Alfred Drake, Chita Rivera, Larry of the Three Stooges and Mickey Cohen. Finished 11th World Open Pairs 1990, 20th World Mixed Pairs 1982; WBF World Master. Grand Life Master with 24,006 MPs as of 3/2001, ranked #14 in ACBL. Won Men's BAM Teams 1986, IMP Pairs 1988, 98; Silver Ribbon Pairs 1995. In 1991 won 3 events a week in 9 consecutive regionals partnered by Mike Passell. When his son Michael became a Life Master, he was the youngest at age 14.

FREEDMAN, Richard N. (Dick) (b. 1945) of Newton MA, computer programmer. With his background as a player and a director, Freedman tired of waiting for scores so he developed the first scoring program. Its first official use was at a sectional in Lexington MA 1977. This program was subsequently used in North American Championships in Chicago, Atlanta and Houston, a couple of regionals in New England and then the World Pairs Olympiad in New Orleans 1978. Has had several regional wins.

FREEDMAN, Robert P. (b. 1926) of Buffalo NY attorney. A member of ACBL Board of Directors 1956-57.

Won Open Pairs 1969, Master Mixed Teams 1956; placed 2nd Master Mixed Teams 1955, Life Master Pairs 1970. Diamond Life Master with numerous regional titles.

FREEMAN, Louise K. (Mrs. Richard, formerly Louise Robinson) of Atlanta GA. Won Master Mixed Teams 1961, has had several regional wins.

FREEMAN, Richard A. (Dick) (b. 1933) of Atlanta GA, managing director Oppenheimer and Co., Inc. Freeman was a "Quiz Kid" of radio fame 1942, 44, 45. Became ACBL's Youngest Life Master in 1952 at age 18. Member ACBL Hall of Fame. Served on Board of Governors 1976-80, directed from 1952-63 and was regionally ranked. Edited *Roth Stone System* and *Bridge is a Partnership Game*. World Grand Master, ranked #29 in world, won Bermuda Bowl 1995, 99, 2nd 97. Grand Life Master with 12,437 MPs as of 3/2001. Won Men's BAM Teams 1955, 62, 66; Master Mixed Teams 1961, Vanderbilt 1979, 2000; Spingold, 1993, 94, 95, 96, 98, 99; Reisinger 1993, 94, 95; USBC Team Trials 1998; Fishbein Trophy 1995. Placed 2nd Spingold 1959, Men's BAM Teams 1958, 77, 83; Reisinger 1965, Blue Ribbon Pairs 1970, Vanderbilt 1975, 96; GNOT 1983; Team Trials 1995, 97; Open BAM Teams 1998, 99.

FREILICH, Edith (formerly Kemp, nee Seamon) of Miami Beach FL, one of the great women players of all time. Member ACBL Hall of Fame. One of only two women (Helen Sobel Smith was the other) who have won all 3 major team championship events — the Reisinger (formerly the Chicago), Spingold and Vanderbilt. Grand Life Master with 11,669 MPs as of 3/2001. Represented ACBL several times in international competition, WBF World Master. Placed 2nd World Women's Pairs 1966, 5th 1986, 18th 1982; 2nd Venice Cup 1981, 5th Olympiad Women's Teams 1988. Her string of more than 30 national titles began in 1941 and includes Chicago (now the Reisinger) 1946, 52; Vanderbilt, Spingold 1963; Master Mixed Teams 1947, 52, 53, 57, 74; Open Pairs 1943, Women's BAM Teams 1951, 62, 65, 69; Women's KO Teams 1979, 80, 82, 84; North American Women's Swiss Teams 1982, Women's Pairs 1941, 42, 43, 46, 66, 79, 86; Life Master Women's Pairs 1967, 77, 79, 81. Placed 2nd Spingold 1953, 72; Reisinger (Chicago) 1964, Master Mixed Teams 1942, 45, 48, 64; Women's BAM Teams 1948, 55, 71; Women's Pairs 1957, 78; Life Master Women's Pairs 1962, 73, 74, 80; GNOT 1980, Life Master Pairs 1962, Women's KO Teams 1996. Won district and zonal GNOT 1976, 1980 and District in 1982.

FRENCH, Capt. Fred G. (1893-1937) of Philadelphia, an Army officer, bridge teacher and writer. Was 1931 president of ABL and member of Advisory Council which drafted and approved the Official System.

FRENCH, Marvin L. (b. 1927) of San Diego CA, retired senior engineer with General Dynamics Corp. A blackjack expert with many articles published under pen name "Marvin L. Master". Contributor to the *Bridge World, Contract Bridge Forum* (currently the editor) and *Popular Bridge*. Author of *Party Bridge* and many conventions and treatments including AmBIGuous Diamond System, 2♣ Game Try, Stoplight, Defense against Precision 1♦ Opening, Unbalanced Heart Convention, Omnibus and Non-Jump Splinters.

FRENDO, Paul (1923-1996) of Udine, Italy, public relations executive. Won European Teams 1969, EEC Senior Teams 1993. Many national titles. Contributor to several magazines.

88

FRENKIEL, Marian (1919-1995) of Warsaw, Poland, journalist. WBF World Master. Won Rosenblum Teams 1978. Represented Poland in many other world and zonal championships. Winner of many national titles. President of Polish Bridge Union 1973-1990. EBL Executive member 1983-1991.

FRESE, Dale H. (b. 1919) of Longwood FL, retired IRS agent. Diamond Life Master, has won more than 50 regionals.

FREW, David (b. 1943) of Edinburgh, Scotland, journalist. Represented Scotland 9 times in Camrose Trophy matches. Many national wins include 3 Scottish Cups.

FREY, Mable (Mrs. Richard L.) (1905-1993) of New York City, editor. Was recorder at many national and international championships, won 2 consecutive Women's Pairs at Eastern States Regional in partnership with her mother, Gussie Planco in 1935-36. Won other regionals with her husband Richard Frey.

FREY, Richard L. (1905-1988) of New York City, writer, editor and champion player. Public relations chief and editor of the ACBL *Bulletin* from 1958-1970, editor-in-chief of the first 3 editions of *Official Encyclopedia of Bridge* and edited 12 World Championship books. Member ACBL Hall of Fame. Put together bridge exhibitions and TV shows and was chief commentator at Bridge-o-Rama or vugraph exhibitions. After retirement in 1970, became president of International Bridge Press Association (IBPA), serving in that post for 11 years. Freelance writer on diverse non-fiction subjects for major magazines. His books on canasta published in 1950 and 1951 sold more than a million copies and his *According to Hoyle* in 1956 nearly three million. He was the author of *How to Win At Contract Bridge in Ten Easy Lessons* and several other books.

The new generation of bridge players who knew Frey as an editor and writer did not link him with personalities such as Culbertson, Sims, Vanderbilt, Jacoby and Schenken. But Frey was right there at the beginning of the heyday of contract bridge. He was an original member of the Bid-Rite Team and the Four Aces. The Bid-Rite team (David Burnstine, Charles Lockridge, Howard Schenken and Frey) was forerunner of the original Four Aces, formed in 1933 when Oswald Jacoby broke free from a Culbertson commitment and replaced Lockridge. At the age of 25 he had his first major tournament victory — the prestigious Goldman Pairs. In a relatively short playing career he won both the Vanderbilt and the Spingold in the same year on two occasions (1934 and 1942) along with several other national events. Some of his other successes include Asbury Park Challenge Teams 1933, Master Pairs, Grand National Teams (1934 and 35). He was second in 7 other NABCs. He had the best tournament record of any player in 1934 with another good year in 1942. He was #8 in the first group of players to be designated Life Masters when the category was created in 1936. For more than 20 years he had the highest percentage of North American Championship victories won out of events entered. In 1935 Frey resigned from the Four Aces to join the Culbertson organization as sales manager for Kem Cards. He was an editor of *The Bridge World* magazine, technical consultant on the Culbertson System and a player on Culbertson teams, often as Culbertson's partner. After the sale of Kem in 1937, Frey returned to the advertising business.

He had begun a daily newspaper bridge column in 1937, took over writing the Four Aces column in 1944

and in 1954 merged the two in collaboration with Howard Schenken. In 1970, when he turned the column over to Schenken, his was the longest continuously published syndicated bridge feature in the United States. From Culbertson to Charles Goren, Frey's writing frequently appeared under the byline of the bridge greats. He had the chameleon-like ability to change the style and flavor of his writing to fit that of the original. Following his retirement from the ACBL, he became chairman of the Goren Editorial Board, editor of the *Precision Club Newsletter* and a consultant on a variety of bridge projects. Frey was boss and mentor to a number of bridge personalities he brought to the League — Alan Truscott, Albert Dormer, Tannah Hirsch, Tom Smith, Steve Becker, Richard Oshlag and Sue Emery.

FRIEDBERG, Joel M. (b. 1954) of Arsdale NY, attorney, real estate investor, options trader, broker and former regional director. Friedberg finished 1st in Pan American Games 1983, 3rd Maccabiah Games 1977 and represented ACBL in World Olympiad New Orleans 1978, Miami 1986. He won Senior/Advanced Senior Master Pairs 1973, Mixed Pairs 1977, placed 2nd Men's Pairs 1984, Swiss Teams 1988, 89. Diamond Life Master, has won more than 50 regionals events.

FRIEDLAND, Dr. Peter (b. 1952) of Los Altos CA, chairman/founder of software company, former chief of Artificial Intelligence Research and Applications at NASA Ames Research Center. Captain of National Champion College Bowl Team-Stanford 1977. Served on both Unit and District Boards, contributor to *Palo Alto Kibitzer*. Won 31 regionals, placed 2nd ACBL Continent-wide Charity Game (1984) but was only 2nd in his local club in same event.

FRIEDLANDER, Jerome (Thumbs, Jerry) (1906-1995) of Jupiter FL, ACBL R4 tournament director since 1950. Was head director for Cavendish Invitational from its inception until 1978. Life Master #102, he was awarded a scroll in 1983 for 25 plus years as a tournament director in 1983 and received an honorary plaque in 1987 at the 50-year anniversary of the ACBL. Placed 2nd in the Golder Cup Pairs 1951. He had several regional wins.

FRIEDMAN, Maurice (Mickey) (b. 1939) of Boca Raton FL, president of art gallery, estate consultant, bridge teacher and managing editor *Goren Bridge Newsletter*. Has 15 regional wins.

FRISCHAUER, Edward (1895-1964) of Hollywood CA, born in Vienna Austria. Served in Austro-Hungarian Army during World War I, emigrated to U.S. in 1938 after Germany annexed Austria. Won world championship for Austria 1937, placed 2nd Spingold 1953. Considered to be one of the great dummy players of all time.

FROME, Si (b. 1928) of Lauderhill FL, retired, past president Louisiana Bridge Association. Placed 2nd Open Swiss Teams 1982; won 15+ regionals.

FRY, Sam, Jr. (1909-1991) of New York City, secretary of the Regency Whist Club. One of the outstanding American bridge players and personalities. Represented North America in the Bermuda Bowl 1959. Fry was Life Master #10 when that category was created in 1936, at 26 the youngest of the ten selected. His writings on bridge and other games include *How to Win at Bridge with Any Partner* and a modern edition of Watson's *Play of the Hand at Bridge*. He was a contributing editor of *The Bridge World* (1932-1966) and of the *Bridge Encyclopedia*. He won AWL Open Teams, Open Pairs 1933, 34; USBA Open Teams 1936, ABL Asbury Challenge Teams

1933, Men's Pairs 1934, Spingold 1937, 41, 45; Vanderbilt 1958. He placed 2nd in the Vanderbilt 1933, 35, 42; Master Mixed Teams 1957, Life Master Pairs 1940, Open Pairs 1933, 47.

FRYDRICH, Julian (b. 1937) born in Poland owner-manager of travel agency and journalist. WBF World Master. 3rd Bermuda Bowl 1976, 85; 2nd European Championships 1975, 85. Represented Israel in 3 other world championships and 12 other European Championships. Won more than 10 national titles. Edited Israel's Bridge Magazine 1971-72. Co-owner Israel's biggest club.

FU, Zhong (b. 1969) of Beijing, China. WBF World Master. Represented China in 2 world championships. Won China Cup Pairs 1998, 99. 2nd Far East Open Teams 1997. Won many national titles.

FUCIK, Jan (b. 1956) of Vienna, Austria, born in Czechoslovakia, insurance clerk and bridge professional. WBF World Life Master. Top Austrian masterpoint winner. Placed 2nd Bermuda Bowl 1985, World Team Olympiad 1988. Won European Open Teams 1985, European Junior Teams 1976. 2nd European Team Cup 1988, European Pairs 1985, and represented Austria on many other occasions. 2nd European Individual 1992. Won Statenbank 1988, 89. 16 national victories include 11 Open Teams.

FUKUSHIMA, Everett A. (b. 1944) of Aiea HI, attorney. Member ACBL Appeals Committee, past president Unit Board, certified director. Diamond Life Master, Hawaii Life Master of the Year 1990, 91, 92, 93, 94, 95, 97. Has over 50 regional wins.

FULWILER, C. H. (1886-deceased) of Albuquerque NM, investment and finance counselor. Was inventor of Fulwiler. President of Western Division ACBL in 1940, he served on ACBL Board of Directors. He had many regional wins.

FUNK, David (b. 1955) of North Garden VA, CFO of software company. Contributor to *Bridge World*. Won Blue Ribbon Pairs 1984. Has 20+ regional wins.

FURBECK, Barbara W. (b. 1924) of Wilmington DE, retired research chemist with one patent. Won Life Master Women's Pairs 1976.

FURMAN, David B. (b. 1941) of Lansdowne PA, financial analyst and collection specialist. Won North American Swiss Teams 1980.

FURNISH, Bradley J. (b. 1951) of Kansas City MO, economist, bridge teacher and club director. Has won 16+ regionals.

FURR, William F. (Bill) (1926-1995) of New Orleans, retired professor of mathematics. Editor of *ABA Bulletin* from 1982. Instrumental in integrating bridge in New Orleans in the early Sixties. Later was president of ABA Unit there. Certified director in ABA and ACBL. Head director of ABA in the Southwest. Life Master in both organizations.

G

GABARRET, Adolfo (1890-1956) of Buenos Aires, Argentina, writer and journalist. Pioneer of bridge in Argentina. Won South American Teams 1954, National Open Teams 1940, 41, 43. Participated in radio match against a Culbertson team in 1936. Columnist in bridge magazines and author of several books. Gabarret Cup was named in his memory.

GABRIEL, Charles P. (Garp, Charlie) (b. 1933) of Irving TX. Won GNOT 1975 and many regionals

GABRILOVITCH, Andrew (Andy) (b. 1925) of Vienna VA, retired director of administration for ITT. Escaped from Paris the day before German occupation, did mine sweeping during the war. Past president Washington Bridge League. The WBL honored him with the status of Life Member. Heavily involved in the fight to desegregate the WBL 1959-64. Retired from serious bridge in protest of cheating. Won Spingold 1961, 2nd 1959, won approximately 20 regionals.

GAER, Gerald W. (Jerry) (b. 1934) of Scottsdale AZ, bridge teacher and professional player. Served on Unit 354 Board and was president District 17 Board of Directors. Has been local and Unit tournament chairman; co-chaired Phoenix NABC 1995. Appointed to ACBL Appeals Committee 1991, regular contributor to Unit newsletter *Shuffle Deal and Play*. Grand Life Master. Won Senior Swiss Teams 1997, more than 100 regionals.

GAER, Margaret (Maggie) (Mrs. Gerald W.) (1921-1996) of Scottsdale AZ, retired bridge teacher and professional player. Grand Life Master with 12,717 MPs as of 3/2001, won Women's Pairs 1954, 64; Women's Teams 1959, Life Master Women's Pairs 1964; placed 2nd Mixed Pairs 1964. Many regional wins.

GALLEY, Dwight (b. 1949) of Sugarland TX, network engineer for Southwestern Bell. Chairman ABA National Appeals Committee 1992, chairman ABA National Tournament Committee 1986-88. Won 18 major ABA national championships (including 7 KOs and 3 Open Pairs), has had 9 KO Teams and 2 Open Pair 2nd place finishes. Won William A. Friend Award 1980, first ABA player to win more than 1000 points in one year. Has won several ACBL regionals.

GANDENBERGER, Dr. Kurt (b. 1951) of Pendleton SC, medical doctor, publisher. Began playing bridge at age 4, has been a certified director since 1974. Diamond Life Master, winner of more than 50 regionals.

GANDHI, Mohandas Karamchand (1869-1948) world-renowned Indian spiritual leader and advocate of the philosophy of active non-violence, not only indulged in occasional games of bridge but even used bridge as a metaphor to illustrate a basic Hindu belief. Gandhi was trained as attorney in England. During his years as a student, he emulated the British gentleman, taking dancing lessons, learning to play the violin and enjoying sessions of bridge. In fact, "Mahatma" (or "Great Soul," as he came to be called) insists that the very first occasion on which he felt the influence of God in his life came during a bridge game at an English resort. According to Gandhi, a female member of his foursome began making lascivious advances toward him. The lonely Gandhi, having left his bride at home in India, was about to succumb to temptation. Then the hand of God stopped him. As he advanced spiritually, Gandhi never denigrated his bridge playing or other youthful experiences, looking upon them as formative. In fact, when he later developed firm theological beliefs, mostly based upon orthodox Hinduism, he used bridge to discuss the relationship between "kharma" (predetermined fate and "dharma" (man's action). "Kharma is analogous to the hand dealt at bridge; Dharma is how man plays the hand. Man is not bound to a predetermined destiny because he may play his hand well or poorly. It is ultimately up to him whether he wins or loses. The final result of a man's life develops from his learning, striving and skill — not just from the hand he is dealt.

GANGULY, Sudhir (b. 1943) of Calcutta, India, clearing agency proprietor. Won Far East Open Teams 1977, 2nd BFAAME Open Teams 1985, won Far East Open Pairs 1979, and represented India in one other zonal championship. 18 national wins.

GARABELLO, Giuseppe (b. 1925) of Italy, businessman. World Life Master, won Bermuda Bowl 1973.

GARBER, Keith E. (b. 1945) of Pelham Manor NY, professional bridge player, day trader in stocks, former rubber bridge club owner. Member of original Precision Team, formed by C.C. Wei. Won Continent-wide Charity Fund Game 1978 and one of only two partnerships to win the Goldman Pairs twice (Roth-Haberman won 3 times). Won 25+ regionals.

GARBER, Ronald A. (1937) of Temecula CA, chemist, magazine editor of *Squeeze Books*, contributor Southern CA *Bridge News*. Has won between 18-20 regional events.

GARCIA, Ribeyro Jaime (b.1942) of Lima, Peru, lawyer and bank president. Represented Peru in 2 world championships and 10 zonal championships. Won many national titles.

GARCIA, Roberto Casalegno (b.1945) of Santiago, Chile, attorney. Represented Chile in 6 world championships and 15 zonal championships. Top player in Chilean rankings.

GARDENER, Nico (formerly Goldinger) (1908-1989) of London, England, born in Latvia, bridge teacher and writer. Won World Mixed Teams 1962. 2nd World Team Olympiad 1960. Won European Teams 1950, 1961; 2nd 1953. Represented Britain in 2 other world championships and 2 other zonal championships. Won Sunday Times 1970. National wins include Gold Cup. Founded and directed London School of Bridge. Co-author of 2 books. Devised Gardener Notrump Overcall. Won medals for ballroom dancing. (see FAMILY.)

GARDENER, Nicola. See SMITH, Nicola.

GARDNER, Craig (b. 1951) of Streamwood IL, chief financial officer. Won 40+ regionals. 3 time winner Art Glatt Award for most points won at the Central States Regional.

GARDNER, Eugene (b. 1936) of Bausman PA, investment adviser. Won North American Swiss Teams 1989 and 25+ regionals.

GARDNER, James L. (b. 1946) of Lansing MI, data processing consultant. Diamond Life Master, placed 2nd Men's Teams 1981. Resigned in protest from tournament play. Had more than 30 regional wins.

GARDNER, Mary of Streamwood IL, bridge teacher. Won more than 30 regionals including 3 District 13 NAOP titles.

GARDNER, Robert R. (b. 1946) of Chicago IL, chief financial officer. Diamond Life Master, won 28 regionals.

GARDNER, Thomas W. (Tom) (b. 1921) of Southfield MI, company vice president. Organizer (winner 2 years) of one University Team of Four championship (BAM), organizer of 1st Big Ten inter-university league of 4 schools. Has played with 5 generations of family from grandparents to grandchildren in tournament competition. Had 41 bombing missions in WW II and was awarded Distinguished Flying Cross and 7 other air medals. Headed the search for the site of the new Detroit Lions stadium. Served as 1st alternate for ACBL Board of Directors and on ACBL Board of Governors. Bridge instructor, gives free classes. Diamond Life Master with many regional wins.

GARGRAVE, Jeffrey J. (Jeff) (b. 1949) of Pasadena CA, tax attorney. Won national convention Battle Plan 1991. Involved in National and District committee work. Directs on bridge cruises. Diamond Life Master, won more than 30 regionals.

GAROFALO, Robert J. (Gazelle) (b. 1942) of Ridgefield NJ, professional bridge player and lecturer; CFO of small financal consulting firm. Manager of New Jersey's largest bridge club and one of the 10 largest ACBL clubs since 1992. Contributor to Unit 106 newsletter and *Bridge Today*. Unit 106 Player of Year 1987, won several regionals.

GAROZZO, Benito (b. 1927) of Wilmington DE, formerly of Rome, Italy and Boca Raton FL, retired jewelry store owner. Considered by many experts as the world's best player during his world championship years. Until 1976 was never on a losing team in international competition. Garozzo and Pietro Forquet formed one of the great partnerships of the world through 1972. From 1972 to 1976 he paired with Georgio Belladonna in what many considered to be the best partnership in the world at the time. Grand Master, ranks 2nd in world behind Bob Hamman through 2000. Member of Lancia Team that toured the United States in 1975. Co-creator (with Belladonna) of "Precision and Superprecision Bidding", "The Blue Club" and *The Italian Blue Team Bridge Book*. Won World Team Olympiad 1964, 68, 72; Bermuda Bowl 1961, 62, 63, 65, 66, 67, 69, 73, 74, 75 and placed 2nd in World Open Pairs 1970, Bermuda Bowl 1976, 79, 83; placed 4th in World Open Pairs 1966, 7th World Mixed Teams 1972, 6th Rosenblum Teams 1982, 7th Olympiad Open Teams 1984. Won World Par Contest in Geneva 1990, placed 2nd World Senior Pairs 1998. European Champion 1969, 71, 73, 75, 79. His Italian national wins include Italian Open Teams 1958, 63, 67, 68 among others. Won the Cap Gemini 1991. In ACBL won Men's Pairs 1971, North American Swiss Teams 1984, Senior KO Teams 1995; placed 2nd in Mixed Pairs 1983, Open Swiss Teams 1993, North American Swiss 1981, 83, 95, 2000. He has also won several regional titles. See BLUE TEAM.

GARRELL, Burton S. (Burt) (b. 1923) of Webster NY, retired mechanical engineer; tournament director 1957-1995.

GARYN, Stephen (b. 1936) of Melville NY, CPA. Placed 5th World Senior Swiss Teams 1994, 98. Has won approximately 60 regional events.

GATES, Bill founder of Microsoft, was richest man in United States. Enjoys playing computer bridge, frequently plays with Fred Gitelman against Warren Buffett and Sharon Osberg. Competed in Mixed BAM Teams 2000 and qualified for final.

GATES, Georgiana (b. 1945) of Houston TX, computer systems analyst. Contributor to *Bridge World*. Diamond Life Master, won Women's Pairs 1988, Women's KO Teams 1994; 2nd Women's KO Teams 1989, 96. Won many regionals.

GAULT, Annalee (b. 1941) of Raleigh NC, office manager, retired English teacher. Diamond Life Master, has won more than 30 regionals.

GAULT, Gregory F. (Greg) (b. 1941) of Raleigh NC, high school psychology teacher; expert in subliminal advertising. Was involved in local bridge in Tucson and has assisted wife running tournaments in Raleigh. A main witness in the Cokin/Sion case. Has won 30-40 regionals.

GAUTHIER, Francois (Frank) (b. 1927) of Montreal PQ, retired accountant and high school teacher. Owner,

managed and directed at his own bridge club. Co-authored *Amiliarons Notre Bridge*.Diamond Life Master, has won more than 15 regionals.

GAWRYS, Piotr (b.1955) of Warsaw, Poland, bridge professional and former architect. World Life Master. Won 1984 World Team Olympiad, 2nd Bermuda Bowl 1991. Won Trans-National Teams 2000. Won Cavendish Invitational Pairs 1990, 2nd 1992. Won European Individual 1992, European Open Teams 1993, European Open Pairs 1995, European Cup 1984, European Junior Pairs 1976. 2nd in European Junior Pairs in 1980. 3rd European Open Teams in 1991. Won Generali Individual 1992. Represented Poland in many World and European Championships. Winner of many Polish championships.

GELEERD, William L., Jr. (Bill) (b. 1930) of Highland Park IL, wine and spirits broker; retired Army Reserve Colonel-Intelligence Branch. Won Senior/Advanced Senior Pairs 1971.

GELLMAN, Adair (b. 1968) of Ashburn VA, programmer. Vice president-Youth Bridge Federation 1989-90, secretary Washington BL 1992-97. She has represented Juniors to ACBL Board of Directors and Board of Governors. Queen of Bridge 1985, became youngest female Life Master 1982 (14 years 6 months 4 days). Placed 2nd Mixed Pairs 1990.

GENUD, Maury (b. 1940) of Tarzana CA, child psychologist and teacher. ACBL analyst of the 1965 Team Trials report, former contributor to *Bridge World* and columnist for *Los Angeles Bridge News*. Won Open Pairs 1967, many regional events.

GEORGE, Noldy (b. 1961) of Jakarta, Indonesia, company employee. Won PABF (Far East) Teams 1991, 92, represented Indonesia in one world championship.

GERARD, Joan Levy (b. 1935) of White Plains NY, former 1st grade teacher, administrator for private boys and girls camps, assistant to general manager of hotel handling personnel, purchasing, advertising, catering and sales. Has served in all aspects of bridge administration starting at the Unit level. Member ACBL Goodwill Committee and Charity Foundation. Unit 188 secretary 1969, tournament chairman 1975, president 1976. District 3 president 1976-85, became District 3 representative to ACBL Board of Directors 1985, was elected ACBL president 1992, chairman of Board 1993, appeals administrator 1995, 96; World Bridge Federation representative 1993-present, vice president WBF 1999-present. Contributor to all Unit and District newsletters, won several regionals.

GERARD, Ronald (Ron) (b. 1944) of White Plains NY, attorney, Contributor to *Bridge World* and authored *1-2-3 Two-Bids*, placed 13th Rosenblum Teams 1982. 12th in world World Simultaneous Pairs 1988. Diamond Life Master, won Spingold, Blue Ribbon Pairs 1981, Men's Teams 1985, Vanderbilt 1990; placed 2nd GNOT 1976, GNOP 1980, 83; Men's Teams 1983; Vanderbilt 1994, 95. Placed 2nd Cavendish Invitational Pairs 1994 and 5th 1990. Numerous regional wins.

GERBER, John (1906-1981) of Houston, famous as the inventor of the Gerber 4♣ ace-asking bid and one of the leading players and personalities in bridge. Member ACBL Hall of Fame. Served 2 years on ACBL Board of Directors and was a highly important and influential power in bridge politics. At North American Championships, an early riser, he could usually be found in a comfortable chair in the hotel lobby, collecting and dispensing information. Npc of North American Teams in Bermuda Bowl competitions of 1962, 63, 65.

He was in the eye of a storm on more than one occasion. In 1962 in New York he split the partnerships of Bobby Nail-Mervin Key and Lew Mathe-Ron von der Porten, putting Mathe and Nail together in an unusual move that worked well and almost took the title from Italy. The next year in St. Vincent, Italy, he again broke up a long established partnership, pairing Nail with Howard Schenken and benching Peter Leventritt and Jim Jacoby. This move was not successful and may have cost the Americans the championship. It followed a little known incident that occurred at the time Gerber arrived at the Grand Hotel Bilia. An anonymous letter written in Italian was delivered to him. He secured a translator, but after the first paragraph was read to him, he asked the translator to stop; to deliver the letter to Italy's captain, Carl' Alberto Perroux and to explain that Gerber had listened only to the first paragraph. The writer had accused the Blue Team of cheating. Perroux, after reading the letter to his team, suggested that the match be played with screens running across the tables (this was 12 years before present-day screens were employed) - but Gerber would have none of it. The goodwill engendered by this exchange inspired Perroux and his team to present their championship trophies to Gerber and the American team in what was described as the greatest act of sportsmanship in bridge history. When Gerber's daring move to pair Schenken with Nail backfired, he faced a lot of flak, but the Board nevertheless appointed him captain of the next Bermuda Bowl team in 1965. That was the time when 2 members of his team brought cheating charges against a British partnership. Gerber spent 10 minutes in the grandstand watching the famous British pair who were accused of using finger signals to tell each other how many hearts were held. The 10 minutes were enough to convince him and he became one of the strongest witnesses against the pair when the World Bridge Federation suspended them.

A very strong captain, Gerber was a great player in his own right. He represented North America in the Bermuda Bowl in Buenos Aires 1961 and won the Chicago (now the Reisinger) 1964, Master Mixed Teams 1964, Men's Pairs 1959, Men's Teams 1953 and placed 2nd in the Spingold 1954, 67; Chicago 1957, 59; Men's Pairs 1957, Master Mixed Teams 1967, Mixed Pairs 1953, 68; Life Master Men's Pairs 1974. (See BUENOS AIRES AFFAIR)

GERENTOPOULOS, Panos (b.1949) of Athens, Greece, university lecturer, land surveyor, bridge administrator. Vice president of World Bridge Federation since 1998; Executive Council member since 1992; chairman Youth Committee since 1992. Honorary secretary of European Bridge League since 1995; member Executive Committee 1985-95; chairman Youth Committee since 1985, and Press and Publications Committee since 1987. Established European Junior Pairs (1991), European Schools Teams (1994), World Junior Pairs and World Junior Camp (both 1995). Established and operated WBF and EBL Internet sites starting in 1995. Editor of *EBL News* and *EBL Review* 1998-2000. Awarded EBL Silver Medal 1991 for services to European bridge. Named Bridge Personality of the Year 1995 for activities in youth bridge. Chief organizer of 1991 European Union Championships in Athens. Member IBPA Executive. Has written, in Greek, on Victory Point Scales and Comparability of Pairs Movements. Magazine contributor and former columnist.

GERK, Carole (formerly MacLean) (b. 1942) of Eden Prairie MN, client relations representative. President Unit 103 1984-88; Unit 178 1944-90; represented both Units on District Board 1983-90; chaired GNOP and GNOT tournament, co-chaired Minneapolis NABC 1994. Has won several regional events.

GERSTMAN, Daniel M. (Dan) (b. 1948) of Buffalo NY, financial planner. Won Open Pairs 1981, Life Master Men's Pairs 1982, placed 2nd Open Pairs 1982, 83. Diamond Life Master, has won numerous regionals.

GHAZI, Rashidul (b. 1948), of Karachi, Pakistan, bank executive. Won BFAAME Open Pairs 1985 and played in 3 world championships. Many national titles.

GHESTEM, Pierre (1929-2000) of Lille, France, retired merchant. Grand Master, won Bermuda Bowl 1956, World Team Olympiad 1960, European Championship 1953, 55, 62, 2nd 1956, 61. Represented France Bermuda Bowl 1954, 61, 63. 3rd PAMP Pairs 1990. Former world checker champion and French chess champion. Inventor of complex Monaco System with which he had many major success with Rene Bacherich.

GHOSE, Santanu (b. 1948) of Calcutta, India, civil engineer, computer programmer and businessman. 4th World Open Teams 1988. Won BFAAME Open Teams 1997, 2nd 1985, 89. 2nd BFAAME Open Pairs 1985. Represented India in 8 other world championships and one other zonal championship. 17 national wins. Won Epson Play Award 1987. Member WBF Laws Committee, Convention Card Committee and several Appeals Committees. Chairman Laws Committees of BFAAME and BFI. Joint Secretary (Technical) Bridge Federation of India 1981-92 and 1994-to date. BFAAME *Daily Bulletin* Editor 1991.

GHOSH, Sukha Ranjan (b. 1935) of Calcutta, India, retired government servant. Won Far East Teams 1977 and represented India in 2 other zonal championships and 4 world championships. 24 national wins.

GIANERA, J. Howard (b.1936) of Wayzata MN, owner of 9 childcare centers; former mayor of La Crescenta CA, former president and vice-present San Diego Unit. Won 21 regionals.

GIBBS, Gordon M. (1898-1968) of Rochester NY. Had the unique distinction of serving as the last president of the ABL and the first president of the ACBL (1937). Also served as ACBL treasurer 7 years. His massive figure — he was a member of the New York Giants football team — was a familiar sight at early tournaments. Won several regionals.

GIDDINGS, Ruth of Dublin, Ireland. The most successful Irish player ever, judged by appearances in international competition. 2nd European Women's Teams 1954, 73, 3rd 1952, 61, 62. Represented Ireland regularly from 1951 for more than 30 years. Represented Ireland in the Camrose in 1951, one of very few women to play in that event.

GIELKENS, Ine (b. 1957), of Monnickendam, The Netherlands, mathematics teacher. WBF World Master. 2nd Venice Cup 1989 and represented The Netherlands in 2 other world championships and 2 European Championships. Won National Women's Pairs 1991.

GILL, Robert J. (1889-1983) of Baltimore, retired attorney. ACBL president 1941, chairman of the ACBL Committee on Membership Eligibility 1952. Honorary Member 1945.Served in both World Wars and received many military decorations. In 1945 he was appointed chief military counsel to Supreme Court Justice Robert Jackson at the War Trials in Nurenburg.

GILPIN, Alfred B. (Big Al) (1915-1984) of Riverside CA, bridge teacher and club director. Was an active member of the ACBL Board of Governors from 1964, its vice chairman 1980-82 and a member of the Board of Directors 1969-75. Served 2 terms as president of the Western Conference and was a member of its assembly for 9 years. Retired from the US Civil Service Commission where he had been project head for the Navy Air-Launched Missile program.

GIMKIEWICZ, Benno (b. 1922) of Bangkok, Thailand, born in Germany, merchant. Won PABF (Far East) Teams 1963, 1966. Represented Thailand in 8 world championships. Won 5 national titles. Former member WBF Executive Council and WBF 3rd vice-president. Former Hon. Secretary Far East Bridge Federation (now PABF). Chief tournament director Far East Championships 1975. Former columnist *Bangkok Nation Review*.

GISH, Robert of El Monte CA, bridge teacher, professional bridge player. Won 15+ regionals.

GITELMAN, Fred (b. 1965) of Toronto ON, computer programmer specializing in bridge software. Creator of Gaming Zone software for online Microsoft bridge game. Creator of Base III, Bridge Master and Pendergraph vugraph program. WBF World Master. Member ACBL Junior team, placed 2nd Bermuda Bowl 1995, World Junior Championships 1991. Regular partner of Microsoft founder Bill Gates on internet. Represented ACBL in Epson International bridge tournament Tokyo 1984, 85. Represented Canada in Maccabiah games 1993. Won Open BAM Teams 1998, placed 2nd Life Master Pairs 1999, Spingold 2000. Won more than 15 regionals.

GLASER, Leo (The Leaper) (b. 1946) of Winfield BC, born in Sweden, bridge professional and teacher. Director on Microsoft Gaming Zone. Has won 40 regionals.

GLASSON, Joann (b. 1946) of Pennington NJ, credit union president Diamond Life Master, placed 2nd in first McConnell Cup 1994. Won Women's KO Teams 1994, 2nd Women's BAM Teams 1996. Won numerous regionals.

GLATT, Arthur (1909-1975) of Lincolnwood IL, financial consultant, was technical adviser to the TV program *Championship Bridge*. Won Men's Pairs, Men's Teams 1946, Open Pairs 1951; was 2nd in Chicago (now the Reisinger) 1936, Mixed Pairs 1936, Spingold 1948, Life Master Pairs 1949, 52; Men's Teams 1962. Won numerous regionals.

GLENN, Bob (b. 1948) of Chicago IL, professional bridge player since 1983, former vice-president of management consulting firm. Grand Life Master with more than 13,000 MPs, won more than 130 regional events.

GLENN, Richard M. (Dick) (b. 1917) of Sarasota FL, retired stock broker, also founded and operated a large personnel placement service. Diamond Life Master, won several regionals. He won his first tournament on board the S.S. France at age 12 in 1930 and played with 27 different partners at the time they become Life Masters.

GLICK, Jefferson (Jeff) (1906-1985) of North Miami Beach, bridge administrator, was instrumental in organizing the Florida Unit, subsequently the largest ACBL unit, was its president 1949-65 and executive manager from 1965-79. Chairman of 2 international tournaments and 4 North American Championships, all held in Miami. ACBL president 1955, ACBL Honorary Member 1964. Npc of U.S. team that placed 2nd in Bermuda Bowl 1956. Won Spingold 1949, Chicago (now the Reisinger) 1949, Men's Teams 1947, 48, 54, 58; Mixed Pairs 1941, Asbury Challenge Teams 1934. Placed 2nd Spingold 1934, 52; Chicago 1952.

GLICK, Vera (Mrs. Jefferson) of Miami Beach, served as co-chairman of the 1975 Summer NABC held in Miami. Won Women's Teams 1953, Mixed Pairs 1941 and many regional titles.

GLUBOK, Brian (Gluby) (b. 1959) of New York City, bridge professional, novelist, rubber bridge player. Since 1985 has divided his time between New York and Sydney, Australia. In 1989 he was granted residency status in Australia (in recognition of his bridge achievements) through the category "Special Talents - Sporting".) He became a Life Master at age 15 and his first "major" win was the prestigious Eastern States KO Teams 1980. At 20 was youngest to win this event. At 17 was a finalist in Reisinger partnered by Oswald Jacoby. At 18 again partnered with Oswald Jacoby he competed in the 5th annual Goldman Pairs. Jacoby who had won the first one in 1927 advised Glubok to "quit bridge and go back to college." Glubok won the International Bridge Press Association Romex Award (for the best bid hand of 1990-91) with Edgar Kaplan. WBF World Master, placed 4th World Open Pairs 1990, 17th Rosenblum Teams 1990. Won Spingold 1987, Reisinger 1991, Open Swiss Teams 1996, 97, 99; placed 2nd Spingold 1980, 83, 86; GNOT 1981, Blue Ribbon Pairs 1990. Was 2nd in Mott-Smith Trophy 1990, Open BAM Teams 1994. Won gold medal in Maccabian Games 1983, won Australian National Open Teams 1990 (2nd in 1987). Has placed high in international money tournaments including being a 4-time winner of the Cavendish Teams, most recent 1993, 3rd 1990, 4th 1991; Canadian Invitational Pairs 1st 1993, 2nd 1992. Has won dozens of regionals. A contributor to the *Bridge World*, ACBL *BULLETIN, Popular Bridge, Australian Bridge, New Zealand Bridge*, he also writes on non-bridge subjects.

GLYNNE, Anthony Christopher (Tony) (b. 1947) of Portland OR, born in United Kingdom, formerly of Birmingham, England; professional bridge player, teacher and director. In 1967 became education producer of Uganda TV in East Africa and while there he climbed Mt. Kilimanjaro. From 1970-75 was the senior producer for BBC radio in Birmingham and interviewed a variety of entertainment stars. Represented England in Camrose Trophy match vs. Wales 1975. Won British University Team Championship 1966; represented ACBL in Pan American Championships 1992. Placed 2nd Open Pairs 1992. Diamond Life Master, has won more than 200 regional events since 1976.

GODED, Federico (b. 1951) of Madrid, Spain, public official and bridge professional. WBF World Master. Represented Spain in 3 world championships and 6 zonals. Columnist. Author of 5 books. National titles include Open Teams and Open Pairs several times.

GODFREY, Kerr M. (Deputy Dog) (b. 1951) of Houston TX, bridge teacher, former deputy constable. Directs locally and at tournaments. Diamond Life Master, has won 21 regionals.

GOENKA, Prem Chand of Guwahati, India, chairman of carbon company. BFAAME founder-president 1978 and now president emeritus, with number of member countries increasing from 5 to 14. President of Indian Bridge Federation 1971-74, 1976-78, 1980-84. President emeritus 1984-to date. During his presidency the number of players rose from 430 to more than 12,000 and the number of organizations from 12 to 27. Pioneered carbon production in India. Chairman of Confederation of Indian Industries. President Assam Manufacturers Association. Former president of Table Tennis Federation of India.

GOKHALE, Avinash S. (b. 1947) of Pune, India, advertising agent. WBF World Master. 4th World Open Teams 1988, represented India in 4 other world championships. 2nd BFAAME Open Teams 1989. 16 national wins. Joint secretary Bridge Federation of India 1980. BFAAME *Daily Bulletin* editor 1983. Former editor of *Bridge Digest*.

GOLD, Sam (1908-1982) of Montreal, retailer, tournament director member of National Laws Commission. Was one of the leading Canadian players. In 1948 became Life Master #132, the 2nd Canadian to achieve that rank. Represented Canada 1964 World Team Olympiad and won Canadian-American Open Teams 1952, 54, 66, 67, Men's Pairs 1956, 57 and was a member of the Montreal Intercity Team that won the Congress Trophy in Montreal 1967 and in New York 1968. Charter member of Montreal Bridge League in early Thirties and was instrumental in having the MBL affiliate with the ACBL in 1946. Contributed many new tournament movements to the ACBL, the most notable being the Three-Quarter Movement, a version or which is used for most one-winner duplicate games.

GOLDBERG, (nee McGinley) Constance S. (Connie) (b. 1956) of Merion Station PA, options trader. Youngest woman Life Master at age 17 in 1974. Played as a teenager in the early Seventies, then quit for 25 years. She restarted in 1995 and after only 4 years back in tournament play she qualified to play in the Venice Cup in 2000. WBF World Master. Won Women's BAM Teams 1997, Women's KO Teams 1999; placed 2nd Women's Swiss Teams 1997; and has about 30 regional wins.

GOLDBERG, Freddie (Mrs. Richard) of Nashville TN, formerly of Memphis, former bridge teacher. Her active bridge career proved a valuable background for her role as wife of the ACBL Executive Secretary (Richard Goldberg 1971-84). Member of the ACBL Goodwill Committee, won several regional events.

GOLDBERG, Richard L. (Dick) (1922-1999) of Nashville TN, formerly of Memphis, was ACBL executive secretary and general manager 1971-1984. His first official connection with the ACBL was as a regional tournament director in 1959, was promoted to national tournament director 1961. He was brought to ACBL National Headquarters in New York to take over tournament scheduling in 1963. He was groomed for ACBL's top job by serving as assistant to Easley Blackwood, Executive Secretary 1965-71. He succeeded Blackwood. The smooth transition of ACBL Headquarters from Greenwich to Memphis was achieved under his aegis. Active in World Bridge Federation affairs, Zone II representative 1972, WBF secretary 1981, later became treasurer and financial director. Member of ACBL Laws Commission, Goodwill Committee and editorial board of the *Bridge Encyclopedia*. Member of WBF Committee of Honor.

GOLDBERG, Steve (b. 1945) of Las Vegas NV, gaming expert. Placed 3rd WBF Continuous Pairs 1990, 5th/8th Rosenblum Teams 1994. Won Reisinger 1972, Spingold 1974, placed 2nd Men's Teams 1973, won approximately 15-20 regionals.

GOLDBERG, Victor (b. 1923) of Glasgow, Scotland, company director. Represented Great Britain in 2 European Championships and one Common Market Championship. Represented Scotland in winning the Camrose Trophy 1964, 65, the first victories by non-English teams. 47 Camrose appearances is a record. Won Gold Cup 1969, 73, 76 and Sunday Times Pairs 1980. Won Scottish Cup 8 times, Scottish National Pairs 3 times.

GOLDER, Benjamin M. (1894-1946) died the day before the close of his term as 1946 ACBL president. Member of Pennsylvania State Legislature 1916-24, later elected to the U.S. House of Representatives, where he served from 1924-33. ACBL Honorary Member 1947. A trophy in his memory, the Golder Cup, was put into play 1947.

GOLDFEIN, Jerome R. (Jerry) (b. 1956) of Chicago IL, office manager for law firm, former options trader. Teaches beginning bridge, became a Life Master at age 18 and won first national championship at 22. Won GNOT 1979, 91; placed 2nd Vanderbilt 1982, Spingold 1983, GNOT 1984, 88, 95; GNOP 1995, 96; North American Swiss Teams 1988, 89; Reisinger 2000. Diamond Life Master with more than 25 regional wins.

GOLDMAN, Robert (Bobby) (1938-1999) of Highland Village TX, bridge professional, former vice president cable television company. Member ACBL Hall of Fame. High school singles tennis champion and as a freshman at Drexel University was captain of Mid-Atlantic Conference basketball champions 1957-58. Seved as ACBL recorder 1986-88. In early Seventies Goldman taught bridge classes, as many as 17 per week; wrote lesson plans, computer bridge practice hands, a computer program to evaluate bidding probabilities and TV scripts for *Play Bridge with the Experts*. Originator of Super Gerber (Kickback), Exclusion Blackwood, Goldman after Stayman and other elements of Aces Scientific System. Author of *Aces Scientific* and *Winners and Losers at the Bridge Table*. Was prominent in President's Advisory Committee activities, i.e. alerts, conventions, slow play, ethics, committee (appeals) precedent book. Was one of world's leading players, Grand Master in both WBF and ACBL (won more than 18,500 MPs). Member of first Aces team put together by Ira Corn in 1968, .remained a member team until 1974. Won Bermuda Bowl 1970, 71, 79; World Mixed Teams 1972. Represented U.S. in Bermuda Bowl 1969, 73, 74; competed in other World Bridge Federation events 1972, 78, 84. He placed 5th-8th in the World Olympiad Teams in Seattle 1984. In 1977 he won both the pair and team event at the Pan-American Invitational Championships. Won Life Master Men's Pairs 1964, Life Master Pairs 1968, Open BAM Teams 1993; Men's Teams 1968, 89, 91; Spingold 1969, 78, 83, 86, 88; Reisinger 1970, 76, 80; Vanderbilt 1971, 73, 78, 98; North American Swiss Teams 1998. Placed 2nd Vanderbilt 1966, 70, 76; Spingold 1970, 90, 94, 96; Reisinger 1968, 86, 90, 93, 95; Blue Ribbon Pairs 1968, Men's Teams 1969; Life Master Pairs 1968; Men's BAM Teams 1984; GNOT 1998. Had won 3 world championships, 2 NABC pair events and many NABC team events before ever winning his first regional pair event in 1974.

GOLDSMITH, Arthur S. (1909-1995) of Lyndhurst OH, retired attorney. Life Master #41. Won Spingold 1949, Chicago (now the Reisinger) 1949, Men's Teams 1947, 54, 58; placed 2nd Spingold 1946, 52; Chicago 1952.

GOLDSMITH, Jeff (b. 1961) of Pasadena CA, computer graphics engineer, internet sofware engineer; inventor internet bridge movies. Author of convention "Puppet Major Raises". Served on District 23 Board of Directors 1992-present and ABCL Appeals Committee 1998-present. Won approximately 40 regionals.

GOLDSTEIN, Abraham M. (Abe) (1902-1982) of Flushing NY, bridge teacher and director for more than 25 years, club owner for 10 years. Mentor of many young players who became successful, notably Robert Levin.

Authored *Common-Sense Bridge for the Intermediate Player*. Won a few regionals.

GOLDSTEIN, Barry (b. 1952) of Yonkers NY, attorney, instructor domestic violence classes. Served as ACBL Area Manager in Westchester for the education program and was a bridge professional. Before retiring from bridge he accumulated 18 regional wins including the first Jerry Machlin Open Pairs 1983. In 1990 when he won Albany Flight A Stratified Pairs, his 85 year-old partner, Manny Dannet, was winning his first regional.

GOLDSTEIN, Fredrick (Rick) (b. 1946) of White Plains NY, New York State parole officer, former special education teacher. Co-owner and full- time manager of The Bridge Deck in Westchester. Diamond Life Master, has won between 50 and 75 regionals.

GOLDSTEIN, Gratian B. (b. 1919) of Coral Gables FL, retired, import business owner. Diamond Life Master, won Women's Pairs 1947, 48; Women's Teams 1948, 53; Life Master Women's Pairs 1969; Master Mixed Teams 1955, 58; placed 2nd Women's Pairs 1953, Blue Ribbon Pairs 1966, Women's Teams 1971, Mixed Pairs 1972, Mixed Teams 1967.

GOLDSTEIN, Lin (b. 1962) of Butte MT, software engineer. Won first NABC Non-Life Master Pairs event 1981.

GOLDSTEIN, Stephen D. (Steve) (b. 1947) of Elkins Park PA, options trader and bridge teacher, former lawyer, newspaper reporter. Wrote daily bridge column for *Washington Times* 1982-96; served on Boards of WBL 1994-95 and GNYBA 1974-76. Diamond Life Master, won Men's Teams 1974, placed 2nd Vanderbilt and Reisinger 1974. Has more than 20 regional titles.

GOLDWATER, Henry A. (Harry) (1901-1995) of Yonkers NY, ACBL national tournament director since 1957. Starting in 1962 he served as an adviser to the ACBL Laws Commission and was a contributing editor to the *Bridge Encyclopedia*. Inventor of Goldwater's Rule: "If he doesn't know whose lead it is, he probably doesn't know what to lead. Accept his lead out of turn."

GOLDWATER, Robert A. (Bob) (b. 1924) of Hartsdale NY, bridge teacher, formerly in public relations. Was sports information director of Fordham University and did promotion work with New York State Olympic Committee. Has served on Unit 188 Board of Directors since 1967 and held various executive positions including president, vice-president, tournament chairman. Has written Sunday bridge column for Gannett Suburban Newspapers since 1976.

GOLIAS, Tipton (b.1941) of Beaumont TX, president Helena Labs; won Spingold 1997; placed 2nd Open Swiss Teams 1994, 99; has won many regionsls.

GOMEZ-DIAZ, Gala de Reschko de of Las Palmas, Canary Islands, tournament organizer. Many national titles include Open Teams Women's Teams and Mixed Pairs. Member of Spanish Open Team in one world championship and 2 European Championships. Represented Spain in women's and mixed play on 21 occasions including 6 other world championships. As delegate for Spain, proposed World Women's Team contest which became Venice Cup. She and husband "Juanfis" Gomez-Diaz were chief organizers of 1974 World Pairs Olympiad in Las Palmas.

GONG, Fang-Wen (b. 1958) of Taipei, Taiwan, civil engineer. WBF World Master. Member Taiwan women's team in 7 zonal championships and 5 world championships since 1990.

GOODEN, George S. (1904-1981) of Carmel CA, bridge writer, lecturer, tour conductor, member ACBL Board of Directors 1959 and president of ABTA 1962-63. Taught more than 250,000 pupils, lectured on radio and in department stores. Authored many books and booklets for teaching purposes including *Contract Bridge Bidding and Play: Self-Teaching Lesson Course for Beginning Players*. Also co-authored *Sherlock Holmes, Bridge Detective*. Won World Olympic Par contest 1941.

GOODMAN, Aaron (b. 1901) of Montreal, born in England, export/import businessman. Served as treasurer and director of Canadian Bridge Federation, director and president of the Montreal BL. Won Men's Pairs 1942 and several regional titles.

GOODMAN, Andy (b. 1946) of San Francisco CA, investment manager. Previously founded and ran Professional Sports Publications, the nation's largest publisher of sports programs. Won his 1st and 2nd regional titles on the same day (1988) and he won 4 events at Wine Country regional in 1991. Won Vanderbilt 1992, Open BAM Teams 1994; placed 2nd Red Ribbon Pairs 1992.

GOODWIN, Jude. See HANSON, Jude Goodwin.

GOPPERT, Clarence H. (1908-99) of Valley Center CA, retired banker who had control of substantial interests in 20 banks. Purchased his first "tiny" bank 1941. Began horse racing business 1982. Honored as "Donor of the Year" 1988, as "Kansas City Donor of the Year" 1991, honorary degrees from Wm. Jewell and Avila Colleges. Established the Goppert Foundation in 1959. Didn't become Life Master until age 65 but then acquired more than 9000 points by age 73 to become a Diamond Life Master. Won McKenney Trophy (now Crane Top 500) in 1979 at age 71 after open-heart surgery and was 2nd in 1976. Won more than 200 regionals.

GORDON, Agnes L. (1906-1967), renowned American bridge player. Born in Ontario, she moved to Buffalo NY but remained a Canadian citizen for life. Placed 2nd World Women's Teams 1964, represented US in Turin, Italy, 1969, New York 1962. Won the Chicago (since 1965 the Reisinger) 1948; Master Mixed Teams 1951, 56, 62; Women's Pairs 1961; Mixed Pairs 1961; Women's Teams 1967; placed 2nd Master Mixed Teams 1955, Mixed Pairs 1956, Women's Teams 1957, 63, 64; Women's Pairs 1959, Life Master Women's Pairs 1964 and had many regional victories. Noted for her grace and courtesy at the bridge table as well as her effervescence away from it. Her score of 506 1/2 on a 325 average (78%) with Eric Murray is one of the highest single-session scores ever recorded at an NABC.

GORDON, Dianna M. (b. 1944) of Toronto, travel agent. WBF World Life Master, Won World Mixed Pairs 1982, 3rd Venice Cup 1989, 4th Women's Teams Olympiad 1976, 88; 7th 1980, 9th 1984; 6th World Women's Pairs 1986; 8th World Mixed Pairs 1978; 5th Swiss Plate 1984. Also represented Canada in world competition Monte Carlo 1976, New Orleans 1978, Valkenburg 1980, Seattle 1984, Venice 1988, Yokohama 1991, Salsomaggiori, Italy, 1992, Santiago, Chile 1993. Won North American Women's Swiss Teams 1985, placed 2nd Women's Teams 1981, North American Women's Swiss Teams 1983. Won Canadian Open Pairs Championship 1982, 2nd 1989. Won all Canadian Women's National championships attended 1975-94. She has also won many regional titles.

GORDON, Fritzi (1916-1992) of London, England, born in Austria. WBF Grand Master. Won World Women's Teams 1964, World Women's Pairs 1962, 74; World Mixed Teams 1962. 2nd World Women's Pairs 1970. Won European Women's Teams 1950, 51, 52, 59, 61, 63, 75. Represented Britain on 8 other occasions. Many national wins include 2 Gold Cups. Partnership with Rixi Markus was once the best in women's play.

GORDON, Irving (b.1940) of Surrey, England, born in Scotland, proprietor of recruitment consultancy. Won World Seniors Pairs 1998. Represented Britain European Championship 1970 and England in Camrose Trophy. Won 2 Gold Cups and other national titles.

GORDON, Linda (b. 1944) of New York City, retired high school guidance counselor. Won IMP Pairs 1987, Mixed Pairs 2000, competed in *Bridge World* Challenge the Champs with husband (Robb Gordon). Won more than 20 regionals.

GORDON, Loula. See ZOUGHEB, Loula.

GORDON, Robert M. (Robb) (b. 1956) of New York City, options trader, former air traffic controller. Was member ACBL Board of Governors, ACBL Appeals Committee for many years. Has been a member *Bridge World* Master Solvers Panel. Diamond Life Master, won IMP Pairs 1987, 2nd Open Pairs 1986, has won 20-30 regionals.

GORDY, Edward L. (1904-1979) of West Palm Beach FL. Was for a long time a driving force in the American Bridge Teachers Association, which he served as president 1975 and as director-at-large 1979. Gordy and his wife, Laura Jane, devised valuable flash cards for teaching the play of the hand and a game kit to improve one's bridge playing ability — "Easy Bridge". They also served as club directors and cruise directors. He produced the ABTA's *Standard American Report* for bridge teachers, contributed many articles to various bridge publications.

GORDY, Laura Jane (b. 1912) of West Palm Beach FL, bridge teacher and writer. With her late husband Edward devised flash cards, the "Easy Bridge" game. Served as regional vice president of ABTA.

GOREN, Barry (Kid Zero) (b. 1960) of Chicago IL, options trader, former bridge teacher and professional. Lived in Tel Aviv, Israel 1970-79, graduated high school and learned to play bridge there. Played in Epson Tournament (collegiate team) Tokyo 1985, competed in international competition Biarritz 1982 and Geneva 1990. Won 15+ regionals.

GOREN, Charles Henry (1901-1991) world's foremost bridge authority for most of the last half of the 20th century. Known to millions as "Mr. Bridge." They bought his books, attended his lectures, took lessons from his accredited teachers, "traveled with Goren" on bridge cruise ships, collected cards and game accessories imprinted with his logo, read his columns and the articles he wrote for *Sports Illustrated* and *McCall's* and for bridge magazines throughout the world.

Born in Philadelphia, Goren was a law student at McGill University when he learned to play bridge in a casual game. He earned an LLB in 1922 and a Masters degree in 1923, the year he was admitted to the Pennsylvania Bar. In his spare time he boned up on Milton Work's classics and laid out and studied hand after hand. When he felt he was ready he entered his first duplicate. He won his direction and was hooked.

Goren attracted the attention of Milton Work, also a Philadelphian. He took a job as his technical assistant, helping to prepare books, lectures and columns. By 1931, Goren was playing tournament bridge. He won his first major events in 1933 - the United States Bridge Asso-

ciation Open Teams and the American Bridge League's Open Teams.

He began to do some teaching on his own and in 1936 he published his first book, *Winning Bridge Made Easy*. *The Chicago Tribune* and *New York Daily News* chose to syndicate his daily newspaper articles as a replacement for Ely Culbertson, who had moved to another syndicate.

After 13 years as a member of the bar, Goren turned to bridge full time. Though still a member of the bar, he never practiced again. Goren was a fine writer and analyst, an excellent speaker and a tireless worker. Starting in 1937 he won so many tournaments that he captured the "McKenney Trophy" (now the Crane Top 500) for best performance on 8 occasions - a record that still stands. Soon he took over the top spot of the masterpoint winners list and held that without interruption from 1944-62. His introduction of point-count valuation, adding points for distribution to high-card values of 4, 3, 2, one for ace, king queen, jack, quickly became the norm, and made his methods into what came to be called Standard American. More important, because this valuation method proved much easier to learn, it helped make millions of new bridge players, giving the game a life it had not enjoyed since the first boom of the early Culbertson years.

The name of Goren became synonymous with bridge to millions. His importance as a world figure was recognized when he was on the front cover of *Time* magazine. His classic *Contract Bridge Complete* ran to 12 editions. His *Point Count Bidding* revolutionized bidding to the extent that "Goren" became a standard recognized worldwide. Culbertson's honor-trick valuation died overnight. It is estimated that Goren books have sold more than 10 million copies. His writings have been translated into a dozen languages. His books include: *Better Bridge for Better Players, Standard Book of Bidding, Contract Bridge Made Easy, A Self-Teacher, Point-Count Bidding in Contract Bridge, Goren Presents the Italian Bridge System, New Contract Bridge in a Nutshell; Sports Illustrated Book of Bridge, Goren's Winning Partnership Bridge, Charles Goren's Bridge Complete,* and *Goren on Play and Defense.*

Goren became a world champion in Bermuda in 1950 when the first Bermuda Bowl World Championship was staged. Placed 2nd 1956 and 1957 Bermuda Bowls, member of U.S. team that finished 4th in first World Team Olympiad in Turin in 1960. Won equivalent of 34 NABC championships and was runner-up on 21 occasions. His television show, *Championship Bridge with Charles Goren,* ran from 1959 to 1964. It was called the first successful bridge program on television and won an award as one of the best new television features. A lifelong bachelor, Goren may genuinely have been married to the game. In spite of his work as writer, lecturer, promoter, TV personality (unlike Culbertson, who grew bored with the game when he became successful), Goren was devoted to tournament play.

He seldom played rubber bridge, and never for high stakes. He considered his playing status amateur and once turned over to the Damon Runyon Cancer Fund the full amount of a $1,500 purse which he won in a charity tournament played in Las Vegas. Before his retirement from active competition in 1966, he captured virtually every major bridge trophy in U.S. tournament play. ACBL Honorary Member 1959, one of first 3 elected to ACBL Hall of Fame (then of *The Bridge World*) in 1963. Member ACBL Laws Commission from 1956, contributing editor

of *The Bridge World,* member of Editorial Advisory Board of *Bridge Encyclopedia*. Awarded the honorary degree of Doctor of Laws by McGill University 1963.

After retiring from the tournament scene in the late Sixties, Goren lived quietly at his home in Miami Beach. For the last 19 years of his life he lived with his nephew, Marvin Goren, in Southern California. Because of poor eyesight and failing health, he was seldom seen in the Seventies. There were rare appearances on the *According to Goren* panel shows at North American Bridge Championships and in 1972 he hosted a party for the press at his Miami Beach home during the Fourth World Bridge Olympiad.

His personal record by events: won Bermuda Bowl 1950, placed 2nd 1956, 57; 3rd World Team Olympiad 1960. On the national level he won the Vanderbilt 1944, 45, placed 2nd 1934, 36, 49, 50, 53, 55, 59, 62; Asbury Park Trophy (later the Spingold) 1937; Spingold Master KO Teams 1943, 47, 51, 56, 60, 2nd 1939, 1950; Reisinger BAM Teams (formerly Chicago) 1937, 38, 39, 42, 43, 50, 57, 63, 2nd 1944, 51; Master Mixed Teams 1938, 41, 43, 44, 48, 54, 2nd 1946, 49, 50, 51; Men's BAM Teams 1952, 2nd 1946, 55; Life Master Pairs 1942, 58, 2nd 1953; Open Pairs 1940; Mixed Pairs 1943, 47, 2nd 1934; Men's Pairs 1938, 43, 49, 2nd in 1935; Masters Individual 1945; McKenney Trophy 1937, 43, 45, 47 48, 49, 50, 51.

GOSLAR, Gerda (1912-87) of Johannesburg, South Africa, born in Germany. 2nd World Women's Teams 1968, 1972, World Women's Pairs 1974. Also represented South Africa in World Open Teams 1960, World Open Pairs 1966, World Women's Pairs 1970. 5 national titles. Founder Women's Bridge Association of South Africa.

GOTHE, Eva-Liss (b. 1941) of Stockholm, Sweden. WBF World Master. Placed 2nd World Mixed Pairs 1990. Won European Women's Pair 1989. Represented Sweden 9 other times.

GOTHE, Hans G. (b. 1937) of Spinga, Sweden, computer expert. WBF World Life Master. 3rd Bermuda Bowl 1987, World Team Olympiad 1988. Represented Sweden in many other world championships. Won European Teams 1977, 1987, 3rd 1989 and played on 6 other occasions. Nordic Champion 1968, 1984 1990. 9 national wins 1967-90.

GOTTLIEB, Michael T. (1902-1980) of Hillsborough CA, held the distinction of playing on both the Culbertson team and the Four Aces, and won deserved recognition when the ACBL designated him Life Master #9. Born in New York City, established a reputation early as a champion, netting some 13 USBA titles in the years 1929-1935, along with 3 second place finishes. One of Ely Culbertson's partners in the famous Culbertson- Lenz match, played on Culbertson's team against England and France in 1933. Key member of Four Aces team that dominated bridge scene in the mid-Thirties. In 1935, with Howard Schenken, launched forth on a successful bridge tour of Europe, taking on, all comers. On their return to America, Gottlieb and Schenken rejoined their teammates to defeat the champions of Europe, France, in the first world championship match. Retiring from tournament play in 1936, Gottlieb devoted his energies to his hotel in Millbrae CA and to Gottlieb Enterprises, which specialized in the development of gas wells. Owned shopping centers and hotels in Phoenix, and for 10 years held a seat on the New York Stock Exchange. Near the end of his life Gottlieb made a pleasant return to the bridge world, winning several sectionals and regionals.

GOUDSMIT, Frits (1899-1971) of Amsterdam, the Netherlands, lawyer and bridge columnist. 2nd European Championships 1932, 33, 34. Represented The Netherlands on many other occasions. Won national Open Teams 11 times. Authored several books on bidding and play, translated many others from English to Dutch.

GOUGH, William L. (1951-1987) of Oreland PA, bridge teacher. Won first regional and played in Blue Ribbon Pairs in 1966 at age of 15, placed 1st in ACBL in Epson Pairs 1986. Won many regional events.

GOULD, Edward A., Jr. (1928-1997) of Hooksett NH., sales representative. Former president District 25, served for 18 years on ACBL Board of Directors, 1973-91, president of ACBL 1990 and Chairman of the Board 1991.

GOULD, Lawrence E. (Larry) (b. 1942) of Raleigh NC, financial officer. Won Spingold 1974, placed 2nd 1977; Men's Teams 1973. Diamond Life Master, won numerous regionals.

GOULD, Susan (Muffin) (b. 1940) of Brookline MA., grower of pitless peach, exporter of 100,000+ fruit trees. Won 21 regionals.

GOW, Robert D. (Bob) (b. 1942) of Midwest City OK, computer programmer and analyst, mathematician. Diamond Life Master, won 17 regionals.

GOWDY, Bruce Douglas (B.G.) (b. 1930) of Toronto ON, retired chartered accountant, vice president of finance (Country Style Donuts), store franchiser. Former president Unit 166. Became a tournament director in 1950 and scored sheets all over the country for Al Sobel, Alvin Landy and Russell Baldwin. Was Director in Charge (DIC) of half of the tournaments in Ontario 1953-60. WBF World Life Master, placed 3rd World Team Olympiad 1972 and also represented Canada in Turin, Italy, 1960, New Orleans 1978 (11th Rosenblum Teams), Monte Carlo 1976 (placed 13th World Team Olympiad). Holds record for being youngest player ever to win a major knockout event — won Spingold at the age of 19 in 1949. 2nd Spingold 1964, won Canadian National Open Teams 1949, 50, 51, 52, 53 and numerous regionals.

GOWER, Craig (b. 1957) of Johannesburg, South Africa, bridge teacher and club owner. WBF World Master. Won BFAME Teams twice. Represented South Africa in 4 World Team Olympiads. Bermuda Bowl quarterfinalist 1995.

GRABEL, Ross D. (b. 1950) of Huntington Beach CA, company owner. Represented ACBL in world play 1986 placing 16th in Rosenblum Teams. Won Men's Teams 1980, North American Men's Swiss Teams 1982, Reisinger 1984 (in the famous 4-way tie), GNOT 1998, placed 2nd Spingold 1989. Diamond Life Master, won numerous regionals.

GRACA, Ella (b. 1918) born in China. Represented Hong Kong in one world championship and many Far East Championships. Top Hong Kong team winner in 1982, only woman ever to win this title.

GRAFT, Larry W. (b. 1934) of Sacramento CA, ACBL tournament director, began directing in 1963 and in 1979 advanced to Regional 4. President Sacramento Unit 1963-64. Former sales executive, rocket engine test coordinator and navigator in U.S. Air Force. 2-handicap golfer.

GRANOVETTER, Matthew (Matt) (b. 1950) of Jerusalem, Israel, formerly of New York City, writer/publisher. Has authored 2 children's musicals and several books: *Murder at the Bridge Table, I Shot my Bridge Partner, The Bridge Team Murders, Bridge Additions,* and co-authored *Tops and Bottoms, Conventions at a Glance and The Ulitmate Club, A Switch in Time, Forgive Me Partner* and *Learn Bridge in 9 Minutes.* Editor of *Bridge Today* magazine, *Bridge Today Digest Online, OKbridge Today* daily e-mail column, the ACBL *Bridge Bulletin* column *Partnership Bridge"*. Bridge editor for *Jerusalem Post* and columnist for OKbridge *Spectator.* One of the originators of the Relay System and was a member of the New York team that defeated the Lancia Team in 1975 (see Lancia Tournaments). In 1981 he appeared in 13 episodes of *Grand Slam*, TV challenge match made for BBC. Placed 2nd World Mixed Teams 1974. Diamond Life Master, won Open Pairs 1972, Men's Teams 1975, 1982; Mixed BAM Teams 1999; placed 2nd Reisinger 1976, 77. Won Cavendish Invitational Pairs, Cavendish Invitational Teams 1993, New Orleans Money Tournament 1982, Bridge Today All-Star Game 1992, National Israel Open Pairs, Mixed Pairs, Open Teams 1993. Producer of Bridge Today All-Star Games.

GRANOVETTER, Pamela (Pam) (b. 1953) of Jerusalem, Israel, formerly of New York City, writer/editor, runs a website "Judaism for Beginners". Author of *Movie Guide for Bridge Players"* and *The Torah Weekly Reader - Wisdon for the Torah.* Member of ACBL Goodwill Committee. Co-editor of *Bridge Today* magazine, ACBL *Bridge Bulletin* column *Partnership Bridge,* the books *Tops and Bottoms, Conventions at a Glance, A Switch in time, Forgive Me Partner,* and *Learn Bridge in 9 Minutes.* Co-produced 4 Bridge Today All-Star games. Represented Canada in New Orleans 1978, Valkenberg 1980. Won Women's BAM Teams 1990, placed 2nd Women's KO Teams 1991. Won Cavendish Invitational Teams, Israeli Open Teams, Mixed Pairs 1993; New Orleans Money Tournament 1983, placed 2nd in Iceland Open Teams.

GRANT, Audrey (b. 1940) of Toronto ON, educator and author. Taught in Toronto school system for many years and was consultant to Toronto School Board before concentrating on bridge. Educational consultant for ACBL for many years. Authored ACBL teaching series — *Club, Diamond, Heart* and *Spade.* Co-authored with husband David Lindop *Joy of Bridge, "Bridge Maxims* with Eric Rodwell. Founder and editor *Better Bridge* newsletter, has authored many other books including several work of fiction. Producer of ACBL TV teaching series including *The Bridge Class, Play Bridge with Audrey Grant I* and *II,* produced many TV bridge shows in Canada starting in 1986. Co-ordinator and lecturer for many bridge cruises with husband David Lindop and son Jason as assistants.

GRANTHAM, John M. (b. 1944) of Amarillo TX, retail store owner, former commodity broker and professional bridge player. Won Blue Ribbon Pairs and Lou Herman Trophy 1971. Won numerous regional titles.

GRAUPERA, Javier (b. 1958) of Barcelona, Spain, computer engineer and enterprise manager. 2nd European Junior Teams 1980. Represented Spain in 4 world championships and 7 other zonal championships.

GRAVES, Allan (b. 1949) of Vancouver BC, bridge professional, former child counselor. Member *Bridge World* Master Solvers panel since 1978. WBF World Master. Represented Canada in Las Palmas 1974, New Orleans 1978, Valkenburg 1980, Biarritz 1982, Seattle 1984, Bal Harbour 1986. Placed 3rd Rosenblum Teams 1982. 9th 1990. Diamond Life Master, won North American Swiss Teams 1986, placed 2nd Reisinger 1978, won Canadian National Teams Championship 1980, 81, 83.

GRAY, Charles (Charlie) (b. 1930) of Philadelphia PA, licensed professional engineer since 1967, semi-retired engineering consultant. Served in various executive positions in Unit 141 and District 4 including president of both, co-chairman of 1972, 80, 89 Fall NABCs and on the committee for the Spring NABC 1991. Began directing 1962, currently non-active. Directed the first Omar Sharif Bridge Circus visit to Philadelphia in 1968 and organized the first KO team event in Philadelphia bridge history, including a vugraph exhibition. Has won more than 30 regional events.

GRECO, Eric Alan (b. 1975) of Philadelphia VA , equity options trader. Developed and plays his own system. In 1991 won Mini-McKenney in NABC Master category. Became Life Master at age 15 and won the youth category (under 20) in 1991 amassing 557 points, was 3rd in the Junior category (under 25). Member of Junior team that competed in the World Junior Championships in Aarhus, Denmark, 1993, became King Of Bridge that year; won Junior Team Trials 1994. Won North American Non-Life Master Pairs 1991, GNOT Flight B 1993 (both with his father, Philip), Open Pairs I 1997, Life Master Pairs 1998. Won the Youth Flight of the Royal Viking/Instant Matchpoint Pairs 1992, Open Pairs I 1997, Life Master Pairs 1998; placed 2nd 1999 World Junior Championships; 4th 1993 World Juniors; placed 4th Cavendish 1999.

GREEN, Farrell B. (Farfel) (b. 1937) of Edina MN, semi-retired financial controller, consultant and accountant. Member ACBL New Systems and Conventions Committee in the Sixties; youngest to become a Life Master in Minnesota 1961; has won 20+ regional events.

GREEN, Mary (b. 1930) of Carlisle MA., formerly of Memphis TN, former college math teacher. Wife of Roy Green, ACBL chief executive officer 1992-1998. Diamond Life Master, has won more than 15 regional events.

GREEN, Roy G. (b. 1930) of Carlisle MA., formerly of Memphis TN, retired executive vice president of OKbridge, retired CEO of ACBL 1992-1998, former banker. Was appointed by President Ford to National Commission on Electronic Fund Transfers. National president of U.S. League of Savings Institutions (1981-1982). Charter trustee and former chairman of the Appraisal Foundation, Washington D.C. Has been a contributor to ACBL *Bridge Bulletin* and OKbridge *Spectator*. Has been active over last 30 years in every aspect of bridge administration and is a long-time member of the ACBL Goodwill Committee. Has won more than 15 regional events.

GREEN, Susan (Mrs. Michael Cappelletti Sr.) (b. 1952) of Alexandria VA, technical editor/writer and consultant. Diamond Life Master, won Women's KO Teams 1991, placed 2nd Mixed Pairs, Women's BAM Teams 1988, has won more than 75 regional titles.

GREENBERG, Byron (Beau) (1927-deceased) of Las Vegas NV, retired restaurateur. Held executive positions several times in Oklahoma bridge. Won Open Pairs 1953, placed 2nd Spingold 1972, Reisinger 1973. Diamond Life Master with numerous regional wins.

GREENBERG, Gail H. (b. 1938) of New York City, bridge teacher and professional player. One of the leading women players of the world. World Grand Master ranked #11 in world among women. ACBL Grand Life Master with 14,810 MPs as of 3/2001. Active in bridge administration, currently a vice-chairman of ACBL Appeals Committee and a member of both the ACBL Goodwill Committee and the ACBL Charity Committee. Past president of Greater New York

B.A. and former District 24 member of the ACBL Board of Governors. Won Venice Cup 1976, 78, (2nd 1985); World Olympiad Women's Teams 1980, 84; 2nd World Mixed Teams 1972. Represented ACBL in other world competition with these results: 1974 - 4th Mixed Pairs, 9th Women's Pairs; 1976 - 3rd Olympiad Women's Teams; 1978 - 7th Mixed Pairs, 8th Women's Pairs; 1982 - 17th Mixed Pairs, 19th Women's Pairs; 1986 - 14th Mixed Pairs; 1990 - 17th Women's Pairs 1990. She won the first Pan American Women's Teams Championship 1992. ACBL national titles include Master Mixed Teams 1967, 72; North American Women's Swiss Teams 1983, 92 (2nd 1985); Women's KO Teams 1971, 74, 75, 76, 83, 90, 93, 95 (2nd 1973, 82); Mixed Pairs 1978; Women's BAM Teams placed 2nd 1986, 88. (see FAMILY.)

GREENBERG, Julie (b. 1938) of Memphis TN, manager ACBL Education Deparment. An ACBL tournament director for 20 years achieving rank of associate national. Authored *Duplicate Decisions* which served as a model for a version created by the European Bridge League. Wrote ACBL *Bridge Bulletin* column *Ruling the Game* for 10 years. Editor of ABCL newsletter, *The Bridge Teacher*. Was the first editor of *The Grapevine*. Created the first Tournament Director manual to help create uniformity in the way the job was performed and developed ACBL's student *Bridge Bulletin* supplements.

GREENBERG, Sherie R. (b. 1932) of Palo Alto CA., bridge teacher and professional player. Presently on Unit 503 Board of Directors and has served several other times in the last 20 years. Diamond Life Master, won Women's BAM Teams 1996 and has won many regional titles.

GREENSPAN, Jonathan (Jon) (b.1950) of New York City bridge professional, former commodity trader. Placed 2nd Reisinger 1989 and won 15+ regionals.

GRENSIDE, Richard (b. 1938) of Sydney, Australia, born in England, tournament director. Chief Director of Australian Bridge Federation since 1976. Directed at many PABF (Far East) Championships. Senior Director of World Bridge Federation, at world championships since 1986.

GRESHAM, William Lindsay (1909-1962) of New Rochelle NY, noted American novelist, used the tarot pack as background material in his macabre story about carnival life, *Nightmare Alley*, from which an excerpt appears in *The Fireside Book of Cards*.

GRIEVE, William P. (Billy) (b. 1929) of White Plains NY, IBM system programmer and mathematician. Retired tournament player, won Men's Pairs 1958, Spingold 1959, Master Mixed Teams 1960, Reisinger 1969,70,71; Men's Teams 1975. Placed 2nd Open Pairs 1959, Spingold 1960, 66, 69; Reisinger, Men's Teams 1972.

GRIFFEY, Candace (Candy) (formerly Fowler) of Palm Beach Gardens, professional bridge player. Placed 2nd Women's KO Teams 1999. Won more than 100 regionals.

GRIFFEY, Larry R. (b. 1944) of Palm Beach Gardens, retired mathematics professor, bridge professional and teacher. Diamond Life Master with more than 10,900 MPs as of 3/2001, has won District 9 GNOP 9 times, GNOT twice and numerous other regionals.

GRIFFIN, Edward Furnival (b. 1947) of Sydney, Australia, company director. Won PABF (Far East) Open Pairs and represented Australia in 4 zonal championships. Won New Zealand Open Teams and 2 Australian titles including Open Teams. Won McCutcheon Trophy for most masterpoints in a year. Legal Counsel to Australian Bridge Federation.

GRIFFIN, Estee (1931-1993) of New York City, sys-

tem manager, served as tournament chairman, vice president and president of the Greater New York B.A. Was former assistant editor of *The Bridge World*, associate editor of *Post Mortem* and promotion director of *The Bridge Journal*. She had several regional wins.

GRIFFIN, James M. (b. 1955) of Austin TX, computer consultant. Won NAOP 1993, 94, 99 and 15+ regionals. Griffin's grandparents, Major General Martin Griffin and wife Lucille, used to play bridge with the Eisenhowers in the Fifties.

GRIGGS, Eloene T. of Memphis TN, formerly of Washington DC, retired bridge teacher, former bridge club owner and director. Served as general secretary of the International Bridge Press Association (IBPA) 1973-1992 and has served in many executive posiions in the ABTA, including president (1976, 77, 78), on editorial staff of *ABTA Quarterly*. Organized many service-connected women's clubs and has been a member of the National Council of Women since 1954. She is listed in *Who's Who of American Women, World's Who's Who of Women* and several other biographical dictionaries. Griggs was given Certificate of Appreciation for Advancement of Human Rights, honored by Business and Professional Women's Clubs as "Woman of the Year" — 1986, was awarded certificate by U.S. Congressional Advisory Board for Outstanding Services, made Honorary Citizen of New Orleans 1978, and awarded "Bridge Personality of the Year" 1990 by the IPBA at World Championships in Geneva.

GRISCOM, Dr. John H. (b. 1929) of Nashville TN, physician, Tennessee state junior golf champion 1947, captain of collegiate golf team. Griscom won GNOP 1983 and competed in international competition in Bal Harbour 1986. Grand Life Master with 11,817 MPs as of 3/2001.

GRISSOM, Bettye (B.J.) (b. 1922) of San Antonio TX, rancher. Was tournament chairman Spring NABC in San Antonio 1984. Member ACBL Board of Governors 1971-83, held many executive positions on Unit and District level. Member District 16 Board 1971-82 serving as president 1974, vice-president 1972, 73; member Ethics Committee 1972, 73, 74. Won a few regionals.

GRODSKY, Mike J. (b. 1957) of Atlanta GA, computer programmer. Won Red Ribbon Pairs 1990. Has won many regionals.

GROETHEIM, Glenn (b. 1959) of Trondheim, Norway, engineer. WBF World Life Master. 2nd Bermuda Bowl 1993, 3rd 1997. 3rd European Teams 1987, 93, 97. Won European Junior Teams 1980. Many national titles. Author of *The Viking Club* (Relay Precision).

GROMOV, Andrei (b.1970) of Moscow, Russia, businessman. 2nd Internet World Championship 1999. Quarterfinalist World Olympiad Teams 1996. Represented Soviet Union and Russia in 2 world championships and 2 zonal championships. 3rd Generali Individual 2000. Won North American Swiss Teams 2000, Vanderbilt 2001. Several national wins.

GRONER, Alexander (Alex) (1914-2001) of Poway CA, retired journalist, former editorial writer for *Cleveland Press*, correspondent for *Time, Life and Fortune magazines*. Creator of duplicate movements for Swiss pairs and multiple teams of multiple pairs . Wrote definitive work for club and tournament directors, *Duplicate Bridge Direction* — it is ACBL mandatory for anyone becoming a director. He also wrote *The History of American Business and Industry* and *Science in the Service of Mankind*.

GRONER, Edward L. (Ed) (b. 1929) of Duncan OK,

retired special products manager. Holds several patents on flow metering devices. Diamond Life Master, placed 2nd Senior Swiss Teams 1997, won more than 30 regional events.

GROSS, Steven H. (b. 1944) of Ventura CA, attorney. Placed 2nd Non-Life Masters Men's Pairs 1965, competed in international play New Orleans 1978, won PAC-10 Bridge Championship 1965 playing for Stanford with partner, Grant Baze. Placed 2nd Zonal Pairs 1994 World Bridge Championship. Diamond Life Master with more than 50 regional wins.

GROSS, William M. (Bill) (b. 1930) of Harrisburg PA, attorney, has strong interest in computer technology. ACBL executive director 1987-1991, ACBL president 1983,chairman of Board 1984, served as ACBL Board member from District 4 (1972-87), member ACBL Board of Governors and ACBL Goodwill Committee, past president of District 4. Co-chairman of Fall NABC in Lancaster PA 1972, 80. Former bridge columnist, wrote regularly for the Harrisburg *Sunday Patriot-News*. Graduate of University of Pennsylvania and Harvard Law School, past president of the American Lung Association and served as a member of its National Board of Directors. Numerous regional wins.

GROSSMAN, David L. (b. 1935) of Livingston NJ, senior director national programs - The House of Seagram. Winner Non-Life Masters Teams 1984.

GROTHUS, Phillip (b. 1949) of San Antonio TX., securities and derivatives trader. Served as local president, District treasurer, vice-president. Has won 15+ regionals.

GRUENTHER, General Alfred M. (1899-1983) of Washington DC, a recognized authority on duplicate contract bridge and the outstanding director of bridge tournaments in America in the Thirties. Acted as chief referee in the Culbertson-Lenz Match 1931-32. He authored *Duplicate Bridge Simplified, Duplicate Bridge Guide* and *Famous Hands of the Culbertson-Lenz Match*. Honorary president of the World Bridge Federation from its inception in 1958 until he resigned from all bridge activities in 1978. Awarded the Wetzlar Trophy 1938, 44 and was named ACBL Honorary Member 1944. Charter member of ACBL Laws Commission and its Honorary Member 1948-78, chairman of the ACBL Charity Foundation 1964-65 and a former member of the Editorial Advisory Board of *Bridge Encyclopedia*. Gruenther served 38 years in the U.S. Army. His final military assignment was Supreme Commander, Allied Powers, Europe, 1953-56. In this capacity he came into contact with General Dwight D. Eisenhower. On occasion they played bridge. He retired December 31, 1956 and from 1957 to 1964 was president of the American Red Cross, serving with particular devotion and special interest in its youth program. He received 9 awards from Red Cross Societies from other countries for International Red Cross league activities. He was decorated by 14 governments other than the United States. He was the recipient of the Distinguished Service Medal with 2 Oak Leaf clusters and the Legion of Merit from this country. He had honorary degrees from 31 American colleges and universities. (see EISENHOWER, Dwight D.)

GRUVER, Nancy G. (1931-1990) of Ellicott City MD. One of the leading American women players, a former elementary school teacher. A past president of the Women's Bridge League of Maryland and Board member of the Maryland B.L., served as co-chairman of the ACBL Appeals Committee for many years and was

elected to the ACBL Laws Commission 1982. A certified director and club manager in Baltimore, she gave private instruction on occasion and was an active member of Bridge Pro organization. Placed 2nd World Women's Pairs 1966, Venice Cup 1981, also represented the U.S. in 1968, 78, 82. Won Women's Pairs 1965, Women's Teams 1966, 73, 78, 80; Master Mixed Teams 1975, Mixed Pairs 1977, Life Master Women's Pairs 1967, 79, 81; North American Women's Swiss 1982, Women's KO Teams 1984. Placed 2nd Master Mixed Teams 1969, Mixed Pairs 1976, Life Master Women's Pairs 1980. She won the USWBC (women's team trials) 1981, 87. Diamond Life Master.

GU, Ling (b. 1959) of Guangzhou, China, company employee. WBF World Life Master. In 2000, 10th in Women's World rankings. 2nd World Olympiad Women's Teams 1996. 2nd Venice Cup 1997, 3rd 1991. Won Far East Women's Teams 1986, 91, 93, 94, 96, 97, 98. Represented China in 13 World championships. Won many national titles.

GUAGLIARDO, Matthew T. (Matt) (b. 1945) financial management adviser and portfolio manager, former manager Education Department of ACBL. Was npc of first ACBL Junior team 1987. Chairman of 1980 Spring NABC in Fresno CA. Creator of many bridge hospitality functions including *The Bridge Gong Show, Bridge All-Star Challenge, ACBL Celebrity Squares*. Edited many regional *Daily Bulletin*s on West Coast, the Fresno Unit publication, District 22 news for the *Contract Bridge Forum* and has contributed to the ACBL *Bridge Bulletin*. Founded and was executive director of the Professional Bridge Association.

GUARNERI, Richard C. (Rick) (b. 1938) of Charleston SC, electronic technician. Served in various capacities on the local level. Diamond Life Master with more than 20 regional wins.

GUDGE, Anna (b. 1946) of Long Melford, England, bridge administrator. Secretary, British Bridge League 1984-99. WBF Liaison since 1999. MSO Worldwide Bridge Editor 1999. Administrator at several world championships. Co-inventor of scoring program for worldwide events. Won EBU Women's Teams 1986.

GUERIN, Donald H. (Don) (b. 1942) of Sacramento CA, independent real estate appraiser. Has written articles for *The Bridge World, The Forum* and *Los Angeles Bridge News*. Diamond Life Master, placed 2nd Senior/Advanced Senior Master Pairs 1965 and has won several regionals.

GUIVER, Harold B. (Squeezer) (b. 1925) of Long Beach CA, mortgage company co-owner, graduate of USC and was a member of its NCAA tennis championship team. Vice president of Los Angeles Rams and assistant general manager of New Orleans Saints. Named Contract Negotiator of the Year in 1980 by *Sports Illustrated* for his role as an agent representing professional football players. Won the Chicago (Reisinger) 1962, Men's Teams 1962, Men's BAM Teams 1983, placed 2nd Chicago (now Reisinger) 1961, Vanderbilt 1961, 63; Men's Teams 1974, Spingold 1975. Diamond Life Master, won numerous regionals.

GULLBERG, Tommy (b. 1943) of Solna, Sweden, representative. WBF World Life Master. 3rd Olympiad Teams 1988, Bermuda Bowl 1987, 91, Rosenblum Teams 1994. European champion 1987, 2nd 1991, 99, 3rd 1989. European Junior champion 1968. Nordic champion 1984, 1990. Represented Sweden on many other occasions.

National tournament chairman 1971-73. Bridge columnist *Svenska Dagbladet*, contributor to *Bridgetidningen,* author of two teaching books.

GUMBY, Pauline (b. 1949) of Mosman, Australia, computer programmer, former mathematics teacher. Won PABF (Far East) Women's Teams 1985. Represented Australia in 4 world championships. Won many national titles.

GUPTA, Subhash (b. 1947) of New Delhi India, formerly of Calgary BC, mechanical engineer, represented Canada in Bermuda Bowl the first time a Canadian team qualified, Sao Paulo 1985. Won tri-country playoff 1985. WBF World Master, also represented Canada in Biarritz 1982, Bal Harbour 1986, Geneva 1990; represented India in world competition Salsomagiorri, Italy 1992. Won Epson Swiss Teams in Japan 1984, Dubai 1990. Has won all major team events in India.

GURVICH, Louis S. (1921-1986) of Metairie LA, was president of a guard and detective agency employing 300 men both nationally and internationally. ACBL president 1977, Chairman of the Board 1978, chairman of the Board of Governors 1967-71 and served on many committees prior to his presidency, including the committee that approved and defined the present day convention chart and convention card. General chairman of 1978 World Olympiad in New Orleans, a member of the WBF executive committee 1977, 79. Served on WBF Appeals Committee. Former president Mid-South Conference and Louisiana B.A. Placed 2nd Master Mixed Teams 1961 and won many regional events. Gurvich's daughter was one of the victims in the Jonestown tragedy. He was one of the few Americans allowed to go look for a body.

GUSTAFSON, Helen R. (Mrs. John) (b. 1923) of Des Moines IA, retired office manager. Chaired numerous tournaments since 1973. Grand Life Master with 10,825 MPs as of 3/2001. Won Mixed Pairs 1983, Senior Swiss Teams 1997; competed in WBF events in Bal Harbour 1986 and placed 15th World Senior Pairs in Geneva 1990. Won more than 70 regionals.

GUSTAFSON, John E. (b. 1924) of Des Moines IA, pediatric cardiologist, medical consultant to life insurance companies. Served Unit 116 and District 14 as president. Member ACBL Board of Governors, vice-chairman ACBL Education Foundation. Grand Life Master with 13,148 MPs, as of 3/2001 won Mixed Pairs 1983, Senior Swiss Teams 1997. Placed 15th World Senior Pairs Geneva 1990. Has more than 80 regional titles.

GUSTAVSSON, Marten (b. 1960) of Stockholm, Sweden, civil engineer. 3rd Rosenblum Teams 1994. Won Swedish Pairs 1996, 97, 98.

GUTOWSKY, Ace, Jr. (1909-1976) of Oklahoma City won acclaim both as a bridge player and as a football star. On the gridiron Gutowsky played professionally from 1931-38 and was fullback for the Detroit Lions when they won the world championship in 1935. After his retirement from football he worked as an aircraft sales representative. His bridge victories came in the Fifties and included Men's Teams 1951. Ace was his given name.

GWIS, Krzysztof (b. 1939) of Olsztyn, Poland, engineer. Won European Senior Teams 1995. Won many Polish championships.

GWOZDZINSKY, G. Margie (The Countess) of New York City, born in Poland, bridge teacher and business systems analyst. Member GNYBA Board of Directors for 14 years. Won Venice Cup 1989. Placed 16th World Women's Pairs 1986. Diamond Life Master, won Women's Swiss Teams 1984, 1989; Women's BAM

Teams 1993, Women's Pairs 1997, Women's KO Teams 1998. She placed 2nd Reisinger 1989, Women's Pairs 1996, Women's KO Teams 1996, Women's BAM Teams 1998.

GYNZ, Detler von (b. 1944) of Munster, Germany, factory employee. Represented Germany in world and zonal championships from 1969-87. Won 22 national titles.

H

HABERMAN, Barbara (Bari) (Mrs. Sigmund, formerly Rappaport) (b. 1935) of New York City, options trader, former English teacher. Was one of the leading American women players in late Sixties and 70's, won Fishbein Trophy 1971, Life Master Pairs 1971, 72; Life Master Women's Pairs 1977; placed 2nd in Women's Teams 1969, 71; Women's Pairs 1978, Master Mixed Teams 1966, 74, 75; Life Master Women's Pairs 1974. Diamond Life Master. Three-time winner of Goldman Pairs. After sweeping the pairs events in a sectional tournament, she was named honorary Men's Pairs champion so that her record would not be flawed.

HABERT, Rhoda (b.1948) of Montreal PQ, high school English teacher. Has been a contributor to *Bridge World*. Placed 2nd Women's Team Olympiad 2000, 4th World Women's Teams 1996. Represented Canada in WBF events 1986 (Rosenblum Teams); Canadian Women's Teams 1990, 92, 93, 94, 96, 97 and 2000.

HACKETT, Jason P. (b. 1970) of Manchester, England, bridge professional. Bungee jumped at original bungee site in New Zealand. WBF World Master. Junior world champion 1995. Junior European champion 1994. Silver EEC Athens 1991. Won Junior Camrose 1990-1995, NEC Cup 1998, 2000, CAC Pairs 1996, 99; Djarum Cup 1995, 96; China Cup 2000, Icelandic Pairs 2001. Many national and worldwide wins. Britain's youngest Grand Master at 24. ACBL successes include 2nd Open BAM Teams North American Swiss Teams 1996. Represented Britain on many occasions with twin brother Justin. When their father Paul played with them in Rhodes 1997 they became the first family to have 3 players on the same team in world play.

HACKETT, Justin T. (b. 1970) of Manchester, England, bridge consultant. WBF World Master. Junior World Champion 1995. Junior European Champion 1994. Silver EEC Athens 1991. Won Junior Camrose 1990-95, NEC Cup 1998, 2000; CAC Pairs 1996, 99; China Cup 2000, Djarum Cup 1995, 96; Icelandic Pairs 2001. ACBL successes include 2nd BAM Teams, North American Swiss Teams1996. Represented Britain on many occasions with twin brother Jason. When their father Paul played with them in Rhodes 1997 they became the first family to have 3 players on the same team in world play. Many national and worldwide wins. Contributor to *Bridge Magazine* and co-author of several books.

HACKETT, Paul D. (b. 1941) of Manchester, England, bridge professional. Placed 2nd European Teams 1981. Gold, silver and bronze European Pairs. Represented Great Britain for 20 years including Rhodes 1997 when played on the same team as his sons Jason and Justin. Winner NEC Cup 1998, 2000, China Cup 2000. ACBL successes include 2nd Open BAM Teams and North American Swiss Teams, both 1996. Many other national and worldwide wins. Magazine contributor and author of several books.

HADDAD, Betty (formerly Windley) (1924-1984) of Arlington VA, painter. Won Mixed Pairs 1954, Women's Pairs 1961 and several regional events.

HADDAD, Louis J. (1900-1980) insurance counselor, born in Iowa. Presided over ACBL in 1935. Won many auction bridge events 1928-32 and the Hilliard Trophy in 1935.

HADDAD, Said (b. 1916) of La Gorce Island FL, contractor. Former director and treasurer of the Washington B.L. Won Mixed Pairs 1954, the Baird Trophy 1956 and several regional events.

HADDEN, David A. (Dave) (b. 1944) of San Antonio TX, engineer/systematic management service, retired U.S. Air Force colonel. Served in several executive positions Unit 172, treasurer for Summer 1999 NABC, editor for Unit newsletter *Winning Finesse*. Won Men's Pairs 1973 and 15+ regionals.

HADI, Khurshid (b. 1944) of Karachi, Pakistan, senior business executive and CEO. President of Pakistan Bridge Federation since 1998.

HAIT, Sharon G. (b. 1944) of Livingston NJ, bookkeeper. Won Life Master Women's Pairs 1998 and several regionals.

HALF, Natalie G. (b. 1941) of Pompano Beach FL, secretary. Has won approximately 30 regionals.

HALL, Clay (b. 1953) of Birmingham AL, computer programmer/analyst. Served as 1st Alternate Director for District 10 1991-96, held several executive positions in Unit and District including president of both, certified director, co-chairman NABC Birmingham 2000 and chaired several local sectionals and regionals. Was Intercollegiate campus winner 1975. Winner nationwide Instant Matchpoint Game (N/S) 1992. Won numerous regionals.

HALL, James M. (Jim) (b. 1940) of Minneapolis MN, insurance salesman. Master Solver panelist for the *Bridge World*. Placed 2nd Reisinger 1988 and Open BAM Teams 1991, 93. Has won more than 90 regionals, Diamond Life Master with more than 10,700 MPs as of 3/2001.

HALL, Jeffrey M. (b. 1951) of Schenectady NY, computer systems manager, won GNOP 1970, placed 2nd Senior/Advanced Senior Master Pairs 1972.

HALL, Robert B. (Burt) of Lake Worth FL, CPA. Authored 1997 ABTA Book of theYear – *How Experts Win at Bridge*. Won at least 20 regionals. As a Junior was selected to play with Charles Goren in a regional event in 1953.

HALLBERG, Gunnar (b. 1945) of Brighton, England, born in Sweden, professional player and teacher. WBF World Master. 4th Olympiad 2000. 6 times Swedish champion. Nordic champion. Numerous tournament wins. Represented Sweden in the 80's.

HALLE, Diana (b. 1924) of Boca Raton FL, lawyer. Won NABC Amateur Women's Pairs 1976.

HALLE, Ranik (1905-1987) of Oslo, Norway. Managing editor of press agency, editor and bridge columnist. Represented Norway 10 times in European Championships, placing 2nd 1938. President International Bridge Press Association 1960-64. Honorary Member and president Norway Bridge Association. Served on *Bridge Encyclopedia* advisory board.

HALLEE, Gerard F. (Jerry) (b. 1940) of Snohomish WA, president of software development and consulting company. Contributor to *Bridge World*. Won Vanderbilt 1969, Senior/Advanced Senior Master Pairs 1963, placed 2nd Men's Pairs 1969. Won several regionals.

HALLEN, Hans-Olof (b. 1929) of Malmo, Sweden, tournament director. 1964 Nordic champion and 1964 Swedish team champion. For many years, one of 4 EBL Chief Tournament Directors. Awarded EBL Honor medal 1981. Co-author of *Movements - a Fair Approach*, a major work of directing and movements.

HALPERIN, Richard M. (Wizard of Odds) (b. 1940) of Skokie IL, semi- retired investor. Nickname came from his facility to calculate odds instantaneously on almost any event. Unofficially known as World's Fastest Adder and The Human Calculator, he added 100 numbers in 30.3 seconds. In 1993 had all-expense trip to Paris to have his brain examined. Won 20+ regional events.

HALPIN, Robert (1896-1972) of Chicago, printing company president. Was one of the founding fathers of the ABL, president 1929. Won Chicago (now the Reisinger) 1929.

HAM, Charles Manini of Montevideo, Uruguay. Won 69 national titles.

HAM, Esther Munoz de of Montevideo, Uruguay. Won South American Women's Teams 1967, 71, 90. Regular member Uruguay Women's team in international competition, has won 79 national titles.

HAMAOUI, Steve (b. 1954) of Caracas, Venezuela, born in Egypt, shirt manufacturer. WBF World Master. Won CAC Teams 1977, 85, 87, 91, 93, 97; CAC Pairs once. Represented Venezuela in 12 world championships and won many national titles. Former president Venezuela Bridge Federation. Bridge teacher.

HAMILTON, Fred (b. 1936) of Encino CA, professional bridge player and teacher. WBF Grand Master, ranked #38 in world. Won Bermuda Bowl 1976, Transnational Senior Pairs 2000. Placed 2nd Bermuda Bowl 1977, World Team Olympiad 1980, World Senior Teams 1994, 4th Rosenblum Teams 1982, 5th World Open Pairs 1978, 7th Olympiad Open Teams 1976. ACBL Grand Life Master with 28,011 MPs as of 3/2001, ranked #8 in ACBL. Won Herman Trophy 1974, Reisinger 1974, 75, 78, 79; Vanderbilt 1977, Spingold 1979, Master Mixed Teams 1976, Team Trials 1975, 79; IMP Pairs 1989, Senior KO Teams 1996, 98; Senior Swiss Teams, GNOT 1998; Silver Ribbon Pairs 2001. Placed 2nd Vanderbilt 1972, 81, 83; GNOT 1974, Men's Teams 1980, 88; North American Swiss Teams 1991, 92; Silver Ribbon Pairs 1992, Mixed Pairs 2000. In 1982 won Cavendish Invitational, placed 2nd Omar Sharif Individual 1990, 3rd All-Star Individual 1992. Invented Hamilton Over Notrump, has won more than 250 regionals.

HAMILTON, John T. (b. 1933) of Columbus OH, retired U.S. Air Force Lt. Col. and ACBL tournament director. A Rhodes Scholar, Hamilton began directing full time in 1965 and three years later was elevated to the rating of national director. Became director-in-charge at North American Bridge Championships in 1976. Served as treasurer of Professional Tournament Directors Association for more than 10 years. Also served as director of the Miami Valley B.A. 1960-62, director and treasurer of the Central Ohio B.A. 1964-69, vice president of the Midwest Conference and chaired several regionals in mid Sixties. With Marc Low he contributed to the Swiss Team Movement.

HAMMAN, Petra (Pete) (b. 1946) of Dallas TX, born in Germany, bridge teacher, former teacher and manufacturer's representative. Member of Board of Governors and vice president of Unit 176, currently president of that body. Won Women's Team Olympiad 2000. Also won Women's BAM Teams 1989, 98, 2000; Women's Swiss Teams 1999, placed 2nd Women's Swiss Teams 1992, Open Pairs I 1999, Women's KO Teams 2000.

HAMMAN, Robert D. (Bob) (b. 1938) of Dallas TX, company president, chartered life insurance underwriter, professional player. One of the world's greatest players, ranks #1 among WBF Grand Masters, also ranks 1st in world performance over past 10 years. Member ACBL Hall of Fame. Has been highest ranked player in the world since 1985. ACBL Grand Life Master with 23,219 MPs as of 3/2001. Ranked #19 in ACBL, world champion many times over. Won Bermuda Bowl 1970, 71, 77, 83, 85, 87, 95, 99; World Team Olympiad 1988, World Open Pairs 1974, placed 2nd Bermuda Bowl 1966, 73, 74, 75, 97; World Team Olympiad 1964, 72, 80, 92; World Mixed Pairs 1986, 94, World Open Pairs 1994, World Par Contest 1990, and many other high finishes in world events. Won ACBL Team Trials (USBC) 1969, 71, 73, 77, 79, 85, 95, 97, 99; Fishbein Trophy 1969, 83; Lou Herman Trophy 1978, 88. Player of the Year 1990, 93. Honorary Member 1991. Won 39 NABC titles including Reisinger 1962, 70, 78, 79, 88, 93, 94, 95; Vanderbilt 1964, 66, 71, 73, 2000; Blue Ribbon Pairs 1964, 86, 91, 93; Spingold 1969, 79, 82, 83, 89, 90, 93, 94, 95, 96, 98, 99; GNOT 1975, 77, 86; Life Master Pairs 1980, 83, 92; Men's Pairs 1986, Master Mixed Teams 1987, Men's BAM Teams 1988, Open Swiss Teams 1990. Placed 2nd in Reisinger 1968, 98, 99; Vanderbilt 1968, 70, 81, 96; Men's Teams 1969, 80; Spingold 1970, Life Master Men's Pairs 1980, 81; Men's BAM Teams 1984, 89; Men's Pairs 1985, Open Pairs 1988, Open Swiss Teams 1992, Open BAM Teams 1998, 99; Open Pairs I 1999.

HAMMERICH, Johannes J. J. (1919-1995) of Copenhagen, Denmark, lawyer, business executive. Resident of Caracas, Venezuela, for many years before moving back to his native country. Represented Venezuela in 3 world championships and 3 zonal championships. Co-founder of Venezuela Bridge Federation, won many Venezuelan titles. Secretary General South American Bridge Federation 1962-69, member WBF Executive Council 1962-78.

HAMPSON, Geoff (b. 1968) of Toronto ON, bridge professional, member ACBL Junior Corps. WBF World Master. Placed 2nd World Junior Championships 1991 and Pan-American Games Open Teams 1992. Grand Life Master with 13,845 MPs as of 3/2001. Won North American Swiss 1992, Mixed Pairs 1994, Open Pairs I 1997, Life Master Pairs 1998, placed 2nd GNOT 1996, won CNTC 1991. More than 50 regional wins.

HAMUI, Jose J. (Johnny) (1935-1983) of Mexico City, company president and director. Represented Mexico in world competition Monte Carlo 1976, New Orleans, Maccabiah Games 1977. Jai-alai champion 1955, 58, 62, 66; member of the Mexican jai-alai Olympic Team 1968. Served as president of Mexican Bridge Unit and treasurer of Mexican Bridge Federation. Won Master Mixed Teams 1980 and several regional events.

HANCOCK, John H. (Jack) (b. 1923) of Deming NM, mathematician. Won Master Mixed Teams and placed 2nd Vanderbilt 1951.

HANDLEY, Michele V. See BARKER, Michele.

HANN, Gary S. of Ann Arbor MI, finance consultant. Served as member Michigan Bridge Association Board of Directors 1981-82; ACBL Board of Directors 1988-89; ACBL Appeals Committee 1981-88, Board of Governors 1980-88 and chairman 1991-95, vice chairman

1995-96. Co-chairman World Junior Championship Committee, contributing editor to Unit publication *Table Talk*. Diamond Life Master, placed 2nd Men's BAM Teams 1979, has won 55+ regionals.

HANNA, William J. (Bill) (b. 1931) of Bethesda MD, professor at University of Maryland. One of the leading players on West Coast until he retired from active play in 1961. Contributed many articles to various publications including *Bridge World*, wrote the monthly column *Western Dateline* for ACBL *Bulletin*. Co-authored *Precision Power Bidding* and the Bull System. Won Spingold 1958, Reisinger 1960.

HANNER, Olof (b. 1922) of V. Frolunda, Sweden, retired professor of mathematics. Inventor and developer of many movements: Pivot Mitchell; Stanza Howell; movement for odd number of teams without bye; several perfectly balanced individual movements with each player having each other player as partner once and opponent twice. Co-author of *Movements - a Fair Approach*, a major work of directing and movements. Contributing editor to *Bridge Encyclopedia*.

HANSON, Jude Goodwin- (b. 1953) of Maple Ridge BC, desktop publishing, graphic design, cartoonist, web master. Canadian Bridge Federation Web Master and magazine editor. Served as Unit 574 sectional co-chairman 1983-86, from 1986-99 was newsletter editor, president, vice president, secretary for Unit 430. Edited District 19 *Bridge Buff* 1989-96 and from 1997 has done District 19 *Tournament Gazette*. Author of *Table Talk Cartoons, Let's Play Cards*, co-authored *Teach Me to Play and Teach Me to Play, Book Two*. Publisher of *Canadian Bridge*, editor of Kootenay, *Trump-it*, Vancouver *Matchpointer* and District 19 *Daily Bulletins*. Has done illustrations for ACBL *Bridge Bulletin* and Devyn Press. Her *Table Talk* cartoons have been published around the world in various bridge publications.

HANSON, Keith V. of Boca Raton FL, bridge teacher, former teacher. Formerly taught college bridge classes for credit. Author of *Winning Bridge Intangibles* (with Mike Lawrence), *Card Play Fundamentals* (with Easley Blackwood), *Fingertip Bridge* and *The Art of Bidding*. Won 17 regionals.

HANSON, Linda (b.1941) of Nashville TN, retired English teacher. Past president local board and Unit board member. Has won more than 75 regional events.

HARASIMOWICZ, Ewa (b.1951) of Krakow, Poland, economist. WBF World Master. Placed 3rd World Mixed Pairs 1994. Won European Mixed Pairs 1992. Won many national titles. Represented Poland many times.

HARDY, Mary E. (Mrs. Max, formerly Senti) (b. 1936) of Las Vegas NV, bridge professional, former business manager for 2 radio stations. Vice-chairman of ACBL Appeals Committee. Original appointee to National Ethical Oversight Committee. *Bridge World* Master Solvers panelist. Worked on *Two-over-One Game Force-revised* with Max Hardy. Placed 2nd Women's BAM Teams 1989. Diamond Life Master with more than 11,800 MPs as of 3/2001, has won more than 100 regionals.

HARDY, Max L. (b. 1932) of Las Vegas NV, associate national tournament director, bridge teacher and professional. Former teacher of theory, composer, conductor, singer and music teacher. Began directing 1961, became regional director 1970, attained present rating 1973, retired 2000. Former faculty member of Los Angeles Conservatory of Music which became California Institute of the Arts. Has served as vice-chairman of ACBL Ap-

peals Committee 1985-93 (resumed in 2000), original appointee to National Ethical Oversight Committee for 5 years. Associate editor *Popular Bridge,* founding editor of *Southern California Bridge News*. Author of *Five Card Majors—Western Style,* which went through 4 printings. Follow-up book was *Two over One Game Force.* Other books include *Play My Card, Forcing NT, 4th Suit, New Minors, Splinters and other Shortness Bids, Two over One Game Force Revised", Two-Over-One Game Force Quiz Book, Competitive Bidding with Two-Suited Hands, The Problems with Major Suit Raises and How to Fix Them, Standard Bridge Bidding.* Has been a *Bridge World and Southern California Bridge News* Master Problem Solvers panelist. Developed Hardy Adjunct to New Minor Forcing. Diamond Life Master with more than 11,200 MPs, has won more than 100 regional events.

HARDY, William Thomas (Bill) (b. 1953) of Portland OR, sports cards and memorabilia retailer, former consultant and social worker for state of Oregon. Placed 2nd ABA Victor Daly Teams 1988, competed in 1989 Goodwill Games, finished 2nd E-W in U.S. in Epson Pairs 1989.

HARFOUCHE, Gaby (b. 1944) of Baabda, Lebanon, Engineer. Represented Lebanon in 7 international championships. Won Gold Cup, Lebanese Festival 1973. Won many national titles.

HARKAVY, Harold (1915-1965) of Miami Beach, native New Yorker, bridge club manager, gained national renown as a player. Was one of the world's greatest at declarer play and a brilliant though unorthodox bidder. Won Master Mixed Teams 1952, 53, 55, 57; Chicago (now the Reisinger) 1952, Vanderbilt 1963, Spingold 1956, 63; placed 2nd Chicago 1945, Master Mixed Teams 1947, 64; Spingold 1953, Blue Ribbon Pairs 1963.

HARKER, William C. (Bill) (b. 1942) of Santa Fe NM, software engineer. Diamond Life Master, has won more than 15 regionals.

HARMON, Leonard B. (Len) (b. 1919) of East Hampton NY, semi-retired insurance company president. Formerly served as president and treasurer of Greater New York BA and chairman of District 24 Judiciary Committee. Retired from bridge in the Seventies. Represented North America in Bermuda Bowl 1959 (placed 2nd) and ACBL in first World Bridge Olympiad 1960. Won McKenney Trophy 1958, Chicago (now the Reisinger), Vanderbilt, Open Pairs 1958; Spingold 1962. Placed 2nd in Spingold 1958, Master Mixed Teams 1959, Vanderbilt 1966.

HARRIS, John T. (Spider) (1930-1994) of Houston, ACBL national tournament director, began his career in 1961. Intercollegiate champion 1952. (see WEB MOVEMENT.)

HARRIS, Marguerite (Tommy) (1896-1987) of New York City, from 1946 to 1969 was an ACBL staff member in charge of Club Department and writer of the ACBL *Bulletin* feature *Club Corner*. Won Women's Teams 1954, placed 2nd in 1952.

HARRIS, Shirlee (b. 1934) of Houston, former teacher. Represented ACBL in World Open Pairs 1962. Won Mixed Pairs 1960, 62; and several regionals.

HARRISON, Broma Lou. See REED, Broma Lou.

HARRISON-GRAY, Maurice (1900-1968) of London, England, bridge writer. Won European Teams 1948, 49, 50, 63; 2nd 1958. Represented Britain in 3 other world championships. National wins include 7 Gold Cups. Helped develop ACOL System, protagonist of Losing Trick Count. Bridge editor of *London Evening Standard, Country Life* and others. Author of 2 books.

HART, Norman de Villiers (1888-1976) of London, England. Won English Inter-county championship. Authored *Daily Telegraph Book of Contract Bridge, Bridge Players' Bedside Book.* Co-authored *Right Through the Pack, Vienna System of Contract Bridge, Quintessence of CAB.*

HARTLEY, Patti (b. 1944) of Kirkland WA, real estate agent. Placed 2nd Women's Swiss Teams 1989, won 15+ regional events.

HATHORN, John B. (1925-1964) of Houston TX. Though stricken by polio in 1954, still achieved Life Master status in 1956. Became bridge writer and leading bridge personality in Southwest. In 1959 Hathorn founded *Texas Bridge* which he published and edited until his death. Writings include several booklets on bidding and play, most written in collaboration with Bobby Nail

HATZIDAKIS, Manos (b. 1943) of Athens, Greece, born in Crete, printer. Represents Greece in international events. National wins include 2 Open Pairs and 3 Open Teams. Formerly presented bridge on national radio and published a magazine that included 8 pages about bridge.

HAUSE, Terry E. (The Reverend) (b. 1947) of San Jose CA, mathematics teacher, selected for *Who's Who Among American Teachers.* Won Open Pairs 1976.

HAUSLER, Helmut (b. 1956) of Saarbrucken, Germany, mathematics and physics teacher. 3rd European Pairs 1980. Represented Germany frequently since 1974. Won more than 30 national titles.

HAVAS, Elizabeth (Liz) (b. 1944) of Canberra, Australia, pharmacist. Won PABF (Far East) Women's Teams 1977, and represented Australia in 2 world championships, 7 other zonal championships. With Barbara Travis, played in 1998 PABF Open Teams, the first women's pair to represent Australia in open competition. Won one South Pacific playoff and 5 national titles.

HAVAS, George (b. 1947) of Brisbane, Australia, born in Hungary, computer scientist and theoretical mathematician. Won Far East Open Pairs 1971, South Pacific playoff 1977. Runner-up PABF (Far East) Teams and PABF (Far East) Pairs 1976. Represented Australia in 4 world championships and one other zonal championship. National wins include 2 Open Teams, 3 Open Pairs, Victor Champion Cup. Author of *The Australian Book of Bridge,* and bridge columnist of *The Australian* 1973-95.

HAWES, Emma Jean (Mrs. David B.) (d. 1987) of Fort Worth TX, graduated from Cornell University at age 18. Former president Fort Worth Unit, was member ACBL Board of Governors. One of the leading American women players. At one time was one of only 8 women WBF Grand Masters. Won Venice Cup 1974, 76, 78, World Olympiad Women's Teams 1980. Also represented ACBL in Deauville 1968 (placed 3rd Women's Teams), Miami Beach 1972 (3rd Women's Teams, 5th Mixed Teams), Las Palmas 1974 (3rd Women's Pairs), Monte Carlo 1976 (3rd Women's Teams). Hawes won Open Pairs 1958, Life Master Women's Pairs 1966, 78; Women's Teams 1967, 70, 72, 74, 75, 76; Women's Pairs 1981, Master Mixed Teams 1964. She placed 2nd Life Master Women's Pairs 1972, Women's Pairs 1968, 76; Master Mixed Teams 1952, 67, 72.

HAWKINS, Allen W., Jr. (Hawk) (b. 1949) of Birmingham AL, bank examiner-FDIC. Placed 2nd Open BAM Teams 1997.

HAXTON, Owen V. (b. 1929) of Novato CA, retired U.S. Army aviator, chairperson ROTC Scholarship selection committee for 6th U.S. Army. Began his career in

bridge administration 1976 at Unit level, became editor of Unit 508 *Double Dummy,* later served 3 terms as Unit president. Also Unit secretary, tournament chairman, representative to the District. Member District 21 executive committee since 1981, district president 1985-87, member ACBL Board of Directors 1993-95.

HAYDEN, Garey (b. 1944) of Tucson AZ, professional bridge instructor and player, owner of retail computer store. Grand Life Master with 22,030 MPs as of 3/2001 ranked #24 in ACBL. Won Men's Teams 1973, Open Pairs 1975, Men's Pairs 1977, North American Swiss Teams 1982, 85, 90; Open BAM Teams 1992, Mixed BAM Teams 1996. Placed 2nd Blue Ribbon Pairs 1972, Life Master Pairs 1976, North American Swiss Teams 1986, Life Master Open Pairs 1997, Spingold 1999. Has won more than 250 regional titles. One of only a few players to have won 5 events at a regional.

HAYS, G. Gard (b. 1933) of Veradale WA, salesman. District board member, Grand Life Master with 12,765 MPs as of 3/2001. Won Men's Pairs 1961, 64 and several regional events.

HAYWARD, Diane (b. 1936) of San Francisco, executive assistant, regional administration manager. Former District 21 *Forum* editor, doing research for genealogy book. Edited 4th edition *Encyclopedia of Bridge,* contributing editor to 5th and 6th editions. Former assistant editor of *Contract Bridge Forum,* has been editor for many West Coast regional *Daily Bulletins,* was *Daily Bulletin* assistant at NABCs for many years.

HAZEN, Lee (1905-1991) of New York City attorney, played professional baseball for the Brooklyn Dodgers. Driving force in modernization of ACBL in late Forties. ACBL Director 1940, served as ACBL counsel 1942-85, ACBL vice president 1945-47, ACBL Honorary Member 1958, member ACBL Laws Commission 1942-73. When he resigned he was named Member Emeritus. Trustee and treasurer ACBL Charity Foundation. Member ACBL Hall of Fame. Was founder and former vice president of Greater New York B.A. Contributing editor *Encyclopedia of Bridge.* WBF Life Master, represented ACBL Bermuda Bowl 1956, 59 (placed 2nd both times). Npc of winning North American team in 1971 Bermuda Bowl and the silver medal team in the World Team Olympiad 1972. Won Spingold 1942, 47, 55; Chicago (now the Reisinger) 1945, 49; Vanderbilt 1939, 42, 49, 58; Men's Pairs 1945, Master Individual 1941. Placed 2nd Spingold 1945, 58; Chicago 1941, 42; Vanderbilt 1944, 47; Master Individual 1940, Life Master Pairs 1946.

HEAD, Cecil (Cece) (1910-1996) of Fort Branch IN, retired attorney. Won Life Master Pairs 1948, several regionals. Set scoring records with S. Garton Churchill when winning Life Master Pairs in 1948.

HEITMANN, Eva Lund (b. 1960) of Alta, Norway, legal secretary. WBF World Master. 4th World Women's Team Olympiad 2000. National wins include Women's Teams.

HEITNER, Paul L. (the Whale) (1939-1988) of Bramalea ON, computer systems consultant. Was a leading bridge theorist. Co-developer with John Lowenthal of the Canary Club System. Co-founder and managing editor of *Bridge Journal,* now out of print. Won Life Master Pairs 1970, Men's Teams 1976, placed 2nd Men's Pairs 1972. Also won events in South Africa 1974.

HELDRING, Ernst (1904-1993) of Amsterdam, the Netherlands, attorney. Served European Bridge League as director 1952-71, secretary 1958-71. President Neth-

erlands Bridge League 1949-59, member editorial advisory board *Bridge Encyhclopedia,*

HELGEMO, Geir (b. 1970) of Trondheim, Norway, bridge professional. WBF World Life Master. Won World Junior Pairs 1995, Generali Individual 1996, European Junior Teams 1990. 3rd European Open Championship 1993, 97, 99. 2nd World Junior Championship 1993. Rated the world's most prominent Junior player 1990-95. 2nd Bermuda Bowl 1993, 4th 2000. Many national titles. With Tor Helness, won several prestigious invitational tournaments: MacAllan (twice), Cap Volmac (twice). 5 North American titles include Reisinger 1998, 99.

HELLEMANN, Anne-Lill (b. 1949) of Oslo, Norway, veterinarian. WBF World Master. 4th World Women's Team Olympiad 2000. Defeated U.S. Women's champions IOC 2000. 2nd Nordic Women's Teams 1998. National wins include Women's Teams.

HELLER, Barbara (b. 1948) of Decatur AL, media specialist. Served in many executive positions at Unit level including president, 2nd alternate to ACBL Board of Directors for District 7 1995-present; president Mid-Atlantic Bridge Conference 1991-92; co-chairman Gatlinburg regionals 1987-22; co-chairman Atlanta NABC 1995. Has won about 20 regionals.

HELMS, Gerald W. (Jerry) (b. 1950) of Charlotte NC, professional bridge player, teacher/trainer for ACBL, former full-time club owner/director. Has served Unit 153 as vice president and president and District 7 as vice president. Contributor to *The Bridge Grapevine* and *The Bridge Teacher.* Hand analyst for N.A. Collegiate Bridge Championship 1990, 91, 93; Novice Championship 1992. As an ACBL teacher trainer has trained more than 2000 teachers. Frequent lecturer at regionals, NABCs and the ABTA. Former member of ACBL Appeals Committee. Diamond Life Master with more than 12,000 MPs, has been on Crane Top 500 list past 16 years. Wrote *Helms to Hello.* Contributor to *Better Bridge* and *Bridge Bulletin.* Placed 2nd Blue Ribbon Pairs 1995, represented district 4 times in NAOP, has won 100+ regional events.

HELNESS, Tor (b.1957) of Oslo, Norway, stockbroker. WBF World Life Master. 2nd Bermuda Bowl 1993, 4th 2000. 3rd World Team Olympiad 1980, European Teams 1993. Won Nordic Teams 1980, 82, European Junior Teams 1980. Represented Norway in 10 world and European Championships. With Geir Helgemo, won several prestigious invitational tournaments: Macallan twice and Cap Volmac twice. Many national titles. Daily bridge column in Norway's biggest newspaper, *Verdens Gang.* Editor of *Bridge-Nytt* 1995-1996.

HENDERSON, Richard B. (Rick) (b. 1933) of Los Angles CA, retired CPA. As of 3/2001 ranked #79 on the ACBL Top 100 list with 12,043 MPs, has won more than 100 regionals.

HENKE, Chuck (b. 1934) of Aurora CO, safety coordinator with the National Child Safety Council. Was bridge professional, teacher and cruise director in the Sixties. Won Blue Ribbon Pairs 1965.

HENNER, Christal (b. 1954) of New York City, director of technology financial services firm. Won 15 regional events.

HENRY, Dr. Joseph L. (b. 1924) of Newton Center MA. Top ranking player of ABA for 12 years until his retirement from tournament competition. Became an ABA Life Master in 9 months and won more than 20 ABA National Championships.

HERBERT, Walter (1902-1975) of San Diego, conduc-

tor of the San Diego Opera, formerly general director of the Houston Opera Company. Originator of Herbert Convention, advocated by Herbert when he was a member of the 1937 Austrian team that defeated Ely and Josephine Culbertson, Helen Sobel and Charles Vogelhofer representing the U.S. to win the World Bridge Team Championship. The convention was applied in many ways in the Vienna System.

HERBST, Ilian (b.1968) of Haifa, Israel, computer engineer. WBF World Master. 5th World Team Olympiad 1992, World Junior Teams 1991, represented Israel on many other occasions. 2nd European Junior Teams 1990. Won European Union Junior Teams 1993. National wins include Junior Pairs 7 times and League Teams 10 times. Brother of Ophir.

HERBST, Ophir (b.1971) of Haifa Israel, computer engineer. WBF World Master. 5th World Team Olympiad 1992, World Junior Teams 1991, represented Israel on many other occasions. 2nd European Junior Teams 1990. Won European Union Junior Teams 1993. National wins include Junior Pairs 7 times, League Teams 10 times, and Open Pairs once. Brother of Ilian.

HEREDIA, Iréne Bajos de (1918-1998) Honorary Chief French Tournament Director, directed many international tournaments including World Pairs Championship Cannes, France, 1962. Co-author of *Le Bridge d'Ecole Francaise.*

HERON, Douglas (Doug) (b. 1943) of Ottawa ON, surgeon; former pilot in Canadian Armed Forces, (awarded Queen's Jubilee Medal). Served as president of Canadian Bridge Federation 1991-, Unit 192 president, District one Judiciary chairman, Unit appeals chairman, member ACBL Appeals Committee. Contributor to *Canadian Bridge,* Unit newsletter and occasionally the *Bridge World.* Won CNTC and Tri-Country Playoffs 1990. He and son Alex are the only father and son to have won the Canadian National Pairs Championship. Won more than 60 regionals.

HERR, Barbara Chase (b. 1920) of Wilmington DE, retired chemist. Appointed by governor of Delaware to chair Delaware State Commission for Women 1977-82. Won Life Masters Women's Pairs 1976.

HERRINGTON, Gaye W. (b. 1938) of Redondo Beach CA, retired municipal court judge. Has served on several unit boards and ALACBU Board. Accredited teacher. Won Life Master Women's Pairs 1987.

HERRMANN, John P. (b. 1945) of Chattanooga TN, bridge professional, former high school mathematics teacher. Served on ACBL Appeals Committee 1983-91, has chaired many appeals committees since 1975. Since 1986 has lectured at NABCs. As a teacher he was nominated to his school's Hall of Fame. Placed 2nd North American Swiss Teams 1977. Diamond Life Master with more than 9,000 MPs.

HERTZ, Dr. Daniel (b. 1934) of Harrison NY, physician. WBF vice-chairman of senior committee for the ACBL from 1999-present. Placed 19th Mixed Pairs 1998 6th Senior Teams. Placed 2nd 1996 Senior MP race. Has won more than 70 regionals.

HERTZ, Natalie (b.1934) of Harrison NY, attorney. Placed 6th in World Senior Teams 1998. Has been a top ten Senior MP winner 1992-98. Has 71 regional wins.

HERTZBERG, Dr. Howard (1936-1999) of Alpine NJ, orthopedic surgeon. Served Alpine as councilman and mayor. Placed 2nd Men's BAM Teams 1988, Senior KO Teams 1994, 96.

HESTHAVEN, Dennis G. (b. 1946) of Louisville KY, first vice president Morgan Keegan. Vice president and board member Unit board 1984-87, 1998-present. Diamond Life Master, won North American Swiss Teams 1991, 17 regional wins.

HEUSDEN, Willy van (1929 -1988) of Culemborg, The Netherlands. Represented The Netherlands in European Championships from 1963 to 1979. Many national titles. (see CONTINENTAL CLUB.)

HEWITT, Richard G. (Dick) (b. 1927) of New York City, attorney. Served on ACBL Board of Directors 1975-85. Member and chairman ACBL Charity Foundation 1983-1991 (2 terms as president). President District 3 Co-ordinating Committee 1965-75. Member ACBL Executive Committee, ACBL Goodwill Committee, ACBL Board of Governors 1985-96, ACBL Laws Commission 1985-97. Treasurer of 1968 Spring and 1974 Summer NABC. Chairman of 1981 Bermuda Bowl Committee. Has run a weekly bridge club since 1957.

HICKS, Karl S. (b. 1943) of Dominion NS, vice-principal and R-3 tournament director. Has served as Zone one director for Canadian B.F., 2 terms as Unit 194 president, the Unit tournament chairman 1974-84. Well-known for his repertoire of "stories". Editor of *Maritime Bridge Line*. Won "Fred Friendly" award 1991. Placed 1st in North America and 3rd in world in 1989 World-Wide Epson Pairs.

HILLIARD, Olga (1891-1979) of New York City. Donated the ABL trophy for Mixed Pairs, which is still given at the ACBL Spring NABC for a two-session event. Won Master Mixed Teams 1932 and Women's Teams 1942, finished 2nd in Women's Pairs 1931, 43.

HINDS, Carreen S. (b. 1944) of Bakersfield CA., math teacher. Diamond Life Master, placed 2nd Women's BAM Teams 1993. Won 15+ regional events.

HINGERTY, Dr. Brian E. (b. 1948) of Knoxville TN, scientist at Oak Ridge National Laboratory. Owner Knox Computer Consultants. Won 15+ regionals.

HIRON, Alan M. (1933-1999) of Marbella, Spain, computer and games consultant. WBF World Master. Won World Senior Pairs 1990. Represented Britain in one zonal championship. 5 national wins. Editor *Bridge Magazine* (1985-1990). Bridge correspondent *The Independent* in England.

HIRON, Maureen (b. 1942) of Marbella, Spain, in England, computer and games consultant. 3rd European Senior Pairs 1993. Represented Britain in one zonal. Bridge columnist of *The Independent* in England. Co-author of 2 bridge books and many trivia books. Inventor of best-selling games including *Continuo* and *Duo*. Voted Londoner of Year 1990 for charitable work.

HIRSCH, Tannah (b. 1933) of New York City, formerly of South Africa and Israel, bridge writer, editor and since 1978 president of Goren International. Co-author of *Tournament Book of the Second World Olympiad Pairs*. Edited *Daily Bulletin* at the European Championships 1965, 74, 76; editor ACBL *Bulletin* 1967-72. Contributed articles to bridge publications around the world. Won South Africa Congress Teams 1957, Natal Teams 1958, Jerusalem Pairs 1962, 63, 64.

HIRSCHBERG, Ralph (1906-1962) of New York City, insurance broker. Set a record by capturing Eastern States Reisinger Trophy 6 times, including 4 consecutive wins, 1956-59. Won Reisinger BAM Teams 1958, Men's BAM Teams 1955; placed 2nd Life Master Pairs, Open Pairs, Men's Pairs 1944, Reisinger 1945, Vanderbilt 1958, Spingold 1960.

HIRSCHHAUT, Fida (b. 1937 in Romania) boutique owner. WBF World Master. Won CAC Women's Teams 1979, 80, 81, 85, 87, 91, 95. Represented Venezuela in world championships and won many national titles. Bridge teacher and director. Quarterfinalist Venice Cup 1995.

HIRSCHMAN, Daniel (Dan) (b. 1984) of Southfield MI, student. Began learning bridge at age 4. Became youngest Life Master at 10 years, 2 months, 20 days in November 1994 — achieved his goal in 15 months. Awarded Homer Shoop Pre-Teen Scholarship Award. When he became Life Master, all members of the family (4) were Life Masters — father Martin, mother Marcia, brother Sam. Believed to be youngest winner of any regional event — won Bracket II KO Teams at age of 9 years, 8 months, 14 days, at the Cleveland regional in May 1994. First unlimited regional win was Cyclone Continuous Pairs at Cedar Rapids, Iowa. 1994 with his mother — he was 9 years, 10 months, and 2 days. See FAMILY.

HIRSCHMAN, Martin A. (b. 1949) of Southfield MI, bridge teacher and professional player, retired attorney, former wire service newsman. Editor Unit 137 *Table Talk* since 1987. Served on Unit Board of Directors. Co-editor *Daily Bulletin* at NEC World Junior Team Championships 1991. Author of *The Bridge Manual* and *Play Your Way into Flight A*. Three-time winner Unit 137 Player of the Year award. Teacher and principal partner of both sons, Sam and Dan, during their respective successful campaigns to become Youngest Life Master. Diamond Life Master with more than 8,600 MPs, has won more than 52 regionals. See FAMILY.

HIRSCHMAN, Samuel A. (Sam) (b. 1976) of Southfield MI, student, enjoys computer and role-playing games. Became the youngest Life Master at the time in July 1988, at age 11 years 9 months, 5 days. His feat was featured in *Sports Illustrated* magazine. King of Bridge. Member ACBL Junior Team 1997. See FAMILY.

HISATOMI, Hiroshi (b. 1946) of Tokyo, Japan, born in China, bridge instructor and publisher. Far East champion 1985, represented Japan in 11 other Far East Championships and 7 world championships. Won 24 national team titles and 2 national pair titles. Author of *Five-Card Major Standard*, and *Seattle 84*.

HOADLEY, Frank M. (b. 1923) of New Orleans LA, retired professor of English, worked in television commercials. Served several terms on New Orleans Board of Directors. Grand Life Master with 13,072 as of 3/2001. Won Men's Pairs 1960 and placed 2nd Spingold 1959, Reisinger 1975, GNOP 1987.

HOBLEY, Susan (b. 1952) of Sydney, Australia, environmental and urban horticultural consultant. Represented Australia Venice Cup 1981, 85. Won PABF (Far East) Women's Teams 1985 and many national titles.

HOBSON, John (b. 1964) of London, England, stock broker. Won World Junior Teams 1989. Won Gold Cup once.

HOCHEKER, Danuta Jolanta (b. 1951) of Olsztyn, Poland, mathematician. WBF World Master. Won World Mixed Pairs 1994. Won many national titles.

HOCHZEIT, Michael (b. 1942) of Tel Aviv, Israel, building contractor and club owner. WBF World Master. Placed 3rd Bermuda Bowl 1976, 85. Represented Israel in 9 world championships, 5 European championships and 8 European Pairs Championships. Co-owner Israel's biggest club.

HODAPP, Thomas (b. 1942) of Cincinnati OH, advertising executive. Won Life Master Men's Pairs 1978 and placed 2nd Blue Ribbon Pairs 1969. Grand Life Master with 10,969 MPs as of 3/2001.

HODGE, Paul (1910-1976), expert player and bridge commentator. Placed 2nd Bermuda Bowl 1961, also was npc of U.S. Women's team in 1964 World Team Olympiad. Won Fishbein Trophy 1954, Herman Trophy 1955. Won Mixed Pairs 1953, Life Master Pairs 1955, Reisinger 1955, 64, Men's BAM Teams 1953, 56. Placed 2 in Reisinger 1956, 57, 59, Men's Pairs 1957, 60; Vanderbilt 1959, Men's BAM Teams 1960, Spingold 1967.

HODLER, Marc (b. 1915) of Bern, Switzerland, retired lawyer. The personal link between the World Bridge Federation and the International Olympic Committee, of which he is a vice president. Has worked for the inclusion of bridge in the Olympic Games, perhaps in Turin 2006. Institution of I.O.C. Grand Prix under his guidance was a step in this direction. Member I.O.C. since 1963. President International Skiing Federation for 47 years, 1951-98. President Swiss Bridge Federation 1955-85, probably a bridge record. Represented Switzerland in one zonal championship. IBPA Personality of the Year 1999.

HOEIE, Erik (b. 1928) of Stavanger, Norway, tailor. Represented Norway 1970 Bermuda Bowl and 4 European Championships. Author of *Stavanger-grangen*, dealing with 1NT opening bids and responses.

HOERSCH, Joel J. (b. 1937) of La Jolla CA, newspaper composition programmer. Member San Diego Unit Board of Directors for many years. Has served on the ACBL Appeals Committee. Contributor to *Contract Bridge Forum*. For 20 years Hoersch has written, directed and acted in bridge skits and shows for regionals and NABCs. Placed 2nd Reisinger 1981, has won more than 30 regionals.

HOFFMAN, Anne Sykes (b. 1947) of Peru VT and Nantucket MA, real estate developer and licensed general contractor. Won a national sailing championship in 1970. District 25 vice president 2000-present, second vice president 1999, Unit 175 representative to District Board 1955-99. District 25 Executive Committee 1995-99, member ACBL Board of Governors 1997-99. Diamond Life Master, has been on the Barry Crane Top 500 since 1992. Won Transnational Mixed Teams 2000, placed 5th WBF Zonal Pairs 1994. Very involved with ACBL Junior program, director of North American Youth Bridge Foundation and has been captain, coach and sponsor of 6 ACBL Junior Teams.

HOFFMAN, Arthur H. (b. 1935) of Maplewood NJ, compliance officer with Prudential Insurance Company. Served as board member of Unit 140 1983-89 and 1992-98; contributor to Unit 140 *Declarer*. Won Men's Pairs 1988.

HOFFMAN, Martin (b. 1932) of London, England, bridge writer and professional. Winner of many European tournaments and one of fastest analysts in the game. Author of *Hoffman on Pairs Play*, and occasional magazine contributor. Survivor of Auschwitz.

HOFFNER, David L. (Lion) of Potomac MD, croupier and entrepreneur. Won Life Master Men's Pairs 1977. Diamond Life Master with many regional wins.

HOLLAND, George T. (Giorgio Bella Holland) (b. 1947) of Dartmouth NS, vice-president real estate development/brokerage firm. Served as local tournament chairman Units 194 and 166, 2 terms as president Unit 194, chairman Can-Am and Can-At regionals 3 times each, was president of Canadian Bridge Federation. Has been regular contributor to *Maritime Bridge Line*. Won several regional events. Has represented Zone I of CBF 11 times in finals of CNTC.

HOLLINGSWORTH, Wayne (Wagney) (1940) of Irmo SC, software consultant and engineer. District 7 secretary 1997-99, vice-president 1999-present, NAOP co-ordinator 1995-present. Member MABC Board of Governors 1997-present. Diamond Life Master with 25 regional wins.

HOLMES, Robert L. (Bob) (b. 1946) of Las Vegas, owner pest control service. Won 20 regionals.

HOLT, Clarice K. (1911-deceased) of Fort Worth TX, oil executive. Won Women's Pairs 1962, Mixed Pairs 1962, placed 2nd in Women's Teams 1964. Diamond Life Master with numerous regional wins.

HOLTSBERRY, Brad C. (b. 1958) of Farmington Hills MI, attorney. Has served as vice president District 12 1996-98 and president 1998-present. Contributor to SMBA newsletter *Echo*. Won 17 regionals.

HOMSY, Marguerite (b. 1951) of Cairo, Egypt, former bank official. WBF World Master. Won BFAAME Women's Teams 1987, 91, 97, runner-up 1989. Represented Egypt in several world and other zonal championships.

HOOKER, Jim L. (b. 1937) of Los Angeles, independent oil operator. Won the GNOT 1975 and numerous regional events in the Seventies.

HORN, Stormy (b. 1929) of El Paso TX, consultant-atmospheric physics, former research scientist at White Sands Missile Range. Co-author of *The System* and *System Update*. Authored *Bidding Magic* and did early presentations of several conventions including Reed/Horn 4NT, Integrated Major Raises, Mini-Splinters, Colorado Relays, Tricolor and StarWars. Won 30+ regionals.

HORNING, Edmund M. (Ted) (1940-1999) of Willowdale ON, syndicated bridge columnist, bridge studio and travel agency owner, professional bridge teacher and player. Served as vice chairman of the Canadian Bridge Federation National Championship Committee 1977. Diamond Life Master, placed 2nd Blue Ribbon Pairs 1978.

HOROBETZ, Helen (1915-1989) of Chula Vista CA, bridge cruise director, lecturer and writer. Struggled against the crippling effects of rheumatoid arthritis from the age of 18 months. Press Room worker at NABCs for 20 years. Managed regional tournaments, edited *Daily Bulletins* at other tournaments, taught classes and devoted hours of volunteer work to advance bridge in San Diego area. Instituted District 22's regional *Daily Bulletin* which she edited. Contributor to ACBL *Bulletin, Southern California Bridge News, Contract Bridge Forum* and *ABTA Quarterly*. Member of American Bridge Teachers Association since 1973, served as its regional vice president 1974-78. Member of committee that edited Report of ABTA Committee on Standard American. Held various executive positions in Unit 519 and District 22, was second alternate to ACBL Board of Directors, member of ACBL Board of Governors. In 1987 at the celebration of the 50th anniversary of the ACBL she received a golden medallion for her lifetime of service to the game and its players, the only one ever to be honored in this manner.

HORTON, Mark H. (b.1950) of Romford, England. Bridge professional, editor of *Bridge Magazine, Daily Bulletin* editor for WBF, European Bridge League and other bridge organizations. Represented Great Britain and England internationally, EBU Grandmaster #94.

Winner of numerous national titles including Crockfords Cup and Grandmasters Pairs, placed 2nd 1996 European Community Mixed Teams. Captained British women's World Olympiad team 1992, finishing 2nd. Author of numerous books including *Step-by-Step Signalling* and the *Mammoth Book of Bridge.*

HORTON, Sally (formerly Sowter; now Brock). See BROCK, Sally.

HORWITZ, Janice C. (Jan) (b. 1924) of Butler PA and Scottsdale AZ, bridge teacher. Won Master Mixed Teams 1969, World-Wide Epson Pairs 1988, won 17-18 regionals.

HOWARD, Denis (b. 1932) of Sydney, Australia, solicitor. President World Bridge Federation 1986-91. WBF World Life Master. Placed 3rd Bermuda Bowl 1971. Represented Australia in 4 other world championships and 3 zonal championships. 19 national titles include Inter-State Teams 12 times. Member WBF Executive Council 1982-86. Former president Australian Bridge Federation. Founding editor of *Australian Bridge.* Bridge columnist of *National Times* for 15 years, of *Sydney Morning Herald* since 1999. Honor Member of IBPA. Interim CEO of ACBL 1992.

HOWARD, Laurence B. III, (Bryan) (b. 1958) of Brentwood TN, attorney. Won 20+ regionals.

HOWARD, Laurence B., Jr. (Larry) (b. 1927) of Nashville TN, retired corporation chairman of the board. Has served in various executive positions on Unit and District levels including unit president. Was partnered by 13-year-old daughter in first legitimate (post litigation) victory by female in Men's Pairs. Has won 20+ regional events all over the Southeast.

HOWARD, Morgan H. (1893-1965) of North Hollywood CA, for many years a top executive of the Hearst publishing enterprise in Pittsburgh and New York. ACBL president 1942.

HOWELL, Edwin Cull (1860-1907), newspaper editor and teacher, credited with the invention of the Howell Movement 1897. Learned whist at Harvard and became its best player. Took a prominent part in the activities of the American Whist League and in 1896 published *Howell's Whist Openings: a systematic treatment of the short-suit game,* and in 1897 the *Howell Method of Duplicate Whist for Pairs.*

HOYLE, Edmond (1672-1769) a London barrister. First authority on whist and other games and first professional teacher of whist. His famous work was perhaps the best seller of the 18th century and had the longest title of any book ever written on cards: *A Short Treatise on the Game of Whist, Containing the Laws of the Game, and also Some Rules Whereby a Beginner May, with Due Attention to Them, Attain to the Playing of It Well.* Published in 1742, it quickly went through several editions as well as being pirated extensively. Hoyle's technique was surprisingly modern. He introduced the idea of inferring the nature of unseen hands from the fall of the cards and discussed matters of probability. He also included a Code of Ethics and Fair Play, which was embodied almost without change in the Laws of Auction nearly 200 years later. He was the first person to establish a tradition of law and order in card games, whence the phrase, now used to describe correct procedure in anything, "according to Hoyle". The book of laws by Hoyle was reprinted verbatim through the years. The prominent London Clubs eventually did make certain changes as to style and working from time to time, especially in the 19th century, but Hoyle's imprimatur remained on most editions. He achieved considerable fame

during his lifetime and his name has since become a household word. Any collection of rules of card, table or board games is still termed a Hoyle.

HSIAO, Chi-Han or Elmer (b. 1941) of Taipei, Taiwan, born in China, English teacher. World Life Master. Placed 2nd Bermuda Bowl 1970, Far East Champion 1969, 1976. Represented Taiwan in 3 world championships and 6 zonal championships.

HSIEH, Douglas (b. 1969) of New York City, corporate finance analyst. Became youngest Life Master in 1981 at age of 11 years 10 months and 4 days, a record that stood for 7 years. Also youngest to win a regional event (age 9) and the youngest Junior Master (age 7). Represented ACBL World Junior Bridge Championships 1993. Won National Youth Championship 1988 and several regionals. Hsieh believes the title of Youngest Life Master has been and will always be the measure of a family's strength and perseverance. See FAMILY.

HSIEH, William C. (Bill) (b. 1966) of San Francisco, investment banker. Youngest Life Master in 1980 at age 13 years 7 months. Placed 3rd World Junior Championships in Amsterdam 1987, and was on the U.S. Junior team in the Epson International in Japan 1985, had several regional wins. See FAMILY.

HSU, Jen-Yuen (1914-83) of Taipei, Taiwan, born in China, textile merchant. Taiwan's "Father of Bridge". Won Far East Open Pairs 1959, 69. Rrepresented Taiwan on 6 other occasions. Coordinator of 1971 Bermuda Bowl and 3 Far East Championships in Taipei. Founded *Chinese Bridge Magazine* and was its chief editor for 22 years. Bridge teacher and coached first women's team in Taiwan. Translated more than 30 bridge books into Chinese.

HU, Jihong (b. 1955) of Shanghai, China, technical employee. WBF World Master. Won Far East Teams 1991, 2nd 1993. Represented China in 5 World championships and 4 zonal championships. Won IOC Grand Prix 1998. Won many national titles.

HU, Sheau-Fong (b. 1952) of Taipei, Taiwan, government employee. Represented Taiwan in 12 zonal championships and 10 world championships. Top ranking woman player in Taiwan.

HUANG, Kuang-Hui or Patrick (b. 1943) of Taipei, Taiwan, born in China, financial executive in plastics corporation. WBF World Life Master. Placed 2nd Bermuda Bowl 1969, 70; represented Taiwan in 15 world championships. Far East Team champion 9 times and Open Pairs champion 5 times in 22 appearances. First played in Far East Championship at age 15. Assisted C. C. Wei in the development of the Precision System, which has been used regularly by Taiwan teams.

HUBERT, Olin (b. 1949) of Atlanta GA, professional player and an Associate National tournament director since early 80's. Hubert has won 40-50 regional titles.

HUDECEK, Carl J. (b. 1934) of Perrysburg OH, technical consultant, former chief physicist of Owens-Illinois Glass Co. Author of many technical papers on glass and international expert on TV tube manufacturing. Served as president many times of Unit 105 and District 12. Member of *Bridge World* Master Solver's Panel for more than 30 years. Won Life Master Men's Pairs 1966 and 50+ regional events. Member of team that defeated the Italians in Omar Sharif's Bridge Circus in Seventies.

HUDGINS, John L. (Jack) (b. 1929) of Memphis TN, retired ACBL national tournament director. Began directing career in 1960 and achieved the rating of national director in 1968. Has won several regionals.

HUGGARD, Marietta (b. 1935) of Naples FL. Won Venice Cup 1974. Won Life Master Women's Pairs 1970, Women's Teams 1971 (2nd in 1973), Master Mixed Teams 1972, numerous regionals.

HULGAARD, Johannes (b 1932) of Aarhus, Denmark, orthopedic surgeon. WBF World Master. Placed 3rd World Team Olympiad 1988. Represented Denmark World Team Olympiad 1960, 84 and European Championships 9 times. 21 Danish titles. With his father-in-law, Axel Voigt, has been a leading theorist for the Danish versions of the Acol system, co-authoring several books.

HULGAARD, Lida (b. 1939) of Aarhus, Denmark, lawyer. Won Nordic Teams 1973. Represented Denmark in one world championship and 5 zonals, including 3 opens. Many national wins.

HUME, Hampton (1924-1969) of Atlanta. Won Open Pairs 1961, placed 2nd Master Mixed Teams 1964. Many regional wins. Published *Modern Bridge* magazine 1964.

HUME, Jean H. of Livermore CA, self-employed tax accountant. Served as Unit 501 president 1993-97 and board member 1990-97. Has won 25 regionals.

HUMER, Norman D. (b. 1940) of Boston MA, scientific programmer. Retired from tournament play to protest the way cheating situations were handled during the early Eighties. Had many regional wins.

HUNT, Richard W. (Dick) (b. 1931) of Las Vegas NV, retired CFO. Diamond Life Master, won the Barry Crane Top 500 race 1994, was 2nd in Senior MP race in same year. Won Senior KO Teams 1994, placed 2nd in Senior KO Teams 1995. He has won 80+ regionals.

HUSKE, William H. (1879-1945) of New York City, native of Quebec, spent 30 years in newspaper business. Bridge editor Cleveland *Plain Dealer* 1927-29. Covered the first famous "grudge" match. It was between Ely Culbertson who played with George Reith (from New York), and Carl Robertson, an editorial writer for the *Plain Dealer* who played with Ralph R. Richards of Detroit. As a result of his coverage became associate editor of *Bridge World,* was made editor 1932. Editor ACBL *Bulletin* 1937-39. Wrote many articles on bridge and towie, the three-handed game he helped sponsor.

HUSSEIN, Dr. Ahmed D. (b. 1941) of Cairo Egypt, formerly of New York City, born in Egypt, investor chairman National Investment Co. Received Cairo University Golden Medal for Social Services 1958. Placed 2nd Egyptian Open Chess Championship 1959, awarded Fulbright in 1965. Won Mixed Pairs 1978, placed 2nd Life Master Pairs 1975. Has had many regional wins.

HUSTON, Michael B. (b. 1941) of Joplin MO, labor arbitrator and bridge professional. Member of ACBL Appeals Committee since 1970,and District Judiciary Chairman 1995-present. Diamond Life Master, has won more than 100 regional events.

HUTCHINSON, Mary L. (b. 1916) of Lethbridge AB and Corvallis OR, company vice president. She and husband (Robert) celebrated their 64th wedding anniversary. One of top women MP holders in Canada. Diamond Life Master, has won many regional events.

HUTCHINSON, Robert (b. 1905) of Lethbridge AB and Corvallis OR, president of land company, retired farmer. Diamond Life Master, ranks among the top MP holders in Canada. Has won 15+ regional events.

HWANG, Frank K. (b. 1940) of Warren NJ, born in China, formerly of Taiwan, mathematics professor. WBF World Life Master. 2nd Bermuda Bowl 1969, represented Taiwan World Team Olympiad 1972. Won first national

title at the age 17, won 1992 national teams with an overseas Chinese squad. Represented Taiwan in Far East Championship when he was 18 and his brother, Patrick Huang, was 15. This was the youngest international partnership ever in a major championship.

HYATT, Irene M. (b.1920) of Arvada CO, retired, former president Boulder Manufacturing Corporation and Hyatt Bridge Enterprises, Inc. Served as Unit 359 president, board member and tournament chairman for 9 years. Has contributed to *The Contract Bridge Forum.* Was weekly bridge columnist in Sixties and Seventies for *The Boulder Daily Camera.* Has played bridge in Mexico, England, Germany, Canada, France, Iran, Japan, Bolivia, Colombia and Kenya. She has won 15+ regional events.

HYLAND, Daniel A. (b. 1929) of Arlington Heights IL, president bank brokerage firm. Won Open Pairs 1975. Won several regionals.

HYMES, Edward, Jr. (1908-1962) of New York City, attorney. Life Master #23, one of leaders among the "Young Turks" who gained their seasoning as members of the Deal Club group. They were closely associated with P. Hal Sims at his summer home in Deal NJ. He won his first major national championship, the 1935 Open Pairs, with fellow Columbia alumnus Oswald Jacoby. Also won one Vanderbilt and 4 Spingolds. Lifetime member and former president Cavendish Club in New York.

I

INCE, Mehmet Ali (b. 1947) of Istanbul, Turkey, businessman. Represented Turkey in 2 world and 3 zonal championships. 6 national wins.

IN DER MAUR, Gangolf (b. 1931) of Klagenfurt, Austria, lawyer. Represented Austria in 5 World Championships and 5 European Championships. Won 7 Austrian Open Teams and 2 Open Pairs.

INGBERMAN, Monroe J. (1935-1985) of White Plains NY, college professor. Inventor of Fragment Bid, 3NT Response as a forcing major raise. Frequent contributor to bidding structure including Splinter Bid, Unusual over Unusual, method for Inverted Minors, Structured Reverses, 3NT to ask for a singleton after a jump major raise (Mathe Asking Bid), modified Roman Keycard Blackwood. Contributing editor, *Bridge Encyclopedia* and ACBL *Bulletin.*

INGRAM, Henry St. John (1888-1974) of Farnborough, Kent, England, printer, bridge writer, editor. Captained some British teams in pre-World War II era. Won Schwab Cup 1936. Contributing editor for 2 encyclopedias, author of bridge books.

INO, Masayuki (b. 1948) of Kanagawa, Japan, manager electronics company. WBF World Master. Represented Japan in 3 world championships and 3 Far East Championships. Won National Open Teams 27 times and 14 other national titles. Expert in game of Go.

INOUE, Shiro (b. 1915) of Tokyo, Japan, securities company adviser, former bank president. National titles include Princess Takamatsu 1968, 72, Prince Takamatsu Cup 1970, Fujiyama Cup 1970, Yamada Cup, 1965, 71, 77. Life Master in both U.S. and Japan. President JCBL 1969-72.

INOUE, Utako (Mrs. Shiro) (1914-83) of Tokyo, Japan, former secretary. Played in Far East Women's Team

Championships, representing Japan 1964, 69, Philippines 1974. National titles include Yamada Cup 1971, Princess Takamatsu Cup 1968. Life Master in 3 countries - Japan, U.S. and Philippines.

IRWIN, Florence (1865-1956) well-known New York City novelist, bridge teacher and expert on auction bridge. Wrote one of the first books on contract bridge in 1927, bridge editor of *New York Times* in early 1900s.

ISAACS, E. Sydney (Syd) (b. 1928) of London ON, retired university associate registrar. Member ACBL Goodwill Committee for 25 years. 4th) Women's Team Olympiad 1976. Won Master Mixed Teams 1975, several regional events.

ITABASHI, Mark M. (b. 1954) of Murrieta CA, bridge teacher and professional player, former computer analyst, former concert clarinet player. Grand Life Master with 25,591 MPs as of 3/2001, #10 in ACBL. Won 4 events at several regionals-Portland, Santa Rosa, Pasadena and Phoenix. Won GNOT 1998, placed 2nd North American Swiss Teams 1986, Master Mixed Teams, Mixed Pairs 1987, Life Master Open Pairs 1995. More than 300 regional wins.

IVASKA, J. Paul, Jr. (b. 1941) of Las Vegas NV, office manager, formerly a control systems engineer, designing and analyzing control and guidance systems for missiles and spacecraft. Has served Culver City and Las Vegas Units as president, District 17 Board member in the early Eighties. Placed 18th World Mixed Pairs 1982. Won Amateur Swiss Teams 1976, North American Swiss Teams 1979, placed 2nd North American Men's Swiss Teams 1982, GNOT 1989. Grand Life Master with 12,675 MPs as of 3/2001, has won dozens of regional events.

IVEY, Ernest (Ernie) (b. 1934) of Santa Maria CA, systems requirements analyst. Has served as president, vice president and chairman of charity committee of District 21. Diamond Life Master, won Open Pairs 1976 and approximately 20 regionals.

IVEY, Joan L. (b. 1939) of Santa Maria CA, retired office manager. Was secretary and vice president of Unit 543, secretary of District 22 and on District 21 judiciary committee. Recipient Unit 503 Sportsmanship Award 1984. Diamond Life Master, has won 15+ regionally rated games.

IWASZKO, Anthony J. (Knute) (b. 1935) of Belmar NJ, retired sales manager, also owner/innkeeper of a seashore bed and breakfast. Author of *The 401(K) Millionaire*. Won Sub-National Masters Pairs (under 50 points) 1966.

J

JABBOUR, Sharon (Lucky) of Boca Raton FL, nurse, bridge teacher, cruise director and lecturer. Finished 2nd Women's KO Teams 1999, has won more than 50 regionals events.

JABBOUR, Zeke of Boca Raton FL, professional player, cruise director and lecturer. Has been associated with all aspects of the theater and has lent his expertise to variety shows at NABCs. Contributor to *The Bridge Bulletin,* panelist *It's Your Call,* hand consultant for *Tall Tales and Short Stories.* Grand Life Master with 24,950 MPs as of 3/2001, #12 in ACBL, won 71 regional events in 1989, the year he won the Barry Crane Top 500. Won Fishbein Trophy 1989, George Burns Trophy for Senior

Player of Year 1995. Placed 2nd World Senior Teams 1994. Won Senior KO Teams 1994, 95, 96, 98, Senior Swiss Teams 1998. Placed 2nd Life Master Men's Pairs, Men's BAM Teams 1979, Senior KO Teams 1997. Has won more than 500 regional events.

JABES, Rina of Rome, Italy, WBF World Life Master, won World Women's Team Olympiad 1972, 76; European Women's Teams 1970, 71, 73, 74.

JABON, Joseph A. (Joe) (b. 1925) of Seattle WA, owner of transportation company. In Sixties introduced musical entertainment to regionals using talent furnished by bridge players. He served two terms as president of Seattle Unit, was columnist for Seattle *Times.* Member of the "Whiz Kids" team that included Sidney Lazard, Ron Dreyfus and Noel Duvic. Grand Life Master with 12,543 MPs as of 3/2001, won Open Swiss Teams 1992, National Open Individual 1959, placed 2nd Open Individual 1950, Open Pairs 1965, GNOP 1992.

JACKSON, Joan S. (b. 1947) of Dallas TX, financial manager, previously in corporate finance with a major retailer. Won Women's Team Olympiad 2000, competed in international competition in New Orleans 1978, Biarritz 1982, Geneva 1990, Albuquerque 1994. Won Women's BAM Teams 1989, 2000; Women's Swiss Teams 1992, 99; placed 2nd in National Amateur Pairs 1976, Women's Swiss Teams, Life Master Women's Pairs 1992, 2000, Women's KO Teams 2000.

JACKSON, Peter (b.1940) of Pretoria, South Africa, scientist. Member of SABF Executive since 1971 and senior tournament director. Maintains masterpoint register and designs movements, using computer expertise.

JACOB, Dan R. (b. 1951) of Burnaby BC, born in Romania, engineer. A Diamond Life Master. Was National Master of the Year 1979, won Canadian National Teams Championship 1999. Won WBF Pairs 1999. Has won more than 15 regionals.

JACOB, Thomas Patrick (Tom) (b. 1958) of Auckland, New Zealand, computer systems manager. Far East Champion 1995. Represented New Zealand in two world championships and two other Far East Championships. Won National Open Teams 3 times, National Open Pairs once and two other titles. With Brian Mace and Denis Humphries, developed Bondage bidding system. It features two-under transfer openings and many relays based on Symmetric principles.

JACOBI, Ernst (b.1914) of Zurich, Switzerland, chemical engineer. Represented Switzerland in one world championship and many zonal championships. 11 national wins.

JACOBS, Bill (b. 1955) of Melbourne, Australia, software development manager. Represented Australia in one Bermuda Bowl and two zonal championships. National wins include interstate teams and open teams. Magazine contributor.

JACOBS, George H. (b.1947) of Burr Ridge IL, executive. Has served as vice president of Unit 123 and board member CCBA since 1992. Received many awards and honors outside the bridge world including "Entrepreneur of the Year" 1992, was inducted in "Entrepreneurial Hall of Fame" (IL.) 1993. NABC vugraph comentator, chief auctioneer for Cavendish Pairs and Teams (as well as participant). He and his team were invited to participate in the 1999 Olympic "showcase" in Lausanne Switzerland - a prelude to bridge being accepted by the Olympic Committee and being recognized as a sport. WBF World Master. Diamond Life Master has competed internationally

and was 9th in Rosenblum 1998. Placed 2nd China Cup 1999, USBC 1999, 3rd 1997. Won Vanderbilt, IMP Pairs 1999; placed 2nd Reisinger 1998. Has won more than 60 regionals.

JACOBS, Hans J. (b.1949) of Aurora ON, born in Germany. Founder and operator Heritage Carpets (1969-89), manages investment properties. Served on Unit 246 Board of Directors for 10 years, 5 of those years as Judiciary Chairperson. District 2 president 1990-2000. Member ACBL Board of Governors for 6 years. Diamond Life Master, won Richmond Trophy 1997. Has been on Barry Crane Top 500 list for past 10 years, has won 40-50 regionals.

JACOBS, Jos (b. 1947), of Amsterdam, The Netherlands. *Daily Bulletin* editor at world and European Championship. Represented The Netherlands 1984 World Teams. National titles include Open Teams 1976. Contributor to *Bridge* as tournament directing expert. Speaks 8 languages.

JACOBS, Walter L. (Wally) (1896-1985) of Bay Harbor Island FL, founder, president and CEO of Hertz Rent-a-Car Corp. 1918-60. Recipient of Horatio Alger Award. Won Open Pairs 1936, 39.

JACOBSON, Ann (b.1940) of Stockton CA, staff accountant. Won North American Swiss Teams 1981 and several regionals.

JACOBSON, James A. (Jake) (b.1951) of Sioux City IA, sales. Has won 20+ regionals.

JACOBSON, Rita (1911-1992) of Sydney, Australia, formerly of Johannesburg, South Africa. 2nd World Women's Teams 1968, 1972, World Women's Pairs 1974. Also represented South Africa World Team Olympiad 1964, 1976, 1980, World Pair Olympiad 1962, 1966, 1970, Maccabi Games 1977. 9 national wins. Bridge columnist *The Star*.

JACOBUS, Marc S. (b. 1951) of Las Vegas, professional player. WBF World Master. Grand Life Master with 15,451 MPs as of 3/2001. Won Life Master Men's Pairs 1972, North American Swiss Teams 1986, placed 2nd Reisinger 1974, Spingold 2000. Has won more than 100 regional titles.

JACOBY, James O. (Jim) (1933-1991) of Richardson TX, stockbroker, graduate of Notre Dame. Outside interests included backgammon, sports and opera. Co-author with his father (Oswald Jacoby) of Jacoby Transfer Bid, Jacoby 2NT and a syndicated bridge column. Frequently served as member of ACBL Board of Governors, past president of Dallas B.A. World Grand Master. Member ACBL Hall of Fame. Won Bermuda Bowl 1970, 71; World Mixed Teams 1972, World Team Olympiad 1988; placed 2nd Bermuda Bowl 1963, 73; World Open Pairs 1966, World Team Olympiad 1972, World Mixed Pairs 1978. Grand Life Master with more than 25,000 MP. Won the McKenney Trophy 1988, Fishbein Trophy 1968. He also won many ACBL nationally rated events including: Spingold 1969, Chicago (now the Reisinger) 1955, Reisinger 1970, 77; Vanderbilt 1965, 67, 71, 82; Men's Pairs 1956, Men's Teams 1968, 72, 73; Master Mixed Teams 1968, GNOT 1981. He placed 2nd in the Spingold 1957, 62, 70, 73, 76; Men's Teams 1954, 68; Mixed Pairs 1963, Blue Ribbon Pairs 1976, Life Master Pairs 1968, 71; Men's Teams 1969, 88.

JACOBY, Mary Zita (Mrs. Oswald) (1909-1987) of Dallas, a former tennis champion. One of two women whose husband and son have won world titles. She placed 2nd in Master Mixed Teams 1935 and won several regionals in the Sixties.

JACOBY, Oswald (Ozzie, Jake) (1902-1984) of Dallas TX, bridge columnist. One of the great players of all time. Member ACBL Hall of Fame. First achieved international preeminence as partner of Sidney Lenz in the famous Culbertson-Lenz Match. Had already established himself as a champion at auction and contract. Next became a member of famed Four Horsemen and Four Aces teams. His selection by Lenz over players of greater experience and with whom Lenz had practiced partnerships was early recognition of the brilliance and skill that were later to bring Jacoby to the top of the ACBL's list of all-time masterpoint winners.

Jacoby had two months of Army service in World War I, when he was 15, and he was awarded the Victory Medal. On Dec. 7, 1941 he was playing in the NABC Open Pairs in Richmond VA. when the attack on Pearl Harbor was announced. He immediately left the tournament and did not play again for 4 years. During most of that time he served as a specialist in the Navy, with the rank of lieutenant commander. When he returned to competition in 1945, he found Charles Goren far ahead in the MP rankings. He had done very little about returning to the top when he again returned to active duty in 1950 for service in the Korean War. He served as a commander in Intelligence and was a member of the original staff at the Panmunjom armistice conference. This return to service cost him his place on the American team in the first Bermuda Bowl matches. He had however, represented the ABL in international competition as far back as 1935, the year when the Four Aces team defeated the French, champions of Europe, in the first official World Championship encounter. Returning from 2 years of Korean service, Jacoby found he had dropped out of the top 19 MP holders. By 1958 he had managed to move back into 6th place, still far behind Goren. At that time he decided to make a determined effort to regain the #1 position. By 1962, he had done so. Between 1959 and 1963, he won the McKenney Trophy 4 times in 5 years; the only player at that time older than 50 to win the trophy. He won it at ages 57, 59, 60 and 61. In 1963 he became the first player to acquire more than 1,000 MPs in a single year. His winning total that year was 1,034. In 1967, he surpassed the 10,000-point mark, at which time he retired from active competition for the McKenney Trophy. Almost exactly one year later he relinquished his position as top masterpoint holder to Barry Crane.

Jacoby pioneered many bidding ideas, including Forcing 2NT, Jacoby Transfer Bids and Weak Jump Overcalls. His innovations have included developments of Gerber and Blackwood and a specialized use of Two Notrump and Three Notrump Responses. His most recent innovations were the use of Two-Way Stayman in connection with Jacoby Transfer Bids after 2NT opening and after 2-anything-2NT. He invented the use of 2♥ as a double negative response to 2♣ with 2NT a positive heart response and 2♦ the usual waiting bid. Among his writings are *"The Four Aces System , What's New in Bridge, Win at Bridge with Oswald Jacoby, Win at Bridge with Jacoby Modern, The Backgammon Book* (with John Crawford). He also had many books on mathematics, gambling, poker and other card games, including canasta, in which he had the two best-selling books.

Jacoby, born in Brooklyn on Dec. 8, 1902, left Columbia in his junior year to become an actuary, completing the examination of the Society of Actuaries in 1924 to become, at age 21, the youngest person ever to do so.

After four years with Metropolitan Life, he went into business for himself, but his success was cut short by the 1929 stock market crash. Jacoby's victory-studded career includes many oddities. He played in (and won) his first auction tournament in July 1929 — the National Team Championship of the American Whist League. But he had already won the first big contract pair tournament ever played, the Goldman Pairs event in the Eastern States Championship held in February of that year. Later on, he set a record by winning the Goldman Trophy 3 times in 20 years. Those were the only occasions on which he entered. Afterward, he became a national champion by winning 2 AWL pair and team events.

After the Culbertson-Lenz match, Jacoby was secretary of the United States Bridge Association for nearly 2 years - thus being associated with Ely Culbertson. Late in 1933, however, he helped to form the original Four Aces team, which dominated the bridge world for the next several years. During this period, in addition to American Bridge League triumphs, he won 2 pair championships and 4 team championships of the USBA.

He won a North American Championship (the Chicago in 1955) with his son, James Jacoby. He also scored many victories with his wife of 50 years, Mary Zita Jacoby. Jacoby was elected to the bridge Hall of Fame 1965 and was named ACBL Honorary Member in 1967. Jacoby was npc of North American teams for 1969, 1970 and 1971. As a result he became captain of the first North American Bermuda Bowl champion teams (1970 and 1971). The United States had not won this coveted title in more than a decade. His North American Championship titles are as follows: Spingold 1934, 36, 38, 39, 45, 50, 59; Vanderbilt 1931, 34, 35, 37, 38, 46, 65; Chicago (now the Reisinger) 1955; Reisinger 1983; Master Individual 1935; Master Mixed Teams 1968; Life Master Pairs 1936; Men's Teams 1952, 59; Open Pairs 1935, 60, 64; Men's Pairs 1934, 39, 49. He also won USBA Grand National Open Teams 1934, 35, 37, Open Pairs 1936, 37. He also won ABL Men's Teams 1931, 32; AWL Team-of-Four 1929, 31, 33, Open Pairs 1933, Herman Trophy 1960. He placed 2nd in many NABC events and won countless regional titles including the prestigious Marcus Cup 1955. In 1973 he won the World Championship of Backgammon.

In 1950, Jacoby became the daily bridge columnist for Newspaper Enterprise Association, serving several hundred newspapers. He established a record on April 22, 1982 when his 10,000th article was printed. (Goren's name appeared on more than this number, but he had not written any columns for many years before his death in 1991.) Jacoby wrote books on poker, canasta, gin rummy and mathematical odds. He also continuously maintained a practice as a consulting actuary, He served for 6 years as a member of the Board of Visitors of Harvard Observatory (for the last 3, under the chairmanship of then Senator John F. Kennedy) He became an expert on computers and was frequently consulted on questions of tournament movements, elimination schedules and scoring.

JAEGER, Henry P. (1888-1971) of Cleveland Heights OH, bridge writer and lecturer. A member of the group which promoted the Official System, he won trophies in whist, auction and contract bridge.

JAEGER, Jane (Mrs. Lewis M.) (b. 1914) of North Bay Village FL, She and her late husband were the first married couple to attain Life Master ranking, #74 and #94

respectively, in 1947. Jaeger is currently semi-retired from competitive bridge. She won the Open Pairs 1945, the Chicago (now the Reisinger) 1947, Master Mixed Teams 1951, GNOT 1973, placed 2nd Vanderbilt 1956.

JAFRI, Mazhar (b. 1941) of Karachi, Pakistan, lawyer. Prominent on international scene since 1979 when he founded the Bridge Federation of Africa and the Middle East (BFAAME). Secretary and CEO of BFAAME 1980-1995 and president from 1995. Represented BFAAME on WBF Executive Council from 1980 and now its longest-serving member. WBF vice-president from 1991. Chairman of WBF Admissions, Zoning and Infrastructure Committee and IOC Liaison Committee. Member of 5 other WBF committees. President Pakistan Bridge Federation 1991-96 and now President Emeritus. Helped China and many other countries to form NCBOs and join the WBF. Launched WBF Infrastructure Development Program. Member of the WBF Committee of Honor, the result of his successful effort to have bridge and the WBF recognized by the International Olympic Committee (IOC).

JAFRI, Syed Saeed (b. 1916) of Karachi, retired senior civil servant. President of the Pakistan Bridge Association for 13 years, now President Emeritus. Vice-president BFAAME for 10 years.

JAIS, Pierre (1913-1988) of Paris, France, physician, Grand Master. Won Bermuda Bowl 1956, World Team Olympiad 1960, World Open Pairs 1962 – a triple that has seldom been duplicated in world bridge history. Won European Teams 1955, 70, 2nd 54, 56, 69. Won London Sunday Times Invitational 1963 and many national titles. Author of many books and a contributor to many magazines. Partnership with Roger Trezel one of strongest in world 1950-70.

JAKOBSDOTTIR, Esther (b. 1944) of Kopavogur, Iceland, cashier. Won Nordic Women's Teams 1990. Represented Iceland in one world championship, 5 European Championships and 5 other Nordic Championships. 21 national wins.

JAMES, Rex (b. 1942 in Antigua) of Kingston, Jamaica, banker, WBF World Master. CACBF National Team champion 1982, 1983 and represented Jamaica on many other occasions including 1983 Bermuda Bowl. Numerous national titles.

JANITSCHKE, Craig (b. 1951) of Olympia WA computer technical specialist for state of WA. Former professional bridge player (1977-84). Won a national award for a computer system that is currently in effect across the state of Washington. Was Colorado state champion pianist (junior high division) in 1966. Youngest Life Master in Colorado in 1971 — a record that held for many years. Janitschke was a frequent partner of the late Barry Crane. He placed 4th World Open Pairs 1982 and is a WBF World Master. Grand Life Master, won GNOT, Life Master Men's Pairs 1980, Open Pairs 1981, 2nd Men's Swiss Teams.

JANITSCHKE, Jan P. (b. 1947) of Littleton CO, bridge professional. An excellent pianist and violinist and performed as a soloist with several orchestras as a teenager. Co-author *Bridge Mini Series* which was ABTA's "Book of the Year". Janitschke, a WBF World Master, placed 4th in World Open Pairs in Biarritz 1982. Grand Life Master with 13,349 MPs as of 3/2001. His North American titles are GNOT, Life Master Men's Pairs 1980; North American Men's Teams 1982, GNOP 1987.

JANNERSTEN, Eric (1912-1982) of Stockholm, Sweden, editor, publisher and teacher. Represented Sweden in one European championship and on other occasions.

Won many national titles. Founded International Bridge Press Association 1958, and was its executive secretary until 1975. Founded *Bridgetidningen*, a major bridge magazine. Bridge columnist from 1940. Edited and published European Bridge Review 1949-51. Published about 40 bridge books, and wrote many. From 1938, headed a bridge school with an estimated 150,000 pupils. Introduced the bidding box, now used in all national and international events, and in many clubs.

JANNERSTEN, Per (b. 1948) of Avesta, Sweden, publisher, printer and auditor. Owner of Jannersten Forlag, a major supplier of bridge books and equipment. Helped invent computerized dealing machine used in major tournaments. Also redesigned the bidding box. Bridge columnist *Svenska Dagbladet*. Co-author of *Movements - a Fair Approach*, a major work of directing and movements. Contributing editor to *Bridge Encyclopedia*.

JANSEN, Piet (b. 1957) of Groningen, the Netherlands, owner of bridge and chess pub. WBF World Life Master. Won Bermuda Bowl 1993, EC Teams 1987.

JANSMA, Jan (b. 1962), of Nijmegen, The Netherlands, mathematics teacher. WBF World Master. World Junior Team champion 1987. European Junior champion 1986.

JANZ, Ricardo (b. 1948) of Rio de Janeiro, Brazil, engineer. WBF World Life Master. Won Bermuda Bowl 1989, second 2000. Won South American Teams 1988, 89, 91. Represented Brazil in one other world championship.

JAQUES, Arturo (b. 1923-1991) of Buenos Aires, Argentina, travel agent and bridge writer. South American champion 1958, 1959, 1961. Represented Argentina in Bermuda Bowl 1959, 1962, in World Team Olympiad 1964, 1972. 43 national titles. Won Gabarret Cup 1959, 1960; top Argentine masterpoint holder 1960-1975. Former editor of *Bridge Argentino*, contributed to many bridge periodicals.

JARIGESE, Jacqueline L. (Jackie) (b. 1931) of Vancouver WA, retired co-owner Portland Bridge Club, former school teacher. In 1990 she drove from Anchorage to Prudhoe Bay on the Arctic Ocean down to Valdez, following the pipeline and back to Anchorage, a feat few people have accomplished. Also drove to Transylvania on Halloween. Diamond Life Master with more than 50 regional events. Placed 2nd ABA Victor R. Daly KO Teams Top Flight 1989 (equivalent to ACBL's Spingold), Diamond Life Master with more than 11,000 MPs as of 3/ 2001.

JARIYANUNTINATE, Panjaroon (b. 1947) of Bangkok, Thailand, state enterprise employee. Won PABF (Far East) Open Pairs 1982, 2nd PABF (Far East) Open Teams 1985. Represented Thailand in 3 world championships and 7 other times.

JASSEM, Krzysztof (b. 1965) of Poznan, Poland, professor of mathematics and computer science, specialist in artificial intelligence, bridge journalist. WBF World Life Master. 2nd World Team Olympiad, World Transnational Open Teams 1997. Won many national titles.

JEFFERSON, Leonard A., Jr. (Len) (b. 1922) of Arlington TX, retired federal employee. ABA Honorary Life Member, ABA Platinum Life Master with more than 12,000 MPs. Chaired the History and Archives Committee for the ABA for many years. Won ABA Summer KO Teams 1969, Spring Round-Robin Teams 1978, 80, 84, 85; ABA KO Teams 1975-89; ABA Spring National Swiss Teams, Open Teams, National Non-Mixed Pairs, National Swiss Teams 1993. From 1946-1993 had more than 500 wins including more than 50 ABA national

championships, with wins in all major events. Served as member ABCL Board of Governors 1962-68. Was a consultant for ABA Nationals and chaired ABA 1995 National. He has held many other bridge administrative postions. Won 50+ ACBL regional events.

JELLINEK, Hans born in Vienna, Austria; deported by the Germans from Norway and died in a concentration camp. Won world championship 1937, Europeans 1936.

JENSEN, Nils E. (b. 1920) of Stockholm, Sweden, owner of Elfa, an electric supplies company. Represented Sweden in 7 world events. 2nd Far East Pairs 1977. Organized 1970 Bermuda Bowl and World Pairs Olympiad in Stockholm, the 1974 World Pairs Olympiad in Las Palmas, and the 1983 Bermuda Bowl in Stockholm. President Swedish Bridge League 1965-70 and 1981-83. President European Bridge League 1981-1987, then President Emeritus. Delegate from Europe to WBF 1971-87. WBF Honorary Member 1982.

JENSEN, Tore (1926-1989) of Oslo, Norway, store owner. Won Nordic Teams 1966. Several national titles. 3rd Bermuda Bowl 1969. 2nd European Teams 1968.

JEPSON, Tom (b. 1951) of Kirkland WA. Won more than 15 regional events.

JERONIMIDIS, Elena D. (b. 1946) of Reading, England, editor, translator and theatrical producer. Editor of *Bridge Plus* since 1989, publisher from 1993. Publisher of *Bridge Plus Practise* series since 1997. Bridge editor *Teletext* from 1993.

JESNER, George (b. 1925 in Scotland), of Canberra, Australia, master draper, bridge teacher and writer. Member of winning Scottish team in 1964 Camrose series. Won first South Pacific playoff and represented Australia on several other occasions. Won several national titles. Former ABF president and columnist for the *Australian*. Co-inventor of Benjamin.

JEZIORO, Aleksander (b. 1939) of Krakow, Poland. WBF World Master. 3rd Bermuda Bowl 1981, 2nd World Senior Teams 1998. Won European Open Teams 1981, 2nd European Senior Teams 1995, 1997. Won many national titles.

JOELSON, Gail (b. 1954) of University Heights OH, programmer/analyst. She was the 1984 Ohio women's state table tennis champion. Served as member Unit 125 Board of Directors. Won Non-Life Master GNOP 1992.

JOHANNSSON, Gudlaugur R. (b. 1944) of Hafnarfjordur, Iceland, certified accountant. Won Bermuda Bowl 1991. Represented Iceland in 6 other world championships, 6 European Championships and one Nordic Championship. 11 national wins.

JOHANNSSON, Helgi (b 1951) of Reykjavik, Iceland, managing director. Former president of the Icelandic Bridge Federation. Major promoter of Icelandic bridge. NPC numerous times. 5 national wins.

JOHNSTON, David Kyle (b. 1936) of Lurgan, Northern Ireland, solicitor. Represented Northern Ireland frequently in Camrose Matches from late 1960s and has won all major national titles.

JOHNSON, Benjamin O. (Ben) (1906-1976) counsel and member of the Executive Committee of the WBF, presided over the ACBL in 1953. An attorney from Spartansburg SC, Johnson served as npc of the ACBL Bermuda Bowl team in 1954 and as chairman of the ACBL Charity Foundation. Johnson won the Chicago (now the Reisinger) in 1949.

JOHNSON, Chester (Chet) (b. 1940) of Chicago, stock chaser. One of the leading ABA players, ranked 3rd in

MPs with more than 17,600. Some of his wins include the ABA National Open Teams 1977, KO Teams 1982, 83, 84, 86, 87, 89, 91; and a few ACBL regionals.

JOHNSON, George W. (b. 1923) of Charlotte N.C., U.S. Postal Service director of finance. Won several American Bridge Association regional and national titles. He has been active in ABA bridge administration since 1968 and served as president 1984.

JOHNSON, Jane (1933-2000) of Memphis TN, manager of ACBL Club Membership Department since 1984. Worked on 4th edition of *Bridge Encyclopedia.* She was a charter member and assistant manager of Parkway Village B.C. from early Seventies through 1982. She was editor of *Club Managers Newsletter.* At NABC's Johnson held the very popular and well attended "Coffee with Jane" for club managers.

JOHNSON, Jared A. (b. 1948) of Golden CO, writer and lawyer, bridge columnist for *Denver Post* since 1977. Author of *Classic Bridge Quotes,* editor and writer for *The Contract Bridge Forum,* District 17 *Scorecard,* contributor to *Bridge World, Popular Bridge, Bridge Today,* and ACBL *Bridge Bulletin.*

JOHNSON, Jean of Bermuda, has taught bridge, has been very active in bridge administration for Bermuda and has served as vice president, ethics officer Unit 198; president Bermuda Bridge Club and chairman Bermuda regional 1988, 89, 90. Represented Bermuda in world competition in Biarritz 1982, Seattle 1984, Bal Harbour 1986, the Tri-Country playoffs 1989 and won the Norman Bach Trophy 1984. Has won 15+ regionals.

JOHNSON, Karl (b. 1924) of Sebring FL, retired in 1988 as an ACBL national tournament director. His directing career began in 1960 and he attained his national status in 1967.

JOHNSON, Marilyn K. (b. 1928) of Houston. Before her retirement from active tournament play she was one of the world's leading women players. World Grand Master, she won the World Women's Pairs 1970, Venice Trophy 1978, Women's Team Olympiad 1980. She represented ACBL in other world competitions 1972 (3rd Women's Olympiad Teams), 1974 (6th Women's Pairs), 1976 (3rd Women's Olympiad Teams), 1978 (9th Women's Pairs). She and her partner Mary Jane Farrell were the first women's pair ever to win the Life Master Pairs (1978). Diamond Life Master. Her ACBL national wins are Mixed Pairs 1968, 73; Women's Teams 1974, 75, 76. 2nd Women's Pairs 1967, Mixed Pairs 1969, Master Mixed Teams 1969, Women's Teams 1973.

JOHNSON, Patty (b. 1949) of Sebring FL, R-4 tournament director. Served in various positions of Professional Tournament Directors Association since 1985. District 9 tournament coordinator 1996-present;. Johnson began directing in 1976 and has worked at world championships in Bal Harbour 1986 and Jamaica 1987. She works at all NABCs as results coordinator.

JOHNSON, Perry L. (b. 1948) of Farmington Hills MI, company president. Author of *Keeping Score* and nine other books on quality. WBF World Master. Won Open Pairs I 1992, placed 2nd Men's Pairs 1979. Won Cavendish Teams 2000.

JOHNSON, Sallie B. of New York City (1925-1999), bridge teacher. Formerly one of the leading American women players. Represented the ACBL in 4 Olympiads — Amsterdam 1966, Stockholm 1970, Las Palmas 1974, Miami Beach 1972. She won the Deauville Individual 1970. Won Women's Teams 1955, 58, 60, 61, 68; placed 2nd in

Women's Pairs 1969, Master Mixed Teams 1957, 74.

JOHNSON, Walter D. (b. 1953) of Columbus OH., administrative officer in health care facility. Won Blue Ribbon Pairs 1985, GNOT 1990; placed 2nd in the Reisinger 1987, USBC (team trials) 1989.

JOLMA, Lawrence N. (Larry) (1923-1996) of Portland OR, a business broker, former CPA. Served on ACBL Board of Directors from 1966-1995, was ACBL treasurer, District 20 Board member, Western Conference Board member, past president of Unit 487. Winner of Men's Teams 1967.

JONES, Dr. Arnold P. (Doc) (b.1930) of Chicago IL, retired psychologist. Served 3 terms as president of ABA 1972-74, 1977-81. First ABA president to be ranked in the top 25 list of ABA MP holders. He has won several ABA national events - Open Pairs, Mixed Pairs, KO Teams, Swiss Teams, Round-Robin.

JONES, Henry (See CAVENDISH.)

JONES, Michael D. (1936-1996) of Burlingame CA, bridge professional. Former member ACBL Board of Directors, Diamond Life Master.

JONES, Richard L. (b.1935) of Sacramento CA., insurance broke. Has won 30 regional events.

JONES, Robert G. (Bob) (1949-1995) of Auburndale NY, born in Lima, Peru, full-time bridge professional - playing, teaching and directing. Served on Unit 242 Board. Placed 5th Rosenblum Cup Teams 1990, won Australian National Mixed Teams 1989, placed 2nd in Men's Swiss Teams 1986. Diamond Life Master. has won more than three dozen regional titles.

JONSSON, Steinar (b. 1972) of Reykjavik, Iceland, carpenter. Won the Nordic Junior Teams 1997. Represented Iceland in 4 European Junior Teams and 3 other Nordic Junior Teams. 8 national wins.

JONSSON, Thorlakur (b. 1956) of Kopavogur, Iceland, mechanical engineer. WBF world Life Master. Won Bermuda Bowl 1991, Nordic Teams 1988. Represented Iceland in 5 other world championships, 5 European Championships, 4 other Nordic Championships, one European Junior Teams and 3 Nordic Junior Teams. 10 national titles.

JORDAN, John S., III (Big John) (b. 1939) of Washington DC, math teacher, former federal government economist. He is an ABA regional director and an ACBL certified club director, frequent contributor to the *ABA Bulletin.* Was president of Banneker B.C. 1979-88, ABA chairman of National Recommendations Committee. For more than 15 years he has been listed as one of the ABA's top 10 players in total points, with more than 12,500. Jordan has won many ABA sectional (equivalent to ACBL regional) titles. His ABA national titles include KO Teams Flt. B 1969, Summer KO Teams Flt. A 1975, Men's Teams 1976, Mixed Teams 1979, Swiss Teams 1980, Spring Open Pairs 1982. Placed 2nd in Summer Mixed Teams 1970, KO Teams 1978, 84, 88, 90; Spring Mixed Pairs 1982, Swiss Teams 1975, 88.

JORDAN, Robert F. (b. 1927) of Cincinnati OH, businessman. Formerly one of the outstanding American bridge players. WBF World Life Master, placed 2nd in the World Team Olympiad 1964, 68. He also represented the ACBL in world play New York 1962 (5th World Championship Open Pairs) and North America in Bermuda Bowl 1963 (placed 2nd). Won McKenney Trophy 1960, Mott-Smith Trophy 1961, 62; Vanderbilt 1961, 68; Reisinger 1966, 67; Master Mixed Teams 1959, Open Pairs 1960, 62. 2nd Vanderbilt 1965, Chicago (now the Reisinger), Mixed Pairs 1961; Men's Pairs 1956. Jordan and Arthur Robinson,

thought by many to be the best American partnership in the Sixties, came out of retirement to play in the "Bicentennial Bridge Match" against Great Britain in 1976.

JORGENSEN, Adalsteinn (b. 1959) of Reykjavik, Iceland, managing director. WBF World Life Master. Won Bermuda Bowl 1991, Transnational Mixed Teams 1996. Represented Iceland in 2 other world championships, 6 European Championships, one Nordic Championship, 2 European Junior Teams and one Nordic Junior Teams. 15 national wins. Currently the highest ranking Icelandic bridge player in WBF masterpoints.

JOTCHAM, Raymond G. (Ray) (b. 1941) of Scarborough ON. retired mathematics teacher. Has been directing since 1959, tournament director 1978-1993 and has rating of R-l. Jotcham placed 2nd in the Spingold 1964. Competed in world play New Orleans 1978, was Canadian Intercollegiate champion 1961. Won 15 regionals.

JOURDAIN, Patrick D. (b. 1942) of Cardiff, Wales, bridge journalist and teacher. Represented Wales more than 66 times in Camrose Trophy, and Scotland twice. Won Gold Cup 1976 and many Welsh titles. President Welsh Bridge Union 1984-85. President British Bridge League 1995-97. Chairman Bridge Great Britain 2001. Editor *IBPA Bulletin* since 1982. Bridge correspondent of *London Daily Telegraph* since 1992. Author of 2 books.

JOURDAN, Roger Founder of Jourdan's in Boca Raton (highly successful club). Won almost 3000 points in 1984, the year Grant Baze set the record. Died while still in his early 30s.

JOYCE, Kay (b. 1949) of Raleigh NC, librarian. Has been secretary/treasurer of Unit 119 1978-94. Was managing editor of Unit newsletter 1980-84 and editor-in-chief since 1984. Served 2 terms as secretary of District 7. Unit GNOP and GNOT coordinator. Diamond Life Master, won Royal Viking Instant Matchpoint Game 1996 and 17+ regional titles.

JOYCE, Randolph (Randy) (b. 1947) of Raleigh NC, salesman. Has served Unit 119 as president, District 7 as recorder. Diamond Life Master with more than 12,700 MPs, placed 2nd in GNOT 1983 and Open Pairs 1990. Has won more than 50 regionals.

K

KACHMAR, Barbara (formerly Collyer) (1911-1982) of Beverly Hills CA. Won USBA Mixed Pairs 1936, Women's Teams 1960, 61, Women's Pairs 1962. Placed 2nd Master Mixed Teams 1934, Women's Teams 1963. Writings included many entertaining contributions to *Bridge World, Modern Bridge* and other periodicals.

KADLEC, Alfred (b. 1953) of Vienna, Austria, systems analyst. WBF World Master. 2nd World Team Olympiad 1988, represented Austria in one other world championship. European Junior Champion 1976. Was 2nd European Team Cup 1982. National wins include 5 Open Teams and one Mixed Pairs.

KAHN, Allen M. (b. 1952) of New York City, partner ISP (computer server). Won 18 regionals.

KAHN, Richard F. (1911-1987) of New York City, retired motion picture sales executive. Co-founder of Card School of New York 1950, served Cavendish Club and Greater New York B.A. for 10 years. Placed 2nd Bermuda Bowl 1956. Won Grand National Mixed Teams 1933,

Mixed Pairs 1939, Chicago (now the Reisinger) 1949, Life Master Pairs 1951, Vanderbilt 1953, Spingold 1955, Master Mixed Teams 1951. Placed 2nd Open Pairs 1951.

KALES, Eugene L. (Gene) (b. 1943) of Arlington VA, bridge teacher and CPA. Diamond Life Master with 22 regional wins.

KALES, Eugene of East Lansing MI, professor of physics and astronomy a Michigan State University; bridge director, teacher and columnist. Former president ACBL Education Foundation, member of Board of Governors, chairman of unit sectionals since 1982.

KALISH, Avi (b. 1952) of Haifa, Israel, civil engineering manager. 3rd World Teams 1994. Represented Israel in 2 other world championships and 4 zonals. Won Maccabiah Teams 1997, Moscow Invitational Pairs 2000. National wins include Open Teams and Open Pairs several times.

KALKERUP, Bettina (b. 1963) of Copenhagen, Denmark, computer programmer. Won Women's World Team Olympiad 1988, 5th 1992. 2nd World Women's Pairs 1986, won Nordic Women's Teams 1988. 16 Danish titles.

KALOW, Gwenn (b. 1972) of New York City, attorney. Member ACBL Junior Corps. Won North American Junior Pairs 1990, 2nd 1991.

KAMB, John G. (b. 1929) of Mount Vernon WA, attorney. Former district court judge. Was presented "The Award of Merit" by Washington State Bar Association 1991. Served 18 years on the public school board, 5 as chairman. Member ACBL Board of Governors, president of Unit 439. Diamond Life Master, won 25+ regionals.

KAMIL, Michael S. (b.1960) of Holmdel NJ, stock options trader. Diamond Life Master, won Vanderbilt 1990, Life Master Open Pairs 1992; placed 2nd Vanderbilt 1995, 1999; Open Pairs I 1998. Placed 2nd Cavendish 1990, won at least 17 regionals.

KAMIYO, Takahiro (b. 1937) of Tokyo, Japan, oil company executive; Represented Japan in one World Olympiad and one Far East Championship. Won 10 national team titles and 2 national pair titles. JCBL librarian 25 years, member of tournament committee 10 years.

KAMSKY, Asya (b. 1965) of Monterey CA, born in Leningrad USSR, computer programmer, bridge teacher. S3 tournament director. Member Junior Corps, has served on Unit 497 Board of Directors and GNYBA board. Editor and publisher of Youth Bridge Federation newsletter. President and founder of Youth Bridge Federation, organizes and runs annual Berkeley Calcutta. Won North American Collegiate Teams 1987, placed 2nd Master Mixed Teams 1991, 3rd World Junior Championships in Amsterdam 1987. As a Junior placed 3rd Life Master Open Pairs 1992.

KANNAVOS, Takis (b. 1956) of Athens, Greece, mathematician. Represented Greece 1988 World Team Olympiad, finished 5th, the best performance ever by a Greek team. Tournament director and top bridge teacher. Many national wins include 5 Open Teams and one Open Pairs.

KANSIL, Prince Joli (formerly Joel D. Gaines) (b. 1943) of Honolulu HI. The inventor of Bridgette and many other card games, word games and board games that have been marketed nationally. He is author of the *Backgammon Quiz Book*. Held Scrabble record for highest score on a single turn for 14 years. Co-founder Eastern Collegiate Bridge League. Retired from tournament bridge after college in 1964. Personal assistant to the late Albert H. Morehead and a close personal friend of Waldemar von Zedwitz, who co-authored the *Official Laws of Bridgette.*

KANTAR, Edwin B. (Eddie) (b. 1932) of Santa Monica CA, bridge teacher, writer, professional player, cruise director and lecturer. Member ACBL Hall of Fame. Minnesota state table tennis champion 1948, competed in the World Table Tennis Championships in Stockholm 1957. Inducted into Minnesota state table tennis Hall of Fame 1996. Invented Kantar Cuebids and several Key-Card innovations (1430, etc.). Kantar has been awarded the ABTA "Book of the Year" 4 times, more than anyone else. A popular and prolific author of many bridge books including: *Introduction to Declarer's Play, Introduction to Defender's Play, Bridge Bidding Made Easy, Bridge Conventions, Bridge Humor, Test Your Bridge Play (Vol. 1 and II), Gamesman Bridge, Improving Your Bidding Skills, Defend With Your Life, Kantar for the Defense (Vol. I and II), Complete Defensive Play, Kantar Lessons (Vol. I and II), Roman Key Card Blackwood, A Treasury of Bridge Tips, The Best of Eddie Kantar, Eddie Kantar Teaches Modern Bridge Defense, Eddie Kantar Teaches Advanced Bridge Defense, Classic Kantar, Bridge for Dummies, Kantar Lessons III* and a video tape *Win at Bridge.*

A regular columnist *for* ACBL *Bridge Bulletin,* frequent contributor to *Bridge World, Bridge Today, The Spectator, Le Bridgeur* and other periodicals around the world, contributing editor to *Bridge Encyclopedia.* Kantar learned to play bridge at 11 and taught his first class at age 17. His teaching is now confined mainly to cruises. One of the outstanding world players and a WBF Grand Master, ranked #36 among Grand Masters. Won Bermuda Bowl 1977, 79, 2nd 1975. He also competed in international play 1969 (3rd Bermuda Bowl), 1970, 1978 (9th Rosenblum Teams), 1982 (9th World Open Pairs), 1986, 1990 (17th Rosenblum Teams). He won Maccabiah Games 1981, placed 3rd 1977; won Pan-American Invitational Championships Open Teams 1977. Grand Life Master. Won Spingold 1961, 62, 74; Chicago (now the Reisinger) 1962, 65; Reisinger 1977, 81; Vanderbilt 1964, 88; GNOT 1974, 76; Life Master Pairs 1983, Men's Swiss Teams 1987. He placed 2nd Vanderbilt 1961, 68, 73, 76, 78, 83, 89; Reisinger 1968, 83, 92; Open Pairs, Men's Pairs 1962, 67; Spingold 1991. Kantar also has won scores of regionals.

KANTOR, Dorothy. See BUCHANAN, DOROTHY.

KANTOR, Simon W. (Eddie) (b. 1925) of Agawam MA, born in Belgium, professor emeritus at University of Massachusetts, Listed in *Who's Who in America* since 1974, has more than two dozen U.S. patents on polymer science. Served on Capital District B.A. Board 1967-72, Western MA, and on District 25 Executive Committee since 1997. Member ACBL Board of Governors for 3 years. Bridge Unit Board 1989-92. Diamond Life Master with more than 10,800 MPs as of 3/2001, placed 2nd World Senior Pairs 1994 Albuquerque, 2nd Senior KO Teams 1996, more than 100 regional wins.

KANZEE, Stephen (b. 1948) of Hayward CA, retired real estate investor. Searched and found his birthparents and through paternal grandmother's lineage, became a member of the General Society of Mayflower Descendants. Has served on Units 497 and 508 Boards and was vice-president for 497 1979-85. Diamond Life Master, placed 2nd North American Swiss Teams 1984, 20 regional wins.

KAPAYANNIDES, Thanos (b. 1963) of Athens, Greece. Won 1987 Common Market Pairs while a junior. Represented Greece many times from 1991. Many national wins include 3 Open Teams, 2 Open Pairs and 2 Master Pairs.

KAPLAN, Alain (b. 1940) of Brussels, Belgium, psychologist manager. WBF World Master. Represented Belgium in 5 European Championships. National wins include 8 Open Teams and 3 Open Pairs.

KAPLAN, Betty (Mrs. Edgar, formerly Mrs. Alfred Sheinwold) (1913-1985) of New York City. Was circulation manager of *The Bridge World.* Former director of a music school. Won Master Mixed Teams 1963, Life Master Women's Pairs 1964, Mixed Pairs 1965, Women's Teams 1965. Placed 2nd Master Mixed Teams 1959, Women's Pairs 1962.

KAPLAN, Edgar (1925-1997) of New York City, bridge writer, teacher. Editor and publisher of *The Bridge World* 1967 till his death. Was one of the world's leading players and outstanding bridge personalities. Member ACBL Hall of Fame. Chief commentator for the WBF Championships for more than a decade. Was known not only for his expert analysis but his delightful wit. World's greatest authority on the laws of duplicate and rubber bridge, served as co-chairman of the ACBL Laws Commission and as a member of the WBF Laws Commission for many years. Named IBPA Bridge Personality of the Year 1979, named ACBL Honorary Member 1993. Represented District 24 (New York City area) on the ACBL Board for many years and was a former partner of the Card School of New York.

Co-inventor of the Kaplan-Sheinwold system, author of several books including *How to Play Winning Bridge* (co-author), *The Complete Italian System of Winning Bridge, Winning Contract Bridge Complete, Competitive Bidding in Modern Bridge, Duplicate Bridge: How to Play, How to Wi.n W*as a contributing editor to the *Encyclopedia of Bridge.* Assistant captain of U.S. team World Team Olympiad1964. Coach many times to North American teams, which benefited from his detailed knowledge of European systems. WBF Life Master. Placed 2nd in the World Team Olympiad 1968, in the International Team Trials 1966, USBC (team trials) 1987. Also competed in world championships in 1966 (11th Mixed Pairs), 1967 (2nd in Bermuda Bowl), 1971, 1978, 1982 (5th World Open Pairs), 1986 (6th Rosenblum Teams), 1990 (4th World Open Pairs, 17th Rosenblum Teams).

Life Master #342, ACBL Grand Life Master. Won McKenney Trophy 1957. Won North American championships in 5 decades - Vanderbilt 1953, 68, 70, 81, 83, 86; Spingold 1967, 68; Chicago (now the Reisinger) 1958, Reisinger 1966, 67, 71, 82, 83, 84, 90; Men's Teams 1955, 1966, Mixed Pairs 1965; Master Individual 1957, Master Mixed Teams 1963, Men's Teams 1966, Open Pairs 1966; Life Master Men's Pairs 1973, Blue Ribbon Pairs 1974, Open Swiss Teams 1997. Placed 2nd in the Vanderbilt 1958, 65, 94, 95 (npc); Men's Teams 1958, 61; Master Mixed Teams 1959, 68; Spingold 1965, 71, 78; Life Master Men's Pairs 1965, Reisinger 1969, Men's Pairs 1970, Men's Teams 1975, Open Swiss Teams 1991.

KAPLAN, Muriel (1920-1970) of New York City. Won Women's Team Trials in 1963 and placed 2nd in the World Women's Teams 1964.

KAPLAN, Peggy (b.1951) of Minnetonka MN, philosophy instructor, realtor. Editor Minnesota *Bridge News* and Minneapolis B.C. newsletter. Diamond Life Master, has won 60+ regionals.

KARAMANLIS, Miltos (b. 1981) of Athens, Greece. The leading Greek junior. Won the 1st World Generali Junior Individual in 2000.

KARLAFTIS, George (b. 1937) of Athens, Greece, civil engineer. 2nd in Greek masterpoint standings. A perma-

nent member of Greek team. Finished 5th in 1988 World Team Olympiad, the highest a Greek team has ever placed in world competition. He is the only Greek with the rank of European Master and has won every national title many times. President of the Hellenic Bridge Federation, steering it in new directions.

KARN, Willard S. (1898-1950) of New York City, executive. Was a member of the Four Horsemen. Wrote *Karn's Bridge Service* as well as articles for the *Bridge World*. Won Vanderbilt 1931, 32, Spingold, Master Individual 1931. 2nd in Spingold 1930.

KARPIN, Fred (1913-1986) of Silver Spring MD, bridge teacher, lecturer and writer. Pioneered development of the 4-3-2-1 point-count method that eventually was popularized by Charles Goren. Bridge editor for *Washington Post* 1965-81, contributing editor to *Encyclopedia of Bridge*. He ghosted books and newspaper columns for many of the game's greats. Some of his many books include *Contract Bridge: the Play of the Cards, Psychological Strategy in Contract Bridge, How to Play (and Misplay) Slam Contracts, Winning Play in Contract Bridge: Strategy at Trick One, The Finesse, The Art of Card Reading, Winning Play in Tournament* and *Duplicate Bridge: How the Experts Triumph, The Complete Book of Duplicate Bridge* (with Norman Kay and Bill Root). His cross-referenced file of hands was reputed to be one of the best in the world.

KARWUR, Franky Steven (b. 1965) of Manado, Indonesia. WBF World Life Master. Won International Olympic Committee Teams 2000. Won PABF (Far East) Teams 1992, 99.

KASDAY, Tony (b. 1936) of Las Vegas, consultant, former bridge club owner. Collecter of old movies, has 16,000 tapes. Won Open Swiss Teams 1993 and placed 2nd GNOT 1989. Diamond Life Master, has won at least 100 regionals.

KASLE, Barbara (b. 1939) of Boca Raton FL, former bridge club owner. Won Mixed BAM Teams 1996 and many regional events.

KASLE, Gaylor L. (b. 1941) of Boca Raton FL, retired bridge professional. Greatly responsible for professional bridge getting bigger and better in the middle Sixties and early Seventies. Grand Life Master with 25,430 MPs as of 3/2001, ranked #11 in ACBL. WBF World Master. Won Rosenblum Teams 1994. Won Men's Teams 1973, North American Swiss 1982, 85, 90; Open Pairs 1993, Vanderbilt 1994, Mixed BAM Teams 1996. Placed 2nd Reisinger 1978, North American Swiss Teams 1986, GNOT, Blue Ribbon Pairs 1989. Won Sunday London Times Invitational 1993, placed 2nd 1994. Has won scores of regionals.

KASLE, Lee (Mrs. Sidney) (1917-1995) of Tucson AZ, mother of Gaylor Kasle. Won Women's Teams 1959 a few months after becoming a Life Master. She had a number of wins with her husband Sidney Kasle, who died in 1960. In 1973 she won District 17 Women's Pairs.

KASS, Irving (Cookie) (1915-1993) of Hollywood FL, retired insurance agent who lectured and ran bridge games on cruise ships for 15 years. Primarily became a rubber bridge player. Won Vanderbilt 1952.

KASSAY, Michael Bela (b. 1924) of Sarasota FL, born in Hungary, senior associate of engineering consulting firm. Was involved in the Hungarian revolution of 1956 and moved to the U.S. afterward. He was part of a group that started the revival of organized bridge activities in Hungary after WWII. Was a member of the Hungarian National Team in 1956 and won 5 Hungarian national titles 1954-56. Kassay proposed a Swiss Team format

for tournaments in the United States in 1966. First to propose in a printed publication the Swiss Team format 1966. Won more than 15 regionals.

KATZ, Harold (b. 1935) of Memphis TN, proofreader for the ACBL *Bridge Bulletin*. Formerly a civil engineer. Katz has been an ACBL staff member since 1973. He is also a sectional director and has run local bridge games for more than 20 years.

KATZ, Martha (b. 1968) of Burr Ridge IL. Was Queen of Bridge 1986. Member of the winning Junior team at the World Junior Team Olympiad in Michigan 1991. Placed 6th World Pairs 1998. Won Non-Life Master Swiss Teams 1983; placed 2nd Mixed BAM Teams 1997 and won approximately 20 regionals.

KATZ, Moshe (b. 1920) of Tel Aviv, Israel, retired sales manager. Won World Senior Teams 1994, 96. Represented Israel in 6 world championships and 3 European Championships. Several national wins.

KATZ, Ralph (b. 1957) of Burr Ridge IL, options trader. WBF World Life Master - placed 2nd World Open Pairs 1990, 7th 1994, 4th 1999. Placed 13th 1982, 11th 1986, 5th 1990 in Rosenblum Teams. Grand Life Master with 14,144 MPs as of 3/2001, won Fishbein Trophy 1981; Life Master Pairs 1979, 94; Master Mixed Teams, Spingold 1981; Men's Teams 1984; Open Pairs 1985; Open Pairs I 1996; Vanderbilt, IMP Pairs 1999; Reisinger 2000, Open Swiss Teams 2001. Placed 2nd GNOT 1986, Reisinger 1987, Life Master Pairs 1989; Mixed BAM Teams 1997; Reisinger 1995, 98. Won more than 100 regionals.

KATZ, Richard H. (Dick) (b. 1942) of Rancho Mirage CA, physician. High school state mathematics winner 1958, Intercollegiate champion 1966. Co-author *Breakthrough in Bridge*. Winner of Fishbein Trophy 1973, 76. Diamond Life Master, won Open Pairs 1967, Blue Ribbon Pairs 1968, Reisinger 1973, Spingold 1973, 76; GNOT 1974, Vanderbilt 1975, 76; Master Mixed Teams 1976, Life Master Pairs 1989, Open BAM Teams 1992, Life Master Open Pairs 1994. Placed 2nd Blue Ribbon Pairs 1969, Vanderbilt 1973. (see HOUSTON AFFAIR, LANCIA TEAMS.)

KATZ, Stanley B. (Steamer) (b. 1949) of Wheeling IL, controller. Helped with the formation of high school bridge program in the Chicago area for which he received Service Award from the city of Chicago. Has 18 regional wins.

KATZ, Susi (b. 1936) of Longwood FL, travel agent and bridge professional. Diamond Life Master. In 1986 she won Ace of Clubs award in the Life Master category. Has been Unit winner of Mini-McKenney. Has won 60+ regionals.

KAUDER, Arnold J. (Arnie) (1908-1990) of Los Angeles, electronics engineer. Won Master Mixed Teams 1949, 50, 55; 2nd Men's Teams 1953, won many regionals.

KAUDER, James S. (b. 1943) of Los Angeles, attorney, bridge writer. Author of *The Bridge Philosopher* and formerly contributed to the ACBL *Bridge Bulletin* and *The Bridge World*. He is the son of Mary Jane Farell and Arnold Kauder. Won many regional events.

KAUFMAN, George S. (1889-1961) famous New York dramatist, a prominent rubber bridge player, honorary member of Cavendish Club, also member of Crockford's Club and Regency Club. Many of his humorous writings about bridge appeared in *The New Yorker* and have often been reprinted. They include *Kibitzers' Revolt* and the ingenious suggestion that bridge clubs should post on the bulletin board the information that North-South (or East-West) are holding good cards.

KAUFMAN, Istvan (1922-1995) of Budapest, Hungary, company manager. Most successful Hungarian player of the Sixties and Seventies. Won national Open Teams 12 times 1954-79, national Open Pairs 7 times 1959-75. Represented Hungary 150 times in various championships.

KAVIN, Craig A. (b. 1952) of Tarzana CA, in retail sales, bridge professional and teacher. Has won 17+ regional events.

KAWAKAMI, Kuniaki (b. 1940), computer software executive. Far East champion 1985 and represented Japan frequently since 1964. Npc Japanese team Bermuda Bowl 1991. Won many national titles. Former member Japan Board of Governors.

KAY, Judy (Mrs. Norman) (b. 1934) of Narberth PA, retired owner/operator wholesale baseball memorabilia business, former bridge teacher. Close personal friend of Edgar Kaplan, won her first regional with him when she was a novice. Coordinated 1971 Omar Sharif Bridge Circus in Philadelphia. Wrote the production for 1972 Lancaster NABC. Has won more than 15 regionals.

KAY, Norman (b. 1927) of Narberth PA, retired account executive, baseball memorabilia business owner/operator with wife, owned horses (harness) from 1970-87. Co-author of *The Complete Book of Duplicate Bridge*. Served as active (and emeritus) member of PCBA for more than 30 years, was president of Keystone Conference in late 60's. Kaplan (Edgar)\Kay had one of the most successful and longest lasting partnerships, spanning more than 40 years. It was ended only by Kaplan's death in 1997. Was named the top performance player for the double decade 1957-1977 (ACBL *Bulletin* Oct. 1977), honored by his Unit for outstanding achievement in bridge as well as for being one of the finest gentlemen the game has known. ACBL Honorary Member 2000, member ACBL Hall of Fame. One of world's leading players and a WBF Life Master. Kay placed 2nd Bermuda Bowl 1961, 67; 2nd World Olympiad Teams 1968; 3rd World Olympiad Open Teams 1960; 5th World Open Pairs 1982; 6th Rosenblum Teams 1986, 10th 1982 and has represented the ACBL in other world competitions. LM #364 and Grand Life Master with 13,308 MPs as of 3/2001. Won McKenney Trophy, Master Individual 1955; Men's BAM Teams 1955, 61, 66; Men's Pairs 1958; Mott-Smith Trophy 1960, 68; Chicago (now the Reisinger) 1961, Vanderbilt 1959, 60, 68, 70, 81, 83, 86; Open Pairs 1963, 66; Reisinger 1966, 67, 71, 82, 83, 84, 90; Spingold 1967, 68; Life Master Men's Pairs 1973; Blue Ribbon Pairs 1974; Open Swiss Teams 1997. Placed 2nd in the Vanderbilt 1958, 65, 94; Men's BAM Teams, Men's Pairs 1958, 65, 70; Chicago 1969, Spingold 1960, 61, 65, 71, 78; Master Mixed Teams 1960, 62, 67; Men's BAM Teams 1968, 63, 75; Men's Swiss Teams 1967, Reisinger 1969, Open Swiss Teams 1991.

KAYE, Dorothy R. (b. 1923) of Denver CO. Won Life Master Women's Pairs 1968. Licensed helicopter pilot.

KAYE, Richard I. (b. 1923) of Denver CO, president of his fur company. Chairman of the Denver Crime Commission and Colorado. State Coordinating Board. Won Men's Pairs 1970 and several regionals.

KEARSE, Judge Amalya (b. 1937) of New York City, United States Court of Appeals circuit judge, attorney and former partner of Wall Street firm of Hughes, Hubbard and Reed. One of her professors called her "the best student, male or female, to come down the pike". First woman to sit on the Federal Appeals court in Manhattan. Served Greater New York BA as counsel to the Board 1970-79, Board member 1966-75, Conduct and Ethics Committee counsel 1970-73, chairman 1973-79 and various other committees. Served the ACBL as member of the Board of Governors 1970-76, member of the ACBL Appeals Committee 1971-75 and as a member of the ACBL Laws Commission since 1975. Editor of 3rd edition of *Encyclopedia of Bridge* and is a member of the Charles Goren Editorial Board. She authored *Bridge Conventions Complete, Bridge at Your Fingertips.* Was co-translator of *Championship Bridge, Bridge a la Une* and *Bridge Analysis* with Jose le Dentu. Her non-bridge writings include several legal publications. Editor of *Law Review* (at University of Michigan.) and she has been listed in *Who's Who in America.*

IBPA Bridge Personality of the Year in 1980. Was taught to play bridge by her parents while in high school and took up duplicate in law school. WBF World Life Master, won World Women's Pairs 1986, and has represented ACBL in other events. Diamond Life Master, won USWBC 1992 and Women's Pairs 1971, Life Master Women's Pairs 1972, Women's KO Teams 1987, Women's BAM Teams 1990, North American Women's Swiss Teams 1991 and 7 ABA national championships 1972-73. She placed 2nd Women's KO Teams 1991, Mixed BAM Teams 1996, Women's Swiss Teams 2001.

KEAVENEY, Gay of Galway, Ireland, university lecturer. WBF World Master. Represented Ireland in 2 world championships and 3 zonals. Member Irish team that won Camrose in 2000, the 1st win by a country other than England and Scotland. Ireland's top-ranked masterpoint holder and winner of many national titles. Pioneered the Irish Schools Championship in 1983.

KEEL, Darrell E. (b. 1940) of Montesano WA, senior account insurance agent. Past president Unit 428, served as tournament chairman for sectionals and regionals. Co-founder of Tri-Cities B.C. and was instrumental in starting sectional and regional tournaments for his unit. He and Steve Bruno are believed to hold the record for the highest two-session Flight A event when they scored $452^1/_2$ on an average of 312. Placed 2nd North American Swiss Teams 1993. Won 26 regionals.

KEHELA, Sami R. (Sammy) (b. 1934) of Toronto ON, born in Baghdad, semi-retired bridge journalist and teacher. Former editor of Ontario *Kibitzer*, bridge columnist for *Toronto Life,* contributor to ACBL *Bridge Bulletin,* contributing editor *Encyclopedia of Bridge.* One of world's great players. WBF World Life Master. Placed 2nd Bermuda Bowl 1974, 3rd Olympiad Teams 1968, 72; Rosenblum Teams 1982; 4th World Olympiad Teams 1964; 5th World Open Pairs 1970, Rosenblum Cup Teams 1978. Represented Canada in other world championships 1960, 66, 67, 72, 76, 80, 86, 88, 90. His partnership with Eric Murray lasted more than 30 years. Kehela was coach for the North American team in the Bermuda Bowl 1962, 63, 65. Won Team Trials 1966, 73; Life Master Men's Pairs 1963, Spingold 1964, 65, 68; Vanderbilt 1966, 70; Blue Ribbon Pairs 1967, Life Master Pairs 1969, Canadian National Teams Championship 1980, 81. 2nd Spingold 1963, Blue Ribbon Pairs 1969, Reisinger 1969, 72.

KEHOE, Robert A. (Bob) (1946-2000) of Orange Park FL, contact representative, bridge professional. Won North American Swiss Teams 1978.

KEIDAN, Bruce (b. 1943) of Monroeville PA, bridge columnist. Keidan was the first to notice unusual foot movements by one Italian pair during the 1975 Bermuda Bowl. Won several regionals. (see BERMUDA INCIDENT.)

KELLER, Brenda (b. 1943) of Boise ID, professional player. Diamond Life Master, placed 2nd Women's KO Teams 1983; North American Women's Swiss Teams 1983, 92; Life Master Women's Pairs 1988.

KELLY, Jack (1916-1970) of Sutton, Ireland, government accountant. Represented Ireland in 3 world championships and 3 zonal championships. Won all Irish national titles. Columnist of *Irish Times* and magazine contributor. IBPA President 1964-70.

KELLY, Nathan (1876-1959) of Boston MA, attorney and bridge teacher. Prominent player of whist, auction and contract. Invented Kelly Solid Suit Signals. Won many AWL national titles and several regional championships at contract.

KELNER, Louis (1907-1989) of Forest Hills NY, accountant, stockbroker. ACBL regional tournament director. Won Spingold 1956 and placed 2nd Life Master Pairs 1956.

KELSEY, Hugh Walter (1926-1995) of Edinburgh Scotland, novelist and bridge writer. Represented Scotland 12 times in Camrose matches. Won Gold Cup 1969 (the 1st Scottish win) and 1980. Won every major Scottish title many times. Bridge columnist of *The Scotsman*. Author of *Killing Defense in Bridge* and 44 other books.

KEMIC, Stephen B. (b. 1946) of Los Alamos NM, physicist. Disciplinary Chairman Unit 381 1992-present and District 17 Appellate Judiciary Committee member 1997-present. Won 20 regionals.

KEMP-FREILICH, Edith. See FREILICH, Edith.

KEMPNER, Alicia (Mrs. Ralph) of Palm Springs CA. Placed 2nd Women's Team Olympiad 1964. Won Master Mixed Teams 1946, 54, 60; Women's Teams 1962, 69; placed 2nd Mixed Pairs 1955, Women's Pairs 1965.

KEMPNER, Ralph of Los Angeles, stockbroker. Won Open Pairs 1936, placed 2nd Spingold 1948. Kempner also won numerous regionals.

KEMPSON, Ewart (1895-1966) of Gainford, England, Army officer and bridge writer. In the Thirties he was the staunchest supporter of the Walter Buller method called *British Bridge* — direct bidding with no forcing bids. Authored 21 books on bridge. Editor and director of *Bridge* magazine, contributing editor *Bridge Encyclopedia*.

KENDRICK, Carmen K. (Boots) (b. 1925) of Lubbock TX, assistant to Director of Institute of *Good Housekeeping* magazine. Placed 2nd Master Mixed Teams 1961 and won several regionals.

KENEDI, Tibor (b. 1915- deceased) of Sao Paulo, Brazil, industrialist. Represented Brazil in 1964 World Team Olympiad and in 4 South American Championships. National successes include 6 Open Teams.

KENNEDY, Betty Ann of Shreveport LA. One of the leading women players of the world. WBF Grand Master, ranked 26th among women Grand Masters. ACBL Grand Life Master with 13,455 MPs as of 3/2001. She has lectured on many bridge cruises and at many NABCs. Recipient of the 1985 Image Award. Was inducted into the Louisiana Hall of Fame 1993 (only the 2nd woman to be so honored). In 1990 she was entered into the Shreveport-Bossier Sports Hall of Fame. Member NABC Appeals Committee, a past vice-president of Unit 170, past member of District 10 Judiciary Committee, served on World Bridge Olympiad Appeals Committee 1992 and was for many years Chairman of Unit 170 Appeals Committee.

A world champion several times over, she won the Venice Cup 1974, 76; World Women's Pairs 1982, Women's Olympiad Teams 1984. Placed 2nd Venice Cup 1981, 85; World Women's Pairs 1978, placed 5th World Women's Pairs and 6th World Mixed Teams 1974. Won USWBC 1993, Master Mixed Teams 1960, Women's KO Teams 1978, 80, 83, 87, 2000; North American Women's Swiss Teams 1983, 95; Life Master Women's Pairs 1990, Women's BAM Teams 1992, 95; Women's Pairs 1993. 2nd in Women's Pairs 1960, 90, 92; Life Master Women's Pairs 1971, 81; Women's KO Teams 1982, 92, 2000; North American Women's Swiss Teams 1985, 2000; Women's BAM Teams 1986, 91. Has made many trips to China and won the Ambassador's Cup in Beijing 1988, Open Teams in Hong Kong 1981, International Bridge Team Championship in Beijing 1993 and placed 3rd in the First International Invitational Chinese Bridge Tournament Open Teams 1981.

KENNEDY, John E. (Jack) (b. 1920) of Shreveport LA., industrialist, retired U.S. Army colonel. In WW II he was awarded 3 U.S., 2 foreign decorations and 4 campaign medals. Kennedy was inducted in Shreveport Sports Hall of Fame. He has served on the ACBL Board of Governors, as president of Unit 170 and as vice president of District 10. Diamond Life Master, placed 6th World Mixed Teams 1974. Won Men's Pairs 1973, Blue Ribbon Pairs 1984 and placed 2nd in Men's Pairs 1976. Won Open Teams in Hong Kong 1981 and was 3rd in First Invitational Chinese Bridge Tournament Open Teams 1981, won Open Pairs 1987.

KENNY, Michael (b. 1954) of Toronto ON, systems analyst. Vice president Canadian Bridge Federation 1984-85, Unit 151 president 1984-85, member ACBL Board of Governors 1983-85. Won CNTC 1993 and more than 20 regionals.

KEOHANE, Ethel (Mrs. William H.) (1901-1995) of Wellesley Hills MA., administrative secretary. Served as secretary of Eastern MA Bridge Association for 18 years; as assistant chairman of the Goodwill Committee for many years; was on the executive board of the New England B.C. Named ACBL Honorary Member 1982, she was also honored in 1991 at the Spring NABC on her 90th birthday. Keohane, LM #151, Grand Life Master. Strong competitor until her death and played in many regionals and at NABC's. In 1990, at the age of 89, won more than 250 points with many strong performances in NABC's and regional competitions. Had many regular partnerships but the most successful was with Frank Westcott. Was member of winning Boston Inter-City Match team 1970, 71, 72, 73. Placed 2nd in Women's KO Teams 1952, 77. Won dozens of regionals starting in the Forties and continuing into the Nineties. In 1981, at the age of 80, Keohane survived a brutal car accident that killed her partner, Ida Bennett. Although practically every bone in her body was broken and she was not expected to live, she somehow managed to pull through. She was told she would never walk again, but after months of exercise and going through physical rehabilitation she regained the use of her legs.

KERR, Robert A. (Bob) (b. 1935) of Los Angeles, supervisor of transportation pricing. Served on Unit ethics committees in Seventies. Diamond Life Master, placed 2nd Men's Pairs 1971 and won several regionals.

KERWIN, Madeleine (1882-1965) introduced bridge in the Cavendish Club in 1926. Was a bitter antagonist of Ely Culbertson. In 1931 she became 2nd president of ABL and helped codify the Official System, which was

designed to replace Culbertson's as the public's favorite. More successful than this effort was her theoretical work as one of the originators of the Forcing Two-Bid. Her writings include the first book on the Sims System (*The One-Over-One for Everyone*) as well as some 5 other books and numerous bridge articles.

KESSLER, Gary D. (b. 1953) of Springfield IL, president Recycled Records Inc. Springfield tournament coordinator 1991-to date. Diamond Life Master, has won 40-50 regionally rated events.

KESSLER, Mark N. (b. 1947) of Springfield IL, coowner Recycled Records Inc. Won 20+ regional events.

KHALIL, Lily (b. 1940) of Cairo, Egypt, bridge teacher. WBF World Master. Won BFAAME Women's Teams 1987, 91, 97, 2nd 1989. Represented Egypt in several world and other zonal championships.

KHAUTIN, Richard L. (1940-1993) of New York City, accountant. Won Blue Ribbon Pairs 1972.

KHIOUPPENEN, Yuri (b. 1971) of St.Petersburg, Russia, manager. WBF World Master. 2nd Internet World Championship 1999. Quarterfinalist World Teams 1996. 3rd World Junior Teams 1997. Represented Russia in one world and 2 zonal championships. Several national wins.

KHOLOMEEV, Vadim (b. 1970) of St. Petersburg, Russia, bridge professional. WBF World Master. 2nd Internet World Championship 1999. Quarterfinalist World Teams 1996. Represented Russia in one world and 2 zonal championships. Several national wins.

KHOURI, Maud (b. 1946) of Cairo, Egypt, bridge teacher. Won BFAAME Women's Teams 1987, 91. 97, 2nd 1989. Represented Egypt in several world and other zonal championships.

KIATCHOKWIWAT, Adisorn (b. 1950) of Bangkok, Thailand, state employee. 2nd PABF (Far East) Open Teams 1977, 85; represented Thailand in 6 other Far East Championships and 4 world championships.

KIERZNOWSKI, Roman (b. 1949) of Olsztyn, Poland, engineer. Won European Open Pairs 1997. Won many national titles.

KILSTRUP, Vivian (b. 1938) of Denver CO, born in Poland, bridge teacher, director and former bridge club owner. Diamond Life Master with 15+ regional wins.

KIMELMAN, Neil D. (b. 1954) of Regina SK, manager with federal government, past president and vice-president Unit 181 1975-78. Has won 18 regionals. Kimelman placed 5th in Epson World-Wide Bidding Contest.

KIMOTO, Hidenobu (b. 1948) of Tokyo, Japan, bridge teacher and director. Represented Japan in World Team Olympiad 1976 and 1984 and in Far East Championships 6 times. Won 14 national team titles including Prince Takamatsu Cup 3 times. Won 3 National Pair events.

KIMURA, Rokuro (b. 1908) of Ashiya, Hyogo Pref., Japan. One of the 11 original members of the JCBL when it was founded in 1953. Vice-president 1972-81. Honorary Life Member 1981.

KINCAID, Arthur R. (b. 1911) of Liberty MO, attorney. Was a member of the Missouri Legislature 1937-43 and city attorney 1945-51. Placed 2nd Spingold 1953.

KING, David W. (b. 1951) of Omaha NE, senior business systems architect, chaired 1987 Omaha regional. Diamond Life Master who started playing bridge at age 10. Has won 19 regionals.

KING, Frank P., Jr. (b. 1933) of Alexandria VA., retired from USAF. While on active duty King was the leading MP holder among members of the Armed Forces. Placed 9th World Senior Pairs 1990 (highest placed U.S. pair). Placed 2nd Silver Ribbon Pairs 1996. Diamond Life Master with more than 200 regional wins.

KING, Malcolm T. (Mac) (b.1929) of Toronto ON, retired systems analyst. Won 15+ regionally rated events.

KING, Philip (b. 1966) of London, England, bridge writer. 9 national wins include 2 Gold Cups. Represented England in 6 Camrose matches, winning each time. Coach of 3 winning British teams in international competition. Co-author, with his father, Robert King, of *The King's Tales* and 5 other successful books of bridge parodies. Bridge editor for Batsford publishers.

KING, Warren R. (b. 1958) of Albuquerque NM, sales representative. Won Non-Life Master GNOP 1989 and a few regionals.

KIRBY, Graham (b. 1955) of Nottingham, England. WBF World Master. Placed 2nd Bermuda Bowl 1987. Won European Teams 1991, 2nd 1987. Represented Britain in 3 other world championships and 3 other zonal championships. Represented England in 30 Camrose matches, won several national titles including 6 Gold Cups.

KIRKHAM, Corinne (b. 1936) of San Bernardino CA., computer programmer, systems analyst, project manager. Unit official and tournament manager. Placed 2nd in a regional event with daughter, Adair Gellman, who was 11 years old and had 5 MPs. Adair went on to become Youngest Life Master and Queen of Bridge. While working full time in 1988 Corinne won 844 MPs. Grand Life Master with 14,628 MPs as of 3/2001, won Women's Pairs 1994, Senior KO Teams, Silver Ribbon Pairs 1999; placed 2nd IMP Pairs 1988, Silver Ribbon Pairs 1993.

KIRKHAM, Jim (b. 1936) of San Bernardino CA., retired U.S. Marine officer, tournament manager. District 22 president, has served 3 terms as Unit president. ACBL Board of Directors member, ACBL President 2001. While working full time in 1988 he won 1056 MPs. Invented Kirkham Over Big Bids (Kobb) and Modified Drury. Placed 17th World Mixed Pairs 1986. Diamond Life Master, won Senior KO Teams, Silver Ribbon Pairs 1999; placed 2nd in IMP Pairs, Silver Ribbon Pairs 1988. Grand Life Master with 17,694 MPs as of 3/2001. Has won dozens of regionals.

KITCHEL, Robert H. (Bob, Kitch or Stanley) (1931-1995) of Union Grove AL, associate national tournament director, former stockbroker. Served as Professional Tournament Directors Association representative to the ACBL Board of Directors, adviser to Chicago CBA, tournament co-ordinator for District 10. Kitchel began his directing career in 1962 and became full time in 1975. Placed 2nd in President's Cup 1962.

KIVEL, Joseph (Joe) (b. 1934) of Newport Coast CA., investment adviser, former nuclear scientist. Diamond Life Master. On the international level placed 9th in Rosenblum Teams 1990. Won Life Master Pairs 1995. placed 2nd GNOT 1990, Open Pairs II 1998, Open Pairs II 2001.

KIVEL, Mickie of Potomac MD, Public Health Advisor for FDA. Listed in *Who's Who in American Women* and *Who's Who in the East*. WBF World Master. 3rd World Women's Teams 1998, 16th World Women's Pairs 1990. Won Life Master Women's Pairs 1986. Diamond Life Master, won approximately 40-50 regionals.

KLAPPER, Wit (b. 1944) of Krakow, Poland, engineer. 2nd European Open Teams 1970. 2nd European Senior Teams 1995. Won many national titles.

KLAR, Robin of Houston TX. Won Women's Team

Olympiad 2000. Won Women's Swiss Teams 1999, Women's BAM Teams 2000, placed 2ⁿᵈ Women's KO Teams 2000, Women's Pairs 2000.

KLAUSNER, Malvine (Mrs. Siegfried) (1902-1997) of Van Nuys CA. Represented U.S. in World Team Olympiad 1960. Won Master Mixed Teams 1953, placed 2ⁿᵈ Mixed Pairs 1965.

KLAUSNER, Siegfried (1890-1949) of Beverly Hills CA, born in Vienna. Was a leading Austrian player in the Thirties. In 1932 he invented plastic playing cards, those manufactured in the United States under the name "Kem Cards".

KLEINMAN, Danny (b. 1937) of Los Angeles CA., computer programmer, bridge and backgammon teacher, songwriter, writer. Designed and programmed the first backgammon computer—Jack Gammon. He has written more than 30 books on bridge some of which are: *Bridge Scandal in Houston, Understanding Bidding: Foundations, Understanding Bidding: Ramifications, Advice to the Bridgelorn, Bridge in the Real World, It's a Bidder's Game, Bridge for Dummies, Defenders and Declarers, Pass is a Four-letter Word.* Author of numerous conventions and of several other books on backgammon. District 23 assistant recorder 1990-92. He won Intercollegiate Championship (E-W) 1957 and other regionals.

KLINGER, Ronald Denny (b. 1941) of Sydney, Australia, born in Shanghai, China, author, publisher, bridge teacher. Former university lecturer in law. Won PABF (Far East) Teams 1970 and PABF (Far East) Open Pairs twice. Represented Australia in 6 world championships, and won almost every Australian national title. Author of more than 20 books, including *Guide to Better Card Play* which won award as 1991 Bridge Book of the Year. Won Bols Brilliancy Prize as player in 1976 and as journalist in 1980.

KLUEWER, Ann C. (b. 1924) of Bakersfield CA., transcriptioner. Diamond Life Master, won Women's Pairs 1994 and 15+ regionally rated events.

KLUKOWSKI, Julian (b.1939) of Warsaw, Poland. Doctor of mathematics. WBF World Life Master. 3ʳᵈ Bermuda Bowl 1989, 1991; 2ⁿᵈ World Senior Teams 1998. Won European Teams 1981, 1989. Won Seniors Teams Bermuda 2000, 2ⁿᵈ European Senior Teams 1997. Represented Poland in many World Championships and European Championships. Winner of many titles in Polish Championships. Author of two bridge books. Bridge journalist and columnist.

KNIEST, Thomas W. (Tom) (b. 1945) of Clayton MO, semi-retired CPA. Placed 2ⁿᵈ in Life Master Pairs 1986, Master Mixed Teams 1995, GNOP 1999. Was 2ⁿᵈ ABA National Mixed Pairs 1986. Has won 40 plus regionals including the first one he ever played in.

KNIGA-LEOSZ, Jerzy (b. 1942) of Warsaw, Poland, engineer. Won European Senior Pairs 1999.

KNIPFEL, Earl C. (b.1939) of Moose Jaw SK, liquor store employee, teacher, won 18 regional events.

KOCH-PALMUND, Charlotte (b. 1965) of Copenhagen, Denmark, computer programmer. WBF World Life Master. Won Women's World Team Olympiad 1988, 2ⁿᵈ World Women's Pairs 1986. Won Women's Nordic Teams 1988, 2ⁿᵈ Nordic Junior Teams 1985, 3ʳᵈ Common Market Women's Pairs 1989. Frequently represented Denmark in world and zonal competitions.

KOCH-PALMUND, Dennis (b. 1959) of Copenhagen, Denmark, clerk. WBF World Master. 3ʳᵈ World Team Olympiad 1996. Represented Denmark in Bermuda Bowl 1993, 97, World Team Olympiad 1992 and 5 European

Championships. Won European Club Cup 1991. 16 Danish titles.

KOCK, Rudolf (Putte) (b. 1901) of Stockholm, Sweden, radio and television executive. Placed 2ⁿᵈ Bermuda Bowl 1950, representing Europe, and 1953, representing Sweden. Won European Teams 1939, 52, 2ⁿᵈ 1948, 49, 50. Won many national titles. Writings included one book. Represented Sweden at soccer. (see KOCK-WERNER REDOUBLES.)

KOISTINEN, Kalervo (b. 1958) of Helsinki, Finland, insurance mathematician. WBF World Master. Represented Finland 10 times, including 4 world championships and 3 European championships. Many national wins.

KOISTINEN, Kauko K. (b. 1960) of Helsinki, Finland, bridge teacher and tournament director. WBF World Master. Represented Finland 12 times, including 4 world championships and 6 European championships. 15 national titles. Chief editor of Finnish bridge magazine, *Bridge-lehti.*

KOKISH, Eric O. (b. 1947) of Toronto ON, bridge professional, writer, teacher, coach, former research analyst. Frequent traveler in his work with international teams, preparing them for world events. Has served as District 1 Judiciary chairman since the early Seventies, as Zone II CBF representative, past president of Unit 151, District 1 GNOT co-ordinator. Wrote large portions of World Championship books 1979-85 and 1988-2000. Editor of Unit 151 *Melange De Bridge,* wrote weekly bridge column for Montreal *Gazette 1977-97,* Toronto Star Syndicate 1998, is editor *e-bridge.* Directs Master Solvers Club for *Bridge World,* regular columnist for ACBL *Bridge Bulletin,* regular contributor to *South African Bridge Bulletin , Bridge World, Imp* magazine (Holland) and most leading bridge publications around the world. Kokish is syndicated daily in *Toronto Star.* Author of several conventions including Kokish (Birthright), Reject and the Montreal Relay. Kokish won a Bols Brilliancy prize 1980 and the Romex Best Bid Hand Award. WBF vugraph commentator and WBF news editor.

WBF World Life Master, placed 2ⁿᵈ Bermuda Bowl 1995, World Open Pairs 1978; 3ʳᵈ Rosenblum Teams 1982, 90; 5ᵗʰ 1978, 9ᵗʰ 1986, has represented Canada in many other world championships. Placed 3ʳᵈ Pan-Am Invitational, Maccabiah Games 1981; won Deauville Tournament of Champions 1979, 2 world Intercity Championships in Tokyo, Calcutta Teams 1985, CDN International Pairs 1989. Diamond Life Master, won Vanderbilt 1974, Men's Teams 1978; placed 2ⁿᵈ Men's Teams 1974, Vanderbilt 1980, Spingold 1982, Reisinger 1982, CNTC 1980, 81, 85.

KOLKER, Larry M. (b. 1928) of St. Louis MO, rubber bridge club owner, professional bridge teacher and player. Won Vanderbilt 1962 and numerous regional titles.

KONERU, Venkatrao (b.1959) of San Antonio TX, born in India, Lieutenant Colonel, U.S. Air Force. Won 50 regionals.

KONSTAM, Kenneth (1906-1968) of London, England, executive and journalist. Won Bermuda Bowl 1955. Won European Teams in 1948, 49, 50, 54, 61, 63 and represented Britain in 5 other world championships and 6 other zonal championships. Many national wins included 4 Gold Cups. Bridge editor *London Sunday Times.*

KONSTANTINOVSKY, Elias (Lucho) (1934-1994) of Mexico, bridge club owner and teacher. Represented Mexico in international competition Las Palmas 1974, New Orleans 1978, Valkenburg 1980, Maccabiah Games

1981. He contributed to Mexican bridge publications. Served as chairman of the 1982 Mexican Nationals and as a Board member of the Mexican Bridge Federation. Won Master Mixed Teams 1980 and several regionals.

KOOIJMAN, Ton (b. 1941) of Gouda, The Netherlands, education inspector and tournament director. WBF operations director since 1991, chairman of WBF Laws Committee.

KOPERA, Michael P. (b. 1953) of New York City, options trader. Placed 2nd North American Swiss Teams 1983. Won numerous regional events.

KOPPANG, Knut (b. 1936) of Oslo, Norway, actuary. Placed 3rd Bermuda Bowl 1969. 2nd European Championship 1968, 3rd 1966. Won 2 national championships.

KORNFELD, Warren (b. 1939) of Jericho NY, owner executive search firm. Served as chairman Conduct and Ethics Committee for N.J. Bridge Association and as treasurer NSBA. Won Blue Ribbon Pairs 1972. Had highest E-W score in North America in Epson 1991 and has won 20+ regionals.

KORTAY, Mehmet (d. 1988) of Istanbul, Turkey. Represented Turkey in 4 world and 6 zonal championships. 10 national wins.

KOVACICH, Michael (Mike) (b. 1945) of Stone Mountain GA., attorney. Has served on ACBL Board of Governors 1999-present, as 1st and 2nd Alternate District (7) Director; president, vice president, and secretary District 7; and various executive positions on the Unit (114) level. Diamond Life Master with 17 regional titles; E/W winner Instant Matchpoint Game 1999.

KOVALENKO, Yuri of Tashkent, Uzbekistan. Leading tournament director of the former Soviet Union. Has directed at several world championships.

KOWALCZYK, Ireneusz (b. 1950) of Katowice, Poland, businessman. WBF World Master. 2nd World Transnational Open Teams 1997. Won many national titles.

KOWALSKI, Apolinary (b. 1948) of Warsaw, Poland, chemistry engineer, bridge professional. WBF World Master. Won World Mixed Pairs 1994, 2nd World Individual 1998. 2nd European Open Teams 1997, 3rd European Open Pairs 1999. 4th World Open Pairs 1994. Won many national titles.

KOYTCHOU, Boris (b. 1919) of New York City, born in Russia, retired bridge teacher and lecturer, co-founder and partner in The Card School. Served as chairman of the Card Committee and Board member of the Regency Whist Club (New York City), one of the outstanding players in France and later in the United States. Represented France in European Championships 1948, 49, 50; North America in the Bermuda Bowl 1957, in Biarritz 1982. He won 3 French national team championships and holds the WBF rank of World Master. Koytchou won the Spingold 1956, 60; Chicago (now the Reisinger) 1963 and placed 2nd Vanderbilt 1955, 62, 65. Now enjoys competitive croquet.

KOZAKOS, George (b. 1956) of Sydney, Australia, computer professional. Won South Pacific Teams 1995. Represented Australia in Bermuda Bowl and other zonal teams. 4 national wins include Interstate Teams, Grand National Teams and Open Pairs. Co-developer of CARDS bridge rating system.

KOZLOVE, Lawrence M. (Larry) (b. 1945) of Louisville KY, bank vice president. Represented ACBL in Rosenblum Teams (placed 11th) 1978. Won Men's Pairs 1978, placed 2nd Men's Pairs 1975, Spingold 1977. Diamond Life Master with numerous regional wins.

KRAFT, Beverly G. (b.1947) of Toronto ON, bridge writer, former retailer. Writes and edits for *The Bridge World* and syndicated daily column for *Toronto Star*. Won Canadian Women's Teams Championships (CWTC) 1985, 92, 95, 96, 98, 99, placed 2nd Women's Team Olympiad 2000, 3rd 1996.

KRANSBERG, Gladys (b. 1910) of North Miami Beach FL. Placed 2nd Mixed Pairs 1960 and won several regional events.

KRATENSTEIN, Rhoda M. (b. 1948) of Schenectady NY, computer systems manager, Y2K project manager. Has been president, vice president, and tournament manager for Unit 115. Won Life Master Women's Pairs and Women's Swiss Teams 1994; was 2nd Women's BAM Teams 1995. Has won many regional events.

KRAUSS, Donald P. (Don) (b. 1937) of Los Angeles CA., stockbroker. Helped to organize the Corporate America vs. Hollywood Celebrities match 1992. Ranked a WBF Life Master, he placed 2nd World Team Olympiad 1964. Represented North America in Bermuda Bowl 1971, in New Orleans 1978. He won the Team Trials 1963, International Playoff matches 1970, Maccabiah Games 1981, Vanderbilt 1964, Chicago (now the Reisinger) 1962, Reisinger 1971, Men's Teams 1970 and placed 2nd Spingold 1971, Men's Teams 1972, Life Master Men's Pairs 1981.

KREHBIEL, Carol (b. 1930) of Owensboro KY, bridge teacher, retired restaurant owner. Club manager of 2 Owensboro duplicate clubs since 1994, *Midwest Monitor* bridge reporter. Unit Education Liaison, long-time member of local and District boards. Won 13-16 regionally rated events.

KREIJNS, Hans (b. 1925) of The Hague, The Netherlands, bridge tour conductor, former painting contractor. WBF World Grand Master. Won World Open Pairs 1966, 2nd European Teams 1965, 66, 3rd World Teams 1980. Represented The Netherlands regularly in international championships until 1987. Winner of 12 major national titles, top Dutch masterpoint winner.

KREKORIAN, James E. (Jim) (b. 1952) of New York City, options trader, bridge professional and teacher. Was 3-time college track letterman. Holds airline transport pilot rating. Grand Life Master, with 12,814 MPs as of 3/2001. Won Life Master Men's Pairs 1986, GNOP 1992, Blue Ribbon Pairs 1996, Open BAM Teams 1997; placed 2nd Men's Swiss Teams 1986, 90, the Vanderbilt 1987. Won Cavendish Invitational Pairs 1987 and has won more than 100 regionals.

KREMER, Norbert A. (Norb) (b. 1941) of Schenectady NY, tax preparer and partner in Neinor Corp. with Neil Chambers. Diamond Life Master, won Master Mixed Teams 1983, placed 2nd GNOT 1973, Master Mixed Teams 1981, Life Master Men's Teams 1985. Has won many regional events.

KRISTINSSON, Jakob (b. 1962) of Kopavogur, Iceland, and Rochester Hills, Michigan, website designer, bridge teacher. Won Nordic Championship 1994. Represented Iceland in one World Championship, 2 European Championships, one other Nordic Championship, one European Junior Teams and one Nordic Junior Teams. 3 national wins. Holds current record of becoming ACBL Life Master in the shortest amount of time, 6 weeks, beating Sabine Auken (formerly Zenkel) by 3 weeks.

KRISTJONSDOTTIR, Valgerdur (b. 1945) of Reykjavik, Iceland, editor and publisher. Won Nordic Women's Teams 1990. Represented Iceland in one world

championship, 4 European Championships and 4 other Nordic Championships. 12 national wins.

KUBAK, Fritz (b. 1949) of Vienna, Austria, croupier. WBF World Master. 2nd World Team Olympiad 1988. Won European Mixed Pairs 1996. Represented Austria in 9 other world championships and 6 European events. Won 8 Austrian Teams, one Open Pairs and 2 Mixed Pairs.

KUBISTA, Dr. Josef (b. 1931) of Jonkoping, Sweden, born in Czechoslovakia, pediatrician. Won Baltic Cup 1963. Represented Czechoslovakia on many occasions, won 6 national titles there before relocating Sweden in 1968.

KUDLA, Marek (b.1939) of Poznan, Poland. World Master. 3rd Bermuda Bowl 1981. Won European Open Pairs 1980, European Open Teams 1981. Won many national titles.

KUNDU, Oindrilla (1951-1991) of Calcutta, India, actress and florist. Won BFAAME Women's Teams 1985 and represented India in 3 world championships. Won 2 national titles. Only woman winner of West Bengal Open Pairs. Won journalist awards including Epson 1987. Child film star as "Tinkoo Tagore", starring in best Indian movie of 1956.

KUNGS, Egon (1912-1985) of Tallinn, Estonia, accountant. A driving force in the development of Estonian and Soviet bridge in Sixties and Seventies. Won Soviet Union Teams 1979, 81; Estonian Teams 1969, 70; Estonian Pairs 1977.

KUO, Che-Kung (b. 1952) of Taipei, Taiwan. WBF World Master. Won Far East Teams 1976, 78, 81, 86, 94, 97; Far East Pairs 1976, 87. Represented Taiwan in 13 zonal championships and 8 world championships. Author of Chinese Precision which is the most popular among Chinese players on both sides of the strait.

KURLAN, Roslyn of Great Neck NY, cruise director and bridge teacher 1970-87. Diamond Life Master, has won 69 regional events.

KURLANDER, Norman A. (b. 1938) of Flushing NY, co-owner of rubber bridge club and bridge teacher, former options trader. Chairperson of Conduct and Ethics Committee for professional bridge union in NY. Placed 2nd Men's Teams 1973 and won several regionals.

KUROKAWA, Akio (b. 1937) of Tokyo, Japan, bridge teacher, club owner, balalaika and mandolin player. Known as ace-king-ten. Far East champion 1985, represented Japan in many other Far East Championships. Won more that 30 national titles. Author of *Introduction to Bridge Play, How to Improve in Bridge* and *Bridge for Beginners*.

KUSHNER, Jack B. (1903-1963) of Longmeadow MA., bridge teacher and writer. Co-inventor of TNT system and author of *The Kushner System* and many booklets. Won Open Pairs 1950 and was president of New England Bridge Conference 1962.

KUTSKA, Michael R. (Mike) (b.1935) of River Forest IL, CPA. Has won approximately 25 regionals. As a bird watcher Kutska has seen 738 species in North America and 2,500 in the world.

KWIECIEN, Michal (b. 1957) of Lublin, Poland, engineer and businessman. WBF World Life Master. Won World Open Pairs 1998, 2nd World Team Olympiad 2000. 2nd European Open Teams 1997. 3rd World Transnational Open Teams 1998. Won European Junior Teams 1982. Won many national titles.

KYRIAKIDOU, Nitsa (b. 1946) of Athens, Greece. 3rd 1989 Common Market Women's Teams and represented Greece on many other occasions. 5 national wins include 3 women's pairs.

KYRIAKOS, Costas (b. 1926) of Athens, Greece, journalist and retired director-general of Automobile Touring Club of Greece and organizer of 1971 European Championships in Athens. Founded a club for junior players and introduced computer scoring to Greece. Columnist for *Ethnos*, author of 3 bridge books, and translator-publisher of 2 Victor Mollo books. Established Kyriakos Trophy for yearly masterpoint winner.

L

LAANEMAE, Tiit (b. 1953) of Tallinn, Estonia, bank employee. WBF World Master. Won Soviet Union Teams 1982, 1986, 1987; Soviet Union Pairs 1981, 1982; Estonian Teams 1980, 86, 87, 90, 92, 95, 97, 98, 99; Estonian Pairs 1984, 87, 88. Represented Soviet Union in one world and 2 zonal championships; Estonia in 2 world and 3 zonal championships. Columnist of *Sonumileht*.

LABINS, Stephen H. (b. 1933) of West Hartford CT, retired, prison volunteer. Won 20+ regionals.

LACY, Jack (b. 1942) of Round Rock TX, independent software consultant. President Unit 207 – 1987, Conduct and Ethics chairman 1997-98, member District 16 Conduct and Ethics 1976. Won 18+ regional events.

LAFOURCADE, Jean-Pierre (b. 1952) of Liege, Belgium, bridge teacher, journalist and writer. Represented Belgium in one World Championship and 3 European Championships. National wins include 3 Open Teams.

LAGUARDIA, Carmen of Paranaque, Philippines. Won Far East Women's Teams, 1968, 79, 82 representing Philippines; in 1971, 72 representing Singapore. Represented Philippines in several world and zonal championships.

LAI, Hui-Ping or Jennifer (b. 1961) of Taipei, Taiwan, computer system analyst. Won Far East Women's Teams 1989. Represented Taiwan in 4 zonal championships and 4 world championships.

LAIR, Mark (b. 1947) of Canyon TX, bridge professional, one of leading American players, ACBL Grand Life Master with 41,641 MPs as of 3/2001. Ranked #3 in ACBL behind Paul Soloway and Mike Passell. WBF World Master. Placed 4th Rosenblum Teams 1982, 5th 1986, 9th 1990. Won Crane Top 500 1990, placed 2nd 1979. Won Master Pairs 1970, Master Mixed Teams 1977, 78, 79, 90; Vanderbilt 1979, 97, 98; Blue Ribbon Pairs 1984, 94; Fishbein Trophy 1986, Men's BAM Teams 1986, 88; Spingold 1986, 89; Reisinger 1988, 92; Open Swiss Teams 1991, 2000; Open BAM Teams 1993, North American Swiss Teams 1998. Placed 2nd Blue Ribbon Pairs 1972, Reisinger 1978, 80, 90, 93, 94, 00; Master Mixed Teams 1984, Spingold 1994, Open BAM Teams 1995. Lair has more than 400 regional titles to his credit.

LaLIBERTE, Andre (b. 1937) of Quebec, life insurance and mutual funds representative. Represented Canada 1979 in Sweden, 1989 in Australia. Has competed many times in CNTC, has won more than 15 regionals.

LALL, Hemant (b. 1951) of Plano TX, born in India, systems analyst. Represented Uttar Pradesh in National Bridge Team Championships of India in 1971 when 19. Won Life Master Pairs 1992, placed 2nd Mixed Pairs 1980, Spingold 1993. Diamond Life Master, won many regionals.

LAMB, Charles (1775-1834). See BATTLE, SARAH in General Information section.

LAMBARDI, Pablo (b. 1961) of Buenos Aires, Argentina, bridge teacher. WBF World Master. Won South American Teams 1979, 80, 95, 96. Represented Argentina in 5 world championships. Has 10 national titles. Won Gabarret Cup 1980, 84, 86.

LAMBERT, Bernie A. (b. 1953) of Viking AB, realtor and property manager, professional bridge player 1987-90. Won more than 30 regionals.

LAMBRINOS, Alex (b. 1950) of Athens, Greece, bridge teacher. WBF World Master. Represented Greece - 1988 World Team Olympiad, finishing 5th. This was the best performance ever by a Greek team. Represented Greece in 2 European Championships. 16 national wins include 5 Open Teams and 3 Open Pairs.

LAMBRINOU, Sofia (b. 1958) born in U.S.S.R. Was 3rd 1989 Common Market Women's Teams, represented Greece on many other occasions. 5 national wins include 3 Women's Pairs.

LAMPERT, Harry (b. 1916) of Deerfield Beach FL, bridge teacher and author. Worked in motion picture industry as an animation cartoonist 1933-53. Later through 1953, had cartoons in many leading magazines and newspapers. Creator of The Flash in *Flash Comics*. The Flash became a TV series in the 60's. His firm (The Lampert Agency) won the Cannes Film Festival Golden Lion Award for the World's Best TV Commercial - 1967. ABTA president 1991-93, member of Executive Board since 1994. Authored *The Fun Way to Learn Serious Bridge, The Fun Way to Serious Bridge, The Fun Way to Advanced Bridge, Declarer Play and Opening Leads, A Fun Way Bridge Book*. His book *A Fun Way to Advanced Bridge* was ABTA's 1985 Bridge Book of the Year. He has twice won the ABTA's Apple Basket Award for the best bridge teaching tip (1991 and 98). Columnist of *A Fun Way Bridge Tip* for ACBL *Bridge Bulletin*.

LAMPREY, Charles V. (Chuck) (b. 1938) of White Plains New York. Placed 13th Rosenblum Teams 1986, 17th 1990. Placed 2nd in GNOT 1979, Men's Teams 1982. Diamond Life Master.

LANDA, Sallie M. (b. 1925) of Boca Raton FL, former bridge teacher and professional player. Past manager and originator of 2 duplicate clubs in Fargo ND and past president of the Fargo C.B.L. Became a director about 30 years ago and began directing on bridge cruises. Author of *Duplicate for Master Points not for Glory*. Landa competed in World Bridge Olympiad 1972 and is a Diamond Life Master. Won more than 50 regionals.

LANDAU, Charles S. (1898-1981) of Mount Lebanon PA, former member ACBL Board of Directors and long-time bridge administrator in the Pittsburgh area. ACBL Honorary Member 1976.

LANDAU, Eric (b. 1945) of Silver MD, software developer. Has contributed to the *Bridge World* and ACBL *Bridge Bulletin*. Author of *Every Hand an Adventure*, codified and popularized the EHAA system.

LANDAU, Judith (Judy) (b. 1947) of Palm Harbor FL, advertising and sales representative. Won Master Mixed Teams 1983 and many regionals.

LANDEN, Stephen W. (b. 1952) of West Bloomfield MI, computer consultant and bridge professional. Served on Unit 137 Board of Directors, contributing editor to Unit *Table Talk*. Named Sportsman of Year 1980. Diamond Life Master, won Open Pairs 1990, Open Pairs II 2000; placed 2nd GNOP 1979, 91; GNOT 1982.

LANDLEY, Wilson W. (1917-1990) of Orlando FL, U.S. Civil Service employee. Won Life Master Pairs 1958.

LANDOW, William (Billy) (b. 1940) of Philadelphia PA, options trader. Won more than 15 regionals.

LANDRETH, George H. (b. 1927) of Norman OK, consulting petroleum engineer. Mini-McKinney Non-Master of the Year 1981, at that time he won with more masterpoints than any other in this category. Won several regionals.

LANDY, Alvin (1905-1967) born in Cleveland Ohio. Landy graduated from Western Reserve University and received his law degree from that school in 1927. After serving in WW II, Landy joined the ACBL as a tournament director, shortly thereafter became the League's business manager (1948). He was top ACBL executive 1950 until his sudden death in 1967. In his capacity as executive secretary, Landy was known for his temperance and wisdom. ACBL Honorary Member 1957, member ACBL Hall of Fame, secretary ACBL Charity Foundation from its inception. He played a key role in creation of that foundation and helped build it into a quarter-million dollar annual project. Member ACBL Laws Commission, secretary from 1956. Helped found and served as one of the original officers of World Bridge Federation - secretary-treasurer 1958-66. Originated the convention bearing his name—2♦ over opponents' 1NT requesting partner to bid one of the majors. Won Spingold in 1949; Men's BAM Teams 1948, 49, 54, 58. He was Life Master #24.

LANDY, Sandra (b. 1938) of Aylesbury, England, manager *Bridge for All*, the English Bridge Union's national teaching scheme. Former professor of computing. WBF World Grand Master, and joint leading woman in WBF 2000 all-time performance list. Won Venice Cup 1981, 85; 2nd 1976; 2nd World Women's Olympiad Teams 1976, 84, 88, 92, 96, was 3rd 1980; 3rd World Women's Pairs 1982, 86. Won European Women's Teams 1975, 79, 81, 97, 99; placed 2nd 1969, 77, 85. Won 5 Common Market titles. Represented Britain in 4 other world championship and 6 other zonal championships. Many national titles including Gold Cup. Chair of Educational Trust for British Bridge. Editor *Really Easy* series of books. Inventor of Standard English System, used in many online games.

LANGELAND, Ase of Norway. WBF World Master. 4th World Women's Team Olympiad 2000. Represented Norway in one zonal.

LANGSTROM, Linda of Stockholm, Sweden, artist. WBF World Master. 3rd Venice Cup 1993. Won European Women's Teams 1993, Nordic Teams 1992, 98. Represented Sweden in 2 other world championships and 4 zonal championships. Has 2 national titles.

LANOUE, Jack (b. 1940) of New Orleans LA. Diamond Life Master, won GNOP 1990, placed 2nd Reisinger 1975, GNOT 1987, won several regional events.

LANTARON, Luis (b. 1959) of Madrid, Spain, economist and bridge professional. WBF World Master. Represented Spain in 6 world championships and 5 zonals. National titles include Open Teams and Open Pairs several times. Placed 2nd ACBL Open Swiss Teams 2001.

LANZAROTTI, Massimo (b. 1959) of Voghera, Italy. WBF World Life Master. Won Rosenblum Teams 1998, European Teams 1995, 97 and 3 Italian titles. 1st in Italian ranking 1995, 97. 2nd European Pairs 1989.

LAPIDES, Steven R. (b. 1943) of Towson MD, data processing sales and consultant. Won Life Master Men's Pairs 1975, 89. Has won numerous regional events.

LaPIERRE, Suzanne (b. 1947) of Longueuil PQ, part-

time bridge professional. Co-authored *La Clef Du Bridge: Les Encheres*, 1st and 2nd editions. Won 21 regionals.

LARDNER, Ring (old) Wilmer (1885-1933) famous American author. Wrote 2 short stories on bridge, both of which appear in anthologies: *Contract* in *Treasury of Gambling Stories* and *Who Dealt* in *Grand Slam*.

LARSEN, Bjorn (1921-1991) of Oslo, Norway, inspector and bridge columnist. Won Nordic Teams 1948, 51. Several national titles. Placed 3rd Bermuda Bowl 1969. 2nd European Championship 1968, 3rd 1966. Honorary Member of Norwegian Bridge Federation, former secretary general and president.

LARSEN, Karl Christian (Chris) (b. 1941) of Costa Mesa CA, born in Norway, accountant, bridge teacher and club director. Graduated from college in Norway with 3 degrees. Placed 9th Rosenblum Teams 1990. ACBL Diamond Life Master, placed 2nd GNOT 1990, Mixed Pairs 1995, Open Pairs II 2001. Has numerous regional wins with 9 or 10 District 22 GNOT wins.

LARSEN, Kyle A. (b. 1950) of San Francisco CA, professional player. Has competed in several world championships. Youngest player ever to win a major North American Championship team title – was only 18 when he won the Reisinger 1968. Became Life Master at age 15, the youngest player to do so at the time. Grand Life Master with 11,747 MPs as of 3/2001. Won Men's Pairs 1968, Reisinger 1977, Spingold 1980, 2000; Open Swiss Teams 2000, GNOT 1982, 96. Placed 2nd Men's Teams 1970, Vanderbilt 1971, North American Swiss Teams 1999, GNOT 2000.

LARSON, Bernice E. (b. 1911) of Greenfield WI, bridge teacher. 1st alternate for ACBL Board of Directors, on ACBL Board of Governors for many years, president of Wisconsin/Upper Michigan B.A., Greater Milwaukee B.A. and has held various other executive positions. Contributes to Unit 222 *Brewer Bridge*. Chaired many sectionals and regionals in Milwaukee. An annual unit award has been created in her name and is given for service and achievement. Won Life Master Women's Pairs 1974, Diamond Life Master.

LASOCKI, Krzysztof (b.1940) of Warsaw, Poland, bridge professional. World Life Master. Placed 2nd Bermuda Bowl 1991, Rosenblum Teams 1994. Won European Open Teams 1993, European Open Pairs 1995, European Senior Pairs 1999. Was 3rd European Teams 1991, 2nd in Cavendish 1992. Represented Poland in many World and European Championships. Won many national titles.

LASUT, Henky (b. 1947) of Manado, Indonesia. WBF World Life Master. Won International Olympic Committee Teams 2000. Won PABF (Far East) Teams 1972, 73, 74, 79, 82, 83, 84, 92, 93, 99. Represented Indonesia in 12 world championships and in other zonal championships.

LaTRAVERSE, Jean Joseph (b. 1939) of Dollard-des-Ormeaux PQ, executive search consultant. Has been very active in the administrative side of bridge. He served as president of District 2, had 2 terms as president Unit 151, member of CBF Board of Directors 1975-78, chairman of District 2 judiciary committee 1977-82 and held several other executive positions. General chairman of 1985 NABC in Montreal. As a tournament director he achieved the rank of R-3.

LATTES, Robert (b.1924) of Paris, France, mathematician. WBF World Life Master. Won Bermuda Bowl 1956, European Teams 1955. Won several national titles. Retired from tournament play 1961. Contributed to vari-

ous periodicals including *Bridge Magazine*.

LAURIA, Lorenzo (b. 1946) of Rome, Italy, insurance broker. WBF Grand Master, ranked #25 in world. With Alfredo Versace forms one of the world's best partnerships. Won Rosenblum Teams 1998, World Team Olympiad 2000; placed 2nd Bermuda Bowl 1979, 83; won European Teams 1979, 95, 97; 2nd 1977. Won Vanderbilt 1999, Open Swiss Teams 2001, Cavendish Teams 1996, 97; Macallan 1998.

LAVINGS, Paul Warwick (b. 1945) of Sydney, Australia, bridge club manager. Represented Australia in 2 world championships and 6 Far East Championships. Won South Pacific playoff 1991. Played internationally with 8 different partners, probably a world record. Won almost all national titles. Editor and consulting editor of *Australian Bridge* 1985-90. Former columnist *Bulletin*.

LAVINTHAL, Hy (1894-1972) invented the suit preference signal that bears his name - 1933-34. A retail store manager and innovative bridge teacher from Trenton NJ. Lavinthal also served as associate editor of *The Bridge World*. His book *Defense Tricks* explained all the stipulations of his theory of defense.

LAWRENCE, I. (Larry) (b. 1935) of Warren NJ, attorney. Served as adviser to ACBL Education Foundation 1987-90 and held various executive positions on Unit and District level. Won Non-Life Master Teams 1983.

LAWRENCE, Michael S. (b. 1940) of Berkeley CA, one of the world's leading player/authors. WBF Grand Master, ranked 15th in world. ACBL Grand Life Master with 21,158 MPs as of 3/2001. Ranked #28 in ACBL. Notable author. Two of his books, *How to Read Your Opponents' Cards* and *The Complete Book on Overcalls in Contract Bridge* were named "Book of the Year" by Alfred Sheinwold and are generally considered to be classics. Some of his others are *Judgment at Bridge*, *The Complete Book on Balancing in Contract Bridge* and *Play a Swiss Teams of Four with Mike Lawrence*. Won Bermuda Bowl 1970, 71, 87; placed 2nd 1973, 89; World Team Olympiad 1972; 5th Rosenblum Teams 1986, 9th World Open Pairs 1982. He won International Playoff Match 1969, Lou Herman Trophy 1965, Vanderbilt 1967, 71, 73, 77, 85; Spingold 1969, Reisinger 1965, 70, 77, 80; GNOT 1978, 79, 87; Men's Teams 1964, 68; Men's Pairs 1983, Life Master Pairs 1984, Master Mixed Teams 1992. Placed 2nd Blue Ribbon Pairs 1965, 68, 71, 83; Men's Teams 1969, Vanderbilt 1970, Spingold 1970, 76, 80 85; Vanderbilt 1970, Life Master Men's Pairs 1978, Reisinger 1983.

LAWRENCE, Richard M. (Dick) (1903-1999) of Ann Arbor MI, retired store owner. Former holder of state record for 500 yard free style for swimmers older than 70. Won Men's Pairs 1967 and several regional events.

LAWRENCE, Stephen J. (b. 1924) of Athens TX, retired subsurface petroleum geologist and research at White Sands. Member ACBL Board of Governors 1970-86, has served District 16 and Unit 159 in various executive positions including president. ACBL Grand Life Master with 14,568 MPs as of 3/2001. ACBL Senior Player of Year 1996. Has won between 75 and 100 regional titles.

LAY, James E. (Spike) (b. 1944) of Ormond Beach FL, bridge club manager, certified director and former CPA. Placed 2nd IMP Pairs 1999 and won approximately 50 regionals.

LAZARD, Sidney H. (b. 1930) of New Orleans LA, oil and gas producer. One of the most successful American players. Member ACBL Hall of Fame. WBF World Life

Master, placed 2nd Bermuda Bowl 1959, 3rd 1969. Member of U.S. team World Team Olympiad 1960. Grand Life Master with 14,621 MPs as of 3/2001. Won Team Trials 1968, Spingold 1958, 68; Chicago (now the Reisinger) 1960, Vanderbilt 1970, 94; Master Mixed Teams 1963, 77, 78, 79, 82; GNOP 1990. Placed 2nd Spingold 1954, 66, 73; Vanderbilt 1967, Reisinger 1968, 69, 75, 97; Men's Teams 1954, 56, 61, 65; Men's Pairs 1967; Master Mixed Teams 1961, Mixed Pairs 1959, North American Men's Swiss Teams 1983, GNOT 1987, Open Pairs II 1997.

LAZARD, Sidney Jr. (Squid) (1958-1999) of Metairie LA, computer consultant. Lazard became a Life Master at age 16 and was the youngest Life Master that Louisiana had produced. Placed 2nd Men's Swiss Teams 1983.

LAZARUS, Diane (b. 1942) of Baltimore MD, retired accountant and travel agent. Has won more than 15 regionals.

LAZARUS, Edmond P. (Ed) (b. 1937) of Baltimore MD, engineering design manager, patent attorney. Has served as local tournament chairman. Member ACBL Appeals Committee. Diamond Life Master, won Men's Pairs 1968 and numerous regionals.

LAZARUS-LERNER, Shirlee (b. 1932) of Woodland Hills CA. Placed 2nd Master Mixed Teams 1975 and won numerous regionals.

LEARY, James Bolton (Jim) (b. 1936) of Irvine CA, attorney (estate planning). Placed 7th World Senior Pairs 1994. ACBL Grand Life Master with more than 10,500 MPs as of 3/2001. Leary won Silver Ribbon Pairs 1992. Won District 14 GNOT 1976 and 75+ other regional events.

LEARY, Patricia L. of Livermore CA. Won Women's Pairs 1974; was 2nd Women's Teams 1980. Numerous regional wins.

LEAVITT, Arnold K. (Arny) (b. 1932) of Lincolnwood IL. Won GNOT 1979, placed 2nd Open Pairs. Won numerous regionals.

LEAVITT, Carol (Toddy, formerly Mrs. J.J. Ruther) (b. 1936) of Chicago IL, bridge teacher. Placed 2nd Women's Teams 1965.

LEAVITT, Sandra (Sandi) (b. 1933) of Highland Park IL, retired editor. Member Board of Directors for CCBA in the 60's. Former associate editor and columnist of *The Kibitzer*. Won Women's Teams 1981, placed 2nd Mixed Pairs 1975, Women's Teams, Life Master Women's Pairs 1979. Diamond Life Master, won scores of regionals.

LEBEL, Michel (b.1944) of Nantes, France, born in Rumania, bridge writer. WBF World Grand Master. Won World Team Olympiad 1980, Rosenblum Teams 1982. 3rd Bermuda Bowl 1997. Won European Teams 1974, 83, 2nd 1973, 95; European Pairs 1976. Represented France in 3 other world championships and 4 other zonal championships. Won 17 national titles. Columnist of *Le Point*. Author or co-author of many books.

LeBENDIG, Alan P. (b. 1948) of Los Angeles CA, property manager, former business owner. Served as member of Board of Governors, its chairman 1984-87 (vice-chairman 1982-84), co-chairman Tournament Appeals Committee, member Goodwill Committee, 1st alternate to Board of Directors. Elected to ACBL Board of Directors 1999. Contributor to Southern CA *Bridge News* and ACBL *Bulletin*. Grand Life Master with more than 12,600 MPs as of 3/2001. Won North American Swiss Teams 1993, placed 2nd Life Master Pairs 1993. Won more than 60 regionals.

LEBENSOLD, Kenneth W. (b. 1947) of Oakland CA,

mathematics professor. Frequently credited with inventing the Lebensold Convention, but disclaims any connection to it. Won several regional events.

LEBHAR, Bertram, Jr. (1907-1972) Bert Lee was his professional name. Had a national reputation as a sportscaster and later as a bridge player and administrator. In private life he owned radio and television stations in Florida. Perhaps his greatest achievements arose from his work as ACBL treasurer (1945-47) and as a member of the Steering Committee. In the late 40's, Lebhar was instrumental in ACBL modernization. He was perhaps the first man to visualize ACBL's vast potential for expansion. His farsighted efforts were recognized when he was made ACBL Honorary Member 1963. A founder of Greater New York B.A. and its first president 1948. Donated Lebhar Trophy to ACBL. Won Spingold 1940, Master Mixed Teams 1946; placed 2nd Men's Pairs 1936, Chicago (now the Reisinger) 1943, Life Master Pairs 1945, Vanderbilt 1946, 47; Spingold 1953.

LEBI, Robert (Extra) (b. 1951) of Toronto ON, born in Paris France, systems analyst. Canadian Intercollegiate Pairs and Team champion 1972. Diamond Life Master won Blue Ribbon Pairs 1989, placed 2nd Reisinger 1982. Won Canadian National Team Championship 1999. Won more than 30 regionals.

LEBIODA, Lukasz (b.1943) of Krakow, Poland, chemist. 2nd European Teams 1970, 3rd 1973; 4th World Open Pairs 1978. Represented Poland in many World and European Championships. Won London Sunday Times Pairs 1971. Won many national titles.

LEBOVIC, Wolf (Willy) (b. 1931) of Toronto ON, born in Czechoslovakia, builder and developer. Originator of Lebovic Asking Bid convention. Npc of Canadian Women's Teams in World Olympiads in Deauville 1968 and Canadian Men's Teams in Monte Carlo 1976. Won Men's Pairs 1963, Individual 1965, Blue Ribbon Pairs 1967.

LEBOW, Howard A. (1957-2000) of Pittsburgh PA, statistician. Served as District 5 Judiciary/Conduct Committee Chairman (since 1976), Unit 142 Charity Committee Chairman and Board member. Diamond Life Master, Intercollegiate Bridge champion 1979. Won District 5 GNOT 1987 and 39 regionals.

LECKIE, Samuel (b. 1930) of Glasgow, Scotland, accountant. Represented Scotland in winning Camrose Trophy 1964, 65; the first victories by non-English teams. 26 Camrose appearances. Represented Great Britain in one European Championship. Won Gold Cup twice, Scottish Cup 3 times and Open Teams twice. Vu-graph commentator and contributor to bridge magazines.

LeDENTU, Jose (1917-1997) of Le Cannet, France, bridge writer and journalist. Won 5 French Open Team Championships. Retired from tournament play in 1957, but returned as a member of the French team in 1961 Bermuda Bowl. Author of *Bridge a La Une; 120 Donnes et Problemes du Bridge.* Co-author of *L'Aristocratie du Bridge; Le Championnat du Monde; Cent Donnes Extraordinaires; Souvenirs et Secrets; 100 Questions - 100 Reponses; Le Bridge.* Columnist of *Le Figaro; Point de Vue; La Montagne; Le Monde.* Contributor to *Le Bridgeur*, and author of many other newspaper and magazine articles. TV commentator. Honorary Member IBPA.

LEDERER, Rhoda Barrow (d. 1990) of Chalfont St. Peter, England, bridge writer and teacher. Author and co-author of many books, including the European version of this *Encyclopedia.* Editor *IBPA Bulletin* 1967-71.

LEDERER, Richard (1894-1941) club owner and writer. He was perhaps the first great figure in British bridge. Represented Great Britain in Schwab Cup 1934, won Gold Cup 3 times. His club was the training ground for many of the finest players produced by Great Britain B Maurice Harrison-Gray, Kenneth Konstam, Adam Meredith, Terence Reese. Wrote several books.

LEE, Edna S. (b. 1922) of Columbia SC, retired teacher. Became the 1st South Carolinian to have won a national event when she won Women's Teams 1966.

LEE, Linda M. (b. 1947) of Toronto ON, management consultant. Co-owner Master Point Press (bridge book publisher), was contibuting editor of *Canadian Master Point* magazine 1992-97 and of Ontario *Kibitzer* in 70's. Placed 2nd Mixed Pairs 1992 and won many regionals.

LEE, Ray (b. 1945) of Toronto ON, book publisher. Bridge columnist for *Toronto Star* 1971-78; editor *Ontario Kibitzer* 1972-75; publisher *Canadian Masterpoint* magazine since 1992; contributor to other bridge publications. Member IBPA. Placed 2nd Mixed Pairs 1992 and has won several regionals.

LEENHARDT, Francois, of Marseilles, France, banker, WBF World Master. Was 3rd Bermuda Bowl 1975, won European Teams 1974. Represented France in 2 other world championships and won several national titles.

LEHMAN, David (b. 1952) of Glenview IL, options trader. Placed 2nd Men's BAM Teams 1977, Men's Pairs 1977, Men's Swiss Teams 1987, Open BAM Teams 1991, 93, Reisinger 1988; 3rd Reisinger 1992.

LEHMAN, Barbara of Glenview IL, macrobiotic consultant and feng shui consultant. Placed 2nd Mixed Pairs 1998; two 3rd places Women's Life Master Pairs, one 3rd place Women's Swiss. Won 30+ regionals.

LEIBENDERFER, Ralph J. (1881-1969) of New York City attorney. Was one of great players of auction bridge, won Eastern Auction Open Teams 1927, 28. A regular member of the famous Knickerbocker Whist Club team which included Sidney Lenz, Winfield Liggett, George Reith and P. Hal Sims. Associated with Ely and Josephine Culbertson in the foundation of *The Bridge World* magazine, acting as its counsel. Official referee for Culbertson in the famous Culbertson-Lenz Match. Leibenderfer wrote articles for *The Bridge World, Vanity Fair, Auction Bridge Magazine*, as well as book reviews and introductions to many books.

LeMAITRE, Andre (1911-1980) of Antwerp, Belgium, business executive, bridge organizer and writer. One of the greatest contributors to the cause of world bridge. Was president European Bridge League, secretary WBF. Outstanding organizer and administrator for 3 decades, first for Germany , then Belgium, then Europe, then the world. Translated rules and established various tournament regulations for the German Bridge Federation. Newspaper columnist and contributor to various bridge periodicals. Founding member of International Bridge Press Association. IBPA Man of Year 1973. Contributing editor *Bridge Encyclopedia*. Captain Belgium team 1959-63, npc 1966, 1969-73. Won German Open Teams 1956, 58, 61, 62, 65; Mixed Pairs 1968; Open Pairs 1955, 56; Belgian Teams II 1966; Knockout Teams 1961.

LEMING, John T. (b. 1938) of Port Hueneme CA, insurance broker. Served in several executive positions including president Oxnard Unit. Won Stoddard Trophy 1990 (most MPs at Bridge Week) and 37 regionals.

LEMON, James H. (1903-1977). ACBL president 1939. Frequent golf partner of President Dwight Eisenhower.

Eisenhower honored Lemon by appointing him special ambassador for the ceremonies celebrating the independence of the Republic of Ghana. Was director of Washington Bridge League and served for many years as member of ABL and ACBL Executive Committees.

LENZ, Sidney S(imon) (1873-1960). Author and champion player of whist and all forms of bridge. Was expert in many other games and sports. Member ACBL Hall of Fame. A series of coups in the lumber business made him prosperous and by the age of 30 he was rich. He promptly retired and devoted the rest of his life to competition, writing, reading and travel. First he took up bowling — one of his records, an average of 240 for 20 consecutive games (1909) stood for nearly 20 years. In 1909 he became engrossed in whist and the next year he won the American Whist League's principal national team championship, the Minneapolis Trophy. Altogether he won more than 600 whist and bridge competitions. These ranged from club duplicate games to his 14 national championships. His Knickerbocker Whist Club auction bridge team (Lenz, Winfield Liggett, P. Hal Sims, George, Ralph J. Leibenberfer) was considered the strongest in the country. He won the last tournament he played in — the Goldman Cup Pairs at the Eastern Championships of 1932, a national event at that time. Lenz had remarkable versatility in intellectual, coordinative and athletic competitions. He played chess against Jose Capablanca and tennis against "Little Bill" Johnston with small odds. He was scratch at golf and "shot his age" at 69. At table tennis he was also of championship caliber. Professional magicians considered him the best amateur ever elected Honorary Member of the American Society of Magicians. His special skill at dealing seconds impelled him to refuse to play card games for stakes.

However, whist and bridge were his greatest loves and he thought of himself primarily as a bridge player. Lenz wrote several books on auction and contract bridge. *Lenz on Bridge* (1926) is ranked as a classic. He wrote many short stories with bridge settings. As a part owner and associate editor of the former humorous magazine *Judge*, Lenz conducted double-dummy problem contests that greatly served to publicize bridge. He contributed articles on bridge to many other magazines including the bridge magazines and occasionally wrote bridge columns for newspapers, including *The New York Times*. In 1931 Lenz joined the advisory council of Bridge Headquarters and contributed to the Official System. He represented this group in the Culbertson-Lenz Match, from which he acquired lasting fame despite his loss. In his later years, Lenz appeared frequently at major tournaments as an honorary referee.

At whist he won the American Whist League Open Pairs Championship 1910, 18, 19, 20; representing the Knickerbocker Whist Club he won the Men's Pairs 1914, 16, 30, 33; Open Teams 1929 and combination Open Teams and Pairs 193. In auction in the American Whist League Championships he won Open Teams 1924, Open Pairs 1927, 28, representing the Knickerbocker Whist Club. In contract he won the Eastern States Open Pairs 1932. The technical contributions of Sidney Lenz to contract bridge are hard to define. His effort to introduce a new call, the "challenge," to replace the takeout double, was unsuccessful. His bidding system at contract bridge, the 1-2-3, gave way to the artificial 2♣ bid with intermediate (strong) two-bids in other suits. The Lenz echo, a distribution-showing high-low from a four-card hold-

ing, remains standard among experts. Lenz disclaimed credit for this, saying it was standard among whist experts and he merely taught auction players to use it. In 1965 he was elected to the Bridge Hall of Fame.

LEON, Philip H. (b. 1927) of Grosse Pointe Shores MI, retired but still does selective interior design projects. Past president (served 2 terms) and tournament chairman of Michigan B.A. Leon served as M.B.A. and Board of Governors member for many years and was vice-chairman of the ACBL Appeals Committee for more than 20 years. Diamond Life Master, won more than 14,700 MPs as of 3/2001. He has won more than 100 regional titles.

LERENA, Raul (b. 1916) of Buenos Aires, Argentina, bank official. 3 national titles. Tournament director of Bermuda Bowl 1961, 65. Editor *Bridge Argentino* since 1966.

LERNER, Dr. Marcelo (b.1923) of Buenos Aires, Argentina, physician and surgeon. WBF World Life Master. Won South American Teams 1957. Represented Argentina in 5 world championships. Won 22 national titles. Won Gabarret Cup 1964, 65.

LERNER, S. Lazarus (Shirl). See LAZARUS-LERNER, Shirley.

LESNIEWSKI, Marcin (b. 1948) of Zakopane, Poland, mathematician and bridge professional. WBF World Life Master. Won World Open Pairs 1994, Transnational Open Teams 1997. Placed 3rd World Mixed Pairs 1994. Won Spingold 1997, 2nd 1998; placed 2nd Reisinger 1997. Won European Cup 1984, European Pairs 1989, European Mixed Pairs 1992, European Open Teams 1993. Represented Poland in many World and European Championships. Won many national titles.

LESTER, Claire (formerly Grigg) of Perth, Australia. Won PABF (Far East) Women's Teams 1977. Represented Australia in 3 world championships and one other zonal championship.

LETIZIA, Marinesa (b. 1954) of Kingston NY, critical care nursing supervisor. Won McConnell Cup 1994, Venice Cup 1997. She also placed 4th Mixed Pairs 1994. Won Pan-American Women's Pairs 1992, Mixed Teams 1990, 92; Women's KO Teams 1992. Placed 2nd Women's Swiss Teams 1995. Grand Life Master with 13,575 MPs as of 3/2001. Won scores of regionals.

LETIZIA, Ralph V., Jr. (b. 1952) of Louisville KY, system analyst. Served on Unit Conduct and Ethics Committee for more than 11 years. Won North American Swiss Teams 1991, and District 11 GNOP.

LEUFKENS, Enri (b. 1963), of De Bilt, The Netherlands, automation expert. Won Bermuda Bowl 1993; WBF World Life Master. Placed 3rd World Olympiad Teams 1992. World Junior champion 1987. European Junior champion 1986. Represented The Netherlands in 2 other world championships and 2 European Championships. National titles include Open Teams twice.

LEV, Sam (b. 1947) of Forest Hills NY. Placed 3rd Bermuda Bowl 1976, 85, 4th 1993; 7th Rosenblum Teams 1978. Won Trans-National Mixed Teams 2000. WBF World Life Master and has competed in other world championships. He has won the Reisinger 1989, 91; Open Swiss Teams, Life Master Pairs 1999. Placed 2nd Blue Ribbon Pairs 1990, Spingold 1991, Vanderbilt 1993, 2001; Life Master Pairs, Open BAM Teams 2000.

LEVENE, Doug (b. 1963) of Birmingham AL, business owner. King of Bridge 1981. At the time he made Life Master (age 16) he was the 4th youngest in the country. Won District 10 GNOP 1989 and 15 other regional events.

LEVENKO, Vassili (b. 1950) of Tallinn, Estonia, math-

ematician. Won Soviet Union Teams 1979, 82, 86, 87; Estonian Teams 1980, 84, 86, 87, 90, 92, 95; Estonian Pairs 1977, 80, 87, 88, 94. Represented both Soviet Union and Estonia in one world and 2 zonal championships.

LEVENTRITT, Peter A. (1916-1998) of NYC. Was one of the outstanding American players teachers and lecturers. 1954 ACBL president, assistant treasurer 1945-46. Past president Greater New York B.A. and of the Card School of New York, which he co-founded. He pioneered the use of the Schenken System in partnership with its inventor. Member ACBL Hall of Fame. WBF World Life Master, placed 2nd Bermuda Bowl 1955 (as npc); placed 2nd 1957, 61, 63, 65. Coach of South African Women's Team in Deuville 1968. He won the Spingold 1956, 60; Chicago (now the Reisinger) 1941, 49; Vanderbilt 1953, 64; Life Master Pairs 1944, 51; Master Mixed Teams 1949, 50, 59; Mixed Pairs 1950, Men's Teams 1966. Placed 2nd in Chicago 1943, 53; Vanderbilt 1947, 48, 55, 59, 62, 67; Men's Teams 1955, Open Pairs 1948, 51; Mixed Pairs 1949; Master Mixed Teams 1947, Master Individual 1952. Many regional successes.

LEVERONE, Anne Marie (b. 1947) of St. Paul MN, retired business manager. Placed 2nd Life Master Women's Pairs 1978. Several other regional wins.

LEVEY, Sydney A., Jr. (Syd) (1927-1999) of North Hollywood CA, CPA. ACBL president 1982, treasurer 1979, 80, chairman of the Board 1983 and District 22 representative to Board of Directors from 1975-87. Chairman ACBL Systems and Convention Committee and Finance Committee. Was a member of Western Conference Board 1962-65, Chairman of the Assembly 1965, president 1984-85; member of Board of Governors and Goodwill Committee. Executive secretary of Bridge PRO. Placed 3rd WBF Swiss Plate Pairs 1986. Grand Life Master. He placed 2nd in Swiss Teams 1983 and won numerous regional events.

LEVIN, Jillian S. (b. 1961) of Bronx NY, attorney and bridge teacher. Member of one of the outstanding bridge families. Instituted a highly publicized lawsuit in an attempt to force ACBL to allow women to play in high-level Men's Pairs events. ACBL now runs women's events opposite some open events and there are no men's events at the North American Championship level. WBF World Life Master. Won World Women's Team Olympiad 1996. Won ACBL Mixed Pairs 1994, Women's KO Teams 2000. Placed 2nd Reisinger 1989, Women's KO Teams 1998, Women's Swiss Teams 2000. (see FAMILY; BLANCHARD CASE)

LEVIN, Muriel (Mutzie) (b. 1922) of Chicago, retired office manager. Won Senior/Advanced Senior Master Pairs 1965.

LEVIN, Robert J. (b. 1957) of Aventura FL, options trader, partner in real estate company, part-time bridge professional. One of the outstanding young American players. WBF World Life Master, won Bermuda Bowl 1981, youngest player ever to win a world championship up to that time. Placed 6th World Mixed Pairs and 9th Rosenblum Teams 1990. Won the Pan American Teams 1992. Became Life Master in 1973, the youngest ever to do so at that time. King of Bridge in 1975. At age 13 played in and won his first event, a sectional Men's Pairs with his bridge teacher, the late Abe Goldstein. Grand Life Master with 23,084 MPs as of 3/2001, ranked #20 in ACBL. Won USBC 1993, Lou Herman Trophy 1979, 1978, Reisinger, Blue Ribbon Pairs 1979; Vanderbilt 1980, 89; Master Mixed Teams, Men's BAM Teams 1987; Life Master Men's

Pairs 1988, Life Master Pairs 1989, 94; Spingold 1992, Open Pairs I 1993, Life Master Open Pairs 1994, Open BAM Teams 1996, GNOT 1997, 99, 2000. Placed 2nd GNOT 1978, 92; Men's BAM Teams 1983, Vanderbilt 1984, 2000; Men's Pairs 1986, Blue Ribbon Pairs 1987, 88, 2000; Spingold 1988, 91; Open BAM Teams 1990, Open Pairs II 1999. Won hundreds of regionals.

LEVINE, Doug, won 15+ regionals including a triple at Space City Regional.

LEVINE, Michael (Mike) (b. 1938) of Boca Raton FL, retired businessman, inventor, scientist, high-tech business owner. Developed over 100 U.S. patents including programmable thermostat. Authored several books on mathematical algorithms. Placed 2nd World Senior Teams 1994. Diamond Life Master, won Senior KO Teams 1995, 98; Senior Swiss Teams 1998. Placed 2nd Senior KO Teams 1997. Has won dozens of regional events.

LEVINSON, Delle (b. 1920) of Glenview IL, retired artisan and artist. Won Senior/Advanced Senior Master Pairs 1965, Life Master Women's Pairs 1971.

LEVINSON, Michael A. (b. 1952) of Daly City CA, computer programmer. Former tournament chess player. Won Life Master Men's Pairs 1981.

LEVIT, Yeshayahu (b. 1943) of Tel Aviv, Israel, owner/manager of bridge club and bridge teacher. WBF World Master. 3rd Bermuda Bowl 1976, 2nd European Teams 1975. Represented Israel 9 other times. Won several national team titles.

LEVIT-PORAT, Ruth of Ramat Gan, Israel, psychologist. Placed 4th Generali Masters Individual 1998. 3rd European Women's Teams 1995, 97. 2nd European Women's Pairs 1993. In 1991 won European Union Women's Teams, 2nd Women's Pairs. Many national titles include Women's Pairs from 1985-98 and National Cup twice.

LEVITT, Evelyn (Mrs. Harold) (1919-1987) of Wilmington DE, bridge teacher, lecturer and director. Was past president of District 4 and Unit 190. Former member ACBL Appeals Committee. WBF World Master and competed internationally on a few occasions. Won Women's Teams 1978, 81; Women's Pairs 1983, Master Mixed Teams 1985, Women's KO Teams 1986. Placed 2nd Mixed Pairs 1969, North American Women's Swiss Teams 1985 and won numerous regional titles.

LEVITT, Jerry (b. 1918) of Clayton MO, bridge teacher and columnist. Won Vanderbilt 1962, placed 2nd GNOT 1973.

LEVITT, Paul A. (1939-1993) of Azle TX, life insurance management consultant. Won Mixed Pairs 1962 and placed 2nd Spingold 1966, Vanderbilt 1967.

LEVITZ, Jerry (b. 1943) of Ventura CA, attorney and businessman. Active in Rotary International. Past vice president Unit 547. Diamond Life Master, won more than 30 regionals.

LEVY, Alain (b. 1948) of Paris, France, born in Morocco, bridge teacher and writer. WBF World Grand Master. In 2000, ranked 10th in WBF world rankings. Won World Team Olympiad 1992, 96; Bermuda Bowl 1997. 3rd European Teams 1981, European Individual 1992. Won Common Market Teams twice. Represented France in 4 other world championships and won many national titles.

LEVY, Alvin (b. 1940) of Stony Brook NY, research aerospace scientist. Received a Special Achievement Award from NASA in 1981 and has been a visiting scholar at the University of Cambridge (England). Was president of District 24 Board of Directors, has served

as president and tournament chairman of Unit 242 and is a regular contributor to the *Islander*. Won Advanced Senior Pairs 1967 and several regionals.

LEVY, David (b. 1934) of Kingston, Jamaica, born in England, radiologist. Won CACBF National Teams 1982, 83. Represented Jamaica in 2 world championships, including Bermuda Bowl in 1983 and 6 other zonal championships. Numerous national titles. Past President of Jockey Club of Jamaica.

LEVY, Louis (b. 1921) of Los Angeles CA, retired businessman. National Open chess co-champion 1972, U.S. Senior chess champion 1984, U.S. Senior co-champion 1991-92. Diamond Life Master, won Life Master Pairs 1958 and has won numerous regionals.

LEVY, Michael (Mike) (b. 1941) of Tucson AZ, born in Kobe Japan, retired systems engineer, Lt. Col. USAF. Won 15 regional events.

LEVY, Rose of Santa Monica CA, professor. Speaks 6 languages, interpreter for French President DeGaulle when he visited U.S. Served in various administrative positions for District 23, certified bridge teacher. Placed 2nd Mixed Pairs, won 17+ regionals.

LEVY, Stephen G. (Steve) (b. 1947) of Las Vegas NV, screenwriter, professional bridge player, author, club owner and director. Directs on cruises, wrote *What the Pros Play* and a screenplay called *Tournament*. Contributor to *Password*. Has won 50 regional events.

LEWIS, Edwin R. (Ed) (b. 1931) of Falls Church VA, bridge club owner/manager, teacher and certified director since 1975; retired USAF colonel. Author of Extended Jacoby Transfer. Co-author of Cappelletti over NT and Cappelletti over One of a Major Doubled. Life Master #8 of the Japan Contract Bridge League and represented Japan in the Far East Championships 1961 (placed 3rd). Won 7 Japanese team championships 1961-1963. Represented Nebraska University in first Big 8 bridge tournament 1950. Won *Bridge World* Chance-of-a-Lifetime contest 1968. Diamond Life Master with more than 14,200 MPs as of 3/2001. Placed 2nd Silver Ribbon Pairs 1996, Senior Swiss Teams 1999. Won more than 160 regionals.

LEWIS, Ellee (b. 1934) of New York City, accountant specializing in Broadway and off Broadway Theatre, bridge professional. Placed 3rd McConnell Cup 1998. In the ACBL she placed 2nd Women's Swiss Teams 1984, Master Mixed Teams 1990. Won more than 20 regionals.

LEWIS, Harlow S., II (b. 1932) of Wynnewood PA, investment advisor. Past president of Philadelphia Whist Association (now Philadelphia Contract B.A.). A *Bridge World* panelist and occasional contributor to *Bridge World* and *Bridge Journal*. Won Life Master Men's Pairs 1967, Men's Pairs 1975, Reisinger 1970; placed 2nd Men's Teams 1967, Reisinger 1971, Spingold 1974. Won several regional titles including Intercollegiate Championship 1953.

LEWIS, Jerry M. (1895-1965) of Dallas TX, sales executive. ACBL president 1963 and chairman of Board of Directors 1962-64. Served under General John Pershing in both the Mexican War and World War I and was decorated with a Distinguished Service citation. Lewis won several regional titles.

LEWIS, John Malcolm (b. 1943) of Broadstairs, Kent UK, mathematics teacher. Served on Bermuda Unit 198 including as vice president 1975 and on organizing committee for Bermuda Bowl 1975. Represented Bermuda in world play Miami 1972, Monte Carlo 1976 and the Pan American 1975. Won the Crockfords Cup 1991 (En-

gland). Lewis designed and made the first screens used in the Bermuda Bowl at its Silver Jubilee in 1975.

LEWIS, Linda Marie (b. 1952) of Las Vegas NV, gambler. Placed 2nd Crane Top 500 with most masterpoints ever in a year by a woman, 2746, in 1983. ACBL Grand Life Master with 13,045 MPs as of 3/2001. Won Master Mixed Teams 1981, Women's KO Teams 1998, Women's Swiss Teams 2000; placed 2nd North American Women's Swiss Teams 1983, 86; Women's KO Teams 1983, Women's BAM Teams 1989, Life Master Women's Pairs 1996, Fast Open Pairs 2000. Grand Life Master with 13,045 MPs as of 3/2001. Has won more than 200 regional titles including all the events at Portland ME regional 1983.

LEWIS, Paul E. (b. 1949) of Hilton Head Island SC, retired CFO/publisher/owner. Won 18 regional events.

LEWIS, Paul J. (b. 1952) of Las Vegas NV, real estate management, former professional bridge player and attorney. Grand Life Master with more than 10,000 MPs, won Open Pairs 1980, Master Mixed Teams 1981; placed 2nd Fast Open Pairs 2000, Reisinger 1982, Men's Swiss Teams 1982, Open Pairs 1988. Has won more than 200 regional events.

LEWIS, Robert N. (b. 1937) of McLean VA, computer specialist. Placed 3rd World Mixed Teams 1974.

LIARAKOS, Spyros (b. 1963) of Athens, Greece. Won 1987 Common Market Pairs while a junior. Represented Greece many times from 1991. Many national wins include 3 Open Teams, 2 Open Pairs, 2 Master Pairs.

LICHTENSTEIN, Princess Nadine von (formerly Nadine Ansay) of Paris, France. Placed 2nd World Women's Team Olympiad 1960. Represented France in several European Championships. Many national titles. Organizer of many international bridge festivals at Deauville and Cannes.

LICHTMAN, Edward L. (Ed) (b. 1949) of Winnipeg MB, chartered accountant. Placed 2nd Amateur Swiss Teams 1976. Won Canadian National Teams Championship 1976, 86, 90, 96.

LIEN, Reidar (b. 1942) of Bergen, Norway, bank manager. Won Nordic Teams 1975, 78, 82. Represented Norway in several European Championships. Many national wins.

LIGGAT, David of Edinburgh, Scotland, government servant. Represented Scotland 9 times in Camrose Trophy matches. Many national wins include Gold Cup once and Scottish Cup 3 times.

LIGGETT, Winfield S., Jr. (1881-1937) executive officer of the U.S.S. Montana in World War I, retired from the Navy and became a bridge writer, teacher and lecturer. One of the leading pre-war American bridge personalities. Liggett partnered Sidney Lenz during the last part of the Culbertson-Lenz Match. Won numerous national championships at whist, auction and contract. Member Advisory Council on Official System, and authored *Contract Bridge Summary*, co-authored *Winning Leads at Contract Bridge*.

LIGGINS, Glyn (b. 1962) of London, England, bridge professional. WBF World Master. 4th Olympiad 2000, won Bonn Cup 2000. Represented Britain in 2 zonals and England in 10 Camrose matches.

LIGHTMAN, M(alcolm) A. (1892-1958) of Memphis TN, was associated with the motion picture business. Won Life Master Pairs 1945 and the Chicago (now the Reisinger) 1947.

LIGHTNER, Theodore A. (1893-1981) of New York City, one of great players of the world and a leading figure in bridge from the earliest days of contract. Life Master # 7, member ACBL Hall of Fame. Born in Grosse Pointe MI, later a resident of Chicago and New York City. Graduate of Yale and of Harvard Law School. He had a seat on the New York Stock Exchange. Contributor to development of Culbertson System and was the inventor of the Lightner Double of slam contracts. His writings include *High Lights of the Culbertson System, Famous Hands of the Culbertson-Lenz Match* (co-author) and he made frequent contributions to *The Bridge World*. Partnered Ely Culbertson during a part of the Culbertson-Lenz Match and was a member of the Culbertson team that won victories over British teams in 1930, 33, 34. Won Bermuda Bowl 1953. Won Spingold 1937, 39, 45; Chicago 1947, Vanderbilt 1930, Life Master Pairs 1932, 35; Open Pairs 1928. Placed 2nd Spingold 1941, Chicago 1932, 34; Vanderbilt 1937, 38, 39, 41, 45; Life Master Pairs 1931, 47 and won numerous regional titles.

LILIE, Harold J. of Las Vegas NV. WBF World Master, placed 6th Rosenblum Teams 1986. An ACBL Diamond Life Master, won Men's Teams, Men's Pairs, Mott-Smith Trophy 1982; Master Mixed Teams 1986, 95; IMP Pairs 1995. Placed 2nd Vanderbilt 1984, GNOT 1995. Won numerous regional events.

LILIE, Joyce of Las Vegas NV, retired schoolteacher, accomplished amateur pianist. WBF World Master. ACBL Diamond Life Master, won Master Mixed Teams 1986, 95; Women's BAM Teams 1986, 90; North American Women's Swiss Teams 1991. Placed 2nd North American Women's Swiss Teams 1985, 98; Women's KO Teams 1989, 91. Has dozens of regional titles.

LILLARD, Edgar of Southern Pines NC, bridge teacher, bridge club operator. Taught more than 3000 students. Played rubber bridge in Dupont Circle with some of America's top players. Won many regionals, almost always while playing with a student.

LILLEY, M. David (b. 1946) of Canberra, Australia, born in Britain, government employee. Won PABF (Far East) Pairs twice, represented Australia in 3 world championships.

LIM, Teong Wah (b. 1932) of Kauala Lumpur, Malaysia, virologist. Represented Malaysia in one world championship and 17 zonals. Malaysia's top Masterpoint winner. Many national wins.

LIN, Hsien-Chu or Harry (b. 1939) of Taiwan, bank auditor. WBF World Life Master. Was 2nd Bermuda Bowl 1970 and represented Taiwan in 2 other world championships. Far East champion 1967, 70, 76, 78.

LIN, Hung Shih or Emerson (b. 1956) of Taipei, Taiwan, textile entrepreneur. WBF World Master. Won Far East Teams 1981, Pacific Asia Teams 1997. Represented Taiwan in 5 zonal championships and 4 world championships.

LIN, Mei-Li or Phoebe (b. 1956) of Taipei, Taiwan, merchandiser. WBF World Master. Won Far East Women's Teams 1989. Represented Taiwan in 6 zonal championships and 3 world championships.

LINAH, Mike (1942-1985) of Covina CA, formerly of New York City. Became an ACBL associate national tournament director in 1975. In 1978 he was a member of the directing staff at the World Pair Olympiad in New Orleans.

LINDEN, Johan C. (b. 1943) of Helsinki, Finland, electrical engineer. Represented Finland 6 times, including one world championship and 4 European Championships. Many national wins. Road-racing motorcyclist.

LINDEN, Siv C. (b. 1932) of Helsinki, Finland, bridge organizer and tournament director. Nordic Women's Team champion 1971 and represented Finland on 13 other occasions including 4 world championships and 5 European Championships. Member EBL Ladies Committee and board member of Bridge League of Finland.

LINDINGER, Barbara (b. 1942) of Salzburg, Austria, teacher of chemistry. WBF World Life Master. Won World Women's Olympiad Teams 1992. Won Velden tournament at age 18.

LINDKVIST, Magnus (b. 1958) of Hoor, Sweden, bridge writer. WBF World Life Master. Placed 3rd in 6 world championships: Rosenblum Teams 1986, 98; World Team Olympiad 1988, Bermuda Bowl 1987, 91; World Pairs 1998. Won European Teams 1987, 3rd 1989. 3rd European Pairs 1997. Won Cavendish Invitational Pairs 1988, European Community Championships 1996, Nordic Championships 1996. Editor of *Bridgetidningen*. Author or co-author of 4 bridge books and author of many articles. Bridge teacher. Organizer of bridge travel.

LINDOP, David (b. 1946) of Toronto ON, born in England, business systems analyst. Past president Canadian Bridge Federation. Represented Canada in world championships New Orleans 1978, Salsomaggiore 1992. 2nd CNTC 1993. Edited many of the books authored by Audrey Grant, co-editor *Better Bridge*.

LINDQVIST, Jorgen (b. 1945) of Stockholm, Sweden, bridge writer. WBF World Life Master. Placed 3rd Bermuda Bowl 1977. Won European Teams 1977. Won Caransa Teams 3 times. Represented Sweden in 2 world championships and 5 other European championships. Many national wins.

LINDSAY, Ian (b. 1942) of Belfast, Northern Ireland, chartered accountant. Represented N. Ireland in 15 Camrose Trophy matches. Won All-Ireland Clubs Pairs 3 times and other major national titles at least twice each. Past president of Irish Bridge Union.

LING, Roger (b. 1951) of Hong Kong, accounting manager. WBF World Master. Won Far East Open Teams 1987. Represented Hong Kong in 4 world championships and 6 other Far East Championships.

LINHART, William James (Jim) (b. 1936) of New York City, professional bridge player, won Master Mixed Teams 1975, placed 2nd Senior KO Teams 1997. Diamond Life Master, won numerous regionals.

LINZ, Rama (b. 1940) of Beverly Hills CA, born in Israel, retired jewelry designer and real estate developer. Was the first to arrange sponsorships to promote tournament bridge in South Africa in 1971. Placed 8th World Women's Pairs 1986. Won Women's KO Teams 1985, Master Mixed Teams 1987. Placed 2nd Life Master Women's Pairs 1985, 86; Women's KO Teams 1986. Won several regionals.

LIPMAN, James O. (Jimmy) (b. 1919) of Arlington VA, retired from U.S. Library of Congress. ACBL regional tournament director for more than 20 years, member Unit 218 Board of Directors. Diamond Life Master, won several regionals.

LIPSCOMB, Shannon of Red Bank TN, professional bridge player. Former member Junior Corps, member Junior team USA II 1996-97.Won Mixed Pairs 1999, placed 2nd Life Master Women's Pairs 1998. Won dozens of regionally rated events.

LIPSITZ, Robert H. (Lipper) (b. 1942) of Palm Harbor FL, computer analyst. WBF World Life Master. ACBL Grand Life Master with 13,177 MPs as of 3/2001.

Won World Mixed Teams 1974, Rosenblum Teams 1986. Won Life Master Pairs 1976, Life Master Men's Pairs 1982, GNOT 1984, 88, 92; Senior KO Teams 1999; placed 2nd Master Mixed Teams 1973, Reisinger 1976, 77; Life Master Pairs 1977, 82; Vanderbilt 1978, GNOT 1985, Senior KO Teams 2000. Won scores of regional titles.

LIPSKER, Aaron (b. 1918) of Olympia WA, retired real estate and investment broker. Club owner since 1967, has served as president of 2 Units, alternate director for District 18 for 3 terms in the 50's.

LIPTON, Dr. William V. (1901-1977) of New York City, dentist. Introduced the magazine *Post Mortem* and was widely thought to be the original author of its famous *Cynical Observer* column. Served as ACBL Board member 1956-1959, as well as presiding over the Greater New York and the New York-New Jersey Bridge Associations. Won Vanderbilt 1953, Men's Pairs 1942 and placed 2nd Chicago 1955.

LISE, Colette (b. 1944) of Paris, France, bridge journalist. WBF World Life Master. 3rd World Women's Team Olympiad 1992. Won European Women's Teams 1983, 95, 2nd 1993. 3rd European Mixed Pairs 1998.

LITVACK, Irving of Toronto, proprietor of the Regal club, the most successful bridge club in Canada. 2nd Bermuda Bowl 1995 as npc. Won Cavendish Invitational 1985 but did not defend 1986. Because of an administrative error Cavendish had one too many pairs. When no pair belonging to Cavendish Club would withdraw, Litvack and partner Joey Silver's offer to withdraw was accepted.

LIU, Gang (b. 1951) of Beijing, China. Executive vice president and secretary general of Chinese Bridge Association. Organizer of PABF Championships in Hangzhou 1999.

LIU, Yiqian (b. 1959) of Shanghai, China, assistant professor. WBF World Master. Placed 3rd Venice Cup 1991. Won Far East Women's Teams 1993. Represented China in 3 World championships and zonal championships. Won one national title.

LIVEZEY, Joseph C. (Joey) (b. 1937) of Paoli PA, options trader, antique dealer, bridge teacher, club director. Youngest Life Master in 1968. Was 1st in North American Zone Epson Pairs 1986 and 7th in the world. In 1997 won North American Zone and was 2nd in the world. Was guest on TV show *What's My Line* in 1969 as the youngest Life Master. Diamond Life Master, has won more than 100 regionals .

LIVINGSTON, Alene F. (Mrs. Milton M.) (b. 1908) of Paducah KY, won Women's Teams 1962; 2nd Team of Four Non-Masters 1958.

LIVSHITS, Vitaly (b.1944) of Kharkov, Ukraine, computer programmer. Represented Ukraine in one world championship. Won USSR Open Teams 1990, 91; Ukrainian Open Pairs 1991.

LOBBEN, Mickey H. (formerly Rosenthal) (1933-1993) of Encino CA, psychologist. Placed 2nd Master Mixed Teams 1970 and won several regionals.

LOCKRIDGE, Charles (1905-1970) president of New York retailing company and bridge teacher. Noted for the brilliance of his dummy play. Was a member of the Bid-Rite Team. Lockridge won U.S. Bridge Association Mixed Teams and placed 2nd USBA Grand Nationals 1936. Also won Vanderbilt 1940, 49; Master Mixed Teams 1931. Placed 2nd Vanderbilt 1937, 38, 44; Spingold 1935, 38, 40; Reisinger 1941.

LODGE, Steve (b. 1958) of London, England, electronics engineer. Was 2nd European Teams 1981. Won Junior European Teams 1978. Represented Britain in 2 world championships and one other zonal championship. Represented England in Camrose Trophy many times. Several national titles include 6 Gold Cups.

LONG, Larry A. (b. 1942) of Canton OH, refinery area manager. Unit 164 Board member and former bridge columnist. Diamond Life Master, has won more than 30 regionals. Was Sectional Player of the Year 1998.

LONG, May Belle (1901-1987) of El Paso TX, former physical education teacher and tennis coach. Won Women's Pairs 1961.

LOOKS, Harry A. (b. 1952) of St. Louis MO, President-Edison Brothers Stores International. Won Senior/Advanced Senior Master Pairs 1973.

LOPUSHINSKY, Jim E. (b. 1945) of Edmonton AB, tournament director, computer programmer. Served as Unit Manager Unit 391 1977-79, 1986-88. Developer of ACBLScore. First developed the scoring program in 1981, under the name Compu-Score. Its first testing was done in 1982 at club games. Over the course of 20 years the program has evolved into the one presently used. It was purchased by ACBL in 1990 and Lopushinsky was retained for enhancements and upgrades. ACBLScore is now used in all ACBL sanctioned tournaments, other major tournaments and many bridge clubs.

LORD, Roger E., III (b. 1941) of St Louis MO, advertising executive. Placed 2nd GNOT 1973 and has won many regional events.

LORENTZ, Gabriel M. (Gaby) (b. 1937) of Sydney, Australia, born in Hungary, solicitor and company director. Represented Australia in 4 world championships and 2 zonal championships. National titles include Open Teams twice.

LORER, Matilda (b. 1954) of Sofia, Bulgaria, now a resident of Israel, microelectronic engineer. Placed 3rd Women's Olympiad Teams 1988. Won European Women's Pairs 1987, 3rd 1989.

LORVAN, Sidney (Sid) (b. 1933) of Pacifica CA, attorney, former mayor and city councilman of Pacifica. Placed 2nd Men's Pairs 1989, participant 1991 US BC Pairs Trails for USA Team #2.

LOVE, Clyde E. (b. 1960) of Ann Arbor MI, professor of mathematics. Specialist on squeeze plays. His writings include *Squeeze Play in Bridge, Bridge Squeeze Complete* and many magazine articles.

LOW, Marc E. (b. 1935) of Centerville OH, Dean, College of Science and mathematics Wright State University. With John Hamilton adapted chess pairings to create the Swiss Movement 1967. Diamond Life Master, Low won Mixed BAM Teams 1997, Senior Swiss Teams 1999; placed 2nd Mixed Pairs 1989, Silver Ribbon Pairs 2000. Won numerous regional titles.

LOW, Sandra (Sandy) (b. 1932) of Centerville OH. Diamond Life Master, Won Mixed BAM Teams 1997, Senior Swiss Teams 1999; placed 2nd Life Master Women's Pairs 1983, Mixed Pairs 1989 and has won between 70 and 80 regional events.

LOW, William S. (b. 1918) of New York City, retired attorney. Author of *Graphic Guide to Duplicate Bridge Directing.*

LOWE, Forest B. (b. 1926) of Eden Prairie MN, retired. Won Senior/Advanced Senior Master Pairs 1960, Senior Swiss Teams 1994 and several regionals.

LOWENTHAL, John (1938-2000) of New York City,

computer software developer. Was a regular panelist on *Bridge World* Master Solvers panel. Author of Borel computer program, a sophisticated hand-generator. Co-developer of the Canary Club and the Ultra Club relay systems. Also developed the computer system which reports U.S. national election returns (1970). Winner of Men's Teams 1976; placed 2nd GNOT 1981. Won numerous regionals.

LOWERY, Sylvester (1914-1985) of Longport NJ, builder and developer. Won U.S. Zone World Bridge Olympics 1940. Past president Philadelphia C.B.A., Philadelphia Whist Association, Cavendish Club of Philadelphia, the Keystone Conference and chairman of ACBL Conduct and Ethics Committee. Referee in first Bermuda Bowl 1950 and was npc of Philadelphia women's team that played against the visiting British women's team 1953. Placed 2nd Mixed Pairs 1966.

LU, Yan of Sichuan, China. WBF World Master. Placed 2nd Venice Cup 1997. Won one national title.

LU, Yulin (b. 1944) of Shanghai, China, technical employee. Placed 2nd Far East Teams 1984, 87. Represented China in 4 world championships. Won many national titles.

LUBLIN, Glenn A. (Iron Man) (b. 1951) of Silver Spring MD, professional bridge instructor. Grand Life Master with 21,374 MPs as of 3/2001, ranked #26 in ACBL. Developed Leaping Flannery, Lublin and Michaels vs Michaels Defense. Placed 2nd North American Swiss Teams 1981, Life Master Men's Pairs 1988, Open Pairs 1990. Has more than 350 regional wins.

LUCARDIE, Anthonie J.E. ("The Colonel") (1875-1954) of The Netherlands. Founder of The Netherlands Bridge Federation. At his instigation, the International Bridge League, forerunner of the World Bridge Federation, was founded.

LUCAS, Beverly of Youngstown OH. Represented U.S. in 2 world championships. High-ranked ABA player. With husband, Sam, the top-ranked married couple in ABA for 45 years. Holds record number of wins in ABA national KO Team events.

LUCAS, Michael H. (b. 1955) of Las Vegas NV, director management information service department. Won Open Pairs II 1992 and several regional events.

LUCAS, Sam of Youngstown OH. Represented U.S. in 2 world championships. High-ranked ABA player. With wife, Beverly, the top-ranked married couple in ABA for 45 years. Holds record number of wins in ABA national KO Team events.

LUCENA, Carlos (b. 1959) of Buenos Aires, Argentina, engineer. WBF World Master. Won South American Teams 1994, 95. Represented Argentina in 2 world championships. Many national wins.

LUDEWIG, Bernhard (b. 1954) of Karlsruhe, Germany, market researcher. WBF World Master. Won Rosenblum Teams 1990 and 4 national titles.

LUDWIG, R. J. (b. 1918) of Schenectady NY, modern languages teacher. Placed 2nd Senior Master Individual 1954.

LUKACS Paul (1915-1982) of Tel Aviv, Israel, actuary. 4th in World Par Contest 1961 and represented Israel in one zonal. Co-author *Spotlight on Cardplay, 2nd Book of Bridge Problems, Bridge Hands for the Connoisseur.* Contributor to many magazines.

LUKASZEWICZ, Krzysztof (b. 1964) of Olsztyn, Poland, engineer. Won European Open Pairs 1997. Won many national titles.

LUND, Peter (b. 1941) of Copenhagen, Denmark, bridge

teacher, author and journalist. Represented Denmark 1972 World Team Olympiad and 2 European Championships. Won 2 Danish Open Teams and 2 Danish Cups. Has authored several books on bridge and other card games. Has written daily column in *Ekstra Bladet* since 1974. Outstanding organizer for the Danish Bridge Federation and Copenhagen bridge district. Member of IBPA board for many years.

LUO, Shaoxing of Jiangsu, China, technical employee. 2nd Far East Teams 1993. Represented China in 2 World championships and one zonal championship. Won many national titles.

LUSK, David (b. 1946) of Adelaide, Australia, bridge teacher, administrator and journalist. His 4 national wins include Interstate Teams twice and Grand National Teams. Co-editor of *ABF Newsletter* (since 1974) and editor of online magazine *BridgeOn.* Chief editor *Daily Bulletin* 1995 PABF championships. Joint ABF Youth Coordinator since 1999.

LUSK, Sue of Adelaide, Australia, computer systems and website developer, co-editor of Australian Bridge Federation newsletter and part-owner of BridgeOn.net, the online bridge magazine. WBF World Master, represented Australia in Venice Cup 1985, 87, 89, 91, 95, 97, 2000; Women's Team Olympiad 1992, 96, 2000. Won Far East Women's 1985, 90; Zone 7 championship 1985, 87, 91, 95, 99. Won many Australian championships.

LUSKY, John A. (b. 1951) of Portland OR, partner in law firm. Climbed Mt. Kilimanjaro. Served as District 20 Appeals Committee chairman, Judiciary Committee chairman. Winner of more than 25 regionals including District 20 GNOT 1979, 84, 85, 87, 91, 92; District 20 GNOP 1980.

LYON, Thomas P. (b. 1936) of Washington DC, bridge club owner/manager 1972. Placed 2nd Open Pairs 1969 and several regionals.

LYONS, Torrence B. (Ted) (1901-1989) of Pittsburgh, bridge teacher, certified director, lecturer and writer. Served American Bridge Teachers Association in various executive positions, including president 1980-81. For many years wrote the column *Lyons Den* for *ABTA Quarterly* and was one of a few to be awarded Master Bridge Teachers Certificate by ABTA.

M

MAAS, Anton (b. 1952) of Amsterdam, the Netherlands, bank manager. WBF World Life Master. 2nd World Open Pairs 1982 after being declared winner as result of serious scoring error; 3rd World Team Olympiad 1980. Many national wins.

Mac NAB, Robin B. (1915-85) of Bozeman MT, hotel owner, cattle rancher. ACBL president 1965, member ACBL Board of Directors 1956-81, former member ACBL Laws Commission and past president of Western Conference. Also served on WBF executive council 1965-73. Interests included writing, trout fishing, model railroading. Was member of U.S. Olympic track and field squad 1936.

MACASLAN, David F. See CASLAN, David F.

MacCRACKEN, Charles M. (Charley) (b. 1941) of Memphis TN, associate national tournament director, ACBL field representative, former ACBL tournament manager, former bridge professional, active in child abuse

prevention. Began directing career 1963; had achieved R3 rating when he joined ACBL headquarters staff in 1972; manager ACBL Tournament Dept 1978-1989. Served on ACBL Laws Commission for many years. Was instrumental in developing ACBL's first computer scoring program. Editor Northern California *Forum* 1970, 71 and technical editor of *World Championship Book* 1977-83. Wrote hand analyses for continent-wide games 1974-87. He competed internationally New Orleans 1978, won ACBL Mixed Pairs 1978. Won many regional titles. Partner of Marty Cohn when Cohn perpetrated his famous psych against Howard Schenken and Peter Leventritt. Cohn preempted on his singleton heart, and there was no longer any way for Schenken and Leventritt to find their great heart fit.

MACE, Dr. Brian Richard (b. 1953) of Auckland, New Zealand, lecturer in engineering. WBF World Master. Far East champion 1995. Represented New Zealand in 2 world championships and 2 other Far East Championships. Won 6 national events. With Tom Jacob and Denis Humphries, developed Bondage bidding system. It features two-under transfer openings and many relays based on Symmetric principles.

MACHLIN, Gertrude (Trudy) (Mrs. Jerome) (b. 1918) of Silver Spring MD, bridge teacher and retired sectional director. Wife of Jerry Machlin for more than 51 years. Editor District 6 and 7 Mid-Atlantic Insert. Won Mixed Pairs 1967.

MACHLIN, Jerome S. (Jerry) (1913-1997) of Silver Spring MD, retired as an ACBL national tournament director. Began his directing career in early 40's when his famous uncle, Al Sobel, asked him to assist at tournaments. Machlin became a full-time director in 1950 and retired in 1979. Mid-Atlantic treasurer for many years. Acted as ACBL tournament coordinator for District 6 and 7 for many years. He originated the District 6 and 7 inserts, and was well known as author of the Washington BL *Bulletin* column *The Poor Man's 30 (& 60) Days* and the book *Tournament Bridge: An Uncensored Memoir.*

MACIESZCZAK, Andrzej (1940-1986) of Warsaw, Poland, bridge professional and journalist. WBF World Life Master. Won Rosenblum Teams 1978, 3rd European Open Teams 1973. Represented Poland in one other World Championship and 5 European Championships. Won many national titles. Author of many bridge books.

MACKENZIE, Greer (b. 1939) of Hillsborough, Northern Ireland, computer software engineer. Represented N. Ireland in more than 50 Camrose Trophy matches, and Ireland in World Team Olympiad, European Championship and Common Market Championship once each. Former president Irish Bridge Union, Chairman Northern Ireland Bridge Union and Irish delegate to WBF.

MACLAREN, John (b. 1926) of Edinburgh, Scotland, retired actuary. Represented Scotland in winning the Camrose Trophy 1964, 65, the first victories by non-English teams. Played in 45 Camrose matches. Several national titles. President Scottish Bridge Union 1967-68.

MacLEAN, Hugh C. (b. 1938) of Bloomington MN, bridge professional and bridge club owner. District 14 tournament coordinator. WBF International Master. ACBL Grand Life Master with 13,424 MPs as of 3/2001. Won 2nd Advanced Senior Masters Pairs 1962, Open Pairs 1974, Blue Ribbon Pairs 1975, Vanderbilt 1977. Has more than 80 regional wins including District 14 GNOT 1987, 88.

MacLEOD, Iain (1913-1970) of London, England, one of the great British players. Chancellor of Exchequer and

Prime Minister candidate at time of his death. One of the originators of ACOL System. Won Gold Cup 1937. Former bridge editor of *London Sunday Times*. Authored *Bridge Is an Easy Game*.

MADDOX, Marilyn A. (b. 1929) of Pleasant Ridge MI, bridge teacher. Diamond Life Master. Won ACBL-Wide Charity Game 1992 (with 3384 tables in play) and more than 30 regional events.

MADDOX, Myles V. (b. 1925) of Pleasant Ridge MI, retired teacher. Board member Michigan B.A. 1958-62, president 1963. Diamond Life Master; won ACBL-Wide Charity Game 1992 (with 3384 tables in play) and 25 regionals.

MADSEN, Lars Lund (b. 1972) of Copenhagen, Denmark, technologist. Won World Junior Teams 1997, 3rd 1995; 3rd World Junior Pairs 1995; 2nd European Junior Teams 1994, 3rd 1996. Won European Union Junior Teams 1996, European Universities Junior Teams 1994. Won 5 national junior titles. Successful partnership with younger brother, Morten. Co-author of one book.

MADSEN, Morten Lund (b. 1974) of Copenhagen, Denmark, mathematician. Won World Junior Teams 1997, 3rd 1995, 99. 3rd World Junior Pairs 1995; 2nd European Junior Teams 1994, 98, 3rd 1996. Won European Union Junior Teams 1996, Junior Pairs 1998. Won European Universities Junior Teams 1994. 2nd place 3 times in Nordic Junior Teams. His 17 junior medals in international competition, (mainly with his older brother Lars) is world record.

MAGERMAN, Paul (b. 1929) of Schilde, Belgium. President of European Community (later Union) Bridge League 1983-85 and from 1989 until its dissolution in 1998. Member of EBL executive 1998-to date. Chairman of WBF and EBL University Committees.

MAHFOOD, Sam (b.1940) of Kingston, Jamaica, business executive. Represented Jamaica in 4 World Championships, including 1987 Bermuda Bowl and 5 CACBF Championships. Won 2 zonal events and several national titles. Past president of Jamaica Bridge Association.

MAHMOOD, Zia (b. 1946) of New York City and London, born in Pakistan, chartered accountant and company executive. WBF World Life Master, one of the leading bridge players and personalities in the world. Represented Pakistan in 1981 Bermuda Bowl and placed 2nd. Also 2nd Rosenblum Teams 1986. ACBL Player of the Year-1991 and won Mott-Smith Trophy 1991, Reisinger 1987, 89, 96; Life Master Open Pairs 1990, 91; Spingold 1991, Open BAM Teams 1991, 96; Blue Ribbon Pairs 1998, Vanderbilt 1994, 96; Life Master Pairs 2000. Also won Omar Sharif Individual. Placed 2nd Men's Pairs 1987, Open Pairs 1991, Open Swiss Teams 1992, Vanderbilt 1988, 90, 91, 2000; Spring Life Master Pairs 1992, Spingold 1993, 95; Open Pairs I 1994, Mixed BAM Teams 1999. Author of *Bridge My Way*, an autobiography; hosted many TV shows.

MAIA, Alcio (b. 1949) of Rio de Janeiro, Brazil, psychologist. Won South American Teams 1983 and represented Brazil in 3 world championships.

MAIER, Merwyn D. (Jimmy) (1909-1942) of New York City, member of Four Aces from 1937-42. Was a leading player of pre-World War II era. Won Vanderbilt 1937, 38; Spingold 1938, 39; Master Individual 1939, Men's Pairs 1940, Life Master Pairs 1941; placed 2nd in the Chicago 1934, Vanderbilt 1935, 41; Master Individual 1936, Spingold 1936, 41.

MALCOLM, Marti L. (b. 1947) of Topeka KS, social service administrator. District 15 secretary/treasurer 1997- to date. Co-chairman 2001 Kansas City NABC and regionals for past 5 years. Won 19+ regional events; placed 5th German National Mixed Pairs.

MALCOLM, Morag of Johnstone, Scotland, retired mathematics teacher. Won Common Market Women's Pairs 1981. Won Lady Milne 3 times, and represented Scotland on 15 other occasions. National wins include Scottish and English Women's Pairs. Secretary Scottish Bridge Union for 10 years, then Honorary Life President. Represented Scotland at field hockey.

MALINOWSKI, Anna Maria (b.1961) of Oslo, Norway, chemistry and mathematics professor. WBF World Master. 4th World Women's Team Olympiad 2000, defeated champion U.S. women's team IOC 2000. 2nd Nordic Women's Team 1998. National wins include Women's Teams twice.

MALLANDER, Antha L. (b. 1917) of Houston TX, certified bridge teacher and director. Held various executive positions in ABTA, including president 1976-78 and 1984-85. Contributor to ABTA *Quarterly* and formerly to newspapers in Colorado and Texas. Author of *Goren-Standard American Point Count Bidding System Student Manual* and *Standard American Bridge for All*. Mallander has actively promoted bridge as a college credit course.

MALOWAN, Walter (1882-1966) originator of the Malowan 6♣ Convention. Was one of the leading players of the pre-World War II period. Born in Austria, Malowan moved to New York City where he was an exporter. Secretary and Honorary Member of Regency Club and secretary of Crockford's Club. Author of many articles, Malowan collaborated with Sidney Lenz on newspaper articles. Won AWL Open Teams 1933.

MAMULA, Donald Elliott (b.1954) of Mill Creek WA, marketing executive and management consultant. Chairman ACBL Board of Governors 2000-to date, vice chairman 1998-2000, member since 1994. Founding member North American Youth Bridge Foundation. Won Mini-McKenney NABC Master 1993, and 30+ regionals.

MANARA, Gabriella (b. 1958) of Catania, Italy, shop owner. WBF World Master. 2nd EEC Women's Teams 1993. Won EEC Mixed Pairs and 2 Italian titles.

MANCHESTER, Max M. (1914-1969) of Portland OR, executive secretary of Oregon Public Employees Retirement System. ACBL Chairman of the Board 1960, 61; president 1962 and named Honorary Member in 1963. Manchester won Men's Pairs 1961.

MANCUSO, Renee C. (b. 1955) of Los Angeles CA, accountant, CPA. Diamond Life Master, won Master Mixed Teams 1994, Women's KO Teams 1997. Placed 2nd Women's BAM Teams 1997.

MANDEL, Larry A. (b. 1947) of Van Nuys CA. Won 1974 Team Trials and several regional events.

MANDELL, Sidney (1907-1990) of Miami Beach FL, attorney. Won Vanderbilt 1952, 54.

MANDELOT, Agota (b. 1941) of Brazil, born in Hungary, artist. WBF World Master. Won South American Women's Teams 1975, 80, 81, 82, 86, 89, 91. Represented Brazil in 10 world championships.

MANFIELD, Edward A. (Ed) (1943-2000) of Hyattsville MD, economist, professional bridge player. World Life Master. Won Rosenblum Teams 1986, placed 2nd 1982. Grand Life Master with more than 11,000 MPs. Won GNOT 1984, 88, 92; Men's Pairs 1985, Open Pairs 1987, 89; Men's BAM Teams 1986, 89; Blue Ribbon Pairs 1990, Vanderbilt 1991; placed 2nd Spingold 1979, 81; Reisinger 1980, Open Pairs 1981, GNOT 1985, Blue Ribbon Pairs 1985, 86; Open Pairs I 1996. Won 1979

Cavendish Invitational Pairs and numerous regionals.

MANFIELD, Jo Ann M. See SPRUNG, Jo Ann M.

MANGAN, Betty of San Antonio TX, bridge club operator. Placed 2nd Life Master Women's Pairs 1970.

MANHARDT, Peter (b. 1936) of Vienna, consultant. WBF World Life Master. World Pair champion 1970. Represented Austria in one other world championship and 8 European Championships. Dominated the European grand prix circuit in the Seventies, winning the Philip Morris Bridge Cup 4 times and finishing 2nd twice. Won 11 Austrian Teams. 3 Open Pairs and 2 Mixed Pairs. Headed Austrian masterpoint rankings for nearly 20 years.

MANLEY, Brent (b. 1947) of Memphis TN, executive editor ACBL *Bridge Bulletin*, former city editor of Houston *Post* and political reporter for *Memphis Press-Scimitar*.Viet Nam veteran, long distance runner whose goal is to run a marathon in each of the 50 states. Certified director. Co-authored *At the Table* with Bob Hamman, *Precision 2000* with David Berkowitz. Worked on *Daily Bulletin* at several world championship events and many North American championships. Contributing editor to *Encyclopedia of Bridge.*

MANNING-FOSTER, Alfred Edye (1874-1939) of London, one of the leading pre-war bridge players. Founder of *Bridge Magazine* and its editor until 1939. Foreign contributing editor of *The Bridge World* and bridge correspondent of London *Times* for many years. Founded and was 1st president of British Bridge League 1933. Two years later he was named ACBL Honorary Member. Writings include *Auction Bridge for All, Contract Bridge for all,* and *Baby Contract Book.*

MANNING, John R. (1925-1998), noted English authority on movements. Author of a paper entitled *Mathematics of Duplicate Bridge Movements*, which was first printed in *Bulletin of Institute of Mathematics and its Applications* in 1979 and author of *EBU Manual of Duplicate Bridge Movements*, 1991, which replaced the earlier standard work by Frank Farrington.

MANOPPO, F. Eddy (b. 1945) of Manado, Indonesia. WBF World Life Master. Won International Olympic Committee Teams 2000. Won PABF (Far East) Teams 1972, 73, 74, 79, 82, 83, 84, 92, 93, 99.

MANRIQUE, Hector (b. 1936) of Caracas, Venezuela, born in Ecuador, civil engineer. Won CAC Teams 1977, 87, 91. Represented Venezuela in 3 world championships. Won many national titles.

MANSELL, Petra (b. 1923) of Durban, South Africa, bridge teacher. WBF World Life Master. 2nd World Women's Teams 1968, 72. Represented South Africa in World Team Olympiad 1964, World Women's Team Olympiad, 1960, 76, 92; Venice Cup 1993, 95, 97. 17 national wins.

MARCUS, Edward N. (1895-1952) for whom the Marcus Cup is named. Clothing manufacturer from Boston. ACBL Board member and president of New England BA. Won the Chicago (now Resinger) 1949.

MARCUS, Melvin L. (b. 1938) of Framingham MA, self-employed bridge teacher. Local and district board member, GNOT coordinator, Conduct and Ethics Committee member. Diamond Life Master with 30+ regional wins.

MAREK, John of Wrexham, Wales, member of Parliament and of Welsh Assembly. Represented Wales in 2 Camrose Trophy matches, defeating England. Represented Wrexham in Parliament since 1983, and member of Parliament bridge team.

MARI, Christian (b. 1945) of Paris France, bridge professional. WBF World Grand Master . In 2000, stood 19th in WBF world rankings. Won World Olympiad Teams 1980, 96; 3rd Bermuda Bowl 1997; 3rd Rosenblum Teams 1978, Bermuda Bowl 1975. Won European Teams 1974, 2nd 1973, 89, 95; 3rd 1981. Won Common Market Teams 1973. Placed 2nd Generali Individual 1994. Represented France in 3 other world championships and 3 other zonal championships.

MARIANI, Carlo (b. 1947) of Florence, Italy, WBF World Master. Won World Transnational Teams 1997, EEC Mixed Pairs 1998, and 7 Italian titles.

MARIANO-TAN, Gemma of Makati, Philippines. Won Asian Mixed Teams 1995, 97. Frequent member of Philippines women's teams. Top woman in Philippines masterpoint rankings.

MARISCAL, Laura (Mrs. Elias Konstantinovsky) (b. 1939) of Mexico DF, bridge club owner and teacher. Won Master Mixed Teams and several regionals.

MARK, Dr. Louis (1893-1954) in whose honor the Mark Memorial Trophy was donated. Was an international authority on chest ailments. 1949 ACBL president, Honorary Member in 1950.

MARK, Louise Fu-Ming (Lulu) (b. 1934) of North York ON, born in Shanghai China, senior systems analyst. Represented Canada in World Women's Teams 1964, 68, won Women's Pairs 1965.

MARKS, Paul N. (1908-1968) of Maywood IL, accountant and teacher of mathematics and bridge, ACBL national tournament director from 1957. He devised Appendix Movements for 7-, 11- and 13-table Rainbow Individual Movements.

MARKUS, Rika (Rixi) (1910-92) of London, England, born in Romania. One of the greatest women players of all time, and the first to become a WBF Grand Master. Top woman in WBF rankings from the beginning (1974) until 1980. Won 14 international titles, more than any other woman: World Women's Teams 1937, 64; World Mixed Teams 1962, World Women's Pairs 1962, 74; European Women's Teams 1935, 36, 51, 52, 59, 61, 63, 66, 75. Pre-war wins were representing Austria, from which she fled to England in 1938. Other wins, mainly with Fritzi Gordon, were for Britain, including 2nd World Mixed Pairs 1970 and World Women's Pairs 1974. Many national titles. Named IBPA Personality of the Year 1974. She was awarded MBE for contributions to bridge by Queen Elizabeth 1975. Organizer of annual matches between House of Commons and House of Lords. Bridge editor of the *Guardian* 1955-92 and columnist of *Evening Standard* 1975-80. Contributor to many magazines and author of 7 books. (see BUENOS AIRES AFFAIR.)

MARSH, Edward I. (Bud) (b. 1927) of Scottsdale AZ, retired businessman. Playing captain of Montreal's championship inter-city bridge team 1967, 68. Member Montreal B.L. board of directors 1950's and 60's. Placed 4th World Senior Teams 1994. Won Amateur Swiss Teams 1977. Won 40+ regional titles.

MARSTON, Paul Hamilton (b. 1949) of Sydney, Australia, born in New Zealand, bridge professional. WBF World Master. Placed 3rd World Pairs 1986, Bermuda Bowl 1989. Won South Pacific playoff 1991. In world and zonal championships, represented New Zealand 8 times 1973-81and Australia 10 times 1983-99. 21 Australia national wins include Open Teams 5 times. Former publisher of *Australian Bridge.* Author of 5 books. One of the world's authorities on Strong Pass and Relay methods. (see Moscito.)

MARTEL, Charles U. (Chip) (b. 1953) of Davis CA, professor of computer science. WBF Grand Master, ranks 12th in world. Chairman of WBF System Rating Committee 1990. Was youngest player to win World Open Pairs - 1982, at age 29. Originally he and Lew Stansby were announced as finishing 2nd but a mammoth set of corrections moved them clearly into 1st place, unseating Max Rebattu and Anton Maas of The Netherlands. Won Bermuda Bowl 1985, 87; placed 2nd Rosenblum Teams 1982, Bermuda Bowl 1989; 4th World Par Contest, 9th World Open Pairs and Rosenblum Teams 1990. In other international competitions he was 2nd in EOE Optebeurs Netherlands 1990, 3rd London Sunday Times Invitational 1991. Won Rosenkranz Best Bid Hand award 1979, 97; Bols Tip competition 1991. Martel was captain and coach of winning World Junior Teams 1991 and captain of bronze medal team 1993. Won USBC 1985, 87, 89; 2nd 1988. Grand Life Master with 13,487 MPs as of 3/2001, won Lou Herman Trophy 1981, Reisinger 1981, 85, 86, 96; GNOT 1982, 83, 85, 87, 93, 96; Vanderbilt 1984, 87, 94, 96; GNOP 1988, Spingold 1990, 2000; Open Swiss Teams 1994, Open BAM Teams 1995. Placed 2nd GNOP 1981, Blue Ribbon Pairs 1981, Vanderbilt 1992, Spingold 1992, 93, 95; Open Swiss Teams and GNOT 2000. His numerous regional wins include District 21 GNOT 1981, 82, 83, 84, 85, 86, 87, 90, 2000. Contributing editor *Bridge Today.*

MARTEL, Jan F. (b. 1943) of Davis CA, retired attorney. Active in Forum for Women in Bridge 1985-1990. Won Women's Pairs 1974, Women's Swiss Teams 1986, Women's BAM Teams 1987, GNOP 1988, Women's KO Teams 1994; placed 2nd Women's KO Teams 1979, 85, 87; Women's Pairs 1988, Women's Swiss Teams 1996. Contributing editor *Bridge Today.* Npc U.S.A. II in World Junior Championships 1993.

MARTENS, Krzysztof (b.1952) of Rzeszew, Poland, engineer, bridge professional. WBF Grandmaster. Won World Team Olympiad 1984, Transnational Open Teams 1997, 2nd Bermuda Bowl 1991, 3rd Bermuda Bowl 1989. Won European Open Teams 1981, 1989, 1993; 3rd 1991. Won European Open Pairs 1989. Won many national titles. Bridge journalist, bridge teacher, coaching representative for teams of many countries from Europe, Africa and Asia. Author of a bridge book.

MARTENSSON, Eva (b. 1924) of Stockholm, Sweden. WBF World Life Master. Won World Women's Teams 1968, Nordic Women's Teams 1957, 66, 68. Many national wins.

MARTIN, Christiane (b. 1914 - deceased) of Paris, France. Won European Women's Teams 1939, 54, 56. Represented France on 7 other occasions. Several national wins.

MARTIN, Phillip (b. 1953) of Bronxville NY, stock options trader. Placed 2nd GNOT 1981. Numerous regional wins include District 24 GNOT 1981, 83.

MARTINO, Michael J. (Mike) (b. 1936) of Hamilton ON, lawyer, executive, won Men's Pairs 1969.

MARX, John C. H. (Jack) (1907-1991) of England, bridge journalist. One of the original Acol quartet (with M. Harrison Gray, S. J. Simon, I. McLeod). Known as the headmaster, he codified the system. Won European Teams 1950, prevented by ill health from playing in 1st Bermuda Bowl. National titles included Gold Cup 1937, 47, 71. Served BBL and EBU in various capacities. Regular contributor to *Contract Bridge Journal, British Bridge World* and *Illustrated News.* Developed Stayman 2♣ response to 1NT independently of George Rapee and Sam Stayman, but his identical version was not published until after World War II. Devised Byzantine Blackwood.

MASOOD, Salim (b. 1940) of Karachi, Pakistan, businessman. Placed 2nd Bermuda Bowl 1981, winner BFAAME Open Teams 1981, 83, 85, 87. Frequent partner of Zia Mahmood.

MASOOD, Tahir (b. 1956) of Karachi, Pakistan, hotel executive. Won BFAAME Open Teams 1981, BFAAME Open Pairs 1985. Represented Pakistan 1991 Bermuda Bowl.

MASTERSON, Marcia W. of Pasadena CA, financial consultant. Diamond Life Master, won Amateur Swiss Teams 1977, Women's BAM Teams 1990. Won approximately 35 regionals.

MATHE, Eugenie M. (Genie, Mrs. Lewis) (1925-1991) of Canoga Park CA, U.S. Census Bureau survey clerk. Chairman ALACBU Publishing Committee from 1979. Edited *Southern California Bridge News* 1979-82 and authored popular monthly column *The LOL* from 1966. She was involved in writing and performing in many shows for bridge tournaments. Won European Open Teams at Lake Balaton, Hungary 1975, ACBL Master Mixed Teams 1970 (2nd 1975), Mixed Pairs 1971.

MATHE, Lewis L. (Lew) (1915-86) of Canoga Park CA, real estate appraiser and broker. Member ACBL Hall of Fame, WBF Grand Master. One of the great bridge players and personalities of the world, noted for adaptability and table presence. Leading exponent of direct method of bidding favored on West Coast. Originator of Mathe Asking Bid. ACBL president 1975, chairman of Board 1976, chairman Board of Governors 1968, WBF representative from ABCL and WBF treasurer 1977-82. Three-time president Western Conference, ACBL Board member from District 23 1958-61 and 1970-1982. Played major role in Bermuda Incident and Houston Affair. Bermuda Bowl champion 1954, also represented North America in Bermuda Bowl 1955, 62, 66, 71; the U.S. in World Team Olympiad 1960. Won International Playoff Match 1970, Herman Trophy 1957, Mott-Smith Trophy 1959, 64, 67; Spingold 1954, Vanderbilt 1964, 66, 67; Chicago 1959, 60, 62; Reisinger 1971, Blue Ribbon Pairs 1964, Men's Teams 1957, 62; Open Pairs 1957, 59; Mixed Pairs 1971, Men's Teams 1970, Life Master Pairs 1963, 67; Master Mixed Teams 1970. Placed 2nd Team Trials 1965, Spingold 1953, 71, 74; Reisinger 1966, Blue Ribbon Pairs 1967, Master Mixed Teams 1953, Men's Pairs 1961, Mixed Pairs 1959, Open Pairs 1964, 67, Men's Teams 1972, Life Master Men's Pairs 1982. Won 1975 European Open Teams at Lake Balaton Hungary.

MATHESON, John (b. 1945) of Glasgow, Scotland, physician. WBF World Master. Represented Scotland 38 times in Camrose Trophy. Won Gold Cup once, Scottish Cup 8 times. Bridge writer.

MATHEWS, Art (b. 1948) of Atlanta GA, HedgeFund manager, real estate broker. Won District GNOP and GNOT 5 times and 20-25 regionals.

MATHIS, James L. (b. 1927) of Williamsville NY, retired bank executive. Served on local board 1987-90 and on Board of Governors 1987-90, president of Unit in early 50's. Represented U.S. in Stockholm 1970. Won Open Pairs 1969. Placed 2nd Life Master Pairs 1970. Grand Life Master with more than xx MPs as of 3/2001, 100+ regional wins.

MATTHEWS, Ben G., Judge (b. 1926) of Shelbyville KY, attorney, former city judge and bank president. Had a 300 in bowling 1963. Matthews scored a clean sweep

of a sectional tournament in 1984 (4 events). Won 15-20 regionals.

MATTHEWS, Grace R. of Las Vegas NV, Western art dealer, runs Las Vegas Western Art Auction. President Unit 373, Co-chairman of NABC 1991, largest in ACBL history with 24,221 tables. Chaired Las Vegas regionals 1988, 90, 92. Has had 20+ regional wins.

MATTHEWS, Jackie A. (b. 1936) of Sacramento CA, S4 tournament director. Matthews has been in charge of all caddies at NABC's for many years. She won several regional events.

MATTHEWS, Lillian Munroe of Marbella, Spain, formerly of Toronto and Boston, journalist. Represented Spain in many world and zonal Women's Pairs and Mixed Pairs. Bridge columnist *Marbella Times* and hotel magazines. Organizer of Marbella Bridge Festival since 1980. Spanish delegate to EBL and WBF 1974-82,

MATZ, Norma (b. 1916) of Miami Beach FL, investment counselor. Won Women's Teams 1952, 54 and many regional titles.

MATZIARIS, Thanassis (b. 1969) of Athens, Greece. Represented Greece many times in Junior events and in 2000 World Bridge Olympiad. Many national wins including Open Pairs and Open Teams. Tournament director, top bridge teacher and journalist. Editor of Greece's official bridge magazine. Worked for WBF Internet site from 1996-2000 and produced Internet presentation in numerous World and European Championships.

MAUGHAM, William Somerset (1874-1965), famous novelist and short story writer, once called bridge "the most intelligent and entertaining card game the wit of man so far has devised." He often used card playing in his settings. He wrote the first play in theater history to feature bridge. A game began his successful comedy *Smith* which opened in 1909. It was later made into a film. In his slightly fictionalized memoirs, *Ashenden*, he records playing contract bridge "with which I was not very familiar" during World War I. The book was not published until 1928 and must have been written at least a year earlier. At that time he would certainly not have heard of Vanderbilt's new version, and it is most improbable that he was committing an anachronism. He was in Switzerland, and it is possible that he was playing "plafond", and used "contract" as a translation into English. In *Three Fat Women of Antibes*, three middle-aged women are looking for a congenial fourth. He wrote the introduction to Charles Goren's *The Standard Book of Bidding*. His verdict on bridge is memorable. "If I had my way, I would have children taught bridge as a matter of course, just as they are taught dancing. In the end it will be more useful to them . . . You can play bridge as long as you can sit at a table and tell one card from another. In fact, when all else fails – sport, love, ambition – bridge remains a solace and an entertainment." His observations on the requirements for playing bridge: "The essentials for playing a good game of bridge are to be truthful, clear-headed, and considerate, prudent but not averse to taking a risk, and not to cry over spilt milk. And incidentally those are perhaps also the essentials for playing the more important game of life."

MAVROMICHALIS, Brigitte (b. 1926) of Switzerland, formerly of Bridgetown, Barbados. Served as president Caribbean-Central America Zone 1987-89, 1991-95. President Barbados Bridge League 1986-88. Won China Cup 1999, competitor in many invitational events.

MAY, Walter R. (b. 1930) of Sarasota FL, bridge teacher,

professional player. Diamond Life Master. Central NYBA Player of Year 4 times, Team Player of Year 5 times. Won GNOT 1975, 78, Zone III 1975; GNOP 1982 and 36 other regional events.

MAYADAS, Lina (b. 1935) of Bombay, India, plastics manufacturer and former journalist. WBF World Master. Won Far East Women's Teams 1978, BFAAME Women's Teams 1983, 85. 2nd BFAAME Open Pairs 1983. Represented India in 4 world championships and 2 other zonal championships.

MAYER, Edward (1901-1980) OF London, England, attorney. Represented Great Britain in Schwab Cup match 1933. Won unofficial matches against American team 1954, 56. Won Gold Cup 1932, English Open Teams 1948. Counsel Member of British Bridge League. Author of *Money Bridge*. Bridge correspondent *London Times* for more than 20 years.

MAYER, Malcolm (b. 1953) of Christ Church, New Zealand. Won World Continuous Pairs 1990. Represented New Zealand in 5 other world championships and 6 zonal championships. 7 national wins include Open Teams once.

MAZZA, Dino (b. 1927) of Vigevano, Italy, journalist. General secretary Italian Bridge Federation 1971-89. Bridge columnist *La Republica,* contributor to *Bridge d'Italia.*

McADAM, John R. (b. 1928) of Ottawa ON, with Department of Industry, Trade and Commerce. Served as president of Unit 192 and is current vice president of District 1. Diamond Life Master with more than 15 regional wins.

McALEAR, Allen L. (Al) (b. 1928) of Bozeman MT, attorney. He has been president of his District, member of Western Conference Board and ACBL Board of Governors. Won District 18 GNOP 1988 and 25+ regionals.

McAVOY, Constance C. (b. 1950) of Victoria BC, teacher, lectures on technology for blind or learning disabled and wrote *Blueprints for Writing* (a special needs technology book). Placed 2nd Canadian Women's Team Championship 1998 and won 17 regionals.

McAVOY, James M. (b. 1950) of Victoria BC, partner in accounting firm. Represented Canada in WBF events Bal Harbour 1986 and in Tri-Country playoff 1993; has been Zone VI CBF representative to CNTC 13 times, won in 1992. Has many regional wins.

McCALLON, Dr. William R. (Bill) (b. 1929) of St. Augustine FL, retired epidemiologist. Made two Atlantic crossings in his sailboat. Diamond Life Master, has won 38 regionals.

McCALLUM, Karen T. (Kate) (b. 1946) of Exeter NH, editor/publisher and bridge professional. Edited *Law of Total Tricks* (Larry Cohen), *Bridge, Zia and Me* (Michael Rosenberg) and others. Contributor or panelist for *Bridge Today, Bridge World, Brig Dunyasi* (Turkish), *Australian Bridge Magazine, Bridge Forum International* and others. WBF Grand Master, ranks #16 among women in world; won Venice Cup 1989, 93, 2nd 1995; won World Women's Pairs 1990; placed 5th Rosenblum Teams 1990. ACBL Diamond Life Master. Won North American Women's Swiss Teams 1989, 90, 93, 98, 99, 2001; Women's Team Trials 1995; Master Mixed Teams, Women's BAM Teams 1999. Was 2nd North American Women's Swiss Teams 1984, 94, 99; Women's KO Teams 1987. McCallum has won many regional events.

McCAMPBELL, Bryan (d. ca 1930) of St Louis MO, claimed invention of Takeout Double as well as 4-3-2-1 Point-Count. There is no reason to doubt that he arrived at

both ideas independently, though perhaps not first. Was one of the most successful players of auction bridge and author of perhaps the first book, *Auction Tactics*, to describe the strategy of the successful rubber-bridge player.

McCAMPBELL, Leavell (1880-1946) of New York City, was chairman of the Whist Club committee that produced the first generally accepted *Laws of Contract Bridge*. He assisted in many later revisions of the Laws.

McCANCE, Ian (b. 1927) of Melbourne, Australia. Editor for Australian Physiological and Pharmacological Society. Represented Australia in one world championship. National titles include Open Teams 4 times, Open Pairs once, Individual once. Devised Specific Trump Cu-bids.

McCONNELL, Ruth (Mrs. Lee W.) (1918-2000) of Columbia City IN. ACBL's first woman president 1974 and first woman Chairman of ACBL Board of Directors 1975. ACBL President Emeritus. Inaugurated Venice Cup matches 1974. After 5-year battle, convinced WBF that the Venice Cup should be a major WBF event -1978. Victorious captain of the first American Venice Cup team - 1974. Also Venice Cup captain in 1976 and 1978 American victories. Captained 1980 Women's Olympiad Teams champions, also 1976 Women's Olympiad captain. Donated McConnell Cup to go to winner of McConnell Cup World Women's Championship (women's equivalent to Rosenblum Teams) when event was added to WBF program 1994. First woman president of the ACBL Charity Foundation 1975, Trustee Emeritus of foundation. First woman elected to WBF Executive Council 1984. First woman to hold WBF office — treasurer 1985-90. Established first District Judiciary Committee — now all ACBL Districts must have such a committee. Founded *Midwest Monitor* and was its first editor 1963-67. Also founded District 8's *Advocate*. Won Spring Continent-wide Charity Pairs 1967. Won many regional championships

McCRACKIN, Nancy P. (Mrs. M. R. McCrackin) (b. 1922) of Albuquerque NM, was once on cover of Life magazine - 1938. Won a few regional events.

McCRARY, Marilyn of Des Moines IA. Won Master Mixed Teams 1971.

McDANIEL, Garner N. of Naples FL, realtor. Diamond Life Master, won Women's Teams 1963, 64; Women's Pairs 1967; placed 2nd Women's Teams 1962, Women's Pairs 1963, 66; Master Mixed Teams 1963. Won many regionals.

McDERMOTT, John D. (b. 1947) of West Roxbury MA, attorney specializing in real estate. First recipient Larry Weiss Trophy (given for "skill and grace at the bridge table"). Authored Eastern Massachusetts B.A. By-Laws in 80's. Won approximately 30 regionals.

McDEVITT, Patrick J. of Brookline MA, company president. Has contributed to *Irish Bridge Journal*. Diamond Life Master. Won N.E. College Championship at University of Massachusetts 1964. Won Senior KO Teams 2000, Money Tournament at 1996 NABC and approximately 20 regional events including GNOP.

McDONALD, June (b. 1920) of Rosebud TX, former bridge club owner and teacher, full time club director 1975-89. Won more than 15 regional events.

McDONALD, Sheryl A. (b. 1933) of Las Vegas NV, former English teacher. Unit Conduct and Ethics chairman. Won 15 regionals.

McDONOUGH, James B. of Billings MT, attorney and former company president. Won North American Swiss Teams 1986.

McGARRY, Dennis J. (b. 1947) of Lauderhill FL, small business owner, part-time bridge professional. Named to ACBL Appeals Committee 1974. Diamond Life Master, placed 2nd Senior/Advanced Senior Masters Pairs 1970, Life Master Men's Pairs 1979, Master Mixed Teams 1980. His 75+ regional wins include District 5 GNOP 1980, 82; District 18 1986.

McGARRY, Linda (b. 1947) of Lauderhill FL, bridge instructor. Won more than 20 regionals including District 18 GNOP 1986, District 9 GNOP 1996.

McGEE, David (b. 1939) of Mason City IA. ACBL president 1991, chairman of Board 1992. Served on Unit board since 1964, past president, for many years ran Grand National events in District 14. He was 2nd alternate to ACBL Board of Directors for 6 years and 1st alternate for 9 years before moving up to the ACBL Board. Edited Iowa State *Bridge Bulletin* for about 6 years. Diamond Life Master, won 30+ regionals.

McGINLEY, Constance S. (Connie) See GOLDBERG, Constance (Connie).

McGINNIN, Coleman (Coley) (b. 1943) of Nashville TN, professor of political science. Served as president of Unit 179 1986-99, District 10 1992-99 and Mid-South B.A. 1985-86. ACBL accredited teacher, certified teacher trainer. Has taught on 25+ cruises. Diamond Life Master, won about 75 regionals.

McGOWAN, Elizabeth (b. 1945) of Edinburgh, Scotland, teacher of Russian and bridge writer. WBF World Grand Master. Won Transnational World Mixed Teams 1996, European Women's Teams 1997, 99. 2nd Women's Team Olympiad 1988, 92. Represented Britain in 7 other world championships, 3 other European championships and 3 Common Market championships. Many national wins. Daily columnist of *The Scotsman*. Won IBPA Hand of the Year 1992.

MacGREGOR, John Atlee (b. 1949) of Georgetown, Guyana, born in Canada, computer specialist, tournament director and bridge teacher. Chief tournament director of CACBF from 1993. Represented Canada in one world championship and Costa Rica in 2 zonal championships.

McGROVER, Raymond J. (1905-1974) of New York City, attorney, ACBL president 1947. Played a major role in 1948 reorganization of ACBL, later assisted in formation of 1963 Laws. President of Long Island B.L. for 7 years.

McHANN, Annette (b. 1937) of Gulf Breeze FL, owner McHann Railroad Services, Inc. Won continent-wide Royal Viking Instant Matchpoint Pairs (E/W) 1993 and more than 40 regionals including District 10 GNOP.

McINTYRE, Glenn (b. 1955) of Bedford MA, computer consultant. Has documented some innovative bidding ideas including "Advanced Lebensohl". Has 21 regional wins including District 25 GNOP 1993.

McKEAN, Joan De Witt of Grosse Pointe MI, stockbroker and bridge teacher. President ABCL Charity Foundation 1987, 88, 91, 92, 93, 94. Won Master Mixed Teams 1977, 78, 79, 82.

McKENNEY, William E. (1891-1950). McKenney Trophy (now Crane Top 500) perpetuated his memory. Gained fame as a bridge columnist, philanthropist and administrator. Contributed daily bridge columns to Scripps-Howard newspapers from 1929-1950. So widely read was his work that in Europe the Suit-Preference Signal became known as the "McKenney Convention" instead of being attributed to its inventor, Hy Lavinthal. His dedication to bridge and its organizations extended well beyond the written word. In 1927 he helped found American Auction Bridge League. He became chairman of its committee on laws and then

executive secretary in 1928. He continued as secretary of both the ABL and ACBL until 1948. McKenney founded National Laws Commission in 1932 and chaired it 1935-48. Several times McKenney contributed his privately earned income to the ABL and ACBL. For example, in 1929 he founded Bridge Supplies, Inc., which sold trophies, scoring supplies and other merchandise. In 1936 he donated this corporation to the ABL. He devoted nearly all his time to the interests of the successive bridge leagues. To a degree McKenney acquired a spirit of proprietary control that became increasingly inconsistent with ACBL interests as ACBL became larger and more financially stable. McKenney was deposed in favor of democratic control of the ACBL in 1948. He founded both the ABL and the ACBL charity programs. Through these channels he led the League to endow the Children's Cancer Ward at Memorial Hospital in New York City and to establish War Orphans Scholarships. He won ABL National Open Pairs 1929.

McMAHON, Mary of Sydney, Australia, investor. Won PABF (Far East) Open Teams 1970, Women's Teams 1973, 1974. Represented Australia in 3 world championships. 11 national wins.

McNEIL, Keith A. (1929-1993) of Adelaide Australia, pharmacist. Received Medal of the Order of Australia for services to bridge. President of Australian Bridge Federation 1986-90, President Emeritus 1990-93. McNeil held almost every committee position in the South Australian B.F. and became a Life Member 1984. Authored *Match Your Bidding Against the Masters*, a compilation of his articles as the sadistic moderator of *Bidding Forum* in *Australian Bridge*.

McPHERRAN, Robert A. (1915-1986) of New York City. Won Spingold 1939, Vanderbilt 1940, 41; Master Mixed Teams 1936, Master Individual 1946; placed 2nd Vanderbilt 1939, Mixed Pairs 1940.

MECKSTROTH, Jeffrey J. (Jeff) (b. 1956) of Reynoldsburg OH, professional bridge player, one of the leading players of the world. WBF World Grand Master, ranks #8 in the world. ACBL Grand Life Master with 39,671 MPs as of 3/2001, ranks #4 in ACBL behind Paul Soloway, Mike Passell and Mark Lair. Rose rapidly from King of Bridge in 1974 to Bermuda Bowl champion in 1981. Also won Bermuda Bowl 1995, 99, placed 2nd 1997. Has represented ACBL in many world championships. He won World Open Pairs 1986, World Team Olympiad 1988. One of a small group of players who have scored victories in the 3 most important world events – Bermuda Bowl, Olympiad, Open Pairs. Placed 2nd World Team Olympiad 1992, 6th World Open Pairs 1982, 4th Bermuda Bowl 1983 and 5th 1991; 5th Rosenblum Teams 1986. ACBL Player of the Year 1992, won USBC (Team Trials) 1991, placed 2nd 1985. Won Mott-Smith Trophy 1979, 80, 85; Lou Herman Trophy 1980, 82. His most regular partner is Eric Rodwell. As a pair they are known as Meckwell. Meckstroth's many national titles include the Reisinger 1979, 85, 93, 94, 95; Life Master Men's Pairs 1979, Open Pairs 1979, Open Pairs I 1992; Mixed Pairs 1980, Vanderbilt 1980, 82, 85, 2000; Blue Ribbon Pairs 1982, Spingold 1984, 88, 91, 93, 94, 95, 96, 98, 99; Men's BAM Teams 1984, Men's Teams 1989, GNOT 1990, 97, 99, 2000; Open Swiss Teams 1994, Open Pairs II 1999. Placed 2nd Vanderbilt 1979, 91, 96; Reisinger 1980, 98, 99; Life Master Pairs 1983, Master Mixed Teams 1983, 92; Spingold 1985, 90; Life Master Men's Pairs 1985, Life Master Open Pairs 1992, GNOT 1994. Won IBPA award for best bid hand 1998, 99.

MEFFLEY, Richard (b. 1950) of Fresno CA, corpo-

rate tax technician. President Fresno Unit 522, editor *Aces, Places and Faces*, member ACBL Board of Governors. Diamond Life Master, won Open Pairs I 2001, 20+ regionals.

MEINL, Wolfgang (b.1947-1997) of Vienna, Austria, merchant. WBF World Life Master. Was 2nd Bermuda Bowl 1985, World Pairs 1986, World Team Olympiad 1988. Won European Teams 1985, European Pairs 1981, European Team Cup 1988, European Junior Teams 1976. Austrian wins include 13 Open Teams and 5 Open Pairs. He has won the Caransa and Hoechst tournaments in The Netherlands.

MELLO, Roberto Figueira de (b. 1950) of Rio de Janeiro, Brazil, engineer. WBF Grand Master. Won Bermuda Bowl 1989, 2nd 2000. Won South American Teams 1968, 78, 83, 87, 89, 91, 93. Represented Brazil in 7 world championships. National wins include 3 open teams.

MELLO, Sylvia Figueira (b. 1958) of Rio de Janeiro, Brazil, economist. Won South American Women's Teams 1968, 80, 81. Represented Brazil in 5 world championships, won 2 national titles.

MELMAN, Fredric L. (Fred) (b. 1935) of Agoura CA, bridge teacher and director. Won Amateur Men's Pairs 1976, Summer NAC secondary Commercial and Industrial Teams 1974, 75, 76.

MELSON, Ellen (nee Ostertag, formerly Pidhajecky, Gryka, Siebert) of Chicago IL, former teacher, college professor and school principal; accredited bridge teacher and certified director. Involved in local/regional theater. Served on ACBL Appeals Committee and Board of Directors Palm Springs Unit. Placed 2nd Life Master Women's Pairs 1999. Won more than 35 regionals.

MELSON, Richard T. (Dick) (b. 1946) of Chicago IL, stock options trader. Diamond Life Master, placed 2nd Men's Pairs 1977, Men's Teams 1978; Reisinger 1988, Men's Open BAM Teams 1991, 93.

MELTON, Murray S. (b. 1939) of Las Vegas NV, poker dealer. Diamond Life Master, placed 2nd Trans-National Senior Pairs 1994. Won at least 50 regionals.

MENG, Sharon E. (b. 1949) of Tampa FL, computer consultant, contracts negotiator. Won Mini-McKenney Rookie of the Year (IL) 1994 and National Master of the Year. Won more than 15 regionals.

MENGES, Cordelia Sykes (b. 1938) of New York City, game inventor, bridge club owner and director. Won Non-Life Master Pairs 1992.

MENG HO, Ching-Shan or Gloria (b. 1944) of Taipei, Taiwan, born in China, bank employee. WBF World Master. Won Far East Women's Teams 1988, 89, Far East Open Pairs 1988. Represented Taiwan in zonal championships since 1969 and in 8 world championships.

MERBLUM, Franklin P. (Frank) (b. 1949) of Bloomfield CT, actuary. Won his first regional at age 18 with his father Frank. Together they won events in 60's, 80's and 90's. Diamond Life Master, won GNOP 2001 and 41 regionals including District 25 GNOP 1989, 90.

MEREDITH, Adam (1913-1976) of New York City, formerly of London, noted for his skill in dummy play, especially in making "unmakable" contracts and for unconventional bidding maneuvers. Won Bermuda Bowl 1955, European champion 1949, 54; also represented Great Britain in European Championship 1955, 57, 59. His British wins include Gold Cup 5 times and Master Pairs 1960. Meredith co-authored (with Leo Baron) *Baron System of Contract Bridge*.

MERHY, Gaby (b. 1928) of Beirut, Lebanon. Repre-

sented Lebanon in 12 international championships. Won many national titles. Secretary of Lebanese Bridge Federation since 1974. Bridge editor of *Magazine Revue*.

MERRILL, James (J) (b. 1955) of Potomac MD, was the first King of Bridge (1973). Placed 2nd Reisinger 1974 and won more than 20 regionals.

MERRY, Philip H. (b. 1924) of Tulsa OK, ACBL national tournament director since 1963. Served as chairman of Conduct, Deportment and Ethics Committee of Professional Tournament Directors Association. Contributing editor *Bridge Encyclopedia*.

MESBUR, Adam (b. 1952) of Dublin, Ireleand, chartered accountant. WBF World Master. Placed 2nd European Junior Pairs 1974, Common Market Pairs 1982. Represented Ireland regularly in world and zonal championshipa since 1975. Won more than 25 national titles. Columnist *Sunday Tribune*.

MESSER, Alan W. (b. 1934) of West Patterson NJ, executive for computer software developer. Won Men's Teams 1960. Pioneered recorder system in Greater New York B.A. A ranked senior tennis player and former referee and chair umpire at major professional tournaments, also a marathon runner.

MESSINA, Giuseppe (b. 1926) of Florence, Italy. WBF World Life Master. Won European Teams 1965, 67, 69,71; 2nd 1962, 63.

METHOL, Raquel Donamari de of Montevideo, Uruguay. Won South American Women's Teams 1967, 71, 74, 90. A regular member of the Uruguay Women's team in international competition and has won 36 national titles.

MEYER, Babe (Mrs. Frank H.) (b. 1908) of Virginia Beach VA. Placed 2nd Mixed Pairs 1948.

MEYER, Mrs. Bert W. (1915-1993) of La Canada CA. Won Amateur Swiss Teams 1977. Had several regional titles.

MEYER, Jean-Paul (b. 1936) of Paris, France, bridge writer. WBF World Master. Won European Pairs 1987. Represented France in 2 world championships and 2 zonal championships. Editor *Revue Francaise de Bridge - Le Bridgeur* 1978-2000, columnist of *l'Express,* and *Journal du Dimanche.* Author of 2 books. Vice president IBPA. Editor World Championship Daily Bulletins and European Bridge League Daily Bulletins.

MEYER, Kenneth C. (Ken) (b. 1947) of Lititz PA, systems analyst. Won North American Swiss Teams 1989 and District 4 GNOT 1977, 81, 89, 90, Zone II 1981; District 4 GNOP 1979.

MEYER, Maria del Carmen of Montevideo, Uruguay. Won South American Women's Teams 1971, 74, 90. A regular member of Uruguay Women's team in international competition and has won 44 national titles.

MEYERS, Jill J. (Mrs. Sid Brownstein) (b. 1950) of Santa Monica CA, attorney and music consultant. WBF Grand Master, ranked #4 among women and tied for 23rd among all Grand Masters. Her performance in past 10 years is 3rd best among all women and 9th among all players. ACBL Grand Life Master with 12,355 MPs as of 3/2001. Early in 2000 she became the top ranked woman bridge player in the world, but Shawn Quinn (U.S.) and Sabine Auken (Germany) passed her during the year. Meyers won Venice Cup 1993, 97; 2nd 1995, 99; won World Women's Pairs 1998, Transnational Mixed Teams 2000. Placed 3rd McConnell Cup 1994. 4th Venice Cup 1991. Won USWBC (Team Trials) 1991, 97; placed 2nd 1993. Won Lou Herman Trophy 1987, Life Master Women's Pairs 1987, Women's KO Teams 1989, 97;

Women's BAM Teams 1991, 99; North American Women's Swiss Teams 1991, 93, 2001; Blue Ribbon Pairs 1999 (first woman to win this event since 1963 when Dorothy Hayden (Truscott) won with B.J. Becker), Life Master Open Pairs 2000 (only woman to win since it became an Open event in 1990). Placed 2nd Women's Swiss Teams 1987, 95, 99; North American Swiss Teams 1987, Women's KO Teams 1990, 93; GNOT 99; NAOP 2001.

MICHAELS, Charles (1884-1962) of New York City, was active in promoting bridge among the younger group. Introduced contract as course of study at Queens College while a teacher there and later taught in the Manhasset and Great Neck high schools, stimulating the juvenile interest in an unusual scientific manner. Founder of Barclay Bridge Supplies, Inc. Michaels co-authored Ideal *Student Textbook*.

MICHAELS, Michael N. (1924-1966) of Miami Beach FL, bridge writer and lecturer. Best known as inventor of Michaels Cuebid and for his long-time association with Charles Goren in various journalistic enterprises. Placed 2nd Spingold 1959, Open Pairs 1962 and his many regional success included the Marcus Cup 1953.

MICHAELS, Terry (b. 1927) of Prairie Village KS, formerly of Washington DC, retired bridge teacher and director. Established Bridge Center of Washington where she had the first club Swiss Team, the first computer scoring. She started many duplicate players and directors including Harry Clark during the period 1968-78. WBF World Master, she placed 3rd McConnell Teams 1994, 14th World Women's Pairs 1982. Won Master Mixed Teams 1955, Women's Teams 1963, 66, 73, 79; Women's Pairs 1967; placed 2nd Master Mixed Teams 1963, Women's Teams 1961, 62, 63, 66; Women's KO Teams 1984, 88; Mixed Pairs 2001. Diamond Life Master.

MICHAUD, Gerald L. (b. 1929) of Derby KS, retired attorney. Represented U.S. in Rosenblum Teams 1978 and was International Team alternate 1963. Won Life Master Pairs, Life Master Men's Pairs 1974; Open Swiss Teams 1990; placed 2nd Spingold 1962, Men's Teams 1962, Men's Swiss Teams 1988. Intercollegiate champion 1951, Diamond Life Master.

MICHELL, Jean Ellen (b. 1925) of Orinda CA, bridge teacher, office manager of law firm. Served as member ACBL Charity Committee, Board of Governors and on District 21 board, as Unit 499 President, vice-president, sectional tournament manager. Diamond Life Master, placed 2nd Women's Swiss Teams 1989, won 25+ regionals.

MIDKIFF, David M. (b. 1953) of St. Louis MO, bridge professional, certified teacher and director. Placed 2nd IMP Pairs 1992, won District 8 GNOT 1987.

MIDSKOG, Caterina (Cat) (b. 1962) of Stockholm, Sweden, bridge teacher. WBF World Master. 3rd Venice Cup 1993. Won European Women's Teams 1993, Nordic Women's Teams 1992, 98. Represented Sweden in one other world championship and one other zonal championship. Won 2 national titles.

MILAVEC, Alexander (b. 1944) of Vienna, Austria, attorney. Represented Austria in 3 world championships and European Junior Teams. Won Austrian Teams 6 times.

MILDE, Andrzej (b.1939) of Poznan, Poland. World Master. 3rd Bermuda Bowl 1981, won European Open Pairs 1980, European Open Teams 1981. Won Transnational Senior Pairs 2000. Won many national titles.

MILES, Marshall (b. 1926) of Redlands CA, retired attorney and bridge writer. Represented U.S. Cannes 1962.

ACBL Grand Life Master with 13,021 MPs as of 3/2001. Miles' books include *How to Win at Duplicate Bridge, All 52 Cards, Marshall Miles Teaches Logical Bridge, Bridge from the Top,* Volumes I and II, *Stronger Competitive Bidding, Competitive Bidding in the 21st Century.* He has written many articles for *The Bridge World, American Bridge Digest, Bridge Today,* ACBL *Bridge Bulletin* and is a contributing editor, *The Official Encyclopedia of Bridge.* Member *Bridge World* Master Solvers panel and bidding panel of *Australian Bridge.* Placed 3rd World Bidding Contest, 2nd in USA. Won Fishbein Trophy 1961, Spingold 1961, 62; Life Masters Pairs 1961, Lou Herman Trophy, Chicago 1962, Reisenger 1965; placed 2nd Vanderbilt 1961, Open Pairs 1962, Men's Pairs 1962, 72. Regional successes included Marcus Cup 1960.

MILES, R(ufus) L., Jr. (Skinny) (1907-1984) of Virginia Beach VA, investment executive. ACBL president 1950, 56, member of many of its administrative committees for nearly 2 decades. Honorary Member 1952. Served as president of Mid-Atlantic Conference, npc North American Bermuda Bowl team 1957 and of U.S. team World Team Olympiad 1960.

MILES, Sidsel K. (Cecile) (b. 1937) of Adelaide, Australia, born in Norway, former secretary. Won PABF (Far East) Women's Teams 1975, 77, 90. Represented Australia in 5 world championships and 3 zonal championships. National wins include Interstate Teams 3 times.

MILLER, Arthur M. (b. 1924) of Beverly Hills CA, manufacturer and importer. Placed 2nd Vanderbilt 1956, Chicago (now the Reisinger) 1958.

MILLER, Bernard A. (Bernie) (b. 1940) of Boca Raton FL, retired attorney. Past president Eastern Massachusetts B.A., former member ACBL Board of Governors, ACBL Rules and Protest Committee, District 25 Board of Directors. Placed 5th Bermuda Bowl 1991. Won USBC (Team Trials) 1991, GNOT 1989, Open Pairs II 1992. Miller, a Diamond Life Master, has won 25-30 regionals.

MILLER, Billy (b. 1956) of Las Vegas NV, writer, former stockbroker. Attended New England Conservatory of Music at ages 3-5 (piano), taught guitar at age 10. Last person to play bridge with Barry Crane (Bridge Week Masters Pairs). He was a member of Crane's KO team that went on to win the event with substitute Kerri Shuman (now Sanborn). Columnist for *Western Contract Bridge Forum* since 1987 and for ACBL *Bridge Bulletin* since 1993. Has written and published a book based on his *Dear Billy* column. Diamond Life Master with more than 13,400 MPs as of 3/2001. Placed 2nd North American Swiss Teams 1999, 2nd Cavendish Pairs 1999, 3rd Cavendish Teams. Won more than 150 regionals including District 21 GNOP 1998, 90, GNOT 1991.

MILLER, Charles (b. 1934) of Houston TX, investment executive. Won Men's Teams 1964.

MILLER, Clifton A., Sr. (Clif, Math Doc) (b. 1947) of Shreveport LA, mathematics tutor, test preparation instructor. Has won 18 regional events.

MILLER, Harvey H. (b. 1929) of Chicago, real estate broker and investor. Won Amateur Men's Pairs 1975, placed 2nd North American Swiss Teams 1979, won several regional events.

MILLER, James D. (Jim) (b. 1946) of Memphis TN, manager ACBL Membership Services Division, former retail store manager. Past president North Colorado Unit.

MILLER, Jeffrey A. (b. 1948) of Naperville IL, research and computer modeling of equity options and other securities, college professor University of WI. Served on

Upper Michigan B.A. board 1975-87, president 1981-83, Chicago Contract B.A. board member. Diamond Life Master, won more than 15 regional events including District 13 GNOP 1993.

MILLER, Martin E. (Marty) (b. 1937) of Rochester NY, college guidance counselor and social worker, former rubber bridge and backgammon club owner. Served as president of Unit 113 and District 21. Placed 2nd Master Mixed Teams 1985, won 35 regionals.

MILLER, Richard A. (Dick) (1911-1983) of York PA, account executive, bridge writer. One of the founders of Keystone Conference (now District 4). Member of its Board from 1951 and president 1960-61. Also one of the founders of Unit 168, president 1963. Member ACBL Board of Governors. Wrote weekly column for *The National Observer* 1962-77, *York Gazette and Daily* 1945-65 and prior to his death a monthly column for *The American Way* - American Airlines' in-flight magazine. One of the early exponents of point-count method of evaluation. He wrote *Point Count Bidding* in 1947, the first application of point-count to suit bidding. Other works by Miller are *It's a Bidder's Game, Bridge Brilliance and Blunders* and *More Bridge Brilliance and Blunders.*

MILLER, Susan J. (Susie) (b. 1943) of Boca Raton FL, travel agent. Has contributed to *Bridge World* and *Bridge Today*. Won Life Master Women's Pairs 1995, placed 2nd Women's Swiss Teams 1998, Women's KO Teams and Women's BAM Teams 1999.

MILLERD, James A. (Jim) (b. 1927) of Dana Point CA, marketing director. Contributor to *The Bridge World* in the 50's. Life Master #753, has won events in 5 consecutive decades beginning in the 50's.

MILLION, Ruth (d. 1990) of Union City CA. Won Master Mixed Teams 1951.

MILNES Eric (1912-1984) of Bradford, York, England, former editor *Bridge Magazine*, bridge author. Won several national titles.

MINTER, Lulu (Lou) (b. 1950) of Glendora CA, born in Romania, engineer. Cruise lecturer and bridge director since 1991. First player born in Romania to achieve Life Master status. Won 20 regionals.

MISK, Alexandre (b. 1952) of Minas Gerais, Brazil, engineer. Won South American Teams 1983 and represented Brazil in 2 world championships.

MITCHELL, Bill of Falkirk, Scotland, retired civil servant. Represented Scotland 14 times in Camrose Trophy matches. Won Gold Cup and Scottish Cup once each. Active as coach and administrator.

MITCHELL, Billie P. (b. 1927) of Ruidoso NM, secretary/bookeeper. Has served locally in executive positions 1988-90; Unit vice-president, secretary 1992-94, 1997-99, tournament chairman many times. Diamond Life Master, won 15+ regionals.

MITCHELL, Jacquelyn M. (Jacqui) (Mrs. Victor) (b. 1936) of New York City, bridge teacher, one of the outstanding women players of the world. WBF Grand Master, ranks #6 among women and #24 among all Grand Masters. ACBL Grand Life Master with 14,106 MPs as of 3/2001. Won Venice Cup 1976, 78; World Olympiad Women's Teams 1980, 84; World Women's Pairs 1986; placed 2nd Venice Cup 1985, World Mixed Teams and World Mixed Pairs 1974. Represented U.S. in international competition 1972 (3rd Olympiad Women's Teams, 5th Mixed Teams), 1974 (9th World Women's Pairs, 1976 (3rd Olympiad Women's Teams) 1978 (8th World Women's Pairs), 1982. Won USWBC 1983, 87, Women's Teams

1965, 70, 74, 75, 76; Women's Pairs 1971, 75, 77, 84; Women's KO Teams 1983, 87; North American Women's Swiss Teams 1983, 91; Women's BAM Teams 1990; placed 2nd Women's Pairs 1962, 70, 74; Women's KO Teams 1973, 82; North American Women's Swiss Teams 1985, 2001; Women's BAM Teams 1986, 97; Master Mixed Teams 1989, 97; Women's KO Teams 1991. Mitchell's numerous regional titles include Eastern States KO Teams 1962, 63, 64; New York Blue Ribbon Individual 1977 and was New York Player of the Year in 1958, her 2nd year of tournament play.

MITCHELL, John Templeton (1854-1914) of Chicago, born in Glasgow, Scotland. Known as "Father of Duplicate Whist" because of the movements of boards and players he designed for tournaments. He invented many schedules for individual, pair and team contests, the most notable of which is the Mitchell Movement. He helped to adapt the matchpoint scoring and used whist for the purposes of duplicate auction. Mitchell was a lineal descendant of Sir Roger Kirkpatrick, a famous Highland chieftain who supported Wallace and Bruce in the struggle for Scottish independence circa 1350. In 1875, Mitchell immigrated to the United States and became a naturalized citizen. In 1888 he took up whist when he saw a clipping from the London *Field* regarding a duplicate whist match. It was between two clubs in his native Glasgow, using James Allison's Automatic Hand Registers. This excited Mitchell and he formed the Chicago Duplicate Whist Club. He wrote the world's first book on duplicate whist, 1892, revised 1896. He joined the Hyde Park team in 1895 that won the 5th American Whist League Congress (national championship). Mitchell, director in the American Whist Leaque, favored the long-suit game and his modified American leads were published in *Whist*,1896.

MITCHELL, Victor (1923-1995) of New York City, bridge teacher, was one of the outstanding American players. Member ACBL Hall of Fame, WBF Life Master, placed 2nd in World Team Olympiad 1964, World Mixed Teams 1974; 5th World Olympiad Teams 1960 and Mixed Teams 1972; 8th Rosenblum Teams 1986. Represented U.S. in other world championships. Named ACBL Honorary Member 1988. ACBL Grand Life Master. Won the Spingold 1956, 59; Life Master Men's Pairs 1962, Men's Teams 1962, 63; placed 2nd Life Master Pairs 1954, 55; Chicago (now the Reisinger), Men's Pairs 1955; Men's Teams, Life Master Men's Pairs 1965; Vanderbilt, Spingold 1969; Men's BAM Teams 1988, Master Mixed Teams 1989. Mitchell was well known for holding court in hotel lobbies at bridge tournaments.

MITTELMAN, George of Toronto, PQ. WBF World Life Master, won World Mixed Pairs 1982, placed 2nd Bermuda Bowl 1995, 3rd Rosenblum Teams 1982, 90. Represented Canada in international competition 1978 (5th Rosenblum Teams, 8th World Championship Mixed Pairs), 1980, 1984, 1986 (9th Rosenblum Teams). ACBL Diamond Life Master, won Richmond Trophy 1981, North American Swiss Teams 1986, Open Swiss Teams 1995, Open BAM Teams 1998. Placed 2nd Reisinger 1978, 82; Men's Pairs 1985. Won CNTC 5 times 1980, 81, 83, 85, 89; placed 2nd 1990.

MIYAISHI, Etsuko (b. 1942) of Tokyo, Japan, bridge teacher. WBF World Master. Was 2nd in Far East Women's Teams 1989. Represented Japan in 5 world championships including Venice Cup 1991. Won more than 20 national titles.

MIYAKUNI, Kenji (b. 1951) of Tokyo, Japan, bridge

professional. WBF World Master. Represented Japan on numerous occasions in FEBF/PABF and 2 World Team Olympiads and Venezuela in one World Team Olympiad. Won Pan-Am Swiss Teams 1992, NEC Cup 1999, CAC (Zone 6) Open Pairs 1993, Asian Cup 1998, Far East Open Teams 1985. 2nd ACBL IMP Pairs 1997, 3rd Spingold 1991, 2nd PABF Open Teams 2000. Won many national titles in both Japan and Venezuela.

MIZUTANI, Eizo (b. 1933) of Tokyo, Japan, bridge teacher, writer and national tournament director. Represented Japan in Far East Championships 1962, 65, 68, 69, 72. National wins include Knockout Teams 5 times, Round-robin Teams 3 times. Co-authored *Contract Bridge Nyumon* and *Contract Bridge no Subete*.

MODLIN, Merle (b. 1940) of Johannesburg, South Africa, bridge teacher. WBF World Master. Represented South Africa in 5 World Women's Team Olympiads and 3 Venice Cups. Won BFAME Women's Teams 1993, 95, 97. Won numerous national titles. Represented South Africa in Maccabi Games as a swimmer.

MOEGEL, Marianne of Hanover, Germany. WBF World Life Master. 2nd Venice Cup 1993. Won European Women's Teams 1989, 2nd 1991. 2nd European Women's Pairs 1993 and has won 6 national titles. Represented Germany in other world championships. Member of winning German team of Venice Cup - 1995.

MOELLER, Donald A. (b. 1925) of Dayton OH, banking executive and CPA. Held numerous positions with ACBL, including: District 11 Director 1973-98, ACBL treasurer 1985-93, ACBL Charity Foundation trustee since 1986, ACBL Charity Foundation treasurer (since 1984), ACBL pension trustee (since 1980). First president District 11, treasurer Midwest Monitor beginning 1974, president Miami Valley BA, Unit 136 1969-70, 1990-present. Current treasurer for District 11, has been Board member since 1970.

MOELLER, Kirsten Steen (b 1947) of Copenhagen, Denmark. Won World Women's Team Olympiad 1988, represented Denmark in 2 other Olympiads and 8 European Championships. Won China Cup 1999, 26 Danish titles.

MOELLER, Steffen Steen (b 1939) of Copenhagen, Denmark, attorney. Since his debut in Nordic Championships - 1966 he has played 426 times for Denmark, including 4 World Team Olympiads and 13 European Championships. 31 Danish titles. Npc of Open Team and Women's Team champions China Cup 1999. Invented several conventions and system gadgets. Regular contributor to *Dansk Bridge*, was bridge columnist of *Berlingske Tidende* for more than a decade and has authored several bridge books. WBF and EBL Appeals Committee member.

MOETI, Dr. Justice Simon (b. 1926) of Gaborone, Botswana, born in South Africa. Represented Botswana in 2 world championships. Chairman of Botswana Bridge Federation since its foundation in 1989.

MOFFAT, John R. (b. 1949) of Bellingham WA, attorney. Served as Unit 439 president 1978-85 and District 19 representative to ACBL Board of Governors 1981-84. 15+ regional wins include District 19 GNOP 1981.

MOGAL, Sol (1911-1989) of Croton on Hudson NY, import company president. Won Spingold 1946, 49 (2nd 1952); Men's Pairs 1947, Men's Teams 1947, 48, 54; the Chicago (now the Reisinger) 1949.

MOHAN, John A. (b. 1939) of Christiansted, St. Croix, owner Bridge Paradise Resorts. One of the leading

American players. ACBL Grand Life Master with 18,276 MPs as of 3/2001, and WBF World Life Master. Won Trans-National Mixed Teams, World Senior Teams 2000, placed 3rd World Open Pairs 1978, represented U.S. in several other events and in Bal Harbour 1986. ACBL wins include Mixed Pairs 1972, Vanderbilt 1975, 76, 88, 92; Spingold 1976, Life Master Men's Pairs 1976, 85; Lou Hermann Trophy 1977, North American Men's Swiss Teams 1985; Men's Swiss Teams 1987, Open BAM Teams 1994, Open Swiss Teams, Life Master Pairs, Blue Ribbon Pairs 1999; placed 2nd Life Master Men's Pairs 1977, Men's BAM Teams 1985, Life Master Pairs 1990, 2000; Open BAM Teams 2000, Vanderbilt 2001. ACBL Player of Year 1999. Npc of Women's Swiss Teams winners 2001. Also won South African National Open Pairs 1988, 89; Open Teams 1989, 90. Won hundreds of regionals.

MOHAN, Dr. Sangarpillai (b. 1941) of Oakbrook IL, born in Sri Lanka, psychiatrist. Won between 15-20 regionally rated events.

MOHR, Arne (b. 1946), of Århus, Denmark, bridge teacher. Represented Denmark World Team Olympiad 1988 and European Championships 1991. 7 Danish titles. Won Nordic Junior Teams 1973, Baltic Cup 1980 and Hoechst 1991.

MOHR, Mark D. (b. 1939) of Union NJ, attorney. Won NAC Senior/Advanced Senior Master Pairs 1961. Past president New Jersey BL and former editor *The Declarer*.

MOLLEMET, Peter D. (b. 1943) of Williamsville NY, former national tournament director and area field representative for Districts 2, 4, 5, 11, 12. Now assistant ACBL web page administrator ACBL Headquarters. Began directing career 1975, achieved national ranking 1988. Won Canadian National Swiss Teams 1975, District 4 Swiss Teams 1977.

MOLLO, Victor (1909-87) of London, England, born in St. Petersburg, bridge writer. Best-known for characters he created as members of the fictional Griffins Club: the Hideous Hog, the Rueful Rabbit and others. They first appeared in *Bridge in the Menagerie*, and in many magazine articles which were collected in book form. Author of more than 25 books. Won 4 national titles. Editor in BBC European service 1939-69.

MOLOCHKO, Daniel Steele (b. 1955) of El Cerrito CA, data processing and business management consultant. Was a state of Connecticut scholar and a prep school All-American swimmer. Won Open BAM Teams 1990.

MOLSON, Markland (Mark) (b. 1949) of Miami FL, formerly of Montreal, professional bridge player. Has represented Canada in international competition, 2nd Bermuda Bowl 1995 and placed 3rd Rosenblum Teams 1990. ACBL Grand Life Master with 15,376 MPs as of 3/2001. Won Richmond Trophy 1979, 80, 82, 83, 84; Canadian National Pairs 1985, Reisinger 1989, Blue Ribbon Pairs 1989, North American Swiss Teams 1992, 94, 95. Placed 2nd Spingold, Reisinger 1982; Open Pairs II 1992. Molson, with partner, Boris Baran, have the best record in the CNTC, having won it 5 times 1983, 85, 87, 89, 91. They came in 2nd 3 times 1986, 88, 90.

MOLSON, Janice. See Seamon-Molson, Janice

MONDOLFO, Renato of Trieste, Italy. WBF World Life Master. Won European Teams 1965, 67, 69, 71. Italian national titles include Open Teams twice.

MONSEGUR, Martin (b. 1941) of Buenos Aires, Argentina, attorney. WBF World Master. Won South American Teams 1985, 94, 95. Represented Argentina in 8 world championships. Won 11 national titles. Won Gabarret Cup 1975, 85, 90, 95.

MONTAIGU, Marie Claire de (1901-1977) of Paris, France. Won European Women's Teams 1939, 53, 54 (captain 1953). Won European Women's Pairs 1935. Represented France on other occasions and won many national titles.

MONTIN, Randi of Napa CA. Won Venice Cup 1997, 2nd Venice Cup 1999. Won Women's KO Teams 1982, 89, 97; Women's Swiss Teams 1982, Women's BAM Teams 1999; placed 2nd Women's BAM Teams 1987, Women's KO Teams 1990, North American Women's Swiss Teams 1995, 99. Ranked 14th in the world, of top women players.

MONZINGO, Ken (b. 1939) of San Diego CA, professional player and teacher, theatrical press agent for national touring shows. District 22 Board of Governors representative, editor and publisher of *Contract Bridge Forum* and has served as Pacific Southwest Regional manager and *Daily Bulletin* editor for many West Coast regionals. Authored *Cruise with Ken, Bridge in Windows: a cruise Guide*. Diamond Life Master, has won approximately 100 regionals.

MOONEY, Guillermo (b. 1941) of Buenos Aires, Argentina, attorney. WBF World Master. Won South American Teams 1985, 94, 95. Represented Argentina in 3 world championships. Won 12 national titles. Won Gabarret Cup 1985, 91.

MOORE, Dorothy H. (1928-2000) of Dallas, TX, retired corporate executive, president Aces International 1968-82. Was listed by *Fortune Magazine* (1978) as one of the top 10 women in big business. Edited bridge column of the late Ira G. Corn Jr.'s, also books published by Aces Team. Assisted Corn in forming and managing the Aces. Was deputy captain of U.S. Women's Team - World Team Olympiad 1980. Won Mixed Pairs 1963, Life Master Women's Pairs 1975.

MOORE, Joan Remey (d. 1998) of Troy MI, retired social worker. Was member ACBL Board of Directors representing District 12. Member Board of Directors and past president of MBA. Grand Life Master with more than 15,000 MPs. Won Open Pairs 1971, Master Mixed Teams 1987, Silver Ribbon Pairs 1993; placed 2nd Women's Teams 1960, 65, Master Mixed Teams 1971, 75, 80; Women's Pairs 1976, 77. Won more than 100 regionals since 1958 including Marcus Cup 1970.

MORAN, Brian J. (1938-1999) of Ellicott City MD, national tournament director. Began his directing career in 1965 and was elevated to national status 1987. Served as president of Virginia State B.A. 1972-77. He won Mid-Atlantic KO Teams 1973, 74, 76. Author of *Ruling the Game* column for ACBL *Bridge Bulletin* for many years.

MORAN, John H. (1909-1977) of Camarillo CA, club director, former bridge instructor and cruise director. Represented North America in Bermuda Bowl 1955. Won Spingold 1954, Blue Ribbon Pairs 1965. Placed 2nd in the Chicago (now the Reisinger) 1958, Men's Teams 1953, Mixed Pairs 1954. Won numerous regionals between 1950 and 1970 including Marcus Cup 1957.

MORATALLA, Marquesa de, (Sol Cabeza de Vaca-Leighton) of Lausanne, Switzerland, horse owner and breeder. She is ranked 1st in France as a horse owner-breeder. 4th World Open Teams 1982, the best performance ever by a woman in the Rosenblum Teams. Also represented Spain in 3 other world championships and 2 zonal championships. Won 2 French national titles.

MORATH, Anders (The Carrot) (b. 1944) of Jarfalla, Sweden, computer systems developer. WBF World Life Master. 3rd Bermuda Bowl 1977, 91. Represented Sweden in many other world championships. Won European Teams 1977, 2nd 1991. Played on 3 other occasions. Won European Junior Teams 1968. Won national Open Teams 8 times, top Swedish masterpoint holder. Co-author of Carrot Club and other systems.

MORCOS, Josephine (b. 1923) of Heliopolis, Egypt. WBF World Life Master. Won World Women's Team Olympiad 1960, when the Egyptian team competed as United Arab Republic. Won BFAAME Women's Teams 1987, 91, 97; 2nd 1985, 89. Represented Egypt regularly in World Women's Team Championship from 1964 and is the highest ranked Egyptian player in WBF rankings. Won more than 30 national titles. Bridge columnist for *Cairo's*, a magazine.

MORDECAI, Daniel (Dan) (b. 1932) of Denver CO, president and chairman U.S. Nursing Corporation. Started program of formal recording (with Judge John Barnard) of behavior and actions detrimental to bridge in the 60's. Won Cavendish Pairs 1979 and 50+ regional events.

MOREHEAD, Albert Hodges (1909-1966) of New York City, League official, bridge author, writer and editor in general fields. Officer and director United States Bridge Association when that organization amalgamated with the American Bridge League 1937. A governor of the ACBL 1937, president 1943, chairman of the Board 1943-45, Honorary . Was in charge of production of the International Laws of Contract Bridge in 1943 and subsequent years. Was only 25 when he played on Culbertson team that defeated the British (1934) in the 2nd international match for the Schwab Cup. Won or placed high in several national and regional tournaments. Ely Culbertson hired him in 1932 because of his outstanding ability as a player and analyst. He was made technical editor of *The Bridge World* 1933. He proved so invaluable that in 1934 he was made general manager of all Culbertson enterprises. He relinquished tournament play in order to handle additional duties. Did editing (and in the case of the *Red Book on Play*, much of the writing) of Culbertson books, the *Bridge Encyclopedia*, 1935. Also did endorsements, the management details of Crockford's Clubs both in New York and Chicago and the executive direction of Kem Playing Cards, Inc. Sold Kem Cards within 4 years for a profit of more than half a million dollars.

First bridge editor of *The New York Times*, with a Sunday column from 1935 and a daily column from 1959. Resigned from *Times* late in 1963. He wanted to devote full time to writing, editing and publishing of the dictionaries, encyclopedias and thesauruses that made him one of the foremost American lexicographers. His works also include many "Hoyle" books giving the rules of card games — he had become the leading modern American authority. Retired from *The Bridge World* 1946, but retained his duties of an advisory capacity and director of the Master Solvers' Club. He now devoted his time to other pursuits. Authored many bridge books, including *Bridge the Expert Way, Contract Bridge Summary,* and *Morehead on Bidding* which won the IBPA "Bridge Book of the Year" award in 1966.

MORENAS, Genevieve (1926-83) of Lyon, France. 2nd World Women's Team Olympiad, European Women's Teams 1966, 81. Won European Mixed Pairs 1976 and many national titles.

MORI, Lawrence K. (Larry) (b. 1948) of Charlton NY,

raised in Tokyo, licensed psychotherapist, currently administrator of family owned business, professional bridge player. Intercollegiate champion 1976. Grand Life Master with 11,045 MPs as of 3/2001. Won North American Swiss Teams 1990, Open Pairs 1991, Mixed Pairs 1992. Placed 2nd GNOP 1979, Mixed BAM Teams 1997. Has won dozens of regionals.

MORRELL, Clinton D. (Clint) (b. 1945) of Marlborough MA, operations research analyst (USAF). Diamond Life Master, placed 2nd Life Master Pairs 1991. Won many regionals including District 3 GNOP 1979, 83.

MORRIS, Anthony G. (Tony) (b. 1940) of Billings MT, retired revenue officer, former bridge professional. Past president Unit 106, wrote monthly column *Ethically Speaking* 1980-83 and contributes regular articles for District 18 *Wasumi*. Multiple winner "Big Sky Trophy" (most sectionals won annually in Minnesota). Won 15-20 regionals.

MORRIS, Robert F. (Tiger) (1922-1998) of Cincinnati OH, advertising agency field representative. Placed 2nd Blue Ribbon Pairs 1969. Diamond Life Master with more than 10,000 MPs. Has won many regionals.

MORSE, Dan (b. 1938) of Houston TX, pharmacist. WBF World Master and ACBL Grand Life Master with 12,974 MPs as of 3/2001. Won World Senior Teams 2000, placed 3rd Rosenblum Teams 1978, 90; 7th World Open Pairs 1986. Npc of the following: winning Bermuda Bowl team 1976, 87; Olympiad Team 1988; 2nd Bermuda Bowl Team 1989, Venice Cup 1985, Olympiad 1992; the Reisinger team winners in Teams Trials 1974, 75; Spingold team 1976. Coach of winners of World Women's Team Olympiad 1984. Honorary Member 1989. ACBL representative to WBF Executive Council. Replaced Bobby Wolff as ACBL District 16 Director 1993. Won Mixed Pairs 1964, GNOT 1977, Spingold 1977, Vanderbilt 1990, 93; Life Master Pairs 1993, Senior KO Teams 1994. Placed 2nd Spingold 1967, Life Master Pairs 1979, Blue Ribbon Pairs 1980, Vanderbilt 1985, GNOP 1989, Open Swiss Teams 1991, North American Swiss Teams 1996.

MORSE, Jo (b. 1932) of Palm Beach Gardens FL, one of the leading North American women players. Served Washington B.L. as board member, secretary and treasurer. WBF World Life Master, won World Mixed Teams 1974, captained winning Venice Cup team 1993 and 2nd place Venice Cup team 1999. Represented ACBL in world competition several other times. Grand Life Master with 19,311 MPs as of 3/2001. Won Women's Teams 1973, 77, 79, 81; Women's Pairs 1983, Women's KO Teams 1986, Women's BAM Teams 1990, 99; Women's Swiss Teams 1998. Placed 2nd Women's Teams 1980, North American Women's Swiss Teams 1985, Women's KO Teams 1988, 89, 91.

MOSCA, Carlo (b. 1945) of Milan, Italy, bridge teacher. WBF World Life Master. Won World Team Olympiad 2000 as npc. Placed 2nd World Team Olympiad 1976, Bermuda Bowl 1983. European champion 1975, 2nd 1974, 83. Represented Italy on many other occastions.

MOSES, Tod (b. 1955) of Glendale MD, CPA. Won about 40 regionals.

MOSS, Andrew B. (b. 1972) of New York City, student at University of Wisconsin, spent 5 weeks in 1990 as volunteer worker in refugee camps in Thailand. Youngest person ever appointed to ACBL Goodwill Committee, member of Junior Corps. Won Non-Life Master Swiss Teams 1988 (he and Martha Benson (now Katz) are the youngest players to win this event), North Ameri-

can Youth Team Championship 1989, 0-2000 KO Teams; placed 2nd Junior Pairs 1991. (see FAMILY)

MOSS, Mary (Mrs. John) (1920-1981) of London, England. Won World Women's Team Olympiad 1964, European Women's Championship 1963. WBF Life Master. Represented Great Britain in other world competition.

MOSS, Michael (Mike) (b. 1935) of New York City, stockbroker. WBF World Master and ACBL Grand Life Master with 12,338 MPs as of 3/2001; 2nd Rosenblum Teams 1990, 4th World Mixed Pairs 1974. Won Master Mixed Teams 1967, 72; Life Master Pairs 1970, Mixed Pairs 1988; Men's Pairs 1989, Open Pairs II 1998; placed 2nd Men's Pairs 1966, Men's BAM Teams 1988. See FAMILY.

MOSS, Michael Brad (Brad) (b. 1971) formerly of Berkeley CA and New York City, now of Florida. National Merit Scholar, member Junior Corps, 1989 King of Bridge, the youngest player to be New York Player of the Year 1991. WBF World Master. Won 1990 World Junior Pair Trials. Placed 4th World Junior Championship 1991. Won Non-Life Master GNOP 1988, Master Mixed Teams 1991, GNOT, Life Master Open Pairs 1993; Open BAM Teams 1998. Placed 2nd Blue Ribbon Pairs 1992, IMP Pairs 1995, Life Master Pairs 1999, Spingold 2000. (See FAMILY.)

MOSZCZYNSKI, Krzysztof (b. 1951), Warsaw, Poland, doctor of mathematics. WBF World Master. Placed 3rd - Bermuda Bowl 1989. Won European Open Teams 1989, European Junior Pairs 1976. Won many national titles.

MOTT-SMITH, Geoffrey (1902-1960) of New York City, born in Honolulu. Co-chairman ACBL Laws Commission, editor of ACBL *Bridge Bulletin* 1935-36, contributor to *The Bridge World*, writer and cryptographer. One of the first to operate a bridge club and to direct bridge tournaments. Director of annual Intercollegiate Tournaments and other "par" bridge events. Worked with Ely Culbertson in organization of the United States Bridge Association and with William E. McKenney in the early years of ACBL. During WW II, he served as chief instructor for the OSS in the training of cryptographers and cryptanalysts. Authored or co-authored more than 29 books on games. Served as games consultant for the Association of American Playing Card Manufacturers. A great player, brilliant theorist and one of the soundest and most lucid of the early writers on contract bridge.

MOUAT, Andrew J. (1870-1956) of Evanston IL, leading personality in whist organization during lifetime of the American Whist League. Was its chief tournament director more than 40 years. Served as its president, secretary and tournament committee chairman. Editor *Whist Review* 1915-1919. ACBL Honorary Member 1948.

MOUIEL, Hervé (b. 1949) of Paris, France, bridge professional. WBF World Grand Master. In 2000, ranked 8th in WBF world rankings. Won World Team Olympiad 1992, 96; 2nd 1984. Won Bermuda Bowl 1997, European Teams 1983, Common Market Teams twice. Represented France in 6 other world championships and won many national titles.

MOUSER, William S. (1912-1963) of Detroit MI, presumed dead when his private plane was lost over Lake Erie. Speech therapist and for 10 years was Sunday bridge columnist for *Detroit News*. Served both as president and treasurer of Michigan B.A. Bercame member of ACBL Board of Directors1963.

MOYSE, Alphonse, Jr. (Sonny) (1898-1973) publisher and editor of *The Bridge World* from 1956-66, a bridge author and champion player. Member ACBL Hall of Fame.

Born in Summit MS. Moyse spent most of his boyhood in Cincinnati then settled in New York City. When the crash of 1929 ended his career as a stockbroker, he adopted bridge as a profession. In 1934 he joined the organization of Ely Culbertson, partly as an associate editor of *The Bridge World* but chiefly as writer of syndicated newspaper articles that were published under the names of Ely and Josephine Culbertson. From that time until 1956 he wrote 2 bridge columns each day, a total of more than 20,000. In addition he did many magazine articles and editorial work on Culbertson books. Moyse was managing editor of *The Bridge World* 1939-43 and was publisher and chief editor 1946-56. On the death of Culbertson in 1955 he bought the *Bridge World*, Inc., from the Culbertson estate. He was president and general manager until 1963, when he sold it to McCall Corp. Remained as publisher and editor of the magazine until his retirement 1966. Moyse was a keen advocate of the 4-3 trump fit. Because of his strong advocacy of this it was given his name — hence the name Moysian Fit. An original member of the Editorial Advisory Board "*Bridge Encyclopedia*. In 1973, a few weeks before his death, he was selected as the first American to be named an IBPA Honorary Member. Perhaps Moyse's most admired writings were humorous articles about the bridge exploits of his wife, Jackie Moyse, whom he depicted as the typical member of ladies' luncheon-club bridge games. Though a comparatively infrequent contestant in tournaments, won Men's Teams 1949, Men's Pairs 1963 and several regionals.

MUELLER, Jane (Mrs. A. H.) of Cincinnati Ohio, former retirement consultant. Represented U.S. in World Women's Pairs 1962. Won Women's Pairs 1960 and several regional events.

MUHSAM, Gertrude (Mrs. Rudolf, formerly Brunner) (1909-1979) of New York City, born in Vienna, was assistant manager of Cavendish Club (New York) and an outstanding player. European Women's Teams champion 1935, 36, 37 and captain 1935-37.

MUKHERJEE, Kamal (b. 1945) of Calcutta, India, government employee. WBF World Master. 4th Open World Teams 1988. Won Far East Open Teams 1977, 2nd BFAAME Open Teams 1985. Represented India in 5 other world championships and 2 other zonal championships. Won 22 national titles. India's top masterpoint holder.

MULDER, Andre (b. 1951) of Alphen, The Netherlands, systems analyst. WBF World Master. 3rd World Team Olympiad 1980. Represented The Netherlands in 6 other world championships and 2 European Championships. Many national titles.

MULLAMPHY, Matthew (b. 1966) of Townsville, Australia, singer and actor. 3rd World Junior Teams 1991, won Far East Junior Teams 1990, 2nd 1991. Represented Australia in one other world championship and won 2 national titles.

MULLER, Bauke (b. 1962) of Hoorn, Netherlands, psychologist. WBF World Life Master. Won Bermuda Bowl 1993. Was 3rd World Olympiad Teams 1992. Many national wins.

MULTON, Franck (b. 1964) of Nice, France, bridge professional. Won World Team Olympiad 1996, Bermuda Bowl 1997. Placed 2nd World Junior Teams 1987. Won European Junior Teams 1988. 2nd Generali World Individual 1996.

MUNAFO, Dr. Paul M. (b. 1939) of Huntsville AL, manager, materials, processes and manufacturing department. Chief metallurgist, NASA, designers of the space shuttle.

His field is prevention of premature structural failure in space vehicles. Recipient of NASA Exceptional Service Medal 1991. Past president District 10, Unit 232, 143 and has served on unit and district boards for the past 25 years. ACBL Grand Life Master. Won North American Swiss Teams 1988, placed 2nd Morehead Cup 1967. Won more than 100 regional events including District 10 GNOT 1982, 92.

MUNOZ, Rafael (b. 1927) of Madrid, Spain, attorney and importer-exporter. Placed 4th World Open Teams 1982. Represented Spain in 4 other world championships and 6 zonal championships. Won many national titles.

MUNSON-COOPER, Kitty (b. 1950) of Albuquerque NM, computer systems analyst. Served on GNYBA Board of Directors for several years. Contributed to *International Bridge Monthly* and *Bridge International*. Bridge teacher. Due to her appeal to the WBF, the rules governing the time period between teams representing different countries internationally were changed. WBF World Life Master, won Venice Cup 1989, 2nd 1995. Placed 5th Rosenblum Teams 1994. Playing for Britain placed 4th World Mixed Pairs in Bal Harbour 1986, won Common Market Mixed Teams, was 3rd European Women's Teams 1987. Won National Advanced Senior Masters Pairs 1975, North American Swiss Teams 1987, 90; Women's Swiss Teams 1989, Mixed Pairs 1992, Women's KO teams 1998. Was 2nd Women's Swiss Teams 1985, 94; Women's BAM Teams 1988, Women's Pairs 1994, 98; Mixed BAM Teams 1998, 2000. Her many regional wins include Pan-Am Pairs Qualifier 1990.

MURDOCH, Elinor (1901-1986) of Birmingham AL, bridge teacher, Life Master #64. Won Women's Pairs, Mixed Pairs 1931, Master Individual 1934, Master Mixed Teams 1933. Past president Alabama B.A.

MURPHY, James (Jim) (b. 1942) of Cheasepeake VA, professional bridge teacher and player. Contributor to *Bridge Today* and *Bridge World*. Diamond Life Master, placed 2nd Senior Swiss Teams 1999, won more than 50 regionals.

MURPHY, John T. (Jack) (1920-1992) of Calgary AB, retired locomotive engineer. Served as Honor Guard for Pope John Paul II 1984. President Canadian Bridge Federation 1975-77. Canada's delegate to Board of Governors to WBF 1976, 80. Served 10 years on CBF Board of Directors and CBF Charitable Trust. Past president Unit 390 and chaired Calgary tournament 1967, 70, 73. In 1972 became first Canadian to be appointed assistant chairman ACBL Goodwill Committee.

MURRAY, David S. (b. 1921) of Alexandria VA, retired statistician. Placed 2nd Mixed Teams 1954.

MURRAY, Eric R. (b. 1928) of Toronto, barrister and solicitor. Member ACBL Hall of Fame, WBF World Life Master, one of world's outstanding bridge players and personalities. Represented North America in Bermuda Bowl 1962, 66, 67, 74; Canada in other world competitions in 1960, 64, 68, 70, 72, 78, 80, 82. Placed 3rd Rosenblum Teams 1982. ACBL Grand Life Master. Won Team Trials 1966, Lou Herman Trophy 1963, Vanderbilt 1961, 70; Spingold 1964, 65, 68; Men's Teams 1962, Life Master Men's Pairs, Mixed Pairs 1963; Men's Pairs 1945, 55, Master Mixed Teams 1956, 62; Life Master Pairs 1969; placed 2nd Master Mixed Teams 1954, the Chicago (now the Reisinger) 1961, Men's Pairs 1965, Blue Ribbon Pairs 1969, Reisinger 1969, 72. Won Canadian National Teams Championship 1980, 81, 87; placed 2nd 1986, 88. Also won Canadian Invitational Pairs

(Calcutta) 1993. Organizing chairman Summer NABC 1967, past president Eastern Canadian B.C. and Ontario Unit, former director of District 2. Devised Murray 2♦ convention. Co-authored Drury convention. Contributing editor *Bridge Encyclopedia*.

MURTHY, Ravindra (1966-2001) of Berkeley CA. Was member of Junior Corps, placed 4th 1991 World Junior Championship, 2nd Junior Team Trials 1990, won Forbo International Teams 1994 (Holland), GNOT, Life Master Open Pairs 1993; placed 2nd Mixed Pairs 1990, Blue Ribbon Pairs 1992. Won 25-35 regional events.

MURTINHO, Maria Elisabeth (Lizzie) (b. 1946-deceased) of Rio de Janeiro, Brazil, clinical psychologist. WBF World Master. Won South American Women's Teams 1972, 73, 75, 80, 81, 83, 90. Represented Brazil in 9 world championships. Former bridge editor of *Jornal do Brasil*.

MUSUMECI, Joseph (b. 1921) of Richardson TX, retired Air Force officer, bridge teacher, writer. Coach and trainer of famed Aces team. Coached numerous U.S. international teams 1970-84, captain of U.S. team 1983. Former president San Antonio B.L. Associated with the late Ira Corn in the bridge column *Aces on Bridge* and ghost contributor to other Aces publications. Won District 16 GNOT and Zonal GNOT 1983.

N

NADAR, Kiran (b. 1951) of Delhi, India. WBF World Master. Won BFAAME Women's Teams 1989, 2nd 1991. Represented India in 9 world championships. Won 4 national titles.

NAGUIB, Sherif of Cairo, Egypt, WBF World Master. Won BFAAME Open Teams 1989, 2nd 1995. Represented Egypt in several world and other international championships.

NAGY, Edward A. (Ed) (b. 1946) of Oakland CA, attorney. Won Master Mixed Teams 1979; placed 2nd Open Pairs 1989, Life Master Open Pairs 1993. Won numerous regionals.

NAGY, Peter I. (b. 1942) of Chicago IL, formerly of Montreal, options trader and professional bridge player. Served as District one representative to ACBL Board of Governors 1979-82. Born in Budapest, escaped Communist Hungary in 1957 with his uncle, immigrating to Canada. Spoke neither French nor English, but by 1958 was at top of his class and was valedictorian of his high school class in 1961. After graduating from Princeton in 1967, Nagy worked in the computer field until 1974. One of the leading players, WBF Life Master, placed 2nd World Championship Open Pairs 1978, 90; 3rd Rosenblum Teams 1982, 5th 1978, 90, 9th 1986. Won Men's BAM Teams 1978, GNOT 1991, Vanderbilt 1993, Open Swiss Teams 1995. 2nd Amateur Swiss Teams 1977, Blue Ribbon Pairs 1978, Vanderbilt 1980, 84; Spingold 1982, Men's Swiss Teams 1989, Reisinger 1994, GNOT 1995. Won CNTC 1980, 81. Won more than 50 regional events. Won IBPA Best Bid Hand of the Year Award 1977 and Bols Brillancy Prize for best defensive hand in World Team Olympiad 1980. (see also IBPA AWARDS.)

NAGY, Zoltan (b. 1946) of Adelaide, Australia, born in Hungary, public servant. Won South Pacific playoff 1974 and represented Australia in 9 Far East Championships. Winner of numerous national titles.

NAIL, Betty (Mrs. G. Robert) (b. 1923) of Houston TX retired, bridge club owner. She and late husband, G.R. (Bobby) Nail opened their club in Houston, 1959, with Julie (now Julie Harding) and Mervin Key. Won Women's Pairs 1958.

NAIL, G. Robert (Bobby) (1925-1995) of Houston TX, bridge teacher and writer. Nail, with wife Betty, Julie (now Julie Harding) and Mervin Key opened duplicate club called The Bridge Studio of Houston. It was sold and Nail opened a rubber bridge club that continued for 30 years (until his death). It is still in operation under name "The Club." One of the most successful American players of the postwar period, WBF Life Master, member ACBL Hall of Fame. Represented North America in Bermuda Bowl 1962, 63 (placed 2nd). Originator of Big Diamond System and co-author of *Winning Duplicate, How to Play the Hand,* and *Revolution in Bridge.* Nail won Team Trials 1962, Men's Teams 1965, Life Master Men's Pairs 1974, Vanderbilt 1967, Life Master Pairs 1974. Placed 2nd Men's Pairs 1949, Spingold 1953, 62; Chicago (now the Reisinger) 1960, Men's Teams 1961, 64, 88; Life Master Pairs 1979, Blue Ribbon Pairs 1980, Vanderbilt 1985, GNOP 1989.

NAIMAN, Jeff (b. 1967) of New York City, radiology resident. Founding member and president Yale Student Bridge Club 1986-89. Won Non-Life Master Pairs 1990.

NAKAMURA, Yoshiyuki (b. 1944) of Tokyo, Japan, bridge teacher. Far East champion 1985. WBF World Master. Represented Japan in 16 other Far East Championships and one World Team Olympiad. Won many national titles.

NANDHABIWAT, Somboon (1922-1996) of Bangkok, Thailand, president of pulp and paper company. Won PABF (Far East) Teams 1961, 63, 65. Represented Thailand in Bermuda Bowl 1966, 67; 5 other world championships and many other zonal championships. Former president Far East Bridge Federation and the Contract Bridge League of Thailand. Originated Bangkok Club System. Was Thailand's top masterpoint winner. Won every national title including Open Teams more than 10 times.

NARTIS, Evangelos (b. 1943) of Athens, Greece, born in Czechoslovakia. Represented Greece in 1988 World Team Olympiad, finishing 5th , the best performance ever by a Greek team. Won many national titles.

NASH, Garrett G. (1919-1997) of University City MO. Was former member U.S. International Table Tennis Team. Was ranked #1 in U.S.- 1939 and 3rd in world 1948. Former professional baseball player and U.S. Army officer. Won Vanderbilt 1962; had several regionals to his credit.

NASH, James L. (Jim) (b. 1946) of Omaha NE, professional bridge player, teacher and certified director (since 1984), former Medicare fraud and abuse investigator. Diamond Life Master, with over 13,600 MPs (3-01). He won all 6 events at Omaha sectional 1991. Staff writer for Unit 241 bridge publication. Has won 100 regional events.

NATHAN, Marc W. (b. 1953) of Miami FL, personnel manager. Won Open Pairs 1981, 2nd 1982.

NATHANSON, Neil L. (b. 1943) of Little Ferry NJ, pension fund auditor. Placed 2nd GNOT 1976 and won several regionals.

NEE, Leland J. (Lee) (b. 1933) of Auburn WA, retired USAF Lt. Col. Diamond Life Master with 16 regional wins.

NEEDHAM, Richard E. (1887-1956) of Greenville PA, bridge writer, tournament organizer and ABL tournament director. Was one of the most active tournament promoters in western Pennsylvania, Ohio, West Virginia and upstate New York for many years. Writings included *Auction Bridge Sidelights, Contract Bridge Condensed* and *Tournament Tactics at Contract Bridge.*

NEHMERT, Beate (Pony) (b. 1952) of Wiesbaden, Germany. WBF World Grand Master. Won Venice Cup 1995, 2nd 1993; 3rd World Women's Team Olympiad 2000. 2nd European Women's Teams 1991, 95; Women's Pairs 1991, 95.

NEIGER, Eugene J. (Gene) (b. 1936) of New York City, stockbroker. Won Spingold 1971, Vanderbilt 1972 and numerous regional titles.

NEILL, Bruce G. of Sydney, Australia, computer systems consultant. Represented Australia in 6 zonal championships. Won 8 national titles. (see RUBINSOHL.)

NELSON, Martin E. (b. 1944) of Annapolis MD, professor of nuclear/mechanical engineering. Diamond Life Master with over 9,000 MPs as of 3/2001. Won 23 regionals.

NEUFFER, Henry Happoldt (Hap) (b. 1950) of Columbia SC, store manager. Won Mixed Pairs 1993 and many regionals.

NEUMAN, Cyrus (b. 1921) of Miami FL, attorney. Won Spingold 1958, placed 2nd 1954.

NEUT, Jaap van der (b. 1959) of Amsterdam, Netherlands, bridge journalist. WBF World Master. Placed 3rd World Olympiad Teams 1992. Won National Open Teams 1991.

NEVINS, Emilie (b. 1912) of Ft. Lauderdale FL, retired social worker. Won Senior/Advanced Senior Masters Pairs 1956; placed 2nd Women's Pairs 1955.

NEWELL, Peter (b. 1962) of Wellington, New Zealand, policy analyst. WBF World Master. Won Far East Teams 1990, Far East Pairs 1991. Represented New Zealand 2 world championships and one other zonal championship. Won New Zealand pairs 4 straight years.

NEWLAND, Martin W. (b. 1945) of Ottawa ON, born in England, chartered accountant, fellow in Institute of Chartered Accountants in both England and Wales. Won Red Ribbon Pairs 1986.

NEWMAN, Peter (b. 1966) of Sydney, Australia, computer programmer. WBF World Master. 3rd World Junior Teams 1991, won PABF (Far East) Junior Teams 1990. Represented Australia in one other world championship and on 2 other occasions. Won several national titles.

NEWTON, Mark of Long Melford, England. Author of program to score world-wide games, network administrator at world championships.

NEXON, Baron Robert de (1892-1967) of Paris, France, perfume company president, racer and breeder of horses. One of the great figures in the world of international bridge. One of the founders of World Bridge Federation in 1958. He served as its first president until 1964 when he became President Emeritus. In 1948, with Herman Dedichen, helped to revive the European Bridge League and was its president 1950-65, then President Emeritus. President of French Bridge Federation 1941-65. Won European Teams 1935 and represented EBL in World Championship match against the Four Aces later that year. Npc of many French teams. Many national wins include Open Teams and Open Pairs. Co-author, with Pierre Albarran, of *Notre Methode de Bridge* (1935), the basis of modern French point-count bidding, and of 3 other books.

NICHOLSON, Joyce (b. 1919) of Melbourne, Australia, journalist, author and publisher. Member of the Order of Australia for services to writing and the book-publishing industry. Won National Women's Individual 1983. Editor and publisher of *Australian Bridge* 1985-1989. Author of *Why Women Lose at Bridge*, a feminist analysis.

NICKELL, Frank T. (Nick) (b. 1947) of Raleigh NC, president and CEO Kelso and Co. WBF Grand Master, ranked #32 in world. Won Bermuda Bowl 1995, 99; placed 2nd 1997. Diamond Life Master with more than 9700 MPs. Won Blue Ribbon Pairs 1991, Spingold 1993, 94, 95, 96, 98, 99; Reisinger 1993, 94, 95; Vanderbilt 2000. He finished 2nd in GNOT 1983, Vanderbilt 1996, Open BAM Teams 1998, 99. Won Cavendish Pairs 1998 and was on winning Corporate America Team when they defeated the team from U.S. Congress 1993; won numerous regional titles.

NIEBERDING, Joseph H. (b. 1908) of St. Louis MO, retired executive. Won bridge events in 7 decades beginning in 1930. Had several regional wins.

NIEMEIJER, Chris (b. 1946) of Broek in Waterland, The Netherlands, project manager, computer systems. WBF World Master. Represented The Netherlands in 3 zonal championships. Several national titles. A notable theorist, he developed the Biedermeier (Dutch) standard of bidding, based on a survey of 100 Dutch experts. Coach of Dutch Women's Team since 1987. Author of 2 books and contributor to Bridge.

NIKOLOV, Ivan (b. 1927) of Sofia, Bulgaria, professor of sociology. Founded Bulgarian Bridge Federation 1979, and served as president until 1989. Dismissed from Bulgarian Communist Party in 1988 after presiding over first public meeting of Bulgaria's dissident organization.

NILSLAND, Mats (b. 1950) of Malmo, Sweden, computer programmer. WBF World Life Master. Was 3rd Bermuda Bowl 1991, Rosenblum Teams 1986, 98. Represented Sweden in 3 other world championships. 2nd European Teams 1991, 93; 2nd Nordic Championships twice, 2nd Vanderbilt 1993. Won 5 Swedish titles. Author or coauthor of 6 books on bridge.

NIPPGEN, George of Karlsruhe, Germany. WBF World Master. Won World Teams 1990.

NIST, Barbara L. (b. 1940) of Bellevue WA, research interviewer Fred Hutchinson Cancer Research Center. President Unit 446 1989-90, President District 19 1992-93, NACB co-chair 1993. Member ACBL Board of Directors since 1998.

NOLAND, Helen (Heitie) (1920-91) of Lake Charles LA. Diamond Life Master, Won World Mixed Teams 1972, placed 2nd World Mixed Pairs 1978, Women's Teams 1973. Numerous regional titles.

NOOIJEN, Marcel (b. 1963) of Amsterdam, The Netherlands, chemist. WBF World Master. 3rd World Teams 1992. World Junior Team champion 1987. European Junior Team champion 1986. Won National Open Teams 1991.

NORANTE, Barbara of Butler PA. World-wide winner of Epson Pairs 1988 and of several regional events.

NORDBY, Harald (b. 1941) of Oslo, Norway, systems analyst. 3rd World Team Olympiad 1980. Won Nordic Teams 1971, 78, 82. Represented Norway in 3 World and 7 European Championships. Many national titles. Top Norwegian masterpoint holder.

NORDENSON, Britt (formerly Blom, Nygren) (b. 1925) of Norrkoping, Sweden. WBF World Life Master. Won World Women's Teams 1968, European Women's Teams 1967, Nordic Women's Teams 6 times. Won 14 national titles.

NORMAN, Barbara B. (b 1931) of La Jolla CA, retired high school teacher. Member ACBL Charity Foundation. Won 20+ regionally rated events.

NORRIS, Georg (b. 1941) of Birkerød, Denmark, engineer. Represented Denmark in Bermuda Bowl 1993 and World Team Olympiads 1972, 80; also 2 European Championships. Won EEC Mixed Teams 1989. Won 3 Danish Open Teams 1992 and 3 Danish Cups. Partners include his wife Judy and their son John with whom he won the Danish Open Teams 1992 and played in Bermuda Bowl 1993.

NORRIS, Judy (1940-1995) of Birkerød, Denmark, correspondent. Won Women's Team Olympiad 1988, Nordic Championship 1988, EEC Mixed Teams 1989. Represented Denmark twice in the World Team Olympiad partnered by her husband Georg. Represented Denmark in 6 European Championships. 19 Danish championships.

NORTH, Frederick (Freddy) of Hove, England, bridge writer and teacher. Bridge cruise director for P&O. Represented Britain in 2 world championships, and England in Camrose Trophy matches. Many national wins. Author and co-author of many books. Magazine contributor.

NORWOOD, Barbara B. (Mrs. Robert) (b. 1938) of Austin TX. Served in various executive positions on Unit and District level. Norwood won Women's Pairs 1980, 2nd 1984. Won several regional titles including District 16 GNOP 1981.

NORWOOD, John W., Jr. (b. 1908) of Greenville SC, attorney. ACBL president 1967, Chairman of Board 1968; member WBF Executive Council in the 60's and of ACBL Board of Directors 1961-76. Won several regionals.

NOSZKA, Gloria E. (1923-1983) of Pittsburgh PA, real estate agent. Represented U.S. in international competition Stockholm 1970, Las Palmas 1974. Won Women's Pairs 1969.

NOVAK, Phyllis (b. 1927) of Seattle WA, real estate investor. Won Women's Pairs, Mixed Pairs 1958, Women's Teams 1962 and many regional events.

NOVAK, Ruth M. (b. 1909) of Camarillo CA, bridge teacher, former full-time director for 10-15 years while living in Illinois. Member ACBL Charity Committee and served in varied positions on Unit and District level. Novak received an Outstanding Service Award for her work for charity 1977. Won Women's Teams 1962.

NOVRUP, Svend (b. 1945) of Denmark. Bridge journalist and author. Bridge columnist for Copenhagen newspaper *Politiken* 1970-2000. Author of more than 70 books of which around half are about bridge. Others include an encyclopedia of chess as well as books on backgammon, poker, snooker, Tour de France. Commentator at Eurosport television since 1996. Keen bridge theorist.

NOWAK, Janusz (b. 1927) of Warsaw, Poland, retired WBF World Life Master. Won European Senior Pairs 1995, European Senior Teams 1995. 2nd European Open Teams 1970, 3rd European Senior Pairs 1993. Won Senior Teams Bermuda 2000. Represented Poland in many World and European Championships. Won many national titles.

NUDELMAN, Barbara N. (b. 1931) of Chicago IL, retired advertising executive. President of ACBL 1993, Chairman of the Board 1994. Served as ACBL repre-

sentative to WBF Executive Council 1994-97. Member ACBL Board of Directors for District 13 from 1985-97, Chairman ACBL Board of Governors 1983, 84; president of ACBL Educational Foundation 1991-92 and has served on many other ACBL committees. Held various executive positions in Chicago Contract B.A. (including president) since 1968. Won numerous regional events.

NUNES, Jack (b. 1912) of London, England, company director. Represented England in numerous Camrose matches. Many national wins include 4 Gold Cups. His book *Improve Your Bridge* was the basis for 2 instructional TV series.

NUTTING, Ann (formerly Jacobson) (b. 1940) of San Francisco CA, CPA. Diamond Life Master, won North American Swiss Teams 1981 and numerous regionals.

NUTTING, Willard H. III (Bill) (b. 1945) of San Francisco CA, vice president; past president of Unit 197 and former treasurer of District 21. Nutting won GNOP 1982.

O

OAKEY, Larry B. (b. 1937) of Minneapolis MN, retired air traffic controller and broker. District 14 recorder 1985-present; R 1 tournament director, president local B.C. Contributor to *Gopher, Viking Bridge News* and was bridge columnist for *Sun* newspapers. A Diamond Life Master, Oakey placed 2nd Men's Teams 1978, played on Minneapolis Inter-City Match Team 1968 (won), 1969 (lost). Has won over 40 regionals including District 14 GNOT 1985, 86, 87.

OAKIE, Donald A. (Don) (formerly Donald Akira Aoki) (1914-1983) of San Jose CA. Was one of the leading American bridge personalities. He was the first of Japanese descent to win Bermuda Bowl (1954) and first ACBL member to become a Life Master with all points (300) being red. He represented the U.S. in international play - Turin 1960. He won Spingold 1953, Chicago (now the Reisinger) 1958 and placed 2nd Men's Pairs 1959. He also won numerous regionals. For many years Oakie was involved with bridge administration. He was ACBL president 1976, chairman of ACBL Board of Directors 1977, a Board member 1967-81, co-chairman of ACBL Laws Commission from 1975, WBF Laws Commission 1974, president of Western Conference 1966. Oakie was principal draftsman of the revised American format of 1974 *ACBL HANDBOOK* 1973, 74, 75. He authored *Simplified Standard American Bridge Bidding* and was named "Sportsman of the Year" by IBPA - 1976 (see IPBA AWARDS.)

OAKS, Alan W. (b. 1938) of Germantown TN, retired director for ACBL Member Services Dept. Former ACBL Operations Manager and executive secretary of ACBL Charity Foundation. Frequent contributor to ACBL *Bulletin*. Some of his many regional wins include Summer NABC secondary Golder Pairs 1987.

O'BRIEN, Patrick L. (P.L.) (1943-1993) of Berkeley CA, counselor for the Hemophilia Foundation. O'Brien, a hemophiliac, was a member of National Hemophilia Society, an honorary member of Royal Hemophilia Society and served as president of Disabled Students Advisory Committee at Yuba College 1986. Won several regionals. (see HANDICAPPED PLAYERS.)

ODLUND, Britt-Marie (Bim) (b. 1945) of Stockholm,

Sweden, civil engineer. WBF World Master. Placed 3rd Venice Cup 1993. Won European Women's Teams 1993, Nordic Women's Teams 1982, 84. Represented Sweden in 2 other world championships and 3 other zonal championships. Won 4 national titles.

O'DOHERTY, Eileen (d. 1992) of Ireland. Won Common Market Women's Teams 1980. Represented Ireland in one world championship and many zonal championships, during an international career spanning 40 years. Won many national titles, including Open Teams and Open Pairs. Reached European Women's Pairs final in an octogenarian partnership with Ann Quinn shortly before her death.

O'DOWD, John (b. 1929) of Hamilton ON, computer operator and bookkeeper. Served on Unit 166 Board of Directors for 5 years and is founder and 1st president of Hamilton and District B.A. 1966-72. Won Canadian National Open Teams 1958.

OEST, John N. (Jack) (b. 1952) of Chicago IL, attorney. Served as Unit president and is presently on District Judiciary Committee. Represented ACBL in international play Bal Harbour 1986, Pan-American Games 1992, Rhodes 1996. Has been a contributor to Chicago *Kibitzer*. Diamond Life Master - won GNOT 1991, 95; International Team Trial 1996. Placed 2nd GNOT 1984, 88. Has won 15-20 regional events. Oest was instrumental in putting together the Eric Rodwell/Jeff Meckstroth partnership.

O'GRADY, Angeline (Andy) of Miami FL, professional bridge teacher and player. Assistant coach and captain for 1999 Junior World Championships -won silver medal. Placed 4th World Senior Teams 1998. Placed 2nd Women's BAM Teams 1988 and won ACBL-Wide International Fund Game 1975. Diamond Life Master with more than 10,800 MPs, has won more than 175 regional titles.

OGUST, Harold A. (1916-1978) of New York City, plastics manufacturer, travel agent. Was president and founder of Goren International, Inc. Originator of Ogust Rebids after Weak Two-Bids and an outstanding player. He represented U.S. in Bermuda Bowl 1957, World Team Olympiad 1960. He won Spingold 1956, 60; Reisinger 1957, 63.

OHNO, Kyoko (b. 1946) of Tokyo, Japan, computer systems engineer. WBF World Master. 2nd Far East Women's Team Championship 1986. Represented Japan in 5 open world championships and one women's world championship. Won national Open Teams 30 times and national Open Pairs 14 times.

OKEN, Daniel (Dan) (b. 1917) of Ajijic, Mexico, retired real estate and land developer. Oken is a certified director, has served as tournament chairman in 2 Units; member Board of Directors for Unit 205. Has won over 20 regionals.

OKEN, Louise (Mrs. Daniel) (1937-1983) of Miami FL, real estate developer. Won Mixed Pairs 1966 and several regional events.

OLDROYD, Rita (1921-2000) of Yorkshire, England. WBF World Life Master. Placed 2nd Venice Cup 1976. Won European Women's Teams 1975, 79. First woman grand master in English rankings and first woman to play for England in a Camrose match.

OLIVEIRA, Manuel Vasques (b. 1944) of Lisbon, Portugal, chemical engineer. Represented Portugal in one World and one European championship. Won European Union Open Teams 1998. Won many national titles.

OLIVIERI, Gabriella (b. 1952) of Valenza, Italy. WBF World Master. 3rd 1987 Venice Cup. Won EEC Women's

Pairs 1998, 2nd European Women's Teams 1987, European Women's Pairs 1997.

OLMEDO ZUMARAN, Alejandro (b. 1902) of Buenos Aires, Argentina, solicitor. Won South American Teams 1951, 53, 57. 8 national titles.

O'LOUGHLIN, Walter K. (1910-1989) of Towson MD, retired executive, graduated Catholic University of America. Served as ACBL president 1978, ACBL Director 1962-65, 1971-80; ACBL Treasurer 1973-75, president Maryland B.A. 1956, president Mid-Atlantic Conference 1970-72. O'Loughlin had several regional credits to his name.

OLSEN, Jack (b. 1925) of Rollinsville CO, journalist and author. Formerly wrote for *Sports Illustrated*. He is author of *The Mad World Of Bridge* and co-author of *A New Approach to Bridge*.

OLSON, Jeffrey A. (b. 1958) of Dallas TX, insurance agent and financial consultant, bridge professional. Diamond Life Master with 35 regional wins.

O'MALIA, Bernard E. (Barney) (1904-1994) of Kailua-Kona HI, casino owner. Placed 2nd Reisinger 1978 and won numerous regional titles.

ONDERWYZER, Steven J. (b. 1941) of Marina Del Ray CA, retired private investor, lingerie manufacturer, electrical engineer. Diamond Life Master with approximately 25 regional wins. Won Pond Point Championship (OKBridge) 1999 (for best tournament record).

ONG, Ah Moy (b. 1909) of Kuala Lumpur, Malaysia. Represented Malaysia in 6 zonal championship. Won 1975 Far East Open Pairs.

ONORATI, Mario (b. 1928) of Caracas, Venezuela, born in Italy, insurance broker. WBF World Master. Won South American Teams 1963, 65, 66. Won CAC Teams 1973, 77, 84, 85, 86, 87, 91, 93. Represented Venezuela in 12 world championships. Won many national titles.

ONSTOTT, John H. (b. 1944) of New Orleans LA, brokerage firm owner. Served on ACBL Board of Governors 1981-87, as vice-president of Louisiana B.A., co-chairman New Orleans Summer NABC 1983. Won North American Swiss Teams 1998; placed 2nd North American Swiss Teams 1983, GNOT 1987, 97; Spingold 1999. Onstott is an ACBL Grand Life Master with 12,768 MPs as of 3/2001 and has won more than 100 regional titles.

OPPEN, Carol G. J. von (b.1935) of Amsterdam, The Netherlands, bridge-tour operator. WBF World Master. Placed 3rd World Teams 1980. Represented The Netherlands in 4 other world championships and 2 European Championships. Won Common Market Teams. Many national titles. Author of 4 books.

OPPENHEIMER, Tom (b. 1949) of Ballwin MO, financial analyst with Anheuser Busch. Served as member of ACBL Board of Governors and District 8 Board of Directors. Placed 2nd IMP Pairs 1992. Won many regional championships including District 8 GNOT 1988.

O'REILLY, Edward C. (Ed) (b. 1936) of Kingston ON, bridge club owner, teacher, director formerly a public health administrator. O'Reilly has served as an executive member of Unit Board for 15 years, District 1 treasurer for 5 years and as member ACBL Board of Governors for 2 years. He founded Brockville D.B.C. and assisted in founding 3 other clubs. He writes weekly bridge column for *Kingston Whig-Standard*. Represented Canada internationally Las Palmas 1974. Won a few regionals.

ORNSTEIN, Alexander J. (Alex) (b. 1962) of Roslyn Heights NY, vice president and managing director of private investment company, attorney. Competed to quarter-finals of Bermuda Bowl 1991. Placed 2nd Epson (Japan) Open Swiss 1984. Won Mixed BAM Teams 2000, college bridge trials 1984. Won 20 or more regionals.

O'ROURKE, Lou Ann of Portola Valley, CA. Placed 3rd Cavendish Teams in first appearance. Won more than 15 regionals in 1998-2001.

ORTIZ-PATINO, Jaime of Marbella, Spain, and London, England, formerly of Geneva, Switzerland. WBF World Life Master. Has business interests throughout the world. President of World Bridge Federation 1976-86, president emeritus 1986-to date. WBF vice president 1974-75, treasurer European Bridge League 1974-75. As WBF president he was instrumental in forming 2 new zones – Central American-Caribbean, Asia and the Middle East. He also added many new countries to the WBF roster, including the People's Republic of China. General chairman and chief organizer of Geneva World Championships 1990.

He was the prime force behind the introduction of bidding screens at international tournaments, despite strong opposition from world figures who insisted that screens would denaturalize and dehumanize tournament bridge. Screens were used for the first time in world competition at the Bermuda Bowl in Southampton, Bermuda in 1975. The competitors were virtually unanimous in their approval. The screens allowed them to relax on their side of the curtain. They didn't have to fear they might be transmitting unwitting messages to partner through body language. He also fostered, along with others, the use of bidding boxes, a move that cut the noise level tremendously. He attempted to do something about destructive bidding systems that were invading international tournaments. He feels he was too late to stop the influx, but he helped design a complex convention card that makes it incumbent on all pairs to explain exactly what their system consists of, including follow-up bids. He also felt very strongly that international bridge should be on the highest possible ethical ground. He took major steps during his presidency to ensure the upgrading of ethics, and he was eminently successful. He also is a strong believer in Junior bridge and has attended almost all major world Junior championships.

Represented Switzerland in World Team Olympiad 1964, 68; World Open Pairs 1962, Rosenblum Teams 1982, European Championships 1955, 56, 59, 61, 62, 63, 65, 67. Placed 5th World Par Point Contest 1961. Swiss national titles include Open Teams 1953, 56, 59, 61; KO Teams 1955, 56, 60, 62, 63.

Patino now has major interests in golf. His own golf course in Spain — Valderrama –was the site of 1997 Ryder Cup and also has been the site of other major world-class tournaments.

OSBERG, Sharon (b. 1949) of San Francisco CA, bank executive. Member ACBL Appeals Committee beginning in 1991. WBF World Master, won Venice Cup 1991, 93; placed 2nd Transnational Mixed Teams 1996. She was semi-finalist in Venice Cup 1987 and placed 13th World Women's Pairs 1986. She has placed 2nd in USWBC (Teams Trials). Won Master Mixed Teams 1979, Women's KO Teams 1986, 91; Women's BAM Teams 1988. Was 2nd Women's Pairs 1986, Women's BAM Teams 1987, Women's Team Trials 1987, 91, 93; Women's Swiss Teams 1990, Open Swiss Teams 1995. She is a frequent partner to Warren Buffett and Bill Gates.

OSBORN, Florence (d. 1985) of Mount Carmen CT, bridge columnist and lecturer in the humanities. Was

bridge editor of New York *Herald Tribune* (from 1936 until the newspaper was discontinued in 1966) and of the New York *American*. Her writings include *How's Your Bridge Game?* Osborn formerly conducted a bridge interview radio program and made many television appearances. She was stabbed to death in her home.

OSHLAG, Mary B. (b. 1942) of Germantown TN, former ACBL headquarters staff member. Finished 2nd Master Mixed Teams 1989, Women's KO Teams 1999. Won several regionals including District 10 GNOP.

OSHLAG, Richard J. (b. 1945) of Germantown TN, ACBL computer programmer/analyst. Oshlag served as business manager for ACBL *Bulletin* from 1969-84, ACBL programmer from 1984-88. He returned to ACBL as computer specialist in 1993.Diamond Life Master, placed 2nd Master Mixed Teams 1989. He has many regional wins including District 10 GNOT 1978, 88, 2000; District 10 GNOP 1986, 90, 91.

OSIE, Judith (b. 1936) of Johannesburg, South Africa, professional kaluki player. WBF World Master. Represented South Africa in World Women's Teams 1976, 80, 2000; Maccabi Games 1977. 6 national wins.

OSOFSKY, Aileen of New York City, has served as Chairman of ACBL Goodwill Committee since 1985, as a Director of ACBL Educational Foundation since 1989, for many years as a member of ACBL Board of Governors and for over 10 years on GNYBA Board. Won several regional events.

OSTRICH, Dr. Nathan (b. 1928) of Lafayette LA, optometrist. Founder of S.W. Louisiana Unit. He produced the TV series *Play Bridge with the Experts*.

OSTROW, Albert A. (1910-1961) of Malverne NY. He was an authority on card games and the author of numerous books, among them, *The Complete Card Player* and *The Bridge Player's Bedside Companion*. He was a consultant on card games to Association of American Playing Card Manufacturers 1960-61.

O'SULLIVAN, James de Courey (1024-1982) of Brisbane, Australia, owner of printing and stationery business. Chairman of WBF Zone 7 from 1973. President of Australian Bridge Federation many times starting in 1971. Member WBF Executive in Seventies. Commemorated in O'Sullivan Trust, which makes loans to Australian clubs.

OTSTAVEL, Ain (b. 1942) of Tartu, Estonia, entrepeneur. Won Soviet Union Teams and Pairs 1984; Estonian Teams 1971, 79, 83, 84, 89; Estonian Pairs 1970, 78, 83. 2nd Cavendish Invitational Pairs 1989. Represented Soviet Union in one zonal championship. Devised Tartu Strong Pass System.

OTTLIK, Geza (1912-1900) of Budapest, Hungary, novelist, essayist, bridge writer. Co-author *Adventures in Card Play* which introduced and developed many new concepts: Entry Squeeze, Backwash Squeeze, Elopement, Elbow-Room, Entry-Shifting Play, Non-Material Plays, Rio Finesse, KO Squeeze. Author of many magazine articles, one of which won IBPA's Article of the Year Award 1968 (the 1st time it was awarded). His novel, *A School at the Frontier,* was translated into many languages. In 1985 received Kossuth Prize for Literature. Represented Hungary in international matches 1936-38, 71-72. In Hungary known as ultimate authority on Hungarian prose.

OUDSHOORN, Nicolaus D. (Nico) (1906-1993) of Rijswijk, The Netherlands. Tournament manager of European Championships 1963, 65, 66; World Team Olympiad 1968, World Pair Olympiad 1974. Honorary EBL

Tournament Director.

OUIMET, Jean G. (b. 1934) of Hollywood FL, born in Montreal, retired from UASF. Won over 20 regionals.

OUTRED, Vi (nee Mitchell) of Kilsyth, Scotland, teacher. Represented Britain in one world championship and one European Championship. Represented Scotland 4 times in Camrose Trophy matches. Many national wins include Scottish Cup 4 times.

OWEN, Ernest D., Jr. (1942-1995) of Warwick Bermuda, permanent secretary, Ministry of Labor and Home Affairs. Served on ACBL Board of Governors and Executive Committee of Bermuda B.C. Owen represented Bermuda in world play Miami 1972, 86; Monte Carlo 1976, Valkenburg 1980, Biarritz 1982. He represented Bermuda in Pan American Games in Mexico City 1975. Won several regional events and was twice the recipient of the Norman Bach Trophy. Killed by a drunk driver when returning home from Bermuda Bridge Club.

OXLEY, John F. (b. 1945) of St. Joseph MO, company president. Diamond Life Master has been on Top 500 list for last 10+ years. Won 45 to 50 regionals including District 15 GNOT 1986, 93; GNOP 1991.

O'YANG, Helen (b. 1955) of Taipei, Taiwan, accountant. WBF World Master. Won Far East Women's Teams 1988. Represented Taiwan in Venice Cup - 1985, 91.

OZORIO, L.A. (b. 1911) of Hong Kong, businessman. Won Far East Open Teams 1959, 60 and represented Hong Kong 2 other times.

P

PABIS-TICCI, Camillo (b. 1920) of Florence, Italy, engineer. WBF Grand Master, 7th in world career listings 1992. Won World Team Olympiad 1964, 68, 72; Bermuda Bowl 1963, 65, 66, 67, 69. Columnist and magazine contributor.

PACHECO, Morella of Caracas, Venezuela. WBF World Master. Won CAC Women's Teams 1979, 80, 81, 82, 87, 91. Represented Venezuela in more than 8 world championships, won many national titles.

PADUA, Letitia de (Letty) formerly of the Philippines, businesswoman. Represented Philippines in world and Far East championships. As president of Philippine CBA, was chief organizer of 1977 Bermuda Bowl and Far East championships.

PADGET, John E. (b. 1948) of Concord CA, consultant. Wrote *Bridge and You* (1975). Placed 10th on Top 500 -1971 and 72. Won 25+ regionals.

PAGAN, Shirley (b. 1932) of Corpus Christi TX. Unit board member for many years. President District 16 1993, member ACBL Education Foundation, ACBL Goodwill Committee. Was chairman WBF Pan-American Championships - Corpus Christi 1992. Chaired many District 16 sectionals and 1 regional.

PALMER, Beth (b. 1952) of Silver Spring MD, attorney. One of the leading women players. WBF Life Master, won Venice Cup 1987, 89; placed 2nd World Championship Women's Pairs 1982, 4th 1990, Transnational Women's Teams 2000. Palmer is an ACBL Grand Life Master with 10,945 MPs as of 3/2001, Her many national credits include Master Mixed Teams 1982, 92, 93; Life Master Women's Pairs 1983, 85; Women's KO Teams 1985, 99; Mixed Pairs 1985, North American Women's

Swiss Teams 1987,95, 96; Women's BAM Teams 1993, 95. She placed 2nd Women's KO Teams 1986, 92, 94 97; Life Master Women's Pairs 1989, Women's BAM Teams 1991.

PANG, Vern (b. 1950) of Walnut CA, senior project manager. Has won over 20 regionals.

PAPP, Balint (b. 1921) of Daytona Beach FL, born in Soviet Union, raised in Hungary, technical interpreter. After a brief stint in Hungarian Army he spent 7 years as POW in the Soviet Union. After his release he worked as an interpreter and was Hungarian National Platform Diving Champion 1952, 53; coach of Hungarian Olympic Diving Team 1956. Papp defected to U.S. in 1956. Diamond Life Master, has won 17 regionals, including FL State Team Campionship.

PARENT, Henri F. (b. 1925) of Montreal, company president. Served as an ACBL District Director 1967-79, representative to WBF Executive Council and past president of Montreal B.L., and District 1. Parent contributed to the organizing and sanctioning of a bridge club in a terminal patient hospital. He won Canadian National Open Teams 1960, Can-Am Men's Pairs, Open Teams 1967.

PARKER, Abner (Ab) (1902-1988) of Los Angeles CA, born in Russia, management consultant. Former Director of ACBL Charity Foundation. He organized the first District-wide Charity game.

PARKER, Joshua B. (b. 1956) of Briarcliff Manor NY, alternative investment manager, attorney. Served GNYBA as president and general counsel, chairman Conduct & Ethics Committee. Competed in world play Bal Harbour 1986, Won Men's BAM Teams 1985 and 18+ regional events. He was the youngest winner of William Keohane Individual.

PARKER, Steven J. (b. 1945) of Brookville MD, human resources director. Served on Washington B.L. Board of Directors 1967-77. Won World Mixed Teams 1974. ACBL wins include the Reisinger 1972, Mixed Pairs 1969, 76; placed 2nd Master Mixed Teams 1973, Reisinger 1976, GNOT 1977. Parker is a Diamond Life Master and has won over 100 regional events and has been Washington B.L. Player of the Year 3 times.

PARNES, Gordon M. (b. 1947) of Flint MI, teacher. Past president EMBA and of District 12. Diamond Life Master, won 20-30 regionally rated events.

PARNES, Susan M. (b. 1944) of Flint MI, teacher. Past president Eastern Michigan BC. Club manager, director (10 years). Won 20-30 regionals.

PARTOS, George (1907-1986) of Miami Beach FL. Owned one of the largest private collections of bridge books and periodicals. Contributing editor, *Bridge Encyclopedia*.

PAS, Marijke van der (b. 1949) of Utrecht, The Netherlands, bridge journalist. WBF World Grand Master, #28 among women in world. Won World Women's Team Olympiad 2000. Placed 2nd Venice Cup 1989, 3rd World Women's Team Olympiad 1984. Won European Women's Pairs 1980, 2nd 1987; 2nd European Women's Teams, 1983, 89. Won Netherlands Women's Pairs many times. Represented Netherlands regularly since 1979. Columnist, author and contributor to *Bridge*.

PASQUINI, Paulo (b. 1944) of Caracas, Venezuela, born in Italy, business executive, bridge teacher. WBF World Master. Won CAC Teams 1977, 84, 85, 86, 87, 91. Represented Venezuela in several world championships. More than 30 national titles.

PASSELL, Michael (Mike) (b. 1947) of Dallas TX, professional bridge player. One of the leading American players. Learned to play bridge during high school vacations by watching his brother William teach bridge classes. Passell ranks #2 in all-time masterpoint holders. ACBL Grand Life Master with 45,315 MPs 3/2001, trailing only Paul Soloway. WBF Grand Master, won Bermuda Bowl 1979, placed 2nd 1977, 4th 1983; 2nd World Team Olympiad 1980, 4th Rosenblum Teams 1982, 9th 1978, 90. He also represented ACBL Biarritz 1982. He and wife Nancy Passell are one of only a handful of couples who are both world champions. Won McKenney Trophy (now the Crane Top 500) 1976, Mott-Smith Trophy 1978, 83; Fishbein Trophy 1978. Won Reisinger 1976, 88, 92; Vanderbilt 1978, 82; Spingold 1978, 86, 87; Open Pairs 1978, 83; GNOT 1981, Men's BAM Teams 1986, 88, 93; IMP Pairs 1988, Open Swiss Teams 1991, 96, Open Pairs I 1999. Placed 2nd Vanderbilt 1976, 97, 98; Life Master Pairs 1976; Reisinger 1980, 90, 93, 94, 96; Mixed Pairs 1982, Men's Pairs 1983, Spingold 94, 97; Open BAM Teams 1995, Mixed BAM Teams 1996, GNOT 1998. Won several hundred regionals.

PASSELL, Nancy L. (b. 1949) of Dallas TX, professional bridge player, former teacher. WBF World Master, won Venice Cup 1991. She and husband Mike Passell are the only U.S. couple to win the Bermuda Bowl and Venice Cup. Won Life Master Women's Pairs 1988, Women's KO Teams 1991, Mixed BAM Teams 1996. Placed 2nd Mixed Pairs 1982, Women's KO Teams 1983; Women's BAM Teams 1988, North American Women's Swiss Teams 1990. She has won 50+ regionals.

PASSELL, William L. (Bill) (b. 1930) of Coral Springs FL, bridge teacher and certified director. Grand Life Master with over 15,638 MPs as of 3/2001. Won Mixed Pairs 1960, Master Mixed Teams 1972, Fishbein Trophy, Spingold 1985. Placed 2nd GNOT 1980, North American Men's Swiss Teams 1984. Was 2nd in World Bidding Contest 1969. He has won over 100 regionals.

PATINO, Jaime Ortiz-. See ORTIZ-PATINO, JAIME.

PATRIAS, Christopher (Chris) (b. 1949) of St. Louis MO, ACBL national tournament director, tournament director field representative, former Director of Tournament Operations (ACBL) Headquarters, ACBL Bridge Administrator. Won Senior/Advanced Senior Masters Pairs 1972, District 14 GNOT 1979.

PATTERSON, Jean M. (formerly Wright) (b. 1947) of Memphis TN, has served ACBL in many capacities including tournament coordinator, marketing coordinator, customer service supervisor, manager of ACBL Sales and Marketing Department. Former associate editor *Bridge Builders Newsletter*.

PATTERSON, Lucille E. (Lucy) of Sacramento CA, secretary. Won Women's Pairs 1964. Diamond Life Master, with numerous regional wins.

PATTON, Major Charles Lee (1851-1941) was a pioneer of bridge organization from 1906. Born in Mississippi, resident of New York City after 1888. Patton was the originator of the Patton movement and one of those who claimed invention of the Takeout Double. (see Team-of-Four Movement.)

PAUL, Abe (b. 1943) of Roswell GA, born in Germany, retired actuary. Served local unit as Appeals Committee Chairman and Recorder, board member. Diamond Life Master, has won 25-30 regional events.

PAUL, Mariana (Mary) (b. 1933) of Toronto ON, born in Romania, accountant, bridge teacher. Board member Unit 116, recorder for Unit and District 2, member Conduct & Ethics Committees at some regionals and NABCs.

Authored *Partnership Bidding*. WBF World Master, placed 3rd Venice Cup 1989, 4th World Olympiad Women's Teams 1988, 7th 1980, 9th 1984; 5th Swiss Plate 1984. Represented Canada in other World Championship events 1968, 72, 78, 82, 86, 91, 92. Member of winning team of the first Canadian National Team Championship (CNTC) 1977, subsequently won it 1993, 2nd 1989. Former president Montreal Team-of-Four B.L. Has won many regional events.

PAUL, Maurice (Moose) (1923-86) of Toronto ON, born in Belgium. Created the first Team-of-Four Bridge League on North American continent, 1956 in Montreal. He served as member of ACBL Charity Foundation and NABC Appeals Committee. Besides his several regional wins he won Intercity Championship (Montreal vs Chicago) 1967.

PAULS, Brian A. (b. 1940) of Winnipeg MB, attorney. Legal counsel for Canadian Bridge Federation (pro tem), bridge editor for Winnipeg *Free Press* since 1962, contributing writer to *CBF News*. Won District 2 GNOT 1974.

PAULSEN, Erik (b. 1926) of Upland CA, born in Norway, aerospace engineer. A leading American player. WBF Life Master. ACBL Grand Life Master with 15,638 MPs as of 3/2001. Won Bermuda Bowl 1976, 2nd 1977; World Open Pairs 1970, 4th World Team Olympiad 1976. His national wins include Reisinger 1962, 68, 74, 75; Blue Ribbon Pairs 1969. Paulsen placed 2nd Men's Pairs 1959, Vanderbilt 1963, Reisinger 1966, Men's Swiss Teams 1988. Won many regional championships.

PAVLICEK, Richard (b. 1945) of Ft. Lauderdale FL, bridge teacher and writer. One of the leading American bridge players. WBF World Master, placed 6th Rosenblum Teams 1986. ACBL Grand Life Master with 15,213 MPs as of 3/2001. Author of a variety of teaching texts and co-author of *Modern Bridge Conventions*; contributor to various bridge publications. Former editor *Gold Coast Bridge News* and *Florida Bridge News*. Analyst for Royal Viking Instant Matchpoint Pairs 1987-93. He is an accomplished organist. He won GNOT 1973; Reisinger 1982, 83, 84, 90; Vanderbilt 1983, 86, 95; Open Swiss Teams 1992, 99; GNOT 1997. Placed 2nd Spingold 1978, GNOP 1982, North American Men's Swiss Teams 1984, GNOT 1992, Life Master Open Pairs 1994, Life Master Pairs 1995, 98.

PEAKE, Lyle R. (the Rhinestone Cowboy) (1944-1994) of Culver City CA, crypto-translator, professional bridge player, teacher, director. Peake ran the first ACBL duplicate club in East Africa, founded the American Bridge College 1985. A Diamond Life Master he won several regionals.

PEARSON, Don B. of Berkeley CA. Devised Pearson Point Count which states that 4th hand should open the bidding if the number of high card points and the number of spades total 15 or more – 14 is optional. Won Men's Teams 1970; placed 2nd Life Master Men's Pairs 1968 and won several regionals.

PECKETT, Heather, District 1 secretary since 1983, past president Unit 192, Diamond Life Master, won 15+ regionals.

PENCHARZ, William (Bill) (b. 1945) of London, England, solicitor. Won 4 national titles including Gold Cup. Past president EBL, member EBL executive. IBPA General Counsel 1991-2000. Member WBF Executive Council, member WBF Laws Commission. Former EBL Laws Committee chairman and EBU vice chairman.

PENDER, Peter A. (1936-1990) of Forestville CA, resort owner and executive director. Member ACBL Hall of Fame. Was one of the leading bridge players of the world. Served as commentator at numerous Team Trials and World Championships. Was a member of numerous Appeals Committees including for the WBF. Pender was a United States Figure Skating Association and Canadian Figure Skating Association gold medalist and former figure skating coach. He was director of Human Rights Foundation 1977, president of Russian Business Association 1980 and an accomplished pianist. In 1966, Pender helped England's Jeremy Flint to set a record in becoming a Life Master. The feat was accomplished in 11 weeks. At the time of his death Pender had become a multi-millionaire and bequeathed more than $2.26 million for Aids research.

A Grand Life Master with more than 10,000 MPs, Pender was a world champion and won Bermuda Bowl 1985, was 2nd in 1989. He was member of 1987 Bermuda Bowl Team but was unable to play because of his illness. Placed 2nd Rosenblum Teams 1982. Won Pan-American Invitational Pairs 1974, 75. He won Team Trials 1985, 87, 89; the McKenney Trophy 1966, the Reisinger 1968, 70, 81, 85, 86; Life Master Men's Pairs 1967, 84; GNOT 1982, 83, 85, 87; Vanderbilt 1984, 87. Was 2nd Mixed Pairs 1964, Reisinger 1971, 83; Spingold 1974, GNOP 1985. Pender was coach of United States World Women's Team 1972, 76 and Venice Cup Team 1976. He represented U.S. in Las Palmas 1974, Biarritz 1982, Geneva 1990.

PEDERSON, Darryl of Mill Creek WA. Served on local board 1975-80, contributor to ACBL *Bulletin*. Won Life Master Pairs 1985, Men's Pairs 1987. Placed 2nd Men's Pairs 1964. Won 20 regional events.

PENICK, Michael P. (b. 1947) of Dallas TX, attorney. Author of *Beginning Bridge Complete, Beginning Bridge Quizzes* and pamphlet *Minor Suit Openings*. Won District 8 GNOT 1985.

PENNARIO, Leonard (b. 1924) of Los Angeles CA, concert pianist, a theatre and film enthusiast and art collector. He has performed as a soloist with all of the major symphony orchestras of Europe and United States under conductors such as Fritz Reiner, Leopold Stokowsky, Otto Klemperer, and Georg Solti. He has played and recorded with Heifetz and Piatigorsky. A Life Master, Pennario won an Open Pairs event in Beijing China 1991 and placed 2nd Fall NAC secondary Swiss Teams 1973, Spring NABC secondary Open Pairs 1980.

PENNINGTON, Lee H. (b. 1926) of Nashville TN, math teacher. Won several ABA national championships including KO Teams 1979, Open Pairs Spring and Summer 1977 and several sectional (equivalent to ABCL regional) titles. An ABA tournament director since 1979, he served as New York City tournament committee chairman and as national coordinator of ABA "point races".

PENROD, Dr. Darrell D. (b. 1936) of Crestview FL, professor of mechanical engineering. Penrod was Intercollegiate Champion 1963; won Summer NAC secondary Marcus Cup 1965 and other regionals.

PERES, Charles (b. 1930) of Chicago, options and futures trader. Won Morehead Trophy 1967, Master Mixed Teams, Men's Pairs 1969; GNOT 1978 and placed 2nd Reisinger 1967, Open Pairs 1973.

PERKINS, Frank K. (1891-1971) of Newton MA, civil engineer and bridge writer. For about 30 years he wrote daily bridge columns for *Boston Herald*. He won wide acclaim for his chess and bridge-playing skills and writings as well as his expertise as a fly fisherman. He wrote numerous instructional texts on bridge, including *Vital Tricks at Contract Bridge, Modern Contract Standards*

and served as bridge consultant to *Grolier's Encyclopedia* and the *American Heritage Dictionary*. An outstanding player, Perkins was 2nd in Reisinger 1931 and won New England KO Teams 7 times. Founder of New England B.L., he acted as its secretary, treasurer and tournament director until 1946.

PERLMAN, Howard M. (b. 1943) of Southfield MI, bridge and backgammon club owner. Placed 2nd Vanderbilt 1972 and GNOT 1974 and won many regionals.

PERLMAN, Linda M. (Red) (b. 1945) of Loxahatchee FL, bridge teacher, director and player. Placed 3rd McConnell Cup 1994. ACBL Diamond Life Master she won Master Mixed Teams 1987; placed 2nd Women's KO Teams 1988, 89; Life Master Women's Pairs 1997 and has won numerous regionals.

PERLSTEIN, Lila E. (1925-1996) of Roslyn Heights NY. Won Women's Pairs, Women's KO Teams, Life Master Women's Pairs 1995. Placed 2nd Women's Teams 1976 and won many regionals. In 1996 was part of women's team that went on to win World Women's Team Olympiad. The team dedicated the victory to her.

PERRIN, Wayne M. (b. 1952) of Gloucester ON, assistant municipal administrator, bridge teacher. Held executive posts in Unit 192 1980-88, tournament chairman 1979-86. Won Red Ribbon Pairs 1986.

PERRON, Michel (b. 1951) of Paris, France, bridge professional. WBF Grand Master, #16 in world. Won World Team Olympiad 1980, 92. Won European Pairs 1982. Won London Sunday Times Invitational Pairs, has represented France in many world championship and other zonal championships.

PERROUX, Carl Alberto (1905-1977) of Italy, trial lawyer. Most famous npc in bridge history. Led Italian Blue Team in a record series of 9 world championship wins 1957-66 and 5 European Championships 1951-1959. Celebrated for tough team discipline, checked to see that each member went to bed on time and by themselves — no wives, no girlfriends.. Players who violated his rules were benched, even when it hurt the team. Former president Italian Bridge Federation. Author of *The Blue Team – Our Story of Bridge*.

PETERS, Carolyn S.(b. 1946) of Grapeland TX, retired accountant, won 18 regional events.

PETERS, Thomas J. (Tom) (b. 1943) of Grapeland TX, retired geophysicist. Has been active in local and district bridge administration since the 70's including president of Louisana B.A. and District 16. Diamond Life Master won Open Pairs II 1994; placed 2nd Open Pairs, Swiss Teams 1978. Diamond Life Master, won 30 regionals including District 16 GNOT 1978.

PETERSON, Dr. Gary H. (b. 1946) of Louisville KY, radiologist. Won North American Swiss Teams 1991.

PETERSON, Harrison V. (Pete) (b. 1914) of Los Angeles CA, credit union general manager, retired. Co-founder of ALACBU and was first chairman of ALACBU Ethics Committee. He set up a question and answer column in *Southern California Bridge News*. Was president of Los Angeles Unit 1959-61, 72, and 73. Peterson won a few regionals.

PETERSON, Olive A. (1894-1965) of St. Davids PA, was an outstanding player and teacher whose career spanned from auction to contract bridge. She was closely associated with Milton C. Work with whom she won many auction and contract championships. She and Work conducted one of the earliest bridge cruises, 1933 on the SS Carinthia.

She was subsequently associated with Charles Goren. She was President Women's National Committee 1939, vice-president Women's Auxiliary of ABL 1936 and ACBL Secretary 1951. Her national auction bridge titles include Women's Pairs 1931, Women's Teams 1932. In contract she won Women's Pairs 1930, 32, 45; Women's Teams 1938, 43; Master Mixed Teams 1940, 42, 43, 44; Mixed Pairs 1943. Placed 2nd Women's Pairs 1935, Women's Teams 1953. Her writings include *Work-Peterson Accurate Valuation System, 101 Celebrated Hands, Simplified Digest of Culbertson System* and *Common-Sense Contract*.

PETTERSON, Kelsey (1911-1983) of Las Vegas NV, retired attorney, was member of ACBL Board of Directors 1967-70 and a former president and attorney of Western Conference. Petterson was npc of Los Angeles team in the *Sports Illustrated* Trophy matches. He represesnted North America in Bermuda Bowl 1965. Won Men's Teams, placed 2nd Vanderbilt and had numerous regional titles.

PETRONELLA, Anthony V. (Tony) (b. 1942) of Kingstown RI, teacher, technical writer. Served in many executive positions of Unit 145 and District 25, including president of both. Former bridge columnist Providence *Journal-Bulletin*. Won 13 regionally rated events.

PETRUNIN, Aleksander of Russia. Won Vanderbilt 2001, North American Swiss Teams 2000; placed 2nd World Internet Championships 1999. Quarter-finalist World Teams 1996. Represented Soviet Union and Russia in 2 world championships and 2 zonal championships.

PETTIJOHN, Fran of Indianapolis IN. Placed 2nd Women's Teams and won many regionals.

PETTIT, Randall S. (Randy) (b. 1943) of Marietta GA, retired financial planner. Served as president of Unit 114. Diamond Life Master with more than 12,700 MPs as of 3/2001. Won Barry Crane Top 500 1997. Has been Player of the Year (Unit 114) 7 times. Placed 2nd Senior Swiss Teams, Senior KO Teams 1999. His 100+ regional wins include District 7 GNOT 1991, 93; GNOP 1992.

PHILLIPS, Duncan R. (b. 1930) of Toronto, attorney. WBF Life Master, placed 3rd World Team Olympiad 1973. Represented Canada in international competition 1962, 66, 86. Placed 2nd Senior KO Teams 1994. He was founder and 1st president of the Metropolitan Toronto B.A.

PHILLIPS, Hubert (1891-1964) of London, England. Editor of *British Bridge World* 1936-1939, one of pioneers of bridge organization in England. The Hubert Phillips Trophy (aggregate Mixed Teams) still is one of the most prestigious Bridtish events. For many years Phillips was internationally the most eminent author of intellectual and mathematical puzzles under the name "Caliban" and "Dogberry" and of cryptic crosswords. Authored some 70 books on various subjects. Resident expert on Britain's most famous quiz program. Essayist and lead writer for *London News Chronicle*. Many bridge writings include *Brush Up Your Bridge, The Elements of Contract, Bridge at Ruff's Club, Bridge with Goren*.

PHILLIPS, L. James (Jim) (b. 1935) of Chicago IL, retired executive, now part-time consultant. Former president Chicago Contract B.A. Served on Conduct and Ethics Committee 1975-80. Winner Harmon Wilkes Sportsmanship Award 1985, accredited teacher and director. Diamond Life Master, won 15 regionals including District 13 GNOT 1976.

PICKETT, Heather of Canada, senior analyst with Canadian Government, former teacher and chartered accountant. District 1 secretary since 1983, past president Unit 192. Diamond Life Master with 15 regional wins.

PICUS, Susan J. (Sue) (b. 1948) of New York City, computer scientist. World Grand Master. Won Venice Cup 1991, 93, 97 (as npc); McConnell Cup 1994; placed 2nd Venice Cup 1995. Also competed internationally Las Palmas 1972, Bal Harbour 1986, Geneva 1990. Her national titles include Master Mixed Teams 1971, Mixed BAM Teams 2000; Women's BAM Teams 1972, 97; North American Women's Swiss Teams 1986, Women's KO Teams 1991; placed 2nd USWBC 1991, Women's Pairs 1983, Women's KO Teams 1985, 91; Women's Swiss Teams 1990, 94; Women's BAM Teams 1986,87. Has also won a number of regionals.

PIETRI, Luis (b. 1931) of Philadelphia PA, insurance salesman. One of the top-ranking players in American Bridge Association. Won ABA Open Teams 1968, 70, 72, 78; Open Pairs 1963, 66, 68, 72, 73. Has won all other major titles at least once. He has had a number of ACBL regional wins also.

PIETSHER, Jerry (b. 1932) of Elk Grove CA, former aerospace engineer, worked on Titan Intercontinental Missile and Apollo moon mission. Won 20+ regionals.

PIGOT, David R. (1900-1965) of Dublin, Ireland, solicitor. Was CBAI champion 1936-49. Represented Ireland in international events as player and npc. Served as president CBAI 1946, vice president 1955, 65. Member of WCB Executive Committee, EBL Executive Committee 1951-65, chairman of EBL tournament committee 1957-65. Contributed to revision of IMP scale and preparation of 1964 Olympiad regulations. Member of advisory board, *Bridge Encyclopedia*.

PIKEN, Dr. Edward P. (b. 1948) of Palos Verdes CA, gastroenterologist. Bridge columnist for New York newspaper 1965-69. Won his 1st bridge event at age 15. Won 20 regionals including Southern California GNOP twice.

PILON, Dominique (b. 1950) of Paris, France, bridge teacher. WBF World Master. Won World Olympiad Teams 1982, European Mixed Teams 1992. Represented France in several other world championships, won several national titles.

PILTCH, Howard J. of Andover MA, licensed real estate and insurance broker. Member ACBL Board of Directors for District 25 for several years, ACBL president 1997, Chairman of the Board 1998. Member ACBL Charity Foundation, co-chairman Boston NABC 1999. Consistently in top100 MP holders. Diamond Life Master with more than 14,466 MPs as of 3/2001 and a regular lecturer at NABCs on "Shape, Beautiful Shape" and "Balance, Baby, Balance!" Author of many articles dealing with competitive and constructive bidding, developed Piltch Over NT. Placed 2nd Men's BAM Teams 1976, won over 300 regional events.

PINCUS, Carol (b. 1930) of Las Vegas NV, business school administrative assistant. WBF World Master, finished 5th World Women's Olympiad Teams, 6th World Championship Women's Pairs and 7th World Mixed Pairs 1982. Also represented ACBL in Sao Paulo 1985, Perth 1989. Pincus, a Diamond Life Master, won Women's KO Teams 1984, 88; North American Women's Swiss Teams 1988; finished 2nd North American Women's Swiss Teams 1986, 87's Women's BAM Teams 1989, 94. Won several regional events.

PIRO, Evelyn (d. 1990) of Federal Way WA, apartment house owner and manager. Was one of the pioneers of bridge organization in the Northwest. She was responsible for the foundation of several tournaments including the Pacific Northwest and various units and clubs. She was chairman of Seattle Unit 1949, 50, Portland Unit 1950, 51, co-chairman ACBL Goodwill Committee 1962, ACBL Director 1958-61, 1964.

PISK, Dr. George M. (Manchaca Fats) (b. 1932) of Manchaca TX, retired university professor. Was a frequent partner of Osward Jacoby toward the end of his life. Diamond Life Master with more than 13,000 MPs as of 3/2001, won scores of regionals.

PITTALA, Vito (b. 1927) of Turin, Italy, professor of mechanical engineering. WBF Grand Master. Won Bermuda Bowl 1973, 75; 2nd 1976, 79. Won European Teams 1979. Won many national titles.

PLATNICK, Brian Scott (b. 1966) of Merion Station PA, stock options trader, former industrial engineer. Became certified club director at age of 17 and was director and club manager of a duplicate B.C. for 2 years while in high school. He is a member of the Junior Corps and is a WBF World Master. Won NEC World Junior Team Championship 1991. Has 2 dozen regional wins.

POE, Edgar Allan (1809-1849) American poet and critic. Wrote a number of stories on mystery and occultism. He was interested in detection, cryptology and whist. In his famous detective story, *The Purloined Letter*, he embodied a fine analysis of the mental aspects of whist in the plot. He also discussed whist at some length in *The Murders in the Rue Morgue*.

POE, Dr. William L. (Lyle) (b. 1947) of Columbia MD, attorney. Served in several capacities in Maryland B.A. Certified director since 1974, contributed to *Bridge World*. Authored *The Millenium Club*. Placed 2nd Open Pairs 1987. Won 15 regionals.

POLAK, Gunther (b. 1933) of Chicago IL, insurance investigator. Placed 2nd Blue Ribbon Pairs 1964 and won Summer NAC Golder Pairs 1961 and many regional events.

POLAK, Milos (b. 1932) of Waterloo ON, born in Czechoslovakia, accountant, bridge club manager and teacher. Represented Czechoslovakia in several international contests. His national titles include Czechoslovakian Open Teams 1960, 61, 62, 63, 64, 65, 67; Open Pairs 1961, 63; Mixed Pairs 1962. Polak was co-founder of the Czechoslovak Bridge Association in 1961, its vice president and secretary general 1961-68. Also co-founder of European Junior Championship 1968. He is the former editor of Czechoslovakian bridge magazine.

POLEC, Janusz (b. 1939) of Warsaw, Poland, mechanical engineer. WBF World Life Master. Won Rosenblum Teams 1978. Won many national titles. Represented Poland in other world and zonal championships.

POLISNER, Jeffrey D. (Jeff) (b. 1939) of Lafayette CA, attorney, counsel general of ACBL 1985-2001 and of WBF counsel general 1992-1994 and since 1999. Was president of Unit 499 1980, 81; president District 21 1983-84, chairman District 21 Judiciary and Conduct and Ethics Committees 1981. Appointed to NABC Appeals Committee 1979 and ACBL Laws Commission 1982. Polisner is a WBF World Master and an ACBL Diamond Life Master. Was npc of winning GNOT 1982, placed 2nd Open Pairs 1989, Life Master Open Pairs 1993; won numerous regional events.

POLLACK, Frederic S. (Fred) (b. 1974) of Cincinnati Ohio, graduate student in mathematics, teaching assistant and bridge professional. Member District 1 board. King of Bridge 1992. Placed 4th World Junior Team Championship 1995, 97; 8th/16th Rosenblum Teams 1994. Placed 2nd Junior Trials 1996, GNOT Flt. B 1994, 95. Won at least 15 regionals.

POLLACK, Rozanne (formerly Marel) (b. 1948) of Warren NJ, sociologist. World Grand Master, won McConnell Cup 1994; placed 2nd Venice Cup 1995, Transnational Mixed Teams 1996; 3rd World Championship Mixed Pairs 1986 and 14th World Championship Women's Pairs 1990. Placed 2nd in *Bridge World* Challenge of the Decade (with husband Bill) and is a Master Solver panelist. Won USWBC 1985, Master Mixed Teams 1985, North American Women's Swiss Teams 1986, Women's BAM Teams 1988, 97; Women's KO Teams 1990, 93, 99. Was 2nd Women's Pairs 1981, Women's KO Teams 1985, Women's BAM Teams 1986, 87; Master Mixed Teams 1991. Pollack has won dozens of regionals and is a Diamond Life Master.

POLLACK, William L. (Bill) (b. 1951) of Warren NJ, telecommunications executive. Served as co-chairman of NABC Appeals Committee 1984-90, member International Team Trials Committee and as a member Board of Directors of Greater New York B.A. 2nd *Bridge World* Challenge of the Decade (with wife Rozanne) and is a *Bridge World* Master Solver Club panelist. Contributor to *Bridge Today*. Authored approved convention Lebensohl over Weak Two-bids. Pollack became the youngest ACBL tournament director ever in 1967 at age 16. WBF World Master, placed 2nd World Transnational Mixed Teams 1996, 3rd World Championship Mixed Pairs 1986, Rosenblum Teams 1998 and is a WBF World Master. In ACBL he was 2nd USBC (Team Trials) 1989, 91; won Master Mixed Teams 1985, Vanderbilt 1990; placed 2nd Reisinger 1987. Winner of the Romex Award: Best Bid Hand of 1992-93. An ACBL Diamond Life Master he has won dozens of regional titles.

POLOWAN, Michael (b. 1958) of New York City, professional bridge player. Won Vanderbilt 1995, Open Swiss Teams 1999. Placed 2nd Life Master Pairs 1990, Life Master Open Pairs 1994.

POLUNSKY, Harry (1895-1972) of San Angelo TX, food merchant. Owned one of the largest private collections of books on playing cards and the games played with them. Contributor to various magazines and a contributing editor, *Bridge Encyclopedia*.

PONTIOUS, Frances (Bitsy) (1911-1988) of Beaumont TX, former medical secretary. First president of Unit 201 in 1957 and its executive secretary 1966-80. Won Mixed Pairs 1962.

POPKIN, Nancy L. (b. 1948) of St. Louis MO, college English teacher. Won 15+ regionals.

POPLAWSKI, Mary McColl (b. 1945) of Albany NY, bridge club owner and ACBL-accredited bridge teacher. Served as president Unit 112. Publisher of area newsletter. Won GNOT Flt B 1991.

POPLAWSKI, Stanley M. (Stan) (1940-1995) of Endicott NY, computer programmer. Won GNOT Flt B 1991 and Summer NAC secondary Commercial and Industrial Teams 1973.

PORTNOY, Eunice B. (b. 1932) of Chesterfield MO and Boca Raton FL, in real estate. Was twice St. Louis area Player of the Year. Placed 2nd Women's BAM Teams 1986 and won many regionally rated events.

PORTNOY, Paul (b. 1923) of Chesterfield MO and Boca Raton FL. Won about 50 regionals.

PORTUGAL, Helen (Mrs. Morris) (1919-1986) of Los Angeles CA, one of the leading American woman players. Placed 2nd World Women's Teams 1964 and represented the U.S.– Turin 1960, Cannes 1962. She won Mixed Pairs 1951, 53; Life Master Pairs 1960, Life Mas-

ter Women's Pairs 1961, Master Mixed Teams 1962, Women's Teams 1969. Placed 2nd Women's Teams 1959, 63, 64; Women's Pairs 1961, Vanderbilt 1964. (see also Life Master.)

PORTUGAL, Morris (Port) (b. 1916-1997) of Los Angeles CA, professional bridge player/teacher, one of the leading players of the West Coast. Served on Los Angeles Unit Board 1947-48, Westwood Unit 1949-59. Competed in international play Amsterdam 1966. Portugal is a Grand Life Master with over 1?,000 MPs. National wins include Mixed Pairs 1953, Master Mixed Teams 1954, Life Master Pairs 1960. Placed 2nd Men's Pairs 1947, Vanderbilt 1964, Mixed Pairs 1965. Portugal has had hundreds of regional wins including the first Los Angeles Bridge Week 4-session Open Pairs 1946. (see Life Master.)

POTTAGE, John F. (b. 1964) of London, England, accountant. Won World Junior Championship 1989, Common Market Junior Championship 1985, 89. Represented England on many occasions in international competition. English national wins include the Crockford Cup, Spring Fours and Tollemache. He is the co-inventor of the Pottage Defense to 1 NT.

POTTAGE, Julian Y. (b. 1962) of Basingstoke England, pension plan manager, photographer, bridge teacher and writer. Won Pachabo Cup 1982, Junior Camrose Trophy 1984. He was captain of the winning Cambridge team in the varsity match vs Oxford in 1983. He is the co-inventor of the Pottage Defense to 1NT. He discovered the Compound Guard Squeeze. Author of *Clues from the Bidding* and co-author with Terence Reese of *Positive Defense, Positive Declarer's Play* and *The Extra Edge in Play.*

POTTER, John R. (Cigar) (b. 1936) of Panama City Beach FL, retired USAF Lt. Col. Diamond Life Master, won Senior Swiss Teams, Senior KO Teams 1999 and over 60 regionally rated events.

POUPART, Marc (b. 1950) of Longueuil PQ, attorney. Co-authored *Le Clef du Bridge: Les Encheres*, 1st and 2nd editions. Won 27 regionals events.

POWELL, Ronald L. (Ron) (b. 1947) of Mountain View CA, psychiatric nursing assistant. Placed 2nd Men's Swiss Teams 1989.

POWELL, Richard P. (Dick) (b. 1908) of Fort Myers FL, novelist, author of *Tickets to the Devil,* a bridge novel published in 1968. Foreign editions have been published in England, Scandinavia, Germany and Italy. A certified director since 1970. Manager (since 1973) and past president of Coconut Duplicate B.C. A writer since 1930, he is author of 19 published novels, 4 of which have been made into movies: *The Philadelphian,* filmed as *The Young Philadelphians; Pioneer, Go Home!,* filmed as *Follow that Dream; Don Quixote, U.S.A.,* filmed as *Bananas;* and *The Build-Up Boys* (published under the pen name Jeremy Kirk) filmed as *Madison Avenue.*

PRALL, Jack W. (b. 1914) of Lakeland FL, retired postal clerk. One of the founders of District 12. Former president and vice president of District 12 and of the Northern Ohio B.A. He was District 12 representative to ABCL Board of Directors 1963-65.

PRAGER, Rhoda of Allentown PA, teacher, data processor. Placed 2nd Mixed BAM Teams 1999.

PRATT, John M. (1904-1997) of Flint MI, scholar, retired teacher and General Motors executive. Graduated from high school at age 16 as class valedictorian with the highest grades ever from that school. Pratt was named chairman of ACBL Goodwill Committee 1979 and

served until 1984. He was a former president of Unit 200, Heart of America B.C. and former vice president of Hartford B.C. Pratt organized other bridge clubs and chaired sectional and regional tournaments. He taught bridge to thousands of people in the Flint area and in 1973 he did a series of 10 bridge lessons on TV.

PRESBERG, Shirley (b. 1935) of Norfolk VA, writer. Wrote *Death by Contract* and will soon have her second book out. A Diamond Life Master, she has won several regional events.

PRICE, Robert J. (Bob) of Chicago IL, real estate broker. Member of barber shop family quartet. Served as member Chicago CBA 1972-78, national vice president of ABA 1988-89, president 1990-91. In 1978 for 7 consecutive months he successfully "Challenged the Champs". Ranked the #1 player in ABA since 1965 with over 28,000 MPs and has played for 25 years with the same partner, Joyce Williams. He has won ABA Victor Daley KO Teams 25 times, ABA National Open Pairs 25 times, Mixed Pairs 15 times, Swiss Teams 7 times. Won the William Friend Award (equivalent to Crane Top 500) 8 straight years 1972-79 and is continuously one of the top finishers each year. Has contributed to *Bridge World* and *Bridge Today*. Winner of Harmon Wilkes Good Sportsmanship Award.

PRICE, Steven T. (b. 1951) of Safety Harbor FL, CFO. Served as District 21 treasurer 1984-87. Price was 2nd Blue Ribbon Pairs 1993. Won several regionals including District 21 GNOT 1980, GNOP 1982.

PRIDAY, Angela Jane (Mrs. Richard A.) (deceased)of London, England. WBF World Life Master. Won World Women's Team Olympiad 1964, World Women's Pairs 1966. Won European Women's Teams 1961, 63, 66. Played in Camrose matches. Among her national victories is Gold Cup 1972. Represented Britain other world and zonal championships.

PRIDAY, Richard A. (Tony) of London, England, chairman of hardwood company. WBF World Life Master. Placed 2nd Bermuda Bowl 1985 as Great Britain npc, 3rd Bermuda Bowl 1962, World Team Olympiad 1976. Won European Teams 1961, 2nd 1971. Won London Sunday Times Invitational Pairs 1970, competed in 28 Camrose matches. His more than 15 national titles include 7 Gold Cups. Held several executive positions including chairman of British League. Columnist for *Sunday Telegraph*. (See BUENOS AIRES AFFAIR.)

PRISYON, Jerome B. (Jerry) (b. 1927) of Valley Stream NY, business person, bridge cruise lecturer, bridge administrator. Board member and former president of Greater New York B.A. He orginated a novice program for GNYBA, which included printed hand analyses. It was later adopted and expanded by the ACBL. Prisyon is a former regional tournament director.

PROTHRO, James Thomason (Tommy) (1920-1995) of Memphis TN, football coach, graduated with 3 degrees from Duke University, in many "Halls of Fame" including the National Football Foundation. Was named national Coach of the Year. He was a blocking back for the Duke team and went on to coach football at Oregon State University, UCLA and subsequently for the Los Angeles Rams and the San Diego Chargers. He retired as executive vice president of the Cleveland Browns in 1982. Prothro won several regionals.

PRZYBORA, Tomasz (b. 1949) of Warsaw, Poland, bridge professional. WBF World Life Master. Won World Team Olympiad 1984, European Teams 1981, European Pairs 1989. Represented Poland in many world and zonal championships. Won many national titles.

PSZCZOLA, Jacek of Poland. World Life Master, ranks 23rd in WBF Open rankings. Won World Open Pairs 1998, placed 2nd World Team Olympiad 2000, Cavendish Invitational 2001; placed 3rd Transnational Open Teams 1997, NEC Teams 2001.

PUTNAM, Roger (b. 1942) of Redmond WA, national tournament director and tournament director field representative. Began his directing career in 1967, became associate national 1977 and achieved his present national rating 1985.

Q

QIN, Lu, Life Master from Hong Kong, member of the original Chinese women's team formed in 1985, represented China in several Zonal and World Champion events, including the 1987 Venice Trophy and the 1986 Far East Championship. Married to Karic Chiu and migrated to Hong Kong in 1991. Numerous national titles in both China and Hong Kong.

QUANTIN, Jean-Christophe (b. 1966) of Paris, France, bridge trainer, WBF World Master. 2nd World Junior Teams 1987, 3rd 1989. Won European Pairs 1991, 93; 2nd European Teams 1989; won European Junior Teams 1988. Represented France in 3 other world championships and won some national titles.

QUEEN, Frank C. (b. 1940) of Englewood CO, retired teacher. Author of *It's Only a Game* in District 17 *Contract Bridge Forum*. Was guest host on Denver radio bridge program with Dan Mordecai. Member District 17 Board of Directors 1985-97, president 1990-94, member Unit 361 Board of Directors 1979-88, president 1980-88, 1st alternate to ACBL Board of Directors 1991 to present, member ACBL Board of Governors 1991 to present.

QUIGGLE, Louis R. (b. 1940) of Redding CA, retired stockbroker. Diamond Life Master, won 16 regional events.

QUIGGLE, Rosalind E. (Roz) (b. 1937) of Redding CA. optometric assistant. Diamond Life Master with 16 regional wins.

QUINLAN, Thomas J. (T.Q.) (b. 1942) of San Mateo CA, retired 1999 as director in charge at NABCs) national tournament director, TD field representative. Began directing career in 1964, attained national ranking 1987. Director-in-charge at NABCs from Anaheim 1987 to Orlando 1998. Past president Professional Tournament Directors Association and served as District 21 GNOP and GNOT coordinator 1974-91. Editor *Contract Bridge Forum* 1970-81 and of District 21 edition 1967-81.

QUINN, Ann (d. 1992) of Dublin, Ireland, civil servant. Won Common Market Women's Teams 1981. Represented Ireland in world and zonal championships from 1959. More than 20 national titles include Open Teams and Open Pairs. Reached European Women's Pairs final in an octogenarian partnership with Eileen O'Doherty shortly before her death.

QUINN, Joe (b. 1950) of Katy TX, engineering manager. Diamond Life Master. Won North American Swiss Teams 1993. His 20 regional wins include District 22 GNOT 1991.

QUINN, Shawn (nee Womack) (b. 1961) of Katy TX, site manager for winBridge.com, certified director, former systems analyst. WBF Grand Master, ranks #10 among women Grand Masters. Ranks #1 among women in world performance over past 10 years. Won World Women's Team Olympiad 1996, World Women's Pairs 1998, placed 2nd Venice Cup 2000 and 3rd McConnell Cup 1998. Diamond Life Master, won Life Master Women's Pairs 1992, 99, 2000; Women's BAM Teams 1993, 98, 2000; Women's Swiss Teams 1994, 97, 99; Women's KO Teams 1995, 96, 97; North American Swiss Teams 1993, Women's International Team Trials 1996, 99, 2000. Placed 2nd Women's Pairs 1993, 99; Women's BAM Teams 1997, Women's KO Teams 2000.

QUINN, Terry (b. 1945) of Washington, novelist, former editor and ghostwriter. Author of *The Great Bridge Conspiracy*, co-author with Kathie Wei-Sender of *Second Daughter*.

R

RABICEW, Elizabeth (formerly Solar) (b. 1935) of Caracas, Venezuela, born in Poland, computer and quality consultant. Won CAC Women's Teams 1979, 80, 81, 87. Represented Venezuela in 8 world championships. Won many national titles. 5th Venice Cup 1995.

RADIN, Judi (formerly Solodar, nee Friedenberg) (b. 1955) of New York City, bridge teacher, professional player. Was contributing editor to *Precision Newsletter*, co-author of *Precision One Club Complete*. One of leading American women players, ranks 9th among women WBF Grand Masters, only woman to have won all 4 major women's world championships. Won World Women's Pairs 1978, World Women's Team Olympiad 1984, Venice Cup 1987, McConnell Cup 1994; placed 2nd Venice Cup 1981, 85; World Women's Pairs 1990. Grand Life Master with 14,611 MPs as of 3/2001, won Women's BAM Teams 1971, 98, Women's KO Teams 1977, 80, 83, 87; Women's Pairs 1978, 98, 2001; North American Women's Swiss Teams 1983, Mixed BAM Teams 2000; placed 2nd Reisinger 1974, Vanderbilt 1979, Women's KO Teams 1982, Master Mixed Teams 1983, Life Master Women's Pairs 1984, North American Women's Swiss Teams 1985, Women's BAM 1986, 95, North American Swiss Teams 1991.

RADIN, Michael (b. 1950) of New York City, attorney. Placed 11th World Mixed Pairs 1982. Placed 2nd Master Mixed Teams 1991. Won dozens of regionals.

RADJEF, Tarek Lucien (b. 1937) of Dallas TX, born in France, entrepreneur, formerly an electrical engineer. Contributor World Championship *Daily Bulletin* 1997, won 22 regionals.

RAFF, Barrett J. (b. 1938) of Johnson City NY, dentist. Won GNOT Flight B 1991.

RAGAZZO, Vincent L. (b. 1938) of Las Vegas NV, retired computer analyst. Won CNTC 1972, 81.

RAINWATER, Ross (b. 1948) of Portland OR, bridge club operator, bridge teacher, former professional bridge player. Diamond Life Master with more than 16,600 MPs, has won more than 100 regional titles. Once placed in KO team overall ranking by losing both matches played. First was in a round-robin where the other team was eliminated on quotient, bye for 2nd round, lost in 3rd round for 5th -place tie.

RALLIS, George (b. 1918) of Athens, Greece. Former prime minister. In 1975 during his time as Minister and due to his efforts, bridge was recognized as a sport in Greece and the Sports Ministry started to subsidize Hellenic Bridge Federation. Still an expert player, contributes regularly to the bi-monthly bridge magazine.

RALPH, Mark P. (b. 1946) of San Francisco CA, US Department of Defense investigator. Diamond Life Master, won 23+ regionals including District 22 GNOT 1973, 76.

RAMSEY, Guy (d. 1959) of London, England, journalist and author. Writings included *Aces All* and many magazine articles. Bridge editor for London *Daily Telegraph*. First president European (now International) Bridge Press Association 1958-1959.

RAND, Alfred (Al) (1907-1998) of New York City, investment manager. Diamond Life Master, won Men's BAM Teams 1982, placed 2nd Men's Swiss 1986.

RAND, Nissan (b. 1930) of Afeka, Israel, born in Czechoslovakia, expert in animal nutrition. Won World Senior Teams 1994, 98 and represented Israel on many other occasions in open and senior competitition. Won many national titles. Chairman WBF Seniors Committee since 1998. Member EBL Executive since 1996, and chairman of its Seniors Committee. Former president and executive chairman of Israel Bridge Federation. Columnist in Haaretz newspaper. Member of International Poultry Hall of Fame.

RAND, Rita L. (Mrs. Alfred) of New York City, investor. Placed 2nd North American Swiss Teams 1988, 89. Invented Rand Club.

RANDALL, Winslow H. (1897-1983) of Redlands CA, ACBL president 1959, president of Western Conference 1955, served as an ACBL Director for many years.

RANDEL, Judith C. (Judy) (b. 1936) of Albuquerque NM, bridge teacher and director. Member ACBL Board of Governors since 1985, president of Unit 374 1976-77, Dist 17 Recorder since 1986 and on ACBL Board of Appeals for 7 years. Grand Life Master with 11,087 MPs as of 3/2001, won Women's BAM Teams 1990, Women's Pairs 1996, 4th Pan American Women's Pairs 1992. Won about 60 regionals.

RANDLES, Janice R. (b. 1934) of Redmond WA, bridge teacher, director and club owner. Won Women's BAM Teams 1987, placed 2nd USWBC (team trials) 1988.

RANK, Peter C. (b. 1938) of Los Angeles, attorney, ACBL counsel 2001, former California State Health Director, former director California Employment Department, breeder, owner, handler of more than 300 champion Toy Manchester terriers. One of leading players of West Coast in the Sixties and Seventies, retired from playing 1978. He and Barry Crane were the top masterpoint winning pair 1964-75. Grand Life Master, won McKenney Trophy 1965, Men's Pairs 1966, Open Pairs 1977; Mixed Pairs 1968; placed 2nd Master Mixed Teams 1969. For almost 3 decades has produced fund-raising shows featuring many major celebrities such as Bob Hope, Betty Ford, Steve Allen, Tommy Tune and Gene Kelly. Former president District 21, commentator at NABCs and international tournaments 1968-80. Developed bridge musicals as entertainment for many NABCs, has written, scored and produced 4 productions that were based on Broadway musicals: *My Fair Little Old Lady, The Lesser Vice (Guys and Dolls), Partnership! Partnership! (Kiss Me Kate), There is Nothing Like a Game* and *Annie Bid your Slam*. Won hundreds of regionals.

RAO, Y. Kamalakara (b. 1928) of Hyderabad, India, tournament director. President of Bridge Federation of India from 1998, and previously its secretary. Chief director 1981 BFAAME Championships, and, in 1982, the first Indian to direct in a world championship. Editor Indian *Bridge World*.

RAPEE, George (1915-1999) of New York City, attorney and real estate investor. WBF Grand Master, Diamond Life Master, Life Master #44, member ACBL Hall of Fame; inventor of Stayman convention, which shares with Blackwood the distinction of being the most widely played convention throughout the world. Won Bermuda Bowl 1950, 51, 53; 3rd Rosenblum Cup Teams 1990, also represented North America in Bermuda Bowl 1958, 59 and the U.S. in first World Team Olympiad 1960. Won Team Trials and Fishbein Trophy 1968. Had best record in the 3 major NABC team championships for years 1942-80; winning 21 and finishing 2nd in 18. Won Spingold 1944, 48, 50, 52, 57, 68; Chicago (now the Reisinger) 1945, 47, 53, 54, 56; Reisinger 1970, 71; Vanderbilt 1946, 50, 51, 55, 56, 57, 59, 70; 2nd in Vanderbilt 1942, 44, 52, 65, 67; Spingold 1943, 47, 55, 60, 61, 66, 76, 80; Chicago 1947, 48, 50; Reisinger 1968, 69, 72. Also won Master Individual 1944, 49; Master Mixed Teams 1960; Men's BAM Teams 1975; placed 2nd Men's BAM Teams 1946, 48, 72; Men's Pairs 1945, 50; Mixed Pairs 1955; Master Mixed Teams 1952, 68.

RAPOPORT, Alexander (b. 1952) of Kharkov, Ukraine, mathematician. Represented Ukraine in 1 world championship and 1 European championship. Won USSR Open Teams 1990, 1991, Ukrainian Open Pairs 1991, Open Teams 1994, 1995, 1996.

RAPPAPORT, Barbara. See HABERMAN, Barbara.

RAPSON, Bryan (b. 1927) of Dartmouth NS, Canada, retired chemical engineer. Founded Saguenay Unit 1999, secretary 1954-1972; 1st alternate Director District 1 1972-1992.

RASKIN, Raymond L. (b. 1943) of King of Prussia PA, compliance chief for regulatory affairs for major pharmaceutical firms. Past president District 4 and Philadelphia CBA, served as District 4 Recorder 1970-80 and chairman ACBL Appeals and Charges Committee 1999, 97, 99. Served on ACBL Board of Governors 1983-86, member of ACBL Board of Directors since 1986. Diamond Life Master, won 25 regionals.

RASMIDATTA, Vibul (b. 1928) of Bangkok, Thailand, retired banker. Won PABF (Far East) Teams 1965. Represented Thailand in 2 world championships and on 4 other occasions. Has won all national titles.

RASMUS, Patricia A. (b. 1948) of Hamburg NY, school teacher, president District 5 1999-2000, won Non-Life Master Swiss Teams 1985.

RASMUS, Richard J. (b. 1942) of Hamburg NY, chemist, won Non-Life Master Swiss Teams 1985.

RASMUSSEN, Arild (b. 1961) of Bergen, Norway, computer consultant. WBF World Master. 2nd Bermuda Bowl 1993, 3rd European Teams 1993, 99.

RAU, John (1908-1982) of Walnut Creek CA, a leading figures in early days of contract bridge. In 1930 Rau and William K. Barrett caused a sensation at their first national tournament by extensive use of psychic bids and by winning the Open Team championship (now the Reisinger) as a pickup team with Ely Culbertson and W. James Carpenter. Won Open Pairs 1934, was 2nd in Vanderbilt (twice) and the Spingold as well as other major victories in important Eastern tournaments. Protege and special assis-

tant to P. Hal Sims in early Thirties when the Sims mansion in Deal NJ was summer headquarters for all the principal bridge experts. When the category of Life Master was created by the American Bridge League in 1936, Rau was not included on the original list, having quit bridge to seek his fortune in the business world. Through the vagaries of the bridge league's bookkeeping system in those days, Rau's early exploits were never recognized with masterpoints, so when he moved to California and resumed playing bridge, he started a 2nd bridge career and became a Life Master in 3 years.

RAUSCHEID, Andrea (b. 1963) of Heidelberg, Germany. WBF World Life Master. Won Venice Cup 1995, 3rd World Women's Team Olympiad 2000. 2nd European Women's Team and Pairs 1995. Won 7 national titles.

RAUTENBERG, Lee H. (b. 1951) of Boca Raton FL, microcomputer systems programmer/designer, placed 2nd Mixed Pairs 1976.

RAYNER, John W. (b. 1951) of Oakville ON, bridge professional, bridge teacher, bridge club manager. Taught students at all levels for 30 years. Won 17 regionals.

REBATTU, Maximiliaan J. (b. 1939) of Amstelveen, The Netherlands, bridge journalist and teacher. WBF World Life Master. 2nd World Open Pairs 1982, after a scoring error made it appear that he and Anton Maas had won. Represented The Netherlands in 3 other world championships and 6 European Championships. Won numerous national titles. Contributor to the biggest Netherlands newspaper *Telegraaf* and to *Bridge* (Dutch bridge magazine). Introduced bridge on Teletext in 1980, and continues it.

REBNER, Stella (1910-1991) of Los Angeles CA, born in Austria. Placed 2nd World Women's Teams 1964, won Women's Team Trials 1963, Master Mixed Teams 1952, 53; Women's Teams 1957, 62; placed 2nd Mixed Pairs 1959.

REED, Broma Lou (formerly Harrison) (b. 1932) of Boulder CO, retired teacher. Placed 20th World Mixed Pairs 1990. Diamond Life Master, won Women's BAM Teams 1990, placed 2nd North American Women's Swiss 1993. Won 60+ regionals.

REESE, D. Ann (b. 1936) of Atlanta GA, professional bridge teacher/player, former teacher, model and TV show host. novice coodinator for District 7, author of *Four Suit Transfers*, columnist Unit 114 *Pip 'n Tips*. Diamond Life Master.

REESE, J. Terence (1913-1996) of Hove, England, bridge writer. Grand Master. Won Bermuda Bowl 1955, World Par 1961. 2nd World Team Olympiad 1960, World Pairs 1962. Won European Teams 1948, 49, 54, 63. Represented Britain in 2 other world championships and 5 other zonal championships. More than 20 national titles including 8 Gold Cups. Won London Sunday Times Invitational 1964. First to write a book about Acol System – which became standard in Britain. Conducted regular radio programs about bridge, and acted as commentator at international championships. Bridge columnist of *London Observer* and *London Evening News*, and other periodicals. Editor *British Bridge World* 1955-62. Author of more than 20 books of which two, *Reese on Play* and *The Expert Game*, are classics that made major contributions to the game. For the accusation of cheating made against him at the 1965 Bermuda Bowl world championships, see BUENOS AIRES AFFAIR.

REEVE, Bruce F. (b. 1946) of Raleigh NC, bridge teacher, professional player. Member Board of Directors from District 7 1997-2000, elected for 2nd 3-year

term 2000; Trustee Educational Foundation. Member of first Board of Directors of U.S. Bridge Federation 2001. Trustee Educational Foundation. Former president District 7 and Unit 119, served on Middle Atlantic board more than 25 years, District 7 recorder 1992-97, assistant national recorder 1995-97, member Board of Governors, member National Appeals Committee 1992-97. Diamond Life Master, won 24 regionals.

REICH, Louis I. (b. 1949) of Wheaton MD, computer programmer. Diamond Life Master, placed 2nd Men's BAM 1976.

REICH, Peggy (formerly Lipsitz, Parker) (b. 1941) of Potomac MD, bridge teacher, volunteer at crisis centers, counsels battered women. Won World Mixed Teams 1974. Won Mixed Pairs 1969, 76; placed 2nd Master Mixed Teams 1973. Won 30+ regionals.

REICHMUTH, Eleanor A. (d. 1990) of Billings MT, bridge teacher and club director, bridge pioneer in Montana. Began directing in 1934 and was instrumental in starting many duplicate clubs, received ACBL Service Award for having directed a club continuously for 25 or more years (35 years as of 1981).

REID, Felicity (b. 1949) of Kingston, Jamaica, born in England, business executive and bridge teacher. Represented Jamaica in 8 CBF Championships and 2 Olympiads. Former president Jamaica Bridge Association. Organizer Bermuda Bowl and Venice Cup championships Ocho Rios 1987. President of Central American and Caribbean Bridge Federation, 1997-2001.

REID, Martin Alexander (b. 1963) of Wellington, New Zealand, computer consultant. WBF World Master. Won Far East Teams 1990, Far East Pairs 1991. Represented New Zealand in 1 other Far East Championship and 2 world championships.

REIMAN, James H. (b. 1949) of Mansfield OH, purchasing vice president. District 11 president 1997-98, 1st alternate Director 1994-98, member from District 11 to ACBL Board of Directors 1999-to date. Diamond Life Master with more than 14,300 MPs as of 3/2001 won 120+ regionals.

REINHOLD, Arthur E. (Bud) (1913-1996) of Highland Park IL, furniture industry consultant, former naval officer. , won Bermuda Bowl 1981. Diamond Life Master, won Spingold 1973, Reisinger 1973, 79; Vanderbilt 1980; placed 2nd Vanderbilt 1973, GNOT 1978, IMP Pairs 1989, Reisinger 1986.

REIPLINGER, Robert (b. 1942) of Paris, France, businessman. WBF World Master. 3rd Bermuda Bowl 1995. 2nd European Teams 1995.

REISIG, Richard H. (b. 1939) of Boynton Beach FL, bridge instructor, computer analyst. Cavendish Club manager 3 years. Won Reisinger 1984, Senior Swiss Teams 1998, Senior KO Teams 1999.

REISINGER, Curt H. (1891-1964) of New York City, a principal patron of contract bridge and the ACBL in early years of both. Reisinger was great-grandson of both Anheuser and Busch, co-founders of the brewery from which he inherited great wealth. That wealth enabled him to become a stalwart financial supporter of the game, as well as a noted philanthropist on a far larger scale. Among the positions in which he served were director of the USBA, president of the Greater New York BA and chairman of ACBL. ACBL Honorary Member 1953. The Reisinger Teams at the New York Eastern Regional is one of the longest running bridge events. See REISINGER TROPHY.

REITH, George (1876-1939) of Yonkers NY, bridge expert and writer, was one of the leading American bridge personalities. Took up bridge in 1927 after he retired from the brokerage business. In 1929 won first Eastern States Pairs championship with Oswald Jacoby. He won many titles including the Chicago Trophy (now the Reisinger) 1932. Reith authored four books on bridge — *The Art of Successful Bidding, Contract, Accurate Contract and Reith's One-Over-One*. He was at one time chief exponent of the one-over-one system of bidding. Reith was chairman of the Knickerbocker Whist Club Card Committee for 15 years, president of Crockford's Club, executive vice-president of the USBA and ACBL Board member. Created and acted as chairman of the Eastern States Championships, which for many years was one of the largest regionals in the United States.

REITMAN, Dr. Nelson R. (b. 1911) of New Milford NJ, dentist, retired regionally rated tournament director, past president of NY/NJ Conference.

REMEN, Solvi Ir (b. 1965) of Bergen, Norway, information technology consultant. WBF World Master. 4th World Women's Teams 2000. National wins include Women's Teams.

REMEY, Joan See MOORE, Joan R.

REMEY, Vincent O. (1911-1988) of Southfield MI, retired company executive. Diamond Life Master and had earned almost 9,000 MPs. Founded and served as editor of the Unit 137 newsletter *Table Talk*. Elected to the ACBL Board of Directors 1974 and served until his death. ACBL representative to WBF. Won Open Pairs 1971, placed 2nd Life Master Pairs 1948, Master Mixed Teams 1971, 75, 80.

RENGSTORFF, John C. (b. 1943) of New York City, retired stock option market maker. Diamond Life Master, won Open BAM Teams 1997, placed 2nd Open Pairs 1986.

RESNICK, Jeffrey L. (b. 1953) of Christiansted, St. Croix, Virgin Islands, born in Brooklyn, U.S., federal magistrate. Represented Virgin Islands in 2 world championships and 12 CAAC zonal championships. Secretary of Virgin Islands B.F.

RETEK, George (b. 1936) of Montreal PQ, born in Hungary, chartered accountant. Member ACBL Board of Directors representing District 1 since 1979, primarily involved in finance, international affairs and appeals committees; previously served as ACBL treasurer. Member of WBF Executive Council since 1988, WBF treasurer since 1990, WBF vice president since 1998.

REUS, Anthony P. (Tony the tuna) (b. 1954) born in London, England, but lived whole life in Montreal, Canada, married to Sharyn. Inventor of EHAA bidding system, tournament player/teacher/pro for more than 25 years, classical music enthusiast. Retired from bridge play for a few years but took up the game again in 2001. OKbridge club manager and tournament director since 1996, took up internet bridge play 1995. Got the name Tuna as a retaliation from a bunch of pals to whom he gave fish names.

REUS, Sharyn (b. 1950) of St Laurent PQ, personal income tax preparer. Began playing in 1969 and by 1972 was in her 1st Olympiad as the youngest player to represent Canada. Assistant director OKbridge. WBF World Life Master, placed 3rd Venice Cup 1989; 3rd World Women's Team Olympiad 1996; 4th World Women's Team Olympiad 1976, 88, 6th 1980, 7th 1972; 6th World Women's Pairs 1986. Also represented Canada 1976, 78, 82, 84, 91, 92, 93. Placed 2nd NTC 1989.

REVELL, A. Richard (1913-1988) of Prospect Heights IL, accountant. Won Men's Pairs, Men's Teams 1950. Director of Chicago CBA 1961-65 and received its Sportsmanship Award.

REX-TAYLOR, David (b. 1947) of Feltham, England, managing editor *IBPA Bulletin*. Discoverer of the word "bridge" from obsolete Russian word "biritch"– meaning declarer.

REYES, Jose (1910-1980) of Pasay City, Philippines, attorney and planter. One of the founders of Far East Bridge Federation, president 1957-63. Delegate to WBF. Won Far East Teams 1958. National titles include Open Teams.

REYES, Vicente (b. 1937) of Makati City, Philippines, mechanical engineer. Won Far East Pairs 1974. Represented Philippines in 3 world championships and 11 zonal championships. More than 20 nationals wins.

REYNOLDS, Robert (1925-1984) of Coral Gables FL, bridge teacher. Won Master Individual 1960, placed 2nd Vanderbilt 1960, Life Master Pairs 1961.

REYSA, Gloria (formerly Turner) (b. 1925) of Dallas TX, secretary. Diamond Life Master, won Master Mixed Teams 1957, 61; placed 2nd Vanderbilt 1951, Master Mixed Teams 1953.

RHATIGAN, Jack K. (b. 1931) of Cottage Grove MN, retired pharmacist. Diamond Life Master, won Open Pairs 1973.

RHODE, George L. (b. 1949) of Duluth GA, retired U.S. Army drug and alcohol detoxification specialist. Served as District 8 college coordinator, District 7 GNOP coordinator 1985-90, Unit 179 bridge school and has been a member of ACBL Appeals Committee since 1986. Feature writer for *Pips and Tips* and the Dist 7, 9 and 10 *Bulletins*.

RHODES, Kathryn M. (Kay) (1910-1996) of Rohnert Park CA, formerly of New York City. Holds 2 unusual records — 4 consecutive wins in Women's Pairs 1955, 56, 57, 58; 7 consecutive seconds in Women's Teams 1952-58. Won the Chicago (now the Reisinger)1949, Women's Pairs 1949; placed 2nd Master Mixed Teams 1942, Women's Pairs 1944.

RIBNER, Paula (formerly Bacher, Levin) (b. 1908) of Palm Beach FL, formerly one of the leading women players of the East Coast, Life Master #65. Ribner and teammates Jane Jaeger, Kay Rhodes, Sally Young, won the Chicago (now the Reisinger) in 1947, the only time in history the event has been won by an all-woman team. Also won Mixed Pairs 1946. Placed 2nd Women's Pairs 1944; Women's Teams 1946; Mixed Pairs 1949, Open Pairs 1952.

RICE, Betty K. (b. 1939) of Sante Fe NM. National Rookie of Year 1985, National Senior Master of Year 1986 (set new record of 633 MPs).

RICE, Shirley J. (b. 1925) of Clearwater FL, bridge teacher. First to author and record bridge lessons on cassette tapes *Anyone for Bridge?* Served 2 terms Unit 111 president.

RICHARDS, Ralph R. (1876-1943) of Detroit, accountant, founder and first president American Bridge League, also bridge teacher, writer, lecturer and leading tournament player. Played bridge at the old Chicago Whist Club and won many honors at whist and auction bridge. Active member of American Whist League and while attending the Congress at Hanover NH in summer of 1927, he proposed an organization to sponsor, promote and develop the game of bridge. The American Auction Bridge League (subsequently American Bridge League) was the first national organization devoted entirely to bridge. At its initial tournament at Chicago in December 1927, Richards and teammates Theodore A. Lightner, Waldemar von Zedtwitz and Ely Culbertson won the team-of-four championship. During the 2nd meeting of the League held in Cleveland 1928, contract bridge was introduced for tournament play. In 1929, the tournament went back to Chicago and Richards and his partner, William E. McKenney, tied for 1st in Open Pairs. Richards authored *Championship Bridge* and co-authored *Common Sense Contract.*

RICHENS, Muriel W. of San Mateo CA, marriage and family therapist, bridge teacher, retired educator. Diamond Life Master, won 19 regionals.

RICHMAN, Robert Alan (Bob) (b. 1950) of Sydney, Australia, born in Cleveland Ohio, options trader. 3rd Bermuda Bowl 1979. Represented Australia on 6 other occasions. Won Maccabiah Games 1985. National wins include Open Teams 4 times and Open Pairs 6 times. The most successful Australian player 1984-1999.

RICHMOND, David G. (1906-1980) of Winnipeg MB, pharmacist. Represented Canada World Open Pairs 1962. Active in promoting bridge in Canada and in 1974 donated the Richmond Trophy, the Canadian equivalent of the Barry Crane Top 500 (formerly McKenney Trophy).

RIEGLE, Jim E. (b. 1950) of Ottawa ON, economist. Diamond Life Master, placed 2nd COPC 1985, won 35+ regionals.

RIELY, Terry P. (b. 1943) of San Antonio TX, corporate executive, served as Unit 172 president 1985-90, president District 16 1986. Diamond Life Master, won 25+ regionals.

RIGAL, Barry (b.1958) of New York City, formerly of London. Writer and player, has worked on vugraph and Daily Bulletins at almost every world championship since 1988. Has written many books and co-operated on most world championships books in the last decade. Regular contributor to ACBL *Bridge Bulletin* and ACBL NABC *Daily Bulletin*s. Contributing editor *Official Bridge Encyclopedia*. Very active in ACBL appeals process. Won Mixed Teams 2000, 4th World Mixed Pairs 1986, won Common Market Mixed Teams 1987 and almost all British major championships including Gold Cup 1990. Represented England in Camrose Trophy 6 times. May be only professional to have failed to declare a single board in a 26-board session with a client!

RIGMAIDEN, Roscoe (b. 1918) of Philadelphia, retired U.S. Postal superintendent. First winner of ABA William A. Friend award for most masterpoints won in a year, and for many years was the leading American Bridge Association masterpoint holder. Top-ranked ABA player 1969-70, 1974-77, won leading player award in the ABA Summer Nationals 1966 and 1968, Spring Nationals 1969. Has won all major ABA titles including Open Pairs 6 times and Open Teams 4 times. Former member ABA Executive Board, chairman of National Ethics Committee, contributor to ABA *Bulletin*.

RIMINGTON, Derek C. (b. 1927) of Beckenham, England, retired computer manager of Greater London Council and bridge writer. Many national wins include Gold Cup 1956. Columnist for *Field* magazine and syndicated columnist. Contributor to many magazines. Author of 1 book and co-author of another. Chief commentator World Junior Bridge Championships 1989.

RIORDAN, Beverly R. (b. 1928) of Ypsilanti MI, college chemistry and biology instructor. Former member

National Appeals Committee, president Michigan BA, vice president District 12, chairman of 1991 World Junior Championship. Won 15+ regionals.

RIPSTRA, Joseph G. (Rip) (1900-1982) of Wichita KS, investor, mechanical contractor; helped develop Kansas State BA. Member ACBL Board of Directors 1945-58, was instrumental in increasing the number of members on Board from 8 to 23 when ACBL merged with Western Conference. ACBL president 1957. Invented Ripstra convention, was npc of Bermuda Bowl team 1958, placed 2nd in the Chicago (now the Reisinger) 1955, Men's Pairs 1949, won numerous regionals.

RISKIN, Alexander (b.1949) of Chelyabinsk, Russia, bridge organizer. Vice president Russian Bridge League. Former president Russian Bridge League (1992-95). Director of Russian Cup tournament. Several national wins.

RITZENBERG, James L.(b. 1957) of Bethesda MD, attorney. Won Red Ribbon Pairs 1987.

RIVAS, Santiago R. (b. 1955) of Bogota, Colombia. WBF World Master. Winner CAC Open Teams 1980, 81, 89; placed 2nd 1985, 87. 2nd South American Junior championships 1979-80. Has won all national titles.

ROBAUDO, Maria Antonietta (b. 1926), of Genoa, Italy. WBF World Life Master. Won World Women's Teams 1972, 76, European Women's Teams 1970, 71, 73, 74, EEC Women's Teams 1971, 1973.

ROBB, Audrey W. (b. 1934) of New York City, real estate agent. Won Non-Life Master Pairs 1992,

ROBB, Paul H. (b. 1923) of Altamonte Springs FL, bridge teacher and professional player, home remodeling. Served as co-chairman Washington NABC 1973. Diamond Life Master with more than 9000 points Placed 3rd Epson Pairs 1998, won 50+ regionals.

ROBBINS, Lawrence (Larry) (b. 1954) of Chicago, physician, won GNOT 1979, 91; placed 2nd 1984, 86. Won Team Trials 1996, represented U.S. in World Team Olympiad 1996. Won Intercollegiate Championship 1976.

ROBINSON, Arthur Guy (b. 1936) of Villanova PA, bridge teacher. WBF Life Master, placed 2nd Bermuda Bowl 1963, World Team Olympiad 1964, 68; 5th World Open Pairs 1962. Won Team Trials 1967, 2nd in 1962. Won Vanderbilt 1961, 68; Open Pairs 1962; Reisinger 1966, 67. Placed 2nd Master Individual 1960; Chicago (now the Reisinger) 1961; Vanderbilt 1965.

ROBINSON, Eric S. (b. 1956) of Scarsdale NY, attorney. Won GNOP 1979.

ROBINSON, Frances E. (1908-1985) of Philadelphia, former teacher. Member of one of U.S. teams that played against the visiting British women's team 1953, won Women's Teams 1947, 49. Mother of Arthur G. Robinson.

ROBINSON, Gary (b. 1943) of Lafayette CA, insurance broker, hypnotherapist; won Non-Life Master Pairs 1965, Inventor of anti-signaling bridge playing cards.

ROBINSON, Maurice (b. 1918) of New York City, attorney and social worker. President American Bridge Association 1964-69 and one of its national tournament directors.

ROBINSON, Steve W. (b. 1941) of Arlington VA, retired computer specialist, bridge professional. Active in WBL since 1971, serving as a Board member 1971-78, 80, 87-88, president 1979, treasurer since 1989, president District 6 1985, vice president 1982-85, was District 6 representative to the ACBL Board of Governors 1975-81, 1st alternate to ACBL Board of Directors (District 6) 1980-86, 1996-99, 2nd alternate 1978-79, 1987-93. WBF Life Master, won World Mixed Teams 1974,

Rosenblum Teams 1986, China Cup 1997. Grand Life Master with 25,791 MPs as of 3/2001, ranked #9 in ACBL. Co-inventor of CRASH convention. Won Herman Trophy, Men's Pairs 1971; Reisinger 1972, 86; Blue Ribbon Pairs 1973, 75; Men's BAM 1978, 89; GNOT 1984, 88, 92; GNOP 1985, Mixed Pairs 1985; Men's Swiss Teams 1986; Mott-Smith Trophy 1987; Vanderbilt 1987, 91, 97, Open BAM Teams 1994. Placed 2nd Life Master Men's Pairs 1971, 72, Men's Teams 1973, 74; Men's Pairs 1973, 74; Master Mixed Teams 1973; GNOT 1977, 85; Spingold 1979, 92, 96; Blue Ribbon Pairs 1982; Life Master Pairs 1987; Men's BAM Teams 1989; Vanderbilt 1992, 99, Life Master Open Pairs 1994.

ROBINSON, William A. (Bill) (1918-1992) of Campbellcroft ON. Unit 166 president 1967, Canadian Bridge Federation president 1969, District 2 president 1972.

ROBISON, James R. (Jim) (b. 1942) of Los Angeles CA, bridge and poker professional. Placed 7th World Mixed Pairs 1982, 16th Rosenblum Cup 1986. Grand Life Master with 14,434 MPs as of 3/2001, won North American Swiss Teams 1979, 90; Reisinger 1984, Open Pairs 1985, IMP Pairs 1998. 2nd Open Pairs 1981, Mixed Pairs 1987; Men's Swiss Teams 1982, Reisinger 1986.

ROBSON, Andrew M. (b. 1964) of London, England, bridge writer, professional player. WBF World Master. Won European Teams 1991, World Junior Teams 1989, Junior EEC Teams 1989. Won Cap Gemini 1990, 2000; London Sunday Times Invitational 1990, Statten Bank 1990. Placed 3rd 1998 Generali World Individual, 5th Bermuda Bowl 1991. ACBL wins include Reisinger 1998, 99; 2nd Mixed BAM Teams 1998. Co-author of *Partnership Bidding*. Columnist of *London Times* and *Country Life*. Owner-manager of a club. Featured *Harper's and Queens*, an English women's magazine, as one of the 4 "Hot Properties of the Month".

ROCCHI, Egisto (1922-1984) of Buenos Aires, Argentina, wholesale furrier. World Life Master. Won South American Teams 1959, 61, 64, 76, 79, 80. Represented Argentina in 8 world championships. 35 national titles. Won Gabarret Cup 1963, 69, 76, 78, 82. Former director Argentine Bridge Association.

ROCHE, Michael J. (b. 1951) of Toronto ON, insurance company regional manager. WBF World Master. Placed 2nd Bermuda Bowl 1995 as npc of Canadian team; won CNTC 1993, 96; won15+ regionals.

ROCK, Lawrence J. (1945-1994) of University Heights OH, pension consultant. Member National Appeals Committee 1984-present, Dist 5 Executive Committee 1987-89, Unit 125 president 1981-83; contributor to District 5 and Unit 125 publications. Won Mixed Pairs 1984, Diamond Life Master

ROCKAWAY, Dr. Harold (Rocky) (1926-1993) of Houston, psychiatrist. Won Herman Trophy 1964, Open Pairs, Men's Teams 1953; Chicago (now the Reisinger) 1964; placed 2nd Men's Teams 1956, Life Master Men's Pairs 1964.

RODRIGUE, Claude (b. 1930) of London, England, born in Egypt, stockbroker. WBF World Life Master. Won World Par Contest 1961, European Teams 1961. Represented Britain in 7 world championships and 9 other zonal championships. Represented Egypt in 1 zonal championship and England in Camrose matches. Won London Sunday Times Invitational 1967. Many national wins include 3 Gold Cups. Magazine contributor.

RODRIGUE, Maria Elena Cucullu de (b. 1930) of

Buenos Aires, Argentina. Won South American Women's Teams 1957, 61, 66. Represented Argentina in 2 world championships. 19 national titles.

RODWELL, Eric V. (b. 1957) of Clearwater FL, professional bridge player, teacher and writer; accomplished pianist; composes music. Member ACBL Laws Commission, Conduct and Ethics Committee. One of leading bridge players in the world and one of a very small group of players to have won all 3 major world championships. World Grand Master, ranked #2 behind Bob Hamman. Won Bermuda Bowl 1981, 95, 99, World Open Pairs 1986, World Team Olympiad 1988; finished 2nd World Team Olympiad 1992, 2nd Bermuda Bowl 1997, 5th Rosenblum Teams 1988, 5th Bermuda Bowl 1991, 4th Bermuda Bowl 1993, 6th World Open Pairs 1982. Also won Macallan Pairs 1995, 96, 3rd Par Contest 1998, World Top Pairs 1988, 2nd Cap Gemini 1994, won Scientist vs Naturalist match in London, Iceland Pairs and Teams 1992, Pan-American Open Pairs 1992, NT Challenge Match 1993; placed 2nd Sunday Times Pairs 1993. Won Cavendish Invitational 2000, Cavendish Teams 2000.

Outstanding theoretician, he designed RM (Rodwell-Meckstroth) Precision System and invented Support Doubles, Serious 3- Notrump and many other bids. Co-author of *Joy of Bridge, The Joy of Bridge Companion, Bridge Maxims*; also a major contributor to the Teaching Series of books authored by Audrey Grant. Grand Life Master with 30,584 MPs, #7 in ACBL. Won Reisinger 1979, 85, 93, 94, 95; Open Pairs 1979, Life Master Men's Pairs 1979; Life Master Pairs 1980, 86, 91; Mott-Smith Trophy 1980; Vanderbilt 1980, 82, 85, 95, 2000; USBC (Team Trials) 1981, 88, 91, 92; Blue Ribbon Pairs 1982, 85, 98; Lou Herman Trophy 1982, 85; Spingold 1984, 88, 91, 93, 94, 95, 96, 98, 99; Men's BAM 1984, Men's Swiss Teams 1989; GNOT 1990, 94, 99, 2000, Fishbein Trophy 1991, Open Pairs II 1999, Open Swiss Teams 1994, Open BAM Teams 1998, 99. Placed 2nd Spingold 1979, 85, 90; Reisinger 1980, Life Master Pairs 1983, Mixed Teams 1983, Life Master Men's Pairs, USBC 1985, 93; Life Master Open Pairs 1992, Vanderbilt 1991, 96, Open BAM Teams 1998, 99; Blue Ribbon Pairs 1999.

ROET, Leo (b. 1903) of Hallandale FL, won Life Master Pairs 1949, Master Mixed Teams 1951; Men's Teams 1949. Placed 2nd Open Pairs 1945, 50, 52.

ROGERS, Michael P. (b. 1939) of Boynton Beach FL, bridge lecturer and tournament director. Has directed on bridge cruises more than 1000 days. Unit 156 president 1980-81, invented Victory Point scale for Chicago.

ROGERS, Rebecca (Becky) (b. 1939) of Las Vegas, former WBF general manager and assistant, former ACBL national tournament director (since 1979), former ACBL director of operations. Coordinator of World Junior Championship 1991; npc of U.S. Women's Olympiad Team 1992. Second woman to achieve national rating as a director. Served on several President's Advisory Committees in which were developed new convention charts, active ethics program, ACBL standard card. Placed 2nd Silver Ribbon Pairs 1997.

ROGERS, Reece D. (1951-1998) of Cordova TN. Diamond Life Master, 2nd GNOT 1974, GNOP 1994.

ROHAN, Karl (b. 1934) of Salzburg, Austria, and Boca Raton FL, entrepreneur and prominent at world level as a bridge administrator; former WBF treasurer. WBF World Life Master. 2nd Bermuda Bowl 1985; won World Senior Teams 1994, 98; 3rd World Senior Pairs 1990; rep-

resented Austria in 3 other world championships. European champion 1985. Played in 4 other European Championships. Twice 3rd in European Senior Pairs. Won CAC Open Pairs, Copa d'Oro (Paris) and Tournoi de Champions du Monde (Deauville, France). Won Austrian Teams 3 times and Open Pairs 2 times.

ROHOWSKY, Roland (b. 1967) of Stuttgart, Germany, bridge teacher. WBF World Master. Won Rosenblum Teams 1990, thus becoming at 22, the youngest ever world bridge champion. Won 5 national titles.

ROMANET, Bertrand (b. 1921) of Paris. WBF World Life Master, won Bermuda Bowl 1956, World Par Championship 1963, European Championship 1955. Won many national titles including Open Teams 4 times. Inventor of Alpha System. Author of 4 bridge books.

ROMANSKI, Jacek (b.1950) of Lublin, Poland, bridge professional. WBF World Life Master. Won World Teams 1984, 2nd European Open Teams 1997, 3rd European Open Pairs 1999; 4th World Open Pairs 1994. Represented Poland in many World and European Championships. Won many national titles.

ROMIK, Pinhas (b. 1946) of Tel Aviv, Israel, born in USSR, physicist. 2nd European Teams 1975, European Junior Teams 1972. Represented Israel in 1 world championship and 2 other European Championships. Won 4 National League titles. Founded e-bridge, a major online bridge service, in 2000.

RON, Jacob (b 1973) of Arhus, Denmark. WBF World Master. Won World Junior Teams 1997, 3rd 1995. 2nd European Junior Teams 1994, 3rd 1996. Won Nordic Junior Teams 1993, European Union Junior Teams 1996. Won 8 Danish championships.

RONA, Gianarrigo, EBL president, member of EBL Executive since 1995. Member WBF Executive Council. President of Italian Bridge Federation.

RONCARELLI, Mimi (1909-1980) of Montreal, bridge club owner. Represented Canada in World Women's Team Olympiad, won Women's Teams 1947.

RONEMUS, Marti of York PA, owns and operates a bridge club and karate studio. Easybridge! field coordinator for ACBL.

RONG, Gaotang (b. 1912) of Beijing, China. President Chinese Bridge Association. Chairman of Chinese organizing committee of 1995 Bermuda Bowl and Venice Cup in Beijing.

ROOSEN, Russell W. (1908-1995) of Hamden CT, formerly of Detroit; bridge club manager, one of Detroit's most prominent bridge figures in early days of contract as a teacher, lecturer, problem composer and instructor via radio. At exhibitions he demonstrated a remarkable memory by playing 10 separate hands simultaneously while blindfolded. Author of *When to Play Bridge and How*; bridge columnist for the Detroit *Free Press*; member *The Bridge World* panel from 1956 to 1995.

ROOT, William S. (Bill) (b. 1923) of Boca Raton FL, bridge teacher, lecturer and writer. Member ACBL Hall of Fame. Served as national tournament director for Intercollegiate Par-Hand Bridge Tournament 1959-1965 for about 400 colleges. During same period represented Association of American Playing Card Manufacturers as its authority on card games. Considered by many to be the foremost teacher on bridge, has taught tens of thousands in past 42 years; probably more than any bridge teacher in history. His bridge cruises have become legendary. Organized many duplicate bridge clubs in the Greater New York area. Contributing editor to the *Cromwell-Collier Ency-*

clopedia, The Official Encyclopedia of Bridge. Authored *Common Sense Bidding, The ABCs of Bridge, How to Play a Bridge Hand, Modern Bridge Conventions* (co-authored with Richard Pavlicek) and *How to Defend a Bridge Hand.* His videos are *Bill Root Teaches Bridge, Volume 1 - Bidding, Volume 2 The Play of the Hand, Volume 3 - Defense, Volume 4 Open Leads, Volume 5 - Non-Competitive Bidding.*

Placed 2nd Bermuda Bowl 1967, World Team Olympiad 1968, 6th Rosenblum Cup 1986; 2nd USBC (Team Trials) 1987, 92. WBF World Life Master. Diamond Life Master, won Men's Pairs 1953, Chicago (now the Reisinger) 1957; Spingold 1961, 66, 67; Reisinger 1967, 82, 83, 84, 90; Vanderbilt 1968, 83, 86, 95. Placed 2nd Spingold 1963, 74, 78; Men's Teams 1963; Reisinger, Open Pairs 1966; North American Men's Swiss Teams 1984; GNOT 1992, Life Master Pairs 1995. Numerous regional titles include Eastern States KO Teams 1960, 61, 66, 68, 88, 89.

ROSE, Albert (1908-1970) of London, England, textile converter. 2nd World Team Olympiad 1960, 3rd Bermuda Bowl 1962. Won European Teams 1961, 2nd 1953. Represented Britain in 2 other world championships and 1 zonal championship. National wins include 7 Gold Cups.

ROSE, Eddie (b. 1938) of Laguna Niguel CA, bridge instructor, city council member. Wrote bridge column for Aliso Viejo/Laguna Niguel *Review* 1991-92, Invented ROSE (Raise Our Suit Effectively) Double, won 15+ regionals.

ROSE, Irving N. (1938-1996), bridge-club manager. 3rd World Team Olympiad 1976. 2nd European Teams 1981. Represented Britain in 2 other world championships and 5 other zonal championships. Played frequently in Camrose Trophy matches, won more than 15 national titles including Gold Cup.

ROSE, Steven M (b. 1949) of Des Plaines IL, data processing consultant, won 25+ regionals

ROSE-HALL, Marilyn J. (b. 1944) of Lake Worth FL, retired computer specialist. Co-authored *How the Experts Win at Bridge*, ABTA Book of the Year 1999. Won about 20 regionals.

ROSEN, Edward L. (Eddie) (b. 1929) of Los Angeles CA, controller. Diamond Life Master, won Life Master Pairs 1959, Mixed Pairs 1960, 62.

ROSEN, Eunice M. (b. 1930) of Highland Park IL, retired free-lance editor. Diamond Life Master, won Master Mixed Teams 1958, 66; finished 2nd Women's BAM Teams 1972.

ROSEN, Robert (Bob) (b. 1941) of Delray Beach FL, bridge professional, bridge club owner. Has served in various executive positions Unit 128 including president 1992, District 9 president, national recorder 1985-95. Placed 4th Senior Teams 1998, 5th as npc U.S. Bermuda Bowl team 1991; (tied 5th/6th); npc USBC (Team Trials) winners 1991. Bermuda Bowl II 1993 (4th), coach of U.S. Junior teams 1995, 97, 99. Diamond Life Master, Rookie of Year 1977. Won 160+ regionals.

ROSEN, William A. (Billy) (b. 1928) of Highland Park IL, options trader. WBF Life Master, won Bermuda Bowl 1954, placed 2nd 1955. Was 25 when he won Bermuda Bowl, youngest player ever to win that title until 1981 when the record was broken by Robert Levin. Diamond Life Master, won McKenney Trophy 1953, Men's Pairs 1952, Spingold 1953, 54; Life Master Pairs 1953, Master Mixed Teams 1958, 66 (2nd in 1965); GNOT 1978, Men's Teams 1980.

ROSENBERG, Beverly of Sherman Oaks CA, bridge teacher, formerly accountant, placed 5th World Olympiad Women's Teams 1988, 7th World Mixed Pairs 1986, 2nd Pan Am Women's Pairs 1992. Grand Life Master with more than 14,000 MPs, won Women's Pairs 1982, Women's KO Teams 1984, 88; North American Women's Swiss Teams 1988; placed 2nd Women's Teams 1973, Women's Pairs 1977, 80, North American Women's Swiss Teams 1987; North American Swiss Teams 1987, Women's BAM Teams 1989, 94. *Bridge World* Master Solver panelist.

ROSENBERG, Debbie (b. 1968) of Westchester NY, bridge teacher and professional player; member of Junior Corps; served as a member Greater New York B.A. board and Education Liaison to ACBL. Won World Junior Championship 1991.

ROSENBERG, Michael (b. 1954) of New York City, formerly of Glasgow, Scotland, stock options trader. Authored *Bridge, Zia and Me.* Contributor to *Bridge Today.* World Grand Master, ranks #38 in world, Won World Par Contest 1998, Rosenblum Teams 1994, placed 2nd World Team Olympiad 1992, Open Pairs 1994, 2nd Rosenblum Teams 1994, 3rd Bermuda Bowl 1999. Won Camrose Trophy 1974, 76, 77, 3 Junior Camrose Trophies, European Junior Championship 1978, London Sunday Times Invitational 1975 and 2nd 1978, Cavendish Invitational 1986, 1992 (2nd 1978), Cap Gemini Pairs 1992, 95 and 3rd 1994-96., represented Great Britain in Common Market Championships 1975. Youngest person ever to win the British Gold Cup 1976 and London Sunday Times Invitational 1975 (age 21); also won Scottish Rayne Trophy 1972, placed 2nd British Team Trials 1976, Scottish Team Trials 1973. Grand Life Master with 14,214 MPs as of 3/2001. Won Team Trials 1991, 97, 99, Vanderbilt 1994, 96; Reisinger 1989, 96; Spingold, Open BAM Teams 1991, 96; Life Master Open Pairs 1992, Blue Ribbon Pairs 1993, Life Master Pairs 2000, Open Pairs I 1994; placed 2nd Team Trials 1996, Spingold 1980, 93, 95; GNOT 1981, Vanderbilt 1990, 91, 2000; Open Swiss Teams 1992. ACBL Player of the Year 1994 with 545 MPs, 2nd 1993, 3rd 1992. Learned chess at age 9, represented Scotland in the World Student Chess Olympiad 1969, 71, 72, 80.

ROSENBERG, Milton (b. 1944) of Winfield IL, precious metals broker. Diamond Life Master, won GNOT 1978, Men's Teams 1980, Men's Swiss 1984; placed 2nd Vanderbilt 1977. Won 50+ regionals.

ROSENBERG, Mortimer (Monty) (b. 1923) of Belfast, Northern Ireland, retired furniture dealer. In a 36-year career has represented Northern Ireland more often than any other player in Camrose Trophy matches. Represented Ireland several times in world and European championships. Many wins in national Open Teams and Open Pairs. Former NIBU competitions secretary and former chairman. Past president Irish Bridge Union.

ROSENBERG, Ronald (b. 1922) of Bronx NY, accountant and purchasing agent. Won Spingold 1956, placed 2nd Men's Teams 1951.

ROSENBLOOM, Edith L. (b. 1903) of Miami Beach FL, former high school teacher. Won Mixed Pairs 1951.

ROSENBLUM, Julius (1906-1978) of New Orleans, a leading American bridge personality. President World Bridge Federation 1970-76, ACBL president 1951. Won Men's Pairs 1960. Captained U.S. team that defeated Italy in 1951 Bermuda Bowl, played briefly thus becoming the only person to have captained and played on a team that defeated the Italians. Also captained U.S. teams in 1963, 66, 67, 68. Became WBF secretary-treasurer 1966

and a voting member of WBF Executive Committee in 1968 when he was appointed to replace Waldemar von Zedtwitz, who retired. Elected to WBF Committee of Honor. International Bridge Press Association bestowed the Charles Goren Man of the Year award on him 1975. In 1977 the Australian Bridge Federation named him to Life Membership, the 1st non-Australian to be so honored. ACBL Honorary Member 1970.

ROSENBLUM, Michael (b.1956) of Moscow, Russia, mathematician. Vice president of Russian Bridge League. Bridge writer and organizer. Represented Soviet Union in 1 world championship and 1 zonal championship. Several national wins.

ROSENBLUM, Robert D. (b. 1927) of San Diego CA, travel agency owner. Past president Unit 539 and District 22; co-chairman Fall NABC 1984, bridge columnist for *San Diego Union* 1968-88, weekly bridge columnist Copley News Service 1975-81. Placed 2nd GNOT 1990.

ROSENDORFF, Hans-Gunther (1910-1983) of Perth, Australia, born in Germany, retired librarian and bridge writer. Many times npc of Australian Women's Teams. National wins include Men's Pairs once, Individual twice. Held many executive positions. Columnist *West Australian* 1956-83 and *Weekend News* 1978-83.

ROSENKRANZ, Edith (Mrs. Jorge) (b. 1924) of Mexico City, born in Austria; represented Mexico World Women's Team Olympiad 1962, 64, 66, 70, 74, 76, 78, 80, 82, 86, 90; served as npc Mexican Olympiad Team 1988. Mexico's leading female masterpoint holder, Mexico's first female Life Master; 4-time winner of John Pike Memorial Trophy for best overall performance at Mexican Nationals. Won Open Swiss Teams 1998,North American Women's Swiss 1990, Master Mixed Teams 1990; placed 2nd Master Mixed Teams 1967, 84.

ROSENKRANZ, Jorge (George) (b. 1916) of Mexico City, chemist and founding chairman of Syntex Corporation, made scientific contributions in the field of steroid hormones, namely cortisone and birth control pills. Leading Mexican player and theorist, has represented Mexico in world championships continuously with few exceptions since 1962, was npc of both Mexican teams 1964 and of a team in the USBC 1984. Placed 3rd Bermuda Bowl 1983. ACBL Honorary Member 1990, member ACBL Hall of Fame. ACBL Grand Life Master with 14,229 MPs as of 3/2001, was Mexico's first Life Master. Established Rosenkranz Award for International Bridge Press Association 1975, won Precision Award 1976. Writings include contributions to the ACBL *Bridge Bulletin* and other bridge periodicals. Has authored 10 bridge books including *The Romex System of Bidding, Win with Romex, Bid Your Way to the Top, Trump Leads, Tips for Tops, More Tips for Tops, Bridge: The Bidders Game,* also *Modern Ideas in Bidding, Bidding on Target* with Alan Truscott and *Bid to Win, Play for Pleasure* with Phillip Alder. Invented Dynamic Notrump, Mexican Two Diamonds, Rosenkranz Doubles; author of the Romex System. Served as president of Mexican Federation of Bridge and Mexican Unit of the ACBL, member of ACBL Laws Commission since 1977. Won Vanderbilt 1975, 76, 82; Spingold 1976, 84; GNOT 1981, Men's BAM Teams 1984, 87; Reisinger 1985, Master Mixed Teams, North American Swiss 1990; Men's Swiss 1991. Placed 2nd Blue Ribbon Pairs 1974, Men's Teams 1975, Vanderbilt 1978, 2001, Reisinger 1980, 1997, Team Trials 1982, Master Mixed Teams 1967, 84, 1994; Open BAM Teams 1990, 2000, Open Swiss Teams 1998, Sil-

ver Ribbon Pairs 1992. Won John Pike Memorial Trophy for best overall performance at the Mexican Nationals 12 times.

ROSETTA, Annalisa (b. 1957) of Busto Arsizio, Italy, dentist. 3rd European Women's Teams 1993, 2nd EEC Women's Teams 1993.

ROSLER, Lawrence (Larry) (b. 1934) of Palo Alto CA, senior scientist - Hewlett-Packard Labs, former physicist. Placed 2nd World Par Championship 1961, won North American Zone World Par Championship 1963; Men's Pairs 1965. Served as vice president and president New Jersey BL 1967-1970. Developed some team-of-four movements and helped introduce and popularize Swiss Teams competitions. Co-authored *Journalist Leads* (with Jeff Rubens) and assisted in writing *Bridge Is a Partnership Game* and *Better Bidding in 15 Minutes.* Was editor of *The Bridge Journal* (no longer published). Contributes articles to *The Bridge World* and is a contributing editor to *The Official Encyclopedia of Bridge.* Co-inventor of Journalist Leads, Astro, Astro Cuebid.

ROSNER, Warren M. (b. 1944) of White Plains NY, systems analyst. WBF World Master. Placed 13th Rosenblum Teams 1982, 86, 12th World Simultaneous Pairs. Won Blue Ribbon Pairs 1980, Men's Pairs 1980, 81; Spingold 1981; placed 2nd GNOT 1979, Vanderbilt 1982. Posted 84.7% game in GNOP qualifying game 1981.

ROSS, Harry (b. 1928) of Des Moines IA, born in Austria, retired salesman. Started or helped to start duplicate bridge in Mason City, Ottawa, LaSalle, Pontiac and Streator, all in Iowa. Grand Life Master with 11,900 MPs as of 3/2001, won GNOP 1979, Senior Swiss Teams 1997, Has contributed articles to *The Bridge World;*

ROSS, Hugh L. (b. 1937) of Oakland CA, born in Montreal, systems analyst. WBF Grand Master, ranks 27th in world, won Bermuda Bowl 1976, 85, 87; placed 2nd Bermuda Bowl 1977, 89; Rosenblum Teams 1982, 7th World Olympiad Open Teams 1976. Npc Bermuda Bowl team USA II 1991. Grand Life Master with 12,695 MPs as of 3/2001. Won Reisinger 1968, 74, 75, 81, 85, 86; Team Trials 1975, 85, 87, 89; GNOT 1982, 83, 85, 87, 93, 96; Vanderbilt 1984, 87; North American Swiss Teams 1996, Open Swiss Teams 1995, Life Masters Open Pairs 1990, 91. Was 2nd Reisinger 1966, 83; GNOP 1985, Open Swiss Teams 1994, Life Master Pairs 1992.

ROSS, John (b. 1948) of Brampton ON, self-employed, founder of Flin Flon DBC, co-founder of Northern Manitoba Unit, served as first president. Invented Low Tolerance Redouble, Good Two Notrump (both published in *The Bridge World).* Won 15+ regionals.

ROSSANO, Enza (b. 1953) of Turin, Italy. Won World Mixed Pairs 1998, EEC Mixed Teams 1998, Mixed Pairs 1996; Italian Mixed Pairs 1997.

ROTH, Alvin L. (Al) (b. 1914) of Boca Raton FL, formerly of New York City, owner and manager of Mayfair Club, one of greatest players of all time, generally considered the most original bidding theorist of his bridge generation. Member ACBL Hall of Fame. Won North American championships with 11 different partners. Represented North America Bermuda Bowl 1955, 58, 67; WBF World Life Master, placed 2nd World Team Olympiad 1968. Co-inventor of Roth-Stone System. Contributions to bidding theory include Unusual Notrump, Weak-Two's, 1NT Forcing, Negative Double. Author of *The Roth-Stone System, Al Roth on Bridge, Picture Bidding,,* co-author of *Bridge is a Partnership Game, Modern Bridge Complete, Bridge for Beginners.* On staff of *Bridge Today,* on the panel of

The Bridge World, Bridge Today, Australian Bridge. Grand Life Master with 12,581 MPs as of 3/2001, won Spingold 1940, 56, 57, 63, 67; Open Pairs 1942, Master Individual 1943, Vanderbilt 1943, 63, 68; Chicago (now the Reisinger)1946, 52; Lou Herman Trophy, Mixed Pairs 1952; Master Mixed Teams 1952, 53, 55, 65; Men's Teams 1955, 61, 69, 71; Life Master Pairs 1956, 71, 72; Open Pairs 1960, Fishbein Trophy 1963, 65, 66; Reisinger 1967. Placed 2nd Chicago (now the Reisinger) 1937, 54; Spingold 1943, 45, 53, 61; Master Mixed Teams 1945, 63, 74, 75; Men's Teams 1957, 73, 77; Open Pairs 1958; Life Master Pairs 1965; Reisinger 1966; Team Trials 1967; Vanderbilt 1975. His numerous regional wins include Eastern States KO Teams (Reisinger) 1946, 60, 61, 66, 68, Open Pairs (Goldman) 1961, 77, 78, 79. During his first world championship, Roth was declaring a 2♠ contract and felt he had played the hand before as a defender. The director, Al Sobel, did not believe him as the hands had been hand-dealt. Sobel made Roth call out the all the cards in each hand, including the spots, before he threw the hand out. No one knows to this day how it happened.

ROTH, Daniel L. M. (b. 1946) of London, author of a number of bridge books, including *Clues to Winning Play, Signal Success in Bridge, Awareness, The Way to Improve your Bridge, Bridge—Groundwork in Play and Defence, Why Women Win at Bridge, Hand Reading in Bridge, The Expert Beginner, The Expert Improver, The Expert Advancer, The Expert Club Player.*

ROTHFIELD, Carole (b. 1933) of Melbourne, Australia. Represented Australia in Bermuda Bowl 1998, 2000, at a record age for a woman player. Won South Pacific Teams 1998 and 2 national titles. Won Maccabiah Teams 1985.

ROTHFIELD, Jessel (b. 1917) of Melbourne, Australia, born in Scotland, company director. Won PABF (Far East) Teams 1968, 1970. Represented Australia in 2000 Bermuda Bowl at the age of 82 (a record) and in 2 other zonal championships. Won Australian Pairs 1970, Maccabiah Teams 1985. President Australian Bridge Federation 1967-71. Organizer of PABF (Far East) Championship 1971. Former member WBF Executive Council. Marathon runner.

ROTHLEIN, Robert R. (1922-1995) of Orlando FL, general contractor, former governor of Florida Unit, founder and president of Central Florida Unit; won Spingold 1958, placed 2nd 1954.

ROTHSCHILD, Donald R. (b. 1931) of Sunnyvale CA, bridge teacher, retired electrical engineer. Won 15+ regionals.

ROTMAN, Daniel (Danny) (b. 1932) of Aventura FL, bridge professional and retired businessman. Placed 5th Rosenblum Teams 1990. Grand Life Master with 11,063 MPs as of 3/2001, won Life Master Pairs 1959, Morehead Trophy 1967, Mixed Teams 1969, 88; GNOT 1978, Men's BAM Teams 1985, Spingold 1987; placed 2nd Open Pairs 1963, 73; Men's Teams 1965, Reisinger 1967, Vanderbilt 1989, North American Swiss 1992.

ROTMAN, Florence (Flo) (b. 1931) of Aventura FL, retired stock options trader, now a day trader. Won Mixed Teams 1969, Women's Pairs 1978, Life Master Women's Pairs 1995.

ROTZELL, Peggy (1929-1969) of Philadelphia, bridge teacher. Edited ACBL *Bridge Bulletin* feature *Hand o' the Month* in the early Sixties and authored 2 books, *Bridge Play and Defense, Bridge Bidding Complete.* Won Women's Teams 1956, 58.

ROUDINESCO Jean-Marc (b. 1932) of Boulogne, France, bridge writer, translator and theoretician. WBF World Life Master. European champion 1966, 70. Represented France in Bermuda Bowl 1967, 1971. National titles include 4 in Open Teams. Inventor of 2♣ Roudi. *Author of Le Dictionnaire des Maniements de Couleurs* 1995, translated into English with the title *The Dictionary of Suit Combinations.* Other books include *La Majeure par Tournoi par paires, L'intelligence du Bridge* and *Initiation au Bridge.* Contributor to *Revue Francaise de Bridge.*

ROUTMAN, Mark J. (b. 1944) of Cleveland MS, professor of sociology. Author of *Club Level Duplicate Bridge: Which Strategies Win?*

ROVERA, Laura (b. 1956) of Pavia, Italy, teacher. WBF World Master. 3rd European Women's Teams 1993, 2nd EEC Women's Teams 1993, 96. Won 2 Italian titles, top woman in Italian rankings 1994.

ROVERE, Ernest (Ernie) (1906-2000) of Carmel CA, journalist, author, director of Contract Bridge Cruises. ACBL Honorary Member 1986. Bridge editor for San Francisco *Chronicle*, bridge columnist San Francisco *Call Bulletin* for 23 years, commentator on radio and TV bridge programs. Conducted one of longest running TV bridge programs, 32 weeks on 2 PBS stations with 12,000 students. Pioneer in changing rules and laws restricting blacks and Jews from being included in the bridge community, served as member of ACBL Board of Directors 1957-60. Contributing editor to *Bridge Encyclopedia*, author of *Leads, Signals and Discards, Modern Point-Count Contract Bridge, Contract Bridge Complete.* Won Master Mixed Teams 1955.

ROWE, Nelson G. (b. 1913) of Atlanta GA, associate national tournament director, began directing career 1946. 4-time president of Georgia Unit, ACBL Board of Directors member 1956-57.

ROY, Debasish (b. 1956) of Calcutta, share-broker. 4th World Open Teams 1988, 2nd BFAAME Open Teams 1989, represented India in 2 other world championships. 7 nationals wins.

ROY, Robi N. (b. 1931) of Calcutta, India, retired government officer. Represented India in 3 world championships and 3 zonal championships. Won Far East Pairs 1979, 80. 22 national wins.

ROZECKI, Aleksander (1912-1975) of Warsaw, Poland, bridge writer and editor. Represented Poland in 1 World Championship and 1 European Championship. Won 2 national titles. Author of 2 bridge books. Former executive editor of *Brydz* magazine.

RUBBRA, Fredrick C. (Fred) (d. 1987) of Nassau, Bahamas, born in Canada, retired stockbroker, represented Bahamas in world play 1970, 72, 76, 80. Founder, honorary president and representative to the World Bridge Federation of the Bahamas Contract Bridge Club. Won many regionals.

RUBENS, Jeff (b. 1941) of Scarsdale NY, editor and co-editor of *The Bridge World* since 1967, mathematician, computer scientist, educator, bridge writer, editor. Collaborated with Bill Root and Larry Rosler in creating and judging par hands for Intercollegiate Par Hand Tournament. Edited *The Bridge Journal* (now defunct) 1963-66, Bols Tip competition winner 1977, won Precision Award twice. Author of *Secrets of Winning Bridge, Swiss Match Challenge*, co-author of *Test your Play as Declarer* (two volumes), *Modern Bridge Bidding Complete* and *Bridge for Beginners, Oddings and Endings*, contributing editor to the *Bridge Encyclopedia.* Repre-

sented North America in Bermuda Bowl 1973, won Team Trials 1972. Won Men's Teams, Men's Pairs 1965; Spingold 1972, Intercollegiate Championship 1958.

RUBIN, Carl B. (1920-1995) of Cincinnati OH, attorney, Chief Judge U.S. District Court for Southern District of Ohio starting in 1969. ACBL president 1971, chairman of Board 1972. Member ACBL Board of Directors 1966-73, ACBL Honorary Member 1981. His vote as ACBL president broke a 12-12 tie and sent ACBL Headquarters from Greenwich CT to Memphis TN.

RUBIN, Ira S. (The Beast) (b. 1930) of Paramus NJ, retired mathematician, computer analyst, consultant and instructor, author of digital computer textbook. Has other interests in stamp collecting (British Colonies) and digital computers (1953-65). Invented Rubin Transfers, Two-Way Two Bids, Gladiator Responses to Notrump, Gladiator, Extended Landy. Ranks 27th among WBF Grand Masters, won Bermuda Bowl 1976, placed 2nd Bermuda Bowl 1966, 77; 2nd World Team Olympiad 1980, 4th World Open Pairs 1970, 5th World Team Olympiad 1960, 7th World Team Olympiad 1976, 8th World Open Pairs 1966. Diamond Life Master, member ACBL Hall of Fame, won Team Trials 1965, 75, 80; Spingold 1956, 59, 66, 79, 85; Men's Pairs 1958, 61, 62; Fishbein Trophy 1959, 62; Open Pairs 1961, Life Master Pairs 1962, Vanderbilt 1965, 66; Reisinger 1969, 74, 75, 78, 79; Lou Herman Trophy, Blue Ribbon Pairs 1970; North American Men's Swiss 1983. Placed 2nd Life Master Pairs 1954, 55, 63; Men's Pairs 1955, Master Mixed Teams 1957, Spingold 1957, 69; Reisinger 1965, Vanderbilt 1968, 69, 71, 81; Men's Teams 1976, 80. Placed 3rd Cavendish Invitational Pairs 1976.

RUBIN, Ronald D. (Ron) (b. 1948) of North Miami Beach FL, stock options trader, became regional tournament director at age 18. WBF World Life Master, won Bermuda Bowl 1983, 5th 1993; placed 5th Rosenblum Teams 1986, 10th 1982. Diamond Life Master, won Men's Teams 1975, Vanderbilt 1977, 81, 85, 89; Spingold 1980, 82, 92; USBC Team Trials 1980, 82; Open Pairs 1988, Life Master Pairs 1990. Placed 2nd Vanderbilt 1978, Team Trials 1980, GNOT 1981, 1992; Reisinger 1983, Spingold 1985, 88. Won *The Bridge World Challenge the Champs* competition 10 months in a row and the Rosenkranz Award in 1976. Co-authored *The Ultimate Club*. Won world championship in backgammon 1983, finished 2nd 1978, 89.

RUBINOW, Morton L. (1927-1962) of New York City, bridge teacher. Faculty member at The Card School, pioneer in giving bridge lessons through phonograph records, *Play Bridge with Morton Rubinow* and *Advanced Bridge Conventions*. Represented U.S. World Team Olympiad 1960, won Herman Trophy, Spingold, Open Pairs 1959; Men's Pairs 1961.

RUDERMAN, David L. (b. 1943) of Burtonsville MD, attorney, accountant. Won IMP Pairs 1993.

RUDMAN, William K., Jr. (Bill) (b. 1948) of Castro Valley CA, engineer. Won17+ regionals.

RUDOLPH, Richard P. (Rudy) (b. 1938) of Pickerington OH, retired engineer, was USAF tactical fighter pilot 1961-66. Diamond Life Master, won more than15 regionals.

RUIA, Ramniwas R. (1900-1979) of Bombay, India. Represented India 1960 World Team Olympiad, won several national titles. Former president Bridge Federation of India, former member WBF Executive.

RUMMEL, Aarne (b. 1953) of Tallinn, Estonia, head of informatics department. Won Soviet Union Teams 1982,

86, 87; Soviet Union Pairs 1981, 82; Estonian Teams 1980, 86, 87, 90, 92, 95, 97, 98, 1999; Estonian Pairs 1994. Represented Estonia in 2 world and 3 zonal championships. Secretary Estonia Tournament Bridge League.

RUNEBERG, Lorenzo (b. 1916) of Helsinki, Finland, doctor of forestry. Represented Finland in 8 European championships between 1938 and 1962. 11 national wins. Honorary president Bridge League of Finland.

RUNEBERT, Ulla (Mrs. Lorenzo) (b. 1916) of Helsinki, Finland. Represented Finland 1962 European championships, open division, and thus one of the few women ever to play in that event. Represented Finland 6 times in European Women's championship. 8 national wins.

RUPP, Henriette (Henree) (b. 1906) of Indianapolis IN, bridge director; one of the early organizers of bridge in Indianapolis area, Life Master #396; placed 2nd Women's Teams 1966.

RUSINOW, Sydney (1907-1953) of Newark NJ, businessman, silver mine owner. Designed system of opening leads that bears his name. Won Vanderbilt 1933. (See RUSINOW LEADS).

RUSKIN, Stanley C. (b. 1940) of Pittsburgh PA, CEO of packaging company. Won 18 regionals.

RUSS, William (Bill) (b. 1945) of Zurich, Switzerland, born in New York City, manager of leading trading and commodities company. Moved to Zurich at age 22 where he has recruited and trained young people. Has returned to U.S. 4 times to compete in ABA Nationals. Won Victor Daley KO Teams 1983, Mixed Teams 1997, C.G. Fredd KO Teams 1999, Men's Pairs 2000; placed 2nd Mixed Pairs 1983, Non-Mixed Pairs 1999, 2000. Co-ordinator of youth bridge in Switzerland; reached Swiss National finals 3 times playing with Juniors. ABA Diamond Life Master with more than 30 regional and national championships, most of which were earned before he moved to Switzerland at age 22. Won several Swiss national titles.

RUSSELL, Clifford (b. 1919-2001) of Coral Gables FL, banker, builder and developer; past chairman of Metropolitan Museum of Art (Coral Gables) and of First National Bank of Hialeah. Placed 3rd Rosenblum Teams 1978; won Pan-Am Open Teams 1992; 4th Bermuda Bowl 1993. Grand Life Master with 11,547 MPs at his death. Won Spingold 1963, 77; Vanderbilt 1963, 75, 79; GNOT 1977, Reisinger 1991. Placed 2nd Spingold 1954, 72, 91; Blue Ribbon Pairs 1963, 70; Reisinger, Master Mixed Teams 1964; Men's Teams 1973, 77; Vanderbilt 1975, 84, 89, 93; GNOT 1980, GNOP 1982, Men's BAM Teams 1983, USBC (Team Trials) 1987.

RUSSELL, John J. (b. 1936) of North Barrington IL, CPA. Diamond Life Master with more than 9,400 points, won Silver Ribbon Pairs 1997, placed 3rd Open BAM Teams 1996, has won 67 regionals.

RUST, Gail H. of Daytona Beach FL, bridge club co-owner and retired home economist, served for 20 years for District 4 and Unit 148 Boards, member ACBL National Appeals Committee, ACBL Board of Governors for District 9. Diamond Life Master, won more than 20 regionals.

RUTLEDGE, Thomas (b. 1939) of Charleston SC, former bank executive. Past president Mid-Atlantic Bridge Conference, South Carolina Unit 160, Diamond Life Master with more than 12,200 MPs, placed 3rd twice GNOT, won 50+ regionals.

RUTSTEIN, Donald I. (b. 1927) of Evanston IL, salesman, former professional jazz musician, interests in thoroughbred racing and breeding. Won ABA National KO

Teams 1978. Awarded Chicago CBA Harmon Wilkes Sportsmanship Award 1997.

RYAN, Marion (1912-1988) of Indianapolis IN. Placed 2nd Women's Pairs 1950, Women's Teams 1966.

RYDER, Robert W. (b. 1935) of Caldwell NJ, consulting actuary, New Jersey BL Player of the Year 1968, 76, 91; Grand Life Master. Won Open Pairs 1969, Senior Teams 2000; placed 2nd Senior Teams 1994, 96. Senior Player of Year 1997.

RYMAN, Mari (b. 1959) of Stockholm, Sweden, economist. WBF World Master. Was 3rd Venice Cup 1993, won European Women's Teams 1993, Nordic Teams 1992, 98. Represented Sweden in 3 other world championships and 2 other zonal championships.

S

SA, Joao Pereira de (b. 1954), of Oporto, Portugal, physician. Represented Portugal in 2 European championships. Won European Union Open Teams 1998.

SABURI, Ken (1901-1985) of Tokyo, Japan, managing director of trading house. Former president and honorary president JCBL. Presided over Far East Championships 1964 and 1979. Contributor *JCBL Bulletin*.

SACHEN, William F. (Bill) (b. 1930) of Lindenhurst IL, retired attorney. Club director 1971-93. Authored *Bridge: A Guide to the Literature*, contributor to *Bridge Buffs' Bulletin*, *ABTA Quarterly* and contributing editor to 4th and 5th editions *Encyclopedia of Bridge*. Bridge book and magazine collector.

SACHS, David S. (Dave) of Baltimore MD, actuary. Former president of Maryland BA. Diamond Life Master, won Mixed BAM Teams 1997. Placed 2nd Open Pairs 1969, Master Mixed Teams 1970, 74, 78; won numerous regional events.

SACHS, Edith of New York City, real estate broker. Won Master Mixed Teams 1973.

SACHS, Suzanne H. (Sue) (Mrs. David S.) of Baltimore MD, travel agency owner. Placed 2nd World Women's Pairs 1966, 3rd World Olympiad Women's Teams 1968, 3rd Venice Cup 1997. Represented ACBL in several other world championships. WBF Life Master and ACBL Grand Life Master with 11,087 MPs (3/2001). Won Women's Pairs 1965, Women's Teams 1966, 77, 79; Life Master Women's Pairs 1967, Mott-Smith Trophy 1969. She was 2nd in Women's Teams, Open Pairs 1969; Master Mixed Teams 1970, 74, 78; Women's KO Teams 1988.

SACKS, David L. (b. 1948) of Los Angeles, owner/operator of discount clothing stores. Placed 2nd Life Master Pairs 1978, Men's BAM Teams 1979, North American Men's Swiss Teams 1985. Won over 25 regional events.

SACUL, Denny J. (b. 1948) of Jakarta, Indonesia, businessman. WBF World Life Master, 2nd World Team Olympiad 1996. Won International Olympic Committee Teams 2000. Won PABF (Far East) Teams 1974, 1979, 1983, 1984, 1993. Represented Indonesia in 10 world championships and in other zonal Championships.

SADEK, Tarek Mohamed of Cairo, Egypt, WBF World Master. Won BFAAME Teams 1989. Quarterfinalist World Olympiad Teams 1992.

SAELENSMINDE, Erik (b. 1964) of Bergen, Norway,

student. WBF World Master. Nordic Team champion 1998. 3rd European Teams 1997, 1999. 3rd Bermuda Bowl 1998, 4th 2000. 2 national titles.

SAID, Chuck (b. 1937) of Nashville TN, born in Baghdad, professional bridge player and teacher. Grand Life Master with 23,549 MPs as of 3/2001, #17 in ACBL. Before he left native country in late Fifties he had stories published in magazines and a collection of short stories published in a book; also an editor for local newspaper. Won Senior KO Teams 1995, 97; Silver Ribbon Pairs 1997. Won more than 400 regionals.

SAKURAI, Tsuneo (b. 1937) of Chiba Pref., Japan, company employee. Represented Japan in 3 Far East Championships. Won 20 national open team titles and three national open pair titles. JCBL tournament committee chairman 10 years.

SALIM, Masood (b. 1940) of Karachi, Pakistan, businessman. WBF World Master. Placed 2nd Bermuda Bowl 1981, winner BFAME zonal championships 1981, 83, 85, 87. Played reguarly as partner of Zia Mahmood.

SALMENKIVI, Eero (b. 1958) of Espoo, Finland, philosopher and journalist. 2nd Nordic Teams 1984, represented Finland 5 other times, including 1 world championship and 2 European Championships. National wins include 7 open teams, 2 open pairs and 2 knockout teams. Former editor *Bridge-lehti*.

SALTSMAN, Barbara J. (Barbie) (b. 1936) of Montreal PQ. WBF World Master. Represented Canada in world play Miami Beach 1972, Bal Harbour 1986, Chile 1993, Bermuda 2000. Placed 2nd Master Mixed Teams 1974.

SALTSMAN, A. David (b. 1936) of Montreal PQ, stockbroker, placed 2nd Open Pairs 1975.

SALTZ, Jack B. (JBS) (b. 1936) of New York City, vice president Bear Stearns, won varsity football state championship. Placed 2nd Master Mixed Teams 1974, won many regionals.

SALVETTI, Sandro of Milan, Italy. Npc Italy's Bermuda Bowl champions 1973, 74, 75; npc Italy's European champions 1973, 75, 79. Chose to continue to use Sergio Zuchelli and Gianfranco Facchini after the 1975 Bermuda Bowl incident in which the pair were reprimanded for foot-tapping. See BERMUDA BOWL INCIDENT.

SANBORN, Kerri (formerly Shuman) (b. 1946) of Stony Point NY, stock trader. Actively involved in thoroughbred breeding and racing. One of leading women players in world, WBF Grand Master, ranks 8th among women Grand Masters and in the top 25 of all Grand Masters (2001). ACBL Grand Life Master with 18,526 MPs (3/2001). Had long and highly successful partnership with Barry Crane. They were quoted at 2-1 odds against field in World Mixed Pairs, won event by 5 boards.

Won World Mixed Pairs 1978, (2nd 1986), Venice Cup 1989, 93 (2nd 1995, 3rd 97); World Women's Pairs 1990. Also 5th Olympiad Women's Teams 1988, Rosenblum Teams 1990; 8th World Women's Pairs 1986. Represented ACBL in Par Contest 1990 in Geneva. (This event was by invitation only, limited to about 10-15 players from throughout the world, she was the only woman to be invited!) Won McKenney Trophy 1974, setting a new record. Won Women's Pairs 1972, Women's Teams 1978, Mixed Pairs 1975, 77, 82; North American Women's Swiss Teams 1989, 90, 93; Master Mixed Teams 1980, 87, 90; finished 2nd Mixed Pairs 1971, 74; Women's Teams 1974, Life Master Women's Pairs 1975, 85, 86; North American Women's Swiss Teams 1983, Women's

KO Teams 1986, Blue Ribbon Pairs 1987, Reisinger 1989, Master Mixed Teams 1994. Sanborn has won hundreds of regional titles.

SANBORN, Steve (b. 1954) of Stony Point NY, former options trader, former computer marketing analyst/consultant. NPC 2nd place Venice Cup team 1995. Won Men's Pairs 1980; placed 2nd GNOP 1983, 5th Cavendish 1986. Won 20-25 regional titles including 6-7 GNOTs. With Warren Rosner in a GNOP qualifier had 84.7% game.

SANDERS, Carol L. (Mamma Bear) (Mrs. Thomas K.) (b. 1932) of Nashville TN. One of world's leading women players, WBF Grand Master. Won Venice Cup 1974, 76; World Women's Pairs 1982, Women's Team Olympiad 1984, npc winning Venice Cup team 1987. Placed 2nd Women's Pairs 1978, Venice Cup 1981, 85, 3rd World Mixed Pairs 1978; 3rd McConnell Cup 1998; 5th Women's Pairs 1974; 6th Olympiad Mixed Teams 1974, 7th World Mixed Pairs, World Women's Pairs 1974. Won Israel Swiss Team Championship 1986, 2nd Israel Women's Pairs 1994. Won Taipei Bridge Week Championships 1979, Beijing International Friendship Cup 1986, Ambassador's Cup 1987. Represented U.S. in world competition on many other occasions. Took leave of absence from bridge competition 1965-70 to tend to family when the oldest of 6 children were becoming teenagers.

Named ACBL co-Honorary Goodwill Member of Year 1997 with husband Tom. Nashville Unit Board member 20 years, appointed Honorary Member 1984. Trustee ACBL Charity Foundation 1989-97, vice chairman ACBL Goodwill Committee since the 80s, District 10 charity coordinator 1979-89. Chaired or co-chaired many Nashville tournaments. With husband was co-panelist on *Bridge World* Master Solvers forum for more than 30 years, past member of the ACBL Appeals Committee. Lecturer aboard cruise ships as well as at Tennessee State Penitentiary for Women.

ACBL Grand Life Master with 17,445 MPs (3/2001).Won Women's Pairs 1962, 93; Open Pairs 1964, Master Mixed Teams 1976, 82; Women's KO Teams 1978, 80, 83, 87, 99; North American Women's Swiss Teams 1983, 95; Life Master Women's Pairs 1990, Women's BAM Teams 1963, 92, 95; Women's Team Trials 1993. Placed 2nd Open Pairs 1960, the Chicago (now the Reisinger) 1961, Life Master Women's Pairs 1971, 81; Mixed Pairs 1979, North American Women's Swiss Teams 1985; Master Mixed Teams 1984, Women's KO Teams 1982, 92, 94; Women's BAM Teams 1986, 91, 2000; Women's Pairs 1990, 92.

SANDERS, Thomas K. (Pappa Bear) (Tom) (b. 1932) of Nashville TN, investor. Npc 1981 Bermuda Bowl champions, placed 2nd World Senior Teams 1994. Represented U.S. in world play Cannes 1962, Miami Beach 1972, Las Palmas 1974 (6th World Mixed Teams, 7th World Mixed Pairs), New Orleans 1978 (7th Rosenblum Teams, 13th World Open Pairs), Biarritz 1982, Bal Harbour 1986 (11th World Mixed Pairs), Geneva 1990. ACBL Grand Life Master with 16,339 MPs as of 3/2001. Won Mixed Pairs 1961, Men's Teams 1962, 72; Spingold, Blue Ribbon Pairs 1977; Vanderbilt 1979, 90, 93; Life Master Pairs, Master Mixed Teams 1982; Men's BAM Teams 1983, Senior KO Teams 1995, 96, 98. Placed 2nd Open Pairs 1960, Chicago (now the Reisinger) 1961; Spingold, Men's Pairs 1963; Reisinger 1973, 86; Vanderbilt 1978, 85; Mixed Pairs 1979; North American Swiss Teams 1982; USBC (Team Trials) 1990. Won Israel Swiss Team championship, Beijing International

Friendship Cup 1986, Beijing Ambassador's Cup 1987, Taipei Bridge Week Championship 1979. Won Cavendish Club Invitational Individual 1979, Open Pairs 1981.

ACBL president 1986, chairman of Board 1987. Founder ACBL Educational Foundation, served as its first president (1987-1990 and was elected President Emeritus in 1990). Member ACBL Board of Directors 1980-89. Lifetime member ACBL Board of Governors, past member of ACBL and WBF Appeals Committees. Only graduate of Vanderbilt University to win Vanderbilt Trophy. Chairman of Fall NABC 1988, has been *Bridge World* co-panelist (with wife, Carol) for more than 30 years. Has been panelist for Italian and Turkish bridge magazines. Received International Bridge Press Romex award for best bid hand of the year 1992-93; was named ACBL Goodwill Co-Honorary Member of Year (with wife Carol) 1997. Participant in Charles Goren's "Championship Bridge" series in Sixties. Traditional jazz buff and co-produces Dixieland jazz albums as a labor of love. Frequently lectures on bridge aboard cruise ships, won hundreds of regional events.

SANDS, Norma (b. 1938) of Denver CO, bridge teacher, writer, member ACBL Conduct & Ethics Committee since 1991. Author of *Standard American Bridge Updated, Playing the Cards*, and *Bridge Helper*. She co-authored (with Jan Janitschke) the *Bridge Mini Series*, which included *Fine Tuning Your Bridge, Later in the Auction, Opening Leads Versus Suits, Double Trouble, Weak Two Bids, Competitive Bidding, Defensive Signals, Negative Doubles, Slam Bidding I, Slam Bidding II*. This series was awarded Book of the Year 1992 by ABTA. Won District 17 GNOT 1990; Colorado Victory Trophy 1989.

SANDSMARK, Tommy (b. 1947) of Oslo, Norway. Bridge columnist, teacher, author and tournament director. Editor of his own bridge press agency, *Bridge & Kryss*, weekly column in *Dagsavisen*, editor of *Daily Bulletins* at many zonal championships. Principal of Norway's biggest bridge school. One of founders of the independent Norwegian bridge magazine, *Bridge i Norge*, which he published and edited 1985 to 1999. One of founders of Norwegian Bridge Press Association. IBPA president 1990-1996.

SANTAMARINA, Agustin (1934-1995) of Buenos Aires, Argentina, landowner. World Life Master. Won South American Teams 1962, 1964, 1976, 1979, 1980, 1981. Represented Argentina in 10 world championships. Many national titles. Won Gabarret Cup 1973, 1974, 1977, 1981.

SANTAMARINA, Marcos (b. 1931) of Buenos Aires, Argentina, landowner. Won South American Teams 1962, 1995 and represented Argentina in two world championships. 14 national titles.

SANTOS, Jorge Monteiro dos (b. 1941), of Lisbon, Portugal, lawyer. Represented Portugal in 3 world and 8 European championships. 4th in European Union Mixed Teams 1993. Won many national titles.

SANTOS, Maria Beatriz Oliveira Monteiro dos (b. 1925), of Lisbon, Portugal, physician. Represented Portugal in 1 world and 3 European championships. 4th European Union Mixed Teams 1993. 5th European Women's Teams 1970. Won many national titles.

SANTOS, Rui Silva (b. 1944), of Lisbon, Portugal, electrical engineer. Represented Portugal in 2 world and 6 European championships. President Portuguese Bridge Federation 1984-1986. Won European Union Open

Teams 1998. Won many national titles.

SAPIRE, Leon (B. 1910) of Johannesburg, South Africa, attorney. Won Open Pairs 1955. Founder and editor of *Bridge Bulletin*. Honorary life vice president South African BF. Former member WBF Executive Council, vice president IBPA.

SARAVIA, Alfredo (1908-91) of Buenos Aires, Argentina, real estate official. Won South American Teams 1964, and represented Argentina in Bermuda Bowl 1963. 16 national titles. Former president Argentine Bridge Association.

SARON, Robert (Bob) (1923-1990) of St. Petersburg FL, stockbroker, former company executive, District 9 representative to ACBL Board of Directors 1977-1990. Four-time president Unit 128, served more than 30 years as member of its Board and served as president of District 9. Bridge editor St. Petersburg *Times* and authored *Medical Directory of Good Bridge*. Won Fall NAC Secondary Commercial and Industrial Pairs 1961.

SARTORIUS, Barbara (b. 1941) of Lake Hiawatha NJ, professional bridge teacher/player. Member NJBL Board of Directors 1970-82. Diamond Life Master, won Open Pairs 1969, Life Master Women's Pairs 1998. Placed 2nd Life Master Women's Pairs 1990. Regional wins include District 3 GNOP 1989.

SARWAT, Safeya (Sophie) (b. 1933) of Cairo, Egypt. WBF World Master. Won BFAAME Women's Teams 1987, 91, 97, 2nd 1985. Represented Egypt in several world championships, won many national mixed pair titles.

SASSON, Esther (born in England) of Caracas, Venezuela. Won CAC Women's Teams 1979, 81, Represented Venezuela in 9 world championships. Won 24 national titles.

SAVAGE, Mike D. (b. 1941) of Downey CA, ACBL associate national director, former technical illustrator and commercial artist. Diamond Life Master, placed 2nd Senior Swiss Teams 2000, won 40+ regionals.

SAWIRUDIN, Munawar (b. 1948) of Jakarta, Indonesia, Staff Secretary of Chamber of Commerce. Won PABF (Far East) Teams 1979, 1982, 1984, 1992, 1993. Represented Indonesia in 6 world championships and in other zonal championships.

SAWYER, Victoria M. (Vicky) (b. 1975) of Occoquan VA, student. 4th youngest female ever to achieve Life Master rating 1990. Member Junior Corps, was appointed Chairman for Junior Activities for Summer NABC 1993. Won Junior Pairs 1992, placed 2nd Youth Pairs 1989, Youth Flight of Viking Pairs 1989, 90.

SAYED, Floyd E. (b. 1925) of Boca Raton FL, insurance agent, past president of Michigan BA, served on its Board more than 20 years. Diamond Life Master, won 20-25 regionals including District 12 GNOT Zone I 1973.

SCAFFIDI, Sam (1935-1988) of Mingo Junction OH, social worker. Described and named, with John Lowenthal, the Striped-Tail Ape Double.

SCANAVINO, Eduardo (b. 1941) of Buenos Aires, Argentina, bridge club manager and teacher. WBF World Master. Won South American Teams 1976, 79, 80, 81, 85, 94. Represented Argentina 9 world championships. 19 national titles. Junior chess champion.

SCHAAB, Gail K. (b. 1941) of Colorado Springs, engineering assistant, designed oil refineries. Won Women's Pairs 1976.

SCHAEFER, Lynne C. (b. 1955) of Southfield MI, vice-president for administrative services. Won Women's BAM Teams 1989.

SCHÄFFER, Lauge (b 1959) of Copenhagen, Denmark, a physician working in the field of diabetes research. WBF World Master. Placed 8th World Pairs 1990. 3rd World Team Olympiad 1996, represented Denmark Bermuda Bowl 1997. Won 3 Danish titles.

SCHALTZ, Dorthe (b 1956), of Odense, Denmark, medical secretary. WBF World Master. Won Women's Team Olympiad 1988. Represented Denmark Bermuda Bowl 1993, World Team Olympiad 1992, and 3 European championships. 12 Danish titles. See FAMILY.

SCHALTZ, Lizzie (b. 1923) of Copenhagen, Denmark, bridge teacher, World Master. 3rd World Women's Olympiad Teams 1960, won European Women's Teams 1955. See FAMILY.

SCHALTZ, Peter (b 1950) of Odense, Denmark, manager of wine company. World Life Master. Won European Junior Championship 1970, Nordic Championship 1986; placed 3rd World Team Olympiad 1984; finished 2nd at European Championships 1979, 93. Also represented Denmark in 4 World Team Olympiads and 9 European Championships. 27 national championships. Son of European women's champion Lizzie Schaltz and national team player Jørgen-Elith Schaltz. Played with cousin, Knud-Aage Boesgaard, early in career with many successes. See FAMILY.

SCHAPIRO, Boris (b 1909) of London, England. WBF Grand Master. Won Bermuda Bowl 1955, 2nd World Team Olympiad 1960, World Pairs 1962. Won European Teams 1948, 49, 54, 63. World Senior Pairs champion 1998 at age 89. Won London Sunday Times Invitational 1964, 2nd 1991 at age of 81. Many national wins include Gold Cup 11 times (last win 1998 at age 89). Author of 2 books, bridge columnist *London Sunday Times*. See BUENOS AIRES AFFAIR.

SCHAUFELBERGER William K.A. (Win) (1902-1972) of Sydney, Australia. Chief director of New South Wales BA, captain of first Australian team to compete in an international event, the World Team Olympiad 1960. Won many national titles.

SCHEINBERG, Martin R. (b. 1930) of New York City, systems engineer. Won Men's Teams 1960. Pioneer in scoring tournament results and predealing hands by electronic data processing equipment. (see COMPUTERS.)

SCHEMEIL, Pierre (b. 1921 in Egypt) of Paris, France, former lawyer and finance counsel. The only person to have represented 4 countries (Lebanon, Egypt, Switzerland, France) in international competition. Won national titles in Lebanon, Egypt and France. Npc of 2 French world champion teams. Considered to be one of the world's great diplomats, often working with French players who were not talking to one another.

SCHENKEN, Bee (Mrs. Howard, formerly Bee Gale) (1916-1993) of New York City, one of the world's most successful women rubber bridge players. Won Mixed Pairs 1957, Fall Women's Teams 1958, 60, 61, 69; Spring Women's Teams 1964, 68. Placed 2nd Master Mixed Teams 1958, Spring Women's Teams 1963, 67; Reisinger 1966, Womens' Pairs 1969. Won several international titles including Deauville Open Pairs 8 times and numerous regional titles.

SCHENKEN, Howard (1904-1979) of New York City, real estate investor, bridge author and columnist. Considered by many to be best player of all time. Member ACBL Hall of Fame. Credited with introduction of several aspects of playing technique and deceptive play that are now standard. That plus the Weak Two-bid, the forc-

ing Two-Over-One, the prepared opening bid ("anticipation"), and other bidding devices helped to establish him as a force to be reckoned with. Schenken's Raymond Club team, 1927-1929, first successfully broke the reign of the established men's clubs in tournament competition. Occasional appearances with Four Horsemen and Bid-Rite teams. Helped found Four Aces, participated in their long series of victories including the victory over the French European champions in 1935, first official World Championship. Then came a winning tour of Europe in pair matches with Michael T. Gottlieb, the next year.

Won Bermuda Bowl 1950, 51, 53; represented U.S. in World Team Olympiad 1960, and North America in Bermuda Bowl 1961, 63, 65. Won Life Master Pairs 1931, 33, 34, 41, 43; Spingold 1934, 36, 38, 39, 43, 45, 48, 50, 52, 60; Vanderbilt 1934, 35, 37, 38, 46, 50, 55, 56, 57, 64. Other national wins include Master Individual 1932, Mixed Teams 1935, Men's Teams 1949, Mixed Pairs 1957, Chicago 1957, 63; Reisinger 1968. He was 2nd in national events 19 times. ACBL Board Member, IBPA honorary member 1973. Writings include *Four Aces System of Contract Bridge, Better Bidding in Fifteen Minutes* and *Howard Schenken's Big Club* and *Education of a Bridge Player*. Took over Four Aces syndicated bridge column 1943. In 1957 he merged it with Richard L. Frey's to become co-author of the longest continuously published nationally syndicated bridge feature. Became sole author of column 1970. Contributing editor, *Bridge Encyclopedia*. See SCHENKEN SYSTEM.

SCHENONE, Mercedes Guerrico de, (d. 1997) of Buenos Aires, Argentina. Won South American Women's Teams 1948, 49, 50, 51, 53, 61, 62, 77, 79, 81. 26 national titles.

SCHEPPS, Joan of Holyoke MA, teacher; foremost collector of trump indicators in the United States. The collection was exhibited at the World Bridge Olympiad in Albuquerque NM 1994, the University Gallery at the University of Massachusetts, the Springfield MA Museum of Fine Arts and the New York City Triple Pier Antique Show 1998. The collection was showcased on the TV program *Personal FX the Collectibles Show* 1996 and has been written up in many antique journals and publications. Founded the international Trump Indicator Collector's Club, and writes for the international publication *Clear The Decks* for the 52 Plus Joker Club. Founded the Holyoke Bridge Club in 1975, writes a bridge column for a regional paper.

SCHERMER, John (b. 1948) of Seattle WA, painting contractor. Won Swiss Teams 1977, Men's BAM Teams 1978, Vanderbilt 1992; placed 2nd Spingold 1986. Diamond Life Master, Won numerous regional events.

SCHEUER, Jerome (1889-1979) of Brookline MA, insurance broker, bridge writer. Lawn tennis official at national and international levels. Won New England KO Teams 12 times 1938-54. His writing included contributions to *Bridge Magazine* and *The Bridge World*. Contributing editor *Bridge Encyclopedia*.

SCHIFF, Martin (Marty) (b. 1938) of Tucson AZ, urologist. Won 15-20 regionally rated events.

SCHIPPERHEYN, Ton (b. 1933) of Amstelveen, The Netherlands, bridge writer and journalist. Former assistant manager of Netherlands Bridge League. Bridge columnist for regional syndicated newspapers, editor of *Bridge*. Author (with Cees Sint) of four TV courses and about 40 books, including *From Start to Finish*. (The first two volumes are the official beginners' course of the Netherlands Bridge League). More than a million copies of Sint/Schipperheyn's books have been sold.

SCHIPPERS, Elly (b. 1943) of Amstelveen, The Netherlands, systems analyst. WBF World Life Master. 2nd Venice Cup 1989, 3rd World Women's Teams 1984. 2nd European Women's Teams 1983, 89. Won European Women's Pairs 1980, 2nd 1987. Represented Netherlands regularly since 1979. Won Netherlands Women's Pairs 4 times.

SCHLEIFER, Meyer (1908-1994) of Los Angeles CA, bridge teacher, member ACBL Hall of Fame. Won Life Master Pairs 1966, Barclay Trophy 1947; a Diamond Life Master, scores of regional events.

SCHNEIDER, Karl (1904-1977) of Vienna, Austria, engineer. World champion 1937, European champion 1936. Represented France in Bermuda Bowl 1952, represented Austria 5 times in European championships, placing 2nd 1951, 57. Won first Austrian Teams in 1968 and then retired from all play.

SCHNEIDER, Rebecca A. (b. 1977) of East Brunswick NJ, student. In 1991 became youngest female (age 14) certified club director, conducted novice bridge sessions at Bethesda regional and at Summer NABC 1991. Directed at Rutgers University Duplicate Bridge Club, ran North American College Bridge Championships there 1991.

SCHODER, Lt./Colonel William J. (Kojak) (b. 1932) of Tampa FL, chief tournament director for WBF, retired ACBL national tournament director, ACBL Field Representative. Began directing career part-time 1959, in 1966 achieved regional rating, promoted to associate national 1980. Contributes to the ACBL *Bridge Bulletin, Florida Bridge News, Gold Coast Bridge News Trumpet*. Past president PTDA. Chief tournament director for Central American and Caribbean Bridge Federation (since 1972), China Cup since 1996. Trainer for China's tournament directing staff. WBF director since 1972, chief director since 1987. Retired USAF pilot, awarded many decorations including Distinguished Service Medal, Distinguished Flying Cross, Bronze Star, Legion of Merit and 10 air medals. Fluent in Spanish, German and French. Accomplished pianist.

SCHOU, Steen (b 1952), of Aarhus, Denmark, computer consultant. WBF World Master. Placed 3rd World Team Olympiad 1984, won Nordic Teams 1984. Represented Denmark in 2 other Olympiads and 2 European Championships.

SCHREIBER, Michael J. (b. 1952) of Costa Mesa CA, investment syndicator. Served for many years on ACBL Appeals Committee. Using the pseudonym Sol I. Taryman, he was the original moderator for Problem Solvers Panel in *Southern California Bridge News*. Grand Life Master with 11,550 MPs (3/2001), won Open Pairs 1980, Intercollegiate champion 1973; placed 2nd Men's Swiss Teams 1987, Life Master Open Pairs 1996. Has won approximately 100 regionals.

SCHROEDER, David A. (b. 1950) of Las Vegas, baseball handicapper. Won Life Master Men's Pairs 1977. Backgammon champion.

SCHROEDER, Dirk (b. 1943) of Wiesbaden, Germany, bridge teacher, journalist, travel organizer. WBF World Master. Won 3 Common Market titles and more than 30 German titles. Represented Germany internationally many times. Developed first European Youth Camp 1975. Former member of EBL Executive and its youth com-

mittee. Board member DBV 1983-89. Magazine columnist, theorist.

SCHROEDER, Kareen (b. 1947) of Wiesbaden, Germany, bridge teacher, journalist and travel organizer. Placed 2nd Venice Cup 1989. Won European Women's Teams 1989, won 15 national titles. Represented Germany in many events since 1975 including 5 world championships. Magazine columnist.

SCHUETT, Jeffrey G. (Jeff) of Riverwoods IL, computer software developer. Diamond Life Master, won Life Master Open Pairs 1997. Placed 2nd Master Mixed Teams 1995. Won more 60 regionals.

SCHUETT, Virginia (Ginny) of Riverwoods IL, bridge teacher, professional player, former teacher. CCBA Board member since 1987 and current president, Unit Education Liaison since 1988, president ABTA 1998-99, 3-star teacher. Diamond Life Master, placed 2nd Master Mixed Teams 1995, won more than 40 regionals.

SCHULD, Diana K. (b. 1938) of Glen Head NY, retired elementary music teacher (34 years), co-owner/operator Vanderbilt BC. Unit 242 Board member 1968-76. Placed 2nd Life Masters Pairs 1967, won several regional events.

SCHULD, Frank P., Jr. (1927-1993) of Glen Head NY, co-owner/president Vanderbilt BC, bridge teacher and director. Member of committee that established District 24, District 24 Judiciary Committee. Instrumental in bringing about separate unit status for Nassau-Suffolk BA. Author of *The Simple Squeeze in Bridge*. Placed 2nd Life Masters Pairs 1967.

SCHULLE, Kay (b. 1950) of Purchase NY, bridge professional. WBF World Life Master, won Venice Cup 1993, placed 4th 1991; won USWBC (Team Trials) 1985, 91, 2nd 1993. ACBL Grand Life Master with 13,096 MPs, won Women's KO Teams 1985, 89; Women's Pairs 1987, North American Women's Swiss Teams 1991, 93; Women's BAM Teams 1991. Placed 2nd North American Women's Swiss Teams 1988, 95; Women's KO Teams 1990, 93; Life Master Pairs 1990, Mixed Pairs 1994. USA Goodwill ambassador to South African Nationals 1985, 88, 89, 90, 91, won National Pairs once and National Teams twice.

SCHUTZE, Kenneth R. (b. 1949) of Austin TX, staff attorney Texas Court of Criminal Appeals. Diamond Life Master, won Life Master Pairs 1979, GNOP 1993, 94, 99. Placed 2nd North American Swiss Teams 1977, 79. Has won 25+ regionals.

SCHWAB, Charles M. (1862-1939) of New York City, a noted financier, steel magnate and patron of bridge. President Whist Club of New York, played on its teams and was ex officio member of committee that participated in the first International Code of Contract Bridge Laws 1932. (see SCHWAB CUP.)

SCHWAB, Irving W. (1903-1984) of Springfield MO, attorney. Instrumental in the formation of the ACBL Goodwill Committee, won several regional events.

SCHWARTZ, Elmer I. (1903-1996) of Shaker Heights OH, practicing attorney. Life Master #96. Past president District 5. *Bridge World* panelist in the Fifties. Won the Chicago (now the Reisinger) 1949, Men's Teams 1958. Placed 2nd Spingold 1946, Chicago 1952.

SCHWARTZ, Eugene (b. 1916) of Mercer Island WA, retired commercial pilot, has piloted all aircraft from DC-3 to B747. Won 15 regionals.

SCHWARTZ, Peter L. (b. 1934) of Cote St. Luc PQ, bridge professional, former corporate executive. A bridge teacher, has taught on cruises for 20+ years. Schwartz authored the book *K.I.S.S. (Keep it Simple, Stupid): A simplified Approach to Learning Bridge.* Previous owner, with Peter Pender, of Montreal School of Bridge. Placed 2nd GNOP 1995. When he became a Life Master in 1958, he was at that time the youngest in Canada.

SCHWARTZ, Richard C. (b. 1943) of East Elmhurst NY, mathematical analyst and computer programmer to solve engineering problems in defense and aerospace industry. Most successful horse race handicapper in country 1975-89. WBF World Master, Diamond Life Master, won IMP Pairs 1989, Open Swiss Teams 1992, Vanderbilt 1997, 98; placed 2nd IMP Pairs 1990, Open Pairs II 1993, Spingold 1996, Life Master Open Pairs 1998, Vanderbilt 2000, U.S. Team Trials 2000. Placed 2nd and 5th Cavendish Pairs.

SCHWARTZ, Sylvia (Mrs. Elmer I.) (1907-1978) of Shaker Heights OH, represented U.S. in World Team Olympiad 1960. Placed 2nd Women's Pairs 1959.

SCHWENCKE, John (Jack) (b. 1916) of North Palm Beach FL, real estate developer. Won Swiss Teams 1978, placed 2nd Vanderbilt 1987. Grand Life Master with 11,355 MPs, won approximately 150 regionals.

SCHWENKREIS, Tomas (b. 1942) of Frankfurt, Germany, corporate accountant. WBF World Master. Represented Germany regularly in world and zonal championships from 1973. Won several national titles. High-ranked chess player.

SCOPE, Ivan H. (b. 1934) of San Francisco, worker's compensation consultant. Diamond Life Master, won GNOP 1982, numerous regionals.

SCOTT, Gratz M. (1882-1935) of New York City, bridge teacher and president of Cavendish Club of New York. Outstanding figure in whist and bridge for 25 years. Scott and teammates, Wilbur C. Whitehead, Edwin A. Wetzlar and Ralph R. Richards, were co-winners of the 1st national contract bridge tournament ever held. It was the 1928 Board-a-Match competition for the Harold S. Vanderbilt Trophy. The following year he placed 2nd. The Vanderbilt event is still being played in 2001.

SCOTT, Joe V. (b. 1947) of Rogers AR, realtor, former director of administration. Past president Unit 247. Won 15+ regionals including District 10 GNOT 1977, 79, 83; District 10 GNOP 1981, 82, 84, 89, 92.

SEAGRAM, Barbara A. (b. 1947) of Toronto ON, born in Barbados West Indies, owner Kate Buckman Bridge Studio, former nursing instructor. Served on Unit 166 Board of Directors (since 1988) as vice president and president, Unit Novice chairman (1988-98), chairman Novice Program/Toronto NABC (1992). Member Blue Ribbon Task Force on future of bridge 1995-96). First alternate ACBL Board of Governors (since 1997). Awarded Master Teacher status by ABTA 1997. Member ABTA Board of Directors (since 1998). One of innovators of Zero Tolerance program. Co-author (with Marc Smith) *25 Bridge Conventions You Should Know*, the ABTA Book of the Year 1999 and *25 Ways to Enter the Bidding.* Recipient of Kate Buckman Award (1995). Teaches more than 1000 students. Accredited ACBL teacher. One of top 5 recruiters of new members for ACBL annually.

SEALY, Larry (b. 1955) of Huntsville AL, strategic defense systems analyst. Coaches youth basketball and baseball. His 20+ regional wins include District 10 GNOT 1982, 86, 88.

SEAMON, Janice. See SEAMON-MOLSON, Janice.

SEAMON, Michael E. (b. 1960) of Miami Beach FL, bridge teacher and professional player. WBF World Master, placed 2nd Rosenblum Teams 1990. ACBL Grand Life Master with 22,854 MPs, #21 in ACBL, won Open Teams 1992, 93 Master Mixed Teams 1994. GNOT 1997, 99, 2000; Open Pairs 1999. Placed 2nd U.S. Bridge Championship 1998, Spingold 1987, IMP Pairs 1989, Reisinger 1996, Vanderbilt 1997, 98; Spingold 1997. His more than 90 regional wins include District 9 GNOT 1989. (See FAMILY.)

SEAMON, Rita (Mrs. William E.) (b. 1924) of North Miami Beach FL, bridge teacher and director. Won Master Mixed Teams 1974; placed 2nd Women's Pairs 1961, 89; Women's KO Teams 1996. Diamond Life Master with numerous regional wins including District 9 GNOP 1980, GNOT 1982. (see FAMILY.)

SEAMON, William E. (Billy) (1917-1992) of Miami Beach FL, retired banking executive. Represented North America in Bermuda Bowl 1957. Contributing editor to *Bridge Encyclopedia* and syndicated bridge columnist. Diamond Life Master, won Spingold 1956, 63; Vanderbilt 1963, GNOT 1973, Master Mixed Teams 1974. Placed 2nd Men's Teams 1952, Chicago (now the Reisinger) 1954, Vanderbilt 1960, Spring Men's Teams 1973, GNOT 1978, 80. Won Israeli Men's Pairs 1988 and numerous regional titles including secondary Mixed Pairs 1968 with his sister Edith Kemp-Freilich. Brother of Anne Burnstein. (see FAMILY.)

SEAMON-MOLSON, Janice of North Miami FL, attorney, bridge teacher. Won Junior Master of Year 1976, her first year of playing. Placed 2nd Venice Cup 1999. Won Women's KO Teams 1988, 92, 2000; Women's Pairs 1992, Life Master Women's Pairs 1993, 97; Women's BAM Teams 1999; placed 2nd North American Women's Swiss Teams 1988, 99, 2000; Women's Pairs 1989, Women's KO Teams 1989, 93; Life Master Women's Pairs 1991. (see FAMILY.)

SEARS, Richard C. (b. 1936) of Palisades NY, retired employee benefits consultant. Attends 20-30 bullfights each year in Spain. Youngest Fellow, Society of Actuaries, since Oswald Jacoby. Won New England Fall Men's Pairs in the late Fifties playing with female fill-in (Connie Kemball).

SEEWALD, Leo J. (1908-1991) of South St. Paul MN, teacher. ACBL president 1964, member ACBL Board of Directors, Board of Governors and chairman of the ACBL Masterpoint Plan Committee. He also served as president of the Minnesota Unit and as director of the Mid-American-Canadian Conference.

SEGANDER, Rut (b. 1917) of Karlsborg, Sweden. WBF World Life Master. Won World Women's Teams 1968, European Women's Teams 1962, 1967. Won Nordic Women's Teams and one national title.

SEIDEL, Tilman (b. 1968) of Innsbruck, Austria, ecologist. Won European Junior Pairs 1991. Represented Austria in four other European events. Won Austrian Open Pairs. Active member of *Greenpeace*.

SEIDMAN, Solomon (Sol) (1909-1995) of Brooklyn NY, social studies teacher and bridge lecturer, educated at NYU and City College of NY. ACBL Honorary Member 1984. Co-chairman NABC Appeals Committee for many years, served on Board of Directors 1974-84. Former president of District 24, associated with Greater New York BA from 1952, held every major office. Chairman of board of GNYBA in 1984, succeeding Ira Zippert,

who succeeded Seidman as District 24 director. Diamond Life Master, won just about every title at sectional and regional tournaments in NY area, New Jersey and Philadelphia, including Von Zedtwitz Teams, Goldman Pairs and Eastern States KO Teams.

SEIFERT, Bogumil (b.1923) of Warsaw, Poland, economist. Helped found Polish Bridge Union, general secretary 1957-1962. Helped to establish Hungarian and Czech NCBOs. Bridge journalist, author of several books. Chief editor of Polish *Bridge Encyclopedia*.

SEKIZAWA, Miho (b. 1962) of Tokyo, translator/editor for investment bank, board member of JCBL from 2000. 2nd ACBL Women's Pairs 1995. Represented Japan in Women's Team Olympiad 2000. Won 2 national titles.

SELIGMAN, Barbara of Dublin, Ireland, barrister. 2nd European Women's Teams 1972, 3rd 1962. Represented Ireland in two world championships and seven other zonal championships. Won all major national titles

SELIGMAN, Dr. Martin E.P. (Marty) (b. 1942) professor of psychology. Contributor to *Bridge Today*. Came 2nd Blue Ribbon Pairs 1998, won 50+ regionally rated events. Won OKBridge Internet World Championship.

SELLERS, Steve (b. 1954) of Arcata CA, real estate consultant. President District 22, member ACBL Board of Governors from District 22. Placed 2nd Masters Division Mini-McKenney 1980, won District 20 GNOP 1986 and several other regional events.

SEMENTA, Antonio (b. 1968) of Parma, Italy, professional player. WBF World Life Master. Won Rosenblum Teams 1998, European Teams 1995, European Junior Teams 1989, 1992; Generali Individual 2000. 3rd European Pairs 1995.

SENDER, Elfreda (b. 1931 in Germany) of Irvine, Calif., formerly of Johannesburg, South Africa, retired secretary. 2nd World Women's Teams 1968, represented South Africa in 2 other world championships.

SENIOR, Brian R. (b. 1953) of Nottingham, England, bridge writer, teacher and professional player. WBF World Master. Represented both Britain and Ireland in world and zonal championships, and both England and Northern Ireland in Camrose Trophy matches. Author of more than 20 books and many magazine articles. Last editor of now defunct *International Popular Bridge Monthly* magazine. Current editor and publisher of official *World Championship Book* series and regular member of *Daily Bulletin* team at World and European Championships.

SENIOR, Nevena M. (b. 1959 as Nevena Deleva), of Nottingham, England, originally of Sofia, Bulgaria, bridge professional. WBF World Master. Represented both Bulgaria and Great Britain, with 3 medals in European Women's Teams (gold 1987, bronze 1989 and 1999), and bronze medalist in World Women's Teams 1988. Many Bulgarian national titles; won Lady Milne Trophy twice for England. Won EBU Women's Teams.

SERES, Thomas Peter (Tim) (b. 1925 in Austria), of Randwick NSW, Australia, horse-racing investor. WBF World Life Master. 3rd Bermuda Bowl 1971, 1979, represented Australia in 10 other world championships. Won Far East Teams 1968, 1970, Far East Pairs 1986, and represented Australia on 7 other occasions. 37 national wins include Inter-State Teams 21 times, Open Pairs 8 times. Contributor to several magazines. Honorary Member of ABF. Awarded Order of Australia for contribution to bridge. See SERES SQUEEZE.

SERF, Marianne (b. 1931) of Paris, France, bridge teacher, World Life Master. 2nd World Women's Pairs 1962, represented France World Women's Team Olympiad 1964, 1968; European Women's Championships 1963, 67, 81. Won many national titles.

SERVER, Lenore (Len) (b. 1937) of River Vale NJ, elementary school teacher, taught and lectured on bridge cruises. Placed 2nd Swiss Teams 1977.

SHAH, Jatindra M. (b. 1950) of Bombay, India, bridge teacher. WBF World Master. Represented India in 5 world championships. 9 national titles.

SHAKOFSKY, Jerry (1945-2000) of Kew Gardens NY, graduate of Mannes College of Music. Began directing 1969, R3 rank.

SHALLON, Marty (b. 1952) of Redondo Beach CA, accountant. Placed 2nd Men's Teams 1974, Spingold 1975, IMP Pairs 1991.

SHANAHAN, Dorothy of London, England. Won World Women's Team Olympiad 1964, European women's champion 1961, 66. Many national titles.

SHANBROM, Helen (b. 1919) of Tamarac FL, retired math teacher. ACBL Grand Life Master with 16,456 MPs (3/2001). Contributor to ACBL *Bridge Bulletin*. LM #973 of the original 1000. Won ACBL Ace of Clubs - Life Master category 1989, 90 (broke record with 369 points), 91, 92, 93, 94, 95, 96, 97, 98. In 1970 was member of Detroit team that beat the Italian Blue Team in a series of closed television sessions. Won Silver Ribbon Pairs 1993, placed 2nd Women's Teams 1960.

SHAPIRO, Ed of Camphill PA, writer. Diamond Life Master, won North American Swiss Teams 1989. Won more than 15 regionals.

SHARIF, Omar (b. 1932) of Paris, France, formerly of Egypt, motion picture star. Won Golden Globe Award 1963, nominated for Oscar for Best Supporting Actor 1963 for *Lawrence of Arabia*. One of the most active promoters of bridge, with many public and TV appearances. His most famous quote: "Acting is my business, bridge is my passion." Organized Sharif Bridge Circus, lent his name to and played in the Sharif Individual, played on Italy's Blue Team and Lancia Team. Won 1974 IBPA Simon Award for sportsmanship. Represented United Arab Republics 1964, playing captain for Egypt World Team Olympiad 1968. Placed 3rd London Sunday Times Invitational 1999. Author of *Ma Vie en Bridge*, since 1975 co-author of Goren syndicated bridge column. Authored playbooks for the Epson World-Wide Pairs for many years. *Observer* columnist since 1996.

SHARP, Robert G. (1910-1990) of Miami Beach FL, real estate broker. Former president Midwest Conference, Cincinnati BA. Florida BA. Won Men's Teams 1959, Mixed Pairs 1966, GNOT 1973; placed 2nd Blue Ribbon Pairs 1964.

SHARPLES, Hendrik W. (b. 1954) of Portland OR, appraiser and custom jewelery designer. District 20 recorder 1988-91, Unit 487 recorder since 1988. Has won 37 regionals.

SHARPLES, James (1908-85) of Caterham, England, retired bank officer. 2nd European Teams 1958, represented Britain in 2 other zonal championships. Represented England in more than 20 Camrose Trophy matches 1950-77. 21 national wins include 6 Gold Cups. Twin brother of Robert.

SHARPLES, Robert (1908-1999) of Caterham, England, retired bank officer. 2nd European Teams 1958, represented Britain in 2 other zonal championships. Rep-

resented England in more than 20 Camrose matches 1950-77. 21 national wins include 6 Gold Cups. Twin brother of James.

SHATILA, Samia of Cairo, Egypt. WBF World Master. Won BFAAME Women's Teams 1997. Represented Egypt on other international occasions.

SHAUFEL, Elyiakim (b. 1945) of Tel Aviv, Israel. WBF World Master. European champion 1975, represented Israel in World Team Olympiad, World Open Pairs, 6 other European championships,. Won many national titles.

SHAW, Shirlee R. (b. 1924) of Concord CA, legal assistant. Past president Unit 499. Won Non-Life Master Pairs 1981.

SHEARDOWN, Percy E. (Shorty) (1911-1993) of Toronto, bridge club owner/manager. Canada's first Life Master (1948) and greatest bridge player of the Thirties, Forties and Fifties. Brilliant card player, teacher and mentor to many of Canada's leading players. Began bridge career while attending University of Toronto 1933. Consistent tournament winner before days of masterpoints. World Life Master, represented Canada internationally World Team Olympiad 1960, Deauville 1968. Won the Chicago (now the Reisinger) 1936, 51; Spingold 1964, 65; Fishbein Trophy 1964; placed 2nd Life Master Pairs 1964.

SHEEHAN, Robert of London, England, computer systems analyst and bridge writer. WBF World Life Master. 2nd Bermuda Bowl 1987, European Teams 1971, 81, 87. Represented Britain in 5 other world championships and 4 other zonals. Won 5 Gold Cups. Bridge columnist *London Times* 1994-99. Author of 3 bridge books. Consultant to spread-betting bookmaker.

SHEFCHIK, Charles Milton (Chuck) (b. 1939) of Las Vegas NV, sales representative. Diamond Life Master, 20+ regional wins include District 14 GNOP 1983, District 17 GNOT 1988.

SHEIKH, Mohammad Aslam (1933-1996) of Karachi, Pakistan, businessman. Secretary of Pakistan Bridge Association and its chief tournament director 1983-96. Supervised all major events in Pakistan, officiated at 1990 world championships and many zonal championships. Represented Pakistan 1982 world championships. Editor of *Bridge Kibitzer*.

SHEIKH, Tufail Mohammad (b. 1939) of Karachi, Pakistan, businessman. Won BFAAME Open Teams 1991, represented Pakistan in Bermuda Bowl 1991.

SHEINWOLD, Alfred (Freddy) (1912-1997) of Los Angeles, formerly of New York City, born in London England; bridge author and columnist. One of the most successful player-writer personalities. Member ACBL Hall of Fame. During World War II was chief code and cipher expert of OSS. From 1945-1955 he sang with the Cantata singers. Npc North American Team in 1975 Bermuda Bowl when two Italian players were accused of cheating. Won Chicago (now Reisinger) 1958, Men's Teams 1964; placed 2nd Vanderbilt 1958, Chicago 1959.

Editor *The Bridge World* 1934-1963, successively as technical editor, managing editor and senior editor, editor of *ACBL Bulletin* 1952-1958, editor-in-chief of *Autobridge* since 1938.

For years he was bridge editor of the *Los Angeles Times*. Contributing editor *Popular Bridge*, games editor for *Argosy,* syndicated bridge and backgammon columnist for Los Angeles Times Syndicate. Pioneered bridge lessons on Pay TV 1963-1964. Chairman ACBL Laws Commission 1964-1975, chairman of Appeals

Committee at North American Championships, chairman of ACBL Board of Governors 1970-1973, member Editorial Advisory Board, *Bridge Encyclopedia*. ACBL Honorary Member 1983. Co-inventor of Kaplan-Sheinwold system, author of 13 bridge books, notably *Five Weeks to Winning Bridge,* which has sold more than 1 million copies, and a series of *Pocket Books of Bridge Quizzes.*

SHEINWOLD, Patricia Fox- (formerly Mrs. Alfred, previously Mrs. Julian Adler) of New York City, author. Retired from tournament play in Mid-Sixties. Won Women's Teams 1963. President Women's Bridge League of MD, chaired Mid-Atlantic Regional. Pulitzer nominee for writing on subject of blindness. Among her 6 published non-fiction books are *Husbands and Other Men I've Played With: Bridge, That Is, Gone But Not Forgotten* and the best seller, *Too Young to Die.*

SHELTON, Gary W. (Big Dog) (b. 1949) of Danvers MA, vice president of computer software company that makes bridge playing software (Base III). Played violin in Carnegie Hall 1967.

SHEN, Chih-Kuo (b. 1958) of Taipei, Taiwan. financial consultant. WBF World Master. Far East champion 1989. Represented Taiwan in 4 world championships. Coached and captained Chinese Taipei Women's Team in world championships since 1991.

SHEN, Chun-Shan (b. 1933 in China) of Hsin Chu, Taiwan, professor of physics and astrophysics, formerly university administrator at Purdue University. WBF World Life Master. 2nd Bermuda Bowl 1969. Far East champion 1976. Represented Taiwan in 3 world championships and 5 zonal championships. National wins include Open Team 6 times, Open Pairs twice. Helped C.C. Wei develop the Precision System, world class player of the Chinese game of Go.

SHEN, Kin Wha (b. 1911) of Bangkok, Thailand, merchant. 2nd Bermuda Bowl 1969 as member of Taiwan team. Won PABF (Far East) Teams 1961, 66. Also represented Thailand in 2 other world championships and 1 zonal.

SHENKIN, Barnet (b. 1950 in Scotland) of Boca Raton, FL, retired carpet importer. Represented Britain in 1 world championship, 3 European Championships and 3 Common Market Championships. Represented Scotland more than 40 times in Camrose Trophy matches 1974-92. Won Sunday Times Pairs 1976, 1980. Many national titles include Gold Cup 1973, 1977.

SHEPARD, Edward V. (1869-1937) of New York City, civil engineer. One of America's leading authorities on bridge mathematics of bridge, devoted many years to studying card probabilities. Called by Ely Culbertson "a giant of the Old Guard." First to establish a college for the teaching of bridge and the qualifying of bridge teachers. First to teach bridge over the radio (1923) and one of the first to teach and write on contract bridge in 1924 and 1925. A member of the advisory council of the ABL, he assisted in drafting and approving the Official System. Contributed articles to numerous magazines, had a syndicated newspaper column, authored several books including *Scientific Auction Bridge, Win at Bridge, Contract Bridge Standardized* and *Correct Contract Bridge.*

SHEPHERD, Richard of Pacific Palisades CA, won Fishbein Trophy 1974, Spingold 1974 and numerous regionals.

SHERIDAN, John K. (b. 1948) of Indianapolis IN, president, Sheridan and Associates, Inc. (attorney). National Merit Scholar 1966. Temporarily retired from bridge 1984. Won Men's Pairs 1978. Placed 2nd Men's Pairs 1975, Spingold 1977, 79. His more than 30 regional wins include District 11 GNOT 1974, 76; GNOP 1979.

SHERMAN, Ruth T. (1903-1965) of New York City, a leading player of East Coast for 30 years. Won USBA Grand Nationals 1934, Master Mixed Teams 1935, 1945, 1951. Won Chicago (now Reisinger) 1944, Women's Pairs 1944, 49; Women's Teams 1942, Master Pairs 1946, Mixed Pairs 1950, Vanderbilt 1953. Placed 2nd Women's Pairs 1934, 44, 47; Life Master Pairs 1946, Women's Teams 1948, 50, 52, 53, 54, 55; Chicago 1953.

SHI, Haojun (b. 1964) of Shanghai, China. Won Far East Open Teams 1998, IOC Grand Prix 1998. Won many national titles.

SHI, Shaomin of Zhejiang, China. 3rd Venice Cup 1991. Won Far East Women's Teams 1991.

SHIBE, Madelyn (Mady) of Lauderhill FL, bridge teacher. Highest scoring pair in 5th Epson Worldwide Bridge Contest in Zone II (U.S., Canada, Mexico, Bermuda) 1990; placed 25th in the world.

SHIMAMURA, Kyoko (formerly Mizutani) of Tokyo, Japan, bridge teacher and violinist. Retired psychologist with Association for Handicapped Children. WBF World Master. Far East champion 1985. Represented Japan World Team Olympiad 1980, 6 other world championships and 10 other Far East Championships. Won more than 20 national titles.

SHIPLEY, Roberta D. (Bobbie) (b. 1933) of Lake Villa IL, ACBL national tournament director, retired 1999. Director since 1965, received associate national rating 1981, national rating 1987. Served as Director in Charge or Assistant DIC of NABCs 1987-99.

SHIREY, Steven A. (b. 1958) of Ft. Worth TX, bridge professional. Diamond Life Master, won 40+ regionals including District 16 GNOT 1989.

SHIVDASANI, Jaggy (b. 1958) of New York City, formerly of Bombay, India, chartered accountant, exporter, travel agent. WBF World Master. 4th World Open Teams 1988, represented India in 8 other world championships. Won Spingold 1987, first non-American to win the event. These were his first two national events. Won Reisinger Teams 1988. Won BFAAME Open Teams, 1997, 2nd 1985 and 1989. 19 national wins.

SHKLYAR, Dmytro (born 1957) of Kiev, Ukraine, mathematician-economist. Playing captain of Ukrainian team in 1 world championship and 1 European championship. Won National Open Teams 1994, 1995, 1996. President Ukrainian Bridge Federation.

SHMUCKLER, Pauline (b. 1913) of Miami Beach FL, former bridge teacher, LM# 114. Placed 2nd Women's Teams 1946, 54. Holds many regional titles. Played on Philadelphia women's team that played the British women's team in unofficial matches in 1953. In 1954 she had an automobile accident that forced her to curtail her bridge playing activities.

SHNEIDER, Alma (1928-1986) of Durban, South Africa, bridge teacher. 2nd World Women's Teams 1968, 1972, and represented South Africa World Women's Pairs. 11 national wins.

SHOOP, Homer (1912-1991) of North Webster IN, banker. Founder of International Palace of Sports Youth Foundation which annually awards the King or Queen of Bridge title. Placed 2nd Life Master Pairs 1980. Won numerous regional titles. Former tennis tournament player.

SHORT, Brian D. (b. 1944) of Edinburgh, Scotland, computer consultant. Represented Britain in 2 world championships, 1 European championship and 1 Common Market Championship. Represented Scotland in 18 Camrose Trophy matches. National titles include 3 Scottish Cups.

SHORT, Karol K. (b. 1934) of Miami FL, tennis professional. Nicknamed Golden Goddess of Tennis, was ranked #5 woman player in U.S. and #6 in world in Fifties. Banned from playing at Wimbledon until she covered her gold lame panties with white lace. Short turned professional 1959, toured with Harlem Globe Trotters and Althea Gibson. Won a few regionals.

SHOUP, Russell O. (Mr. Bridge) (b. 1947) of Dayton OH, bridge teacher, club manager and professional player. Competitive long distance runner and semi-professional basso. Diamond Life Master, finished 2nd Swiss Teams 1979, has won more than 40 regional titles including District 11 GNOT 1973, 85, 86; GNOP 1983, 91. Editor of *Valley Talley* since 1988, member MVBA Board of Directors.

SHUDNEV, Andrei (b.1963) of Riga, Latvia, bridge professional. WBF World Master. Quarterfinalist World Teams 1996. Represented Russia in 1 world and 1 zonal championship. Several national wins.

SHUGART, Rita K. of Pebble Beach CA, active in both business and community activities on Monterey Peninsula, president of Monterey Airplane Company, an aircraft charter and management company; proprietor and operator of R.K. Shugart, a women's fashion boutique in Carmel, and general partner in Pebble Beach Ventures, an investment and asset management organization. Became active in community educational activities in 1982 when she started a kindergarten-through-eighth-grade private school in Carmel, using a recently closed facility she purchased from the local school district. The school, Briarcliff Academy, was donated to Robert Louis Stevenson School in Pebble Beach and is still in operation. Won Reisinger 1998, 99; Open BAM Teams 1999; placed 2nd Mixed BAM Teams 1998.

SHUMAN, Kerri. See SANBORN, Kerri.

SHUMAN, Michael (b. 1931) of Pasadena CA, professional bridge player. Owns and races thoroughbred horses. Ran bridge cruises since the Sixties, has been *Bridge World* Master Solvers panelist for 30 years. Grand Life Master with 21,984 MPs (3/2001). Former managing editor of *Contract Bridge Forum*. Writings include *Dummy Play Technique* in *The Contract Bridge Forum* and contributions to *The Bridge World* and other magazines and tabloids. Won Men's Teams 1962, Senior Swiss Teams 2000; placed 2nd Men's Pairs 1959, Chicago (now the Reisinger) 1961, Open Pairs 1962, Men's Teams 1974, North American Men's Swiss Teams 1985, North American Swiss 1991, 92. Won approximately 140 regionals.

SIDELL, Steven G. (b. 1947) of Seattle WA, travel consultant. Former president Seattle Unit and District 19. His 20+ regional wins include District 19 GNOT, District 19 GNOT 1973, 83, 85, 87.

SIDES, William C. (Bill) of Burbank CA, bank executive. Won Silver Ribbon Pairs 1998; placed 2nd Men's Teams 1974, Spingold 1975. One of top-ranking ABA players, set record at 1969 ABA Summer Nationals by winning 5 major events and finishing 2nd in another.

SIEBERT, Allan P. (b. 1942) of North Little Rock AR, company president. He and brother (David) are 2nd highest masterpoint holders (as brothers) behind Mike and

Bill Passell. Grand Life Master with 20,800 MPs as of 3/2001, #29 in ACBL, won North American Swiss 1988, Life Master Pairs 1995 and finished 2nd in Life Master Pairs 1985, Senior KO Teams, Senior Swiss Teams 1999. Has won nearly 100 regional titles.

SIEBERT, David A. (b. 1940) of Las Vegas NV, company executive. member ACBL Board of Governors for District 10, past president Unit 161, tournament chairman 1986, 89. He and brother (Alan) are 2nd highest masterpoint holders (as brothers) behind Mike and Bill Passell. Represented ACBL in World Championships Bal Harbour 1986, Geneva 1990. Won North American Swiss 1988; placed 2nd Life Master Pairs 1985. Grand Life Master with 19,155 MPs as of 3/2001, won more than 100 regionals.

SIEBERT, Ellen. See MELSON, Ellen.

SIERON, Gloria (b.1928) of Milford CT, retired, currently teaches bridge. Director since 1984, she manages and directs a regular bridge club. Member Connecticut BA board since 1989. She has accumulated 20 regional wins.

SIGURDSSON, Valur (b. 1949) of Reykjavik, Iceland, mason. Won Nordic Open Teams 1988. Represented Iceland in 2 world championships, 2 European Championships and 2 other Nordic Championships. 13 national wins.

SIGURHJARTARSON, Karl (b. 1941) of Reykjavik, Iceland, manager. Won Nordic Teams 1988 and 1992. Represented Iceland in 3 world championships, 3 European Championships and 3 other Nordic Championships. 12 national wins.

SILBER, Albert J. (Al) (b. 1912) of Southfield MI, attorney and corporate director. At 14 became youngest athlete in country to earn a varsity letter. Between 1928-33 won 9 state championships in high jump and long jump. In 1993 he was inducted into the Michigan Jewish Sports Hall of Fame. At 20 he became the youngest law graduate from the University of Michigan and at 21 he was admitted to practice. Past president Michigan BA, former member ACBL Board of Governors. Recipient MBA Goodwill award 1985. Placed 2nd Marcus Cup 1964, won 16 regional events. Captain of District 12 team that defeated Sharif Bridge Circus in 1970.

SILBER, David O. (b. 1943) of Memphis TN, formerly of London, England. Earned degrees at Oxford and Harvard. Became American citizen 1976, Chief executive officer American Contract Bridge League 1998-2001 and United States Bridge Federation since 2001. Former marketing director and publisher, marketing lecturer Golden Gate University, president Golden Turtle Press. Board member, diverse charitable and not-for-profit organizations. Hobbies: Choral singing, soccer, performing arts. Accredited bridge teacher.

SILBERSTEIN, David S. (b. 1951) of Medfield MA, research assistant. Won Senior/Advanced Senior Master Pairs 1974; New England Individual 1973.

SILBORN, Gunborg (b. 1924) of Norrkoping, Sweden. WBF World Life Master. Won World Women's Teams 1968, European Women's Teams 1967. Won Nordic Women's Teams 5 times, won 11 national titles.

SILODOR, Sidney (1906-1963) of Havertown PA, lawyer, bridge lecturer, writer and instructor. Was one of the world's top players. Member ACBL Hall of Fame. Member of North American team that won the World Championship in first Bermuda Bowl 1950, also represented North America in Bermuda Bowl 1958, 61, played

for U.S. World Team Olympiad 1960. Won McKenney Trophy 1946, Master Mixed Teams 1941, 43, 44, 54; Reisinger 1942, 43, 50, 54, 56, 61; Spingold 1943, 51, 57; Vanderbilt 1944, 45, 50, 55, 56, 57, 59, 60; Life Master Pairs 1946; Mixed Pairs 1951, 55, 56; Master Individual 1951; Men's BAM Teams 1952, 56, 61; Men's Pairs 1958; Open Pairs 1963. He was 2nd Spingold 1936, 47, 50, 55, 60, 61; Open Pairs 1941; Men's Pairs 1941, 50, 58, 62; Life Master Pairs 1943, 56; Reisinger 1944, 51; Master Mixed Teams 1946, 52, 60, 62; Men's BAM Teams 46, 59, 63; Vanderbilt 1953. At his death was member of ACBL Board of Directors and holder of the Open Pairs Championship. Was 3rd highest on list of all-time masterpoint winners, with a total of 6,450 — a figure great enough to hold that place until a year after his death. At that time his total was surpassed by Norman Kay, who had been his regular partner. Silodor authored a newspaper column and many articles for *The Bridge World*. His books included *Silodor Says*, *Contract Bridge According to Silodor and Tiernery* and *The Complete Book of Duplicate Bridge*.

SILVER, Joseph (Joey) (b. 1941) of Hampstead PQ, criminal defense trial lawyer. WBF World Master. Active member ACBL Board of Governors more than 20 years. Represented Canada in world competition 1974, 78, 82, 90, 94, 95, 96, 98, 2000. Placed 2nd Bermuda Bowl 1995. Won Cavendish Invitational Pairs 1985. Representing Montreal, won Epson Inter-City Team Championship 1983, 85 and NEC Cup (Japan) 1996. Placed 3rd Maccabiah Games 1981. Diamond Life Master, in top 10 Canadian masterpoint holders. Won Vanderbilt 1974, Men's BAM Teams 1981, Open Pairs 1985, North American Swiss Teams 1986; CNTC 1994, 95, 97; placed 2nd Men's Teams 1973, Master Mixed Teams 1974, CNTC 1984, North American Men's Swiss Teams 1989, Vanderbilt 1995. In 1986, as the defending champions of the Cavendish, he and his partner, Irving Litvack, withdrew to allow a British pair to play. For that action he was awarded the John Simon Trophy for Bridge Sportsman of the Year. Contributor to the *Bridge World, Bridge Today, Australian Bridge, Melange De Bridge, New Zealand Bridge, German Bridge, British Bridge Magazine* and *International Popular Bridge*.

SILVERMAN, Gloria (b. 1948) of Toronto ON, born in Germany, educational program developer for Addiction Research Foundation of Ontario. WBF World Life Master, placed 3rd Venice Cup 1989, 4th Women's Team Olympiad 1988. Also represented Canada in international competition 1982, 1986, 1991, 1992, 2000. Won Canadian Women's Team Championship 1986, 87, 88, 89, 91; placed 2nd CWTC 1982, CNTC 1988. Won District 2 GNOT 1982, 94 and has many other regional titles to her credit.

SILVERMAN, Harry J. (b. 1927) of Rye Brook NY, president, Barclay Bridge Supplies, Inc. 1965-90, now retired. Represented District 3 on ACBL Board of Governors 1985-95. Served on Unit 188 board 1975-95. Editor, *Silverman 5-Card Major Teachers Manual* and *Texts*.

SILVERMAN, Jerome R. (Jerry) (1912-1985) of Mill Valley CA, attorney and account executive, graduate of Rutgers University School of Law. ACBL president 1973, ACBL treasurer 1970-72, chairman of ACBL Goodwill Committee 1975, ACBL representative to WBF 1973-76, trustee of ACBL Charity Foundation 1974, president ACBL Charity Foundation 1980-82, vice president WBF

1976-78, member ACBL Board of Directors 1966-75, member of the Laws Commission of the ACBL. Former president New Jersey BL, NY-NJ Bridge Conference, and District 21. He served as npc of the North American team in the 1977 Bermuda Bowl. directed on bridge cruises. Father of Neil Silverman.

SILVERMAN, Neil (b. 1949) of Ft. Lauderdale FL, options trader, former genealogical researcher. WBF World Master, won Rosenblum Teams 1986, placed 3rd Bermuda Bowl 1999. ACBL Diamond Life Master, won Life Master Pairs 1976, Men's Pairs 1980, GNOT 1997, North American Swiss Teams 1999. Placed 2nd Reisinger 1977, Men's Pairs 1981, Open Pairs 1990, Vanderbilt, Spingold 1992, GNOT 1997, North American Swiss Teams 1999. Won gold medal at the Maccabiah Games, placed 3rd in Invitational Pairs Championship. Appeared on a 13-segment TV show on bridge for BBC 1981.

SILVERMAN, Shirley Seiner (Mrs. Harry J.) (1928-1992) of White Plains NY, bridge writer and administrator. Served as chairman ACBL Board of Governors 1975-78. President, vice president, tournament chairman, publication editor for Unit 188. Former co-owner of bridge supply company. Member ABTA and IBPA. Author of the *Five Card Major Bridge Teachers' Manual, Elementary Bridge Five Card Major Student Text, Intermediate Bridge Five Card Major Student Text, Play of the Hand as Declarer* and *Defender Student Text, Advanced and Duplicate Bridge Student Text, Chicago Bridge, Point Count Bidding Guide*, editor of *Expert Bridge*.

SILVERSTEIN, Dr. Bruce M. (b. 1951) of Lancaster PA, physician. Won North American Swiss 1989; approximately 10 regional events plus District 4 GNOT 5 times, GNOP 3 times.

SILVERSTEIN, Nate (1909-1992) of Memphis TN, born in Poland, bridge club manager. For more than 30 years a devoted promoter of bridge. Member ACBL Board of Directors 1968-71, had much to do with move of ACBL Headquarters to Memphis. Tireless worker for charity, because of his drive, Unit 144 had highest donations per capita for many years. Unit president many times, served as vice president of ACBL Charity Foundation. Won dozens of regionals, Diamond Life Master.

SILVERSTONE, Victor (b. 1940) of London, England, formerly of Glasgow Scotland, chartered accountant. Won Camrose Trophy once, represented Scotland in 24 Camrose matches. Several national titles.

SIMMONDS, Alan (b.1940) of Cape Town, South Africa, journalist. Represented South Africa in 1 world championship and on other international occasions. Won 3 national titles. Editor of *S.A.Bridge Bulletin* 1974-81. Daily bridge columnist for *Cape Town The Argus*, and is syndicated.

SIMON, Adaline (Mrs. John E.) (1901-1985) of St. Louis MO. Won Women's Teams 1959 and numerous regional titles.

SIMON, Allan K. (b. 1945) of Calgary AB, born in Denmark, casino employer, former systems analyst. Zone V representative to CBF since 1991. Editor *Canadian Bridge Digest* 1985-90. Won 1988 Epson World-Wide Bidding Challenge.

SIMON, Carol WBF World Master. Placed 2nd Venice Cup 1995. Won Women's Knockouts 1998. placed 2nd Women's Swiss 1994, Women's Pairs 1998.

SIMON, Edith (1914-1998) of Memphis TN, ACBL librarian 1972-83, administrative secretary for Chicago CBA 1964-72.

SIMON, John E. (1897-1993) of St. Louis MO, limited partner in brokerage firm. ACBL Honorary Member 1962, Life Master #641. Was chairman of ACBL Goodwill Committee. Donor of Simon Award. Won Men's Teams 1972, 73; placed 2nd Open Pairs 1961. (See IBPA AWARDS.)

SIMON, S.J. (Skidelsky or Skid) (1904-1948), novelist and bridge writer. One of best-loved British bridge personalities. One of originators of ACOL System. European champion 1948, also represented Great Britain in European championships 1939. National wins include Gold Cup 1937, 47. Wrote many successful humorous novels in collaboration with ballet expert Carol Brahms including *Bullet in the Ballet, No Bed for Bacon* and *Trottie True*. A contributor *The Bridge World*. Simon wrote the classic *Why You Lose at Bridge, Design for Bidding* and *Cut for Partners*.

SIMONS, Anneke (b. 1951) of Amsterdam, Netherlands. WBF World Life Master. Won Venice Cup 2000. Won European Union Women's Pairs 1998. Represented Netherlands in 3 other world championships and 5 zonals.

SIMPSON, Colin (b 1948) of Buckinghamshire, England. Scotland Yard detective. WBF World Master. Represented England in Olympiad 2000, finishing fourth. Represented England in Camrose series. Winner 1999 South Africa Teams. 5 time winner of Lederer Invitation tournament, winner Spring Fours 2000 and other major English competitions.

SIMPSON, Gene (b. 1942) of Pacific Palisades CA, advertising salesman, Grand Life Master with 17,301 MPs (3/2001). Won North American Swiss 1983, GNOT 1998, Senior Swiss Teams 1999. Placed 2nd Men's BAM Teams 1986, Life Master Open Pairs 1996.

SIMPSON, Howard (b. 1941) of Bluffton SC, manager-PacBell. Vice president and tournament manager for Whittier Unit and District 23 1978-82. District 23 representative to ALACBU 1978-82, president LA Commercial Bridge Association, member ALACBU Appeals Committee 1978-83. Won 17 regionals.

SIMS, Dorothy Rice (1889-1960) of Deal NJ, one of leading personalities of early days of bridge. Daughter of Isaac L. Rice, first manufacturer of the submarine and patron of chess and other recreational activities. From her teens she was active in competition and held the U.S. motorcycle speed championship for women (1911). Sims was one of the first U.S. aviatrixes when she met and married P. Hal Sims. Noted sculptress, designed City of Asbury Park Trophy. Writings include several bridge books as well as work in fields other than bridge. Acquired interest in bridge through husband and became a successful player. Won ABL Auction Women's Pairs 1929; AWL Open Teams 1929, Open Pairs 1930; ABL Mixed Teams 1930. In 1935 she was her husband's principal partner in 150-rubber match against Ely and Josephine Culbertson. Widely credited with inventing the psychic bid, but probably just initiated the popular name for it. However, she wrote the first book on the subject, *Psychic Bidding*. After her husband's death, she toured the world several times as a political correspondent for various newspapers. (see CULBERTSON-SIMS MATCH.)

SIMS P(hillip) Hal (1886-1949) of Deal NJ. Member ACBL Hall of Fame. One of the great American players, his system had the largest expert following prior to 1935. Born in Selma AL, Sims represented U.S. banks in foreign countries from 1906-1916. While a member of the

U.S. Army Air Corps in 1917 he met Dorothy Rice, U.S. aviatrix in transport service, whom he married. After World War I Sims devoted himself chiefly to competitive sports, in which he excelled, and to bridge. He held a national trapshooting record and won the Artists' and Writers' Golf Tournament in 1937. In auction bridge was member of highest-ranked team, the Knickerbocker Whist Club team, which included Sydney S. Lenz, Winfield S. Liggett, George Reith, and Ralph J. Leibenderfer. Captain of contract bridge team called the Four Horsemen whose other members were Williard S. Karn, Oswald Jacoby and David Burnstine. This team won most of the principal American tournaments 1931-1933.

The Sims System, a subjective approach based on Sim's desire to dominate every pair and team of which he was a member, left little impression on contract bridge methods used by experts from 1935 on. First- and 2nd-hand opening one-bids were stronger than 3rd- and 4th-hand bids; notrump bids were always strong but had wide limits; psychic bids were used freely; high preemptive bids were eschewed. In 1935 Hal and Dorothy Sims tested this system in a 150-rubber match against Ely and Josephine Culbertson, and were defeated. Sims' books included *Money Contract, Master Contract* (his definitive work, largely by Sir Derrick Wernher) and several lesser works.

Sims was one of the most colorful characters in bridge history. Called "the shaggy giant", his commanding presence (6'4" in height, more than 300 pounds in weight, big-boned and muscular) augmented his claim to authority. For more than 5 years his mansion in Deal NJ was summer headquarters for the principal experts and promising new players. He controlled the ABL for several years without holding formal office. He founded the Deal Club, a bridge club at which the principal U.S. and international experts played from 1930-1935. His skill as a raconteur and his personal charm were proverbial. He died of a heart attack while bidding a hand in a game at the Havana Country Club, where he and his wife spent their winters after 1946.(see CULBERTSON-SIMS MATCH.)

SIMSON, Douglas A. (Doug) (b. 1940) of Bexley OH, president/owner First City Bank and First Investment Company. WBF World Master. Won Life Master Pairs 1986, 91; GNOT 1990. Placed 2nd GNOT 1994, Open Pairs I 2000. He also won Pan American Pairs 1992 and OKBridge World Championship Teams 1999.

SINGHA, Govinda (b. 1934) of Calcutta, India, retired. Won Far East Open Teams 1977, represented India in 2 other zonal championships and 3 world championships. 15 national wins.

SINISCALCO, Guglielmo (b. 1921) of Naples, Italy, professor of civil engineering. WBF World Grand Master. Won Bermuda Bowl 1957, 58, 59; European Teams 1955, 56, 57, 58, 2nd 1952

SINT, Cornelis J. (Cees) (b. 1940) of Broek in Waterland, the Netherlands, bridge writer and journalist. WBF World Master. Represented The Netherlands in 4 world championships and 7 zonal championships. Won many national titles. Author (with Ton Schipperheyn) of 4 TV courses and about 40 books, including *From Start to Finish*. (The first two volumes are the official beginners course of the Netherlands Bridge League). More than a million copies of Sint/Schipperheyn's books have been sold. Contributor to *Bridge* and *Algemeen Dagblad*.

SITHISARIPUTRA, Boonita (b. 1946) of Bangkok, Thailand, company executive and director. 2nd PABF (Far East) Women's Teams 1979. Represented Thailand in 2 world championships and on 10 other occasions. Won 5 ASEAN team titles. Won 1961 Mixed Pairs, at 17 the youngest winner in Thai bridge history.

SKAANNING-NORRIS, Lotte (b 1963) of Copenhagen, Denmark, computer programmer. WBF World Master. 5th World Women's Team Olympiad 1992. 2nd Nordic Women's Teams 1988, 92. Many national wins.

SKINNER, Richmond H. (Dick) (1898-1986) of Dallas TX, ACBL president 1944, member ACBL Executive Committee from its formation through 1944. President Mid-Atlantic BA, Keystone Conference, New England BA. Civil engineer by training, had varied career. U.S. Army officer, pipe organ builder and installer, pilot and flying instructor, top flight tennis player and referee (awarded the McGovern Cup for national tennis umpire of the year 1972) and longtime member of the New Hampshire Legislature. Invented Skinner Psychic Controls, Skinner Responses to a 1NT Opening, Skinner Two-Bids and originated a point-count method in 1932 in which an ace was assigned 5 points, king 3 points, queen 2 points and jack 1 point. Won Eastern States KO Teams 1940 and several other regionals.

SKIPPER, Jane (formerly Evitt) (b. 1949), of Christchurch N.Z., science and mathematics teacher. Won Far East Women's Teams 1981, 2nd 1978. Represented New Zealand in one world championship and one other zonal championship. Top masterpoint winner in New Zealand 1978. Bridge teacher.

SKOLNIK, Mel D. (b. 1940) of New York City, real estate developer, investor and entrepreneur. Advocate of animal rights, protection of environment and free enterprise. Won McKenney Trophy 1981 over Barry Crane in hardest fought and most bitterly contested fight for that trophy in history It went right down to the wire, including the midnight zip swiss in the last tournament of the year. Won 38 regional events in 1981, a record at that time. He also won 183 MPs at the Calgary regional, another record for that time.

SKOROUPO, Roman (1900-1971 of Helsingfors, Finland, businessman, bridge writer, bridge administrator. Member of Executive of WBF and European Bridge League, secretary-general Finnish Bridge League, contributing editor to *Bridge Encyclopedia.*

SKOTTE, Gulle (1917-1994) of Odense, Denmark. 3rd World Women's Olympiad Teams 1960, won European Women's Teams 1948, 49, 55, 57, 2nd 1951. Many national titles.

SLAGER, Hilda K. (Mrs. Julian H.) (b. 1908) of Montgomery AL. Won International North-South Pairs Championship in 1933 World Bridge Olympic, the United States North-South Pair championship in 1932 World Bridge Olympic and several regionals.

SLAGER, Julian H. (b. 1902) of Montgomery AL. ACBL Goodwill Member of Year 1991. Won several regional events.

SLAVENBURG, Cornelis (Bob) of Rotterdam, the Netherlands. WBF Grand Master. Won Sunday Times 1971. Won World Open Pairs 1966, represented Netherlands 1966 Bermuda Bowl, 1970 World Open Pairs. Also European Championships 1951, 59, 65, 66, 67. Many national titles. Also represented Morocco internationally.

SLEMMONS, George W. of Bellevue WA. Won Men's Pairs 1974 and many regionals.

SLOAN, Jesse (1913-1989) of Van Nuys CA, real estate loan broker, former bridge club owner. Won Vanderbilt 1952.

SMART, Diana Frances of Melbourne, Australia, research psychologist. WBF World Master. Won PABF (Far East) Women's Teams 1984, 90, 95. Represented Australia in 6 world championships and 7 other zonal championships. Won numerous national titles.

SMILDE, Roelof (b. 1930) of Sydney, Australia, bridge teacher. WBF World Life Master. 3rd Bermuda Bowl 1971. Won PABF (Far East) Teams 1968, 1970. Represented Australia in 4 other world championships. National titles include open teams 6 times.

SMITH, Allan W. (b. 1950) of Peterborough ON, parole officer. Won 15+ regionals.

SMITH, Curtis (b. 1925) of Conroe TX, engineer. Grand Life Master. Contributor to ACBL *Bridge Bulletin*, authored *Bidding Through Logic* and invented Smith convention (not Smith Echo). Won Open Pairs 1960, Spingold 1966, 77; GNOT 1977. Placed 2nd Open Pairs 1953, Chicago (now the Reisinger) 1960, 64; Life Master Pairs 1963, Life Master Men's Pairs 1970, Spingold 1972.

SMITH, David L. (b. 1949 in England) of Melbourne, Australia, computing manager. Won South Pacific playoff 1991. Represented Australia in one world championship, one zonal championship and one zonal playoff. 7 national wins.

SMITH, David W. (Dave) (b. 1944) of Newark DE, computer programmer/analyst. Represented Korea in Far East Championships 1969. Diamond Life Master, placed 2nd GNOT 1973, won about 75 regional events. Encyclopedia proofreader.

SMITH, Duncan H. (Slam Dunk) (b. 1948) of Victoria BC, hospital housekeeper, bridge teacher and club director. Diamond Life Master, contributor Victoria newsletter. Won approximately 35 regionals which include District 19 GNOT 1978; Canadian National Teams, Zone 6 1981.

SMITH, Glenn F. (b. 1932) of Creve Coeur MO, retired senior vice-president, graduate of St. Louis University. President of the ACBL 1999, Chairman of the Board of Directors 2000. District 8 representative to ACBL Board of Directors, member ACBL Goodwill committee and has served on Unit 143 Board. Won several regionals including District 8 GNOT (twice).

SMITH, Helen of Philadelphia PA, insurance broker. Placed 2nd Mixed Pairs 1973, Spring Women's KO Teams 1976, won many regional events.

SMITH, Helen Martin (Mrs. Stanley, formerly Mrs. Al Sobel and Mrs. Jack White) (1910-1969) of Detroit was universally ranked as probably the greatest woman bridge player of all time. Member ACBL Hall of Fame. Became Life Master #25 in 1941. Born in Philadelphia, and after a long residence in New York City moved to Miami Beach 1963. After her marriage to Smith, she moved to Detroit. She enjoyed a brief stage career as a chorus girl and appeared in several stage shows including *Animal Crackers* with the Marx Brothers. Another chorus girl taught her how to play bridge and she rocketed to stardom at the card table. In 1934, as Mrs. Jack White, she won the Women's Pairs Championship, the first of her many titles.

Shortly after her marriage to Al Sobel ended in divorce (1937-1945), she was invited by Ely Culbertson to represent the United States. She played with the Culbertsons and Charles Vogelhofer in a World Championship conducted by the International Bridge League (1937) in

Budapest. It was won by Austria. This was tacit recognition that Culbertson, like many other experts, considered her the equal of any male player, a view which became that of Charles Goren in 1940 when they won the Open Pair title, their first of many to come. This was to become one of the most enduring and successful partnerships in the history of bridge. Together they won the De La Rue International Invitation Pairs Tournament in London 1957. They represented North America in the Bermuda Bowl 1957 where they came in 2nd; the U.S. in the World Team Olympiad of 1960.

Many of her 33 titles were won with Goren including Life Master Pairs twice 1942, 58. She won the McKenney 1941, 42, 44, and the Fishbein Trophy 1958. She won the Spingold 5 times 1944, 47, 51, 56, 60; Chicago (now the Reisinger) 4 times 1941, 43, 50, 57; the Vanderbilt 1944, 45; Women's Pairs 1938, 39; Women's Teams 1935, 36, 39, 43, 44, 45, 46; Master Mixed Teams 1941, 43, 33 38, 54, 68; Mixed Pairs 1955, 56. She placed 2nd Women's Teams 1937, 41, 42, 50, 52, 54, 55, 56, 57, 58; Vanderbilt 1942, 49, 50, 53, 59, 62; Spingold 1943, 50; Reisinger 1944, 51; Master Mixed Teams 1946, 49, 50, 51; Women's Pairs 1947, 65; Life Master Pairs 1953. By 1948 she had amassed the greatest number of master-points of any woman. She took over the top spot from Sally Young and held it uninterruptedly until 1964. Author of *All the Tricks* and several magazine articles.

SMITH, Herbert L. (b. 1932) of San Mateo CA, born in Austria, accountant. ACBL president 1988, District 21 representative to ACBL Board of Directors 1981-89. ACBL treasurer 22 years. Served several terms as president Unit 506, District 21 and Western Conference. Chairman Fall NABC 1981. Diamond Life Master.

SMITH, Ivy Mary (b. in New York City) of Caracas, Venezuela, teacher of English. WBF World Master. Won CAC Women's Teams 1980, 81, 85, 91, 95. Represented Venezuela in 8 world championships. Won many national titles. Quarterfinalist Venice Cup 1995.

SMITH, Linda S. (b. 1947) of Chattanooga TN, data processor. Diamond Life Master. Won Zonal Open Teams 1994, Zonal Open Pairs 1998. Won 75+ regionals.

SMITH, Marc (b 1960) of Southampton, England, bridge writer. Winner 1985 European Union Junior Teams, represented England successfully in 3 Junior Camroses. Played numerous zonal and one world championship. National titles include Swiss Teams (3 times), Two Stars Pairs (twice), Four Stars Teams at the Summer Nationals (twice), the Autumn Teams (3 times), the Pachabo Cup and the Tollemache Cup. Author of numerous books including *25 Conventions You Should Know, Over Hoffman's Shoulder* and *World Class*. Regular columnist in various bridge magazines and online publications.

SMITH, Nicola P. (b. 1949) of London, England, bridge teacher. WBF World Grand Master. Won Venice Cup 1981, 1985; 2nd 1976; 2nd World Women's Team Olympiad 1976, 84, 88. 92, 3rd 1980. Won European Women's Teams 1975, 79, 81, 97, 99, 2nd 1969, 77, 85. Won Generali World Individual 1994. Won 5 Common Market titles. Represented Britain in 1 other world championship and 6 other zonals. More than 20 national victories include 3 Gold Cups. Awarded MBE for services to bridge 1995.

SMITH, Ronald (Ron) of San Francisco CA, Hedge Fund manager, options trader, professional bridge player. Has performed as a concert pianist. Grand Life Master

with 16,272 MPs, *Bridge World* panelist. Won Blue Ribbon Pairs 1979, Reisinger 1987, North American Swiss Teams 1993, GNOT, Life Master Open Pairs 1996; Open Swiss Teams 1998; placed 2nd GNOT 1973, Reisinger 1978, Vanderbilt, Blue Ribbon Pairs 1988, Open BAM Teams 1994, 97; Spingold 1996, Life Master Open Pairs 1998, GNOT 2000. Placed 2nd and 3rd Cavendish. Won more than 100 regionals.

SMITH, Ronald L. (b. 1947) of Hixson TN, mathematics professor. District GNOP co-ordinator 1985-95. Grand Life Master with 15,490 MPs. Won Men's BAM Teams 1977, Life Master Open Pairs 1996; finished 2nd GNOT 1975, Open BAM Teams 1997. Won more than 100 regionals.

SMITH, Terry (b. 1936) of Los Angeles CA, general administrator, former regional tournament director. Was ACBL tournament coordinator 1968-70, ACBL executive assistant 1970-74, member of drafting committee of 1975 Laws of Duplicate, ACBL organizer 1972 World Olympiad. Contributed to ACBL *Bulletin* and *Bridge Encyclopedia*.

SMITH, Thomas M. (b. 1938) of Greenwich CT, bridge editor and writer, vice-president of Goren International; editorial manager 2nd edition *Official Encyclopedia of Bridge*, World Championship Handbooks 1966-72. Contributor to *ACBL Bridge Bulletin, Bridge Journal* and *The Bridge World*. Editor Greater New York BA *Post-Mortem* 1973-78, 1985-91. Business manager ACBL *Bulletin* 1970-72. Managed Cavendish Club 1973-87, elected honorary member 1988 and president 1990. Placed 12th Rosenblum Teams 1986. Diamond Life Master, original member of Precision Team that won Spingold 1970, 71; Vanderbilt 1972. Other ACBL national placings were 2nd Life Master Men's Pairs 1976; Spingold 1978, Men's BAM Teams 1982. Intercollegiate champion 1965.

SMITH, William H. (Bill) (1909-1993) of Fort Meyers FL, retired teacher. Associate editor ACBL *Bulletin* 1958-64. Became tournament director 1944, directed on many cruises.

SMITH, William P. (Willie, Smitty) (b. 1948) of Endicott NY; driver. Won GNOT Flt B 1991.

SMOLEN, Michael (Mike) (1940-92) of Alamo CA, attorney and commodity trader. WBF World Master, placed 5th Rosenblum Teams, 13th World Open Pairs 1990. Grand Life Master with 17,421 MPs. #16 on list of all-time masterpoint holders at time of death. Devised Smolen Transfer Bid. Known for his ability to help develop new players and for being a good partner. Won Men's Teams 1976, North American Swiss Teams 1978, Mixed Pairs 1979, Fishbein Trophy, Men's Swiss Teams 1982; North American Men's Swiss, npc North American Women's Swiss 1982; Reisinger 1984. Placed 2nd Men's Teams 1974, Open Pairs, Open Swiss Teams 1990.

SMOLEN, Steven F. (Steve) of Manhattan Beach CA, computer consultant. Won Amateur Swiss Teams 1977.

SMOLSKI, Roman (b. 1950 in England) of Bermuda, computer programmer. WBF World Master. Won European Teams 1991, Common Market Teams 1980. Represented Britain in 5 world championships and 1 other zonal. Represented England in 15 Camrose matches.

SNITE, Fred, Jr. (d. 1955) of Miami Beach. Lived last 19 years of his life in iron lung. Regular competitor in ACBL tournaments. Honorary Member 1954. (see HANDICAPPED PLAYERS.)

SNYDER, Marion D. (formerly Weed) of Dallas TX, interior decorator. Won Life Master Women's Pairs 1975,

Master Mixed Teams 1976 and many regional events.

SOBEL, Alexander M. (Al) (1901-1972) of New York City, a leading bridge personality. Member ACBL Hall of Fame. Won greatest fame as a director, but he was also noted as a writer, a quizmaster and a wit. 3rd person to be North American Championships Tournament Manager for ACBL, following Alfred M. Gruenther and Russell Baldwin, held that position from 1942 until his retirement in 1969. Sobel, MIT graduate engineer, turned to bridge during the Depression "rather than sell apples." Directed tournaments from September 1934 in U.S., Canada, Mexico, Argentina, France, Italy, England, and Brazil. Made other guest appearances in Hong Kong, Tokyo, and the Philippines. Debut as major tournament manager 1935 —substituted for Gruenther at Eastern States Championships, then a national tournament.

The craze for quizzes resulted in the bridge experts playing a game similar to the popular, *Ask Me Another*. They played late at night after almost every tournament session. Sobel became their unofficial quiz master. For three years, 1948-1951, he wrote the questions for the Bob Hawk *Lemac* radio quiz. His commanding voice created a tournament directorial style. Until the great crowds of the Fifties Sobel seldom needed a microphone. In 1937 he married Helen Martin White. They divorced in 1945. He became a member of the ACBL Laws Commission 1943, was the first Honorary Member of Japan Contract Bridge League, was ACBL Honorary Member 1949.

Sobel was one of a group of four talented writers who worked for Ely Culbertson in the early Thirties. Culbertson's summonses to "Al" regularly created confusion, since, in addition to Sobel, the others were Albert Morehead, Alfred Sheinwold and Alphonse Moyse Jr. Was associate editor *ACBL Bulletin*, and as such Sobel authored *60 Days*, a popular bi-monthly diary column. It became a monthly column *30 Days* and later returned to *60 Days*. He was also a former editor of the West Coast publication, *Contract Bridge Forum* and a contributing editor, *Bridge Encyclopedia*.

SOBEL, Helen Martin. See SMITH, Helen Martin.

SOKOLOW, Tobi (nee Levine, formerly Deutch) (Mrs. David) (b. 1942) of Austin TX, realtor, former social worker, headhunter. WBF Grand Master, #29 among women in world; ranks 9th among women in world in performance over last 10 years; won Venice Cup 1997; placed 2nd 1999, 5th 1995; was 3rd McConnell Cup 1994, 98. Placed 5th Women's Pairs 1994. Won Women's Team Trials 1992, 97, 99; 2nd 1995. Also represented ACBL in world championship play 1986, 1992. Won USWBTC 1992 and competed in USBC 1991. Grand Life Master, has won each of the 5 women's national titles at least once. Won Women's Swiss Teams 1984, 85; Women's Pairs 1987, 1990; Life Master Women's Pairs 1991, Women's BAM Teams 1994, 99; Women's KO Teams 1997, 2000. Placed 2nd Women's Swiss Teams 1988, 95, 99, 2000; Women's BAM Teams 1997. Was Board member and editor for newsletter in Phoenix Unit, currently active locally. Has won more than 150 regional events.

SOKOLOWER, Lester (b. 1931) of Verona NJ, retired retailing executive. Diamond Life Master, won at least 15 regional events.

SOLAR, Elizabeth See RABICEW, Elizabeth

SOLER, Rosa (b. 1920) of Barcelona, Spain. Represented Spain in 20 zonal championships and 6 world championships. Won 6 national titles.

SOLODAR, John (b. 1940) of New York City, retired director of systems and programming. Was Bermuda Bowl champion 1981; WBF World Life Master placed 3rd Rosenblum Teams 1990, 11th 1986, 13th 1978; 14th World Mixed Pairs 1978. New York manager for the Sharif Bridge Circus 1968. Diamond Life Master won Life Master Men's Pairs 1968, Vanderbilt 1980; placed 2nd Spingold 1976, 1980; Men's BAM Teams 1983.

SOLOMON, Charles J. (1906-1975) of Philadelphia, attorney, bridge administrator, teacher and author, a leading figure in bridge. Member ACBL Hall of Fame. Life Master #16 in 1939, he amassed a lifetime total of 6594 masterpoints and won 12 national titles, including the Chicago (now the Reisinger) 1937, 1938, 1939, 1944; Men's Pairs 1943, Life Master Pairs 1946, Master Individual 1947, Master Mixed Teams 1949, 1950, 1959; Men's BAM Teams 1952, 1965; Spingold 1955. In addition to 16 2nd places — Life Master Pairs 1938, Spingold 1939, Master Mixed Teams 1939, 40; Master Individual 1943, Reisinger 53, 59; Vanderbilt 1954, 58; Men's BAM Teams 1955, 60; Open Pairs 1959, 68; Mixed Pairs 1961, Life Master Men's Pairs 1963 and numerous regional wins.

Member U.S. International team 1956, npc Open Team 1959 and U.S. Women's Team 1960. Donated the Charles J. Solomon Trophy to the World Bridge Federation in 1966, to be given to the country with the best record in pair events at World Pair Championship. ACBL president 1958, chairman of Board 1944, 55, 57; ACBL Honorary Member 1961.

On international level, was on organizing committee and helped to found the World Bridge Federation. WBF vice president 1958-1964, president 1964-1968, chairman of the Board 1968-1972, honorary chairman 1972 until his death. Also served with distinction on ACBL Laws Commission 1940-60, on Editorial Advisory Board *Bridge Encyclopedia*. Author *Slam Bidding and Point Count* and *No Trump Bidding*; bridge editor of *Philadelphia Inquirer* 30 years. Sponsored IBPA Solomon Award, given annually for best description of a bridge deal in world press. (See BUENOS AIRES AFFAIR.)

SOLOMON, Eliezer N. (Ely) (b. 1944) of Riviera Beach MD, born in India, software engineer, placed 2nd Swiss Teams 1978 and has won several regionals.

SOLOMON, Peggy (Mrs. Charles J.) (1909-1995) of Philadelphia PA, a leading women player for 3 decades, Life Master #33. Won Chicago (now Reisinger) 1944, Master Mixed Teams 1949, 50, 59; Women's Teams 1957, 64, 68, 70; Women's Pairs 1960; placed 2nd Master Mixed Teams 1939, 40; Spingold 1944, Women's Teams 1948, 53, 54, 61, 67; Chicago 1953, Vanderbilt 1954, Mixed Pairs 1961, Life Master Women's Pairs 1965, 66, 67. Diamond Life Master.

SOLOWAY, Paul (b. 1941) of Mill Creek WA, professional player, WBF Grand Master. Won Bermuda Bowl 1976, 77, 79, 99; placed 2nd World Team Olympiad 1972, 80; 2nd Bermuda Bowl 1975, 4th 1973; 6th World Team Olympiad 1984, 7th 1976; 9th Rosenblum Teams 1978. Represented ACBL in several other world competitions. Grand Life Master, leading ACBL masterpoint holder with 53,843 MPs as of 3/2001. Won Lazard Sportsmanship Award 2001.

Won Pan American Invitational Championship 1977, McKenney Trophy 1968, 69; Team Trials (now USBC) 1975, 77, 79, 80, 84; Lou Herman Trophy 1976, Life Master Men's Pairs 1965, Master Mixed Teams 1966, 87; Vanderbilt 1969, 78, 97, 98, 2000; Spingold 1978, 83, 86, 88, 98, 99; Reisinger 1976, 80, 94; GNOT 1974, 76;

Men's Swiss Teams 1989, Open Swiss Teams 1991, Life Master Open Pairs 1999. Soloway placed 2nd Men's Pairs 1969, Men's Teams 1970, Vanderbilt 1971, 76; Spingold 1973, 90, 94, 96; Men's BAM Teams 1984, Reisinger 1986, 90, 93; Open BAM Teams 1995, 98, 99.

SONTAG, Alan (b. 1946) of Gaithersburg MD, professional player, Sportsman of the Year 1975. Author of *The Bridge Bum*, *Power Precision* and co-author of *Improve Your Bridge Fast*. WBF World Life Master, Bermuda Bowl champion 1983, 5th 1991; placed 7th Rosenblum Teams 1978, 8th World Open Pairs 1974, 78. Won USBC (Team Trials) 1983, 91; Men's Teams 1971, 79; Life Master Men's Pairs 1971, Vanderbilt 1972, 88, 99; Reisinger 1973, Life Master Pairs 1977, Spingold 1980, 82, 2000; Men's Swiss Teams 1985, 87; Master Mixed Teams 1989, GNOT 1994. Placed 2nd Life Master Pairs 1972, 84; Vanderbilt 1975, 81, 83, 89, 97; Reisinger 1977, 92, 96, 98; Spingold 1979, 91,, 96, 97; Men's BAM Teams 1985, Open Swiss Teams 2000. Grand Life Master with 20,498 MPs as of 3/2001, #30 in ACBL. Won the Invitational Pairs Championship 1973, 75, Cavendish Club Invitational 1976, 77.

SOPHONPANICH, Khunying Chodchoy Esther (b. 1944) of Bangkok, Thailand, business executive. President Pacific Asia Bridge Federation and Contract Bridge League of Thailand. Represented Thailand in 2 World Olympiads and 11 zonal championships. Won 5 Asean titles Championships.

SORENSEN, Dennis E. (b. 1946) of Portland OR, bridge professional, retired teacher, hortculturalist. Served on ACBL Conduct and Ethics Committee in 80s and 90s. Past president District 20, coordinator GNOT and GNOP events. Grand Life Master with 15,861 MPs (3/2001), won Crane Top 500 1992, Intercollegiate Bridge Championship 1978; finished 2nd North American Swiss Teams 1991, Open Pairs I 1993. His 150+ regional wins include District 20 GNOT, Zone VIII 1980.

SORRI, Kalevi (b. 1924) of Helsinki, Finland. Represented Finland in 4 European championships. Many national titles.

SORRI, Keijo (b. 1926) of Helsinki, Finland. Represented Finland in 5 European championships. Many national wins.

SOULET, Philippe (b. 1954) of Paris, France, bridge teacher. WBF World Life Master. Won World Team Olympiad 1980, Rosenblum Teams 1982. 3rd Bermuda Bowl 1995. Won European Teams 1983, 2nd 1995. Represented France in 3 other world championships and 1 other zonal championship. Many national titles.

SOWTER, Anthony P. (Tony) (b. 1946) of Nottingham, England. WBF World Master. Won European Teams 1991, 2nd 1981. Represented Britain in 9 world championships. National titles include 3 Gold Cups. Managing editor *International Popular Bridge Monthly* 1976-1998. Editor of *World Championship Books* 1990-94. Series Editor Batsford Bridge Books 1994-1998. Author of 8 books including *The Takeout Double* and *It's Your Bid*.

SPIEGEL, Bernard M. (Buddy) (b. 1947) of Boca Raton FL, National Change-of-Address Program Project Manager for U.S. Postal service. Former ACBL Director of Administration, ACBL tournament coordinator, ACBL associate national tournament director, secretary to the ACBL Laws Commission, author of *Ruling the Game* for ACBL *Bulletin*.

SPINGOLD, Nathan B. (Nate) (1886-1958) of New York City, publicist, motion picture executive, patron of the arts. Most influential man in bridge administration 1937-43. Born in Chicago, he became a reporter on *The Chicago Examiner*, *The Chicago Record Herald* and *The Chicago Tribune*. Spingold's interest in show business brought him to New York City. In 1932 he joined Columbia Pictures in a public relations capacity and continued his association with the company until his death. In 1940 he was named to the Board of Directors and three years later was appointed vice president in charge of advertising, publicity and development. In 1954 he became vice president of the company. Nate and Frances Spingold were leading art collectors and owned an outstanding gallery of French impressionist paintings and contempory American art. Active in bridge from its earliest days, Spingold donated the prestigious trophy which bears his name. In 1936 he was named ABL Honorary Member. In 1937 he was influential in effecting a peaceful merger between the American Bridge League and the United States Bridge Association. He became president of the newly formed American Contract Bridge League the following year. He served for many years on the League's Board of Governors and Board of Directors. Spingold was also president of the Cavendish Club in New York.

SPINN, Rosi (b. 1928) of Kitzbhel, Austria, retired English teacher. WBF World Master. Runner-up 1991 Venice Cup; represented Austria in one other world championship and one European Championship.

SPITALNICK, Richard L. (b. 1944) of Sunnyvale CA, CPA. Treasurer for District 21 1980-85, Fall NABC 1981. Placed 2nd Amateur Swiss Teams 1977. His 50+ regional wins include District 21 GNOT 1980; District 21 GNOT 1991, 92.

SPITZ, Marshall R. (b. 1943) of Chestnut Hill MA, senior vice president investments. Won 21 regional events.

SPIVACK, Leo J. (b. 1926) of Miami FL, formerly of Chicago, retired attorney and investment banker. ACBL President 1979, Member Board of Directors 1970-86, chairman ACBL Appeals and Charges Committee, 1974, 75, 77, 78, 82. Chairman of the Board 1980, chairman of WBF Appeals Committee 1980-81. Board member of Chicago CBA for many years, president 1968-70.

SPOONER, John Richard (b. 1965) of Canberra, Australia, systems administrator. 3rd World Junior Teams 1991, won Far East Junior Teams 1990, and represented Australia in one other world championship. Junior chess champion.

SPOTTS, Robert L. (b. 1937) of Oakley CA, retired project manager. Placed 2nd Men's Teams 1967 and has won 16 regional events. Retired from tournament play 1976.

SPRUNG, Danny (b. 1965) of Philadelphia PA, stock option trader. Won Mixed Pairs 1991 and has several regional wins to his credit.

SPRUNG, JoAnn M. (b. 1950) of Philadelphia PA, regional sales manager, member Unit 141 Board. Won Master Mixed Teams 1988; Mixed Pairs 1990, 91; North American Swiss Teams 1994; placed 2nd Women's Teams 1984. Won numerous regionals.

SQUIRE, Norman (1907-1991) of London, England, bridge writer. Won De La Rue International par tournament 1957. National wins include 3 Gold Cups. Author of 12 books. Competition editor of *Bridge Magazine* for many years, and author of many magazine articles. Made important contributions to bidding theory, including

Fourth-Suit Forcing and Out-Of-The-Blue Cuebid.

ST. LUCE, Dr. Ralph (b. 1934) of Miami FL, formerly of Jamaica, physician. Represented Jamaica in international play Deauville 1968, Central American-Caribbean Championships 1971, 72, 73, 74 winning 3 times and placing 2nd once. St. Luce, temporarily retired from tournament play, has won every major Jamaican title.

ST. PIERRE, George R. (b. 1930) Of Columbus OH, university professor and chairman emeritus. Has received a number of awards for distinguished research and teaching in materials science. Won 15+ regionals.

STABELL, Leif-Erik (b. 1954) of Harare, Zimbabwe, formerly of Oslo, Norway, computer consultant. 3rd World Team Olympiad 1980. Won Nordic Junior Teams 1975, 1978 and 1979. Won Nordic Teams 1980 and 1982. Many national titles. Won 6 Zimbabwe titles. Founder of magazine *Bridge i Norge*.

STACK, Don (b. 1939) of Overland Park KS, full-time chemist and part-time computer programmer. District recorder for Unit 131 and District 15. Diamond Life Master with 11,622 MPS (3/2001). Has won more than 200 regionals, including District 15 GNOT 1979, 81, Zone V 1981, GNOP 1981.

STAKGOLD, Alice (1924-1994) of Newark DE. Won Master Mixed Teams 1969.

STAKGOLD, Ivar (b. 1925) of Wilmington DE, born in Norway, Professor Emeritus University of Delaware, former chairman of mathematics department. Placed 2nd Bermuda Bowl 1959, represented U.S. in World Team Olympiad 1960. Won Mott-Smith Trophy, Chicago (now the Reisinger), Vanderbilt, Open Pairs 1958; Spingold 1962; Levintritt Pairs 1964, Master Mixed Teams 1969. Placed 2nd Men's Teams 1957, Spingold 1958, Open Pairs 1963. Won English Melville Smith Teams 1968 and placed 2nd Crockford's Cup 1968.

STALLARD, M. Berl (1913-1997) of Miles City MT, retired accountant. Creator of First-Up, a method of bidding that uses no conventions. In the Seventies he hired professional players to play only his system in a regional in Helena MT — they beat out Barry Crane's team. Author of several books on this subject. He and his wife Helen also introduced Instant Bridge, a bridge-like game that requires no bidding. Treasurer and business manager IBPA, Honor Member 1991. ABTA treasurer several years.

STANSBY, Lew (b. 1940) of Castro Valley CA, commodity trader. Member ACBL Hall of Fame. WBF Grand Master, #11 in world, won World Open Pairs 1982, placed 9th 1990. Won Bermuda Bowl 1985, 87, placed 2nd 1989, 3rd 2000. Won Rosenblum Teams 1994, placed 2nd 1982, 9th 1990. Grand Life Master with 16,269 MPs (3/2001) won Fishbein Trophy 2000, Reisinger 1965, 81, 85, 86, 96; Vanderbilt 1967, 84, 87, 94, 96; Spingold 1975, 90, 2000; GNOT 1982, 83, 85, 87, 93, 96; Mott-Smith Trophy 1984, 86; Open Pairs 1986, Open BAM Teams 1995, Life Master Open Pairs 1998. Placed 2nd Blue Ribbon Pairs 1981, Reisinger 1983, Mens BAM Teams 1989, Open Pairs 1991, Vanderbilt 1992, Spingold 1992, 93, 95; Open BAM Teams 1994, GNOT, GNOP 1997; Life Master Open Pairs 1999, Open Swiss Teams 2000. Won the Rosenkranz Romex Award 1979, 97.

STAPPENBECK, Harry A. (b. 1939) of Uniondale NY, bridge teacher. Diamond Life Master, won Spingold 1987, 2nd 1974. Won 40+ regionals. Standing 6 feet, 11 inches, world's tallest expert.

STARK, Dr. Gary (b. 1931) of Portland OR, dentist. Won Men's Teams 1967.

STARR, Jeffrey C. (b. 1949) of Las Vegas NV, stock and options trader, poker player. Diamond Life Master, placed 2nd GNOT 1974, 82. Won 40+ regionals.

STARR, Robert E. (Bob) (b. 1919) of Centerville MA, retired bridge club owner/manager. Life Master #330. Won Summer NAC secondary President's Pairs 1947 and won at least 15 other regionals. Began directing 1953 and became full time 1965. He retired and sold his bridge club in 1976 due to complications from multiple sclerosis. Retired bridge columnist who wrote for several newspapers and magazines.

STAUBER, Allan G. (b. 1944) of Cross River NY, collectibles broker. Diamond Life Master, won Blue Ribbon Pairs 1980; Mott-Smith Trophy, Spingold, Men's Teams 1981; Men's Pairs 1981, 83; North American Men's Swiss Teams 1982, Reisinger 1984. Placed 2nd GNOT 1979.

STAWOWY, Barbara (b. 1968) of Munster, Germany. WBF World Master. 2nd in 1998 World Women's Teams, 3rd World Women's Team Olympiad 2000. Won China Cup 1999.

STAYMAN, Josephine L. (Tubby, Mrs. Samuel) (b. 1924) of Palm Beach FL, former gift shop owner. Placed 2nd World Mixed Teams 1974 and won several regional events.

STAYMAN, Samuel M. (1909-1993) of Palm Beach FL, portfolio manager, investor and bridge author. Life Master #48, Member ACBL Hall of Fame. In June 1945 issue of *The Bridge World* he described a convention, invented by his then partner George Rapee, which subsequently became known as the Stayman Convention. He made other contributions to the theory of the game, including NAMYATS (Stayman spelled backwards). WBF Grand Master, was Bermuda Bowl champion 1950, 51, 53 and placed 2nd World Team Olympiad 1964, 5th 1960; 8th Rosenblum Teams 1986. Represented North America in several other world championships.

ACBL Diamond Life Master with more than 8,000 MPs at time of death. Won Spingold 1942, 44, 48, 50, 52, 55, 59; Vanderbilt 1942, 46, 50, 51; Chicago (now Reisinger) 1945, 47; Men's Teams 1952, 62, 63, 80; Open Pairs 1959; Life Master Pairs 1965, Reisinger 1984. Placed 2nd Vanderbilt 1944, 45, 52, 69; Men's Pairs 1945, Spingold 1947, 69; Men's Teams 1948, 55, 65; Chicago, Life Master Pairs 1950; Reisinger 1976, 77. Won numerous regional titles, including Eastern States KO Teams 1939, 40, 51, 63. President Cavendish Club New York, ACBL treasurer 1966)69, trustee ACBL Charity Foundation, ACBL Honorary Member 1969, Honorary Member ABTA 1979. Author of *Expert Bidding, The Complete Stayman System of Contract Bidding*, and *Do You Play Stayman?* Contributing editor to the *Official Encyclopedia of Bridge*.

STEARNS, Sherman (1900-1965) of New York City, real estate broker. A leading American players of the Thirties, member of Four Aces Team during its later years. Won USBA Open Teams, Open Pairs 1935; 2nd USBA Open Pairs 1936. Won Vanderbilt 1935, 37, 38, 41; Life Master Pairs 1938. He placed 2nd Vanderbilt 1931, Spingold, Reisinger 1934; Master Mixed Teams 1941.

STEDEM, Joseph J. (1899-1983) of Palm Springs CA, executive vice president of Hertz Corporation. ACBL president 1968, member of ACBL Board of Directors 1949-50 and 1964-69; president of ACBL Charity Foundation 1973-74, trustee 1972-75. ACBL Honorary Mem-

ber 1971. President Midwest Bridge Conference and Chicago CBA. Stedem helped initiate the ACBL policy, begun in 1949, of holding North American Championships in many centers. Previously all such tournaments had been held in the Greater New York area. The experiment of attempting a national in Chicago in 1949 proved most successful. As a result, players in all sections of the ACBL have had the opportunity to play in NABCs at not too great a distance from their homes. Instrumental in the reorganization of the ACBL, working with Waldemar Von Zedtwitz. Stedem placed 2nd NAC Senior Master Individual 1952 and won several regionals.

STEEN, Douglas (b. 1927) of Los Angles CA, division head with CIA, primary scientist to discover astropsychology via statistical studies in finance. WBF Life Master, Bermuda Bowl champion 1954. ACBL Life Master #331. Won Master Mixed Teams 1952, Spingold 1953 and placed 2nd Men's Teams 1953, Men's Pairs 1954. Co-inventor of the Bulldog System and co-author of *Precision Power Bidding*. Retired from bridge 1956.

STEHLY, Paul E. (Fred) (1925-1985) of Minneapolis MN, associate national tournament director since 1968. Represented tournament directors at ACBL Board meetings. The Fred Friendly Award was established in his honor. It is given to the tournament director who most epitomizes Stehly's character of friendliness and concern for the players.

STEIN, Ethan (b. 1946) of Irvington NY, attorney, bridge teacher-professional. Contributor to District 3 publication *Bridging the Counties*. Placed 5th Rosenblum Teams 1986. Won Gold Medal Maccabiah Games 1983. ACBL diamond Life Master, placed 2nd Senior/Advanced Senior Master Pairs 1974, Men's Pairs 1984, North American Men's Swiss Teams 1986, North American Swiss Teams 1988, 89. He was 5th Cavendish Pairs. Has won 40-50 regional events.

STEIN, Joan S. (b. 1934) of River Hills WI, businesswoman. Has served on Unit board, ACBL Board of Governors and been regional chairman. Grand Life Master with 11,205 MPs (3/2001). Won Life Master Women's Pairs 1974, Women's Pairs 2000; placed 2nd Life Master Women's Pairs 1983. Has won more than 80 regional events.

STEIN, Mark (b. 1934) of Aventura FL, born in China, retired company president. Represented Canada in international competition 1978, 86, as npc in 1988, 89, 90, Venice Trophy team 1993. Won CNTC 1985, npc of 2nd place teams 1988, 90. Stein won GNOP 1991, North American Swiss Teams 1992, 94, 95; placed 2nd GNOP 1990. Won World Epson Towers 1990 and approximately 70 regional events.

STEIN, Sylvia A. (1921-1995) of Southfield MI, former bridge club owner. Represented U.S. in World Women's Pairs 1962, 70. Diamond Life Master, won Life Master Individual 1958; Lou Herman Trophy 1958, 69; Women's Pairs 1962, Women's Teams 1965, 68; Life Master Women's Pairs 1969; placed 2nd Mixed Pairs 1958; Women's Teams 1960, 65, 71; Master Mixed Teams 1960, 62, 65, 67; Life Master Women's Pairs 1964.

STEINBERG, Charles (b. 1931) of Memphis TN, retired CEO of small chain of retail stores. Served on Unit 144 Board of Directors including as president. Member Unit Hall of Fame. Kidney transplant patient and competes in Transplant Olympiad Games. Does volunteer work in this area. His mother, Ruth, was Life Master #270 and his father, Philip, #350. Won 15+ regional events.

STEINBERG, Jonathan (b. 1950) of Toronto ON, private investor. Represented Canada in world play Bal Harbour 1986, Geneva 1990. Was npc winning Team Canada, 7th Hero International Youth Bridge Festival's-Hertogenbosh 1999, npc Canada I World Junior Teams 1999. District 2 representative to ACBL Board of Directors 1994 to present. Served as member District 2 and Unit 166 Board of Directors; member ACBL Board of Governors 1990-93, vice president ACBL Educational Foundation 1998-99. Diamond Life Master, placed 2nd North American Swiss Teams 1985 and has won more than 50 regionals.

STEINER, Albert (1901-1977) of Cincinnati, president of toy manufacturing company. Won Chicago (now Reisinger) 1933. Co-donor of the Steiner Trophy.

STEINER, Carlyn J. (b. 1945) of Seattle WA, attorney. Co-chairman Organizing Committee 1984 World Olympiad. Placed 2nd Women's Pairs 1987. Has won many regionals including District 19 GNOT 1985, 87.

STEINER, George M. (b. 1945) of Seattle WA, investment broker. Grand Life Master with 11,650 MPs (3/2001). Won Men's Pairs 1985, 87; Life Master Pairs 1985, Vanderbilt 1994, IMP Pairs 2000; placed 2nd Vanderbilt 1994, 95; and has won numerous regionals.

STEINER, Harry L. (b. 1958) of Seattle WA, bridge teacher and professional. Served as Unit treasurer 1984-88. Club director for 8 years. Writes column *Ask Harry* for Unit publication. Placed 2nd GNOP 1992, Won 25-30 regional events.

STEINER, Phillip (1901-1993) of Cincinnati OH, company executive. ABL vice president 1936, member of Board 1930-38, committee chairman 1934, ACBL Honorary Member 1937. Co-donor of Steiner Trophy, which for more than a quarter century was one of the most important events on the ACBL calendar. Won the Chicago (now Reisinger) 1933. With Albert and another brother, Joseph, Steiner founded the toy-making firm Kenner Products in 1945.

STEINFELDT, Sherman I. (Irv) (b. 1918) of Minneapolis MN, Board chairman, former president Clearr Corp. Won inaugural Silver Ribbon Pairs 1992. Numerous regional wins.

STENGER, Charles A. (b. 1922) of Bethesda MD, national consultant for American Ex-Prisoners of War Association since 1980, clinical psychologist. Was POW 1944-45 (Battle of the Bulge). In Veterans Administration he headed the planning for return of Viet Nam veterans and POWs. Member ACBL Board of Directors (1980-92), past president District 6, Mid-Atlantic Conference and Washington BL. Chaired District 6 Judiciary Committee for many years. Chaired committee that led to national no-smoking policy and committee on professionalism. Chairman and Master of Ceremonies of 1st United States vs. British Parliament bridge event. Recognized as an international expert on hostages and POWs, he retired following a long career in the Veteran's Administration, in which he served as national director of a staff of 1,400 psychologists. Diamond Life Master with more than 10,000 MPs, and numerous regional wins.

STENGER, E. Jeanne (Mrs. Charles A.) (b. 1924) of Bethesda MD, retired. Treasurer for Washington DC NABCs 1973 and 1984. Diamond Life Master. She and her husband, Charles, have been married 53 years. They are probably the only couple married 50+ years who each have more than 10,000 MPs.

STEPHENS, Daisy W. (1907-1988) of Shreveport LA.

Won Amateur Women's Pairs 1975 and several regionals.

STERN, Roger D. (b. 1934) of Baltimore MD, financial corporation president, attorney. Npc Bermuda Bowl champions 1977 and of North American team in 1973 Bermuda Bowl. Placed 2nd World Par Contest 1961, won U.S. Zone World Par Contest 1963, Men's Teams 1965, Mixed Pairs 1969, Blue Ribbon Pairs 1989. First president of District 24, president Greater New York BA. Member ACBL Board of Governors for several years, member ACBL Laws Commission, vice-chairman NABC Appeals Committee. Co-inventor of Astro and Astro Cuebid and co-author of several *Bridge World* articles, including a series outlining a modern style of defensive bidding.

STERNBERG, James H. (Dr. J.) (b. 1937) of Jupiter FL, physician, radiologist. Rookie of the Year 1977, became Life Master that same year with 377 MPs, a record that held for 19 years. Won Men's BAM Teams 1979, placed 2nd Spingold 1984. Won 21 regional events including District 9 GNOT 1979, 90.

STETTEN, Jacques (b. 1926) of Paris, France, builder, World Life Master. European champion 1962, 2nd 1961, represented France in Bermuda Bowl 1963, 67, 69, European Championships 1966. Won several national titles.

STEUER, Joseph B. (Joe) (d. 2000) of Memphis TN, placed 2nd Amateur Men's Pairs 1975, won 15+ regional events. Diamond Life Master.

STEVENSON, David (b.1947) of Liverpool, England, tournament director and professional player. Former chief tournament director Welsh Bridge Union. Authority on laws and their interpretation. Co-founder of internet laws mailing list. Co-author of *Duplicate Bridge Rules Simplified*. 3rd Common Market Junior Championships 1973.

STEWART, B. (b. 1927) of Regina SK, attorney, judge, land developer, farmer. Has 16 regional wins.

STEWART, Frank R. (b. 1946) of Fayette AL, formerly of Memphis TN and Birmingham AL. One of the world's leading bridge journalists. Repesented South Korea in 1968 Far East Championship while serving in U.S. Army. Won many tournament events in Seventies. Discontinued tournament play to devote full time to writing about bridge. Syndicated columnist, author and editor. Managing editor *The Contract Bridge Bulletin* 1984-89, continues to contribute through the column he began in 1981. Edited ACBL's *World Championship Book* 1983-87 and was a principal contributor 1986-89. Major contributor to Fifth Edition *Encyclopedia of Bridge*. In 1986 began a collaboration with Alfred Sheinwold to produce the syndicated newspaper column *Sheinwold on Bridge*. After Sheinwold's death in 1997, the column continued under Stewart's byline as *Sheinwold's Bridge* and eventually became *Stewart on Bridge*. It appears in more than 180 newspapers and on several internet sites. Stewart has published hundreds of articles appearing in most of the world's leading bridge magazines and on-line publications. These include technical pieces, tournament reports, fiction and humor. Author of 17 books, among them *The Bridge Player's Comprehensive Guide to Defense, Better Bridge for the Advancing player, The Devyn Press Bridge Teacher's Manuals and Student Texts, The Bridge Today 2001 Workbook, My Bridge and Yours, the Bidder's bible* and *A Christmas Stocking*. Frequent analyst for ACBL-wide and District-wide charity events. Well known for his recall of bridge deals and facts. Frequent lecturer and teacher. Former member of NABC Appeals Committee, former professional player. Low-

handicap golfer and chairman of the Fayette Christian Center of Concern, a food bank. His wife, Charlotte is a pediatric speech-language pathologist.

STEWART, Frederick M. (b. 1948) of Kingston NY, stockbroker, WBF World Master. Placed 5th Bermuda Bowl 1991, 14th World Open Pairs 1986. Won Pan-American Pairs 1991. Won Life Master Pairs 1981, Reisinger 1984, Blue Ribbon Pairs 1987, 94; Open Swiss Teams 1992, Open BAM Teams, Open Pairs II 1995. Placed 2nd GNOT 1991, Reisinger 1995, Vanderbilt 1999. Won Cavendish Invitational 1993, 96.

STEWART, John G. (b. 1951) of Halifax NS, attorney, bridge teacher and club manager. Placed 2nd CNTC 1982. Won several regionals including District 1 GNOT 1978. Founding member of *Halifax Bridge World* and one of its contributors, columnist for *Halifax Daily News*.

STIEFEL, John D. (b. 1944) of Wethersfield CT, actuary, (Fellow of the Society of Actuaries). Wrote Sunday bridge column for *Hartford Courant* 1979-84. Grand Life Master, with 10,503 MPs. Won Amateur Swiss Teams 1976, and mlre than 50 regional events including District 25 GNOT 1981, 88, 90, 92; GNOP 1984, 85, 88, 90.

STIEFSOHN, Helga (b. 1959) of Vienna, Austria, social worker. European Women's Team champion 1991.

STOBER, Ruth L. (b. 1935) of Great Neck NY, retired CFO and business manager. Won Pan American Mixed Pairs 1992, more than 40 regional events.

STOBIECKI, Wlodzimierz (b. 1941) of Kielce, Poland, civil servant, World Master. Won European Senior Teams 1995, European Senior Pairs 1995. Won many national titles.

STODDARD, Peggy (Mrs. Thomas W.) of Atlanta GA, formerly of Laguna Hills CA, retired real estate broker, assisted her husband in many Pacific Bridge League and ACBL Western Division activities. PBL secretary 1936-37 and a contributor to *The Contract Bridge Forum*. Member ACBL Goodwill Committee since 1952, awarded a silver card for Outstanding Services to Bridge by ACBL 1969.

STODDARD, Tom (1896-1976) of Laguna Hills CA, "Father of Bridge on the West Coast." One of outstanding personalities of American bridge. Pioneer in bridge teaching and bridge club management, founder of the Pacific Bridge League, former ACBL executive. In 1931 Stoddard owned a Los Angeles hotel at a time when most hotels were going bankrupt. He conceived the idea of making his hostelry a center for bridge lessons and duplicate gmes. The project was a sensational success, at its peak there were 11 teachers conducting games daily from 9:20 a.m. to midnight. Founded PBL 1933, was responsible for wildfire growth of bridge on West Coast. The PBL included the 11 Far Western states, the territories of Hawaii and Alaska and the Canadian provinces of British Columbia and Alberta. It rapidly reached a membership in the thousands, promoting two major tournaments (the All-Western and Bridge Week) and many minor ones. Founded *Contract Bridge Forum* in early Thirties. Collaboration between the ACBL and the PBL began in 1940 when they agreed on a uniform masterpoint system. In 1946 Stoddard turned over his bridge business to his associates. In 1948 he agreed to amalgamation of the PBL and national organizations, an arrangement consummated in 1956. At this time he was elected President Emeritus of ACBL, Western Division and ACBL Board member. ACBL Honorary Mem-

ber 1960. In May of 1976 he was awarded the rare "Certificate of Service" citation by the ACBL Board of Directors. Stoddard was a regional correspondent for the *ACBL Bulletin.*

STOLITSA, Evgeny (1905-1985) of Sofia, Bulgaria, born Russia, pianist and astrologer. Introduced duplicate bridge to Bulgaria and became its leading theorist, creating the natural bidding system *ERS* and *Ultra-Texas*.

STONE, Janice G. (Jan) (Mrs. David H. Fulton) (1920-1992) of Miami Beach FL, formerly of New York City. Became Life Master in 7 months, the first to attain that status in such a short time. Also a backgammon champion. A radio and TV actress from childhood, she starred on many nationally prominent TV dramatic and variety shows. Between 1974-78 she was an executive in a family owned mining operation. Former wife of Tobias Stone. The year after they married the couple finished 1st and 2nd in the McKenney race. They were also the only married couple to win the New York City Goldman Pairs (1957) in the 64-year history of the event. Stone placed 2nd World Women's Teams 1964 and won Women's Team Trials 1963. Won Women's Teams 1956, 69; Life Master Women's Pairs, Master Mixed Teams 1965; placed 2nd Master Mixed Teams 1956, Spingold 1959, Women's Teams 1961, 62.

STONE, Kenneth (Sky King) (1910-1988) of Fort Worth TX, associate national tournament director since 1965, began directing in 1950. Owner\manager of air and cruise travel agency.

STONE, Tobias (Stoney) (b. 1921) of Las Vegas NV, bridge author, WBF World Life Master, placed 2nd Bermuda Bowl 1958, 3rd World Team Olympiad 1960, also competed internationally Amsterdam 1966, Miami Beach 1972, Las Palmas 1974. Diamond Life Master. Won McKenney Trophy 1956, Open Pairs 1942, Vanderbilt 1949, 59, 60; Chicago (now Reisinger) 1952, 61; Master Individual 1953, Spingold 1956, 57; Fishbein Trophy, Life Master Pairs 1956; Men's Teams 1961, 63; Men's Pairs 1961, Master Mixed Teams 1965. He placed 2nd in the Life Master Pairs 1942, 65; Men's Pairs 1952, Spingold 1953, 61, 63; Master Mixed Teams 1956; Fall Open Pairs 1958, Spring Open Pairs 1958, 1965; Men's Teams 1959, Vanderbilt 1969. Won dozens of regional titles including the prestigious Eastern States KO Teams 1942, 44, 61, 63, 67, 73, 74, Open Pairs (Goldman) 1957, 1961; Marcus Cup 1960.

He and partner Al Roth were the first Americans to win the Deauville Invitation pair event; they scored a record-breaking 82% game. Stone also is an international backgammon champion. Co-inventor of the Roth-Stone System, has made many contributions to bidding theory. Co-author of *Bridge is a Partnership Game* and *The Bridge World* department *What Do You Play and Why?*

STOPPA, Jean-Louis (b. 1932) of Paris, France, physician, World Life Master. 2nd Bermuda Bowl 1971, won European Teams 1970. Represented France in 6 other world championships and 3 other zonals. Won many national titles. Npc of many victorious French teams.

STOUT, Alan F. (Herman) (b. 1949) of Cedar Rapids IA, field auditor for the State of IA; runs the state Medicaid program. Diamond Life Master with over 19,992 (3/2001). Has won over 200 regionals including District 14 GNOP 1981. Stout is a specialist at sectionals, having won more than 1000. Has had several sectionals where he won every event, has won almost 3000 silver points at sectionals.

STRAFNER, Michael (b. 1952 in Austria) of Munich, Germany. European Junior Team champion 1976. WBF World Master. Represented Austria in 3 world championships and 3 European Championships. Won Austrian Teams 4 times, Open Pairs 3 times. First-class badminton player.

STRASBERG, David I. (b. 1928) of Ft Lauderdale FL, semi-retired executive recruiter. Diamond Life Master. Won Spingold, Fishbein Trophy 1970; placed 2nd Chicago (now the Reisinger) 1958, Men's Pairs 1968; Master Mixed Teams 1970, GNOT 1980.

STRAUSS, Richard P. of Northbrook IL, regional tournament director, club manager. Directing since 1986, club manager since 1980. Recipient of Tom Weeks Award.

STRICKLAND, Fred E., III (b. 1945) of Marietta GA, bridge teacher, writer; former attorney. Past president Unit 114, Unit Player of the Year 1980. Author and publisher of books used in classes - *Intermediate Bidding, Advanced Bidding* (Books 1, 2, & 3). Diamond Life Master, won at least 15 regionals.

STROM, Louis Andr (b. 1927) of Stavanger, Norway, meteorologist. Former editor of *Norsk Bridge*. Represented Norway 1970 Bermuda Bowl and 4 European Championships.

STUART, Joel H. (b. 1927) of Rego Park NY, options trader. Won Spingold 1970, 71; Vanderbilt 1972; placed 2nd Men's Teams 1968. (See PRECISION TEAM.)

STUART, B. Wayne, III (b. 1965) of Raleigh NC, systems analyst, won World Junior Team Championship 1991, NABC Junior Pairs 1991. Member of Junior Corps, won several regionals. Has Master ranking in U.S. Chess Federation but no longer competes.

STURM, Charlotte G. (Char) (b. 1927) of Whittier CA, bridge club teacher and director. Directs on cruise ships. Diamond Life Master, placed 2nd Senior Master Pairs 1965. Won 20+ regionally rated events. Past president Unit 564. She and son (Steve Sturm) are one of the highest ranking mother\sons in total masterpoints.

STURM, Corrine (b. 1923) of Kailua-Kona HI, retired accountant and auditor. Won 1974 ACBL-wide Olympiad Fund Game with 77% game, 15+ regionals.

STURM, Stephen F. (Steve) (b. 1951) of Whittier CA, mail processing, Chicago Conservatory of Music graduate. Diamond Life Master, won North American Swiss Teams 1983. Also won 15+ regionals. Accomplished pianist, plays for entertainment at bridge tournaments. He and his mother (Charlotte Sturm) are one of the highest ranking mother/sons in total masterpoints.

STURM, Walter A. (Walt) (b. 1930) of Kailua Kona, HI, retired electrical engineer, computer architecture and APL programmer. Won 15+ regionals, and ACBL-wide Olympiad Fund Game with 77% game, 1974.

SUBECK, Stanton I. (Stan) (b. 1949) of Olympia Fields IL, financial consultant, actuary. Contributor to CCBA *Kibitzer*. Diamond Life Master, with more than 50 regional wins.

SUBECK, Susan R. (Suzi) (b. 1949) of Olympia Fields IL, consultant. Served on CCBA Board in 80's. Editor District 13 *Bulletin,* contributor to CCBA *Kibitzer*. Diamond Life Master with more than 50 regional wins.

SUCHARITKUL, Kovit (b. 1920) of Bangkok, Thailand, tin miner. 2nd Bermuda Bowl 1969 as member of Taiwan team. Representing Thailand, won PABF (Far East) Teams 1961, 1963.

SUEMATU, Shigehisa (b. 1910) of Tokyo, Japan, math-

ematics teacher. Lt. Colonel in World War II. First member of JCBL, and its first tournament director. Represented Japan first Japan-U.S.A. match 1950. Member JCBL Board of Directors for many years. Recipient Fifth Class Order of the Sacred Treasure.

SUGAR, Paul (b. 1928) of Chicago IL, attorney, CPA, former bank president. Placed 2nd Mixed Pairs 1975. Won numerous regionals. Sugar was Chicago CBA Player of the Year 1962. Former director, treasurer and legal counsel of the Chicago Contract B.A.

SUKHORUKOV, Alexander (b.1956) of Moscow, Russia, bridge writer and promoter. Chief editor of *Bridge in Russia* magazine. Owner of the bridge shop. Inventor of the Sukhty bidding system.

SUKONECK, Ronald M. (Ron) (b. 1949) of Annandale VA, professional player, bridge teacher, financial consultant, CFO. Member ACBL Appeals Committee 1977-1984. WBF World Master, placed 3rd Rosenblum Teams 1990. Also represented ACBL in world play Bal Harbour 1986, Santiago 1993. Won USBC (Team Trials) 1993. ACBL Grand Life Master with 13,940 MPS, (3/2001). Won North American Men' Swiss Teams 1988, Spingold 1992, GNOP 1998; placed 2nd Life Master Pairs 1982, GNOP 1987. Placed 1/2 Toronto Calcutta, 4th Cavendish.

SULAIMAN AL-SALEH, Sa'id (b. 1935) of Ahmadi, Kuwait, bridge organizer and tournament director. Bridge pioneer in Kuwait, founder of Kuwait Bridge Committee and now its president. Active in supporting WBF effort to secure IOC recognition of bridge as an Olympic sport.

SULGROVE, Kathleen J. (b. 1952) of Twinsburg OH, restaurant owner. Won Mixed Pairs 1984. Won a number of regionals.

SULLIVAN, John L. (Sully) (1917-2000) of Corpus Christi TX, retired attorney, former city manager of several cities. Served 2 terms as president South Texas Unit. Diamond Life Master with more than 15 regional wins.

SULLIVAN, Michael J. (Mick) (1894-1974) of Brisbane, Australia, accountant. Pioneer of bridge in Australia 1932. Co-founder World Bridge Federation 1958, chairman WBF Constitution Committee, member WBF Executive Board. Organized Jubilee Year Olympic 1951, 1954 bidding championship, 1961 and 1963 Global Par championships. Joint formulator Laws of Par Point Contract Bridge. World Par zonal winner 1939,40,41. National titles include Par wins 1937, 39, 43, 50, 57. Honorary Life Member Australian Bridge Federation. Contributed many double dummy problems to *Bridge*.

SUMMERS, Sylvia F. (b. 1954) of Long Beach CA, professional bridge player. Senior Master of the Year 1982. Won North American Swiss Teams 1983, 88. Has won a number of regionals.

SUN, Ming (b. 1955) of Beijing, China, company employee. WBF World Life Master. In 2000, 13th in Women's World rankings. 2nd Women's Team Olympiad 1996, 2nd Venice Cup 1997, 3rd 1991. Won Far East Women's Teams 1986, 91, 93, 94, 96, 97, 98. Represented China in 13 World championships. Won many national titles.

SUNDBY, Robert D. (1925-1998) of Madison WI, judge. Authored *Breakthrough in Bridge*; *Bridge in the '80s*; past president Wisconsin/Upper Michigan BA.

SUNDELIN, P.O. (b. 1937) of Stockholm, Sweden, computer analyst and consultant. WBF World Life Master. 3rd in 4 world championships, World Team Olympiad 1988, Bermuda Bowl 1977, 87, 91. Won European Teams

1977, 1987, 2nd 1991, 3rd 1989. Represented Sweden in 10 other world championships and 10 other European Championships. Many national wins. Won Sunday Times 1978, 1981. Won 1984 ACBL Life Master Pairs. Contributes to bridge magazines.

SUNG, Leslie L. of Hong Kong, newspaper editor and lawyer. Represented Hong Kong in Far East Championships 4 times. Former chairman of Hong Kong CBA for 20 years.

SUNSER, Larry (b. 1960) of Syracuse NY, manager - New York State. Club manager, director, instructor. Won more than 25 regionals.

SUSSEL, Andree (1914-2000) of Paris, France, antique dealer, World Master. Won European Women's Teams 1956, 65, 69; represented France in European Championships 1958, 59, 62, 66, 75.

SUSSKIND, Alan L. (Tuss) (b. 1952), former professional bridge player/instructor. Served on Chicago Contract B.A. Won 40+ regionals.

SUTHERLAND, Eric R. (b. 1972) of Waterloo ON, bridge teacher. Represented Canada and won silver medal in World Junior Bridge Championship 1991. At age of 16, Sutherland was one of the youngest Canadians to achieve Life Master status.

SUTHERLIN, John C. (b. 1936) of Dallas TX, retired bank vice president. Co-chairman Ethical Oversight Committee 1999-2001, national recorder 1986-96, International Team trial Executive Committee 1999-to date. WBF World Master, won Senior Transnational Teams 2000. Placed 2nd World Mixed Pairs 1982, 3rd Rosenblum Teams 1990, 7th World Open Pairs 1986. Grand Life Master with 19,901 MPs (3-2001), ranks 32nd on all-time masterpoint list. Placed 2nd Crane Top 500 1990. Won Master Mixed Teams 1976, Spingold 1981, Men's BAM Teams 1983, Mott-Smith Trophy, Open Swiss 1990; Vanderbilt 1990, 93; Life Master Pairs 1993; Fishbein Trophy 1993, Senior KO Teams 1994, Life Master Open Pairs 1995. Placed 2nd Mixed Pairs 1962, 94; Men's Teams 1967, North American Swiss Teams 1982, Vanderbilt 1985, Open Swiss Teams 1991, Mixed Pairs 1994, North American Swiss Teams 1996, Open BAM Teams 1997, Blue Ribbon Pairs 1999. His win of the Mott-Smith Trophy (300 MPs) in 1990 set a record that wasn't broken until 2000. Npc of victorious Venice Cup team 1987.

SUTHERLIN, Peggy (nee Berry) (b. 1937) of Dallas TX, retired flight attendant. Represented District 21 on Board of Governors 1988-91 and District 16 1993-96. Member ACBL Laws Commission 1993-to date; Competition and Conventions Committee 1999-to date, Ethical Oversight Committee 1992-to date, co-chairman National Appeals Committee 1990-96. WBF World Life Master, won World Women's Team Olympiad 2000. Placed 2nd World Mixed Pairs 1982, 4th Venice Cup 1987, 13th World Women's Pairs 1986. Diamond Life Master, with more than 9000 MPs. Won Mixed Pairs 1972, Master Mixed Teams 1976, Women's KO Teams 1986, 2000; Women's BAM Teams 1998, 99, 2000; Women's Swiss Teams 1999, Women's Team Trials 2000. Placed 2nd Mixed Pairs 1962, Women's Pairs 1986. Amateur genealogist, contributing editor to *The Official Encyclopedia of Bridge*.

SVEINDAL, Jon (b. 1946) of Bergen, Norway, teacher. WBF World Master. 2nd Bermuda Bowl 1993. 3rd European Teams 1993, 1999. Won Nordic Teams 1980. Many national titles. Bridge columnist in *Aftenposten*, one of Norway's main national newspapers. Has won several

national and international journalist awards.

SVERRISSON, Sigurdur (b. 1953) of Kopavogur, Iceland, aviation engineer. WBF World Master. Won Nordic Teams 1988. Represented Iceland in 3 world championships, 2 European Championships, 2 other Nordic Championships, 3 European Junior Teams, and 1 Nordic Junior Teams. 16 national wins.

SWAN, Mary Margaret of Houston TX, publisher. Won Mixed Pairs 1964.

SWANDER, Shirley A. (b. 1930) of Mission KS, artist. Won Women's Teams 1955 and several regionals.

SWANSON, Elizabeth G. (Liz) (b. 1939) of Athens GA, District 7 GNOT coordinator. Diamond Life Master with 16 regional wins.

SWANSON, John C., Jr. (b. 1937) of Mission Viejo CA, computer programmer. WBF World Life Master, Bermuda Bowl champion 1977, 2nd 1975, 4th 1973; placed 5th World Open Pairs 1978. Also represented North America in Bermuda Bowl 1971. Diamond Life Master, won Men's Pairs 1959, Vanderbilt 1969, 77; Men's Teams 1970, GNOT 1974, 76. Placed 2nd Life Master Men's Pairs 1968, Spingold 1973. Contributor to *Southern California Bridge News*, *The Bridge World*, and ACBL *Bulletin*. Co-authored *Recap Bridge*, (computer dealt hands with analysis), and co-developed the Walsh System.

SWANSON, Paul (b. 1932) of Morgantown WV, company president. Diamond Life Master, won Mott-Smith Trophy, Men's Teams 1972; Life Master Pairs 1973, Master Mixed Teams 1976, Men's Pairs 1979, 86. Placed 2nd Chicago (now Reisinger) 1963, Life Master Men's Pairs 1968, Vanderbilt 1972, Reisinger 1973, 80; Men's Pairs 1978.

SWANSTROM, Madeleine P.B. (B. 1942, of Solna, Sweden, district attorney. WBF World Master. Won European Women's Pairs 1989, Nordic Women's Teams 1980. Represented Sweden in several world and European championships.

SWEARINGEN, Gladys (b. 1913) of St. Louis MO, retired secretary. Won Women's Pairs 1953.

SWEENEY, Frank Henderson, Jr. (b. 1919) of La Jolla CA, retired CPA, Former member ACBL Board of Directors. Served on District 22 Board 1982-87, Western Conference president 1991, past president Unit 526.

SWIMER, Ralph (1914-1997) of London, England, company director. WBF World Life Master. 2nd World Team Olympiad 1960, npc of British team two members of which were accused of cheating in 1965 Bermuda Bowl in Buenos Aires, Argentina, forfeited the matches. Represented Britain in 1 other world championship and 2 zonal championships. National wins include Gold Cup once. See BUENOS AIRES AFFAIR.

SYDNOR, Caroline of Naples FL, bridge teacher and writer. Lectured on many cruises. Author of *Bridge Made Easy series*, *Book One* (Basics), *Book Two* (Intermediate), *Book Three (How to Win More Tricks)*, *Book Four (How to Set Your Opponents)*. Each volume has a special deck of cards coded to deal 40 lesson hands. *Book Three* won Book of the Year award from ABTA 1981; *Book Four* won in 1993. She also wrote *Teaching Bridge — How To Do It Better*.

SZENBERG, Stefan (b.1937) of Poland, living in Milan, Italy, businessman. Won World Senior Teams 2000. 2nd World Senior Teams 1998, 2nd European Senior Teams 1995, 1997.

SZURIG, Zbigniew (1938-1984) of Warsaw, Poland, mathematician, bridge professional. 2nd World Pairs 1963.

Represented Poland in many World and European Championships. Won many national titles. Bridge theorist, exponent of forcing pass, editor, author of a bridge book.

SZWARC, Henri (b. 1930 in Poland) of Paris, France, textile company director. WBF World Grand Master, #20 in world. Won World Team Olympiad 1980, 1996, 2nd 1984. Won European Teams 1966, 1970, 1974, 1983, 2nd 1967. Represented France in 6 other world championships and 7 other zonal championships. With Jean-Michel Boulenger, named best pair in Europe in 1966. Won Sunday Times 1977. Many national titles.

SZYMANOWSKI, Marek (b.1955) of Warsaw, Poland, economist and bridge professional. WBF World Life Master. Won World Open Pairs 1994, 2nd Bermuda Bowl 1991, 3rd Bermuda Bowl 1989. Won Spingold Teams 1997, 2nd Spingold Teams 1998, 2nd Reisinger Teams 1997. Won European Teams 1989, 3rd 1991. Represented Poland in many world and European Championships. Won many national titles.

T

TAI, Min-Fan (b. 1938) of Taipei, Taiwan, chemical engineer. World Life Master. 2nd Bermuda Bowl 1969, 70. Represented Taiwan in 14 world championships. Chief tournament director of several international events.

TAI TENN, Quee Ronald (b. 1933) of Kingston, Jamaica. CACBF National Team champion 1983. Represented Jamaica in 2 world championships including 1987 Bermuda Bowl. Numerous national titles.

TAKAHASHI, Satoru (b. 1913) of Tokyo, Japan, foreign service officer. Former ambassador to Spain. Represented Japan in Far East Championships. Won Takamatsu Cup 1958. Former president JCBL.

TAMMENS, Kees (b.1950) of Amsterdam, The Netherlands, bridge journalist and barman. WBF World Master. Coach of Dutch Junior team. Represented Netherlands in 3 world championships and 3 European Championships. Many national titles. Columnist, staff member and contributor to *Bridge*.

TAN, Allen L. (b. 1947) of Makati, Philippines, psychologist. Won Asean Mixed Teams 1995, 97. Represented Philippines in 2 world championships and 4 zonal championships. Invented Matchpoint Teams.

TANG, Houzu (b. 1935) of Shanghai, China, teacher. 2nd Far East Teams 1984. Represented China in 4 World championships and 4 zonal championships. Won many national titles.

TANG, Jizu (b. 1940) of Shanghai, China, technical employee. 2nd Far East Teams 1984. Represented China in 4 world championships and 4 zonal championships. Won many national titles.

TARLO, Joel (1905-1991) of Marbella, Spain, formerly of London, England, retired solicitor. Won European Teams 1960. Represented Britain in 2 world championships and 4 zonal championships. Represented Spain in a zonal at 82, perhaps a record. National wins include 2 Gold Cups.

TARLO, Louis (1911-1997) of Hove, England, solicitor. Won European Teams 1950. 2nd World Team Olympiad as npc 1960. Represented Britain in 8 zonal championships. Former EBU Chairman.

TAUBE, Richard (b. 1938) of Marietta GA, retired at-

torney, bridge professional, national junior bowling champion 1949. As member of White House Commission on Emergency Medical Services 1969-79, developed telemetry and roadside telephone emergency communication systems. Chairman 1973 Summer NABC, member ACBL National Appeals Committee, has been active in bridge administration since 1965. Diamond Life Master with more than 11,000 MPs, has won 100+ regionals.

TAYLOR, Edward O. (1912-1984) of Glendale CA, marketing director, Life Master #83; won Open Pairs 1957, Chicago (now the Reisinger) 1959, 62; Men's Teams 1959, 62; Open Pairs 1959, Life Master Pairs 1963; placed 2nd Vanderbilt 1963.

TAYLOR, Jeffrey (b. 1941) of Eugene OR, chemistry teacher, tax practitioner. Won Intercollegiate Par contest 1964.

TAYLOR, Pauline J. of Detroit, retired decorative arts curator, first woman president American Bridge Association (1969-73). Active promoter of bridge since 1949, president Detroit Unit 1956-61, founder of first women's duplicate there. ABA titles include Mixed Teams 1952, Women's Pairs 1957, Individual 1974.

TAYLOR, Tony of Auckland, New Zealand (born in England) WBF World Master. Represented New Zealand in 5 world championships and 2 zonal championships. National wins include Open Teams once.

TCHAMITCH, Haig G. (b. 1951) of Peoria AZ, born in Lebanon, semi-retired salesman. Won Lou Herman Trophy, Blue Ribbon Pairs 1992, many regionals.

TEAGUE, Terry (1904-1987) of Birmingham AL, insurance agent, member ACBL Board of Directors 1957-60; won several regional events.

TEIXEIRA, Carlos Spinola (b. 1939) of Lisbon, Portugal, company director. Represented Portugal in 1 world and 10 European championships. 2nd European Junior Teams 1968, 5th Sunday Times Invitational Pairs 1990, 5th European Teams 1966, 6th 1974. Won many national titles.

TEMMERMAN, Simone de (b. 1917) of Paris, France, musician. Won European Women's Team Championship 1956, 65, 69. Represented France European Championships 1955, 59, 61, 65, 74. Won many national titles.

TENCH, Stanley (Stan) (b. 1929) of Ottawa ON, retired director of government computer center, ACBL associate national tournament director; developed Tench movement.

TEPPER, Barbara (b. 1930) of Verona NJ, medical group administrator; Diamond Life Master, won Women's Teams 1969.

TERRANEO, Franz (b. 1953) of Vienna, Austria, project manager. WBF World Life Master. Placed 2nd Bermuda Bowl 1985, World Team Olympiad 1988. Won European Teams 1985, 2nd European Pairs 1985, European Mixed Pairs 1990. Won Statenbank Invitational (Netherlands) 1987, 89. Won 7 Austrian Teams, 2 Mixed Pairs.

TEUKOLSKY, Roselyn (Ros) (b. 1948) of Ithaca NY, born in South Africa, math and computer science teacher. Author of *How to Play Bridge with your Spouse...and Survive,* a contributor to the ACBL *Bridge Bulletin* under the title *As I See It,* to *Bridge Today* under the title *Undertricks,* also contributes to *Canadian Masterpoint,* Had highest ACBL E-W score in Epson Pairs 1988,

THEIMER, Dr. Ernst T. (b. 1910) of Rumson NJ, retired company vice president. President, tournament

chairman of New Jersey BL. Wrote weekly bridge column for *Newark News.* Author of *The Bridge Adventures of Androcles MacThick,* has contributed to *The Bridge World* and *Bridge Today.*

THEOBALDS, Vaughn (b. 1927) of Kingston, Jamaica, born in Grenada, architect, bridge teacher, former honorary secretary and former honorary treasurer Central American and Caribbean Bridge Federation. More than 35 years of service to bridge administration in Jamaica and Zone 5.

THERON, Georges (1922-1970) of Paris, France, physician and bridge writer. Won European championship 1962, 2nd 1967. Represented France World Open Pairs 1962, Bermuda Bowl 1963, 69; World Team Olympiad 1964, European Championships 1965. Won London Sunday Times Invitational 1966. Contributed to many bridge magazines.

THEUS, Edgar G. (1913-1994) of Oklahoma City OK, attorney, member ACBL Board of Directors 1961-88; ACBL president 1969; chairman of Board 1970, President Emeritus. Member ACBL Laws Commission, member WBF Executive Council 1969-86; served as 1st vice president of WBF, co-captain of defending Bermuda Bowl team in 1977, captain of champion North American Bermuda Bowl team 1979. Placed 2nd Life Master Men's Pairs 1966.

THOMAS, Frank of Los Angeles, syndicated bridge columnist, former leading boy actor of stage and screen, playwright, scriptwrter, actor for radio and TV, retired from theater 1962 to begin bridge teaching in association with George Gooden, reaching as many as 18,000 students a year in department stores. Editor and publisher of *ABTA Quarterly* since 1969. Author of several books including *Sherlock Holmes, Bridge Detective* (in collaboration with Gooden) and *Sherlock Holmes, Bridge Detective, Returns.* Past president American Bridge Teachers Association.

THOMAS, Jayne (b. 1931) of Lutz FL, executive manager Unit 128, retired 30-year math teacher. Diamond Life Master, won Silver Ribbon Pairs 1994, numerous regionals, 2 of which were Men's Pairs (as fill-in). Member ACBL Board of Directors, ACBL Educational Foundation (president twice, treasurer once), ACBL Charity Foundation, ACBL Goodwill Committee. Served for years as member Board of Directors of District 9 and Unit 128, served as president of both. Contributes to *Florida Bridge Bulletin.*

THOMAS, Robert (Bob) (1911-1996) of Philadelphia PA, investments company executive, won national events 50 years apart — Rothschild Teams 1940, Open Pairs 1991, placed 2nd the Chicago (now the Reisinger) 1940.

THOMPSON, Benjamin John Polya (b. 1965) of Melbourne, Australia, born in California, computer scientist. 3rd World Junior Teams 1991, won PABF (Far East) Junior Teams 1990, represented Australia in 1 other world championship. Won 3 national titles. Magazine contributor.

THOMSON, Matthew (b. 1962) of Sydney, Australia, electrical engineer and financial project manager. Placed 2nd Pacific-Asia Teams 1995. Represented Australia in 1 other zonal and 4 world championships. Winner 9 national teams titles. System theorist.

THOMSON, Robert D. (Bob) (b. 1957) of Half Moon Bay CA, computer consultant. Won North American Swiss 1981, BAM Teams 1990; placed 2nd Master Mixed Teams 1991.

THORBJORNSSON, Saevar (b. 1956) of Reykjavik, Iceland, civil engineer. Won Nordic Teams 1988, 92, 94. Represented Iceland in 2 world championships, 2 European Championships, 4 other Nordic Championships, 2 European Junior Teams and 2 Nordic Junior Teams. 9 national wins.

THORESEN, Siv (b.1960) of Oslo, Norway, economics teacher. WBF World Master. 4th World Women's Team Olympiad 2000, defeated U.S. women's champions in IOC 2000. 2nd Nordic Women's Teams 1998.

THORFINNSSON, Einar (1906-1980) of Reykjavik, Iceland, banker. Represented Ireland World Team Olympiad 1960, European Championships 1950, 51, 58, 71; represented Europe in 1st Bermuda Bowl 1950. Won many national titles.

THORNTON, Susan M. (b. 1932) of Crescent Springs KY, bridge director. District 11 president 1983, placed 2nd Master Mixed Teams 1977.

THORPE, Catherine C. (Katie) (b. 1948) of Toronto ON, born in England, data base administrator. Canadian Bridge Federation Zone III Director since 1987, member ACBL Laws Commission; CBF president 1989-91, Unit 166 Board member 1976-81 (past president), member ACBL Board of Governors, alternate Director District 2. WBF World Master, placed 3rd Venice Cup 1989, 4th Olympiad Women's Teams 1988, 9th 1984, 5th Swiss Plate 1984. Won CWTC 1984, 86, 87, 90, 91, COPC 1990, Master Mixed Teams 1991; placed 2nd CNTC 1987.

THORVALDSSON, Matthias (b. 1966) of Reykjavik, Iceland, psychologist. Won Nordic Teams in 1992, 94. Represented Iceland in 2 world championships, 2 European Championships, 2 European Junior Teams and 3 Nordic Junior Teams. 14 national wins.

TIBREWALA, N.S. (b. 1918) of Bombay, India, pediatrician. Represented India in 4 world championships and one zonal championship. Won Far East Pairs 1978. 11 national wins. President Bridge Federation of India 1978-79 and 1990-93.

TIERNAN, Agatha D. (1884-1981) of Brandon VT, bridge teacher, writer, lecturer. Got first club sanction for monthly masterpoint game for Cavendish Club, New York. ACBL Honorary Secretary 1960, placed 2nd Women's Teams 1951.

TIERNAN, Mary Elizabeth (b. 1907) of Brandon VT. Won Women's Teams 1956, 2nd 1951.

TIERNEY, Dr. John A. (b. 1917) of Atlantic Beach FL, retired mathematics professor. Co-author *Contract Bridge: According to Silodor and Tierney,* contributor to *The Bridge World.*

TILL, Daniel J. (b. 1938) of Lincoln NE, retired physician. Won 18 regionals.

TILLES, Jules (1907-1976) of New York City, bridge teacher, club owner and tournament director, business manager Greater New York BA 1957-72. Placed 2nd Mixed Pairs 1952.

TINTNER, Leon (b. 1910) of Paris, France, born in Austria, retired publisher. World Life Master. European champion 1962, 66, represented France Bermuda Bowl 1962, 67, 69. Won London Sunday Times Invitational 1971, many national titles.

TOBIN, E. J. (Ned) (1868-1953) of Miami and Chicago, one of founders of the American Bridge League, served as its first secretary 1927-28, became treasurer in 1929, and was made an Honorary Member in 1932. Contributor to the Chicago *Record Herald* and the *Daily Journal,* was the holder of many whist championships,

author of *Sound Principles of Auction Bridge.*

TOH, Chee Kian (b. 1947) of Singapore, school teacher. Represented Singapore in 7 zonal championships. Several national wins.

TOIBIN, Niall (b. 1959) of Dublin, Ireland, administrator of Irish aid to East Africa. Won Common Market Open Pairs and Junior Teams 1981. Represented Ireland in 2 world championships and 1 zonal championship. Member Irish team that won Camrose in 2000, the 1st win by a country other than England and Scotland. Won 10 national titles.

TOLEDANO, John H. (Buster) (b. 1907) of New Orleans LA, bridge teacher. With wife Dotty organized and developed Unit 134, celebrated 50 years of continuous service with Unit 1992. Finished 2nd Men's Teams 1956.

TOLLIVER, Mark H. (b. 1953) of Portland OR, CPA, financial analyst. Master chess player. placed 2nd Blue Ribbon Pairs 1991, won 30 regionals.

TOM, Merle H. (b. 1935) of Cos Cob CT, attorney, Diamond Life Master with more than 6500 MPs, won Open Pairs 1972, Men's Teams 1974; placed 2nd Vanderbilt 1974, Men's Teams 1977. Member original Precision Team, won 40+ regionals..

TOMASZEWSKA, Wieslawa (b. 1939) of Warsaw, Poland. 2nd European Mixed Pairs 1996. Won many national titles.

TOMCHIN, Stanley of Orinda CA, won Master Mixed Teams 1973, placed 2nd Vanderbilt 1975.

TOMCZYK, Gary (b. 1953) of Sunrise FL, Richmond Trophy winner 1987, 89 (Canadian equivalent of Top 500); Diamond Life Master with approximately 50 regional wins.

TORLONTANO, Anna Maria (b. 1930) of Pescara, Italy. Member of WBF Executive Council, EBL vice-president, Italian Bridge Federation Executive Committee. Very influential in WBF women's bridge.

TORNAY, Claire J. (c. Belle, Clara Belle) (b. 1940) of New York City, born in Belgium, psychotherapist, professional bridge player, formerly school teacher. Vice-chairman ACBL Appeals Committee for many years. Major organizer of Battle of Sexes 1969. Served as president of Greater NYBA 1986-90, past president Cavendish Club (NY), has served on WBF Appeals Committee. WBF World Master, placed 3rd McConnell Teams 1994, 1998, 4th World Women's Pairs 1982. Won Women's Pairs 1980, Mixed Pairs 1988; placed 2nd Swiss 1981, Women's Pairs 1991.

TORNAY, George F., Jr. (b. 1936) of New York City, consulting actuary, Won Swiss Plate 1986, placed 8th Rosemblum Teams 1986. Won Senior and Advanced Senior Master Pairs 1962, Men's BAM Teams 1980, Reisinger 1984.

TORRENCE, Anita C. (b. 1942) of Bexley OH, bridge teacher, professional player, served many terms on Unit and District board including 2 terms as president of Central Ohio BA. Diamond Life Master, authored ACBL partnership brochure.

TORRES, J. Ignacio Gutierrez (b. 1955) of Madrid, Spain, computer scientist. 3rd European Community Pairs 1999, represented Spain in 10 zonals. 2nd European Junior Teams 1980, also represented Spain 1978.

TOUCHTIDIS, Stelios (b. 1947) of Sherman Oaks CA, born in Greece, advertising executive, with interests in archery, astronomy, comic book collecting, fine wines. Panel member Southern CA *Bridge News.* Placed 7th World Mixed Pairs 1986, npc US II Women's team 1985

Venice Cup. Won Reisinger 1984; placed 2nd Open Pairs 1980, Men's Swiss Teams 1982, North American Swiss Teams 1987. ACBL Diamond Life Master.

TOWNSEND, Mary B. (McBeth, MB) of Baton Rouge LA, bridge teacher and director, records books for the blind in spare time. Member National Appeals Committee. Diamond Life Master, won Women's Swiss Teams 1984, placed 2nd Women's KO Teams 1968. Won 30+ regionals.

TOY, John O. (b. 1944) of Buffalo NY, high school teacher. President Unit 116 1971-79, president Upper New York State Conference 1987-89, member National Appeals Committee, 1975-90, chairman Buffalo NABC 1988, co-chairman Niagara Falls NABC 1982. Won 25+ regionals.

TRACY, Robert D. (b. 1940) of Troy MI, retired supervisory analyst. Diamond Life Master, won 49 regionals.

TRAD, Tony (b 1928) of Cairo, Egypt, longtime Swiss resident. Won World Mixed Pairs 1974. Represented Egypt in 4 European championships and Switzerland in 1. Many national wins include Egyptian Open Teams 10 times. Former technical adviser to Egyptian Bridge Federation.

TRAUB, Alexander A. (Alec) (b. 1911) of Capetown, South Africa, wool merchant, bridge writer. Won South African par event 1953, Open Teams 1955, 62, 2nd 1956. 57. IBPA awards secretary 1975-1982. Contributed to *Le Bridgeur*, translated *Mathematical Theory of Bridge,* authored *Point Count Expectancy Tables, Trump Technique,* co-authored *Probabilities at Contract Bridge.* Editor *Practical Odds at Bridge,* contributing editor *Bridge Encyclopedia.*

TRAVIS, Barbara (b. 1959) of Adelaide, Australia. WBF World Master. Won PABF (Far East) Women's Teams 1985, represented Australia in 5 world championships, many zonal championships. Won many national titles. Youngest winner McCutcheon Trophy 1979. With Liz Havas played in 1998 PABF Open Teams, 1st women's pair to represent Australia in open competition.

TREADWELL, David (b. 1912) of Wilmington DE, retired chemical engineer. ACBL Honorary Member 1985, member ACBL Hall of Fame. Has served in various executive positions including chairman ACBL Board of Governors 1979, 80, 81, co-chairman ACBL Appeals Committee 1975-91, past president Unit 190 and District 4, chairman Hall of Fame Committee 1995-1998. Grand Life Master with 22,617 MPs as of 3/2001 won North American Swiss Teams 1982, Master Mixed Teams 1985; placed 2nd Presidents Pairs 1936; Men's BAM Teams 1960; Mixed Pairs 1969. Won more than 100 regionals.

TREDINNICK, Gerald A. (b. 1963) of Beckenham, England, actuary. WBF World Master. Won World Junior Teams 1989. Represented Britain in 4 zonals. Won several national titles. Twin brother of Stuart.

TREDINNICK, Stuart P. (b. 1963) of Beckenham, England, computer programmer. WBF World Master. Won World Junior Teams 1989. Represented Britain in 4 zonals. Won several national titles. Twin brother of Gerald.

TREITEL, David H. (b. 1954) of New York City, transportation consultant, won Swiss Teams 1980.

TRENT, Paul (b. 1936) of New York City, attorney. Won Men's Teams 1969, 71; Intercollegiate Par champion 1957.

TREUIL, Pierre W. (b. 1934) of Ottawa ON, retired actuary. Won COPC 1992, 93, 95. Won 17 regionals.

TRÉZEL, Roger (1918-1986) of Paris, France, journalist, WBF Grand Master. Won Bermuda Bowl 1956, World Team Olympiad 1960, World Pairs 1962, a triple matched by very few players. Won European Teams 1955, 70; 2nd 1954, 56, 59. Won London Sunday Times Individual 1963 and many national titles. Partnership with Pierre Jais one of world's strongest 1950-1970. Author of booklets later translated into English by Terence Reese.

TRITT, James F. (b. 1946) of Fresno CA, attorney. National Appeals Committee 1980-84. Won Open Pairs I 2001. 3rd Pairs Plate 1986, GNOP 1981, 95, 96. Won 25 regionals.

TROY, Anita E. of Henderson NV, retired purchasing agent. Held numerous executive positions in American Bridge Association including president 1992-95, vice-president 1990-91, Great Lakes Section vice president 1973-74, Western Section vice-president 1986-89, national tournament chairperson 1974, 77, consultant for 1986 national. ABA wins include Mixed Pairs 1967, Women's Teams 1971, Flight B KO Teams 1971, 80, Swiss Teams 1982, 85, BAM Teams 1987, 90; placed 2nd Women's Teams 1972, Women's Pairs 1982, 92, Mixed Teams 1991.

TRUSCOTT, Alan (b. 1925) of New York City, formerly of England, leading international bridge writer, member ACBL Hall of Fame. Bridge editor *New York Times* since 1964. Former president, (1981-86) now president emeritus, of International Bridge Press Association Frequent contributor to *The Bridge World,* ACBL *Bridge Bulletin, Bridge* and other magazines throughout the world. Executive editor first 3 editions of *The Official Encyclopedia of Bridge,* editor of 4th, 5th, 6th editions. After serving as secretary British Bridge League 1957-62, worked as associate editor ACBL *Bridge Bulletin* 1963-64. European champion 1961, represented Great Britain in European Championships 1951, 58. Represented Great Britain 1962 Bermuda Bowl, finished 3rd. Represented U.S. World Mixed Pairs 1970, 74, 78, 82, 86, 90; Mixed Teams 1972, 74; Open Pairs 1974, 76; Rosenblum Teams 1982.

Invented Truscott Card, now widely used to prevent seating errors in team play. Authored several conventions, including: Truscott defense to strong club, Truscott relay 2-way Stayman, 2NT over a takeout double of partner's opening bid to show a limit raise. Contributions to theory include restricted choice. Written many books including *Contract Bridge, Bridge from First Principles, Practical Bridge, The Great Bridge Scandal, Master Bridge By Question and Answer, Teach Yourself Basic Bridge (with Dorothy Truscott), Basic Bridge in Three Weeks, Intermediate Bridge in Three Weeks.* Npc Bermuda team 1964 World Team Olympiad and of Brazilian team 1971 Bermuda Bowl. British successes include Masters Individual 1953, 58. American national wins include Master Mixed Teams 1985, North American Swiss Teams 1987, Mixed Pairs 1989. President Greater New York Bridge Association 1977-79, president District 24 (New York area) 1980-90. President International Bridge Academy. Devised and organized Bridge Battle of the Sexes. Completed 1986 New York Marathon at 61, plays tennis. Oxford University chess champion, defeated several top-ranked British players while a student.

TRUSCOTT, Dorothy Hayden (Mrs. Alan) of New York City, bridge teacher, author, mathematician. Member ACBL Hall of Fame. WBF World Open Life Master

(only woman with this title), has been selected 13 times to represent the United States in international competition including 1st Women's Olympiad team 1960 (placed 5th). Truscott and Helen Sobel Smith are the only 2 women to have played on a North American Team for Bermuda Bowl. She won 4 world titles — Venice Cup 1974, 76, 78, World Women's Team Olympiad 1980. Finished 2nd Bermuda Bowl 1965, 3rd World Open Pairs 1966 (the only woman ever to have finished in the top 10 in this event). 3rd World Women's Team Olympiad 1968, 72, 76, World Women's Pairs 1962, 74; placed 5th World Mixed Teams 1972. Won Pan-Am Women's Teams 1992, npc of winning Venice Cup team 1989.

Won 25 NABC titles (including 4 playing with partners with whom she had never played a session of bridge before) Mixed Pairs 1959, 89; Women's Pairs 1959, 61, 66, 78, 81; Open Pairs 1962; Blue Ribbon Pairs 1963; Life Master Pairs 1964; Women's Teams 1967, 70, 72, 74, 75, 76, 82; Women's Swiss Teams 1982, 84; Master Mixed Teams 1985, Women's BAM Teams 1986; North American Swiss Teams 1987, 92; Women's KO Teams 1990, 93. Placed 2nd Master Mixed Teams 1957, 60, 67, 72; Women's Pairs 1961, 68, 72, 76, 88; Women's Teams 1963, 64; Vanderbilt 1964, Spingold 1965, 68; Women's KO Teams 1987; Women's BAM Teams 1988. Contributions to bridge theory include Unusual Jump to show a singleton (now called Splinter Bid) and responses to Blackwood after Interference (now called DOPI). Author of *Bid Better, Play Better, Winning Declarer Play*, co-author with Alan Truscott of *Teach Yourself Basic Bidding*. Contributes to various magazines, contributing editor to *Official Encyclopedia of Bridge*. Is writing a historical novel about New Amsterdam. See BUENOS AIRES AFFAIR.

TSCHEKALOFF, Alex (1927-1995) of Las Vegas NV, computer programmer. Diamond Life Master, won Life Master Men's Pairs 1965, Blue Ribbon Pairs 1969; placed 2nd Men's Pairs 1961.

TSIANG, George Y.C. (b. 1919) of Hong Kong, business executive. Far East champion 1959, 2nd 1963. Former vice-chairman Hong Kong CBA.

TU, Ya-Pin (b. 1950) of San Francisco, born in Taiwan, computer software specialist. Won Far East Teams 1978, represented Taiwan in 2 world championships.

TUASON, Severo (1909-1973) of Manila, Philippines, civil engineer. Represented Philippines in WBF Executive Council, leading administrator in Philippines and Far East.

TUBBS, Lewis G. (1902-1971) of Arlington VA, bridge instructor and club director, ACBL Board member 1965-68, former president Washington BA. Placed 2nd Master Mixed Teams 1954. Author of *How We Teach and Play Contract Bridge*.

TUCKER, Jacqueline (Jacque) (b. 1932) of San Antonio TX, retired high school teacher. Member ACBL Board of Governors. Diamond Life Master with more than 7000 MPs, won 15+ regionals.

TUCKER, Judy (1946-1998) of New York City, bridge professional and travel agent. 2nd alternate District 24, served many years on Nassau\Suffolk BA Board and as member of NABC Appeals Committee. WBF World Master, placed 5th World Mixed Pairs 1978, 8th World Women's Pairs 1990. Won the Pan Am Games Women's Teams, placed 3rd Women's Pairs 1992. Diamond Life Master, won Women's Pairs 1984, North American Women's Swiss 1992, Women's KO Teams 1993; placed

2nd Women's BAM Teams 1986, 87; Mixed Pairs 1991.

TUCKER, Patricia (Patty) (b. 1954) of Chamblee GA, owner used book store, bridge teacher. Won NAOP 2000.

TUDOR, Harry H. (The King) (b. 1951) of Miami FL. Professional gambler. Diamond Life Master. Won Cavendish Invitational Pairs 1995, 1997, 2nd Cavendish Teams 1998. 5th tie Rosenblum Teams 1994. Won more than 70 regional events.

TUELL, David R. Jr. (Dave) (b. 1936) of Tacoma WA, lawyer, professional bowler Senior PBA Tour. Served in various executive capacities for District 19 and Unit 451 including president, former president of Western Conference. Won 40+ regionals.

TUERAH, Donny (b. 1951) of Jakarta, Indonesia. Won PABF (Far East) Teams 1982, National Open Teams once.

TURNER, Alan George (b. 1947) of Tauranga, New Zealand, born in South Africa, chemical engineer and high school mathematics teacher. Won zonal "test match" against Australia 1987. Represented New Zealand in 1 Bermuda Bowl and 2 Far East Championships. Won 10 national titles. Top masterpoint winner 1982, 89. Former president New Zealand CBA.

TUSZYNSKI, Piotr (b.1955) of Warsaw, Poland, bridge professional. WBF World Life Master. Won World Team Olympiad 1984 and 2nd 2000: 2nd World Transnational Open Teams 1997, 2nd European Junior Pairs 1980. Represented Poland in many World and European Championships. Won many national titles.

U

UKKONEN, Petri (b. 1960) of Helsinki, Finland, waiter. Represented Finland 7 times, including 1 world championship and 2 European Championships. Several national wins. Board member Bridge League of Finland. Contributor to *Finnish Bridge Magazine*. Member Laws Committee of Bridge League of Finland and former member of EBL Systems Committee.

ULKE, Asim (b. 1940) of Monroeville PA, mechanical engineer. Placed 2nd GNOT 1993.

ULTIS, Mark M. (b. 1957) of Cedar Rapids Iowa, chemist, former club manager. Placed 2nd Mini-McKenney Club Master 1981. Won 18 regionals.

UNGER, Gavriel (b. 1943) of Vienna, Austria, born in Israel, teacher. Represented Austria in several European Pair Championships. Won 5 Austrian Teams and 1 Open Pairs. Editor of *Austrian Bridge Magazine.*

UNSON, Rosemarie (b. 1934) of Quezon City, retired property owner. Won Far East Women's Teams 1979, represented Philippines in 1 world championship and 8 zonal championships.

UTEGAARD, Helen S. of Las Vegas NV, born in Beijing, China; WBF World Master, placed 5th World Women's Teams 1988, 6th World Mixed Teams 1974, 7th 1972. She also represented ACBL internationally Venice Cup 1985, 93; Women's Team Olympiad 1988. Grand Life Master with 11,100 MPs as of 3/2001. Won Women's Teams 1971, 73, 81; Mixed Pairs 1974; Master Mixed Teams 1975, 88; Women's KO Teams 1984, 88; Fishbein Trophy, North American Women's Swiss Teams 1988; Women's BAM Teams 1992; placed 2nd Master Mixed Teams 1980; North American Women's Swiss Teams 1987, Women's BAM Teams 1991; Women's KO Teams 1992.

V

VAKIL, Piyush (b. 1941) of Wooster OH, born in India, chemical engineer, nationally ranked table tennis player in India during the Sixties. Won Spingold 1975, placed 2nd GNOT 1993.

VALENTI, Anna (Mrs. Paolo) (b.1917) of Leghorn, Italy, WBF World Grand Master. Won World Women's Olympiad Teams 1972, 2nd 1980; 2nd Venice Cup 1974, 78. Won European Women's Teams 1970, 71, 73, 74. Many other titles included EEC Women's Teams twice and Italian Open Teams twice.

VALENZUELA, Gonzalo (b. 1932 in Chile) of Montevideo, Uruguay, engineer. 2nd South American Teams 1979, 1989. Represented Uruguay regularly in zonal championships since 1980 and earlier represented Chile. Won 36 national titles.

VALENZUELA, Loly of Montevideo, Uruguay. Won South American Women's Teams 1967, 71, 74, 90. A regular member of the Uruguay Women's team in international competition and has won 96 national titles.

VAN COURT, Wendell A. (Woody) (b. 1926) of Memphis TN, bridge teacher and director, retired high school teacher. President Unit 111 1991-92. Won more than 50 regionals.

VANDERBILT, Harold Stirling (1884-1970) of Newport RI, was a bridge authority whose revisions of auction bridge scoring principles created modern contract bridge, also a system-maker and champion player. Member ACBL Hall of Fame. For many years he was a successful business executive. His greatest fame in competitive fields is as a yachtsman – his revision of right-of-way rules is still known as the Vanderbilt Rules. Nevertheless, his lasting fame is more likely to come from his contributions to bridge. Vanderbilt took up bridge seriously in 1906, and his partnership with J. B. Elwell was considered the strongest in the U.S. from 1910 to 1920. During that period the contract bridge principle – counting only bid tricks toward game – was often proposed and as often rejected, except for the limited success of Plafond. Experimenting with the proposed new game while on a cruise late in 1925, Vanderbilt originated the factors of vulnerability and inflated slam bonuses. He produced a scoring table so balanced as to make nearly every aggressive or sacrifice bid an approximately even bet, allowing just enough differential to permit the exercise of nice judgment.

The rapid spread of contract bridge from 1926 to 1929 is largely attributable to Vanderbilt's espousal of it; his social standing made the game fashionable. Vanderbilt's technical contribution was even greater. He devised the first unified system of bidding, and was solely responsible for the artificial 1♣ bid to show a strong hand; the negative 1♦ response, the strong (16- to 18-point) notrump on balanced hands only, and the weak two-bid opening. These and his other principles were presented in his books, *Contract Bridge Bidding and the Club Convention*; *The New Contract Bridge*; *Contract by Hand Analysis*; and *The Club Convention Modernized*. Vanderbilt was a member of the Laws Committee of the Whist Club of New York that made the American laws of contract bridge (1927, 1931) and the first international code (1932). He then became chairman of that committee and largely drafted the international code of 1935, the American code of 1943, and the international codes of 1948 and 1949. He remained co-chairman of the National Laws Commission of the ACBL for the 1963 laws.

In 1928 Vanderbilt presented the Harold S. Vanderbilt Cup for a national team-of-four championship. This became and remained for many years the most coveted American team trophy, mainly because the replicas were donated personally by Vanderbilt to the winners. In 1960 Vanderbilt supplied the permanent trophy for the World Bridge Federation's Olympiad Team tournaments, again adopting the policy of giving replicas to the winners. As a player, Vanderbilt always ranked high. In 1932 and 1940 he won his own Vanderbilt Cup. He played by choice only in the strongest money games, and was a consistent winner. His regular partnership with Waldemar von Zedtwitz was among the strongest and most successful in the U.S.

In 1941 he retired from tournament bridge, but he continued to play in the most expert rubber bridge games, in clubs and at home. In 1968, Vanderbilt spent more than $50,000 to recreate the lost molds for the replicas of the American trophy and to provide a quantity of replicas of both trophies sufficient to last from 20 to 40 years. To perpetuate this practice of awarding individual replicas, Vanderbilt further bequeathed to the ACBL a trust fund of $100,000, a gift that wisely foresaw the possibility of inflation, but provided that excess funds, if any, can be donated in Vanderbilt's name to a charity of ACBL's choice. In 1969, the World Bridge Federation made Vanderbilt its first honorary member. When a Bridge Hall of Fame was inaugurated in 1964, Vanderbilt was one of the first three persons elected. Member Advisory Board *Bridge Encyclopedia*. (See HISTORY OF BRIDGE)

VAN GELDER, Jacques (Jacq) (1902-1993) of Ft. Lauderdale FL, accountant; wrote column *Mixed Masters* for the ACBL *Bridge Bulletin* and contributed to other bridge publications. Directed bridge activities on more than 100 cruises 1972-1993.

VANIJAKA, Naina (b. 1948) of Bangkok, Thailand, bank manager. 2nd PABF (Far East) Women's Teams 1979. Represented Thailand in 3 world championships and 20 zonal championships. Won 4 Asean titles.

VAN MIDDELEM, Guy (b. 1959) of Brussels, Belgium, bridge teacher. World Master. Represented Belgium in 3 World Championships and 4 European Championships. National wins include 7 open teams.

VAN NESS, John P. (b. 1940) of Aspen CO, attorney. President District 17 1998, president Western Conference 1996-97. Won NABC Amateur Pairs 1976.

VAN VLECK, Charles Edward (1896-1950) of New York City, pioneer of new bidding methods in the Thirties. Originated Weak Jump Shift Responses subsequently adopted by the Roth-Stone System and advocated ultra weak Weak Two-Bids. His system, which was based on the Vanderbilt Club System, was probably the first to use the Three-Quarter Notrump. Placed 2nd Vanderbilt 1943.

VAN WYK, Rod (b.1938) of Alton IL, retired research director. Won 15+ regionals.

VAN ZANDT, Esta V. of Houston, born in India, bridge teacher. Placed 2nd Far East Women's Championships (represented Okinawa) 1966. Won Master Mixed Teams, Mixed Pairs 1981; placed 2nd Women's Teams 1973. Diamond Life Master.

VAUCROSSON, Charles H. B. (b. 1934) of Pembroke Parish, Bermuda, retired attorney. District 2 Board member for 6 years and president Unit 198 for 10 years. Represented Bermuda in world competition and in Tri-Coun-

try playoffs. Was a prime mover for Tri-Country play-offs to determine representatives to Bermuda Bowl and Venice Cup.

VELARDE, Ernesto (b.1938) of Lima, Peru, lawyer. President of South American Bridge Federation since 1989. Member WBF Executive Council since 1991. President Peruvian Bridge Commission 1984-89. Represented Peru in 1 world championship and 2 zonal championships.

VENTIN, Carlos (b. 1957) of Barcelona Spain, actuary. Placed 2nd European Junior Teams 1980. Represented Spain in 2 world championships, 2 zonal championships and 3 other zonal junior championships. Won many national titles.

VENTURINI, Maria Vittoria (b.1928) of Rome, Italy. WBF World Life Master. Won World Women's Team Olympiad 1972, European Women's Teams 1970, 71, 73.

VERBEEK, Martine (b. 1962) of Rotterdam, Netherlands, bookkeeper. Won Venice Cup 2000, European Union Women's Teams 1998. Represented Netherlands in 1 other world championship and 1 zonal.

VERGARA, Etelvina (1905-1983) of Buenos Aires, Argentina. Won South American Women's Teams 1948, 49, 50, 51, 53, 57, 61, 62, 64. Represented Argentina in 2 world championships. 8 national titles.

VERGOED, F.J. (Hans) (b. 1948) of Delft, The Netherlands, pharmacist. WBF World Master. Placed 3rd World Team Olympiad 1980. Represented The Netherlands in 3 other world championships and 3 European Championships. Won many national titles. Bridge columnist.

VERNAY, Colby K. (b. 1942) of Lacon IL, basketball coach, avid golfer, has had three holes-in-one. Was editor of the *Central Illinois Duplicate Bulletin* 1973-76, VP of Unit 208 1975-76, and a member of the ACBL Board of Governors 1985-91. Diamond Life Master with more than 12,200 MPs, has won more than 125 regionals including District 8 GNOP 1982, 88, GNOT 1990, 91.

VERNE, Jules (1828-1905) famous French author of *Voyages Extraordinaires*. His 43-year output of 60-odd volumes, is called "The Father of modern science fiction." In his most successful "voyage" novel, *Around the World in Eighty Days*, his hero, Phileas Fogg, makes his extraordinary wager over the whist table at the Reform Club with his whist partners. Throughout the course of the voyage, Phileas Fogg plays whist with fellow travelers.

VERNOFF, Milton (1905-1989) of Los Angeles CA, retired attorney, won Master Mixed Teams 1938 and numerous regional events. Vernoff pioneered bridge on television in Florida and served as president of the Florida Unit.

VERNON, Francis (b. 1934) of Caracas, Venezuela, civil engineer, bridge teacher, writer and director. WBF World Master. Won South American Teams 1965, 66; CAC Teams 1973, 77, 85, 97. Represented Venezuela in 10 world championships. Won many national titles.

VERSACE, Alfredo (b. 1969) of Rome, Italy. WBF World Life Master, professional player. Together with Lorenzo Lauria forms one of the world's best partnerships. Won World Team Olympiad 2000, Rosenblum Teams 1998, European Teams 1995, 97; European Junior Teams 1990. Won Cavendish Teams 1996, 97; Macallan 1998, Vanderbilt 1999. Won many Italian titles.

VIEDMA, Rafael G. (b. 1934) of Saudi Arabia, formerly of Madrid, Spain, engineer. Placed 4th World Open Teams

1982. Represented Spain in 2 other world championships and 2 zonal championships. Won many national titles.

VILAS BOAS, Miguel (b. 1968) of Salvador, Brazil, economist. WBF World Life Master. Placed 2nd Rosenblum Teams 1998, Bermuda Bowl 2000. Won IOC Teams 1998. Represented Brazil in 2 other world championships. Won South American Teams 1990, 96, 98. Won 2 national team titles.

VINE, Frank (1927-1987) of Hamilton ON, attorney. Won Men's Pairs 1969 and was a contributor to *The Bridge World*, ACBL *Bridge Bulletin* and other publications.

VIOLIN, Lois C. (b. 1927) of Palm Desert CA, bridge teacher, retired factory representative. Placed 2nd Women's BAM Teams 1975, won 20 regionals.

VIOLIN, Roxy R. (b. 1929) of Palm Desert CA, air conditioning engineer/consultant. Served on ACBL Board of Governors 9 years. Won Mixed Pairs 1970, placed 2nd Life Master Men's Pairs 1973. Was playing with Ed Weiner as teammates of Marty Cohn and Charles MacCracken when Cohn made his famous psychic bid against Howard Schenken and Peter Leventritt.

VON ZEDTWITZ, Waldemar K. (1896-1984) linguist and lexicographer, ACBL president emeritus, one of the great players and personalities of all time. Member ACBL Hall of Fame. He was born in Berlin, the son of a German (Saxon) baron, to whose title he succeeded when his father died a few months after his birth, and of an American mother. He thereby acquired dual citizenship; after World War I he adopted United States citizenship, relinquishing his title. Von Zedtwitz was president of the ACBL in 1948 and of its parent organization, the American Bridge League, in 1932. He was named Honorary Member by the ABL in 1931. When dissension threatened to break up the ACBL in 1948, the contesting factions agreed to keep him as president and chairman with carte blanche, and he is credited with saving the ACBL. In 1949, upon the League's rehabilitation, he immediately returned his carte blanche power to the Board of Directors. He was a charter member of the ACBL Laws Commission and as co-chairman played an active role in preparing the international code in 1963.

He helped found the World Bridge Federation, was a WBF director, chairman of its committee on International Matchpoints and chairman of the Rules Committee for the 1964 World Team Olympiad. He also played a major role in the formation of the ACBL Charity Foundation. Von Zedtwitz was noted for versatility in playing with exponents of different systems. He was an early contributor to the Culbertson System, a contributor and consultant in connection with the Four Aces System, a member of the Bridge World Team that won the first international matches (1930) in England and France. He had one of the most successful all-time partnerships with Harold S. Vanderbilt playing the club convention, and was a regular partner of P. Hal Sims, S. Garton Churchill, the Four Aces, Charles E. Van Vleck and many others. Later his regular partners included Harold Harkavy, Edith Kemp and Barbara Brier.

He was one of the first 10 to be named Life Master (No. 4) when that category was created by the ABL in 1936. Von Zedtwitz began his tournament bridge career in 1923, won many national auction bridge championships and won nearly all the contract bridge championships. In 1930 he donated the Gold Cup for Master Pairs (now Life Master Pairs) and won it the first year. His

other tournament successes are World Mixed Pairs 1970 (at age 74), USBA Grand National Teams, Mixed Pairs 1936; Spingold 1937, 1941, 1947; Chicago (now the Reisinger) 1932, 1945; Vanderbilt 1930, 1932, 1940; Master Mixed Teams 1940, 1942, 1945, 1965; Life Master Pairs 1930; Open Pairs 1928, 1937; Men's Pairs 1946; Master Individual 1936. He placed 2nd USBA Mixed Teams 1936; Spingold 1936, 1940, 1949, 1953, 1963; Chicago 1930, 1933, 1936, 1941, 1942; Vanderbilt 1937, 1938, 1943, 1945, 1960; Reisinger 1964, Master Mixed Teams 1933, 1935, 1956; Life Master Pairs 1933, 1939; Open Pairs 1935, Men's Pairs 1938, 1953. Von Zedtwitz won a major backgammon tournament in Hawaii at age 82. His other interests included Bridgette, travel, tennis and golf.

VRIEND, Bep (b. 1946) of Amstelveen, The Netherlands, secretary and bridge teacher. WBF World Grand Master, #4 in world women's rankings. Best record of any Dutch woman player. Won Venice Cup 2000, 2nd 1989. Won World Women's Pairs 1994, 3rd 1990. 3rd World Women's Teams 1984. Won European Women's Pairs 1993, European Mixed Teams 1994. 2nd European Women's Teams, 1983, 1989, 3rd, 1979, 1991. Won European Union Women's Teams, 1989, 1997, 1998. 3rd European Mixed Teams 1992. National wins include Open Pairs 3 times and Women's Pairs 9 times. Appointed a member of the Order of Orange-Nassau by Queen Beatrix.

W

WACHSMAN, David P. (b. 1942) of East Meadow NY, vice president of investments at Salomon Smith Barney. Former president of North Jersey Bridge Association. Board of Governors member, certified bridge director; lecturer and director on cruise ships. Won many regional events, including District 4 1995 North American Pairs and Grand National Teams.

WACHSMAN, Janis L. (b. 1948) of East Meadow NY, math teacher. Won many regional events including District 4 1995 North American Pairs and Grand National Teams. Winner of 7 Mini-McKenney awards. Teaches ACBL School Bridge Lesson Series.

WADAS, Judith L. (Judy) (b. 1936) of Chicago IL, insurance company executive, co-founder Insurance Consumer Affairs Exchange. 1st president and co-founder of Forum for Women in Bridge; won Women's Swiss Teams 1997, 2000; Women's KO Teams 1996; placed 2nd Mixed Pairs 1981, Women's BAM Teams 2000; North American Women's Swiss Teams 1988. Won ACBL-wide East-West Epson Pairs 1990.

WAGAR, Margaret (April 6, 1902-Jan 6, 1990) of Delaware OH, formerly of Atlanta GA, bridge teacher and writer, served on ACBL Board of Directors 1960-72, ACBL Honorary Member 1979, member ACBL Hall of Fame. Life Master #37 and one of the great American woman players of all time; npc of U.S. World Women's Olympiad teams 1968, 72. With Kay Rhodes, she shares one of the most remarkable achievements in ACBL history — they won the Women's Pairs 4 straight times 1955, 56, 57, 58. Wagar also won the same event in 1944. Impressive record also includes Women's Teams 1940, 43, 44, 45, 46, 64, 65; the Chicago (now the Reisinger) 1941; Master Mixed Teams 1942, 45, 48, 54, 64; Spingold 1946,

48; Open Pairs 1947, 48; Mixed Pairs 1948, 49; Life Master Women's Pairs 1962. Wagar placed 2nd Master Mixed Teams 1933, 49, 50, 62, 67; Life Master Pairs 1943; Women's Teams 1952, 53, 54, 55, 56, 57, 58, 64. Also won the Hilliard Trophy 1933, 45 and Marcus Cup 1958.

WAGNER, Willem M. (Wim) (1926-1991) of Amsterdam, The Netherlands, chemist and marine biologist. Chief organizer 1980 World Team Olympiad. Appointed assistant chief tournament director of the European Bridge League in 1982. WBF operations director 1986-1991.

WAINWRIGHT, Louise (Mrs. Stuyvesant) (1902-1986) of Southampton NY, antique shop owner. Placed 2nd Master Mixed Teams 1941; Hilliard Trophy 1939, Mixed Teams 1940, 41, 44.

WAINWRIGHT, Stuyvesant (1891-1975) of New York City and Naples FL, stockbroker. Member Vanderbilt Cup Tournament Committee 1928-57, member of the Whist Club Committee on laws for international codes of 1932 and 1935 and vice president of the Regency Club, New York. Placed 2nd Mixed Teams 1943.

WAKEFIELD, Joseph E. (Joe) (b. 1943) of Southampton Bermuda, born in England, attorney. Represented Bermuda 1976 ,80, 84 in the Tri-Country playoffs 1989, 91. Served as president Bermuda Unit 1977, 78 and tournament chairman 1975,76.

WAKEMAN, Robert P. (1913-1981) of Upper Montclair NJ, systems engineer, former director, bridge editor New Jersey BL and former bridge editor of *Newark Evening News*. Contributing editor *Bridge Encyclopedia*. Won Men's Teams 1960.

WAKEN, Harvard C. (b. 1917) of Arcadia CA, CPA, real estate. Won North American Swiss Teams 1983.

WALDMANN, Arthur J. (b. 1933) of Rocky Hill CT, investments. Diamond Life Master, won Men's Pairs 1975; placed 2nd Spingold 1974, Men's Teams 1977.

WALETZKY, Niel (b. 1949) of Shaker Heights OH, revenue officer, attorney. Wrote, directed and performed in 2 bridge shows. Won 18 regionals.

WALKER, Abbey (b. 1976) of Oxford, England, pensions adviser. WBF World Master. Youngest competitor in a major world championship, playing in the Venice Cup in 1995 at age 19. Won European Women's Teams 1999. 3rd European Under-20 Women's Teams 1996. Also represented Britain in one other Venice Cup.

WALKER, Karen S. (b. 1951) of Champaign IL, ad copywriter and college English teacher. District 8 *Advocate* editor since 1980; author of *Bridge for Beginners and Beyond*. Placed 2nd Life Master Pairs 1986. Her regional wins include District 8 GNOT 1980, 90, 91.

WALLACE, Charlton (1904-1979) of Cincinnati OH, bridge writer, was a founder-member of the International Bridge Press Association and in 1978 was elected honorary member. Bridge associate of Ely Culbertson, P. Hal Sims and other greats. Director of AWL, Midwest president USBA 1936, bridge editor *Cincinnati Post-Times-Star* from 1933 until his death; contributing editor *Bridge Encyclopedia*.

WALLACE, Jane V. (Mrs. Charlton) of Cincinnati OH, won Women's Teams 1947.

WALLACE, Wilfrid (b. 1908) of Summer Hill, Australia, chemist. Won World Par Contest 1937 with perfect score. Many national titles.

WALLIS, Peter James (Jim) (b. 1965) of Brisbane, Australia. Placed 3rd World Junior Teams 1991, won PABF

(Far East) Junior Teams 1990, and represented Australia in 1 other world championship. Won 2 national titles.

WALSH, Alan D. (b. 1945) of Sydney, Australia, systems analyst. Won PABF (Far East) Open Pairs 1972 and zonal play-off 1983. Represented Australia in 1 world championships and 9 other zonal championships. Won 7 national titles.

WALSH, Rhoda of Henderson NV, attorney, former bridge professional. WBF World Master, placed 3rd World Women's Teams 1968, 5th 1988, 9th World Mixed Pairs 1986. Grand Life Master with 16,077 MPs as of 3/2001. Co-author *Recap Bridge*. In 1968, Walsh won all 3 women's national events held that year, Women's Teams, Women's Pairs, Life Master Women's Pairs. Also won Women's Pairs, Life Master Women's Pairs 1972; Master Mixed Teams 1976; North American Swiss 1984, 85; North American Women's Swiss 1985, 88; Life Master Women's Pairs 1989, Silver Ribbon Pairs 2000; placed 2nd in Life Master Women's Pairs 1982, North American Swiss 1986; North American Women's Swiss 1987.

WALSH, Richard R. (b. 1936) of Zurich, Switzerland, commodities and currencies analyst, before retiring from tournament play was one of the leading American players and competed internationally. Diamond Life Master, invented the WALSH SYSTEM. Won Vanderbilt 1969; Team Trials, Men's Teams, Men's Pairs 1970; placed 2nd Spingold 1959 and had more than 50 regional wins.

WALSHE, Col. George Gordon J. (1873-1959) of London, England. Represented England in the Anglo-American match 1934 and was one of the referees in the Culbertson-Lenz match 1932. Co-inventor of the CAB system. Wrote under the pseudonym "Yarborough" for the London *Daily Times*. Wrote several books.

WALSHE, Pat (b. 1954) of Dublin, Ireland, born in Listowel, Ireland, computer analyst. WBF World Master. Placed 2nd European Junior Teams 1974. Won Common Market Pairs 1981. 2nd Common Market Open Teams 1983, Mixed Teams 1989. Won more than 30 national titles

WALTERS, Florine W. of Pittsburgh PA, real estate agent, former bridge club owner, director, teacher. Placed 2nd Women's Teams 1978, 79; North American Women's Swiss 1985, GNOT 1993.

WALUYAN, Ferdinand (b. 1946) of Jakarta, Indonesia, management consultant. WBF World Master. Won PABF (Far East) Teams 1979, 82, 83, 84. Represented Indonesia in 4 world championships and in other zonal championships.

WALVICK, Katharine H. (Kathie) (Mrs. Walter J.) (b. 1942) of McLean VA, senior legal editor. WBF World Master, placed 3rd World Mixed Teams 1974, World Mixed Pairs 1990, 4th World Women's Pairs 1982. Was the only woman to reach the World Open Pairs finals 1978, placed 15th 1974. Diamond Life Master with more than 9000 MPs, won Master Mixed Teams 1967; Life Master Women's Pairs 1980; placed 2nd Mixed Pairs 1967, Blue Ribbon Pairs 1973, 77, Master Mixed Teams 1983; Women's Pairs 1991.

WALVICK, Walter J. (Crab) (b. 1942) of McLean VA, attorney. WBF World Master, placed 3rd World Mixed Pairs 1990, won Swiss Plate 1986. Diamond Life Master, won Lou Herman Trophy 1975, Life Master Men's Pairs 1975, 89; placed 2nd Life Master Pairs 1974; Men's Swiss 1988.

WAN, Li of Beijing, China. Retired Chairman of People's Congress. Won IBPA Solomon Award 1984. Placed 2nd Epson 1990. President Emeritus of Chinese Bridge Association. Winner of Gold Medal awarded by WBF 1993 and Presidential citation ACBL 1993. Chairman Wan was responsible for building the 10 famous architectural structures in 12 months, including the Great Hall of the People in the Fifties. Responsible for the rapid growth of bridge in China today.

WAN, Samuel S.K. (b. 1951) of Hong Kong, executive recruitment consultant. WBF World Master. Won Far East Open Teams 1987. Represented Hong Kong in 4 world championships and 6 other Far East Championships.

WANG, Chia-Chi (b. 1925) of Taipei, Taiwan, born in China, Air Force retiree. Represented Taiwan in 2 Far East Championships. Headed Taiwan's tournament committee since 1961. Managed the International Bridge Center of Taipei 1978-1998. Author of *Natural Bidding System* and *Bridge for Beginners*.

WANG, Hongli (b. 1968) of Shaanxi, China. WBF Life Master. Placed 2nd World Olympiad Women's Teams 1996. Won Far East Women's Teams 1993, 94, 96, 97, 98. Represented China in 5 World championships. Won many national titles.

WANG, Junren (b. 1947) of Shanghai, China, company employee. WBF World Master. 2nd Far East Teams 1984, 1987. Represented China in 4 world championships and 3 zonal championships. Won many national titles.

WANG, Ping of Zhejiang, China. WBF World Master. Placed 3rd Venice Cup 1991. Won Far East Women's Teams 1991. Represented China in 4 World championships and 2 zonal championships. Won 2 national titles.

WANG, Weimin (b. 1968) of Shanghai, China. WBF World Master. Won Far East Open Teams 1998, 2nd 1997. Won IOC Grand Prix 1998. Represented China in 1 world championship. Won many national titles.

WANG, Wenfei (b. 1970) of Shanghai, China. WBF Life Master. Placed 2nd World Olympiad Women's Teams 1996. 2nd Venice Cup 1997. Won Far East Women's Teams 1996, 97, 98. Represented China in 5 world championships. Won many national titles.

WANG, Xiaojing (b. 1964) of Jiangshu, China. WBF World Master. Represented China in 2 world championships. Won Far East Open Teams 1998, 2nd 1997. Won many national titles.

WANUFEL, Christian (b. 1944) of Liege, Belgium, engineer. WBF World Master. Represented Belgium in 2 World Championships and 6 European Championships. National wins include 5 Open Teams and 2 Open Pairs.

WARADIA, Dadan (b. 1967) of Jakarta, Indonesia, government employee. Won PABF (Far East) Junior Teams 1990, 1991. Won one national title.

WARDEN, Mary L. (b. 1951) of Madison WI, teacher, business manager. Served on Board of Governors 1990-99, won 25 regionals.

WARDEN, Phillip J. (Phil) (b. 1947) of Madison WI, painting contractor. Member National Appeals Committee 1990-99, Diamond Life Master with more than 8500 MPs, won 75 regionals.

WARNER, Caroline N. (b. 1922) of Fort Lauderdale FL, bridge director, teacher, professional. Won 16 regionals.

WARNER, David (1911-1987) of Bala-Cynwyd PA, stockbroker. Former ACBL vice president, former president of Philadelphia CBA; placed 2nd Master Mixed Teams 1947, Mixed Pairs 1957.

WARNER, Janet M. (1901-1991) of Pampa TX, secretary, won Women's Pairs 1962.

WARNER, Stephen R. (b. 1927) of Fort Lauderdale FL,

retired dentist. District 9 recorder; Diamond Life Master, 20+ regional wins.

WARREN, Emily (Mrs. Prescott) (1876-deceased) of Newton MA, prominent New England bridge teacher, bridge writer and radio lecturer in the Twenties and Thirties. Columnist for *Boston Transcript,* authored several books on games including *Auction and Contract Bridge Condensed* and co-authored *Contract Bridge of 1930.*

WARSHAUER, Judge Bernard J. (1920-1998) of Sumter SC, family court judge. Was District 7 representative on ACBL Board of Directors 1979-94; past president of Unit 160. Contributor to District 7 newsletter, had weekly column in *Sumter Daily Item.* Diamond Life Master.

WASIK, Artur (b. 1965) of Madrid, Spain, born in Poland, engineer and bridge professional. WBF World Master. Represented Spain in 1 world championship and 4 zonals. National titles include Open Team several times.

WATANABE, Fumio (b. 1917) of Kanagawa Prefect, Japan. Formerly CEO of, and later adviser to, Tokyo Marine and Fire Insurance and Japan Air Lines. Represented Japan in 1st Japan-U.S.A. match 1950. JCBL President 1981-91, Worked for JCBL incorporation, for 3 Epson international tournaments, and the 1991 staging of the Bermuda Bowl and Venice Cup in Yokohama. JCBL Honorary Life Member. Recipient First Class Order of the Sacred Treasure.

WATSON, Alan D. (b. 1952) of Malvern PA, pharmaceutical management. Developed seeding point plan for major team events with Edgar Kaplan, won 30 regionals.

WATSON, Louis H. (1907-1936) of New York City, was a leading player of the Thirties. *Collier's* magazine of March 24, 1934, ranked Watson as 4th greatest player in the world. Won AWL Open Teams and Open Pairs 1933, 34; Asbury Challenge Teams 1932, Cavendish Club Individual 1933; and placed 2nd in 4 major events including the Vanderbilt 1933. Daily columnist for *New York Post* and technical editor for *The Bridge World.* His writings included the classic *Watson on the Play of the Hand* and *Contract Bridge.*

WATULINGAS, Giovani (b. 1959) of Jakarta, Indonesia. WBF World Master. Won PABF (Far East) Teams 1993 and National Open Teams 3 times.

WEBBER, Robert F. (Bob) (b. 1946) of Waterford MI, CPA and financial planner. Served as president and tournament chairman for Michigan BA. Diamond Life Master, won 40 regionals. See also HIGHEST SCORE.

WEBER, Lynne J. (formerly Pollenz) (b. 1955) of Redwood City CA, management consultant. Won Women's Swiss 1986, placed 2nd Women's Pairs 1983.

WEBSTER, Harold Tucker (1885-1952) noted syndicated cartoonist, was best known for the character "The Timid Soul," which he created. He used bridge as the topic of many of his humorous pictures. He co-authored cartoon books on bridge with Ely Culbertson, Caswell Adams, Philo Clark Calhoun, William Johnston and authored *Grand Slams.*

WEED, Charles E. (b. 1931) of Shreveport LA, retired business consultant, served as president of Dallas BA; won GNOT 1975, Swiss Teams 1978; won 50+ regionals.

WEEMS, Kyle R. (b. 1937) of Chattanooga TN, attorney. President Unit 206 1972-77, Diamond Life Master, won 35+ regionals.

WEI, Charles C. (C.C.) (1914-Feb. 20, 1987) of New York City, born in Shanghai, China, shipbuilding magnate. In the Mid-Sixties he devised the Precision bid-

ding system which was used successfully by the Taiwan team in the Bermuda Bowl 1969, 70, by the Precision Team in winning the Spingold 1970, 71, the Vanderbilt 1972, and by the Italian Team in winning World Team Olympiad 1972 and the Bermuda Bowl 1973, 74. Wei was a former trustee of the ACBL Charity Foundation. He was npc of the Taiwan team in the World Team Olympiad 1964, Bermuda Bowl 1969, and npc of North American Venice Cup 1981. Authored many books and articles on Precision and Super Precision. Playing with Ron Andersen at the New York Winter regional 1974 he had the biggest game ever recorded in an ACBL regional on a 156 average — 260, (83.3%)! (See also HIGHEST SCORE, PRECISION CLUB, PRECISION TEAM, SPONSORS.)

WEI-SENDER, Katherine (Kathie) (formerly Mrs. Charles C. Wei) of Nashville TN, formerly of New York City, born in China, writer and lecturer on the Precision Club system, formerly a nurse, medical facility administrator for 15 years before retiring in 1972. Was appointed adviser to the Shanghai Bridge League while attending the first international bridge tournament ever held in China (March 1981). Makes frequent trips there to advise and assist in various bridge activities and endeavors, now official adviser to Chinese Bridge League. Ambassador of Bridge for WBF and ACBL. Served as mistress of ceremonies at all matches between Corporate America and U.S. Congress.

International Bridge Press Association Personality of the Year 1986, member ACBL Hall of Fame, ACBL Honorary Member 1997. Charter member WBF Friends of Bridge 1987. In 1981 the International Bridge Press Association awarded the Goren Personality of the Year award to Deng Xiaoping, premier of the People's Republic of China. Wei-Sender delivered the award to Mr. Deng in Beijing, and during that visit she played bridge with Mr. Deng as his partner.

WBF Grand Master ranked #12 in world among women, one of a very small number of women to have won three different major world Women's titles — World Women's Pairs 1978, World Olympiad Women's Teams 1984, Venice Cup 1987. Placed 2nd Venice Cup 1981, 85, Women's Pairs 1990. Won USWBC 1983, 87; ACBL Honorary Member 1987, member ACBL Hall of Fame. Made first major mark in bridge as co-captain and manager of Taiwan team in 1971 Bermuda Bowl. Taiwan surprised the world by finishing 2nd to the then all-powerful Blue Team from Italy. Wei-Sender also captained Taiwan in the 1972 World Team Olympiad.

Served as Board member of Greater New York BA, trustee and president of ACBL Charity Foundation. Contributor to various national and international bridge publications, with a regular weekly column with Alan Truscott in China's *People's Daily*; co-author of her autobiography *Second Daughter* and co-author of *Action for the Defense* and *One Club Complete.* Also has hosted television series in China entitled *Yang Xiao-Yen Presents.* Yang Xiao-Yen is her Chinese name.

ACBL Grand Life Master with 14,652 MPs as of 3/2001. Won Women's Teams 1971, 80; North American Women's Swiss 1983 95, 96; Women's KO Teams 1983, 87, 94, 2000; Women's BAM Teams 1992, 95; placed 2nd Women's Teams 1973, 82; Vanderbilt 1974, 77, 79; Life Master Women's Pairs 1984; North American Women's Swiss 1985, 2000; Women's BAM Teams 1986, 91; Women's KO Teams 1992, 97,98.

WEI, Stella (b. 1946) of Taipei, Taiwan, born in China, computer network specialist for a bank. WBF World Master. Won Far East Women's Teams 1988, 89; Far East Open Pairs 1988. Represented Taiwan in 4 world championships and 12 Far East Championships.

WEICHSEL, Nancy E. (Mrs. Arthur Blaustein) (b. 1945) of Encinitas CA, former backgammon and bridge professional, won Master Mixed Teams 1976 and numerous regionals.

WEICHSEL, Peter M. (b. 1943) of Encinitas CA, professional bridge player, WBF Life Master, won Bermuda Bowl 1983, World Mixed Pairs 1990, World Transnational Teams 1999; placed 5th Rosenblum Teams 1986, 7th 1978, 9th 1990; 8th World Open Pairs 1974, 78. Won Pan-Am Teams 1992 and the International Team Trials 1982. Grand Life Master with 23,570 MPs as of 3/2001, #16 in ACBL. Won Spingold 1970, 71, 80, 82, 92; Life Master Men's Pairs 1971; Vanderbilt 1972, 85, 89, 99; Reisinger 1973; Master Mixed Teams 1976, 89; Life Master Pairs 1977; Men's Teams 1979; Men's Pairs 1980, 84; Open BAM Teams 1996; Mens BAM Teams 1987, Open Pairs II 1993; placed 2nd Men's Teams 1968, Vanderbilt 1975, 81; Reisinger 1983, 98; Blue Ribbon Pairs 1983; Spingold 1985, 88, 91; IMP Pairs 1987; Life Master Men's Pairs 1989; Open BAM Teams 1990; Open Swiss Teams 2000; GNOT 2000. Won Cavendish Invitational 1976, 77; London Sunday Times Pairs 1975 (2nd in 1973). Placed 2nd U.S. Team Trials 1999. (See LANCIA TEAMS and PRECISION TEAM.)

WEIGKRICHT, Terry (b.1958) of Vienna, Austria, mathematics and French teacher. WBF World Grand Master. In 2000, 20th in Women's World rankings. Won Women's World Team Olympiad 1992, McConnell Teams 1998, placed 2nd Venice Cup 1991. Won European Women's Teams 1991. Has represented Austria on several other occasions.

WEIK, Thomas W. (b. 1942) of Wyomissing PA, president of investment advisory firm, past member ACBL Board of Governors. Placed 2nd Life Master Pairs 1974.

WEIL, Frank P. (b. 1918) of Sacramento CA, retired; founder and for 25 years editor of Unit 505 publication *The Overcall*; for 17 years was a columnist to *Contract Bridge Forum* and has been a contributor to ACBL *Bridge Bulletin*; has been directing bridge activities aboard cruise ships for 17 years.

WEINER, Barbara L. (b. 1930) of Joplin MO, retired secretary, won Women's Pairs 1953.

WEINER, Howard (b. 1944) of Southfield MI, attorney. Diamond Life Master; placed 2nd GNOP 1992.

WEINER, Leo B. (1906-1993) of Chicago IL, insurance claims manager, club director and manager. LM #135, Diamond Life Master.

WEINROTT, Joan B. (b. 1932) of Bryn Mawr PA, bridge coach, teacher. Goodwill Member of Year 2000, Unit 141 president 1987-88, business manager 1993-, co-chair Philadelphia NABC 1996, founded bridge school 1973.

WEINSTEIN, Arthur (Art) (b. 1927) of San Mateo CA, bridge teacher and certified director; author of *Bridge Poems for your Partner, Art of Bridge (Bridge Poems for your Ex Partner), Bridge the Gap, Art Weinstein Talks Bridge*. Former bridge columnist for several weekly newspapers.

WEINSTEIN, Howard M. (b. 1953) of Chicago IL, retired options trader, member ACBL Ethical Oversight Committee, ACBL Appeals Committee. chair of Conventions and Competition Committee 1997-99. WBF World Master, placed 3rd World Team Olympiad 2000, Rosenblum Teams 1998, 5th Rosenblum Teams 1990. Won USBC 2000, 2nd 1989. Grand Life Master, won GNOT 1991, Vanderbilt 1993, Open Pairs I 1996, Life Master Pairs 1997, Blue Ribbon Pairs 1998, Reisinger 1997; placed 2nd GNOT 1986, 88, Reisinger 1987, 95, Men's BAM Teams 1987, Life Master Pairs 1988, 89. Won Cavendish Teams 2001, won Forbes National Cup 2001; placed 2nd Cavendish Invitational 2000, 2nd Cap Gemini 2001.

WEINSTEIN, Jerrold (b. 1936) of Las Vegas, CPA. Past president Chicago CBA, won 16 regionals.

WEINSTEIN, Sol (b. 1949) of Yonkers NY, born in Montreal; ACBL field representative and national tournament director, began directing 1969 and achieved his current rating in 1979.

WEINSTEIN, Steven M. (Steve) (b. 1964) of Upper Montclair NJ, stock options trader. WBF World Master, placed 5th Bermuda Bowl 1991, 14th World Open Pairs 1986. At age 17 he was the youngest player ever to win an NABC. King of Bridge 1982. Won Life Master Pairs 1981, Reisinger 1984; Blue Ribbon Pairs 1987; Open Swiss Teams 1992; Open BAM Teams 1995; Open Pairs II 1995; placed 2nd GNOT 1991; Vanderbilt 2000; Open Pairs II 1999; Reisinger 1995; Blue Ribbon Pairs 1994, 2000. Won Pan Am Pair Trials 1991, Cavendish Invitational Pairs 1993, 96, 99. Won Cavendish Teams 1009, 99, placed 2nd U.S. Team Trials 2000, Cap Gemini 2000.

WEINSTEIN, Sue A. (b. 1938) of Glenview IL, administrative secretary for Chicago Contract BA 1975-97, former teacher of the blind and partially sighted. Placed 10th World Women's Pairs 1986. ACBL Diamond Life Master, won North American Women's Swiss 1984, 97; Women's KO Teams 1988, 96; Life Master Women's Pairs 1991; placed 2nd Women's KO Teams 1978, 79, 81.

WEINSTEIN-GORSEY, Carole (b. 1947), of Acton MA, insurance broker. District 25 recorder 1998, won 16 regionals.

WEISBACH, Dean (Mrs. Frank) (1911-1998) of Redmond WA, ACBL Operations Division manager 1970-1976; was first women to achieve the rank of national tournament director 1956-1970.

WEISBACH, Frank (1906-1981) of Cincinnati OH, was a leading Midwest player and expert analyst. Life Master #80, won the Life Master Pairs 1947, placed 2nd Spingold 1951.

WEISS, Albert (Dingy) (1900-1981) of Miami Beach FL. Won Open Pairs 1939, 51; Men's Teams 1946; Vanderbilt 1963, 65; placed 2nd Master Individual 1945; Life Master Pairs 1949, 62; Men's Teams 1952; Spingold 1953, 72.

WEISS, David J. (b. 1944) of Pasadena CA, psychology professor, author of *BRIDGE: Parity Leads in Defence;* contributor to *International Popular Bridge Monthly, Bridge World, Southern California Bridge News,* and *Australian Bridge.* Placed 2nd Reisinger 1981, won more than 20 regionals..

WEISS, Larry A. of Vista CA, retired attorney, former ACBL photographer; author of several *Bridge World* articles and is the originator of the Weiss Convention and Simplified Club System. which is described in his book *The Simplified Club.* Diamond Life Master, placed 2nd Mixed Pairs 1970.

WEISS, Lawrence (Larry) (1905-1979) of Brookline

MA, attorney. Was chairman of the committee to revise ACBL bylaws in 1949 and is credited with devising administrative methods used by the ACBL since then. A former ACBL vice president and president of the New England Bridge Conference, he authored *Contract Bridge: The Bidding Structure.*

WEL, Rob van (b. 1962), of Sittard, The Netherlands, tax employee. WBF World Master. World Junior Team champion 1987. European Junior Team champion 1986.

WELCH, Lawrence J. (Larry) (b. 1895) of Indianapolis IN, retired realtor and appraiser, LM #79; won the Chicago (now the Reisinger) 1935 and many regionals.

WELLAND, Roy of New York City, options trader. 2nd Spingold 2000, Rookie of Year 1986. Won Cavendish Teams 2001, won 17 regionals.

WELLS, Nell (formerly Childs) (d. 1987) of San Francisco CA, bridge teacher. LM #168 in 1949, 1st woman Life Master on Pacific coast. Won Barclay Trophy 1946, 51, 55. Won numerous regionals.

WELTMAN, Dr. Harold S. (b. 1931) of Kingston PA, dentist, past president of Unit 120 and District 4; placed 2nd Amateur Men's Pairs 1976.

WENDT, Edward G. Jr. (Jay) (b. 1928) of New York City, insurance company executive, placed 2nd the Chicago (now the Reisinger) 1961.

WERDELIN, Stig (b. 1937) of Copenhagen, Denmark, Supreme Court attorney. WBF World Master. Placed 3rd World Team Olympiad 1984, 2nd European Teams 1979, 3rd 1961. Represented Denmark more often than any other person. More than 30 national titles including Open Teams 16 times and Open Pairs 8 times.

WERNER, Einar of Stockholm, Sweden, doctor of mathematics. Placed 2nd Bermuda Bowl 1950, representing Europe, and 1953, representing Sweden. Won European Teams 1939, 1952, 2nd 1948, 49, 50. Many national titles. Secretary Swedish Bridge League 1939-1964. Chairman WBF Committee on international matchpoints and assisted in their subsequent 1961 revision. (see KOCK-WERNER REDOUBLES.)

WERNZ, Timothy C. (b. 1943) of Minneapolis MN. Editor *Viking, Gopher Bridge News,* won 30 regionals.

WESTCOTT, Frank (1901-1974) of North Attleboro MA, engineer and contractor. ACBL president 1960, chairman of Board 1961, Honorary Member 1968, former member of the ACBL Board of Directors, president New England Bridge Conference and Eastern Massachusetts BA. Life Master #152, npc of the North American international team 1961, 64; placed 2nd Men's Teams 1964. Won Inter-City matches 1970, 71, 72, 73 for Boston.

WESTERHOF, Jan (b. 1954) of Groningen, the Netherlands, economics teacher. WBF World Life Master. Won Bermuda Bowl 1993. Won several national titles.

WESTFALL, David L. (b. 1950) of Spokane WA, wine dealer, owns bridge studio. President District 19 1983-84, president Spokane Unit 1980-82, member Board of Governors 1980-82, won 25+ regionals.

WESTHEIMER, Gerald J. (Jeff) (b. 1934) of New York City, commodity specialist. Won Reisinger 1969, placed 2nd Vanderbilt 1968, 69; Spingold 1969. Won Cavendish Invitational 1976.

WESTHEIMER, Valerie of New York City. Won Women1s Pairs 1998; Women1s Swiss Teams 2000, 2nd 1997.

WESTRA, Berry (b. 1961) of Rotterdam, The Netherlands, bridge teacher and author. Won Bermuda Bowl 1993. WBF World Life Master. 3rd World Teams 1992. One of Europe's leading players. World Junior Team champion 1987. European Junior Team champion 1986. Represented The Netherlands in 1 other world championship and 3 European Championships. Many national titles. Contributor to *IMP Bridge.*

WESTROM, Ann B. of Monroe LA. District 10 president, Unit 211 president, 15+ regionals.

WETZLAR, Edwin A. (d. 1934) of New York City, a leading personality in the early years of whist and bridge. Won Vanderbilt 1928, Master Mixed Teams 1933; placed 2nd Vanderbilt 1929; won AWL Open Pairs 1931, 33. Board member of the American Whist League.

WEXLER, Susan M. (b. 1951) of New York City, bridge teacher, bridge professional, formerly legal administrator. Won Women's KO Teams 1998, Women's Pairs 1997; placed 2nd Women's BAM Teams 1998, Women's KO Teams 1996, Women's Pairs 1996.

WEYANT, William S. (Bill) (b. 1920) of Cincinnati, ACBL associate national tournament director, began directing in 1962 and achieved current rating in 1972. A former scientist in charge of Antarctic atmospheric research, he was awarded a Congressional medal in 1960. Mount Weyant, Antarctica, was named for him.

WHALEN, Vivian (formerly Lavery) of Jupiter FL, bridge club owner, placed 2nd Women's Teams 1976, North American Women's Swiss 1984; Master Mixed Teams 1990.

WHEELER, Sally D. (b. 1954) of The Woodlands TX, CPA. Won Women's Pairs 1988, Women's KO Teams 1986; placed 2nd Women's KO 1988; 4th Venice Cup 1987.

WHITE, Charles H. (1908-1984) of Ft Lauderdale FL, retired advertising agency executive, won Open Pairs 1949; ACBL Board of Directors member 1951-77, president of Florida Unit 1961, 63. Sunday columnist of *Ft. Lauderdale News* for many years, formerly edited and published *Florida Bridge News.*

WHITE, Edward (b. 1937) of Grand Blanc MI, president management company. Diamond Life Master, won 20 regionals.

WHITE, Effie L. (formerly Long) (1918-1989) of Mason TX, tournament director and Goren bridge teacher, associated with Charles H. Goren for many years, she conducted the Goren national forums in New York 1968-70 and numerous cruises 1965-77; was selected as coordinator of the Goren Teacher Society in 1965; co-authored with Goren *Introduction to Bridge* and was associate editor of *Goren Teacher Manual.* Past president of ABTA, wrote articles for the ABTA *Quarterly, Popular Bridge*; was columnist for local newspapers.

WHITE, Paul of Edmond OK, retired chemical engineer. Diamond Life Master, won 16 regionals.

WHITE, Robert (b. 1946) of Raleigh NC, investment manager. Diamond Life Master, former president Middle Atlantic Bridge Conference, won 30+ regionals.

WHITEHEAD, Wilbur C. (Herier) (1866-1931) of New York City, was one of the world's greatest bridge authorities. He was president of the Simplex Automobile Company, but bridge held such a fascination for him that he retired from business to devote his whole life to bridge in 1910. At that time he was living in France and wrote his first publication, *Royal Spades.* A second book was published in London in 1913. His first book appearing in America was *Whitehead's Convention of Auction Bridge* in 1914. Inventor of many of outstanding conventions of bidding and play, quick trick table of card

values, Whitehead system of requirements for original bids and responses, Whitehead table of preferential leads. Instrumental in standardizing procedures in auction bridge and later in contract bridge. Member of team that won Vanderbilt 1928, the first year it was in play, 2nd following year. Contributing editor *The Bridge World.* Published several books including *Auction Bridge Standard,* which explained the Whitehead System.

WHITESEL, William F. (b. 1940) of Coeur d'Alene ID, bridge professional, farm manager. Diamond Life Master, won 50 regionals.

WHITMAN, Michael R. V. (b. 1944) of San Francisco, investment executive, fisherman, motorcycling enthusiast. West Coast rubber bridge fixture since late Sixties. Won Open BAM Teams 1998, WBF Zonal Open Pairs 1994; 2nd Spingold 1998. Played on 5-man pickup team which won 1992 Open BAM Teams but was relegated to npc when unable to return from business detour in time to play final session. Won more than 30 regionals.

WHITWORTH, George F. (1949) of Coarsegold CA, retired systems analyst. Diamond Life Master, placed 2nd Mixed Pairs 1997, won 41 regionals.

WHOLEY, Jack (b. 1946) of Albany CA, attorney, Peace Corps volunteer to the Philippines 1968-70; won Open BAM Teams 1990.

WIDENGREN, Britta (b. 1913) of Kitzbhel, Austria, born in Sweden, retired managing director. Placed 2nd Venice Cup 1991, represented Austria on 3 other occasions. Nordic Women's Team champion 1948. Retired from bridge 1958-72, when she moved to Austria and resumed play. Her Venice Cup silver medal in Yokohama in 1991 seems to make her, at 78, the oldest person ever to finish 1st or 2nd in a major world championship.

WIDMAN, Nancy R. (b. 1945) of Briarcliff Manor NY, computer and software marketing. Won Women's Pairs 1991, 96.

WIEBE, Lavern E. (b. 1960) of Madison WI, project manager, won Non-Life Master Swiss

WIGNALL John (b. 1932) of Christchurch, New Zealand, born in England, sharebroker. WBF World Master. Represented New Zealand in 3 World Team Olympiads, 3 Bermuda Bowls and 8 Far East Championships. Won all New Zealand national titles, many more than once. President Zone 7 (South Pacific) since 1986. Vice president WBF Executive Council and member of WBF Laws Commission. Member of WBF Committee of Honor, former president New Zealand CBA. Bridge correspondent *Christchurch Press* since 1966 and *Otago Daily Times* since 1970. Member New Zealand Order of Merit for services to the sport of bridge.

WIJAYA, Yasin (b. 1940) of Jakarta, Indonesia, billiard center manager. Won PABF (Far East) Teams 1972, 79, 84. Represented Indonesia in 6 world championships and more than 7 other zonal championships. Won more than 9 national titles including Open Teams 4 times.

WILDAVSKY, Adam (b. 1960) of Jackson Heights NY, independent computer consultant. A student of Objectivism, believes the philosophy of Ayn Rand is superb for bridge players and that it produces positive results at the table. Won Blue Ribbon Pairs 1992, 97, 3/4 in Vanderbilt 2000. Greater New York Team Player of Year 2000, won more than 50 regionals. Chairman of GNYBA Board 3 years. District 25 recorder 1983-1985. Contributor to NABC daily bulletins, *The Bridge Bulletin, Bridge Today.*

WILDY, Marion Edwin (1910-1978) of Aiea HI, bridge

teacher and tournament director. First black ACBL Life Master (#1225, 1956). President Honolulu Unit 1964.

WILEY, Lois (Mrs. Kent) of Beverly Hills FL, chiropractic physician, the most successful blind player, was a familiar sight at tournaments with her seeing-eye dog. Won numerous regional events. See HANDICAPPED PLAYERS.

WILKERSON, Dale C. of Lafayette CA, travel agent, retired bridge club manager. 25+ regionals.

WILKINS, Robert H. (Bob) (1911-1993) of Memphis TN, ACBL executive, served organized bridge in various capacities for many years. Became a tournament director in 1952 and held the rating of national tournament director in 1965 when he was appointed ACBL tournament coordinator. From 1968 to 1978 he was director of ACBL elections and director of communications for the ACBL Board of Directors. He also served as executive secretary of the ACBL Charity Foundation 1969-1973. Wilkins contributed to many bridge publications, including the Chicago CBA *Kibitzer* and the ACBL *Bridge Bulletin.* Past president of Chicago CBA.

WILKINSON, Charles D. (Chuck) (b. 1944) of Ridgeland MS, investment advisor (CFA), bridge club owner/manager. Member ACBL Board of Directors, was the founder and editor of the Jackson Bridge Club newsletter, past president of District 10 and Mississippi Bridge Association. Won District 10 GNOP 1985.

WILKINSON, Jenny of New Zealand. WBF World Master. Won PABF (Far East) 1985, 90; Zone 7 playoff 1985, 87, 91. Won many national titles.

WILKOSZ, Andrzej (b.1935) of Krakow, Poland, retired scientist. WBF World Life Master. Won Rosenblum Teams 1978, 2nd World Senior Teams 1998, 2nd European Teams 1970, 4th World Open Pairs 1978. 2nd European Senior Teams 1995, 1997. Won World Senior Teams 2000. Represented Poland in many World and European Championships. Author of one bridge book, journalist *Brydz* magazine. Won many national titles.

WILLARD, Sylvie (b.1952) of Paris, France, bridge organizer. WBF World Life Master, 2nd World Women's Teams 1987, 3rd 1985; 3rd Venice Cup 1995. Won European Women's Teams 1983, 85, 87, 95. Represented France in 3 other world championships and 4 other zonal championships. Many national titles.

WILLIAMS, Alice M. (b. 1931) of Turtle Creek PA. Won 22 regionals.

WILLIAMS, Don R. (b. 1931) of Kansas City MO, economist, placed 2nd Men's Teams 1962.

WILLIAMS, Joyce of Chicago, retired schoolteacher, bridge teacher (often to children). Represented U.S. in world championship events. 4th in overall ABA masterpoint rankings. Top ABA woman player more than times in masterpoint rankings. Annual award named for her. 7 consecutive wins in *The Bridge World Challenge the Champs.*

WILLIAMS, Mary C. (formerly Philley) (b. 1927) of Leander TX, retired attorney. In the Fifties she worked on the National Laws Commission with John Gerber, formulating the new Laws of Bridge and with Emma Jean Hawes on the New Conventions Committee; former secretary and vice president of District 16 and was the first editor of its publication, *Scorecard;* served as first alternate to ACBL Board of Directors from District 16 for many years; one of the founders and first vice president The Forum for Women in Bridge. Recipient in 1991 of the Oswald and James Jacoby Service Award for Dis-

trict 16. Placed 2nd Master Mixed Teams 1964, Women's KO Teams 1984.

WILLIAMS, Margaret of New York City, pharmaceutical division manager. Served on Board of Governors and as first alternate district director. Won more than 50 regionals including Goldman Pairs.

WILLIAMS, Phyllis (1907-1990) of London, England. Won European Women's Teams 1950, 51, 52 and represented Britain in 6 other zonal championships. Won several national titles. As Phyllis Fletcher, represented Wales in Camrose Trophy 1938-39.

WILLIAMS, Robert Edward (1917-1974) of Sydney, Australia. Represented Australia 1960. National wins included Open Teams 6 times. Handsetter and organizer of World Par Championships 1961, 1963. Joint author of Laws of Par Point Contract Bridge 1963. Vice-president Australian Bridge Council.

WILLIAMSON, Mrs. Vivian (b. 1912) of Roswell NM, bridge teacher, won Women's Pairs 1973, won with her daughter, Ann Economidy, the only mother-daughter to have won this event.

WILLIS, Dave G. (b. 1947) of Orleans ON, bridge teacher, bridge club manager, runs land and sea cruises. Won CNTC 1990, COPC 1988, 96; represented Canada 1991 Bermuda Bowl, has had same partner John Valliant, since 1966, bridge columnist *Ottawa Citizen,* editor of Unit 192 *The Recap* for 6 years, won 15+ regionals.

WILSON, Bertram S. (Bert) (b. 1915) of Clearwater FL, magazine editor, freelance writer, bridge columnist and lecturer, Travel with Goren cruise ship lecturer since 1965. Co-author of *Hold our Bridge Hands* and the originator of Wilson 2 ♦.

WILSON, Chris H. of Phoenix AZ. ACBL president 1985, chairman of the Board 1986; member of the ACBL Board of Directors 1977-89; president of the Western Conference and Phoenix Unit for four terms each. One of the founders of District 17 Association in 1969, she was a member of its Board and executive committee until 1989. Wilson served the longest term as president, presiding over 4 NABCs instead of 3 when the Board changed the time of the presidency. Chairperson of 1971 Fall North American Championships.

WILSON, Keith A. (b. 1949) of Louisville KY, corporate executive, won North American Swiss 1991, won 35+ regionals..

WILSON, Mike A. (b. 1950) of Vancouver BC, stockbroker, won several regionals. Plays bridge with his toes. (see HANDICAPPED PLAYERS.)

WILSON, Walter T. (b. 1910) of Auburndale FL, bridge teacher and writer, ACBL associate national tournament director since the mid-Fifties.

WILTON, Betty (b. 1928) of Lutz, Florida. Retired mechanical engineer, currently bridge director. 2nd Silver Ribbon Pairs 1994, won many regional events.

WILTON, Herbert C. (b. 1933) of Cincinnati OH, born in Vienna; retired computer scientist, former president and secretary of Cincinnati BA. Diamond Life Master. Placed 2nd Master Mixed Teams 1958, Silver Ribbon Pairs 1994. Won 35+ regionals.

WINGEARD, Robert O. (b. 1939) of Colorado Springs CO, assistant director, operations support, headquarters NORAD, member ACBL Board of Directors since 1990, president Western Conference 1983-84, District 17 1976-79, Unit 360 1972-75, 1988. Writes column for the District 17 *Scorecard*, Western Conference *Forum* and served as editor of the *Peak Kibitzer* during the 1960s and 70s.

WINKLER, Dr. Peter (b. 1946) of Madison NJ, director of research group in mathematics and theoretical computer science for Bell Communications; discovered Encrypted Signals and has written a number of articles for the *Bridge World* and *Bridge Magazine*. Former Navy cryptographer.

WINSLOW, Thomas Newby (1861-1942) of East Orange NJ, bridge author and system-maker. His system, introduced in a series of booklets beginning in 1930 and in the book *Win with Winslow*, anticipated the Four Aces System in its 1 1\2 -1-1\2 point-count and canape in showing the lowest four-card suit first, regardless of the strength of that suit.

WIRGREN, Anders (b. 1951) of Lund, Sweden, bridge writer and editor. WBF World Master. Placed 3rd Rosenblum Teams 1986. Represented Sweden in 2 other world championships. 2nd 1976 European Junior Teams, 1973 Nordic Junior Teams, 1988 Nordic Teams. Won Cavendish Invitational 1991. 11 national wins. Bridge columnist *Arbetet Nyheterna, Hallandsposten* and *Helsingbors Dagblad*. Contributes to many bridge magazines and twice won IBPA Award for best article of year. Authored 8 bridge books and 2 chess books. Swedish junior chess champion 1968.

WISDOM, William E. (b. 1949) of Salisbury NC, Social Security claims representative. Past president Central Caroline Unit, Diamond Life Master with more than 10,800 MPs, placed 2nd Intercollegiates 1971, won 15+ regionals.

WISE, William G. (b. 1945} of Warren MI, material management. Won 16 regionals.

WISEMILLER, James P. (b. 1943) of Fountain Valley CA, systems consultant; won Open Pairs 1965.

WISER, John (b. 1926) of Beaconsfield PQ, former bridge club owner and retired ACBL national tournament director, a rank achieved in 1979. From 1961-1963 was director of bridge TV show. Wiser began his bridge career in 1950, and with his even temper and quiet demeanor spent many years specializing in appeals at NABCs and other tournaments. Accredited WBF tournament director since 1972. Contributed several articles to ACBL *Bridge Bulletin* column *Ruling the Game*.

WITEK, Marek (b. 1957) of Katowice, Poland, engineer, owner of a construction firm. WBF World Master. 2nd World Transnational Open Teams 1997. Won many national titles.

WITTES, Jon (b. 1942) of Claremont CA, school psychologist, member ACBL Appeals Committee. WBF World Master, won World Mixed Pairs 1986, placed 7th 1990. Grand Life Master with 13,227 MPs as of 3/2001 Won Reisinger 1985, GNOT 1998; placed 2nd North American Men's Swiss 1982, 83; Spingold 1989. Won 50+ regionals.

WITTES, Pamela S. (Pam) (b. 1944) of Huntington Beach CA, clothing store owner, WBF World Master, won World Mixed Pairs 1986, 7th 1990, placed 4th Venice Cup 1991, won Pan-Am Women's Teams 1992. Diamond Life Master, won USWBC (Women's Team Trials) 1991; Women's KO Teams 1989, 96, North American Women's Swiss 1991, 97; placed 2nd North American Swiss, Women's BAM Teams 1987; Women's KO Teams 1990, 97.

WODNIANSKY, Alexander (Axi) (b. 1967) of Vienna, mathematician. European Junior Pair champion 1991. Represented Austria n European Teams 1991 and 3 other European events. Won Austrian Life Master Individual 1986, Mixed Pairs 1992.

WOHLIN, Jan (1924-1999) of Stockholm, Sweden, bridge teacher. WBF World Life Master. Placed 2nd Bermuda Bowl 1950, representing Europe, and 1953, representing Sweden. Won European Teams 1952, 2nd 1948, 49, 50 and represented Sweden on other occasions. Won many Nordic titles and 9 Swedish titles. Co-inventor of Efos System. Co-author of 2 books. Regular IBPA contributor.

WOLD, Edward M. (Eddie) (b. 1951) of Houston TX, bridge professional. WBF World Master, placed 3rd Rosenblum Teams 1978, 9th 1990; 4th Bermuda Bowl 1983, World Open Pairs 1986. Won McKenney Trophy (now the Barry Crane Top 500) and the International Team Trials 1982, tied with Jeff Meckstroth in Barry Crane Top 500 1996. Won 2nd USBC 1985. Grand Life Master with 37,829 MPs as of 3/2001, #5 in ACBL behind Paul Soloway, Mike Passell, Mark Lair and Jeff Meckstroth. Won GNOT 1977, 81; Spingold 1977, 84; Vanderbilt 1979, 82; Men's BAM Teams 1984, 87; Reisinger 1985; Mott-Smith Trophy 1989; Lou Herman Trophy, Master Mixed Teams 1990; Open Swiss 1991; placed 2nd Reisinger 1980, 90, 97; Master Mixed Teams 1984, 94; Open BAM Teams 1990, 2000; Open Pairs I 1993; Open Swiss Teams 1998; Life Master Pairs 1994; GNOT 1998. Won Mott-Smith Trophy 1998. Won more than 600 regionals.

WOLFE, Edward C. (1883-1972) of Cleveland OH, was expert writer whose success at whist and auction bridge helped make him one of the earliest of the recognized authorities on contract bridge. A member of the Advisory Council of Bridge Headquarters, he helped draft the Official System. After Culbertson's defeat of Lenz, he joined the Culbertson staff, organizing teachers' conventions and lecturing. Former contributing editor to *The Bridge World* and *Bridge*, authored *The Play of the Cards at Contract Bridge*.

WOLFF, Betsey Y. (b. 1937) of Dallas TX, consultant and bridge professional. Won World Mixed Teams 1972; placed 2nd Women's Pairs 1971, 82; Women's Teams 1973; North American Women's Swiss 1988.

WOLFF, Robert S. (Bobby) of Dallas TX, business consultant, professional bridge player, syndicated bridge columnist, author. Member ACBL Hall of Fame. WBF Grand Master, ranked #3 in world. Grand Life Master with 24,410 MPs as of 3/2001, #13 in ACBL, member ACBL of Fame, member ACBL Board of Directors representing District 16 1981-1992 and served as ACBL president 1987, chairman of the Board 1988. Served on WBF Executive Council 1988-94, was WBF president 1992-94. Has also served as tournament recorder at NABCs and is the author of the ACBL Active Ethics program. Has won 11 world titles - Bermuda Bowl 1970, 71, 77, 83, 85, 87, 95; World Mixed Teams 1972; Open Pairs 1974; Open Teams 1988; World Senior Teams 2000; the only player to have won world championships in 5 different categories. Placed 2nd World Open Teams 1972, 80, 92; Bermuda Bowl 1973, 74, 75, 97; 3rd Rosenblum Teams 1978, 1982 and has had other high finishes in world events.

Won Pan-American Invitational 1974, 76, 77; USBC (Team Trials) 1983, 85, 87, 92, 93, 95, 97; Spingold 1969, 79, 82, 83, 89, 90, 93, 94, 95; Reisinger 1970, 78, 79, 88, 93, 94, 95; Vanderbilt 1971, 73, 96; Men's BAM Teams 1972, 73, 1984, 88; Mott-Smith Trophy 1973; GNOT 1975, 77, 86; Fishbein Trophy 1979; Blue Ribbon Pairs 1984. Placed 2nd Life Master Pairs 1960, 68; Reisinger

1964; Spingold 1967, 70; Men's Teams 1969, 80; Vanderbilt 1981; Men's BAM Teams 1989; Open Swiss 1992. Wrote, programmed and developed *Bridge Bidding* and *Bridgetrix* programs with Neil Cohen for use on home computers, developed the Wolff Sign-Off Convention. Has been on 3 TV bridge programs and contributed to *Play Bridge With the Aces* and *Winning Bridge*, and the videos *Secrets of Successful Bridge*. See ACES TEAM.

WOLFSON, Don of Aurora OH, won Open Individual 1960.

WOLFSON, Jeffrey (Jeff) of Northbrook IL, options securities trader. WBF World Master. Placed 3rd Bermuda Bowl 1999, won USBC 1999. Won Life Master Pairs 1994, GNOT 1997, North American Swiss Teams 1999. Npc U.S. team Bermuda Bowl 1993.

WOLNY, Henryk (1947- 1993) of Slupsk, Poland, bridge professional and teacher. WBF World Master. Won World Team Olympiad 1984. Represented Poland in many World and European Championships. Won many national titles.

WOLPERT, Charles M. (b. 1921), bridge teacher, director. President Unit 210 1985-86, has directed more than 200 bridge cruises

WOMACK, Paul (1835) of Bella Vista AR, retired director of international sales U.S. Army Aviation. Diamond Life Master, won 45+ regionals.

WOMACK, Shawn Y. See QUINN, Shawn.

WONG, John P. (b. 1928) of Rowland Heights CA, born in China, formerly of Japan and Taiwan, computer specialist, bridge teacher; Japan's first Life Master. Former vice-chairman of Japan Contract Bridge League and former editor of its publication. He represented Taiwan in the World Olympiad 1964 and represented Japan in the Far East Championships 1958-1964, winning Far East Open Pairs 1961 and placing second in Open Teams 1958, 64. Won the Takamatsu Open Teams 1955, 56, 62; *Japan Times* Cup 1959, 60, 61, 63, Mixed Pairs 1960; Master Individual 1961, Trial Pairs 1962. Diamond Life Master, won 40+ regionals.

WONG, Thomas (b. 1943) of Singapore, born in China, engineer. President Singapore CBA since 1983. Represented Singapore in 1 world championships and 2 zonal championships. Several national wins.

WOOD, Nadine K. (b. 1935) of Silver Spring MD, caterer, bridge club director, member ACBL Board of Directors representing District 6; member ACBL Board of Governors, served as chairman 1988-90, ACBL representative to WBF Executive. Has served as president of Mid-Atlantic Bridge Conference 1990-92, president Washington BL 1983-86, tournament chairman of Summer NABCs 1984 and 1993, and as tournament chairman for Washington BL since 1980. WBF World Master. Diamond Life Master, won Women's Pairs 1989, placed 2nd Women's Swiss 1982, North American Swiss, Women's Pairs 1985.

WOOD, Philip A. (Phil) (b. 1921) of Richmond BC, retired ACBL national tournament director, a former baseball writer and statistician, Wood began his directing career in 1954. In 1968 he became the first Canadian to achieve the rating of national tournament director. He has served as tournament manager for District 18 since 1971. Wood also manages country club bridge activity in greater Vancouver, averaging more than 400 tables per month. Manager Vancouver NABC 2000.

WOODS, Jo (1899-1977) of Little Rock AR, bridge

teacher and writer, first president of American Bridge Teachers' association. Wrote many books and booklets for bridge teachers and students including *At the Bridge Table* and *Little Green Book*.

WOODSON, William B. (1921-1989) of Charlotte NC, computer consultant, served as a member of the ACBL Board of Directors 1973-79, president of the Mid-Atlantic BA for two terms and as president and treasurer of Unit 153. He was a special consultant to the ACBL in 1967, was awarded a Certificate of Service by the Board in 1968 and was elected to the South Carolina Bridge Hall of Fame. Inventor of Woodson Two-Way Notrump and the author of *Woodson Two-Way Notrump* and *Woodson Electronic Bidding System*.

WOODWORTH, Robert M. (Woody) (b. 1911) of St. Petersburg FL, attorney, bridge lecturer, teacher, writer; bridge columnist for *St. Petersburg Times* for 20 years and a contributor to bridge publications. Woodworth, was Special Agent, Counter Intelligence Corp, ETO WW II. Life Master #219, past president of Florida Unit, was awarded a prize for bridge articles by IBPA. Diamond Life Master.

WOOLDRIDGE, Jill H. (b. 1939) of Buffalo NY, IRS employee, editor Unit 116 *Bridge Buff*; 2nd in ACBL and 5th world-wide in Epson Pairs 1991;

WOOLDRIDGE, Joel P. (b. 1979) of Buffalo NY, student, won Toronto Mixed Pairs 1990, District 5 NLM-NAOP 1991. Placed 2nd World Junior Teams 1999. Won IMP Pairs 1997. At 11 years and 4 months, Wooldridge became the youngest player ever to achieve the rank of Life Master (Dec. 2, 1990). 1990 ACBL Rookie of the Year with the second highest total ever and believed to be the youngest player to make the Barry Crane Top 500. Also won Homer Schoop youth scholarship 1990.

WOOLES, Kris G. (b. 1950) of Christchurch, New Zealand, solicitor. WBF World Master. Represented New Zealand in 3 world championships and one zonal championship. 12 national wins. World Women's Team Olympiad 2000.

WOOLSEY, Christopher R. (Kit) (b. 1943) of Kensington CA, systems analyst. WBF World Life Master, won Rosenblum Teams 1986, placed 2nd 1982; won World Senior Teams 2000; 6th World Mixed Teams 1974, 12th World Open Pairs 1978; placed 2nd USBC 1989. Woolsey. Grand Life Master with 17,576 MPs as of 3/2001 MPs. Won Blue Ribbon Pairs 1978, 75, 90; Men's BAM Teams 1978, 86, 89; GNOT 1984, Men's Pairs 1985; Lou Herman Trophy, Men's Swiss 1986; Open Pairs 1987, 89; placed 2nd Life Master Men's Pairs 1971, 72; Men's Pairs 1973, 74; GNOT 1977; Spingold 1979, 81, 92; Reisinger 1980; Open Pairs 1981; Vanderbilt 1992. He has also won the Cavendish Invitational Pairs 1979. Author of *Modern Defensive Signals*, *Partnership Defense in Bridge*, *Matchpoints* and co-author of *Clobber Their Artificial Club*.

WOOLSEY, Sally L. (b. 1943) of Kensington CA, retired teacher. Placed 2nd McConnell Teams 1994. Diamond Life Master, won Women's KO Teams 1995, Women's BAM Teams; placed 2nd Mixed BAM Teams 1997, Women's BAM Teams.

WORK, Milton C. (1864-1934) was the outstanding American authority on auction bridge, a noted player and authority on whist and contract bridge. Member ACBL Hall of Fame. From 1887 to 1917 Work practiced law in Philadelphia. In 1917 he took a leave of absence to tour the U.S. with Wilbur C. Whitehead, organizing bridge

competitions and lecturing on bridge, to promote the sale of Liberty bonds. The success of the tour induced him to quit the practice of law and adopt bridge as a career.

Work's whist career began as president of the U of Pennsylvania's whist club where he organized and played in the first duplicate whist team-of-four match ever held between clubs (1881). He helped found the American Whist League (1893), and was captain of the Hamilton Club team of Philadelphia, which won several whist tournaments. Work's first book, *Whist of Today* (1895), demonstrated the clarity of style for which his later books were so admired. He turned to bridge and then to auction bridge as those games became preeminent. His first book on auction bridge (1913) began a series that outsold all other bridge books by a wide margin until the appearance of Ely Culbertson's *Blue Book* in 1930.

From 1917 through 1931, Work was acknowledged the greatest bridge authority. He became a member of the laws committee of the Whist Club (New York) in 1909. He largely wrote and controlled the 1915 auction bridge laws, which revolutionized the scoring, and the 1917 laws, for which the contract bridge principle was first considered and rejected. He was 1927 ACBL Honorary Member , Honorary Chairman of its Laws Committee. Was president of United States Bridge Association (1933-1934) Work was founder and chief editor of the earliest auction bridge magazines, the *Work-Whitehead Auction Bridge Bulletin* (1924-1926) and its successor, the *Auction Bridge Magazine* (1927-29). Assisted by Whitehead, served as chief authority on the first series of bridge games broadcast on radio (1926-29). In 1928 he was paid $7,000 per week to give brief lectures on bridge in the course of vaudeville presentations.

Work's considerable fortune was substantially lost in the stock market crashes of 1929-30, and he resumed some bridge activities from which he had retired. In 1931 he participated in the founding of Bridge Headquarters and the promulgation of the Official System, being chief architect of the system and principal author of its official books. In 1933-34 he resumed tournament play in contract bridge and won 5 consecutive sectional tournaments as a member of a team that included Goren, Olive Peterson, and Fred French.

WRIGHT, Lionel (b. 1953) of London, England. Had a long playing career as a resident of Auckland, New Zealand. WBF World Master. Won WBF Continuous Pairs 1990. Represented New Zealand in 5 other world championships and 5 zonal championships. 7 national wins.

WU, Chia-Hsiang (b. 1954) of Taipei, Taiwan, chemical engineer. WBF World Master. Won Far East Teams 1986, 89, 94, 97, Far East Open Pairs 1989. Represented Taiwan in 8 world championships and 9 zonal Championships.

WYNSTON, Linda (b. 1937) of Toronto ON, secretary, travel agent. Won Canadian Women's Team Championship twice.

X

XIAOPING, Deng. See DENG Xiaoping.

XU, Hongjun (b. 1952) of Shanghai, China, technical employee. WBF World Master. Won Far East Teams 1991,

98; 2nd 1993. Represented China in 6 World championships and 4 zonal championships. Won IOC Grand Prix 1998. Won many national titles.

Y

YAMADA, Akihiko (b. 1946) of Tokyo, Japan, bridge teacher. WBF World Master. Far East champion 1985. Represented Japan in 1 world championship. Won 51 national team titles and 19 national open pair titles.

YANAGIYA, Kensuke (b. 1924) of Tokyo, Japan, foreign affairs officer. Former ambassador to Australia. In 1992, with Japan International Cooperation Agency. JCBL President from 1991.

YANINE, Odette (b. 1945) of Santiago, Chile, bridge teacher. Won South American Women's Teams 1978, 94. Represented Chile in 1 world championship and 11 zonal championships. 2nd-ranked Chilean woman player.

YANKO, Richard F. (b. 1939) of Scottsdale AZ, attorney. Diamond Life Master, placed 2nd GNOT 1974, has won numerous regionals.

YAP, Florence of Makati, Philippines, interpreter. Won Far East Teams 1957, Far East Women's Teams 1979, 82. Represented Philippines in several world and zonal championships. National wins include several Open Teams.

YAP, Robert (b. 1919) of Makati, Philippines, manufacturer. Won Far East Teams 1957. Represented Philippines in 3 world championships and many zonal championships.

YARINGTON, Richard B. (Dick) (b. 1952) of Seattle WA, property manager and bridge teacher. Diamond Life Master, won 15+ regionals.

YAVITZ, Jerome A. of Bay Harbor Island FL, real estate developer. Won Master Mixed Teams 1974, placed 2nd Master Mixed Teams 1964.

YELTON, Carey M., Jr. (b. 1934) of Glencoe IL, financial consultant and restaurateur, Intercollegiate champion 1953, 54.

YI, Hougao (b.1933) of Beijing, China. Chief organizer of 1995 Bermuda Bowl and Venice Cup in Beijing.

YOMTOV, Bernard D. (Bernie) (b. 1946) of Nashville TN, born in Germany, private investor, edited *Partnership Defense*, *Matchpoints* and *Dynamic Defense* and assisted in the editing of the 1980, 81 *World Championship Book*. Won Non-Life Master Men's Pairs 1969; placed 2nd GNOT 1975. Regional wins include District 10 GNOT 1981, Zonal 1975, 81.

YOST, E. Lowell (b. 1922) of Wichita KS, manufacturing company president, WW II Naval pilot; placed 2nd Life Master Men's Pairs 1970.

YOUNG, Sally (Mrs. R. C.) (1906-1970) of Narberth PA, one of the great woman players of all time. Life Master #17, 1st woman to earn Life Master status, member ACBL Hall of Fame. Between 1937 and 1958, set a record by winning the Spring Women's Teams 7 times and finishing 2nd 3 times. Among her other successes were 4 wins in the Chicago (now the Reisinger); 4 wins in the Women's Pairs; 5 wins in the Master Mixed Teams, and one each in the Fall Open and Mixed Pairs. Young's win of the Chicago in 1947 was the only time it was won by a team of all women. The others on that team were Paula Bacher, Jane Jaeger and Kay Rhodes. During the late Thirties she was among the favorite partners of Charles Goren.

YUDIN, Mark E. (b. 1947) of Montreal QB, bridge teacher and tournament director, past president of the Montreal BL. Co-founder of the Sectional-in-Clubs idea. Helped formulate rules for bidding boxes.

YUE, Dr. Wen Y. (b. 1918) of Excelsior MN, born in China, anesthesiologist, won Senior/Advanced Senior Master Pairs 1972.

YUNGMING Chu (b. 1922) of Irvine CA, formerly of Hong Kong, born in Shanghai, China, accountant. Served on board of directors of Hong Kong CBA as masterpoint and prize director, also top masterpoint holder until immigration to U.S. in 1973. Far East Championship Open Teams winner 1959, 2nd 1963, 65, 69; Open Pairs 2nd 1971. Interport Teams winner 1957, 59, 60, 66, 67. 13 Hong Kong championships. Many North American regional championships.

Z

ZALUSKI, Edward (b. 1941) of Ottawa ON, retired computer systems consultant. Authored *Rate Your Team Play*, articles on 2♣ bidding structure for ACBL *Bridge Bulletin*, won CNTC 1990, competed for Canada in Bermuda Bowl 1991. Won 15+ regionals.

ZALUSKI, John (b. 1963) of Nepean ON, system analyst for Environment Canada. Won COPC 1992-93. Won 25 regionals.

ZANKAY, Peter (b. 1919) of Budapest, Hungary, retired catering manager. His book, *Bridge,* published in 1957, revived bridge in Hungary in face of Communist regime which regarded bridge as a capitalistic game. This book, and his later works, caused Hungarian players to adopt Standard American bidding, which became normal in Hungary, with Precision gaining some ground later.

ZAWISZA, Jerzy (1908-1986) of Wilmington DE, retired bridge club manager, placed 2nd Men's Teams 1960.

ZECKHAUSER, Richard J. (b. 1940) of Cambridge MA, professor of political economy. Won Blue Ribbon Pairs 1966; placed 2nd Men's Teams 1968; won Intercollegiate Championships 1961.

ZENKEL, Sabine. See AUKEN, Sabine.

ZEVE, Vic D. (1899-1985) of Wilton Manors FL, retired mortgage broker, won Open Pairs 1952, Men's Teams 1958. Served as president of District 9, author of *Method Bidding.*

ZHANG, Weili (b. 1954) of Beijing, China. WBF World Master, Far East Teams 1991. Represented China in 4 World championships and 2 zonal championships. Npc Chinese Women's Team that placed 2nd Women's Team Olympiad 1996. Won many national titles.

ZHANG, Yalan (b. 1957) of Guangzhou, China, company employee. WBF World Life Master. In 2000, 11th in World Women's rankings. 2nd World Olympiad Women's Teams 1996. 2nd Venice Cup 1997, 3rd 1991. Won Far East Women's Teams 1986, 91, 93, 94, 96, 97, 98. Represented China in 12 World championships. Won many national titles.

ZHANG, Yu (b. 1964) of Zhejiang, China. WBF Life Master, 28th in world women's rankings 2000. 2nd World Olympiad Women's Teams 1996. 2nd Venice Cup 1997. Won Far East Women's Teams 1997, 1998. Represented

China in 3 World championships. Won many national titles.

ZHOU, Jiahong of Shanghai, China, technical employee. WBF World Master. Won Far East Teams 1991. Represented China in 3 World championships and 4 zonal championships. Won many national titles.

ZHU, Xiaoying (b. 1957) of Beijing, China, teacher. WBF World Master. Won Far East Women's Teams 1986. Won many national titles.

ZHUANG, Zejun (b. 1969) of Shanghai, China. WBF World Master. Won Far East Open Teams 1998, IOC Grand Prix 1998. Won many national titles.

ZIA, Mahmood. See MAHMOOD, Zia.

ZIADIE, Victor (b. 1954) of Kingston, Jamaica, attorney. Won 4 CAC titles including Open Teams 1980, 81. Represented Jamaica internationally. Leading Jamaican masterpoint winner 1990-91. Caribbean badminton champion.

ZILIC, John P. (b. 1939) of Houston TX, bridge professional, bridge club owner/manager, teacher, director and insurance underwriter. Houston NABC co-chairman 1978. Grand Life Master with 16,280 MPs as of 3/2001, won Open Pairs 1966, North American Swiss 1988; placed 2nd in Swiss Teams 1978, North American Men's Swiss 1983.

ZILIC, Virginia A. (b. 1939) of Houston TX, born in Venezuela, bridge club director and bridge teacher, co-chairman Houston NABC 1978; placed 2nd Swiss Teams 1978.

ZIMMERMAN, James E. (b. 1942) of Shaker Heights OH, 1st vice president Raymond James Investments, former attorney. ACBL Distinguished Member 1995, one of only two to receive this honor (Lou Bluhm was the other). Member ACBL Board of Directors representing District 5 1973-94, ACBL president 1981, chairman of Board 1982, ACBL representative to WBF Executive 1983-94, WBF vice president 1986-94, president Northern Ohio Unit 1973, chairman National Appeals Committee 1978-80, 1983-90, president ACBL Charity Foundation 1995-99, member ACBL Charity Foundation 1991-99, member Goodwill Committee. As ACBL president he led a group of ACBL members to the first major bridge tournament on Chinese soil in Shanghai 1981. Represented ACBL in world play 1978, 82, 86, 90 94; won 1985 Venice Cup as npc. Grand Life Master with 12,037 MPs as of 3/2001. Won Mixed Pairs 1981, placed 2nd Life Master Men's Pairs 1973, Master Mixed Teams 1975. Has won more than 200 regionals.

ZIPPERT, Ira (b. 1922) of Fort Lee NJ, business executive. Member ACBL Board of Directors for District 24 1984-95, member ACBL Charity Foundation; served 3 terms as president of Greater New York B.A., 2 as president of Nassau/Suffolk BA. Member ACBL Goodwill Committee.

ZIADIE, Victor (b. 1954) of Kingston, Jamaica, attorney. Won five CACBF titles including Open Teams 1980, 82, 97. Represented Jamaica in 1987 Bermuda Bowl. Former Caribbean badminton champion and comic-book collector.

ZIRINSKY, Victor J. (b. 1920) of Hong Kong, merchant. Won Far East Open Teams 1959, represnted Hong Kong on other occasions. Co-founder Far East Bridge Federation and Hong Kong CBA. Originator of Zirinsky Formula and some bidding conventions.

ZMUDZINSKI, Adam (b. 1956) of Katowice, Poland, electronic engineer and bridge trainer. WBF World Life Master. Placed 2nd World Team Olympiad 2000, Bermuda

Bowl 1991, Rosenblum Teams 1994. Won European Teams 1989, 93; London Sunday Times Pairs 1994. Has represented Poland in many world and zonal championships. Won many national titles.

ZOLLER, Raymond G. (Ray) of Prescott AZ, therapist and professional poker player. won Life Master Men's Pairs 1966. A panelist for *The Bridge World* Master Solvers' Club and *You Be the Judge* for many years. Won 20+ regionals.

ZORLU, Nafiz (b. 1954) of Izmir, Turkey, businessman. Represented Turkey in 4 world and 4 zonal championships. 9 national wins.

ZOUGHEB, Loula de See GORDON, Loula de.

ZUCHELLI, Sergio (b. 1934) of Bologna, Italy, pharmaceutical representative, bridge journalist. Won Bermuda Bowl 1975, London Sunday Times Invitational 1974. During 1975 Bermuda Bowl accused of illicit communication through foot signals. (see BERMUDA INCIDENT.)

ZUCKER, Richard N. (b. 1952) of Dobbs Ferry NY, bridge teacher, professional player. Won NAOP 1992, more than 50 regionals including Goldman Pairs twice and Von Zedwitz Teams several times.

ZUCKERBERG, Debbie See ROSENBERG, Debbie.

ZURFLUH, William M. (Willie) (b. 1944) of West Allis WI, bridge professional, retired computer programmer. Editor *Brewer Bridge*, member Greater Milwaukee board of Directors since 1972, 2nd alternate to Board of Directors District 13 1987-90, 1999-. Certified director and club manager.

APPENDIX I
North American Championships
Spring Championships

VANDERBILT KNOCKOUT TEAMS. This originally was a double elimination Open Team event scored by international matchpoints; usually nine or ten sessions. In 1966 the double elimination method was replaced by three qualifying sessions (subsequently reduced to two), followed by single elimination knockout matches. The preliminary qualifying sessions were dropped in 1970. In 1928 it was scored by Board-a-Match, hence the tie.

1928	1-2.	Ralph R. Richards, Gratz M. Scott, Edwin A.Wetzlar, Wilbur C. Whitehead
	1-2.	Abraham Brown, Mrs. Sidney Lovell, Caroline Taylor, Nils M. Wester
1929	1.	Michael T. Gottlieb, Lee Langdon, Jean P.Mattheys, Harry B. Raffel
	2.	Ralph J. Leibenderfer, Gratz M. Scott,Edwin A. Wetzlar, Wilbur C. Whitehead
1930	1.	Ely Culbertson, Josephine Culbertson,Theodore A. Lightner, Waldemar K. von Zedtwitz
	2-3.	Winfield S. Liggett, Walter Malowan,George Reith, Howard Schenken
	2-3.	H. Huber Boscowitz, Oswald Jacoby, Willard S. Karn, P. Hal Sims
1931	1.	David Burnstine, Oswald Jacoby, Willard S. Karn, P. Hal Sims
	2.	Walter Malowan, Jean P. Mattheys, Howard Schenken, Sherman Stearns
1932	1.	Willard S. Karn, P. Hal Sims, Harold S. Vanderbilt, Waldemar K. von Zedtwitz
	2.	David Burnstine, Richard L. Frey, Charles S. Lockridge, Howard Schenken
1933	1.	Phil Abramsohn, Benjamin Feuer, Francis A. Rendon, Sydney Rusinow
	2.	A. Mitchell Barnes, Richard L. Frey, Sam Fry, Jr., Louis H. Watson
1934	1.	David Burnstine, Richard L. Frey, Michael Gottlieb, Oswald Jacoby, Howard Schenken
	2.	H. Huber Boscowitz, Charles H. Goren, Charles S. Lockridge, Johnny Rau
1935	1.	David Burnstine, Michael T. Gottlieb, Oswald Jacoby, Howard Schenken, Sherman Stearns
	2.	Sam Fry, Jr., Edward Hymes, Jr., Merwyn D. Maier, Louis H. Watson
1936	1.	Phil Abramsohn, Irving Epstein, Harry J. Fishbein, Fred D. Kaplan
	2.	Walter Beinicke, Charles H. Goren, Lee Langdon, Jean P. Mattheys
1937	1.	David Burnstine, Oswald Jacoby, Merwyn D. Maier, Howard Schenken, Sherman Stearns
	2.	B. Jay Becker, Theodore A. Lightner, Charles S. Lockridge, Harold S. Vanderbilt, Waldemar K. von Zedtwitz
1938	1.	David Burnstine, Oswald Jacoby, Merwyn D. Maier, Howard Schenken, Sherman Stearns
	2.	B. Jay Becker, Edward Hymes, Jr., Theodore A. Lightner, Charles S. Lockridge, Waldemar K. von Zedtwitz
1939	1.	Melville Alexander, Sigmund Dornbusch, Syl Gintell, Lee Hazen, Harry B. Raffel
	2.	Wingate Bixby, Theodore A. Lightner, Robert A. McPherran, Mrs. S. W. Peck
1940	1.	Edward Hymes, Jr., Charles S. Lockridge, Robert A. McPherran, Harold S. Vanderbilt, Waldemar K. von Zedtwitz
	2.	Al Brodsky, Louis Lipschitz, Herbert Rosenzweig, Alexander Schultz
1941	1.	John R. Crawford, Myron Fuchs, Robert A. McPherran, Sherman Stearns
	2.	B. Jay Becker, Oswald Jacoby, Theodore A. Lightner, Merwyn D. Maier, Howard Schenken
1942	1.	Lester R. Bachner, Sigmund Dornbusch, Richard L. Frey, Lee Hazen, Samuel M. Stayman
	2.	Sam Fry, Jr., Benedict Jarmel, George Rapee, Helen Sobel

1943	1.	Harry Fagin, Harry J. Fishbein, Fred D. Kaplan, Alvin Roth, Tobias Stone
	2.	Phil Abramsohn, Morrie Elis, E. O. Keller, Charles E. Van Vleck, Waldemar K. von Zedtwitz
1944	1.	B. Jay Becker, Charles H. Goren, Sidney Silodor, Helen Sobel
	2.	Richard L. Frey, Lee Hazen, Charles S. Lockridge, George Rapee, Samuel M. Stayman
1945	1.	B. Jay Becker, Charles H. Goren, Sidney Silodor, Helen Sobel
	2.	Edward Hymes, Jr., Theodore A. Lightner, Howard Schenken, Samuel M. Stayman, Waldemar K. von Zedtwitz
1946	1.	John R. Crawford, Oswald Jacoby, George Rapee, Howard Schenken, Samuel M. Stayman
	2.	Samuel Katz, Bertram Lebhar, Jr., Peter A. Leventritt, Simon Rossant, Waldemar K. von Zedtwitz
1947	1.	David B. Clarren, Harry Feinberg, Harry J. Fishbein, Larry Hirsch, Joseph E. Low
	2.	Lee Hazen, Samuel Katz, Bertram Lebhar, Jr., Peter Leventritt
1948	1.	Robert Appleyard, Jay T. Feigus, William M. Lichtenstein, Harry Sonnenblick, Albert Weiss
	2.	Ambrose Casner, Herman H. Goldberg, Fred Hirsch, Mrs. Ira Strasser, Albert Wolfe
1949	1.	Morrie Elis, Harry J. Fishbein, Lee Hazen, Larry Hirsch, Charles S. Lockridge
	2.	B. Jay Becker, Myron Field, Charles H. Goren, Oswald Jacoby, Helen Sobel
1950	1.	John R. Crawford, George Rapee, Howard Schenken, Sidney Silodor, Samuel M. Stayman
	2.	B. Jay Becker, Myron Field, Charles H. Goren, Helen Sobel
1951	1.	B. Jay Becker, John R. Crawford, George Rapee, Samuel M. Stayman
	2.	Barry Crane, Jack Hancock, Emanuel Hochfield, Gloria Turner, Hortense Evans
1952	1.	Ned Drucker, Irvin Kass, Sidney Mandell, Milton Moss, Jesse Sloan
	2.	B. Jay Becker, John R. Crawford, George Rapee, Howard Schenken, Samuel M. Staymen
1953	1.	Richard Kahn, Edgar Kaplan, Peter A. Leventritt, William V. Lipton, Ruth Sherman
	2.	Myron Field, Charles H. Goren, Alvin Roth, Sidney Silodor, Helen Sobel
1954	1.	Dr. Kalman Apfel, Francis P. Begley, Ned Drucker, Sidney Mandell, Milton Moss
	2.	Morrie Elis, Stanley Fenkel, Simon Rossant, Peggy Solomon, Charles S. Solomon
1955	1.	B. Jay Becker, John R. Crawford, George Rapee, Howard Schenken, Sidney Silodor
	2.	Charles H. Goren, Boris Koytchou, Peter A. Leventritt, Harold A. Ogust, Helen Sobel
1956	1.	B. Jay Becker, John R. Crawford, George Rapee, Howard Schenken, Sidney Silodor
	2.	Leonard Hess, Jane Jaeger, Lewis M. Jaeger, William M. Lichtenstein, Joseph E. Low
1957	1.	B. Jay Becker, John R. Crawford, George Rapee, Howard Schenken, Sidney Silodor
	2.	Rudolf Bortstiber, Raoul Lichtenstein, Ozzie J. Ray, Moe Rubenfeld
1958	1.	Harry J. Fishbein, Sam Fry, Jr., Leonard B. Harmon, Lee Hazen, Ivar Stakgold
	2.	Ralph Hirschberg, Richard Kahn, Edgar Kaplan, Norman Kay, Alfred Sheinwold, Charles J. Solomon
1959	1.	B. Jay Becker, John R. Crawford, Norman Kay, George Rapee, Sidney Silodor, Tobias Stone
	2.	Charles H. Goren, Paul Hodge, Peter A. Leventritt, Harold A. Ogust, Howard Schenken, Helen Sobel
1960	1.	John R. Crawford, Norman Kay, Sidney Silodor, Tobias Stone
	2.	Russell Arnold, Edith Kemp, Robert Reynolds, William Seamon, Albert Weiss, Waldemar K. von Zedtwitz
1961	1.	Charles Coon, Robert F. Jordan, Eric R. Murray, Arthur G. Robinson

	2.	Ollie Adams, Harold B. Guiver, Eddie Kantar, Marshall Miles, Ron Von der Porten
1962	1.	Larry Kolker, Carolyn Levitt, Jerry Levitt, Garrett Nash, George de Runtz
	2.	Charles H. Goren, Boris Koytchou, Peter A. Leventritt, Harold A. Ogust, Howard Schenken, Helen Sobel
1963	1.	Harold Harkavy, Edith Kemp, Alvin Roth, Clifford Russell, William Seamon, Albert Weiss
	2.	Harold B. Guiver, Lewis L. Mathe, Erik Paulsen, Ron Von der Porten, Edward O. Taylor
1964	1.	Robert D. Hamman, Eddie Kantar, Donald P. Krauss, Peter A. Leventritt, Lewis L. Mathe, Howard Schenken
	2.	B. Jay Becker, Ivan Erdos, Dorothy Hayden, Kelsey Petterson, Helen Portugal, Morris Portugal
1965	1.	Philip Feldesman, John Fisher, James Jacoby, Oswald Jacoby, Ira S. Rubin, Albert Weiss
	2.	Robert F. Jordan, Edgar Kaplan, Norman Kay, Boris Koytchou, George Rapee, Arthur G. Robinson
1966	1.	Philip Feldesman, Robert D. Hamman, Sami R. Kehela, Lewis L. Mathe, Ira S. Rubin
	2.	Bill Eisenberg, Ivan Erdos, Bobby Goldman, Leonard B. Harmon, Tobias Stone
1967	1.	James Jacoby, Michael S. Lawrence, Lewis L. Mathe, G. Robert Nail, Ron Von der Porten, Lew Stansby
	2.	Sidney H. Lazard, Peter A. Leventritt, Paul Levitt, George Rapee, Howard Schenken
1968	1.	Robert F. Jordan, Edgar Kaplan, Norman Kay, Arthur G. Robinson, William S. Root, Alvin Roth
	2.	Robert D. Hamman, Eddie Kantar, Ira S. Rubin, Gerald J. Westheimer
1969	1.	Gerard F. Hallee, Paul Soloway, John Swanson, Richard Walsh
	2.	Philip Feldesman, Victor Mitchell, Ira S. Rubin, Samuel M. Stayman, Tobias Stone, Gerald J. Westheimer
1970	1.	Edgar Kaplan, Norman Kay, Sami R. Kehela, Sidney H. Lazard, Eric R. Murray, George Rapee
	2.	Bill Eisenberg, Bobby Goldman, Robert D. Hamman, James Jacoby, Michael S. Lawrence, Bobby Wolff
1971	1.	Bill Eisenberg, Bobby Goldman, Robert D. Hamman, James Jacoby, Michael S. Lawrence, Bobby Wolff
	2.	Chuck F. Burger, Eddie Kantar, Kyle Larsen, Ron Von der Porten, Ira S. Rubin, Paul Soloway
1972	1.	Steven Altman, Eugene Neiger, Thomas M. Smith, Alan Sontag, Joel H. Stuart, Peter Weichsel
	2.	Jack Blair, Fred Hamilton, Howard M. Perlman, Paul Soloway
1973	1.	Mark E. Blumenthal, Bobby Goldman, Robert D. Hamman, Michael S. Lawrence, Bobby Wolff
	2.	Larry Cohen, Bill Eisenberg, Eddie Kantar, Dr. Richard H. Katz, Bud Reinhold
1974	1.	David M. Crossley, Robert E. Crossley, Eric Kokish, Joseph Silver
	2.	Ron E. Andersen, Mark D. Feldman, Stephen Goldstein, Merle Tom, Kathie Wei
1975	1.	Roger Bates, Larry Cohen, Dr. Richard H. Katz, John Mohan, George Rosenkranz
	2.	Richard Freeman, Alvin Roth, Clifford Russell, Alan Sontag, Stan Tomchin, Peter Weichsel
1976	1.	Roger Bates, Larry Cohen, Dr. Richard H. Katz, John Mohan, George Rosenkranz
	2.	Malcolm Brachman, Bill Eisenberg, Bobby Goldman, Eddie Kantar, Mike Passell, Paul Soloway
1977	1.	Mike Becker, Mark E. Blumenthal, Fred Hamilton, Michael E. Lawrence, Ron Rubin, John Swanson
	2.	Ron E. Andersen, Gerald Caravelli, Hugh C. MacLean, Milt Rosenberg, Kathie Wei
1978	1.	Malcolm Brachman, Bobby Goldman, Eddie Kantar, Bill Eisenberg, Mike Passell, Paul Soloway
	2.	Mike Becker, Lou Bluhm, George Rosenkranz, Ron Rubin, Thomas K. Sanders
1979	1.	Lou Bluhm, Richard Freeman, Mark Lair, Clifford Russell, Thomas K. Sanders, Eddie Wold
	2.	Ron E. Andersen, Dave Berkowitz, Jeff Meckstroth, Judi Radin, Kathie Wei
1980	1.	Russ Arnold, Robert Levin, Jeff Meckstroth, Bud

		Reinhold, Eric Rodwell
	2.	Ron E. Andersen, Mark Feldman, Eric Kokish, Peter Nagy
1981	1.	B. Jay Becker, Michael Becker, Edgar Kaplan, Norman Kay, Ron Rubin
	2.	Ira Corn, Robert D. Hamman, Fred Hamilton, Ira Rubin, Alan Sontag, Peter Weischsel, Bobby Wolff
1982	1.	James Jacoby, Jeff Meckstroth, Mike Passell, Eric Rodwell, George Rosenkranz, Eddie Wold
	2.	Marty Bergen, Mark Cohen, Jerry Goldfein, Warren Rosner, Luella Slaner
1983	1.	Bill Root, Richard Pavlicek, Norman Kay, Edgar Kaplan
	2.	Eddie Kantar, Bill Eisenberg, Fred Hamilton, Jim Cayne, Alan Sontag
1984	1.	Chip Martel, Lew Stansby, Hugh Ross, Peter Pender
	2.	Cliff Russell, Robert Levin, Curtis Smith, Peter Nagy, Dave Berkowitz, Harold Lilie
1985	1.	Eric Rodwell, Jeff Meckstroth, Ron Rubin, Mike Lawrence, Michael Becker, Peter Weichsel
	2.	Barry Crane, Bobby Nail, Dan Morse, Ira Chorush, Tom Sanders, John Sutherlin
1986	1.	Edgar Kaplan, Norman Kay, Bill Root, Richard Pavlicek
	2.	Jim Whitaker, Chris Compton, Ira Corush, Bart Bramley, Lou Bluhm
1987	1.	Peter Pender, Peter Boyd, Lew Stansby, Hugh Ross, Steve Robinson, Chip Martel
	2.	Jack Schwencke, Drew Casen, Jim Krekorian, Jim Becker, Howard Chandross
1988	1.	Eddie Kantar, Alan Sontag, John Mohan, Roger Bates
	2.	Dave Berkowitz, Billy Cohen, Ron Smith, Zia Mahmood
1989	1.	Ron Rubin, Michael Becker, Bart Bramley, Robert Levin, Lou Bluhm, Peter Weichsel
	2.	Eddie Kantar, Alan Sontag, Dan Rotman, Bill Eisenberg, Larry Cohen, Cliff Russell
1990	1.	Dan Morse, John Sutherlin, Michael Kamil, Ron Gerard, Tom Sanders, Bill Pollack
	2.	Zia Mahmood, Michael Rosenberg, Seymon Deutsch, Dave Berkowitz, Larry N. Cohen, Marty Bergen
1991	1.	Steve Robinson, Peter Boyd, Kit Woolsey, Ed Manfield
	2.	Zia Mahmood, Michael Rosenberg, Seymon Deutsch, Eric Rodwell, Jeff Meckstroth
1992	1.	Andy Goodman, John Mohan, Roger Bates, John Schermer, Neil Chambers
	2.	Steve Robinson, Peter Boyd, Kit Woolsey, Neil Silverman, Chip Martel, Lew Stansby
1993	1.	Howard Weinstein, Peter Nagy, Dan Morse, John Sutherlin, Tommy Sanders, Russ Arnold
	2.	Cliff Russell, Sam Lev, Dave Berkowitz, Bjorn Fallenius, Mats Nilsland, Larry N. Cohen
1994	1.	Seymon Deutsch, Gaylor Kasle, Michael Rosenberg, Zia Mahmood, Chip Martel, Lew Stansby
	2.	Ron Gerard, George Steiner, Edgar Kaplan, Norman Kay, Sidney Lazard
1995	1.	Bill Root, Richard Pavlicek, Michael Polowan, Marc Jacobus
	2.	Edgar Kaplan npc; George Steiner, Joey Silver, Ron Gerard, Michael Kamil
1996	1.	Zia Mahmood, Michael Rosenberg, Seymon Deutsch, Chip Martel, Lew Stansby
	2.	Nick Nickell, Richard Freeman, Bobby Wolff, Bob Hamman, Jeff Meckstroth, Eric Rodwell
1997	1.	Richard Schwartz, Mark Lair, Steve Robinson, Peter Boyd, Paul Soloway, Bobby Goldman
	2.	James Cayne, Mark Feldman, Chuck Burger, Mike Passell, Michael Seamon, Alan Sontag
1998	1.	Richard Schwartz, Mark Lair, Steve Robinson, Peter Boyd, Paul Soloway, Bobby Goldman
	2.	James Cayne, Chuck Burger, Michael Seamon, Mike Passell, David Berkowitz, Larry Cohen
1999	1.	George Jacobs, Ralph Katz, Peter Weichsel, Alan Sontag, Alfredo Versace, Lorenzo Lauria
	2.	Steve Robinson, Peter Boyd, Michael Becker, Mike Kamil, Fred Stewart, Kit Woolsey
2000	1.	Nick Nickell, Bob Hamman, Richard Freeman, Paul Soloway, Eric Rodwell, Jeff Meckstroth
	2.	Steve Weinstein, Zia Mahmood, Robert Levin, Richard Schwartz, Drew Casen, Michael

Rosenberg
2001	1.	Andrew Gromov, Aleksander Petrunin, Cezary Balicki, Adam Zmudzinski
	2.	George Rosenkranz, Sam Lev, John Mohan, Piotr Gawrys, Jacek Pszczola

NORTH AMERICAN PAIRS FLIGHT A.

This is a grassroots event, with the first stage conducted strictly at the club level. Qualifiers then advance to the Unit competition, and the qualifiers advance to the District finals. Two pairs qualify at the District level for the North American final, which is held just prior to the Spring North American Championships.

1979	1.	Arthur Moore, Eric Robinson
	2.	Steve Landen, Larry Mori
1980	1.	Bob Feller, Jeffrey Hall
	2.	Larry N. Cohen, Ron Gerard
1981	1.	Helen Blakey, Robert Blakey
	2.	Mark Feldman, Chip Martel
1982	1.	Bill Nuttig, Ivan Scope
	2.	Richard Pavlicek, Cliff Russell
1983	1.	John Griscom, Jim Felts
	2.	Ron Gerard, Stephen Sanborn
1984	1.	Steve Sion, Harold Stengel
	2.	Marty Bergen, Larry N. Cohen
1985	1.	Peter Boyd, Steve Robinson
	2.	Hugh Ross, Peter Pender
1986	1.	Drew Cannell, G. Sekhar
	2.	Craig Cordes, Tom Daniel
1987	1.	Jan Janitschke, Dick Reed
	2.	Ron Sukoneck, Judi Cody
1988	1.	Jan Martel, Chip Martel
	2.	Mark Cohen, Stasha Cohen
1989	1.	David Caslan, Dennis Clerkin
	2.	Bobby Nail, Dan Morse
1990	1.	Sidney Lazard, Jack La Noue
	2.	Mark Stein, Boris Baran
1991	1.	Mark Stein, Boris Baran
	2.	Pratap Rajadhyaksha, Steve Landen
1992	1.	Jim Krekorian, Rick Zucker
	2-3.	Joe Jabon, Harry Steiner
	2-3.	Howard Weiner, Robert Crafton
1993	1.	James Griffin, Kenneth Schutze
	2.	Iftikar Baque, Mitch Aunitz
1994	1.	James Griffin, Kenneth Schutze
	2.	Ralph Cohen, Reece Rogers
1995	1.	David Berkowitz, Lisa Berkowitz
	2.	Gary Cohler, Jerry Goldfein
1996	1.	Marshall Tuly, James Cunningham
	2.	Gary Cohler, Jerry Goldfein
1997	1.	Aidan Ballantyne, Gordon McOrmond
	2.	Joanna Stansby, Lew Stansby
1998	1.	Ron Sukoneck, Bill Cole
	2.	Marshall Tuly, Jim Cunningham
1999	1.	Ken Schutze, Jim Griffin
	2.	Tom Kniest, Karen Walker
2000	1.	Patty Tucker, Kevin Collins
	2.	Victor King, John Stiefel
2001	1.	Frank Merblum, Doug Doub
	2.	Jill Meyers, Ed Davis

NORTH AMERICAN PAIRS FLIGHT B.

A grass-roots event conducted in the same way as Flight A — limited to players with 2000 masterpoints.

1992	1.	Peter Worley, Kevin Young
	2.	Kathie Blumenthal, Patricia Goldfein
1993	1.	Robert Sewell, Paul Janicki
	2.	Lawrence Gibbons, Gregory Jecker
1994	1.	Brendan Dempsey, Ian Crowe
	2.	Jack Kilby, Ernest Lambertsen
1995	1.	Jay Levy, William Rushmore
	2.	Bill Archambo, Richard Bender
1996	1.	Robert Johnson, David Rosenstein
	2.	Daniel Levi, Samuel Ehrlichman
1997	1.	Bill Drewett, Kirk Twiss
	2.	David Green, Donald Tofte
1998	1.	Brian Gilbert, Adam Beneschan
	2.	Ronald Zajak, Mark Burkhammer
1999	1.	Andy Kaufman, Greg Burch

	2.	Patricia Griffin, Stephen Wood
2000	1.	Mark Chen, Hal Hindman
	2.	Tien-Chun Yang; Fang Wu
2001	1.	Jonathan Weinstein, Walter Lee
	2.	Mike Ralston, Mahesh Rathi

NORTH AMERICAN PAIRS FLIGHT C.

A grass-roots event conducted in the same way as Flight A — open only to non-Life Masters.

1987	1-2.	Bill Thomas, David Deaderick
	1-2.	Bernard Pollack, Leo Austern
1988	1.	Brad Moss, Aaron Silverstein
	2.	Geoffrey O'Connor, Charles Bilick
1989	1.	Warren King, Jeffrey Brown
	2.	Sylvian Descoteauz, Guy Belisle
1990	1.	Philip Leung, Moske Harel
	2.	Deborah Hart, Nate Ward
1991	1.	Eric Greco, Philip Greco
	2.	Bruce Graff, Steve Castellino
1992	1.	Gail Joelson, Alan Kasner
	2.	J. Greg Fowler, Don Herring
1993	1.	Mark Michele, Everett Boyer
	2.	Gabrida Rabiega, Leszek Rabiega
1994	1.	Weizhong Bao, Jingdong Guo
	2.	Duane Tilden, Grace Jeklin
1995	1.	Edward Lee, Brett Roby
	2.	Philip Feng Lu, Xiaodong Zhang
1996	1.	Yue Zuo, Ruoyo Fan
	2.	Carlos Bichara, Rita Bichara
1997	1.	Thomas Franklin, Michael Corker
	2.	Weiming Hu, Alex Lo
1998	1.	Tien-Chun Wang, Fang Wu
	2.	Paul Coulter, Matt Just
1999	1.	James Gun, Harry Schaffer
	2.	Judith Hallowell, Norman Cannon
2000	1.	Meredith Beck, John Johnson
	2.	Rachel Chittaro, Edward Nield
2001	1.	Hailong Ao, Jian-Jian Wang
	2.	David Pettit, Doris Suojanen

OPEN PAIRS.

This four-session event consisting of two qualifying sessions and two final sessions is contested for the SILODOR TROPHY. It became Open Pairs I in 1992.

1958	1.	Leonard B. Harmon, Ivar Stakgold
	2.	Alvin Roth, Tobias Stone
1959	1.	Lewis L. Mathe, Edward O. Taylor
	2.	Harry J. Fishbein, Charles J. Solomon
1960	1.	Robert F. Jordan, Alvin Roth
	2.	Carol Sanders, Thomas K. Sanders
1961	1.	Mark Hodges, Hampton Hume
	2.	Jack Denny, John E. Simon
1962	1.	Robert F. Jordan, Arthur G. Robinson
	2.	Michael N. Michaels, Mike Shuman
1963	1.	Norman Kay, Sidney Silodor
	2.	Daniel Rotman, Ivar Stakgold
1964	1.	Barry Crane, Oswald Jacoby
	2.	Ivan Erdos, Lewis L. Mathe
1965	1.	John Biddle, James P. Wisemiller
	2.	Ivan Erdos, Tobias Stone
1966	1.	Edgar Kaplan, Norman Kay
	2.	Alvin Roth, William Root
1967	1.	Harvey Cohen, Maury Genud
	2.	Philip Feldesman, Lewis L. Mathe
1968	1.	Ronald Blau, Richard Spero
	2.	Harry F. Fishbein, Charles J. Solomon
1969	1.	Richard Freedman, James L. Mathis
	2.	David Sachs, Sue Sachs
1970	1.	Barry Crane, Dr. John Fisher
	2.	Gerald L. Michaud, G. Robert Nail
1971	1-2.	Barry Crane, Dr. John Fisher
	1-2.	Joan Remey, Vincent Remey
1972	1-2.	Barry Crane, Dr. John Fisher
	1-2.	Matt Granovetter, Merle Tom
1973	1.	Michael Hoffman, Jack Rhatigan
	2.	Charlie Peres, Daniel Rotman
1974	1.	Barry Crane, Dr. John Fisher
	2.	Ron E. Andersen, Hugh C. MacLean
1975	1.	Garey Hayden, Daniel Hyland
	2.	Don Piafsky, Dave Saltsman

1976	1.	Terry Hause, Ernest Ivey
	2.	Barry Crane, Dr. John Fisher
1977	1.	Barry Crane, Peter Rank
	2.	John Ashton, Troy Horton
1978	1.	Robert Levin, Mike Passell
	2.	Marty Arndt, Thomas Peters
1979	1.	Jeff Meckstroth, Eric Rodwell
	2.	Larry N. Cohen, Dan Zirker
1980	1.	Paul J. Lewis, Michael Schreiber
	2.	Jim Robison, Stelios Touchtidis
1981	1.	Dan Gertsman, Marc Nathan
	2.	Ed Manfield, Kit Woolsey
1982	1.	Gerald Caravelli, V. Craig Janitschke
	2.	Dan Gertsman, Marc Nathan
1983	1.	Barry Crane, Mike Passell
	2.	Dave Berkowitz, Dan Gerstman
1984	1.	Lou Bluhm, Bart Bramley
	2.	Barry Crane, Gerald Caravelli
1985	1.	Jim Robison, Joey Silver
	2.	John Roberts, Dave Berkowitz
1986	1.	Lew Stansby, Ralph Katz
	2.	Robb Gordon, John Rengstorff
1987	1.	Ed Manfield, Kit Woolsey
	2.	Lyle Poe, Steve Carton
1988	1.	Ron Rubin, Michael Becker
	2.	Bob Hamman, Paul Lewis
1989	1.	Kit Woolsey, Ed Manfield
	2.	Ed Nagy, Jeff Polisner
1990	1.	Don Campbell, Barry Harper
	2.	Randy Joyce, Glenn Lublin
1991	1.	Larry Mori, Henry Bethe
	2.	Zia Mahmood, Fred Chang

(became Open Pairs I)

1992	1.	Jeff Meckstroth, Perry Johnson
	2.	Tony Glynne, S. James Elliott
1993	1.	Russ Ekeblad, Peter Weichsel
	2.	Richard Schwartz, Drew Casen
1994	1.	Lloyd Arvedon, Allan Falk
	2.	Michael Rosenberg, Zia Mahmood
1995	1.	John Strauch, Evan Bailey
	2.	Seymon Deutsch, Tony Forrester
1996	1.	Ralph Katz, Howard Weinstein
	2.	Kit Woolsey, Ed Manfield
1997	1.	Eric Greco, Geoff Hampson
	2.	Geir Helgemo, Tony Forrester
1998	1.	Geir Helgemo, Tony Forrester
	2.	Michael Becker, Mike Kamil
1999	1.	Michael Seamon, Mike Passell
	2.	Petra Hamman, Bob Hamman
2000	1.	Mike Cappelletti Jr., Larry Hicks
	2.	Walter Johnson, Doug Simson
2001	1.	Jim Tritt, Richard Meffley
	2.	Henry Bethe, Varis Carey

OPEN PAIRS II, formerly MEN'S PAIRS.

This four-session event consisting of two qualifying rounds and two final rounds is contested for the WERNHER TROPHY. From 1969 through 1971 it was contested as a three-session championship. In 1992 the event became Open Pairs II instead of Men's Pairs.

1934	1.	David Burnstine, Oswald Jacoby
	2.	Morrie Elis, George Kennedy
1935	1.	Edward M. Cook, Jr., Fred French
	2.	Charles H. Goren, Louis H. Watson
1936	1.	Dr. Richard H. Ecker, Fred D. Kaplan
	2.	Bertram Lebhar, Jr., Samuel Katz
1937	1.	Edward M. Cook, Jr., John C. Kunkle
	2.	Philip Abramsohn, Morrie Elis
1938	1.	B. Jay Becker, Charles H. Goren
	2.	Morrie Elis, Waldemar K. von Zedtwitz
1939	1.	John R. Crawford, Oswald Jacoby
	2.	Henry Chanin, Morrie Elis
1940	1.	Merwyn D. Maier, Robert A. McPherran
	2.	Morrie Elis, Harry J. Fishbein
1941	1.	Joseph E. Low, Simon Rossant
	2.	Joseph Davis, Sidney Silodor
1942	1.	Robert von Engel, Aaron Goodman
	2.	Murray Gross, Dr. William Lipton
1943	1.	Charles H. Goren, Charles J. Solomon
	2.	Dr. Richard H. Ecker, Jr., Fred D. Kaplan

1944	1.	Sigmund Dornbusch, Herman Goldberg
	2.	Ambrose Casner, Ralph Hirschberg
1945	1.	Sylvester Gintell, Lee Hazen
	2.	George Rapee, Samuel M. Stayman
1946	1.	A. Mitchell Barnes, Waldemar K. von Zedtwitz
	2.	Lewis A. Bernard, Jr., Frank Weisbach
1947	1.	Sol Mogal, Tobias Stone
	2.	Morrie Elis, Morris Portugal
1948	1.	Fred Hirsch, Samuel Katz
	2.	Lewis A. Bernard, Jr., Harold Feldstein
1949	1.	Charles H. Goren, Oswald Jacoby
	2.	G. Robert Nail, Joseph G. Ripstra
1950	1.	Phillip A. Briggs, A. Richard Revell
	2.	George Rapee, Sidney Silodor
1951	1.	Milton Q. Ellenby, Emanuel Hochfield
	2.	Clifford Bishop, Alexander Nusinoff
1952	1.	Arthur C. Grau, William A. Rosen
	2.	Harold Harkavy, Tobias Stone
1953	1.	Harold Harkavy, William Root
	2.	John R. Crawford, Waldemar K. von Zedtwitz
1954	1.	Douglas Drury, Eric R. Murray
	2.	Milton Q. Ellenby, Douglas Steen
1955	1.	Douglas Drury, Eric R. Murray
	2.	Ira S. Rubin, Victor Mitchell
1956	1.	Paul Allinger, James Jacoby
	2.	Robert F. Jordan, Robert Sitnek
1957	1.	David C. Carter, John W. Hubbell
	2.	John Gerber, Paul H. Hodge
1958	1.	William Grieve, Ira S. Rubin
	2.	Norman Kay, Sidney Silodor
1959	1.	Harry J. Fishbein, John Gerber
	2.	Erik Paulsen, Mike Shuman
1960	1.	Jack Blair, William Christian
	2.	David C. Carter, Paul H. Hodge
1961	1.	Philip Feldesman, Ira S. Rubin
	2.	Paul Allinger, Lewis L. Mathe
1962	1.	Philip Feldesman, Ira S. Rubin
	2.	Eddie Kantar, Marshall Miles
1963	1.	Sami R. Kehela, B. Wolf Lebovic
	2.	Alphonse Moyse, Jr., Thomas K. Sanders
1964	1.	Ed Don Weiner, G. Gard Hays
	2.	Darryl Pedersen, Don Nemiro
1965	1.	Lawrence Rosler, Jeff Rubens
	2.	Eric R. Murray, Norman Kay
1966	1.	Barry Crane, Peter C. Rank
	2.	Mark Blumenthal, Michael Moss
1967	1.	Richard Lawrence, Art Price
	2.	Eddie Kantar, Sidney Lazard
1968	1.	Kyle Larsen, Edmond Lazarus
	2.	William Passell, David Strasberg
1969	1.	Michael J. Martino, Frank Vine
	2.	Gerald Hallee, Paul Soloway
1970	1.	Richard Kaye, Richard Walsh
	2.	Edgar Kaplan, Norman Kay
1971	1.	Giorgio Belladonna, Benito Garozzo
	2.	Robert Kerr, Jay T. McKee
1972	1.	Stephen W. Robinson, Kit Woolsey
	2.	Paul Heitner, Marshall Miles
1973	1.	Jack E. Kennedy, David Hadden
	2.	Stephen W. Robinson, Kit Woolsey
1974	1.	George Slemmons, George Steiner
	2.	Stephen W. Robinson, Kit Woolsey
1975	1.	Harlow Lewis, Art Waldmann
	2.	Larry Kozlove, John Sheridan
1976	1.	Gerald Caravelli, Larry Cohen
	2.	Jack E. Kennedy, Bobby Wolff
1977	1.	Joseph Fox, Garey Hayden
	2.	David Lehman, Dick Melson
1978	1.	Larry Kozlove, John Sheridan
	2.	Roy Fox, Paul Swanson
1979	1.	Roy Fox, Paul Swanson
	2.	Perry Johnson, Michael Zerbini
1980	1.	Neil Silverman, Peter Weichsel
	2.	Warren Rosner, Stephen Sanborn
1981	1.	Warren Rosner, Allan Stauber
	2.	Bill Eisenberg, Neil Silverman
1982	1.	David Berkowitz, Harold Lilie
	2.	James Barlow, Chuck Carroll
1983	1.	Marty Bergen, Allan Stauber
	2.	Mike Passell, Ron Andersen
1984	1.	Mike Lawrence, Peter Weichsel
	2.	Joel Friedberg, Ethan Stein
1985	1.	Ed Manfield, Kit Woolsey
	2.	Bob Hamman, George Mittelman
1986	1.	Bob Hamman, Paul Swanson

	2.	Robert Levin, Fred Hamilton
1987	1.	Darryl Pedersen, George Steiner
	2.	Zia Mahmood, Chris Compton
1988	1.	Arthur Hoffman, Stephen Shane
	2.	Ken Kranyak, Harry Stratton
1989	1.	Mike Moss, Charles Coon
	2.	Robert Beiles, Sidney Lorvan
1990	1.	Steve Sion, Steve Landen
	2.	Neil Silverman, Mike Smolen
1991	1.	Bob Thomas, Ken Cohen
	2.	JoAnna Stansby, Lew Stansby
		(became Open Pairs II)
1992	1.	Bernie Miller, Mike Lucas
	2.	Geoff Hampson, Mark Molson
1993	1.	Gaylor Kasle, Robert Levin
	2.	Eddie Wold, Dennis Sorensen
1994	1.	Thomas Peters, John Zilic
	2.	Steve Beatty, Curtis Cheek
1994	1.	Thomas Peters, John Zilic
	2.	Steve Beatty, Curtis Cheek
1995	1.	Steve Weinstein, Fred Stewart
	2.	Martin Caley, Peter Schwartz
1996	1.	David Berkowitz, Larry Cohen
	2.	Jackie Buroker, Dick Yarington
1997	1.	Lloyd Arvedon, Allan Falk
	2.	Bart Bramley, Sidney Lazard
1998	1.	Mike Moss, Bjorn Fallenius
	2.	Evan Bailey, Joe Kivel
1999	1.	Eric Rodwell, Jeff Meckstroth
	2.	Robert Levin, Steve Weinstein
2000	1.	Pratap Rajadhyaksha, Steve Landen
	2.	Ken Kranyak, Harry Stratton
2001	1.	Chris Willenkin, Ron Smith
	2.	Joe Kivel, Chris Larsen

This event was held in the Summer North American Championships until 1963. A similar event was held at the Spring NABCs 1958-1962 with the following results:

1958	1.	Norman Kay, Sidney Silodor
	2.	Jack Denny, Richard Harrison
1959	1.	James Pestaner, John Swanson
	2.	Donald A. Oakie, Meyer Schleifer
1960	1.	Frank Hoadley, Julius L. Rosenblum
	2.	Harold Creed, S. Samuel Gould, Jr.
1961	1.	Morton Rubinow, Tobias Stone
	2.	Erik Paulsen, Alex Tschekaloff
1962	1.	Ivan Erdos, Philip Feldesman
	2.	Norman Kay, Sidney Silodor

WOMEN'S PAIRS. This four-session event consisting of two qualifying rounds and two final rounds is contested for the WHITEHEAD TROPHY. From 1969 through 1971 it was contested as a three-session championship.

1930	1.	Olive Peterson, Maud S. Zontlein
	2.	Josephine Culbertson, Elinor Murdoch
1931	1.	Vivi Hanson, Elinor Murdoch
	2.	Mary Clement, Olga Hilliard
1932	1.	Mrs. Jay S. Jones, Olive Peterson
	2.	Florence Fitch, Maud S. Zontlein
1933	1.	Doris Fuller, Mrs. Courtand Smith
	2.	Marie Black, Mary Clement
1934	1.	Helen Bonwit, Matie White
	2.	Ruth Sherman, Mrs. Thomas Stern
1935	1.	Bertine Teichman, Mable Ulbrich
	2.	Doris Fuller, Olive Peterson
1936	1.	Mrs. Jay S. Jones, Sally Young
	2.	Mable Ervin, Doris Fuller
1937	1.	Mable Ervin, Doris Fuller
	2.	Martha Lemon, Mrs. Martin R. West
1938	1.	Helen Sobel, Sally Young
	2.	Phyllis Gardner, Dorothy Roberts
1939	1.	Helen Sobel, Sally Young
	2.	Doris Fuller, Millicent Tansill
1940	1.	Edith Atkinson, Mrs. John Waidlich
	2.	Estelle Drescher, Gussie Planco
1941	1.	Mae P. Rosen, Edith Seligman
	2.	Ruth Horn, Gussie Planco

1942	1.	Mae P. Rosen, Edith Seligman
	2.	Helen Bonwit, Mrs. D. P. Hanson
1943	1.	Mae P. Rosen, Edith Seligman
	2.	Olga Hilliard, Evelyn Lebhar
1944	1.	Ruth Sherman, Margaret Wagar
	2.	Paula Bacher, Kay Rhodes
1945	1.	Peggy Golder, Olive Peterson
	2.	Ruth Sherman, Margaret Wagar
1946	1.	Edith Seligman, Sally Young
	2.	Anne Burnstein, Mrs. G. Rosenbaum
1947	1.	Gratian Goldstein, Josephine Gutman
	2.	Ruth Sherman, Helen Sobel
1948	1.	Gratian Goldstein, Josephine Gutman
	2.	Mildred Cunningham, Mrs. Harry Mason Smith
1949	1.	Kay Rhodes, Ruth Sherman
	2.	Mildred Cunningham, Mrs. Harry Mason Smith
1950	1.	Mrs. John Kelly, Dorothy Thompson
	2.	Reba Buck, Mrs. George P. Ryan
1951	1.	Alwina M. Dunphy, Mrs. Edward Minear
	2.	Mrs. Frank Fooshe, Mrs. Henry C. Wolfe
1952	1.	Shirley Fairchild, Elaine Lee
	2.	Mildred Betzler, Mrs. Michael Hoffman
1953	1.	Mrs. Harold P. Swearingen, Barbara Weiner
	2.	Gretchen Feldstein, Gratian Goldstein
1954	1.	Margaret Alcorn, Sally Neely
	2.	Paula Levin, Mrs. Max Ritter
1955	1.	Kay Rhodes, Margaret Wagar
	2.	Mrs. Carl I. Conklin, Paula Nevins
1956	1.	Kay Rhodes, Margaret Wagar
	2.	Wynne Ecker, Mrs. P. Halbestadt
1957	1.	Kay Rhodes, Margaret Wagar
	2.	Edith Kemp, Terry Michaels
1958	1.	Betty Nail, Phyllis Novak
	2.	Alberta Albersheim, Mrs. M. J. Root
1959	1.	Betty Adler, Dorothy Hayden
	2.	Agnes Gordon, Sylvia Schwartz
1960	1.	Mary Jane Farell, Peggy Solomon
	2.	Mabel Mahoney, Mrs. James Welch
1961	1.	Agnes Gordon, Betty Haddad
	2.	Mrs. Seymour Keith, Rita Seamon
1962	1.	Carol Sanders, Sylvia Stein
	2.	Betty Kaplan, Jacqui Mitchell
1963	1.	Mrs. K. L. Sargent, Mrs. Ray Tobin
	2.	Garner McDaniel, Terry Michaels
1964	1.	Margaret Alcorn, Lucille Patterson
	2.	Ruth Ballantyne, Mrs. Lloyd Scott
1965	1.	Nancy Gruver, Sue Sachs
	2.	Alicia Kempner, Helen Sobel
1966	1.	Virginia Heckel, Edith Kemp
	2.	Garner McDaniel, Terry Michaels
1967	1.	Garner McDaniel, Terry Michaels
	2.	Hermine Baron, Marilyn Johnson
1968	1.	Hermine Baron, Rhoda Walsh
	2-3.	Emma Jean Hawes, Dorothy Hayden
	2-3.	Gloria Cohen, Belle Kauffman
1969	1.	Gale Clarke, Gloria Noszka
	2.	Sallie Johnson, Bee Schenken
1970	1.	Robin Klar, Tina Rockaway
	2.	Jacqui Mitchell, Gail Moss
1971	1.	Amalya L. Kearse, Jacqui Mitchell
	2.	Barbara Brier, Betsey Wolff
1972	1.	Kerri Davis, Rhoda Walsh
	2.	Gail Moss, Judi Solodar
1973	1.	Ann Economidy, Vivian Williamson
	2.	Mary Anderson, Pamela Eckard
1974	1.	Pat Leary, Jan Stansby
	2.	Jacqui Mitchell, Gail Moss
1975	1.	Jacqui Mitchell, Gail Moss
	2.	Hermine Baron, Carol Greenhut
1976	1.	Gail Schaab, Barbara Staton
	2.	Emma Jean Hawes, Dorothy Hayden Truscott
1977	1.	Jacqui Mitchell, Gail Moss
	2.	Hermine Baron, Beverly Rosenberg
1978	1.	Babs Charney, Flo Rotman
	2.	Edith Kemp, Barbara Rappaport
1979	1.	Anne Burnstein, Edith Kemp
	2.	Ann Roberts, Genne Winter
1980	1.	Mildred Boyce, Barbara Norwood
	2.	Hermine Baron, Beverly Rosenberg
1981	1.	Emma Jean Hawes, Dorothy Hayden Truscott
	2.	Roberta Epstein, Rozanne Marel
1982	1.	Hermine Baron, Beverly Rosenberg
	2.	Nancy Alpaugh, Betsey Wolff
1983	1.	Evelyn Levitt, Jo Morse
	2.	Lynne Pollenz, Sue Picus

1984	1.	Judy Tucker, Jacqui Mitchell
	2.	Mildred Breed, Barbara Norwood
1985	1.	Dale Dermer, JoAnne Caplan
	2.	Nadine Wood, Robin Taylor
1986	1.	Edith Freilich, Nancy Gruver
	2.	Peggy Sutherlin, Sharon Osberg
1987	1.	Tobi Deutsch, Kay Schulle
	2.	Carlyn Steiner, Janet Daling
1988	1.	Sally Wheeler, Georgiana Gates
	2.	Jan Martel, Dorothy Truscott
1989	1.	Nadine Wood, Jeanne Elkner
	2.	Janice Seamon, Rita Seamon
1990	1.	Tobi Deutsch, June Deutsch
	2.	Carol Sanders, Betty Ann Kennedy
1991	1.	Leslie Paryzer, Nancy Widman
	2.	Claire Tornay, Kathie Walvick
1992	1.	Cheri Bjerkan, Janice Seamon
	2.	Carol Sanders, Betty Ann Kennedy
1993	1.	Carol Sanders, Betty Ann Kennedy
	2.	Shawn Womack, Jan Cohen
1994	1.	Corinne Kirkham, Ann Kluewer
	2.	Bernace De Young, Ellasue Chaitt
1995	1.	Lila Perlstein, Juanita Chambers
	2.	Ayako Amano, Miho Sekizawa
1996	1.	Nancy Widman, Leslie Paryzer
	2.	Susan Wexler, Margie Gwozdzinsky
1997	1.	Susan Wexler, Margie Gwozdzinsky
	2.	Suzy Burger, Barbara Sion
1998	1.	Judi Radin, Valerie Westheimer
	2.	Carol Simon, Kitty Munson
1999	1.	Ellen Crawford, Harriet Eaton
	2.	Mildred Breed, Shawn Quinn
2000	1.	Joan Stein, Eunice Rosen
	2.	Marilyn Hemenway, Barbara Fellows
2001	1.	Judi Radin, Sylvia Moss
	2.	Tobi Sokolow, Janice Seamon-Molson

This event was held at the Summer North American Championships until 1962. A similar event was held at the Spring NABC 1958-1962 with the following results:

1958	1.	Kay Rhodes, Margaret Wagar
	2.	Mrs. N. L. Cassibry, Ann Smith
1959	1.	Bert Epstein, Blossom Grossblatt
	2.	Betty Coombs, Malvine Klausner
1960	1.	Gretchen Feldstein, Jane Mueller
	2.	Gertrude Eberson, Mrs. M. Jones
1961	1.	May Belle Long, Effie Woods
	2.	Dorothy Hayden, Helen Portugal
1962	1.	Clarice Holt, Mrs. Greeley Warner
	2.	Kay Carter, Mrs. G. M. Sharum

MIXED PAIRS. This event is contested for the ROCKWELL TROPHY. It is a four-session event with two qualifying sessions and two final sessions.

1946	1.	Anne Burnstein, Alvin Roth
	2.	David C. Carter, Frances Carter
1947	1.	Evelyn Ansin, Charles H. Goren
	2.	John R. Crawford, Margaret Wagar
1948	1.	John R. Crawford, Margaret Wagar
	2.	Charles C. Johnson, Mrs. Frank Myer
1949	1.	John R. Crawford, Margaret Wagar
	2.	Paula Bacher, Peter A. Leventritt
1950	1.	Peter A. Leventritt, Ruth Sherman
	2.	William Thiemann, Mrs. William Thiemann
1951	1.	Edith Rosenbloom, Sidney Silodor
	2.	Edward Burns, Shirley Fairchild
1952	1.	Anne Burnstein, Alvin Roth
	2.	Ella Tilles, Jules Tilles
1953	1.	Jewel Hodge, Paul H. Hodge
	2.	John Gerber, Celeste Mounce
1954	1.	Said Haddad, Betty Windley
	2.	Zenobia Allen, John H. Moran
1955	1.	Sidney Silodor, Helen Sobel
	2.	Alicia Kempner, George Rapee
1956	1.	Sidney Silodor, Helen Sobel
	2.	Donald G. Farquharson, Agnes Gordon
1957	1.	Bee Gale, Howard Schenken
	2.	Frances Carter, David Warner
1958	1.	Carol Ross, Edwin J. Smith
	2.	Louis J. Cohen, Sylvia Stein

1959	1.	John R. Crawford, Dorothy Hayden
	2.	Sidney H. Lazard, Stella Rebner
1960	1.	Elsie Abrams, William L. Passell
	2.	Peter Johnson, Gladys Kransberg
1961	1.	Art Comstock, Margaret Muirhead
	2.	Charles J. Solomon, Peggy Solomon
1962	1.	Clarice K. Holt, Paul Levitt
	2.	Peggy Jean Berry, John C. Sutherlin
1963	1.	Agnes Gordon, Eric R. Murray
	2.	Barbara Brier, Jerry Brier
1964	1.	Dan Morse, Mary Margaret Swan
	2.	Margaret Alcorn, Peter A. Pender
1965	1.	Betty Kaplan, Edgar Kaplan
	2.	Malvine Klausner, Morris Portugal
1966	1.	Robert G. Sharp, Louise Sharp
	2.	Gertrude Blasband, Sylvester Lowery
1967	1.	Gertrude Machlin, Kit Woolsey
	2.	Kathie Cappelletti, Mike Cappelletti
1968	1.	Marilyn Johnson, Peter C. Rank
	2.	John Gerber, Carol Klar
1969	1.	Peggy Parker, Steve Parker
	2.	Evelyn Levitt, David R. Treadwell
1970	1.	George S. Dawkins, Carolyn C. Flournoy
	2.	Mary Chilcote, Larry Weiss
1971	1.	Eugenie Mathe, Lewis L. Mathe
	2.	Barry Crane, Kerri Davis
1972	1.	John A. Mohan, Peggy Sutherlin
	2.	Leland Ferer, Gratian Goldstein
1973	1.	Bernie Chazen, Marilyn Johnson
	2.	Kenneth L. Cohen, Helen Smith
1974	1.	Gerald A. Caravelli, Helen Utegaard
	2.	Barry Crane, Kerri Shuman
1975	1.	Barry Crane, Kerri Shuman
	2.	Sandi Leavitt, Paul Sugar
1976	1.	Peggy Lipsitz, Steve Parker
	2.	Nancy Gruver, Lee Rautenberg
1977	1.	Joel Friedberg, Nancy Gruver
	2.	Barry Crane, Kerri Shuman
1978	1.	Ahmed Hussein, Gail Moss
	2.	Dave McClintock, Janet McClintock
1979	1.	Juanita Skelton, Mike Smolen
	2.	Carol Sanders, Thomas K. Sanders
1980	1.	Jeff Meckstroth, Patty Meckstroth
	2.	Hemant Lall, Jan Lall
1981	1.	Esta Van Zandt, James E. Zimmerman
	2-3.	Charlie Dorn, Bonnie LaRochelle
	2-3.	Bart Bramley, Judy Wadas
1982	1.	Barry Crane, Kerri Shuman
	2.	Mike Passell, Nancy Passell
1983	1.	John Gustafson, Helen Gustafson
	2.	Benito Garozzo, Lea duPont
1984	1.	Kathy Sulgrove, Larry Rock
	2.	Audrey Rennels, Ron Von der Porten
1985	1.	Beth Palmer, Steve Robinson
	2.	Patricia Hassett, Steve Garner
1986	1.	Lisa Berkowitz, David Berkowitz
	2.	Laurie Kranyak, Phil Becker
1987	1.	Lisa Berkowitz, David Berkowitz
	2.	Juanita Chambers, Jim Robison
1988	1.	Claire Tornay, Michael Moss
	2.	Susan Green, Mike Cappelletti
1989	1.	Dorothy Truscott, Alan Truscott
	2.	Sandra Low, Marc Low
1990	1.	Jo Ann Manfield, Ken Cohen
	2.	Adair Gellman, Ravindra Murthy
1991	1.	Jo Ann Manfield, Danny Sprung
	2.	Judy Tucker, Jim Becker
1992	1.	Kitty Bethe, Larry Mori
	2.	Linda Lee, Ray Lee
1993	1.	Libby Fernandez, Happoldt Neuffer
	2.	Sabine Zenkel, Ron Andersen
1994	1.	Jillian Blanchard, Geoff Hampson
	2.	Kay Schulle, John Sutherlin
1995	1.	Cindy Bernstein, Bob Bernstein
	2.	Kay Larsen, Chris Larsen
1996	1.	Margery Tamres, Joseph Brady
	2.	Anne Simon, Arnie Fisher
1997	1.	Phyllis Quinn, Wafik Abdou
	2.	Shirley Blum, George Whitworth
1998	1.	Joan Eaton, Leslie Amoils
	2.	Barbara Lehman, Craig Jacobson
1999	1.	Michael Cappelletti Jr., Shannon Lipscomb
	2.	Anne Arndt, Godfrey Chang
2000	1.	Linda Gordon, Bernie Chazen
	2.	Rhoda Walsh, Fred Hamilton

2001 1. Barbara Shaw, Mark Shaw
   2. Terry Michaels, Gary Roberts

OPEN SWISS TEAMS, formerly NORTH AMERICAN MEN'S SWISS TEAMS. This four-session event consists of two qualifying and two final sessions.

1982 1. Allan Stauber, Jan Janitschke, Ross Grabel, Mike Smolen
   2-3. Si Frome, Marc Renson, Hamish Bennett, Bob Etter
   2-3. Jim Robison, Stelios Touchtidis, Jon Wittes, Steve Cohen, Paul Ivaska, Paul Lewis
1983 1. Mike Albert, Ira Rubin, Grant Baze, Barry Crane
   2. George Ateljevich, Sidney Lazard, Sidney Lazard, Jr., John Zilic, Norb Kremer
1984 1. Bart Bramley, Mark Cohen, Milt Rosenberg, Ralph Katz
   2. Tom Mahaffey, Andy Bernstein, Richard Pavlicek, Bill Passell, Bill Root
1985 1. John Devine, Alan Sontag, John Mohan, Roger Bates
   2. David Ashley, David Sacks, Mike Shuman, Ed Davis, Jon Wittes, Steve Cohen
1986 1. Mark Cohen, Peter Boyd, Steve Robinson, Kit Woolsey
   2. Bob Jones, Jim Krekorian, Ethan Stein, Drew Casen, Al Rand
1987 1. Eddie Kantar, Alan Sontag, Roger Bates, John Mohan, John Devine
   2. Claude Vogel, David Lehman, Tom Fox, Michael Schreiber
1988 1. Ron Sukoneck, Doug Fraser, Kamel Fergani, Bill Pettis
   2. Jim Jacoby, Gerald Michaud, Bobby Nail, Fred Hamilton, Walt Walvick, Erik Paulsen
1989 1. Jim Mahaffey, Ron Andersen, Paul Soloway, Bobby Goldman, Jeff Meckstroth, Eric Rodwell
   2-3. Rob Stevens, Ron Powell, Sidney Brownstein, Mark Singer
   2-3. Jan Janitschke, Craig Janitschke, Marc Jacobus, Peter Nagy, Joey Silver
(became Open Swiss)
1990 1. John Sutherlin, Bart Bramley, Gerald Michaud, Larry Richardson, Bob Hamman
   2. Grant Baze, Jim Krekorian, Drew Casen, Mike Smolen
1991 1. George Rosenkranz, Eddie Wold, Mark Lair, Mike Passell, Paul Soloway, Bobby Goldman
   2. Bart Bramley, Per Olov Sundelin, John Sutherlin, Dan Morse, Edgar Kaplan, Norman Kay
1992 1. Richard Schwartz, Drew Casen, Michael Seamon, Richard Pavlicek, Fred Stewart, Steve Weinstein
   2. Morris Chang, Bob Hamman, Bobby Wolff, Michael Rosenberg, Zia Mahmood
1993 1. Tony Kasday, Michael Seamon, Steve Sion, Bill Cohen, Ron Smith
   2. Martin Scheinberg, Benito Garozzo, Lea duPont, Bill Eisenberg
1994 1. Perry Johnson, Jeff Meckstroth, Chip Martel, Eric Rodwell
   2. Grant Baze, Tipton Golias, Hugh Ross, Bart Bramley, Mike Lawrence
1995 1. Ralph Cohen, Billy Cohen, Peter Nagy, George Mittelman, Marty Sklar, Hugh Ross
   2. Mark Feldman, Jim Looby, Sharon Osberg, Cameron Doner
1996 1. Jimmy Cayne, Bjorn Fallenius, Brian Glubok, Chuck Burger, Mats Nisland, Mike Passell
   2. Paul Hackett, Jason Hackett, Justin Hackett, Brigitte Mavromichalis
1997 1. Edgar Kaplan, Norman Kay, Brian Glubok, Bart Bramley, Walter Schafer, Geir Helgemo
   2. Varis Carey, Nicolas Ecuyer, Jeffrey Blond, Michael Shuster, Curtis Cheek, Michael Schreiber
1998 1. Edith Rosenkranz, Ralph Cohen, Ron Smith, Bob Etter, Bob Morris
   2. Eddie Wold, George Rosenkranz, Henri Leufkens, Berry Westra, Magnus Magnusson, Jon Baldursson
1999 1. Sam Lev, Barnet Shenkin, John Mohan, Michael

Polowan, Brian Glubok
   2. Cezary Balicki, Adam Zmudzinski, Krzysztof Martens, Mark Szymanowski, Grant Baze, Tipton Golias
2000 1. Mark Lair, Richard Finberg, Gary Cohler, Mike Cappelletti Jr.
   2. Rose Meltzer, Chip Martel, Alan Sontag, Peter Weichsel, Kyle Larsen, Lew Stansby
2001 1. George Jacobs, Ralph Katz, Norberto Bocchi, Lorenzo Lauria, Alfredo Versace, Giorgio Duboin
   2. Gerald Sosler, Kay Schulle, Massimo Lanzarotti, Andrea Buratti, Antonio Sementa, Benito Garozzo

NORTH AMERICAN WOMEN'S SWISS TEAMS. This four-session event has two qualifying and two final sessions with Victory Point scoring.

1982 1. Dorothy Truscott, Stasha Cohen, Edith Kemp, Nancy Gruver, Mary Jane Farell, Randi Montin, Mike Smolen (npc)
   2. Jo Ann Manfield, Nadine Wood, Marilyn Eber, Bonnie Smith, Jan Janitschke (npc)
1983 1. Kathie Wei, Judi Radin, Gail Moss, Jacqui Mitchell, Betty Ann Kennedy, Carol Sanders
   2. Dianna Gordon, Brenda Keller, Mary Albert, Sandra Fraser, Linda Peterson, Kerri Shuman
1984 1. June Deutsch, Tobi Deutsch, Cheri Bjerkan, Margie Gwozdzinsky, Dorothy Truscott, Sue Halperin
   2. Karen McCallum, Ellee Lewis, Vivian Whalen, Kitty Bethe
1985 1. Sue Farino, Dianna Gordon, June Deutsch, Tobi Deutsch, Rhoda Walsh
   2-3. Kathie Wei, Jacqui Mitchell, Judi Radin, Gail Greenberg, Carol Sanders, Betty Ann Kennedy
   2-3. Jo Morse, Cindy Bernstein, Joyce Lilie, Evelyn Levitt, Sally Wheeler, Florine Kuehl
1986 1. Jan Martel, Rozanne Pollack, Lynne Pollenz, Lynne Feldman, Roberta Epstein, Sue Picus
   2. Sally Woolsey, Linda Peterson, Carol Pincus, Ann Jacobson, Nell Cahn, Kitty Poldosky
1987 1. Cheri Bjerkan, Juanita Chambers, Lynn Deas, Beth Palmer
   2. Helen Utegaard, Helene Gingiss, Rhoda Walsh, Jill Meyers, Beverly Rosenberg
1988 1. Helen Utegaard, Rhoda Walsh, Carol Pincus, Beverly Rosenberg
   2-3. Judy Wadas, Sandra Fraser, Janice Seamon, Renee Mancuso
   2-3. Tobi Deutsch, Betsey Wolff, Nancy Alpaugh, Kay Schulle
1989 1. Kerri Shuman, Kitty Bethe, Margie Gwozdzinsky, Karen McCallum
   2. Jean Michell, Patti Hartley, Shirley Blum, Janet Robertson
1990 1. Kerri Shuman, Karen McCallum, Edith Rosenkranz, Sabine Zenkel, Daniela von Arnim
   2. Nell Cahn, Sharon Osberg, Sue Picus, Nancy Passell
1991 1-2. Jacqui Mitchell, Joyce Lilie, Amalya Kearse, Jo Morse
   1-2. Ron Andersen (npc), Kay Schulle, Jill Meyers, Randi Montin, Pam Wittes, Juanita Chambers, Cheri Bjerkan
1992 1. Gail Greenberg, Judy Tucker, Dorothy Truscott, Lisa Berkowitz, Sandra Landy, Michele Handley
   2. Renee Mancuso, Brenda Keller, Joan Jackson, Petra Hamman, Judi Cody, Ellasue Chaitt
1993 1. Kay Schulle, Jill Meyers, Kerri Shuman, Karen McCallum
   2. Jean Anderson, Janet Daling, Sharon Colson, Broma Lou Reed
1994 1. Juanita Chambers, Rhoda Kratenstein, Shawn Womack, Jan Cohen, Hjordis Eythorsdottir
   2. Karen McCallum, Kitty Munson, Carol Simon, Sue Picus
1995 1. Kathie Wei-Sender, Carol Sanders, Betty Ann Kennedy, Sue Sachs, Lynn Deas, Beth Palmer
   2. Marinesa Letizia, Kay Schulle, Jill Meyers, Randi Montin, Dorothy Truscott, Tobi Deutsch
1996 1. Kathie Wei-Sender, Sue Sachs, Beth Palmer, Lynn Deas, Juanita Chambers
   2. Sally Woolsey, JoAnne Casen, Jan Martel, Georgiana Gates

1997 1. Pam Wittes, Shawn Quinn, Cheri Bjerkan, Sue Weinstein, Stasha Cohen, Judy Wadas
2. Judi Radin, Sylvia Moss, Valerie Westheimer, Connie Goldberg
1998 1. Jo Morse, Karen McCallum, Rose Johnson-Meltzer, Hjordis Eythorsdottir, Lynn Baker
2. Suzy Burger, Barbara Sion, Susie Miller, Joyce Lilie
1999 1. Robin Klar, Joan Jackson, Petra Hamman, Peggy Sutherlin, Shawn Quinn, Mildred Breed
2. Randi Montin, Lynn Baker, Jill Meyers, Janice Molson-Seamon, Karen McCallum, Tobi Sokolow
2000 1. Linda Lewis, Karen Barrett, Hjordis Eythorsdottir, Valerie Westheimer, Judy Wadas
2. Kathie Wei-Sender, Betty Ann Kennedy, Jill Levin, Juanita Chambers, Janice Seamon-Molson, Tobi Sokolow
2001 1. John Mohan, npc; Lynn Baker, Karen McCallum, Kerri Sanborn, Jill Meyers, Irina Levitina, Randi Montin
2. Lynne Tarnapol, Laurie Vogel, Gail Greenberg, Amalya Kearse, Jacqui Mitchell

SILVER RIBBON PAIRS. This event, consisting of two qualifying and two final sessions, is open only to players at least 55 years of age. Pre-quali-

fication is required and may be earned by placing first or second in a regionally or nationally-rated senior event.

1992 1. James Leary, S. Irving Steinfeldt
2. George Rosenkranz, Fred Hamilton
1993 1. Joan Remey Moore, Helen Shanbrom
2. Corinne Kirkham, Jim Kirkham
1994 1. Virgil Anderson, Jayne Thomas
2. Betty Wilton, Herb Wilton
1995 1. Gene Freed, Peter Benjamin
2. Marge Cox, Lloyd Loux
1996 1. Phil Karani, Martin Hoffman
2. Ed Lewis, Frank King
1997 1. John Russell, Chuck Said
2. Becky Rogers, Nell Cahn
1998 1. Bill Sides, Eli Borok
2. Dudley Brown, Richard Budd
1999 1. Corinne Kirkham, Jim Kirkham
2. Gerald Caravelli, Godfrey Chang
2000 1. Rhoda Walsh, Charles Coon
2. Gerald Caravelli, Marc Low
2001 1. Fred Hamilton, Steve Catlett
2. Ethan Stein, Gerry Caravelli

Summer Championships

SPINGOLD MASTER KNOCKOUT TEAMS. First known as the Challenge Knockout Teams, the event was contested for the ASBURY PARK TROPHY. The runner-up team in the regularly scheduled portion of the event had the right to challenge the winners to a playoff. This right was never utilized. In 1934, 1936 and 1937 the MASTERS TEAMS-of-FOUR and the Asbury Park Trophy were separate events, providing two sets of winners. In 1938 the event became the Spingold Master Knockout Teams. At one time the Spingold was a double elimination event scored by international matchpoints, usually lasting nine or ten sessions, restricted to players of Senior Master rank and higher. In 1965, the double elimination method was replaced by three qualifying sessions (subsequently reduced to two), followed by single elimination knockout matches. The preliminary qualifying sessions were dropped in 1970.

WINNERS ASBURY PARK TROPHY
1930 1. Ely Culbertson, Josephine Culbertson, Theodore A. Lightner, Waldemar K. von Zedtwitz
2. Michael T. Gottlieb, Williard S. Karn, Lee Langdon, P. Hal Sims
1931 1. David Burnstine, Oswald Jacoby, Williard S. Karn, P. Hal Sims
2. S. Garton Churchill, Travers J. LeGros, Dorothy Roberts, A. Phillip Stockvis
1932 1. Michael T. Gottlieb, Oswald Jacoby, Theodore A. Lightner, Louis H. Watson
2. B. Jay Becker, Herbert D. Lent, George Reith, Anne Rosenfeld
1933 1. David Burnstine, Oswald Jacoby, Richard L. Frey, Howard Schenken
2. Sam Fry, Jr., Edward Hymes, Louis H. Watson, Waldemar K. von Zedtwitz
1934 1. Aaron Frank, Jeff Glick, William Hopkins, Charles H. Porter
2. Josephine Culbertson, Theodore A. Lightner, Alphonse Moyse, Jr., Sherman Stearns
1935 1. Sam Fry, Jr., Edward Hymes, Jr., Theodore A. Lightner, Merwyn D. Maier, Louis H. Watson
2. A. Mitchell Barnes, H. Huber Boscowitz, Charles S. Lockridge, Johnny Rau

1936 1. Lewis A. Bernard, Louis J. Haddad, Alvin Landy, Matthew S. Reilly, Philip Steiner
2. E. Melvin Goddard, Sidney Silodor, Dr. Henry J. Vogel, Sir Derrick Wernher
1937 1. David Burnstine, Charles H. Goren, Oswald Jacoby, Merwyn D. Maier, Howard Schenken
2. Phil Abramsohn, A. Mitchell Barnes, Henry H. Chanin, Morrie Elis, Fred D. Kaplan
WINNERS MASTERS TEAMS-of-FOUR
1934 1. David Burnstine, Richard L. Frey, Michael T. Gottlieb, Oswald Jacoby, Howard Schenken
2. Aaron Frank, Jeff Glick, Louis J. Haddad, Charles A. Hall
1936 1. B. Jay Becker, David Burnstine, Oswald Jacoby, Howard Schenken
2. Sam Fry, Jr., Edward Hymes, Jr., Merwyn D. Maier, Waldemar K. von Zedtwitz
1937 1. Sam Fry, Jr., Edward Hymes, Jr., Theodore A. Lightner, Waldemar K. von Zedtwitz
2. Phil Abramsohn, Lewis Bernard, Morrie Elis, Harry Fishbein, Herbert Goldberg
WINNERS SPINGOLD KNOCKOUT TEAMS
1938 1. B. Jay Becker, David Burnstine, Oswald Jacoby, Merwyn D. Maier, Howard Schenken
2. A. Mitchell Barnes, Morrie Elis, Fred D. Kaplan, Charles S. Lockridge
1939 1. Oswald Jacoby, Theodore A. Lightner, Merwyn D. Maier, Robert A. McPherran, Howard Schenken
2. John R. Crawford, Myron Fuchs, Charles H. Goren, Charles J. Solomon, Sally Young
1940 1. Oscar J. Brotman, Bertram Lebhar, Samuel Katz, Alvin Roth
2. Sam Fry, Jr., Myron Fuchs, Edward Hymes, Jr., Charles S. Lockridge, Waldemar K. von Zedtwitz
1941 1. A. Mitchell Barnes, Sam Fry, Jr., Edward Hymes, Jr., Waldemar K. von Zedtwitz
2. B. Jay Becker, Oswald Jacoby, Theodore A. Lightner, Merwyn D. Maier, Howard Schenken
1942 1. Sigmund Dornbusch, Richard L. Frey, Lee Hazen, Samuel M. Stayman
2. Jay T. Feigus, Charles Harvey, Samuel Katz, Edward Marcus
1943 1. John R. Crawford, Charles H. Goren, Edward Hymes, Jr., Howard Schenken, Sidney Silodor
2. B. Jay Becker, Harry J. Fishbein, George Rapee, Alvin Roth, Helen Sobel
1944 1. B. Jay Becker, George Rapee, Helen Sobel, Samuel M. Stayman
2. Simon Becker, Edward G. Ellenbogen, Stanley Frenkel, Peggy Golder
1945 1. Sam Fry, Jr., Edward Hymes, Jr., Oswald Jacoby, Theodore A. Lightner, Howard Schenken
2. Harry Fishbein, Lee Hazen, Alvin Roth, Waldemar

K. von Zedtwitz

1946 1. William Christian, Mark Hodges, Sol Mogal, Margaret Wagar
2. Jeff Glick, Arthur S. Goldsmith, Alvin Landy, Elmer I. Schwartz

1947 1. B. Jay Becker, Charles H. Goren, Lee Hazen, Helen Sobel, Waldemar K. von Zedtwitz
2. John R. Crawford, George Rapee, Howard Schenken, Sidney Silodor, Samuel M. Stayman

1948 1. John R. Crawford, George Rapee, Howard Schenken, Samuel M. Stayman, Margaret Wagar
2. Julius Bank, Arthur Glatt, Robert W. Halpin, Oswald Jacoby, Ralph Kempner

1949 1. Jeff Glick, Arthur S. Goldsmith, Bruce Gowdy, Alvin Landy, Sol Mogal
2. Henry H. Chanin, David Clarren, Oswald Jacoby, Jack Krause, Waldemar K. von Zedtwitz

1950 1. John R. Crawford, Oswald Jacoby, George Rapee, Howard Schenken, Samuel M. Stayman
2. B. Jay Becker, Charles H. Goren, Sidney Silodor, Helen Sobel, Waldemar K. von Zedtwitz

1951 1. Myron Field, Charles H. Goren, Sidney Silodor, Helen Sobel
2. Ambrose Casner, Charles A. Hall, Allen P. Harvey, Frank Weisbach

1952 1. B. Jay Becker, John R. Crawford, George Rapee, Howard Schenken, Samuel M. Stayman
2. Jeff Glick, Arthur S. Goldsmith, Alvin Landy, Sol Mogal, Edwin J. Smith, Jr.

1953 1. Clifford Bishop, Milton Q. Ellenby, Donald A. Oakie, William Rosen, Doug Steen
2-5. Ed Burns, David Clarren, Bertram Lebhar Jr., Sam Katz, Albert Weiss
2-5. F. Ayers Bombeck, David C. Carter, John W. Hubbell, Arthur Kincaid, G. Robert Nail
2-5. Harold Harkavy, Edith Kemp, Alvin Roth, Tobias Stone, Walemar K. von Zedtwitz
2-5. Ivan E. Erdos, Dr. Edward Fischauer, Lewis L. Mathe, Meyer Schleifer

1954 1. Clifford Bishop, Milton Q. Ellenby, Lewis L. Mathe, John Moran, William Rosen
2-4. F. Ayers Bombeck, David C. Carter, John Gerber, John W. Hubbell, Harold Rockaway
2-4. Eddie Burns, Ambrose Casner, Allen P. Harvey, Cliff Russell
2-4. Sidney Lazard, Cyrus Neuman, Lewis Rosen, Julius L. Rosenblum, Robert Rothlein

1955 1. Myron Field, Lee Hazen, Richard Kahn, Charles J. Solomon, Samuel M. Stayman
2. B. Jay Becker, John R. Crawford, George Rapee, Howard Schenken, Sidney Silodor

1956 1-3. Charles H. Goren, Peter A. Leventritt, Boris Koytchou, Harold Ogust, William Seamon, Helen Sobel
1-3. Harold Harkavy, Victor Mitchell, Alvin Roth, Ira S. Rubin, Tobias Stone
1-3. Robert Abeles, Dr. Kalman Apfel, Francis P. Begley, Louis Kelner, Ronald Rosenberg

1957 1. B. Jay Becker, John R. Crawford, George Rapee, Alvin Roth, Sidney Silodor, Tobias Stone
2. Milton Q. Ellenby, Ivan E. Erdos, Emanuel Hochfeld, James Jacoby, Oswald Jacoby, Ira S. Rubin

1958 1. Paul Allinger, William Hanna, Sidney Lazard, Cyrus Neuman, Robert Rothlein
2. Harry Fishbein, Sam Fry, Jr., Leonard B. Harmon, Lee Hazen, Ivar Stakgold

1959 1. William Grieve, Oswald Jacoby, Victor Mitchell, Ira S. Rubin, Morton Rubinow, Samuel M. Stayman
2. Richard Freeman, Andy Gabrilovitch, Frank Hoadley, Mike Michaels, Jan Stone, Richard Walsh

1960 1. Charles H. Goren, Peter A. Leventritt, Boris Koytchou, Harold Ogust, Howard Schenken, Helen Sobel
2. B. Jay Becker, William Grieve, Ralph Hirschberg, Norman Kay, George Rapee, Sidney Silodor

1961 1. Andy Gabrilovitch, Eddie Kantar, Marshall Miles, William Root
2. John R. Crawford, Norman Kay, Alvin Roth, George Rapee, Sidney Silodor, Tobias Stone

1962 1. Leonard B. Harmon, Eddie Kantar, Marshall Miles, Ivar Stakgold
2. David C. Carter, John W. Hubbell, James Jacoby,

Gerald Michaud, G. Robert Nail

1963 1. Russell Arnold, Harold Harkavy, Edith Kemp, Alvin Roth, Cliff Russell, William Seamon
2. Sami R. Kehela, Richard Kahn, William Root, Thomas K. Sanders, Tobias Stone, Waldemar K. von Zedtwitz

1964 1. Bruce Elliott, Sami R. Kehela, Eric R. Murray, Percy Sheardown
2. Marvin Altman, Bruce Gowdy, Fred Hoffer, Ray Jotcham

1965 1. Bruce Elliott, Sami R. Kehela, Eric R. Murray, Percy Sheardown
2. B. Jay Becker, Dorothy Hayden, Norman Kay, Edgar Kaplan

1966 1. William Root, Alvin Roth, Ira S. Rubin, Curtis K. Smith
2. William Grieve, Sidney Lazard, Paul Levitt, Harold Ogust, George Rapee

1967 1. Edgar Kaplan, Norman Kay, William Root, Alvin Roth
2. John Gerber, Paul H. Hodge, Dan Morse, George Rosenkranz, Bobby Wolff

1968 1. Sami R. Kehela, Edgar Kaplan, Norman Kay, Sidney Lazard, Eric R. Murray, George Rapee
2. Steve Altman, B. Jay Becker, Michael Becker, Dorothy Hayden

1969 1. Bill Eisenberg, Bobby Goldman, Robert D. Hamman, Michael S. Lawrence, James Jacoby, Bobby Wolff
2. Phil Feldesman, William Grieve, Victor Mitchell, Ira S. Rubin, Samuel M. Stayman, Jeff Westheimer

1970 1. Steve Altman, Thomas M. Smith, Dave Strasberg, Joel Stuart, Peter Weichsel
2. Bill Eisenberg, Bobby Goldman, Robert D. Hamman, James Jacoby, Michael S. Lawrence, Bobby Wolff

1971 1. Steve Altman, Eugene Neiger, Thomas M. Smith, Joel Stuart, Peter Weichsel
2. Edgar Kaplan, Norman Kay, Donald P. Krauss, Lewis L. Mathe

1972 1. B. Jay Becker, Michael Becker, Andy Bernstein, Jeff Rubens
2. Pat Brennan, Byron Greenberg, Edith Kemp, Cliff Russell, Curtis K. Smith, Albert Weiss

1973 1. Larry Cohen, Bill Eisenberg, Eddie Kantar, Richard H. Katz, Bud Reinhold
2. Minda Brachman, Sidney Lazard, James Jacoby, Paul Soloway, John Swanson

1974 1. Lou Bluhm, Larry Gould, Steve Goldberg, Richard Shepherd
2. Harlow Lewis, Lewis L. Mathe, Peter A. Pender, William Root, Harry Stappenbeck, Arthur Waldmann

1975 1. Grant S. Baze, John Fejervary, Lew Stansby, Piyush Vakil, Ron Von der Porten
2. Ira Cohen, Harold Guiver, Marty Shallon, Bill Sides

1976 1. Roger Bates, Larry Cohen, Richard H. Katz, John Mohan, George Rosenkranz
2. Dave Berkowitz, Mark E. Blumenthal, James Jacoby, Michael S. Lawrence, George Rapee, John Solodar

1977 1. Lou Bluhm, Dan Morse, Cliff Russell, Curtis K. Smith, Thomas K. Sanders, Eddie Wold
2. Ken Cohen, Larry Gould, Larry Kozlove, John Sheridan

1978 1. Malcolm Brachman, Bobby Goldman, Eddie Kantar, Mike Passell, Paul Soloway
2. Steve Altman, Edgar Kaplan, Norman Kay, Richard Pavlicek, William Root, Thomas M. Smith

1979 1. Fred Hamilton, Robert D. Hamman, Ira S. Rubin, Bobby Wolff
2. Ed Manfield, Stephen W. Robinson, Eric Rodwell, John Sheridan, Kit Woolsey

1980 1. Mike Becker, Kyle Larsen, Ron Rubin, Alan Sontag, Ron Von der Porten, Peter Weichsel
2. Rich Freisner, Brian Glubok, Michael S. Lawrence, George Rapee, Michael Rosenberg, John Solodar

1981 1. Larry N. Cohen, Ron Gerard, Ralph Katz, Warren Rosner, Allan Stauber, John Sutherlin
2. Bart Bramley, Rich Freisner, Ed Manfield, Kit Woolsey

1982 1. Ron Rubin, Mike Becker, Bob Hamman, Bobby Wolff, Alan Sontag, Peter Weichsel
2. Mark Molson, Billy Cohen, Eric Kokish, Peter Nagy
1983 1. Malcolm Brachman, Bobby Wolff, Bobby Goldman, Bob Hamman, Paul Soloway, Ron Andersen
2. Luella Slaner, Marty Bergen, Brian Glubok, Larry N. Cohen, Mark Cohen, Jerry Goldfein
1984 1. George Rosenkranz, Eddie Wold, Jeff Meckstroth, Eric Rodwell, Marty Bergen, Larry N. Cohen
2. Alan Sontag, Allan Cokin, Jim Sternberg, Bernie Chazen, Steve Sion
1985 1. Tom Mahaffey, Jack Denny, Bill Passell, Russ Arnold, Ira Rubin, Chuck Burger
2. Ron Rubin, Jeff Meckstroth, Eric Rodwell, Mike Lawrence, Peter Weichsel
1986 1. Malcolm Brachman, Bobby Goldman, Ron Andersen, Mike Passell, Mark Lair, Paul Soloway
2. Brian Glubok, Billy Cohen, John Schermer, Neil Chambers
1987 1. Brian Glubok, Dan Rotman, Harry Stappenbeck, Jaggy Shivdasani
2. Tom Mahaffey, Jack Denny, Russ Arnold, Bernie Chazen, Roy Fox, Michael Seamon
1988 1. Jim Mahaffey, Ron Andersen, Paul Soloway, Bobby Goldman, Eric Rodwell, Jeff Meckstroth
2. Ron Rubin, Michael Becker, Peter Weichsel, Bart Bramley, Robert Levin, Lou Bluhm
1989 1. Jim Cayne, Chuck Burger, Bob Hamman, Bobby Wolff, Mike Passell, Mark Lair
2. Jon Wittes, Ross Grabel, Mark Cohen, Mark Feldman
1990 1. Jim Cayne, Chuck Burger, Chip Martel, Lew Stansby, Bob Hamman, Bobby Wolff
2. Jim Mahaffey, Paul Soloway, Bobby Goldman, Ron Andersen, Jeff Meckstroth, Eric Rodwell
1991 1. Zia Mahmood, Michael Rosenberg, Seymon Deutsch, Jeff Meckstroth, Eric Rodwell
2. Cliff Russell, Peter Weichsel, Robert Levin, Sam Lev, Alan Sontag, Eddie Kantar
1992 1. Ron Rubin, Russ Ekeblad, Mike Becker, Ron Sukoneck, Robert Levin, Peter Weichsel
2. Steve Robinson, Peter Boyd, Lew Stansby, Kit Woolsey, Neil Silverman, Chip Martel
1993 1. Richard Freeman, Nick Nickell, Eric Rodwell, Jeff Meckstroth, Bobby Wolff, Bob Hamman
2. Zia Mahmood, Michael Rosenberg, Seymon Deutsch, Hemant Lall, Chip Martel, Lew Stansby
1994 1. Richard Freeman, Nick Nickell, Bob Hamman, Bobby Wolff, Jeff Meckstroth, Eric Rodwell
2. Jimmy Cayne, Chuck Burger, Mark Lair, Mike Passell, Paul Soloway, Bobby Goldman
1995 1. Richard Freeman, Nick Nickell, Bob Hamman, Bobby Wolff, Jeff Meckstroth, Eric Rodwell
2. Zia Mahmood, Michael Rosenberg, Chip Martel, Lew Stansby
1996 1. Richard Freeman, Nick Nickell, Bob Hamman, Bobby Wolff, Jeff Meckstroth, Eric Rodwell
2. Richard Schwartz, Paul Soloway, Bobby Goldman, Steve Robinson, Alan Sontag, Ron Smith
1997 1. Grant Baze, Tipton Golias, Adam Zmudzinski, Marek Szymanowski, Marcin Lesniewski, Cezary Balicki
2. Jimmy Cayne, Chuck Burger, Mike Passell, Michael Seamon, Mark Feldman, Alan Sontag
1998 1. Nick Nickell, Richard Freeman, Bob Hamman, Paul Soloway, Jeff Meckstroth, Eric Rodwell
2. Grant Baze, Michael Whitman, Adam Zmudzinski, Marek Szymanowski, Marcin Lesniewski, Cezary Balicki
1999 1. Nick Nickell, Richard Freeman, Bob Hamman, Paul Soloway, Jeff Meckstroth, Eric Rodwell
2. Steve Beatty, John Onstott, Bill Eisenberg, Gary Hayden
2000 1. Rose Meltzer, Peter Weichsel, Kyle Larsen, Lew Stansby, Alan Sontag, Chip Martel
2. Ray Welland, Brad Moss, Marc Jacobus, Fred Gitelman, Magnus Lindkvist, Peter Fredin

WOMEN'S TEAMS. This event is contested for the COFFIN TROPHY. Until 1976 it was a four-session event scored by Board-a-Match; contested as a three-session championship until 1972 and in 1975; held at the Fall North American Championships until 1963. In 1976 the event became a North American Championship Women's Knockout with Swiss qualifying.

1933 1. Mrs. Greene Fenley, Jr., Mrs. Richard Field, Mrs. John W. Friedlander, Jane Wallace
2. Mollie Funk, Ethel Gardner, Marguerite Hoffmeier, Marie White
1934 1. Gail Hamilton, Marguerite Hoffmeier, Helen Pendelton Rockwell, Anne Rosenfeld
2. Elizabeth Banfield, Phyllis Gardner, Eva Gross, Dorothy Roberts
1935 1. Doris Fuller, Angela Quigley, Florence Stratford, Helen White
2. Gail Hamilton, Marguerite Hoffmeier, Helen Pendelton Rockwell, Anne Rosenfeld
1936 1. Doris Fuller, Angela Quigley, Florence Stratford, Helen White
2. Marge Anderson, Mrs. J. A. Faulkner, Marjorie Haldeman, Mrs. G. Keedick
1937 1. Martha Lemon, Mrs. A. Philip Stockvis, Mrs. Martin West, Sally Young
2. Doris Fuller, Angela Quigley, Helen Sobel, Florence Stratford
1938 1. Mrs. Galloway Morris, Lillian Peck, Olive Peterson, Mrs. Donald B. Tansill
2. Mariquita Fullerton, Mollie Funk, Ann Rosenfeld, Lucille Schwarz
1939 1. Mable Ervin, Doris Fuller, Helen Mitchell, Helen Sobel, Sally Young
2. Sylvia DeYoung, Margaret Katzen, Catherine W. Samberg, Florence Stratford
1940 1. Helen Levy, Adelaide Neuwirth, Margaret Wagar, Lottie Zetosch
2. Ruth Horn, Olga Hilliard, Marguerite McKenney, Gussie Planco
1941 1. Inez Buchannan, Mae Dickens, Mabel Scott, Linda Terry
2. Doris Fuller, Mrs. Joseph M. Rothschild, Helen Sobel, Sally Young
1942 1. Peggy Golder, Olga Hilliard, Olive Peterson, Ruth Sherman
2. Emily Folline, Doris Fuller, Ethel Gardner, Helen Sobel
1943 1. Emily Folline, Helen Sobel, Margaret Wagar, Sally Young
2. Eleanor Hirsch, Evelyn Lebhar, Marguerite McKenney, Florence Stratford
1944 1. Emily Folline, Helen Sobel, Margaret Wagar, Sally Young
2. Mrs. M. Godfrey, Mrs. C. W. Neeld, Dorothy Sullivan, Anne H. Todd
1945 1. Emily Folline, Helen Sobel, Margaret Wagar, Sally Young
2. Josephine Gutman, Gratian Goldstein, Marjorie Perlmutter, Gretchen Schildmiller
1946 1. Emily Folline, Helen Sobel, Margaret Wagar, Sally Young
2. Paula Bacher, Marie Basher, Jane Jaeger, Pauline Schmuckler
1947 1-2. Marge Anderson, Ruby Lyons, Mimi Roncarelli, Jane Wallace
1-2. Cass Illig, Frances Robinson, Alma Stewart, Carolyn Sondheim
1948 1. Ruth Gordon, Gratian Goldstein, Josephine Gutman, Charlotte Sidway
2. Ruth Gilbert, Olive Peterson, Edith Seligman, Ruth Sherman, Peggy Solomon
1949 1-2. Hortense Evans, Frances Robinson, Mrs. Henry Sabatt, Carolyn Sondheim
1-2. Marianne Boschan, Catherine Cotter, Gertrude Eberson, Katherine McNutt
1950 1. Marge Anderson, Mary Bowden, Ruth Gordon, G. Eloise Neil
2-5. Olive Peterson, Ruth Sherman, Helen Sobel, Margaret Wagar
2-5. Shirley Fairchild, Mrs. Ezra Feldman, Rose Groves, Luise Mathews, Claire Meyer
2-5. Margaret Byrd, Isabelle Garn, Virginia Ploehn, Billy Traveletti
2-5. Inez Buchanan, Zodie Glover, Sally Herman, Mabel Scott
1951 1. Paula Bacher, Anne Burnstein, Dolly Rosenfeld,

         Edith Seligman, Sally Young
2. Thelma Hathorn, Mollie Steiner, Agatha Tiernan, Clara Tiernan, Mary Elizabeth Tiernan

1952 1. Jackie Begin, Sally Herman, Jessie S. Moore, Norma Matz
2-3. Peggy Adams, Helen Baker, Marguerite Harris, Ethel Keohane
2-3. Kay Rhodes, Ruth Sherman, Helen Sobel, Margaret Wagar

1953 1. Gretchen Feldstein, Vera Glick, Gratian Goldstein, Lucille Schwarz
2-3. Mary Jane Kauder, Kay Rhodes, Ruth Sherman, Margaret Wagar
2-3. Elaine Lee, Olive Peterson, Roberta Sheronas, Peggy Solomon

1954 1. Wynne Ecker, Doris Fuller, Marguerite Harris, Norma Matz
2-5. Marguerite Bouldin, Lillian Hassler, Ann Jervis, Dorothy Payne
2-5. Marie Cohn, Olive Peterson, Pauline Schmuckler, Peggy Solomon
2-5. Kay Rhodes, Ruth Sherman, Helen Sobel, Margaret Wagar
2-5. Margaret Alcorn, Louise Eisenman, Emily Folline, Sue Reith

1955 1. Peggy Adams, Carlyn Brall, Louise Eisenman, Shirley Johnson, Juanita Strich
2-4. Kay Rhodes, Ruth Sherman, Helen Sobel, Margaret Wagar
2-4. Anne Burnstein, Edith Kemp, Paula Levin, Ruth Steinberg, Sally Young
2-4. Ruth Gordon, Josephine Gutman, Evelyn Engleman, Margaret Katzen, G. Eloise Neil

1956 1. Peggy Rotzell, Jan Stone, Charlotte Sidway, Mary Elizabeth Tiernan
2. Kay Rhodes, Helen Sobel, Margaret Wagar, Sally Young

1957 1. Marie Cohn, Mary Jane Kauder, Stella Rebner, Peggy Solomon
2. Agnes Gordon, Kay Rhodes, Helen Sobel, Margaret Wagar

1958 1. Carolyn Brall, Bee Gale, Sally Johnson, Peggy Rotzell
2. Kay Rhodes, Helen Sobel, Margaret Wagar, Sally Young

1959 1. Margaret Alcorn, Lee Kasle, Josephine Sharp, Adaline Simon, Garner McDaniel
2. Kay Dunn, Jane Herb, Malvine Klausner, Helen Portugal, Rose Reif

1960 1. Roberta Erde, Sally Johnson, Barbara Kachmar, Bee Schenken
2. Joan Remey, Helen Shanbrom, Sylvia Stein, Marge Stone

1961 1. Roberta Erde, Sally Johnson, Barbara Kachmar, Bee Schenken
2. Mary Jane Farell, Terry Michaels, Peggy Solomon, Jan Stone

1962 1. Anne Burnstein, Edith Kemp, Alicia Kempner, Stella Rebner, Teddie Warner
2. Muriel Kaplan, Terry Michaels, Garner McDaniel, Jan Stone

1963 1. Pat Adler, Terry Michaels, Garner McDaniel, Cora Sanders, Sylvia Stein
2. Dorothy Hayden, Barbara Kachmar, Agnes Gordon, Helen Portugal, Margaret Wagar

1964 1. Hermine Baron, Mary Jane Farell, Peggy Solomon, Bee Schenken
2. Agnes Gordon, Dorothy Hayden, Helen Portugal, Margaret Wagar

1965 1. Virginia Heckel, Betty Kaplan, Edith Kemp, Jacqui Mitchell
2. Debbie Polak, Joan Remey, Carol Ruther, Sylvia Stein

1966 1-2. Freida Arst, June Deutsch, Sylvia Stein, Carol Stoklin
1-2. Nancy Gruver, Garner McDaniel, Terry Michaels, Sue Sachs

1967 1. Dorothy Hayden, Emma Jean Hawes, Agnes Gordon, Margaret Wagar
2-3. Hermine Baron, Mary Jane Farell, Bee Schenken, Peggy Solomon
2-3. Dolores Bick, Jude Ballard, Ruth Needham, Viola Kirkwood

1968 1. Hermine Baron, Mary Jane Farell, Sally Johnson, Bee Schenken, Peggy Solomon, Rhoda Walsh

2. Jean Frankel, Teddy O'Brien, Mary Beth Townsend, Esta Van Zandt

1969 1. Karen Allison, Virginia Heckel, Edith Kemp, Alicia Kempner, Helen Portugal, Jan Stone
2. Nancy Gruver, Barbara Rappaport, Sue Sachs, Barbara Tepper

1970 1. Mary Jane Farell, Emma Jean Hawes, Dorothy Hayden, Marilyn Johnson, Jacqui Mitchell, Peggy Solomon
2. Dorothy Cowger, Diane Hawes, Florence Van Winkle, Freda Van Cleve

1971 1. Judi Friedenberg, Gail Moss, Marietta Passell, Helen Utegaard, Kathie Wei
2. Roberta Epstein, Gretchen Goldstein, Edith Kemp, Barbara Rappaport, Sylvia Stein

1972 1. Mary Jane Farell, Emma Jean Hawes, Dorothy Hayden, Sue Picus
2. Frieda Arst, June Deutsch, Eunice Rosen, Carol Stoklin

1973 1. Nancy Gruver, Terry Michaels, Jo Morse, Helen Utegaard
2-4. Nancy Alpaugh, Fran Beard, Heitie Noland, Betsey Wolff, Esta Van Zandt
2-4. Mary Jane Farell, Marilyn Johnson, Jacqui Mitchell, Gail Moss, Marietta Passell, Kathie Wei
2-4. Jean Christopher, Muriel Peterson, Beverly Rosenberg, Elaine Sternberg

1974 1. Mary Jane Farell, Emma Jean Hawes, Marilyn Johnson, Jacqui Mitchell, Gail Moss, Dorothy Hayden Truscott
2. Hermine Baron, Carol Greenhut, Trudi Nugit, Kerri Shuman

1975 1. Mary Jane Farell, Emma Jean Hawes, Marilyn Johnson, Jacqui Mitchell, Gail Moss, Dorothy Hayden Truscott
2. Anita Davis, Mildred Freedman, Robin Grantham, Carol Klar

1976 1. Mary Jane Farell, Emma Jean Hawes, Marilyn Johnson, Jacqui Mitchell, Gail Moss, Dorothy Hayden Truscott
2. Evelyn Levitt, Lila Perlstein, Helen Smith, Vivian Whalen

1977 1. Betty Adler, Jo Morse, Judi Radin, Sue Sachs
2. Ida Bennett, Mary Lou Cushner, Carole Felczer, Ethel Keohane

1978 1. Nancy Alpaugh, Nancy Gruver, Betty Ann Kennedy, Evelyn Levitt, Carol Sanders, Kerri Shuman
2. Cheri Bjerkan, Sue Halperin, Beverly Nelson, Florine Walters

1979 1. Betty Adler, Anne Burnstein, Edith Kemp, Terry Michaels, Jo Morse, Sue Sachs
2. Cheri Bjerkan, June Deutsch, Sue Halperin, Sandy Leavitt, Beverly Nelson, Florine Walters

1980 1. Nancy Gruver, Edith Kemp, Betty Ann Kennedy, Judi Radin, Carol Sanders, Kathi Wei
2. Betty Adler, Pat Lapides, Pat Leary, Terry Michaels, Jo Morse, Jan Stansby

1981 1. June Deutsch, Pat Lapides, Sandy Leavitt, Evelyn Levitt, Jo Morse, Helen Utegaard
2. Karen Allison, Cheri Bjerkan, Lynn Deas, Dianna Gordon, Sue Halperin, Sharyn Kokish

1982 1. Stasha Cohen, Mary Jane Farell, Nancy Gruver, Edith Kemp, Randi Montin, Dorothy Hayden Truscott
2. Betty Ann Kennedy, Jacqui Mitchell, Gail Moss, Judi Radin, Carol Sanders, Kathie Wei

1983 1. Kathie Wei, Judi Radin, Jacqui Mitchell, Gail Moss, Carl Sanders, Betty Ann Kennedy, Jim Zimmerman (npc)
2. Brenda Keller, Linda Peterson, Nancy Passell, Patsy Arnett, Nell Cahn

1984 1. Edith Kemp Frelich, Nancy Gruver, Mary Jane Farell, Helen Utegaard, Beverly Rosenberg, Carol Pincus
2. Terry Michaels, Garner McDaniel, Mary Williams, Sally Wheeler, Cindy Bernstein

1985 1. Rama Linz, Beth Palmer, Kay Schulle, Barbara Hamman, Juanita Skelton, Lynn Deas
2. Roberta Epstein, Jan Martel, Lisa Berkowitz, Rozanne Pollack, Lynn Feldman, Sue Picus

1986 1. Jo Morse, Evelyn Levitt, Sharon Osberg, Peggy Sutherlin, Cindy Bernstein, Sally Wheeler
2. Rama Linz, Beth Palmer, Lynn Deas, Juanita Chambers, Kerri Shuman, Cheri Bjerkan

1987	1.	Kathie Wei, Judi Radin, Jacqui Mitchell, Amalya Kearse, Carol Sanders, Betty Ann Kennedy
	2.	Mary Jane Farell, Roberta Epstein, Jan Martel, Dorothy Truscott, Carol Simon, Karen McCallum
1988	1.	Beverly Rosenberg, Helen Utegaard, Sue Weinstein, Janice Seamon, Carol Pincus, Pat Schor
	2.	Terry Michaels, Cindy Bernstein, Linda Perlman, Sue Sachs, Sally Wheeler, Jo Morse
1989	1.	Juanita Chambers, Kay Schulle, Cheri Bjerkan, Randi Montin, Pam Wittes, Jill Meyers
	2.	Jo Morse, Joyce Lilie, Cindy Bernstein, Georgiana Gates, Janice Seamon, Linda Perlman
1990	1.	Mary Jane Farell, Roberta Epstein, Dorothy Truscott, Gail Greenberg, Lisa Berkowitz, Rozanne Pollack
	2.	Juanita Chambers, Cheri Bjerkan, Kay Schulle, Jill Meyers, Pam Wittes, Randi Montin
1991	1.	Nancy Passell, Nell Cahn, Sue Picus, Stasha Cohen, Susan Green, Sharon Osberg
	2.	Jacqui Mitchell, Amalya Kearse, Joyce Lilie, Jo Morse, Pamela Granovetter, Nancy Alpaugh
1992	1.	Juanita Chambers, Cheri Bjerkan, Marinesa Letizia, Janice Seamon
	2.	Kathie Wei, Helen Utegaard, Carol Sanders, Betty Ann Kennedy, Lynn Deas, Beth Palmer
1993	1.	Gail Greenberg, Dorothy Truscott, Judy Tucker, Stasha Cohen, Irina Levitina, Rozanne Pollack
	2.	Kay Schulle, Jill Meyers, Cheri Bjerkan, Janice Seamon
1994	1.	Sally Woolsey, Georgiana Gates, Jo Anne Casen, Jan Martel, Joann Glasson, Jo Ann Manfield
	2.	Kathie Wei-Sender, Carol Sanders, Lisa Berkowitz, Lynn Deas, Beth Palmer
1995	1.	Juanita Chambers, Lila Perlstein, Gail Greenberg, Jillian Levin, Irina Levitina, Shawn Womack
	2.	Sun Ming, Gu Ling, Zhang Yalan, Liu Yiqian
1996	1.	Pam Wittes, Cheri Bjerkan, Sue Weinstein, Stasha Cohen, Shawn Quinn, Judy Wadas
	2.	Edith Freilich, June Deutsch, Rita Seamon, Janice Seamon, Susan Wexler, Margie Gwozdzinsky
1997	1.	Jill Meyers, Randi Montin, Mildred Breed, Tobi Sokolow, Renee Mancuso, Shawn Quinn
	2.	Kathie Wei-Sender, Juanita Chambers, Lynn Deas, Beth Palmer, Stasha Cohen
1998	1.	Kitty Munson, Carol Simon, Margie Gwozdzinsky, Susan Wexler, Linda Lewis, Karen Barrett
	2.	Kathie Wei-Sender, Juanita Chambers, Stasha Cohen, Pam Wittes, Irina Levitina, Jill Levin
1999	1.	Carol Sanders, Lynn Deas, Connie Goldberg, Rozanne Pollack, Lisa Berkowitz, Beth Palmer; Karen Allison npc
	2.	Sharon Jabbour, Jan Assini, Susan Miller, Candace Fowler, Mary Oshlag, Laurie Kranyak
2000	1.	Kathie Wei-Sender, Juanita Chambers, Jill Levin, Betty Ann Kennedy, Janice Seamon-Molson, Tobi Sokolow
	2.	Joan Jackson, Petra Hamman, Peggy Sutherlin, Robin Klar, Mildred Breed, Shawn Quinn

GRAND NATIONAL TEAMS.

The competition is contested for the ALBERT MOREHEAD TROPHY. The initial stages are contested over the course of several months. Originally this was a North American contest with all 25 ACBL districts participating. Now it is a United States event, with only the 23 U.S. districts participating. The district winners play off for the championship at the Summer North American Championships. In 1985 the event was subdivided into three separate events and this event became Flight A.

1973	1.	Russell Arnold, James Beery, Jane Jaeger, Richard Pavlicek, William Seamon, Robert G. Sharp
	2.	Brian Economidy, Jerry Levitt, Roger Lord, Norb Kremer, Dave Smith, Ron Smith
1974	1.	Larry Cohen, Bill Eisenberg, Eddie Kantar, Richard Katz, Paul Soloway, John Swanson
	2.	Chuck Burger, Fred Hamilton, Howard Perlman, Stanley Smith, Jeffrey Starr, Dick Yanko

1975	1.	John Fisher, Charles Gabriel, Robert Hamman, Jim Hooker, Charles Weed, Bobby Wolff
	2.	Mike Cook, Jim Felts, Doug Hill, Reece Rogers, Ron Smith, Bernie Yomtov
1976	1.	Bill Eisenberg, Eddie Kantar, Paul Soloway, John Swanson
	2.	Marty Fleisher, Charlie Friedman, Ron Gerard, Halina Jamner, Archie McKellar, Neil Nathanson
1977	1.	Robert Hamman, Dan Morse, Curtis Smith, Eddie Wold, Bobby Wolff
	2.	Bobby Lipsitz, Steve Parker, Steve Robinson, Kit Woolsey
1978	1.	Gerald Caravelli, Charles Peres, William Rosen, Milton Rosenberg, Dan Rotman
	2.	Allan Cokin, Robert Levin, Bud Reinhold, William Seamon, Steve Sion
1979	1.	Greg DeFotis, Jerry Goldfein, Arnold Leavitt, Larry Robbins, Claude Vogel
	2.	Marty Bergen, Chuck Lamprey, Warren Rosner, Allan Stauber
1980	1.	Jack Bitman, Jan Janitschke, Craig Janitschke, Dick Lesko
	2.	Russell Arnold, Edith Kemp, William Passell, Cliff Russell, William Seamon, Dave Strasberg
1981	1.	Ira Chorush, James Jacoby, Mike Passell, George Rosenkranz, Eddie Wold
	2.	Mike Becker, Brian Glubok, John Lowenthal, Phillip Martin, Michael Rosenberg, Ron Rubin
1982	1.	Ron Von der Porten, Hugh Ross, Chip Martel, Lew Stansby, Kyle Larsen, Peter Pender
	2.	Steve Landen, Pratap Rajadhyaksha, Jeff Starr, Frank Bell, Chuck Burger
1983	1.	Chip Martel, Hugh Ross, Peter Pender, Lew Stansby
	2.	Lou Bluhm, Richard Freeman, Larry Gould, Randy Joyce, Nick Nickell
1984	1.	Kit Woolsey, Ed Manfield, Peter Boyd, Bob Lipsitz, Steve Robinson
	2.	Greg DeFotis, Larry Robbins, Jerry Goldfein, Hal Mouser, Jack Oest, Gerry Caravelli
1985	1.	Chip Martel, Hugh Ross, Lew Stansby, Peter Pender
	2.	Steve Robinson, Ed Manfield, Peter Boyd, Bob Lipsitz
1986	1.	Seymon Deutsch, Bobby Wolff, Bob Hamman, Jim Jacoby
	2.	Milt Rosenberg, Ralph Katz, Hal Mouser, Greg DeFotis, Larry Robbins, Howard Weinstein
1987	1.	Chip Martel, Hugh Ross, Peter Pender, Lew Stansby, Mike Lawrence
	2.	Frank Hoadley, Sidney Lazard, John Onstott, Jack LaNoue
1988	1.	Steve Robinson, Ed Manfield, Peter Boyd, Robert Lipsitz
	2.	Jack Oest, Steve Garner, Jerry Goldfein, Bart Bramley, Gerry Caravelli, Howard Weinstein
1989	1.	Steve Sion, Robert Barr, Harold Stengel, Bernie Miller
	2.	Tony Kasday, Paul Ivaska, Gaylor Kasle, Garey Hayden, Roger Bates
1990	1.	Doug Simson, Walter Johnson, Jeff Meckstroth, Eric Rodwell, Dennis Clerkin
	2.	Kay Larsen, Chris Larsen, Joe Kivel, Robert Rosenblum, Evan Bailey
1991	1.	Larry Robbins, Jerry Goldfein, Jack Oest, Peter Nagy, Steve Garner, Howard Weinstein
	2.	Marty Bergen, Fred Stewart, Larry Cohen, Steve Weinstein
1992	1.	Steve Robinson, Peter Boyd, Robert Lipsitz, Ed Manfield
	2.	Michael Becker, Ron Rubin, Richard Pavlicek, William Root, Robert Levin, Jeff Wolfson
1993	1.	Ravindra Murthy, Brad Moss, Lew Stansby, Chip Martel, Hugh Ross, Jeff Ferro
	2.	Brian Ellis, Asim Ulke, Florine Walters, Richard Finberg, Jay Apfelbaum, Piyush Vakil
1994	1.	Jimmy Cayne, Alan Sontag, Dave Berkowitz, Larry Cohen
	2.	Doug Simson, Walter Johnson, Eric Rodwell, Jeff Meckstroth
1995	1.	Steve Garner, Jack Oest, Larry Robbins, Jerry Goldfein, Gerald Caravelli, Gary Cohler
	2.	Billy Cohen, Marc Jacobus, Harold Lilie, Peter Nagy

1996	1.	Ralph Buchalter, Hugh Ross, Kyle Larsen, Ron Smith, Chip Martel, Lew Stansby
	2.	Chuck Burger, Geoff Hampson, Allan Falk, Perry Johnson
1997	1.	Jeffrey Wolfson, Robert Levin, Jeff Meckstroth, Neil Silverman, Richard Pavlicek, Michael Seamon
	2.	Hjordis Eythorsdottir, Curtis Cheek, Steve Beatty, John Onstott
1998	1.	Ross Grabel, Jon Wittes, Mark Itabashi, Fred Hamilton, Gene Simpson
	2.	Bobby Goldman, John Sutherlin, Malcolm Brachman, Mike Passell, Eddie Wold
1999	1.	Robert Levin, Eric Rodwell, Jeff Meckstroth, Joseph Shay, Michael Seamon
	2.	Iftikhar Baqai, Jill Meyers, Mitch Dunitz, Ed Davis
2000	1.	Joseph Shay, Michael Seamon, Eric Rodwell, Jeff Meckstroth, Robert Levin
	2.	Rose Meltzer, Peter Weichsel, Ron Smith, Kyle Larsen, Chip Martel, Lew Stansby

NORTH AMERICAN TEAMS, FLIGHT B.

This event is a grass-roots competition, with games at various levels eventually leading to each of the 25 ACBL districts sending its champion to the Summer North American Bridge Championships to compete for the championship. It is open only to players with fewer than 2000 masterpoints.

1985	1.	Irving Goodman, Floyd Dyson, Leo Takefman, Tim McPhail, Louis Richardson
	2.	Sally Grace, Linda Weinstein, Sharon Meng, Jennifer James, Jerry Poliquin, Robert Buchner
1986	1.	Paul McGowan, George Towner, Winston Edwards, Regena Jones
	2.	Ken Connell, Linda Connell, Carla Eisenhauer, S. K. Carruthers, Claire Jones, Dennis Nelson
1987	1.	Dwight Hunt, Ed Horwitz, Ken Kadis, Claude LeFeuvre
	2.	Bob Webb, Pat Webb, Kevin Chen, Joseph Blalock
1988	1.	Steven Beck, Michael Camp, Win Allegaert, Fred Chang
	2.	Jean Molnar, Michael Weber, Donn Holmer, Walter Riddle, Joseph Rubin
1989	1.	George Runyan, Tim Joder, Iype Koshy, Robert Dupont
	2.	Paul Nickerson, William Goldsmith, Denise Goldsmith, Cheryl Porter
1990	1.	Judy Hughes, Karen Miller, Robert Seaholm, John Morano, Goutam Chakraborty, Krishnanand Maillacheruvu
	2.	Jim Adams, John Edmunds, Dan Feldman, Larry Kahn, Usuf Ismail
1991	1.	Mary Poplawski, Stanley Poplawski, William Smith, Barrett Raff
	2.	Bruce Norman, Fred Gitelman, Sheri Winestock, Geoff Hampson
1992	1.	Otto Rothenberg, Richard Baumer, Arthur Haley, Bert Kulic
	2.	Nielih Cheng, Peter Kalat, Jeffery Allen, Carlos Munoz, L. P. Calahan, Bruce Platt
1993	1.	Eric Greco, Philip Greco, Kefer Xu, Harry Zhou, David Better
	2.	Jack Jessop, Morrie Kleinplatz, Barry Onslow, Elaine Morrison
1994	1.	Larry Crevier, Marc-Andre Fourcaudot, Sylvain Descoteaux, Frederic Pollack
	2.	Glen Holman, Warren Wolpert, Hazel Wolpert, Eric Sutherland
1995	1.	Larry Crevier, Marc-Andre Fourcaudot, Sylvain Descoteaux, Frederic Pollack
	2.	Sam Yoga, Gordon Brown, Warren Wolpert, Hazel Wolpert
1996	1.	David Green, Edward Lee, Chien Huang, Robert Johnson
	2.	David Walker, Robert Moore, Jim Hawkins, Geoffrey Mallette
1997	1.	Sigridur Kristjansdottir, Harold Jordan, Andy Kaufman, Greg Burch
	2.	Steve Albin, Julia Ehlers, Mike McNamara, Elaine Pittius

1998	1.	Robert Latulippe, Rene Pelletier, Jocelyn Bernier, Richard Wildi, Jacques Carel, Herve Chatagnier;
	2.	Richard Wegman, Kefu Xu, Yi Zhong, Weizhong Boo
1999	1.	Claude King, Henry Caspar, Tom Buttle, Ringo Chung, Helen DeWeld, Vinray Sarin
	2.	Steve Albin, Dennis Thompson, David Liss, Jack Brauner
2000	1.	Gilbert Lambert, Tai Eng, Insa Fricker, Mike Moffet
	2.	John Turner, Ralph Russo, Mark de Garcia, David Shipman

NORTH AMERICAN TEAMS, FLIGHT C.

This event is a grass-roots competition, with games at various levels eventually leading to each of the 25 ACBL districts sending its champion to the Summer North American Bridge Championships to compete for the championship. It is open only to non-Life Masters with fewer than 500 masterpoints.

1991	1.	Bob Fashingbauer, Kenneth Wolf, Thomas Dressing, David Marker
	2.	Albert Tom, Dennis Erani, Valentin Carciu, Gary Gottleib
1992	1.	Richard Unger, Charles Morrin, Andrew Ware, Martin Wewerka
	2.	J. Michael Hill, Kevin Kadmus, Carol Wisemiller, Marty Lobdale
1993	1.	Stephen Arshan, Richard Ross, Feng Liu, Steve Pessin, George Shamy
	2.	Sardarsinh Gohel, Jack Shartsis, Joyce Bell, Nathan Banker
1994	1.	Sundar Atre, Jiabin Luo, Zheng Zhang, Ariel Kaushal
	2.	Gregory Bieber, Betsy Wellington, Arthur Steinberg, Roman Shapiro
1995	1.	William Chen, Andrew Lewis, Nathaniel Thurston, David Shao
	2.	Jeffrey Jacob, David Rosenstein, Judi Hager, Yiping Wang
1996	1.	Mark Edeburn, Susan Ostrowski, Dan Berlowitz, Joseph Seo
	2.	Mark de Garcia, Marcus Redhouse, Steven Erickson, Sheng-Hung Wang
1997	1.	Tim Barrett, Joe Grue, Joe Barrett, Chengwei Lee, Tom Monikowsky
	2.	Curtis Ruder, Atul Rae, Dennis Alfholter, Jonathan Davidson
1998	1.	Jerzy Jelen, Marek Dalecki, Ted Ryll, Romuald Mindak, Weislaw Kalita, Zbigniew Muszynski
	2.	Ed Williams, Kurt Dasher, Thomas Reband, Bill Gliesman
1999	1.	Jon Kurasch, Dave Hemmer, Roger Soleman, Roger Alps
	2.	Jim Boardman, Tom Allen, Paul Hazzard, Bruce Scott
2000	1.	Marian Kowalewski, Zbigniew Muszynski, Robert Boruta, Michael Omielski, Eugenisk Babiarz, Pavel Boruta
	2.	Leo Zelevinsky, Otis Bricker, Suresh Adina, Barry Margolin

LIFE MASTER PAIRS.

This six-session event with two qualifying, two semifinal and two final rounds, restricted to Life Masters, is contested for the VON ZEDTWITZ GOLD CUP.

1930	1.	P. Hal Sims, Waldemar K. von Zedtwitz
	2.	Ely Culbertson, Josephine Culbertson
1931	1.	David Burnstine, Howard Schenken
	2.	Michael T. Gottlieb, Theodore A. Lightner
1932	1.	Michael T. Gottlieb, Theodore A. Lightner
	2.	David Burnstine, Howard Schenken
1933	1.	David Burnstine, Howard Schenken
	2.	P. Hal Sims, Waldemar K. von Zedtwitz
1934	1.	Richard L. Frey, Howard Schenken
	2.	Walter Malowan, Sydney Rusinow
1935	1.	B. Jay Becker, Theodore A. Lightner
	2.	Louis J. Haddad, Charles A. Hall

1936	1.	David Burnstine, Oswald Jacoby
	2.	Robert Appleyard, Isadore Epstein
1937	1.	S. Garton Churchill, Charles L. Lockridge
	2.	Doris Fuller, Dr. Henry J. Vogel
1938	1.	Morrie Elis, Sherman Stearns
	2.	John R. Crawford, Charles J. Solomon
1939	1.	Robert Appleyard, Harry J. Fishbein
	2.	Oswald Jacoby, Waldemar K. von Zedtwitz
1940	1.	Harry J. Fishbein, Morrie Elis
	2.	Sam Fry, Jr., Myron Fuchs
1941	1.	Merwyn D. Maier, Howard Schenken
	2.	John R. Crawford, Oswald Jacoby
1942	1.	Charles H. Goren, Helen Sobel
	2.	Philip Abramsohn, Tobias Stone
1943	1.	John R. Crawford, Howard Schenken
	2.	Sidney Silodor, Margaret Wagar
1944	1.	Samuel Katz, Peter A. Leventritt
	2.	Ambrose Casner, Ralph Hirschberg
1945	1.	Robert Appleyard, Malcolm A. Lightman
	2.	Bertram Lebhar, Jr., Simon Rossant
1946	1.	Sidney Silodor, Charles J. Solomon
	2.	Lee Hazen, Ruth Sherman
1947	1.	Allen P. Harvey, Frank Weisbach
	2.	John R. Crawford, Theodore A. Lightner
1948	1.	S. Garton Churchill, Cecil Head
	2.	Erik Coon, Vincent Remey
1949	1.	Ruth Gilbert, Leo Roet
	2.	Arthur Glatt, Albert Weiss
1950	1.	Manuel Sherwin, Dr. C. W. Yorke
	2.	Edward N. Marcus, Samuel M. Stayman
1951	1.	Richard Kahn, Peter A. Leventritt
	2.	Ned Drucker, Edgar Kaplan
1952	1.	William W. Jackson, William Joseph
	2-3.	Arthur Glatt, Albert Weiss
	2-3.	John R. Crawford, Howard Schenken
1953	1.	Milton Q. Ellenby, William A. Rosen
	2.	Charles H. Goren, Helen Sobel
1954	1.	David C. Carter, John W. Hubbell
	2.	Victor Mitchell, Ira S. Rubin
1955	1.	Ben Fain, Paul H. Hodge
	2.	Victor Mitchell, Ira S. Rubin
1956	1.	Alvin Roth, Tobias Stone
	2.	John R. Crawford, Sidney Silodor
1957	1.	H. Sanborn Brown, Martin Cohn
	2.	Francis P. Begley, Louis Kelner
1958	1-2.	Charles H. Goren, Helen Sobel
	1-2.	Wilson Landley, Louis Levy
1959	1.	Ed Rosen, Dan Rotman
	2.	Sidney Aronson, Larry Weiss
1960	1.	Helen Portugal, Morris Portugal
	2.	Curtis K. Smith, Bobby Wolff
1961	1.	Philip Feldesman, Marshall Miles
	2.	Paul Kibler, Robert Reynolds
1962	1.	Philip Feldesman, Ira S. Rubin
	2.	Edith Kemp, Albert Weiss
1963	1.	Lewis L. Mathe, Edward O. Taylor
	2.	Ira Rubin, Curtis Smith
1964	1.	B. Jay Becker, Dorothy Hayden
	2.	Bruce Elliott, Percy E. Sheardown
1965	1.	Victor Mitchell, Samuel M. Stayman
	2.	Alvin Roth, Tobias Stone
1966	1.	Hermine Baron, Meyer Schleifer
	2.	Morrie Freier, Robert Reynolds
1967	1.	Philip Feldesman, Lewis L. Mathe
	2.	Diana Schuld, Frank Schuld
1968	1.	Bill Eisenberg, Bobby Goldman
	2.	James Jacoby, Bobby Wolff
1969	1.	Sami R. Kehela, Eric R. Murray
	2.	Chuck F. Burger, James Cayne
1970	1.	Paul Heitner, Michael Moss
	2.	Robert Freedman, James Mathis
1971	1.	Alvin Roth, Barbara Rappaport
	2.	James Jacoby, Minda Brachman
1972	1.	Alvin Roth, Barbara Rappaport
	2.	Alan Sontag, Peter Weichsel
1973	1.	Jack Blair, Paul Swanson
	2.	Chuck F. Burger, James Cayne
1974	1.	Gerald Michaud, G. Robert Nail
	2.	Walter Walvick, Thomas Weik
1975	1.	Roy Fox, Eugene O'Neill
	2.	Michael Becker, Ahmed Hussein
1976	1.	Robert Lipsitz, Neil Silverman
	2.	Garey Hayden, Mike Passell
1977	1.	Alan Sontag, Peter Weichsel
	2.	Ken Cohen, Robert Lipsitz

1978	1.	Mary Jane Farell, Marilyn Johnson
	2.	Ron Feldman, David Sacks
1979	1.	Ralph Katz, Ken Schutze
	2.	Dan Morse, G. Robert Nail
1980	1.	Robert D. Hamman, Eric Rodwell
	2.	Don Caton, Homer Shoop
1981	1.	Fred Stewart, Steve Weinstein
	2.	Paul Lavings, Bob Richman
1982	1.	Tom Sanders, Ron Andersen
	2.	Robert Lipsitz, Ron Sukoneck
1983	1.	Bob Hamman, Eddie Kantar
	2.	Eric Rodwell, Jeff Meckstroth
1984	1.	Mike Lawrence, Peter Weichsel
	2.	Alan Sontag, Steve Sion
1985	1.	George Steiner, Darryl Pedersen
	2.	David Siebert, Allan Siebert
1986	1.	Eric Rodwell, Douglas Simson
	2.	Tom Kniest, Karen Walker
1987	1.	Larry N. Cohen, Dave Berkowitz
	2.	Steve Robinson, Peter Boyd
1988	1.	Marty Bergen, Larry N. Cohen
	2.	Howard Weinstein, John Carruthers
1989	1.	Richard Katz, Robert Levin
	2.	Howard Weinstein, Ralph Katz
1990	1.	Ron Rubin, Michael Becker
	2.	John Mohan, Kay Schulle
1991	1.	Doug Simson, Eric Rodwell
	2.	Steve Sion, Clint Morrell
1992	1.	Bob Hamman, Hemant Lall
	2.	Hugh Ross, Zia Mahmood
1993	1.	Dan Morse, John Sutherlin
	2.	Tom Clarke, Alan LeBendig
1994	1.	Robert Levin, Jeff Wolfson
	2.	Eddie Wold, Steve Sion
1995	1.	Joe Knivel, Allan Siebert
	2.	William Root, Richard Pavlicek
1996	1.	David Berkowitz, Larry Cohen
	2.	Tony Forrester, Geir Helgemo
1997	1.	Steve Garner, Howard Weinstein
	2.	Tony Forrester, Geir Helgemo
1998	1.	Eric Greco, Geoff Hampson
	2.	Richard Pavlicek, Rich Pavlicek Jr.
1999	1.	John Mohan, Sam Lev
	2.	Fred Gitelman, Brad Moss
2000	1.	Zia Mahmood, Michael Rosenberg
	2.	John Mohan, Sam Lev

IMP PAIRS. This event, consisting of two qualifying and two final sessions, is scored by International Match Points.

1987	1.	Robb Gordon, Linda Danas
	2.	Peter Weichsel, Richard Katz
1988	1.	Gene Freed, Mike Passell
	2.	Corinne Gellman, Jim Kirkham
1989	1.	Richard Schwartz, Fred Hamilton
	2.	Bud Reinhold, Michael Seamon
1990	1.	Ralph Cohen, Renee Mancuso
	2.	Richard Schwartz, Drew Casen
1991	1.	Harvey Brody, Ralph Buchalter
	2.	Ron Feldman, Marty Shallon
1992	1.	Vera Gama, Marcelo Branco
	2.	David Midkiff, Tom Oppenheimer
1993	1.	Bob Klein, David Ruderman
	2.	Win Allegaert, Gary Gottlieb
1994	1.	Tom Fox, Walter Schafer
	2.	Howard Chandross, Lee Rautenberg
1995	1.	Steve Sion, Harold Lilie
	2.	Brad Moss, Elizabeth Reich
1996	1.	Mike Albert, Marilyn Hemenway
	2.	Steve Beatty, Adam Wildavsky
1997	1.	Tom Carmichael, Joel Wooldridge
	2.	Dick Bruno, Kenji Miyakuni
1998	1.	Jim Robison, Gene Freed
	2.	Jeanne Rahmey, Gary Cohler
1999	1.	George Jacobs, Ralph Katz
	2.	Rob Crawford, Spike Lay
2000	1.	Aschley Back, Stephen Burgess
	2.	Steve Beatty, George Steiner

MIXED BOARD-A-MATCH TEAMS, formerly *MASTER MIXED TEAMS. This event is contested for the LEBHAR TROPHY (originally for

the BARCLAY TROPHY until 1945). A four-session Board-a-Match event, with two qualifying rounds and two final rounds, it is restricted to players who have won at least 100 masterpoints. In 1969 this event was played in three sessions.

1929   1.   Max M. Cohen, Mrs. M. K. Alexander, Rose Fleischer, R. Frankenstein
1930   1.   Cmdr. Winfield W. Liggett, Jr., Dorothy Rice Sims, P. Hal Sims, Sir Derrick J. Wernher
      2.   W. Cleveland Cogswell, J. Arnold Farrar, Doris Fuller, George Reith
1931   1.   Mrs. G. A. Bennett, Doris Fuller, Charles S. Lockridge, George Reith
      2.   E. M. Baker, Margaret Beech, William McKenney, Mrs. H. D. Stahl
1932   1.   Marie Black, H. Huber Boscowitz, Sam Fry, Jr., Olga Hilliard
      2.   Mrs. L. Bloomberg, Bernard Cone, A. Louis Gotthelf, Mrs. Thomas Stern
1933   1.   David Burnstine, Elinor Murdoch, Mrs. Ivan Stengel, Edwin A. Wetzler
      2.   Dorothy Rice Sims, P. Hal Sims, Margaret Wagar, Waldemar K. von Zedtwitz
1934   1.   Lester R. Bachner, Mrs. Lester R. Bachner, James H. Lemon, Martha Lemon
      2.   A. Mitchell Barnes, Barbara Collyer, Doris Fuller, Dr. Henry J. Vogel
1935   1.   Helen Bonwit, Howard Schenken, Ruth Sherman, Louis H. Watson
      2.   Mary Clement, Mary Zita Jacoby, Oswald Jacoby, Waldemar K. von Zedtwitz
1936   1.   Hortense Evans, Louis J. Haddad, Robert McPherran, Elizabeth Whitney
      2.   B. Jay Becker, Helen Bonwit, Howard Schenken, Sally Young
1937   1.   Philip Abramsohn, Estelle Drescher, Morrie Elis, Ann Naiman
      2.   S. Garton Churchill, Phyllis Gardner, Travers LeGros, Dorothy Roberts
1938   1.   Doris Fuller, Charles H. Goren, Dr. Henry J. Vogel, Sally Young
      2.   Eleanor Hirsch, John C. Kunkel, Helen Pendelton Rockwell, Milton Vernoff
1939   1.   Robert Chatkin, Valerie Klein, Alvin Landy, Florence Stratford
      2.   Edward G. Ellenbogen, Peggy Golder, Helen Mitchell, Charles J. Solomon
1940   1.   Marie Black, Henry H. Chanin, Olive Peterson, Waldemar K. von Zedtwitz
      2.   Edward G. Ellenbogen, Peggy Golder, Helen Mitchell, Charles J. Solomon
1941   1.   Charles H. Goren, Sidney Silodor, Helen Sobel, Sally Young
      2.   Oswald Jacoby, Louise Wainwright, Sherman Stearns, Mrs. William A. Tucker
1942   1.   John R. Crawford, Olive Peterson, Margaret Wagar, Waldemar K. von Zedtwitz
      2.   Philip Abramson, Kay Rhodes, Edith Seligman, Tobias Stone
1943   1.   Charles H. Goren, Olive Peterson, Sidney Silodor, Helen Sobel
      2.   Edith Hammond, Pat Lightner, Walter Malowan, Stuyvesant Wainwright
1944   1.   Charles H. Goren, Olive Peterson, Sidney Silodor, Helen Sobel
      2.   Marie Basher, Edward Cohn, John R. Crawford, Margaret Wagar
1945   1.   John R. Crawford, Ruth Sherman, Margaret Wagar, Waldemar K. von Zedtwitz
      2.   Morrie Elis, Harry J. Fishbein, Alvin Roth, Edith Seligman
1946   1.   Samuel Katz, Alicia Kempner, Evelyn Lebhar, Bertram Lebhar, Jr.
      2.   Charles H. Goren, Emily Folline, Sidney Silodor, Helen Sobel
1947   1.   Harry J. Fishbein, Ruth Goldberg, Ludwig Kabakjian, Edith Seligman
      2-3.   Emily Folline, Peter A. Leventritt, David Warner, Sally Young
      2-3.   Harold Harkavy, Jane Jaeger, Lewis M. Jaeger, Mrs. G. Strasser
1948   1.   John R. Crawford, Charles H. Goren, Helen Sobel, Margaret Wagar
      2.   Harry J. Fishbein, Ruth Goldberg, Ludwig Kabakjian, Edith Seilgman
1949   1.   Peter A. Leventritt, Charles J. Solomon, Peggy Solomon, Sally Young
      2.   John R. Crawford, Charles H. Goren, Helen Sobel, Margaret Wagar
1950   1.   Peter A. Leventritt, Charles J. Solomon, Peggy Solomon, Sally Young
      2.   John R. Crawford, Charles H. Goren, Helen Sobel, Margaret Wagar
1951   1.   Jane Jaeger, Ruth Kahn, Leo Roet, Ruth Sherman
      2.   Myron Field, Agnes Gordon, Charles H. Goren, Helen Sobel
1952   1.   Anne Burnstein, Harold Harkavy, Alvin Roth, Edith Seligman
      2.   John R. Crawford, Emma Jean Hawes, George Rapee, Olive Peterson, Sidney Silodor
1953   1.   Anne Burnstein, Harold Harkavy, Edith Kemp, Alvin Roth
      2.   Emanuel Hochfeld, Mary Jane Kauder, Lewis L. Mathe, Gloria Turner
1954   1.   Charles H. Goren, Sidney Silodor, Helen Sobel, Margaret Wagar
      2.   Marianne Boschan, Gertrude Eberson, David Murray, Lewis Tubbs
1955   1.   Gratian Goldstein, Harold Harkavy, Terry Michaels, Alvin Roth
      2.   Mary Bowden, Douglas Drury, Richard Freedman, Agnes Gordon, Eric R. Murray
1956   1.   Mary Bowden, Douglas Drury, Robert Freedman, Agnes Gordon, Eric R. Murray
      2.   Barbara Brier, Jan Stone, Tobias Stone, Waldemar K. von Zedtwitz
1957   1.   John R. Crawford, Milton Q. Ellenby, Harold Harkavy, Edith Kemp, Gloria Turner
      2.   Sam Fry, Jr., Dorothy Hayden, Sally Johnson, Ira S. Rubin
1958   1.   Leland Ferer, Gratian Goldstein, Eunice Rosen, William Rosen
      2.   B. Jay Becker, Bee Gale, Betty Goldberg, Howard Schenken
1959   1.   Peter A. Leventritt, Robert F. Jordan, Charles J. Solomon, Peggy Solomon, Sally Young
      2.   Leonard B. Harmon, Edgar Kaplan, Peggy Rotzell, Alfred Sheinwold, Betty Sheinwold
1960   1.   William Grieve, Alicia Kempner, George Rapee, Betty Ann Welch
      2.   B. Jay Becker, Dorothy Hayden, Norman Kay, Sidney Silodor, Sylvia Stein
1961   1.   Richard Freeman, Emanuel Hochfield, Louise Robinson, Gloria Turner
      2.   John Fisher, Jean Frankel, Lou Gurvich, Boots Kendrick, Sidney Lazard
1962   1.   Charles Coon, Agnes Gordon, Eric Murray, Helen Portugal
      2.   Norman Kay, Sidney Silodor, Sylvia Stein, Margaret Wagar
1963   1.   Sidney Lazard, Betty Kaplan, Edgar Kaplan, Stella Rebner
      2.   Israel Cohen, Garner McDaniel, Terry Michaels, Alvin Roth
1964   1.   John Fisher, John Gerber, Emma Jean Hawes, Margaret Wagar
      2-3.   Martin J. Cohn, Hampton Hume, Bernadine Jenkins, Mary Philley
      2-3.   Harold Harkavy, Virginia Heckel, Edith Kemp, Clifford Russell, Jerome Yavitz, Jr.
1965   1.   Barbara Brier, Alvin Roth, Jan Stone, Tobias Stone, Waldemar K. von Zedtwitz
      2.   Burt Norton, Carol Norton, Alan Press, William Rosen, Sylvia Stein, Carol Stolkin
1966   1.   James Cayne, Judy Dryer, Paul Soloway, Eunice Rosen, William Rosen
      2.   Barbara Rappaport, Alvin Roth, Bee Schenken, Howard Schenken
1967   1.   Mike Cappelletti, Kathie Cappelletti, Michael Moss, Gail Shane
      2-4.   John Gerber, Norman Kay, Carol Klar, George Rosenkranz, Edith Rosenkranz
      2-4.   B. Jay Becker, John Fisher, Dorothy Hayden, Emma Jean Hawes
      2-4.   Leland Ferer, Gratian Goldstein, Fred Hamilton, Sylvia Stein
1968   1.   Minda Brachman, James Jacoby, Oswald Jacoby,

Helen Sobel Smith
2. Betty Kaplan, Edgar Kaplan, George Rapee, Carol Stolkin
1969 1. Janice Cohn, Flo Orner, Charles Peres, Dan Rotman, Ivar Stakgold, Alice Stakgold
2. Barry Crane, Jules Farell, Mary Jane Farell, Marilyn Johnson, Peter Rank
1970 1. Dorothy Bare, Gerald Bare, Eugenie Mathe, Lewis L. Mathe
2-3. Ken Barbour, William Daly, Mickey Rosenthal, Helen Strasberg, Dave Strasberg
2-3. Betty Adler, Julian Adler, Dave Sachs, Sue Sachs
1971 1. John Anderson, Ron E. Andersen, Marilyn McCrary, Sue Picus
2. Dorsey Brooks, Zerrene Brooks, Joan Remey, Vincent Remey
1972 1. Gail Moss, Michael Moss, Marietta Passell, William Passell
2. B. Jay Becker, John Fisher, Emma Jean Hawes, Alan Truscott, Dorothy Hayden Truscott
1973 1. Ellen Alfandre, Philip Feldesman, Edith Sachs, Stanley Tomchin
2-5. Betty Adler, Julian Adler, Dave Sachs, Sue Sachs
2-5. Doug Fraser, Sandra Fraser, Barbara Saltsman, Joe Silver
2-5. Mark Berger, Sallie Johnson, Amos Kaminsky, Jack Saltz, Mona Stocknoff
2-5. Carol Crawford, John R. Crawford, Barbara Rappaport, Alvin Roth
1974 1. Edith Kemp, Jerome Yavitz, Rita Seamon, William Seamon
2. Robert Lipsitz, Jo Morse, Peggy Parker, Steve Parker, Steve Robinson
1975 1. Gerald Caravelli, Nancy Gruver, Jim Linhart, Helen Utegaard
2-3. Shirlee Lazarus, Eugenie Mathe, Lewis L. Mathe, Joan Remey, Vincent Remey, James E. Zimmerman
2-3. Carol Crawford, John R. Crawford, Barbara Rappaport, Alvin Roth
1976 1-2. Richard H. Katz, Carol Sanders, Paul Swanson, Marion Weed
1-2. Fred Hamilton, John C. Sutherlin, Peggy Sutherlin, Rhoda Walsh, Nancy Weichsel, Peter Weichsel
1977 1. Nancy Alpaugh, Joan DeWitt, Mark Lair, Sidney Lazard
2. Ethel Dayboch, Morrie Freier, Richard Paulsen, Sue Thornton
1978 1. Nancy Alpaugh, Joan DeWitt, Mark Lair, Sidney Lazard
2. Betty Adler, Julian Adler, David Sachs, Sue Sachs
1979 1-3. Betty Bloom, Steven Bloom, Mark Cohen, Edith Sachs
1-3. Nancy Alpaugh, Joan DeWitt, Mark Lair, Sidney Lazard
1-3. Lynne Feldman, Mark Feldman, Ed Nagy, Sharon Smith
1980 1. Barry Crane, Jose John Hamui, Elias Konstantinovsky, Laura Mariscal, Kerri Shuman
2. Gerald Caravelli, Dennis McGarry, Joan Remey, Vincent Remey, Helen Utegaard
1981 1. Doug Fraser, Sandra Fraser, Ralph Katz, Paul Lewis, Linda Peterson, Esta Van Zandt
2. Bill Cole, Lynn Deas, Norb Kremer, Beth Palmer
1982 1-2. Tommy Sanders, Carol Sanders, Sidney Lazard, Joan DeWitt
1-2. Lynn Deas, Norb Kremer, Beth Palmer, Bill Cole
1983 1. Alan Kudisch, Judy Landau, Drew Casen, Karen Allison
2. Kathie Wei, Judi Radin, Eric Rodwell, Jeff Meckstroth
1984 1. Susan Sternberg, Bernie Chazen, Juanita Skelton, Allan Cokin, Barbara Sion, Steve Sion
2. Edith Rosenkranz, George Rosenkranz, Carol Sanders, Mark Lair, Lynn Deas, Eddie Wold
1985 1. Bill Pollack, Rozanne Pollack, Alan Truscott, Dorothy Truscott, Evelyn Levitt, Dave Treadwell
2. Rich Schmieder, Jyme Tropila, Martin Miller, Carole Dietz
1986 1. Mark Cohen, Stasha Cohen, Harold Lilie, Joyce Lilie, David Berkowitz, Lisa Berkowitz
2. Carol Simon, Bob Etter, Min Ross, Hugh Ross, Paul Kern, Claire Kern
1987 1-2. Jim Mahaffey, Linda Perlman, Joan Remey, Paul

Soloway
1-2. Bob Hamman, Kerri Shuman, Rama Linz, Robert Levin
1988 1-2. Robert Radwin, Helen Utegaard, Flo Rotman, Dan Rotman
1-2. Ken Cohen, Jo Anne Manfield, Robert Woodard, Ev Cogan
1989 1. Alan Sontag, Peter Weichsel, Gladys Collier, Juanita Chambers
2-3. Marty Bergen, Dori Cohen, Mary Oshlag, Richard Oshlag
2-3. Chester Hirsch, Mary Jane Farell, Jacqui Mitchell, Victor Mitchell
1990 1. Edith Rosenkranz, George Rosenkranz, Eddie Wold, Marinesa Letizia, Kerri Shuman, Mark Lair
2. Jim Becker, Ellee Lewis, Howard Chandross, Vivian Whalen
1991 1. John Carruthers, Katie Thorpe, Brad Moss, Bronia Gmach, Jared Lilienstein
2. Robert Thomson, Asya Kamsky, Rozanne Pollack, Michael Radin, Marty Bergen, Dori Cohen
1992 1. Gabriel Chagas, Marinesa Letizia, Dennis Clerkin, Juanita Chambers, Mike Lawrence, Beth Palmer
2. Bjorn Fallenius, Kathy Anday, Shirlee Meckstroth, Jeff Meckstroth
1993 1. Lisa Berkowitz, David Berkowitz, Beth Palmer, William Pettis
2. Nancy Molesworth, Stephen Schneer, Robbie Hopkins, Joan Lewis
1994 1. Mike Lucas, Michael Seamon, Renee Mancuso, Steve Sion, Barbara Sion
2. George Rosenkranz, Sabine Zenkel, Eddie Wold, Kerri Sanborn , Larry Cohen
1995 1. Joyce Lilie, Harold Lilie, David Berkowitz, Lisa Berkowitz
2. Jeff Schuett, Ginny Schuett, Tom Kniest, Karen Walker, Florine Walters, Mark Feldman

In 1996, the event became the Mixed Board --A-Match Teams.
1996 1. Gaylor Kasle, Barbara Kasle, Nancy Passell, Garey Hayden
2. Jimmy Cayne, Jacqui Mitchell, Amalya Kearse, Mike Passell, Chuck Burger, Suzy Burger
1997 1. Marc Low, Sandra Low, Sue Sachs, David Sachs
2. Kit Woolsey, Sal Woolsey, Jo Anne Casen, Larry Mori, Martha Katz, Ralph Katz
1998 1. David Berkowitz, Lisa Berkowitz, Jim Bjerkan, Cheri Bjerkan
2. Rita Shugart, Geir Helgemo, Tony Forrester, Andrew Robson
1999 1. Matt Granovetter, Lynn Baker, Karen McCallum, Zia Mahmood
2. Richard Gabriel, Ellen Gabriel, Brian Ellis, Rhoda Prager
2000 1. Judi Radin, Alex Ornstein, Sue Picus, Jeff Ferro, Sylvia Moss, Barry Rigal
2. Stephen Cooper, Kitty Munson-Cooper, Betty Bloom, Steve Bloom, Mel Colchamiro, Janet Colchamiro

From 1946-1955 a separate event with national rating was held on the West Coast.
1946 1. Nell Wells, George Wells, Kay Dunn, James Dunn
1947 1. Rose Eidem, Meyer Schleifer, Betty Bysshe, Detmar Walther
1948 1. Alma Rosekrans, Waldemar von Zedtwitz, Maurice Seiler, Mrs. Maurice Seiler
1949 1. Arnold Kauder, Mary Jane Kauder, Helen Cale, Jack Ehrlenbach
1950 1. Arnold Kauder, Mary Jane Kauder, Helen Cale, Jack Ehrlenbach
1951 1. Ruth Smith, Casey Million, Nell Wells, John Hancock
1952 1. Don Oakie, Mrs. James Moffatt, Stella Rebner, Doug Steen
1953 1. Barry Cohen, Stella Rebner, Malvine Klausner, Dr. Eddie Frischauer
1954 1. Harriet Rethers, Clarence Strouse, Alicia Kempner, Barry Crane
1955 1. Arnold Kauder, Mary Jane Kauder, Nell Wells, Ernest Rovere

RED RIBBON PAIRS. This event, with two quali-fying and two final sessions, is open only to pairs that qualify by winning or placing second in two-

session regional-rated events. Both members of the pair must have fewer than 2000 masterpoints.

1986	1.	Wayne Perrin, Martin Newland
	2.	Hugh Ogle, Charlie Cargile
1987	1.	Jim Gaarder, Jimmy Ritzenberg
	2.	Charles Moser, Paul Bratton
1988	1.	Leni Holtz, Guy Green
	2.	Anthony Trafecanty, Michael Trafecanty
1989	1.	Lu Kohutiak, Yvonne Hernandez
	2-3.	Warren Haynie, Charlie Cargile
	2-3.	Bill Goldberg, Bill McKenna
1990	1.	Philip Gordon, Mike Grodsky
	2.	Rajendra Agarwal, Don Chillrud
1991	1.	Dan Marthaler, Robert Johnstone
	2.	Steven Gaynor, Art Ardy Bakshian
1992	1.	Duncan McCallum, Peter Peng
	2.	Andy Goodman, Steve Zolotow
1993	1.	Ron Weinstock, John Gillette
	2.	Hank Meyer, Marty Graf
1994	1.	T.C. Petty, Steve Altus
	2.	Grant Robinson, Joe Waldon
1995	1.	Marc Umeno, Hank Youngerman
	2.	Bernie Greenspan, Keith Sechler
1996	1.	Vinay Sarin, Ringo Chung
	2.	Burton Lipsky, Arnold Goldstein
1997	1.	Diane Miller, Tony Miller
	2.	Mark Bumgardner, Nagy Kamel
1998	1.	Paul Spear, Jim Johnson
	2.	Mike Nadler, Davd Halasi
1999	1.	Jennifer-Jo Hartsman, Andrew Rosenthal
	2.	Andy Stark, Martin Hunter
2000	1.	Nie Wei Ping, Christopher Leung
	2.	Xiaodong Shi, David Yang

SENIOR AND ADVANCED SENIOR MASTER PAIRS.

This four-session event with two qualifying sessions and two final sessions was contested for the R. L. MILES TROPHY through 1975.

1950	1.	John Winsten, Mrs. John Winsten
	2-3.	Dorothy E. Berning, Sims Gaynor
	2-3.	Dorsey W. Brooks, Fred Gregorich
1951	1.	Ben Fain, Julius L. Rosenblum
	2.	Dorothy Glick, Aaron Ritter

1952	1.	Elaine Lee, Harry Feinburg
	2.	Betty Harding, Mrs. Allan E. van Ness
1953	1-2.	Dr. Robert M. Lloyd, Elfric H. Martin
	1-2.	Margaret L. Fisher, Kiffin Rockwell
1954	1.	Armand Fahrer, Richard B. Troxel
	2.	Richard G. Lesko, Paul A. Schwarz
1955	1.	Stanley Rappaport, Herschel Wolpert
	2.	Robert Sitnek, Betty Windley
1956	1.	Nat Gerstman, Mrs. Marshall Nevins
	2.	George Ateljevich, Robert E. Herb
1957	1-2.	Arnold Levine, Harold Solof
	1-2.	Daniel J. Conroy, William T. Dean
1958	1.	Fritz J. Hopf, Mrs. Fritz J. Hopf
	2.	Allan R. Cohen, Herbert C. Wilton
1959	1.	Victor Lohmann, Robert L. Muyres
	2.	Ira Ewen, Thomas C. Griffin
1960	1.	Lillian Hilbert, Forest Lowe
	2.	Ruth Row, Stephens Roe
1961	1.	Amos Brown, Mark D. Mohr
	2.	Dr. Ronald Forbes, Jack Howell
1962	1.	Leon Shore, George Tornay
	2.	Richard Dufour, Hugh C. MacLean
1963	1.	Gerard Hallee, Paul Soloway
	2.	Frank Adams, Max Neiman
1964	1.	Mrs. R. Gust, Jr., Mrs. Leslie Wilcox
	2.	Gerald A. Caravelli, Alan Levine
1965	1.	Muriel Levin, Delle Levinson
	2.	Don Guerin, Charlotte Sturm
1966	1.	Carla Gross, H. E. Pries
	2.	Steve Goldstein, Ron Rubin
1967	1.	Alvin Levy, Harold Thaw
	2.	Maryanne Drury, Kenneth Kadis
1968	1.	Henry Greenberg, John Landon
	2.	Howard Abrams, Jim Crumpacker
1969	1.	Col. William B. Foster, Bobbie Foster
	2.	Judy Carmena, Proctor Hawkins
1970	1.	Michael Krevor, James Lewis
	2.	Dennis McGarry, Louis Reich
1971	1.	William L. Geleerd, Jr., Marc S. Passman
	2.	Bert Newman, Dave Turner
1972	1.	Chris Patrias, Dr. Wen Y. Yue
	2.	Robert Bell, Jeff Hall
1973	1.	Joel Friedberg, Harry Looks
	2.	William Post, Alvin Swonger
1974	1.	Dale Beers, Dave Silberstein
	2.	Ethan Stein, Karen Swenson
1975	1.	Kitty Munson, Robert Schachter
	2.	John Brady, Patricia Murphy

Fall Championships

REISINGER BOARD-A-MATCH TEAMS.

This event is contested for the REISINGER TROPHY (originally the CHICAGO TROPHY until 1965). It is a six-session Open Team-of-Four event scored by Board-a-Match with two qualifying sessions, two semifinal sessions and two final sessions. It was contested as a four-session championship until 1966.

1929	1.	Max M. Cohen, Louis J. Haddad, Robert W. Halpin, Nils M. Wester
	2.	Carlton R. Drake, James Kelly, Paul D. Parcells, Charles Rilling
1930	1.	William K. Barrett, W. James Carpenter, Ely Culbertson, Johnny Rau
	2.	Mary Clement, Dorothy Rice Sims, P. Hal Sims, Waldemar K. von Zedtwitz
1931	1.	Elizabeth Banfield, Cmdr. Winfield S. Liggett, Jr., Frances Newman, George Unger
	2.	David Burnstine, Oswald Jacoby, Willard S. Karn, P. Hal Sims
1932	1.	B. Jay Becker, S. Garton Churchill, George Reith, Waldemar K. von Zedtwitz
	2.	Ely Culbertson, Michael T. Gottlieb, Oswald Jacoby, Theodore A. Lightner
1933	1.	Charles A. Hall, Albert Steiner, Philip Steiner, Richard M. Wildberg
	2.	B. Jay Becker, S. Garton Churchill, P. Hal Sims,

		Waldemar K. von Zedtwitz
1934	1.	Henry S. Dinkelspiel, Jr., Lewis Jaeger, Bernard Rabinowitz, Maurice Seiler
	2.	Theodore A. Lightner, Merwyn D. Maier, Jean P. Mattheys, Sherman Stearns
1935	1.	F. Roland Buck, Joseph E. Cain, Lawrence J. Welch, Edson T. Wood
	2.	Ely Culbertson, Josephine Culbertson, Richard L. Frey, Albert H. Morehead
1936	1.	Marge Anderson, Donald G. Farquharson, Mrs. J. A. Faulkner, Percy E. Sheardown
	2.	Arthur Glatt, Laura Heiner, John R. Smith, Albert Weiss
1937	1.	John R. Crawford, Charles H. Goren, Charles J. Solomon, Sally Young
	2.	Oscar J. Brotman, William Perry, Alvin Roth, S. S. Vorzimer
1938	1.	John R. Crawford, Charles H. Goren, Charles J. Solomon, Sally Young
	2.	A. Mitchell Barnes, Mary Clement, Benedict Jarmel, Waldemar K. von Zedtwitz
1939	1.	B. Jay Becker, John R. Crawford, Charles H. Goren, Charles J. Solomon, Sally Young
	2-4.	Jay Cushing, Seymour Kaplan, Al Leibowitz, Edward N. Marcus
	2-4.	Oswald Jacoby, Merwyn D. Maier, Robert A. McPherran, Waldemar K. von Zedtwitz
	2-4.	Henry Auslander, Joseph Davis, Jacob D. Lindy, Catherine W. Samberg
1940	1.	Henry Feinberg, Jeff Glick, Maury J. Glick, Louis Newman
	2.	Alfred R. Dick, C. William Potts, James Sheern,

		Edward R. Thomas
1941	1.	Peter A. Leventritt, Simon Rossant, Helen Sobel, Margaret Wagar
	2.	A. Mitchel Barnes, S. Garton Churchill, Lee Hazen, Charles S. Lockridge, Waldemar K. von Zedtwitz
1942	1.	B. Jay Becker, Charles H. Goren, Sidney Silodor, John R. Crawford
	2.	S. Garton Churchill, Harry J. Fishbein, Lee Hazen, Waldemar K. von Zedtwitz
1943	1.	B. Jay Becker, Charles H. Goren, Sidney Silodor, Helen Sobel
	2.	Samuel Katz, Bertram Lebhar, Jr., Peter A. Leventritt, Simon Rossant
1944	1.	Simon Becker, Peggy Golder, Ruth Sherman, Charles J. Solomon
	2.	B. Jay Becker, Charles H. Goren, Sidney Silodor, Helen Sobel
1945	1.	Lee Hazen, George Rapee, Samuel M. Stayman, Waldemar K. von Zedtwitz
	2.	Ambrose Casner, Harold J. Harkavy, Ralph Hirschberg, Harold A. Ogust, Jack Shore
1946	1.	A. Mitchel Barnes, John R. Crawford, Alvin Roth, Edith Seligman
	2.	Simon Becker, Stanley O. Fenkel, Fred D. Karpin, Louis Newman
1947	1-3.	Paula Bacher, Jane Jaeger, Kay Rhodes, Sally Young
	1-3.	John R. Crawford, Theodore A. Lightner, George Rapee, Samuel M. Stayman
	1-3.	Robert Appleyard, Morris Berliant, Malcolm A. Lightman, Simon Rossant
1948	1.	George Boeckh, C. Bruce Elliott, Agnes Gordon, Charlotte Sidway
	2.	John R. Crawford, George Rapee, Sidney Silodor, Samuel M. Stayman
1949	1.	Lee Hazen, Larry Hirsch, Richard Kahn, Peter A. Leventritt, Jack Shore
	2-3.	Sidney Aronson, Emily Folline, Benjamin O. Johnson, Ludwig J. Kabakjian, Edward N. Marcus
	2-3.	Jeff Glick, Arthur S. Goldsmith, Alvin Landy, Sol Mogal, Elmer I. Schwartz
1950	1.	B. Jay Becker, Myron F. Field, Charles H. Goren, Sidney Silodor, Helen Sobel
	2.	John R. Crawford, George Rapee, Edward N. Marcus, Howard Schenken, Samuel M. Stayman
1951	1.	Corti Boland, C. Bruce Elliot, Micky M. Miller, Percy E. Sheardown
	2.	B. Jay Becker, Charles H. Goren, Myron F. Field, Sidney Silodor, Helen Sobel
1952	1.	Harold Harkavy, Edith Kemp, Alvin Roth, Tobias Stone
	2.	Edward H. Cohen, Jeff Glick, Arthur S. Goldsmith, Elmer I. Schwartz
1953	1.	B. Jay Becker, John R. Crawford, George Rapee, Samuel M. Stayman
	2.	Harry J. Fishbein, Peter A. Leventritt, Ruth Sherman, Charles J. Solomon, Peggy Solomon
1954	1.	B. Jay Becker, John R. Crawford, George Rapee, Sidney Silodor
	2.	Israel Cohen, Paul Kibler, Alvin Roth, William Seamon
1955	1.	Ben Fain, George Heath, Paul Hodge, James Jacoby, Oswald Jacoby
	2.	William V. Lipton, Victor Mitchell, W. Miller Nelson, Joseph G. Ripstra
1956	1.	B. Jay Becker, John R. Crawford, George Rapee, Sidney Silodor
	2.	Ben Fain, Paul Hodge, Oswald Jacoby, Dick Sutton
1957	1.	Charles H. Goren, Harold A. Ogust, William S. Root, Howard Schenken, Helen Sobel
	2.	Robert Y. Barrett, Ben Fain, Harry J. Fishbein, John Gerber, Paul Hodge
1958	1.	Leonard B. Harmon, Ralph Hirschberg, Edgar Kaplan, Alfred Sheinwold, Ivar Stakgold
	2.	Arthur M. Miller, John H. Moran, David Strasberg, Jay Wendt
1959	1.	Lewis L. Mathe, Donald A. Oakie, Meyer Schleifer, Edward O. Taylor
	2.	Harry J. Fishbein, John Gerber, Paul Hodge, Charles J. Solomon
1960	1.	Ollie Adams, William Hanna, Sidney H. Lazard, Lewis L. Mathe

	2.	Oswald Jacoby, Mervin Key, G. Robert Nail, Curtis Smith
1961	1.	John R. Crawford, Norman Kay, Alvin Roth, Sidney Silodor, Tobias Stone
	2-3.	Charles Coon, Robert F. Jordan, Eric R. Murray, Arthur G. Robinson
	2-3.	Harold B. Guiver, Carol Sanders, Thomas K. Sanders, Michael Shuman
1962	1-2.	Paul Allinger, Harold B. Guiver, Lewis L. Mathe, Ron Von der Porten, Erik Paulsen, Edward O. Taylor
	1-2.	Robert D. Hamman, Eddie Kantar, Donald P. Krauss, Marshall Miles, Bill Eisenberg
1963	1.	Charles H. Goren, Peter A. Leventritt, Harold A. Ogust, Howard Schenken
	2.	Donald R. Faskow, William L. Flannery, Herbert Sachs, Paul Swanson
1964	1.	John Gerber, Paul Hodge, Mervin Key, Harold Rockaway
	2.	Harold Harkavy, Edith Kemp, Cliff Russell, Curtis K. Smith, Bobby Wolff, Waldemar K. von Zedtwitz
1965	1.	Eddie Kantar, Michael S. Lawrence, Marshall Miles, Lew Stansby
	2.	Michael Engel, Phil Feldesman, Richard Freeman, Ira S. Rubin
1966	1.	Robert F. Jordan, Edgar Kaplan, Norman Kay, Arthur G. Robinson
	2-3.	Gerald W. Bare, Harold B. Guiver, Lewis L. Mathe, Mike McMahan, Erik Paulsen, Hugh Ross
	2-3.	William S. Root, Alvin Roth, Bee Schenken, Howard Schenken
1967	1.	Robert F. Jordan, Edgar Kaplan, Norman Kay, Arthur G. Robinson, William S. Root, Alvin Roth
	2.	Steve Altman, Michael M. Becker, Charles Peres, Daniel Rotman
1968	1.	Kyle Larsen, Erik Paulsen, Peter A. Pender, Hugh Ross, Howard Schenken
	2.	Bill Eisenberg, Bobby Goldman, Robert D. Hamman, Eddie Kantar, Sidney Lazard, George Rapee
1969	1.	Philip Feldesman, William Grieve, Ira Rubin, Jeff Westheimer
	2.	Edgar Kaplan, Norman Kay, Sami R. Kehela, Sidney Lazard, Eric R. Murray, George Rapee
1970	1-2.	Bill Eisenberg, Bobby Goldman, Robert D. Hamman, James Jacoby, Michael S. Lawrence, Bobby Wolff
	1-2.	Grant S. Baze, Anthony H. Dionisi, William P. Grieve, Harlow S. Lewis, Peter A. Pender, George Rapee
1971	1.	William Grieve, Edgar Kaplan, Norman Kay, Donald P. Krauss, Lewis L. Mathe, George Rapee
	2.	Grant S. Baze, Anthony H. Dionisi, Harlow S. Lewis, Peter A. Pender
1972	1.	Lou Bluhm, Steve Goldberg, Steven J. Parker, Stephen W. Robinson
	2.	William Grieve, Sami R. Kehela, Eric R. Murray, George Rapee
1973	1.	Larry Cohen, Dr. Richard H. Katz, Bud Reinhold, Alan Sontag, Peter Weichsel
	2.	Jack Blair, Byron L. Greenberg, Thomas K. Sanders, Paul Swanson
1974	1.	Fred Hamilton, Erik Paulsen, Hugh Ross, Ira S. Rubin
	2.	Stephen Goldstein, Marc S. Jacobus, J. Merrill, Steve Sion, John Solodar
1975	1.	Fred Hamilton, Erik Paulsen, Hugh Ross, Ira S. Rubin
	2.	Richard E. Doughty, Frank M. Hoadley, Jack LaNoue, Sidney H. Lazard
1976	1.	Malcolm K. Brachman, Bill Eisenberg, Bobby Goldman, Eddie Kantar, Mike Passell, Paul Soloway
	2.	Matt Granovetter, Robert H. Lipsitz, Steven J. Parker, Samuel M. Stayman
1977	1.	Jim Cayne, Alan Greenberg, James Jacoby, Kyle Larsen, Michael S. Lawrence
	2.	Matt Granovetter, Robert H. Lipsitz, Neil Silverman, Samuel M. Stayman
1978	1.	Ira G. Corn, Jr., Fred Hamilton, Robert D. Hamman, Ira S. Rubin, Bobby Wolff

	2.	Allan Graves, Gaylor Kasle, Mark Lair, George Mittelman, Barney O'Malia, Ron Smith
1979	1-2.	Russ Arnold, Robert Levin, Jeff Meckstroth, Bud Reinhold, Eric Rodwell
	1-2.	Ira G. Corn, Jr., Fred Hamilton, Robert D. Hamman, Ira S. Rubin, Bobby Wolff
1980	1.	Ron E. Andersen, Malcolm K. Brachman, Bobby Goldman, Eddie Kantar, Michael S. Lawrence, Paul Soloway
	2-3.	Mark Lair, Jeff Meckstroth, Mike Passell, Eric Rodwell, George Rosenkranz, Eddie Wold
	2-3.	Roy Fox, Ed Manfield, Paul Swanson, Kit Woolsey
1981	1.	Chip Martel, Peter A. Pender, Hugh Ross, Lew Stansby
	2-3.	Roger Bates, Chuck F. Burger, Jim Cayne, Bill Eisenberg, Alan Greenberg
	2-3.	Evan Bailey, L. Andrew Campbell, Joel Hoersch, David J. Weiss
1982	1.	Bill Root, Richard Pavlicek, Edgar Kaplan, Norman Kay
	2.	Mark Molson, Eric Kokish, Paul Lewis, Robert Lebi, George Mittelman, Drew Cannell
1983	1.	Oswald Jacoby, Edgar Kaplan, Norman Kay, Bill Root, Richard Pavlicek
	2-3	Ron Rubin, Mike Becker, Bill Eisenberg, Eddie Kantar, Mike Lawrence, Peter Weichsel
	2-3.	Chip Martel, Lew Stansby, Peter Pender, Hugh Ross
1984	1-4.	Bill Root, Richard Pavlicek, Edgar Kaplan, Norman Kay
	1-4.	Fred Stewart, Steve Weinstein, Allan Stauber, Mike Smolen
	1-4.	Sam Stayman, Richard Reisig, George Tornay, Saul Bronstein
	1-4.	Jim Robison, Jon Wittes, Ross Grabel, Stelios Touchtidis
1985	1-2.	Chip Martel, Peter Pender, Hugh Ross, Lew Stansby
	1-2.	George Rosenkranz, Eddie Wold, Jeff Meckstroth, Eric Rodwell, Marty Bergen, Larry N. Cohen
1986	1.	Steve Robinson, Chip Martel, Hugh Ross, Peter Boyd, Peter Pender, Lew Stansby
	2.	Bud Reinhold, Ron Andersen, Tom Sanders, Paul Soloway, Bobby Goldman
1987	1.	Zia Mahmood, Jaggy Shivdasani, Billy Cohen, Ron Smith
	2.	Walter Johnson, Mark Cohen, Ralph Katz, Bill Pollack, Dave Berkowitz, Howard Weinstein
1988	1.	Jimmy Cayne, Bob Hamman, Mike Passell, Mark Lair, Chuck Berger, Bobby Wolff
	2.	Tom Fox, Dick Melson, Jim Hall, David Lehman
1989	1.	Zia Mahmood, Michael Rosenberg, Sam Lev, Chris Compton, Mark Molson
	2.	Jillian Blanchard, Robert Blanchard, Jon Greenspan, Kerri Shuman, Margie Gwozdzinsky, Glenn Eisenstein
1990	1.	Richard Pavlicek, William Root, Edgar Kaplan, Norman Kay, Brian Glubok
	2.	Malcolm Brachman, Mike Passell, Paul Soloway, Bobby Goldman, Mark Lair, Eddie Wold
1991	1.	Cliff Russell, Sam Lev, Larry N. Cohen, David Berkowitz, Marty Bergen, Bjorn Fallenius
	2.	Mike Cappelletti, Jr., Mike Cappelletti, Sr., Lawrence Hicks, Rob Crawford
1992	1.	James Cayne, Mike Passell, Mark Lair, Chuck Burger, Gabriel Chagas, Marcelo Branco
	2.	Jim Mahaffey, Alan Sontag, Eddie Kantar, Ron Andersen, Tony Forrester
1993	1.	Nick Nickell, Richard Freeman, Bob Hamman, Bobby Wolff, Jeff Meckstroth, Eric Rodwell
	2.	Jimmy Cayne, Chuck Burger, Mike Passell, Paul Soloway, Bobby Goldman, Mark Lair
1994	1.	Nick Nickell, Richard Freeman, Bob Hamman, Bobby Wolff, Jeff Meckstroth, Eric Rodwell
	2.	James Cayne, Bobby Goldman, Mark Lair, Mike Passell, Chuck Burger, Paul Soloway
1995	1.	Nick Nickell, Richard Freeman, Bob Hamman, Bobby Wolff, Jeff Meckstroth, Eric Rodwell
	2.	Peter Nagy, Bruce Ferguson, Howard Weinstein, Ralph Katz, Fred Stewart, Steve Weinstein
1996	1.	Zia Mahmood, Michael Rosenberg, Chip Martel,

		Lew Stansby
	2.	James Cayne, Mark Feldman, Chuck Burger, Michael Seamon, Mike Passell, Alan Sontag
1997	1.	Bart Bramley, Howard Weinstein, Sidney Lazard, Steve Garner
	2.	George Rosenkranz, Eddie Wold, Adam Zmudzinski, Marek Szymanowski, Marcin Lesniewski, Cezary Balicki
1998	1.	Rita Shugart, Andrew Robson, Geir Helgemo, Tony Forrester
	2.	George Jacobs, Ralph Katz, Lorenzo Lauria, Alfredo Versace, PeterWeichsel, Alan Sontag
1999	1.	Rita Shugart, Andrew Robson, Geir Helgemo, Tony Forrester
	2.	Dano DeFalco, Giorgio Duboin, Guido Ferraro, Norberto Bocchi
2000	1.	George Jacobs, Alfredo Versace, Lorenzo Lauria, Ralph Katz, Norberto Bocchi, Giorgio Duboin
	2.	Mike Cappelletti Jr., Gary Cohler, Richard Finberg, Mark Lair, Jerry Goldfein

BLUE RIBBON PAIRS. This event is contested for the CAVENDISH TROPHY. It is a six-session pair event with two qualifying sessions. Entry is restricted to winners and runners-up in regional championships and high finishers in North American Championships, members of current Grand National District Championship teams, members of current official teams representing the ACBL or member countries of the ACBL, together with the top 100 lifetime masterpoint holders.

1963	1.	B. Jay Becker, Dorothy Hayden
	2.	Harold Harkavy, Cliff Russell
1964	1.	Robert D. Hamman, Lewis L. Mathe
	2.	Gunther Polak, Robert G. Sharp
1965	1.	Chuck Henke, John H. Moran
	2.	Michael S. Lawrence, Ron Von der Porten
1966	1.	Charles Coon, Richard Zeckhauser
	2.	Leland Ferer, Gratian Goldstein
1967	1.	Sami R. Kehela, Baron Wolf Lebovic
	2.	Phil Feldesman, Lewis L. Mathe
1968	1.	Larry Cohen, Richard H. Katz
	2.	Bobby Goldman, Michael S. Lawrence
1969	1.	Erik Paulsen, Alex Tschekaloff
	2-4.	Sami R. Kehela, Eric R. Murray
	2-4.	Tom Hodapp, Robert F. Morris
	2-4.	Larry Cohen, Richard H. Katz
1970	1.	Chuck F. Burger, Ira S. Rubin
	2.	Richard Freeman, Cliff Russell
1971	1.	Roger Bates, John M. Grantham
	2.	Hermine Baron, Michael S. Lawrence
1972	1.	Richard Khautin, Warren Kornfeld
	2.	Garey Hayden, Mark Lair
1973	1.	Steve Robinson, Kit Woolsey
	2.	Kathie Cappelletti, Mike Cappelletti
1974	1.	Edgar Kaplan, Norman Kay
	2.	Roger Bates, George Rosenkranz
1975	1.	Steve Robinson, Kit Woolsey
	2.	Ron E. Andersen, Hugh C. MacLean
1976	1.	Jay Apfelbaum, Bill Edelstein
	2.	James Jacoby, David Berkowitz
1977	1.	Lou Bluhm, Thomas K. Sanders
	2.	Kathie Cappelletti, Mike Cappelletti
1978	1.	Ron E. Andersen, David Berkowitz
	2.	Ted Horning, Peter Nagy
1979	1.	Robert Levin, Ron Smith
	2.	James Bennett, Chester Davis
1980	1.	Warren Rosner, Allan Stauber
	2.	Dan Morse, G. Robert Nail
1981	1.	Larry N. Cohen, Ron Gerard
	2.	Chip Martel, Lew Stansby
1982	1.	Eric Rodwell, Jeff Meckstroth
	2-3.	Robert Blanchard, Drew Casen
	2-3.	Peter Boyd, Steve Robinson
1983	1.	Marty Bergen, Larry N. Cohen
	2.	Peter Weichsel, Mike Lawrence
1984	1-2.	Jack Kennedy, Bobby Wolff
	1-2.	David Funk, Mark Lair
1985	1.	Eric Rodwell, Walter Johnson

		(left column)
	2.	Kit Woolsey, Ed Manfield
1986	1.	Bob Hamman, Ron Von der Porten
	2.	Kit Woolsey, Ed Manfield
1987	1.	Fred Stewart, Steve Weinstein
	2.	Kerri Shuman, Robert Levin
1988	1.	Marty Bergen, Larry N. Cohen
	2.	Robert Levin, Ron Smith
1989	1.	Mark Molson, Robert Lebi
	2.	Gaylor Kasle, Roger Bates
1990	1.	Kit Woolsey, Ed Manfield
	2.	Brian Glubok, Sam Lev
1991	1.	Bob Hamman, Nick Nickell
	2.	Mark Tolliver, Marc Zwerling
1992	1.	Haig Tchamitch, Adam Wildavsky
	2.	Brad Moss, Ravindra Murthy
1993	1.	Bob Hamman, Michael Rosenberg
	2.	Martin De Bruin, Steve Price
1994	1.	Mark Lair, Alexander Weiland
	2.	Fred Stewart, Steve Weinstein
1995	1.	David Berkowitz, Larry Cohen
	2.	Paul Kiefer, Jerry Helms
1996	1.	Jim Krekorian, Bob Blanchard
	2.	Larry Cohen. David Berkowitz
1997	1.	Adam Wildavsky, Allan Falk
	2.	Geir Helgemo, Tony Forrester
1998	1.	Zia Mahmood, Howard Weinstein
	2.	Eric Rodwell, Marty Seligman
1999	1.	Jill Meyers, John Mohan
	2.	John Sutherlin, Russ Ekeblad
2000	1.	Richard Coren, Marc Jacobus
	2.	Robert Levin, Steve Weinstein

LIFE MASTER OPEN PAIRS, formerly LIFE MASTER MEN'S PAIRS.

It is a four-session event with two qualifying sessions and two final sessions, restricted to Life Masters. Before 1963 it was restricted to National Masters and players of higher rank. It was a men's event until 1990 when it became an open event.

1961	1.	G. Gard Hays, Max Manchester
	2.	Martin J. Cohn, Hampton Hume
1962	1.	Sam Fuoto, Victor Mitchell
	2.	Hal Kandler, Kelsey Petterson
1963	1.	Sami R. Kehela, Eric R. Murray
	2.	Harry J. Fishbein, Charles J. Solomon
1964	1.	Charles Coon, Bobby Goldman
	2-3.	Mervin Key, Harold Rockaway
	2-3.	Jack Blair, Col. William Christian
1965	1.	Paul Soloway, Alex Tschekaloff
	2.	Edgar Kaplan, Victor Mitchell
1966	1.	Carl J. Hudeck, Ray Zoller
	2.	Gaylor Kasle, Ed Theus
1967	1.	Harlow S. Lewis, Peter A. Pender
	2.	Donald R. Faskow, William L. Flannery
1968	1.	Henry Bethe, John Solodar
	2.	Don Pearson, John Swanson
1969	1.	Chuck F. Burger, James Cayne
	2.	Norman H. Fischer, Christopher G. Jeans
1970	1.	Ron E. Andersen, Hugh C. MacLean
	2.	Curtis K. Smith, E. Lowell Yost
1971	1.	Alan Sontag, Peter Weichsel
	2.	Stephen W. Robinson, Kit Woolsey
1972	1.	Leslie C. Bart, Marc S. Jacobus
	2.	Stephen W. Robinson, Kit Woolsey
1973	1.	Edgar Kaplan, Norman Kay
	2.	Roxy Violin, Ed Weiner
1974	1.	Gerald L. Michaud, G. Robert Nail
	2.	John Gerber, Daniel Kaim
1975	1.	Steve Lapides, Walt Walvick
	2.	Marc Culbertson, Robert Visokey
1976	1.	Roger Bates, John Mohan
	2.	Steve Altman, Thomas M. Smith
1977	1.	David Hoffner, David Schroeder
	2.	Roger Bates, John Mohan
1978	1.	Norm Coombs, Tom Hodapp
	2.	Kevin Castner, Michael S. Lawrence
1979	1.	Jeff Meckstroth, Eric Rodwell
	2.	Zeke Jabbour, Dennis McGarry
1980	1.	V. Craig Janitschke, Jan Janitschke
	2.	Robert D. Hamman, Paul Swanson
1981	1.	Roger Abelson, Mike Levinson

	2.	Robert D. Hamman, Donald P. Krauss
1982	1.	Robert Lipsitz, Dan Gerstman
	2.	Lew Mathe, Harold Guiver
1983	1.	Marty Bergen, Larry N. Cohen
	2.	Mitch Chandler, Cliff Bishop
1984	1.	Per Olov Sundelin, Peter Pender
	2.	Jim Becker, Howard Chandross
1985	1.	John Mohan, Roger Bates
	2.	Eric Rodwell, Jeff Meckstroth
1986	1.	Jim Krekorian, Paul Kiefer
	2.	Marty Bergen, Larry N. Cohen
1987	1.	Bart Bramley, Lou Bluhm
	2.	Leslie West, David Ashley
1988	1.	Robert Levin, Larry Cohen
	2.	Glen Lublin, Peter Boyd
1989	1.	Steve Lapides, Walt Walvick
	2.	Peter Weichsel, Roger Stern

In 1990 the event became the LIFE MASTER OPEN PAIRS.

1990	1.	Zia Mahmood, Hugh Ross
	2.	Tommy Gullberg, Michael Polowan
1991	1.	Zia Mahmood, Hugh Ross
	2.	Larry N. Cohen, David Berkowitz
1992	1.	Mike Kamil, Michael Rosenberg
	2.	Jeff Meckstroth, Eric Rodwell
1993	1.	Brad Moss, Ravindra Murthy
	2.	Ed Nagy, Jeff Polisner
1994	1.	Robert Levin, Richard Katz
	2.	Michael Polowan, Steve Robinson
1995	1.	John Sutherlin, Bart Bramley
	2.	Mark Itabashi, Gene Simpson
1996	1.	Walter Schafer, Ron Smith
	2.	Michael Schreiber, Curtis Cheek
1997	1.	Kerry Smith, Jeff Schuett
	2.	Dennis Kasle, Garey Hayden
1998	1.	JoAnna Stansby, Lew Stansby
	2.	Ron Smith, Richard Schwartz
1999	1.	Paul Soloway, Steve Catlett
	2.	Lew Stansby, JoAnna Stansby
2000	1.	Jill Meyers, Steve Garner
	2.	Zia Mahmood, Chuck Burger

LIFE MASTER WOMEN'S PAIRS.

This event is contested for the HELEN SOBEL SMITH TROPHY. It is a four-session event with two qualifying sessions and two final sessions, restricted to Life Masters. Prior to 1963 it was restricted to National Masters and players of higher rank.

1961	1.	Dorothy Hayden, Helen Portugal
	2.	Gratian Goldstein, Jane Mueller
1962	1.	Barbara Kachmar, Margaret Wagar
	2.	Anne Burnstein, Edith Kemp
1963	1.	Anne Burnstein, Hermine Baron
	2.	Carrie Arnold, Neva L. Gray
1964	1.	Margaret Alcorn, Betty Kaplan
	2.	Agnes Gordon, Sylvia Stein
1965	1.	Ann Sheaber, Jan Stone
	2.	Mary Jane Farell, Peggy Solomon
1966	1.	Emma Jean Hawes, Dorothy Hayden
	2.	Mary Jane Farell, Peggy Solomon
1967	1.	Nancy Gruver, Edith Sachs
	2.	Mary Jane Farell, Peggy Solomon
1968	1.	Dorothy Talmage, Rhoda Walsh
	2.	Katherine Blanchard, Mary Jane Farell
1969	1.	Gratian Goldstein, Sylvia Stein
	2.	Karen Allison, Gladys W. Collier
1970	1.	Bette L. Cohn, Marietta Passell
	2.	Louise Krauss, Betty Mangan
1971	1.	Ruth Bloomfield, Delle Levinson
	2.	Betty Ann Kennedy, Carol Sanders
1972	1.	Amalya Kearse, Rhoda Walsh
	2.	Emma Jean Hawes, Dorothy Hayden Truscott
1973	1.	Frieda Arst, June Deutsch
	2.	Edith Kemp, Barbara Rappaport
1974	1.	Bernice Larson, Joan Stein
	2.	Edith Kemp, Barbara Rappaport
1975	1.	Dorothy Moore, Marion Weed
	2.	Nancy Gruver, Helen Utegaard
1976	1.	Barbara Furbeck, Barbara Herr

	2.	Carol Crawford, Joan Remey
1977	1.	Edith Kemp, Barbara Rappaport
	2.	Bernadine Jenkins, Joan Remey
1978	1.	Emma Jean Hawes, Dorothy Hayden Truscott
	2.	Ann Economidy, Anne Leverone
1979	1.	Nancy Gruver, Edith Kemp
	2.	June Deutsch, Sandi Leavitt
1980	1.	Kathie Cappelletti, Claire Tornay
	2.	Nancy Gruver, Edith Kemp
1981	1.	Nancy Gruver, Edith Kemp
	2.	Betty Ann Kennedy, Carol Sanders
1982	1.	Dorothy Buchanan, Barbara Morris
	2.	Mary Albert, Rhoda Walsh
1983	1.	Beth Palmer, Lynn Deas
	2.	Sandra Low, Joan Stein
1984	1.	Karen Singer, Sharon Soules
	2.	Kathie Wei, Judi Radin
1985	1.	Lynn Deas, Beth Palmer
	2.	Rama Linz, Kerri Shuman
1986	1.	Mickie Kivel, Judi Cody
	2.	Rama Linz, Kerri Shuman
1987	1.	Jill Meyers, Gaye Herrington
	2.	Mary Ann Coyle, Jackie Hess
1988	1.	Nancy Passell, Nell Cahn
	2.	Brenda Keller, Renee Mancuso
1989	1.	Rhoda Walsh, Sabine Zenkel
	2.	Lynn Deas, Beth Palmer
1990	1.	Carol Sanders, Betty Ann Kennedy
	2.	Barbara Sartorius, Marla Chaikin
1991	1.	Sue Weinstein, Tobi Deutsch
	2.	Janice Seamon, Cheri Bjerkan
1992	1.	Shawn Womack, Jan Cohen
	2.	Sabine Zenkel, Joan Jackson
1993	1.	Janice Seamon, Sabine Zenkel
	2.	Sharon David, Trudi Nugit
1994	1.	Lynn Deas, Rhoda Kratenstein
	2.	Cynthia Balderson, Peg Waller
1995	1.	Flo Rotman, Susan Miller
	2.	Lila Perlstein, Juanita Chambers
1996	1.	Suzy Burger, Barbara Sion
	2.	Judy Randel, Linda Lewis
1997	1.	Janice Seamon, Sylvia Moss
	2.	Linda Perlman, Hjordis Eythorsdottir
1998	1.	Sharon Hait, Barbara Sartorius
	2.	Shannon Lipscomb, Rhoda Walsh
1999	1.	Mildred Breed, Shawn Quinn
	2.	Nell Cahn, Ellen Siebert
2000	1.	Mildred Breed, Shawn Quinn
	2.	Joan Jackson, Robin Klar

OPEN BOARD-A-MATCH TEAMS, formerly MEN'S BOARD-A-MATCH TEAMS.

This four-session event consists of two qualifying and two final sessions. It was a men's event until 1990 when it became an open event. This event is contested for the GOREN TROPHY. It was contested as a three-session championship until 1972.

1946	1.	Maynard Adams, Julius Bank, Arthur Glatt, William McGhee, Albert Weiss
	2.	A. Mitchell Barnes, John R. Crawford, Charles H. Goren, George Rapee, Sidney Silodor
1947	1.	Jeff Glick, Arthur S. Goldsmith, Jack Kravatz, Alvin Landy, Sol Mogal
	2.	Joseph Cohan, Dr. Louis Mark, Dr. H. Russ Storr, George Unger
1948	1.	Jack L. Ankus, Jeff Glick, Alvin Landy, John H. Law, Sol Mogal
	2.	John R. Crawford, Edward N. Marcus, George Rapee, Samuel M. Stayman
1949	1.	Muriel Levin, Alphonse Moyse, Jr., Leo Roet, Howard Schenken
	2.	Joseph Cohan, Herbert J. Gerst, Jack L. Ankus, William Joseph, Dr. H. Russ Storr
1950	1.	Edward Burns, John F. Carlin, David Carter, A. Richard Revell
	2.	Robert Appleyard, Ned Drucker, Fred Hirsch, Milton Moss, Milton Vernoff
1951	1.	J. Van Brooks, Eugene Dautell, Jack Denny, Ace Gutowsky, Edwin J. Smith
	2.	Fred L. Bickel, Joseph J. Foreacre, Robert Lattomus, Ronald Rosenberg

1952	1.	Charles H. Goren, Oswald Jacoby, Sidney Silodor, Charles Solomon, Samuel M. Stayman
	2-3.	Samuel Katz, Charles Kuhn, William Seamon, Albert Weiss
	2-3.	Harry J. Fishbein, Harold Harkavy, Alvin Roth, Tobias Stone, Waldemar K. von Zedtwitz
1953	1.	Ben Fain, John Gerber, George Heath, Paul Hodge, Harold Rockaway
	2.	Clifford W. Bishop, Harry J. Fishbein, Arnold Kauder, John H. Moran, Douglas Steen
1954	1.	Aaron J. Frank, Jeff Glick, Arthur S. Goldsmith, Alvin Landy, Sol Mogal
	2.	Henry Chanin, Dr. John W. Fisher, James Jacoby, Oswald Jacoby, Sidney H. Lazard
1955	1.	Richard Freeman, Edgar Kaplan, Ralph Hirschberg, Norman Kay, Alvin Roth
	2.	Charles H. Goren, Peter A. Leventritt, Charles J. Solomon, Samuel M. Stayman
1956	1.	John R. Crawford, Ben Fain, Paul H. Hodge, Sidney Silodor
	2-3.	Paul Allinger, Dr. John W. Fisher, Emanuel Hochfeld, Oswald Jacoby, Sidney H. Lazard
	2-3.	Barry Crane, Harold Rockaway, Clarence A. Strouse, John H. Toledano
1957	1.	Lewis L. Mathe, Donald A. Oakie, Meyer Schleifer, Edward O. Taylor
	2.	Israel Cohen, Richard Freeman, John C. Kunkel, Alvin Roth, Ivar Stakgold
1958	1.	Jeff Glick, Arthur S. Goldsmith, Alvin Landy, Elmer I. Schwartz, Vic D. Zeve
	2.	Richard Freeman, Edgar Kaplan, Norman Kay, Ralph Hirschberg
1959	1.	Ollie Adams, Ivan Erdos, Oswald Jacoby, Robert G. Sharp
	2.	B. Jay Becker, John R. Crawford, Sidney Silodor, Tobias Stone
1960	1.	Charles Denby, Burrell I. Humphreys, Alan W. Messer, Marty Scheinberg, Robert P. Wakeman
	2-4.	Harry J. Fishbein, John Gerber, Paul H. Hodge, Charles J. Solomon
	2-4	Wilfred Dumas, Donald McGee, John Siverts, Jerzy Zawisza
	2-4.	James R. Hughes, Marvin Paulshock, Eli Reich, David R. Treadwell
1961	1.	John R. Crawford, Norman Kay, Alvin Roth, Sidney Silodor, Tobias Stone
	2.	Edgar Kaplan, Mervin Key, Sidney H. Lazard, G. Robert Nail
1962	1-2.	Phil Feldesman, Richard Freeman, Victor Mitchell, Eric R. Murray, Samuel M. Stayman
	1-2.	Paul Allinger, Harold G. Guiver, Lewis L. Mathe, Edward O. Taylor
1963	1.	Phil Feldesman, Victor Mitchell, Samuel M. Stayman, Tobias Stone
	2.	B. Jay Becker, Norman Kay, William Root, Sol Rubinow, Sidney Silodor
1964	1.	Ivan Erdos, Harold B. Guiver, Michael S. Lawrence, Alfred Sheinwold
	2.	Charles Coon, G. Robert Nail, Robert Stucker, Frank T. Westcott
1965	1.	Harry J. Fishbein, Jeff Rubens, Charles J. Solomon, Roger D. Stern
	2.	Phil Feldesman, Sidney H. Lazard, Victor Mitchell, Daniel Rotman, Samuel M. Stayman
1966	1.	Philip Feldesman, Richard Freeman, Edgar Kaplan, Norman Kay
	2.	Anthony Dionisi, Jeremy Flint, Harlow S. Lewis, Peter A. Pender
1967	1.	Thomas E. Bussey, Jim R. Dunlap, Lawrence Jolma, Robert P. Patterson, Gary Stark
	2.	Edward J. Barlow, Phil Read, Robert Spotts, John C. Sutherlin
1968	1.	Ira G. Corn, Jr., Bill Eisenberg, Bobby Goldman, James Jacoby, Michael S. Lawrence, Bobby Wolff
	2.	Michael M. Becker, Charles Coon, Joel H. Stuart, Peter Weichsel, Richard J. Zeckhauser
1969	1.	Chuck F. Burger, James Cayne, Alvin Roth, Paul Trent
	2-3.	Bill Eisenberg, Bobby Goldman, Robert D. Hamman, James Jacoby, Michael S. Lawrence, Bobby Wolff
	2-3.	Martin J. Cohn, Norman H. Fischer, Charles M. MacCracken, Bill Reister
1970	1.	Bernie Bergovoy, Donald P. Krauss, Lewis L.

        Mathe, Don Pearson, John Swanson, Richard Walsh
- 2. Eddie Kantar, Kyle Larsen, Paul Soloway, Ron Von der Porten

1971 1. Bernie Chazen, Alvin Roth, Alan Sontag, Paul Trent
- 2. Gerald Caravelli, Larry Cohen, Barry Crane, Dr. John Fisher

1972 1. Jack Blair, James Jacoby, John Simon, Paul Swanson, Bobby Wolff
- 2. Grant S. Baze, William Grieve, Donald P. Krauss, Lewis L. Mathe, Peter A. Pender, George Rapee

1973 1. Garey Hayden, James Jacoby, Gaylor Kasle, John Simon, Bobby Wolff
- 2-3. Lou Bluhm, Steve Goldberg, Lawrence Gould, Stephen Robinson
- 2-3. John R. Crawford, Norm Kurlander, Alvin Roth, Clifford Russell, William Seamon

1974 1. Ron E. Andersen, Mark Feldman, Stephen Goldstein, Hugh C. MacLean, Merle Tom
- 2-3. Eric Kokish, Stephen Robinson, Mike Shuman, Joseph Silver
- 2-3. Harold B. Guiver, Marty Shallon, William Sides, Mike Smolen

1975 1. Matt Granovetter, William Grieve, George Rapee, Ron Rubin
- 2. Roger Bates, Edgar Kaplan, Norman Kay, George Rosenkranz

1976 1. David Ashley, Paul Heitner, John Lowenthal, Mike Smolen
- 2. Bart Bramley, Marvin Herbert, Howard Piltch, Lou Reich, Ira S. Rubin

1977 1. Lou Bluhm, Richard Doughty, Bruce Ferguson, Irv Kostal, Sidney H. Lazard, Ron Smith, Leslie West
- 2. Richard Freeman, Alvin Roth, Clifford Russell, Curtis K. Smith, Merle Tom, Art Waldmann

1978 1. Neil Chambers, Eric Kokish, Peter Nagy, Stephen Robinson, John Schermer, Kit Woolsey
- 2. Steve Garner, Dave Lehman, Dick Melson, Larry Oakey

1979 1. Allan Cokin, Steve Sion, Alan Sontag, Jim Sternberg, Peter Weichsel
- 2. Mike Cappelletti, Ron Feldman, Gary Hann, David Hoffner, Zeke Jabbour, David Sacks

1980 1. Bart Bramley, Ross Grabel, William Rosen, Milton Rosenberg, Samuel Stayman, George Tornay
- 2. Ira Corn, Fred Hamilton, Robert D. Hamman, Ira Rubin, Bobby Wolff

1981 1. Marty Bergen, Neil Chambers, Joseph Silver, Allan Stauber
- 2. Michael Aliotta, Marc Culbertson, Jim Gardner, Bert Newman

1982 1. Dave Berkowitz, Matt Granovetter, Harold Lilie, Al Rand
- 2. Robert Blanchard, Drew Casen, Chuck Lamprey, Thomas M. Smith

1983 1. Tom Sanders, Harold Guiver, Grant Baze, John Sutherlin
- 2. Cliff Russell, Robert Levin, Richard Freeman, Lou Bluhm, John Solodar, Ron Gerard

1984 1. George Rosenkranz, Eddie Wold, Jeff Meckstroth, Eric Rodwell, Marty Bergen, Larry N. Cohen
- 2. Malcolm Brachman, Bobby Wolff, Bob Hamman, Paul Soloway, Ron Andersen, Bobby Goldman

1985 1. Hal Mouse, Josh Parker, Ron Gerard, Dan Rotman
- 2. Roger Bates, John Mohan, Alan Sontag, John Devine

1986 1. Gene Freed, Mike Passell, Ed Manfield, Kit Woolsey, Mark Lair
- 2. Don Caton, Robert Kehoe, Gene Simpson, Robert Teel

1987 1. George Rosenkranz, Eddie Wold, Ira Chorush, Peter Weichsel, Robert Levin
- 2. Bart Bramley, Steve Garner, Howard Weinstein, Lou Bluhm

1988 1. Jimmy Cayne, Bob Hamman, Bobby Wolff, Mike Passell, Chuck Burger, Mark Lair
- 2. Vic Mitchell, Albert Rahmey, Michael Moss, Drew Casen, Howard Hertzberg

1989 1. Steve Robinson, Ed Manfield, Peter Boyd, Kit Woolsey
- 2. James Cayne, Chuck Burger, Bobby Wolff, Bob Hamman, Lew Stansby, Dave Berkowitz

In 1990 the Men's Board-a-Match Teams became the Open Board-a-Match Teams.

1990 1. Mark Moss, Robert Thompson, Daniel Molochko, Jack Wholey
- 2. George Rosenkranz, Eddie Wold, Peter Weichsel, Robert Levin, Marty Bergen, Larry N. Cohen

1991 1. Zia Mahmood, Michael Rosenberg, Jeffrey Wolfson, David Berkowitz, Larry N. Cohen
- 2. Jim Hall, Tom Fox, Dick Melson, David Lehman

1992 1. Richard Katz, Garey Hayden, Wafik Abdou, Ira Cohen, Mike Whitman (npc)
- 2. Drew Cannell, Jeffrey Hand, Claudio Caponi, Steve Hamaoui

1993 1. Paul Soloway, Bobby Goldman, Mark Lair, Mike Passell, Jimmy Cayne (npc)
- 2. Jim Hall, Tom Fox, Dave Lehman, Dick Melson

1994 1. Andy Goodman, Peter Boyd, Ed Manfield, John Mohan, Steve Robinson, Kit Woolsey
- 2. Brian Glubok, Steve Zolotow, Chris Compton, Lew Stansby, Ron Smith

1995 1. Chip Martel, Lew Stansby, Steve Weinstein, Fred Stewart
- 2. Jimmy Cayne; Chuck Burger, Paul Soloway, Mike Passell, Mark Lair, Bobby Goldman

1996 1. Robert Baldwin, Robert Levin, Peter Weichsel, Zia Mahmood, Michael Rosenberg
- 2. David Messop, Paul Hackett, Justin Hackett, Jason Hackett

1997 1. Bob Blanchard, Jim Krekorian, Doug Doub, John Rengstorff
- 2. Allen Hawkins, Russ Ekeblad, Jim Foster, John Sutherlin, Ron Smith

1998 1. Grant Baze, Fred Gitelman, George Mittelman, Brad Moss, Michael Whitman
- 2. Nick Nickell, Eric Rodwell, Bob Hamman, Paul Soloway, Jeff Meckstroth, Richard Freeman

1999 1. Rita Shugart, Geir Helgemo, Tony Forrester, Andrew Robson
- 2. Nick Nickell, Richard Freeman, Eric Rodwell, Jeff Meckstroth, Paul Soloway, Bob Hamman

2000 1. Andrew Gromov, Aleksander Petrunin, Cezary Balicki, Adam Zmudzinski
- 2. Eddie Wold, George Rosenkranz, Sam Lev, John Mohan, Piotr Gawrys, Jacek Pszczola

WOMEN'S BOARD-A-MATCH TEAMS. This four-session event has two qualifying and two final sessions.

1986 1. Lisa Berkowitz, Dorothy Truscott, Joyce Lilie, Jan Martel
- 2-4. Eunice Portnoy, Halina Jamner, Genevieve Geiger, Madelynn Treitel
- 2-4. Kathie Wei, Judi Radin, Jacqui Mitchell, Gail Greenberg, Carol Sanders, Betty Ann Kennedy
- 2-4. Rozanne Pollack, Roberta Epstein, Judy Tucker, Stasha Cohen, Sue Picus, Karen Allison

1987 1. Shirley Edelson, Donna Bailey, Lynn Blumenthal, Janice Randles
- 2-3. Rozanne Pollack, Randi Montin, Stasha Cohen, Pam Wittes, Judy Tucker
- 2-3. Lynne Feldman, Ellasue Chaitt, Sharon Osberg, Judi Cody

1988 1. Lynne Feldman, Rozanne Pollack, Lisa Berkowitz, Sharon Osberg
- 2-3. Mary Jane Farell, Roberta Epstein, Dorothy Truscott, Gail Greenberg, Kitty Bethe, Susan Green
- 2-3. Elspeth Moore, Andy O'Grady, Nancy Passell, Nell Cahn

1989 1. Lynne Schaefer, Suzy Burger, Petra Hamman, Joan Jackson
- 2. Beverly Rosenberg, Linda Lewis, Mary Hardy, Carol Pincus

1990 1-2. Jacqui Mitchell, Amalya Kearse, Joyce Lilie, Nancy Alpaugh, Pamela Granovetter, Jo Morse
- 1-2. Judy Randel, Sally Woolsey, Broma Lou Reed, Marcia Masterson

1991 1. Juanita Chambers, Cheri Bjerkan, Jill Meyers, Kay Schulle
2. Kathie Wei, Helen Utegaard, Betty Ann Kennedy, Carol Sanders, Lynn Deas, Beth Palmer
1992 1. Kathie Wei, Helen Utegaard, Betty Ann Kennedy, Carol Sanders, Beth Palmer, Lynn Deas
2. Sally Woolsey, Karen Singer, Dori Cohen, Karen Allison
1993 1. Juanita Chambers, Jan Cohen, Margie Gwozdzinsky, GerriAnne Klafter, Shawn Womack
2. Sharon Colson, Judy Pede, Jean Anderson, Carreen Hinds
1994 1. Dorothy Truscott, Hjordis Eythorsdottir, Mildred Breed, Tobi Deutsch
2. June Deutsch, Beverly Rosenberg, Carol Pincus, Lynne Feldman
1995 1. Kathie Wei-Sender, Sue Sachs, Carol Sanders, Betty Ann Kennedy, Lynn Deas, Beth Palmer
2. Judi Radin, Jacqui Mitchell, Lynn Tarnopol, Rhoda Kratenstein
1996 1. Sherie Greenberg, Jyme Schmieder, Fran Dickman, Diane Shannon
2. Joann Glasson, Jo Ann Spring, Sue Picus, JoAnna Stansby
1997 1. Sue Picus, Connie Goldberg, Rozanne Pollack, Lisa Berkowitz
2. Tobi Sokolow, Mildred Breed, Shawn Quinn, Renee Mancuso
1998 1. Judi Radin, Sylvia Moss, Mildred Breed, Shawn Quinn, Petra Hamman, Peggy Sutherlin
2. Margie Gwozdzinsky, Linda Lewis, Karen Barrett, Susan Wexler
1999 1. Lynn Baker, Tobi Sokolow, Karen McCallum, Jill Meyers, Randi Montin, Janice Seamon-Molson
2. Susan Miller, Jo Morse, Barbara Sion, Suzy Berger
2000 1. Petra Hamman, Peggy Sutherlin, Joan Jackson, Robin Klar, Shawn Quinn, Mildred Breed
2. Hjordis Eythorsdottir, Carol Sanders, Libby Fernandez, Judy Wadas, Valerie Westheimer

NORTH AMERICAN SWISS TEAMS.

This six-session event has two qualifying sessions, two semifinal sessions and a two-session final with Victory Point scoring.

1977 1. Neil Chambers, Jim Donaldson, Bruce Ferguson, Clarence Goppert, John Schermer
2. Dennis Clerkin, Jerry Clerkin, John Herrmann, Ken Schutze
1978 1. Barry Crane, Bob Kehoe, Mike Smolen, Charles Weed, Billy Cohen
2. Ira Chorush, Thomas Peters, Ely Solomon, John Zilic, Virginia Zilic
1979 1. Hermine Baron, R. Jay Becker, Paul Ivaska, Jim Robison
2. Gerald Caravelli, Mark Cohen, Ralph Katz, Harvey Miller, Ken Schutze, Russell Shoup
1980 1-2. Steve Becker, Philip Cowan, Rich DeMartino, Judy Rich
1-2. Dale Beers, William Epperson, Dave Furman, Dave Treitel
1981 1. Ron Beall, Bob Etter, Ann Jacobson, Bob Thomson
2. Lea duPont, Benito Garozzo, Glenn Lublin, Claire Tornay
1982 1. Gaylor Kasle, Garey Hayden, Garnet Snyder, Martha Beecher, David Ashley, Dave Treadwell
2. Andy Bernstein, Jim Foster, Tom Sanders, John Sutherlin
1983 1. Sylvia Summers, Harve Waken, Robert Radwin, Gene Simpson, Steve Sturm
2-3. Philip Cowan, Michael Kapera, Alan Miller, John Heller, George Berger
2-3. Richard Capps, John Onstott, Dan Requard, Syd Levey
1984 1. Grant Baze, Rhoda Walsh, Lea duPont, Benito Garozzo
2. William Laubenheimer, Stephen Kanzee, Marc Renson, Hamish Bennett

1985 1. Jack Coleman, Rhoda Walsh, Jim Jacoby, Gaylor Kasle, Garey Hayden
2. Nadine Wood, Jonathan Steinberg, Eric Hochman, Mike Cappelletti
1986 1. Marc Jacobus, Joey Silver, Jim McDonough, George Mittelman, Allan Graves
2. Jack Coleman, Rhoda Walsh, Mark Itabashi, Gaylor Kasle, Garey Hayden
1987 1. Henry Bethe, Kitty Bethe, Alan Truscott, Dorothy Hayden Truscott
2. Jill Meyers, Beverly Rosenberg, Stelios Touchtidis, Steve Cohen, Pan Wittes, Carol Pincus
1988 1. John Zilic, David Siebert, Allan Siebert, Sylvia Summers, Paul Munafo
2. Rita Rand, Gerald Caravelli, Joel Friedberg, Ethan Stein, Jerry Goldfein
1989 1. Eugene Gardner, Kenneth Meyer, Ed Shapiro, Bruce Silverstein
2. Joel Friedberg, Rita Rand, Ethan Stein, Gerald Caravelli, Jerry Goldfein
1990 1-2. Larry Mori, Kitty Bethe, Juanita Chambers, Jim Robison
1-2. George Rosenkranz, Miguel Reygadas, Gaylor Kasle, Garey Hayden, Roger Bates, John Grantham
1991 1. Keith Wilson, Gary Peterson, Dennis Hesthaven, Ralph Letizia, Benton Wheeler
2. Jack Coleman, Judi Radin, Fred Hamilton, Dennis Sorensen, Mike Shuman
1992 1. Lewis Kaplan, Boris Baran, Geoff Hampson, Mark Molson, Mark Stein
2. Jack Coleman, Mike Shuman, Larry Cohen, Dan Rotman, Fred Hamilton
1993 1. Alan Le Bendig, Tom Clarke, Joe Quinn, Shawn Womack
2. Lynn Blumenthal, Steve Bruno, Loren Hawkins, Darrell Keel, Sue Lyski
1994 1. Jack Coleman, Drew Cannell, Mark Molson, Boris Baran, Mark Stein
2. Barry Rigal, JoAnn Manfield, Alan Truscott, Dorothy Truscott
1995 1. Jack Coleman, Drew Cannell, Mark Molson, Boris Baran, Mark Stein
2. Irina Levitina, Judy Tucker, Benito Garozzo, Lea Dupont, Karen Allison, Mike Ledeen
1996 1. Rita Rand, Gerald Caravelli, Arnie Fisher, Steve Garner, Richard Colker
2. John Begley, Mike Lawrence, John Sutherlin, Dan Morse, Hugh Ross
1997 1. John Malley, Dan Colatosti, Bill Hunter, Shome Mukherjee
2. Jacob Podbilevich, Gonzalo Herrera, Jim Looby, Cameron Doner
1998 1. Steve Beatty, John Onstott, Bobby Goldman, Mark Lair
2. Jack Coleman, Chris Compton, Boris Baran, Mike Shuman, Mark Molson Henry
1999 1. David Berkowitz, Larry Cohen, Jeff Wolfson, Neil Silverman
2. Billy Miller, Curtis Cheek, Brian Gunnell, Kyle Larsen
2000 1. Steven Cooper, Kitty Munson-Cooper, Mel Colchamiro, Janet Colchamiro, Betty Bloom, Steve Bloom
2. Benito Garozzo, Lea Dupont, Steve Levinson, Barnet Shenkin

MASTER INDIVIDUAL.

This event was contested for the KARN TROPHY (1931-1933) and the STEINER TROPHY from 1934.

1931	1. Willard S. Karn	2. Richard L. Frey
1932	1. Howard Schenken	2. David Burnstine
1933	1. David Burnstine	2. Elinor Murdoch
1934	1. Elinor Murdoch	2. B. Jay Becker
1935	1. Oswald Jacoby	2. David Burnstine
1936	1. Waldemar K. von Zedtwitz	2. Merwyn D. Maier
1937	1. B. Jay Becker	2. George Unger
1938	1. Richard Ecker, Jr.	2. Harry Fishbein
1939	1. Merwyn D. Maier	2. Alvin Landy
1940	1. Morrie Elis	2. Lee Hazen
1941	1. Lee Hazen	2. B. Jay Becker
1942	1. Harry J. Fishbein	2. Olive Peterson

1943	1. Alvin Roth	2. Charles Solomon
1944	1. George Rapee	2. Robert D. Chatkin
1945	1. Charles H. Goren	2. Albert Weiss
1946	1. Robert A. McPherran	2. Morrie Ellis
1947	1. Charles J. Solomon	2. Jack Cushing
1948	1. B. Jay Becker	2. Myron Field
1949	1. George Rapee	2. B. Jay Becker
1950	1. Morrie Elis	2. Robert Appleyard
1951	1. Sidney Silodor	2. John Crawford
1952	1. Harry J. Fishbein	2. Peter Leventritt
1953	1. Tobias Stone	2. Larry Hirsch
1954	1. Edward Burns	2. F. Ayers Bombeck
1955	1. Norman Kay	2-3. Alvin Roth, B. Jay Becker
1956	1. John R. Crawford	2. Robert Appleyard
1957	1. Edgar Kaplan	2. Dr. Ernest E. Karshmer
1958	1. Sylvia Stein	2. John Crawford
1959	1. Leo Pressburg	2. Frank L. Jackson
1960	1. Robert Reynolds	2. Arthur Robinson

UNITED STATES BRIDGE ASSOCIATION GRAND NATIONALS

OPEN TEAMS

YEAR	WINNERS	RUNNERS-UP
1934	Howard Schenken	Walter Malowan
	Michael Gottlieb	Lee Landon
	David Burnstine	Lester Bachner
	Richard L. Frey	Sydney Rusinow
1935	Howard Schenken	Walter Beinecke
	Michael Gottlieb	Jean (John) Matthews
	Oswald Jacoby	Hugh Jackson
	Sherman Stearns	Charles Van Vleck
	Richard L. Frey	
1936	Josephine Culbertson	Edward Hymes
	Waldemar von Zedtwitz	B. Jay Becker
	Sam Fry	Merwyn Maier

AMERICAN BRIDGE ASSOCIATION CHAMPIONSHIPS

OPEN TEAMS

1934 Egbert Clarke, J.C. Graham, Dr. Louis P. Rolerfort, D. Edward Smith

1935 Dr. E. Brandon, Lawrence Grant, Bernard Gray, George Gilmer, Dr. B. Withers

1936 Gilhooly F. Benoit, William A. Friend, Clyde L. Long, Allan Parkinson, Percy E. Thomas

1937 James P. Holt, Othello A. Moore, Lawrence Buser, Oliver Landry

1938 James P. Holt, Othello A. Moore, Lawrence Buser, Oliver Landry

1939 Gilhooly F. Benoit, William A. Friend, Albert E. Hawkins, Joseph Niles

1940 Lawrence Buser, James P. Holt, Oliver Landry, Othello A. Moore

1941 Roscoe Alexander, Caesar E. Barron, Leon A. Jones, Kermit D. Ross

1942 Caesar E. Barron, Dewey M. Carr, Kermit D. Ross, Allan L. Woolridge

1943 Robert Banks, Dr. William Richie, Glenn Stewart, Alvin Wilkes

1944 Zach H. Brooks, Kelly C. Brown, Louis Clay, Othello A. Moore, Lola Scales

1946 Kenneth F. Cox, Richard Cunningham, Charles Hanson, Samuel White

1947 Zach H. Brooks, Kelly C. Brown, Louis Clay, Othello A. Moore, Lola Scales

1949 Dorothy Alexander, Roscoe Alexander, Leon A. Jones, Caesar E. Barron, Morris Garrett

1950 Dorothy Alexander, Roscoe Alexander, Leon A. Jones, Caesar E. Barron, Morris Garrett

1952 Alfred A. Bishop, Kenneth F. Cox, James H. Smith, Samuel White

1953 William Chapman, Lyda Goggins, George Hall, Allan L. Woolridge, Mrs. Clyde Woolridge

1954 Howard M. Bowman, Martin Gertler, Kai Larson, Ruth Million

1955 Roscoe Alexander, Robert Friend, William A. Friend, Dr. Joseph Henry, Leon A. Jones

1956 Roscoe Alexander, Robert Friend, William A. Friend, Dr. Joseph Henry, Leon A. Jones

1957 Roscoe Alexander, Robert Friend, William A. Friend,

	Mitchell Barnes	Charles Lockridge
1937	David Burnstine	Edward Burns
	Merwyn Maier	Stanley Sanders
	Howard Schenken	Morris Schoenfield
	B. Jay Becker	Len Reiter

MIXED TEAMS

YEAR	WINNERS	RUNNERS-UP
1935	John Sherman	M. Kalman
	Ruth Sherman	Richard L. Frey
	Richard Kahn	Gussie Planco
	Mrs. Fred Greenbaum	J. Arnold Farrar
1936	Mrs. George Harris	Doris Fuller
	Jean (John) Mattheys	Mitchell Barnes
	Mrs. Josiah Thaw	Barbara Collyer
	Raymond Balfe	Waldemar von Zedtwitz
1937	Henry Chanin	Mrs. S. A. Herzog
	Mary Clement	Doris Fuller
	Charles Lockridge	Robert Appleyard
	Mrs. N. Demarest	Jack Shore

OPEN PAIRS

YEAR	WINNERS	RUNNERS UP
1934	Howard Schenken	A. Mitchell Barnes
	Michael Gottlieb	Edward Hymes, Jr
1935	Merwyn Maier	Morrie Elis
	Sherman Stearns	Fred Kaplan
1936	Oswald Jacoby	Sherman Stearns
	David Burnstine	Merwyn Maier
1937	Oswald Jacoby	Waldemar von Zedtwitz
	Lester Bachner	Merwyn Maier

MIXED PAIRS

YEAR	WINNERS	RUNNERS UP
1936	Waldemar von Zedtwitz	M. Lovejoy
	Barbara Collyer	Winfield Liggett
1937	Henry Chanin Millie Tansill	Mary Clement
	Raymond Balfe	

1958 Dr. Joseph Henry, Leon A. Jones
Alfred A. Bishop, Kenneth F. Cox, James Garcia, Samuel White

1959 Caesar E. Barron, Oliver Cassell, Frederick O. Petite, Allan L. Woolridge, Mrs. Clyde Woolridge

1960 Caesar E. Barron, Oliver Cassell, Walter Mann, Frederick O. Petite

1961 Jim Becheley, Robert D. Hamman, William Hanna, Stella Rebner

1962 Robert Bratcher, Mary Cocherell, Dr. Guy Ginn, Robert Landry (tied with) Doris Brooks, Dr. Joseph Henry, Stanley Jarrett, Ronald Searcy

1963 Jean Haley, Andrew Mells, Charles Pyant, Janice Wilkins

1964 Roscoe Alexander, Dr. Joseph Henry, Leon A. Jones, Mrs. Clyde Woolridge

1965 Zenobia Allen, Andrew Mells, Samuel White, Bertram Hudson, Daniel Scrivens

1966 Zenobia Allen, Andrew Mells, Samuel White, Bertram Hudson, Daniel Scrivens

1967 Dr. Arthur R. Flowers, Glenn Fowlkes, George Hall, J.Herbert Kerr, Charles Pyant, Arthur Wills

1968 James Garcia, Dr. Guy A. Ginn, Luis Pietri, Roscoe Rigmaiden, Ronald Smith, Hollis Steed

1969 Doris Brooks, Leonard Jefferson, Dr. William Lipton, J. Prisyon, Murray Schnee, Sol Seidman

1970 Dr. Arthur R. Flowers, Douglas Fullwood, Andrew Mells, Luis Pietri, Roscoe Rigmaiden, William Sides

1971 Robert Becker, Mark Blumenthal, Oscar Cohen, William Landow, Harlow Lewis, Alan Sontag

1972 Dr. Arthur R. Flowers, Douglas Fullwood, Amalya Kearse, Andrew Mells, Luis Pietri, William Sides

1973 Zenobia Allen, Richard Halperin, Harvey Miller, Robert Price, Roscoe Rigmaiden, Joyce Williams

1974 Zenobia Allen, Claudius G. Fredd, Robert Landry, Beverly Lucas, Samuel Lucas

1975 *¹Herbert Bryan, Orlando Croft, John S. Jordan III, Robert Seymour

1976 *Douglas Fullwood, Beverly Lucas, Samuel Lucas, Louis Sutherland

1977 Reginald Chapman, Leonard Jefferson, Chester Johnson, Arnold Jones (Spring)
Marv Dauer, Ed Davis, Al Okuneff, David Sachs,

George Siegel, Perry Van Hook (Summer)
1978 Alfred Bishop, Douglas Fullwood, Samuel Lucas, Beverly Lucas, Luis Pietri, Louis Sutherland (Spring)
Richard Halperin, Harvey Miller, Paul Sugar, Don Rutstein, Claude Vogel, Carey Yelton (Summer)
1979 Dr. Arthur R. Flowers, Chester Johnson, Andrew Mells, Herbert Taylor, Arthur Wills (Spring)
Lawrence Berkley, Lee Pennington, Jeffrey Stroud, John Washington, William E. Williams (Summer)
1980 Kenneth Cox, Clinton Elmore, Charles Hanson, Leonard Jefferson, Robert Seymour (Spring)
Robert Canty, Theodore Griffith, Sandra Stevenson, Norma Sweeting (Summer)
1981 Paul Ivaska, Tony Kasday, William Sides, Eddie Thomas (Spring)
Lionel Barton, Dwight Galley, Samuel Lucas, Beverly Lucas, Robert Price, Joyce Williams (Summer)
1982 Lionel Barton, Dwight Galley, Samuel Lucas, Beverly Lucas, Robert Price, Joyce Williams (Summer)
1983 Bill Sides, Louis Sutherland, Luis Pietri, Chester Johnson (Spring)
David Berkowitz, Lisa Berkowitz, Ira Herman, Robert Blanchard, Jilliam Blanchard (*tied with*) William Russ, Eric Robinson, James Becker, James Hamilton, James Garcia, Jeffrey Stroud (Summer)
1984 Bob Price, Joyce Williams, Lionel Barton, Dwight Galley (Spring)
Daniel Page, Norma Sweeting, Vernette Wills, Robert Canty (Summer)
1985 Robert Price, Joyce Williams, Samuel Lucas, Beverly Lucas, Dwight Galley, Lionel Barton (Spring)
Robert Landry, Bobbye Caldwell, Dan Requard, Herbert Taylor, Bernice Laster, Joan Williams (Summer)
1986 Chester Johnson, Herbert Taylor, Joan Williams, Dan Requard (Spring)
Chester Johnson, Herbert Taylor, Dan Requard, Joan Williams (Summer)
1987 Chester Johnson, Herbert Taylor, Dan Requard, Joan Williams (Spring)
Bob Price, Joyce Williams, Beverly Lucas, Samuel Lucas, Bill Sides, Louis Sutherland (Summer)
1988 Robert Price, Joyce Williams, Louis Sutherland, Samuel Lucas, Beverly Lucas (Spring)
Luis Pietri, Dwight Galley, Lionel Barton, Sara Pearson (Summer)
1989 Roscoe Rigmaiden, Reginald Chapman, Sandra Stevenson, Clarice Reid, Dorothy Sides (Spring)
Chester Johnson, Herbert Taylor, Joan Williams, Luis Pietri (Summer)
1990 Sara Pearson, Dwight Galley, Mae Clark, Lela Wilson (Spring)
Chester Johnson, Herbert Taylor, Luis Pietri, Bill Sides (Summer)
1991 William M. Troy, Robert Friend, Edward West, Henry Bell (Spring)
Luis Pietri, Chester Johnson, Herbert Taylor, Joan Williams (Summer)
1992 Chester Johnson, Joan Williams, Herbert Taylor, Luis Pietri (Spring)
Dwight Galley, Lionel Barton, Sara Pearson, Luis Pietri, Eddie Thomas Jr., Bill Furr (Summer)
1993 Naomi Ballard, Heywood Ballard, William Thompson, Berrie Johnson, Taylor Cox (Spring)
1994 Edward West, George Johnson, Edna Cravanas, Lela Wilson, Henry Bell, Robert Friend (Spring)
1995 Chester Johnson, Herbert Taylor, Daniel C. Requard, Gary Kessler, Lela Wilson, Dwight Galley (Spring)
Chester G. Johnson, Daniel C. Requard, Herbert Taylor, Gary Kessler, Dwight Galley, Lela M. Wilson (Summer)
1996 Chester Johnson, Herbert Taylor, Daniel Requard, Gary Kessler, Dwight Galley, Lela Wilson (Spring)
Lionel O. Barton, Reginald O. Chapman, Jeffrey Stroud, Harold R. Bickham, Mae Clark (Summer)
1997 Chester G. Johnson, Daniel C. Requard, Herbert Taylor, Gary Kessler, Dwight Galley, Lela M. Wilson (Spring)
Lionel O. Barton, Reginald O. Chapman, Jeffrey Stroud, Harold R. Bickham, Mae Clark (Summer)
1998 Chester G. Johnson, Daniel C. Requard, Herbert Taylor, Gary Kessler, Dwight Galley, Lela M. Wilson (Spring)
Reginald O. Chapman, Jeffrey Stroud, Luis F. Pietri, Harold R. Bickham, Lionel O. Barton, Mae Clark (Summer)
1999 Arthur L. Wills, Robert W. Wallace, Sylvia J. Christian, Sandra A. Stevenson, Bessie W. Haley, William M. Russ

(Spring)
Reginold O. Chapman, Harold R. Bickham, Lionel O. Barton, Mae Clark (Summer)
2000 Chester Johnson, Herbert Taylor, Sara J. Pearson, Dwight Galley, Lela M. Wilson (Spring)
Chester Johnson, Herbert Taylor, Sara J. Pearson, Dwight Galley, Lela M. Wilson, Bill Sides (Summer)

OPEN PAIRS

1934 Louis Collins, Mrs. Louis Collins
1935 Dr. A. Maurice Curtis, Dr. W. Wethers
1936 Lyda Goggins, Horace R. Milles
1937 James P. Holt, Othello A. Moore
1938 Leon A. Jones, James McDougald
1940 Hazel Facey, Lucius Fields
1941 Dr. A. Maurice Curtis, Allan Parkinson
1942 William A. Friend, Lyda Goggins
1943 Courtland Booker, Lewis White
1944 Eloise Landry, Elvert Marsh
1946 Roscoe Alexander, Leon A. Jones
1947 Kelly C. Brown, Louis Clay
1948 Elvert Marsh, Rexcell Watkins
1949 William A. Friend, Dr. Fred Slaughter
1950 Richard Cunningham, Zenobia Rucker
1951 Alexander Herndon, Evelyn Herndon
1952 William A. Friend, Dr. Fred Slaughter
1953 Louis Clay, Zenobia Rucker
1954 William A. Friend, Hollis Steed
1955 Robert Friend, William A. Friend
1956 James Garcia, Elvert Marsh
1957 Sandy Gholston, Marion Griffis
1958 Alfred A. Bishop, Dr. Joseph Henry
1959 Roscoe Alexander, Zenobia Hall
1960 James Lee, Carlisle Pratt
1961 Kenneth F. Cox, Samuel White
1962 Walter Hampton, Frank Tucker
1963 Luis Pietri, Roscoe Rigmaiden
1964 Alfred A. Bishop, Dr. Joseph Henry
1965 Bertram Hudson, Andrew Mells
1966 Luis Pietri, Roscoe Rigmaiden
1967 Robert Price, William Sides
1968 Luis Pietri, Roscoe Rigmaiden
1969 Lawrence Berkley, Arthur Wills (Spring)
Dr. Milton Haley, Arthur Reid (Summer)
1970 Robert Canty, Sylvester Lee (*tied with*) Theodore Griffith, Ben Siegel (Spring)
William Sides, Douglas Fullwood (Summer)
1971 F. Maxine Davis, James Dozier (Spring)
Robert Price, Joyce Williams (Summer)
1972 Amalya Kearse, Luis Pietri (Spring)
Dr. Guy A. Ginn, Theodore Griffith (Summer)
1973 Amalya Kearse, Luis Pietri (Spring)
Dr. Felix Dunn, Sarah Dunn (Summer)
1974 Dr. Arthur F. Flowers, Andrew Mells (Spring)
Vivian Banks, Franklyn Taylor (Summer)
1975 Reginald Chapman, Roscoe Rigmaiden (Spring)
Dr. Arthur R. Flowers, Andrew Mells (Summer)
1976 Douglas Fullwood, Louis Sutherland (Spring)
Bobby Caldwell, Robert Landry (Summer)
1977 Lee Pennington, William E. Williams (Spring)
Lee Pennington, William E. Williams (Summer)
1978 James Garcia, Dr. Milton Haley (Spring)
Taylor Cox, Vernette Wills (Summer)
1979 Reginald Chapman, Roscoe Rigmaiden (Spring)
Reginald Chapman, Roscoe Rigmaiden (Summer)
1980 Douglas Fullwood, Louis Sutherland (Spring)
Dwight Galley, Lionel Barton (Summer)
1981 Paul Ivaska, William Sides (Spring)
Douglas Fullwood, Louis Sutherland (Summer)
1982 Mildred Anderson, John S. Jordan III (Spring)
1983 Leonard Jefferson, Arnold Jones (Spring)
Not played (black out) (New York) (Summer)
1984 Robert Price, Joyce Williams (Spring)
Dwight Galley, Lionel Barton (Summer)
1985 Norm Coombs, Herbert Taylor (Spring)
Chester Johnson, Herbert Taylor (Summer)
1986 Andrew Mells, Arthur Wills (Spring)
Joan Williams, Dan Requard (Summer)
1987 Joyce Williams, Louis Sutherland (Spring)
Dwight Galley, Lionel Barton (Summer)
1988 William F. Furr, James Garcia (Spring)
Robert Price, Bill Sides (Summer)
1989 Melvin Rone, Harold Bickham (Spring)
Joyce Williams, Louis Sutherland (Summer)
1990 Luis Pietri, Chester Johnson (Spring)

Eddie Thomas, Sara Pearson (Summer)
1991 Joyce Williams, Robert Price (Spring)
Arthur Wills, Julius Fields (Summer)
1992 George Johnson, Edna Cravanas (Spring)
Reginald Chapman, Roscoe Rigmaiden (Summer)
1993 Lionel Barton, Sara Pearson (Spring)
1994 Marvin Comer, Theodore Griffith (Spring)
1995 Edward West, Henry Bell (Spring)
Dwight Galley, Chester Johnson (Summer)

1996 Arthur Wills, Sandra Stevenson(Spring)
Dwight Galley, Chester G. Johnson (Summer)
1997 Dwight Galley, Lela M. Wilson (Spring)
Naomi Ballard, Heywood Ballard (Summer)
1998 Chester Johnson, Herert Taylor (Spring)
Ola C. Parks, John W. Phoenix (Summer)
1999 W.E. Richardson Jr., Bill Sides (Spring)
Robert Price, Bill Turner (Summer)
2000 Louis Sutherland, Lawrence H. Berkley (Spring)
Arnold P. Jones Jr., Arthur J. Reid Jr. (Summer)

CANADIAN CHAMPIONSHIPS

NATIONAL TEAM CHAMPIONSHIPS (CNTC)

The first official Canadian National Team Championship was held in Toronto in 1980. However, there were three previous playoffs to select a team for international competition.

1968 Eric Murray, Sami Kehela, Percy Sheardown, Bruce Elliott, Al Lando npc, Wolf Lebovic anpc
1971 Bruce Gowdy, Duncan Phillips, Gerry Charney, Bill Crissey
1977 Don Cowan, Mike Cummings, Maurice Paul, Mary Paul
1980 Allan Graves, George Mittelman, Eric Kokish, Peter Nagy, Eric Murray, Sami Kehela
1981 Allan Graves, George Mittelman, Eric Kokish, Peter Nagy, Eric Murray, Sami Kehela
1982 Nick Gartaganis, Zygmunt Marcinski, Gordon Crispin, Vojtech Pomykalski
1983 Mark Molson, Boris Baran, Allan Graves, George Mittelman, John Guoba, John Carruthers
1984 Subhash Gupta, Doran Flock, Gordon Campbell, Mike Chomyn, Bryan Maksymetz, Drew Cannell
1985 Boris Baran, Mark Molson, Eric Kokish, George Mittelman, Pascal Menachi, Mark Stein
1986 Michael Schoenborn, Harmon Edgar, Arno Hobart, Martin Kirr, Greg Carroll, David Turner, Laurie McIntyre npc
1987 Mark Molson, Boris Baran, John Guoba, John Carruthers, Eric Murray
1988 Maurice Larochelle, Jean Bernier, Andre Laliberte, Jacques Laliberte, Raymond Fortin, Kamel Fergani
1989 Mark Molson, Boris Baran, George Mittelman, Arno Hobart, Martin Kirr, Billy Cohen
1990 Doug Heron, David Willis, John Valliant, Mike Betts, Randy Bennett, Ed Zaluski
1991 Ed Bridson, John Gowdy, David Lindop, Geoff Hampson, Boris Baran, Mark Molson
1992 Jim McAvoy, Duncan Smith, Michael Strebinger, Peter Herold, Jim Dickie, Bruce Ferguson
1993 Mike Cafferata, Mike Kenny, Mary Paul, David Colbert, Michael Roche, Chris Hough
1994 Joseph Silver, Fred Gitelman, George Mittelman, Mark Molson, Eric Kokish
1995 Joseph Silver, Fred Gitelman, George Mittelman, Mark Molson, Eric Kokish, Boris Baran
1996 Nader Hanna, Doug Fraser, Michael Roche, Jim Green, Paul Thurston, Rick Delogu
1997 Gordon McOrmond, Michael Hargreaves, Allan Graves, Joseph Silver
1998 Gordon McOrmond, Michael Hargreaves, Allan Graves, Joseph Silver, Bryan Maksymetz
1999 Ted Horning, Honorary captain; Robert Lebi, Nader Hanna, Drew Cannell, John Carruthers
2000 Kamel Fergani, Nicolas L'Ecuyer, Doug Fraser, Jeffrey Blond, Darren Wolpert, Jurek Czyzowicz

WOMEN'S TEAM CHAMPIONSHIPS (CWTC)

1984 Dianna Gordon, Sharyn Kokish, Francine Cimon, Sandra Fraser, Catherine Thorpe, Mary Paul, George Mittelman npc
1985 Anna Boivin, Renee Mancuso, Rhoda Habert, Beverly Kraft, Nancy Koffler, Barbara Saltsman
1986 Mary Paul, Francine Cimon, Katie Thorpe, Gloria Silverman, Sharyn Reus, Dianna Gordon
1987 Mary Paul, Francine Cimon, Katie Thorpe, Gloria Silverman, Sharyn Reus, Dianna Gordon, George Mittelman npc
1988 Mary Paul, Francine Cimon, Katie Thorpe, Gloria Silverman, Sharyn Reus, Dianna Gordon, George Mittelman npc
1989 Kathy Adachi, Ina Anderson, Pat Landau, Joyce Peters, Marge Neate, Alison Dorosh
1990 Mary Paul, Francine Cimon, Katie Thorpe, Gloria Silverman, Sharyn Reus, Dianna Gordon
1991 Mary Paul, Francine Cimon, Katie Thorpe, Gloria Silverman, Sharyn Reus, Dianna Gordon, John Carruthers npc
1992 Sharyn Reus, Dianna Gordon, Beverly Kraft, Rhoda Habert
1993 Judy Harris, Barbara Kupkee, Anne Pilon, Diane Christianson
1994 Barbara Clinton, Joan Eaton, Roisin O'Hara, Gloria Silverman
1995 Francine Cimon, Barbara Saltsman, Sharyn Reus, Dianna Gordon, Beverly Kokish, Rhoda Habert
1996 George Holland, npc, Sharyn Reus, Dianna Gordon, Rhoda Habert, Beverly Kraft, Barbara Saltsman, Francine Cimon
1997 June Pocock, Marylou Bert, Kathy Adachi, Leslie Gold
1998 Diana Gordon, Sheri Winestock, Beverly Kraft, Rhoda Habert, Francine Cimon, Barbara Saltsman
1999 Dianna Gordon, Katie Thorpe, Beverly Kraft, Francine Cimon, Martine Lacroix, Rhoda Habert
2000 Dianna Gordon, Katie Thorpe, Beverly Kraft, Francine Cimon, Martine Lacroix, Rhoda Habert

OPEN PAIRS CHAMPIONSHIP (COPC)

1985 Boris Baran, Mark Molson
1986 Gary Whiteman, Ken Warren
1987 Maurice de la Salle, Mark Chalfin
1988 John Valliant, David Willis
1989 Ron Borg, Michael Strebinger
1990 Katie Thorpe, John Carruthers
1991 Michael Cafferata, Ken Warren
1992 Pierre Treuil, John Zaluski
1993 Pierre Treuil, John Zaluski
1994 Dick Anderson, Peter Basarsky
1995 Jim Riegle, Pierre Treuil
1996 Dave Willis, John Valliant
1997 Michael Betts, Randy Bennett
1998 Doug Heron, Alex Heron
1999 Dan Jacob, Lawrence Hicks
2000 David McLellan, Bill Treble

APPENDIX II
WBF, ACBL and ABA Masterpoint and Rankings Lists

WORLD OPEN RANKINGS 2000

1.	Bob Hamman, USA	4026
2.	Eric Rodwell, USA	3762
3.	Jeff Meckstroth, USA	3714
4.	Gabriel Chagas, Brazil	2953
5.	Marcello Branco, Brazil	2610
6.	Lorenzo Lauria, Italy	2565
7.	Robert Wolff, USA	2491
8.	Herve Mouiel, France	2456
9.	Cezary Balicki, Poland	2455
10.	Adam Zmudzinski, Poland	2455
11.	Giorgio Duboin, Italy	2436
12.	Alfredo Versace, Italy	2354
13.	Lewis Stansby, USA	2320
14.	Norberto Bocchi, Italy	2283
15.	Charles Martel, USA	2281
16.	Alain Levy, France	2198
17.	Paul Chemla, France	2151
18.	David Berkowitz, USA	1955
19.	Richard Freeman, USA	1891
20.	Nick Nickell, USA	1891
21.	Ralph Katz, USA	1871
22.	Michal Kwiecien, Poland	1828
23.	Jacek Pszczola, Poland	1817
24.	Larry Cohen, USA	1754
25.	Piotr Tuszynski, Poland	1696
26.	Magnus Lindkvist, Sweden	1695
27.	Dano DeFalco, Italy	1692
28.	Michael Rosenberg, USA	1683
29.	Krzysztof Martens, Poland	1683
30.	Michel Perron, France	1663
31.	Peter Weichsel, USA	1579
32.	Bjorn Fallenius, Sweden	1576
33.	Zia Mahmood, USA	1548
34.	Christian Mari, France	1517
35.	Paul Soloway, USA	1498
36.	Miguel Villas-Boas, Brazil	1494
37.	Tor Helness, Norway	1480
38.	Piotr Gawrys, Poland	1477
39.	Roberto Mello, Brazil	1435
40.	Henky Lasut, Indonesia	1411
41.	Eddy Manoppo, Indonesia	1411
42.	Denny Jacob Sacul, Indonesia	1391
43.	Franck Multon, France	1386
44.	Geir Helgemo, Norway	1384
45.	Joao Paulo Campos, Brazil	1373
46.	Marek Szymanowski, Poland	1314
47.	Peter Fredin, Sweden	1287
48.	Mats Nilsland, Sweden	1280
49.	Jens Auken, Denmark	1279
50.	Anton Maas, Netherlands	1264

WBF OPEN GRAND MASTERS 2000

1.	Bob Hamman, USA
2.	Benito Garozzo, USA
3.	Robert Wolff, USA
4.	Pietro Forquet, Italy
5.	Eric Rodwell, USA
6.	Gabriel Chagas, Brazil
7.	Camillo Pabis Ticci, Italy
8.	Jeff Meckstroth, USA
9.	Marcelo Branco, Brazil
10.	Paul Soloway, USA
11.	Lewis Stansby, USA
12.	Charles Martel, USA
13.	Paul Chemla, France
14.	William Eisenberg, USA
15.	Michael Lawrence, USA
16.	Michel Perron, France
17.	Hugh Ross, USA
18.	Herve Mouiel, France
19.	Christian Mari, France
20.	Henri Szwarc, France
21.	Cezary Balicki, Poland
22.	Adam Zmudzinski, Poland
23.	Michel Lebel, France
24.	Arturo Franco, Italy
25.	Lorenzo Lauria, Italy

26.	Gabino Cintra, Brazil
27.	Ira Rubin, USA
28.	Michael Rosenberg, USA
29.	Richard Freeman, USA
30.	Roberto Mello, Brazil
31.	Alain Levy, France
32.	Nick Nickell, USA
33.	Krzysztof Martens, Poland
34.	Pedro Paulo Assumpcao, Brazil
35.	Piotr Gawrys, Poland
36.	Edwin Kantar, USA
37.	Boris Schapiro, GBR
38.	Fred Hamilton, USA
39.	Michael Passell, USA
40.	Dano De Falco, Italy
41.	Alfredo Versace, Italy
42.	Peter Weichsel, USA
43.	Pedro Paulo Branco, Brazil
44.	Piotr Tuszynski, Poland
45.	Franck Multon, France
46.	Seymon Deutsch, USA
47.	Christiano Fanseca, Brazil
48.	Hans Krejins, Netherlands
49.	Claude Demouly, France
50.	Gerard Bourchtoff, France
51.	Guglielmo Sinsicalco, Italy

2000 WORLD WOMEN'S RANKINGS

1.	Shawn Quinn, USA	2698
2.	Sabine Auken, Germany	2676
3.	Jill Meyers, USA	2598
4.	Bep Vriend, Netherlands	2555
5.	Daniela von Arnim, Germany	2455
6.	Veronique Bessis, France	2189
7.	Marijke van der Pas, Netherlands	2099
8.	Catherine D'Ovidio (Saul), France	2065
9.	Tobi Sokolow, USA	2049
10.	Gu Ling, China	1948
11.	Zhang, Yalan, China	1935
12.	Mildred Breed, USA	1903
13.	Lynn Deas, USA	1824
14.	Sun Ming, China	1804
15.	Pony Nehmert, Germany	1786
16.	Jet Pasman, Netherlands	1750
17.	Anneke Simons, Netherlands	1729
18.	Dianna Gordon, Canada	1637
19.	Doris Fischer, Austria	1628
20.	Wietske van Zwol, Netherlands	1528
21.	Randi Montin, USA	1465
22.	Nicola Smith, England	1464
23.	Wang Wenfei, China	1457
24.	Francine Cimon, Canada	1445
25.	Andrea Rauscheid, Germany	1439
26.	Maria Erhart, Austria	1413
27.	Martine Verbeek, Netherlands	1396
28.	Zhang Yu, China	1387
29.	Kerri Sanborn, USA	1371
30.	Terry Weigkricht, Austria	1335
31.	Sylvie Willard, France	1331
32.	Juanita Chambers, USA	1296
33.	Sandra Landy, England	1279
34.	Beth Palmer, USA	1244
35.	Gail Greenberg, USA	1238
36.	Wang Hongli, China	1224
37.	Pat Davies, England	1217
38.	Kathie Wei-Sender, USA	1210
39.	Benedicte Cronier, France	1175
40.	Elizabeth McGowan, Scotland	1161
41.	Sue Picus, USA	1145
42.	Peggy Sutherlin, USA	1073
43.	Rhoda Habert, Canada	1069
44.	Beverly Kraft, Canada	1069
45.	Irina Levitina, USA	1047
46.	Migri Tzur-Campanile, Israel	1019
47.	Petra Hannam, USA	1004
48.	Lisa Berkowitz, USA	978
49.	Sharyn Reus, Canada	962
50.	Karen McCallum, USA	957

WBF WOMEN GRAND MASTERS 2000
(Listed in order of Placng Points)

1. Lynn Deas, USA
2. Sandra Landy, England
3. Nicola Smith, England
4. Jill Meyers, USA
5. Sabine Auken, Germany
6. Jacqui Mitchell, USA
7. Daniela von Arnim, Germany
8. Kerri Sanborn, USA
9. Judi Radin, USA
10. Shawn Quinn, USA
11. Gail Greenberg, USA
12. Katherine Wei-Sender, USA
13. Pat Davies, England
14. Sue Picus, USA
15. Bep Vriend, Netherlands
16. Karen McCallum, USA
17. Dorothy Truscott, USA
18. Doris Fischer, Austria
19. Juanita Chambers, USA
20. Beth Palmer, USA
21. Maria Erhart, Austria
22. Terry Weigkricht, Austria
23. Carot Sanders, USA
24. Pony Nehmert, Germany
25. Mary Jane Farell, USA
26. Betty Ann Kennedy, USA
27. Sally Brock, England
28. Marijke van der Pas, Netherlands
29. Tobi Sokolow, USA
30. Mildred Breed, USA
31. Marisa Bianchi, Italy
32. Marilyn Johnson, USA
33. Dianna Gordon, Canada
34. Randi Montin, USA
35. Elizabeth McGowan, Scotland
36. Marisa D'Andrea, Italy
37. Luciana Capodanno, Italy
38. Rozanne Pollack, USA
39. Marinesa Letizia, USA
40. Sharon Osberg, USA

BARRY CRANE TOP 500

This trophy is presented to the ACBL member who has accumulated the most masterpoints during the calendar year. Originally the McKenney Trophy, it was put into play by William E. McKenney, ACBL executive secretary. It was known as the **McKenney Trophy** contest from 1937-1981. When the list was expanded to include the leading 500 players it was called the **Top 500** from 1982-1985. It became the **Barry Crane Top 500** in 1986. Crane, who was murdered in July 1985, was ACBL's top masterpoint holder and was acknowledged by his peers to be unequalled as a masterpoint winner and a matchpoint player. His influence on the race was dominant for more than three decades. The winners from 1937 through 1947:

1937	Charles Goren
1938	Morrie Elis
1939	Merwyn Maier
1940	Morrie Elis
1941	Helen Sobel
1942	Helen Sobel
1943	Charles Goren
1944	Helen Sobel
1945	Charles Goren
1946	Sidney Silodor
1947	Charles Goren

The following are the victors since 1947, together with their point totals. An asterisk indicates the record was broken that year.

1948	Charles Goren	378
1949	Charles Goren	440*
1950	Charles Goren	399
1951	Charles Goren	457*
1952	Barry Crane	604*
1953	William Rosen	470
1954	David Carter	468
1955	Norman Kay	519
1956	Tobias Stone	791*
1957	Edgar Kaplan	808*
1958	Len Harmon	768
1959	Oswald Jacoby	784
1960	Robert Jordan	873*
1961	Oswald Jacoby	735
1962	Oswald Jacoby	713
1963	Oswald Jacoby	1034*
1964	Hermine Baron	1370*
1965	Peter Rank	1141
1966	Peter Pender	1282
1967	Barry Crane	1309
1968	Paul Soloway	981
1969	Paul Soloway	1434*
1970	Hermine Baron	1399
1971	Barry Crane	1443*
1972	John Fisher	1387
1973	Barry Crane	1562*
1974	Kerri Shuman	1619*
1975	Barry Crane	1547
1976	Mike Passell	1815*
1977	Ron Andersen	2009*
1978	Barry Crane	1790
1979	Clarence Goppert	2118*
1980	Ron Andersen	2725*
1981	Mel Skolnik	2421
1982	Eddie Wold	2016
1983	Ron Andersen	2994*
1984	Grant Baze	3270*
1985	Grant Baze	2209
1986	Ron Andersen	2521
1987	Grant Baze	1923
1988	Jim Jacoby	2223
1989	Zeke Jabbour	2468
1990	Mark Lair	2624
1991	Jim Becker	2914
1992	Dennis Sorensen	2745
1993	Jeff Meckstroth	1950
1993	Jeff Meckstroth	1950
1994	Richard Hunt	3146
1995	Jeff Meckstroth	2385
	Eddie Wold	2385
1996	Ron Andersen	2370
1997	Randy Pettit	2117
1998	Paul Soloway	2564
1999	Jim Barrow	3584*
2000	Jeff Meckstroth	2493

ACBL PLAYER OF THE YEAR

This recognition goes to the contestant who earns the most masterpoints at *nationally-rated* championships at the three NABC tournaments each year. The winners through 2000:

1990	Bob Hamman
1991	Zia Mahmood
1992	Jeff Meckstroth
1993	Bob Hamman
1994	Michael Rosenberg
1995	Steve Weinstein, Fred Stewart
1996	Zia Mahmood
1997	Bart Bramley
1998	Paul Soloway
1999	John Mohan
2000	Zia Mahmood

ACBL TOP 200 MASTERPOINT HOLDERS

1.	Paul Soloway, Mill Creek WA	53,999
2.	Mike Passell, Plano TX	45,425
3.	Mark Lair, Canyon TX	41,733
4.	Jeff Meckstroth, Tampa FL	39,875
5.	Eddie Wold, Houston TX	38,049
6.	Grant Baze, La Jolla CA	33,243

7.	Eric Rodwell, Clearwater FL	30,744	92.	Charles Coon, Marshfield MA	14,219
8.	Fred Hamilton, Las Vegas NV	28,150	93.	Jerry Clerkin, North Vernon IN	14,212
9.	Steve Robinson, Arlington VA	25,936	94.	Ellen Allen, Summerville SC	14,128
10.	Mark Itabashi, Murrieta CA	25,764	95.	Geoff Hampson, Los Angeles CA	14,020
11.	Gaylor Kasle, Boca Raton FL	25,457	96.	Ron Sukoneck, Annandale VA	13,970
12.	Zeke Jabbour, Boca Raton FL	25,032	97.	Mike Cappelletti Jr., Red Bank TN	13,820
13.	Bobby Wolff, Fort Worth TX	24,226	98.	Russ Arnold, Miami FL	13,777
14.	Gene Freed, Los Angeles CA	24,087	99.	Hamish Bennett, Menlo Park CA	13,721
15.	Peter Weichsel, Los Gatos CA	23,648	100.	Larry Allen, Summerville SC	13,655
16.	Chuck Said, Nashville TN	23,640	101.	James Nash, Omaha NE	13,643
17.	David Adams, Kennesaw GA	23,632	102.	Marinesa Letizia, Kingston NY	13,619
18.	Mary Jane Farell, Los Angeles CA	23,340	103.	Chip Martel, Davis CA	13,560
19.	Bob Hamman, Dallas TX	23,323	104.	Betty Ann Kennedy, Shreveport LA	13,515
20.	Robert Levin, Bronx NY	23,181	105.	Billy Miller, Las Vegas NV	13,509
21.	Michael Seamon, Miami Beach FL	22,977	106.	Hugh Maclean, Gonzales TX	13,424
22.	David Treadwell, Wilmington DE	22,632	107.	Ellasue Chaitt, Palm Beach Gardens FL	13,393
23.	Lynn Deas, Schenectady NY	22,501	108.	Arnold Fisher, Clementon NJ	13,366
24.	Garey Hayden, Tucson AZ	22,093	109.	Jon Wittes, Claremont CA	13,362
25.	Michael Shuman, Pasadena CA	22,043	110.	Gerald Bare, Pacific Palisades CA	13,358
26.	Glenn Lublin, Silver Spring MD	21,384	111.	Jan Janitschke, Littleton CO	13,352
27.	Alan Bell, Anaheim CA	21,265	112.	George Dawkins, Austin TX	13,333
28.	Mike Lawrence, Berkeley CA	21,176	113.	Norman Kay, Narberth PA	13,312
29.	Allan Siebert, Little Rock AR	20,873	114.	Kay Schulle, Purchase NY	13,284
30.	Alan Sontag, Gaithersburg MD	20,574	115.	Robert Lipsitz, Palm Harbor FL	13,241
31.	Alan Stout, Lisbon IA	20,009	116.	John Gustafson, Des Moines IA	13,221
32.	John Sutherlin, Dallas TX	19,937	117.	Bart Bramley, Chicago IL	13,219
33.	Jo Morse, Palm Beach Gardens FL	19,354	118.	Mike Aliotta, Oklahoma City OK	13,202
34.	David Berkowitz, Old Tappan NJ	19,318	119.	Veronica McMurdie, Sacramento CA	13,158
35.	David Siebert, Little Rock AR	19,225	120.	Marshall Miles, Redlands CA	13,148
36.	Peter Boyd, Silver Spring MD	19,095	121.	Linda Lewis, Las Vegas NV	13,132
37.	Kerri Sanborn, Stony Point NY	18,731	122.	Lloyd Arvedon, Bedford MA	13,104
38.	John Mohan, Christiansted VI	18,486	123.	Frank Hoadley, New Orleans LA	13,076
39.	John Fisher, Dallas TX	17,938	124.	George Pisk, Manchaca TX	13,044
40.	Jim Kirkham, San Bernardino CA	17,769	125.	Dan Morse, Houston TX	13,039
41.	Kit Woolsey, Kensington CA	17,709	126.	Mary Chilcote, Delray Beach FL	12,955
42.	Carol Sanders, Nashville TN	17,486	127.	Jim Krekorian, New York NY	12,891
43.	Gene Simpson, Pacific Palisades CA	17,395	128.	Randy Pettit, Marietta GA	12,861
44.	Roger Bates, Mesa AZ	17,186	129.	Jerry Gaer, Scottsdale AZ	12,813
45.	Bernie Chazen, Tamarac FL	17,134	130.	Gard Hays, Veradale WA	12,791
46.	Dennis Clerkin, Bloomington IN	17,030	131.	Randy Joyce, Raleigh NC	12,773
47.	George Bloomer, Pittsboro NC	16,958	132.	John Onstott, New Orleans LA	12,768
48.	Mike Cappelletti Sr., Alexandria VA	16,786	133.	Alan Le Bendig, Los Angeles CA	12,736
49.	Gerald Caravelli, Des Plaines IL	16,739	134.	Hugh Ross, Oakland CA	12,695
50.	Ross Rainwater, Vancouver WA	16,661	135.	Paul Ivaska, Las Vegas NV	12,675
51.	Jim Linhart, Delray Beach FL	16,660	136.	Marty Bergen, West Palm Beach FL	12,644
52.	Helen Shanbrom, Tamarac FL	16,468	137.	Jill Meyers, Santa Monica CA	12,625
53.	Ron Smith, San Francisco CA	16,449	138.	Evan Bailey, San Diego CA	12,583
54.	Allan Cokin, Palm Beach FL	16,444	139.	Alvin Roth, Boca Raton FL	12,581
55.	John Zilic, Houston TX	16,388	140.	Joseph Jabon, Bellevue WA	12,544
56.	Lew Stansby, Castro Valley CA	16,377	141.	Richard Freeman, Atlanta GA	12,537
57.	Tom Sanders, Nashville TN	16,339	142.	Michael Moss, New York NY	12,364
58.	Rhoda Walsh, Henderson NV	16,133	143.	Juanita Chambers, Boca Raton FL	12,362
59.	Dennis Sorensen, Portland OR	15,862	144.	Colby Vernay, Lacon IL	12,357
60.	Martin Baff, Beachwood OH	15,723	145.	Tom Rutledge, Charleston SC	12,287
61.	Bill Passell, Coral Springs FL	15,645	146.	John Fox, Whittier CA	12,269
62.	Marc Jacobus, Las Vegas NV	15,588	147.	Jerry Helms, Charlotte NC	12,125
63.	Ron Smith, Hixson TN	15,558	148.	Jim Zimmerman, Shaker Heights OH	12,058
64.	Mark Molson, Miami FL	15,448	149.	Harvey Brody, San Francisco CA	12,041
65.	Frank King, Heavener OK	15,443	150.	Allen Childs Jr., Little Rock AR	11,972
66.	Curtis Cheek, Huntsville AL	15,360	151.	Harry Ross, Winter Springs FL	11,966
67.	Bruce Ferguson, Boise ID	15,273	152.	Chuck Burger, West Bloomfield MI	11,908
68.	Richard Pavlicek, Fort Lauderdale FL	15,270	153.	Dorothy Truscott, Bronx NY	11,890
69.	Jim Barrow, Lake Charles LA	15,258	154.	Mary Hardy, Las Vegas NV	11,866
70.	Malcolm Brachman, Dallas TX	15,257	155.	Kyle Larsen, San Francisco CA	11,846
71.	Chris Compton, Dallas TX	14,934	156.	John Griscom, Boca Raton FL	11,833
72.	Gail Greenberg, New York NY	14,910	157.	Boris Baran, Cote Saint-Luc PQ	11,793
73.	Larry Cohen, Boca Raton FL	14,896	158.	Ed Davis, Seal Beach CA	11,783
74.	Phil Leon, Grosse Pointe MI	14,805	159.	Donald Stack, Shawnee Mission KS	11,765
75.	Kathie Wei-Sender, Nashville TN	14,765	160.	Erik Paulsen, Upland CA	11,760
76.	Sidney Lazard, New Orleans LA	14,745	161.	Liane Turner, Muskegon MI	11,731
77.	Judi Radin, New York NY	14,738	162.	George Steiner, Seattle WA	11,705
78.	Corinne Kirkham, San Bernardino CA	14,681	163.	Mark Blumenthal, Chicago IL	11,692
79.	Steve Lawrence, Athens TX	14,577	164.	Edith Freilich, Miami Beach FL	11,676
80.	Jim Robison, Las Vegas NV	14,532	165.	Janet Daling, Seattle WA	11,664
81.	Howard Piltch, Andover MA	14,477	166.	Russ Ekeblad, Providence RI	11,657
82.	Rick Henderson, Los Angeles CA	14,457	167.	Richard De Martino, Riverside CT	11,640
83.	George Rosenkranz, Mexico City	14,406	168.	Larry Cohen, Las Vegas NV	11,628
84.	Jim Reiman, Mansfield OH	14,364	169.	J. David King, Miami Beach FL	11,627
85.	Ralph Katz, Hinsdale IL	14,331	170.	Bob Etter, Sacramento CA	11,592
86.	Ed Lewis, Falls Church VA	14,326	171.	Shome Mukherjee, Randolph MA	11,587
87.	David Ashley, Las Vegas NV	14,309	172.	Michael Schreiber, Costa Mesa CA	11,578
88.	Jan Weyant, Cincinnati OH	14,306	173.	Harold Feldheim, Hamden CT	11,563
89.	Norman Coombs, Brookville IN	14,257	174.	Cliff Russell, Coral Gables FL	11,547
90.	Jacqui Mitchell, New York NY	14,247	175.	Richard Taube, Marietta GA	11,428
91.	Beverly Rosenberg, Sherman Oaks CA	14,238	176.	Steve Garner, Northfield IL	11,420

177.	Jack Schwencke, North Palm Beach FL	11,367
178.	Max Hardy, Las Vegas NV	11,321
179.	Joan Stein, Milwaukee WI	11,305
180.	Dick Yarington, Seattle WA	11,295
181.	Howard Weinstein, St. Charles IL	11,257
182.	Mike Albert, Omaha NE	11,241
183.	Gary Ullman, Sherman Oaks CA	11,174
184.	Bert Newman, West Bloomfield MI	11,155
185.	Daniel Rotman, Aventura FL	11,154
186.	Brenda Keller, Boise ID	11,151
187.	Judy Randel, Albuquerque NM	11,144
188.	Robert Teel Jr., Rockford AL	11,128
189.	Helen Utegaard, Las Vegas NV	11,100
190.	Larry Mori, Clearwater FL	11,094
191.	Sue Sachs, Owings Mills MD	11,089
192.	Jackie Jarigese, Vancouver WA	11,076
193.	Wayne Hascall, Grandville MI	11,070
194.	William Cole, Silver Spring MD	11,063
195.	Larry Washington, Carmichael CA	11,020
196.	Phil Brady, Philadelphia PA	11,017
197.	Tom Hodapp, Cincinnati OH	10,969
198.	Claude Vogel, Chicago IL	10,968
199.	Beth Palmer, Silver Spring MD	10,965
200.	Simon Kantor, Agawam MA	10,944
201.	Jeanne Stenger, Bethesda MD	10,939
202.	William Pettis, Silver Spring MD	10,930
203.	Larry Griffey, Palm Beach Gardens FL	10,924
204.	Bill Wisdom, Salisbury NC	10,910
205.	Helen Gustafson, Des Moines IA	10,886
206.	James Murphy, Chesapeake VA	10,865
207.	James Fellows, Omaha NE	10,846
208.	Stephen Swearingen, Arlington VA	10,842
209.	Andy O'Grady, Miami FL	10,821
210.	William Hunter, Reading MA	10,819

ABA TOP 100 MASTERPOINT HOLDERS

1	Robert Price, Chicago, IL	28,144
2	Chester Johnson, Chicago, IL	26,864
3	Lionel Barton, Missouri City, TX	26,842
4	Reginald Chapman, Washington, DC	24,353
5	Arnold Jones Jr, Chicago, IL	20,895
6	Dwight Galley, Sugar Land, TX	20,128
7	Lee Pennington, Nashville, TN	19,407
8	Julius Fields, New York, NY	18,868
9	Mae Clark, Arlington, TX	18,799
10	Arthur Wills, Southfield, MI	18,212
11	Beverly Lucas, Yellow Springs, OH	17,910
12	George Johnson, Charlotte, NC	17,848
13	Lawrence Berkley, Columbus, OH	17,160
14	Samuel Lucas, Yellow Springs, OH	17,061
15	Sandra Stevenson, Columbus, OH	16,760
16	Arthur Reid Jr, Bethesda, MD	16,651
17	Naomi Ballard, Southfield, MI	16,149
18	Joyce Williams, Chicago, IL	15,416
19	John Washington, New York, NY	15,073
20	Lela Wilson, Beaumont, TX	14,979
21	Heywood Ballard, Southfield, MI	14,882
22	John Jordan III, Washington, DC	14,797
23	Luis Pietri, Philadelphia, PA	14,709
24	W E Richardson Jr, Brooklyn, NY	14,626
26	Mary Moragne, Raleigh, NC	14,624
27	Harold Bickham, Indianapolis, IN	13,539
28	Thomas Hunt, Henderson, NC	13,412
29	Herbert Taylor, Chicago, IL	13,270
30	Sara Pearson, Los Angeles, CA	13,074
31	Taylor Cox, Southfield, MI	12,950
32	William Thompson, Souhtfield, MI	12,911
33	Clarice Reid, Bethesda, MD	12,735
34	Calvin Morris, New York, NY	12,333
35	Berrye Thompson, Southfield, MI	12,039
36	Bobbye Caldwell, Chicago, IL	11,992
37	Gloria Christler, Atlanta, GA	11,913
38	Worth Christler, Atlanta, GA	11,589
39	Bill Turner, Calumet City, IL	11,549
40	Edna Cravanas, Antioch, CA	11,530
41	Henry Bell, Des Moines, WA	11,479
42	Earline E Winn, Houston, TX	11,392
43	Daniel Requard, Chicago, IL	11,293
44	Bessie Haley, Dayton, OH	11,176
45	Vernette Wills, Southfield, MI	11,164
46	Leonard Jefferson, Arlington, TX	11,068
47	Louis Sutherland, Louisville, KY	10,630
48	Sylvia Christian, Southfield, MI	10,391
49	Winston Edwards, Columbia, MD	10,125

50	Freddie Jones, Chicago, IL	10,029
51	Faye Burke, Silver Spring, MD	9,986
52	Mary Green, Philadelphia, PA	9,830
53	Edward West Sr, Federal Way, WA	9,739
54	Richard Bowling, Greensboro, NC	9,714
55	Melvin Rone, Chicago, IL	9,287
56	Robert Wallace, Indianapolis, IN	9,121
57	George Hudson Jr, Creve Coeur, MO	8,957
58	Robert Friend, Irvine, CA	8,798
59	Verna Scott, Los Angeles, CA	8,782
60	Clyde Gulston, Brooklyn, NY	8,426
61	Edith Morgan, Las Vegas, NV	8,100
62	Jimmy Pelham, Baldwin, NY	7,964
63	Victor Stewart, Columbia, MD	7,946
64	Martin Phipps, Ocala, FL	7,909
65	Joan Williams, Homewood, IL	7,902
66	Anderson Williams, Atlanta, GA	7,778
67	Anita Troy, Henderson, NV	7,645
68	Charles Ferguson, Durham, NC	7,593
69	Bill Sides, Burbank, CA	7,569
70	Robert Seymour, Lake Mary, FL	7,518
71	Alton Moman Jr, Chicago, IL	7,371
72	Allie Raines, Southfield, MI	7,309
73	Marian Womack, Houston, TX	7,277
74	Dolores Thomas, West Orange, NJ	7,241
75	Gladys Randall, Chicago, IL	7,238
76	Patricia Abney, Los Angeles, CA	7,238
77	Mildred Anderson, Washington, DC	7,050
78	Wanda Mc-Wills, Southfield, MI	7,024
79	Louise Harris, Conyers, GA	7,016
80	Willis Troy Jr, Henderson, NV	6,960
81	Benjamin Williams, Philadelphia, PA	6,922
82	Mary Coleman, New Orleans, LA	6,903
83	Regena Edwards, Columbia, MD	6,766
84	Jerri Thomas, Ft Washington, MD	6,718
85	Janice Van Buren, St Louis, MO	6,691
86	Helen Furr, New Orleans, LA	6,676
87	James Harris, Conyers, GA	6,554
88	Evelyn Gilliard, East Point, GA	6,532
89	Loisteen Murff, Punta Gorda, FL	6,530
90	Robert Williams, Chicago, IL	6,482
91	Jeffrey Stroud, New York, NY	6,383
92	Leola Rucker, Virginia Beach, VA	6,360
93	Marvin Comer, Cincinnati, OH	6,356
94	Jacqueline Southern, Rex, GA	6,126
95	Seymour Bibuld, Rahway, NY	6,057
96	William Johnson, Inglewood, CA	5,934
97	Barbara Hutson, Detroit, MI	5,932
98	Willetta Phipps, Atlanta, GA	5,929
99	Peggy Jones, Springfield, OH	5,876
100	Edward Jackson, Atlanta, GA	5,841

NORTH AMERICAN CHAMPIONSHIP TROPHY WINNERS

MOTT-SMITH TROPHY. This trophy is awarded every year to the player with the best overall individual performance record in the Spring North American Bridge Championships. Donated by friends in memory of Geoffrey Mott-Smith in 1961, it was made retroactive to 1958 to include all the winners. The winners 1958 through 1968 were:

1958	Ivar Stakgold
1959	Lew Mathe
1960	Norman Kay
1961	Robert Jordan
1962	Robert Jordan
1963	Sidney Silodor tied with Norman Kay
1964	Lew Mathe
1965	Phil Feldesman
1966	Phil Feldesman
1967	Lew Mathe
1968	Norman Kay

The following are the Mott-Smith Trophy winners since 1969 together with their point totals. An asterisk indicates the record was broken that year.

1969	Sue Sachs	168
1970	Barry Crane	155
1971	Barry Crane	135
1972	Paul Swanson tied	159
	with Jack Blair	159
1973	Robert Wolff	233*
1974	Ron Andersen	250*
1975	Roger Bates	203
1976	Larry Cohen	225
1977	Mark Blumenthal	200
1978	Mike Passell	250*
1979	Jeff Meckstroth	215
1980	Jeff Meckstroth tied	173
	with Eric Rodwell	173
1981	Allan Stauber	166
1982	Dave Berkowitz tied	198
	with Harold Lilie	198
1983	Mike Passell	214
1984	Lew Stansby	172
1985	Jeff Meckstroth	196
1986	Lew Stansby	207
1987	Steve Robinson tied	200
	with Peter Boyd	200
1988	Roger Bates	193
1989	Eddie Wold	167
1990	John Sutherlin	300*
1991	Zia Mahmood	183
1992	Roger Bates	186
1993	Michael Seamon	196
1994	Chip Martel	250
1995	Michael Polowan	242
1996	Zia Mahmood	252
1997	Bart Bramley	292
1998	Eddie Wold	243
1999	Petra Hamman	265
2000	Jeff Meckstroth	313*

FISHBEIN TROPHY. This trophy is awarded every year to the player with the best overall individual performance record in the Summer North American Bridge Championships. The trophy, in memory of Sally Fishbein, was donated by ACBL in recognition of the untiring efforts of Harry Fishbein who served as Treasurer of ACBL and refused to accept the customary compensation. He insisted that the trophy honor his late wife. The winners 1952-1963 are:

1952	John Crawford
1953	Milton Ellenby
1954	David Carter
1955	Paul Hodge
1956	Tobias Stone
1957	John Crawford
1958	Helen Sobel
1959	Ira Rubin
1960	Boris Koytchou
1961	Marshall Miles
1962	Ira Rubin
1963	Alvin Roth

The following are the Fishbein Trophy winners since 1964 together with their point totals. An asterisk indicates the record was broken that year.

1964	Percy Sheardown	223*
1965	Alvin Roth	210
1966	Alvin Roth	186
1967	Phil Feldesman	177
1968	Jim Jacoby	205
1969	Robert Hamman	180
1970	Dave Strasberg	155
1971	Barbara Rappaport	187
1972	B.Jay Becker	179
1973	Richard Katz	199
1974	Richard Shepherd	162
1975	Grant Baze	176
1976	Richard Katz	219
1977	Ken Cohen	198

1978	Mike Passell	215
1979	Bobby Wolff	179
1980	Peter Weichsel	194
1981	Ralph Katz	236*
1982	Mike Smolen	221
1983	Bob Hamman	280*
1984	Steve Sion	271
1985	Bill Passell	225
1986	Mark Lair	187
1987	Danny Rotman	188
1988	Helen Utegaard	168
1989	Zeke Jabbour	198
1990	Ron Rubin tied	
	with Michael Becker	227
1991	Eric Rodwell	278
1992	Juanita Chambers	182
1993	John Sutherlin	233
1994	Lynn Deas	238
1995	Nick Nickell	253
	Dick Freeman	253
1996	Jeff Meckstroth	269
1997	Steve Garner	247
1998	Paul Soloway	281*
1999	Eric Rodwell	348*
2000	Rose Meltzer	315
	Kyle Larsen	315
	Peter Weichsel	315
	Lew Stansby	315
	Chip Martel	315

LOU HERMAN TROPHY. This trophy is awarded to the player with the best overall individual performance record at the Fall North American Championships. It was donated in 1951 by Sally Lipton, formerly Mrs. Lou Herman, of New York, in memory of her husband. The recipients of this award 1952 through 1962 were:

1952	Al Roth
1953	John Crawford
1954	Paul Hodge
1955	Milt Ellenby
1956	Paul Hodge
1957	Lew Mathe
1958	Sylvia Stein
1959	Mort Rubinow
1960	Oswald Jacoby
1961	Phil Feldesman
1962	Marshall Miles

The following are the Herman Trophy winners since 1962 with their point totals. An asterisk indicates the record was broken that year.

1963	Eric Murray	211
1964	Harold Rockaway	180
1965	Mike Lawrence	211
1966	Charles Coon	144
1967	Sami Kehela	155
1968	Henry Bethe	144
1969	Sylvia Stein	150
1970	Ira Rubin tied with Chuck Burger	154
1971	John Grantham	150
1972	Steve Robinson	181
1973	Larry Cohen	207
1974	Fred Hamilton	202
1975	Walt Walvick	171
1976	Paul Soloway	199
1977	John Mohan	160
1978	Bob Hamman	165
1979	Robert Levin	233*
1980	Jeff Meckstroth	225
1981	Chip Martel	224
1982	Jeff Meckstroth tied with Eric Rodwell	191
1983	Marty Bergen	233*
1984	Grant Baze	200
1985	Eric Rodwell	365*
1986	Kit Woolsey tied with Ed Manfield	212
1987	Jill Meyers	176
1988	Bob Hamman	270

1989	Mark Molson	254
1990	Eddie Wold	276
1991	David Berkowitz	357
1992	Haig Tchamitch	202
1993	Bob Hamman	355
1994	Mark Lair	365*
1995	Jeff Meckstroth	407*
1996	Michael Rosenberg	445*
1997	Bart Bramley, tied with Sidney Lazard	320
1998	Eric Rodwell	329
1999	Geir Helgemo	449*
2000	George Jacobs	365

ACBL MINI-McKENNEY CONTESTS

Rookie (0-5 Masterpoints)

1975	Robert Blanchard, New York NY	164
1976	Carolyn Behr, Orlando FL	176
1977	Jim Sternberg, Fort Lauderdale FL	377
1978	Bob Rosen, North Miami FL	216
1979	Cameron Cotton, Sacramento CA	190
1980	Alan Kleist, Cheverly MD	262
1981	Rick Purdy, Duluth MN	123
1982	Arif Janjua, San Jose CA	146
1983	Joe Barnard, Marysville OH	295
1984	Barbara Larson, Madison WI	116
1985	Elizabeth Rice, Huntington Valley OH	156
	Harry Falk, East Greenbush NY	156
1986	Richard Kennedy, East Cleveland OH	148
1987	John Blubaugh, Independence MO	141
1988	Norris "Pete" Peterson, Gaithersburg MD	119
1989	Donald Geerhart, Arlington VA	137
1990	Joel Wooldridge, Snyder NY	301
1991	John Cook, Gloucester ON	129
1992	Leslie Shafer, Silver Spring MD	181
1993	Niles Brown, New Orleans LA	328
1994	Jay Gibson, Plano TX	320
1995	John Kokubo, Royal Oak MI	457
1996	James Satterfield, Marietta GA	273
1997	Nick Bykov, Carmichael CA	363
1998	Brad Campbell, Smyrna GA	187
1999	Greg Bruce, Santa Barbara CA	236
2000	Mac Busby, San Diego CA	416

Junior Master (5-20 Masterpoints)

1975	Jim Prentice, Santa Monica CA	161
1976	Janice Seamon, Gainesville FL	153
1977	Craig Harrison, Seattle WA	265
1978	Marc Arbour, Scarborough ON	201
1979	Elisabeth Brenhouse, Newport Beach CA	255
1980	Mary Wolf, Philadelphia PA	183
1981	George Landreth, Blackduck MN	388
1982	Alan Watson, Cambridge MA	291
1983	Robert Batoff, Philadelphia PA	148
1984	Paul Ford, Los Angeles CA	201
1985	Connie Hicks, Brentwood TN	167
1986	Yvonne Hernandez, Fort Lauderdale FL	224
1987	Michel Bertrand, Dorval PQ	133
1988	Manuel Urrizola, Los Angeles CA	204
1989	Tom Barlow, Little Rock AR	215
1990	John Fout, Fairfield CA	228
1991	Yann Ozenne, Bonsecours, France	159
1992	Charles Donahue, Glendora CA	289
1993	Nancy Freeman, El Cajon CA	226
1994	Michael Papangelis	384
1995	Jsames Barry, Twain Harte CA	209
1996	Jeff Smith, Ottawa ON	335
1997	Michael Lohman, Baton Rouge LA	188
1998	Betty Haggard, Norfolk VA	170
1999	James Welch, Ketchum ID	370
2000	Ahmed Sorothia, Chino CA	266

Club Master (20-50 Masterpoints)

1975	Jeff Overby, St. Augustine FL	231
1976	Milton Stern, Dallas TX	306
1977	John D. Jones, Redondo Beach CA	364
1978	Ross Taylor, Hamilton ON	282
1979	Bruce Rogoff, Great Neck NY	223
1980	Bill Weakley, Nashville TN	237
1981	Robert Bobker, Wheeling IL	262
1982	Lele Dean, Greenville DE	166
1983	Moses Ma, Cambridge MA	335
1984	Cynthia Handy, Villa Park CA	254
1985	Charlie Cargile, Toney AL	205
1986	Robert Cohen, Minneapolis MN	239
1987	Sorin Samanta, Downey CA	190
1988	Earle Davidoff, New York NY	234
1989	Robert Cranor, Panorama City CA	166
1990	David Yang, Agoura Hills CA	313
1991	Sean Ganness, Ottawa ON	326
1992	Charles James, Salem OR	223
1993	Jeffrey Figgins, La Mesa CA	241
1994	Gerald Collier, Westlake Village CA	291
1995	Gaylord Bermaas, Portland OR	273
1996	Elwin Brown, Gloucester ON	288
1997	Amelia Fraser, Miami FL	243
1998	Ron Rose, Dayton OH	308
1999	Federico Kladt, Torrance CA	312
2000	Elizabeth Dressler, Cleveland OH	310

Sectional Master (50-100 Masterpoints)

1975	Claudia Zucker, Atlanta GA	214
1976	Stasha Wroblewski, Garnerville NY	365
1977	Lynn Deas, Norfolk VA	360
1978	Mark Bartusek, Anaheim CA	479
1979	Dan Jacob, Vancouver BC	296
1980	Keith Woolf, Mentor OH	422
1981	Andrew Kaufman, Bowie MD	304
1982	Charlie Ju, Rochester NY	309
1983	Mark Lewis, Charlotte NC	244
1984	Sharon Meng, Shaumburg IL	224
1985	Alan Benaroya, Kirkland WA	460
1986	Christopher Bohan, Berkeley CA	372
1987	Robert Crawford, Vancouver BC	401
1988	Michael Klein, Albany NY	357
1989	Jaf Chiang, South Windsor CT	350
1990	Hirsch Davis, Rockville MD	251
1991	Stephen Williams, Lawrenceville NJ	339
1992	Murray Johnstone, Chino Hills CA	289
1993	Marshall Hall, Boston MA	340
1994	Mark McCarthy, Mill Valley CA	311
1995	Everett Wong, Scarsdale NY	411
1996	Sam Graham, Oakland CA	349
1997	Thompson Jin, Alhambra CA	302
1998	Lev Pinsky, Columbus OH	310
1999	Tim Crank, Wheaton MD	374
2000	Carole Stuenkel, Landrum SC	350

Regional Master (100-200 Masterpoints)

1975	Allan Feineman, St. Petersburg FL	508
1976	Shirley Boice, Cheyenne WY	359
1977	Jeff Corbin, Wichita KS	427
1978	Keith Balcombe, Oshawa ON	426
1979	Juanita Skelton, Dallas TX	628
1980	Chris Kaufman, Bowie MD	305
1981	Mary Wolf, Philadelphia PA	363
1982	Sylvia Summers, Santa Monica CA	356
1983	David Funk, Norman OK	321
1984	Robert Batoff, Philadelphia PA	322
1985	Andrew Greenberg, Ithaca NY	397
1986	Elizabeth Rice, Huntington Valley OH	633
1987	Brenda Wiseman, Lincoln NE	281
1988	John Blubaugh, Independence MO	329
1989	Jade Barrett, Reading MA	214
1990	Qiang Wang, Woodside NY	309
1991	Gary Brown, Philadelphia PA	644
1992	Vicki Smith, Morro Bay CA	278
1993	Mary Keeler, Basalt CO	396
1994	Lynda Hempel, Emmett ID	415
1995	John Atteridg, San Francisco CA	668
1996	John Anderson, Baton Rouge LA	440
1997	Jean Cole, Richards TX	638
1998	Wildon Barker, Walker LA	455
1999	James Breihan, Austin TX	351
2000	Jim Eastham, Atlanta GA	538

NABC Master (200-Life Master)

1975	Troy Horton, Beaverton OR	493
1976	Claudia Zucker Feagin, Atlanta GA	442
1977	Fran Dolmage, Clovis NM	380
1978	Mike Hansen, Vancouver WA	342
1979	Ken Chen, Charlotte NC	401
1980	Elisabeth Brenhouse, Newport Beach CA	781

1981	Chris Hough, Ann Arbor MI	342
1982	Sally Alsfelder, Cincinnati OH	483
1983	Alan Kleist, Cheverly MD	540
1984	Emily Oglesby, Knoxville TN	473
1985	Jack Coleman, San Francisco CA	676
1986	Charlie Cargile, Toney AL	514
1987	Mary Keenan, Napa CA	548
1988	Dale Andersen, Busby AB	295
1989	Geoff Hampson, North York ON	464
1990	Lin-Huan Chen, Santa Monica CA	463
1991	Eric Greco, Annandale VA	557
1992	George Jacobs, Burr Ridge IL	482
1993	Donald Mamula, Kirkland WA	336
1994	Shannon Lipscomb, Red Bank TN	475
1995	Peter Cheung, Fremont CA	678
1996	James Barry Twain Harte CA	641
1997	Max Limbocker, Louisville KY	416
1998	Ed Hagerman, Las Vegas NV	491
1999	Michael Lucy, Red Lion PA	446
2000	Raymond Spalding, Atlanta GA	488

LIFE MASTER RACES

Life Master

1993	Not awarded	
1994	John Paul McNamee, Boston MA	336
1995	John Bridgewater, Columbus IN	649
1996	Barbara Benbow, Laurel MD	605
1997	Sam Graham, Oakland CA	753
1998	Phil Hook, Atlanta GA	563
1999	Scott Stearns, Clemson SC	613
2000	James Welch, Ketchum ID	618

Bronze Life Master

1993	Sean Ganness, Aventura FL	997
1994	Sheila Gabay, Newton MA	617
1995	Mark Novisoff, Las Vegas NV	1958
1996	Jason Ciano, New York NY	590
1997	Paul Lewis, Powell OH	804
1998	James Barry, Twain Harte CA	1117
1999	Alan Goldenberg, Oak Ridge TN	720
2000	John Villman, Yorbo Linda CA	1213

Silver Life Master

1993	Paul Kinney, Cambridge MA	867
1994	Richard Hunt, Las Vegas	3146
1995	John Fout, Fairfield CA	1206
1996	Gerald Sosler, Purchase NY	837
1997	Brian Gunnell, Jacksonville FL	916
1998	Robin Klar, Spring TX	1147
1999	Joseph Shea, Ponte Vedro FL	913
2000	Andy Stark, Hamilton ON	1083

Gold Life Master

1993	Jim Reiman, Mansfield OH	1189
1994	Geoff Hampson, Fenton MI	1574
1995	Stephen Levy, Las Vegas NV	1884
1996	John Fout, Fairfield CA	2199
1997	Hans Jacobs, Aurora ON	1145
1998	Richard Holmes, Wichita KS	1193
1999	Sheila Gabay, Newton MA	1074
2000	Kathy Newman, West Bloomfield MI	1718

Diamond Life Master

1993	Not awarded	
1994	Alan Susskind, Deerfield Beach FL	1571
1995	Mike Cappelletti Jr., Red Bank TN	1580
1996	Geoff Hampson, Fenton MI	1451
1997	Randy Pettit, Marietta GA	2117
1998	Geoff Hampson, Fenton MI	1820
1999	Jim Barrow, Lake Charles LA	3584
2000	Bert Newman, West Bloomfield MI	1719

ACBL ACE OF CLUBS CONTESTS

Rookie (0-5 Masterpoints)

1984	Myrna Blaufarb, Culver City CA	60
1985	Lapt Chan, Woodside NY	72

1986	Roy Welland, New York NY	94
1987	Richard Gamble, Ottawa ON	87
1988	Norris Peterson, Gaithersburg MD	65
1989	Robert Kast, Fort Lauderdale FL	95
1990	Ralph Mastrangelo, Cranston RI	90
1991	Wayne Karson, Culver City CA	59
1992	Gregory Robbins, New York NY	80
1993	Rod Organt, Salt Lake City UT	109
1994	Anand Nuggihalli, Dorval PQ	92
1995	Gilbert Guydos, Hollywood FL	81
1996	Tom Harbin, Hobe Sound FL	137
1997	Rene Jobin, Neufchatel PQ	90
1998	James Quibley, Pittsburgh PA	97
1999	Terrence Griffin, Sillery PQ	129
2000	Claude Cote, Sillery PQ	125

Junior Master (5-20 Masterpoints)

1984	Alice Lahoud, Newport RI	60
1985	Charles Marsh, Venice FL	60
1986	Ralph McAuley, Sarasota FL	71
1987	Michel Bertrand, Dorval PQ	93
1988	Manuel Urrizola, Los Angeles CA	118
1989	Tom Koch, Pembroke Pines FL	93
1990	Tom Cannon, Clearwater FL	141
1991	Martin Saffian, Orange CA	60
1992	Martin Marinov, New York NY	113
1993	David Brown, Brookline MA	77
1994	Michael Papangelis, Evanston IL	156
1995	Robert Walsh, Falls Church VA	100
1996	Barney Oppedahl, Vero Beach FL	114
1997	Gary Sullivan, Plantation FL	95
1998	Dan Kosman, Van Nuys CA	83
1999	Louis Sucheston, Clearwater FL	93
2000	Bill Linskey, Seal Beach CA	82

Club Master (20-50 Masterpoints)

1984	Donald Gifford, Seffner FL	80
1985	Manny Kussack, New York NY	91
1986	Ron Lucas, Long Beach CA	111
1987	Sorin Samanta, Downey CA	149
1988	Earle Davidoff, New York NY	118
1989	Jeffrey Baillet, Atlanta GA	89
1990	David Gurvich, New York NY	97
1991	Hugh Morrison, Harahan LA	92
1992	Greg Reich, New York NY	120
1993	Jeffrey Figgins, La Mesa CA	141
1994	Harry Wesley, Los Angeles CA	123
1995	William Clegg, San Antonio TX	193
1996	Claire Alpert, New York NY	156
1997	Therese Samson, Sillery PQ	116
1998	Lionel Venditti, Quebec PQ	162
1999	Jacques Gagnon, Quebec PQ	144
2000	Faylene Shark, Charleston SC	141

Sectional Master (50-100 Masterpoints)

1984	Jay Goldman, Thousand Oaks CA	99
1985	Esther Bigio, Miami Beach FL	102
1986	Marc Poupart, Longueuil PQ	117
1987	Sandra Nyman, Weston MA	106
1988	Paul Streigle, Clearwater FL	90
1989	Henry Barksdale, Riverview FL	131
1990	Madeleine Taeni, Cape Coral FL	112
1991	Tom Finley, Omaha NE	133
1992	Jack Chao, Vista CA	142
1993	Irving Klein, Montreal PQ	139
1994	Michel Duval, Repentigny, PQ	143
1995	Carl Wolinsky, Marietta GA	171
1996	John McNamara, Clearwater FL	155
1997	Bob Durand, Ormond Beach FL	144
1998	Jeffrey Myers, Medford NJ	125
1999	Lionel Venditti, Quebec PQ	236
2000	Terrence Griffin, Sillery PQ	201

Regional Master (100-200 Masterpoints)

1984	Sadru Visram, Toronto ON	140
1985	John Sensale, Hyde Park NY	92
1986	Esther Bigio, Miami Beach FL	120
1987	Andrea Hayman, New York NY	149
1988	Morris Biale, Queens Village NY	160
1989	Joyce Collos, Pembroke Pines FL	149
1990	Joyce Collos, Pembroke Pines FL	172

1991	Ralph Mastrangelo, Cranston RI	201
1992	Hugh Morrison, Harahan LA	162
1993	Jackie Rowe, Sun City Center FL	161
1994	David Brown, Jamaica Plain MA	183
1995	Janette Carter, Huntington Beach CA	212
1996	Roger Maurer, Pompano Beach FL	239
1997	John McNamara, Clearwater FL	260
1998	Rachid Benzakour, Hampstead PQ	162
1999	Gilbert April, Ste. Foy PQ	150
2000	Robert Kenney, Ottawa ON	168

NABC Master (200-Life Master)

1984	Aaron Brody, Riverdale NY	139
1985	Sadru Visram, Toronto ON	153
1986	Earl Ziskin, Los Angeles CA	138
1987	Marc Poupart, Longueuil PQ	176
1988	Malle Andrade, New York NY	191
1989	Morris Biale, Queens Village NY	158
1990	Alan Hayman, New York NY	188
1991	Dixie Hsu, San Luis Obispo CA	168
1992	Madeleine Taeni, Cape Coral FL	157
1993	Hugh Morrison, Harahan LA	183
1994	Robert Mault, Los Alamitos CA	190
1995	Terry Byrne, Jamestown RI	176
1996	Charles Clarke, Ventura CA	177
1997	William Clegg, San Antonio TX	190
1998	William Clegg, San Antonio TX	205
1999	Jon Yinger, Brea CA	201
2000	Lionel Venditti, Quebec PQ	234

Life Master
Through 1992 ALL Life Master were included.

1984	Sallie Landa, Boca Raton FL	174
1985	Gayle Rubens, Bay Harbor Island FL	199
1986	Susi Katz, Orlando FL	231
1987	Hugh Montagne, West Babylon NY	274
1988	Andy Tarkington, Dallas TX	254
1989	Helen Shanbrom, Tamarac FL	356
1990	Helen Shanbrom, Tamarac FL	356
1991	Helen Shanbrom, Tamarac FL	326
1992	Helen Shanbrom, Tamarac FL	351

Starting in 1993, this category included only those Life Masters who had not yet advanced to Bronze Life Master.

1993	Claude Rouleau, Ste. Adele PQ	165
1994	Yannis Yannakis, Athens, Greece	172
1995	Michael Papangelis, Evanston IL	207
1996	Adruen Boisclair, Montreal PQ	212
1997	William White, Arlington TX	179
1998	Edwin Siegel, New York NY	170
1999	Leon Kluger, Toronto ON	138
2000	Vincent Grande, Jupiter FL	170

Bronze Life Master

1993	Christian Chantigny, Montreal PQ	220
1994	Brad Stevens, Florissant MO	236
1995	Sam Yoga, Scarborough ON	253
1996	John Laufer, Montreal PQ	232
1997	R.J. Mourer, Pompano Beach FL	272
1998	R.J. Maurer, Pompano Beach FL	253
1999	Bernard Turenne, Charlesbourg PQ	305
2000	Claude Morissette, Quebec PQ	279

Silver Life Master

1993	Paul Kinney, Cambridge MA	289
1994	Christian Chantigny, Montreal PQ	316
1995	Claude Laberge, Longueil ON	287
1996	Sheila Gabay, Newton MA	351
1997	James Polites, Maple Shade NJ	247
1998	R.F. Smith, Don Mills ON	304
1999	Normand Houle, Momtreal PQ	280
2000	Bernard Turenne, Charlesbourg PQ	305

Gold Life Master

1993	Charles Drum, Brookline MA	265
1994	Paul Kinney, Cambridge MA	292
1995	Dudley Camacho, Toronto ON	343
1996	Claude Laberge, Longueil PQ	320
1997	Sheila Gabay, Newton MA	362
1998	Sheila Gabay, Newton MA	372
1999	Sheila Gabay, Newton MA	394
2000	Shelly Salvi, Lighthouse Point FL	414

Diamond Life Master

1993	Frances Silby, Fort Lauderdale FL	291
1994	Frances Silby, Fort Lauderdale FL	345
1995	Frances Silby, Fort Lauderdale FL	342
1996	Frances Silby, Fort Lauderdale FL	330
1997	Paul Kinney, Roxbury MA	363
1998	Paul Kinney, Cambridge MA	320
1999	Paul Kinney, Jamaica Plain MA	348
2000	Sheila Gabay, Newton MA	430

Grand Life Master

1993	Helen Shanbrom, Tamarac FL	419
1994	Helen Shanbrom, Tamarac FL	427
1995	Helen Shanbrom, Tamarac FL	448
1996	Helen Shanbrom, Tamarac FL	401
1997	Helen Shanbrom, Tamarac FL	362
1998	Helen Shanbrom, Tamarac FL	267
1999	Helen Shanbrom, Tamarac FL	296
2000	Helen Shanbrom, Tamarac FL	304

SENIOR PLAYER OF THE YEAR. George Burns, an all-time great of television, radio and the cinema – and an avid bridge player – donated the George Burns Trophy in 1993. The award is given annually to the Senior player (at least 55 years old) who wins the most masterpoints in Senior competition in that calendar year. The first to receive the award was Liane Slack in 1993.

1989	Homer Shoop, North Miami FL	233
1990	Homer Shoop, North Miami FL	819
1991	Homer Shoop, North Miami FL	638
1992	Loren Lange, Hurley SD	616
1993	Liane Slack, Kansas City MO	547
1994	Wayne Hascall, Grandville MI	1249
1995	Zeke Jabbour, Boca Raton FL	654
1996	Steve Lawrence, Athens TX	591
1997	Robert Ryder, Caldwell NJ	989
1998	Ed Weiss, Chesterfield MO	498
1999	Donald Turner, Overland Park KS	571
2000	Lowell Andrews, Huntington Beach CA	384

JUNIOR PLAYER OF THE YEAR. The Junior Player of the Year award was established in 1990. The competition to determine the junior player who can win the most materpoints in a single year is restricted to contestants 25 or younger who had not reached their 26th birthday as of Dec. 31 of the previous year. The winners:

1990	Sabine Zenkel, Chicago IL	633
1991	Leni Holtz, Los Angeles CA	688
1992	Geoff Hampson, Toronto ON	658
1993	Eric Greco, Charlottesville VA	770
1994	Geoff Hampson, Fenton MI	1574
1995	Shannon Lipscomb, Red Bank TN	896
1996	Michael Schuster, San Francisco CA	803
1997	Michael Schuster, San Francisco CA	685
1998	Kent Mignocchi, Bronx NY	1040
1999	Kent Mignocchi, Bronx NY	732
2000	Kent Mignocchi, Bronx NY	820

YOUTH PLAYER OF THE YEAR. The Youth Player of the Year award was established in 1990. The competition to determine the youth who can win the most masterpoints in a single year is restricted to contestants 19 or younger who had not reached their 20th birthday as of Dec. 31 of the previous year. The winners:

1990	Brad Moss, New York NY	385
1991	Eric Greco, Annandale VA	557
1992	Eric Greco, Annandale VA	608
1993	Eric Greco, Charlottesville VA	770

1994	Eric Greco, Charlottesville VA	897
1995	Eric Greco, Charlottesville VA	753
1996	Joel Wooldridge, Williamsville NY	598
1997	Kent Mignocchi, Glendale CA	590
1998	Kent Mignocchi, Bronx NY	1040
1999	John Kranyak, Bay Village OH	693
2000	John Kranyak, Bay Village OH	422

RICHMOND TROPHY

1974	John Carruthers, Toronto	522
1975	Mike Schoenborn, Toronto	524
1976	Bruce Ferguson, New Westminster BC	929
1977	Bruce Ferguson, New Westminster BC	671
1978	Bruce Ferguson, Calgary AB	610
1979	Mark Molson, Montreal	819
1980	Mark Molson, Montreal	599
1981	George Mittelman, Toronto	681
1982	Mark Molson, Montreal	689
1983	Mark Molson, Montreal	784
1984	Mark Molson, Montreal	679
1985	Cliff Campbell, Thunder Bay ON	552
1986	Cliff Campbell, Thunder Bay ON	493
1987	Gary Tomczyk, Parksville BC	1071
1988	Robert Crawford, Vancouver BC	1400
1989	Gary Tomczyk, Parksville BC	1214
1990	Robert Crawford, Vancouver	1399
1991	Cameron Doner, Richmond BC	944
1992	Cliff Campbell, Thunder Bay ON	1561
1993	Cliff Campbell, Thunder Bay ON	957
1994	Martin Caley, Montreal PQ	791
1995	Ken Warren, Pickering ON	1040
1996	Martin Caley, Montreal PQ	772
1997	Hans Jacobs, Aurora ON	1145
1998	Ken Gee, Regina SK	1328
1999	Ken Gee, Regina SK	1028
2000	Ken Gee, Regina SK	1346

APPENDIX III
ZONAL CHAMPIONSHIPS

EUROPEAN OPEN TEAMS (Zone 1)

Winners	Runners-up
1932 Scheveningen, Holland	
Austria	*Holland*
Dr. Paul Stern	Ernst C. Goudsmit
Edmond R. H. Pollak	Frits W. Goudsmit
Louis Urvater	Bolo Einhorn
Simon Fleischmann	Jacques Borel
	J. R. Cor van Bemmel Suyck
1933 London, England	
Austria	*Holland*
Simon Fleischmann	Ernst C. Goudsmit
Walter Herbert	Frits W. Goudsmit
Dr. Paul von Kaltenegger	Bolo Einhorn
Edmond R. H. Pollak	Jean de Kuyper
Dr. Paul Stern	
1934 Vienna, Austria	
Hungary	*Holland*
Emeric Alpar	Ernst C. Goudsmit
Rafael Cohen	Frits W. Goudsmit
Laslo Decsi	Bolo Einhorn
Francis von Leitner	J. R. Cor van Bemmel Suyck
Andor Keleti	Sam van Houten
Laszlo Klor	Lion B. Zeldenrust
1935 Brussels, Belgium	
France	*Hungary*
Baron Robert de Nexon	Emeric Alpar
Pierre Albarran	Rafael Cohen
Adrien Aron	Laslo Decsi
Joseph Broutin	George Ferenczy
M. Georges Rousset	Laszlo Klor
Sophocles Venizelos	Andor Keleti
1936 Stockholm, Sweden	
Austria	*Hungary*
Hans Jellinek	Emeric Alpar
Dr. Paul von Kaltenegger	Rafael Cohen
Edmond R. H. Pollak	Laslo Decsi
Karl Schneider	Andor Keleti
1938 Oslo, Norway	
Hungary	*Norway*
G. E. Zichy	R. Abrahamsen
E. Bokor	Leif Christiansen
George Ferenczy	Ranik Halle
Laszlo Klor	Odd Larsson
A. Por	Jens Magnussen
Dr. Lajos Widder	Trygve Sommervelt
1939 The Hague, Holland	
Sweden	*Yugoslavia*
Rudolf Kock	Dr. Nicholas Singer
Jac Neumann	Dr. Josef Fischer
Tore Sandgren	Geza Klein
Dr. Einar Werner	Ing. Marjanovic
	G. Stern
	Julius Klein
1948 Copenhagen, Denmark	
Great Britain	*Sweden*
Leslie W. Dodds	Dr. Einar Werner
Kenneth W. Konstam	Rudolf Kock
Edward Rayne	Nils-Olof Lilliehook
Boris Schapiro	Jan Wohlin
Terence Reese	Solve Sundin
S. J. Simon	Tom Wennberg
Maurice Harrison-Gary (capt.)	
1949 Paris, France	
Great Britain	*Sweden*
Kenneth Konstam	Rudolf Kock
Adam Meredith	Dr. Einar Werner
Boris Schapiro	Jan Wohlin
Terence Reese	Nils-Olof Lilliehook
S. J. Simon	Elis Brome
Maurice Harrison-Gray (capt.)	Bertil Kjelldahl
1950 Brighton, England	
Great Britain	*Sweden*
John C. H. Marx	Rudolf Kock
Kenneth W. Konstam	Dr. Einar Werner
Leslie W. Dodds	Jan Wohlin
Nico Gardener	P. Brome
Louis Tarlo	Bertil Kjelldahl
Maurice Harrison-Gray (capt.)	

1951 Venice, Italy	
Italy	*Austria*
Paolo Baroni	Hans Eisler
Eugenio Chiaradia	Laszlo Gulyas
Pietro Forquet	Karl Klimt
Augusto Ricci	Dr. Max Reithoffer
Mario Franco	Karl Schneider
Guglielmo Siniscalco	
1952 DunLaoghaire, Ireland	
Sweden	*Italy*
Gunnar Anulf	Engenio Chiaradia
Rudolf Kock	Mario Franco
Robert Larsen	Michele Giovine
Dr. Einer Werner	Guglielmo Siniscalco
Nils-Olof Lilliehook	Paolo Baroni
Jan Wohlin	Celestino Zeuli
1953 Helsinki, Finland	
France	*Great Britain*
Jacques Amouraben	Leslie W. Dodds
Marcel Kornblum	Kenneth W. Konstam
Dr. F. Hervouet	Nico Gardener
Pierre Ghestem	Albert Rose
Robert Schiltz	Peter F. Swinnerton-Dyer
Rene Bacherich	Dimmie Fleming
1954 Montreaux, Switzerland	
Great Britain	*France*
Leslie W. Dodds	Pierre Jais
Kenneth W. Konstam	F. Bodier
Boris Schapiro	P. Figeac
Terence Reese	P. J. Guerin
Adam Meredith	Henri Svarc
Jordanis Pavlides	Roger Trezel
1955 Amsterdam, Holland	
France	*Italy*
Pierre Jais	Eugenio Chiaradia
Roger Trezel	N. Sabetti
Pierre Ghestem	Massimo d'Alelio
Robert Lattes	Mario Franco
Rene Bacherich	Michele Giovine
Bertrand Romanet	Augusto Ricci
1956 Stockholm, Sweden	
Italy	*France*
Walter Avarelli	Pierre Ghestem
Giorgio Belladonna	Rene Bacherich
Eugenio Chiaradia	Henry Svarc
Massimo d'Alelio	Gerard Bourchtoff
Pietro Forquet	Pierre Jais
Guglielmo Siniscalco	Roger Trezel
1957 Vienna, Austria	
Italy	*Austria*
Walter Avarelli	Dr. Max Reithoffer
Giorgio Belladonna	Hans Eisler
Eugenio Chiaradia	Karl Klimt
Massimo d'Alelio	Hans Hartwich
Pietro Forquet	Dr. Erich Gluttig
Guglielmo Siniscalco	Karl Schneider (capt.)
1958 Oslo, Norway	
Italy	*Great Britain*
Walter Avarelli	Terence Reese
Giorgio Belladonna	Boris Schapiro
Eugenio Chiaradia	James Sharples
Massimo d'Alelio	Robert Sharples
Pietro Forquet	Maurice Harrison-Gray
Guglielmo Siniscalo	Alan Truscott
1959 Palermo, Italy	
Italy	*France*
Walter Avarelli	Pierre Jais
Georgio Belladonna	Roger Trezel
Benito Bianchi	Gerald Bourchtoff
R. Manca	Claude Delmouly
Pietro Forquet	Dr. Jacques Pariente
Eugenio Chiaradia	Henri Svarc
1961 Torquay, England	
Great Britain	*France*
Nico Gardener	Pierre Ghestem
Albert Rose	Rene Bacherich
Claude Rodrigue	Louis Malabat
Kenneth W. Konstam	Claude Deruy
R. Anthony Priday	J. Herschmann
Alan Truscott	Jacques Stetten

1962 Beirut, Lebanon

France
Rene Bacherich
Pierre Ghestem
Gerard Desrousseaux
Dr. Georges Theron
Jacques Stetten
Leon Tinter

Italy
Giorgio Belladonna
Massimo d'Alelio
Benito Bianchi
Giovan Battista Brogi
Giuseppe Messina
Camillo Pabis-Ticci

1963 Baden-Baden, Germany

Great Britain
Jeremy Flint
Maurice Harrison-Gray
Kenneth W. Konstam
Terence Reese
Boris Schapiro
Joel Tarlo

Italy
Benito Bianchi
Giovan Battista Brogi
Eugenio Chiaradia
Massimo d'Alelio
Dr. Guiseppe Messina
Camillo Pabis-Ticci

1965 Ostend, Belgium

Italy
Piero Astolfi
Giorgio Belladonna
Benito Bianchi
Vito Gandolfi
Dr. Giuseppe Messina
Renato Mondolfo

The Netherlands
Moritz Blitzblum
Pieter Boender
J. T. M. (Hans) Kreyns
C. Leo Oudshoorn
Anton Rijke
Cornelis (Bob) Slavenburg

1966 Warsaw, Poland

France
Jean-Michel Boulenger
Henri Svarc
Jean-Marc Roudinesco
Jacques Pariente
Jacques Stetten

The Netherlands
Martijn Cats
Cornelis Kaiser
Jacobus C. Kokkes
Jut Kramer
Cornelis (Bob) Slavenburg

1967 Dublin, Ireland

Italy
Giorgio Belladonna
Renato Mondolfo
Benito Bianchi
Dr. Giuseppe Messina
Cesale Bresciani
Oscar Bellentani

France
Henri Svarc
Jean-Michel Boulenger
Jacques Pariente
Jean-Marc Roudinesco
Dr. Georges Theron
Gerard Desrousseaux

1969 Oslo, Norway

Italy
Giorgio Belladona
Benito Bianchi
Paolo Frendel
Benito Garrozzo
Dr. Giuseppe Messina
Renato Mondolfo

Norway
Eric Hoie
Tore Jensen
Knut Koppang
Bjorn Larsen
Louis Andre Strom
Willy Varnas

1970 Estoril, Portugal

France
Jean-Michel Boulenger
Pierre Jais
Jean-Marc Roudinesco
Jean-Louis Stoppa
Henri Svarc
Roger Trezel

Poland
Wit Klapper
Lukasz Lebioda
Janusz Nowak
Janusz Pietruk
Andrzej Wilkosz
Adam Zimnielski

1971 Athens, Greece

Italy
Giorgio Belladonna
Benito Bianchi
Benito Garozzo
Dr. Guiseppe Messina
Frederico Mayer
Renato Mondolfo

Great Britain
Jonathan Cansino
Chris Dixon
Jeremy Flint
R. Anthony Priday
Claude Rodrigue
Rob Sheehan

1973 Ostend, Belgium

Italy
Giorgio Belladona
Dano de Falco
Arturo Franco
Benito Garozzo
Rodolfo Pedrini
Antonio Vivaldi

France
Jean-Michel Boulenger
Charles Guiton
Pierre Jais
Michel Lebel
Christian Mari
Henri Svarc

1974 Herzliya, Israel

France
Jean-Michel Boulenger
Michel Lebel
Francois Leenhardt
Christian Mari
Henri Svarc
Edmond Vial

Italy
Oscar Bellentani
Benito Bianchi
Cesare Besciani
Giorgio Matteucci
Carlo Mosca
Silvio Sbarigia

1975 Brighton, England

Italy
S. Di Stefano
Arturo Franco
Benito Garozzo

Israel
Julian Frydrich
Michael Hochzeit
Schmuel Lev

Ottorino Milani
Carlo Mosca
Silvio Sbarigia

1977 Elsinore, Demnark

Sweden
Sven-Olov Flodqvist
P. O. Sundelin
Hans Gothe
Anders Morath
Anders Brunzell
Jorgen Lindqvist

1979 Lausanne, Switzerland

Italy
Vito Pittala
Loranzo Lauria
Giorgio Belladonna
Dano de Falco
Benito Garozzo
Arturo Franco

1981 Birmingham, England

Poland
Alexander Jezioro
Julian Klukowski
Tomasz Przybora
Krzysztof Martens
Andrzej Milde
Marek Kudla

1983 Wiesbaden, Germany

France
Michel Corn
Philippe Cronier
Michel Lebel
Hervé Mouiel
Philippe Soulet
Henri Szwarc

1985 Salsomaggiore, Italy

Austria
Heinrich Berger
Kurt Feichtinger
Jan Fucik
Wolfgang Meinl
Karl Rohan
Franz Terraneo

1987 Brighton, England

Sweden
Magnus Lindkvist
Bjorn Fallenius
Sven-Olov Flodqvist
Hans Gothe
Tommy Gullberg
P.O. Sundelin

1989 Turku, Finland

Poland
Krzysztof Martens
Cezary Balicki
Julian Klukowski
K. Moszczynski
Marek Szymanowski
Adam Zmudzinski

1991 Killarney, Ireland

Britain
John Armstrong
Anthony Forrester
Graham Kirby
Andy Robson
Roman Smolski
Tony Sowter

1993 Menton, France

Poland
Cezary Balicki
Krzysztof Lasocki
Piotr Tuszynski
Piotr Gawrys
Wojoiech Olanski
Adam Zmudzinski

1995 Vilamoura, Portugal

Italy
Andrea Buratti
Massimo Lanzarotti
Lorenzo Lauria
Alfredo Versace
Antonio Sementa
Maurizio Pataccini

Yeshayha Levit
Pinhas Romik
Eliakim Shaufel

Italy
Vittorio Fellegara
Benito Garozzo
Giorgio Belladonna
Vito Pittala
Antonio Vivaldi
Arturo Franco

Denmark
Stig Werdelin
Steffen Steen Moller
Peter Schaltz
Knud Aage Boesgaard
Hans Werge
Eric Grande

Great Britain
Irving Rose
Robert Sheehan
John Collings
Paul Hackett
Tony Sowter
Steve Lodge

Italy
Giorgio Belladonna
Dano de Falco
Arturo Franco
Benito Garozzo
Lorenzo Lauria
Carlo Mosca

Israel
Michael Hochzeit
David Birman
Julian Frydrich
Eliakim Shaufel
Shalom Zeligman

Great Britain
John Armstrong
Raymond Brock
Anthony Forrester
Graham Kirby
Robert Sheehan
Jeremy Flint

France
Eric Eisenberg
Christian Mari
Dominique Poubeau
Jean-Christophe
Quantin
Maurice Salama
Patrick Sussel

Sweden
Sven-Ake Bjerregard
Bjorn Fallenius
Tommy Gullberg
Anders Morath
Mats Nilsland
P.O. Sundelin

Denmark
Jens Auken
Georg Norris
Peter Schaltz
Dennis Koch-Palmund
John Norris
Dorthe Schaltz

France
Paul Chemla
Michel Lebel
Christian Mari
Michel Perron
Robert Reiplinger
Philippe Soulet

1997 Montecatini, Italy

Italy	Poland
Andrea Buratti	Adam Zmudzinski
Massimo Lanzarotti	Cezary Balicki
Lorenzo Lauria	Apolinary Kowalski
Alfredo Versace	Jacek Romanski
Norberto Bocchi	Jacek Pszczola
Giorgio Duboin	Michal Kwiecin

1999 Malta

Italy	Sweden
Andrea Buratti	Lars Andersson
Massimo Lanzarotti	Bjorn Fallenius
Lorenzo Lauria	Peter Fredin
Alfredo Versace	Tommy Gullberg
Norberto Bocchi	Magnus Lindkvist
Giorgio Duboin	Mats Milsland

2001 Arona, Tenerife, Canary Islands, Spain

Italy	Norway
Norberto Bocchi	Aa Terje
Dano DeFalco	Boye Brogeland
George Duboin	Glenn Grotheim
Guido Ferraro	Geir Helgemo
Lorenzo Lauria	Tor Helness
Alfredo Versace	Eric Saelensminde

EUROPEAN WOMEN'S TEAMS
(Zone 1)

1935 Brussels, Belgium

Austria
Gertrude Brunner
Marianne Boschan
Ethel Ernst
Gretl Joseffy
Hella Mandl
Rixi Markus

1936 Stockholm, Sweden

Austria
Gertrude Brunner
Marianne Boschan
Ethel Ernst
Gretl Joseffy
Hella Mandl
Rixi Markus

1938 Oslo, Norway

Denmark
Mrs. K. Kolle
Mrs. E. Lundsteen
Mrs. A. Hillerup
Demly Wilming

1939 The Hague, Holland

France
Moussia Behr
Marie de Montaigu
Christianne Martin
Esmerian Pouldjian

1948 Copenhagen, Denmark

Denmark
Else Dam
Rigmor Fraenckel
Gurli Kieldsen
Vera Thostrup
Demly Wilming

1949 Paris, France

Denmark
Rigmor Fraenckel
Otti Damm
Else Dam
Demly Wilming

1950 Brighton, England

Great Britain
Mrs. N. Renshaw
Phyllis M. Williams
Penguin Evans
Fritzi Gordon
Alison B. Crisford
Mrs. A. N. Carr

1951 Venice, Italy

Great Britain
Penguin Evans
Fritzi Gordon
Dimmie Fleming
Rixi Markus
Lady Doris Rhodes
Phyllis M. Williams

1952 Dun Laoghaire, Ireland

Great Britain
Penguin Evans
Fritzi Gordon
Dimmie Fleming
Lady Doris Rhodes
Rixi Markus
Phyllis Williams

1953 Helsinki, Finland

France
Suzanne Baldon
Mrs. M. de Vries
Andree Bourchtoff
Mrs. Morand

1954 Montreus, Switzerland

France
Suzalle Baldon
Andree Bourchtoff
Mrs. M. de Vries
Christianne Martin
Marie de Montaigu
Mrs. Morand

1955 Amsterdam, Holland

Denmark
Otti Damm
Lizzie Schaltz
Vibeke Petersen
Rigmor Fraenckel
Gulli Skotte

1956 Stockholm, Sweden

France
Mrs. C. Bedin
Christianne Martin
Mrs. M. de Vries
Simone de Temmermann
Esmerian Pouldjian
Andree Sussel

1957 Vienna, Austria

Denmark
Otti Damm
Mrs. Detlevsen
Rigmor Fraenckel
Vibeke Peterson
Gulle Skotte

1958 Oslo, Norway

Denmark
Annelise Faber
Rigmor Fraenckel
Gerda Ljungberg
Otti Damm
Mis Nyholm

1959 Palermo, Italy

Great Britain
Fritzi Gordon
Dimmie Fleming
Rixi Markus
Marjorie Whitaker
Mary Edwards
Mrs. G. R. Higginson

1961 Torquay, England

Great Britain
Fritzi Gordon
Rixi Markus
Jane Juan
Dorothy Shanahan
Joan Durran
Marjorie Hiron

1962 Beirut, Lebanon

Sweden
Inga Lisa Larsson
Maj Rex
Rut Segander
Britta Werner
Elna Friberg
Lotty Saabye-Christiansen

1963 Baden-Baden, Germany

Great Britain
Dimmie Fleming
Fritzi Gordon
Jane Juan
Rixi Marcus
Mary Moss
Dorothy Shanahan

1965 Ostend, Belgium

France
Mrs. de Gailherd
Christianne Martin
Esmerian Pouldjian
Andree Sussel
Simone de Temmermann
Jacqueline Velut

1966 Warsaw, Poland

Great Britain
Joan Durran
Fritzi Gordon
Betty Harris
Jane Juan
Rixi Markus
Dorothy Shanahan

1967 Dublin, Ireland

Sweden
Britt Blom
Gunilla Jarpner
May Moore
Rut Segander
Gunborg Silborn
Britta Werner

1969 Oslo, Norway

France
Mrs. C. Brochot
Mrs. M. de Vries
Mrs. M. Kitabji
Marianne Serf
Andree Sussel
Simone de Temmermann

1970 Estoril, Portugal

Italy
Marisa Bianchi
Rina Jabes
Antoinetta Robaudo
Luciana C. Romanelli
Anna Valenti
Maria Venturini

1971 Athens, Greece

Italy
Marisa Bianchi
Rina Jabes
Maria Antonia Robaudo
Luciana C. Romanelli
Anna Valenti
Maria Venturini

1973 Ostend, Belgium

Italy
Marisa Bianchi
Luciana Canessa
Rina Jabes
Maria Antonia Robaudo
Anna Valenti
Maria Venturini

1974 Herzliya, Israel

Italy
Marisa Bianchi
Luciana Capodanno
Marisa D'Andrea
Rina Jabes
Maria Antonia Robaudo
Anna Valenti

1975 Brighton, England

Great Britain
Charley Esterson
Nicola Gardener
Fritzi Gordon
Sandra Landy
Rixi Markus
Rita Oldroyd

1976 No Contest

(After 1975 held
only in odd years.)

1977 Elsinore, Denmark

Italy
Marisa Bianchi
Luciana Capodanno
Marisa D'Andrea
Enrichetta Gut
Andreina Morini
Anna Valenti

1979 Lausanne, Switzerland

Great Britain
Nicola Gardener
Rita Oldroyd
Sally Sowter
Sandra Landy
Michelle Brunner
Rosemary Hudson

1981 Birmingham, England

Great Britain
Pat Davies
Nicola Gardener
Sandra Landy
Sally Sowter
Maureen Dennison
Diana Williams

1983 Wiesbaden, Germany

France
Danielle Allouche
Colette Lise
Ginette Chevalley
Veronique Bessis
Sylvie Willard

1985 Salsomaggiore, Italy

France
Veronique Bessis
Sylvie Willard
Danielle Allouche
Ginette Chevalley
Catherine Saul
Fabienne Pigeaud

1987 Brighton, England

France
Danielle Allouche
Ginette Chevalley
Helene Bordenave

1989 Turku, Finland

Germany
Daniela von Arnim
Sabine Zenkel
Waltraud Vogt

Veronique Bessis
Sylvie Willard
Benedicte Cronier
1991 Killarney, Ireland
Austria
Gabriele Bamberger
Doris Fischer
Rosi Spinn
Maria Erhart
Terry Weigkricht
Britta Widengren
1995 Vilamoura, Portugal
France
Veronique Bessis
Benedicte Cronier
Colette Lise
Catherine Saul
Claude Blouquit
Sylvie Willard
1999 Malta

Great Britain
Nicola Smith
Pat Davies
Sandra Landy
Abbey Walker
Liz McGowan

Kareen Schroeder
Karin Caesar
Marianne Moegel
1993 Menton, France
Sweden
Linda Lanstrom
Pyttsi Flodqvist
Bim Odlund
Catarina Midskog
Mari Ryman
Lisbeth Astrom
1997 Montecatini, Italy
Great Britain
Nicola Smith
Pat Davies
Sandra Landy
Michele Handley
Liz McGowan
Heather Dhondy
2001 Tenerife, Canary Islands
England
Sally Brock
Michelle Brunner
Margaret Courtney
Heather Dhondy
Rhona Goldenfield
Nicola Smith

EUROPEAN OPEN PAIRS

1993, Bielefeld, Germany
1. **France:** Jean-Christophe Quantin – Michel Abecassis
2. **France:** Jean-Paul Meyer – Francois Stretz
1995, Rome, Italy
1. **Poland:** Piotr Gawrys – Krzysztof Lasocki
2. **Great Britain:** Tony Waterlow – Paul Hackett
1997, Hague, The Netherlands
1. **Poland:** Roman Kierznowski – Krzysztof Lukaszewicz
2. **France:** Jean-Cristophe Quantin – Michel Abecassis
1999, Warsaw, Poland
1. **France:** Paul Chemla – Alain Levy
2. **Italy:** Giorgio Duboin – Guido Ferraro

EUROPEAN WOMEN'S PAIRS

1993, Bielefeld, Germany
1. **The Netherlands:** Carla Arnolds – Bep Vriend
2. **Germany:** Marianne Moegel – Karin Caesar
1995, Villamoura, Portugal
1. **Germany:** Sabine Auken – Daniela von Arnim
2. **Germany:** Pony Nehmert – Andrea Rauscheid
1997, Montecatini, Italy
1. **Germany:** Sabine Auken – Daniela von Arnim
2. **France:** Cristina Golin & Gabriella Olivieri
1999, Malta
1. **France:** Elisabeth Lacroix - Catherine Poulain
2. **France:** Nadine Cohen - Catherine Multon
2001, Arona, Tenerife, Canary Islands, Spain
1. **Germany:** Sabine Auken – Daniela von Arnim
2. **Italy:** Tiziani Rosi – Anton Bacaccoli

EUROPEAN SENIOR PAIRS

1993 Switzerland: Gerry Link – Max Saesseli
1995 Poland: Janusz Nowek – Wlodzimierz Stobiecki
1997 France: Nadine Cohen – Marie France Renoux
1999 Poland: Jerzy Kuiga-Leosz – Krystzof Lasocki

EUROPEAN SENIOR TEAMS

2000 Poland: Wit Klapper, Andrzeg Milde, Wlodzimierz Stobiecki, W. Wala, Jerzy Russyan, Andrzeg Wilkosz

EUROPEAN MIXED TEAMS

1994, Paris, France
Netherlands: Marijke Van Der Pas, Kees Tammens, Anton Maas, Bep Vriend
1996, Monte Carlo
France : Veronique Bessis, Michel Bessis, Paul Chemla, Catherine d'Ovidio Saul
1998, Ballaria, Italy
France: Veronique Bessis, Michel Bessis, Paul Chemla, Catherine d'Ovidio Saul
2000, Rimini
Denmark: Peter Schaltz, Dorthe Schaltz, Jens Auken, Sabine Auken

EUROPEAN MIXED PAIRS

1994 Germany: Sabine Auken – Georg Nippgen
1996 Austria: Marie Erhart – Fritz Kubac
1998 Sweden: Pia Anderson - Arne Larsson
2000 Italy: Carlo Mariani – Monica Buratti

EUROPEAN JUNIOR TEAMS (Zone 1)

1968 (Prague)	Sweden
1970 (Dublin)	Denmark
1972 (Delft)	Poland
1974 (Copenhagen)	Sweden
1976 (Lund)	Austria
1978 (Stirling)	Great Britain
1980 (Tel Aviv)	Norway
1982 (Salsomaggiore)	Poland
1984 (Hasselt)	France
1986 (Budapest)	Netherlands
1988 (Plovdiv)	France
1990 (Neumunster)	Norway
1992 (Paris)	Italy

1994, Arnhem, The Netherlands
1. **Great Britain**: NPC Raymond Brock, Justin Hackett, Jason Hackett, Jeff Allerton, Danny Davies, Phil Souter, Tom Townsend
1996, Cardiff, Wales, Great Britain
1. **Norway**: NPC Espen Kvam, Boye Brogeland, Thomas Charlsen, Espen Erichsen, Christer Kristoffersen, Bjorn Morten Mathisen, Oyvind Saur
1998, Vienna, Austria
1. **Italy**: NPC Gianpaolo Rinaldi, Daniele Pagani, Paolo Marino, Bernardo Biondo, Riccardo Intonti, Mario d'Avossa, Matteo Mallardi
2000, Antalya, Turkey
1. **Norway**: Thomas Charlsen, Stig Roar Hakkebo, Gunnar Harr, Ronny Jorstad, Nils Kare Kvangraven, Olav Ellestad

EUROPEAN SCHOOLS TEAMS

1994, Arnhem, The Netherlands
France: NPC Jean-Cristophe Quantin, Laurent Bouscarel, Julien Geitner, Dominique Fonteneau, Jérôme Rombaut
1996, Cardiff, Wales, Great Britain
Germany: NPC Roland Rohowsky, Raoul Balschun, Matthias Felmy, Daniela Kehl, Julius Linde, Martin Moeller, Matthias Schueller
1998, Vienna, Austria
Italy: NPC Enrico Guerra, Furio di Bello, Stelio di Bello, Ruggero Guariglia, Fabio Lo Presti, Leonardo Magrini, Stefano Uccelo
2000, Antalya, Turkey
Poland: Konrad Araszkiewicz, Krzysztof Buras, Szymon Kapala, Jakub Kotorowicz, Krzysztof Kotorowicz, Piotr Madry

European Junior Pairs

1991, Fiesch, Switzerland
1. **Austria**: Tilmann Seidel – Axel Wodniansky
2. **Germany**: Julia Korus – Michael Tomski
1993, Obereifenberg, Germany
1. **Denmark**: Jesper Dall – Jesper Thomsen
2. **Poland**: Mariusz Puczynski – Tomasz Puczynski
(then incorporated into World Junior Pairs)

NORTH AMERICAN CHAMPIONSHIPS
(Zone 2)

BERMUDA BOWL QUALIFIERS

1950	John Crawford, Charles Goren, George Rapee, Howard Schenken, Sidney Silodor, Samuel Stayman
1951	B. Jay Becker, John Crawford, George Rapee, Howard Schenken, Samuel Stayman, npc Julius Rosenblum
1953	B. Jay Becker, John Crawford, Theodore Lightner, George Rapee, Howard Schenken, Samuel Stayman, npc Joseph Cohan
1954	Cliff Bishop, Milton Ellenby, Lew Mathe, Don Oakie, William Rosen, Douglas Steen, npc Benjamin Johnson
1955	Cliff Bishop, Milton Ellenby, Lew Mathe, John Moran, William Rosen, Alvin Roth, npc Peter Leventritt
1956	Myron Field, Charles Goren, Lee Hazen, Richard Kahn, Charles Solomon, Samuel Stayman, npc Jeff Glick
1957	Charles Goren, Boris Koytchou, Peter Leventritt, Harold Ogust, William Seamon, Helen Sobel, npc Rufus Miles
1958	B. Jay Becker, John Crawford, George Rapee, Alvin Roth, Sidney Silodor, Tobias Stone, npc J.G. Ripstra

1959 Harry Fishbein, Sam Fry, Leonard Harmon, Lee Hazen, Sidney Lazard, Ivan Stakgold, npc Charles Solomon

1961 John Gerber, Paul Hodge, Norman Kay, Peter Leventritt, Sidney Silodor, Howard Schenken, npc Frank Westcott

1962 Charles Coon, Mervin Key, Lew Mathe, Bobby Nail, Eric Murray, Ron von der Porten, npc John Gerber

1963 James Jacoby, Robert Jordan, Peter Leventritt, Bobby Nail, Arthur Robinson, Howard Schenken, npc John Gerber

1965 Howard Schenken, Peter Leventritt, Ivan Erdos, Kelsey Petterson, B. Jay Becker, Dorothy Hayden, npc John Gerber

1966 Phil Feldesman, Bob Hamman, Sami Kehela, Lew Mathe, Eric Murray, Ira Rubin, npc Julius Rosenblum

1967 Edgar Kaplan, Norman Kay, Sami Kehela, Eric Murray, William Root, Alvin Roth, npc Julius Rosenblum

1969 Bill Eisenberg, Bobby Goldman, Bob Hamman, Eddie Kantar, Sidney Lazard, George Rapee, npc Oswald Jacoby

1970 Bill Eisenberg, Bobby Goldman, Bob Hamman, James Jacoby, Mike Lawrence, Bobby Wolff, npc Oswald Jacoby

1971 Defending champion North America: Bill Eisenberg, Bobby Goldman, Mike Lawrence, James Jacoby, Bob Hamman, Bobby Wolff, npc Oswald Jacoby. United States: Edgar Kaplan, Norman Kay, Don Krauss, Lew Mathe, John Swanson, Richard Walsh, npc Lee Hazen

1973 Defending champion North America: Mark Blumenthal, Bobby Goldman, Mike Lawrence, James Jacoby, Bob Hamman, Bobby Wolff, npc Ira Corn. United States: B. Jay Becker, Michael Becker, Jeff Rubens, John Swanson, Paul Soloway, Andrew Bernstein, npc Roger Stern

1975 Bill Eisenberg, Bob Hamman, Eddie Kantar, Paul Soloway, John Swanson, Bobby Wolff, npc Alfred Sheinwold

1976 Bill Eisenberg, Fred Hamilton, Erik Paulsen, Hugh Ross, Ira Rubin, Paul Soloway, npc Dan Morse

1977 Defending champion North America: Fred Hamilton, Mike Passell, Erik Paulsen, Hugh Ross, Ira Rubin, Ron von der Porten, npc Jerome Silverman. United States: Bill Eisenberg, Bob Hamman, Eddie Kantar, Paul Soloway, John Swanson, Bobby Wolff, npc Roger Stern

1979 Malcolm Brachman, Bill Eisenberg, Bobby Goldman, Eddie Kantar, Mike Passell, Paul Soloway, npc Ed Theus

1981 Russ Arnold, Robert Levin, Jeff Meckstroth, Bud Reinhold, Eric Rodwell, John Solodar, npc Thomas Sanders

1983 North America I: Michael Becker, Bob Hamman, Ron Rubin, Alan Sontag, Peter Weichsel, Bobby Wolff, npc Joe Musurneci. North America II: James Jacoby, Jeff Meckstroth, George Rosenblum, Eric Rodwell, Mike Passell, Eddie Wold, npc James Zimmerman

1985 United States: Bob Hamman, Bobby Wolff, Chip Martel, Lew Stansby, Peter Pender, Hugh Ross, npc Alfred Sheinwold. Canada Drew Cannell, Gordon Campbell, Bryan Maksymetz, Mike Chomyn, Doran Flock, Subhash Gupta, npc John Carruthers

1987 United States: Mike Lawrence, Hugh Ross, Bob Hamman, Lew Stansby, Chip Martel, Bobby Wolff, npc Dan Morse. Canada Harmon Edgar, Michael Schoenborn, Arno Hobart, Greg Carroll, David Turner, Martin Kirr, npc George Mittelman

1989 United States: Hugh Ross, Peter Pender, Chip Martel, Lew Stansby, Mike Lawrence, Kit Woolsey. Canada Andre Laliberte, Jacques LaLiberte, Raymond Fortin, Kamel Fergani, Maurice Larochelle, Jean Bernier

1991 United States I: Bart Bramley, Mark Feldman, Fred Stewart, Steve Weinstein, Alexander Ornstein, Jeff Ferro, npc Hugh Ross. United States II: Robert Barr, Harold Stengel, Bernard Miller, Alan Sontag, Jeff Meckstroth, Eric Rodwell, npc Robert Rosen. Canada' Doug Heron, Ed Zaluski, Mike Belts, David Willis, Randy Bennett, John Valliant, npc Dave Kent

1993 United States I: Mike Becker, Ron Rubin, Robert Levin, Peter Weichsel, Russ Ekeblad, Ron Sukoneck, npc Jeff Wolfson. United States II: Cliff Russell, Sam Lev, David Berkowitz, Larry Cohen, Eric Rodwell, Marty Bergen, npc Bob Rosen; Mexico' Gonzalo Herrara, Miriam Rosenberg, Nancy Gerson, Alicia Duran, npc Beatriz Herrara

1995 United States I: Edgar Kaplan, npc ; Nick Nickell, Richard Freeman, Bob Hamman, Bobby Wolff, Jeff Meckstroth, Eric Rodwell. United States II: James Cayne, Chuck Burger, Mike Passell, Mark Lair, Paul Soloway, Bobby Goldman. Canada: Eric Kokish, Joey Silver, George Mittelman, Fred Gitelman, Boris Baran, Mark Molson

1997 United States I: Seymon Deutsch, Lew Stansby, Chip Martel, Zia Mahmood, Michael Rosenberg, United States II Nick Nickell, Richard Freeman, Bob Hamman, Bobby Wolff, Eric Rodwell, Jeff Meckstroth. Nador Hanna, Michael Roche, Jim Green, Paul Thurston, Rick Delogu,

Doug Fraser, npc George Mittelman

1999 Nick Nickell, Richard Freeman, Eric Rodwell, Jeff Meckstroth, Bob Hamman, Paul Soloway, Jeff Wolfson, Neil Silverman, Zia Mahmood, Michael Rosenberg, Chip Martel, Lew Stansby. Canada: Fred Gitelman, Joey Silver, Brian Maksymetz, Allan Graves, M. Hargreaves, Gord McCormond

2001 United States I: Nick Nickell, Richard Freeman, Eric Rodwell, Jaff Meckstroth, Bob Hamman, Paul Soloway. United States II Rose Meltzer, Kyle Larsen, Peter Weichsel, Alan Sontag, Chip Martel Lew Stansby. There was no Tri-Country Playoff because Canada, Mexico and Bermuda all finished in the lower half of the standings in the 2000 World Team Olympiad.

OPEN TEAM OLYMPIAD QUALIFIERS

1960 United States: John Crawford, Tobias Stone, B. Jay Becker, George Rapee, Sidney Silodor, Norman Kay, npc Julius Rosenbloom; Oswald Jacoby, Ira Rubin, Samuel Stayman, Morton Rubinow, Victor Mitchell, William Grieve, npc Ben Johnson; Charles Goren, Helen Sobel, Howard Schenken, Harold Ogust, Lew Mathe, Paul Allinger, npc R.L. Miles; Don Oakie, Meyer Schleifer, Leonard Harmon, Ivar Stakgold, Sidney Lazard, William Hanna, npc Harry Fishbein. Canada: Eric Murray, Percy Sheardown, C.B. Elliott, Harry Bork, Sami Kehela, Bruce Gowdy, npc N.M Burns

1964 United States: Bob Hamman, Robert Jordan, Donald Krauss, Victor Mitchell, Arthur Robinson, Samuel Stayman, npc Frank Westcott. Canada: Ralph Cohen, R. Forbes, Sam Gold, Jack Howell, Sami Kehela, Eric Murray, npc A.M. Lando. Bermuda: Norman Bach, Malcolm Martin, W.G. Rosner, Tony Saunders, Bill Tucker, Peter Willcocks, npc Alan Truscott

1968 United States: Robert Jordan, Norman Kay, William Root, Edgar Kaplan, Arthur Robinson, Alvin Roth, npc Julius Rosenblum. Canada: Bruce Elliott, William Crissey, Eric Murray, Gerald Charney, Sami Kehela, Percy Sheardown, npc Albert Lando. Bermuda: Mrs. Norman Bach, Hugh Barr, Thomas Lines, Norman Bach, Tracy Denninger, Malcolm Martin, npc Dudley Cooper

1972 United States: Bobby Goldman, Bob Hamman, James Jacoby, Mike Lawrence, Paul Soloway, Bobby Wolff. Canada: Gerry Charney, Bill Crissey, Bruce Gowdy, Sami Kehela, Eric Murray, Duncan Phillips, npc Al Lando. Bermuda: Tracy Denninger, H.B. Eve, M. M. Lewis, M.V.D. Martin, Ernie Owen, Tony Saunders, npc D.G. Cooper

1976 United States: Bill Eisenberg, Fred Hamilton, Paul Soloway, Ira Rubin, Hugh Ross, Erik Paulsen, npc Dan Morse. Canada: Bruce Gowdy, Karen Allison, Franco Bandoni, Don Cowan, Eric Murray, Sami Kehela, npc Baron Wolf Lebovic. Bermuda: Mal Martin, Tracy Denninger, Malcolm Lewis, Ernie Owen, Joe Wakefield, Colin Millington, npc Tony Saunders.

1980 United States: Fred Hamilton, Bob Hamman, Mike Passell, Ira Rubin, Paul Soloway, Bobby Wolff, npc Ira Corn. Canada: Allan Graves, Sami Kehela, Eric Kokish, George Mittelman, Eric Murray, Peter Nagy, npc Gerald Charney. Bermuda: Alan Douglas, David Ezekiel, Colin Millington, Ernie Owen, Charles Vaucrosson, Joe Wakefield, npc Jack Rhind.

1984 United States: Ron Andersen, Bob Hamman, Bobby Wolff, Malcolm Brachman, Bobby Goldman, Paul Soloway, npc Ed Theus. Canada: Mark Molson, Boris Baran, John Carruthers, John Guoba, George Mittelman, Allan Graves, npc Steve Aarons. Bermuda: David Ezekiel, Colin Millington, Alan Douglas, Charles Vaucrosson, Jean Johnson, Frank Wharton, npc Jack Rhind

1988 United States: Seymon Deutsch, Bob Hamman, James Jacoby, Jeff Meckstroth, Eric Rodwell, Bobby Wolff, npc Dan Morse. Canada: Boris Baran, John Carruthers, John Guoba, Sami Kehela, Mark Molson, Eric Murray, npc Mark Stein. Bermuda: Paul Below, John Burville, Alan Douglas, Ian Harvey, David Pereira, Charles Vaucrosson, npc Jack Rhind

1992 United States: Seymon Deutsch, Bob Hamman, Jeff Meckstroth, Eric Rodwell, Michael Rosenberg, Bobby Wolff, npc Dan Morse. Canada: Ed Bridson, David Lindop, Geoff Hampson, John Gowdy, Mark Molson, Boris Baran

1996 United States: Gerald Caravelli, Gary Cohler, Steve Garner, Jerry Goldfein, Jack Oest, Larry Robbins. Canada: Boris Baran, Fred Gitelman, Eric Kokish, George Mittelman, Mark Molson, Joey Silver. Mexico: Gonzalo Herrera, Baran, Miguel Reygadas, George Rosenkranz, Edith Rosenkranz. Bermuda: John Burrville, Jean Johnson,

David Pereira, Vera Petty, Joe Wakefield, Margie Way
2000 United States: George Jacobs, Ralph Katz, Steve Garner, Steve Weinstein, David Berkowitz, Larry Cohen. Canada: Martin Kirr, npc; Drew Cannell, John Carruthers, Nader Hanna, Eric Kokish, Robert Lebi, George Mittleman. Mexico: Ana Luisa Hernandez, npc; Moises Ades, Gonzalo Herrera, Enrico Pagani, Jacobo Podbilewicz, Mauricio Smid. Bermuda: Edna Clay, npc; David Cordon, Vera Petty, David Schroeder, Roman Smolski, David Sykes, Charles Vaucrosson.

VENICE CUP QUALIFIERS

1974 Bette Cohn, Emma Jean Hawes, Betty Ann Kennedy, Marietta Passell, Carol Sanders, Dorothy Truscott, npc Ruth McConnell
1976 Emma Jean Hawes, Betty Ann Kennedy, Jacqui Mitchell, Gail Moss, Carol Sanders, Dorothy Truscott, npc Ruth McConnell
1978 Mary Jane Farell, Emma Jean Hawes, Marilyn Johnson, Jacqui Mitchell, Gail Moss, Dorothy Truscott, npc Ruth McConnell
1981 Nancy Gruver, Edith Kemp, Betty Ann Kennedy, Judi Radin, Carol Sanders, Kathie Wei, npc Ron Andersen
1985 North America I: Kathie Wei, Judi Radin, Jacqui Mitchell, Gail Greenberg, Carol Sanders, Betty Ann Kennedy, npc Dan Morse. North America II: Edith Freilich, Nancy Gruver, Mary Jane Farell, Helen Utegaard, Beverly Rosenberg, Carol Pincus, npc Stelios Touchtidis
1987 North America I: Jo Morse, Sue Sachs, Cindy Bernstein, Sally Wheeler, Sharon Osberg, Peggy Sutherlin, npc John Sutherlin. North America II: Lynn Deas, Beth Palmer, Juanita Chambers, Cheri Bjerkan, Kathie Wei, Judi Radin, npc Carol Sanders
1989 United States: Beth Palmer, Lynn Deas, Kitty Bethe, Margie Gwozdzinsky, Karen McCallum, Kerri Shuman, npc Dorothy Truscott. Canada: Dianna Gordon, Sharyn Reus, Mary Paul, Francine Cimon, Gloria Silverman, Katie Thorpe, npc George Mittelman.
1991 United States I: Juanita Chambers, Cheri Bjerkan, Kay Schulle, Jill Meyers, Pam Wittes, Randi Montin, npc Ron Andersen. United States II: Lynn Deas, Stasha Cohen, Sharon Osberg, Sue Picus, Nell Cahn, Nancy Passell, npc Kathie Wei. Canada: Francine Cimon, Dianna Gordon, Mary Paul, Sharyn Reus, Gloria Silverman, Katie Thorpe, npc John Carruthers
1993 United States I: Lynn Deas, Beth Palmer, Helen Utegaard, Kathie Wei-Sender, Carol Sanders, Betty Ann Kennedy, npc Sue Sachs. United States II: Jill Meyers, Kay Schulle, Kerri Sanborn, Karen McCallum, Sharon Osberg, Sue Picus, npc Jo Morse. Canada: Francine Cimon, Rhoda Habert, Dianna Gordon, Sharyn Reus, Barbara Saltsman, Beverly Kraft, npc Mark Stein.
1995 United States I: Karen McCallum, Kitty Munson-Cooper, Rozanne Pollack, Carol Simon, Sue Picus, Kerri Sanborn, npc Steve Sanborn. United States II: Mildred Breed, Amalya Kearse, Jacqui Mitchell, Jo Morse, Joyce Lilie, Tobi Sokolow, npc Phillip Alder. Canada:
1997 United States I: Marinesa Letizia, Lisa Berkowitz,, Jill Meyers, Randi Montin, Tobi Sokolows, Mildred Breed, npc Sue Picus. United States II: Kathie Wei-Sender, Sue Sachs, Juanita Sanders, Lynn Deas, Beth Palmer, Kerri Sanborn. Canada: Dianna Gordon, Sharyn Reus, Beverly Kraft, Francine Cimon, Rhoda Habert, Barbara Saltsman, npc George Holland
1999 United States I: Jill Meyers, Randi Montin, Tobi Sokolow, Janice Seamon-Molson, Renee Mancuso, Shawn Quinn, npc Ron Smith. United States II: Lynn Deas, Beth Palmer, Sue Picus, Lisa Berkowitz, Rozanne Pollack, Connie Goldberg, npc Karen Allison
2001 United States I: Lynn Baker, Irina Levitina, Randi Montin, Karen McCallum, Kerri Sanborn, Jill Myers. United States II: Petra Hamman, Joan Jackson, Robin Klar, Kay Schulle, Shawn Quinn, Mildred Breed. Canada: Sharyn Reus, Dinana Gordon, Ina Demme, Katie Thorpe (playing captain), Francine Cimon, Martine Lacroix, npc Ralph Cohen

WOMEN'S TEAM OLYMPIAD QUALIFIERS

1960 United States: Malvine Klausner, Helen Portugal, Sylvia Schwartz, Agnes Gordon, Dorothy Hayden, Jo Sharp, npc Charles Solomon
1964 United States: Agnes Gordon, Muriel Kaplan, Alicia Kempner, Helen Portugal, Stella Rebner, Jan Stone, npc Paul Hodge. Canada: Cecile Fisher, Louise Mark, Joyce

Philips, Frances Pielsticker, Mimi Roncarelli, Helen Smith, npc Baron Wolf Lebovic. Bermuda: Mrs. Colin Anderson, Mrs. Norman Bach, Mrs. Brownlow Eve, Mrs. Roland Lines, Mrs. T.H. Lines, Mrs. W.G. Rosser, npc Dudley Cooper
1968 United States: Hermine Baron, Emma Jean Hawes, Sue Sachs, Nancy Gruver, Dorothy Hayden, Rhoda Walsh, npc Margaret Wagar. Canada: Mary Bowden, Maureen O'Brien, Mary Paul, Louise Mark, Jackie Begin, Vi Broad, npc Baron Wolf Lebovic. Bermuda: Captain Mrs. Roland Lines, Mrs. Hugh Barr, Mrs. Brownlow Eve, Mrs. James Murray, Mrs. Dudley Cooper, Mrs. Thomas Lines
1972 United States: Mary Jane Farell, Emma Jean Hawes, Marilyn Johnson, Jacqui Mitchell, Peggy Solomon, Dorothy Truscott, npc Margaret Wagar. Canada: Jackie Begin, Moselle Berger, Irene Hodgson, Sharyn Linkovsky, Mary Paul, Mrs. David Saltsman, npc Aaron Goodman. Bermuda: Mrs. Brownlow Eve, Mrs. F. Jackson, Mrs. B. Kahn, Mrs. Roland Lines, Mrs. Thomas Lines, Mrs. W.A. Rosser, npc Arthur Eccles
1976 United States: Mary Jane Farell, Emma Jean Hawes, Marilyn Johnson, Jacqui Mitchell, Gail Moss, Dorothy Truscott, npc Ruth McConnell. Canada: Dianna Gordon, Irene Hodsdon, Sydney Isaacs, Marilyn Pearce, Sharyn Kokish, Francine Cimon, npc Peter Nagy.
1980 United States: Dorothy Truscott, Emma Jean Hawes, Gail Moss, Jacqui Mitchell, Mary Jane Farell, Marilyn Johnson, npc Ruth McConnell. Canada: Karen Allison, Pamela Bridson, Francine Cimon, Dianna Gordon, Sharyn Kokish, Mary Paul, npc Georges Hania.
1984 United States: Gail Moss, Judi Radin, Kathie Wei, Betty Ann Kennedy, Carol Sanders, Jacqui Mitchell, npc Jim Zimmerman. Canada: Dianna Gordon, Mary Paul, Katie Thorpe, Sharyn Kokish, Francine Cimon, Sandra Fraser, npc Eric Kokish
1988 United States: Edith Freilich, Carol Pincus, Beverly Rosenberg, Kerri Shuman, Helen Utegaard, Rhoda Walsh, npc Grant Baze. Canada: Francine Cimon, Dianna Gordon, Mary Paul, Sharyn Reus, Gloria Silverman, Katie Thorpe, npc George Mittelman.
1992 United States: Jo Morse, Joyce Lilie, Jacqui Mitchell, Amalya Kearse, Tobi Deutsch, Mildred Breed, npc Rebecca Rogers.
1996 United States: Gail Greenberg, Jill Levin, Irina Levitina, Shawn Quinn, Lynn Deas, Juanita Chambers. Canada: Francine Cimon, Dianna Gordon, Rhoda Habert, Beverly Kraft, Barbara Saltsman, Sharyn Reus. Mexico: Miriam Rosenberg, Margarita Rosenberg, Benusillo, Bronia Nosnik, Montelongo.
2000 United States: Bob Hamman, npc; Petra Hamman, Shawn Quinn, Mildred Breed, Peggy Sutherlin, Joan Jackson, Robin Klar. Canada: Jim Green, npc; Francine Cimon, Dianna Gordon, Rhoda Habert, Beverly Kraft, Catherine Thorpe, Martine LaCroix. Mexico: Nancy Lira, npc; Nancy Gerson, Bronia Nosnik, Margarita Rosenberg, Miriam Rosenberg, Adriana Salinas.

WORLD JUNIOR TEAMS QUALIFIERS

1987 Guy Doherty, Jon Heller, Asya Kamsky, Aaron Silverstein, Bill Hsieh, npc Matt Guagliardo
1989 Larry Hicks, Mike Cappelletti, James Baker, David Williams, Michael Klein, David Rowntree, npc Bill Eisenberg
1991 U.S.A. I: Brad Moss, Leni Holtz, Ravindra Murthy, Mike Cappelletti, David Rowntree, Michael Klein, npc Bobby Wolff; U.S.A. II: Jeff Ferro, Wayne Stuart, John Diamond, Brian Platnick, Martha Benson, Tricia Thomas, npc Chip Martel; Canada: Mark Caplan, Eric Sutherland, Fred Gitelman, Geoff Hampson, Bronia Gmach, Mike Roberts, npc John Carruthers
1993 U.S.A. I: Eric Greco, Kevin Wilson, Jeff Ferro, Leni Holtz, Debbie Zuckerberg, Rich Pavlicek, npc Chip Martel; U.S.A. II: Sam Dinkin, Michael Shuster, Albert Tom, Doug Hsieh, Eric Secan, John Fout, npc Jan Martel; Canada: Geoff Hampson, Bronia Gmach, Eric Sutherland, Mike Roberts, Jeffrey Blond, Nicholas L'Ecuyer, npc John Carruthers

SOUTH AMERICAN CHAMPIONSHIPS
(Zone 3)

OPEN WINNERS	WOMEN'S WINNERS
1948 Buenos Aires, Argentina	
Argentina	*Argentina*
Ricardo M. Argerich	Celia M. de Basavilbaso
Alberto J. Blousson	Josefina M. de Cramer
Carlos Cabanne	Celia de Luro
Alejandro Castro	Sara R. de Pianentini
Carlos Ottolenghi	Etelvina S. de Vergara
Dr. Louis A. Schenone	Mercedes Guerrico
1949 Sao Paulo and Rio de Janeiro, Brazil	
Brazil	
Milton Alvarenga	
Mauricio de Couver	
Renato Cusano	
A. Figueredo	
Alaerte Frugoli	
Dr. Samuel Leite Ribeiro	
1950 Montevideo, Uruguay	
Argentina	*Argentina*
Carlos Cabanne	Ines M. G. de Casado
Fernando de Corral	Mercedes Guerrico
Alejandro Zumarin Olmedo	Esther Perez Mendoza
Julio Quesada	Maria Elvira Quesada
Marcus Ugarte	
1951 Santiago, Chile	
Chile	*Argentina*
Alfonso Aguero	Ines M.G. de Casado
Antonio Carrasco	Maria Laura V. de Mihura
Carlos Doren	Etelvina S. de Vergara
Jorge Guzman	Elsa C. de Vidal
Arturo Herrera	Mercedes Guerrico
Jorge Ovalle	Esther Perez Mendoza
Jorge Suarez	
Julio Subercasseaux	
1953 Puenta del Este, Uruguay	
Argentina	*Argentina*
Ricardo M. Argerich	Ines M. G. de Casado
Carlos Cabanne	Maria Laura V. de Mihura
Alejandro Castro	Mercedes Guerro
Alejandro Olmedo	Esther Perez Mendoza
Dr. Luis A. Schenone	Leonor Vivot
	Etelvina S. de Vergara
1954 São Paulo, Brazil	
Argentina	*Brazil*
Miguel Alfredo Denedit	France Estella
Carlos Cabanne	Doris Machado
Alejandro Castro	Sylvia Salles Godoy
Hector Cramer	Lucia Stefani
Carlos F. Dibar	Dolores Vasconcelios
Adolfo Gabarret	Margarita Villalobos
1955 Buenos Aires, Argentina	
Brazil	*Brazil*
Eros Amaral	Marina Farias
Milton Alvarenga	Eddy Lessa Dos Santos
Laslo Desci	Doris Machado
Norberto Mandler	Rosa Fitueira de Mello
Joao Murtinho	Lucia Stefani
Carlos Soute	Dolores Vasconcelios
1956 Lima, Peru	
Brazil	*Brazil*
Milton Alvarenga	Marina Farias
Mario Giorgetti	Eddy Lessa Dos Santos
Caio Luis Pereira de Sousa	Doris Machado
Norberto Mandler	Lucia Stefani
Nelson Martins	Dolores Vasconcelios
Joao Murtinho	
1957 Santiago, Chile	
Argentina	*Argentina*
Alberto J. Blousson	Ines M. G. de Casado
Carlos Cabanne	Maria Elena C. de Rodrigue
Alejandro Castro	Etelvina S. de Vergara
Hector Cramer	Esther Perez Mendoza
Dr. Marcelo H. Lerner	Maria Elvira Quesada
Alejandro Olmedo	Leonor Vivot
1958 Punta del Este, Uruguay	
Argentina	*Brazil*
Alberto Berisso	Sylvia Godoy
Alberto J. Blousson	Eddy Lessa Dos Santos
Alejandro Castro	Esther Rodrigues
Carlos F. Dibar	Regina Schmieder
Arturo Jacques	Lea Sigueira
Carlos Ottolenghi	Lucia Stefani

1959 Santos, Brazil	
Argentina	*Brazil*
Alberto Berisso	Selda Almeida
Desidero Blum	Marina Farias
Carlos Cabanne	Rosa Figueira de Mello
Ricardo Calvente	Doris Machado
Arturo Jacques	Ria Petzold
Egisto Rocchi	Dolores Vasconcelios
1960 Not Contested	
1961 Lima, Peru	
Argentina	*Argentina*
Luis Attaguile	Ines M. G. de Casado
Alberto Berisso	Maria Elena C. de Rodrigue
Carlos Cabanne	Mercedes G. de Schenone
Ricardo Calvente	Etelvina S. de Vergara
Arturo Jacque	Esther Perez Mendoza
Egisto Rocchi	Maria Elvira Quesada
1962 Buenos Aires, Argentina	
Argentina	*Argentina*
Luis Attaguile	Ines M. G. de Casado
Alberto Berisso	Maria Elena C. de Rodrigue
Desidero Blum	Mercedes G. de Schenone
Carlos Cabanne	Etelvina S. de Vergara
Agustin Santamarina	Maria Teresa de Espinosa Paz
Marcos Santamarina	Maria Elvira Quesada
1963 Caracas, Venezuela	
Venezuela	*Peru*
Edgar Lloynaz	Pauline de Alaez
Manuel Gonzalez-Vaie	Elena de Bozzo
Mario Onorati	Maruja de Foccaci
Renato Straziota	Elena de Carbone
Roger Rossignol	Zita de Fleischman
David A. Berah	Ana de Isnardi
1964 Montevideo and Punta del Este, Uruguay	
Argentina	*Argentina*
Luis Attaguile	Esther Claret de Aguirre
Desidero Blum	Ines M. G. de Casado
Carlos Cabanne	Adela N. de Engel
Egisto Rocchi	Hildegaard S. de Lippstadt
Agustin Santamarina	Etelvina S. de Vergara
Alfredo Saravia	Maria Elvira Quesada
1965 Santiago, Chile	
Venezuela	*Brazil*
Roberto Benaim	Sybil Jung
David A. Berah	Maria Elena Mirando Jordao
Mario Onorati	Yolanda Paez de Barros
Roger Rossignol	Vera Sampaio
Renato Straziota	Lea Sequeira
Francis Vernon	Dolores Vasconcelios
1966 Sao Paulo, Brazil	
Venezuela	*Brazil*
Roberto Benaim	Teresa Chammas
David A. Berah	Marina Farias
Edgar Lloynaz	Marina Elena Mirando
Jordao Roberto Romanelli	Sylvia Figueira de Mello
Roger Rossignol	Sylvia Salles Godoy
Frank Vernon	Dolores Vasconcelios
	(tied with)
	Uruguay
	Marta Brito del Pino
	Lola P. de Castillo
	Esther M. de Ham
	Raquel D. de Methol
	Brigida Philipstal
	Elena Maria G. de Zumaran
1967 Lima, Peru	
Brazil	*Uruguay*
Pedro Paulo Assumpcao	Marta Brito del Pino
Mario Giorgetti	Lola P. de Castillo
George S. Golefarf	Esther M. de Ham
Eduardo Nahmias	Raquel D. de Methol
Gabriel Pinheiro	Brigid Philipstal
Adelstano Porto D'Ave	Elena Maria G. de Zumaran
1968 Bogota, Colombia	
Brazil	*Colombia*
Marcello Castelo Branco	Angela Echeverri Gonzalez
Roberto Figueira de Mello	Marta Marulanda de Ferrer
Decio Martins Coutinho	Marta Olga Velez de Hortet
Pedro Paulo Assumpcao	Maria Cristina Rivas de Rivas
Gabriel Pinheiro Chagas	Ana Pinzon de Soto
Adelstano Porto D'Ave	Emilia Osorio de Velez
1969 Buenos Aires, Argentina	
Brazil	*Peru*
Pedro Paulo Assumpcao	Maria Delfina de Denegri
Pablo Pino de Barros	Zita de Fleischman

Educado Bastos
Pedro Paulo Castelo Branco
Gabriel Pinheiro Chagas
Synesio Martina Ferreira

1970 Caracas, Venezuela
Brazil
Eros Amaral
Pedro Paulo Assumpcao
Gabriel Pinheiro Chagas
Gabino Cintra
Christiano G. Fonseca
Tibor Kenedi

1971 Montevideo, Uruguay
Brazil
Pedro Paulo Assumpcao
Adelstano Porto D'Ave
Sergio Barbosa
Marcelo Castelo Branco
Octavio G. de Faria
Christiano G. Fonseca

1972 Santiago, Chile
Brazil
Pedro Paulo Assumpcao
Marcelo Castelo Branco
Pedro Paulo Castelo Branco
Gabriel Pinheiro Chagas
Gabino Cintra
Christiano G. Fonseca

1973 Rio de Janeiro, Brazil
Brazil
Pedro Paulo Assumpcao
Marcelo Castelo Branco
Pedro Paulo Castelo Branco
Gabriel Pinheiro Chagas
Gabino Cintra
Christiano G. Fonseca

1974 Lima, Peru
Brazil
Eros Amaral
Pedro Paulo Assumpcao
Pablo Plinio de Barros
Gabriel Pinheiro Chagas
Nelson Martins Ferreira
Synesio Martins Ferreira

1975 Bogota, Colombia
Brazil
Pedro Paulo Assumpcao
Gabriel Pinheiro Chagas
Pedro Paulo Castelo Branco
Marcelo Castelo Branco
Gabino Cintra
Christiano G. Fonseca

1976 Buenos Aires, Argentina
Argentina
Luis Attaguile
Jaime Braceras
Carlos Cabanne
Egisto Rocchi
Agustin Santamarina
Eduardo Scanavino

1977 Montevideo, Uruguay
Brazil
Pedro Paulo Assumpcao
Gabriel Pinheiro Chagas
Gabino Cintra
Marcelo Castelo Branco
Jose Barbosa Oliveira
Roberto Figueira de Mello

1978 Isla Margarita, Venezuela
Brazil
Pedro Paulo Assumpcao
Gabriel Pinheiro Chagas
Gabino Cintra
Marcelo Castelo Branco
Jose Barbosa Oliveira
Roberto Figueira de Mello

1979 Santiago, Chile
Argentina
Luis Attaguile
Hector Camberos
Pablo Lombardi
Egisto Rocchi
Agustin Santamarina
Eduardo Scanavino

Blanca de Magnani
Eda de Piana
Alicia de Flucker
Pilar de Velarde

Colombia
Tania de Mandowsky
Rosario de Nunez
Marina de Prieto
Maria Cristina Rivas de Rivas
Ana P. de Soto
Olga de Zuloaga

Uruguay
Esther M. de Ham
Raquel D. de Methol
Maria del Carmen C. de Meyer
Marta Britto del Pino
Brigida Philipsthal
Lola de Pineyrua

Brazil
Lia Cintra
Gilda Leal
Doris Machado
Elizabeth Murtinho
Maria Helena de Oliveira
Dolores Vasconcelios

Brazil
Lia Cintra
Suzy Fujihura
Gerry Gramegna
Lucia Gil
Elizabeth Murtinho
Heloisa Nogueira

Uruguay
Vera B. de Beer
Raquel D. de Methol
Maria del Carmen C. de Meyer
Marta Brito del Pino
Brigida Philipsthal
Lola de Pineyrua

Brazil
Sylvia Figueira de Mello
Gertie Gramegna
Heloisa L. Nogueira
Agota Mandelot
Elizabeth Murtinho
Vera Schaffer

Colombia
Josefina de Bennet
Angela Echeverry Gonzalez
Marta Marulanda de Ferrer
Marta O. Velez de Hortet
Blanca de Jaramillo
Silva de Vazquez

Argentina
Delia C. de Biquard
Matilde I. de Espiasse
Adriana C. Martinez de Hoz
Anke M.J. de Moirano
Mary Ann M. de Monsegur
Mercedes G. de Schenone

Chile
Adriana D. de Aguad
Odette Y. de Yanine
Samira B. de Awad
Dare Turenne
Carla P. de Pariatore
Sonia R. de Ready

Argentina
Ana Maria G. de Alonso
Martha J. Matienzo
Clara Monsegur
Lucrecia T. Monsegur
Mercedes G. de Schenone
Christina de Suaya

1980 Bahia, Brazil
Argentina
Luis Attaguile
Hector Camberos
Pablo Lombardi
Egisto Rocchi
Agustin Santamarina
Eduardo Scanavino

1981 Lima, Peru
Argentina
Gustavo Alujas
Luis Attaguile
Hector Camberos
Agustin Santamarina
Eduardo Scanavino
David Zanalda

1983 Buenos Aires, Argentina
Brazil
Alcio Maia
Sergio Barbosa
Marcelo Branco
Gabriel Chagas
Alexandre Misk
Roberto de Mello

1984 Santiago, Chile
Brazil
Sergio Barbosa
Gabriel Chagas
Pedro-Paulo Assumpcao
Gabino Cintra
Adelstano Porto D'Ave
Marcelo Branco

1985 Uruguay
Argentina
Martin Monsegur
Eduardo Scanavino
Luiz Attaguile
Hector Camberos
Carlo de Miguel
Guillermo Mooney

1986 Beuenos Aires, Argentina
Brazil
Gabriel Chagas
Pedro-Paulo Assumpcao
Paulo Barbelos
Rolando Evelino
Marcelo Branco
José Barbosa Oliveira

1987 Santiago, Chile
Brazil
Ronaldo Avelino
Eduardo Barcellos
Carlos Camacho
Gabriel Chagas
Roberto de Mello
Jose Barbosa Oliviera

1988 Brazil
Brazil
Carlos Camacho
Marcelo Branco
Luis Fetter
Flavio Moreira
Sergio Aranha
Marcelo Amaral

1989 Bolivia
Brazil
Carlos Camacho
Marcelo Branco
Pedro Branco
Gabriel Chagas
Ricardo Janz
Roberto de Mello

1990 Paraguay
Brazil
Gabriel Chagas
Pedro-Paulo Assumpcao
Marcelo Amaral
Sergio Aranha
Miguel Villasboas

1991 Peru
Brazil
Carlos Camacho
Gabino Cintra
Marcelo Branco

Brazil
Heloisa Nogueira
Gertie Gaamegna
Ana Maria Assumpcao
Agota Mandelot
Maria Elizabeth Murtinho
Sylvia Figueira de Mello

Brazil
Agota Mandelot
Sylvia Figueira de Mello
Maria Elizabeth Murtinho
Susy Powidzer
Alice Saade
Maria Elena Brito E. Silva

Argentina
Marta Matienzo
Diana Budkin
Mary Ann Monsegur
Ines A. de Gonzalez Pini
Maria I. Iacapraro
Mercedes G. de Schenone

Argentina
Diana Budkin
Maria T.B. de Diaz
Lucrecia Monsegur
Ana M. de Blum
Maria T.P. de Espinosa Paz
Grace C. de Camberos

Argentina
Maria Teresa Diaz
Diana Budkin
Marisu Llauro
Lucrezia Monsegur
Victoria Merdinger
Ana Maria de Alonso

Brazil
Heloise Nogueira
Agota Mandelot
Elizabeth Murtinho
Susy Powidzer
Sylvia F. de Mello
Vera Amaral

Argentina
Marta Matienzo
Diana Budkin
Graciela Lucchini
Gloria de Rosenfeld
Lucrecia Monsegur
Monica Borstein

Argentina
Diana Budkin
Marta Matienzo
Maria Iacapraro
Marisu I. De Lauro
Marta D. de Tiscornia
Charo Garateguy

Brazil
Lucia Gil
Vera Amaral
Suzy Powidzer
Agota Mandelot
Suely Sampaio
Lia Cintra

Uruguay
Loly P. de Valenzuela
Raquel D. de Methol
Esther M. de Ham
Carmen A. de Meyer
Martha D. de Raffo
Ana C. de Castro

Brazil
Agota Mandelot
Sylvia de Mello
Elizabeth Murtinho

Gabriel Chagas
Ricardo Janz
Roberto de Mello

Heloisa Noguera
Ana-Maria Assumpcao
Lia Cintra

(From 1992, official championships, with one entry from each country, were held only in odd-numbered years, with qualification for the Bermuda Bowl. Competitions continued to be held in even-numbered years, with open entries.)

1993 Sao Paulo, Brazil

Brazil	*Argentina*
Marcelo Amaral	Marta Matienzo
Jose Barbosa	Marylin Hernandez
Marcelo Branco	Ana M. de Blum
Pedro Branco	Marta de Tiscornia
Carlos Camacho	Gloria de Rosenfeld
Gabriel Chagas	Cristina de Suaya

1995 Buenos Aires, Argentina

Argentina	*Brazil*
Horacio Elijovich	Agota Mandelot
Pablo Lambardi	Elizabeth Murtinho
Carlos Lucena	Lia Cintra
Martin Monsegur	Lucia Gil
Guillermo Mooney	Heloisa Nogueira
Marcos Santamarina	Sylvia de Mello

1997 Asuncion, Paraguay

Brazil	*Argentina*
Gabriel Chagas	Ana M. de Blum
Marcelo Branco	Marta de Tiscornia
Pedro Branco	Graciela Lucchini
Gabino Cintra	Lucrecia Monsegur
Roberto Mello	Cristina de Suaya
Christiano Fonseca	Maria de Espinosa Paz

1999 Lima, Peru

Brazil	*Brazil*
Gabriel Chagas	Agota Mandelot
Marcelo Branco	Marta Sampaio
Miguel Villas Boas	Irene De Fatima
Joao Paulo Campos	Marina Amaral
Roberto de Mello	Lia Tajtelbaum
Ricardo Janz	Lucia Gil

2001 Cochabamba, Bolivia

Argentina	*Brazil*
Christobal Aguierre	Isabelle Andrade
Jorge Estavarena	Ana Maria Assumpcao
Agustin Madala	Sylvia DeMello
Ernesto Muzzio	Agota Mandelot
Pablo Ravenna	Heloisa Nogueira
Marcelo Villegas	Leda Pain
Alexis Pejacsevich, npc	Demaio Paez, npc

ASIA AND MIDDLE EAST CHAMPIONSHIPS (Zone 4)

Open	Women's
1981 *Pakistan*	
Nishat Abedi	
Nisar Ahmed	
Gaffa Cochinwalla	
Zia Mahmood	
Masood Salim	
1983 *Pakistan*	*India*
Nishat Abedi	Rita Choksi
Nisar Ahmad	Nina Bonerji
Munir Ataullah	Lina Mayadas
Jan-E-Alam Fazli	Ursula Garg
Zia Mahmood	Prabha Kanetkar
Masood Salim	Prabha Joshi
1985 *Pakistan*	*India*
Nishat Abedi	Lina Mayadas
Nisar Ahmad	Nina Bonerji
Munir Ataullah	Rita Choksi
Jan-E-Alan Fazli	Sheelu Thadani
Zia Mahmood	Kalpana Misra
Masood Salim	Oindrilla Kundu
1987 *Pakistan*	*Egypt*
Nisar Ahmad	Marguerite Homsy
Munir Ataullah	Lily Khalil
Iftikhar Baqui	Maud Khouri
Jan-E-Alam Fazli	J. Morcos
Zia Mahmood	Safia Sarwat

Masood Salim

Josephine Hanna

1989 *Egypt*	*India*
Samih Khalil	Shailaja Mahajan
Tarek Sadek	Snehlata Singha
Abdel Raouf	Nina Bonerji
Ashraf Sadek	Kiran Nadar
Ahmed Abass	Bimal Sicka
	Ursula Garg
1991 *Pakistan*	*Egypt*
Abdul Rehman Allana	Marguerite Homsy
Tahir Masood	Lily Khalil
Kamal Shoib	Maud Khouri
Javed Ahmed	J. Morcos
Tufail Mohammed Sheikh	Safia Sarwat
	Marie Assouad-Doche
1993 *India*	*India*
Avinash Gokhale	Shailaja Mahajan
Alihas Vaidya	Bimal Sicka
Keshav Samant	Hilda Raymonds
Rajesh Dalal	Marianne Karmarkar
Ramamurthy Sridharan	Yvette Singapure
Ashok Vaidya	Greta Lakhani

MIDDLE EAST, ASIA, AFRICA (Zone 4)

1995 Jordan

South Africa	*Egypt*
Leon Boolkin	Lily Khalil
Bernard Donde	Maud Khouri
Chris Convery	Marguerite Homsy
Craig Gower	Josephine Morcos
Tim Cope	Sophie Sarwat
Henry Mansell	Samia Shatila
Maurice Joffe, npc	

1997

India	*Egypt*
Arvind Poddar	Lily Khalil
Santanu Ghose	Randa Elostaz
Jaggy Shivdasani	Marguerite Homsy
Subhash Gupta	Maud Khouri
Rajeslo Dalal	Nada Wattar
Anil Padye	Shamya Shatila
Amand Mehta, npc	

1999 Sri Lanka

The Open final between South Africa and Pakistan was never played because a member of the Pakistan team died suddenly. The result was declared a tie for the championship, and both teams qualified for the Bermuda Bowl.

South Africa	*India*
Tim Cope	Subu Chinikrishnan
Chris Convery	Padmini Divakaran
Craig Gower	Hema Deora
Neville Eber	Pramilla Shivdasani
Les Amoils	Geeta Lakhani
Maurice Joffe, npc	B. Mal
Kamalakara Roa npc	
Pakistan	
Masood Salim	
Sultan Siddiqui	
Shahin Iqbal	
Rashid Jafer	
Nishat Abedi	
Khurshid Hadi	
Muhammed Ismail	

CENTRAL AMERICA-CARIBBEAN TEAMS (Zone 5)

Open	Women's
1983 *Jamaica*	
Cecil Chuck	
Rex James	
Ronald Tai Tenquee	
David Levy	
Lenny Chin	
Don DaCosta	
1985 *Venezuela*	*Venezuela*
Claudio Caponi	Fida Hirschhaut
Steve Hamaoui	Ivy Smith
Paulo Pasquini	Alice Lerch
Francisco Vernon	Rosario Nunez
Memo Danese	Juana Lawnern
Roberto Benaim	Lucy Rodriguez
1987 *Venezuela*	*Venezuela*
Ricardo Solomon	Fida Hirschhaut

Claudio Caponi
Steve Hamaoui
Hector Manrique
Mario Onorati
Paulo Pasquini
1989 *Colombia*
Jorge Barrera
Anton Cahn-Speyer
Santiago Rivas
J.C. Alvarez

1991 *Venezuela*
Claudio Caponi
Alberto Dhers
Steve Hamaoui
Hector Manrique
Mario Onorati
Paulo Pasquini
1993 *Venezuela*
Alejandro Bianchedi
Claudio Caponi
Alberto Calvo
Steve Hamaoui
Mario Onorati
Paulo Pasquini
1994 *Costa Rica*
Connie Almy
Chuck Paparigian
Lee Karam
Richard Karam
1995
Venezuela
Paolo Pasquini
Franco Gusso
Steve Hamaoui
Claudio Caponi
Mario Onorati
Alejandro Bianchedi
1997
Venezuela
Pedro Pasquini
Franco Gusso
Adolfo Mendoza
Francis Vernon
Steve Hamaoui
Claudio Caponi
1999
Guadeloupe
Philippe Mathieu
Jeannine Moers
Dominique Guerin
Jean-Paul Bouveresse
Daniel Veron
Charles Garnier

Morella Pacheco
Elisabeth Solar
Maria-Grazia deBettini
Guilia Fornari
Alice Lerch
Colombia
Gloria deVargas
Tobina Choitoru
Flor Macias
Ana deSoto
Gloria deArboleda
Cilia Khoudari
Venezuela
Morella Pacheco
Ivy Smith
Rosario Nunez
Gania Mandowski
Tania de Mandowsky
Alejandra Piontkowski
Venezuela
Ayako Amano
Tania deMandowsky
Morella Pacheco
Alexandra Pointkowski
Elisabeth Solar
Esther Sasson

Colombia
Elizabeth Rabicew (Solar)
Alexandra Piontowsky
Fida Hirschhaut
Ivy Smith
Morella Pacheco
Ayako Amano

Colombia
Ana Soto
Toby Croitoru
Zita Lechter
Flor Macias
Sara Wasserman
Cilia Khoudari

Colombia
Zita Lechter
Patricia Ramirez
Tobi Eisenstein
Flor Macias
Beatriz Angel
Giorgio Helmsdorff, npc

PACIFIC ASIA BRIDGE FEDERATION
(Zone 6)
FORMERLY FAR EAST CHAMPIONSHIPS
OPEN   *WOMEN'S*
1957 Manila, Philippines
Philippines
Stephen Chua
Antonio Zamora
Lionel de Silva
Robert Yap
Carmen Ballesteros
Florence Leung
1958 Tokyo, Japan
Philippines
Jose J. Reyes
Stephen Chua
Lionel de Silva
R. Hernandez
Eligio Teehankee
Vincent Reyes
1959 Taipei, Formosa
Hong Kong
Y.T. Fong
L.A. Ozorio
Henry S. Y. Kuai
Victor Zirinsky
George Tsiang
Y.M. Chu

1960 Hong Kong
Hong Kong
Y.T. Fong
L.A. Ozorio
William Wong
Dodge Chen
Henry S.Y. Kuai
Andre Ouan
1961 Bankok, Thailand
Thailand
Oei Keng Hian
Tan Hok San
M.W. Hasnam
Mr. Djanwar
Thio Oen Gei
Tan Kiong Say
1963 Taipei, Formosa
Thailand
Kovit Suchartkul
Boontham Nantaterm
Ua Isrankul
Somboon Nandhabiwat
Manoo Veeraburus
Benno Gimkiewicz
1964 Tokyo, Japan
Indonesia
Liem Hok Po
Boris Hutagalung
P. Sanbudhi
K. Sudianto
J. Alex Fraser
Oey Tek Goan
1965 Hong Kong
Thailand
Kovit Suchartkul
Ananta Boonsupa
Manoo Veeraburus
Vibal Rasmidatta
Patama Narabhallobh
Ua Israngkul
1966 Bangkok, Thailand
Thailand
K.W. Shen
Benno Gimkiewicz
Reggie Gaan
Somboon Nandhabiwat
Sara Pothisuwan
Prakorb Vanigbandhu
1967 Manila, Philippines
Taiwan
Y.J. Hsi
Min-Fan Tai
Patrick Kuang-Hui Huang
Harry T. Lin
C.W. Liaw

1968 Kuala Lumpur, Malaysia
Australia
Jessel Rothfield
Nat Rothfield
Tim Seres
Roelof Smilde
Wally Scott
Jim Borin
1969 Taipei, Taiwan
Taiwan
Conrad K.R. Cheng
V. Chow
C. Hsois
Patrick Kuang-Hui-Huang
C. Lee
Min-Fan Tai
1970 Jakarta, Indonesia
Australia
Ron Klinger
Mary McMahon
Jessel Rothfield
Tim Seres
Roelof Smilde

1971 Melbourne, Australia
Taiwan
C. Chen
Conrad Cheng
Ching-Po Huang

Thailand
Saisawart Chang
Gladys Huang
Promari Pibulsonggram
Cherdsri Sooksawasdi

Malaysia
Gladys Loh
Lorraine Lim
Mrs. R.G. Fraser
Mrs. G.W. Arnott
Shirley Bradley
Doreen Peddie

Thailand
Saisawart Chang
Gladys Huang
Manee Dibavadi
Inthira Chandarasomboon
Cherdsri Sooksawasdi
Promari Pibulsonggram

Philippines
Mrs. M. Cacho
Helen Small
R. Cacho
Imelda Tubangui
Helen Tubangui
Margaut Yu

Philippines
Carmen LaGuardia
Mrs. L. Galpert
Mrs. C. Palmer
Paz A. de Tuason
Imelda Tubangui

Singapore
Josephine Crane
Lotta Pahverk
Sybil Holloway
Emily Hee
Jenny Han

Indonesia
Joan Shariff
Indra Widowo
Netty Suparto
E. Gontha
A. Raturandang
M. Djajawikadj

Singapore
Josephine Crane
Lotta Pahverk
Sybil Holloway

Harry Lin
C. Lu
Min-Fan Tai
1972 Singapore
Indonesia
Max Aguw
J. Alex Fraser
Hengky Lasut
Frank Manoppo
M.F. Manoppo
E. Najoan
Denny Sacul
Felix Walujan
1973 Hongkong
Indonesia
Hengky Lasut
Max Aguw
Frank E. Manoppo
M.F. Manoppo
B. Mutagalune

1974 Manila, Philippines
Indonesia
Frank Manoppo
M.F. Manoppo
I. Arwin
Hengky Lasut
W. A. Montaga
Denny Sacul
1975 Hong Kong
Hong Kong
Leslie Sung
T.S. Lo
Anthony Chow
Raymond S.P. Chow
Derek Zen

1976 Auckland, New Zealand
Taiwan
Min-Fan Tai
Harry Shien-Chu Lin
Patrick Kuang-Hui Huang
Che Hung Kuo
Conrad Cheng

1977 Manila, Philippines
India
A. Brahmachari
S. Ganguly
S.K. Ghosh
S.R. Ghosh
Kamal Mukherjee
G. Singha
1978 New Delhi, India
Taiwan
Patrick Kuang-Hui Huang
Dr. Chun Shan Shen
Che-Hung Kuo
Conrad Cheng
Harry Lin
Ya Pin Tu
1979 Tokyo, Japan
Indonesia
Hengky Lasut
Max Aguw
Denny Sacul
Munawar Sawirudin
Felix Waluyan
Yasin Wijaya
1980 Not Contended
1981 Taipei, Taiwan
Taipei
Harry S.C. Lin
Patrick K.H. Huang
Yin-Tsun Chang
Che-Hung Kuo
K.R. Chen
H.T. Chang
1982 Bangkok, Thailand
Indonesia
Denny Sacul
Hengky Lasut
FelixWaluyan
Munawar Sawirudin
Donny Tuerah

Carmen LaGuardia
Emily Hee
Jenny Han

Singapore
Josephine Crane
Lotta Pahverk
Sybil Holloway
Carmen LaGuardia
Emily Hee
Jenny Han

Australia
Felicity Beale
Ruth Eaton
Gerda Stern
Winsome Lipscomb
Mary McMahon
Gabay Tabak

Australia
P. Brown
Ruth Eaton
Gerda Stern
Winsome Lipscomb
Mary McMahon
Elaine Poulsen

Australia
Margaret Choate
Mary McMahon
Mrs. G. Reynolds
Cecile Miles
Val Cummings
Ivy Dahler

New Zealand
Eileen Taylor
Zelda Morris
Val Bell
Nola Mather
Marion Hill
Frances Ewington

Australia
Ivy Dahler
Elizabeth Havas
Fay Landy
Claire Lester
Barbara McDonald
Cecile Miles

India
Rita Choksi
Lina Mayadas
Suhhadra Krishna
Mrs. S. Thadani
Mrs. S. Mahajan
Jane Merma

Philippines
Helen Tubangui
Rose Unson
Florence Yap
Tina del Gallego
Rudi Santiago
Carmen LaGuardia

New Zealand
Kathy Boardman
Jane Evitt
Jan Cormack
Jocelyn Kinsella
Stella Secker
Rosalie Cunningham

Philippines
Tina del Gallego
Lydia Jalbuena
Carmen LaGuardia
Rudi Santiago
Helen Tubangui
Florence Yap

1983 Hong Kong
Indonesia
Denny Sacul
Hengky Lasut
FelixWaluyan
Munawar Sawirudin
Donny Tuerah
Max Aguw
1984 Macao
Indonesia
Denny Sacul
Hengky Lasut
FelixWaluyan
Munawar Sawirudin
Yasin Wijawa
E. Manoppo
1985 Sydney, Australia
Japan
Hiroshi Hisatomi
Kuniaki Kawakami
Akio Kurokawa
Yoshiyuki Nakamura
Kyoko Shimamura
Akihiko Yamada
1986 Panang, Malaysia
Taiwan
C.S. Chen
C.H. Kuo
Patrick Huang
M.F. Tai
C.H. Wu
C.C. Chen
1987 Shanghai, China
Hong Kong
David Chan
Karic Chiu
Peter Chun
Roger Ling
Samuel Wan

1988 Not contested.
1989 Jakarta, Indonesia
Taiwan
C.C. Chen
Patrick Huang
C.K. Shen
Min-Fan Tai
C.H. Wu
Antonio Chong
1990 Singapore
New Zealand
Stephen Blackstock
Peter Newell
Dwayne Crombie
Martin Reid
Malcolm Mayer
Lionel Wright
1991 Guangzhou, China
China
Zhang Weili
Hu Jihong
Xu Hong Jun
Zhou Jiahang
Chen Rongchang

1992 Singapore
Indonesia
Henky Lasut
Danny Sacul
Santje Panelewen
Munawar Sawiruddin
Giovanni Watulingas

New Zealand
Kathy Boardman
Jan Cormack
Lyn Bishop
Zelda Morris
Jane Evitt
Joyce Kerr

Australia
Rosemary Atherton
Margaret Drake
Lindy Vincent
Diana Smart
Felicity Beale

Australia
Pauline Gumby
Sue Hobley
Barbara Travis
Paula Schroor
Margaret Bourke
Sue Lusk

China
Gu Ling
Zhang Yalan
Li Manling
Lu Qin
Zhu Xiao Yin
Sun Ming

Japan
Kazuko Banno
Makiko Hayashi
Kyoko Mizutani
Setsuko Ogihara
Yukiko Yoshimori
Kaoru Kotani

Taiwan
Amy Chen
Jennifer Lai
Phoebe Lin
Gloria Meng
Stella Wei
Tze-Ying Chen

Australia
Norma Borin
Cathy Chua
Felicity Beale
Diana Smart
Sue Lusk
Cecile Miles

China
Gu Ling
Liu Yiquian
Sun Ming
Wang Ping
Zhang Yalan
Shi Shaomin

China
Sun Ming
Wang Liping
Zhang Yalan
Wang Wenfei
Gu Ling
Wang Hongli

1993 Singapore

Open	Women's	Youth
Indonesia	*China*	*Australia*
Denny Sacul	Gu Ling	Ben Hutchinson
Munawar Sawirudin	Zhang Yalan	Rob Fruewirth
Henky Lasut	Sun Ming	David Appleton
Giovani Watulingas	Wang Hongli	David Thompson
Santje Panelewen	Wang Liping	Murray Green
Adam Sarten	Wang Wenfei	

1994 Wellington, New Zealand

Chinese Taipei	*China*	*China*
Patrick Huang	Sun Ming	Zhuang Zejun

C.H.Kuo	Wang Hongli	Huang Ye
S.R.Wu	Gu Ling	Chen Jien
C.H.Wu	Zhang Yalan	Li Yongchuan
M.F.Tai	Wang Liping	Zhang Guangyang
Liu Yiqian	He Weiwei	

1995 Perth, Australia

New Zealand	*Australia*	*China*
Brian Mace	Lidia Beech	Wein Fei Wang
Tom Jacob	Sue Lusk	Jien Chen
Martin Reid	Felicity Beale	Ziqiu Xie
Peter Newell	Alida Clark	Ye Huang
Ken Yule	Margaret Bourke	Yong Chuan Li
Stephen Blackstock	Diana Smart	Jianyong You

1996 not contested

1997 Hong Kong

Chinese Taipei	*China*	*China*
Patrick Huang	Gu Ling	Chen Jien
C.H.Kuo	Sun Ming	Jiang Qing
H.S.Lin	Wang Hongli	Lei Ming
M.F.Tai	Wang Wenfei	Li Yongchuan
C.H.Wu	Zhang Yalan	Yan Shi
S.R.Wu	Zhang Yu	Zhang Guoxu

1998 Kobe, Japan

China	*China*	*Chinese Taipei*
Wang Xiaojing	Gu Ling Jim Wu	Eric Wu
Wang Weimin	Wang Wenfei	Tony Yung
Xu Hongjun	Zhang Yu	Dave Sun
Zhuang Zejun	Zhang Yalan	Wayne Choe
Shi Haojun	Sun Ming	Fred Chen
Dai Jianming	Wang Hongli	

1999 Hangzhou, China

Indonesia	*China*	*China*
Henky Lasut	Gu Ling	Wei Yu
Eddy Manoppo	Wang Wenfei	Ma Yi
Denny Sacul	Zhang Yu	Hou Jian
Santje Panelewen	Zhang Yalan	Xu Haomin
Robert Tobing	Sun Ming	Shen Chen
Franky Karwur	Wang Hongli	Chen Yinglei

Ron Klinger	Jan Cormack
Terry Brown	Jan Alabaster
David Lilley	Jane Skipper
George Bilski	Shirley Newton
Warren Lazer	Rosie Don
Peter Gill	Jenny Wilkinson

1995 *Australia*	*Australia*
Paul Marston	Sue Lusk
George Kozakos	Alida Clark
John Roberts	Felicity Beale
Matthew Thomson	Diana Smart
Hugh Grosvenor	Lidia Beech
Phil Gue	Margaret Bourke

1997 *Indonesia*	*New Zealand*
T. Asbi	Karen Cumpstone
W. Dadan	Kathryn Yule
F. Karwur	Shirley Newton
S. Munawar	Jenny Wilkinson
S. Panalewen	Judy Pawson
Denny Sacul	Sue Veal

Carol Rothfield, Jessel Rothfield, Kokhin Bagshi, Seamus Browne, Stephen Burgess, Bobby Richman of Australia won the right to represent Zone 7 in the Bermuda Bowl. Indonesia was not eligible because it is not a member of Zone 7. Teams from Zones 6 and 7 frequently compete in each other's championships.

1999 *Australia*	*Australia*
Kokhin Bagchi	Lydia Beech
Seamus Browne	Margaret Bourke
I. delMonte	Felicity Beale
Bobby Richman	Diana Smart
Carol Rothfield	Sue Lusk
Jessel Rothfield	Terresa Tully

2001 *Australia*	*Australia*
George Bilski	Jan Cormack
Phil Gue	Debbie Muir
Terry Browne	Marilyn Chadwick
Barry Noble	Alida Clark
Peter Fordham	Liz Havas
Micheal Prescott	Barbara Travis

SOUTH PACIFIC (Zone 7)

Open	Women's
1981 *Australia*	*Australia*
Dick Cummings	Felicity Beale
Bill Jacobs	Sue Edwards
Paul Lavings	Barbara Travis
Gabby Lorentz	Pauline Gumby
Tim Seres	Sue Hobley
Davis Smith	Diana Smart
1983 *New Zealand*	
Michael Cornell	
Malcolm Mayer	
Tony Taylor	
John Wignall	
Kris Wooles	
Lionel Wright	
1985 *New Zealand*	*Australia*
Michael Cornell	Pauline Gumby
Malcolm Mayer	Sue Hobley
Tony Taylor	Margaret Bourke
John Wignall	Paula Schroor
Kris Wooles	Sue Lusk
Lionel Wright	Barbara Travis
1987 *New Zealand*	*Australia*
Alan Turner	Felicity Beale
Bill Haughie	Claire Lester
Dwayne Crombie	Jill Courtney
Stephen Blackstock	Barbara Travis
Peter Newell	Sue Lusk
Martin Reid	Diana Smart
1989 *New Zealand*	*New Zealand*
Michael Cornell	Jan Alabaster
Tony Taylor	Rose Don
Andy Braithwaite	Tina McVeigh
Lionel Wright	Jenny Wilkinson
Pat Carter	Emma Barrack
Ken Yule	Shirley Newton
1991 *Australia*	*Australia*
Paul Lavings	Felicity Beale
Paul Marston	Sue Lusk
Terry Brown	Diana Smart
George Bilski	Norma Borin
Aldur Kaljo	Rae Branicki
Wally Malaczynski	Cecile Miles
1993 *Australia*	*New Zealand*

AFRICA (Zone 8)

2000

Open	Women's
Egypt	*South Africa*
Hany Dagher	Cherrie Schwartz
Sherif Naguib	Petra Mansell
Tarek Sadek	Margie Hulett
Waleed Elahmady	Merle Narunsky
Samir Saleb	Joan Fihrer
Adel El-Kordy	Di Adrain
Ashraf Sadek, npc	

APPENDIX IV
Special Events

IOC CUP Lausanne, Switzerland.

1998 Brazil tied China

Gabriel Chagas	Dai Jianming
Marcelo Branco	Shi Haiojun
Miguel Villas-Boas	Wang Weimin
Joao Campos	Xu Hongjun
Zhang Zejun	
Hu Jihong	

1999 Italy
Lorenzo Lauria
Alfredo Versace
Andrea Buratti
Massimo Lanzarotti
Francesco Angelini
Antonio Sementa

2000 Indonesia
Denny Sacul
Franky Karwar
Henky Lasut
Eddy Manoppo

Women's Teams : Europe (Jet Pasman – Carla Simons, Netherlands; Pony Nehmert – Andrea Rauscheid, Germany; Anne Lill Helleman-Anna Maria Malinowski, Norway; Veronique Bessis-Catherine D'Ovidio, France) defeated North America

EPSON WORLDWIDE BRIDGE CONTEST
Worldwide and ACBL winners/high score %:

1986 — France (Worldwide) Francis Frainais,	
Jann Bouteille	78.79
ACBL 1st Billy Gough, Joe Livezey	76.58
ACBL 2nd Marty Bergen, Larry Cohen	76.29
1987 — Great Britain (Worldwide) Peter Thompson,	
Robin Stretch	79.50
ACBL 1st David Harrison, Alan Roebuck	76.25
ACBL 2nd Frank MacEntee, William Isaacs	75.33
1988 — USA (Worldwide) Jan Horwitz,	
Barbara Norante	76.29
ACBL N/S Horwitz, Norante	76.29
ACBL E/W Roselyn Teukolsky,	
Saul Teukolsky	74.95
1989 — Poland (Worldwide) Wojciech Biegajlo,	
Dariusz Zembruzuski	79.17
ACBL N/S Karl Hicks, Ron Macdonald	78.19
ACBL E/W Marvin Schatz, Ronald Perry	71.50
1990 — Denmark (Worldwide) Soren Godtfredsen,	
Sorin Lupan	88.54
ACBL N/S Marilyn Shibe, Harold Shibe	73.54
ACBL E/W Bart Bramley, Judy Wadas	71.25
1991 — Poland (Worldwide) Miroslaw Kopowski,	
Wieslaw Maczkowski	79.58
ACBL N/S Kay Harrison, John Gilliatt	75.41
ACBL E/W Warren Kornfeld, Paul Markarian	74.91
1992 — France (Worldwide) Patrice Baverel,	
Francois Hazard	77.00
ACBL N/S Ralph Katz, Richard Halperin	74.00
ACBL E/W Steve Garner, Gerald Caravelli	73.12
1993 — China (Worldwide) Zho Bao Qi,	
Wang Zuo Lei	78.17
ACBL N/S Julius Fields, Calvin Morris	78.04
ACBL E/W Peter Gostovic, Jacques Cloutier	71.17
1994 — (Worldwide) New Zealand - Albert Bouwer, John	
Ruddell	80.50
ACBL Friday 1st - Richard Chan, Dennis Hsu	74.40
Saturday 1st - Sue Cooper, Hugh Hughes	74.67
1995 — (Worldwide) China - Mia Okuan, Lei	79.60
ACBL Friday 1st Linda Peterson,	
Eugene White	78.40
ACBL Saturday 1st Barbara Petty,	
Patricia Hartman	74.29
1996 — (Worldwide) China - Wang Weidon,	
He Weidong	81.37
ACBL Friday 1st - Patrick McCannon,	
Richard Bender	78.50
ACBL Saturday 1st - David Halasi,	
Ben Zeidenberg	75. 67
1997 — (Worldwide) China - Zhang Jie, Zhao Jinlong	79.08
ACBL Friday - Mary Edney, Richard Edney	74.70
ACBL Saturday - Connie Goldberg,	
Joe Livesey	77.00

1998 — (Worldwide) USA - Ray Boehne,	
James Coventry	77.70
ACBL Friday - Mark Hupert, Mark Lombard	75.80
ACBL Saturday - Ray Boehne,	
James Coventry	77.70
1999 — Millenium I - Friday - Nancy Koffler,	
Ady Koffler	74.00
Millenium II - Saturday -	
Jim Wattenbarger, Tom Mori	72.50
2000 — No game	

ACBL-WIDE INSTANT MATCHPOINT PAIRS

		Open winners	Score %
1987	1st	Grady Gravel, Bob Ayers	77.73
	2nd	Helen Furbee, Maggie Wilson	74.38
1988	NS	Markland Jones, Howard Segel	80.50
	EW	Robert Michaels, Robert Quinn	75.60
1989	EW	Gordon Ezekiel, Randy Bennett	79.64
	NS	Robert Dolliver, Mike Inkpen	72.38
1990	NS	Bill Kass, Robert Bernstein	75.50
	EW	Suzanne Lapierre, Marc Poupart	74.50
1991	NS	Bob Hill, Ken Cable	73.75
	EW	Dr. Muin Haddad, George Laubacher	71.08
1992	NS	Clay Hall, Steve Beatty	75.50
	EW	Raymond Lothian, Wilma Lothian	71.70
1993	NS	Jeanne Rahmey, Albert Rahmey	73.46
	EW	Annette McHann, Bill Cook	73.38
1994	N/S	John Lyddon, William Budd	75.46
	E/W	Patricia Civale, Vincent Civale (1699)	
1995	N/S	Clara Rogers, Gopal Tejwani	74.83
	E/W	Dorothy Corbett, Joyce Lamm	74.83
1996	N/S	Shirley Hill Bradley, Leonard Lehman	73.25
	E/W	Kay Joyce, Randy Joyce	74.58
1997	N/S	Richard Grant, Jacques Ribeyre	71.00
	E/W	Shaila Mahajan, Patrick Thompson	72.21
1998	N/S	Kaye McCandle, Sally Kemp	73.00
	E/W	Mary Jane Orock, Jeff Daniel	73.40
1999	N/S	Tong Zhao, Xiaodong Shi	77.21
	E/W	Michael Kovacich, Sam Marks (1772)	
2000	N/S	Malca Langer, Joseph Fenton	73.83
	E/W	David Hunt, Stephen DeSmitt	69.04
		Youth Flight winners	
1989		Andrew Kalish, Daniel Kalish	56.14
1990		Andrew Kalish, Daniel Kalish	56.88
1991		Brian Denninger, Jonathan Rodney	62.50
1992		Eric Greco, Vicky Sawyer	71.50
1993		Brian Kregor, Diane Kregor	66.46
		Daniel Rodney, Lewis Steckler	58.13
		Darren Wolpert , David Halasi	75.57

EUROPEAN COMMON MARKET CHAMPIONSHIPS
Also known as European Community Championships

TEAMS

	Open	Women	Mixed	Junior
1991 Athens (Greece)				
	France	Israel	Belgium	Denmark
	Levy	Zur-Albu	V.Polet	Krojgaard
	Mouiel	Porat-Levit	G.Polet	Jepsen
	Duchon	Birman	Cypres	Caspersen
	Bessis	Abramov	Coenraets	Clemmensen
	Melech		Munksgaard	
	Naveh		Bruun	
1993 Montechoro (Portugal)				
	Israel	Gt.Britain	France	Israel
	Birman	Landy	Willard	I.Herbst
	Zeligman	Handley	Levy	O.Herbst
	Frydrich	Smith	Mouiel	Levin
	Hochzeit	Horton	Allouche	Hermelstein
	Porat	Gaviard	Perlmutter	Fohrer
	Barel			

PAIRS

1967 Overall: Italy
Open Monk-Silberwasser, Belgium; Women's Devries-

Sussel, France; Mixed Peck-Schroeder, Germany
1969 Overall: France
Open Saulino-Zanasi, Italy; Women's Goldschmidt-Kover,
Belgium; Mixed Deutsch-Gille, France
1971 Overall: France
Open Saulino-Zanasi, Italy; Women's DeGailherd-Sussel,
France; Mixed Valenti-Facchini, Italy
1973 Overall: Italy
Open Garozzo-Mayer, Italy; Women's Van Heusden-DeKater,
Netherlands; Mixed Moscati-Sticotti, Italy; Junior Capri -
Faina, Italy
1975 Overall: France
Open Aujaleu-Majoux, France; Women's Gardener-Landy,
Great Britain; Mixed Schroeder-Schroeder, Germany; Junior
Schoofs-Polet, Belgium
1977 Overall: Italy
Open Von Cirlacy-VonCirlacy, Germany; Women's Kennis-
Segers, Belgium; Mixed Cyprés-Polet, Belgium; Junior
Pattacini-Matson, Germany
1979 Overall: Italy
Open Lauria-Rosati, Italy; Women's Arrigoni-Felcini, Italy;
Mixed Mondolfo-Belladonna, Italy; Junior Bellefroid-
Schick, France
1981 Overall: Italy
Open Walshe-Tobin, Ireland; Women's Quinn-O'Doherty,
Ireland; Mixed Van Mechelin-Rebattu, Netherlands; Junior
Roger-Sahal, France
1983 Overall: Netherlands
Open Fauconnier-Wanuffel, Belgium; Women's Malcom-
Mitchell, Great Britain; Mixed Pasman-Niemeyer,
Netherlands; Junior Girollet-Eisenberg, France
1985 Overall: Italy
Open Duboin-Ferraro, Italy; Women's Moeller-Zenkel,
Germany; Mixed Manara-Atttanasio, Italy; Junior
Krijgsman-Ter Laare, Netherlands
1987 Overall: France
Open Duboin-Ferraro, Italy; Women's Lise-Delor, France;
Mixed Nahmens-Solari, France; Junior Kapaiannidis-Liarak,
Greece
1989 Overall: Netherlands
Open Buratti-Bocchi, Italy; Women's Guillaumin-Saul,
France; Women's Quevy-Zadikyan, Belgium; Junior Bilde-
Larsen, Denmark
1991 Overall: France
Open Pietri-DiMaio, Italy; Women's Handley-Landy, Great
Britain; Mixed Allouche-Gaviard, France; Junior
Munksgaard-Bruun, Denmark
1993 Overall: Italy
Open Ricciarelli-DeFalco, Italy; Women's DaRos-Favas,
France; Mixed Guillaumin-Quantin, France; Junior Versace-
Nunes, Italy

AUSTRALIAN NATIONAL OPEN TEAMS

1973	E.Auerbach, M.Hitter, G.Lorentz, O.Minc
1974	R.Cummings, D.Howard, T.Seres, R.Smilde
1975	R.Klinger, P.Lavings, N.Mathieson, A.Reiner, R.Richman
1976	R.Smilde, P.Lavings, A.Reiner, R.Richman, T.Seres
1977	R.Smilde, P.Lavings, T.Seres, A.Reiner, R.Richman, N.Mathieson
1978	T.Brown, M.Shieff, J.Newman, C.Hughes, K.Hume, A.Kanetkar
1979	W.Scott, T.Bourke, R.Cook, C.Hughes, G.Kilvington, R.vanRiel
1980	T.Bourke, J.Lathbury, P.Schroor, W.Scott, R.vanRiel
1981	T.Seres, R.Cummings, G.Lorentz, P.Lavings, W.Jacobs, D.Smith
1982	M.Watson, M.Borewicz, J.Lester, A.Marcovics, M.Stampf, P.Wyer
1983	F.Theeman, S.Browne, S.Burgess, P.Marston, B.Neill, A.Walsh
1984	G.Lorentz, J.Lester, S.Burgess, P.Marston, P.Gill, R.Klinger
1985	B.Neill, P.Fordham, E.Griffin, M.Hughes, A.Walsh, D.Zines
1986	R.Smilde, T.Seres, D.Anderson, Z.Nagy
1987	M.Watson, M.Borewicz, J.Lester, P.Marston, M.Courtney, P.Wyer
1988	M.Cornell, L.Wright, K.Boardman, A.Taylor
1989	M.Cornell, L.Wright, A.Braithwaite, A.Taylor
1990	J.Roberts, M.Thomson, B.Glubok, G.Eggins, J.Lowe
1991	E.Otvosi, S.Burgess, R.Richman, J.Borin, Z.Nagy, G.Smolanko
1992	J.Roberts, R.Brightling, S.Lester, S.Snow, M.Thomson

1993	A.Reiner, S.Burgess, D.Middleton, Z.Nagy, T.Seres, G.Smolanko
1994	P.Marston, S.Burgess, D.Middleton, Z.Nagy, T.Seres, G.Smolanko
1995	D.Sacul, F.Karwur, H.Lasut, E.Manoppo, S.Panelewen, G.Watulingas
1996	D.Sacul, F.Karwur, S.Panelewen, G.Watulingas
1997	D.Sacul, T.Asbi, F.Karwur, S.Panelewen, G.Watulingas
1998	S.Burgess, M.Cornell, D.Crombie, B.Jones, P.Marston, M.Mayer
1999	B.Noble, G.Bilski, T.Brown, P.Gue, A.Peake
2000	B.Neill, M.Hughes, P.Gumby, W.Lazer, B.McDonald, A.Walsh
2001	M.Lavazza, N.Bocchi, G.Duboin, G.Ferraro, A.Versace, P.Russo

AUSTRALIAN WOMEN'S BUTLER TEAMS

1967	R.Eaton, M.McMahon, W.Lipscomb, G.Stern, J.Gillespie, L.Fraser
1969	Creasy, V.Ramsay, J.Allen, W.Lipscomb, F.Landy, Groom
1970	M.Choate, C.Miles, V.Cummings, G.Stern, Fowler, D.Jesner
1971	W.Golding, C.Grigg, I.Dahler, F.Landy, M.Freedman, V.Vahala
1972	Bell, G.Reynolds, S.Hobley, U.Husten, M.Freedman, V.Vahala
1973	W.Lipscomb, G.Stern, R.Eaton, M.McMahon, F.Beale, G.Tabak
1974	W.Lipscomb, G.Stern, R.Eaton, M.McMahon, P.Brown, E.Poulson
1975	M.Choate, C.Miles, I.Dahler, G.Reynolds, V.Cummings, M.McMahon
1976	M.McMahon, G.Stern, N.Borin, E.Havas, P.Schroor, A.Tandy
1977	C.Grigg, C.Miles, E.Havas, B.McDonald, I.Dahler, F.Landy
1978	E.Havas, B.McDonald, F.Beale, D.Smart, R.Eaton, W.Lipscomb
1979	P.Gumby, S.Hobley, F.Beale, D.Smart, M.Bourke, A.Tandy
1980	P.Gumby, S.Hobley, F.Beale, D.Smart, M.Bourke, A.Tandy
1981	L.Kilvington, P.Schroor, M.Bourke, A.Tandy, S.Edwards, B.Gill
1982	V.Cummings, E.Havas, G.Stern, K.Moses, D.McKinnon, M.Scudder
1984	M.Bourke, P.Schroor, S.Lusk, B.Travis, P.Gumby, S.Hobley
1985	S.Lusk, B.Travis, F.Beale, D.Smart, M.Bourke, P.Schroor
1986	S.Lusk, B.Travis, J.Courtney, C.Lester, M.Scudder, T.Zines
1987	S.Lusk, B.Travis, C.Chua, D.McKinnon, H.Bunning, P.Schroor
1988	S.Lusk, B.Travis, H.Bunning, P.Schroor, J.Butts, T.Tully
1989	P.McCartney, R.Walcott, M.Bourke, L.Kilvington, K.Moses, G.Stern
1990	L.Beech, M.Bourke, V.Cummings, J.Wyer, S.Lusk, C.Miles
1991	N.Borin, R.Branicki, N.Church, J.Hoffman, K.Moses, G.Stern
1992	J.Butts, T.Tully, L.Beech, M.Bourke, F.Beale, D.Smart
1993	J.Butts, T.Tully, D.Rogers, G.Tucker, F.Beale, D.Smart
1994	L.Beech, M.Bourke, K.Robb, M.Robb, P.Crittle, B.Folkard
1995	S.Collins, L.Richards, P.Evans, J.Faranda, L.Beech, M.Bourke
1996	L.Beech, M.Bourke, R.Clayton, M.Millar, L.Kalmin, E.Urbach
1997	K.Moses, B.Folkard, T.Lloyd, P.McCartney, N.Church, J.Hoffman
1998	F.Beale, D.Smart, R.Clayton, M.Millar, D.Dodd, G.Tucker
1999	S.Lusk, T.Tully, M.Brown, R.Kaplan, L.Beech, M.Bourke
2000	S.Lusk, T.Tully, J.Hay, D.Moir, N.Bashar, M.Robb

AUSTRALIAN OPEN PAIRS
(formerly BLUE-RIBBON PAIRS)

1978   M.Mayer, M.Sims
1979   P.Marston, M.Sims
1980   R.Richman, C.Surany
1981   P.Lavings, G.Lorentz
1982   P.Lavings, G.Lorentz
1983   S.Burgess, P.Marston
1984   R.Cummings, R.Richman
1985   R.Cummings, R.Richman
1986   R.Cummings, R.Richman
1987   P.Herold, A.Skuce
1988   M.Courtney, P.Wyer
1989   P.Gill, W.Lazer
1990   M.Mayer, L.Wright
1991   J.Borin, R.Richman
1992   G.Bilski, T.Brown
1993   C.Balicki, A.Zmudzinski
1994   W.Izdebski, W.Siewiec
1995   R.Fruewirth, R.Richman
1996   M.Prescott, M.Ware
1997   B.Kat, K.Kat
1998   P.Gumby, W.Lazer
1999   D.Beauchamp, A.Peake
2000   G.Gaspar, B.Tencer
2001   A.Bach, K.Dyke

AUSTRALIAN OPEN BUTLER TEAMS

1967   R.Cummings, R.Smilde, I.McCance, F.Altman,
     G.Jesner, F.Jarvis
1969   J.Borin, N.Borin, D.Howard, R.Smilde, R.Cummings,
     T.Seres
1970   R.Cummings, T.Seres, D.Howard, R.Smilde, J.Borin,
     N.Borin
1971   J.Borin, N.Borin, A.Hancock, D.Hoffman, T.Seres,
     R.Smilde
1972   R.Cummings, D.Howard, D.Anderson, Z.Nagy,
     F.Altman, I.McCance
1973   P.Lavings, A.Reiner, D.Middleton, R.Robertson,
     A.Jackman, M.Robson
1974   P.Lavings, A.Markovics, D.Anderson, Z.Nagy,
     F.Altman, M.Kent
1975   L.Longhurst, R.Klinger, R.Cummings, R.Smilde,
     P.Lavings, N.Mathieson
1976   J.Borin, G.Havas, J.Lathbury, J.Lester, E.Griffin,
     G.Smith
1977   J.Lathbury, J.Lester, J.Borin, G.Havas, T.Bourke,
     D.Smith
1978   P.Lavings, M.McMahon, R.Cummings, T.Seres,
     G.Lorentz, O.Minc
1979   N.Perry, A.Wolframs, R.Evans, R.Grynberg, J.Borin,
     N.Borin
1980   J.Borin, N.Borin, R.Morrish, R.Richman,
     N.Rosendorff, L.Summers
1981   J.Borin, N.Borin, R.Davis, P.Gill, N.Rosendorff,
     L.Summers
1982   M.Courtney, R.Richman, S.Burgess, P.Marston,
     I.McCance, V.Muntz
1983   P.Gill, R.Klinger, J.Borin, N.Borin, S.Burgess,
     P.Marston
1984   P.Gill, R.Klinger, M.Courtney, N.Rosendorff,
     M.Hughes, D.Zines
1985   R.Januszke, G.Sargent, P.Lavings, N.Hughes, R.Gallus,
     S.Henbest
1986   R.Klinger, D.Lilley, J.Borin, N.Borin, N.Rosendorff,
     P.Smith
1987   J.Borin, N.Borin, R.Richman, J.Wallis, M.Courtney,
     P.Wyer
1988   P.Gue, N.Rosendorff, P.Newman, M.Thomson, J.Borin,
     N.Borin
1989   H.Grosvenor, I.Thomson, R.Klinger, D.Lilley,
     K.Bagchi, P.Lavings
1990   M.Courtney, P.Gill, S.Burgess, E.Otvosi, D.Middleton,
     G.Smolanko
1991   S.Snow, T.Snow, P.Gue, Z.Nagy, J.Roberts, M.Thomson
1992   P.Fordham, B.Neill, P.Gill, R.Klinger, H.Grosvenor,
     P.Gue
1993   D.Beauchamp, E.Chadwick, S.Hinge, B.Thompson,
     S.Browne, R.Mann
1994   J.Roberts, M.Thomson, D.Beauchamp, E.Chadwick,
     H.Christie, R.Cooper

1995   K.Bagchi, P.Newman, G.Kozakos, P.Marston,
     H.Christie, R.Cooper
1996   K.Bagchi, S.Browne, J.Lester, G.Lorentz, H.Christie,
     R.Cooper
1997   K.Bagchi, S.Browne, B.Neill, M.Hughes, S.Burgess,
     M.Mayer
1998   K.Bagchi, S.Browne, H.Grosvenor, R.Richman,
     T.Brown, P.Gue
1999   P.Newman, M.Thomson, T.Brown, P.Gue, S.Browne,
     I.DelMonte
2000   A.Bach, K.Dyke, T.Brown, P.Gue, S.Browne,
     I.DelMonte

AUSTRALIAN GOLD COAST TEAMS

1962   G.McCutcheon, H.Hiley, A.Jackman, B.Meares,
     D.Priest, R.Williams
1963   G.McCutcheon, A.Jackman, D.Priest, T.Seres,
     R.Smilde
1964   E.Auerbach, M.Coltheart, R.Eaton, M.McMahon
1965   M.McMahon, R.Eaton, D.Evans, T.Seres, I.Weiss
1966   M.McMahon, R.Eaton, D.Evans, T.Seres, I.Weiss
1967   J.Fahrer, A.Jackman, D.Priest, J.Selinger, G.Westcott
1968   N.Rothfield, M.McMahon, J.Rothfield, W.Scott,
     T.Seres, R.Smilde
1969   A.Jackman, F.Jarvis, B.Meares, M.Robson
1970   R.Smilde, M.McMahon, J.Rothfield, W.Scott, T.Seres
1971   R.Smilde, M.McMahon, J.Rothfield, W.Scott, T.Seres
1972   D.Evans, A.Jackman, F.Jarvis, J.Lathbury, I.Weiss
1973   D.Evans, A.Jackman, F.Jarvis, I.Weiss
1974   M.McMahon, R.Cummings, R.Klinger, T.Seres
1975   M.McMahon, R.Cummings, R.Klinger, T.Seres
1976   M.McMahon, R.Klinger, R.Richman, T.Seres
1977   M.Pemberton, A.Jackman, I.Morris, M.Robson
1978   F.Theeman, D.Evans, P.Lavings, T.Ong
1979   R.Klinger, M.McMahon, R.Richman, T.Seres
1980   M.McMahon, R.Klinger, R.Richman, T.Seres
1981   A.Walsh, V.Cummings, E.Havas, W.Scott
1982   M.McMahon, T.Bourke, D.Smith, T.Seres
1983   V.Cummings, E.Havas, W.Scott, A.Walsh
1984   S.Burgess, P.Marston, M.Borewicz, R.Richman
1985   J.Lowe, G.Eggins, J.Free, A.Webb
1986   A.Walsh, V.Cummings, E.Havas, W.Scott
1987   M.McMahon, K.Hume, T.Seres, T.Tully
1988   E.Otvosi, S.Burgess, R.Cummings, R.Richman
1989   R.Dalley, A.Dalley, R.Cummings, T.Ong
1990   E.Otvosi, S.Browne, S.Burgess, R.Richman
1991   D.Beech, L.Beech, T.Bourke, R.Gallus, D.Smith
1992   R.Brightling, S.Lester, C.Quail, I.Robinson, S.Snow
1993   A.Bach, I.DelMonte, M.Mullamphy, R.Richman
1994   A.Bach, I.DelMonte, R.Richman, L.Wright
1995   A.Bach, I.DelMonte, M.Mullamphy, R.Richman
1996   T.Antoff, A.Delivera, K.Dyke, R.Hills, D.Jesner,
     G.Jesner
1997   H.Grosvenor, R.Richman, C.Rothfield, J.Rothfield
1998   F.Beale, D.McLeish, A.Mill, A.Silver, R.vanRiel
1999   M.Mullamphy, P.Newman, J.Spooner, P.Yovich
2000   P.Hackett, J.Hackett, J.Hackett, R.Harper, R.Harper
2001   I.Delmonte, E.Erichsen, C.Gower, C.Convery

AUSTRALIAN GRAND NATIONAL OPEN TEAMS

1986   P.Marston, P.Buchen, R.Grynberg, G.Kozakos,
     R.Smilde, D.Stern
1987   F.Theeman, K.Bagchi, S.Browne, A.Kanetkar,
     J.Lathbury
1988   B.Neill, P.Buchen, P.Fordham, E.Griffin, M.Hughes,
     A.Walsh
1989   J.Roberts, P.Gill, W.Lazer, P.Newman, M.Thomson
1990   P.Crittle, G.Bilski, R.Brightling, T.Brown, S.Lester,
     R.Moore
1991   Z.Nagy, P.Gue, D.Middleton, G.Smolanko
1992   R.Harms, J.Chan, K.Hocking, J.Zollo
1993   D.Evans, T.Antoff, G.Bilski, L.Bornecrantz, T.Brown,
     M.Lalov
1994   K.Dyke, D.Lusk, S.Lusk, A.Peake
1995   D.Beauchamp, E.Chadwick, M.Chadwick, R.Klinger,
     K.Morrison, P.Newman
1996   C.Chua, R.Gallus, S.Hinge, D.Smith
1997   P.Chan, P.Gue, R.Januszke, G.Sargent
1998   J.Haffer, D.Horton, P.Markey, G.Smolanko
1999   V.Cummings, K.Dyke, R.Klinger, M.Mullamphy,
     P.Newman, M.Thomson

2000 V.Cummings, K.Dyke, R.Klinger, M.Mullamphy,
      P.Newman, M.Thomson

AUSTRALIAN GOLD COAST PAIRS

1962	H.Hiley, R.Williams
1963	T.Seres, R.Smilde
1964	R.Eaton, M.McMahon
1965	D.Evans, I.Weiss
1966	T.Landy, D.Neill
1967	A.Selinger, G.Westcott
1968	M.McMahon, T.Seres
1969	M.McMahon, T.Seres
1970	G.Stern, R.Stern
1971	D.Evans, I.Weiss
1972	F.Bell'ham, H.Hochmuth
1973	D.Evans, I.Weiss
1974	M.McMahon, T.Seres
1975	I.McCance, W.Scott
1976	M.McMahon, T.Seres
1977	M.McMahon, T.Seres
1978	D.Evans, P.Lavings
1979	B.Gill, P.Jamieson
1980	J.Borin, N.Borin
1981	R.Richman, D.Smith
1982	J.Lester, R.Richman
1983	S.Burgess, P.Marston
1984	S.Burgess, P.Marston
1985	B.Glubok, D.Greenwald
1986	S.Burgess, R.Richman
1987	R.Klinger, D.Lilley
1988	J.Borin, N.Borin
1989	E.Havas, A.Walsh
1990	S.Browne, R.Richman
1991	J.Borin, R.Richman
1992	D.Beauchamp, U.Durmus
1993	I.DelMonte, R.Richman
1994	A.Bach, I.DelMonte
1995	R.Bentley, P.King
1996	M.Horton, B.Senior
1997	B.Polii, C.Watulingas
1998	H.Grosvenor, R.Richman
1999	S.Browne, R.Brightling
2000	Z.Huilin, T.Ong
2001	T.Jacob, R.Jedrychowsky

ANGLO-AMERICAN MATCHES

Results of semi-official or unofficial matches:

London, 1930. America (Ely and Josephine Culbertson, Theodore A. Lightner, and Waldemar K. von Zedtwitz) beat England (Lt. Col. Walter Buller, Alice G. Evers, Cedric Kehoe, and Nelson Wood-Hill) by 4,845 total points over 300 boards.

London, 1933. For the SCHWAB CUP. America (Ely and Josephine Culbertson, Theodore A. Lightner, and Michael T. Gottlieb) beat England (Lt. Col. Henry M. Beasley, Gerald G. Domville, P.V. Tabbush, George Morris, Graham F. Mathieson, and Lady Doris Rhodes) by 11,110 total points over 300 boards.

London, 1934. For the SCHWAB CUP. America (Ely and Josephine Culbertson, Theodore A. Lightner, and Albert H. Morehead) beat England (Richard Lederer, William Rose, Henry St. John Ingram, and Stanley Hughes; with Col. George G. J. Walshe [capt.] and A. Frost as alternates) by 3,600 total points over 300 boards.

London, 1949. For the Crowninshield cup. England beat America by 330 total points, the net result of two matches. England (Maurice Harrison-Gray [capt.], Kenneth W. Konstam, Terence Reese, and Boris Schapiro) beat America (Johnny R. Crawford, George Rapee, Samuel M. Stayman, and Peter A. Leventritt) by 2,950 total points. The same American team beat England (Ewart Kempson [capt.], Rixi Markus, Kenneth W. Konstam, Leslie Dodds, Edward Rayne, Jordanis T. Pavlides, and Graham F. Mathieson) by 2,620 total points. Both matches were of 96 boards.

London, 1954. England (Terence Reese, Boris Schapiro, Kenneth W. Konstam, Adam Meredith, and Edward Mayer) beat America (Clifford W. Bishop, Milton Q. Ellenby, Douglas Steen, Lewis L. Mathe, and Don Oakie; William Rosen was absent) by 81 IMPs over 100 boards.

Miami, 1955. America (Waldemar K. von Zedtwitz, Harold Harkavy, William S. Root, Albert Weiss, Edward Burns, William Seamon, Harold Vanderbilt, Charles Goren, and Charles

Whitebrook) beat Great Britain (Terence Reese, Kenneth W. Konstam, Leslie Dodds, Adam Meredith, and Jordanis T. Pavlides) by 150 total points over 100 boards.

London, 1956. England (Terence Reese, Boris Schapiro, Kenneth W. Konstam, Leslie Dodds, and Edward Mayer) beat America (Samuel M. Stayman, Charles Goren, Charles J. Solomon, Myron Field, Lee Hazen, and Richard Kahn) by 79 IMPs over 100 boards.

Philadelphia, 1976. Bicentennial challenge match. The U.S. (Colonists) (Edgar Kaplan, Norman Kay, Bobby Goldman, Mark Blumenthal, Robert Jordan, Arthur Robinson with Simon [Skippy] Becker as npc) defeated Great Britain (Redcoats) (Claude Rodrigue, Tony Priday, Barnet Shenkin and Michael Rosenberg) 90 IMPs to 65 over 40 boards.

FRANCO-AMERICAN MATCHES

There have been 18 official meetings in world championship competition.

1936 - New York United States won	1968 - Deauville, France United States won
1954 - Monte Carlo United States won	1969 - Rio de Janeiro, Brazil North America won
1956 - Paris France won	1971 - Taipei United States won
1960 - Turin France won	1972 - Miami United States won
1961 - Buenos Aires North America won	1974 - Venice, Italy North America won
1963 - St.Vincent, Italy North America won	1975 - Bermuda North America won
1964 - New York United States won	1976 - Monte Carlo France won
1967 - Miami Beach North America won	1980 - Valkenburg, Netherlands France won
	1992 - Salsomaggiore, Italy France won
	1997 - Hammamet, Tunisia France won

The following semiofficial or unofficial matches have been played:

(1) Paris 1933. United States (Ely and Josephine Culbertson, Theodore Lightner, Waldemar von Zedtwitz) drew with France (Pierre Bellanger, Pierre Albarran, A. B. de Puchesse, Robert de Nexon, Georges Rousset, Emanuel Tulumaris, Sophocles Venizelos). The match was played at PLAFOND, the forerunner of contract bridge, and, after a dispute, was abandoned as a draw shortly before the end when the scores were almost level.

(2) Paris 1954. France beat the United States (Cliff Bishop, Milton Ellenby, Lewis Mathe, Don Oakie, Doug Steen) by 17 IMPS.

PAN AMERICAN BRIDGE CHAMPIONSHIPS

Held in Corpus Christi TX in 1992, the medal winners were:

OPEN PAIRS
1. USA: Eric Rodwell and Doug Simson
2. Brazil: Gabriel Chagas and Marcelo Branco
WOMENS PAIRS
1. USA: Marinesa Letizia and Juanita Chambers
2. USA: June Deutsch and Beverly Rosenberg
OPEN TEAMS
1. USA: Cliff Russell, Robert Levin, Sam Lev, David Berkowitz, Larry Cohen, Peter Weichsel
2. Canada: Ed Bridson, David Lindop, Geoff Hampson, John Gowdy, Mark Molson, Boris Baran
WOMENS TEAMS
1. USA: Gail Greenberg, Dorothy Truscott, Judy Tucker, Lisa Berkowitz, Randi Montin, Pam Wittes
2. Colombia: Tobi Croitoru, Flor Macias, Sara Wasserman, Cilia Khoudari, Zita Lechter, Deisl Gould

CAVENDISH INVITATIONAL PAIRS

1975	James Jacoby, Gerald Westheimer
1976	Alan Sontag, Peter Weichsel
1977	Alan Sontag, Peter Weichsel
1978	Roy Fox, Paul Swanson
1979	Roger Bates, Daniel Mordecai

1980	Lou Bluhm, Thomas Sanders
1981	James Cayne, Fred Hamilton
1982	Ed Manfield, Kit Woolsey
1983	Robert Lipsitz, Neil Silverman
1984	Marty Bergen, Larry Cohen
1985	Irving Litvack, Joseph Silver
1986	Matt Granovetter, Michael Rosenberg
1987	Drew Casen, Jim Krekorian
1988	Bjorn Fallenius, Magnus Lindkvist
1989	Marty Bergen, Larry Cohen
1990	Piotr Gawrys, Elyakim Shoufel
1991	Johan Bennet, Anders Wirgren
1992	Amos Kaminski, Shmuel Lev
1993	Fred Stewart, Steve Weinstein
1994	Kit Woolsey, Neil Silverman
1995	Paul Soloway, Harry Tudor
1996	Fred Stewart, Steve Weinstein
1997	Michael Seamon, Harry Tudor
1998	Bob Hamman, Nick Nickell
1999	Robert Levin, Steve Weinstein
2000	Marty Fleisher, Eric Rodwell
2001	Michal Kwiecien, Jacek Pszczola

CAVENDISH TEAMS

1995	Piotr Gawrys, Krzysztof Lasocki, Sam Lev, Michael Polowan
1996	Alfredo Versace, Lorenzo Lauria, Andrea Buratti, Massimo Lanzarotti
1997	Alfredo Versace, Lorenzo Lauria, Andrea Buratti, Massimo Lanzarotti
1998	Jan Van Cleeff, Jan Jansma, Bauke Muller, Wubbo de Boer
1999	Steve Weinstein, Robert Levin, Chip Martel, Lew Stansby
2000	Geoff Hampson, Eric Greco, Eric Rodwell, Jeff Meckstroth, Perry Johnson
2001	Fred Gitelman, Brad Moss, Roy Welland, Bjorn Fallenius, Steve Garner, Howard Weinstein

SUNDAY TIMES PAIRS

1963	Pierre Jais, Roger Trezel (France)
1964	Terence Reese, Boris Schapiro (England)
1965	No contest
1966	Gerard Desrousseaux, Dr. George Theron (France)
1967	Claude Rodrigue, Louis Tarlo (England)
1968	Claude Delmouly, Leon Yallouze (France, Egypt)
1969	Jean Besse, John D. Collings (Switzerland, England)
1970	Nico Gardener, Richard Anthony Priday (England)
1971	Lukasz Lebioda, Andrzej Wilkosz (Poland)
1972	Steven Altman, Alan Sontag (U.S.A.)
1974	Gianfranco Facchini, Sergio Zucchelli (Italy)
1975	Alan Sontag, Peter Weichsel (U.S.A.)
1976	Michael Rosenberg, Barnet Shenkin (Scotland)
1977	Jean-Michel Boulenger, Henri Szwarc (France)
1978	Sven-Olov Flodqvist, Per Olof Sundelin (Sweden)
1979	Pedro Paulo Assumpcao, Gabriel Chagas (Brazil)
1980	Victor Goldberg, Barnet Shenkin (Scotland)
1981	Sven-Olov Flodqvist, Per Olof Sundelin (Sweden)
1990	Tony Forrester, Andrew Robson (England)
1991	Paul Chemla, Michel Perron (France)
1992	Gabriel Chagas, Marcelo Branco (Brazil)
1993	Robert Levin, Gaylor Kasle (U.S.A.)
1994	Adam Zmudzinski, Cezary Balicki (Poland)

Sponsored by Macallan Malt Whisky 1995-99

1995	Jeff Meckstroth, Eric Rodwell
1996	Jeff Meckstroth, Eric Rodwell
1997	Lorenzo Lauria, Alfredo Versace
1998	Geir Helgemo, Tor Helness
1999	Geir Helgemo, Tor Helness
2000	Not held

CAP GEMINI PAIRS

1987 —	Jan Fucik - Franz Terraneo (Austria)
1988 —	Jeff Meckstroth - Eric Rodwell (US)
1989 —	Jan Fucik - Franz Terraneo (Austria)
1990 —	Tony Forrester - Andy Robson (Great Britain)
1991 —	Billy Eisenberg - Benito Garozzo (US)
1992 —	Zia Mahmood (Pakistan) - Michael Rosenberg (US)
1993 —	Gabriel Chagas - Marcelo Branco (Brazil)
1994 —	Geir Helgemo - Tor Helness (Norway)

1995 —	Zia Mahmood, Michael Rosenberg
1996 —	Geir Helgemo, Tor Helness
1997 —	Gabriel Chagas, Marcelo Branco
1998 —	Zia Mahmood, Tony Forrester
1999 —	Berkowitz, Larry Cohen
2000 —	Zia Mahmood, Andrew Robson
2001 —	Zia Mahmood, Andrew Robson

PHILIP MORRIS EUROPEAN MIXED CHAMPIONSHIPS

1990 *Bordeaux* MIXED PAIRS Saul-Quantin, France
MIXED TEAMS 1. France (Captain G. Chevalley)
1992 *Ostend* MIXED PAIRS Harasimowiz-Lesniewsky, Poland MIXED TEAMS France (Captain D. Pilon)
1994 *Barcelona* MIXED PAIRS Zenkel-Nippgen, Germany
MIXED TEAMS Netherlands (Captain van der Pas)
1996 MIXED PAIRS Erhart-Kubak, Austria; MIXED TEAMS France (Captain Bessis)
1998 MIXED PAIRS Andersson-Larsson, Sweden. MIXED TEAMS France (Captain Bessis)

NORDIC CHAMPIONSHIP

The Nordic Championships, contested by six Scandinavian countries, is one of the oldest international competitions. The nations are Denmark, Farse Islands, Finland, Iceland, Norway and Sweden. The winners are:

Year	Open	Women's
1946	Norway	Sweden
1947	Sweden	Denmark
1948	Norway	Sweden
1949	Sweden	Sweden
1951	Norway	Denmark
1953	Sweden	Sweden
1955	Sweden	Denmark
1957	Sweden	Sweden
1962	Sweden	Denmark
1964	Sweden	Sweden
1966	Norway	Sweden
1968	Sweden	Sweden
1971	Norway	Finland
1973	Denmark	Norway
1975	Norway	Sweden
1978	Norway	Sweden
1980	Norway	Sweden
1982	Norway	Sweden
1984	Sweden	Sweden
1986	Denmark	Norway
1988	Iceland	Denmark
1990	Sweden	Iceland
1992	Iceland	Sweden
1994	Iceland	Denmark
1996	Sweden	Sweden
1998	Norway	Sweden
2000	Sweden	Finland

GENERALI EUROPE INDIVIDUAL CHAMPIONSHIP

	Men	Women
1992	Piotrys Gawrys, Poland	Maria Erhart, Austria
1994	Jon Baldursson, Iceland	Nicola Smith, Great Britain
1996	Geir Helgemo, Norway	Elisabeth Delor, France
1998	Paul Chemla, France	Migri Zur-Albu, Israel
2000	Antonio Sementa, Italy	Benedicte Cronier, France

OKBRIDGE INTERNET WORLD BRIDGE CHAMPIONSHIP

1999 – United States: Marty Seligman, Paul Soloway, Doug Simson, Eric Rodwell, John Schuler, Mike Crawford
2000 – Romania: Catalin Popescu, Darin Musat, Serban Criscota, Alexandre Feber, Dorin Chergulescu, Marion Radulescu

FORBO INTERNATIONAL TEAMS

The Hague, Netherlands

1996	Germany – Steve Haas, Michael Elinescu, Andrzej Holowski, Thomasz Gotarel
1997	Italy – Norberto Bocchi, Alfredo Versace, Andrew Buratti, Massimo Lanzarotti
1998	Germany – Michael Elinescu, Peter Splettstosser, Dr. Wladlow, Helmut Hausler
1999	Netherlands – Schelte Wijma, Jaap Brulleman, Franz ten Brink, Hans de Vrind
2000	Canada – John Carruthers, George Mittelman, Drew Cannell, Eric Kokish
2001	Italy – Norberto Bocchi, Giorgio Duboin, Lorenzo Lauria, Alfredo Versace

FORBO NATIONS CUP

The Hague, Netherlands

1993	TVM — René Coppens, Geert Jansen, Harm Everts, Rieks Mulder
1994	USA — Michael Polowan, Sam Lev, Brad Moss, Ravindra Murthy
1995	Denmark — Niels Krojgaard, Jes Bank, Mads Krojgaard, Henrik Caspersen
1996	Italy — Lorenzo Lauria, Alfredo Versace, Andrea Buratti, Massimo Lanzarotti
1997	Italy — Norberto Bocchi, Alfredo Versace, Andrew Buratti, Massimo Lanzarotti
1998	France – Paul Chemla, Michel Perron, Christian Mari, Alain Levy
1999	China – Fu Zhong, Sun Shaolin, Wang Weiman, Li Xin
2000	Netherlands – Bauke Muller, Piet Jansen, Jan Westerhof, Wubbo du Boer
2001	North America – Fred Gitelman, Brad Moss, John Carruthers, Howard Weinstein

CHINA CUP OPEN TEAMS

1996	China Bridge Association (Luo Yunhong, Hu Jihong, Xu Hongiun, He Zhengyi, Zhuang Zejun, Chen Rongchang, Li Xin
1997	North America (Boris Baran, George Mittleman, Mark Molson, Canada; Peter Boyd, Steve Robinson, Peter Nagy, United States)
1998	France (Paul Chemla, Christian Mari, Frank Multon, Alain Levy)
1999	Europe (Jens Auken, Dennis Koch-Palmund, Denmark; Peter Fredin, Magnus Lindkvist, Soren Christiansen, Morten Andersen, Sweden; Steen Moller, Denmark, npc)
2000	Mavromichalis (Brigitte Mavromichalis, Switzerland; Paul Hackett, Jason Hackett, Justin Hackett, Great Britain; Mark Lair, United States; Geir Helgemo, Norway)

CHINA CUP WOMEN'S TEAMS

1996	United States (Kathie Wei-Sender, Sue Sachs, Lynn Deas, Juanita Chambers)
1997	North America (Kathie Wei-Sender, Sue Sachs, Lynn Deas, Juanita Chambers, Irina Levitina, Stasha Cohen)
1998	China Bridge Association (Zhang Yalan, Gu Ling, Wang Wenfei, Zhang Yu)
1999	World Stars (Sabine Auken, Kirsten Moller, Denmark; Barbara Stawowy, Katrin Farwig, Germany; Sylvie Willard, Benedicte Cronier, France; Steen Moller, Denmark, npc)
2000	Not contested

CHINA CUP OPEN PAIRS

1996	Lynn Deas, Juanita Chambers, United States
1997	Sun Ming, Lu Yan, China
1998	Fu Zhong, Ju Chuanchang, China
1999	Fu Zhong, Ju Chuanchang, China
2000	Ju Chuanchang, Shi Jhengjun, China

EPSON INTERCITY CHAMPIONSHIP

Tokyo, Japan

1983	Montreal, Canada: Sami Kehela, Eric Kokish, Beverly Kraft, Irv Litvack, Joey Silver
1984	Taipei, Taiwan: C.H. Kuo, H.S. Lin, C.K. Shen, W.T. Hsu
1985	Montreal, Canada:Gerald Charney-Zia Mahmood, Irving Litvack-Joey Silver, Beverly Kraft-Eric Kokish

NEC BRIDGE FESTIVAL

Tokyo and Yokohama, Japan

1995	Jenn-Wah, Lee Cheng-Tao, Chang Wei-Ming, Yen Yung-Nan, Shen Nai-Jeng, Lai Hui-Ping, all of Taiwan
1996	No tournament
1997	Eric Kokish, Canada; Richard Colker, United States; Henky Lasut, Eddy Manoppo, Denny Sacul, Taufik Asbi, Indonesia
1998	Brigitte Mavromichalis, Switzerland; John Armstrong, Canada; Paul Hackett, Jason Hackett, Justin Hackett, Great Britain
1999	Masayuki Ino, Dawei Chen, Tadashi Imakura, Kenji Miyakuni, Hiroshi Hisatomi, Tadashi Teramoto, all of Japan
2000	Brigitte Mavromichalis, Switzerland; John Armstrong, Canada; Paul Hackett, Jason Hackett, Justin Hackett, Great Britain
2001	Sam Lev, John Mohan, United States; Piotr Gawrys, Jacek Pszczola, Poland; Pinhas Romik, Israel, npc

POLITIKEN WORLD PAIRS

Copenhagen, Denmark

1995	Zia Mahmood, Peter Weichsel, United States
1997	Geir Helgemo, Norway, Krzysztof Martens, Poland
1999	Norberto Bocchi, Giorgio Duboin

ASEAN BRIDGE CLUB CHAMPIONSHIPS

Date	Open	Women	Youth	Mixed
1979	Indonesia			Singapore
1980	Indonesia	Thailand	Indonesia	
1981	Indonesia	Singapore	Indonesia	Singapore
1982	Indonesia	Singapore	Indonesia	Thailand
1983	Indonesia	Indonesia	Thailand	Thailand
1984	Indonesia	Thailand	Indonesia	
1985	Indonesia	Singapore	Thailand	Thailand
1986	Indonesia	Indonesia	Thailand	Thailand
1987	Indonesia	Indonesia	Indonesia	Thailand
1988	Indonesia	Indonesia		Thailand
1989	Indonesia	Malaysia	Indonesia	Thailand
1990	Indonesia	Thailand	Indonesia	Malaysia
1991	Indonesia	Thailand	Indonesia	Indonesia
1992	Indonesia	Singapore	Indonesia	Singapore
1993	Indonesia	Indonesia	Indonesia	Indonesia
1994	Indonesia	Singapore		Indonesia
1995	Thailand	Indonesia	Thailand	Philippines
1996	Thailand	Thailand	Thailand	Indonesia
1997	Indonesia	Singapore	Indonesia	Philippines
1998	Indonesia	Singapore	Thailand	Thailand
1999	Indonesia	Singapore	Thailand	Thailand

WORLD COMPUTER CHAMPIONSHIPS

Albuquerque NM
1 Bridge Baron; 2 Q-Plus
Chicago
1 GIB; 2 Q-Plus
Bermuda
1 GIB 2 Wbridge5
2000 Maastricht

NORTH AMERICAN COLLEGE TEAM CHAMPIONSHIPS

Competition began in 1987 at the Spring NABC in St. Louis and the winners (except Barry Goren, who was not eligible) represented ACBL in the first World Junior Championships in Amsterdam, the Netherlands. Guy Doherty, Jon Heller and Asya Kamsky – joined by Bill Hsieh and Aaron Silverstein – finished third in the World Junior championships.

The championships were played at the Spring NABCs in 1988 and 1989. In 1990, the competition was moved to ACBL headquarters in Memphis where it was co-sponsored by ACBL and the Association of College Unions-International.

The competition moved back to the Spring NABC in 1991 but the following year it returned to Mem-

phis, where it became a part of the annual "Memphis in May" festivities.

1987   New York University: Guy Doherty, Barry Goren, Jon Heller, Asya Kamsky.
1988   University of Illinois: Brian Blackmore, Dennis Carney, Justin Graver, Michael Steigmann.
1989   University of Tennessee: Jim Baker, Mike Cappelletti Jr., Michael White, David Williams.
1990   Harvard: Bill Cole, Michael Mitzenbacher, Franco Baseggio, James Colen.
1991   University of Virginia: John Miller, John Prince, Hank Strauch, Scott Tumperi.
1992   Rensselaer Polytechnic Institute: Scott Bieber, Brady Richter, Andrew Skolnick, Ron Sperber.
1993   Yale University: Matt Hastings, Douglas Koltenuk, Malik Madon-Ismail, Tony Tang.
1994   Harvard University: Mark Paltrowitz, Barry Piafsky, Michael Steigmann, Tom Rozinski.
1995   Stanford: Steve Altus, Scott Benson, Bert Hackney, Joel Singer
1996   Texas A & M:Hank Eng, Eric Wolff, Patricia Lozano, Marc Whinery
(Canceled after 1996)

OKBRIDGE/ACBL INTERNET COLLEGE TEAM CHAMPIONSHIP

1997   Harvard: Barry Piafsky, Shawn Samuel, Jenni Hartsman, Joel Singer
1998   University of Kentucky: Daniel Neill, Gilbert Busby, Ali Vaezy, Todd Anderson
1999   University of California - San Diego: Michael Davis, Dan Harting, Jeremy Martin, Eugene Hung, Richard Wang
2000   University of Technology - Vienna, Austria: (no names available)
2001   Harvard: Li-Chung Chen, captain; Andrew Cotton. Qixiang Sun (Stanford), Theodore Hwa (Stanford), Jason Woolever (MIT).

NORTH AMERICAN COLLEGE PAIR CHAMPIONSHIPS

1940   Radcliffe College
1941   Harvard University
1942   Princeton University
1943-45   (cancelled due to World War II)
1946   Cornell University
1947   University of California (first time on national basis)
     Charles W. Drake, Philip J. Smith
1948   Capital University, Columbus, OH
     Charles Krueger, Luther Schleisser, Jr.
1949   Wayne University, Detroit
     Clifford Bishop, Dorsey Brooks
1950   Massachussetts Institute of Technology
     Martin Cornish, Jr., Richard Lesser
1951   Washburn University, Topeka, KS
     Gerald Michaud, Bradley Post
1952   Rice Institute, Houston, TX
     John "Spider" Harris, Richard Sutton
1953   Purdue University (N-S)
     Frank McClure, Carey Yelton, Jr.
     Princeton University (E-W)
     David Bradley, Harlow Lewis
1954   Purdue University (N-S)
     Herman Rose, Carey Yelton, Jr.
     Dartmouth College (E-W)
     Harry Connaro, Robert Sokolsky
1955   Whitman College (N-S)
     William Click, Robert Luther
     University of Texas (E-W)
     Charles Callery, Charles Miller
1956   Harvard University (N-S)
     Franklin Bunn, Boyd Everett, Jr.
     Dartmouth College (E-W)
     Frank Barteaux, Jr., John Strong, Jr.
1957   Cornell University (N-S)
     Frank Goldring, Paul Trent
     Oberlin College (E-W)
     Danny Kleinman, Dick Recht

1958   University of Iowa (N-S)
     Terry Campbell, Peter Kemble
     Cornell University (E-W)
     Robert Ewen, Jeff Rubens
1959   Columbia University (N-S)
     James Becker, Sanford Reder
     Princeton University (E-W)
     John O'Neil, Willard Speakman
1960   Columbia University (N-S)
     James Becker, Sanford Reder
     North Carolina State College (E-W)
     Robert Smith, Richard Stanton
1961   Harvard University (N-S)
     Roman Weil, Richard Zeckhauser
     Stanford University (E-W)
     Mort Goerman, Roger Tippy
1962   University of Iowa (N-S)
     Larry Friedman, Robert Pugh
     Lake Forest College, Illinois (E-W)
     Richard Berger, James Berg
1963   Lake Forest College, Illinois (N-S)
     Richard Berger, James Berg
     University of Illinois (E-W)
     Robert Ewen, Darrell Penrod
     tied with
     University of California at Berkeley
     Bill Nutting, Hugh Ross
1964   University of Texas (N-S)
     George Kirkwood, Dan Leightman
     University of Oregon (E-W)
     Dale Forster, Jeff Taylor
     tied with
     State University of Buffalo
     Richard Flieshman, Robert Lipsitz
1965   1.   Cornell University
     Thomas M. Smith, Emil Tobenfeld
   2.   University of Wisconsin
     Larry Cohen, Richard H. Katz
1966   1.   University of Wisconsin
     Larry Cohen, RIchard H. Katz
   2.   University of Minnesota
     Richard Dufour, Morrie Freier
1967   1.   Rensselaer Ploytechnic Institute
     Gerald Cohen, Tony Rosenstein
   2.   University of Colorado
     Michael Copeland, Robert Wherry
1968   1.   University of Maryland
     Jeff Hand, John Richards II
   2.   University of Michigan
     Ron Gerard, Daniel Suty
     tied with
     Rensselaer Polytechnic Institute
     Frank Hacker, Gary Weldin
1969   1.   Rice University
     Michael Finch, Delmas Parker
   2.   University of Utah
     Reed Coray, Ron Rosenthal
1970   1.   University of Virginia
     E. Craig Kennedy, Jr., Bruce Platt
   2.   University of Florida
     Markland Jones, Patricia Sprague
1971   1.   Louisiana State University
     Dennis Conlon, Charles Crosby
   2.   University of North Carolina
     Douglas Stewart, William Wisdom
1972   1.   State University of New York at Stoney Brook
     Raghunath Khetan, Sheo Khetan
   2.   University of Washington
     Neil Chambers, John Schermer
1973   1.   Loyola University of Los Angeles
     Bill Schreiber, Mike Schreiber
   2.   University of Alabama
     Bob Dennard, Ann Hubmaier
1974   1.   University of California at San Diego
     Douglas DePoister, Barry Rothstein
   2.   University of Pennsylvania
     Max Bazerman, Marc Nathan
1975   1.   University of Missouri
     Thomas Allen, Lee Goodman
   2.   Yale University
     Jeff Juster, Andrew Markowitz
1976   1.   University of Michigan
     Larry Mori, Larry Robbins
   2.   University of Colordao
     Stephen Strauss, Michael Zeitlin

1977	1.	Swarthmore College in Pennsylvania
		Marty Fleisher, Alan Heubert
	2.	Washington University in St. Louis
		William Doroshow, Robert Alan Portnoy
1978	1.	University of Texas
		Charles Sterling Darrin, Dennis Sorensen
	2.	Swarthmore College in Pennsylvania
		Marty Fleisher, Alan Heubert
1979	1.	University of Pennsylvania
		Saul Gross, Howard Lebow
	2.	University of Wisconsin
		Jim Elliott, Mark Kinzer

SCHOOL BRIDGE LESSON SERIES INSTANT MATCHPOINT GAME

1995	Josh Silver and Mandy Revzen - Toronto (overall winner only)
1996	N/S - Stephen Cartwright and Bessie Legault; E/W Robert Usiskin and Jake Yocom-Piatt
1997	N/S - Dan Hall and Jon Greenman; E/W - Owen Jones and Adam Ross
1998	N/S - Phil Chan and Roger Huang; E/W Daniel Barry and Ryan Adrian
1999	N/S - Lois Kooh and Woon Joo Lee; E/W Josh Kueker and Nate Miller
2000	N/S - Alana Awad and Emily Neamtz; E/W Justin May and James Hogendoorn

WORLD PAR CONTESTS

International events using prepared deals. Par tournaments conducted throughout the world were initiated in 1932, and the event was called the World Bridge Olympic. The event was abandoned in 1941 because of World War II. The World Par Contest was revived by Australia in 1951, and the World Bridge Federation took over sponsorship in 1961, intending to run the event every two years. However, the event has not taken place since 1963.

1932	N-S Byrne Baldwin, Ruth Baldwin, East Orange, NJ
	E-W Lewis Frank, Robert Mayer, Detroit, MI
1933	N-S Hilda Slager, Fred Levy, Montgomery, AL
	E-W Leo Craine, J. Fredrick Benedict, Sherburne, NJ (tied with) Otto Krefting, Isak Nielson, Oslo, Norway
1934	N-S Dr Eugene Hilb, Robert Darvas, Budapest, Hungary
	E-W Mrs. Gene Hill, Mrs. George Whitaker, Winston-Salem, NC
1935	N-S Dr L.L. von Barkow, Mrs. C. von Kamensky, Dresden, Germany
	E-W Popy Lotou, Stephen Zotos, Athens, Greece
1936	N-S R. E. Horner, Alfred Harris, Ottawa, Canada (tied with) S Rivlin, Capt. W. H. Ricardo, Cardiff, Wales
	E-W Dr Paul Stern, Dr Paul Kaltenegger, Vienna, Austria
1937	N-S Dr O. P. Hampton, Jr, Walter Boeger, University City, MO
	E-W William Savery, Jr, J. E. Muckley, Seattle, WA
1938	N-S Tore Sandgren, Bertil Fant, Stockholm, Sweden
	E-W Irwin Fisher, Harold Karp, Baltimore, MD
1939	E-W Dr. W. Konigsberger and W. Nye, Netherlands.
1940	N-S J.M.Learmonth, E.Learmonth, Maracaibo, Venezuela
	E-W Mrs A. C. Bryant, Mrs. C. H. Drury, Ketchikan, AK
1941	N-S Robert Wilson, George Gooden, San Francisco, CA
	E-W Marjorie Foote, Charles Miller Jr, Phoenix, AZ
1961	Terence Reese, Claude Rodrigue, London, England
1963	Gerard Desrousseaux, Dr. Bernard Romanet, Paris, France
	United States winners when not listed above were:
1934	N-S Elsieh Powell, Robert Powell, Freeport, TX
1935	N-S Cecile Guthrie, G A Smith, Conneaut, OH
	E-W Mrs. Theodore Ahrenbeck Jr., M. O. McDonald, Houston, TX
1936	N-S Arthur Cowperthwait, Tucson, AZ, Ralph Cash, Phoenix, AZ
	E-W George Sherbaum, Memphis, TN, Larry Shurlds, Shelby, TN
1938	N-S Mr. and Mrs. W. H. Gharrity, Chippewa Falls, WI
1939	N-S Marcella Miller, Dr Mandel Shimberg, Leavenworth, KS
	E-W Anton Bugge, Mrs. C. C. Covington, Houston, TX

1940	N-S G. R. Trimmer, Dell Keating, Glasgow, MT
1961	Lawrence Rosler, Murray Hill, NJ, Roger Stern, New York, NY
1963	Lawrence Rosler, Murray Hill, NJ, Roger Stern, New York, NY

GABARRET CUP

This Argentine award donated in memory of Adolfo Gabarret is the equivalent of the ACBL McKENNEY TROPHY or now the BARRY CRANE TOP 500. The winners:

1956	Carlos Ottolenghi	1979	Hector Camberos
1957	Alejandro Castro	1980	Pablo Lambardi
1958	Alberto Berisso	1981	Agustin Santamarina
1959	Arturo Jaques	1982	Egisto Rocchi
1960	Arturo Jaques	1983	Carlos Cabanne
1961	Luis Attaguile	1984	Pablo Lambardi
1962	Alberto Berisso	1985	Martin Monsegur and
1963	Egisto Rocchi		Guillermo Mooney
1964	Marcelo Lerner	1986	Pablo Lambardi
1965	Marcelo Lerner	1987	Alejandro Orzábal
1966	Eduardo Diaz	1988	Rafael Benaderette
1967	Ricardo Calvente	1989	Daniel González
1968	Alberto Berisso	1990	Martín Monsegur
1969	Egisto Rocchi	1991	Guillermo Mooney
1970	David Zanalda	1992	Ricardo Poleschi
1971	Alberto Berisso	1993	Ricardo Poleschi
1972	Carlos Cabanne	1994	Ricardo Poleschi
1973	AgustinSantamarina	1995	Martin Monsegur
1974	Agustin Santamarina	1996	Ernesto Muzzio
1975	Martin Monsegur	1997	Ricardo Poleschi
1976	Egisto Rocchi	1998	Pierre Pejacsevich
1977	Agustin Santamarina	1999	Walter Fornasar
1978	Egisto Rocchi		

BRIDGE TODAY ALL-STAR GAMES

Game 1, Albany NY
1. Michael Rosenberg, tied with Zia Mahmood — $4500 prize split between them
Game 2, Boca Raton FL
1. Richard Pavlicek, $4000; 2, Zia Mahmood — $2000
Game 3, Albany NY
1. Dorothy Truscott, $3000; 2. Marcelo Branco — $2000
Game 4, Novato CA
1. Matt Granovetter, $4000; 2, Zia Mahmood — $2000

CAMROSE SERIES

This is an annual contest among England, Scotland, Wales and Northern Ireland. The Republic of Ireland rejoined the series in 1998. The Camrose Trophy was in play for the 57th time in 1999. England has been the winner 42 times, including 1994. Scotland has won 12 times – 1964, 65, 67, 70, 71, 74, 76, 77, 79, 89, 97, 98. England and Scotland tied for the title in 1972 and 1973.

The most successful player in the Camrose is Monty Rosenberg of Northern Ireland with 67 caps. Patrick Jourdain has been the most successful in Wales (56), Victor Goldberg in Scotland (49) and Tony Forrester in England (36).

LADY MILNE SERIES

This is an annual contest for women among England, Scotland, Wales and Northern Ireland. Over the 45-year history of the event, England has won 39 times, Scotland (1956, 79, 90, 84, 86, 92 and 94), Wales 3 (1967, 68, 88) and Northern Ireland 2 (1981, 85).

The most successful player is Jessie Newton of Wales with 23 caps, closely followed by Mary Nimmons of Northern Ireland. Nicola Gardener-

Smith has had nine caps for England, all wins.

JUNIOR CAMROSE AND
PEGGY BAYER SERIES

This is an annual contest for Junior players among England, Scotland, Wales and Northern Ireland. Over the past 30 years England has won 23 times and Scotland 7.

In 1990 an event for under-20s was added. Scotland won the first year, and England won the next four.

APPENDIX V
WORLD CHAMPIONSHIPS
BERMUDA BOWL

1950. Played in Bermuda. United States defeated Great Britain by 3,660 points and Sweden-Iceland by 4,720 points. Sweden-Iceland defeated Great Britan by 1940 points. UNITED STATES: John R. Crawford, Charles H. Goren, George Rapee, Howard Schenken, Sidney Silodor, Samuel M. Stayman. GREAT BRITAIN: Maurice Harrison-Gray (captain), Leslie Dodds, Nico Gardener, Kenneth Konstam, Joel Tarlo, Louis Tarlo. SWEDEN-ICELAND: Dr. Einar Werner (captain), Gunnar Gudmundsson, Rudolf Kock, Nils-Olof Lilliehook, Einar Thorfinnsson, Jan Wohlin.

1951. Played in Naples. United States defeated Italy by 116 IMPs. UNITED STATES: B. Jay Becker, John R. Crawford, George Rapee, Howard Schenken, Samuel M. Stayman, npc Julius Rosenblum. ITALY: Paolo Baroni, Eugenio Chiaradia, Pietro Forquet, Mario Franco, Augusto Ricci, Guglielmo Siniscalco, npc Carl'Alberto Perroux.

1953. Played in New York. United States defeated Sweden by 8,260 points. UNITED STATES: B. Jay Becker, John R. Crawford, Theodore A. Lightner, George Rapee, Howard Schenken, Samuel M. Stayman, npc Joseph M. Cohan. SWEDEN: Dr. Einar Werner (captain): Gunnar Anulf, Rudolf Kock, Robert Larsen, Nils-Olof Lilliehook, Jan Wohlin.

1954. Played in Monte Carlo. United States defeated France by 49 IMPs.UNITED STATES: Clifford Bishop, Milton Q. Ellenby, Lewis Mathe, Don Oakie, William A. Rosen, Douglas Steen, npc Benjamin O. Johnson. FRANCE: Jacques Amouraben, Rene Bacherich, Jean Besse (Switzerland), Pierre Ghestem, Marcel Kornblum, Karl Schneider (Austria).

1955. Played in New York. Great Britain defeated the United States by 5,420 points. GREAT BRITAIN: Leslie Dodds, Kenneth Konstam, Adam Meredith, Jordanis Pavlides, Terence Reese, Boris Schapiro, npc Reginald Corwen. UNITED STATES: Clifford Bishop, Milton Q. Ellenby, Lewis Mathe, John H. Moran, William A. Rosen, Alvin Roth, npc Peter A. Leventritt.

1956. Played in Paris. France defeated United States 342-288 IMPs. FRANCE: Rene Bacherich, Pierre Ghestem, Pierre Jaïs, Robert Lattes, Bertrand Romanet, Roger Trezel, npc Baron Robert de Nexon. UNITED STATES: Myron Field, Charles H. Goren, Lee Hazen, Richard F. Kahn, Charles J. Solomon, Samuel M. Stayman, npc Jeff Glick.

1957. Played in New York. Italy defeated United States by 10,150 points. ITALY: Walter Avarelli, Giorgio Belladonna, Eugenio Chiaradia, Massimo D'Alelio, Pietro Forquet, Guglielmo Siniscalco, npc Carl'Alberto Perroux. UNITED STATES: Charles H. Goren, Boris Koytchou, Peter A. Leventritt, Harold Ogust, William Seamon, Helen Sobel, npc Rufus L. Miles Jr.

1958. Played in Como, Italy. Italy defeated United States 211-174 and Argentina 239-167. ITALY: Walter Avarelli, Giorgio Belladonna, Eugenio Chiaradia, Massimo D'Alelio, Pietro Forquet, Guglielmo Siniscalco, npc Carl'Alberto Perroux. UNITED STATES: B. Jay Becker, John Crawford, George Rapee, Alvin Roth, Sidney Silodor, Tobias Stone, npc J.G. Ripstra. ARGENTINA: Carlos Cabanne (co-captain), Alejandro Castro (co-captain), Alberto Blousson, Ricardo Calvente, Marcelo Lerner.

1959. Played in New York. Italy defeated United States 233-183 and Argentina 218-178. ITALY: Walter Avarelli, Giorgio Belladonna, Eugenio Chiaradia, Massimo D'Alelio, Pietro Forquet, Guglielmo Siniscalco, npc Carl'Alberto Perroux. UNITED STATES: Harry Fishbein, Sam Fry Jr., Leonard Harmon, Lee Hazen, Sidney Lazard, Ivar Stakgold, npc Charles J. Solomon. ARGENTINA: Alberto Berisso, Ricardo Calvente, Alejandro Castro, Carlos Dibar, Arturo Jaques, Egisto Rocchi, npc Dr. Luis Santa Coloma.

1961. Played in Buenos Aires. Italy defeated Argentina 422-282; France 371-261; North America 382-262. North America defeated Argentina, 411-284; France 262-236. France defeated Argentina 339-287. ITALY: Walter Avarelli, Giorgio Belladonna, Eugenio Chiaradia, Massimo D'Alelio, Pietro Forquet, Benito Garozzo, npc Carl'Alberto Perroux. NORTH AMERICA: John

Gerber, Paul Hodge, Norman Kay, Peter A. Leventritt, Sidney Silodor, Howard Schenken, npc Frank Westcott.

1962. Played in New York. Italy defeated Argentina 420-308; Great Britain 365-286, North America 331-305. North America defeated Argentina 400-242; Great Britain 345-332. Great Britain defeated Argentina 318-311. ITALY: Walter Avarelli, Giorgio Belladonna, Eugenio Chiaradia, Massimo D'Alelio, Pietro Forquet, Benito Garozzo, npc Carl'Alberto Perroux. NORTH AMERICA: Charles Coon, Mervin Key, Lewis Mathe, Eric Murray, G. Robert Nail, Ron Von der Porten, npc John Gerber.

1963. Played in St. Vincent, Italy. Italy defeated Argentina 372-282; France 421-236; North America 313-294. North America defeated France 340-251; Argentina 496-261. France defeated Argentina 453-319. ITALY: Giorgio Belladonna, Eugenio Chiaradia, Massimo D'Alelio, Pietro Forquet, Benito Garozzo, Camillo Pabis Ticci, npc Carl'Alberto Perroux. NORTH AMERICA: James Jacoby, Robert Jordan, Peter Leventritt, G. Robert Nail, Arthur Robinson, Howard Schenken, npc John Gerber.

1965. Played in Buenos Aires. Italy defeated Argentina 325-237; Great Britain 354-233; North America 304-230. North America defeated Argentina 359-250; Great Britain (forfeit). Argentina defeated Great Britain (forfeit). ITALY: Walter Avarelli, Giorgio Belladonna, Massimo D'Alelio, Pietro Forquet, Benito Garozzo, Camillo Pabis Ticci, npcs Sergio Osella, Carl'Alberto Perroux. NORTH AMERICA: Howard Schenken, Peter Leventritt, Ivan Erdos, Kelsey Petterson, B. Jay Becker, Dorothy Hayden, npc John Gerber.

1966. Played in St. Vincent, Italy. Italy defeated North America 319-262; Venezuela 362-203; Netherlands 326-198; Thailand 486-143. North America defeated Venezuela 398-260; Netherlands 477-243; Thailand 359-234. Venezuela defeated Netherlands 331-247; Thailand 326-290. Netherlands defeated Thailand 293-230. ITALY: Walter Avarelli, Giorgio Belladonna, Massimo D'Alelio, Pietro Forquet, Benito Garozzo, Camillo Pabis Ticci, npc Carl'Alberto Perroux. NORTH AMERICA: Phil Feldesman, Robert Hamman, Sami Kehela, Lewis Mathe, Eric Murray, Ira Rubin, npc Julius Rosenblum.

1967. Played in Miami Beach. Italy defeated North America 338-227 in the final; in the playoff for third place France defeated Thailand 182-133. ITALY: Walter Avarelli, Giorgio Belladonna, Massimo D'Alelio, Pietro Forquet, Benito Garozzo, Camillo Pabis Ticci, npc Guido Barbone. NORTH AMERICA: Edgar Kaplan, Norman Kay, Sami Kehela, Eric Murray, William Root, Alvin Roth, npc Julius Rosenblum. FRANCE: Jean-Michel Boulenger, Jacques Pariente, Jean-Marc Roudinesco, Jacques Stetten, Henri Svarc, Leon Tintner, npc René Huni.

1969. Played in Rio de Janeiro. Italy defeated Chinese Taipei 429-182 in the final. In the playoff for third place North America defeated France 150-115. ITALY: Walter Avarelli, Giorgio Belladonna, Massimo D'Alelio, Pietro Forquet, Benito Garozzo, Camillo Pabis Ticci, npc Angelo Tracanella. CHINESE TAIPEI: Frank Huang, Patrick Huang, C.S. Shen, K.W. Shen, Kovit Suchartkul, M.F. Tai, npc C.C. Wei. NORTH AMERICA: William Eisenberg, Robert Goldman, Robert Hamman, Edwin Kantar, Sidney Lazard, George Rapee, npc Oswald Jacoby.

1970. Played in Stockholm. United States defeated Chinese Taipei 308-167. In the playoff for third place, Norway defeated Brazil 137-114. UNITED STATES: William Eisenberg, Robert Goldman, Robert Hamman, James Jacoby, Michael Lawrence, Robert Wolff, npc Oswald Jacoby. CHINESE TAIPEI: Conrad Cheng, Elmer Hsiao, Patrick Huang, Harry Lin, M.F. Tai, npc David Mao. NORWAY: Erik Hoie, Tore Jensen, Knut Koppans, Bjorn Larsen, Louis Andre Strom, Willy Varnas, npc Baard Baardsen.

1971. Played in Taipei. The Aces defeated France 243-181. In the playoff for third place, Australia defeated Chinese Taipei, 174-134. Brazil defeated North America in the clash for fifth place, 79-63. ACES: William Eisenberg. Robert Goldman, Robert Hamman, James Jacoby, Michael Lawrence, Robert Wolff, npc Oswald Jacoby. FRANCE: Jean-Michel Boulenger, Pierre Jaïs, Jean-Marc Roudinesco, Jean-Louis Stoppa, Henri Svarc, Roger Trezel, npc Rene Huni. AUSTRALIA: Jim Borin, Norma

Borin, Dick Cummings, Denis Howard, Tim Seres, Roelof Smilde, npc Jessel Rothfield.

1973. Played in Guaruja, Brazil. Italy defeated the Aces 333-205 IMPs. ITALY: Giorgio Belladonna, Benito Bianchi, Pietro Forquet, Benito Garozzo, Giuseppe Garabello, Vito Pittala, npc Sandro Salvetti. ACES: Mark Blumenthal, Robert Goldman, Robert Hamman, James Jacoby, Michael Lawrence, Robert Wolff, npc Ira G. Corn Jr.

1974. Played in Venice. Italy defeated North America 195-166. Brazil defeated Indonesia in the playoff for third place, 182-181. ITALY: Giorgio Belladonna, Benito Bianchi, Soldano de Falco, Pietro Forquet, Arturo Franco, Benito Garozzo, npc Sandro Salvetti. NORTH AMERICA: Mark Blumenthal, Robert Goldman, Robert Hamman, Sami Kehela, Eric Murray, Robert Wolff, npc Ira G. Corn Jr. BRAZIL: Pedro Paulo Assumpcao, Marcelo Branco, Pedro Branco, Gabriel Chagas, Gabino Cintra, Christiano Fonseca, npc Georges Vero.

1975. Played in Bermuda. Italy defeated North America 215-189 in the final. In the semifinals, Italy defeated Indonesia 280-134 and North America defeated France 159-147. ITALY: Giorgio Belladonna, Gianfranco Facchini, Arturo Franco, Benito Garozzo, Vito Pittala, Sergio Zucchelli, npc Sandro Salvetti. NORTH AMERICA: William Eisenberg, Robert Hamman, Edwin Kantar, Paul Soloway, John Swanson, Robert Wolff, npc Alfred Sheinwold. FRANCE: Jean-Michel Boulenger, Michel Lebel, Francois Leenhardt, Christian Mari, Henri Svarc, Edmond Vial, npc René Bacherich. INDONESIA: I. Arwin, Hengky Lasut, Frank Manoppo, M. Manoppo, W. Moniaga, Denny Sacul, npc O. Wullur.

1976. Played in Monte Carlo. North America defeated Italy 232-198 in the final. NORTH AMERICA: William Eisenberg, Fred Hamilton, Erik Paulsen, Hugh Ross, Ira Rubin, Paul Soloway, npc Dan Morse. ITALY: Giorgio Belladonna, Pietro Forquet, Benito Garozzo, Arturo Franco, Vito Pittala, Antonio Vivaldi, npc Sandro Salvetti.

1977. Played in Manila. The North American challengers defeated the North American defenders 245-214.5 in the final. NORTH AMERICA: William Eisenberg, Robert Hamman, Edwin Kantar, Paul Soloway, John Swanson, Robert Wolff, npc Roger Stern, Steve Altman (coach). DEFENDING CHAMPIONS: Fred Hamilton, Mike Passell, Erik Paulsen, Hugh Ross, Ira Rubin, Ron Von der Porten, npc Jerome Silverman, npc Ed Theus.

1979. Played in Rio de Janeiro. North America defeated Italy 253-248 in the final. NORTH AMERICA: Malcolm Brachman, William Eisenberg, Robert Goldman, Edwin Kantar, Mike Passell, Paul Soloway, npc Ed Theus. ITALY: Giorgio Belladonna, Soldano de Falco, Arturo Franco, Benito Garozzo, Lorenzo Lauria, Vito Pittala, npc Guido Barbone; npc Sandro Salvetti.

1981. Played in Port Chester, New York. United States defeated Pakistan 271-182$\frac{1}{2}$. In the semifinals United States defeated Poland 178-119; Pakistan beat Argentina 174-113/₃.UNITED STATES: Russ Arnold; Robert Levin, Jeff Meckstroth, A.E. (Bud) Reinhold, Eric Rodwell, John Solodar; npc Thomas K. Sanders. PAKISTAN: Nishat Abedi, Nisar Ahmed, Jan-e-Alam Fazli, Munir Ata-Ullah, Zia Mahmood, Masood Salim, npc Sattar Cochinwala. POLAND: Alexsander Jezioro, Julian Klukowski, Marek Kudla, Krzysztof Martens, Andrzej Milde, Tomasz Przybora, npc Marian Frenkiel. ARGENTINA: Gustavo Alujas, Luis Attaguile, Hector Camberos, Agustin Santamarina, Eduardo Scanavino, David Zanalda, npc Gonzalo Araujo.

1983. Played in Stockholm, Sweden. United States I defeated Italy 413-408. In the semifinals U.S. I defeated U.S. 2, 440-338; Italy beat France 346-335. Under the new Bermuda Bowl format, the No. 1 teams from both North America and Europe automatically advanced to the semifinals, while the No. 2 teams from those continents had to battle through the round-robin. France won the European Championship. U.S. I won the North American Team Trials. U.S. I: Michael Becker, Robert Hamman, Ron Rubin, Alan Sontag, Peter Weichsel, Bobby Wolff, npc Joe Musumeci. ITALY: Giorgio Belladonna, Dano DeFalco, Arturo Franco, Benito Garozzo, Lorenzo Lauria, Carlo Mosca, npc Filippo Palma. FRANCE: Phillippe Cronier, Michel Corn, Michel Lebel, Hervé Mouiel, Phillipe Soulet, Henri Szwarc, npc Pierre Schemeil. U.S. 2: Jim Jacoby, Jeff Meckstroth, Mike Passell, Eric Rodwell, George Rosenkranz, Eddie Wold, npc Jim Zimmerman.

1985. Played in Sao Paulo, Brazil. United States defeated European champion Austria 399-324. In the semifinals the U.S. defeated Brazil 351-342 and Austria defeated Israel 434-346. In the playoff for third place, Israel defeated Brazil 174-142. UNITED STATES: Bob Hamman, Bobby Wolff, Chip Martel, Hugh Ross, Lew Stansby, Peter Pender, npc Alfred Sheinwold. AUSTRIA: Heinrich Berger, Kurt Feichtinger, Jan Fucik, Wolfgang Meinl, Karl Rohan, Franz Terraneo, npc Franz Baratta. ISRAEL: David Birman, Julian Frydrich, Michael Hochzeit, Shmuel Lev, Shalom Zeligman, Eliakim Shaufel, npc Avrick Peleg.

1987. At Ocho Rios, Jamaica. In the final United States defeated Great Britain 354-290. In the semifinals United States defeated Chinese Taipei 421-290 and Great Britain defeated Sweden 358-311. UNITED STATES: Mike Lawrence, Hugh Ross, Bob Hamman, Lew Stansby, Bobby Wolff, Chip Martel, npc Dan Morse. GREAT BRITAIN: Tony Forrester, Graham Kirby, John Armstrong, Rob Sheehan, Jeremy Flint, Raymond Brock, npc Tony Priday. SWEDEN: Hans Gothe, Tommy Gullberg, Magnus Lindkvist, Bjorn Fallenius, Sven-Olov Flodqvist, P. O. Sundelin, npc P.D. Lindeberg. CHINESE TAIPEI: C.H. Wu, C.C. Chen, C.H. Kuo, M.F. Tai, Patrick Huang, C.S. Shen, npc Tony Chong.

1989. Played in Perth, West Australia. Brazil defeated U.S.A. 442-338 in the final. In the semifinals Brazil defeated Poland 369-327 and U.S.A. defeated Australia 387-327. BRAZIL: Gabriel Chagas, Marcelo Branco, Pedro Branco, Roberto Mello, Carlos Camacho, Ricardo Janz. UNITED STATES: Hugh Ross, Peter Pender, Chip Martel, Lew Stansby, Mike Lawrence, Kit Woolsey. POLAND: Cezary Balicki, Adam Zmudzinski, Krzysztof Moszczynski, Julian Klukowski, Krzysztof Martens, Marek Szymanowski. AUSTRALIA: Gaby Lorentz, John Lester, Ron Klinger, David Lilley, Paul Marston, Stephen Burgess.

1991. Played in Yokohama, Japan. Iceland defeated Poland 415-376 in the final. In the semifinals Iceland defeated Sweden 211-199 and Poland defeated Brazil 261-209. In the playoff for third place Sweden defeated Brazil 151-122. ICELAND: Orn Arnthorsson, Gudlaugur Johannsson, Gudmundur Arnarson, Thorlakur Jonsson, Jon Baldursson, Adalsteinn Jorgensen, npc Bjorn Eysteinsson. POLAND: Krzysztof Martens, Marek Szymanowski, Piotr Gawrys, Krzysztof Lasocki, Cezary Balicki, Adam Zmudzinski, npc Andrzej Orlow. SWEDEN: P. O. Sundelin, Tommy Gullberg, Bjorn Fallenius, Mats Nilsland, Anders Morath, Sven-Ake Bjerregard, npc Svante Ryman.

1993. Played in Santiago, Chile. Netherlands defeated Norway 350-316 in the final. In the semifinals Netherlands defeated USA II 202-199 and Norway defeated Brazil 208-205. NETHERLANDS: Bauke Muller, Wubbo deBoer, Piet Jansen, Jan Westerhof, Enri Leufkens, Berry Westra, npc Jaap Trouwborst. NORWAY: Glenn Groetheim, Terje Aa, Arild Rasmussen, Jon Sveindal, Geir Helgemo, Tor Helness, npc Runar Lillevik. UNITED STATES II: Cliff Russell, Sam Lev, David Berkowitz, Larry Cohen, Eric Rodwell, Marty Bergen, npc Bob Rosen. BRAZIL: Oliviera Barbosa, Marcelo Branco, Carlos Camacho, Pedro Paulo Branco, Gabriel Chagas, Roberto Mello, npc Pedro Paulo Assumpçao.

1995. Played in Beijing, China. United States defeated Canada, 339-296. United States: Bob Hamman, Bobby Wolff, Jeff Meckstroth, Eric Rodwell, Richard Freeman, Nick Nickell, Edgar Kaplan npc. Canada: Joey Silver, Eric Kokish, Mark Molson, Fred Gitelman, George Mittelman, Boris Baran, Irving Litvack, npc.

1997. Played in Hammamet, Tunisia. France defeated United States, 327-301. France: Paul Chemla, Michel Perron, Alain Levy, Herve Mouiel, Christian Mari, Frank Multon, Jean-Louis Stoppa npc. United States: Bob Hamman, Bobby Wolff, Jeff Meckstroth, Eric Rodwell, Richard Freeman, Nick Nickell. Norway won the bronze medal: Geir Helgemo, Boye Brogeland, Erik Saelensminde, Tor Helness, Glenn Groetheim, Terje Aa, Einar Brenne, npc.

1999. Played in Bermuda in January 2000. United States defeated Brazil, 506-288. United States: Bob Hamman, Paul Soloway, Eric Rodwell, Jeff Meckstroth, Richard Freeman, Nick Nickell, Sidney Lazard npc. Brazil: Gabriel Chagas, Marcelo Branco, Miguel Villas-Boas, Joao Paulo Campos, Ricardo Janz, Roberto Mello, Pedro-Paulo Assumpcao, npc. United States won the bronze medal: Zia Mahmood, Chip Martel, Michael Rosenberg, Neil Silverman, Lew Stansby, Jeff Wolfson, Michael Becker npc.

OPEN TEAM OLYMPIAD

WINNERS	RUNNERS-UP
1960 Turin, Italy	
FRANCE (16 V.P.)	GREAT BRITAIN (15 V.P.)
Pierre Jais	Terence Reese
Roger Trezel	Boris Schapiro
Gerard Bourchtoff	Albert Rose
Claude Delmouly	Nico Gardener
Rene Bacherich	Jeremy Flint
Pierre Ghestem	Ralph Swimer
Baron Robert de Nexon (npc)	Louis Tarlo (npc)
1964 New York, USA	
ITALY	UNITED STATES
Walter Avarelli	Robert Hamman
Giorgio Belladonna	Robert Jordan
Massimo d'Alelio	Donald Krauss
Pietro Forquet	Victor Mitchell
Benito Garozzo	Arthur Robinson
Camillo Pabis Ticci	Samuel Stayman
Sergio Osella (npc)	Frank Westcott (npc)
1968 Deauville, France	
ITALY	UNITED STATES
Walter Avarelli	Robert Jordan
Giorgio Belladonna	Edgar Kaplan
Massimo d'Alelio	Norman Kay
Pietro Forquet	Arthur Robinson
Benito Garozzo	William Root
Camillo Pabis Ticci	Alvin Roth
Angelo Tracanella (npc)	Julius Rosenblum (npc)
1972 Miami Beach, Florida, USA	
ITALY	UNITED STATES
Walter Avarelli	Bobby Goldman
Pietro Forquet	Jim Jacoby
Massimo d'Alelio	Robert Hamman
Benito Garozzo	Paul Soloway
Giorgio Belladonna	Mike Lawrence
Camillo Pabis Ticci	Bobby Wolff
Umberto Barsotti (npc)	Lee Hazen (npc)
1976, Monte Carlo	
BRAZIL	ITALY
Gabino Cintra	Giorgio Belladonna
Christiano Fonseca	Pietro Forquet
Marcelo Branco	Benito Garozzo
Pedro Paulo Assumpcao	Arturo Franco
Gabriel Chagas	Carlo Mosca
Sergio Barbosa	Silvio Sbarigia
Serge Apoteker (npc)	Sandro Salvetti (npc)
1980, Valkenburg, The Netherlands	
FRANCE	UNITED STATES
Paul Chemla	Paul Soloway
Christian Mari	Ira Rubin
Michel Lebel	Robert Hamman
Michel Perron	Bobby Wolff
Henri Svarc	Fred Hamilton
Philippe Soulet	Mike Passell
	Ira Corn (npc)
1984 Seattle, Washington, USA	
POLAND	FRANCE
Jacek Romanski	Paul Chemla
Krzysztof Martens	Michel Perron
Tomasz Przybora	Herve Mouiel
Piotr Gawrys	Henri Szwarc
Piotr Tuszynski	Fivo Paladimo
Marian Trnkiel (npc)	Felix Covo
	Pierre Schemeil (npc)
1988 Venice, Italy	
UNITED STATES	AUSTRIA
Seymon Deutsch	Heinrich Berger
Jeff Meckstroth	Jan Fucik
Eric Rodwell	Alfred Kadlec
Bob Hamman	Friedrick Kubac
Jim Jacoby	Wolfgang Meinl
Bobby Wolff	Franz Terranao
Dan Morse (npc)	Franz Baratta (npc)
1992 Salsomaggiore, Italy	
FRANCE	UNITED STATES
Paul Chemla	Bob Hamman
Michel Perron	Bobby Wolff
Herve Mouiel	Jeff Meckstroth
Alain Levy	Eric Rodwell
Pierre Adad	Michael Rosenberg
Maurice Aujaleu	Seymon Deutch
Jose Damiani (npc)	Dan Morse (npc)

1996 Rhodes, Greece

FRANCE	INDONESIA
Christian Mari	Henky Lasut
Frank Multon	Denny Sacul
Alain Levy	Eddy Manoppo
Herve Mouiel	Franky Karwur
Henri Szwarc	Giovanni Watulingas
Marc Bompis	Sance Panelewen

2000 Maastricht, the Netherlands

ITALY	POLAND
Norberto Bocchi	Cezary Balicki
Giorgio Duboin	Krzysztof Jassem
Dano DeFalco	Michal Kwiecien
Guido Ferraro	Jacek Pszczola
Lorenzo Lauria	Piotr Tuszynski
Alfredo Versace	Adam Zmudzinski
Carlo Mosca, npc	Jan Rogowski, npc

VENICE CUP

1974. Played in Venice, Italy. United States defeated Italy 297-262. UNITED STATES: Bette Cohn, Emma Jean Hawes, Betty Ann Kennedy, Marietta Passell, Carol Sanders, Dorothy Hayden Truscott, npc Ruth McConnell. ITALY: Marisa Bianchi, Luciana Canessa, Rina Jabes, Antonietta Robaudo, Anna Valenti, Maria Venturini, npc Giovannl Pelucchi.

1976. Played in Monte Carlo. United States defeated Great Britain 395-211. UNITED STATES: Emma Jean Hawes, Betty Ann Kennedy, Jacqui Mitchell, Gail Moss, Carol Sanders, Dorothy Hayden Truscott, npc Ruth McConnell, Peter Pender (coach). GREAT BRITAIN: Charley Esterson, Nicola Gardener, Fritzi Gordon, Sandra Landy, Rixi Markus, Rita Oldroyd, npc Graham Cooke.

1978. Played in New Orleans, Louisiana. In the final the United States defeated Italy 229 1/2-140. UNITED STATES: Mary Jane Farell, Emma Jean Hawes, Marilyn Johnson, Jacqui Mitchell, Gail Moss, Dorothy Hayden Truscott, npc Ruth McConnell. ITALY: Marisa Bianchi, Luciana Capodanno, Marisa D'Andrea, Enrica Gut, Andreina Morini, Anna Valenti, npc Guido Barbone.

1981. Played in Port Chester, New York. In the final Great Britain defeated the United States, 160 2/3-122. GREAT BRITAIN: Pat Davies, Maureen Dennison, Nicola Gardener, Sandra Landy, Sally Sowter, Diana Williams, npc Derek Rimington. UNITED STATES: Nancy Gruver, Edith Kemp, Betty Ann Kennedy, Judi Radin, Carol Sanders, Kathie Wei, npc C.C. Wei, coach Ron Andersen.

1985. Played in Sao Paulo, Brazil. In the final Great Britain defeated United States I 323-213. In the semifinals U.S. I defeated Chinese Taipei 342-246 and Great Britain defeated France 276-241. In the playoff for third place, France defeated Chinese Taipei 188-149. GREAT BRITAIN: Sandra Landy, Sally Horton, Pat Davies, Nicola Smith, Gillian Scott-Jones, Michelle Brunner, npc Grattan Endicott. UNITED STATES I: Gail Greenberg, Kathie Wei, Betty Ann Kennedy, Carol Sanders, Judi Radin, Jacqui Mitchell, npc Dan Morse. FRANCE: Veronique Bessis, Danielle Gaviard, Ginette Chevalley, Fabienne Pigeaud, Catherine Saul, Sylvie Willard, npc Alain Lévy.

1987. Played in Ocho Rios, Jamaica. In the final United States II defeated France 251-219. In the semifinals U.S. II defeated U.S. I 277-251 and France defeated Italy 276-227. UNITED STATES II: Kathie Wei, Judi Radin, Juanita Chambers, Cheri Bjerkan, Beth Palmer, Lynn Deas, npc Carol Sanders. FRANCE: Veronique Bessis, Helene Bordenave, Sylvie Willard, Benedicte Cronier, Danielle Gaviard, Ginette Chevalley, npc Gerard LeRoyer. ITALY: Luciana Capodanno, Marisa D'Andrea, Carla Gianardi, Marisa Bianchi, Anna Valenti, Gabriella Olivieri, npc Guido Resta. UNITED STATES I: Jo Morse, Sue Sachs, Cindy Bernstein, Sharon Osberg, Peggy Sutherlin, Sally Wheeler, npc John Sutherlin.

1989. Played in Perth, West Australia. U.S.A. defeated the Netherlands 353-319 in the final. In the semifinals U.S.A. defeated Canada 344.5-197.5 and Netherlands defeated Germany 310-289. UNITED STATES: Beth Palmer, Lynn Deas, Kitty Bethe, Margie Gwozdzinsky, Karen McCallum, Kerri Shuman, npc Dorothy Truscott. NETHERLANDS: Ellen Bakker, Ina Gielkens, Carla Arnolds, Bep Vriend, Marijke van der Pas, Elly Schippers. CANADA: Dianna Gordon, Sharyn Reus, Mary Paul, Francine Cimon, Gloria Silverman, Katie Thorpe. GERMANY:

Sabine Zenkel, Daniela von Arnim, Waltraud Vogt, Kareen Schroeder, Karin Caesar, Marianne Moegel.

1991. Played in Yokohama, Japan. USA II defeated Austria 360-258 in the final. In the semifinals USA II defeated USA I 219-125 and Austria defeated China 254-166. UNITED STATES II: Lynn Deas, Stasha Cohen, Sharon Osberg, Sue Picus, Nell Cahn, Nancy Passell, npc Kathie Wei. AUSTRIA: Maria Erhart, Gabriele Bamberger, Doris Fischer, Terry Weigkricht, Britta Widengren, Rosi Spinn, npc Ernst Pichler. UNITED STATES I: Juanita Chambers, Cheri Bjerkan, Kay Schulle, Jill Meyers, Pam Wittes, Randi Montin, npc Ron Andersen. CHINA: Gu Ling, Zhang Yalan, Wang Ping, Shi Shaomin, Sun Ming, Liu Yiquian, npc Yi Hougao.

1993. Played in Santiago, Chile. USA II defeated Germany 304.5-240 in the final. In the semifinals USA II defeated Argentina 333.5-180 and Germany defeated Sweden 257-237. UNITED STATES II: Kay Schulle, Jill Meyers, Kerri Sanborn, Karen McCallum, Sue Picus, Sharon Osberg, npc Jo Morse. GERMANY: Daniela von Arnim, Sabine Zenkel, Karin Caesar, Marianne Moegel, Beate Nehmert, Waltraud Vogt, npc Klaus Reps. ARGENTINA: Ana Blum, Marta Tiscornia, Marta Matienzo, Marilyn Hernandez, Christina Suaya, Gloria Rosenfeld, npc Gonzalo Valenzuela. SWEDEN: Linda Langstrom, Catharina Midskog, Pyttsi Flodqvist, Mari Ryman, Bim Odlund, Lisbeth Astrom, npc Kerstin Strandberg.

1995. Played in Beijing, China. Germany defeated United States, 312-248. Germany: Daniela von Arnim, Sabine Auken, Karin Caesar, Marianne Moegel, Pony Nehmert, Andrea Rauscheid, Klaus Reps npc. United States: Karen McCallum, Kerri Sanborn, Kitty Munson, Carol Simon, Sue Picus, Rozanne Pollack, Steve Sanborn npc.

1997. Played in Hammamet, Tunisia. United States defeated China, 249-184. United States: Jill Meyers, Randi Montin, Tobi Sokolow, Mildred Breed, Marinesa Letizia, Lisa Berkowitz, Sue Picus npc. China: Sun Ming, Gu Ling, Lu Yan, Zhang Yalan, Zhang Yu, Wang Wenfei, Harry Lin npc. USA II won the bronze medal: Sue Sachs (npc), Kathie Wei-Sender, Kerri Sanborn, Irina Levitina, Juanita Chambers, Beth Palmer, Lynn Deas.

1999. Played in Bermuda in January 2000. Netherlands defeated United States, 249.75-249.25. Netherlands: Jet Pasman, Anneke Simons, Bep Vriend, Marijke van der Pas, Wietske Van Zwol, Martine Verbeek, Ed Franken npc. United States: Renee Mancuso, Jill Meyers, Randi Montin, Shawn Quinn, Janice Season-Molson, Tobi Sokolow, Jo Morse npc. Denmark won the bronze medal: Dorte Cilleborg, Mette Drogmuller, Bettina Kalkerup, Charlotte Koch-Palmund, Trine Bilde Kofoed, Kirsten Steen Moeller, Lotte Skaaning-Norris npc.

WOMEN'S TEAM OLYMPIAD

1960 Turin, Italy	1972 Miami Beach, Florida
UNITED ARAB	ITALY
REPUBLICS	Anna Valenti
Helen Camara	Marisa Bianchi
Aida Choucry	Rina Jabes
Samika Fathy	Antonietta Robaudo
Loula Gordon	Luciana Romanelli
Josephine Morcos	Maria Venturini
Suzanne Naguib	Giovanni Pelucchi (npc)
Sergio de Polo (npc)	

1964 New York City	1976 Monte Carlo
GREAT BRITAIN	ITALY
Irene (Dimmie) Fleming	Anna Valenti
Fritzi Gordon	Rina Jabes
Jane Juan	Maria Rabaudo
Rixi Markus	Luciana Capodanno
Mary Moss	Marisa D'Andrea
Dorothy Shanahan	Marisa Bianchi
Harold Franklin (npc)	Giovanni Pelucchi (npc)

1968 Deauville, France	1980 Valkenburg, the Netherlands
SWEDEN	UNITED STATES
Britt Blom	Dorothy Hayden Truscott
Karin Eriksson	Emma Jean Hawes
Eva Martensson	Gail Moss
Rut Segander	Jacqui Mitchell
Gunborg Silborn	Mary Jane Farell
Britta Werner	Marilyn Johnson
Lotty Saabye (npc)	Ruth McConnell (npc)

1984 Seattle, Washington

WINNERS	RUNNERS-UP
UNITED STATES	GREAT BRITAIN
Gail Moss	Nicola Smith
Judi Radin	Pat Davies
Kathie Wei	Sally Horton
Betty Ann Kennedy	Sandra Landy
Carol Sanders	Sarah Scarborough
Jacqui Mitchell	Gillian Scott-Jones
Jim Zimmerman (npc)	Hugh Kelsey (npc)

1988 Venice, Italy

DENMARK	GREAT BRITAIN
Kristin Moeller	Elizabeth McGowan
Dorthe Schaltz	Sandra Penfold
Bettina Kalkerup	Michelle Brunner
Charlotte Palmund	Nicola Smith
Trine Dahl	Pat Davies
Judy Norris	Sandra Landy
Inger Lindegaard, npc	Grattan Endicott (npc)

1992 Salsomaggiore, Italy

AUSTRIA	GREAT BRITAIN
Terry Weigkricht	Pat Davies
Doris Fischer	Michelle Handley
Maria Erhart	Sandra Landy
Barbara Lindinger	Elizabeth McGowan
Jovanka Smederevac	Sandra Penfold
Herta Gyimesi	Nicola Smith
	Mark Horton (npc)

1996 Rhodes, Greece

UNITED STATES	CHINA
Gail Greenberg	Gu Ling
Jill Levin	Zhang Yalan
Irina Levitina	Sun Ming
Shawn Quinn	Wang Hongli
Lynn Deas	Wang Wenfei
Juanita Chambers	Zhang Yu
Eddie Wold, npc	Zhang Weili, npc

2000 Maastricht, the Netherlands

UNITED STATES	CANADA
Mildred Breed	Francine Cimon
Petra Hamman	Dianna Gordon
Joan Jackson	Rhoda Habert
Robin Klar	Beverly Kraft
Shawn Quinn	Martine LaCroix
Peggy Sutherlin	Katie Thorpe

ROSENBLUM CUP TEAMS

1978 Played in New Orleans, Louisiana. Poland defeated Brazil 164-80.

POLAND	BRAZIL
Marian Frenkiel	Gabriel Chagas
Andrzej Macieszczak	Pedro Paulo Assumpcao
Andrezej Wilkosz	Gabino Cintra
Janusz Polec	Marcelo Branco
	Roberto Taunay
	Sergio Barbosa

1982 Played in Biarritz, France. France defeated the United States 178-161.

FRANCE	UNITED STATES
Michel Lebel	Chip Martel
Philippe Soulet	Lew Stansby
Dominique Pilon	Peter Pender
Albert Feigenbaum	Hugh Ross
Pierre Schemeil (npc)	Kit Woolsey
	Ed Manfield

1986 Played in Miami Beach, Florida. United States defeated Pakistan, 357-207.

UNITED STATES	PAKISTAN
Neil Silverman	Nishat Abedi
Ed Manfield	Nisar Ahmed
Peter Boyd	Zia Mahmood
Steve Robinson	Jan-e-Alam Fazli
Bob Lipsitz	
Kit Woolsey	

1990 Played in Geneva, Switzerland. Germany defeated United States, 145-132.

GERMANY	UNITED STATES
Bernhard Ludwig	Mike Moss
Jochen Bitschene	Charles Coon
Georg Nippgen	Michael Seamon
Roland Rohowsky	Drew Casen

1994

UNITED STATES	POLAND
Seymon Deutsch	Erwin Otvosi
Chip Martel	Marek Borewicz
Lew Stansby	Krzyzstof Lasocki
Gaylor Kasle	Piotr Gawrys
Roger Bates	Cezary Balicki
Michael Rosenberg	Adam Zmudzinski

1998

ITALY	BRAZIL
Antonio Sementa	Gabriel Chagas
Alfredo Versace	Marcelo Branco
Andrea Buratti	Miguel Vilas Boas
Lorenzo Lauria	Joao Paulo Campos
Massimo Lanzarotti	
Francesco Angelini	

McCONNELL WOMEN'S TEAMS

1994

UNITED STATES	UNITED STATES
Marinesa Letizia	Sally Woolsey
Sue Picus	JoAnn Manfield
Judi Radin	Dori Cohen
Rozanne Pollack	Joann Glasson
Jillian Levin	Karen Allison
	JoAnne Casen

1998

AUSTRIA	GERMANY
Maria Erhart	Sabine Auken
Doris Fischer	Daniela von Arnim
Terri Weigkricht	Barbara Stawowy
Sylvia Terraneo	Katrin Farwig

WORLD OPEN PAIRS

	Winners	Runners-up
1962	FRANCE	GREAT BRITAIN
	Pierre Jais	Terence Reese
	Roger Trezel	Boris Schapiro
1966	NETHERLANDS	UNITED STATES
	Bob Slavenburg	Dr. John Fisher
	Hans Kreyns	James Jacoby
1970	AUSTRIA	ITALY
	Fritz Babsch	Benito Garozzo
	Peter Manhardt	Frederico Mayer
1974	UNITED STATES	ITALY
	Robert Hamman	Leandro Burgay
	Bobby Wolff	Antonio Abato
1978	BRAZIL	CANADA
	Marcelo Branco	Eric Kokish
	Gabino Cintra	Peter Nagy
1982	UNITED STATES	THE NETHERLANDS
	Chip Martel	Max Rebattu
	Lew Stansby	Anton Maas
1986	UNITED STATES	AUSTRIA
	Eric Rodwell	Heinrich Berger
	Jeff Meckstroth	Wolfgang Meinl
1990	BRAZIL	UNITED STATES
	Gabriel Chagas	Ralph Katz
	Marcela Branco	Peter Nagy
1994	POLAND	UNITED STATES
	Marcin Lesniewski	Bob Hamman
	Marek Szymanowski	Michael Rosenberg
1998	POLAND	UNITED STATES
	Michal Kwiecien	Larry Cohen
	Jacek Pszczola	David Berkowitz

WORLD WOMEN'S PAIRS

	Winners	Runners-up
1962	GREAT BRITAIN	FRANCE
	Rixi Markus	Fanny Pariente
	Fritzi Gordon	C. Serf
1966	GREAT BRITAIN	UNITED STATES
	Joan Durran	Sue Sachs
	Jane Juan	Nancy Gruver
1970	UNITED STATES	GREAT BRITAIN
	Mary Jane Farell	Rixi Markus
	Marilyn Johnson	Fritzi Gordon
1974	GREAT BRITAIN	SOUTH AFRICA
	Fritzi Gordon	Gerda Goslar
	Rixi Markus	Rita Jacobson
1978	UNITED STATES	UNITED STATES
	Kathie Wei	Betty Ann Kennedy
	Judi Radin	Carol Sanders

1982	UNITED STATES	UNITED STATES
	Carol Sanders	Lynn Deas
	Betty Ann Kennedy	Beth Palmer
1986	UNITED STATES	DENMARK
	Amalya Kearse	Charlotte Palmund
	Jacqui Mitchell	Bettina Kalkerup
1990	UNITED STATES	UNITED STATES
	Kerri Shuman	Kathie Wei
	Karen McCallum	Judi Radin
1994	NETHERLANDS	FRANCE
	Bep Vriend	Veronique Bessis
	Carla Arnolds	Catherine Saul
1998	UNITED STATES	GERMANY
	Jill Meyers	Sabine Auken
	Shawn Quinn	Daniela von Arnim

WORLD MIXED PAIRS

	Winners	Runners-up
1966	UNITED STATES	GREAT BRITAIN
	Mary Jane Farell	Joan Durran
	Ivan Erdos	Maurice Weissberger
1970	UNITED STATES	GREAT BRITAIN
	Barbara Brier	Rixi Markus
	Waldemar von Zedwitz	Georges Catzeflis
1974	SWITZERLAND	UNITED STATES
	Loula Gordon	Jacqui Mitchell
	Tony Trad	James Cayne
1978	UNITED STATES	UNITED STATES
	Barry Crane	James Jacoby
	Kerri Shuman	Heitie Noland
1982	CANADA	UNITED STATES
	Dianna Gordon	Peggy Sutherlin
	George Mittelman	John Sutherlin
1986	UNITED STATES	UNITED STATES
	Pam Wittes	Bob Hamman
	Jon Wittes	Kerri Shuman
1990	UNITED STATES	SWEDEN
	Juanita Chambers	Lars Andersson
	Peter Weichsel	Eva-Liss Gothe
1994	POLAND	GERMANY-USA
	Danuta Hocheker	Sabine Zenkel
	Apolinare Kowalski	Bob Hamman
1998	ITALY	FRANCE
	Antonio Vivaldi	Claude Blouquit
	Enza Rossano	Marc Bompis

WORLD MIXED TEAMS

1962	GREAT BRITAIN	THE NETHERLANDS
	Rixi Markus	Mme. Westerfield
	Fritzi Gordon	Mme. Hoogenkamp
	Boris Schapiro	Herman Filarski
	Nico Gardener	A. Kornlijnsliper
1974	UNITED STATES	UNITED STATES
	Jo Morse	Tubby Stayman
	Steve Robinson	Vic Mitchell
	Steve Parker	Jacqui Mitchell
	Bob Lipsitz	James Cayne
	Peggy Lipsitz	Matt Granovetter

WORLD IMP PAIRS

1998	UNITED STATES	FRANCE
	Michael Seamon	D. Masure
	Russ Ekeblad	M. Leflon

TRANSNATIONAL WORLD SENIOR TEAMS

1994. 1. Karl Rohan, Franz Baratta, Austria; Nissan Rand, Moshe Katz, Israel; Kees Kaiser, Bob Kaiser, The Netherlands; 2. Mike Levine, Zeke Jabbour, Bill Eisenberg, Tom Sanders, Russ Arnold, Fred Hamilton, United States
1998. 1. Karl Rohan, Franz Baratta, Austria; Nissan Rand, Moshe Katz, Israel; Christo Drumev, Bulgaria; 2. Szenberg, Klukowski, Wilkosz, Jezioro, Poland
2000:. 1. United States: John Mohan, John Sutherlin, Steve Robinson, Kit Woolsey, Dan Morse, Bobby Wolff; 2. France: F. Leenhardt, Christian Mari, Claude Delmouly, Jean-Marc Roudinesco, Z. Janza, M. Polak

TRANSNATIONAL OPEN TEAMS

1997. 1. Leandro Burgay, Dano DeFalco, Franco Mariani, Italy; Marcin Lesniewski, Krzyzstof Martens, Poland. 2. Tomasz Przybora, Jacek Pszczola, Michael Kwiecin, Gardynik Jasem, Tuszynski
2000. 1. Rose Meltzer, Peter Weichsel, Alan Sontag, United States; Adam Zmudzinski, Cezary Balicki, Poland; 2, Reese Milner, Robert Levin, Marc Jacobus, Brad Moss, United States; Fred Gitelman, Canada.

TRANSNATIONAL MIXED TEAMS

1996. 1. Heather Dhondy, England; Elizabeth McGowan, Scotland; Jon Baldursson, Adalsteinn Jorgensen, Bjorn Eysteinsson, Ragnar Hermansson, Iceland. 2. Mark Feldman, Sharon Osberg, Bill Pollack, Rozanne Pollack, United States.
2000. 1. e-bridge: Jill Meyers, Irina Levitina, Sam Lev, John Mohan, USA; Migry Tzur-Campanile, Israel; Piotr Gawrys, Poland; 2. France: Michel Bessis, Veronique Bessis, Catherine D'Ovidio, Paul Chemla

TRANSNATIONAL WOMEN'S TEAMS

2000. 1. Dorthy Francis, Sharon Jabbour, Lynn Deas, Beth Palmer, Jeannie Fisher, Hjordis Eythorsdottir, United States.

TRANSNATIONAL SENIOR PAIRS

1990. 1. Albert Dormer, Great Britain; Alan Hiron, Spain
1994. 1. Hamish Bennett, Fred Hamilton, United States; 2. Simon Kantar, Murray Melton, United States
1998. 1. Boris Shapiro, Irving Gordon, England; 2. Benito Garozzo, Lea Dupont, United States
2000. 1. Andrzej Milde, Poland, and Hans Humberg, Germany; 2, Charles Schutte and Ad Oskam, Netherlands

WORLD SENIORS EXHIBITION

2000. 1. Poland: Janusz Nowak, Aleksander Jezioro, Julian Klukowski, Stefan Szenberg, \andrzej Wilkosz, Jan Prochowski, npc. 2. France: Pierre Adad, Maurice Aujaleu, Claude Delmouly, Jean-Marc Roudinesco

WORLD JUNIOR TEAMS

1987	Amsterdam, Netherlands

Netherlands — Wubbo de Boer, Marcel Nooyen, Berry Westra, Enri Leufkens

1989 Nottingham, England

England — John Pottage, Andy Robson, Derrick Patterson, John Hobson, Gerald Tredinnick, Stuart Tredinnick

1991 Ann Arbor MI, USA

United States — John Diamond, Jeff Ferro, Martha Benson (Katz), Brian Platnick, Wayne Stuart, Debbie Zuckerberg

1993 Arhus, Denmark

Germany — Klaus Reps, Markus Joest, Guido Hopfenheit, Roland Rohowsky

1995 Bali, Indonesia

Great Britain — Justin Hackett, Jason Hackett, Jeff Allerton, Danny Davies, Phil Souter, Tom Townsend

1997 Hamilton, Ontario, Canada

Denmark — Freddi Brøndum, Mik Kristensen, Lars Lund Madsen, Morten Lund Madsen, Mikkel Bensby Nohr, Jacob Røn

1999 Fort Lauderdale, Florida, USA

Italy — Bernardo Biondo, Riccardo Intonti, Mario d'Avossa, Matteo Mallardi

WORLD JUNIOR PAIRS

1995 Boye Brogeland-Geir Helgemo, Norway
1997 Solbrandt-O. Wademack, Sweden
1999 A. Gloyer-B. Saura, Austria

UNIVERSITY TEAMS

2000 Austria: Bernd Saurer, Arno Lindermann, Andreas Gloyr, Martin Schifko, Hamelone Thomasberger npc

WORLD JUNIOR TRIATHLON

1998 Overall: ITALY – Paolo Marino tied with Daniele Pagani
Teams: ITALY – Riccardo Intonti, Paolo Marino, Daniele Pagani, Medusei
Pairs: POLAND – T. Przyjemski, M. Zaremba
Individual: POLAND – R. Jagniewski

ZONAL MIXED PAIRS

1994 UNITED STATES – Garey Hayden, Barbara Kasle
1998 FRANCE – Isabelle Chilaud, Jacques Chilaud

EARLY CHAMPIONSHIPS

1935 (the first official meeting between the champions of Europe and the American Bridge League.) The UNITED STATES defeated FRANCE by 2,810 points over 300 boards.

UNITED STATES	FRANCE
David Burnstine	Pierre Albarran
Michael Gottlieb	Baron Robert de Nexon
Oswald Jacoby	M. Georges Rousset
Howard Schenken	Emanuel Tulumaris

1937 (under the auspices of the International Bridge League) Budapest, Hungary, AUSTRIA defeated UNITED STATES by 4,740 points.

AUSTRIA	UNITED STATES
Karl von Bluhdorn	Ely Culbertson
Dr. Edward Frischauer	Josephine Culbertson
Walter Herbert	Helen Sobel
Hans Jellinek	Charles C. Vogelhofer
Udo von Meissel	
Karl Schneider	
Dr. Paul Stern (npc)	

WOMEN'S WINNERS

AUSTRIA	
Mariane Boschan	Lisi Klauber
Gertrude Brunner	Rixi Markus
Ethel Ernst	Ditta Riemer
Gretl Joseffy	Gertrude Schlesinger

B I B L I O G R A P H Y

KEY: Many thousands of books have been written on bridge. This bibliography attempts to list these books under 29 subdivisions. In each category the books are listed alphabetically by author.

A HISTORY (Bridge Whist)
B HISTORY (Auction Bridge)
C HISTORY (contract Bridge, non-Vanderbilt scoring)
D HISTORY (Auction and Contract Bridge)
E MATERIAL FOR NEWCOMERS
F TEACHER'S MATERIAL
G BIDDING SYSTEMS
H SUMMARIES OF BIDDING SYSTEMS BOOKS AND POPULAR SYSTEMS
I BIDDING CONVENTIONS AND TREATMENTS
J COMPETITIVE BIDDING
K HAND EVALUATION, BIDDING PRINCIPLES, BIDDING THEORY AND SPECIAL SITUATIONS
L BIDDING PRACTICE AND QUIZZES
M PLAY (including play and defense)
N BIDDING AND PLAY PLUS GENERAL DISCUSSION OF GAME
O PROBLEMS AND QUIZZES AT LEAST PARTLY ON PLAY (including Par hands)

P DEFENSE, LEADS AND SIGNALS
Q POETRY, HUMOR AND WHIMSY
R COLLECTIONS OF COLUMNS, ARTICLES, TIPS, HANDS AND HANDS PLAYED
S TOURNAMENT BRIDGE (including direction, organization and replaying of hands)
T RUBBER BRIDGE
U BIBLIOGRAPHIES, DICTIONARIES AND ENCYCLOPEDIAS
V LAWS AND THEIR INTERPRETATION
W HISTORY AND BIOGRAPHY
X ANNOTATED HAND RECORDS AND REPORTS ON TOURNAMENTS
Y MATHEMATICS AND ODDS
Z FICTION AND NOVELS
AA MEMORY
BB VARIATIONS OF CONTRACT BRIDGE
CC COOKING AND BRIDGE

Books of historic significance and books of importance for the purposes of a modern technical bridge library have been separately identified as follows:

* Books marked thus made a major contribution to the technical development of the game.

† Books marked thus are optional requirements for a modern technical bridge library

‡ Books marked thus are mandatory requirements for a modern technical bridge library.

AUTHOR	TITLE	PUBLISHER	YEAR	PAGES

A. HISTORICAL – BRIDGE WHIST

Title	(Publisher, Year, Pages)			
Ace	Bridge And Whist *(Fox, 1906, 127p.)*			
Ace Of Spades	Epitome Of Bridge *(Webster, 1903, 6p.)*			
Ace Of Spades	Rules For Playing Bridge Whist *(Woolley, 1903, 3p.)*			
Ace Of Spades	The Theory And Practice Of Bridge *(Times Of India, 1903, 75p.)*			
Agacy, H A	Correct Bridge, Or How To Play To The Best Advantage *(Simpkin, Marshall, 1905-06, 99p.)*			
Allen, Bessie E	Bridge Talks *(Burdick & Allen, 1907, 108p.)*			
Ames, Fisher	Bridge Whist In Brief *(Carter, 1904, 54p.)*			
Ames, Fisher	The Game Of Bridge *(Little Brown, 1906, 190p.)*			
Anonymous	"Myskore" Bridge Table *(Private, 1902, 1p.)*			
Anonymous	A Guide To The Game Of Bridge *(Norman & Stacey, 1903, 43p.)*			
Anonymous	Bridge *(Johnson Bros, 1907, 8p.)*			
Anonymous	Bridge And Progressive Bridge *(The International Card Co, 1904, 31p.)*			
Anonymous	Bridge Hints *(Goodall, 1906, 6p.)*			
Anonymous	Bridge Or Bridge Whist, Pocket Guide *(Ayres, 1903, 8p.)*			
Anonymous	Bridge Rules *(The International Card Co, 1903, 16p.)*			
Anonymous	Progressive Bridge (Rules) *(Anti-Rheu-Gem, 1903, 1p.)*			
Anonymous	The Laws Of Bridge (1902) *(U S Playing Card Co, 1902, 9p.)*			
Anonymous	The Laws Of Bridge (1905) *(Mudie, 1905, 27p.)*			
Argus	Bridge Rhymes For Beginners *(Glaisher, 1904, 2p.)*			
Association Of U.S. Clubs	The American Laws Of Bridge *(Scribner, 1902-05, 37- 39p.)*			
Atchison, George T & Lindsell, Arthur J	The Why And Wherefore Of Bridge *(Longmans Green, 1905, 113p.)*			
Atherton, George E	Bridge Up-to-Date *(Private, 1905, ?p.)*			
Avery, Mabel Allen	Mother Goose On Bridge *(Lyman Bros, 1909, 79p.)*			
Ayres, Steven B	Bridge *(Brentano's, 1909, 125p.)*			
Badsworth	A Defence Of Bridge *(Putnam's, 1904, 16p.)*			
Badsworth	Badsworth On Bridge *(Putnam's, 1903-09, 283p.)*			
Badsworth & Boaz	The Laws Of Bridge And A Guide To The Game By Boaz And How To Play Bridge By Badsworth *(De La Rue, 1895-1905, 39p.)*			
Barbey, Henry	*A Short Precis Of The Game *(Private, 1892, ?p.)*			
Barton, Frederick P	Bridge Simplified, With Remarks On The New Laws *(Simpkin, Marshall, 1905, 105p.)*			
Bassett, Sare Ware	Mrs. Christy's Bridge Party *(Private, 1907, 31p.)*			

AUTHOR	TITLE
Beasley, Col. H M	*London Bridge And How It Is Played *(Heinemann, 1905, 132p.)*
Beekay	Bridge In Brief, With Advanced Hints *(Simkin Marshall/Mudie, 1911, 21p.)*
Bergholt, Ernest	Double Dummy Bridge *(Thos. De La Rue, 1906, 150p.)*
Bergholt, Ernest	On The Cards To Lead At Bridge *(Tollitt & Harvey, 1902, 8p.)*
Bergholt, Ernest	The Leads At Bridge *(Tollitt & Harvey, 1901, 4p.)*
Bergholt, Ernest	The Original Lead At Bridge *(Tollitt & Harvey, 1901-02, 4-8p.)*
Bergholt, Ernest & George Bincke	Rover Bridge *(Chas Goodall & Sons, 1917, 42p.)*
Bethell, Victor	Bridge Reflections *(Heinemann, 1908, 165p.)*
Blackburn, Lucy	Bridge Helps *(Armstrong News, 1905, ?p.)*
Blackburn, Lucy	Helps On The Popular Game Bridge Whist *(Armstrong News, 1906, ?p.)*
Bland, John	Bridge Sins *(Private, 1909, 11p.)*
Blenheim Club	The Leads At Bridge Adopted And Recommended By The Blenheim Club *(Blenheim Club, 1903, 2p.)*
Boaz	*Laws Of Bridge And A Guide To The Game *(De La Rue, 1895, 37p.)*
Boaz	The Pocket Guide To Bridge *(De La Rue, 1894-1905, 18p.)*
Boston	Bridge And How To Play It *(Penn Pub, 1908, 160p.)*
Braine, Woodhouse	Index To The Laws Of Bridge *(Glaiser, 1901-05, 8p.)*
Bruce, Arthur Loring	The Bridge-Fiend: A Cheerful Book For Bridge-Whisters *(Moffett Yard, 1909, 289p.)*
Bruck, L J	The House Of Lords Book Of Bridge *(Private, 1907, ?p.)*
Brydges, R H	Bridge Catechism *(Chatto & Windus, 1907-08, 286p.)*
Camp, Walter C	Bridge Don'ts: Condensed Bridge For the Busy Man *(Collier, 1909, 34p.)*
Campbell, Herbert	Bridge For Bridgettes *(Black & White, 1909, 48p.)*
Clifford, Frank E	Authentic Manual Of X-L, Or Three-Hand Bridge *(Private, 1903, 32p.)*
Collinson, John	*Biritch, Or Russian Whist *(Private, 1886, 4p.) (Reprinted by Bibliagora in 1977, 14p.)*
Crawfurd, Oswald	The Laws Of Misery Bridge *(Buchanan, 1902/03, 3-8p.)*
Crawfurd, Oswald	The Laws Of Opposition Bridge *(Buchanan, 1906, 8p.)*
Cut-Cavendish	How To Win At Bridge *(Upcott Gill, 1904-12, 104p.)*
Cut-Cavendish	Popular Bridge Player *(Werner Laurie, 1907, 280p.)*
Cut-Cavendish	The Bridge Winner: A Guide To Success At The Game Of Bridge *(Cassell, 1906, 77p.)*
Cut-Cavendish	The Complete Bridge Player *(Lippencott/Werner Laurie, 1905-10, 232p.)*
Cut-Cavendish	The Game Of Bridge *(Werner Laurie, 1909, 103p.)*
Dalton, William	*Saturday Bridge *(West Strand, 1906-10, 231p.)*
Dalton, William	Bridge Abridged, Or Practical Bridge *(Scribner/De La Rue, 1901-12, 139p.)*
Dalton, William	Bridge At A Glance. An Alphabetical Synopsis Of Bridge *(De La Rue, 1904-05, 99-100p.)*
Dalton, William	Dalton's Complete Bridge (Saturday Bridge) *(Stokes, 1906, 319p.)*
Dalton, William	Inferences At Bridge *(West Strand, 1908, 86p.)*
Dalton, William	The Laws Of Bridge, With Cases And Decisions *(La Rue, 1905-10, 54-63p.)*
Dickinson, Bessie	Bridge Abridged *(Wolcott/Private, 1902-05, 24p.)*
Dickinson, Bessie	Bridge Essentials *(Hall & McCresney, 1907, 40p.)*
Diehl, C Vidal & Gates, J W	Draw-Bridge *(Chas Goodall & Sons, 1904-12, 4-11p.)*
Doe, John	*The Bridge Manual Illustrated *(Warne/Mudie, 1900-06, 122p.)*
Doe, John	Bridge Conventions *(Pioneer Press, 1899, 204p.)*
Dunn, Archibald Jr.	Bridge And How To Play It *(Routledge, 1899-1913, 74p.)*
Dunn, Archibald Jr.	Club Bridge *(Mills & Boon, 1909-10, 245p.)*
Dunn, Archibald Jr.	New Ideas On Bridge *(Scott, 1902, 106p.)*
Dunn, Archibald Jr.	The Bridge Book: A Complete Treatise On Bridge *(Routledge, 1907, 234p.)*
Dunn, Archibald Jr.	The Bridge Book: Practical Talks About Bridge *(Routledge, 1902-07, 228p.)*
DuVal, H C	Bridge Rules In Rhyme *(Pafraets, 1902, 7p.)*
Ecryb Eiram	Bridge In Brief, Do's And Don't *(Dutton/The Jerseyman Press, 1904, 40p.)*
Elwell, Joseph Bowne	*Advanced Bridge *(Newnes, 1904, 277p.)*
Elwell, Joseph Bowne	*Bridge Axioms And Laws *(Dutton, 1907, 89p.)*
Elwell, Joseph Bowne	*Elwell On Bridge *(Scribner/Newnes, 1902-08, 136p.)*
Elwell, Joseph Bowne	*Practical Bridge *(Scribner, 1906-08, 249p.)*
Elwell, Joseph Bowne	*The Analysis And Complete Play Of The Bridge Tournament Hands *(Scribner, 1904, 69p.)*
Elwell, Joseph Bowne	Bridge Lessons *(Private, 1906, 16p.)*
Emery, Bell Bowman	Dont's In Bridge *(Emerson/Jenkins, 1906-10, 32p.)*
Fitch, George	Bridge Whist *(Collier/Gibson, 1908-10, 35p.)*
Foster, Robert F	Bridge Maxims *(De La Rue/ Brentano, 1904-5, 97p.)*
Foster, Robert F	Foster's Bridge (Manual) *(Laurence /Brentano's, 1900-08, 186p.)*
Foster, Robert F	Foster's Bridge Tactics *(Warne/Mudie, 1903-06, 215p.)*
Foster, Robert F	Foster's Complete Bridge *(McClure-Phillips, 1905-10, 324p.)*
Foster, Robert F	The Gist Of Bridge *(Dick & Fitzgerald, 1904, 86p.)*
Foster, Robert F	The Pocket Laws Of Bridge, With Hints To Beginners *(The Chas Elliot Co, 1908, 25p.)*
Gluckstein, S M	Bridge And Bridge Playing *(Francis Griffiths, 1911, 126p.)*
Grant, W Forsyth	Bridge In Canada *(Morang & Co Ltd, 1910, 150p.)*
Grim	Elementary Bridge - A Note Book For Beginners *(Thacker, Spink, 1904, 62p.)*
H.W.H.	Point Bridge *(Mortimer, 1911, 8p.)*
Hammond, Robert	Bridge Catechism: Questions And Answers *(Chatto & Windus, 1912, 287p.)*
Harrison, C B	The Laws Of Bridge (1902) *(U S Playing Card Co, 1902, 9p.)*
Hellespont	*The Laws And Principles Of Bridge *(De La Rue, 1901-10, 317p.)*
Hess, Minnie Stevens	Correct Bridge *(Rand, McNally, 1906, 111p.)*
Hill, Frank P	Hill's Bridge And How To Play It *(McKay, 1906, 247p.)*
Hingley, Samual H	Hints On Advanced Bridge *(Bell, 1910, 94p.)*
Hoffman	Bridge *(Goodall, 1904-08, 41p.)*
Hoffman	Bridge Whist *(Goodall, 1900-03, 15p.)*
Hoffman, Professor	Bridge Varieties *(Chas Goodall & Sons/Musson, 1908-09, 45p.)*
Hulme-Beaman, Ardern G	English And Continental Bridge *(The Charterhouse Press, 1902, 12p.)*
Hulme-Beaman, Ardern G	The Pons Asinorum, Or Bridge For Beginners *(Methuen/ Scribner, 1899, 103p.)*
Leather, Ernest	Oruba, The New Bridge *(Private, 1913, 4p.)*
Leigh, Lennard	Bridge Whist:How To Play It *(Coates, 1901-02, 158p.)*
Leigh, Lennard	The Blue Book Of Bridge And Auction *(Winston, 1911, 229p.)*
Leikeze	Kindergarten Bridge Whist *(Private, 1906, 19p.)*

Lewis, Angelo John — Bridge *(Goodall, 1899-1903, 41p.)*
Lewis, Angelo John — Bridge Whist *(Goodall, 1899, 15p.)*
Lynx — A Guide To The Game Of Bridge *(Norman & Stacey, 1903, ?p.)*
Lynx — Bridge Topics *(Newman, 1903, 91p.)*
Mainwaring, Arthur E — Cut Cavendish, Or Whist In A Few Whiffs Together With The Foundation Of Bridge *(Bradbury/Routledge, 1899-1900, 54p.)*
McColl, Florence Linder — Helps For Bridge Players *(Pulis Printing, 1906-09, 37p.)*
McHardy, McL — Brief Bridge By-Words *(Private, 1903, 4p.)*
McTear, J S — Abecedary Of Nuhlo, The Improved Bridge *(Private, 1906, 34p.)*
McTear, J S — Nuhlo (The Improved Bridge: Synopsis Of The Game) *(Private, 1906, 2p.)*
Melrose, C J — Bridge Whist: Its Whys And Wherefores *(Upcott Gill, 1901-04, 224p.)*
Metcalfe, Arthur Ready — Bridge That Wins, With Thirty Illustrative Deals *(Hathaway, 1905, 131p.)*
Meyer, Virginia May Keller — Enlarged Small Talks On Bridge *(Ruledge Playing Card Co., 1909, 40p.)*
Meyer, Virginia May Keller — Small Talks On Bridge *(Private, 1908, 11p.)*
Meyer, Virginia May Keller — Virginia Cards *(Ruledge, 1908, ?p.)*
Montagu, J H — Bridge Pocket Book *(Mudie, 1906, 39p.)*
Mottelay, Paul Fleury — *The Blue Book Of Bridge *(Scribner, 1906, 152p.)*
O'F, E — Essentials Of Sound Bridge *(Ponsonby, 1906, 20p.)*
Oliver, Edwin — The Pocket 'Bridge' *(Spicer, 1906, 103p.)*
Page, Mrs. W E — Bridge Helps *(Private, 1907, 20p.)*
Philp, Carolyn Howard — Bridge For Beginners *(Ulrich, 1906, 11p.)*
Pontifex — A Book Of Bridge *(Blackie, 1905, 375p.)*
Pontoon — A Manual Of Bridge *(Thacker, 1905, 88p.)*
Problematicus — Leads At Bridge *(Private, 1904, 4p.)*
Quilon — Confessions Of A Bridge Player *(Harrison, 1910, 129p.)*
Red Lancer — Cosmopolitan Bridge *(Times Of Ceylon, 1906, 115p.)*
A. Revoke — *The Grand Slam - A Modern Bridge Guyed *(Hodges Figgis/Mudie/Simpkin Marshall, 1906-07, 56-67p.)*
Rice, Lilian S — Bridge "In A Nutshell" *(Private, 1906, 12p.)*
Robertson, Edmund & Hyde-Wollaston, A — *Bridge Developments From The 'Higher Grammar Of Bridge' *(Brentano's, 1904-06, 127p.)*
Robertson, Edmund & Hyde-Wollaston, A — The Robertson Rule And Other Bridge Axioms *(Private, 1902-06, 122p.)*
Roome, Henry A — Hints On Bridge *(Dutton/Routledge, 1901-06, 74p.)*
Rowe, Louise Jopling — The Tete-a-Tete Bridge *(Lamley & Co, 1916, 22p.)*
Rundell, Edwin A — Mental Relief In Bridge Whist Or Auction Bridge *(Albert Co, 1914, 12p.)*
Shelby, Annie Blanche — Bridge Abridged *(Duffield/Whittaker, 1905-6, 171p.)*
Simpson, J — Bridge For Beginners *(Thacker, 1908, 79p.)*
Simpson, J — Notes On Bridge *(Myles Standish, 1911, 112p.)*
Slam — Modern Bridge *(Longmans Green, 1901-05, 151p.)*
Smith, Colin — Bridge Condensed *(Leadenhall Press, 1902, 32p.)*
Springer, John E — Bridge Mastery *(Private, 1914, 44p.)*
Steele, Kate N — Simple Rules For Bridge *(Jenkins, 1902-04, 32p.)*
Street, Charles Stuart — Bridge Up-to-Date *(Private/Dodd, Mead/Robinson, 1900-09, 111p.)*
Street, Charles Stuart — Good Bridge *(Dodd, Mead, 1907, 122p.)*
Street, Charles Stuart — Sixty Bridge Hands *(Dodd, Mead, 1903, 116p.)*
Stuart, Herbert — Six-Handed Bridge *(Bell, 1907, 8p.)*
Templar — Bridge *(Bell, 1904, 82p.)*
Tennant, Eleanor A — Bridge Up-to-Date *(Hutchinson, 1905-15, 122p.)*
Tennant, Eleanor A — The ABC Of Bridge *(Drane/ McKay, 1901-07, 80p.)*
The Kernel — Bridge In A Nutshell *(Private, 1908-10, 8p.)*
Tinkham, E A — How To Play Bridge *(Private, 1909, 141p.)*
Wallace, Lula Haines — Winning Bridge Plays *(Private, 1907, 16p.)*
Wells, Carolyn — The Rubaiyat Of Bridge *(Harper & Brothers, 1909, 40p.)*
Wheler, Colonel C S — Bridge Notes *(Crowther & Goodman, 1908, 16p.)*
Whist Club, The — The Laws Of Bridge *(Whist Club/N.Y. Consolidated Card Co, 1897-1908, 32-62p.)*
Whitfeld, William H — The Pocket Laws Of Bridge, With Hints To Beginners *(De La Rue, 1904, 31p.)*
Winner — Bridge Tips *(Hill & Kirkwood, 1904, 6p.)*
Yarborough & Hoffman — Bridge: An Elementary Handbook Of The Game *(Goodall, 1912, ?p.)*

B. HISTORICAL – AUCTION BRIDGE

A.C.B. — Auction Bridge For Beginners/Everybody *(Stanley Paul, 1924-29, 204p.)*
Ace High — Auction Bridge Simplified *(Private, 1931, 15p.)*
Ace High — Auction Bridge: How To Bid *(Private, 1930, 23p.)*
Ace High — How To Play Auction Bridge *(Green, 1932, 23p.)*
Adams, Charles True — Auction Bridge At Sight *(Bruce-Roberts, 1928, ?p.)*
Adams, J R — *Defence At Auction Bridge *(Bodley Head, 1930, 140p.)*
Adams, Nancy H — Auction Bridge In Twelve Lessons *(Waverley, 1925, ?p.)*
American Auction Bridge League — Official Laws Of Progressive Auction Bridge And Pivot Bridge *(Metcalfe, 1928, 19p.)*
Anonymous — Auction Bridge Made Easy *(Daily News, 1923, 63p.)*
Anonymous — Auction Bridge: 25 Cigarette Cards *(Imperial Tobacco, 1925, 50p.)*
Anonymous — Auction Pitfalls By One Who Has Fallen *(Private, 1916, 1p.)*
Anonymous — Easy Lessons In Auction Bridge *(US Playing Card Co, 1922-29, 120p.)*
Anonymous — How To Play Auction Bridge *(US Playing Card Co, 1920, 120p.)*
Anonymous — Miller's Auction Bridge *(Beecher, Miller, 1926, p.)*
Anonymous — Rules For Buccaneer Bridge *(Private, 1924, 11p.)*
Anonymous — Rules Of 'Buccaneer' Bridge *(Waddington, 1924, 12p.)*
Anonymous — The Gist Of Auction *(Southam Press, 1913, 16p.)*
Anonymous — The Laws Of Auction Bridge (1909) *(De La Rue, 1909, 21p.)*
Anonymous — The Laws Of Auction Bridge (1911) *(N.Y. Consolidated Card, 1911, 31p.)*
Anonymous — The Laws Of Duplicate Auction Bridge Of The Knickerbocker Whist Club *(Auction Bridge Bulletin, 1926, 14p.)*
Anonymous — The Laws Of Royal Auction Bridge *(De La Rue, 1913-14, 29p.)*
Anonymous — The Rules Of Royal Auction Bridge *(Gibson, 1920, 31p.)*

AUTHOR	TITLE, PUBLISHER, YEAR, PAGES
Anthony, Edwin	How To Win At Auction Bridge *(Jacobs, 1919, 202p.)*
Atherton, George E	The ABC Of Auction Bridge *(McKay, 1913-16, 82p.)*
Auctioneer	Auction Bridge For Three Or Four Players *(Sampson Low, Marston & Co Ltd, 1908, 31p.)*
Badsworth	Auction Bridge And Royal Auction *(Putnam, 1913, 304p.)*
Badsworth	Badsworth On Auction Bridge *(Putnam, 1910, 292p.)*
Badsworth	Royal Auction Bridge *(Putnam, 1914-20, 286p.)*
Barron, A A	Auction Bridge For Beginners And Others *(Virginia Water, 1929, 15p.)*
Barton, Frederick P	Auction Bridge Simplified *(Simpkin, Marshall, 1911, 116p.)*
Bascule	Advanced Auction Bridge *(Longmans Green, 1917-24, 271p.)*
Bascule	Hints On Auction Bridge *(Smith & Son Ltd, 1911-12, 34p.)*
Bascule	Royal Auction Bridge *(Longmans Green, 1915-24, 184p.)*
Bascule	Royal Spades Auction Bridge *(Longmans Green, 1913-15, 180p.)*
Bascule	The Rules And Principles Of Auction Bridge *(Longmans Green, 1911-12, 178p.)*
Bath Club	The Laws Of Auction Bridge *(De La Rue, 1908, 29p.)*
Bath Club	The Laws Of Auction Bridge As Played At The Bath Club *(De La Rue, 1907, 4p.)*
Beachcroft, C P	Auction Bridge Nuts *(Hutchinson, 1927, 296p.)*
Bergholt, Ernest	Bergholt's Modern Auction *(Hutchinson, 1924, 358p.)*
Bergholt, Ernest	Guide To Royal Auction Bridge *(De La Rue, 1924-31, 54p.)*
Bergholt, Ernest	Royal Auction Bridge - The Art And Practice *(Routledge, 1916-18, 219p.)*
Bergholt, Ernest	Royal Auction Bridge - The Laws And Principles *(Routledge/Dutton, 1916-18, 156p.)*
Bergholt, Ernest	Royal Auction Bridge *(Goodall, 1917, 84p.)*
Bergholt, Ernest	Royal Spades, Or Lily Auction Bridge And Royal Auction Bridge *(Goodall, 1913-15, 78p.)*
Bergholt, Ernest & Manning-Foster, A E	Auction Bridge: Laws And Principles, Art And Practise *(Routledge /Dutton, 1929, 360p.)*
Bignold, H B	Auction Simplified *(Angus & Robertson, 1922, 26p.)*
Black, Paul W	Auction Bridge Outline *(Private, 1928, ?p.)*
Blackburn, Lucy	Helps On The Popular Game Of Auction Bridge *(Private, 1916-20, 77p.)*
Bluet, Walter	Twenty-One Bridge Fallacies *(Jarrolds, 1921, 92p.)*
Boyden, Elizabeth Clark & Warren, Mrs. Prescott	Practical Auction Principles *(Private, 1925, 16p.)*
Browning, H S	Auction Bridge And How To Play It *(Routledge/Dutton, 1909-13, 191p.)*
Browning, H S	Auction Bridge Hands *(Hutchinson, 1927, 255p.)*
Browning, H S	Royal Auction Bridge And Poker *(Routledge, 1920, 64p.)*
Browning, H S	The Auction Bridge Book *(Routledge, 1913, 284p.)*
Bruelheide, Frank E	Party Bridge *(Buzza, 1927, 104p.)*
Bruelheide, Frank Elmer	A Bridge Questionnaire *(Buzza, 1927, 125p.)*
Buccaneer	Practical Auction Bridge *(Werner Laurie, 1917-25, 303p.)*
Butler & Brevitas	Auction Bridge In A Nutshell, Royal Spades *(Simpkin, Marshall, 1913-19, 67p.)*
Buxton, William H	Auction Bridge Blue Book *(Private, 1926-8, 36p.)*
Camp, Walter C	A Pocket Bridge Book: Why Not Win? *(Doubleday, Page, 1923, 42p.)*
Camp, Walter C	Auction Bridge Don'ts *(Doubleday, 1912, 56p.)*
Camp, Walter C	Auction Up-to-Date, Including Nullos *(Private, 1914, 89p.)*
Camp, Walter C	Condensed Auction For The Busy Man *(Platt & Peck, 1912, 58p.)*
Campbell, Murray & Campbell, Virginia	Sidelights Of Auction Bridge *(Casper, 1928, ?p.)*
Carney, Helen Carroll	Eight Lessons In Auction Bridge *(Private, 1921, 22p.)*
Carrington, Hereward	Bridge Simplified, A Book For Beginners *(Copeland, 1928, 322p.)*
Carson, H A H	The Economy Of Auction Bridge *(Methuen, 1926, 120p.)*
Carson, Harry	How To Play Auction Bridge *(Waddington, 1926-7, 14p.)*
Carvalho, Solomon S	Complete Auction Bridge For 1922 *(Current Book, 1922, 93p.)*
Cavendish Hoyle	The A.B.C Of Royal Auction Bridge *(Drane, 1920, 64p.)*
Chamberlain, Bernard P	Miscellaneous Sine Qua Nons Of Bridge *(J H Furst, 1923, 29p.)*
Chatterji, Jogini	Royal Auction Bridge: Its Principles And Practice *(J Callarman, 1916, 223p.)*
Clark, Harriet Pickert	Auction Bridge Condensed *(Private, 1911, 12p.)*
Clark, Harriet Pickert	Auction Bridge, Including A Synopsis Of Bridge *(Dodd, Mead, 1912, 139p.)*
Clark, Harriet Pickert	Modern Auction Bridge (1916) *(Wycil, 1916, 106p.)*
Clark, Harriet Pickert	Royal Auction Bridge Up-to-Date, Including Nullos *(Dodd, Mead, 1914, 146p.)*
Clark, Harriet Pickert	Royal Auction Bridge, Up-to-Date *(Dodd, Mead, 1913, 125p.)*
Clark, William	Royal Auction Bridge: New Facts And A New System *(De La Rue, 1923, 127p.)*
Claxton, A G B	Notes On Auction For The Average Player *(Private, 1920, 32p.)*
Cochran, Thomas C	Auction Bridge Handbook *(Holt, 1926, 115p.)*
Cochran, Thomas C	Auction Bridge Hints *(Holt, 1923, 58p.)*
Coffin, Charles Emmet	Gist Of Auction Bridge *(McClurg, 1917, 147p.)*
Coffin, Charles Emmet	Gist Of Auction Bridge *(McClurg, 1921, 157p.)*
Crane, Joshua	Common Sense In Auction Bidding *(Hinkley, 1916-23, 23p.)*
Cross-Ruff	Auction-Bridge Essentials *(Hutchinson, 1928, 218p.)*
Crothers, E M	Auction Bridge In Brief *(Private, 1927, 32p.)*
Culbertson, Ely & Culbertson, Josephine	Lesson Sheets On The Approach Forcing System *(Private, 1927, ?p.)*
Cut-Cavendish	How To Win At Auction Bridge (Royal Spades) *(Werner Laurie, 1912-3, 194p.)*
Cut-Cavendish	How To Win At Royal Auction Bridge *(Werner Laurie, 1915-19, 215p.)*
Dalton, Basil	Auction Bridge For Beginners *(Richards Press, 1922-29, 64p.)*
Dalton, William	Auction Bridge *(De La Rue, 1928, 231p.)*
Dalton, William	Auction Bridge Containing The Laws Of Auction Bridge *(De La Rue, 1908, 149p.)*
Dalton, William	Auction Bridge Up-to-Date *(De La Rue/Wycil, 1909-13, 210p.)*
Dalton, William	Auction Bridge With Cases And Decisions *(De La Rue, 1924-5, 229p.)*
Dalton, William	Bridge And Auction Bridge *(Stokes, 1910, 363p.)*
Dalton, William	Royal Auction Bridge *(De La Rue, 1913-16, 114p.)*
Dalton, William	Royal Auction Bridge, With Cases And Decisions Of The Portland Club Committee *(De La Rue, 1918-23, 202p.)*
Davis, Charlotte Cotton	Rules In Rhyme For Auction Bridge *(Cleve Penton, 1927, ?p.)*
Denison, Edward Elias	*The Play Of Auction Hands *(Lothrop/Harrap, 1922-3, 284p.)*
Doe, John	*Auction Bridge *(Pioneer Press, 1904, 14p.)*
Doe, John	*The Auction Bridge Manual Of John Doe *(Thacker & Co, 1910, 144p.)*

JV   Royal Auction Bridge *(Private, 1925, 23p.)*
Keene, Clemence Cooke   The Essentials Of Auction Bridge *(Bridge Publishing, 1925, 25p.)*
Khanhoo   Bridge Maxims *(Kelly & Walsh, 1918, 12p.)*
Kirwan, M Lydia   Auction Points Abridged *(Private, 1915, 39p.)*
Knickerbocker Whist Club   The Laws Of Auction Bridge *(Knickerbocker Whist Club, 1925, 23p.)*
Latakia   Royal Auction *(Barrell, 1914, 43p.)*
Leigh, Lennard   The Blue Book Of Bridge And Auction For Beginners And Experts *(Winston, 1911, 229p.)*
Lenz, Sidney S   Lenz On Bridge *(Simon & Schuster, 1926-27, 372p.)*
Lenz, Sidney S   Lenz On Bridge, Volume Two/ More Lenz On Bridge *(Simon & Schuster/Allen & Unwin, 1927-30, 456p.)*
Lewin, Lt-Col.   Rules Of Auction Bridge *(London Opinion, 1908, 24p.)*
Lilies, W G   Lilies' Auction Bridge *(Barse & Hopkins, 1913, 100p.)*
Linet, Henry A   Auction Bridge Made Simple For Beginners *(Shields, 1928, 63p.)*
Littlefield, Louis   High Points Of Auction Bridge *(Mississippi Sun et al, 1923-27, 128p.)*
Lyman, V B   Auction Bridge Bidding *(Bley And Lyman, 1925, 4p.)*
MacBeth, J C H   Auction Bridge Simplified *(Butterworth, 1925, 320p.)*
MacBeth, J C H   Common Sense In Auction Bridge *(Dutton, 1924, 322p.)*
MacMahon, Freda   Stepping Stones To Better Auction *(Private, 1924, 45p.)*
Maginn, Mary Peali   Auction Made Easy For Beginners *(Miller Press, 1921-24, 20p.)*
Major Tenace   Auction Bridge: Lessons For The Unskilled *(Longmans Green, 1928, 125p.)*
Manning-Foster, A E   *Auction Bridge Made Clear *(Nash & Grayson, 1921-31, 191p.)*
Manning-Foster, A E   Auction Bridge Dialogues *(Methuen, 1926, 106p.)*
Manning-Foster, A E   Auction Bridge Do's And Don'ts *(Methuen, 1924-33, 152p.)*
Manning-Foster, A E   Auction Bridge For All *(Benn, 1928-20, 317p.)*
Manning-Foster, A E   Auction Bridge Play And Problems *(Methuen, 1925-28, 152-158p.)*
Manning-Foster, A E   Auction Bridge Table Talk *(Routledge, 1919, 168p.)*
Manning-Foster, A E   Auction Bridge Variations *(Nash & Grayson, 1923, 186p.)*
Manning-Foster, A E   Baby Bridge Book *(Waddington, 1928, 80p.)*
Manning-Foster, A E   The ABC Of Auction Bridge Penalties *(Waddington, 1926, 24p.)*
Manning-Foster, A E   The Light Side Of Auction Bridge *(Putnam, 1922-24, 166p.)*
Manning-Foster, A E &
  Hervey, George F   *Auction Bridge Informatory Doubles *(Bles, 1926, 158p.)*
Mastbaum, Stanley V   Auction Bridge *(Private, 1911, 17p.)*
McCampbell, Bryant   *Auction Tactics *(Dodd, Mead, 1916-20, 148p.)*
McColl, Florence Linder   Helps For Players Of Auction Bridge *(Private, 1910-15, 28p.)*
McKinlay, Major L H   Auction Bridge Mathematics *(Private, 1926, 19p.)*
McNeil, Keith A   Winning Auction *(Private, 1964, 10p.)*
Meagher, George E   Short Cuts To Good Bridge *(Private, 1930, 14p.)*
Metcalfe, Arthur Ready   Auction Bridge *(De Clerque, 1911-13, 94p.)*
Metcalfe, Arthur Ready   Auction Bridge With Nullos *(Browne & Howell, 1910, -p.)*
Metcalfe, Arthur Ready   Common Sense Bidding *(McClurg, 1922, 148p.)*
Metcalfe, Arthur Ready   Complete Auction Bridge *(Browne & Howell, 1914, 188p.)*
Metcalfe, Arthur Ready   Real Auction Bridge *(McClurg, 1915, 53p.)*
Metcalfe, Arthur Ready   The Game Of Lilies (Auction Bridge) *(Browne & Howell, 1913, 33p.)*
Meyer, Virginia May Keller   Auction Bridge Quiz Jingles *(Private, 1920, ?p.)*
Meyer, Virginia May Keller   Ideal Auction Bridge *(Private, 1923, 107p.)*
Meyer, Virginia May Keller   New Bids And Don'ts Of Auction Bridge *(Private, 1916, 20p.)*
Meyer, Virginia May Keller   Revised Auction Bridge Quiz Jingles, Don'ts Etc. *(Private, 1922, 24p.)*
Meyer, Virginia May Keller   Royal Or 'Lily' Aucton In A Nutshell And Small Talks On Auction *(Paul Elder & Co, 1915, 30p.)*
Meyer, Virginia May Keller   Small Talks On Auction Bridge *(Private/Paul Elder & Co, 1910,23- 30p.)*
Meyer, Virginia May Keller   Small Talks On Royal Or 'Lily' Auction *(Paul Elder & Co, 1913, 26p.)*
Meyer, Virginia May Keller   Sure Winners At Auction Bridge - New Jingles Etc. *(Private1921, 24p.)*
Midwood   Midwood On Royal Auction Bridge *(Hutchinson, 1924, 92p.)*
Miles, P L   Epitome Of A System Of Bidding At Auction Bridge *(Private, 1912, 3p.)*
Mitchell, Samuel   Solitaire Bridge *(Sears, 1928, 144p.)*
Moeller, Ernest Henry   Auction Bridge Sense And Nonsense *(Private, 1928, 32p.)*
Montgomery, Grace G   Auction Bridge In Ten Lessons *(Scribner /Newnes, 1912-14, 120p.)*
Montgomery, Grace G   Modern Auction *(Scribner, 1923-26, 220p.)*
Montgomery, Grace G   Modern Auction In Ten Lessons *(Scribner, 1915-21, 184p.)*
Morris, William C   First Steps To Auction Bridge *(Mills & Boon, 1924, 61p.)*
Morris, William C   Pithy Points In Auction Bridge *(Reilly & Lee, 1923, 67p.)*
Morrison, Murphy M   Auction Bridge *(Sunday Gazetter Pub., 1927, 35p.)*
Mott-Smith, Geoffrey   Pencil Bridge *(Putnam, 1928, 161p.)*
Muller-Thym, Lambert A J   The Common-Sense System Of Bidding At Auction (The Nullo Bid Included) *(Lowman & Hanford, 1915, 22p.)*
Needham, Richard Edgar   Auction Bridge Sidelights *(Vinal/ Humphries, 1927-33, 147p.)*
Nyvall, Albert   The Theory Of Correct Bidding *(Dragner Nyvall, 1925, 133p.)*
Oliver, Edwin   The ABC Of Auction Bridge *(Drane, 1909-12, 83p.)*
Oliver, Edwin &
  Atherton, George E   The ABC Of Auction Bridge *(McKay, 1912, 83p.)*
One Who Has Fallen   Auction Pitfalls *(Mudie, 1913-16, 2p.)*
Owen, Major A G L   Modern Bridge *(Heath Cranton, 1920-21, 95p.)*
Pachabo   Royal Auction Bridge Summarised *(Anderson, 1918, 48p.)*
Pachabo   Twelve Keys To Auction Bridge Play *(Routledge, 1920, 184p.)*
Pachabo   Wrinkles On Royal Auction Bridge *(Routledge, 1919-20, 95p.)*
Passmore, Umus   Bridgework Or Sumpin' *(Evans, 1920, 20p.)*
Pedagogue   Every Man's Bridge *(Lothian, 1933, 19p.)*
Pennell, Vane   Auction Bridge *(Brown Langham, 1908, 100p.)*
Phelan, Alfred   Auction Bridge Latest Bidding *(Cowan, 1924, 49p.)*
Pimm, Ella G   Auction Bridge From A To Z *(Musson, 1926, 204p.)*
Pimm, Ella G   Auction Bridge In Ten Lessons *(Harper Brothers, 1923, 140p.)*
Portland Club   The Laws Of Auction Bridge (1909) *(Portland Club, 1909, 36p.)*
Portland Club   The Laws Of Auction Bridge *(De La Rue, 1924-29, 32-47p.)*

Portland Club	The Laws Of Auction Bridge, With Cases And Decisions (1926) *(De La Rue, 1926, 80p.)*			
Powell, Robert Lee	The Code Of The Defense … At Contract/Auction Bridge *(Southwestern Publising, 1935, 62p.)*			
Rawls, Elizabeth S	What Do You Know About Bridge? (Three Hundred Questions And Answers) *(Ready Reference, 1927, 64p.)*			
Raymond, Col. Henry I	Auction Bridge In Its Simplest Terms *(Professional Press, 1928, 86p.)*			
Raymond, Col. Henry I	Why's Of Auction Bridge *(Bobbs Merrill, 1926, 203p.)*			
Reith, George	The Art Of Successful Bidding *(Doubleday Doran, 1928, 227p.)*			
Richey, Anna Gertrude	Auction Bridge Couplets, The ABC Of Bridge In Rhyme *(McElvany, 1926, 40p.)*			
Robertson, Edmund	Pocket Guide To The Laws And Penalties Of Royal Auction Bridge *(Field & Queen/ Wheeler, 1916-20, 192p.)*			
Robertson, Edmund	Royal Auction Bridge *(Field & Queen/ Laird & Lee, 1914, 268p.)*			
Robertson, Edmund & Hyde-Wollaston, A	Bridge Developments, With A Chapter On Auction Bridge By 'Auctioneer' *(Kegan Paul Trench, 1909, 138p.)*			
Rundell, Edwin A	Mental Relief In Bridge Whist Or Auction Bridge *(Albert, 1914, 12p.)*			
S C	Bridge *(Private, 1923, 17p.)*			
Sanders, Grace W	Practical Hints On Royal Auction Bidding *(Private, 1912-13, 27p.)*			
Scott, Gratz M	Changes In The Laws Of Auction Bridge *(Holt, 1926, 7p.)*			
Seabury, Katharine Emerson	Royal Auction - Suggestions On The Game *(Grafton, 1912, 30p.)*			
Seymour, Paul H	Auction Bridge For Beginners *(McClurg, 1925, 99p.)*			
Seymour, Paul H	Auction Bridge Simplified *(Private, 1927, 32p.)*			
Seymour, Paul H	Highlights On Auction Bridge *(Saul Bros, 1926-28, 32p.)*			
Shelby, Annie Blanche	Auction Bridge: A Clear Concise, And Up-to-Date Statement *(Duffield, 1911, 120p.)*			
Shepard, Edward V	Auction To Win *(Reynolds, 1923, 262p.)*			
Shepard, Edward V	Correct Auction *(Harper Brothers, 1920, 258p.)*			
Shepard, Edward V	Expert Auction *(Harper Brothers, 1917, 247p.)*			
Shepard, Edward V	Scientific Auction Bridge *(Harper/Chapman & Hall, 1913-14,241- 254p.)*			
Shepard, Edward V	Win At Bridge *(Reynolds, 1927, 150p.)*			
Simonton, Sue Gunning	Auction Bridge Made Easy *(Gibson, 1923, 21p.)*			
Smith, Dr. Melville	Auction Bridge Up-to-Date *(Foulsham, 1932-39, 77p.)*			
Solus	Auction Bridge *(Private, 1924, 64p.)*			
Solus	Auction Bridge Up-to-Date *(Foulsham, 1926, 90p.)*			
Solus	Royal Auction Bridge Condensed *(Private, 1923,38-p.)*			
Staples, Thomas L	The Heart Of Auction Bridge *(Better-Bridge, 1929, 93p.)*			
Staples, Thomas L	The Heart Of Bridge *(Professional Press, 1926, 96p.)*			
Stedman, John Harry	Auction Bridge Compendium *(Rochester Democrat & Chronicle Print, 1910, 8p.)*			
Steele, W F	Sound Auction Bridge *(Grove City, 1928, 139p.)*			
Street, Charles Stuart	Auction Bidding With Leads *(Private, 1925, 74p.)*			
Street, Charles Stuart	Outlines Of Auction Bridge *(Private, 1909, 29p.)*			
Street, Charles Stuart	Street On Auction *(Private, 1912-13, 120p.)*			
Street, Charles Stuart	The Clysmic Book Of Auction Bridge *(Clysmic Spring, 1911, 80p.)*			
Sykes, Brigadier General C A	The Bridge Mind *(Methuen, 1924, 76p.)*			
Tattersall, W B	Royal Auction Bridge: Rules Of The Game *(Smith & Son Ltd, 1922, 39p.)*			
Taylor, Mrs. Agnes M & Hervey, George F	Taylor And Hervey On Auction Bridge *(Putnam, 1928, 212p.)*			
Tenace	Bridge For Beginners *(Jenkins, 1924, 160p.)*			
Tennant, Eleanor A	Bridge Up-to-Date *(Hutchinson, 1909-15, 122p.)*			
Thompson, Lawrence Dudley	The One-Two-Three Of Auction Bridge Bidding *(Private, 1929, 8p.)*			
Tobin, E J	Sound Principles Of Auction Bridge *(McKiernan, 1927, 95p.)*			
Tuite, Hugh	Iris Plays Better Bridge *(Bles, 1928-30, 112p.)*			
Tuite, Hugh	Mrs. Pottleton's Bridge Parties *(Bles/Simon & Schuster, 1926-28, 156p.)*			
Tuite, Hugh	Teaching Iris Auction Bridge *(Bles, 1926-32, 108p.)*			
Tuite, Hugh	The Pottleton Bridge Club/So They Played Bridge - And How *(Bles/Simon & Schuste, 1925-26, 159-156p.)*			
Valet De Pique	Bridge And Auction Bridge *(Eveleigh Nash, 1912, 318p.)*			
Viator	Royal Auction Draw-Bridge *(Chas Goodall & Sons, 1913, 8p.)*			
Wagner, Mary Swain	Auction Bridge Abridged For Busy People *(Private, 1925, 20p.)*			
Wagner, Mary Swain	Auction Bridge Rhyme And Reason *(Private, 1928, 32p.)*			
Warren, Mencil	Royal Auction For Beginners And Others *(Combridge, 1926, ?p.)*			
Warren, Mencil	The Hay, B, C Of Royal Auction Bridge *(Combridges, 1924, 46p.)*			
Watkinson, A B	Royal Auction Bridge: The Laws And Play *(Private, 1922, 36p.)*			
Webster, H T & Johnston, William	*Webster's Bridge *(Stokes, 1924, 112p.)*			
Wentworth, W W	Bridge Made Easy: No. 1, Bidding *(Ready Reference, 1928, 64p.)*			
Wentworth, W W	What Do You Know About Bridge *(Ready Reference, 1927, 64p.)*			
Wheelock, Kate	Auction Bridge Suggestions, Including Royal Count *(Ebbert And Richardson, 1912, 56p.)*			
Wheelock, Kate	Auction High Spade Bids *(Ebbert And Richardson, 1913, 20p.)*			
Wheelock, Kate	Kate Wheelcock's New Auction Bridge Suggestions *(Private, 1922, 89p.)*			
Wheler, Colonel C S	Auction Bridge Notes *(Crowther & Goodman, 1912, 46p.)*			
Wheler, Colonel C S	Auction Bridge Offshoots, Including Royal Spades *(Crowther & Goodman, 1913, 64p.)*			
Whist Club, The	The Laws Of Auction *(Whist Club/Winston, 1910-26, 39-44p.)*			
White, True W	Auction 1916 Manual *(Boston Bridge Club, 1916, 40p.)*			
White, True W	Auction Bridge Manual *(Palmer, 1926-27, 48p.)*			
Whitehead, Wilbur C	*Auction Bridge Standards *(Stokes et al, 1918-26, 314p.)*			
Whitehead, Wilbur C	*Authoritative Leads And Conventions Of Play *(John H Smith, 1923-27, 38p.)*			
Whitehead, Wilbur C	*Whitehead's Complete Auction Bridge *(Stokes, 1926-27, 308p.)*			
Whitehead, Wilbur C	Auction Bridge Summary *(Stokeset al, 1925-30, 54p.)*			
Whitehead, Wilbur C	New Picture Method Bridge - Bridge *(Experimenter, 1928, 93p.)*			
Whitehead, Wilbur C	Royal Spades Auction Bridge Conventions *(Mudie, 1913, 56p.)*			
Whitehead, Wilbur C	Studio Lessons In Auction Bridge *(De Bower Pub, 1928, 384p.)*			
Whitehead, Wilbur C	Whitehead's Auction Bridge For Beginners *(Stokes, 1928, 120p.)*			
Whitehead, Wilbur C	Whitehead's Conventions Of Auction Bridge *(Stokes, 1914, 243p.)*			
Whitehead, Wilbur C	Whitehead's Winning Bridge *(Stokes, 1929, 186p.)*			
Wilkinson, Sir William Henry	Bridge Maxims *(Goodall, 1920, 18p.)*			

Wilkinson, Sir William Henry   Royal Auction Bridge Maxims *(Kelly & Walsh, 1921, 36p.)*
Williams, Taunton   Royal Auction Bridge Including Nullos *(MacBride Nast, 1915-16, 115p.)*
Williamson, E I F   Auction Bridge With Royal Spades *(Drane, 1913, 78p.)*
Wood, Clement   Auction Bridge For Beginners *(Haldeman-Julius, 1924, 63p.)*
Woods, Edward F   Short-Cut To Standard Auction Bridge *(Woods, 1926-27, 70p.)*
Work, Milton Cooper   *Auction Bridge Complete *(Winston et al, 1926-29, 500p.)*
Work, Milton Cooper   *Auction Developments *(Houghton Mifflin et al, 1913, 612p.)*
Work, Milton Cooper   *Auction Of To-Day *(Houghton Mifflin, 1913, 300p.)*
Work, Milton Cooper   *Auction Under The Laws Of 1915 *(Winston, 1915, 104p.)*
Work, Milton Cooper   Auction Bridge For Beginners *(Winston, 1928, 136p.)*
Work, Milton Cooper   Auction Bridge In Twelve Lessons *(Milton Bradley, 1922, 270p.)*
Work, Milton Cooper   Auction Bridge Of 1924 *(Winston, 1923, 507p.)*
Work, Milton Cooper   Auction Declarations *(Winston, 1917-19, 288p.)*
Work, Milton Cooper   Auction For Two Or Three *(Winston et al, 1921, 222p.)*
Work, Milton Cooper   Auction Methods Up-to-Date *(Winstonet al, 1920, 332p.)*
Work, Milton Cooper   Bridge By Radio 1927-28 *(U S Playing Card Co, 1927, 146p.)*
Work, Milton Cooper   Bridge Pointers And Tests *(Winston, 1927, 186p.)*
Work, Milton Cooper   Par Auction Analysis Of Bids And Play, Series B, Packs 3 And 4 *(Milton Bradley, 1922, 61p.)*
Work, Milton Cooper   Par Auction Analysis Of Play, Series A, Packs One And Two *(Milton Bradley, 1921, 59p.)*
Work, Milton Cooper   Radio Auction Bridge Games - Fifth Series, 1929-1930 *(U S Playing Card Co, 1930, 213p.)*
Work, Milton Cooper   Radio Auction Bridge Games - Fourth Series, 1928-1929 *(U S Playing Card Co, 1930, 146p.)*
Yarborough   Royal Auction Bridge: Problems Of Analysis *(Routledge, 1921, 128p.)*
Yarborough   Royal Auction Bridge: Problems Of Inference And Perception *(Routledge, 1921, 96p.)*

C. HISTORICAL - CONTRACT BRIDGE: NON-VANDERBILT SCORING

Bergholt, Ernest   A Description Of The Variant Of Royal Auction Bridge *(Goodall, 1920, 38p.)*
Bergholt, Ernest   Contract Bridge: A Description Of The Variant Of Royal Auction Bridge *(Goodall, 1920, 38p.)*
Foster, Robert F   Foster's Contract Bridge *(Greenberg, 1927, 114p.)*
Foster, Robert F   Foster's Contract Bridge Score Card *(Greenberg, 1927, 2p.)*
Headen, T P   Contract Bridge Made Easy *(Haldeman, 1927, 64p.)*
Irwin, Florence   Contract Bridge *(Stokes, 1927, 30p.)*
Lenz, Sidney Samuel   Lenz On Contract Bridge *(Simon & Schuster/Allen & Unwin, 1927, 131-87p.)*
MacKay, Donald   Plafond Or Contract Bridge *(Private, 1927, 68p.)*
Manning-Foster, A E   *Contract Bridge *(Routledge, 1920, 64p.)*
Monteith, E   *Contract Bridge *(Medici Soc, 1926, 151p.)*
Pimm, Ella G   Contract Bridge Simplified *(Musson, 1926, 120p.)*
Shepard, Edward V   Contract Bridge *(Private, 1926, 8p.)*

D. HISTORICAL – AUCTION AND CONTRACT BRIDGE

Ace High   Complete Rules For Auction And Contract Bridge *(Green, 1930, 15p.)*
Ace High   New International Laws Of Contract And Auction Bridge, The *(Private, 1932, 23p.)*
Adams, Charles True   Auction And Contract Bridge Pointers *(Bruce-Roberts, 1929, 52p.)*
Adams, Nancy H   Auction And Contract Bridge *(Waverley, 1926-27, 56p.)*
Adams, Nancy H   The Little Blue Teacher A-B-C And X-Y-Z Of Auction Bridge Including Contract *(Private, 1926-29, 56p.)*
American Bridge League   Official Laws Of Duplicate Auction and Duplicate Contract Etc. *(A.B.L., 1929, 64p.)*
Anonomous   Bridge: Auction And Contract At A Glance *(U.S. Card Playing Co., 1930, 20p.)*
Anonymous   Better Bridge, Auction Contract *(Lane, 1929, 60p.)*
Anonymous   Bridge - Auction And Contract At A Glance *(Sloan, 1930, 20p.)*
Anonymous   Contract And Auction Bridge *(Private, 1933, 80p.)*
Anonymous   Contract And Auction Bridge Including Three-Handed Auction And Two-Handed Auction *(Private, 1933, 80p.)*
Anonymous   Contract Bridge For The Auction Bridge Player *(Keystone Press, 1934, 39p.)*
Anonymous   Corona Keys To Contract Bridge, Written For Those Who Understand Auction Bridge *(Revalk-Perry Company, 1933, 5p.)*
Black, Mary Nimmo   ABC Of Auction And Contract Bridge *(McKay, 1926-7, 144p.)*
Blossom, Robert   Bridge, Contract And Auction *(Fedelin, 1931, 63p.)*
Boyden, Elizabeth Clark &
  Warren, Mrs. Prescott   Auction And Contract Bridge Condensed *(Private, 1927, 24p.)*
Boyden, Elizabeth Clark &
  Warren, Mrs. Prescott   Principles Of Auction Bridge Condensed *(Private, 1926, 60p.)*
Brannon, Robert M   Simplified Self-Teacher, Contract And Auction Bridge *(Taylor Press, 1940, 37p.)*
Brett (Lucy Brett Andrews)   Quickies, The ABC Of Contract Bridge For The Auction Player *(Private, 1930, 10p.)*
Brown, Bernard   Principles Of Auction And Contract Bridge *(Sully, 1928, 200p.)*
Bryant, Mary P   Bridge, Contract And Auction *(Private, 1929, 126p.)*
Buller, Col. Walter   From Auction To Contract: The Logic Of British Bridge *(Methuen, 1932, 184p.)*
Buller, Col. Walter   Reflections Of A Bridge Player *(Methuen, 1929, 197p.)*
Crayford, James   Auction To Contract In Four Lessons *(Judson, 1933, 19p.)*
Culbertson, Ely   *Contract Bridge For Auction Players *(Garden City/Faber, 1932, 192p.)*
Cut-Cavendish   How To Win At Royal Auction Bridge With A Chapter On Contract Bridge *(Werner Laurie, 1920, 244p.)*
Dalton, Basil   Contract Bridge And Its Development From Auction *(Richards, 1929-31, 94p.)*
Davis, Charlotte Cotton   Rules In Rhyme For Bridge And Contract *(Private, 1928, 32p.)*
De La Mater, Edgar De Witt   Bridge You Should Know: Auction Bridge, Contract Bridge *(Private, 1931, 32p.)*
Ellicott, John Morris   Valuation Bridge - A New And Accurate Method Of Bidding In Contract And Auction *(Private, 1930, 32p.)*
Ferguson, Wynne   1927 Rules And Laws Of Auction Bridge And Authorized Laws Of Contract Bridge, The *(Private, 1927, 143p.)*
Foster, Robert F   Bridge For Advanced Players *(Greenberg, 1929, 324p.)*
Foster, Robert F   Foster's Auction Bridge *(De La Rue, 1929, 279p.)*
Frederick, Byron C   Summary Play Of The Hands For Auction And Contract Bridge Players *(Keystone, 1931, 62p.)*
Fritch, Edward H   Simplified Auction Bridge Complete In A Nutshell: Including Contract Bridge *(Private, 1926-28, 58p.)*
Hattersley, Lelia   Auction And Contract Bridge Clarified *(McBride, 1927, 400p.)*
Hattersley, Lelia   Contract And Auction Bridge Clarified *(McBride, 1927, 400p.)*

AUTHOR	TITLE	PUBLISHER	YEAR	PAGES

Hollyday, J Steuart — How To Play Contract Or Auction Bridge For Amateur Or Novice *(Private, 1938, 4p.)*
Jones, Ellis O — Bridge, Auction And Contract With Bidding And Play That Wins *(Westbrook, 1928-29, 110p.)*
Kandl, Norman — Auction And Contract In 10 Lessons *(Auction Bridge Studio, 1930, 34p.)*
Kelley, Ada Campbell — Abridged Auction And Contract Bridge *(Private, 1928, 85p.)*
Kelley, Ada Campbell — Abridged Auction And Contract Bridge *(Private/Allen & Unwin, 1928-30, 85p.)*
Kelley, Ada Campbell — Auction And Contract Bridge, Complete - Condensed *(Day, 1930, 120p.)*
Kerwin, Madeleine — Improve Your Card-Play At Contract Or Auction Bridge *(Century/Knopf, 1930, 137p.)*
Keston, Mrs. C B & Jackson, B — Few Random Hints On Auction And Contract Bridge, A *(Business Office Service, 1929, 11p.)*
Kling, Alpha H — Ideal Self-Teacher On The Play Of The Hand, Auction Or Contract, The *(Taylor Press, 1933-50, 63p.)*
Knickerbocker Whist Club — The Laws Of Duplicate Auction And Duplicate Contract Of The Knickerbocker Whist Club *(Knickerbocker Whist Club, 1929, 30p.)*
Langer, Jacob — Bridge The Easy Way: Auction, Contract *(Humphries /Daniel, 1933, 40p.)*
Lenz, Sidney Samuel — Lenz On Contract Bridge *(Simon & Schuster/Allen & Unwin, 1927-29, 131p.)*
Manning-Foster, A E — Auction And Contract Bridge Made Clear *(Grayson, 1933, 327p.)*
Manning-Foster, A E — Auction And Contract Bridge With Illustrative Hands *(Liverpool & London & Globe, 1930, 48p.)*
Mathey, Fabyan & Hallahan, Harry T — Bridge Puzzles For Auction & Contract Players *(Dutton, 1929, 228p.)*
Merrill, William J — Auction And Contract Bridge Combined And Simplified. The Merrill System *(Dorrance, 1930, 162p.)*
Mott-Smith, Geoffrey — Contract Bridge And Advanced Auction Bidding *(Minton Balch, 1927, 281p.)*
Nafe, Muriel — The Key To Contract Bridge: Opens The Door For All Auction Players Who Want To Play Contract *(Private, 1930, 11p.)*
Nield, Dorathy — Bridge Auction And Contract *(Thornquest Press, 1935, 9p.)*
Reeve, Edward Gordon & Craigie, John — Reevu System Of Auction And Contract Bridge, The *(Lane, 1933, 61p.)*
Reith, George — Auction And Contract Compared *(Private, 1928, 16p.)*
Rendel, Robert — Squeeze Play For Auction And Contract Bridge: An Analysis *(Allen & Unwin, 1934, 93p.)*
Russell, Carlton & Bonney, Norman — Common Sense Bridge: Auction-Contract: The Play Of The Cards *(Private, 1935, 95p.)*
Russell, Edward C — Bridge At A Glance, Auction - Contract *(Liggett & Myers, 1930, 28p.)*
Seymour, Paul H — Simplified Bridge (Auction And Contract) *(Reilly & Lee, 1929-30, 96p.)*
Sheafe — Mechanical Contract And Auction Bridge *(Technical, 1935, 8p.)*
Slam-It — Bridge In Brevity: Slamit's Speedy Guide To Contract Auction And Play Of The Hand *(Private, 1932, 23p.)*
Snipes, Mrs. J J — Bridge Leads And Plays, Auction Or Contract *(Private, 1930, 25p.)*
Speyer, Edwin J — Contract And Auction Bridge Featuring The Play Of The Cards Applicable To Any System *(Private, 1932, 32p.)*
Stanley, Enos — Individual Contract - Individual Auction *(Private, 1927, 12p.)*
Steers, Alfred E — All-Point System Of Contract And Auction Bridge, The *(Private, 1933, ?p.)*
Taylor, Mrs. A M & Hervey, George F — Advanced Auction Bridge With A Chapter On Contract Bridge *(Putnam, 1929, 256p.)*
Taylor, Mrs. Agnes Mundell — A Guide To Contract Bridge For Beginners And Teachers With A Few Notes On Auction *(London School Auction/Contract, 1930, 33p.)*
Thornely, H L — Advanced Auction And Contract Bridge Tactics For The Keen Player *(Foulsham, 1929, 159p.)*
Van Alen, M A — Correct Leads For Winning Play At Contract And Auction Bridge *(Taylor Press, 1934-40, 29p.)*
Warren, Mrs. Prescott — Auction And Contract Bridge Condensed *(Houghton Mifflin, 1927, 247p.)*
Wester, Nils M — *Auction To Contract Including The Laws Of Contract Bridge *(Columbian Colortype, 1929, 152p.)*
Whitehead, Wilbur C — Bridge Made Easy, Contract And Auction: Series No. 1 *(Jones, 1930, 72p.)*
Whitehead, Wilbur C — Teaching Of Auction And Contract Bridge, The *(Stokes, 1930, 10p.)*
Work, Milton Cooper — Celebrated Contract Hands With Their Auction Bidding *(Ile, 1931, 46p.)*
Work, Milton Cooper — Play-A-Hand: Auction Or Contract Bridge - The Newest Thing In Bridge *(Carson Pirie Scott, 1930, 24p.)*
Work, Milton Cooper — Playing Problems In Auction And Contract *(Private, 1930, 24p.)*

E. MATERIAL FOR NEWCOMERS

A.C.B.L. — E-Z Guide Companion: Club/Diamond/Heart Play Courses *(A.C.B.L., 1995, 75p. each)*
Abramsohn, Phil & Gotthelf, A Lewis — Contract For Beginners *(Bridge-O-Matic, 1938, 30p.)*
Aiston, Neil — Bridge Year 4 *(Private, 1999, 432p.)*
Alder, Phillip — You Can Play Bridge *(Thames Methuen, 1983, 214p.)*
Andersen, Ronald E — Counting *(Devyn Press, 1985, 10p.)*
Anderton, Philip — Bridge In Twenty Lessons *(Bell, 1961, 127p.)*
Anderton, Philip — Contract Bridge Simplified *(Thorsons, 1954, 63p.)*
Anonymous — A Short Cut To Contract *(Simpkin Marshall, 1930, 32p.)*
Anonymous — Basic Bridge *(Page Publications, 1970, 64p.)*
Anonymous — How To Learn Bridge The Easy Way *(Ace Playing Card, 1975, 48p.)*
Anonymous — How To Play Bridge *(Stancraft, 1975, 34p.)*
Anonymous — How To Play Contract Bridge *(Gainsborough Press, 1929, 40p.)*
Anonymous — How To Start Playing Bridge In Twenty-Two Minutes *(American Playing Card Mfrs, 1957, 20p.)*
Anonymous — How To Start Playing Bridge In Twenty-Two Minutes *(U.S. Playing Card Co, 1957, 20p.)*
Austin, W B — Welcome To Bridge *(Austin, 1977, 94p.)*
B(anks), M — Simple Way Of Learning Contract Bridge *(Private/Whitcomb Tombs, 1932-48, 28-39p.)*
Bailey, J R — Bridge, A Beginner's Simplified Guide On How To Enjoy The Game *(Shelwing, 1997, 8p.)*
Banfield, Mrs. Elizabeth B — Lesson Sheets In The A B C Of Contract Bridge *(Private, 1949, 37p.)*
Banfield, Mrs. Elizabeth B & Newman, Frances B — A B C Of Contract Bridge: The Approach Forcing System As Played And Taught By *(Welling & Welling, 1932, 23p.)*
Barclay, Shepard — Learn Bridge Fast *(David McKay, 1944-50, 126p.)*
Barclay, Shepard — Playing At Bridge *(Livingston Press, 1934, 24p.)*
Bardwell, Getrude S — Contract Bridge Lessons *(Private, 1932, 39p.)*
Bart, Belle & Frank, Lewis C — When To Play Bridge And How *(Frank, 1933, 345p.)*
Barton, Frederick P — Contract Bridge For Beginners Only *(Joiner & Steele, 1937, 75p.)*
Barton, Frederick P — Contract Bridge For Beginners Only *(Joiner & Steele, 1938-46, 75p.)*

Bayone, Jeff &
Beesley, Amanda — It's Bridge, Baby: How To Be A Player In Ten Easy Lessons *(Riverhead Books, 1998, 349p.)*
Beard, John — Develop Your Bridge The Acol Way *(J.B. Bridge Courses, 1978-, 63p.)*
Beard, John — The Play Way *(J.B. Bridge Courses, 1985, 93p.)*
Becker, Jim — The Biggest Little Bridge Book In The World: Play And Defense In Suit Contracts *(Beverly Card School, 1999, 55p.)*
Belsey, Margery — The Play-Easy Contract Lessons *(Stockwell, 1935, 66p.)*
Bissett, Mrs. Clyde A — Compact Of Contract Bridge … *(Private, 1931, 40p.)*
Black, Paul W — E-Z Contract Bridge Condensed *(Private, 1930, 20p.)*
Black, Paul W — The Ten Commandments In Contract Bridge Are Ten Times Ten *(Private, 1930, 20p.)*
Blackwood, Easley — Introduction To Declarer Play *(Devyn Press, 1989, 8p.)*
Blackwood, Easley &
Hanson, Keith — Card Play Fundamentals *(Devyn Press, 1987, 114p.)*
Bleasdale, Winefride — The Streets Of Dublin: A Personal Guide To The Game Of Bridge *(Minerva Press, 1995, 103p.)*
Blessing, Leonard C — Crossing Your Bidding Bridges *(Item Press, 1959-66, 89p.)*
Bloom, I H — Culbertson System Self-Teacher: Contract Bridge Plays And Leads *(Steel City Pub, 1936, 80p.)*
Bonney, C Jack — Home Work For Bridge Beginners (To Supplement Class Lessons) *(Idea Treasury, 1958-66, 43p.)*
Bonney, C Jack — Home Work For Intermediate-Advanced Bridge Students (To Supplement Class Lessons) *(Idea Treasury, 1959, 28p.)*
Bonney, Norman — Norman Bonney's New Deal Leaflets On The Play Of The Cards: Number One *(New Deal Club, 1935, 16p.)*
Booty, June & Hurst, Richard — The Wendy And Colin Bridge Kit *(Private, 1996, 38p.)*
Bosshart, Mrs. Marie J — Self-Teacher Golden Rule Book On Contract Bridge: Easy Point Count *(Private, 1950, 26p.)*
Bramley, T E — Bridge *(Black, 1990-95, 36-48p.)*
Breeser, Robert — Bridge Flashcards: Delightful Mix/Quick Review/Just For Beginners/ Opening Bid/Suit Bids *(Mindracer Publishing, 1997-, 60p. each)*
Brewster, Henry Sturgeon — Contract Bridge Simplified *(Private, 1933, 23p.)*
Brill, Tobias — Contract Bridge Simplified *(Private, 1930, 46p.)*
Bristowe — Contract Bridge Simplified *(St Catherine Press, 1929-30, 44-55p.)*
Brock, Raymond — Notrump Play: How To Play Bridge *(Batsford, 1998, 96p.)*
Brock, Sally — Playing With Trumps - How To Play Bridge *(Batsford, 1998, 96p.)*
Brooke, Mrs. Doris — Contract Bridge *(Private, 1930, 16p.)*
Brooke, Mrs. Doris — Contract Bridge And The Play Of The Cards *(Private, 1930, 23p.)*
Browne, Derrick — Beginner's Bridge *(Trumps Publishing, 1998, 112p.)*
Bruelheide, Frank Elmer — Contract Bridge Self-Teacher *(Bruelheide, 1936, 32p.)*
Bruelheide, Frank Elmer — Culbertson System, A Self-Teacher *(Bruelheide, 1938-40, 40p.)*
Bruelheide, Frank Elmer — How To Play Contract Bridge *(Bruelheide, 1938, 32p.)*
Bruelheide, Frank Elmer — New Simplified Culbertson System *(Bruelheide, 1941-48, 64p.)*
Buller, Col. Walter — How To Play Contract Bridge: A Complete Guide For For British Players *(The Star, 1932, 144p.)*
Buntman, Vera — Bridge Fun Book *(Private, 2000, 56p.)*
Burrows, Ena — Contract Bridge *(Australian Book Pub, 1932, 63p.)*
Buxton, William H — Contract Bridge 1929/1930 *(Private, 1929, 36p. each)*
Cade, Lawrence H — Commonsense Contract *(Hurst & Blackett, 1933, 240p.)*
Campbell, Horace — Fundamentals Of Contract Bridge *(Hobson Book Press, 1946, 96p.)*
Campbell, Virgina — Fundamentals Of Contract Bridge *(Campbell, 1930, 28p.)*
Card School — The Biggest Little Bridge Book In The World *(Card School Inc, 1958-93, 32-60p.)*
Carew, Mrs. T P — Contract Calls Simplified. A Synopsis Of The Culbertson Approach-Forcing System *(Mills & Boon, 1931, 54p.)*
Carney, Helen Carroll — Twelve Lessons In Contract Bridge *(Private, 1928, 24p.)*
Cayley, Frank — Bridge Play Made Easy *(Reed, 1980, 88p.)*
Cayley, Frank — Contract Bridge - Play *(Rigby, 1978, 64p.)*
Cayley, Frank — Contract Bridge-Bidding *(Rigby, 1970-78, 64p.)*
Cayley, Frank — Modern Contract Bridge *(Auto Press, 1933, 108p.)*
Cobb, Ruth S — Cobb To Win - Contract Bridge For The Beginner *(Harvard Sq Press, 1934, 187p.)*
Coe, Montgomery — The Basics Of Bridge *(Gambling Research Institute, 1988-2000, 64p.)*
Coffin, George Sturgis — Bridge On Deck *(Coffin, 1959-69, 52-66p.)*
Coffin, George Sturgis — Contract Bridge Self-Teacher *(Manthorne & Burack, 1936, 48p.)*
Coffin, George Sturgis — Learn Bridge The Easy Way *(Branford/ Joiner & Steele, 1950, 128p.)*
Coffin, George Sturgis — Little Drill Book, George Coffin's Bridge Quizzes For Use With Bridge On Deck *(Private, 1961, 16p.)*
Coffin, George Sturgis — Pocket Self-Teacher *(Coffin, 1933-36, 33p.)*
Coffin, George Sturgis — Self-Teaching Contract Cards - Culbertson System *(Thompson & Smith, 1933, ?p.)*
Cohen, Ben & Barrow, Rhoda — Contract Bridge For Beginners *(Collins, 1974, 142p.)*
Cohen, Ben &
Barrow/Lederer, Rhoda — The ABC Of Contract Bridge *(Barnes/Blond/Collins/Unwin, 1964-79, 287p.)*
Cohen, Louis J — Learn To Enjoy Bridge *(Cen Bridge School, 1968, 12p.)*
Cohen, Ruth M — The Elements Of Play *(Barclay, 1958-, 63p.)*
Conway, Mrs. Stephen — The Open Book Of Contract Bridge *(Private, 1931, 75p.)*
Cook, Dorothy Jane — Contract Bridge *(Private, 1959, 50p.)*
Cook, Dorothy Jane — Contract Bridge Lessons *(Private, 1962, 56p.)*
Cooper, Joan (Place, Lucille) — Bridge Basics *(Coles, 1976, 152p.)*
Cotter, E P C — Contract Bridge *(Teach Yourself Books, 1975, 128p.)*
Cotter, E P C — Tackle Contract Bridge This Way /Tackle Bridge *(Stanley Paul, 1962-73, 128p.)*
Cotter, E P C — Teach Yourself Contract Bridge *(E.U.P., 1969, 128p.)*
Courtenay, F Dudley — Play Bridge And Like It *(Courtcraft, 1938-51, 48p.)*
Courtenay, F Dudley — Supplement To The System The Experts Play: Courtenay On The Essentials Of Play *(Bridge Headquarters, 1934, 95p.)*
Courtenay, F Dudley — The Standard Manual Of Play In Self-Teacher Question And Answer Form *(Bridge Headquarters, 1938, 96p.)*
Courtenay, F Dudley &
Courtenay, Mrs. Amy D — Contract Bridge: Learn To Play The Easy Way- Books No. 1-5 *(Courtcraft, 1954, 40p each.)*
Courtenay, F Dudley &
Courtenay, Mrs. Amy D — The Student's Self-Teacher On Bidding And Play *(Bridge Headquarters, 1935-38, 80-96p.)*
Cox, Jean — Bridge With Jean Cox - The Bidding *(Private, 1963-70, 66p.)*

Cox, Jean	Bridge With Jean Cox - The Play *(Private, 1964-70, 55p.)*	
Cramer, Hannah Jean	Bridge Light *(Private, 1939, 88p.)*	
Crans, Lillian Pettit	What You Must Know To Play Contract Bridge *(Private, 1934, 31p.)*	
Creel, Maude	Point Count Bidding Based On Charles Goren's Contract Bridge *(Private, 1955, 8p.)*	
Cromelin, Paul L	Bridge As It Seems To Me: Volume 1, Basic Bridge *(Cromelin, 1974, 302p.)*	
Cromelin, Paul L	Bridge Is Beautiful *(Cromelin, 1977, 400p.)*	
Cron, Bea & Rosen, Fern	Advanced Bridge Five Card Major Student Text *(Private, 1985, 90p.)*	
Cron, Bea & Rosen, Fern	Beginning Bridge Five Card Major Student Text *(Private, 1985, 78p.)*	
Cron, Bea & Rosen, Fern	Intermediate Bridge Five Card Major Student Text *(Private, 1985, 74p.)*	
Culbertson, Ely	Contract Bridge Self-Teacher *(Winston/Faber, 1933-65, 80p.)*	
Culbertson, Ely	Contract In Ten Minutes *(Faber, 1932, 42p.)*	
Culbertson, Ely	Ely Culbertson Tells You How To Become A Good Bridge Player: In His Own Bridge School *(The Bridge World, 1953, 15p.)*	
Culbertson, Ely	How To Lead And Play Self-Instructor *(The Bridge World/Faber, 1934, 64p.)*	
Culbertson, Ely	How To Play Contract Bridge With Thrilling Hands From The Famous Culbertson-Lenz Match *(The Bridge World, 1932, 29p.)*	
Culbertson, Josephine	Contract Bridge For Beginners *(Winston/Faber, 1938-49, 223p.)*	
Culbertson, Josephine	Contract Bridge Made Easy The New Point Count Way *(Winston/Faber, 1955-65, 148/176p.)*	
Dallas, Gus	Bridge: How To Play, How To Win *(Gambing International, 1965, 64p.)*	
Daniels, Mark	The Bettabridge Handbook *(Ariel, 1957, 194p.)*	
Davies, Lola S	Contract Bridge *(Private, 1930, 22p.)*	
Davis, Jonathan & Ward, Matthew	Learn Bridge In A Weekend *(Knopf/Dorling Kindersley etc., 1993, 96p.)*	
Davy, Kenneth L	Let's Learn Bridge *(Rockliff, 1946, 47p.)*	
De Cordova, Rudolph	Contract In A Nutshell *(Grayson & Grayson, 1932, 107p.)*	
De Noument, Jules & De Noument, Beatrice	Clear And Concise Contract *(Columbia, 1932, 92p.)*	
De Satnick, Shelley	Bridge For Everyone *(Avon, 1982, 152p.)*	
De Straelborn, D	Contract Bridge - The Science Of Bidding Based On The Culbertson System *(Private, 1935, 20p.)*	
Dersnah, Ruth K	Basic Bridge For The Casual, Unsure Or Rusty Player *(Picton Gazette, 1969, 31p.)*	
Deschamps, M M & Ford, W L	Bridge To Enjoy *(Private, 1982, 98p.)*	
Downes, E Hall	Answer Book For All Problems Contained In 'Playing Your Hand' (Self-Taught) *(Bridge Publications, 1933, 32p.)*	
Downes, E Hall	Contract Bridge Self-Teacher *(Bridge Publications, 1932-33, 48-64p.)*	
Downes, E Hall	Contract Bridge: Lesson No. 1-6, *(Gulf Refining Co., 1933, 8p. each)*	
Downes, E Hall	Leads And Plays: The Original Self-Teacher *(Bridge Publications, 1934, 64p.)*	
Downes, E Hall	Playing Your Hand: Self-Teacher *(Bridge Publications, 1933, 63p.)*	
Downes, E Hall	The Original Contract Bridge Self-Teacher: Culbertson System *(Bridge Publications, 1934, 64p.)*	
Dummy	The ABC Of Contract Bridge *(Dow & Lester, 1933, 76p.)*	
Echo	Concise Contract, Plafond And Play: All Systems In Brief: Notes On The Laws *(Joiner & Steele, 1935, 97p.)*	
Ehrlenbach, J J	Discourse Number 1 –10: Contract Bridge *(Private, 1950, 150p.)*	
Eichenbaum, Ken	What Do I Bid Now? *(Private, 1999, 157p.)*	
Emporos	Contract - It's Charm And Principles *(Warne, 1930, 79p.)*	
English Bridge Union	Really Easy Bidding *(E.B.U., 1998, 135p.)*	
English Bridge Union	Really Easy Mistakes *(E.B.U., 2000, 124p.)*	
English Bridge Union	Really Easy Play In Notrumps *(E.B.U., 1999, 138p.)*	
English Bridge Union	Really Easy Practice *(E.B.U., 1999, 136p.)*	
English Bridge Union	Really Easy Practice 2 *(E.B.U., 2000, 138p.)*	
English Bridge Union	Standard English System Summary: Foundation Level *(E.B.U., 1998, 7p.)*	
Etherington, Lew	Simplified Bidding For Contract Bridge (Weak-Club System) *(Private, 1985, 90p.)*	
Ewen, Robert B	The Teenager's Guide To Bridge/ Beginner's Guide *(Dodd Mead/Hale, 1976/1980, 214p.)*	
Ferguson, Wynne	Contract Bridge Lessons *(Bristol, 1932, 31p.)*	
Ferguson, Wynne	Wynne Ferguson's Contract Bridge *(Private, 1930-31, 105-130p.)*	
Fitzsimmons, Cortland	Contract Bridge For The Beginner And Average Player *(McBride, 1931, 56p.)*	
Flasher, Mary	You Too Can Play Bridge *(Private, 1947, 39p.)*	
Flint, Jeremy	How To Play Bridge *(Hamlyn/ Treasure Press, 1977-88, 62p.)*	
Flint, Jeremy & Gullick, John	The First Bridge Book *(Pan/Hale, 1984-94, 223p.)*	
Flintom, Frances Young	Contract Bridge In Twelve Lessons *(Private, 1932, 13p.)*	
Forrester, Tony	The Daily Telegraph Improve Your Bridge At Home *(Batsford, 1995, 128p.)*	
Forrester, Tony	The Daily Telegraph Play Bridge At Home *(Batsford, 1994, 127p.)*	
Foster, Robert Frederic	Contract Bridge Simplified *(Greenberg, 1930, 45p.)*	
Fox, Colin	The Good Bridge Guide *(Solar Publishing, 1995, 60p.)*	
Fox, Colin	Your Perfect Bridge Partner *(Private, 1997, 65p.)*	
Fox, George Clive Henry	Begin Bridge/How To Play Bridge *(Elliot Rightway/ Coles, 1973/1979, 125p.)*	
Fox, Gerald L	Partnership Bridge - An Easy Guide To Standard American Bidding *(Grand Slam Press, 1972-96, 35-117p.)*	
Fox, Gerald L	Partnership Defense - An Easy Guide To Defender's Play At Contract Bridge *(Grand Slam Press, 1982-93, 94p.)*	
Fox, Gerald L	Tricks For The Taking - An Easy Guide To Declarer's Play At Contract Bridge *(Grand Slam Press,1976- 1990, 125-137p.)*	
Gardener, Nico	Bridge Advanced Course *(London School Of Bridge, 1952, ?p.)*	
Gardener, Nico	Bridge Beginner Course *(London School Of Bridge, 1952, ?p.)*	
Garvey, Ruth	Who Dealt? 100 Guideposts To Bridge Bidding *(K.E.T.C.-T.V., 1977, 24p.)*	
Gemmill	Contract Bridge In Three Lessons *(Private, 1939, 16p.)*	
George, Dan	Play Bridge By George *(Private, 1983-87, 35p.)*	
Glover, Deborah Norris	Outline For Contract Bridge Bidding Based On The Goren Point Count Method *(Private, 1963, 48p.)*	
Goldsmith, M A	Contract Bridge Made Easy: A Book For Beginners *(Modern Sports, 1930, 64p.)*	
Gooden, George S	Contract Bridge Bidding And Play Self-Teaching Lesson Course For Beginning Players *(Private, 1966-69, 133-152p.)*	
Gooden, George S	Contract Bridge Lesson Course *(Gooden, 1969-74, 90-124p.)*	
Gooden, George S	Lesson Sheets *(Private, 1946, 32p.)*	

AUTHOR	TITLE	PUBLISHER	YEAR	PAGES
Hiron, Alan & Hiron, Maureen	Easy Guide To Bridge *(Cadogan, 1994, 159p.)*			
Hiron, Alan & Hiron, Maureen	The Eleven Plus Bridge Book *(Crowood Press, 1983, 144p.)*			
Hirschowitz, Sam & Eber, Neville	You Too Can Play Bridge Well *(Private, 1972, 294p.)*			
Horrocks, W V	Contract Bridge Explained *(Conquest, 1932, 41p.)*			
Horton, Mark	Simple Conventions - How To Play Bridge *(Batsford, 2000, 96p.)*			
Hyde, Edward P	Multiple-Purpose Lesson Hands *(The Bridge World, 1935, 64p.)*			
Ibsen, Hannah	It's Been A Pleasure, Partner! *(Private, 1976, 25p.)*			
Inman, Marshall	Inman's Beginning Bridge And Beyond *(Melbourne Bridge Centre, 1982, 96p.)*			
Isralsky, Emanuel & Isralsky, Jeff	Manny Sez'': The Complete Intermediate Bridge Course *(Private, 1965, 49p.)*			
Jacka, R F	Social Contract Bridge Made Easy *(Vantage Press, 1994, 169p.)*			
Jacoby, James	Instant Bridge *(Stancraft, 1964, 135p.)*			
Jameson, Henry Allen	Contract Bridge *(Private, 1930, 172p.)*			
Johnson, Norman	Bridge (Contract) For Boobs *(Private, 1930, 43p.)*			
Johnson, Robert Lee	1940 Contract Bridge *(Private, 1940, 0p.)*			
Johnson, Robert Lee	Bridgeasy: A Simplified Method Of Learning Contract Bridge *(Modern Living, 1958-62, 16p.)*			
Johnson, Robert Lee	Contract Bridge Simplified *(Private, 1940, ?p.)*			
Johnson, Robert Lee	Learn The New Point Count Bridge Bidding *(Bridgeasy/ Modern Living, 1954, 12p.)*			
Johnson, Robert Lee	The Play Of Your Cards At Contract Bridge *(Private, 1958-62, 47p.)*			
Jourdain, Patrick	Play The Game Bridge *(Ward Lock, 1990-83, 80p.)*			
Kantar, Edwin B	A Comprehensive Bridge Manual *(Private, 1965-67, 122-143p.)*			
Kantar, Edwin B	A New Lesson Series *(Private, 1960, 47p.)*			
Kantar, Edwin B	Bridge For Dummies *(I.D.G. Books, 1997, 382p.)*			
Kantar, Edwin B	Introduction To Declarer's Play *(Prentice Hall et al., 1968-, 147p.)*			
Kantar, Edwin B	Introduction To Defender's Play *(Prentice Hall et al, 1968-, 153p.)*			
Kantar, Edwin B	Play Of The Hand Complete *(Private, 1965, 108p.)*			
Kaplan, Edgar	Card Play At Contract Bridge *(Faber, 1965, 187p.)*			
Kayser, Mrs. Carl	Simplified Notes On Contract Bridge *(W H Allen, 1930, 94p.)*			
Keene, Clemence Cooke	Sane And Sound Contract Bridge *(Bridge Publications, 1929-30, 69p.)*			
Kelsey, Hugh Walter	Instant Bridge *(Coles, 1979, 70p.)*			
Kelsey, Hugh Walter	Learn Bridge For Fun *(Ward Lock, 1976, 96p.)*			
Kelsey, Hugh Walter	Start Bridge The Easy Way *(Gollancz, 1983-89, 96p.)*			
Kelsey, Hugh Walter & Kambites, Andrew	Acol Bridge For Bright Beginners *(Gollancz, 1995-, 144p.)*			
Kelsey, Hugh Walter & Kambites, Andrew	Acol Bridge For Bright Improvers *(Gollancz, 1996-, 144p.)*			
Kempson, Ewart	Contract Bridge Hints *(Liverpool & London & Globe, 1947, 44p.)*			
Kempson, Ewart	Contract Bridge: How To Play It *(Star/Kaye/Emerson Books, 1949-57, 160-164p.)*			
Kilmer, J C	Basic Bridge For Beginners *(Private, 1958, ?p.)*			
King, James B	Back To Basics With … Simple Minded Bridge *(Private, 1999, 122p.)*			
Kling, Alpha H	Playing Winning Bridge *(Private, 1933, 63p.)*			
Klinger, Ron	Acol Bridge Made Easy *(Gollancz, 1986-, 95p.)*			
Klinger, Ron	Acol Bridge Made Easy *(Gollancz, 1997, 96p.)*			
Klinger, Ron	Basic Bridge: The Guide To Good Acol Bidding And Play *(Ward Lock/Gollancz, 1978, 127p.)*			
Klinger, Ron	Bridge Basics *(Reld/ A.B. Publications/Modern Bridge Publication, 1974-, 129-86p.)*			
Klinger, Ron	Bridge For Children / Teach Your Child Bridge *(Modern Bridge Publications/Gollancz, 1989-90, 96p.)*			
Klinger, Ron	Bridge In Easy Stages *(Modern Bridge Publications, 1989, 32p.)*			
Klinger, Ron	Bridge Made Easy *(Modern Bridge Publications, 1985, 92p.)*			
Klinger, Ron	Exercise Book For Use In Conjunction With Bridge Basics *(Modern Bridge Publications, 1985, 12p.)*			
Klinger, Ron	Exercise Book For Use In Conjunction With Bridge Made Easy *(Modern Bridge Publications, 1985, 12p.)*			
Klinger, Ron	How To Play Contract Bridge *(Thorpe, 1981, 72p.)*			
Klinger, Ron	The Beginners' Pack *(Gollancz, 1985, 151p.)*			
Klinger, Ron	The Bridge Beginners' Pack *(Gollancz, 1997, 151p.)*			
Klinger, Ron & Husband, Pat	Basic Bridge: The Guide To Good Acol Bidding And Play *(Gollancz, 1994, 127p.)*			
Konstam, Kenneth	Contract Bridge *(Educational Productions, 1958-76, 32-36p.)*			
Kosuga, Mineko	Contract Bridge For Madame *(Stockwell, 1975, 164p.)*			
Kushner, Jack	Hands For Supervised Duplicate Bidding And Play. First & Second Series *(Private, 1960, 12 & 16p.)*			
Kushner, Jack	Play Of The Hand, Contract Bridge Lessons 1-10 *(Private, 1950, 30p.)*			
Kushner, Jack	Point Count Methods Of Contract Bridge *(Private, 1963, 11p.)*			
Lamford, Paul	Improve Your Game: Fifty Bridge Puzzles *(Chameleon Books, 1999, 128p.)*			
Lampert, Harry	Declarer Play And Opening Leads: A Fun Way Bridge Book *(Private, 1988, 207p.)*			
Lampert, Harry	Fun Way To Learn Serious Bridge *(Hardel Publishing/ Cornerstone Library, 1978-80, 136-160p.)*			
Lawrence, Mike	Overcalls And Takeout Doubles *(Devyn Press, 1989, 8p.)*			
Lawrence, Mike & Fox, Gerald L	Bridge-O-Matic. The Modern Approach To Contract Bridge. *(Bridge-O-Matic, 1975, 0p.)*			
Layne, Ed	Your First Bridge Book: An Introductory Text To Contract Bridge *(Layne, 1993, 52p.)*			
Lederer, Anthony & Lederer, Rhoda *(see Barrow, Rhoda)*	Learn Bridge With The Lederers *(Cassell/Unwin/Collins Willow, 1977-93, 202p.)*			
Lefebvre, Earl	An Introduction To Winning Bridge *(Private, 1961-65, 131p.)*			
Levinson, William A	Basic Bridge *(Dell/Mayflower, 1964-67, 64p.)*			
Levitt, Carolyn & Levitt, Jerry	The Language Of Bidding *(Private, 1964, 30p.)*			
Levitt, Jerry	The Language Of Bidding *(Private, 1982, 130p.)*			
Liddell, K C	Contract And Plafond Bridge Self-Taught *(Pitman, 1936, 72p.)*			
Liggett, Commander Winfield C	The Easy Road To Contract Bridge *(World Syndicate Pub Corp, 1932, 189p.)*			
Lind, Betty	Are Bridge Players People? *(Ryda/Private, 1965-78, 78p.)*			
Longmeyer, Carole	Six Puppy Feet: Bridge For Kids *(Unknown, 1985, 0p.)*			
Lynn, James E	Contract Bridge For Beginners *(Encyclopaedia Britannica, 1963, 0p.)*			

MacKey, Thomas M — Eight Easy Lessons In Contract Bridge *(Private, 1932, 64p.)*
Mahmood, Zia — Collins Bridge For Beginners : Bidding *(Collins Willow, 1994, 175p.)*
Mahmood, Zia — Collins Bridge For Beginners : Declarer Play *(Collins Willow, 1994, 158p.)*
Mahmood, Zia — Collins Bridge For Beginners : Defence *(Collins Willow, 1994, 174p.)*
Mahmood, Zia &
  Grant, Audrey — Breakthrough Bridge: Bidding For Beginners *(Virgin, 1990, 184p.)*
Mahmood, Zia &
  Grant, Audrey — Breakthrough Bridge: Declarer Play For Beginners *(Virgin, 1990, 144p.)*
Mahmood, Zia &
  Grant, Audrey — Breakthrough Bridge: Defence For Beginners *(Virgin, 1990, 151p.)*
Mahmood, Zia &
  Grant, Audrey — Bridge For Beginners: A Complete Course *(Batsford, 1998, 460p.)*
Malkind, Samuel L — How To Win At Contract *(Crown Heights Bridge Academy, 1932, 24p.)*
Manning-Foster, A E — Contract Bridge For All *(Benn, 1929-30, 127-221p.)*
Manning-Foster, A E — Contract Without Conventions *(Seeley Service, 1935, 255p.)*
Margulies, Ray — Hello! I'm A Game Called Bridge *(Private, 2000, 88p.)*
Margulies, Ray — The Genie That Hovers Over The Bridge Table *(Private, 2000, 58p.)*
Marston, Paul — All About Notrumps *(Grand Slam Books, 1989, 69p.)*
Marston, Paul — Contract Bridge: The Principles Of Card Play *(Hamilton/Grand Slam Books, 1986-, 263p.)*
Marston, Paul — Paul Marston's Introduction To Bridge *(Grand Slam Books, 1989-, 81-114p.)*
Marston, Paul — PM's Introduction To Bridge - Practice Hands - Acol Edition *(Grand Slam Books, 1997, 34p.)*
Marston, Paul — PM's Introduction To Bridge - Practice Hands - Standard Edition *(Grand Slam Books, 1997, 34p.)*
Marston, Paul &
  Brightling, Richard — The Bridge Workbook For Beginners *(Contract Bridge Supplies, 1985, 125p.)*
Marston, Paul & Smith, Peter — Paul Marston's Introduction To Bridge - Acol Edition *(Grand Slam Books, 1990, 85p.)*
Matsukis, Lyn — Take It Easy : Bridge Lessons, Ideal For Beginners And Intermediate Bridge Players *(Private, 1995, 81p.)*
Maurice, Brian A — Bridge Conversations *(Fore Golf Publications, 1996, 90p.)*
Maxwell, Douglas — A Simpler Way To Better Bridge *(Angus & Robertson, 1968, 141p.)*
McIlrath, John — Listen To Your Partner: A Collection Of Notes For The Bridge Beginner *(Private, 1991, 10p.)*
McKee, Judi — Contract Bridge: Pastime Or Lifestyle *(Flinders Bridge Centre, 1982, 84p.)*
McKenney, William E — Contract Bridge: Bridge Bidding With Instructions For Scoring *(Bridge Bureau, 1931, 36p.)*
McMullin, Edith — Easybridge! 1 1/2: Can Count To 13? Play Of The Hand *(Private, 1998, 14p.)*
McMullin, Edith — Easybridge! 1, The Comic Book - Presenters Manual *(Private, 1997, 85p.)*
McMullin, Edith — Easybridge! 2: Ten Lessons All Intermediate /Novice Players Should Know *(Private, 1997, 60p.)*
McMullin, Edith — Easybridge! Lite, The Comic Book. HowTo Bid, Play And Have Fun Playing Bridge! *(Private, 1999, 64p.)*
McMullin, Edith — Easybridge! The Comic Book *(Private, 1997, 85p.)*
McVey, Mary — Bridge Basics *(Ket, 1982, 120p.)*
Medley, H Anthony — The Complete Idiot's Guide To Bridge *(Alpha Books, 1997, 364p.)*
Michaels, Charles — It's Fun To Play Bridge *(Private, 1948, 37p.)*
Michaels, Charles — The Four-Three-Two-One Point Count System - A Manual Of Contract Bridge Bidding *(Barclay, 1952, 40p.)*
Michaels, Charles &
  Cohen, Ruth M — Ideal Student Textbook - Four-Three-Two-One Manual *(Barclay, 1957-, 48p.)*
Mill, Andrew & Borin, Jim — Bridge And Beyond. A Complete Guide To Standard American Five Card Majors *(Private, 1999, 42p.)*
Milnes, Eric Charles &
  Franklin, Harold — Play And Learn Bridge *(Waddington, 1976, 0p.)*
Milnes, Eric Charles &
  Lukacs, Paul — Learn To Play Bridge *(Kaye & Ward, 1977, 153p.)*
Mollo, Victor &
  Gardener, Nico — Bridge For Beginners *(Duckworth/Barnes/Pan, 1956-96, 160p.)*
Mulholland, Harry — Pick Up The Tricks Of Bridge *(Mulholland-Wirral, 1987, 120p.)*
Muntz, Sylvia — Contract By Contact *(Private, 1941-49, 82-86p.)*
Muntz, Sylvia — Culbertson System Of Contract Bridge: 90 New Deals From Contract By Contact *(Private, 1949, 90p.)*
Muntz, Sylvia — Today's Point Count Bidding Lesson Sheets *(Private, 1950, 9p.)*
Nash, Garrett — Bridge Institute Lesson Manual *(Coffin, 1968, 96p.)*
Newman, John — Beginner's Bridge *(Private, 1982, 76p.)*
North, Freddie — Bridge Players Handbooks: Learning Bridge: The Right Path *(Probray Press, 1988-92, 44p.)*
North, Freddie — Bridge: Basic Defence *(Batsford, 1997, 112p.)*
North, Freddie — Getting Started: How To Play Bridge *(Batsford, 1998, 96p.)*
North, Freddie — Learning Bridge: The Right Path *(Apsbridge, 1997, 64p.)*
North, Freddie — Plan Your Defence *(Batsford, 1998, 96p.)*
Norwood, Robert E &
  Pisk, George M — Bridge Digest, An Outline Of Standard American Bidding Methods For Beginning Players *(Private, 1975-82, 47p.)*
Novrup, Svend &
  Kelsey, Hugh Walter — First Steps In Card Play *(Gollancz, 1989, 64p.)*
O'Neil, Daniel — Contract Bridge Made Simple *(Made Simplebook/Doubleday, 1957-61, 159-197p.)*
Orchard, Barbara — Introducing Bridge To A Beginner *(Private, 1981, 65-126p.)*
Ostdiek, Mabelle — The Culbertson Point Count Method Of Contract Bridge Bidding *(Bruelheide, 1952, 48p.)*
Ostrow, Albert A — Contract Bridge Made Easy *(Atwater Press, 1959, 15p.)*
Ostrow, Albert A — Pocket Guide To Contract Bridge *(Stephens Publications, 1961, 15p.)*
Ozaki, Milton — Bridge For Absolute Beginners/ The Fundamentals Of Contract Bridge *(Grafo Art/World's Work etc., 1963-80, 100-102p.)*
Parker, May M — Contract Bridge As Taught By May M. Parker … *(Private, 1953, 63p.)*
Parker, May M — Contract Bridge: Complete Course *(Private, 1933-40, 118-135p.)*
Pavlicek, Richard — Advanced Review I & II*(Private, 1983, 13p each.)*
Pavlicek, Richard — Beginning Bridge *(Private, 1984, 46p.)*
Pavlicek, Richard — Play And Defense At Bridge *(Baron, 1976, 20p.)*
Peach, Josephine C — Contract Bridge Step By Step *(Private, 1933, 67p.)*
Pedagogue — Every Man's Contract Primer - Easy Bidding For Beginners *(Lothian, 1933, 17p.)*

AUTHOR	TITLE
Penick, Michael	Beginning Bridge Complete *(Devyn Press, 1985, 172p.)*
Penick, Michael	Beginning Bridge Quizzes *(Devyn Press, 1989, 133p.)*
Peterson, Bette	Learn … Better Bridge *(Private, 1960, 16p.)*
Pezzaro, Judy	Judy Pezzaro School Of Contract Bridge *(Private, 1960, 21p.)*
Phillips, Hubert & Reese, Terence	How To Play Bridge *(Penguin/Parrish, 1945-58, 128-152p.)*
Phillips, Hubert & Reese, Terence	The Elements Of Contract *(British Bridge World/ Eyre & Spottiswoode, 1937, 271-266p.)*
Pierson, Les	Bridge For Beginning Beginners *(Private, 1969, 86p.)*
Place, Lucille	Beginning Bridge For All Ages/ Fell's Beginner's Guide To Bridge For All Ages /BridgeBasics *(Place/Fell/Coles, 1961-81, 132-152p.)*
Plager, Morris	Classroom Method Of Teaching Bridge *(Private, 1980, 64p.)*
Ploen, Virginia	Contract Bridge - First & Second Course *(Private, 1961, 24 & 17p.)*
Pyros, Liberty Zabetakis	Bridge And Baklava, A Complete Bridge Education For Beginning And Intermediate Players *(Private, 1987, 204p.)*
Raath, S Arnold	Logical Bridge For Beginners *(Private, 1994-96, 144-148p.)*
Rabach, Joshua M	Basic Bridge *(Dell, 1973, 64p.)*
Randle, Ralph	Instant Bridge *(Private, 1961, 26p.)*
Randle, Ralph	Instant Bridge And Tips To Win *(Private/Stancraf, 1963-64, 135p.)*
Raymond, Col. Henry I	Contract Bridge *(Professional Press, 1930, 0p.)*
Raymond, Col. Henry I	The Gist Of Contract Bridge *(Professional Press, 1928, 40p.)*
Reese, Terence	Begin Bridge With Reese *(Sterling/Bodley Head/Penguin, 1977-84, 128-133p.)*
Reese, Terence	Bridge *(Penguin, 1961-72, 208p.)*
Reese, Terence	Bridge For Bright Beginners *(Oak Tree Press/Sterling/Dover, 1965-73, 151p.)*
Reese, Terence	Bridge: Teach Yourself Books *(Hodder & Stoughton, 1980-96, 138p.)*
Reese, Terence	Contract Bridge *(Liverpool & London & Globe, 1938, 44p.)*
Reese, Terence	Learn Bridge In Five Days *(Batsford, 1995, 128p.)*
Reese, Terence	Learn Bridge With Reese *(Faber/Hamlyn, 1962-78, 164p.)*
Reese, Terence	The Game Of Bridge *(Constable, 1962, 208p.)*
Reese, Terence	Your Book Of Contract Bridge *(Faber, 1965, 80p.)*
Reese, Terence & Bird, David L	Bridge: Teach Yourself Books *(Hodder & Stoughton, 1998, 148p.)*
Reese, Terence & Bird, David L	Make A Start At Bridge *(Faber, 1994, 148p.)*
Reese, Terence & Schapiro, Boris	Bridge Card By Card *(Hamlyn, 1969, 88p.)*
Reford, John Hope	Contract In Six Lessons *(Hutchinson, 1932, 94p.)*
Reznik, Anne	Teach Yourself Bridge *(Private, 1985, 30p.)*
Richardson, H Du P	Contract Bridge In 13 Lessons *(MacMillan, 1960, 122p.)*
Rimington, Derek	Bridge Conventions: Contract Bridge: The Basics *(Probray Press, 1985, 36p.)*
Root, William S	Introduction To Bidding *(Prentice Hall/Muller, 1967-70, 154p.)*
Root, William S	The ABCs Of Bridge *(Three Rivers Press, 1998, 281p.)*
Rosen, Edward L	Bidding And Response For Contract Bridge *(Duncan, 1958, 6p.)*
Rosendorff, Nigel	Learn How To Play Bridge *(Rosendorff's Bridge School, 1982, 68p.)*
Ross, MacYe B	Easy Bridge For Pupil, Player And Instructor *(Private/Vantage, 1961-62, 176p.)*
Roth, Alvin & Rubens, Jeff	Bridge For Beginners *(Funk & Wagnalls, 1970, 216p.)*
Roth, Milton S	Contract Bridge Primer And Review *(Private, 1945, 56p.)*
Rothenberg, Joy	Bridge From Beginners To Advanced *(Private, 1998, 77p.)*
Rovere, Ernest W	Contract Bridge Self-Taught *(Cal Bulletin, 1952, 378p.)*
Rowe, Owen	First Class Bidding *(Bridge Press, 1984, 48p.)*
Rowe, Owen	First Class Play *(Bridge Press, 1983, 48p.)*
Rubinow, Morton	Play Bridge With Morton Rubinow *(Contract Bridge Institute, 1959, 71p.)*
Russell, Carlton	Dollar Bridge, The Birth Of New Champions *(Private, 1945, 27p.)*
Ryan, George	The Bones Of Bridge *(Temple Printing, 1966-86, 62p.)*
Sahai, Rameshwar	Practical Pocket Guide On Contract Bridge For Beginners And Tournament Players *(Private, 1966, 60p.)*
Salob, Roberta	Roberta Sez Bridge Series: Books 1-7 *(Private, 1995, 7-8p each.)*
Salob, Roberta	The Roberta Sez Bridge Guide, The Easy Way To Bridge Fame: Basic, Standard & Advanced *(Private, 1995, 7p. each)*
Sands, Norma & Janitschke, Jan	Bridge Mini Series, Volumes I – X *(Rocky Mountain Books/Devyn Press, 1992,20- 24p. each)*
Schambelan, B O & Fisher, Arnold	Building Bridge *(Simon & Schuster, 1993, 239p.)*
Schryver, Geo H & Boland, Vincent F	Contract Bridge Instructions *(Monarch Fire Insurance Company, 1932, 32p.)*
Schwanbeck, Bea	A Concise Basic Contract Bridge Course *(Private, 1985, 21p.)*
Scott, Eddie	Contract Bridge For Beginners And Improvers *(Foulsham, 1992, 94p.)*
Seligman, Edith	How To Bid Your Best In Bridge *(Bridge Travel, 1990, 0p.)*
Senior, Brian	Bridge Players Handbooks: Begin Declarer Play *(Probray Press, 1985, 32p.)*
Senior, Brian	Competitive Bidding - How To Play Bridge *(Batsford, 2000, 96p.)*
Senior, Brian	The Amazing Book Of Bridge *(Tiger Books International, 1995, 125p.)*
Sheinwold, Alfred	Bridge Play (For Beginners) *(Sterling/Faber/Cornerstone, 1953-78, 159p.)*
Sheinwold, Alfred	Pocket Guide To Bridge *(General Features Corp, 1969-75, 36p.)*
Sheinwold, Alfred	Sheinwold On Bridge: Basic Bidding *(General Features Corp, 1958, 28p.)*
Shepard, Edward Valentine	Correct Contract Bridge *(Doubleday/Douglas, 1929-30, 265p.)*
Shinner, Ernest Gardner	The Streamlined System Of Contract Bridge *(Dorrance, 1941, 84p.)*
Silberstang, Edwin	Handbook Of Winning Bridge *(Cardoza, 1995, 122p.)*
Silberstang, Edwin	Play Bridge Tonight *(Gambler's Book Club, 1976, 64p.)*
Silverman, Shirley	Advanced And Duplicate Bridge Student Text *(Barclay, 1976-96, 64p.)*
Silverman, Shirley	Elementary Five Card Major Student Text *(Barclay, 1976-96, 48p.)*
Silverman, Shirley	Intermediate Bridge Five Card Major Student Text *(Barclay, 1976-96, 48p.)*
Silverman, Shirley	Play Of The Hand As Declarer And Defender *(Barclay, 1980-96, 64p.)*
Silverstein, Nate	Point Count Bidding *(Private, 1983, 35p.)*
Simmons, Carolyn O	Carolyn's Contract Complete *(The Bridge World, 1936, 24p.)*

F. TEACHER'S MATERIAL

A.C.B.L. — Information Manual For A.C.B.L. Accredited Teachers *(A.C.B.L., 1993-97, 155p.)*

Anonymous — Bridge: A Guide Of Forty Playing Lessons *(Private, 1975, 94p.)*

Baron, Randall & Stewart, Frank — The Bridge Teacher's Manual - Volumes 1 to 4 - For Beginning Players *(Devyn Press, 1988-90, 141-146p.)*

Berg, Lynn — Using Computers To Teach Bridge *(A.C.B.L., 1997, 80p.)*

Bonney, C Jack — Bridge Teacher's Guide For Elementary And Intermediate Students *(Lev Gleason Printing, 1951, 76p.)*

Bonney, C Jack — Master Bridge Teaching Guide For Elementary And Intermediate Classes *(Barclay, 1957, 128p.)*

Burnstine, David & Gottleib, Michael — Teacher Outline Of 4 Aces System *(Four Aces Bridge Studio, 1935, 28p.)*

Campbell, Lilian H — Twelve Lessons In Contract Bidding Based On The Four Aces' System *(Private, 1936, 12p.)*

Culbertson, Ely — How To Become A Contract Bridge Teacher *(Culbertson National Studios, 1933, 16p.)*

Culbertson, Ely — Lesson Sheets On The Culbertson System *(Culbertson National Studio/The Bridge World, 1930-36, 100-48p.)*

English Bridge Union — Duplicate Bridge: A Resource Pack For Teachers, Volumes I & II *(Apsbridge, 1991, 172-165p.)*

Gooden, George S — Contract Bridge Teacher's Blue Book *(Private, 1960-61, 200p.)*

Goren, Charles H — Bridge Teacher's Manual *(Goren Enterprises, 1955-58, 175p.)*

Grant, Audrey — Bridge: A.C.B.L. Introduction To Bridge Bidding, Club/Diamond/Heart/Spade Series Teacher's Manual *(A.C.B.L., 1987-94, 132-316p.)*

Grant, Audrey — Handbook For Supervised Play *(A.C.B.L., 1992, 22p.)*

Grant, Audrey — Teacher's Manual For The A.C.B.L. Intermediate Lesson Series: Better Bridge - Defense *(A.C.B.L., 1996, 107p.)*

Hamilton, Betty — Teacher's Manual (To Be Used In Conjunction With Bridge One, Two And Three Textbooks) *(Private, 1969, 20p.)*

Havner, Roy R — The Point Count System Teacher's Manual *(Private, 1948, 139p.)*

Henry, Lee & Jacobwitz, Norman — Lee Henry's Intermediate-Advanced Lesson Series: Special Bidding Problems *(Private, 1976, 24p.)*

Kantar, Edwin B — Kantar Lessons I-IV *(Private, 1989-2000, 300-182p.)*

Kushner, Jack — Culbertson Teachers Lesson Charts *(Private, 1950, 0p.)*

Kushner, Jack — Point Count Teachers Lesson Charts *(Private, 1950, 0p.)*

Kushner, Jack — Ten Pamphlets On Play: Teacher's Lesson Sheets *(Private, 1952, 30p.)*

Lampert, Harry — Teacher's Guide For Lesson Plans *(Private, 1988, 11p.)*

Long, Effie Lindsay — American Bridge Teachers' Association Handbook On Teaching Techniques *(A.B.T.A, 1978, 30p.)*

McMullin, Edith — Easybridge Introduction Packet *(Private, 2000, 72p.)*

McMullin, Edith — Easybridge! 1 1/2: Director's Manual *(Private, 1998, 11p.)*

McMullin, Edith — Easybridge! Lite, Presenter's Manual *(Private, 1999, 25p.)*

Michaels, Charles — Master Bridge Teacher's Training Course & Manual, The Basic-Intermediate Course *(Barclay, 1959-65, 172p.)*

Parmer, Mrs. Allan — Compact And Simplified Lesson Notes On Contract Bridge *(Gate City Stationery Co, 1930, 23p.)*

Peterson, Gerald — Preparation For Bridge Lessons *(Vantage Press, 1962, 50p.)*

Place, Lucille — Teacher's Manual *(Place Publications, 1960-61, 24p.)*

Randle, Ralph & Spann, Marcella — Teacher's Manual For Instant Bridge: Twenty Complete Lesson Plans *(Private, 1960, 23p.)*

Rathburn, Mrs. Merle C R — Lesson Notes On Contract Bridge *(Private, 1930, 18p.)*

Sands, Norma — Lesson Plans For Chapters I-VI Of Playing The Cards *(Rocky Mountain Books, 1984, 9p.)*

Silverman, Shirley — Five Card Major Teacher's Manual *(Barclay/ Baron-Barclay, 1976-96, 250-334p.)*

Silverman, Shirley — Play Of The Hand Lesson Plans *(Barclay, 1981, 79p.)*

Sydnor, Caroline — Teaching Bridge: How To Do It Better *(Bridge Made Easy, 1988, 177p.)*

Taylor, Mrs. Agnes Mundell — Contract Bridge - Further Notes For Beginners And Teachers *(London School Of Bridge, 1931, 36p.)*

Wei, C C & Silverman, Shirley — Official Precision Teacher's Manual *(Barclay/ Devyn Press, 1972-98, 65p.)*

Woods, Jo — Jo Woods Bridge Teacher's Manual Basic Course *(Private, 1960, 185p.)*

Woods, Jo — Jo Woods Manual On Defensive Play Of The Hands *(Private, 1958-60, 112p.)*

Work, Milton Cooper & Richards, Ralph Reed — Lesson Hands For The Use Of Bridge Teachers Of The Common Sense System *(Winston, 1930, 25p.)*

G. BIDDING SYSTEMS (INCLUDING SURVEYS OF THEM)

Abbey, L H — The Abbey System *(Abbey, 1941, 11p.)*

Abramsohn, Phil — The Modern One-Over-One System Of Contract Bridge *(Rothchild-Fink Corporation, 1933, 32p.)*

Ace Trumper — Contract Concentrated *(H.W. Smith, 1935, 56p.)*

Agnew, Herbert C — Game In Contract Bridge Is 26 Points *(Private, 1954-58, 21-29p.)*

Albano, Helen D — Analysis And Practical Application Of The Goren Method (1962-72) *(Private, 1962, 22p.)*

Alder, Phillip — Singleton System *(Private, 1979, 22p.)*

Allard, J Gordon — Outline Of Culbertson Contract Bridge *(Sutton House, 1937, 122p.)*

Allen, David *see Marsh-Smith, David*

Amsbury, Joe — Bridge: Bidding Naturally *(Batsford, 1979, 152p.)*

Anderson, Chalmers & Gale, Harry — The Eighteen System *(Adshead, 1934, 20p.)*

Anderson, J W — Redcastle Acol *(Montrose Review Press, 1979, 28p.)*

Anonymous — Bridge Club Contract As Experts Play It *(Bassett, 1936, 40p.)*

Anonymous — The Bidding Guide *(Smith Advertising, 1933, 4p.)*

Anonymous — The Vienna System Of Contract Bridge Bidding *(Vienna System Ltd, 1934, 32p.)*

Anonymous — The Weak Openings Systems In The European Championships1979 *(Polish Bridge Assoc., 1979, 4p.)*

Antoff, Theo — Tanc Bidding: The Offensive *(Glomar, 2000, 351p.)*

Atkinson, Charlie — Charlie Atkinson's Simple System *(Private, 1978, 22p.)*

August, William J — A Logical Approach To Standard Bidding: Course No. 1 & 2 *(Private, 1973, 10-37p.)*

August, William J — Bridge: Light Up Your Understanding Of Bidding *(Rutledge, 1995, 248p.)*

Bailey, Edward — The Bailey System Of Contract Bidding *(Private, 1937, 8p.)*

Bailey, Maureen O'Brien & Oeschger, Ivy — Bridge For The Joneses *(Morrow, 1947, 331p.)*

Baldursson, Jon — Icelandic Precision *(Private, 1992, 0p.)*

Bancroft, Griffing — Natural Contract Bidding *(Private, 1936, 56p.)*

Bangs, Fred T — Basic Bidding In Contract Bridge *(Phoenix Pub, 1955, 128p.)*

Barclay, Shepard — The Pocket Charts On All Systems Of Contract Bridge *(Barclay, 1930, 32p.)*

Baron, Leo & Meredith, Adam — Contract Bridge - The Baron System Outlined *(Nicholson & Watson, 1946, 30p.)*

Baron, Leo & Meredith, Adam — The Baron System Of Contract Bridge *(Contract Bridge Equipment, 1948, 180p.)*

Barton, F D — Contract Bridge - The Bidding Simplified *(Private, 1935, 22p.)*

Barton, Frederick P — American Contract Bridge *(Jackson, 1928, 48p.)*

Barton, Frederick P — Barton On Contract Bridge *(Jackson/Joiner & Steele, 1929-31, 16-126p.)*

Barton, Frederick P — The Barton Variation *Joiner & Steele, 1933-46, 87-89p.)*

Barton, Frederick P — The Barton Variation More Fully Explained *(Joiner & Steele, 1934, 33p.)*

Barton, Frederick P & Blake, Middleton — The Barton System Of Bidding At Contract Bridge *(Farrar & Reinhart, 1934, 80p.)*

Battaglia, Anthony — New Battaglia Contract Bridge Bidding System *(Morris Graphics, 1964, 28p.)*

Batten, Howard W — Simplified Contract Bridge And The Simplified System *(Record Roches, 1933, 28p.)*

Beard, John & Cummings, Vic — The Precision Way *(J.B. Bridge Courses, 1987, 84p.)*

Beasley, Col. Henry Mountifort — Simple Contract *(Mudie, 1938, 99p.)*

Beasley, Col. Henry Mountifort — The Beasley Contract Bridge System *(Associated Newspapers, 1935-36, 128p.)*

Becker, Mike & Ginsberg, Matt — The Ultimate Club *(Ultimate Club, 1981, 127p.)*

Beinecke, Walter & Richard, Harold — The Manhattan Whist Club System 1935 (The Vanderbilt Club System Modified) *(Winston, 1935, 26p.)*

Belladonna, Giorgio — Roman Club (1969) *(Private, 1972, 107p.)*

Belladonna, Giorgio & Avarelli, Walter — *The Roman Club System Of Distributional Bidding *(Simon & Schuster/Cassell, 1959-60, 162p.)*

Belladonna, Giorgio & Garozzo, Benito — *Precision And Superprecision Bidding *(Putnam's/Cassell, 1975-76, 237p.)*

Bennett, H W — Better Bridge For Busy People *(Private, 1940, 47p.)*

Bentfield, H R — Bridge Naturally *(Private, 1979, 99p.)*

Beresford, Elizabeth — Complete Contract Bidding For All Four Players Together With Their Response *(Beresford, 1934, 34p.)*

Beynon, George W — Sims System Of Contract Bidding *(Private, 1933, 0p.)*

Beyrouti, Michael G — Contrast, A First Approach To Indirect Bidding *(Private, 1998, 200p.)*

Bird, David L & Bourke, Tim — *Tournament Acol - A System For Winners *(Gollancz, 1995, 158p.)*

Bissell, Harold W — *The Bissell System: The Distributional Method Of Contract Bidding *(Columbia University Press, 1936, 317p.)*

Blackwood, Easley — Blackwood On Bidding *(Bobbs Merrill/ Eyre & Spottiswoode, 1956-57, 215p.)*

Blackwood, Easley — The Blackwood System Of Contract Bridge *(Private, 1937, 20p.)*

Blake, Edwin G — The Blake System Of Contract Bridge *(Private, 1934, 64p.)*

Blake, Middleton — The Barton System Of Bidding Contract Bridge *(Farrar & Reinhart, 1934, 80p.)*

Boardman, Paul K — The Churchill Bidding Style *(Private, 1961, 34p.)*

Boblett, Marge — It Takes Two To Bid *(Maric Enterprises, 1983, 76p.)*

Boland, Vincent F — Boland System Of Contract Bridge Bidding *(Penton Press, 1935, 88p.)*

Boland, Vincent F & Law, John H — Accurate Contract Bidding - The Boland Club *(Harris Printing, 1931, 84p.)*

Booker, Courtland S — Atomic Club System *(Cotton Printing, 1948, 37p.)*

Boone, Lemuel D — Stepping Stones To Sterling Bridge *(Private, 1941, 63p.)*

Borin, Jim — Bridge Borin Style - Baronised Acol *(Private, 1978, 48p.)*

Borin, Jim & Borin, Norma — Our Precision Style *(Thorpe, 1981, 72p.)*

Bourget, Frank E & Tobin, E J — A Digest Of Popular Systems Of Contract Bridge (Red Book Of Contract Bridge) *(Whitman, 1933, 60p.)*

Bourke, Tim — The Red Club *(Australian Bridge Institute, 1975, 15p.)*

Brannon, Robert M — Foolproof Contract 1933 *(Brannon, 1933, 166p.)*

Brannon, Robert M — The Incomparable Club Convention *(News Printing House, 1935, 88p.)*

Brannon, Robert M — The Professor Does His Stuff - Foolproof Contract Bridge *(Play Bridge/Paragon Duplex, 1930-31, 117p.)*

Breeser, Robert — The Bridge Memopad: Notrumps *(Mindracer Publishing, 1997, 58p.)*

Bridge Headquarters — The New Standardized Official System Of Contract Bridge *(Winston, 1932, 289-313p.)*

Bridge Headquarters — The Official System Of Contract Bridge *(Winston/Putnam's, 1931-33, 236-292p.)*

Brinig, Liz — Bridge Bidding: The Golden Rules *(Crowood Press, 1991, 149p.)*

Brinker, P A — The Brinker System *(Private, 1946, 16p.)*

Broomfield, D — Acol Flow Chart *(Private, 1997, 4p.)*

Brown, John — Bidding Craft *(Duckworth, 1962, 133p.)*

Brown, Rick — Natural Precision: Effective, Aggressive, But Natural Precision Bidding *(Private, 1998, 93p.)*

Bruelheide, Frank Elmer — The American System *(Bruelheide, 1941, 17p.)*

Bruelheide, Frank Elmer — The Culbertson System: Abridged For The Average Player *(Bruelheide, 1935-39, 64p.)*

Brunner, Michelle — Bridge With Brunner: Acol Bidding For Improvers *(Batsford, 2000, 192p.)*

Buckley, Joseph J — The Roxbury Point Bidding System Of Contract Bridge *(Independent Press, 1961, 64p.)*

Buller, Col. Walter — The Way To Play The Buller System Of Contract Bridge *(The Star, 1936, 128p.)*

Bunch, Gienn I — Subtract Two: The Simplified System Of Contract Bridge And How To Play Bridge Simplified *(Private, 1934, 48p.)*

Burgay, Leandro — Bridge: The Burgay Diamond *(Private, 1979, 87p.)*

Burns, Margery — The Nottingham Club System Of Contract Bridge *(Nottingham B C, 1954-58, 47-107p.)*

Burns, Margery — The Nottingham System Of Contract Bridge *(Educational Productions, 1969, 107p.)*

Burnstine, David — *The Four Horsemen's One-Over-One Method Of Contract Bidding *(Black/Blue Ribbon, 1932, 118p.)*

Burnstine, David &
  Gottlieb, Michael   Lectures On The Four Aces System *(Four Aces Bridge Studio, 1935, 31p.)*
Burtenshaw, Mrs. James H.   Contract Bridge Questionnaire *(Private, 1933-36, 12-20p.)*
Busby, Mrs. Oscar E   Contract Partnership Bidding, Compiled From The Lectures Of The Busby School Of Bridge *(Private, 1929, 48p.)*

Butler, Geoffrey &
  Stern, Dr. Paul   The Two Club System Of Bidding *(Faber, 1940-46, 300p.)*
Butler, Grant A   Trump Control Bridge *(Private, 1960, 32p.)*
Campbell, Allan   Clarified Contract Bridge *(Simpkin Marshall, 1937, 68p.)*
Carpenter, Kim   How To Become A Professional Money Bridge Player - The Stat System *(Educator Books, 1969, 162p.)*
Carter, John Thomas   The Carter System - Contract *(Private, 1936, 32p.)*
Charron, George O   The A-B-C Contract Bridge System *(Regal Press, 1938, 5p.)*
Chazen, Bernie   Avoiding The Traps *(Club Letter, 1997, 32p.)*
Chazen, Bernie   Club Letter Standard, The Official Two-Over-One Bidding System Of The Club Letter *(Club Letter, 1996, 32p.)*
Churchill, S Garton   Churchill Natural Bidding Style At Contract Bridge *(Private, 1979, 743p.)*
Churchill, S Garton &
  Ferguson, Albert B   *Contract Bidding Tactics At Matchpoint Play *(A.D. Press, 1936, 323p.)*
Clark, Morris   The Four Leafed Club *(Tom's Technical Pubs, 1983, 165p.)*
Coffin, George Sturgis   Acol And The New Point Count *(Duckworth, 1953-70, 56p.)*
Coffin, George Sturgis   American Canapé *(Coffin, 1962, 9p.)*
Coffin, George Sturgis   Canapé Bidding, Your Pass Book To More Master Points *(Private, 1960, 24p.)*
Coffin, George Sturgis   Canapé Club System *(Private, 1965, 16p.)*
Coffin, George Sturgis   Culbertson System Point Count For 1953 *(Branford, 1953, 15p.)*
Coffin, George Sturgis   Natural Big Club *(Parsonfield, 1969, 192p.)*
Coffin, Kathryne P   The ABC's Of The Official System Of Contract Bridge And The Play Of The Hand *(Bobbs Merrill, 1932, 90p.)*
Cohen, Ben   Change To Acol *(Allen & Unwin, 1953-57, 126-158p.)*
Cohen, Ben & Barrow, Rhoda   Calling A Spade A Spade *(Blond/Barnes, 1965, 142p.)*
Cohen, Ben & Barrow,
  Rhoda/Lederer, Rhoda   Acol Without Tears/Bidding Better Bridge - Acol For Americans *(Allen & Unwin/Barnes, 1962-65, 287-293p.)*
Cohen, Ben & Barrow,
  Rhoda/Lederer, Rhoda   All About Acol *(Allen & Unwni/ Unwin/Collins Willow, 1969-93, 264-304p.)*
Cohen, Ben & Barrow,
  Rhoda/Lederer, Rhoda   Basic Acol *(Allen & Unwni/ Unwin/Collins Willow, 1969-93, 63-120p.)*
Cohen, Ben & Reese, Terence   *The Acol System Of Contract Bridge *(Joiner & Steele, 1939-56, 64-148p.)*
Cohen, Ben & Reese, Terence   *The Acol Two Club *(British Bridge World, 1938, 55p.)*
Cohen, Lawrence & Katz,
  Richard & Sundby, Robert   Breakthrough In Bridge *(Breakthrough Bridge, 1973-74, 168-186p.)*
Collins, J H   The Archer System *(Private, 1955, 303p.)*
Conot, Robert   Pattern Relay Organised System *(Private, 1967, 141p.)*
Conover, David M &
  Joslin, Bernard F   Conover-Joslin Point System Of Contract Bridge *(Private, 1946, 12p.)*
Courtenay, F Dudley   The Standardized Code Of Contract Bridge Bidding *(Bridge Headquarters/Methuen, 1937, 108p.)*
Courtenay, F Dudley   The System The Experts Play *(Bridge Headquarters, 1934-36, 90-95p.)*
Courtenay, F Dudley &
  Walshe, G G J   The Losing Trick Count: *(Methuen, 1935-47, 176p.)*
Cox, Mrs. Spencer &
  Meldon, W W   Contract Bridge - The Combined Count *(Belsey & Copp/Devonshire Club/Private, 1936-52, 12-44p.)*
Crane, Joshua   Common Sense In Contract Bidding *(Pearson, 1932-36, 126p.)*
Crane, Joshua   The Crane System Of Contract Bidding *(Lewes Press, 1937, 118p.)*
Crane, Joshua   The Crane System Of Modern Contract Bidding *(East Anglia Times, 1948, 106p.)*
Criticus   Contract Simplicitas *(Jenkins, 1933, 332p.)*
Crowhurst, Eric   *Precision Bidding In Acol *(Pelham, 1974-, 240p.)*
Crowhurst, Eric &
  Kambites, Andrew   Understanding Acol *(Gollancz, 1990-97, 157-176p.)*
Culbertson, Ely   *Contract Bridge Blue Book *(The Bridge World/Faber, 1930-35, 344-599p.)*
Culbertson, Ely   Culbertson Point-Count Bidding *(Winston/Faber, 1954,171- 222p.)*
Culbertson, Ely
  (& Culbertson, Josephine)   Contract Bridge For Everyone *(Winston/Signet/Faber/Penguin, 1948-49, 117-118p.)*
Dalton, Basil   Contract Bridge Conventions, Collected, Compared And Criticised *(Richards, 1932, 80p.)*
Danielson, Robert J   Danielson's Precision *(Private, 1976, 27p.)*
Danielson, Robert J   Relay Precision - Book One to Five *(Private, 1977-79,80-106p.)*
Davies, G H & Norris, V E   The Gorvic System *(England, 1985, 274p.)*
Davis, Frank Maxie   Precision Bridge *(Dorrance, 1976, 425p.)*
Deedler, Kenneth   Kenkard Basic Bidding Series *(Private, 1954, 200p.)*
Delmain, A V   Hand Pattern System *(Medulla Press, 1993, 271p.)*
Dennison, Maureen &
  Samuels, John   Acol Bidding Made Easy *(Decision Tree, 1986, 48p.)*
Desai, Gaurang & Desai, G R   Contract Bridge: Not Without Pattern Points, Not Without Pattern Controls *(Mehta, 1996, 136p.)*
Desante, Gilbert &
  Desante, David   Exact Point Count: A System For Bidding Contract Bridge *(Slate Creek Press, 1988, 176p.)*
Dettman, H V   Simplified Precision Bidding *(Dorrance, 1972, 145p.)*
Dewhurst, Victor   The Two Club System *(Faber, 1965, 220p.)*
Discher, Raymond H   Contract Rapid-Handy Direct Bridge *(Cosmopolitan Bridge Pub, 1934, 283p.)*
Discher, Raymond H   Point Contract-Bridge *(Union Tribune Print, 1931, 47p.)*
Dlugatch, Irving   Bridge. A Simple, Easy To Learn Precision Bidding System *(Modern Science, 1970, 84p.)*
Dobereiner, A E   Winning Contract As Played By National Champions In Fourteen Easy Lessons *(Private, 1934, 47p.)*
Donovan, Peter &
  MacLeod, Iain   Bridge Is Still An Easy Game *(Wheaton, 1988, 246p.)*

Graham, H E — Contract Bridge: How To Improve Your Game *(Clowes, 1937, 80p.)*

Graham, J — Contract Bridge: The Watson-Glenny One Club Forcing System *(Private, 1953, 8p.)*

Greene, Ernest — Now You Can Play Contract In Half An Hour In Seven Complete Lessons *(Fletcher, 1935, 64p.)*

Greene, Ernest — The Greene Book On Contract *(Joiner & Steele, 1935, 96p.)*

Greenhalgh, F &
  Greenhalgh, R N — VA-SK: A New Approach To Slam Bidding *(S.I. Libraries, 1948, 89p.)*

Griffiths, David C — The Little Black Bridge Book, A Pocket Guide To Acol Bidding *(Vaughan Bridge Guides, 1994, 55p.)*

Groetheim, Glenn &
  Sontag, Alan — The Viking Precision Club: A Relay System For The 21st Century *(Devyn Press, 2000, 253p.)*

Grunden, William O — The Weak Two System *(Carlton, 1975, 40p.)*

Gutman, Sid — Major Five Bridge Bidding Handbook *(Private, 1985, 189p.)*

Guzy, Saul C — Positive Response System Of Contract Bridge *(Sandra Distributing, 1933, 80p.)*

Hamied, K A — Hoc System Precise Bidding At Bridge *(Splalvani Pub, 1970, 107p.)*

Hamilton, Fraser B — How To Bid And Win At Bridge: The Canadian Contract Bidding System *(Private, 1960, 64p.)*

Hamilton-Gordon, Comdr. H — Standard Contract *(Houghton & Scott-Snell, 1935, 116p.)*

Hankin, Sam — Bridge: The Simple System For Intermediate Students *(Private, 1988, 115p.)*

Hanna, William &
  Steen, Douglas — Precision Power Bidding *(Coffin, 1956, 104p.)*

Hardy, Max — *+Two Over One Game Force, Revised - Expanded, Updated For The 1990's *(Hardy, 1989-97, 322p.)*

Hardy, Max — *Five Card Majors, Western Style *(Hardy, 1974-80, 94-95p.)*

Hardy, Max — *Standard Bridge Bidding For The Twenty-First Century *(Squeeze Books, 2000, 279p.)*

Hardy, Max — *Two Over One Game Force *(Hardy, 1982-84, 147p.)*

Hardy, Max — *Two Over One Game Force Quiz Book *(Devyn Press, 1993, 180p.)*

Hargrove, Wanda R — Having A Conversation In Bridge Language *(Private, 1971, 123p.)*

Hart, Norman De Vere — Daily Telegraph And Morning Post Book Of Contract Bridge *(Daily Telegraph-Morning Post, 1938, 205p.)*

Hartmann, John — The Modest Club: The Fastest Way To Find The Card *(Private, 1990, 200p.)*

Hasney,Chris & Pottier, Jerry — The Basic American Bidding System *(Trafford Pub, 1998, 189p.)*

Hasney,Chris & Pottier, Jerry — The Intermediate American Bidding System *(Trafford Pub, 1998, 170p.)*

Hattersley, Lelia — Contract Developments *(McBride, 1928, 205p.)*

Hattersley, Lelia — How To Play The Culbertson System *(The Bridge World, 1931, 200p.)*

Hattersley, Lelia — Up-to-The-Minute Contract *(McBride, 1930, 75p.)*

Havner, Roy R — The Point Count System *(Private, 1950, 23p.)*

Havner, Roy R — Twenty-Five Points Is Game: The Point-Count Bidding System *(Private, 1947, 73p.)*

Heath, Forrest A &
  Beebe, Henry W — Seven-Eleven: A Manual Of The Heath System Of Bidding At Contract Bridge *(Private, 1933, 55p.)*

Henderson, Arthur Lyonell — Q Systems: Two Quintessential Kiss Methods For Bidding Bridge Hands *(Private, 1998, 116p.)*

Hermansen, J V V — Danish Bridge System *(Private, 1932, 8p.)*

Hermon, G M — Contract Bridge In Six Lessons *(Private, 1932, 38p.)*

Heron, Charles B — Heron Club System Of Contract Bridge *(Clonmore & Reynolds, 1947, 86p.)*

Hester, A R — The Hester Winning Count System *(Guardian Press, 1951, 32p.)*

Hester, A R — The Winning Count *(Private, 1950, 18p.)*

Hickey, Ina & Peart, Noel — Modern Contract Bridge: Bidding And Play Made Easy *(Browne & Nolan, 1944, 62p.)*

Hira, K L — The Bridge Book - Hand Pattern Bidding System *(Sterling, 1979, 131p.)*

Hollender, Bertie — Contract Bridge Up-To-Date *(Bazaar Exchange, 1931, 72p.)*

Hollis, Maude &
  Riggs, Marjorie — A Complete Synopsis Of Improvements And Finer Points Of The Culbertson System For 1933 *(Private, 1933, 5p.)*

Holmes, C Ellwood — Acol But - *(Bander Press, 1967, 55p.)*

Holmes, C Ellwood — Acol Limited *(Private, 1956, 60p.)*

Holmes, C Ellwood — Bid To Win On Two Way Approach *(Private, 1955, 26p.)*

Holmes, C Ellwood — Bidding For Two *(Bander Press, 1967, 55p.)*

Holmes, C Ellwood — Two Way Approach *(Bander Press, 1958, 24p.)*

Holveck, Joseph Emil — Presenting A Bidding System In Contract Bridge *(Mathias, 1934, 30p.)*

Hopkins, William F &
  Hall, Charles A — Winning Contract - The Hall System *(Rosenthal, 1934, 94p.)*

Horn, A C — Contract Bridge: Limited Opening Bids *(Private, 1977, 167p.)*

Horne, Lawrence W — Handy Guide Books To Contract Bridge With Summary Of Popular Bidding Systems *(Clement, 1933, 70p.)*

Howard, Denis — The New South Wales System (1970) *(Reldt, 1970, 70p.)*

Howard, Denis — The New South Wales System *(Private, 1964, 83p.)*

Hummel, John & Lee, Peggy — Kushner System, As Revised By … *(Private, 1965, 39p.)*

Humphreys, Ivan L'e — Contract Bridge - Basic Bidding *(Private, 1942, 0p.)*

Humphreys, Ivan L'e — The Basic Principles Of Bidding Common To All Systems *(Private, 1945, 96p.)*

Huo, P T — Bidding With Confidence (For Advanced Players) *(Private, 1958, 78p.)*

Husband, Pat & Klinger, Ron — Introduction To Acol Bidding *(Gollancz, 1991, 24p.)*

Huston, Irvin &
  Roosen, Russell — The Detroit System Of Contract Bridge *(Huston College Of Bridge, 1932, 32p.)*

Ingram, H St John — The Ingram One Club Or Simplified Bridge *(Eyre & Spottiswoode, 1935, 96p.)*

Ingram, H St John — The Leading Bidding Systems In Brief *(Cotton, 1935, 31p.)*

Jacobi, Ernst &
  Hartland, Stanley — Acol The Swiss Way *(Vantage Press, 1992, 80p.)*

Jacobson, Bob — St. Peter's Just For Fun Bridge In Five Easy Lessons *(Dorrance, 1994, 77p.)*

Jacoby, O & Burnstine, D &
  Gottleib, M & Schenken, H — *The Four Aces System Of Contract Bridge *(Random House, 1935, 302p.)*

Jacoby, Oswald — Point Count Bidding *(Nea Service/Arco, 1955-60, 32p.)*

Jaeger, Henry P — Bidding Chart - Official System *(Bruelheide, 1932, 0p.)*

Jago, Willie — Most - Major Oriented Standard *(Beads D.T.P., 1995, 132p.)*

Jamieson, P D — Blue Club Notes *(Australian Bridge Institute, 1976, 16p.)*

Janik, Francis J — Contract Bridge: The 2096 System *(Private, 1941-46, 32-56p.)*

AUTHOR	TITLE
Jannersten, Eric & Lederer, Rhoda	*Precision Bridge (Precision Bidding) *(Allen & Unwin/Scribner/(Devyn), 1972-92, 224-227p.)
Jarboe, Robert J	A Different Concept Of Bridge *(Private, 1990-92, 9p.)*
Jarboe, Robert J	The Jarboe Concept - Point Count Response *(Private, 1992, 2p.)*
Jarman, Kara J	Two Over One - Game Force: Simplified *(Sun Graphics, 1994-95, 147-48p.)*
Jayarajan, P M	The Weak Notrump With Strong Opening Bids In Every Suit *(Private, 1972-76, 76-92p.)*
Jensen, Anker	Anchor Contract Bridge *(Private, 1936, 16p.)*
Jensen, Anker & Lyman, Edward D	Anchor Contract Bidding *(Chatto & Windus/O.U.P., 1934, 48-60p.)*
Joannides, Dinos C H R	A Complete Bidding System For Advanced Players *(Private, 1985, 75p.)*
Johnson, Paul M	Would You Like To Play Bridge. An Explanation Of A Simplified System By A Non-Expert. *(Vantage Press, 1966, 41p.)*
Joshi, K D	Contract Bridge: Simple System Of Bidding *(Private, 1959, 41p.)*
Joshi, V R	Precise Bidding In Contract Bridge *(Joshi, 1959, 222p.)*
Kane, Lawrence	Normal Bridge Bidding: Finding Your Bid In The Modern Game *(Vantage Press, 1999, 34p.)*
Kantar, Edwin B	An Expert's Guide To Improving Your Bidding Skills *(Wilshire, 1980, 151p.)*
Kantar, Edwin B	Bidding *(Private, 1963-65, 37-52p.)*
Kantar, Edwin B	Bridge Bidding Made Easy *(Wilshire, 1972, 256p.)*
Kantar, Edwin B	How To Win At Bridge *(Collier/Wilshire, 1962-67, 143p.)*
Kaplan, Edgar	Complete Italian System Of Winning Bridge *(Ives Washburn/Signet, 1959, 159p.)*
Kaplan, Edgar	Kaplan-Sheinwold Updated *(The Bridge World/Nella, 1972-80, 42p.)*
Kaplan, Edgar	Notes On Three Italian Systems *(The Bridge World, 1967, 19p.)*
Kaplan, Edgar	The Leghorn Diamond *(The Bridge World, 1970, 15p.)*
Kaplan, Edgar	The New South Wales System *(The Bridge World, 1971, 21p.)*
Kaplan, Edgar	The Roman Club *(The Bridge World, 1968, 19p.)*
Kaplan, Edgar & Sheinwold, Alfred	*How To Play Winning Bridge *(Collie/Fleet/Allenr, 1958-1962, 256- 224p.)
Kaplan, Edgar & Sheinwold, Alfred	*The Kaplan-Sheinwold System Of Winning Bridge *(Fleet/Signet, 1963-83, 283p.)
Kearse, Amalya	Bridge At Your Fingertips *(Visual Library, 1979, 320p.)*
Keith, Ronald L G	Bidding By Numbers - The Matic System *(Edurec, 1974, 40p.)*
Keith, Ronald L G	The Matic System Or Bidding By Numbers At Contract Bridge *(Edurec, 1996, 88p.)*
Kemmer, Charles B	The Combination System: Contract Bridge Bidding *(Private, 1947, 24p.)*
Kempson, Ewart	British Bridge *(Aberdeen Journal, 1935-36, 151-159p.)*
Kempson, Ewart	Kempson On Bidding *(Aberdeen Journal, 1936, 172p.)*
Kempson, Ewart & Hart, Norman De Vere	The Quintessence Of CAB: The CAB System Of Bridge *(Kaye, 1959, 160p.)*
Kennedy, George	Kennedy System Of Bridge *(Arco, 1965, 284p.)*
Kerr, R P & Jones, W L	*The Symmetric Relay *(Private, 1980, 98p.)
Kerwin, Madeleine	How To Bid: Contract Bridge *(Private/Knopf, 1929-30, 58-62p.)*
Kerwin, Madeleine	How To Bid: Contract Bridge In 1931 *(Knopf, 1930, 69p.)*
Kerwin, Madeleine	Kerwin On Contract - The Official System *(Century, 1931, 89p.)*
Kerwin, Madeleine	One-Over-One For Every One (The Philip Hal Sims System) *(Kerwin, 1932, 116p.)*
Kierein, John	Big Clubs Little Notrump *(Private, 1990, 4p.)*
Klein, Emil	Enjoy Your Bridge *(Nicholson & Watson, 1947, 191p.)*
Klein, Emil	What System Partner? *(Nicholson & Watson, 1940, 23p.)*
Klinger, Ron	1976 Bermuda Bowl Systems *(Australian Bridge Institute, 1976, 12p.)*
Klinger, Ron	Five-Card Majors *(Gollancz/Houghton, 1992-2000, 126-128p.)*
Klinger, Ron	Simplified N.S.W. After One Club-One Notrump *(Australian Bridge Institute, 1976, 8p.)*
Klinger, Ron	The Power System *(Modern Bridge Publications, 1993, 384p.)*
Koenig, Thomas W	The Koenig System Of Bidding *(Private, 1943, 56p.)*
Konstam, Kenneth	The C.A.B. System Of Bidding At Bridge *(Sunday Times, 1959, 7p.)*
Kroll, Harris E	Official Ace Over Ace System *(Private, 1944, 36p.)*
Kunac, Peter	The Kunac Approach To Acol *(Private, 1992-97, 56p.)*
Kushner, Jack	Kushner System-The Partnership System *(Private, 1960, 39p.)*
Kushner, Jack	The T.N.T. System Of Bidding *(Private, 1952, 8p.)*
Kyle, H M	Elements Of Contract Bridge Volume 1. Theory And Practice Of Sound Bidding *(Private, 1932, 32p.)*
Landau, Eric & Baron, Randall	Every Hand An Adventure *(Devyn Press, 1996, 62p.)*
Langness, Cleveland W	Triple's Simple Simon System: Contract Bridge *(Wakefield Park, 1939, 30p.)*
Lawhorn, Melvin C	Lawhorn System Of Bidding *(Private, 1949, 26p.)*
Lawrence, Mike	*Mike Lawrence's Workbook On The Two Over One System *(Hardy, 1987-93, 189p.)
Lea, Robert H	Bridge Is Easy With The Lea System *(Lea Enterprises, 1965, 144p.)*
Lederer, Richard	Lederer Bids Two Clubs *(Williams & Norgate, 1934-35, 220p.)*
Ledvina, J P	How To Win At Bridge *(Plaza, 1948, 61p.)*
Lenz, Sidney Samuel	Contract Bidding *(Allen & Unwin, 1931, 96p.)*
Lenz, Sidney Samuel	My System Of Contract Bidding *(Simon & Schuster, 1930, 93p.)*
Levinrew, George E	Stallard's First Up The Line Bridge Bidding *(Private, 1982-83, 80-146p.)*
Levinrew, George E	The Levinrew System *(Private, 1966, 2p.)*
Levinson, W B	How To Win: Contract Bridge Simplified By Experts *(Private, 1932, 34p.)*
Levy, Harry L	The Control System, Contract Bridge *(Weiss Printing, 1932, 82p.)*
Lewis, William	Data-4 *(Private, 1995, 16p.)*
Lightner, Theodore	Highlights Of The Culbertson System *(The Bridge World, 1931, 238-242p.)*
Lindsay, Kenneth L	Three-D And The Mafia Club *(Aiga, 1981, 228p.)*
Littler, Malcolm	Strong Club (An Entire System) *(Private, 2000, 74p.)*
Loper, Walter	The No Trump Forcing System *(Private, 1932, 40p.)*
Lucian	The First Bid *(Falcon Press, 1934, 64p.)*
Lucian	The Straight Bid Or Standard Hand Bidding (+Extra Chapter) *(Benn, 1936+37, 137+11p.)*
Lutz, Joe & Fink, Jerry	American Forcing Minor Bidding System *(Private/Devyn Press, 1994-5, 230p.)*
Lynch, Edgar	Bridge - The Diamond System *(Littlebury, 1948, 57p.)*
MacKay, Donald	The MacKay System: Presenting An Honour Count System In Contract *(Stokes, 1934, 34p.)*
MacLean, Bob	Thank You Partner *(Private, 1993, 83p.)*
MacLeod, Iain	*Bridge Is An Easy Game *(Falcon/Muller/Gollancz, 1952-80, 244p.)
MacMillan, W S	Simply Blue:*(Bibliagora, 1985, 256p.)*

Mallon, John — Bridge Bidding *(Abelard-Schuman/Collier, 1957-75, 192p.)*
Manning-Foster, A E — Baby Contract Book *(Waddington, 1930-32, 70-73p.)*
Manning-Foster, A E — English Contract Bridge *(Benn, 1932, 206p.)*
Marchione, Richard V — Power Precision Updated And Expanded *(Barclay, 1982, 132p.)*
Marr, Chester A &
   Marr, Margaret B — The Marr 'FM' Contract Bidding System *(Private, 1952, 25p.)*
Marr, Col — Bid Your Suit Hands As Accurately As Notrump Hands *(Private, 1952, 21p.)*
Marsh-Smith,
   David (Allen, David) — The Phoney Club: The Cleveland Club System *(Dorrance(Hale), 1993, 77(125)p.)*
Marston, Paul — Forcing Pass Relay *(Private, 1983, 27p.)*
Matthews, Charles H — Essentials Of A Contract System *(Minden Press, 1931, 71p.)*
Matula, Greg — The Polish Club *(Scania Bridgekonsult, 1994, 183p.)*
McCabe, Aileen — Contract Without Tears (The ABC Of Culbertson) *(Faber, 1933, 165p.)*
McNeil, Keith A — The New South Wales System (With A Few Improvements) *(Private, 1971, 20p.)*
McNeil, Keith A — The Roman Club System *(Private, 1964, 12p.)*
McOsker, Joseph A — Controlled Bidding *(Private/Humpries, 1936-37, 32-48p.)*
McOsker, Joseph A — How To Bid *(Christopher, 1934, 32p.)*
McOsker, Joseph A — International Contract Bridge *(Private, 1970, 22p.)*
McOsker, Joseph A — The Standard System *(Humphries, 1935, 48p.)*
McPherson, Kenneth — The A To Z Of Contract Bridge (Culbertson System) *(Lane, 1932, 326p.)*
Merlino, Salvatore — The Philadelphia Contract Bridge Bidding System *(Dorrance, 1977, 40p.)*
Merritt, Ronald K — Play Bridge For Fun *(Private, 1989, 39p.)*
Meyer, Harlan — The Meyer System For Bidding Contract Bridge *(Private, 1961-63, 33-91p.)*
Miller, B — Point Count Bidding System *(Private, 1978, 40p.)*
Miller, Richard A — It's A Bidder's Game *(Private, 1955, 47p.)*
Millingen, Myra A — Contract Kernels *(Angus & Robertson, 1931-33, 40-172p.)*
Millingen, Myra A — Contract Kernels Up-to-Date *(Angus & Robertson, 1937, 158p.)*
Moeller, Henry — Three C System.Contract Bridge, An Abridged Outline - Compensation, Control, Count *(Private, 1935, 16p.)*
Mollo, Victor — Bridge: Modern Bidding *(Faber, 1961-78, 124-145p.)*
Mollo, Victor — Streamlined Bridge *(C Johnson/Prentice-Hall/Marlowe/Newnes, 1948-60, 256-270p.)*
Mollo, Victor &
   Culbertson, Ely — Culbertson's Contract Bridge For Everyone *(Faber, 1969, 123p.)*
Moore, Alfred R — Contract Bridge For Pleasure. A Simple Treatise On Contract Bridge *(Shackleton, 1935, 38p.)*
Morrison, Logie — The Combined Count System Of Contract Bridge *(Smith, 1950, 71p.)*
Moss, Tom — Moss One Club Forcing *(Private, 1970, 7p.)*
Mottershead, W A — The Mottershead System *(Private, 1950, 6p.)*
Mulholland, Harry — Tricks Of Bridge For Improvers: Expand And Strengthen Your Acol Bidding *(Mulholland-Wirral, 1992-96, 64p.)*
Mullick, S G Bose — The Relay Club *(Allied Publishers, 1975, 344p.)*
Mundy, Lindsay — Contract Calling Or Finger Posts To Finer Play *(Methuen, 1931, 118p.)*
Mundy, Lindsay — The Direct (British) System Of Contract Bidding *(Rich & Cowans, 1932, 174p.)*
Nail, G Robert &
   Stucker, Robert — Revolution In Bridge *(Naylor, 1965, 325p.)*
Nelson, Hugh W — Contract Bridge - Simplified For You And Me *(Harrison, 1933, 95p.)*
Nilsland, Mats — *Strong Club - The Scanian Way *(Scania Bridgekonsult, 1995, 83p.)*
Noall, William — Contract Bridge - The Australian One Club System *(Angus & Robertson, 1959, 109p.)*
Noall, William — Contract Bridge - The Australian Pachabo System *(Robertson & Mullens, 1936-38, 62p.)*
Oakie, Donald — Simplified Standard American Bridge Bidding *(B.P.A. Pub, 1976, 339p.)*
Oakley, Peter — The Diamond Major *(Private, 1992-98, 42-65p.)*
O'Brien, Maureen &
   Oeschger, Ivy — Culbertson For The Joneses *(Morrow/Faber, 1942,206- 287.)*
Opp, Dr Paul F — Value-Showing First-Round Bidding For Contract Bridge *(Private, 1963, 22p.)*
Ostrow, Albert A — Modern Basis Of Contract Bidding *(Private, 1948, 33p.)*
Oystragh, Geoff — A Relay Club System *(Private, 1980, 34p.)*
Palmer, Roy — Quit Guessing At Contract Bridge Bidding *(Lucas, 1933, 108p.)*
Paquin, William Thomas — The International Contract Bridge System *(International, 1934, 1p.)*
Paradiso, E Jerry — Instant Bridge *(Paradiso Development, 1978, 59p.)*
Parker, Rutledge Benedict — The Totally New And Simple Pin Point Bidding In Bridge *(Barry, 1982, 43p.)*
Pavlicek, Richard — Bridge Basics *(Private, 1991, 62p.)*
Pavlicek, Richard — Bridge Bidding Guide *(Private, 1991, 36p.)*
Pavlicek, Richard — Standard Bridge *(Private, 1985, 38p.)*
Pavlides, Jordanis — One-Page Guide To Bidding *(Games Pubs Ltd, 1946, 24p.)*
Payne, Dick — The Pragmatic Club *(Private, 1999, 126p.)*
Pejsa, Arthur J — Strong Club Standard Bidding In Contract Bridge *(Kenwood Publishing, 1991, 34p.)*
Peters, L — The Palooka Two Suit Contract Bridge System (1957) *(Private, 1957, 7p.)*
Petersen, Nis C — Petersen System Of Contract Bridge *(Private, 1940-49, 88-78p.)*
Peterson, Olive A — Simplified Digest Of The Four Aces System *(Private, 1935, 63p.)*
Phillips, John S — Phillips Precision Contract Bridge Bidding System *(Army Times, 1948, 75p.)*
Phillips, Travis O — The Phillips Bridge Bidding Procedure *(Private, 1935, 23p.)*
Pinto, Louis — A System For Duplicate *(Private, 1986, 84p.)*
Pitts, R C — Contract Bridge: Bidding To Show Distribution *(Private, 1946, 21p.)*
Plummer, Constance B &
   Plummer, Risque W — The Small Club: A Unique Bidding System *(Private, 1987, 93p.)*
Porter, Victor W — Logical System Of Contract Bidding *(Logical Publishing, 1938, 64p.)*
Pottier, Jerry & Hasney,Chris — The Advanced American Bidding System *(Trafford Pub, 1998, 161p.)*
Radner, Sidney — Radner On Bridge *(Padell, 1961, 96p.)*
Reed, Dick & Horn, A C — The System Bidding Techniques Of Reed-Horn *(B.P.A. Pub, 1976, 51p.)*
Reese, Terence — *Modern Bidding And The Acol System *(Nicholson & Watson, 195-602, 128p.)*
Reese, Terence — *Precision Bidding And Precision Play *(Hale/Sterling/Cornerstone Library, 1973-90, 153-154p.)*
Reese, Terence — C.C. Wei's Precision System *(Private, 1976, 98p.)*
Reese, Terence — Stallard's First Up - A Revolution In Bridge Bidding *(Private, 1977, 73p.)*
Reese, Terence — Stallard's First Up Acol Bidding - A Revolution In Bridge Bidding *(Private, 1978, 73p.)*

Reese, Terence &
Bird, David L — Acol In The 90s *(Hale, 1990-94, 153-157p.)*

Reese, Terence &
Bird, David L — All You Need To Know About Bidding *(Gollancz, 1992, 128p.)*

Reese, Terence &
Dormer, Albert — *The Acol System Today/Blueprint For Bidding *(Edward Arnold(Sterling), 1961, 163p.)*

Reese, Terence &
Dormer, Albert — Bridge: The Acol System Of Bidding *(Pan/Hale, 1978-80, 156p.)*

Reeve, Edgar T Jr. &
Rixey, William W — The New Definitive Bidding System For Contract Bridge *(Private, 1965, 24p.)*

Reeve, Edward Gordon — Contract Bridge: Bidding And Play. Including The Evolution Of Two Club Bidding *(Joiner & Steele, 1936, 132p.)*

Reford, John Hope — Contract Up-To-Date *(Hutchinson, 1931-33, 255-315p.)*

Reilly, Mrs. Ottie — Your Approved Simplified Pocket Bridge-Guide *(Pocket Books, 1963, 6p.)*

Reiter, Len — The Reiter System Of Contract Bridge Bidding *(Private, 1932, 28p.)*

Reith, George — *Accurate Contract *(Day, 1931, 241p.)*

Reith, George — *Contract *(Day/Allen & Unwin, 1929-31, 250p.)*

Reith, George — *One-Over-One System Of Contract Bidding *(The Bridge World, 1932-33, 128p.)*

Reith, George — Contract Bidding - Handy Pocket Edition *(Day, 1930, 37p.)*

Reith, George — George Reith's One-Over-One System Of Contract Bridge Bidding *(Knickerbocker Whist Club, 1932, 51p.)*

Rhodes, G I — The Rack System *(Private, 1955, 29p.)*

Rigal, Barry — *Precision In The 90s *(Hale, 1997, 272p.)*

Roberts, A Carson — Pocket Guide To The Step System *(Harrison, 1934, 11p.)*

Roberts, Loyd O — Robert's Rules For Bidding And Playing Winning Bridge *(Exposition, 1974, 144p.)*

Roberts, R B Bernard — The Bristol System Of Bidding In Contract Bridge *(Bristol Lodge, 1937, 0p.)*

Robinson, Steve — Washington Standard *(Private, 1989, 11p.)*

Robinson, Steve — Washington Standard, Five Card Majors, Two-Over-One Game Forcing *(Devyn Press, 1996, 300p.)*

Rogers, Frank L — Barton System – Plus *Private, 1935, 4p.)*

Roman, John — Learn Bridge At Home Playing Solitary Bridge With The New 44-Fff-F Step System *(Roman Publications, 1981, 75p.)*

Roosen, Coord — Clarified Contract: 1934 Concealed Bidding Tactics As Used By Leading Experts *(Private, 1933, 32p.)*

Root, William S — *Commonsense Bidding *(Crown, 1986-, 216p.)*

Root, William S — Standard Bidding *(Crown, 1979, 96p.)*

Rosenfeld, Louis M — Pocket Guide To Opening Bids And Rebids At Bridge *(Ottenheimer, 1957, 61p.)*

Rosenkranz, George — Bid Your Way To The Top *(Chancellor Hall-Barclay, 1978, 214p.)*

Rosenkranz, George — Bridge: The Bidder's Game *(Devyn Press, 1985, 488p.)*

Rosenkranz, George — Godfrey's Stairway To The Stars *(Devyn Press, 1998, 130p.)*

Rosenkranz, George — The Romex System Of Bidding *(World Publ, 1970, 327p.)*

Rosenkranz, George — Win With Romex *(Crown, 1975, 402p.)*

Roth, Alvin — *Al Roth On Bridge: The Roth-Stone System *(Melville, 1953, 176p.)*

Roth, Alvin — The Art Of Painting A Bridge Hand: Picture Bidding *(Granovetter, 1991, 317p.)*

Roth, Alvin & Rubens, Jeff — Modern Bridge Bidding Complete *(Funk & Wagnalls, 1968, 512p.)*

Roth, Alvin & Stone, Tobias — *Bridge Is A Partnership Game - The Roth-Stone System *(Dutton/Granovetter, 1958-89, 237p.)*

Rothschild, Joseph M — The Rothschild Contract Bridge Bidding System *(Private, 1931, 11p.)*

Rotzell, Peggy — Bridge Bidding Complete *(Private, 1964, 43p.)*

Rowson, Herbert — A Key To Contract Bridge *(Private, 1938, 52p.)*

Rowson, Herbert — Picture Echo Calling - The 'Open Sesame' To Contract Bridge *(Private, 1933, 63p.)*

Rubbra, Fred — The Forcing Club And Canapé System- Used Quite Often And Mis-Used By *(Private, 1977, 10p.)*

Ruminski, Stanislaw — No Name System *(Private, 1978, 63p.)*

Rush, Adolph — Weak Notrump System *(Private, 1944, 40p.)*

Ryan, Mrs. William C — Modern Contract Bridge *(Naylor, 1932, 120p.)*

Sands, David C — The Step System: Step One An Introduction To A New Bidding System *(Superior Printing, 1990, 57p.)*

Sands, Norma — Standard American Bridge Updated - Five Card Majors *(Rocky Mountain Books, 1980-, 85p.)*

Saxe, J & Beinecke, W &
Johnson, J & Richard, H — Vanderbilt One Club Bid With One Diamond Response - Modified System *(Private, 1939-41, 27-36p.)*

Scarfi, Pablo — Basic Contract Bridge: How To Play Well And Enjoy It. *(John, 1947, 110p.)*

Schenken, Howard — Better Bidding In Fifteen Minutes *(Simon & Schuste /Hodder & Stoughton, 1965-68, 192p.)*

Schenken, Howard — Howard Schenken's Big Club *(Simon & Schuster/Hale, 1968-71, 223p.)*

Schenley Bridge Club — Schenley System - Book I-V, Contract Fundamentals *(Private, 1933, 16p. each)*

Scholz, George — Simple Bidding To Win *(Private, 1977, 22p.)*

Scott, William — Contract Bridge (Five Count Easy Advance System) *(Lincolnwood Printing Co, 1933, 22p.)*

Sergeant, Roy L — Contract Bridge Illustrated *(Private, 1928-29, 72-102p.)*

Sewell, Antony — Bridge Made Easy: The Kenilworth Club *(Monterey, 1995, 232p.)*

Sharif, Omar — How To Play The Blue Team Club *(Stancraft, 1970, 48p.)*

Sharpsteen, Harold — Key To Contract (Culbertson) *(Baird-Ward, 1936-42, 97p.)*

Sharpsteen, Harold — Key To The Culbertson System For 1935 *(Frigidaire Corp, 1935, 32p.)*

Sheinwold, Alfred — Fourth Book Of Bridge/Bridge Players' Guide To Bidding/ Improve Your Bridge/ How To Improve Your Bridge *(Sterling/Bantam/Barnse/Constable/Wilshire, 1956-75, 192p.)*

Shepard, Edward Valentine — Contract Bridge - Synopsis Of Bidding *(Private, 1927, 4p.)*

Silley, P G — The Seven-Thirteen System Of Bidding At Contract *(Douglas, 1932, 120p.)*

Silodor, Sidney — Silodor Says, The Grand Slam Of Bridge Literature *(Pageant Press, 1952-61, 240p.)*

Silodor, Sidney &
Tierney, John A — Contract Bridge According To Silodor And Tierney *(Stanley Allen, 1961, 442p.)*

Simon, F Lester — Bidding Harmony In A Minor Key: The Fm (Forcing Minors) System *(Baltimore, 1964, 28p.)*

Simpson, L W — The Revised Nottingham Club *(Private, 1980, 76p.)*

Sims, P Hal — *Master Contract *(Simon & Schuster, 1934, 302p.)*

Sims, P Hal — *Money Contract (U.K. title was Master Contract) *(Simon & Schuster (Lane), 1932, 250p.)*

Sims, P Hal — One-Over-One System *(Bruelheide, 1933, 2p.)*

Six Club, The — Strain's Contract Bridge With The Simple Six System For Calling To The Limit *(Strain, 1932, 13p.)*

Slawinski, Lukasz — The Singleton System 'Delta' *(Private, 1979-87, 30-32p.)*

Slawinski, Lukasz &
Ruminski, Stanislaw — *Introduction To Weak Openings System And Regres System *(Private, 1976-79, 102p.)*

Slawinski, Lukasz &
Ruminski, Stanislaw — Systems Of Weak Opening Bids - Regres System *(Private, 1974, 65p.)*

Slawinski, Lukasz &
Ruminski, Stanislaw — Weak Openings System And Regres System *(Private, 1976, 91p.)*

Smith, Arthur Joseph — The Vienna System Of Bidding *(Faber, 1942-47, 64p.)*

Smith, Curtis K — Bidding Through Logic *(Private/Doubleday/Baxter, 1964, 186-174p.)*

Smith, Dr. Melville — Contract Bridge Up-to-Date *(Foulsham, 1932, 77p.)*

Smith, Victor R — The Distributional System Of Contract Bridge *(Dodd Mead, 1932, 221p.)*

Smith, William Sherman &
Smith, Gertrude S — Smith's Simplified Contract *(Stigberg, 1935, 90p.)*

Snam — Bidding At Bridge: The Vienna Scheme Of Bidding Analyzed And Simplified *(Private, 1950, 180p.)*

Soloway, Paul &
Chazen, Bernie — Two-Over-One, Part I – III *(Club Letter, 1995, 16p. each)*

Sontag, Alan — *Power Precision *(Morrow/Faber, 1979-80, 319p.)*

Southmayd, Leon Nutting — The Scotch System *(Private, 1933, 40p.)*

Spear, John A — The Spear System Of Contract Bidding *(Private, 1933, 12p.)*

Squire, Norman — Contract Bridge: Bidding Today *(Pitman, 1976, 133p.)*

Stallard, M Berl — Bridgette: The Cut And Dried Bidding System *(Carlton, 1967, 80p.)*

Stallard, M Berl — First Up: International Bridge Bidding Winner *(Private/I.B.P.A., 1974-76, 118-70p.)*

Stallard, M Berl — Stallard's First Up The Line Standard American Bridge Bidding *(Private, 1977, 70p.)*

Stallard, M Berl &
Stallard, Helen M — Stallard's First Up: International Bridge Bidding *(Private, 1977, 70p.)*

Stanley, Enos — Theories Of Contract Bidding *(Private, 1934, 37p.)*

Stayman, Samuel M — *The Complete Stayman System Of Contract Bridge *(Rinehart/Rockliff, 1956, 223p.)*

Stayman, Samuel M — Expert Bidding At Contract Bridge *(Wellington Associates/Faber, 1951-52, 144-168p.)*

Steckoll, Simon — Purfect Precision *(Private, 1990, 62p.)*

Stein, W Eduard — Contract Bridge - The Standard System Of Contract Bidding *(Keystone, 1935-38, 55-58p.)*

Stephenson, C W — The Master Method Of Slam Bidding For Contract Bridge *(Stephenson, 1934, 61p.)*

Stern, Dr. Paul — *The Stern Austrian System *(Harrop/David McKay, 1938, 192p.)*

Stern, Dr. Paul &
Hart, Norman De Vere — *The Vienna System Of Contract Bridge *(Contract Bridge Equipment, 1947-48, 243-249p.)*

Stoddard, Thomas Wren — Contract Bridge: Five Popular Systems *(Private, 1934, 33p.)*

Street, Charles Stuart — Street On Contract *(Private, 1928, 129p.)*

Strong, Theron R — Thumbnail Sketch Of Contract Bidding *(Contract Publishers, 1930, 40p.)*

Stub — The Stub System *(Allied Printing, 1930, 12p.)*

Stupica, Joe L — Trick Bidding - The Pompano Club *(J Lawrence, 1967, 24p.)*

Sundby, Robert D — Bridge In The '80s, Featuring The Comfortable Club *(Breakthrough Bridge, 1984, 571p.)*

Taylor, F W — From No Bid To Grand Slam *(Holywell Press, 1946, 40p.)*

Taylor, Frank L — Canadian Contract Bridge System Featuring The Forcing Two Club Bid *(Private, 1932, 32p.)*

Teague, E D &
Smith, Arthur Joseph — Streamlined Vienna System *(World's Work, 1954, 72p.)*

Templeman, John D — Contract Bridge: Danish System Of Bidding: A Simple Method *(Private, 1934, 12p.)*

Terlizzi, Count Fausto — The Millenniumn Revolution Bridge *(Private, 2000, 9p.)*

Thomas, Fred R — Better Bidding At Contract Bridge: Universal Club - The System For Everyone *(Uniclub Press, 1980, 127p.)*

Thomas, Fred R — Universal Club Instant Bidding Guide *(Uniclub Press, 1979, 11p.)*

Thompson, Toby — The Simplified System For Contract Bridge *(Simplified Systems, 1946, 48p.)*

Thorne, Harold — Culbertson Vs. The Offical System: The Strong And Weak Points Of Each *(Dutton, 1931, 64p.)*

Tollemache, Lord — The Chronological Order System - The Key To Safe Calling In Contract Bridge *(Phillipson & Golder, 1930, 69p.)*

Tollemache, Lord — The Key To Safe Slam Calling In Contract: The Chronological Order System Inter Alia *(Phillipson & Golder, 1930, 69p.)*

Tompson, Angela — Bridge With Angela *(Fleming, 1996-97, 68p.)*

Troyer, Mrs. Robert R — Notes On Contract - Official System *(Private, 1931, 39p.)*

Turner, Walter S — Common Sense Bridge *(Private, 1954, 171p.)*

Turner, Walter S &
Bumgarner, Tom — Natural Contract Bidding *(Private, 1935, 36p.)*

Uncut Cavendish — Contract Bridge Bidding Systems And Points Of Law In A Nutshell *(Faber, 1942, 23p.)*

Uncut Cavendish — Contract Bridge Systems In A Nuttshelle *(Joiner & Steeler, 1938-40, 12-16p.)*

Van Vleck, C E — The V V Or Victory System *(Private, 1942, 1p.)*

Van Zak, Martin — The Monday Morning Bridge Book *(Private, 1979, 49-58p.)*

Vanderbilt, Harold — *Contract Bridge Bidding And The Club Convention *(Scribner, 1929, 251p.)*

Vanderbilt, Harold — *The New Contract Bridge: Club Convention Bidding And Forcing Overbids *(Scribner, 1930, 333p.)*

Vanderbilt, Harold — Contract By Hand Analysis: A Synopsis Of 1933 Club Convention Bidding *(The Bridge World, 1933, 165p.)*

Vanderbilt, Harold — The Club Convention System Of Bidding At Contract Bridge *(Scribner, 1964, 186p.)*

Vickery, Ronald W — The Hybrid Club *(Private, 1981, 115p.)*

Victor, A D J — The Victory System Of Modern Bidding At Contract Bridge *(Roxy Paper Co, 1976, 87p.)*

Victor, A D J — Veejay System Of Modern Bidding At Contract Bridge *(Devyn Press, 1983, 271p.)*

Wahltuch, V L — Contract Bridge - Current Bidding Systems Explained *(Printing Craft, 1937, 35p.)*

Wakeman, Robert P — Modern Bidding Techniques: How To Improve Your Partnership Communication *(Essex Bridge Centre, 1972, 111p.)*

Walshe, G G J — Let's Play CAB *(Methuen, 1945-47, 71p.)*

Walter, A Charles — Walter's Esperanto Bridge System *(Private, 1937, 85p.)*

Warner, Charles — Contract Bridge Simplified *(Best Rose, 1930, 92p.)*

Washburn, Abbott McC. — Bidding In Contract Bridge (And Feminine Failings By Mildred Washburn McClean) *(Dodd Mead, 1929, 132p.)*

Washburn, Abbott McC. — Bidding In Contract Bridge *(Private, 1928, 59p.)*

Watkins, Allen — Partnerproof Contract *(Joiner & Steele, 1937, 104p.)*

H. SUMMARIES OF BIDDING SYSTEM BOOKS AND POPULAR SYSTEMS

AUTHOR	TITLE
Anonymous	Point-Count Bidding *(American Playing Card Mfrs, 1955, 8p.)*
Anonymous	Select-A-Bid. A Bidding Aid In Contract Bridge, A Gift From Pommac. *(Dalympic Of Texas, 1964, 4p.)*
Anonymous	Summary Of The Official System Of Contract Bridge *(U.S. Playing Card Co, 1932, 8p.)*
Anonymous	The Official System Of Contract Bridge *(Private, 1930, 8p.)*
Avondale, Cyril	Contract Bridge In Brief *(Toohey's Ltd, 1935, 16p.)*
Baird, Milly S	Contract Bidding *(Private, 1930, 3p.)*
Baird, Milly S	Rules Abridged And Bridge Jingles *(Hungerford Holbrook, 1928, 47p.)*
Banfield, Mrs. Elizabeth B & Wood, Alice D	Learn Contract Easily: Lesson Sheets Based On Culbertson Approach Forcing System *(The Bridge World, 1931, 20p.)*
Bard, George L	Contract Made Easy *(Approach Forcing System Standard Throughout The World) (Columbia Publishing, 1935, 32p.)*
Bard, George L	Culbertson System Of Contract Bridge: A Handy Reference Outline *(Private/ Bridge World Accessories, 1941-48, 24p.)*
Bard, George L	Culbertson System Of Point Count Bidding *(The Bridge World, 1953, 24p.)*
Bard, George L	Pocket Summary Of Contract Bridge, Approach-Forcing System *(Columbia Publishing, 1933, 8p.)*
Bardach, Milton	Contract Bridge: The Correct Bids And Responses *(Private, 1931-33, 15p.)*
Baron, Randall	Bridge Wheel *(Devyn Press, 1992, 1p.)*
Bernstein, Andrew & Baron, Randall	Popular Systems I & II *(Devyn Press, 1985, 10p. each)*
Blackmon, May Ritchie	Contract Bridge: Culbertson One-Over-One *(Manhattan Storage, 1934, 3p.)*
Blackmon, May Ritchie	Opening Bids And Contract Score *(Manhattan Storage, 1934, 7p.)*
Blackwood, Easley	Ten Quick Ways To Win At Bridge *(Droke House, 1949, 5p.)*
Blake, Edwin G	Summary Of Contract Bridge *(Private, 1932, 0p.)*
Bloom, I H	Contract Bridge Summary. Culbertson System. *(Steel City Pub, 1937, 37p.)*
Bloom, I H & Watson, Louis H	Culbertson System Summary *(Steel City Pub, 1937, 29p.)*
Boothe, Mr. E V & Boothe, Mrs. E V	The Complete Bidding Guide Contract Bridge *(Standard American - The Direct Method) (Private, 1978, 8p.)*
Booty, June & Hurst, Richard	Beginner's Guide To Acol *(Private, 1998, 6p.)*
Bosshart, Mrs. Marie J	Official Blue Book On Contract Bridge: Simplified Standard Point Count *(Private, 1937, 8p.)*
Bosshart, Mrs. Marie J	Self-Teacher Golden Rule Book On Contract Bridge: Easy Point Count *(Private, 1950, 26p.)*
Bourget, Frank E & Tobin, E J	High Points On Contract Bridge *(Century, 1932, 31p.)*
Boyden, Elizabeth Clark & Warren, Mrs. Prescott	Pocket Contract Bridge - The Culbertson Forcing System [Official] *(Harcourt Brac /Faber, 1931, 17p.)*
Boyton, Mrs. Guy E	Concentrated Contract *(Private, 1931, 26p.)*
Brannon, Robert M	Brannon's Foolproof Summary: Approach Forcing System *(American Ptg, 1932, 18p.)*
Brannon, Robert M	Contract Bridge In Brief. Based On The Approach Forcing System *(Bridge Headquarters, 1932, 18p.)*
Brannon, Robert M	Contract Step By Step Summary *(Dutton, 1931, 40p.)*
Bridge Headquarters	Notes On Contract For 1933 Including The One-Over-One *(Bridge Headquarters, 1933, 52p.)*
Bridge Headquarters	Pocket Summary Of The Standardized Code Of Contract Bridge Bidding *(Bridge Headquarters, 1938, 16p.)*
Bridge Headquarters	The Automatic Bridge Summary On The Official System System Of Contract Bridge *(Bridge Headquarters, 1931, 4p.)*
Brown, R G	Memorandum Culbertson System *(Private, 1931, 4p.)*
Browne, Derrick	Five Card Majors Flipper *(Trumps Publishing, 1998, 24p.)*
Bruelheide, Frank Elmer	Contract Bidding *(Gibson Art, 1934-35, 16p.)*
Bruelheide, Frank Elmer	Contract Bidding Culbertson System *(Bruelheide, 1935-39, 24p.)*
Bruelheide, Frank Elmer	Culbertson System *(Bruelheide, 1935-39, 8-15p.)*
Bruelheide, Frank Elmer	Digest Of The Sims System *(Bruelheide, 1934, 16p.)*
Bruelheide, Frank Elmer	How To Play The Culbertson System, A Complete Summary Of The Culbertson System *(Gibson Art, 1932-35, 8p.)*
Bruelheide, Frank Elmer	Simplified Culbertson System *(Bruelheide, 1941-52, 15-32p.)*
Bruelheide, Frank Elmer	Simplified Culbertson System, Finger-Tipped For Quick Reference *(Bruelheide, 1941-48, 30-33p.)*
Bruelheide, Frank Elmer	The Brains Of Contract Bridge *(Hollycrafte/Bruelheide, 1930-31, 16p.)*
Bruelheide, Frank Elmer	The Culbertson-Offical Alliance *(Bruelheide, 1935, 2p.)*
Bruelheide, Frank Elmer	The Latest Culbertson System *(Bruelheide, 1936, 8p.)*
Bruelheide, Frank Elmer	The New Simplified Culbertson System, Abridged For The Average Player *(Bruelheide, 1941-53, 64p.)*
Bruno, Steve & Hardy, Max	Two Over One Game Force: An Introduction *(Devyn Press, 1993, 141p.)*
Burns, Margery	A Simple Guide To Contract Bridge *(Rae Features, 1968, 6p.)*
Burns, Margery	The Nottingham Club System Of Contract Bridge - A Simple Guide To The Bidding *(Private, 1969, 4p.)*
Burnstine, David	The Four Horsemen's One-Over-One Method Of Contract Bidding: Pocket Summary *(Blue Ribbon And Black, 1932, 16-29p.)*
Burnstine, David & Gottleib, Michael	Pocket Outline Of 4 Aces System Of Contract Bridge *(Four Aces Bridge Studio, 1936, 8p.)*
Buxton, William H	Contract Bridge *(Approach-Forcing System) (Private, 1931-32, 37-32p.)*
Buxton, William H	Standardized Contract Bridge 1931 *(Private, 1931, 37p.)*
Callaway, John L	Bridge *(Private, 1974, 23p.)*
Cantrell, James E	Contract Bridge: How To Be A Winner *(Wetzel, 1933, 62p.)*
Clark, Grace	Outline Of The Culbertson Forcing System *(Lincoln Warehouse, 1933, 7p.)*
Clark, Sylvia	Complete Summary Of Point Count Bidding As Taught By Mrs. Richard W Beck *(Private, 1969, 7p.)*
Coffin, George Sturgis	Bridge Summary Complete *(International Pocket Library, 1964, 96p.)*
Coffin, Kathryne P & Rawls, Elizabeth S	ABC Of Contract Bridge *(Private, 1932, 9p.)*
Cohen, Ben & Reese, Terence	A Summary Of The Acol System Of Contract Bridge *(Joiner & Steele, 1938-43, 12p.)*

Cohen, Ruth M &
Silverman, Shirley — Contract Bridge - Point Count Bidding Guide *(Barclay, 1970-80, 8p.)*

Conway, Mrs. Stephen — Complete Culbertson System For 1935 *(Private, 1935, 20p.)*

Cooney, Eunice L — Complete Summary Of 1935 Contract Bridge *(Johnson Cox, 1935, 74p.)*

Cooper, Dr R D — Learn To Play Bridge Like An Expert: Instruction Book For The Select-A-Bidder *(Cooper Enterprises, 1959, 12p.)*

Cooper, Dr R D — Select-A-Bidder *(Cooper Enterprises, 1959, 4p.)*

Courtenay, F Dudley — Pocket Summary: Contract Bridge Bidding - Culbertson System - Checked And Revised *(Bridge Headquarters, 1937, 16p.)*

Courtenay, F Dudley — Pocket Summary: The System The Experts Play *(Bridge Headquarters, 1936, 16p.)*

Courtenay, F Dudley &
Brannon, Robert M — Contract Bridge Simplified - The Official System Of Contract Bridge *(Bridge Headquarters, 1932, 47p.)*

Courtenay, F Dudley &
Brannon, Robert M — Contract Bridge Simplified For 1933 *(Bridge Headquarters, 1933, 47p.)*

Crane, Joshua — The Crane System Of Contract Bidding *(Summary Card) (Lewes Press, 1937, 2p.)*

Crane, Joshua — The Crane System Of Modern Contract Bidding *(Summary Card) (East Anglia Times, 1948, 2p.)*

Crews, Ray — Contract Bridge Simplified *(Private, 1931, 2p.)*

Crowhurst, Eric — Summary Of The Acol System Of Contract Bridge *(Mr. Bridge, 1994, 22p.)*

Culbertson, Ely — About Bridge - Instruction In Bidding And Play *(Liggett & Myers, 1934, 28p.)*

Culbertson, Ely — Bridge At A Glance: Instruction In Bidding And Play *(Liggett & Myers, 1935-36, 29-32p.)*

Culbertson, Ely — Contract At A Glance *(Musson, 1934, 45p.)*

Culbertson, Ely — Contract Bridge *(Chicago Daily News, 1932, 16p.)*

Culbertson, Ely — Culbertson's Summary Of Contract Bridge *(The Bridge World/Winston.Faber, 1931-54, 47-64p.)*

Culbertson, Ely — Hallmark Bridge Bidder *(Hall Brothers Inc, 1935, 4p.)*

Culbertson, Ely — Pocket Guide To Contract Bridge *(The Bridge World, 1933-34, 2p.)*

Culbertson, Ely — Point Count Summary Of 1954 Culbertson Contract Bridge *(Private, 1954, 5p.)*

Culbertson, Ely — Simplified Outline Of The Culbertson System Of Contract Bridge *(The Bridge World, 1941-49, 16p.)*

Demarest, Nelva — Nutshell Notes On The Four Aces System *(Private, 1937, 14p.)*

Dendy, Dr. Julius — Play Dandy Bridge *(Private, 1957, 26p.)*

Dunlop, Newell Fraser — Bridge In Brief *(Private, 1931, 32p.)*

Duschak, Herbert W — Outline Of Contract Bridge *(Eliicott Press, 1930, 6p.)*

Eady, Kenneth Charles — The Bridge Buddy *(Alken, 1993, 0p.)*

Ehlbert, Mark K — Bidrite Pocket Dictionary Of Contract Bridge Bidding *(Private, 1935, 23p.)*

Ellicott, John Morris — Synopsis Of Ellicott Contract Bridge, 1935 *(Private, 1935, 4p.)*

Embee — To Bid Or Not To Bid? *(Norman Bros, 1933, 24p.)*

Fletcher, John &
Lederer, Rhoda — The Fletcher-Lederer Bridge Bidding Guide *(Fyfe Carnegie, 1976-81, 4p.)*

Flintom, Frances Young — Easyway Contract Bridge Culbertson System Simplified *(Easyway Publishing, 1932-34, 29p.)*

Foley, Joseph P — ABC's Of Contract Bridge *(Private, 1937, 10p.)*

Fox, Colin — The Tricks Of Bridge *(Treasure Leisure Company, 1992-96, 50p.)*

Fox, L E — Condensed Contract *(Thacker & Co, 1945, 29p.)*

Furstner,Michael — Contract Bridge Bidding Guide For Standard Bidding With 5 Card Majors *(Private, 1986, 10p.)*

Geissler, Charles Mrs. — Radio Contract *(Private, 1935, 36p.)*

Glassman, Lucille — Howard Schenken's Big Club System Summarized *(Private, 1965, 5p.)*

Glenn, Myrtis — Summary Of The Sims System *(Private, 1932, 16p.)*

Glenn, Myrtis — The 1933 Summary Of The P Hal Sims System *(Taylor Press, 1933, 34p.)*

Glynn, Sean — A Guide To The Acol System Of Bidding *(Glynn, 1983-91, 6p.)*

Glynn, Sean — A Guide To The Precision System Of Bidding *(Glynn, 1987, 6p.)*

Gooden, George S — Contract Bridge Bidding Chart *(Private, 1960, 2p.)*

Gooden, George S — Contract Bridge Simplified Including Leads And Signals *(Private, 1960, 22p.)*

Goren, Charles H — An Entirely New Bridge Summary *(Heines, 1953-60, 64p.)*

Goren, Charles H — Basic Bridge For Novice Players - Introduction To Bridge *(T.D.C.-Heines, 1975, 16p.)*

Goren, Charles H — Bridge At Your Fingertips *(Heines, 1970-76, 24p.)*

Goren, Charles H — Bridge Bidding - Outline For Successful Contracts *(Heines, 1975, 16p.)*

Goren, Charles H — Bridge For The Novice *(Post & Times Herald, 1950, 15p.)*

Goren, Charles H — Bridge Guide And Scorepad *(Heines, 1976, 66p.)*

Goren, Charles H — Charles Goren's Eight Easy Steps To Winning Bridge *(Heines, 1960, 48p.)*

Goren, Charles H — Charles Goren's Shortcut To Expert Bridge *(Trend Development Corporation, 1956, 9p.)*

Goren, Charles H — Charles H Goren Presents The Italian Systems *(Bridge Master, 1959, 5p.)*

Goren, Charles H — Charles H Goren's New Contract Bridge In A Nutshell *(Doubleday/Fireside/W H ALlen, 1957-72, 137-142p.)*

Goren, Charles H — Contract Bridge In A Nutshell *(Doubleday/Edwards, 1947-52, 128p.)*

Goren, Charles H — Easy Steps: Eight Steps To Winning Bridge *(T.D.C., 1975, 48p.)*

Goren, Charles H — Easy Way To Better Bridge: Goren Official Point Count Bridge Tips *(Bruelheid/Heinese, 1954-70, 6p.)*

Goren, Charles H — Goren Point Count Bidding Wheel *(Bridge Master/T.D.C.-Heines, 1954-75, 2p.)*

Goren, Charles H — Goren Point Counter *(Newly Revised) (Taylor Press, 1955, 24p.)*

Goren, Charles H — Goren Twin Guide To Modern Point Count Bidding *(Goren Enterprises, 1956, 36p.)*

Goren, Charles H — Goren's Point Count System Made Easy *(Doubleday, 1960, 97p.)*

Goren, Charles H — Grand Slam! *(Heines, 1960, 7p.)*

Goren, Charles H — Highlights Of Winning Bridge *(Arrco, 1938, 42p.)*

Goren, Charles H — How To Play Better Bridge *(Tribune Company, 1949, 23p.)*

Goren, Charles H — How To Play Bridge The Winning Way *(Viceroy, 1960, 64p.)*

Goren, Charles H — Instant Answers: Official Goren Shortcut To Expert Bridge *(T.D.C.-Heines, 1976, 9p.)*

Goren, Charles H — Let's Play Bridge With Charles H Goren *(Schwayder Bros, 1956, 36p.)*

Goren, Charles H — New Revised Point Count Bidding Summary At A Glance For Your Partner *(Goren Enterprises, 1960, 7p.)*

Goren, Charles H — Play Bridge With Goren *(Bruelheide/Heines, 1950-56, 24p.)*

Goren, Charles H — Play Bridge With Goren: Improve Your Game With Proper Opening Leads *(Tayl;or Press/ Barclay, 1940-50, 72p.)*

Goren, Charles H — Point Count Bidding *(Goren Enterprises et al, 1956, 6p.)*

Goren, Charles H — Point Count-Er With Ten New Commandments *(Goren Enterprises, 1958, 24p.)*

Goren, Charles H — The New Contract Bridge Featuring Point Count Bidding *(Arrco et al., 1950, 47p.)*
Goren, Charles H — Winning Bridge In Fifteen Minutes *(Goren Enterprises, 1955-77, 6-12p.)*
Goren, Charles H &
  Sharif, Omar — Bridge Bidding Wheel. Official Charles H Goren, Omar Sharif *(Hoyle Products, 1976, 2p.)*
Goren, Charles H &
  Sharif, Omar — Bridge Pocket Guide. Pocket Pal For Bidding *(Hoyle Products, 1979, 24p.)*
Gowen, Albert Y — A Brief Summary Of The Crane System In Contract Bidding *(Private, 1944, 13p.)*
Grant, Audrey — E-Z Guide To Bidding Bridge The A.C.B.L. Way *(A.C.B.L., 1993, 36p.)*
Greene, Ernest — Greene's Pocket Guide *(Joiner & Steele, 1935, 4p.)*
Habib, David P &
  Manley, Brent — Contract Bridge For Social Players - A Quick Reference *(Deem Publishing, 1993, 40p.)*
Haddad, Louis H — The New 1935 Methods For Original Bidding At Contract Bridge *(Lincoln Warehouse, 1935, 5p.)*
Hall, John S — Concise Contract *(Private, 1936, 12p.)*
Hanson, Keith — Fingertip Bridge *(Devyn Press, 1989, 10p.)*
Holloway, Toni — Table Cloth Summary Of Contract Bridge *(Private, 1957, 1p.)*
Humphery, H H — Bridge, Contract: Important Points *(Eldon Bridge Parlour, 1945, 6p.)*
Hunt, Mrs. Marion — How To Lead, How To Play Contract Bridge *(Hunt & Hunt, 1934, 48p.)*
Huttig, William D H — Quick Contract: Forcing System *(Bruce-Roberts, 1931, 28p.)*
Hyers, Earl W — Contract Bridge Summary *(Approach Forcing System)* With Digest Of Leads And Laws *(Private, 1935, 39p.)*
Irvine, S Margie — Contract Bridge *(Avery, 1933, 25p.)*
Jarboe, Robert J — Romance Language Courses: Bridge *(Private, 1990, 12p.)*
Johnson, Alice &
  Johnson, Thayer — Bid Grid For Novices *(Private, 1993, 10p.)*
Johnson, Robert Lee — A Complete Course In Charles Goren's Point Count Method Of Bidding *(Private, 1950, 35p.)*
Johnson, Robert Lee — A Complete Course Of Instruction In Contract Bridge Bidding *(Private, 1947, 43p.)*
Johnson, Robert Lee — A Complete Course Of Instruction In The Latest Culbertson System Of Contract Bridge *(Private, 1944, 36p.)*
Johnson, Robert Lee — An Easy To Understand Summary Of The New Culbertson System *(Private, 1941, 32p.)*
Johnson, Robert Lee — Bridge Bidding At A Glance Based On Latest Goren Point Count *(Grandslam Records, 1960, 4p.)*
Johnson, Robert Lee — Contract Bridge Bidding, The Latest Point Count Bidding *(Private, 1952-53, 36p.)*
Johnson, Robert Lee — The Latest Summary Point Count Bidding *(Modern Living, 1959, 16p.)*
Kaback, Edwin Rice — Bidding Index. A Quick Guide To Point Bidding In Contract Bridge *(Private, 1960, 48p.)*
Kaplan, Edgar — Contract Bridge Summary *(Bantam, 1970, 96p.)*
Kapp, Spencer S — Contract Bridge Synopsis: 98 Percent Of Contract-Bidding, Plays And Leads Of 1932 *(Private, 1931, 15p.)*
Kapp, Spencer S — Richfield: How To Play Contract Bridge - Comparison Of Official And Culbertson Systems *(Hitt/Richfield, 1931, 2p.)*
Kelsey, Hugh Walter — Instant Guide To Bridge *(Ward Lock/Gollancz/Coles, 1975-94, 70-80p.)*
Kelsey, Hugh Walter &
  Klinger, Ron — Instant Guide To Bridge: Standard American Edition *(Houghton Mifflin, 1991, 80p.)*
Kelsey, Hugh Walter &
  Klinger, Ron — Instant Guide To Standard Bridge *(Gollancz, 1991, 80p.)*
Kerwin, Madeleine — Summary Of One Over One And P Hal Sims System *(Private, 1932, 24p.)*
Klinger, Ron — Basic Acol Bridge Flipper *(Gollancz, 1986-96, 24p.)*
Klinger, Ron — Basic Bridge Flipper *(Modern Bridge Publications, 1985, 30p.)*
Klinger, Ron — Fingertip Bridge Finder *(Castle Books, 1978, 50p.)*
Klinger, Ron — The Standard Bridge Flipper *(Gollancz/Houghton Mifflin, 1984, 30p.)*
Klinger, Ron &
  Brightling, Richard — Bridge Flipper Fast Fact Finder For Modern Five-Card Majors *(Modern Bridge Publications, 1984, 30p.)*
Klinger, Ron &
  Brightling, Richard — Fast Fact Finder For Standard Bridge *(A.B. Publications/Modern Bridge, 1983-90, 32p.)*
Klinger, Ron &
  Brightling, Richard — Fast Fact Finder The For Acol System *(A.B. Publications/Modern Bridge 1983-90. 32p.)*
Klinger, Ron &
  Kelsey, Hugh Walter — Five-Card Majors Bidding Flipper *(Gollancz, 1987-98, 20p.)*
Klinger, Ron &
  Kelsey, Hugh Walter — The Acol Bridge Flipper - The Fast Fact Finder *(Gollancz, 1983-94, 30p.)*
Knight, M — A Simple Guide To Contract Bridge - Culbertson System *(Willis, 1935, 26p.)*
Konstam, Kenneth — De La Rue Hints On Contract Bridge *(De La Rue, 1955, 6p.)*
Kussman, Robert — Guide To Standard American Bidding, Four And Five Card Majors *(Puget Bridge Suppy, 1985, 16p.)*
L, R E — Bridge Table Side Guide *(For Beginners) (Propwash Press, 1977, 2p.)*
Lapointe, T — Basic Bridge Info At Your Finger Tip … *(Private, 1985, 10p.)*
Lenz, Sidney Samuel — One-Two-Three, Sidney S. Lenz's Book On The Official System Of Contact Bidding *(Simon & Schuster, 1931, 35p.)*
Liddell, K C — Daily Express Contract Bridge Card *(Daily Express, 1933, 14p.)*
Liddell, K C — Everybodies Contract Bridge Handbook *(Foulsham, 1935, 16p.)*
Liddell, K C — Pocket Contract Bridge Chart *(Houghton, 1933-35, 2p.)*
Liggett, Commander
  Winfield C — Contract Bridge Summary: The Official System *(Stokes, 1931, 20p.)*
Loper, Walter — The Forcing Feature Of The No Trump Forcing System *(Private, 1932, 1p.)*
Lowery, Sylvester A Mrs. — Annual Manual On Bridge: Convenient, Compact Contract *(Private, 1937-41, 79p.)*
Lowery, Sylvester A Mrs. — Convenient, Compact Contract *(Private, 1946, 79p.)*
Lyman, V B — Contract Bridge *(Bley And Lyman, 1927, 4p.)*
MacNicholl, Florence White — Point Count Contract Bridge *(Private, 1950, 25p.)*
Marks, Richard L B — A Concise And Complete Digest Of The Culbertson System Of Contract Bridge *(Private, 1932, 5p.)*
Marks, Richard L B — A Concise And Complete Digest Of The Official System *(Private, 1932, 3p.)*
Marston, Paul — Cheat Sheet: Acol System *(Grand Slam Books, 1997-99, 22p.)*
Marston, Paul — Cheat Sheet: Five Card Majors *(Grand Slam Books, 1997-99, 22p.)*
Marston, Paul &
  Brightling, Richard — Cheat Sheet: Four Card Majors With Limit Raises *(Bridge Shop-Grand Slam Books, 1992-95, 20-22p.)*

Marston, Paul &
  Brightling, Richard — Easy Access Cheat Sheet … The Expert At Your Elbow *(Contract Bridge Supplies, 1985-92, 22p.)*

Martin, Christopher — The Bridge-Learner's Table-Side Reference *(Private, 1978-83, 32p.)*

Matsukis, Lyn — On Table Simple Study Aid For Bridge Beginners *(Private, 1990, 8-10p.)*

McElroy, Hugh F — Contract Bridge Summary *(McGill-Warner Company, 1933, 31p.)*

Meade, Beatrice — The Why And Wherefore Of Contract Bridge *(Barrell, 1930-32, 35p.)*

Mertens, Hugo — Contract Bridge Summary *(Fort Pitt Brewing, 1935, 32p.)*

Mollo, Victor — Acol - Victor Mollo's Pocket Guide To The Winning System Of Point Count Bidding *(Literary Services, 1960, 7p.)*

Mollo, Victor — Bridge - Victor Mollo's Pocket Guide To Winning *(Acol)* Bidding *(L.S.P., 1968, 7p.)*

Mollo, Victor &
  North, Freddie — Win At Bridge *(Series 1)* Key To Modern Bidding *(Rexard/Smith & Ebbs, 1955-64, 7p.)*

Moore, Godfrey B — Contract At A Glance *(Proper Press, 1930, 12p.)*

Morehead, Albert H — Contract Bridge Summary *(MacMillan/Signe/The Bridge World, 1963, 124p.)*

Morehead, Albert H — Pocket Outline Of The Culbertson System *(The Bridge World, 1938-39, 16p.)*

Morrow, J Edward — 1937 Contract Bridge: Bids-Leads-Plays-Laws *(Dallas Morning News, 1937, 64p.)*

Morrow, J Edward — Winning Contract Bridge Bids, Leads, Plays And Laws *(Dallas Morning News, 1939, 0p.)*

Muntz, Sylvia — Comprehensive Digest Of Today's Contract Bridge *(R W Bruelheid, 1950, 5p.)*

Nield, Dorathy — Contract Bridge Point Count From Goren *(Thornquest Press, 1963, 8p.)*

O'Hara, Russell Ernest — Contract Bidding In A Nut-Shell *(Private, 1931, 16p.)*

Ohaver, Mrs.Laura Frahm — Contract Bridge Summary *(Banknote Printing, 1930, 40p.)*

Osborn, Lewis — Expert Bidding *(Private, 1934, 31p.)*

Osborne, Winifred — Winifred Osborne Presents Her Summary Of The Official System Of Contract Bridge *(Private, 1931, 68p.)*

Ostdiek, Mabelle — The Culbertson Point Count Method Outlined *(Bruelheide, 1952, 5p.)*

Ostdiek, Mabelle — The Goren Point Count Method Of Contract Bridge Bidding *(Bruelheide, 1954-55, 20p.)*

Ostdiek, Mabelle — The Point Count Method Of Contract Bridge Bidding *(Heines, 1960, 20p.)*

Ostrow, Albert A — Bridge: Combination Scorepad And Bidding Summary *(Atwater Press, 1959, 13p.)*

Parker, Vera — Bridge Communication, As Taught By Lucille Place *(VIP Enterprises, 1979, 46p.)*

Pavlicek, Richard — Modern Bridge *(Baron, 1976, 20p.)*

Perkins, Lee — Contract Bidding, Valuation Of Hands, Bidding Requirements *(Private, 1932, 41p.)*

Pescott-Day, John — The Easy Guide To Bridge Playing The Acol System *(Private, 1990, 5p.)*

Peterson, Olive A — Better Bridge In Brief *(Private, 1940, 71p.)*

Peterson, Olive A — Common Sense Contract *(Private, 1934-43, 79-80p.)*

Phillips, Morris Mondle — Contracted Contract *(Lothian, 1933, 36p.)*

Platt, A G — Contract Bridge Memory Tickler *(Delgado, 1930, 2p.)*

Purdy, Mrs. Guy U — Mrs. Guy U. Purdy's Latest Contract Ideas For 1933 *(Private, 1933, 52p.)*

Railsback, Paul W &
  O'Rourke, Martha L — Contract Bridge Quick Reference Guide *(Quick Reference Press, 1990, 29p.)*

Reich, Marion Louise — Bridge-It, The Goren Point Count System Summary Form *(Bridge-It, 1954, 6p.)*

Rice, Raymond A — Contract Bridge Bidding Charts In Point Count Based On The Goren Method *(Glo-Lite Dist, 1954, 24p.)*

Rimington, Derek — Contract Bridge: Type-Acol Bidding Guide *(Private, 1993, 8p.)*

Roedel,Mrs. Alice Morgan — An Outline Of The 1938 Culbertson System, Based On Contract Bridge Complete *(Private, 1938, 32p.)*

Root, William S — Contract Bridge Outlines On Standard Bidding Plus Modern Bidding Conventions *(Private, 1965-66, 54p.)*

Root, William S — New Contract Bridge Outlines On Standard Bidding *(Crown, 1971, 64p.)*

Russell, Carlton — Rapid Contract Bridge, Thumbnail Chart, Complete For Bidding And Play *(Brookline/Humphries/Private, 1931, 16-31p.)*

Russell, Carlton — Russell R-A-P-I-D Contract Bridge *(Private, 1932, 20p.)*

Sands, Norma — Bridge Helper *(Rocky Mountain Books, 1988, 9p.)*

Schenken, Howard — Howard Schenken's Big Club Summarized *(Simon & Schuster, 1968, 4p.)*

Schenken, Howard — The Schenken's System Summarized *(Simon & Schuster, 1963, 4p.)*

Sell, Naomi & Treanor, Anne — Anaheim Ebell Club - 1949 Notes On Contract Bridge *(Private, 1949, 8p.)*

Senk, Ernest — The Acol System Bridge Summary *(Private, 1995, 4p.)*

Seymour, Paul H — Contract Simplified *(Private, 1941, 32p.)*

Shaw, H C &
  Carlton, George A — Bids, Rebids And Responses *(Summary Culbertson Bluebook)* *(Private/Reilly & Lee/Index Pub, 1931-35, 35p.)*

Shaw, Walter — Bridge Made Easy *(Castell, 1933, 28p.)*

Sheardown, P E — Rapid Tally Digest Of Bridge Conventions Including Tips On Bidding And Play *(Private, 1950, 9p.)*

Sheinwold, Alfred — It's Your Bid *(Plain Dealer, 1970, 28p.)*

Shermet, Bee — Bridge Made Easy The Silodor Way *(Sidbee, 1953-55, 30p.)*

Shirlee Company — Dial-A-Bid *(Private, 1980, 2p.)*

Sims, P Hal — The Sims Summary Of Money Contract *(Simon & Schuster, 1933, 69p.)*

Slam-It — Bridge In Brevity *(Dewdney, 1930-31, 7p.)*

Sneezum, George — A Concise Summary Of Contract Bridge And The Culbertson System *(Cowell, 1935, 29p.)*

Staples, Thomas L — Heart Of Contract Bridge *(Professional Press/Better-Bridge, 1928-30, 93-111p.)*

Stewart, Frank — Bridge Abridged: A Pocket Guide To Good Bidding And Play *(A.C.B.L., 1993, 18p.)*

Stoddard, Thomas Wren — Complete Contract Bridge *(Hit/Privatet, 1945-49, 49p.)*

Stoddard, Thomas Wren — Contract Bridge, A Complete Summary Of Culbertson System Of Bidding *(Hitt, 1933-34, 24p.)*

Stoddard, Thomas Wren — Culbertson System, Easy-Way Contract Bridge *(Private, 1940, 32p.)*

Taylor, Arthur M — Bridge Simplified To Better Your Game *(Private, 1941, 32p.)*

Taylor, Charles Hammond — Quickies On The Play Of The Hand *(Taylor Press, 1930, 6p.)*

Taylor, Charles Hammond — Taylor's Digest Of Culbertson One-over-One *(Taylor Press, 1930, 25p.)*

Taylor, Charles Hammond — The Last Word On Contract Bridge *(Taylor Press, 1935-48, 23-36p.)*

Thorne, Harold — Contract Prompter *(Thorne School Of Bridge, 1933, 5p.)*

Thorne, Harold — Thorne's Ready Reference Contract *(Dutton, 1931, 35p.)*

Tiernan, Agatha D — How To Value Your Hand For Contract Bridge *(Taylor Press, 1933-39, 24p.)*

Tilley, H A — A Complete Summary Of Contract Bridge *(Private, 1933, 12p.)*

Trippe, Mrs. Fedora S — Contract Bridge: Pointers For Points With The Distributional Count And Forcing System

          (Norman, 1930, 29p.)

Truscott, Alan F &
  Harrison-Gray, Maurice Short Cut To Expert Bridge *(Foulsham, 1966, 1p.)*
Tyler, Frances G New Culbertson System Of 1935 *(Private, 1935, 24p.)*
Van Court, Georgine Sickels An Outline Of The Culbertson System *(Vanco, 1935, 8p.)*
Van Court, Georgine Sickels Outline Of The Improved Culbertson System Of Contract Bridge *(Vanco, 1947, 15p.)*
Vandyke, Clifford Contract Contracted: A Simple Summary *(Routledge, 1933, 48p.)*
Vernon, M Bridge In Brief *(Klopp, 1927, 31p.)*
Walsh, R I Contract At A Glance Based On Culbertson *(Private, 1934, 4p.)*
Wei, C C Revised Summary Of The Precision System *(Precision System Hq., 1978, 9p.)*
Wei, C C Summary Of The Precision System *(Precision System Hq., 1970-73, 8p.)*
Wei, C C & Belladonna, G
  & Garrozzo, B Bridge Club Elite Presents - Precision Club *(Private, 1972, 24p.)*
Wei, C C & Belladonna, G
  & Garrozzo, B New, Revised Summary Of The Super Precision System *(Monna Lisa, 1975, 39p.)*
Wei, C C & Belladonna, G
  & Garrozzo, B Summary Of The Super Precision System *(Monna Lisa, 1975, 27p.)*
Whitehead, Wilbur Cherrier Whitehead's Contract At A Glance, Complete In Twenty Pages *(Stokes, 1930, 26p.)*
Willson, James A The Table-Side Bidding Companion *(Private, 1975, 8p.)*
Wohlgemuth, Albert J Contract Bidding Chart Based On The Culbertson Standard System *(Bobbs Merrill, 1931, 7p.)*
Woodard, Kenneth E M Pocket Tabular Contract With Examples *(Cranmore, 1938, 22p.)*
Woods, Edward F Shortcut To Standard Contract Bridge *(Private, 1927, 0p.)*
Woods, Jo At The Bridge Table *(Private, 1952-76, 40p.)*
Woods, Jo Little Green Book: Artificial Bids, Leads, Signals, Discards And Many Other Subjects *(Private, 1958, 68p.)*
Work, Milton Cooper The Official Summary Of New Standardized Official System Of Contract Bridge *(Winston, 1933, 80p.)*
Work, Milton Cooper The Official System Of Contract Bridge In A Nutshell *(Winston, 1931, 52p.)*
Zorn, Bill Bridge Abridged: Modern Bidding Based On Goren With 4 Card Majors *(Sydney Bridge Publishing, 1985, 8p.)*

I. BIDDING CONVENTIONS AND TREATMENTS

A.C.B.L. A.C.B.L. Guide To Conventions *(A.C.B.L., 1964, 19p.)*
A.C.B.L. A.C.B.L. Guide To Conventions With Suggested Defenses *(A.C.B.L., 1966-74, 22-30p.)*
Ainger, Simon Simple Conventions For The Acol System *(Mr. Bridge, 1995, 24p.)*
Amsbury, Joe Bridge Conventions: Control Asking (Or Blackwood And All That Jazz) *(Bridge Players Handbooks, 1980, 32p.)*
August, William J The August Two Diamond Bid *(Private, 1962, 4p.)*
Baker, Bob Bridge Conventions: The Swiss Convention *(Bridge Players Handbooks, 1980-85, 31p.)*
Baron, Randall More Popular Conventions *(Devyn Press, 1981, 10p.)*
Baron, Randall Popular Conventions *(Devyn Press, 1979, 10p.)*
Baron, Randall The One Notrump Opening Bid And Responses *(Devyn Press, 1989, 8p.)*
Beard, John The New Conventional Way *(Beard, 1996, 99p.)*
Beard, John & Keech, Ray The Conventional Way *(J & R Bridge Enterprises, 1981-87, 64p.)*
Bergen, Marty Better Bidding With Bergen - Volume One - Uncontested Auctions *(Hardy, 1985, 199p.)*
Bergen, Marty Minor Suit Raises *(Devyn Press, 1985, 10p.)*
Bernstein, Andrew Splinter Bids *(Devyn Press, 1979, 10p.)*
Blackwood, Easley The Blackwood Convention *(Devyn Press, 1981, 10p.)*
Blubaugh, John Game Tries *(Private, 1992, 19p.)*
Blubaugh, John Inverted Minor Suit Raises *(Private, 1992, 28p.)*
Blubaugh, John Jacoby And Texas Transfer Bids *(Private, 1992, 32p.)*
Blubaugh, John Minor Suit Transfer Bids *(Private, 1992, 28p.)*
Blubaugh, John The Forcing Notrump *(Private, 1992, 30p.)*
Bourke, Tim A System Of Responding To One Notrump *(Australian Bridge Institute, 1976, 2p.)*
Bourke, Tim An Alternative NT Structure For Precision *(Australian Bridge Institute, 1976, 4p.)*
Bourke, Tim Blackout - Conventional Responses After Partner's Reverse *(Australian Bridge Institute, 1975, 3p.)*
Bourke, Tim Comparison Of Transfer And Stayman After Precision Two Clubs *(Australian Bridge Institute, 1975, 10p.)*
Brashler, Ted Bidding Conventions Book One *(Private, 1985, 24p.)*
Breeser, Robert Bridge Flashcards: Notrumps And Stayman And Jacoby Transfers *(Mindracer Publishing, 1999, 50p.)*
Breeser, Robert Bridge Flashcards: Notrumps, Stayman And Piece Of Mind *(Mindracer Publishing, 1995, 50p.)*
Browne, Derrick Benjamin Twos *(Bridge Shop, 1993, 63p.)*
Budin, Barnett &
  Kornfeld, Morris Bridge Players Digest Of Conventions *(Budin Press, 1962-63, 32-48p.)*
Coffin, George Sturgis Asking Bids Complete *(Coffin, 1936, 16p.)*
Coffin, George Sturgis The O'Donnell Mandate Bids *(Private, 1958, 8p.)*
Coffin, George Sturgis The Weak Notrump *(Coffin, 1956, 32p.)*
Cohen, Ben & Barrow, Rhoda
  (see Lederer, Rhoda) Conventions Made Clear *(Blond, 1966, 133p.)*
Cohen, Ben & Lederer, Rhoda Current Conventions Made Clear *(Allen & Unwin, 1973, 161p.)*
Culbertson, Ely Asking Bids And The Two-Way Three Bid. *(Culbertson National Studios, 1936, 16p.)*
De Satnick, Shelley Everyone's Introduction To Bridge Conventions *(Avon, 1984, 137p.)*
Drury, Douglas The Drury Two Club Convention *(Souvenir De Mexico, 1962, 46p.)*
Duke, J Dan Foundations Of Bidding V, Conventions In Vogue *(Land Cruise, 1997, 123p.)*
Duke, J Dan Modern Popular Conventions *(Land Cruise, 1988, 152p.)*
Ernst, Leonard Conventions In A Nutshell *(Nella Bridge Supplies, 1973, 7p.)*
Farell, Mary Jane Two Clubs - Strong, Artificial And Forcing *(Devyn Press, 1985, 10p.)*
Field, Leslie O The Field Convention For Sound Bidding In The Slam Zone *(Private, 1947-48, 20p.)*
Field, Leslie O The Field Slam Convention *(Private, 1957, 32p.)*
Flannery, William L Flannery *(Devyn Press, 1981, 10p.)*
Flannery, William L The Complete Flannery Two Diamond Opener *(Nella Bridge Supplies, 1979, 16p.)*
Flannery, William L The Flannery 2 Diamond Opening *(Devyn Press, 1984, 190p.)*
Glynn, Sean A Guide To Popular Bridge Conventions *(Glynn, 1990, 6p.)*

AUTHOR	TITLE	PUBLISHER	YEAR	PAGES

Glynn, Sean — A Guide To Transfer Responses To Opening Bids Of One Notrump And Two Notrump *(Glynn, 1987, 6p.)*

Goren, Charles H — Handbook Of The Most Widely Used Bridge Conventions *(Goren Enterprises/Heines, 1960-64, 44p.)*

Granovetter, Matthew &
Granovetter, Pamela — Conventions At A Glance *(Granovetter, 1993, 92p.)*

Hardy, Max — Forcing Notrump Responses *(Hardy, 1984, 36p.)*

Hardy, Max — Fourth Suit Forcing *(Hardy, 1984, 45p.)*

Hardy, Max — New Minor Forcing *(Hardy, 1984, 22p.)*

Hardy, Max — Splinters And Other Shortness Bids *(Hardy, 1987-90, 88p.)*

Hardy, Max — The Problems With Major Suit Raises And How To Fix Them *(Devyn Press, 1998, 93p.)*

Hart, Norman De Vere — The Culbertson Asking Bids And New 5NT Bid *(Joiner & Steele, 1936, 36p.)*

Helms, Jerry — Helms To Hello *(Private, 1996, 44p.)*

Hodgins, Don &
Hodgins, Maurine — Hodgins Convention *(Thomas Industries, 1981, 34p.)*

Horton, Mark — Bridge Conventions: Defences To A Strong Club *(Probray Press, 1982, 32p.)*

Horton, Sally — Bridge Conventions: Transfers After One No-Trump *(Bridge Players Handbooks, 1984, 32p.)*

Horton, Sally
(see Sowter/Brock, Sally) — Bridge Conventions: Responding To Two Notrump *(Probray Press, 1982, 32p.)*

Hunt, William Montague — Play To Win: Contract Bridge, Improved Bidding Methods *(Private, 1941, 72p.)*

Jacoby, James — The Major-Suit Opening Bids And Responses *(Devyn Press, 1989, 8p.)*

Jacoby, James & Falk, Allan — Bridge Toolkit *(Zookeeper, 1992, 247p.)*

Jacoby, Oswald — Jacoby Transfer Bids *(Devyn Press, 1979, 10p.)*

Jacoby, Oswald — Major Suit Raises *(Devyn Press, 1981, 10p.)*

Jacoby, Oswald — What's New In Bridge *(Hanover House, 1954, 158p.)*

Jason, Marvin — Jason Mix Two Way Notrump Convention *(Jason Crafts, 1996, 28p.)*

Jason, Marvin — Jason Splinter Bridge Convention *(Jason Crafts, 1995, 30p.)*

Jason, Marvin — Jason Two Way Majors Bridge Convention *(Jason Crafts, 1997, 55p.)*

Kantar, Edwin B — *+Roman Key Card Blackwood *(Granovetter/C & T Bridge Supplies/Hale, 1991-98, 118-215p.)*

Kantar, Edwin B — Bridge Conventions: A Guide To Understanding Techniques Of Modern Bidding *(Wilshire, 1972-76, 133p.)*

Kantar, Edwin B — Everything You Wanted To Know About Conventions *(Private, 1971, 100p.)*

Kearse, Amalya — Bridge Conventions Complete *(Hart/Black/Devyn Press, 1975-1990, 624-1121p.)*

Keenan, Mary — Roman Key Card Blackwood *(Devyn Press, 1989, 8p.)*

Kerns, Walter — Kernsy: Alias = Zero-One; Short-Two; Short-Two *(Private, 1996, 34p.)*

Kierein, John — You Ought To Bid An Average Hand, Featuring The Kamikaze Notrump *(Private, 1977, 45p.)*

Kleinman, Danny — A Cornucopia Of Conventions *(Private, 1998, 134p.)*

Kleinman, Danny — Not Your Daddy's Blackwood *(Private, 1999, 116p.)*

Kleinman, Danny — The Notrump Bidder's Bible *(Private, 1997, 66p.)*

Klinger, Ron — Benjamin Twos *(Modern Bridge Publications, 1986, 8p.)*

Klinger, Ron — Bid Better, Much Better *(Modern Bridge Publications, 2000, 128p.)*

Klinger, Ron — Bridge Conventions, Defences And Countermeasures *(Gollancz, 1993-99, 143-160p.)*

Klinger, Ron — Multi-Twos, Including RCO Twos *(Modern Bridge Publications, 1988, 8p.)*

Klinger, Ron — One Notrump: Two Clubs - Extended Stayman, Lavings Or Power *(Modern Bridge Publications, 1986, 8p.)*

Klinger, Ron — Relay Slam Bidding Over Balanced Hand Openings *(Australian Bridge Institute, 1976, 7p.)*

Klinger, Ron — Roman Key Card Blackwood, The Key To Better Slam Bidding *(Modern Bridge Publications, 1988, 8p.)*

Klinger, Ron — Ten Great Conventions *(Modern Bridge Publications, 1986, 8p.)*

Klinger, Ron — Transfers Over One Notrump *(Modern Bridge Publications, 1988, 8p.)*

Klinger, Ron — Twelve More Great Conventions *(Modern Bridge Publications, 1998, 8p.)*

Klinger, Ron &
Kambites, Andrew — Bridge Conventions For You *(Gollancz, 1994-99, 128-144p.)*

Kornfeld, Morris — Bridge Player's Digest Of Conventions *(Suburbn Offset, 1968, 48p.)*

Kushner, Jack — Distributional, Or Weak 2 Bids *(Private, 1953, 10p.)*

Kushner, Jack — One No Trump With Stayman Check-Back And Kushner Slam *(Private, 1960, 36p.)*

Lawrence, Mike — Major Suit Raises *(Texas Bridge Supplies, 1983, 86p.)*

Lawrence, Mike — The Jacoby And Texas Transfers Convention *(Texas Bridge Supplies, 1983, 22p.)*

Lederer, Rhoda
(see Barrow, Rhoda) — Bridge Conventions Made Clear *(Bibliagora, 1982, 128p.)*

Lindqvist, Magnus &
Nilsland, Mats — Notrump Bidding - The Scanian Way: Swedish Expert Methods, Volume Two *(Scania Bridgekonsult, 1990, 63p.)*

Lowden, Reed C — The Lowden Cue Bid Over The Strong Two Club Open *(Lowden, 1993, 37p.)*

Marston, Paul & Hughes, Nick — Opening Two Bids *(Hamilton, 1992, 59p.)*

Marston, Paul & Hughes, Nick — Weak Twos And Strong Two Clubs *(Grand Slam Books, 1991, 30p.)*

McMath, Virginia — Reliable Rebids For One Heart Openings *(Baron-Barclay, 1992, 4p.)*

Meckstroth, Jeff — New Minor And Fourth Suit Forcing And Artificial *(Devyn Press, 1985, 10p.)*

Megary, Leo & Mernin, Emy — The San Francisco System - Contract Bridge *(Decarr, 1958, 76p.)*

Mollo, Victor — Bridge - Victor Mollo's Pocket Guide To Winning Conventions *(Rexard/L.S.P., 1960-70, 7-8p.)*

Morehead, Albert H — Bidding Conventions Of 1951-52 *(New York Times, 1952, 23p.)*

Morehead, Albert H — Bidding Conventions Of 1959-60 *(New York Times, 1960, 19p.)*

Munger, Robert — The Roman Two Diamond Opening And Variations *(Devyn Press, 1998, 64p.)*

Nilsland, Mats &
Wirgren, Anders — Major Suit Raises - The Scanian Way: Swedish Expert Methods, Volume One *(Scania Bridgekonsult, 1989, 53p.)*

North, Freddie — Conventional Bidding Explained *(Batsford, 1994, 144p.)*

O'Brien, Maureen &
Oeschger, Ivy — The New Culbertson Asking Bids And The Two-Way Three Bids *(Private, 1935, 61p.)*

Palmer, Frank H — The Palmer Code *(Private, 1948, 20p.)*

Palmer, Frank H — The Palmer Conventional System *(Private, 1947, 4p.)*

Reese, Anne — Four Suit Transfers *(Anne Reese, 1993, 32p.)*

Root, William S &

Pavlicek, Richard — *+Modern Bridge Conventions *(Crown, 1981, 244p.)*

Rosenkranz, George &
Truscott, Alan F — Bidding On Target *(Devyn Press, 1992, 292p.)*

Rosenkranz, George &
Truscott, Alan F — Modern Ideas In Bidding *(Devyn Press, 1982, 236p.)*

Rosenthal, Al — Some Issues Of Intermediate Bridge And The Montreal Relay Plus System *(Private, 1992, 80p.)*

Rubens, Jeff — The Useful Space Principle And Transfer Advances Of Overcalls *(The Bridge World, 1995, 40p.)*

Schenken, Howard — Weak Two Bids *(Devyn Press, 1979, 10p.)*

Seagram, Barbara &
Smith, Marc — Twenty-Five Conventions You Should Know *(Master Point Press, 1999, 190p.)*

Senior, Brian — Bridge Conventions: Fourth Suit Forcing *(Probray Press, 1985, 32p.)*

Senior, Brian — Bridge Conventions: The Multi-Coloured 2d *(Probray Press, 1982, 32p.)*

Senior, Brian — Bridge Conventions: Weak Two Bids *(Apsbridge, 1991, 30p.)*

Senior, Brian — Bridge Players Handbooks: Roman Keycard Blackwood *(Apsbridge, 1993, 28p.)*

Senior, Brian — The Transfer Principle *(Probray Press, 1986, 124p.)*

Shuman, Kerri — Drury *(Devyn Press, 1981, 10p.)*

Silverman, Shirley — Popular Bridge Conventions *(Barclay, 1970-, 8p.)*

Smith, F D &
Braham, Vivian G — Victorian Blackwood Slam Convention *(Private, 1939, 48p.)*

Smith, William Sherman &
Smith, Gertrude S — The Smith Slam Convention *(Private, 1941, 16p.)*

Soloway, Paul — Strong Opening Bids *(Devyn Press, 1989, 8p.)*

Soloway, Paul — The Stayman Convention *(Devyn Press, 1979, 10p.)*

Sontag, Alan — One No Trump Forcing *(Devyn Press, 1981, 10p.)*

Sowter, Sally — Bridge Conventions: Transfers After One No-Trump *(Bridge Players Handbooks, 1980, 32p.)*

Squire, Norman — A Guide To Bridge Conventions *(Duckworth, 1958-79, 136-100p.)*

Stayman, Samuel M — A Short Guide To Better Notrump Bidding *(Odyssey, 1965, 6p.)*

Thwaites, Marje B — Victorian Blackwood Convention Slam Bidding Revised And Compiled *(Private, 1955, 4p.)*

Tierney, Edgar F — TNT: Tierney No Trump Bridge System *(Private, 1935, 47p.)*

Weaver, G A — The Club Forcing Convention For Duplicate Players *(Private, 1963, 48p.)*

Wei, C C &
Andersen, Ronald E — Perfect Your No Trump Bidding: Bidding Precisely - Volume 4 *(Monna Lisa Precision, 1978, 232p.)*

Wolff, Bobby &
Musumeci, Joe — Jacoby Transfer Bids: For Intermediate And Advanced Players *(Aces, 1992, 26p.)*

Wolff, Bobby &
Musumeci, Joe — Limit Raises' Forcing Raises' Splinter Bids And The Forcing Notrump *(Aces, 1992, 26p.)*

Woodson, William B — Woodson Two-Way No Trump *(Private, 1953, 31p.)*

J. COMPETITIVE BIDDING

Amsbury, Joe — Bridge Conventions: Doubles In Competition *(Probray Press, 1985, 31p.)*

Andersen, Ronald E — Killing Their Notrump *(Devyn Press, 1979, 10p.)*

Andersen, Ronald E — The Lebensohl Convention Complete In Contract Bridge *(Barclay, 1987, 105p.)*

August, William J — Defensive Bidding: Part I - III. *(Graphics Plus, 1992-93, 28-67p.)*

Baron, Randall &
Champney, Ken — Clobber Their Artificial Club *(Baron, 1979-90, 20-32p.)*

Bergen, Marty — Better Bidding With Bergen - Volume Two - Competitive Bidding *(Hardy, 1988, 149p.)*

Bergen, Marty — Introduction To Negative Doubles *(Magnus, 2000, 64p.)*

Bergen, Marty — Negative Doubles *(Magnus, 2000, 118p.)*

Blackmon, May Ritchie — Defense Overcalls *(Manhattan Storage, 1934, 3p.)*

Blackmon, May Ritchie — Takeout And Penalty Doubles *(Manhattan Storage, 1934, 3p.)*

Blubaugh, John — Escaping One Notrump Doubled *(Private, 1992, 20p.)*

Blubaugh, John — Lebensohl Vs. Weak Two Bids *(Private, 1992, 24p.)*

Blubaugh, John — Negative And Responsive Doubles *(Private, 1992, 32p.)*

Blubaugh, John — New Minor Forcing *(Private, 1992, 20p.)*

Blubaugh, John — Overcalls *(Private, 1992, 36p.)*

Blubaugh, John — Take-Out Doubles *(Private, 1992, 28p.)*

Blubaugh, John — The Law Of Total Tricks *(Private, 1992, 32p.)*

Blubaugh, John — The Lebensohl Convention *(Private, 1992, 32p.)*

Booty, June & Hurst, Richard — Guide To Overcalling *(Private, 1998, 6p.)*

Breeser, Robert — Bridge Flashcards: Overcalls Overeasy *(Mindracer Publishing, 1995, 48p.)*

Brock, Sally — Step-By-Step: Overcalls *(Batsford, 1995, 142p.)*

Brock, Sally — The Complete Book Of Bols Bridge Tips *(Chess & Bridge, 1997, 168p.)*

Cappelletti, Mike &
Lewis, E D — Cappelletti Over One Notrump *(Private, 1989, 12p.)*

Cappelletti, Mike &
Lewis, E D — Cappelletti Over One-Of-A-Major Doubled (C/1mx) *(Private, 1990, 12p.)*

Cohen, Larry — *+To Bid Or Not To Bid: The Law Of Total Tricks *(Natco Press/Gollancz, 1992-, 272p.)*

Cohen, Larry — Following The Law: The Total Tricks Sequel *(Natco Press, 1994, 244p.)*

Cohen, Larry — Introduction To The Law: The Law Of Total Tricks Simplified *(Devyn Press, 1997, 62p.)*

Crowhurst, Eric — *Acol In Competition *(Pelham, 1980, 383p.)*

Delmain, A V — The Misunderstood Takeout Double, Defensive Bidding *(Medulla Press, 1996, 67p.)*

Dinkel, Jeanne & Dinkel, Rich — Enjoying Your Tiger Bridge *(Private, 1996, 162p.)*

Duke, J Dan — Competitive Bidding *(Land Cruise, 1988-91, 136p.)*

Duke, J Dan — Foundations Of Bidding III & IV, Competitive Bidding I & II *(Land Cruise, 1997, 103p. each)*

Ernst, Leonard — Michaels Cue Bid *(Nella Bridge Supplies, 1978, 6p.)*

Ewen, Robert B — *Doubles For Takeout, Penalties And Profit At Contract Bridge *(Prentice Hall/Hale/M.B. Books, 1974-85, 278p.)*

Ewen, Robert B — The Defensive Bidding Quiz Book *(Monna Lisa, 1980, 105p.)*

Feldheim, Harold — Negative And Responsive Doubles In Bridge *(Barclay, 1980, 64p.)*

Feldheim, Harold — Negative, Responsive, And Other Competitive Doubles *(C & T Bridge Supplies, 1993, 77p.)*

Feldheim, Harold — Tactical Bidding *(C & T Bridge Supplies, 1992, 228p.)*

Flint, Jeremy & Sharp, Richard — Competitive Bidding *(Cassell, 1980, 202p.)*

Flint, Jeremy & Sharp, Richard — Competitive Bidding *(Hale, 1987, 202p.)*

Frank, D S — A Systematic Orbit For Sputnik *(Australian Bridge Institute, 1975, 8p.)*

Goldman, Bobby — Doubles *(Devyn Press, 1981, 10p.)*
Goren, Charles H — Winning Doubles: Doubling To Win At Contract Bridge *(T.D.C.-Heines, 1975, 47p.)*
Hall, Peter — Competitive Bidding At Pairs *(South Bucks Bridge Club, 1996, 182p.)*
Hardy, Max — Competitive Bidding With Two-Suited Hands *(Devyn Press, 1996, 154p.)*
Hayden (Truscott), Dorothy — Competitive Bidding *(Barclay, 1971, 8p.)*
Horton, Sally
  (see Sowter/Brock, Sally) — Double Trouble *(Faber, 1993, 273p.)*
Husband, Pat &
  Kambites, Andrew — Overcalling In Acol *(Gollancz, 1991, 24p.)*
Kaplan, Edgar — Competitive Bidding In Modern Bridge *(Barrie & Rockliff, 1966, 192p.)*
Kaplan, Edgar — Competitive Bidding In Modern Bridge *(Cornerstone Library, 1968, 192p.)*
Kaplan, Edgar — Competitive Bidding In Modern Bridge *(Fleet, 1965, 192p.)*
Kleinman, Danny — Doubles: Sputnik And The Axe *(Private, 1992, 54p.)*
Klinger, Ron — Competitive Bidding *(Modern Bridge Publications, 1998, 8p.)*
Klinger, Ron — Doubles *(Modern Bridge Publications, 1986, 8p.)*
Klinger, Ron — Negative Doubles *(Modern Bridge Publications, 1986, 8p.)*
Klinger, Ron — The Law Of Total Tricks Flipper *(Gollancz, 1999, 32p.)*
Klinger, Ron &
  Kelsey, Hugh Walter — Master Doubles *(Gollancz, 1988, 10p.)*
Kushner, Jack — Defense Against Slams, Doubled *(Private, 1950, 7p.)*
Kushner, Jack — Defense Against Takeout Doubles *(Private, 1950, 14p.)*
Kushner, Jack — Defense Against Three No-Trump Doubled *(Private, 1950, 9p.)*
Kushner, Jack — Takeout Doubles, Traps And Balances *(Private, 1953, 0p.)*
Lawrence, Mike — *+The Complete Book On Overcalls In Contract Bridge *(Hardy/Pelham, 1979-, 202-256p.)*
Lawrence, Mike — *Disturbing Opponents Notrump *(C & T Bridge Supplies, 1995, 45p.)*
Lawrence, Mike — *The Complete Book On Balancing In Contract Bridge *(Hardy, 1981-, 209p.)*
Lawrence, Mike — Balancing *(Devyn Press, 1981, 10p.)*
Lawrence, Mike — Book One In The Series On Doubles: The Complete Book On Takeout Doubles *(Magnus, 1994, 222p.)*
Lawrence, Mike — Overcalls *(Devyn Press, 1981, 10p.)*
Lawrence, Mike — The Complete Guide To Contested Auctions *(Lawrence & Leong, 1992, 360p.)*
Lawrence, Mike — The Lebensohl Convention *(Texas Bridge Supplies, 1983, 23p.)*
Marston, Paul — *General Defence To Forcing Pass And Other Artificial Bids *(Contract Bridge Supplies, 1985, 15p.)*
Marston, Paul — *Winning Decisions In Competitive Bidding *(Grand Slam Books, 1995, 89p.)*
Mendelson, Paul — *Mendelson's Guide To The Bidding Battle *(Colt Books, 1998, 197p.)*
Miles, Marshall — *Competitive Bidding In The Twenty-First Century *(Master Point Press, 2000, 254p.)*
Miles, Marshall — Stronger Competitive Bidding *(Lawrence & Leong, 1992, 318p.)*
Nilsland, Mats — *Absolute Doubles - The Scanian Way: Swedish Expert Methods Volume Four *(Scania Bridgekonsult, 1998, 56p.)*
Passell, Michael — Michaels Cue Bid *(Devyn Press, 1979, 10p.)*
Pavlicek, Richard — Competitive Bidding *(Private, 1983, 13p.)*
Payne, Dick & Amsbury, Joe — *Bridge: TNT And Competitive Bidding *(Batsford, 1981, 175p.)*
Peche, George — Interventions At The Bridge Table *(Private, 1986, 67p.)*
Robson, Andrew &
  Segal, Oliver — *+Partnership Bidding At Bridge: The Contested Auction *(Faber/C & T Bridge Supplies, 1993, 406p.)*
Rodwell, Eric — Lebensohl *(Devyn Press, 1985, 10p.)*
Rosen, Edward L — The Negative Double *(Nella Bridge Supplies, 1973, 7p.)*
Roth, Alvin — Negative Doubles *(Devyn Press, 1979, 10p.)*
Roth, Alvin — The Unusual Notrump *(Devyn Press, 1979, 10p.)*
Seagram, Barbara &
  Smith, Marc — Bridge: Twenty-Five Ways To Compete In The Bidding *(Master Point Press, 2000, 220p.)*
Senior, Brian — Bridge Conventions: Defending Against Pre-Empts *(Probray Press, 1984, 32p.)*
Senior, Brian — Bridge Players Handbooks: Balancing After I-Level Openings *(Probray Press, 1986, 32p.)*
Senior, Brian — Bridge Players Handbooks: Lebensohl *(Apsbridge, 1993, 31p.)*
Smolski, Roman — *Bridge Conventions: Defences To One Notrump *(Probray Press, 1982-91, 32p.)*
Sowter, Tony — Bridge Conventions: The Take-Out Double *(Bridge Players Handbooks, 1980-83, 32p.)*
Sowter, Tony — Step-By-Step: Competitive Bidding *(Batsford, 1996, 143p.)*
Stephens, George R — Takeout Double Pointers *(Contract Bridge Supplies, 1979, 2p.)*
Truscott, Dorothy Hayden — Competitive Bidding *(Barclay, 1973, 8p.)*
Wei, Kathie — Defense Against Strong Club Openings *(Devyn Press, 1979, 10p.)*
Wei, Kathie &
  Andersen, Ronald E — Action For The Defense *(Monna Lisa, 1980, 247p.)*
Wolff, Bobby &
  Musumeci, Joe — Negative Doubles Responsive Double Maximal Doubles *(Aces, 1992, 26p.)*

K. HAND EVALUATION, BIDDING PRINCIPLES, BIDDING THEORY AND SPECIAL SITUATIONS

Andersen, Ronald E — The Bidding Messages *(Devyn Press, 1989, 8p.)*
Andersen, Ronald E — Where And How High: For People Who Hate To Read Bridge Books *(Wisconsin Bridge Assoc., 1970, 92p.)*
Andersen, Ronald E &
  Zenkel, Sabine — Preempts From A To Z *(Magnus, 1993-96, 290-307p.)*
Anonymous — Gulf Bridge Lessons: Number 4, Slam Bidding *(Gulf Refining Co., 1933, 6p.)*
Bangs, Fred T — Hon-Suit Bidding *(Hon-Suit, 1945, 48p.)*
Blackwood, Easley — Dynamic Point Counter *(Bobbs Merrill, 1956, 4p.)*
Blubaugh, John — The Losing Trick Count *(Private, 1992, 28p.)*
Bomar, Bob — The Bomar T.P.C.B. (Total Point Count Bidding) System *(Vantage Press, 1968, 41p.)*
Desai, G R &
  Mehta, Ravindra C — Contract Bridge And High Card Points: A New Look *(Mehta, 1985, 144p.)*
Desai, Gaurang — Revolution In Contract Bridge *(Navdeep Prakashan, 1981, 556p.)*
Desai, Gaurang & Desai, G R — Contract Bridge: The Absolute Measure Of Trick Potential Of A Hand *(Mehta, 1990, 94p.)*
Desai, Gaurang &
  Mehta, Ravindra C — Contract Bridge Bidding Technique Through High Card And Pattern Points: Book I-III *(Mehta, 1988, 86p. each)*
Desai, Gaurang &

AUTHOR	TITLE	PUBLISHER	YEAR	PAGES
Mehta, Ravindra C	Elements Of Modern Contract Bridge Or Primer Of Card Points And Pattern Points *(Mehta, 1988, 117p.)*			
Fenton, Estil Irvin	Contract Bridge Success: Simplified System For Slam Bidding *(Private, 1941, 8p.)*			
Frank, D S	Four-Four-Four-One Hand Patterns *(Australian Bridge Institute, 1976, 2p.)*			
Fry, Sam Jr.	*How To Win At Bridge With Any Partner *(Golden Press/Faber/Cornerstone Library, 1961-65, 144p.)*			
Gerber, John	The Four-Club Bid: A Slam Convention - As Easy As ABC *(Private, 1942, 28p.)*			
Gerber, John	The Gerber Four Club Slam Convention *(Texas Bridge, 1963, 24p.)*			
Gordy, Ed	Standard American 1987 *(Private, 1967, 8p.)*			
Gorski, Andrew	The Art Of Logical Bidding *(Devyn Press, 1985, 87p.)*			
Griffiths, David C	Bridge Conventions: The Losing Trick Count *(Probray Press, 1984, 32p.)*			
Grose, J	Slam Bidding At Contract Bridge *(Allen & Unwin, 1934, 66p.)*			
Hackett, Paul & Hackett, Jason	Practise Your Pre-Emptive Bidding *(Bridge Plus, 1997, 16p.)*			
Hamman, Robert	Opening Preempts *(Devyn Press, 1981, 10p.)*			
Hanson, Eugene	Bridge By The Winner Method *(Private, 1960, 104p.)*			
Harrison-Gray, Maurice	Losing Trick Count *(Private/Bibliagora, 1961-83, 4-8p.)*			
Hart, Norman De Vere	Slams A La Culbertson: A Manual Of Modern Slam Bidding *(Joiner & Steele, 1937, 99p.)*			
Hathorn, John B	The Secrets Of Tactical Bridge *(Texas Bridge, 1961, 85p.)*			
Immick, H P A	A Bridge Contractor Becomes A Contract Player *(Private, 1935, 14p.)*			
Jacoby, James	Is It Forcing? *(Devyn Press, 1985, 10p.)*			
Johnson, Robert Lee	Cue Bidding *(Private, 1946, 15p.)*			
Kambites, Andrew	Slam Bidding For You *(Gollancz, 1992, 128p.)*			
Kambites, Andrew	Strategic Acol Bidding *(Gollancz, 1991, 24p.)*			
Kambites, Andrew & Husband, Pat	Improve Your Acol Bidding: By Understanding Its Logical Basis *(Gollancz, 1990, 24p.)*			
Kambites, Andrew & Husband, Pat	Strong Twos, Pre-Empts And Slams *(Gollancz, 1990, 24p.)*			
Kantar, Edwin B	The Forcing Pass *(Barclay, 1983, 72p.)*			
Karpin, Fred L	The Point Count System Of Bidding In Contract Bridge *(Kaufman Press, 1949, 50-88p.)*			
Kelsey, Hugh Walter	Master Slam Bidding *(Gollancz, 1987, 10p.)*			
Kelsey, Hugh Walter	Slam Bidding *(Faber/Gollabcz, 1973-91, 200-192p.)*			
Kleinman, Danny	The Goldsmith Lectures: Slam Bidding *(Private, 1992, 62p.)*			
Kleinman, Danny	Understanding Bidding Volume 1 - Foundations *(Private, 1981, 177p.)*			
Klinger, Ron	Cue Bidding To Slams *(Thorpe/Modern Bridge Publications/Gollancz, 1986-1992, 80p.)*			
Klinger, Ron	Cue Bidding To Slams/Master Cue Bidding To Slams *(Modern Bridge Publications/Gollancz, 1986, 8/16p.)*			
Klinger, Ron	Modern Losing Trick Count *(Modern Bridge Publications/Gollancz, 1986-93, 122-143p.)*			
Klinger, Ron	Modern Losing Trick Count Flipper *(Gollancz, 1990-98, 32p.)*			
Klinger, Ron	Practical Slam Bidding *(Modern Bridge Publications/Gollancz, 1997-98, 96p.)*			
Klinger, Ron & Kambites, Andrew	How Good Is Your Bridge Hand? *(Gollancz, 2000, 96p.)*			
Lagron, E M	Making The Most Of Contract: Volume 1 & 2 *(Private, 1933, 23p.)*			
Lawrence, Mike	*The Complete Guide To Passed Hand Bidding *(Lawrence & Leong, 1989, 216p.)*			
Lawrence, Mike	The Complete Book On Hand Evaluation In Contract Bridge *(Hardy/Devyn Press,1983-93, 194p.)*			
Lederer, Rhoda & Griffiths, David C	Fits And Misfits *(Unwin, 1989, 163p.)*			
Lindelof, Edvin Torbjorn	The Computer - Designed Bidding System Cobra *(Gollancz, 1983, 280p.)*			
Marston, Paul	The Language Of Bidding *(Hamilton, 1987-92, 309-298p.)*			
Miles, Marshall	Bridge From The Top - Book I & II *(Tamarind, 1987-89, 299-260p.)*			
Miller, Richard A	Point Count Bidding *(Private, 1947, 30p.)*			
Morehead, Albert H	*Morehead On Bidding *(McMillan/Faber, 1964, 374-344p.)*			
Morehead, Albert H	Bridge The Expert Way *(The Bridge World, 1943, 62p.)*			
Morehead, Albert H & Frey, Richard L	*Morehead On Bidding: Albert H Morehead's Classic Book Revised And Modernized *(Simon & Schuster, 1974, 447p.)*			
Mould, Alan	Step-By-Step Pre-Empts *(Batsford, 1997, 143p.)*			
Mould, Alan	Step-By-Step Slam Bidding *(Batsford, 1995, 143p.)*			
Muntz, Sylvia	Slam Bidding *(Bruelheide, 1950, 16p.)*			
Oeschger, Ivy	Key To Point Count Bidding Valuation *(Private, 1950, 15p.)*			
Oeschger, Ivy	Point Count For Contract Bidding *(Private, 1950, 15p.)*			
Patterson, Derek & Howarth, Mark	Alert! – 1) Pre-Emption *(Fleming, 1992, 134p.)*			
Penick, Michael	The Minor-Suit Opening Bids And Responses *(Devyn Press, 1989, 8p.)*			
Perkins, Frank K	Simplified Contract Standards *(Coffin, 1939, 80p.)*			
Poppet, Patsy	Trumps And To Spare *(Private, 1960, 130p.)*			
Radin, Judi	The Weak No Trump *(Devyn Press, 1981, 10p.)*			
Randle, Ralph	Point Count Bidding In Bridge *(Nea Service, 1963, 32p.)*			
Randle, Ralph	Point Count Bridge - A Digest Of Bridge Fundamentals *(Private, 1960, 8p.)*			
Reese, Terence & Bird, David L	The Art Of Good Bidding *(Faber, 1992, 138p.)*			
Rosenkranz, George	Slam Bidding *(Devyn Press, 1985, 10p.)*			
Roth, Danny	Focus On Bidding *(Master Point Press, 1999, 167p.)*			
Sapire, M	Accurate Slam Bidding At Contract Bridge *(The Bridge World, 1948, 63p.)*			
Senior, Brian	Bread And Butter Bidding *(Maxwell MacMillan Bridge, 1991, 214p.)*			
Senior, Brian	Hand Evaluation In Bridge *(Batsford, 1998, 141p.)*			
Senior, Brian	Raising Partner *(Faber/Batsford, 199-951, 140-128p.)*			
Shows, George A	Slam Bidding *(Private, 1987, 465p.)*			
Simon, S J	*Design For Bidding *(Nicholson & Watson, 1949-51, 268p.)*			
Sims, Dorothy Rice	Psychic Bidding *(Vanguard Press/Allen & Unwin, 1932, 87p.)*			
Slam-It	Supplement To The Slam-It Bridge Guides *(Dewdney, 1931, 3p.)*			
Smyth, P M	Contract Bridge Principles - Modern Approach And Forcing Bids With Epitome *(Lane, 1931, 95p.)*			

Solomon, Charles J   No Trump Bidding *(Philadelphia Inquirer/Private, 1946-47, 40-48p.)*

Solomon, Charles J &
   Disbrow, Bennett L   Slam Bidding And Point Count *(MacRae Smith, 1951, 281p.)*

Sowter, Tony   Step-By-Step: Constructive Bidding *(Batsford, 1994, 144p.)*

Squire, Norman   *The Theory Of Bidding *(Duckworth, 1959-79, 280-233p.)*

Squire, Norman   Bidding At Bridge *(Penguin/Duckworth, 1964-79, 191-182p.)*

Stanley, Enos   Valuing Hands, With Hands Demonstrating Bidding Theories *(Private, 1934, 0p.)*

Stanley, Enos &
   Stanley, Mrs. E   Correcting The Mathematical Bridge Count *(Private, 1955, 2p.)*

Stanley, Enos &
   Stanley, Mrs. E   Three Times Thirteen Equals Thirty-Nine *(Private, 1955, 2p.)*

Stayman, Samuel M   Do You Play Stayman? *(Odyssey/Faber, 1965, 207-237p.)*

Stayman, Samuel M   High Road To Winning Bridge: Do You Play Stayman? *(Cornerstone Library, 1970, 192p.)*

Stewart, Frank   The Bidder's Bible - How To Reach Winning Contracts At Bridge *(C & T Bridge Supplies, 1994, 294p.)*

Tambling, Charles W   Tam's Slam Convention: Quick Pocket Reference *(Private, 1952, 2p.)*

Templeton, K R   Bridge - Count Up To Three With L T C - Losing Trick Count *(Private, 1960, 17p.)*

Trippett, Bernard L   Psychic Bidding *(Miami Valley Bridge Assoc., 1996-97, 20p.)*

Truscott, Alan F   *The Bidding Dictionary *(Lawrence & Leong, 1996, 272p.)*

Truscott, Alan F &
   Alder, Phillip   *On Bidding: Albert Morehead's Classic Work Revised And Updated *(Simon & Schuster, 1990, 399p.)*

Van Dernoot, Julia   Postgraduate Contract Bridge: Advanced Points For Advanced Players *(Appleton, 1931, 52p.)*

Van Zak, Martin   Bridge Bidding *(Private, 1968, 10p.)*

Walshe, G G J   Contract Bridge: Bidding Principles *(De La Rue, 1932, 117p.)*

Walshe, G G J   Slams Made Simple: How To Use Cuebids *(Methuen, 1938, 67p.)*

Watkins, Allen   Slam Skill In One Lesson *(Joiner & Steele, 1938, 46p.)*

Wei, C C &
   Andersen, Ronald E   Profits From Preempts: Bidding Precisely Volume 3 *(Monna Lisa/ Devyn Press, 1977-92, 162p.)*

Weiss, Lawrence   *Contract Bridge: The Bidding Structure *(Garden City, 1942, 376p.)*

White, H W   New Departure, H. W. White's Point Count For Bridge *(Private, 1950, 16p.)*

White, H W   Point Count System For Bridge *(Private, 1950, 5p.)*

Wolff, Bobby   Sacrifices *(Devyn Press, 1985, 10p.)*

Wolff, Bobby &
   Musumeci, Joe   Modern Slam Bidding Simplified For Intermediate And Advanced Players *(Aces, 1992, 33p.)*

Work, Milton Cooper &
   Peterson, Olive A   Work-Peterson Accurate Valuation System Of Contract Bridge *(Winston, 1934, 101p.)*

Yang, Cliff   The Yang's Jump Shifts - A Powerful Approach For Slams! *(Abridge Publisher, 1996, 188p.)*

L. BIDDING PRACTICE AND QUIZZES

Aces, The   *Bid-Em-Up Series A-K: Strong Opening Bids *(Barclay/Bridge Shop, 1970-90, 16p each.)*

Alexander, Ben   Alexander's Bridge Bidding Hands *(Private, 1980, 4p.)*

Bird, David L   Practise Your Defence Against Pre-Empts *(Bridge Plus, 1999, 16p.)*

Bridge World, The   Challenge The Champs - Book 1-VIII *(The Bridge World, 1978-96, 48p. each)*

Bridge World, The   Rate Your Own Game *(The Bridge World, 1981, 48p.)*

Brock, Raymond &
   Brock, Sally   Bridge Quiz: Bidding *(Batsford, 2000, 128p.)*

Chubb, Edith Taft &
   Johnson, Laurence B   How's Your 1933 Culbertson: An Easy Way To Better Contract *(The Bridge World, 1933, 128p.)*

Chubb, Edith Taft &
   Johnson, Laurence B   Test Your Bids In Contract *(Winston, 1931, 44p.)*

Cohen, Ben   Bridge Quiz *(Foyle/Magna Print, 1960-75, 77-102p.)*

Cohen, Ben & Barrow, Rhoda
   (see Lederer, Rhoda)   Acol Quiz *(Allen & Unwin, 1963, 96p.)*

Crowhurst, Eric   Practise Your Crowhurst Two Clubs *(Bridge Plus, 1997, 16p.)*

Forrester, Tony   Practise Your Re-Opening And Rebalancing *(Bridge Plus, 1999, 16p.)*

Goldman, Bobby   Slam Challenges *(Private, 1980, 25p.)*

Goren, Charles H   Charles H Goren's Bridge Quiz Book *(Permabooks, 1949, 184p.)*

Hackett, Paul & Hackett, Jason   Practise Your Benjamin Two Bids *(Bridge Plus, 2000, 16p.)*

Hackett, Paul & Hackett, Jason   Practise Your Negative Doubles *(Bridge Plus, 1997, 16p.)*

Hackett, Paul & Hackett, Jason   Practise Your Roman Key-Card Blackwood *(Bridge Plus, 1997, 16p.)*

Hackett, Paul & Hackett, Jason   Practise Your Weak Twos *(Bridge Plus, 1997, 16p.)*

Hanson, Keith   The Art Of Bidding *(Private, 1990, 224p.)*

Holmes, C Ellwood   Test Your Bidding - 40 Interesting Hands From Play *(T & G Allen/Private, 1950-60, 8p.)*

Huggett, Dave   Practise Your Transfer Bidding *(Bridge Plus, 1997, 16p.)*

International Bridge Academy   Bidding Contest 1983 *(Australian Bridge, 1983, 2p.)*

Jeronimidis, Elena   Practise Your Bidding Of 4-4-4-1 Hands *(Bridge Plus, 2000, 16p.)*

Kelley, Truman L   Cooperative Bridge: Part 2 - Practice *(Private, 1955, 153p.)*

Kleinman, Danny   Master Solvers' Archives 1985-1987 *(Private, 1988, 228p.)*

Kleinman, Danny   Master Solvers' Archives 1988-1990 *(Private, 1991, 234p.)*

Kleinman, Danny   Master Solvers' Archives 1991-1993 *(Private, 1994, 234p.)*

Kleinman, Danny   Master Solvers' Archives 1994-1996 *(Private, 1997, 228p.)*

Kleinman, Danny   Master Solvers' Archives 1997-1999 *(Private, 1997, 180p.)*

Larone, J N   Two-Over-One Game Force Bidding Problems No. 1 *(Aegean Park Press, 1996, 82p.)*

Lawrence, Mike   Mike Lawrence's Bidding Quizzes Volume 1: The Uncontested Auction *(Lawrence & Leong, 1990, 280p.)*

Lederer, Rhoda
   (see Barrow, Rhoda)   Acol-Ites Quiz *(Allen & Unwin/Collins Willow, 1970-93, 197-232p.)*

Magee, Bernard   Practise Your Fourth Suit Forcing *(Bridge Plus, 1997, 16p.)*

Mallon, John   Bridge Bidding Guide *(Snibbe Sports, 1967-72, 96p.)*

McNeil, Keith A   Match Your Bidding Against The Masters *(Modern Bridge Publications, 1991, 176p.)*

McNeil, Keith A &
   Reese, Terence   Bid Against The Masters - The Best Of Bidding Forum *(Gollancz, 1993, 128p.)*

Mendelson, Paul   Practise Your Law Of Total Tricks *(Bridge Plus, 2000, 16p.)*

Meyer, Harlan   Analysis Of Bidding *(Private, 1966, 88p.)*

Meyer, Harlan — Test Your Bidding #1-216 *(Private, 1960, 18p.)*
Mollo, Victor — Streamline Your Bidding With 1100 Quizzes *(Faber, 1979, 217p.)*
Mollo, Victor — Will You Be My Partner?/Bridge With A Master *(Duckworth/Barnes, 1959-60, 102p.)*
Parry, David — Practise Your Lebensohl *(Bridge Plus, 1999, 16p.)*
Price, David — Practise Your Wriggle (A Defence To One Notrump Doubled) *(Bridge Plus, 1997, 16p.)*
Reese, Terence — *Develop Your Bidding Judgment/Bidding A Bridge Hand *(Oak Tree Press /Cornerstone/Dover, 1962-72, 254p.)*
Reese, Terence — What Would You Bid? *(Faber, 1986, 160p.)*
Reese, Terence &
  Bird, David L — *Famous Bidding Decisions - Test Your Skill Against The Experts *(Gollancz, 1996, 128p.)*
Rigal, Barry — Practise Your Doubling (After The Opponents Have Opened) *(Bridge Plus, 2000, 16p.)*
Rigal, Barry — Test Your Bridge Judgement *(Cadogan/Hale, 1993-97, 174-186p.)*
Rimington, Derek — Practise Your Reverse Bidding *(Bridge Plus, 1997, 16p.)*
Rowlands, Bob &
  Hawthorn, Amanda — Test Your Acol Bidding *(Bridge Plus, 1995, 127p.)*
Rowlands, Bob &
  Townsend, Tom — Practise Your Acol Bidding *(Bridge Plus, 1998, 127p.)*
Senior, Brian — It's Your Call: Bidding Problems Answered By International Panel *(Five Aces Books, 2000, 122p.)*
Senior, Brian — Practise Your Cue Bidding *(Bridge Plus, 1999, 16p.)*
Senior, Nevena — Practise Your Asptro (A Defence To 1NT) *(Bridge Plus, 1999, 16p.)*
Sheardown, P E — One Hundred Bridge Hands For Let's Play Bridge *(C.B.C. Dominion Network, 1948, 3p.)*
Smith, Marc — Practise Your Overcalling *(Bridge Plus, 2000, 16p.)*
Sowter, Tony — The First IPBM Book Of Bidding Hands *(Probray Press, 1984, 32p.)*
Swanson, Mike — Practise Your Splinter Bids *(Bridge Plus, 1997, 16p.)*
Townsend, Tom — Practise Your Losing Trick Count *(Bridge Plus, 1997, 16p.)*
Townsend, Tom — Practise Your Stayman Two Clubs *(Bridge Plus, 1997, 16p.)*
Townsend, Tom — Practise Your Two-Suited Overcalls *(Bridge Plus, 1999, 16p.)*
Van Alen, M A — Bridge Quiz/Contract Bridge Quiz *(Taylor Press, 1934-51, 29-32p.)*
Wolff, Bobby & Aces, The — Bidding Challenge*(Devyn Press, 1986, 43p.)*

M. PLAY (INCLUDING PLAY AND DEFENSE)

Ace High — How To Play Your Cards *(Private, 1932, 23p.)*
Bard, George L — Play Of The Hand Made Easy *(Columbia Publishing, 1934, 32p.)*
Berthe, Robert &
  Lebely, Norbert — Bridge: Step By Step Cardplay - No-Trumps *(Batsford, 1981-96, 167-144p.)*
Bird, David L — Practise Your Suit Combinations *(Bridge Plus, 2000, 16p.)*
Bird, David L &
  Forrester, Tony — Secrets Of Expert Card Play *(Batsford, 1997, 144p.)*
Bird, David L & Smith, Marc — Deceptive Card Play *(Master Point Press, 2000, 64p.)*
Bird, David L & Smith, Marc — Eliminations And Throw-Ins *(Master Point Press, 2000, 64p.)*
Bird, David L & Smith, Marc — Entry Management *(Master Point Press, 2000, 64p.)*
Bird, David L & Smith, Marc — Planning In Suit Contracts *(Master Point Press, 2000, 64p.)*
Bird, David L & Smith, Marc — Planning The Play Notrump *(Master Point Press, 2001, 61p.)*
Bird, David L & Smith, Marc — Safety Plays *(Master Point Press, 2000, 64p.)*
Bird, David L & Smith, Marc — Squeezes Made Simple *(Master Point Press, 2001, 61p.)*
Bird, David L & Smith, Marc — Tricks With Trumps *(Master Point Press, 2000, 64p.)*
Black, Paul W — My Bridge Opponents Are Between The Devil And The Deep Blue Sea *(Private, 1930, 0p.)*
Blackmon, May Ritchie — Contract Bridge, Endplays And Coups *(Manhattan Storage, 1934, 2p.)*
Blackmon, May Ritchie — Contract Bridge, The Play Of The Hand *(Manhattan Storage, 1934, 2p.)*
Blackwood, Easley — Play Of The Hand With Blackwood *(Corwin Books/Hale, 1978, 458p.)*
Bourke, Tim & Smith, Marc — *Countdown To Winning Bridge *(Master Point Press, 1999, 214p.)*
Brannon, Robert M — Brannon's Contract Play By Play *(Private, 1931, 78p.)*
Brock, Sally — Suit Combinations In Bridge *(Batsford, 1998, 126p.)*
Brown, John — *Winning Tricks *(Duckworth, 1947-55, 300p.)*
Bruelheide, Frank Elmer — Fundamentals Of Play, How To Play Your Hand At Contract Bridge *(Bruelheide, 1939-40, 64p.)*
Burt, Harold W — Contract Bridge: Control Of The Hand *(Private, 1980, 304p.)*
Cashmore, Stephen — Practise Your Finessing *(Bridge Plus, 1999, 16p.)*
Coffin, George Sturgis — *Endplays *(A.D. Press/Duckworth/Dover, 1938-81, 236-211p.)*
Coffin, George Sturgis — Bridge Play Four Classics *(Duckworth, 1975, 918p.)*
Coffin, George Sturgis — Bridge Play From A To Z *(Faber/Dover, 1954-79, 352p.)*
Coffin, George Sturgis — Endplays At Bridge Explained *(Coffin/Humphries, 1932, 64-96p.)*
Coffin, George Sturgis — File S Safety Plays *(Private, 1953, 27p.)*
Cotter, E P C &
  Rimington, Derek — The Country Life Book Of Bridge Play Technique/Bridge Play Technique *(Country Life Books/ Hale, 1982-88, 176p.)*
Culbertson, Ely — *Contract Bridge Red Book On Play *(Winston/Faber, 1934, 616p.)*
Culbertson, Ely — A Double Finesse Or A Double Squeeze *(The Bridge World, 1933, 12p.)*
De Barra, Risteard P — Improve Your Bridge Play *(Private, 1970, 64p.)*
Donnelly, John L — Happiness Is A Squeeze *(Vantage Press, 1972, 121p.)*
Dormer, Albert — *Dormer On Deduction *(Gollancz, 1995, 143p.)*
Downes, E Hall — Squeezes, Coups And Endplays *(Bridge Publications/Cresset Press, 1934, 64p.)*
Duke, J Dan — Play Of The Hand *(Land Cruise, 1989-97, 150-263p.)*
Eng, Fook H — Bridge Squeezes Illustrated *(Private, 1973, 185p.)*
England, Frank &
  Reford, John Hope — The Play Of The Cards *(De La Rue, 1930-34, 163-224p.)*
Flintom, Frances Young — Winningway Contract Bridge: Golden Rules *(Lash, 1936-38, 52-57p.)*
Fox, George Clive Henry — Bridge: The Basic Elements Of Play And Defence *(Hale, 1994, 346p.)*
Fox, George Clive Henry — Bridge: The Elements Of Play *(Hale, 1980, 176p.)*
Freehill, H G — The Squeeze At Bridge *(Faber, 1949, 126p.)*
Gooden, George S — Contract Bridge - Play Of The Cards *(Private, 1966, 2p.)*
Gooden, George S &
  Hansen, Harold — Contract Bridge: Play Of The Cards - Declarer's Hand *(Hansen, 1933, 109p.)*
Goren, Charles H — *Better Bridge For Better Players *(Doubleday Doran/Rockliff/Barrie & Jenkins, 1942-71, 538p.)*
Goren, Charles H — *Goren On Play And Defense *(Doubleday/Hale, 1974-76, 489p.)*

Goren, Charles H — Goren ... Helps You Improve Your Play Of The Cards *(Heines, 1965, 8p.)*

Goren, Charles H — Goren's Winning Play *(Taylor Press/Heines, 1956-65, 8p.)*

Goren, Charles H — Twelve Newest Winning Bridge Tips *(North American Van Lines, 1959, 20p.)*

Gould, Francis Lewis — The Play's The Thing *(Barnstead, 1934, 24p.)*

Greenberg, Gail — Introduction To Card Combinations *(Devyn Press, 1989, 8p.)*

Hamman, Robert — Squeeze Play *(Devyn Press, 1985, 10p.)*

Hayden (Truscott), Dorothy — Winning Declarer Play *(Harper & Row/Hale/Tandem/Award Books, 1969, 280-318p.)*

Hoffman, Martin &
Smith, Marc — Over Hoffman's Shoulder *(Finesse Bridge, 2001, 159p.)*

Hoffman, Martin &
Wei-Sender, Kathie — On The Other Hand *(C & T Bridge Supplies, 1994, 135p.)*

Husband, Pat & Klinger, Ron — Play Your Cards Right *(Gollancz, 1991, 24p.)*

Jannersten, Eric &
Barrow, Rhoda — *Cards On The Table/Card Reading (Allen & Unwin/Hart, 1971, 207p.)*

Jannersten, Eric &
Wohlin, Jan — Play Safe - And Win *(Gollancz, 1981, 160p.)*

Johnson, Robert Lee — How To Play The Cards At Contract Bridge *(Private, 1940, 63p.)*

Kambites, Andrew — Card Placing For You *(Gollancz, 1995, 95p.)*

Kantar, Edwin B — Take Your Tricks: Over 550 Declarer Play Tips *(Griffin, 1993, 210p.)*

Kantar, Edwin B &
Stanley, Jackson — Gamesman Bridge *(Barker/Liveright/Bantam, 1973-74, 177p.)*

Karpin, Fred L — Contract Bridge: The Play Of The Cards *(Bridge Quarterly, 1958, 506p.)*

Karpin, Fred L — How To Play (And Misplay) Slam Contracts *(Harper & Brothers/Collier/ Collier-MacMillan, 1962-65, 171-191p.)*

Karpin, Fred L — The Art Of Card Reading At Bridge *(Harper & Row/Black/Dover, 1973-82, 232p.)*

Karpin, Fred L — The Drawing Of Trumps And Its Postponement *(Hardy, 1981-90, 178p.)*

Karpin, Fred L — The Finesse: How To Win More Tricks More Often *(Prentice Hall, 1972, 273p.)*

Karpin, Fred L — Winning Play In Contract Bridge: Strategy At Trick One/Bridge Strategy At Trick One *(Mayflowe/Del/Constable/Dover, 1967-76, 288p.)*

Kauder, James A — Creative Card Play: The Cure For Unimaginative Bridge *(Lawrence & Leong, 1989, 226p.)*

Kauder, James A — The Bridge Philosopher *(Private, 1972, 144p.)*

Kelsey, Hugh Walter — *Kelsey On Squeeze Play: Double Squeezes (Gollancz, 1987, 125p.)*

Kelsey, Hugh Walter — *Kelsey On Squeeze Play: Simple Squeezes (Gollancz/Houghton Mifflin, 1985-95, 120p.)*

Kelsey, Hugh Walter — *Kelsey On Squeeze Play: Strip Squeezes (Gollancz, 1986, 120p.)*

Kelsey, Hugh Walter — *Kelsey On Squeeze Play: Triple Squeezes (Gollancz, 1990, 120p.)*

Kelsey, Hugh Walter — +*Bridge: The Mind Of The Expert/Sharpen Your Bridge Technique (Faber/Gollancz, 1981-93, 160p.)*

Kelsey, Hugh Walter — Bridge For The Connoisseur *(Gollancz, 1991, 141p.)*

Kelsey, Hugh Walter — Bridge Wizardry *(Methuen, 1986, 139p.)*

Kelsey, Hugh Walter — Countdown To Better Bridge *(Devyn Press, 1986, 184p.)*

Kelsey, Hugh Walter — Master Finessing *(Gollancz, 1987, 10p.)*

Kelsey, Hugh Walter — Master Squeeze Play *(Gollancz, 1990, 16p.)*

Kelsey, Hugh Walter — The Tricky Game/Deceptive Plays In Bridge *(Hardy/Hale, 1982, 198/187p.)*

Kelsey, Hugh Walter — Winning Card Play *(Gollancz, 1979-89, 234p.)*

Kichline, J Peter — Bridging The Gap *(Granovetter, 1989, 139p.)*

King, Jack Q — The Squeeze In Valhalla *(Carlton, 1964, 300p.)*

Kleinman, Danny — Advice To The Bridgelorn *(Private, 1981, 152p.)*

Kleinman, Danny — Bridge For Dummies, Defenders And Declarers *(Private, 1997, 256p.)*

Kleinman, Danny — Contracts Are For Tricks *(Private, 1998, 130p.)*

Klinger, Ron — *Guide To Better Card Play (Modern Bridge Publications/Gollancz, 1990, 186-192p.)*

Klinger, Ron — Best Play At Trick One/Master Play At Trick One *(Modern Bridge Publications/Gollancz, 1986-88, 8p.)*

Klinger, Ron &
Kambites, Andrew — Card Play Made Easy Four: Timing And Communication *(Gollancz, 1999, 96p.)*

Klinger, Ron &
Kambites, Andrew — Card Play Made Easy One: Safety Plays And Endplays *(Gollancz, 1996, 96p.)*

Klinger, Ron &
Kambites, Andrew — Card Play Made Easy Three: Trump Management *(Gollancz, 1998, 96p.)*

Klinger, Ron &
Kambites, Andrew — Card Play Made Easy Two: Know Your Suit Combinations *(Gollancz, 1997, 96p.)*

Lawrence, Mike — +*How To Read Your Opponents' Cards (Prentice Hall/Hale.Devyn Press, 1973-, 175p.)*

Lawrence, Mike — Falsecards *(Devyn Press, 1986, 214p.)*

Lawrence, Mike — How To Play Card Combinations *(Devyn Press, 1988, 227p.)*

Le Dentu, José — Bridge: Triumphs And Disasters *(Gollancz, 1990, 143p.)*

Love, Clyde E — +*Bridge Squeezes Complete (Barclay/ Mayflower/Constable/Dover, 1959-, 260p.)*

Love, Clyde E — Squeeze Play In Bridge *(Richard R Smith, 1951, 183p.)*

Lownds, E H — The Play's The Thing *(Private, 1932, 69p.)*

Mallon, John — How To Play Your Cards When You Are The Declarer At Contract Bridge *(Chilton, 1976, 119p.)*

Marston, Paul — First Principles Of Card Play *(Faber/Batsford, 1990-95, 152p.)*

Miles, Marshall — *All Fifty Two Cards/Card Reading At Contract (Exposition/Kaye/Cornerstone Library/C & T Bridge Supplies, 1963-92, 142-221p.)*

Mollo, Victor &
Gardener, Nico — +*Card Play Technique (Newnes/Faber/Batsford, 1955-, 381p.)*

Nail, G Robert &
Hathorn, John B — How To Play The Hand *(Texas Bridge, 1961, 73p.)*

North, Freddie — Cards At Play *(Batsford, 1995, 144p.)*

North, Freddie — Practise Your Elimination Play *(Bridge Plus, 1999, 16p.)*

Ostrow, Albert A — The Play Summary *(Atwater Press, 1959, 15p.)*

Ottlik, Geza &
Kelsey, Hugh Walter — +*Adventures In Card Play (Gollancz, 1979-, 285p.)*

Pavlicek, Richard — Squeezes And Endplays *(Private, 1983, 21p.)*

Reese, Terence — *Bridge For Ambitious Players (Gollancz, 1988-92, 143p.)*

Reese, Terence — *Play These Hands With Me (W H Allen/Devyn Press, 1976-83, 195p.)*

Reese, Terence — +*Play Bridge With Reese (Mayflower/Barnes & Noble/Sterling/Dover, 1960-69, 252p.)*

Reese, Terence	+*Reese On Play *(Edward Arnold/Longmans Greene/Conerstone/Hale, 1947-75, 232p.)*			
Reese, Terence	+*The Expert Game/Master Play *(Edward Arnold/Hale/Coffin/Simon & Schuster/Dover, 1958-84, 190p.)*			
Reese, Terence	Do You Really Want To Win At Bridge? *(Gollancz, 1989, 159p.)*			
Reese, Terence	Master Deceptive Plays *(Gollancz, 1989, 10p.)*			
Reese, Terence	Master Plays In A Single Suit *(Gollancz, 1987, 10p.)*			
Reese, Terence & Bird, David L	*All You Need To Know About Play *(Gollancz, 1993, 128p.)*			
Reese, Terence & Bird, David L	*Bridge - Tricks Of The Trade *(Gollancz, 1989-91, 144p.)*			
Reese, Terence & Bird, David L	*How The Experts Do It: Improving Your Bridge *(Faber, 1985, 215p.)*			
Reese, Terence & Bird, David L	+*That Elusive Extra Trick *(Gollancz, 1994, 128p.)*			
Reese, Terence & Bird, David L	+*The Hidden Side Of Bridge *(Faber/Batsford, 1988-93, 136p.)*			
Reese, Terence & Dormer, Albert	The Play Of The Cards *(Penguin/Hale, 1967-92, 224p.)*			
Reese, Terence & Jourdain, Patrick	Squeeze Play Is Easy/Squeeze Play Made Easy *(Allen & Unwin/Sterling/Hale, 1980-88, 145p.)*			
Reese, Terence & Rigal, Barry	*The Expert Game *(Hale, 1997, 208p.)*			
Reese, Terence & Trezel, Roger	Blocking And Unblocking Plays In Bridge *(Ward Lock/Fell/Gollancz, 1976-90, 64p.)*			
Reese, Terence & Trezel, Roger	Elimination Play In Bridge *(Ward Lock/Fell/Gollancz, 1976-90, 77p.)*			
Reese, Terence & Trezel, Roger	Safety Plays In Bridge *(Ward Lock/Fell/Gollancz, 1976-90, 64p.)*			
Reese, Terence & Trezel, Roger	Snares And Swindles In Bridge *(Ward Lock/Fell/Gollancz, 1976-86, 64p.)*			
Reese, Terence & Trezel, Roger	Those Extra Chances In Bridge *(Ward Lock/Fell/Gollancz, 1978-90, 64p.)*			
Reese, Terence & Trezel, Roger	When To Win, When To Duck In Bridge *(Ward Lock/Fell/Gollancz, 1978-90, 64p.)*			
Reich, Marion Louise	Play-It: Bridge Play In Summary Form *(Bridge-It, 1954, 6p.)*			
Rendel, Robert	That Extra Trick *(Allen & Unwin/Houghton Mifflin, 1932, 126p.)*			
Rigal, Barry	*Step-By-Step: Deceptive Declarer Play *(Batsford, 1996, 144p.)*			
Root, William S	*How To Play A Bridge Hand/The Play Of The Hand *(Crown/Hale, 1990-91, 310p.)*			
Rosecrans Publishing Co	Squeezes, Coups And Endplays *(Private, 1965, 68p.)*			
Roth, Danny	Clues To Winning Play: Detective Work In Bridge *(Gollancz, 1987, 136p.)*			
Roth, Danny	Focus On Declarer Play *(Master Point Press, 1997, 128p.)*			
Roth, Danny	Hand Reading In Bridge - How To Improve Your Card Play *(Gollancz, 1993, 125p.)*			
Roth, Danny	Practise Your Counting *(Bridge Plus, 1999, 16p.)*			
Roudinesco, Jean-Marc	+*The Dictionary Of Suit Combinations *(Guy Tredaniel, 1995, 477p.)*			
Rubens, Jeff	The Moysian Fit *(Australian Bridge Institute, 1975, 20p.)*			
Sands, Norma	Playing The Cards *(Rocky Mountain Books, 1984, 127p.)*			
Schuld, Frank P	The Simple Squeeze In Bridge *(Drake, 1974-77, 223-220p.)*			
Seabrook, Barry	Bridge: Expert Dummy Play *(Batsford, 1981, 175p.)*			
Senior, Brian	+*Clever Bridge Tricks *(Faber, 1988, 170p.)*			
Senior, Brian	Bridge Players Handbooks: Intermediate Declarer Play *(Probray Press, 1993, 31p.)*			
Senior, Brian	IPBM Book Of Suit Combinations *(Probray Press, 1984, 32p.)*			
Senior, Brian	Master Counting *(Gollancz, 1989, 16p.)*			
Senior, Brian	Play These Hands With Brian Senior *(Batsford, 1996, 127p.)*			
Senior, Brian	Step-By-Step: Card Play In Suits *(Batsford, 1994, 144p.)*			
Sheinwold, Alfred	Second Book Of Bridge – The Play Of The Hand *(Sterling, 1953, 159p.)*			
Smith, Arthur Joseph	Handbook Of Safety Plays *(Private, 1954, 78p.)*			
Smith, Forrest G	The Elementary Squeeze *(Canterbury Press, 1989, 51p.)*			
Smith, Forrest G	Tidbits *(Canterbury Press, 1989, 120p.)*			
Smith, Marc	Bridge Card Play: Attack And Defence *(Finesse Bridge, 2000, 160p.)*			
Smith, Thomas M	Winning Play At Bridge *(Barclay, 1969, 8p.)*			
Smith, Victor R	Play Of The Cards At Contract Bridge *(Private, 1937, 132p.)*			
Sobel, Helen	*All The Tricks/ Winning Bridge *(Greenberg/Cornerstone Library/Davies, 1949-61, 186p.)*			
Squire, Norman	Contract Bridge: Card Play Technique *(Pitman, 1976, 147p.)*			
Squire, Norman	Contract Bridge: Squeeze Play Simplified *(Duckworth, 1979, 184p.)*			
Stanley, Enos	The Play Of The Hand By The Stanleys *(Private, 1955, 20p.)*			
Stanley, Enos	Theories Of Play *(Private, 1934, 0p.)*			
Taylor, Charles Hammond	Play Of The Hand *(Taylor Press, 1948, 64p.)*			
Traub, Alec	Trump Technique *(Private, 1981, 363p.)*			
Truscott, Dorothy Hayden	Winning Declarer Play *(Wilshire, 1978, 280p.)*			
Wang, Chien-Hwa	Practical Bridge Endings *(Batsford, 1997, 127p.)*			
Wang, Chien-Hwa	The Squeeze At Bridge *(Cadogan, 1993, 203p.)*			
Watson, Louis H	*Watson On The Play Of The Hand At Contract Bridge *(Sterling/Copeland, 1934, 492p.)*			
Watson, Louis H	*Watson's Classic Book On The Play Of The Hand At Bridge *(Sterling/Bailey & Swinfen/Barnes & Noble, 1958-, 475p.)*			
Wentworth, W W	Playing Your Hand - Bridge Made Easy No. 2 *(Ready Reference, 1928, 64p.)*			
White, Travis	Odd Tricks *(The Bridge World/Gambler's Book Club, 1934-78, 105-141p.)*			
Wolfe, Edward C	The Play Of The Cards At Contract Bridge *(Winston, 1932-34, 251-285p.)*			
Wolfe, Edward C	The Play Of The Hand At A Suit Declaration *(Lyon Metal Products, 1933, 37p.)*			

N. BIDDING AND PLAY ALONG WITH GENERAL DISCUSSION OF THE GAME

Abrahams, Gerald	Brains In Bridge *(Constable/ Horizon House/Teach Yourself Books, 1962-77, 262p.)*			
Aces, The	Learn Winning Bridge In As Little As Eight Hours *(Kodo Enterprises, 1969, 47p.)*			
Adams, Charles True	Contract Bridge Standardized *(Hawkins & Loomis, 1928-29, 73p.)*			
Adams, Charles True	Modern Contract Bridge *(Hawkins & Loomis, 1930, 75p.)*			
Alder, Phillip	Get Smarter At Bridge *(Alder, 1994, 232p.)*			

AUTHOR	TITLE	PUBLISHER	YEAR	PAGES

Allgood, Ralph H — Bridge Abridged *(Banks Upshaw, 1945, 69p.)*
Anderton, Philip — Play Bridge *(Gallery, 1967, 111p.)*
Anonymous — Better Auction Bridge *(Lane, 1929, 59p.)*
Anonymous — Better Bridge - Auction Contract (Completely Revised) *(Lane, 1929, 60p.)*
Arthur, Jimmy — King Arthur And The Square Table *(Probray Press, 1989, 36p.)*
Aydin, I Rami — My Bridge Book *(Private, 1999, 180p.)*
Baikie, Ken R — Ken Baikie's Lazy Man's Guide To Better Bridge *(Dorrance/Private, 1972-79, 99-104p.)*
Ballantyne, Robin — Punish Your Partner *(Reno Bridge Club Unit 473, 2000, 64p.)*
Barton, Frederick P — Concentrated Contract *(Joiner & Steele, 1933, 118p.)*
Beisiegel, Gretta Ruppert — The Cloister Sixth Annual Bridge Festival Handbook *(Private, 1983, 111p.)*
Bergen, Marty — More Points Schmoints! *(Magnus, 1999, 210p.)*
Bergen, Marty — Points Schmoints! Bergen's Winning Bridge Secrets *(Magnus, 1995, 210p.)*
Bird, David L — Ten Ways To Improve Your Bridge *(Gollancz, 2000, 128p.)*
Bird, David L — Win At Bridge In Thirty Days/How To Win At Bridge In Thirty Days *(Faber/Batsford, 1990-98, 121p.)*
Bodington, Oliver E — Bridge Wisdom For Beginners And Others *(Hutchinson, 1933, 108p.)*
Bourget, Frank E — Standardized Contract Bridge: 1936 Edition *(Century, 1935, 64p.)*
Boyden, Elizabeth Clark & Warren, Mrs. Prescott — Contract Bridge Of 1929 *(Garden City, 1928, 140p.)*
Boyden, Elizabeth Clark & Warren, Mrs. Prescott — Contract Bridge Of 1930 *(Harcourt Brace, 1930, 200p.)*
Boyden, Elizabeth Clark & Warren, Mrs. Prescott — Contract Bridge Of 1931 *(Harcourt Brace, 1931, 218p.)*
Bridge World, The — Bridge Movies And Post Mortems *(The Bridge World, 1979, 48p.)*
Bruelheide, Frank Elmer — Bridge Forum *(Bruelheide, 1935, 15p.)*
Bruelheide, Frank Elmer — Contract Digest *(Bruelheide, 1932, 0p.)*
Buenano, Eduardo A — Family Bridge *(Private, 1946, 59p.)*
Buller, Col. Walter — *Reflections Of A Bridge Player: With A Chapter On How To Bid At Contract *(Methuen, 1929, 197p.)*
Campbell, Murray & Campbell, Virginia — ABC's Of Contract Bridge *(Casper/Homestead, 1928, 108p.)*
Cantrell, James E — The Golden Key To Contract Bridge *(Haynes, 1932, 158p.)*
Carew, Maurice N — The New Contract For Culbertson, Official And Standard *(Arnold & Co, 1932, 88p.)*
Cederborg, Warren & Farell, Mary Jane — Coffee With Mary Jane Farell *(B.P.A. Pub, 1974, 142p.)*
Courtenay, F Dudley — Standardised Contract Bridge Complete *(Bartholomew, 1941, 161p.)*
Courtenay, F Dudley & Courtenay, Mrs. Amy D — Back To The Dark Ages In Contract Bridge *(Courtcraft, 1955, 32p.)*
Crawford, John R & Karpin, Fred L — Crawford's Contract Bridge *(Grosset & Dunlap, 1953, 367p.)*
Culbertson, Ely — *Contract Bridge Complete - The Gold Book Of Bidding And Play *(Winston/Faber, 1936-65, 563-610p.)*
Culbertson, Ely — The Official Book Of Contract Bridge *(Winston/Faber, 1941-46,279-402p.)*
Dalton, Basil — Basil Dalton On Contract *(Richards, 1931, 176p.)*
Dooley, John L M — Contract Bridge For Social Player *(Private, 1991-96, 45-87p.)*
Dormer, Albert & Klinger, Ron — The New Complete Book Of Bridge *(Gollancz, 1996-97, 448p.)*
Downey, Ned — Just Plain Bridge, A Book For The Average Player *(Sug Harbor Enterprises, 1997, 151p.)*
Dutta, Prabhat K — Bridge Puzzle *(N.E. Publishers, 1990, 131p.)*
Ewen, Robert B — Contract Bridge: How To Improve Your Technique *(Watts/Hale, 1975-77, 64-124p.)*
Farrelly, Mrs. Charles T & Coleman, Milton Leonard — Contract Bridge *(Boni And Liveright, 1927-28, 216p.)*
Flint, Jeremy & Horak — Bridge *(Chancerel/Rigby, 1975, 96p.)*
Flint, Jeremy & Horak — Jeremy Flint's Bridge Class *(Beaverbrook News, 1969, 80p.)*
Flint, Jeremy & North, Freddie — *Tiger Bridge *(Hodder & Stoughton/ Simon & Schuster, 1970, 191-184p.)*
Flint, Jeremy & North, Freddie — Tiger Bridge Revisited *(MacMillan, 1991, 152p.)*
Fontaine, Hosford L — Eleven Shortcuts To Winning Contract Bridge *(Scrivener King, 1933, 95p.)*
Forrester, Tony — Secrets Of Success *(Faber/Batsford, 1993-97, 151p.)*
Forrester, Tony — The Daily Telegraph Winning Bridge At Home *(Batsford, 1996, 128p.)*
Forrester, Tony & Senior, Brian — Over Your Shoulder : Learn From The Experts *(Batsford, 1994, 144p.)*
Fry, Sam Jr. — How To Improve Your Bridge *(Sunday Mirror Magazine, 1939, 30p.)*
Goldstein, Abraham M — Common Sense Bridge *(Arco, 1959, 80p.)*
Gordon, Sam — Horse Sense Bridge *(Rudolph Tkuhn/Register And Tribune Syndicate, 1941-45, 24p.)*
Goren, Charles H — *Contract Bridge Complete *(Doubleday/Barrie & Rockliff/Cresset, 1951-93, 498-706p.)*
Goren, Charles H — Charles H Goren's New Way To Better Bridge *(Simon & Schuster, 1958, 96p.)*
Goren, Charles H — Goren's Easy Steps To Winning Bridge *(Watts, 1963, 287p.)*
Goren, Charles H — Goren's Winning Partnership Bridge/Play Winning Bridge With Any Partner *(Random House/ Cornerstone 1961-70, 183p.)*
Goren, Charles H & Olsen, Jack — Bridge Is My Game, Lessons Of A Lifetime *(Doubleday/Cornerstone Library/Barrie & Rockliff, 1965-70, 190p.)*
Graham, H E — How To Play Better Bridge *(Clowes, 1947, 156p.)*
Granovetter, Matthew — Bridge Additions 96 *(Granovetter, 1996, 144p.)*
Gray, Elsie — Human Side Of Bridge *(Westminster Press, 1939, 34p.)*
Green, Linda J — Bridge Wise (For Tournament Players Only) *(Private, 1995, 56p.)*
Hale, Glorya & Starr, Nancy — *Bridge *(Black Dog And Leventhal, 1998, 647p.)*
Hall, Burt & Rose-Hall, Lynn — How The Experts Win At Bridge *(Jordan Press, 1996, 264p.)*
Hamilton-Gordon, Comdr. H — Contract Bridge: Reprint Of Articles By Jack King *(County Press, 1932, 24p.)*
Harris, Larry — Bridge Player's Companion *(C & T Bridge Supplies, 1991, 320p.)*
Hattersley, Lelia — Contract Developments *(McBride, 1928-30, 205-220p.)*
Hayden (Truscott), Dorothy — *Bid Better, Play Better *(Award Books/Harper & Rowe, 1967-86, 254p.)*
Holmes, F L & Brinsmade, Estelle — Your Bridge Psychology *(Bridge Headquarters, 1932, 95p.)*

AUTHOR	TITLE
Horton, Mark & Sowter, Tony	Bridge: Learn From The Stars *(Batsford, 1998, 125p.)*
Ingram, H St John	How To Win At Bridge *(Eyre & Spottiswoode, 1950, 126p.)*
Inman, Marshall	Contract Bridge - The Global Game *(Private, 1980, 46p.)*
International Bridge Academy & Traub, Alec	Annals - Volume 1 & II*(I.B.A., 1966, 88 & 102p.)*
Jacoby, James	Jacoby On Bridge *(Pharo Books/Pocket Book, 1987-89, 208p.)*
Jacoby, Oswald & Jacoby, James	Win At Bridge With Jacoby And Son *(Putnam's/Faber, 1966-68, 222-243p.)*
Jago, Willie	Team Tactics At Bridge *(Beads D.T.P., 1994, 176p.)*
Kaplan, Edgar	Improve Your Bridge 1 & 2 *(Doop Bridge Supplies, 1970, 27p each.)*
Kaplan, Edgar	Winning Contract Bridge Complete/Winning Contract Bridge *(Fleet/Bantam/Dover, 1964-83, 436p.)*
Karn, Willard	Willard Karn's Bridge Service *(Long & Smith, 1933, 363p.)*
Karpin, Fred L	Psychological Strategy In Contract Bridge *(Harper & Brothers/Hamilton/Dover, 1960-73, 325p.)*
Kelley, Truman L	Cooperative Bridge: Part 1 - Principles *(Private, 1955, 73p.)*
Kelsey, Hugh Walter	How To Improve Your Bridge/Improve Your Bridge *(Faber/Hart/Gollancz, 1971-93, 191p.)*
Kempson, Ewart	Kempson On Contract *(Hodder & Stoughton, 1935, 180p.)*
Kerwin, Madeleine	Partnership Contract *(Morrow, 1934, 180p.)*
Kleinman, Danny	Bids Are For Contracts *(Private, 1995, 192p.)*
Kleinman, Danny	Bridge 95 *(Private, 1996, 304p.)*
Kleinman, Danny	Bridge Fifty Years After *(Private, 1994, 180p.)*
Kleinman, Danny	Bridge For Smart Players *(Private, 1997, 226p.)*
Kleinman, Danny	Bridge In The Devil's Own Year *(Private, 1999, 271p.)*
Kleinman, Danny	Bridge In The Real World *(Private, 1980, 217p.)*
Kleinman, Danny	Bridge In The Tower Of Babel *(Private, 1989, 358p.)*
Kleinman, Danny	Bridge In Theory And Practice *(Private, 1986, 190p.)*
Kleinman, Danny	Bridge You Don't Learn On Your Daddy's Knee *(Private, 1994, 322p.)*
Kleinman, Danny	Building Better Bridge *(Private, 1991, 210p.)*
Kleinman, Danny	Drumming Bridge Basics Into Your Head *(Private, 1982, 156p.)*
Kleinman, Danny	It's A Bidder's Game *(Private, 1986, 192p.)*
Kleinman, Danny	It's Not The End Of Bridge *(Private, 1999, 230p.)*
Kleinman, Danny	Newbridge *(Private, 1990, 438p.)*
Kleinman, Danny	Pass Is A Four-Letter Word *(Private, 1992, 354p.)*
Kleinman, Danny	Review, Please *(Private, 1987, 416p.)*
Kleinman, Danny	The Bridge Weird Anthology *(Private, 1981, 160p.)*
Kleinman, Danny	Understanding Bidding V2 - Ramifications *(Private, 1981, 149p.)*
Klinger, Ron	Ron Klinger's Guide To Better Bridge/Guide To Better Bridge *(Modern Bridge Publications/ Houghton, 1987-91, 184-191p.)*
Klinger, Ron & Kambites, Andrew	Guide To Better Acol Bridge *(Gollancz, 1988-89/'96, 184p.)*
Lampert, Harry	The Fun Way To Advanced Bridge *(Simon & Schuster/Devyn Press, 1985-90, 158p.)*
Lawrence, Mike	+*Judgement At Bridge *(Hardy, 1976-, 151p.)*
Lawrence, Mike	Topics On Bridge 1 to 30 *(Lawrence, 1992, 24p. each)*
Le Geyt, P S	One Hundred And One Pillars And Planks Of Bridge *(Government Press, 1956, 30p.)*
Lederer, Rhoda & Hawthorn, Amanda	Improve Your Bridge The Lederer Way/Improve Your Bridge *(Bibliagora Collins Willow, 1982- 93, 223-219p.)*
Lipkin, Mike	Invitation To Annihilation *(Devyn Press, 1991, 144p.)*
Lloyd, William	How To Win At Contract Bridge *(Private, 1948, 20p.)*
Lozowick, Lee & Hoy, Alexandra	Zen Gamesmanship: The Art Of Bridge *(Hohm Press, 1980, 139p.)*
Mahmood, Zia & Rice, Jonathan	Play Bridge With Zia *(B.B.C., 1991, 128p.)*
Markus, Rixi	Bid Boldly, Play Safe *(Blond/Hawthorn/Bodley Head/Unwin, 1966-82, 212-288p.)*
Markus, Rixi	Bridge Around The World *(Bodley Head, 1979, 239p.)*
Markus, Rixi	Bridge Table Tales *(David & Charles/Unwin, 1980-83, 96p.)*
Markus, Rixi	Common-Sense Bridge *(Bodley Head/Random House/Pan, 1972-74, 171p.)*
Markus, Rixi	Improve Your Bridge *(Bodley Head, 1979, 104p.)*
Markus, Rixi	More Deadly Than The Male *(Faber, 1984, 155p.)*
Markus, Rixi	Play Better Bridge With Rixi Markus *(Octopus Books, 1979, 157p.)*
Markus, Rixi	The Rixi Markus Book Of Bridge *(Willow Books, 1985, 208p.)*
Martin, Neil (G C H Fox)	Play Winning Bridge *(Coles, 1976, 118p.)*
McKesson, John H	Contract Bridge Simplified And Standardized *(Colewell Press, 1934, 70p.)*
McVey, Mary	Play Bridge *(Ket, 1983, 196p.)*
McVey, Mary	Play More Bridge *(Ket, 1985, 229p.)*
Mendelson, Paul	The Right Way To Play Bridge *(Right Way, 1994, 192p.)*
Miles, Marshall	Marshall Miles Teaches Logical Bridge *(Exposition, 1967, 319p.)*
Mollo, Victor	Bridge Basics And Beyond *(Hart, 1976, 155p.)*
Mollo, Victor	Bridge Course Complete *(Faber, 1977, 237p.)*
Mollo, Victor	Bridge Psychology *(Duckworth/Barclay, 1958, 127p.)*
Mollo, Victor	Instant Bridge: A Textbook From B To Z - You Know A Little? Here's The Rest. *(Faber, 1975, 155p.)*
Mollo, Victor	Success At Bridge *(Newnes/Cornerstone Library, 1964-66, 125-128p.)*
Mollo, Victor	The Other Side Of Bridge *(Methuen, 1984, 148p.)*
Mollo, Victor	Tomorrow's Textbook - A View In The Crystal Ball *(Methuen, 1985, 137p.)*
Nagel, Richard	Play Bridge Like An Expert *(Private, 1983, 189p.)*
Nail, G Robert & Hathorn, John B	Bidding And Play Complete *(Texas Bridge, 1960, 0p.)*
Nicholson, Joyce	Why Women Lose At Bridge *(Gollancz, 1985, 95p.)*
North, Freddie	Bridge: The Vital Principles *(Batsford, 1996, 144p.)*
Nunes, Jack	Improve Your Bridge - For Players Of All Levels *(Stanley Paul, 1974, 197p.)*
Peart, Noel	Sixpence A Hundred *(Cahill, 1943, 38p.)*
Phillips, Hubert	Thorne's Complete Contract Bridge *(Eyre & Spottiswoode, 1948, 256p.)*
Plaat, Charles C	Better Your Bridge *(Crowell, 1946, 71p.)*

AUTHOR	TITLE
Plaat, Charles C	Contract Bridge To-Day *(Private, 1943-45, 56-49p.)*
Plaat, Charles C	Winning Ways In Contract Bridge *(Private, 1930, 83p.)*
Reese, Terence & Bird, David L	Bridge: The Modern Game *(Faber, 1983-98, 200p.)*
Reese, Terence & Dormer, Albert	*How To Play A Good Game Of Bridge/How To Play A Better Game Of Bridge *(Heinemann/ Stein & Day, 1969, 181p.)*
Reese, Terence & Dormer, Albert	The Complete Book Of Bridge *(Faber/ Saturday Review, 1973-85, 485p.)*
Reese, Terence & Markus, Rixi	*Better Bridge For Club Players *(Gollancz, 1989, 125p.)*
Reese, Terence & Trezel, Roger	*The Mistakes You Make At Bridge *(Gollancz, 1984-94, 168p.)*
Roberts, A Carson	The Future Of Bridge *(The Times, 1934, 15p.)*
Roche, W L & Kearsey, W L	Bridge For Ladies *(Littlebury, 1948, 94p.)*
Rosenberg, Michael	Bridge, Zia … And Me *(Master Point Press, 1999, 191p.)*
Rosendorff, Nigel	Develop Your Bridge *(Rosendorff's Bridge School, 1982, 83p.)*
Rosenkranz, George & Alder, Phillip	Bid To Win - Play For Pleasure *(Devyn Press, 1990, 428p.)*
Roth, Danny	Awareness - The Way To Improve Your Bridge *(Gollancz, 1991, 127p.)*
Roth, Danny	The Expert Advancer *(Collins Willow, 1993, 285p.)*
Roth, Danny	The Expert Beginner *(Collins Willow, 1992, 304p.)*
Roth, Danny	The Expert Club Player *(Collins Willow, 1993, 301p.)*
Roth, Danny	The Expert Improver *(Collins Willow, 1992, 350p.)*
Roth, Danny	Why Women Win At Bridge *(Faber, 1992, 114p.)*
Rovere, Ernest W	Contract Bridge Complete *(Simon & Schuster, 1963-73, 834-844p.)*
Rovere, Ernest W	Modern Point Count Contract Bridge *(Nourse, 1963, 780p.)*
Rovere, Ernest W	Point Count Contract Bridge (Complete) *(San Francisco Cal-Bulletin/Random House, 1954, 674-710p.)*
Rubens, Jeff	+*The Secrets Of Winning Bridge *(Grosset & Dunlap/Hale/Dover, 1969-1980, 241p.)*
Rubens, Jeff	Improve Your Bridge # 4 *(Doop Bridge Supplies, 1974, 27p.)*
Rush, Adolph	Better Bridge For You. Contract Bridge Analysis And Practice *(Pageant Press, 1957, 128p.)*
Russell, Carlton & Bonney, Norman	Common Sense Bridge: Auction-Contract: The Play Of The Cards *(Russell, 1935, 95p.)*
Ryan, George	Some Of The Flesh *(Temple Printing, 1975, 40p.)*
Sapire, Leon	Bridge Clinic 1965 *(Johannesburg Bridge Club, 1966, 74p.)*
Sapire, Leon	Bridge: Lectures And Notes On Play *(Private, 1962, 48p.)*
Seabrook, Barry	Bridge: From Average To Expert *(Batsford, 1979, 172p.)*
Sharif, Omar	Play Bridge With Omar Sharif *(Express Books, 1990, 156p.)*
Sharif, Omar	Play More Bridge With Omar Sharif *(MacMillan, 1994, 322p.)*
Sheinwold, Alfred	A Short Cut To Winning Bridge *(Fleet/Jenkins/Bantam, 1961-63, 160p.)*
Sheinwold, Alfred	Complete Bridge Course *(Sterling, 1959, 640p.)*
Sheinwold, Alfred	First Book Of Bridge *(Barnes & Noble/Sterling/Faber, 1952-54, 153-166p.)*
Sheinwold, Alfred	Five Weeks To Winning Bridge *(Simon & Schuster/Permabooks etc., 1962-,498-548p.)*
Shepard, Edward Valentine	Contract Bridge Standardized *(Cosmopolitan Book Corp, 1931, 209p.)*
Simon, S J	+*Why You Lose At Bridge *(Nicholson & Watson/Simon & Schuster/Devyn Press etc, 1945-, 154-160p.)*
Smith, Dr. Melville	Advanced Contract Bridge Up-to-Date *(Foulsham, 1933, 62p.)*
Smith, Victor R	Contract Bridge Simplified *(Smith Bridge Studios, 1930, 262p.)*
Smyth, G M Watson	Basic Bridge - Secrets Of Good Play *(Citizen Press, 1940, 32p.)*
Solomon, Charles J & Disbrow, Bennett L	How To Bid And What To Lead *(MacRae Smith, 1953, 128p.)*
Sommerville, Rufus J	Winning Ways In Contract Plays. *(Newlife Pub Corp, 1935, 349p.)*
Sontag, Alan & Steinberg, Peter	Improve Your Bridge - Fast *(Hardy, 1982, 153p.)*
Squire, Norman	Contract Bridge: How To Become A Champion *(Luscombe, 1974, 122p.)*
Steel, Christopher	The Theory Of Modern Contract *(Allen & Unwin, 1934, 192p.)*
Stewart, Frank	*Becoming A Bridge Expert *(Master Point Press, 2001, 300p.)*
Stewart, Frank	*Better Bridge For The Advancing Player *(Prentice Hall, 1984, 234p.)*
Swisher, Carl S	Bridge, Its Language And Logic *(Private, 1947, 39p.)*
Thorne, Harold (& Petronius)	Contract Bridge Omnibus/ Thorne's Complete Contract Bridge *(Eyre & Spottiswoode/Holt/, 1933, 256-275p.)*
Wagner, Mary Swain	Pros And Cons Of Contract Bridge *(Private, 1929, 32p.)*
Watson, Louis H	The Outline Of Contract Bridge *(Grosset & Dunlap, 1934, 333p.)*

O. PROBLEMS AND QUIZZES AT LEAST PARTLY ON PLAY (INCLUDING PAR HANDS)

AUTHOR	TITLE
Adams, J R	The Contract Bridge World Olympic Of 1933 *(Sydney News, 1933, 31p.)*
Andersson, Ivar & Coffin, George Sturgis	*Sure Tricks *(Coffin/David McKay, 1948-50, 255-256p.)*
Anonymous	Australian Pairs Championships: Hands 1937 - 1951 With Accomanying Notes*(Barclay, 1952, 46+7p.)*
Anonymous	Par Contract Cards For The Home - Series A & B *(Waddington, 1939, 25p each.)*
Anonymous	Solo-Bridge: Books 1 - 3 *(Luse Syndicate, 1948, 31p each.)*
Anonymous	World Wide Bridge Contest *(Foreign Affairs Recreation, 1991, 38p.)*
Australian Bridge Council	Australian Jubilee Year 1951 World Olympiad *(A.B.C., 1951, 52p.)*
Badger, Terry M	A Full Deck Of Double-Dummy Problems *(Oldcastle, 1996, 127p.)*
Barclay, Shepard	Par-Score Contract Bridge *(Par-Score Inc., 1936, 20p.)*
Bernasconi, Pietro	Bridge World Championship: Jean Besse Trophy, Lille - August 21-22, 1998 *(W.B.F., 1998, 55p.)*
Bernasconi, Pietro	Bridge World Championship: Par Hands Contest *(W.B.F., 1990, 47p.)*
Bishoric, Allison J R	Solution: Vaniva Prize Bridge Contest *(Bardon, 1929, 4p.)*
Brecher, Erwin	Hocus-Pocus:A Bridge Book With A Difference *(Panacea Press, 2001, 202p.)*
Bridge World, The	Rate Your Own Game *(The Bridge World, 1981, 48p.)*
Brock, Raymond & Brock, Sally	Bridge Quiz: Slam Play *(Batsford, 2000, 128p.)*
Brown, Herbert L	What's Your Bridge IQ? *(Campbellsville Pub, 1962, 73p.)*

Chatteriee, Shome Nath	Play Super Bridge *(C.F.E., 1993, 160p.)*			
Cioffi, Raphael	Bridge Endings *(Coffin/Joiner & Steele, 1953, 128p.)*			
Cioffi, Raphael	Bridge Endings *(Joiner & Steele, 1953, 128p.)*			
Coffin, George Sturgis	Bridge Perfect Plays And Matchpoint Ways (Sure Tricks) *(Coffin, 1973, 160p.)*			
Coffin, George Sturgis	Double Dummy Bridge, The Complete Book Of Endplays *(Private, 1967, 192p.)*			
Coffin, George Sturgis	Sure Tricks *(Faber, 1952, 240p.)*			
Cohen, Ben	Bridge Quiz *(Foyle/Magna Print, 1960-75, 77-102p.)*			
Cohen, Ben	Cardograms *(Foyle, 1960, 90p.)*			
Cohen, Ben	Test Your Bridge/Playing Better Bridge *(Arco/Barnes, 1962-64, 227p.)*			
Cotter, E P C &				
Rimington, Derek	Bridge Quiz From A New Angle *(Elliot Rightway, 1972, 159p.)*			
Darvas, Robert &				
Lukacs, Paul	*Spotlight On Card Play *(Kaye/Barclay/Gollancz/Devyn Press, 1960-99, 160p.)*			
Darwen, Hugh	Bridge Magic *(Faber, 1973, 213p.)*			
Diosy, Andrew	There Must Be A Way *(Master Point Press, 1995, 88p.)*			
Diosy, Andrew & Lee, Linda	You Have To See This *(Master Point Press, 1998, 96p.)*			
Elks National				
Bridge Tournament	Analyses Of The Sixteen Hands Provided For The Elks National Bridge Tournament *(Private, 1933, 16p.)*			
England, Frank	Bridge Tips And Test Hands *(Bodley Head, 1932, 100p.)*			
Falk, Allan	Bermuda Bowl Challenge *(Zookeeper, 1997, 182p.)*			
Falk, Allan	Spingold Challenge *(Granovetter, 1988, 154p.)*			
Falk, Allan	Team Trial *(Zookeeper, 1991, 156p.)*			
Flint, Jeremy & North, Freddie	*Bridge In The Looking Glass/Match Your Skill Against The Masters *(Cassell/Stein & Day, 1971-72, 208p.)*			
Flint, Jeremy & North, Freddie	Bridge: The First Principles *(Pan, 1985, 224p.)*			
Flint, Jeremy & North, Freddie	Bridge: The Golden Principles *(Pan, 1985-92, 218p.)*			
Flint, Jeremy & North, Freddie	Bridge: The Golden Principles Of Dummy Play *(Zephy House, 1979, 106p.)*			
Foster, Robert Frederic	Vanity Fair's Bridge Problems *(Liveright, 1932, 198p.)*			
Fox, George Clive Henry	The Daily Telegraph Bridge Quiz *(Hale/Sphere, 1977-78, 115p.)*			
Fox, George Clive Henry	The Second Daily Telegraph Bridge Quiz *(Hale, 1979, 123p.)*			
Goren, Charles H	Bridge Mystery Deals *(Heines, 1960, 64p.)*			
Goren, Charles H	Championship Bridge With Charles Goren: Championship Bridge Quiz *(North American Van Lines, 1960, 3p.)*			
Goren, Charles H	Charles H Goren's Bridge Quiz Book *(Permabooks, 1949, 184p.)*			
Goren, Charles H	Goren's Bridge Quizzes *(Dolphin/Hale, 1966-71, 142p.)*			
Gregory, C O	Improve Your Game At Contract Bridge *(Some Works Howrah, 1945, 78p.)*			
Grosser, Paul	Individual Par Contest 1954 *(L.C.B.A., 1954, 40p.)*			
Havas, George	Australian Book Of Bridge *(Horwitz, 1979, 128p.)*			
Huggett, Dave &				
Cashmore, Stephen	Plan The Play: Problems In Declarer Play For Intermediate Players *(Gollancz, 1998, 128p.)*			
Humes, Mae R	The Culbertson System In Questions And Answers *(Bridge World Accessories, 1939, 55p.)*			
Jannersten, Eric	With Open Cards: One Hundred And Ten Double Dummy Problems *(Bibliagora, 1980, 279p.)*			
Jannersten, Eric &				
Kelsey, Hugh Walter	Find The Mistakes: A Bridge Quiz *(Gollancz, 1982, 160p.)*			
Jannersten, Eric &				
Kelsey, Hugh Walter	The Only Chance *(Bodley Head, 1980, 171p.)*			
Jeronimidis, Elena	The Joy Of Bridge *(Bridge Plus, 2000, 96p.)*			
Johnson, Robert Lee	Quiz Book *(Grandslam Records, 1960, 9p.)*			
Kantar, Edwin B	*Test Your Bridge Play *(Wilshire, 1974, 202p.)*			
Kantar, Edwin B	*Test Your Bridge Play Volume 2 *(Wilshire, 1981, 234p.)*			
Kantar, Edwin B	A New Approach To Play And Defense *(H.D.L., 1986, 204p.)*			
Kantar, Edwin B	A New Approach To Play And Defense Volume 2 *(H.D.L., 1987, 205p.)*			
Karpin, Fred L	The Play Of The Cards Self Quizzes At Bridge *(Hardy, 1982, 210p.)*			
Kelsey, Hugh Walter	*Challenge Match *(Faber, 1983, 188p.)*			
Kelsey, Hugh Walter	*Test Your Match Play *(Faber, 1977, 190p.)*			
Kelsey, Hugh Walter	*The Needle Match *(Faber, 1982, 190p.)*			
Kelsey, Hugh Walter	*The Tough Game *(Faber, 1979, 190p.)*			
Kelsey, Hugh Walter	+*Advanced Play At Bridge *(Faber/Hart/Devyn Press/Gollancz, 1968-92, 192p.)*			
Kelsey, Hugh Walter	Advanced Play At Bridge *(Devyn Press, 1984, 192p.)*			
Kelsey, Hugh Walter	Logical Bridge Play/Bridge Logic *(Faber/Hart/Gollancz, 1976-88, 192p.)*			
Kelsey, Hugh Walter	Test Your Card Play – 1 to 6 *(Gollancz, 1990-92, 80p each.)*			
Kelsey, Hugh Walter	Test Your Card Play *(Houghton, 1993, 156p.)*			
Kelsey, Hugh Walter	Test Your Card Reading *(Gollancz, 1982, 80p.)*			
Kelsey, Hugh Walter	Test Your Communications *(Gollancz, 1982-89, 80p.)*			
Kelsey, Hugh Walter	Test Your Defensive Play *(Gollancz, 1985, 80p.)*			
Kelsey, Hugh Walter	Test Your Elimination Play *(Gollancz, 1984-89, 80p.)*			
Kelsey, Hugh Walter	Test Your Finessing *(Gollancz, 1981, 80p.)*			
Kelsey, Hugh Walter	Test Your Pairs Play *(Gollancz, 1985-91, 80p.)*			
Kelsey, Hugh Walter	Test Your Percentages *(Gollancz, 1983-89, 80p.)*			
Kelsey, Hugh Walter	Test Your Safety Play *(Gollancz, 1984-89, 80p.)*			
Kelsey, Hugh Walter	Test Your Timing *(Gollancz, 1983, 80p.)*			
Kelsey, Hugh Walter	Test Your Trump Control *(Gollancz, 1981-88, 80p.)*			
Kelsey, Hugh Walter &				
Bourke, Tim	*Bridge Quiz For Improving Players *(Gollancz, 1993, 128p.)*			
Kempson, Ewart	First Pocket Book Of Bridge Problems *(Nicholas Vane/Barclay/Kaye & Ward, 1961-69, 79p.)*			
Kempson, Ewart	More Bridge Quizzes *(Joiner & Steele, 1952, 109p.)*			
Kempson, Ewart &				
Lukacs, Paul	*Second Book Of Bridge Problems [Single Dummy Plays] *(Nicholas Vane, 1962, 80p.)*			
Kempson, Ewart & Ritch, J H	Bridge Quiz - Three Hundred Problems In Play *(Contract Bridge Equipment, 1949, 215p.)*			
Klinger, Ron	*Playing To Win At Bridge *(Ward Lock/Gollancz, 1976-99, 125-128p.)*			
Klinger, Ron	Bridge Without Error *(Gollancz, 1981-92, 128p.)*			
Klinger, Ron	Winning Bridge - Trick By Trick *(Gollancz, 1980-93, 127p.)*			

AUTHOR	TITLE
Krohngold, Jacob B & Leary, G H	Grand Slam Bridge Puzzles *(Conkey, 1933, 64p.)*
Lawrence, Mike	*Play A Swiss Teams Of Four With Mike Lawrence *(Hardy/Hardy, 1982-93, 99p.)*
Lawrence, Mike	Play Bridge With Mike Lawrence *(Devyn Press, 1983, 232p.)*
Le Dentu, José	Championship Bridge *(Harper & Row/Black, 1974-75, 308p.)*
Le Dentu, José & Kearse, Amalya	Bridge Analysis *(Hart/Hale, 1978-79, 287p.)*
Lenz, Sidney Samuel & Rendel, Robert	How's Your Bridge? *(Simon & Schuster, 1929, 227p.)*
Lukacs, Paul & Rubens, Jeff	*Test Your Play As Declarer *(Hart/Hale, 1977-78, 189p.)*
Magee, Bernard	Collins Bridge Quiz Book *(Collins Willow, 1996, 192p.)*
Magee, Bernard	Mr. Bridge's Quiz And Puzzle Book *(Foulsham, 1997, 192p.)*
Manning-Foster, A E	Abdulla Bridge Problems *(Abdulla, 1930, 16p.)*
Mansfield, Eric & Rimington, Derek	Bridge: The Ultimate Limits *(Hale, 1986, 208p.)*
Miles, Marshall	Reisinger Challenge *(C & T Bridge Supplies, 1997, 126p.)*
Milnes, Eric Charles & Lukacs, Paul	*Bridge Hands For The Connoisseur *(Kaye & Ward/Barclay, 1974, 127p.)*
Milnes, Eric Charles & Lukacs, Paul	*Improve Your Dummy Play*(Kaye & Ward/Barclay, 1969, 80p.)*
Mollo, Victor	I Challenge You *(Methuen/Fireside, 1984, 150p.)*
Mollo, Victor	Streamline Your Cardplay *(Pelham, 1981, 208p.)*
Mollo, Victor	Test Your Bridge *(Hart, 1975, 190p.)*
Mollo, Victor	Victor Mollo's Winning Double/How Good Is Your Bridge? *(Faber/Hart, 1968-73, 149-162p.)*
Mollo, Victor & Jannersten, Eric	*The Best Of Bridge *(Faber, 1973, 223p.)*
Mott-Smith, Geoffrey	1953-60 National Intercollegiate Bridge Tournament *(Barclay, 1953-60, 16-19p.)*
National Bridge Association	Olympic Bridge Hands *(N.B.A., 1933-39, 6p. each)*
Osborn, Florence	How's Your Bridge Game?/How's Your Bridge? *(McGraw Hill/Faber, 1948-49, 201-211p.)*
Parson, Donald	Fall Of The Cards *(Little Brown And Company, 1959, 280p.)*
Pates, Frederick Beckwith	New Way To Expert Bridge *(Clarence Clark, 1932, 2p.)*
Pates, Frederick Beckwith	The New Way To Expert Bridge - The Wonder Bridge Player - Explanation Of Hands *(Clarence Clark, 1932, 14p.)*
Payne, Dick	Bridge Single Dummy Problems *(Hale, 1984, 197p.)*
Perkins, Frank K	Vital Tricks At Contract Bridge *(Coffin/Joiner & Steele, 1937, 96p.)*
Pottage, Julian	Bridge Problems For A New Millenium *(Master Point Press, 2001, 160p.)*
Pottage, Julian	Clues From The Bidding *(Gollancz, 1990, 128p.)*
Priest, Denis	Problems In Play - First Book Of Bridge Problems *(U.Q.P., 1982, 167p.)*
Priest, Denis	Problems In Play - Second Book Of Bridge Problems *(U.Q.P., 1983, 197p.)*
Reese, Terence	*Bridge By Question And Answer *(Barker/Key, 1976, 150p.)*
Reese, Terence	*The Most Puzzling Situations In Bridge Play *(Sterling/New American Library/Allen & Unwin, 1978-79, 160p.)*
Reese, Terence	Advanced Bridge *(Sterling, 1973, 464p.)*
Reese, Terence	Practical Bidding And Practical Play *(W H Allen, 1972-74, 292p.)*
Reese, Terence & Bird, David L	*Famous Play Decisions- Test Your Skill Against The Experts *(Gollancz, 1997, 128p.)*
Reese, Terence & Franklin, Harold	The Listener Book Of Bridge - The Best Of Bridge On The Air *(B.B.C., 1965, 176p.)*
Reese, Terence & Hoffman, Martin	Play It Again Sam *(Devyn Press, 1986, 158p.)*
Reese, Terence & Pottage, Julian	*The Extra Edge In Play *(Gollancz, 1994, 108p.)*
Reese, Terence & Pottage, Julian	Positive Declarer Play *(Gollancz, 1986, 128p.)*
Reese, Terence & Simon, S J	*Par Contract: Official Hand Analyis Bulletin Of Waddington's Par Contest. Vol. I No. 1-4 *(Waddington, 1938, 18p. each)*
Rimington, Derek	Learn Bridge From The Experts/Play Bridge With The Experts *(Pelham/Hale, 1981-91, 208p.)*
Rimington, Derek & Klinger, Ron	*Improve Your Bidding And Play *(Gollancz, 1999, 128p.)*
Root, William S	National Intercollegiate Bridge Tournament 1961-62 *(Barclay, 1961-62, 18p each.)*
Root, William S & Rosler, Lawrence	National Industrial Recreation Association Bridge Tournament *(Nira, 1964, 8p.)*
Root, William S & Rubens, Jeff	1963 National Intercollegiate Bridge Tournament 1963-65 *(Barclay, 1963, 18p. each)*
Roth, Danny	Challenge Your Declarer Play *(Master Point Press, 2000, 124p.)*
Roudinesco, Jean-Marc	Play Bridge With Me *(Gollancz, 1980, 95p.)*
Rubens, Jeff	North American Collegiate Bridge Championship Par Contest -1986-88 *(A.C.B.L., 1986-88,30-26p.)*
Rubens, Jeff	The Bridge World Magazine Swiss Match Challenge *(Lawrence & Leong, 1992, 234p.)*
Rubens, Jeff & Lukacs, Paul	*Test Your Play As Declarer, Volume 2 *(Devyn Press, 1982, 222p.)*
Rubens, Jeff & Rosler, Lawrence	National Intercollegiate Bridge Tournament *(Barclay, 1966-67, 18-24p.)*
Sarma, P S N	One Trick Short *(Vantage Press, 1995, 222p.)*
Sheinwold, Alfred	Pocket Book Of Bridge Puzzles No. 1 – 6/The Devyn Press Book Of Bridge Puzzles No. 1 - 3 *(Devyn Press, 1970-80,191p.)*
Smith, Forrest G	Sixty Hands: Through The Mind Of Declarer *(Canterbury Press, 1989, 97p.)*
Sowter, Tony	First IPBM Book Of Play Problems *(Probray Press, 1984, 32p.)*
Stewart, Frank	Frank Stewart's Contract Bridge Quiz Book *(Prentice Hall, 1986, 234p.)*
Stewart, Frank	My Bridge And Yours *(Stewart, 1992, 208p.)*
Stewart, Frank	The Bridge Today One Thousand And One Workbook *(Granovetter, 1990, 263p.)*
Stewart, Frank	Two Minute Bridge Tips *(Private/Cresent, 1992-95, 191p.)*
Tait, James William	Bridge Challenge *(Wolfe, 1974, 141p.)*
Tait, James William	Bridge Match *(Faber, 1976, 133p.)*
Truscott, Alan F	Master Bridge By Question And Answer *(Quadrangle/Allen & Unwin, 1971, 252-260p.)*

Van Damm, David H — Bridge Decisions: How Fast Can You Make Them? *(Putnam's, 1931, 122p.)*
Wentworth, W W — Bridge-Me Another? The Bridge-Question-Answer Book *(Ready Reference, 1927, 117p.)*
Willemsens, Henk — It's All In The Smalls *(Willemsens, 1996, 220p.)*
Work, Milton Cooper — Bridge For One: Game No. 1-4 *(Bridge For One, 1930, 3p. each)*
Work, Milton Cooper — Bridge Strategy *(Dille, 1932, 52p.)*
Work, Milton Cooper — Play-A-Hand: Auction Or Contract Bridge - The Newest Thing In Bridge *(Carson Pirie Scott, 1930, 24p.)*
Work, Milton Cooper — Solo-Bridge *(Solo Bridge, 1931, 26p.)*
World Bridge Federation — Global Par Point Championships 1963 *(W.B.F., 1963, 40p.)*
Zaluski, Edward — Rate Your Team Play And Improve Your Analytical Techniques *(Lin-Mar, 1987, 124p.)*

P. DEFENSE (INCLUDING DEFENSIVE QUIZZES), LEADS AND SIGNALS

Andrew, Lucy Brett — Quickies, A Self Teacher On Correct Leads *(Taylor Press, 1935, 11p.)*
Anonymous — Gulf Bridge Lessons: Number 6, Conventional Signals Used In Contract Bridge *(Gulf Refining Co., 1933, 6p.)*
Bird, David L — *Famous Leads And Defences - Test Your Skill Against The Experts *(Gollancz, 1998, 128p.)*
Bird, David L & Forrester, Tony — *Secrets Of Expert Defence *(Batsford, 1999, 144p.)*
Bird, David L & Smith, Marc — Bridge Technique Series: Defensive Signalling *(Master Point Press, 2001, 62p.)*
Blackmon, May Ritchie — The Defending Hand *(Manhattan Storage, 1934, 3p.)*
Blackwood, Easley — *The Complete Book Of Opening Leads *(Devyn Press, 1983-93, 475p.)*
Bridge Headquarters — Winning Leads At Contract Bridge *(Bridge Headquarters, 1932, 56p.)*
Brock, Raymond — Expert Defence *(Batsford, 1997, 144p.)*
Brock, Raymond — Step-By-Step: Planning The Defence *(Batsford, 1995, 144p.)*
Brock, Raymond & Brock, Sally — Bridge Quiz: Defence *(Batsford, 2000, 128p.)*
Brown, John — *Winning Defence *(Duckworth, 1952-66, 343p.)*
Brown, R G — Modern Leads *(Private, 1931, 3p.)*
Bruelheide, Frank Elmer — Contract Bridge Leads *(Bruelheide, 1935-38, 16p.)*
Bruelheide, Frank Elmer — Leads And Conventions, Authoritative *(Bruelheide, 1931, 38p.)*
Bruelheide, Frank Elmer — The Gold Book Of Leads And Conventions *(Bruelheide, 1932-34, 24p.)*
Cayley, Frank — Pocket Guide To Opening Leads *(P & O, 1975, 7p.)*
Cohen, Ben & Barrow, Rhoda/Lederer, Rhoda — Your Lead, Partner/Opening Leads To Better Bridge *(Allen & Unwin, 1964-84, 96-92p.)*
Cohn, Judy A & Fink, Jerry A — Power Defensive Carding *(Private/Devyn Press, 1989, 117-204p.)*
Duke, J Dan — Defensive Play Of The Hand *(Land Cruise, 1990-97, 152-138p.)*
Eckel, Julia — Leads *(Private, 1930, 2p.)*
Eichenbaum, Ken — Keys To Winning Defense *(Private, 1999, 114p.)*
Ernst, Leonard — Opening Lead And Signals In Bridge *(Nella Bridge Supplies, 1976, 16p.)*
Ewen, Robert B — *Opening Leads *(Prentice Hal/Halel, 1970-71, 226p.)*
Ewen, Robert B — Opening Leads (Championship Bridge Series) *(Devyn Press, 1979, 10p.)*
Flint, Jeremy & Greenwood, David — Instructions For The Defence *(Bodley Head/Unwin, 1980-83, 125p.)*
Fox, George Clive Henry — Bridge: The Elements Of Defence *(Hale, 1984, 171p.)*
Glynn, Sean — A Guide To Leads Signals And Discards *(Glynn, 1990, 6p.)*
Gooden, George S — Leads And Signals At Contract Bridge *(Private, 1944, 32p.)*
Goren, Charles H — Opening Leads/Leading To Win/Leads/Correct Opening Leads *(Bruelheide/Vanco/Heines/T.D.C., 1938-75, 32-44p.)*
Goren, Charles H — Winning Play (Leads And Play) /General Principles Of Leading *(Goren Enterprises/T.D.C.-Heine, 1960-75, 7p.)*
Goulash — Defence At Contract Bridge *(Thorsons, 1950, 188p.)*
Granovetter, Matthew & Granovetter, Pamela — +*A Switch In Time *(Granovetter, 1994, 192p.)*
Hackett, Paul & Hackett, Jason — Practise Your Opening Leads *(Bridge Plus, 1997, 16p.)*
Hathorn, John B — It's Your Lead *(Texas Bridge, 1958, 34p.)*
Hathorn, John B — Your Best Defense *(Texas Bridge, 1960-62, 40p.)*
Hillson, Nathanial J — Leads And Defensive Play At Contract Bridge *(Pacific Coast Bridge Institute, 1932, 27p.)*
Hoffman, Martin — *Defence In Depth *(Faber, 1985, 144p.)*
Horton, Mark — Step-By-Step Signalling *(Batsford, 1994, 128p.)*
Johnson, Robert Lee — Contract Bridge - Leads, Signals, Discards *(Private, 1946, 35p.)*
Kambites, Andrew — *Defensive Skills For You *(Gollancz, 1993, 144p.)*
Kambites, Andrew — Signals And Discards For You *(Gollancz, 1994, 96p.)*
Kantar, Edwin B — *Defensive Bridge Play Complete *(Wilshire, 1974, 528p.)*
Kantar, Edwin B — *Defensive Tips For Bad Card Holders *(Griffin Publishing, 1994, 278p.)*
Kantar, Edwin B — *Kantar For The Defense Volume 1 *(Wilshire, 1983, 204p.)*
Kantar, Edwin B — *Kantar For The Defense Volume 2 *(Wilshire, 1984, 200p.)*
Kantar, Edwin B — +*Eddie Kantar Teaches Advanced Bridge Defense *(Master Point Press, 1999, 240p.)*
Kantar, Edwin B — +*Eddie Kantar Teaches Modern Bridge Defense *(Master Point Press, 1999, 240p.)*
Kantar, Edwin B — Defensive Play *(Private, 1964-67, 29-51p.)*
Kelsey, Hugh Walter — *Improve Your Partner's Defence *(Gollancz, 1988, 124p.)*
Kelsey, Hugh Walter — +*Killing Defence At Bridge *(Faber/Hart/Gollancz/Houghton Mifflin, 1966-97, 191p.)*
Kelsey, Hugh Walter — Master Signals *(Gollancz, 1988, 10p.)*
Kelsey, Hugh Walter — More Killing Defence At Bridge *(Faber/Hart/Gollancz, 1972-92, 192p.)*
Kelsey, Hugh Walter — Test Your Defensive Play *(Gollancz, 1990, 80p.)*
Kelsey, Hugh Walter & Matheson, John — *Improve Your Opening Leads *(Gollancz, 1979-91, 124p.)*
Klinger, Ron — Opening Leads/Master Opening Leads *(Modern Bridge Publications/Gollancz, 1985-92, 8p.)*
Lagron, E M — Defensive Bridge *(Bobbs Merrill, 1933, 162p.)*
Lampert, Harry — Introduction To Defensive Play *(Devyn Press, 1989, 8p.)*
Lavinthal, Hy — Defense Tricks/Suit Preference Signals In Contract Bridge/Defense Strategy In Bridge *(Coffin/Faber/Dover, 1963, 192p.)*
Lawrence, Mike — +*Mike Lawrence's Opening Leads *(C & T Bridge Supplies, 1996, 289p.)*
Lawrence, Mike — Dynamic Defense *(Devyn Press, 1982, 226p.)*

Lawrence, Mike &
  Klinger, Ron — Opening Leads Flipper *(Gollancz, 1998, 32p.)*
Lawrence, Mike &
  Klinger, Ron — Opening Leads For Acol Players *(Gollancz, 1997, 160p.)*
Liggett, Commander Winfield
  C & Brannon, Robert M — Winning Leads At Contract Bridge *(Bridge Headquarters, 1932, 56p.)*
Magee, Bernard — Practise Your Discarding *(Bridge Plus, 1999, 16p.)*
Mallon, John — Opening Leads And Signals *(Abelard-Schuman/Collier, 1964-69, 159p.)*
Miles, Marshall — Defensive Signals *(C & T Bridge Supplies, 1995, 215p.)*
Mollo, Victor — Bridge - Victor Mollo's Pocket Guide To Winning Defence *(Rexard, 1960, 8p.)*
Mollo, Victor — Bridge: Case For The Defence/Test Your Defense *(Faber/Prentice Hall, 1970-86, 311p.)*
Mollo, Victor &
  Nielsen, Aksel J — Defence At Bridge/How Good Is Your Defense? *(Faber/Hart, 1976, 256p.)*
Mollo, Victor &
  Nielsen, Aksel J — How Good Is Your Defense? *(Hart, 1976, 256p.)*
Muntz, Sylvia — Leads *(Bruelheide, 1950, 13p.)*
Nielsen, Aksel J — Focus On Bridge Defence *(Kaye & Ward, 1980, 196p.)*
Reese, Terence &
  Kantar, Edwin B — Defend With Your Life *(Faber, 1981, 160p.)*
Reese, Terence &
  Pottage, Julian — Positive Defence *(Gollancz, 1985-89, 128p.)*
Reese, Terence &
  Trezel, Roger — The Art Of Defence In Bridge *(Gollancz/Fell, 1979-88, 79p.)*
Rigal, Barry — *Step-By-Step: Deception In Defence *(Batsford, 1997, 144p.)*
Rigal, Barry — Practise Your Signalling *(Bridge Plus, 1999, 16p.)*
Root, William S — *How To Defend A Bridge Hand/Defensive Bridge Complete *(Crown/Hale, 1994, 410p.)*
Rosenkranz, George — Everything You Always Wanted To Know About Trump Leads And Were Not Afraid To Ask *(Devyn Press, 1986, 158p.)*
Rosler, Lawrence &
  Rubens, Jeff — Journalist Leads *(Pando, 1988, 198p.)*
Roth, Danny — Bridge: Groundwork For Play And Defence *(Hale, 1992, 156p.)*
Roth, Danny — Focus On Defence *(Master Point Press, 1997, 127p.)*
Roth, Danny — Signal Success In Bridge *(Gollancz, 1989, 142p.)*
Roth, Danny — Step By Step Discarding *(Batsford, 2000, 144p.)*
Rotzell, Peggy — Bridge Play And Defense *(Private, 1964, 72p.)*
Rovere, Ernest W — Leads, Signals And Discards *(Hearst Publications, 1941, 36p.)*
Sherman, Noah — All There Is To Know - About Leads / Play To Leads / Card Language / Signals *(Sears Roebuck, 1935, 6p.)*
Slawinski, Lukasz — +*Systems In Defence *(Private, 1983, 74p.)*
Smith, Marc & Pottage, Julian — *The Golden Rules Of Defence *(Gollancz, 2000, 160p.)*
Smith, Thomas M — Opening Leads In Bridge *(Barclay, 1969, 8p.)*
Snipes, Mrs. J J — Bridge Leads And Plays, Auction Or Contract *(Private, 1930, 25p.)*
Sowter, Tony — Bridge: Improve Your Defence *(Batsford/Probray, 1979-86, 168-160p.)*
Sowter, Tony — Opening Leads In Bridge *(Batsford, 1998, 127p.)*
Stewart, Frank — *The Bridge Players Comprehensive Guide To Defense/ Bridge: The Complete Guide To Defensive Play *(Dodd Mead/Simon & Schuster/Hale, 1988-94, 404p.)*
Stewart, Frank — Winning Defense For The Advancing Player *(Prentice Hall, 1985, 324p.)*
Sydnor, Caroline — Flash Card On Opening Leads *(Bridge Made Easy, 1994, 9p.)*
Sydnor, Caroline — Introduction To Defensive Signals *(Devyn Press, 1989, 8p.)*
Taylor, Charles Hammond — Winning Leads For Defensive Play *(Taylor Press, 1930-48, 15p.)*
Thomas, Frank Jr. — Introduction To Opening Leads *(Devyn Press, 1989, 8p.)*
Thorne, Harold — Thorne's Contract Prompter No. 2, Leads And Covering An Honour *(Toter, 1938, 11p.)*
Truscott, Dorothy Hayden — Defensive Play *(Barclay, 1971-, 8p.)*
Van Alen, M A — Try This Bridge Quiz And Test Your Knowledge Of Correct Leads *(Taylor Press, 1945, 29p.)*
Victor, A D J — Effective Defence At Contract Bridge *(Roxy Paper, 1982, 218p.)*
Vinje, Helge — *New Ideas In Defensive Play/ Defensive Play In Bridge *(Hale/Sterling, 1979-90, 192-184p.)*
Watson, Louis H — Pocket Guide Of Modern Leads *(Bard Bridge Bureau, 1935, 5p.)*
Weiss, David J &
  Rimington, Derek — Bridge: Parity Leads In Defence *(Hale, 1994, 181p.)*
Wolfe, Edward C — Leads And Partnership Leads - Book Number Three *(Private, 1933, 21p.)*
Woolsey, Kit — +*Partnership Defense In Bridge *(Devyn Press, 1980, 303p.)*
Woolsey, Kit — Modern Defensive Signalling In Contract Bridge *(Barclay/Devyn Press, 1981-92, 64p.)*

Q. POETRY, HUMOR AND WIMSY, INCLUDING HANDS PLAYED IN HUMOROUS SETTINGS

Abern, Wendell &
  Fielder, Jarvis — Bridge Is A Contact Sport *(Carolivia Press, 1995, 59p.)*
Ackerley, Chris — The Bridging Of Troy Or Tales From The Trojan Tournament *(Gollancz, 1986, 124p.)*
Adams, David B — The Reproach System Of Contract Bridge *(Stone Hall Craftsman, 1933, 47p.)*
Adler, Bill — Bridge Players Write The Funniest Letters To Charles Goren *(Doubleday, 1968, 148p.)*
Akers, K N — How Not To Play Contract *(Centaur Press, 1934, 22p.)*
Ames, Delano L — Contract Bridge Rhymes *(Ritz, 1933, 89p.)*
Anonymous — Bridge Players' Coloring Book *(Heines, 1962, 48p.)*
Anonymous — Camera Night 1966 At Kingsley Bridge Club *(Ivan Erdos, 1966, 25p.)*
Anonymous — How To Play Bridge (Simplified Rules) *(Buzza, 1929, 21p.)*
Anonymous — Points Of Contact *(Burford Press, 1932, 29p.)*
Arkell, Reginald — Bridge Without Sighs, A Harmless Handbook To The Game *(Jenkins, 1934, 79p.)*
Ashby, William — Slam! - A Ga-Ga History Of The Culbertson-Lenz Bridge War *(The Bridge World, 1932, 83p.)*
Barclay, Shepard — Bridge Fun - Verse And Worse, With An Offer To Win Fame And Fortune *(Drey, 1934, 95p.)*
Barclay, Shepard — Bridge Verses *(Private, 1931, 18p.)*
Beker, Harold — Poet's Guide To Contract Bridge *(Dorrance, 1972, 35p.)*
Bird, David L — *All Hands On Deck! *(Gollancz, 2000, 128p.)*
Bird, David L — *Having Nun Partner? *(Finesse Bridge, 2000, 160p.)*
Bird, David L — *Robin Hood's Bridge Memoirs *(Batsford, 1997, 144p.)*
Bird, David L — *The Abbot And The Sensational Squeeze *(Gollancz, 1999, 128p.)*
Bird, David L — The Bridge Adventures Of Robin Hood *(Batsford, 1995-2000, 128p.)*

AUTHOR	TITLE	PUBLISHER	YEAR	PAGES

Bird, David L & Bourke, Tim   *Saints And Sinners: The St Titus Bridge Challenge *(Master Point Press, 2000, 192p.)*

Bird, David L &
Cocheme, Simon   *Bridge With A Feminine Touch *(Gollancz, 1996, 128p.)*

Bird, David L &
Cocheme, Simon   Bachelor Bridge: The Amorous Adventures Of Jack O'Hearts *(Gollancz, 1994, 139p.)*

Bird, David L & Klinger, Ron   *Kosher Bridge *(Gollancz, 1992, 128p.)*

Bird, David L & Klinger, Ron   *Kosher Bridge Two *(Gollancz, 1994, 127p.)*

Bird, David L & Klinger, Ron   *The Rabbi's Magic Trick - More Kosher Bridge *(Gollancz, 1998, 128p.)*

Braley, Berton   Bonehead Bridge Or Contract In Cement Circles *(Sears, 1932, 107p.)*

Brannon, Robert M   And They Call The Game Contract *(Play Bridge Co., 1930, 32p.)*

Bridge World, The   *Bridge World Humor *(The Bridge World, 1980, 48p.)*

Brown, Curtis L   Partnerslips And Other Bridge Nonsense *(Private, 1995, 60p.)*

Burkoff, Stanley   Short Tall Bridge Tales: Funny Stories About Trick Hands *(Private, 1996, 189p.)*

Clark, Cumberland   The Humours Of Bridge *(Wass Pritchard/Jenkins, 1926-28,133-134p.)*

Closerson, Uli   Closerson's Own Summary Of The Game Of Contract Bridge *(Private, 1932-81, 7-21p.)*

Cole, Bill   Fishheads *(Devyn Press, 1991, 144p.)*

Crawford, Richard   Men, Women And Bridge *(Sterling, 1978, 191p.)*

Crawford, Richard   People Play Bridge *(Vantage Press, 1976, 167p.)*

Culbertson, Ely &
Webster, H T   *The Culbertson Webster Contract System *(Stokes/Allen & Unwin, 1932-33, 152p.)*

Darvas, Robert &
Hart, Norman De Vere   +*Right Through The Pack *(Contract Bridge Equipment/Stuyvesant/Unwin/Allen & Unwin/Devyn Press, 1947-, 220p.)*

Dixey, Marmaduke   The Beauties Of Bridge *(Faber, 1938, 64p.)*

Dorfman, Nat   Grand Slams And Other Slams *(Samuel Pub, 1934, 32p.)*

Duncan, Sanford   Basic Bridge In Rhyme *(Logic Press, 1956, 12p.)*

Eber, Patty & Freeman, Mike   Have I Got A Story For You *(Devyn Press, 1984, 228p.)*

Ely, E Ward   The Water Below The Bridge And The Bridge Above The Water. A Poem On Contract Bridge. *(Geo. M. Allen, 1936, 31p.)*

Fein, Phyllis M   Lighter Side Of Bridge *(A.B.D.T., 1991, 67p.)*

Frankau, Gilbert   The X Y Z Of Bridge *(King, 1906, 47p.)*

Goit, Kenneth E   Two Fisted Contract In Fifteen Rounds *(Bridge Hindquarters, 1932, 61p.)*

Goldman, Bobby   Winners And Losers At The Bridge Table *(Hardy, 1979, 103p.)*

Goodwin, Jude   Table Talk *(Devyn Press, 1982, 128p.)*

Gordon, D William   Rhyming Guide To Contract Bridge *(Private, 1942, 31p.)*

Grapewin, Charles   Squawk Bridge *(Young & McAllister, 1930, 23p.)*

Gray, Howard   Bridge Mitt. A New Deal For Cold Hands With B.S* (*Bridge Secrets) *(Private, 1975, 13p.)*

Gray, Robert   *The Best Of Robert Gray Book One & Two *(The Bridge World, 1992, 40p. each)*

Greenberg, Sherry   Mixed Deal *(Private, 1977, 53p.)*

Hellman, Sam   Low Bridge And Punk Pungs *(Little Brown And Company, 1924, 112p.)*

Hellman, Sam   Toll Bridge *(Harper & Brothers, 1930, 25p.)*

Hoffman, Martin &
Granovetter, Matthew   The Adventures Of Jenny Mae The Bridge Pro *(Granovetter, 1994, 128p.)*

Holmes, Leah Britton &
Britton, J G   The Nonsense System Of Contract Bridge *(Garrett & Mossie/Private, 1936-40, 51-40p.)*

Howe, Dan   A Collection Of Tales *(Private, 1966, 55p.)*

Hughes, Spike   The Art Of Coarse Bridge *(Hutchinson, 1970-72, 118p.)*

James, Joe   What The Hell Is Trumps *(Barnes/Thomas Yoseloff, 1969, 91p.)*

Johnson, Jared   Classic Bridge Quotes *(Devyn Press, 1989, 119p.)*

Johnson, Ken & Scheetz, Fred   I Bid Ten Spades *(Private, 1960, 32p.)*

Kantar, Edwin B   *Bridge Humor *(Wilshire, 1977, 151p.)*

Kantar, Edwin B   *Classic Kantar - A Collection Of Bridge Humor *(Master Point Press, 1999, 190p.)*

Kantar, Edwin B   *The Best Of Eddie Kantar *(Granovetter, 1989, 214p.)*

Kempson, Ewart   Bridge Magazine Picture Book *(Waddington, 1956, 64p.)*

Kempson, Ewart &
Sims, Dorothy Rice   *Just Bridge *(Allen & Unwin, 1935, 95p.)*

Kilpatrick, James J   A Bestiary Of Bridge *(Universal Press, 1986, 119p.)*

King, Phillip & King, Robert   *Contract Killers *(Batsford, 1995, 144p.)*

King, Phillip & King, Robert   *The Hog In The Twenty-First Century *(Batsford, 1999, 144p.)*

King, Phillip & King, Robert   *The King's Tales *(Batsford, 1994, 142p.)*

King, Phillip & King, Robert   Farewell My Dummy *(Batsford, 1996, 128p.)*

King, Phillip & King, Robert   Play It Again Slam *(Batsford, 1998, 128p.)*

King, Phillip & King, Robert   Your Deal, Mr. Bond *(Batsford, 1997, 128p.)*

Klinger, Ron   The Bridge Player Who Laughed *(Hutchinson/Modern Bridge Publications, 1984-94, 124-144p.)*

Lawrence, Mike   True Bridge Humor *(Hardy, 1980, 60p.)*

Levett, Benjamin A   Culbertson In Rime *(The Bridge World, 1934, 63p.)*

Lind, Betty   Psychotics, Neurotics And Bridge Players *(Burt Freireicht/Simons, 1961, 58p.)*

Lord, Frank B   The Rubaiyat Of Bridge *(Ruby Pub, 1930, 29p.)*

Lyman, Helen   Bridge Rhymes And Reasons *(Professional Press, 1928, 43p.)*

Lyman, Helen   Suspension Bridge [Contract Bridge] *(Private, 1929, 48p.)*

Lynch, Warren J   Culbertson For Morons: A Bridge Primer *(The Bridge World, 1931, 79p.)*

Machlin, Jerome S   Tournament Bridge: An Uncensored Memoir *(Hardy, 1980, 121p.)*

McCullough, W D H &
Fougasse   Aces Made Easy ('Pons Asinorum In A Nutshell') *(Methuen, 1934-51, 134p.)*

Michaels, Charles   Professional Listening And Advisory Rates For Bridge Players *(Private, 1953, 4p.)*

Mollo, Victor   *Bridge In The Fourth Dimension *(Faber/Batsford, 1974-96, 160p.)*

Mollo, Victor   *Destiny At Bay *(Methuen, 1987, 206p.)*

Mollo, Victor   *Masters And Monsters/ Victor Mollo's Bridge Club *(Faber/Fireside, 1979-87, 242p.)*

Mollo, Victor   *You Need Never Lose At Bridge *(Methuen/ Simon & Schuster, 1983-87, 163p.)*

Mollo, Victor   +*Bridge In The Menagerie *(Faber/Hawthorn etc., 1965-, 152p.)*

Moyse, Alphonse Jr.   *Bridge With Jackie: Book One & Two *(The Bridge World, 1993, 40p. each)*

Natalie, George S   Dear Bridge Partner. A Book Of Verses For The Bridge Table *(Private, 1985, 27p.)*

Neill, Gilbert William   Beware Bridge Players *(Private, 1936, 23p.)*

North, Freddie   Aunt Agatha Plays Tournament Bridge *(Faber, 1984, 181p.)*

North, Freddie — Bridge With Aunt Agatha *(Faber, 1983, 207p.)*

Olsen, Jack — The Mad World Of Bridge *(Holt Rinehart & Winston/Pyramid, 1960-62, 239-192p.)*

Otis, Margaret R — Bridge. Enjoyable Misery For Bewildered Beginners And Others *(Private, 1971, 27p.)*

Passmore, Umus — Bridgework Or Sumpin' *(Evans, 192?, 20p.)*

Phillips, Hubert — Bridge At Ruff's Club *(Batchworth, 1951, 248p.)*

Phillips, Hubert — Brush Up Your Bridge *(Dent, 1939, 119p.)*

Phillips, Hubert &
Reese, Terence — Bridge With Mr. Playbetter *(Batchworth, 1952, 221p.)*

Raines, Halsey — The Bridge Battle Of The Century *(Sollinge Pub, 1932, 105p.)*

Rebholz, L J & Rebholz, W J — Bridge Toasts *(Heines, 1965, 32p.)*

Reese, Terence &
Bird, David L — *Cardinal Sins (Gollancz, 1991-, 156p.)*

Reese, Terence &
Bird, David L — *Divine Intervention (Gollancz, 1995-, 126p.)*

Reese, Terence &
Bird, David L — *Doubled And Venerable (Gollancz, 1987-, 183p.)*

Reese, Terence &
Bird, David L — *Miracles Of Card Play (Gollancz, 1982-, 160p.)*

Reese, Terence &
Bird, David L — *Unholy Tricks - More Miracles Of Card Play (Gollancz, 1984-, 160p.)*

Rubens, Jeff — *Bridge In Muttropolis Book One & Two (The Bridge World, 1987, 40p. each)*

Rubens, Jeff — *Bridge In Wonderland (The Bridge World, 1986, 40p.)*

Saunders, Philip Frederick — Bridge With A Perfect Partner *(Ward Lock, 1976, 128p.)*

Saunders, Philip Frederick — Bridge With My Granddaughter *(Mr. Bridge, 1992, 71p.)*

Saunders, Philip Frederick — Bridge With My Wife *(Probray Press, 1987, 143p.)*

Sefi, E — A Pack Of Cards, Contract Bridge - Verses And Reverses *(Rowley & Rowley, 1931, 36p.)*

Sheinwold, Alfred — Bridge With Algy *(The Bridge World, 1997, 32p.)*

Sibbett, Cecil James — The Rubaiyat Of Bridge *(Private, 1953, 40p.)*

Silver, David — A Study In Silver *(Master Point Press, 1998, 128p.)*

Silver, David — Tales Out Of School *(Master Point Press, 1995, 121p.)*

Silver, David & Bourke, Tim — Bridge The Silver Way *(Master Point Press, 2000, 189p.)*

Simon, S J — *Cut For Partners (Nicholson & Watson/Devyn Press, 1950-1999, 128p.)*

Singer, George &
Theimer, Ernst — Shrinks' Contract Bridge *(Private, 1985, 68p.)*

Sohl, Jerry — Underhanded Bridge *(Hawthorn Books, 1975, 115p.)*

Spaeth, Sigmund — Sing A Song Of Contract *(Fisher, 1931, 16p.)*

Spitz, Phyllis — Sam's Slams 1978-79 Dirt And Date Book *(Sam Slam Enterprises, 1978, 30p.)*

Spurlock, Grace M — Bridge Bits *(Tuttle, 1953, 159p.)*

Stein, Clem Jr. & Ross, A L — Bridge And Gin Gambitry *(Home Library Press/Cornerstone Library, 1963, 157p.)*

Stoddard, Susan &
Winkler, Larry — Running From A Double *(Bridge Gallery, 1972, 50p.)*

Sundby, Robert D — Breakthrough Bridge Monograph Number 1: Heresey In Wonderland, A Bedtime Bridge Fable *(Breakthrough Bridge, 1978, 12p.)*

Tait, James William — Tales Of The Club Expert *(Faber, 1987, 116p.)*

Tait, James William — The Devil's Coup And Other Bridge Stories *(Gollancz, 1990, 157p.)*

Teukolsky, Roselyn — How To Play Bridge With Your Spouse And Survive *(Granovetter, 1991, 192p.)*

Theimer, Ernst — The Bridge Adventures Of Androcles MacThick *(Private, 1981, 247p.)*

Thompson, Wesley — Doubled And Vulnerable *(Swarthmore Press/Heines, 1958, 46p.)*

Vine, Frank — The Best Of Frank Vine *(The Bridge World, 1989, 48p.)*

Webster, H T — *Grand Slams (Horizon House, 1938, 61p.)*

Webster, H T &
Calhoun, Philo — *Who Dealt This Mess? (Doubleday, 1948, 174p.)*

Weinstein, Art — Bridge Laffs *(Private, 1993, 56p.)*

Weinstein, Art — Bridge Poems For Your Ex-Partner *(Devyn Press, 1989, 31p.)*

Weinstein, Art — Bridge Poems For Your Partner *(Private/Coffin, 1970-75, 42- 24p.)*

Weinstein, Art — You Play Like An Ass *(San Mateo Bridge Center, 1978, 12p.)*

West, Lou — Why Play Bridge To Lose *(Private, 1930, 57p.)*

Wilson, Dorothy W — Bridge Babies *(Heines, 1961, 44p.)*

Wilson, Prof L M — Contract Bridge *(Private, 1945, 32p.)*

Wright, C Watts — C. Watts Wright On Contract Bridge *(Central States Book, 1931, 34p.)*

Wylie, Michael — Shakespeare At The Bridge Table *(Password Publishing & Design, 1993, 64p.)*

Young, Lillian — Harvard Bridge *(International Publicity, 1911, 3p.)*

R. COLLECTIONS OF COLUMNS, ARTICLES, TIPS, HANDS AND HANDS PLAYED

Allard, J Gordon — Illustrative Hands Demonstrating The Culbertson System *(Lellaway-Ide, 1938, 86p.)*

Becker, B J — Becker On Bridge *(Grosset & Dunlap/White Lion, 1971-73, 128p.)*

Benjamin, Albert — The Lion Of The North *(Apsbridge, 1996, 44p.)*

Bird, David L — *Famous Bridge Disasters (Gollancz, 1999, 128p.)*

Bird, David L &
Helgemo, Geir — +*Bridge With Imagination (Finesse Bridge, 2000, 160p.)*

Blackwood, Easley — Bridge Humanics/The Human Element In Bridge *(Droke House/Faber, 1949-51, 255-246p.)*

Blackwood, Easley — How You Can Play Winning Bridge With Blackwood/ Winning Bridge With Blackwood *(Pinnacle/Hale, 1977-80, 281-191p.)*

Boekorst, Andre — Bols Brilliancy Prize Tenth Anniversary Booklet *(Bols/I.B.P.A., 1985-86, 27p.)*

Boekorst, Andre — The Second Bols Book Of Bridge Tips *(Hale, 1993, 183p.)*

Boyden, Elizabeth Clark &
Warren, Mrs. Prescott — Forty Hands Illustrating The Culbertson Standard System *(The Bridge World, 1931-32, 216p.)*

Bridge World, The — The Bridge World: Best Of The Early Sixties *(The Bridge World, 1982, 48p.)*

Brock, Raymond &
Harrison-Gray, M — The Best Of Gray: The Country Life Book Of Bridge Revisited *(Five Aces Books, 1999, 186p.)*

Brock, Sally & Rigal, Barry — Fit For A King: A Collection Of Bridge Brilliancies *(Five Aces Books, 2000, 136p.)*

Brown, John — Bridge With Dora *(Duckworth, 1965, 172p.)*

C.B.A. Of Ireland — Irish Bridge Annual 1947-48, '48-49, '49-50 *(C.B.A. Of Ireland, 1947, 75-64p.)*

Clark, Frank — Fifty Classic Bridge Hands Played At Tavistock *(Private, 1999, 56p.)*

Corn, Ira Jr. — Play Bridge With The Aces *(Fawcett/Coronet, 1972-73, 224p.)*

AUTHOR	TITLE	PUBLISHER	YEAR	PAGES
Cotter, E P C & Rimington, Derek	Financial Times Book Of Bridge *(Hale, 1977-95, 176p.)*			
Courtney, Michael	*Play Cards With Tim Seres *(Ludus, 1995, 137p.)*			
Culbertson, Ely	Sixty Contract Lesson Hands Illustrating Correct Bidding And Play *(The Bridge World, 1933, 160p.)*			
Culbertson, Ely	The 1932 World Bridge Olympic Hands *(The Bridge World, 1932, 96p.)*			
Culbertson, Ely	The Bridge World: Volume 25, October 1953 - September 1954 *(Arno, 1969, 576p.)*			
De L'Argent, La Comptesse Marie	Contract Bridge Do's And Don'ts *(Private, 1931, 18p.)*			
Dickel, C E	A Bridge Phantasmagoria Or Green Baize Knavery *(Private, 1999, 280p.)*			
Dinkel, Rich & Dinkel, Jeanne	A Bridge Player Comes Of Age *(Private, 1999, 196p.)*			
Dodd, Charles C	Bridge At The Old Soldiers Club *(Private, 1980, 84p.)*			
Erdos, Ivan	Bridge A La Carte *(American Press, 1966, 232p.)*			
Flint, Jeremy	*Bridge With The Times *(Country Life Books, 1983, 175p.)*			
Flint, Jeremy	*The Winning Edge *(Faber, 1986, 176p.)*			
Flint, Jeremy & Buckland, John	Bid With The Perfect Partner - Yourself *(Private, 1985, 28p.)*			
Flint, Jeremy & Reese, Terence	*Bridge With The Professional Touch *(Gollancz, 1991, 141p.)*			
Flintom, Frances Young	Check Your Bridge, Contract Without Brain-Fag *(Pilot, 1932, 72p.)*			
Forquet, Pietro	+*Bridge With The Blue Team *(Australian Bridge/Gollancz, 1983-97, 384p.)*			
Forrester, Tony	The Bridge Player's Bedside Book *(Colt/Master Point Press, 1997-98, 243p.)*			
Forrester, Tony	Vintage Forrester: Selected Writings From The Daily Telegraph *(Batsford, 1998, 144p.)*			
Fox, George Clive Henry	Grand Master Of Bridge: Foxy, The Autobiography Of G C H Fox *(G & T Books, 1999, 107p.)*			
Fox, George Clive Henry	Master Play - The Best Of International Bridge *(Hale/St Martin's, 1976, 186p.)*			
Fox, George Clive Henry	The Daily Telegraph Book Of Bridge *(Hale/Sphere, 1975-78, 237p.)*			
Fox, George Clive Henry	The Second Daily Telegraph Book Of Bridge *(Hale, 1982, 176p.)*			
Frey, Richard L	Bridge For Women *(Doubleday/Funk & Wagnalls/Souvenir, 1967-68, 221p.)*			
Glatt, Arthur	Ten Hands That Can Make You A Bridge Expert *(National Bank Of Chicago, 1960, 15p.)*			
Gooden, George S & Thomas, Frank Jr.	Sherlock Holmes, Bridge Detective *(Frank Thomas/Hale/Devyn Press, 1973, 122p.)*			
Goren, Charles H	*Charles H Goren's One Hundred Challenging Bridge Hands *(Doubleday/Hale/Shere, 1976-80, 100-207p.)*			
Goren, Charles H	Championship Bridge With Charles H Goren *(Doubleday, 1964, 254p.)*			
Goren, Charles H	Evening Of Bridge With Charles Goren *(Simon & Schuster, 1959, 121p.)*			
Goren, Charles H	I-Deal *(Bridge Hand Of The Month, 1955, 48p.)*			
Goren, Charles H	The Best Of Championship Bridge *(North American Van Lines, 1959, 25p.)*			
Goren, Charles H	The Sports Illustrated Book Of Bridge *(Time Inc, 1961, 518p.)*			
Graham, H E	Contract Bridge: Some Do - Some Don't *(Clowes, 1948, 77p.)*			
Granovetter, Matthew & Granovetter, Pamela	For Experts Only: Selected Essays On Bridge *(Granovetter, 1993, 207p.)*			
Granovetter, Matthew & Granovetter, Pamela	Tops And Bottoms *(Granovetter, 1992, 180p.)*			
Griffiths, J N R	The Golden Years Of Bridge *(Gollancz, 1981, 127p.)*			
Gross, Steve	How I Won 0.63 Masterpoints And Was Ahead $4.00 Until Jackie Bought A Flower Pot *(Private, 1977, 35p.)*			
Harris, Goodman J	Trumpet Pocket Solitaire Bride - Play Your Own Game *(Private, 1933, 20p.)*			
Harrison-Gray, Maurice	*Country Life Book Of Bridge *(Hamlyn, 1972, 159p.)*			
Hart, Norman De Vere	*Bridge Players' Bedside Book *(Eyre & Spottiswoode, 1939-40, 160p.)*			
Heaton, Rose & Bosworth, Phyllis	Contract With James *(Elkin Matthews & Marrot, 1933-35, 288p.)*			
Hervey, George F	The Bridge Player's Bedside Book *(Faber, 1964, 116p.)*			
Holmes, C Ellwood	But Is This Bridge? *(Bander Press, 1960, 202p.)*			
Horton, Mark	*The Mammoth Book Of Bridge *(Robinson, 1999, 536p.)*			
Horton, Mark & Senior, Brian	For Love Or Money: The Life Of A Bridge Journalist *(Master Point Press, 2000, 188p.)*			
I.B.P.A.	Bridge Writer's Choice 1964 *(I.B.P.A., 1964, 177p.)*			
I.B.P.A.	Bridge Writer's Choice 1968 *(I.B.P.A., 1968, 240p.)*			
Jacoby, Oswald	Win At Bridge With Oswald Jacoby *(Newspaper Enterprise Ass, 1963, 64p.)*			
Jacoby, Oswald & Jacoby, James	Improve Your Bridge With Oswald Jacoby *(McGraw Hill, 1983, 140p.)*			
Jacoby, Oswald & Jacoby, James	Win At Bridge With Jacoby Modern *(Enterprise Pub, 1970-73, 128-112p.)*			
Jeronimidis, Elena	Bedside Book Of Bridge *(Collins Willow, 1993, 224p.)*			
Jeronimidis, Elena	More Bedside Bridge *(Collins Willow, 1996, 224p.)*			
Jeronimidis, Elena	The Bridge Plus Annual (1991/1992/1993) *(Mr. Bridge, 1990, 128p.each)*			
Kantar, Edwin B	A Treasury Of Bridge Tips *(Howland, 1992, 163p.)*			
Kantar, Edwin B	Fifty-Two Facts Of Bridge Life *(Popular Bridge/Granovetter, 1975-91, 5-18p.)*			
Kaplan, Jim	Raising Your Bridge: Valuable Tips For Improving Players *(Devyn Press, 1993, 177p.)*			
Kaplan, William	Bridge For The Developing Player, 1990-1991/1992-1993 *(Private, 1990/93, 70/116p.)*			
Kelsey, Hugh Walter	One Hundred And One Bridge Maxims *(Devyn Press, 1983, 209p.)*			
Kempson, Ewart	Contract Bridge Hands *(Faber, 1950, 96p.)*			
Klinger, Ron	*One Hundred Winning Bridge Tips *(Gollancz, 1987, 128p.)*			
Klinger, Ron	Fifty More Winning Bridge Tips *(Gollancz, 1996, 96p.)*			
Klinger, Ron	Fifty Winning Duplicate Tips For Improving Players *(Gollancz, 1991, 128p.)*			
Lacey, David	Essays On Bridge *(Private, 1979, 0p.)*			
Lawrence, Mike & Hanson, Keith	Winning Bridge Intangibles *(Devyn Press, 1985, 57p.)*			
Lederer, Rhoda & Griffiths, David C	Winning Ways At Bridge *(Unwin/Collins Willow, 1987-93, 184-173p.)*			
Lind, Betty	Box-Car Annie At The Bridge Table *(Rydal, 1966, 60p.)*			
MacKinnon, Alan	The Bridge Of Alan MacKinnon *(Century, 1976, 111p.)*			
Mahmood, Zia & Burn, David	*Around The World In Eighty Hands *(Master Point Press, 1999, 254p.)*			
Margulies, Ray	Kibitzing Ivan: A Book On Bridge *(Private, 2000, 41p.)*			
Markus, Rixi	Aces And Places: The International Bridge Circuit *(Drake/Secker & Warburg/Unwin, 1973-84,*			

140-144p.)

Markus, Rixi — Best Bridge Hands *(Unwin, 1985, 154p.)*

Martin, Ira — The Ins And Outs And Wins Of Contract Bridge *(Exposition, 1977, 127p.)*

McDill, Harriet &
  Williams, Marguerite — One Hundred And One Best Of The Best Bridge Hands At Hilton Head Island Bridge Club *(Island Packet, 1974, 214p.)*

McKenney, William E — Contract Bridge (Bidding And Play Of 750 Hands) *(American Merchandise, 1935, 108p.)*

Mendelson, Paul — The MacAllan Malt One Hundred Tips For Better Bridge *(Stanley Paul, 1994, 106p.)*

Mesbur, Adam — Homegame Bridge On The Downhill Run *(Homegame International, 1992, 121p.)*

Miller, Billy — Dear Billy *(Miller, 1992, 144p.)*

Miller, Richard A — Bridge Brilliance And Blunders *(Dow Jones, 1974, 222p.)*

Miller, Richard A — More Bridge Brilliance And Blunders *(Dow Jones, 1976, 217p.)*

Mollo, Victor — Bridge A La Carte *(Pelham, 1982, 158p.)*

Mollo, Victor — Bridge Unlimited/Bridge Saga *(Faber/Hart, 1976, 210p.)*

Mollo, Victor — The Compleat Bridge Player *(Methuen, 1986, 162p.)*

Mollo, Victor — The Finer Arts Of Bridge *(Faber, 1978, 201p.)*

Morehead, Albert H — 1947 Bridge *(New York Times, 1947, 29p.)*

Mortimer, Lynn — Trumps And Tips *(Private, 1981, 84p.)*

Newman, John — Bridge For Developing Players *(Private, 1984, 72p.)*

Nielsen, Aksel J — Bridge With The Three Musketeers *(Kaye & Ward, 1978, 233p.)*

O'Keefe, John &
  O'Keefe, Aileen — Homegame Bridge On The Nursery Slopes *(Homegame International, 1992, 163p.)*

Ostrow, Albert A — *The Bridge Player's Bedside Companion *(Prentice Hall/Bodley Head, 1955-56, 391p.)*

Paranjape, Prakash K — Easier Done Than Said: Brilliancies At The Bridge Table *(Master Point Press, 1998, 127p.)*

Phillips, Hubert — Bridge Is Only A Game *(Parrish/Sterling, 1959, 96p.)*

Phillips, Hubert — Bridge With Goren/Bridge With Mr. Goren *(Citadel Press/Arco, 1960, 128p.)*

Phillips, Hubert — One Hundred Contract Bridge Hands *(Faber, 1932, 146p.)*

Phillips, Hubert — You Can Play And Laugh *(De La Rue & Faber, 1934, 268p.)*

Phillips, Hubert &
  Westall, Bernard C — Two Hundred Hands From Match Play *(De La Rue & Faber, 1934, 401p.)*

Reese, Terence — *Bridge Tips By World Masters/ Bridge Tips From The Masters *(Hale/Crown, 1980-81, 174-236p.)*

Reese, Terence — Your Bridge Questions Answered *(Jordan & Sons, 1951, 136p.)*

Reese, Terence &
  Bird, David L — Famous Hands From Famous Matches *(Maxwell MacMillan Bridge, 1991, 156p.)*

Rosenkranz, George — Our Man Godfrey: Tales From The Bridge Table *(Devyn Press, 1994, 227p.)*

Rosenkranz, George &
  Alder, Phillip — Godfrey's Bridge Challenge *(Devyn Press, 1996, 157p.)*

Saunders, L G — Contract Bridge Primer - 55 Rules With Logical Reasons *(David McKay, 1931, 198p.)*

Schapiro, Boris — Boris Schapiro On Bridge/Bridge Analysis *(Pitman, 1976, 190p.)*

Sheehan, Robert — *The Times Book Of Bridge One *(Batsford, 1997, 144p.)*

Sheehan, Robert — The Times Book Of Bridge Two *(Batsford, 1998, 112p.)*

Shenkin, Barnet — Playing With The Bridge Legends *(Master Point Press, 2000, 225p.)*

Slam — Fifty Cigarette Cards With Hands *(Churchmans, 1935, 0p.)*

Smith, Arthur Joseph — Contract Chronicles *(Grayson & Grayson, 1936, 52p.)*

Smith, Dr. Herbert Bell — Mae B. Rongg's Illustrated History Of Duplicate Bridge *(Dorrance, 1975, 131p.)*

Smith, Marc — Enterprising Tales *(Damien, 1990, 273p.)*

Smith, Nick — Bridge Literature *(Cadogan, 1993, 198p.)*

Solomon, Charles J &
  Wilson, Bert — Hold Our Bridge Hands *(Lefax, 1969, 140p.)*

Stern, Dr. Paul &
  Smith, Arthur Joseph — Sorry Partner *(Faber, 1945-47, 141p.)*

Stern, Milton L — Expert Bridge: From Novice To Superstar In Ninety Days - Perhaps *(Hardy, 1978, 136p.)*

Stewart, Frank — A Christmas Stocking *(Prentice Hall, 1985, 64p.)*

Stokes, H F Scott — Pons Asinorum, Or Bridge Without Brains - The Amateur Game *(Private, 1962, 72p.)*

Story, Mrs. Henry &
  Briggs, Luta — Common Sense Contract Bridge *(Irwin-Hodson, 1930, 64p.)*

The Times Bridge
  Correspondent (J G Hartley) — Bridge From The Times *(Times Pub, 1950, 237p.)*

Thomas, Frank Jr. — Sherlock Holmes, Bridge Detective, Returns *(Private/Pinnacle, 1975, 232-200p.)*

Thompson, Phillipa Newton — Pip's Tips, A Guide To Social Bridge *(Private, 1990, 20p.)*

Thorne, Harold &
  Culbertson, Ely — Pocket Bridge *(Cassell, 1948, 23p.)*

Tislevoll, Geo &
  Helgemo, Geir — Helgemo's World Of Bridge: The Maestro Reveals His Secrets *(Five Aces Books, 2000, 102p.)*

Truscott, Alan F — Grand Slams *(Times Books/Unwin, 1985-87, 133p.)*

Truscott, Alan F — The New York Times Bridge Series: Doubles And Redoubles *(Times Books, 1987, 152p.)*

Vourkas, Rudy — Look Before You Leap: A Guide To Winning Bridge *(Private, 1992, 52p.)*

Wentworth, W W — Fifty-One Common Errors In Bridge And How To Correct Them/Bridge Made Easy: No. 3 *(Ready Reference, 1928, 64p.)*

Work, Milton Cooper &
  Peterson, Olive A — *One Hundred And One Celebrated Hands In Contract Bridge *(Winston, 1933, 215p.)*

S. TOURNAMENT BRIDGE INCLUDING DIRECTION, ORGANIZATION AND REPLAYING OF HANDS

A.C.B.L. — A.C.B.L. Duplicate Instant Scorer *(A.C.B.L., 1991, 2p.)*

A.C.B.L. — A.C.B.L. Guide For Swiss Teams *(A.C.B.L., 1993, 14p.)*

A.C.B.L. — A.C.B.L. Handbook *(A.C.B.L., 1948, 70p.)*

A.C.B.L. — A.C.B.L. Handbook For Intermediate-Newcomer Coordinators *(A.C.B.L., 1995, 32p.)*

A.C.B.L. — A.C.B.L. Handbook Of Regulations *(A.C.B.L., 1946, 70p.)*

A.C.B.L. — Bridge Cruise Director's Handbook *(A.C.B.L., 1984, 8p.)*

A.C.B.L. — Caddy Master's Guide For Training Tournament Caddies *(A.C.B.L., 1999, 21p.)*

A.C.B.L. — Duplicate Bridge - How To Play It *(A.C.B.L., 1976, 18p.)*

A.C.B.L. — Duplicate Bridge For Small Clubs *(A.C.B.L., 1975-83, 7-8p.)*

AUTHOR	TITLE
A.C.B.L.	Easy Guide To Duplicate Bridge *(A.C.B.L., 1965-84, 31p.)*
A.C.B.L.	Factoring *(A.C.B.L., 1975, 10p.)*
A.C.B.L.	Half Table Movements For Mitchell Games *(A.C.B.L., 1978, 2p.)*
A.C.B.L.	Handbook On Rules And Regulations *(A.C.B.L., 1946-, 70-250p.)*
A.C.B.L.	Mechanics For Duplicate Clubs With Small Games *(A.C.B.L., 1987, 10p.)*
A.C.B.L.	New Member Guide: The ACBL From A To Z *(A.C.B.L., 1998, 64p.)*
A.C.B.L.	Planning And Organizing An Intermediate/Newcomer Sectional Or Regional Tournament *(A.C.B.L., 2000, 60p.)*
A.C.B.L.	The Non-Playing Captain *(A.C.B.L., 1990, 8p.)*
A.C.B.L.	Tournament Chairman's Guide For Planning Your Sectional Or Regional Tournament *(A.C.B.L., 1987-98, 43-44p.)*
A.C.B.L.	Two-Table Duplicate *(A.C.B.L., 1995, 16p.)*
Ace High	Bridge - Methods Of Play For Two, Three Or Eight Players/Tournaments, Parties And Teams *(Robertson & Mullens, 1930, 15p.)*
Ainger, Angela & Ainger, Simon	Simple Menus And Movements For Social Bridge *(Mr. Bridge, 1995, 48p.)*
Ainger, Simon	Introduction To Duplicate Bridge *(Mr. Bridge, 1997-99, 47p.)*
Andersen, Ronald E	Match Point Tactics *(Devyn Press, 1981, 10p.)*
Anonymous	Better Bridge In Britain *(Private, 1986, 8p.)*
Anonymous	Bridge For Four, Series A., J.& R. 48 Hands Each *(Cardinal Co, 1977, 100p. each)*
Anonymous	How To Pivot At Card Parties - So That Each Player Draws Every Other Player As A Partner *(U.S. Playing Card Co, 1932, 4p.)*
Anonymous	How To Play Duplicate Bridge: Auction Or Contract *(Valparaiso Novelty Company, 1930, 16p.)*
Anonymous	How To Play Duplicate Contract *(Private, 1940, 22p.)*
Anonymous	Tournament Director's Manual *(Private, 1980, 25p.)*
Ashley, Jerry J & Oatway, Eric A	Tournament Bridge At Home *(McIndoe, 1970, 229p.)*
August, William J	Director's Set-Up Manual For Club Duplicates And Pair Games *(Private, 1973, 7p.)*
Bernstein, Andrew & Baron, Randall	Do You Know Your Partner? *(Devyn Press, 1979, 18p.)*
Beynon, George W	Bridge Director's Manual For Duplicate Games *(Coffin, 1955-65, 184-192p.)*
Beynon, George W	Duplicate Bridge Direction *(Stuyvesant, 1944, 117p.)*
Beynon, George W	Duplicate Bridge Guide *(Bruelheide, 1937, 48p.)*
Beynon, George W	Tournament And Duplicate Bridge *(Stuyvesant, 1944, 270p.)*
Boeder, John	Thinking About Imps *(Devyn Press, 1994, 269p.)*
Boone, Lemuel D	Percentage Tables: Appendix And Twin Howell Movements For Duplicate Bridge *(The Bridge World, 1941, 27p.)*
Brandly, Michael S	Schedules For Balanced Optimized Cyclic Arrangements Of Matched Pairs *(Beck & Orr, 1993, 124p.)*
Bridge Headquarters	How To Play Duplicate In The Home *(Bridge Headquarters, 1930, 18p.)*
Brock, Raymond & Brock, Sally	Expert Tuition For Tournament Bridge *(Batsford, 1998, 128p.)*
Bruelheide, Frank Elmer	Duplicate Bridge Guide With Complete Instructions And Diagrams *(Bruelheide, 1938, 64p.)*
Bruelheide, Frank Elmer	Progressive Contract Bridge *(Bruelheide, 1933, 16p.)*
Burger, Robert E & McClain, Guthrie	Pro Bridge *(Cameron, 1970, 167p.)*
Burn, David	How To Survive Your First Tournament *(Faber, 1993, 133p.)*
Caprera, Dave	Matchpoint Standard *(Private, 1980, 0p.)*
Cardwell, Fowler H	A Primer For Duplicate Beginners *(Vanco, 1934, 24p.)*
Coffin, George Sturgis	Bridge Director's Logistics For Duplicate Games *(Coffin, 1981, 128p.)*
Coffin, George Sturgis	Bridge Musical Chairs For Tournament Pairs *(Private, 1974, 63p.)*
Coffin, George Sturgis	Bridge Twenty-Four. A Bridge Director's Manual With Table Guide Cards To Play 24 Boards *(Private, 1978, 34p.)*
Coffin, George Sturgis	Instant Matchpoints *(Private, 1968-69, 10p.)*
Coffin, George Sturgis	Multiple Twinning *(Private, 1957, 4p.)*
Coffin, George Sturgis	New Mitchells For Everyone In 1971 *(Private, 1971, 40p.)*
Coffin, George Sturgis & Magner, James M Jr.	Winning Duplicate *(Humphries, 1933, 149p.)*
Cook, Mary	Confessions Of A Bridge Addict *(Private, 1979, 215p.)*
Craven, Jay A	Duplicate Bridge Movements *(Private, 1933, 43p.)*
Culbertson, Ely & Culbertson, Josephine	*Bidding And Play In Duplicate Contract Bridge *(Winston/Faber, 1946-51, 271-253p.)*
Dawson, Eric H	Rules And Instructions For Playing Duplicate Contract And Auction Bridge *(Gibson, 1932, ?p.)*
Dowdeswell, R J	An Introduction To Duplicate Bridge *(E.B.U., 1983, 8p.)*
Edwards, Brian	Convention Card: Basic Acol, Incorporating Class Method Of Bidding *(Private, 2000, 2p.)*
Eichorn, Arthur M	Duplicate Bridge In The Home *(Eichorn, Virchow & Yates, 1932, 8p.)*
English Bridge Union	Handbook Of The Master Points Scheme *(E.B.U., 1968, 28p.)*
English Bridge Union	Introduction To Duplicate Bridge *(E.B.U., 1966, 11p.)*
Erickson, Bonnie H	The Allocation Of Esteem And Disesteem : A Test Of Goode's Theory *(Dept. Of Sociology U Of Toronto, 1983, 51p.)*
Farrington, Frank	*Duplicate Bridge Movements *(Private/Smith & Ebbs/E.B.U., 1960-79, 98-179p.)*
Farrington, Frank	Duplicate Bridge Pairs Movements *(Stanford Print, 1969, 30p.)*
Feldheim, Harold	Winning Swiss Team Tactics In Bridge *(Barclay/Lorold, 1976-93, 236-273p.)*
Fox, George Clive Henry	Duplicate Bridge *(Edward Arnold/Hale/St. Martin's, 1955-75, 143-160p.)*
Gleason, Joseph H	Gleason Rating Standards For Contract Bridge *(Taylor Press, 1935, 8p.)*
Gooden, George S	Home Duplicate Instruction Book *(Coffin, 1960, 78p.)*
Goren, Charles H	Duplicate Bridge Tips *(Goren Enterprises/Heines/T.D.C., 1955-75, 30p.)*
Gracy, Leonard R	Duplicate Contract Bridge In The Home And Simple Tournament Procedure *(Winston, 1933, 68p.)*
Granovetter, Matthew & Granovetter, Pamela	Forgive Me, Partner - The Guide To A Successful Partner *(Granovetter, 1997, 168p.)*
Grant, Audrey	A.C.B.L. Introduction To Duplicate Bridge *(A.C.B.L., 1994-97, 305-342p.)*
Greenwood, David	The Pairs Game *(Cassell/Faber, 1978-82, 150p.)*
Groner, Alex	*Duplicate Bridge Direction *(Barclay/Devyn Press, 1967-99, 236-237p.)*

Groner, Alex — Directing Swiss Movements *(Barclay, 1971, 14p.)*

Gruenther, Alfred M — *Duplicate Contract Complete *(The Bridge World, 1933, 328p.)*

Gruenther, Alfred M — Duplicate Contract Simplified *(Private/The Bridge World, 1931, 40p.)*

Gruenther, Alfred M — How To Play Progressive Contract *(The Bridge World, 1930, 5p.)*

Gullick, John — Understand Duplicate, With A Hilarious Look At Bridge Clubs And Players *(Wimbledon Bridge Enterprises, 1990, 95p.)*

Gurr, Dr C E — *Simple Directing At The Bridge Club *(Private, 1984-93, 32-40p.)*

Hallen, Hans-Olof & Hanner, Olof & Jannersten, Per — +*Movements - A Fair Approach *(Nederlandse Bridge, 1994, 607p.)*

Hamill, R Madison — Your Contract Ability *(Private, 1933, 6p.)*

Harris, Larry — +*Bridge Director's Companion *(Devyn Press, 1988-99, 102-306p.)*

Harris, Larry — Director's Quick Reference Companion *(Devyn Press, 1996-2000, 70-78p.)*

Harrison, Ruth — The Player's Guide To The Rules Of Duplicate Bridge *(Devyn Press, 1989, 169p.)*

Hartman, Dewight — Cures For Relay Troubles At Duplicate *(Kutztown Pub, 1935, 39p.)*

Hasler, Alexander T — Duplicate Bridge *(Waddington, 1930, 8p.)*

Hasler, Alexander T — Duplicate Bridge Simplified *(Harrap & Waddington, 1935, 134p.)*

Hasler, Alexander T — Duplicate Bridge, Auction Or Contract *(Foulsham, 1933, 62p.)*

Hoffman, Martin — Hoffman On Pairs Play *(Faber, 1983, 184p.)*

Hoffman, Martin — More Tales Of Hoffman *(Faber, 1983, 187p.)*

Hughes, Boyd R — Amateur Director's Guide *(Private, 1973, 14p.)*

Hughes, Boyd R & Woodson, William B — New Amateur Director's Guide *(Woodson, 1975, 32p.)*

Husband, Pat — Master Duplicate Bridge, An Intoduction *(Gollancz, 1988, 10p.)*

Jacoby, Oswald — Oswald Jacoby's Master Bridge *(Private, 1963, 32p.)*

Jannersten, Eric & Partavlinsteknik, Vinnan — Winning Pairs Technique *(Gollancz, 1980, 160p.)*

Jelks, Edward & Schmitt, Raymond — Trick Taking Potential *(Jett, 1974, 67p.)*

Jourdan, Catherine R — ABC Of Duplicate Bridge Direction *(Coffin, 1967, 96p.)*

Kambites, Andrew — Duplicate Pairs For You *(Gollancz, 1991, 144p.)*

Kaplan, Edgar — Director's Guide *(A.C.B.L., 1976, 32p.)*

Kaplan, Edgar — Duplicate Bridge, How To Play, How To Win *(Hearthside/Bantam/Faber, 1967-68, 146-152p.)*

Karpin, Fred L — Winning Play In Tournament And Duplicate Bridge *(Signet/Dover, 1968-76, 237-242p.)*

Kay, Norman & Karpin, Fred L — The Complete Book Of Duplicate Bridge *(Putnam's/Barnes & Noble/Devyn Press, 1965-93, 496p.)*

Kelsey, Hugh Walter — Match Point Bridge *(Faber/Gollancz, 1970-95, 239p.)*

Kempson, Ewart — Duplicate Bridge *(Waddington, 1960, 12p.)*

Kempson, Ewart & Benjamin, Albert — Tournament Bridge For Everyone *(Faber, 1963, 200p.)*

Kingsbury, Edward J — Duplicate Bridge Guide Cards For 4 Through 17 Pairs: Director's Handbook *(Private, 1979, 8p.)*

Kleinman, Danny — Rough And Tumble Teams *(Private, 1999, 164p.)*

Kling, Alpha H & Taylor, Charles Hammond — How To Play Duplicate Bridge *(Taylor Press, 1938, 41p.)*

Klinger, Ron — Guide To Better Duplicate Bridge *(Modern Bridge Publications/Gollancz, 1995, 168p.)*

Klinger, Ron — World Championship Pairs Bridge *(Gollancz, 1983, 167p.)*

Klinger, Ron & Brightling, Richard — Modern Duplicate Methods Flipper/Duplicate Bridge Flipper *(A.B. Publications/Contract Bridge Supplies, 1983-95, 32p.)*

Klinger, Ron & Kelsey, Hugh Walter — Duplicate Bridge Flipper *(Gollancz, 1983-95, 30p.)*

Lawrence, Mike — Partnership Understandings *(Devyn Press, 1983-, 59p.)*

Lederer, Richard — *Modern Contract And Duplicate *(Williams & Norgate, 1936, 149p.)*

Lennon, Jacob — Championship Defensive Bidding *(Private, 1987, 97p.)*

Lenz, Sidney Samuel — How To Play Duplicate Bridge *(Lowell-Kelly, 1927, 30p.)*

Low, William S — Graphic Guide To Duplicate Bridge Directing *(Private, 1978, 57p.)*

Manning, J R — +*The EBU Manual Of Duplicate Bridge Movements *(E.B.U., 1992, 185p.)*

Manning-Foster, A E — Baby Tournament Guide *(Waddington, 1930, 93p.)*

Marchione, Richard V — Filling Out Your Duplicate Bridge Convention Card *(Barclay, 1980, 16p.)*

Marr, Chester A — A Research Student Looks At Duplicate Bridge *(Greenwich Book, 1959, 42p.)*

McIlrath, John — A Director Is Called: A Handbook For The Director At The Local Bridge Centre *(Private, 1991-98, 28p.)*

McKee, Judi — Bridge Director's Handbook Of Movements And Scoring *(Private, 1995, 47p.)*

McKenney, William E & Baldwin, Russell J — How To Play Duplicate Bridge *(Taylor Press, 1934, 22p.)*

McKinnon, Ian — *Bridge Directing Complete *(Private, 1979, 293p.)*

McMullin, Edith — Adventures In Duplicate Bridge *(A.C.B.L., 1988-93, 51-56p.)*

McMullin, Edith — Easybridge At A Tournament *(Private, 2000, 12p.)*

McMullin, Edith — Easybridge! 2: Director's Manual *(Private, 1997, 25p.)*

McMullin, Edith — Easybridge! 3: The Duplicate Condition *(Private, 1997, 84p.)*

McMullin, Edith — The Convention Card *(Private, 1998, 40p.)*

Michaels, Charles — Your Half Table Headaches Are Over *(Barclay, 1957, 24p.)*

Miles, Marshall — *How To Win At Duplicate Bridge *(Exposition/Collier, 1962-70, 442p.)*

Mott-Smith, Geoffrey — Duplicate Bridge: Contract & Auction, Duplicate Games For One, Two, And Three Tables *(Bridge World, 1935, 16p.)*

Mott-Smith, Geoffrey — Duplicate Bridge: Contract & Auction, Duplicate Scoring: Accuracy And Speed *(Bridge World, 1935, 32p.)*

Nail, G Robert & Hathorn, John B — How To Play Championship Duplicate Bridge *(Texas Bridge, 1963, 69p.)*

Nail, G Robert & Hathorn, John B — Winning Duplicate *(Texas Bridge, 1962, 28p.)*

National Bridge Association — First Semi Annual National Rating Of Master Contract Players In The United States *(National Bridge Assoc., 1936, 10p.)*

Needham, Richard Edgar — Tournament Tactics At Contract Bridge *(Needham, 1934, 16p.)*

Osborn, Lewis — How To Play Duplicate In Clubs Or Homes *(Bridge World, 1932, 31p.)*
Parker, Allan E &
  Quarles, Miller Jr. — Lets Play Duplicate: Volumes 1-3 *(Miller Quarles, 1962, 270p.)*
Parry, David — Passport To Duplicate Bridge *(Mr. Bridge, 1990-94, 31p.)*
Paul, Mary — Partnership Bidding *(Master Point Press, 1994, 86p.)*
Pennebaker, C B — Tournament Bridge Hands *(Tournament Bridge Corp, 1938, 40p.)*
Porteus, Bob — Bridge From Your Living Room To The Duplicate Club *(Boport, 1980, 97p.)*
Powell, James H &
  Stokes, Derek L — Tournament Direction For Bridge Clubs: An Introduction To Tournament Direction *(Private, 1978, 110p.)*
Quarles, Miller Jr. — Percentage - The Modern Bridge (Set A) *(Miller Quarles, 1963, 64p.)*
Reese, Terence — Brilliancies And Blunders In The European Bridge Championship *(McMillan, 1991, 132p.)*
Reese, Terence &
  Dormer, Albert — *Bridge For Tournament Players *(Hale, 1968-72, 173p.)*
Robinson, Cecil E — Robinson's Manual Of Duplicate Movement For The Club Director *(Private, 1964, 40p.)*
Rodwell, Eric — How To Fill Out The New ACBL Convention Card *(A.C.B.L., 1994, 12p.)*
Roney, Bill & Hardy, Max — Play My Card *(Hardy, 1980, 136p.)*
Rosen, Edward L — Duplicate Bridge Made Easy *(Arrco, 1966, 32p.)*
Rosen, Edward L — How To Play, How To Win Swiss Teams *(Nella Bridge Supplies, 1973, 15p.)*
Rosenkranz, George — More Tips For Tops *(Devyn Press, 1991, 224p.)*
Rosenkranz, George — Tips For Tops *(Devyn Press, 1988, 224p.)*
Routman, Mark J — Club Level Duplicate Bridge: Which Strategies Win *(Daring Books, 1986, 331p.)*
Rovere, Ernest W — How To Play And Score Duplicate Bridge *(San Francisco Chronicle, 1963, 15p.)*
Samuelson, Carl G &
  Brock, Sally — A New Approach To Matchpointed Pairs *(Apsbridge, 1997, 36p.)*
Sanders, Carol &
  Sanders, Tommy — Swiss Team Tactics *(Devyn Press, 1981, 10p.)*
Saxon, Burt — Go For The Gold - Becoming An A.C.B.L. Life Master *(D B M, 1996, 58p.)*
Senior, Brian — Bridge Players Handbooks: Directing A Club Duplicate *(Apsbridge, 1990, 28p.)*
Senior, Brian — Master Pairs Technique *(Gollancz, 1990, 15p.)*
Senior, Brian &
  Robson, Andrew — Bridge Players Handbooks: Matchpoint Bidding *(Probray Press, 1992, 32p.)*
Sheinwold, Alfred — Duplicate Bridge *(Sterling/Dover, 1954-71, 159p.)*
Simmelkjaer, Harold Eustace — Handbook On The Theory And Play Of Championship Contract Bridge *(Worthwhile Books, 1941-52, 88-80p.)*
Sneden, Lawrence — Popular Culture As Metaphor : Duplicate Bridge As A Way Of Life *(Ginn Press, 1993, 86p.)*
Spiro, Richard C — Twenty Minutes To Duplicate Bridge *(Parker Brother, 1965, 30p.)*
Squire, Norman &
  Harrison-Gray, Maurice — Winning Points At Match Point Bridge *(Faber, 1959, 151p.)*
Stewart, Frank &
  Baron, Randall — How To Be A Good Partner *(Devyn Press, 1989, 8p.)*
Stone, Leonard — Howell Progressive Duplicate Bridge Games *(Private, 1934, 16p.)*
Tait, James William — Master Pairs Technique *(Hale, 1982, 123p.)*
Thorne, Harold — The Blue Book Of Duplicate Bridge *(Eyre & Spottiswoode, 1937, 95p.)*
Van Der Krol, Rijk — Play Duplicate Bridge At Home Volume 1 *(Cobwebs, 1993, 255p.)*
Walker, Karen — Discovering The Fun And Challenge Of Duplicate Bridge *(Private, 1996, 14p.)*
Walsh, Donald E — Partnership Misunderstandings In Contract Bridge *(Walsh Pub, 1966, 52p.)*
Wei, Kathie — Start Playing Duplicate Bridge *(Private, 1990, 0p.)*
Weir, Richard Lloyd — Practical Duplicate Bridge, A Quick Reference To Popular Conventions … *(Private, 1987, 20p.)*
Weisz, Harry &
  Whitcomb, Ken — How To Run Duplicate Bridge At Home *(Private, 1972-94, 27-48p.)*
Welter, Leo — Welter's Duplicate Summary *(Private, 1969, 64p.)*
Whitcomb, Ken — Charting The Game: A Flow Chart Quide To Ruling The Game Of Duplicate Bridge *(Geometrix, 1993, 27p.)*
White, Clarence R &
  White, Richie D — A Sure Winner At Bridge : (For Winning Contract And Duplicate Play) *(W & W Publishers, 1977, 115p.)*
White, Clarence R &
  White, Richie D — Bid Your Way To Winning Bridge … Made Easy, A Strategy For Winning Bids *(W & W Publishers, 1984, 74p.)*
White, Richie D &
  White, Clarence R — Two Mathematicians Play Contract Bridge (For Winning Duplicate Play) *(W & W Publishers, 1975, 78p.)*
Whitehead, Wilbur C &
  Cook, F A — *Whitehead's Duplicate Auction Bridge Including Duplicate Contract Bridge *(Stokes, 1928, 145p.)*
Williams, Llewellyn — Duplicate Contract - Procedure And Play *(Gowan & Gray, 1935, 122p.)*
Willison, J R — Instructions For One Table Dupicate: Duplicate For Four Players *(Private, 1954, 3p.)*
Woolsey, Kit — Matchpoints *(Devyn Press, 1982-93, 343p.)*
Work, Milton Cooper — How To Play Duplicate Contract *(Temme-Daller, 1930, 22p.)*
World Bridge Federation — 1988 World Team Olympiad: Guide To Completion Of The WBF Convention Card *(W.B.F., 1988, 18p.)*

T. RUBBER BRIDGE

A.C.B.L. — Four Deal Bridge: Chicago *(A.C.B.L., 1963, 8p.)*
A.C.B.L. — Laws Of 4 Deal Bridge (Chicago) *(A.C.B.L., 1970, 4p.)*
Ainger, Simon — Chicago Bridge *(Mr. Bridge, 1995, 15p.)*
Albarran, Pierre & Jais, Pierre — How To Win At Rubber Bridge *(Barrie & Rockliff, 1961, 191p.)*
Anonymous — Bridge Secrets Of A Winner *(Tred, 1971, 114p.)*
Anonymous — S-T-R-E-T-C-H The Rubber Or Bridge On The River Flat *(Michigan Leffel Pubs, 1983, 12p.)*
Goren, Charles H — Chicago Bridge: Expert Guide To Four Deal Bridge *(T.D.C.-Heines, 1975, 16p.)*
Larson, William A — The Bridge Life Of The American Male *(Pageant Press, 1954, 173p.)*
Mayer, Edward — Money Bridge *(Eyre & Spottiswoode/Van Nostrand, 1954, 258p.)*
Mayer, Edward — Winning At Rubber Bridge *(Batsford, 1975, 195p.)*
Miller, Peter Otey — Win Twice As Much At Bridge Or The Bidding And Play Of Goulashes *(Private, 1940, 16p.)*

Ostrow, Albert A — Bridge At Home *(Kingsbridge, 1959, 17p.)*
Ostrow, Albert A — How To Entertain With Bridge *(Atwater Press, 1959, 24p.)*
Pearson, N W — Chicago Bridge *(Cricket Press/Heines, 1963, 62p.)*
Phillips, Hubert — Making Bridge Pay *(Parrish, 1962, 448p.)*
Sheehan, Robert — The Big Game: Rubber Bridge In A London Club *(Five Aces Books, 1999, 108p.)*
Silverman, Shirley — Chicago Bridge: How To Play Four - Deal Contract Bridge *(Barclay/Mr. Bridge, 1983-97, 15p.)*
Stanley, Enos &
  Stanley, Mrs. E — Stanley Bidding System - Devoted Entirely To Rubber Bridge *(Private, 1953, 24p.)*
Stanley, Enos &
  Stanley, Mrs. E — Stanley Bidding System, The Betting Odds For Rubber Bridge *(Private, 1955, 2p.)*
Thompson, Lawrence Dudley — Sociable Bridge *(Private, 1935, 8p.)*
Thorne, Harold — Eight-Deal Bridge In Twenty Minutes *(Eyre & Spottiswoode, 1959, 40p.)*
Wertheimer, Philip M — Ghoulie (Train Bridge) - A New, Faster, More Exciting Game Of Bridge *(Sterling, 1952, 63p.)*
Young, Ray — Bridge For Blood *(Follett, 1966, 113p.)*

U. BIBLIOGRAPHIES, DICTIONARIES AND ENCYCLOPEDIAS

Baron, Randall — The Bridge Player's Dictionary *(Devyn Press, 1993, 279p.)*
Bergen, Marty — Everyone's Guide To The New Convention Card *(Natco Press, 1994, 152p.)*
Cohen, Ben & Barrow, Rhoda — The Bridge Players Encyclopedia *(Hamlyn, 1967, 674p.)*
Culbertson, Ely — *The Encyclopedia Of Bridge *(The Bridge World, 1935, 477p.)*
Donovan, Peter &
  Parry, David — Collins Dictionary Of Bridge Terms *(Collins Willow, 1991, 176p.)*
Filarski, Herman &
  Oudshoorn, Nico — Dictionary Of Bridge *(W.B.F., 1964, 47p.)*
Fisher, Russell — Dictionary Of Contract Bridge *(Colonial, 1933, 32p.)*
Fisher, Russell — Dictionary Of Contract Bridge *(Elliot, 1933, 32p.)*
Frey, Richard & Truscott,
  Alan & Smith, Thomas — +*The Official Encyclopedia of Bridge, Editions I and II *(Crown, 1964, 1971, 691 and 793p.)*
Francis, Henry & Truscott,
  Alan & Kearse, Amalya — +*The Official Encyclopedia of Bridge, Edition III *(Crown, 1976, 858p.)*
Francis, Henry & Truscott,
  Alan & Hayward, Diane — +*The Official Encyclopedia of Bridge, Edition IV *(Crown, 1984, 922p.)*
Francis, Henry & Truscott,
  Alan & Francis, Dorthy — +*The Official Encyclopedia of Bridge, Editions V and VI *(A.C.B.L., 1994, 2001, 861 and 886p.)*
Grosse, Philip — El Bridge (English-Spanish Vocabulary) *(Private, 1978-85, 16-28p.)*
Grosse, Philip — Le Bridge (English-French Vocabulary) *(Private, 1981, 16p.)*
Hervey, George F — Contract Bridge Dictionary *(Arrowsmith, 1934, 159p.)*
Jessel, Frederic — A Bibliography Of The Game Of Auction Bridge *(Parris, 1980, 7p.)*
Parris, Leslie — *Contract Bridge Books - An Annotated Bibliography For The British Isles 1920 - 1969 *(Private, 1975, 65p.)*
Parry, David &
  Thompson, Giles — The Bridge Player's Dictionary *(Mr. Bridge, 1991, 127p.)*
Reese, Terence &
  Dormer, Albert — Bridge Players Dictionary/Bridge Conventions, Finesses And Coups *(Mayflower et al., 1959-70, 252-192p.)*
Reese, Terence &
  Dormer, Albert — The Bridge Player's Alphabetical Handbook *(Faber, 1981, 223p.)*
Sachen, William — Bridge: A Guide To The Literature *(Garland, 1984, 171p.)*

V. LAWS AND THEIR INTERPRETATION

A.C.B.L. — ACBL Summary Of Changes In The New 1963 Duplicate Laws *(A.C.B.L., 1963, 11p.)*
A.C.B.L. — Duplicate Decisions: A Club Director's Guide To Ruling At The Table *(A.C.B.L., 1991-98, 135p.)*
A.C.B.L. — Laws Of Duplicate Contract Bridge *(A.C.B.L., 1990, 103p.)*
A.C.B.L. — Ruling The Game *(A.C.B.L., 1974-78, 30-75p.)*
Ace High — Complete Rules For Auction And Contract Bridge *(Green, 1930, 15p.)*
Ace High — The New International Laws Of Contract And Auction Bridge *(Private, 1932, 23p.)*
American Bridge League — Laws Of Duplicate Bridge *(A.B.L., 1933, 64p.)*
American Bridge League — Official Laws Of Duplicate Auction, Duplicate Contract etc. *(A.B.L., 1929, 64p.)*
Anonymous — By-Laws And Code Of Ethics, American Contract Bridge League (Western Division) *(A.C.B.L., 1950, 24p.)*
Anonymous — Duplicate Bridge Club: Rules Of Competitions 1934-35 *(Duplicate Bridge Club, 1934, 15p.)*
Anonymous — Gulf Bridge Lessons: Number 5, Laws Of Pivot Bridge *(Gulf Refining Co., 1933, 6p.)*
Anonymous — International Contract Bridge *(Andersons, 1933, 12p.)*
Anonymous — Progressive Contract Bridge *(De La Rue, 1930, 4p.)*
Apfelbaum, Jay — Reno 1998 Spring NABC Appeals Committee Decisions *(A.C.B.L., 1998, 126p.)*
Apsimon, Hugh — Educating Evelyn: Conversations On The Curious Laws Of Rubber Bridge *(Smythe, 1996, 98p.)*
Bard, George L — Summary Of The 1948 Laws Of Contract Bridge *(The Bridge World, 1948, 20p.)*
Blubaugh, John — Appeals Committee Decisions From The 1994 NEC World Championships In Albuquerque *(Devyn Press, 1994, 185p.)*
Blubaugh, John — Cincinnati 1994 Appeals Committee Decisions *(A.C.B.L., 1994, 128p.)*
Blubaugh, John — Indianapolis Appeals Committee Decisions *(A.C.B.L., 1991, 32p.)*
Blubaugh, John — Kansas City 1993 Appeals Committee Decisions *(A.C.B.L., 1993, 64p.)*
Blubaugh, John — Minneapolis 1994 Appeals Committee Decisions *(A.C.B.L., 1994, 72p.)*
Blubaugh, John — New Orleans 1995 Appeals Decisions *(A.C.B.L., 1994, 132p.)*
Blubaugh, John — Orlando Appeals Committee Decisions *(A.C.B.L., 1992, 36p.)*
Blubaugh, John — Pasadena Appeals Committee Decisions *(A.C.B.L., 1992, 42p.)*
Blubaugh, John — Phoenix 1995 Appeals Committee Decisions *(A.C.B.L., 1995, 146p.)*
Blubaugh, John — San Diego 1994 Appeals Committee Decisions *(A.C.B.L., 1994, 144p.)*
Blubaugh, John — Seattle 1993 Appeals Committee Decisions *(A.C.B.L., 1993, 108p.)*
Blubaugh, John — Washington D. C. 1993 Appeals Committee Decisions *(A.C.B.L., 1993, 112p.)*
Brannon, Robert M — Brannon's Clear-Concise-Complete Digest Of The Laws Of Contract Bridge *(Taylor Press, 1940, 16p.)*
Bridge World, The — Appeals Committee Volume 1 & 2 *(The Bridge World, 1983-84, 48-40p.)*
Bridge World, The — How Would You Rule *(The Bridge World, 1978, 52p.)*

Whist Club, The — The Laws Of Duplicate Contract Bridge And Party Contract Bridge *(Winston, 1935, 91p.)*

Work, Milton Cooper — Summary Of The New International Code Of Contract Bridge *(Russell Playing Card Co., 1932, 7p.)*

World Bridge Federation — Laws Of Par Point Bridge (1963) *(W.B.F., 1963, 16p.)*

World Bridge Federation — The International Laws Of Contract Bridge (1981) *(Gollancz, 1993, 64p.)*

W. HISTORY AND BIOGRAPHY

A.C.B.L. — ACBL Twentieth Anniversary Yearbook - 1947 *(A.C.B.L., 1947, 120p.)*

Ackerley, Chris — A History Of The Otago Bridge Club *(Otago Bridge Club, 1996, 371p.)*

Anonymous — Margaret Wilkinson Wagar *(Private, 1982, 4p.)*

Barton, Frederick P — We'll Go No More A-Roving: An Autobiography *(Joiner & Steele, 1937, 288p.)*

Cameron, Judson J — Cheating At Bridge: Go Home With The Winners *(Gambler's Book Club, 1973, 188p.)*

Chua, Cathy — *The History Of Australian Bridge *(Australian Bridge Federation, 1993, 290p.)*

Chua, Cathy — Fair Play Or Foul? - Cheating Scandals In Bridge *(Pioneer Books, 1998, 127p.)*

Clay, John — Culbertson: The Man Who Made Contract Bridge *(Weidenfeld & Nicholson, 1985, 242p.)*

Clay, John — Tales From The Bridge Table: Contract Bridge 1925 To 1995 *(Hodder & Stoughton, 1998, 284p.)*

Corbett, Helen G — A Brief History Of Duplicate Bridge In Oak Ridge *(Oak Ridge Bridge Assoc., 1992, 8p.)*

Culbertson, Ely — *The Strange Lives Of One Man *(Winston/Faber, 1940, 693-542p.)*

Daniels, David — *The Golden Age Of Contract Bridge *(Stein & Day, 1980, 212p.)*

Dunne, J Patrick &
Ostrow, Albert A — Championship Bridge *(Whittlesey House/Bodley Head, 1949-52, 251-188p.)*

Emery, Sue — *No Passing Fancy - Fifty Years Of Contract Bridge *(A.C.B.L., 1977, 128p.)*

Goodman, Jonathan — The Slaying Of Joseph Bowne Elwell *(Harrap, 1987, 224p.)*

Hamman, Robert &
Manley, Brent — *At The Table My Life And Times *(D B M, 1994-96, 314p.)*

Haring, Robert C &
Munday, Robert — Market Characteristics Of The American Contract Bridge League *(Bureau Of Business, 1978, 129p.)*

Horton, Sally — A Fistful Of Honours *(Bridge Players Handbooks, 1985, 162p.)*

Kleinman, Danny — Bridge Scandal In Houston *(Private/Nella Bridge Supplies, 1978-99, 139-166p.)*

Klinger, Leslie S &
Bourke, Tim — What Game Is Afoot In The Red-Headed League? *(Daypark Press, 1997, 8p.)*

MacKey, Rex — The Walk Of The Oysters *(Prentice Hall, 1965, 217p.)*

MacKey, Rex — The Walk Of The Oysters *(W H Allen, 1964-86, 197p.)*

Mahmood, Zia — Bridge My Way *(Faber/Granovetter, 1992, 192p.)*

Markus, Rixi &
Mountfield, David — A Vulnerable Game: The Memoirs Of Rixi Markus *(Collins, 1988, 151p.)*

Masters, Colin — Mind Games: A Biographical History Of Bridge In Queensland *(Queensland Bridge Assoc., 1999, 279p.)*

Mollo, Victor — Confessions Of An Addict *(Faber/Newnes, 1966, 142-199p.)*

Mollo, Victor — The Bridge Immortals *(Faber/Hart, 1967, 191-256p.)*

Ohman, August R — *Historical Sketch Of The Knickerboker Whist Club *(Knickerbocker Whist Club, 1926, 21p.)*

Phillips, Hubert — Journey To Nowhere - A Discursive Autobiography *(MacGibbon & Kee, 1960, 336p.)*

Preece, Edgar — A History Of The South Australian Bridge Association 1933-1983 *(South Australian Bridge Assoc., 1983, 21p.)*

Ramsey, Guy — *Aces All *(Museum Press, 1955, 205p.)*

Reese, Terence — *Story Of An Accusation *(Heinemann/Simon & Schuster, 1966, 244p.)*

Reese, Terence — Bridge At The Top *(Faber, 1977, 143p.)*

Reese, Terence &
Sharif, Omar — Omar Sharif's Life In Bridge *(Faber, 1983, 146p.)*

Rubens, Jeff — Scandal At Buenos Aires *(Bridge Journal, 1966, 48p.)*

Schenken, Howard — The Education Of A Bridge Player *(Simon & Schuster/Hale, 1973, 286p.)*

Sharif, Omar &
Guinchard, Marie-Therese — The Eternal Male *(Doubleday, 1976, 184p.)*

Sheinwold, Patricia Fox — Husbands And Other Men I've Played With *(Houghton Mifflin/Allen & Unwin, 1976-79, 196p.)*

Smith, Marc — *World Class: Conversations With Bridge Masters *(Master Point Press, 1999, 287p.)*

Sontag, Alan — *The Bridge Bum - My Life And Play *(Morrow, 1977, 240p.)*

Stephens, Jack J — A Functional Analysis Of The Duplicate Bridge Group *(Private, 1963, 116p.)*

Swanson, John — *Inside The Bermuda Bowl *(Private, 1998, 250p.)*

Truscott, Alan F — *The Great Bridge Scandal *(Yarborough, 1969, 331p.)*

Wei, Kathie & Quinn, Terry — Second Daughter *(Little Brown And Company, 1984, 243p.)*

X. ANNOTATED HAND RECORDS AND REPORTS ON TOURNAMENTS

Alder, Phillip &
Jourdain, Patrick — Thirty-Fifth European Bridge Championships: Daily Bulletins *(Polish Bridge Assoc., 1981, 124p.)*

Anonymous — Australian National Congress 1980 – Open Teams & Women's Teams Finals *(T.B.A., 1980, 60p.)*

Anonymous — Fifth World Bridge Team Olympiad Board By Board, Monaco 1976 *(Private, 1976, 364p.)*

Anonymous — Fifth World Bridge Team Olympiad Line-Up *(Monaco, 1976, 45p.)*

Anonymous — International Bridge Test *(News Chronicle Publications Department, 1930, 222p.)*

Beasley, Col.
Henry Mountifort — Beasley V. Culbertson: The International Bridge Match 1933 *(Hutchinson, 1933, 288p.)*

Bourke, Tim — 1976 Australian Open Interstate Teams *(Australian Bridge Institute, 1976, 15p.)*

Bourke, Tim — 1979 Open Interstate Final *(Private, 1979, 16p.)*

Bourke, Tim — Australia v. Lancia *(Australian Bridge Institute/Indian Bridge World, 1976-77, 16-37p.)*

Bourke, Tim — Australian National Open Teams Final 1979 *(Private, 1979, 16p.)*

Bourke, Tim — Australian National Open Teams Final 1980 *(Private, 1980, 32p.)*

Bourke, Tim — Australian Open Interstate Teams 1974 *(Australian Bridge Institute, 1976, 15p.)*

Bourke, Tim — Australian Open Teams Playoff Final *(Australian Bridge Federation, 1992, 50p.)*

Bourke, Tim — Australian Teams Playoff Finals *(Australian Bridge Federation, 1994, 100p.)*

Bourke, Tim — Australian Women's Playoff To Select The Olympiad Bridge Team *(Australian Bridge Federation, 1992, 125p.)*

Bourke, Tim — Grand National Teams Final *(Australian Bridge Federation, 1991, 34p.)*

Bourke, Tim — Interstate Teams Finals *(Australian Bridge Federation, 1991-93, 74-65p. each)*

Bourke, Tim — National Open Teams Final *(Australian Bridge Federation, 1991-95, 34p. each)*

AUTHOR	TITLE	PUBLISHER	YEAR	PAGES

Bourke, Tim — National Women's Teams Final *(Australian Bridge Federation, 1991-94, 34p. each)*
Bourke, Tim — Open Interstate Teams Final *(Australian Bridge Federation, 1990, 32p.)*
Bourke, Tim — Selected Hands From The Australian Interstate 1978 *(Australian Bridge Federation, 1978, 12p.)*
Bourke, Tim — South Pacific Teams Championships Final *(Australian Bridge Federation, 1993, 98p.)*
Bourke, Tim — Spingold Final *(Australian Bridge Federation, 1993, 34p.)*
Bourke, Tim — Spring National Open Teams Final *(Australian Bridge Federation, 1991, 34p. each)*
Bourke, Tim — Spring National Women's Teams Final *(Australian Bridge Federation, 1990-93, 34p. each)*
Bourke, Tim — The 1986 Open Interstate Teams Championship *(Private, 1986, 16p.)*
Bourke, Tim — Victor Champion Cup 1980 *(Private, 1980, 33p.)*
Bourke, Tim — Victor Champion Cup Final *(Australian Bridge Federation, 1991, 18p.)*
Bourke, Tim — Zone 7 South Pacific Championship Finals *(Australian Bridge Federation, 1991, 132p.)*
Buller, Col. Walter — Colonel Buller On The Beasley-Culbertson Bridge Contest Of 1933 *(The Star, 1933, 128p.)*
Buller, Col. Walter & Kempson, Ewart — The Buller-Almacks Bridge Contest *(Private, 1934, 108p.)*
Criticus — A Critical Survey Of The Anglo-American Contract Bridge Contest And Its Lessons *(Mudie, 1933, 28p.)*
Culbertson, Ely — Britain v. America: Contract Bridge Championship Of 1933 *(News Chronicle Publications Department, 1933, 390p.)*
Culbertson, Ely — New Winningway Reversible Score Pad *(Winningway, 1937, 57p.)*
Culbertson, Ely — Three Hundred Contract Bridge Hands - The First World Championship *(The Bridge World, 1933, 390p.)*
Culbertson, Ely & Josephine & Jacoby, Oswald etc. — Famous Hands Of The Culbertson-Lenz Match *(The Bridge World, 1932, 438p.)*
Cummings, Richard — Australia At The World Bridge Olympiad, New York, May 1964: A Personal Report *(Private, 1964, 33p.)*
Cummings, Richard & Howard, Denis — The Australian Open Team At The Third World Bridge Olympiad: Deauville 1968 *(Private, 1968, 76p.)*
England, Frank & Harris, A F Stapleton — Crockford's Club v. The Dutch And German Teams *(Bodley Head, 1932, 104p.)*
English Bridge Union — Bermuda Bowl, Venice Cup 1981 *(E.B.U., 1981, 16p.)*
Filarski, Herman & Hirsch, Tannah — Tournament Book Of The Second Olympiad Pairs *(Elseviers Weekblad, 1966, 206p.)*
Flint, Jeremy — The Canberra Cruises World Bridge Trophy *(B.B.C., 1986, 56p.)*
Flint, Jeremy & James, Jeremy — Grand Slam: An International Bridge Tournament *(Country Life Books, 1983, 175p.)*
Francis, Henry G — 1973 Contract Bridge Team World Championship, Casa Grande Hotel, Guaruja, Brazil *(A.C.B.L., 1973, 215p.)*
Francis, Henry G — 1976 World Championships, Monte Carlo, Monaco, May 2-22, 1976 *(A.C.B.L., 1976, 191p.)*
Francis, Henry G — 1995 World Bridge Championships *(A.C.B.L., 1996, 170p.)*
Francis, Henry G — Contract Bridge Pairs And Knockout Teams Open Pairs 1982 *(A.C.B.L., 1983, 176p.)*
Francis, Henry G — Contract Bridge Pairs And Knockout Teams Open Pairs 1986 *(A.C.B.L., 1987, 144p.)*
Francis, Henry G — Contract Bridge Team World Championship 1974 *(A.C.B.L., 1974, 192p.)*
Francis, Henry G — Contract Bridge Team World Championship 1975 *(A.C.B.L., 1975, 205p.)*
Francis, Henry G — Contract Bridge Team World Championships 1985 *(A.C.B.L., 1986, 238p.)*
Francis, Henry G — Contract Bridge Team World Championships 1987 *(A.C.B.L., 1988, 224p.)*
Francis, Henry G — Contract Bridge Team World Championships 1989 *(A.C.B.L., 1990, 336p.)*
Francis, Henry G — Eighth Contract Bridge World Bridge Team Olympiad 1988 *(A.C.B.L., 1989, 143p.)*
Francis, Henry G — Fifth World Pair Olympiad 1978 *(A.C.B.L., 1979, 159p.)*
Francis, Henry G — Seventh Contract Bridge World Bridge Team Olympiad 1984 *(A.C.B.L., 1985, 189p.)*
Francis, Henry G — Sixth Contract Bridge World Bridge Team Olympiad 1980 *(A.C.B.L., 1981, 190p.)*
Francis, Henry G — Third NEC Junior World Team Championship *(A.C.B.L., 1991, 72p.)*
Francis, Henry G — Twenty-Fifth Contract Bridge Team World Championships 1981 *(A.C.B.L., 1982, 176p.)*
Francis, Henry G — Twenty-Fourth Contract Bridge Team World Championship 1979 *(A.C.B.L., 1980, 238p.)*
Francis, Henry G — Twenty-Sixth Contract Bridge Team World Championships 1983 *(A.C.B.L., 1984, 256p.)*
Francis, Henry G — Twenty-Third Contract Bridge Team World Championship, October 20-28, 1977 *(A.C.B.L., 1978, 187p.)*
Francis, Henry G & Senior, Brian — *The Bermuda Bowl: History And All The Best Deals *(Five Aces Books, 1999, 252p.)*
Frey, Richard L — 1958 World Championship Contract Bridge Team Matches *(A.C.B.L., 1958, 162p.)*
Frey, Richard L — 1959 World Championship Contract Bridge Team Matches, New York, N.Y. - February 7-15 *(A.C.B.L., 1959, 160p.)*
Frey, Richard L — 1961 World Championship Contract Bridge Team Matches, Buenos Aires, Argentina April15-23 *(A.C.B.L., 1961, 136p.)*
Frey, Richard L — 1962 World Championship Contract Bridge Team Matches *(A.C.B.L., 1962, 120p.)*
Frey, Richard L — 1963 World Championship Contract Bridge Team Matches *(A.C.B.L., 1963, 120p.)*
Frey, Richard L — 1965 Contract Bridge Team World Championship *(A.C.B.L., 1965, 192p.)*
Frey, Richard L — 1966 Contract Bridge Team World Championship *(A.C.B.L., 1966, 219p.)*
Frey, Richard L — 1967 Contract Bridge Team World Championship *(A.C.B.L., 1967, 224p.)*
Frey, Richard L — 1969 Contract Bridge Team World Championship, Rio Country Club, Rio Di Janeiro, May 8-17 *(A.C.B.L., 1969, 224p.)*
Frey, Richard L — First World Bridge Olympiad Contract Bridge Team Matches 1960 *(A.C.B.L., 1960, 144p.)*
Frey, Richard L — International Team Trials, Dallas, Texas, November 20 - 26, 1964 *(A.C.B.L., 1964, 144p.)*
Frey, Richard L — Report On The 1966 International Team Trials, San Francisco - Nov. 13-18, 1965 *(A.C.B.L., 1966, 388p.)*
Frey, Richard L — Report On The 1967 International Teams Trials *(A.C.B.L., 1966, 144p.)*
Frey, Richard L — Selecting The American Team For The 1970 World Championships *(A.C.B.L., 1969, 96p.)*
Frey, Richard L — The Second World Bridge Team Olympiad 1964 *(A.C.B.L., 1964, 192p.)*
Frey, Richard L — The Third World Bridge Team Olympiad 1968 *(A.C.B.L., 1968, 192p.)*
Gardener, Nicola — Master Bridge *(MacMillan, 1983, 140p.)*
Hirsch, Tannah — 1970 World Contract Bridge Team Championship *(A.C.B.L., 1970, 224p.)*
Hirsch, Tannah — 1971 Contract Bridge Team World Championship, Mandarin Hotel Tapei, Taiwan, May 6-17 *(A.C.B.L., 1971, 223p.)*
Hoof, Toine Van — The Staten Bank World Top Invitational Pairs Tournament Of Bridge 1987 *(Bridgesoft, 1987, 71p.)*

AUTHOR	TITLE	PUBLISHER	YEAR	PAGES

Smith, Thomas M — The Fourth World Bridge Team Olympiad 1972 *(A.C.B.L., 1972, 224p.)*
Sowter, Tony — 1993 World Championship Book *(Apsbridge, 1994, 192p.)*
Sowter, Tony — 1994 World Championship Book *(Apsbridge, 1995, 132p.)*
Sowter, Tony — The 1991 World Bridge Championships, The NEC Bermuda Bowl, The NEC Venice Cup *(Apsbridge, 1992, 160p.)*
Sowter, Tony — The 1992 World Championship Book, The 9th NEC World Bridge Teams Olympiad *(Apsbridge, 1993, 176p.)*
Sowter, Tony — World Bridge Championships, Mixed Pairs, Open Pairs, Women's Pairs, Knockout Teams 1990 *(Apsbridge, 1991, 160p.)*
Starworth, Irving J — Contract Bridge Score Totalizer *(Totalizer Co, 1948, 22p.)*
Stern, Dr. Paul — Beating The Culbertsons: How The Austrians Won The World Contract Bridge Championship *(Rodale Press, 1938, 128p.)*
Stern, Dr. Paul — Beating The Culbertsons: How The Austrians Won The World Contract Bridge Championship *(Werner Laurie, 1938, 128p.)*
Whitehead, Wilbur Cherrier — Championship Bridge Hands (What The Experts Did With Them!) *(Stokes, 1929, 120p.)*

Y. MATHEMATICS AND ODDS

Bailey, Edward — Contract Bridge Suit Divisions *(Private, 1936, 14p.)*
Borel, Emile & Cheron, Andre — +*The Mathematical Theory Of Bridge *(Monna Lisa, 1974, 434p.)*
Bourke, Tim — Tables Of Bridge Hand Patterns *(Private, 1987, 179p.)*
Brink, Glen — What Are Your Odds At Bridge? *(Radiant Expression, 1977, 10p.)*
Cowan, Richard — Hand Evaluation In The Game Of Contract Bridge *(Private, 1987, 14p.)*
Frost, Frederick H & Kibler, Robert E — +*Bridge Odds Complete: Probabilities In Contract Bridge *(Coffin/Aegean Park Press, 1976, 96p.)*
Gibson, Campbell — What's The Deal?: Chances Of Common And Uncommon Hands In Bridge *(Private, 1982, 30p.)*
Kelsey, Hugh Walter — Master Percentages In Bridge *(Gollancz, 1989, 16p.)*
Kelsey, Hugh Walter & Glauert, Michael — +*Bridge Odds For Practical Players *(Gollancz, 1980-94, 125p.)*
Kibler, Robert E & Telfer, Roy L — Probabilities In Contract Bridge: A Reference Text *(Coffin, 1963, 103p.)*
Northrop, Eugene & Stein, Arthur — *Mathematical Odds In Contract Bridge *(Vanguard/Williams & Norgate, 1934, 93p.)*
Powell, E W — Should I Finesse? *(Electric City Press, 1937, 6p.)*
Reese, Terence & Trezel, Roger — Master The Odds In Bridge *(Fell/Gollancz, 1979-86, 79p.)*
Telfer, Roy L — Practical Odds At Bridge *(Private/Traub, 1961, 106-114p.)*
Traub, Alec — Point Count Expectancy Tables *(Coffin, 1960, 21p.)*
Traub, Alec & Desai, Gaurang — Role Of Combinations In Contract Bridge Vis-A-Vis Point Count Distribution *(Mehta, 1990, 273p.)*
Zimmerman, Arnold W — Pure Mathematical Bridge *(Century, 1936, 40p.)*

Z. FICTION AND NOVELS

Armstrong, Len — The Final Deal *(Apsbridge, 1999, 147p.)*
Bloom, Thomas — The Nova Affair *(Ravenhaus, 1999, 207p.)*
Boden, Hilda — Bridge Club *(Ronald, 1952, 223p.)*
Cohen, Larry & Davis, Liz — Bridge Below The Belt *(Natco Press, 1997, 238p.)*
Cole, E R — Grand Slam - 13 Great Short Stories About Bridge *(Putnam's/Bodley Head, 1975, 224p.)*
Corbett, Andrea — Passionate Obsession *(Private, 1990, 122p.)*
Deserpa, Allan — The Mexican Contract *(Hardy, 1981, 148p.)*
Duncan, Walter — The Fourth At Bridge And Other Short Stories *(Shakespeare Press, 1912, 168p.)*
Eichenbaum, Ken — Bridge Without A Partner *(Private, 1993, 200p.)*
Forrester, Stan — Fool Deck Or A Bridge Triumph *(Private, 1997, 146p.)*
Friedman, B H — Yarborough *(World, 1964, 374p.)*
Gerontopoulos, Panos — Proceedings Of The First Bridge Promotion Week *(European Bridge League, 1989, 96p.)*
Granovetter, Matthew — I Shot My Bridge Partner *(Granovetter/Master Point Press, 1989, 370-372p.)*
Granovetter, Matthew — Murder At The Bridge Table *(Granovetter/Master Point Press, 1988-99, 310p.)*
Granovetter, Matthew — The Bridge Team Murders *(Granovetter/Master Point Press, 1992, 400p.)*
Gross, Jacqui — Henrietta Kingsley Bridge Pro - A Bridge Novel *(Private, 1999, 105p.)*
Halloran, Julia — Murder At The Nationals *(Bookcrafters, 1986, 115p.)*
Herts, B Russell — Grand Slam *(Pratt, 1932, 288p.)*
Heyer, Georgette — Duplicate Death *(Dutton, 1969, 233p.)*
Nicolet, C C — Death Of A Bridge Expert *(Simon & Schuster, 1932, 235p.)*
Powell, Richard — Tickets To The Devil *(Scribner/Hodder & Stoughton/Devyn Press, 1968-85, 306-200p.)*
Presberg, Shirley — Death By Contract *(Zookeeper, 1997, 247p.)*
Quinn, Terry — The Great Bridge Conspiracy *(St Martin's, 1979, 196p.)*
Reese, Terence & Flint, Jeremy — Trick Thirteen *(Weidenfeld & Nicholson/Bibliagora, 1979, 172p.)*
Von Elsner, Donald — Ace Of Spies *(Award Books/Hardy, 1966-82, 192p.)*
Von Elsner, Donald — Cruise Bridge *(Hardy, 1980, 187p.)*
Von Elsner, Donald — Everything's Jake With Me *(Hardy, 1980, 105p.)*
Von Elsner, Donald — How To Succeed In Murder Without Really Trying *(Signet, 1963, 144p.)*
Von Elsner, Donald — The Ace Of Spades *(Universal Pub & Dist Corp, 1966, 192p.)*
Von Elsner, Donald — The Best Of Jake Winkman *(Hardy, 1981, 117p.)*
Von Elsner, Donald — The Jack Of Hearts *(Award Books, 1968-82, 188-129p.)*
Von Elsner, Donald — The Jack Of Diamonds *(Award Books/Hardy, 1963, 192-111p.)*
Von Elsner, Donald — The Jake Winkman Trilogy *(Hardy, 1982, 370p.)*
Von Elsner, Donald — You Can't Do Business With Murder *(Signet, 1962, 143p.)*
Wiss, Mike Dorn — Shadow In The Bridge World *(J.B.F., 1993, 200p.)*

AA. MEMORY

Dendy, Dr. Julius — Memory Bridge: Instant Learning Through Organisation, Classification And Association *(Exposition, 1971, 165p.)*
Klinger, Ron — Better Bridge With A Better Memory: How Mnemonics Will Improve Your Game *(Gollancz, 1998, 96p.)*
Klinger, Ron — Improve Your Bridge Memory *(Gollancz/Houghton Mifflin, 1984-93, 93p.)*
Sheafe — Mechanical Contract And Auction Bridge *(Technical, 1935, 8p.)*

BB. VARIATIONS OF CONTRACT BRIDGE

Anonymous — Equal Suit Bridge *(Bridge Products Inc, 1959, 20p.)*

Anonymous — Equal Suit Bridge Scoring - Equal Suit Bridge *(Bridge Products Inc, 1959, 4p.)*

Anonymous — Equal Suit Bridge Scoring - Equal Suit Bridge Rules (Including Scorecard) *(Bridge Products Inc, 1959, 4p.)*

Anonymous — Jogo: Modern Bridge *(Jogo Co, 1950, 12p.)*

Anonymous — Maximum-Contract Bridge *(Bridge Products Inc, 1962, 6p.)*

Beasley, Col. Henry Mountifort
& Westall, Bernard C — Five-suit Bridge *(De La Rue, 1938, 32p.)*

Bondet, Edwin L — Winning Five-suit Bridge *(Ructor Pub, 1938, 32p.)*

Bourget, Frank E — An Outline Of Bidding-Playing-Scoring Super-Contract Bridge *(Arrco, 1938, 11p.)*

Bourget, Frank E — Green Book Of Super Contract Five-suit Bridge *(Arrco, 1938, 64p.)*

Bridge Headquarters — Hy-Lo Contract Bridge *(Bridge Headquarters, 1938, 11p.)*

Bridge World, The — Five-suit Bridge *(The Bridge World, 1938, 47p.)*

Buckley, Joseph J — Advanced Contract Bridge (No Dummy) *(Angel Guardian Press, 1933, 41p.)*

Burnstine, David &
Jacoby, Oswald — Five-suit Bridge (Bidding And Play) *(Simon & Schuster, 1938, 96p.)*

Coffin, George Sturgis — Bridge For Three/Contract Bridge For Three *(Faber/ Ives Washburn, 1955-56, 64p.)*

Coffin, George Sturgis — Triangle Contract *(Humphries, 1934, 64p.)*

Courtenay, F Dudley &
Gracy, Leonard R — Elective Contract *(Bridge Headquarters, 1935, 61p.)*

Culbertson, Ely — Outline Of The Culbertson System Of Five-suit Bridge *(Bard Bridge Bureau, 1938, 29p.)*

Ellicott, John Morris — Ellicott Three-Handed Contract Bridge *(Private, 1931, 10p.)*

Ellicott, John Morris — Super-Contract Bridge *(Coffin, 1940, 32p.)*

Ferguson, Albert B — Poker Bridge *(Malba, 1934-35, 27p.)*

Finst, Rudy — Three-handed Bridge *(Private, 1967, 15p.)*

Fishburne, S B — Cut-throat Contract *(Private, 1936-37, 16-37p.)*

Fry, Sam Jr. &
Hymes, Edward Jr. — How To Win At Five-suit Bridge *(Knight/Foulsham, 1938, 61p.)*

Guest, Freddie — Fifteen - The Advanced Game Of Contract Bridge *(Stanley Paul, 1960, 72p.)*

Huske, William J &
Replogle, J Leonard — Towie *(Towie, 1934-35, 77p.)*

Jensen, Anker — Five-suit Bridge *(Private, 1938, 0p.)*

Kling, Alpha H — The Regal Self-Teacher For Five-suit Contract - Showing Card Valuation. *(Taylor Press, 1938, 27p.)*

Manion, James S — Culbertson's Contract Golf *(The Bridge World/Allen & Unwin, 1932-33, 64p.)*

Manning-Foster, A E — Bridge-Plafond, The Original Game Of Contract Bridge: The Game With A Past And A Future *(Benn, 1933, 93p.)*

Momsen, Vice Admiral
Charles B — Push Contract Bridge For Fun, Simplicity And Excitement *(Great Outdoors, 1965, 59p.)*

Monte, Du Bose — Game Contract Bridge *(Monahan, 1947, 28p.)*

Packer, Alfred Herbert &
Seymour, Paul H — Bridge For Six Or Seven *(Private, 1931, 47p.)*

Phillips, Hubert — Contract Whist *(Faber, 1932, 200p.)*

Stallard, Helen M — Instant Bidless Bridge *(Private, 1978, 30p.)*

Stallard, Helen M — Instant Bridge: An Exciting Game For 3 Or 4 Players, Ages 8 To 88. *(Private, 1977, 4p.)*

Stallard, M Berl &
Stallard, Helen M — Bridge For Two Or Three Players *(Private, 1978, 6p.)*

Stanley, Enos &
Stanley, Mrs. E — Three Hand Bridge *(Private, 1954, 2p.)*

Wainwright, Stuyvesant K — Towie Tactics *(Stuyvesant, 1946, 33p.)*

Walters, Linwood A — Lindy Bridge - Bridge For Three *(Mountain Press, 1945, 25p.)*

CC. COOKING AND BRIDGE

ACT Bridge Association — The Bridge Players' Cook Book *(A.C.B.T.A, 1981, 60p.)*

Anderson, Molly — Bridge Party Hostess *(Foulsham, 1995, 160p.)*

Cook, Dorothy Jane — Cook And Deal 1 & II *(Private, 1982-93, 210-286p.)*

Cox, Nicola — Bridge Player's Supper Book *(Gollancz, 1995, 96p.)*

Delineator Home Institute &
Bentley, Mildred Maddocks — How To Give A Bridge Party, Prepared By Delineator Home Institute *(Delineator Service, 1929, 32p.)*

Lutes, Della T — Bridge Food For Bridge Fans *(Barrows, 1932, 70p.)*

Ryan, Margaret — Play Bridge And Cook Too *(Carlton, 1966, 64p.)*

Stibolt, Hoppie &
Bishop, Barbara — Grand Slam *(Grand Slam, 1987, 126p.)*

NOTES

NOTES

NOTES

NOTES